FEDERAL INDIVIDUAL INCOME TAX

2008-20

MW00611595

EDITORIAL ADVISORS

ASPEN PUBLISHERS

FEDERAL INDIVIDUAL INCOME TAX

WITH COMMENTARY

2008-2009

George Mundstock
Professor of Law
University of Miami

and

Kyle Siebrecht
Editor

Wolters Kluwer
Law & Business

AUSTIN   BOSTON   CHICAGO   NEW YORK   THE NETHERLANDS

To contact Customer Care, e-mail customer.care@aspenpublishers.com,
call 1-800-234-1660, fax 1-800-901-9075, or mail correspondence to:

Aspen Publishers
Attn: Order Department
PO Box 990
Frederick, MD 21705

Printed in the United States of America.

1 2 3 4 5 6 7 8 9 0

ISBN 978-0-7355-7231-7

About Wolters Kluwer Law & Business

Wolters Kluwer Law & Business is a leading provider of research information and workflow solutions in key specialty areas. The strengths of the individual brands of Aspen Publishers, CCH, Kluwer Law International and Loislaw are aligned within Wolters Kluwer Law & Business to provide comprehensive, in-depth solutions and expert-authored content for the legal, professional and education markets.

CCH was founded in 1913 and has served more than four generations of business professionals and their clients. The CCH products in the Wolters Kluwer Law & Business group are highly regarded electronic and print resources for legal, securities, antitrust and trade regulation, government contracting, banking, pension, payroll, employment and labor, and healthcare reimbursement and compliance professionals.

Aspen Publishers is a leading information provider for attorneys, business professionals and law students. Written by preeminent authorities, Aspen products offer analytical and practical information in a range of specialty practice areas from securities law and intellectual property to mergers and acquisitions and pension/benefits. Aspen's trusted legal education resources provide professors and students with high-quality, up-to-date and effective resources for successful instruction and study in all areas of the law.

Kluwer Law International supplies the global business community with comprehensive English-language international legal information. Legal practitioners, corporate counsel and business executives around the world rely on the Kluwer Law International journals, loose-leafs, books and electronic products for authoritative information in many areas of international legal practice.

Loislaw is a premier provider of digitized legal content to small law firm practitioners of various specializations. Loislaw provides attorneys with the ability to quickly and efficiently find the necessary legal information they need, when and where they need it, by facilitating access to primary law as well as state-specific law, records, forms and treatises.

Wolters Kluwer Law & Business, a unit of Wolters Kluwer, is headquartered in New York and Riverwoods, Illinois. Wolters Kluwer is a leading multinational publisher and information services company.

Table of Contents

Table of Contents

Table of Contents

Table of Contents

ix

Table of Contents

Table of Contents

Table of Contents

Table of Contents

Table of Contents

xiv

TECHNICAL NOTE

Obviously, this volume is intended solely for student use. Deletions and other features make it unsuitable for other uses.

Note that the key non-Code statutory transition rules are reprinted after Section 1. The table at the beginning of the text should help the student see the structure of the Code.

Much of the current 26 C.F.R. dates back to the mother of all Treasury Decisions, the post-1954 monster consolidating Treasury Decision: T.D. 6500, 25 FR 11402, Nov. 26, 1960; 25 FR 14021, Dec. 21, 1960. In this volume, when no history is indicated for a regulation, that means that the regulation dates back to T.D. 6500 and has not been amended. (This is the practice in the C.F.R.) Any subsequent amendments and the source of later-promulgated regulations are indicated at the end of a regulations section. However, in the interests of saving space, the history of a group of regulations under the same Code section with overlapping amendments is indicated at the end of the group.

We have tried to conform as much as possible to the respective conventions on things like spacing, capitalization, hyphens, and the like used in the printed versions of the U.S.C.A. and the C.F.R.

Current through December 31, 2007.

The author and editor prepared this volume into an almost camera ready form using OpenOffice.org Writer exclusively

FEDERAL INDIVIDUAL INCOME TAX

2008-2009

Outline of the Internal Revenue Code

TITLE 26 - INTERNAL REVENUE CODE

Parts are shown only for subchapters of particular interest to the student.

5

Starting Code Sec.

Outline of the Internal Revenue Code

Outline of the Internal Revenue Code

Outline of the Internal Revenue Code

Sec. 1. Tax imposed

(a) Married individuals filing joint returns and surviving spouses. -- There is hereby imposed on the taxable income of--

    (1) every married individual (as defined in section 7703) who makes a single return jointly with his spouse under section 6013, and

    (2) every surviving spouse (as defined in section 2(a)), a tax determined in accordance with **5** the following table:

If taxable income is:	The tax is:	
Not over $36,900	15% of taxable income.	
Over $36,900 but not over $89,150	$5,535, plus 28% of the excess over $36,900.	10
Over $89,150 but not over $140,000	$20,165, plus 31% of the excess over $89,150.	
Over $140,000 but not over $250,000	$35,928.50, plus 36% of the excess over $140,000.	
Over $250,000	$75,528.50, plus 39.6% of the excess over $250,000.	

    (b) Heads of households. -- There is hereby imposed on the taxable income of every head of a **15** household (as defined in section 2(b)) a tax determined in accordance with the following table:

If taxable income is:	The tax is:	
Not over $29,600	15% of taxable income.	
Over $29,600 but not over $76,400	$4,440, plus 28% of the excess over $$29,600.	20
Over $76,400 but not over $127,500	$17,544, plus 31% of the excess over $76,400.	
Over $127,500 but not over $250,000	$33,385, plus 36% of the excess over $127,500.	
Over $250,000	$77,485, plus 39.6% of the excess over $250,000.	

    (c) Unmarried individuals (other than surviving spouses and heads of households). -- There **25** is hereby imposed on the taxable income of every individual (other than a surviving spouse as defined in section 2(a) or the head of a household as defined in section 2(b)) who is not a married individual (as defined in section 7703) a tax determined in accordance with the following table:

If taxable income is:	The tax is:	
		30
Not over $22,100	15% of taxable income.	
Over $22,100 but not over $53,500	$3,315, plus 28% of the excess over $22,100.	
Over $53,500 but not over $115,000	$12,107, plus 31% of the excess over $53,500.	
Over $115,000 but not over $250,000	$31,172, plus 36% of the excess over $115,000.	
Over $250,000	$79,772, plus 39.6% of the excess over $250,000.	35

    (d) Married individuals filing separate returns. -- There is hereby imposed on the taxable income of every married individual (as defined in section 7703) who does not make a single return jointly with his spouse under section 6013, a tax determined in accordance with the following table: **40**

If taxable income is:	The tax is:	
Not over $18,450	15% of taxable income.	
Over $18,450 but not over $44,575	$2,767.50, plus 28% of the excess over $18,450.	
Over $44,575 but not over $70,000	$10,082.50, plus 31% of the excess over $44,575.	45
Over $70,000 but not over $125,000	$17,964.25, plus 36% of the excess over $70,000.	
Over $125,000	$37,764.25, plus 39.6% of the excess over $125,000.	

    (e) Estates and trusts. -- There is hereby imposed on the taxable income of--

    (1) every estate, and **50**

    (2) every trust,

Sec. 1. Tax imposed

taxable under this subsection a tax determined in accordance with the following table:

If taxable income is:	The tax is:
Not over $1,500	15% of taxable income.
Over $1,500 but not over $3,500	$225, plus 28% of the excess over$1,500.
Over $3,500 but not over $5,500	$785, plus 31% of the excess over $3,500.
Over $5,500 but not over $7,500	$1,405, plus 36% of the excess over $5,500.
Over $7,500	$2,125, plus 39.6% of the excess over $7,500.

(f) Phaseout of marriage penalty in 15-percent bracket; adjustments in tax tables so that inflation will not result in tax increases. --

(1) In general. -- Not later than December 15 of 1993, and each subsequent calendar year, the Secretary shall prescribe tables which shall apply in lieu of the tables contained in subsections (a), (b), (c), (d), and (e) with respect to taxable years beginning in the succeeding calendar year.

(2) Method of prescribing tables. -- The table which under paragraph (1) is to apply in lieu of the table contained in subsection (a), (b), (c), (d), or (e), as the case may be, with respect to taxable years beginning in any calendar year shall be prescribed--

(A) except as provided in paragraph (8), by increasing the minimum and maximum dollar amounts for each rate bracket for which a tax is imposed under such table by the cost-of-living adjustment for such calendar year,

(B) by not changing the rate applicable to any rate bracket as adjusted under subparagraph (A), and

(C) by adjusting the amounts setting forth the tax to the extent necessary to reflect the adjustments in the rate brackets.

(3) Cost-of-living adjustment. -- For purposes of paragraph (2), the cost-of-living adjustment for any calendar year is the percentage (if any) by which--

(A) the CPI for the preceding calendar year, exceeds

(B) the CPI for the calendar year 1992.

(4) CPI for any calendar year. -- For purposes of paragraph (3), the CPI for any calendar year is the average of the Consumer Price Index as of the close of the 12-month period ending on August 31 of such calendar year.

(5) Consumer Price Index. -- For purposes of paragraph (4), the term "Consumer Price Index" means the last Consumer Price Index for all-urban consumers published by the Department of Labor. For purposes of the preceding sentence, the revision of the Consumer Price Index which is most consistent with the Consumer Price Index for calendar year 1986 shall be used.

(6) Rounding. --

(A) In general. -- If any increase determined under paragraph (2)(A), section 63(c)(4), section 68(b)(2) or section 151(d)(4) is not multiple of $50, such increase shall be rounded to the next lowest multiple of $50.

(B) Table for married individuals filing separately. -- In the case of a married individual filing a separate return, subparagraph (A) (other than with respect to sections 63(c)(4) and 151(d)(4)(A)) shall be applied by substituting "$25" for "$50" each place it appears.

Sec. 1. Tax imposed

(7) Special rule for certain brackets. --

(A) Calendar year 1994. -- In prescribing the tables under paragraph (1) which apply with respect to taxable years beginning in calendar year 1994, the Secretary shall make no adjustment to the dollar amounts at which the 36 percent rate bracket begins or at which the 39.6 percent rate begins under any table contained in subsection (a), (b), (c), (d), or (e). 5

(B) Later calendar years. -- In prescribing tables under paragraph (1) which apply with respect to taxable years beginning in a calendar year after 1994, the cost-of-living adjustment used in making adjustments to the dollar amounts referred to in subparagraph (A) shall be determined under paragraph (3) by substituting "1993" for "1992".

(8) Elimination of marriage penalty in 15-percent bracket. -- With respect to taxable 10 years beginning after December 31, 2003, in prescribing the tables under paragraph (1)--

(A) the maximum taxable income in the 15-percent rate bracket in the table contained in subsection (a) (and the minimum taxable income in the next higher taxable income bracket in such table) shall be 200 percent of the maximum taxable income in the 15-percent rate bracket in the table contained in subsection (c) (after any other adjustment under this 15 subsection), and

(B) the comparable taxable income amounts in the table contained in subsection (d) shall be 1/2 of the amounts determined under subparagraph (A).

(g) Certain unearned income of minor children taxed as if parent's income. --

(1) In general. -- In the case of any child to whom this subsection applies, the tax imposed 20 by this section shall be equal to the greater of

(A) the tax imposed by this section without regard to this subsection, or

(B) the sum of--

(i) the tax which would be imposed by this section if the taxable income of such child for the taxable year were reduced by the net unearned income of such child, plus 25

(ii) such child's share of the allocable parental tax.

(2) Child to whom subsection applies. -- This subsection shall apply to any child for any taxable year if--

(A) such child --

(i) has not attained age 18 before the close of the taxable year, or 30

(ii)((I) has attained age 18 before the close of the taxable year and meets the age requirements of section 152(c)(3) (determined without regard to subparagraph (B) thereof), and

(II) whose earned income (as defined in section 911(d)(2)) for such taxable year does not exceed one-half of the amount of the individual's support (within the meaning of 35 section 152(c)(1)(D) after the application of section 152(f)(5) (without regard to subparagraph (A) thereof)) for such taxable year,

(B) either parent of such child is alive at the close of the taxable year, and

(C) such child does not file a joint return for the taxable year.

(3) Allocable parental tax. -- For purposes of this subsection-- 40

(A) In general. -- The term "allocable parental tax" means the excess of--

(i) the tax which would be imposed by this section on the parent's taxable income if such income included the net unearned income of all children of the parent to whom this subsection applies, over

(ii) the tax imposed by this section on the parent without regard to this subsection. 45

Sec. 1. Tax imposed

For purposes of clause (i), net unearned income of all children of the parent shall not be taken into account in computing any exclusion, deduction, or credit of the parent.

(B) Child's share. -- A child's share of any allocable parental tax of a parent shall be equal to an amount which bears the same ratio to the total allocable parental tax as the child's net unearned income bears to the aggregate net unearned income of all children of such parent to whom this subsection applies.

(C) Special rule where parent has different taxable year. -- Except as provided in regulations, if the parent does not have the same taxable year as the child, the allocable parental tax shall be determined on the basis of the taxable year of the parent ending in the child's taxable year.

(4) Net unearned income. -- For purposes of this subsection--

(A) In general. -- The term "net unearned income" means the excess of--

(i) the portion of the adjusted gross income for the taxable year which is not attributable to earned income (as defined in section 911(d)(2)), over

(ii) the sum of--

(I) the amount in effect for the taxable year under section 63(c)(5)(A) (relating to limitation on standard deduction in the case of certain dependents), plus

(II) the greater of the amount described in subclause (I) or, if the child itemizes his deductions for the taxable year, the amount of the itemized deductions allowed by this chapter for the taxable year which are directly connected with the production of the portion of adjusted gross income referred to in clause (i).

(B) Limitation based on taxable income. -- The amount of the net unearned income for any taxable year shall not exceed the individual's taxable income for such taxable year.

***

(5) Special rules for determining parent to whom subsection applies. -- For purposes of this subsection, the parent whose taxable income shall be taken into account shall be--

(A) in the case of parents who are not married (within the meaning of section 7703), the custodial parent (within the meaning of section 152(e)) of the child, and

(B) in the case of married individuals filing separately, the individual with the greater taxable income.

(6) Providing of parent's TIN. -- The parent of any child to whom this subsection applies for any taxable year shall provide the TIN of such parent to such child and such child shall include such TIN on the child's return of tax imposed by this section for such taxable year.

(7) Election to claim certain unearned income of child on parent's return. --

(A) In general. -- If--

(i) any child to whom this subsection applies has gross income for the taxable year only from interest and dividends (including Alaska Permanent Fund dividends),

(ii) such gross income is more than the amount described in paragraph (4)(A)(ii)(I) and less than 10 times the amount so described,

(iii) no estimated tax payments for such year are made in the name and TIN of such child, and no amount has been deducted and withheld under section 3406, and

(iv) the parent of such child (as determined under paragraph (5)) elects the application of subparagraph (B), such child shall be treated (other than for purposes of this paragraph) as having no gross income for such year and shall not be required to file a return under section 6012.

8

Sec. 1. Tax imposed

(B) Income included on parent's return. -- In the case of a parent making the election under this paragraph--

(i) the gross income of each child to whom such election applies (to the extent the gross income of such child exceeds twice the amount described in paragraph (4)(A)(ii) (I)) shall be included in such parent's gross income for the taxable year,   5

(ii) the tax imposed by this section for such year with respect to such parent shall be the amount equal to the sum of--

(I) the amount determined under this section after the application of clause (i), plus

(II) for each such child, 10 percent of the lesser of the amount described in   10 paragraph (4)(A)(ii)(I) or the excess of the gross income of such child over the amount so described, and

(iii) any interest which is an item of tax preference under section 57(a)(5) of the child shall be treated as an item of tax preference of such parent (and not of such child).

(C) Regulations. -- The Secretary shall prescribe such regulations as may be necessary   15 or appropriate to carry out the purposes of this paragraph.

(h) Maximum capital gains rate. --

(1) In general. -- If a taxpayer has a net capital gain for any taxable year, the tax imposed by this section for such taxable year shall not exceed the sum of--

(A) a tax computed at the rates and in the same manner as if this subsection had not   20 been enacted on the greater of -

(i) taxable income reduced by the net capital gain; or

(ii) the lesser of -

(I) the amount of taxable income taxed at a rate below 25 percent; or

(II) taxable income reduced by the adjusted net capital gain;   25

(B) 5 percent (0 percent in the case of taxable years beginning after 2007) of so much of the adjusted net capita gain (or, if less, taxable income) as does not exceed the excess (if any) of--

(i) the amount of taxable income which would (without regard to this paragraph) be taxed at a rate below 25 percent, over   30

(ii) the taxable income reduced by the adjusted net capital gain;

(C) 15 percent of the adjusted net capital gain (or, if less, taxable income) in excess of the amount on which a tax is determined under subparagraph (B);

(D) 25 percent of the excess (if any) of--

(i) the unrecaptured section 1250 gain (or, if less, the net capital gain (determined   35 without regard to paragraph (11))), over

(ii) the excess (if any) of--

(I) the sum of the amount on which tax is determined under subparagraph (A) plus the net capital gain, over

(II) taxable income; and   40

(E) 28 percent of the amount of taxable income in excess of the sum of the amounts on which tax is determined under the preceding subparagraphs of this paragraph.

Sec. 1. Tax imposed

(2) Net capital gain taken into account as investment income. -- For purposes of this subsection, the net capital gain for any taxable year shall be reduced (but not below zero) by the amount which the taxpayer takes into account as investment income under section 163(d)(4)(B)(iii).

(3) Adjusted net capital gain. -- For purposes of this subsection, the term "adjusted net capital gain" means the sum of--

  (A) net capital gain (determined without regard to paragraph (11)) reduced (but not below zero) by the sum of--

    (i) unrecaptured section 1250 gain, and

    (ii) 28-percent rate gain, plus

  (B) qualified dividend income (as defined in paragraph (11)).

(4) 28-percent rate gain. -- For purposes of this subsection, the term "28-percent rate gain" means the excess (if any) of--

  (A) the sum of--

    (i) collectibles gain; and

    (ii) section 1202 gain, over

  (B) the sum of--

    (i) collectibles loss;

    (ii) the net short-term capital loss; and

    (iii) the amount of long-term capital loss carried under section 1212(b)(1)(B) to the taxable year.

(5) Collectibles gain and loss. -- For purposes of this subsection--

  (A) In general. -- The terms "collectibles gain" and "collectibles loss" mean gain or loss (respectively) from the sale or exchange of a collectible (as defined in section 408(m) without regard to paragraph (3) thereof) which is a capital asset held for more than 1 year but only to the extent such gain is taken into account in computing gross income and such loss is taken into account in computing taxable income.

***

(6) Unrecaptured section 1250 gain. -- For purposes of this subsection--

  (A) In general. -- The term "unrecaptured section 1250 gain" means the excess (if any) of--

    (i) the amount of long-term capital gain (not otherwise treated as ordinary income) which would be treated as ordinary income if section 1250(b)(1) included all depreciation and the applicable percentage under section 1250(a) were 100 percent, over

    (ii) the excess (if any) of--

      (I) the amount described in paragraph (4)(B); over

      (II) the amount described in paragraph (4)(A).

  (B) Limitation with respect to section 1231 property. -- The amount described in subparagraph (A)(i) from sales, exchanges, and conversions described in section 1231(a)(3)(A) for any taxable year shall not exceed the net section 1231 gain (as defined in section 1231(c)(3)) for such year.

(7) Section 1202 gain.--For purposes of this subsection, the term "section 1202 gain"

Sec. 1. Tax imposed

means the excess of--

    (A) the gain which would be excluded from gross income under section 1202 but for the percentage limitation in section 1202(a), over

    (B) the gain excluded from gross income under section 1202.

(8) Coordination with recapture of net ordinary losses under section 1231. -- If any amount is treated as ordinary income under section 1231(c), such amount shall be allocated among the separate categories of net section 1231 gain (as defined in section 1231(c)(3)) in such manner as the Secretary may by forms or regulations prescribe.

(9) Regulations. -- The Secretary may prescribe such regulations as are appropriate (including regulations requiring reporting) to apply this subsection in the case of sales and exchanges by pass-thru entities and of interests in such entities.

(10) Pass-thru entity defined. -- For purposes of this subsection, the term "pass-thru entity" means--

    (A) a regulated investment company;

    (B) a real estate investment trust;

    (C) an S corporation;

    (D) a partnership;

    (E) an estate or trust;

    (F) a common trust fund; and

    (G) a qualified electing fund (as defined in section 1295).

(11) Dividends taxed as net capital gain. --

    (A) In general. -- For purposes of this subsection, the term "net capital gain" means net capital gain (determined without regard to this paragraph) increased by qualified dividend income.

    (B) Qualified dividend income. -- For purposes of this paragraph--

        (i) In general. -- The term "qualified dividend income" means dividends received during the taxable year from--

            (I) domestic corporations, and

            (II) qualified foreign corporations.

        (ii) Certain dividends excluded. -- Such term shall not include--

            (I) any dividend from a corporation which for the taxable year of the corporation in which the distribution is made, or the preceding taxable year, is a corporation exempt from tax under section 501 or 521,

            (II) any amount allowed as a deduction under section 591 (relating to deduction for dividends paid by mutual savings banks, etc.), and

            (III) any dividend described in section 404(k).

        (iii) Coordination with section 246(c). -- Such term shall not include any dividend on any share of stock--

            (I) with respect to which the holding period requirements of section 246(c) are not met (determined by substituting in section 246(c) "60 days" for "45 days" each place it appears and by substituting "121-day period" for "91-day period"), or

            (II) to the extent that the taxpayer is under an obligation (whether pursuant to a short sale or otherwise) to make related payments with respect to positions in substantially similar or related property.

Sec. 1. Tax imposed

(C) Qualified foreign corporations. --

    (i) In general. -- Except as otherwise provided in this paragraph, the term "qualified foreign corporation" means any foreign corporation if--

        (I) such corporation is incorporated in a possession of the United States, or

        (II) such corporation is eligible for benefits of a comprehensive income tax treaty with the United States which the Secretary determines is satisfactory for purposes of this paragraph and which includes an exchange of information program.

    (ii) Dividends on stock readily tradable on United States securities market. -- A foreign corporation not otherwise treated as a qualified foreign corporation under clause (i) shall be so treated with respect to any dividend paid by such corporation if the stock with respect to which such dividend is paid is readily tradable on an established securities market in the United States.

    (iii) Exclusion of dividends of certain foreign corporations. -- Such term shall not include any foreign corporation which for the taxable year of the corporation in which the dividend was paid, or the preceding taxable year, is a passive foreign investment company (as defined in section 1297).

    (iv) Coordination with foreign tax credit limitation. -- Rules similar to the rules of section 904(b)(2)(B) shall apply with respect to the dividend rate differential under this paragraph.

(D) Special rules. --

    (i) Amounts taken into account as investment income. -- Qualified dividend income shall not include any amount which the taxpayer takes into account as investment income under section 163(d)(4)(B).

    (ii) Extraordinary dividends. -- If a taxpayer to whom this section applies receives, with respect to any share of stock, qualified dividend income from 1 or more dividends which are extraordinary dividends (within the meaning of section 1059(c)), any loss on the sale or exchange of such share shall, to the extent of such dividends, be treated as long-term capital loss.

    (iii) Treatment of dividends from regulated investment companies and real estate investment trusts.--A dividend received from a regulated investment company or a real estate investment trust shall be subject to the limitations prescribed in sections 854 and 857.

(i) Rate reductions after 2000. --

    (1) 10-percent rate bracket. --

        (A) In general. -- In the case of taxable years beginning after December 31, 2000 -

        (i) the rate of tax under subsections (a), (b), (c), and (d) on taxable income not over the initial bracket amount shall be 10 percent, and

        (ii) the 15 percent rate of tax shall apply only to taxable income over the initial bracket amount but not over the maximum dollar amount for the 15-percent rate bracket.

        (B) Initial bracket amount. -- For purposes of this paragraph, the initial bracket amount is--

        (i) $14,000 in the case of subsection (a),

        (ii) $10,000 in the case of subsection (b), and

        (iii) 1/2 the amount applicable under clause (i) (after adjustment, if any, under subparagraph (C)) in the case of subsections (c) and (d).

Sec. 1. Tax imposed

(C) Inflation adjustment. -- In prescribing the tables under subsection (f) which apply with respect to taxable years beginning in calendar years after 2003--

(i) the cost-of-living adjustment shall be determined under subsection (f)(3) by substituting "2002" for "1992" in subparagraph (B) thereof, and

(ii) the adjustments under clause (i) shall not apply to the amount referred to in subparagraph (B)(iii).

If any amount after adjustment under the preceding sentence is not a multiple of $50, such amount shall be rounded to the next lowest multiple of $50.

(D) Coordination with acceleration of 10 percent rate bracket benefit for 2001. -- This paragraph shall not apply to any taxable year to which section 6428 applies.

(2) Reductions in rates after June 30, 2001. -- In the case of taxable years beginning in a calendar year after 2000, the corresponding percentage specified for such calendar year in the following table shall be substituted for the otherwise applicable tax rate in the tables under subsections (a), (b), (c), (d), and (e).

The corresponding percentages shall be substituted				for the following percentages:			
	28%	31%	36%	39.6%
2001............................	27.5%	30.5%	35.5%	39.1%
2002............................	27.0%	30.0%	35.0%	38.6%
2003 and thereafter....	25.0%	28.0%	33.0%	35.0%

(3) Adjustment of tables. -- The Secretary shall adjust the tables prescribed under subsection (f) to carry out this subsection.

TERMINATION DATES OF 2001 AND 2003 AMENDMENTS

Pub. L. 107-16, title IX, Sec. 901, June 7, 2001, 115 Stat. 150, as amended by Pub. L. 107-358, Sec. 2, Dec. 17, 2002, 116 Stat. 3015, provided that:

(a) In General. - All provisions of, and amendments made by, this Act shall not apply -
 (1) to taxable, plan, or limitation years beginning after December 31, 2010, or
 (2) in the case of title V [see Tables for classification], to estates of decedents dying, gifts made, or generation skipping transfers, after December 31, 2010.
(b) Application of Certain Laws. - The Internal Revenue Code of 1986 and the Employee Retirement Income Security Act of 1974 [29 U.S.C. 1001 et seq.] shall be applied and administered to years, estates, gifts, and transfers described in subsection (a) as if the provisions and amendments described in subsection (a) had never been enacted.

Pub. L. 108-27, title III, Sec. 303, May 28, 2003, 117 Stat. 764, provided that:

All provisions of, and amendments made by, this title [amending this section, sections 55, 57, 163, 301, 306, 338, 467, 531, 541, 584, 702, 854, 857, 1255, 1257, 1445, and 7518 of this title, and section 1177 of Title 46, Appendix, Shipping, repealing section 341 of this title, and enacting provisions set out as notes under this section] shall not apply to taxable years beginning after December 31, 2008, and the Internal Revenue Code of 1986 shall be applied and administered to such years as if such provisions and amendments had never been enacted.

13

TERMINATION DATES OF 2001 AND 2003 AMENDMENTS

Pub. L. 109-222, Sec. 102, May 17, 2006, 120 Stat. 345, provided that:

Section 303 of the Jobs and Growth Tax Relief Reconciliation Act of 2003 is amended by striking `December 31, 2008' and inserting `December 31, 2010'.

Sec. 2. Definitions and special rules

(a) Definition of surviving spouse. --

(1) In general. -- For purposes of section 1, the term "surviving spouse" means a taxpayer -

(A) whose spouse died during either of his two taxable years immediately preceding the taxable year, and

(B) who maintains as his home a household which constitutes for the taxable year the principal place of abode (as a member of such household) of a dependent (i) who (within the meaning of section 152, determined without regard to subsections (b)(1), (b)(2), and (d)(1)(B) thereof) is a son, stepson, daughter, or stepdaughter of the taxpayer, and (ii) with respect to whom the taxpayer is entitled to a deduction for the taxable year under section 151.

For purposes of this paragraph, an individual shall be considered as maintaining a household only if over half of the cost of maintaining the household during the taxable year is furnished by such individual.

(2) Limitations. -- Notwithstanding paragraph (1), for purposes of section 1 a taxpayer shall not be considered to be a surviving spouse--

(A) if the taxpayer has remarried at any time before the close of the taxable year, or

(B) unless, for the taxpayer's taxable year during which his spouse died, a joint return could have been made under the provisions of section 6013 (without regard to subsection (a)(3) thereof).

(3) Special rule where deceased spouse was in missing status. -- If an individual was in a missing status (within the meaning of section 6013(f)(3)) as a result of service in a combat zone (as determined for purposes of section 112) and if such individual remains in such status until the date referred to in subparagraph (A) or (B), then, for purposes of paragraph (1)(A), the date on which such individual died shall be treated as the earlier of the date determined under subparagraph (A) or the date determined under subparagraph (B):

(A) the date on which the determination is made under section 556 of title 37 of the United States Code or under section 5566 of title 5 of such Code (whichever is applicable) that such individual died while in such missing status, or

(B) except in the case of the combat zone designated for purposes of the Vietnam conflict, the date which is 2 years after the date designated under section 112 as the date of termination of combatant activities in that zone.

(b) Definition of head of household. --

(1) In general. -- For purposes of this subtitle, an individual shall be considered a head of a household if, and only if, such individual is not married at the close of his taxable year, is not a surviving spouse (as defined in subsection (a)), and either--

(A) maintains as his home a household which constitutes for more than one-half of such taxable year the principal place of abode, as a member of such household, of--

(i) a qualifying child of the individual (as defined in section 152(c), determined without regard to section 152(e)), but not if such child--

(I) is married at the close of the taxpayer's taxable year, and

Sec. 2. Definitions and special rules

(II) is not a dependent of such individual by reason of section 152(b)(2) or 152(b)(3), or both, or

(ii) any other person who is a dependent of the taxpayer, if the taxpayer is entitled to a deduction for the taxable year for such person under section 151, or

(B) maintains a household which constitutes for such taxable year the principal place of abode of the father or mother of the taxpayer, if the taxpayer is entitled to a deduction for the taxable year for such father or mother under section 151.

For purposes of this paragraph, an individual shall be considered as maintaining a household only if over half of the cost of maintaining the household during the taxable year is furnished by such individual.

(2) Determination of status. -- For purposes of this subsection--

(A) an individual who is legally separated from his spouse under a decree of divorce or of separate maintenance shall not be considered as married;

(B) a taxpayer shall be considered as not married at the close of his taxable year if at any time during the taxable year his spouse is a nonresident alien; and

(C) a taxpayer shall be considered as married at the close of his taxable year if his spouse (other than a spouse described in subparagraph (C)) (!1) died during the taxable year.

(3) Limitations. -- Notwithstanding paragraph (1), for purposes of this subtitle a taxpayer shall not be considered to be a head of a household--

(A) if at any time during the taxable year he is a nonresident alien; or

(B) by reason of an individual who would not be a dependent for the taxable year but for--

(i) subparagraph (H) of section 152(d)(2), or

(ii) paragraph (3) of section 152(d).

(c) Certain married individuals living apart. -- For purposes of this part, an individual shall be treated as not married at the close of the taxable year if such individual is so treated under the provisions of section 7703(b).

(d) Nonresident aliens. -- In the case of a nonresident alien individual, the taxes imposed by sections 1 and 55 shall apply only as provided by section 871 or 877.

(e) Cross reference. -- For definition of taxable income, see section 63.

Sec. 3. Tax tables for individuals

(a) Imposition of tax table tax. --

(1) In general. -- In lieu of the tax imposed by section 1, there is hereby imposed for each taxable year on the taxable income of every individual -

(A) who does not itemize his deductions for the taxable year, and

(B) whose taxable income for such taxable year does not exceed the ceiling amount,

a tax determined under tables, applicable to such taxable year, which shall be prescribed by the Secretary and which shall be in such form as he determines appropriate. In the table so prescribed, the amounts of the tax shall be computed on the basis of the rates prescribed by section 1.

(2) Ceiling amount defined. -- For purposes of paragraph (1), the term "ceiling amount" means, with respect to any taxpayer, the amount (not less than $20,000) determined by the Secretary for the tax rate category in which such taxpayer falls.

Sec. 3. Tax tables for individuals

(3) Authority to prescribe tables for taxpayers who itemize deductions. -- The Secretary may provide that this section shall apply also for any taxable year to individuals who itemize their deductions. Any tables prescribed under the preceding sentence shall be on the basis of taxable income.

5

Sec. 11. Tax imposed

(a) Corporations in general. -- A tax is hereby imposed for each taxable year on the taxable income of every corporation.

(b) Amount of tax. --

10   **(1) In general.** -- The amount of the tax imposed by subsection (a) shall be the sum of--

(A) 15 percent of so much of the taxable income as does not exceed $50,000,

(B) 25 percent of so much of the taxable income as exceeds $50,000 but does not exceed $75,000,

15   **(C)** 34 percent of so much of the taxable income as exceeds $75,000 but does not exceed $10,000,000, and

(D) 35 percent of so much of the taxable income as exceeds $10,000,000.

In the case of a corporation which has taxable income in excess of $100,000 for any taxable year, the amount of tax determined under the preceding sentence for such taxable 20   year shall be increased by the lesser of (i) 5 percent of such excess, or (ii) $11,750. In the case of a corporation which has taxable income in excess of $15,000,000, the amount of the tax determined under the foregoing provisions of this paragraph shall be increased by an additional amount equal to the lesser of (i) 3 percent of such excess, or (ii) $100,000.

(2) Certain personal service corporations not eligible for graduated rates. -- 25   Notwithstanding paragraph (1), the amount of the tax imposed by subsection (a) on the taxable income of a qualified personal service corporation (as defined in section 448(d)(2)) shall be equal to 35 percent of the taxable income.

Sec. 21. Expenses for household and dependent care services necessary for gainful employment

30   **(a) Allowance of credit.** --

(1) In general. -- In the case of an individual for which there are 1 or more qualifying individuals (as defined in subsection (b)(1)) with respect to such individual, there shall be allowed as a credit against the tax imposed by this chapter for the taxable year an amount equal to the applicable percentage of the employment-related expenses (as defined in subsection (b) 35   (2)) paid by such individual during the taxable year.

(2) Applicable percentage defined. -- For purposes of paragraph (1), the term "applicable percentage" means 35 percent reduced (but not below 20 percent) by 1 percentage point for each $2,000 (or fraction thereof) by which the taxpayer's adjusted gross income for the taxable year exceeds $15,000.

40   **(b) Definitions of qualifying individual and employment-related expenses.** -- For purposes of this section -

16

Sec. 21. Expenses for household and dependent care services necessary for gainful employment

(1) Qualifying individual. -- The term "qualifying individual" means --

(A) a dependent of the taxpayer (as defined in section 152(a)(1)) who has not attained age 13,

(B) a dependent of the taxpayer who is physically or mentally incapable of caring for himself or herself and who has the same principal place of abode as the taxpayer for more 5 than one-half of such taxable year, or (C) the spouse of the taxpayer, if the spouse is physically or mentally incapable of caring for himself or herself and who has the same principal place of abode as the taxpayer for more than one-half of such taxable year.

(2) Employment-related expenses. --

(A) In general. -- The term "employment-related expenses" means amounts paid for the 10 following expenses, but only if such expenses are incurred to enable the taxpayer to be gainfully employed for any period for which there are 1 or more qualifying individuals with respect to the taxpayer:

(i) expenses for household services, and

(ii) expenses for the care of a qualifying individual. 15

Such term shall not include any amount paid for services outside the taxpayer's household at a camp where the qualifying individual stays overnight.

(B) Exception. -- Employment-related expenses described in subparagraph (A) which are incurred for services outside the taxpayer's household shall be taken into account only if incurred for the care of-- 20

(i) a qualifying individual described in paragraph (1)(A), or

(ii) a qualifying individual (not described in paragraph (1)(A) who regularly spends at least 8 hours each day in the taxpayer's household.

(C) Dependent care centers. -- Employment-related expenses described in subparagraph (A) which are incurred for services provided outside the taxpayer's household 25 by a dependent care center (as defined in subparagraph (D)) shall be taken into account only if--

(i) such center complies with all applicable laws and regulations of a State or unit of local government, and

(ii) the requirements of subparagraph (B) are met. 30

(D) Dependent care center defined. -- For purposes of this paragraph, the term "dependent care center" means any facility which--

(i) provides care for more than six individuals (other than individuals who reside at the facility), and

(ii) receives a fee, payment, or grant for providing services for any of the individuals 35 (regardless of whether such facility is operated for profit).

(c) Dollar limit on amount creditable. -- The amount of the employment-related expenses incurred during any taxable year which may be taken into account under subsection (a) shall not exceed--

(1) $3,000 if there is 1 qualifying individual with respect to the taxpayer for such taxable 40 year, or

(2) $6,000 if there are 2 or more qualifying individuals with respect to the taxpayer for such taxable year.

The amount determined under paragraph (1) or (2) (whichever is applicable) shall be reduced by the aggregate amount excludable from gross income under section 129 for the taxable year. 45

17

Sec. 21. Expenses for household and dependent care services necessary for gainful employment

(d) Earned income limitation. --

(1) In general. -- Except as otherwise provided in this subsection, the amount of the employment-related expenses incurred during any taxable year which may be taken into account under subsection (a) shall not exceed--

(A) in the case of an individual who is not married at the close of such year, such individual's earned income for such year, or

(B) in the case of an individual who is married at the close of such year, the lesser of such individual's earned income or the earned income of his spouse for such year.

(2) Special rule for spouse who is a student or incapable of caring for himself. -- In the case of a spouse who is a student or a qualifying individual described in subsection (b)(1)(C), for purposes of paragraph (1), such spouse shall be deemed for each month during which such spouse is a full-time student at an educational institution, or is such a qualifying individual, to be gainfully employed and to have earned income of not less than--

(A) $250 if subsection (c)(1) applies for the taxable year, or

(B) $500 if subsection (c)(2) applies for the taxable year.

In the case of any husband and wife, this paragraph shall apply with respect to only one spouse for any one month.

(e) Special rules. -- For purposes of this section--

(1) Place of abode. -- An individual shall not be treated as having the same principal place of abode of the taxpayer if at any time during the taxable year of the taxpayer the relationship between the individual and the taxpayer is in violation of local law.

(2) Married couples must file joint return. -- If the taxpayer is married at the close of the taxable year, the credit shall be allowed under subsection (a) only if the taxpayer and his spouse file a joint return for the taxable year.

(3) Marital status. -- An individual legally separated from his spouse under a decree of divorce or of separate maintenance shall not be considered as married.

(4) Certain married individuals living apart. -- If--

(A) an individual who is married and who files a separate return--

(i) maintains as his home a household which constitutes for more than one-half of the taxable year the principal place of abode of a qualifying individual, and

(ii) furnishes over half of the cost of maintaining such household during the taxable year

(B) during the last 6 months of such taxable year such individual's spouse is not a member of such household, such individual shall not be considered as married.

(5) Special dependency test in case of divorced parents, etc. -- If--

(A) section 152(e) applies to any child with respect to any calendar year, and

(B) such child is under the age of 13 or is physically or mentally incapable of caring for himself,

in the case of any taxable year beginning in such calendar year, such child shall be treated as a qualifying individual described in subparagraph (A) or (B) of subsection (b)(1) (whichever is appropriate) with respect to the custodial parent (as defined in section 152(e)(4)(A)), and shall not be treated as a qualifying individual with respect to the noncustodial parent.

(6) Payments to related individuals. -- No credit shall be allowed under subsection (a) for any amount paid by the taxpayer to an individual--

(A) with respect to whom, for the taxable year, a deduction under section 151(c)

Sec. 21. Expenses for household and dependent care services necessary for gainful employment

(relating to deduction for personal exemptions for dependents) is allowable either to the taxpayer or his spouse, or

(B) who is a child of the taxpayer (within the meaning of section 152(f)(1)) who has not attained the age of 19 at the close of the taxable year.

For purposes of this paragraph, the term "taxable year" means the taxable year of the taxpayer in which the service is performed.

(7) Student. -- The term "student" means an individual who during each of 5 calendar months during the taxable year is a full-time student at an educational organization.

(8) Educational organization. -- The term "educational organization" means an educational organization described in section 170(b)(1)(A)(ii).

(9) Identifying information required with respect to service provider. -- No credit shall be allowed under subsection (a) for any amount paid to any person unless--

(A) the name, address, and taxpayer identification number of such person are included on the return claiming the credit, or(

B) if such person is an organization described in section 501(c)(3) and exempt from tax under section 501(a), the name and address of such person are included on the return claiming the credit.In the case of a failure to provide the information required under the preceding sentence, the preceding sentence shall not apply if it is shown that the taxpayer exercised due diligence in attempting to provide the information so required.

(10) Identifying information required with respect to qualifying individuals. -- No credit shall be allowed under this section with respect to any qualifying individual unless the TIN of such individual is included on the return claiming the credit.

(f) Regulations. -- The Secretary shall prescribe such regulations as may be necessary to carry out the purposes of this section.

Reg. § 1.21-1. Expenses for household and dependent care services necessary for gainful employment.

(a) *In general.*--(1) Section 21 allows a credit to a taxpayer against the tax imposed by chapter 1 for employment-related expenses for household services and care (as defined in paragraph (d) of this section) of a qualifying individual (as defined in paragraph (b) of this section). The purpose of the expenses must be to enable the taxpayer to be gainfully employed (as defined in paragraph (c) of this section). For taxable years beginning after December 31, 2004, a qualifying individual must have the same principal place of abode (as defined in paragraph (g) of this section) as the taxpayer for more than one-half of the taxable year. For taxable years beginning before January 1, 2005, the taxpayer must maintain a household (as defined in paragraph (h) of this section) that includes one or more qualifying individuals.

(2) The amount of the credit is equal to the applicable percentage of the employment-related expenses that may be taken into account by the taxpayer during the taxable year (but subject to the limits prescribed in §1.21-2). Applicable percentage means 35 percent reduced by 1 percentage point for each $2,000 (or fraction thereof) by which the taxpayer's adjusted gross income for the taxable year exceeds $15,000, but not less than 20 percent. For example, if a taxpayer's adjusted gross income is $31,850, the applicable percentage is 26 percent.

(3) Expenses may be taken as a credit under section 21, regardless of the taxpayer's method of accounting, only in the taxable year the services are performed or the taxable year the expenses are paid, whichever is later.

(4) The requirements of section 21 and §§ 1.21-1 through 1.21-4 are applied at the

Sec. 21. Expenses for household and dependent care services necessary for gainful employment

time the services are performed, regardless of when the expenses are paid.

(5) *Examples.* The provisions of this paragraph (a) are illustrated by the following examples.

Example 1. In December 2007, B pays for the care of her child for January 2008.
5 Under paragraph (a)(3) of this section, B may claim the credit in 2008, the later of the years in which the expenses are paid and the services are performed.

Example 2. The facts are the same as in Example 1, except that B's child turns 13 on February 1, 2008, and B pays for the care provided in January 2008 on February 3, 2008. Under paragraph (a)(4) of this section, the determination of whether the expenses are
10 employment-related expenses is made when the services are performed. Assuming other requirements are met, the amount B pays will be an employment-related expense under section 21, because B's child is a qualifying individual when the services are performed, even though the child is not a qualifying individual when B pays the expenses.

(b) *Qualifying individual*--(1) In general. For taxable years beginning after December
15 31, 2004, a qualifying individual is--

(i) The taxpayer's dependent (who is a qualifying child within the meaning of section 152) who has not attained age 13;

(ii) The taxpayer's dependent (as defined in section 152, determined without regard to subsections (b)(1), (b)(2), and (d)(1)(B)) who is physically or mentally incapable of self-
20 care and who has the same principal place of abode as the taxpayer for more than one-half of the taxable year; or

(iii) The taxpayer's spouse who is physically or mentally incapable of self-care and who has the same principal place of abode as the taxpayer for more than one-half of the taxable year.

25   ***

(3) *Qualification on a daily basis.* The status of an individual as a qualifying individual is determined on a daily basis. An individual is not a qualifying individual on the day the status terminates.

(4) *Physical or mental incapacity.* An individual is physically or mentally incapable of
30 self-care if, as a result of a physical or mental defect, the individual is incapable of caring for the individual's hygiene or nutritional needs, or requires full-time attention of another person for the individual's own safety or the safety of others. The inability of an individual to engage in any substantial gainful activity or to perform the normal household functions of a homemaker or care for minor children by reason of a physical or mental condition
35 does not of itself establish that the individual is physically or mentally incapable of self-care.

(5) *Special test for divorced or separated parents or parents living apart*--(i) *Scope.* This paragraph (b)(5) applies to a child (as defined in section 152(f)(1) for taxable years beginning after December 31, 2004, and in section 151(c)(3) for taxable years beginning
40 before January 1, 2005) who--

(A) Is under age 13 or is physically or mentally incapable of self-care;

(B) Receives over one-half of his or her support during the calendar year from one or both parents who are divorced or legally separated under a decree of divorce or separate maintenance, are separated under a written separation agreement, or live apart at all
45 times during the last 6 months of the calendar year; and

(C) Is in the custody of one or both parents for more than one-half of the calendar year.

(ii) *Custodial parent allowed the credit.* A child to whom this paragraph (b)(5) applies is the qualifying individual of only one parent in any taxable year and is the qualifying
50 child of the custodial parent even if the noncustodial parent may claim the dependency

Sec. 21.   Expenses for household and dependent care services necessary for gainful employment

exemption for that child for that taxable year. See section 21(e)(5). The custodial parent is the parent having custody for the greater portion of the calendar year. See section 152(e)(4)(A).

(6) *Example.* The provisions of this paragraph (b) are illustrated by the following examples.

Example. C pays $420 for the care of her child, a qualifying individual, to be provided from January 2 through January 31, 2008 (21 days of care). On January 20, 2008, C's child turns 13 years old. Under paragraph (b)(3) of this section, C's child is a qualifying individual from January 2 through January 19, 2008 (13 days of care). C may take into account $260, the pro rata amount C pays for the care of her child for 13 days, under section 21. See §1.21-2(a)(4).

(c) *Gainful employment*--(1) *In general.* Expenses are employment-related expenses only if they are for the purpose of enabling the taxpayer to be gainfully employed. The expenses must be for the care of a qualifying individual or household services performed during periods in which the taxpayer is gainfully employed or is in active search of gainful employment. Employment may consist of service within or outside the taxpayer's home and includes self-employment. An expense is not employment-related merely because it is paid or incurred while the taxpayer is gainfully employed. The purpose of the expense must be to enable the taxpayer to be gainfully employed. Whether the purpose of an expense is to enable the taxpayer to be gainfully employed depends on the facts and circumstances of the particular case. Work as a volunteer or for a nominal consideration is not gainful employment.

(2) *Determination of period of employment on a daily basis*--(i) *In general.* Expenses paid for a period during only part of which the taxpayer is gainfully employed or in active search of gainful employment must be allocated on a daily basis.

(ii) *Exception for short, temporary absences.* A taxpayer who is gainfully employed is not required to allocate expenses during a short, temporary absence from work, such as for vacation or minor illness, provided that the care-giving arrangement requires the taxpayer to pay for care during the absence. An absence of 2 consecutive calendar weeks is a short, temporary absence. Whether an absence longer than 2 consecutive calendar weeks is a short, temporary absence is determined based on all the facts and circumstances.

(iii) *Part-time employment.* A taxpayer who is employed part-time generally must allocate expenses for dependent care between days worked and days not worked. However, if a taxpayer employed part-time is required to pay for dependent care on a periodic basis (such as weekly or monthly) that includes both days worked and days not worked, the taxpayer is not required to allocate the expenses. A day on which the taxpayer works at least 1 hour is a day of work.

(3) *Examples.* The provisions of this paragraph (c) are illustrated by the following examples:

Example 1. D works during the day and her husband, E, works at night and sleeps during the day. D and E pay for care for a qualifying individual during the hours when D is working and E is sleeping. Under paragraph (c)(1) of this section, the amount paid by D and E for care may be for the purpose of allowing D and E to be gainfully employed and may be an employment-related expense under section 21.

Example 2. F works at night and pays for care for a qualifying individual during the hours when F is working. Under paragraph (c)(1) of this section, the amount paid by F for care may be for the purpose of allowing F to be gainfully employed and may be an employment-related expense under section 21.

Example 3. G, the custodial parent of two children who are qualifying individuals, hires

Sec. 21. Expenses for household and dependent care services necessary for gainful employment

a housekeeper for a monthly salary to care for the children while G is gainfully employed. G becomes ill and as a result is absent from work for 4 months. G continues to pay the housekeeper to care for the children while G is absent from work. During this 4-month period, G performs no employment services, but receives payments under her employer's

5   wage continuation plan. Although G may be considered to be gainfully employed during her absence from work, the absence is not a short, temporary absence within the meaning of paragraph (c)(2)(ii) of this section, and her payments for household and dependent care services during the period of illness are not for the purpose of enabling her to be gainfully employed. G's expenses are not employment-related expenses, and

10 she may not take the expenses into account under section 21.

Example 4. To be gainfully employed, H sends his child to a dependent care center that complies with all state and local requirements. The dependent care center requires payment for days when a child is absent from the center. H takes 8 days off from work as vacation days. Because the absence is less than 2 consecutive calendar weeks, under

15 paragraph (c)(2)(ii) of this section, H's absence is a short, temporary absence. H is not required to allocate expenses between days worked and days not worked. The entire fee for the period that includes the 8 vacation days may be an employment-related expense under section 21.

Example 5. J works 3 days per week and her child attends a dependent care center

20 (that complies with all state and local requirements) to enable her to be gainfully employed. The dependent care center allows payment for any 3 days per week for $150 or 5 days per week for $250. J enrolls her child for 5 days per week, and her child attends the care center for 5 days per week. Under paragraph (c)(2)(iii) of this section, J must allocate her expenses for dependent care between days worked and days not worked.

25 Three-fifths of the $250, or $150 per week, may be an employment-related expense under section 21.

Example 6. The facts are the same as in Example 5, except that the dependent care center does not offer a 3-day option. The entire $250 weekly fee may be an employment-related expense under section 21.

30 (d) *Care of qualifying individual and household services--*(1) *In general.* To qualify for the dependent care credit, expenses must be for the care of a qualifying individual. Expenses are for the care of a qualifying individual if the primary function is to assure the individual's well-being and protection. Not all expenses relating to a qualifying individual are for the individual's care. Amounts paid for food, lodging, clothing, or education are not

35 for the care of a qualifying individual. If, however, the care is provided in such a manner that the expenses cover other goods or services that are incidental to and inseparably a part of the care, the full amount is for care.

(2) *Allocation of expenses.* If an expense is partly for household services or for the care of a qualifying individual and partly for other goods or services, a reasonable

40 allocation must be made. Only so much of the expense that is allocable to the household services or care of a qualifying individual is an employment-related expense. An allocation must be made if a housekeeper or other domestic employee performs household duties and cares for the qualifying children of the taxpayer and also performs other services for the taxpayer. No allocation is required, however, if the expense for the

45 other purpose is minimal or insignificant or if an expense is partly attributable to the care of a qualifying individual and partly to household services.

(3) *Household services.* Expenses for household services may be employment-related expenses if the services are performed in connection with the care of a qualifying individual. The household services must be the performance in and about the taxpayer's

50 home of ordinary and usual services necessary to the maintenance of the household and

22

Sec. 21. Expenses for household and dependent care services necessary for gainful employment

attributable to the care of the qualifying individual. Services of a housekeeper are household services within the meaning of this paragraph (d)(3) if the services are provided, at least in part, to the qualifying individual. Such services as are performed by chauffeurs, bartenders, or gardeners are not household services.

(4) *Manner of providing care.* The manner of providing care need not be the least **5** expensive alternative available to the taxpayer. The cost of a paid caregiver may be an expense for the care of a qualifying individual even if another caregiver is available at no cost.

(5) *School or similar program.* Expenses for a child in nursery school, pre-school, or similar programs for children below the level of kindergarten are for the care of a **10** qualifying individual and may be employment-related expenses. Expenses for a child in kindergarten or a higher grade are not for the care of a qualifying individual. However, expenses for before- or after-school care of a child in kindergarten or a higher grade may be for the care of a qualifying individual.

(6) *Overnight camps.* Expenses for overnight camps are not employment-related **15** expenses.

(7) *Day camps.*--(i) The cost of a day camp or similar program may be for the care of a qualifying individual and an employment-related expense, without allocation under paragraph (d)(2) of this section, even if the day camp specializes in a particular activity. Summer school and tutoring programs are not for the care of a qualifying individual and **20** the costs are not employment-related expenses.

(ii) A day camp that meets the definition of dependent care center in section 21(b)(2) (D) and paragraph (e)(2) of this section must comply with the requirements of section 21(b)(2)(C) and paragraph (e)(2) of this section.

(8) *Transportation.* The cost of transportation by a dependent care provider of a **25** qualifying individual to or from a place where care of that qualifying individual is provided may be for the care of the qualifying individual. The cost of transportation not provided by a dependent care provider is not for the care of the qualifying individual.

(9) *Employment taxes.* Taxes under sections 3111 (relating to the Federal Insurance Contributions Act) and 3301 (relating to the Federal Unemployment Tax Act) and similar **30** state payroll taxes are employment-related expenses if paid in respect of wages that are employment-related expenses.

(10) *Room and board.* The additional cost of providing room and board for a caregiver over usual household expenditures may be an employment-related expense.

(11) *Indirect expenses.* Expenses that relate to, but are not directly for, the care of a **35** qualifying individual, such as application fees, agency fees, and deposits, may be for the care of a qualifying individual and may be employment-related expenses if the taxpayer is required to pay the expenses to obtain the related care. However, forfeited deposits and other payments are not for the care of a qualifying individual if care is not provided.

(12) *Examples.* The provisions of this paragraph (d) are illustrated by the following **40** examples:

Example 1. To be gainfully employed, K sends his 3-year old child to a pre-school. The pre-school provides lunch and snacks. Under paragraph (d)(1) of this section, K is not required to allocate expenses between care and the lunch and snacks, because the lunch and snacks are incidental to and inseparably a part of the care. Therefore, K may **45** treat the full amount paid to the pre-school as for the care of his child.

Example 2. L, a member of the armed forces, is ordered to a combat zone. To be able to comply with the orders, L places her 10-year old child in boarding school. The school provides education, meals, and housing to L's child in addition to care. Under paragraph (d)(2) of this section, L must allocate the cost of the boarding school between expenses **50**

Sec. 21. Expenses for household and dependent care services necessary for gainful employment

for care and expenses for education and other services not constituting care. Only the part of the cost of the boarding school that is for the care of L's child is an employment-related expense under section 21.

Example 3. To be gainfully employed, M employs a full-time housekeeper to care for
5 M's two children, aged 9 and 13 years. The housekeeper regularly performs household services of cleaning and cooking and drives M to and from M's place of employment, a trip of 15 minutes each way. Under paragraph (d)(3) of this section, the chauffeur services are not household services. M is not required to allocate a portion of the expense of the housekeeper to the chauffeur services under paragraph (d)(2) of this
10 section, however, because the chauffeur services are minimal and insignificant. Further, no allocation under paragraph (d)(2) of this section is required to determine the portion of the expenses attributable to the care of the 13-year old child (not a qualifying individual) because the household expenses are in part attributable to the care of the 9-year old child. Accordingly, the entire expense of employing the housekeeper is an employment-
15 related expense. The amount that M may take into account as an employment-related expense under section 21, however, is limited to the amount allowable for one qualifying individual.

Example 4. To be gainfully employed, N sends her 9-year old child to a summer day camp that offers computer activities and recreational activities such as swimming and arts
20 and crafts. Under paragraph (d)(7)(i) of this section, the full cost of the summer day camp may be for care.

Example 5. To be gainfully employed, O sends her 9-year old child to a math tutoring program for two hours per day during the summer. Under paragraph (d)(7)(i) of this section, the cost of the tutoring program is not for care.

25 *Example 6.* To be gainfully employed, P hires a full-time housekeeper to care for her 8-year old child. In order to accommodate the housekeeper, P moves from a 2-bedroom apartment to a 3-bedroom apartment that otherwise is comparable to the 2-bedroom apartment. Under paragraph (d)(10) of this section, the additional cost to rent the 3-bedroom apartment over the cost of the 2-bedroom apartment and any additional utilities
30 attributable to the housekeeper's residence in the household may be employment-related expenses under section 21.

Example 7. Q pays a fee to an agency to obtain the services of an au pair to care for Q's children, qualifying individuals, to enable Q to be gainfully employed. An au pair from the agency subsequently provides care for Q's children. Under paragraph (d)(11) of this
35 section, the fee may be an employment-related expense.

Example 8. R places a deposit with a pre-school to reserve a place for her child. R sends the child to a different pre-school and forfeits the deposit. Under paragraph (d)(11) of this section, the forfeited deposit is not an employment-related expense.

(e) *Services outside the taxpayer's household--(1) In general.* The credit is allowable
40 for expenses for services performed outside the taxpayer's household only if the care is for one or more qualifying individuals who are described in this section at--

(i) Paragraph (b)(1)(i) or (b)(2)(i); or

(ii) Paragraph (b)(1)(ii), (b)(2)(ii), (b)(1)(iii), or (b)(2)(iii) and regularly spend at least 8 hours each day in the taxpayer's household.

45 (2) *Dependent care centers--(i) In general.* The credit is allowable for services performed by a dependent care center only if--

(A) The center complies with all applicable laws and regulations, if any, of a state or local government, such as state or local licensing requirements and building and fire code regulations; and

50 (B) The requirements provided in this paragraph (e) are met.

24

Sec. 21. Expenses for household and dependent care services necessary for gainful employment

(ii) *Definition.* The term dependent care center means any facility that provides full-time or part-time care for more than six individuals (other than individuals who reside at the facility) on a regular basis during the taxpayer's taxable year, and receives a fee, payment, or grant for providing services for the individuals (regardless of whether the facility is operated for profit). For purposes of the preceding sentence, a facility is 5 presumed to provide full-time or part-time care for six or fewer individuals on a regular basis during the taxpayer's taxable year if the facility has six or fewer individuals (including the taxpayer's qualifying individual) enrolled for full-time or part-time care on the day the qualifying individual is enrolled in the facility (or on the first day of the taxable year the qualifying individual attends the facility if the qualifying individual was enrolled in 10 the facility in the preceding taxable year) unless the Internal Revenue Service demonstrates that the facility provides full-time or part-time care for more than six individuals on a regular basis during the taxpayer's taxable year.

(f) *Reimbursed expenses.* Employment-related expenses for which the taxpayer is reimbursed (for example, under a dependent care assistance program) may not be taken 15 into account for purposes of the credit.

(g) *Principal place of abode.* For purposes of this section, the term principal place of abode has the same meaning as in section 152.

***

(j) *Expenses qualifying as medical expenses*--(1) *In general.* A taxpayer may not take 20 an amount into account as both an employment-related expense under section 21 and an expense for medical care under section 213.

(2) *Examples.* The provisions of this paragraph (j) are illustrated by the following examples:

Example 1. S has $6,500 of employment-related expenses for the care of his child 25 who is physically incapable of self-care. The expenses are for services performed in S's household that also qualify as expenses for medical care under section 213. Of the total expenses, S may take into account $3,000 under section 21. S may deduct the balance of the expenses, or $3,500, as expenses for medical care under section 213 to the extent the expenses exceed 7.5 percent of S's adjusted gross income. 30

Example 2. The facts are the same as in Example 1, however, S first takes into account the $6,500 of expenses under section 213. S deducts $500 as an expense for medical care, which is the amount by which the expenses exceed 7.5 percent of his adjusted gross income. S may not take into account the $6,000 balance as employment-related expenses under section 21, because he has taken the full amount of the 35 expenses into account in computing the amount deductible under section 213.

(k) *Substantiation.* A taxpayer claiming a credit for employment-related expenses must maintain adequate records or other sufficient evidence to substantiate the expenses in accordance with section 6001 and the regulations thereunder.

40

Reg. § 1.21-2 Limitations on amount creditable.

(a) *Annual dollar limitation.*--(1) The amount of employment-related expenses that may be taken into account under §1.21-1(a) for any taxable year cannot exceed--

(i) $2,400 ($3,000 for taxable years beginning after December 31, 2002, and before January 1, 2011) if there is one qualifying individual with respect to the taxpayer at any 45 time during the taxable year; or

(ii) $4,800 ($6,000 for taxable years beginning after December 31, 2002, and before January 1, 2011) if there are two or more qualifying individuals with respect to the taxpayer at any time during the taxable year.

(2) The amount determined under paragraph (a)(1) of this section is reduced by the 50

25

Sec. 21. Expenses for household and dependent care services necessary for gainful employment

aggregate amount excludable from gross income under section 129 for the taxable year.

(3) A taxpayer may take into account the total amount of employment-related expenses that do not exceed the annual dollar limitation although the amount of employment-related expenses attributable to one qualifying individual is disproportionate
5 to the total employment-related expenses. For example, a taxpayer with expenses in 2007 of $4,000 for one qualifying individual and $1,500 for a second qualifying individual may take into account the full $5,500.

(4) A taxpayer is not required to prorate the annual dollar limitation if a qualifying individual ceases to qualify (for example, by turning age 13) during the taxable year.
10 However, the taxpayer may take into account only amounts that qualify as employment-related expenses before the disqualifying event. See also §1.21-1(b)(6).

(b) *Earned income limitation*--(1) *In general*. The amount of employment-related expenses that may be taken into account under section 21 for any taxable year cannot exceed--
15 (i) For a taxpayer who is not married at the close of the taxable year, the taxpayer's earned income for the taxable year; or

(ii) For a taxpayer who is married at the close of the taxable year, the lesser of the taxpayer's earned income or the earned income of the taxpayer's spouse for the taxable year.
20 (2) *Determination of spouse*. For purposes of this paragraph (b), a taxpayer must take into account only the earned income of a spouse to whom the taxpayer is married at the close of the taxable year. The spouse's earned income for the entire taxable year is taken into account, however, even though the taxpayer and the spouse were married for only part of the taxable year. The taxpayer is not required to take into account the earned
25 income of a spouse who died or was divorced or separated from the taxpayer during the taxable year. See §1.21-3(b) for rules providing that certain married taxpayers legally separated or living apart are treated as not married.

(3) *Definition of earned income*. For purposes of this section, the term earned income has the same meaning as in section 32(c)(2) and the regulations thereunder.
30 (4) *Attribution of earned income to student or incapacitated spouse*. (i) For purposes of this section, a spouse is deemed, for each month during which the spouse is a full-time student or is a qualifying individual described in §1.21-1(b)(1)(iii) or (b)(2)(iii), to be gainfully employed and to have earned income of not less than--

(A) $200 ($250 for taxable years beginning after December 31, 2002, and before
35 January 1, 2011) if there is one qualifying individual with respect to the taxpayer at any time during the taxable year; or

(B) $400 ($500 for taxable years beginning after December 31, 2002, and before January 1, 2011) if there are two or more qualifying individuals with respect to the taxpayer at any time during the taxable year.
40 (ii) For purposes of this paragraph (b)(4), a full-time student is an individual who, during each of 5 calendar months of the taxpayer's taxable year, is enrolled as a student for the number of course hours considered to be a full-time course of study at an educational organization as defined in section 170(b)(1)(A)(ii). The enrollment for 5 calendar months need not be consecutive.
45 (iii) Earned income may be attributed under this paragraph (b)(4), in the case of any husband and wife, to only one spouse in any month.

(c) *Examples*.--The provisions of this section are illustrated by the following examples:

Example 1. In 2007, T, who is married to U, pays employment-related expenses of $5,000 for the care of one qualifying individual. T's earned income for the taxable year is
50 $40,000 and her husband's earned income is $2,000. T did not exclude any dependent

care assistance under section 129. Under paragraph (b)(1) of this section, T may take into account under section 21 only the amount of employment-related expenses that does not exceed the lesser of her earned income or the earned income of U, or $2,000.

Example 2. The facts are the same as in Example 1 except that U is a full-time student at an educational organization within the meaning of section 170(b)(1)(A)(ii) for 9 months of the taxable year and has no earned income. Under paragraph (b)(4) of this section, U is deemed to have earned income of $2,250. T may take into account $2,250 of employment-related expenses under section 21.

Example 3. For all of 2007, V is a full-time student and W, V's husband, is an individual who is incapable of self-care (as defined in §1.21-1(b)(1)(iii)). V and W have no earned income and pay expenses of $5,000 for W's care. Under paragraph (b)(4) of this section, either V or W may be deemed to have $3,000 of earned income. However, earned income may be attributed to only one spouse under paragraph (b)(4)(iii) of this section. Under the limitation in paragraph (b)(1)(ii) of this section, the lesser of V's and W's earned income is zero. V and W may not take the expenses into account under section 21.

(d) *Cross-reference.* For an additional limitation on the credit under section 21, see section 26

Reg. § 1.21-3 Special rules applicable to married taxpayers.

(a) *Joint return requirement.* No credit is allowed under section 21 for taxpayers who are married (within the meaning of section 7703 and the regulations thereunder) at the close of the taxable year unless the taxpayer and spouse file a joint return for the taxable year. See section 6013 and the regulations thereunder relating to joint returns of income tax by husband and wife.

(b) *Taxpayers treated as not married.* The requirements of paragraph (a) of this section do not apply to a taxpayer who is legally separated under a decree of divorce or separate maintenance or who is treated as not married under section 7703(b) and the regulations thereunder (relating to certain married taxpayers living apart). A taxpayer who is treated as not married under this paragraph (b) is not required to take into account the earned income of the taxpayer's spouse for purposes of applying the earned income limitation on the amount of employment-related expenses under §1.21-2(b).

(c) *Death of married taxpayer.* If a married taxpayer dies during the taxable year and the survivor may make a joint return with respect to the deceased spouse under section 6013(a)(3), the credit is allowed for the year only if a joint return is made. If, however, the surviving spouse remarries before the end of the taxable year in which the deceased spouse dies, a credit may be allowed on the decedent spouse's separate return.

Reg. § 1.21-4 Payments to certain related individuals

(a) In general. A credit is not allowed under section 21 for any amount paid by the taxpayer to an individual--

(1) For whom a deduction under section 151(c) (relating to deductions for personal exemptions for dependents) is allowable either to the taxpayer or the taxpayer's spouse for the taxable year;

(2) Who is a child of the taxpayer (within the meaning of section 152(f)(1) for taxable years beginning after December 31, 2004, and section 151(c)(3) for taxable years beginning before January 1, 2005) and is under age 19 at the close of the taxable year;

(3) Who is the spouse of the taxpayer at any time during the taxable year; or

(4) Who is the parent of the taxpayer's child who is a qualifying individual described in §1.21-1(b)(1)(i) or (b)(2)(i).

Sec. 21. Expenses for household and dependent care services necessary for gainful employment

(b) *Payments to partnerships or other entities.*--In general, paragraph (a) of this section does not apply to services performed by partnerships or other entities. If, however, the partnership or other entity is established or maintained primarily to avoid the application of paragraph (a) of this section to permit the taxpayer to claim the credit, for
5 purposes of section 21, the payments of employment-related expenses are treated as made directly to each partner or owner in proportion to that partner's or owner's ownership interest. Whether a partnership or other entity is established or maintained to avoid the application of paragraph (a) of this section is determined based on the facts and circumstances, including whether the partnership or other entity is established for the
10 primary purpose of caring for the taxpayer's qualifying individual or providing household services to the taxpayer.

(c) *Examples.* The provisions of this section are illustrated by the following examples:

Example 1. During 2007, X pays $5,000 to her mother for the care of X's 5-year old child who is a qualifying individual. The expenses otherwise qualify as employment-
15 related expenses. X's mother is not her dependent. X may take into account under section 21 the amounts paid to her mother for the care of X's child.

Example 2. Y is divorced and has custody of his 5-year old child, who is a qualifying individual. Y pays $6,000 during 2007 to Z, who is his ex-wife and the child's mother, for the care of the child. The expenses otherwise qualify as employment-related expenses.
20 Under paragraph (a)(4) of this section, Y may not take into account under section 21 the amounts paid to Z because Z is the child's mother.

Example 3. The facts are the same as in Example 2, except that Z is not the mother of Y's child. Y may take into account under section 21 the amounts paid to Z.

25 [T.D. 9354. 5/4/2006]

Sec. 22. Credit for the elderly and the permanently and totally disabled

(a) **General rule.** -- In the case of a qualified individual, there shall be allowed as a credit against the tax imposed by this chapter for the taxable year an amount equal to 15 percent of such individual's section 22 amount for such taxable year.

30 (b) **Qualified individual.** -- For purposes of this section, the term "qualified individual" means any individual--

(1) who has attained age 65 before the close of the taxable year, or

(2) who retired on disability before the close of the taxable year and who, when he retired, was permanently and totally disabled.

35 (c) **Section 22 amount.** -- For purposes of subsection (a)--

(1) **In general.** -- An individual's section 22 amount for the taxable year shall be the applicable initial amount determined under paragraph (2), reduced as provided in paragraph (3) and in subsection (d).

(2) **Initial amount.** --

40 (A) **In general.** -- Except as provided in subparagraph (B), the initial amount shall be -

(i) $5,000 in the case of a single individual, or a joint return where only one spouse is a qualified individual,

(ii) $7,500 in the case of a joint return where both spouses are qualified individuals, or

45 (iii) $3,750 in the case of a married individual filing a separate return.

28

Sec. 22. Credit for the elderly and the permanently and totally disabled

(B) Limitation in case of individuals who have not attained age 65. --

(i) In general. -- In the case of a qualified individual who has not attained age 65 before the close of the taxable year, except as provided in clause (ii), the initial amount shall not exceed the disability income for the taxable year.

(ii) Special rules in case of joint return. -- In the case of a joint return where both spouses are qualified individuals and at least one spouse has not attained age 65 before the close of the taxable year-- 5

(I) if both spouses have not attained age 65 before the close of the taxable year, the initial amount shall not exceed the sum of such spouses' disability income, or

(II) if one spouse has attained age 65 before the close of the taxable year, the initial amount shall not exceed the sum of $5,000 plus the disability income for the taxable year of the spouse who has not attained age 65 before the close of the taxable year. 10

(iii) Disability income. -- For purposes of this subparagraph, the term "disability income" means the aggregate amount includable in the gross income of the individual for the taxable year under section 72 or 105(a) to the extent such amount constitutes wages (or payments in lieu of wages) for the period during which the individual is absent from work on account of permanent and total disability. 15

(3) Reduction. --

(A) In general. -- The reduction under this paragraph is an amount equal to the sum of the amounts received by the individual (or, in the case of a joint return, by either spouse) as a pension or annuity or as a disability benefit-- 20

(i) which is excluded from gross income and payable under--

(I) title II of the Social Security Act,

(II) the Railroad Retirement Act of 1974, or 25

(III) a law administered by the Veterans' Administration, or

(ii) which is excluded from gross income under any provision of law not contained in this title.

No reduction shall be made under clause (i)(III) for any amount described in section 104(a)(4). 30

(B) Treatment of certain workmen's compensation benefits. -- For purposes of subparagraph (A), any amount treated as a social security benefit under section 86(d)(3) shall be treated as a disability benefit received under title II of the Social Security Act.

(d) Adjusted gross income limitation. -- If the adjusted gross income of the taxpayer exceeds -

(1) $7,500 in the case of a single individual, 35

(2) $10,000 in the case of a joint return, or

(3) $5,000 in the case of a married individual filing a separate return,

the section 22 amount shall be reduced by one-half of the excess of the adjusted gross income over $7,500, $10,000, or $5,000, as the case may be.

(e) Definitions and special rules. -- For purposes of this section-- 40

(1) Married couple must file joint return. -- Except in the case of a husband and wife who live apart at all times during the taxable year, if the taxpayer is married at the close of the taxable year, the credit provided by this section shall be allowed only if the taxpayer and his spouse file a joint return for the taxable year.

(2) Marital status. -- Marital status shall be determined under section 7703. 45

Sec. 22. Credit for the elderly and the permanently and totally disabled

(3) Permanent and total disability defined. -- An individual is permanently and totally disabled if he is unable to engage in any substantial gainful activity by reason of any medically determinable physical or mental impairment which can be expected to result in death or which has lasted or can be expected to last for a continuous **period** of not less than 12 months. An individual shall not be considered to be permanently and totally disabled unless he furnishes proof of the existence thereof in such form and manner, and at such times, as the Secretary may require.

Sec. 23. Adoption expenses

(a) Allowance of credit. --

(1) In general. -- In the case of an individual, there shall be allowed as a credit against the tax imposed by this chapter the amount of the qualified adoption expenses paid or incurred by the taxpayer.

(2) Year credit allowed. -- The credit under paragraph (1) with respect to any expense shall be allowed--

(A) in the case of any expense paid or incurred before the taxable year in which such adoption becomes final, for the taxable year following the taxable year during which such expense is paid or incurred, and

(B) in the case of an expense paid or incurred during or after the taxable year in which such adoption becomes final, for the taxable year in which such expense is paid or incurred.

(3) $10,000 credit for adoption of child with special needs regardless of expenses. -- In the case of an adoption of a child with special needs which becomes final during a taxable year, the taxpayer shall be treated as having paid during such year qualified adoption expenses with respect to such adoption in an amount equal to the excess (if any) of $10,000 over the aggregate qualified adoption expenses actually paid or incurred by the taxpayer with respect to such adoption during such taxable year and all prior taxable years.

(b) Limitations. --

(1) Dollar limitation. -- The aggregate amount of qualified adoption expenses which may be taken into account under subsection (a) for all taxable years with respect to the adoption of a child by the taxpayer shall not exceed $10,000.

(2) Income limitation. --

(A) The amount allowable as a credit under subsection (a) for any taxable year (determined without regard to subsection (c)) shall be reduced (but not below zero) by an amount which bears the same ratio to the amount so allowable (determined without regard to this paragraph but with regard to paragraph (1)) as--

(i) the amount (if any) by which the taxpayer's adjusted gross income exceeds $150,000, bears to

(ii) $40,000.

(B) Determination of adjusted gross income. -- For purposes of subparagraph (A), adjusted gross income shall be determined without regard to sections 911, 931, and 933.

(3) Denial of double benefit. --

(A) In general. -- No credit shall be allowed under subsection (a) for any expense for which a deduction or credit is allowed under any other provision of this chapter.

(B) Grants. -- No credit shall be allowed under subsection (a) for any expense to the extent that funds for such expense are received under any Federal, State, or local program.

Sec. 23. Adoption expenses

(4) Limitation based on amount of tax. -- The credit allowed under subsection (a) for any taxable year shall not exceed the excess of--

    (A) the sum of the regular tax liability (as defined in section 26(b)) plus the tax imposed by section 55, over

    (B) the sum of the credits allowable under this subpart (other than this section) and 5 section 27 for the taxable year.

(c) Carryforwards of unused credit. -- If the credit allowable under subsection (a) for any taxable year exceeds the limitation imposed by subsection (b)(4) for such taxable year, such excess shall be carried to the succeeding taxable year and added to the credit allowable under subsection (a) for such taxable year. No credit may be carried forward under this subsection to 10 any taxable year following the fifth taxable year after the taxable year in which the credit arose. For purposes of the preceding sentence, credits shall be treated as used on a first- in first-out basis.

(d) Definitions. -- For purposes of this section--

    (1) Qualified adoption expenses. -- The term "qualified adoption expenses" means 15 reasonable and necessary adoption fees, court costs, attorney fees, and other expenses--

        (A) which are directly related to, and the principal purpose of which is for, the legal adoption of an eligible child by the taxpayer,

        (B) which are not incurred in violation of State or Federal law or in carrying out any surrogate parenting arrangement, 20

        (C) which are not expenses in connection with the adoption by an individual of a child who is the child of such individual's spouse, and

        (D) which are not reimbursed under an employer program or otherwise.

    (2) Eligible child. -- The term "eligible child" means any individual who--

        (A) has not attained age 18, or 25

        (B) is physically or mentally incapable of caring for himself.

    (3) Child with special needs. -- The term "child with special needs" means any child if--

        (A) a State has determined that the child cannot or should not be returned to the home of his parents,

        (B) such State has determined that there exists with respect to the child a specific factor 30 or condition (such as his ethnic background, age, or membership in a minority or sibling group, or the presence of factors such as medical conditions or   physical, mental, or emotional handicaps) because of which it is reasonable to conclude that such child cannot be placed with adoptive parents without providing adoption assistance, and

        (C) such child is a citizen or resident of the United States (as defined in section 217(h) 35 (3)).

(e) Special rules for foreign adoptions. -- In the case of an adoption of a child who is not a citizen or resident of the United States (as defined in section 217(h)(3))

    (1) subsection (a) shall not apply to any qualified adoption expense with respect to such adoption unless such adoption becomes final, and 40

    (2) any such expense which is paid or incurred before the   taxable year in which such adoption becomes final shall be taken into account under this section as if such expense were paid or incurred during such year.

(f) Filing requirements. --

    (1) Married couples must file joint returns. -- Rules similar to the rules of paragraphs (2), 45 (3), and (4) of section 21(e) shall apply for purposes of this section.

Sec. 23.   Adoption expenses

(2) Taxpayer must include TIN. --

    (A) In general. -- No credit shall be allowed under this section with respect to any eligible child unless the taxpayer includes (if known) the name, age, and TIN of such child on the return of tax for the taxable year.

    (B) Other methods. -- The Secretary may, in lieu of the information referred to in subparagraph (A), require other information meeting the purposes of subparagraph (A), including identification of an agent assisting with the adoption.

(g) Basis adjustments. -- For purposes of this subtitle, if a credit is allowed under this section for any expenditure with respect to any property, the increase in the basis of such property which would (but for this subsection) result from such expenditure shall be reduced by the amount of the credit so allowed.

(h) Adjustments for inflation. -- In the case of a taxable year beginning after December 31, 2002, each of the dollar amounts in subsection (a)(3) and paragraphs (1) and (2)(A)(i) of subsection (b) shall be increased by an amount equal to -

(1) such dollar amount, multiplied by

(2) the cost-of-living adjustment determined under section 1(f)(3) for the calendar year in which the taxable year begins, determined by substituting "calendar year 2001" for "calendar year 1992" in subparagraph (B) thereof.

If any amount as increased under the preceding sentence is not a multiple of $10, such amount shall be rounded to the nearest multiple of $10.

(i) Regulations. -- The Secretary shall prescribe such regulations as may be appropriate to carry out this section and section 137, including regulations which treat unmarried individuals who pay or incur qualified adoption expenses with respect to the same child as 1 taxpayer for purposes of applying the dollar amounts in subsections (a)(3) and (b)(1) of this section and in section 137(b)(1).

Sec. 24.   Child tax credit

(a) Allowance of credit. -- There shall be allowed as a credit against the tax imposed by this chapter for the taxable year with respect to each qualifying child of the taxpayer an amount equal to $1,000.

(b) Limitations. --

    (1) Limitation based on adjusted gross income. -- The amount of the credit allowable under subsection (a) shall be reduced (but not below zero) by $50 for each $1,000 (or fraction thereof) by which the taxpayer's modified adjusted gross   income exceeds the threshold amount. For purposes of the preceding sentence, the term "modified adjusted gross income" means adjusted gross income increased by any amount excluded from gross income under section 911, 931, or 933.

    (2) Threshold amount. -- For purposes of paragraph (1), the term "threshold amount" means--

    (A) $110,000 in the case of a joint return,

    (B) $75,000 in the case of an individual who is not married, and

    (C) $55,000 in the case of a married individual filing a separate return

For purposes of this paragraph, marital status shall be determined under section 7703.

    (3) Limitation based on amount of tax. -- The credit allowed under subsection (a) for any taxable year shall not exceed the excess of--

Sec. 24. Child tax credit

(A) the sum of the regular tax liability (as defined in section 26(b)) plus the tax imposed by section 55, over

(B) the sum of the credits allowable under this subpart (other than this section and sections 23 and 25B) and section 27 for the taxable year.

(c) Qualifying child. -- For purposes of this section--

(1) In general. -- The term "qualifying child" means a qualifying child of the taxpayer (as defined in section 152(c)) who has not attained age 17.

(2) Exception for certain noncitizens. -- The term "qualifying child" shall not include any individual who would not be a dependent if subparagraph (A) of section 152(b)(3) were applied without regard to all that follows "resident of the United States".

(d) Portion of credit refundable. --

(1) In general. -- The aggregate credits allowed to a taxpayer under subpart C shall be increased by the lesser of--

(A) the credit which would be allowed under this section without regard to this subsection and the limitation under subsection (b)(3), or

(B) the amount by which the amount of credit allowed by this section (determined without regard to this subsection) would increase if the limitation imposed by subsection (b)(3) were increased by the greater of--

(i) 15 percent of so much of the taxpayer's earned income (within the meaning of section 32) which is taken into account in computing taxable income for the taxable year as exceeds $10,000, or

(ii) in the case of a taxpayer with 3 or more qualifying children, the greater of--

(I) the taxpayer's social security taxes for the taxable year, over

(II) the credit allowed under section 32 for the taxable year.

The amount of the credit allowed under this subsection shall not be treated as a credit allowed under this subpart and shall reduce the amount of credit otherwise allowable under subsection (a) without regard to subsection (b)(3). For purposes of subparagraph (B), any amount excluded from gross income by reason of section 112 shall be treated as earned income which is taken into account in computing taxable income for the taxable year.

(2) Social security taxes. -- For purposes of paragraph (1)--

(A) In general. -- The term "social security taxes" means, with respect to any taxpayer for any taxable year--

(i) the amount of the taxes imposed by sections 3101 and 3201(a) on amounts received by the taxpayer during the calendar year in which the taxable year begins,

(ii) 50 percent of the taxes imposed by section 1401 on the self-employment income of the taxpayer for the taxable year, and

(iii) 50 percent of the taxes imposed by section 3211(a) on amounts received by the taxpayer during the calendar year in which the taxable year begins.

(B) Coordination with special refund of social security taxes. -- The term "social security taxes" shall not include any taxes to the extent the taxpayer is entitled to a special refund of such taxes under section 6413(c).

(C) Special rule. -- Any amounts paid pursuant to an agreement under section 3121(l) (relating to agreements entered into by American employers with respect to foreign affiliates) which are equivalent to the taxes referred to in subparagraph (A)(i) shall be treated as taxes referred to in such subparagraph.

33

Sec. 24. Child tax credit

(3) Inflation adjustment. -- In the case of any taxable year beginning in a calendar year after 2001, the $10,000 amount contained in paragraph (1)(B) shall be increased by an amount equal to--

    (A) such dollar amount, multiplied by

    (B) the cost-of-living adjustment determined under section 1(f)(3) for the calendar year in which the taxable year begins, determined by substituting "calendar year 2000" for "calendar year 1992" in subparagraph (B) thereof. Any increase determined under the preceding sentence shall be rounded to the nearest multiple of $50.

(e) Identification requirement. -- No credit shall be allowed under this section to a taxpayer with respect to any qualifying child unless the taxpayer includes the name and taxpayer identification number of such qualifying child on the return of tax for the taxable year.

(f) Taxable year must be full taxable year. -- Except in the case of a taxable year closed by reason of the death of the taxpayer, no credit shall be allowable under this section in the case of a taxable year covering a period of less than 12 months.

Sec. 25A. Hope and Lifetime Learning credits

(a) Allowance of credit. -- In the case of an individual, there shall be allowed as a credit against the tax imposed by this chapter for the taxable year the amount equal to the sum of--

    (1) the Hope Scholarship Credit, plus

    (2) the Lifetime Learning Credit.

(b) Hope Scholarship Credit. --

    (1) Per student credit. -- In the case of any eligible student for whom an election is in effect under this section for any taxable year, the Hope Scholarship Credit is an amount equal to the sum of--

        (A) 100 percent of so much of the qualified tuition and related expenses paid by the taxpayer during the taxable year (for education furnished to the eligible student during any academic period beginning in such taxable year) as does not exceed $1,000, plus

        (B) 50 percent of such expenses so paid as exceeds $1,000 but does not exceed the applicable limit.

    (2) Limitations applicable to Hope Scholarship Credit. --

        (A) Credit allowed only for 2 taxable years. -- An election to have this section apply with respect to any eligible student for purposes of the Hope Scholarship Credit under subsection (a)(1) may not be made for any taxable year if such an election (by the taxpayer or any other individual) is in effect with respect to such student for any 2 prior taxable years.

        (B) Credit allowed for year only if individual is at least 1/2 time student for portion of year. -- The Hope Scholarship Credit under subsection (a)(1) shall not be allowed for a taxable year with respect to the qualified tuition and related expenses of an individual unless such individual is an eligible student for at least one academic period which begins during such year.

        (C) Credit allowed only for first 2 years of postsecondary education. -- The Hope Scholarship Credit under subsection (a)(1) shall not be allowed for a taxable year with respect to the qualified tuition and related expenses of an eligible student if the student has completed (before the beginning of such taxable year) the first 2 years of postsecondary education at an eligible educational institution.

Sec. 25A. Hope and Lifetime Learning credits

(D) Denial of credit if student convicted of a felony drug offense. -- The Hope Scholarship Credit under subsection (a)(1) shall not be allowed for qualified tuition and related expenses for the enrollment or attendance of a student for any academic period if such student has been convicted of a Federal or State felony offense consisting of the possession or distribution of a controlled substance before the end of the taxable year with 5 or within which such period ends.

(3) Eligible student. -- For purposes of this subsection, the term "eligible student" means, with respect to any academic period, a student who--

(A) meets the requirements of section 484(a)(1) of the Higher Education Act of 1965 (20 U.S.C. 1091(a)(1)), as in effect on the date of the enactment of this section, and 10

(B) is carrying at least 1/2 the normal full-time work load for the course of study the student is pursuing.

(4) Applicable limit. -- For purposes of paragraph (1)(B), the applicable limit for any taxable year is an amount equal to 2 times the dollar amount in effect under paragraph (1)(A) for such taxable year. 15

(c) Lifetime Learning Credit. --

(1) Per taxpayer credit. -- The Lifetime Learning Credit for any taxpayer for any taxable year is an amount equal to 20 percent of so much of the qualified tuition and related expenses paid by the taxpayer during the taxable year (for education furnished during any academic period beginning in such taxable year) as does not exceed $10,000 ($5,000 in the case of 20 taxable years beginning before January 1, 2003).

(2) Special rules for determining expenses. --

(A) Coordination with Hope Scholarship. -- The qualified tuition and related expenses with respect to an individual who is an eligible student for whom a Hope Scholarship Credit under subsection (a)(1) is allowed for the taxable year shall not be taken into 25 account under this subsection.

(B) Expenses eligible for Lifetime Learning Credit. -- For purposes of paragraph (1), qualified tuition and related expenses shall include expenses described in subsection (f)(1) with respect to any course of instruction at an eligible educational institution to acquire or improve job skills of the individual. 30

(d) Limitation based on modified adjusted gross income. --

(1) In general. -- The amount which would (but for this subsection) be taken into account under subsection (a) for the taxable year shall be reduced (but not below zero) by the amount determined under paragraph (2).

(2) Amount of reduction. -- The amount determined under this paragraph is the amount 35 which bears the same ratio to the amount which would be so taken into account as--

(A) the excess of--

(i) the taxpayer's modified adjusted gross income for such taxable year, over

(ii) $40,000 ($80,000 in the case of a joint return), bears to

(B) $10,000 ($20,000 in the case of a joint return). 40

(3) Modified adjusted gross income. -- The term "modified adjusted gross income" means the adjusted gross income of the taxpayer for the taxable year increased by any amount excluded from gross income under section 911, 931, or 933.

(e) Election not to have section apply. -- A taxpayer may elect not to have this section apply with respect to the qualified tuition and related expenses of an individual for any taxable year. 45

(f) Definitions. -- For purposes of this section--

Sec. 25A. Hope and Lifetime Learning credits

(1) Qualified tuition and related expenses. --

(A) In general. -- The term "qualified tuition and related expenses" means tuition and fees required for the enrollment or attendance of--

(i) the taxpayer,

(ii) the taxpayer's spouse, or

(iii) any dependent of the taxpayer with respect to whom the taxpayer is allowed a deduction under section 151,at an eligible educational institution for courses of instruction of such individual at such institution.

(B) Exception for education involving sports, etc. -- Such term does not include expenses with respect to any course or other education involving sports, games, or hobbies, unless such course or other education is part of the individual's degree program.

(C) Exception for nonacademic fees. -- Such term does not include student activity fees, athletic fees, insurance expenses, or other expenses unrelated to an individual's academic course of instruction.

(2) Eligible educational institution. -- The term "eligible educational institution" means an institution--

(A) which is described in section 481 of the Higher Education Act of 1965 (20 U.S.C. 1088), as in effect on the date of the enactment of this section, and

(B) which is eligible to participate in a program under title IV of such Act.

(g) Special rules. --

(1) Identification requirement. -- No credit shall be allowed under subsection (a) to a taxpayer with respect to the qualified tuition and related expenses of an individual unless the taxpayer includes the name and taxpayer identification number of such individual on the return of tax for the taxable year.

(2) Adjustment for certain scholarships, etc. -- The amount of qualified tuition and related expenses otherwise taken into account under subsection (a) with respect to an individual for an academic period shall be reduced (before the application of subsections (b), (c), and (d)) by the sum of any amounts paid for the benefit of such individual which are allocable to such period as--

(A) a qualified scholarship which is excludable from gross income under section 117,

(B) an educational assistance allowance under chapter 30, 31, 32, 34, or 35 of title 38, United States Code, or under chapter 1606 of title 10, United States Code, and

(C) a payment (other than a gift, bequest, devise, or inheritance within the meaning of section 102(a)) for such individual's educational expenses, or attributable to such individual's enrollment at an eligible educational institution, which is excludable from gross income under any law of the United States.

(3) Treatment of expenses paid by dependent. -- If a deduction under section 151 with respect to an individual is allowed to another taxpayer for a taxable year beginning in the calendar year in which such individual's taxable year begins--

(A) no credit shall be allowed under subsection (a) to such individual for such individual's taxable year, and

(B) qualified tuition and related expenses paid by such individual during such individual's taxable year shall be treated for purposes of this section as paid by such other taxpayer.

(4) Treatment of certain prepayments. -- If qualified tuition and related expenses are paid by the taxpayer during a taxable year for an academic period which begins during the first 3

months following such taxable year, such academic period shall be treated for purposes of this section as beginning during such taxable year.

(5) Denial of double benefit. -- No credit shall be allowed under this section for any expense for which a deduction is allowed under any other provision of this chapter.

(6) No credit for married individuals filing separate returns. -- If the taxpayer is a married individual (within the meaning of section 7703), this section shall apply only if the taxpayer and the taxpayer's spouse file a joint return for the taxable year.

(7) Nonresident aliens. -- If the taxpayer is a nonresident alien individual for any portion of the taxable year, this section shall apply only if such individual is treated as a resident alien of the United States for purposes of this chapter by reason of an election under subsection (g) or (h) of section 6013.

(h) Inflation adjustments. --

(1) Dollar limitation on amount of credit. --

(A) In general. -- In the case of a taxable year beginning after 2001, each of the $1,000 amounts under subsection (b)(1) shall be increased by an amount equal to--

(i) such dollar amount, multiplied by

(ii) the cost-of-living adjustment determined under section 1(f)(3) for the calendar year in which the taxable year begins, determined by substituting "calendar year 2000" for "calendar year 1992" in subparagraph (B) thereof.

(B) Rounding. -- If any amount as adjusted under subparagraph (A) is not a multiple of $100, such amount shall be rounded to the next lowest multiple of $100.

(2) Income limits. --

(A) In general. -- In the case of a taxable year beginning after 2001, the $40,000 and $80,000 amounts in subsection (d)(2) shall each be increased by an amount equal to--

(i) such dollar amount, multiplied by

(ii) the cost-of-living adjustment determined under section 1(f)(3) for the calendar year in which the taxable year begins, determined by substituting "calendar year 2000" for "calendar year 1992" in subparagraph (B) thereof.

(B) Rounding. -- If any amount as adjusted under subparagraph (A) is not a multiple of $1,000, such amount shall be rounded to the next lowest multiple of $1,000.

(i) Regulations. -- The Secretary may prescribe such regulations as may be necessary or appropriate to carry out this section, including regulations providing for a recapture of the credit allowed under this section in cases where there is a refund in a subsequent taxable year of any amount which was taken into account in determining the amount of such credit.

Reg. § 1.25A-1   Calculation of education tax credit and general eligibility requirements.

(a) *Amount of education tax credit.* An individual taxpayer is allowed a nonrefundable education tax credit against income tax imposed by chapter 1 of the Internal Revenue Code for the taxable year. The amount of the education tax credit is the total of the Hope Scholarship Credit (as described in § 1.25A-3) plus the Lifetime Learning Credit (as described in § 1.25A-4). For limitations on the credits allowed by subpart A of part IV of subchapter A of chapter 1 of the Internal Revenue Code, see section 26.

(b) *Coordination of Hope Scholarship Credit and Lifetime Learning Credit*--(1) *In general.* In the same taxable year, a taxpayer may claim a Hope Scholarship Credit for each eligible student's qualified tuition and related expenses (as defined in § 1.25A-2(d)) and a Lifetime Learning Credit for one or more other students' qualified tuition and related

Sec. 25A. Hope and Lifetime Learning credits

expenses. However, a taxpayer may not claim both a Hope Scholarship Credit and a Lifetime Learning Credit with respect to the same student in the same taxable year.

(2) *Hope Scholarship Credit.* Subject to certain limitations, a Hope Scholarship Credit may be claimed for the qualified tuition and related expenses paid during a taxable year
5 with respect to each eligible student (as defined in § 1.25A-3(d)). Qualified tuition and related expenses paid during a taxable year with respect to one student may not be taken into account in computing the amount of the Hope Scholarship
Credit with respect to any other student. In addition, qualified tuition and related expenses paid during a taxable year with respect to any student for whom a Hope
10 Scholarship Credit is claimed may not be taken into account in computing the amount of the Lifetime Learning Credit.

(3) *Lifetime Learning Credit.* Subject to certain limitations, a Lifetime Learning Credit may be claimed for the aggregate amount of qualified tuition and related expenses paid during a taxable year with respect to students for whom no Hope Scholarship Credit is
15 claimed.

(4) *Examples.* The following examples illustrate the rules of this paragraph (b):

Example 1. In 1999, Taxpayer A pays qualified tuition and related expenses for his dependent, B, to attend College Y during 1999. Assuming all other relevant requirements are met, Taxpayer A may claim either a Hope Scholarship Credit or a Lifetime Learning
20 Credit with respect to dependent B, but not both. See § 1.25A-3(a) and § 1.25A-4(a).

Example 2. In 1999, Taxpayer C pays $2,000 in qualified tuition and related expenses for her dependent, D, to attend College Z during 1999. In 1999, Taxpayer C also pays $500 in qualified tuition and related expenses to attend a computer course during 1999 to improve Taxpayer C's job skills. Assuming all other relevant requirements are met,
25 Taxpayer C may claim a Hope Scholarship Credit for the $2,000 of qualified tuition and related expenses attributable to dependent D (see § 1.25A-3(a)) and a Lifetime Learning Credit (see § 1.25A-4(a)) for the $500 of qualified tuition and related expenses incurred to improve her job skills.

Example 3. The facts are the same as in Example 2, except that Taxpayer C pays
30 $3,000 in qualified tuition and related expenses for her dependent, D, to attend College Z during 1999. Although a Hope Scholarship Credit is available only with respect to the first $2,000 of qualified tuition and related expenses paid with respect to D (see § 1.25A-3(a)), Taxpayer C may not add the $1,000 of excess expenses to her $500 of qualified tuition and related expenses in computing the amount of the Lifetime Learning Credit.

35 (c) *Limitation based on modified adjusted gross income--*(1) *In general.* The education tax credit that a taxpayer may otherwise claim is phased out ratably for taxpayers with modified adjusted gross income between $40,000 and $50,000 ($80,000 and $100,000 for married individuals who file a joint return). Thus, taxpayers with modified adjusted gross income above $50,000 (or $100,000 for joint filers) may not claim an education tax
40 credit.

(2) *Modified adjusted gross income defined.* The term modified adjusted gross income means the adjusted gross income (as defined in section 62) of the taxpayer for the taxable year increased by any amount excluded from gross income under section 911, 931, or 933 (relating to income earned abroad or from certain U.S. possessions or Puerto
45 Rico).

(3) *Inflation adjustment.* For taxable years beginning after 2001, the amounts in paragraph (c)(1) of this section will be increased for inflation occurring after 2000 in accordance with section 1(f)(3). If any amount adjusted under this paragraph (c)(3) is not a multiple of $1,000, the amount will be rounded to the next lowest multiple of
50 $1,000.***

Sec. 25A. Hope and Lifetime Learning credits

(f) Claiming the credit in the case of a dependent--(1) In general. If a student is a claimed dependent of another taxpayer, only that taxpayer may claim the education tax credit for the student's qualified tuition and related expenses. However, if another taxpayer is eligible to, but does not, claim the student as a dependent, only the student may claim the education tax credit for the student's qualified tuition and related expenses. 5

(2) *Examples.* The following examples illustrate the rules of this paragraph (f):

Example 1. In 1999, Taxpayer A pays qualified tuition and related expenses for his dependent, B, to attend University Y during 1999. Taxpayer A claims B as a dependent on his federal income tax return. Therefore, assuming all other relevant requirements are met, Taxpayer A is allowed an education tax credit on his federal income tax return, and B 10 is not allowed an education tax credit on B's federal income tax return. The result would be the same if B paid the qualified tuition and related expenses. See § 1.25A-5(a).

Example 2. In 1999, Taxpayer C has one dependent, D. In 1999, D pays qualified tuition and related expenses to attend University Z during 1999. Although Taxpayer C is eligible to claim D as a dependent on her federal income tax return, she does not do so. 15 Therefore, assuming all other relevant requirements are met, D is allowed an education tax credit on D's federal income tax return, and Taxpayer C is not allowed an education tax credit on her federal income tax return, with respect to D's education expenses. The result would be the same if C paid the qualified tuition and related expenses on behalf of D. See § 1.25A-5(b). 20

(g) *Married taxpayers.* If a taxpayer is married (within the meaning of section 7703), no education tax credit is allowed to the taxpayer unless the taxpayer and the taxpayer's spouse file a joint Federal income tax return for the taxable year.

***

Reg. § 1.25A-2 Definitions. 25

(a) *Claimed dependent.* A claimed dependent means a dependent (as defined in section 152) for whom a deduction under section 151 is allowed on a taxpayer's federal income tax return for the taxable year. Among other requirements under section 152, a nonresident alien student must be a resident of a country contiguous to the United States in order to be treated as a dependent. 30

***

(c) *Academic period.* Academic period means a quarter, semester, trimester, or other period of study as reasonably determined by an eligible educational institution. In the case of an eligible educational institution that uses credit hours or clock hours, and does not have academic terms, each payment period (as defined in 34 CFR 668.4, revised as 35 of July 1, 2002) may be treated as an academic period.

(d) *Qualified tuition and related expenses*--(1) *In general.* Qualified tuition and related expenses means tuition and fees required for the enrollment or attendance of a student for courses of instruction at an eligible educational institution.

(2) *Required fees*--(i) *In general.* Except as provided in paragraph (d)(3) of this section, 40 the test for determining whether any fee is a qualified tuition and related expense is whether the fee is required to be paid to the eligible educational institution as a condition of the student's enrollment or attendance at the institution.

(ii) *Books, supplies, and equipment.* Qualified tuition and related expenses include fees for books, supplies, and equipment used in a course of study only if the fees must be 45 paid to the eligible educational institution for the enrollment or attendance of the student at the institution.

(iii) *Nonacademic fees.* Except as provided in paragraph (d)(3) of this section, qualified tuition and related expenses include fees charged by an eligible educational institution that are not used directly for, or allocated to, an academic course of instruction only if the 50 fee must be paid to the eligible educational institution for the enrollment or attendance of the student at the institution.

(3) *Personal expenses.* Qualified tuition and related expenses do not include the costs of room and board, insurance, medical expenses (including student health fees),
5 transportation, and similar personal, living, or family expenses, regardless of whether the fee must be paid to the eligible educational institution for the enrollment or attendance of the student at the institution.

(4) *Treatment of a comprehensive or bundled fee.* If a student is required to pay a fee (such as a comprehensive fee or a bundled fee) to an eligible educational institution that
10 combines charges for qualified tuition and related expenses with charges for personal expenses described in paragraph (d)(3) of this section, the portion of the fee that is allocable to personal expenses is not included in qualified tuition and related expenses. The determination of what portion of the fee relates to qualified tuition and related expenses and what portion relates to personal expenses must be made by the institution
15 using a reasonable method of allocation.

(5) *Hobby courses.* Qualified tuition and related expenses do not include expenses that relate to any course of instruction or other education that involves sports, games, or hobbies, or any noncredit course, unless the course or other education is part of the student's degree program, or in the case of the Lifetime Learning Credit, the student
20 takes the course to acquire or improve job skills.

(6) *Examples.* The following examples illustrate the rules of this paragraph (d). In each example, assume that the institution is an eligible educational institution and that all other relevant requirements to claim an education tax credit are met. The examples are as follows:
25 *Example 1.* University V offers a degree program in dentistry. In addition to tuition, all students enrolled in the program are required to pay a fee to University V for the rental of dental equipment. Because the equipment rental fee must be paid to University V for enrollment and attendance, the tuition and the equipment rental fee are qualified tuition and related expenses.
30 *Example 2.* First-year students at College W are required to obtain books and other reading materials used in its mandatory first-year curriculum. The books and other reading materials are not required to be purchased from College W and may be borrowed from other students or purchased from off-campus bookstores, as well as from College W's bookstore. College W bills students for any books and materials purchased from
35 College W's bookstore. The fee that College W charges for the first-year books and materials purchased at its bookstore is not a qualified tuition and related expense because the books and materials are not required to be purchased from College W for enrollment or attendance at the institution.

Example 3. All students who attend College X are required to pay a separate student
40 activity fee in addition to their tuition. The student activity fee is used solely to fund on-campus organizations and activities run by students, such as the student newspaper and the student government (no portion of the fee covers personal expenses). Although labeled as a student activity fee, the fee is required for enrollment or attendance at College X. Therefore, the fee is a qualified tuition and related expense.
45 *Example 4.* The facts are the same as in Example 3, except that College X offers an optional athletic fee that students may pay to receive discounted tickets to sports events. The athletic fee is not required for enrollment or attendance at College X. Therefore, the fee is not a qualified tuition and related expense.

Example 5. College Y requires all students to live on campus. It charges a single
50 comprehensive fee to cover tuition, required fees, and room and board. Based on College Y's reasonable allocation, sixty percent of the comprehensive fee is allocable to

tuition and other required fees not allocable to personal expenses, and the remaining forty percent of the comprehensive fee is allocable to charges for room and board and other personal expenses. Therefore, only sixty percent of College Y's comprehensive fee is a qualified tuition and related expense.

Example 6. As a degree student at College Z, Student A is required to take a certain 5 number of courses outside of her chosen major in Economics. To fulfill this requirement, Student A enrolls in a square dancing class offered by the Physical Education Department. Because Student A receives credit toward her degree program for the square dancing class, the tuition for the square dancing class is included in qualified tuition and related expenses.   10

Reg. § 1.25A-3   Hope Scholarship Credit.

***

(b) *Per student credit*--(1) *In general.* A Hope Scholarship Credit may be claimed for the qualified tuition and related expenses of each eligible student (as defined in 15 paragraph (d) of this section).

***

(c) *Credit allowed for only two taxable years.* For each eligible student, the Hope Scholarship Credit may be claimed for no more than two taxable years.

(d) *Eligible student*--(1) *Eligible student defined.* For purposes of the Hope Scholarship 20 Credit, the term eligible student means a student who satisfies all of the following requirements--

(i) *Degree requirement.* For at least one academic period that begins during the taxable year, the student enrolls at an eligible educational institution in a program leading toward a postsecondary degree, certificate, or other recognized postsecondary 25 educational credential;

(ii) *Work load requirement.* For at least one academic period that begins during the taxable year, the student enrolls for at least one-half of the normal full-time work load for the course of study the student is pursuing. The standard for what is half of the normal full-time work load is determined by each eligible educational institution. However, the 30 standard for half-time may not be lower than the applicable standard for half-time established by the Department of Education under the Higher Education Act of 1965 and set forth in 34 CFR 674.2(b) (revised as of July 1, 2002) for a half-time undergraduate student;

(iii) *Year of study requirement.* As of the beginning of the taxable year, the student has 35 not completed the first two years of postsecondary education at an eligible educational institution. Whether a student has completed the first two years of postsecondary education at an eligible educational institution as of the beginning of a taxable year is determined based on whether the institution in which the student is enrolled in a degree program (as described in paragraph (d)(1)(i) of this section) awards the student two years 40 of academic credit at that institution for postsecondary course work completed by the student prior to the beginning of the taxable year. Any academic credit awarded by the eligible educational institution solely on the basis of the student's performance on proficiency examinations is disregarded in determining whether the student has completed two years of postsecondary education; and   45

(iv) *No felony drug conviction.* The student has not been convicted of a Federal or State felony offense for possession or distribution of a controlled substance as of the end of the taxable year for which the credit is claimed.

***

(e) *Academic period for prepayments*--(1) *In general.* For purposes of determining 50

Sec. 25A.   Hope and Lifetime Learning credits

whether a student meets the requirements in paragraph (d) of this section for a taxable year, if qualified tuition and related expenses are paid during one taxable year for an academic period that begins during January, February or March of the next taxable year (for taxpayers on a fiscal taxable year, use the first three months of the next taxable year), the academic period is treated as beginning during the taxable year in which the payment is made.

***

Reg. § 1.25A-4   Lifetime Learning Credit.

(a) *Amount of the credit--*

***

(3) *Coordination with the Hope Scholarship Credit.* Expenses paid with respect to a student for whom the Hope Scholarship Credit is claimed are not eligible for the Lifetime Learning Credit.

[T.D. 9034, 67 FR 78691, Dec. 26, 2002; 68 FR 15940, Apr. 2, 2003]

Sec. 25B.   Elective deferrals and IRA contributions by certain individuals

(a) **Allowance of credit.** -- In the case of an eligible individual, there shall be allowed as a credit against the tax imposed by this subtitle for the taxable year an amount equal to the applicable percentage of so much of the qualified retirement savings contributions of the eligible individual for the taxable year as do not exceed $2,000.

(b) **Applicable percentage.** -- For purposes of this section, the applicable percentage is the percentage determined in accordance with the following table:

Adjusted Gross Income						Applicable
Joint return		Head of a household		All other cases		Percentage
Over	Not over	Over	Not over	Over	Not over	
	$30,000		$22,500		$15,000	50
30,000	32,500	22,500	24,375	15,000	16,250	20
32,500	50,000	24,375	37,500	16,250	25,000	10
50,000		37,500		25,000		0

(c) **Eligible individual.** -- For purposes of this section--

(1) **In general.** -- The term "eligible individual" means any individual if such individual has attained the age of 18 as of the close of the taxable year.

(2) **Dependents and full-time students not eligible.** -- The term "eligible individual" shall not include -

(A) any individual with respect to whom a deduction under section 151 is allowed to another taxpayer for a taxable year beginning in the calendar year in which such individual's taxable year begins, and

(B) any individual who is a student (as defined in section152(f)(2)).

(d) **Qualified retirement savings contributions.** -- For purposes of this section--

(1) **In general.** -- The term "qualified retirement savings contributions" means, with respect to any taxable year, the sum of--

(A) the amount of the qualified retirement contributions (as defined in section 219(e)) made by the eligible individual,

    (B) the amount of -

        (i) any elective deferrals (as defined in section 402(g)(3)) of such individual, and

        (ii) any elective deferral of compensation by such individual under an eligible deferred compensation plan (as defined in section 457(b)) of an eligible employer described in section 457(e)(1)(A), and

    (C) the amount of voluntary employee contributions by such individual to any qualified retirement plan (as defined in section 4974(c)).

  (2) Reduction for certain distributions.---

    (A) In general. -- The qualified retirement savings contributions determined under paragraph (1) shall be reduced (but not below zero) by the aggregate distributions received by the individual during the testing period from any entity of a type to which contributions under paragraph (1) may be made. The preceding sentence shall not apply to the portion of any distribution which is not includible in gross income by reason of a trustee-to-trustee transfer or a rollover distribution.

    (B) Testing period. -- For purposes of subparagraph (A), the testing period, with respect to a taxable year, is the period which includes--

        (i) such taxable year,

        (ii) the 2 preceding taxable years, and

        (iii) the period after such taxable year and before the due date (including extensions) for filing the return of tax for such taxable year.

    (C) Excepted distributions. -- There shall not be taken into account under subparagraph (A)--

        (i) any distribution referred to in section 72(p), 401(k)(8), 401(m)(6), 402(g)(2), 404(k), or 408(d)(4), and

        (ii) any distribution to which section 408A(d)(3) applies.

    (D) Treatment of distributions received by spouse of individual. -- For purposes of determining distributions received by an individual under subparagraph (A) for any taxable year, any distribution received by the spouse of such individual shall be treated as received by such individual if such individual and spouse file a joint return for such taxable year and for the taxable year during which the spouse receives the distribution.

  (e) Adjusted gross income. -- For purposes of this section, adjusted gross income shall be determined without regard to sections 911, 931, and 933.

  (f) Investment in the contract. --   Notwithstanding any other provision of law, a qualified retirement savings contribution shall not fail to be included in determining the investment in the contract for purposes of section 72 by reason of the credit under this section.

  (g) Limitation based on amount of tax. -- In the case of a taxable year to which section 26(a)(2) does not apply, the credit allowed under subsection (a) for the taxable year shall not exceed the excess of--

    (1) the sum of the regular tax liability (as defined in section 26(b)) plus the tax imposed by section 55, over

    (2) the sum of the credits allowable under this subpart (other than this section and section 23) and section 27 for the taxable year.

  (h) Termination. -- This section shall not apply to taxable years beginning after December 31, 2006.

Sec. 25C. Nonbusiness energy property

(a) Allowance of Credit. -- In the case of an individual, there shall be allowed as a credit against the tax imposed by this chapter for the taxable year an amount equal to the sum of--

(1) 10 percent of the amount paid or incurred by the taxpayer for qualified energy efficiency improvements installed during such taxable year, and

(2) the amount of the residential energy property expenditures paid or incurred by the taxpayer during such taxable year.

(b) Limitations. --

(1) Lifetime limitation. -- The credit allowed under this section with respect to any taxpayer for any taxable year shall not exceed the excess (if any) of $500 over the aggregate credits allowed under this section with respect to such taxpayer for all prior taxable years.

(2) Windows. -- In the case of amounts paid or incurred for components described in subsection (c)(3)(B) by any taxpayer for any taxable year, the credit allowed under this section with respect to such amounts for such year shall not exceed the excess (if any) of $200 over the aggregate credits allowed under this section with respect to such amounts for all prior taxable years.

(3) Limitation on residential energy property expenditures. -- The amount of the credit allowed under this section by reason of subsection (a)(2) shall not exceed--

(A) $50 for any advanced main air circulating fan,

(B) $150 for any qualified natural gas, propane,
or oil furnace or hot water boiler, and

(C) $300 for any item of energy-efficient building property.

(c) Qualified Energy Efficiency Improvements. -- For purposes of this section--

(1) In general. -- The term `qualified energy efficiency improvements' means any energy efficient building envelope component which meets the prescriptive criteria for such component established by the 2000 International Energy Conservation Code, as such Code (including supplements) is in effect on the date of the enactment of this section (or, in the case of a metal roof with appropriate pigmented coatings which meet the Energy Star program requirements), if--

(A) such component is installed in or on a dwelling unit located in the United States and owned and used by the taxpayer as the taxpayer's principal residence (within the meaning of section 121),

(B) the original use of such component commences with the taxpayer, and

(C) such component reasonably can be expected to remain in use for at least 5 years.

***

(d) Residential Energy Property Expenditures. -- For purposes of this section--

(1) In general. -- The term `residential energy property expenditures' means expenditures made by the taxpayer for qualified energy property which is--

(A) installed on or in connection with a dwelling unit located in the United States and owned and used by the taxpayer as the taxpayer's principal residence (within the meaning of section 121), and

(B) originally placed in service by the taxpayer. Such term includes expenditures for labor costs properly allocable to the onsite preparation, assembly, or original installation of the property.

Sec. 25C. Nonbusiness energy property

(2) Qualified energy property. --

    (A) In general. -- The term `qualified energy property' means--

        (i) energy-efficient building property,

        (ii) a qualified natural gas, propane, or oil furnace or hot water boiler, or

        (iii) an advanced main air circulating fan.   5

    (B) Performance and quality standards. -- Property described under subparagraph (A) shall meet the performance and quality standards, and the certification requirements (if any), which--

        (i) have been prescribed by the Secretary by regulations (after consultation with the Secretary of Energy or the Administrator of the Environmental Protection Agency, as 10 appropriate), and

        (ii) are in effect at the time of the acquisition of the property, or at the time of the completion of the construction, reconstruction, or erection of the property, as the case may be.

***

    15

(3) Energy-efficient building property. -- The term `energy- efficient building property' means--

    (A) an electric heat pump water heater which yields an energy factor of at least 2.0 in the standard Department of Energy test procedure,

    (B) an electric heat pump which has a heating seasonal performance factor (HSPF) of at 20 least 9, a seasonal energy efficiency ratio (SEER) of at least 15, and an energy efficiency ratio (EER) of at least 13,

    (C) a geothermal heat pump which--

        (i) in the case of a closed loop product, has an energy efficiency ratio (EER) of at least 14.1 and a heating coefficient of performance (COP) of at least 3.3,   25

        (ii) in the case of an open loop product, has an energy efficiency ratio (EER) of at least 16.2 and a heating coefficient of performance (COP) of at least 3.6, and

        (iii) in the case of a direct expansion (DX) product, has an energy efficiency ratio (EER) of at least 15 and a heating coefficient of performance (COP) of at least 3.5,

    (D) a central air conditioner which achieves the highest efficiency tier established by the 30 Consortium for Energy Efficiency, as in effect on January 1, 2006, and

    (E) a natural gas, propane, or oil water heater which has an energy factor of at least 0.80.

(4) Qualified natural gas, propane, or oil furnace or hot water boiler. -- The term qualified natural gas, propane, or oil furnace or hot water boiler' means a natural gas, propane, or oil furnace or hot water boiler which achieves an annual fuel utilization efficiency rate of 35 not less than 95.

(5) Advanced main air circulating fan. -- The term `advanced main air circulating fan' means a fan used in a natural gas, propane, or oil furnace and which has an annual electricity use of no more than 2 percent of the total annual energy use of the furnace (as determined in the standard Department of Energy test procedures).   40

  (f) Basis Adjustments. -- For purposes of this subtitle, if a credit is allowed under this section for any expenditure with respect to any property, the increase in the basis of such property which would (but for this subsection) result from such expenditure shall be reduced by the amount of the credit so allowed.

  (g) Termination. -- This section shall not apply with respect to any property placed in service 45 after December 31, 2007.

Sec. 25C. Nonbusiness energy property

Sec. 25D. Residential energy efficient property

(a) **Allowance of Credit.** -- In the case of an individual, there shall be allowed as a credit against the tax imposed by this chapter for the taxable year an amount equal to the sum of--

5   (1) 30 percent of the qualified solar electric property expenditures made by the taxpayer during such year,

(2) 30 percent of the qualified solar water heating property expenditures made by the taxpayer during such year, and

(3) 30 percent of the qualified fuel cell property expenditures made by the taxpayer during
10   such year.

(b) **Limitations.** --

(1) **Maximum credit.** -- The credit allowed under subsection (a) for any taxable year shall not exceed--

(A) $2,000 with respect to any qualified solar electric property expenditures,

15   (B) $2,000 with respect to any qualified solar water heating property expenditures, and

(C) $500 with respect to each half kilowatt of capacity of qualified fuel cell property (as defined in section 48(c)(1)) for which qualified fuel cell property expenditures are made.

(2) **Certification of solar water heating property.** -- No credit shall be allowed under this section for an item of property described in subsection (d)(1) unless such property is certified
20   for performance by the non-profit Solar Rating Certification Corporation or a comparable entity endorsed by the government of the State in which such property is installed.

(c) **Carryforward of Unused Credit.** -- If the credit allowable under subsection (a) exceeds the limitation imposed by section 26(a) for such taxable year reduced by the sum of the credits allowable under this subpart (other than this section), such excess shall be carried to the
25   succeeding taxable year and added to the credit allowable under subsection (a) for such succeeding taxable year.

(d) **Definitions.**--For purposes of this section--

(1) **Qualified solar water heating property expenditure.** -- The term `qualified solar water heating property expenditure' means an expenditure for property to heat water for use in a
30   dwelling unit located in the United States and used as a residence by the taxpayer if at least half of the energy used by such property for such purpose is derived from the sun.

(2) **Qualified solar electric property property expenditure.** -- The term `qualified solar electric property property expenditure' means an expenditure for property which uses solar energy to generate electricity for use in a dwelling unit located in the United States and used as
35   a residence by the taxpayer.

(3) **Qualified fuel cell property expenditure.** -- The term qualified fuel cell property expenditure' means an expenditure for qualified fuel cell property (as defined in section 48(c)(1)) installed on or in connection with a dwelling unit located in the United States and used as a principal residence (within the meaning of section 121) by the taxpayer.

40   (e) **Special Rules.** -- For purposes of this section--

***

(7) **Allocation in certain cases.** -- If less than 80 percent of the use of an item is for nonbusiness purposes, only that portion of the expenditures for such item which is properly allocable to use for nonbusiness purposes shall be taken into account.

Sec. 25D.   Residential energy efficient property

***

(f) Basis Adjustments. -- For purposes of this subtitle, if a credit is allowed under this section for any expenditure with respect to any property, the increase in the basis of such property which would (but for this subsection) result from such expenditure shall be reduced by the amount of the credit so allowed. 5

(g) Termination. -- The credit allowed under this section shall not apply to property placed in service after December 31, 2008.

Sec. 26.   Limitation based on tax liability; definition of tax liability

(a) Limitation based on amount of tax. -- 10

(1) In general. -- The aggregate amount of credits allowed by this subpart (other than sections 23, 24, and 25B) for the taxable year shall not exceed the excess (if any) of--

(A) the taxpayer's regular tax liability for the taxable year, over

(B) the tentative minimum tax for the taxable year (determined without regard to the alternative minimum tax foreign tax credit). 15

For purposes of subparagraph (B), the taxpayer's tentative minimum tax for any taxable year beginning during 1999 shall be treated as being zero.

(2) Special rule for taxable years 2000 through 2007. -- For purposes of any taxable year beginning during 2000, 2001, 2002, 2003, 2004, 2005, 2006, or 2007, the aggregate amount of credits allowed by this subpart for the taxable year shall not exceed the sum of-- 20

(A) the taxpayer's regular tax liability for the taxable year reduced by the foreign tax credit allowable under section 27(a), and

(B) the tax imposed by section 55(a) for the taxable year.

(b) Regular tax liability. -- For purposes of this part--

(1) In general. -- The term "regular tax liability" means the tax imposed by this chapter for 25 the taxable year.

(2) Exception for certain taxes. -- For purposes of paragraph (1), any tax imposed by any of the following provisions shall not be treated as tax imposed by this chapter:

(A) section 55 (relating to minimum tax),

(B) section 59A (relating to environmental tax), 30

(C) subsection (m)(5)(B), (q), (t), or (v) of section 72 (relating to additional taxes on certain distributions),

(D) section 143(m) (relating to recapture of proration of Federal subsidy from use of mortgage bonds and mortgage credit certificates),

(E) section 530(d)(3) (relating to additional tax on certain distributions from Coverdell 35 education savings accounts),

(F) section 531 (relating to accumulated earnings tax),

(G) section 541 (relating to personal holding company tax),

(H) section 1351(d)(1) (relating to recoveries of foreign expropriation losses),

(I) section 1374 (relating to tax on certain built-in gains of S corporations), 40

(J) section 1375 (relating to tax imposed when passive investment income of corporation having subchapter C earnings and profits exceeds 25 percent of gross receipts),

Sec. 26.   Limitation based on tax liability; definition of tax liability

(**K**) subparagraph (A) of section 7518(g)(6) (relating to nonqualified withdrawals from capital construction funds taxed at highest marginal rate),

(**L**) sections 871(a) and 881 (relating to certain income of nonresident aliens and foreign corporations),

(**M**) section 860E(e) (relating to taxes with respect to certain residual interests),

(**N**) section 884 (relating to branch profits tax),

(**O**) sections 453(l)(3) and 453A(c) (relating to interest on certain deferred tax liabilities),

(**P**) section 860K (!1) (relating to treatment of transfers of high-yield interests to disqualified holders),

(**Q**) section 220(f)(4) (relating to additional tax on Archer MSA distributions not used for qualified medical expenses),

(**R**) section 138(c)(2) (relating to penalty for distributions from Medicare Advantage MSA not used for qualified medical expenses if minimum balance not maintained),

(**S**) sections 106(e)(3)(A)(ii), 223(b)(8)(B)(i)(II), and 408(d)(9)(D)(i)(II) (relating to certain failures to maintain high deductible health plan coverage),

(**T**) section 170(o)(3)(B) (relating to recapture of certain deductions for fractional gifts),

(**U**) section 223(f)(4) (relating to additional tax on health savings account distributions not used for qualified medical expenses). and

(**V**) subsections (a)(1)(B)(i) and (b)(4)(A) of section 409 (relating to interest and additional tax with respect to certain deferred compensation).

(**c**) **Tentative minimum tax.** -- For purposes of this part, the term "tentative minimum tax" means the amount determined under section 55(b)(1).

Sec. 30B.   Alternative motor vehicle credit

(**a**) **Allowance of Credit.** -- There shall be allowed as a credit gainst the tax imposed by this chapter for the taxable year an amount equal to the sum of--

(**1**) the new qualified fuel cell motor vehicle credit determined under subsection (b),

(**2**) the new advanced lean burn technology motor vehicle credit determined under subsection (c),

(**3**) the new qualified hybrid motor vehicle credit determined under subsection (d), and

(**4**) the new qualified alternative fuel motor vehicle credit determined under subsection (e).

(**b**) **New Qualified Fuel Cell Motor Vehicle Credit.** --

(**1**) **In general**. -- For purposes of subsection (a), the new qualified fuel cell motor vehicle credit determined under this subsection with respect to a new qualified fuel cell motor vehicle placed in service by the taxpayer during the taxable year is--

(**A**) $8,000 ($4,000 in the case of a vehicle placed in service after December 31, 2009), if such vehicle has a gross vehicle weight rating of not more than 8,500 pounds,

(**B**) $10,000, if such vehicle has a gross vehicle weight rating of more than 8,500 pounds but not more than 14,000 pounds,

(**C**) $20,000, if such vehicle has a gross vehicle weight rating of more than 14,000 pounds but not more than 26,000 pounds, and

Sec. 30B. Alternative motor vehicle credit

(D) $40,000, if such vehicle has a gross vehicle weight rating of more than 26,000 pounds.

(2) Increase for fuel efficiency. --

(A) In general. -- The amount determined under paragraph (1)(A) with respect to a new qualified fuel cell motor vehicle which is a passenger automobile or light truck shall be increased by--

(i) $1,000, if such vehicle achieves at least 150 percent but less than 175 percent of the 2002 model year city fuel economy,

(ii) $1,500, if such vehicle achieves at least 175 percent but less than 200 percent of the 2002 model year city fuel economy,

(iii) $2,000, if such vehicle achieves at least 200 percent but less than 225 percent of the 2002 model year city fuel economy,

(iv) $2,500, if such vehicle achieves at least 225 percent but less than 250 percent of the 2002 model year city fuel economy,

(v) $3,000, if such vehicle achieves at least 250 percent but less than 275 percent of the 2002 model year city fuel economy,

(vi) $3,500, if such vehicle achieves at least 275 percent but less than 300 percent of the 2002 model year city fuel economy, and

(vii) $4,000, if such vehicle achieves at least 300 percent of the 2002 model year city fuel economy.

(B) 2002 model year city fuel economy. -- For purposes of subparagraph (A), the 2002 model year city fuel economy with respect to a vehicle shall be determined in accordance with the following tables:

(i) In the case of a passenger automobile:

If vehicle inertia fuel economy is:	The 2002 model year city class is:
1,500 or 1,750 lbs.............................	45.2 mpg
2,000 lbs...	39.6 mpg
2,250 lbs...	35.2 mpg
2,500 lbs...	31.7 mpg
2,750 lbs...	28.8 mpg
3,000 lbs...	26.4 mpg
3,500 lbs...	22.6 mpg
4,000 lbs...	19.8 mpg
4,500 lbs...	17.6 mpg
5,000 lbs...	15.9 mpg
5,500 lbs...	14.4 mpg
6,000 lbs...	13.2 mpg
6,500 lbs...	12.2 mpg
7,000 to 8,500 lbs.............................	11.3 mpg.

Sec. 30B. Alternative motor vehicle credit

(ii) In the case of a light truck:

If vehicle inertia fuel economy is:	The 2002 model year city class is:
1,500 or 1,750 lbs............................	39.4 mpg
2,000 lbs..	35.2 mpg
2,250 lbs..	31.8 mpg
2,500 lbs..	29.0 mpg
2,750 lbs..	26.8 mpg
3,000 lbs..	24.9 mpg
3,500 lbs..	21.8 mpg
4,000 lbs..	19.4 mpg
4,500 lbs..	17.6 mpg
5,000 lbs..	16.1 mpg
5,500 lbs..	14.8 mpg
6,000 lbs..	13.7 mpg
6,500 lbs..	12.8 mpg
7,000 to 8,500 lbs.............................	12.1 mpg.

(C) **Vehicle inertia weight class.** -- For purposes of subparagraph (B), the term `vehicle inertia weight class' has the same meaning as when defined in regulations prescribed by the Administrator of the Environmental Protection Agency for purposes of the administration of title II of the Clean Air Act (42 U.S.C. 7521 et seq.).

(3) **New qualified fuel cell motor vehicle.** -- For purposes of this subsection, the term `new qualified fuel cell motor vehicle' means a motor vehicle--

(A) which is propelled by power derived from 1 or more cells which convert chemical energy directly into electricity by combining oxygen with hydrogen fuel which is stored on board the vehicle in any form and may or may not require reformation prior to use,

(B) which, in the case of a passenger automobile or light truck, has received on or after the date of the enactment of this section a certificate that such vehicle meets or exceeds the Bin 5 Tier II emission level established in regulations prescribed by the Administrator of the Environmental Protection Agency under section 202(i) of the Clean Air Act for that make and model year vehicle,

(C) the original use of which commences with the taxpayer,

(D) which is acquired for use or lease by the taxpayer and not for resale, and

(E) which is made by a manufacturer.

(c) **New Advanced Lean Burn Technology Motor Vehicle Credit.** --

(1) **In general.** -- For purposes of subsection (a), the new advanced lean burn technology motor vehicle credit determined under this subsection for the taxable year is the credit amount determined under paragraph (2) with respect to a new advanced lean burn technology motor vehicle placed in service by the taxpayer during the taxable year.

(2) **Credit amount.** --

(A) **Fuel economy.** --

(i) **In general.** -- The credit amount determined under this paragraph shall be

Sec. 30B. Alternative motor vehicle credit

determined in accordance with the following table:

In the case of a vehicle which achieves a fuel economy (expressed as a percentage of the 2002 model year city fuel economy) of--	The credit amount is--
At least 125 percent but less than 150 percent..	$400
At least 150 percent but less than 175 percent..	$800
At least 175 percent but less than 200 percent..	$1,200
At least 200 percent but less than 225 percent..	$1,600
At least 225 percent but less than 250 percent..	$2,000
At least 250 percent..	$2,400.

(ii) 2002 model year city fuel economy. -- For purposes of clause (i), the 2002 model year city fuel economy with respect to a vehicle shall be determined on a gasoline gallon equivalent basis as determined by the Administrator of the Environmental Protection Agency using the tables provided in subsection (b)(2)(B) with respect to such vehicle.

(B) Conservation credit. -- The amount determined under subparagraph (A) with respect to a new advanced lean burn technology motor vehicle shall be increased by the conservation credit amount determined in accordance with the following table:

In the case of a vehicle which achieves a lifetime fuel savings (expressed in gallons of gasoline) of--	The conservation credit amount is--
At least 1,200 but less than 1,800.............................	$250
At least 1,800 but less than 2,400.............................	$500
At least 2,400 but less than 3,000.............................	$750
At least 3,000...	$1,000.

(3) New advanced lean burn technology motor vehicle. -- For purposes of this subsection, the term `new advanced lean burn technology motor vehicle' means a passenger automobile or a light truck--

(A) with an internal combustion engine which--

(i) is designed to operate primarily using more air than is necessary for complete combustion of the fuel,

(ii) incorporates direct injection,

(iii) achieves at least 125 percent of the 2002 model year city fuel economy,

51

Sec. 30B. Alternative motor vehicle credit

(iv) for 2004 and later model vehicles, has received a certificate that such vehicle meets or exceeds--

(I) in the case of a vehicle having a gross vehicle weight rating of 6,000 pounds or less, the Bin 5 Tier II emission standard established in regulations prescribed by the Administrator of the Environmental Protection Agency under section 202(i) of the Clean Air Act for that make and model year vehicle, and (II) in the case of a vehicle having a gross vehicle weight rating of more than 6,000 pounds but not more than 8,500 pounds, the Bin 8 Tier II emission standard which is so established,

(B) the original use of which commences with the taxpayer,

(C) which is acquired for use or lease by the taxpayer and not for resale, and

(D) which is made by a manufacturer.

(4) **Lifetime fuel savings.** -- For purposes of this subsection, the term `lifetime fuel savings' means, in the case of any new advanced lean burn technology motor vehicle, an amount equal to the excess (if any) of--

(A) 120,000 divided by the 2002 model year city fuel economy for the vehicle inertia weight class, over

(B) 120,000 divided by the city fuel economy for such vehicle.

(d) New Qualified Hybrid Motor Vehicle Credit. --

(1) **In general.** -- For purposes of subsection (a), the new qualified hybrid motor vehicle credit determined under this subsection for the taxable year is the credit amount determined under paragraph (2) with respect to a new qualified hybrid motor vehicle placed in service by the taxpayer during the taxable year.

(2) **Credit amount.** --

(A) Credit amount for passenger automobiles and light trucks.--In the case of a new qualified hybrid motor vehicle which is a passenger automobile or light truck and which has a gross vehicle weight rating of not more than 8,500 pounds, the amount determined under this paragraph is the sum of the amounts determined under clauses (i) and (ii).

(i) **Fuel economy.** -- The amount determined under this clause is the amount which would be determined under subsection (c)(2)(A) if such vehicle were a vehicle referred to in such subsection.

(ii) **Conservation credit.** -- The amount determined under this clause is the amount which would be determined under subsection (c)(2)(B) if such vehicle were a vehicle referred to in such subsection.

(B) **Credit amount for other motor vehicles.** --

(i) **In general.** -- In the case of any new qualified hybrid motor vehicle to which subparagraph (A) does not apply, the amount determined under this paragraph is the amount equal to the applicable percentage of the qualified incremental hybrid cost of the vehicle as certified under clause (v).

(ii) **Applicable percentage.** -- For purposes of clause (i), the applicable percentage is--

(I) 20 percent if the vehicle achieves an increase in city fuel economy relative to a comparable vehicle of at least 30 percent but less than 40 percent,

(II) 30 percent if the vehicle achieves such an increase of at least 40 percent but less than 50 percent, and

  (III) 40 percent if the vehicle achieves such an increase of at least 50 percent.

  (iii) Qualified incremental hybrid cost. -- For purposes of this subparagraph, the qualified incremental hybrid cost of any vehicle is equal to the amount of the excess of the manufacturer's suggested retail price for such vehicle over such price for a comparable vehicle, to the extent such amount does not exceed-- 5

  (I) $7,500, if such vehicle has a gross vehicle weight rating of not more than 14,000 pounds,

  (II) $15,000, if such vehicle has gross vehicle weight rating of more than 14,000 pounds but not more than 26,000 pounds, and 10

  (III) $30,000, if such vehicle has a gross vehicle weight rating of more than 26,000 pounds.

(3) New qualified hybrid motor vehicle. -- For purposes of this subsection--

  (A) In general. -- The term `new qualified hybrid motor vehicle' means a motor vehicle-- 15

  (i) which draws propulsion energy from onboard sources of stored energy which are both--

  (I) an internal combustion or heat engine using consumable fuel, and

  (II) a rechargeable energy storage system,

  (ii) which, in the case of a vehicle to which paragraph (2)(A) applies, has received a 20 certificate of conformity under the Clean Air Act and meets or exceeds the equivalent qualifying California low emission vehicle standard under section 243(e)(2) of the Clean Air Act for that make and model year, and

  (I) in the case of a vehicle having a gross vehicle weight rating of 6,000 pounds or less, the Bin 5 Tier II emission standard established in regulations 25 prescribed by the Administrator of the Environmental Protection Agency under section 202(i) of the Clean Air Act for that make and model year vehicle, and

  (II) in the case of a vehicle having a gross vehicle weight rating of more than 6,000 pounds but not more than 8,500 pounds, the Bin 8 Tier II emission standard which is so established, 30

  (iii) which has a maximum available power of at least--

  (I) 4 percent in the case of a vehicle to which paragraph (2)(A) applies,

  (II) 10 percent in the case of a vehicle which has a gross vehicle weight rating of more than 8,500 pounds and not more than 14,000 pounds, and

  (III) 15 percent in the case of a vehicle in excess of 14,000 pounds, 35

  (iv) which, in the case of a vehicle to which paragraph (2)(B) applies, has an internal combustion or heat engine which has received a certificate of conformity under the Clean Air Act as meeting the emission standards set in the regulations prescribed by the Administrator of the Environmental Protection Agency for 2004 through 2007 model year diesel heavy duty engines or motorcycle heavy duty engines, as applicable, 40

  (v) the original use of which commences with the taxpayer,

  (vi) which is acquired for use or lease by the taxpayer and not for resale, and

  (vii) which is made by a manufacturer.

Such term shall not include any vehicle which is not a passenger automobile or light truck if such vehicle has a gross vehicle weight rating of less than 8,500 pounds. 45

Sec. 30B. Alternative motor vehicle credit

(B) Consumable fuel. -- For purposes of subparagraph (A)(i)(I), the term `consumable fuel' means any solid, liquid, or gaseous matter which releases energy when consumed by an auxiliary power unit.

(C) Maximum available power. --

(i) Certain passenger automobiles and light trucks. -- In the case of a vehicle to which paragraph (2)(A) applies, the term `maximum available power' means the maximum power available from the rechargeable energy storage system, during a standard 10 second pulse power or equivalent test, divided by such maximum power and the SAE net power of the heat engine.

(ii) Other motor vehicles. -- In the case of a vehicle to which paragraph (2)(B) applies, the term `maximum available power' means the maximum power available from the rechargeable energy storage system, during a standard 10 second pulse power or equivalent test, divided by the vehicle's total traction power. For purposes of the preceding sentence, the term `total traction power' means the sum of the peak power from the rechargeable energy storage system and the heat engine peak power of the vehicle, except that if such storage system is the sole means by which the vehicle can be driven, the total traction power is the peak power of such storage system.

(e) New Qualified Alternative Fuel Motor Vehicle Credit . --

(1) Allowance of credit. -- Except as provided in paragraph (5), the new qualified alternative fuel motor vehicle credit determined under this subsection is an amount equal to the applicable percentage of the incremental cost of any new qualified alternative fuel motor vehicle placed in service by the taxpayer during the taxable year.

(2) Applicable percentage. -- For purposes of paragraph (1), the applicable percentage with respect to any new qualified alternative fuel motor vehicle is--

(A) 50 percent, plus

(B) 30 percent, if such vehicle--

(i) has received a certificate of conformity under the Clean Air Act and meets or exceeds the most stringent standard available for certification under the Clean Air Act for that make and model year vehicle (other than a zero emission standard), or

(ii) has received an order certifying the vehicle as meeting the same requirements as vehicles which may be sold or leased in California and meets or exceeds the most stringent standard available for certification under the State laws of California (enacted in accordance with a waiver granted under section 209(b) of the Clean Air Act) for that make and model year vehicle (other than a zero emission standard).

For purposes of the preceding sentence, in the case of any new qualified alternative fuel motor vehicle which weighs more than 14,000 pounds gross vehicle weight rating, the most stringent standard available shall be such standard available for certification on the date of the enactment of the Energy Tax Incentives Act of 2005.

(3) Incremental cost. -- For purposes of this subsection, the incremental cost of any new qualified alternative fuel motor vehicle is equal to the amount of the excess of the manufacturer's suggested retail price for such vehicle over such price for a gasoline or diesel fuel motor vehicle of the same model, to the extent such amount does not exceed--

(A) $5,000, if such vehicle has a gross vehicle weight rating of not more than 8,500 pounds,

(B) $10,000, if such vehicle has a gross vehicle weight rating of more than 8,500 pounds but not more than 14,000 pounds,

(C) $25,000, if such vehicle has a gross vehicle weight rating of more than 14,000

Sec. 30B. Alternative motor vehicle credit

pounds but not more than 26,000 pounds, and

(D) $40,000, if such vehicle has a gross vehicle weight rating of more than 26,000 pounds.

(4) **New qualified alternative fuel motor vehicle.** -- For purposes of this subsection--

(A) **In general.** -- The term `new qualified alternative fuel motor vehicle' means any motor vehicle--

(i) which is only capable of operating on an alternative fuel,

(ii) the original use of which commences with the taxpayer,

(iii) which is acquired by the taxpayer for use or lease, but not for resale, and

(iv) which is made by a manufacturer.

(B) **Alternative fuel.** -- The term `alternative fuel' means compressed natural gas, liquefied natural gas, liquefied petroleum gas, hydrogen, and any liquid at least 85 percent of the volume of which consists of methanol.

(5) **Credit for mixed-fuel vehicles.** --

(A) **In general.** -- In the case of a mixed-fuel vehicle placed in service by the taxpayer during the taxable year, the credit determined under this subsection is an amount equal to--

(i) in the case of a 75/25 mixed-fuel vehicle, 70 percent of the credit which would have been allowed under this subsection if such vehicle was a qualified alternative fuel motor vehicle, and

(ii) in the case of a 90/10 mixed-fuel vehicle, 90 percent of the credit which would have been allowed under this subsection if such vehicle was a qualified alternative fuel motor vehicle.

(B) **Mixed-fuel vehicle.** -- For purposes of this subsection, the term `mixed-fuel vehicle' means any motor vehicle described in subparagraph (C) or (D) of paragraph (3), which--

(i) is certified by the manufacturer as being able to perform efficiently in normal operation on a combination of an alternative fuel and a petroleum-based fuel,

(ii) either--

(I) has received a certificate of conformity under the Clean Air Act, or

(II) has received an order certifying the vehicle as meeting the same requirements as vehicles which may be sold or leased in California and meets or exceeds the low emission vehicle standard under section 88.105-94 of title 40, Code of Federal Regulations, for that make and model year vehicle,

(iii) the original use of which commences with the taxpayer,

(iv) which is acquired by the taxpayer for use or lease, but not for resale, and

(v) which is made by a manufacturer.

(C) **75/25 mixed-fuel vehicle**. -- For purposes of this subsection, the term `75/25 mixed-fuel vehicle' means a mixed-fuel vehicle which operates using at least 75 percent alternative fuel and not more than 25 percent petroleum-based fuel.

(D) **90/10 mixed-fuel vehicle**. -- For purposes of this subsection, the term `90/10 mixed-fuel vehicle' means a mixed-fuel vehicle which operates using at least 90 percent alternative fuel and not more than 10 percent petroleum-based fuel.

(f) **Limitation on Number of New Qualified Hybrid and Advanced Lean-Burn Technology Vehicles Eligible for Credit**. --

(1) **In general.** -- In the case of a qualified vehicle sold during the phaseout period, only the applicable percentage of the credit otherwise allowable under subsection (c) or (d) shall be

Sec. 30B. Alternative motor vehicle credit

allowed.

    (2) Phaseout period. -- For purposes of this subsection, the phaseout period is the period beginning with the second calendar quarter following the calendar quarter which includes the first date on which the number of qualified vehicles manufactured by the manufacturer of the vehicle referred to in paragraph (1) sold for use in the United States after December 31, 2005, is at least 60,000.

    (3) Applicable percentage. -- For purposes of paragraph (1), the applicable percentage is--

        (A) 50 percent for the first 2 calendar quarters of the phaseout period,

        (B) 25 percent for the 3d and 4th calendar quarters of the phaseout period, and

        (C) 0 percent for each calendar quarter thereafter.

    (4) Controlled groups. --

        (A) In general. -- For purposes of this subsection, all persons treated as a single employer under subsection (a) or (b) of section 52 or subsection (m) or (o) of section 414 shall be treated as a single manufacturer.

        (B) Inclusion of foreign corporations. -- For purposes of subparagraph (A), in applying subsections (a) and (b) of section 52 to this section, section 1563 shall be applied without regard to subsection (b)(2)(C) thereof.

    (5) Qualified vehicle. -- For purposes of this subsection, the term `qualified vehicle' means any new qualified hybrid motor vehicle (described in subsection (d)(2)(A)) and any new advanced lean burn technology motor vehicle.

(g) Application With Other Credits. --

    (1) Business credit treated as part of general business credit. -- So much of the credit which would be allowed under subsection (a) for any taxable year (determined without regard to this subsection) that is attributable to property of a character subject to an allowance for depreciation shall be treated as a credit listed in section 38(b) for such taxable year (and not allowed under subsection (a)).

    (2) Personal credit. -- The credit allowed under subsection (a) (after the application of paragraph (1)) for any taxable year shall not exceed the excess (if any) of--

        (A) the regular tax reduced by the sum of the credits allowable under subpart A and sections 27 and 30, over

        (B) the tentative minimum tax for the taxable year.

(h) Other Definitions and Special Rules. -- For purposes of this section--

***

    (4) Reduction in basis. -- For purposes of this subtitle, the basis of any property for which a credit is allowable under subsection (a) shall be reduced by the amount of such credit so allowed (determined without regard to subsection (g)).

    (5) No double benefit. -- The amount of any deduction or other credit allowable under this chapter--

        (A) for any incremental cost taken into account in computing the amount of the credit determined under subsection (e) shall be reduced by the amount of such credit attributable to such cost, and

        (B) with respect to a vehicle described under subsection (b) or (c), shall be reduced by the amount of credit allowed under subsection (a) for such vehicle for the taxable year.

***

    (8) Recapture. -- The Secretary shall, by regulations, provide for recapturing the benefit of

Sec. 30B. Alternative motor vehicle credit

any credit allowable under subsection (a) with respect to any property which ceases to be property eligible for such credit (including recapture in the case of a lease period of less than the economic life of a vehicle).

(9) Election to not take credit. -- No credit shall be allowed under subsection (a) for any vehicle if the taxpayer elects to not have this section apply to such vehicle.

***

(j) Termination. -- This section shall not apply to any property purchased after--

(1) in the case of a new qualified fuel cell motor vehicle (as described in subsection (b)), December 31, 2014,

(2) in the case of a new advanced lean burn technology motor vehicle (as described in subsection (c)) or a new qualified hybrid motor vehicle (as described in subsection (d)(2)(A)), December 31, 2010,

(3) in the case of a new qualified hybrid motor vehicle (as described in subsection (d)(2)(B)), December 31, 2009, and

(4) in the case of a new qualified alternative fuel vehicle (as described in subsection (e)), December 31, 2010.

Sec. 31. Tax withheld on wages

(a) Wage withholding for income tax purposes. --

(1) In general. -- The amount withheld as tax under chapter 24 shall be allowed to the recipient of the income as a credit against the tax imposed by this subtitle.

(2) Year of credit. -- The amount so withheld during any calendar year shall be allowed as a credit for the taxable year beginning in such calendar year. If more than one taxable year begins in a calendar year, such amount shall be allowed as a credit for the last taxable year so beginning.

(b) Credit for special refunds of social security tax. --

(1) In general. -- The Secretary may prescribe regulations providing for the crediting against the tax imposed by this subtitle of the amount determined by the taxpayer or the Secretary to be allowable under section 6413(c) as a special refund of tax imposed on wages. The amount allowed as a credit under such regulations shall, for purposes of this subtitle, be considered an amount withheld at source as tax under section 3402.

(2) Year of credit. -- Any amount to which paragraph (1) applies shall be allowed as a credit for the taxable year beginning in the calendar year during which the wages were received. If more than one taxable year begins in the calendar year, such amount shall be allowed as a credit for the last taxable year so beginning.

(c) Special rule for backup withholding. -- Any credit allowed by subsection (a) for any amount withheld under section 3406 shall be allowed for the taxable year of the recipient of the income in which the income is received.

Sec. 32. Earned income

(a) Allowance of credit. --

(1) In general. -- In the case of an eligible individual, there shall be allowed as a credit against the tax imposed by this subtitle for the taxable year an amount equal to the credit percentage of so much of the taxpayer's earned income for the taxable year as does not exceed the earned income amount.

Sec. 32. Earned income

(2) Limitation. -- The amount of the credit allowable to a taxpayer under paragraph (1) for any taxable year shall not exceed the excess (if any) of -

(A) the credit percentage of the earned income amount, over

(B) the phaseout percentage of so much of the adjusted gross income (or, if greater, the earned income) of the taxpayer for the taxable year as exceeds the phaseout amount.

(b) Percentages and amounts. -- For purposes of subsection (a) -

(1) Percentages. -- The credit percentage and the phaseout percentage shall be determined as follows:

(A) In general. -- In the case of taxable years beginning after 1995:

In the case of an eligible individual with:	The credit percentage is:	The phaseout percentage is:
1 qualifying child.................,...........	34	15.98
2 or more qualifying children.........	40	21.06
No qualifying children...................	7.65	7.65

***

(2) Amounts. --

(A) In general. -- Subject to subparagraph (B), the earned income amount and the phaseout amount shall be determined as follows:

In the case of an eligible individual with:	The earned income amount is:	The phaseout amount is:
1 qualifying child...........................	$6,330	$11,610
2 or more qualifying children.........	$8,890	$11,610
No qualifying children...................	$4,220	$5,280

(B) Joint returns. -- In the case of a joint return filed by an eligible individual and such individual's spouse, the phaseout amount determined under subparagraph (A) shall be increased by -

***

(iii) $3,000 in the case of taxable years beginning after 2007.

(c) Definitions and special rules. -- For purposes of this section--

(1) Eligible individual. --

(A) In general. -- The term "eligible individual" means--

(i) any individual who has a qualifying child for the taxable year, or

(ii) any other individual who does not have a qualifying child for the taxable year, if--

(I) such individual's principal place of abode is in the United States for more than one-half of such taxable year,

(II) such individual (or, if the individual is married, either the individual or the individual's spouse) has attained age 25 but not attained age 65 before the close of the taxable year, and

(III) such individual is not a dependent for whom a deduction is allowable under section 151 to another taxpayer for any taxable year beginning in the same calendar year as such taxable year.

Sec. 32. Earned income

For purposes of the preceding sentence, marital status shall be determined under section 7703.

(B) Qualifying child ineligible. -- If an individual is the qualifying child of a taxpayer for any taxable year of such taxpayer beginning in a calendar year, such individual shall not be treated as an eligible individual for any taxable year of such individual beginning in 5 such calendar year.

(C) Exception for individual claiming benefits under section 911. -- The term "eligible individual" does not include any individual who claims the benefits of section 911 (relating to citizens or residents living abroad) for the taxable year.

(D) Limitation on eligibility of nonresident aliens. -- The term "eligible individual" 10 shall not include any individual who is a nonresident alien individual for any portion of the taxable year unless such individual is treated for such taxable year as a resident of the United States for purposes of this chapter by reason of an election under subsection (g) or (h) of section 6013.

(E) Identification number requirement. -- No credit shall be allowed under this 15 section to an eligible individual who does not include on the return of tax for the taxable year--

(i) such individual's taxpayer identification number, and

(ii) if the individual is married (within the meaning of section 7703), the taxpayer identification number of such individual's spouse. 20

(F) Individuals who do not include TIN, etc., of any qualifying child. -- No credit shall be allowed under this section to any eligible individual who has one or more qualifying children if no qualifying child of such individual is taken into account under subsection (b) by reason of paragraph (3)(D).

(2) Earned income. -- 25

(A) The term "earned income" means--

(i) wages, salaries, tips, and other employee compensation, but only if such amounts are includible in gross income for the taxable year, plus

(ii) the amount of the taxpayer's net earnings from self-employment for the taxable year (within the meaning of section 1402(a)), but such net earnings shall be determined 30 with regard to the deduction allowed to the taxpayer by section 164(f).

(B) For purposes of subparagraph (A)--

(i) the earned income of an individual shall be computed without regard to any community property laws,

(ii) no amount received as a pension or annuity shall be taken into account, 35

(iii) no amount to which section 871(a) applies (relating to income of nonresident alien individuals not connected with United States business) shall be taken into account,

(iv) no amount received for services provided by an individual while the individual is an inmate at a penal institution shall be taken into account,

(v) no amount described in subparagraph (A) received for service performed in work 40 activities as defined in paragraph (4) or (7) of section 407(d) of the Social Security Act to which the taxpayer is assigned under any State program under part A of title IV of such Act shall be taken into account, but only to the extent such amount is subsidized under such State program, and

(vi) in the case of any taxable year ending-- 45

(I) after the date of the enactment of this clause, and

59

Sec. 32.   Earned income

(II) before January 1, 2008,

a taxpayer may elect to treat amounts excluded from gross income by reason of section 112 as earned income.

(3) Qualifying child. --

(A) In general. -- The term "qualifying child" means a qualifying child of the taxpayer (as defined in section 152(c), determined without regard to paragraph (1)(D) thereof and section 152(e)).

(B) Married individual. -- The term "qualifying child" shall not include an individual who is married as of the close of the taxpayer's taxable year unless the taxpayer is entitled to a deduction under section 151 for such taxable year with respect to such individual (or would be so entitled but for section 152(e)).

(C) Place of abode. -- For purposes of subparagraph (A), the requirements of section 152(c)(1)(B) shall be met only if the principal place of abode is in the United States.

(D) Identification requirements. --

(i) In general. -- A qualifying child shall not be taken into account under subsection (b) unless the taxpayer includes the name, age, and TIN of the qualifying child on the return of tax for the taxable year.

(ii) Other methods. -- The Secretary may prescribe other methods for providing the information described in clause (i).

(4) Treatment of military personnel stationed outside the United States. -- For purposes of paragraphs (1)(A)(ii)(I) and (3)(C), the principal place of abode of a member of the Armed Forces of the United States shall be treated as in the United States during any period during which such member is stationed outside the United States while serving on extended active duty with the Armed Forces of the United States. For purposes of the preceding sentence, the term "extended active duty" means any period of active duty pursuant to a call or order to such duty for a period in excess of 90 days or for an indefinite period.

(d) Married individuals. -- In the case of an individual who is married (within the meaning of section 7703), this section shall apply only if a joint return is filed for the taxable year under section 6013.

(e) Taxable year must be full taxable year. -- Except in the case of a taxable year closed by reason of the death of the taxpayer, no credit shall be allowable under this section in the case of a taxable year covering a period of less than 12 months.

(f) Amount of credit to be determined under tables. --

(1) In general. -- The amount of the credit allowed by this section shall be determined under tables prescribed by the Secretary.

(2) Requirements for tables. -- The tables prescribed under paragraph (1) shall reflect the provisions of subsections (a) and (b) and shall have income brackets of not greater than $50 each--

(A) for earned income between $0 and the amount of earned income at which the credit is phased out under subsection (b), and

(B) for adjusted gross income between the dollar amount at which the phaseout begins under subsection (b) and the amount of adjusted gross income at which the credit is phased out under subsection (b).

(g) Coordination with advance payments of earned income credit. --

(1) Recapture of excess advance payments. -- If any payment is made to the individual by an employer under section 3507 during any calendar year, then the tax imposed by this chapter for the individual's last taxable year beginning in such calendar year shall be increased by the

Sec. 32. Earned income

aggregate amount of such payments.

(2) Reconciliation of payments advanced and credit allowed. -- Any increase in tax under paragraph (1) shall not be treated as tax imposed by this chapter for purposes of determining the amount of any credit (other than the credit allowed by subsection (a)) allowable under this part. 5

***

(i) Denial of credit for individuals having excessive investment income. --

(1) In general. -- No credit shall be allowed under subsection (a) for the taxable year if the aggregate amount of disqualified income of the taxpayer for the taxable year exceeds $2,200.

(2) Disqualified income. -- For purposes of paragraph (1), the term "disqualified income" 10 means--

(A) interest or dividends to the extent includible in gross income for the taxable year,

(B) interest received or accrued during the taxable year which is exempt from tax imposed by this chapter,

(C) the excess (if any) of-- 15

(i) gross income from rents or royalties not derived in the ordinary course of a trade or business, over

(ii) the sum of--

(I) the deductions (other than interest) which are clearly and directly allocable to such gross income, plus 20

(II) interest deductions properly allocable to such gross income,

(D) the capital gain net income (as defined in section 1222) of the taxpayer for such taxable year, and

(E) the excess (if any) of--

(i) the aggregate income from all passive activities for the taxable year (determined 25 without regard to any amount included in earned income under subsection (c)(2) or described in a preceding subparagraph), over

(ii) the aggregate losses from all passive activities for the taxable year (as so determined).

For purposes of subparagraph (E), the term "passive activity" has the meaning given such 30 term by section 469.

(j) Inflation adjustments. --

(1) In general. -- In the case of any taxable year beginning after 1996, each of the dollar amounts in subsections (b)(2) and (i)(1) shall be increased by an amount equal to---

(A) such dollar amount, multiplied by 35

(B) the cost-of-living adjustment determined under section 1(f)(3) for the calendar year in which the taxable year begins, determined---

(i) in the case of amounts in subsections (b)(2)(A) and (i)(1), by substituting "calendar year 1995" for "calendar year 1992" in subparagraph (B) thereof, and

(ii) in the case of the $3,000 amount in subsection (b)(2)(B)(iii), by substituting 40 "calendar year 2007" for "calendar year 1992" in subparagraph (B) of such section 1.

(2) Rounding. --

(A) In general. -- If any dollar amount in subsection (b)(2)(A) (after being increased under subparagraph (B) thereof), after being increased under paragraph (1), is not a multiple of $10, such dollar amount shall be rounded to the nearest multiple of $10. 45

Sec. 32. Earned income

(B) **Disqualified income threshold amount.** -- If the dollar amount in subsection (i)(1), after being increased under paragraph (1), is not a multiple of $50, such amount shall be rounded to the next lowest multiple of $50.

(k) Restrictions on taxpayers who improperly claimed credit in prior year. --

5   **(1) Taxpayers making prior fraudulent or reckless claims.** --

(A) **In general.** -- No credit shall be allowed under this section for any taxable year in the disallowance period.

(B) **Disallowance period.** -- For purposes of paragraph (1), the disallowance period is -

(i) the period of 10 taxable years after the most recent taxable year for which there
10   was a final determination that the taxpayer's claim of credit under this section was due to fraud, and

(ii) the period of 2 taxable years after the most recent taxable year for which there was a final determination that the taxpayer's claim of credit under this section was due to reckless or intentional disregard of rules and regulations (but not due to fraud).

15   **(2) Taxpayers making improper prior claims.** -- In the case of a taxpayer who is denied credit under this section for any taxable year as a result of the deficiency procedures under subchapter B of chapter 63, no credit shall be allowed under this section for any subsequent taxable year unless the taxpayer provides such information as the Secretary may require to demonstrate eligibility for such credit.

20   **(l) Coordination with certain means-tested programs.** -- For purposes of--

(1) the United States Housing Act of 1937,

(2) title V of the Housing Act of 1949,

(3) section 101 of the Housing and Urban Development Act of 1965,

(4) sections 221(d)(3), 235, and 236 of the National Housing Act, and

25   **(5)** the Food Stamp Act of 1977,

any refund made to an individual (or the spouse of an individual) by reason of this section, and any payment made to such individual (or such spouse) by an employer under section 3507, shall not be treated as income (and shall not be taken into account in determining resources for the month of its receipt and the following month).

30   **(m) Identification numbers.** -- Solely for purposes of subsections (c)(1)(E) and (c)(3)(D), a taxpayer identification number means a social security number issued to an individual by the Social Security Administration (other than a social security number issued pursuant to clause (II) (or that portion of clause (III) that relates to clause (II)) of section 205(c)(2)(B)(i) of the Social Security Act).

35

Sec. 35. Health insurance costs of eligible individuals

(a) **In general.** -- In the case of an individual, there shall be allowed as a credit against the tax imposed by subtitle A an amount equal to 65 percent of the amount paid by the taxpayer for coverage of the taxpayer and qualifying family members under qualified health insurance for eligible coverage months beginning in the taxable year.

40   (b) **Eligible coverage month.** -- For purposes of this section---

(1) In general. -- The term "eligible coverage month" means any month if---

(A) as of the first day of such month, the taxpayer---

(i) is an eligible individual,

Sec. 35. Health insurance costs of eligible individuals

      (ii) is covered by qualified health insurance, the premium for which is paid by the taxpayer,

      (iii) does not have other specified coverage, and

      (iv) is not imprisoned under Federal, State, or local authority, and

  (B) such month begins more than 90 days after the date of the enactment of the Trade Act of 2002.

(2) Joint returns. -- In the case of a joint return, the requirements of paragraph (1)(A) shall be treated as met with respect to any month if at least 1 spouse satisfies such requirements.

(c) Eligible individual. -- For purposes of this section--

  (1) In general. -- The term "eligible individual" means--

    (A) an eligible TAA recipient,

    (B) an eligible alternative TAA recipient, and

    (C) an eligible PBGC pension recipient.

  (2) Eligible TAA recipient. -- The term "eligible TAA recipient" means, with respect to any month, any individual who is receiving for any day of such month a trade readjustment allowance under chapter 2 of title II of the Trade Act of 1974 or who would be eligible to receive such allowance if section 231 of such Act were applied without regard to subsection (a) (3)(B) of such section. An individual shall continue to be treated as an eligible TAA recipient during the first month that such individual would otherwise cease to be an eligible TAA recipient by reason of the preceding sentence.

  (3) Eligible alternative TAA recipient. -- The term "eligible alternative TAA recipient" means, with respect to any month, any individual who--

    (A) is a worker described in section 246(a)(3)(B) of the Trade Act of 1974 who is participating in the program established under section 246(a)(1) of such Act, and

    (B) is receiving a benefit for such month under section 246(a)(2) of such Act.

An individual shall continue to be treated as an eligible alternative TAA recipient during the first month that such individual would otherwise cease to be an eligible alternative TAA recipient by reason of the preceding sentence.

  (4) Eligible PBGC pension recipient. -- The term "eligible PBGC pension recipient" means, with respect to any month, any individual who--

    (A) has attained age 55 as of the first day of such month, and

    (B) is receiving a benefit for such month any portion of which is paid by the Pension Benefit Guaranty Corporation under title IV of the Employee Retirement Income Security Act of 1974.

(d) Qualifying family member. -- For purposes of this section -

  (1) In general. -- The term "qualifying family member" means--

    (A) the taxpayer's spouse, and

    (B) any dependent of the taxpayer with respect to whom the taxpayer is entitled to a deduction under section 151(c).

Such term does not include any individual who has other specified coverage.

  (2) Special dependency test in case of divorced parents, etc. -- If section 152(e) applies to any child with respect to any calendar year, in the case of any taxable year beginning in such calendar year, such child shall be treated as described in paragraph (1)(B) with respect to the custodial parent (as defined in section 152(e)(4)(A)) and not with respect to the noncustodial parent.

Sec. 35. Health insurance costs of eligible individuals

(e) Qualified health insurance. -- For purposes of this section--

(1) In general. -- The term "qualified health insurance" means any of the following:

(A) Coverage under a COBRA continuation provision (as defined in section 9832(d)(1)).

(B) State-based continuation coverage provided by the State under a State law that requires such coverage.

(C) Coverage offered through a qualified State high risk pool (as defined in section 2744(c)(2) of the Public Health Service Act).

(D) Coverage under a health insurance program offered for State employees.

(E) Coverage under a State-based health insurance program that is comparable to the health insurance program offered for State employees.

(F) Coverage through an arrangement entered into by a State and -

(i) a group health plan (including such a plan which is a multiemployer plan as defined in section 3(37) of the Employee Retirement Income Security Act of 1974),

(ii) an issuer of health insurance coverage,

(iii) an administrator, or

(iv) an employer.

(G) Coverage offered through a State arrangement with a private sector health care coverage purchasing pool.

(H) Coverage under a State-operated health plan that does not receive any Federal financial participation.

(I) Coverage under a group health plan that is available through the employment of the eligible individual's spouse.

(J) In the case of any eligible individual and such individual's qualifying family members, coverage under individual health insurance if the eligible individual was covered under individual health insurance during the entire 30- day period that ends on the date that such individual became separated from the employment which qualified such individual for--

(i) in the case of an eligible TAA recipient, the allowance described in subsection (c)(2),

(ii) in the case of an eligible alternative TAA recipient, the benefit described in subsection (c)(3)(B), or

(iii) in the case of any eligible PBGC pension recipient, the benefit described in subsection (c)(4)(B).

For purposes of this subparagraph, the term "individual health insurance" means any insurance which constitutes medical care offered to individuals other than in connection with a group health plan and does not include Federal- or State-based health insurance coverage.

(2) Requirements for state-based coverage. --

(A) In general. -- The term "qualified health insurance" does not include any coverage described in subparagraphs (B) through (H) of paragraph (1) unless the State involved has elected to have such coverage treated as qualified health insurance under this section and such coverage meets the following requirements:

(i) Guaranteed issue. -- Each qualifying individual is guaranteed enrollment if the individual pays the premium for enrollment or provides a qualified health insurance costs credit eligibility certificate described in section 7527 and pays the remainder of

Sec. 35. Health insurance costs of eligible individuals

such premium.

(ii) No imposition of preexisting condition exclusion. -- No pre-existing condition limitations are imposed with respect to any qualifying individual.

(iii) Nondiscriminatory premium. -- The total premium (as determined without regard to any subsidies) with respect to a qualifying individual may not be greater than 5 the total premium (as so determined) for a similarly situated individual who is not a qualifying individual.

(iv) Same benefits. -- Benefits under the coverage are the same as (or substantially similar to) the benefits provided to similarly situated individuals who are not qualifying individuals. 10

(B) Qualifying individual. -- For purposes of this paragraph, the term "qualifying individual" means -

(i) an eligible individual for whom, as of the date on which the individual seeks to enroll in the coverage described in subparagraphs (B) through (H) of paragraph (1), the aggregate of the periods of creditable coverage (as defined in section 9801(c)) is 3 15 months or longer and who, with respect to any month, meets the requirements of clauses (iii) and (iv) of subsection (b)(1)(A); and

(ii) the qualifying family members of such eligible individual.

(3) Exception. -- The term "qualified health insurance" shall not include--

(A) a flexible spending or similar arrangement, and 20

(B) any insurance if substantially all of its coverage is of excepted benefits described in section 9832(c).

(f) Other specified coverage. -- For purposes of this section, an individual has other specified coverage for any month if, as of the first day of such month--

(1) Subsidized coverage. -- 25

(A) In general. -- Such individual is covered under any insurance which constitutes medical care (except insurance substantially all of the coverage of which is of excepted benefits described in section 9832(c)) under any health plan maintained by any employer (or former employer) of the taxpayer or the taxpayer's spouse and at least 50 percent of the cost of such coverage (determined under section 4980B) is paid or incurred 30 by the employer.

(B) Eligible alternative TAA recipients. -- In the case of an eligible alternative TAA recipient, such individual is either--

(i) eligible for coverage under any qualified health insurance (other than insurance described in subparagraph (A), (B), or (F) of subsection (e)(1)) under which at least 50 35 percent of the cost of coverage (determined under section 4980B(f)(4)) is paid or incurred by an employer (or former employer) of the taxpayer or the taxpayer's spouse, or

(ii) covered under any such qualified health insurance under which any portion of the cost of coverage (as so determined) is paid or incurred by an employer (or former 40 employer) of the taxpayer or the taxpayer's spouse.

(C) Treatment of cafeteria plans. -- For purposes of subparagraphs (A) and (B), the cost of coverage shall be treated as paid or incurred by an employer to the extent the coverage is in lieu of a right to receive cash or other qualified benefits under a cafeteria plan (as defined in section 125(d)). 45

(2) Coverage under Medicare, Medicaid, or SCHIP. -- Such individual--

Sec. 35.   Health insurance costs of eligible individuals

        (A) is entitled to benefits under part A of title XVIII of the Social Security Act or is enrolled under part B of such title, or

        (B) is enrolled in the program under title XIX or XXI of such Act (other than under section 1928 of such Act).

        (3) Certain other coverage. -- Such individual--

        (A) is enrolled in a health benefits plan under chapter 89 of title 5, United States Code, or

        (B) is entitled to receive benefits under chapter 55 of title 10, United States Code.

(g) Special rules. --

        (1) Coordination with advance payments of credit. -- With respect to any taxable year, the amount which would (but for this subsection) be allowed as a credit to the taxpayer under subsection (a) shall be reduced (but not below zero) by the aggregate amount paid on behalf of such taxpayer under section 7527 for months beginning in such taxable year.

        (2) Coordination with other deductions. -- Amounts taken into account under subsection (a) shall not be taken into account in determining any deduction allowed under section 162(l) or 213.

        (3) Medical and health savings accounts. -- Amounts distributed from an Archer MSA (as defined in section 220(d)) or from a health savings account (as defined in section 223(d)) shall not be taken into account under subsection (a).

        (4) Denial of credit to dependents. -- No credit shall be allowed under this section to any individual with respect to whom a deduction under section 151 is allowable to another taxpayer for a taxable year beginning in the calendar year in which such individual's taxable year begins.

        (5) Both spouses eligible individuals. -- The spouse of the taxpayer shall not be treated as a qualifying family member for purposes of subsection (a), if--

        (A) the taxpayer is married at the close of the taxable year,

        (B) the taxpayer and the taxpayer's spouse are both eligible individuals during the taxable year, and

        (C) the taxpayer files a separate return for the taxable year.

        (6) Marital status; certain married individuals living apart. -- Rules similar to the rules of paragraphs (3) and (4) of section 21(e) shall apply for purposes of this section.

        (7) Insurance which covers other individuals. -- For purposes of this section, rules similar to the rules of section 213(d)(6) shall apply with respect to any contract for qualified health insurance under which amounts are payable for coverage of an individual other than the taxpayer and qualifying family members.

        (8) Treatment of payments. -- For purposes of this section--

        (A) Payments by Secretary. -- Payments made by the Secretary on behalf of any individual under section 7527 (relating to advance payment of credit for health insurance costs of eligible individuals) shall be treated as having been made by the taxpayer on the first day of the month for which such payment was made.

        (B) Payments by taxpayer. -- Payments made by the taxpayer for eligible coverage months shall be treated as having been made by the taxpayer on the first day of the month for which such payment was made.

        (9) Regulations. -- The Secretary may prescribe such regulations and other guidance as may be necessary or appropriate to carry out this section, section 6050T, and section 7527.

Sec. 35. Health insurance costs of eligible individuals

Sec. 38. General business credit

(a) **Allowance of credit.** -- There shall be allowed as a credit against the tax imposed by this chapter for the taxable year an amount equal to the sum of--

    (1) the business credit carryforwards carried to such taxable year,

    (2) the amount of the current year business credit, plus   5

    (3) the business credit carrybacks carried to such taxable year.

(b) **Current year business credit.** -- For purposes of this subpart, the amount of the current year business credit is the sum of the following credits determined for the taxable year:

    (1) the investment credit determined under section 46,

    (2) the work opportunity credit determined under section 51(a),   10

***

(c) **Limitation based on amount of tax.** --

    (1) In general. -- The credit allowed under subsection (a) for any taxable year shall not exceed the excess (if any) of the taxpayer's net income tax over the greater of--

        (A) the tentative minimum tax for the taxable year, or   15

        (B) 25 percent of so much of the taxpayer's net regular tax liability as exceeds $25,000. For purposes of the preceding sentence, the term "net income tax" means the sum of the regular tax liability and the tax imposed by section 55, reduced by the credits allowable under subparts A and B of this part, and the term "net regular tax liability" means the regular tax liability reduced by the sum of the credits allowable under subparts A and B of this part.   20

    (2) Empowerment zone employment credit may offset 25 percent of minimum tax. --

        (A) In general. -- In the case of the empowerment zone employment credit credit--

            (i) this section and section 39 shall be applied separately with respect to such credit, and

            (ii) for purposes of applying paragraph (1) to such credit--   25

                (I) 75 percent of the tentative minimum tax shall be substituted for the tentative minimum tax under subparagraph (A) thereof, and

                (II) the limitation under paragraph (1) (as modified by subclause (I)) shall be reduced by the credit allowed under subsection (a) for the taxable year (other than the empowerment zone employment credit or the New York Liberty Zone business 30 employee credit or the specified credits).

        (B) Empowerment zone employment credit. -- For purposes of this paragraph, the term "empowerment zone employment credit" means the portion of the credit under subsection (a) which is attributable to the credit determined under section 1396 (relating to empowerment zone employment credit).   35

    (3) Special rules for New York Liberty Zone business employee credit. --

        (A) In general. -- In the case of the New York Liberty Zone business employee credit -

            (i) this section and section 39 shall be applied separately with respect to such credit, and

            (ii) in applying paragraph (1) to such credit -   40

                (I) the tentative minimum tax shall be treated as being zero, and

                (II) the limitation under paragraph (1) (as modified by subclause (I)) shall be reduced by the credit allowed under subsection (a) for the taxable year (other than

Sec. 38. General business credit

the New York Liberty Zone business employee credit or the specified credits).

(B) New York Liberty Zone business employee credit. -- For purposes of this subsection, the term "New York Liberty Zone business employee credit" means the portion of work opportunity credit under section 51 determined under section 1400L(a).

(4) Special rules for specified credits. --

   (A) In general. -- In the case of specified credits--

      (i) this section and section 39 shall be applied separately with respect to such credits, and

      (ii) in applying paragraph (1) to such credits -

         (I) the tentative minimum tax shall be treated as being zero, and

         (II) the limitation under paragraph (1) (as modified by subclause (I)) shall be reduced by the credit allowed under subsection (a) for the taxable year (other than the specified credits).

   (B) Specified credits. -- For purposes of this subsection, the term "specified credits" includes -

      (i) for taxable years beginning after December 31, 2004, the credit determined under section 40,

      (ii) the credit determined under section 45 to the extent that such credit is attributable to electricity or refined coal produced--

         (I) at a facility which is originally placed in service after the date of the enactment of this paragraph, and

         (II) during the 4-year period beginning on the date that such facility was originally placed in service

(5) Special rules. --

   (A) Married individuals. -- In the case of a husband or wife who files a separate return, the amount specified under subparagraph (B) of paragraph (1) shall be $12,500 in lieu of $25,000. This subparagraph shall not apply if the spouse of the taxpayer has no business credit carryforward or carryback to, and has no current year business credit for, the taxable year of such spouse which ends within or with the taxpayer's taxable year.

   (B) Controlled groups. -- In the case of a controlled group, the $25,000 amount specified under subparagraph (B) of paragraph (1) shall be reduced for each component member of such group by apportioning $25,000 among the component members of such group in such manner as the Secretary shall by regulations prescribe. For purposes of the preceding sentence, the term "controlled group" has the meaning given to such term by section 1563(a).

   (C) Limitations with respect to certain persons. -- In the case of a person described in subparagraph (A) or (B) of section 46(e)(1) (as in effect on the day before the date of the enactment of the Revenue Reconciliation Act of 1990), the $25,000 amount specified under subparagraph (B) of paragraph (1) shall equal such person's ratable share (as determined under section 46(e)(2) (as so in effect) of such amount.

   (D) Estates and trusts. -- In the case of an estate or trust, the $25,000 amount specified under subparagraph (B) of paragraph (1) shall be reduced to an amount which bears the same ratio to $25,000 as the portion of the income of the estate or trust which is not allocated to beneficiaries bears to the total income of the estate or trust.

(d) Ordering rules. -- For purposes of any provision of this title where it is necessary to

Sec. 38. General business credit

ascertain the extent to which the credits determined under any section referred to in subsection (b) are used in a taxable year or as a carryback or carryforward--

  (1) In general. -- The order in which such credits are used shall be determined on the basis of the order in which they are listed in subsection (b) as of the close of the taxable year in which the credit is used.

  (2) Components of investment credit. -- The order in which the credits listed in section 46 are used shall be determined on the basis of the order in which such credits are listed in section 46 as of the close of the taxable year in which the credit is used.

  (3) Credits no longer listed. -- For purposes of this subsection--

    (A) the credit allowable by section 40, as in effect on the day before the date of the enactment of the Tax Reform Act of 1984, (relating to expenses of work incentive programs) and the credit allowable by section 41(a), as in effect on the day before the date of the enactment of the Tax Reform Act of 1986, (relating to employee stock ownership credit) shall be treated as referred to in that order after the last paragraph of subsection (b), and

    (B) the credit determined under section 46--

      (i) to the extent attributable to the employee plan percentage (as defined in section 46(a)(2)(E) as in effect on the day before the date of the enactment of the Tax Reform Act of 1984) shall be treated as a credit listed after paragraph (1) of section 46, and

      (ii) to the extent attributable to the regular percentage (as defined in section 46(b)(1) as in effect on the day before the date of the enactment of the Revenue Reconciliation Act of 1990) shall be treated as the first credit listed in section 46.

Sec. 39. Carryback and carryforward of unused credits

  (a) In general. --

  (1) 1-year carryback and 20-year carryforward. -- If the sum of the business credit carryforwards to the taxable year plus the amount of the current year business credit for the taxable year exceeds the amount of the limitation imposed by subsection (c) of section 38 for such taxable year (hereinafter in this section referred to as the "unused credit year"), such excess (to the extent attributable to the amount of the current year business credit) shall be--

    (A) a business credit carryback to each of the 1 taxable years (!1) preceding the unused credit year, and

    (B) a business credit carryforward to each of the 20 taxable years following the unused credit year, and, subject to the limitations imposed by subsections (b) and (c), shall be taken into account under the provisions of section 38(a) in the manner provided in section 38(a).

  (2) Amount carried to each year. --

    (A) Entire amount carried to first year. -- The entire amount of the unused credit for an unused credit year shall be carried to the earliest of the 21 taxable years to which (by reason of paragraph (1)) such credit may be carried.

    (B) Amount carried to other 20 years. -- The amount of the unused credit for the unused credit year shall be carried to each of the other 20 taxable years to the extent that such unused credit may not be taken into account under section 38(a) for a prior taxable year because of the limitations of subsections (b) and (c).

  (3) 5-year carryback for marginal oil and gas well production credit. -- Notwithstanding subsection (d), in the case of the marginal oil and gas well production credit--

Sec. 39.   Carryback and carryforward of unused credits

    (A) this section shall be applied separately from the business credit (other than the marginal oil and gas well   production credit),

    (B) paragraph (1) shall be applied by substituting "5 taxable years" for "1 taxable years" in subparagraph (A) thereof, and

5   (C) paragraph (2) shall be applied -

        (i) by substituting "25 taxable years" for "21 taxable years" in subparagraph (A) thereof, and

        (ii) by substituting "24 taxable years" for "20 taxable years" in subparagraph (B) thereof.

10 **(b) Limitation on carrybacks.** -- The amount of the unused credit which may be taken into account under section 38(a)(3) for any preceding taxable year shall not exceed the amount by which the limitation imposed by section 38(c) for such taxable year exceeds the sum of--

    (1) the amounts determined under paragraphs (1) and (2) of section 38(a) for such taxable year, plus

15   (2) the amounts which (by reason of this section) are carried back to such taxable year and are attributable to taxable years preceding the unused credit year.

  (c) Limitation on carryforwards. -- The amount of the unused credit which may be taken into account under section 38(a)(1) for any succeeding taxable year shall not exceed the amount by which the limitation imposed by section 38(c) for such taxable year exceeds the sum of the

20 amounts which, by reason of this section, are carried to such taxable year and are attributable to taxable years preceding the unused credit year.

  (d) Transitional rule. -- No portion of the unused business credit for any taxable year which is attributable to a credit specified in section 38(b) or any portion thereof may be carried back to any taxable year before the first taxable year for which such specified credit or such portion is

25 allowable (without regard to subsection (a)).

Sec. 41.   Credit for increasing research activities

  (a) General rule. -- For purposes of section 38, the research credit determined under this section for the taxable year shall be an amount equal to the sum of--

30   (1) 20 percent of the excess (if any) of--

        (A) the qualified research expenses for the taxable year,over

        (B) the base amount,

    (2) 20 percent of the basic research payments determined under subsection (e)(1)(A), and

    (3) 20 percent of the amounts paid or incurred by the taxpayer in carrying on any trade or

35 business of the taxpayer during the taxable year (including as contributions) to an energy research consortium for energy research .

  (b) Qualified research expenses. -- For purposes of this section--

    (1) Qualified research expenses. -- The term "qualified research expenses" means the sum of the following amounts which are paid or incurred by the taxpayer during the taxable year in

40 carrying on any trade or business of the taxpayer--

        (A) in-house research expenses, and

        (B) contract research expenses.

    (2) In-house research expenses. --

        (A) In general. -- The term "in-house research expenses" means--

Sec. 41. Credit for increasing research activities

(i) any wages paid or incurred to an employee for qualified services performed by such employee,

(ii) any amount paid or incurred for supplies used in the conduct of qualified research, and

(iii) under regulations prescribed by the Secretary, any amount paid or incurred to 5 another person for the right to use computers in the conduct of qualified research.

Clause (iii) shall not apply to any amount to the extent that the taxpayer (or any person with whom the taxpayer must aggregate expenditures under subsection (f)(1)) receives or accrues any amount from any other person for the right to us substantially identical personal property. 10

(B) Qualified services. -- The term "qualified services" means services consisting of--

(i) engaging in qualified research, or

(ii) engaging in the direct supervision or direct support of research activities which constitute qualified research.

If substantially all of the services performed by an individual for the taxpayer during the 15 taxable year consists of services meeting the requirements of clause (i) or (ii), the term "qualified services" means all of the services performed by such individual for the taxpayer during the taxable year.

(C) Supplies. -- The term "supplies" means any tangible property other than--

(i) land or improvements to land, and 20

(ii) property of a character subject to the allowance for depreciation.

(D) Wages. --

(i) **In general.** -- The term "wages" has the meaning given such term by section 3401(a).

(ii) **Self-employed individuals and owner-employees.** -- In the case of an employee 25 (within the meaning of section 401(c)(1)), the term "wages" includes the earned income (as defined in section 401(c)(2)) of such employee.

(iii) **Exclusion for wages to which work opportunity credit applies.** -- The term "wages" shall not include any amount taken into account in determining the work opportunity credit under section 51(a). 30

(3) Contract research expenses. --

(A) In general. -- The term "contract research expenses" means 65 percent of any amount paid or incurred by the taxpayer to any person (other than an employee of the taxpayer) for qualified research.

(B) Prepaid amounts. -- If any contract research expenses paid or incurred during any 35 taxable year are attributable to qualified research to be conducted after the close of such taxable year, such amount shall be treated as paid or incurred during the period during which the qualified research is conducted.

(C) Amounts paid to certain research consortia. --

(i) **In general.** -- Subparagraph (A) shall be applied by substituting "75 percent" for 40 "65 percent" with respect to amounts paid or incurred by the taxpayer to a qualified research consortium for qualified research on behalf of the taxpayer and 1 or more unrelated taxpayers. For purposes of the preceding sentence, all persons treated as a single employer under subsection (a) or (b) of section 52 shall be treated as related taxpayers. 45

(ii) **Qualified research consortium.** -- The term "qualified research consortium"

Sec. 41. Credit for increasing research activities

means any organization (other than an energy research consortium) which--

    (I) is described in section 501(c)(3) or 501(c)(6) and is exempt from tax under section 501(a),

    (II) is organized and operated primarily to conduct scientific research, and

    (III) is not a private foundation.

(D) Amounts paid to eligible small businesses, universities, and federal laboratories. --

    (i) In general.--In the case of amounts paid by the taxpayer to--

        (I) an eligible small business,

        (II) an institution of higher education (as defined in section 3304(f)), or

        (III) an organization which is a Federal laboratory, for qualified research which is energy research, subparagraph (A) shall be applied by substituting `100 percent' for `65 percent'.

    (ii) Eligible small business. -- For purposes of this subparagraph, the term `eligible small business' means a small business with respect to which the taxpayer does not own (within the meaning of section 318) 50 percent or more of--

        (I) in the case of a corporation, the outstanding stock of the corporation (either by vote or value), and

        (II) in the case of a small business which is not a corporation, the capital and profits interests of the small business.

    (iii) Small business. -- For purposes of this subparagraph--

        (I) In general. -- The term `small business' means, with respect to any calendar year, any person if the annual average number of employees employed by such person during either of the 2 preceding calendar years was 500 or fewer. For purposes of the preceding sentence, a preceding calendar year may be taken into account only if the person was in existence throughout the year.

        (II) Startups, controlled groups, and predecessors. -- Rules similar to the rules of subparagraphs (B) and (D) of section 220(c)(4) shall apply for purposes of this clause.

***

(4) Trade or business requirement disregarded for in-house research expenses of certain startup ventures. -- In the case of in-house research expenses, a taxpayer shall be treated as meeting the trade or business requirement of paragraph (1) if, at the time such in-house research expenses are paid or incurred, the principal purpose of the taxpayer in making such expenditures is to use the results of the research in the active conduct of a future trade or business -

    (A) of the taxpayer, or

    (B) of 1 or more other persons who with the taxpayer are treated as a single taxpayer under subsection (f)(1).

(c) Base amount. --

    (1) In general. -- The term "base amount" means the product of--

        (A) the fixed-base percentage, and

        (B) the average annual gross receipts of the taxpayer for the 4 taxable years preceding the taxable year for which the credit is being determined (hereinafter in this subsection referred to as the "credit year").

Sec. 41. Credit for increasing research activities

(2) Minimum base amount. -- In no event shall the base amount be less than 50 percent of the qualified research expenses for the credit year.

(3) Fixed-base percentage. --

(A) In general. -- Except as otherwise provided in this paragraph, the fixed-base percentage is the percentage which the aggregate qualified research expenses of the taxpayer for taxable years beginning after December 31, 1983, and before January 1, 1989, is of the aggregate gross receipts of the taxpayer for such taxable years.

(B) Start-up companies. --

(i) Taxpayers to which subparagraph applies. -- The fixed-base percentage shall be determined under this subparagraph if--

(I) the first taxable year in which a taxpayer had both gross receipts and qualified research expenses begins after December 31, 1983, or

(II) there are fewer than 3 taxable years beginning after December 31, 1983, and before January 1, 1989, in which the taxpayer had both gross receipts and qualified research expenses.

(ii) Fixed-base percentage. -- In a case to which this subparagraph applies, the fixed- base percentage is--

(I) 3 percent for each of the taxpayer's 1st 5 taxable years beginning after December 31, 1993, for which the taxpayer has qualified research expenses,

(II) in the case of the taxpayer's 6th such taxable year, 1/6 of the percentage which the aggregate qualified research expenses of the taxpayer for the 4th and 5th such taxable years is of the aggregate gross receipts of the taxpayer for such years,

(III) in the case of the taxpayer's 7th such taxable year, 1/3 of the percentage which the aggregate qualified research expenses of the taxpayer for the 5th and 6th such taxable years is of the aggregate gross receipts of the taxpayer for such years,

(IV) in the case of the taxpayer's 8th such taxable year, 1/2 of the percentage which the aggregate qualified research expenses of the taxpayer for the 5th, 6th, and 7th such taxable years is of the aggregate gross receipts of the taxpayer for such years,

(V) in the case of the taxpayer's 9th such taxable year, 2/3 of the percentage which the aggregate qualified research expenses of the taxpayer for the 5th, 6th, 7th, and 8th such taxable years is of the aggregate gross receipts of the taxpayer for such years,

(VI) in the case of the taxpayer's 10th such taxable year, 5/6 of the percentage which the aggregate qualified research expenses of the taxpayer for the 5th, 6th, 7th, 8th, and 9th such taxable years is of the aggregate gross receipts of the taxpayer for such years, and

(VII) for taxable years thereafter, the percentage which the aggregate qualified research expenses for any 5 taxable years selected by the taxpayer from among the 5th through the 10th such taxable years is of the aggregate gross receipts of the taxpayer for such selected years.

(iii) Treatment of de minimis amounts of gross receipts and qualified research expenses. -- The Secretary may prescribe regulations providing that de minimis amounts of gross receipts and qualified research expenses shall be disregarded under clauses (i) and (ii).

(C) Maximum fixed-base percentage. -- In no event shall the fixed-base percentage exceed 16 percent.

Sec. 41. Credit for increasing research activities

(D) Rounding. -- The percentages determined under subparagraphs (A) and (B)(ii) shall be rounded to the nearest 1/100th of 1 percent.

(4) Election of alternate incremental credit. --

(A) In general. -- At the election of the taxpayer, the credit determined under subsection (a)(1) shall be equal to the sum of --

(i) 3 percent of so much of the qualified research expenses for the taxable year as exceeds 1 percent of the average described in subsection (c)(1)(B) but does not exceed 1.5 percent of such average,

(ii) 4 percent of so much of such expenses as exceeds 1.5 percent of such average but does not exceed 2 percent of such average, and

(iii) 5 percent of so much of such expenses as exceeds 2 percent of such average.

(B) Election. --An election under this paragraph shall apply to the taxable year for which made and all succeeding taxable years unless revoked with the consent of the Secretary.

(5) Election of alternative simplified credit. --

(A) In general. --At the election of the taxpayer, the credit determined under subsection (a)(1) shall be equal to 12 percent of so much of the qualified research expenses for the taxable year as exceeds 50 percent of the average qualified research expenses for the 3 taxable years preceding the taxable year for which the credit is being determined.

***

(C) Election. -- An election under this paragraph shall apply to the taxable year for which made and all succeeding taxable years unless revoked with the consent of the Secretary. An election under this paragraph may not be made for any taxable year to which an election under paragraph (4) applies.

(6) Consistent treatment of expenses required. --

(A) In general. -- Notwithstanding whether the period for filing a claim for credit or refund has expired for any taxable year taken into account in determining the fixed-base percentage, the qualified research expenses taken into account in computing such percentage shall be determined on a basis consistent with the determination of qualified research expenses for the credit year.

***

(d) Qualified research defined. -- For purposes of this section--

(1) In general. -- The term "qualified research" means research--

(A) with respect to which expenditures may be treated as expenses under section 174,

(B) which is undertaken for the purpose of discovering information--

(i) which is technological in nature, and

(ii) the application of which is intended to be useful in the development of a new or improved business component of the taxpayer, and

(C) substantially all of the activities of which constitute elements of a process of experimentation for a purpose described in paragraph (3).

Such term does not include any activity described in paragraph (4).

(2) Tests to be applied separately to each business component. -- For purposes of this subsection--

(A) In general. -- Paragraph (1) shall be applied separately with respect to each business component of the taxpayer.

74

Sec. 41. Credit for increasing research activities

(B) **Business component defined.** -- The term "business component" means any product, process, computer software, technique, formula, or invention which is to be -

    (i) held for sale, lease, or license, or

    (ii) used by the taxpayer in a trade or business of the taxpayer.

(C) **Special rule for production processes.** -- Any plant process, machinery, or technique for commercial production of a business component shall be treated as a separate business component (and not as part of the business component being produced).

(3) **Purposes for which research may qualify for credit.** -- For purposes of paragraph (1) (C)--

(A) **In general.** -- Research shall be treated as conducted for a purpose described in this paragraph if it relates to--

    (i) a new or improved function,

    (ii) performance, or

    (iii) reliability or quality.

(B) **Certain purposes not qualified.** -- Research shall in no event be treated as conducted for a purpose described in this paragraph if it relates to style, taste, cosmetic, or seasonal design factors.

(4) **Activities for which credit not allowed.** -- The term "qualified research" shall not include any of the following:

(A) **Research after commercial production.** -- Any research conducted after the beginning of commercial production of the business component.

(B) **Adaptation of existing business components.** -- Any research related to the adaptation of an existing business component to a particular customer's requirement or need.

(C) **Duplication of existing business component.** -- Any research related to the reproduction of an existing business component (in whole or in part) from a physical examination of the business component itself or from plans, blueprints, detailed specifications, or publicly available information with respect to such business component.

(D) **Surveys, studies, etc.** -- Any -

    (i) efficiency survey,

    (ii) activity relating to management function or technique,

    (iii) market research, testing, or development (including advertising or promotions),

    (iv) routine data collection, or

    (v) routine or ordinary testing or inspection for quality control.

(E) **Computer software.** -- Except to the extent provided in regulations, any research with respect to computer software which is developed by (or for the benefit of) the taxpayer primarily for internal use by the taxpayer, other than for use in--

    (i) an activity which constitutes qualified research (determined with regard to this subparagraph), or

    (ii) a production process with respect to which the requirements of paragraph (1) are met.

(F) **Foreign research.** -- Any research conducted outside the United States, the Commonwealth of Puerto Rico, or any possession of the United States.

(G) **Social sciences, etc.** -- Any research in the social sciences, arts, or humanities.

(H) **Funded research.** -- Any research to the extent funded by any grant, contract, or

Sec. 41. Credit for increasing research activities

otherwise by another person (or governmental entity).

(e) Credit allowable with respect to certain payments to qualified organizations for basic research. -- For purposes of this section--

(1) In general. -- In the case of any taxpayer who makes basic research payments for any taxable year--

(A) the amount of basic research payments taken into account under subsection (a)(2) shall be equal to the excess of--

(i) such basic research payments, over

(ii) the qualified organization base period amount, and

(B) that portion of such basic research payments which does not exceed the qualified organization base period amount shall be treated as contract research expenses for purposes of subsection (a)(1).

(2) Basic research payments defined. -- For purposes of this subsection--

(A) In general. -- The term "basic research payment" means, with respect to any taxable year, any amount paid in cash during such taxable year by a corporation to any qualified organization for basic research but only if--

(i) such payment is pursuant to a written agreement between such corporation and such qualified organization, and

(ii) such basic research is to be performed by such qualified organization.

(B) Exception to requirement that research be performed by the organization. -- In the case of a qualified organization described in subparagraph (C) or (D) of paragraph (6), clause (ii) of subparagraph (A) shall not apply.

(3) Qualified organization base period amount. -- For purposes of this subsection, the term "qualified organization base period amount" means an amount equal to the sum of--

(A) the minimum basic research amount, plus

(B) the maintenance-of-effort amount.

(4) Minimum basic research amount. -- For purposes of this subsection--

(A) In general. -- The term "minimum basic research amount" means an amount equal to the greater of--

(i) 1 percent of the average of the sum of amounts paid or incurred during the base period for--

(I) any in-house research expenses, and

(II) any contract research expenses, or

(ii) the amounts treated as contract research expenses during the base period by reason of this subsection (as in effect during the base period).

(B) Floor amount. -- Except in the case of a taxpayer which was in existence during a taxable year (other than a short taxable year) in th base period, the minimum basic research amount for any base period shall not be less than 50 percent of the basic research payments for the taxable year for which a determination is being made under this subsection.

(5) Maintenance-of-effort amount. -- For purposes of this subsection--

(A) In general. -- The term "maintenance-of-effort amount" means, with respect to any taxable year, an amount equal to the excess (if any) of--

(i) an amount equal to--

(I) the average of the nondesignated university contributions paid by the taxpayer

Sec. 41. Credit for increasing research activities

during the base period, multiplied by

 (II) the cost-of-living adjustment for the calendar year in which such taxable year begins, over

 (ii) the amount of nondesignated university contributions paid by the taxpayer during such taxable year. 5

(B) Nondesignated university contributions. -- For purposes of this paragraph, the term "nondesignated university contribution" means any amount paid by a taxpayer to any qualified organization described in paragraph (6)(A)--

 (i) for which a deduction was allowable under section 170, and

 (ii) which was not taken into account-- 10

  (I) in computing the amount of the credit under this section (as in effect during the base period) during any taxable year in the base period, or

  (II) as a basic research payment for purposes of this section.

(C) Cost-of-living adjustment defined. --

 (i) In general. -- The cost-of-living adjustment for any calendar year is the cost-of- 15 living adjustment for such calendar year determined under section 1(f)(3), by substituting "calendar year 1987" for "calendar year 1992" in subparagraph (B) thereof.

 (ii) Special rule where base period ends in a calendar year other than 1983 or 1984. -- If the base period of any taxpayer does not end in 1983 or 1984, section 1(f)(3) (B) shall, for purposes of this paragraph, be applied by substituting the calendar year in 20 which such base period ends for 1992. Such substitution shall be in lieu of the substitution under clause (i).

(6) Qualified organization. -- For purposes of this subsection, the term "qualified organization" means any of the following organizations:

(A) Educational institutions. -- Any educational organization which-- 25

 (i) is an institution of higher education (within the meaning of section 3304(f)), and

 (ii) is described in section 170(b)(1)(A)(ii).

(B) Certain scientific research organizations. -- Any organization not described in subparagraph (A) which--

 (i) is described in section 501(c)(3) and is exempt from tax under section 501(a), 30

 (ii) is organized and operated primarily to conduct scientific research, and

 (iii) is not a private foundation.

(C) Scientific tax-exempt organizations. -- Any organization which -

 (i) is described in--

  (I) section 501(c)(3) (other than a private foundation),or 35

  (II) section 501(c)(6),

 (ii) is exempt from tax under section 501(a),

 (iii) is organized and operated primarily to promote scientific research by qualified organizations described in subparagraph (A) pursuant to written research agreements, and 40

 (iv) currently expends--

  (I) substantially all of its funds, or

  (II) substantially all of the basic research payments received by it, for grants to, or contracts for basic research with, an organization described in subparagraph (A).

Sec. 41. Credit for increasing research activities

(D) Certain grant organizations. -- Any organization not described in subparagraph (B) or (C) which--

(i) is described in section 501(c)(3) and is exempt from tax under section 501(a) (other than a private foundation),

(ii) is established and maintained by an organization established before July 10, 1981, which meets the requirements of clause (i),

(iii) is organized and operated exclusively for the purpose of making grants to organizations described in subparagraph (A) pursuant to written research agreements for purposes of basic research, and

(iv) makes an election, revocable only with the consent of the Secretary, to be treated as a private foundation for purposes of this title (other than section 4940, relating to excise tax based on investment income).

(7) Definitions and special rules. -- For purposes of this subsection--

(A) Basic research. -- The term "basic research" means any original investigation for the advancement of scientific knowledge not having specific commercial objective, except that such term shall not include--

(i) basic research conducted outside of the United States, and

(ii) basic research in the social sciences, arts, or humanities.

(B) Base period. -- The term "base period" means the 3-taxable-year period ending with the taxable year immediately preceding the 1st taxable year of the taxpayer beginning after December 31, 1983.

(C) Exclusion from incremental credit calculation. -- For purposes of determining the amount of credit allowable under subsection (a)(1) for any taxable year, the amount of the basic research payments taken into account under subsection (a)(2)--

(i) shall not be treated as qualified research expenses under subsection (a)(1)(A), and

(ii) shall not be included in the computation of base amount under subsection (a)(1)(B).

(D) Trade or business qualification. -- For purposes of applying subsection (b)(1) to this subsection, any basic research payments shall be treated as an amount paid in carrying on a trade or business of the taxpayer in the taxable year in which it is paid (without regard to the provisions of subsection (b)(3)(B)).

(E) Certain corporations not eligible. -- The term "corporation" shall not include--

(i) an S corporation,

(ii) a personal holding company (as defined in section 542), or

(iii) a service organization (as defined in section 414(m)(3)).

(f) Special rules. -- For purposes of this section--

(1) Aggregation of expenditures. --

(A) Controlled group of corporations. -- In determining the amount of the credit under this section--

(i) all members of the same controlled group of corporations shall be treated as a single taxpayer, and

(ii) the credit (if any) allowable by this section to each such member shall be its proportionate shares of the qualified research expenses, basic research payments, and amounts paid or incurred to energy research consortiums, giving rise to the credit.

(B) Common control. -- Under regulations prescribed by the Secretary, in determining

Sec. 41. Credit for increasing research activities

the amount of the credit under this section--

> **(i)** all trades or businesses (whether or not incorporated) which are under common control shall be treated as a single taxpayer, and

> **(ii)** the credit (if any) allowable by this section to each such person shall be its proportionate shares of the qualified research expenses, basic research payments, and amounts paid or incurred to energy research consortiums, giving rise to the credit. 5

The regulations prescribed under this subparagraph shall be based on principles similar to the principles which apply in the case of subparagraph (A).

(2) Allocations. --

> **(A) Pass-thru in the case of estates and trusts.** -- Under regulations prescribed by the Secretary, rules similar to the rules of subsection (d) of section 52 shall apply. 10

> **(B) Allocation in the case of partnerships.** -- In the case of partnerships, the credit shall be allocated among partners under regulations prescribed by the Secretary.

(3) Adjustments for certain acquisitions, etc. -- Under regulations prescribed by the Secretary-- 15

> **(A) Acquisitions.** -- If, after December 31, 1983, a taxpayer acquires the major portion of a trade or business of another person (hereinafter in this paragraph referred to as the "predecessor") or the major portion of a separate unit of a trade or business of a predecessor, then, for purposes of applying this section for any taxable year ending after such acquisition, the amount of qualified research expenses paid or incurred by the 20 taxpayer during periods before such acquisition shall be increased by so much of such expenses paid or incurred by the predecessor with respect to the acquired trade or business as is attributable to the portion of such trade or business or separate unit acquired by the taxpayer, and the gross receipts of the taxpayer for such periods shall be increased by so much of the gross receipts of such predecessor with respect to the acquired trade or 25 business as is attributable to such portion.

> **(B) Dispositions.** -- If, after December 31, 1983--

>> **(i)** a taxpayer disposes of the major portion of any trade or business or the major portion of a separate unit of a trade or business in a transaction to which subparagraph (A) applies, and 30

>> **(ii)** the taxpayer furnished the acquiring person such information as is necessary for the application of subparagraph (A),

> then, for purposes of applying this section for any taxable year ending after such disposition, the amount of qualified research expenses paid or incurred by the taxpayer during periods before such disposition shall be decreased by so much of such expenses as 35 is attributable to the portion of such trade or business or separate unit disposed of by the taxpayer, and the gross receipts of the taxpayer for such periods shall be decreased by so much of the gross receipts as is attributable to such portion.

***

(4) Short taxable years. -- In the case of any short taxable year, qualified research expenses 40 and gross receipts shall be annualized in such circumstances and under such methods as the Secretary may prescribe by regulation.

(5) Controlled group of corporations. -- The term "controlled group of corporations" has the same meaning given to such term by section 1563(a), except that--

> **(A)** "more than 50 percent" shall be substituted for "at least 80 percent" each place it 45 appears in section 1563(a)(1), and

> **(B)** the determination shall be made without regard to subsections (a)(4) and (e)(3)(C)

79

of section 1563.

(6) Energy research consortium. --

    (A) In general. -- The term `energy research consortium' means any organization--

        (i) which is--

            (I) described in section 501(c)(3) and is exempt from tax under section 501(a) and is organized and operated primarily to conduct energy research, or

            (II) organized and operated primarily to conduct energy research in the public interest (within the meaning of section 501(c)(3)),

        (ii) which is not a private foundation,

        (iii) to which at least 5 unrelated persons paid or incurred during the calendar year in which the taxable year of the organization begins amounts (including as contributions) to such organization for energy research, and

        (iv) to which no single person paid or incurred (including as contributions) during such calendar year an amount equal to more than 50 percent of the total amounts received by such organization during such calendar year for energy research.

    (B) Treatment of persons. -- All persons treated as a single employer under subsection (a) or (b) of section 52 shall be treated as related persons for purposes of subparagraph (A) (iii) and as a single person for purposes of subparagraph (A)(iv).

***

    (E) Energy research. -- The term "energy research" does not include any research which is not qualified research

(g) Special rule for pass-thru of credit. -- In the case of an individual who--

    (1) owns an interest in an unincorporated trade or business,

    (2) is a partner in a partnership,

    (3) is a beneficiary of an estate or trust, or

    (4) is a shareholder in an S corporation,

the amount determined under subsection (a) for any taxable year shall not exceed an amount (separately computed with respect to such person's interest in such trade or business or entity) equal to the amount of tax attributable to that portion of a person's taxable income which is allocable or apportionable to the person's interest in such trade or business or entity. If the amount determined under subsection (a) for any taxable year exceeds the limitation of the preceding sentence, such amount may be carried to other taxable years under the rules of section 39; except that the limitation of the preceding sentence shall be taken into account in lieu of the limitation of section 38(c) in applying section 39.

(h) Termination. --

    (1) In general. -- This section shall not apply to any amount paid or incurred--

        (A) after June 30, 1995, and before July 1, 1996, or

        (B) after December 31, 2010.

    (2) Computation of base amount. -- In the case of any taxable year with respect to which this section applies to a number of days which is less than the total number of days in such taxable year, the base amount with respect to such taxable year shall be the amount which bears the same ratio to the base amount for such year (determined without regard to this paragraph) as the number of days in such taxable year to which this section applies bears to the total number of days in such taxable year.

Sec. 42. Low-income housing credit

(a) In general. -- For purposes of section 38, the amount of the low-income housing credit determined under this section for any taxable year in the credit period shall be an amount equal to-

(1) the applicable percentage of

(2) the qualified basis of each qualified low-income building.

(b) Applicable percentage: 70 percent present value credit for certain new buildings; 30 percent present value credit for certain other buildings. -- For purposes of this section -

***

(2) Buildings placed in service after 1987. --

(A) In general. -- In the case of any qualified low-income building placed in service by the taxpayer after 1987, the term "applicable percentage" means the appropriate percentage prescribed by the Secretary for the earlier of--

(i) the month in which such building is placed in service, or

(ii) at the election of the taxpayer -

(I) the month in which the taxpayer and the housing credit agency enter into an agreement with respect to such building (which is binding on such agency, the taxpayer, and all successors in interest) as to the housing credit dollar amount to be allocated to such building, or

(II) in the case of any building to which subsection (h)(4)(B) applies, the month in which the tax-exempt obligations are issued.

A month may be elected under clause (ii) only if the election is made not later than the 5th day after the close of such month. Such an election, once made, shall be irrevocable.

(B) Method of prescribing percentages. -- The percentages prescribed by the Secretary for any month shall be percentages which will yield over a 10-year period amounts of credit under subsection (a) which have a present value equal to--

(i) 70 percent of the qualified basis of a building described in paragraph (1)(A), and

(ii) 30 percent of the qualified basis of a building described in paragraph (1)(B).

(C) Method of discounting. -- The present value under subparagraph (B) shall be determined--

(i) as of the last day of the 1st year of the 10-year period referred to in subparagraph (B),

(ii) by using a discount rate equal to 72 percent of the average of the annual Federal mid-term rate and the annual Federal long-term rate applicable under section 1274(d) (1) to   the month applicable under clause (i) or (ii) of subparagraph (A) and compounded annually, and

(iii) by assuming that the credit allowable under this section for any year is received on the last day of such year.

(3) Cross references. --

(A) For treatment of certain rehabilitation expenditures as separate new buildings, see subsection (e).

(B) For determination of applicable percentage for increases in qualified basis after the 1st year of the credit period, see subsection (f)(3).

(C) For authority of housing credit agency to limit applicable percentage and qualified basis which may be taken into account under this section with respect to any building, see

Sec. 42. Low-income housing credit

subsection (h)(7).

(c) Qualified basis; qualified low-income building. -- For purposes of this section--

(1) Qualified basis. --

(A) Determination. -- The qualified basis of any qualified low-income building for any taxable year is an amount equal to--

(i) the applicable fraction (determined as of the close of such taxable year) of

(ii) the eligible basis of such building (determined under subsection (d)(5)).

(B) Applicable fraction. -- For purposes of subparagraph (A), the term "applicable fraction" means the smaller of the unit fraction or the floor space fraction.

(C) Unit fraction. -- For purposes of subparagraph (B), the term "unit fraction" means the fraction--

(i) the numerator of which is the number of low-income units in the building, and

(ii) the denominator of which is the number of residential rental units (whether or not occupied) in such building.

(D) Floor space fraction. -- For purposes of subparagraph (B), the term "floor space fraction" means the fraction--

(i) the numerator of which is the total floor space of the low-income units in such building, and

(ii) the denominator of which is the total floor space of the residential rental units (whether or not occupied) in such building.

(E) Qualified basis to include portion of building used to provide supportive services for homeless. -- In the case of a qualified low-income building described in subsection (i)(3)(B)(iii), the qualified basis of such building for any taxable year shall be increased by the lesser of--

(i) so much of the eligible basis of such building as is used throughout the year to provide supportive services designed to assist tenants in locating and retaining permanent housing, or

(ii) 20 percent of the qualified basis of such building (determined without regard to this subparagraph).

(2) Qualified low-income building. -- The term "qualified low-income building" means any building--

(A) which is part of a qualified low-income housing project at all times during the period -

(i) beginning on the 1st day in the compliance period on which such building is part of such a project, and

(ii) ending on the last day of the compliance period with respect to such building, and

(B) to which the amendments made by section 201(a) of the Tax Reform Act of 1986 apply.

Such term does not include any building with respect to which moderate rehabilitation assistance is provided, at any time during the compliance period, under section 8(e)(2) (!1) of the United States Housing Act of 1937 (other than assistance under the McKinney-Vento Homeless Assistance Act (as in effect on the date of the enactment of this sentence)).

(d) Eligible basis. -- For purposes of this section--

(1) New buildings. -- The eligible basis of a new building is its adjusted basis as of the close of the 1st taxable year of the credit period.

Sec. 42. Low-income housing credit

(2) Existing buildings. --

(A) In general. -- The eligible basis of an existing building is--

(i) in the case of a building which meets the requirements of subparagraph (B), its adjusted basis as of the close of the 1st taxable year of the credit period, and

(ii) zero in any other case.

(B) Requirements. -- A building meets the requirements of this subparagraph if--

(i) the building is acquired by purchase (as defined in section 179(d)(2)),

(ii) there is a period of at least 10 years between the date of its acquisition by the taxpayer and the later of -

(I) the date the building was last placed in service, or

(II) the date of the most recent nonqualified substantial improvement of the building,

(iii) the building was not previously placed in service by the taxpayer or by any person who was a related person with respect to the taxpayer as of the time previously placed in service, and

(iv) except as provided in subsection (f)(5), a credit is allowable under subsection (a) by reason of subsection (e) with respect to the building.

(C) Adjusted basis. -- For purposes of subparagraph (A), the adjusted basis of any building shall not include so much of the basis of such building as is determined by reference to the basis of other property held at any time by the person acquiring the building.

(D) Special rules for subparagraph (B). --

(i) Nonqualified substantial improvement. -- For purposes of subparagraph (B) (ii)--

(I) In general. -- The term "nonqualified substantial improvement" means any substantial improvement if section 167(k) (as in effect on the day before the date of the enactment of the Revenue Reconciliation Act of 1990) was elected with respect to such improvement or section 168 (as in effect on the day before the date of the enactment of the Tax Reform Act of 1986) applied to such improvement.

(II) Date of substantial improvement. -- The date of a substantial improvement is the last day of the 24-month period referred to in subclause (III).

(III) Substantial improvement. -- The term "substantial improvement" means the improvements added to capital account with respect to the building during any 24-month period, but only if the sum of the amounts added to such account during such period equals or exceeds 25 percent of the adjusted basis of the building (determined without regard to paragraphs (2) and (3) of section 1016(a)) as of the 1st day of such period.

(ii) Special rules for certain transfers. -- For purposes of determining under subparagraph (B)(ii) when a building was last placed in service, there shall not be taken into account any placement in service--

(I) in connection with the acquisition of the building in a transaction in which the basis of the building in the hands of the person acquiring it is determined in whole or in part by reference to the adjusted basis of such building in the hands of the person from whom acquired,

(II) by a person whose basis in such building is determined under section 1014(a) (relating to property acquired from a decedent),

Sec. 42.   Low-income housing credit

(III) by any governmental unit or qualified nonprofit organization (as defined in subsection (h)(5)) if the requirements of subparagraph (B)(ii) are met with respect to the placement in service by such unit or organization and all the income from such property is exempt from Federal income taxation,

(IV) by any person who acquired such building by foreclosure (or by instrument in lieu of foreclosure) of any purchase-money security interest held by such person if the requirements of subparagraph (B)(ii) are met with respect to the placement in service by such person and such building is resold within 12 months after the date such building is placed i n service by such person after such foreclosure, or

(V) of a single-family residence by any individual who owned and used such residence for no other purpose than as his principal residence.

(iii) Related person, etc. --

(I) Application of section 179. -- For purposes of subparagraph (B)(i), section 179(d) shall be applied by substituting "10 percent" for "50 percent" in section (!2) 267(b) and 707(b) and in section 179(d)(7).

(II) Related person. -- For purposes of subparagraph (B)(iii), a person (hereinafter in this subclause referred to as the "related   person") is related to any person if the related person bears a relationship to such person specified in section 267(b) or 707(b)(1), or the related person and such person are engaged in trades or businesses under common control (within the meaning of subsections (a) and (b) of section 52). For purposes of the preceding sentence, in applying section 267(b) or 707(b)(1), "10 percent" shall be substituted for "50 percent".

(3) Eligible basis reduced where disproportionate standards for units. --

(A) In general. -- Except as provided in subparagraph (B), the eligible basis of any building shall be reduced by an amount equal to the portion of the adjusted basis of the building which is attributable to residential rental units in the building which are not low income units and which are above the average quality standard of the low-income units in the building.

(B) Exception where taxpayer elects to exclude excess costs. --

(i) In general. -- Subparagraph (A) shall not apply with respect to a residential rental unit in a building which is not a low-income unit if--

(I) the excess described in clause (ii) with respect to such unit is not greater than 15 percent of the cost described in clause (ii)(II), and

(II) the taxpayer elects to exclude from the eligible basis of such building the excess described in clause (ii) with respect to such unit.

(ii) Excess. -- The excess described in this clause with respect to any unit is the excess of--

(I) the cost of such unit, over

(II) the amount which would be the cost of such unit if the average cost per square foot of low-income units in the building were substituted for the cost per square foot of such unit.

The Secretary may by regulation provide for the determination of the excess under this clause on a basis other than square foot costs.

(4) Special rules relating to determination of adjusted basis. -- For purposes of this subsection--

(A) In general. -- Except as provided in subparagraphs (B) and (C), the adjusted basis of any building shall be determined without regard to the adjusted basis of any property which

84

Sec. 42. Low-income housing credit

is not residential rental property.

(B) Basis of property in common areas, etc., included. -- The adjusted basis of any building shall be determined by taking into account the adjusted basis of property (of a character subject to the allowance for depreciation) used in common areas or provided as comparable amenities to al residential rental units in such building. 5

(C) Inclusion of basis of property used to provide services for certain nontenants. --

(i) In general. -- The adjusted basis of any building located in a qualified census tract (as defined in paragraph (5)(C)) shall be determined by taking into account the adjusted basis of property (of a character subject to the allowance for depreciation and not otherwise taken into account) used throughout the taxable year in providing any 10 community service facility.

(ii) Limitation. -- The increase in the adjusted basis of any building which is taken into account by reason of clause (i) shall not exceed 10 percent of the eligible basis of the qualified low-income housing project of which it is a part. For purposes of the preceding sentence, all community service facilities which are part of the same 15 qualified low-income housing project shall be treated as one facility.

(iii) Community service facility. -- For purposes of this subparagraph, the term "community service facility" means any facility designed to serve primarily individuals whose income is 60 percent or less of area median income (within the meaning of subsection (g)(1)(B)). 20

(D) No reduction for depreciation. -- The adjusted basis of any building shall be determined without regard to paragraphs (2) and (3) of section 1016(a).

(5) Special rules for determining eligible basis. --

(A) Eligible basis reduced by Federal grants. -- If, during any taxable year of the compliance period, a grant is made with respect to any building or the operation thereof 25 and any portion of such grant is funded with Federal funds (whether or not includible in gross income), the eligible basis of such building for such taxable year and all succeeding taxable years shall be reduced by the portion of such grant which is so funded.

(B) Eligible basis not to include expenditures where section 167(k) elected. -- The eligible basis of any building shall not include any portion of its adjusted basis which is 30 attributable to amount with respect to which an election is made under section 167(k) (as in effect on the day before the date of the enactment of the Revenue Reconciliation Act of 1990).

(C) Increase in credit for buildings in high cost areas. --

(i) In general. -- In the case of any building located in a qualified census tract or 35 difficult development area which is designated for purposes of this subparagraph--

(I) in the case of a new building, the eligible basis of such building shall be 130 percent of such basis determined without regard to this subparagraph, and

(II) in the case of an existing building, the rehabilitation expenditures taken into account under subsection (e) shall be 130 percent of such expenditures determined without regard 40 to this subparagraph.

(ii) Qualified census tract. --

(I) In general. -- The term "qualified census tract" means any census tract which is designated by the Secretary of Housing and Urban Development and, for the most recent year for which census data are available on household income in such tract, either in which 45 50 percent or more of the households have an income which is less than 60 percent of the area median gross income for such year or which has a poverty rate of at least 25 percent.

Sec. 42. Low-income housing credit

If the Secretary of Housing and Urban   Development determines that sufficient data for any period are not available to apply this clause on the basis of census tracts, such Secretary shall apply this clause for such period on the basis of enumeration districts.

(II) Limit on MSA's designated. -- The portion of a metropolitan statistical area which may be designated for purposes of this subparagraph shall not exceed an area having 20 percent of the population of such metropolitan statistical area.

(III) Determination of areas. -- For purposes of this clause, each metropolitan statistical area shall be treated as a separate area and all nonmetropolitan areas in a State shall be treated as 1 area.

(iii) Difficult development areas. --

(I) In general. -- The term "difficult development areas" means any area designated by the Secretary of Housing and Urban Development as an area which has high construction, land, and utility costs relative to area median gross income.

(II) Limit on areas designated. -- The portions of metropolitan statistical areas which may be designated for purposes of this subparagraph shall not exceed an aggregate area having 20 percent of the population of such metropolitan statistical areas. A comparable rule shall apply to nonmetropolitan areas.

(iv) Special rules and definitions. -- For purposes of this subparagraph--

(I) population shall be determined on the basis of the most recent decennial census for which data are available,

(II) area median gross income shall be determined in accordance with subsection (g)(4),

(III) the term "metropolitan statistical area" has the same meaning as when used in section 143(k)(2)(B), and

(IV) the term "nonmetropolitan area" means any county (or portion thereof) which is not within a metropolitan statistical area.

(6) Credit allowable for certain federally-assisted buildings acquired during 10-year period described in paragraph (2)(B)(ii). --

(A) In general. -- On application by the taxpayer, the Secretary (after consultation with the appropriate Federal official) may waive paragraph (2)(B)(ii) with respect to any federally-assisted building if the Secretary determines that such waiver is necessary--

(i) to avert an assignment of the mortgage secured by property in the project (of which such building is a part) to the Department of Housing and Urban Development or the Farmers Home Administration, or

(ii) to avert a claim against a Federal mortgage insurance fund (or such Department or Administration) with respect to a mortgage which is so secured.

The preceding sentence shall not apply to any building described in paragraph (7)(B).

(B) Federally-assisted building. -- For purposes of subparagraph (A), the term "federally-assisted building" means any building which is substantially assisted, financed, or operated under--

(i) section 8 of the United States Housing Act of 1937,

(ii) section 221(d)(3) or 236 of the National Housing Act, or

(iii) section 515 of the Housing Act of 1949, as such Acts are in effect on the date of the enactment of the Tax Reform Act of 1986.

(C) Low-income buildings where mortgage may be prepaid. -- A waiver may be granted under subparagraph (A) (without regard to any clause thereof) with respect to a

Sec. 42. Low-income housing credit

federally- assisted building described in clause (ii) or (iii) of subparagraph (B) if--

 (i) the mortgage on such building is eligible for prepayment under subtitle B of the Emergency Low Income Housing Preservation Act of 1987 or under section 502(c) of the Housing Act of 1949 at any time within 1 year after the date of the application for such a waiver, 5

 (ii) the appropriate Federal official certifies to the Secretary that it is reasonable to expect that, if the waiver is not granted, such building will cease complying with its low-income occupancy requirements, and

 (iii) the eligibility to prepay such mortgage without the approval of the appropriate Federal official is waived by all 10
persons who are so eligible and such waiver is binding on all successors of such persons.

(D) Buildings acquired from insured depository institutions in default. -- A waiver may be granted under subparagraph (A) (without regard to any clause thereof) with respect to any building acquired from an insured depository institution in default (as defined in section 3 of the Federal Deposit Insurance Act) or from a receiver or conservator of such an 15 institution.

(E) Appropriate Federal official. -- For purposes of subparagraph (A), the term "appropriate Federal official" means--

 (i) the Secretary of Housing and Urban Development in the case of any building described in subparagraph (B) by reason of clause (i) or (ii) thereof, and 20

 (ii) the Secretary of Agriculture in the case of any building described in subparagraph (B) by reason of clause (iii) thereof.

(7) Acquisition of building before end of prior compliance period. --

 (A) In general. -- Under regulations prescribed by the Secretary, in the case of a building described in subparagraph (B) (or interest therein) which is acquired by the 25 taxpayer--

 (i) paragraph (2)(B) shall not apply, but

 (ii) the credit allowable by reason of subsection (a) to the taxpayer for any period after such acquisition shall be equal to the amount of credit which would have been allowable under subsection (a) for such period to the prior owner referred to in 30 subparagraph (B) had such owner not disposed of the building.

 (B) Description of building. -- A building is described in this subparagraph if--

 (i) a credit was allowed by reason of subsection (a) to any prior owner of such building, and

 (ii) the taxpayer acquired such building before the end of the compliance period for such 35 building with respect to such prior owner (determined without regard to any disposition by such prior owner).

(e) Rehabilitation expenditures treated as separate new building. --

 (1) In general. -- Rehabilitation expenditures paid or incurred by the taxpayer with respect to any building shall be treated for purposes of this section as a separate new building. 40

***

(f) Definition and special rules relating to credit period. --

 (1) Credit period defined. -- For purposes of this section, the term "credit period" means, with respect to any building, the period of 10 taxable years beginning with--

 (A) the taxable year in which the building is placed in service, or 45

 (B) at the election of the taxpayer, the succeeding taxable year, but only if the building

87

Sec. 42. Low-income housing credit

is a qualified low-income building as of the close of the 1st year of such period. The election under subparagraph (B), once made, shall be irrevocable.

***

(g) Qualified low-income housing project. -- For purposes of this section--

(1) In general. -- The term "qualified low-income housing project" means any project for residential rental property if the project meets the requirements of subparagraph (A) or (B) whichever is elected by the taxpayer:

(A) 20-50 test. -- The project meets the requirements of this subparagraph if 20 percent or more of the residential units in such project are both rent-restricted and occupied by individuals whose income is 50 percent or less of area median gross income.

(B) 40-60 test. -- The project meets the requirements of this subparagraph if 40 percent or more of the residential units in such project are both rent-restricted and occupied by individuals whose income is 60 percent or less of area median gross income.

Any election under this paragraph, once made, shall be irrevocable. For purposes of this paragraph, any property shall not be treated as failing to be residential rental property merely because part of the building in which such property is located is used for purposes other than residential rental purposes.

***

(h) Limitation on aggregate credit allowable with respect to projects located in a State. --

(1) Credit may not exceed credit amount allocated to building. --

(A) In general. -- The amount of the credit determined under this section for any taxable year with respect to any building shall not exceed the housing credit dollar amount allocated to such building under this subsection.

***

(i) Definitions and special rules. -- For purposes of this section -

(1) Compliance period. -- The term "compliance period" means, with respect to any building, the period of 15 taxable years beginning with the 1st taxable year of the credit period with respect thereto.

***

(j) Recapture of credit. --

(1) In general. -- If--

(A) as of the close of any taxable year in the compliance period, the amount of the qualified basis of any building with respect to the taxpayer is less than

(B) the amount of such basis as of the close of the preceding taxable year, then the taxpayer's tax under this chapter for the taxable year shall be increased by the credit recapture amount.

(2) Credit recapture amount. -- For purposes of paragraph (1), the credit recapture amount **is an amount equal to the sum of--**

(A) the aggregate decrease in the credits allowed to the taxpayer under section 38 for all prior taxable years which would have resulted if the accelerated portion of the credit allowable by reason of this section were not allowed for all prior taxable years with respect to the excess of the amount described in paragraph (1)(B) over the amount described in paragraph (1)(A), plus

(B) interest at the overpayment rate established under section 6621 on the amount determined under subparagraph (A) for each prior taxable year for the period beginning on the due date for filing the return for the prior taxable year involved.

Sec. 42. Low-income housing credit

No deduction shall be allowed under this chapter for interest described in subparagraph (B).

(3) Accelerated portion of credit. -- For purposes of paragraph (2), the accelerated portion of the credit for the prior taxable years with respect to any amount of basis is the excess of--

(A) the aggregate credit allowed by reason of this section (without regard to this subsection) for such years with respect to such basis, over 5

(B) the aggregate credit which would be allowable by reason of this section for such years with respect to such basis if the aggregate credit which would (but for this subsection) have been allowable for the entire compliance period were allowable ratably over 15 years.

*** 10

(k) Application of at-risk rules. -- For purposes of this section--

(1) In general. -- Except as otherwise provided in this subsection, rules similar to the rules of section 49(a)(1) (other than subparagraphs (D)(ii)(II) and (D)(iv)(I) thereof), section 49(a)(2), and section 49(b)(1) shall apply in determining the qualified basis of any building in the same manner as such sections apply in determining the credit base of property. 15

(2) Special rules for determining qualified person. -- For purposes of paragraph (1)--

(A) In general. -- If the requirements of subparagraphs (B), (C), and (D) are met with respect to any financing borrowed from a qualified nonprofit organization (as defined in subsection (h)(5)), the determination of whether such financing is qualified commercial financing with respect to any qualified low-income building shall be made without regard 20 to whether such organization--

(i) is actively and regularly engaged in the business of lending money, or

(ii) is a person described in section 49(a)(1)(D)(iv)(II).

***

(l) Certifications and other Reports to the Secretary. -- 25

(1) Certification with respect to 1st year of credit period. -- Following the close of the 1st taxable year in the credit period with respect to any qualified low-income building, the taxpayer shall certify to the Secretary (at such time and in such form and in such manner as the Secretary prescribes)--

(A) the taxable year, and calendar year, in which such building was placed in service, 30

(B) the adjusted basis and eligible basis of such building as of the close of the 1st year of the credit period,

(C) the maximum applicable percentage and qualified basis permitted to be taken into account by the appropriate housing credit agency under subsection (h),

(D) the election made under subsection (g) with respect to the qualified low-income 35 housing project of which such building is a part, and

(E) such other information as the Secretary may require.
In the case of a failure to make the certification required by the preceding sentence on the date prescribed therefor, unless it is shown that such failure is due to reasonable cause and not to willful neglect, no credit shall be allowable by reason of subsection (a) with respect to such 40 building for any taxable year ending before such certification is made.

(2) Annual reports to the Secretary. -- The Secretary may require taxpayers to submit an information return (at such time and in such form and manner as the Secretary prescribes) for each taxable year setting forth--

(A) the qualified basis for the taxable year of each qualified low-income building of the 45 taxpayer,

89

Sec. 42. Low-income housing credit

(B) the information described in paragraph (1)(C) for the taxable year, and

(C) such other information as the Secretary may require.

The penalty under section 6652(j) shall apply to any failure to submit the return required by the Secretary under the preceding sentence on the date prescribed therefor.

(3) Annual reports from housing credit agencies. -- Each agency which allocates any housing credit amount to any building for any calendar year shall submit to the Secretary (at such time and in such manner as the Secretary shall prescribe) an annual report specifying -

(A) the amount of housing credit amount allocated to each building for such year,

(B) sufficient information to identify each such building and the taxpayer with respect thereto, and

(C) such other information as the Secretary may require.

The penalty under section 6652(j) shall apply to any failure to submit the report required by the preceding sentence on the date prescribed therefor.

***

Sec. 46. Amount of credit

For purposes of section 38, the amount of the investment credit determined under this section for any taxable year shall be the sum of--

(1) the rehabilitation credit,

(2) (2) the energy credit.

***

Sec. 47. Rehabilitation credit

(a) General rule. -- For purposes of section 46, the rehabilitation credit for any taxable year is the sum of--

(1) 10 percent of the qualified rehabilitation expenditures with respect to any qualified rehabilitated building other than a certified historic structure, and

(2) 20 percent of the qualified rehabilitation expenditures with respect to any certified historic structure.

(b) When expenditures taken into account. --

(1) In general. -- Qualified rehabilitation expenditures with respect to any qualified rehabilitated building shall be taken into account for the taxable year in which such qualified rehabilitated building is placed in service.

***

(c) Definitions. -- For purposes of this section -

(1) Qualified rehabilitated building. --

(A) In general. -- The term "qualified rehabilitated building" means any building (and its structural components) if--

(i) such building has been substantially rehabilitated,

(ii) such building was placed in service before the beginning of the rehabilitation,

(iii) in the case of any building other than a certified historic structure, in the rehabilitation process--

(I) 50 percent or more of the existing external walls of such building are retained in place as external walls,

Sec. 47. Rehabilitation credit

(II) 75 percent or more of the existing external walls of such building are retained in place as internal or external walls, and

(III) 75 percent or more of the existing internal structural framework of such building is retained in place, and

(iv) depreciation (or amortization in lieu of depreciation) is allowable with respect to such building.

(B) Building must be first placed in service before 1936. -- In the case of a building other than a certified historic structure, a building shall not be a qualified rehabilitated building unless the building was first placed in service before 1936.

(C) Substantially rehabilitated defined. --

(i) In general. -- For purposes of subparagraph (A)(i), a building shall be treated as having been substantially rehabilitated only if the qualified rehabilitation expenditures during the 24-month period selected by the taxpayer (at the time and in the manner prescribed by regulation) and ending with or within the taxable year exceed the greater of--

(I) the adjusted basis of such building (and its structural components), or

(II) $5,000.

The adjusted basis of the building (and its structural components) shall be determined as of the beginning of the 1st day of such 24-month period, or of the holding period of the building, whichever is later. For purposes of the preceding sentence, the determination of the beginning of the holding period shall be made without regard to any reconstruction by the taxpayer in connection with the rehabilitation.

***

(2) Qualified rehabilitation expenditure defined. --

(A) In general. -- The term "qualified rehabilitation expenditure" means any amount properly chargeable to capital account--

(i) for property for which depreciation is allowable under section 168 and which is -

(I) nonresidential real property,

(II) residential rental property,

(III) real property which has a class life of more than 12.5 years, or

(IV) an addition or improvement to property described in subclause (I), (II), or (III), and

(ii) in connection with the rehabilitation of a qualified rehabilitated building.

(B) Certain expenditures not included. -- The term "qualified rehabilitation expenditure" does not include--

(i) Straight line depreciation must be used. -- Any expenditure with respect to which the taxpayer does not use the straight line method over a recovery period determined under subsection (c) or (g) of section 168. The preceding sentence shall not apply to any expenditure to the extent the alternative depreciation system of section 168(g) applies to such expenditure by reason of subparagraph (B) or (C) of section 168(g)(1).

(ii) Cost of acquisition. -- The cost of acquiring any building or interest therein.

(iii) Enlargements. -- Any expenditure attributable to the enlargement of an existing building.

***

Sec. 47. Rehabilitation credit

(D) **Nonresidential real property; residential rental property; class life.** -- For purposes of subparagraph (A), the terms "nonresidential real property," "residential rental property," and "class life" have the respective meanings given such terms by section 168.

(3) **Certified historic structure defined.** --

(A) **In general.** -- The term "certified historic structure" means any building (and its structural components) which--

(i) is listed in the National Register, or

(ii) is located in a registered historic district and is certified by the Secretary of the Interior to the Secretary as being of historic significance to the district.

***

Sec. 48. Energy credit

(a) **Energy credit.** --

(1) **In general.** -- For purposes of section 46, except as provided in paragraph (1)(B) or (2) (B) of subsection (d), the energy credit for any taxable year is the energy percentage of the basis of each energy property placed in service during such taxable year.

(2) **Energy percentage.** --

(A) **In general. -- The energy percentage is--**

(i) 30 percent in the case of--

(I) qualified fuel cell property,

(II) energy property described in paragraph (3)(A)(i) but only with respect to periods ending before January 1, 2009, and

(III) energy property described in paragraph (3)(A)(ii), and

(ii) in the case of any energy property to which clause (i) does not apply, 10 percent.

(B) **Coordination with rehabilitation credit.** -- The energy percentage shall not apply to that portion of the basis of any property which is attributable to qualified rehabilitation expenditures.

(3) **Energy property.** -- For purposes of this subpart, the term "energy property" means any property--

(A) which is--

(i) equipment which uses solar energy to generate electricity, to heat or cool (or provide hot water for use in) a structure, or to provide solar process heat, excepting property used to generate energy for the purposes of heating a swimming pool,

(ii) equipment which uses solar energy to illuminate the inside of a structure using fiber-optic distributed sunlight but only with respect to periods ending before January 1, 2009,

(iii) equipment used to produce, distribute, or use energy derived from a geothermal deposit (within the meaning of section 613(e)(2)), but only, in the case of electricity generated by geothermal power, up to (but not including) the electrical transmission stage, or`

(iv) qualified fuel cell property or qualified microturbine property,

(B)(i) the construction, reconstruction, or erection of which is completed by the taxpayer, or

(ii) which is acquired by the taxpayer if the original use of such property commences with the taxpayer,

(C) with respect to which depreciation (or amortization in lieu of depreciation) is allowable, and

(D) which meets the performance and quality standards (if any) which--

(i) have been prescribed by the Secretary by regulations (after consultation with the Secretary of Energy), and

(ii) are in effect at the time of the acquisition of the property.

***

(c) **Qualified Fuel Cell Property; Qualified Microturbine Property**. -- For purposes of this section --

(1) **Qualified fuel cell property.** --

(A) **In general.** -- The term `qualified fuel cell property' means a fuel cell power plant which--

(i) has a nameplate capacity of at least 0.5 kilowatt of electricity using an electrochemical process, and

(ii) has an electricity-only generation efficiency greater than 30 percent.

(B) **Limitation**. -- In the case of qualified fuel cell property placed in service during the taxable year, the credit otherwise determined under subsection (a) for such year with respect to such property shall not exceed an amount equal to $500 for each 0.5 kilowatt of capacity of such property.

***

(E) **Termination.** -- The term `qualified fuel cell property' shall not include any property for any period after December 31, 2008.

(2) **Qualified microturbine property.** --

(A) **In general.** -- The term `qualified microturbine property' means a stationary microturbine power plant which--

(i) has a nameplate capacity of less than 2,000 kilowatts, and

(ii) has an electricity-only generation efficiency of not less than 26 percent at International Standard Organization conditions.

(B) **Limitation.** -- In the case of qualified microturbine property placed in service during the taxable year, the credit otherwise determined under subsection (a) for such year with respect to such property shall not exceed an amount equal $200 for each kilowatt of capacity of such property.

(C) **Stationary microturbine power plant.** -- The term `stationary microturbine power plant' means an integrated system comprised of a gas turbine engine, a combustor, a recuperator or regenerator, a generator or alternator, and associated balance of plant components which converts a fuel into electricity and thermal energy. Such term also includes all secondary components located between the existing infrastructure for fuel delivery and the existing infrastructure for power distribution, including equipment and controls for meeting relevant power standards, such as voltage, frequency, and power factors.

***

(E) **Termination.** -- The term `qualified microturbine property' shall not include any property for any period after December 31, 2008.

***

5

10

15

20

25

30

35

40

45

Sec. 50. Other special rules

(a) Recapture in case of dispositions, etc. -- Under regulations prescribed by the Secretary--

(1) Early disposition, etc. --

(A) General rule. -- If, during any taxable year, investment credit property is disposed of, or otherwise ceases to be investment credit property with respect to the taxpayer, before the close of the recapture period, then the tax under this chapter for such taxable year shall be increased by the recapture percentage of the aggregate decrease in the credits allowed under section 38 for all prior taxable years which would have resulted solely from reducing to zero any credit determined under this subpart with respect to such property.

(B) Recapture percentage. -- For purposes of subparagraph (A), the recapture percentage shall be determined in accordance with the following table:

If the property ceases to be investment credit property within -	The recapture percentage is:
(i) One full year after placed in service............................	100
(ii) One full year after the close of the period described in clause (i).............................	80
(iii) One full year after the close of the period described in clause (ii)...........................	60
(iv) One full year after the close of the period described in clause (iii)..........................	40
(v) One full year after the close of the period described in clause (iv)..........................	20

***

(4) Subsection not to apply in certain cases. -- Paragraphs (1) and (2) shall not apply to--

(A) a transfer by reason of death, or

(B) a transaction to which section 381(a) applies.

For purposes of this subsection, property shall not be treated as ceasing to be investment credit property with respect to the taxpayer by reason of a mere change in the form of conducting the trade or business so long as the property is retained in such trade or business as investment credit property and the taxpayer retains a substantial interest in such trade or business.

(5) Definitions and special rules. --

(A) Investment credit property. -- For purposes of this subsection, the term "investment credit property" means any property eligible for a credit determined under this subpart.

(B) Transfer between spouses or incident to divorce. -- In the case of any transfer described in subsection (a) of section 1041--

(i) the foregoing provisions of this subsection shall not apply, and

(ii) the same tax treatment under this subsection with respect to the transferred property shall apply to the transferee as would have applied to the transferor.

(C) Special rule. -- Any increase in tax under paragraph (1) or (2) shall not be treated as tax imposed by this chapter for purposes of determining the amount of any credit allowable under this chapter.

***

(c) Basis adjustment to investment credit property. --

Sec. 50. Other special rules

(1) In general. -- For purposes of this subtitle, if a credit is determined under this subpart with respect to any property, the basis of such property shall be reduced by the amount of the credit so determined.

(2) Certain dispositions. -- If during any taxable year there is a recapture amount determined with respect to any property the basis of which was reduced under paragraph (1), the basis of such property (immediately before the event resulting in such recapture) shall be increased by an amount equal to such recapture amount. For purposes of the preceding sentence, the term "recapture amount" means any increase in tax (or adjustment in carrybacks or carryovers) determined under subsection (a).

(3) Special rule. -- In the case of any energy credit--

    (A) only 50 percent of such credit shall be taken into account under paragraph (1), and

    (B) only 50 percent of any recapture amount attributable to such credit shall be taken into account under paragraph (2).

(4) Recapture of reductions. --

    (A) In general. -- For purposes of sections 1245 and 1250, any reduction under this subsection shall be treated as a deduction allowed for   depreciation.

    (B) Special rule for section 1250. -- For purposes of section 1250(b), the determination of what would have been the depreciation adjustments under the straight line method shall be made as if there had been no reduction under this section.

***

Sec. 51. Amount of credit

(a) Determination of amount. -- For purposes of section 38, the amount of the work opportunity credit determined under this section for the taxable year shall be equal to 40 percent of the qualified first-year wages for such year.

(b) Qualified wages defined. -- For purposes of this subpart--

    (1) In general. -- The term "qualified wages" means the wages paid or incurred by the employer during the taxable year to individuals who are members of a targeted group.

***

Sec. 53. Credit for prior year minimum tax liability

(a) Allowance of credit. -- There shall be allowed as a credit against the tax imposed by this chapter for any taxable year an amount equal to the minimum tax credit for such taxable year.

(b) Minimum tax credit. -- For purposes of subsection (a), the minimum tax credit for any taxable year is the excess (if any) of--

    (1) the adjusted net minimum tax imposed for all prior taxable years beginning after 1986, over

    (2) the amount allowable as a credit under subsection (a) for such prior taxable years.

(c) Limitation. -- The credit allowable under subsection (a) for any taxable year shall not exceed the excess (if any) of--

    (1) the regular tax liability of the taxpayer for such taxable year reduced by the sum of the credits allowable under subparts A, B, D, E, and F of this part, over

    (2) the tentative minimum tax for the taxable year.

(d) Definitions. -- For purposes of this section--

    (1) Net minimum tax. --

95

Sec. 53.   Credit for prior year minimum tax liability

(A) **In general.** -- The term "net minimum tax" means the tax imposed by section 55.

(B) **Credit not allowed for exclusion preferences.** --

(i) **Adjusted net minimum tax.** -- The adjusted net minimum tax for any taxable year is--

(I) the amount of the net minimum tax for such taxable year, reduced by

(II) the amount which would be the net minimum tax for such taxable year if the only adjustments and items of tax preference taken into account were those specified in clause (ii).

(ii) **Specified items.** -- The following are specified in this clause--

(I) the adjustments provided for in subsection (b)(1) of section 56, and

(II) the items of tax preference described in paragraphs (1), (5), and (7) of section 57(a).

(iii) **Special rule.** -- The adjusted net minimum tax for the taxable year shall be increased by the amount of the credit not allowed under section 30 solely by reason of the application of section 30(b)(3)(B).

(iv) **Credit allowable for exclusion preferences of corporations.** -- In the case of a corporation--

(I) the preceding provisions of this subparagraph shall not apply, and

(II) the adjusted net minimum tax for any taxable year is the amount of the net minimum tax for such year increased in the manner provided in clause (iii).

(2) **Tentative minimum tax.** -- The term "tentative minimum tax" has the meaning given to such term by section 55(b).

(e) **Special Rule for Individuals With Long-Term Unused Credits.** --

(1) **In general.** -- If an individual has a long-term unused minimum tax credit for any taxable year beginning before January 1, 2013, the amount determined under subsection (c) for such taxable year shall not be less than the AMT refundable credit amount for such taxable year.

(2) **AMT refundable credit amount.** -- For purposes of paragraph (1)--

(A) **In general.** -- The term "AMT refundable credit amount" means, with respect to any taxable year, the amount (not in excess of the long-term unused minimum tax credit for such taxable year) equal to the greater of --

(i) $5,000,

(ii) 20 percent of the long-term unused minimum tax credit for such taxable year, or

(iii) the amount (if any) of the AMT refundable credit amount determined under this paragraph for the taxpayer's preceding taxable year (as determined before any reduction under subparagraph (B))

(B) **Phaseout of amt refundable credit amount.** --

(i) **In general.** -- In the case of an individual whose adjusted gross income for any taxable year exceeds the threshold amount (within the meaning of section 151(d)(3) (C)), the AMT refundable credit amount determined under subparagraph (A) for such taxable year shall be reduced by the applicable percentage (within the meaning of section 151(d)(3)(B)).

(ii) **Adjusted gross income.** -- For purposes of clause (i), adjusted gross income shall be determined without regard to sections 911, 931, and 933.

(3) **Long-term unused minimum tax credit.** --

Sec. 53. Credit for prior year minimum tax liability

(A) In general. -- For purposes of this subsection, the term `long-term unused minimum tax credit' means, with respect to any taxable year, the portion of the minimum tax credit determined under subsection (b) attributable to the adjusted net minimum tax for taxable years before the 3rd taxable year immediately preceding such taxable year.

(B) First-in, first-out ordering rule. -- For purposes of subparagraph (A), credits shall be treated as allowed under subsection (a) on a first-in, first-out basis.

(4) Credit refundable. -- For purposes of this title (other than this section), the credit allowed by reason of this subsection shall be treated as if it were allowed under subpart C.

Sec. 55. Alternative minimum tax imposed

(a) General rule. -- There is hereby imposed (in addition to any other tax imposed by this subtitle) a tax equal to the excess (if any) of--

(1) the tentative minimum tax for the taxable year, over

(2) the regular tax for the taxable year.

(b) Tentative minimum tax. -- For purposes of this part--

(1) Amount of tentative tax. --

(A) Noncorporate taxpayers. --

(i) In general. -- In the case of a taxpayer other than a corporation, the tentative minimum tax for the taxable year is the sum of--

(I) 26 percent of so much of the taxable excess as does not exceed $175,000, plus

(II) 28 percent of so much of the taxable excess as exceeds $175,000.

The amount determined under the preceding sentence shall be reduced by the alternative minimum tax foreign tax credit for the taxable year.

(ii) Taxable excess. -- For purposes of this subsection, the term "taxable excess" means so much of the alternative minimum taxable income for the taxable year as exceeds the exemption amount.

(iii) Married individual filing separate return. -- In the case of a married individual filing a separate return, clause (i) shall be applied by substituting "$87,500" for "$175,000" each place it appears. For purposes of the preceding sentence, marital status shall be determined under section 7703.

(B) Corporations. -- In the case of a corporation, the tentative minimum tax for the taxable year is--

(i) 20 percent of so much of the alternative minimum taxable income for the taxable year as exceeds the exemption amount, reduced by

(ii) the alternative minimum tax foreign tax credit for the taxable year.

(2) Alternative minimum taxable income. -- The term "alternative minimum taxable income" means the taxable income of the taxpayer for the taxable year--

(A) determined with the adjustments provided in section 56 and section 58, and

(B) increased by the amount of the items of tax preference described in section 57.

If a taxpayer is subject to the regular tax, such taxpayer shall be subject to the tax imposed by this section (and, if the regular tax is determined by reference to an amount other than taxable income, such amount shall be treated as the taxable income of such taxpayer for purposes of the preceding sentence).

(3) Maximum rate of tax on net capital gain of noncorporate taxpayers. -- The amount

Sec. 55. Alternative minimum tax imposed

determined under the first sentence of paragraph (1)(A)(i) shall not exceed the sum of--

   (A) the amount determined under such first sentence computed at the rates and in the same manner as if this paragraph had not been enacted on the taxable excess reduced by the lesser of-

      (i) the net capital gain; or

      (ii) the sum of--

         (I) the adjusted net capital gain, plus

         (II) the unrecaptured section 1250 gain, plus

   (B) 5 percent (0 percent in the case of taxable years beginning after 2007) of so much of the adjusted net capital gain (or, if less, taxable excess) as does not exceed an amount equal to the excess described in section 1(h)(1)(B), plus

   (C) 15 percent of the adjusted net capital gain (or, if less, taxable excess) in excess of the amount on which tax determined under subparagraph (B), plus

   (D) 25 percent of the amount of taxable excess in excess of the sum of the amounts on which tax is determined under the preceding subparagraphs of this paragraph.

Terms used in this paragraph which are also used in section 1(h) shall have the respective meanings given such terms by section 1(h) but computed with the adjustments under this part.

(c) Regular tax. --

   (1) In general. -- For purposes of this section, the term "regular tax" means the regular tax liability for the taxable year (as defined in section 26(b))

***

(d) Exemption amount. -- For purposes of this section--

   (1) Exemption amount for taxpayers other than corporations. -- In the case of a taxpayer other than a corporation, the term "exemption amount" means -

      (A) $45,000 ($66,250 in the case of taxable years beginning in 2007) in the case of--

         (i) a joint return, or

         (ii) a surviving spouse,

      (B) $33,750 ($44,350 in the case of taxable years beginning in 2007) in the case of an individual who -

         (i) is not a married individual, and

         (ii) is not a surviving spouse,

      (C) 50 percent of the dollar amount applicable under paragraph (1)(A) in the case of a married individual who files a separate return, and

      (D) $22,500 in the case of an estate or trust.

For purposes of this paragraph, the term "surviving spouse" has the meaning given to such term by section 2(a), and marital status shall be determined under section 7703.

   (2) Corporations. -- In the case of a corporation, the term "exemption amount" means $40,000.

   (3) Phase-out of exemption amount. -- The exemption amount of any taxpayer shall be reduced (but not below zero) by an amount equal to 25 percent of the amount by which the alternative minimum taxable income of the taxpayer exceeds -

      (A) $150,000 in the case of a taxpayer described in paragraph (1)(A) or (2),

      (B) $112,500 in the case of a taxpayer described in paragraph (1)(B), and

Sec. 55. Alternative minimum tax imposed

(C) $75,000 in the case of a taxpayer described in subparagraph (C) or (D) of paragraph (1).

In the case of a taxpayer described in paragraph (1)(C), alternative minimum taxable income shall be increased by the lesser of (i) 25 percent of the excess of alternative minimum taxable income (determined without regard to this sentence) over the minimum amount of such income (as so determined) for which the exemption amount under paragraph (1)(C) is zero, or (ii) such exemption amount (determined without regard to this paragraph). 5

(e) Exemption for small corporations. --

    (1) In general. --

        (A) $7,500,000 gross receipts test. -- The tentative minimum tax of a corporation shall be zero for any taxable year if the corporation's average annual gross receipts for all 3-taxable-year periods ending before such taxable year does not exceed $7,500,000. For purposes of the preceding sentence, only taxable years beginning after December 31, 1993, shall be taken into account. 10

        (B) $5,000,000 gross receipts test for first 3-year period. -- Subparagraph (A) shall be applied by substituting "$5,000,000" for "$7,500,000" for the first 3-taxable-year period (or portion thereof) of the corporation which is taken into account under subparagraph (A). 15

        (C) First taxable year corporation in existence. -- If such taxable year is the first taxable year that such corporation is in existence, the tentative minimum tax of such corporation for such year shall be zero. 20

        (D) Special rules. -- For purposes of this paragraph, the rules of paragraphs (2) and (3) of section 448(c) shall apply.

Sec. 56. Adjustments in computing alternative minimum taxable income

(a) Adjustments applicable to all taxpayers. -- In determining the amount of the alternative minimum taxable income for any taxable year the following treatment shall apply (in lieu of the treatment applicable for purposes of computing the regular tax): 25

    (1) Depreciation. --

        (A) In general. --

            (i) Property other than certain personal property. -- Except as provided in clause (ii), the depreciation deduction allowable under section 167 with respect to any tangible property placed in service after December 31, 1986, shall be determined under the alternative system of section 168(g). In the case of property placed in service after December 31, 1998, the preceding sentence shall not apply but clause (ii) shall continue to apply. 30 ... 35

            (ii) 150-percent declining balance method for certain property. -- The method of depreciation used shall be--

                (I) the 150 percent declining balance method,

                (II) switching to the straight line method for the 1st taxable year for which using the straight line method with respect to the adjusted basis as of the beginning of the year will yield a higher allowance. 40

The preceding sentence shall not apply to any section 1250 property (as defined in section 1250(c)) (and the straight line method shall be used for such section 1250 property) or to any other property if the depreciation deduction determined under section 168 with respect to such other property for purposes of the regular tax is determined by using the straight line method. 45

99

Sec. 56. Adjustments in computing alternative minimum taxable income

(B) Exception for certain property. -- This paragraph shall not apply to property described in paragraph (1), (2), (3), or (4) of section 168(f).

(2) Mining exploration and development costs. --

(A) In general. -- With respect to each mine or other natural deposit (other than an oil, gas, or geothermal well) of the taxpayer, the amount allowable as a deduction under section 616(a) or 617(a) (determined without regard to section 291(b)) in computing the regular tax for costs paid or incurred after December 31, 1986, shall be capitalized and amortized ratably over the 10-year period beginning with the taxable year in which the expenditures were made.

(B) Loss allowed. -- If a loss is sustained with respect to any property described in subparagraph (A), a deduction shall be allowed for the expenditures described in subparagraph (A) for the taxable year in which such loss is sustained in an amount equal to the lesser of--

(i) the amount allowable under section 165(a) for the expenditures if they had remained capitalized, or

(ii) the amount of such expenditures which have not previously been amortized under subparagraph (A).

(3) Treatment of certain long-term contracts. -- In the case of any long-term contract entered into by the taxpayer on or after March 1, 1986, the taxable income from such contract shall be determined under the percentage of completion method of accounting (as modified by section 460(b)). For purposes of the preceding sentence, in the case of a contract described in section 460(e)(1), the percentage of the contract completed shall be determined under section 460(b)(1) by using the simplified procedures for allocation of costs prescribed under section 460(b)(3). The first sentence of this paragraph shall not apply to any home construction contract (as defined in section 460(e)(6)).

(4) Alternative tax net operating loss deduction. -- The alternative tax net operating loss deduction shall be allowed in lieu of the net operating loss deduction allowed under section 172.

(b) Adjustments applicable to individuals. -- In determining the amount of the alternative minimum taxable income of any taxpayer (other than a corporation), the following treatment shall apply (in lieu of the treatment applicable for purposes of computing the regular tax):

(1) Limitation on deductions. --

(A) In general. -- No deduction shall be allowed--

(i) for any miscellaneous itemized deduction (as defined in section 67(b)), or

(ii) for any taxes described in paragraph (1), (2), or (3) of section 164(a).

Clause (ii) shall not apply to any amount allowable in computing adjusted gross income.

(B) Medical expenses. -- In determining the amount allowable as a deduction under section 213, subsection (a) of section 213 shall be applied by substituting "10 percent" for "7.5 percent".

(C) Interest. -- In determining the amount allowable as a deduction for interest, subsections (d) and (h) of section 163 shall apply, except that--

(i) in lieu of the exception under section 163(h)(2)(D), the term "personal interest" shall not include any qualified housing interest (as defined in subsection (e)),

(ii) sections 163(d)(6) and 163(h)(5) (relating to phase-ins) shall not apply,

(iii) interest on any specified private activity bond (and any amount treated as interest on a specified private activity bond under section 57(a)(5)(B)), and any deduction

Sec. 56. Adjustments in computing alternative minimum taxable income

referred to in section 57(a)(5)(A), shall be treated as includible in gross income (or as deductible) for purposes of applying section 163(d),

    (iv) in lieu of the exception under section163(d)(3)(B)(i), the term "investment interest" shall not include any qualified housing interest (as defined in subsection (e)), and

    (v) the adjustments of this section and sections 57 and 58 shall apply in determining net investment income under section 163(d).

(D) Treatment of certain recoveries. -- No recovery of any tax to which subparagraph (A)(ii) applied shall be included in gross income for purposes of determining alternative minimum taxable income.

(E) Standard deduction and deduction for personal exemptions not allowed. -- The standard deduction under section 63(c), the deduction for personal exemptions under section 151, and the deduction under section 642(b) shall not be allowed.

(F) Section 68 not applicable. -- Section 68 shall not apply.

(2) Circulation and research and experimental expenditures. --

(A) In general. -- The amount allowable as a deduction under section 173 or 174(a) in computing the regular tax for amounts paid or incurred after December 31, 1986, shall be capitalized and--

    (i) in the case of circulation expenditures described in section 173, shall be amortized ratably over the 3-year period beginning with the taxable year in which the expenditures were made, or

    (ii) in the case of research and experimental expenditures described in section 174(a), shall be amortized ratably over the 10-year period beginning with the taxable year in which the expenditures were made.

(B) Loss allowed. -- If a loss is sustained with respect to any property described in subparagraph (A), a deduction shall be allowed for the expenditures described in subparagraph (A) for the taxable year in which such loss is sustained in an amount equal to th lesser of--

    (i) the amount allowable under section 165(a) for the expenditures if they had remained capitalized, or

    (ii) the amount of such expenditures which have not previously been amortized under subparagraph (A).

(3) Treatment of incentive stock options. -- Section 421 shall not apply to the transfer of stock acquired pursuant to the exercise of an incentive stock option (as defined in section 422). Section 422(c)(2) shall apply in any case where the disposition and the inclusion for purposes of this part are within the same taxable year and such section shall not apply in any other case. The adjusted basis of any stock so acquired shall be determined on the basis of the treatment prescribed by this paragraph.

(c) Adjustments applicable to corporations. -- In determining the amount of the alternative minimum taxable income of a corporation, the following treatment shall apply:

(1) Adjustment for adjusted current earnings. -- Alternative minimum taxable income shall be adjusted as provided in subsection (g).

(d) Alternative tax net operating loss deduction defined. --

(1) In general. -- For purposes of subsection (a)(4), the term "alternative tax net operating loss deduction" means the net operating loss deduction allowable for the taxable year under section 172, except that--

Sec. 56. Adjustments in computing alternative minimum taxable income

(A) the amount of such deduction shall not exceed the sum of--

(i) the lesser of--

(I) the amount of such deduction attributable to net operating losses (other than the deduction described in clause (ii)(I)), or

(II) 90 percent of alternative minimum taxable income determined without regard to such deduction, plus

(ii) the lesser of--

(I) the amount of such deduction attributable to the sum of carrybacks of net operating losses from taxable years ending during 2001 or 2002 and carryovers of net operating losses to taxable years ending during 2001 and 2002, or

(II) alternative minimum taxable income determined without regard to such deduction reduced by the amount determined under clause (i), and

(B) in determining the amount of such deduction--

(i) the net operating loss (within the meaning of section 172(c)) for any loss year shall be adjusted as provided in paragraph (2), and

(ii) appropriate adjustments in the application of section 172(b)(2) shall be made to take into account the limitation of subparagraph (A).

(2) Adjustments to net operating loss computation. --

(A) Post-1986 loss years. -- In the case of a loss year beginning after December 31, 1986, the net operating loss for such year under section 172(c) shall--

(i) be determined with the adjustments provided in this section and section 58, and

(ii) be reduced by the items of tax preference determined under section 57 for such year.

An item of tax preference shall be taken into account under clause (ii) only to the extent such item increased the amount of the net operating loss for the taxable year under section 172(c).

(e) Qualified housing interest. -- For purposes of this part--

(1) In general. -- The term "qualified housing interest" means interest which is qualified residence interest (as defined in section 163(h)(3)) and is paid or accrued during the taxable year on indebtedness which is incurred in acquiring, constructing, or substantially improving any property which--

(A) is the principal residence (within the meaning of section 121) of the taxpayer at the time such interest accrues, or

(B) is a qualified dwelling which is a qualified residence (within the meaning of section 163(h)(4)).

Such term also includes interest on any indebtedness resulting from the refinancing of indebtedness meeting the requirements of the preceding sentence; but only to the extent that the amount of the indebtedness resulting from such refinancing does not exceed the amount of the refinanced indebtedness immediately before the refinancing.

(2) Qualified dwelling. -- The term "qualified dwelling" means any--

(A) house,

(B) apartment,

(C) condominium, or

(D) mobile home not used on a transient basis (within the meaning of section 7701(a) (19)(C)(v)), including all structures or other property appurtenant thereto.

Sec. 56. Adjustments in computing alternative minimum taxable income

(g) Adjustments based on adjusted current earnings. --

(1) In general. -- The alternative minimum taxable income of any corporation for any taxable year shall be increased by 75 percent of the excess (if any) of--

(A) the adjusted current earnings of the corporation, over

(B) the alternative minimum taxable income (determined without regard to this subsection and the alternative tax net operating loss deduction).

(2) Allowance of negative adjustments. --

(A) In general. -- The alternative minimum taxable income for any corporation of any taxable year, shall be reduced by 75 percent of the excess (if any) of--

(i) the amount referred to in subparagraph (B) of paragraph (1), over

(ii) the amount referred to in subparagraph (A) of paragraph (1).

(B) Limitation. -- The reduction under subparagraph (A) for any taxable year shall not exceed the excess (if any) of--

(i) the aggregate increases in alternative minimum taxable income under paragraph (1) for prior taxable years, over

(ii) the aggregate reductions under subparagraph (A) of this paragraph for prior taxable years.

(3) Adjusted current earnings. -- For purposes of this subsection, the term "adjusted current earnings" means the alternative minimum taxable income for the taxable year -

(A) determined with the adjustments provided in paragraph (4), and

(B) determined without regard to this subsection and the alternative tax net operating loss deduction.

(4) Adjustments. -- In determining adjusted current earnings, the following adjustments shall apply:

(A) Depreciation. --

(i) Property placed in service after 1989. -- The depreciation deduction with respect to any property placed in service in a taxable year beginning after 1989 shall be determined under the alternative system of section 168(g). The preceding sentence shall not apply to any property placed in service after December 31, 1993, and the depreciation deduction with respect to such property shall be determined under the rules of subsection (a)(1)(A).

***

(v) Special rule for certain property. -- In the case of any property described in paragraph (1), (2), (3), or (4) of section 168(f), the amount of depreciation allowable for purposes of the regular tax shall be treated as the amount allowable under the alternative system of section 168(g).

(B) Inclusion of items included for purposes of computing earnings and profits. --

(i) In general. -- In the case of any amount which is excluded from gross income for purposes of computing alternative minimum taxable income but is taken into account in determining the amount of earnings and profits--

(I) such amount shall be included in income in the same manner as if such amount were includible in gross income for purposes of computing alternative minimum taxable income, and

(II) the amount of such income shall be reduced by any deduction which would have been allowable in computing alternative minimum taxable income if such amount were includible in gross income.

The preceding sentence shall not apply in the case of any amount excluded from gross income under section 108 (or the corresponding provisions of prior law) or under section 139A or 1357. In the case of any insurance company taxable under section 831(b), this clause shall not apply to any amount not described in section 834(b).

(ii) Inclusion of buildup in life insurance contracts. -- In the case of any life insurance contract--

(I) the income on such contract (as determined under section 7702(g)) for any taxable year shall be treated includible in gross income for such year, and

(II) there shall be allowed as a deduction that portion of any premium which is attributable to insurance coverage.

(C) Disallowance of items not deductible in computing earnings and profits. --

(i) In general. -- A deduction shall not be allowed for any item if such item would not be deductible for any taxable year for purposes of computing earnings and profits.

(ii) Special rule for certain dividends. --

(I) In general. -- Clause (i) shall not apply to any deduction allowable under section 243 or 245 for any dividend which is a 100-percent dividend or which is received from a 20-percent owned corporation (as defined in section 243(c)(2)), but only to the extent such dividend is attributable to income of the paying corporation which is subject to tax under this chapter (determined after the application of sections 30A, 936 (including subsections (a)(4), (i), and (j) thereof) and 921 (as in effect before its repeal by the FSC Repeal and Extraterritorial Income Exclusion Act of 2000)).

(II) 100-percent dividend. -- For purposes of subclause (I), the term "100 percent dividend" means any dividend if the percentage used for purposes of determining the amount allowable as a deduction under section 243 or 245 with respect to such dividend is 100 percent.

***

(D) Certain other earnings and profits adjustments. --

(i) Intangible drilling costs. -- The adjustments provided in section 312(n)(2)(A) shall apply in the case of amounts paid or incurred in taxable years beginning after December 31, 1989. In the case of a taxpayer other than an integrated oil company (as defined in section 291(b)(4)), in the case of any oil or gas well, this clause shall not apply in the case of amounts paid or incurred in taxable years beginning after December 31, 1992.

(ii) Certain amortization provisions not to apply. -- Sections 173 and 248 shall not apply to expenditures paid or incurred in taxable years beginning after December 31, 1989.

(iv) Installment sales. -- In the case of any installment sale in a taxable year beginning after December 31, 1989, adjusted current earnings shall be computed as if the corporation did not use the installment method. The preceding sentence shall not apply to the applicable percentage (as determined under section 453A) of the gain from any installment sale with respect to which section 453A(a)(1) applies.

(E) Disallowance of loss on exchange of debt pools. -- No loss shall be recognized on the exchange of any pool of debt obligations for another pool of debt obligations having substantially the same effective interest rates and maturities.

Sec. 56. Adjustments in computing alternative minimum taxable income

(F) Depletion. --

(i) In general. -- The allowance for depletion with respect to any property placed in service in a taxable year beginning after December 31, 1989, shall be cost depletion determined under section 611.

(ii) Exception for independent oil and gas producers and royalty owners. -- 5 In the case of any taxable year beginning after December 31, 1992, clause (i) (and subparagraph (C)(i)) shall not apply to any deduction for depletion computed in accordance with section 613A(c).

***

(H) Adjusted basis. -- The adjusted basis of any property with respect to which an 10 adjustment under this paragraph applies shall be determined by applying the treatment prescribed in this paragraph.

(I) Treatment of charitable contributions. -- Notwithstanding subparagraphs (B) and (C), no adjustment related to the earnings and profits effects of any charitable contribution shall be made in computing adjusted current earnings. 15

(5) Other definitions. -- For purposes of paragraph (4)--

(A) Earnings and profits. -- The term "earnings and profits" means earnings and profits computed for purposes of subchapter C.

(B) Treatment of alternative minimum taxable income. -- The treatment of any item for purposes of computing alternative minimum taxable income shall be determined 20 without regard to this subsection.

Sec. 57. Items of tax preference

(a) General rule. -- For purposes of this part, the items of tax preference determined under this section are-- 25

(1) Depletion. -- With respect to each property (as defined in section 614), the excess of the deduction for depletion allowable under section 611 for the taxable year over the adjusted basis of the property at the end of the taxable year (determined without regard to the depletion deduction for the taxable year). Effective with respect to taxable years beginning after December 31, 1992, this paragraph shall not apply to any deduction for depletion computed in 30 accordance with section 613A(c).

(2) Intangible drilling costs. --

(A) In general. -- With respect to all oil, gas, and geothermal properties of the taxpayer, the amount (if any) by which the amount of the excess intangible drilling costs arising in the taxable year is greater than 65 percent of the net income of the taxpayer from oil, gas, 35 and geothermal properties for the taxable year.

(B) Excess intangible drilling costs. -- For purposes of subparagraph (A), the amount of the excess intangible drilling costs arising in the taxable year is the excess of--

(i) the intangible drilling and development costs paid or incurred in connection with oil, gas, and geothermal wells (other than costs incurred in drilling a nonproductive 40 well) allowable under section 263(c) or 291(b) for the taxable year, over

(ii) the amount which would have been allowable for the taxable year if such costs had been capitalized and straight line recovery of intangibles (as defined in subsection (b)) had been used with respect to such costs.

(C) Net income from oil, gas, and geothermal properties. -- For purposes of 45

Sec. 57. Items of tax preference

subparagraph (A), the amount of the net income of the taxpayer from oil, gas, and geothermal properties for the taxable year is the excess of--

> (i) the aggregate amount of gross income (within the meaning of section 613(a)) from all oil, gas, and geothermal properties of the taxpayer received or accrued by the taxpayer during the taxable year, over

> (ii) the amount of any deductions allocable to such properties reduced by the excess described in subparagraph (B) for such taxable year.

(D) Paragraph applied separately with respect to geothermal properties and oil and gas properties. -- This paragraph shall be applied separately with respect to--

> (i) all oil and gas properties which are not described in clause (ii), and

> (ii) all properties which are geothermal deposits (as defined in section 613(e)(2)).

(E) Exception for independent producers. -- In the case of any oil or gas well--

> **(i) In general.** -- In the case of any taxable year beginning after December 31, 1992, this paragraph shall not apply to any taxpayer which is not an integrated oil company (as defined in section 291(b)(4)).

> **(ii) Limitation on benefit.** -- The reduction in alternative minimum taxable income by reason of clause (i) for any taxable year shall not exceed 40 percent (30 percent in case of taxable years beginning in1993) of the alternative minimum taxable income for such year determined without regard to clause (i) and the alternative tax net operating loss deduction under section 56(a)(4).

(5) Tax-exempt interest. --

(A) In general. -- Interest on specified private activity bonds reduced by any deduction (not allowable in computing the regular tax) which would have been allowable if such interest were includible in gross income.

(B) Treatment of exempt-interest dividends. -- Under regulations prescribed by the Secretary, any exempt-interest dividend (as defined in section 852(b)(5)(A)) shall be treated as interest on a specified private activity bond to the extent of its proportionate share of the interest on such bonds received by the company paying such dividend.

(C) Specified private activity bonds. --

> **(i) In general.** -- For purposes of this part, the term "specified private activity bond" means any private activity bond (as defined in section 141) which is issued after August 7, 1986, and the interest on which is not includible in gross income under section 103.

> **(ii) Exception for qualified 501(c)(3) bonds.** -- For purposes of clause (i), the term "private activity bond" shall not include any qualified 501(c)(3) bond (as defined in section 145).

(7) Exclusion for gains on sale of certain small business stock. -- An amount equal to 7 percent of the amount excluded from gross income for the taxable year under section 1202.

(b) Straight line recovery of intangibles defined. -- For purposes of paragraph (2) of subsection (a)--

(1) In general. -- The term "straight line recovery of intangibles", when used with respect to intangible drilling and development costs for any well, means (except in the case of an election under paragraph (2)) ratable amortization of such costs over the 120-month period beginning with the month in which production from such well begins.

106

Sec. 57. Items of tax preference

(2) Election. -- If the taxpayer elects with respect to the intangible drilling and development costs for any well, the term "straight line recovery of intangibles" means any method which would be permitted for purposes of determining cost depletion with respect to such well and which is selected by the taxpayer for purposes of subsection (a)(2).

Sec. 58. Denial of certain losses

(a) Denial of farm loss. --

(1) In general. -- For purposes of computing the amount of the alternative minimum taxable income for any taxable year of a taxpayer other than a corporation--

(A) Disallowance of farm loss. -- No loss of the taxpayer for such taxable year from any tax shelter farm activity shall be allowed.

(B) Deduction in succeeding taxable year. -- Any loss from a tax shelter farm activity disallowed under subparagraph (A) shall be treated as a deduction allocable to such activity in the 1st succeeding taxable year.

(2) Tax shelter farm activity. -- For purposes of this subsection, the term "tax shelter farm activity" means--

(A) any farming syndicate as defined in section 464(c), and

(B) any other activity consisting of farming which is a passive activity (within the meaning of section 469(c)).

(3) Application to personal service corporations. -- For purposes of paragraph (1), a personal service corporation (within the meaning of section 469(j)(2)) shall be treated as a taxpayer other than a corporation.

(4) Determination of loss. -- In determining the amount of the loss from any tax shelter farm activity, the adjustments of sections 56 and 57 shall apply.

(b) Disallowance of passive activity loss. -- In computing the alternative minimum taxable income of the taxpayer for any taxable year, section 469 shall apply, except that in applying section 469 -

(1) the adjustments of sections 56 and 57 shall apply,

(2) the provisions of section 469(m) (relating to phase-in of disallowance) shall not apply, and

(3) in lieu of applying section 469(j)(7), the passive activity loss of a taxpayer shall be computed without regard to qualified housing interest (as defined in section 56(e)).

(c) Special rules. -- For purposes of this section--

(1) Special rule for insolvent taxpayers. --

(A) In general. -- The amount of losses to which subsection (a) or (b) applies shall be reduced by the amount (if any) by which the taxpayer is insolvent as of the close of the taxable year.

(B) Insolvent. -- For purposes of this paragraph, the term "insolvent" means the excess of liabilities over the fair market value of assets.

(2) Loss allowed for year of disposition of farm shelter activity. -- If the taxpayer disposes of his entire interest in any tax shelter farm activity during any taxable year, the amount of the loss attributable to such activity (determined after carryovers under subsection (a)(1)(B)) shall (to the extent otherwise allowable) be allowed for such taxable year in computing alternative minimum taxable income and not treated as a loss from a tax shelter farm activity.

Sec. 59. Other definitions and special rules

(e) Optional 10-year writeoff of certain tax preferences. --

  (1) In general. -- For purposes of this title, any qualified expenditure to which an election under this paragraph applies shall be allowed as a deduction ratably over the 10-year period (3-year period in the case of circulation expenditures described in section 173) beginning with the taxable year in which such expenditure was made (or, in the case of a qualified expenditure described in paragraph (2)(C), over the 60-month period beginning with the month in which such expenditure was paid or incurred).

  (2) Qualified expenditure. -- For purposes of this subsection, the term "qualified expenditure" means any amount which, but for an election under this subsection, would have been allowable as a deduction (determined without regard to section 291) for the taxable year in which paid or incurred under--

   (A) section 173 (relating to circulation expenditures),

   (B) section 174(a) (relating to research and experimental expenditures),

   (C) section 263(c) (relating to intangible drilling and development expenditures),

   (D) section 616(a) (relating to development expenditures), or

   (E) section 617(a) (relating to mining exploration expenditures).

  (3) Other sections not applicable. -- Except as provided in this subsection, no deduction shall be allowed under any other section for any qualified expenditure to which an election under this subsection applies.

  (4) Election. --

   (A) In general. -- An election may be made under paragraph (1) with respect to any portion of any qualified expenditure.

   (B) Revocable only with consent. -- Any election under this subsection may be revoked only with the consent of the Secretary.

  (5) Dispositions. --

   (A) Application of section 1254. -- In the case of any disposition of property to which section 1254 applies (determined without regard to this section), any deduction under paragraph (1) with respect to amounts which are allocable to such property shall, for purposes of section 1254, be treated as a deduction allowable under section 263(c), 616(a), or 617(a), whichever is appropriate.

   (B) Application of section 617(d). -- In the case of any disposition of mining property to which section 617(d) applies (determined without regard to this subsection), any deduction under paragraph (1) with respect to amounts which are allocable to such property shall, for purposes of section 617(d), be treated as a deduction allowable under section 617(a).

  (6) Amounts to which election apply not treated as tax preference. -- Any portion of any qualified expenditure to which an election under paragraph (1) applies shall not be treated as an item of tax preference under section 57(a) and section 56 shall not apply to such expenditure.

 (f) Coordination with section 291. -- Except as otherwise provided in this part, section 291 (relating to cutback of corporate preferences) shall apply before the application of this part.

 (g) Tax benefit rule. -- The Secretary may prescribe regulations under which differently treated items shall be properly adjusted where the tax treatment giving rise to such items will not result in the reduction of the taxpayer's regular tax for the taxable year for which the item is taken into account or for any other taxable year.

***

Sec. 59. Other definitions and special rules

(i) Special rule for amounts treated as tax preference. -- For purposes of this subtitle (other than this part), any amount shall not fail to be treated as wholly exempt from tax imposed by this subtitle solely by reason of being included in alternative minimum taxable income.

(j) Treatment of unearned income of minor children. --

(1) In general. -- In the case of a child to whom section 1(g) applies, the exemption amount for purposes of section 55 shall not exceed the sum of--

(A) such child's earned income (as defined in section 911(d)(2)) for the taxable year, plus

(B) $5,000.

(2) Inflation adjustment. -- In the case of any taxable year beginning in a calendar year after 1998, the dollar amount in paragraph (1)(B) shall be increased by an amount equal to the product of--

(A) such dollar amount, and

(B) the cost-of-living adjustment determined under section 1(f)(3) for the calendar year in which the taxable year begins, determined by substituting "1997" for "1992" in subparagraph (B) thereof.

If any increase determined under the preceding sentence is not a multiple of $50, such increase shall be rounded to the nearest multiple of $50.

Sec. 61. Gross income defined

(a) General definition. -- Except as otherwise provided in this subtitle, gross income means all income from whatever source derived, including (but not limited to) the following items:

(1) Compensation for services, including fees, commissions, fringe benefits, and similar items;

(2) Gross income derived from business;

(3) Gains derived from dealings in property;

(4) Interest;

(5) Rents;

(6) Royalties;

(7) Dividends;

(8) Alimony and separate maintenance payments;

(9) Annuities;

(10) Income from life insurance and endowment contracts;

(11) Pensions;

(12) Income from discharge of indebtedness;

(13) Distributive share of partnership gross income;

(14) Income in respect of a decedent; and

(15) Income from an interest in an estate or trust.

(b) Cross references. -- For items specifically included in gross income, see part II (sec. 71 and following). For items specifically excluded from gross income, see part III (sec. 101 and following).

Reg. § 1.61-1 Gross income.

(a) *General definition.* Gross income means all income from whatever source derived,

Sec. 61. Gross income defined

unless excluded by law. Gross income includes income realized in any form, whether in money, property, or services. Income may be realized, therefore, in the form of services, meals, accommodations, stock, or other property, as well as in cash. Section 61 lists the more common items of gross income for purposes of illustration. For purposes of further
5   illustration, § 1.61-14 mentions several miscellaneous items of gross income not listed specifically in section 61. Gross income, however, is not limited to the items so enumerated.

(b) *Cross references.* Cross references to other provisions of the Code are to be found throughout the regulations under section 61. The purpose of these cross references is to
10 direct attention to the more common items which are included in or excluded from gross income entirely, or treated in some special manner. To the extent that another section of the Code or of the regulations thereunder, provides specific treatment for any item of income, such other provision shall apply notwithstanding section 61 and the regulations thereunder. The cross references do not cover all possible items.
15   (1) For examples of items specifically included in gross income, see Part II (section 71 and following), Subchapter B, Chapter 1 of the Code.

(2) For examples of items specifically excluded from gross income, see part III (section 101 and following), Subchapter B, Chapter 1 of the Code.

(3) For general rules as to the taxable year for which an item is to be included in gross
20 income, see section 451 and the regulations thereunder.

Reg. § 1.61-2   Compensation for services, including fees, commissions, and similar items.

(a) *In general.* (1) Wages, salaries, commissions paid salesmen, compensation for
25 services on the basis of a percentage of profits, commissions on insurance premiums, tips, bonuses (including Christmas bonuses), termination or severance pay, rewards, jury fees, marriage fees and other contributions received by a clergyman for services, pay of persons in the military or naval forces of the United States, retired pay of employees, pensions, and retirement allowances are income to the recipients unless excluded by law.
30 Several special rules apply to members of the Armed Forces, National Oceanic and Atmospheric Administration, and Public Health Service of the United States; see paragraph (b) of this section.

(2) The Code provides special rules including the following items in gross income:

(i) Distributions from employees' trusts, see sections 72, 402, and 403, and the
35 regulations thereunder;

(ii) Compensation for child's services (in child's gross income), see section 73 and the regulations thereunder;

(iii) Prizes and awards, see section 74 and the regulations thereunder.

(3) Similarly, the Code provides special rules excluding the following items from gross
40 income in whole or in part:

(i) Gifts, see section 102 and the regulations thereunder;

(ii) Compensation for injuries or sickness, see section 104 and the regulations thereunder;

(iii) Amounts received under accident and health plans, see section 105 and the
45 regulations thereunder;

(iv) Scholarship and fellowship grants, see section 117 and the regulations thereunder;

(v) Miscellaneous items, see section 122.

***

50   (c) *Payment to charitable, etc., organization on behalf of person rendering services.*
The value of services is not includible in gross income when such services are rendered

Sec. 61. Gross income defined

directly and gratuitously to an organization described in section 170(c). Where, however, pursuant to an agreement or understanding, services are rendered to a person for the benefit of an organization described in section 170(c) and an amount for such services is paid to such organization by the person to whom the services are rendered, the amount so paid constitutes income to the person performing the services. 5

(d) *Compensation paid other than in cash--(1) In general.* Except as otherwise provided in paragraph (d)(6)(i) of this section (relating to certain property transferred after June 30, 1969), if services are paid for in property, the fair market value of the property taken in payment must be included in income as compensation. If services are paid for in exchange for other services, the fair market value of such other services taken in 10 payment must be included in income as compensation. If the services are rendered at a stipulated price, such price will be presumed to be the fair market value of the compensation received in the absence of evidence to the contrary. For special rules relating to certain options received as compensation, see §§ 1.61-15, 1.83-7, and section 421 and the regulations thereunder. For special rules relating to premiums paid by an 15 employer for an annuity contract which is not subject to section 403(a), see section 403(c) and the regulations thereunder and § 1.83-8(a). For special rules relating to contributions made to an employees' trust which is not exempt under section 501, see section 402(b) and the regulations thereunder and § 1.83-8(a).

(2) *Property transferred to employee or independent contractor.* (i) Except as otherwise 20 provided in section 421 and the regulations thereunder and § 1.61-15 (relating to stock options), and paragraph (d)(6)(i) of this section, if property is transferred by an employer to an employee or if property is transferred to an independent contractor, as compensation for services, for an amount less than its fair market value, then regardless of whether the transfer is in the form of a sale or exchange, the difference between the 25 amount paid for the property and the amount of its fair market value at the time of the transfer is compensation and shall be included in the gross income of the employee or independent contractor. In computing the gain or loss from the subsequent sale of such property, its basis shall be the amount paid for the property increased by the amount of such difference included in gross income 30

(ii)(A) *Cost of life insurance on the life of the employee.* Generally, life insurance premiums paid by an employer on the life of his employee where the proceeds of such insurance are payable to the beneficiary of such employee are part of the gross income of the employee. However, the amount includible in the employee's gross income is determined with regard to the provisions of section 403 and the regulations thereunder in 35 the case of an individual contract issued after December 31, 1962, or a group contract, which provides incidental life insurance protection and which satisfies the requirements of section 401(g) and § 1.401-9, relating to the nontransferability of annuity contracts. For example, if an employee or independent contractor is the owner (as defined in § 1.61-22(c)(1)) of a life insurance contract and the payments with regard to such 40 contract are not split-dollar loans under § 1.7872-15(b)(1), the employee or independent contractor must include in income the amount of any such payments by the employer or service recipient with respect to such contract during any year to the extent that the employee's or independent contractor's rights to the life insurance contract are substantially vested (within the meaning of § 1.83-3(b)). This result is the same 45 regardless of whether the employee or independent contractor has at all times been the owner of the life insurance contract or the contract previously has been owned by the employer or service recipient as part of a split-dollar life insurance arrangement (as defined in § 1.61-22(b)(1) or (2)) and was transferred by the employer or service recipient to the employee or independent contractor under § 1.61-22(g). For the special rules 50 relating to the includibility in an employee's gross income of an amount equal to the cost

111

Sec. 61. Gross income defined

of certain group term life insurance on the employee's life which is carried directly or indirectly by his employer, see section 79 and the regulations thereunder. For special rules relating to the exclusion of contributions by an employer to accident and health plans for the employee, see section 106 and the regulations thereunder.

5   (B) *Cost of group-term life insurance on the life of an individual other than an employee.* The cost (determined under paragraph (d)(2) of § 1.79-3) of group-term life insurance on the life of an individual other than an employee (such as the spouse or dependent of the employee) provided in connection with the performance of services by the employee is includible in the gross income of the employee.

10   (3) *Meals and living quarters.* The value of living quarters or meals which an employee receives in addition to his salary constitutes gross income unless they are furnished for the convenience of the employer and meet the conditions specified in section 119 and the regulations thereunder. For the treatment of rental value of parsonages or rental allowance paid to ministers, see section 107 and the regulations

15 thereunder; for the treatment of statutory subsistence allowances received by police, see section 120 and the regulations thereunder.

(4) *Stock and notes transferred to employee or independent contractor.* Except as otherwise provided by section 421 and the regulations thereunder and § 1.61-15 (relating to stock options), and paragraph (d)(6)(i) of this section, if a corporation transfers its own

20 stock to an employee or independent contractor as compensation for services, the fair market value of the stock at the time of transfer shall be included in the gross income of the employee or independent contractor. Notes or other evidences of indebtedness received in payment for services constitute income in the amount of their fair market value at the time of the transfer. A taxpayer receiving as compensation a note regarded

25 as good for its face value at maturity, but not bearing interest, shall treat as income as of the time of receipt its fair discounted value computed at the prevailing rate. As payments are received on such a note, there shall be included in income that portion of each payment which represents the proportionate part of the discount originally taken on the entire note.

30

Reg. § 1.61-3 Gross income derived from business.

(a) *In general.* In a manufacturing, merchandising, or mining business, ``gross income'' means the total sales, less the cost of goods sold, plus any income from investments and from incidental or outside operations or sources. Gross income is determined without

35 subtraction of depletion allowances based on a percentage of income to the extent that it exceeds cost depletion which may be required to be included in the amount of inventoriable costs as provided in § 1.471-11 and without subtraction of selling expenses, losses or other items not ordinarily used in computing costs of goods sold or amounts which are of a type for which a deduction would be disallowed under section 162 (c), (f),

40 or (g) in the case of a business expense. The cost of goods sold should be determined in accordance with the method of accounting consistently used by the taxpayer. Thus, for example, an amount cannot be taken into account in the computation of cost of goods sold any earlier than the taxable year in which economic performance occurs with respect to the amount (see § 1.446-1(c)(1)(ii)).

45   ***

Reg. § 1.61-4 Gross income of farmers.

(a) *Farmers using the cash method of accounting.* A farmer using the cash receipts and disbursements method of accounting shall include in his gross income for the taxable year--

50   (1) The amount of cash and the value of merchandise or other property received during the taxable year from the sale of livestock and produce which he raised,

Sec. 61. Gross income defined

(2) The profits from the sale of any livestock or other items which were purchased,

(3) All amounts received from breeding fees, fees from rent of teams, machinery, or land, and other incidental farm income,

(4) All subsidy and conservation payments received which must be considered as income, and

(5) Gross income from all other sources.

The profit from the sale of livestock or other items which were purchased is to be ascertained by deducting the cost from the sales price in the year in which the sale occurs, except that in the case of the sale of purchased animals held for draft, breeding, or dairy purposes, the profits shall be the amount of any excess of the sales price over the amount representing the difference between the cost and the depreciation allowed or allowable (determined in accordance with the rules applicable under section 1016(a) and the regulations thereunder). However, see section 162 and the regulations thereunder with respect to the computation of taxable income on other than the crop method where the cost of seeds or young plants purchased for further development and cultivation prior to sale is involved. Crop shares (whether or not considered rent under State law) shall be included in gross income as of the year in which the crop shares are reduced to money or the equivalent of money. See section 263A for rules regarding costs that are required to be capitalized.

(b) *Farmers using an accrual method of accounting.* A farmer using an accrual method of accounting must use inventories to determine his gross income. His gross income on an accrual method is determined by adding the total of the items described in subparagraphs (1) through (5) of this paragraph and subtracting therefrom the total of the items described in subparagraphs (6) and (7) of this paragraph. These items are as follows:

(1) The sales price of all livestock and other products held for sale and sold during the year;

(2) The inventory value of livestock and products on hand and not sold at the end of the year;

(3) All miscellaneous items of income, such as breeding fees, fees from the rent of teams, machinery, or land, or other incidental farm income;

(4) Any subsidy or conservation payments which must be considered as income;

(5) Gross income from all other sources;

(6) The inventory value of the livestock and products on hand and not sold at the beginning of the year; and

(7) The cost of any livestock or products purchased during the year (except livestock held for draft, dairy, or breeding purposes, unless included in inventory).

All livestock raised or purchased for sale shall be added in the inventory at their proper valuation determined in accordance with the method authorized and adopted for the purpose. Livestock acquired for draft, breeding, or dairy purposes and not for sale may be included in the inventory (see subparagraphs (2), (6), and (7) of this paragraph) instead of being treated as capital assets subject to depreciation, provided such practice is followed consistently from year to year by the taxpayer. When any livestock included in an inventory are sold, their cost must not be taken as an additional deduction in computing taxable income, because such deduction is reflected in the inventory. See the regulations under section 471. See section 263A for rules regarding costs that are required to be capitalized. Crop shares (whether or not considered rent under State law) shall be included in gross income as of the year in which the crop shares are reduced to money or the equivalent of money.

***

(d) *Definition of ``farm''.* As used in this section, the term ``farm'' embraces the farm in

Sec. 61. Gross income defined

the ordinarily accepted sense, and includes stock, dairy, poultry, fruit, and truck farms; also plantations, ranches, and all land used for farming operations. All individuals, partnerships, or corporations that cultivate, operate, or manage farms for gain or profit, either as owners or tenants, are designated as farmers. For more detailed rules with respect to the determination of whether or not an individual is engaged in farming, see § 1.175-3. For rules applicable to persons cultivating or operating a farm for recreation or pleasure, see sections 162 and 165, and the regulations thereunder.

(e) *Cross references.* (1) For election to include Commodity Credit Corporation loans as income, see section 77 and regulations thereunder.

(2) For definition of gross income derived from farming for purposes of limiting deductibility of soil and water conservation expenditures, see section 175 and regulations thereunder.

(3) For definition of gross income from farming in connection with declarations of estimated income tax, see section 6073 and regulations thereunder.

Reg. § 1.61-6 Gains derived from dealings in property.

(a) *In general.* Gain realized on the sale or exchange of property is included in gross income, unless excluded by law. For this purpose property includes tangible items, such as a building, and intangible items, such as goodwill. Generally, the gain is the excess of the amount realized over the unrecovered cost or other basis for the property sold or exchanged. The specific rules for computing the amount of gain or loss are contained in section 1001 and the regulations thereunder. When a part of a larger property is sold, the cost or other basis of the entire property shall be equitably apportioned among the several parts, and the gain realized or loss sustained on the part of the entire property sold is the difference between the selling price and the cost or other basis allocated to such part. The sale of each part is treated as a separate transaction and gain or loss shall be computed separately on each part. Thus, gain or loss shall be determined at the time of sale of each part and not deferred until the entire property has been disposed of. This rule may be illustrated by the following examples:

Example (1). A, a dealer in real estate, acquires a 10-acre tract for $10,000, which he divides into 20 lots. The $10,000 cost must be equitably apportioned among the lots so that on the sale of each A can determine his taxable gain or deductible loss.

Example (2). B purchases for $25,000 property consisting of a used car lot and adjoining filling station. At the time, the fair market value of the filling station is $15,000 and the fair market value of the used car lot is $10,000. Five years later B sells the filling station for $20,000 at a time when $2,000 has been properly allowed as depreciation thereon. B's gain on this sale is $7,000, since $7,000 is the amount by which the selling price of the filling station exceeds the portion of the cost equitably allocable to the filling station at the time of purchase reduced by the depreciation properly allowed.

(b) *Nontaxable exchanges.* Certain realized gains or losses on the sale or exchange of property are not ``recognized", that is, are not included in or deducted from gross income at the time the transaction occurs. Gain or loss from such sales or exchanges is generally recognized at some later time. Examples of such sales or exchanges are the following:

***

(3) Exchange of certain property held for productive use or investment for property of like kind, see section 1031;

***

(5) Certain involuntary conversions of property if replaced, see section 1033;

***

(c) *Character of recognized gain.* Under Subchapter P, Chapter 1 of the Code, relating

Sec. 61. Gross income defined

to capital gains and losses, certain gains derived from dealings in property are treated specially, and under certain circumstances the maximum rate of tax on such gains is 25 percent, as provided in section 1201. Generally, the property subject to this treatment is a ``capital asset'', or treated as a ``capital asset''. For definition of such assets, see sections 1221 and 1231, and the regulations thereunder. For some of the rules either 5 granting or denying this special treatment, see the following sections and the regulations thereunder:

***

    (2) Sale or exchange of property used in the trade or business and involuntary conversions, section 1231; 10
      (3) Payment of bonds and other evidences of indebtedness, section 1232 [1271];
      (4) Gains and losses from short sales, section 1233;
      (5) Options to buy or sell, section 1234;
      (6) Sale or exchange of patents, section 1235;
      (7) Securities sold by dealers in securities, section 1236; 15
      (8) Real property subdivided for sale, section 1237;

***

Reg. § 1.61-8 Rents and royalties.

    (a) *In general.* Gross income includes rentals received or accrued for the occupancy of real estate or the use of personal property. For the inclusion of rents in income for the 20 purpose of the retirement income credit, see section 37 and the regulations thereunder. Gross income includes royalties. Royalties may be received from books, stories, plays, copyrights, trademarks, formulas, patents, and from the exploitation of natural resources, such as coal, gas, oil, copper, or timber. Payments received as a result of the transfer of patent rights may under some circumstances constitute capital gain instead of ordinary 25 income. See section 1235 and the regulations thereunder. For special rules for certain income from natural resources, see Subchapter I (section 611 and following), Chapter 1 of the Code, and the regulations thereunder.

    (b) *Advance rentals; cancellation payments.* Except as provided in section 467 and the regulations thereunder and except as otherwise provided by the Commissioner in 30 published guidance (see § 601.601(d)(2) of this chapter), gross income includes advance rentals, which must be included in income for the year of receipt regardless of the period covered or the method of accounting employed by the taxpayer. An amount received by a lessor from a lessee for cancelling a lease constitutes gross income for the year in which it is received, since it is essentially a substitute for rental payments. As to amounts 35 received by a lessee for the cancellation of a lease, see section 1241 and the regulations thereunder.

    (c) *Expenditures by lessee.* As a general rule, if a lessee pays any of the expenses of his lessor such payments are additional rental income of the lessor. If a lessee places improvements on real estate which constitute, in whole or in part, a substitute for rent, 40 such improvements constitute rental income to the lessor. Whether or not improvements made by a lessee result in rental income to the lessor in a particular case depends upon the intention of the parties, which may be indicated either by the terms of the lease or by the surrounding circumstances. For the exclusion from gross income of income (other than rent) derived by a lessor of real property on the termination of a lease, representing 45 the value of such property attributable to buildings erected or other improvements made by a lessee, see section 109 and the regulations thereunder. For the exclusion from gross income of a lessor corporation of certain of its income taxes on rental income paid by a lessee corporation under a lease entered into before January 1, 1954, see section 110 and the regulations thereunder. 50

Sec. 61. Gross income defined

Reg. § 1.61-11 Pensions.

(a) *In general.* Pensions and retirement allowances paid either by the Government or by private persons constitute gross income unless excluded by law. Usually, where the taxpayer did not contribute to the cost of a pension and was not taxable on his employer's
5 contributions, the full amount of the pension is to be included in his gross income. But see sections 72, 402, and 403, and the regulations thereunder. When amounts are received from other types of pensions, a portion of the payment may be excluded from gross income. Under some circumstances, amounts distributed from a pension plan in excess of the employee's contributions may constitute long-term capital gain, rather than
10 ordinary income.

***

Reg. § 1.61-12 Income from discharge of indebtedness.

(a) *In general.* The discharge of indebtedness, in whole or in part, may result in the realization of income. If, for example, an individual performs services for a creditor, who
15 in consideration thereof cancels the debt, the debtor realizes income in the amount of the debt as compensation for his services. A taxpayer may realize income by the payment or purchase of his obligations at less than their face value. In general, if a shareholder in a corporation which is indebted to him gratuitously forgives the debt, the transaction amounts to a contribution to the capital of the corporation to the extent of the principal of
20 the debt.

(b) *Proceedings under Bankruptcy Act.* (1) Income is not realized by a taxpayer by virtue of the discharge, under section 14 of the Bankruptcy Act (11 U.S.C. 32), of his indebtedness as the result of an adjudication in bankruptcy, or by virtue of an agreement among his creditors not consummated under any provision of the Bankruptcy Act, if
25 immediately thereafter the taxpayer's liabilities exceed the value of his assets. Furthermore, unless one of the principal purposes of seeking a confirmation under the Bankruptcy Act is the avoidance of income tax, income is not realized by a taxpayer in the case of a cancellation or reduction of his indebtedness under--

(i) A plan of corporate reorganization confirmed under Chapter X of the Bankruptcy Act
30 (11 U.S.C., ch. 10);

(ii) An ``arrangement'' or a ``real property arrangement'' confirmed under Chapter XI or XII, respectively, of the Bankruptcy Act (11 U.S.C., ch. 11, 12); or

(iii) A ``wage earner's plan'' confirmed under Chapter XIII of the Bankruptcy Act (11 U.S.C., ch. 13).

35 (2) For adjustment of basis of certain property in the case of cancellation or reduction of indebtedness resulting from a proceeding under the Bankruptcy Act, see the regulations under section 1016.

(c) Issuance and repurchase of debt instruments--(1) Issuance. An issuer does not realize gain or loss upon the issuance of a debt instrument. For rules relating to an
40 issuer's interest deduction for a debt instrument issued with bond issuance premium, see § 1.163-13.

(2) *Repurchase--(i) In general.* An issuer does not realize gain or loss upon the repurchase of a debt instrument. However, if a debt instrument provides for payments denominated in, or determined by reference to, a nonfunctional currency, an issuer may
45 realize a currency gain or loss upon the repurchase of the instrument. See section 988 and the regulations thereunder. For purposes of this paragraph (c)(2), the term repurchase includes the retirement of a debt instrument, the conversion of a debt instrument into stock of the issuer, and the exchange (including an exchange under section 1001) of a newly issued debt instrument for an existing debt instrument.

50 (ii) *Repurchase at a discount.* An issuer realizes income from the discharge of indebtedness upon the repurchase of a debt instrument for an amount less than its

Sec. 61. Gross income defined

adjusted issue price (within the meaning of § 1.1275-1(b)). The amount of discharge of indebtedness income is equal to the excess of the adjusted issue price over the repurchase price. See section 108 and the regulations thereunder for additional rules relating to income from discharge of indebtedness. For example, to determine the repurchase price of a debt instrument that is repurchased through the issuance of a new 5 debt instrument, see section 108(e)(10).

(iii) *Repurchase at a premium.* An issuer may be entitled to a repurchase premium deduction upon the repurchase of a debt instrument for an amount greater than its adjusted issue price (within the meaning of § 1.1275-1(b)). See § 1.163-7(c) for the treatment of repurchase premium. 10

***

Reg. § 1.61-14 Miscellaneous items of gross income.

(a) *In general.* In addition to the items enumerated in section 61(a), there are many other kinds of gross income. For example, punitive damages such as treble damages under the antitrust laws and exemplary damages for fraud are gross income. Another 15 person's payment of the taxpayer's income taxes constitutes gross income to the taxpayer unless excluded by law. Illegal gains constitute gross income. Treasure trove, to the extent of its value in United States currency, constitutes gross income for the taxable year in which it is reduced to undisputed possession.

20

Reg. § 1.61-21 Taxation of fringe benefits.

(a) *Fringe benefits*--(1) *In general.* Section 61(a)(1) provides that, except as otherwise provided in subtitle A of the Internal Revenue Code of 1986, gross income includes compensation for services, including fees, commissions, fringe benefits, and similar items. For an outline of the regulations under this section relating to fringe benefits, see 25 paragraph (a)(7) of this section. Examples of fringe benefits include: an employer-provided automobile, a flight on an employer-provided aircraft, an employer-provided free or discounted commercial airline flight, an employer-provided vacation, an employer-provided discount on property or services, an employer-provided membership in a country club or other social club, and an employer-provided ticket to an entertainment or 30 sporting event.

(2) *Fringe benefits excluded from income.* To the extent that a particular fringe benefit is specifically excluded from gross income pursuant to another section of subtitle A of the Internal Revenue Code of 1986, that section shall govern the treatment of that fringe benefit. Thus, if the requirements of the governing section are satisfied, the fringe 35 benefits may be excludable from gross income. Examples of excludable fringe benefits include qualified tuition reductions provided to an employee (section 117(d)); meals or lodging furnished to an employee for the convenience of the employer (section 119); benefits provided under a dependent care assistance program (section 129); and no-additional-cost services, qualified employee discounts, working condition fringes, and de 40 minimis fringes (section 132). Similarly, the value of the use by an employee of an employer-provided vehicle or a flight provided to an employee on an employer-provided aircraft may be excludable from income under section 105 (because, for example, the transportation is provided for medical reasons) if and to the extent that the requirements of that section are satisfied. Section 134 excludes from gross income ``qualified military 45 benefits." An example of a benefit that is not a qualified military benefit is the personal use of an employer-provided vehicle. The fact that another section of subtitle A of the Internal Revenue Code addresses the taxation of a particular fringe benefit will not preclude section 61 and the regulations thereunder from applying, to the extent that they are not inconsistent with such other section. For example, many fringe benefits 50 specifically addressed in other sections of subtitle A of the Internal Revenue Code are

117

Sec. 61. Gross income defined

excluded from gross income only to the extent that they do not exceed specific dollar or percentage limits, or only if certain other requirements are met. If the limits are exceeded or the requirements are not met, some or all of the fringe benefit may be includible in gross income pursuant to section 61. See paragraph (b)(3) of this section.

5   (3) *Compensation for services.* A fringe benefit provided in connection with the performance of services shall be considered to have been provided as compensation for such services. Refraining from the performance of services (such as pursuant to a covenant not to compete) is deemed to be the performance of services for purposes of this section.

10   (4) *Person to whom fringe benefit is taxable--(i) In general.* A taxable fringe benefit is included in the income of the person performing the services in connection with which the fringe benefit is furnished. Thus, a fringe benefit may be taxable to a person even though that person did not actually receive the fringe benefit. If a fringe benefit is furnished to someone other than the service provider such benefit is considered in this section as

15 furnished to the service provider, and use by the other person is considered use by the service provider. For example, the provision of an automobile by an employer to an employee's spouse in connection with the performance of services by the employee is taxable to the employee. The automobile is considered available to the employee and use by the employee's spouse is considered use by the employee.

20   (ii) *All persons to whom benefits are taxable referred to as employees.* The person to whom a fringe benefit is taxable need not be an employee of the provider of the fringe benefit, but may be, for example, a partner, director, or an independent contractor. For convenience, the term ``employee" includes any person performing services in connection with which a fringe benefit is furnished, unless otherwise specifically provided

25 in this section.

    (5) *Provider of a fringe benefit referred to as an employer.* The ``provider" of a fringe benefit is that person for whom the services are performed, regardless of whether that person actually provides the fringe benefit to the recipient. The provider of a fringe benefit need not be the employer of the recipient of the fringe benefit, but may be, for example, a

30 client or customer of the employer or of an independent contractor. For convenience, the term ``employer" includes any provider of a fringe benefit in connection with payment for the performance of services, unless otherwise specifically provided in this section.

***

    (b) *Valuation of fringe benefits--(1) In general.* An employee must include in gross

35 income the amount by which the fair market value of the fringe benefit exceeds the sum of--

    (i) The amount, if any, paid for the benefit by or on behalf of the recipient, and

    (ii) The amount, if any, specifically excluded from gross income by some other section of subtitle A of the Internal Revenue Code of 1986.Therefore, for example, if the

40 employee pays fair market value for what is received, no amount is includible in the gross income of the employee. In general, the determination of the fair market value of a fringe benefit must be made before subtracting out the amount, if any, paid for the benefit and the amount, if any, specifically excluded from gross income by another section of subtitle A. See paragraphs (d)(2)(ii) and (e)(1)(iii) of this section.

45   (2) *Fair market value.* In general, fair market value is determined on the basis of all the facts and circumstances. Specifically, the fair market value of a fringe benefit is the amount that an individual would have to pay for the particular fringe benefit in an arm's-length transaction. Thus, for example, the effect of any special relationship that may exist between the employer and the employee must be disregarded. Similarly, an employee's

50 subjective perception of the value of a fringe benefit is not relevant to the determination of the fringe benefit's fair market value nor is the cost incurred by the employer

Sec. 61. Gross income defined

determinative of its fair market value. For special rules relating to the valuation of certain fringe benefits, see paragraph (c) of this section.

(3) *Exclusion from income based on cost.* If a statutory exclusion phrased in terms of cost applies to the provision of a fringe benefit, section 61 does not require the inclusion in the recipient's gross income of the difference between the fair market value and the 5 excludable cost of that fringe benefit. For example, section 129 provides an exclusion from an employee's gross income for amounts contributed by an employer to a dependent care assistance program for employees. Even if the fair market value of the dependent care assistance exceeds the employer's cost, the excess is not subject to inclusion under section 61 and this section. However, if the statutory cost exclusion is a 10 limited amount, the fair market value of the fringe benefit attributable to any excess cost is subject to inclusion. This would be the case, for example, where an employer pays or incurs a cost of more than $5,000 to provide dependent care assistance to an employee.

(4) F*air market value of the availability of an employer-provided vehicle--*(i) *In general.* If the vehicle special valuation rules of paragraph (d), (e), or (f) of this section do not 15 apply with respect to an employer-provided vehicle, the value of the availability of that vehicle is determined under the general valuation principles set forth in this section. In general, that value equals the amount that an individual would have to pay in an arm's-length transaction to lease the same or comparable vehicle on the same or comparable conditions in the geographic area in which the vehicle is available for use. An example of 20 a comparable condition is the amount of time that the vehicle is available to the employee for use, e.g., a one-year period. Unless the employee can substantiate that the same or comparable vehicle could have been leased on a cents-per-mile basis, the value of the availability of the vehicle cannot be computed by applying a cents-per-mile rate to the number of miles the vehicle is driven.   25

(ii) *Certain equipment excluded.* The fair market value of a vehicle does not include the fair market value of any specialized equipment not susceptible to personal use or any telephone that is added to or carried in the vehicle, provided that the presence of that equipment or telephone is necessitated by, and attributable to, the business needs of the employer. However, the value of specialized equipment must be included, if the employee 30 to whom the vehicle is available uses the specialized equipment in a trade or business of the employee other than the employee's trade or business of being an employee of the employer.

(5) F*air market value of chauffeur services--*(i) *Determination of value--*(A) *In general.* The fair market value of chauffeur services provided to the employee by the employer is 35 the amount that an individual would have to pay in an arm's-length transaction to obtain the same or comparable chauffeur services in the geographic area for the period in which the services are provided. In determining the applicable fair market value, the amount of time, if any, the chauffeur remains on-call to perform chauffeur services must be included. For example, assume that A, an employee of corporation M, needs a chauffeur to be on- 40 call to provide services to A during a twenty-four hour period. If during that twenty-four hour period, the chauffeur actually drives A for only six hours, the fair market value of the chauffeur services would have to be the value of having a chauffeur on-call for a twenty-four hour period. The cost of taxi fare or limousine service for the six hours the chauffeur actually drove A would not be an accurate measure of the fair market value of chauffeur 45 services provided to A. Moreover, all other aspects of the chauffeur's services (including any special qualifications of the chauffeur (e.g., training in evasive driving skills) or the ability of the employee to choose the particular chauffeur) must be taken into consideration.

(B) *Alternative valuation with reference to compensation paid.* Alternatively, the fair 50 market value of the chauffeur services may be determined by reference to the compensation (as defined in paragraph (b)(5)(ii) of this section) received by the chauffeur from the employer.

(C) *Separate valuation for chauffeur services.* The value of chauffeur services is determined separately from the value of the availability of an employer-provided vehicle.

5   (ii) Definition of compensation--(A) In general. For purposes of this paragraph (b)(5) (ii), the term ``compensation" means compensation as defined in section 414(q)(7) and the fair market value of nontaxable lodging (if any) provided by the employer to the chauffeur in the current year.

(B) *Adjustments to compensation.* For purposes of this paragraph (b)(5)(ii), a
10   chauffeur's compensation is reduced proportionately to reflect the amount of time during which the chauffeur performs substantial services for the employer other than as a chauffeur and is not on-call as a chauffeur. For example, assume a chauffeur is paid $25,000 a year for working a ten-hour day, five days a week and also receives $5,000 in nontaxable lodging. Further assume that during four hours of each day, the chauffeur is
15   not on-call to perform services as a chauffeur because that individual is performing secretarial functions for the employer. Then, for purposes of determining the fair market value of this chauffeur's services, the employer may reduce the chauffeur's compensation by 4/10 or $12,000 (.4x($25,000+$5,000) = $12,000). Therefore, in this example, the fair market value of the chauffeur's services is $18,000 ($30,000 -$12,000). However, for
20   purposes of this paragraph (b)(5)(ii), a chauffeur's compensation is not to be reduced by any amounts paid to the chauffeur for time spent ``on-call," even though the chauffeur actually performs other services for the employer during such time. For purposes of this paragraph (b)(5)(ii), a determination that a chauffeur is performing substantial services for the employer other than as a chauffeur is based upon the facts and circumstances of
25   each situation. An employee will be deemed to be performing substantial services for the employer other than as a chauffeur if a certain portion of each working day is regularly spent performing other services for the employer.

(iii) *Calculation of chauffeur services for personal purposes of the employee.* The fair market value of chauffeur services provided to the employee for personal purposes may
30   be determined by multiplying the fair market value of chauffeur services, as determined pursuant to paragraph (b)(5)(i) (A) or (B) of this section, by a fraction, the numerator of which is equal to the sum of the hours spent by the chauffeur actually providing personal driving services to the employee and the hours spent by the chauffeur in ``personal on-call time," and the denominator of which is equal to all hours the chauffeur spends in
35   driving services of any kind paid for by the employer, including all hours that are ``on-call."

(iv) *Definition of on-call time.* For purposes of this paragraph, the term ``on-call time" means the total amount of time that the chauffeur is not engaged in the actual performance of driving services, but during which time the chauffeur is available to
40   perform such services. With respect to a round-trip, time spent by a chauffeur waiting for an employee to make a return trip is generally not treated as on-call time; rather such time is treated as part of the round-trip.

(v) *Definition of personal on-call time.* For purposes of this paragraph, the term ``personal on-call time" means the amount of time outside the employee's normal
45   working hours for the employer when the chauffeur is available to the employee to perform driving services.

***

(f) *Commuting valuation rule--(1) In general.* Under the commuting valuation rule of this paragraph (f), the value of the commuting use of an employer-provided vehicle may
50   be determined pursuant to paragraph (f)(3) of this section if the following criteria are met by the employer and employees with respect to the vehicle:

Sec. 61. Gross income defined

(i) The vehicle is owned or leased by the employer and is provided to one or more employees for use in connection with the employer's trade or business and is used in the employer's trade or business;

(ii) For bona fide noncompensatory business reasons, the employer requires the employee to commute to and/or from work in the vehicle;

(iii) The employer has established a written policy under which neither the employee, nor any individual whose use would be taxable to the employee, may use the vehicle for personal purposes, other than for commuting or de minimis personal use (such as a stop for a personal errand on the way between a business delivery and the employee's home);

(iv) Except for de minimis personal use, the employee does not use the vehicle for any personal purpose other than commuting; and

(v) The employee required to use the vehicle for commuting is not a control employee of the employer (as defined in paragraphs (f)(5) and (6) of this section).

Personal use of a vehicle is all use of the vehicle by an employee that is not used in the employee's trade or business of being an employee of the employer. An employer-provided vehicle that is generally used each workday to transport at least three employees of the employer to and from work in an employer-sponsored commuting vehicle pool is deemed to meet the requirements of paragraphs (f)(1)(i) and (ii) of this section.

(2) *Special rules.* Notwithstanding anything in paragraph (f)(1) of this section to the contrary, the following special rules apply--

(i) Chauffeur-driven vehicles. If a vehicle is chauffeur-driven, the commuting valuation rule of this paragraph (f) may not be used to value the commuting use of any person (other than the chauffeur) who rides in the vehicle. (See paragraphs (d) and (e) of this section for other vehicle special valuation rules.) The special rule of this paragraph (f) may be used to value the commuting-only use of the vehicle by the chauffeur if the conditions of paragraph (f)(1) of this section are satisfied. For purposes of this paragraph (f)(2), an individual will not be considered a chauffeur if he or she performs non-driving services for the employer, is not available to perform driving services while performing such other services and whose only driving services consist of driving a vehicle used for commuting by other employees of the employer.

(ii) *Control employee exception.* If the vehicle in which the employee is required to commute is not an automobile as defined in paragraph (d)(1)(ii) of this section, the restriction of paragraph (f)(1)(v) of this section (relating to control employees) does not apply.

(3) *Commuting value--*(i) *$1.50 per one-way commute.* If the requirements of this paragraph (f) are satisfied, the value of the commuting use of an employer-provided vehicle is $1.50 per one-way commute (e.g., from home to work or from work to home). The value provided in this paragraph (f)(3) includes the value of any goods or services directly related to the vehicle (e.g., fuel).

(ii) V*alue per employee.* If there is more than one employee who commutes in the vehicle, such as in the case of an employer-sponsored commuting vehicle pool, the amount includible in the income of each employee is $1.50 per one-way commute. Thus, the amount includible for each round-trip commute is $3.00 per employee. See paragraphs (d)(7)(vi) and (e)(5)(vi) of this section for use of the automobile lease valuation and vehicle cents-per-mile valuation special rules for valuing the use or availability of the vehicle in the case of an employer-sponsored vehicle or automobile commuting pool.

(4) *Definition of vehicle.* For purposes of this paragraph (f), the term ``vehicle" means any motorized wheeled vehicle manufactured primarily for use on public streets, roads,

Sec. 61. Gross income defined

and highways. The term ``vehicle" includes an automobile as defined in paragraph (d)(1)(ii) of this section.

(5) *Control employee defined--Non-government employer.* For purposes of this paragraph (f), a control employee of a non-government employer is any employee--

5   (i) Who is a Board- or shareholder-appointed, confirmed, or elected officer of the employer whose compensation equals or exceeds $50,000,

(ii) Who is a director of the employer,

(iii) Whose compensation equals or exceeds $100,000, or

(iv) Who owns a one-percent or greater equity, capital, or profits interest in the 10 employer.

For purposes of determining who is a one-percent owner under paragraph (f)(5)(iv) of this section, any individual who owns (or is considered as owning under section 318(a) or principles similar to section 318(a) for entities other than corporations) one percent or more of the fair market value of an entity (the ``owned entity") is considered a one-15 percent owner of all entities which would be aggregated with the owned entity under the rules of section 414(b), (c), (m), or (o). For purposes of determining who is an officer or director with respect to an employer under this paragraph (f)(5), notwithstanding anything in this section to the contrary, if an entity would be aggregated with other entities under the rules of section 414(b), (c), (m), or (o), the officer definition (but not the compensation 20 requirement) and the director definition apply to each such separate entity rather than to the aggregated employer. An employee who is an officer or a director of an entity (the ``first entity") shall be treated as an officer or a director of all entities aggregated with the first entity under the rules of section 414(b), (c), (m), or (o). Instead of applying the control employee definition of this paragraph (f)(5), an employer may treat all, and only, 25 employees who are ``highly compensated" employees (as defined in § 1.132-8(g)) as control employees for purposes of this paragraph (f).

(6) *Control employee defined--Government employer.* For purposes of this paragraph (f), a control employee of a government employer is any--

(i) Elected official, or

30   (ii) Employee whose compensation equals or exceeds the compensation paid to a Federal Government employee holding a position at Executive Level V, determined under Chapter 11 of title 2, United States Code, as adjusted by section 5318 of Title 5 United States Code.

For purposes of this paragraph (f), the term ``government" includes any Federal, state or 35 local governmental unit, and any agency or instrumentality thereof. Instead of applying the control employee definition of paragraph (f)(6), an employer may treat all and only employees who are ``highly compensated" employees (as defined in § 1.132-8(f)) as control employees for purposes of this paragraph (f).

(7) *``Compensation" defined.* For purposes of this paragraph (f), the term 40 ``compensation" has the same meaning as in section 414(q)(7). Compensation includes all amounts received from all entities treated as a single employer under section 414 (b), (c), (m), or (o). Levels of compensation shall be adjusted at the same time and in the same manner as provided in section 415(d). The first such adjustment shall be for calendar year 1988.

45   (g) *Non-commercial flight valuation rule--(1) In general.* Under the non-commercial flight valuation rule of this paragraph (g), except as provided in paragraph (g)(12) of this section, if an employee is provided with a flight on an employer-provided aircraft, the value of the flight is calculated using the aircraft valuation formula of paragraph (g)(5) of this section. For purposes of this paragraph (g), the value of a flight on an employer-50 provided aircraft by an individual who is less than two years old is deemed to be zero. See paragraph (b)(1) of this section for rules relating to the amount includible in income

Sec. 61. Gross income defined

when an employee reimburses the employee's employer for all or part of the fair market value of the benefit provided.

(2) *Eligible flights and eligible aircraft.* The valuation rule of this paragraph (g) may be used to value flights on all employer-provided aircraft, including helicopters. The valuation rule of this paragraph (g) may be used to value international as well as domestic flights. 5 The valuation rule of this paragraph (g) may not be used to value a flight on any commercial aircraft on which air transportation is sold to the public on a per-seat basis. For a special valuation rule relating to certain flights on commercial aircraft, see paragraph (h) of this section.

(3) *Definition of a flight*--(i) *General rule.* Except as otherwise provided in paragraph (g) 10 (3)(iii) of this section (relating to intermediate stops), for purposes of this paragraph (g), a flight is the distance (in statute miles, i.e., 5,280 feet per statute mile) between the place at which the individual boards the aircraft and the place at which the individual deplanes.

(ii) Valuation of each flight. Under the valuation rule of this paragraph (g), value is determined separately for each flight. Thus, a round-trip is comprised of at least two 15 flights. For example, an employee who takes a personal trip on an employer-provided aircraft from New York City to Denver, then Denver to Los Angeles, and finally Los Angeles to New York City has taken three flights and must apply the aircraft valuation formula separately to each flight. The value of a flight must be determined on a passenger-by-passenger basis. For example, if an individual accompanies an employee 20 and the flight taken by the individual would be taxed to the employee, the employee would be taxed on the special rule value of the flight by the employee and the flight by the individual.

(iii) *Intermediate stop.* If a landing is necessitated by weather conditions, by an emergency, for purposes of refueling or obtaining other services relating to the aircraft or 25 for any other purpose unrelated to the personal purposes of the employee whose flight is being valued, that landing is an intermediate stop. Additional mileage attributable to an intermediate stop is not considered when determining the distance of an employee's flight.

*** 30

(k) *Commuting valuation rule for certain employees*--(1) I*n general.* Under the rule of this paragraph (k), the value of the commuting use of employer-provided transportation may be determined under paragraph (k)(3) of this section if the following criteria are met by the employer and employee with respect to the transportation:

(i) The transportation is provided, solely because of unsafe conditions, to an employee 35 who would ordinarily walk or use public transportation for commuting to or from work;

(ii) The employer has established a written policy (e.g., in the employer's personnel manual) under which the transportation is not provided for the employee's personal purposes other than for commuting due to unsafe conditions and the employer's practice in fact corresponds with the policy; 40

(iii) The transportation is not used for personal purposes other than commuting due to unsafe conditions; and

(iv) The employee receiving the employer-provided transportation is a qualified employee of the employer (as defined in paragraph (k)(6) of this section).

(2) *Trip-by-trip basis.* The special valuation rule of this paragraph (k) applies on a trip- 45 by-trip basis. If an employer and employee fail to meet the criteria of paragraph (k)(1) of this section with respect to any trip, the value of the transportation for that trip is not determined under paragraph (k)(3) of this section and the amount includible in the employee's income is determined by reference to the fair market value of the transportation. 50

(3) *Commuting value*--(i) *$1.50 per one-way commute.* If the requirements of this

Sec. 61. Gross income defined

paragraph (k) are satisfied, the value of the commuting use of the employer-provided transportation is $1.50 per one-way commute (i.e., from home to work or from work to home).

(ii) *Value per employee.* If transportation is provided to more than one qualified
5 employee at the same time, the amount includible in the income of each employee is $1.50 per one-way commute.

(4) *Definition of employer-provided transportation.* For purposes of this paragraph (k), ``employer-provided transportation" means transportation by vehicle (as defined in paragraph (f)(4) of this section) that is purchased by the employer (or that is purchased
10 by the employee and reimbursed by the employer) from a party that is not related to the employer for the purpose of transporting a qualified employee to or from work. Reimbursements made by an employer to an employee to cover the cost of purchasing transportation (e.g., hiring cabs) must be made under a bona fide reimbursement arrangement.

15 (5) *Unsafe conditions.* Unsafe conditions exist if a reasonable person would, under the facts and circumstances, consider it unsafe for the employee to walk to or from home, or to walk to or use public transportation at the time of day the employee must commute. One of the factors indicating whether it is unsafe is the history of crime in the geographic area surrounding the employee's workplace or residence at the time of day the employee
20 must commute.

(6) *Qualified employee defined--*(i) *In general.* For purposes of this paragraph (k), a qualified employee is one who meets the following requirements with respect to the employer:

(A) The employee performs services during the current year, is paid on an hourly
25 basis, is not claimed under section 213(a)(1) of the Fair Labor Standards Act of 1938 (as amended), 29 U.S.C. 201-219 (FLSA), to be exempt from the minimum wage and maximum hour provisions of the FLSA, and is within a classification with respect to which the employer actually pays, or has specified in writing that it will pay, compensation for overtime equal to or exceeding one and one-half times the regular rate as provided by
30 section 207 of the FLSA; and

(B) The employee does not receive compensation from the employer in excess of the amount permitted by section 414(q)(1)(C) of the Code.

(ii) ``*Compensation" and ``paid on an hourly basis" defined.* For purposes of this paragraph (k), ``compensation" has the same meaning as in section 414(q)(7).
35 Compensation includes all amounts received from all entities treated as a single employer under section 414(b), (c), (m), or (o). Levels of compensation shall be adjusted at the same time and in the same manner as provided in section 415(d). If an employee's compensation is stated on an annual basis, the employee is treated as ``paid on an hourly basis" for purposes of this paragraph (k) as long as the employee is not claimed to
40 be exempt from the minimum wage and maximum hour provisions of the FLSA and is paid overtime wages either equal to or exceeding one and one-half the employee's regular hourly rate of pay.

***

(v) *Non-qualified employees.* If an employee is not a qualified employee within the
45 meaning of this paragraph (k)(6), no portion of the value of the commuting use of employer-provided transportation is excluded under this paragraph (k).

***

[T.D. 6500, 25 FR 11402, Nov. 26, 1960; T.D. 6696, 28 FR 13450, Dec. 12, 1963; T.D.
50 6856, 30 FR 13316, Oct. 20, 1965; T.D. 6984, 33 FR 19174, Dec. 24, 1968; T.D. 7207, 37

Sec. 61. Gross income defined

FR 20767, Oct. 5, 1972; T.D. 7285, 38 FR 26184, Sept. 19, 1973; T.D. 7544, 43 FR 31913, July 24, 1978; T.D. 7623, 44 FR 28800, May 17, 1979; T.D. 7741, 45 1870, Jan. 16, 1992; T.D. 8408, 57 FR 12419, Apr. 10, 1992; T.D. 8457, 57 FR 62195, Dec. 30, 1992; T.D. 8491, 58 FR 53127, Oct. 14, 1993; T.D. 8607, 60 FR 40076, Aug. 7, 1995; T.D. 8729, 62 FR 44546, Aug. 22, 1997; T.D. 8746, 62 FR 68175, Dec. 31, 1997; T.D. 8820, 64 FR 26851, May 18, 1999; T.D. 9092, 68 FR 54344, Sept. 17, 2003; T.D. 9135, 69 FR 41192, July 8, 2004]

Sec. 62. Adjusted gross income defined

(a) **General rule.** -- For purposes of this subtitle, the term "adjusted gross income" means, in the case of an individual, gross income minus the following deductions:

(1) Trade and business deductions. -- The deductions allowed by this chapter (other than by part VII of this subchapter) which are attributable to a trade or business carried on by the taxpayer, if such trade or business does not consist of the performance of services by the taxpayer as an employee.

(2) Certain trade and business deductions of employees. --

(A) Reimbursed expenses of employees. -- The deductions allowed by part VI (section 161 and following) which consist of expenses paid or incurred by the taxpayer, in connection with the performance by him of services as an employee, under a reimbursement or other expense allowance arrangement with his employer. The fact that the reimbursement may be provided by a third party shall not be determinative of whether or not the preceding sentence applies.

(B) Certain expenses of performing artists. -- The deductions allowed by section 162 which consist of expenses paid or incurred by a qualified performing artist in connection with the performances by him of services in the performing arts as an employee.

(C) Certain expenses of officials. -- The deductions allowed by section 162 which consist of expenses paid or incurred with respect to services performed by an official as an employee of a State or a political subdivision thereof in a position compensated in whole or in part on a fee basis.

(D) Certain expenses of elementary and secondary school teachers. -- In the case of taxable years beginning during 2002, 2003, 2004, 2005, 2006, or 2007 the deductions allowed by section 162 which consist of expenses, not in excess of $250, paid or incurred by an eligible educator in connection with books, supplies (other than nonathletic supplies for courses of instruction in health or physical education), computer equipment (including related software and services) and other equipment, and supplementary materials used by the eligible educator in the classroom.

(E) Certain expenses of members of reserve components of the Armed Forces of the United States. -- The deductions allowed by section 162 which consist of expenses, determined at a rate not in excess of the rates for travel expenses (including per diem in lieu of subsistence) authorized for employees of agencies under subchapter I of chapter 57 of title 5, United States Code, paid or incurred by the taxpayer in connection with the performance of services by such taxpayer as a member of a reserve component of the Armed Forces of the United States for any period during which such individual is more than 100 miles away from home in connection with such services.

(3) Losses from sale or exchange of property. -- The deductions allowed by part VI (sec. 161 and following) as losses from the sale or exchange of property.

(4) Deductions attributable to rents and royalties. -- The deductions allowed by part VI (sec. 161 and following), by section 212 (relating to expenses for production of income), and

Sec. 62. Adjusted gross income defined

by section 611 (relating to depletion) which are attributable to property held for the production of rents or royalties.

(5) Certain deductions of life tenants and income beneficiaries of property. -- In the case of a life tenant of property, or an income beneficiary of property held in trust, or an heir, legatee, or devisee of an estate, the deduction for depreciation allowed by section 167 and the deduction allowed by section 611.

(6) Pension, profit-sharing, and annuity plans of self-employed individuals. -- In the case of an individual who is an employee within the meaning of section 401(c)(1), the deduction allowed by section 404.

(7) Retirement savings. -- The deduction allowed by section 219 (relating to deduction of certain retirement savings).

***

(9) Penalties forfeited because of premature withdrawal of funds from time savings accounts or deposits. -- The deductions allowed by section 165 for losses incurred in any transaction entered into for profit, though not connected with a trade or business, to the extent that such losses include amounts forfeited to a bank, mutual savings bank, savings and loan association, building and loan association, cooperative bank or homestead association as a penalty for premature withdrawal of funds from a time savings account, certificate of deposit, or similar class of deposit.

(10) Alimony. -- The deduction allowed by section 215.

(11) Reforestation expenses. -- The deduction allowed by section 194.

***

(13) Jury duty pay remitted to employer. -- Any deduction allowable under this chapter by reason of an individual remitting any portion of any jury pay to such individual's employer in exchange for payment by the employer of compensation for the period such individual was performing jury duty. For purposes of the preceding sentence, the term "jury pay" means any payment received by the individual for the discharge of jury duty.

(14) Deduction for clean-fuel vehicles and certain refueling property. -- The deduction allowed by section 179A.

(15) Moving expenses. -- The deduction allowed by section 217.

(16) Archer MSAs. -- The deduction allowed by section 220.

(17) Interest on education loans. -- The deduction allowed by section 221.

(18) Higher education expenses. -- The deduction allowed by section 222.

(19) Health savings accounts. -- The deduction allowed by section 223.

(20) Costs involving discrimination suits, etc. -- Any deduction allowable under this chapter for attorney fees and court costs paid by, or on behalf of, the taxpayer in connection with any action involving a claim of unlawful discrimination (as defined in subsection (e)) or a claim of a violation of subchapter III of chapter 37 of title 31, United States Code (!2) or a claim made under section 1862(b)(3)(A) of the Social Security Act (42 U.S.C. 1395y(b)(3) (A)). The preceding sentence shall not apply to any deduction in excess of the amount includible in the taxpayer's gross income for the taxable year on account of a judgment or settlement (whether by suit or agreement and whether as lump sum or periodic payments) resulting from such claim.

***

Nothing in this section shall permit the same item to be deducted more than once.

(b) Qualified performing artist. --

Sec. 62.   Adjusted gross income defined

(1) In general. -- For purposes of subsection (a)(2)(B), the term "qualified performing artist" means, with respect to any taxable year, any individual if--

   (A) such individual performed services in the performing arts as an employee during the taxable year for at least 2 employers,

   (B) the aggregate amount allowable as a deduction under section 162 in connection with 5 the performance of such services exceeds 10 percent of such individual's gross income attributable to the performance of such services, and

   (C) the adjusted gross income of such individual for the taxable year (determined without regard to subsection (a)(2)(B)) does not exceed $16,000.

(2) Nominal employer not taken into account. -- An individual shall not be treated as 10 performing services in the performing arts as an employee for any employer during any taxable year unless the amount received by such individual from such employer for the performance of such services during the taxable year equals or exceeds $200.

(3) Special rules for married couples. --

   (A) In general. -- Except in the case of a husband and wife who lived apart at all times 15 during the taxable year, if the taxpayer is married at the close of the taxable year, subsection (a)(2)(B) shall apply only if the taxpayer and his spouse file a joint return for the taxable year.

   (B) Application of paragraph (1). -- In the case of a joint return--

      (i) paragraph (1) (other than subparagraph (C) thereof) shall be applied separately 20 with respect to each spouse, but

      (ii) paragraph (1)(C) shall be applied with respect to their combined adjusted gross income.

   (C) Determination of marital status. -- For purposes of this subsection, marital status shall be determined under section 7703(a).   25

   (D) Joint return. -- For purposes of this subsection, the term "joint return" means the joint return of a husband and wife made under section 6013.

(c) Certain arrangements not treated as reimbursement arrangements. -- For purposes of subsection (a)(2)(A), an arrangement shall in no event be treated as a reimbursement or other expense allowance arrangement if--   30

   (1) such arrangement does not require the employee to substantiate the expenses covered by the arrangement to the person providing the reimbursement, or

   (2) such arrangement provides the employee the right to retain any amount in excess of the substantiated expenses covered under the arrangement.

The substantiation requirements of the preceding sentence shall not apply to any expense to the 35 extent that substantiation is not required under section 274(d) for such expense by reason of the regulations prescribed under the 2nd sentence thereof.

(d) Definition; special rules. --

   (1) Eligible educator. --

      (A) In general. -- For purposes of subsection (a)(2)(D), the term "eligible educator" 40 means, with respect to any taxable year, an individual who is a kindergarten through grade 12 teacher, instructor, counselor, principal, or aide in a school for at least 900 hours during a school year.

      (B) School. -- The term "school" means any school which provides elementary education or secondary education (kindergarten through grade 12), as determined under 45 State law.

Sec. 62. Adjusted gross income defined

(2) Coordination with exclusions. -- A deduction shall be allowed under subsection (a)(2) (D) for expenses only to the extent the amount of such expenses exceeds the amount excludable under section 135, 529(c)(1), or 530(d)(2) for the taxable year.

(e) Unlawful discrimination defined. -- For purposes of subsection (a)(19), the term "unlawful 5 discrimination" means an act that is unlawful under any of the following:

***

Reg. §. 1.62-2 Reimbursements and other expense allowance arrangements.

***

10   (b) *Scope.* For purposes of determining ``adjusted gross income," section 62(a)(2)(A) allows an employee a deduction for expenses allowed by part VI (section 161 and following), subchapter B, chapter 1 of the Code, paid by the employee, in connection with the performance of services as an employee of the employer, under a reimbursement or other expense allowance arrangement with a payor (the employer, its agent, or a third 15 party). Section 62(c) provides that an arrangement will not be treated as a reimbursement or other expense allowance arrangement for purposes of section 62(a)(2)(A) if--
    (1) Such arrangement does not require the employee to substantiate the expenses covered by the arrangement to the payor, or
    (2) Such arrangement provides the employee the right to retain any amount in excess 20 of the substantiated expenses covered under the arrangement.
This section prescribes rules relating to the requirements of section 62(c).
    (c) *Reimbursement or other expense allowance arrangement*--(1) *Defined.* For purposes of §§ 1.62-1, 1.62-1T, and 1.62-2, the phrase ``reimbursement or other expense allowance arrangement" means an arrangement that meets the requirements of 25 paragraphs (d) (business connection, (e) (substantiation), and (f) (returning amounts in excess of expenses) of this section. A payor may have more than one arrangement with respect to a particular employee, depending on the facts and circumstances. See paragraph (d)(2) of this section (payor treated as having two arrangements under certain circumstances).
30   (2) *Accountable plans*--(i) *In general.* Except as provided in paragraph (c)(2)(ii) of this section, if an arrangement meets the requirements of paragraphs (d), (e), and (f) of this section, all amounts paid under the arrangement are treated as paid under an ``accountable plan."
    (ii) *Special rule for failure to return excess.* If an arrangement meets the requirements 35 of paragraphs (d), (e), and (f) of this section, but the employee fails to return, within a reasonable period of time, any amount in excess of the amount of the expenses substantiated in accordance with paragraph (e) of this section, only the amounts paid under the arrangement that are not in excess of the substantiated expenses are treated as paid under an accountable plan.
40   (3) *Nonaccountable plans*--(i) *In general.* If an arrangement does not satisfy one or more of the requirements of paragraphs (d), (e), or (f) of this section, all amounts paid under the arrangement are treated as paid under a ``nonaccountable plan." If a payor provides a nonaccountable plan, an employee who receives payments under the plan cannot compel the payor to treat the payments as paid under an accountable plan by 45 voluntarily substantiating the expenses and returning any excess to the payor.
    (ii) *Special rule for failure to return excess.* If an arrangement meets the requirements of paragraphs (d), (e), and (f) of this section, but the employee fails to return, within a reasonable period of time, any amount in excess of the amount of the expenses substantiated in accordance with paragraph (e) of this section, the amounts paid under 50 the arrangement that are in excess of the substantiated expenses are treated as paid

Sec. 62. Adjusted gross income defined

under a nonaccountable plan.

(4) *Treatment of payments under accountable plans.* Amounts treated as paid under an accountable plan are excluded from the employee's gross income, are not reported as wages or other compensation on the employee's Form W-2, and are exempt from the withholding and payment of employment taxes (Federal Insurance Contributions Act (FICA), Federal Unemployment Tax Act (FUTA), Railroad Retirement Tax Act (RRTA), Railroad Unemployment Repayment Tax (RURT), and income tax.) See paragraph (l) of this section for cross references.

(5) *Treatment of payments under nonaccountable plans.* Amounts treated as paid under a nonaccountable plan are included in the employee's gross income, must be reported as wages or other compensation on the employee's Form W-2, and are subject to withholding and payment of employment taxes (FICA, FUTA, RRTA, RURT, and income tax). See paragraph (h) of this section. Expenses attributable to amounts included in the employee's gross income may be deducted, provided the employee can substantiate the full amount of his or her expenses (i.e., the amount of the expenses, if any, the reimbursement for which is treated as paid under an accountable plan as well as those for which the employee is claiming the deduction) in accordance with §§ 1.274-5T and 1.274(d)-1 or § 1.162-17, but only as a miscellaneous itemized deduction subject to the limitations applicable to such expenses (e.g., the 80-percent limitation on meal and entertainment expenses provided in section 274(n) and the 2-percent floor provided in section 67).

(d) *Business connection*--(1) *In general.* Except as provided in paragraphs (d)(2) and (d)(3) of this section, an arrangement meets the requirements of this paragraph (d) if it provides advances, allowances (including per diem allowances, allowances only for meals and incidental expenses, and mileage allowances), or reimbursements only for business expenses that are allowable as deductions by part VI (section 161 and the following), subchapter B, chapter 1 of the Code, and that are paid or incurred by the employee in connection with the performance of services as an employee of the employer. The payment may be actually received from the employer, its agent, or a third party for whom the employee performs a service as an employee of the employer, and may include amounts charged directly or indirectly to the payor through credit card systems or otherwise. In addition, if both wages and the reimbursement or other expense allowance are combined in a single payment, the reimbursement or other expense allowance must be identified either by making a separate payment or by specifically identifying the amount of the reimbursement or other expense allowance.

(2) *Other bona fide expenses.* If an arrangement provides advances, allowances, or reimbursements for business expenses described in paragraph (d)(1) of this section (i.e., deductible employee business expenses) and for other bona fide expenses related to the employer's business (e.g., travel that is not away from home) that are not deductible under part VI (section 161 and the following), subchapter B, chapter 1 of the Code, the payor is treated as maintaining two arrangements. The portion of the arrangement that provides payments for the deductible employee business expenses is treated as one arrangement that satisfies this paragraph (d). The portion of the arrangement that provides payments for the nondeductible employee expenses is treated as a second arrangement that does not satisfy this paragraph (d) and all amounts paid under this second arrangement will be treated as paid under a nonaccountable plan. See paragraphs (c)(5) and (h) of this section.

(3) *Reimbursement requirement*--(i) *In general.* If a payor arranges to pay an amount to an employee regardless of whether the employee incurs (or is reasonably expected to incur) business expenses of a type described in paragraph (d)(1) or (d)(2) of this section, the arrangement does not satisfy this paragraph (d) and all amounts paid under the

Sec. 62. Adjusted gross income defined

arrangement are treated as paid under a nonaccountable plan. See paragraphs (c)(5) and (h) of this section.

 (ii) *Per diem allowances.* An arrangement providing a per diem allowance for travel expenses of a type described in paragraph (d)(1) or (d)(2) of this section that is computed
5 on a basis similar to that used in computing the employee's wages or other compensation (e.g., the number of hours worked, miles traveled, or pieces produced) meets the requirements of this paragraph (d) only if, on December 12, 1989, the per diem allowance was identified by the payor either by making a separate payment or by specifically identifying the amount of the per diem allowance, or a per diem allowance computed on
10 that basis was commonly used in the industry in which the employee is employed. See section 274(d) and § 1.274(d)-1. A per diem allowance described in this paragraph (d)(3) (ii) may be adjusted in a manner that reasonably reflects actual increases in employee business expenses occurring after December 12, 1989.

 (e) *Substantiation*--(1) *In general.* An arrangement meets the requirements of this
15 paragraph (e) if it requires each business expense to be substantiated to the payor in accordance with paragraph (e)(2) or (e)(3) of this section, whichever is applicable, within a reasonable period of time. See § 1.274-5T or § 1.162-17.

 (2) *Expenses governed by section 274(d).* An arrangement that reimburses travel, entertainment, use of a passenger automobile or other listed property, or other business
20 expenses governed by section 274(d) meets the requirements of this paragraph (e)(2) if information sufficient to satisfy the substantiation requirements of section 274(d) and the regulations thereunder is submitted to the payor. See § 1.274-5. Under section 274(d), information sufficient to substantiate the requisite elements of each expenditure or use must be submitted to the payor. For example, with respect to travel away from home, §
25 1.274-5(b)(2) requires that information sufficient to substantiate the amount, time, place, and business purpose of the expense must be submitted to the payor. Similarly, with respect to use of a passenger automobile or other listed property, § 1.274-5(b)(6) requires that information sufficient to substantiate the amount, time, use, and business purpose of the expense must be submitted to the payor. See § 1.274-5(g) and (j), which
30 grant the Commissioner the authority to establish optional methods of substantiating certain expenses. Substantiation of the amount of a business expense in accordance with rules prescribed pursuant to the authority granted by § 1.274-5(g) or (j) will be treated as substantiation of the amount of such expense for purposes of this section.

 (3) *Expenses not governed by section 274(d).* An arrangement that reimburses
35 business expenses not governed by section 274(d) meets the requirements of this paragraph (e)(3) if information is submitted to the payor sufficient to enable the payor to identify the specific nature of each expense and to conclude that the expense is attributable to the payor's business activities. Therefore, each of the elements of an expenditure or use must be substantiated to the payor. It is not sufficient if an employee
40 merely aggregates expenses into broad categories (such as ``travel") or reports individual expenses through the use of vague, nondescriptive terms (such as ``miscellaneous business expenses"). See § 1.162-17(b).

 (f) *Returning amounts in excess of expenses*--(1) *In general.* Except as provided in paragraph (f)(2) of this section, an arrangement meets the requirements of this paragraph
45 (f) if it requires the employee to return to the payor within a reasonable period of time may amount paid under the arrangement in excess of the expenses substantiated in accordance with paragraph (e) of this section. The determination of whether an arrangement requires an employee to return amounts in excess of substantiated expenses will depend on the facts and circumstances. An arrangement whereby money
50 is advanced to an employee to defray expenses will be treated as satisfying the requirements of this paragraph (f) only if the amount of money advanced is reasonably

Sec. 62. Adjusted gross income defined

calculated not to exceed the amount of anticipated expenditures, the advance of money is made on a day within a reasonable period of the day that the anticipated expenditures are paid or incurred, and any amounts in excess of the expenses substantiated in accordance with paragraph (e) of this section are required to be returned to the payor within a reasonable period of time after the advance is received.   5

(2) *Per diem or mileage allowances.* The Commissioner may, in his discretion, prescribe rules in pronouncements of general applicability under which a reimbursement or other expense allowance arrangement that provides per diem allowances providing for ordinary and necessary expenses of traveling away from home (exclusive of transportation costs to and from destination) or mileage allowances providing for ordinary 10 and necessary expenses of local travel and transportation while traveling away from home will be treated as satisfying the requirements of this paragraph (f), even though the arrangement does not require the employee to return the portion of such an allowance that relates to the days or miles of travel substantiated and that exceeds the amount of the employee's expenses deemed substantiated pursuant to rules prescribed under 15 section 274(d), provided the allowance is paid at a rate for each day or mile of travel that is reasonably calculated not to exceed the amount of the employee's expenses or anticipated expenses and the employee is required to return to the payor within a reasonable period of time any portion of such allowance which relates to days or miles of travel not substantiated in accordance with paragraph (e) of this section.   20

(g) *Reasonable period*--(1) *In general.* The determination of a reasonable period of time will depend on the facts and circumstances.

(2) *Safe harbors*--(i) *Fixed date method.* An advance made within 30 days of when an expense is paid or incurred, an expense substantiated to the payor within 60 days after it is paid or incurred, or an amount returned to the payor within 120 days after an expense 25 is paid or incurred will be treated as having occurred within a reasonable period of time.

(ii) *Periodic statement method.* If a payor provides employees with periodic statements (no less frequently than quarterly) stating the amount, if any, paid under the arrangement in excess of the expenses the employee has substantiated in accordance with paragraph (e) of this section, and requesting the employee to substantiate any 30 additional business expenses that have not yet been substantiated (whether or not such expenses relate to the expenses with respect to which the original advance was paid) and/or to return any amounts remaining unsubstantiated within 120 days of the statement, an expense substantiated or an amount returned within that period will be treated as being substantiated or returned within a reasonable period of time.   35

(3) *Pattern of overreimbursements.* If, under a reimbursement or other expense allowance arrangement, a payor has a plan or practice to provide amounts to employees in excess of expenses substantiated in accordance with paragraph (e) of this section and to avoid reporting and withholding on such amounts, the payor may not use either of the safe harbors provided in paragraph (g)(2) of this section for any years during which such 40 plan or practice exists.

***

(i) *Application.* The requirements of paragraphs (d) (business connection), (e) (substantiation), and (f) (returning amounts in excess of expenses) of this section will be applied on an employee-by-employee basis. Thus, for example, the failure by one 45 employee to substantiate expenses under an arrangement in accordance with paragraph (e) of this section will not cause amounts paid to other employees to be treated as paid under a nonaccountable plan.

[T.D. 8324, 55 FR 51691, Dec. 17, 1990; 56 FR 8911, Mar. 4, 1991; T.D. 8451, 57 FR 50 57668, Dec. 7, 1992; T.D. 8666, 61 FR 27005, May 30, 1996; T.D. 8784, 63 FR 52600,

131

Sec. 62. Adjusted gross income defined

Oct. 1, 1998; T.D. 8864, 65 FR 4122, Jan. 26, 2000; T.D. 9064, 68 FR 39011, July 1, 2003]

Sec. 63. Taxable income defined

    (a) In general. -- Except as provided in subsection (b), for purposes of this subtitle, the term
5 "taxable income" means gross income minus the deductions allowed by this chapter (other than the standard deduction).

    (b) Individuals who do not itemize their deductions. -- In the case of an individual who does not elect to itemize his deductions for the taxable year, for purposes of this subtitle, the term "taxable income" means adjusted gross income, minus--

10   **(1)** the standard deduction, and

    (2) the deduction for personal exemptions provided in section151.

    (c) Standard deduction. -- For purposes of this subtitle--

    (1) In general. -- Except as otherwise provided in this subsection, the term "standard deduction" means the sum of--

15   **(A)** the basic standard deduction, and

    (B) the additional standard deduction.

    (2) Basic standard deduction. -- For purposes of paragraph (1), the basic standard deduction is--

    (A) 200 percent of the dollar amount in effect under subparagraph (C) for the taxable
20   year in the case of--

    (i) a joint return, or

    (ii) a surviving spouse (as defined in section 2(a)),

    (B) $4,400 in the case of a head of household (as defined in section 2(b)), or

    (C) $3,000 in any other case.

25   **(3) Additional standard deduction for aged and blind.** -- For purposes of paragraph (1), the additional standard deduction is the sum of each additional amount to which the taxpayer is entitled under subsection (f).

    (4) Adjustments for inflation. -- In the case of any taxable year beginning in a calendar year after 1988, each dollar amount contained in paragraph (2)(B), (2)(C), or (5) or subsection
30 (f) shall be increased by an amount equal to--

    (A) such dollar amount, multiplied by

    (B) the cost-of-living adjustment determined under section 1(f)(3) for the calendar year in which the taxable year begins, by substituting for "calendar year 1992" in subparagraph (B) thereof -

35   **(i)** "calendar year 1987" in the case of the dollar amounts contained in paragraph (2) (B), (2)(C), or (5)(A) or subsection (f), and

    (ii) "calendar year 1997" in the case of the dollar amount contained in paragraph (5) (B).

    (5) Limitation on basic standard deduction in the case of certain dependents. -- In the
40 case of an individual with respect to whom a deduction under section 151 is allowable to another taxpayer for a taxable year beginning in the calendar year in which the individual's taxable year begins, the basic standard deduction applicable to such individual for such individual's taxable year shall not exceed the greater of--

    (A) $500, or

Sec. 63. Taxable income defined

(B) the sum of $250 and such individual's earned income.

(6) Certain individuals, etc., not eligible for standard deduction. -- In the case of--

(A) a married individual filing a separate return where either spouse itemizes deductions,

(B) a nonresident alien individual,

(C) an individual making a return under section 443(a)(1) for a period of less than 12 months on account of a change in his annual accounting period, or

(D) an estate or trust, common trust fund, or partnership, the standard deduction shall be zero.

(d) Itemized deductions. -- For purposes of this subtitle, the term "itemized deductions" means the deductions allowable under this chapter other than--

(1) the deductions allowable in arriving at adjusted gross income, and

(2) the deduction for personal exemptions provided by section 151.

(e) Election to itemize. --

(1) In general. -- Unless an individual makes an election under this subsection for the taxable year, no itemized deduction shall be allowed for the taxable year. For purposes of this subtitle, the determination of whether a deduction is allowable under this chapter shall be made without regard to the preceding sentence.

(2) Time and manner of election. -- Any election under this subsection shall be made on the taxpayer's return, and the Secretary shall prescribe the manner of signifying such election on the return.

(3) Change of election. -- Under regulations prescribed by the Secretary, a change of election with respect to itemized deductions for any taxable year may be made after the filing of the return for such year. If the spouse of the taxpayer filed a separate return for any taxable year corresponding to the taxable year of the taxpayer, the change shall not be allowed unless, in accordance with such regulation--

(A) the spouse makes a change of election with respect to itemized deductions, for the taxable year covered in such separate return, consistent with the change of treatment sought by the taxpayer, and

(B) the taxpayer and his spouse consent in writing to the assessment (within such period as may be agreed on with the Secretary) of any deficiency, to the extent attributable to such change of election, even though at the time of the filing of such consent the assessment of such deficiency would otherwise be prevented by the operation of any law or rule of law.

This paragraph shall not apply if the tax liability of the taxpayer's spouse for the taxable year corresponding to the taxable year of the taxpayer has been compromised under section 7122.

(f) Aged or blind additional amounts. --

(1) Additional amounts for the aged. -- The taxpayer shall be entitled to an additional amount of $600--

(A) for himself if he has attained age 65 before the close of his taxable year, and

(B) for the spouse of the taxpayer if the spouse has attained age 65 before the close of the taxable year and an additional exemption is allowable to the taxpayer for such spouse under section 151(b).

(2) Additional amount for blind. -- The taxpayer shall be entitled to an additional amount of $600--

(A) for himself if he is blind at the close of the taxable year, and

(B) for the spouse of the taxpayer if the spouse is blind as of the close of the taxable year

Sec. 63. Taxable income defined

and an additional exemption is allowable to the taxpayer for such spouse under section 151(b).

For purposes of subparagraph (B), if the spouse dies during the taxable year the determination of whether such spouse is blind shall be made as of the time of such death.

(3) Higher amount for certain unmarried individuals. -- In the case of an individual who is not married and is not a surviving spouse, paragraphs (1) and (2) shall be applied by substituting "$750" for "$600".

(4) Blindness defined. -- For purposes of this subsection, an individual is blind only if his central visual acuity does not exceed 20/200 in the better eye with correcting lenses, or if his visual acuity is greater than 20/200 but is accompanied by a limitation in the fields of vision such that the widest diameter of the visual field subtends an angle no greater than 20 degrees.

(g) Marital status. -- For purposes of this section, marital status shall be determined under section 7703.

Sec. 64. Ordinary income defined

For purposes of this subtitle, the term "ordinary income" includes any gain from the sale or exchange of property which is neither a capital asset nor property described in section 1231(b). Any gain from the sale or exchange of property which is treated or considered, under other provisions of this subtitle, as "ordinary income" shall be treated as gain from the sale or exchange of property which is neither a capital asset nor property described in section 1231(b).

Sec. 65. Ordinary loss defined

For purposes of this subtitle, the term "ordinary loss" includes any loss from the sale or exchange of property which is not a capital asset. Any loss from the sale or exchange of property which is treated or considered, under other provisions of this subtitle, as "ordinary loss" shall be treated as loss from the sale or exchange of property which is not a capital asset.

Sec. 66. Treatment of community income

(a) Treatment of community income where spouses live apart. -- If--

(1) 2 individuals are married to each other at any time during a calendar year;

(2) such individuals--

(A) live apart at all times during the calendar year, and

(B) do not file a joint return under section 6013 with each other for a taxable year beginning or ending in the calendar year;

(3) one or both of such individuals have earned income for the calendar year which is community income; and

(4) no portion of such earned income is transferred (directly or indirectly) between such individuals before the close of the calendar year,

then, for purposes of this title, any community income of such individuals for the calendar year shall be treated in accordance with the rules provided by section 879(a).

(b) Secretary may disregard community property laws where spouse not notified of community income. -- The Secretary may disallow the benefits of any community property law to any taxpayer with respect to any income if such taxpayer acted as if solely entitled to such income and failed to notify the taxpayer's spouse before the due date (including extensions) for filing the

Sec. 66.   Treatment of community income

return for the taxable year in which the income was derived of the nature and amount of such income.

(c) Spouse relieved of liability in certain other cases. -- Under regulations prescribed by the Secretary, if--

    (1) an individual does not file a joint return for any taxable year,   5

    (2) such individual does not include in gross income for such taxable year an item of community income properly includible therein which, in accordance with the rules contained in section 879(a), would be treated as the income of the other spouse,

    (3) the individual establishes that he or she did not know of, and had no reason to know of, such item of community income, and   10

    (4) taking into account all facts and circumstances, it is inequitable to include such item of community income in such individual's gross income,

then, for purposes of this title, such item of community income shall be included in the gross income of the other spouse (and not in the gross income of the individual). Under procedures prescribed by the Secretary, if, taking into account all the facts and circumstances, it is inequitable 15 to hold the individual liable for any unpaid tax or any deficiency (or any portion of either) attributable to any item for which relief is not available under the preceding sentence, the Secretary may relieve such individual of such liability.

(d) Definitions. -- For purposes of this section--

    (1) Earned income. -- The term "earned income" has the meaning given to such term by 20 section 911(d)(2).

    (2) Community income. -- The term "community income" means income which, under applicable community property laws, is treated as community income.

    (3) Community property laws. -- The term "community property laws" means the community property laws of a State, a foreign country, or a possession of the United States.   25

Sec. 67.   2-percent floor on miscellaneous itemized deductions

(a) General rule. -- In the case of an individual, the miscellaneous itemized deductions for any taxable year shall be allowed only to the extent that the aggregate of such deductions exceeds 2 percent of adjusted gross income.   30

(b) Miscellaneous itemized deductions. -- For purposes of this section, the term "miscellaneous itemized deductions" means the itemized deductions other than--

    (1) the deduction under section 163 (relating to interest),

    (2) the deduction under section 164 (relating to taxes),

    (3) the deduction under section 165(a) for casualty or theft losses described in paragraph (2) 35 or (3) of section 165(c) or for losses described in section 165(d),

    (4) the deductions under section 170 (relating to charitable, etc., contributions and gifts) and section 642(c) (relating to deduction for amounts paid or permanently set aside for a charitable purpose),

    (5) the deduction under section 213 (relating to medical, dental, etc., expenses),   40

    (6) any deduction allowable for impairment-related work expenses,

    (7) the deduction under section 691(c) (relating to deduction for estate tax in case of income in respect of the decedent),

    (8) any deduction allowable in connection with personal property used in a short sale,

Sec. 67. 2-percent floor on miscellaneous itemized deductions

(9) the deduction under section 1341 (relating to computation of tax where taxpayer restores substantial amount held under claim of right),

(10) the deduction under section 72(b)(3) (relating to deduction where annuity payments cease before investment recovered),

(11) the deduction under section 171 (relating to deduction for amortizable bond premium), and

(12) the deduction under section 216 (relating to deductions in connection with cooperative housing corporations).

(c) Disallowance of indirect deduction through pass-thru entity. --

(1) In general. -- The Secretary shall prescribe regulations which prohibit the indirect deduction through pass-thru entities of amounts which are not allowable as a deduction if paid or incurred directly by an individual and which contain such reporting requirements as may be necessary to carry out the purposes of this subsection.

(2) Treatment of publicly offered regulated investment companies. --

(A) In general. -- Paragraph (1) shall not apply with respect to any publicly offered regulated investment company.

(B) Publicly offered regulated investment companies. -- For purposes of this subsection--

(i) In general. -- The term "publicly offered regulated investment company" means a regulated investment company the shares of which are--

(I) continuously offered pursuant to a public offering (within the meaning of section 4 of the Securities Act of 1933, as amended (15 U.S.C. 77a to 77aa)),

(II) regularly traded on an established securities market, or

(III) held by or for no fewer than 500 persons at all times during the taxable year.

(ii) Secretary may reduce 500 person requirement. -- The Secretary may by regulation decrease the minimum shareholder requirement of clause (i)(III) in the case of regulated investment companies which experience a loss of shareholders through net redemptions of their shares.

(d) Impairment-related work expenses. -- For purposes of this section, the term "impairment-related work expenses" means expenses--

(1) of a handicapped individual (as defined in section 190(b)(3)) for attendant care services at the individual's place of employment and other expenses in connection with such place of employment which are necessary for such individual to be able to work, and

(2) with respect to which a deduction is allowable under section 162 (determined without regard to this section).

(e) Determination of adjusted gross income in case of estates and trusts. -- For purposes of this section, the adjusted gross income of an estate or trust shall be computed in the same manner as in the case of an individual, except that--

(1) the deductions for costs which are paid or incurred in connection with the administration of the estate or trust and which would not have been incurred if the property were not held in such trust or estate, and

(2) the deductions allowable under sections 642(b), 651, and 661, shall be treated as allowable in arriving at adjusted gross income.

Under regulations, appropriate adjustments shall be made in the application of part I of subchapter J of this chapter to take into account the provisions of this section.

(f) Coordination with other limitation. -- This section shall be applied before the application

Sec. 67. 2-percent floor on miscellaneous itemized deductions

of the dollar limitation of the second sentence of section 162(a) (relating to trade or business expenses).

Reg. § 1.67-1T   2-percent floor on miscellaneous itemized deductions (temporary).

(a) *Type of expenses subject to the floor*--(1) *In general.* With respect to individuals, 5 section 67 disallows deductions for miscellaneous itemized deductions (as defined in paragraph (b) of this section) in computing taxable income (i.e., so-called ``below-the-line" deductions) to the extent that such otherwise allowable deductions do not exceed 2 percent of the individual's adjusted gross income (as defined in section 62 and the regulations thereunder). Examples of expenses that, if otherwise deductible, are 10 subject to the 2-percent floor include but are not limited to--

(i) Unreimbursed employee expenses, such as expenses for transportation, travel fares and lodging while away from home, business meals and entertainment, continuing education courses, subscriptions to professional journals, union or professional dues, professional uniforms, job hunting, and the business use of the employee's home.   15

(ii) Expenses for the production or collection of income for which a deduction is otherwise allowable under section 212(1) and (2), such as investment advisory fees, subscriptions to investment advisory publications, certain attorneys' fees, and the cost of safe deposit boxes,

(iii) Expenses for the determination of any tax for which a deduction is otherwise 20 allowable under section 212(3), such as tax counsel fees and appraisal fees, and

(iv) Expenses for an activity for which a deduction is otherwise allowable under section 183.

See section 62 with respect to deductions that are allowable in computing adjusted gross income (i.e., so-called ``above-the-line" deductions).   25

(2) *Other limitations.* Except as otherwise provided in paragraph (d) of this section, to the extent that any limitation or restriction is placed on the amount of a miscellaneous itemized deduction, that limitation shall apply prior to the application of the 2-percent floor. For example, in the case of an expense for food or beverages, only 80 percent of which is allowable as a deduction because of the limitations provided in section 274(n), 30 the otherwise deductible 80 percent of the expense is treated as a miscellaneous itemized deduction and is subject to the 2-percent limitation of section 67.

(b) *Definition of miscellaneous itemized deductions.* For purposes of this section, the term ``miscellaneous itemized deductions" means the deductions allowable from adjusted gross income in determining taxable income, as defined in section 63, other 35 than--

(1) The standard deduction as defined in section 63(c),

(2) Any deduction allowable for impairment-related work expenses as defined in section 67(d),

(3) The deduction under section 72(b)(3) (relating to deductions if annuity payments 40 cease before the investment is recovered),

(4) The deductions allowable under section 151 for personal exemptions,

(5) The deduction under section 163 (relating to interest),

(6) The deduction under section 164 (relating to taxes),

(7) The deduction under section 165(a) for losses described in subsection (c)(3) or (d) 45 of section 165,

(8) The deduction under section 170 (relating to charitable contributions and gifts),

(9) The deduction under section 171 (relating to deductions for amortizable bond premiums),

(10) The deduction under section 213 (relating to medical and dental expenses),   50

`(11) The deduction under section 216 (relating to deductions in connection with

Sec. 67. 2-percent floor on miscellaneous itemized deductions

cooperative housing corporations),

    (12) The deduction under section 217 (relating to moving expenses),

    (13) The deduction under section 691(c) (relating to the deduction for estate taxes in the case of income in respect of the decedent),

5   (14) The deduction under 1341 (relating to the computation of tax if a taxpayer restores a substantial amount held under claim of right), and

    (15) Any deduction allowable in connection with personal property used in a short sale.

    (c) Allocation of expenses. If a taxpayer incurs expenses that relate to both a trade or 10 business activity (within the meaning of section 162) and a production of income or tax preparation activity (within the meaning of section 212), the taxpayer shall allocate such expenses between the activities on a reasonable basis.

    (d) *Members of Congress*--(1) *In general.* With respect to the deduction for living expenses of Members of Congress referred to in section 162(a), the 2-percent floor 15 described in section 67 and paragraph (a) of this section shall be applied to the deduction before the application of the $3,000 limitation on deductions for living expenses referred to in section 162(a). (For purposes of this paragraph (d), the term ``Member(s) of Congress" includes any Delegate or Resident Commissioner.) The amount of miscellaneous itemized deductions of a Member of Congress that is disallowed pursuant 20 to section 67 and paragraph (a) of this section shall be allocated between deductions for living expenses (within the meaning of section 162(a)) and other miscellaneous itemized deductions. The amount of deductions for living expenses of a Member of Congress that is disallowed pursuant to section 67 and paragraph (a) of this section is determined by multiplying the aggregate amount of such living expenses (determined without regard to 25 the $3,000 limitation of section 162(a) but with regard to any other limitations) by a fraction, the numerator of which is the aggregate amount disallowed pursuant to section 67 and paragraph (a) of this section with respect to miscellaneous itemized deductions of the Member of Congress and the denominator of which is the amount of miscellaneous itemized deductions (including deductions for living expenses) of the Member of 30 Congress (determined without regard to the $3,000 limitation of section 162(a) but without regard to any other limitations). The amount of deductions for miscellaneous itemized deductions (other than deductions for living expenses) of a Member of Congress that are disallowed pursuant to section 67 and paragraph (a) of this section is determined by multiplying the amount of miscellaneous itemized deductions (other than deductions 35 for living expenses) of the Member of Congress (determined with regard to any limitations) by the fraction described in the preceding sentence.

    (2) *Example.* The provisions of this paragraph (d) may be illustrated by the following example:

    Example For 1987 A, a Member of Congress, has adjusted gross income of $100,000, 40 and miscellaneous itemized deductions of $10,750 of which $3,750 is for meals, $3,000 is for other living expenses, and $4,000 is for other miscellaneous itemized deductions (none of which is subject to any percentage limitations other than the 2-percent floor of section 67). The amount of A's business meal expenses that are disallowed under section 274(n) is $750 ($3,750x20%). The amount of A's miscellaneous itemized deductions that 45 are disallowed under section 67 is $2,000 ($100,000x2%). The portion of the amount disallowed under section 67 that is allocated to A's living expenses is $1,200. This portion is equal to the amount of A's deductions for living expenses allowable after the application of section 274(n) and before the application of section 67 ($6,000) multiplied by the ratio of A's total miscellaneous itemized deductions disallowed under section 67 to 50 A's total miscellaneous itemized deductions, determined without regard to the $3,000 limitation of section 162(a) ($2,000/$10,000). Thus, after application of section 274(n)

Sec. 67. 2-percent floor on miscellaneous itemized deductions

and section 67, A's deduction for living expenses is $4,800 ($6,750-$750-$1,200). However, pursuant to section 162(a), A may deduct only $3,000 of such expenses. The amount of A's other miscellaneous itemized deductions that are disallowed under section 67 is $800 ($4,000x$2,000/$10,000). Thus, $3,200 ($4,000-$800) of A's miscellaneous itemized deductions (other than deductions for living expenses) are allowable after application of section 67. A's total allowable miscellaneous itemized deductions are $6,200 ($3,000+$3,200).

***

[T.D. 8189, 53 FR 9875, Mar. 28, 1988]

Sec. 68. Overall limitation on itemized deductions

(a) **General rule.** -- In the case of an individual whose adjusted gross income exceeds the applicable amount, the amount of the itemized deductions otherwise allowable for the taxable year shall be reduced by the lesser of--

    (1) 3 percent of the excess of adjusted gross income over the applicable amount, or

    (2) 80 percent of the amount of the itemized deductions otherwise allowable for such taxable year.

(b) **Applicable amount.** --

    (1) **In general.** -- For purposes of this section, the term "applicable amount" means $100,000 ($50,000 in the case of a separate return by a married individual within the meaning of section 7703).

    (2) **Inflation adjustments.** -- In the case of any taxable year beginning in a calendar year after 1991, each dollar amount contained in paragraph (1) shall be increased by an amount equal to--

        (A) such dollar amount, multiplied by

        (B) the cost-of-living adjustment determined under section 1(f)(3) for the calendar year in which the taxable year begins, by substituting "calendar year 1990" for "calendar year 1992" in subparagraph (B) thereof.

(c) **Exception for certain itemized deductions.** -- For purposes of this section, the term "itemized deductions" does not include -

    (1) the deduction under section 213 (relating to medical, etc. expenses),

    (2) any deduction for investment interest (as defined in section 163(d)), and

    (3) the deduction under section 165(a) for casualty or theft losses described in paragraph (2) or (3) of section 165(c) or for losses described in section 165(d).

(d) **Coordination with other limitations.** -- This section shall be applied after the application of any other limitation on the allowance of any itemized deduction.

(e) **Exception for estates and trusts.** -- This section shall not apply to any estate or trust.

(f) **Phaseout of limitation.** --

    (1) **In general.** -- In the case of taxable years beginning after December 31, 2005, and before January 1, 2010, the reduction under subsection (a) shall be equal to the applicable fraction of the amount which would (but for this subsection) be the amount of such reduction.

    (2) **Applicable fraction.** -- For purposes of paragraph (1), the applicable fraction shall be determined in accordance with the following table:

For taxable years beginning in calendar year -	The applicable fraction is -

139

| 2006 and 2007 | 2/3 |
| 2008 and 2009 | 1/3 |

5   **(g) Termination.** -- This section shall not apply to any taxable year beginning after December 31, 2009.

Sec. 71. Alimony and separate maintenance payments

(a) General rule. -- Gross income includes amounts received as alimony or separate
10 maintenance payments.

(b) Alimony or separate maintenance payments defined. -- For purposes of this section--

(1) In general. -- The term "alimony or separate maintenance payment" means any payment in cash if--

(A) such payment is received by (or on behalf of) a spouse under a divorce or separation
15 instrument,

(B) the divorce or separation instrument does not designate such payment as a payment which is not includible in gross income under this section and not allowable as a deduction under section 215,

(C) in the case of an individual legally separated from his spouse under a decree of
20 divorce or of separate maintenance, the payee spouse and the payor spouse are not members of the same household at the time such payment is made, and

(D) there is no liability to make any such payment for any period after the death of the payee spouse and there is no liability to make any payment (in cash or property) as a substitute for such payments after the death of the payee spouse.

25 **(2) Divorce or separation instrument.** -- The term "divorce or separation instrument" means--

(A) a decree of divorce or separate maintenance or a written instrument incident to such a decree,

(B) a written separation agreement, or

30 **(C)** a decree (not described in subparagraph (A)) requiring a spouse to make payments for the support or maintenance of the other spouse.

(c) Payments to support children. --

(1) In general. -- Subsection (a) shall not apply to that part of any payment which the terms of the divorce or separation instrument fix (in terms of an amount of money or a part of the
35 payment) as a sum which is payable for the support of children of the payor spouse.

(2) Treatment of certain reductions related to contingencies involving child. -- For purposes of paragraph (1), if any amount specified in the instrument will be reduced--

(A) on the happening of a contingency specified in the instrument relating to a child (such as attaining a specified age, marrying, dying, leaving school, or a similar
40 contingency), or

(B) at a time which can clearly be associated with a contingency of a kind specified in subparagraph (A),
an amount equal to the amount of such reduction will be treated as an amount fixed as payable for the support of children of the payor spouse.

45 **(3) Special rule where payment is less than amount specified in instrument.** -- For

Sec. 71. Alimony and separate maintenance payments

purposes of this subsection, if any payment is less than the amount specified in the instrument, then so much of such payment as does not exceed the sum payable for support shall be considered a payment for such support.

(d) Spouse. -- For purposes of this section, the term "spouse" includes a former spouse.

(e) Exception for joint returns. -- This section and section 215 shall not apply if the spouses make a joint return with each other.

(f) Recomputation where excess front-loading of alimony payments. --

(1) In general. -- If there are excess alimony payments--

(A) the payor spouse shall include the amount of such excess payments in gross income for the payor spouse's taxable year beginning in the 3rd post-separation year, and

(B) the payee spouse shall be allowed a deduction in computing adjusted gross income for the amount of such excess payments for the payee's taxable year beginning in the 3rd post- separation year.

(2) Excess alimony payments. -- For purposes of this subsection, the term "excess alimony payments" mean the sum of--

(A) the excess payments for the 1st post-separation year, and

(B) the excess payments for the 2nd post-separation year.

(3) Excess payments for 1st post-separation year. -- For purposes of this subsection, the amount of the excess payments for the 1st post-separation year is the excess (if any) of--

(A) the amount of the alimony or separate maintenance payments paid by the payor spouse during the 1st post-separation year, over

(B) the sum of--

(i) the average of--

(I) the alimony or separate maintenance payments paid by the payor spouse during the 2nd post-separation year, reduced by the excess payments for the 2nd post-separation year, and

(II) the alimony or separate maintenance payments paid by the payor spouse during the 3rd post-separation year, plus

(ii) $15,000.

(4) Excess payments for 2nd post-separation year. -- For purposes of this subsection, the amount of the excess payments for the 2nd post-separation year is the excess (if any) of--

(A) the amount of the alimony or separate maintenance payments paid by the payor spouse during the 2nd post- separation year, over

(B) the sum of -

(i) the amount of the alimony or separate maintenance payments paid by the payor spouse during the 3rd post- separation year, plus

(ii) $15,000.

(5) Exceptions. --

(A) Where payment ceases by reason of death or remarriage. -- Paragraph (1) shall not apply if--

(i) either spouse dies before the close of the 3rd post-separation year, or the payee spouse remarries before the close of the 3rd post-separation year, and

(ii) the alimony or separate maintenance payments cease by reason of such death or remarriage.

Sec. 71. Alimony and separate maintenance payments

(B) Support payments. -- For purposes of this subsection, the term "alimony or separate maintenance payment" shall not include any payment received under a decree described in subsection (b)(2)(C).

(C) Fluctuating payments not within control of payor spouse. -- For purposes of this subsection, the term "alimony or separate maintenance payment" shall not include any payment to the extent it is made pursuant to a continuing liability (over a period of not less than 3 years) to pay a fixed portion or portions of the income from a business or property or from compensation for employment or self-employment.

(6) Post-separation years. -- For purposes of this subsection, the term "1st post-separation years" means the 1st calendar year in which the payor spouse paid to the payee spouse alimony or separate maintenance payments to which this section applies. The 2nd and 3rd post-separation years shall be the 1st and 2nd succeeding calendar years, respectively.

(g) Cross references. --

(1) For deduction of alimony or separate maintenance payments, see section 215.

***

Reg. § 1.71-1T Alimony and separate maintenance payments (temporary).

(a) *In general.*

Q-1 What is the income tax treatment of alimony or separate maintenance payments?

A-1 Alimony or separate maintenance payments are, under section 71, included in the gross income of the payee spouse and, under section 215, allowed as a deduction from the gross income of the payor spouse.

Q-2 What is an alimony or separate maintenance payment?

A-2 An alimony or separate maintenance payment is any payment received by or on behalf of a spouse (which for this purpose includes a former spouse) of the payor under a divorce or separation instrument that meets all of the following requirements:

(a) The payment is in cash (see A-5).

(b) The payment is not designated as a payment which is excludible from the gross income of the payee and nondeductible by the payor (see A-8).

(c) In the case of spouses legally separated under a decree of divorce or separate maintenance, the spouses are not members of the same household at the time the payment is made (see A-9).

(d) The payor has no liability to continue to make any payment after the death of the payee (or to make any payment as a substitute for such payment) and the divorce or separation instrument states that there is no such liability (see A-10).

(e) The payment is not treated as child support (see A-15).

(f) To the extent that one or more annual payments exceed $10,000 during any of the 6-post-separation years, the payor is obligated to make annual payments in each of the 6-post-separation years (see A-19).

***

(b) *Specific requirements.*

Q-5 May alimony or separate maintenance payments be made in a form other than cash?

A-5 No. Only cash payments (including checks and money orders payable on demand) qualify as alimony or separate maintenance payments. Transfers of services or property (including a debt instrument of a third party or an annuity contract), execution of a debt instrument by the payor, or the use of property of the payor do not qualify as alimony or separate maintenance payments.

Q-6 May payments of cash to a third party on behalf of a spouse qualify as alimony or separate maintenance payments if the payments are pursuant to the terms of a divorce

Sec. 71.   Alimony and separate maintenance payments

or separation instrument?

A-6 Yes. Assuming all other requirements are satisfied, a payment of cash by the payor spouse to a third party under the terms of the divorce or separation instrument will qualify as a payment of cash which is received ``on behalf of a spouse''. For example, cash payments of rent, mortgage, tax, or tuition liabilities of the payee spouse made under the terms of the divorce or separation instrument will qualify as alimony or separate maintenance payments. Any payments to maintain property owned by the payor spouse and used by the payee spouse (including mortgage payments, real estate taxes and insurance premiums) are not payments on behalf of a spouse even if those payments are made pursuant to the terms of the divorce or separation instrument. Premiums paid by the payor spouse for term or whole life insurance on the payor's life made under the terms of the divorce or separation instrument will qualify as payments on behalf of the payee spouse to the extent that the payee spouse is the owner of the policy.

Q-7 May payments of cash to a third party on behalf of a spouse qualify as alimony or separate maintenance payments if the payments are made to the third party at the written request of the payee spouse?

A-7 Yes. For example, instead of making an alimony or separate maintenance payment directly to the payee, the payor spouse may make a cash payment to a charitable organization if such payment is pursuant to the written request, consent or ratification of the payee spouse. Such request, consent or ratification must state that the parties intend the payment to be treated as an alimony or separate maintenance payment to the payee spouse subject to the rules of section 71, and must be received by the payor spouse prior to the date of filing of the payor's first return of tax for the taxable year in which the payment was made.

Q-8 How may spouses designate that payments otherwise qualifying as alimony or separate maintenance payments shall be excludible from the gross income of the payee and nondeductible by the payor?

A-8 The spouses may designate that payments otherwise qualifying as alimony or separate maintenance payments shall be nondeductible by the payor and excludible from gross income by the payee by so providing in a divorce or separation instrument (as defined in section 71(b)(2)). If the spouses have executed a written separation agreement (as described in section 71(b)(2)(B)), any writing signed by both spouses which designates otherwise qualifying alimony or separate maintenance payments as nondeductible and excludible and which refers to the written separation agreement will be treated as a written separation agreement (and thus a divorce or separation instrument) for purposes of the preceding sentence. If the spouses are subject to temporary support orders (as described in section 71(b)(2)(C)), the designation of otherwise qualifying alimony or separate payments as nondeductible and excludible must be made in the original or a subsequent temporary support order. A copy of the instrument containing the designation of payments as not alimony or separate maintenance payments must be attached to the payee's first filed return of tax (Form 1040) for each year in which the designation applies.

Q-9 What are the consequences if, at the time a payment is made, the payor and payee spouses are members of the same household?

A-9 Generally, a payment made at the time when the payor and payee spouses are members of the same household cannot qualify as an alimony or separate maintenance payment if the spouses are legally separated under a decree of divorce or of separate maintenance. For purposes of the preceding sentence, a dwelling unit formerly shared by both spouses shall not be considered two separate households even if the spouses physically separate themselves within the dwelling unit. The spouses will not be treated as members of the same household if one spouse is preparing to depart from the

Sec. 71. Alimony and separate maintenance payments

household of the other spouse, and does depart not more than one month after the date the payment is made. If the spouses are not legally separated under a decree of divorce or separate maintenance, a payment under a written separation agreement or a decree described in section 71(b)(2)(C) may qualify as an alimony or separate maintenance
5 payment notwithstanding that the payor and payee are members of the same household at the time the payment is made.

Q-10 Assuming all other requirements relating to the qualification of certain payments as alimony or separate maintenance payments are met, what are the consequences if the payor spouse is required to continue to make the payments after the death of the
10 payee spouse?

A-10 None of the payments before (or after) the death of the payee spouse qualify as alimony or separate maintenance payments.

Q-11 What are the consequences if the divorce or separation instrument fails to state that there is no liability for any period after the death of the payee spouse to continue to
15 make any payments which would otherwise qualify as alimony or separate maintenance payments?

A-11 If the instrument fails to include such a statement, none of the payments, whether made before or after the death of the payee spouse, will qualify as alimony or separate maintenance payments.
20 Example (1). A is to pay B $10,000 in cash each year for a period of 10 years under a divorce or separation instrument which does not state that the payments will terminate upon the death of B. None of the payments will qualify as alimony or separate maintenance payments.

Example (2). A is to pay B $10,000 in cash each year for a period of 10 years under a
25 divorce or separation instrument which states that the payments will terminate upon the death of B. In addition, under the instrument, A is to pay B or B's estate $20,000 in cash each year for a period of 10 years. Because the $20,000 annual payments will not terminate upon the death of B, these payments will not qualify as alimony or separate maintenance payments. However, the separate $10,000 annual payments will qualify as
30 alimony or separate maintenance payments.

Q-12 Will a divorce or separation instrument be treated as stating that there is no liability to make payments after the death of the payee spouse if the liability to make such payments terminates pursuant to applicable local law or oral agreement?

A-12 No. Termination of the liability to make payments must be stated in the terms of
35 the divorce or separation instrument.

Q-13 What are the consequences if the payor spouse is required to make one or more payments (in cash or property) after the death of the payee spouse as a substitute for the continuation of pre-death payments which would otherwise qualify as alimony or separate maintenance payments?
40 A-13 If the payor spouse is required to make any such substitute payments, none of the otherwise qualifying payments will qualify as alimony or separate maintenance payments. The divorce or separation instrument need not state, however, that there is no liability to make any such substitute payment.

Q-14 Under what circumstances will one or more payments (in cash or property)
45 which are to occur after the death of the payee spouse be treated as a substitute for the continuation of payments which would otherwise qualify as alimony or separate maintenance payments?

A-14 To the extent that one or more payments are to begin to be made, increase in amount, or become accelerated in time as a result of the death of the payee spouse,
50 such payments may be treated as a substitute for the continuation of payments terminating on the death of the payee spouse which would otherwise qualify as alimony

Sec. 71. Alimony and separate maintenance payments

or separate maintenance payments. The determination of whether or not such payments are a substitute for the continuation of payments which would otherwise qualify as alimony or separate maintenance payments, and of the amount of the otherwise qualifying alimony or separate maintenance payments for which any such payments are a substitute, will depend on all of the facts and circumstances. 5

Example (1). Under the terms of a divorce decree, A is obligated to make annual alimony payments to B of $30,000, terminating on the earlier of the expiration of 6 years or the death of B. B maintains custody of the minor children of A and B. The decree provides that at the death of B, if there are minor children of A and B remaining, A will be obligated to make annual payments of $10,000 to a trust, the income and corpus of which 10 are to be used for the benefit of the children until the youngest child attains the age of majority. These facts indicate that A's liability to make annual $10,000 payments in trust for the benefit of his minor children upon the death of B is a substitute for $10,000 of the $30,000 annual payments to B. Accordingly, $10,000 of each of the $30,000 annual payments to B will not qualify as alimony or separate maintenance payments. 15

Example (2). Under the terms of a divorce decree, A is obligated to make annual alimony payments to B of $30,000, terminating on the earlier of the expiration of 15 years or the death of B. The divorce decree provides that if B dies before the expiration of the 15 year period, A will pay to B's estate the difference between the total amount that A would have paid had B survived, minus the amount actually paid. For example, if B dies 20 at the end of the 10th year in which payments are made, A will pay to B's estate $150,000 ($450,000-$300,000). These facts indicate that A's liability to make a lump sum payment to B's estate upon the death of B is a substitute for the full amount of each of the annual $30,000 payments to B. Accordingly, none of the annual $30,000 payments to B will qualify as alimony or separate maintenance payments. The result would be the same if 25 the lump sum payable at B's death were discounted by an appropriate interest factor to account for the prepayment.

(c) *Child support payments.*

Q-15 What are the consequences of a payment which the terms of the divorce or separation instrument fix as payable for the support of a child of the payor spouse? 30

A-15 A payment which under the terms of the divorce or separation instrument is fixed (or treated as fixed) as payable for the support of a child of the payor spouse does not qualify as an alimony or separate maintenance payment. Thus, such a payment is not deductible by the payor spouse or includible in the income of the payee spouse.

Q-16 When is a payment fixed (or treated as fixed) as payable for the support of a 35 child of the payor spouse?

A-16 A payment is fixed as payable for the support of a child of the payor spouse if the divorce or separation instrument specifically designates some sum or portion (which sum or portion may fluctuate) as payable for the support of a child of the payor spouse. A payment will be treated as fixed as payable for the support of a child of the payor spouse 40 if the payment is reduced (a) on the happening of a contingency relating to a child of the payor, or (b) at a time which can clearly be associated with such a contingency. A payment may be treated as fixed as payable for the support of a child of the payor spouse even if other separate payments specifically are designated as payable for the support of a child of the payor spouse. 45

Q-17 When does a contingency relate to a child of the payor?

A-17 For this purpose, a contingency relates to a child of the payor if it depends on any event relating to that child, regardless of whether such event is certain or likely to occur. Events that relate to a child of the payor include the following: the child's attaining a specified age or income level, dying, marrying, leaving school, leaving the spouse's 50 household, or gaining employment.

Sec. 71. Alimony and separate maintenance payments

Q-18 When will a payment be treated as to be reduced at a time which can clearly be associated with the happening of a contingency relating to a child of the payor?

A-18 There are two situations, described below, in which payments which would otherwise qualify as alimony or separate maintenance payments will be presumed to be reduced at a time clearly associated with the happening of a contingency relating to a child of the payor. In all other situations, reductions in payments will not be treated as clearly associated with the happening of a contingency relating to a child of the payor.

The first situation referred to above is where the payments are to be reduced not more than 6 months before or after the date the child is to attain the age of 18, 21, or local age of majority. The second situation is where the payments are to be reduced on two or more occasions which occur not more than one year before or after a different child of the payor spouse attains a certain age between the ages of 18 and 24, inclusive. The certain age referred to in the preceding sentence must be the same for each such child, but need not be a whole number of years.

The presumption in the two situations described above that payments are to be reduced at a time clearly associated with the happening of a contingency relating to a child of the payor may be rebutted (either by the Service or by taxpayers) by showing that the time at which the payments are to be reduced was determined independently of any contingencies relating to the children of the payor. The presumption in the first situation will be rebutted conclusively if the reduction is a complete cessation of alimony or separate maintenance payments during the sixth post-separation year (described in A-21) or upon the expiration of a 72-month period. The presumption may also be rebutted in other circumstances, for example, by showing that alimony payments are to be made for a period customarily provided in the local jurisdiction, such as a period equal to one-half the duration of the marriage.

Example: A and B are divorced on July 1, 1985, when their children, C (born July 15, 1970) and D (born September 23, 1972), are 14 and 12, respectively. Under the divorce decree, A is to make alimony payments to B of $2,000 per month. Such payments are to be reduced to $1,500 per month on January 1, 1991 and to $1,000 per month on January 1, 1995. On January 1, 1991, the date of the first reduction in payments, C will be 20 years 5 months and 17 days old. On January 1, 1995, the date of the second reduction in payments, D will be 22 years 3 months and 9 days old. Each of the reductions in payments is to occur not more than one year before or after a different child of A attains the age of 21 years and 4 months. (Actually, the reductions are to occur not more than one year before or after C and D attain any of the ages 21 years 3 months and 9 days through 21 years 5 months and 17 days.) Accordingly, the reductions will be presumed to clearly be associated with the happening of a contingency relating to C and D. Unless this presumption is rebutted, payments under the divorce decree equal to the sum of the reduction ($1,000 per month) will be treated as fixed for the support of the children of A and therefore will not qualify as alimony or separate maintenance payments.

(d) *Excess front-loading rules.*

Q-19 What are the excess front-loading rules?

A-19 The excess front-loading rules are two special rules which may apply to the extent that payments in any calendar year exceed $10,000. The first rule is a minimum term rule, which must be met in order for any annual payment, to the extent in excess of $10,000, to qualify as an alimony or separate maintenance payment (see A-2(f)). This rule requires that alimony or separate maintenance payments be called for, at a minimum, during the 6 ``post-separation years". The second rule is a recapture rule which characterizes payments retrospectively by requiring a recalculation and inclusion in income by the payor and deduction by the payee of previously paid alimony or separate maintenance payment to the extent that the amount of such payments during any of the 6

Sec. 71. Alimony and separate maintenance payments

``post-separation years" falls short of the amount of payments during a prior year by more than $10,000.

Q-20 Do the excess front-loading rules apply to payments to the extent that annual payments never exceed $10,000?

A-20 No. For example, A is to make a single $10,000 payment to B. Provided that the other requirements of section 71 are met, the payment will qualify as an alimony or separate maintenance payment. If A were to make a single $15,000 payment to B, $10,000 of the payment would qualify as an alimony or separate maintenance payment and $5,000 of the payment would be disqualified under the minimum term rule because payments were not to be made for the minimum period.

Q-21 Do the excess front-loading rules apply to payments received under a decree described in section 71(b)(2)(C)?

A-21 No. Payments under decrees described in section 71(b)(2)(C) are to be disregarded entirely for purposes of applying the excess front-loading rules.

Q-22 Both the minimum term rule and the recapture rule refer to 6 ``post-separation years". What are the 6 ``post separation years"?

A-22 The 6 ``post-separation years" are the 6 consecutive calendar years beginning with the first calendar year in which the payor pays to the payee an alimony or separate maintenance payment (except a payment made under a decree described in section 71(b)(2)(C)). Each year within this period is referred to as a ``post-separation year". The 6-year period need not commence with the year in which the spouses separate or divorce, or with the year in which payments under the divorce or separation instrument are made, if no payments during such year qualify as alimony or separate maintenance payments. For example, a decree for the divorce of A and B is entered in October, 1985. The decree requires A to make monthly payments to B commencing November 1, 1985, but A and B are members of the same household until February 15, 1986 (and as a result, the payments prior to January 16, 1986, do not qualify as alimony payments). For purposes of applying the excess front-loading rules to payments from A to B, the 6 calendar years 1986 through 1991 are post-separation years. If a spouse has been making payments pursuant to a divorce or separation instrument described in section 71(b)(2)(A) or (B), a modification of the instrument or the substitution of a new instrument (for example, the substitution of a divorce decree for a written separation agreement) will not result in the creation of additional post-separation years. However, if a spouse has been making payments pursuant to a divorce or separation instrument described in section 71(b)(2)(C), the 6-year period does not begin until the first calendar year in which alimony or separate maintenance payments are made under a divorce or separation instrument described in section 71(b)(2)(A) or (B).

Q-23 How does the minimum term rule operate?

A-23 The minimum term rule operates in the following manner. To the extent payments are made in excess of $10,000, a payment will qualify as an alimony or separate maintenance payment only if alimony or separate maintenance payments are to be made in each of the 6 post-separation years. For example, pursuant to a divorce decree, A is to make alimony payments to B of $20,000 in each of the 5 calendar years 1985 through 1989. A is to make no payment in 1990. Under the minimum term rule, only $10,000 will qualify as an alimony payment in each of the calendar years 1985 through 1989. If the divorce decree also required A to make a $1 payment in 1990, the minimum term rule would be satisfied and $20,000 would be treated as an alimony payment in each of the calendar years 1985 through 1989. The recapture rule would, however, apply for 1990. For purposes of determining whether alimony or separate maintenance payments are to be made in any year, the possible termination of such payments upon the happening of a contingency (other than the passage of time) which has not yet

147

Sec. 71. Alimony and separate maintenance payments

occurred is ignored (unless such contingency may cause all or a portion of the payment to be treated as a child support payment).

Q-24 How does the recapture rule operate?

A-24 The recapture rule operates in the following manner. If the amount of alimony or
5 separate maintenance payments paid in any post-separation year (referred to as the ``computation year'') falls short of the amount of alimony or separate maintenance payments paid in any prior post-separation year by more than $10,000, the payor must compute an ``excess amount'' for the computation year. The excess amount for any computation year is the sum of excess amounts determined with respect to each prior
10 post-separation year. The excess amount determined with respect to a prior post-separation year is the excess of (1) the amount of alimony or separate maintenance payments paid by the payor spouse during such prior post-separation year, over (2) the amount of the alimony or separate maintenance payments paid by the payor spouse during the computation year plus $10,000. For purposes of this calculation, the amount of
15 alimony or separate maintenance payments made by the payor spouse during any post-separation year preceding the computation year is reduced by any excess amount previously determined with respect to such year. The rules set forth above may be illustrated by the following example. A makes alimony payments to B of $25,000 in 1985 and $12,000 in 1986. The excess amount with respect to 1985 that is recaptured in 1986
20 is $3,000 ($25,000- ($12,000+$10,000)). For purposes of subsequent computation years, the amount deemed paid in 1985 is $22,000. If A makes alimony payments to B of $1,000 in 1987, the excess amount that is recaptured in 1987 will be $12,000. This is the sum of an $11,000 excess amount with respect to 1985 ($22,000-$1,000+$10,000)) and a $1,000 excess amount with respect to 1986 ($12,000-($1,000+$10,000)). If, prior to the
25 end of 1990, payments decline further, additional recapture will occur. The payor spouse must include the excess amount in gross income for his/her taxable year beginning with or in the computation year. The payee spouse is allowed a deduction for the excess amount in computing adjusted gross income for his/her taxable year beginning with or in the computation year. However, the payee spouse must compute the excess amount by
30 reference to the date when payments were made and not when payments were received.

Q-25 What are the exceptions to the recapture rule?

A-25 Apart from the $10,000 threshold for application of the recapture rule, there are three exceptions to the recapture rule. The first exception is for payments received under temporary support orders described in section 71(b)(2)(C) (see A-21). The second
35 exception is for any payment made pursuant to a continuing liability over the period of the post-separation years to pay a fixed portion of the payor's income from a business or property or from compensation for employment or self-employment. The third exception is where the alimony or separate maintenance payments in any post-separation year cease by reason of the death of the payor or payee or the remarriage (as defined under
40 applicable local law) of the payee before the close of the computation year. For example, pursuant to a divorce decree, A is to make cash payments to B of $30,000 in each of the calendar years 1985 through 1990. A makes cash payments of $30,000 in 1985 and $15,000 in 1986, in which year B remarries and A's alimony payments cease. The recapture rule does not apply for 1986 or any subsequent year. If alimony or separate
45 maintenance payments made by A decline or cease during a post-separation year for any other reason (including a failure by the payor to make timely payments, a modification of the divorce or separation instrument, a reduction in the support needs of the payee, or a reduction in the ability of the payor to provide support) excess amounts with respect to prior post-separation years will be subject to recapture.

50
***

[T.D. 7973, 49 FR 34455, Aug. 31, 1984; 49 FR 36645, Sept. 19, 1984]

Sec. 72. Annuities; certain proceeds of endowment and life insurance contracts

(a) **General rule for annuities.** -- Except as otherwise provided in this chapter, gross income includes any amount received as an annuity (whether for a period certain or during one or more lives) under an annuity, endowment, or life insurance contract.

(b) **Exclusion ratio.** --

(1) **In general.** -- Gross income does not include that part of any amount received as an 5 annuity under an annuity, endowment, or life insurance contract which bears the same ratio to such amount as the investment in the contract (as of the annuity starting date) bears to the expected return under the contract (as of such date).

(2) **Exclusion limited to investment.** -- The portion of any amount received as an annuity which is excluded from gross income under paragraph (1) shall not exceed the unrecovered 10 investment in the contract immediately before the receipt of such amount.

(3) **Deduction where annuity payments cease before entire investment recovered.** --

(A) **In general.** -- If--

(i) after the annuity starting date, payments as an annuity under the contract cease by reason of the death of an annuitant, and   15

(ii) as of the date of such cessation, there is unrecovered investment in the contract,

the amount of such unrecovered investment (in excess of any amount specified in subsection (e)(5) which was not included in gross income) shall be allowed as a deduction to the annuitant for his last taxable year.

(B) **Payments to other persons.** -- In the case of any contract which provides for 20 payments meeting the requirements of subparagraphs (B) and (C) of subsection (c)(2), the deduction under subparagraph (A) shall be allowed to the person entitled to such payments for the taxable year in which such payments are received.

(C) **Net operating loss deductions provided.** -- For purposes of section 172, a deduction allowed under this paragraph shall be treated as if it were attributable to a trade 25 or business of the taxpayer.

(4) **Unrecovered investment.** -- For purposes of this subsection, the unrecovered investment in the contract as of any date is--

(A) the investment in the contract (determined without regard to subsection (c)(2)) as of the annuity starting date, reduced by   30

(B) the aggregate amount received under the contract on or after such annuity starting date and before the date as of which the determination is being made, to the extent such amount was excludable from gross income under this subtitle.

(c) **Definitions.** --

(1) **Investment in the contract.** -- For purposes of subsection (b), the investment in the 35 contract as of the annuity starting date is--

(A) the aggregate amount of premiums or other consideration paid for the contract, minus

(B) the aggregate amount received under the contract before such date, to the extent that such amount was excludable from gross income under this subtitle or prior income tax 40 laws.

(2) **Adjustment in investment where there is refund feature.** -- If--

Sec. 72. Annuities; certain proceeds of endowment and life insurance contracts

(A) the expected return under the contract depends in whole or in part on the life expectancy of one or more individuals;

(B) the contract provides for payments to be made to a beneficiary (or to the estate of an annuitant) on or after the death of the annuitant or annuitants; and

(C) such payments are in the nature of a refund of the consideration paid, then the value (computed without discount for interest) of such payments on the annuity starting date shall be subtracted from the amount determined under paragraph (1). Such value shall be computed in accordance with actuarial tables prescribed by the Secretary. For purposes of this paragraph and of subsection (e)(2)(A), the term "refund of the consideration paid" includes amounts payable after the death of an annuitant by reason of a provision in the contract for a life annuity with minimum period of payments certain, but (if part of the consideration was contributed by an employer) does not include that part of any payment to a beneficiary (or to the estate of the annuitant) which is not attributable to the consideration paid by the employee for the contract as determined under paragraph (1)(A).

(3) Expected return. -- For purposes of subsection (b), the expected return under the contract shall be determined as follows:

(A) Life expectancy. -- If the expected return under the contract, for the period on and after the annuity starting date, depends in whole or in part on the life expectancy of one or more individuals, the expected return shall be computed with reference to actuarial tables prescribed by the Secretary.

(B) Installment payments. -- If subparagraph (A) does not apply, the expected return is the aggregate of the amounts receivable under the contract as an annuity.

(4) Annuity starting date. -- For purposes of this section, the annuity starting date in the case of any contract is the first day of the first period for which an amount is received as an annuity under the contract; except that if such date was before January 1, 1954, then the annuity starting date is January 1, 1954.

(d) Special rules for qualified employer retirement plans. --

(1) Simplified method of taxing annuity payments. --

(A) In general. -- In the case of any amount received as an annuity under a qualified employer retirement plan--

(i) subsection (b) shall not apply, and

(ii) the investment in the contract shall be recovered as provided in this paragraph.

(B) Method of recovering investment in contract. --

(i) In general. -- Gross income shall not include so much of any monthly annuity payment under a qualified employer retirement plan as does not exceed the amount obtained by dividing--

(I) the investment in the contract (as of the annuity starting date), by

(II) the number of anticipated payments determined under the table contained in clause (iii) (or, in the case of a contract to which subsection (c)(3)(B) applies, the number of monthly annuity payments under such contract).

(ii) Certain rules made applicable. -- Rules similar to the rules of paragraphs (2) and (3) of subsection (b) shall apply for purposes of this paragraph.

(iii) Number of anticipated payments. -- If the annuity is payable over the life of a single individual, the number of anticipated payments shall be determined as follows:

Sec. 72. Annuities; certain proceeds of endowment and life insurance contracts

If the age of the annuitant on the annuity starting date is:	The number of anticipated payments is:
Not more than 55...	360
More than 55 but not more than 60....................	310
More than 60 but not more than 65....................	260
More than 65 but not more than 70....................	210
More than 70...	160.

(iv) Number of anticipated payments where more than one life. -- If the annuity is payable over the lives of more than 1 individual, the number of anticipated payments shall be determined as follows:

If the combined ages of annuitants are:	The number is:
Not more than 110..	410
More than 110 but not more than 120.................	360
More than 120 but not more than 130.................	310
More than 130 but not more than 140.................	260
More than 140...	210.

(C) Adjustment for refund feature not applicable. -- For purposes of this paragraph, investment in the contract shall be determined under subsection (c)(1) without regard to subsection (c)(2).

(D) Special rule where lump sum paid in connection with commencement of annuity payments. -- If, in connection with the commencement of annuity payments under any qualified employer retirement plan, the taxpayer receives a lump-sum payment--

(i) such payment shall be taxable under subsection (e) as if received before the annuity starting date, and

(ii) the investment in the contract for purposes of this paragraph shall be determined as if such payment had been so received.

(E) Exception. -- This paragraph shall not apply in any case where the primary annuitant has attained age 75 on the annuity starting date unless there are fewer than 5 years of guaranteed payments under the annuity.

(F) Adjustment where annuity payments not on monthly basis. -- In any case where the annuity payments are not made on a monthly basis, appropriate adjustments in the application of this paragraph shall be made to take into account the period on the basis of which such payments are made.

(G) Qualified employer retirement plan. -- For purposes of this paragraph, the term "qualified employer retirement plan" means any plan or contract described in paragraph (1), (2), or (3) of section 4974(c).

(2) Treatment of employee contributions under defined contribution plans. -- For purposes of this section, employee contributions (and any income allocable thereto) under a defined contribution plan may be treated as a separate contract.

(e) Amounts not received as annuities. --

(1) Application of subsection. --

151

Sec. 72. Annuities; certain proceeds of endowment and life insurance contracts

(A) In general. -- This subsection shall apply to any amount which -

(i) is received under an annuity, endowment, or life insurance contract, and

(ii) is not received as an annuity,

if no provision of this subtitle (other than this subsection) applies with respect to such amount.

(B) Dividends. -- For purposes of this section, any amount received which is in the nature of a dividend or similar distribution shall be treated as an amount not received as an annuity.

(2) General rule. -- Any amount to which this subsection applies -

(A) if received on or after the annuity starting date, shall be included in gross income, or

(B) if received before the annuity starting date--

(i) shall be included in gross income to the extent allocable to income on the contract, and

(ii) shall not be included in gross income to the extent allocable to the investment in the contract.

(3) Allocation of amounts to income and investment. -- For purposes of paragraph (2)(B)-

(A) Allocation to income. -- Any amount to which this subsection applies shall be treated as allocable to income on the contract to the extent that such amount does not exceed the excess (if any) of--

(i) the cash value of the contract (determined without regard to any surrender charge) immediately before the amount is received, over

(ii) the investment in the contract at such time.

(B) Allocation to investment. -- Any amount to which this subsection applies shall be treated as allocable to investment in the contract to the extent that such amount is not allocated to income under subparagraph (A).

(4) Special rules for application of paragraph (2)(B). -- For purposes of paragraph (2)(B)--

(A) Loans treated as distributions. -- If, during any taxable year, an individual -

(i) receives (directly or indirectly) any amount as a loan under any contract to which this subsection applies, or

(ii) assigns or pledges (or agrees to assign or pledge) any portion of the value of any such contract,

such amount or portion shall be treated as received under the contract as an amount not received as an annuity. The preceding sentence shall not apply for purposes of determining investment in the contract, except that the investment in the contract shall be increased by any amount included in gross income by reason of the amount treated as received under the preceding sentence.

(B) Treatment of policyholder dividends. -- Any amount described in paragraph (1)(B) shall not be included in gross income under paragraph (2)(B)(i) to the extent such amount is retained by the insurer as a premium or other consideration paid for the contract.

(C) Treatment of transfers without adequate consideration. --

(i) In general. -- If an individual who holds an annuity contract transfers it without full and adequate consideration, such individual shall be treated as receiving an amount equal to the excess of--

152

(I) the cash surrender value of such contract at the time of transfer, over

(II) the investment in such contract at such time, under the contract as an amount not received as an annuity.

(ii) Exception for certain transfers between spouses or former spouses. -- Clause (i) shall not apply to any transfer to which section 1041(a) (relating to transfers 5 of property between spouses or incident to divorce) applies.

(iii) Adjustment to investment in contract of transferee. -- If under clause (i) an amount is included in the gross income of the transferor of an annuity contract, the investment in the contract of the transferee in such contract shall be increased by the amount so included. 10

(5) Retention of existing rules in certain cases. --

(A) In general. -- In any case to which this paragraph applies -

(i) paragraphs (2)(B) and (4)(A) shall not apply, and

(ii) if paragraph (2)(A) does not apply,

the amount shall be included in gross income, but only to the extent it exceeds the 15 investment in the contract.

(B) Existing contracts. -- This paragraph shall apply to contracts entered into before August 14, 1982. Any amount allocable to investment in the contract after August 13, 1982, shall be treated as from a contract entered into after such date.

(C) Certain life insurance and endowment contracts. -- Except as provided in 20 paragraph (10) and except to the extent prescribed by the Secretary by regulations, this paragraph shall apply to any amount not received as an annuity which is received under a life insurance or endowment contract.

(D) Contracts under qualified plans. -- Except as provided in paragraph (8), this paragraph shall apply to any amount received-- 25

(i) from a trust described in section 401(a) which is exempt from tax under section 501(a),

(ii) from a contract--

(I) purchased by a trust described in clause (i),

(II) purchased as part of a plan described in section 403(a), 30

(III) described in section 403(b), or

(IV) provided for employees of a life insurance company under a plan described in section 818(a)(3), or

(iii) from an individual retirement account or an individual retirement annuity. -- Any dividend described in section 404(k) which is received by a participant 35 or beneficiary shall, for purposes of this subparagraph, be treated as paid under a separate contract to which clause (ii)(I) applies.

(E) Full refunds, surrenders, redemptions, and maturities. -- This paragraph shall apply to--

(i) any amount received, whether in a single sum or otherwise, under a contract in 40 full discharge of the obligation under the contract which is in the nature of a refund of the consideration paid for the contract, and

(ii) any amount received under a contract on its complete surrender, redemption, or maturity.

Sec. 72. Annuities; certain proceeds of endowment and life insurance contracts

In the case of any amount to which the preceding sentence applies, the rule of paragraph (2)(A) shall not apply.

(6) Investment in the contract. -- For purposes of this subsection, the investment in the contract as of any date is--

(A) the aggregate amount of premiums or other consideration paid for the contract before such date, minus

(B) the aggregate amount received under the contract before such date, to the extent that such amount was excludable from gross income under this subtitle or prior income tax laws.

(8) Extension of paragraph (2)(B) to qualified plans. --

(A) In general. -- Notwithstanding any other provision of this subsection, in the case of any amount received before the annuity starting date from a trust or contract described in paragraph (5)(D), paragraph (2)(B) shall apply to such amounts.

(B) Allocation of amount received. -- For purposes of paragraph (2)(B), the amount allocated to the investment in the contract shall be the portion of the amount described in subparagraph (A) which bears the same ratio to such amount as the investment in the contract bears to the account balance. The determination under the preceding sentence shall be made as of the time of the distribution or at such other time as the Secretary may prescribe.

(C) Treatment of forfeitable rights. -- If an employee does not have a nonforfeitable right to any amount under any trust or contract to which subparagraph (A) applies, such amount shall not be treated as part of the account balance.

(9) Extension of paragraph (2)(B) to qualified tuition programs and Coverdell education savings accounts. -- Notwithstanding any other provision of this subsection, paragraph (2)(B) shall apply to amounts received under a qualified tuition program (as defined in section 529(b)) or under a Coverdell education savings account (as defined in section 530(b)). The rule of paragraph (8)(B) shall apply for purposes of this paragraph.

(10) Treatment of modified endowment contracts. --

(A) In general. -- Notwithstanding paragraph (5)(C), in the case of any modified endowment contract (as defined in section 7702A)--

(i) paragraphs (2)(B) and (4)(A) shall apply, and

(ii) in applying paragraph (4)(A), "any person" shall be substituted for "an individual".

(B) Treatment of certain burial contracts. -- Notwithstanding subparagraph (A), paragraph (4)(A) shall not apply to any assignment (or pledge) of a modified endowment contract if such assignment (or pledge) is solely to cover the payment of expenses referred to in section 7702(e)(2)(C)(iii) and if the maximum death benefit under such contract does not exceed $25,000.

(11) Special rules for certain combination contracts providing long-term care insurance. -- Notwithstanding paragraphs (2), (5)(C), and (10), in the case of any charge against the cash value of an annuity contract or the cash surrender value of a life insurance contract made as payment for coverage under a qualified long-term care insurance contract which is part of or a rider on such annuity or life insurance contract--

(A) the investment in the contract shall be reduced (but not below zero) by such charge, and

(B) such charge shall not be includible in gross income.

Sec. 72. Annuities; certain proceeds of endowment and life insurance contracts

(12) Anti-abuse rules. --

(A) In general. -- For purposes of determining the amount includible in gross income under this subsection--

(i) all modified endowment contracts issued by the same company to the same policyholder during any calendar year shall be treated as 1 modified endowment 5 contract, and

(ii) all annuity contracts issued by the same company to the same policyholder during any calendar year shall be treated as 1 annuity contract.

The preceding sentence shall not apply to any contract described in paragraph (5)(D).

(B) Regulatory authority. -- The Secretary may by regulations prescribe such additional 10 rules as may be necessary or appropriate to prevent avoidance of the purposes of this subsection through serial purchases of contracts or otherwise.

(f) Special rules for computing employees' contributions. -- In computing, for purposes of subsection (c)(1)(A), the aggregate amount of premiums or other consideration paid for the contract, and for purposes of subsection (e)(6), the aggregate premiums or other consideration 15 paid, amounts contributed by the employer shall be included, but only to the extent that--

(1) such amounts were includible in the gross income of the employee under this subtitle or prior income tax laws; or

(2) if such amounts had been paid directly to the employee at the time they were contributed, they would not have been includible in the gross income of the employee under 20 the law applicable at the time of such contribution.

Paragraph (2) shall not apply to amounts which were contributed by the employer after December 31, 1962, and which would not have been includible in the gross income of the employee by reason of the application of section 911 if such amounts had been paid directly to the employee at the time of contribution. The preceding sentence shall not apply to amounts which were 25 contributed by the employer, as determined under regulations prescribed by the Secretary, to provide pension or annuity credits, to the extent such credits are attributable to services performed before January 1, 1963, and are provided pursuant to pension or annuity plan provisions in existence on March 12, 1962, and on that date applicable to such services, or to the extent such credits are attributable to services performed as a foreign missionary (within the meaning of 30 section 403(b)(2)(D)(iii), as in effect before the enactment of the Economic Growth and Tax Relief Reconciliation Act of 2001).

(g) Rules for transferee where transfer was for value. -- Where any contract (or any interest therein) is transferred (by assignment or otherwise) for a valuable consideration, to the extent that the contract (or interest therein) does not, in the hands of the transferee, have a basis which is 35 determined by reference to the basis in the hands of the transferor, then--

(1) for purposes of this section, only the actual value of such consideration, plus the amount of the premiums and other consideration paid by the transferee after the transfer, shall be taken into account in computing the aggregate amount of the premiums or other consideration paid for the contract;   40

(2) for purposes of subsection (c)(1)(B), there shall be taken into account only the aggregate amount received under the contract by the transferee before the annuity starting date, to the extent that such amount was excludable from gross income under this subtitle or prior income tax laws; and

(3) the annuity starting date is January 1, 1954, or the first day of the first period for which 45 the transferee received an amount under the contract as an annuity, whichever is the later.

Sec. 72. Annuities; certain proceeds of endowment and life insurance contracts

For purposes of this subsection, the term "transferee" includes a beneficiary of, or the estate of, the transferee.

(h) Option to receive annuity in lieu of lump sum. -- If--

(1) a contract provides for payment of a lump sum in full discharge of an obligation under the contract, subject to an option to receive an annuity in lieu of such lump sum;

(2) the option is exercised within 60 days after the day on which such lump sum first became payable; and

(3) part or all of such lump sum would (but for this subsection) be includible in gross income by reason of subsection (e)(1),

then, for purposes of this subtitle, no part of such lump sum shall be considered as includible in gross income at the time such lump sum first became payable.

(j) Interest. -- Notwithstanding any other provision of this section, if any amount is held under an agreement to pay interest thereon, the interest payments shall be included in gross income.

***

(l) Face-amount certificates. -- For purposes of this section, the term "endowment contract" includes a face-amount certificate, as defined in section 2(a)(15) of the Investment Company Act of 1940 (15 U.S.C., sec. 80a-2), issued after December 31, 1954.

(m) Special rules applicable to employee annuities and distributions under employee plans

***

(2) Computation of consideration paid by the employee. -- In computing--

(A) the aggregate amount of premiums or other consideration paid for the contract for purposes of subsection (c)(1)(A) (relating to the investment in the contract), and

(B) the aggregate premiums or other consideration paid for purposes of subsection (e)(6) (relating to certain amounts not received as an annuity),

any amount allowed as a deduction with respect to the contract under section 404 which was paid while the employee was an employee within the meaning of section 401(c)(1) shall be treated as consideration contributed by the employer, and there shall not be taken into account any portion of the premiums or other consideration for the contract paid while the employee was an owner-employee which is properly allocable (as determined under regulations prescribed by the Secretary) to the cost of life, accident, health, or other insurance.

(3) Life insurance contracts. --

(A) This paragraph shall apply to any life insurance contract--

(i) purchased as a part of a plan described in section 403(a), or

(ii) purchased by a trust described in section 401(a) which is exempt from tax under section 501(a) if the proceeds of such contract are payable directly or indirectly to a participant in such trust or to a beneficiary of such participant.

(B) Any contribution to a plan described in subparagraph (A)(i) or a trust described in subparagraph (A)(ii) which is allowed as a deduction under section 404, and any income of a trust described in subparagraph (A)(ii), which is determined in accordance with regulations prescribed by the Secretary to have been applied to purchase the life insurance protection under a contract described in subparagraph (A), is includible in the gross income of the participant for the taxable year when so applied.

(C) In the case of the death of an individual insured under a contract described in subparagraph (A), an amount equal to the cash surrender value of the contract immediately before the death of the insured shall be treated as a payment under such plan or a

Sec. 72. Annuities; certain proceeds of endowment and life insurance contracts

distribution by such trust, and the excess of the amount payable by reason of the death of the insured over such cash surrender value shall not be includible in gross income under this section and shall be treated as provided in section 101.

***

(5) Penalties applicable to certain amounts received by 5-percent owners. --   5

(A) This paragraph applies to amounts which are received from a qualified trust described in section 401(a) or under a plan described in section 403(a) at any time by an individual who is, or has been, a 5-percent owner, or by a successor of such an individual, but only to the extent such amounts are determined, under regulations prescribed by the Secretary, to exceed the benefits provided for such individual under the plan formula.   10

(B) If a person receives an amount to which this paragraph applies, his tax under this chapter for the taxable year in which such amount is received shall be increased by an amount equal to 10 percent of the portion of the amount so received which is includible in his gross income for such taxable year.

(C) For purposes of this paragraph, the term "5-percent owner" means any individual   15 who, at any time during the 5 plan years preceding the plan year ending in the taxable year in which the amount is received, is a 5-percent owner (as defined in section 416(i)(1)(B)).

(6) Owner-employee defined. -- For purposes of this subsection, the term "owner-employee" has the meaning assigned to it by section 401(c)(3) and includes an individual for whose benefit an individual retirement account or annuity described in section 408(a) or (b) is   20 maintained. For purposes of the preceding sentence, the term "owner-employee" shall include an employee within the meaning of section 401(c)(1).

(7) Meaning of disabled. -- For purposes of this section, an individual shall be considered to be disabled if he is unable to engage in any substantial gainful activity by reason of any medically determinable physical or mental impairment which can be expected to result in   25 death or to be of long-continued and indefinite duration. An individual shall not be considered to be disabled unless he furnishes proof of the existence thereof in such form and manner as the Secretary may require.

***

(10) Determination of investment in the contract in the case of qualified domestic   30 **relations orders.** -- Under regulations prescribed by the Secretary, in the case of a distribution or payment made to an alternate payee who is the spouse or former spouse of the participant pursuant to a qualified domestic relations order (as defined in section 414(p)), the investment in the contract as of the date prescribed in such regulations shall be allocated on a pro rata basis between the present value of such distribution or payment and the present value of all   35 other benefits payable with respect to the participant to which such order relates.

(o) Special rules for distributions from qualified plans to which employee made deductible contributions. --

(1) Treatment of contributions. -- For purposes of this section and sections 402 and 403, notwithstanding section 414(h), any deductible employee contribution made to a qualified   40 employer plan or government plan shall be treated as an amount contributed by the employer which is not includible in the gross income of the employee.

***

(3) Amounts constructively received. --

(A) In general. -- For purposes of this subsection, rules similar to the rules provided by   45 subsection (p) (other than the exception contained in paragraph (2) thereof) shall apply.

Sec. 72. Annuities; certain proceeds of endowment and life insurance contracts

(B) Purchase of life insurance. -- To the extent any amount of accumulated deductible employee contributions of an employee are applied to the purchase of life insurance contracts, such amount shall be treated as distributed to the employee in the year so applied.

(4) Special rule for treatment of rollover amounts. -- For purposes of sections 402(c), 403(a)(4), and 403(b)(8), 408(d)(3), and 457(e)(16), the Secretary shall prescribe regulations providing for such allocations of amounts attributable to accumulated deductible employee contributions, and for such other rules, as may be necessary to insure that such accumulated deductible employee contributions do not become eligible for additional tax benefits (or freed from limitations) through the use of rollovers.

(5) Definitions and special rules. -- For purposes of this subsection -

(A) Deductible employee contributions. -- The term "deductible employee contributions" means any qualified voluntary employee contribution (as defined in section 219(e)(2)) made after December 31, 1981, in a taxable year beginning after such date and made for a taxable year beginning before January 1, 1987, and allowable as a deduction under section 219(a) for such taxable year.

(B) Accumulated deductible employee contributions. -- The term "accumulated deductible employee contributions" means the deductible employee contributions--

(i) increased by the amount of income and gain allocable to such contributions, and

(ii) reduced by the sum of the amount of loss and expense allocable to such contributions and the amounts distributed with respect to the employee which are attributable to such contributions (or income or gain allocable to such contributions).

(C) Qualified employer plan. -- The term "qualified employer plan" has the meaning given to such term by subsection (p)(3)(A)(i).

(D) Government plan. -- The term "government plan" has the meaning given such term by subsection (p)(3)(B).

(6) Ordering rules. -- Unless the plan specifies otherwise, any distribution from such plan shall not be treated as being made from the accumulated deductible employee contributions, until all other amounts to the credit of the employee have been distributed.

(p) Loans treated as distributions. -- For purposes of this section--

(1) Treatment as distributions. --

(A) Loans. -- If during any taxable year a participant or beneficiary receives (directly or indirectly) any amount as a loan from a qualified employer plan, such amount shall be treated as having been received by such individual as a distribution under such plan.

(B) Assignments or pledges. -- If during any taxable year a participant or beneficiary assigns (or agrees to assign) or pledges (or agrees to pledge) any portion of his interest in a qualified employer plan, such portion shall be treated as having been received by such individual as a loan from such plan.

(2) Exception for certain loans. --

(A) General rule. -- Paragraph (1) shall not apply to any loan to the extent that such loan (when added to the outstanding balance of all other loans from such plan whether made on, before, or after August 13, 1982), does not exceed the lesser of--

(i) $50,000, reduced by the excess (if any) of--

(I) the highest outstanding balance of loans from the plan during the 1-year period ending on the day before the date on which such loan was made, over

Sec. 72. Annuities; certain proceeds of endowment and life insurance contracts

(II) the outstanding balance of loans from the plan on the date on which such loan was made, or

(ii) the greater of (I) one-half of the present value of the nonforfeitable accrued benefit of the employee under the plan, or (II) $10,000.

For purposes of clause (ii), the present value of the nonforfeitable accrued benefit shall be determined without regard to any accumulated deductible employee contributions (as defined in subsection (o)(5)(B)). 5

(B) Requirement that loan be repayable within 5 years. --

(i) In general. -- Subparagraph (A) shall not apply to any loan unless such loan, by its terms, is required to be repaid within 5 years. 10

(ii) Exception for home loans. -- Clause (i) shall not apply to any loan used to acquire any dwelling unit which within a reasonable time is to be used (determined at the time the loan is made) as the principal residence of the participant.

(C) Requirement of level amortization. -- Except as provided in regulations, this paragraph shall not apply to any loan unless substantially level amortization of such loan 15 (with payments not less frequently than quarterly) is required over the term of the loan.

(D) Related employers and related plans. -- For purposes of this paragraph -

(i) the rules of subsections (b), (c), and (m) of section 414 shall apply, and

(ii) all plans of an employer (determined after the application of such subsections) shall be treated as 1 plan. 20

(3) Denial of interest deductions in certain cases. --

(A) In general. -- No deduction otherwise allowable under this chapter shall be allowed under this chapter for any interest paid or accrued on any loan to which paragraph (1) does not apply by reason of paragraph (2) during the period described in subparagraph (B).

(B) Period to which subparagraph (A) applies. -- For purposes of subparagraph (A), 25 the period described in this subparagraph is the period--

(i) on or after the 1st day on which the individual to whom the loan is made is a key employee (as defined in section 416(i)), or

(ii) such loan is secured by amounts attributable to elective deferrals described in subparagraph (A) or (C) of section 402(g)(3). 30

(4) Qualified employer plan, etc. -- For purposes of this subsection--

(A) Qualified employer plan. --

(i) In general. -- The term "qualified employer plan" means--

(I) a plan described in section 401(a) which includes a trust exempt from tax under section 501(a), 35

(II) an annuity plan described in section 403(a), and

(III) a plan under which amounts are contributed by an individual's employer for an annuity contract described in section 403(b).

(ii) Special rule. -- The term "qualified employer plan" shall include any plan which was (or was determined to be) a qualified employer plan or a government plan. 40

(B) Government plan. -- The term "government plan" means any plan, whether or not qualified, established and maintained for its employees by the United States, by a State or political subdivision thereof, or by an agency or instrumentality of any of the foregoing.

(5) Special rules for loans, etc., from certain contracts. -- For purposes of this subsection,

Sec. 72. Annuities; certain proceeds of endowment and life insurance contracts

any amount received as a loan under a contract purchased under a qualified employer plan (and any assignment or pledge with respect to such a contract) shall be treated as a loan under such employer plan.

(q) 10-percent penalty for premature distributions from annuity contracts. --

(1) Imposition of penalty. -- If any taxpayer receives any amount under an annuity contract, the taxpayer's tax under this chapter for the taxable year in which such amount is received shall be increased by an amount equal to 10 percent of the portion of such amount which is includible in gross income.

(2) Subsection not to apply to certain distributions. -- Paragraph 1 shall not apply to any distribution--

(A) made on or after the date on which the taxpayer attains age 59 1/2 ,

(B) made on or after the death of the holder (or, where the holder is not an individual, the death of the primary annuitant (as defined in subsection (s)(6)(B))),

(C) attributable to the taxpayer's becoming disabled within the meaning of subsection (m)(7),

(D) which is a part of a series of substantially equal periodic payments (not less frequently than annually) made for the life (or life expectancy) of the taxpayer or the joint lives (or joint life expectancies) of such taxpayer and his designated beneficiary,

(E) from a plan, contract, account, trust, or annuity described in subsection (e)(5)(D),

(F) allocable to investment in the contract before August 14, 1982, or (!2)

(G) under a qualified funding asset (within the meaning of section 130(d), but without regard to whether there is a qualified assignment),

(H) to which subsection (t) applies (without regard to paragraph (2) thereof),

(I) under an immediate annuity contract (within the meaning of section 72(u)(4)), or

(J) which is purchased by an employer upon the termination of a plan described in section 401(a) or 403(a) and which is held by the employer until such time as the employee separates from service.

(3) Change in substantially equal payments. -- If--

(A) paragraph (1) does not apply to a distribution by reason of paragraph (2)(D), and

(B) the series of payments under such paragraph are subsequently modified (other than by reason of death or disability)--

(i) before the close of the 5-year period beginning on the date of the first payment and after the taxpayer attains age 59 1/2 , or

(ii) before the taxpayer attains age 59 1/2 ,

the taxpayer's tax for the 1st taxable year in which such modification occurs shall be increased by an amount, determined under regulations, equal to the tax which (but for paragraph (2)(D)) would have been imposed, plus interest for the deferral period (within the meaning of subsection (t)(4)(B)).

(r) Certain railroad retirement benefits treated as received under employer plans. --

(1) In general. -- Notwithstanding any other provision of law, any benefit provided under the Railroad Retirement Act of 1974 (other than a tier 1 railroad retirement benefit) shall be treated for purposes of this title as a benefit provided under an employer plan which meets the requirements of section 401(a).

(2) Tier 2 taxes treated as contributions. --

Sec. 72. Annuities; certain proceeds of endowment and life insurance contracts

(A) In general. -- For purposes of paragraph (1)--

(i) the tier 2 portion of the tax imposed by section 3201 (relating to tax on employees) shall be treated as an employee contribution,

(ii) the tier 2 portion of the tax imposed by section 3211 (relating to tax on employee representatives) shall be treated as an employee contribution, and

(iii) the tier 2 portion of the tax imposed by section 3221 (relating to tax on employers) shall be treated as an employer contribution.

(B) Tier 2 portion. -- For purposes of subparagraph (A)--

(i) **After 1984.** -- With respect to compensation paid after 1984, the tier 2 portion shall be the taxes imposed by sections 3201(b), 3211(b), and 3221(b).

***

(C) Contributions not allocable to supplemental annuity or windfall benefits. -- For purposes of paragraph (1), no amount treated as an employee contribution under this paragraph shall be allocated to--

(i) any supplemental annuity paid under section 2(b) of the Railroad Retirement Act of 1974, or

(ii) any benefit paid under section 3(h), 4(e), or 4(h) of such Act.

(3) Tier 1 railroad retirement benefit. -- For purposes of paragraph (1), the term "tier 1 railroad retirement benefit" has the meaning given such term by section 86(d)(4).

(s) Required distributions where holder dies before entire interest is distributed. --

(1) In general. -- A contract shall not be treated as an annuity contract for purposes of this title unless it provides that--

(A) if any holder of such contract dies on or after the annuity starting date and before the entire interest in such contract has been distributed, the remaining portion of such interest will be distributed at least as rapidly as under the method of distributions being used as of the date of his death, and

(B) if any holder of such contract dies before the annuity starting date, the entire interest in such contract will be distributed within 5 years after the death of such holder.

(2) Exception for certain amounts payable over life of beneficiary. -- If--

(A) any portion of the holder's interest is payable to (or for the benefit of) a designated beneficiary,

(B) such portion will be distributed (in accordance with regulations) over the life of such designated beneficiary (or over a period not extending beyond the life expectancy of such beneficiary), and

(C) such distributions begin not later than 1 year after the date of the holder's death or such later date as the Secretary may by regulations prescribe,

then for purposes of paragraph (1), the portion referred to in subparagraph (A) shall be treated as distributed on the day on which such distributions begin.

(3) Special rule where surviving spouse beneficiary. -- If the designated beneficiary referred to in paragraph (2)(A) is the surviving spouse of the holder of the contract, paragraphs (1) and (2) shall be applied by treating such spouse as the holder of such contract.

(4) Designated beneficiary. -- For purposes of this subsection, the term "designated beneficiary" means any individual designated a beneficiary by the holder of the contract.

(5) Exception for certain annuity contracts. -- This subsection shall not apply to any annuity contract--

Sec. 72. Annuities; certain proceeds of endowment and life insurance contracts

(A) which is provided--

    (i) under a plan described in section 401(a) which includes a trust exempt from tax under section 501, or

    (ii) under a plan described in section 403(a),

(B) which is described in section 403(b),

(C) which is an individual retirement annuity or provided under an individual retirement account or annuity, or

(D) which is a qualified funding asset (as defined in section 130(d), but without regard to whether there is a qualified assignment).

(6) Special rule where holder is corporation or other non-individual. --

    (A) In general. -- For purposes of this subsection, if the holder of the contract is not an individual, the primary annuitant shall be treated as the holder of the contract.

    (B) Primary annuitant. -- For purposes of subparagraph (A), the term "primary annuitant" means the individual, the events in the life of whom are of primary importance in affecting the timing or amount of the payout under the contract.

(7) Treatment of changes in primary annuitant where holder of contract is not an individual. -- For purposes of this subsection, in the case of a holder of an annuity contract which is not an individual, if there is a change in a primary annuitant (as defined in paragraph (6)(B)), such change shall be treated as the death of the holder.

(t) 10-percent additional tax on early distributions from qualified retirement plans. --

(1) Imposition of additional tax. -- If any taxpayer receives any amount from a qualified retirement plan (as defined in section 4974(c)), the taxpayer's tax under this chapter for the taxable year in which such amount is received shall be increased by an amount equal to 10 percent of the portion of such amount which is includible in gross income.

(2) Subsection not to apply to certain distributions. -- Except as provided in paragraphs (3) and (4), paragraph (1) shall not apply to any of the following distributions:

    (A) In general. -- Distributions which are--

        (i) made on or after the date on which the employee attains age 59 1/2 ,

        (ii) made to a beneficiary (or to the estate of the employee) on or after the death of the employee,

        (iii) attributable to the employee's being disabled within the meaning of subsection (m)(7),

        (iv) part of a series of substantially equal periodic payments (not less frequently than annually) made for the life (or life expectancy) of the employee or the joint lives (or joint life expectancies) of such employee and his designated beneficiary,

        (v) made to an employee after separation from service after attainment of age 55,

        (vi) dividends paid with respect to stock of a corporation which are described in section 404(k), or

        (vii) made on account of a levy under section 6331 on the qualified retirement plan.

    (B) Medical expenses. -- Distributions made to the employee (other than distributions described in subparagraph (A), (C), or (D)) to the extent such distributions do not exceed the amount allowable as a deduction under section 213 to the employee for amounts paid during the taxable year for medical care (determined without regard to whether the employee itemizes deductions for such taxable year).

162

Sec. 72. Annuities; certain proceeds of endowment and life insurance contracts

(C) Payments to alternate payees pursuant to qualified domestic relations orders. -- Any distribution to an alternate payee pursuant to a qualified domestic relations order (within the meaning of section 414(p)(1)).

(D) Distributions to unemployed individuals for health insurance premiums. --

(i) In general. -- Distributions from an individual retirement plan to an individual 5 after separation from employment--

(I) if such individual has received unemployment compensation for 12 consecutive weeks under any Federal or State unemployment compensation law by reason of such separation,

(II) if such distributions are made during any taxable year during which such 10 unemployment compensation is paid or the succeeding taxable year, and

(III) to the extent such distributions do not exceed the amount paid during the taxable year for insurance described in section 213(d)(1)(D) with respect to the individual and the individual's spouse and dependents (as defined in section 152, determined without regard to subsections (b)(1), (b)(2), and (d)(1)(B) thereof). 15

(ii) Distributions after reemployment. -- Clause (i) shall not apply to any distribution made after the individual has been employed for at least 60 days after the separation from employment to which clause (i) applies.

(iii) Self-employed individuals. -- To the extent provided in regulations, a self-employed individual shall be treated as meeting the requirements of clause (i)(I) if, 20 under Federal or State law, the individual would have received unemployment compensation but for the fact the individual was self-employed.

(E) Distributions from individual retirement plans for higher education expenses. -- Distributions to an individual from an individual retirement plan to the extent such distributions do not exceed the qualified higher education expenses (as defined in 25 paragraph (7)) of the taxpayer for the taxable year. Distributions shall not be taken into account under the preceding sentence if such distributions are described in subparagraph (A), (C), or (D) or to the extent paragraph (1) does not apply to such distributions by reason of subparagraph (B).

(F) Distributions from certain plans for first home purchases. -- Distributions to an 30 individual from an individual retirement plan which are qualified first-time homebuyer distributions (as defined in paragraph (8)). Distributions shall not be taken into account under the preceding sentence if such distributions are described in subparagraph (A), (C), (D), or (E) or to the extent paragraph (1) does not apply to such distributions by reason of subparagraph (B). 35

(3) Limitations. --

(A) Certain exceptions not to apply to individual retirement plans. -- Subparagraphs (A)(v) and (C) of paragraph (2) shall not apply to distributions from an individual retirement plan.

(B) Periodic payments under qualified plans must begin after separation. -- 40 Paragraph (2)(A)(iv) shall not apply to any amount paid from a trust described in section 401(a) which is exempt from tax under section 501(a) or from a contract described in section 72(e)(5)(D)(ii) unless the series of payments begins after the employee separates from service.

(4) Change in substantially equal payments. -- 45

(A) In general. -- If--

163

Sec. 72. Annuities; certain proceeds of endowment and life insurance contracts

(i) paragraph (1) does not apply to a distribution by reason of paragraph (2)(A)(iv), and

(ii) the series of payments under such paragraph are subsequently modified (other than by reason of death or disability) -

(I) before the close of the 5-year period beginning with the date of the first payment and after the employee attains age 59 1/2 , or

(II) before the employee attains age 59 1/2 , the taxpayer's tax for the 1st taxable year in which such modification occurs shall be increased by an amount, determined under regulations, equal to the tax which (but for paragraph(2)(A)(iv)) would have been imposed, plus interest for the deferral period.

(B) Deferral period. -- For purposes of this paragraph, the term "deferral period" means the period beginning with the taxable year in which (without regard to paragraph (2)(A)(iv)) the distribution would have been includible in gross income and ending with the taxable year in which the modification described in subparagraph (A) occurs.

(5) Employee. -- For purposes of this subsection, the term "employee" includes any participant, and in the case of an individual retirement plan, the individual for whose benefit such plan was established.

(6) Special rules for simple retirement accounts. -- In the case of any amount received from a simple retirement account (within the meaning of section 408(p)) during the 2-year period beginning on the date such individual first participated in any qualified salary reduction arrangement maintained by the individual's employer under section 408(p)(2), paragraph (1) shall be applied by substituting "25 percent" for "10 percent".

(7) Qualified higher education expenses. -- For purposes of paragraph (2)(E)--

(A) In general. -- The term "qualified higher education expenses" means qualified higher education expenses (as defined in section 529(e)(3)) for education furnished to -

(i) the taxpayer,

(ii) the taxpayer's spouse, or

(iii) any child (as defined in section 152(f)(1)) or grandchild of the taxpayer or the taxpayer's spouse, at an eligible educational institution (as defined in section 529(e)(5)).

(B) Coordination with other benefits. -- The amount of qualified higher education expenses for any taxable year shall be reduced as provided in section 25A(g)(2).

(8) Qualified first-time homebuyer distributions. -- For purposes of paragraph (2)(F)--

(A) In general. -- The term "qualified first-time homebuyer distribution" means any payment or distribution received by an individual to the extent such payment or distribution is used by the individual before the close of the 120th day after the day on which such payment or distribution is received to pay qualified acquisition costs with respect to a principal residence of a first-time homebuyer who is such individual, the spouse of such individual, or any child, grandchild, or ancestor of such individual or the individual's spouse.

(B) Lifetime dollar limitation. -- The aggregate amount of payments or distributions received by an individual which may be treated as qualified first-time homebuyer distributions for any taxable year shall not exceed the excess (if any) of -

(i) $10,000, over

(ii) the aggregate amounts treated as qualified first-time homebuyer distributions with respect to such individual for all prior taxable years.

Sec. 72. Annuities; certain proceeds of endowment and life insurance contracts

(C) **Qualified acquisition costs.** -- For purposes of this paragraph, the term "qualified acquisition costs" means the costs of acquiring, constructing, or reconstructing a residence. Such term includes any usual or reasonable settlement, financing, or other closing costs.

(D) **First-time homebuyer; other definitions.** -- For purposes of this paragraph--

(i) **First-time homebuyer.** -- The term "first-time homebuyer" means any individual if--

(I) such individual (and if married, such individual's spouse) had no present ownership interest in a principal residence during the 2-year period ending on the date of acquisition of the principal residence to which this paragraph applies, and

(II) subsection (h) or (k) of section 1034 (!3) (as in effect on the day before the date of the enactment of this paragraph) did not suspend the running of any period of time specified in section 1034 (!3) (as so in effect) with respect to such individual on the day before the date the distribution is applied pursuant to subparagraph (A).

(ii) **Principal residence.** -- The term "principal residence" has the same meaning as when used in section 121.

(iii) **Date of acquisition.** -- The term "date of acquisition" means the date -

(I) on which a binding contract to acquire the principal residence to which subparagraph (A) applies is enteredinto, or

(II) on which construction or reconstruction of such a principal residence is commenced.

(E) **Special rule where delay in acquisition.** -- If any distribution from any individual retirement plan fails to meet the requirements of subparagraph (A) solely by reason of a delay or cancellation of the purchase or construction of the residence, the amount of the distribution may be contributed to an individual retirement plan as provided in section 408(d)(3)(A)(i) (determined by substituting "120th day" for "60th day" in such section), except that -

(i) section 408(d)(3)(B) shall not be applied to such contribution, and

(ii) such amount shall not be taken into account in determining whether section 408(d)(3)(B) applies to any other amount.

(u) **Treatment of annuity contracts not held by natural persons.** --

(1) **In general.** -- If any annuity contract is held by a person who is not a natural person -

(A) such contract shall not be treated as an annuity contract for purposes of this subtitle (other than subchapter L), and

(B) the income on the contract for any taxable year of the policyholder shall be treated as ordinary income received or accrued by the owner during such taxable year.
For purposes of this paragraph, holding by a trust or other entity as an agent for a natural person shall not be taken into account.

(2) **Income on the contract.** --

(A) **In general.** -- For purposes of paragraph (1), the term "income on the contract" means, with respect to any taxable year of the policyholder, the excess of--

(i) the sum of the net surrender value of the contract as of the close of the taxable year plus all distributions under the contract received during the taxable year or any prior taxable year, reduced by

(ii) the sum of the amount of net premiums under the contract for the taxable year and prior taxable years and amounts includible in gross income for prior taxable years

Sec. 72. Annuities; certain proceeds of endowment and life insurance contracts

with respect to such contract under this subsection.

Where necessary to prevent the avoidance of this subsection, the Secretary may substitute "fair market value of the contract" for "net surrender value of the contract" each place it appears in the preceding sentence.

(B) Net premiums. -- For purposes of this paragraph, the term "net premiums" means the amount of premiums paid under the contract reduced by any policyholder dividends.

(3) Exceptions. -- This subsection shall not apply to any annuity contract which--

(A) is acquired by the estate of a decedent by reason of the death of the decedent,

(B) is held under a plan described in section 401(a) or 403(a), under a program described in section 403(b), or under an individual retirement plan,

(C) is a qualified funding asset (as defined in section130(d), but without regard to whether there is a qualified assignment),

(D) is purchased by an employer upon the termination of a plan described in section 401(a) or 403(a) and is held by the employer until all amounts under such contract are distributed to the employee for whom such contract was purchased or the employee's beneficiary, or

(E) is an immediate annuity.

(4) Immediate annuity. -- For purposes of this subsection, the term "immediate annuity" means an annuity--

(A) which is purchased with a single premium or annuity consideration,

(B) the annuity starting date (as defined in subsection (c)(4)) of which commences no later than 1 year from the date of the purchase of the annuity, and

(C) which provides for a series of substantially equal periodic payments (to be made not less frequently than annually) during the annuity period.

(v) 10-percent additional tax for taxable distributions from modified endowment contracts. --

(1) Imposition of additional tax. -- If any taxpayer receives any amount under a modified endowment contract (as defined in section 7702A), the taxpayer's tax under this chapter for the taxable year in which such amount is received shall be increased by an amount equal to 10 percent of the portion of such amount which is includible in gross income.

(2) Subsection not to apply to certain distributions. -- Paragraph (1) shall not apply to any distribution--

(A) made on or after the date on which the taxpayer attains age 59 1/2 ,

(B) which is attributable to the taxpayer's becoming disabled (within the meaning of subsection (m)(7)), or

(C) which is part of a series of substantially equal periodic payments (not less frequently than annually) made for the life (or life expectancy) of the taxpayer or the joint lives (or joint life expectancies) of such taxpayer and his beneficiary.

(w) Application of basis rules to nonresident aliens. --

(1) In general. -- Notwithstanding any other provision of this section, for purposes of determining the portion of any distribution which is includible in gross income of a distributee who is a citizen or resident of the United States, the investment in the contract shall not include any applicable nontaxable contributions or applicable nontaxable earnings.

(2) Applicable nontaxable contribution. -- For purposes of this subsection, the term "applicable nontaxable contribution" means any employer or employee contribution -

166

Sec. 72. Annuities; certain proceeds of endowment and life insurance contracts

(A) which was made with respect to compensation--

 (i) for labor or personal services performed by an employee who, at the time the labor or services were performed, was a nonresident alien for purposes of the laws of the United States in effect at such time, and

 (ii) which is treated as from sources without the United States, and   5

(B) which was not subject to income tax (and would have been subject to income tax if paid as cash compensation when the services were rendered) under the laws of the United States or any foreign country.

(3) Applicable nontaxable earnings. -- For purposes of this subsection, the term "applicable nontaxable earnings" means earnings--   10

 (A) which are paid or accrued with respect to any employer or employee contribution which was made with respect to compensation for labor or personal services performed by an employee,

 (B) with respect to which the employee was at the time the earnings were paid or accrued a nonresident alien for purposes of the laws of the United States, and   15

 (C) which were not subject to income tax under the laws of the United States or any foreign country.

(4) Regulations. -- The Secretary shall prescribe such regulations as may be necessary to carry out the provisions of this subsection, including regulations treating contributions and earnings as not subject to tax under the laws of any foreign country where appropriate to carry   20 out the purposes of this subsection.

(x) Cross reference. -- For limitation on adjustments to basis of annuity contracts sold, see section 1021.

Reg. § 1.72-2 Applicability of section.   25

(a) *Contracts.* (1) The contracts under which amounts paid will be subject to the provisions of section 72 include contracts which are considered to be life insurance, endowment, and annuity contracts in accordance with the customary practice of life insurance companies. For the purposes of section 72, however, it is immaterial whether such contracts are entered into with an insurance company. The term ``endowment   30 contract'' also includes the ``face-amount certificates'' described in section 72(1).

***

(b) *Amounts.* (1)(i) In general, the amounts to which section 72 applies are any amounts received under the contracts described in paragraph (a)(1) of this section. However, if such amounts are specifically excluded from gross income under other   35 provisions of Chapter 1 of the Code, section 72 shall not apply for the purpose of including such amounts in gross income. For example, section 72 does not apply to amounts received under a life insurance contract if such amounts are paid by reason of the death of the insured and are excludable from gross income under section 101(a). See also sections 101(d), relating to proceeds of life insurance paid at a date later than death,   40 and 104(a)(4), relating to compensation for injuries or sickness.

(ii) Section 72 does not exclude from gross income any amounts received under an agreement to hold an amount and pay interest thereon. See paragraph (a) of § 1.72-14. However, section 72 does apply to amounts received by a surviving annuitant under a joint and survivor annuity contract since such amounts are not considered to be paid by   45 reason of the death of an insured. For a special deduction for the estate tax attributable to the inclusion of the value of the interest of a surviving annuitant under a joint and

Sec. 72. Annuities; certain proceeds of endowment and life insurance contracts

survivor annuity contract in the estate of the deceased primary annuitant, see section 691(d) and the regulations thereunder.

(2) Amounts subject to section 72 in accordance with subparagraph (1) of this paragraph are considered ``amounts received as an annuity" only in the event that all of
5 the following tests are met:

(i) They must be received on or after the ``annuity starting date" as that term is defined in paragraph (b) of § 1.72-4;

(ii) They must be payable in periodic installments at regular intervals (whether annually, semiannually, quarterly, monthly, weekly, or otherwise) over a period of more
10 than one full year from the annuity starting date; and

(iii) Except as indicated in subparagraph (3) of this paragraph, the total of the amounts payable must be determinable at the annuity starting date either directly from the terms of the contract or indirectly by the use of either mortality tables or compound interest computations, or both, in conjunction with such terms and in accordance with sound
15 actuarial theory.

For the purpose of determining whether amounts subject to section 72(d) and § 1.72-13 are ``amounts received as an annuity", however, the provisions of subdivision (i) of this subparagraph shall be disregarded. In addition, the term ``amounts received as an annuity" does not include amounts received to which the provisions of paragraph (b) or
20 (c) of § 1.72-11 apply, relating to dividends and certain amounts received by a beneficiary in the nature of a refund. If an amount is to be paid periodically until a fund plus interest at a fixed rate is exhausted, but further payments may be made thereafter because of earnings at a higher interest rate, the requirements of subdivision (iii) of this subparagraph are met with respect to the payments determinable at the outset by means
25 of computations involving the fixed interest rate, but any payments received after the expiration of the period determinable by such computations shall be taxable as dividends received after the annuity starting date in accordance with paragraph (b)(2) of § 1.72-11.

(3)(i) Notwithstanding the requirement of subparagraph (2)(iii) of this paragraph, if amounts are to be received for a definite or determinable time (whether for a period
30 certain or for a life or lives) under a contract which provides:

(a) That the amount of the periodic payments may vary in accordance with investment experience (as in certain profit-sharing plans), cost of living indices, or similar fluctuating criteria, or

(b) For specified payments the value of which may vary for income tax purposes, such
35 as in the case of any annuity payable in foreign currency, each such payment received shall be considered as an amount received as an annuity only to the extent that it does not exceed the amount computed by dividing the investment in the contract, as adjusted for any refund feature, by the number of periodic payments anticipated during the time that the periodic payments are to be made. If payments are to be made more frequently
40 than annually, the amount so computed shall be multiplied by the number of periodic payments to be made during the taxable year for the purpose of determining the total amount which may be considered received as an annuity during such year. To this extent, the payments received shall be considered to represent a return of premium or other consideration paid and shall be excludable from gross income in the taxable year in
45 which received. See paragraph (d) (2) and (3) of § 1.72-4. To the extent that the payments received under the contract during the taxable year exceed the total amount thus considered to be received as an annuity during such year, they shall be considered to be amounts not received as an annuity and shall be included in the gross income of the recipient. See section 72(e) and paragraph (b)(2) of § 1.72-11.
50 (ii) For purposes of subdivision (i) of this subparagraph, the number of periodic

168

Sec. 72. Annuities; certain proceeds of endowment and life insurance contracts

payments anticipated during the time payments are to be made shall be determined by multiplying the number of payments to be made each year (a) by the number of years payments are to be made, or (b) if payments are to be made for a life or lives, by the multiple found by the use of the appropriate tables contained in § 1.72-9, as adjusted in accordance with the table in paragraph (a)(2) of § 1.72-5.   5

(iii) For an example of the computation to be made in accordance with this subparagraph and a special election which may be made in a taxable year subsequent to a taxable year in which the total payments received under a contract described in this subparagraph are less than the total of the amounts excludable from gross income in such year under subdivision (i) of this subparagraph, see paragraph (d)(3) of § 1.72-4.   10

Reg. § 1.72-4 Exclusion ratio.

(a) *General rule.* (1)(i) To determine the proportionate part of the total amount received each year as an annuity which is excludable from the gross income of a recipient in the taxable year of receipt (other than amounts received under (a) certain employee   15 annuities described in section 72(d) and § 1.72-13, or (b) certain annuities described in section 72(o) and § 1.122-1), an exclusion ratio is to be determined for each contract. In general, this ratio is determined by dividing the investment in the contract as found under § 1.72-6 by the expected return under such contract as found under § 1.72-5. Where a single consideration is given for a particular contract which provides for two or more   20 annuity elements, an exclusion ratio shall be determined for the contract as a whole by dividing the investment in such contract by the aggregate of the expected returns under all the annuity elements provided thereunder. However, where the provisions of paragraph (b)(3) of § 1.72-2 apply to payments received under such a contract, see paragraph (b)(3) of § 1.72-6. In the case of a contract to which § 1.72-6(d) (relating to   25 contracts in which amounts were invested both before July 1, 1986, and after June 30, 1986) applies, the exclusion ratio for purposes of this paragraph (a) is determined in accordance with § 1.72-6(d) and, in particular, § 1.72-6(d)(5)(i).

(ii) The exclusion ratio for the particular contract is then applied to the total amount received as an annuity during the taxable year by each recipient. See, however,   30 paragraph (e)(3) of § 1.72-5. Any excess of the total amount received as an annuity during the taxable year over the amount determined by the application of the exclusion ratio to such total amount shall be included in the gross income of the recipient for the taxable year of receipt.

(2) The principles of subparagraph (1) may be illustrated by the following example: 35
Example. Taxpayer A purchased an annuity contract providing for payments of $100 per month for a consideration of $12,650. Assuming that the expected return under this contract is $16,000 the exclusion ratio to be used by A is $12,650/16,000; or 79.1 percent (79.06 rounded to the nearest tenth). If 12 such monthly payments are received by A during his taxable year, the total amount he may exclude from his gross income in   40 such year is $949.20 ($1,200x79.1 percent).The balance of $250.80 ($1,200 less $949.20) is the amount to be included in gross income. If A instead received only five such payments during the year, he should exclude $395.50 (500x79.1 percent) of the total amounts received.

For examples of the computation of the exclusion ratio in cases where two annuity   45 elements are acquired for a single consideration, see paragraph (b)(1) of § 1.72-6.

(3) The exclusion ratio shall be applied only to amounts received as an annuity within the meaning of that term under paragraph (b) (2) and (3) of § 1.72-2. Where the periodic payments increase in amount after the annuity starting date in a manner not provided by the terms of the contract at such date, the portion of such payments representing the   50

169

Sec. 72. Annuities; certain proceeds of endowment and life insurance contracts

increase is not an amount received as an annuity. For the treatment of amounts not received as an annuity, see section 72(e) and § 1.72-11. For special rules where paragraph (b)(3) of § 1.72-2 applies to amounts received, see paragraph (d)(3) of this section.

5   (4) After an exclusion ratio has been determined for a particular contract, it shall be applied to any amounts received as an annuity thereunder unless or until one of the following occurs:

    (i) The contract is assigned or transferred for a valuable consideration (see section 72(g) and paragraph (a) of § 1.72-10);

10   (ii) The contract matures or is surrendered, redeemed, or discharged in accordance with the provisions of paragraph (c) or (d) of § 1.72-11;

    (iii) The contract is exchanged (or is considered to have been exchanged) in a manner described in paragraph (e) of § 1.72-11.

***

15   (d) *Exceptions to the general rule.* (1) Where the provisions of section 72 would otherwise require an exclusion ratio to be determined, but the investment in the contract (determined under § 1.72-6) is an amount of zero or less, no exclusion ratio shall be determined and all amounts received under such a contract shall be includible in the gross income of the recipient for the purposes of section 72.

20   (2) Where the investment in the contract is equal to or greater than the total expected return under such contract found under § 1.72-5, the exclusion ratio shall be considered to be 100 percent and all amounts received as an annuity under such contract shall be excludable from the recipient's gross income. See, for example, paragraph (f)(1) of § 1.72-5. In the case of a contract to which § 1.72-6(d) (relating to contracts in which

25 amounts were invested both before July 1, 1986, and after June 30, 1986) applies, this paragraph (d)(2) is applied in the manner prescribed in § 1.72-6(d) and, in particular, § 1.72-6(d)(5)(ii).

    (3)(i) If a contract provides for payments to be made to a taxpayer in the manner described in paragraph (b)(3) of § 1.72-2, the investment in the contract shall be

30 considered to be equal to the expected return under such contract and the resulting exclusion ratio (100%) shall be applied to all amounts received as an annuity under such contract. For any taxable year, payments received under such a contract shall be considered to be amounts received as an annuity only to the extent that they do not exceed the portion of the investment in the contract which is properly allocable to that

35 year and hence excludable from gross income as a return of premiums or other consideration paid for the contract. The portion of the investment in the contract which is properly allocable to any taxable year shall be determined by dividing the investment in the contract (adjusted for any refund feature in the manner described in paragraph (d) of § 1.72-7) by the applicable multiple (whether for a term certain, life, or lives) which would

40 otherwise be used in determining the expected return for such a contract under § 1.72-5. The multiple shall be adjusted in accordance with the provisions of the table in paragraph (a)(2) of § 1.72-5, if any adjustment is necessary, before making the above computation. If payments are to be made more frequently than annually and the number of payments to be made in the taxable year in which the annuity begins are less than the number of

45 payments to be made each year thereafter, the amounts considered received as an annuity (as otherwise determined under this subdivision) shall not exceed, for such taxable year (including a short taxable year), an amount which bears the same ratio to the portion of the investment in the contract considered allocable to each taxable year as the number of payments to be made in the first year bears to the number of payments to

50 be made in each succeeding year. Thus, if payments are to be made monthly, only seven

170

payments will be made in the first taxable year, and the portion of the investment in the contract allocable to a full year of payments is $600, the amounts considered received as an annuity in the first taxable year cannot exceed $350 ($600x7/12). See subdivision (iii) of this subparagraph for an example illustrating the determination of the portion of the investment in the contract allocable to one taxable year of the taxpayer. 5

(ii) If subdivision (i) of this subparagraph applies to amounts received by a taxpayer and the total amount of payments he receives in a taxable year is less than the total amount excludable for such year under subdivision (i) of this subparagraph, the taxpayer may elect, in a succeeding taxable year in which he receives another payment, to redetermine the amounts to be received as an annuity during the current and succeeding 10 taxable years. This shall be computed in accordance with the provisions of subdivision (i) of this subparagraph except that:

(a) The difference between the portion of the investment in the contract allocable to a taxable year, as found in accordance with subdivision (i) of this subparagraph, and the total payments actually received in the taxable year prior to the election shall be divided 15 by the applicable life expectancy of the annuitant (or annuitants), found in accordance with the appropriate table in § 1.72-9 (and adjusted in accordance with paragraph (a)(2) of § 1.72-5), or by the remaining term of a term certain annuity, computed as of the first day of the first period for which an amount is received as an annuity in the taxable year of the election; and 20

(b) The amount determined under (a) of this subdivision shall be added to the portion of the investment in the contract allocable to each taxable year (as otherwise found). To the extent that the total periodic payments received under the contract in the taxable year of the election or any succeeding taxable year does not equal this total sum, such payments shall be excludable from the gross income of the recipient. To the extent such 25 payments exceed the sum so found, they shall be fully includible in the recipient's gross income. See subdivision (iii) of this subparagraph for an example illustrating the redetermination of amounts to be received as an annuity and subdivision (iv) of this subparagraph for the method of making the election provided by this subdivision.

30

Reg. § 1.72-6 Investment in the contract.

(a) *General rule.* (1) For the purpose of computing the ``investment in the contract'', it is first necessary to determine the ``aggregate amount of premiums or other consideration paid'' for such contract. See section 72(c)(1). This determination is made as of the later of the annuity starting date of the contract or the date on which an amount is 35 first received thereunder as an annuity. The amount so found is then reduced by the sum of the following amounts in order to find the investment in the contract:

(i) The total amount of any return of premiums or dividends received (including unpaid loans or dividends applied against the principal or interest on such loans) on or before the date on which the foregoing determination is made, and 40

(ii) The total of any other amounts received with respect to the contract on or before such date which were excludable from the gross income of the recipient under the income tax law applicable at the time of receipt.

Amounts to which subdivision (ii) of this subparagraph applies shall include, for example, amounts considered to be return of premiums or other consideration paid under section 45 22(b)(2) of the Internal Revenue Code of 1939 and amounts considered to be an employer-provided death benefit under section 22(b)(1)(B) of such Code. For rules relating to the extent to which an employee or his beneficiary may include employer contributions in the aggregate amount of premiums or other consideration paid, see § 1.72-8. If the aggregate amount of premiums or other consideration paid for the contract 50 includes amounts for which deductions were allowed under section 404 as contributions on behalf of a self-employed individual, such amounts shall not be included in the investment in the contract.

(2) For the purpose of subparagraph (1) of this paragraph, amounts received
5 subsequent to the receipt of an amount as an annuity or subsequent to the annuity starting date, whichever is the later, shall be disregarded. See, however, § 1.72-11.

(3) The application of this paragraph may be illustrated by the following examples:

Example (1). In 1950, B purchased an annuity contract for $10,000 which was to provide him with an annuity of $1,000 per year for life. He received $1,000 in each of the
10 years 1950, 1951, 1952, and 1953, prior to the annuity starting date (January 1, 1954). Under the Internal Revenue Code of 1939, $300 of each of these payments (3 percent of $10,000) was includible in his gross income, and the remaining $700 was excludable therefrom during each of the taxable years mentioned. In computing B's investment in the contract as of January 1, 1954, the total amount excludable from his gross income during
15 the years 1950 through 1953 ($2,800) must be subtracted from the consideration paid ($10,000). Accordingly, B's investment in the contract as of January 1, 1954, is $7,200 ($10,000 less $2,800).

Example (2). In 1945, C contracted for an annuity to be paid to him beginning December 31, 1960. In 1945 and in each successive year until 1960, he paid a premium
20 of $5,000. Assuming he receives no payments of any kind under the contract until the date on which he receives the first annual payment as an annuity (December 31, 1960), his investment in the contract as of the annuity starting date (December 31, 1959) will be $75,000 ($5,000 paid each year for the 15 years from 1945 to 1959, inclusive).

Example (3). Assume the same facts as in example (2), except that prior to the annuity
25 starting date C has already received from the insurer dividends of $1,000 each in 1949, 1954, and 1959, such dividends not being includible in his gross income in any of those years. C's investment in the contract, as of the annuity starting date, will then be $72,000 ($75,000-$3,000).

30 **Reg. § 1.72-7   Adjustment in investment where a contract contains a refund feature.**

(a) *Definition of a contract containing a refund feature.* A contract to which section 72 applies, contains a refund feature if:

(1) The total amount receivable as an annuity under such contract depends, in whole
35 or in part, on the continuing life of one or more persons,

(2) The contract provides for payments to be made to a beneficiary or the estate of an annuitant on or after the death of the annuitant if a specified amount or a stated number of payments has not been paid to the annuitant or annuitants prior to death, and

(3) Such payments are in the nature of a refund of the consideration paid. See
40 paragraph (c)(1) of § 1.72-11.

***

Reg. § 1.72-9 Tables.

The following tables are to be used in connection with computations under section 72
45 and the regulations thereunder.

***

Sec. 72. Annuities; certain proceeds of endowment and life insurance contracts

Table I--Ordinary Life Annuities--One Life--Expected Return Multiples

Ages		Multiples
Male	Female	
6	11	65.0
7	12	64.1
8	13	63.2
9	14	62.3
10	15	61.4
11	16	60.4
12	17	59.5
13	18	58.6
14	19	57.7
15	20	56.7
16	21	55.8
17	22	54.9
18	23	53.9
19	24	53.0
20	25	52.1
21	26	51.1
22	27	50.2
23	28	49.3
24	29	48.3
25	30	47.4
26	31	46.5
27	32	45.6
28	33	44.6
29	34	43.7
30	35	42.8
31	36	41.9
32	37	41.0
33	38	40.0
34	39	39.1
35	40	38.2
36	41	37.3
37	42	36.5
38	43	35.6
39	44	34.7
40	45	33.8
41	46	33.0
42	47	32.1
43	48	31.2
44	49	30.4
45	50	29.6
46	51	28.7
47	52	27.9
48	53	27.1
49	54	26.3
50	55	25.5
51	56	24.7
52	57	24.0
53	58	23.2
54	59	22.4
55	60	21.7
56	61	21.0
57	62	20.3
58	63	19.6
59	64	18.9
60	65	18.2
61	66	17.5
62	67	16.9
63	68	16.2
64	69	15.6
65	70	15.0
66	71	14.4
67	72	13.8
68	73	13.2
69	74	12.6
70	75	12.1
71	76	11.6
72	77	11.0
73	78	10.5
74	79	10.1
75	80	9.6
76	81	9.1
77	82	8.7
78	83	8.3
79	84	7.8
80	85	7.5
81	86	7.1
82	87	6.7

173

Sec. 72. Annuities; certain proceeds of endowment and life insurance contracts

83	88	6.3
84	89	6.0
85	90	5.7
86	91	5.4
87	92	5.1
88	93	4.8
89	94	4.5
90	95	4.2
91	96	4.0
92	97	3.7
93	98	3.5
94	99	3.3
95	100	3.1
96	101	2.9
97	102	2.7
98	103	2.5
99	104	2.3
100	105	2.1
101	106	1.9
102	107	1.7
103	108	1.5
104	109	1.3
105	110	1.2
106	111	1.0
107	112	.8
108	113	.7
109	114	.6
110	115	.5
111	116	0

Table V--Ordinary Life Annuities One Life--Expected Return Multiples

Age	Multiple
5	76.6
6	75.6
7	74.7
8	73.7
9	72.7
10	71.7
11	70.7
12	69.7
13	68.8
14	67.8
15	66.8
16	65.8
17	64.8
18	63.9
19	62.9
20	61.9
21	60.9
22	59.9
23	59.0
24	58.0
25	57.0
26	56.0
27	55.1
28	54.1
29	53.1
30	52.2
31	51.2
32	50.2
33	49.3
34	48.3
35	47.3
36	46.4
37	45.4
38	44.4
39	43.5
40	42.5
41	41.5
42	40.6
43	39.6
44	38.7
45	37.7
46	36.8
47	35.9
48	34.9
49	34.0
50	33.1
51	32.2
52	31.3

Sec. 72. Annuities; certain proceeds of endowment and life insurance contracts

Age	Value
53	30.4
54	29.5
55	28.6
56	27.7
57	26.8
58	25.9
59	25.0
60	24.2
61	23.3
62	22.5
63	21.6
64	20.8
65	20.0
66	19.2
67	18.4
68	17.6
69	16.8
70	16.0
71	15.3
72	14.6
73	13.9
74	13.2
75	12.5
76	11.9
77	11.2
78	10.6
79	10.0
80	9.5
81	8.9
82	8.4
83	7.9
84	7.4
85	6.9
86	6.5
87	6.1
88	5.7
89	5.3
90	5.0
91	4.7
92	4.4
93	4.1
94	3.9
95	3.7
96	3.4
97	3.2
98	3.0
99	2.8
100	2.7
101	2.5
102	2.3
103	2.1
104	1.9
105	1.8
106	1.6
107	1.4
108	1.3
109	1.1
110	1.0
111	.9
112	.8
113	.7
114	.6
115	.5

Table VI--Ordinary Joint Life and Last Survivor Annuities; Two Lives--Expected Return Multiples

Ages	5	6	7	8	9	10	11	12	13	14
5	83.8	83.3	82.8	82.4	82.0	81.6	81.2	80.9	80.6	80.3
6	83.3	82.8	82.3	81.8	81.4	81.0	80.6	80.3	79.9	79.6
7	82.8	82.3	81.8	81.3	80.9	80.4	80.0	79.6	79.3	78.9
8	82.4	81.8	81.3	80.8	80.3	79.9	79.4	79.0	78.6	78.3
9	82.0	81.4	80.9	80.3	79.8	79.3	78.9	78.4	78.0	77.6
10	81.6	81.0	80.4	79.9	79.3	78.8	78.3	77.9	77.4	77.0
11	81.2	80.6	80.0	79.4	78.9	78.3	77.8	77.3	76.9	76.4
12	80.9	80.3	79.6	79.0	78.4	77.9	77.3	76.8	76.3	75.9
13	80.6	79.9	79.3	78.6	78.0	77.4	76.9	76.3	75.8	75.3
14	80.3	79.6	78.9	78.3	77.6	77.0	76.4	75.9	75.3	74.8
15	80.0	79.3	78.6	77.9	77.3	76.6	76.0	75.4	74.9	74.3
16	79.8	79.0	78.3	77.6	76.9	76.3	75.6	75.0	74.4	73.9
17	79.5	78.8	78.0	77.3	76.6	75.9	75.3	74.6	74.0	73.4
18	79.3	78.5	77.8	77.0	76.3	75.6	74.9	74.3	73.6	73.0
19	79.1	78.3	77.5	76.8	76.0	75.3	74.6	73.9	73.3	72.6

Sec. 72. Annuities; certain proceeds of endowment and life insurance contracts

	Age									
	20	78.9	78.1	77.3	76.5	75.8	75.0	74.3	73.6	72.9	72.3
	21	78.7	77.9	77.1	76.3	75.5	74.8	74.0	73.3	72.6	71.9
	22	78.6	77.7	76.9	76.1	75.3	74.5	73.8	73.0	72.3	71.6
	23	78.4	77.6	76.7	75.9	75.1	74.3	73.5	72.8	72.0	71.3
5	24	78.3	77.4	76.6	75.7	74.9	74.1	73.3	72.6	71.8	71.1
	25	78.2	77.3	76.4	75.6	74.8	73.9	73.1	72.3	71.6	70.8
	26	78.0	77.2	76.3	75.4	74.6	73.8	72.9	72.1	71.3	70.6
	27	77.9	77.1	76.2	75.3	74.4	73.6	72.8	71.9	71.1	70.3
	28	77.8	76.9	76.1	75.2	74.3	73.4	72.6	71.8	70.9	70.1
10	29	77.7	76.8	76.0	75.1	74.2	73.3	72.5	71.6	70.8	70.0
	30	77.7	76.8	75.9	75.0	74.1	73.2	72.3	71.5	70.6	69.8
	31	77.6	76.7	75.8	74.9	74.0	73.1	72.2	71.3	70.5	69.6
	32	77.5	76.6	75.7	74.8	73.9	73.0	72.1	71.2	70.3	69.5
	33	77.5	76.5	75.6	74.7	73.8	72.9	72.0	71.1	70.2	69.3
15	34	77.4	76.5	75.5	74.6	73.7	72.8	71.9	71.0	70.1	69.2
	35	77.3	76.4	75.5	74.5	73.6	72.7	71.8	70.9	70.0	69.1
	36	77.3	76.3	75.4	74.5	73.5	72.6	71.7	70.8	69.9	69.0
	37	77.2	76.3	75.4	74.4	73.5	72.6	71.6	70.7	69.8	68.9
	38	77.2	76.2	75.3	74.4	73.4	72.5	71.6	70.6	69.7	68.8
20	39	77.2	76.2	75.3	74.3	73.4	72.4	71.5	70.6	69.6	68.7
	40	77.1	76.2	75.2	74.3	73.3	72.4	71.4	70.5	69.6	68.6
	41	77.1	76.1	75.2	74.2	73.3	72.3	71.4	70.4	69.5	68.6
	42	77.0	76.1	75.1	74.2	73.2	72.3	71.3	70.4	69.4	68.5
	43	77.0	76.1	75.1	74.1	73.2	72.2	71.3	70.3	69.4	68.5
25	44	77.0	76.0	75.1	74.1	73.1	72.2	71.2	70.3	69.3	68.4
	45	77.0	76.0	75.0	74.1	73.1	72.2	71.2	70.2	69.3	68.4
	46	76.9	76.0	75.0	74.0	73.1	72.1	71.2	70.2	69.3	68.3
	47	76.9	75.9	75.0	74.0	73.1	72.1	71.1	70.2	69.2	68.3
	48	76.9	75.9	75.0	74.0	73.0	72.1	71.1	70.1	69.2	68.2
30	49	76.9	75.9	74.9	74.0	73.0	72.0	71.1	70.1	69.1	68.2
	50	76.9	75.9	74.9	73.9	73.0	72.0	71.0	70.1	69.1	68.2
	51	76.8	75.9	74.9	73.9	73.0	72.0	71.0	70.1	69.1	68.1
	52	76.8	75.9	74.9	73.9	72.9	72.0	71.0	70.0	69.1	68.1
	53	76.8	75.8	74.9	73.9	72.9	71.9	71.0	70.0	69.0	68.1
35	54	76.8	75.8	74.8	73.9	72.9	71.9	71.0	70.0	69.0	68.1
	55	76.8	75.8	74.8	73.9	72.9	71.9	70.9	70.0	69.0	68.0
	56	76.8	75.8	74.8	73.8	72.9	71.9	70.9	69.9	69.0	68.0
	57	76.8	75.8	74.8	73.8	72.9	71.9	70.9	69.9	69.0	68.0
	58	76.8	75.8	74.8	73.8	72.8	71.9	70.9	69.9	68.9	68.0
40	59	76.7	75.8	74.8	73.8	72.8	71.9	70.9	69.9	68.9	68.0
	60	76.7	75.8	74.8	73.8	72.8	71.8	70.9	69.9	68.9	67.9
	61	76.7	75.7	74.8	73.8	72.8	71.8	70.9	69.9	68.9	67.9
	62	76.7	75.7	74.8	73.8	72.8	71.8	70.8	69.9	68.9	67.9
	63	76.7	75.7	74.8	73.8	72.8	71.8	70.8	69.9	68.9	67.9
45	64	76.7	75.7	74.7	73.8	72.8	71.8	70.8	69.8	68.9	67.9
	65	76.7	75.7	74.7	73.8	72.8	71.8	70.8	69.8	68.9	67.9
	66	76.7	75.7	74.7	73.7	72.8	71.8	70.8	69.8	68.9	67.9
	67	76.7	75.7	74.7	73.7	72.8	71.8	70.8	69.8	68.8	67.9
	68	76.7	75.7	74.7	73.7	72.8	71.8	70.8	69.8	68.8	67.9
50	69	76.7	75.7	74.7	73.7	72.7	71.8	70.8	69.8	68.8	67.8
	70	76.7	75.7	74.7	73.7	72.7	71.8	70.8	69.8	68.8	67.8
	71	76.7	75.7	74.7	73.7	72.7	71.8	70.8	69.8	68.8	67.8
	72	76.7	75.7	74.7	73.7	72.7	71.8	70.8	69.8	68.8	67.8
	73	76.7	75.7	74.7	73.7	72.7	71.7	70.8	69.8	68.8	67.8
55	74	76.7	75.7	74.7	73.7	72.7	71.7	70.8	69.8	68.8	67.8
	75	76.7	75.7	74.7	73.7	72.7	71.7	70.8	69.8	68.8	67.8
	76	76.6	75.7	74.7	73.7	72.7	71.7	70.8	69.8	68.8	67.8
	77	76.6	75.7	74.7	73.7	72.7	71.7	70.8	69.8	68.8	67.8
	78	76.6	75.7	74.7	73.7	72.7	71.7	70.7	69.8	68.8	67.8
60	79	76.6	75.7	74.7	73.7	72.7	71.7	70.7	69.8	68.8	67.8
	80	76.6	75.7	74.7	73.7	72.7	71.7	70.7	69.8	68.8	67.8
	81	76.6	75.7	74.7	73.7	72.7	71.7	70.7	69.8	68.8	67.8
	82	76.6	75.7	74.7	73.7	72.7	71.7	70.7	69.8	68.8	67.8
	83	76.6	75.7	74.7	73.7	72.7	71.7	70.7	69.8	68.8	67.8
65	84	76.6	75.7	74.7	73.7	72.7	71.7	70.7	69.8	68.8	67.8
	85	76.6	75.7	74.7	73.7	72.7	71.7	70.7	69.8	68.8	67.8
	86	76.6	75.7	74.7	73.7	72.7	71.7	70.7	69.8	68.8	67.8
	87	76.6	75.7	74.7	73.7	72.7	71.7	70.7	69.8	68.8	67.8
	88	76.6	75.7	74.7	73.7	72.7	71.7	70.7	69.8	68.8	67.8
70	89	76.6	75.7	74.7	73.7	72.7	71.7	70.7	69.7	68.8	67.8
	90	76.6	75.6	74.7	73.7	72.7	71.7	70.7	69.7	68.8	67.8
	91	76.6	75.6	74.7	73.7	72.7	71.7	70.7	69.7	68.8	67.8
	92	76.6	75.6	74.7	73.7	72.7	71.7	70.7	69.7	68.8	67.8
	93	76.6	75.6	74.7	73.7	72.7	71.7	70.7	69.7	68.8	67.8
75	94	76.6	75.6	74.7	73.7	72.7	71.7	70.7	69.7	68.8	67.8
	95	76.6	75.6	74.7	73.7	72.7	71.7	70.7	69.7	68.8	67.8
	96	76.6	75.6	74.7	73.7	72.7	71.7	70.7	69.7	68.8	67.8
	97	76.6	75.6	74.7	73.7	72.7	71.7	70.7	69.7	68.8	67.8
	98	76.6	75.6	74.7	73.7	72.7	71.7	70.7	69.7	68.8	67.8
80	99	76.6	75.6	74.7	73.7	72.7	71.7	70.7	69.7	68.8	67.8
	100	76.6	75.6	74.7	73.7	72.7	71.7	70.7	69.7	68.8	67.8
	101	76.6	75.6	74.7	73.7	72.7	71.7	70.7	69.7	68.8	67.8
	102	76.6	75.6	74.7	73.7	72.7	71.7	70.7	69.7	68.8	67.8
	103	76.6	75.6	74.7	73.7	72.7	71.7	70.7	69.7	68.8	67.8

Sec. 72. Annuities; certain proceeds of endowment and life insurance contracts

Age										
104	76.6	75.6	74.7	73.7	72.7	71.7	70.7	69.7	68.8	67.8
105	76.6	75.6	74.7	73.7	72.7	71.7	70.7	69.7	68.8	67.8
106	76.6	75.6	74.7	73.7	72.7	71.7	70.7	69.7	68.8	67.8
107	76.6	75.6	74.7	73.7	72.7	71.7	70.7	69.7	68.8	67.8
108	76.6	75.6	74.7	73.7	72.7	71.7	70.7	69.7	68.8	67.8
109	76.6	75.6	74.7	73.7	72.7	71.7	70.7	69.7	68.8	67.8
110	76.6	75.6	74.7	73.7	72.7	71.7	70.7	69.7	68.8	67.8
111	76.6	75.6	74.7	73.7	72.7	71.7	70.7	69.7	68.8	67.8
112	76.6	75.6	74.7	73.7	72.7	71.7	70.7	69.7	68.8	67.8
113	76.6	75.6	74.7	73.7	72.7	71.7	70.7	69.7	68.8	67.8
114	76.6	75.6	74.7	73.7	72.7	71.7	70.7	69.7	68.8	67.8
115	76.6	75.6	74.7	73.7	72.7	71.7	70.7	69.7	68.8	67.8

Table VI--Ordinary Joint Life and Last Survivor Annuities; Two Lives--Expected Return Multiples

Ages	15	16	17	18	19	20	21	22	23	24
15	73.8	73.3	72.9	72.4	72.0	71.6	71.3	70.9	70.6	70.3
16	73.3	72.8	72.3	71.9	71.4	71.0	70.7	70.3	70.0	69.6
17	72.9	72.3	71.8	71.3	70.9	70.5	70.0	69.7	69.3	69.0
18	72.4	71.9	71.3	70.8	70.4	69.0	69.5	69.9	68.7	68.3
19	72.0	71.4	70.9	70.4	69.8	69.4	68.9	68.5	68.1	67.7
20	71.6	71.0	70.5	69.9	69.4	68.8	68.4	67.9	67.5	67.1
21	71.3	70.7	70.0	69.5	68.9	68.4	67.9	67.4	66.9	66.5
22	70.9	70.3	69.7	69.0	68.5	67.9	67.4	66.9	66.4	65.9
23	70.6	70.0	69.3	68.7	68.1	67.5	66.9	66.4	65.9	65.4
24	70.3	69.6	69.0	68.3	67.7	67.1	66.5	65.9	65.4	64.9
25	70.1	69.3	68.6	68.0	67.3	66.7	66.1	65.5	64.9	64.4
26	69.8	69.1	68.3	67.6	67.0	66.3	65.7	65.1	64.5	63.9
27	69.6	68.8	68.1	67.3	66.7	66.0	65.3	64.7	64.1	63.5
28	69.3	68.6	67.8	67.1	66.4	65.7	65.0	64.3	63.7	63.1
29	69.1	68.4	67.6	66.8	66.1	65.4	64.7	64.0	63.3	62.7
30	69.0	68.2	67.4	66.6	65.8	65.1	64.4	63.7	63.0	62.3
31	68.8	68.0	67.2	66.4	65.6	64.8	64.1	63.4	62.7	62.0
32	68.6	67.8	67.0	66.2	65.4	64.6	63.8	63.1	62.4	61.7
33	68.5	67.6	66.8	66.0	65.2	64.4	63.6	62.8	62.1	61.4
34	68.3	67.5	66.6	65.8	65.0	64.2	63.4	62.6	61.9	61.1
35	68.2	67.4	66.5	65.6	64.8	64.0	63.2	62.4	61.6	60.9
36	68.1	67.2	66.4	65.5	64.7	63.8	63.0	62.2	61.4	60.6
37	68.0	67.1	66.2	65.4	64.5	63.7	62.8	62.0	61.2	60.4
38	67.9	67.0	66.1	65.2	64.4	63.5	62.7	61.8	61.0	60.2
39	67.8	66.9	66.0	65.1	64.2	63.4	62.5	61.7	60.8	60.0
40	67.7	66.8	65.9	65.0	64.1	63.3	62.4	61.5	60.7	59.9
41	67.7	66.7	65.8	64.9	64.0	63.1	62.3	61.4	60.5	59.7
42	67.6	66.7	65.7	64.8	63.9	63.0	62.2	61.3	60.4	59.6
43	67.5	66.6	65.7	64.8	63.8	62.9	62.1	61.2	60.3	59.4
44	67.5	66.5	65.6	64.7	63.8	62.9	62.0	61.1	60.2	59.3
45	67.4	66.5	65.5	64.6	63.7	62.8	61.9	61.0	60.1	59.2
46	67.4	66.4	65.4	64.6	63.6	62.7	61.8	60.9	60.0	59.1
47	67.3	66.4	65.4	64.5	63.6	62.6	61.7	60.8	59.9	59.0
48	67.3	66.3	65.4	64.4	63.5	62.6	61.6	60.7	59.8	58.9
49	67.2	66.3	65.3	64.4	63.5	62.5	61.6	60.7	59.7	58.8
50	67.2	66.2	65.3	64.3	63.4	62.5	61.5	60.6	59.7	58.8
51	67.2	66.2	65.3	64.3	63.4	62.4	61.5	60.5	59.6	58.7
52	67.1	66.2	65.2	64.3	63.3	62.4	61.4	60.5	59.6	58.6
53	67.1	66.2	65.2	64.2	63.3	62.3	61.4	60.4	59.5	58.6
54	67.1	66.1	65.2	64.2	63.2	62.3	61.3	60.4	59.5	58.5
55	67.1	66.1	65.1	64.2	63.2	62.3	61.3	60.4	59.4	58.5
56	67.0	66.1	65.1	64.1	63.2	62.2	61.3	60.3	59.4	58.4
57	67.0	66.1	65.1	64.1	63.2	62.2	61.2	60.3	59.3	58.4
58	67.0	66.0	65.1	64.1	63.1	62.2	61.2	60.3	59.3	58.4
59	67.0	66.0	65.0	64.1	63.1	62.1	61.2	60.2	59.3	58.3
60	67.0	66.0	65.0	64.1	63.1	62.1	61.2	60.2	59.2	58.3
61	67.0	66.0	65.0	64.0	63.1	62.1	61.1	60.2	59.2	58.3
62	66.9	66.0	65.0	64.0	63.1	62.1	61.1	60.2	59.2	58.2
63	66.9	66.0	65.0	64.0	63.0	62.1	61.1	60.1	59.2	58.2
64	66.9	65.9	65.0	64.0	63.0	62.1	61.1	60.1	59.2	58.2
65	66.9	65.9	65.0	64.0	63.0	62.0	61.1	60.1	59.1	58.2
66	66.9	65.9	64.9	64.0	63.0	62.0	61.1	60.1	59.1	58.2
67	66.9	65.9	64.9	64.0	63.0	62.0	61.1	60.1	59.1	58.1
68	66.9	65.9	64.9	64.0	63.0	62.0	61.0	60.1	59.1	58.1
69	66.9	65.9	64.9	63.9	63.0	62.0	61.0	60.0	59.1	58.1
70	66.9	65.9	64.9	63.9	63.0	62.0	61.0	60.0	59.1	58.1
71	66.9	65.9	64.9	63.9	62.9	62.0	61.0	60.0	59.1	58.1
72	66.9	65.9	64.9	63.9	62.9	62.0	61.0	60.0	59.0	58.1
73	66.8	65.9	64.9	63.9	62.9	62.0	61.0	60.0	59.0	58.1
74	66.8	65.9	64.9	63.9	62.9	62.0	61.0	60.0	59.0	58.1
75	66.8	65.9	64.9	63.9	62.9	61.9	61.0	60.0	59.0	58.1
76	66.8	65.9	64.9	63.9	62.9	61.9	61.0	60.0	59.0	58.0
76	66.8	65.9	64.9	63.9	62.9	61.9	61.0	60.0	59.0	58.0
77	66.8	65.9	64.9	63.9	63.9	62.9	61.0	60.0	59.0	58.0
78	66.8	65.8	64.9	63.9	62.9	61.9	61.0	60.0	59.0	58.0
79	66.8	65.8	64.9	63.9	62.9	61.9	61.0	60.0	59.0	58.0

177

Age										
80	66.8	65.9	64.9	63.9	62.9	61.9	60.9	60.0	59.0	58.0
81	66.8	65.8	64.9	63.9	62.9	61.9	60.9	60.0	59.0	58.0
82	66.8	65.8	64.9	63.9	62.9	61.9	60.9	60.0	59.0	58.0
83	66.8	65.8	64.9	63.9	62.9	61.9	60.9	60.0	59.0	58.0
84	66.8	65.8	64.8	63.9	62.9	61.9	60.9	60.0	59.0	58.0
85	66.8	65.8	64.8	63.9	62.9	61.9	60.9	60.0	59.0	58.0
86	66.8	65.8	64.8	63.9	62.9	61.9	60.9	60.0	59.0	58.0
87	66.8	65.8	64.8	63.9	62.9	61.9	60.9	60.0	59.0	58.0
88	66.8	65.8	64.8	63.9	62.9	61.9	60.9	60.0	59.0	58.0
89	66.8	65.8	64.8	63.9	62.9	61.9	60.9	60.0	59.0	58.0
90	66.8	65.8	64.8	63.9	62.9	61.9	60.9	60.0	59.0	58.0
91	66.8	65.8	64.8	63.9	62.9	61.9	60.9	60.0	59.0	58.0
92	66.8	65.8	64.8	63.9	62.9	61.9	60.9	59.9	59.0	58.0
93	66.8	65.8	64.8	63.9	62.9	61.9	60.9	59.9	59.0	58.0
94	66.8	65.8	64.8	63.9	62.9	61.9	60.9	59.9	59.0	58.0
95	66.8	65.8	64.8	63.9	62.9	61.9	60.9	59.9	59.0	58.0
96	66.8	65.8	64.8	63.9	62.9	61.9	60.9	59.9	59.0	58.0
97	66.8	65.8	64.8	63.9	62.9	61.9	60.9	59.9	59.0	58.0
98	66.8	65.8	64.8	63.9	62.9	61.9	60.9	59.9	59.0	58.0
99	66.8	65.8	64.8	63.9	62.9	61.9	60.9	59.9	59.0	58.0
100	66.8	65.8	64.8	63.9	62.9	61.9	60.9	59.9	59.0	58.0
101	66.8	65.8	64.8	63.9	62.9	61.9	60.9	59.9	59.0	58.0
102	66.8	65.8	64.8	63.9	62.9	61.9	60.9	59.9	59.0	58.0
103	66.8	65.8	64.8	63.9	62.9	61.9	60.9	59.9	59.0	58.0
104	66.8	65.8	64.8	63.9	62.9	61.9	60.9	59.9	59.0	58.0
105	66.8	65.8	64.8	63.9	62.9	61.9	60.9	59.9	59.0	58.0
106	66.8	65.8	64.8	63.9	62.9	61.9	60.9	59.9	59.0	58.0
107	66.8	65.8	64.8	63.9	62.9	61.9	60.9	59.9	59.0	58.0
108	66.8	65.8	64.8	63.9	62.9	61.9	60.9	59.9	59.0	58.0
109	66.8	65.8	64.8	63.9	62.9	61.9	60.9	59.9	59.0	58.0
110	66.8	65.8	64.8	63.9	62.9	61.9	60.9	59.9	59.0	58.0
111	66.8	65.8	64.8	63.9	62.9	61.9	60.9	59.9	59.0	58.0
112	66.8	65.8	64.8	63.9	62.9	61.9	60.9	59.9	59.0	58.0
113	66.8	65.8	64.8	63.9	62.9	61.9	60.9	59.9	59.0	58.0
114	66.8	65.8	64.8	63.9	62.9	61.9	60.9	59.9	59.0	58.0
115	66.8	65.8	64.8	63.9	62.9	61.9	60.9	59.9	59.0	58.0

Table VI--Ordinary Joint Life and Last Survivor Annuities; Two Lives--Expected Return Multiples

Ages	25	26	27	28	29	30	31	32	33	34
25	63.9	63.4	62.9	62.5	62.1	61.7	61.3	61.0	60.7	60.4
26	63.4	62.9	62.4	61.9	61.5	61.1	60.7	60.4	60.0	59.7
27	62.9	62.4	61.9	61.4	60.9	60.5	60.1	59.7	59.4	59.0
28	62.5	61.9	61.4	60.9	60.4	60.0	59.5	59.1	58.7	58.4
29	62.1	61.5	60.9	60.4	59.9	59.4	59.0	58.5	58.1	57.7
30	61.7	61.1	60.5	60.0	59.4	58.9	58.4	58.0	57.5	57.1
31	61.3	60.7	60.1	59.5	59.0	58.4	57.9	57.4	57.0	56.5
32	61.0	60.4	59.7	59.1	58.5	58.0	57.4	56.9	56.4	56.0
33	60.7	60.0	59.4	58.7	58.1	57.5	57.0	56.4	55.9	55.5
34	60.4	59.7	59.0	58.4	57.7	57.1	56.5	56.0	55.5	54.9
35	60.1	59.4	58.7	58.0	57.4	56.7	56.1	55.6	55.0	54.5
36	59.9	59.1	58.4	57.7	57.0	56.4	55.8	55.1	54.6	54.0
37	59.6	58.9	58.1	57.4	56.7	56.0	55.4	54.8	54.2	53.6
38	59.4	58.6	57.9	57.9	56.4	55.7	55.1	54.4	53.8	53.2
39	59.2	58.4	57.7	56.9	56.2	55.4	54.7	54.1	53.4	52.8
40	59.0	58.2	57.4	56.7	55.9	55.2	54.5	53.8	53.1	52.4
41	58.9	58.0	57.2	56.4	55.7	54.9	54.2	53.5	52.8	52.1
42	58.7	57.9	57.1	56.2	55.5	54.7	53.9	53.2	52.5	51.8
43	58.6	57.7	56.9	56.1	55.3	54.5	53.7	52.9	52.2	51.5
44	58.4	57.6	56.7	55.9	55.1	54.3	53.5	52.7	52.0	51.2
45	58.3	57.4	56.6	55.7	54.9	54.1	53.3	52.5	51.7	51.0
46	58.2	57.3	56.5	55.6	54.8	53.9	53.1	52.3	51.5	50.7
47	58.1	57.2	56.3	55.5	54.6	53.8	52.9	52.1	51.3	50.5
48	58.0	57.1	56.2	55.3	54.5	53.6	52.8	51.9	51.1	50.3
49	57.9	57.0	56.1	55.2	54.4	53.5	52.6	51.8	51.0	50.1
50	57.8	56.9	56.0	55.1	54.2	53.4	52.5	51.7	50.8	50.0
51	57.8	56.9	55.9	55.0	54.1	53.3	52.4	51.5	50.7	49.8
52	57.7	56.8	55.9	55.0	54.1	53.2	52.3	51.4	50.5	49.7
53	57.6	56.7	55.8	54.9	54.0	53.1	52.2	51.3	50.4	49.6
54	57.6	56.7	55.7	54.8	53.9	53.0	52.1	51.2	50.3	49.4
55	57.5	56.6	55.7	54.7	53.8	52.9	52.0	51.1	40.2	49.3
56	57.5	56.5	55.6	54.7	53.8	52.8	51.9	51.0	50.1	49.2
57	57.4	56.5	55.6	54.6	53.7	52.8	51.9	50.9	50.0	49.1
58	57.4	56.5	55.5	54.6	53.6	52.7	51.8	50.9	50.0	49.1
59	57.4	56.4	55.5	54.5	53.6	52.7	51.7	50.8	49.9	49.0
60	57.3	56.4	55.4	54.5	53.6	52.6	51.7	50.8	49.8	48.9
61	57.3	56.4	55.4	54.5	53.5	52.6	51.6	50.7	49.8	48.9
62	57.3	56.3	55.4	54.4	53.5	52.5	51.6	50.7	49.7	48.8
63	57.3	56.3	55.3	54.4	53.4	52.5	51.6	50.6	49.7	48.7
64	57.2	56.3	55.3	54.4	53.4	52.5	51.5	50.6	49.6	48.7
65	57.2	56.3	55.3	54.3	53.4	52.4	51.5	50.5	49.6	48.7
66	57.2	56.2	55.3	54.3	53.4	52.4	51.5	50.5	49.6	48.6

Sec. 72. Annuities; certain proceeds of endowment and life insurance contracts

67	57.2	56.2	55.3	54.3	53.3	52.4	51.4	50.5	49.5	48.6
68	57.2	56.2	55.2	54.3	53.3	52.4	51.4	50.4	49.5	48.6
69	57.1	56.2	55.2	54.3	53.3	52.3	51.4	50.4	49.5	48.5
70	57.1	56.2	55.2	54.2	53.3	52.3	51.4	50.4	49.4	48.5
71	57.1	56.2	55.2	54.2	53.3	52.3	51.3	50.4	49.4	48.5
72	57.1	56.1	55.2	54.2	53.2	52.3	51.3	50.4	49.4	48.5
73	57.1	56.1	55.2	54.2	53.2	52.3	51.3	50.3	49.4	48.4
74	57.1	56.1	55.2	54.2	53.2	52.3	51.3	50.3	49.4	48.4
75	57.1	56.1	55.1	54.2	53.2	52.2	51.3	50.3	49.4	48.4
76	57.1	56.1	55.1	54.2	53.2	52.2	51.3	50.3	49.3	48.4
77	57.1	56.1	55.1	54.2	53.2	52.2	51.3	50.3	49.3	48.4
78	57.1	56.1	55.1	54.2	53.2	52.2	51.3	50.3	49.3	48.4
79	57.1	56.1	55.1	54.1	53.2	52.2	51.2	50.3	49.3	48.4
80	57.1	56.1	55.1	54.1	53.2	52.2	51.2	50.3	49.3	48.3
81	57.0	56.1	55.1	54.1	53.2	52.2	51.2	50.3	49.3	48.3
82	57.0	56.1	55.1	54.1	53.2	52.2	51.2	50.3	49.3	48.3
83	57.0	56.1	55.1	54.1	53.2	52.2	51.2	50.3	49.3	48.3
84	57.0	56.1	55.1	54.1	53.2	52.2	51.2	50.3	49.3	48.3
85	57.0	56.1	55.1	54.1	53.2	52.2	51.2	50.2	49.3	48.3
86	57.0	56.1	55.1	54.1	53.1	52.2	51.2	50.2	49.3	48.3
87	57.0	56.1	55.1	54.1	53.1	52.2	51.2	50.2	49.3	48.3
88	57.0	56.1	55.1	54.1	53.1	52.2	51.2	50.2	49.3	48.3
89	57.0	56.1	55.1	54.1	53.1	52.2	51.2	50.2	49.3	48.3
90	57.0	56.1	55.1	54.1	53.1	52.2	51.2	50.2	49.3	48.3
91	57.0	56.1	55.1	54.1	53.1	52.2	51.2	50.2	49.3	48.3
92	57.0	56.1	55.1	54.1	53.1	52.2	51.2	50.2	49.3	48.3
93	57.0	56.1	55.1	54.1	53.1	52.2	51.2	50.2	49.3	48.3
94	57.0	56.0	55.1	54.1	53.1	52.2	51.2	50.2	49.3	48.3
95	57.0	56.0	55.1	54.1	53.1	52.2	51.2	50.2	49.3	48.3
96	57.0	56.0	55.1	54.1	53.1	52.2	51.2	50.2	49.3	48.3
97	57.0	56.0	55.1	54.1	53.1	52.2	51.2	50.2	49.3	48.3
98	57.0	56.0	55.1	54.1	53.1	52.2	51.2	50.2	49.3	48.3
99	57.0	56.0	55.1	54.1	53.1	52.2	51.2	50.2	49.3	48.3
100	57.0	56.0	55.1	54.1	53.1	52.2	51.2	50.2	49.3	48.3
101	57.0	56.0	55.1	54.1	53.1	52.2	51.2	50.2	49.3	48.3
102	57.0	56.0	55.1	54.1	53.1	52.2	51.2	50.2	49.3	48.3
103	57.0	56.0	55.1	54.1	53.1	52.2	51.2	50.2	49.3	48.3
104	57.0	56.0	55.1	54.1	53.1	52.2	51.2	50.2	49.3	48.3
105	57.0	56.0	55.1	54.1	53.1	52.2	51.2	50.2	49.3	48.3
106	57.0	56.0	55.1	54.1	53.1	52.2	51.2	50.2	49.3	48.3
107	57.0	56.0	55.1	54.1	53.1	52.2	51.2	50.2	49.3	48.3
108	57.0	56.0	55.1	54.1	53.1	52.2	51.2	50.2	49.3	48.3
109	57.0	56.0	55.1	54.1	53.1	52.2	51.2	50.2	49.3	48.3
110	57.0	56.0	55.1	54.1	53.1	52.2	51.2	50.2	49.3	48.3
111	57.0	56.0	55.1	54.1	53.1	52.2	51.2	50.2	49.3	48.3
112	57.0	56.0	55.1	54.1	53.1	52.2	51.2	50.2	49.3	48.3
113	57.0	56.0	55.1	54.1	53.1	52.2	51.2	50.2	49.3	48.3
114	57.0	56.0	55.1	54.1	53.1	52.2	51.2	50.2	49.3	48.3
115	57.0	56.0	55.1	54.1	53.1	52.2	51.2	50.2	49.3	48.3

Table VI--Ordinary Joint Life and Last Survivor Annuities; Two Lives--Expected Return Multiples

Ages	35	36	37	38	39	40	41	42	43	44
35	54.0	53.5	53.0	52.6	52.2	51.8	51.4	51.1	50.8	50.5
36	53.5	53.0	52.5	52.0	51.6	51.2	50.8	50.4	50.1	49.8
37	53.0	52.5	52.0	51.5	51.0	50.6	50.2	49.8	49.5	49.1
38	52.6	52.0	51.5	51.0	50.5	50.0	49.6	49.2	48.8	48.5
39	52.2	51.6	51.0	50.5	50.0	49.5	49.1	48.6	48.2	47.8
40	51.8	51.2	50.6	50.0	49.5	49.0	48.5	48.1	47.6	47.2
41	51.4	50.8	50.2	49.6	49.1	48.5	48.0	47.5	47.1	46.7
42	51.1	50.4	49.8	49.2	48.6	48.1	47.5	47.0	46.6	46.1
43	50.8	50.1	49.5	48.8	48.2	47.6	47.1	46.6	46.0	45.6
44	50.5	49.8	49.1	48.5	47.8	47.2	46.7	46.1	45.6	45.1
45	50.2	49.5	48.8	48.1	47.5	46.9	46.3	45.7	45.1	44.6
46	50.0	49.2	48.5	47.8	47.2	46.5	45.9	45.3	44.7	44.1
47	49.7	49.0	48.3	47.5	46.8	46.2	45.5	44.9	44.3	43.7
48	49.5	48.8	48.0	47.3	46.6	45.9	45.2	44.5	43.9	43.3
49	49.3	48.5	47.8	47.0	46.3	45.6	44.9	44.2	43.6	42.9
50	49.2	48.4	47.6	46.8	46.0	45.3	44.6	43.9	43.2	42.6
51	49.0	48.2	47.4	46.6	45.8	45.1	44.3	43.6	42.9	42.2
52	48.8	48.0	47.2	46.4	45.6	44.8	44.1	43.3	42.6	41.9
53	48.7	47.9	47.0	46.2	45.4	44.6	43.9	43.1	42.4	41.7
54	48.6	47.7	46.9	46.0	45.2	44.4	43.6	42.9	42.1	41.4
55	48.5	47.6	46.7	45.9	45.1	44.2	43.4	42.7	41.9	41.2
56	48.3	47.5	46.6	45.8	44.9	44.1	43.3	42.5	41.7	40.9
57	48.3	47.4	46.5	45.6	44.8	43.9	43.1	42.3	41.5	40.7
58	48.2	47.3	46.4	45.5	44.7	43.8	43.0	42.1	41.3	40.5
59	48.1	47.2	46.3	45.4	44.5	43.7	42.8	42.0	41.2	40.4
60	48.0	47.1	46.2	45.3	44.4	43.6	42.7	41.9	41.0	40.2
61	47.9	47.0	46.1	45.2	44.3	43.5	42.6	41.7	40.9	40.0
62	47.9	47.0	46.0	45.1	44.2	43.4	42.5	41.6	40.8	39.9
63	47.8	46.9	46.0	45.1	44.2	43.3	42.4	41.5	40.6	39.8

Age										
64	47.8	46.8	45.9	45.0	44.1	43.2	42.3	41.4	40.5	39.7
65	47.7	46.8	45.9	44.9	44.0	43.1	42.2	41.3	40.4	39.6
66	47.7	46.7	45.8	44.9	44.0	43.1	42.2	41.3	40.4	39.5
67	47.6	46.7	45.8	44.8	43.9	43.0	42.1	41.2	40.3	39.4
68	47.6	46.7	45.7	44.8	43.9	42.9	42.0	41.1	40.2	39.3
69	47.6	46.6	45.7	44.8	43.8	42.9	42.0	41.1	40.2	39.3
70	47.5	46.6	45.7	44.7	43.8	42.9	41.9	41.0	40.1	39.2
71	47.5	46.6	45.6	44.7	43.8	42.8	41.9	41.0	40.1	39.1
72	47.5	46.6	45.6	44.7	43.7	42.8	41.9	40.9	40.0	39.1
73	47.5	46.5	45.6	44.6	43.7	42.8	41.8	40.9	40.0	39.0
74	47.5	46.5	45.6	44.6	43.7	42.7	41.8	40.9	39.9	39.0
75	47.4	46.5	45.5	44.6	43.6	42.7	41.7	40.8	39.9	39.0
76	47.4	46.5	45.5	44.6	43.6	42.7	41.7	40.8	39.9	38.9
77	47.4	46.5	45.5	44.6	43.6	42.7	41.7	40.8	39.8	38.9
78	47.4	46.4	45.5	44.5	43.6	42.6	41.7	40.7	39.8	38.9
79	47.4	46.4	45.5	44.5	43.6	42.6	41.7	40.7	39.8	38.9
80	47.4	46.4	45.5	44.5	43.6	42.6	41.7	40.7	39.8	38.8
81	47.4	46.4	45.5	44.5	43.5	42.6	41.6	40.7	39.8	38.8
82	47.4	46.4	45.4	44.5	43.5	42.6	41.6	40.7	39.7	38.8
83	47.4	46.4	45.4	44.5	43.5	42.6	41.6	40.7	39.7	38.8
84	47.4	46.4	45.4	44.5	43.5	42.6	41.6	40.7	39.7	38.8
85	47.4	46.4	45.4	44.5	43.5	42.6	41.6	40.7	39.7	38.8
86	47.3	46.4	45.4	44.5	43.5	42.5	41.6	40.6	39.7	38.8
87	47.3	46.4	45.4	44.5	43.5	42.5	41.6	40.6	39.7	38.7
88	47.3	46.4	45.4	44.5	43.5	42.5	41.6	40.6	39.7	38.7
89	47.3	46.4	45.4	44.4	43.5	42.5	41.6	40.6	39.7	38.7
90	47.3	46.4	45.4	44.4	43.5	42.5	41.6	40.6	39.7	38.7
91	47.3	46.4	45.4	44.4	43.5	42.5	41.6	40.6	39.7	39.7
92	47.3	46.4	45.4	44.4	44.4	43.5	42.5	41.6	40.6	38.7
93	47.3	46.4	45.4	43.5	42.5	42.5	41.6	40.6	39.7	39.7	38.7
94	47.3	46.4	45.4	44.4	43.5	42.5	41.6	40.6	39.7	38.7
95	47.3	46.4	45.4	44.4	43.5	42.5	41.6	40.6	39.7	38.7
96	47.3	46.4	45.4	44.4	43.5	42.5	41.6	40.6	39.7	38.7
97	47.3	46.4	45.4	44.4	43.5	42.5	41.6	40.6	39.6	38.7
98	47.3	46.4	45.4	44.4	43.5	42.5	41.6	40.6	39.6	38.7
99	47.3	46.4	45.4	44.4	43.5	42.5	41.5	40.6	39.6	38.7
100	47.3	46.4	45.4	44.4	43.5	42.5	41.5	40.6	39.6	38.7
101	47.3	46.4	45.4	44.4	43.5	42.5	41.5	40.6	39.6	38.7
102	47.3	46.4	45.4	44.4	43.5	42.5	41.5	40.6	39.6	38.7
103	47.3	46.4	45.4	44.4	43.5	42.5	41.5	40.6	39.6	38.7
104	47.3	46.4	45.4	44.4	43.5	42.5	41.5	40.6	39.6	38.7
105	47.3	46.4	45.4	44.4	43.5	42.5	41.5	40.6	39.6	38.7
106	47.3	46.4	45.4	44.4	43.5	42.5	41.5	40.6	39.6	38.7
107	47.3	46.4	45.4	44.4	43.5	42.5	41.5	40.6	39.6	38.7
108	47.3	46.4	45.4	44.4	43.5	42.5	41.5	40.6	39.6	38.7
109	47.3	46.4	45.4	44.4	43.5	42.5	41.5	40.6	39.6	38.7
110	47.3	46.4	45.4	44.4	43.5	42.5	41.5	40.6	39.6	38.7
111	47.3	46.4	45.4	44.4	43.5	42.5	41.5	40.6	39.6	38.7
112	47.3	46.4	45.4	44.4	43.5	42.5	41.5	40.6	39.6	38.7
113	47.3	46.4	45.4	44.4	43.5	42.5	41.5	40.6	39.6	38.7
114	47.3	46.4	45.4	44.4	43.5	42.5	41.5	40.6	39.6	38.7
114	47.3	46.4	45.4	44.4	43.5	42.5	41.5	40.6	39.6	38.7
115	47.3	46.4	45.4	44.4	43.5	42.5	41.5	40.6	39.6	38.7

Table VI--Ordinary Joint Life and Last Survivor Annuities; Two Lives--Expected Return Multiples

Ages	45	46	47	48	49	50	51	52	53	54
45	44.1	43.6	43.2	42.7	42.3	42.0	41.6	41.3	41.0	40.7
46	43.6	43.1	42.6	42.2	41.8	41.4	41.0	40.6	40.3	40.0
47	43.2	42.6	42.1	41.7	41.2	40.8	40.4	40.0	39.7	39.3
48	42.7	42.2	41.7	41.2	40.7	40.2	39.8	39.4	39.0	38.7
49	42.3	41.8	41.2	40.7	40.2	39.7	39.3	38.8	38.4	38.1
50	42.0	41.4	40.8	40.2	39.7	39.2	38.7	38.3	37.9	37.5
51	41.6	41.0	40.4	39.8	39.3	38.7	38.2	37.8	37.3	36.9
52	41.3	40.6	40.0	39.4	38.8	38.3	37.8	37.3	36.8	36.4
53	41.0	40.3	39.7	39.0	38.4	37.9	37.3	36.8	36.3	35.8
54	40.7	40.0	39.3	38.7	38.1	37.5	36.9	36.4	35.8	35.3
55	40.4	39.7	39.0	38.4	37.7	37.1	36.5	35.9	35.4	34.9
56	40.2	39.5	38.7	38.1	37.4	36.8	36.1	35.6	35.0	34.4
57	40.0	39.2	38.5	37.8	37.1	36.4	35.8	35.2	34.6	34.0
58	39.7	39.0	38.2	37.5	36.8	36.1	35.5	34.8	34.2	33.6
59	39.6	38.8	38.0	37.3	36.6	35.9	35.2	34.5	33.9	33.3
60	39.4	38.6	37.8	37.1	36.3	35.6	34.9	34.2	33.6	32.9
61	39.2	38.4	37.6	36.9	36.1	35.4	34.6	33.9	33.3	32.6
62	39.1	38.3	37.5	36.7	35.9	35.1	34.4	33.7	33.0	32.3
63	38.9	38.1	37.3	36.5	35.7	34.9	34.2	33.5	32.7	32.0
64	38.8	38.0	37.2	36.3	35.5	34.8	34.0	33.2	32.5	31.8
65	38.7	37.9	37.0	36.2	35.4	34.6	33.8	33.0	32.3	31.6
66	38.6	37.8	36.9	36.1	35.2	34.4	33.6	32.9	32.1	31.4
67	38.5	37.7	36.8	36.0	35.1	34.3	33.5	32.7	31.9	31.2
68	38.4	37.6	36.7	35.8	35.0	34.2	33.4	32.5	31.8	31.0
69	38.4	37.5	36.6	35.7	34.9	34.1	33.2	32.4	31.6	30.8

70	38.3	37.4	36.5	35.7	34.8	34.0	33.1	32.3	31.5	30.7
71	38.2	37.3	36.5	35.6	34.7	33.9	33.0	32.2	31.4	30.5
72	38.2	37.3	36.4	35.5	34.6	33.8	32.9	32.1	31.2	30.4
73	38.1	37.2	36.3	35.4	34.6	33.7	32.8	32.0	31.1	30.3
74	38.1	37.2	36.3	35.4	34.5	33.6	32.8	31.9	31.1	30.2
75	38.1	37.1	36.2	35.3	34.5	33.6	32.7	31.8	31.0	30.1
76	38.0	37.1	36.2	35.3	34.4	33.5	32.6	31.8	30.9	30.1
77	38.0	37.1	36.2	35.3	34.4	33.5	32.6	31.7	30.8	30.0
78	38.0	37.0	36.1	35.2	34.3	33.4	32.5	31.7	30.8	29.9
79	37.9	37.0	36.1	35.2	34.3	33.4	32.5	31.6	30.7	29.9
80	37.9	37.0	36.1	35.2	34.2	33.4	32.5	31.6	30.7	29.8
81	37.9	37.0	36.0	35.1	34.2	33.3	32.4	31.5	30.7	29.8
82	37.9	36.9	36.0	35.1	34.2	33.3	32.4	31.5	30.6	29.7
83	37.9	36.9	36.0	35.1	34.2	33.3	32.4	31.5	30.6	29.7
84	37.8	36.9	36.9	35.0	34.2	33.2	32.3	31.4	30.6	29.7
85	37.8	36.9	36.0	35.1	34.1	33.2	32.3	31.4	30.5	29.6
86	38.8	36.9	36.0	35.0	34.1	33.2	32.3	31.4	30.5	29.6
87	37.8	36.9	35.9	35.0	34.1	33.2	32.3	31.4	30.5	29.6
88	37.8	36.9	35.9	35.0	34.1	33.2	32.3	31.4	30.5	29.6
89	37.8	36.9	35.9	35.0	34.1	33.2	32.3	31.4	30.5	29.6
90	37.8	36.9	35.9	35.0	34.1	33.2	32.3	31.3	30.5	29.6
91	37.8	36.8	35.9	35.0	34.1	33.2	32.2	31.3	30.4	29.5
92	37.8	36.8	35.9	35.0	34.1	33.2	32.2	31.3	30.4	29.5
93	37.8	36.8	35.9	35.0	34.1	33.1	32.2	31.3	30.4	29.5
94	37.8	36.8	35.9	35.0	34.1	33.1	32.2	31.3	30.4	29.5
95	37.8	36.8	35.9	35.0	34.0	33.1	32.2	31.3	30.4	29.5
96	37.8	36.8	35.9	35.0	34.0	33.1	32.2	31.3	30.4	29.5
97	37.8	36.8	35.9	35.0	34.0	33.1	32.2	31.3	30.4	29.5
98	37.8	36.8	35.9	35.0	34.0	33.1	32.2	31.3	30.4	29.5
99	37.8	36.8	35.9	35.0	34.0	33.1	32.2	31.3	30.4	29.5
101	37.8	36.8	35.9	35.0	34.0	33.1	32.2	31.3	30.4	29.5
102	37.8	36.8	35.9	35.0	34.0	33.1	32.2	31.3	30.4	29.5
103	37.7	36.8	35.9	34.9	34.0	33.1	32.2	31.3	30.4	29.5
104	37.7	36.8	35.9	34.9	34.0	33.1	32.2	31.3	30.4	29.5
105	37.7	36.8	35.9	34.9	34.0	33.1	32.2	31.3	30.4	29.5
106	37.7	36.8	35.9	34.9	34.0	33.1	32.2	31.3	30.4	29.5
107	37.7	36.8	35.9	34.9	34.0	33.1	32.2	31.3	30.4	29.5
108	37.7	36.8	35.9	34.9	34.0	33.1	32.2	31.3	30.4	29.5
109	37.7	36.8	35.9	34.9	34.0	33.1	32.2	31.3	30.4	29.5
110	37.7	36.8	35.9	34.9	34.0	33.1	32.2	31.3	30.4	29.5
111	37.7	36.8	35.9	34.9	34.0	33.1	32.2	31.3	30.4	29.5
112	37.7	36.8	35.9	34.9	34.0	33.1	32.2	31.3	30.4	29.5
113	37.7	36.8	35.9	34.9	34.0	33.1	32.2	31.3	30.4	29.5
114	37.7	36.8	35.9	34.9	34.0	33.1	32.2	31.3	30.4	29.5
115	37.7	36.8	35.9	34.9	34.0	33.1	32.2	31.3	30.4	29.5

Table VI--Ordinary Joint Life and Last Survivor Annuities; Two Lives--Expected Return Multiples

Ages	55	56	57	58	59	60	61	62	63	64
55	34.4	33.9	33.5	33.1	32.7	32.3	32.0	31.7	31.4	31.1
56	33.9	33.4	33.0	32.5	32.1	31.7	31.4	31.0	30.7	30.4
57	33.5	33.0	32.5	32.0	31.6	31.2	30.8	30.4	30.1	29.8
58	33.1	32.5	32.0	31.5	31.1	30.6	30.2	29.9	29.5	29.2
59	32.7	32.1	31.6	31.1	30.6	30.1	29.7	29.3	28.9	28.6
60	32.3	31.7	31.2	30.6	30.1	29.7	29.2	28.8	28.4	28.0
61	32.0	31.4	30.8	30.2	29.7	29.2	28.7	28.3	27.8	27.4
62	31.7	31.0	30.4	29.9	29.3	28.8	28.3	27.8	27.3	26.9
63	31.4	30.7	30.1	29.5	28.9	28.4	27.8	27.3	26.9	26.4
64	31.1	30.4	29.8	29.2	28.6	28.0	27.4	26.9	26.4	25.9
65	30.9	30.2	29.5	28.9	28.2	27.6	27.1	26.5	26.0	25.5
66	30.6	29.9	29.2	28.6	27.9	27.3	26.7	26.1	25.6	25.1
67	30.4	29.7	29.0	28.3	27.6	27.0	26.4	25.8	25.2	24.7
68	30.2	29.5	28.8	28.1	27.4	26.7	26.1	25.5	24.9	24.3
69	30.1	29.3	28.6	27.8	27.1	26.5	25.8	25.2	24.6	24.0
70	29.9	29.1	28.4	27.6	26.9	26.2	25.6	24.9	24.3	23.7
71	29.7	29.0	28.2	27.5	26.7	26.0	25.3	24.7	24.0	23.4
72	29.6	28.8	28.1	27.3	26.5	25.8	25.1	24.4	23.8	23.1
73	29.5	28.7	27.9	27.1	26.4	25.6	24.9	24.2	23.5	22.9
74	29.4	28.6	27.8	27.0	26.2	25.5	24.7	24.0	23.3	22.7
75	29.3	28.5	27.7	26.9	26.1	25.3	24.6	23.8	23.1	22.4
76	29.2	28.4	27.6	26.8	26.0	25.2	24.4	23.7	23.0	22.3
77	29.1	28.3	27.5	26.7	25.9	25.1	24.3	23.5	22.8	22.1
78	29.1	28.2	27.4	26.6	25.8	25.0	24.2	23.4	22.7	21.9
79	29.0	28.2	27.3	26.5	25.7	24.9	24.1	23.3	22.6	21.8
80	29.0	28.1	27.3	26.4	25.6	24.8	24.0	23.2	22.4	21.7
81	28.9	28.1	27.2	26.4	25.5	24.7	23.9	23.1	22.3	21.6
82	28.9	28.0	27.2	26.3	25.5	24.6	23.8	23.0	22.3	21.5
83	28.8	28.0	27.1	26.3	25.4	24.6	23.8	23.0	22.2	21.4
84	28.8	27.9	27.1	26.2	25.4	24.5	23.7	22.9	22.1	21.3
85	28.8	27.9	27.0	26.2	25.3	24.5	23.7	22.8	22.0	21.3
86	28.7	27.9	27.0	26.1	25.3	24.5	23.6	22.8	22.0	21.2
87	28.7	27.8	27.0	26.1	25.3	24.4	23.6	22.8	21.9	21.1

Age										
88	28.7	27.8	27.0	26.1	25.2	24.4	23.5	22.7	21.9	21.1
89	28.7	27.8	26.9	26.1	25.2	24.4	23.5	22.7	21.9	21.1
90	28.7	27.8	26.9	26.1	25.2	24.3	23.5	22.7	21.8	21.0
91	28.7	27.8	26.9	26.0	25.2	24.3	23.5	22.6	21.8	21.0
92	28.6	27.8	26.9	26.0	25.2	24.3	23.5	22.6	21.8	21.0
93	28.6	27.8	26.9	26.0	25.1	24.3	23.4	22.6	21.8	20.9
94	28.6	27.7	26.9	26.0	25.1	24.3	23.4	22.6	21.7	20.9
95	28.6	27.7	26.9	26.0	25.1	24.3	23.4	22.6	21.7	20.9
96	28.6	27.7	26.9	26.0	25.1	24.2	23.4	22.6	21.7	20.9
97	28.6	27.7	26.8	26.0	25.1	24.2	23.4	22.5	21.7	20.9
98	28.6	27.7	26.8	26.0	25.1	24.2	23.4	22.5	21.7	20.9
99	28.6	27.7	26.8	26.0	25.1	24.2	23.4	22.5	21.7	20.9
100	28.6	27.7	26.8	26.0	25.1	24.2	23.4	22.5	21.7	20.8
101	28.6	27.7	26.8	25.9	25.1	24.2	23.4	22.5	21.7	20.8
102	28.6	27.7	26.8	25.9	25.1	24.2	23.3	22.5	21.7	20.8
103	28.6	27.7	26.8	25.9	25.1	24.2	23.3	22.5	21.7	20.8
104	28.6	27.7	26.8	25.9	25.1	24.2	23.3	22.5	21.6	20.8
105	28.6	27.7	26.8	25.9	25.1	24.2	23.3	22.5	21.6	20.8
106	28.6	27.7	26.8	25.9	25.1	24.2	23.3	22.5	21.6	20.8
107	28.6	27.7	26.8	25.9	25.1	24.2	23.3	22.5	21.6	20.8
108	28.6	27.7	26.8	25.9	25.1	24.2	23.3	22.5	21.6	20.8
109	28.6	27.7	26.8	25.9	25.1	24.2	23.3	22.5	21.6	20.8
110	28.6	27.7	26.8	25.9	25.1	24.2	23.3	22.5	21.6	20.8
111	28.6	27.7	26.8	25.9	25.0	24.2	23.3	22.5	21.6	20.8
112	28.6	27.7	26.8	25.9	25.0	24.2	23.3	22.5	21.6	20.8
113	28.6	27.7	26.8	25.9	25.0	24.2	23.3	22.5	21.6	20.8
114	28.6	27.7	26.8	25.9	25.0	24.2	23.3	22.5	21.6	20.8
115	28.6	27.7	26.8	25.9	25.0	24.2	23.3	22.5	21.6	20.8

Table VI--Ordinary Joint Life and Last Survivor Annuities; Two Lives--Expected Return Multiples

Ages	65	66	67	68	69	70	71	72	73	74
65	25.0	24.6	24.2	23.8	23.4	23.1	22.8	22.5	22.2	22.0
66	24.6	24.1	23.7	23.3	22.9	22.5	22.2	21.9	21.6	21.4
67	24.2	23.7	23.2	22.8	22.4	22.0	21.7	21.3	21.0	20.8
68	23.8	23.3	22.8	22.3	21.9	21.5	21.2	20.8	20.5	20.2
69	23.4	22.9	22.4	21.9	21.5	21.1	20.7	20.3	20.0	19.6
70	23.1	22.5	22.0	21.5	21.1	20.6	20.2	19.8	19.4	19.1
71	22.8	22.2	21.7	21.2	20.7	20.2	19.8	19.4	19.0	18.6
72	22.5	21.9	21.3	20.8	20.3	19.8	19.4	18.9	18.5	18.2
73	22.2	21.6	21.0	20.5	20.0	19.4	19.0	18.5	18.1	17.7
74	22.0	21.4	20.8	20.2	19.6	19.1	18.6	18.2	17.7	17.3
75	21.8	21.1	20.5	19.9	19.3	18.8	18.3	17.8	17.3	16.9
76	21.6	20.9	20.3	19.7	19.1	18.5	18.0	17.5	17.0	16.5
77	21.4	20.7	20.1	19.4	18.8	18.3	17.7	17.2	16.7	16.2
78	21.2	20.5	19.9	19.2	18.6	18.0	17.5	16.9	16.4	15.9
79	21.1	20.4	19.7	19.0	18.4	17.8	17.2	16.7	16.1	15.6
80	21.0	20.2	19.5	18.9	18.2	17.6	17.0	16.4	15.9	15.4
81	20.8	20.1	19.4	18.7	18.1	17.4	16.8	16.2	15.7	15.1
82	20.7	20.0	19.3	18.6	17.9	17.3	16.6	16.0	15.5	14.9
83	20.6	19.9	19.2	18.5	17.8	17.1	16.5	15.9	15.3	14.7
84	20.5	19.8	19.1	18.4	17.7	17.0	16.3	15.7	15.1	14.5
85	20.5	19.7	19.0	18.3	17.6	16.9	16.2	15.6	15.0	14.4
86	20.4	19.6	18.9	18.2	17.5	16.8	16.1	15.5	14.8	14.2
87	20.4	19.6	18.8	18.1	17.4	16.7	16.0	15.4	14.7	14.1
88	20.3	19.5	18.8	18.0	17.3	16.6	15.9	15.3	14.6	14.0
89	20.3	19.5	18.7	18.0	17.2	16.5	15.8	15.2	14.5	13.9
90	20.2	19.4	18.7	17.9	17.2	16.5	15.8	15.1	14.5	13.8
91	20.2	19.4	18.6	17.9	17.1	16.4	15.7	15.0	14.4	13.7
92	20.2	19.4	18.6	17.8	17.1	16.4	15.7	15.0	14.3	13.7
93	20.1	19.3	18.6	17.8	17.1	16.3	15.6	14.9	14.3	13.6
94	20.1	19.3	18.5	17.8	17.0	16.3	15.6	14.9	14.2	13.6
95	20.1	19.3	18.5	17.8	17.0	16.3	15.6	14.9	14.2	13.5
96	20.1	19.3	18.5	17.7	17.0	16.2	15.5	14.8	14.2	13.5
97	20.1	19.3	18.5	17.7	17.0	16.2	15.5	14.8	14.1	13.5
98	20.1	19.3	18.5	17.7	16.9	16.2	15.5	14.8	14.1	13.4
99	20.0	19.2	18.5	17.7	16.9	16.2	15.5	14.7	14.1	13.4
100	20.0	19.2	18.4	17.7	16.9	16.2	15.4	14.7	14.0	13.4
101	20.0	19.2	18.4	17.7	16.9	16.1	15.4	14.7	14.0	13.3
102	20.0	19.2	18.4	17.6	16.9	16.1	15.4	14.7	14.0	13.3
103	20.0	19.2	18.4	17.6	16.9	16.1	15.4	14.7	14.0	13.3
104	20.0	19.2	18.4	17.6	16.9	16.1	15.4	14.7	14.0	13.3
105	20.0	19.2	18.4	17.6	16.8	16.1	15.4	14.6	13.9	13.3
106	20.0	19.2	18.4	17.6	16.8	16.1	15.3	14.6	13.9	13.3
107	20.0	19.2	18.4	17.6	16.8	16.1	15.3	14.6	13.9	13.2
108	20.0	19.2	18.4	17.6	16.8	16.1	15.3	14.6	13.9	13.2
109	20.0	19.2	18.4	17.6	16.8	16.1	15.3	14.6	13.9	13.2
110	20.0	19.2	18.4	17.6	16.8	16.1	15.3	14.6	13.9	13.2
111	20.0	19.2	18.4	17.6	16.8	16.0	15.3	14.6	13.9	13.2
112	20.0	19.2	18.4	17.6	16.8	16.0	15.3	14.6	13.9	13.2
113	20.0	19.2	18.4	17.6	16.8	16.0	15.3	14.6	13.9	13.2
114	20.0	19.2	18.4	17.6	16.8	16.0	15.3	14.6	13.9	13.2
115	20.0	19.2	18.4	17.6	16.8	16.0	15.3	14.6	13.9	13.2

Table VI--Ordinary Joint Life and Last Survivor Annuities; Two Lives--Expected Return Multiples

Ages	75	76	77	78	79	80	81	82	83	84
75	16.5	16.1	15.8	15.4	15.1	14.9	14.6	14.4	14.2	14.0
76	16.1	15.7	15.4	15.0	14.7	14.4	14.1	13.9	13.7	13.5
77	15.8	15.4	15.0	14.6	14.3	14.0	13.7	13.4	13.2	13.0
78	15.4	15.0	14.6	14.2	13.9	13.5	13.2	13.0	12.7	12.5
79	15.1	14.7	14.3	13.9	13.5	13.2	12.8	12.5	12.3	12.0
80	14.9	14.4	14.0	13.5	13.2	12.8	12.5	12.2	11.9	11.6
81	14.6	14.1	13.7	13.2	12.8	12.5	12.1	11.8	11.5	11.2
82	14.4	13.9	13.4	13.0	12.5	12.2	11.8	11.5	11.1	10.9
83	14.2	13.7	13.2	12.7	12.3	11.9	11.5	11.1	10.8	10.5
84	14.0	13.5	13.0	12.5	12.0	11.6	11.2	10.9	10.5	10.2
85	13.8	13.3	12.8	12.3	11.8	11.4	11.0	10.6	10.2	9.9
86	13.7	13.1	12.6	12.1	11.6	11.2	10.8	10.4	10.0	9.7
87	13.5	13.0	12.4	11.9	11.4	11.0	10.6	10.1	9.8	9.4
88	13.4	12.8	12.3	11.8	11.3	10.8	10.4	10.0	9.6	9.2
89	13.3	12.7	12.2	11.6	11.1	10.7	10.2	9.8	9.4	9.0
90	13.2	12.6	12.1	11.5	11.0	10.5	10.1	9.6	9.2	8.8
91	13.1	12.5	12.0	11.4	10.9	10.4	9.9	9.5	9.1	8.7
92	13.1	12.5	11.9	11.3	10.8	10.3	9.8	9.4	8.9	8.5
93	13.0	12.4	11.8	11.3	10.7	10.2	9.7	9.3	8.8	8.4
94	12.9	12.3	11.7	11.2	10.6	10.1	9.6	9.2	8.7	8.3
95	12.9	12.3	11.7	11.1	10.6	10.1	9.6	9.1	8.6	8.2
96	12.9	12.2	11.6	11.1	10.5	10.0	9.5	9.0	8.5	8.1
97	12.8	12.2	11.6	11.0	10.5	9.9	9.4	8.9	8.5	8.0
98	12.8	12.2	11.5	11.0	10.4	9.9	9.4	8.9	8.4	8.0
99	12.7	12.1	11.5	10.9	10.4	9.8	9.3	8.8	8.3	7.9
100	12.7	12.1	11.5	10.9	10.3	9.8	9.2	8.7	8.3	7.8
101	12.7	12.1	11.4	10.8	10.3	9.7	9.2	8.7	8.2	7.8
102	12.7	12.0	11.4	10.8	10.2	9.7	9.2	8.7	8.2	7.7
103	12.6	12.0	11.4	10.8	10.2	9.7	9.1	8.6	8.1	7.7
104	12.6	12.0	11.4	10.8	10.2	9.6	9.1	8.6	8.1	7.6
105	12.6	12.0	11.3	10.7	10.2	9.6	9.1	8.5	8.0	7.6
106	12.6	11.9	11.3	10.7	10.1	9.6	9.0	8.5	8.0	7.5
107	12.6	11.9	11.3	10.7	10.1	9.6	9.0	8.5	8.0	7.5
108	12.6	11.9	11.3	10.7	10.1	9.5	9.0	8.5	8.0	7.5
109	12.6	11.9	11.3	10.7	10.1	9.5	9.0	8.4	7.9	7.5
110	12.6	11.9	11.3	10.7	10.1	9.5	9.0	8.4	7.9	7.4
111	12.5	11.9	11.3	10.7	10.1	9.5	8.9	8.4	7.9	7.4
112	12.5	11.9	11.3	10.6	10.1	9.5	8.9	8.4	7.9	7.4
113	12.5	11.9	11.2	10.6	10.0	9.5	8.9	8.4	7.9	7.4
114	12.5	11.9	11.2	10.6	10.0	9.5	8.9	8.4	7.9	7.4
115	12.5	11.9	11.2	10.6	10.0	9.5	8.9	8.4	7.9	7.4

Table VI--Ordinary Joint Life and Last Survivor Annuities; Two Lives--Expected Return Multiples

Ages	85	86	87	88	89	90	91	92	93	94
85	9.6	9.3	9.1	8.9	8.7	8.5	8.3	8.2	8.0	7.9
86	9.3	9.1	8.8	8.6	8.3	8.2	8.0	7.8	7.7	7.6
87	9.1	8.8	8.5	8.3	8.1	7.9	7.7	7.5	7.4	7.2
88	8.9	8.6	8.3	8.0	7.8	7.6	7.4	7.2	7.1	6.9
89	8.7	8.3	8.1	7.8	7.5	7.3	7.1	6.9	6.8	6.6
90	8.5	8.2	7.9	7.6	7.3	7.1	6.9	6.7	6.5	6.4
91	8.3	8.0	7.7	7.4	7.1	6.9	6.7	6.5	6.3	6.2
92	8.2	7.8	7.5	7.2	6.9	6.7	6.5	6.3	6.1	5.9
93	8.0	7.7	7.4	7.1	6.8	6.5	6.3	6.1	5.9	5.8
94	7.9	7.6	7.2	6.9	6.6	6.4	6.2	5.9	5.8	5.6
95	7.8	7.5	7.1	6.8	6.5	6.3	6.0	5.8	5.6	5.4
96	7.7	7.3	7.0	6.7	6.4	6.1	5.9	5.7	5.5	5.3
97	7.6	7.3	6.9	6.6	6.3	6.0	5.8	5.5	5.3	5.1
98	7.6	7.2	6.8	6.5	6.2	5.9	5.6	5.4	5.2	5.0
99	7.5	7.1	6.7	6.4	6.1	5.8	5.5	5.3	5.1	4.9
100	7.4	7.0	6.6	6.3	6.0	5.7	5.4	5.2	5.0	4.8
101	7.3	6.9	6.6	6.2	5.9	5.6	5.3	5.1	4.9	4.7
102	7.3	6.9	6.5	6.2	5.8	5.5	5.3	5.0	4.8	4.6
103	7.2	6.8	6.4	6.1	5.8	5.5	5.2	4.9	4.7	4.5
104	7.2	6.8	6.4	6.0	5.7	5.4	5.1	4.8	4.6	4.4
105	7.1	6.7	6.3	6.0	5.6	5.3	5.0	4.8	4.5	4.3
106	7.1	6.7	6.3	5.9	5.6	5.3	5.0	4.7	4.5	4.2
107	7.1	6.6	6.2	5.9	5.5	5.2	4.9	4.6	4.4	4.2
108	7.0	6.6	6.2	5.8	5.5	5.2	4.9	4.6	4.3	4.1
109	7.0	6.6	6.2	5.8	5.5	5.1	4.8	4.5	4.3	4.1
110	7.0	6.6	6.2	5.8	5.4	5.1	4.8	4.5	4.3	4.0
111	7.0	6.5	6.1	5.7	5.4	5.1	4.8	4.5	4.2	4.0
112	7.0	6.5	6.1	5.7	5.4	5.0	4.7	4.4	4.2	3.9
113	6.9	6.5	6.1	5.7	5.4	5.0	4.7	4.4	4.2	3.9
114	6.9	6.5	6.1	5.7	5.3	5.0	4.7	4.4	4.1	3.9
115	6.9	6.5	6.1	5.7	5.3	5.0	4.7	4.4	4.1	3.9

Sec. 72. Annuities; certain proceeds of endowment and life insurance contracts

Ages	95	96	97	98	99	100	101	102	103	104
95	5.3	5.1	5.0	4.8	4.7	4.6	4.5	4.4	4.3	4.2
96	5.1	5.0	4.8	4.7	4.5	4.4	4.3	4.2	4.1	4.0
97	5.0	4.8	4.7	4.5	4.4	4.3	4.1	4.0	3.9	3.8
98	4.8	4.7	4.5	4.4	4.2	4.1	4.0	3.9	3.8	3.7
99	4.7	4.5	4.4	4.2	4.1	4.0	3.8	3.7	3.6	3.5
100	4.6	4.4	4.3	4.1	4.0	3.8	3.7	3.6	3.5	3.3
101	4.5	4.3	4.1	4.0	3.8	3.7	3.6	3.4	3.3	3.2
102	4.4	4.2	4.0	3.9	3.7	3.6	3.4	3.3	3.2	3.1
103	4.3	4.1	3.9	3.8	3.6	3.5	3.3	3.2	3.0	2.9
104	4.2	4.0	3.8	3.7	3.5	3.3	3.2	3.1	2.9	2.8
105	4.1	3.9	3.7	3.6	3.4	3.2	3.1	2.9	2.8	2.7
106	4.0	3.8	3.6	3.5	3.3	3.1	3.0	2.8	2.7	2.5
107	4.0	3.8	3.6	3.4	3.2	3.1	2.9	2.7	2.6	2.4
108	3.9	3.7	3.5	3.3	3.1	3.0	2.8	2.7	2.5	2.3
109	3.8	3.6	3.4	3.3	3.1	2.9	2.7	2.6	2.4	2.3
110	3.8	3.6	3.4	3.2	3.0	2.8	2.7	2.5	2.3	2.2
111	3.8	3.5	3.3	3.2	3.0	2.8	2.6	2.4	2.3	2.1
112	3.7	3.5	3.3	3.1	2.9	2.8	2.6	2.4	2.2	2.1
113	3.7	3.5	3.3	3.1	2.9	2.7	2.5	2.4	2.2	2.0
114	3.7	3.5	3.3	3.1	2.9	2.7	2.5	2.3	2.1	2.0
115	3.7	3.4	3.2	3.0	2.8	2.7	2.5	2.3	2.1	1.9

Table VI--Ordinary Joint Life and Last Survivor Annuities; Two Lives--Expected Return Multiples

Ages	105	106	107	108	109	110	111	112	113	114	115
105	2.5	2.4	2.3	2.2	2.1	2.0	2.0	1.9	1.8	1.8	1.8
106	2.4	2.3	2.2	2.1	2.0	1.9	1.8	1.7	1.7	1.6	1.6
107	2.3	2.2	2.1	1.9	1.8	1.7	1.7	1.6	1.5	1.5	1.4
108	2.2	2.1	1.9	1.8	1.7	1.6	1.5	1.5	1.4	1.3	1.3
109	2.1	2.0	1.8	1.7	1.6	1.5	1.4	1.3	1.3	1.2	1.1
110	2.0	1.9	1.7	1.6	1.5	1.4	1.3	1.2	1.1	1.1	1.0
111	2.0	1.8	1.7	1.5	1.4	1.3	1.2	1.1	1.0	.9	.9
112	1.9	1.7	1.6	1.5	1.3	1.2	1.1	1.0	.9	.8	.8
113	1.8	1.7	1.5	1.4	1.3	1.1	1.0	.9	.8	.7	.7
114	1.8	1.6	1.5	1.3	1.2	1.1	.9	.8	.7	.6	.6
115	1.8	1.6	1.4	1.3	1.1	1.0	.9	.8	.7	.6	.5

Table VIa--Annuities for Joint Life Only; Two Lives--Expected Return Multiples

Ages	5	6	7	8	9	10	11	12	13	14
5	69.5	69.0	68.4	67.9	67.3	66.7	66.1	65.5	64.8	64.1
6	69.0	68.5	68.0	67.5	66.9	66.4	65.8	65.1	64.5	63.8
7	68.4	68.0	67.5	67.0	66.5	66.0	65.4	64.8	64.2	63.5
8	67.9	67.5	67.0	66.6	66.1	65.5	65.0	64.4	63.8	63.2
9	67.3	66.9	66.5	66.1	65.6	65.1	64.6	64.0	63.4	62.8
10	66.7	66.4	66.0	65.5	65.1	64.6	64.1	63.6	63.0	62.5
11	66.1	65.8	65.4	65.0	64.6	64.1	63.6	63.1	62.6	62.1
12	65.5	65.1	64.8	64.4	64.0	63.6	63.1	62.7	62.2	61.7
13	64.8	64.5	64.2	63.8	63.4	63.0	62.6	62.2	61.7	61.2
14	64.1	63.8	63.5	63.2	62.8	62.5	62.1	61.7	61.2	60.7
15	63.4	63.1	62.9	62.6	62.2	61.9	61.5	61.1	60.7	60.2
16	62.7	62.4	62.2	61.9	61.6	61.3	60.9	60.5	60.1	59.7
17	61.9	61.7	61.5	61.2	60.9	60.6	60.3	59.9	59.6	59.2
18	61.2	61.0	60.7	60.5	60.2	60.0	59.7	59.3	59.0	58.6
19	60.4	60.2	60.0	59.8	59.5	59.3	59.0	58.7	58.4	58.0
20	59.6	59.4	59.2	59.0	58.8	58.6	58.3	58.0	57.7	57.4
21	58.8	58.7	58.5	58.3	58.1	57.8	57.6	57.3	57.1	56.8
22	58.0	57.8	57.7	57.5	57.3	57.1	56.9	56.6	56.4	56.1
23	57.2	57.0	56.9	56.7	56.5	56.4	56.1	55.9	55.7	55.4
24	56.3	56.2	56.1	55.9	55.8	55.6	55.4	55.2	55.0	54.7
25	55.5	55.4	55.2	55.1	55.0	54.8	54.6	54.4	54.2	54.0
26	54.6	54.5	54.4	54.3	54.1	54.0	53.8	53.7	53.5	53.3
27	53.8	53.7	53.6	53.4	53.3	53.2	53.0	52.9	52.7	52.5
28	52.9	52.8	52.7	52.6	52.5	52.4	52.2	52.1	51.9	51.7
29	52.0	51.9	51.8	51.7	51.6	51.5	51.4	51.3	51.1	51.0
30	51.1	51.0	51.0	50.9	50.8	50.7	50.6	50.4	50.3	50.2
31	50.2	50.2	50.1	50.0	50.0	49.9	49.8	49.7	49.6	49.5
32	49.3	49.3	49.2	49.1	49.0	49.0	48.9	48.8	48.6	48.5
33	48.4	48.4	48.3	48.2	48.2	48.1	48.0	47.9	47.8	47.7
34	47.5	47.5	47.4	47.4	47.3	47.2	47.1	47.0	47.0	46.8
35	46.6	46.6	46.5	46.5	46.4	46.3	46.3	46.2	46.1	46.0
36	45.7	45.7	45.6	45.6	45.5	45.4	45.4	45.3	45.2	45.1
37	44.8	44.7	44.7	44.7	44.6	44.6	44.5	44.5	44.4	44.3
38	43.9	43.8	43.8	43.7	43.7	43.6	43.6	43.5	43.5	43.4
39	42.9	42.9	42.9	42.8	42.8	42.7	42.7	42.6	42.6	42.5
40	42.0	42.0	42.0	41.9	41.9	41.8	41.8	41.7	41.7	41.6
41	41.1	41.1	41.0	41.0	41.0	40.9	40.9	40.8	40.8	40.7
42	40.2	40.1	40.1	40.1	40.1	40.0	40.0	39.9	39.9	39.8
43	39.2	39.2	39.2	39.2	39.1	39.1	39.1	39.0	39.0	39.0
44	38.3	38.3	38.3	38.3	38.2	38.2	38.2	38.1	38.1	38.1

Age										
45	37.4	37.4	37.4	37.3	37.3	37.3	37.3	37.2	37.2	37.2
46	36.5	36.5	36.5	36.4	36.4	36.4	36.4	36.3	36.3	36.3
47	35.6	35.6	35.5	35.5	35.5	35.5	35.5	35.4	35.4	35.4
48	34.7	34.7	34.6	34.6	34.6	34.6	34.6	34.5	34.5	34.5
49	33.8	33.8	33.7	33.7	33.7	33.7	33.7	33.7	33.6	33.6
50	32.9	32.9	32.8	32.8	32.8	32.8	32.8	32.8	32.7	32.7
51	32.0	32.0	31.9	31.9	31.9	31.9	31.9	31.9	31.9	31.8
52	31.1	31.1	31.1	31.0	31.0	31.0	31.0	31.0	31.0	30.9
53	30.2	30.2	30.2	30.2	30.1	30.1	30.1	30.1	30.1	30.1
54	29.3	29.3	29.3	29.3	29.3	29.2	29.2	29.2	29.2	29.2
55	28.4	28.4	28.4	28.4	28.4	28.4	28.4	28.3	28.3	28.3
56	27.5	27.5	27.5	27.5	27.5	27.5	27.5	27.5	27.5	27.5
57	26.7	26.7	26.7	26.6	26.6	26.6	26.6	26.6	26.6	26.6
58	25.8	25.8	25.8	25.8	25.8	25.8	25.8	25.7	25.7	25.7
59	24.9	24.9	24.9	24.9	24.9	24.9	24.9	24.9	24.9	24.9
60	24.1	24.1	24.1	24.1	24.1	24.0	24.0	24.0	24.0	24.0
61	23.2	23.2	23.2	23.2	23.2	23.2	23.2	23.2	23.2	23.2
62	22.4	22.4	22.4	22.4	22.4	22.4	22.3	22.3	22.3	22.3
63	21.5	21.5	21.5	21.5	21.5	21.5	21.5	21.5	21.5	21.5
64	20.7	20.7	20.7	20.7	20.7	20.7	20.7	20.7	20.7	20.7
65	19.9	19.9	19.9	19.9	19.9	19.9	19.9	19.9	19.9	19.9
66	19.1	19.1	19.1	19.1	19.1	19.1	19.1	19.1	19.1	19.1
67	18.3	18.3	18.3	18.3	18.3	18.3	18.3	18.3	18.3	18.3
68	17.5	17.5	17.5	17.5	17.5	17.5	17.5	17.5	17.5	17.5
69	16.8	16.8	16.8	16.7	16.7	16.7	16.7	16.7	16.7	16.7
70	16.0	16.0	16.0	16.0	16.0	16.0	16.0	16.0	16.0	16.0
71	15.3	15.3	15.3	15.3	15.3	15.3	15.3	15.3	15.3	15.2
72	14.6	14.6	14.5	14.5	14.5	14.5	14.5	14.5	14.5	14.5
73	13.9	13.9	13.8	13.8	13.8	13.8	13.8	13.8	13.8	13.8
74	13.2	13.2	13.2	13.2	13.2	13.2	13.2	13.2	13.2	13.2
75	12.5	12.5	12.5	12.5	12.5	12.5	12.5	12.5	12.5	12.5
76	11.9	11.9	11.8	11.8	11.8	11.8	11.8	11.8	11.8	11.8
77	11.2	11.2	11.2	11.2	11.2	11.2	11.2	11.2	11.2	11.2
78	10.6	10.6	10.6	10.6	10.6	10.6	10.6	10.6	10.6	10.6
79	10.0	10.0	10.0	10.0	10.0	10.0	10.0	10.0	10.0	10.0
80	9.5	9.5	9.5	9.5	9.5	9.5	9.5	9.5	9.4	9.4
81	8.9	8.9	8.9	8.9	8.9	8.9	8.9	8.9	8.9	8.9
82	8.4	8.4	8.4	8.4	8.4	8.4	8.4	8.4	8.4	8.4
83	7.9	7.9	7.9	7.9	7.9	7.9	7.9	7.9	7.9	7.9
84	7.4	7.4	7.4	7.4	7.4	7.4	7.4	7.4	7.4	7.4
85	6.9	6.9	6.9	6.9	6.9	6.9	6.9	6.9	6.9	6.9
86	6.5	6.5	6.5	6.5	6.5	6.5	6.5	6.5	6.5	6.5
87	6.1	6.1	6.1	6.1	6.1	6.1	6.1	6.1	6.1	6.1
88	5.7	5.7	5.7	5.7	5.7	5.7	5.7	5.7	5.7	5.7
89	5.3	5.3	5.3	5.3	5.3	5.3	5.3	5.3	5.3	5.3
90	5.0	5.0	5.0	5.0	5.0	5.0	5.0	5.0	5.0	5.0
91	4.7	4.7	4.7	4.7	4.7	4.7	4.7	4.7	4.7	4.7
92	4.4	4.4	4.4	4.4	4.4	4.4	4.4	4.4	4.4	4.4
93	4.1	4.1	4.1	4.1	4.1	4.1	4.1	4.1	4.1	4.1
94	3.9	3.9	3.9	3.9	3.9	3.9	3.9	3.9	3.9	3.9
95	3.7	3.7	3.7	3.7	3.7	3.7	3.6	3.6	3.6	3.6
96	3.4	3.4	3.4	3.4	3.4	3.4	3.4	3.4	3.4	3.4
97	3.2	3.2	3.2	3.2	3.2	3.2	3.2	3.2	3.2	3.2
98	3.0	3.0	3.0	3.0	3.0	3.0	3.0	3.0	3.0	3.0
99	2.8	2.8	2.8	2.8	2.8	2.8	2.8	2.8	2.8	2.8
100	2.7	2.7	2.7	2.7	2.7	2.7	2.7	2.7	2.7	2.7
101	2.5	2.5	2.5	2.5	2.5	2.5	2.5	2.5	2.5	2.5
102	2.3	2.3	2.3	2.3	2.3	2.3	2.3	2.3	2.3	2.3
103	2.1	2.1	2.1	2.1	2.1	2.1	2.1	2.1	2.1	2.1
104	1.9	1.9	1.9	1.9	1.9	1.9	1.9	1.9	1.9	1.9
105	1.8	1.8	1.8	1.8	1.8	1.8	1.8	1.8	1.8	1.8
106	1.6	1.6	1.6	1.6	1.6	1.6	1.6	1.6	1.6	1.6
107	1.4	1.4	1.4	1.4	1.4	1.4	1.4	1.4	1.4	1.4
108	1.3	1.3	1.3	1.3	1.3	1.3	1.3	1.3	1.3	1.3
109	1.1	1.1	1.1	1.1	1.1	1.1	1.1	1.1	1.1	1.1
110	1.0	1.0	1.0	1.0	1.0	1.0	1.0	1.0	1.0	1.0
111	.9	.9	.9	.9	.9	.9	.9	.9	.9	.9
112	.8	.8	.8	.8	.8	.8	.8	.8	.8	.8
113	.7	.7	.7	.7	.7	.7	.7	.7	.7	.7
114	.6	.6	.6	.6	.6	.6	.6	.6	.6	.6
115	.5	.5	.5	.5	.5	.5	.5	.5	.5	.5

Table VIa--Annuities for Joint Life Only; Two Lives--Expected Return Multiples

Ages	15	16	17	18	19	20	21	22	23	24
15	59.8	59.3	58.8	58.2	57.6	57.0	56.4	55.8	55.1	54.5
16	59.3	58.8	58.3	57.8	57.2	56.7	56.1	55.5	54.8	54.2
17	58.8	58.3	57.8	57.3	56.8	56.3	55.7	55.1	54.5	53.9
18	58.2	57.8	57.3	56.9	56.4	55.9	55.3	54.7	54.2	53.5
19	57.6	57.2	56.8	56.4	55.9	55.4	54.9	54.4	53.8	53.2
20	57.0	56.7	56.3	55.9	55.4	54.9	54.5	53.9	53.4	52.8
21	56.4	56.1	55.7	55.3	54.9	54.5	54.0	53.5	53.0	52.4

185

Sec. 72. Annuities; certain proceeds of endowment and life insurance contracts

Age										
22	55.8	55.5	55.1	54.7	54.4	53.9	53.5	53.0	52.5	52.0
23	55.1	54.8	54.5	54.2	53.8	53.4	53.0	52.5	52.1	51.6
24	54.5	54.2	53.9	53.5	53.2	52.8	52.4	52.0	51.6	51.1
25	53.8	53.5	53.2	52.9	52.6	52.2	51.9	51.5	51.1	50.6
26	53.0	52.8	52.5	52.3	52.0	51.6	51.3	50.9	50.5	50.1
27	52.3	52.1	51.8	51.6	51.3	51.0	50.7	50.3	50.0	49.6
28	51.5	51.3	51.1	50.9	50.6	50.3	50.0	49.7	49.4	49.0
29	50.8	50.6	50.4	50.2	49.9	49.7	49.4	49.1	48.8	48.4
30	50.0	49.8	49.6	49.4	49.2	49.0	48.7	48.4	48.1	47.8
31	49.2	49.0	48.9	48.7	48.5	48.3	48.0	47.8	47.5	47.2
32	48.4	48.2	48.1	47.9	47.7	47.5	47.3	47.1	46.8	46.5
33	47.6	47.4	47.3	47.1	47.0	46.8	46.6	46.3	46.1	45.9
34	46.7	46.6	46.5	46.3	46.2	46.0	45.8	45.6	45.4	45.2
35	45.9	45.8	45.7	45.5	45.4	45.2	45.1	44.9	44.7	44.4
36	45.0	44.9	44.8	44.7	44.6	44.4	44.3	44.1	43.9	43.7
37	44.2	44.1	44.0	43.9	43.8	43.6	43.5	43.3	43.2	43.0
38	43.3	43.2	43.1	43.0	42.9	42.8	42.7	42.5	42.4	42.2
39	42.4	42.4	42.3	42.2	42.1	42.0	41.9	41.7	41.6	41.4
40	41.6	41.5	41.4	41.3	41.2	41.1	41.0	40.9	40.8	40.6
41	40.7	40.6	40.5	40.5	40.4	40.3	40.2	40.1	40.0	39.8
42	39.8	39.7	39.7	39.6	39.5	39.4	39.4	39.3	39.1	39.0
43	38.9	38.9	38.8	38.7	38.7	38.6	38.5	38.4	38.3	38.2
44	38.0	38.0	37.9	37.9	37.8	37.7	37.7	37.6	37.5	37.4
45	37.1	37.1	37.0	37.0	36.9	36.9	36.8	36.7	36.6	36.5
46	36.2	36.2	36.2	36.1	36.1	36.0	35.9	35.9	35.8	35.7
47	35.3	35.3	35.3	35.2	35.2	35.1	35.1	35.0	34.9	34.9
48	34.5	34.4	34.4	34.4	34.3	34.3	34.2	34.2	34.1	34.0
49	33.6	33.5	33.5	33.5	33.4	33.4	33.4	33.3	33.2	33.2
50	32.7	32.7	32.6	32.6	32.6	32.5	32.5	32.4	32.4	32.3
51	31.8	31.8	31.8	31.7	31.7	31.7	31.6	31.6	31.5	31.5
52	30.9	30.9	30.9	30.9	30.8	30.8	30.8	30.7	30.7	30.6
53	30.0	30.0	30.0	30.0	30.0	29.9	29.9	29.9	29.8	29.8
54	29.2	29.2	29.1	29.1	29.1	29.1	29.0	29.0	29.0	28.9
55	28.3	28.3	28.3	28.3	28.2	28.2	28.2	28.2	28.1	28.1
56	27.4	27.4	27.4	27.4	27.4	27.3	27.3	27.3	27.3	27.2
57	26.6	26.6	26.5	26.5	26.5	26.5	26.5	26.5	26.4	26.4
58	25.7	25.7	25.7	25.7	25.7	25.6	25.6	25.6	25.6	25.6
59	24.9	24.8	24.8	24.8	24.8	24.8	24.8	24.8	24.7	24.7
60	24.0	24.0	24.0	24.0	24.0	23.9	23.9	23.9	23.9	23.9
61	23.2	23.2	23.1	23.1	23.1	23.1	23.1	23.1	23.1	23.0
62	22.3	22.3	22.3	22.3	22.3	22.3	22.3	22.2	22.2	22.2
63	21.5	21.5	21.5	21.5	21.5	21.4	21.4	21.4	21.4	21.4
64	20.7	20.7	20.7	20.6	20.6	20.6	20.6	20.6	20.6	20.6
65	19.9	19.8	19.8	19.8	19.8	19.8	19.8	19.8	19.8	19.8
66	19.1	19.0	19.0	19.0	19.0	19.0	19.0	19.0	19.0	19.0
67	18.3	18.3	18.3	18.3	18.2	18.2	18.2	18.2	18.2	18.2
68	17.5	17.5	17.5	17.5	17.5	17.5	17.5	17.5	17.4	17.4
69	16.7	16.7	16.7	16.7	16.7	16.7	16.7	16.7	16.7	16.7
70	16.0	16.0	16.0	16.0	16.0	16.0	15.9	15.9	15.9	15.9
71	15.2	15.2	15.2	15.2	15.2	15.2	15.2	15.2	15.2	15.2
72	14.5	14.5	14.5	14.5	14.5	14.5	14.5	14.5	14.5	14.5
73	13.8	13.8	13.8	13.8	13.8	13.8	13.8	13.8	13.8	13.8
74	13.2	13.1	13.1	13.1	13.1	13.1	13.1	13.1	13.1	13.1
75	12.5	12.5	12.5	12.5	12.5	12.5	12.5	12.5	12.5	12.5
76	11.8	11.8	11.8	11.8	11.8	11.8	11.8	11.8	11.8	11.8
77	11.2	11.2	11.2	11.2	11.2	11.2	11.2	11.2	11.2	11.2
78	10.6	10.6	10.6	10.6	10.6	10.6	10.6	10.6	10.6	10.6
79	10.0	10.0	10.0	10.0	10.0	10.0	10.0	10.0	10.0	10.0
80	9.4	9.4	9.4	9.4	9.4	9.4	9.4	9.4	9.4	9.4
81	8.9	8.9	8.9	8.9	8.9	8.9	8.9	8.9	8.9	8.9
82	8.4	8.4	8.4	8.4	8.4	8.4	8.4	8.4	8.4	8.4
83	7.9	7.9	7.9	7.9	7.9	7.9	7.9	7.9	7.8	7.8
84	7.4	7.4	7.4	7.4	7.4	7.4	7.4	7.4	7.4	7.4
85	6.9	6.9	6.9	6.9	6.9	6.9	6.9	6.9	6.9	6.9
86	6.5	6.5	6.5	6.5	6.5	6.5	6.5	6.5	6.5	6.5
87	6.1	6.1	6.1	6.1	6.1	6.1	6.1	6.1	6.1	6.1
88	5.7	5.7	5.7	5.7	5.7	5.7	5.7	5.7	5.7	5.7
89	5.3	5.3	5.3	5.3	5.3	5.3	5.3	5.3	5.3	5.3
90	5.0	5.0	5.0	5.0	5.0	5.0	5.0	5.0	5.0	5.0
91	4.7	4.7	4.7	4.7	4.7	4.7	4.7	4.7	4.7	4.7
92	4.4	4.4	4.4	4.4	4.4	4.4	4.4	4.4	4.4	4.4
93	4.1	4.1	4.1	4.1	4.1	4.1	4.1	4.1	4.1	4.1
94	3.9	3.9	3.9	3.9	3.9	3.9	3.9	3.9	3.9	3.9
95	3.6	3.6	3.6	3.6	3.6	3.6	3.6	3.6	3.6	3.6
96	3.4	3.4	3.4	3.4	3.4	3.4	3.4	3.4	3.4	3.4
97	3.2	3.2	3.2	3.2	3.2	3.2	3.2	3.2	3.2	3.2
98	3.0	3.0	3.0	3.0	3.0	3.0	3.0	3.0	3.0	3.0
99	2.8	2.8	2.8	2.8	2.8	2.8	2.8	2.8	2.8	2.8
100	2.7	2.7	2.7	2.7	2.7	2.7	2.7	2.7	2.7	2.7
101	2.5	2.5	2.5	2.5	2.5	2.5	2.5	2.5	2.5	2.5
102	2.3	2.3	2.3	2.3	2.3	2.3	2.3	2.3	2.3	2.3
103	2.1	2.1	2.1	2.1	2.1	2.1	2.1	2.1	2.1	2.1
104	1.9	1.9	1.9	1.9	1.9	1.9	1.9	1.9	1.9	1.9
105	1.8	1.8	1.8	1.8	1.8	1.8	1.8	1.8	1.8	1.8

Sec. 72. Annuities; certain proceeds of endowment and life insurance contracts

106	1.6	1.6	1.6	1.6	1.6	1.6	1.6	1.6	1.6	1.6
107	1.4	1.4	1.4	1.4	1.4	1.4	1.4	1.4	1.4	1.4
108	1.3	1.3	1.3	1.3	1.3	1.3	1.3	1.3	1.3	1.3
109	1.1	1.1	1.1	1.1	1.1	1.1	1.1	1.1	1.1	1.1
110	1.0	1.0	1.0	1.0	1.0	1.0	1.0	1.0	1.0	1.0
111	.9	.9	.9	.9	.9	.9	.9	.9	.9	.9
112	.8	.8	.8	.8	.8	.8	.8	.8	.8	.8
113	.7	.7	.7	.7	.7	.7	.7	.7	.7	.7
114	.6	.6	.6	.6	.6	.6	.6	.6	.6	.6
115	.5	5	.5	.5	.5	.5	.5	.5	.5	.5

Table VIa--Annuities for Joint Life Only; Two Lives--Expected Return Multiples

Ages	25	26	27	28	29	30	31	32	33	34
25	50.2	49.7	49.2	48.6	48.1	47.5	46.9	46.2	45.6	44.9
26	49.7	49.2	48.7	48.2	47.7	47.1	46.5	45.9	45.3	44.6
27	49.2	48.7	48.3	47.8	47.3	46.7	46.2	45.6	45.0	44.3
28	48.6	48.2	47.8	47.3	46.8	46.3	45.8	45.2	44.6	44.0
29	48.1	47.7	47.3	46.8	46.4	45.9	45.4	44.8	44.3	43.7
30	47.5	47.1	46.7	46.3	45.9	45.4	44.9	44.4	43.9	43.3
31	46.9	46.5	46.2	45.8	45.4	44.9	44.5	44.0	43.5	42.9
32	46.2	45.9	45.6	45.2	44.8	44.4	44.0	43.5	43.0	42.5
33	45.6	45.3	45.0	44.6	44.3	43.9	43.5	43.0	42.6	42.1
34	44.9	44.6	44.3	44.0	43.7	43.3	42.9	42.5	42.1	41.6
35	44.2	44.0	43.7	43.4	43.1	42.7	42.4	42.0	41.6	41.1
36	43.5	43.3	43.0	42.7	42.4	42.1	41.8	41.4	41.0	40.6
37	42.8	42.5	42.3	42.1	41.8	41.5	41.2	40.8	40.5	40.1
38	42.0	41.8	41.6	41.4	41.1	40.8	40.6	40.2	39.9	39.5
39	41.3	41.1	40.9	40.7	40.4	40.2	39.9	39.6	39.3	39.0
40	40.5	40.3	40.1	39.9	39.7	39.5	39.2	39.0	38.7	38.4
41	39.7	39.5	39.4	39.2	39.0	38.8	38.5	38.3	38.0	37.7
42	38.9	38.8	38.6	38.4	38.3	38.1	37.8	37.6	37.4	37.1
43	38.1	38.0	37.8	37.7	37.5	37.3	37.1	36.9	36.7	36.4
44	37.3	37.2	37.0	36.9	36.7	36.6	36.4	36.2	36.0	35.8
45	36.5	36.3	36.2	36.1	36.0	35.8	35.6	35.5	35.3	35.1
46	35.6	35.5	35.4	35.3	35.2	35.0	34.9	34.7	34.5	34.4
47	34.8	34.7	34.6	34.5	34.4	34.3	34.1	34.0	33.8	33.6
48	34.0	33.9	33.8	33.7	33.6	33.5	33.4	33.2	33.1	32.9
49	33.1	33.0	33.0	32.9	32.8	32.7	32.6	32.4	32.3	32.2
50	32.3	32.2	32.1	32.1	32.0	31.9	31.8	31.7	31.5	31.4
51	31.4	31.4	31.3	31.2	31.2	31.1	31.0	30.9	30.8	30.6
52	30.6	30.5	30.5	30.4	30.3	30.3	30.2	30.1	30.0	29.9
53	29.7	29.7	29.6	29.6	29.5	29.5	29.4	29.3	29.2	29.1
54	28.9	28.9	28.8	28.8	28.7	28.6	28.6	28.5	28.4	28.3
55	28.1	28.0	28.0	27.9	27.9	27.8	27.8	27.7	27.6	27.5
56	27.2	27.2	27.1	27.1	27.0	27.0	26.9	26.9	26.8	26.7
57	26.4	26.3	26.3	26.3	26.2	26.2	26.2	26.1	26.0	25.9
58	25.5	25.5	25.5	25.4	25.4	25.4	25.3	25.3	25.2	25.1
59	24.7	24.7	24.6	24.6	24.6	24.5	24.5	24.5	24.4	24.3
60	23.9	23.8	23.8	23.8	23.8	23.7	23.7	23.6	23.6	23.5
61	23.0	23.0	23.0	23.0	22.9	22.9	22.9	22.8	22.8	22.7
62	22.2	22.2	22.2	22.1	22.1	22.1	22.1	22.0	22.0	21.9
63	21.4	21.4	21.3	21.3	21.3	21.3	21.3	21.2	21.2	21.2
64	20.6	20.6	20.5	20.5	20.5	20.5	20.5	20.4	20.4	20.4
65	19.8	19.8	19.7	19.7	19.7	19.7	19.7	19.6	19.6	19.6
66	19.0	19.0	19.0	18.9	18.9	18.9	18.9	18.9	18.8	18.8
67	18.2	18.2	18.2	18.2	18.2	18.1	18.1	18.1	18.1	18.1
68	17.4	17.4	17.4	17.4	17.4	17.4	17.4	17.3	17.3	17.3
69	16.7	16.7	16.7	16.6	16.6	16.6	16.6	16.6	16.6	16.6
70	15.9	15.9	15.9	15.9	15.9	15.9	15.9	15.9	15.8	15.8
71	15.2	15.2	15.2	15.2	15.2	15.2	15.2	15.1	15.1	15.1
72	14.5	14.5	14.5	14.5	14.5	14.5	14.5	14.4	14.4	14.4
73	13.8	13.8	13.8	13.8	13.8	13.8	13.8	13.8	13.7	13.7
74	13.1	13.1	13.1	13.1	13.1	13.1	13.1	13.1	13.1	13.1
75	12.5	12.5	12.5	12.4	12.4	12.4	12.4	12.4	12.4	12.4
76	11.8	11.8	11.8	11.8	11.8	11.8	11.8	11.8	11.8	11.8
77	11.2	11.2	11.2	11.2	11.2	11.2	11.2	11.2	11.2	11.1
78	10.6	10.6	10.6	10.6	10.6	10.6	10.6	10.6	10.6	10.5
79	10.0	10.0	10.0	10.0	10.0	10.0	10.0	10.0	10.0	10.0
80	9.4	9.4	9.4	9.4	9.4	9.4	9.4	9.4	9.4	9.4
81	8.9	8.9	8.9	8.9	8.9	8.9	8.9	8.9	8.9	8.9
82	8.4	8.4	8.3	8.3	8.3	8.3	8.3	8.3	8.3	8.3
83	7.8	7.8	7.8	7.8	7.8	7.8	7.8	7.8	7.8	7.8
84	7.4	7.4	7.4	7.4	7.4	7.4	7.4	7.4	7.4	7.4
85	6.9	6.9	6.9	6.9	6.9	6.9	6.9	6.9	6.9	6.9
86	6.5	6.5	6.5	6.5	6.5	6.5	6.5	6.5	6.5	6.5
87	6.1	6.1	6.1	6.1	6.1	6.1	6.1	6.1	6.1	6.1
88	5.7	5.7	5.7	5.7	5.7	5.7	5.7	5.7	5.7	5.7
89	5.3	5.3	5.3	5.3	5.3	5.3	5.3	5.3	5.3	5.3
90	5.0	5.0	5.0	5.0	5.0	5.0	5.0	5.0	5.0	5.0
91	4.7	4.7	4.7	4.7	4.7	4.7	4.7	4.7	4.7	4.7
92	4.4	4.4	4.4	4.4	4.4	4.4	4.4	4.4	4.4	4.4

93	4.1	4.1	4.1	4.1	4.1	4.1	4.1	4.1	4.1	4.1
94	3.9	3.9	3.9	3.9	3.9	3.9	3.9	3.9	3.9	3.9
95	3.6	3.6	3.6	3.6	3.6	3.6	3.6	3.6	3.6	3.6
96	3.4	3.4	3.4	3.4	3.4	3.4	3.4	3.4	3.4	3.4
5 97	3.2	3.2	3.2	3.2	3.2	3.2	3.2	3.2	3.2	3.2
98	3.0	3.0	3.0	3.0	3.0	3.0	3.0	3.0	3.0	3.0
99	2.8	2.8	2.8	2.8	2.8	2.8	2.8	2.8	2.8	2.8
100	2.7	2.7	2.7	2.7	2.7	2.7	2.7	2.7	2.7	2.7
101	2.5	2.5	2.5	2.5	2.5	2.5	2.5	2.5	2.5	2.5
10 102	2.3	2.3	2.3	2.3	2.3	2.3	2.3	2.3	2.3	2.3
103	2.1	2.1	2.1	2.1	2.1	2.1	2.1	2.1	2.1	2.1
104	1.9	1.9	1.9	1.9	1.9	1.9	1.9	1.9	1.9	1.9
105	1.8	1.8	1.8	1.8	1.8	1.8	1.8	1.8	1.8	1.8
106	1.6	1.6	1.6	1.6	1.6	1.6	1.6	1.6	1.6	1.6
15 107	1.4	1.4	1.4	1.4	1.4	1.4	1.4	1.4	1.4	1.4
108	1.3	1.3	1.3	1.3	1.3	1.3	1.3	1.3	1.3	1.3
109	1.1	1.1	1.1	1.1	1.1	1.1	1.1	1.1	1.1	1.1
110	1.0	1.0	1.0	1.0	1.0	1.0	1.0	1.0	1.0	1.0
111	.9	.9	.9	.9	.9	.9	.9	.9	.9	.9
20 112	.8	.8	8	.8	.8	.8	.8	.8	.8	.8
113	.7	.7	.7	.7	.7	.7	.7	.7	.7	.7
114	.6	.6	.6	.6	.6	.6	.6	.6	.6	.6
115	.5	.5	.5	.5	.5	.5	.5	.5	.5	.5

25

Table VIa--Annuities for Joint Life Only; Two Lives--Expected Return Multiples

Ages	35	36	37	38	39	40	41	42	43	44
30 35	40.7	40.2	39.7	39.2	38.6	38.0	37.4	36.8	36.2	35.5
36	40.2	39.7	39.3	38.7	38.2	37.7	37.1	36.5	35.9	35.2
37	39.7	39.3	38.8	38.3	37.8	37.3	36.7	36.2	35.6	34.9
38	39.2	38.7	38.3	37.9	37.4	36.9	36.3	35.8	35.2	34.6
39	38.6	38.2	37.8	37.4	36.9	36.4	35.9	35.4	34.9	34.3
35 40	38.0	37.7	37.3	36.9	36.4	36.0	35.5	35.0	34.5	34.0
41	37.4	37.1	36.7	36.3	35.9	35.5	35.1	34.6	34.1	33.6
42	36.8	36.5	36.2	35.8	35.4	35.0	34.6	34.1	33.7	33.2
43	36.2	35.9	35.6	35.2	34.9	34.5	34.1	33.7	33.2	32.8
44	35.5	35.2	34.9	34.6	34.3	34.0	33.6	33.2	32.8	32.3
40 45	34.8	34.6	34.3	34.0	33.7	33.4	33.0	32.7	32.3	31.8
46	34.1	33.9	33.7	33.4	33.1	32.8	32.5	32.1	31.8	31.4
47	33.4	33.2	33.0	32.8	32.5	32.2	31.9	31.6	31.2	30.8
48	32.7	32.5	32.3	32.1	31.8	31.6	31.3	31.0	30.7	30.3
49	32.0	31.8	31.6	31.4	31.2	30.9	30.7	30.4	30.1	29.8
45 50	31.3	31.1	30.9	30.7	30.5	30.3	30.0	29.8	29.5	29.2
51	30.5	30.4	30.2	30.0	29.8	29.6	29.4	29.2	28.9	28.6
52	29.7	29.6	29.5	29.3	29.1	28.9	28.7	28.5	28.3	28.0
53	29.0	28.9	28.7	28.6	28.4	28.2	28.1	27.9	27.6	27.4
54	28.2	28.1	28.0	27.8	27.7	27.5	27.4	27.2	27.0	26.8
50 55	27.4	27.3	27.2	27.1	27.0	26.8	26.7	26.5	26.3	26.1
56	26.7	26.6	26.5	26.3	26.2	26.1	26.0	25.8	25.6	25.4
57	25.9	25.8	25.7	25.6	25.5	25.4	25.2	25.1	24.9	24.8
58	25.1	25.0	24.9	24.8	24.7	24.6	24.5	24.4	24.2	24.1
59	24.3	24.2	24.1	24.1	24.0	23.9	23.8	23.6	23.5	23.4
55 60	23.5	23.4	23.4	23.3	23.2	23.1	23.0	22.9	22.8	22.7
61	22.7	22.6	22.6	22.5	22.4	22.4	22.3	22.2	22.1	22.0
62	21.9	21.9	21.8	21.7	21.7	21.6	21.5	21.4	21.3	21.2
63	21.1	21.1	21.0	21.0	20.9	20.8	20.8	20.7	20.6	20.5
64	20.3	20.3	20.2	20.2	20.1	20.1	20.0	20.0	19.9	19.8
60 65	19.6	19.5	19.5	19.4	19.4	19.3	19.3	19.2	19.1	19.1
66	18.8	18.8	18.7	18.7	18.6	18.6	18.5	18.5	18.4	18.4
67	18.0	18.0	18.0	17.9	17.9	17.9	17.8	17.8	17.7	17.6
68	17.3	17.3	17.2	17.2	17.2	17.1	17.1	17.0	17.0	16.9
69	16.5	16.5	16.5	16.5	16.4	16.4	16.4	16.3	16.3	16.2
65 70	15.8	15.8	15.8	15.7	15.7	15.7	15.6	15.6	15.6	15.5
71	15.1	15.1	15.1	15.0	15.0	15.0	15.0	14.9	14.9	14.9
72	14.4	14.4	14.4	14.3	14.3	14.3	14.3	14.2	14.2	14.2
73	13.7	13.7	13.7	13.7	13.7	13.6	13.6	13.6	13.6	13.5
74	13.1	13.0	13.0	13.0	13.0	13.0	13.0	12.9	12.9	12.9
70 75	12.4	12.4	12.4	12.4	12.3	12.3	12.3	12.3	12.3	12.2
76	11.8	11.8	11.7	11.7	11.7	11.7	11.7	11.7	11.6	11.6
77	11.1	11.1	11.1	11.1	11.1	11.1	11.1	11.1	11.0	11.0
78	10.5	10.5	10.5	10.5	10.5	10.5	10.5	10.5	10.5	10.4
79	10.0	10.0	9.9	9.9	9.9	9.9	9.9	9.9	9.9	9.9
75 80	9.4	9.4	9.4	9.4	9.4	9.4	9.4	9.3	9.3	9.3
81	8.9	8.8	8.8	8.8	8.8	8.8	8.8	8.8	8.8	8.8
82	8.3	8.3	8.3	8.3	8.3	8.3	8.3	8.3	8.3	8.3
83	7.8	7.8	7.8	7.8	7.8	7.8	7.8	7.8	7.8	7.8
84	7.3	7.3	7.3	7.3	7.3	7.3	7.3	7.3	7.3	7.3
80 85	6.9	6.9	6.9	6.9	6.9	6.9	6.9	6.9	6.9	6.9
86	6.5	6.5	6.5	6.5	6.4	6.4	6.4	6.4	6.4	6.4
87	6.1	6.0	6.0	6.0	6.0	6.0	6.0	6.0	6.0	6.0
88	5.7	5.7	5.7	5.7	5.7	5.7	5.7	5.6	5.6	5.6
89	5.3	5.3	5.3	5.3	5.3	5.3	5.3	5.3	5.3	5.3

Sec. 72.   Annuities; certain proceeds of endowment and life insurance contracts

90	5.0	5.0	5.0	5.0	5.0	5.0	5.0	5.0	5.0	5.0	
91	4.7	4.7	4.7	4.7	4.7	4.7	4.7	4.7	4.6	4.6	
92	4.4	4.4	4.4	4.4	4.4	4.4	4.4	4.4	4.4	4.4	
93	4.1	4.1	4.1	4.1	4.1	4.1	4.1	4.1	4.1	4.1	
94	3.9	3.9	3.9	3.9	3.9	3.9	3.9	3.9	3.9	3.9	5
95	3.6	3.6	3.6	3.6	3.6	3.6	3.6	3.6	3.6	3.6	
96	3.4	3.4	3.4	3.4	3.4	3.4	3.4	3.4	3.4	3.4	
97	3.2	3.2	3.2	3.2	3.2	3.2	3.2	3.2	3.2	3.2	
98	3.0	3.0	3.0	3.0	3.0	3.0	3.0	3.0	3.0	3.0	
99	2.8	2.8	2.8	2.8	2.8	2.8	2.8	2.8	2.8	2.8	10
100	2.7	2.7	2.7	2.7	2.7	2.7	2.7	2.7	2.6	2.6	
101	2.5	2.5	2.5	2.5	2.5	2.5	2.5	2.5	2.5	2.5	
102	2.3	2.3	2.3	2.3	2.3	2.3	2.3	2.3	2.3	2.3	
103	2.1	2.1	2.1	2.1	2.1	2.1	2.1	2.1	2.1	2.1	
104	1.9	1.9	1.9	1.9	1.9	1.9	1.9	1.9	1.9	1.9	15
105	1.8	1.8	1.8	1.8	1.8	1.8	1.8	1.8	1.8	1.8	
106	1.6	1.6	1.6	1.6	1.6	1.6	1.6	1.6	1.6	1.6	
107	1.4	1.4	1.4	1.4	1.4	1.4	1.4	1.4	1.4	1.4	
108	1.3	1.3	1.3	1.3	1.3	1.3	1.3	1.3	1.3	1.3	
109	1.1	1.1	1.1	1.1	1.1	1.1	1.1	1.1	1.1	1.1	20
110	1.0	1.0	1.0	1.0	1.0	1.0	1.0	1.0	1.0	1.0	
111	.9	.9	.9	.9	.9	.9	.9	.9	.9	.9	
112	.8	.8	.8	.8	.8	.8	.8	.8	.8	.8	
113	.7	.7	.7	.7	.7	.7	.7	.7	.7	.7	
114	.6	.6	.6	.6	.6	.6	.6	.6	.6	.6	25
115	.5	.5	.5	.5	.5	.5	.5	.5	.5	.5	

Table VIa--Annuities for Joint Life Only; Two Lives--Expected Return Multiples

Ages	45	46	47	48	49	50	51	52	53	54	
											30
45	31.4	30.9	30.5	30.0	29.4	28.9	28.3	27.7	27.1	26.5	
46	30.9	30.5	30.0	29.6	29.1	28.5	28.0	27.4	26.9	26.3	
47	30.5	30.0	29.6	29.2	28.7	28.2	27.7	27.1	26.6	26.0	
48	30.0	29.6	29.2	28.7	28.3	27.8	27.3	26.8	26.3	25.7	35
49	29.4	29.1	28.7	28.3	27.9	27.4	26.9	26.5	25.9	25.4	
50	28.9	28.5	28.2	27.4	27.4	27.0	26.5	26.1	25.6	25.1	
51	28.3	28.0	27.7	27.3	26.9	26.5	26.1	25.7	25.2	24.7	
52	27.7	27.4	27.1	26.8	26.5	26.1	25.7	25.3	24.8	24.4	
53	27.1	26.9	26.6	26.3	25.9	25.6	25.2	24.8	24.4	24.0	40
54	26.5	26.3	26.0	25.7	25.4	25.1	24.7	24.4	24.0	23.6	
55	25.9	25.7	25.4	25.1	24.9	24.6	24.2	23.9	23.5	23.2	
56	25.2	25.0	24.8	24.6	24.3	24.0	23.7	23.4	23.1	22.7	
57	24.6	24.4	24.2	24.0	23.7	23.5	23.2	22.9	22.6	22.2	
58	23.9	23.7	23.5	23.3	23.1	22.9	22.6	22.4	22.1	21.7	45
59	23.2	23.1	22.9	22.7	22.5	22.3	22.1	21.8	21.5	21.2	
60	22.5	22.4	22.2	22.1	21.9	21.7	21.5	21.2	21.0	20.7	
61	21.8	21.7	21.6	21.4	21.2	21.1	20.9	20.6	20.4	20.2	
62	21.1	21.0	20.9	20.7	20.6	20.4	20.2	20.0	19.8	19.6	
63	20.4	20.3	20.2	20.1	19.9	19.8	19.6	19.4	19.2	19.0	50
64	19.7	19.6	19.5	19.4	19.3	19.1	19.0	18.8	18.6	18.5	
65	19.0	18.9	18.8	18.7	18.6	18.5	18.3	18.2	18.0	17.9	
66	18.3	18.2	18.1	18.0	17.9	17.8	17.7	17.6	17.4	17.3	
67	17.6	17.5	17.4	17.3	17.3	17.2	17.1	16.9	16.8	16.7	
68	16.9	16.8	16.7	16.7	16.6	16.5	16.4	16.3	16.2	16.1	55
69	16.2	16.1	16.1	16.0	15.9	15.8	15.8	15.7	15.6	15.4	
70	15.5	15.4	15.4	15.3	15.3	15.2	15.1	15.0	14.9	14.8	
71	14.8	14.8	14.7	14.7	14.6	14.5	14.5	14.4	14.3	14.2	
72	14.1	14.1	14.1	14.0	14.0	13.9	13.8	13.8	13.7	13.6	
73	13.5	13.5	13.4	13.4	13.3	13.3	13.2	13.2	13.1	13.0	60
74	12.8	12.8	12.8	12.7	12.7	12.7	12.6	12.6	12.5	12.4	
75	12.2	12.2	12.2	12.1	12.1	12.1	12.0	12.0	11.9	11.9	
76	11.6	11.6	11.6	11.5	11.5	11.5	11.4	11.4	11.3	11.3	
77	11.0	11.0	11.0	10.9	10.9	10.9	10.8	10.8	10.8	10.7	
78	10.4	10.4	10.4	10.4	10.3	10.3	10.3	10.2	10.2	10.2	65
79	9.9	9.8	9.8	9.8	9.8	9.8	9.7	9.7	9.7	9.6	
80	9.3	9.3	9.3	9.3	9.2	9.2	9.2	9.2	9.1	9.1	
81	8.8	8.8	8.7	8.7	8.7	8.7	8.7	8.7	8.6	8.6	
82	8.3	8.2	8.2	8.2	8.2	8.2	8.2	8.2	8.1	8.1	
83	7.8	7.8	7.7	7.7	7.7	7.7	7.7	7.7	7.7	7.6	70
84	7.3	7.3	7.3	7.3	7.3	7.2	7.2	7.2	7.2	7.2	
85	6.8	6.8	6.8	6.8	6.8	6.8	6.8	6.8	6.8	6.7	
86	6.4	6.4	6.4	6.4	6.4	6.4	6.4	6.4	6.3	6.3	
87	6.0	6.0	6.0	6.0	6.0	6.0	6.0	6.0	6.0	5.9	
88	5.6	5.6	5.6	5.6	5.6	5.6	5.6	5.6	5.6	5.6	75
89	5.3	5.3	5.3	5.3	5.3	5.3	5.3	5.2	5.2	5.2	
90	5.0	4.9	4.9	4.9	4.9	4.9	4.9	4.9	4.9	4.9	
91	4.6	4.6	4.6	4.6	4.6	4.6	4.6	4.6	4.6	4.6	
92	4.4	4.4	4.4	4.3	4.3	4.3	4.3	4.3	4.3	4.3	
93	4.1	4.1	4.1	4.1	4.1	4.1	4.1	4.1	4.1	4.1	80
94	3.9	3.9	3.8	3.8	3.8	3.8	3.8	3.8	3.8	3.8	
95	3.6	3.6	3.6	3.6	3.6	3.6	3.6	3.6	3.6	3.6	
96	3.4	3.4	3.4	3.4	3.4	3.4	3.4	3.4	3.4	3.4	
97	3.2	3.2	3.2	3.2	3.2	3.2	3.2	3.2	3.2	3.2	

98	3.0	3.0	3.0	3.0	3.0	3.0	3.0	3.0	3.0	3.0
99	2.8	2.8	2.8	2.8	2.8	2.8	2.8	2.8	2.8	2.8
100	2.6	2.6	2.6	2.6	2.6	2.6	2.6	2.6	2.6	2.6
101	2.5	2.5	2.5	2.5	2.5	2.5	2.5	2.5	2.5	2.5
102	2.3	2.3	2.3	2.3	2.3	2.3	2.3	2.3	2.3	2.3
103	2.1	2.1	2.1	2.1	2.1	2.1	2.1	2.1	2.1	2.1
104	1.9	1.9	1.9	1.9	1.9	1.9	1.9	1.9	1.9	1.9
105	1.8	1.8	1.8	1.8	1.8	1.8	1.8	1.8	1.8	1.8
106	1.6	1.6	1.6	1.6	1.6	1.6	1.6	1.6	1.6	1.6
107	1.4	1.4	1.4	1.4	1.4	1.4	1.4	1.4	1.4	1.4
108	1.3	1.3	1.3	1.3	1.3	1.3	1.3	1.3	1.3	1.3
109	1.1	1.1	1.1	1.1	1.1	1.1	1.1	1.1	1.1	1.1
110	1.0	1.0	1.0	1.0	1.0	1.0	1.0	1.0	1.0	1.0
111	.9	.9	.9	.9	.9	.9	.9	.9	.9	.9
112	.8	.8	.8	.8	.8	.8	.8	.8	.8	.8
113	.7	.7	.7	.7	.7	.7	.7	.7	.7	.7
114	.6	.6	.6	.6	.6	.6	.6	.6	.6	.6
115	.5	.5	.5	.5	.5	.5	.5	.5	.5	.5

Table VIa--Annuities for Joint Life Only; Two Lives--Expected Return Multiples

Ages	55	56	57	58	59	60	61	62	63	64
55	22.7	22.3	21.9	21.4	20.9	20.4	19.9	19.4	18.8	18.3
56	22.3	21.9	21.5	21.1	20.6	20.1	19.6	19.1	18.6	18.0
57	21.9	21.5	21.1	20.7	20.3	19.8	19.3	18.8	18.3	17.8
58	21.4	21.1	20.7	20.3	19.9	19.5	19.0	18.5	18.0	17.5
59	20.9	20.6	20.3	19.9	19.5	19.1	18.7	18.2	17.7	17.3
60	20.4	20.1	19.8	19.5	19.1	18.7	18.3	17.9	17.4	17.0
61	29.9	19.6	19.3	19.0	18.7	18.3	17.9	17.5	17.1	16.7
62	19.4	19.1	18.8	18.5	18.2	17.9	17.5	17.1	16.8	16.3
63	18.8	18.6	18.3	18.0	17.7	17.4	17.1	16.8	16.4	16.0
64	18.3	18.0	17.8	17.5	17.3	17.0	16.7	16.3	16.0	15.6
65	17.7	17.5	17.3	17.0	16.8	16.5	16.2	15.9	15.6	15.3
66	17.1	16.9	16.7	16.5	16.3	16.0	15.8	15.5	15.2	14.9
67	16.5	16.3	16.2	16.0	15.8	15.5	15.3	15.0	14.7	14.5
68	15.9	15.8	15.6	15.4	15.2	15.0	14.8	14.6	14.3	14.0
69	15.3	15.2	15.0	14.9	14.7	14.5	14.3	14.1	13.9	13.6
70	14.7	14.6	14.5	14.3	14.2	14.0	13.8	13.6	13.4	13.2
71	14.1	14.0	13.9	13.8	13.6	13.5	13.3	13.1	12.9	12.7
72	13.5	13.4	13.3	13.2	13.1	12.9	12.8	12.6	12.4	12.3
73	13.0	12.9	12.8	12.7	12.5	12.4	12.3	12.1	12.0	11.8
74	12.4	12.3	12.2	12.1	12.0	11.9	11.8	11.6	11.5	11.3
75	11.8	11.7	11.7	11.6	11.5	11.4	11.3	11.1	11.0	10.9
76	11.2	11.2	11.1	11.0	10.9	10.9	10.8	10.6	10.5	10.4
77	10.7	10.6	10.6	10.5	10.4	10.3	10.3	10.2	10.0	9.9
78	10.1	10.1	10.0	10.0	9.9	9.8	9.8	9.7	9.6	9.5
79	9.6	9.6	9.5	9.5	9.4	9.3	9.3	9.2	9.1	9.0
80	9.1	9.0	9.0	9.0	8.9	8.9	8.8	8.7	8.7	8.6
81	8.6	8.5	8.5	8.5	8.4	8.4	8.3	8.3	8.2	8.1
82	8.1	8.1	8.0	8.0	8.0	7.9	7.9	7.8	7.8	7.7
83	7.6	7.6	7.6	7.5	7.5	7.5	7.4	7.4	7.3	7.3
84	7.2	7.1	7.1	7.1	7.1	7.0	7.0	7.0	6.9	6.9
85	6.7	6.7	6.7	6.7	6.6	6.6	6.6	6.5	6.5	6.5
86	6.3	6.3	6.3	6.3	6.2	6.2	6.2	6.2	6.1	6.1
87	5.9	5.9	5.9	5.9	5.9	5.8	5.8	5.8	5.8	5.7
88	5.6	5.5	5.5	5.5	5.5	5.5	5.5	5.4	5.4	5.4
89	5.2	5.2	5.2	5.2	5.2	5.1	5.1	5.1	5.1	5.1
90	4.9	4.9	4.9	4.9	4.9	4.8	4.8	4.8	4.8	4.8
91	4.6	4.6	4.6	4.6	4.6	4.5	4.5	4.5	4.5	4.5
92	4.3	4.3	4.3	4.3	4.3	4.3	4.3	4.2	4.2	4.2
93	4.1	4.1	4.0	4.0	4.0	4.0	4.0	4.0	4.0	4.0
94	3.8	3.8	3.8	3.8	3.8	3.8	3.8	3.8	3.8	3.7
95	3.6	3.6	3.6	3.6	3.6	3.6	3.6	3.6	3.5	3.5
96	3.4	3.4	3.4	3.4	3.4	3.4	3.4	3.3	3.3	3.3
97	3.2	3.2	3.2	3.2	3.2	3.2	3.2	3.2	3.1	3.1
98	3.0	3.0	3.0	3.0	3.0	3.0	3.0	3.0	3.0	3.0
99	2.8	2.8	2.8	2.8	2.8	2.8	2.8	2.8	2.8	2.8
100	2.6	2.6	2.6	2.6	2.6	2.6	2.6	2.6	2.6	2.6
101	2.5	2.4	2.4	2.4	2.4	2.4	2.4	2.4	2.4	2.4
102	2.3	2.3	2.3	2.3	2.3	2.3	2.3	2.3	2.3	2.2
103	2.1	2.1	2.1	2.1	2.1	2.1	2.1	2.1	2.1	2.1
104	1.9	1.9	1.9	1.9	1.9	1.9	1.9	1.9	1.9	1.9
105	1.8	1.8	1.8	1.8	1.8	1.8	1.7	1.7	1.7	1.7
106	1.6	1.6	1.6	1.6	1.6	1.6	1.6	1.6	1.6	1.6
107	1.4	1.4	1.4	1.4	1.4	1.4	1.4	1.4	1.4	1.4
108	1.3	1.3	1.3	1.3	1.3	1.3	1.3	1.3	1.3	1.3
109	1.1	1.1	1.1	1.1	1.1	1.1	1.1	1.1	1.1	1.1
110	1.0	1.0	1.0	1.0	1.0	1.0	1.0	1.0	1.0	1.0
111	.9	.9	.9	.9	.9	.9	.9	.9	.9	.9
112	.8	.8	.8	.8	.8	.8	.8	.8	.8	.8
113	.7	.7	.7	.7	.7	.7	.7	.7	.7	.7
114	.6	.6	.6	.6	.6	.6	.6	.6	.6	.6
115	.5	.5	.5	.5	.5	.5	.5	.5	.5	.5

Sec. 72. Annuities; certain proceeds of endowment and life insurance contracts

Table VIa--Annuities for Joint Life Only; Two Lives--Expected Return Multiples

Ages	65	66	67	68	69	70	71	72	73	74
65	14.9	14.5	14.1	13.7	13.3	12.9	12.5	12.0	11.6	11.2
66	14.5	14.2	13.8	13.4	13.1	12.6	12.2	11.8	11.4	11.0
67	14.1	13.8	13.5	13.1	12.8	12.4	12.0	11.6	11.2	10.8
68	13.7	13.4	13.1	12.8	12.5	12.1	11.7	11.4	11.0	10.6
69	13.3	13.1	12.8	12.5	12.1	11.8	11.4	11.1	10.7	10.4
70	12.9	12.6	12.4	12.1	11.8	11.5	11.2	10.8	10.5	10.1
71	12.5	12.2	12.0	11.7	11.4	11.2	10.9	10.5	10.2	9.9
72	12.0	11.8	11.6	11.4	11.1	10.8	10.5	10.2	9.9	9.6
73	11.6	11.4	11.2	11.0	10.7	10.5	10.2	9.9	9.7	9.4
74	11.2	11.0	10.8	10.6	10.4	10.1	9.9	9.6	9.4	9.1
75	10.7	10.5	10.4	10.2	10.0	9.8	9.5	9.3	9.1	8.8
76	10.3	10.1	9.9	9.8	9.6	9.4	9.2	9.0	8.8	8.5
77	9.8	9.7	9.5	9.4	9.2	9.0	8.8	8.6	8.4	8.2
78	9.4	9.2	9.1	9.0	8.8	8.7	8.5	8.3	8.1	7.9
79	8.9	8.8	8.7	8.6	8.4	8.3	8.1	8.0	7.8	7.6
80	8.5	8.4	8.3	8.2	8.0	7.9	7.8	7.6	7.5	7.3
81	8.0	8.0	7.9	7.9	7.7	7.5	7.4	7.3	7.1	7.0
82	7.6	7.5	7.5	7.4	7.3	7.2	7.1	6.9	6.8	6.7
83	7.2	7.1	7.1	7.0	6.9	6.8	6.7	6.6	6.5	6.4
84	6.8	6.7	6.7	6.6	6.5	6.4	6.4	6.3	6.2	6.0
85	6.4	6.4	6.3	6.2	6.2	6.1	6.0	5.9	5.8	5.7
86	6.0	6.0	5.9	5.9	5.8	5.8	5.7	5.6	5.5	5.4
87	5.7	5.6	5.6	5.6	5.5	5.4	5.4	5.3	5.2	5.2
88	5.3	5.3	5.3	5.2	5.2	5.1	5.1	5.0	5.0	4.9
89	5.0	5.0	5.0	4.9	4.9	4.8	4.8	4.7	4.7	4.6
90	4.7	4.7	4.7	4.6	4.6	4.6	4.5	4.5	4.4	4.4
91	4.5	4.4	4.4	4.4	4.3	4.3	4.3	4.2	4.2	4.1
92	4.2	4.2	4.1	4.1	4.1	4.1	4.0	4.0	3.9	3.9
93	3.9	3.9	3.9	3.9	3.9	3.8	3.8	3.8	3.7	3.7
94	3.7	3.7	3.7	3.7	3.6	3.6	3.6	3.6	3.5	3.5
95	3.5	3.5	3.5	3.5	3.5	3.4	3.4	3.4	3.3	3.3
96	3.3	3.3	3.3	3.3	3.3	3.2	3.2	3.2	3.2	3.1
97	3.1	3.1	3.1	3.1	3.1	3.1	3.0	3.0	3.0	3.0
98	2.9	2.9	2.9	2.9	2.9	2.9	2.9	2.9	2.8	2.8
99	2.8	2.8	2.8	2.7	2.7	2.7	2.7	2.7	2.7	2.6
100	2.6	2.6	2.6	2.6	2.6	2.5	2.5	2.5	2.5	2.5
101	2.4	2.4	2.4	2.4	2.4	2.4	2.4	2.4	2.3	2.3
102	2.2	2.2	2.2	2.2	2.2	2.2	2.2	2.2	2.2	2.2
103	2.1	2.1	2.1	2.1	2.1	2.0	2.0	2.0	2.0	2.0
104	1.9	1.9	1.9	1.9	1.9	1.9	1.9	1.9	1.9	1.9
105	1.7	1.7	1.7	1.7	1.7	1.7	1.7	1.7	1.7	1.7
106	1.6	1.6	1.6	1.6	1.6	1.6	1.6	1.6	1.5	1.5
107	1.4	1.4	1.4	1.4	1.4	1.4	1.4	1.4	1.4	1.4
108	1.3	1.3	1.3	1.3	1.3	1.3	1.3	1.3	1.3	1.3
109	1.1	1.1	1.1	1.1	1.1	1.1	1.1	1.1	1.1	1.1
110	1.0	1.0	1.0	1.0	1.0	1.0	1.0	1.0	1.0	1.0
111	.9	.9	.9	.9	.9	.9	.9	.9	.9	.9
112	.8	.8	.8	.8	.8	.8	.8	.8	.8	.8
113	.7	.7	.7	.7	.7	.6	.6	.6	.6	.6
114	.6	.6	.6	.6	.6	.6	.5	.5	.5	.5
115	.5	.5	.5	.5	.5	.5	.5	.5	.5	.5

Table VIa--Annuities for Joint Life Only; Two Lives--Expected Return Multiples

Ages	75	76	77	78	79	80	81	82	83	84
75	8.6	8.3	8.0	7.7	7.4	7.1	6.8	6.5	6.2	5.9
76	8.3	8.0	7.8	7.5	7.2	6.9	6.7	6.4	6.1	5.8
77	8.0	7.8	7.5	7.3	7.0	6.8	6.5	6.2	5.9	5.7
78	7.7	7.5	7.3	7.0	6.8	6.6	6.3	6.0	5.8	5.5
79	7.4	7.2	7.0	6.8	6.6	6.3	6.1	5.9	5.6	5.4
80	7.1	6.9	6.8	6.6	6.3	6.1	5.9	5.7	5.5	5.2
81	6.8	6.7	6.5	6.3	6.1	5.9	5.7	5.5	5.3	5.1
82	6.5	6.4	6.2	6.0	5.9	5.7	5.5	5.3	5.1	4.9
83	6.2	6.1	5.9	5.8	5.6	5.5	5.3	5.1	4.9	4.7
84	5.9	5.8	5.7	5.5	5.4	5.2	5.1	4.9	4.7	4.6
85	5.6	5.5	5.4	5.3	5.2	5.0	4.9	4.7	4.6	4.4
86	5.4	5.3	5.1	5.0	4.9	4.8	4.7	4.5	4.4	4.2
87	5.1	5.0	4.9	4.8	4.7	4.6	4.4	4.3	4.2	4.1
88	4.8	4.7	4.6	4.5	4.4	4.3	4.2	4.1	4.0	3.9
89	4.5	4.5	4.4	4.3	4.2	4.1	4.0	3.9	3.8	3.7
90	4.3	4.2	4.2	4.1	4.0	3.9	3.8	3.8	3.7	3.5
91	4.1	4.0	4.0	3.9	3.8	3.7	3.7	3.6	3.5	3.4
92	3.9	3.8	3.7	3.7	3.6	3.6	3.5	3.4	3.3	3.2
93	3.7	3.6	3.6	3.5	3.4	3.4	3.3	3.2	3.2	3.1
94	3.5	3.4	3.4	3.3	3.3	3.2	3.2	3.1	3.0	3.0
95	3.3	3.2	3.2	3.2	3.1	3.1	3.0	3.0	2.9	2.8
96	3.1	3.1	3.0	3.0	3.0	2.9	2.9	2.8	2.8	2.7
97	2.9	2.9	2.9	2.9	2.8	2.8	2.7	2.7	2.6	2.6

98	2.8	2.8	2.7	2.7	2.7	2.6	2.6	2.6	2.5	2.5
99	2.6	2.6	2.6	2.6	2.5	2.5	2.5	2.4	2.4	2.3
100	2.5	2.5	2.4	2.4	2.4	2.4	2.3	2.3	2.3	2.2
101	2.3	2.3	2.3	2.3	2.2	2.2	2.2	2.2	2.1	2.1
102	2.2	2.1	2.1	2.1	2.1	2.1	2.0	2.0	2.0	2.0
103	2.0	2.0	2.0	2.0	1.9	1.9	1.9	1.9	1.9	1.8
104	1.8	1.8	1.8	1.8	1.8	1.8	1.8	1.7	1.7	1.7
105	1.7	1.7	1.7	1.7	1.6	1.6	1.6	1.6	1.6	1.6
106	1.5	1.5	1.5	1.5	1.5	1.5	1.5	1.5	1.5	1.4
107	1.4	1.4	1.4	1.4	1.4	1.4	1.3	1.3	1.3	1.3
108	1.3	1.2	1.2	1.2	1.2	1.2	1.2	1.2	1.2	1.2
109	1.1	1.1	1.1	1.1	1.1	1.1	1.1	1.1	1.1	1.1
110	1.0	1.0	1.0	1.0	1.0	1.0	1.0	1.0	1.0	1.0
111	.9	.9	.9	.9	.9	.9	.9	.9	.8	.8
112	.8	.8	.8	.7	.7	.7	.7	.7	.7	.7
113	.6	.6	.6	.6	.6	.6	.6	.6	.6	.6
114	.5	.5	.5	. 5	.5	.5	.5	.5	.5	.5
115	.5	.5	.5	.5	.5	.5	.5	.5	.5	. 5

Table VIa--Annuities for Joint Life Only; Two Lives--Expected Return Multiples

Ages	85	86	87	88	89	90	91	92	93	94
85	4.2	4.1	3.9	3.8	3.6	3.4	3.3	3.2	3.0	2.9
86	4.1	3.9	3.8	3.6	3.5	3.3	3.2	3.1	2.9	2.8
87	3.9	3.8	3.6	3.5	3.4	3.2	3.1	3.0	2.8	2.7
88	3.8	3.6	3.5	3.4	3.2	3.1	3.0	2.9	2.8	2.6
89	3.6	3.5	3.4	3.2	3.1	3.0	2.9	2.8	2.7	2.6
90	3.4	3.3	3.2	3.1	3.0	2.9	2.8	2.7	2.6	2.5
91	3.3	3.2	3.1	3.0	2.9	2.8	2.7	2.6	2.5	2.4
92	3.2	3.1	3.0	2.9	2.8	2.7	2.6	2.5	2.4	2.3
93	3.0	2.9	2.8	2.8	2.7	2.6	2.5	2.4	2.3	2.3
94	2.9	2.8	2.7	2.6	2.6	2.5	2.4	2.3	2.3	2.2
95	2.8	2.7	2.6	2.5	2.5	2.4	2.3	2.2	2.2	2.1
96	2.6	2.6	2.5	2.4	2.4	2.3	2.2	2.2	2.1	2.0
97	2.5	2.5	2.4	2.3	2.3	2.2	2.2	2.1	2.0	2.0
98	2.4	2.4	2.3	2.2	2.2	2.1	2.1	2.0	2.0	1.9
99	2.3	2.2	2.2	2.1	2.1	2.0	2.0	1.9	1.9	1.8
100	2.2	2.1	2.1	2.0	2.0	1.9	1.9	1.9	1.8	1.8
101	2.1	2.0	2.0	1.9	1.9	1.9	1.8	1.8	1.7	1.7
102	1.9	1.9	1.9	1.8	1.8	1.8	1.7	1.7	1.6	1.6
103	1.8	1.8	1.8	1.7	1.7	1.7	1.6	1.6	1.5	1.5
104	1.7	1.7	1.6	1.6	1.6	1.5	1.5	1.5	1.5	1.4
105	1.6	1.5	1.5	1.5	1.5	1.4	1.4	1.4	1.4	1.3
106	1.4	1.4	1.4	1.4	1.4	1.3	1.3	1.3	1.3	1.2
107	1.3	1.3	1.3	1.3	1.2	1.2	1.2	1.2	1.2	1.2
108	1.2	1.2	1.2	1.1	1.1	1.1	1.1	1.1	1.1	1.1
109	1.1	1.1	1.0	1.0	1.0	1.0	1.0	1.0	1.0	1.0
110	.9	.9	.9	.9	.9	.9	.9	.9	.9	.9
111	.8	.8	.8	.8	.8	.8	.8	.8	.8	.8
112	.7	.7	.7	.7	.7	.7	.7	.7	.7	.7
113	.6	.6	.6	.6	.6	.6	.6	.6	.6	.6
114	.5	.5	.5	.5	.5	.5	. 5	.5	.5	.5
115	.5	.5	.5	.5	.5	.5	. 5	.5	.5	.5

Table VIa--Annuities for Joint Life Only; Two Lives--Expected Return Multiples

Ages	95	96	97	98	99	100	101	102	103	104
95	2.0	2.0	1.9	1.8	1.8	1.7	1.6	1.6	1.5	1.4
96	2.0	1.9	1.9	1.8	1.7	1.7	1.6	1.5	1.5	1.4
97	1.9	1.9	1.8	1.7	1.7	1.6	1.6	1.5	1.4	1.3
98	1.8	1.8	1.7	1.7	1.6	1.6	1.5	1.5	1.4	1.3
99	1.8	1.7	1.7	1.6	1.6	1.5	1.5	1.4	1.4	1.3
100	1.7	1.7	1.6	1.6	1.5	1.5	1.4	1.4	1.3	1.3
101	1.6	1.6	1.6	1.5	1.5	1.4	1.4	1.3	1.3	1.2
102	1.6	1.5	1.5	1.5	1.4	1.4	1.3	1.3	1.2	1.2
103	1.5	1.5	1.4	1.4	1.4	1.3	1.3	1.2	1.2	1.1
104	1.4	1.4	1.3	1.3	1.3	1.3	1.2	1.2	1.1	1.1
105	1.3	1.3	1.3	1.2	1.2	1.2	1.2	1.1	1.1	1.0
106	1.2	1.2	1.2	1.2	1.1	1.1	1.1	1.1	1.0	1.0
107	1.1	1.1	1.1	1.1	1.1	1.0	1.0	1.0	1.0	.9
108	1.0	1.0	1.0	1.0	1.0	1.0	1.0	.9	.9	.9
109	1.0	.9	.9	.9	.9	.9	.9	.9	.8	.8
110	.9	.9	.8	.8	.8	.8	.8	.8	.8	.8
111	.8	.8	.8	.8	.8	.7	.7	.7	.7	.7
112	.7	.7	.7	. 7	.7	.7	.7	.7	.6	.6
113	.6	.6	.6	. 6	.6	.6	.6	.6	.6	.6
114	.5	.5	.5	.5	.5	.5	.5	.5	.5	.5
115	.5	.5	.5	.5	.5	.5	. 5	.5	.5	.5

Sec. 72. Annuities; certain proceeds of endowment and life insurance contracts

Table VIaa--Annuities for Joint Life Only; Two Lives--Expected Return Multiples

Ages	105	106	107	108	109	110	111	112	113	114	115
105	1.0	1.0	.9	.9	.8	.7	.7	.6	.6	.5	.5
106	1.0	.9	.9	.8	.8	.7	.7	.6	.6	.5	.5
107	.9	.9	.8	.8	.7	.7	.7	.6	.6	.5	.5
108	.9	.8	8	.8	.7	.7	.6	.6	.5	.5	.5
109	.8	.8	.7	.7	.7	.7	.6	.6	.5	.5	.5
110	.7	.7	.7	.7	.7	.6	.6	.6	.5	.5	.5
111	.7	.7	.7	.6	.6	.6	.6	.5	.5	.5	.5
112	.6	.6	.6	.6	.6	.6	.5	.5	.5	.5	.5
113	.6	.6	.6	.5	.5	.5	.5	.5	.5	.5	.5
114	.5	.5	.5	.5	.5	.5	.5	.5	.5	.5	.5
115	.5	.5	.5	.5	.5	.5	.5	.5	.5	.5	.5

Table VII--Percent Value of Refund Feature; Duration of Guaranteed Amount

Age	Years--									
	1	2	3	4	5	6	7	8	9	10
5	0	0	0	0	0	0	0	0	0	0
6	0	0	0	0	0	0	0	0	0	0
7	0	0	0	0	0	0	0	0	0	0
8	0	0	0	0	0	0	0	0	0	0
9	0	0	0	0	0	0	0	0	0	0
10	0	0	0	0	0	0	0	0	0	0
11	0	0	0	0	0	0	0	0	0	0
12	0	0	0	0	0	0	0	0	0	0
13	0	0	0	0	0	0	0	0	0	0
14	0	0	0	0	0	0	0	0	0	0
15	0	0	0	0	0	0	0	0	0	0
16	0	0	0	0	0	0	0	0	0	0
17	0	0	0	0	0	0	0	0	0	0
18	0	0	0	0	0	0	0	0	0	0
19	0	0	0	0	0	0	0	0	0	0
20	0	0	0	0	0	0	0	0	0	0
21	0	0	0	0	0	0	0	0	0	0
22	0	0	0	0	0	0	0	0	0	0
23	0	0	0	0	0	0	0	0	0	0
24	0	0	0	0	0	0	0	0	0	0
25	0	0	0	0	0	0	0	0	0	0
26	0	0	0	0	0	0	0	0	0	0
27	0	0	0	0	0	0	0	0	0	0
28	0	0	0	0	0	0	0	0	0	0
29	0	0	0	0	0	0	0	0	0	0
30	0	0	0	0	0	0	0	0	0	0
31	0	0	0	0	0	0	0	0	0	0
32	0	0	0	0	0	0	0	0	0	0
33	0	0	0	0	0	0	0	0	0	0
34	0	0	0	0	0	0	0	0	0	0
35	0	0	0	0	0	0	0	0	0	0
36	0	0	0	0	0	0	0	0	0	0
37	0	0	0	0	0	0	0	0	0	1
38	0	0	0	0	0	0	0	0	0	1
39	0	0	0	0	0	0	0	0	1	1
40	0	0	0	0	0	0	0	1	1	1
41	0	0	0	0	0	0	0	1	1	1
42	0	0	0	0	0	0	1	1	1	1
43	0	0	0	0	0	0	1	1	1	1
44	0	0	0	0	0	1	1	1	1	1
45	0	0	0	0	0	1	1	1	1	1
46	0	0	0	0	1	1	1	1	1	1
47	0	0	0	0	1	1	1	1	1	1
48	0	0	0	0	1	1	1	1	1	1
49	0	0	0	1	1	1	1	1	1	2
50	0	0	0	1	1	1	1	1	1	2
51	0	0	0	1	1	1	1	1	2	2
52	0	0	0	1	1	1	1	1	2	2
53	0	0	1	1	1	1	1	2	2	2
54	0	0	1	1	1	1	1	2	2	2
55	0	0	1	1	1	1	2	2	2	2
56	0	0	1	1	1	1	2	2	2	3
57	0	0	1	1	1	2	2	2	3	3
58	0	1	1	1	1	2	2	2	3	3
59	0	1	1	1	1	2	2	3	3	4
60	0	1	1	1	2	2	2	3	3	4
61	0	1	1	1	2	2	3	3	4	4
62	0	1	1	2	2	2	3	4	4	5
63	0	1	1	2	2	3	3	4	5	5
64	0	1	1	2	2	3	4	4	5	6
65	0	1	2	2	3	3	4	5	6	6

	66	1	1	2	2	3	4	5	5	6	7
	67	1	1	2	3	3	4	5	6	7	8
	68	1	1	2	3	4	5	6	7	8	9
	69	1	1	2	3	4	5	6	7	8	10
5	70	1	2	3	4	5	6	7	8	9	11
	71	1	2	3	4	5	6	8	9	10	12
	72	1	2	3	4	6	7	8	10	11	13
	73	1	2	4	5	6	8	9	11	13	14
	74	1	3	4	5	7	9	10	12	14	16
10	75	1	3	4	6	8	9	11	13	15	17
	76	2	3	5	7	9	10	12	15	17	19
	77	2	4	5	7	9	12	14	16	18	21
	78	2	4	6	8	10	13	15	18	20	23
	79	2	4	7	9	11	14	17	19	22	25
15	80	2	5	7	10	13	15	18	21	24	27
	81	3	5	8	11	14	17	20	23	26	29
	82	3	6	9	12	15	19	22	25	28	32
	83	3	7	10	13	17	20	24	27	31	34
	84	4	7	11	15	19	22	26	30	33	37
20	85	4	8	12	16	20	24	28	32	36	40
	86	4	9	13	18	22	27	31	35	39	42
	87	5	10	15	20	24	29	33	37	41	45
	88	5	11	16	21	26	31	36	40	44	48
	89	6	12	18	23	28	33	38	43	47	50
25	90	7	13	19	25	31	36	41	45	49	53
	91	7	14	21	27	33	38	43	48	52	55
	92	8	15	22	29	35	40	45	50	54	58
	93	9	17	24	31	37	43	48	52	56	60
	94	9	18	26	33	39	45	50	54	58	62
30	95	10	19	27	35	41	47	52	57	60	64
	96	11	20	29	36	43	49	54	59	62	66
	97	11	21	30	38	45	51	56	61	64	68
	98	12	23	32	40	47	53	58	63	66	69
	99	13	24	34	42	49	55	60	65	68	71
35	100	14	26	36	44	52	58	63	67	70	73
	101	14	27	38	47	54	60	65	69	72	75
	102	15	29	40	49	56	62	67	71	74	77
	103	17	31	42	52	59	65	69	73	76	78
	104	18	33	45	55	62	67	72	75	78	80
40	105	19	36	48	58	65	70	74	77	80	82
	106	21	38	51	61	68	73	77	79	82	84
	107	23	42	55	64	71	75	79	81	84	85
	108	25	45	58	67	73	78	81	83	85	87
	109	28	49	62	71	76	80	83	85	87	88
45	110	31	52	66	74	79	82	85	87	88	89
	111	34	57	70	77	82	85	87	88	90	91
	112	37	61	73	80	84	87	88	90	91	92
	113	41	66	77	83	86	88	90	91	92	93
	114	45	70	80	85	88	90	92	93	93	94
50	115	50	75	83	88	90	92	93	94	94	95

Table VII--Percent Value of Refund Feature; Duration of Guaranteed Amount

	Age	Years--									
55		11	12	13	14	15	16	17	18	19	20
	5	0	0	0	0	0	0	0	0	0	0
	6	0	0	0	0	0	0	0	0	0	0
60	7	0	0	0	0	0	0	0	0	0	0
	8	0	0	0	0	0	0	0	0	0	0
	9	0	0	0	0	0	0	0	0	0	0
	10	0	0	0	0	0	0	0	0	0	0
	11	0	0	0	0	0	0	0	0	0	0
65	12	0	0	0	0	0	0	0	0	0	0
	13	0	0	0	0	0	0	0	0	0	0
	14	0	0	0	0	0	0	0	0	0	0
	15	0	0	0	0	0	0	0	0	0	0
	16	0	0	0	0	0	0	0	0	0	0
70	17	0	0	0	0	0	0	0	0	0	0
	18	0	0	0	0	0	0	0	0	0	0
	19	0	0	0	0	0	0	0	0	0	0
	20	0	0	0	0	0	0	0	0	0	1
	21	0	0	0	0	0	0	0	0	0	1
75	22	0	0	0	0	0	0	0	0	1	1
	23	0	0	0	0	0	0	0	1	1	1
	24	0	0	0	0	0	0	0	1	1	1
	25	0	0	0	0	0	0	1	1	1	1
	26	0	0	0	0	0	0	1	1	1	1
80	27	0	0	0	0	0	1	1	1	1	1
	28	0	0	0	0	1	1	1	1	1	1
	29	0	0	0	0	1	1	1	1	1	1
	30	0	0	0	1	1	1	1	1	1	1
	31	0	0	0	1	1	1	1	1	1	1

Sec. 72. Annuities; certain proceeds of endowment and life insurance contracts

Age										
32	0	0	1	1	1	1	1	1	1	1
33	0	0	1	1	1	1	1	1	1	1
34	0	1	1	1	1	1	1	1	1	1
35	0	1	1	1	1	1	1	1	1	1
36	1	1	1	1	1	1	1	1	1	1
37	1	1	1	1	1	1	1	1	1	1
38	1	1	1	1	1	1	1	1	1	2
39	1	1	1	1	1	1	1	1	2	2
40	1	1	1	1	1	1	1	2	2	2
41	1	1	1	1	1	1	2	2	2	2
42	1	1	1	1	1	2	2	2	2	2
43	1	1	1	1	2	2	2	2	2	3
44	1	1	1	2	2	2	2	2	3	3
45	1	1	2	2	2	2	2	3	3	3
46	1	2	2	2	2	2	3	3	3	3
47	1	2	2	2	2	2	3	3	3	4
48	2	2	2	2	2	3	3	3	4	4
49	2	2	2	2	3	3	3	4	4	4
50	2	2	2	3	3	3	3	4	4	5
51	2	2	3	3	3	3	4	4	4	5
52	2	2	3	3	3	4	4	5	5	5
53	2	3	3	3	4	4	5	5	5	6
54	3	3	3	4	4	4	5	5	6	7
55	3	3	4	4	4	5	5	6	7	7
56	3	3	4	4	5	5	6	7	7	8
57	3	4	4	5	5	6	6	7	8	9
58	4	4	5	5	6	6	7	8	9	9
59	4	5	5	6	6	7	8	9	9	10
60	4	5	6	6	7	8	9	10	10	11
61	5	6	6	7	8	9	10	10	11	13
62	5	6	7	8	9	10	11	12	13	14
63	6	7	8	9	10	11	12	13	14	15
64	7	8	8	9	10	12	13	14	15	17
65	7	8	9	10	12	13	14	15	17	18
66	8	9	10	12	13	14	15	17	18	20
67	9	10	11	13	14	15	17	18	20	22
68	10	11	13	14	15	17	19	20	22	24
69	11	12	14	15	17	19	20	22	24	26
70	12	14	15	17	19	20	22	24	26	28
71	13	15	17	18	20	22	24	26	28	30
72	15	17	18	20	22	24	26	28	30	32
73	16	18	20	22	24	26	28	31	33	35
74	18	20	22	24	26	28	31	33	35	37
75	19	22	24	26	28	31	33	35	38	40
76	21	24	26	28	31	33	36	38	40	43
77	23	26	28	31	33	36	38	41	43	45
78	25	28	31	33	36	38	41	43	46	48
79	28	30	33	36	38	41	44	46	48	51
80	30	33	36	38	41	44	46	49	51	53
81	32	35	38	41	44	47	49	51	54	56
82	35	38	41	44	47	49	52	54	56	58
83	38	41	44	47	49	52	54	57	59	61
84	40	44	47	49	52	55	57	59	61	63
85	43	46	49	52	55	57	59	62	63	65
86	46	49	52	55	57	60	62	64	66	67
87	48	52	55	57	60	62	64	66	68	69
88	51	54	57	60	62	64	66	68	70	71
89	54	57	60	62	65	67	68	70	72	73
90	56	59	62	64	67	69	70	72	74	75
91	59	62	64	67	69	71	72	74	75	76
92	61	64	66	69	71	72	74	75	77	78
93	63	66	68	70	72	74	75	77	78	79
94	65	68	70	72	74	75	77	78	79	80
95	67	69	72	74	75	77	78	79	81	82
96	69	71	73	75	77	78	80	81	82	83
97	70	73	75	77	78	80	81	82	83	84
98	72	74	76	78	79	81	82	83	84	85
99	74	76	78	79	81	82	83	84	85	86
100	75	78	79	81	82	83	84	85	86	86
101	77	79	81	82	83	84	85	86	87	87
102	79	81	82	83	84	85	86	87	88	88
103	80	82	83	85	86	87	87	88	89	89
104	82	84	85	86	87	88	88	89	90	90
105	84	85	86	87	88	89	89	90	90	91
106	85	86	87	88	89	90	90	91	91	92
107	87	88	89	89	90	91	91	92	92	93
108	88	89	90	90	91	92	92	93	93	93
109	89	90	91	92	92	93	93	94	94	94
110	90	91	92	92	93	93	94	94	94	95
111	92	92	93	93	94	94	95	95	95	95
112	93	93	94	94	95	95	95	96	96	96
113	94	94	95	95	95	96	96	96	96	97
114	95	95	95	96	96	96	97	97	97	97
115	95	96	96	96	97	97	97	97	97	98

Sec. 72. Annuities; certain proceeds of endowment and life insurance contracts

Table VII--Percent Value of Refund Feature; Duration of Guaranteed Amount

Age	Years--									
	21	22	23	24	25	26	27	28	29	30
5	0	0	0	0	0	0	0	0	0	0
6	0	0	0	0	0	0	0	0	0	0
7	0	0	0	0	0	0	0	0	0	0
8	0	0	0	0	0	0	0	0	0	1
9	0	0	0	0	0	0	0	0	1	1
10	0	0	0	0	0	0	0	1	1	1
11	0	0	0	0	0	0	1	1	1	1
12	0	0	0	0	0	0	1	1	1	1
13	0	0	0	0	0	1	1	1	1	1
14	0	0	0	0	1	1	1	1	1	1
15	0	0	0	1	1	1	1	1	1	1
16	0	0	1	1	1	1	1	1	1	1
17	0	0	1	1	1	1	1	1	1	1
18	0	1	1	1	1	1	1	1	1	1
19	1	1	1	1	1	1	1	1	1	1
20	1	1	1	1	1	1	1	1	1	1
21	1	1	1	1	1	1	1	1	1	1
22	1	1	1	1	1	1	1	1	1	1
23	1	1	1	1	1	1	1	1	1	1
24	1	1	1	1	1	1	1	1	1	1
25	1	1	1	1	1	1	1	1	1	1
26	1	1	1	1	1	1	1	1	1	1
27	1	1	1	1	1	1	1	1	1	2
28	1	1	1	1	1	1	1	1	2	2
29	1	1	1	1	1	1	1	2	2	2
30	1	1	1	1	1	1	2	2	2	2
31	1	1	1	1	1	2	2	2	2	2
32	1	1	1	1	2	2	2	2	2	2
33	1	1	1	2	2	2	2	2	2	2
34	1	1	2	2	2	2	2	2	2	3
35	1	2	2	2	2	2	2	2	3	3
36	2	2	2	2	2	2	2	3	3	3
37	2	2	2	2	2	2	3	3	3	3
38	2	2	2	2	2	3	3	3	3	4
39	2	2	2	2	3	3	3	3	4	4
40	2	2	3	3	3	3	3	4	4	4
41	2	3	3	3	3	3	4	4	4	5
42	3	3	3	3	3	4	4	4	5	5
43	3	3	3	4	4	4	4	5	5	6
44	3	3	4	4	4	4	5	5	6	6
45	3	4	4	4	5	5	5	6	6	7
46	4	4	4	5	5	5	6	6	7	7
47	4	4	5	5	5	6	6	7	7	8
48	4	5	5	5	6	6	7	7	8	9
49	5	5	5	6	6	7	8	8	9	10
50	5	5	6	6	7	8	8	9	10	10
51	5	6	6	7	8	8	9	10	11	11
52	6	7	7	8	8	9	10	11	11	12
53	7	7	8	8	9	10	11	12	13	14
54	7	8	8	9	10	11	12	13	14	15
55	8	9	9	10	11	12	13	14	15	16
56	9	9	10	11	12	13	14	15	16	18
57	9	10	11	12	13	14	15	17	18	19
58	10	11	12	13	14	16	17	18	19	21
59	11	12	13	15	16	17	18	20	21	22
60	12	14	15	16	17	19	20	21	23	24
61	14	15	16	17	19	20	22	23	25	26
62	15	16	18	19	20	22	23	25	27	28
63	16	18	19	21	22	24	25	27	29	30
64	18	19	21	23	24	26	28	29	31	33
65	20	21	23	25	26	28	30	31	33	35
66	21	23	25	27	28	30	32	34	35	37
67	23	25	27	29	31	32	34	36	38	40
68	25	27	29	31	33	35	37	38	40	42
69	28	29	31	33	35	37	39	41	43	44
70	30	32	34	36	38	40	42	43	45	47
71	32	34	36	38	40	42	44	46	47	49
72	35	37	39	41	43	45	46	48	50	51
73	37	39	41	43	45	47	49	51	52	54
74	40	42	44	46	48	50	51	53	54	56
75	42	44	46	48	50	52	54	55	57	58
76	45	47	49	51	53	54	56	58	59	60
77	47	50	51	53	55	57	58	60	61	62
78	50	52	54	56	57	59	61	62	63	64
79	53	55	56	58	60	61	63	64	65	66
80	55	57	59	60	62	63	65	66	67	68

196

81	58	59	61	63	64	66	67	68	69	70
82	60	62	63	65	66	68	69	70	71	72
83	62	64	66	67	68	70	71	72	73	74
84	65	66	68	69	70	71	72	73	74	75
85	67	68	70	71	72	73	74	75	76	77
86	69	70	72	73	74	75	76	77	77	78
87	71	72	73	75	76	76	77	78	79	80
88	73	74	75	76	77	78	79	80	80	81
89	74	76	77	78	79	79	80	81	81	82
90	76	77	78	79	80	81	81	82	83	83
91	78	79	79	80	81	82	83	83	84	84
92	79	80	81	82	82	83	84	84	85	85
93	80	81	82	83	83	84	85	85	86	86
94	81	82	83	84	84	85	85	86	86	87
95	82	83	84	85	85	86	86	87	87	88
96	83	84	85	86	86	87	87	88	88	88
97	84	85	86	86	87	87	88	88	89	89
98	85	86	87	87	88	88	89	89	89	90
99	86	87	87	88	88	89	89	90	90	90
100	87	88	88	89	89	90	90	90	91	91
101	88	89	89	90	90	90	91	91	91	92
102	89	89	90	90	91	91	91	92	92	92
103	90	90	91	91	91	92	92	92	93	93
104	91	91	91	92	92	92	93	93	93	93
105	91	92	92	92	93	93	93	94	94	94
106	92	93	93	93	93	94	94	94	94	95
107	93	93	94	94	94	94	95	95	95	95
108	94	94	94	94	95	95	95	95	95	96
109	94	95	95	95	95	95	96	96	96	96
110	95	95	95	96	96	96	96	96	96	96
111	96	96	96	96	96	96	97	97	97	97
112	96	96	96	97	97	97	97	97	97	97
113	97	97	97	97	97	97	97	98	98	98
114	97	97	97	98	98	98	98	98	98	98
115	98	98	98	98	98	98	98	98	98	98

Table VII--Percent Value of Refund Feature; Duration of Guaranteed Amount

Age	Years--									
	31	32	33	34	35	36	37	38	39	40
5	0	1	1	1	1	1	1	1	1	1
6	0	1	1	1	1	1	1	1	1	1
7	1	1	1	1	1	1	1	1	1	1
8	1	1	1	1	1	1	1	1	1	1
9	1	1	1	1	1	1	1	1	1	1
10	1	1	1	1	1	1	1	1	1	1
11	1	1	1	1	1	1	1	1	1	1
12	1	1	1	1	1	1	1	1	1	1
13	1	1	1	1	1	1	1	1	1	1
14	1	1	1	1	1	1	1	1	1	1
15	1	1	1	1	1	1	1	1	1	1
16	1	1	1	1	1	1	1	1	1	1
17	1	1	1	1	1	1	1	1	1	1
18	1	1	1	1	1	1	1	1	1	2
19	1	1	1	1	1	1	1	1	2	2
20	1	1	1	1	1	1	1	2	2	2
21	1	1	1	1	1	1	2	2	2	2
22	1	1	1	1	1	2	2	2	2	2
23	1	1	1	2	2	2	2	2	2	2
24	1	1	2	2	2	2	2	2	2	2
25	1	2	2	2	2	2	2	2	2	3
26	2	2	2	2	2	2	2	2	3	3
27	2	2	2	2	2	2	2	3	3	3
28	2	2	2	2	2	2	3	3	3	3
29	2	2	2	2	2	3	3	3	3	4
30	2	2	2	3	3	3	3	3	4	4
31	2	2	3	3	3	3	3	4	4	4
32	2	3	3	3	3	3	4	4	4	5
33	3	3	3	3	3	4	4	4	5	5
34	3	3	3	3	4	4	4	5	5	5
35	3	3	3	4	4	4	5	5	5	6
36	3	4	4	4	4	5	5	5	6	6
37	4	4	4	4	5	5	6	6	6	7
38	4	4	5	5	5	6	6	7	7	8
39	4	5	5	5	6	6	7	7	8	8
40	5	5	5	6	6	7	7	8	8	9
41	5	5	6	6	7	7	8	9	9	10
42	6	6	6	7	7	8	9	9	10	11
43	6	7	7	8	8	9	9	10	11	12
44	7	7	8	8	9	10	10	11	12	13
45	7	8	8	9	10	10	11	12	13	14
46	8	9	9	10	11	11	12	13	14	15

47	9	9	10	11	12	12	13	14	15	16
48	9	10	11	12	13	14	15	16	17	18
49	10	11	12	13	14	15	16	17	18	19
50	11	12	13	14	15	16	17	18	20	21
51	12	13	14	15	16	17	19	20	21	22
52	13	14	15	17	18	19	20	21	23	24
53	15	16	17	18	19	20	22	23	24	26
54	16	17	18	19	21	22	23	25	26	28
55	17	18	20	21	22	24	25	27	28	30
56	19	20	21	23	24	26	27	29	30	32
57	20	22	23	25	26	28	29	31	32	34
58	22	24	25	27	28	30	31	33	34	36
59	24	25	27	28	30	32	33	35	36	38
60	26	27	29	31	32	34	35	37	38	40
61	28	29	31	33	34	36	37	39	40	42
62	30	32	33	35	36	38	40	41	42	44
63	32	34	35	37	39	40	42	43	45	46
64	34	36	38	39	41	42	44	45	47	48
65	37	38	40	42	43	45	46	47	49	50
66	39	41	42	44	45	47	48	50	51	52
67	41	43	45	46	48	49	50	52	53	54
68	44	45	47	48	50	51	52	54	55	56
69	46	48	49	51	52	53	54	56	57	58
70	48	50	51	53	54	55	57	58	59	60
71	51	52	54	55	56	57	59	60	61	62
72	53	54	56	57	58	59	60	62	62	63
73	55	57	58	59	60	61	62	63	64	65
74	57	59	60	61	62	63	64	65	66	67
75	59	61	62	63	64	65	66	67	68	69
76	62	63	64	65	66	67	68	69	69	70
77	64	65	66	67	68	69	70	70	71	72
78	66	67	68	69	70	70	71	72	73	73
79	67	68	69	70	71	72	73	73	74	75
80	69	70	71	72	73	74	74	75	76	76
81	71	72	73	74	74	75	76	76	77	78
82	73	74	74	75	76	77	77	78	78	79
83	74	75	76	77	77	78	79	79	80	80
84	76	77	77	78	79	79	80	80	81	81
85	78	78	79	79	80	81	81	82	82	83
86	79	80	80	81	81	82	82	83	83	84
87	80	81	81	82	83	83	83	84	84	85
88	82	82	83	83	84	84	85	85	85	86
89	83	83	84	84	85	85	85	86	86	87
90	84	84	85	85	86	86	86	87	87	87
91	85	85	86	86	87	87	87	88	88	88
92	86	86	87	87	87	88	88	88	89	89
93	87	87	87	88	88	88	89	89	89	90
94	87	88	88	88	89	89	89	90	90	90
95	88	88	89	89	89	90	90	90	91	91
96	89	89	89	90	90	90	91	91	91	91
97	89	90	90	90	91	91	91	91	92	92
98	90	90	91	91	91	91	92	92	92	92
99	91	91	91	92	92	92	92	92	93	93
100	91	92	92	92	92	92	93	93	93	93
101	92	92	92	93	93	93	93	93	94	94
102	92	93	93	93	93	94	94	94	94	94
103	93	93	93	94	94	94	94	94	94	95
104	94	94	94	94	94	95	95	95	95	95
105	94	94	95	95	95	95	95	95	95	95
106	95	95	95	95	95	95	96	96	96	96
107	95	95	96	96	96	96	96	96	96	96
108	96	96	96	96	96	96	96	96	97	97
109	96	96	96	97	97	97	97	97	97	97
110	97	97	97	97	97	97	97	97	97	97
111	97	97	97	97	97	97	98	98	98	98
112	97	97	98	98	98	98	98	98	98	98
113	98	98	98	98	98	98	98	98	98	98
114	98	98	98	98	98	98	98	98	98	99
115	98	98	98	99	99	99	99	99	99	99

Table VIII--Temporary Life Annuities; \1\ One Life--Expected Return Multiples
[See footnote at end of tables]
Temporary Period--Maximum Duration of Annuity

Age	Years--									
	1	2	3	4	5	6	7	8	9	10
5	1.0	2.0	3.0	4.0	5.0	6.0	7.0	8.0	9.0	10.0
6	1.0	2.0	3.0	4.0	5.0	6.0	7.0	8.0	9.0	10.0
7	1.0	2.0	3.0	4.0	5.0	6.0	7.0	8.0	9.0	10.0
8	1.0	2.0	3.0	4.0	5.0	6.0	7.0	8.0	9.0	10.0
9	1.0	2.0	3.0	4.0	5.0	6.0	7.0	8.0	9.0	10.0

	1.0	2.0	3.0	4.0	5.0	6.0	7.0	8.0	9.0	10.0	
10	1.0	2.0	3.0	4.0	5.0	6.0	7.0	8.0	9.0	10.0	
11	1.0	2.0	3.0	4.0	5.0	6.0	7.0	8.0	9.0	10.0	
12	1.0	2.0	3.0	4.0	5.0	6.0	7.0	8.0	9.0	10.0	
13	1.0	2.0	3.0	4.0	5.0	6.0	7.0	8.0	9.0	10.0	
14	1.0	2.0	3.0	4.0	5.0	6.0	7.0	8.0	9.0	10.0	5
15	1.0	2.0	3.0	4.0	5.0	6.0	7.0	8.0	9.0	10.0	
16	1.0	2.0	3.0	4.0	5.0	6.0	7.0	8.0	9.0	10.0	
17	1.0	2.0	3.0	4.0	5.0	6.0	7.0	8.0	9.0	10.0	
18	1.0	2.0	3.0	4.0	5.0	6.0	7.0	8.0	9.0	10.0	
19	1.0	2.0	3.0	4.0	5.0	6.0	7.0	8.0	9.0	10.0	10
20	1.0	2.0	3.0	4.0	5.0	6.0	7.0	8.0	9.0	10.0	
21	1.0	2.0	3.0	4.0	5.0	6.0	7.0	8.0	9.0	10.0	
22	1.0	2.0	3.0	4.0	5.0	6.0	7.0	8.0	9.0	10.0	
23	1.0	2.0	3.0	4.0	5.0	6.0	7.0	8.0	9.0	10.0	
24	1.0	2.0	3.0	4.0	5.0	6.0	7.0	8.0	9.0	10.0	15
25	1.0	2.0	3.0	4.0	5.0	6.0	7.0	8.0	9.0	10.0	
26	1.0	2.0	3.0	4.0	5.0	6.0	7.0	8.0	9.0	10.0	
27	1.0	2.0	3.0	4.0	5.0	6.0	7.0	8.0	9.0	10.0	
28	1.0	2.0	3.0	4.0	5.0	6.0	7.0	8.0	9.0	10.0	
29	1.0	2.0	3.0	4.0	5.0	6.0	7.0	8.0	9.0	10.0	20
30	1.0	2.0	3.0	4.0	5.0	6.0	7.0	8.0	9.0	10.0	
31	1.0	2.0	3.0	4.0	5.0	6.0	7.0	8.0	9.0	10.0	
32	1.0	2.0	3.0	4.0	5.0	6.0	7.0	8.0	9.0	10.0	
33	1.0	2.0	3.0	4.0	5.0	6.0	7.0	8.0	9.0	10.0	
34	1.0	2.0	3.0	4.0	5.0	6.0	7.0	8.0	9.0	10.0	25
35	1.0	2.0	3.0	4.0	5.0	6.0	7.0	8.0	9.0	10.0	
36	1.0	2.0	3.0	4.0	5.0	6.0	7.0	8.0	9.0	10.0	
37	1.0	2.0	3.0	4.0	5.0	6.0	7.0	8.0	9.0	9.9	
38	1.0	2.0	3.0	4.0	5.0	6.0	7.0	8.0	9.0	9.9	
39	1.0	2.0	3.0	4.0	5.0	6.0	7.0	8.0	9.0	9.9	30
40	1.0	2.0	3.0	4.0	5.0	6.0	7.0	8.0	8.9	9.9	
41	1.0	2.0	3.0	4.0	5.0	6.0	7.0	8.0	8.9	9.9	
42	1.0	2.0	3.0	4.0	5.0	6.0	7.0	8.0	8.9	9.9	
43	1.0	2.0	3.0	4.0	5.0	6.0	7.0	7.9	8.9	9.9	
44	1.0	2.0	3.0	4.0	5.0	6.0	7.0	7.9	8.9	9.9	35
45	1.0	2.0	3.0	4.0	5.0	6.0	7.0	7.9	8.9	9.9	
46	1.0	2.0	3.0	4.0	5.0	6.0	6.9	7.9	8.9	9.9	
47	1.0	2.0	3.0	4.0	5.0	6.0	6.9	7.9	8.9	9.9	
48	1.0	2.0	3.0	4.0	5.0	6.0	6.9	7.9	8.9	9.9	
49	1.0	2.0	3.0	4.0	5.0	6.0	6.9	7.9	8.9	9.8	40
50	1.0	2.0	3.0	4.0	5.0	5.9	6.9	7.9	8.9	9.8	
51	1.0	2.0	3.0	4.0	5.0	5.9	6.9	7.9	8.9	9.8	
52	1.0	2.0	3.0	4.0	5.0	5.9	6.9	7.9	8.8	9.8	
53	1.0	2.0	3.0	4.0	5.0	5.9	6.9	7.9	8.8	9.8	
54	1.0	2.0	3.0	4.0	4.9	5.9	6.9	7.9	8.8	9.8	45
55	1.0	2.0	3.0	4.0	4.9	5.9	6.9	7.8	8.8	9.7	
56	1.0	2.0	3.0	4.0	4.9	5.9	6.9	7.8	8.8	9.7	
57	1.0	2.0	3.0	4.0	4.9	5.9	6.9	7.8	8.8	9.7	
58	1.0	2.0	3.0	4.0	4.9	5.9	6.9	7.8	8.7	9.7	
59	1.0	2.0	3.0	4.0	4.9	5.9	6.8	7.8	8.7	9.6	50
60	1.0	2.0	3.0	3.9	4.9	5.9	6.8	7.8	8.7	9.6	
61	1.0	2.0	3.0	3.9	4.9	5.9	6.8	7.7	8.7	9.6	
62	1.0	2.0	3.0	3.9	4.9	5.8	6.8	7.7	8.6	9.5	
63	1.0	2.0	3.0	3.9	4.9	5.8	6.8	7.7	8.6	9.5	
64	1.0	2.0	3.0	3.9	4.9	5.8	6.7	7.6	8.5	9.4	55
65	1.0	2.0	3.0	3.9	4.9	5.8	6.7	7.6	8.5	9.3	
66	1.0	2.0	2.9	3.9	4.8	5.8	6.7	7.6	8.4	9.3	
67	1.0	2.0	2.9	3.9	4.8	5.7	6.6	7.5	8.4	9.2	
68	1.0	2.0	2.9	3.9	4.8	5.7	6.6	7.5	8.3	9.1	
69	1.0	2.0	2.9	3.9	4.8	5.7	6.6	7.4	8.2	9.0	60
70	1.0	2.0	2.9	3.9	4.8	5.6	6.5	7.3	8.1	8.9	
71	1.0	2.0	2.9	3.8	4.7	5.6	6.5	7.3	8.1	8.8	
72	1.0	2.0	2.9	3.8	4.7	5.6	6.4	7.2	8.0	8.7	
73	1.0	2.0	2.9	3.8	4.7	5.5	6.3	7.1	7.9	8.6	
74	1.0	1.9	2.9	3.8	4.6	5.5	6.3	7.0	7.7	8.4	65
75	1.0	1.9	2.9	3.8	4.6	5.4	6.2	6.9	7.6	8.3	
76	1.0	1.9	2.8	3.7	4.6	5.4	6.1	6.8	7.5	8.1	
77	1.0	1.9	2.8	3.7	4.5	5.3	6.0	6.7	7.3	7.9	
78	1.0	1.9	2.8	3.7	4.5	5.2	5.9	6.6	7.2	7.7	
79	1.0	1.9	2.8	3.6	4.4	5.1	5.8	6.4	7.0	7.5	70
80	1.0	1.9	2.8	3.6	4.4	5.1	5.7	6.3	6.8	7.3	
81	1.0	1.9	2.8	3.6	4.3	5.0	5.6	6.1	6.6	7.0	
82	1.0	1.9	2.7	3.5	4.2	4.9	5.4	6.0	6.4	6.8	
83	1.0	1.9	2.7	3.5	4.1	4.8	5.3	5.8	6.2	6.5	
84	1.0	1.8	2.7	3.4	4.1	4.6	5.2	5.6	6.0	6.3	75
85	1.0	1.8	2.6	3.3	4.0	4.5	5.0	5.4	5.7	6.0	
86	1.0	1.8	2.6	3.3	3.9	4.4	4.8	5.2	5.5	5.7	
87	.9	1.8	2.5	3.2	3.8	4.3	4.7	5.0	5.3	5.5	
88	.9	1.8	2.5	3.1	3.7	4.1	4.5	4.8	5.0	5.2	
89	.9	1.8	2.5	3.1	3.6	4.0	4.3	4.6	4.8	4.9	80
90	.9	1.7	2.4	3.0	3.4	3.8	4.1	4.4	4.5	4.7	
91	.9	1.7	2.4	2.9	3.3	3.7	4.0	4.2	4.3	4.4	
92	.9	1.7	2.3	2.8	3.2	3.5	3.8	4.0	4.1	4.2	
93	.9	1.7	2.3	2.7	3.1	3.4	3.6	3.8	3.9	4.0	

94	.9	1.6	2.2	2.7	3.0	3.3	3.5	3.6	3.7	3.8
95	.9	1.6	2.2	2.6	2.9	3.1	3.3	3.4	3.5	3.6
96	.9	1.6	2.1	2.5	2.8	3.0	3.2	3.3	3.3	3.4
97	.9	1.6	2.1	2.4	2.7	2.9	3.0	3.1	3.2	3.2
98	.9	1.5	2.0	2.4	2.6	2.8	2.9	3.0	3.0	3.0
99	.9	1.5	2.0	2.3	2.5	2.6	2.7	2.8	2.8	2.8
100	9	1.5	1.9	2.2	2.4	2.5	2.6	2.6	2.6	2.7
101	8	1.4	1.8	2.1	2.3	2.4	2.4	2.5	2.5	2.5
102	8	1.4	1.8	2.0	2.1	2.2	2.3	2.3	2.3	2.3
103	8	1.4	1.7	1.9	2.0	2.1	2.1	2.1	2.1	2.1
104	8	1.3	1.6	1.8	1.9	1.9	1.9	1.9	1.9	1.9
105	8	1.3	1.5	1.7	1.7	1.8	1.8	1.8	1.8	1.8
106	8	1.2	1.4	1.5	1.6	1.6	1.6	1.6	1.6	1.6
107	7	1.1	1.3	1.4	1.4	1.4	1.4	1.4	1.4	1.4
108	7	1.1	1.2	1.3	1.3	1.3	1.3	1.3	1.3	1.3
109	7	1.0	1.1	1.1	1.1	1.1	1.1	1.1	1.1	1.1
110	7	.9	1.0	1.0	1.0	1.0	1.0	1.0	1.0	1.0
111	6	.8	.9	.9	.9	.9	.9	.9	.9	.9
112	6	.7	.8	8	.8	.8	.8	.8	.8	.8
113	6	.6	.7	.7	.7	.7	.7	.7	.7	.7
114	5	.6	.6	.6	.6	.6	.6	.6	.6	.6
115	5	.5	.5	.5	.5	.5	.5	.5	.5	.5

Table VIII--Temporary Life Annuities;\1\ One Life--Expected Return Multiples
[See footnote at end of tables]
Temporary Period--Maximum Duration of Annuity

Age	Years--									
	11	12	13	14	15	16	17	18	19	20
5	11.0	12.0	13.0	14.0	15.0	16.0	17.0	18.0	19.0	19.9
6	11.0	12.0	13.0	14.0	15.0	16.0	17.0	18.0	19.0	19.9
7	11.0	12.0	13.0	14.0	15.0	16.0	17.0	18.0	19.0	19.9
8	11.0	12.0	13.0	14.0	15.0	16.0	17.0	18.0	18.9	19.9
9	11.0	12.0	13.0	14.0	15.0	16.0	17.0	18.0	18.9	19.9
10	11.0	12.0	13.0	14.0	15.0	16.0	17.0	18.0	18.9	19.9
11	11.0	12.0	13.0	14.0	15.0	16.0	17.0	17.9	18.9	19.9
12	11.0	12.0	13.0	14.0	15.0	16.0	17.0	17.9	18.9	19.9
13	11.0	12.0	13.0	14.0	15.0	16.0	17.0	17.9	18.9	19.9
14	11.0	12.0	13.0	14.0	15.0	16.0	16.9	17.9	18.9	19.9
15	11.0	12.0	13.0	14.0	15.0	16.0	16.9	17.9	18.9	19.9
16	11.0	12.0	13.0	14.0	15.0	16.0	16.9	17.9	18.9	19.9
17	11.0	12.0	13.0	14.0	15.0	15.9	16.9	17.9	18.9	19.9
18	11.0	12.0	13.0	14.0	15.0	15.9	16.9	17.9	18.9	19.9
19	11.0	12.0	13.0	14.0	15.0	15.9	16.9	17.9	18.9	19.9
20	11.0	12.0	13.0	14.0	14.9	15.9	16.9	17.9	18.9	19.9
21	11.0	12.0	13.0	14.0	14.9	15.9	16.9	17.9	18.9	19.9
22	11.0	12.0	13.0	14.0	14.9	15.9	16.9	17.9	18.9	19.9
23	11.0	12.0	13.0	13.9	14.9	15.9	16.9	17.9	18.9	19.9
24	11.0	12.0	13.0	13.9	14.9	15.9	16.9	17.9	18.9	19.9
25	11.0	12.0	13.0	13.9	14.9	15.9	16.9	17.9	18.9	19.9
26	11.0	12.0	12.9	13.9	14.9	15.9	16.9	17.9	18.9	19.9
27	11.0	12.0	12.9	13.9	14.9	15.9	16.9	17.9	18.9	19.9
28	11.0	12.0	12.9	13.9	14.9	15.9	16.9	17.9	18.9	19.8
29	11.0	12.0	12.9	13.9	14.9	15.9	16.9	17.9	18.9	19.8
30	11.0	11.9	12.9	13.9	14.9	15.9	16.9	17.9	18.8	19.8
31	11.0	11.9	12.9	13.9	14.9	15.9	16.9	17.9	18.8	19.8
32	11.0	11.9	12.9	13.9	14.9	15.9	16.9	17.8	18.8	19.8
33	11.0	11.9	12.9	13.9	14.9	15.9	16.9	17.8	18.8	19.8
34	10.9	11.9	12.9	13.9	14.9	15.9	16.8	17.8	18.8	19.8
35	10.9	11.9	12.9	13.9	14.9	15.9	16.8	17.8	18.8	19.7
36	10.9	11.9	12.9	13.9	14.9	15.8	16.8	17.8	18.8	19.7
37	10.9	11.9	12.9	13.9	14.9	15.8	16.8	17.8	18.7	19.7
38	10.9	11.9	12.9	13.9	14.8	15.8	16.8	17.8	18.7	19.7
39	10.9	11.9	12.9	13.9	14.8	15.8	16.8	17.7	18.7	19.6
40	10.9	11.9	12.9	13.8	14.8	15.8	16.7	17.7	18.7	19.6
41	10.9	11.9	12.9	13.8	14.8	15.8	16.7	17.7	18.6	19.6
42	10.9	11.9	12.8	13.8	14.8	15.7	16.7	17.6	18.6	19.5
43	10.9	11.9	12.8	13.8	14.8	15.7	16.7	17.6	18.6	19.5
44	10.9	11.8	12.8	13.8	14.7	15.7	16.6	17.6	18.5	19.4
45	10.9	11.8	12.8	13.8	14.7	15.7	16.6	17.5	18.5	19.4
46	10.9	11.8	12.8	13.7	14.7	15.6	16.6	17.5	18.4	19.3
47	10.8	11.8	12.8	13.7	14.7	15.6	16.5	17.5	18.4	19.3
48	10.8	11.8	12.7	13.7	14.6	15.6	16.5	17.4	18.3	19.2
49	10.8	11.8	12.7	13.7	14.6	15.5	16.4	17.4	18.3	19.2
50	10.8	11.7	12.7	13.6	14.6	15.5	16.4	17.3	18.2	19.1
51	10.8	11.7	12.7	13.6	14.5	15.4	16.3	17.2	18.1	19.0
52	10.8	11.7	12.6	13.6	14.5	15.4	16.3	17.2	18.0	18.9
53	10.7	11.7	12.6	13.5	14.4	15.3	16.2	17.1	18.0	18.8
54	10.7	11.6	12.6	13.5	14.4	15.3	16.2	17.0	17.9	18.7
55	10.7	11.6	12.5	13.4	14.3	15.2	16.1	16.9	17.8	18.6
56	10.7	11.6	12.5	13.4	14.3	15.1	16.0	16.8	17.6	18.4
57	10.6	11.5	12.4	13.3	14.2	15.1	15.9	16.7	17.5	18.3

Sec. 72. Annuities; certain proceeds of endowment and life insurance contracts

Age										
58	10.6	11.5	12.4	13.3	14.1	15.0	15.8	16.6	17.4	18.1
59	10.6	11.4	12.3	13.2	14.0	14.9	15.7	16.4	17.2	17.9
60	10.5	11.4	12.3	13.1	13.9	14.7	15.5	16.3	17.0	17.7
61	10.5	11.3	12.2	13.0	13.8	14.6	15.4	16.1	16.8	17.5
62	10.4	11.3	12.1	12.9	13.7	14.5	15.2	15.9	16.6	17.2
63	10.3	11.2	12.0	12.8	13.6	14.3	15.0	15.7	16.3	17.0
64	10.3	11.1	11.9	12.7	13.4	14.1	14.8	15.5	16.1	16.7
65	10.2	11.0	11.8	12.5	13.2	13.9	14.6	15.2	15.8	16.3
66	10.1	10.9	11.6	12.4	13.1	13.7	14.4	14.9	15.5	16.0
67	10.0	10.8	11.5	12.2	12.9	13.5	14.1	14.7	15.2	15.6
68	9.9	10.6	11.4	12.0	12.7	13.3	13.8	14.3	14.8	15.3
69	9.8	10.5	11.2	11.8	12.4	13.0	13.5	14.0	14.4	14.8
70	9.6	10.3	11.0	11.6	12.2	12.7	13.2	13.7	14.0	14.4
71	9.5	10.2	10.8	11.4	11.9	12.4	12.9	13.3	13.6	13.9
72	9.4	10.0	10.6	11.2	11.7	12.1	12.5	12.9	13.2	13.5
73	9.2	9.8	10.4	10.9	11.4	11.8	12.1	12.5	12.7	13.0
74	9.0	9.6	10.1	10.6	11.0	11.4	11.7	12.0	12.3	12.5
75	8.8	9.4	9.9	10.3	10.7	11.0	11.3	11.6	11.8	12.0
76	8.6	9.1	9.6	10.0	10.3	10.6	10.9	11.1	11.3	11.4
77	8.4	8.9	9.3	9.7	10.0	10.2	10.5	10.6	10.8	10.9
78	8.2	8.6	9.0	9.3	9.6	9.8	10.0	10.2	10.3	10.4
79	7.9	8.3	8.7	9.0	9.2	9.4	9.5	9.7	9.8	9.8
80	7.7	8.0	8.3	8.6	8.8	9.0	9.1	9.2	9.3	9.3
81	7.4	7.7	8.0	8.2	8.4	8.5	8.6	8.7	8.8	8.8
82	7.1	7.4	7.6	7.8	8.0	8.1	8.2	8.2	8.3	8.3
83	6.8	7.1	7.3	7.4	7.5	7.6	7.7	7.8	7.8	7.8
84	6.5	6.7	6.9	7.0	7.1	7.2	7.3	7.3	7.3	7.4
85	6.2	6.4	6.6	6.7	6.7	6.8	6.8	6.9	6.9	6.9
86	5.9	6.1	6.2	6.3	6.4	6.4	6.4	6.5	6.5	6.5
87	5.6	5.8	5.9	5.9	6.0	6.0	6.0	6.1	6.1	6.1
88	5.3	5.4	5.5	5.6	5.6	5.6	5.7	5.7	5.7	5.7
89	5.1	5.1	5.2	5.3	5.3	5.3	5.3	5.3	5.3	5.3
90	4.8	4.9	4.9	4.9	5.0	5.0	5.0	5.0	5.0	5.0
91	4.5	4.6	4.6	4.6	4.7	4.7	4.7	4.7	4.7	4.7
92	4.3	4.3	4.3	4.4	4.4	4.4	4.4	4.4	4.4	4.4
93	4.0	4.1	4.1	4.1	4.1	4.1	4.1	4.1	4.1	4.1
94	3.8	3.8	3.9	3.9	3.9	3.9	3.9	3.9	3.9	3.9
95	3.6	3.6	3.6	3.6	3.7	3.7	3.7	3.7	3.7	3.7
96	3.4	3.4	3.4	3.4	3.4	3.4	3.4	3.4	3.4	3.4
97	3.2	3.2	3.2	3.2	3.2	3.2	3.2	3.2	3.2	3.2
98	3.0	3.0	3.0	3.0	3.0	3.0	3.0	3.0	3.0	3.0
99	2.8	2.8	2.8	2.8	2.8	2.8	2.8	2.8	2.8	2.8
100	2.7	2.7	2.7	2.7	2.7	2.7	2.7	2.7	2.7	2.7
101	2.5	2.5	2.5	2.5	2.5	2.5	2.5	2.5	2.5	2.5
102	2.3	2.3	2.3	2.3	2.3	2.3	2.3	2.3	2.3	2.3
103	2.1	2.1	2.1	2.1	2.1	2.1	2.1	2.1	2.1	2.1
104	1.9	1.9	1.9	1.9	1.9	1.9	1.9	1.9	1.9	1.9
105	1.8	1.8	1.8	1.8	1.8	1.8	1.8	1.8	1.8	1.8
106	1.6	1.6	1.6	1.6	1.6	1.6	1.6	1.6	1.6	1.6
107	1.4	1.4	1.4	1.4	1.4	1.4	1.4	1.4	1.4	1.4
108	1.3	1.3	1.3	1.3	1.3	1.3	1.3	1.3	1.3	1.3
109	1.1	1.1	1.1	1.1	1.1	1.1	1.1	1.1	1.1	1.1
110	1.0	1.0	1.0	1.0	1.0	1.0	1.0	1.0	1.0	1.0
111	.9	.9	.9	.9	.9	.9	.9	.9	.9	.9
112	.8	.8	.8	.8	.8	.8	.8	.8	.8	.8
113	.7	.7	.7	.7	.7	.7	.7	.7	.7	.7
114	.6	.6	.6	.6	.6	.6	.6	.6	.6	.6
115	.5	.5	.5	.5	.5	.5	.5	.5	.5	.5

Table VIII--Temporary Life Annuities; \1\ One Life--Expected Return Multiples
[See footnote at end of tables]

Age	Years--									
	21	22	23	24	25	26	27	28	29	30
5	20.9	21.9	22.9	23.9	24.9	25.9	26.9	27.9	28.9	29.9
6	20.9	21.9	22.9	23.9	24.9	25.9	26.9	27.9	28.9	29.9
7	20.9	21.9	22.9	23.9	24.9	25.9	26.9	27.9	28.9	29.9
8	20.9	21.9	22.9	23.9	24.9	25.9	26.9	27.9	28.9	29.8
9	20.9	21.9	22.9	23.9	24.9	25.9	26.9	27.9	28.9	29.8
10	20.9	21.9	22.9	23.9	24.9	25.9	26.9	27.9	28.8	29.8
11	20.9	21.9	22.9	23.9	24.9	25.9	26.9	27.9	28.8	29.8
12	20.9	21.9	22.9	23.9	24.9	25.9	26.9	27.8	28.8	29.8
13	20.9	21.9	22.9	23.9	24.9	25.9	26.9	27.8	28.8	29.8
14	20.9	21.9	22.9	23.9	24.9	25.9	26.8	27.8	28.8	29.8
15	20.9	21.9	22.9	23.9	24.9	25.9	26.8	27.8	28.8	29.8
16	20.9	21.9	22.9	23.9	24.9	25.8	26.8	27.8	28.8	29.8
17	20.9	21.9	22.9	23.9	24.9	25.8	26.8	27.8	28.8	29.8
18	20.9	21.9	22.9	23.9	24.8	25.8	26.8	27.8	28.8	29.7
19	20.9	21.9	22.9	23.9	24.8	25.8	26.8	27.8	28.8	29.7
20	20.9	21.9	22.9	23.8	24.8	25.8	26.8	27.8	28.7	29.7
21	20.9	21.9	22.9	23.8	24.8	25.8	26.8	27.8	28.7	29.7

5 10 15 20 25 30 35 40 45 50 55 60 65 70 75 80

Sec. 72. Annuities; certain proceeds of endowment and life insurance contracts

	Age										
	22	20.9	21.9	22.8	23.8	24.8	25.8	26.8	27.7	28.7	29.7
	23	20.9	21.9	22.8	23.8	24.8	25.8	26.7	27.7	28.7	29.7
	24	20.9	21.8	22.8	23.8	24.8	25.8	26.7	27.7	28.7	29.6
	25	20.9	21.8	22.8	23.8	24.8	25.7	26.7	27.7	28.6	29.6
5	26	20.8	21.8	22.8	23.8	24.8	25.7	26.7	27.7	28.6	29.6
	27	20.8	21.8	22.8	23.8	24.7	25.7	26.7	27.6	28.6	29.5
	28	20.8	21.8	22.8	23.7	24.7	25.7	26.6	27.6	28.6	29.5
	29	20.8	21.8	22.8	23.7	24.7	25.7	26.6	27.6	28.5	29.5
	30	20.8	21.8	22.7	23.7	24.7	25.6	26.6	27.5	28.5	29.4
10	31	20.8	21.8	22.7	23.7	24.6	25.6	26.6	27.5	28.4	29.4
	32	20.8	21.7	22.7	23.7	24.6	25.6	26.5	27.5	28.4	29.3
	33	20.8	21.7	22.7	23.6	24.6	25.5	26.5	27.4	28.4	29.3
	34	20.7	21.7	22.7	23.6	24.6	25.5	26.4	27.4	28.3	29.2
	35	20.7	21.7	22.6	23.6	24.5	25.5	26.4	27.3	28.2	29.2
15	36	20.7	21.6	22.6	23.5	24.5	25.4	26.3	27.3	28.2	29.1
	37	20.7	21.6	22.6	23.5	24.4	25.4	26.3	27.2	28.1	29.0
	38	20.6	21.6	22.5	23.4	24.4	25.3	26.2	27.1	28.0	28.9
	39	20.6	21.5	22.5	23.4	24.3	25.2	26.1	27.0	27.9	28.8
	40	20.6	21.5	22.4	23.3	24.3	25.2	26.1	27.0	27.8	28.7
20	41	20.5	21.4	22.4	23.3	24.2	25.1	26.0	26.9	27.7	28.6
	42	20.5	21.4	22.3	23.2	24.1	25.0	25.9	26.8	27.6	28.5
	43	20.4	21.3	22.2	23.2	24.0	24.9	25.8	26.6	27.5	28.3
	44	20.4	21.3	22.2	23.1	24.0	24.8	25.7	26.5	27.3	28.2
	45	20.3	21.2	22.1	23.0	23.9	24.7	25.6	26.4	27.2	28.0
25	46	20.2	21.1	22.0	22.9	23.8	24.6	25.4	26.2	27.0	27.8
	47	20.2	21.1	21.9	22.8	23.6	24.5	25.3	26.1	26.8	27.6
	48	20.1	21.0	21.8	22.7	23.5	24.3	25.1	25.9	26.6	27.4
	49	20.0	20.9	21.7	22.6	23.4	24.2	25.0	25.7	26.4	27.1
	50	19.9	20.8	21.6	22.4	23.2	24.0	24.8	25.5	26.2	26.9
30	51	19.8	20.7	21.5	22.3	23.1	23.8	24.6	25.3	25.9	26.6
	52	19.7	20.6	21.4	22.1	22.9	23.6	24.3	25.0	25.7	26.3
	53	19.6	20.4	21.2	22.0	22.7	23.4	24.1	24.7	25.3	25.9
	54	19.5	20.3	21.0	21.8	22.5	23.2	23.8	24.4	25.0	25.6
	55	19.3	20.1	20.8	21.6	22.2	22.9	23.5	24.1	24.6	25.2
35	56	19.2	19.9	20.6	21.3	22.0	22.6	23.2	23.7	24.3	24.7
	57	19.0	19.7	20.4	21.1	21.7	22.3	22.8	23.4	23.8	24.3
	58	18.8	19.5	20.2	20.8	21.4	21.9	22.5	22.9	23.4	23.8
	59	18.6	19.3	19.9	20.5	21.1	21.6	22.0	22.5	22.9	23.2
	60	18.4	19.0	19.6	20.2	20.7	21.2	21.6	22.0	22.4	22.7
40	61	18.1	18.7	19.3	19.8	20.3	20.7	21.1	21.5	21.8	22.1
	62	17.8	18.4	18.9	19.4	19.9	20.3	20.6	21.0	21.2	21.5
	63	17.5	18.1	18.5	19.0	19.4	19.8	20.1	20.4	20.6	20.8
	64	17.2	17.7	18.1	18.6	18.9	19.3	19.5	19.8	20.0	20.2
	65	16.8	17.3	17.7	18.1	18.4	18.7	18.9	19.2	19.3	19.5
45	66	16.5	16.9	17.3	17.6	17.9	18.1	18.3	18.5	18.7	18.8
	67	16.1	16.4	16.8	17.1	17.3	17.5	17.7	17.9	18.0	18.1
	68	15.6	16.0	16.3	16.5	16.7	16.9	17.1	17.2	17.3	17.4
	69	15.2	15.5	15.7	16.0	16.1	16.3	16.4	16.5	16.6	16.7
	70	14.7	15.0	15.2	15.4	15.5	15.7	15.8	15.8	15.9	15.9
50	71	14.2	14.4	14.6	14.8	14.9	15.0	15.1	15.2	15.2	15.2
	72	13.7	13.9	14.1	14.2	14.3	14.4	14.4	14.5	14.5	14.5
	73	13.2	13.3	13.5	13.6	13.7	13.7	13.8	13.8	13.8	13.9
	74	12.6	12.8	12.9	13.0	13.0	13.1	13.1	13.1	13.2	13.2
	75	12.1	12.2	12.3	12.4	12.4	12.5	12.5	12.5	12.5	12.5
55	76	11.5	11.6	11.7	11.8	11.8	11.8	11.8	11.9	11.9	11.9
	77	11.0	11.1	11.1	11.2	11.2	11.2	11.2	11.2	11.2	11.2
	78	10.4	10.5	10.5	10.6	10.6	10.6	10.6	10.6	10.6	10.6
	79	9.9	9.9	10.0	10.0	10.0	10.0	10.0	10.0	10.0	10.0
	80	9.4	9.4	9.4	9.4	9.5	9.5	9.5	9.5	9.5	9.5
60	81	8.8	8.9	8.9	8.9	8.9	8.9	8.9	8.9	8.9	8.9
	82	8.3	8.4	8.4	8.4	8.4	8.4	8.4	8.4	8.4	8.4
	83	7.8	7.9	7.9	7.9	7.9	7.9	7.9	7.9	7.9	7.9
	84	7.4	7.4	7.4	7.4	7.4	7.4	7.4	7.4	7.4	7.4
	85	6.9	6.9	6.9	6.9	6.9	6.9	6.9	6.9	6.9	6.9
65	86	6.5	6.5	6.5	6.5	6.5	6.5	6.5	6.5	6.5	6.5
	87	6.1	6.1	6.1	6.1	6.1	6.1	6.1	6.1	6.1	6.1
	88	5.7	5.7	5.7	5.7	5.7	5.7	5.7	5.7	5.7	5.7
	89	5.3	5.3	5.3	5.3	5.3	5.3	5.3	5.3	5.3	5.3
	90	5.0	5.0	5.0	5.0	5.0	5.0	5.0	5.0	5.0	5.0
70	91	4.7	4.7	4.7	4.7	4.7	4.7	4.7	4.7	4.7	4.7
	92	4.4	4.4	4.4	4.4	4.4	4.4	4.4	4.4	4.4	4.4
	93	4.1	4.1	4.1	4.1	4.1	4.1	4.1	4.1	4.1	4.1
	94	3.9	3.9	3.9	3.9	3.9	3.9	3.9	3.9	3.9	3.9
	95	3.7	3.7	3.7	3.7	3.7	3.7	3.7	3.7	3.7	3.7
75	96	3.4	3.4	3.4	3.4	3.4	3.4	3.4	3.4	3.4	3.4
	97	3.2	3.2	3.2	3.2	3.2	3.2	3.2	3.2	3.2	3.2
	98	3.0	3.0	3.0	3.0	3.0	3.0	3.0	3.0	3.0	3.0
	99	2.8	2.8	2.8	2.8	2.8	2.8	2.8	2.8	2.8	2.8
	100	2.7	2.7	2.7	2.7	2.7	2.7	2.7	2.7	2.7	2.7
80	101	2.5	2.5	2.5	2.5	2.5	2.5	2.5	2.5	2.5	2.5
	102	2.3	2.3	2.3	2.3	2.3	2.3	2.3	2.3	2.3	2.3
	103	2.1	2.1	2.1	2.1	2.1	2.1	2.1	2.1	2.1	2.1
	104	1.9	1.9	1.9	1.9	1.9	1.9	1.9	1.9	1.9	1.9
	105	1.8	1.8	1.8	1.8	1.8	1.8	1.8	1.8	1.8	1.8

Sec. 72. Annuities; certain proceeds of endowment and life insurance contracts

106	1.6	1.6	1.6	1.6	1.6	1.6	1.6	1.6	1.6	1.6	
107	1.4	1.4	1.4	1.4	1.4	1.4	1.4	1.4	1.4	1.4	
108	1.3	1.3	1.3	1.3	1.3	1.3	1.3	1.3	1.3	1.3	
109	1.1	1.1	1.1	1.1	1.1	1.1	1.1	1.1	1.1	1.1	
110	1.0	1.0	1.0	1.0	1.0	1.0	1.0	1.0	1.0	1.0	5
111	.9	.9	.9	.9	.9	.9	.9	.9	.9	.9	
112	.8	.8	.8	.8	.8	.8	.8	.8	.8	.8	
113	.7	.7	.7	.7	.7	.7	.7	.7	.7	.7	
114	.6	.6	.6	.6	.6	.6	.6	.6	.6	.6	
115	.5	.5	.5	.5	.5	.5	.5	.5	.5	.5	10

Table VIII--Temporary Life Annuities;\1\ One Life--Expected Return Multiples
[See footnote at end of tables]
Temporary Period--Maximum Duration of Annuity

Years--

Age	31	32	33	34	35	36	37	38	39	40
5	30.8	31.8	32.8	33.8	34.8	35.8	36.8	37.7	38.7	39.7
6	30.8	31.8	32.8	33.8	34.8	35.8	36.8	37.7	38.7	39.7
7	30.8	31.8	32.8	33.8	34.8	35.8	36.7	37.7	38.7	39.7
8	30.8	31.8	32.8	33.8	34.8	35.7	36.7	37.7	38.7	39.7
9	30.8	31.8	32.8	33.8	34.8	35.7	36.7	37.7	38.7	39.6
10	30.8	31.8	32.8	33.8	34.7	35.7	36.7	37.7	38.6	39.6
11	30.8	31.8	32.8	33.8	34.7	35.7	36.7	37.6	38.6	39.6
12	30.8	31.8	32.8	33.7	34.7	35.7	36.7	37.6	38.6	39.6
13	30.8	31.8	32.7	33.7	34.7	35.7	36.6	37.6	38.6	39.5
14	30.8	31.8	32.7	33.7	34.7	35.7	36.6	37.6	38.6	39.5
15	30.8	31.7	32.7	33.7	34.7	35.6	36.6	37.6	38.5	39.5
16	30.8	31.7	32.7	33.7	34.6	35.6	36.6	37.5	38.5	39.4
17	30.7	31.7	32.7	33.7	34.6	35.6	36.5	37.5	38.5	39.4
18	30.7	31.7	32.7	33.6	34.6	35.6	36.5	37.5	38.4	39.4
19	30.7	31.7	32.6	33.6	34.6	35.5	36.5	37.4	38.4	39.3
20	30.7	31.7	32.6	33.6	34.5	35.5	36.4	37.4	38.3	39.3
21	30.7	31.6	32.6	33.6	34.5	35.5	36.4	37.4	38.3	39.2
22	30.6	31.6	32.6	33.5	34.5	35.4	36.4	37.3	38.2	39.2
23	30.6	31.6	32.5	33.5	34.4	35.4	36.3	37.3	38.2	39.1
24	30.6	31.5	32.5	33.5	34.4	35.3	36.3	37.2	38.1	39.0
25	30.6	31.5	32.5	33.4	34.3	35.3	36.2	37.1	38.1	39.0
26	30.5	31.5	32.4	33.4	34.3	35.2	36.2	37.1	38.0	38.9
27	30.5	31.4	32.4	33.3	34.2	35.2	36.1	37.0	37.9	38.8
28	30.5	31.4	32.3	33.3	34.2	35.1	36.0	36.9	37.8	38.7
29	30.4	31.4	32.3	33.2	34.1	35.0	35.9	36.8	37.7	38.6
30	30.4	31.3	32.2	33.1	34.1	35.0	35.8	36.7	37.6	38.5
31	30.3	31.2	32.2	33.1	34.0	34.9	35.8	36.6	37.5	38.3
32	30.3	31.2	32.1	33.0	33.9	34.8	35.6	36.5	37.4	38.2
33	30.2	31.1	32.0	32.9	33.8	34.7	35.5	36.4	37.2	38.0
34	30.1	31.0	31.9	32.8	33.7	34.6	35.4	36.2	37.1	37.9
35	30.1	31.0	31.8	32.7	33.6	34.4	35.3	36.1	36.9	37.7
36	30.0	30.9	31.7	32.6	33.5	34.3	35.1	35.9	36.7	37.4
37	29.9	30.8	31.6	32.5	33.3	34.1	34.9	35.7	36.5	37.2
38	29.8	30.7	31.5	32.3	33.2	34.0	34.7	35.5	36.2	37.0
39	29.7	30.5	31.4	32.2	33.0	33.8	34.5	35.3	36.0	36.7
40	29.6	30.4	31.2	32.0	32.8	33.6	34.3	35.0	35.7	36.4
41	29.4	30.2	31.0	31.8	32.6	33.3	34.1	34.7	35.4	36.0
42	29.3	30.1	30.9	31.6	32.4	33.1	33.8	34.4	35.1	35.7
43	29.1	29.9	30.7	31.4	32.1	32.8	33.5	34.1	34.7	35.3
44	28.9	29.7	30.5	31.2	31.9	32.5	33.2	33.8	34.3	34.9
45	28.8	29.5	30.2	30.9	31.6	32.2	32.8	33.4	33.9	34.4
46	28.5	29.3	30.0	30.6	31.3	31.9	32.4	33.0	33.5	33.9
47	28.3	29.0	29.7	30.3	30.9	31.5	32.0	32.5	33.0	33.4
48	28.1	28.7	29.4	30.0	30.6	31.1	31.6	32.1	32.5	32.9
49	27.8	28.4	29.0	29.6	30.2	30.7	31.1	31.5	31.9	32.3
50	27.5	28.1	28.7	29.2	29.7	30.2	30.6	31.0	31.4	31.7
51	27.2	27.8	28.3	28.8	29.3	29.7	30.1	30.4	30.7	31.0
52	26.8	27.4	27.9	28.4	28.8	29.2	29.5	29.8	30.1	30.3
53	26.5	27.0	27.4	27.9	28.3	28.6	28.9	29.2	29.4	29.6
54	26.1	26.5	27.0	27.4	27.7	28.0	28.3	28.5	28.7	28.9
55	25.6	26.1	26.5	26.8	27.1	27.4	27.6	27.8	28.0	28.1
56	25.2	25.6	25.9	26.2	26.5	26.7	26.9	27.1	27.2	27.3
57	24.7	25.0	25.3	25.6	25.8	26.0	26.2	26.3	26.5	26.5
58	24.1	24.4	24.7	25.0	25.2	25.3	25.5	25.6	25.7	25.7
59	23.6	23.8	24.1	24.3	24.4	24.6	24.7	24.8	24.9	24.9
60	23.0	23.2	23.4	23.6	23.7	23.8	23.9	24.0	24.0	24.1
61	22.3	22.5	22.7	22.9	23.0	23.1	23.1	23.2	23.2	23.3
62	21.7	21.9	22.0	22.1	22.2	22.3	22.3	22.4	22.4	22.4
63	21.0	21.1	21.3	21.4	21.4	21.5	21.5	21.6	21.6	21.6
64	20.3	20.4	20.5	20.6	20.6	20.7	20.7	20.7	20.8	20.8
65	19.6	19.7	19.8	19.8	19.9	19.9	19.9	19.9	19.9	20.0
66	18.9	19.0	19.0	19.1	19.1	19.1	19.1	19.1	19.1	19.1
67	18.2	18.2	18.3	18.3	18.3	18.3	18.3	18.3	18.4	18.4
68	17.4	17.5	17.5	17.5	17.5	17.6	17.6	17.6	17.6	17.6

15
20
25
30
35
40
45
50
55
60
65
70
75
80

Age										
69	16.7	16.7	16.8	16.8	16.8	16.8	16.8	16.8	16.8	16.8
70	16.0	16.0	16.0	16.0	16.0	16.0	16.0	16.0	16.0	16.0
71	15.3	15.3	15.3	15.3	15.3	15.3	15.3	15.3	15.3	15.3
72	14.6	14.6	14.6	14.6	14.6	14.6	14.6	14.6	14.6	14.6
73	13.9	13.9	13.9	13.9	13.9	13.9	13.9	13.9	13.9	13.9
74	13.2	13.2	13.2	13.2	13.2	13.2	13.2	13.2	13.2	13.2
75	12.5	12.5	12.5	12.5	12.5	12.5	12.5	12.5	12.5	12.5
76	11.9	11.9	11.9	11.9	11.9	11.9	11.9	11.9	11.9	11.9
77	11.2	11.2	11.2	11.2	11.2	11.2	11.2	11.2	11.2	11.2
78	10.6	10.6	10.6	10.6	10.6	10.6	10.6	10.6	10.6	10.6
79	10.0	10.0	10.0	10.0	10.0	10.0	10.0	10.0	10.0	10.0
80	9.5	9.5	9.5	9.5	9.5	9.5	9.5	9.5	9.5	9.5
81	8.9	8.9	8.9	8.9	8.9	8.9	8.9	8.9	8.9	8.9
82	8.4	8.4	8.4	8.4	8.4	8.4	8.4	8.4	8.4	8.4
83	7.9	7.9	7.9	7.9	7.9	7.9	7.9	7.9	7.9	7.9
84	7.4	7.4	7.4	7.4	7.4	7.4	7.4	7.4	7.4	7.4
85	6.9	6.9	6.9	6.9	6.9	6.9	6.9	6.9	6.9	6.9
86	6.5	6.5	6.5	6.5	6.5	6.5	6.5	6.5	6.5	6.5
87	6.1	6.1	6.1	6.1	6.1	6.1	6.1	6.1	6.1	6.1
88	5.7	5.7	5.7	5.7	5.7	5.7	5.7	5.7	5.7	5.7
89	5.3	5.3	5.3	5.3	5.3	5.3	5.3	5.3	5.3	5.3
90	5.0	5.0	5.0	5.0	5.0	5.0	5.0	5.0	5.0	5.0
91	4.7	4.7	4.7	4.7	4.7	4.7	4.7	4.7	4.7	4.7
92	4.4	4.4	4.4	4.4	4.4	4.4	4.4	4.4	4.4	4.4
93	4.1	4.1	4.1	4.1	4.1	4.1	4.1	4.1	4.1	4.1
94	3.9	3.9	3.9	3.9	3.9	3.9	3.9	3.9	3.9	3.9
95	3.7	3.7	3.7	3.7	3.7	3.7	3.7	3.7	3.7	3.7
96	3.4	3.4	3.4	3.4	3.4	3.4	3.4	3.4	3.4	3.4
97	3.2	3.2	3.2	3.2	3.2	3.2	3.2	3.2	3.2	3.2
98	3.0	3.0	3.0	3.0	3.0	3.0	3.0	3.0	3.0	3.0
99	2.8	2.8	2.8	2.8	2.8	2.8	2.8	2.8	2.8	2.8
100	2.7	2.7	2.7	2.7	2.7	2.7	2.7	2.7	2.7	2.7
101	2.5	2.5	2.5	2.5	2.5	2.5	2.5	2.5	2.5	2.5
102	2.3	2.3	2.3	2.3	2.3	2.3	2.3	2.3	2.3	2.3
103	2.1	2.1	2.1	2.1	2.1	2.1	2.1	2.1	2.1	2.1
104	1.9	1.9	1.9	1.9	1.9	1.9	1.9	1.9	1.9	1.9
105	1.8	1.8	1.8	1.8	1.8	1.8	1.8	1.8	1.8	1.8
106	1.6	1.6	1.6	1.6	1.6	1.6	1.6	1.6	1.6	1.6
107	1.4	1.4	1.4	1.4	1.4	1.4	1.4	1.4	1.4	1.4
108	1.3	1.3	1.3	1.3	1.3	1.3	1.3	1.3	1.3	1.3
109	1.1	1.1	1.1	1.1	1.1	1.1	1.1	1.1	1.1	1.1
110	1.0	1.0	1.0	1.0	1.0	1.0	1.0	1.0	1.0	1.0
111	.9	.9	.9	.9	.9	.9	.9	.9	.9	.9
112	.8	.8	.8	.8	.8	.8	.8	.8	.8	.8
113	.7	.7	.7	.7	. 7	.7	.7	. 7	.7	.7
114	.6	.6	.6	.6	.6	.6	.6	.6	.6	.6
115	.5	.5	.5	.5	.5	.5	.5	. 5	. 5	.5

\1\ The multiples in this table are not applicable to annuities for a term certain; for such cases see paragraph (c) of § 1.72-5.

***

Reg. § 1.72-11 Amounts not received as annuity payments.

***

(d) *Amounts received upon the surrender, redemption, or maturity of a contract.* (1) Any amount received upon the surrender, redemption, or maturity of a contract to which section 72 applies, which is not received as an annuity under the regulations of paragraph (b) of § 1.72-2, shall be included in the gross income of the recipient to the extent that it, when added to amounts previously received under the contract and which were excludable from the gross income of the recipient under the law applicable at the time of receipt, exceeds the aggregate of premiums or other consideration paid. See section 72(e)(2)(B). If amounts are to be received as an annuity, whether in lieu of or in addition to amounts described in the preceding sentence, such amounts shall be included in the gross income of the recipient in accordance with the provisions of paragraph (e) or (f) of this section, whichever is applicable. The rule stated in the first sentence of this paragraph shall not apply to payments received as an annuity or otherwise after the date of the first receipt of an amount as an annuity subsequent to the maturity, redemption, or surrender of the original contract. If amounts are so received and are other than amounts

Sec. 72. Annuities; certain proceeds of endowment and life insurance contracts

received as an annuity, they are includible in the gross income of the recipient. See section 72(e)(1)(A) and paragraph (b)(2) of this section.

(2) For the purpose of applying the rule contained in subparagraph (1) of this paragraph, it is immaterial whether the recipient of the amount received upon the surrender, redemption, or maturity of the contract is the same as the recipient of amounts 5 previously received under the contract which were excludable from gross income, except in the case of a contract transferred for a valuable consideration, with respect to which see paragraph (a) of § 1.72-10. For the limit on the amount of tax, for taxable years beginning before January 1, 1964, attributable to the receipt of certain lump sums to which this paragraph applies, see paragraph (g) of this section. 10

[T.D. 6500, 25 FR 11402, Nov. 26, 1960; T.D. 6497, 25 FR 10019, Oct. 20, 1960; T.D. 6885, 31 FR 7798, June 2, 1966; 7352, 40 FR 16663, Apr. 14, 1975; T.D. 8115, 51 FR 45691, Dec. 19, 1986; 52 FR 10223, Mar. 31, 1987; 60 FR 16381, Mar. 30, 1995]

15

Sec. 73. Services of child

(a) **Treatment of amounts received.** -- Amounts received in respect of the services of a child shall be included in his gross income and not in the gross income of the parent, even though such amounts are not received by the child.

(b) **Treatment of expenditures.** -- All expenditures by the parent or the child attributable to 20 amounts which are includible in the gross income of the child (and not of the parent) solely by reason of subsection (a) shall be treated as paid or incurred by the child.

(c) **Parent defined.** -- For purposes of this section, the term "parent" includes an individual who is entitled to the services of a child by reason of having parental rights and duties in respect of the child. 25

Sec. 74. Prizes and awards

(a) **General rule.** -- Except as otherwise provided in this section or in section 117 (relating to qualified scholarships), gross income includes amounts received as prizes and awards.

(b) **Exception for certain prizes and awards transferred to charities.** -- Gross income does 30 not include amounts received as prizes and awards made primarily in recognition of religious, charitable, scientific, educational, artistic, literary, or civic achievement, but only if--

(1) the recipient was selected without any action on his part to enter the contest or proceeding;

(2) the recipient is not required to render substantial future services as a condition to 35 receiving the prize or award; and

(3) the prize or award is transferred by the payor to a governmental unit or organization described in paragraph (1) or (2) of section 170(c) pursuant to a designation made by the recipient.

(c) **Exception for certain employee achievement awards.** -- 40

(1) **In general.** -- Gross income shall not include the value of an employee achievement award (as defined in section 274(j)) received by the taxpayer if the cost to the employer of the employee achievement award does not exceed the amount allowable as a deduction to the employer for the cost of the employee achievement award.

(2) **Excess deduction award.** -- If the cost to the employer of the employee achievement 45

Sec. 74. Prizes and awards

award received by the taxpayer exceeds the amount allowable as a deduction to the employer, then gross income includes the greater of--

   (A) an amount equal to the portion of the cost to the employer of the award that is not allowable as a deduction to
the employer (but not in excess of the value of the award), or

   (B) the amount by which the value of the award exceeds the amount allowable as a deduction to the employer.
The remaining portion of the value of such award shall not be included in the gross income of the recipient.

   (3) Treatment of tax-exempt employers. -- In the case of an employer exempt from taxation under this subtitle, any reference in this subsection to the amount allowable as a deduction to the employer shall be treated as a reference to the amount which would be allowable as a deduction to the employer if the employer were not exempt from taxation under this subtitle.

Reg. § 1.74-1 Prizes and awards.

   (a) *Inclusion in gross income.* (1) Section 74(a) requires the inclusion in gross income of all amounts received as prizes and awards, unless such prizes or awards qualify as an exclusion from gross income under subsection (b), or unless such prize or award is a scholarship or fellowship grant excluded from gross income by section 117. Prizes and awards which are includible in gross income include (but are not limited to) amounts received from radio and television giveaway shows, door prizes, and awards in contests of all types, as well as any prizes and awards from an employer to an employee in recognition of some achievement in connection with his employment.

   (2) If the prize or award is not made in money but is made in goods or services, the fair market value of the goods or services is the amount to be included in income.

   (b) *Exclusion from gross income.* Section 74(b) provides an exclusion from gross income of any amount received as a prize or award, if (1) such prize or award was made primarily in recognition of past achievements of the recipient in religious, charitable, scientific, educational, artistic, literary, or civic fields; (2) the recipient was selected without any action on his part to enter the contest or proceedings; and

   (3) the recipient is not required to render substantial future services as a condition to receiving the prize or award. Thus, such awards as the Nobel prize and the Pulitzer prize would qualify for the exclusion. Section 74(b) does not exclude prizes or awards from an employer to an employee in recognition of some achievement in connection with his employment.

   (c) *Scholarships and fellowship grants.* See section 117 and the regulations thereunder for provisions relating to scholarships and fellowship grants.

Proposed § 1.74-1 Prizes and awards. (1/9/89)

   (b) *Exclusion from gross income.*

***

   (4) the payor transfers the prize or award (and the prize or award is, in fact, transferred) to one or more governmental units or organizations described in paragraph (1) or (2) of section 170(c) pursuant to a designation by the recipient. Accordingly, awards such as the Nobel prize and the Pulitzer prize will qualify for the exclusion if the award is transferred by the payor to one or more qualifying organizations pursuant to a qualified designation by the recipient.

   (c) *Designation by recipient*--(1) *In general.* To qualify for the exclusion under this section, the recipient must make a qualifying designation, in writing, within 45 days of the

206

Sec. 74. Prizes and awards

date the prize or award is granted (see paragraph (e)(3) of this section for a definition of "granted"). A qualifying designation is required to indicate only that a designation is being made. The document does not need to state on its face that the organization(s) are entities described in paragraph (1) and/or (2) of section 170(c) to result in a qualified designation. Furthermore, it is not necessary that the document do more than identify a 5
class of entities from which the payor may select a recipient. However, designation of a specific nonqualified donee organization or designation of a class of recipients that may include nonqualified donee organizations is not a qualified designation. The following example illustrates the application of this section: A distinguished ophthalmologist, S, is awarded the Nobel prize for medicine. S may designate that the prize money be given to 10
a particular university that is described in section 170(c)(1), or to any university that is described in that section. However, S cannot designate that the award be given to a donee that is not described in section 170(c)(1), such as a foreign medical school. Selection of such a donee or inclusion of such a donee on a list of possible donees on S's designation would disqualify the designation. 15

(2) Prizes and awards granted before 60 days after date of publication of final regulations. In the case of prizes and awards granted before 60 days after date of publication of final regulations, a qualifying designation may be made at any time prior to 105 days after date of publication of final regulations.

(d) *Transferred by payor.* An exclusion will not be available under this section unless 20
the designated items or amounts are transferred by the payor to one or more qualified donee organizations. The provisions of this paragraph shall not be satisfied unless the items or amounts are transferred by the payor to one or more qualifying donee organizations no later than the due date of the return (without regard to extensions) for the taxable year in which the items or amounts would otherwise be includible in the 25
recipient's gross income. A transfer may be accomplished by any method that results in the receipt of the items or amounts by one or more qualified donee organizations from the payor and does not involve a disqualifying use of the items or amounts. Delivery of items or amounts by a person associated with a payor (e.g., a contractual agent, licensee, or other representative of the payor) will satisfy the requirements of this section 30
so long as the items or amounts are received by, or on behalf of, one or more qualified donee organizations. Possession of a prize or an award by any person before a designation is made will not result in the disallowance of an exclusion unless a disqualifying use of the items or amounts is made before the items or amounts are returned to the payor for transfer to one or more qualified donee organizations (see 35
paragraph (e)(2) of this section for a definition of "disqualifying use"). Accordingly, transfer of an item or amount to a nonqualified donee organization will not result in an ineffective transfer under this section if the item or amount is timely returned to the payor by the nonqualified donee organization before a disqualifying use of the item or amount is made and the item or amount is then transferred to a qualifying organization. 40

(e) *Definitions.*--(1) For purposes of this section, "qualified donee organizations" means entities defined in section 170(c)(1) or (2) of the Code.

(2) For purposes of this section, the term "disqualifying use" means, in the case of cash or other intangibles, spending, depositing, investing or otherwise using the prize or award so as to enure to the benefit of the recipient or any person other than the grantor 45
or an entity described in section 170 (c)(1) or (2). In the case of tangible items, the term "disqualifying use" means physical possession of the item for more than a brief period of time by any person other than the grantor or an entity described in section 170(c)(1) or (2). Thus, physical possession by the recipient or a person associated with the recipient may constitute a disqualifying use if the item is kept for more than a brief period of time. 50
For example, receipt of an unexpected tangible award at a ceremony that otherwise

Sec. 74. Prizes and awards

comports with the requirements of this section will not constitute a disqualifying use unless the recipient fails to return the item to the payor as soon as practicable after receipt.

(3) For purposes of this section, an item will be considered "granted" when it is subject
5 to the recipient's dominion and control to such an extent that it otherwise would be includible in the recipient's gross income.

(f) *Charitable deduction not allowable.* Neither the payor nor the recipient will be allowed a charitable deduction for the value of any prize or award that is excluded under this section.

10 (g) *Qualified scholarships.* See section 117 and the regulations thereunder for provisions relating to qualified scholarships.

Proposed § 1.74-2. Special exclusion for certain employee achievement awards. (1/9/89)

15 (a) *General rule.*--(1) Section 74(c) provides an exclusion from gross income for the value of an employee achievement award (as defined in section 274(j)) received by an employee if the cost to the employer of the award does not exceed the amount allowable as a deduction to the employer for the cost of the award. Thus, where the cost to the employer of an employee achievement award is fully deductible after considering the
20 limitation under section 274(j), the value representing the employer's cost of the award is excludable from the employee's gross income.

(2) Where the cost of an award to the employer is so disproportionate to the fair market value of the award that there is a significant likelihood that the award was given as disguised compensation, no portion of the award will qualify as an employee
25 achievement award excludable under the provisions of this section (see also §1.274-8(c) (1) and (4)).

(b) *Excess deduction award.* Where the cost to the employer of an employee achievement award exceeds the amount allowable as a deduction to the employer, the recipient must include in gross income an amount which is the greater of (1) the excess
30 of such cost over the amount that is allowable as a deduction (but not to exceed the fair market value of the award) or (2) the excess of the fair market value of the award over the amount allowable as a deduction to the employer.

(c) *Examples.* The operation of this section may be illustrated by the following examples:

35 *Example (1).* An employer makes a qualifying length of service award to an employee in the form of a television set. Assume that the deduction limitation under §274(j)(2) applicable to the award is $400. Assume also that the cost of the television set to the employer was $350, and that the fair market value of the television set is $475. The amount excludable is $475 (the full fair market value of the television set). This is true
40 even though the fair market value exceeds both the cost of the television set to the employer and the $400 deduction allowable to the employer for nonqualified plan awards under section 274(j)(2)(A).

Example (2). Assume the same facts as in example (1) except that the fair market value of the television set is $900. Under these circumstances, the fair market value of
45 the television set is so disproportionate to the cost of the item to the employer that the item will be considered payment of disguised compensation. As a result, no portion of the award will qualify as an employee achievement award. Since no portion of the award is excludable by the employee, the employer must report the full fair market value of the award as compensation on the employee's Form W-2.

50 *Example (3).* An employer makes a qualifying safety achievement award to an employee in the form of a pearl necklace. Assume that the deduction limitation under

Sec. 74. Prizes and awards

section 274(j) is $400. Assume also that the cost of the necklace to the employer is $425 and that the fair market value of the necklace is $475. The amount includible by the employee in gross income is the greater of (a) $25 (the difference between the cost of the item ($425) and the employer's deductible amount of $400) or (b) $75 (the amount by which the fair market value of the award ($475) exceeds the employer's deductible 5 amount of $400). Accordingly, $75 is the amount includible in the employee's gross income. The remaining portion of the fair market value of the award (i.e., the $400 amount allowable as a deduction to the employer) is not included in the gross income of the employee. If the cost of the pearl necklace to the employer was $500 instead of $425, then $100 would be includible in the employee's gross income because the excess of the 10 cost of the award over $400 (i.e., $100) is greater than the excess of the fair market value of the award over $400 (i.e., $75). The employer must report the $75, which is includible in the employee's gross income, as compensation on the employee's Form W-2.

Example (4). An employer invites its employees to attend a party it is sponsoring to benefit a charity. In order to encourage the employees to attend the party and to make 15 contributions to the charity, the employer promises to match the employees' contributions and also provides expensive prizes to be awarded to contributing employees selected at random. Each employee receiving a prize must include the full fair market value of the prize in gross income because the prizes are not qualifying achievement awards under section 274(j) or de minimis fringe benefits under section 132(e). Since the prizes are not 20 excludable, the employer must report the full fair market value of the prize as compensation on the employee's Form W-2.

(d) *Special rules.*--(1) The exclusion provided by this section shall not be available for any award made by a sole proprietorship to the sole proprietor.

(2) In the case of an employer exempt from taxation under Subtitle A of the Code, any 25 reference in this section to the amount allowable as a deduction to the employer shall be treated as a reference to the amount which would be allowable as a deduction to the employer if the employer were not exempt from taxation under Subtitle A of the Code.

(e) *Exclusion for certain de minimis fringe benefits.* Nothing contained in this section shall preclude the exclusion of the value of an employee award that is otherwise qualified 30 for exclusion under section 132(e).

Sec. 79. Group-term life insurance purchased for employees

(a) **General rule.** -- There shall be included in the gross income of an employee for the taxable year an amount equal to the cost of group-term life insurance on his life provided for part or all of 35 such year under a policy (or policies) carried directly or indirectly by his employer (or employers); but only to the extent that such cost exceeds the sum of--

(1) the cost of $50,000 of such insurance, and

(2) the amount (if any) paid by the employee toward the purchase of such insurance.

40

Sec. 82. Reimbursement for expenses of moving

Except as provided in section 132(a)(6), there shall be included in gross income (as compensation for services) any amount received or accrued, directly or indirectly, by an individual as a payment for or reimbursement of expenses of moving from one residence to another residence which is attributable to employment or self- employment. 45

Sec. 82. Reimbursement for expenses of moving

Sec. 83. Property transferred in connection with performance of services

(a) **General rule.** -- If, in connection with the performance of services, property is transferred to any person other than the person for whom such services are performed, the excess of--

(1) the fair market value of such property (determined without regard to any restriction other than a restriction which by its terms will never lapse) at the first time the rights of the person having the beneficial interest in such property are transferable or are not subject to a substantial risk of forfeiture, whichever occurs earlier, over

(2) the amount (if any) paid for such property, shall be included in the gross income of the person who performed such services in the first taxable year in which the rights of the person having the beneficial interest in such property are transferable or are not subject to a substantial risk of forfeiture, whichever is applicable. The preceding sentence shall not apply if such person sells or otherwise disposes of such property in an arm's length transaction before his rights in such property become transferable or not subject to a substantial risk of forfeiture.

(b) **Election to include in gross income in year of transfer.** --

(1) In general. -- Any person who performs services in connection with which property is transferred to any person may elect to include in his gross income for the taxable year in which such property is transferred, the excess of--

(A) the fair market value of such property at the time of transfer (determined without regard to any restriction other than a restriction which by its terms will never lapse), over

(B) the amount (if any) paid for such property.
If such election is made, subsection (a) shall not apply with respect to the transfer of such property, and if such property is subsequently forfeited, no deduction shall be allowed in respect of such forfeiture.

(2) Election. -- An election under paragraph (1) with respect to any transfer of property shall be made in such manner as the Secretary prescribes and shall be made not later than 30 days after the date of such transfer. Such election may not be revoked except with the consent of the Secretary.

(c) **Special rules.** -- For purposes of this section--

(1) Substantial risk of forfeiture. -- The rights of a person in property are subject to a substantial risk of forfeiture if such person's rights to full enjoyment of such property are conditioned upon the future performance of substantial services by any individual.

(2) Transferability of property. -- The rights of a person in property are transferable only if the rights in such property of any transferee are not subject to a substantial risk of forfeiture.

(3) Sales which may give rise to suit under section 16(b) of the Securities Exchange Act of 1934. -- So long as the sale of property at a profit could subject a person to suit under section 16(b) of the Securities Exchange Act of 1934, such person's rights in such property are-

(A) subject to a substantial risk of forfeiture, and

(B) not transferable.

(4) For purposes of determining an individual's basis in property transferred in connection with the performance of services, rules similar to the rules of section 72(w) shall apply.

(d) **Certain restrictions which will never lapse.** --

(1) Valuation. -- In the case of property subject to a restriction which by its terms will never lapse, and which allows the transferee to sell such property only at a price determined under a formula, the price so determined shall be deemed to be the fair market value of the property unless established to the contrary by the Secretary, and the burden of proof shall be on the

210

Sec. 83. Property transferred in connection with performance of services

Secretary with respect to such value.

(2) Cancellation. -- If, in the case of property subject to a restriction which by its terms will never lapse, the restriction is canceled, then, unless the taxpayer establishes--

(A) that such cancellation was not compensatory, and

(B) that the person, if any, who would be allowed a deduction if the cancellation were treated as compensatory, will treat the transaction as not compensatory, as evidenced in such manner as the Secretary shall prescribe by regulations, the excess of the fair market value of the property (computed without regard to the restrictions) at the time of cancellation over the sum of--

(C) the fair market value of such property (computed by taking the restriction into account) immediately before the cancellation, and

(D) the amount, if any, paid for the cancellation,

shall be treated as compensation for the taxable year in which such cancellation occurs.

(e) Applicability of section. -- This section shall not apply to--

(1) a transaction to which section 421 applies,

(2) a transfer to or from a trust described in section 401(a) or a transfer under an annuity plan which meets the requirements of section 404(a)(2),

(3) the transfer of an option without a readily ascertainable fair market value,

(4) the transfer of property pursuant to the exercise of an option with a readily ascertainable fair market value at the date of grant, or

(5) group-term life insurance to which section 79 applies.

(f) Holding period. -- In determining the period for which the taxpayer has held property to which subsection (a) applies, there shall be included only the period beginning at the first time his rights in such property are transferable or are not subject to a substantial risk of forfeiture, whichever occurs earlier.

(h) Deduction by employer. -- In the case of a transfer of property to which this section applies or a cancellation of a restriction described in subsection (d), there shall be allowed as a deduction under section 162, to the person for whom were performed the services in connection with which such property was transferred, an amount equal to the amount included under subsection (a), (b), or (d)(2) in the gross income of the person who performed such services. Such deduction shall be allowed for the taxable year of such person in which or with which ends the taxable year in which such amount is included in the gross income of the person who performed such services.

Reg. § 1.83-1 Property transferred in connection with the performance of services.

(a) *Inclusion in gross income*--(1) *General rule.* Section 83 provides rules for the taxation of property transferred to an employee or independent contractor (or beneficiary thereof) in connection with the performance of services by such employee or independent contractor. In general, such property is not taxable under section 83(a) until it has been transferred (as defined in § 1.83-3(a)) to such person and become substantially vested (as defined in § 1.83-3(b)) in such person. In that case, the excess of--

(i) The fair market value of such property (determined without regard to any lapse restriction, as defined in § 1.83-3(i)) at the time that the property becomes substantially vested, over

(ii) The amount (if any) paid for such property, shall be included as compensation in the gross income of such employee or independent contractor for the taxable year in which the property becomes substantially vested. Until such property becomes substantially vested, the transferor shall be regarded as the owner of such property, and any income from such property received by the employee or independent contractor (or

Sec. 83. Property transferred in connection with performance of services

beneficiary thereof) or the right to the use of such property by the employee or independent contractor constitutes additional compensation and shall be included in the gross income of such employee or independent contractor for the taxable year in which such income is received or such use is made available. This paragraph applies to a
5 transfer of property in connection with the performance of services even though the transferor is not the person for whom such services are performed.

(2) *Life insurance.* The cost of life insurance protection under a life insurance contract, retirement income contract, endowment contract, or other contract providing life insurance protection is taxable generally under section 61 and the regulations thereunder
10 during the period such contract remains substantially nonvested (as defined in § 1.83-3(b)). For the taxation of life insurance protection under a split-dollar life insurance arrangement (as defined in § 1.61-22(b)(1) or (2)), see § 1.61-22.

(3) *Cross references.* For rules concerning the treatment of employers and other transferors of property in connection with the performance of services, see section 83(h)
15 and § 1.83-6. For rules concerning the taxation of beneficiaries of an employees' trust that is not exempt under section 501(a), see section 402(b) and the regulations thereunder.

(b) *Subsequent sale, forfeiture, or other disposition of nonvested property.* (1) If substantially nonvested property (that has been transferred in connection with the
20 performance of services) is subsequently sold or otherwise disposed of to a third party in an arm's length transaction while still substantially nonvested, the person who performed such services shall realize compensation in an amount equal to the excess of--

(i) The amount realized on such sale or other disposition, over

(ii) The amount (if any) paid for such property.
25 Such amount of compensation is includible in his gross income in accordance with his method of accounting. Two preceding sentences also apply when the person disposing of the property has received it in a non-arm's length transaction described in paragraph (c) of this section. In addition, section 83(a) and paragraph (a) of this section shall thereafter cease to apply with respect to such property.
30 (2) If substantially nonvested property that has been transferred in connection with the performance of services to the person performing such services is forfeited while still substantially nonvested and held by such person, the difference between the amount paid (if any) and the amount received upon forfeiture (if any) shall be treated as an ordinary gain or loss. This paragraph (b)(2) does not apply to property to which §
35 1.83-2(a) applies.

(3) This paragraph (b) shall not apply to, and no gain shall be recognized on, any sale, forfeiture, or other disposition described in this paragraph to the extent that any property received in exchange therefor is substantially nonvested. Instead, section 83 and this section shall apply with respect to such property received (as if it were substituted for the
40 property disposed of).

(c) *Dispositions of nonvested property not at arm's length.* If substantially nonvested property (that has been transferred in connection with the performance of services) is disposed of in a transaction which is not at arm's length and the property remains substantially nonvested, the person who performed such services realizes compensation
45 equal in amount to the sum of any money and the fair market value of any substantially vested property received in such disposition. Such amount of compensation is includible in his gross income in accordance with his method of accounting. However, such amount of compensation shall not exceed the fair market value of the property disposed of at the time of disposition (determined without regard to any lapse restriction), reduced by the
50 amount paid for such property. In addition, section 83 and these regulations shall continue to apply with respect to such property, except that any amount previously

Sec. 83.   Property transferred in connection with performance of services

includible in gross income under this paragraph (c) shall thereafter be treated as an amount paid for such property. For example, if in 1971 an employee pays $50 for a share of stock which has a fair market value of $100 and is substantially monvested at that time and later in 1971 (at a time when the property still has a fair market value of $100 and is still substantially nonvested) the employee disposes of, in a transaction not at arm's length, the share of stock to his wife for $10, the employee realizes compensation of $10 in 1971. If in 1972, when the share of stock has a fair market value of $120, it becomes substantially vested, the employee realizes additional compensation in 1972 in the amount of $60 (the $120 fair market value of the stock less both the $50 price paid for the stock and the $10 taxed as compensation in 1971). For purposes of this paragraph, if substantially nonvested property has been transferred to a person other than the person who performed the services, and the transferee dies holding the property while the property is still substantially nonvested and while the person who performed the services is alive, the transfer which results by reason of the death of such transferee is a transfer not at arm's length.

(d) *Certain transfers upon death.* If substantially nonvested property has been transferred in connection with the performance of services and the person who performed such services dies while the property is still substantially nonvested, any income realized on or after such death with respect to such property under this section is income in respect of a decedent to which the rules of section 691 apply. In such a case the income in respect of such property shall be taxable under section 691 (except to the extent not includible under section 101(b)) to the estate or beneficiary of the person who performed the services, in accordance with section 83 and the regulations thereunder. However, if an item of income is realized upon such death before July 21, 1978, because the property became substantially vested upon death, the person responsible for filing decedent's income tax return for decedent's last taxable year may elect to treat such item as includible in gross income for decedent's last taxable year by including such item in gross income on the return or amended return filed for decedent's last taxable year.

(e) *Forfeiture after substantial vesting.* If a person is taxable under section 83(a) when the property transferred becomes substantially vested and thereafter the person's beneficial interest in such property is nevertheless forfeited pursuant to a lapse restriction, any loss incurred by such person (but not by a beneficiary of such person) upon such forfeiture shall be an ordinary loss to the extent the basis in such property has been increased as a result of the recognition of income by such person under section 83(a) with respect to such property.

(f) *Examples.* The provisions of this section may be illustrated by the following examples:

Example (1). On November 1, 1978, X corporation sells to E, an employee, 100 shares of X corporation stock at $10 per share. At the time of such sale the fair market value of the X corporation stock is $100 per share. Under the terms of the sale each share of stock is subject to a substantial risk of forfeiture which will not lapse until November 1, 1988. Evidence of this restriction is stamped on the face of E's stock certificates, which are therefore nontransferable (within the meaning of § 1.83-3(d)). Since in 1978 E's stock is substantially nonvested, E does not include any of such amount in his gross income as compensation in 1978. On November 1, 1988, the fair market value of the X corporation stock is $250 per share. Since the X corporation stock becomes substantially vested in 1988, E must include $24,000 (100 shares of X corporation stock x $250 fair market value per share less $10 price paid by E for each share) as compensation for 1988. Dividends paid by X to E on E's stock after it was transferred to E on November 1, 1973, are taxable to E as additional compensation during the period E's stock is substantially nonvested and are deductible as such by X.

Example (2). Assume the facts are the same as in example (1), except that on November 1, 1985, each share of stock of X corporation in E's hands could as a matter of law be transferred to a bona fide purchaser who would not be required to forfeit the stock if the risk of forfeiture materialized. In the event, however, that the risk materializes, E
5 would be liable in damages to X. On November 1, 1985, the fair market value of the X corporation stock is $230 per share. Since E's stock is transferable within the meaning of § 1.83-3(d) in 1985, the stock is substantially vested and E must include $22,000 (100 shares of X corporation stock x $230 fair market value per share less $10 price paid by E for each share) as compensation for 1985.
10 *Example (3).* Assume the facts are the same as in example (1) except that, in 1984 E sells his 100 shares of X corporation stock in an arm's length sale to I, an investment company, for $120 per share. At the time of this sale each share of X corporation's stock has a fair market value of $200. Under paragraph (b) of this section, E must include $11,000 (100 shares of X corporation stock x $120 amount realized per share less $10
15 price paid by E per share) as compensation for 1984 notwithstanding that the stock remains nontransferable and is still subject to a substantial risk of forfeiture at the time of such sale. Under § 1.83-4(b)(2), I's basis in the X corporation stock is $120 per share.

Reg. § 1.83-2 Election to include in gross income in year of transfer.
20 (a) *In general.* If property is transferred (within the meaning of § 1.83-3(a)) in connection with the performance of services, the person performing such services may elect to include in gross income under section 83(b) the excess (if any) of the fair market value of the property at the time of transfer (determined without regard to any lapse restriction, as defined in § 1.83-3(i)) over the amount (if any) paid for such property, as
25 compensation for services. The fact that the transferee has paid full value for the property transferred, realizing no bargain element in the transaction, does not preclude the use of the election as provided for in this section. If this election is made, the substantial vesting rules of section 83(a) and the regulations thereunder do not apply with respect to such property, and except as otherwise provided in section 83(d)(2) and the regulations
30 thereunder (relating to the cancellation of a nonlapse restriction), any subsequent appreciation in the value of the property is not taxable as compensation to the person who performed the services. Thus, property with respect to which this election is made shall be includible in gross income as of the time of transfer, even though such property is substantially nonvested (as defined in § 1.83-3(b)) at the time of transfer, and no
35 compensation will be includible in gross income when such property becomes substantially vested (as defined in § 1.83-3(b)). In computing the gain or loss from the subsequent sale or exchange of such property, its basis shall be the amount paid for the property increased by the amount included in gross income under section 83(b). If property for which a section 83(b) election is in effect is forfeited while substantially
40 nonvested, such forfeiture shall be treated as a sale or exchange upon which there is realized a loss equal to the excess (if any) of--
(1) The amount paid (if any) for such property, over,
(2) The amount realized (if any) upon such forfeiture.
If such property is a capital asset in the hands of the taxpayer, such loss shall be a capital
45 loss. A sale or other disposition of the property that is in substance a forfeiture, or is made in contemplation of a forfeiture, shall be treated as a forfeiture under the two immediately preceding sentences.
(b) *Time for making election.* Except as provided in the following sentence, the election referred to in paragraph (a) of this section shall be filed not later than 30 days
50 after the date the property was transferred (or, if later, January 29, 1970) and may be filed prior to the date of transfer. Any statement filed before February 15, 1970, which was

Sec. 83. Property transferred in connection with performance of services

amended not later than February 16, 1970, in order to make it conform to the requirements of paragraph (e) of this section, shall be deemed a proper election under section 83(b).

(c) *Manner of making election.* The election referred to in paragraph (a) of this section is made by filing one copy of a written statement with the internal revenue office with 5 whom the person who performed the services files his return. In addition, one copy of such statement shall be submitted with this income tax return for the taxable year in which such property was transferred.

(d) *Additional copies.* The person who performed the services shall also submit a copy of the statement referred to in paragraph (c) of this section to the person for whom the 10 services are performed. In addition, if the person who performs the services and the transferee of such property are not the same person, the person who performs the services shall submit a copy of such statement to the transferee of the property.

(e) *Content of statement.* The statement shall be signed by the person making the election and shall indicate that it is being made under section 83(b) of the Code, and shall 15 contain the following information:

(1) The name, address and taxpayer identification number of the taxpayer;

(2) A description of each property with respect to which the election is being made;

(3) The date or dates on which the property is tansferred and the taxable year (for example, ``calendar year 1970'' or ``fiscal year ending May 31, 1970'') for which such 20 election was made;

(4) The nature of the restriction or restrictions to which the property is subject;

(5) The fair market value at the time of transfer (determined without regard to any lapse restriction, as defined in § 1.83-3(i)), of each property with respect to which the election is being made; 25

(6) The amount (if any) paid for such property; and

(7) With respect to elections made after July 21, 1978, a statement to the effect that copies have been furnished to other persons as provided in paragraph (d) of this section.

(f) *Revocability of election.* An election under section 83(b) may not be revoked except with the consent of the Commissioner. Consent will be granted only in the case where the 30 transferee is under a mistake of fact as to the underlying transaction and must be requested within 60 days of the date on which the mistake of fact first became known to the person who made the election. In any event, a mistake as to the value, or decline in the value, of the property with respect to which an election under section 83(b) has been made or a failure to perform an act contemplated at the time of transfer of such property 35 does not constitute a mistake of fact.

Reg. § 1.83-3 Meaning and use of certain terms.

(a) *Transfer*--(1) *In general.* For purposes of section 83 and the regulations thereunder, a transfer of property occurs when a person acquires a beneficial ownership 40 interest in such property (disregarding any lapse restriction, as defined in § 1.83-3(i)). For special rules applying to the transfer of a life insurance contract (or an undivided interest therein) that is part of a split-dollar life insurance arrangement (as defined in § 1.61-22(b) (1) or (2)), see § 1.61-22(g).

(2) *Option.* The grant of an option to purchase certain property does not constitute a 45 transfer of such property. However, see § 1.83-7 for the extent to which the grant of the option itself is subject to section 83. In addition, if the amount paid for the transfer of property is an indebtedness secured by the transferred property, on which there is no personal liability to pay all or a substantial part of such indebtedness, such transaction may be in substance the same as the grant of an option. The determination of the 50 substance of the transaction shall be based upon all the facts and circumstances. The

Sec. 83. Property transferred in connection with performance of services

factors to be taken into account include the type of property involved, the extent to which the risk that the property will decline in value has been transferred, and the likelihood that the purchase price will, in fact, be paid. See also § 1.83-4(c) for the treatment of forgiveness of indebtedness that has constituted an amount paid.

5   (3) *Requirement that property be returned.* Similarly, no transfer may have occurred where property is transferred under conditions that require its return upon the happening of an event that is certain to occur, such as the termination of employment. In such a case, whether there is, in fact, a transfer depends upon all the facts and circumstances. Factors which indicate that no transfer has occurred are described in paragraph (a)(4),
10 (5), and (6) of this section.

   (4) *Similarity to option.* An indication that no transfer has occurred is the extent to which the conditions relating to a transfer are similar to an option.

   (5) *Relationship to fair market value.* An indication that no transfer has occurred is the extent to which the consideration to be paid the transferee upon surrendering the
15 property does not approach the fair market value of the property at the time of surrender. For purposes of paragraph (a) (5) and (6) of this section, fair market value includes fair market value determined under the rules of § 1.83-5(a)(1), relating to the valuation of property subject to nonlapse restrictions. Therefore, the existence of a nonlapse restriction referred to in § 1.83-5(a)(1) is not a factor indicating no transfer has occurred.
20 (6) *Risk of loss.* An indication that no transfer has occurred is the extent to which the transferee does not incur the risk of a beneficial owner that the value of the property at the time of transfer will decline substantially. Therefore, for purposes of this (6), risk of decline in property value is not limited to the risk that any amount paid for the property may be lost.

25 (7) *Examples.* The provisions of this paragraph may be illustrated by the following examples:

   Example (1). On January 3, 1971, X corporation sells for $500 to S, a salesman of X, 10 shares of stock in X corporation with a fair market value of $1,000. The stock is nontransferable and subject to return to the corporation (for $500) if S's sales do not
30 reach a certain level by December 31, 1971. Disregarding the restriction concerning S's sales (since the restrictions is a lapse restriction), S's interest in the stock is that of a beneficial owner and therefore a transfer occurs on January 3, 1971.

   Example (2). On November 17, 1972, W sells to E 100 shares of stock in W corporation with a fair market value of $10,000 in exchange for a $10,000 note without
35 personal liability. The note requires E to make yearly payments of $2,000 commencing in 1973. E collects the dividends, votes the stock and pays the interest on the note. However, he makes no payments toward the face amount of the note. Because E has no personal liability on the note, and since E is making no payments towards the face amount of the note, the likelihood of E paying the full purchase price is in substantial
40 doubt. As a result E has not incurred the risks of a beneficial owner that the value of the stock will decline. Therefore, no transfer of the stock has occurred on November 17, 1972, but an option to purchase the stock has been granted to E.

   Example (3). On January 3, 1971, X corporation purports to transfer to E, an employee, 100 shares of stock in X corporation. The X stock is subject to the sole
45 restriction that E must sell such stock to X on termination of employment for any reason for an amount which is equal to the excess (if any) of the book value of the X stock at termination of employment over book value on January 3, 1971. The stock is not transferable by E and the restrictions on transfer are stamped on the certificate. Under these facts and circumstances, there is no transfer of the X stock within the meeting of
50 section 83.

   Example (4). Assume the same facts as in example (3) except that E paid $3,000 for

216

Sec. 83. Property transferred in connection with performance of services

the stock and that the restriction required E upon termination of employment to sell the stock to M for the total amount of dividends that have been declared on the stock since September 2, 1971, or $3,000 whichever is higher. Again, under the facts and circumstances, no transfer of the X stock has occurred.

  Example (5). On July 4, 1971, X corporation purports to transfer to G, an employee, 100 shares of X stock. The stock is subject to the sole restriction that upon termination of employment G must sell the stock to X for the greater of its fair market value at such time or $100, the amount G paid for the stock. On July 4, 1971 the X stock has a fair market value of $100. Therefore, G does not incur the risk of a beneficial owner that the value of the stock at the time of transfer ($100) will decline substantially. Under these facts and circumstances, no transfer has occurred.

  (b) *Substantially vested and substantially nonvested property.* For purposes of section 83 and the regulations thereunder, property is substantially nonvested when it is subject to a substantial risk of forfeiture, within the meaning of paragraph (c) of this section, and is nontransferable, within the meaning of paragraph (d) of this section. Property is substantially vested for such purposes when it is either transferable or not subject to a substantial risk of forfeiture.

  (c) *Substantial risk of forfeiture--*(1) *In general.* For purposes of section 83 and the regulations thereunder, whether a risk of forfeiture is substantial or not depends upon the facts and circumstances. A substantial risk of forfeiture exists where rights in property that are transferred are conditioned, directly or indirectly, upon the future performance (or refraining from performance) of substantial services by any person, or the occurrence of a condition related to a purpose of the transfer, and the possibility of forfeiture is substantial if such condition is not satisfied. Property is not transferred subject to a substantial risk of forfeiture to the extent that the employer is required to pay the fair market value of a portion of such property to the employee upon the return of such property. The risk that the value of property will decline during a certain period of time does not constitute a substantial risk of forfeiture. A nonlapse restriction, standing by itself, will not result in a substantial risk of forfeiture.

  (2) *Illustrations of substantial risks of forfeiture.* The regularity of the performance of services and the time spent in performing such services tend to indicate whether services required by a condition are substantial. The fact that the person performing services has the right to decline to perform such services without forfeiture may tend to establish that services are insubstantial. Where stock is transferred to an underwriter prior to a public offering and the full enjoyment of such stock is expressly or impliedly conditioned upon the successful completion of the underwriting, the stock is subject to a substantial risk of forfeiture. Where an employee receives property from an employer subject to a requirement that it be returned if the total earnings of the employer do not increase, such property is subject to a substantial risk of forfeiture. On the other hand, requirements that the property be returned to the employer if the employee is discharged for cause or for committing a crime will not be considered to result in a substantial risk of forfeiture. An enforceable requirement that the property be returned to the employer if the employee accepts a job with a competing firm will not ordinarily be considered to result in a substantial risk of forfeiture unless the particular facts and circumstances indicate to the contrary. Factors which may be taken into account in determining whether a covenant not to compete constitutes a substantial risk of forfeiture are the age of the employee, the availability of alternative employment opportunities, the likelihood of the employee's obtaining such other employment, the degree of skill possessed by the employee, the employee's health, and the practice (if any) of the employer to enforce such covenants. Similarly, rights in property transferred to a retiring employee subject to the sole requirement that it be returned unless he renders consulting services upon the request of

217

Sec. 83. Property transferred in connection with performance of services

his former employer will not be considered subject to a substantial risk of forfeiture unless he is in fact expected to perform substantial services.

(3) *Enforcement of forfeiture condition.* In determining whether the possibility of forfeiture is substantial in the case of rights in property transferred to an employee of a
5 corporation who owns a significant amount of the total combined voting power or value of all classes of stock of the employer corporation or of its parent corporation, there will be taken into account (i) the employee's relationship to other stockholders and the extent of their control, potential control and possible loss of control of the corporation, (ii) the position of the employee in the corporation and the extent to which he is subordinate to
10 other employees, (iii) the employee's relationship to the officers and directors of the corporation, (iv) the person or persons who must approve the employee's discharge, and (v) past actions of the employer in enforcing the provisions of the restrictions. For example, if an employee would be considered as having received rights in property subject to a substantial risk of forfeiture, but for the fact that the employee owns 20
15 percent of the single class of stock in the transferor corporation, and if the remaining 80 percent of the class of stock is owned by an unrelated individual (or members of such an individual's family) so that the possibility of the corporation enforcing a restriction on such rights is substantial, then such rights are subject to a substantial risk of forfeiture. On the other hand, if 4 percent of the voting power of all the stock of a corporation is owned by
20 the president of such corporation and the remaining stock is so diversely held by the public that the president, in effect, controls the corporation, then the possibility of the corporation enforcing a restriction on rights in property transferred to the president is not substantial, and such rights are not subject to a substantial risk of forfeiture.

(4) *Examples.* The rules contained in paragraph (c)(1) of this section may be
25 illustrated by the following examples. In each example it is assumed that, if the conditions on transfer are not satisfied, the forfeiture provision will be enforced.

Example (1). On November 1, 1971, corporation X transfers in connection with the performance of services to E, an employee, 100 shares of corporation X stock for $90 per share. Under the terms of the transfer, E will be subject to a binding commitment to resell
30 the stock to corporation X at $90 per share if he leaves the employment of corporation X for any reason prior to the expiration of a 2-year period from the date of such transfer. Since E must perform substantial services for corporation X and will not be paid more than $90 for the stock, regardless of its value, if he fails to perform such services during such 2-year period, E's rights in the stock are subject to a substantial risk of forfeiture
35 during such period.

Example (2). On November 10, 1971, corporation X transfers in connection with the performance of services to a trust for the benefit of employees, $100x. Under the terms of the trust any child of an employee who is an enrolled full-time student at an accredited educational institution as a candidate for a degree will receive an annual grant of cash for
40 each academic year the student completes as a student in good standing, up to a maximum of four years. E, an employee, has a child who is enrolled as a full-time student at an accredited college as a candidate for a degree. Therefore, E has a beneficial interest in the assets of the trust equaling the value of four cash grants. Since E's child must complete one year of college in order to receive a cash grant, E's interest in the
45 trust assets are subject to a substantial risk of forfeiture to the extent E's child has not become entitled to any grants.

Example (3). On November 25, 1971, corporation X gives to E, an employee, in connection with his performance of services to corporation X, a bonus of 100 shares of corporation X stock. Under the terms of the bonus arrangement E is obligated to return
50 the corporation X stock to corporation X if he terminates his employment for any reason. However, for each year occurring after November 25, 1971, during which E remains

218

Sec. 83.   Property transferred in connection with performance of services

employed with corporation X, E ceases to be obligated to return 10 shares of the corporation X stock. Since in each year occurring after November 25, 1971, for which E remains employed he is not required to return 10 shares of corporation X's stock, E's rights in 10 shares each year for 10 years cease to be subject to a substantial risk of forfeiture for each year he remains so employed.　5

Example (4). (a) Assume the same facts as in example (3) except that for each year occurring after November 25, 1971, for which E remains employed with corporation X, X agrees to pay, in redemption of the bonus shares given to E if he terminates employment for any reason, 10 percent of the fair market value of each share of stock on the date of such termination of employment. Since corporation X will pay E 10 percent of the value of　10 his bonus stock for each of the 10 years after November 25, 1971, in which he remains employed by X, and the risk of a decline in value is not a substantial risk of forfeiture, E's interest in 10 percent of such bonus stock becomes substantially vested in each of those years.

(b) The following chart illustrates the fair market value of the bonus stock and the　15 fairmarket value of the portion of bonus stock that becomes substantially vested on November 25, for the following years:

Year	All stock	Fair market value of: Portion of stock that becomes vested	
1972..	$200	$20	20
1973..	300	30	
1974..	150	15	25
1975..	150	15	
1976..	100	10	

If E terminates his employment on July 1, 1977, when the fair market value of the bonus stock is $100, E must return the bonus stock to X, and X must pay, in redemption of the　30 bonus stock, $50 (50 percent of the value of the bonus stock on the date of termination of employment). E has recognized income under section 83(a) and § 1.83-1(a) with respect to 50 percent of the bonus stock, and E's basis in that portion of the stock equals the amount of income recognized, $90. Under § 1.83-1(e), the $40 loss E incurred upon forfeiture ($90 basis less $50 redemption payment) is an ordinary loss.　35

Example (5). On January 7, 1971, corporation X, a computer service company, transfers to E, 100 shares of corporation X stock for $50. E is a highly compensated salesman who sold X's products in a three-state area since 1960. At the time of transfer each share of X stock has a fair market value of $100. The stock is transferred to E in connection with his termination of employment with X. Each share of X stock is subject to　40 the sole condition that E can keep such share only if he does not engage in competition with X for a 5-year period in the three-state area where E had previously sold X's products. E, who is 45 years old, has no intention of retiring from the work force. In order to earn a salary comparable to his current compensation, while preventing the risk of forfeiture from arising, E will have to expend a substantial amount of time and effort in　45 another industry or market to establish the necessary business contacts. Thus, under these facts and circumstances E's rights in the stock are subject to a substantial risk of forfeiture.

(d) Transferability of property. For purposes of section 83 and the regulations thereunder, the rights of a person in property are transferable if such person can transfer　50 any interest in the property to any person other than the transferor of the property, but

Sec. 83. Property transferred in connection with performance of services

only if the rights in such property of such transferee are not subject to a substantial risk of forfeiture. Accordingly, property is transferable if the person performing the services or receiving the property can sell, assign, or pledge (as collateral for a loan, or as security for the performance of an obligation, or for any other purpose) his interest in the property
5   to any person other than the transferor of such property and if the transferee is not required to give up the property or its value in the event the substantial risk of forfeiture materializes. On the other hand, property is not considered to be transferable merely because the person performing the services or receiving the property may designate a beneficiary to receive the property in the event of his death.
10   (e) *Property.* For purposes of section 83 and the regulations thereunder, the term ``property'' includes real and personal property other than either money or an unfunded and unsecured promise to pay money or property in the future. The term also includes a beneficial interest in assets (including money) which are transferred or set aside from the claims of creditors of the transferor, for example, in a trust or escrow account. See,
15   however, § 1.83-8(a) with respect to employee trusts and annuity plans subject to section 402(b) and section 403(c). In the case of a transfer of a life insurance contract, retirement income contract, endowment contract, or other contract providing life insurance protection, or any undivided interest therein, the policy cash value and all other rights under such contract (including any supplemental agreements thereto and whether or not
20   guaranteed), other than current life insurance protection, are treated as property for purposes of this section. However, in the case of the transfer of a life insurance contract, retirement income contract, endowment contract, or other contract providing life insurance protection, which was part of a split-dollar arrangement (as defined in § 1.61-22(b)) entered into (as defined in § 1.61-22(j)) on or before September 17, 2003,
25   and which is not materially modified (as defined in § 1.61-22(j)(2)) after September 17, 2003, only the cash surrender value of the contract is considered to be property. Where rights in a contract providing life insurance protection are substantially nonvested, see § 1.83-1(a)(2) for rules relating to taxation of the cost of life insurance protection.
        (f) *Property transferred in connection with the performance of services.* Property
30   transferred to an employee or an independent contractor (or beneficiary thereof) in recognition of the performance of, or the refraining from performance of, services is considered transferred in connection with the performance of services within the meaning of section 83. The existence of other persons entitled to buy stock on the same terms and conditions as an employee, whether pursuant to a public or private offering may,
35   however, indicate that in such circumstances a transfer to the employee is not in recognition of the performance of, or the refraining from performance of, services. The transfer of property is subject to section 83 whether such transfer is in respect of past, present, or future services.
        (g) *Amount paid.* For purposes of section 83 and the regulations thereunder, the term
40   ``amount paid'' refers to the value of any money or property paid for the transfer of property to which section 83 applies, and does not refer to any amount paid for the right to use such property or to receive the income therefrom. Such value does not include any stated or unstated interest payments. For rules regarding the calculation of the amount of unstated interest payments, see § 1.483-1(c). When section 83 applies to the transfer of
45   property pursuant to the exercise of an option, the term ``amount paid'' refers to any amount paid for the grant of the option plus any amount paid as the exercise price of the option. For rules regarding the forgiveness of indebtedness treated as an amount paid, see § 1.83-4(c).
        (h) *Nonlapse restriction.* For purposes of section 83 and the regulations thereunder, a
50   restriction which by its terms will never lapse (also referred to as a ``nonlapse restriction'') is a permanent limitation on the transferability of property--

Sec. 83. Property transferred in connection with performance of services

(1) Which will require the transferee of the property to sell, or offer to sell, such property at a price determined under a formula, and

(2) Which will continue to apply to and be enforced against the transferee or any subsequent holder (other than the transferor).
A limitation subjecting the property to a permanent right of first refusal in a particular 5 person at a price determined under a formula is a permanent nonlapse restriction. Limitations imposed by registration requirements of State or Federal security laws or similar laws imposed with respect to sales or other dispositions of stock or securities are not nonlapse restrictions. An obligation to resell or to offer to sell property transferred in connection with the performance of services to a specific person or persons at its fair 10 market value at the time of such sale is not a nonlapse restriction. See § 1.83-5(c) for examples of nonlapse restrictions.

(i) *Lapse restriction.* For purposes of section 83 and the regulations thereunder, the term ``lapse restriction" means a restriction other than a nonlapse restriction as defined in paragraph (h) of this section, and includes (but is not limited to) a restriction that carries a 15 substantial risk of forfeiture.

(j) *Sales which may give rise to suit under section 16(b) of the Securities Exchange Act of 1934*--(1) *In general.* For purposes of section 83 and the regulations thereunder if the sale of property at a profit within six months after the purchase of the property could subject a person to suit under section 16(b) of the Securities Exchange Act of 1934, the 20 person's rights in the property are treated as subject to a substantial risk of forfeiture and as not transferable until the earlier of (i) the expiration of such six-month period, or (ii) the first day on which the sale of such property at a profit will not subject the person to suit under section 16(b) of the Securities Exchange Act of 1934. However, whether an option is ``transferable by the optionee" for purposes of § 1.83-7(b)(2)(i) is determined without 25 regard to section 83(c)(3) and this paragraph (j).

(2) *Examples.* The provisions of this paragraph may be illustrated by the following examples:

Example (1). On January 1, 1983, X corporation sells to P, a beneficial owner of 12% of X corporation stock, in connection with P'sperformance of services, 100 shares of X 30 corporation stock at $10 per share. At the time of the sale the fair market value of the X corporation stock is $100 per share. P, as a beneficial owner of more 10% of X corporation stock, is liable to suit under section 16(b) of the Securities Exchange Act of 1934 for recovery of any profit from any sale and purchase or purchase and sale of X corporation stock within a six-month period, but no other restrictions apply to the stock. 35 Because the section 16(b) restriction is applicable to P, P's rights in the 100 shares of stock purchased on January 1, 1983, are treated as subject to a substantial risk of forfeiture and as not transferable through June 29, 1983. P chooses not to make an election under section 83 (b) and therefore does not include any amount with respect to the stock purchase in gross income as compensation on the date of purchase. On June 40 30, 1983, the fair market value of X corporation stock is $250 per share. P must include $24,000 (100 shares of X corporation stock x $240 ($250 fair market value per share less $10 price paid by P for each share)) in gross income as compensation on June 30, 1983. If, in this example, restrictions other than section 16(b) applied to the stock, such other restrictions (but not section 16(b)) would be taken into account in determining whether 45 the stock is subject to a substantial risk of foreiture and is nontransferable for periods after June 29, 1983.

Example (2). Assume the same facts as in example (1) except that P is not an insider on or after May 1, 1983, and the section 16(b) restriction does not apply beginning on that date. On May 1, 1983, P must include in gross income as compensation the 50 difference between the fair market value of the stock on that date and the amount paid for the stock.

Example (3). Assume the same facts as in example (1) except that on June 1, 1983, X corporation sells to P an additional 100 shares of X corporation stock at $20 per share. At the time of the sale the fair market value of the X corporation stock is $150 per share. On
5 June 30, 1983, P must include $24,000 in gross income as compensation with respect to the January 1, 1983 purchase. On November 30, 1983, the fair market value of X corporation stock is $200 per share. Accordingly, on that date P must include $18,000 (100 shares of X corporation stock x $180 ($200 fair market value per share less $20 price paid by P for each share)) in gross income as compensation with respect to the
10 June 1, 1983 purchase.

***

(k) *Special rule for certain accounting rules.* (1) For purposes of section 83 and the regualtions thereunder, property is subject to substantial risk of forfeiture and is not transferable so long as the property is subject to a restriction on transfer to comply with
15 the ``Pooling-of-Interests Accounting" rules set forth in Accounting Series Release Numbered 130 ((10/5/72) 37 FR 20937; 17 CFR 211.130) and Accounting Series Release Numbered 135 ((1/18/73) 38 FR 1734; 17 CFR 211.135).

***

Reg. § 1.83-4 Special rules.
20   (a) *Holding period.* Under section 83(f), the holding period of transferred property to which section 83(a) applies shall begin just after such property is substantially vested. However, if the person who has performed the services in connection with which property is transferred has made an election under section 83(b), the holding period of such property shall begin just after the date such property is transferred. If property to which
25 section 83 and the regulations thereunder apply is transferred at arm's length, the holding period of such property in the hands of the transferee shall be determined in accordance with the rules provided in section 1223.

(b) *Basis.* (1) Except as provided in paragraph (b)(2) of this section, if property to which section 83 and the regulations thereunder apply is acquired by any person
30 (including a person who acquires such property in a subsequent transfer which is not at arm's length), while such property is still substantially nonvested, such person's basis for the property shall reflect any amount paid for such property and any amount includible in the gross income of the person who performed the services (including any amount so includible as a result of a disposition by the person who acquired such property.) Such
35 basis shall also reflect any adjustments to basis provided under sections 1015 and 1016.

(2) If property to which § 1.83-1 applies is transferred at arm's length, the basis of the property in the hands of the transferee shall be determined under section 1012 and the regulations thereunder.

(c) Forgiveness of indebtedness treated as an amount paid. If an indebtedness that
40 has been treated as an amount paid under § 1.83-1(a)(1)(ii) is subsequently canceled, forgiven or satisfied for an amount less than the amount of such indebtedness, the amount that is not, in fact, paid shall be includible in the gross income of the service provider in the taxable year in which such cancellation, forgiveness or satisfaction occurs.

45

Sec. 83. Property transferred in connection with performance of services

Reg. § 1.83-6 Deduction by employer.

(a) *Allowance of deduction*--(1) *General rule.* In the case of a transfer of property in connection with the performance of services, or a compensatory cancellation of a nonlapse restriction described in section 83(d) and § 1.83-5, a deduction is allowable under section 162 or 212 to the person for whom the services were performed. The 5 amount of the deduction is equal to the amount included as compensation in the gross income of the service provider under section 83(a), (b), or (d)(2), but only to the extent the amount meets the requirements of section 162 or 212 and the regulations thereunder. The deduction is allowed only for the taxable year of that person in which or with which ends the taxable year of the service provider in which the amount is included as 10 compensation. For purposes of this paragraph, any amount excluded from gross income under section 79 or section 101(b) or subchapter N is considered to have been included in gross income.

(2) *Special Rule.* For purposes of paragraph (a)(1) of this section, the service provider is deemed to have included the amount as compensation in gross income if the person 15 for whom the services were performed satisfies in a timely manner all requirements of section 6041 or section 6041A, and the regulations thereunder, with respect to that amount of compensation. For purposes of the preceding sentence, whether a person for whom services were performed satisfies all requirements of section 6041 or section 6041A, and the regulations thereunder, is determined without regard to § 1.6041-3(c) 20 (exception for payments to corporations). In the case of a disqualifying disposition of stock described in section 421(b), an employer that otherwise satisfies all requirements of section 6041 and the regulations thereunder will be considered to have done so timely for purposes of this paragraph (a)(2) if Form W-2 or Form W-2c, as appropriate, is furnished to the employee or former employee, and is filed with the federal government, on or 25 before the date on which the employer files the tax return claiming the deduction relating to the disqualifying disposition.

(3) *Exceptions.* Where property is substantially vested upon transfer, the deduction shall be allowed to such person in accordance with his method of accounting (in conformity with sections 446 and 461). In the case of a transfer to an employee benefit 30 plan described in § 1.162-10(a) or a transfer to an employees' trust or annuity plan described in section 404(a)(5) and the regulations thereunder, section 83(h) and this section do not apply.

(4) *Capital expenditure, etc.* No deduction is allowed under section 83(h) to the extent that the transfer of property constitutes a capital expenditure, an item of deferred 35 expense, or an amount properly includible in the value of inventory items. In the case of a capital expenditure, for example, the basis of the property to which such capital expenditure relates shall be increased at the same time and to the same extent as any amount includible in the employee's gross income in respect of such transfer. Thus, for example, no deduction is allowed to a corporation in respect of a transfer of its stock to a 40 promoter upon its organization, notwithstanding that such promoter must include the value of such stock in his gross income in accordance with the rules under section 83.

(5) *Transfer of life insurance contract (or an undivided interest therein)*--(i) *General rule.* In the case of a transfer of a life insurance contract (or an undivided interest therein) described in § 1.61-22(c)(3) in connection with the performance of services, a deduction 45 is allowable under paragraph (a)(1) of this section to the person for whom the services were performed. The amount of the deduction, if allowable, is equal to the sum of the amount included as compensation in the gross income of the service provider under § 1.61-22(g)(1) and the amount determined under § 1.61-22(g)(1)(ii).

(ii) *Effective date*--(A) *General rule.* Paragraph (a)(5)(i) of this section applies to any 50 split-dollar life insurance arrangement (as defined in § 1.61-22(b)(1) or (2)) entered into

Sec. 83. Property transferred in connection with performance of services

after September 17, 2003. For purposes of this paragraph (a)(5), an arrangement is entered into as determined under § 1.61-22(j)(1)(ii).

(B) *Modified arrangements treated as new arrangements.* If an arrangement entered into on or before September 17, 2003 is materially modified (within the meaning of §
5 1.61-22(j)(2)) after September 17, 2003, the arrangement is treated as a new arrangement entered into on the date of the modification.

***

(b) *Recognition of gain or loss.* Except as provided in section 1032, at the time of a transfer of property in connection with the performance of services the transferor
10 recognizes gain to the extent that the transferor receives an amount that exceeds the transferor's basis in the property. In addition, at the time a deduction is allowed under section 83(h) and paragraph (a) of this section, gain or loss is recognized to the extent of the difference between (1) the sum of the amount paid plus the amount allowed as a deduction under section 83(h), and (2) the sum of the taxpayer's basis in the property
15 plus any amount recognized pursuant to the previous sentence.

(c) *Forfeitures.* If, under section 83(h) and paragraph (a) of this section, a deduction, an increase in basis, or a reduction of gross income was allowable (disregarding the reasonableness of the amount of compensation) in respect of a transfer of property and such property is subsequently forfeited, the amount of such deduction, increase in basis
20 or reduction of gross income shall be includible in the gross income of the person to whom it was allowable for the taxable year of forfeiture. The basis of such property in the hands of the person to whom it is forfeited shall include any such amount includible in the gross income of such person, as well as any amount such person pays upon forfeiture.

(d) *Special rules for transfers by shareholders--(1) Transfers.* If a shareholder of a
25 corporation transfers property to an employee of such corporation or to an independent contractor (or to a beneficiary thereof), in consideration of services performed for the corporation, the transaction shall be considered to be a contribution of such property to the capital of such corporation by the shareholder, and immediately thereafter a transfer of such property by the corporation to the employee or independent contractor under
30 paragraphs (a) and (b) of this section. For purposes of this (1), such a transfer will be considered to be in consideration for services performed for the corporation if either the property transferred is substantially nonvested at the time of transfer or an amount is includible in the gross income of the employee or independent contractor at the time of transfer under § 1.83-1a(1) or § 1.83-2(a). In the case of such a transfer, any money or
35 other property paid to the shareholder for such stock shall be considered to be paid to the corporation and transferred immediately thereafter by the corporation to the shareholder as a distribution to which section 302 applies. For special rules that may apply to a corporation's transfer of its own stock to any person in consideration of services performed for another corporation or partnership, see § 1.1032-3. The preceding
40 sentence applies to transfers of stock and amounts paid for such stock occurring on or after May 16, 2000.

(2) *Forfeiture.* If, following a transaction described in paragraph (d)(1) of this section, the transferred property is forfeited to the shareholder, paragraph (c) of this section shall apply both with respect to the shareholder and with respect to the corporation. In
45 addition, the corporation shall in the taxable year of forfeiture be allowed a loss (or realize a gain) to offset any gain (or loss) realized under paragraph (b) of this section. For example, if a shareholder transfers property to an employee of the corporation as compensation, and as a result the shareholder's basis of $200x in such property is allocated to his stock in such corporation and such corporation recognizes a short-term
50 capital gain of $800x, and is allowed a deduction of $1,000x on such transfer, upon a subsequent forfeiture of the property to the shareholder, the shareholder shall take $200x

into gross income, and the corporation shall take $1,000x into gross income and be allowed a short-term capital loss of $800x.

***

Reg. § 1.83-7 Taxation of nonqualified stock options.

(a) *In general.* If there is granted to an employee or independent contractor (or 5 beneficiary thereof) in connection with the performance of services, an option to which section 421 (relating generally to certain qualified and other options) does not apply, section 83(a) shall apply to such grant if the option has a readily ascertainable fair market value (determined in accordance with paragraph (b) of this section) at the time the option is granted. The person who performed such services realizes compensation upon such 10 grant at the time and in the amount determined under section 83(a). If section 83(a) does not apply to the grant of such an option because the option does not have a readily ascertainable fair market value at the time of grant, sections 83(a) and 83(b) shall apply at the time the option is exercised or otherwise disposed of, even though the fair market value of such option may have become readily ascertainable before such time. If the 15 option is exercised, sections 83(a) and 83(b) apply to the transfer of property pursuant to such exercise, and the employee or independent contractor realizes compensation upon such transfer at the time and in the amount determined under section 83(a) or 83(b). If the option is sold or otherwise disposed of in an arm's length transaction, sections 83(a) and 83(b) apply to the transfer of money or other property received in the same manner 20 as sections 83(a) and 83(b) would have applied to the transfer of property pursuant to an exercise of the option. The preceding sentence does not apply to a sale or other disposition of the option to a person related to the service provider that occurs on or after July 2, 2003. For this purpose, a person is related to the service provider if--

(1) The person and the service provider bear a relationship to each other that is 25 specified in section 267(b) or 707(b)(1), subject to the modifications that the language ``20 percent'' is used instead of ``50 percent'' each place it appears in sections 267(b) and 707(b)(1), and section 267(c)(4) is applied as if the family of an individual includes the spouse of any member of the family; or

(2) The person and the service provider are engaged in trades or businesses under 30 common control (within the meaning of section 52(a) and (b)); provided that a person is not related to the service provider if the person is the service recipient with respect to the option or the grantor of the option.

(b) *Readily ascertainable defined*--(1) *Actively traded on an established market.* Options have a value at the time they are granted, but that value is ordinarily not readily 35 ascertainable unless the option is actively traded on an established market. If an option is actively traded on an established market, the fair market value of such option is readily ascertainable for purposes of this section by applying the rules of valuation set forth in § 20.2031-2.

(2) *Not actively traded on an established market.* When an option is not actively 40 traded on an established market, it does not have a readily ascertainable fair market value unless its fair market value can otherwise be measured with reasonable accuracy. For purposes of this section, if an option is not actively traded on an established market, the option does not have a readily ascertainable fair market value when granted unless the taxpayer can show that all of the following conditions exist: 45

(i) The option is transferable by the optionee;

(ii) The option is exerciseable immediately in full by the optionee;

(iii) The option or the property subject to the option is not subject to any restriction or condition (other than a lien or other condition to secure the payment of the purchase price) which has a significant effect upon the fair market value of the option; and   50

(iv) The fair market value of the option privilege is readily in accordance with

225

paragraph (b)(3) of this section.

    (3) *Option privilege.* The option privilege in the case of an option to buy is the opportunity to benefit during the option's exercise period from any increase in the value of property subject to the option during such period, without risking any capital. Similarly, the
5 option privilege in the case of an option to sell is the opportunity to benefit during the exercise period from a decrease in the value of property subject to the option. For example, if at some time during the exercise period of an option to buy, the fair market value of the property subject to the option is greater than the option's exercise price, a profit may be realized by exercising the option and immediately selling the property so
10 acquired for its higher fair market value. Irrespective of whether any such gain may be realized immediately at the time an option is granted, the fair market value of an option to buy includes the value of the right to benefit from any future increase in the value of the property subject to the option (relative to the option exercise price), without risking any capital. Therefore, the fair market value of an option is not merely the difference that may
15 exist at a particular time between the option's exercise price and the value of the property subject to the option, but also includes the value of the option privilege for the remainder of the exercise period. Accordingly, for purposes of this section, in determining whether the fair market value of an option is readily ascertainable, it is necessary to consider whether the value of the entire option privilege can be measured with reasonable
20 accuracy. In determining whether the value of the option privilege is readily ascertainable, and in determining the amount of such value when such value is readily ascertainable, it is necessary to consider--

    (i) Whether the value of the property subject to the option can be ascertained;

    (ii) The probability of any ascertainable value of such property increasing or
25 decreasing; and

    (iii) The length of the period during which the option can be exercised.

***

[T.D. 7554, 43 FR 31913, July 24, 1978; T.D. 8042, 50 FR 31713, Aug. 6, 1985; T.D. 8599, July 19, 1995; 50 FR 31713, Aug. 6, 1985; T.D. 8883, 65 FR 31076, May 16, 2000;
30 T.D. 9067, 68 FR 39454, July 2, 2003; T.D. 9092, 68 FR 54351, Sept. 17, 2003; T.D. 9148, 69 FR 48392, Aug. 10, 2004 T.D. 9223, 70 FR 50971, Aug. 29, 2005]

Sec. 84. Transfer of appreciated property to political organization

    (a) General rule. -- If--

35   **(1)** any person transfers property to a political organization, and

      (2) the fair market value of such property exceeds its adjusted basis,

then for purposes of this chapter the transferor shall be treated   as having sold such property to the political organization on the date of the transfer, and the transferor shall be treated as having realized an amount equal to the fair market value of such property on such date.
40

Sec. 85. Unemployment compensation

    (a) General rule. -- In the case of an individual, gross income includes unemployment compensation.

    (b) Unemployment compensation defined. -- For purposes of this section, the term
45 "unemployment compensation" means any amount received under a law of the United States or of a State which is in the nature of unemployment compensation.

Sec. 85. Unemployment compensation

Sec. 86. Social security and tier 1 railroad retirement benefits

(a) In general. --

(1) In general. -- Except as provided in paragraph (2), gross income for the taxable year of any taxpayer described in subsection (b) (notwithstanding section 207 of the Social Security 5 Act) includes social security benefits in an amount equal to the lesser of--

(A) one-half of the social security benefits received during the taxable year, or

(B) one-half of the excess described in subsection (b)(1).

(2) Additional amount. -- In the case of a taxpayer with respect to whom the amount determined under subsection (b)(1)(A) exceeds the adjusted base amount, the amount included 10 in gross income under this section shall be equal to the lesser of--

(A) the sum of--

(i) 85 percent of such excess, plus

(ii) the lesser of the amount determined under paragraph (1) or an amount equal to one-half of the difference between the adjusted base amount and the base amount of 15 the taxpayer, or

(B) 85 percent of the social security benefits received during the taxable year.

(b) Taxpayers to whom subsection (a) applies. --

(1) In general. -- A taxpayer is described in this subsection if--

(A) the sum of-- 20

(i) the modified adjusted gross income of the taxpayer for the taxable year, plus

(ii) one-half of the social security benefits received during the taxable year, exceeds

(B) the base amount.

(2) Modified adjusted gross income. -- For purposes of this subsection, the term "modified adjusted gross income" means adjusted gross income-- 25

(A) determined without regard to this section and sections 135, 137, 199, 221, 222, 911, 931, and 933, and

(B) increased by the amount of interest received or accrued by the taxpayer during the taxable year which is exempt from tax.

(c) Base amount and adjusted base amount. -- For purposes of this section-- 30

(1) Base amount. -- The term "base amount" means--

(A) except as otherwise provided in this paragraph, $25,000,

(B) $32,000 in the case of a joint return, and

(C) zero in the case of a taxpayer who--

(i) is married as of the close of the taxable year (within the meaning of section 7703) 35 but does not file a joint return for such year, and

(ii) does not live apart from his spouse at all times during the taxable year.

(2) Adjusted base amount. -- The term "adjusted base amount" means--

(A) except as otherwise provided in this paragraph, $34,000,

(B) $44,000 in the case of a joint return, and 40

(C) zero in the case of a taxpayer described in paragraph (1)(C).

(d) Social security benefit. --

227

Sec. 86. Social security and tier 1 railroad retirement benefits

(1) In general. -- For purposes of this section, the term "social security benefit" means any amount received by the taxpayer by reason of entitlement to--

    (A) a monthly benefit under title II of the Social Security Act, or

    (B) a tier 1 railroad retirement benefit.

(2) Adjustment for repayments during year. --

    (A) In general. -- For purposes of this section, the amount of social security benefits received during any taxable year shall be reduced by any repayment made by the taxpayer during the taxable year of a social security benefit previously received by the taxpayer (whether or not such benefit was received during the taxable year).

    (B) Denial of deduction. -- If (but for this subparagraph) any portion of the repayments referred to in subparagraph (A) would have been allowable as a deduction for the taxable year under section 165, such portion shall be allowable as a deduction only to the extent it exceeds the social security benefits received by the taxpayer during the taxable year (and not repaid during such taxable year).

(3) Workmen's compensation benefits substituted for social security benefits. -- For purposes of this section, if, by reason of section 224 of the Social Security Act (or by reason of section 3(a)(1) of the Railroad Retirement Act of 1974), any social security benefit is reduced by reason of the receipt of a benefit under a workmen's compensation act, the term "social security benefit" includes that portion of such benefit received under the workmen's compensation act which equals such reduction.

(4) Tier 1 railroad retirement benefit. -- For purposes of paragraph (1), the term "tier 1 railroad retirement benefit" means--

    (A) the amount of the annuity under the Railroad Retirement Act of 1974 equal to the amount of the benefit to which the taxpayer would have been entitled under the Social Security Act if all of the service after December 31, 1936, of the employee (on whose employment record the annuity is being paid) had been included in the term "employment" as defined in the Social Security Act, and

    (B) a monthly annuity amount under section 3(f)(3) of the Railroad Retirement Act of 1974.

(5) Effect of early delivery of benefit checks. -- For purposes of subsection (a), in any case where section 708 of the Social Security Act causes social security benefit checks to be delivered before the end of the calendar month for which they are issued, the benefits involved shall be deemed to have been received in the succeeding calendar month.

(e) Limitation on amount included where taxpayer receives lump-sum payment. --

(1) Limitation. -- If--

    (A) any portion of a lump-sum payment of social security benefits received during the taxable year is attributable to prior taxable years, and

    (B) the taxpayer makes an election under this subsection for the taxable year, then the amount included in gross income under this section for the taxable year by reason of the receipt of such portion shall not exceed the sum of the increases in gross income under this chapter for prior taxable years which would result solely from taking into account such portion in the taxable years to which it is attributable.

(2) Special rules. --

    (A) Year to which benefit attributable. -- For purposes of this subsection, a social security benefit is attributable to a taxable year if the generally applicable payment date for such benefit occurred during such taxable year.

    (B) Election. -- An election under this subsection shall be made at such time and in such

Sec. 86. Social security and tier 1 railroad retirement benefits

manner as the Secretary shall by regulations prescribe. Such election, once made, may be revoked only with the consent of the Secretary.

(f) Treatment as pension or annuity for certain purposes. -- For purposes of--

    (1) section 22(c)(3)(A) (relating to reduction for amounts received as pension or annuity),

    (2) section 32(c)(2) (defining earned income),

    (3) section 219(f)(1) (defining compensation), and

    (4) section 911(b)(1) (defining foreign earned income),

any social security benefit shall be treated as an amount received as a pension or annuity.

Sec. 101. Certain death benefits

(a) Proceeds of life insurance contracts payable by reason of death. --

    (1) General rule. -- Except as otherwise provided in paragraph (2), subsection (d), subsection (f), and subsection (j), gross income does not include amounts received (whether in a single sum or otherwise) under a life insurance contract, if such amounts are paid by reason of the death of the insured.

    (2) Transfer for valuable consideration. -- In the case of a transfer for a valuable consideration, by assignment or otherwise, of a life insurance contract or any interest therein, the amount excluded from gross income by paragraph (1) shall not exceed an amount equal to the sum of the actual value of such consideration and the premiums and other amounts subsequently paid by the transferee. The preceding sentence shall not apply in the case of such a transfer--

        (A) if such contract or interest therein has a basis for determining gain or loss in the hands of a transferee determined in whole or in part by reference to such basis of such contract or interest therein in the hands of the transferor, or

        (B) if such transfer is to the insured, to a partner of the insured, to a partnership in which the insured is a partner, or to a corporation in which the insured is a shareholder or officer.

The term "other amounts" in the first sentence of this paragraph includes interest paid or accrued by the transferee on indebtedness with respect to such contract or any interest therein if such interest paid or accrued is not allowable as a deduction by reason of section 264(a)(4).

***

(c) Interest. -- If any amount excluded from gross income by subsection (a) is held under an agreement to pay interest thereon, the interest payments shall be included in gross income.

(d) Payment of life insurance proceeds at a date later than death. --

    (1) General rule. -- The amounts held by an insurer with respect to any beneficiary shall be prorated (in accordance with such regulations as may be prescribed by the Secretary) over the period or periods with respect to which such payments are to be made. There shall be excluded from the gross income of such beneficiary in the taxable year received any amount determined by such proration. Gross income includes, to the extent not excluded by the preceding sentence, amounts received under agreements to which this subsection applies.

    (2) Amount held by an insurer. -- An amount held by an insurer with respect to any beneficiary shall mean an amount to which subsection (a) applies which is--

        (A) held by any insurer under an agreement provided for in the life insurance contract, whether as an option or otherwise, to pay such amount on a date or dates later than the death of the insured, and

Sec. 101. Certain death benefits

(B) equal to the value of such agreement to such beneficiary

(i) as of the date of death of the insured (as if any option exercised under the life insurance contract were exercised at such time), and

(ii) as discounted on the basis of the interest rate used by the insurer in calculating payments under the agreement and mortality tables prescribed by the Secretary.

(3) **Application of subsection.** -- This subsection shall not apply to any amount to which subsection (c) is applicable.

***

(g) Treatment of certain accelerated death benefits. --

(1) **In general.** -- For purposes of this section, the following amounts shall be treated as an amount paid by reason of the death of an insured:

(A) Any amount received under a life insurance contract on the life of an insured who is a terminally ill individual.

(B) Any amount received under a life insurance contract on the life of an insured who is a chronically ill individual.

(2) **Treatment of viatical settlements. --**

(A) **In general.** -- If any portion of the death benefit under a life insurance contract on the life of an insured described in paragraph (1) is sold or assigned to a viatical settlement provider, the amount paid for the sale or assignment of such portion shall be treated as an amount paid under the life insurance contract by reason of the death of such insured.

***

(3) **Special rules for chronically ill insureds.** -- In the case of an insured who is a chronically ill individual--

(A) **In general.** -- Paragraphs (1) and (2) shall not apply to any payment received for any period unless--

(i) such payment is for costs incurred by the payee (not compensated for by insurance or otherwise) for qualified long- term care services provided for the insured for such period, and

(ii) the terms of the contract giving rise to such payment satisfy -

(I) the requirements of section 7702B(b)(1)(B), and

(II) the requirements (if any) applicable under subparagraph (B).

For purposes of the preceding sentence, the rule of section 7702B(b)(2)(B) shall apply.

(B) **Other requirements.** -- The requirements applicable under this subparagraph are--

(i) those requirements of section 7702B(g) and section 4980C which the Secretary specifies as applying to such a purchase, assignment, or other arrangement,

(ii) standards adopted by the National Association of Insurance Commissioners which specifically apply to chronically ill individuals (and, if such standards are adopted, the analogous requirements specified under clause (i) shall cease to apply), and

(iii) standards adopted by the State in which the policyholder resides (and if such standards are adopted, the analogous requirements specified under clause (i) and (subject to section 4980C(f)) standards under clause (ii), shall cease to apply).

(C) **Per diem payments.** -- A payment shall not fail to be described in subparagraph (A) by reason of being made on a per diem or other periodic basis without regard to the expenses incurred during the period to which the payment relates.

Sec. 101. Certain death benefits

(D) Limitation on exclusion for periodic payments. -- For limitation on amount of periodic payments which are treated as described in paragraph (1), see section 7702B(d).

(4) Definitions. -- For purposes of this subsection--

(A) Terminally ill individual. -- The term "terminally ill individual" means an individual who has been certified by a physician as having an illness or physical condition 5 which can reasonably be expected to result in death in 24 months or less after the date of the certification.

(B) Chronically ill individual. -- The term "chronically ill individual" has the meaning given such term by section 7702B(c)(2); except that such term shall not include a terminally ill individual. 10

(C) Qualified long-term care services. -- The term "qualified long-term care services" has the meaning given such term by section 7702B(c).

(D) Physician. -- The term "physician" has the meaning given to such term by section 1861(r)(1) of the Social Security Act (42 U.S.C. 1395x(r)(1)).

(5) Exception for business-related policies. -- This subsection shall not apply in the case of 15 any amount paid to any taxpayer other than the insured if such taxpayer has an insurable interest with respect to the life of the insured by reason of the insured being a director, officer, or employee of the taxpayer or by reason of the insured being financially interested in any trade or business carried on by the taxpayer.

(h) Survivor benefits attributable to service by a public safety officer who is killed in the 20 line of duty. --

(1) In general. -- Gross income shall not include any amount paid as a survivor annuity on account of the death of a public safety officer (as such term is defined in section 1204 of the Omnibus Crime Control and Safe Streets Act of 1968) killed in the line of duty--

(A) if such annuity is provided, under a governmental plan which meets the requirements 25 of section 401(a), to the spouse (or a former spouse) of the public safety officer or to a child of such officer; and

(B) to the extent such annuity is attributable to such officer's service as a public safety officer.

(2) Exceptions. -- Paragraph (1) shall not apply with respect to the death of any public 30 safety officer if, as determined in accordance with the provisions of the Omnibus Crime Control and Safe Streets Act of 1968 -

(A) the death was caused by the intentional misconduct of the officer or by such officer's intention to bring about such officer's death;

(B) the officer was voluntarily intoxicated (as defined in section 1204 of such Act) at the 35 time of death;

(C) the officer was performing such officer's duties in a grossly negligent manner at the time of death; or

(D) the payment is to an individual whose actions were a substantial contributing factor to the death of the officer. 40

(i) Certain employee death benefits payable by reason of death of certain terrorist victims or astronauts. --

(1) In general. -- Gross income does not include amounts (whether in a single sum or otherwise) paid by an employer by reason of the death of an employee who is a specified terrorist victim (as defined in section 692(d)(4)). 45

(2) Limitation. --

Sec. 101. Certain death benefits

    (A) In general. -- Subject to such rules as the Secretary may prescribe, paragraph (1) shall not apply to amounts which would have been payable after death if the individual had died other than as a specified terrorist victim (as so defined).

    (B) Exception. -- Subparagraph (A) shall not apply to incidental death benefits paid from a plan described in section 401(a) and exempt from tax under section 501(a).

    (3) Treatment of self-employed individuals. -- For purposes of paragraph (1), the term "employee" includes a self-employed individual (as defined in section 401(c)(1))

(j) Treatment of Certain Employer-Owned Life Insurance Contracts.--

    (1) General rule.-- In the case of an employer-owned life insurance contract, the amount excluded from gross income of an applicable policyholder by reason of paragraph (1) of subsection (a) shall not exceed an amount equal to the sum of the premiums and other amounts paid by the policyholder for the contract.

    (2) Exceptions. -- In the case of an employer-owned life insurance contract with respect to which the notice and consent requirements of paragraph (4) are met, paragraph (1) shall not apply to any of the following:

    (A) Exceptions based on insured's status. -- Any amount received by reason of the death of an insured who, with respect to an applicable policyholder--

    (i) was an employee at any time during the 12-month period before the insured's death, or (ii) is, at the time the contract is issued--

    (I) a director,

    (II) a highly compensated employee within the meaning of section 414(q) (without regard to paragraph (1)(B)(ii) thereof), or (III) a highly compensated individual within the meaning of section 105(h)(5), except that `35 percent' shall be substituted for `25 percent' in subparagraph (C) thereof.

    (B) Exception for amounts paid to insured's heirs. -- Any amount received by reason of the death of an insured to the extent--

    (i) the amount is paid to a member of the family (within the meaning of section 267(c)(4)) of the insured, any individual who is the designated beneficiary of the insured under the contract (other than the applicable policyholder), a trust established for the benefit of any such member of the family or designated beneficiary, or the estate of the insured, or (ii) the amount is used to purchase an equity (or capital or profits) interest in the applicable policyholder from any person described in clause (i).

    (3) Employer-owned life insurance contract. --

    (A) In general. -- For purposes of this subsection, the term `employer-owned life insurance contract' means a life insurance contract which--

    (i) is owned by a person engaged in a trade or business and under which such person (or a related person described in subparagraph (B)(ii)) is directly or indirectly a beneficiary under the contract, and

    (ii) covers the life of an insured who is an employee with respect to the trade or business of the applicable policyholder on the date the contract is issued. For purposes of the preceding sentence, if coverage for each insured under a master contract is treated as a separate contract for purposes of sections 817(h), 7702, and 7702A, coverage for each such insured shall be treated as a separate contract.

    (B) Applicable policyholder. -- For purposes of this subsection--

    (i) In general. -- The term `applicable policyholder' means, with respect to any employer-owned life insurance contract, the person described in subparagraph (A)(i) which owns the contract.

Sec. 101. Certain death benefits

        (ii) Related persons. -- The term `applicable policyholder' includes any person which--

            (I) bears a relationship to the person described in clause (i) which is specified in section 267(b) or 707(b)(1), or (II) is engaged in trades or businesses with such person which are under common control (within the meaning of subsection (a) or (b) of section 52).

    (4) Notice and consent requirements. -- The notice and consent requirements of this paragraph are met if, before the issuance of the contract, the employee--

        (A) is notified in writing that the applicable policyholder intends to insure the employee's life and the maximum face amount for which the employee could be insured at the time the contract was issued,

        (B) provides written consent to being insured under the contract and that such coverage may continue after the insured terminates employment, and

(C) is informed in writing that an applicable policyholder will be a beneficiary of any proceeds payable upon the death of the employee.

    (5) Definitions. -- For purposes of this subsection--

        (A) Employee. -- The term `employee' includes an officer, director, and highly compensated employee (within the meaning of section 414(q)).

        (B) Insured. -- The term `insured' means, with respect to an employer-owned life insurance contract, an individual covered by the contract who is a United States citizen or resident. In the case of a contract covering the joint lives of 2 individuals, references to an insured include both of the individuals.

Reg. § 1.101-1 Exclusion from gross income of proceeds of life insurance contracts payable by reason of death.

    (a)(1) *In general.* Section 101(a)(1) states the general rule that the proceeds of life insurance policies, if paid by reason of the death of the insured, are excluded from the gross income of the recipient. Death benefit payments having the characteristics of life insurance proceeds payable by reason of death under contracts, such as workmen's compensation insurance contracts, endowment contracts, or accident and health insurance contracts, are covered by this provision. For provisions relating to death benefits paid by or on behalf of employers, see section 101(b) and § 1.101-2. The exclusion from gross income allowed by section 101(a) applies whether payment is made to the estate of the insured or to any beneficiary (individual, corporation, or partnership) and whether it is made directly or in trust. The extent to which this exclusion applies in cases where life insurance policies have been transferred for a valuable consideration is stated in section 101(a)(2) and in paragraph (b) of this section. In cases where the proceeds of a life insurance policy, payable by reason of the death of the insured, are paid other than in a single sum at the time of such death, the amounts to be excluded from gross income may be affected by the provisions of section 101(c) (relating to amounts held under agreements to pay interest) or section 101(d) (relating to amounts payable at a date later than death). See §§ 1.101-3 and 1.101-4. However, neither section 101(c) nor section 101(d) applies to a single sum payment which does not exceed the amount payable at the time of death even though such amount is actually paid at a date later than death.

    (2) *Cross references.* For rules governing the taxability of insurance proceeds constituting benefits payable on the death of an employee--

    (i) Under pension, profit-sharing, or stock bonus plans described in section 401(a) and

Sec. 101. Certain death benefits

exempt from tax under section 501(a), or under annuity plans described in section 403(a), see section 72 (m)(3) and paragraph (c) of § 1.72-16;

(ii) Under annuity contracts to which paragraph (a) or (b) of § 1.403(b)-1 applies, see paragraph (c)(3) of § 1.403(b)-1; or

5 (iii) Under eligible State deferred compensation plans described in section 457(b), see paragraph (c) of § 1.457-1.

For the definition of a life insurance company, see section 801.

(b) *Transfers of life insurance policies.* (1) In the case of a transfer, by assignment or otherwise, of a life insurance policy or any interest therein for a valuable consideration, 10 the amount of the proceeds attributable to such policy or interest which is excludable from the transferee's gross income is generally limited to the sum of (i) the actual value of the consideration for such transfer, and (ii) the premiums and other amounts subsequently paid by the transferee (see section 101(a)(2) and example (1) of subparagraph (5) of this paragraph). However, this limitation on the amount excludable 15 from the transferee's gross income does not apply (except in certain special cases involving a series of transfers), where the basis of the policy or interest transferred, for the purpose of determining gain or loss with respect to the transferee, is determinable, in whole or in part, by reference to the basis of such policy or interest in the hands of the transferor (see section 101(a)(2)(A) and examples (2) and (4) of subparagraph (5) of this 20 paragraph). Neither does the limitation apply where the policy or interest therein is transferred to the insured, to a partner of the insured, to a partnership in which the insured is a partner, or to a corporation in which the insured is a shareholder or officer (see section 101(a)(2)(B)). For rules relating to gratuitous transfers, see subparagraph (2) of this paragraph. For special rules with respect to certain cases where a series of 25 transfers is involved, see subparagraph (3) of this paragraph.

(2) In the case of a gratuitous transfer, by assignment or otherwise, of a life insurance policy or any interest therein, as a general rule the amount of the proceeds attributable to such policy or interest which is excludable from the transferee's gross income under section 101(a) is limited to the sum of (i) the amount which would have been excludable 30 by the transferor (in accordance with this section) if no such transfer had taken place, and (ii) any premiums and other amounts subsequently paid by the transferee. See example (6) of subparagraph (5) of this paragraph. However, where the gratuitous transfer in question is made by or to the insured, a partner of the insured, a partnership in which the insured is a partner, or a corporation in which the insured is a shareholder or officer, the 35 entire amount of the proceeds attributable to the policy or interest transferred shall be excludable from the transferee's gross income (see section 101(a)(2)(B) and example (7) of subparagraph (5) of this paragraph).

(3) In the case of a series of transfers, if the last transfer of a life insurance policy or an interest therein is for a valuable consideration--

40 (i) The general rule is that the final transferee shall exclude from gross income, with respect to the proceeds of such policy or interest therein, only the sum of--

(a) The actual value of the consideration paid by him, and

(b) The premiums and other amounts subsequently paid by him;

(ii) If the final transfer is to the insured, to a partner of the insured, to a partnership in 45 which the insured is a partner, or to a corporation in which the insured is a shareholder or officer, the final transferee shall exclude the entire amount of the proceeds from gross income;

(iii) Except where subdivision (ii) of this subparagraph applies, if the basis of the policy or interest transferred, for the purpose of determining gain or loss with respect to the final 50 transferee, is determinable, in whole or in part, by reference to the basis of such policy or interest therein in the hands of the transferor, the amount of the proceeds which is

Sec. 101. Certain death benefits

excludable by the final transferee is limited to the sum of--

(a) The amount which would have been excludable by his transferor if no such transfer had taken place, and

(b) Any premiums and other amounts subsequently paid by the final transferee himself.

(4) For the purposes of section 101(a)(2) and subparagraphs (1) and (3) of this paragraph, a ``transfer for a valuable consideration" is any absolute transfer for value of a right to receive all or a part of the proceeds of a life insurance policy. Thus, the creation, for value, of an enforceable contractual right to receive all or a part of the proceeds of a policy may constitute a transfer for a valuable consideration of the policy or an interest therein. On the other hand, the pledging or assignment of a policy as collateral security is not a transfer for a valuable consideration of such policy or an interest therein, and section 101 is inapplicable to any amounts received by the pledgee or assignee.

(5) The application of this paragraph may be illustrated by the following examples:

Example (1). A pays premiums of $500 for an insurance policy in the face amount of $1,000 upon the life of B, and subsequently transfers the policy to C for $600. C receives the proceeds of $1,000 upon the death of B. The amount which C can exclude from his gross income is limited to $600 plus any premiums paid by C subsequent to the transfer.

Example (2). The X Corporation purchases for a single premium of $500 an insurance policy in the face amount of $1,000 upon the life of A, one of its employees, naming the X Corporation as beneficiary. The X Corporation transfers the policy to the Y Corporation in a tax-free reorganization (the policy having a basis for determining gain or loss in the hands of the Y Corporation determined by reference to its basis in the hands of the X Corporation). The Y Corporation receives the proceeds of $1,000 upon the death of A. The entire $1,000 is to be excluded from the gross income of the Y Corporation.

Example (3). The facts are the same as in example (2) except that, prior to the death of A, the Y Corporation transfers the policy to the Z Corporation for $600. The Z Corporation receives the proceeds of $1,000 upon the death of A. The amount which the Z Corporation can exclude from its gross income is limited to $600 plus any premiums paid by the Z Corporation subsequent to the transfer of the policy to it.

Example (4). The facts are the same as in example (3) except that, prior to the death of A, the Z Corporation transfers the policy to the M Corporation in a tax-free reorganization (the policy having a basis for determining gain or loss in the hands of the M Corporation determined by reference to its basis in the hands of the Z Corporation). The M Corporation receives the proceeds of $1,000 upon the death of A. The amount which the M Corporation can exclude from its gross income is limited to $600 plus any premiums paid by the Z Corporation and the M Corporation subsequent to the transfer of the policy to the Z Corporation.

Example (5). The facts are the same as in example (3) except that, prior to the death of A, the Z Corporation transfers the policy to the N Corporation, in which A is a shareholder. The N Corporation receives the proceeds of $1,000 upon the death of A. The entire $1,000 is to be excluded from the gross income of the N Corporation.

Example (6). A pays premiums of $500 for an insurance policy in the face amount of $1,000 upon his own life, and subsequently transfers the policy to his wife B for $600. B later transfers the policy without consideration to C, who is the son of A and B. C receives the proceeds of $1,000 upon the death of A. The amount which C can exclude from his gross income is limited to $600 plus any premiums paid by B and C subsequent to the transfer of the policy to B.

Example (7). The facts are the same as in example (6) except that, prior to the death of A, C transfers the policy without consideration to A, the insured. A's estate receives the proceeds of $1,000 upon the death of A. The entire $1,000 is to be excluded from the

Sec. 101. Certain death benefits

gross income of A's estate.

Reg. § 1.101-3 Interest payments.

(a) *Applicability of section 101(c).* Section 101(c) provides that if any amount excluded
5 from gross income by section 101(a) (relating to life insurance proceeds) or section
101(b) (relating to employees' death benefits) is held under an agreement to pay interest
thereon, the interest payments shall be included in gross income. This provision applies
to payments made (either by an insurer or by or on behalf of an employer) of interest
earned on any amount so excluded from gross income which is held without substantial
10 diminution of the principal amount during the period when such interest payments are
being made or credited to the beneficiaries or estate of the insured or the employee. For
example, if a monthly payment is $100, of which $99 represents interests and $1
represents diminution of the principal amount, the principal amount shall be considered
held under an agreement to pay interest thereon and the interest payment shall be
15 included in the gross income of the recipient. Section 101(c) applies whether the election
to have an amount held under an agreement to pay interest thereon is made by the
insured or employee or by his beneficiaries or estate, and whether or not an interest rate
is explicitly stated in the agreement. Section 101(d), relating to the payment of life
insurance proceeds at a date later than death, shall not apply to any amount to which
20 section 101(c) applies. See section 101(d)(4). However, both section 101(c) and section
101(d) may apply to payments received under a single life insurance contract. For
provisions relating to the application of this rule to payments received under a permanent
life insurance policy with a family income rider attached, see paragraph (h) of § 1.101-4.

(b) *Determination of ``present value".* For the purpose of determining whether section
25 101(c) or section 101(d) applies, the present value (at the time of the insured's death) of
any amount which is to be paid at a date later than death shall be determined by the use
of the interest rate and mortality tables used by the insurer in determining the size of the
payments to be made.

30 **Reg. § 1.101-4 Payment of life insurance proceeds at a date later than death.**

(a) *In general.* (1)(i) Section 101(d) states the provisions governing the exclusion from
gross income of amounts (other than those to which section 101(c) applies) received
under a life insurance contract and paid by reason of the death of the insured which are
paid to a beneficiary on a date or dates later than the death of the insured. However, if
35 the amounts payable as proceeds of life insurance to which section 101(a)(1) applies
cannot in any event exceed the amount payable at the time of the insured's death, such
amounts are fully excludable from the gross income of the recipient (or recipients) without
regard to the actual time of payment and no further determination need be made under
this section. Section 101(d)(1)(A) provides an exclusion from gross income of any
40 amount determined by a proration, under applicable regulations, of ``an amount held by
an insurer with respect to any beneficiary". The quoted phrase is defined in section
101(d)(2). For the regulations governing the method of computation of this proration, see
paragraphs (c) through (f) of this section. The prorated amounts are to be excluded from
the gross income of the beneficiary regardless of the taxable year in which they are
45 actually received (see example (2) of subparagraph (2) of this paragraph).

(ii) Section 101(d)(1)(B) provides an additional exclusion where life insurance
proceeds are paid to the surviving spouse of an insured. For purposes of this exclusion,
the term ``surviving spouse" means the spouse of the insured as of the date of death,
including a spouse legally separated, but not under a decree of absolute divorce (section
50 101(d)(3)). To the extent that the total payments, under one or more agreements, made in
excess of the amounts determined by proration under section 101(d)(1)(A) do not exceed

Sec. 101. Certain death benefits

$1,000 in the taxable year of receipt, they shall be excluded from the gross income of the surviving spouse (whether or not payment of any part of such amounts is guaranteed by the insurer). Amounts excludable under section 101(d)(1)(B) are not ``prorated'' amounts.

(2) The principles of this paragraph may be illustrated by the following examples:

Example (1). A surviving spouse elects to receive all of the life insurance proceeds with respect to one insured, amounting to $150,000, in ten annual installments of $16,500 each, based on a certain guaranteed interest rate. The prorated amount is $15,000 ($150,000/10). As the second payment, the insurer pays $17,850, which exceeds the guaranteed payment by $1,350 as the result of earnings of the insurer in excess of those required to pay the guaranteed installments. The surviving spouse shall include $1,850 in gross income and exclude $16,000--determined in the following manner:

Fixed payment (including guaranteed interest)................	$16,500
Excess interest...	1,350
Total payment...	17,850
Prorated amount..	15,000
Excess over prorated amount......................	2,850
Annual excess over prorated amount excludable under section 101(d)(1)(B)......	1,000
Amount includible in gross income..................	1,850

Example (2). Assume the same facts as in example (1), except that the third and fourth annual installments, totalling $33,000 (2x$16,500), are received in a single subsequent taxable year of the surviving spouse. The prorated amount of $15,000 of each annual installment, totalling $30,000, shall be excluded even though the spouse receives more than one annual installment in the single subsequent taxable year. However, the surviving spouse is entitled to only one exclusion of $1,000 under section 101(d)(1)(B) for each taxable year of receipt. The surviving spouse shall include $2,000 in her gross income for the taxable year with respect to the above installment payments ($33,000 less the sum of $30,000 plus $1,000).

Example (3). Assume the same facts as in example (1), except that the surviving spouse dies before receiving all ten annual installments and the remaining installments are paid to her estate or beneficiary. In such a case, $15,000 of each installment would continue to be excludable from the gross income of the recipient, but any amounts received in excess thereof would be fully includible.

(b) *Amount held by an insurer.* (1) For the purpose of the proration referred to in section 101(d)(1), an ``amount held by an insurer with respect to any beneficiary'' means an amount equal to the present value to such beneficiary (as of the date of death of the insured) of an agreement by the insurer under a life insurance policy (whether as an option or otherwise) to pay such beneficiary an amount or amounts at a date or dates later than the death of the insured (section 101(d)(2)). The present value of such agreement is to be computed as if the agreement under the life insurance policy had been entered into on the date of death of the insured, except that such value shall be determined by the use of the mortality table and interest rate used by the insurer in calculating payments to be made to the beneficiary under such agreement. Where an insurance policy provides an option for the payment of a specific amount upon the death of the insured in full discharge of the contract, such lump sum is the amount held by the insurer with respect to all beneficiaries (or their beneficiaries) under the contract. See, however, paragraph (e) of this section.

(2) In the case of two or more beneficiaries, the ``amount held by the insurer'' with

Sec. 101. Certain death benefits

respect to each beneficiary depends on the relationship of the different benefits payable to such beneficiaries. Where the amounts payable to two or more beneficiaries are independent of each other, the ``amount held by the insurer with respect to each beneficiary'' shall be determined and prorated over the periods involved independently.

5 Thus, if a certain amount per month is to be paid to A for his life, and, concurrently, another amount per month is to be paid to B for his life, the ``amount held by the insurer'' shall be determined and prorated for both A and B independently, but the aggregate shall not exceed the total present value of such payments to both. On the other hand, if the obligation to pay B was contingent on his surviving A, the ``amount held by the insurer''

10 shall be considered an amount held with respect to both beneficiaries simultaneously. Furthermore, it is immaterial whether B is a named beneficiary or merely the ultimate recipient of payments for a term of years. For the special rules governing the computation of the proration of the ``amount held by an insurer'' in determining amounts excludable under the provisions of section 101(d), see paragraphs (c) to (f), inclusive, of this section.

15 (3) Notwithstanding any other provision of this section, if the policy was transferred for a valuable consideration, the total ``amount held by an insurer'' cannot exceed the sum of the consideration paid plus any premiums or other consideration paid subsequent to the transfer if the provisions of section 101(a)(2) and paragraph (b) of § 1.101-1 limit the excludability of the proceeds to such total.

20 (c) *Treatment of payments for life to a sole beneficiary.* If the contract provides for the payment of a specified lump sum, but, pursuant to an agreement between the beneficiary and the insurer, payments are to be made during the life of the beneficiary in lieu of such lump sum, the lump sum shall be divided by the life expectancy of the beneficiary determined in accordance with the mortality table used by the insurer in determining the

25 benefits to be paid. However, if payments are to be made to the estate or beneficiary of the primary beneficiary in the event that the primary beneficiary dies before receiving a certain number of payments or a specified total amount, such lump sum shall be reduced by the present value (at the time of the insured's death) of amounts which may be paid by reason of the guarantee, in accordance with the provisions of paragraph (e) of this

30 section, before making this calculation. To the extent that payments received in each taxable year do not exceed the amount found from the above calculation, they are ``prorated amounts'' of the ``amount held by an insurer'' and are excludable from the gross income of the beneficiary without regard to whether he lives beyond the life expectancy used in making the calculation. If the contract in question does not provide for

35 the payment of a specific lump sum upon the death of the insured as one of the alternative methods of payment, the present value (at the time of the death of the insured) of the payments to be made the beneficiary, determined in accordance with the interest rate and mortality table used by the insurer in determining the benefits to be paid, shall be used in the above calculation in lieu of a lump sum.

40 ***

(h) *Applicability of both section 101(c) and 101(d) to payments under a single life insurance contract--*(1) *In general.* Section 101(d) shall not apply to interest payments on any amount held by an insurer under an agreement to pay interest thereon (see sections 101(c) and 101(d)(4) and § 1.101-3). On the other hand, both section 101(c) and section

45 101(d) may be applicable to payments received under a single life insurance contract, if such payments consist both of interest on an amount held by an insurer under an agreement to pay interest thereon and of amounts held by the insurer and paid on a date or dates later than the death of the insured. One instance when both section 101(c) and section 101(d) may be applicable to payments received under a single life insurance

50 contract is in the case of a permanent life insurance policy with a family income rider attached. A typical family income rider is one which provides additional term insurance

Sec. 101. Certain death benefits

coverage for a specified number of years from the register date of the basic policy. Under the policy with such a rider, if the insured dies at any time during the term period, the beneficiary is entitled to receive (i) monthly payments of a specified amount commencing as of the date of death and continuing for the balance of the term period, and (ii) a lump sum payment of the proceeds under the basic policy to be paid at the end of the term period. If the insured dies after the expiration of the term period, the beneficiary receives only the proceeds under the basic policy. If the insured dies before the expiration of the term period, part of each monthly payment received by the beneficiary during the term period consists of interest on the proceeds of the basic policy (such proceeds being retained by the insurer until the end of the term period). The remaining part consists of an installment (principal plus interest) of the proceeds of the terms insurance purchased under the family income rider. The amount of term insurance which is provided under the family income rider is, therefore, that amount which, at the date of the insured's death, will provide proceeds sufficient to fund such remaining part of each monthly payment. Since the proceeds under the basic policy are held by the insurer until the end of the term period, that portion of each monthly payment which consists of interest on such proceeds is interest on an amount held by an insurer under an agreement to pay interest thereon and is includible in gross income under section 101(c). On the other hand, since the remaining portion of each monthly payment consists of an installment payment (principal plus interest) of the proceeds of the term insurance, it is a payment of an amount held by the insurer and paid on a date later than the death of the insured to which section 101(d) and this section applies (including the $1,000 exclusion allowed the surviving spouse under section 101(d)(1)(B)). The proceeds of the basic policy, when received in a lump sum at the end of the term period, are excludable from gross income under section 101(a).

(2) *Example of tax treatment of amounts received under a family income rider.* The following example illustrates the application of the principles contained in subparagraph (1) of this paragraph to payments received under a permanent life insurance policy with a family income rider attached:

Example. The sole life insurance policy of the insured provides for the payment of $100,000 to the beneficiary (the insured's spouse) on his death. In addition, there is attached to the policy a family income rider which provides that, if the insured dies before the 20th anniversary of the basic policy, the beneficiary shall receive (i) monthly payments of $1,000 commencing on the date of the insured's death and ending with the payment prior to the 20th anniversary of the basic policy, and (ii) a single payment of $100,000 payable on the 20th anniversary of the basic policy. On the date of the insured's death, the beneficiary (surviving spouse of the insured) is entitled to 36 monthly payments of $1,000 and to the single payment of $100,000 on the 20th anniversary of the basic policy. The value of the proceeds of the term insurance at the date of the insured's death is $28,409.00 (the present value of the portion of the monthly payments to which section 101(d) applies computed on the basis that the interest rate used by the insurer in determining the benefits to be paid under the contract is 2-1/4 percent). The amount of each monthly payment of $1,000 which is includible in the beneficiary's gross income is determined in the following manner:

Sec. 101. Certain death benefits

(a)	Total amount of monthly payment..	$1,000.00
(b)	Amount includible in gross income under section 101(c) as interest on the $100,000 proceeds under the basic policy held by the insurer until 20th anniversary of the basic policy (computed on the basis that the interest rate used by the insurer in determining the benefits to be paid under the contract is 2\1/4\ percent)..	185.00
(c)	Amount to which section 101(d) applies ((a) minus (b)).........	815.00
(d)	Amount excludable from gross income under section 101(d) ($28,409/36)..	789.14
(e)	Amount includible in gross income under section 101(d) without taking into account the $1,000 exclusion allowed the beneficiary as the surviving spouse ((c) minus (d))............	25.86

The beneficiary, as the surviving spouse of the insured, is entitled to exclude the amounts otherwise includible in gross income under section 101(d) (item (e)) to the extent such amounts do not exceed $1,000 in the taxable year of receipt. This exclusion is not applicable, however, with respect to the amount of each payment which is includible in gross income under section 101(c) (item (b)). In this example, therefore, the beneficiary must include $185 of each monthly payment in gross income (amount includible under section 101(c)), but may exclude the $25.86 which is otherwise includible under section 101(d). The payment of $100,000 which is payable to the beneficiary on the 20th anniversary of the basic policy will be entirely excludable from gross income under section 101(a).

(3) *Limitation on amount considered to be an ``amount held by an insurer".* See paragraph (b)(3) of this section for a limitation on the amount which shall be considered an ``amount held by an insurer" in the case of proceeds of life insurance which are paid subsequent to the transfer of the policy for a valuable consideration.

***

[T.D. 6500, 25 FR 11402, Nov. 26, 1960; T.D. 6577, 26 FR 10127, Oct. 28, 1961; 26 FR 10275, Nov. 2, 1961; T.D. 6783, 29 FR 18356, Dec. 24, 1964; T.D. 7836, 47 FR 42337, Sept. 27, 1982]

Sec. 102. Gifts and inheritances

(a) **General rule.** -- Gross income does not include the value of property acquired by gift, bequest, devise, or inheritance.

(b) **Income.** -- Subsection (a) shall not exclude from gross income--

(1) the income from any property referred to in subsection (a); or

(2) where the gift, bequest, devise, or inheritance is of income from property, the amount of such income.

Where, under the terms of the gift, bequest, devise, or inheritance, the payment, crediting, or distribution thereof is to be made at intervals, then, to the extent that it is paid or credited or to be distributed out of income from property, it shall be treated for purposes of paragraph (2) as a gift, bequest, devise, or inheritance of income from property. Any amount included in the gross income of a beneficiary under subchapter J shall be treated for purposes of paragraph (2) as a gift, bequest, devise, or inheritance of income from property.

(c) **Employee gifts.** --

(1) **In general.** -- Subsection (a) shall not exclude from gross income any amount

Sec. 102. Gifts and inheritances

transferred by or for an employer to, or for the benefit of, an employee.

(2) Cross references. --

For provisions excluding certain employee achievement awards from gross income, see section 74(c).

For provisions excluding certain de minimis fringes from gross income, see section 132(e).   5

Reg. § 1.102-1 Gifts and inheritances.

(a) **General rule.** Property received as a gift, or received under a will or under statutes of descent and distribution, is not includible in gross income, although the income from 10 such property is includible in gross income. An amount of principal paid under a marriage settlement is a gift. However, see section 71 and the regulations thereunder for rules relating to alimony or allowances paid upon divorce or separation. Section 102 does not apply to prizes and awards (see section 74 and § 1.74-1) nor to scholarships and fellowship grants (see section 117 and the regulations thereunder).   15

(b) *Income from gifts and inheritances.* The income from any property received as a gift, or under a will or statute of descent and distribution shall not be excluded from gross income under paragraph (a) of this section.

(c) *Gifts and inheritances of income.* If the gift, bequest, devise, or inheritance is of income from property, it shall not be excluded from gross income under paragraph (a) of 20 this section. Section 102 provides a special rule for the treatment of certain gifts, bequests, devises, or inheritances which by their terms are to be paid, credited, or distributed at intervals. Except as provided in section 663(a)(1) and paragraph (d) of this section, to the extent any such gift, bequest, devise, or inheritance is paid, credited, or to be distributed out of income from property, it shall be considered a gift, bequest, devise, 25 or inheritance of income from property. Section 102 provides the same treatment for amounts of income from property which is paid, credited, or to be distributed under a gift or bequest whether the gift or bequest is in terms of a right to payments at intervals (regardless of income) or is in terms of a right to income. To the extent the amounts in either case are paid, credited, or to be distributed at intervals out of income, they are not 30 to be excluded under section 102 from the taxpayer's gross income.

(d) *Effect of Subchapter J.* Any amount required to be included in the gross income of a beneficiary under sections 652, 662, or 668 shall be treated for purposes of this section as a gift, bequest, devise, or inheritance of income from property. On the other hand, any amount excluded from the gross income of a beneficiary under section 663(a)(1) shall be 35 treated for purposes of this section as property acquired by gift, bequest, devise, or inheritance.

(e) *Income taxed to grantor or assignor.* Section 102 is not intended to tax a donee upon the same income which is taxed to the grantor of a trust or assignor of income under section 61 or sections 671 through 677, inclusive.   40

Proposed § 1.102-1. Gifts and Inheritances. (1/9/89)

***

(f) *Exclusions*--(1) *In general.* Section 102 does not apply to prizes and awards (including employee achievement awards) (see section 74); certain de minimis fringe 45 benefits (see section 132); any amount transferred by or for an employer to, or for the benefit of, an employee (see section 102(c)); or to qualified scholarships (see section 117).

(2) *Employer/Employee transfers.* For purposes of section 102(c), extraordinary transfers to the natural objects of an employer's bounty will not be considered transfers 50

241

to, or for the benefit of, an employee if the employee can show that the transfer was not made in recognition of the employee's employment. Accordingly, section 102(c) shall not apply to amounts transferred between related parties (e.g., father and son) if the purpose of the transfer can be substantially attributed to the familial relationship of the parties and
5 not to the circumstances of their employment.

Sec. 103. Interest on State and local bonds

    (a) Exclusion. -- Except as provided in subsection (b), gross income does not include interest on any State or local bond.

10   **(b) Exceptions.** -- Subsection (a) shall not apply to--

        (1) Private activity bond which is not a qualified bond. -- Any private activity bond which is not a qualified bond (within the meaning of section 141).

        (2) Arbitrage bond. -- Any arbitrage bond (within the meaning of section 148).

        (3) Bond not in registered form, etc. -- Any bond unless such bond meets the applicable
15   requirements of section 149.

    (c) Definitions. -- For purposes of this section and part IV--

        (1) State or local bond. -- The term "State or local bond" means an obligation of a State or political subdivision thereof.

        (2) State. -- The term "State" includes the District of Columbia and any possession of the
20   United States.

Sec. 104. Compensation for injuries or sickness. --

    (a) In general. -- Except in the case of amounts attributable to (and not in excess of) deductions allowed under section 213 (relating to medical, etc., expenses) for any prior taxable year, gross
25   income does not include--

        (1) amounts received under workmen's compensation acts as compensation for personal injuries or sickness;

        (2) the amount of any damages (other than punitive damages) received (whether by suit or agreement and whether as lump sums or as periodic payments) on account of personal physical
30   injuries or physical sickness;

        (3) amounts received through accident or health insurance (or through an arrangement having the effect of accident or health insurance) for personal injuries or sickness (other than amounts received by an employee, to the extent such amounts (A) are attributable to contributions by the employer which were not includible in the gross income of the employee,
35   or (B) are paid by the employer);

        (4) amounts received as a pension, annuity, or similar allowance for personal injuries or sickness resulting from active service in the armed forces of any country or in the Coast and Geodetic Survey or the Public Health Service, or as a disability annuity payable under the provisions of section 808 of the Foreign Service Act of 1980; and

40   **(5)** amounts received by an individual as disability income attributable to injuries incurred as a direct result of a terroristic or military action (as defined in section 692(c)(2)).

For purposes of paragraph (3), in the case of an individual who is, or has been, an employee within the meaning of section 401(c)(1) (relating to self-employed individuals), contributions made on behalf of such individual while he was such an employee to a trust described in section 401(a)

Sec. 104. Compensation for injuries or sickness. --

which is exempt from tax under section 501(a), or under a plan described in section 403(a), shall, to the extent allowed as deductions under section 404, be treated as contributions by the employer which were not includible in the gross income of the employee. For purposes of paragraph (2), emotional distress shall not be treated as a physical injury or physical sickness. The preceding sentence shall not apply to an amount of damages not in excess of the amount paid for medical 5 care (described in subparagraph (A) or (B) of section 213(d)(1)) attributable to emotional distress.

(b) Termination of application of subsection (a)(4) in certain cases. --

(1) In general. -- Subsection (a)(4) shall not apply in the case of any individual who is not described in paragraph (2).

(2) Individuals to whom subsection (a)(4) continues to apply. -- An individual is 10 described in this paragraph if--

(A) on or before September 24, 1975, he was entitled to receive any amount described in subsection (a)(4),

(B) on September 24, 1975, he was a member of any organization (or reserve component thereof) referred to in subsection (a)(4) or under a binding written commitment to become 15 such a member,

(C) he receives an amount described in subsection (a)(4) by reason of a combat-related injury, or

(D) on application therefor, he would be entitled to receive disability compensation from the Veterans' Administration. 20

(3) Special rules for combat-related injuries. -- For purposes of this subsection, the term "combat-related injury" means personal injury or sickness--

(A) which is incurred--

(i) as a direct result of armed conflict,

(ii) while engaged in extrahazardous service, or 25

(iii) under conditions simulating war; or

(B) which is caused by an instrumentality of war.

In the case of an individual who is not described in subparagraph (A) or (B) of paragraph (2), except as provided in paragraph (4), the only amounts taken into account under subsection (a) (4) shall be the amounts which he receives by reason of a combat-related injury. 30

(4) Amount excluded to be not less than veterans' disability compensation. -- In the case of any individual described in paragraph (2), the amounts excludable under subsection (a)(4) for any period with respect to any individual shall not be less than the maximum amount which such individual, on application therefor, would be entitled to receive as disability compensation from the Veterans' Administration. 35

(c) Application of prior law in certain cases. -- The phrase "(other than punitive damages)" shall not apply to punitive damages awarded in a civil action--

(1) which is a wrongful death action, and

(2) with respect to which applicable State law (as in effect on September 13, 1995 and without regard to any modification after such date) provides, or has been construed to provide 40 by a court of competent jurisdiction pursuant to a decision issued on or before September 13, 1995, that only punitive damages may be awarded in such an action.

This subsection shall cease to apply to any civil action filed on or after the first date on which the applicable State law ceases to provide (or is no longer construed to provide) the treatment described in paragraph (2). 45

(d) Cross references. --

Sec. 104. Compensation for injuries or sickness. --

(1) For exclusion from employee's gross income of employer contributions to accident and health plans, see section 106.

(2) For exclusion of part of disability retirement pay from the application of subsection (a) (4) of this section, see section 1403 of title 10, United States Code (relating to career compensation laws).

Sec. 105. Amounts received under accident and health plans

(a) Amounts attributable to employer contributions. -- Except as otherwise provided in this section, amounts received by an employee through accident or health insurance for personal injuries or sickness shall be included in gross income to the extent such amounts (1) are attributable to contributions by the employer which were not includible in the gross income of the employee, or (2) are paid by the employer.

(b) Amounts expended for medical care. -- Except in the case of amounts attributable to (and not in excess of) deductions allowed under section 213 (relating to medical, etc., expenses) for any prior taxable year, gross income does not include amounts referred to in subsection (a) if such amounts are paid, directly or indirectly, to the taxpayer to reimburse the taxpayer for expenses incurred by him for the medical care (as defined in section 213(d)) of the taxpayer, his spouse, and his dependents (as defined in section 152, determined without regard to subsections (b)(1), (b)(2), and (d)(1)(B) thereof). Any child to whom section 152(e) applies shall be treated as a dependent of both parents for purposes of this subsection.

(c) Payments unrelated to absence from work. -- Gross income does not include amounts referred to in subsection (a) to the extent such amounts--

(1) constitute payment for the permanent loss or loss of use of a member or function of the body, or the permanent disfigurement, of the taxpayer, his spouse, or a dependent (as defined in section 152, determined without regard to subsections (b)(1), (b)(2), and (d)(1)(B) thereof), and

(2) are computed with reference to the nature of the injury without regard to the period the employee is absent from work.

***

(e) Accident and health plans. -- For purposes of this section and section 104--

(1) amounts received under an accident or health plan for employees, and

(2) amounts received from a sickness and disability fund for employees maintained under the law of a State or the District of Columbia, shall be treated as amounts received through accident or health insurance.

(f) Rules for application of section 213. -- For purposes of section 213(a) (relating to medical, dental, etc., expenses) amounts excluded from gross income under subsection (c) or (d) shall not be considered as compensation (by insurance or otherwise) for expenses paid for medical care.

(g) Self-employed individual not considered an employee. -- For purposes of this section, the term "employee" does not include an individual who is an employee within the meaning of section 401(c)(1) (relating to self-employed individuals).

(h) Amount paid to highly compensated individuals under a discriminatory self-insured medical expense reimbursement plan. --

(1) In general. -- In the case of amounts paid to a highly compensated individual under a self-insured medical reimbursement plan which does not satisfy the requirements of paragraph (2) for a plan year, subsection (b) shall not apply to such amounts to the extent they constitute an excess reimbursement of such highly compensated individual.

Sec. 105. Amounts received under accident and health plans

(2) Prohibition of discrimination. -- A self-insured medical reimbursement plan satisfies the requirements of this paragraph only if--

    (A) the plan does not discriminate in favor of highly compensated individuals as to eligibility to participate; and

    (B) the benefits provided under the plan do not discriminate in favor of participants who are highly compensated individuals.

(3) Nondiscriminatory eligibility classifications. --

    (A) In general. -- A self-insured medical reimbursement plan does not satisfy the requirements of subparagraph (A) of paragraph (2) unless such plan benefits--

        (i) 70 percent or more of all employees, or 80 percent or more of all the employees who are eligible to benefit under the plan if 70 percent or more of all employees are eligible to benefit under the plan; or

        (ii) such employees as qualify under a classification set up by the employer and found by the Secretary not to be discriminatory in favor of highly compensated individuals.

    (B) Exclusion of certain employees. -- For purposes of subparagraph (A), there may be excluded from consideration--

        (i) employees who have not completed 3 years of service;

        (ii) employees who have not attained age 25;

        (iii) part-time or seasonal employees;

        (iv) employees not included in the plan who are included in a unit of employees covered by an agreement between employee representatives and one or more employers which the Secretary finds to be a collective bargaining agreement, if accident and health benefits were the subject of good faith bargaining between such employee representatives and such employer or employers; and

        (v) employees who are nonresident aliens and who receive no earned income (within the meaning of section 911(d)(2)) from the employer which constitutes income from sources within the United States (within the meaning of section 861(a)(3)).

(4) Nondiscriminatory benefits. -- A self-insured medical reimbursement plan does not meet the requirements of subparagraph (B) of paragraph (2) unless all benefits provided for participants who are highly compensated individuals are provided for all other participants.

(5) Highly compensated individual defined. -- For purposes of this subsection, the term "highly compensated individual" means an individual who is--

    (A) one of the 5 highest paid officers,

    (B) a shareholder who owns (with the application of section 318) more than 10 percent in value of the stock of the employer, or

    (C) among the highest paid 25 percent of all employees (other than employees described in paragraph (3)(B) who are not participants).

(6) Self-insured medical reimbursement plan. -- The term "self-insured medical reimbursement plan" means a plan of an employer to reimburse employees for expenses referred to in subsection (b) for which reimbursement is not provided under a policy of accident and health insurance.

(7) Excess reimbursement of highly compensated individual. -- For purposes of this section, the excess reimbursement of a highly compensated individual which is attributable to a self-insured medical reimbursement plan is--

    (A) in the case of a benefit available to highly compensated individuals but not to all

Sec. 105. Amounts received under accident and health plans

other participants (or which otherwise fails to satisfy the requirements of paragraph (2)(B)), the amount reimbursed under the plan to the employee with respect to such benefit, and

(B) in the case of benefits (other than benefits described in subparagraph (A) (!1) paid to a highly compensated individual by a plan which fails to satisfy the requirements of paragraph(2), the total amount reimbursed to the highly compensated individual for the plan year multiplied by a fraction -

(i) the numerator of which is the total amount reimbursed to all participants who are highly compensated individuals under the plan for the plan year, and

(ii) the denominator of which is the total amount reimbursed to all employees under the plan for such plan year.

In determining the fraction under subparagraph (B), there shall not be taken into account any reimbursement which is attributable to a benefit described in subparagraph (A).

(8) Certain controlled groups, etc. -- All employees who are treated as employed by a single employer under subsection (b), (c), or (m) of section 414 shall be treated as employed by a single employer for purposes of this section.

(9) Regulations. -- The Secretary shall prescribe such regulations as may be necessary to carry out the provisions of this section.

(10) Time of inclusion. -- Any amount paid for a plan year that is included in income by reason of this subsection shall be treated as received or accrued in the taxable year of the participant in which the plan year ends.

Reg. § 1.105-1 Amounts attributable to employer contributions.

(a) *In general.* Under section 105(a), amounts received by an employee through accident or health insurance for personal injuries or sickness must be included in his gross income to the extent that such amounts (1) are attributable to contributions of the employer which were not includible in the gross income of the employee, or (2) are paid by the employer, unless such amounts are excluded therefrom under section 105(b), (c), or (d). For purposes of this section, the term ``amounts received by an employee through an accident or health plan" refers to any amounts received through accident or health insurance, and also to any amounts which, under section 105(e), are treated as being so received. See § 1.105-5. In determining the extent to which amounts received for personal injuries or sickness by an employee through an accident or health plan are subject to the provisions of section 105(a), rather than section 104(a)(3), the provisions of paragraphs (b), (c), (d), and (e) of this section shall apply. A self-employed individual is not an employee for purposes of section 105 and §§ 1.105-1 through 1.105-5. See paragraph (g) of § 1.72-15. Thus, such an individual will not be treated as an employee with respect to benefits described in section 105 received from a plan in which he participates as an employee within the meaning of section 401(c)(1) at the time he, his spouse, or any of his dependents becomes entitled to receive such benefits.

***

Reg. § 1.105-3 Payments unrelated to absence from work.

Section 105(c) provides an exclusion from gross income with respect to the amounts referred to in section 105(a) to the extent that such amounts (a) constitute payments for the permanent loss or permanent loss of use of a member or function of the body, or the permanent disfigurement, of the taxpayer, his spouse, or a dependent (as defined in section 152), and (b) are computed with reference to the nature of the injury without regard to the period the employee is absent from work. Loss of use or disfigurement shall be considered permanent when it may reasonably be expected to continue for the life of the individual. For purposes of section 105(c), loss or loss of use of a member or function

Sec. 105. Amounts received under accident and health plans

of the body includes the loss or loss of use of an appendage of the body, the loss of an eye, the loss of substantially all of the vision of an eye, and the loss of substantially all of the hearing in one or both ears. The term ``disfigurement'' shall be given a reasonable interpretation in the light of all the particular facts and circumstances. Section 105(c) does not apply if the amount of the benefits is determined by reference to the period the employee is absent from work. For example, if an employee is absent from work as a result of the loss of an arm, and under the accident and health plan established by his employer, he is to receive $125 a week so long as he is absent from work for a period not in excess of 52 weeks, section 105(c) is not applicable to such payments. See, however, section 105(d) and § 1.105-4. However, for purposes of section 105(c), it is immaterial whether an amount is paid in a lump sum or in installments. Section 105(c) does not apply to amounts which are treated as workmen's compensation under paragraph (b) of § 1.104-1, or to amounts paid by reason of the death of the employee (see section 101).

[T.D. 6500, 25 FR 11402, Nov. 26, 1960, as amended by T.D. 6722, 29 FR 5071, Apr. 14, 1964]

Sec. 106. Contributions by employer to accident and health plans

(a) **General rule.** -- Except as otherwise provided in this section, gross income of an employee does not include employer-provided coverage under an accident or health plan.

(b) **Contributions to Archer MSAs.** --

(1) **In general.** -- In the case of an employee who is an eligible individual, amounts contributed by such employee's employer to any Archer MSA of such employee shall be treated as employer-provided coverage for medical expenses under an accident or health plan to the extent such amounts do not exceed the limitation under section 220(b)(1) (determined without regard to this subsection) which is applicable to such employee for such taxable year.

(2) **No constructive receipt.** -- No amount shall be included in the gross income of any employee solely because the employee may choose between the contributions referred to in paragraph (1) and employer contributions to another health plan of the employer.

(3) **Special rule for deduction of employer contributions.** -- Any employer contribution to an Archer MSA, if otherwise allowable as a deduction under this chapter, shall be allowed only for the taxable year in which paid.

(4) **Employer MSA contributions required to be shown on return.** -- Every individual required to file a return under section 6012 for the taxable year shall include on such return the aggregate amount contributed by employers to the Archer MSAs of such individual or such individual's spouse for such taxable year.

***

(6) **Definitions.** -- For purposes of this subsection, the terms "eligible individual" and "Archer MSA" have the respective meanings give to such terms by section 220.

(c) **Inclusion of long-term care benefits provided through flexible spending arrangements.**--

(1) **In general.** -- Effective on and after January 1, 1997, gross income of an employee shall include employer-provided coverage for qualified long-term care services (as defined in section 7702B(c)) to the extent that such coverage is provided through a flexible spending or similar arrangement.

(2) **Flexible spending arrangement.** -- For purposes of this subsection, a flexible spending arrangement is a benefit program which provides employees with coverage under which--

(A) specified incurred expenses may be reimbursed (subject to reimbursement

Sec. 106. Contributions by employer to accident and health plans

maximums and other reasonable conditions), and

(B) the maximum amount of reimbursement which is reasonably available to a participant for such coverage is less than 500 percent of the value of such coverage.

In the case of an insured plan, the maximum amount reasonably available shall be determined on the basis of the underlying coverage.

(d) Contributions to health savings accounts. --

(1) In general. -- In the case of an employee who is an eligible individual (as defined in section 223(c)(1)), amounts contributed by such employee's employer to any health savings account (as defined in section 223(d)) of such employee shall be treated as employer-provided coverage for medical expenses under an accident or health plan to the extent such amounts do not exceed the limitation under section 223(b) (determined without regard to this subsection) which is applicable to such employee for such taxable year.

Reg. § 1.106-1 Contributions by employer to accident and health plans.
The gross income of an employee does not include contributions which his employer makes to an accident or health plan for compensation (through insurance or otherwise) to the employee for personal injuries or sickness incurred by him, his spouse, or his dependents, as defined in section 152. The employer may contribute to an accident or health plan either by paying the premium (or a portion of the premium) on a policy of accident or health insurance covering one or more of his employees, or by contributing to a separate trust or fund (including a fund referred to in section 105(e)) which provides accident or health benefits directly or through insurance to one or more of his employees. However, if such insurance policy, trust, or fund provides other benefits in addition to accident or health benefits, section 106 applies only to the portion of the employer's contribution which is allocable to accident or health benefits. See paragraph (d) of § 1.104-1 and §§ 1.105-1 through 1.105-5, inclusive, for regulations relating to exclusion from an employee's gross income of amounts received through accident or health insurance and through accident or health plans.

Sec. 107. Rental value of parsonages

In the case of a minister of the gospel, gross income does not include--

(1) the rental value of a home furnished to him as part of his compensation; or

(2) the rental allowance paid to him as part of his compensation, to the extent used by him to rent or provide a home and to the extent such allowance does not exceed the fair rental value of the home, including furnishings and appurtenances such as a garage, plus the cost of utilities.

Reg. § 1.107-1 Rental value of parsonages.
(a) In the case of a minister of the gospel, gross income does not include (1) the rental value of a home, including utilities, furnished to him as a part of his compensation, or (2) the rental allowance paid to him as part of his compensation to the extent such allowance is used by him to rent or otherwise provide a home. In order to qualify for the exclusion, the home or rental allowance must be provided as remuneration for services which are ordinarily the duties of a minister of the gospel. In general, the rules provided in § 1.1402(c)-5 will be applicable to such determination. Examples of specific services the performance of which will be considered duties of a minister for purposes of section 107 include the performance of sacerdotal functions, the conduct of religious worship, the administration and maintenance of religious organizations and their integral agencies, and the performance of teaching and administrative duties at theological seminaries. Also, the service performed by a qualified minister as an employee of the United States

248

Sec. 107. Rental value of parsonages

(other than as a chaplain in the Armed Forces, whose service is considered to be that of a commissioned officer in his capacity as such, and not as a minister in the exercise of his ministry), or a State, Territory, or possession of the United States, or a political subdivision of any of the foregoing, or the District of Columbia, is in the exercise of his ministry provided the service performed includes such services as are ordinarily the 5 duties of a minister.

(b) For purposes of section 107, the term ``home" means a dwelling place (including furnishings) and the appurtenances thereto, such as a garage. The term ``rental allowance" means an amount paid to a minister to rent or otherwise provide a home if such amount is designated as rental allowance pursuant to official action taken prior to 10 January 1, 1958, by the employing church or other qualified organization, or if such amount is designated as rental allowance pursuant to official action taken in advance of such payment by the employing church or other qualified organization when paid after December 31, 1957. The designation of an amount as rental allowance may be evidenced in an employment contract, in minutes of or in a resolution by a church or 15 other qualified organization or in its budget, or in any other appropriate instrument evidencing such official action. The designation referred to in this paragraph is a sufficient designation if it permits a payment or a part thereof to be identified as a payment of rental allowance as distinguished from salary or other remuneration.

(c) A rental allowance must be included in the minister's gross income in the taxable 20 year in which it is received, to the extent that such allowance is not used by him during such taxable year to rent or otherwise provide a home. Circumstances under which a rental allowance will be deemed to have been used to rent or provide a home will include cases in which the allowance is expended (1) for rent of a home, (2) for purchase of a home, and (3) for expenses directly related to providing a home. Expenses for food and 25 servants are not considered for this purpose to be directly related to providing a home. Where the minister rents, purchases, or owns a farm or other business property in addition to a home, the portion of the rental allowance expended in connection with the farm or business property shall not be excluded from his gross income.

30

[T.D. 6500, 25 FR 11402, Nov. 26, 1960; T.D. 6691, 28 FR 12817, Dec. 3, 1963]

Sec. 108. Income from discharge of indebtedness

(a) **Exclusion from gross income.** --

(1) **In general.** -- Gross income does not include any amount which (but for this subsection) 35 would be includible in gross income by reason of the discharge (in whole or in part) of indebtedness of the taxpayer if--

(A) the discharge occurs in a title 11 case,

(B) the discharge occurs when the taxpayer is insolvent,

(C) the indebtedness discharged is qualified farm indebtedness 40

(D) in the case of a taxpayer other than a C corporation, the indebtedness discharged is qualified real property business indebtedness, or

(E) the indebtedness discharged is qualified principal residence indebtedness which is discharged before January 1, 2010.

(2) **Coordination of exclusions.** -- 45

(A) **Title 11 exclusion takes precedence.** -- Subparagraphs (B), (C), (D), and (E) of paragraph (1) shall not apply to a discharge which occurs in a title 11 case.

249

Sec. 108. Income from discharge of indebtedness

(B) Insolvency exclusion takes precedence over qualified farm exclusion and qualified real property business exclusion. -- Subparagraphs (C) and (D) of paragraph (1) shall not apply to a discharge to the extent the taxpayer is insolvent.

(C) Principal residence exclusion takes precedent over insolvency exclusion unless elected otherwise. -- Paragraph (1)(B) shall not apply to a discharge to which paragraph (1)(E) applies unless the taxpayer elects to apply paragraph (1)(B) in lieu of paragraph (1)(E).

(3) Insolvency exclusion limited to amount of insolvency. -- In the case of a discharge to which paragraph (1)(B) applies, the amount excluded under paragraph (1)(B) shall not exceed the amount by which the taxpayer is insolvent.

(b) Reduction of tax attributes. --

(1) In general. -- The amount excluded from gross income under subparagraph (A), (B), or (C) of subsection (a)(1) shall be applied to reduce the tax attributes of the taxpayer as provided in paragraph (2).

(2) Tax attributes affected; order of reduction. -- Except as provided in paragraph (5), the reduction referred to in paragraph (1) shall be made in the following tax attributes in the following order:

(A) NOL. -- Any net operating loss for the taxable year of the discharge, and any net operating loss carryover to such taxable year.

(B) General business credit. -- Any carryover to or from the taxable year of a discharge of an amount for purposes for determining the amount allowable as a credit under section 38 (relating to general business credit).

(C) Minimum tax credit. -- The amount of the minimum tax credit available under section 53(b) as of the beginning of the taxable year immediately following the taxable year of the discharge.

(D) Capital loss carryovers. -- Any net capital loss for the taxable year of the discharge, and any capital loss carryover to such taxable year under section 1212.

(E) Basis reduction. --

(i) In general. -- The basis of the property of the taxpayer.

(ii) Cross reference. -- For provisions for making the reduction described in clause (i), see section 1017.

(F) Passive activity loss and credit carryovers. -- Any passive activity loss or credit carryover of the taxpayer under section 469(b) from the taxable year of the discharge.

(3) Amount of reduction. --

(A) In general. -- Except as provided in subparagraph (B), the reductions described in paragraph (2) shall be one dollar for each dollar excluded by subsection (a).

(B) Credit carryover reduction. -- The reductions described in subparagraphs (B), (C), and (G) shall be 33 1/3 cents for each dollar excluded by subsection (a). The reduction described in subparagraph (F) in any passive activity credit carryover shall be 33 1/3 cents for each dollar excluded by subsection (a).

(4) Ordering rules. --

(A) Reductions made after determination of tax for year. -- The reductions described in paragraph (2) shall be made after the determination of the tax imposed by this chapter for the taxable year of the discharge.

(B) Reductions under subparagraph (A) or (D) of paragraph (2). -- The reductions

Sec. 108.   Income from discharge of indebtedness

described in subparagraph (A) or (D) of paragraph (2) (as the case may be) shall be made first in the loss for the taxable year of the discharge and then in the carryovers to such taxable year in the order of the taxable years from which each such carryover arose.

(C) Reductions under subparagraphs (B) and (G) of paragraph (2). -- The reductions described in subparagraphs (B) and (G) of paragraph (2) shall be made in the order in which carryovers are taken into account under this chapter for the taxable year of the discharge.

(5) Election to apply reduction first against depreciable property. --

(A) In general. -- The taxpayer may elect to apply any portion of the reduction referred to in paragraph (1) to the reduction under section 1017 of the basis of the depreciable property of the taxpayer.

(B) Limitation. -- The amount to which an election under subparagraph (A) applies shall not exceed the aggregate adjusted bases of the depreciable property held by the taxpayer as of the beginning of the taxable year following the taxable year in which the discharge occurs.

(C) Other tax attributes not reduced. -- Paragraph (2) shall not apply to any amount to which an election under this paragraph applies.

(c) Treatment of discharge of qualified real property business indebtedness. --

(1) Basis reduction. --

(A) In general. -- The amount excluded from gross income under subparagraph (D) of subsection (a)(1) shall be applied to reduce the basis of the depreciable real property of the taxpayer.

(2) Limitations. --

(A) Indebtedness in excess of value. -- The amount excluded under subparagraph (D) of subsection (a)(1) with respect to any qualified real property business indebtedness shall not exceed the excess (if any) of--

(i) the outstanding principal amount of such indebtedness (immediately before the discharge), over

(ii) the fair market value of the real property described in paragraph (3)(A) (as of such time), reduced by the outstanding principal amount of any other qualified real property business indebtedness secured by such property (as of such time).

(B) Overall limitation. -- The amount excluded under subparagraph (D) of subsection (a)(1) shall not exceed the aggregate adjusted bases of depreciable real property (determined after any reductions under subsections (b) and (g)) held by the taxpayer immediately before the discharge (other than depreciable real property acquired in contemplation of such discharge).

(3) Qualified real property business indebtedness. -- The term "qualified real property business indebtedness" means indebtedness which--

(A) was incurred or assumed by the taxpayer in connection with real property used in a trade or business and is secured by such real property,

(B) was incurred or assumed before January 1, 1993, or if incurred or assumed on or after such date, is qualified acquisition indebtedness, and

(C) with respect to which such taxpayer makes an election to have this paragraph apply. Such term shall not include qualified farm indebtedness. Indebtedness under subparagraph (B) shall include indebtedness resulting from the refinancing of indebtedness under subparagraph (B) (or this sentence), but only to the extent it does not exceed the amount of the indebtedness being refinanced.

Sec. 108.   Income from discharge of indebtedness

(4) Qualified acquisition indebtedness. -- For purposes of paragraph (3)(B), the term "qualified acquisition indebtedness" means, with respect to any real property described in paragraph (3)(A), indebtedness incurred or assumed to acquire, construct, reconstruct, or substantially improve such property.

(5) Regulations. -- The Secretary shall issue such regulations as are necessary to carry out this subsection, including regulations preventing the abuse of this subsection through cross-collateralization or other means.

(d) Meaning of terms; special rules relating to certain provisions. --

(1) Indebtedness of taxpayer. -- For purposes of this section, the term "indebtedness of the taxpayer" means any indebtedness--

(A) for which the taxpayer is liable, or

(B) subject to which the taxpayer holds property.

(2) Title 11 case. -- For purposes of this section, the term "title 11 case" means a case under title 11 of the United States Code (relating to bankruptcy), but only if the taxpayer is under the jurisdiction of the court in such case and the discharge of indebtedness is granted by the court or is pursuant to a plan approved by the court.

(3) Insolvent. -- For purposes of this section, the term "insolvent" means the excess of liabilities over the fair market value of assets. With respect to any discharge, whether or not the taxpayer is insolvent, and the amount by which the taxpayer is insolvent, shall be determined on the basis of the taxpayer's assets and liabilities immediately before the discharge.

***

(5) Depreciable property. -- The term "depreciable property" has the same meaning as when used in section 1017.

***

(8) Reductions of tax attributes in title 11 cases of individuals to be made by estate. -- In any case under chapter 7 or 11 of title 11 of the United States Code to which section 1398 applies, for purposes of paragraphs (1) and (5) of subsection (b) the estate (and not the individual) shall be treated as the taxpayer. The preceding sentence shall not apply for purposes of applying section 1017 to property transferred by the estate to the individual.

(9) Time for making election, etc. --

(A) Time. -- An election under paragraph (5) of subsection (b) or under paragraph (3)(C) of subsection (c) shall be made on the taxpayer's return for the taxable year in which the discharge occurs or at such other time as may be permitted in regulations prescribed by the Secretary.

(B) Revocation only with consent. -- An election referred to in subparagraph (A), once made, may be revoked only with the consent of the Secretary.

(C) Manner. -- An election referred to in subparagraph (A) shall be made in such manner as the Secretary may by regulations prescribe.

(e) General rules for discharge of indebtedness (including discharges not in title 11 cases or insolvency). -- For purposes of this title--

(1) No other insolvency exception. -- Except as otherwise provided in this section, there shall be no insolvency exception from the general rule that gross income includes income from the discharge of indebtedness.

(2) Income not realized to extent of lost deductions. -- No income shall be realized from the discharge of indebtedness to the extent that payment of the liability would have given rise to a deduction.

Sec. 108.   Income from discharge of indebtedness

(3) Adjustments for unamortized premium and discount. -- The amount taken into account with respect to any discharge shall be properly adjusted for unamortized premium and unamortized discount with respect to the indebtedness discharged.

(4) Acquisition of indebtedness by person related to debtor. --

(A) Treated as acquisition by debtor. -- For purposes of determining income of the debtor from discharge of indebtedness, to the extent provided in regulations prescribed by the Secretary, the acquisition of outstanding indebtedness by a person bearing a relationship to the debtor specified in section 267(b) or 707(b)(1) from a person who does not bear such a relationship to the debtor shall be treated as the acquisition of such indebtedness by the debtor. Such regulations shall provide for such adjustments in the treatment of any subsequent transactions involving the indebtedness as may be appropriate by reason of the application of the preceding sentence.

(B) Members of family. -- For purposes of this paragraph, sections 267(b) and 707(b)(1) shall be applied as if section 267(c)(4) provided that the family of an individual consists of the individual's spouse, the individual's children, grandchildren, and parents, and any spouse of the individual's children or grandchildren.

(C) Entities under common control treated as related. -- For purposes of this paragraph, two entities which are treated as a single employer under subsection (b) or (c) of section 414 shall be treated as bearing a relationship to each other which is described in section 267(b).

(5) Purchase-money debt reduction for solvent debtor treated as price reduction. -- If--

(A) the debt of a purchaser of property to the seller of such property which arose out of the purchase of such property is reduced,

(B) such reduction does not occur--

(i) in a title 11 case, or

(ii) when the purchaser is insolvent, and

(C) but for this paragraph, such reduction would be treated as income to the purchaser from the discharge of indebtedness, then such reduction shall be treated as a purchase price adjustment.

(6) Indebtedness contributed to capital. -- Except as provided in regulations, for purposes of determining income of the debtor from discharge of indebtedness, if a debtor corporation acquires its indebtedness from a shareholder as a contribution to capital--

(A) section 118 shall not apply, but

(B) such corporation shall be treated as having satisfied the indebtedness with an amount of money equal to the shareholder's adjusted basis in the indebtedness.

(f) Student loans. --

(1) In general. -- In the case of an individual, gross income does not include any amount which (but for this subsection) would be includible in gross income by reason of the discharge (in whole or in part) of any student loan if such discharge was pursuant to a provision of such loan under which all or part of the indebtedness of the individual would be discharged if the individual worked for a certain period of time in certain professions for any of a broad class of employers.

(2) Student loan. -- For purposes of this subsection, the term "student loan" means any loan to an individual to assist the individual in attending an educational organization described in section 170(b)(1)(A)(ii) made by--

(A) the United States, or an instrumentality or agency thereof,

Sec. 108. Income from discharge of indebtedness

(B) a State, territory, or possession of the United States, or the District of Columbia, or any political subdivision thereof,

(C) a public benefit corporation--

(i) which is exempt from taxation under section 501(c)(3),

(ii) which has assumed control over a State, county, or municipal hospital, and

(iii) whose employees have been deemed to be public employees under State law, or

(D) any educational organization described in section 170(b)(1)(A)(ii) if such loan is made-

(i) pursuant to an agreement with any entity described in subparagraph (A), (B), or (C) under which the funds from which the loan was made were provided to such educational organization, or

(ii) pursuant to a program of such educational organization which is designed to encourage its students to serve in occupations with unmet needs or in areas with unmet needs and under which the services provided by the students (or former students) are for or under the direction of a governmental unit or an organization described in section 501(c)(3) and exempt from tax under section 501(a).

The term "student loan" includes any loan made by an educational organization described in section 170(b)(1)(A)(ii) or by an organization exempt from tax under section 501(a) to refinance a loan to an individual to assist the individual in attending any such educational organization but only if the refinancing loan is pursuant to a program of the refinancing organization which is designed as described in subparagraph (D)(ii).

(3) Exception for discharges on account of services performed for certain lenders. -- Paragraph (1) shall not apply to the discharge of a loan made by an organization described in paragraph (2)(D) if the discharge is on account of services performed for either such organization.

(g) Special rules for discharge of qualified farm indebtedness. --

(1) Discharge must be by qualified person. --

(A) In general. -- Subparagraph (C) of subsection (a)(1) shall apply only if the discharge is by a qualified person.

(B) Qualified person. -- For purposes of subparagraph (A), the term "qualified person" has the meaning given to such term by section 49(a)(1)(D)(iv); except that such term shall include any Federal, State, or local government or agency or instrumentality thereof.

(2) Qualified farm indebtedness. -- For purposes of this section, indebtedness of a taxpayer shall be treated as qualified farm indebtedness if--

(A) such indebtedness was incurred directly in connection with the operation by the taxpayer of the trade or business of farming, and

(B) 50 percent or more of the aggregate gross receipts of the taxpayer for the 3 taxable years preceding the taxable year in which the discharge of such indebtedness occurs is attributable to the trade or business of farming.

(3) Amount excluded cannot exceed sum of tax attributes and business and investment assets. --

(A) In general. -- The amount excluded under subparagraph (C) of subsection (a)(1) shall not exceed the sum of--

(i) the adjusted tax attributes of the taxpayer, and

(ii) the aggregate adjusted bases of qualified property held by the taxpayer as of the beginning of the taxable year following the taxable year in which the discharge occurs.

Sec. 108.   Income from discharge of indebtedness

(B) Adjusted tax attributes. -- For purposes of subparagraph (A), the term "adjusted tax attributes" means the sum of the tax attributes described in subparagraphs (A), (B), (C), (D), (F), and (G) of subsection (b)(2) determined by taking into account $3 for each $1 of the attributes described in subparagraphs (B), (C), and (G) of subsection (b)(2) and the attribute described in subparagraph (F) of subsection (b)(2) to the extent attributable to any 5 passive activity credit carryover.--

(C) Qualified property. -- For purposes of this paragraph, the term "qualified property" means any property which is used or is held for use in a trade or business or for the production of income.

(D) Coordination with insolvency exclusion. -- For purposes of this paragraph, the 10 adjusted basis of any qualified property and the amount of the adjusted tax attributes shall be determined after any reduction under subsection (b) by reason of amounts excluded from gross income under subsection (a)(1)(B).

(h) Special rules relating to qualified principal residence indebtedness. --

(1) Basis Reduction. -- The amount excluded from gross income by reason of subsection (a) 15 (1)(E) shall be applied to reduce (but not below zero) the basis of the principal residence of the taxpayer.

(2) Qualified principal residence indebtedness. -- For purposes of this section, the term "qualified principal residence indebtedness"'means acquisition indebtedness (within the meaning of section 163(h)(3)(B), applied by substituting `$2,000,000 ($1,000,000' for ` 20 $1,000,000 ($500,000' in clause (ii) thereof) with respect to the principal residence of the taxpayer.

(3) Exception for certain discharges not related to taxpayer's financial condition. -- Subsection (a)(1)(E) shall not apply to the discharge of a loan if the discharge is on account of services performed for the lender or any other factor not directly related to a decline in the 25 value of the residence or to the financial condition of the taxpayer.

(4) Ordering rule. -- If any loan is discharged, in whole or in part, and only a portion of such loan is qualified principal residence indebtedness, subsection (a)(1)(E) shall apply only to so much of the amount discharged as exceeds the amount of the loan (as determined immediately before such discharge) which is not qualified principal residence indebtedness.   30

(5) Principal Residence. -- For purposes of this subsection, the term "principal residence" has the same meaning as when used in section 121.

Sec. 109.   Improvements by lessee on lessor's property

Gross income does not include income (other than rent) derived by a lessor of real property on 35 the termination of a lease, representing the value of such property attributable to buildings erected or other improvements made by the lessee.

Sec. 111.   Recovery of tax benefit items

(a) Deductions. -- Gross income does not include income attributable to the recovery during the 40 taxable year of any amount deducted in any prior taxable year to the extent such amount did not reduce the amount of tax imposed by this chapter.

***

(c) Treatment of carryovers. -- For purposes of this section, an increase in a carryover which has not expired before the beginning of the taxable year in which the recovery or adjustment takes 45

Sec. 111.   Recovery of tax benefit items

place shall be treated as reducing tax imposed by this chapter.

Sec. 112.   Certain combat zone compensation of members of the Armed Forces

(a) **Enlisted personnel.** -- Gross income does not include compensation received for active service as a member below the grade of commissioned officer in the Armed Forces of the United States for any month during any part of which such member--

(1) served in a combat zone, or

(2) was hospitalized as a result of wounds, disease, or injury incurred while serving in a combat zone; but this paragraph shall not apply for any month beginning more than 2 years after the date of the termination of combatant activities in such zone.

With respect to service in the combat zone designated for purposes of the Vietnam conflict, paragraph (2) shall not apply to any month after January 1978.

Sec. 117.   Qualified scholarships

(a) **General rule.** -- Gross income does not include any amount received as a qualified scholarship by an individual who is a candidate for a degree at an educational organization described in section 170(b)(1)(A)(ii).

(b) **Qualified scholarship.** -- For purposes of this section--

(1) **In general.** -- The term "qualified scholarship" means any amount received by an individual as a scholarship or fellowship grant to the extent the individual establishes that, in accordance with the conditions of the grant, such amount was used for qualified tuition and related expenses.

(2) **Qualified tuition and related expenses.** -- For purposes of paragraph (1), the term "qualified tuition and related expenses" means--

(A) tuition and fees required for the enrollment or attendance of a student at an educational organization described in section 170(b)(1)(A)(ii), and

(B) fees, books, supplies, and equipment required for courses of instruction at such an educational organization.

(c) **Limitation.** --

(1) **In general.** -- Except as provided in paragraph (2), subsections (a) and (d) shall not apply to that portion of any amount received which represents payment for teaching, research, or other services by the student required as a condition for receiving the qualified scholarship or qualified tuition reduction.

(d) **Qualified tuition reduction.** --

(1) **In general.** -- Gross income shall not include any qualified tuition reduction.

(2) **Qualified tuition reduction.** -- For purposes of this subsection, the term "qualified tuition reduction" means the amount of any reduction in tuition provided to an employee of an organization described in section 170(b)(1)(A)(ii) for the education (below the graduate level) at such organization (or another organization described in section170(b)(1)(A)(ii)) of -

(A) such employee, or

(B) any person treated as an employee (or whose use is treated as an employee use) under the rules of section 132(h).

Sec. 117. Qualified scholarships

(3) Reduction must not discriminate in favor of highly compensated, etc. -- Paragraph (1) shall apply with respect to any qualified tuition reduction provided with respect to any highly compensated employee only if such reduction is available on substantially the same terms to each member of a group of employees which is defined under a reasonable classification set up by the employer which does not discriminate in favor of highly 5 compensated employees (within the meaning of section 414(q)). For purposes of this paragraph, the term "highly compensated employee" has the meaning given such term by section 414(q).

***

(5) Special rules for teaching and research assistants. -- In the case of the education of an 10 individual who is a graduate student at an educational organization described in section 170(b) (1)(A)(ii) and who is engaged in teaching or research activities for such organization, paragraph (2) shall be applied as if it did not contain the phrase "(below the graduate level)".

Reg. § 1.117-1 Exclusion of amounts received as a scholarship or fellowship grant. 15
(a) *In general.* Any amount received by an individual as a scholarship at an educational institution or as a fellowship grant, including the value of contributed services and accommodations, shall be excluded from the gross income of the recipient, subject to the limitations set forth in section 117(b) and § 1.117-2. The exclusion from gross income of an amount which is a scholarship or fellowship grant is controlled solely by 20 section 117. Accordingly, to the extent that a scholarship or a fellowship grant exceeds the limitations of section 117(b) and § 1.117-2, it is includible in the gross income of the recipient notwithstanding the provisions of section 102 relating to exclusion from gross income of gifts, or section 74(b) relating to exclusion from gross income of certain prizes and awards. For definitions, see § 1.117-3. 25
(b) *Exclusion of amounts received to cover expenses.*--(1) Subject to the limitations provided in subparagraph (2) of this paragraph, any amount received by an individual to cover expenses for travel (including meals and lodging while traveling and an allowance for travel of the individual's family), research, clerical help, or equipment is excludable from gross income provided that such expenses are incident to a scholarship or 30 fellowship grant which is excludable from gross income under section 117(a)(1). If, however, only a portion of a scholarship or fellowship grant is excludable from gross income under section 117(a)(1) because of the part-time employment limitation contained in section 117(b)(1) or because of the expiration of the 36-month period described in section 117(b)(2)(B), only the amount received to cover expenses incident to such 35 excludable portion is excludable from gross income. The requirement that these expenses be incident to the scholarship or the fellowship grant means that the expenses of travel, research, clerical help, or equipment must be incurred by the individual in order to effectuate the purpose for which the scholarship or the fellowship grant was awarded.
(2)(i) In the case of a scholarship or fellowship grant which is awarded after July 28, 40 1956, the exclusion provided under subparagraph (1) of this paragraph is not applicable unless the amount received by the individual is specifically designated to cover expenses for travel, research, clerical help, or equipment.

***

(3) The portion of any amount received to cover the expenses described in 45 subparagraph (1) of this paragraph which is not actually expended for such expenses within the exclusion period described in subparagraph (2) of this paragraph shall, if not returned to the grantor within this period, be included in the gross income of the recipient for the taxable year in which such exclusion period expires.

Sec. 117.   Qualified scholarships

***

Reg. § 117-2   Definitions.
   (a) *Scholarship.* A scholarship generally means an amount paid or allowed to, or for
5 the benefit of, a student, whether an undergraduate or a graduate, to aid such individual
in pursuing his studies. The term includes the value of contributed services and
accommodations (see paragraph (d) of this section) and the amount of tuition,
matriculation, and other fees which are furnished or remitted to a student to aid him in
pursuing his studies. The term also includes any amount received in the nature of a
10 family allowance as a part of a scholarship. However, the term does not include any
amount provided by an individual to aid a relative, friend, or other individual in pursuing
his studies where the grantor is motivated by family or philanthropic considerations. If an
educational institution maintains or participates in a plan whereby the tuition of a child of
a faculty member of such institution is remitted by any other participating educational
15 institution attended by such child, the amount of the tuition so remitted shall be
considered to be an amount received as a scholarship.
   (b) *Educational organization.* For definition of ``educational organization" paragraphs
(a) and (b) of section 117 adopt the definition of that term which is prescribed in section
151(e)(4). Accordingly, for purposes of section 117 the term ``educational organization"
20 means only an educational organization which normally maintains a regular faculty and
curriculum and normally has a regularly organized body of students in attendance at the
place where its educational activities are carried on. See section 151(e)(4) and
regulations thereunder.
   (c) *Fellowship grant.* A fellowship grant generally means an amount paid or allowed to,
25 or for the benefit of, an individual to aid him in the pursuit of study or research. The term
includes the value of contributed services and accommodations (see paragraph (d) of this
section) and the amount of tuition, matriculation, and other fees which are furnished or
remitted to an individual to aid him in the pursuit of study or research. The term also
includes any amount received in the nature of a family allowance as a part of a fellowship
30 grant. However, the term does not include any amount provided by an individual to aid a
relative, friend, or other individual in the pursuit of study or research where the grantor is
motivated by family or philanthropic considerations.
   (d) *Contributed services and accommodations.* The term ``contributed services and
accommodations" means such services and accommodations as room, board, laundry
35 service, and similar services or accommodations which are received by an individual as a
part of a scholarship or fellowship grant.
   (e) *Candidate for a degree.* The term ``candidate for a degree" means an individual,
whether an undergraduate or a graduate, who is pursuing studies or conducting research
to meet the requirements for an academic or professional degree conferred by colleges
40 or universities. It is not essential that such study or research be pursued or conducted at
an educational institution which confers such degrees if the purpose thereof is to meet
the requirements for a degree of a college or university which does confer such degrees.
A student who receives a scholarship for study at a secondary school or other
educational institution is considered to be a ``candidate for a degree."
45
[T.D. 6500, 25 FR 11402, Nov. 26, 1960; 25 FR 14021, Dec. 21, 1960; T.D. 6782, 29 FR
18355, Dec. 24, 1964;T.D. 8032, 50 FR 27232, July 2, 1985]

Proposed § 1.117-6.   Qualified scholarships. (6/9/88)
50   (b) *Exclusion of qualified scholarships.*--(1) Gross income does not include any
amount received as a qualified scholarship by an individual who is a candidate for a

Sec. 117. Qualified scholarships

degree at an educational organization described in section 170(b)(1)(A)(ii), subject to the rules set forth in paragraph (d) of this section. Generally, any amount of a scholarship or fellowship grant that is not excludable under section 117 is includable in the gross income of the recipient for the taxable year in which such amount is received, notwithstanding the provisions of section 102 (relating to exclusion from gross income of gifts). However, see section 127 and the regulations thereunder for rules permitting an exclusion from gross income for certain educational assistance payments. See also section 162 and the regulations thereunder for the deductibility as a trade or business expense of the educational expenses of an individual who is not a candidate for a degree.

(2) If the amount of a scholarship or fellowship grant eligible to be excluded as a qualified scholarship under this paragraph cannot be determined when the grant is received because expenditures for qualified tuition and related expenses have not yet been incurred, then that portion of any amount received as a scholarship or fellowship grant that is not used for qualified tuition and related expenses within the academic period to which the scholarship or fellowship grant applies must be included in the gross income of the recipient for the taxable year in which such academic period ends.

(c) *Definitions*--(1) *Qualified scholarship.*--For purposes of this section, a qualified scholarship is any amount received by an individual as a scholarship or fellowship grant (as defined in paragraph (c)(3) of this section), to the extent the individual establishes that, in accordance with the conditions of the grant, such amount was used for qualified tuition and related expenses (as defined in paragraph (c)(2) of this section). To be considered a qualified scholarship, the terms of the scholarship or fellowship grant need not expressly require that the amounts received be used for tuition and related expenses. However, to the extent that the terms of the grant specify that any portion of the grant cannot be used for tuition and related expenses or designate any portion of the grant for purposes other than tuition and related expenses (such as for room and board, or for a meal allowance), such amounts are not amounts received as a qualified scholarship. See paragraph (e) of this section for rules relating to recordkeeping requirements for establishing amounts used for qualified tuition and related expenses.

(2) *Qualified tuition and related expenses.*--For purposes of this section, qualified tuition and related expenses are--

(i) Tuition and fees required for the enrollment or attendance of a student at an educational organization described in section 170(b)(1)(A)(ii); and

(ii) Fees, books, supplies, and equipment required for courses of instruction at such an educational organization.
In order to be treated as related expenses under this section, the fees, books, supplies, and equipment must be required of all students in the particular course of instruction. Incidental expenses are not considered related expenses. Incidental expenses include expenses incurred for room and board, travel, research, clerical help, and equipment and other expenses that are not required for either enrollment or attendance at an educational organization, or in a course of instruction at such educational organization. See paragraph (c)(6), Example (1) of this section.

(3) *Scholarship or fellowship grant*--(i) *In general.*--Generally, a scholarship or fellowship grant is a cash amount paid or allowed to, or for the benefit of, an individual to aid such individual in the pursuit of study or research. A scholarship or fellowship grant also may be in the form of a reduction in the amount owed by the recipient to an educational organization for tuition, room and board, or any other fee. A scholarship or fellowship grant may be funded by a governmental agency, college or university, charitable organization, business, or any other source. To be considered a scholarship or fellowship grant for purposes of this section, any amount received need not be formally designated as a scholarship. For example, an "allowance" is treated as a scholarship if it

Sec. 117. Qualified scholarships

meets the definition set forth in this paragraph. However, a scholarship or fellowship grant does not include any amount provided by an individual to aid a relative, friend, or other individual in the pursuit of study or research if the grantor is motivated by family or philanthropic considerations.

5   (ii) Items not considered as scholarships or fellowship grants. --The following payments or allowances are not considered to be amounts received as a scholarship or fellowship grant for purposes of section 117:

    (A) Educational and training allowances to a veteran pursuant to section 400 of the Servicemen's Readjustment Act of 1944 (58 Stat. 287) or pursuant to 38 U.S.C. 1631
10 (formerly section 231 of the Veterans' Readjustment Assistance Act of 1952).

    (B) Tuition and subsistence allowances to members of the Armed Forces of the United States who are students at an educational institution operated by the United States or approved by the United States for their education and training, such as the United States Naval Academy and the United States Military Academy.

15   (4) *Candidate for a degree.*--For purposes of this section, a candidate for a degree is--

    (i) A primary or secondary school student;

    (ii) An undergraduate or graduate student at a college or university who is pursuing studies or conducting research to meet the requirement for an academic or professional degree; or

20   (iii) A full-time or part-time student at an educational organization described in section 170(b)(1)(A)(ii) that--

    (A) Provides an educational program that is acceptable for full credit towards a bachelor's or higher degree, or offers a program of training to prepare students for gainful employment in a recognized occupation, and

25   (B) Is authorized under Federal or State law to provide such a program and is accredited by a nationally recognized accreditation agency.

The student may pursue studies or conduct research at an educational organization other than the one conferring the degree provided that such study or research meets the requirements of the educational organization granting the degree. See paragraph (c)(6),
30 Examples (2) and (3) of this section.

    (5) *Educational organization.*--For purposes of this section, an educational organization is an organization described under section 170(b)(1)(A)(ii) and the regulations thereunder. An educational organization is described in section 170(b)(1)(A)(ii) if it has as its primary function the presentation of formal instruction, and it normally
35 maintains a regular faculty and curriculum and normally has a regularly enrolled body of pupils or students in attendance at the place where its educational activities are regularly carried on. See paragraph (c)(6), Example (4) of this section.

    (6) *Examples.*--The provisions of this paragraph may be illustrated by the following examples:

40   *Example (1).* On September 1, 1987, A receives a scholarship from University U for academic year 1987-1988. A is enrolled in a writing course at U. Suggested supplies for the writing course in which A is enrolled include a word processor, but students in the course are not required to obtain a word processor. Any amount used for suggested supplies is not an amount used for qualified tuition and related expenses for purposes of
45 this section. Thus, A may not include the cost of a word processor in determining the amount received by A as a qualified scholarship.

    Example (2). B is a scholarship student during academic year 1987-1988 at Technical School V located in State W. B is enrolled in a program to train individuals to become data processors. V is authorized by State W to provide this program and is accredited by
50 an appropriate accreditation agency. B is a candidate for a degree for purposes of this section. Thus, B may exclude from gross income any amount received as a qualified

Sec. 117. Qualified scholarships

scholarship, subject to the rules set forth in paragraph (d) of this section.

Example (3). C holds a Ph.D. in chemistry. On January 31, 1988, Foundation X awards C a fellowship. During 1988 C pursues chemistry research at Research Foundation Y, supported by the fellowship grant from X. C is not an employee of either foundation. C is not a candidate for a degree for purposes of this section. Thus, the fellowship grant from X must be included in C's gross income.

Example (4). On July 1, 1987, D receives a $500 scholarship to take a correspondence course from School Z. D receives and returns all lessons to Z through the mail. No students are in attendance at Z's place of business. D is not attending an educational organization described in section 170(b)(1)(A)(ii) for purposes of this section. Thus, the $500 scholarship must be included in D's gross income.

(d) *Inclusion of qualified scholarships and qualified tuition reductions representing payment for services*--(1) *In general.*--The exclusion from gross income under this section does not apply to that portion of any amount received as a qualified scholarship or qualified tuition reduction (as defined under section 117(d)) that represents payment for teaching, research, or other services by the student required as a condition to receiving the qualified scholarship or qualified tuition reduction, regardless of whether all candidates for the degree are required to perform such services. The provisions of this paragraph (d) apply not only to cash amounts received in return for such services, but also to amounts by which the tuition or related expenses of the person who performs services are reduced, whether or not pursuant to a tuition reduction plan described in section 117(d).

(2) *Payment for services.*--For purposes of this section, a scholarship or fellowship grant represents payment for services when the grantor requires the recipient to perform services in return for the granting of the scholarship or fellowship. A requirement that the recipient pursue studies, research, or other activities primarily for the benefit of the grantor is treated as a requirement to perform services. A requirement that a recipient furnish periodic reports to the grantor for the purpose of keeping the grantor informed as to the general progress of the individual, however, does not constitute the performance of services. A scholarship or fellowship grant conditioned upon either past, present, or future teaching, research, or other services by the recipient represents payment for services under this section. See paragraph (d)(5), Examples (1), (2), (3) and (4) of this section.

(3) *Determination of amount of scholarship or fellowship grant representing payment for services.*--If only a portion of a scholarship or fellowship grant represents payment for services, the grantor must determine the amount of the scholarship or fellowship grant (including any reduction in tuition or related expenses) to be allocated to payment for services. Factors to be taken into account in making this allocation include, but are not limited to, compensation paid by--

(i) The grantor for similar services performed by students with qualifications comparable to those of the scholarship recipient, but who do not receive scholarship or fellowship grants;

(ii) The grantor for similar services performed by full-time or part-time employees of the grantor who are not students; and

(iii) Educational organizations, other than the grantor of the scholarship or fellowship, for similar services performed either by students or other employees.

If the recipient includes in gross income the amount allocated by the grantor to payment for services and such amount represents reasonable compensation for those services, then any additional amount of a scholarship or fellowship grant received from the same grantor that meets the requirements of paragraph (b) of this section is excludable from gross income. See paragraph (d)(5), Examples (5) and (6) of this section.

(4) *Characterization of scholarship or fellowship grants representing payment for*

Sec. 117. Qualified scholarships

services for purposes of the reporting and withholding requirements.--Any amount of a scholarship or fellowship grant that represents payment for services (as defined in paragraph (d)(2) of this section) is considered wages for purposes of sections 3401 and 3402 (relating to withholding for income taxes), section 6041 (relating to returns of
5   information), and section 6051 (relating to reporting wages of employees). The application of sections 3101 and 3111 (relating to the Federal Insurance Contributions Act (FICA)), or section 3301 (relating to the Federal Unemployment Tax Act (FUTA)) depends upon the nature of the employment and the status of the organization. See sections 3121(b), 3306(c), and the regulations thereunder.
10   (5) *Examples.*--The provisions of this paragraph may be illustrated by the following examples:

Example (1). On November 15, 1987, A receives a $5,000 qualified scholarship (as defined in paragraph (c)(1) of this section) for academic year 1988-1989 under a federal program requiring A's future service as a federal employee. The $5,000 scholarship
15   represents payment for services for purposes of this section. Thus, the $5,000 must be included in A's gross income as wages.

Example (2). B receives a $10,000 scholarship from V Corporation on June 4, 1987, for academic year 1987-1988. As a condition to receiving the scholarship, B agrees to work for V after graduation. B has no previous relationship with V. The $10,000
20   scholarship represents payment for future services for purposes of this section. Thus, the $10,000 scholarship must be included in B's gross income as wages.

Example (3). On March 15, 1987, C is awarded a fellowship for academic year 1987-1988 to pursue a research project the nature of which is determined by the grantor, University W. C must submit a paper to W that describes the research results. The paper
25   does not fulfill any course requirements. Under the terms of the grant, W may publish C's results, or otherwise use the results of C's research. C is treated as performing services for W. Thus, C's fellowship from W represents payment for services and must be included in C's gross income as wages.

Example (4). On September 27, 1987, D receives a qualified scholarship (as defined
30   in paragraph (c)(1) of this section) from University X for academic year 1987-1988. As a condition to receiving the scholarship, D performs services as a teaching assistant for X. Such services are required of all candidates for a degree at X. The amount of D's scholarship from X is equal to the compensation paid by X to teaching assistants who are part-time employees and not students at X. D's scholarship from X represents payment
35   for services. Thus, the entire amount of D's scholarship from X must be included in D's gross income as wages.

Example (5). On June 11, 1987, E receives a $6,000 scholarship for academic year 1987-1988 from University Y. As a condition to receiving the scholarship, E performs services as a researcher for Y. Other researchers who are not scholarship recipients
40   receive $2,000 for similar services for the year. Therefore, Y allocates $2,000 of the scholarship amount to compensation for services performed by E. Thus, the portion of the scholarship that represents payment for services, $2,000, must be included in E's gross income as wages. However, if E establishes expenditures of $4,000 for qualified tuition and related expenses (as defined in paragraph (c)(2) of this section), then $4,000 of E's
45   scholarship is excludable from E's gross income as a qualified scholarship.

Example (6). During 1987 F is employed as a research assistant to a faculty member at University Z. F receives a salary from Z that represents reasonable compensation for the position of research assistant. In addition to salary, F receives from Z a qualified tuition reduction (as defined in section 117(d)) to be used to enroll in an undergraduate
50   course at Z. F includes the salary in gross income. Thus, the qualified tuition reduction does not represent payment for services and therefore, is not includable in F's gross

Sec. 117. Qualified scholarships

income.

Sec. 119. Meals or lodging furnished for the convenience of the employer

(a) Meals and lodging furnished to employee, his spouse, and his dependents, pursuant to employment. -- There shall be excluded from gross income of an employee the value of any meals or lodging furnished to him, his spouse, or any of his dependents by or on behalf of his employer for the convenience of the employer, but only if--

(1) in the case of meals, the meals are furnished on the business premises of the employer, or

(2) in the case of lodging, the employee is required to accept such lodging on the business premises of his employer as a condition of his employment.

(b) Special rules. -- For purposes of subsection (a)--

(1) Provisions of employment contract or State statute not to be determinative. -- In determining whether meals or lodging are furnished for the convenience of the employer, the provisions of an employment contract or of a State statute fixing terms of employment shall not be determinative of whether the meals or lodging are intended as compensation.

(2) Certain factors not taken into account with respect to meals. -- In determining whether meals are furnished for the convenience of the employer, the fact that a charge is made for such meals, and the fact that the employee may accept or decline such meals, shall not be taken into account.

(3) Certain fixed charges for meals. --

(A) In general. -- If--

(i) an employee is required to pay on a periodic basis a fixed charge for his meals, and

(ii) such meals are furnished by the employer for the convenience of the employer, there shall be excluded from the employee's gross income an amount equal to such fixed charge.

(B) Application of subparagraph (A). -- Subparagraph (A) shall apply--

(i) whether the employee pays the fixed charge out of his stated compensation or out of his own funds, and

(ii) only if the employee is required to make the payment whether he accepts or declines the meals.

(4) Meals furnished to employees on business premises where meals of most employees are otherwise excludable. -- All meals furnished on the business premises of an employer to such employer's employees shall be treated as furnished for the convenience of the employer if, without regard to this paragraph, more than half of the employees to whom such meals are furnished on such premises are furnished such meals for the convenience of the employer.

Reg. § 1.119-1 Meals and lodging furnished for the convenience of the employer.

(a) *Meals*--(1) *In general.* The value of meals furnished to an employee by his employer shall be excluded from the employee's gross income if two tests are met: (i) The meals are furnished on the business premises of the employer, and (ii) the meals are furnished for the convenience of the employer. The question of whether meals are furnished for the convenience of the employer is one of fact to be determined by analysis of all the facts and circumstances in each case. If the tests described in subdivisions (i) and (ii) of this subparagraph are met, the exclusion shall apply irrespective of whether under an employment contract or a statute fixing the terms of employment such meals

263

are furnished as compensation.

(2) *Meals furnished without a charge.*--(i) Meals furnished by an employer without charge to the employee will be regarded as furnished for the convenience of the employer if such meals are furnished for a substantial noncompensatory business reason
5 of the employer. If an employer furnishes meals as a means of providing additional compensation to his employee (and not for a substantial noncompensatory business reason of the employer), the meals so furnished will not be regarded as furnished for the convenience of the employer. Conversely, if the employer furnishes meals to his employee for a substantial noncompensatory business reason, the meals so furnished
10 will be regarded as furnished for the convenience of the employer, even though such meals are also furnished for a compensatory reason. In determining the reason of an employer for furnishing meals, the mere declaration that meals are furnished for a noncompensatory business reason is not sufficient to prove that meals are furnished for the convenience of the employer, but such determination will be based upon an
15 examination of all the surrounding facts and circumstances. In subdivision (ii) of this subparagraph, there are set forth some of the substantial noncompensatory business reasons which occur frequently and which justify the conclusion that meals furnished for such a reason are furnished for the convenience of the employer. In subdivision (iii) of this subparagraph, there are set forth some of the business reasons which are
20 considered to be compensatory and which, in the absence of a substantial noncompensatory business reason, justify the conclusion that meals furnished for such a reason are not furnished for the convenience of the employer. Generally, meals furnished before or after the working hours of the employee will not be regarded as furnished for the convenience of the employer, but see subdivision (ii)(d) and (f) of this subparagraph
25 for some exceptions to this general rule. Meals furnished on nonworking days do not qualify for the exclusion under section 119. If the employee is required to occupy living quarters on the business premises of his employer as a condition of his employment (as defined in paragraph (b) of this section), the exclusion applies to the value of any meal furnished without charge to the employee on such premises.

30 (ii)(a) Meals will be regarded as furnished for a substantial noncompensatory business reason of the employer when the meals are furnished to the employee during his working hours to have the employee available for emergency call during his meal period. In order to demonstrate that meals are furnished to the employee to have the employee available for emergency call during the meal period, it must be shown that emergencies have
35 actually occurred, or can reasonably be expected to occur, in the employer's business which have resulted, or will result, in the employer calling on the employee to perform his job during his meal period.

(b) Meals will be regarded as furnished for a substantial noncompensatory business reason of the employer when the meals are furnished to the employee during his working
40 hours because the employer's business is such that the employee must be restricted to a short meal period, such as 30 or 45 minutes, and because the employee could not be expected to eat elsewhere in such a short meal period. For example, meals may qualify under this subdivision when the employer is engaged in a business in which the peak work load occurs during the normal lunch hours. However, meals cannot qualify under
45 this subdivision (b) when the reason for restricting the time of the meal period is so that the employee can be let off earlier in the day.

(c) Meals will be regarded as furnished for a substantial noncompensatory business reason of the employer when the meals are furnished to the employee during his working hours because the employee could not otherwise secure proper meals within a
50 reasonable meal period. For example, meals may qualify under this subdivision (c) when there are insufficient eating facilities in the vicinity of the employer's premises.

Sec. 119. Meals or lodging furnished for the convenience of the employer

(d) A meal furnished to a restaurant employee or other food service employee for each meal period in which the employee works will be regarded as furnished for a substantial noncompensatory business reason of the employer, irrespective of whether the meal is furnished during, immediately before, or immediately after the working hours of the employee. 5

(e) If the employer furnishes meals to employees at a place of business and the reason for furnishing the meals to each of substantially all of the employees who are furnished the meals is a substantial noncompensatory business reason of the employer, the meals furnished to each other employee will also be regarded as furnished for a substantial noncompensatory business reason of the employer. 10

(f) If an employer would have furnished a meal to an employee during his working hours for a substantial noncompensatory business reason, a meal furnished to such an employee immediately after his working hours because his duties prevented him from obtaining a meal during his working hours will be regarded as furnished for a substantial noncompensatory business reason. 15

(iii) Meals will be regarded as furnished for a compensatory business reason of the employer when the meals are furnished to the employee to promote the morale or goodwill of the employee, or to attract prospective employees.

(3) *Meals furnished with a charge.*--(i) If an employer provides meals which an employee may or may not purchase, the meals will not be regarded as furnished for the 20 convenience of the employer. Thus, meals for which a charge is made by the employer will not be regarded as furnished for the convenience of the employer if the employee has a choice of accepting the meals and paying for them or of not paying for and providing his meals in another manner.

(ii) If an employer furnishes an employee meals for which the employee is charged an 25 unvarying amount (for example, by subtraction from his stated compensation) irrespective of whether he accepts the meals, the amount of such flat charge made by the employer for such meals is not, as such, part of the compensation includible in the gross income of the employee; whether the value of the meals so furnished is excludable under section 119 is determined by applying the rules of subparagraph (2) of this paragraph. If 30 meals furnished for an unvarying amount are not furnished for the convenience of the employer in accordance with the rules of subparagraph (2) of this paragraph, the employee shall include in gross income the value of the meals regardless of whether the value exceeds or is less than the amount charged for such meals. In the absence of evidence to the contrary, the value of the meals may be deemed to be equal to the 35 amount charged for them.

(b) *Lodging.* The value of lodging furnished to an employee by the employer shall be excluded from the employee's gross income if three tests are met:

(1) The lodging is furnished on the business premises of the employer,

(2) The lodging is furnished for the convenience of the employer, and 40

(3) The employee is required to accept such lodging as a condition of his employment. The requirement of subparagraph (3) of this paragraph that the employee is required to accept such lodging as a condition of his employment means that he be required to accept the lodging in order to enable him properly to perform the duties of his employment. Lodging will be regarded as furnished to enable the employee properly to 45 perform the duties of his employment when, for example, the lodging is furnished because the employee is required to be available for duty at all times or because the employee could not perform the services required of him unless he is furnished such lodging. If the tests described in subparagraphs (1), (2), and (3) of this paragraph are met, the exclusion shall apply irrespective of whether a charge is made, or whether, 50 under an employment contract or statute fixing the terms of employment, such lodging is

Sec. 119. Meals or lodging furnished for the convenience of the employer

furnished as compensation. If the employer furnishes the employee lodging for which the employee is charged an unvarying amount irrespective of whether he accepts the lodging, the amount of the charge made by the employer for such lodging is not, as such, part of the compensation includible in the gross income of the employee; whether the
5 value of the lodging is excludable from gross income under section 119 is determined by applying the other rules of this paragraph. If the tests described in subparagraph (1), (2), and (3) of this paragraph are not met, the employee shall include in gross income the value of the lodging regardless of whether it exceeds or is less than the amount charged. In the absence of evidence to the contrary, the value of the lodging may be deemed to be
10 equal to the amount charged.

(c) *Business premises of the employer*--(1) *In general.* For purposes of this section, the term "business premises of the employer" generally means the place of employment of the employee. For example, meals and lodging furnished in the employer's home to a domestic servant would constitute meals and lodging furnished on the business premises
15 of the employer. Similarly, meals furnished to cowhands while herding their employer's cattle on leased land would be regarded as furnished on the business premises of the employer.

(2) *Certain camps.* For taxable years beginning after December 31, 1981, in the case of an individual who is furnished lodging by or on behalf of his employer in a camp (as
20 defined in paragraph (d) of this section) in a foreign country (as defined in § 1.911-2(h)), the camp shall be considered to be part of the business premises of the employer.

(d) *Camp defined*--(1) *In general.* For the purposes of paragraph (c)(2) of this section, a camp is lodging that is all of the following:

(i) Provided by or on behalf of the employer for the convenience of the employer
25 because the place at which the employee renders services is in a remote area where satisfactory housing is not available to the employee on the open market within a reasonable commuting distance of that place;

(ii) Located, as near as practicable, in the vicinity of the place at which the employee renders services; and
30 (iii) Furnished in a common area or enclave which is not available to the general public for lodging or accommodations and which normally accommodates ten or more employees.

(2) *Satisfactory housing.* For purposes of paragraph (d)(1)(i) of this section, facts and circumstances that may be relevant in determining whether housing available to the
35 employee is satisfactory include, but are not limited to, the size and condition of living space and the availability and quality of utilities such as water, sewers or other waste disposal facilities, electricity, or heat. The general environment in which housing is located (e.g., climate, prevalence of insects, etc.) does not of itself make housing unsatisfactory. The general environment is relevant, however, if housing is inadequate to
40 protect the occupants from environmental conditions. The individual employee's income level is not relevant in determining whether housing is satisfactory; it may, however, be relevant in determining whether satisfactory housing is available to the employee (see paragraph (d)(3)(i)(B) of this section).

(3) *Availability of satisfactory housing*--(i) *Facts and circumstances.* For purposes of
45 paragraph (d)(1)(i) of this section, facts and circumstances to be considered in determining whether satisfactory housing is available to the employee on the open market include but are not limited to:

(A) The number of housing units available on the open market in relation to the number of housing units required for the employer's employees;
50 (B) The cost of housing available on the open market;

(C) The quality of housing available on the open market; and

Sec. 119. Meals or lodging furnished for the convenience of the employer

(D) The presence of warfare or civil insurrection within the area where housing would be available which would subject U.S. citizens to unusual risk of personal harm or property loss.

(ii) *Presumptions.* Satisfactory housing will generally be considered to be unavailable to the employee on the open market if either of the following conditions is satisfied: 5
(A) The foreign government requires the employer to provide housing for its employees other than housing available on the open market; or
(B) An unrelated person awarding work to the employer requires that the employer's employees occupy housing specified by such unrelated person.The condition of either paragraph (d)(3)(ii)(A) or (B) of this section is not satisfied if the requirement described 10 therein and imposed either by a foreign government or unrelated person applies primarily to U.S. employers and not to a significant number of third country employers or applies primarily to employers of U.S. employees and not to a significant number of employers of third country employees.

(4) *Reasonable commuting distance.* For purposes of paragraph (d)(1)(i) of this 15 section, in determining whether a commuting distance is reasonable, the accessibility of the place at which the employee renders services due to geographic factors, the quality of the roads, the customarily available transportation, and the usual travel time (at the time of day such travel would be required) to the place at which the employee renders services shall be taken into account. 20

(5) *Common area or enclave.* A cluster of housing units does not satisfy paragraph (d) (1)(iii) of this section if it is adjacent to or surrounded by substantially similar housing available to the general public. Two or more common areas or enclaves that house employees who work on the same project (for example, a highway project) are considered to be one common area or enclave in determining whether they normally 25 accommodate ten or more employees.

(e) *Rules.* The exclusion provided by section 119 applies only to meals and lodging furnished in kind by or on behalf of an employer to his employee. If the employee has an option to receive additional compensation in lieu of meals or lodging in kind, the value of such meals and lodging is not excludable from gross income under section 119. 30 However, the mere fact that an employee, at his option, may decline to accept meals tendered in kind will not of itself require inclusion of the value thereof in gross income. Cash allowances for meals or lodging received by an employee are includible in gross income to the extent that such allowances constitute compensation.

(f) *Examples.* The provisions of section 119 may be illustrated by the following 35 examples:

Example (1). A waitress who works from 7 a.m. to 4 p.m. is furnished without charge two meals a work day. The employer encourages the waitress to have her breakfast on his business premises before starting work, but does not require her to have breakfast there. She is required, however, to have her lunch on such premises. Since the waitress 40 is a food service employee and works during the normal breakfast and lunch periods, the waitress is permitted to exclude from her gross income both the value of the breakfast and the value of the lunch.

Example (2). The waitress in example (1) is allowed to have meals on the employer's premises without charge on her days off. The waitress is not permitted to exclude the 45 value of such meals from her gross income.

Example (3). A bank teller who works from 9 a.m. to 5 p.m. is furnished his lunch without charge in a cafeteria which the bank maintains on its premises. The bank furnishes the teller such meals in order to limit his lunch period to 30 minutes since the bank's peak work load occurs during the normal lunch period. If the teller had to obtain 50 his lunch elsewhere, it would take him considerably longer than 30 minutes for lunch, and the bank strictly enforces the 30-minute time limit. The bank teller may exclude from his gross income the value of such meals obtained in the bank cafeteria.

Example (4). Assume the same facts as in example (3), except that the bank charges the bank teller an unvarying rate per meal regardless of whether he eats in the cafeteria.
5 The bank teller is not required to include in gross income such flat amount charged as part of his compensation, and he is entitled to exclude from his gross income the value of the meals he receives for such flat charge.

Example (5). A Civil Service employee of a State is employed at an institution and is required by his employer to be available for duty at all times. The employer furnishes the
10 employee with meals and lodging at the institution without charge. Under the applicable State statute, his meals and lodging are regarded as part of the employee's compensation. The employee would nevertheless be entitled to exclude the value of such meals and lodging from his gross income.

Example (6). An employee of an institution is given the choice of residing at the
15 institution free of charge, or of residing elsewhere and receiving a cash allowance in addition to his regular salary. If he elects to reside at the institution, the value to the employee of the lodging furnished by the employer will be includible in the employee's gross income because his residence at the institution is not required in order for him to perform properly the duties of his employment.

20 *Example (7)*. A construction worker is employed at a construction project at a remote job site in Alaska. Due to the inaccessibility of facilities for the employees who are working at the job site to obtain food and lodging and the prevailing weather conditions, the employer is required to furnish meals and lodging to the employee at the camp site in order to carry on the construction project. The employee is required to pay $40 a week for
25 the meals and lodging. The weekly charge of $40 is not, as such, part of the compensation includible in the gross income of the employee, and under paragraphs (a) and (b) of this section the value of the meals and lodging is excludable from his gross income.

Example (8). A manufacturing company provides a cafeteria on its premises at which
30 its employees can purchase their lunch. There is no other eating facility located near the company's premises, but the employee can furnish his own meal by bringing his lunch. The amount of compensation which any employee is required to include in gross income is not reduced by the amount charged for the meals, and the meals are not considered to be furnished for the convenience of the employer.

35 *Example (9)*. A hospital maintains a cafeteria on its premises where all of its 230 employees may obtain a meal during their working hours. No charge is made for these meals. The hospital furnishes such meals in order to have each of 210 of the employees available for any emergencies that may occur, and it is shown that each such employee is at times called upon to perform services during his meal period. Although the hospital
40 does not require such employees to remain on the premises during meal periods, they rarely leave the hospital during their meal period. Since the hospital furnishes meals to each of substantially all of its employees in order to have each of them available for emergency call during his meal period, all of the hospital employees who obtain their meals in the hospital cafeteria may exclude from their gross income the value of such
45 meals.

[T.D. 6745, 29 FR 9380, July 9, 1964; T.D. 8006, 50 FR 2964, Jan. 23, 1985]

Sec. 121. Exclusion of gain from sale of principal residence

(a) **Exclusion.** -- Gross income shall not include gain from the sale or exchange of property if, during the 5-year period ending on the date of the sale or exchange, such property has been owned and used by the taxpayer as the taxpayer's principal residence for periods aggregating 2 years or more.

(b) **Limitations.** --

> (1) **In general.** -- The amount of gain excluded from gross income under subsection (a) with respect to any sale or exchange shall not exceed $250,000.

> (2) **Special rules for joint returns.** -- In the case of a husband and wife who make a joint return for the taxable year of the sale or exchange of the property--

>> (A) **$500,000 Limitation for certain joint returns.** -- Paragraph (1) shall be applied by substituting "$500,000" for "$250,000" if--

>>> (i) either spouse meets the ownership requirements of subsection (a) with respect to such property;

>>> (ii) both spouses meet the use requirements of subsection (a) with respect to such property; and

>>> (iii) neither spouse is ineligible for the benefits of subsection (a) with respect to such property by reason of paragraph (3).

>> (B) **Other joint returns.** -- If such spouses do not meet the requirements of subparagraph (A), the limitation under paragraph (1) shall be the sum of the limitations under paragraph (1) to which each spouse would be entitled if such spouses had not been married. For purposes of the preceding sentence, each spouse shall be treated as owning the property during the period that either spouse owned the property.

> (3) **Application to only 1 sale or exchange every 2 years.** --

>> (A) **In general.** -- Subsection (a) shall not apply to any sale or exchange by the taxpayer if, during the 2-year period ending on the date of such sale or exchange, there was any other sale or exchange by the taxpayer to which subsection (a) applied.

***

> (4) **Special rule for certain sales by surviving spouses.** -- In the case of a sale or exchange of property by an unmarried individual whose spouse is deceased on the date of such sale, paragraph (1) shall be applied by substituting "$500,000" for "$250,000"'if such sale occurs not later than 2 years after the date of death of such spouse and the requirements of paragraph (2)(A) were met immediately before such date of death.

(c) **Exclusion for taxpayers failing to meet certain requirements.** --

> (1) **In general.** -- In the case of a sale or exchange to which this subsection applies, the ownership and use requirements of subsection (a), and subsection (b)(3), shall not apply; but the dollar limitation under paragraph (1) or (2) of subsection (b), whichever is applicable, shall be equal to--

>> (A) the amount which bears the same ratio to such limitation (determined without regard to this paragraph) as

>> (B)(i) the shorter of--

>>> (I) the aggregate periods, during the 5-year period ending on the date of such sale or exchange, such property has been owned and used by the taxpayer as the taxpayer's principal residence; or

Sec. 121. Exclusion of gain from sale of principal residence

(II) the period after the date of the most recent prior sale or exchange by the taxpayer to which subsection (a) applied and before the date of such sale or exchange, bears to

(ii) 2 years.

(2) Sales and exchanges to which subsection applies. -- This subsection shall apply to any sale or exchange if--

(A) subsection (a) would not (but for this subsection) apply to such sale or exchange by reason of -

(i) a failure to meet the ownership and use requirements of subsection (a), or

(ii) subsection (b)(3), and

(B) such sale or exchange is by reason of a change in place of employment, health, or, to the extent provided in regulations, unforeseen circumstances.

(d) Special rules. --

(1) Joint returns. -- If a husband and wife make a joint return for the taxable year of the sale or exchange of the property, subsections (a) and (c) shall apply if either spouse meets the ownership and use requirements of subsection (a) with respect to such property.

(2) Property of deceased spouse. -- For purposes of this section, in the case of an unmarried individual whose spouse is deceased on the date of the sale or exchange of property, the period such unmarried individual owned and used such property shall include the period such deceased spouse owned and used such property before death.

(3) Property owned by spouse or former spouse. -- For purposes of this section--

(A) Property transferred to individual from spouse or former spouse. -- In the case of an individual holding property transferred to such individual in a transaction described in section 1041(a), the period such individual owns such property shall include the period the transferor owned the property.

(B) Property used by former spouse pursuant to divorce decree, etc. -- Solely for purposes of this section, an individual shall be treated as using property as such individual's principal residence during any period of ownership while such individual's spouse or former spouse is granted use of the property under a divorce or separation instrument (as defined in section 71(b)(2)).

(4) Tenant-stockholder in cooperative housing corporation. -- For purposes of this section, if the taxpayer holds stock as a tenant-stockholder (as defined in section 216) in a cooperative housing corporation (as defined in such section), then--

(A) the holding requirements of subsection (a) shall be applied to the holding of such stock, and

(B) the use requirements of subsection (a) shall be applied to the house or apartment which the taxpayer was entitled to occupy as such stockholder.

(5) Involuntary conversions. --

(A) In general. -- For purposes of this section, the destruction, theft, seizure, requisition, or condemnation of property shall be treated as the sale of such property.

(B) Application of section 1033. -- In applying section 1033 (relating to involuntary conversions), the amount realized from the sale or exchange of property shall be treated as being the amount determined without regard to this section, reduced by the amount of gain not included in gross income pursuant to this section.

(C) Property acquired after involuntary conversion. -- If the basis of the property sold or exchanged is determined (in whole or in part) under section 1033(b) (relating to basis of property acquired through involuntary conversion), then the holding and use by the

Sec. 121. Exclusion of gain from sale of principal residence

taxpayer of the converted property shall be treated as holding and use by the taxpayer of the property sold or exchanged.

(6) **Recognition of gain attributable to depreciation.** -- Subsection (a) shall not apply to so much of the gain from the sale of any property as does not exceed the portion of the depreciation adjustments (as defined in section 1250(b)(3)) attributable to periods after May 6, 1997, in respect of such property.

(7) **Determination of use during periods of out-of-residence care.** -- In the case of a taxpayer who--

(A) becomes physically or mentally incapable of self-care, and

(B) owns property and uses such property as the taxpayer's principal residence during the 5-year period described in subsection (a) for periods aggregating at least 1 year,

then the taxpayer shall be treated as using such property as the taxpayer's principal residence during any time during such 5-year period in which the taxpayer owns the property and resides in any facility (including a nursing home) licensed by a State or political subdivision to care for an individual in the taxpayer's condition.

(8) **Sales of remainder interests.** -- For purposes of this section--

(A) **In general.** -- At the election of the taxpayer, this section shall not fail to apply to the sale or exchange of an interest in a principal residence by reason of such interest being a remainder interest in such residence, but this section shall not apply to any other interest in such residence which is sold or exchanged separately.

(B) **Exception for sales to related parties.** -- Subparagraph (A) shall not apply to any sale to, or exchange with, any person who bears a relationship to the taxpayer which is described in section 267(b) or 707(b).

(9) **Uniformed services, foreign service, and intelligence community.** --

(A) **In general.** -- At the election of an individual with respect to a property, the running of the 5-year period described in subsections (a) and (c)(1)(B) and paragraph (7) of this subsection with respect to such property shall be suspended during any period that such individual or such individual's spouse is serving on qualified official extended duty--

(i) as a member of the uniformed services,

(ii) as a member of the Foreign Service of the United States, or

(iii) as an employee of the intelligence community.

(B) **Maximum period of suspension.** -- The 5-year period described in subsection (a) shall not be extended more than 10 years by reason of subparagraph (A).

(C) **Qualified official extended duty.** -- For purposes of this paragraph--

(i) **In general.** -- The term "qualified official extended duty" means any extended duty while serving at a duty station which is at least 50 miles from such property or while residing under Government orders in Government quarters.

(ii) **Uniformed services.** -- The term "uniformed services" has the meaning given such term by section 101(a)(5) of title 10, United States Code, as in effect on the date of the enactment of this paragraph.

(iii) **Foreign Service of the United States.** -- The term "member of the Foreign Service of the United States" has the meaning given the term "member of the Service" by paragraph (1), (2), (3), (4), or (5) of section 103 of the Foreign Service Act of 1980, as in effect on the date of the enactment of this paragraph.

(iv) **Employee of intelligence community.** -- The term `employee of the intelligence community' means an employee (as defined by section 2105 of title 5, United States

Sec. 121. Exclusion of gain from sale of principal residence

Code) of--

> (I) the Office of the Director of National Intelligence,
>
> (II) the Central Intelligence Agency,
>
> (III) the National Security Agency,
>
> (IV) the Defense Intelligence Agency,
>
> (V) the National Geospatial- Intelligence Agency,
>
> (VI) the National Reconnaissance Office,
>
> (VII) any other office within the Department of Defense for the collection of specialized national intelligence through reconnaissance programs,
>
> (VIII) any of the intelligence elements of the Army, the Navy, the Air Force, the Marine Corps, the Federal Bureau of Investigation, the Department of Treasury, the Department of Energy, and the Coast Guard,
>
> (IX) the Bureau of Intelligence and Research of the Department of State, or
>
> (X) any of the elements of the Department of Homeland Security concerned with the analyses of foreign intelligence information.

(v) Extended duty. -- The term "extended duty" means any period of active duty pursuant to a call or order to such duty for a period in excess of 90 days or for an indefinite period.

(vi) Special rule relating to intelligence community. -- An employee of the intelligence community shall not be treated as serving on qualified extended duty unless such duty is at a duty station located outside the United States.

(D) Special rules relating to election. --

(i) Election limited to 1 property at a time. -- An election under subparagraph (A) with respect to any property may not be made if such an election is in effect with respect to any other property.

(ii) Revocation of election. -- An election under subparagraph (A) may be revoked at any time.

(E) Termination with respect to employees of intelligence community. -- Clause (iii) of subparagraph (A) shall not apply with respect to any sale or exchange after December 31, 2010

(10) Property acquired in like-kind exchange. -- If a taxpayer acquired property in an exchange to which section 1031 applied, subsection (a) shall not apply to the sale or exchange of such property if it occurs during the 5-year period beginning with the date of the acquisition of such property.

(f) Election to have section not apply. -- This section shall not apply to any sale or exchange with respect to which the taxpayer elects not to have this section apply.

(g) Residences acquired in rollovers under section 1034. -- For purposes of this section, in the case of property the acquisition of which by the taxpayer resulted under section 1034 (as in effect on the day before the date of the enactment of this section) in the nonrecognition of any part of the gain realized on the sale or exchange of another residence, in determining the period for which the taxpayer has owned and used such property as the taxpayer's principal residence, there shall be included the aggregate periods for which such other residence (and each prior residence taken into account under section 1223(7) in determining the holding period of such property) had been so owned and used.

Sec. 121. Exclusion of gain from sale of principal residence

Reg. § 1.121-1   Exclusion of gain from sale or exchange of a principal residence.

(a) *In general*. Section 121 provides that, under certain circumstances, gross income does not include gain realized on the sale or exchange of property that was owned and used by a taxpayer as the taxpayer's principal residence. Subject to the other provisions of section 121, a taxpayer may exclude gain only if, during the 5-year period ending on 5 the date of the sale or exchange, the taxpayer owned and used the property as the taxpayer's principal residence for periods aggregating 2 years or more.

(b) *Residence*--(1) *In general*. Whether property is used by the taxpayer as the taxpayer's residence depends upon all the facts and circumstances. A property used by the taxpayer as the taxpayer's residence may include a houseboat, a house trailer, or the 10 house or apartment that the taxpayer is entitled to occupy as a tenant-stockholder in a cooperative housing corporation (as those terms are defined in section 216(b)(1) and (2)). Property used by the taxpayer as the taxpayer's residence does not include personal property that is not a fixture under local law.

(2) *Principal residence*. In the case of a taxpayer using more than one property as a 15 residence, whether property is used by the taxpayer as the taxpayer's principal residence depends upon all the facts and circumstances. If a taxpayer alternates between 2 properties, using each as a residence for successive periods of time, the property that the taxpayer uses a majority of the time during the year ordinarily will be considered the taxpayer's principal residence. In addition to the taxpayer's use of the property, relevant 20 factors in determining a taxpayer's principal residence, include, but are not limited to--

(i) The taxpayer's place of employment;

(ii) The principal place of abode of the taxpayer's family members;

(iii) The address listed on the taxpayer's federal and state tax returns, driver's license, automobile registration, and voter registration card;   25

(iv) The taxpayer's mailing address for bills and correspondence;

(v) The location of the taxpayer's banks; and

(vi) The location of religious organizations and recreational clubs with which the taxpayer is affiliated.

(3) *Vacant land*--(i) *In general*. The sale or exchange of vacant land is not a sale or 30 exchange of the taxpayer's principal residence unless--

(A) The vacant land is adjacent to land containing the dwelling unit of the taxpayer's principal residence;

(B) The taxpayer owned and used the vacant land as part of the taxpayer's principal residence;   35

(C) The taxpayer sells or exchanges the dwelling unit in a sale or exchange that meets the requirements of section 121 within 2 years before or 2 years after the date of the sale or exchange of the vacant land; and

(D) The requirements of section 121 have otherwise been met with respect to the vacant land.   40

(ii) *Limitations*--(A) *Maximum limitation amount*. For purposes of section 121(b)(1) and (2) (relating to the maximum limitation amount of the section 121 exclusion), the sale or exchange of the dwelling unit and the vacant land are treated as one sale or exchange. Therefore, only one maximum limitation amount of $250,000 ($500,000 for certain joint returns) applies to the combined sales or exchanges of vacant land and the dwelling unit. 45 In applying the maximum limitation amount to sales or exchanges that occur in different taxable years, gain from the sale or exchange of the dwelling unit, up to the maximum limitation amount under section 121(b)(1) or (2), is excluded first and each spouse is treated as excluding one-half of the gain from a sale or exchange to which section 121(b) (2)(A) and § 1.121-2(a)(3)(i) (relating to the limitation for certain joint returns) apply.   50

(B) *Sale or exchange of more than one principal residence in 2-year period*. If a

273

Sec. 121. Exclusion of gain from sale of principal residence

dwelling unit and vacant land are sold or exchanged in separate transactions that qualify for the section 121 exclusion under this paragraph (b)(3), each of the transactions is disregarded in applying section 121(b)(3) (restricting the application of section 121 to only 1 sale or exchange every 2 years) to the other transactions but is taken into account as a
5 sale or exchange of a principal residence on the date of the transaction in applying section 121(b)(3) to that transaction and the sale or exchange of any other principal residence.

(C) *Sale or exchange of vacant land before dwelling unit.* If the sale or exchange of the dwelling unit occurs in a later taxable year than the sale or exchange of the vacant
10 land and after the date prescribed by law (including extensions) for the filing of the return for the taxable year of the sale or exchange of the vacant land, any gain from the sale or exchange of the vacant land must be treated as taxable on the taxpayer's return for the taxable year of the sale or exchange of the vacant land. If the taxpayer has reported gain from the sale or exchange of the vacant land as taxable, after satisfying the requirements
15 of this paragraph (b)(3) the taxpayer may claim the section 121 exclusion with regard to the sale or exchange of the vacant land (for any period for which the period of limitation under section 6511 has not expired) by filing an amended return.

(4) *Examples.* The provisions of this paragraph (b) are illustrated by the following examples:
20   *Example 1.* Taxpayer A owns 2 residences, one in New York and one in Florida. From 1999 through 2004, he lives in the New York residence for 7 months and the Florida residence for 5 months of each year. In the absence of facts and circumstances indicating otherwise, the New York residence is A's principal residence. A would be eligible for the section 121 exclusion of gain from the sale or exchange of the New York
25 residence, but not the Florida residence.

Example 2. Taxpayer B owns 2 residences, one in Virginia and one in Maine. During 1999 and 2000, she lives in the Virginia residence. During 2001 and 2002, she lives in the Maine residence. During 2003, she lives in the Virginia residence. B's principal residence during 1999, 2000, and 2003 is the Virginia residence. B's principal residence
30 during 2001 and 2002 is the Maine residence. B would be eligible for the 121 exclusion of gain from the sale or exchange of either residence (but not both) during 2003.

Example 3. In 1991 Taxpayer C buys property consisting of a house and 10 acres that she uses as her principal residence. In May 2005 C sells 8 acres of the land and realizes a gain of $110,000. C does not sell the dwelling unit before the due date for filing C's
35 2005 return, therefore C is not eligible to exclude the $110,000 of gain. In March 2007 C sells the house and remaining 2 acres realizing a gain of $180,000 from the sale of the house. C may exclude the $180,000 of gain. Because the sale of the 8 acres occurred within 2 years from the date of the sale of the dwelling unit, the sale of the 8 acres is treated as a sale of the taxpayer's principal residence under paragraph (b)(3) of this
40 section. C may file an amended return for 2005 to claim an exclusion for $70,000 ($250,000-$180,000 gain previously excluded) of the $110,000 gain from the sale of the 8 acres.

Example 4. In 1998 Taxpayer D buys a house and 1 acre that he uses as his principal residence. In 1999 D buys 29 acres adjacent to his house and uses the vacant land as
45 part of his principal residence. In 2003 D sells the house and 1 acre and the 29 acres in 2 separate transactions. D sells the house and 1 acre at a loss of $25,000. D realizes $270,000 of gain from the sale of the 29 acres. D may exclude the $245,000 gain from the 2 sales.

(c) *Ownership and use requirements*--(1) *In general.* The requirements of ownership
50 and use for periods aggregating 2 years or more may be satisfied by establishing ownership and use for 24 full months or for 730 days (365 x 2). The requirements of

Sec. 121. Exclusion of gain from sale of principal residence

ownership and use may be satisfied during nonconcurrent periods if both the ownership and use tests are met during the 5-year period ending on the date of the sale or exchange.

(2) *Use.*--(i) In establishing whether a taxpayer has satisfied the 2-year use requirement, occupancy of the residence is required. However, short temporary absences, such as for vacation or other seasonal absence (although accompanied with rental of the residence), are counted as periods of use.

(ii) Determination of use during periods of out-of-residence care. If a taxpayer has become physically or mentally incapable of self-care and the taxpayer sells or exchanges property that the taxpayer owned and used as the taxpayer's principal residence for periods aggregating at least 1 year during the 5-year period preceding the sale or exchange, the taxpayer is treated as using the property as the taxpayer's principal residence for any period of time during the 5-year period in which the taxpayer owns the property and resides in any facility (including a nursing home) licensed by a State or political subdivision to care for an individual in the taxpayer's condition.

***

(4) *Examples.* The provisions of this paragraph (c) are illustrated by the following examples. The examples assume that § 1.121-3 (relating to the reduced maximum exclusion) does not apply to the sale of the property. The examples are as follows:

Example 1. Taxpayer A has owned and used his house as his principal residence since 1986. On January 31, 1998, A moves to another state. A rents his house to tenants from that date until April 18, 2000, when he sells it. A is eligible for the section 121 exclusion because he has owned and used the house as his principal residence for at least 2 of the 5 years preceding the sale.

Example 2. Taxpayer B owns and uses a house as her principal residence from 1986 to the end of 1997. On January 4, 1998, B moves to another state and ceases to use the house. B's son moves into the house in March 1999 and uses the residence until it is sold on July 1, 2001. B may not exclude gain from the sale under section 121 because she did not use the property as her principal residence for at least 2 years out of the 5 years preceding the sale.

Example 3. Taxpayer C lives in a townhouse that he rents from 1993 through 1996. On January 18, 1997, he purchases the townhouse. On February 1, 1998, C moves into his daughter's home. On May 25, 2000, while still living in his daughter's home, C sells his townhouse. The section 121 exclusion will apply to gain from the sale because C owned the townhouse for at least 2 years out of the 5 years preceding the sale (from January 19, 1997 until May 25, 2000) and he used the townhouse as his principal residence for at least 2 years during the 5-year period preceding the sale (from May 25, 1995 until February 1, 1998).

Example 4. Taxpayer D, a college professor, purchases and moves into a house on May 1, 1997. He uses the house as his principal residence continuously until September 1, 1998, when he goes abroad for a 1-year sabbatical leave. On October 1, 1999, 1 month after returning from the leave, D sells the house. Because his leave is not considered to be a short temporary absence under paragraph (c)(2) of this section, the period of the sabbatical leave may not be included in determining whether D used the house for periods aggregating 2 years during the 5-year period ending on the date of the sale. Consequently, D is not entitled to exclude gain under section 121 because he did not use the residence for the requisite period.

Example 5. Taxpayer E purchases a house on February 1, 1998, that he uses as his principal residence. During 1998 and 1999, E leaves his residence for a 2-month summer vacation. E sells the house on March 1, 2000. Although, in the 5-year period preceding the date of sale, the total time E used his residence is less than 2 years (21 months), the

275

section 121 exclusion will apply to gain from the sale of the residence because, under paragraph (c)(2) of this section, the 2-month vacations are short temporary absences and are counted as periods of use in determining whether E used the residence for the requisite period.

5   (d) *Depreciation taken after May 6, 1997--(1) In general.* The section 121 exclusion does not apply to so much of the gain from the sale or exchange of property as does not exceed the portion of the depreciation adjustments (as defined in section 1250(b)(3)) attributable to the property for periods after May 6, 1997. Depreciation adjustments allocable to any portion of the property to which the section 121 exclusion does not apply

10 under paragraph (e) of this section are not taken into account for this purpose.

    (2) *Example.* The provisions of this paragraph (d) are illustrated by the following example:

    Example. On July 1, 1999, Taxpayer A moves into a house that he owns and had rented to tenants since July 1, 1997. A took depreciation deductions totaling $14,000 for

15 the period that he rented the property. After using the residence as his principal residence for 2 full years, A sells the property on August 1, 2001. A's gain realized from the sale is $40,000. A has no other section 1231 or capital gains or losses for 2001. Only $26,000 ($40,000 gain realized--$14,000 depreciation deductions) may be excluded under section 121. Under section 121(d)(6) and paragraph (d)(1) of this section, A must recognize

20 $14,000 of the gain as unrecaptured section 1250 gain within the meaning of section 1(h).

    (e) *Property used in part as a principal residence--(1) Allocation required.* Section 121 will not apply to the gain allocable to any portion (separate from the dwelling unit) of property sold or exchanged with respect to which a taxpayer does not satisfy the use

25 requirement. Thus, if a portion of the property was used for residential purposes and a portion of the property (separate from the dwelling unit) was used for non-residential purposes, only the gain allocable to the residential portion is excludable under section 121. No allocation is required if both the residential and non-residential portions of the property are within the same dwelling unit. However, section 121 does not apply to the

30 gain allocable to the residential portion of the property to the extent provided by paragraph (d) of this section.

    (2) *Dwelling unit.* For purposes of this paragraph (e), the term dwelling unit has the same meaning as in section 280A(f)(1), but does not include appurtenant structures or other property.

35   (3) *Method of allocation.* For purposes of determining the amount of gain allocable to the residential and non-residential portions of the property, the taxpayer must allocate the basis and the amount realized between the residential and the non-residential portions of the property using the same method of allocation that the taxpayer used to determine depreciation adjustments (as defined in section 1250(b)(3)), if applicable.

40   (4) *Examples.* The provisions of this paragraph (e) are illustrated by the following examples:

    Example 1. Non-residential use of property not within the dwelling unit. (i) Taxpayer A owns a property that consists of a house, a stable and 35 acres. A uses the stable and 28 acres for non-residential purposes for more than 3 years during the 5-year period

45 preceding the sale. A uses the entire house and the remaining 7 acres as his principal residence for at least 2 years during the 5-year period preceding the sale. For periods after May 6, 1997, A claims depreciation deductions of $9,000 for the non-residential use of the stable. A sells the entire property in 2004, realizing a gain of $24,000. A has no other section 1231 or capital gains or losses for 2004.

50   (ii) Because the stable and the 28 acres used in the business are separate from the dwelling unit, the allocation rules under this paragraph (e) apply and A must allocate the

Sec. 121. Exclusion of gain from sale of principal residence

basis and amount realized between the portion of the property that he used as his principal residence and the portion of the property that he used for non-residential purposes. A determines that $14,000 of the gain is allocable to the non-residential-use portion of the property and that $10,000 of the gain is allocable to the portion of the property used as his residence. A must recognize the $14,000 of gain allocable to the 5 non-residential-use portion of the property ($9,000 of which is unrecaptured section 1250 gain within the meaning of section 1(h), and $5,000 of which is adjusted net capital gain). A may exclude $10,000 of the gain from the sale of the property.

Example 2. Non-residential use of property not within the dwelling unit and rental of the entire property. (i) In 1998 Taxpayer B buys a property that includes a house, a barn, 10 and 2 acres. B uses the house and 2 acres as her principal residence and the barn for an antiques business. In 2002, B moves out of the house and rents it to tenants. B sells the property in 2004, realizing a gain of $21,000. Between 1998 and 2004 B claims depreciation deductions of $4,800 attributable to the antiques business. Between 2002 and 2004 B claims depreciation deductions of $3,000 attributable to the house. B has no 15 other section 1231 or capital gains or losses for 2004.

(ii) Because the portion of the property used in the antiques business is separate from the dwelling unit, the allocation rules under this paragraph (e) apply. B must allocate basis and amount realized between the portion of the property that she used as her principal residence and the portion of the property that she used for non-residential 20 purposes. B determines that $4,000 of the gain is allocable to the non-residential portion of the property and that $17,000 of the gain is allocable to the portion of the property that she used as her principal residence.

(iii) B must recognize the $4,000 of gain allocable to the non-residential portion of the property (all of which is unrecaptured section 1250 gain within the meaning of section 25 1(h)). In addition, the section 121 exclusion does not apply to the gain allocable to the residential portion of the property to the extent of the depreciation adjustments attributable to the residential portion of the property for periods after May 6, 1997 ($3,000). Therefore, B may exclude $14,000 of the gain from the sale of the property.

Example 3. Non-residential use of a separate dwelling unit. (i) In 2002 Taxpayer C 30 buys a 3-story townhouse and converts the basement level, which has a separate entrance, into a separate apartment by installing a kitchen and bathroom and removing the interior stairway that leads from the basement to the upper floors. After the conversion, the property constitutes 2 dwelling units within the meaning of paragraph (e) (2) of this section. C uses the first and second floors of the townhouse as his principal 35 residence and rents the basement level to tenants from 2003 to 2007. C claims depreciation deductions of $2,000 for that period with respect to the basement apartment. C sells the entire property in 2007, realizing gain of $18,000. C has no other section 1231 or capital gains or losses for 2007.

(ii) Because the basement apartment and the upper floors of the townhouse are 40 separate dwelling units, C must allocate the gain between the portion of the property that he used as his principal residence and the portion of the property that he used for non-residential purposes under paragraph (e) of this section. After allocating the basis and the amount realized between the residential and non-residential portions of the property, C determines that $6,000 of the gain is allocable to the non-residential portion of the 45 property and that $12,000 of the gain is allocable to the portion of the property used as his residence. C must recognize the $6,000 of gain allocable to the non-residential portion of the property ($2,000 of which is unrecaptured section 1250 gain within the meaning of section 1(h), and $4,000 of which is adjusted net capital gain). C may exclude $12,000 of the gain from the sale of the property. 50

Example 4. Separate dwelling unit converted to residential use. The facts are the

same as in Example 3 except that in 2007 C incorporates the basement of the townhouse into his principal residence by eliminating the kitchen and building a new interior stairway to the upper floors. C uses all 3 floors of the townhouse as his principal residence for 2 full years and sells the townhouse in 2010, realizing a gain of $20,000. Under section
5   121(d)(6) and paragraph (d) of this section, C must recognize $2,000 of the gain as unrecaptured section 1250 gain within the meaning of section 1(h). Because C used the entire 3 floors of the townhouse as his principal residence for 2 of the 5 years preceding the sale of the property, C may exclude the remaining $18,000 of the gain from the sale of the house.

10   *Example 5.* Non-residential use within the dwelling unit, property depreciated. Taxpayer D, an attorney, buys a house in 2003. The house constitutes a single dwelling unit but D uses a portion of the house as a law office. D claims depreciation deductions of $2,000 during the period that she owns the house. D sells the house in 2006, realizing a gain of $13,000. D has no other section 1231 or capital gains or losses for 2006. Under
15   section 121(d)(6) and paragraph (d) of this section, D must recognize $2,000 of the gain as unrecaptured section 1250 gain within the meaning of section 1(h). D may exclude the remaining $11,000 of the gain from the sale of her house because, under paragraph (e) (1) of this section, she is not required to allocate gain to the business use within the dwelling unit.

20   *Example 6.* Non-residential use within the dwelling unit, property not depreciated. The facts are the same as in Example 5, except that D is not entitled to claim any depreciation deductions with respect to her business use of the house. D may exclude $13,000 of the gain from the sale of her house because, under paragraph (e)(1) of this section, she is not required to allocate gain to the business use within the dwelling unit.

25   ***

Reg. § 1.121-2   Limitations.
        (a) *Dollar limitations*--(1) *In general.* A taxpayer may exclude from gross income up to $250,000 of gain from the sale or exchange of the taxpayer's principal residence. A
30   taxpayer is eligible for only one maximum exclusion per principal residence.
        (2) *Joint owners.* If taxpayers jointly own a principal residence but file separate returns, each taxpayer may exclude from gross income up to $250,000 of gain that is attributable to each taxpayer's interest in the property, if the requirements of section 121 have otherwise been met.
35   (3) *Special rules for joint returns*--(i) *In general.* A husband and wife who make a joint return for the year of the sale or exchange of a
principal residence may exclude up to $500,000 of gain if--
        (A) Either spouse meets the 2-year ownership requirements of § 1.121-1(a) and (c);
        (B) Both spouses meet the 2-year use requirements of § 1.121-1(a) and (c); and
40   (C) Neither spouse excluded gain from a prior sale or exchange of property under section 121 within the last 2 years (as determined under paragraph (b) of this section).
        (ii) *Other joint returns.* For taxpayers filing jointly, if either spouse fails to meet the requirements of paragraph (a)(3)(i) of this section, the maximum limitation amount to be claimed by the couple is the sum of each spouse's limitation amount determined on a
45   separate basis as if they had not been married. For this purpose, each spouse is treated as owning the property during the period that either spouse owned the property.
        (4) *Examples.* The provisions of this paragraph (a) are illustrated by the following examples. The examples assume that § 1.121-3 (relating to the reduced maximum exclusion) does not apply to the sale of the property. The examples are as follows:
50   *Example 1.* Unmarried Taxpayers A and B own a house as joint owners, each owning a 50 percent interest in the house. They sell the house after owning and using it as their

principal residence for 2 full years. The gain realized from the sale is $256,000. A and B are each eligible to exclude $128,000 of gain because the amount of realized gain allocable to each of them from the sale does not exceed each taxpayer's available limitation amount of $250,000.

Example 2. The facts are the same as in Example 1, except that A and B are married 5 taxpayers who file a joint return for the taxable year of the sale. A and B are eligible to exclude the entire amount of realized gain ($256,000) from gross income because the gain realized from the sale does not exceed the limitation amount of $500,000 available to A and B as taxpayers filing a joint return.

Example 3. During 1999, married Taxpayers H and W each sell a residence that each 10 had separately owned and used as a principal residence before their marriage. Each spouse meets the ownership and use tests for his or her respective residence. Neither spouse meets the use requirement for the other spouse's residence. H and W file a joint return for the year of the sales. The gain realized from the sale of H's residence is $200,000. The gain realized from the sale of W's residence is $300,000. Because the 15 ownership and use requirements are met for each residence by each respective spouse, H and W are each eligible to exclude up to $250,000 of gain from the sale of their individual residences. However, W may not use H's unused exclusion to exclude gain in excess of her limitation amount. Therefore, H and W must recognize $50,000 of the gain realized on the sale of W's residence. 20

Example 4. Married Taxpayers H and W sell their residence and file a joint return for the year of the sale. W, but not H, satisfies the requirements of section 121. They are eligible to exclude up to $250,000 of the gain from the sale of the residence because that is the sum of each spouse's dollar limitation amount determined on a separate basis as if they had not been married ($0 for H, $250,000 for W). 25

Example 5. Married Taxpayers H and W have owned and used their principal residence since 1998. On February 16, 2001, H dies. On September 24, 2001, W sells the residence and realizes a gain of $350,000. Pursuant to section 6013(a)(3), W and H's executor make a joint return for 2001. All $350,000 of the gain from the sale of the residence may be excluded. 30

Example 6. Assume the same facts as Example 5, except that W does not sell the residence until January 31, 2002. Because W's filing status for the taxable year of the sale is single, the special rules for joint returns under paragraph (a)(3) of this section do not apply and W may exclude only $250,000 of the gain.

*** 35

Reg. § 1.121-3 Reduced maximum exclusion for taxpayers failing to meet certain requirements.

(a) *In general.* In lieu of the limitation under section 121(b) and § 1.121-2, a reduced maximum exclusion limitation may be available for a taxpayer who sells or exchanges 40 property used as the taxpayer's principal residence but fails to satisfy the ownership and use requirements described in § 1.121-1(a) and (c) or the 2-year limitation described in § 1.121-2(b).

(b) *Primary reason for sale or exchange.* In order for a taxpayer to claim a reduced maximum exclusion under section 121(c), the sale or exchange must be by reason of a 45 change in place of employment, health, or unforeseen circumstances. If a safe harbor described in this section applies, a sale or exchange is deemed to be by reason of a change in place of employment, health, or unforeseen circumstances. If a safe harbor described in this section does not apply, a sale or exchange is by reason of a change in place of employment, health, or unforeseen circumstances only if the primary reason for 50 the sale or exchange is a change in place of employment (within the meaning of

Sec. 121. Exclusion of gain from sale of principal residence

paragraph (c) of this section), health (within the meaning of paragraph (d) of this section), or unforeseen circumstances (within the meaning of   paragraph (e) of this section). Whether the requirements of this section are satisfied depends upon all the facts and circumstances. Factors that may be relevant in determining the taxpayer's primary reason
5   for the sale or exchange include (but are not limited to) the extent to which--

(1) The sale or exchange and the circumstances giving rise to the sale or exchange are proximate in time;

(2) The suitability of the property as the taxpayer's principal residence materially changes;

10   (3) The taxpayer's financial ability to maintain the property is materially impaired;

(4) The taxpayer uses the property as the taxpayer's residence during the period of the taxpayer's ownership of the property;

(5) The circumstances giving rise to the sale or exchange are not reasonably foreseeable when the taxpayer begins using the property as the taxpayer's principal
15   residence; and

(6) The circumstances giving rise to the sale or exchange occur during the period of the taxpayer's ownership and use of the property as the taxpayer's principal residence.

(c) *Sale or exchange by reason of a change in place of employment*--(1) *In general*. A sale or exchange is by reason of a change in place of employment if, in the case of a
20   qualified individual described in paragraph (f) of this section, the primary reason for the sale or exchange is a change in the location of the individual's employment.

(2) *Distance safe harbor*. A sale or exchange is deemed to be by reason of a change in place of employment (within the meaning of paragraph (c)(1) of this section) if--

(i) The change in place of employment occurs during the period of the taxpayer's
25   ownership and use of the property as the taxpayer's principal residence; and

(ii) The qualified individual's new place of employment is at least 50 miles farther from the residence sold or exchanged than was the former place of employment, or, if there was no former place of employment, the distance between the qualified individual's new place of employment and the residence sold or exchanged is at least 50 miles.

30   (3) *Employment*. For purposes of this paragraph (c), employment includes the commencement of employment with a new employer, the continuation of employment with the same employer, and the commencement or continuation of self-employment.

(4) *Examples*. The following examples illustrate the rules of this paragraph (c):

Example 1. A is unemployed and owns a townhouse that she has owned and used as
35   her principal residence since 2003. In 2004 A obtains a job that is 54 miles from her townhouse, and she sells the townhouse. Because the distance between A's new place of employment and the townhouse is at least 50 miles, the sale is within the safe harbor of paragraph (c)(2) of this section and A is entitled to claim a reduced maximum exclusion under section 121(c)(2).

40   *Example 2*. B is an officer in the United States Air Force stationed in Florida. B purchases a house in Florida in 2002. In May 2003 B moves out of his house to take a 3-year assignment in Germany. B sells his house in January 2004. Because B's new place of employment in Germany is at least 50 miles farther from the residence sold than is B's former place of employment in Florida, the sale is within the safe harbor of paragraph (c)
45   (2) of this section and B is entitled to claim a reduced maximum exclusion under section 121(c)(2).

Example 3. C is employed by Employer R at R's Philadelphia office. C purchases a house in February 2002 that is 35 miles from R's Philadelphia office. In May 2003 C begins a temporary assignment at R's Wilmington office that is 72 miles from C's house,
50   and moves out of the house. In June 2005 C is assigned to work in R's London office. C sells her house in August 2005 as a result of the assignment to London. The sale of the

Sec. 121. Exclusion of gain from sale of principal residence

house is not within the safe harbor of paragraph (c)(2) of this section by reason of the change in place of employment from Philadelphia to Wilmington because the Wilmington office is not 50 miles farther from C's house than is the Philadelphia office. Furthermore, the sale is not within the safe harbor by reason of the change in place of employment to London because C is not using the house as her principal residence when she moves to 5 London. However, C is entitled to claim a reduced maximum exclusion under section 121(c)(2) because, under the facts and circumstances, the primary reason for the sale is the change in C's place of employment.

Example 4. In July 2003 D, who works as an emergency medicine physician, buys a condominium that is 5 miles from her place of employment and uses it as her principal 10 residence. In February 2004, D obtains a job that is located 51 miles from D's condominium. D may be called in to work unscheduled hours and, when called, must be able to arrive at work quickly. Because of the demands of the new job, D sells her condominium and buys a townhouse that is 4 miles from her new place of employment. Because D's new place of employment is only 46 miles farther from the condominium 15 than is D's former place of employment, the sale is not within the safe harbor of paragraph (c)(2) of this section. However, D is entitled to claim a reduced maximum exclusion under   section 121(c)(2) because, under the facts and circumstances, the primary reason for the sale is the change in D's place of employment.

(d) *Sale or exchange by reason of health*--(1) *In general.* A sale or exchange is by 20 reason of health if the primary reason for the sale or exchange is to obtain, provide, or facilitate the diagnosis, cure, mitigation, or treatment of disease, illness, or injury of a qualified individual described in paragraph (f) of this section, or to obtain or provide medical or personal care for a qualified individual suffering from a disease, illness, or injury. A sale or exchange that is merely beneficial to the general health or well-being of 25 an individual is not a sale or exchange by reason of health.

(2) *Physician's recommendation safe harbor.* A sale or exchange is deemed to be by reason of health if a physician (as defined in section 213(d)(4)) recommends a change of residence for reasons of health (as defined in paragraph (d)(1) of this section).

(3) *Examples.* The following examples illustrate the rules of this paragraph (d):   30

Example 1. In 2003 A buys a house that she uses as her principal residence. A is injured in an accident and is unable to care for herself. A sells her house in 2004 and moves in with her daughter so that the daughter can provide the care that A requires as a result of her injury. Because, under the facts and circumstances, the primary reason for the sale of A's house is A's health, A is entitled to claim a reduced maximum exclusion 35 under section 121(c)(2).

Example 2. H's father has a chronic disease. In 2003 H and W purchase a house that they use as their principal residence. In 2004 H and W sell their house in order to move into the house of H's father so that they can provide the care he requires as a result of his disease. Because, under the facts and circumstances, the primary reason for the sale of 40 their house is the health of H's father, H and W are entitled to claim a reduced maximum exclusion under section 121(c)(2).

Example 3. H and W purchase a house in 2003 that they use as their principal residence. Their son suffers from a chronic illness that requires regular medical care. Later that year their son begins a new treatment that is available at a hospital 100 miles 45 away from their residence. In 2004 H and W sell their house so that they can be closer to the hospital to facilitate their son's treatment. Because, under the facts and circumstances, the primary reason for the sale is to facilitate the treatment of their son's chronic illness, H and W are entitled to claim a reduced maximum exclusion under section 121(c)(2).   50

Example 4. B, who has chronic asthma, purchases a house in Minnesota in 2003 that

Sec. 121. Exclusion of gain from sale of principal residence

he uses as his principal residence. B's doctor tells B that moving to a warm, dry climate would mitigate B's asthma symptoms. In 2004 B sells his house and moves to Arizona to relieve his asthma symptoms. The sale is within the safe harbor of paragraph (d)(2) of this section and B is entitled to claim a reduced maximum exclusion under section 121(c)
5 (2).

Example 5. In 2003 H and W purchase a house in Michigan that they use as their principal residence. H's doctor tells H that he should get more outdoor exercise, but H is not suffering from any disease that can be treated or mitigated by outdoor exercise. In 2004 H and W sell their house and move to Florida so that H can increase his general
10 level of exercise by playing golf year-round. Because the sale of the house is merely beneficial to H's general health, the sale of the house is not by reason of H's health. H and W are not entitled to claim a reduced maximum exclusion under section 121(c)(2).

(e) *Sale or exchange by reason of unforeseen circumstances*--(1) *In general.* A sale or exchange is by reason of unforeseen circumstances if the primary reason for the sale or
15 exchange is the occurrence of an event that the taxpayer anticipated before purchasing and occupying the residence. A sale or exchange by reason of unforeseen circumstances (other than a sale or exchange deemed to be by reason of unforeseen circumstances under paragraph (e)(2) or (3) of this section) does not qualify for the reduced maximum exclusion if the primary reason for the sale or exchange is a preference for a different
20 residence or an improvement in financial circumstances.

(2) *Specific event safe harbors.* A sale or exchange is deemed to be by reason of unforeseen circumstances (within the meaning of paragraph (e)(1) of this section) if any of the events specified in paragraphs (e)(2)(i) through (iii) of this section occur during the period of the taxpayer's ownership and use of the residence as the taxpayer's principal
25 residence:

(i) The involuntary conversion of the residence.

(ii) Natural or man-made disasters or acts of war or terrorism resulting in a casualty to the residence (without regard to deductibility under section 165(h)).

(iii) In the case of a qualified individual described in paragraph (f) of this section--
30 (A) Death;

(B) The cessation of employment as a result of which the qualified individual is eligible for unemployment compensation (as defined in section 85(b));

(C) A change in employment or self-employment status that results in the taxpayer's inability to pay housing costs and reasonable basic living expenses for the taxpayer's
35 household (including amounts for food, clothing, medical expenses, taxes, transportation, court-ordered payments, and expenses reasonably necessary to the production of income, but not for the maintenance of an affluent or luxurious standard of living);

(D) Divorce or legal separation under a decree of divorce or separate maintenance; or

(E) Multiple births resulting from the same pregnancy.
40 (3) *Designation of additional events as unforeseen circumstances.* The Commissioner may designate other events or situations as unforeseen circumstances in published guidance of general applicability and may issue rulings addressed to specific taxpayers identifying other events or situations as unforeseen circumstances with regard to those taxpayers (see § 601.601(d)(2) of this chapter).
45 (4) *Examples.* The following examples illustrate the rules of this paragraph (e):

Example 1. In 2003 A buys a house in California. After A begins to use the house as her principal residence, an earthquake causes damage to A's house. A sells the house in 2004. The sale is within the safe harbor of paragraph (e)(2)(ii) of this section and A is entitled to claim a reduced maximum exclusion under section 121(c)(2).
50 *Example 2.* H works as a teacher and W works as a pilot. In 2003 H and W buy a house that they use as their principal residence. Later that year W is furloughed from her

Sec. 121. Exclusion of gain from sale of principal residence

job for six months. H and W are unable to pay their mortgage and reasonable basic living expenses for their household during the period W is furloughed. H and W sell their house in 2004. The sale is within the safe harbor of paragraph (e)(2)(iii)(C) of this section and H and W are entitled to claim a reduced maximum exclusion under section 121(c)(2).

Example 3. In 2003 H and W buy a two-bedroom condominium that they use as their 5 principal residence. In 2004 W gives birth to twins and H and W sell their condominium and buy a four-bedroom house. The sale is within the safe harbor of paragraph (e)(2)(iii) (E) of this section, and H and W are entitled to claim a reduced maximum exclusion under section 121(c)(2).

Example 4. In 2003 B buys a condominium in a high-rise building and uses it as his 10 principal residence. B's monthly condominium fee is $X. Three months after B moves into the condominium, the condominium association replaces the building's roof and heating system. Six months later, B's monthly condominium fee doubles in order to pay for the repairs. B sells the condominium in 2004 because he is unable to afford the new condominium fee along with a monthly mortgage payment. The safe harbors of 15 paragraph (e)(2) of this section do not apply. However, under the facts and circumstances, the primary reason for the sale, the doubling of the condominium fee, is an unforeseen circumstance because B could not reasonably have anticipated that the condominium fee would double at the time he purchased and occupied the property. Consequently, the sale of the condominium is by reason of unforeseen circumstances 20 and B is entitled to claim a reduced maximum exclusion under section 121(c)(2).

Example 5. In 2003 C buys a house that he uses as his principal residence. The property is located on a heavily traveled road. C sells the property in 2004 because C is disturbed by the traffic. The safe harbors of paragraph (e)(2) of this section do not apply. Under the facts and circumstances, the primary reason for the sale, the traffic, is not an 25 unforeseen circumstance because C could reasonably have anticipated the traffic at the time he purchased and occupied the house. Consequently, the sale of the house is not by reason of unforeseen circumstances and C is not entitled to claim a reduced maximum exclusion under section 121(c)(2).

Example 6. In 2003 D and her fiance E buy a house and live in it as their principal 30 residence. In 2004 D and E cancel their wedding plans and E moves out of the house. Because D cannot afford to make the monthly mortgage payments alone, D and E sell the house in 2004. The safe harbors of paragraph (e)(2) of this section do not apply. However, under the facts and circumstances, the primary reason for the sale, the broken engagement, is an unforeseen circumstance because D and E could not reasonably have 35 anticipated the broken engagement at the time they purchased and occupied the house. Consequently, the sale is by reason of unforeseen circumstances and D and E are each entitled to claim a reduced maximum exclusion under section 121(c)(2).

Example 7. In 2003 F buys a small condominium that she uses as her principal residence. In 2005 F receives a promotion and a large increase in her salary. F sells the 40 condominium in 2004 and purchases a house because she can now afford the house. The safe harbors of paragraph (e)(2) of this section do not apply. Under the facts and circumstances, the primary reason for the sale of the house, F's salary increase, is an improvement in F's financial circumstances. Under paragraph (e)(1) of this section, an improvement in financial circumstances, even if the result of unforeseen circumstances, 45 does not qualify for the reduced maximum exclusion by reason of unforeseen circumstances under section 121(c)(2).

Example 8. In April 2003 G buys a house that he uses as his principal residence. G sells his house in October 2004 because the house has greatly appreciated in value, mortgage rates have substantially decreased, and G can afford a bigger house. The safe 50 harbors of paragraph (e)(2) of this section do not apply. Under the facts and

Sec. 121. Exclusion of gain from sale of principal residence

circumstances, the primary reasons for the sale of the house, the changes in G's house value and in the mortgage rates, are an improvement in G's financial circumstances. Under paragraph (e)(1) of this section, an improvement in financial circumstances, even if the result of unforeseen circumstances, does not qualify for the reduced maximum
5   exclusion by reason of unforeseen circumstances under section 121(c)(2).

Example 9. H works as a police officer for City X. In 2003 H buys a condominium that he uses as his principal residence. In 2004 H is assigned to City X's K-9 unit and is required to care for the police service dog at his home. Because H's condominium association does not permit H to have a dog in his condominium, in 2004 he sells the
10   condominium and buys a house. The safe harbors of paragraph (e)(2) of this section do not apply. However, under the facts and circumstances, the primary reason for the sale, H's assignment to the K-9 unit, is an unforeseen circumstance because H could not reasonably have anticipated his assignment to the K-9 unit at the time he purchased and occupied the condominium. Consequently, the sale of the condominium is by reason of
15   unforeseen circumstances and H is entitled to claim a reduced maximum exclusion under section 121(c)(2).

Example 10. In 2003, J buys a small house that she uses as her principal residence. After J wins the lottery, she sells the small house in 2004 and buys a bigger, more expensive house. The safe harbors of paragraph (e)(2) of this section do not apply. Under
20   the facts and circumstances, the primary reason for the sale of the house, winning the lottery, is an improvement in J's financial circumstances. Under paragraph (e)(1) of this section, an improvement in financial circumstances, even if the result of unforeseen circumstances, does not qualify for the reduced maximum exclusion under section 121(c) (2).

25   (f) *Qualified individual.* For purposes of this section, qualified individual means--

(1) The taxpayer;

(2) The taxpayer's spouse;

(3) A co-owner of the residence;

(4) A person whose principal place of abode is in the same household as the taxpayer;
30   or

(5) For purposes of paragraph (d) of this section, a person bearing a relationship specified in sections 152(a)(1) through 152(a)(8) (without regard to qualification as a dependent) to a qualified individual described in paragraphs (f)(1) through (4) of this section, or a descendant of the taxpayer's grandparent.

35   (g) *Computation of reduced maximum exclusion.* (1) The reduced maximum exclusion is computed by multiplying the maximum dollar limitation of $250,000 ($500,000 for certain joint filers) by a fraction. The numerator of the fraction is the shortest of the period of time that the taxpayer owned the property during the 5-year period ending on the date of the sale or exchange; the period of time that the taxpayer used the property as the
40   taxpayer's principal residence during the 5-year period ending on the date of the sale or exchange; or the period of time between the date of a prior sale or exchange of property for which the taxpayer excluded gain under section 121 and the date of the current sale or exchange. The numerator of the fraction may be expressed in days or months. The denominator of the fraction is 730 days or 24 months (depending on the measure of time
45   used in the numerator).

(2) *Examples.* The following examples illustrate the rules of this paragraph (g):

Example 1. Taxpayer A purchases a house that she uses as her principal residence. Twelve months after the purchase, A sells the house due to a change in place of her employment. A has not excluded gain under section 121 on a prior sale or exchange of
50   property within the last 2 years. A is eligible to exclude up to $125,000 of the gain from the sale of her house (12/24 x $250,000).

284

Sec. 121. Exclusion of gain from sale of principal residence

Example 2. (i) Taxpayer H owns a house that he has used as his principal residence since 1996. On January 15, 1999, H and W marry and W begins to use H's house as her principal residence. On January 15, 2000, H sells the house due to a change in W's place of employment. Neither H nor W has excluded gain under section 121 on a prior sale or exchange of property within the last 2 years.

(ii) Because H and W have not each used the house as their principal residence for at least 2 years during the 5-year period preceding its sale, the maximum dollar limitation amount that may be claimed by H and W will not be $500,000, but the sum of each spouse's limitation amount determined on a separate basis as if they had not been married. (See § 1.121-2(a)(3)(ii).)

(iii) H is eligible to exclude up to $250,000 of gain because he meets the requirements of section 121. W is not eligible to exclude the maximum dollar limitation amount. Instead, because the sale of the house is due to a change in place of employment, W is eligible to claim a reduced maximum exclusion of up to $125,000 of the gain (365/730 x $250,000). Therefore, H and W are eligible to exclude up to $375,000 of gain ($250,000 + $125,000) from the sale of the house.

***

Reg. § 1.121-4 Special rules.

(a) *Property of deceased spouse--*(1) *In general.* For purposes of satisfying the ownership and use requirements of section 121, a taxpayer is treated as owning and using property as the taxpayer's principal residence during any period that the taxpayer's deceased spouse owned and used the property as a principal residence before death if--

(i) The taxpayer's spouse is deceased on the date of the sale or exchange of the property; and

(ii) The taxpayer has not remarried at the time of the sale or exchange of the property.

(2) *Example.* The provisions of this paragraph (a) are illustrated by the following example. The example assumes that § 1.121-3 (relating to the reduced maximum exclusion) does not apply to the sale of the property. The example is as follows:

Example. Taxpayer H has owned and used a house as his principal residence since 1987. H and W marry on July 1, 1999 and from that date they use H's house as their principal residence. H dies on August 15, 2000, and W inherits the property. W sells the property on September 1, 2000, at which time she has not remarried. Although W has owned and used the house for less than 2 years, W will be considered to have satisfied the ownership and use requirements of section 121 because W's period of ownership and use includes the period that H owned and used the property before death.

(b) *Property owned by spouse or former spouse--*(1) *Property transferred to individual from spouse or former spouse.* If a taxpayer obtains property from a spouse or former spouse in a transaction described in section 1041(a), the period that the taxpayer owns the property will include the period that the spouse or former spouse owned the property.

(2) *Property used by spouse or former spouse.* A taxpayer is treated as using property as the taxpayer's principal residence for any period that the taxpayer has an ownership interest in the property and the taxpayer's spouse or former spouse is granted use of the property under a divorce or separation instrument (as defined in section 71(b)(2)), provided that the spouse or former spouse uses the property as his or her principal residence.

(c) *Tenant-stockholder in cooperative housing corporation.* A taxpayer who holds stock as a tenant-stockholder in a cooperative housing corporation (as those terms are defined in section 216(b)(1) and (2)) may be eligible to exclude gain under section 121 on the sale or exchange of the stock. In determining whether the taxpayer meets the requirements of section 121, the ownership requirements are applied to the holding of the stock and the use requirements are applied to the house or apartment that the taxpayer

Sec. 121. Exclusion of gain from sale of principal residence

is entitled to occupy by reason of the taxpayer's stock ownership.

(d) *Involuntary conversions*--(1) *In general.* For purposes of section 121, the destruction, theft, seizure, requisition, or condemnation of property is treated as a sale of the property.

5 (2) *Application of section 1033.* In applying section 1033 (relating to involuntary conversions), the amount realized from the sale or exchange of property used as the taxpayer's principal residence is treated as being the amount determined without regard to section 121, reduced by the amount of gain excluded from the taxpayer's gross income under section 121.

10 (3) *Property acquired after involuntary conversion.* If the basis of the property acquired as a result of an involuntary conversion is determined (in whole or in part) under section 1033(b) (relating to the basis of property acquired through an involuntary conversion), then for purposes of satisfying the requirements of section 121, the taxpayer will be treated as owning and using the acquired property as the taxpayer's principal residence

15 during any period of time that the taxpayer owned and used the converted property as the taxpayer's principal residence.

(4) *Example.* The provisions of this paragraph (d) are illustrated by the following example:

Example. (i) On February 18, 1999, fire destroys Taxpayer A's house which has an

20 adjusted basis of $80,000. A had owned and used this property as her principal residence for 20 years prior to its destruction. A's insurance company pays A $400,000 for the house. A realizes a gain of $320,000 ($400,000--$80,000). On August 27, 1999, A purchases a new house at a cost of $100,000.

(ii) Because the destruction of the house is treated as a sale for purposes of section

25 121, A will exclude $250,000 of the realized gain from A's gross income. For purposes of section 1033, the amount realized is then treated as being $150,000 ($400,000--$250,000) and the gain realized is $70,000 ($150,000 amount realized--$80,000 basis). A elects under section 1033 to recognize only $50,000 of the gain ($150,000 amount realized--$100,000 cost of new house). The remaining $20,000 of gain is deferred and

30 A's basis in the new house is $80,000 ($100,000 cost--$20,000 gain not recognized).

(iii) A will be treated as owning and using the new house as A's principal residence during the 20-year period that A owned and used the destroyed house.

(e) *Sales or exchanges of partial interests*--(1) *Partial interests other than remainder interests*--(i) *In general.* Except as provided in paragraph (e)(2) of this section (relating to

35 sales or exchanges of remainder interests), a taxpayer may apply the section 121 exclusion to gain from the sale or exchange of an interest in the taxpayer's principal residence that is less than the taxpayer's entire interest if the interest sold or exchanged includes an interest in the dwelling unit. For rules relating to the sale or exchange of vacant land, see § 1.121-1(b)(3).

40 (ii) *Limitations*--(A) *Maximum limitation amount.* For purposes of section 121(b)(1) and (2) (relating to the maximum limitation amount of the section 121 exclusion), sales or exchanges of partial interests in the same principal residence are treated as one sale or exchange. Therefore, only one maximum limitation amount of $250,000 ($500,000 for certain joint returns) applies to the combined sales or exchanges of the partial interests.

45 In applying the maximum limitation amount to sales or exchanges that occur in different taxable years, a taxpayer may exclude gain from the first sale or exchange of a partial interest up to the taxpayer's full maximum limitation amount and may exclude gain from the sale or exchange of any other partial interest in the same principal residence to the extent of any remaining maximum limitation amount, and each spouse is treated as

50 excluding one-half of the gain from a sale or exchange to which section 121(b)(2)(A) and § 1.121-2(a)(3)(i)(relating to the limitation for certain joint returns) apply.

Sec. 121. Exclusion of gain from sale of principal residence

(B) *Sale or exchange of more than one principal residence in 2-year period.* For purposes of applying section 121(b)(3) (restricting the application of section 121 to only 1 sale or exchange every 2 years), each sale or exchange of a partial interest is disregarded with respect to other sales or exchanges of partial interests in the same principal residence, but is taken into account as of the date of the sale or exchange in applying section 121(b)(3) to that sale or exchange and the sale or exchange of any other principal residence.

(2) *Sales or exchanges of remainder interests--(i) In general.* A taxpayer may elect to apply the section 121 exclusion to gain from the sale or exchange of a remainder interest in the taxpayer's principal residence.

(ii) *Limitations--(A) Sale or exchange of any other interest.* If a taxpayer elects to exclude gain from the sale or exchange of a remainder interest in the taxpayer's principal residence, the section 121 exclusion will not apply to a sale or exchange of any other interest in the residence that is sold or exchanged separately.

(B) *Sales or exchanges to related parties.* This paragraph (e)(2) will not apply to a sale or exchange to any person that bears a relationship to the taxpayer that is described in section 267(b) or 707(b).

(iii) *Election.* The taxpayer makes the election under this paragraph (e)(2) by filing a return for the taxable year of the sale or exchange that does not include the gain from the sale or exchange of the remainder interest in the taxpayer's gross income. A taxpayer may make or revoke the election at any time before the expiration of a 3-year period beginning on the last date prescribed by law (determined without regard to extensions) for the filing of the return for the taxable year in which the sale or exchange occurred.

(3) *Example.* The provisions of this paragraph (e) are illustrated by the following example:

Example. In 1991 Taxpayer A buys a house that A uses as his principal residence. In 2004 A's friend B moves into A's house and A sells B a 50% interest in the house realizing a gain of $136,000. A may exclude the $136,000 of gain. In 2005 A sells his remaining 50% interest in the home to B realizing a gain of $138,000. A may exclude $114,000 ($250,000--$136,000 gain previously excluded) of the $138,000 gain from the sale of the remaining interest.

***

(g) *Election to have section not apply.* A taxpayer may elect to have the section 121 exclusion not apply to a sale or exchange of property. The taxpayer makes the election by filing a return for the taxable year of the sale or exchange that includes the gain from the sale or exchange of the taxpayer's principal residence in the taxpayer's gross income. A taxpayer may make an election under this paragraph (g) to have section 121 not apply (or revoke an election to have section 121 not apply) at any time before the expiration of a 3-year period beginning on the last date prescribed by law (determined without regard to extensions) for the filing of the return for the taxable year in which the sale or exchange occurred.

***

[T.D. 9030, 67 FR 78361, Dec. 24, 2002; 68 FR 6350, Feb. 7, 2003; T.D. 9152, 69 FR 50306, Aug. 16, 2004]

Sec. 123. Amounts received under insurance contracts for certain living expenses

(a) **General rule.** -- In the case of an individual whose principal residence is damaged or destroyed by fire, storm, or other casualty, or who is denied access to his principal residence by governmental authorities because of the occurrence or threat of occurrence of such a casualty,

Sec. 123. Amounts received under insurance contracts for certain living expenses

gross income does not include amounts received by such individual under an insurance contract which are paid to compensate or reimburse such individual for living expenses incurred for himself and members of his household resulting from the loss of use or occupancy of such residence.

(b) Limitation. -- Subsection (a) shall apply to amounts received by the taxpayer for living expenses incurred during any period only to the extent the amounts received do not exceed the amount by which--

(1) the actual living expenses incurred during such period for himself and members of his household resulting from the loss of use or occupancy of their residence, exceed

(2) the normal living expenses which would have been incurred for himself and members of his household during such period.

Sec. 125. Cafeteria plans

(a) General rule. -- Except as provided in subsection (b), no amount shall be included in the gross income of a participant in a cafeteria plan solely because, under the plan, the participant may choose among the benefits of the plan.

(b) Exception for highly compensated participants and key employees. --

(1) Highly compensated participants. -- In the case of a highly compensated participant, subsection (a) shall not apply to any benefit attributable to a plan year for which the plan discriminates in favor of--

(A) highly compensated individuals as to eligibility to participate, or

(B) highly compensated participants as to contributions and benefits.

(2) Key employees. -- In the case of a key employee (within the meaning of section 416(i)(1)), subsection (a) shall not apply to any benefit attributable to a plan for which the statutory nontaxable benefits provided to key employees exceed 25 percent of the aggregate of such benefits provided for all employees under the plan. For purposes of the preceding sentence, statutory nontaxable benefits shall be determined without regard to the second sentence of subsection (f).

(3) Year of inclusion. -- For purposes of determining the taxable year of inclusion, any benefit described in paragraph (1) or (2) shall be treated as received or accrued in the taxable year of the participant or key employee in which the plan year ends.

(c) Discrimination as to benefits or contributions. -- For purposes of subparagraph (B) of subsection (b)(1), a cafeteria plan does not discriminate where qualified benefits and total benefits (or employer contributions allocable to qualified benefits and employer contributions for total benefits) do not discriminate in favor of highly compensated participants.

(d) Cafeteria plan defined. -- For purposes of this section--

(1) In general. -- The term "cafeteria plan" means a written plan under which--

(A) all participants are employees, and

(B) the participants may choose among 2 or more benefits consisting of cash and qualified benefits.

(2) Deferred compensation plans excluded. --

(A) In general. -- The term "cafeteria plan" does not include any plan which provides for deferred compensation.

(B) Exception for cash and deferred arrangements. -- Subparagraph (A) shall not

Sec. 125. Cafeteria plans

apply to a profit-sharing or stock bonus plan or rural cooperative plan (within the meaning of section 401(k)(7)) which includes a qualified cash or deferred arrangement (as defined in section 401(k)(2)) to the extent of amounts which a covered employee may elect to have the employer pay as contributions to a trust under such plan on behalf of the employee.

(C) **Exception for certain plans maintained by educational institutions.** -- Subparagraph (A) shall not apply to a plan maintained by an educational organization described in section 170(b)(1)(A)(ii) to the extent of amounts which a covered employee may elect to have the employer pay as contributions for post-retirement group life insurance if--

(i) all contributions for such insurance must be made before retirement, and

(ii) such life insurance does not have a cash surrender value at any time.

For purposes of section 79, any life insurance described in the preceding sentence shall be treated as group-term life insurance.

(D) **Exception for health savings accounts.** -- Subparagraph (A) shall not apply to a plan to the extent of amounts which a covered employee may elect to have the employer pay as contributions to a health savings account established on behalf of the employee.

(e) **Highly compensated participant and individual defined.** -- For purposes of this section--

(1) **Highly compensated participant.** -- The term "highly compensated participant" means a participant who is -

(A) an officer,

(B) a shareholder owning more than 5 percent of the voting power or value of all classes of stock of the employer,

(C) highly compensated, or

(D) a spouse or dependent (within the meaning of section 152, determined without regard to subsections (b)(1), (b)(2), and (d)(1)(B) thereof) of an individual described in subparagraph (A), (B), or (C).

(2) **Highly compensated individual.** -- The term "highly compensated individual" means an individual who is described in subparagraphs (!1) (A), (B), (C), or (D) of paragraph (1).

(f) **Qualified benefits defined.** -- For purposes of this section, the term "qualified benefit" means any benefit which, with the application of subsection (a), is not includible in the gross income of the employee by reason of an express provision of this chapter (other than section 106(b), 117, 127, or 132). Such term includes any group term life insurance which is includible in gross income only because it exceeds the dollar limitation of section 79 and such term includes any other benefit permitted under regulations. Such term shall not include any product which is advertised, marketed, or offered as long-term care insurance.

Sec. 127. Educational assistance programs

(a) **Exclusion from gross income.** --

(1) **In general.** -- Gross income of an employee does not include amounts paid or expenses incurred by the employer for educational assistance to the employee if the assistance is furnished pursuant to a program which is described in subsection (b).

(2) **$5,250 maximum exclusion.** -- If, but for this paragraph, this section would exclude from gross income more than $5,250 of educational assistance furnished to an individual during a calendar year, this section shall apply only to the first $5,250 of such assistance so furnished.

Sec. 127. Educational assistance programs

(b) Educational assistance program. --

    (1) In general. -- For purposes of this section an educational assistance program is a separate written plan of an employer for the exclusive benefit of his employees to provide such employees with educational assistance. The program must meet the requirements of paragraphs (2) through (6) of this subsection.

    (2) Eligibility. -- The program shall benefit employees who qualify under a classification set up by the employer and found by the Secretary not to be discriminatory in favor of employees who are highly compensated employees (within the meaning of section 414(q)) or their dependents. For purposes of this paragraph, there shall be excluded from consideration employees not included in the program who are included in a unit of employees covered by an agreement which the Secretary of Labor finds to be a collective bargaining agreement between employee representatives and one or more employers, if there is evidence that educational assistance benefits were the subject of good faith bargaining between such employee representatives and such employer or employers.

    (3) Principal shareholders or owners. -- Not more than 5 percent of the amounts paid or incurred by the employer for educational assistance during the year may be provided for the class of individuals who are shareholders or owners (or their spouses or dependents), each of whom (on any day of the year) owns more than 5 percent of the stock or of the capital or profits interest in the employer.

    (4) Other benefits as an alternative. -- A program must not provide eligible employees with a choice between educational assistance and other remuneration includible in gross income. For purposes of this section, the business practices of the employer (as well as the written program) will be taken into account.

    (5) No funding required. -- A program referred to in paragraph (1) is not required to be funded.

    (6) Notification of employees. -- Reasonable notification of the availability and terms of the program must be provided to eligible employees.

(c) Definitions; special rules. -- For purposes of this section--

    (1) Educational assistance. -- The term "educational assistance" means--

        (A) the payment, by an employer, of expenses incurred by or on behalf of an employee for education of the employee (including, but not limited to, tuition, fees, and similar payments, books, supplies, and equipment), and

        (B) the provision, by an employer, of courses of instruction for such employee (including books, supplies, and equipment), but does not include payment for, or the provision of, tools or supplies which may be retained by the employee after completion of a course of instruction, or meals, lodging, or transportation. The term "educational assistance" also does not include any payment for, or the provision of any benefits with respect to, any course or other education involving sports, games, or hobbies.

    (2) Employee. -- The term "employee" includes, for any year, an individual who is an employee within the meaning of section 401(c)(1) (relating to self-employed individuals).

    (3) Employer. -- An individual who owns the entire interest in an unincorporated trade or business shall be treated as his own employer. A partnership shall be treated as the employer of each partner who is an employee within the meaning of paragraph (2).

    (4) Attribution rules. --

        (A) Ownership of stock. -- Ownership of stock in a corporation shall be determined in accordance with the rules provided under subsections (d) and (e) of section 1563 (without regard to section 1563(e)(3)(C)).

290

Sec. 127. Educational assistance programs

(B) Interest in unincorporated trade or business. -- The interest of an employee in a trade or business which is not incorporated shall be determined in accordance with regulations prescribed by the Secretary, which shall be based on principles similar to the principles which apply in the case of subparagraph (A).

(5) Certain tests not applicable. -- An educational assistance program shall not be held or considered to fail to meet any requirements of subsection (b) merely because--

(A) of utilization rates for the different types of educational assistance made available under the program; or

(B) successful completion, or attaining a particular course grade, is required for or considered in determining reimbursement under the program.

(6) Relationship to current law. -- This section shall not be construed to affect the deduction or inclusion in income of amounts (not within the exclusion under this section) which are paid or incurred, or received as reimbursement, for educational expenses under section 117, 162 or 212.

(7) Disallowance of excluded amounts as credit or deduction. -- No deduction or credit shall be allowed to the employee under any other section of this chapter for any amount excluded from income by reason of this section.

Sec. 129. Dependent care assistance programs

(a) Exclusion. --

(1) In general. -- Gross income of an employee does not include amounts paid or incurred by the employer for dependent care assistance provided to such employee if the assistance is furnished pursuant to a program which is described in subsection (d).

(2) Limitation of exclusion. --

(A) In general. -- The amount which may be excluded under paragraph (1) for dependent care assistance with respect to dependent care services provided during a taxable year shall not exceed $5,000 ($2,500 in the case of a separate return by a married individual).

(B) Year of inclusion. -- The amount of any excess under subparagraph (A) shall be included in gross income in the taxable year in which the dependent care services were provided (even if payment of dependent care assistance for such services occurs in a subsequent taxable year).

(C) Marital status. -- For purposes of this paragraph, marital status shall be determined under the rules of paragraphs (3) and (4) of section 21(e).

(b) Earned income limitation. --

(1) In general. -- The amount excluded from the income of an employee under subsection (a) for any taxable year shall not exceed--

(A) in the case of an employee who is not married at the close of such taxable year, the earned income of such employee for such taxable year, or

(B) in the case of an employee who is married at the close of such taxable year, the lesser of -

(i) the earned income of such employee for such taxable year, or

(ii) the earned income of the spouse of such employee for such taxable year.

(2) Special rule for certain spouses. -- For purposes of paragraph (1), the provisions of section 21(d)(2) shall apply in determining the earned income of a spouse who is a student or

Sec. 129. Dependent care assistance programs

incapable of caring for himself.

(c) Payments to related individuals. -- No amount paid or incurred during the taxable year of an employee by an employer in providing dependent care assistance to such employee shall be excluded under subsection (a) if such amount was paid or incurred to an individual--

    (1) with respect to whom, for such taxable year, a deduction is allowable under section 151(c) (relating to personal exemptions for dependents) to such employee or the spouse of such employee, or

    (2) who is a child of such employee (within the meaning of section 152(f)(1)) under the age of 19 at the close of such taxable year.

(d) Dependent care assistance program. --

    (1) In general. -- For purposes of this section a dependent care assistance program is a separate written plan of an employer for the exclusive benefit of his employees to provide such employees with dependent care assistance which meets the requirements of paragraphs (2) through (8) of this subsection. If any plan would qualify as a dependent care assistance program but for a failure to meet the requirements of this subsection, then, notwithstanding such failure, such plan shall be treated as a dependent care assistance program in the case of employees who are not highly compensated employees.

    (2) Discrimination. -- The contributions or benefits provided under the plan shall not discriminate in favor of employees who are highly compensated employees (within the meaning of section 414(q)) or their dependents.

    (3) Eligibility. -- The program shall benefit employees who qualify under a classification set up by the employer and found by the Secretary not to be discriminatory in favor of employees described in paragraph (2), or their dependents.

    (4) Principal shareholders or owners. -- Not more than 25 percent of the amounts paid or incurred by the employer for dependent care assistance during the year may be provided for the class of individuals who are shareholders or owners (or their spouses or dependents), each of whom (on any day of the year) owns more than 5 percent of the stock or of the capital or profits interest in the employer.

    (5) No funding required. -- A program referred to in paragraph (1) is not required to be funded.

    (6) Notification of eligible employees. -- Reasonable notification of the availability and terms of the program shall be provided to eligible employees.

    (7) Statement of expenses. -- The plan shall furnish to an employee, on or before January 31, a written statement showing the amounts paid or expenses incurred by the employer in providing dependent care assistance to such employee during the previous calendar year.

    (8) Benefits. --

        (A) In general. -- A plan meets the requirements of this paragraph if the average benefits provided to employees who are not highly compensated employees under all plans of the employer is at least 55 percent of the average benefits provided to highly compensated employees under all plans of the employer.

        (B) Salary reduction agreements. -- For purposes of subparagraph (A), in the case of any benefits provided through a salary reduction agreement, a plan may disregard any employees whose compensation is less than $25,000. For purposes of this subparagraph, the term "compensation" has the meaning given such term by section 414(q)(4), except that, under rules prescribed by the Secretary, an employer may elect to determine compensation on any other basis which does not discriminate in favor of highly compensated employees.

Sec. 129. Dependent care assistance programs

(9) Excluded employees. -- For purposes of paragraphs (3) and (8), there shall be excluded from consideration--

(A) subject to rules similar to the rules of section 410(b)(4), employees who have not attained the age of 21 and completed 1 year of service (as defined in section 410(a)(3)), and 5

(B) employees not included in a dependent care assistance program who are included in a unit of employees covered by an agreement which the Secretary finds to be a collective bargaining agreement between employee representatives and 1 or more employees, if there is evidence that dependent care benefits were the subject of good faith bargaining between such employee representatives and such employer or employers. 10

(e) Definitions and special rules. -- For purposes of this section--

(1) Dependent care assistance. -- The term "dependent care assistance" means the payment of, or provision of, those services which if paid for by the employee would be considered employment-related expenses under section 21(b)(2) (relating to expenses for household and dependent care services necessary for gainful employment). 15

(2) Earned income. -- The term "earned income" shall have the meaning given such term in section 32(c)(2), but such term shall not include any amounts paid or incurred by an employer for dependent care assistance to an employee.

(3) Employee. -- The term "employee" includes, for any year, an individual who is an employee within the meaning of section 401(c)(1) (relating to self-employed individuals). 20

(4) Employer. -- An individual who owns the entire interest in an unincorporated trade or business shall be treated as his own employer. A partnership shall be treated as the employer of each partner who is an employee within the meaning of paragraph (3).

(5) Attribution rules. --

(A) **Ownership of stock.** -- Ownership of stock in a corporation shall be determined in 25 accordance with the rules provided under subsections (d) and (e) of section 1563 (without regard to section 1563(e)(3)(C)).

(B) **Interest in unincorporated trade or business.** -- The interest of an employee in a trade or business which is not incorporated shall be determined in accordance with regulations prescribed by the Secretary, which shall be based on principles similar to the 30 principles which apply in the case of subparagraph (A).

(6) Utilization test not applicable. -- A dependent care assistance program shall not be held or considered to fail to meet any requirements of subsection (d) (other than paragraphs (4) and (8) thereof) merely because of utilization rates for the different types of assistance made available under the program. 35

(7) Disallowance of excluded amounts as credit or deduction. -- No deduction or credit shall be allowed to the employee under any other section of this chapter for any amount excluded from the gross income of the employee by reason of this section.

(8) Treatment of onsite facilities. -- In the case of an onsite facility maintained by an employer,   except to the extent provided in regulations, the amount of dependent care 40 assistance provided to an employee excluded with respect to any dependent shall be based on -

(A) utilization of the facility by a dependent of the employee, and

(B) the value of the services provided with respect to such dependent.

(9) Identifying information required with respect to service provider. -- No amount paid or incurred by an employer for dependent care assistance provided to an employee shall be 45 excluded from the gross income of such employee unless--

(A) the name, address, and taxpayer identification number of the person performing the

Sec. 129. Dependent care assistance programs

services are included on the return to which the exclusion relates, or

(B) if such person is an organization described in section 501(c)(3) and exempt from tax under section 501(a), the name and address of such person are included on the return to which the exclusion relates.

5 In the case of a failure to provide the information required under the preceding sentence, the preceding sentence shall not apply if it is shown that the taxpayer exercised due diligence in attempting to provide the information so required.

Sec. 132. Certain fringe benefits

10 **(a) Exclusion from gross income.** -- Gross income shall not include any fringe benefit which qualifies as a--

(1) no-additional-cost service,

(2) qualified employee discount,

(3) working condition fringe,

15 (4) de minimis fringe,

(5) qualified transportation fringe,

(6) qualified moving expense reimbursement,

(7) qualified retirement planning services, or

(8) qualified military base realignment and closure fringe.

20 **(b) No-additional-cost service defined.** -- For purposes of this section, the term "no-additional-cost service" means any service provided by an employer to an employee for use by such employee if -

(1) such service is offered for sale to customers in the ordinary course of the line of business of the employer in which the employee is performing services, and

25 (2) the employer incurs no substantial additional cost (including forgone revenue) in providing such service to the employee (determined without regard to any amount paid by the employee for such service).

(c) Qualified employee discount defined. -- For purposes of this section--

(1) **Qualified employee discount.** -- The term "qualified employee discount" means any 30 employee discount with respect to qualified property or services to the extent such discount does not exceed -

(A) in the case of property, the gross profit percentage of the price at which the property is being offered by the employer to customers, or

(B) in the case of services, 20 percent of the price at which the services are being offered 35 by the employer to customers.

(2) **Gross profit percentage.** --

(A) **In general.** -- The term "gross profit percentage" means the percent which--

(i) the excess of the aggregate sales price of property sold by the employer to customers over the aggregate cost of such property to the employer, is of

40 (ii) the aggregate sale price of such property.

(B) **Determination of gross profit percentage.** -- Gross profit percentage shall be determined on the basis of--

(i) all property offered to customers in the ordinary course of the line of business of the employer in which the employee is performing services (or a reasonable

294

Sec. 132.   Certain fringe benefits

classification of property selected by the employer), and

(ii) the employer's experience during a representative period.

(3) Employee discount defined. -- The term "employee discount" means the amount by which--

(A) the price at which the property or services are provided by the employer to an employee for use by such employee, is less than

(B) the price at which such property or services are being offered by the employer to customers.

(4) Qualified property or services. -- The term "qualified property or services" means any property (other than real property and other than personal property of a kind held for investment) or services which are offered for sale to customers in the ordinary course of the line of business of the employer in which the employee is peforming (sic.) services.

(d) Working condition fringe defined. -- For purposes of this section, the term "working condition fringe" means any property or services provided to an employee of the employer to the extent that, if the employee paid for such property or services, such payment would be allowable as a deduction under section 162 or 167.

(e) De minimis fringe defined. -- For purposes of this section--

(1) In general. -- The term "de minimis fringe" means any property or service the value of which is (after taking into account the frequency with which similar fringes are provided by the employer to the employer's employees) so small as to make accounting for it unreasonable or administratively impracticable.

(2) Treatment of certain eating facilities. -- The operation by an employer of any eating facility for employees shall be treated as a de minimis fringe if--

(A) such facility is located on or near the business premises of the employer, and

(B) revenue derived from such facility normally equals or exceeds the direct operating costs of such facility.

The preceding sentence shall apply with respect to any highly compensated employee only if access to the facility is available on substantially the same terms to each member of a group of employees which is defined under a reasonable classification set up by the employer which does not discriminate in favor of highly compensated employees. For purposes of subparagraph (B), an employee entitled under section 119 to exclude the value of a meal provided at such facility shall be treated as having paid an amount for such meal equal to the direct operating costs of the facility attributable to such meal.

(f) Qualified transportation fringe. --

(1) In general. -- For purposes of this section, the term "qualified transportation fringe" means any of the following provided by an employer to an employee:

(A) Transportation in a commuter highway vehicle if such transportation is in connection with travel between the employee's residence and place of employment.

(B) Any transit pass.

(C) Qualified parking.

(2) Limitation on exclusion. -- The amount of the fringe benefits which are provided by an employer to any employee and which may be excluded from gross income under subsection (a) (5) shall not exceed--

(A) $100 per month in the case of the aggregate of the benefits described in subparagraphs (A) and (B) of paragraph (1), and

(B) $175 per month in the case of qualified parking.

295

Sec. 132.   Certain fringe benefits

(3) Cash reimbursements. -- For purposes of this subsection, the term "qualified transportation fringe" includes a cash reimbursement by an employer to an employee for a benefit described in paragraph (1). The preceding sentence shall apply to a cash reimbursement for any transit pass only if a voucher or similar item which may be exchanged only for a transit pass is not readily available for direct distribution by the employer to the employee.

(4) No constructive receipt. -- No amount shall be included in the gross income of an employee solely because the employee may choose between any qualified transportation fringe and compensation which would otherwise be includible in gross income of such employee.

(5) Definitions. -- For purposes of this subsection---

(A) Transit pass. -- The term "transit pass" means any pass, token, farecard, voucher, or similar item entitling a person to transportation (or transportation at a reduced price) if such transportation is---

(i) on mass transit facilities (whether or not publicly owned), or

(ii) provided by any person in the business of transporting persons for compensation or hire if such transportation is provided in a vehicle meeting the requirements of subparagraph (B)(i).

(B) Commuter highway vehicle. -- The term "commuter highway vehicle" means any highway vehicle---

(i) the seating capacity of which is at least 6 adults (not including the driver), and

(ii) at least 80 percent of the mileage use of which can reasonably be expected to be---

(I) for purposes of transporting employees in connection with travel between their residences and their place of employment, and

(II) on trips during which the number of employees transported for such purposes is at least 1/2 of the adult seating capacity of such vehicle (not including the driver).

(C) Qualified parking. -- The term "qualified parking" means parking provided to an employee on or near the business premises of the employer or on or near a location from which the employee commutes to work by transportation described in subparagraph (A), in a commuter highway vehicle, or by carpool. Such term shall not include any parking on or near property used by the employee for residential purposes.

(D) Transportation provided by employer. -- Transportation referred to in paragraph (1)(A) shall be considered to be provided by an employer if such transportation is furnished in a commuter highway vehicle operated by or for the employer.

(E) Employee. -- For purposes of this subsection, the term "employee" does not include an individual who is an employee within the meaning of section 401(c)(1).

(6) Inflation adjustment. --

(A) In general. -- In the case of any taxable year beginning in a calendar year after 1999, the dollar amounts contained in subparagraphs (A) and (B) of paragraph (2) shall be increased by an amount equal to--

(i) such dollar amount, multiplied by

(ii) the cost-of-living adjustment determined under section 1(f)(3) for the calendar year in which the taxable year begins, by substituting "calendar year 1998" for "calendar year 1992".

In the case of any taxable year beginning in a calendar year after 2002, clause (ii) shall be applied by substituting "calendar year 2001" for "calendar year 1998" for purposes of

Sec. 132. Certain fringe benefits

adjusting the dollar amount contained in paragraph (2)(A).

(B) Rounding. -- If any increase determined under subparagraph (A) is not a multiple of $5, such increase shall be rounded to the next lowest multiple of $5.

(7) Coordination with other provisions. -- For purposes of this section, the terms "working condition fringe" and "de minimis fringe" shall not include any qualified transportation fringe (determined without regard to paragraph (2)).

(g) Qualified moving expense reimbursement. -- For purposes of this section, the term "qualified moving expense reimbursement" means any amount received (directly or indirectly) by an individual from an employer as a payment for (or a reimbursement of) expenses which would be deductible as moving expenses under section 217 if directly paid or incurred by the individual. Such term shall not include any payment for (or reimbursement of) an expense actually deducted by the individual in a prior taxable year.

(h) Certain individuals treated as employees for purposes of subsections (a)(1) and (2). -- For purposes of paragraphs (1) and (2) of subsection (a)---

(1) Retired and disabled employees and surviving spouse of employee treated as employee. -- With respect to a line of business of an employer, the term "employee" includes--

(A) any individual who was formerly employed by such employer in such line of business and who separated from service with such employer in such line of business by reason of retirement or disability, and

(B) any widow or widower of any individual who died while employed by such employer in such line of business or while an employee within the meaning of subparagraph (A).

(2) Spouse and dependent children. --

(A) In general. -- Any use by the spouse or a dependent child of the employee shall be treated as use by the employee.

(B) Dependent child. -- For purposes of subparagraph (A), the term "dependent child" means any child (as defined in section 152(f)(1)) of the employee--

(i) who is a dependent of the employee, or

(ii) both of whose parents are deceased and who has not attained age 25.

For purposes of the preceding sentence, any child to whom section 152(e) applies shall be treated as the dependent of both parents.

(3) Special rule for parents in the case of air transportation. -- Any use of air transportation by a parent of an employee (determined without regard to paragraph (1)(B)) shall be treated as use by the employee.

(i) Reciprocal agreements. -- For purposes of paragraph (1) of subsection (a), any service provided by an employer to an employee of another employer shall be treated as provided by the employer of such employee if--

(1) such service is provided pursuant to a written agreement between such employers, and

(2) neither of such employers incurs any substantial additional costs (including foregone revenue) in providing such service or pursuant to such agreement.

(j) Special rules. --

(1) Exclusions under subsection (a)(1) and (2) apply to highly compensated employees only if no discrimination. -- Paragraphs (1) and (2) of subsection (a) shall apply with respect to any fringe benefit described therein provided with respect to any highly compensated employee only if such fringe benefit is available on substantially the same terms to each member of a group of employees which is defined under a reasonable classification set up by

Sec. 132. Certain fringe benefits

the employer which does not discriminate in favor of highly compensated employees.

(2) Special rule for leased sections of department stores. --

(A) In general. -- For purposes of paragraph (2) of subsection (a), in the case of a leased section of a department store -

(i) such section shall be treated as part of the line of business of the person operating the department store, and

(ii) employees in the leased section shall be treated as employees of the person operating the department store.

(B) Leased section of department store. -- For purposes of subparagraph (A), a leased section of a department store is any part of a department store where over- the-counter sales of property are made under a lease or similar arrangement where it appears to the general public that individuals making such sales are employed by the person operating the department store.

(3) Auto salesmen. --

(A) In general. -- For purposes of subsection (a)(3), qualified automobile demonstration use shall be treated as a working condition fringe.

(B) Qualified automobile demonstration use. -- For purposes of subparagraph (A), the term "qualified automobile demonstration use" means any use of an automobile by a full-time automobile salesman in the sales area in which the automobile dealer's sales office is located if--

(i) such use is provided primarily to facilitate the salesman's performance of services for the employer, and

(ii) there are substantial restrictions on the personal use of such automobile by such salesman.

(4) On-premises gyms and other athletic facilities. --

(A) In general. -- Gross income shall not include the value of any on-premises athletic facility provided by an employer to his employees.

(B) On-premises athletic facility. -- For purposes of this paragraph, the term "on-premises athletic facility" means any gym or other athletic facility--

(i) which is located on the premises of the employer,

(ii) which is operated by the employer, and

(iii) substantially all the use of which is by employees of the employer, their spouses, and their dependent children (within the meaning of subsection (h)).

(5) Special rule for affiliates of airlines. --

(A) In general. -- If--

(i) a qualified affiliate is a member of an affiliated group another member of which operates an airline, and

(ii) employees of the qualified affiliate who are directly engaged in providing airline-related services are entitled to no-additional-cost service with respect to air transportation provided by such other member,

then, for purposes of applying paragraph (1) of subsection (a) to such no-additional-cost service provided to such employees, such qualified affiliate shall be treated as engaged in the same line of business as such other member.

(B) Qualified affiliate. -- For purposes of this paragraph, the term "qualified affiliate" means any corporation which is predominantly engaged in airline-related services.

(C) Airline-related services. -- For purposes of this paragraph, the term "airline-related services" means any of the following services provided in connection with air transportation:

(i) Catering.

(ii) Baggage handling.

(iii) Ticketing and reservations.

(iv) Flight planning and weather analysis.

(v) Restaurants and gift shops located at an airport.

(vi) Such other similar services provided to the airline as the Secretary may prescribe.

(D) Affiliated group. -- For purposes of this paragraph, the term "affiliated group" has the meaning given such term by section 1504(a).

(6) Highly compensated employee. -- For purposes of this section, the term "highly compensated employee" has the meaning given such term by section 414(q).

(7) Air cargo. -- For purposes of subsection (b), the transportation of cargo by air and the transportation of passengers by air shall be treated as the same service.

(8) Application of section to otherwise taxable educational or training benefits. -- Amounts paid or expenses incurred by the employer for education or training provided to the employee which are not excludable from gross income under section 127 shall be excluded from gross income under this section if (and only if) such amounts or expenses are a working condition fringe.

(k) Customers not to include employees. -- For purposes of this section (other than subsection (c)(2)), the term "customers" shall only include customers who are not employees.

(l) Section not to apply to fringe benefits expressly provided for elsewhere. -- This section (other than subsections (e) and (g)) shall not apply to any fringe benefits of a type the tax treatment of which is expressly provided for in any other section of this chapter.

(m) Qualified retirement planning services. --

(1) In general. -- For purposes of this section, the term "qualified retirement planning services" means any retirement planning advice or information provided to an employee and his spouse by an employer maintaining a qualified employer plan.

(2) Nondiscrimination rule. -- Subsection (a)(7) shall apply in the case of highly compensated employees only if such services are available on substantially the same terms to each member of the group of employees normally provided education and information regarding the employer's qualified employer plan.

(3) Qualified employer plan. -- For purposes of this subsection, the term "qualified employer plan" means a plan, contract, pension, or account described in section 219(g)(5).

(n) Qualified military base realignment and closure fringe. -- For purposes of this section --

(1) In general. -- The term "qualified military base realignment and closure fringe" means 1 or more payments under the authority of section 1013 of the Demonstration Cities and Metropolitan Development Act of 1966 (42 U.S.C. 3374) (as in effect on the date of the enactment of this subsection) to offset the adverse effects on housing values as a result of a military base realignment or closure.

(2) Limitation. -- With respect to any property, such term shall not include any payment referred to in paragraph (1) to the extent that the sum of all of such payments related to such property exceeds the maximum amount described in clause (1) of subsection (c) of such section (as in effect on such date).

Sec. 132. Certain fringe benefits

Reg. § 1.132-1   Exclusion from gross income for certain fringe benefits.
(a) *In general*. Gross income does not include any fringe benefit which qualifies as a--
(1) No-additional-cost service,
5   (2) Qualified employee discount,
(3) Working condition fringe, or
(4) De minimis fringe.
Special rules apply with respect to certain on-premises gyms and other athletic facilities
(§ 1.132-1(e)), demonstration use of employer-provided automobiles by full-time
10   automobile salesmen (§ 1.132-5(o)), parking provided to an employee on or near the
business premises of the employer (§ 1.132-5(p)), and on-premises eating facilities (§
1.132-7).
(b) *Definition of employee--*(1) *No-additional-cost services and qualified employee
discounts.* For purposes of section 132(a)(1) (relating to no-additional-cost services) and
15   section 132(a)(2) (relating to qualified employee discounts), the term ``employee'' (with
respect to a line of business of an employer means--
(i) Any individual who is currently employed by the employer in the line of business,
(ii) Any individual who was formerly employed by the employer in the line of business
and who separated from service with the employer in the line of business by reason of
20   retirement or disability, and
(iii) Any widow or widower of an individual who died while employed by the employer
in the line of business or who separated from service with the employer in the line of
business by reason of retirement or disability. For purposes of this paragraph (b)(1), any
partner who performs services for a partnership is considered employed by the
25   partnership. In addition, any use by the spouse or dependent child (as defined in
paragraph (b)(5) of this section) of the employee will be treated as use by the employee.
For purposes of section 132(a)(1) (relating to no-additional-cost services), any use of air
transportation by a parent of an employee (determined without regard to section 132(f)(1)
(B) and paragraph (b)(1)(iii) of this section) will be treated as use by the employee.
30   (2) *Working condition fringes*. For purposes of section 132(a)(3) (relating to working
condition fringes), the term ``employee'' means--
(i) Any individual who is currently employed by the employer,
(ii) Any partner who performs services for the partnership,
(iii) Any director of the employer, and
35   (iv) Any independent contractor who performs services for the employer.
Notwithstanding anything in this paragraph (b)(2) to the contrary, an independent
contractor who performs services for the employer cannot exclude the value of parking or
the use of consumer goods provided pursuant to a product testing program under §
1.132-5(n); in addition, any director of the employer cannot exclude the value of the use
40   of consumer goods provided pursuant to a product testing program under § 1.132-5(n).
(3) *On-premises athletic facilities*. For purposes of section 132(h)(5) (relating to on-
premises athletic facilities), the term ``employee'' means--
(i) Any individual who is currently employed by the employer,
(ii) Any individual who was formerly employed by the employer and who separated
45   from service with the employer by reason of retirement or disability, and
(iii) Any widow or widower of an individual who died while employed by the employer
or who separated from service with the employer by reason of retirement or disability.
For purposes of this paragraph (b)(3), any partner who performs services for a
partnership is considered employed by the partnership. In addition, any use by the
50   spouse or dependent child (as defined in paragraph (b)(5) of this section) of the
employee will be treated as use by the employee.

300

Sec. 132. Certain fringe benefits

(4) *De minimis fringes*. For purposes of section 132(a)(4) (relating to de minimis fringes), the term ``employee" means any recipient of a fringe benefit.

(5) *Dependent child*. The term ``dependent child" means any son, stepson, daughter, or stepdaughter of the employee who is a dependent of the employee, or both of whose parents are deceased and who has not attained age 25. Any child to whom section 152(e) applies will be treated as the dependent of both parents.

(c) *Special rules for employers--Effect of section 414*. All employees treated as employed by a single employer under section 414 (b), (c), (m), or (o) will be treated as employed by a single employer for purposes of this section. Thus, employees of one corporation that is part of a controlled group of corporations may under certain circumstances be eligible to receive section 132 benefits from the other corporations that comprise the controlled group. However, the aggregation of employers described in this paragraph (c) does not change the other requirements for an exclusion, such as the line of business requirement. Thus, for example, if a controlled group of corporations consists of two corporations that operate in different lines of business, the corporations are not treated as operating in the same line of business even though the corporations are treated as one employer.

(d) *Customers not to include employees*. For purposes of section 132 and the regulations thereunder, the term ``customer" means any customer who is not an employee. However, the preceding sentence does not apply to section 132(c)(2) (relating to the gross profit percentage for determining a qualified employee discount). Thus, an employer that provides employee discounts cannot exclude sales made to employees in determining the aggregate sales to customers.

(e) *Treatment of on-premises athletic facilities--(1) In general*. Gross income does not include the value of any on-premises athletic facility provided by an employer to its employees. For purposes of section 132(h)(5) and this paragraph (e), the term ``on-premises athletic facility" means any gym or other athletic facility (such as a pool, tennis court, or golf course)--

(i) Which is located on the premises of the employer,

(ii) Which is operated by the employer, and

(iii) Substantially all of the use of which during the calendar year is by employees of the employer, their spouses, and their dependent children.

For purposes of paragraph (e) (1) (iii) of this section, the term ``dependent children" has the same meaning as the plural of the term ``dependent child" in paragraph (b)(5) of this section. The exclusion of this paragraph (e) does not apply to any athletic facility if access to the facility is made available to the general public through the sale of memberships, the rental of the facility, or a similar arrangement.

(2) *Premises of the employer*. The athletic facility need not be located on the employer's business premises. However, the athletic facility must be located on premises of the employer. The exclusion provided in this paragraph (e) applies whether the premises are owned or leased by the employer; in addition, the exclusion is available even if the employer is not a named lessee on the lease so long as the employer pays reasonable rent. The exclusion provided in this paragraph (e) does not apply to any athletic facility that is a facility for residential use. Thus, for example, a resort with accompanying athletic facilities (such as tennis courts, pool, and gym) would not qualify for the exclusion provided in this paragraph (e). An athletic facility is considered to be located on the employer's premises if the facility is located on the premises of a voluntary employees' beneficiary association funded by the employer.

(3) *Application of rules to membership in an athletic facility*. The exclusion provided in this paragraph (e) does not apply to any membership in an athletic facility (including health clubs or country clubs) unless the facility is owned (or leased) and operated by the

Sec. 132. Certain fringe benefits

employer and substantially all the use of the facility is by employees of the employer, their spouses, and their dependent children. Therefore, membership in a health club or country club not meeting the rules provided in this paragraph (e) would not qualify for the exclusion.

5   (4) *Operation by the employer.* An employer is considered to operate the athletic facility if the employer operates the facility through its own employees, or if the employer contracts out to another to operate the athletic facility. For example, if an employer hires an independent contractor to operate the athletic facility for the employer's employees, the facility is considered to be operated by the employer. In addition, if an athletic facility
10   is operated by more than one employer, it is considered to be operated by each employer. For purposes of paragraph (e) (1) (iii) of this section, substantially all of the use of a facility that is operated by more than one employer must be by employees of the various employers, their spouses, and their dependent children. Where the facility is operated by more than one employer, an employer that pays rent either directly to the
15   owner of the premises or to a sublessor of the premises is eligible for the exclusion. If an athletic facility is operated by a voluntary employees' beneficiary association funded by an employer, the employer is considered to operate the facility.

        (5) *Nonapplicability of nondiscrimination rules.* The nondiscrimination rules of section 132 and § 1.132-8 do not apply to on-premises athletic facilities.
20   (f) *Nonapplicability of section 132 in certain cases--*(1) *Tax treatment provided for in another section.* If the tax treatment or a particular fringe benefit is expressly provided for in another section of Chapter 1 of the Internal Revenue Code of 1986, section 132 and the applicable regulations (except for section 132(e) and the regulations thereunder) do not apply to such fringe benefit. For example, because section 129 provides an exclusion
25   from gross income for amounts paid or incurred by an employer for dependent care assistance for an employee, the exclusions under section 132 and this section do not apply to the provision by an employer to an employee of dependent care assistance. Similarly, because section 117(d) applies to tuition reductions, the exclusions under section 132 do not apply to free or discounted tuition provided to an employee by an
30   organization operated by the employer, whether the tuition is for study at or below the graduate level. Of course, if the amounts paid by the employer are for education relating to the employee's trade or business of being an employee of the employer so that, if the employee paid for the education, the amount paid could be deducted under section 162, the costs of the education may be eligible for exclusion as a working condition fringe.
35   (2) *Limited statutory exclusions.* If another section of Chapter 1 of the Internal Revenue Code of 1986 provides an exclusion from gross income based on the cost of the benefit provided to the employee and such exclusion is a limited amount, section 132 and the regulations thereunder may apply to the extent the cost of the benefit exceeds the statutory exclusion.

40   ***

Reg. § 1.132-2   No-additional-cost services.
        (a) *In general--*(1) *Definition.* Gross income does not include the value of a no-additional-cost service. A ``no-additional-cost service" is any service provided by an employer to an employee for the employee's personal use if--
45   (i) The service is offered for sale by the employer to its customers in the ordinary course of the line of business of the employer in which the employee performs substantial services, and
        (ii) The employer incurs no substantial additional cost in providing the service to the employee (including foregone revenue and excluding any amount paid by or on behalf of
50   the employee for the service).For rules relating to the line of business limitation, see § 1.132-4. For purposes of this section, a service will not be considered to be offered for

sale by the employer to its customers if that service is primarily provided to employees and not to the employer's customers.

(2) *Excess capacity services*. Services that are eligible for treatment as no-additional-cost services include excess capacity services such as hotel accommodations; transportation by aircraft, train, bus, subway, or cruise line; and telephone services. Services that are not eligible for treatment as no-additional-cost services are non-excess capacity services such as the facilitation by a stock brokerage firm of the purchase of stock. Employees who receive non-excess capacity services may, however, be eligible for a qualified employee discount of up to 20 percent of the value of the service provided. See § 1.132-3.

(3) *Cash rebates*. The exclusion for a no-additional-cost service applies whether the service is provided at no charge or at a reduced price. The exclusion also applies if the benefit is provided through a partial or total cash rebate of an amount paid for the service.

(4) *Applicability of nondiscrimination rules*. The exclusion for a no-additional-cost service applies to highly compensated employees only if the service is available on substantially the same terms to each member of a group of employees that is defined under a reasonable classification set up by the employer that does not discriminate in favor of highly compensated employees. See § 1.132-8.

(5) *No substantial additional cost*--(i) *In general*. The exclusion for a no-additional-cost service applies only if the employer does not incur substantial additional cost in providing the service to the employee. For purposes of the preceding sentence, the term ``cost'' includes revenue that is forgone because the service is provided to an employee rather than a nonemployee. (For purposes of determining whether any revenue is forgone, it is assumed that the employee would not have purchased the service unless it were available to the employee at the actual price charged to the employee.) Whether an employer incurs substantial additional cost must be determined without regard to any amount paid by the employee for the service. Thus, any reimbursement by the employee for the cost of providing the service does not affect the determination of whether the employer incurs substantial additional cost.

(ii) *Labor intensive services*. An employer must include the cost of labor incurred in providing services to employees when determining whether the employer has incurred substantial additional cost. An employer incurs substantial additional cost, whether non-labor costs are incurred, if a substantial amount of time is spent by the employer or its employees in providing the service to employees. This would be the result whether the time spent by the employer or its employees in providing the services would have been ``idle,'' or if the services were provided outside normal business hours. An employer generally incurs no substantial additional cost, however, if the services provided to the employee are merely incidental to the primary service being provided by the employer. For example, the in-flight services of a flight attendant and the cost of in-flight meals provided to airline employees traveling on a space-available basis are merely incidental to the primary service being provided (i.e., air transportation). Similarly, maid service provided to hotel employees renting hotel rooms on a space-available basis is merely incidental to the primary service being provided (i.e., hotel accommodations).

(6) *Payments for telephone service*. Payment made by an entity subject to the modified final judgment (as defined in section 559(c)(5) of the Tax Reform Act of 1984) of all or part of the cost of local telephone service provided to an employee by a person other than an entity subject to the modified final judgment shall be treated as telephone service provided to the employee by the entity making the payment for purposes of this section. The preceding sentence also applies to a rebate of the amount paid by the employee for the service and a payment to the person providing the service. This paragraph (a)(6) applies only to services and employees described in § 1.132-4 (c). For a

Sec. 132. Certain fringe benefits

special line of business rule relating to such services and employees, see § 1.132-4 (c).

(b) *Reciprocal agreements.* For purposes of the exclusion from gross income for a no-additional-cost service, an exclusion is available to an employee of one employer for a no-additional-cost service provided by an unrelated employer only if all of the following
5 requirements are satisfied--

(1) The service provided to such employee by the unrelated employer is the same type of service generally provided to nonemployee customers by both the line of business in which the employee works and the line of business in which the service is provided to such employee (so that the employee would be permitted to exclude from gross income
10 the value of the service if such service were provided directly by the employee's employer);

(2) Both employers are parties to a written reciprocal agreement under which a group of employees of each employer, all of whom perform substantial services in the same line of business, may receive no-additional-cost services from the other employer; and

15 (3) Neither employer incurs any substantial additional cost (including forgone revenue) in providing such service to the employees of the other employer, or pursuant to such agreement. If one employer receives a substantial payment from the other employer with respect to the reciprocal agreement, the paying employer will be considered to have incurred a substantial additional cost pursuant to the agreement, and consequently
20 services performed under the reciprocal agreement will not qualify for exclusion as no-additional-cost services.

(c) *Example.* The rules of this section are illustrated by the following example:

Example. Assume that a commercial airline permits its employees to take personal flights on the airline at no charge and receive reserved seating. Because the employer
25 forgoes potential revenue by permitting the employees to reserve seats, employees receiving such free flights are not eligible for the no-additional-cost exclusion.

Reg. § 1.132-3 Qualified employee discounts.

(a) *In general--*(1) *Definition.* Gross income does not include the value of a qualified
30 employee discount. A ``qualified employee discount" is any employee discount with respect to qualified property or services provided by an employer to an employee for use by the employee to the extent the discount does not exceed--

(i) The gross profit percentage multiplied by the price at which the property is offered to customers in the ordinary course of the employer's line of business, for discounts on
35 property, or

(ii) Twenty percent of the price at which the service is offered to customers, for discounts on services.

(2) *Qualified property or services--*(i) *In general.* The term ``qualified property or services" means any property or services that are offered for sale to customers in the
40 ordinary course of the line of business of the employer in which the employee performs substantial services. For rules relating to the line of business limitation, see § 1.132-4.

(ii) *Exception for certain property.* The term ``qualified property" does not include real property and it does not include personal property (whether tangible or intangible) of a kind commonly held for investment. Thus, an employee may not exclude from gross
45 income the amount of an employee discount provided on the purchase of securities, commodities, or currency, or of either residential or commercial real estate, whether or not the particular purchase is made for investment purposes.

(iii) *Property and services not offered in ordinary course of business.* The term ``qualified property or services" does not include any property or services of a kind that is
50 not offered for sale to customers in the ordinary course of the line of business of the employer. For example, employee discounts provided on property or services that are

304

Sec. 132. Certain fringe benefits

offered for sale primarily to employees and their families (such as merchandise sold at an employee store or through an employer-provided catalog service) may not be excluded from gross income. For rules relating to employer-operated eating facilities, see § 1.132-7, and for rules relating to employer-operated on-premises athletic facilities, see § 1.132-1(e).

(3) *No reciprocal agreement exception.* The exclusion for a qualified employee discount does not apply to property or services provided by another employer pursuant to a written reciprocal agreement that exists between employers to provide discounts on property and services to employees of the other employer.

(4) *Property or services provided without charge, at a reduced price, or by rebates.* The exclusion for a qualified employee discount applies whether the property or service is provided at no charge (in which case only part of the discount may be excludable as a qualified employee discount) or at a reduced price. The exclusion also applies if the benefit is provided through a partial or total cash rebate of an amount paid for the property or service.

(5) *Property or services provided directly by the employer or indirectly through a third party.* A qualified employee discount may be provided either directly by the employer or indirectly through a third party. For example, an employee of an appliance manufacturer may receive a qualified employee discount on the manufacturer's appliances purchased at a retail store that offers such appliances for sale to customers. The employee may exclude the amount of the qualified employee discount whether the employee is provided the appliance at no charge or purchases it at a reduced price, or whether the employee receives a partial or total cash rebate from either the employer-manufacturer or the retailer. If an employee receives additional rights associated with the property that are not provided by the employee's employer to customers in the ordinary course of the line of business in which the employee performs substantial services (such as the right to return or exchange the property or special warranty rights), the employee may only receive a qualified employee discount with respect to the property and not the additional rights. Receipt of such additional rights may occur, for example, when an employee of a manufacturer purchases property manufactured by the employee's employer at a retail outlet.

(6) *Applicability of nondiscrimination rules.* The exclusion for a qualified employee discount applies to highly compensated employees only if the discount is available on substantially the same terms to each member of a group of employees that is defined under a reasonable classification set up by the employer that does not discriminate in favor of highly compensated employees. See § 1.132-8.

(b) *Employee discount*--(1) *Definition.* The term ``employee discount'' means the excess of--

(i) The price at which the property or service is being offered by the employer for sale to customers, over

(ii) The price at which the property or service is provided by the employer to an employee for use by the employee. A transfer of property by an employee without consideration is treated as use by the employee for purposes of this section. Thus, for example, if an employee receives a discount on property offered for sale by his employer to customers and the employee makes a gift of the property to his parent, the property will be considered to be provided for use by the employee; thus, the discount will be eligible for exclusion as a qualified employee discount.

(2) *Price to customers*--(i) *Determined at time of sale.* In determining the amount of an employee discount, the price at which the property or service is being offered to customers at the time of the employee's purchase is controlling. For example, assume that an employer offers a product to customers for $20 during the first six months of a

Sec. 132. Certain fringe benefits

calendar year, but at the time the employee purchases the product at a discount, the price at which the product is being offered to customers is $25. In this case, the price from which the employee discount is measured is $25. Assume instead that, at the time the employee purchases the product at a discount, the price at which the product is being
5 offered to customers is $15 and the price charged the employee is $12. The employee discount is measured from $15, the price at which the product is offered for sale to customers at the time of the employee purchase. Thus, the employee discount is $15 - $12, or $3.

(ii) *Quantity discount not reflected.* The price at which a property or service is being
10 offered to customers cannot reflect any quantity discount unless the employee actually purchases the requisite quantity of the property or service.

(iii) Price to employer's customers controls. In determining the amount of an employee discount, the price at which a property or service is offered to customers of the employee's employer is controlling. Thus, the price at which the property is sold to the
15 wholesale customers of a manufacturer will generally be lower than the price at which the same property is sold to the customers of a retailer. However, see paragraph (a)(5) of this section regarding the effect of a wholesaler providing to its employees additional rights not provided to customers of the wholesaler in the ordinary course of its business.

(iv) Discounts to discrete customer or consumer groups. Subject to paragraph (2)(ii) of
20 this section, if an employer offers for sale property or services at one or more discounted prices to discrete customer or consumer groups, and sales at all such discounted prices comprise at least 35 percent of the employer's gross sales for a representative period, then in determining the amount of an employee discount, the price at which such property or service is being offered to customers for purposes of this section is a discounted price.
25 The applicable discounted price is the current undiscounted price, reduced by the percentage discount at which the greatest percentage of the employer's discounted gross sales are made for such representative period. If sales at different percentage discounts equal the same percentage of the employer's gross sales, the price at which the property or service is being provided to customers may be reduced by the average of the
30 discounts offered to each of the two groups. For purposes of this section, a representative period is the taxable year of the employer immediately preceding the taxable year in which the property or service is provided to the employee at a discount. If more than one employer would be aggregated under section 414 (b), (c), (m), or (o), and not all of the employers have the same taxable year, the employers required to be
35 aggregated must designate the 12-month period to be used in determining gross sales for a representative period. The 12-month period designated, however, must be used on a consistent basis.

(v) *Examples.* The rules provided in this paragraph (b)(2) are illustrated by the following examples:
40 *Example (1).* Assume that a wholesale employer offers property for sale to two discrete customer groups at differing prices. Assume further that during the prior taxable year of the employer, 70 percent of the employer's gross sales are made at a 15 percent discount and 30 percent at no discount. For purposes of this paragraph (b)(2), the current undiscounted price at which the property or service is being offered by the employer for
45 sale to customers may be reduced by the 15 percent discount.

Example (2). Assume that a retail employer offers a 20 percent discount to members of the American Bar Association, a 15 percent discount to members of the American Medical Association, and a ten percent discount to employees of the Federal Government. Assume further that during the prior taxable year of the employer, sales to
50 American Bar Association members equal 15 percent of the employer's gross sales, sales to American Medical Association members equal 20 percent of the employer's

Sec. 132. Certain fringe benefits

gross sales, and sales to Federal Government employees equal 25 percent of the employer's gross sales. For purposes of this paragraph (b)(2), the current undiscounted price at which the property or service is being offered by the employer for sale to customers may be reduced by the ten percent Federal Government discount.

(3) *Damaged, distressed, or returned goods.* If an employee pays at least fair market value for damaged, distressed, or returned property, such employee will not have income attributable to such purchase.

(c) *Gross profit percentage--*(1) *In general--*(i) *General rule.* An exclusion from gross income for an employee discount on qualified property is limited to the price at which the property is being offered to customers in the ordinary course of the employer's line of business, multiplied by the employer's gross profit percentage. The term ``gross profit percentage" means the excess of the aggregate sales price of the property sold by the employer to customers (including employees) over the employer's aggregate cost of the property, then divided by the aggregate sales price.

(ii) *Calculation of gross profit percentage.* The gross profit percentage must be calculated separately for each line of business based on the aggregate sales price and aggregate cost of property in that line of business for a representative period. For purposes of this section, a representative period is the taxable year of the employer immediately preceding the taxable year in which the discount is available. For example, if the aggregate amount of sales of property in an employer's line of business for the prior taxable year was $800,000, and the aggregate cost of the property for the year was $600,000, the gross profit percentage would be 25 percent ($800,000 minus $600,000, then divided by $800,000). If two or more employers are required to aggregate under section 414 (b), (c), (m), or (o) (aggregated employer), and if all of the aggregated employers do not share the same taxable year, then the aggregated employers must designate the 12-month period to be used in determining the gross profit percentage. The 12-month period designated, however, must be used on a consistent basis. If an employee performs substantial services in more than one line of business, the gross profit percentage of the line of business in which the property is sold determines the amount of the excludable employee discount.

(iii) *Special rule for employers in their first year of existence.* An employer in its first year of existence may estimate the gross profit percentage of a line of business based on its mark-up from cost. Alternatively, an employer in its first year of existence may determine the gross profit percentage by reference to an appropriate industry average.

(iv) *Redetermination of gross profit percentage.* If substantial changes in an employer's business indicate at any time that it is inappropriate for the prior year's gross profit percentage to be used for the current year, the employer must, within a reasonable period, redetermine the gross profit percentage for the remaining portion of the current year as if such portion of the year were the first year of the employer's existence.

(2) *Line of business.* In general, an employer must determine the gross profit percentage on the basis of all property offered to customers (including employees) in each separate line of business. An employer may instead select a classification of property that is narrower than the applicable line of business. However, the classification must be reasonable. For example, if an employer computes gross profit percentage according to the department in which products are sold, such classification is reasonable. Similarly, it is reasonable to compute gross profit percentage on the basis of the type of merchandise sold (such as high mark-up and low mark-up classifications). It is not reasonable, however, for an employer to classify certain low mark-up products preferred by certain employees (such as highly compensated employees) with high mark-up products or to classify certain high mark-up products preferred by other employees with low mark-up products.

Sec. 132. Certain fringe benefits

(3) *Generally accepted accounting principles.* In general, the aggregate sales price of property must be determined in accordance with generally accepted accounting principles. An employer must compute the aggregate cost of property in the same manner in which it is computed for the employer's Federal income tax liability; thus, for example, section 263A and the regulations thereunder apply in determining the cost of property.

(d) *Treatment of leased sections of department stores*--(1) *In general*--(i) *General rule.* For purposes of determining whether employees of a leased section of a department store may receive qualified employee discounts at the department store and whether employees of the department store may receive qualified employee discounts at the leased section of the department store, the leased section is treated as part of the line of business of the person operating the department store, and employees of the leased section are treated as employees of the person operating the department store as well as employees of their employer. The term ``leased section of a department store" means a section of a department store where substantially all of the gross receipts of the leased section are from over-the-counter sales of property made under a lease, license, or similar arrangement where it appears to the general public that individuals making such sales are employed by the department store. A leased section of a department store which, in connection with the offering of beautician services, customarily makes sales of beauty aids in the ordinary course of business is deemed to derive substantially all of its gross receipts from over-the-counter sales of property.

(ii) *Calculation of gross profit percentage.* For purposes of paragraph (d) of this section, when calculating the gross profit percentage of property and services sold at a department store, sales of property and services sold at the department store, as well as sales of property and services sold at the leased section, are considered. The rule provided in the preceding sentence does not apply, however, if it is more reasonable to calculate the gross profit percentage for the department store and leased section separately, or if it would be inappropriate to combine them (such as where either the department store or the leased section but not both provides employee discounts).

(2) *Employees of the leased section*--(i) *Definition.* For purposes of this paragraph (d), ``employees of the leased section" means all employees who perform substantial services at the leased section of the department store regardless of whether the employees engage in over-the-counter sales of property or services. The term ``employee" has the same meaning as in section 132(f) and § 1.132-1(b)(1).

(ii) Discounts offered to either department store employees or employees of the leased section. If the requirements of this paragraph (d) are satisfied, employees of the leased section may receive qualified employee discounts at the department store whether or not employees of the department store are offered discounts at the leased section. Similarly, employees of the department store may receive a qualified employee discount at the leased section whether or not employees of the leased section are offered discounts at the department store.

(e) *Excess discounts.* Unless excludable under a provision of the Internal Revenue Code of 1986 other than section 132(a)(2), an employee discount provided on property is excludable to the extent of the gross profit percentage multiplied by the price at which the property is being offered for sale to customers. If an employee discount exceeds the gross profit percentage, the excess discount is includible in the employee's income. For example, if the discount on employer-purchased property is 30 percent and the employer's gross profit percentage for the period in the relevant line of business is 25 percent, then 5 percent of the price at which the property is being offered for sale to customers is includible in the employee's income. With respect to services, an employee discount of up to 20 percent may be excludable. If an employee discount exceeds 20

308

Sec. 132. Certain fringe benefits

percent, the excess discount is includible in the employee's income. For example, assume that a commercial airline provides a pass to each of its employees permitting the employees to obtain a free round-trip coach ticket with a confirmed seat to any destination the airline services. Neither the exclusion of section 132(a)(1) (relating to no-additional-cost services) nor any other statutory exclusion applies to a flight taken 5 primarily for personal purposes by an employee under this program. However, an employee discount of up to 20 percent may be excluded as a qualified employee discount. Thus, if the price charged to customers for the flight taken is $300 (under restrictions comparable to those actually placed on travel associated with the employee airline ticket), $60 is excludible from gross income as a qualified employee discount and 10 $240 is includible in gross income.

Reg. § 1.132-5 Working condition fringes.

(a) *In general*--(1) *Definition*. Gross income does not include the value of a working condition fringe. A ``working condition fringe" is any property or service provided to an 15 employee of an employer to the extent that, if the employee paid for the property or service, the amount paid would be allowable as a deduction under section 162 or 167.

(i) A service or property offered by an employer in connection with a flexible spending account is not excludable from gross income as a working condition fringe. For purposes of the preceding sentence, a flexible spending account is an agreement (whether or not 20 written) entered into between an employer and an employee that makes available to the employee over a time period a certain level of unspecified non-cash benefits with a pre-determined cash value.

(ii) If, under section 274 or any other section, certain substantiation requirements must be met in order for a deduction under section 162 or 167 to be allowable, then those 25 substantiation requirements apply when determining whether a property or service is excludable as a working condition fringe.

(iii) An amount that would be deductible by the employee under a section other than section 162 or 167, such as section 212, is not a working condition fringe.

(iv) A physical examination program provided by the employer is not excludable as a 30 working condition fringe even if the value of such program might be deductible to the employee under section 213. The previous sentence applies without regard to whether the employer makes the program mandatory to some or all employees.

(v) A cash payment made by an employer to an employee will not qualify as a working condition fringe unless the employer requires the employee to-- 35

(A) Use the payment for expenses in connection with a specific or pre-arranged activity or undertaking for which a deduction is allowable under section 162 or 167,

(B) Verify that the payment is actually used for such expenses, and

(C) Return to the employer any part of the payment not so used.

(vi) The limitation of section 67(a) (relating to the two-percent floor on miscellaneous 40 itemized deductions) is not considered when determining the amount of a working condition fringe. For example, assume that an employer provides a $1,000 cash advance to Employee A and that the conditions of paragraph (a)(1)(v) of this section are not satisfied. Even to the extent A uses the allowance for expenses for which a deduction is allowable under section 162 and 167, because such cash payment is not a working 45 condition fringe, section 67(a) applies. The $1,000 payment is includible in A's gross income and subject to income and employment tax withholding. If, however, the conditions of paragraph (a)(1)(v) of this section are satisfied with respect to the payment, then the amount of A's working condition fringe is determined without regard to section 67(a). The $1,000 payment is excludible from A's gross income and not subject to income 50 and employment tax reporting and withholding.

Sec. 132. Certain fringe benefits

(2) *Trade or business of the employee*--(i) *General.* If the hypothetical payment for a property or service would be allowable as a deduction with respect to a trade or business of an employee other than the employee's trade or business of being an employee of the employer, it cannot be taken into account for purposes of determining the amount, if any,
5 of the working condition fringe.

(ii) *Examples.* The rule of paragraph (a)(2)(i) of this section may be illustrated by the following examples:

Example (1). Assume that, unrelated to company X's trade or business and unrelated to employee A's trade or business of being an employee of company X, A is a member of
10 the board of directors of company Y. Assume further that company X provides A with air transportation to a company Y board of director's meeting. A may not exclude from gross income the value of the air transportation to the meeting as a working condition fringe. A may, however, deduct such amount under section 162 if the section 162 requirements are satisfied. The result would be the same whether the air transportation was provided in the
15 form of a flight on a commercial airline or a seat on a company X airplane.

Example (2). Assume the same facts as in example (1) except that A serves on the board of directors of company Z and company Z regularly purchases a significant amount of goods and services from company X. Because of the relationship between Company Z and A's employer, A's membership on Company Z's board of directors is related to A's
20 trade or business of being an employee of Company X. Thus, A may exclude from gross income the value of air transportation to board meetings as a working condition fringe.

Example (3). Assume the same facts as in example (1) except that A serves on the board of directors of a charitable organization. Assume further that the service by A on the charity's board is substantially related to company X's trade or business. In this case,
25 A may exclude from gross income the value of air transportation to board meetings as a working condition fringe.

Example (4). Assume the same facts as in example (3) except that company X also provides A with the use of a company X conference room which A uses for monthly meetings relating to the charitable organization. Also assume that A uses company X's
30 copy machine and word processor each month in connection with functions of the charitable organization. Because of the substantial business benefit that company X derives from A's service on the board of the charity, A may exclude as a working condition fringe the value of the use of company X property in connection with the charitable organization.

35 (b) *Vehicle allocation rules*--(1) *In general*--(i) *General rule.* In general, with respect to an employer-provided vehicle, the amount excludable as a working condition fringe is the amount that would be allowable as a deduction under section 162 or 167 if the employee paid for the availability of the vehicle. For example, assume that the value of the availability of an employer-provided vehicle for a full year is $2,000, without regard to any
40 working condition fringe (i.e., assuming all personal use). Assume Further that the employee drives the vehicle 6,000 miles for his employer's business and 2,000 miles for reasons other than the employer's business. In this situation, the value of the working condition fringe is $2,000 multiplied by a fraction, the numerator of which is the business-use mileage (6,000 miles) and the denominator of which is the total mileage (8,000
45 miles). Thus, the value of the working condition fringe is $1,500. The total amount includible in the employee's gross income on account of the availability of the vehicle is $500 ($2,000-$1,500). For purposes of this section, the term ``vehicle" has the meaning given the term in § 1.61-21(e)(2). Generally, when determining the amount of an employee's working condition fringe, miles accumulated on the vehicle by all employees
50 of the employer during the period in which the vehicle is available to the employee are considered. For example, assume that during the year in which the vehicle is available to

Sec. 132. Certain fringe benefits

the employee in the above example, other employees accumulate 2,000 additional miles on the vehicle (while the employee is not in the automobile). In this case, the value of the working condition fringe is $2,000 multiplied by a fraction, the numerator of which is the business-use mileage by the employee (including all mileage (business and personal) accumulated by other employees) (8,000 miles) and the denominator of which is the total 5 mileage (including all mileage accumulated by other employees) (10,000 miles). Thus, the value of the working condition fringe is $1,600; the 6total amount includible in the employee's gross income on account of the availability of the vehicle is $400 ($2,000- $1,600). If, however, substantially all of the use of the automobile by other employees in the employer's business is limited to a certain period, such as the last three months of the 10 year, the miles driven by the other employees during that period would not be considered when determining the employee's working condition fringe exclusion. Similarly, miles driven by other employees are not considered if the pattern of use of the employer- provided automobiles is designed to reduce Federal taxes. For example, assume that an employer provides employees A and B each with the availability of an employer-provided 15 automobile and that A uses the automobile assigned to him 80 percent for the employer's business and that B uses the automobile assigned to him 30 percent for the employer's business. If A and B alternate the use of their assigned automobiles each week in such a way as to achieve a reduction in federal taxes, then the employer may count only miles placed on the automobile by the employee to whom the automobile is assigned when 20 determining each employee's working condition fringe.

(ii) *Use by an individual other than the employee*. For purposes of this section, if the availability of a vehicle to an individual would be taxed to an employee, use of the vehicle by the individual is included in references to use by the employee.

(iii) *Provision of an expensive vehicle for personal use*. If an employer provides an 25 employee with a vehicle that an employee may use in part for personal purposes, there is no working condition fringe exclusion with respect to the personal miles driven by the employee; if the employee paid for the availability of the vehicle, he would not be entitled to deduct under section 162 or 167 any part of the payment attributable to personal miles. The amount of the inclusion is not affected by the fact that the employee would have 30 chosen the availability of a less expensive vehicle. Moreover, the result is the same even though the decision to provide an expensive rather than an inexpensive vehicle is made by the employer for bona fide noncompensatory business reasons.

(iv) *Total value inclusion*. In lieu of excluding the value of a working condition fringe with respect of an automobile, an employer using the automobile lease valuation rule of § 35 1.61-21(d) may include in an employee's gross income the entire Annual Lease Value of the automobile. Any deduction allowable to the employee under section 162 or 167 with respect to the automobile may be taken on the employee's income tax return. The total inclusion rule of this paragraph (b)(1)(iv) is not available if the employer is valuing the use or availability of a vehicle under general valuation principles or a special valuation rule 40 other than the automobile lease valuation rule. See §§ 1.162-25 and 1.162-25T for rules relating to the employee's deduction.

(v) *Shared usage*. In calculating the working condition fringe benefit exclusion with respect to a vehicle provided for use by more than one employee, an employer shall compute the working condition fringe in a manner consistent with the allocation of the 45 value of the vehicle under § 1.61-21(c)(2)(ii)(B).

(2) *Use of different employer-provided vehicles*. The working condition fringe exclusion must be applied on a vehicle-by-vehicle basis. For example, assume that automobile Y is available to employee D for 3 days in January and for 5 days in March, and automobile Z is available to D for a week in July. Assume further that the Daily Lease 50 Value, as defined in § 1.61-21(d)(4)(ii), of each automobile is $50. For the eight days of

311

Sec. 132. Certain fringe benefits

availability of Y in January and March, D uses Y 90 percent for business (by mileage). During July, D uses Z 60 percent for business (by mileage). The value of the working condition fringe is determined separately for each automobile. Therefore, the working condition fringe for Y is $360 ($400x.90) leaving an income inclusion of $40. The working
5   condition fringe for Z is $210 ($350x.60), leaving an income inclusion of $140. If the value of the availability of an automobile is determined under the Annual Lease Value rule for one period and Daily Lease Value rule for a second period (see § 1.61-21(d)), the working condition fringe exclusion must be calculated separately for the two periods.

   (3) *Provision of a vehicle and chauffeur services--*(i) *General rule.* In general, with
10   respect to the value of chauffeur services provided by an employer, the amount excludable as a working condition fringe is the amount that would be allowable as a deduction under section 162 and 167 if the employee paid for the chauffeur services. The working condition fringe with respect to a chauffeur is determined separately from the working condition fringe with respect to the vehicle. An employee may exclude from gross
15   income the excess of the value of the chauffeur services over the value of the chauffeur services for personal purposes (such as commuting) as determined under § 1.61-21(b) (5). See § 1.61-21(b)(5) for additional rules and examples concerning the valuation of chauffeur services. See § 1.132-5(m)(5) for rules relating to an exclusion from gross income for the value of bodyguard/chauffeur services. When determining whether miles
20   placed on the vehicle are for the employer's business, miles placed on the vehicle by a chauffeur between the chauffeur's residence and the place at which the chauffeur picks up (or drops off) the employee are with respect to the employee (but not the chauffeur) considered to be miles placed on the vehicle for the employer's business and thus eligible for the working condition fringe exclusion. Thus, because miles placed on the vehicle by
25   a chauffeur between the chauffeur's residence and the place at which the chauffeur picks up (or drops off) the employee are not considered business miles with respect to the chauffeur, the value of the availability of the vehicle for commuting is includible in the gross income of the chauffeur. For general and special rules concerning the valuation of the use of employer-provided vehicles, see paragraphs (b) through (f) of § 1.61-21.
30   (ii) *Examples.* The rules of paragraph (b)(3)(i) of this section are illustrated by the following examples:

   Example (1). Assume that an employer makes available to an employee an automobile and a chauffeur. Assume further that the value of the chauffeur services determined in accordance with § 1.61-21 is $30,000 and that the chauffeur spends 30
35   percent of each workday driving the employee for personal purposes. There may be excluded from the employee's income 70 percent of $30,000, or $21,000, leaving an income inclusion with respect to the chauffeur services of $9,000.

   Example (2). Assume that the value of the availability of an employer-provided vehicle for a year is $4,850 and that the value of employer-provided chauffeur services with
40   respect to the vehicle for the year is $20,000. Assume further that 40 percent of the miles placed on the vehicle are for the employer's business and that 60 percent are for other purposes. In addition, assume that the chauffeur spends 25 percent of each workday driving the employee for personal purposes (i.e., 2 hours). The value of the chauffeur services includible in the employee's income is 25 percent of $20,000, or $5,000. The
45   excess of $20,000 over $5,000 or $15,000 is excluded from the employee's income as a working condition fringe. The amount excludable as a working condition fringe with respect to the vehicle is 40 percent of $4,850, or $1,940 and the amount includible is $4,850-$1,940, or $2,910.

   (c) *Applicability of substantiation requirements of sections 162 and 274 (d)--(1) In*
50   *general.* The value of property or services provided to an employee may not be excluded from the employee's gross income as a working condition fringe, by either the employer

Sec. 132. Certain fringe benefits

or the employee, unless the applicable substantiation requirements of either section 274(d) or section 162 (whichever is applicable) and the regulations thereunder are satisfied. The substantiation requirements of section 274(d) apply to an employee even if the requirements of section 274 do not apply to the employee's employer for deduction purposes (such as when the employer is a tax-exempt organization or a governmental 5 unit).

(2) *Section 274(d) requirements.* The substantiation requirements of section 274(d) are satisfied by ``adequate records or sufficient evidence corroborating the [employee's] own statement". Therefore, such records or evidence provided by the employee, and relied upon by the employer to the extent permitted by the regulations promulgated under 10 section 274(d), will be sufficient to substantiate a working condition fringe exclusion.

(d) *Safe harbor substantiation rules*--(1) *In general.* Section 1.274-6T provides that the substantiation requirements of section 274(d) and the regulations thereunder may be satisfied, in certain circumstances, by using one or more of the safe harbor rules prescribed in § 1.274-6T. If the employer uses one of the safe harbor rules prescribed in 15 § 1.274-6T during a period with respect to a vehicle (as defined in § 1.61-21(e)(2)), that rule must be used by the employer to substantiate a working condition fringe exclusion with respect to that vehicle during the period. An employer that is exempt from Federal income tax may still use one of the safe harbor rules (if the requirements of that section are otherwise met during a period) to substantiate a working condition fringe exclusion 20 with respect to a vehicle during the period. If the employer uses one of the methods prescribed in § 1.274-6T during a period with respect to an employer-provided vehicle, that method may be used by an employee to substantiate a working condition fringe exclusion with respect to the same vehicle during the period, as long as the employee includes in gross income the amount allocated to the employee pursuant to § 1.274-6T 25 and this section. (See § 1.61-21(c)(2) for other rules concerning when an employee must include in income the amount determined by the employer.) If, however, the employer uses the safe harbor rule prescribed in § 1.274-6T(a) (2) or (3) and the employee without the employer's knowledge uses the vehicle for purposes other than de minimis personal use (in the case of the rule prescribed in § 1.274-6T(a)(2)), or for purposes other than de 30 minimis personal use and commuting (in the case of the rule prescribed in § 1.274-6T(a) (3)), then the employees must include an additional amount in income for the unauthorized use of the vehicle.

(2) *Period for use of safe harbor rules.* The rules prescribed in this paragraph (d) assume that the safe harbor rules prescribed in § 1.274-6T are used for a one-year 35 period. Accordingly, references to the value of the availability of a vehicle, amounts excluded as a working condition fringe, etc., are based on a one-year period. If the safe harbor rules prescribed in § 1.274-6T are used for a period of less than a year, the amounts referred to in the previous sentence must be adjusted accordingly. For purposes of this section, the term ``personal use" has the same meaning as prescribed in § 40 1.274-6T (e)(5).

(e) Safe harbor substantiation rule for vehicles not used for personal purposes. For a vehicle described in § 1.274-6T(a)(2) (relating to certain vehicles not used for personal purposes), the working condition fringe exclusion is equal to the value of the availability of the vehicle if the employer uses the method prescribed in § 1.274-6T(a)(2). 45

(f) *Safe harbor substantiation rule for vehicles not available to employees for personal use other than commuting.* For a vehicle described in § 1.274-6T(a)(3) (relating to certain vehicles not used for personal purposes other than commuting), the working condition fringe exclusion is equal to the value of the availability of the vehicle for purposes other than commuting if the employer uses the method prescribed in § 1.274-6T(a)(3). This rule 50 applies only if the special rule for valuing commuting use, as prescribed in § 1.61-21(f),

Sec. 132. Certain fringe benefits

is used and the amount determined under the special rule is either included in the employee's income or reimbursed by the employee.

(g) *Safe harbor substantiation rule for vehicles used in connection with the business of farming that are available to employees for personal use--*(1) *In general.* For a vehicle
5 described in § 1.274-6T(b) (relating to certain vehicles used in connection with the business of farming), the working condition fringe exclusion is calculated by multiplying the value of the availability of the vehicle by 75 percent.

(2) *Vehicles available to more than one individual.* If the vehicle is available to more than one individual, the employer must allocate the gross income inclusion attributable to
10 the vehicle (25 percent of the value of the availability of the vehicle) among the employees (and other individuals whose use would not be attributed to an employee) to whom the vehicle was available. This allocation must be done in a reasonable manner to reflect the personal use of the vehicle by the individuals. An amount that would be allocated to a sole proprietor reduces the amounts that may be allocated to employees
15 but is otherwise to be disregarded for purposes of this paragraph (g). For purposes of this paragraph (g), the value of the availability of a vehicle may be calculated as if the vehicle were available to only one employee continuously and without regard to any working condition fringe exclusion.

(3) *Examples.* The following examples illustrate a reasonable allocation of gross
20 income with respect to an employer-provided vehicle between two employees:

Example (1). Assume that two farm employees share the use of a vehicle that for a calendar year is regularly used directly in connection with the business of farming and qualifies for use of the rule in § 1.274-6T(b). Employee A uses the vehicle in the morning directly in connection with the business of farming and employee B uses the vehicle in
25 the afternoon directly in connection with the business of farming. Assume further that employee B takes the vehicle home in the evenings and on weekends. The employer should allocate all the income attributable to the availability of the vehicle to employee B.

Example (2). Assume that for a calendar year, farm employees C and D share the use of a vehicle that is regularly used directly in connection with the business of farming and
30 qualifies for use of the rule in § 1.274-6T(b). Assume further that the employees alternate taking the vehicle home in the evening and alternate the availability of the vehicle for personal purposes on weekends. The employer should allocate the income attributable to the availability of the vehicle for personal use (25 percent of the value of the availability of the vehicle) equally between the two employees.
35 *Example (3).* Assume the same facts as in example (2) except that C is the sole proprietor of the farm. Based on these facts, C should allocate the same amount of income to D as was allocated to D in example (2). No other income attributable to the availability of the vehicle for personal use should be allocated.

(h) *Qualified nonpersonal use vehicles--*(1) *In general.* Except as provided in
40 paragraph (h)(2) of this section, 100 percent of the value of the use of a qualified nonpersonal use vehicle (as described in § 1.274-5T(k)) is excluded from gross income as a working condition fringe, provided that, in the case of a vehicle described in paragraph (k) (3) through (8) of that section, the use of the vehicle conforms to the requirements of that paragraph.
45 (2) *Shared usage of qualified nonpersonal use vehicles.* In general, a working condition fringe under paragraph (h) of this section is available to the driver and all passengers of a qualified nonpersonal use vehicle. However, a working condition fringe under this paragraph (h) is available only with respect to the driver and not with respect to any passengers of a qualified nonpersonal use vehicle described in § 1.274-5T(k)(2)(ii)
50 (L) or (P). In this case, the passengers must comply with provisions of this section (excluding this paragraph (h)) to determine the applicability of the working condition fringe

Sec. 132. Certain fringe benefits

exclusion. For example, if an employer provides a passenger bus with a capacity of 25 passengers to its employees for purposes of transporting employees to and/or from work, the driver of the bus may exclude from gross income as a working condition fringe 100 percent of the value of the use of the vehicle. The value of the commuting use of the employer-provided bus by the employee-passengers is includible in their gross incomes. 5 See § 1.61-21(f) for a special rule to value the commuting-only use of employer-provided vehicles.

(i) [Reserved]

(j) *Application of section 280F.* In determining the amount, if any, of an employee's working condition fringe, section 280F and the regulations thereunder do not apply. For 10 example, assume that an employee has available for a calendar year an employer-provided automobile with a fair market value of $28,000. Assume further that the special rule provided in § 1.61-21(d) is used yielding an Annual Lease Value, as defined in § 1.61-21(d), of $7,750, and that all of the employee's use of the automobile is for the employer's business. The employee would be entitled to exclude as a working condition 15 fringe the entire Annual Lease Value, despite the fact that if the employee paid for the availability of the automobile, an income inclusion would be required under § 1.280F-6(d) (1). This paragraph (j) does not affect the applicability of section 280F to the employer with respect to such employer-provided automobile, nor does it affect the applicability of section 274 to either the employer or the employee. For rules concerning substantiation 20 of an employee's working condition fringe, see paragraph (c) of this section.

(k) *Aircraft allocation rule.* In general, with respect to a flight on an employer-provided aircraft, the amount excludable as a working condition fringe is the amount that would be allowable as a deduction under section 162 or 167 if the employee paid for the flight on the aircraft. For example, if employee P and P's spouse fly on P's employer's airplane 25 primarily for business reasons of P's employer so that P could deduct the expenses relating to the trip to the extent of P's payments, the value of the flights is excludable from gross income as a working condition fringe. However, if P's children accompany P on the trip primarily for personal reasons, the value of the flights by P's children are includible in P's gross income. See § 1.61-21 (g) for special rules for valuing personal flights on 30 employer-provided aircraft.

(l) [Reserved]

(m) *Employer-provided transportation for security concerns--(1) In general.* The amount of a working condition fringe exclusion with respect to employer-provided transportation is the amount that would be allowable as a deduction under section 162 or 35 167 if the employee paid for the transportation. Generally, if an employee pays for transportation taken for primarily personal purposes, the employee may not deduct any part of the amount paid. Thus, the employee may not generally exclude the value of employer-provided transportation as a working condition fringe if such transportation is primarily personal. If, however, for bona fide business-oriented security concerns, the 40 employee purchases transportation that provides him or her with additional security, the employee may generally deduct the excess of the amount actually paid for the transportation over the amount the employee would have paid for the same mode of transportation absent the bona fide business-oriented security concerns. This is the case whether or not the employee would have taken the same mode of transportation absent 45 the bona fide business-oriented security concerns. With respect to a vehicle, the phrase ``the same mode of transportation" means use of the same vehicle without the additional security aspects, such as bulletproof glass. With respect to air transportation, the phrase ``the same mode of transportation" means comparable air transportation. These same rules apply to the determination of an employee's working condition fringe exclusion. For 50 example, if an employer provides an employee with a vehicle for commuting and,

Sec. 132. Certain fringe benefits

because of bona fide business-oriented security concerns, the vehicle is specially designed for security, then the employee may exclude from gross income the value of the special security design as a working condition fringe. The employee may not exclude the value of the commuting from income as a working condition fringe because commuting is
5 a nondeductible personal expense. However, if an independent security study meeting the requirements of paragraph (m)(2)(v) of this section has been performed with respect to a government employee, the government employee may exclude the value of the personal use (other than commuting) of the employer-provided vehicle that the security study determines to be reasonable and necessary for local transportation. Similarly, if an
10 employee travels on a personal trip in an employer-provided aircraft for bona fide business-oriented security concerns, the employee may exclude the excess, if any, of the value of the flight over the amount the employee would have paid for the same mode of transportation, but for the bona fide business-oriented security concerns. Because personal travel is a nondeductible expense, the employee may not exclude the total value
15 of the trip as a working condition fringe.

   (2) *Demonstration of bona fide business-oriented security concerns*--(i) *In general.* For purposes of this paragraph (m), a bona fide business-oriented security concern exists only if the facts and circumstances establish a specific basis for concern regarding the safety of the employee. A generalized concern for an employee's safety is not a bona fide
20 business-oriented security concern. Once a bona fide business-oriented security concern is determined to exist with respect to a particular employee, the employer must periodically evaluate the situation for purposes of determining whether the bona fide business-oriented security concern still exists. Example of factors indicating a specific basis for concern regarding the safety of an employee are--
25   (A) A threat of death or kidnapping of, or serious bodily harm to, the employee or a similarly situated employee because of either employee's status as an employee of the employer; or
   (B) A recent history of violent terrorist activity (such as bombings) in the geographic area in which the transportation is provided, unless that activity is focused on a group of
30 individuals which does not include the employee (or a similarly situated employee of an employer), or occurs to a significant degree only in a location within the geographic area where the employee does not travel.
   (ii) *Establishment of overall security program.* Notwithstanding anything in paragraph (m)(2)(i) of this section to the contrary, no bona fide business-oriented security concern
35 will be deemed to exist unless the employee's employer establishes to the satisfaction of the Commissioner that an overall security program has been provided with respect to the employee involved. An overall security program is deemed to exist if the requirements of paragraph (m)(2)(iv) of this section are satisfied (relating to an independent security study).
40   (iii) *Overall security program*--(A) *Defined.* An overall security program is one in which security is provided to protect the employee on a 24-hour basis. The employee must be protected while at the employee's residence, while commuting to and from the employee's workplace, and while at the employee's workplace. In addition, the employee must be protected while traveling both at home and away from home, whether for
45 business or personal purposes. An overall security program must include the provision of a bodyguard/chauffeur who is trained in evasive driving techniques; an automobile specially equipped for security; guards, metal detectors, alarms, or similar methods of controlling access to the employee's workplace and residence; and, in appropriate cases, flights on the employer's aircraft for business and personal reasons.
50   (B) *Application.* There is no overall security program when, for example, security is provided at the employee's workplace but not at the employee's residence. In addition,

Sec. 132. Certain fringe benefits

the fact that an employer requires an employee to travel on the employer's aircraft, or in an employer-provided vehicle that contains special security features, does not alone constitute an overall security program. The preceding sentence applies regardless of the existence of a corporate or other resolution requiring the employee to travel in the employer's aircraft or vehicle for personal as well as business reasons.   5

(iv) Effect of an independent security study. An overall security program with respect to an employee is deemed to exist if the conditions of this paragraph (m)(2)(iv) are satisfied:

(A) A security study is performed with respect to the employer and the employee (or a similarly situated employee of the employer) by an independent security consultant;   10

(B) The security study is based on an objective assessment of all facts and circumstances;

(C) The recommendation of the security study is that an overall security program (as defined in paragraph (m)(2)(iii) of this section) is not necessary and the recommendation is reasonable under the circumstances; and   15

(D) The employer applies the specific security recommendations contained in the security study to the employee on a consistent basis.
The value of transportation-related security provided pursuant to a security study that meets the requirements of this paragraph (m)(2)(iv) may be excluded from income if the security study conclusions are reasonable and, but for the bona fide business-oriented 20 security concerns, the employee would not have had such security. No exclusion from income applies to security provided by the employer that is not recommended in the security study. Security study conclusions may be reasonable even if, for example, it is recommended that security be limited to certain geographic areas, as in the case in which air travel security is provided only in certain foreign countries.   25

(v) *Independent security study with respect to government employees.* For purposes of establishing the existence of an overall security program under paragraph (m)(2)(ii) of this section with respect to a particular government employee, a security study conducted by the government employer (including an agency or instrumentality thereof) will be treated as a security study pursuant to paragraph (m)(2)(iv) of this section if, in lieu of the 30 conditions of paragraphs (m)(2)(iv)(A) through (D) of this section, the following conditions are satisfied:

(A) The security study is conducted by a person expressly designated by the government employer as having the responsibility and independent authority to determine both the need for employer-provided security and the appropriate protective 35 services in response to that determination;

(B) The security study is conducted in accordance with written internal procedures that require an independent and objective assessment of the facts and circumstances, such as the nature of the threat to the employee, the appropriate security response to that threat, an estimate of the length of time protective services will be necessary, and the 40 extent to which employer-provided transportation may be necessary during the period of protection;

(C) With respect to employer-provided transportation, the security study evaluates the extent to which personal use, including commuting, by the employee and the employee's spouse and dependents may be necessary during the period of protection and makes a 45 recommendation as to what would be considered reasonable personal use during that period; and

(D) The employer applies the specific security recommendations contained in the study to the employee on a consistent basis.

(3) *Application of security rules to spouses and dependents--(i) In general.* If a bona 50 fide business-oriented security concern exists with respect to an employee (because, for

Sec. 132.   Certain fringe benefits

example, threats are made on the life of an employee), the bona fide business-oriented security concern is deemed to exist with respect to the employee's spouse and dependents to the extent provided in this paragraph (m)(3).

(ii) *Certain transportation.* If a working condition fringe exclusion is available under this
5 paragraph (m) for transportation in a vehicle or aircraft provided for a bona fide business-oriented security concern with respect to an employee, the requirements of this paragraph (m) are deemed to be satisfied with respect to transportation in the same vehicle or aircraft provided at the same time to the employee's spouse and dependent children.

10 (iii) *Other.* Except as provided in paragraph (m)(3)(ii) of this section, a bona fide business oriented security concern is deemed to exist for the spouse and dependent children of the employer only if the requirements of paragraph (m)(2) (iii) or (iv) of this section are applied independently to such spouse and dependent children.

(iv) *Spouses and dependents of government employees.* The security rules of this
15 paragraph (m)(3) apply to the spouse and dependents of a government employee. However, the value of local vehicle transportation provided to the government employee's spouse and dependents for personal purposes, other than commuting, during the period that a bona fide business-oriented security concern exists with respect to the government employee will not be included in the government employee's gross income if the personal
20 use is determined to be reasonable and necessary by the security study described in paragraph (m)(2)(v) of this section.

(4) *Working condition safe harbor for travel on employer-provided aircraft.* Under the safe harbor rule of this paragraph (m)(4), if, for a bona fide business-oriented security concern, the employer requires that an employee travel on an employer-provided aircraft
25 for a personal trip, the employer and the employee may exclude from the employee's gross income, as a working condition fringe, the excess value of the aircraft trip over the safe harbor airfare without having to show what method of transportation the employee would have flown but for the bona fide business-oriented security concern. For purposes of the safe harbor rule of this paragraph (m)(4), the value of the safe harbor airfare is
30 determined under the non-commercial flight valuation rule of § 1.61-21(g) (regardless of whether the employer or employee elects to use such valuation rule) by multiplying an aircraft multiple of 200-percent by the applicable cents-per-mile rates and the number of miles in the flight and then adding the applicable terminal charge. The value of the safe harbor airfare determined under this paragraph (m)(4) must be included in the
35 employee's income (to the extent not reimbursed by the employee) regardless of whether the employee or the employer uses the special valuation rule of § 1.61-21(g). The excess of the value of the aircraft trip over this amount may be excluded from gross income as a working condition fringe. If, for a bona fide business-oriented security concern, the employer requires that an employee's spouse and dependents travel on an employer-
40 provided aircraft for a personal trip, the special rule of this paragraph (m)(4) is available to exclude the excess value of the aircraft trips over the safe harbor airfares.

(5) *Bodyguard/chauffeur provided for a bona fide business-oriented security concern.* If an employer provides an employee with vehicle transportation and a bodyguard/chauffeur for a bona fide business-oriented security concern, and but for the
45 bona fide business-oriented security concern the employee would not have had a bodyguard or a chauffeur, then the entire value of the services of the bodyguard/chauffeur is excludable from gross income as a working condition fringe. For purposes of this section, a bodyguard/chauffeur must be trained in evasive driving techniques. An individual who performs services as a driver for an employee is not a
50 bodyguard/chauffeur if the individual is not trained in evasive driving techniques. Thus, no part of the value of the services of such an individual is excludable from gross income

Sec. 132.   Certain fringe benefits

under this paragraph (m)(5). (See paragraph (b)(3) of this section for rules relating to the determination of the working condition fringe exclusion for chauffeur services.)

(6) *Special valuation rule for government employees.* If transportation is provided to a government employee for commuting during the period that a bona fide business-oriented security concern under § 1.132-5(m) exists, the commuting use may be valued by reference to the values set forth in § 1.61-21(e)(1)(i) or (f)(3) (vehicle cents-per-mile or commuting valuation of $1.50 per one-way commute, respectively) without regard to the additional requirements contained in § 1.61-21(e) or (f) and is deemed to have met the requirements of § 1.61-21(c). 5

(7) *Government employer and employee defined.* For purposes of this paragraph (m), ``government employer'' includes any Federal, State, or local government unit, and any agency or instrumentality thereof. A ``government employee'' is any individual who is employed by the government employer. 5

(8) *Examples.* The provisions of this paragraph (m) may be illustrated by the following examples: 5

Example (1). Assume that in response to several death threats on the life of A, the president of X a multinational company, X establishes an overall security program for A, including an alarm system at A's home and guards at A's workplace, the use of a vehicle that is specially equipped with alarms, bulletproof glass, and armor plating, and a bodyguard/chauffeur. Assume further that A is driven for both personal and business reasons in the vehicle. Also, assume that but for the bona fide business-oriented security concerns, no part of the overall security program would have been provided to A. With respect to the transportation provided for security reasons, A may exclude as a working condition fringe the value of the special security features of the vehicle and the value attributable to the bodyguard/chauffeur. Thus, if the value of the specially equipped vehicle is $40,000, and the value of the vehicle without the security features is $25,000, A may determine A's inclusion in income attributable to the vehicle as if the vehicle were worth $25,000. A must include in income the value of the availability of the vehicle for personal use. 5 10 15

Example (2). Assume that B is the chief executive officer of Y, a multinational corporation. Assume further that there have been kidnapping attempts and other terrorist activities in the foreign countries in which B performs services and that at least some of such activities have been directed against B or similarly situated employees. In response to these activities, Y provides B with an overall security program, including an alarm system at B's home and bodyguards at B's workplace, a bodyguard/chauffeur, and a vehicle specially designed for security during B's overseas travels. In addition, assume that Y requires B to travel in Y's airplane for business and personal trips taken to, from, and within these foreign countries. Also, assume that but for bona fide business-oriented security concerns, no part of the overall security program would have been provided to B. B may exclude as a working condition fringe the value of the special security features of the automobile and the value attributable to the bodyguards and the bodyguard/chauffeur. B may also exclude the excess, if any, of the value of the flights over the amount A would have paid for the same mode of transportation but for the security concerns. As an alternative to the preceding sentence, B may use the working condition safe harbor described in paragraph (m)(4) of this section and exclude as a working condition fringe the excess, if any, of the value of personal flights in the Y airplane over the safe harbor airfare determined under the method described in paragraph (m)(4) of this section. If this alternative is used, B must include in income the value of the availability of the vehicle for personal use and the value of the safe harbor. 10 15 20 25

Example (3). Assume the same facts as in example (2) except that Y also requires B to travel in Y's airplane within the United States, and provides B with a chauffeur-driven

Sec. 132. Certain fringe benefits

limousine for business and personal travel in the United States. Assume further that Y also requires B's spouse and dependents to travel in Y's airplane for personal flights in the United States. If no bona fide business-oriented security concern exists with respect to travel in the United States, B may not exclude from income any portion of the value of
5 the availability of the chauffeur or limousine for personal use in the United States. Thus, B must include in income the value of the availability of the vehicle and chauffeur for personal use. In addition, B may not exclude any portion of the value attributable to personal flights by B or B's spouse and dependents on Y's airplane. Thus, B must include in income the value attributable to the personal use of Y's airplane. See § 1.61-21 for
10 rules relating to the valuation of an employer-provided vehicle and chauffeur, and personal flights on employer-provided airplanes.

Example (4). Assume that company Z retains an independent security consultant to perform a security study with respect to its chief executive officer. Assume further that, based on an objective assessment of the facts and circumstances, the security
5 consultant reasonably recommends that 24-hour protection is not necessary but that the employee be provided security at his workplace and for ground transportation, but not for air transportation. If company Z follows the recommendations on a consistent basis, an overall security program will be deemed to exist with respect to the workplace and ground transportation security only.

Example (5). Assume the same facts as in example (4) except that company Z only
5 provides the employee security while commuting to and from work, but not for any other ground transportation. Because the recommendations of the independent security study are not applied on a consistent basis, an overall security program will not be deemed to exist. Thus, the value of commuting to and from work is not excludable from income. However, the value of a bodyguard with professional security training who does not
10 provide chauffeur or other personal services to the employee or any member of the employee's family may be excludable as a working condition fringe if such expense would be otherwise allowable as a deduction by the employee under section 162 or 167.

5 *Example (6)*. J is a United States District Judge. At the beginning of a 3-month criminal trial in J's court, a member of J's family receives death threats. M, the division (within government agency W) responsible for evaluating threats and providing protective services to the Federal judiciary, directs its threat analysis unit to conduct a security study with respect to J and J's family. The study is conducted pursuant to internal written
10 procedures that require an independent and objective assessment of any threats to members of the Federal judiciary and their families, a statement of the requisite security response, if any, to a particular threat (including the form of transportation to be furnished to the employee as part of the security program), and a description of the circumstances under which local transportation for the employee and the employee's spouse and
15 dependents may be necessary for personal reasons during the time protective services are provided. M's study concludes that a bona fide business-oriented security concern exists with respect to J and J's family and determines that 24-hour protection of J and J's family is not necessary, but that protection is necessary during the course of the criminal trial whenever J or J's family is away from home. Consistent with that recommendation, J
20 is transported every day in a government vehicle for both personal and business reasons and is accompanied by two bodyguard/chauffeurs who have been trained in evasive driving techniques. In addition, J's spouse is driven to and from work and J's children are driven to and from school and occasional school activities. Shortly after the trial is concluded, M's threat analysis unit determines that J and J's family no longer need
25 special protection because the danger posed by the threat no longer exists and, accordingly, vehicle transportation is no longer provided. Because the security study conducted by M complies with the conditions of § 1.132-5(m)(2)(v), M has satisfied the

Sec. 132.   Certain fringe benefits

requirement for an independent security study and an overall security program with respect to J is deemed to exist. Thus, with respect to the transportation provided for security concerns, J may exclude as a working condition fringe the value of any special security features of the government vehicle and the value attributable to the two bodyguard/chauffeurs. See Example (1) of this paragraph (m)(8). The value of vehicle transportation provided to J and J's family for personal reasons, other than commuting, may also be excluded during the period of protection, because its provision was consistent with the recommendation of the security study.

Example (7). Assume the same facts as in Example (6) and that J's one-way commute between home and work is 10 miles. Under paragraph (m)(6) of this section, the Federal Government may value transportation provided to J for commuting purposes pursuant to the value set forth in either the vehicle cents-per-mile rule of § 1.61-21(e) or the commuting valuation rule of § 1.61-21(f). Because the commuting valuation rule yields the least amount of taxable income to J under the circumstances, W values the transportation provided to J for commuting at $1.50 per one-way commute, even though J is a control employee within the meaning of § 1.61-21(f)(6).

(n) *Product testing*--(1) *In general*. The fair market value of the use of consumer goods, which are manufactured for sale to nonemployees, for product testing and evaluation by an employee of the manufacturer outside the employer's workplace, is excludible from gross income as a working condition fringe if--

(i) Consumer testing and evaluation of the product is an ordinary and necessary business expense of the employer;

(ii) Business reasons necessitate that the testing and evaluation of the product be performed off the employer's business premises by employees (i.e., the testing and evaluation cannot be carried out adequately in the employer's office or in laboratory testing facilities);

(iii) The product is furnished to the employee for purposes of testing and evaluation;

(iv) The product is made available to the employee for no longer than necessary to test and evaluate its performance and (to the extent not exhausted) must be returned to the employer at completion of the testing and evaluation period;

(v) The employer imposes limits on the employee's use of the product that significantly reduce the value of any personal benefit to the employee; and

(vi) The employee must submit detailed reports to the employer on the testing and evaluation. The length of the testing and evaluation period must be reasonable in relation to the product being tested.

(2) *Employer-imposed limits*. The requirement of paragraph (n)(1)(v) of this section is satisfied if--

(i) The employer places limits on the employee's ability to select among different models or varieties of the consumer product that is furnished for testing and evaluation purposes; and

(ii) The employer generally prohibits use of the product by persons other than the employee and, in appropriate cases, requires the employee, to purchase or lease at the employee's own expense the same type of product as that being tested (so that personal use by the employee's family will be limited). In addition, any charge by the employer for the personal use by an employee of a product being tested shall be taken into account in determining whether the requirement of paragraph (n)(1)(v) of this section is satisfied.

(3) *Discriminating classifications*. If an employer furnishes products under a testing and evaluation program only, or presumably, to certain classes of employees (such as highly compensated employees, as defined in § 1.132-8(g)), this fact may be relevant when determining whether the products are furnished for testing and evaluation purposes

321

or for compensation purposes, unless the employer can show a business reason for the classification of employees to whom the products are furnished (e.g., that automobiles are furnished for testing and evaluation by an automobile manufacturer to its design engineers and supervisory mechanics).

(4) Factors that negate the existence of a product testing program. If an employer fails to tabulate and examine the results of the detailed reports submitted by employees within a reasonable period of time after expiration of the testing period, the program will not be considered a product testing program for purposes of the exclusion of this paragraph (n). Existence of one or more of the following factors may also establish that the program is not a bona fide product testing program for purposes of the exclusion of this paragraph (n):

(i) The program is in essence a leasing program under which employees lease the consumer goods from the employer for a fee;

(ii) The nature of the product and other considerations are insufficient to justify the testing program; or

(iii) The expense of the program outweighs the benefits to be gained from testing and evaluation.

(5) Failure to meet the requirements of this paragraph (n). The fair market value of the use of property for product testing and evaluation by an employee outside the employee's workplace, under a product testing program that does not meet all of the requirements of this paragraph (n), is not excludable from gross income as a working condition fringe under this paragraph (n).

(6) Example. The rules of this paragraph (n) may be illustrated by the following example:

Example. Assume that an employer that manufactures automobiles establishes a product testing program under which 50 of its 5,000 employees test and evaluate the automobiles for 30 days. Assume further that the 50 employees represent a fair cross-section of all of the employees of the employer, such employees submit detailed reports to the employer on the testing and evaluation, the employer tabulates and examines the test results within a reasonable time, and the use of the automobiles is restricted to the employees. If the employer imposes the limits described in paragraph (n)(2) of this section, the employees may exclude the value of the use of the automobile during the testing and evaluation period.

k(o) Qualified automobile demonstration use--(1) In general. The value of qualified automobile demonstration use is excludable from gross income as a working condition fringe. ``Qualified automobile demonstration use" is any use of a demonstration automobile by a full-time automobile salesman in the sales area in which the automobile dealer's sales office is located if--

(i) Such use is provided primarily to facilitate the salesman's performance of services for the employer; and

(ii) There are substantial restrictions on the personal use of the automobile by the salesman.

(2) Full-time automobile salesman--(i) Defined. The term ``full-time automobile salesman" means any individual who--

(A) Is employed by an automobile dealer;

(B) Customarily spends at least half of a normal business day performing the functions of a floor salesperson or sales manager;

(C) Directly engages in substantial promotion and negotiation of sales to customers;

(D) Customarily works a number of hours considered full-time in the industry (but at a rate not less than 1,000 hours per year); and

(E) Derives at least 25 percent of his or her gross income from the automobile

Sec. 132. Certain fringe benefits

dealership directly as a result of the activities described in paragraphs (o)(2)(i)(B) and (C) of this section.

For purposes of paragraph (o)(2)(i) (E) of this section, income is not considered to be derived directly as a result of activities described in paragraphs (o)(2)(i)(B) and (C) of this section to the extent that the income is attributable to an individual's ownership interest in the dealership. An individual will not be considered to engage in direct sales activities if the individual's sales-related activities are substantially limited to review of sales price offers from customers. An individual, such as the general manager of an automobile dealership, who receives a sales commission on the sale of an automobile is not a full-time automobile salesman unless the requirements of this paragraph (o)(2)(i) are met. The exclusion provided in this paragraph (o) is available to an individual who meets the definition of this paragraph (o)(2)(i) whether the individual performs services in addition to those described in this paragraph (o)(2)(i). For example, an individual who is an owner of the automobile dealership but who otherwise meets the requirements of this paragraph (o)(2)(i) may exclude from gross income the value of qualified automobile demonstration use. However, the exclusion of this paragraph (o) is not available to owners of large automobile dealerships who do not customarily engage in significant sales activities.

(ii) *Use by an individual other than a full-time automobile salesman.* Personal use of a demonstration automobile by an individual other than a full-time automobile salesman is not treated as a working condition fringe. Therefore, any personal use, including commuting use, of a demonstration automobile by a part-time salesman, automobile mechanic, or other individual who is not a full-time automobile salesman is not ``qualified automobile demonstration use'' and thus not excludable from gross income. This is the case whether or not the personal use is within the sales area (as defined in paragraph (o) (5) of this section).

(3) *Demonstration automobile.* The exclusion provided in this paragraph (o) applies only to qualified use of a demonstration automobile. A demonstration automobile is an automobile that is--

(i) Currently in the inventory of the automobile dealership; and

(ii) Available for test drives by customers during the normal business hours of the employee.

(4) Substantial restrictions on personal use. Substantial restrictions on the personal use of a demonstration automobile exist when all of the following conditions are satisfied:

(i) Use by individuals other than the full-time automobile salesmen (e.g., the salesman's family) is prohibited;

(ii) Use for personal vacation trips is prohibited;

(iii) The storage of personal possessions in the automobile is prohibited; and

(iv) The total use by mileage of the automobile by the salesman outside the salesman's normal working hours is limited.

(5) *Sales area--*(i) *In general.* Qualified automobile demonstration use consists of use in the sales area in which the automobile dealer's sales office is located. The sales area is the geographic area surrounding the automobile dealer's sales office from which the office regularly derives customers.

(ii) *Sales area safe harbor.* With respect to a particular full-time salesman, the automobile dealer's sales area may be treated as the area within a radius of the larger of--

(A) 75 miles or

(B) The one-way commuting distance (in miles) of the particular salesman from the dealer's sales office.

(6) *Applicability of substantiation requirements of sections 162 and 274(d).* Notwithstanding anything in this section to the contrary, the value of the use of a

Sec. 132. Certain fringe benefits

demonstration automobile may not be excluded from gross income as a working condition fringe, by either the employer or the employee, unless, with respect to the restrictions of paragraph (o)(4) of this section, the substantiation requirements of section 274(d) and the regulations thereunder are satisfied. See § 1.132-5(c) for general and safe harbor rules relating to the applicability of the substantiation requirements of section 274(d).

(7) *Special valuation rules.* See § 1.61-21(d)(6)(ii) for special rules that may be used to value the availability of demonstration automobiles.

(p) *Parking--*(1) *In general.* The value of parking provided to an employee on or near the business premises of the employer is excludable from gross income as a working condition fringe under the special rule of this paragraph (p). If the rules of this paragraph (p) are satisfied, the value of parking is excludable from gross income whether the amount paid by the employee for parking would be deductible under section 162. The working condition fringe exclusion applies whether the employer owns or rents the parking facility or parking space.

(2) *Reimbursement of parking expenses.* A reimbursement to the employee of the ordinary and necessary expenses of renting a parking space on or near the business premises of the employer is excludable from gross income as a working condition fringe, if, but for the parking expense, the employee would not have been entitled to receive and retain such amount from the employer. If, however an employee is entitled to retain a general transportation allowance or a similar benefit whether or not the employee has parking expenses, no portion of that allowance is excludable from gross income under this paragraph (p) even if it is used for parking expenses.

(3) *Parking on residential property.* With respect to an employee, this paragraph (p) does not apply to any parking facility or space located on property owned or leased by the employee for residential purposes.

(4) *Dates of applicability.* This paragraph (p) applies to benefits provided before January 1, 1993. For benefits provided after December 31, 1992, see § 1.132-9.

(q) *Nonapplicability of nondiscrimination rules.* Except to the extent provided in paragraph (n)(3) of this section (relating to discriminating classifications of a product testing program), the nondiscrimination rules of section 132 (h)(1) and § 1.132-8 do not apply in determining the amount, if any, of a working condition fringe.

(r) *Volunteers--*(1) *In general.* Solely for purposes of section 132(d) and paragraph (a) (1) of this section, a bona fide volunteer (including a director or officer) who performs services for an organization exempt from tax under section 501(a), or for a government employer (as defined in paragraph (m)(7) of this section), is deemed to have a profit motive under section 162.

(2) *Limit on application of this paragraph.* This paragraph (r) shall not be used to support treatment of the bona fide volunteer as having a profit motive for purposes of any provision of the Internal Revenue Code of 1986 (Code) other than section 132(d). Nothing in this paragraph (r) shall be interpreted as determining the employment status of a bona fide volunteer for purposes of any section of the Code other than section 132(d).

(3) *Definitions--*(i) *Bona fide volunteer.* For purposes of this paragraph (r), an individual is considered a ``bona fide volunteer'' if the individual does not have a profit motive for purposes of section 162. For example, an individual is considered a ``bona fide volunteer'' if the total value of the benefits provided with respect to the volunteer services is substantially less than the total value of the volunteer services the individual provides to an exempt organization or government employer.

(ii) *Liability insurance coverage for a bona fide volunteer.* For purposes of this paragraph (r), the receipt of liability insurance coverage by a volunteer, or an exempt organization or government employer's undertaking to indemnify the volunteer for liability,

324

Sec. 132. Certain fringe benefits

does not by itself confer a profit motive on the volunteer, provided the insurance coverage or indemnification relates to acts performed by the volunteer in the discharge of duties, or the performance of services, on behalf of the exempt organization or government employer.

(4) *Example.* The following example illustrates the provisions of paragraph (r) of this section.

Example. A is a manager and full-time employee of P, a tax-exempt organization described in section 501(c)(3). B is a member of P's board of directors. Other than $25 to defray expenses for attending board meetings, B receives no compensation for serving 5 as a director and does not have a profit motive. Therefore, B is a bona fide volunteer by application of paragraph (r)(3)(i) of this section and is deemed to have a profit motive under paragraph (r)(1) of this section for purposes of section 132(d). In order to provide liability insurance coverage, P purchases a policy that covers actions arising from A's and B's activities performed as part of their duties to P. The value of the policy and payments 10 made to or on behalf of A under the policy are excludable for A's gross income as a working condition fringe, because A has a profit motive under section 162 and would be able to deduct payments for liability insurance coverage had he paid for it himself. The receipt of liability insurance coverage by B does not confer a profit motive on B by application of paragraph (r)(3)(ii) of this section. Thus, the value of the policy and 15 payments made to or on behalf of B under the policy are excludable from B's income as a working condition fringe. For the year in which the liability insurance coverage is provided to A and B, P may exclude the value of the benefit on the Form W-2 it issues to A or on any Form 1099 it might otherwise issue to B.

(s) *Application of section 274(a)(3)*--(1) *In general.* If an employer's deduction under section 162(a) for dues paid or incurred for membership in any club organized for 5 business, pleasure, recreation, or other social purpose is disallowed by section 274(a)(3), the amount, if any, of an employee's working condition fringe benefit relating to an employer-provided membership in the club is determined without regard to the application of section 274(a) to the employee. To be excludible as a working condition fringe benefit, however, the amount must otherwise qualify for deduction by the employee 10 under section 162(a). If an employer treats the amount paid or incurred for membership in any club organized for business, pleasure, recreation, or other social purpose as compensation under section 274(e)(2), then the expense is deductible by the employer as compensation and no amount may be excluded from the employee's gross income as a working condition fringe benefit. See § 1.274-2(f)(2)(iii)(A). 15

(2) *Treatment of tax-exempt employers.* In the case of an employer exempt from 5 taxation under subtitle A of the Internal Revenue Code, any reference in this paragraph (s) to a deduction disallowed by section 274(a)(3) shall be treated as a reference to the amount which would be disallowed as a deduction by section 274(a)(3) to the employer if the employer were not exempt from taxation under subtitle A of the Internal Revenue Code. 10

Example 1. Assume that Company X provides Employee B with a country club membership for which it paid $20,000. B substantiates, within the meaning of paragraph (c) of this section, that the club was used 40 percent for business purposes. The business use of the club (40 percent) may be considered a working condition fringe benefit, notwithstanding that the employer's deduction for the dues allocable to the business use 10 is disallowed by section 274(a)(3), if X does not treat the club membership as compensation under section 274(e)(2). Thus, B may exclude from gross income $8,000 (40 percent of the club dues, which reflects B's business use). X must report $12,000 as wages subject to withholding and payment of employment taxes (60 percent of the value of the club dues, which reflects B's personal use). B must include $12,000 in gross 15

325

income. X may deduct as compensation the amount it paid for the club dues which reflects B's personal use provided the amount satisfies the other requirements for a salary or compensation deduction under section 162.

Example 2. Assume the same facts as Example 1 except that Company X treats the $20,000 as compensation to B under section 274(e)(2). No portion of the $20,000 will be considered a working condition fringe benefit because the section 274(a)(3) disallowance
5 will apply to B. Therefore, B must include $20,000 in gross income.

(t) *Application of section 274(m)(3)*--(1) *In general.* If an employer's deduction under section 162(a) for amounts paid or incurred for the travel expenses of a spouse,
5 dependent, or other individual accompanying an employee is disallowed by section 274(m)(3), the amount, if any, of the employee's working condition fringe benefit relating to the employer-provided travel is determined without regard to the application of section 274(m)(3). To be excludible as a working condition fringe benefit, however, the amount must otherwise qualify for deduction by the employee under section 162(a). The amount
10 will qualify for deduction and for exclusion as a working condition fringe benefit if it can be adequately shown that the spouse's, dependent's, or other accompanying individual's presence on the employee's business trip has a bona fide business purpose and if the employee substantiates the travel within the meaning of paragraph (c) of this section. If the travel does not qualify as a working condition fringe benefit, the employee must
15 include in gross income as a fringe benefit the value of the employer's payment of travel expenses with respect to a spouse, dependent, or other individual accompanying the employee on business travel. See §§ 1.61-21(a)(4) and 1.162-2(c). If an employer treats as compensation under section 274(e)(2) the amount paid or incurred for the travel expenses of a spouse, dependent, or other individual accompanying an employee, then
20 the expense is deductible by the employer as compensation and no amount may be excluded from the employee's gross income as a working condition fringe benefit. See § 1.274-2(f)(2)(iii)(A).

(2) *Treatment of tax-exempt employers.* In the case of an employer exempt from
5 taxation under subtitle A of the Internal Revenue Code, any reference in this paragraph (t) to a deduction disallowed by section 274(m)(3) shall be treated as a reference to the amount which would be disallowed as a deduction by section 274(m)(3) to the employer if the employer were not exempt from taxation under subtitle A of the Internal Revenue Code.

5

Reg. § 1.132-6   De minimis fringes.

(a) *In general.* Gross income does not include the value of a de minimis fringe provided to an employee. The term ``de minimis fringe" means any property or service the value of which is (after taking into account the frequency with which similar fringes
10 are provided by the employer to the employer's employees) so small as to make accounting for it unreasonable or administratively impracticable.

(b) *Frequency*--(1) *Employee-measured frequency.* Generally, the frequency with which similar fringes are provided by the employer to the employer's employees is
10 determined by reference to the frequency with which the employer provides the fringes to each individual employee. For example, if an employer provides a free meal in kind to one employee on a daily basis, but not to any other employee, the value of the meals is not de minimis with respect to that one employee even though with respect to the employer's entire workforce the meals are provided ``infrequently."

(2) *Employer-measured frequency.* Notwithstanding the rule of paragraph (b)(1) of this
10 section, except for purposes of applying the special rules of paragraph (d)(2) of this section, where it would be administratively difficult to determine frequency with respect to individual employees, the frequency with which similar fringes are provided by the

Sec. 132. Certain fringe benefits

employer to the employer's employees is determined by reference to the frequency with which the employer provides the fringes to the workforce as a whole. Therefore, under this rule, the frequency with which any individual employee receives such a fringe benefit is not relevant and in some circumstances, the de minimis fringe exclusion may apply with respect to a benefit even though a particular employee receives the benefit 5 frequently. For example, if an employer exercises sufficient control and imposes significant restrictions on the personal use of a company copying machine so that at least 85 percent of the use of the machine is for business purposes, any personal use of the copying machine by particular employees is considered to be a de minimis fringe.

(c) *Administrability*. Unless excluded by a provision of chapter 1 of the Internal Revenue Code of 1986 other than section 132(a)(4), the value of any fringe benefit that would not be unreasonable or administratively impracticable to account for is includible in the employee's gross income. Thus, except as provided in paragraph (d)(2) of this 5 section, the provision of any cash fringe benefit is never excludable under section 132(a) as a de minimis fringe benefit. Similarly except as otherwise provided in paragraph (d) of this section, a cash equivalent fringe benefit (such as a fringe benefit provided to an employee through the use of a gift certificate or charge or credit card) is generally not excludable under section 132(a) even if the same property or service acquired (if 10 provided in kind) would be excludable as a de minimis fringe benefit. For example, the provision of cash to an employee for a theatre ticket that would itself be excludable as a de minimis fringe (see paragraph (e)(1) of this section) is not excludable as a de minimis fringe.

(d) *Special rules*--(1) *Transit passes*. A public transit pass provided at a discount to defray an employee's commuting costs may be excluded from the employee's gross income as a de minimis fringe if such discount does not exceed $21 in any month. The 5 exclusion provided in this paragraph (d)(1) also applies to the provision of tokens or fare cards that enable an individual to travel on the public transit system if the value of such tokens and fare cards in any month does not exceed by more than $21 the amount the employee paid for the tokens and fare cards for such month. Similarly, the exclusion of this paragraph (d)(1) applies to the provision of a voucher or similar instrument that is 10 exchangeable solely for tokens, fare cards, or other instruments that enable the employee to use the public transit system if the value of such vouchers and other instruments in any month does not exceed $21. The exclusion of this paragraph (d)(1) also applies to reimbursements made by an employer to an employee after December 31, 1988, to cover the cost of commuting on a public transit system, provided the 15 employee does not receive more than $21 in such reimbursements for commuting costs in any given month. The reimbursement must be made under a bona fide reimbursement arrangement. A reimbursement arrangement will be treated as bona fide if the employer establishes appropriate procedures for verifying on a periodic basis that the employee's use of public transportation for commuting is consistent with the value of the benefit 20 provided by the employer for that purpose. The amount of in-kind public transit commuting benefits and reimbursements provided during any month that are excludible under this paragraph (d)(1) is limited to $21. For months ending before July 1, 1991, the amount is $15 per month. The exclusion provided in this paragraph (d)(1) does not apply to the provision of any benefit to defray public transit expenses incurred for personal 25 travel other than commuting.

Sec. 132.   Certain fringe benefits

(2) *Occasional meal money or local transportation fare*--(i) *General rule*. Meals, meal money or local transportation fare provided to an employee is excluded as a de minimis fringe benefit if the benefit provided is reasonable and is provided in a manner that satisfies the following three conditions:

(A) *Occasional basis*. The meals, meal money or local transportation fare is provided to the employee on an occasional basis. Whether meal money or local transportation fare is provided to an employee on an occasional basis will depend upon the frequency i.e., the availability of the benefit and regularity with which the benefit is provided by the employer to the employee. Thus, meals, meal money, or local transportation fare or a combination of such benefits provided to an employee on a regular or routine basis is not provided on an occasional basis.

(B) *Overtime*. The meals, meal money or local transportation fare is provided to an employee because overtime work necessitates an extension of the employee's normal work schedule. This condition does not fail to be satisfied merely because the circumstances giving rise to the need for overtime work are reasonably foreseeable.

(C) *Meal money*. In the case of a meal or meal money, the meal or meal money is provided to enable the employee to work overtime. Thus, for example, meals provided on the employer's premises that are consumed during the period that the employee works overtime or meal money provided for meals consumed during such period satisfy this condition. In no event shall meal money or local transportation fare calculated on the basis of the number of hours worked (e.g., $1.00 per hour for each hour over eight hours) be considered a de minimis fringe benefit.

(ii) *Applicability of other exclusions for certain meals and for transportation provided for security concerns*. The value of meals furnished to an employee, an employee's spouse, or any of the employee's dependents by or on behalf of the employee's employer for the convenience of the employer is excluded from the employee's gross income if the meals are furnished on the business premises of the employer (see section 119). (For purposes of the exclusion under section 119, the definitions of an employee under § 1.132-1(b) do not apply.) If, for a bona fide business-oriented security concern, an employer provides an employee vehicle transportation that is specially designed for security (for example, the vehicle is equipped with bulletproof glass and armor plating), and the conditions of § 1.132-5(m) are satisfied, the value of the special security design is excludable from gross income as a working condition fringe if the employee would not have had such special security design but for the bona fide business-oriented security concern.

(iii) *Special rule for employer-provided transportation provided in certain circumstances*. (A) *Partial exclusion of value*. If an employer provides transportation (such as taxi fare to an employee for use in commuting to and/or from work because or unusual circumstances and because, based on the facts and circumstances, it is unsafe for the employee to use other available means of transportation, the excess of the value of each one-way trip over $1.50 per one-way commute is excluded from gross income. The rule of this paragraph (d)(2)(iii) is not available to a control employee as defined in § 1.61-21(f) (5) and (6).

(B) ``*Unusual circumstances*''. Unusual circumstances are determined with respect to the employee receiving the transportation and are based on all facts and circumstances. An example of unusual circumstances would be when an employee is asked to work outside of his normal work hours (such as being called to the workplace at 1:00 am when the employee normally works from 8:00 am to 4:00 pm). Another example of unusual circumstances is a temporary change in the employee's work schedule (such as working from 12 midnight to 8:00 am rather than from 8:00 am to 4:00 pm for a two-week period).

(C) "*Unsafe conditions*". Factors indicating whether it is unsafe for an employee to use

Sec. 132. Certain fringe benefits

other available means of transportation are the history of crime in the geographic area surrounding the employee's workplace or residence and the time of day during which the employee must commute.

(3) *Use of special rules or examples to establish a general rule.* The special rules provided in this paragraph (d) or examples provided in paragraph (e) of this section may not be used to establish any general rule permitting exclusion as a de minimis fringe. For example, the fact that $252 (i.e., $21 per month for 12 months) worth of public transit 5 passes can be excluded from gross income as a de minimis fringe in 1992 does not mean that any fringe benefit with a value equal to or less than $252 may be excluded as a de minimis fringe. As another example, the fact that the commuting use of an employer-provided vehicle more than one day a month is an example of a benefit not excludable as a de minimis fringe (see paragraph (e)(2) of this section) does not mean that the 10 commuting use of a vehicle up to 12 times per year is excludable from gross income as a de minimis fringe.

(4) *Benefits exceeding value and frequency limits.* If a benefit provided to an employee is not de minimis because either the value or frequency exceeds a limit provided in this paragraph (d), no amount of the benefit is considered to be a de minimis 5 fringe. For example, if, in 1992, an employer provides a $50 monthly public transit pass, the entire $50 must be included in income, not just the excess value over $21.

(e) *Examples--(1) Benefits excludable from income.* Examples of de minimis fringe benefits are occasional typing of personal letters by a company secretary; occasional 5 personal use of an employer's copying machine, provided that the employer exercises sufficient control and imposes significant restrictions on the personal use of the machine so that at least 85 percent of the use of the machine is for business purposes; occasional cocktail parties, group meals, or picnics for employees and their guests; traditional birthday or holiday gifts of property (not cash) with a low fair market value; occasional 10 theater or sporting event tickets; coffee, doughnuts, and soft drinks; local telephone calls; and flowers, fruit, books, or similar property provided to employees under special circumstances (e.g., on account of illness, outstanding performance, or family crisis).

(2) *Benefits not excludable as de minimis fringes.* Examples of fringe benefits that are 5 not excludable from gross income as de minimis fringes are: season tickets to sporting or theatrical events; the commuting use of an employer-provided automobile or other vehicle more than one day a month; membership in a private country club or athletic facility, regardless of the frequency with which the employee uses the facility; employer-provided group-term life insurance on the life of the spouse or child of an employee; and 10 use of employer-owned or leased facilities (such as an apartment, hunting lodge, boat, etc.) for a weekend. Some amount of the value of certain of these fringe benefits may be excluded from income under other statutory provisions, such as the exclusion for working condition fringes. See § 1.132-5.

(f) *Nonapplicability of nondiscrimination rules.* Except to the extent provided in § 1.132-7, the nondiscrimination rules of section 132(h)(1) and § 1.132-8 do not apply in determining the amount, if any, of a de minimis fringe. Thus, a fringe benefit may be excludable as a de minimis fringe even if the benefit is provided exclusively to highly compensated employees of the employer.   10

Reg § 1.132-8 Fringe benefit nondiscrimination rules.

(a) *Application of nondiscrimination rules--(1) General rule.* A highly compensated employee who receives a no-additional cost service, a qualified employee discount or a 10 meal provided at an employer-operated eating facility for employees shall not be permitted to exclude such benefit from his or her income unless the benefit is available on substantially the same terms to:

Sec. 132. Certain fringe benefits

(i) All employees of the employer; or

(ii) A group of employees of the employer which is defined under a reasonable classification set up by the employer that does not discriminate in favor of highly compensated employees. See paragraph (f) of this section for the definition of a highly
5 compensated employee.

(2) *Consequences of discrimination*--(i) *In general.* If an employer maintains more than one fringe benefit program, i.e., either different fringe benefits being provided to the same group of employees, or different classifications of employees or the same fringe benefit being provided to two or more classifications of employees, the nondiscrimination
10 requirements of section 132 will generally be applied separately to each such program. Thus, a determination that one fringe benefit program discriminates in favor of highly compensated employees generally will not cause other fringe benefit programs covering the same highly compensated employees to be treated as discriminatory. If the fringe benefits provided to a highly compensated individual do not satisfy the nondiscrimination
15 rules provided in this section, such individual shall be unable to exclude from gross income any portion of the benefit. For example, if an employer offers a 20 percent discount (which otherwise satisfies the requirements for a qualified employee discount) to all non-highly compensated employees and a 35 percent discount to all highly compensated employees, the entire value of the 35 percent discount (not just the excess
20 over 20 percent) is includible in the gross income and wages of the highly compensated employees who make purchases at a discount.

(ii) *Exception*--(A) *Related fringe benefit programs.* If one of a group of fringe benefit programs discriminates in favor of highly compensated employees, no related fringe benefit provided to such highly compensated employees under any other fringe benefit
25 program may be excluded from the gross income of such highly compensated employees. For example, assume a department store provides a 20 percent merchandise discount to all employees under one fringe benefit program. Assume further that under a second fringe benefit program, the department store provides an additional 15 percent merchandise discount to a group of employees defined under a classification which
30 discriminates in favor of highly compensated employees. Because the second fringe benefit program is discriminatory, the 15 percent merchandise discount provided to the highly compensated employees is not a qualified employee discount. In addition, because the 20 percent merchandise discount provided under the first fringe benefit program is related to the fringe benefit provided under the second fringe benefit program,
35 the 20 percent merchandise discount provided the highly compensated employees is not a qualified employee discount. Thus, the entire 35 percent merchandise discount provided to the highly compensated employees is includible in such employees' gross incomes.

(B) *Employer operated eating facilities for employees.* For purposes of paragraph (a)
40 (2)(ii)(A) of this section, meals at different employer-operated eating facilities for employees are not related fringe benefits, so that a highly compensated employee may exclude from gross income the value of a meal at a nondiscriminatory facility even though any meals provided to him or her at a discriminatory facility cannot be excluded.

(3) *Scope of the nondiscrimination rules provided in this section.* The nondiscrimination
45 rules provided in this section apply only to fringe benefits provided pursuant to section 132 (a)(1), (a)(2), and (e)(2). These rules have no application to any other employee benefit that may be subject to nondiscrimination requirements under any other section of the Code.

(b) *Aggregation of employees*--(1) *Section 132(a)(1) and (2).* For purposes of
50 determining whether the exclusions for no-additional-cost services and qualified employee discounts are available to highly compensated employees, the

Sec. 132. Certain fringe benefits

nondiscrimination rules of this section are applied by aggregating the employees of all related employers (as defined in § 1.132-1(c)), except that employees in different lines of business (as defined in § 1.132-4) are not to be aggregated. Thus, in general, for purposes of this section, the term ``employees of the employer" refers to all employees of the employer and any other entity that is a member of a group described in sections 5 414(b), (c), (m), or (o) and that performs services within the same line of business as the employer which provides the particular fringe benefit. Employees in different lines of business will be aggregated, however, if the line of business limitation has been relaxed pursuant to paragraphs (b) through (g) of § 1.132-4.

(2) *Section 132 (e) (2).* For purposes of determining whether the exclusions for meals 10 provided at employer-operated eating facilities are available to highly compensated, the nondiscrimination rules of this section are applied by aggregating the employees of all related employers (as defined in section § 1.132-1(c)) who regularly work at or near the premises on which the eating facility is located, except that employees in different lines of business (as defined in § 1.132-4) are not to be aggregated. The nondiscrimination rules 15 of this section are applied separately to each eating facility. Each dining room or cafeteria in which meals are served is treated as a separate eating facility, regardless of whether each such dining room or cafeteria has its own kitchen or other food-preparation area.

(3) *Classes of employees who may be excluded.* For purposes of applying the nondiscrimination rules of this section to a particular fringe benefit program, there may be 20 excluded from consideration employees who may be excluded from consideration under section 89(h), as enacted by the Tax Reform Act of 1986, Pub. L. 99-514, 100 Stat. 2085 (1986) and amended by the Technical and Miscellaneous Revenue Act of 1988, Pub. L. 100-647, 102 Stat. 3342 (1988).

(c) *Availability on substantially the same terms*--(1) *General rule.* The determination of 25 whether a benefit is available on substantially the same terms shall be made upon the basis of the facts and circumstances of each situation. In general, however, if any one of the terms or conditions governing the availability of a particular benefit to one or more employees varies from any one of the terms or conditions governing the availability of a benefit made available to one or more other employees, such benefit shall not be 30 considered to be available on substantially the same terms except to the extent otherwise provided in paragraph (c)(2) of this section. For example, if a department store provides a 20 percent qualified employee discount to all of its employees on all merchandise, the substantially the same terms requirement will be satisfied. Similarly, if the discount provided to all employees is 30 percent on certain merchandise (such as apparel), and 35 20 percent on all other merchandise, the substantially the same terms requirement will be satisfied. However, if a department store provides a 20 percent qualified employee discount to all employees, but as to the employees in certain departments, the discount is available upon hire, and as to the remaining departments, the discount is only available when an employee has completed a specified term of services, the 20 percent discount is 40 not available on substantially the same terms to all of the employees of the employer. Similarly, if a greater discount is given to employees with more seniority, full-time work status, or a particular job description, such benefit (i.e., the discount) would not be available to all employees eligible for the discount on substantially the same terms, except to the extent otherwise provided in paragraph (c)(2) of this section. These 45 examples also apply to no-additional-cost-services. Thus, if an employer charges non-highly compensated employees for a no-additional-cost service and does not charge highly compensated employees (or charges highly compensated employees a lesser amount), the substantially the same terms requirement will not be satisfied.

(2) *Certain terms relating to priority.* Certain fringe benefits made available to 50 employees are available only in limited quantities that may be insufficient to meet

Sec. 132. Certain fringe benefits

employee demand. This situation may occur either because of employer policy (such as where an employer determines that only a certain number of units of a specific product will be made available to employees each year) or because of the nature of the fringe benefit (such as where an employer provides a no-additional-cost transportation service
5 that is limited to the number of seats available just before departure). Under these circumstances, an employer may find it necessary to establish some method of allocating the limited fringe benefits among the employees eligible to receive the fringe benefits. The employer may establish the priorities described below.

(i) *Priority on a first come, first served, or similar basis.* A benefit shall not fail to be
10 treated as available to a group of employees on substantially the same terms merely because the employer allocates the benefit among such employees on a ``first come, first served" or lottery basis, provided that the same notice of the terms of availability is given to all employees in the group and the terms under which the benefit is provided to employees within the group are otherwise the same with respect to all employees. For
15 purposes of the preceding sentence, a program that gives priority to employees who are the first to submit written requests for the benefit will constitute priority on a ``first come, first served" basis. Similarly, if the employer regularly engages in the practice of allocating benefits on a priority basis to employees demonstrating a critical need, such benefit shall not fail to be treated as available on substantially the same terms to all of the employees
20 with respect to whom such priority status is available as long as the determination is based upon uniform and objective criteria which have been communicated to all employees in the group of eligible employees. An example of a critical need would be priority transportation given to an employee in the event of a medical emergency involving the employee (or a member of the employee's immediate family) or a recent
25 death in the employee's immediate family. Frustrated vacation plans or forfeited deposits would not be treated as giving rise to particularly critical needs.

(ii) *Priority on the basis of seniority.* Solely for purposes of § 1.132-8, a benefit shall not fail to be treated as available to a group of employees of the employer on substantially the same terms merely because the employer allocates the benefit among
30 such employees on a seniority basis provided that:

(A) The same notice of the terms of availability is given to all employees in the group; and

(B) The average value of the benefit provided for each nonhighly compensated employee is at least 75% of that provided for each highly compensated employee. For
35 purposes of this test, the average value of the benefit provided for each nonhighly compensated (highly compensated) employee is determined by taking the sum of the fair market values of such benefit provided to all the nonhighly compensated (highly compensated) employees, determined in accordance with § 1.61-21, and then dividing that sum by the total number of nonhighly compensated (highly compensated) employees
40 of the employer. For purposes of determining the average value of the benefit provided for each employee, all employee's of the employer are counted, including those who are not eligible to receive the benefit from the employer.

(d) *Testing for discrimination--(1) Classification test.* In the event that a benefit described in section 132 (a)(1), (a)(2) or (e)(2) is not available on substantially the same
45 terms to all of the employees of the employer, no exclusion shall be available to a highly compensated employee for such benefit unless the program under which the benefit is provided satisfies the nondiscrimination standards set forth in this section. The nondiscrimination standard of this section will be satisfied only if the benefit is available on substantially the same terms to a group of employees of the employer which is
50 defined under a reasonable classification established by the employer that does not discriminate in favor of highly compensated employees. The determination of whether a

Sec. 132. Certain fringe benefits

particular classification is discriminatory will generally depend upon the facts and circumstances involved, based upon principles similar to those applied for purposes of section 410(b)(2)(A)(i) or, for years commencing prior to January 1, 1988, section 410(b)(1)(B). Thus, in general, except as otherwise provided in this section, if a benefit is available on substantially the same terms to a group of employees which, when compared with all of the other employees of the employer, constitutes a nondiscriminatory classification under section 410(b)(2)(A)(i) (or, if applicable, section 410(b)(1)(B)), it shall be deemed to be nondiscriminatory.

(2) *Classifications that are per se discriminatory.* A classification that, on its face, makes fringe benefits available principally to highly compensated employees is per se discriminatory. In addition, a classification that is based on either an amount or rate of compensation is per se discriminatory if it favors those with the higher amount or rate of compensation. On the other hand, a classification that is based on factors such as seniority, full-time vs. part-time employment, or job description is not per se discriminatory but may be discriminatory as applied to the workforce of a particular employer.

(3) *Former employees.* When determining whether a classification is discriminatory, former employees shall be tested separately from other employees of the employer. Therefore, a classification is not discriminatory solely because the employer does not make fringe benefits available to any former employee. Whether a classification of former employees discriminates in favor of highly compensated employees will depend upon the particular facts and circumstances.

(4) *Restructuring of benefits.* For purposes of testing whether a particular group of employees would constitute a discriminatory classification for purposes of this section, an employer may restructure its fringe benefit program as described in this paragraph. If a fringe benefit is provided to more than one group of employees, and one or more such groups would constitute a discriminatory classification if considered by itself, then for purposes of this section, the employer may restructure its fringe benefit program so that all or some of the members of such group may be aggregated with another group, provided that each member of the restructured group will have available to him or her the same benefit upon the same terms and conditions. For example, assume that all highly compensated employees of an employer have fewer than five years of service and all nonhighly compensated employees have over five years of service. If the employer provided a five percent discount to employees with under five years of service and a ten percent discount to employees with over five years of service, the discount program available to the highly compensated employees would not satisfy the nondiscriminatory classification test; however, as a result of the rule described in this paragraph (d)(4), the employer could structure the program to consist of a five percent discount for all employees and a five percent additional discount for nonhighly compensated employees.

(5) *Employer-operated eating facilities for employees*--(i) *General rule.* If access to an employer-operated eating facility for employees is available to a classification of employees that discriminates in favor of highly compensated employees, then the classification will not be treated as discriminating in favor of highly compensated employees unless the facility is used by one or more executive group employees more than a de minimis amount.

(ii) *Executive group employee.* For purposes of this paragraph (d)(5), an employee is an ``executive group employee" if the definition of paragraph (f)(1) of this section is satisfied. For purposes of identifying such employees, the phrase ``top one percent of the employees" is substituted for the phrase ``top ten percent of the employees" in section 414(q)(4) (relating to the definition of ``top-paid group").

(e) *Cash bonuses or rebates.* A cash bonus or rebate provided to an employee by an employer that is determined with reference to the value of employer-provided property or

333

Sec. 132. Certain fringe benefits

services purchased by the employee, is treated as an equivalent employee discount. For example, assume a department store provides a 20 percent merchandise discount to all employees under a fringe benefit program. In addition, assume that the department store provides cash bonuses to a group of employees defined under a classification which
5 discriminates in favor of highly compensated employees. Assume further that such cash bonuses equal 15 percent of the value of merchandise purchased by each employee. This arrangement is substantively identical to the example described in paragraph (e)(2) (i) of this section concerning related fringe benefit programs. Thus, both the 20 percent merchandise discount and the 15 percent cash bonus provided to the highly
10 compensated employees are includible in such employees' gross incomes.

(f) *Highly compensated employee*--(1) *Government and nongovernment employees.* A highly compensated employee of any employer is any employee who, during the year or the preceding year--

(i) Was a 5-percent owner,
15 (ii) Received compensation from the employer in excess of $75,000,

(iii) Received compensation from the employer in excess of $50,000 and was in the top-paid group of employees for such year, or

(iv) Was at any time an officer and received compensation greater than 150 percent of the amount in effect under section 415(c)(1)(A) for such year.
20 For purposes of determining whether an employee is a highly compensated employee, the rules of sections 414 (q), (s), and (t) apply.

(2) *Former employees.* A former employee shall be treated as a highly compensated employee if--

(i) The employee was a highly compensated employee when the employee separated
25 from service, or

(ii) The employee was a highly compensated employee at any time after attaining age 55.

[T.D. 8256, 54 FR 28608, July 6, 1989; T.D. 8389, 57 FR 1871, Jan 16, 1992; 57 FR
30 5982, Feb. 19, 1992; T.D. 8451, 57 FR 57669, Dec. 7, 1992; T.D. 8457, 57 FR 62196, Dec. 30, 1992; T.D. 8666, 61 FR 27006, May 30, 1996; T.D. 8933, 66 FR 2244, Jan. 11, 2001]

Sec. 134. Certain military benefits

(a) General rule. -- Gross income shall not include any qualified military benefit.
35 **(b) Qualified military benefit.** -- For purposes of this section--

(1) In general. -- The term "qualified military benefit" means any allowance or in-kind benefit (other than personal use of a vehicle) which--

(A) is received by any member or former member of the uniformed services of the United States or any dependent of such member by reason of such member's status or
40 service as a member of such uniformed services, and

(B) was excludable from gross income on September 9, 1986, under any provision of law, regulation, or administrative practice which was in effect on such date (other than a provision of this title).

Sec. 135. Income from United States savings bonds used to pay higher education tuition and fees

(a) **General rule.** -- In the case of an individual who pays qualified higher education expenses during the taxable year, no amount shall be includible in gross income by reason of the redemption during such year of any qualified United States savings bond.

(b) **Limitations.** --

(1) **Limitation where redemption proceeds exceed higher education expenses.** --   5

(A) **In general.** -- If--

(i) the aggregate proceeds of qualified United States savings bonds redeemed by the taxpayer during the taxable year exceed

(ii) the qualified higher education expenses paid by the taxpayer during such taxable year, the amount excludable from gross income under subsection (a) shall not exceed   10 the applicable fraction of the amount excludable from gross income under subsection (a) without regard to this subsection.

(B) **Applicable fraction.** -- For purposes of subparagraph (A), the term "applicable fraction" means the fraction the numerator of which is th amount described in subparagraph (A)(ii) and the denominator of which is the amount described in subparagraph (A)(i).   15

(2) **Limitation based on modified adjusted gross income.** --

(A) **In general.** -- If the modified adjusted gross income of the taxpayer for the taxable year exceeds $40,000 ($60,000 in the case of a joint return), the amount which would (but for this paragraph) be excludable from gross income under subsection (a) shall be reduced (but not below zero) by the amount which bears the same ratio to the amount which would   20 be so excludable as such excess bears to $15,000 ($30,000 in the case of a joint return).

(B) **Inflation adjustment.** -- In the case of any taxable year beginning in a calendar year after 1990, the $40,000 and $60,000 amounts contained in subparagraph (A) shall be increased by an amount equal to--

(i) such dollar amount, multiplied by   25

(ii) the cost-of-living adjustment under section 1(f)(3) for the calendar year in which the taxable year begins determined by substituting "calendar year 1989" for "calendar year 1992" in subparagraph (B) thereof.

(C) **Rounding.** -- If any amount as adjusted under subparagraph (B) is not a multiple of $50, such amount shall be rounded to the nearest multiple of $50 (or if such amount is a   30 multiple of $25, such amount shall be rounded to the next highest multiple of $50).

(d) **Special rules.** --

(1) **Adjustment for certain scholarships and veterans benefits.** -- The amount of qualified higher education expenses otherwise taken into account under subsection (a) with respect to the education of an individual shall be reduced (before the application of subsection (b)) by the   35 sum of the amounts received with respect to such individual for the taxable year as--

(A) a qualified scholarship which under section 117 is not includable in gross income,

(B) an educational assistance allowance under chapter 30, 31, 32, 34, or 35 of title 38, United States Code,

(C) a payment (other than a gift, bequest, devise, or inheritance within the meaning of   40 section 102(a)) for educational expenses, or attributable to attendance at an eligible educational institution, which is exempt from income taxation by any law of the United States, or

Sec. 135. Income from United States savings bonds used to pay higher education tuition and fees

    (D) a payment, waiver, or reimbursement of qualified higher education expenses under a qualified tuition program (within the meaning of section 529(b)).

    (2) Coordination with other higher education benefits. -- The amount of the qualified higher education expenses otherwise taken into account under subsection (a) with respect to the education of an individual shall be reduced (before the application of subsection (b)) by--

    (A) the amount of such expenses which are taken into account in determining the credit allowed to the taxpayer or any other person under section 25A with respect to such expenses; and

    (B) the amount of such expenses which are taken into account in determining the exclusions under sections 529(c)(3)(B) and 530(d)(2).

    (3) No exclusion for married individuals filing separate returns. -- If the taxpayer is a married individual (within the meaning of section 7703), this section shall apply only if the taxpayer and his spouse file a joint return for the taxable year.

Sec. 137. Adoption assistance programs

(a) Exclusion. --

    (1) In general. -- Gross income of an employee does not include amounts paid or expenses incurred by the employer for qualified adoption expenses in connection with the adoption of a child by an employee if such amounts are furnished pursuant to an adoption assistance program.

    (2) $10,000 exclusion for adoption of child with special needs regardless of expenses. -- In the case of an adoption of a child with special needs which becomes final during a taxable year, the qualified adoption expenses with respect to such adoption for such year shall be increased by an amount equal to the excess (if any) of $10,000 over the actual aggregate qualified adoption expenses with respect to such adoption during such taxable year and all prior taxable years.

(b) Limitations. --

    (1) Dollar limitation. -- The aggregate of the amounts paid or expenses incurred which may be taken into account under subsection (a) for all taxable years with respect to the adoption of a child by the taxpayer shall not exceed $10,000.

    (2) Income limitation. -- The amount excludable from gross income under subsection (a) for any taxable year shall be reduced (but not below zero) by an amount which bears the same ratio to the amount so excludable (determined without regard to this paragraph but with regard to paragraph (1)) as--

    (A) the amount (if any) by which the taxpayer's adjusted gross income exceeds $150,000, bears to

    (B) $40,000.

Sec. 139B. Benefits provided to volunteer firefighters and emergency medical providers.

    (a) In general. -- In the case of any member of a qualified volunteer emergency response organization, gross income shall not include--

    (1) any qualified State and local tax benefit, and

Sec. 139B. Benefits provided to volunteer firefighters and emergency medical providers.

(2) any qualified payment.

(b) Denial of double benefits. -- In the case of any member of a qualified volunteer emergency response organization—

(1) the deduction under 164 shall be determined with regard to any qualified State and local tax benefit, and

(2) expenses paid or incurred by the taxpayer in connection with the performance of services as such a member shall be taken into account under section 170 only to the extent such expenses exceed the amount of any qualified payment excluded from gross income under subsection (a).

(c) Definitions. -- For purposes of this section--

(1) **Qualified state and local tax benefit.** -- The term "qualified state and local tax benefit" means any reduction or rebate of a tax described in paragraph (1), (2), or (3) of section 164(a) provided by a State or political division thereof on account of services performed as a member of a qualified volunteer emergency response organization.

(2) **Qualified payment.** --

(A) **In general.** -- The term "qualified payment" means any payment (whether reimbursement or otherwise) provided by a State or political division thereof on account of the performance of services as a member of a qualified volunteer emergency response organization.

(B) **Applicable dollar limitation.** -- The amount determined under subparagraph (A) for any taxable year shall not exceed $30 multiplied by the number of months during such year that the taxpayer performs such services.

(3) **Qualified volunteer emergency response organization.** -- The term "qualified volunteer emergency response organization' means any volunteer organization --

(A) which is organized and operated to provide firefighting or emergency medical services for persons in the State or political subdivision, as the case may be, and

(B) which is required (by written agreement) by the State or political subdivision to furnish firefighting or emergency medical services in such State or political subdivision.

Sec. 141. Private activity bond; qualified bond

(a) **Private activity bond.** -- For purposes of this title, the term "private activity bond" means any bond issued as part of an issue--

(1) **which meets--**

(A) the private business use test of paragraph (1) of subsection (b), and

(B) the private security or payment test of paragraph (2) of subsection (b), or

(2) **which meets the private loan financing test of subsection (c).** --

(b) **Private business tests.** --

(1) **Private business use test.** -- Except as otherwise provided in this subsection, an issue meets the test of this paragraph if more than 10 percent of the proceeds of the issue are to be used for any private business use.

(2) **Private security or payment test.** -- Except as otherwise provided in this subsection, an issue meets the test of this paragraph if the payment of the principal of, or the interest on, more than 10 percent of the proceeds of such issue is (under the terms of such issue or any

Sec. 141. Private activity bond; qualified bond

underlying arrangement) directly or indirectly--

    (A) secured by any interest in--

        (i) property used or to be used for a private business use, or

        (ii) payments in respect of such property, or

    (B) to be derived from payments (whether or not to the issuer) in respect of property, or borrowed money, used or to be used for a private business use.

***

(e) Qualified bond. -- For purposes of this part, the term "qualified bond" means any private activity bond if--

    (1) In general. -- Such bond is--

    (A) an exempt facility bond,

    (B) a qualified mortgage bond,

    (C) a qualified veterans' mortgage bond,

    (D) a qualified small issue bond,

    (E) a qualified student loan bond,

    (F) a qualified redevelopment bond, or

    (G) a qualified 501(c)(3) bond.

    (2) Volume cap. -- Such bond is issued as part of an issue which meets the applicable requirements of section 146, and

    (3) Other requirements. -- Such bond meets the applicable requirements of each subsection of section 147.

Sec. 142. Exempt facility bond

(a) General rule. -- For purposes of this part, the term "exempt facility bond" means any bond issued as part of an issue 95 percent or more of the net proceeds of which are to be used to provide--

    (1) airports,

    (2) docks and wharves,

    (3) mass commuting facilities,

    (4) facilities for the furnishing of water,

    (5) sewage facilities,

    (6) solid waste disposal facilities,

    (7) qualified residential rental projects,

    (8) facilities for the local furnishing of electric energy or gas,

    (9) local district heating or cooling facilities,

    (10) qualified hazardous waste facilities,

    (11) high-speed intercity rail facilities,

    (12) environmental enhancements of hydroelectric generating facilities,

    (13) qualified public educational facilities, or

    (14) qualified green building and sustainable design projects.

Sec. 142.   Exempt facility bond

Sec. 143.   Mortgage revenue bonds: qualified mortgage bond and qualified veterans' mortgage bond

(a) Qualified mortgage bond. --

(1) Qualified mortgage bond defined. -- For purposes of this title, the term "qualified mortgage bond" means a bond which is issued as part of a qualified mortgage issue.

(2) Qualified mortgage issue defined. --   5

(A) Definition. -- For purposes of this title, the term "qualified mortgage issue" means an issue by a State or political subdivision thereof of 1 or more bonds, but only if--

(i) all proceeds of such issue (exclusive of issuance costs and a reasonably required reserve) are to be used to finance owner-occupied residences,

(ii) such issue meets the requirements of subsections (c), (d), (e), (f), (g), (h), (i), and 10 (m)(7),

(iii) such issue does not meet the private business tests of paragraphs (1) and (2) of section 141(b), and

(iv) except as provided in subparagraph (D)(ii), repayments of principal on financing provided by the issue are used not later than the close of the 1st semiannual period 15 beginning after the date the prepayment (or complete repayment) is received to redeem bonds which are part of such issue.

(b) Qualified veterans' mortgage bond defined. -- For purposes of this part, the term "qualified veterans' mortgage bond" means any bond--

(1) which is issued as part of an issue 95 percent or more of the net proceeds of which are to 20 be used to provide residences for veterans,

(2) the payment of the principal and interest on which is secured by the general obligation of a State,

(3) which is part of an issue which meets the requirements of subsections (c), (g), (i)(1), and (l), and   25

(4) which is part of an issue which does not meet the private business tests of paragraphs (1) and (2) of section 141(b).

Sec. 144.   Qualified small issue bond; qualified student loan bond; qualified redevelopment bond

(a) Qualified small issue bond. --

(1) In general. -- For purposes of this part, the term "qualified small issue bond" means any 30 bond issued as part of an issue the aggregate authorized face amount of which is $1,000,000 or less and 95 percent or more of the net proceeds of which are to be used--

(A) for the acquisition, construction, reconstruction, or improvement of land or property of a character subject to the allowance for depreciation, or

(B) to redeem part or all of a prior issue which was issued for purposes described in 35 subparagraph (A) or this subparagraph.

***

(b) Qualified student loan bond. -- For purposes of this part--

(1) In general. -- The term "qualified student loan bond" means any bond issued as part of an issue the applicable percentage or more of the net proceeds of which are to be used directly 40 or indirectly to make or finance student loans .

Sec. 144. Qualified small issue bond; qualified student loan bond; qualified redevelopment bond

***

(c) Qualified redevelopment bond. -- For purposes of this part--

(1) In general. -- The term "qualified redevelopment bond" means any bond issued as part of an issue 95 percent or more of the net proceeds of which are to be used for 1 or more redevelopment purposes in any designated blighted area.

Sec. 145. Qualified 501(c)(3) bond

(a) In general. -- For purposes of this part, except as otherwise provided in this section, the term "qualified 501(c)(3) bond" means any private activity bond issued as part of an issue if--

(1) all property which is to be provided by the net proceeds of the issue is to be owned by a 501(c)(3) organization or a governmental unit.

***

Sec. 146. Volume cap

(a) General rule. -- A private activity bond issued as part of an issue meets the requirements of this section if the aggregate face amount of the private activity bonds issued pursuant to such issue, when added to the aggregate face amount of tax-exempt private activity bonds previously issued by the issuing authority during the calendar year, does not exceed such authority's volume cap for such calendar year.

Sec. 148. Arbitrage

(a) Arbitrage bond defined. -- For purposes of section 103, the term "arbitrage bond" means any bond issued as part of an issue any portion of the proceeds of which are reasonably expected (at the time of issuance of the bond) to be used directly or indirectly-

(1) to acquire higher yielding investments, or

(2) to replace funds which were used directly or indirectly to acquire higher yielding investments.

(b) Higher yielding investments. -- For purposes of this section--

(1) In general. -- The term "higher yielding investments" means any investment property which produces a yield over the term of the issue which is materially higher than the yield on the issue.

***

(f) Required rebate to the United States. --

(1) In general. -- A bond which is part of an issue shall be treated as an arbitrage bond if the requirements of paragraphs (2) and (3) are not met with respect to such issue. The preceding sentence shall not apply to any qualified veterans' mortgage bond.

(2) Rebate to United States. -- An issue shall be treated as meeting the requirements of this paragraph only if an amount equal to the sum of--

(A) the excess of--

(i) the amount earned on all nonpurpose investments (other than investments attributable to an excess described in this subparagraph), over

(ii) the amount which would have been earned if such nonpurpose investments were invested at a rate equal to the yield on the issue, plus

Sec. 148. Arbitrage

(B) any income attributable to the excess described in subparagraph (A), is paid to the United States by the issuer in accordance with the requirements of paragraph (3).

Sec. 149. Bonds must be registered to be tax exempt; other requirements

***

(b) Federally guaranteed bond is not tax exempt. --

(1) In general. -- Section 103(a) shall not apply to any State or local bond if such bond is federally guaranteed.

Sec. 151. Allowance of deductions for personal exemptions

(a) Allowance of deductions. -- In the case of an individual, the exemptions provided by this section shall be allowed as deductions in computing taxable income.

(b) Taxpayer and spouse. -- An exemption of the exemption amount for the taxpayer; and an additional exemption of the exemption amount for the spouse of the taxpayer if a joint return is not made by the taxpayer and his spouse, and if the spouse, for the calendar year in which the taxable year of the taxpayer begins, has no gross income and is not the dependent of another taxpayer.

(c) Additional exemption for dependents. -- An exemption of the exemption amount for each individual who is a dependent (as defined in section 152) of the taxpayer for the taxable year.

(d) Exemption amount. -- For purposes of this section--

(1) In general. -- Except as otherwise provided in this subsection, the term "exemption amount" means $2,000.

(2) Exemption amount disallowed in case of certain dependents. -- In the case of an individual with respect to whom a deduction under this section is allowable to another taxpayer for a taxable year beginning in the calendar year in which the individual's taxable year begins, the exemption amount applicable to such individual for such individual's taxable year shall be zero.

(3) Phaseout. --

(A) In general. -- In the case of any taxpayer whose adjusted gross income for the taxable year exceeds the threshold amount, the exemption amount shall be reduced by the applicable percentage.

(B) Applicable percentage. -- For purposes of subparagraph (A), the term "applicable percentage" means 2 percentage points for each $2,500 (or fraction thereof) by which the taxpayer's adjusted gross income for the taxable year exceeds the threshold amount. In the case of a married individual filing a separate return, the preceding sentence shall be applied by substituting "$1,250" for "$2,500". In no event shall the applicable percentage exceed100 percent.

(C) Threshold amount. -- For purposes of this paragraph, the term "threshold amount" means--

(i) $150,000 in the case of a joint return or a surviving spouse (as defined in section 2(a)),

(ii) $125,000 in the case of a head of a household (as defined in section 2(b),

(iii) $100,000 in the case of an individual who is not married and who is not a surviving spouse or head of a household, and

(iv) $75,000 in the case of a married individual filing a separate return.

341

Sec. 151. Allowance of deductions for personal exemptions

For purposes of this paragraph, marital status shall be determined under section 7703.

(D) Coordination with other provisions. -- The provisions of this paragraph shall not apply for purposes of determining whether a deduction under this section with respect to any individual is allowable to another taxpayer for any taxable year.

(4) Inflation adjustments. --

(A) Adjustment to basic amount of exemption. -- In the case of any taxable year beginning in a calendar year after 1989, the dollar amount contained in paragraph (1) shall be increased by an amount equal to--

(i) such dollar amount, multiplied by

(ii) the cost-of-living adjustment determined under section (1)(f)(3) for the calendar year in which the taxable year begins, by substituting "calendar year 1988" for "calendar year 1992" in subparagraph (B) thereof.

(B) Adjustment to threshold amounts for years after 1991. -- In the case of any taxable year beginning in a calendar year after 1991, each dollar amount contained in paragraph (3)(C) shall be increased by an amount equal to--

(i) such dollar amount, multiplied by

(ii) the cost-of-living adjustment determined under section 1(f)(3) for the calendar year in which the taxable year begins, by substituting "calendar year 1990" for "calendar year 1992" in subparagraph (B) thereof.

(e) Identifying information required. -- No exemption shall be allowed under this section with respect to any individual unless the TIN of such individual is included on the return claiming the exemption.

Sec. 152. Dependent defined

(a) In general. -- For purposes of this subtitle, the term "dependent" means--

(1) a qualifying child, or

(2) a qualifying relative.

(b) Exceptions. -- For purposes of this section -

(1) Dependents ineligible. -- If an individual is a dependent of a taxpayer for any taxable year of such taxpayer beginning in a calendar year, such individual shall be treated as having no dependents for any taxable year of such individual beginning in such calendar year.

(2) Married dependents. -- An individual shall not be treated as a dependent of a taxpayer under subsection (a) if such individual has made a joint return with the individual's spouse under section 6013 for the taxable year beginning in the calendar year in which the taxable year of the taxpayer begins.

(3) Citizens or nationals of other countries. --

(A) In general. -- The term "dependent" does not include an individual who is not a citizen or national of the United States unless such individual is a resident of the United States or a country contiguous to the United States.

(B) Exception for adopted child. -- Subparagraph (A) shall not exclude any child of a taxpayer (within the meaning of subsection (f)(1)(B)) from the definition of "dependent" if--

(i) for the taxable year of the taxpayer, the child has the same principal place of abode as the taxpayer and is a member of the taxpayer's household, and

342

Sec. 152.   Dependent defined

(ii) the taxpayer is a citizen or national of the United States.

(c) Qualifying child. -- For purposes of this section--

(1) In general. -- The term "qualifying child" means, with respect to any taxpayer for any taxable year, an individual--

(A) who bears a relationship to the taxpayer described in paragraph (2),

(B) who has the same principal place of abode as the taxpayer for more than one-half of such taxable year,

(C) who meets the age requirements of paragraph (3), and

(D) who has not provided over one-half of such individual's own support for the calendar year in which the taxable year of the taxpayer begins.

(2) Relationship. -- For purposes of paragraph (1)(A), an individual bears a relationship to the taxpayer described in this paragraph if such individual is--

(A) a child of the taxpayer or a descendant of such a child,or

(B) a brother, sister, stepbrother, or stepsister of the taxpayer or a descendant of any such relative.

(3) Age requirements. --

(A) In general. -- For purposes of paragraph (1)(C), an individual meets the requirements of this paragraph if such individual--

(i) has not attained the age of 19 as of the close of the calendar year in which the taxable year of the taxpayer begins, or

(ii) is a student who has not attained the age of 24 as of the close of such calendar year.

(B) Special rule for disabled. -- In the case of an individual who is permanently and totally disabled (as defined in section 22(e)(3)) at any time during such calendar year, the requirements of subparagraph (A) shall be treated as met with respect to such individual.

(4) Special rule relating to 2 or more claiming qualifying child. --

(A) In general. -- Except as provided in subparagraph (B), if (but for this paragraph) an individual may be and is claimed as a qualifying child by 2 or more taxpayers for a taxable year beginning in the same calendar year, such individual shall be treated as the qualifying child of the taxpayer who is--

(i) a parent of the individual, or

(ii) if clause (i) does not apply, the taxpayer with the highest adjusted gross income for such taxable year.

(B) More than 1 parent claiming qualifying child. -- If the parents claiming any qualifying child do not file a joint return together, such child shall be treated as the qualifying child of--

(i) the parent with whom the child resided for the longest period of time during the taxable year, or

(ii) if the child resides with both parents for the same amount of time during such taxable year, the parent with the highest adjusted gross income.

(d) Qualifying relative. -- For purposes of this section--

(1) In general. -- The term "qualifying relative" means, with respect to any taxpayer for any taxable year, an individual--

(A) who bears a relationship to the taxpayer described in paragraph (2),

(B) whose gross income for the calendar year in which such taxable year begins is less

Sec. 152.   Dependent defined

than the exemption amount (as defined in section 151(d)),

    (C) with respect to whom the taxpayer provides over one-half of the individual's support for the calendar year in which such taxable year begins, and

    (D) who is not a qualifying child of such taxpayer or of any other taxpayer for any taxable year beginning in the calendar year in which such taxable year begins.

    (2) Relationship. -- For purposes of paragraph (1)(A), an individual bears a relationship to the taxpayer described in this paragraph if th individual is any of the following with respect to the taxpayer:

    (A) A child or a descendant of a child.

    (B) A brother, sister, stepbrother, or stepsister.

    (C) The father or mother, or an ancestor of either.

    (D) A stepfather or stepmother.

    (E) A son or daughter of a brother or sister of the taxpayer.

    (F) A brother or sister of the father or mother of the taxpayer.

    (G) A son-in-law, daughter-in-law, father-in-law, mother-in- law, brother-in-law, or sister-in-law.

    (H) An individual (other than an individual who at any time during the taxable year was the spouse, determined without regard to section 7703, of the taxpayer) who, for the taxable year of the taxpayer, has the same principal place of abode as the taxpayer and is a member of the taxpayer's household.

    (3) Special rule relating to multiple support agreements. -- For purposes of paragraph (1)(C), over one-half of the support of an individual for a calendar year shall be treated as received from the taxpayer if--

    (A) no one person contributed over one-half of such support,

    (B) over one-half of such support was received from 2 or more persons each of whom, but for the fact that any such person alone did not contribute over one-half of such support, would have been entitled to claim such individual as a dependent for a taxable year beginning in such calendar year,

    (C) the taxpayer contributed over 10 percent of such support, and

    (D) each person described in subparagraph (B) (other than the taxpayer) who contributed over 10 percent of such support files a written declaration (in such manner and form as the Secretary may by regulations prescribe) that such person will not claim such individual as a dependent for any taxable year beginning in such calendar year.

    (4) Special rule relating to income of handicapped dependents. --

    (A) In general. -- For purposes of paragraph (1)(B), the gross income of an individual who is permanently and totally disabled (as defined in section 22(e)(3)) at any time during the taxable year shall not include income attributable to services performed by the individual at a sheltered workshop if--

    (i) the availability of medical care at such workshop is the principal reason for the individual's presence there, and

    (ii) the income arises solely from activities at such workshop which are incident to such medical care.

    (B) Sheltered workshop defined. -- For purposes of subparagraph (A), the term "sheltered workshop" means a school--

    (i) which provides special instruction or training designed to alleviate the disability

Sec. 152.   Dependent defined

of the individual, and

    (ii) which is operated by an organization described in section 501(c)(3) and exempt from tax under section 501(a), or by a State, a possession of the United States, any political subdivision of any of the foregoing, the United States, or the District of Columbia.   5

(5) Special rules for support. -- For purposes of this subsection--

    (A) payments to a spouse which are includible in the gross income of such spouse under section 71 or 682 shall not be treated as a payment by the payor spouse for the support of any dependent, and

    (B) in the case of the remarriage of a parent, support of a child received from the parent's 10 spouse shall be treated as received from the parent.

(e) Special rule for divorced parents. --

    (1) In general. -- Notwithstanding subsection (c)(1)(B), (c)(4), or (d)(1)(C), if--

    (A) a child receives over one-half of the child's support during the calendar year from the child's parents--   15

        (i) who are divorced or legally separated under a decree of divorce or separate maintenance,

        (ii) who are separated under a written separation agreement, or

        (iii) who live apart at all times during the last 6 months of the calendar year, and

    (B) such child is in the custody of 1 or both of the child's parents for more than one-half 20 of the calendar year, such child shall be treated as being the qualifying child or qualifying relative of the noncustodial parent for a calendar year if the requirements described in paragraph (2) are met.

    (2) Requirements. -- For purposes of paragraph (1), the requirements described in this paragraph are met if--   25

    (A) a decree of divorce or separate maintenance or written separation agreement between the parents applicable to the taxable year beginning in such calendar year provides that--

        (i) the noncustodial parent shall be entitled to any deduction allowable under section 151 for such child, or   30

        (ii) the custodial parent will sign a written declaration (in such manner and form as the Secretary may prescribe) that such parent will not claim such child as a dependent for such taxable year,

***

    (3) Custodial parent and noncustodial parent. -- For purposes of this subsection--   35

    (A) Custodial parent. -- The term "custodial parent" means the parent with whom a child shared the same principal place of abode for the greater portion of the calendar year.

    (B) Noncustodial parent. -- The term "noncustodial parent" means the parent who is not the custodial parent.

***

        40

    (E) Mortgage insurance premiums treated as interest. --

        (i) In general. -- Premiums paid or accrued for qualified mortgage insurance by a taxpayer during the taxable year in connection with acquisition indebtedness with respect to a qualified residence of the taxpayer shall be treated for purposes of this section as interest which is qualified residence interest.   45

Sec. 152. Dependent defined

(ii) Phaseout. -- The amount otherwise treated as interest under clause (i) shall be reduced (but not below zero) by 10 percent of such amount for each $1,000 ($500 in the case of a married individual filing a separate return) (or fraction thereof) that the taxpayer's adjusted gross income for the taxable year exceeds $100,000 ($50,000 in the case of a married individual filing a separate return).

(iii) Limitation. -- Clause (i) shall not apply with respect to any mortgage insurance contracts issued before January 1, 2007

(iv) Termination. -- Clause (i) shall not apply to amounts--

(I) paid or accrued after December 31, 2007, or

(II) properly allocable to any period after such date.

(4) Exception for multiple-support agreements. -- This subsection shall not apply in any case where over one-half of the support of the child is treated as having been received from a taxpayer under the provision of subsection (d)(3).

(f) Other definitions and rules. -- For purposes of this section -

(1) Child defined. --

(A) In general. -- The term "child" means an individual who is--

(i) a son, daughter, stepson, or stepdaughter of the taxpayer, or

(ii) an eligible foster child of the taxpayer.

(B) Adopted child. -- In determining whether any of the relationships specified in subparagraph (A)(i) or paragraph (4) exists, a legally adopted individual of the taxpayer, or an individual who is lawfully placed with the taxpayer for legal adoption by the taxpayer, shall be treated as a child of such individual by blood.

(C) Eligible foster child. -- For purposes of subparagraph (A)(ii), the term "eligible foster child" means an individual who is placed with the taxpayer by an authorized placement agency or by judgment, decree, or other order of any court of competent jurisdiction.

(2) Student defined. -- The term "student" means an individual who during each of 5 calendar months during the calendar year in which the taxable year of the taxpayer begins--

(A) is a full-time student at an educational organization described in section 170(b)(1)(A)(ii), or

(B) is pursuing a full-time course of institutional on-farm training under the supervision of an accredited agent of an educational organization described in section 170(b)(1)(A)(ii) or of a State or political subdivision of a State.

(3) Determination of household status. -- An individual shall not be treated as a member of the taxpayer's household if at any time during the taxable year of the taxpayer the relationship between such individual and the taxpayer is in violation of local law.

(4) Brother and sister. -- The terms "brother" and "sister" include a brother or sister by the half blood.

(5) Special support test in case of students. -- For purposes of subsections (c)(1)(D) and (d)(1)(C), in the case of an individual who is--

(A) a child of the taxpayer, and

(B) a student,

amounts received as scholarships for study at an educational organization described in section 170(b)(1)(A)(ii) shall not be taken into account.

(6) Treatment of missing children. --

Sec. 152. Dependent defined

(A) In general. -- Solely for the purposes referred to in subparagraph (B), a child of the taxpayer--

> **(i)** who is presumed by law enforcement authorities to have been kidnapped by someone who is not a member of the family of such child or the taxpayer, and

> **(ii)** who had, for the taxable year in which the kidnapping occurred, the same principal place of abode as the taxpayer for more than one-half of the portion of such year before the date of the kidnapping,

shall be treated as meeting the requirement of subsection (c)(1)(B) with respect to a taxpayer for all taxable years ending during the period that the child is kidnapped.

(B) Purposes. -- Subparagraph (A) shall apply solely for purposes of determining--

> **(i)** the deduction under section 151(c),

> **(ii)** the credit under section 24 (relating to child tax credit),

> **(iii)** whether an individual is a surviving spouse or a head of a household (as such terms are defined in section 2), and

> **(iv)** the earned income credit under section 32.

(C) Comparable treatment of certain qualifying relatives. -- For purposes of this section, a child of the taxpayer--

> **(i)** who is presumed by law enforcement authorities to have been kidnapped by someone who is not a member of the family of such child or the taxpayer, and

> **(ii)** who was (without regard to this paragraph) a qualifying relative of the taxpayer for the portion of the taxable year before the date of the kidnapping,

shall be treated as a qualifying relative of the taxpayer for all taxable years ending during the period that the child is kidnapped.

(D) Termination of treatment. -- Subparagraphs (A) and (C) shall cease to apply as of the first taxable year of the taxpayer beginning after the calendar year in which there is a determination that the child is dead (or, if earlier, in which the child would have attained age 18).

(7) Cross references. -- For provision treating child as dependent of both parents for purposes of certain provisions, see sections 105(b) 132(h)(2)(B), and 213(d)(5).

Sec. 161. Allowance of deductions

In computing taxable income under section 63, there shall be allowed as deductions the items specified in this part, subject to the exceptions provided in part IX (sec. 261 and following, relating to items not deductible).

Reg. § 1.161-1 Allowance of deductions.
Section 161 provides for the allowance as deductions, in computing taxable income under section 63(a), of the items specified in Part VI (section 161 and following), Subchapter B, Chapter 1 of the Code, subject to the exceptions provided in Part IX (section 261 and following), of such Subchapter B, relating to items not deductible. Double deductions are not permitted. Amounts deducted under one provision of the Internal Revenue Code of 1954 cannot again be deducted under any other provision thereof. See also section 7852(c), relating to the taking into account, both in computing a tax under Subtitle A of the Internal Revenue Code of 1954 and a tax under Chapter 1 or 2 of the Internal Revenue Code of 1939, of the same item of deduction.

Sec. 162. Trade or business expenses

Sec. 162. Trade or business expenses

(a) **In general.** -- There shall be allowed as a deduction all the ordinary and necessary expenses paid or incurred during the taxable year in carrying on any trade or business, including -

    (1) a reasonable allowance for salaries or other compensation for personal services actually rendered;

    (2) traveling expenses (including amounts expended for meals and lodging other than amounts which are lavish or extravagant under the circumstances) while away from home in the pursuit of a trade or business; and

    (3) rentals or other payments required to be made as a condition to the continued use or possession, for purposes of the trade or business, of property to which the taxpayer has not taken or is not taking title or in which he has no equity.

For purposes of the preceding sentence, the place of residence of a Member of Congress (including any Delegate and Resident Commissioner) within the State, congressional district, or possession which he represents in Congress shall be considered his home, but amounts expended by such Members within each taxable year for living expenses shall not be deductible for income tax purposes in excess of $3,000. For purposes of paragraph (2), the taxpayer shall not be treated as being temporarily away from home during any period of employment if such period exceeds 1 year. The preceding sentence shall not apply to any Federal employee during any period for which such employee is certified by the Attorney General (or the designee thereof) as traveling on behalf of the United States in temporary duty status to investigate or prosecute, or provide support services for the investigation or prosecution of, a Federal crime.

(b) **Charitable contributions and gifts excepted.** -- No deduction shall be allowed under subsection (a) for any contribution or gift which would be allowable as a deduction under section 170 were it not for the percentage limitations, the dollar limitations, or the requirements as to the time of payment, set forth in such section.

(c) **Illegal bribes, kickbacks, and other payments.** --

    (1) **Illegal payments to government officials or employees.** -- No deduction shall be allowed under subsection (a) for any payment made, directly or indirectly, to an official or employee of any government, or of any agency or instrumentality of any government, if the payment constitutes an illegal bribe or kickback or, if the payment is to an official or employee of a foreign government, the payment is unlawful under the Foreign Corrupt Practices Act of 1977. The burden of proof in respect of the issue, for the purposes of this paragraph, as to whether a payment constitutes an illegal bribe or kickback (or is unlawful under the Foreign Corrupt Practices Act of 1977) shall be upon the Secretary to the same extent as he bears the burden of proof under section 7454 (concerning the burden of proof when the issue relates to fraud).

    (2) **Other illegal payments.** -- No deduction shall be allowed under subsection (a) for any payment (other than a payment described in paragraph (1)) made, directly or indirectly, to any person, if the payment constitutes an illegal bribe, illegal kickback, or other illegal payment under any law of the United States, or under any law of a State (but only if such State law is generally enforced), which subjects the payor to a criminal penalty or the loss of license or privilege to engage in a trade or business. For purposes of this paragraph, a kickback includes a payment in consideration of the referral of a client, patient, or customer. The burden of proof in respect of the issue, for purposes of this paragraph, as to whether a payment constitutes an illegal bribe, illegal kickback, or other illegal payment shall be upon the Secretary to the same extent as he bears the burden of proof under section 7454 (concerning the burden of proof when the issue relates to fraud).

    (3) **Kickbacks, rebates, and bribes under medicare and medicaid.** -- No deduction shall

Sec. 162.   Trade or business expenses

be allowed under subsection (a) for any kickback, rebate, or bribe made by any provider of services, supplier, physician, or other person who furnishes items or services for which payment is or may be made under the Social Security Act, or in whole or in part out of Federal funds under a State plan approved under such Act, if such kickback, rebate, or bribe is made in connection with the furnishing of such items or services or the making or receipt of such payments. For purposes of this paragraph, a kickback includes a payment in consideration of the referral of a client, patient, or customer.

***

(e) Denial of deduction for certain lobbying and political expenditures. --

(1) In general. -- No deduction shall be allowed under subsection (a) for any amount paid or incurred in connection with--

(A) influencing legislation,

(B) participation in, or intervention in, any political campaign on behalf of (or in opposition to) any candidate for public office,

(C) any attempt to influence the general public, or segments thereof, with respect to elections, legislative matters, or referendums, or

(D) any direct communication with a covered executive branch official in an attempt to influence the official actions or positions of such official.

(2) Exception for local legislation. -- In the case of any legislation of any local council or similar governing body--

(A) paragraph (1)(A) shall not apply, and

(B) the deduction allowed by subsection (a) shall include all ordinary and necessary expenses (including, but not limited to, traveling expenses described in subsection (a)(2) and the cost of preparing testimony) paid or incurred during the taxable year in carrying on any trade or business--

(i) in direct connection with appearances before, submission of statements to, or sending communications to the committees, or individual members, of such council or body with respect to legislation or proposed legislation of direct interest to the taxpayer, or

(ii) in direct connection with communication of information between the taxpayer and an organization of which the taxpayer is a member with respect to any such legislation or proposed legislation which is of direct interest to the taxpayer and to such organization,

and that portion of the dues so paid or incurred with respect to any organization of which the taxpayer is a member which is attributable to the expenses of the activities described in clauses (i) and (ii) carried on by such organization.

(3) Application to dues of tax-exempt organizations. -- No deduction shall be allowed under subsection (a) for the portion of dues or other similar amounts paid by the taxpayer to an organization which is exempt from tax under this subtitle which the organization notifies the taxpayer under section 6033(e)(1)(A)(ii) is allocable to expenditures to which paragraph (1) applies.

(4) Influencing legislation. -- For purposes of this subsection--

(A) In general. -- The term "influencing legislation" means any attempt to influence any legislation through communication with any member or employee of a legislative body, or with any government official or employee who may participate in the formulation of legislation.

Sec. 162. Trade or business expenses

(B) Legislation. -- The term "legislation" has the meaning given such term by section 4911(e)(2).

(5) Other special rules. --

(A) Exception for certain taxpayers. -- In the case of any taxpayer engaged in the trade or business of conducting activities described in paragraph (1), paragraph (1) shall not apply to expenditures of the taxpayer in conducting such activities directly on behalf of another person (but shall apply to payments by such other person to the taxpayer for conducting such activities).

(B) De minimis exception. --

(i) In general. -- Paragraph (1) shall not apply to any in-house expenditures for any taxable year if such expenditures do not exceed $2,000. In determining whether a taxpayer exceeds the $2,000 limit under this clause, there shall not be taken into account overhead costs otherwise allocable to activities described in paragraphs (1)(A) and (D).

(ii) In-house expenditures. -- For purposes of clause (i), the term "in-house expenditures" means expenditures described in paragraphs (1)(A) and (D) other than--

(I) payments by the taxpayer to a person engaged in the trade or business of conducting activities described in paragraph (1) for the conduct of such activities on behalf of the taxpayer, or

(II) dues or other similar amounts paid or incurred by the taxpayer which are allocable to activities described in paragraph (1).

(C) Expenses incurred in connection with lobbying and political activities. -- Any amount paid or incurred for research for, or preparation, planning, or coordination of, any activity described in paragraph (1) shall be treated as paid or incurred in connection with such activity.

(6) Covered executive branch official. -- For purposes of this subsection, the term "covered executive branch official" means--

(A) the President,

(B) the Vice President,

(C) any officer or employee of the White House Office of the Executive Office of the President, and the 2 most senior level officers of each of the other agencies in such Executive Office, and

(D)(i) any individual serving in a position in level I of the Executive Schedule under section 5312 of title 5, United States Code, **(ii)** any other individual designated by the President as having Cabinet level status, and **(iii)** any immediate deputy of an individual described in clause (i) or (ii).

(7) Special rule for Indian tribal governments. -- For purposes of this subsection, an Indian tribal government shall be treated in the same manner as a local council or similar governing body.

(f) Fines and penalties. -- No deduction shall be allowed under subsection (a) for any fine or similar penalty paid to a government for the violation of any law.

(g) Treble damage payments under the antitrust laws. -- If in a criminal proceeding a taxpayer is convicted of a violation of the antitrust laws, or his plea of guilty or nolo contendere to an indictment or information charging such a violation is entered or accepted in such a proceeding, no deduction shall be allowed under subsection (a) for two-thirds of any amount paid or incurred--

(1) on any judgment for damages entered against the taxpayer under section 4 of the Act . . .

Sec. 162. Trade or business expenses

(commonly known as the Clayton Act), on account of such violation or any related violation of the antitrust laws which occurred prior to the date of the final judgment of such conviction, or

(2) in settlement of any action brought under such section 4 on account of such violation or related violation.

The preceding sentence shall not apply with respect to any conviction or plea before January 1, 1970, or to any conviction or plea on or after such date in a new trial following an appeal of a conviction before such date.   5

(h) State legislators' travel expenses away from home. --

(1) In general. -- For purposes of subsection (a), in the case of any individual who is a State 5 legislator at any time during the taxable year and who makes an election under this subsection for the taxable year--

(A) the place of residence of such individual within the legislative district which he represented shall be considered his home,

(B) he shall be deemed to have expended for living expenses (in connection with his trade or business as a legislator) an amount equal to the sum of the amounts determined by multiplying each legislative day of such individual during the taxable year by the greater of--   10

(i) the amount generally allowable with respect to such day to employees of the State of which he is a legislator for per diem while away from home, to the extent such amount does not exceed 110 percent of the amount described in clause (ii) with respect 10 to such day, or

(ii) the amount generally allowable with respect to such day to employees of the executive branch of the Federal Government for per diem while away from home but 10 serving in the United States, and

(C) he shall be deemed to be away from home in the pursuit of a trade or business on 10 each legislative day.

***

(l) Special rules for health insurance costs of self-employed individuals. --

(1) Allowance of deduction. --

(A) In general. -- In the case of an individual who is an employee within the meaning of section 401(c)(1), there shall be allowed as a deduction under this section an amount equal 15 to the applicable percentage of the amount paid during the taxable year for insurance which constitutes medical care for the taxpayer, his spouse, and dependents.

(B) Applicable percentage. -- For purposes of subparagraph (A), the applicable 15 percentage shall be determined under the following table:

For taxable years beginning in calendar year -	The applicable percentage is -

***

2003 and thereafter.................................... 100.   20

(2) Limitations. --

(A) Dollar amount. -- No deduction shall be allowed under paragraph (1) to the extent that the amount of such deduction exceeds the taxpayer's earned income (within the meaning of section 401(c)) derived by the taxpayer from the trade or business with respect to which the plan providing the medical care coverage is established.   25

(B) Other coverage. -- Paragraph (1) shall not apply to any taxpayer for any calendar

351

Sec. 162.   Trade or business expenses

month for which the taxpayer is eligible to participate in any subsidized health plan maintained by any employer of the taxpayer or of the spouse of the taxpayer. The preceding sentence shall be applied separately with respect to--

(i) plans which include coverage for qualified long-term care services (as defined in section 7702B(c)) or are qualified long-term care insurance contracts (as defined in section 7702B(b)), and

(ii) plans which do not include such coverage and are not such contracts.

(C) **Long-term care premiums.** -- In the case of a qualified long-term care insurance contract (as defined in section 7702B(b)), only eligible long-term care premiums (as defined in section 213(d)(10)) shall be taken into account under paragraph (1).

(3) **Coordination with medical deduction.** -- Any amount paid by a taxpayer for insurance to which paragraph (1) applies shall not be taken into account in computing the amount allowable to the taxpayer as a deduction under section 213(a).

(m) **Certain excessive employee remuneration.** --

(1) **In general.** -- In the case of any publicly held corporation, no deduction shall be allowed under this chapter for applicable employee remuneration with respect to any covered employee to the extent that the amount of such remuneration for the taxable year with respect to such employee exceeds $1,000,000.

(2) **Publicly held corporation.** -- For purposes of this subsection, the term "publicly held corporation" means any corporation issuing any class of common equity securities required to be registered under section 12 of the Securities Exchange Act of 1934.

(3) **Covered employee.** -- For purposes of this subsection, the term "covered employee" means any employee of the taxpayer if--

(A) as of the close of the taxable year, such employee is the chief executive officer of the taxpayer or is an individual acting in such a capacity, or

(B) the total compensation of such employee for the taxable year is required to be reported to shareholders under the Securities Exchange Act of 1934 by reason of such employee being among the 4 highest compensated officers for the taxable year (other than the chief executive officer).

(4) **Applicable employee remuneration.** -- For purposes of this subsection--

(A) **In general.** -- Except as otherwise provided in this paragraph, the term "applicable employee remuneration" means, with respect to any covered employee for any taxable year, the aggregate amount allowable as a deduction under this chapter for such taxable year (determined without regard to this subsection) for remuneration for services performed by such employee (whether or not during the taxable year).

(B) **Exception for remuneration payable on commission basis.** -- The term "applicable employee remuneration" shall not include any remuneration payable on a commission basis solely on account of income generated directly by the individual performance of the individual to whom such remuneration is payable.

(C) **Other performance-based compensation.** -- The term "applicable employee remuneration" shall not include any remuneration payable solely on account of the attainment of one or more performance goals, but only if--

(i) the performance goals are determined by a compensation committee of the board of directors of the taxpayer which is comprised solely of 2 or more outside directors,

(ii) the material terms under which the remuneration is to be paid, including the performance goals, are disclosed to shareholders and approved by a majority of the vote in a separate shareholder vote before the payment of such remuneration, and

Sec. 162. Trade or business expenses

(iii) before any payment of such remuneration, the compensation committee referred to in clause (i) certifies that the performance goals and any other material terms were in fact satisfied.

***

(E) Remuneration. -- For purposes of this paragraph, the term "remuneration" includes any remuneration (including benefits) in any medium other than cash, but shall not include-

(i) any payment referred to in so much of section 3121(a)(5) as precedes subparagraph (E) thereof, and

(ii) any benefit provided to or on behalf of an employee if at the time such benefit is provided it is reasonable to believe that the employee will be able to exclude such benefit from gross income under this chapter.

For purposes of clause (i), section 3121(a)(5) shall be applied without regard to section 3121(v)(1).

(F) Coordination with disallowed golden parachute payments. -- The dollar limitation contained in paragraph (1) shall be reduced (but not below zero) by the amount (if any) which would have been included in the applicable employee remuneration of the covered employee for the taxable year but for being disallowed under section 280G.

Reg. § 162-1 Business expenses.

(a) **In general.** Business expenses deductible from gross income include the ordinary and necessary expenditures directly connected with or pertaining to the taxpayer's trade or business, except items which are used as the basis for a deduction or a credit under provisions of law other than section 162. The cost of goods purchased for resale, with proper adjustment for opening and closing inventories, is deducted from gross sales in computing gross income. See paragraph (a) of § 1.161-3. Among the items included in business expenses are management expenses, commissions (but see section 263 and the regulations thereunder), labor, supplies, incidental repairs, operating expenses of automobiles used in the trade or business, traveling expenses while away from home solely in the pursuit of a trade or business (see § 1.162-2), advertising and other selling expenses, together with insurance premiums against fire, storm, theft, accident, or other similar losses in the case of a business, and rental for the use of business property. No such item shall be included in business expenses, however, to the extent that it is used by the taxpayer in computing the cost of property included in its inventory or used in determining the gain or loss basis of its plant, equipment, or other property. See section 1054 and the regulations thereunder. A deduction for an expense paid or incurred after December 30, 1969, which would otherwise be allowable under section 162 shall not be denied on the grounds that allowance of such deduction would frustrate a sharply defined public policy. See section 162(c), (f), and (g) and the regulations thereunder. The full amount of the allowable deduction for ordinary and necessary expenses in carrying on a business is deductible, even though such expenses exceed the gross income derived during the taxable year from such business.

***

Reg. § 1.162-2 Traveling expenses.

(a) *Traveling expenses include travel fares, meals and lodging, and expenses incident to travel such as expenses for sample rooms, telephone and telegraph, public stenographers, etc.* Only such traveling expenses as are reasonable and necessary in the conduct of the taxpayer's business and directly attributable to it may be deducted. If the trip is undertaken for other than business purposes, the travel fares and expenses incident to travel are personal expenses and the meals and lodging are living expenses.

Sec. 162. Trade or business expenses

If the trip is solely on business, the reasonable and necessary traveling expenses, including travel fares, meals and lodging, and expenses incident to travel, are business expenses. For the allowance of traveling expenses as deductions in determining adjusted gross income, see section 62(2)(B) and the regulations thereunder.

(b)(1) If a taxpayer travels to a destination and while at such destination engages in both business and personal activities, traveling expenses to and from such destination are deductible only if the trip is related primarily to the taxpayer's trade or business. If the trip is primarily personal in nature, the traveling expenses to and from the destination are not deductible even though the taxpayer engages in business activities while at such destination. However, expenses while at the destination which are properly allocable to the taxpayer's trade or business are deductible even though the traveling expenses to and from the destination are not deductible.

(2) Whether a trip is related primarily to the taxpayer's trade or business or is primarily personal in nature depends on the facts and circumstances in each case. The amount of time during the period of the trip which is spent on personal activity compared to the amount of time spent on activities directly relating to the taxpayer's trade or business is an important factor in determining whether the trip is primarily personal. If, for example, a taxpayer spends one week while at a destination on activities which are directly related to his trade or business and subsequently spends an additional five weeks for vacation or other personal activities, the trip will be considered primarily personal in nature in the absence of a clear showing to the contrary.

(c) Where a taxpayer's wife accompanies him on a business trip, expenses attributable to her travel are not deductible unless it can be adequately shown that the wife's presence on the trip has a bona fide business purpose. The wife's performance of some incidental service does not cause her expenses to qualify as deductible business expenses. The same rules apply to any other members of the taxpayer's family who accompany him on such a trip.

(d) Expenses paid or incurred by a taxpayer in attending a convention or other meeting may constitute an ordinary and necessary business expense under section 162 depending upon the facts and circumstances of each case. No distinction will be made between self-employed persons and employees. The fact that an employee uses vacation or leave time or that his attendance at the convention is voluntary will not necessarily prohibit the allowance of the deduction. The allowance of deductions for such expenses will depend upon whether there is a sufficient relationship between the taxpayer's trade of business and his attendance at the convention or other meeting so that he is benefiting or advancing the interests of his trade or business by such attendance. If the convention is for political, social or other purposes unrelated to the taxpayer's trade or business, the expenses are not deductible.

(e) Commuters' fares are not considered as business expenses and are not deductible.

***

Reg. § 1.162-4 Repairs.

The cost of incidental repairs which neither materially add to the value of the property nor appreciably prolong its life, but keep it in an ordinarily efficient operating condition, may be deducted as an expense, provided the cost of acquisition or production or the gain or loss basis of the taxpayer's plant, equipment, or other property, as the case may be, is not increased by the amount of such expenditures. Repairs in the nature of replacements, to the extent that they arrest deterioration and appreciably prolong the life of the property, shall either be capitalized and depreciated in accordance with section 167 or charged against the depreciation reserve if such an account is kept.

354

Sec. 162. Trade or business expenses

Reg. § 1.162-5 Expenses for education.

(a) *General rule*. Expenditures made by an individual for education (including research undertaken as part of his educational program) which are not expenditures of a type described in paragraph (b) (2) or (3) of this section are deductible as ordinary and necessary business expenses (even though the education may lead to a degree) if the 5 education--

(1) Maintains or improves skills required by the individual in his employment or other trade or business, or

(2) Meets the express requirements of the individual's employer, or the requirements of applicable law or regulations, imposed as a condition to the retention by the individual 10 of an established employment relationship, status, or rate of compensation.

(b) Nondeductible educational expenditures--(1) In general. Educational expenditures described in subparagraphs (2) and (3) of this paragraph are personal expenditures or constitute an inseparable aggregate of personal and capital expenditures and, therefore, are not deductible as ordinary and necessary business expenses even though the 15 education may maintain or improve skills required by the individual in his employment or other trade or business or may meet the express requirements of the individual's employer or of applicable law or regulations.

(2) *Minimum educational requirements*. (i) The first category of nondeductible educational expenses within the scope of subparagraph (1) of this paragraph are 20 expenditures made by an individual for education which is required of him in order to meet the minimum educational requirements for qualification in his employment or other trade or business. The minimum education necessary to qualify for a position or other trade or business must be determined from a consideration of such factors as the requirements of the employer, the applicable law and regulations, and the standards of 25 the profession, trade, or business involved. The fact that an individual is already performing service in an employment status does not establish that he has met the minimum educational requirements for qualification in that employment. Once an individual has met the minimum educational requirements for qualification in his employment or other trade or business (as in effect when he enters the employment or 30 trade or business), he shall be treated as continuing to meet those requirements even though they are changed.

(ii) The minimum educational requirements for qualification of a particular individual in a position in an educational institution is the minimum level of education (in terms of aggregate college hours or degree) which under the applicable laws or regulations, in 35 effect at the time this individual is first employed in such position, is normally required of an individual initially being employed in such a position. If there are no normal requirements as to the minimum level of education required for a position in an educational institution, then an individual in such a position shall be considered to have met the minimum educational requirements for qualification in that position when he 40 becomes a member of the faculty of the educational institution. The determination of whether an individual is a member of the faculty of an educational institution must be made on the basis of the particular practices of the institution. However, an individual will ordinarily be considered to be a member of the faculty of an institution if (a) he has tenure or his years of service are being counted toward obtaining tenure; (b) the institution is 45 making contributions to a retirement plan (other than Social Security or a similar program) in respect of his employment; or (c) he has a vote in faculty affairs.

(iii) The application of this subparagraph may be illustrated by the following examples:

Example (1). General facts:State X requires a bachelor's degree for beginning secondary school teachers which must include 30 credit hours of professional 50 educational courses. In addition, in order to retain his position, a secondary school

Sec. 162. Trade or business expenses

teacher must complete a fifth year of preparation within 10 years after beginning his employment. If an employing school official certifies to the State Department of Education that applicants having a bachelor's degree and the required courses in professional education cannot be found, he may hire individuals as secondary school teachers if they

5 have completed a minimum of 90 semester hours of college work. However, to be retained in his position, such an individual must obtain his bachelor's degree and complete the required professional educational courses within 3 years after his employment commences. Under these facts, a bachelor's degree, without regard to whether it includes 30 credit hours of professional educational courses, is considered to

10 be the minimum educational requirement for qualification as a secondary school teacher in State X. This is the case notwithstanding the number of teachers who are actually hired without such a degree. The following are examples of the application of these facts in particular situations:

Situation 1. A, at the time he is employed as a secondary school teacher in State X,

15 has a bachelor's degree including 30 credit hours of professional educational courses. After his employment, A completes a fifth college year of education and, as a result, is issued a standard certificate. The fifth college year of education undertaken by A is not education required to meet the minimum educational requirements for qualification as a secondary school teacher. Accordingly, the expenditures for such education are

20 deductible unless the expenditures are for education which is part of a program of study being pursued by A which will lead to qualifying him in a new trade or business.

Situation 2. Because of a shortage of applicants meeting the stated requirements, B, who has a bachelor's degree, is employed as a secondary school teacher in State X even though he has only 20 credit hours of professional educational courses. After his

25 employment, B takes an additional 10 credit hours of professional educational courses. Since these courses do not constitute education required to meet the minimum educational requirements for qualification as a secondary school teacher which is a bachelor's degree and will not lead to qualifying B in a new trade or business, the expenditures for such courses are deductible.

30 *Situation 3.* Because of a shortage of applicants meeting the stated requirements, C is employed as a secondary school teacher in State X although he has only 90 semester hours of college work toward his bachelor's degree. After his employment, C undertakes courses leading to a bachelor's degree. These courses (including any courses in professional education) constitute education required to meet the minimum educational

35 requirements for qualification as a secondary school teacher. Accordingly, the expenditures for such education are not deductible.

Situation 4. Subsequent to the employment of A, B, and C, but before they have completed a fifth college year of education, State X changes its requirements affecting secondary school teachers to provide that beginning teachers must have completed 5

40 college years of preparation. In the cases of A, B, and C, a fifth college year of education is not considered to be education undertaken to meet the minimum educational requirements for qualifications as a secondary school teacher. Accordingly, expenditures for a fifth year of college will be deductible unless the expenditures are for education which is part of a program being pursued by A, B, or C which will lead to qualifying him in

45 a new trade or business.

Example (2). D, who holds a bachelor's degree, obtains temporary employment as an instructor at University Y and undertakes graduate courses as a candidate for a graduate degree. D may become a faculty member only if he obtains a graduate degree and may continue to hold a position as instructor only so long as he shows satisfactory progress

50 towards obtaining this graduate degree. The graduate courses taken by D constitute education required to meet the minimum educational requirements for qualification in D's

Sec. 162. Trade or business expenses

trade or business and, thus, the expenditures for such courses are not deductible.

Example (3). E, who has completed 2 years of a normal 3-year law school course leading to a bachelor of laws degree (LL.B.), is hired by a law firm to do legal research and perform other functions on a full-time basis. As a condition to continued employment, E is required to obtain an LL.B. and pass the State bar examination. E completes his law school education by attending night law school, and he takes a bar review course in order to prepare for the State bar examination. The law courses and bar review course constitute education required to meet the minimum educational requirements for qualification in E's trade or business and, thus, the expenditures for such courses are not deductible.

(3) *Qualification for new trade or business*. (i) The second category of nondeductible educational expenses within the scope of subparagraph (1) of this paragraph are expenditures made by an individual for education which is part of a program of study being pursued by him which will lead to qualifying him in a new trade or business. In the case of an employee, a change of duties does not constitute a new trade or business if the new duties involve the same general type of work as is involved in the individual's present employment. For this purpose, all teaching and related duties shall be considered to involve the same general type of work. The following are examples of changes in duties which do not constitute new trades or businesses:

(a) Elementary to secondary school classroom teacher.

(b) Classroom teacher in one subject (such as mathematics) to classroom teacher in another subject (such as science).

(c) Classroom teacher to guidance counselor.

(d) Classroom teacher to principal.

(ii) The application of this subparagraph to individuals other than teachers may be illustrated by the following examples:

Example (1). A, a self-employed individual practicing a profession other than law, for example, engineering, accounting, etc., attends law school at night and after completing his law school studies receives a bachelor of laws degree. The expenditures made by A in attending law school are nondeductible because this course of study qualifies him for a new trade or business.

Example (2). Assume the same facts as in example (1) except that A has the status of an employee rather than a self-employed individual, and that his employer requires him to obtain a bachelor of laws degree. A intends to continue practicing his nonlegal profession as an employee of such employer. Nevertheless, the expenditures made by A in attending law school are not deductible since this course of study qualifies him for a new trade or business.

Example (3). B, a general practitioner of medicine, takes a 2-week course reviewing new developments in several specialized fields of medicine. B's expenses for the course are deductible because the course maintains or improves skills required by him in his trade or business and does not qualify him for a new trade or business.

Example (4). C, while engaged in the private practice of psychiatry, undertakes a program of study and training at an accredited psychoanalytic institute which will lead to qualifying him to practice psychoanalysis. C's expenditures for such study and training are deductible because the study and training maintains or improves skills required by him in his trade or business and does not qualify him for a new trade or business.

(c) *Deductible educational expenditures*--(1) *Maintaining or improving skills*. The deduction under the category of expenditures for education which maintains or improves skills required by the individual in his employment or other trade or business includes refresher courses or courses dealing with current developments as well as academic or vocational courses provided the expenditures for the courses are not within either

357

Sec. 162. Trade or business expenses

category of nondeductible expenditures described in paragraph (b) (2) or (3) of this section.

(2) M*eeting requirements of employer.* An individual is considered to have undertaken education in order to meet the express requirements of his employer, or the requirements
5 of applicable law or regulations, imposed as a condition to the retention by the taxpayer of his established employment relationship, status, or rate of compensation only if such requirements are imposed for a bona fide business purpose of the individual's employer. Only the minimum education necessary to the retention by the individual of his established employment relationship, status, or rate of compensation may be considered
10 as undertaken to meet the express requirements of the taxpayer's employer. However, education in excess of such minimum education may qualify as education undertaken in order to maintain or improve the skills required by the taxpayer in his employment or other trade or business (see subparagraph (1) of this paragraph). In no event, however, is a deduction allowable for expenditures for education which, even though for education
15 required by the employer or applicable law or regulations, are within one of the categories of nondeductible expenditures described in paragraph (b) (2) and (3) of this section.

(d) *Travel as a form of education.* Subject to the provisions of paragraph (b) and (e) of this section, expenditures for travel (including travel while on sabbatical leave) as a form of education are deductible only to the extent such expenditures are attributable to a
20 period of travel that is directly related to the duties of the individual in his employment or other trade or business. For this purpose, a period of travel shall be considered directly related to the duties of an individual in his employment or other trade or business only if the major portion of the activities during such period is of a nature which directly maintains or improves skills required by the individual in such employment or other trade
25 or business. The approval of a travel program by an employer or the fact that travel is accepted by an employer in the fulfillment of its requirements for retention of rate of compensation, status or employment, is not determinative that the required relationship exists between the travel involved and the duties of the individual in his particular position.
30 (e) *Travel away from home.* (1) If an individual travels away from home primarily to obtain education the expenses of which are deductible under this section, his expenditures for travel, meals, and lodging while away from home are deductible. However, if as an incident of such trip the individual engages in some personal activity such as sightseeing, social visiting, or entertaining, or other recreation, the portion of the
35 expenses attributable to such personal activity constitutes nondeductible personal or living expenses and is not allowable as a deduction. If the individual's travel away from home is primarily personal, the individual's expenditures for travel, meals and lodging (other than meals and lodging during the time spent in participating in deductible education pursuits) are not deductible. Whether a particular trip is primarily person or
40 primarily to obtain education the expenses of which are deductible under this section depends upon all the facts and circumstances of each case. An important factor to be taken into consideration in making the determination is the relative amount of time devoted to personal activity as compared with the time devoted to educational pursuits. The rules set forth in this paragraph are subject to the provisions of section 162(a)(2),
45 relating to deductibility of certain traveling expenses, and section 274 (c) and (d), relating to allocation of certain foreign travel expenses and substantiation required, respectively, and the regulations thereunder.

(2) *Examples.* The application of this subsection may be illustrated by the following examples:
50 *Example (1).* A, a self-employed tax practitioner, decides to take a 1-week course in new developments in taxation, which is offered in City X, 500 miles away from his home.

Sec. 162. Trade or business expenses

His primary purpose in going to X is to take the course, but he also takes a side trip to City Y (50 miles from X) for 1 day, takes a sightseeing trip while in X, and entertains some personal friends. A's transportation expenses to City X and return to his home are deductible but his transportation expenses to City Y are not deductible. A's expenses for meals and lodging while away from home will be allocated between his educational pursuits and his personal activities. Those expenses which are entirely personal, such as sightseeing and entertaining friends, are not deductible to any extent.

Example (2). The facts are the same as in example (1) except that A's primary purpose in going to City X is to take a vacation. This purpose is indicated by several factors, one of which is the fact that he spends only 1 week attending the tax course and devotes 5 weeks entirely to personal activities. None of A's transportation expenses are deductible and his expenses for meals and lodging while away from home are not deductible to the extent attributable to personal activities. His expenses for meals and lodging allocable to the week attending the tax course are, however, deductible.

Example (3). B, a high school mathematics teacher in New York City, in the summertime travels to a university in California in order to take a mathematics course the expense of which is deductible under this section. B pursues only one-fourth of a full course of study and the remainder of her time is devoted to personal activities the expense of which is not deductible. Absent a showing by B of a substantial nonpersonal reason for taking the course in the university in California, the trip is considered taken primarily for personal reasons and the cost of traveling from New York City to California and return would not be deductible. However, one-fourth of the cost of B's meals and lodging while attending the university in California may be considered properly allocable to deductible educational pursuits and, therefore, is deductible.

Reg. § 1.162-6 Professional expenses.

A professional man may claim as deductions the cost of supplies used by him in the practice of his profession, expenses paid or accrued in the operation and repair of an automobile used in making professional calls, dues to professional societies and subscriptions to professional journals, the rent paid or accrued for office rooms, the cost of the fuel, light, water, telephone, etc., used in such offices, and the hire of office assistance. Amounts currently paid or accrued for books, furniture, and professional instruments and equipment, the useful life of which is short, may be deducted.

Reg. § 1.162-7 Compensation for personal services.

(a) There may be included among the ordinary and necessary expenses paid or incurred in carrying on any trade or business a reasonable allowance for salaries or other compensation for personal services actually rendered. The test of deductibility in the case of compensation payments is whether they are reasonable and are in fact payments purely for services.

(b) The test set forth in paragraph (a) of this section and its practical application may be further stated and illustrated as follows:

(1) Any amount paid in the form of compensation, but not in fact as the purchase price of services, is not deductible. An ostensible salary paid by a corporation may be a distribution of a dividend on stock. This is likely to occur in the case of a corporation having few shareholders, practically all of whom draw salaries. If in such a case the salaries are in excess of those ordinarily paid for similar services and the excessive payments correspond or bear a close relationship to the stockholdings of the officers or employees, it would seem likely that the salaries are not paid wholly for services rendered, but that the excessive payments are a distribution of earnings upon the stock. An ostensible salary may be in part payment for property. This may occur, for example,

Sec. 162.   Trade or business expenses

where a partnership sells out to a corporation, the former partners agreeing to continue in the service of the corporation. In such a case it may be found that the salaries of the former partners are not merely for services, but in part constitute payment for the transfer of their business.

5   (2) The form or method of fixing compensation is not decisive as to deductibility. While any form of contingent compensation invites scrutiny as a possible distribution of earnings of the enterprise, it does not follow that payments on a contingent basis are to be treated fundamentally on any basis different from that applying to compensation at a flat rate. Generally speaking, if contingent compensation is paid pursuant to a free

10 bargain between the employer and the individual made before the services are rendered, not influenced by any consideration on the part of the employer other than that of securing on fair and advantageous terms the services of the individual, it should be allowed as a deduction even though in the actual working out of the contract it may prove to be greater than the amount which would ordinarily be paid.

15   (3) In any event the allowance for the compensation paid may not exceed what is reasonable under all the circumstances. It is, in general, just to assume that reasonable and true compensation is only such amount as would ordinarily be paid for like services by like enterprises under like circumstances. The circumstances to be taken into consideration are those existing at the date when the contract for services was made, not

20 those existing at the date when the contract is questioned.

    (4) For disallowance of deduction in the case of certain transfers of stock pursuant to employees stock options, see section 421 and the regulations thereunder.

Reg. § 1.162-8   Treatment of excessive compensation.

25   The income tax liability of the recipient in respect of an amount ostensibly paid to him as compensation, but not allowed to be deducted as such by the payor, will depend upon the circumstances of each case. Thus, in the case of excessive payments by corporations, if such payments correspond or bear a close relationship to stockholdings, and are found to be a distribution of earnings or profits, the excessive payments will be

30 treated as a dividend. If such payments constitute payment for property, they should be treated by the payor as a capital expenditure and by the recipient as part of the purchase price. In the absence of evidence to justify other treatment, excessive payments for salaries or other compensation for personal services will be included in gross income of the recipient.

35

Reg. § 1.162-9   Bonuses to employees.

    Bonuses to employees will constitute allowable deductions from gross income when such payments are made in good faith and as additional compensation for the services actually rendered by the employees, provided such payments, when added to the

40 stipulated salaries, do not exceed a reasonable compensation for the services rendered. It is immaterial whether such bonuses are paid in cash or in kind or partly in cash and partly in kind. Donations made to employees and others, which do not have in them the element of compensation or which are in excess of reasonable compensation for services, are not deductible from gross income.

45

Reg. § 1.162-11   Rentals.

    (a) *Acquisition of a leasehold*. If a leasehold is acquired for business purposes for a specified sum, the purchaser may take as a deduction in his return an aliquot part of such sum each year, based on the number of years the lease has to run. Taxes paid by a

50 tenant to or for a landlord for business property are additional rent and constitute a deductible item to the tenant and taxable income to the landlord, the amount of the tax

being deductible by the latter. For disallowance of deduction for income taxes paid by a lessee corporation pursuant to a lease arrangement with the lessor corporation, see section 110 and the regulations thereunder. See section 178 and the regulations thereunder for rules governing the effect to be given renewal options in amortizing the costs incurred after July 28, 1958 of acquiring a lease. See § 1.197-2 for rules governing 5 the amortization of costs to acquire limited interests in section 197 intangibles.

(b) *Improvements by lessee on lessor's property.* (1) The cost to a lessee of erecting buildings or making permanent improvements on property of which he is the lessee is a capital investment, and is not deductible as a business expense. If the estimated useful life in the hands of the taxpayer of the building erected or of the improvements made, 10 determined without regard to the terms of the lease, is longer than the remaining period of the lease, an annual deduction may be made from gross income of an amount equal to the total cost of such improvements divided by the number of years remaining in the term of the lease, and such deduction shall be in lieu of a deduction for depreciation. If, on the other hand, the useful life of such buildings or improvements in the hands of the taxpayer 15 is equal to or shorter than the remaining period of the lease, this deduction shall be computed under the provisions of section 167 (relating to depreciation).

(2) If the lessee began improvements on leased property before July 28, 1958, or if the lessee was on such date and at all times thereafter under a binding legal obligation to make such improvements, the matter of spreading the cost of erecting buildings or 20 making permanent improvements over the term of the original lease, together with the renewal period or periods depends upon the facts in the particular case, including the presence or absence of an obligation of renewal and the relationship between the parties. As a general rule, unless the lease has been renewed or the facts show with reasonable certainty that the lease will be renewed, the cost or other basis of the lease, or the cost of 25 improvements shall be spread only over the number of years the lease has to run without taking into account any right of renewal. The provisions of this subparagraph may be illustrated by the following examples:

Example (1). A subsidiary corporation leases land from its parent at a fair rental for a 25-year period. The subsidiary erects on the land valuable factory buildings having an 30 estimated useful life of 50 years. These facts show with reasonable certainty that the lease will be renewed, even though the lease contains no option of renewal. Therefore, the cost of the buildings shall be depreciated over the estimated useful life of the buildings in accordance with section 167 and the regulations thereunder.

Example (2). A retail merchandising corporation leases land at a fair rental from an 35 unrelated lessor for the longest period that the lessor is willing to lease the land (30 years). The lessee erects on the land a department store having an estimated useful life of 40 years. These facts do not show with reasonable certainty that the lease will be renewed. Therefore, the cost of the building shall be spread over the remaining term of the lease. An annual deduction may be made of an amount equal to the cost of the 40 building divided by the number of years remaining in the term of the lease, and such deduction shall be in lieu of a deduction for depreciation.

(3) See section 178 and the regulations thereunder for rules governing the effect to be given renewal options where a lessee begins improvements on leased property after July 28, 1958, other than improvements which on such date and at all times thereafter, the 45 lessee was under a binding legal obligation to make.

Reg. § 1.162-12 Expenses of farmers.

(a) *Farms engaged in for profit.* A farmer who operates a farm for profit is entitled to deduct from gross income as necessary expenses all amounts actually expended in the 50 carrying on of the business of farming. The cost of ordinary tools of short life or small cost, such as hand tools, including shovels, rakes, etc., may be deducted. The purchase of feed and other costs connected with raising livestock may be treated as expense deductions insofar as such costs represent actual outlay, but not including the value of farm produce grown upon the farm or the labor of the taxpayer. For rules regarding the

5 capitalization of expenses of producing property in the trade or business of farming, see section 263A and the regulations thereunder. For taxable years beginning after July 12, 1972, where a farmer is engaged in producing crops and the process of gathering and disposal of such crops is not completed within the taxable year in which such crops were planted, expenses deducted may, with the consent of the Commissioner (see section 446

10 and the regulations thereunder), be determined upon the crop method, and such deductions must be taken in the taxable year in which the gross income from the crop has been realized. For taxable years beginning on or before July 12, 1972, where a farmer is engaged in producing crops which take more than a year from the time of planting to the process of gathering and disposal, expenses deducted may, with the

15 consent of the Commissioner (see section 446 and the regulations thereunder), be determined upon the crop method, and such deductions must be taken in the taxable year in which the gross income from the crop has been realized. If a farmer does not compute income upon the crop method, the cost of seeds and young plants which are purchased for further development and cultivation prior to sale in later years may be

20 deducted as an expense for the year of purchase, provided the farmer follows a consistent practice of deducting such costs as an expense from year to year. The preceding sentence does not apply to the cost of seeds and young plants connected with the planting of timber (see section 611 and the regulations thereunder). For rules regarding the capitalization of expenses of producing property in the trade or business of

25 farming, see section 263A of the Internal Revenue Code and § 1.263A-4. The cost of farm machinery, equipment, and farm buildings represents a capital investment and is not an allowable deduction as an item of expense. Amounts expended in the development of farms, orchards, and ranches prior to the time when the productive state is reached may, at the election of the taxpayer, be regarded as investments of capital. For the treatment of

30 soil and water conservation expenditures as expenses which are not chargeable to capital account, see section 175 and the regulations thereunder. For taxable years beginning after December 31, 1959, in the case of expenditures paid or incurred by farmers for fertilizer, lime, etc., see section 180 and the regulations thereunder. Amounts expended in purchasing work, breeding, dairy, or sporting animals are regarded as

35 investments of capital, and shall be depreciated unless such animals are included in an inventory in accordance with § 1.61-4. The purchase price of an automobile, even when wholly used in carrying on farming operations, is not deductible, but is regarded as an investment of capital. The cost of gasoline, repairs, and upkeep of an automobile if used wholly in the business of farming is deductible as an expense; if used partly for business

40 purposes and partly for the pleasure or convenience of the taxpayer or his family, such cost may be apportioned according to the extent of the use for purposes of business and pleasure or convenience, and only the proportion of such cost justly attributable to business purposes is deductible as a necessary expense.

***

45

Reg. § 1.162-14 Expenditures for advertising or promotion of good will.

   A corporation which has, for the purpose of computing its excess profits tax credit under Subchapter E, Chapter 2, or Subchapter D, Chapter 1 of the Internal Revenue Code of 1939, elected under section 733 or section 451 (applicable to the excess profits

50 tax imposed by Subchapter E of Chapter 2, and Subchapter D of Chapter 1, respectively) to charge to capital account for taxable years in its base period expenditures for

Sec. 162. Trade or business expenses

advertising or the promotion of good will which may be regarded as capital investments, may not deduct similar expenditures for the taxable year. See section 263(b). Such a taxpayer has the burden of proving that expenditures for advertising or the promotion of good will which it seeks to deduct in the taxable year may not be regarded as capital investments under the provisions of the regulations prescribed under section 733 or 5 section 451 of the Internal Revenue Code of 1939. See 26 CFR, 1938 ed., 35.733-2 (Regulations 112) and 26 CFR (1939) 40.451-2 (Regulations 130). For the disallowance of deductions for the cost of advertising in programs of certain conventions of political parties, or in publications part of the proceeds of which directly or indirectly inures (or is intended to inure) to or for the use of a political party or political candidate, see § 1.276-1. 10

Reg. § 1.162-17   Reporting and substantiation of certain business expenses of employees.

(a) *Introductory.* The purpose of the regulations in this section is to provide rules for the reporting of information on income tax returns by taxpayers who pay or incur ordinary 15 and necessary business expenses in connection with the performance of services as an employee and to furnish guidance as to the type of records which will be useful in compiling such information and in its substantiation, if required. The rules prescribed in this section do not apply to expenses paid or incurred for incidentals, such as office supplies for the employer or local transportation in connection with an errand. Employees 20 incurring such incidental expenses are not required to provide substantiation for such amounts. The term ``ordinary and necessary business expenses" means only those expenses which are ordinary and necessary in the conduct of the taxpayer's business and are directly attributable to such business. The term does not include nondeductible personal, living or family expenses. 25

(b) *Expenses for which the employee is required to account to his employer*--(1) *Reimbursements equal to expenses.* The employee need not report on his tax return (either itemized or in total amount) expenses for travel, transportation, entertainment, and similar purposes paid or incurred by him solely for the benefit of his employer for which he is required to account and does account to his employer and which are charged 30 directly or indirectly to the employer (for example, through credit cards) or for which the employee is paid through advances, reimbursements, or otherwise, provided the total amount of such advances, reimbursements, and charges is equal to such expenses. In such a case the taxpayer need only state in his return that the total of amounts charged directly or indirectly to his employer through credit cards or otherwise and received from 35 the employer as advances or reimbursements did not exceed the ordinary and necessary business expenses paid or incurred by the employee.

(2) *Reimbursements in excess of expenses.* In case the total of amounts charged directly or indirectly to the employer and received from the employer as advances, reimbursements, or otherwise, exceeds the ordinary and necessary business expenses 40 paid or incurred by the employee and the employee is required to and does account to his employer for such expenses, the taxpayer must include such excess in income and state on his return that he has done so.

(3) Expenses in excess of reimbursements. If the employee's ordinary and necessary business expenses exceed the total of the amounts charged directly or indirectly to the 45 employer and received from the employer as advances, reimbursements, or otherwise, and the employee is required to and does account to his employer for such expenses, the taxpayer may make the statement in his return required by subparagraph (1) of this paragraph unless he wishes to claim a deduction for such excess. If, however, he wishes to secure a deduction for such excess, he must submit a statement showing the following 50 information as part of his tax return:

363

Sec. 162. Trade or business expenses

(i) The total of any charges paid or borne by the employer and of any other amounts received from the employer for payment of expenses whether by means of advances, reimbursements or otherwise; and

(ii) The nature of his occupation, the number of days away from home on business,
5 and the total amount of ordinary and necessary business expenses paid or incurred by him (including those charged directly or indirectly to the employer through credit cards or otherwise) broken down into such broad categories as transportation, meals and lodging while away from home overnight, entertainment expenses, and other business expenses.

(4) To ``account'' to his employer as used in this section means to submit an expense
10 account or other required written statement to the employer showing the business nature and the amount of all the employee's expenses (including those charged directly or indirectly to the employer through credit cards or otherwise) broken down into such broad categories as transportation, meals and lodging while away from home overnight, entertainment expenses, and other business expenses. For this purpose, the
15 Commissioner in his discretion may approve reasonable business practices under which mileage, per diem in lieu of subsistence, and similar allowances providing for ordinary and necessary business expenses in accordance with a fixed scale may be regarded as equivalent to an accounting to the employer.

(c) *Expenses for which the employee is not required to account to his employer.* If the
20 employee is not required to account to his employer for his ordinary and necessary business expenses, e.g., travel, transportation, entertainment, and similar items, or, though required, fails to account for such expenses, he must submit, as a part of his tax return, a statement showing the following information:

(1) The total of all amounts received as advances or reimbursements from his
25 employer in connection with the ordinary and necessary business expenses of the employee, including amounts charged directly or indirectly to the employer through credit cards or otherwise; and

(2) The nature of his occupation, the number of days away from home on business, and the total amount of ordinary and necessary business expenses paid or incurred by
30 him (including those charged directly or indirectly to the employer through credit cards or otherwise) broken down into such broad categories as transportation, meals and lodging while away from home overnight, entertainment expenses, and other business expenses.

(d) *Substantiation of items of expense.* (1) Although the Commissioner may require any taxpayer to substantiate such information concerning expense accounts as may
35 appear to be pertinent in determining tax liability, taxpayers ordinarily will not be called upon to substantiate expense account information except those in the following categories:

(i) A taxpayer who is not required to account to his employer, or who does not account;
40 (ii) A taxpayer whose expenses exceed the total of amounts charged to his employer and amounts received through advances, reimbursements or otherwise and who claims a deduction on his return for such excess;

(iii) A taxpayer who is related to his employer within the meaning of section 267(b); and
45 (iv) Other taxpayers in cases where it is determined that the accounting procedures used by the employer for the reporting and substantiation of expenses by employees are not adequate.

(2) The Code contemplates that taxpayers keep such records as will be sufficient to enable the Commissioner to correctly determine income tax liability. Accordingly, it is to
50 the advantage of taxpayers who may be called upon to substantiate expense account information to maintain as adequate and detailed records of travel, transportation,

Sec. 162. Trade or business expenses

entertainment, and similar business expenses as practical since the burden of proof is upon the taxpayer to show that such expenses were not only paid or incurred but also that they constitute ordinary and necessary business expenses. One method for substantiating expenses incurred by an employee in connection with his employment is through the preparation of a daily diary or record of expenditures, maintained in sufficient detail to enable him to readily identify the amount and nature of any expenditure, and the preservation of supporting documents, especially in connection with large or exceptional expenditures. Nevertheless, it is recognized that by reason of the nature of certain expenses or the circumstances under which they are incurred, it is often difficult for an employee to maintain detailed records or to preserve supporting documents for all his expenses. Detailed records of small expenditures incurred in traveling or for transportation, as for example, tips, will not be required.

(3) Where records are incomplete or documentary proof is unavailable, it may be possible to establish the amount of the expenditures by approximations based upon reliable secondary sources of information and collateral evidence. For example, in connection with an item of traveling expense a taxpayer might establish that he was in a travel status a certain number of days but that it was impracticable for him to establish the details of all his various items of travel expense. In such a case rail fares or plane fares can usually be ascertained with exactness and automobile costs approximated on the basis of mileage covered. A reasonable approximation of meals and lodging might be based upon receipted hotel bills or upon average daily rates for such accommodations and meals prevailing in the particular community for comparable accommodations. Since detailed records of incidental items are not required, deductions for these items may be based upon a reasonable approximation. In cases where a taxpayer is called upon to substantiate expense account information, the burden is on the taxpayer to establish that the amounts claimed as a deduction are reasonably accurate and constitute ordinary and necessary business expenses paid or incurred by him in connection with his trade or business. In connection with the determination of factual matters of this type, due consideration will be given to the reasonableness of the stated expenditures for the claimed purposes in relation to the taxpayer's circumstances (such as his income and the nature of his occupation), to the reliability and accuracy of records in connection with other items more readily lending themselves to detailed recordkeeping, and to all of the facts and circumstances in the particular case.

(e) Applicability.

***

(2) With respect to taxable years ending after December 31, 1962, but only in respect of periods after such date, the provisions of the regulations in this section are superseded by the regulations under section 274(d) to the extent inconsistent therewith. See § 1.274-5.

(3) For taxable years beginning on or after January 1, 1989, the provisions of this section are superseded by the regulations under section 62(c) to the extent this section is inconsistent with those regulations. See § 1.62-2.

Reg. § 1.162-20   Expenditures attributable to lobbying, political campaigns, attempts to influence legislation, etc., and certain advertising.

(a) *In general--*(1) *Scope of section.* This section contains rules governing the deductibility or nondeductibility of expenditures for lobbying purposes, for the promotion or defeat of legislation, for political campaign purposes (including the support of or opposition to any candidate for public office) or for carrying on propaganda (including advertising) related to any of the foregoing purposes. For rules applicable to such expenditures in respect of taxable years beginning before January 1, 1963, and for

Sec. 162. Trade or business expenses

taxable years beginning after December 31, 1962, see paragraphs (b) and (c), respectively, of this section. This section also deals with expenditures for institutional or ``good will'' advertising.

(2) *Institutional or ``good will'' advertising.* Expenditures for institutional or ``good will'' advertising which keeps the taxpayer's name before the public are generally deductible as ordinary and necessary business expenses provided the expenditures are related to the patronage the taxpayer might reasonably expect in the future. For example, a deduction will ordinarily be allowed for the cost of advertising which keeps the taxpayer's name before the public in connection with encouraging contributions to such organizations as the Red Cross, the purchase of United States Savings Bonds, or participation in similar causes. In like fashion, expenditures for advertising which presents views on economic, financial, social, or other subjects of a general nature, but which does not involve any of the activities specified in paragraph (b) or (c) of this section for which a deduction is not allowable, are deductible if they otherwise meet the requirements of the regulations under section 162.

***

(c) *Taxable years beginning after December 31, 1962--*(1) *In general.* For taxable years beginning after December 31, 1962, certain types of expenses incurred with respect to legislative matters are deductible under section 162(a) if they otherwise meet the requirements of the regulations under section 162. These deductible expenses are described in subparagraph (2) of this paragraph. All other expenditures for lobbying purposes, for the promotion or defeat of legislation (see paragraph (b)(2) of this section), for political campaign purposes (including the support of or opposition to any candidate for public office), or for carrying on propaganda (including advertising) relating to any of the foregoing purposes are not deductible from gross income for such taxable years. For the disallowance of deductions for bad debts and worthless securities of a political party, see § 1.271-1. For the disallowance of deductions for certain indirect political contributions, such as the cost of certain advertising and the cost of admission to certain dinners, programs, and inaugural events, see § 1.276-1.

(2) *Appearances, etc., with respect to legislation--*(i) *General rule.* Pursuant to the provisions of section 162(e), expenses incurred with respect to legislative matters which may be deductible are those ordinary and necessary expenses (including, but not limited to, traveling expenses described in section 162(a)(2) and the cost of preparing testimony) paid or incurred by the taxpayer during a taxable year beginning after December 31, 1962, in carrying on any trade or business which are in direct connection with--

(a) Appearances before, submission of statements to, or sending communications to, the committees, or individual members of Congress or of any legislative body of a State, a possession of the United States, or a political subdivision of any of the foregoing with respect to legislation or proposed legislation of direct interest to the taxpayer, or

(b) Communication of information between the taxpayer and an organization of which he is a member with respect to legislation or proposed legislation of direct interest to the taxpayer and to such organization.

For provisions relating to dues paid or incurred with respect to an organization of which the taxpayer is a member, see subparagraph (3) of this paragraph.

(ii) *Legislation or proposed legislation of direct interest to the taxpayer--*(a) *Legislation or proposed legislation.* The term ``legislation or proposed legislation'' includes bills and resolutions introduced by a member of Congress or other legislative body referred to in subdivision (i)(a) of this subparagraph for consideration by such body as well as oral or written proposals for legislative action submitted to the legislative body or to a committee or member of such body.

(b) *Direct interest--*(1) *In general.* (i) Legislation or proposed legislation is of direct

Sec. 162.   Trade or business expenses

interest to a taxpayer if the legislation or proposed legislation is of such a nature that it will, or may reasonably be expected to, affect the trade or business of the taxpayer. It is immaterial whether the effect, or expected effect, on the trade or business will be beneficial or detrimental to the trade or business or whether it will be immediate. If legislation or proposed legislation has such a relationship to a trade or business that the 5 expenses of any appearance or communication in connection with the legislation meets the ordinary and necessary test of section 162(a), then such legislation ordinarily meets the direct interest test of section 162(e). However, if the nature of the legislation or proposed legislation is such that the likelihood of its having an effect on the trade or business of the taxpayer is remote or speculative, the legislation or proposed legislation 10 is not of direct interest to the taxpayer. Legislation or proposed legislation which will not affect the trade or business of the taxpayer is not of direct interest to the taxpayer even though such legislation will affect the personal, living, or family activities or expenses of the taxpayer. Legislation or proposed legislation is not of direct interest to a taxpayer merely because it may affect business in general; however, if the legislation or proposed 15 legislation will, or may reasonably be expected to, affect the taxpayer's trade or business it will be of direct interest to the taxpayer even though it also will affect the trade or business of other taxpayers or business in general. To meet the direct interest test, it is not necessary that all provisions of the legislation or proposed legislation have an effect, or expected effect, on the taxpayer's trade or business. The test will be met if one of the 20 provisions of the legislation has the specified effect. Legislation or proposed legislation will be considered to be of direct interest to a membership organization if it is of direct interest to the organization, as such, or if it is of direct interest to one or more of its members.

(ii) Legislation which would increase or decrease the taxes applicable to the trade or 25 business, increase or decrease the operating costs or earnings of the trade or business, or increase or decrease the administrative burdens connected with the trade or business meets the direct interest test. Legislation which would increase the social security benefits or liberalize the right to such benefits meets the direct interest test because such changes in the social security benefits may reasonably be expected to affect the 30 retirement benefits which the employer will be asked to provide his employees or to increase his taxes. Legislation which would impose a retailer's sales tax is of direct interest to a retailer because, although the tax may be passed on to his customers, collection of the tax will impose additional burdens on the retailer, and because the increased cost of his products to the consumer may reduce the demand for them. 35 Legislation which would provide an income tax credit or exclusion for shareholders is of direct interest to a corporation, because those tax benefits may increase the sources of capital available to the corporation. Legislation which would favorably or adversely affect the business of a competitor so as to affect the taxpayer's competitive position is of direct interest to the taxpayer. Legislation which would improve the school system of a 40 community is of direct interest to a membership organization comprised of employers in the community because the improved school system is likely to make the community more attractive to prospective employees of such employers. On the other hand, proposed legislation relating to Presidential succession in the event of the death of the President has only a remote and speculative effect on any trade or business and 45 therefore does not meet the direct interest test. Similarly, if a corporation is represented before a congressional committee to oppose an appropriation bill merely because of a desire to bring increased Government economy with the hope that such economy will eventually cause a reduction in the Federal income tax, the legislation does not meet the direct interest test because any effect it may have upon the corporation's trade or 50 business is highly speculative.

Sec. 162. Trade or business expenses

(2) *Appearances, etc., by expert witnesses.* (i) An appearance or communication (of a type described in paragraph (c)(2)(i)(a) of this section) by an individual in connection with legislation or proposed legislation shall be considered to be with respect to legislation of direct interest to such individual if the legislation is in a field in which he specializes as an
5 employee, if the appearance or communication is not on behalf of his employer, and if it is customary for individuals in his type of employment to publicly express their views in respect of matters in their field of competence. Expenses incurred by such an individual in connection with such an appearance of communication, including traveling expenses properly allocable thereto, represent ordinary and necessary business expenses and are,
10 therefore, deductible under section 162. For example, if a university professor who teaches in the field of money and banking appears, on his own behalf, before a legislative committee to testify on proposed legislation regarding the banking system, his expenses incurred in connection with such appearance are deductible under section 162 since university professors customarily take an active part in the development of the law in their
15 field of competence and publicly communicate the results of their work.

(ii) An appearance or communication (of a type described in paragraph (c)(2)(i)(a) of this section) by an employee or self-employed individual in connection with legislation or proposed legislation shall be considered to be with respect to legislation of direct interest to such person if the legislation is in the field in which he specializes in his business (or
20 as an employee) and if the appearance or communication is made pursuant to an invitation extended to him individually for the purpose of receiving his expert testimony. Expenses incurred by an employee or self-employed individual in connection with such an appearance or communication, including traveling expenses properly allocable thereto, represent ordinary and necessary business expenses and are, therefore,
25 deductible under section 162. For example, if a self-employed individual is personally invited by a congressional committee to testify on proposed legislation in the field in which he specializes in his business, his expenses incurred in connection with such appearance are deductible under section 162. If a self-employed individual makes an appearance, on his own behalf, before a legislative committee without having been
30 extended an invitation his expenses will be deductible to the extent otherwise provided in this paragraph.

(3) *Nominations, etc.* A taxpayer does not have a direct interest in matters such as nominations, appointments, or the operation of the legislative body.

(iii) *Allowable expenses.* To be deductible under section 162(a), expenditures which
35 meet the tests of deductibility under the provisions of this paragraph must also qualify as ordinary and necessary business expenses under section 162(a) and, in addition, be in direct connection with the carrying on of the activities specified in subdivision (i)(a) or (i)(b) of this subparagraph. For example, a taxpayer appearing before a committee of the Congress to present testimony concerning legislation or proposed legislation in which he
40 has a direct interest may deduct the ordinary and necessary expenses directly connected with his appearance, such as traveling expenses described in section 162(a)(2), and the cost of preparing testimony.

(3) *Deductibility of dues and other payments to an organization.* If a substantial part of the activities of an organization, such as a labor union or a trade association, consists of
45 one or more of the activities to which this paragraph relates (legislative matters, political campaigns, etc.), exclusive of any activity constituting an appearance or communication with respect to legislation or proposed legislation of direct interest to the organization (see subparagraph (c)(2)(ii)(b)(1)), a deduction will be allowed only for such portion of the dues or other payments to the organization as the taxpayer can clearly establish is
50 attributable to activities to which this paragraph does not relate and to any activity constituting an appearance or communication with respect to legislation or proposed

Sec. 162. Trade or business expenses

legislation of direct interest to the organization. The determination of whether a substantial part of an organization's activities consists of one or more of the activities to which this paragraph relates (exclusive of appearances or communications with respect to legislation or proposed legislation of direct interest to the organization) shall be based on all the facts and circumstances. In no event shall a deduction be allowed for that 5 portion of a special assessment or similar payment (including an increase in dues) made to any organization for any activity to which this paragraph relates if the activity does not constitute an appearance or communication with respect to legislation or proposed legislation of direct interest to the organization. If an organization pays or incurs expenses allocable to legislative activities which meet the tests of subdivisions (i) and (ii) 10 of subparagraph (2) of this paragraph (appearances or communications with respect to legislation or proposed legislation of direct interest to the organization), on behalf of its members, the dues paid by a taxpayer are deductible to the extent used for such activities. Dues paid by a taxpayer will be considered to be used for such an activity, and thus deductible, although the legislation or proposed legislation involved is not of direct 15 interest to the taxpayer, if, pursuant to the provisions of subparagraph (2)(ii)(b)(1) of this paragraph, the legislation or proposed legislation is of direct interest to the organization, as such, or is of direct interest to one or more members of the organization. For other provisions relating to the deductibility of dues and other payments to an organization, such as a labor union or a trade association, see paragraph (c) of § 1.162-15. 20

(4) *Limitations.* No deduction shall be allowed under section 162(a) for any amount paid or incurred (whether by way of contribution, gift, or otherwise) in connection with any attempt to influence the general public, or segments thereof, with respect to legislative matters, elections, or referendums. For example, no deduction shall be allowed for any expenses incurred in connection with ``grassroot'' campaigns or any other attempts to 25 urge or encourage the public to contact members of a legislative body for the purpose of proposing, supporting, or opposing legislation.

(5) Expenses paid or incurred after December 31, 1993, in connection with influencing legislation other than certain local legislation. The provisions of paragraphs (c)(1) through (3) of this section are superseded for expenses paid or incurred after December 31, 30 1993, in connection with influencing legislation (other than certain local legislation) to the extent inconsistent with section 162(e)(1)(A) (as limited by section 162(e)(2)) and §§ 1.162-20(d) and 1.162-29.

(d) *Dues allocable to expenditures after 1993.* No deduction is allowed under section 162(a) for the portion of dues or other similar amounts paid by the taxpayer to an 35 organization exempt from tax (other than an organization described in section 501(c)(3)) which the organization notifies the taxpayer under section 6033(e)(1)(A)(ii) is allocable to expenditures to which section 162(e)(1) applies. The first sentence of this paragraph (d) applies to dues or other similar amounts whether or not paid on or before December 31, 1993. Section 1.162-20(c)(3) is superseded to the extent inconsistent with this paragraph 40 (d).

Reg. § 1.162-21 Fines and penalties.

(a) In general. No deduction shall be allowed under section 162(a) for any fine or similar penalty paid to-- 45

(1) The government of the United States, a State, a territory or possession of the United States, the District of Columbia, or the Commonwealth of Puerto Rico;

(2) The government of a foreign country; or

(3) A political subdivision of, or corporation or other entity serving as an agency or instrumentality of, any of the above. 50

(b) *Definition.* (1) For purposes of this section a fine or similar penalty includes an

369

Sec. 162. Trade or business expenses

amount--

(i) Paid pursuant to conviction or a plea of guilty or nolo contendere for a crime (felony or misdemeanor) in a criminal proceeding;

(ii) Paid as a civil penalty imposed by Federal, State, or local law, including additions to tax and additional amounts and assessable penalties imposed by chapter 68 of the Internal Revenue Code of 1954;

(iii) Paid in settlement of the taxpayer's actual or potential liability for a fine or penalty (civil or criminal); or

(iv) Forfeited as collateral posted in connection with a proceeding which could result in imposition of such a fine or penalty.

(2) The amount of a fine or penalty does not include legal fees and related expenses paid or incurred in the defense of a prosecution or civil action arising from a violation of the law imposing the fine or civil penalty, nor court costs assessed against the taxpayer, or stenographic and printing charges. Compensatory damages (including damages under section 4A of the Clayton Act (15 U.S.C. 15a), as amended) paid to a government do not constitute a fine or penalty.

(c) *Examples.* The application of this section may be illustrated by the following examples:

Example (1). M Corp. was indicted under section 1 of the Sherman Anti-Trust Act (15 U.S.C. 1) for fixing and maintaining prices of certain electrical products. M Corp. was convicted and was fined $50,000. The United States sued M Corp. under section 4A of the Clayton Act (15 U.S.C. 15a) for $100,000, the amount of the actual damages resulting from the price fixing of which M Corp. was convicted. Pursuant to a final judgment entered in the civil action. M Corp. paid the United States $100,000 in damages. Section 162(f) precludes M Corp. from deducting the fine of $50,000 as a trade or business expense. Section 162(f) does not preclude it from deducting the $100,000 paid to the United States as actual damages.

Example (2). N Corp. was found to have violated 33 U.S.C. 1321(b)(3) when a vessel it operated discharged oil in harmful quantities into the navigable waters of the United States. A civil penalty under 33 U.S.C. 1321(b)(6) of $5,000 was assessed against N Corp. with respect to the discharge. N Corp. paid $5,000 to the Coast Guard in payment of the civil penalty. Section 162(f) precludes N Corp. from deducting the $5,000 penalty.

Example (3). O Corp., a manufacturer of motor vehicles, was found to have violated 42 U.S.C. 1857f-2(a)(1) by selling a new motor vehicle which was not covered by the required certificate of conformity. Pursuant to 42 U.S.C. 1857f-4, O Corp. was required to pay, and did pay, a civil penalty of $10,000. In addition, pursuant to 42 U.S.C. 1857f-5a(c) (1), O Corp. was required to expend, and did expend, $500 in order to remedy the nonconformity of that motor vehicle. Section 162(f) precludes O Corp. from deducting the $10,000 penalty as a trade or business expense, but does not preclude it from deducting the $500 which it expended to remedy the nonconformity.

Example (4). P Corp. was the operator of a coal mine in which occurred a violation of a mandatory safety standard prescribed by the Federal Coal Mine Health and Safety Act of 1969 (30 U.S.C. 801 et seq.). Pursuant to 30 U.S.C. 819(a), a civil penalty of $10,000 was assessed against P Corp., and P Corp. paid the penalty. Section 162(f) precludes P Corp. from deducting the $10,000 penalty.

Example (5). Q Corp., a common carrier engaged in interstate commerce by railroad, hauled a railroad car which was not equipped with efficient hand brakes, in violation of 45 U.S.C. 11. Q Corp. was found to be liable for a penalty of $250 pursuant to 45 U.S.C. 13. Q Corp. paid that penalty. Section 162(f) precludes Q Corp. from deducting the $250 penalty.

Example (6). R Corp. owned and operated on the highways of State X a truck weighing

370

Sec. 162. Trade or business expenses

in excess of the amount permitted under the law of State X. R Corp. was found to have violated the law and was assessed a fine of $85 which it paid to State X. Section 162(f) precludes R Corp. from deducting the amount so paid.

Example (7). S Corp. was found to have violated a law of State Y which prohibited the emission into the air of particulate matter in excess of a limit set forth in a regulation promulgated under that law. The Environmental Quality Hearing Board of State Y assessed a fine of $500 against S Corp. The fine was payable to State Y, and S Corp. paid it. Section 162(f) precludes S Corp. from deducting the $500 fine.

Example (8). T Corp. was found by a magistrate of City Z to be operating in such city an apartment building which did not conform to a provision of the city housing code requiring operable fire escapes on apartment buildings of that type. Upon the basis of the magistrate's finding, T Corp. was required to pay, and did pay, a fine of $200 to City Z. Section 162(f) precludes T Corp. from deducting the $200 fine.

[T.D. 6500, 25 FR 11402, Nov. 26, 1960; T.D. 6520, 25 FR 13692, Dec. 24, 1960; T.D. 6630, 27 FR 12935, Dec. 29, 1962; T.D. 6690, 28 FR 12253, Nov. 19, 1963; T.D. 6819, 30 FR 5581, Apr. 20, 1965; T.D. 6918, 32 FR 6679, May 2, 1967; T.D. 6996, 34 FR 835, Jan. 18, 1969; T.D. 7198, 37 FR 13679, July 13, 1972; T.D. 7315, 39 FR 20203, June 7, 1974; T.D. 7345, 40 FR 7437, Feb. 20, 1975; T.D. 7366, 40 FR 29290, July 11, 1975; T.D. 8189, 53 FR 9881, Mar. 28, 1988; T.D. 8276, 54 FR 51026, Dec. 12, 1989; T.D. 8324, 55 FR 51695, Dec. 17, 1990; T.D. 8491, 58 FR 53128, Oct. 14, 1993; T.D. 8602, 60 FR 37573, July 21, 1995; T.D. 8729, 62 FR 44546, Aug. 22, 1997; T.D. 8867, 65 FR 3825, Jan. 25, 2000; T.D. 8897, 65 FR 50643, Aug. 21, 2000]

Sec. 163. Interest

(a) **General rule.** -- There shall be allowed as a deduction all interest paid or accrued within the taxable year on indebtedness.

(b) **Installment purchases where interest charge is not separately stated.** --

(1) **General rule.** -- If personal property or educational services are purchased under a contract--

(A) which provides that payment of part or all of the purchase price is to be made in installments, and

(B) in which carrying charges are separately stated but the interest charge cannot be ascertained, then the payments made during the taxable year under the contract shall be treated for purposes of this section as if they included interest equal to 6 percent of the average unpaid balance under the contract during the taxable year. For purposes of the preceding sentence, the average unpaid balance is the sum of the unpaid balance outstanding on the first day of each month beginning during the taxable year, divided by 12. For purposes of this paragraph, the term "educational services" means any service (including lodging) which is purchased from an educational organization described in section 170(b)(1)(A)(ii) and which is provided for a student of such organization.

(2) **Limitation.** -- In the case of any contract to which paragraph (1) applies, the amount treated as interest for any taxable year shall not exceed the aggregate carrying charges which are properly attributable to such taxable year.

(c) **Redeemable ground rents.** -- For purposes of this subtitle, any annual or periodic rental under a redeemable ground rent (excluding amounts in redemption thereof) shall be treated as interest on an indebtedness secured by a mortgage.

(d) **Limitation on investment interest.** --

Sec. 163. Interest

(1) In general. -- In the case of a taxpayer other than a corporation, the amount allowed as a deduction under this chapter for investment interest for any taxable year shall not exceed the net investment income of the taxpayer for the taxable year.

(2) Carryforward of disallowed interest. -- The amount not allowed as a deduction for any taxable year by reason of paragraph (1) shall be treated as investment interest paid or accrued by the taxpayer in the succeeding taxable year.

(3) Investment interest. -- For purposes of this subsection--

    (A) In general. -- The term "investment interest" means any interest allowable as a deduction under this chapter (determined without regard to paragraph (1)) which is paid or accrued on indebtedness properly allocable to property held for investment.

    (B) Exceptions. -- The term "investment interest" shall not include--

        (i) any qualified residence interest (as defined in subsection (h)(3)), or

        (ii) any interest which is taken into account under section 469 in computing income or loss from a passive activity of the taxpayer.

    (C) Personal property used in short sale. -- For purposes of this paragraph, the term "interest" includes any amount allowable as a deduction in connection with personal property used in a short sale.

(4) Net investment income. -- For purposes of this subsection--

    (A) In general. -- The term "net investment income" means the excess of--

        (i) investment income, over

        (ii) investment expenses.

    (B) Investment income. -- The term "investment income" means the sum of--

        (i) gross income from property held for investment (other than any gain taken into account under clause (ii)(I)),

        (ii) the excess (if any) of -

            (I) the net gain attributable to the disposition of property held for investment, over

            (II) the net capital gain determined by only taking into account gains and losses from dispositions of property held for investment, plus

        (iii) so much of the net capital gain referred to in clause (ii)(II) (or, if lesser, the net gain referred to in clause (ii)(I)) as the taxpayer elects to take into account under this clause.

Such term shall include qualified dividend income (as defined in section 1(h)(11)(B)) only to the extent the taxpayer elects to treat such income as investment income for purposes of this subsection.

    (C) Investment expenses. -- The term "investment expenses" means the deductions allowed under this chapter (other than for interest) which are directly connected with the production of investment income.

    (D) Income and expenses from passive activities. -- Investment income and investment expenses shall not include any income or expenses taken into account under section 469 in computing income or loss from a passive activity.

    (E) Reduction in investment income during phase-in of passive loss rules. -- Investment income of the taxpayer for any taxable year shall be reduced by the amount of the passive activity loss to which section 469(a) does not apply for such taxable year by reason of section 469(m). The preceding sentence shall not apply to any portion of such passive activity loss which is attributable to a rental real estate activity with respect to which the taxpayer actively participates (within the meaning of section 469(i)(6)) during such taxable year.

(5) Property held for investment. -- For purposes of this subsection--

(A) In general. -- The term "property held for investment" shall include--

(i) any property which produces income of a type described in section 469(e)(1), and 5

(ii) any interest held by a taxpayer in an activity involving the conduct of a trade or business -

(I) which is not a passive activity, and

(II) with respect to which the taxpayer does not materially participate.

(B) Investment expenses. -- In the case of property described in subparagraph (A)(i), 10 expenses shall be allocated to such property in the same manner as under section 469.

(C) Terms. -- For purposes of this paragraph, the terms "activity", "passive activity", and "materially participate" have the meanings given such terms by section 469.

(e) Original issue discount. --

(1) In general. -- In the case of any debt instrument issued after July 1, 1982, the portion of 15 the original issue discount with respect to such debt instrument which is allowable as a deduction to the issuer for any taxable year shall be equal to the aggregate daily portions of the original issue discount for days during such taxable year.

(2) Definitions and special rules. -- For purposes of this subsection--

(A) Debt instrument. -- The term "debt instrument" has the meaning given such term by 20 section 1275(a)(1).

(B) Daily portions. -- The daily portion of the original issue discount for any day shall be determined under section 1272(a) (without regard to paragraph (7) thereof and without regard to section 1273(a)(3)).

***   25

(4) Exceptions. -- This subsection shall not apply to any debt instrument described in--

***

(B) subparagraph (E) of section 1272(a)(2) (relating to loans between natural persons)

(f) Denial of deduction for interest on certain obligations not in registered form. --

(1) In general. -- Nothing in subsection (a) or in any other provision of law   30 shall be construed to provide a deduction for interest on any registration-required obligation unless such obligation is in registered form.

(2) Registration-required obligation. -- For purposes of this section--

(A) In general. -- The term "registration-required obligation" means any obligation 35 (including any obligation issued by a governmental entity) other than an obligation which--

(i) is issued by a natural person,

(ii) is not of a type offered to the public,

(iii) has a maturity (at issue) of not more than 1 year, or

(iv) is described in subparagraph (B).   40

***

(h) Disallowance of deduction for personal interest. --

(1) In general. -- In the case of a taxpayer other than a corporation, no deduction shall be allowed under this chapter for personal interest paid or accrued during the taxable year.

Sec. 163. Interest

(2) Personal interest. -- For purposes of this subsection, the term "personal interest" means any interest allowable as a deduction under this chapter other than--

(A) interest paid or accrued on indebtedness properly allocable to a trade or business (other than the trade or business of performing services as an employee),

(B) any investment interest (within the meaning of subsection (d)),

(C) any interest which is taken into account under section 469 in computing income or loss from a passive activity of the taxpayer,

(D) any qualified residence interest (within the meaning of paragraph (3)),

(E) any interest payable under section 6601 on any unpaid portion of the tax imposed by section 2001 for the period during which an extension of time for payment of such tax is in effect under section 6163, and

(F) any interest allowable as a deduction under section 221 (relating to interest on educational loans).

(3) Qualified residence interest. -- For purposes of this subsection--

(A) In general. -- The term "qualified residence interest" means any interest which is paid or accrued during the taxable year on--

(i) acquisition indebtedness with respect to any qualified residence of the taxpayer, or

(ii) home equity indebtedness with respect to any qualified residence of the taxpayer.

For purposes of the preceding sentence, the determination of whether any property is a qualified residence of the taxpayer shall be made as of the time the interest is accrued.

(B) Acquisition indebtedness. --

(i) In general. -- The term "acquisition indebtedness" means any indebtedness which--

(I) is incurred in acquiring, constructing, or substantially improving any qualified residence of the taxpayer, and

(II) is secured by such residence.

Such term also includes any indebtedness secured by such residence resulting from the refinancing of indebtedness meeting the requirements of the preceding sentence (or this sentence); but only to the extent the amount of the indebtedness resulting from such refinancing does not exceed the amount of the refinanced indebtedness.

(ii) $1,000,000 limitation. -- The aggregate amount treated as acquisition indebtedness for any period shall not exceed $1,000,000 ($500,000 in the case of a married individual filing a separate return).

(C) Home equity indebtedness. --

(i) In general. -- The term "home equity indebtedness" means any indebtedness (other than acquisition indebtedness) secured by a qualified residence to the extent the aggregate amount of such indebtedness does not exceed -

(I) the fair market value of such qualified residence, reduced by

(II) the amount of acquisition indebtedness with respect to such residence.

(ii) Limitation. -- The aggregate amount treated as home equity indebtedness for any period shall not exceed $100,000 ($50,000 in the case of a separate return by a married individual).

***

(E) Mortgage insurance premiums treated as interest. --

(i) In general. -- Premiums paid or accrued for qualified mortgage insurance by a

374

Sec. 163. Interest

taxpayer during the taxable year in connection with acquisition indebtedness with respect to a qualified residence of the taxpayer shall be treated for purposes of this section as interest which is qualified residence interest.

(ii) Phaseout. -- The amount otherwise treated as interest under clause (i) shall be reduced (but not below zero) by 10 percent of such amount for each $1,000 ($500 in the case of a married individual filing a separate return) (or fraction thereof) that the taxpayer's adjusted gross income for the taxable year exceeds $100,000 ($50,000 in the case of a married individual filing a separate return).

(iii) Limitation. -- Clause (i) shall not apply with respect to any mortgage insurance contracts issued before January 1, 2007.

(iv) Termination. -- Clause (i) shall not apply to amounts--

(I) paid or accrued after December 31, 2010, or

(II) properly allocable to any period after such date.

(4) Other definitions and special rules. -- For purposes of this subsection--

(A) Qualified residence. --

(i) In general. -- The term "qualified residence" means--

(I) the principal residence (within the meaning of section 121) of the taxpayer, and

(II) 1 other residence of the taxpayer which is selected by the taxpayer for purposes of this subsection for the taxable year and which is used by the taxpayer as a residence (within the meaning of section 280A(d)(1)).

(ii) Married individuals filing separate returns. -- If a married couple does not file a joint return for the taxable year--

(I) such couple shall be treated as 1 taxpayer for purposes of clause (i), and

(II) each individual shall be entitled to take into account 1 residence unless both individuals consent in writing to 1 individual taking into account the principal residence and 1 other residence.

(iii) Residence not rented. -- For purposes of clause (i)(II), notwithstanding section 280A(d)(1), if the taxpayer does not rent a dwelling unit at any time during a taxable year, such unit may be treated as a residence for such taxable year.

(B) Special rule for cooperative housing corporations. -- Any indebtedness secured by stock held by the taxpayer as a tenant-stockholder (as defined in section 216) in a cooperative housing corporation (as so defined) shall be treated as secured by the house or apartment which the taxpayer is entitled to occupy as such a tenant-stockholder. If stock described in the preceding sentence may not be used to secure indebtedness, indebtedness shall be treated as so secured if the taxpayer establishes to the satisfaction of the Secretary that such indebtedness was incurred to acquire such stock.

(C) Unenforceable security interests. -- Indebtedness shall not fail to be treated as secured by any property solely because, under any applicable State or local homestead or other debtor protection law in effect on August16, 1986, the security interest is ineffective or the enforceability of the security interest is restricted.

***

(E) Qualified mortgage insurance. -- The term `qualified mortgage insurance' means--

(i) mortgage insurance provided by the Veterans Administration, the Federal Housing Administration, or the Rural Housing Administration, and

(ii) private mortgage insurance (as defined by section 2 of the Homeowners

375

Sec. 163. Interest

Protection Act of 1998 (12 U.S.C. 4901), as in effect on the date of the enactment of this subparagraph).

(F) Special rules for prepaid qualified mortgage insurance. -- Any amount paid by the taxpayer for qualified mortgage insurance that is properly allocable to any mortgage the payment of which extends to periods that are after the close of the taxable year in which such amount is paid shall be chargeable to capital account and shall be treated as paid in such periods to which so allocated. No deduction shall be allowed for the unamortized balance of such account if such mortgage is satisfied before the end of its term. The preceding sentences shall not apply to amounts paid for qualified mortgage insurance provided by the Veterans Administration or the Rural Housing Administration.

***

Reg. § 1.163-1   Interest deduction in general.

(a) Except as otherwise provided in sections 264 to 267, inclusive, interest paid or accrued within the taxable year on indebtedness shall be allowed as a deduction in computing taxable income. For rules relating to interest on certain deferred payments, see section 483 and the regulations thereunder.

(b) Interest paid by the taxpayer on a mortgage upon real estate of which he is the legal or equitable owner, even though the taxpayer is not directly liable upon the bond or note secured by such mortgage, may be deducted as interest on his indebtedness. Pursuant to the provisions of section 163(c), any annual or periodic rental payment made by a taxpayer on or after January 1, 1962, under a redeemable ground rent, as defined in section 1055(c) and paragraph (b) of § 1.1055-1, is required to be treated as interest on an indebtedness secured by a mortgage and, accordingly, may be deducted by the taxpayer as interest on his indebtedness. Section 163(c) has no application in respect of any annual or periodic rental payment made prior to January 1, 1962, or pursuant to an arrangement which does not constitute a ``redeemable ground rent" as defined in section 1055(c) and paragraph (b) of § 1.1055-1. Accordingly, annual or periodic payments of Pennsylvania ground rents made before, on, or after January 1, 1962, are deductible as interest if the ground rent is redeemable. An annual or periodic rental payment under a Maryland redeemable ground rent made prior to January 1, 1962, is deductible in accordance with the rules and regulations applicable at the time such payment was made. Any annual or periodic rental payment under a Maryland redeemable ground rent made by the taxpayer on or after January 1, 1962, is, pursuant to the provisions of section 163(c), treated as interest on an indebtedness secured by a mortgage and, accordingly, is deductible by the taxpayer as interest on his indebtedness. In any case where the ground rent is irredeemable, any annual or periodic ground rent payment shall be treated as rent and shall be deductible only to the extent that the payment constitutes a proper business expense. Amounts paid in redemption of a ground rent shall not be treated as interest. For treatment of redeemable ground rents and real property held subject to liabilities under redeemable ground rents, see section 1055 and the regulations thereunder.

(c) Interest calculated for costkeeping or other purposes on account of capital or surplus invested in the business which does not represent a charge arising under an interest-bearing obligation, is not an allowable deduction from gross income. Interest paid by a corporation on scrip dividends is an allowable deduction. So-called interest on preferred stock, which is in reality a dividend thereon, cannot be deducted in computing taxable income. (See, however, section 583.) In the case of banks and loan or trust companies, interest paid within the year on deposits, such as interest paid on moneys received for investment and secured by interest-bearing certificates of indebtedness

Sec. 163. Interest

issued by such bank or loan or trust company, may be deducted from gross income.

***

Reg. § 1.163-8T Allocation of interest expense among expenditures (temporary).

(a) In general--(1) Application. This section prescribes rules for allocating interest expense for purposes of applying sections 469 (the ``passive loss limitation") and 163 (d) and (h) (the ``nonbusiness interest limitations").

(2) Cross-references. This paragraph provides an overview of the manner in which interest expense is allocated for the purposes of applying the passive loss limitation and nonbusiness interest limitations and the manner in which interest expense allocated under this section is treated. See paragraph (b) of this section for definitions of certain terms, paragraph (c) for the rules for allocating debt and interest expense among expenditures, paragraphs (d) and (e) for the treatment of debt repayments and refinancings, paragraph (j) for the rules for reallocating debt upon the occurrence of certain events, paragraph (m) for the coordination of the rules in this section with other limitations on the deductibility of interest expense, and paragraph (n) of this section for effective date and transitional rules.

(3) Manner of allocation. In general, interest expense on a debt is allocated in the same manner as the debt to which such interest expense relates is allocated. Debt is allocated by tracing disbursements of the debt proceeds to specific expenditures. This section prescribes rules for tracing debt proceeds to specific expenditures.

(4) Treatment of interest expenses--(i) General rule. Except as otherwise provided in paragraph (m) of this section (relating to limitations on interest expense other than the passive loss and nonbusiness interest limitations), interest expense allocated under the rules of this section is treated in the following manner:

(A) Interest expense allocated to a trade or business expenditure (as defined in paragraph (b)(7) of this section) is taken into account under section 163 (h)(2)(A);

(B) Interest expense allocated to a passive activity expenditure (as defined in paragraph (b)(4) of this section) or a former passive activity expenditure (as defined in paragraph (b)(2) of this section) is taken into account for purposes of section 469 in determining the income or loss from the activity to which such expenditure relates;

(C) Interest expense allocated to an investment expenditure (as defined in paragraph (b)(3) of this section) is treated for purposes of section 163(d) as investment interest;

(D) Interest expense allocated to a personal expenditure (as defined in paragraph (b) (5) of this section) is treated for purposes of section 163(h) as personal interest; and

(E) Interest expense allocated to a portfolio expenditure (as defined in paragraph (b) (6) of this section) is treated for purposes of section 469(e)(2)(B)(ii) as interest expense described in section 469(e)(1)(A)(i)(III).

(ii) Examples. The following examples illustrate the application of this paragraph (a) (4):

Example (1). Taxpayer A, an individual, incurs interest expense allocated under the rules of this section to the following expenditures:

$6,000 Passive activity expenditure.
$4,000 Personal expenditure.

The $6,000 interest expense allocated to the passive activity expenditure is taken into account for purposes of section 469 in computing A's income or loss from the activity to which such interest relates. Pursuant to section 163(h), A may not deduct the $4,000 interest expense allocated to the personal expenditure (except to the extent such interest is qualified residence interest, within the meaning of section 163(h)(3)).

Example (2). (i) Corporation M, a closely held C corporation (within the meaning of

Sec. 163. Interest

section 469 (j)(1)) has $10,000 of interest expense for a taxable year. Under the rules of this section, M's interest expense is allocated to the following expenditures:

5

$2,000 Passive activity expenditure.
$3,000 Portfolio expenditure.
$5,000 Other expenditures.

(ii) Under section 163(d)(3)(D) and this paragraph (a)(4), the $2,000 interest expense allocated to the passive activity expenditure is taken into account in computing M's

10 passive activity loss for the taxable year, but, pursuant to section 469(e)(1) and this paragraph (a)(4), the interest expense allocated to the portfolio expenditure and the other expenditures is not taken into account for such purposes.

(iii) Since M is a closely held C corporation, its passive activity loss is allowable under section 469(e)(2)(A) as a deduction from net active income. Under section 469(e)(2)(B)

15 and this paragraph (a)(4), the $5,000 interest expense allocated to other expenditures is taken into account in computing M's net active income, but the interest expense allocated to the passive activity expenditure and the portfolio expenditure is not taken into account for such purposes.

(iv) Since M is a corporation, the $3,000 interest expense allocated to the portfolio

20 expenditure is allowable without regard to section 163(d). If M were an individual, however, the interest expense allocated to the portfolio expenditure would be treated as investment interest for purposes of applying the limitation of section 163(d).

(b) *Definitions.* For purposes of this section--

(1) ``Former passive activity" means an activity described in section 469(f)(3), but only

25 if an unused deduction or credit (within the meaning of section 469(f)(1) (A) or (B)) is allocable to the activity under section 469(b) for the taxable year.

(2) ``Former passive activity expenditure" means an expenditure that is taken into account under section 469 in computing the income or loss from a former passive activity of the taxpayer or an expenditure (including an expenditure properly chargeable to capital

30 account) that would be so taken into account if such expenditure were otherwise deductible.

(3) ``Investment expenditure" means an expenditure (other than a passive activity expenditure) properly chargeable to capital account with respect to property held for investment (within the meaning of section 163(d)(5)(A)) or an expenditure in connection

35 with the holding of such property.

(4) ``Passive activity expenditure" means an expenditure that is taken into account under section 469 in computing income or loss from a passive activity of the taxpayer or an expenditure (including an expenditure properly chargeable to capital account) that would be so taken into account if such expenditure were otherwise deductible. For

40 purposes of this section, the term ``passive activity expenditure" does not include any expenditure with respect to any low-income housing project in any taxable year in which any benefit is allowed with respect to such project under section 502 of the Tax Reform Act of 1986.

(5) ``Personal expenditure" means an expenditure that is not a trade or business

45 expenditure, a passive activity expenditure, or an investment expenditure.

(6) ``Portfolio expenditure" means an investment expenditure properly chargeable to capital account with respect to property producing income of a type described in section 469(e)(1)(A) or an investment expenditure for an expense clearly and directly allocable to such income.

50 (7) ``Trade or business expenditure" means an expenditure (other than a passive activity expenditure or an investment expenditure) in connection with the conduct of any

Sec. 163. Interest

trade or business other than the trade or business of performing services as an employee.

(c) *Allocation of debt and interest expense--*(1) *Allocation in accordance with use of proceeds.* Debt is allocated to expenditures in accordance with the use of the debt proceeds and, except as provided in paragraph (m) of this section, interest expense 5 accruing on a debt during any period is allocated to expenditures in the same manner as the debt is allocated from time to time during such period. Except as provided in paragraph (m) of this section, debt proceeds and related interest expense are allocated solely by reference to the use of such proceeds, and the allocation is not affected by the use of an interest in any property to secure the repayment of such debt or interest. The 10 following example illustrates the principles of this paragraph (c)(1):

Example. Taxpayer A, an individual, pledges corporate stock held for investment as security for a loan and uses the debt proceeds to purchase an automobile for personal use. Interest expense accruing on the debt is allocated to the personal expenditure to purchase the automobile even though the debt is secured by investment property. 15

(2) *Allocation period--*(i) *Allocation of debt.* Debt is allocated to an expenditure for the period beginning on the date the proceeds of the debt are used or treated as used under the rules of this section to make the expenditure and ending on the earlier of--

(A) The date the debt is repaid; or

(B) The date the debt is reallocated in accordance with the rules in paragraphs (c)(4) 20 and (j) of this section.

(ii) *Allocation of interest expense--*(A) *In general.* Except as otherwise provided in paragraph (m) of this section, interest expense accruing on a debt for any period is allocated in the same manner as the debt is allocated from time to time, regardless of when the interest is paid. 25

(B) *Effect of compounding.* Accrued interest is treated as a debt until it is paid and any interest accruing on unpaid interest is allocated in the same manner as the unpaid interest is allocated. For the taxable year in which a debt is reallocated under the rules in paragraphs (c)(4) and (j) of this section, however, compound interest accruing on such debt (other than compound interest accruing on interest that accrued before the 30 beginning of the year) may be allocated between the original expenditure and the new expenditure on a straight-line basis (i.e., by allocating an equal amount of such interest expense to each day during the taxable year). In addition, a taxpayer may treat a year as consisting of 12 30-day months for purposes of allocating interest on a straight-line basis.

(C) *Accrual of interest expense.* For purposes of this paragraph (c)(2)(ii), the amount of 35 interest expense that accrues during any period is determined by taking into account relevant provisions of the loan agreement and any applicable law such as sections 163(e), 483, and 1271 through 1275.

(iii) *Examples.* The following examples illustrate the principles of this paragraph (c)(2):

Example (1). (i) On January 1, taxpayer B, a calendar year taxpayer, borrows $1,000 40 at an interest rate of 11 percent, compounded semiannually. B immediately uses the debt proceeds to purchase an investment security. On July 1, B sells the investment security for $1,000 and uses the sales proceeds to make a passive activity expenditure. On December 31, B pays accrued interest on the $1,000 debt for the entire year.

(ii) Under this paragraph (c)(2) and paragraph (j) of this section, the $1,000 debt is 45 allocated to the investment expenditure for the period from January 1 through June 30, and to the passive activity expenditure from July 1 through December 31. Interest expense accruing on the $1,000 debt is allocated in accordance with the allocation of the debt from time to time during the year even though the debt was allocated to the passive activity expenditure on the date the interest was paid. Thus, the $55 interest expense for 50 the period from January 1 through June 30 is allocated to the investment expenditure. In

Sec. 163. Interest

addition, during the period from July 1 through December 31, the interest expense allocated to the investment expenditure is a debt, the proceeds of which are treated as used to make an investment expenditure. Accordingly, an additional $3 of interest expense for the period from July 1 through December 31 ($55x.055) is allocated to the
5 investment expenditure. The remaining $55 of interest expense for the period from July 1 through December 31 ($1,000x.055) is allocated to the passive activity expenditure.

(iii) Alternatively, under the rule in paragraph (c)(2)(ii)(B) of this section, B may allocate the interest expense on a straight-line basis and may also treat the year as consisting of 12 30-day months for this purpose. In that case, $56.50 of interest expense (180/360x
10 $113) would be allocated to the investment expenditure and the remaining $56.50 of interest expense would be allocated to the passive activity expenditure.

Example (2). On January 1, 1988, taxpayer C borrows $10,000 at an interest rate of 11 percent, compounded annually. All interest and principal on the debt is payable in a lump sum on December 31, 1992. C immediately uses the debt proceeds to make a passive
15 activity expenditure. C materially participates in the activity in 1990, 1991, and 1992. Therefore, under paragraphs (c)(2) (i) and (j) of this section, the debt is allocated to a passive activity expenditure from January 1, 1988, through December 31, 1989, and to a former passive activity expenditure from January 1, 1990, through December 31, 1992. In accordance with the loan agreement (and consistent with § 1.1272-1(d)(1) of the
20 proposed regulations, 51 FR 12022, April 8, 1986), interest expense accruing during any period is determined on the basis of annual compounding. Accordingly, the interest expense on the debt is allocated as follows:

Year	Amount	Expenditure	
1988..............................	$10,000 x .11	$1,100	Passive activity.
1989..............................	11,100 x .11	1,221	Passive activity.
1990..............................	12,321 x .11 = 1,355	----------	
	1,355 x 2,321/12,321	255	Passive activity.
	1,355 x 10,000/12,321	1,100	Former passive activity.
		1,355	
1991..............................	13,676 x .11 = 1,504	---------	
	1,504 x 2,576/13,676	283	Passive activity.
	1,504 x 11,100/13,676	1,221	Former passive activity.
		1,504	
1992..............................	15,180 x .11 = 1,670	---------	
	1,670 x 2,859/15,180	315	Passive activity.
	1,670 x 12,321/15,180	1,355	Former passive activity.
		1,670	

(3) *Allocation of debt; proceeds not disbursed to borrower--(i) Third-party financing.* If a lender disburses debt proceeds to a person other than the borrower in consideration for the sale or use of property, for services, or for any other purpose, the debt is treated for
45 purposes of this section as if the borrower used an amount of the debt proceeds equal to such disbursement to make an expenditure for such property, services, or other purpose.

(ii) *Debt assumptions not involving cash disbursements.* If a taxpayer incurs or assumes a debt in consideration for the sale or use of property, for services, or for any other purpose, or takes property subject to a debt, and no debt proceeds are disbursed to
50 the taxpayer, the debt is treated for purposes of this section as if the taxpayer used an amount of the debt proceeds equal to the balance of the debt outstanding at such time to make an expenditure for such property, services, or other purpose.

(4) *Allocation of debt; proceeds deposited in borrower's account--(i) Treatment of deposit.* For purposes of this section, a deposit of debt proceeds in an account is treated

Sec. 163. Interest

as an investment expenditure, and amounts held in an account (whether or not interest bearing) are treated as property held for investment. Debt allocated to an account under this paragraph (c)(4)(i) must be reallocated as required by paragraph (j) of this section whenever debt proceeds held in the account are used for another expenditure. This paragraph (c)(4) provides rules for determining when debt proceeds are expended from 5 the account. The following example illustrates the principles of this paragraph (c)(4)(i):

Example. Taxpayer C, a calendar year taxpayer, borrows $100,000 on January 1 and immediately uses the proceeds to open a noninterest-bearing checking account. No other amounts are deposited in the account during the year, and no portion of the principal amount of the debt is repaid during the year. On April 1, C uses $20,000 of the debt 10 proceeds held in the account for a passive activity expenditure. On September 1, C uses an additional $40,000 of the debt proceeds held in the account for a personal expenditure. Under this paragraph (c)(4)(i), from January 1 through March 31 the entire $100,000 debt is allocated to an investment expenditure for the account. From April 1 through August 31, $20,000 of the debt is allocated to the passive activity expenditure, 15 and $80,000 of the debt is allocated to the investment expenditure for the account. From September 1 through December 31, $40,000 of the debt is allocated to the personal expenditure, $20,000 is allocated to the passive activity expenditure, and $40,000 is allocated to an investment expenditure for the account.

(ii) Expenditures from account; general ordering rule. Except as provided in paragraph 20 (c)(4)(iii)(B) or (C) of this section, debt proceeds deposited in an account are treated as expended before--

(A) Any unborrowed amounts held in the account at the time such debt proceeds are deposited; and

(B) Any amounts (borrowed or unborrowed) that are deposited in the account after 25 such debt proceeds are deposited.

The following example illustrates the application of this paragraph (c)(4)(ii):

Example. On January 10, taxpayer E opens a checking account, depositing $500 of proceeds of Debt A and $1,000 of unborrowed funds. The following chart summarizes the transactions which occur during the year with respect to the account: 30

Date	Transaction	
Jan. 10.....................................	$500 proceeds of Debt A and	
	$1,000 unborowed funds deposited.	35
Jan. 11.....................................	$500 proceeds of Debt B	
	deposited.	
Feb. 17.....................................	$800 personal expenditure.	
Feb. 26.....................................	$700 passive activity	
	expenditure.	40
June 21....................................	$1,000 proceeds of Debt C	
	deposited.	
Nov. 24....................................	$800 investment expenditure.	
Dec. 20....................................	$600 personal expenditure.	
		45

The $800 personal expenditure is treated as made from the $500 proceeds of Debt A and $300 of the proceeds of Debt B. The $700 passive activity expenditure is treated as made from the remaining $200 proceeds of Debt B and $500 of unborrowed funds. The $800 investment expenditure is treated as made entirely from the proceeds of Debt C. The $600 personal expenditure is treated as made from the remaining $200 proceeds of Debt 50 C and $400 of unborrowed funds. Under paragraph (c)(4)(i) of this section, debt is

Sec. 163. Interest

allocated to an investment expenditure for periods during which debt proceeds are held in the account.

(iii) *Expenditures from account; supplemental ordering rules*--(A) *Checking or similar accounts.* Except as otherwise provided in this paragraph (c)(4)(iii), an expenditure from a checking or similar account is treated as made at the time the check is written on the account, provided the check is delivered or mailed to the payee within a reasonable period after the writing of the check. For this purpose, the taxpayer may treat checks written on the same day as written in any order. In the absence of evidence to the contrary, a check is presumed to be written on the date appearing on the check and to be delivered or mailed to the payee within a reasonable period thereafter. Evidence to the contrary may include the fact that a check does not clear within a reasonable period after the date appearing on the check.

(B) *Expenditures within 15 days after deposit of borrowed funds.* The taxpayer may treat any expenditure made from an account within 15 days after debt proceeds are deposited in such account as made from such proceeds to the extent thereof even if under paragraph (c)(4)(ii) of this section the debt proceeds would be treated as used to make one or more other expenditures. Any such expenditures and the debt proceeds from which such expenditures are treated as made are disregarded in applying paragraph (c)(4)(ii) of this section. The following examples illustrate the application of this paragraph (c)(4)(iii)(B):

Example (1). Taxpayer D incurs a $1,000 debt on June 5 and immediately deposits the proceeds in an account (``Account A''). On June 17, D transfers $2,000 from Account A to another account (``Account B''). On June 30, D writes a $1,500 check on Account B for a passive activity expenditure. In addition, numerous deposits of borrowed and unborrowed amounts and expenditures occur with respect to both accounts throughout the month of June. Notwithstanding these other transactions, D may treat $1,000 of the deposit to Account B on June 17 as an expenditure from the debt proceeds deposited in Account A on June 5. In addition, D may similarly treat $1,000 of the passive activity expenditure on June 30 as made from debt proceeds treated as deposited in Account B on June 17.

Example (2). The facts are the same as in the example in paragraph (c)(4)(ii) of this section, except that the proceeds of Debt B are deposited on February 11 rather than on January 11. Since the $700 passive activity expenditure occurs within 15 days after the proceeds of Debt B are deposited in the account, E may treat such expenditure as being made from the proceeds of Debt B to the extent thereof. If E treats the passive activity expenditure in this manner, the expenditures from the account are treated as follows: The $800 personal expenditure is treated as made from the $500 proceeds of Debt A and $300 of unborrrowed funds. The $700 passive activity expenditure is treated as made from the $500 proceeds of Debt B and $200 of unborrowed funds. The remaining expenditures are treated as in the example in paragraph (c)(4)(ii) of this section.

(C) *Interest on segregated account.* In the case of an account consisting solely of the proceeds of a debt and interest earned on such account, the taxpayer may treat any expenditure from such account as made first from amounts constituting interest (rather than debt proceeds) to the extent of the balance of such interest in the account at the time of the expenditure, determined by applying the rules in this paragraph (c)(4). To the extent any expenditure is treated as made from interest under this paragraph (c)(4)(iii) (C), the expenditure is disregarded in applying paragraph (c)(4)(ii) of this section.

(iv) *Optional method for determining date of reallocation.* Solely for the purpose of determining the date on which debt allocated to an account under paragraph (c)(4)(i) of this section is reallocated, the taxpayer may treat all expenditures made during any calendar month from debt proceeds in the account as occurring on the later of the first day of such month or the date on which such debt proceeds are deposited in the account.

This paragraph (c)(4)(iv) applies only if all expenditures from an account during the same calendar month are similarly treated. The following example illustrates the application of this paragraph (c)(4)(iv):

Example. On January 10, taxpayer G opens a checking account, depositing $500 of proceeds of Debt A and $1,000 of unborrowed funds. The following chart summarizes the transactions which occur during the year with respect to the account (note that these facts are the same as the facts of the example in paragraph (c)(4)(ii) of this section):

Date	Transaction
Jan. 10.................................	$500 proceeds of Debt A and $1,000 unborrowed funds deposited.
Jan. 11.................................	$500 proceeds of Debt B deposited.
Feb. 17.................................	$800 personal expenditure.
Feb. 26.................................	$700 passive activity expenditure.
June 21.................................	$1,000 proceeds of Debt C deposited.
Nov. 24.................................	$800 investment expenditure.
Dec. 20.................................	$600 personal expenditure.

Assume that G chooses to apply the optional rule of this paragraph (c)(4)(iv) to all expenditures. For purposes of determining the date on which debt is allocated to the $800 personal expenditure made on February 17, the $500 treated as made from the proceeds of Debt A and the $300 treated as made from the proceeds of Debt B are treated as expenditures occurring on February 1. Accordingly, Debt A is allocated to an investment expenditure for the account from January 10 through January 31 and to the personal expenditure from February 1 through December 31, and $300 of Debt B is allocated to an investment expenditure for the account from January 11 through January 31 and to the personal expenditure from February 1 through December 31. The remaining $200 of Debt B is allocated to an investment expenditure for the account from January 11 through January 31 and to the passive activity expenditure from February 1 through December 31. The $800 of Debt C used to make the investment expenditure on November 24 is allocated to an investment expenditure for the account from June 21 through October 31 and to an investment expenditure from November 1 through December 31. The remaining $200 of Debt C is allocated to an investment expenditure for the account from June 21 through November 30 and to a personal expenditure from December 1 through December 31.

(v) *Simultaneous deposits*--(A) *In general*. If the proceeds of two or more debts are deposited in an account simultaneously, such proceeds are treated for purposes of this paragraph (c)(4) as deposited in the order in which the debts were incurred.

(B) Order in which debts incurred. If two or more debts are incurred simultaneously or are treated under applicable law as incurred simultaneously, the debts are treated for purposes of this paragraph (c)(4)(v) as incurred in any order the taxpayer selects.

(C) *Borrowings on which interest accrues at different rates*. If interest does not accrue at the same fixed or variable rate on the entire amount of a borrowing, each portion of the borrowing on which interest accrues at a different fixed or variable rate is treated as a separate debt for purposes of this paragraph (c)(4)(v).

(vi) *Multiple accounts*. The rules in this paragraph (c)(4) apply separately to each account of a taxpayer.

Sec. 163. Interest

(5) *Allocation of debt; proceeds received in cash--*(i) *Expenditure within 15 days of receiving debt proceeds.* If a taxpayer receives the proceeds of a debt in cash, the taxpayer may treat any cash expenditure made within 15 days after receiving the cash as made from such debt proceeds to the extent thereof and may treat such expenditure as made on the date the taxpayer received the cash. The following example illustrates the rule in this paragraph (c)(5)(i):

Example. Taxpayer F incurs a $1,000 debt on August 4 and receives the debt proceeds in cash. F deposits $1,500 cash in an account on August 15 and on August 27 writes a check on the account for a passive activity expenditure. In addition, F engages in numerous other cash transactions throughout the month of August, and numerous deposits of borrowed and unborrowed amounts and expenditures occur with respect to the account during the same period. Notwithstanding these other transactions, F may treat $1,000 of the deposit on August 15 as an expenditure made from the debt proceeds on August 4. In addition, under the rule in paragraph (c)(4)(v)(B) of this section, F may treat the passive activity expenditure on August 27 as made from the $1,000 debt proceeds treated as deposited in the account.

(ii) *Other expenditures.* Except as provided in paragraphs (c)(5) (i) and (iii) of this section, any debt proceeds a taxpayer (other than a corporation) receives in cash are treated as used to make personal expenditures. For purposes of this paragraph (c)(5), debt proceeds are received in cash if, for example, a withdrawal of cash from an account is treated under the rules of this section as an expenditure of debt proceeds.

(iii) *Special rules for certain taxpayers.* [Reserved]

(6) *Special rules--*(i) *Qualified residence debt.* [Reserved]

(ii) *Debt used to pay interest.* To the extent proceeds of a debt are used to pay interest, such debt is allocated in the same manner as the debt on which such interest accrued is allocated from time to time. The following example illustrates the application of this paragraph (c)(6)(ii):

Example. On January 1, taxpayer H incurs a debt of $1,000, bearing interest at an annual rate of 10 percent, compounded annually, payable at the end of each year (``Debt A''). H immediately opens a checking account, in which H deposits the proceeds of Debt A. No other amounts are deposited in the account during the year. On April 1, H writes a check for a personal expenditure in the amount of $1,000. On December 31, H borrows $100 (``Debt B'') and immediately uses the proceeds of Debt B to pay the accrued interest of $100 on Debt A. From January 1 through March 31, Debt A is allocated, under the rule in paragraph (c)(4)(i) of this section, to the investment expenditure for the account. From April 1 through December 31, Debt A is allocated to the personal expenditure. Under the rule in paragraph (c)(2)(ii) of this section, $25 of the interest on Debt A for the year is allocated to the investment expenditure, and $75 of the interest on Debt A for the year is allocated to the personal expenditure. Accordingly, for the purpose of allocating the interest on Debt B for all periods until Debt B is repaid, $25 of Debt B is allocated to the investment expenditure, and $75 of Debt B is allocated to the personal expenditure.

(iii) *Debt used to pay borrowing costs--*(A) *Borrowing costs with respect to different debt.* To the extent the proceeds of a debt (the ``ancillary debt'') are used to pay borrowing costs (other than interest) with respect to another debt (the ``primary debt''), the ancillary debt is allocated in the same manner as the primary debt is allocated from time to time. To the extent the primary debt is repaid, the ancillary debt will continue to be allocated in the same manner as the primary debt was allocated immediately before its repayment. The following example illustrates the rule in this paragraph (c)(6)(iii)(A):

Example. Taxpayer I incurs debts of $60,000 (``Debt A'') and $10,000 (``Debt B''). I immediately uses $30,000 of the proceeds of Debt A to make a trade or business expenditure, $20,000 to make a passive activity expenditure, and $10,000 to make an investment expenditure. I immediately use $3,000 of the proceeds of Debt B to pay borrowing costs (other than interest) with respect to Debt A (such as loan origination, loan commitment, abstract, and recording fees) and deposits the remaining $7,000 in an account. Under the rule in this paragraph (c)(6)(iii)(A), the $3,000 of Debt B used to pay 5 expenses of incurring Debt A is allocated $1,500 to the trade or business expenditure ($3,000 x $30,000/$60,000), $1,000 to the passive activity expenditure ($3,000 x $20,000/$60,000), and $500 ($3,000 x $10,000/$60,000) to the investment expenditure. The manner in which the $3,000 of Debt B used to pay expenses of incurring Debt A is allocated may change if the allocation of Debt A changes, but such allocation will be 10 unaffected by any repayment of Debt A. The remaining $7,000 of Debt B is allocated to an investment expenditure for the account until such time, if any, as this amount is used for a different expenditure.

(B) *Borrowing costs with respect to same debt.* To the extent the proceeds of a debt are used to pay borrowing costs (other than interest) with respect to such debt, such debt 15 is allocated in the same manner as the remaining debt is allocated from time to time. The remaining debt for this purpose is the portion of the debt that is not used to pay borrowing costs (other than interst) with respect to such debt. Any repayment of the debt is treated as a repayment of the debt allocated under this paragraph (c)(6)(iii)(B) and the remaining debt is the same proportion as such amount bear to each other. The following example 20 illustrates the application of this paragraph (c)(6)(iii)(B):

Example. (i) Taxpayer J borrows $85,000. The lender disburses $80,000 of this amount to J, retaining $5,000 for borrowing costs (other than interest) with respect to the loan. J immediately uses $40,000 of the debt proceeds to make a personal expenditure, $20,000 to make a passive activity expenditure, and $20,000 to make an investment 25 expenditure. Under the rule in this paragraph (c)(6)(iii)(B), the $5,000 used to pay borrowing costs is allocated $2,500 ($5,000 x $40,000/$80,000) to the personal expenditure, $1,250 ($5,000 x $20,000/$80,000) to the investment expenditure. The manner in which this $5,000 is allocated may change if the allocation of the remaining $80,000 of debt is changed.

(ii) Assume that J repays $50,000 of the debt. The repayment is treated as a repayment of $2,941 ($50,000 x $5,000/$85,000) of the debt used to pay borrowing costs and a repayment of $47,059 ($50,000 x $80,000/$85,000) of the remaining debt. Under paragraph (d) of this section, J is treated as repaying the $42,500 of debt allocated to the personal expenditure ($2,500 of debt used to pay borrowing costs and $40,000 of 35 remaining debt). In addition, assuming that under paragraph (d)(2) J chooses to treat the allocation to the passive activity expenditure as having occurred before the allocation to the investment expenditure, J is treated as repaying $7,500 of debt allocated to the passive activity expenditure ($441 of debt used to pay borrowing costs and $7,059 of remaining debt). 40

(iv) *Allocation of debt before actual receipt of debt proceeds.* If interest properly accrues on a debt during any period before the debt proceeds are actually received or used to make an expenditure, the debt is allocated to an investment expenditure for such period.

(7) *Antiabuse rules.* [Reserved] 45

(d) *Debt repayments--(1) General ordering rule.* If, at the time any portion of a debt is repaid, such debt is allocated to more than one expenditure, the debt is treated for purposes of this section as repaid in the following order:

(i) Amounts allocated to personal expenditures;

(ii) Amounts allocated to investment expenditures and passive activity expenditures 50 (other than passive activity expenditures described in paragraph (d)(1)(iii) of this section);

Sec. 163. Interest

(iii) Amounts allocated to passive activity expenditures in connection with a rental real estate activity with respect to which the taxpayer actively participates (within the meaning of section 469(i));

(iv) Amounts allocated to former passive activity expenditures; and

5   (v) Amounts allocated to trade or business expenditures and to expenditures described in the last sentence of paragraph (b)(4) of this section.

(2) *Supplemental ordering rules for expenditures in same class.* Amounts allocated to two or more expenditures that are described in the subdivision of paragraph (d)(1) of this section (e.g., amounts allocated to different personal expenditures) are treated as repaid 10 in the order in which the amounts were allocated (or reallocated) to such expenditures. For purposes of this paragraph (d)(2), the taxpayer may treat allocations and reallocations that occur on the same day as occurring in any order (without regard to the order in which expenditures are treated as made under paragraph (c)(4)(iii)(A) of this section).

15   (3) *Continuous borrowings.* In the case of borrowings pursuant to a line of credit or similar account or arrangement that allows a taxpayer to borrow funds periodically under a single loan agreement--

(i) All borrowings on which interest accrues at the same fixed or variable rate are treated as a single debt; and

20   (ii) Borrowings or portions of borrowings on which interest accrues at different fixed or variable rates are treated as different debts, and such debts are treated as repaid for purposes of this paragraph (d) in the order in which such borrowings are treated as repaid under the loan agreement.

(4) *Examples.* The following examples illustrate the application of this paragraph (d):

25   *Example (1).* Taxpayer B borrows $100,000 (``Debt A'') on July 12, immediately deposits the proceeds in an account, and uses the debt proceeds to make the following expenditures on the following dates:

30
August 31--$40,000 passive activity expenditure 1.
October 5--$20,000 passive activity expenditure 2.
December 24--$40,000 personal expenditure.

On January 19 of the following year, B repays $90,000 of Debt A (leaving $10,000 of Debt A outstanding). The $40,000 of Debt A allocated to the personal expenditure, the $40,000 35 allocated to passive activity expenditure 1, and $10,000 of the $20,000 allocated to passive activity expenditure 2 are treated as repaid.

Example (2). (i) Taxpayer A obtains a line of credit. Interest on any borrowing on the line of credit accrues at the lender's ``prime lending rate" on the date of the borrowing plus two percentage points. The loan documents provide that borrowings on the line of 40 credit are treated as repaid in the order the borrowings were made. A borrows $30,000 (``Borrowing 1") on the line of credit and immediately uses $20,000 of the debt proceeds to make a personal expenditure (``personal expenditure 1") and $10,000 to make a trade or business expenditure (``trade or business expenditure 1"). A subsequently borrows another $20,000 (``Borrowing 2") on the line of credit and immediately uses $15,000 of 45 the debt proceeds to make a personal expenditure (``personal expenditure 2") and $5,000 to make a trade or business expenditure (``trade or business expenditure 2"). A then repays $40,000 of the borrowings.

(ii) If the prime lending rate plus two percentage points was the same on both the date of Borrowing 1 and the date of Borrowing 2, the borrowings are treated for purposes of 50 this paragraph (d) as a single debt, and A is treated as having repaid $35,000 of debt allocated to personal expenditure 1 and personal expenditure 2, and $5,000 of debt allocated to trade or business expenditure 1.

(iii) If the prime lending rate plus two percentage points was different on the date of Borrowing 1 and Borrowing 2, the borrowings are treated as two debts, and, in accordance with the loan agreement, the $40,000 repaid amount is treated as a repayment of Borrowing 1 and $10,000 of Borrowing 2. Accordingly, A is treated as   5 having repaid $20,000 of debt allocated to personal expenditure 1, $10,000 of debt allocated to trade or business expenditure 1, and $10,000 of debt allocated to personal expenditure 2.

(e) *Debt refinancings*--(1) *In general.* To the extent proceeds of any debt (the ``replacement debt") are used to repay any portion of a debt, the replacement debt is   10 allocated to the expenditures to which the repaid debt was allocated. The amount of replacement debt allocated to any such expenditure is equal to the amount of debt allocated to such expenditure that was repaid with proceeds of the replacement debt. To the extent proceeds of the replacement debt are used for expenditures other than repayment of a debt, the replacement debt is allocated to expenditures in accordance   15 with the rules of this section.

(2) *Example.* The following example illustrates the application of this paragraph (e):

Example. Taxpayer C borrows $100,000 (``Debt A") on July 12, immediately deposits the debt proceeds in an account, and uses the proceeds to make the following expenditures on the following dates (note that the facts of this example are the same as   20 the facts of example (1) in paragraph (d)(4) of this section):

> August 31--$40,000 passive activity expenditure 1.
> October 5--$20,000 passive activity expenditure 2.
> December 24--$40,000 personal expenditure 1.   25

On January 19 of the following year, C borrows $120,000 (``Debt B") and uses $90,000 of the proceeds of repay $90,000 of Debt A (leaving $10,000 of Debt A outstanding). In addition, C uses $30,000 of the proceeds of Debt B to make a personal expenditure (``personal expenditure 2"). Debt B is allocated $40,000 to personal expenditure 1,   30 $40,000 to passive activity expenditure 1, $10,000 to passive activity expenditure 2, and $30,000 to personal expenditure 2. Under paragraph (d)(1) of this section, Debt B will be treated as repaid in the following order: (1) amounts allocated to personal expenditure 1, (2) amounts allocated to personal expenditure 2, (3) amounts allocated to passive activity expenditure 1, and (4) amounts allocated to passive activity expenditure 2.   35

***

(j) *Reallocation of debt*--(1) *Debt allocated to capital expenditures*--(i) *Time of reallocation.* Except as provided in paragraph (j)(2) of this section, debt allocated to an expenditure properly chargeable to capital account with respect to an asset (the ``first expenditure") is reallocated to another expenditure on the earlier of--   40

(A) The date on which proceeds from a disposition of such asset are used for another expenditure; or

(B) The date on which the character of the first expenditure changes (e.g., from a passive activity expenditure to an expenditure that is not a passive activity expenditure) by reason of a change in the use of the asset with respect to which the first expenditure   45 was capitalized.

(ii) *Limitation on amount reallocated.* The amount of debt reallocated under paragraph (j)(1)(i)(A) of this section may not exceed the proceeds from the disposition of the asset. The amount of debt reallocated under paragraph (j)(1)(i)(B) of this section may not exceed the fair market value of the asset on the date of the change in use. In applying   50 this paragraph (j)(1)(ii) with respect to a debt in any case in which two or more debts are

Sec. 163. Interest

allocable to expenditures properly chargeable to capital account with respect to the same asset, only a ratable portion (determined with respect to any such debt by dividing the amount of such debt by the aggregate amount of all such debts) of the fair market value or proceeds from the disposition of such asset shall be taken into account.

5   (iii) *Treatment of loans made by the taxpayer.* Except as provided in paragraph (j)(1) (iv) of this section, an expenditure to make a loan is treated as an expenditure properly chargeable to capital account with respect to an asset, and for purposes of paragraph (j) (1)(i)(A) of this section any repayment of the loan is treated as a disposition of the asset. Paragraph (j)(3) of this section applies to any repayment of a loan in installments.

10   (iv) *Treatment of accounts.* Debt allocated to an account under paragraph (c)(4)(i) of this section is treated as allocated to an expenditure properly chargeable to capital account with respect to an asset, and any expenditure from the account is treated as a disposition of the asset. See paragraph (c)(4) of this section for rules under which debt proceeds allocated to an account are treated as used for another expenditure.

15   (2) *Disposition proceeds in excess of debt.* If the proceeds from the disposition of an asset exceed the amount of debt reallocated by reason of such disposition, or two or more debts are reallocated by reason of the disposition of an asset, the proceeds of the disposition are treated as an account to which the rules in paragraph (c)(4) of this section apply.

20   (3) *Special rule for deferred payment sales.* If any portion of the proceeds of a disposition of an asset are received subsequent to the disposition--

(i) The portion of the proceeds to be received subsequent to the disposition is treated for periods prior to the receipt as used to make an investment expenditure; and

(ii) Debt reallocated by reason of the disposition is allocated to such investment 25 expenditure to the extent such debt exceeds the proceeds of the disposition previously received (other than proceeds used to repay such debt).

(4) *Examples.* The following examples illustrate the application of this paragraph (j):

Example (1). On January 1, 1988, taxpayer D sells an asset for $25,000. Immediately before the sale, the amount of debt allocated to expenditures properly chargeable to 30 capital account with respect to the asset was $15,000. The proceeds of the disposition are treated as an account consisting of $15,000 of debt proceeds and $10,000 of unborrowed funds to which paragraph (c)(4) of this section applies. Thus, if D immediately makes a $10,000 personal expenditure from the proceeds and within 15 days deposits the remaining proceeds in an account, D may, pursuant to paragraph (c)(4) 35 (iii)(B) of this section, treat the entire $15,000 deposited in the account as proceeds of a debt.

Example (2). The facts are the same as in example (1) except that, instead of receiving all $25,000 of the sale proceeds on January 1, 1988, D receives 5,000 on that date, $10,000 on January 1, 1989, and $10,000 on January 1, 1990. D does not use any 40 portion of the sale proceeds to repay the debt. Between January 1, 1988, and December 31, 1988, D is treated under paragraph (j)(3) of this section as making an investment expenditure of $20,000 to which $10,000 of debt is allocated. In addition, the remaining $5,000 of debt is reallocated on January 1, 1988, in accordance with D's use of the sales proceeds received on that date. Between January 1, 1989, and December 31, 1989, D is 45 treated as making an investment expenditure of $10,000 to which no debt is allocated. In addition, as of January 1, 1989, $10,000 of debt is reallocated in accordance with D's use of the sales proceeds received on that date.

Example 3. The facts are the same as in example (2), except that D immediately uses the $5,000 sale proceeds received on January 1, 1988, to repay $5,000 of the $15,000 50 debt. Between January 1, 1988, and December 31, 1988, D is treated as making an investment expenditure of $20,000 to which the remaining balance ($10,000) of the debt

388

Sec. 163.   Interest

is reallocated. The results in 1989 are as described in example (2).

***

(m) *Coordination with other provisions*--(1) *Effect of other limitations*--(i) *In general.* All debt is allocated among expenditures pursuant to the rules in this section, without regard to any limitations on the deductibility of interest expense on such debt. The applicability of 5 the passive loss and nonbusiness interest limitations to interest on such debt, however, may be affected by other limitations on the deductibility of interest expense.

(ii) *Disallowance provisions.* (Interest expense that is not allowable as a deduction by reason of a disallowance provision (within the meaning of paragraph (m)(7)(ii) of this section) is not taken into account for any taxable year for purposes of applying the 10 passive loss and nonbusiness interest limitations.

(iii) *Deferral provisions.* Interest expense that is not allowable as a deduction for the taxable year in which paid or accrued by reason of a deferral provision (within the meaning of paragraph (m)(7)(iii) of this section) is allocated in the same manner as the debt giving rise to the interest expense is allocated for such taxable year. Such interest 15 expense is taken into account for purposes of applying the passive loss and nonbusiness interest limitations for the taxable year in which such interest expense is allowable under such deferral provision.

(iv) *Capitalization provisions.* Interest expense that is capitalized pursuant to a capitalization provision (within the meaning of paragraph (m)(7)(i) of this section) is not 20 taken into account as interest for any taxable year for purposes of applying the passive loss and nonbusiness interest limitations.

(2) *Effect on other limitations*--(i) *General rule.* Except as provided in paragraph (m)(2)(ii) of this section, any limitation on the deductibility of an item (other than the passive loss and nonbusiness interest limitations) applies without regard to the manner in which 25 debt is allocated under this section. Thus, for example, interest expense treated under section 265(a)(2) as interest on indebtedness incurred or continued to purchase or carry obligations the interest on which is wholly exempt from Federal income tax is not deductible regardless of the expenditure to which the underlying debt is allocated under this section. 30

(ii) *Exception.* Capitalization provisions (within the meaning of paragraph (m)(7)(i) of this section) do not apply to interest expense allocated to any personal expenditure under the rules of this section.

(3) *Qualified residence interest.* Qualified residence interest (within the meaning of section 163(h)(3)) is allowable as a deduction without regard to the manner in which such 35 interest expense is allocated under the rules of this section. In addition, qualified residence interest is not taken into account in determining the income or loss from any activity for purposes of section 469 or in determining the amount of investment interest for purposes of section 163(d). The following example illustrates the rule in this paragraph (m)(3): 40

Example. Taxpayer E, an individual, incurs a $20,000 debt secured by a residence and immediately uses the proceeds to purchase an automobile exclusively for E's personal use. Under the rules in this section, the debt and interest expense on the debt are allocated to a personal expenditure. If, however, the interest on the debt is qualified residence interest within the meaning of section 163(h)(3), the interest is not treated as 45 personal interest for purposes of section 163(h).

(4) Interest described in section 163(h)(2)(E). Interest described in section 163(h)(2)(E) is allowable as a deduction without regard to the rules of this section.

(5) Interest on deemed distributee debt. [Reserved]

(6) *Examples.* The following examples illustrate the relationship between the passive 50

389

Sec. 163. Interest

loss and nonbusiness interest limitations and other limitations on the deductibility of interest expense:

Example (1). Debt is allocated pursuant to the rules in this section to an investment expenditure for the purchase of taxable investment securities. Pursuant to section 265(a)
5 (2), the debt is treated as indebtedness incurred or continued to purchase or carry obligations the interest on which is wholly exempt from Federal income tax, and, accordingly, interest on the debt is disallowed. If section 265(a)(2) subsequently ceases to apply (because, for example, the taxpayer ceases to hold any tax-exempt obligations), and the debt at such time continues to be allocated to an investment expenditure, interest
10 on the debt that accrues after such time is subject to section 163(d).

Example (2). An accrual method taxpayer incurs a debt payable to a cash method lender who is related to the taxpayer within the meaning of section 267(b). During the period in which interest on the debt is not deductible by reason of section 267(a)(2), the debt is allocated to a passive activity expenditure. Thus, interest that accrues on the debt
15 for such period is also allocated to the passive activity expenditure. When such interest expense becomes deductible under section 267(a)(2), it will be allocated to the passive activity expenditure, regardless of how the debt is allocated at such time.

Example (3). A taxpayer incurs debt that is allocated under the rules of this section to an investment expenditure. Under section 263A(f), however, interest expense on such
20 debt is capitalized during the production period (within the meaning of section 263A(f)(4)(B)) of property used in a passive activity of the taxpayer. The capitalized interest expense is not allocated to the investment expenditure, and depreciation deductions attributable to the capitalized interest expense are subject to the passive loss limitation as long as the property is used in a passive activity. However, interest expense on the debt
25 for periods after the production period is allocated to the investment expenditure as long as the debt remains allocated to the investment expenditure.

(7) *Other limitations on interest expense--*(i) *Capitalization provisions.* A capitalization provision is any provision that requires or allows interest expense to be capitalized. Capitalization provisions include sections 263(g), 263A(f), and 266.
30 (ii) *Disallowance provisions.* A disallowance provision is any provision (other than the passive loss and nonbusiness interest limitations) that disallows a deduction for interest expense for all taxable years and is not a capitalization provision. Disallowance provisions include sections 163(f)(2), 264(a)(2), 264(a)(4), 265(a)(2), 265(b)(2), 279(a), 291(e)(1)(B)(ii), 805(b)(1), and 834(c)(5).
35 (iii) *Deferral provisions.* A deferral provision is any provision (other than the passive loss and nonbusiness interest limitations) that disallows a deduction for interest expense for any taxable year and is not a capitalization or disallowance provision. Deferral provisions include sections 267(a)(2), 465, 1277, and 1282.

***

40 **Reg. § 1.163-10T   Qualified residence interest (temporary).**

(a) *Table of contents.* This paragraph (a) lists the major paragraphs that appear in this § 1.163-10T.

(a) Table of contents.

(b) Treatment of qualified residence interest.
45 (c) Determination of qualified residence interest when secured debt does not exceed the adjusted purchase price.

(1) In general.

(2) Examples.

(d) Determination of qualified residence interest when secured debt exceeds adjusted
50 purchase price--Simplified method.

(1) In general.

Sec. 163. Interest

(b) *Treatment of qualified residence interest.* Except as provided below, qualified residence interest is deductible under section 163(a). Qualified residence interest is not subject to limitation or otherwise taken into account under section 163(d) (limitation on investment interest), section 163(h)(1) (disallowance of deduction for personal interest), section 263A (capitalization and inclusion in inventory costs of certain expenses) or section 469 (limitations on losses from passive activities). Qualified residence interest is subject to the limitation imposed by section 263(g) (certain interest in the case of straddles), section 264(a)(2) and (4) (interest paid in connection with certain insurance), section 265(a)(2) (interest relating to tax-exempt income), section 266 (carrying charges), section 267(a)(2) (interest with respect to transactions between related taxpayers) section 465 (deductions limited to amount at risk), section 1277 (deferral of interest deduction allocable to accrued market discount), and section 1282 (deferral of interest deduction allocable to accrued discount).

(c) *Determination of qualified residence interest when secured debt does not exceed adjusted purchase price--*(1) *In general.* If the sum of the average balances for the taxable year of all secured debts on a qualified residence does not exceed the adjusted purchase price (determined as of the end of the taxable year) of the qualified residence, all of the interest paid or accrued during the taxable year with respect to the secured debts is qualified residence interest. If the sum of the average balances for the taxable year of all secured debts exceeds the adjusted purchase price of the qualified residences (determined as of the end of the taxable year), the taxpayer must use either the simplified method (see paragraph (d) of this section) or the exact method (see paragraph (e) of this section) to determine the amount of interest that is qualified residence interest.

(2) *Examples.*

Example (1). T purchases a qualified residence in 1987 for $65,000. T pays $6,500 in cash and finances the remainder of the purchase with a mortgage of $58,500. In 1988, the average balance of the mortgage is $58,000. Because the average balance of the mortgage is less than the adjusted purchase price of the residence ($65,000), all of the interest paid or accrued during 1988 on the mortgage is qualified residence interest.

Example (2). The facts are the same as in example (1), except that T incurs a second mortgage on January 1, 1988, with an initial principal balance of $2,000. The average balance of the second mortgage in 1988 is $1,900. Because the sum of the average balance of the first and second mortgages ($59,900) is less than the adjusted purchase price of the residence ($65,000), all of the interest paid or accrued during 1988 on both the first and second mortgages is qualified residence interest.

5 *Example (3).* P borrows $50,000 on January 1, 1988 and secures the debt by a qualified residence. P pays the interest on the debt monthly, but makes no principal payments in 1988. There are no other debts secured by the residence during 1988. On December 31, 1988, the adjusted purchase price of the residence is $40,000. The average balance of the debt in 1988 is $50,000. Because the average balance of the debt exceeds the adjusted purchase price ($10,000), some of the interest on the debt is not qualified residence interest. The portion of the total interest that is qualified residence

10 interest must be determined in accordance with the rules of paragraph (d) or paragraph (e) of this section.

(d) *Determination of qualified residence interest when secured debt exceeds adjusted purchase price--Simplified method--(1) In general.* Under the simplified method, the amount of qualified residence interest for the taxable year is equal to the total interest

15 paid or accrued during the taxable year with respect to all secured debts multiplied by a fraction (not in excess of one), the numerator of which is the adjusted purchase price (determined as of the end of the taxable year) of the qualified residence and the denominator of which is the sum of the average balances of all secured debts.

(2) *Treatment of interest paid or accrued on secured debt that is not qualified*

20 *residence interest.* Under the simplified method, the excess of the total interest paid or accrued during the taxable year with respect to all secured debts over the amount of qualified residence interest is personal interest.

(3) *Example.*

Example. R's principal residence has an adjusted purchase price on December 31,

25 1988, of $105,000. R has two debts secured by the residence, with the following average balances and interest payments:

Debt	Date secured	Average balance	Interest
Debt 1	June 1983	$80,000	$8,000
Debt 2	May 1987	40,000	4,800
Total	....	120,000	12,800

The amount of qualified residence interest is determined under the simplified method by

35 multiplying the total interest ($12,800) by a fraction (expressed as a decimal amount) equal to the adjusted purchase price ($105,000) of the residence divided by the combined average balances ($120,000). For 1988, this fraction is equal to 0.875 ($105,000/$120,000). Therefore, $11,200 ($12,800 x 0.875) of the total interest is qualified residence interest. The remaining $1,600 in interest ($12,800-$11,200) is

40 personal interest, even if (under the rules of § 1.163-8T) such remaining interest would be allocated to some other category of interest.

(e) *Determination of qualified residence interest when secured debt exceeds adjusted purchase price--Exact method--(1) In general.* Under the exact method, the amount of qualified residence interest for the taxable year is determined on a debt-by-debt basis by

45 computing the applicable debt limit for each secured debt and comparing each such applicable debt limit to the average balance of the corresponding debt. If, for the taxable year, the average balance of a secured debt does not exceed the applicable debt limit for that debt, all of the interest paid or accrued during the taxable year with respect to the debt is qualified residence interest. If the average balance of the secured debt exceeds

50 the applicable debt limit for that debt, the amount of qualified residence interest with respect to the debt is determined by multiplying the interest paid or accrued with respect

to the debt by a fraction, the numerator of which is the applicable debt limit for that debt and the denominator of which is the average balance of the debt.

(2) *Determination of applicable debt limit.* For each secured debt, the applicable debt limit for the taxable year is equal to

(i) The lesser of--

(A) The fair market value of the qualified residence as of the date the debt is first secured, and

(B) The adjusted purchase price of the qualified residence as of the end of the taxable year,

(ii) Reduced by the average balance of each debt previously secured by the qualified residence.

For purposes of paragraph (e)(2)(ii) of this section, the average balance of a debt shall be treated as not exceeding the applicable debt limit of such debt. See paragraph (n)(1)(i) of this section for the rule that increases the adjusted purchase price in paragraph (e)(2)(i) (B) of this section by the amount of any qualified indebtedness (certain medical and educational debt). See paragraph (f) of this section for special rules relating to the determination of the fair market value of the qualified residence.

(3) *Example.* (i) R's principal residence has an adjusted purchase price on December 31, 1988, of $105,000. R has two debts secured by the residence. The average balances and interest payments on each debt during 1988 and fair market value of the residence on the date each debt was secured are as follows:

Debt	Date secured	Fair market value	Average balance	Interest
Debt 1	June 1983	$100,000	$80,000	$8,000
Debt 2	May 1987	140,000	40,000	4,800
Total	....		120,000	12,800

(ii) The amount of qualified residence interest for 1988 under the exact method is determined as follows. Because there are no debts previously secured by the residence, the applicable debt limit for Debt 1 is $100,000 (the lesser of the adjusted purchase price as of the end of the taxable year and the fair market value of the residence at the time the debt was secured). Because the average balance of Debt 1 ($80,000) does not exceed its applicable debt limit ($100,000), all of the interest paid on the debt during 1988 ($8,000) is qualified residence interest.

(iii) The applicable debt limit for Debt 2 is $25,000 ($105,000 (the lesser of $140,000 fair market value and $105,000 adjusted purchase price) reduced by $80,000 (the average balance of Debt 1)). Because the average balance of Debt 2 ($40,000) exceeds its applicable debt limit, the amount of qualified residence interest on Debt 2 is determined by multiplying the amount of interest paid on the debt during the year ($4,800) by a fraction equal to its applicable debt limit divided by its average balance ($25,000/$40,000 = 0.625). Accordingly, $3,000 ($4,800 x 0.625) of the interest paid in 1988 on Debt 2 is qualified residence interest. The character of the remaining $1,800 of interest paid on Debt 2 is determined under the rules of paragraph (e)(4) of this section.

(4) *Treatment of interest paid or accrued with respect to secured debt that is not qualified residence interest*--(i) *In general.* Under the exact method, the excess of the interest paid or accrued during the taxable year with respect to a secured debt over the amount of qualified residence interest with respect to the debt is allocated under the rules of § 1.163-8T.

(ii) *Example.* T borrows $20,000 and the entire proceeds of the debt are disbursed by

Sec. 163. Interest

the lender to T's broker to purchase securities held for investment. T secures the debt with T's principal residence. In 1990, T pays $2,000 of interest on the debt. Assume that under the rules of paragraph (e) of this section, $1,500 of the interest is qualified residence interest. The remaining $500 in interest expense would be allocated under the rules of § 1.163-8T. Section 1.163-8T generally allocates debt (and the associated interest expense) by tracing disbursements of the debt proceeds to specific expenditures. Accordingly, the $500 interest expense on the debt that is not qualified residence interest is investment interest subject to section 163(d).

(iii) *Special rule if debt is allocated to more than one expenditure.* If--

(A) The average balance of a secured debt exceeds the applicable debt limit for that debt, and

(B) Under the rules of § 1.163-8T, interest paid or accrued with respect to such debt is allocated to more than one expenditure, the interest expense that is not qualified residence interest may be allocated among such expenditures, to the extent of such expenditures, in any manner selected by the taxpayer.

(iv) *Example.* (i) C borrows $60,000 secured by a qualified residence. C uses (within the meaning of § 1.163-8T) $20,000 of the proceeds in C's trade or business, $20,000 to purchase stock held for investment and $20,000 for personal purposes. In 1990, C pays $6,000 in interest on the debt and, under the rules of § 1.163-8T, $2,000 in interest is allocable to trade or business expenses, $2,000 to investment expenses and $2,000 to personal expenses. Assume that under paragraph (e) of this section, $2,500 of the interest is qualified residence interest and $3,500 of the interest is not qualified residence interest.

(ii) Under paragraph (e)(4)(iii) of this section, C may allocate up to $2,000 of the interest that is not qualified residence interest to any of the three categories of expenditures up to a total of $3,500 for all three categories. Therefore, for example, C may allocate $2,000 of such interest to C's trade or business and $1,500 of such interest to the purchase of stock.

(f) *Special rules--*(1) *Special rules for personal property--*(i) *In general.* If a qualified residence is personal property under State law (e.g., a boat or motorized vehicle)--

(A) For purposes of paragraphs (c)(1) and (d)(1) of this section, if the fair market value of the residence as of the date that any secured debt (outstanding during the taxable year) is first secured by the residence is less than the adjusted purchase price as of the end of the taxable year, the lowest such fair market value shall be substituted for the adjusted purchase price.

(B) For purposes of paragraphs (e)(2)(i)(A) and (f)(1)(i)(A) of this section, the fair market value of the residence as of the date the debt is first secured by the residence shall not exceed the fair market value as of any date on which the taxpayer borrows any additional amount with respect to the debt.

(ii) *Example.* D owns a recreational vehicle that is a qualified residence under paragraph (p)(4) of this section. The adjusted purchase price and fair market value of the recreational vehicle is $20,000 in 1989. In 1989, D establishes a line of credit secured by the recreational vehicle. As of June 1, 1992, the fair market value of the vehicle has decreased to $10,000. On that day, D borrows an additional amount on the debt by using the line of credit. Although under paragraphs (e)(2)(i) and (f)(1)(i)(A) of this section, fair market value is determined at the time the debt is first secured, under paragraph (f)(1)(i) (B) of this section, the fair market value is the lesser of that amount or the fair market value on the most recent date that D borrows any additional amount with respect to the line of credit. Therefore, the fair market value with respect to the debt is $10,000.

(2) *Special rule for real property--*(i) *In general.* For purposes of paragraph (e)(2)(i)(A) of this section, the fair market value of a qualified residence that is real property under

Sec. 163. Interest

State law is presumed irrebuttably to be not less than the adjusted purchase price of the residence as of the last day of the taxable year.

(ii) *Example*. (i) C purchases a residence on August 11, 1987, for $50,000, incurring a first mortgage. The residence is real property under State law. During 1987, C makes $10,000 in home improvements. Accordingly, the adjusted purchase price of the residence as of December 31, 1988, is $60,000. C incurs a second mortgage on May 19, 1988, as of which time the fair market value of the residence is $55,000.

(ii) For purposes of determining the applicable debt limit for each debt, the fair market value of the residence is generally determined as of the time the debt is first secured. Accordingly, the fair market value would be $50,000 and $55,000 with respect to the first and second mortgage, respectively. Under the special rule of paragraph (f)(2)(i) of this section, however, the fair market value with respect to both debts in 1988 is $60,000, the adjusted purchase price on December 31, 1988.

(g) *Selection of method*. For any taxable year, a taxpayer may use the simplified method (described in paragraph (d) of this section) or the exact method (described in paragraph (e) of this section) by completing the appropriate portion of Form 8598. A taxpayer with two qualified residences may use the simplified method for one residence and the exact method for the other residence.

(h) *Average balance*--(1) *Average balance defined*. For purposes of this section, the term ``average balance" means the amount determined under this paragraph (h). A taxpayer is not required to use the same method to determine the average balance of all secured debts during a taxable year or of any particular secured debt from one year to the next.

(2) Average balance reported by lender. If a lender that is subject to section 6050H (returns relating to mortgage interest received in trade or business from individuals) reports the average balance of a secured debt on Form 1098, the taxpayer may use the average balance so reported.

(3) Average balance computed on a daily basis--(i) In general. The average balance may be determined by--

(A) Adding the outstanding balance of a debt on each day during the taxable year that the debt is secured by a qualified residence, and

(B) Dividing the sum by the number of days during the taxable year that the residence is a qualified residence.

(ii) *Example*. Taxpayer A incurs a debt of $10,000 on September 1, 1989, securing the debt with A's principal residence. The residence is A's principal residence during the entire taxable year. A pays current interest on the debt monthly, but makes no principal payments. The debt is, therefore, outstanding for 122 days with a balance each day of $10,000. The residence is a qualified residence for 365 days. The average balance of the debt for 1989 is $3,342 (122 x $10,000/365).

(4) *Average balance computed using the interest rate*--(i) *In general*. If all accrued interest on a secured debt is paid at least monthly, the average balance of the secured debt may be determined by dividing the interest paid or accrued during the taxable year while the debt is secured by a qualified residence by the annual interest rate on the debt. If the interest rate on a debt varies during the taxable year, the lowest annual interest rate that applies to the debt during the taxable year must be used for purposes of this paragraph (h)(4). If the residence securing the debt is a qualified residence for less than the entire taxable year, the average balance of any secured debt may be determined by dividing the average balance determined under the preceding sentence by the percentage of the taxable year that the debt is secured by a qualified residence.

(ii) *Points and prepaid interest*. For purposes of paragraph (h)(4)(i) of this section, the amount of interest paid during the taxable year does not include any amount paid as points and includes prepaid interest only in the year accrued.

(iii) *Examples.*

Example (1). B has a line of credit secured by a qualified residence for the entire taxable year. The interest rate on the debt is 10 percent throughout the taxable year. The
5 principal balance on the debt changes throughout the year. B pays the accrued interest on the debt monthly. B pays $2,500 in interest on the debt during the taxable year. The average balance of the debt ($25,000) may be computed by dividing the total interest paid by the interest rate ($25,000 = $2,500/0.10).

Example (2). Assume the same facts as in example 1, except that the residence is a
10 qualified residence, and the debt is outstanding, for only one-half of the taxable year and B pays only $1,250 in interest on the debt during the taxable year. The average balance of the debt may be computed by first dividing the total interest paid by the interest rate ($12,500 = $1,250/0.10). Second, because the residence is not a qualified residence for the entire taxable year, the average balance must be determined by dividing this amount
15 ($12,500) by the portion of the year that the residence is qualified (0.50). The average balance is therefore $25,000 ($12,500/0.50).

(5) *Average balance computed using average of beginning and ending balances--(i) In general.* If--

(A) A debt requires level payments at fixed equal intervals (e.g., monthly, quarterly) no
20 less often than semi-annually during the taxable year,

(B) The taxpayer prepays no more than one month's principal on the debt during the taxable year, and

(C) No new amounts are borrowed on the debt during the taxable year, the average balance of the debt may be determined by adding the principal balance as of the first day
25 of the taxable year that the debt is secured by the qualified residence and the principal balance as of the last day of the taxable year that the debt is secured by the qualified residence and dividing the sum by 2. If the debt is secured by a qualified residence for less than the entire period during the taxable year that the residence is a qualified residence, the average balance may be determined by multiplying the average balance
30 determined under the preceding sentence by a fraction, the numerator of which is the number of days during the taxable year that the debt is secured by the qualified residence and the denominator of which is the number of days during the taxable year that the residence is a qualified residence. For purposes of this paragraph (h)(5)(i), the determination of whether payments are level shall disregard the fact that the amount of
35 the payments may be adjusted from time to time to take into account changes in the applicable interest rate.

(ii) *Example.* C borrows $10,000 in 1988, securing the debt with a second mortgage on a principal residence. The terms of the loan require C to make equal monthly payments of principal and interest so as to amortize the entire loan balance over 20
40 years. The balance of the debt is $9,652 on January 1, 1990, and is $9,450 on December 31, 1990. The
average balance of the debt during 1990 may be computed as follows:

Balance on first day of the year: $9,652
45   Balance on last day of the year: $9,450

Average balance = $\dfrac{\$9652 + \$9450}{2}$ = $9551

50   (6) *Highest principal balance.* The average balance of a debt may be determined by taking the highest principal balance of the debt during the taxable year.

Sec. 163.   Interest

(7) *Other methods provided by the Commissioner.* The average balance may be determined using any other method provided by the Commissioner by form, publication, revenue ruling, or revenue procedure. Such methods may include methods similar to (but with restrictions different from) those provided in paragraph (h) of this section. 5

(8) *Anti-abuse rule.* If, as a result of the determination of the average balance of a debt using any of the methods specified in paragraphs (h) (4), (5), or (6) of this section, there is a significant overstatement of the amount of qualified residence interest and a principal purpose of the pattern of payments and borrowing on the debt is to cause the amount of such qualified residence interest to be overstated, the district director may 10 redetermine the average balance using the method specified under paragraph (h)(3) of this section.

(i) [Reserved]

(j) *Determination of interest paid or accrued during the taxable year--*(1) *In general.* For purposes of determining the amount of qualified residence interest with respect to a 15 secured debt, the amount of interest paid or accrued during the taxable year includes only interest paid or accrued while the debt is secured by a qualified residence.

(2) *Special rules for cash-basis taxpayers--*(i) *Points deductible in year paid under section 461(g)(2).* If points described in section 461(g)(2) (certain points paid in respect of debt incurred in connection with the purchase or improvement of a principal residence) 20 are paid with respect to a debt, the amount of such points is qualified residence interest.

(ii) *Points and other prepaid interest described in section 461(g)(1).* The amount of points or other prepaid interest charged to capital account under section 461(g)(1) (prepaid interest) that is qualified residence interest shall be determined under the rules of paragraphs (c) through (e) of this section in the same manner as any other interest 25 paid with respect to the debt in the taxable year to which such payments are allocable under section 461(g)(1).

(3) *Examples.*

Example (1). T designates a vacation home as a qualified residence as of October 1, 1987. The home is encumbered by a mortgage during the entire taxable year. For 30 purposes of determining the amount of qualified residence interest for 1987, T may take into account the interest paid or accrued on the secured debt from October 1, 1987, through December 31, 1987.

Example (2). R purchases a principal residence on June 17, 1987. As part of the purchase price, R obtains a conventional 30-year mortgage, secured by the residence. At 35 closing, R pays 2\1/2\ points on the mortgage and interest on the mortgage for the period June 17, 1987 through June 30, 1987. The points are actually paid by R and are not merely withheld from the loan proceeds. R incurs no additional secured debt during 1987. Assuming that the points satisfy the requirements of section 461(g) (2), the entire amount of points and the interest paid at closing are qualified residence interest. 40

Example (3). (i) On July 1, 1987, W borrows $120,000 to purchase a residence to use as a vacation home. W secures the debt with the residence. W pays 2 points, or $2,400. The debt has a term of 10 years and requires monthly payments of principal and interest. W is permitted to amortize the points at the rate of $20 per month over 120 months. W elects to treat the residence as a second residence. W has no other debt secured by the 45 residence. The average balance of the debt in each taxable year is less than the adjusted purchase price of the residence. W sells the residence on June 30, 1990, and pays off the remaining balance of the debt.

(ii) W is entitled to treat the following amounts of the points as interest paid on a debt secured by a qualified residence-- 50

399

1987..	$120 = $20x6 months;
1988..	$240 = $20x12 months;
1989..	$120 = $20x6 months.
Total.......................................	$480

5

All of the interest paid on the debt, including the allocable points, is qualified residence interest. Upon repaying the debt, the remaining $1,920 ($2,400-$480) in unamortized points is treated as interest paid in 1990 and, because the average balance of the secured debt in 1990 is less than the adjusted purchase price, is also qualified residence
10 interest.

(k) *Determination of adjusted purchase price and fair market value--(1) Adjusted purchase price--(i) In general.* For purposes of this section, the adjusted purchase price of a qualified residence is equal to the taxpayer's basis in the residence as initially determined under section 1012 or other applicable sections of the Internal Revenue
15 Code, increased by the cost of any improvements to the residence that have been added to the taxpayer's basis in the residence under section 1016(a)(1). Any other adjustments to basis, including those required under section 1033(b) (involuntary conversions), and 1034(e) (rollover of gain or sale of principal residence) are disregarded in determining the taxpayer's adjusted purchase price. If, for example, a taxpayer's second residence is
20 rented for a portion of the year and its basis is reduced by depreciation allowed in connection with the rental use of the property, the amount of the taxpayer's adjusted purchase price in the residence is not reduced. See paragraph (m) of this section for a rule that treats the sum of the grandfathered amounts of all secured debts as the adjusted purchase price of the residence.

25 (ii) *Adjusted purchase price of a qualified residence acquired incident to divorce.* [Reserved]

(iii) *Examples.*

Example (1). X purchases a residence for $120,000. X's basis, as determined under section 1012, is the cost of the property, or $120,000. Accordingly, the adjusted purchase
30 price of the residence is initially $120,000.

Example (2). Y owns a principal residence that has a basis of $30,000. Y sells the residence for $100,000 and purchases a new principal residence for $120,000. Under section 1034, Y does not recognize gain on the sale of the former residence. Under section 1034(e), Y's basis in the new residence is reduced by the amount of gain not
35 recognized. Therefore, under section 1034(e), Y's basis in the new residence is $50,000 ($120,000-$70,000). For purposes of section 163(h), however, the adjusted purchase price of the residence is not adjusted under section 1034(e). Therefore, the adjusted purchase price of the residence is initially $120,000.

Example (3). Z acquires a residence by gift. The donor's basis in the residence was
40 $30,000. Z's basis in the residence, determined under section 1015, is $30,000. Accordingly, the adjusted purchase price of the residence is initially $30,000.

(2) *Fair market value--(i) In general.* For purposes of this section, the fair market value of a qualified residence on any date is the fair market value of the taxpayer's interest in the residence on such date. In addition, the fair market value determined under this
45 paragraph (k)(2)(i) shall be determined by taking into account the cost of improvements to the residence reasonably expected to be made with the proceeds of the debt.

(ii) *Example.* In 1988, the adjusted purchase price of P's second residence is $65,000 and the fair market value of the residence is $70,000. At that time, P incurs an additional debt of $10,000, the proceeds of which P reasonably expects to use to add two
50 bedrooms to the residence. Because the fair market value is determined by taking into account the cost of improvements to the residence that are reasonably expected to be

made with the proceeds of the debt, the fair market value of the residence with respect to the debt incurred in 1988 is $80,000 ($70,000+$10,000).

(3) *Allocation of adjusted purchase price and fair market value.* If a property includes both a qualified residence and other property, the adjusted purchase price and the fair market value of such property must be allocated between the qualified residence and the other property. See paragraph (p)(4) of this section for rules governing such an allocation.

***

(n) *Qualified indebtedness (secured debt used for medical and educational purposes--* (1) *In general--*(i) *Treatment of qualified indebtedness.* The amount of any qualified indebtedness resulting from a secured debt may be added to the adjusted purchase price under paragraph (e)(2)(i)(B) of this section to determine the applicable debt limit for that secured debt and any other debt subsequently secured by the qualified residence.

(ii) *Determination of amount of qualified indebtedness.* If, as of the end of the taxable year (or the last day in the taxable year that the debt is secured), at least 90 percent of the proceeds of a secured debt are used (within the meaning of paragraph (n)(2) of this section) to pay for qualified medical and educational expenses (within the meaning of paragraphs (n)(3) and (n)(4) of this section), the amount of qualified indebtedness resulting from that debt for the taxable year is equal to the average balance of such debt for the taxable year.

(iii) *Determination of amount of qualified indebtedness for mixed-use debt.* If, as of the end of the taxable year (or the last day in the taxable year that the debt is secured), more than ten percent of the proceeds of a secured debt are used to pay for expenses other than qualified medical and educational expenses, the amount of qualified indebtedness resulting from that debt for the taxable year shall equal the lesser of--

(A) The average balance of the debt, or

(B) The amount of the proceeds of the debt used to pay for qualified medical and educational expenses through the end of the taxable year, reduced by any principal payments on the debt before the first day of the current taxable year.

(iv) *Example.* (i) C incurs a $10,000 debt on April 20, 1987, which is secured on that date by C's principal residence. C immediately uses (within the meaning of paragraph (n) (2) of this section) $4,000 of the proceeds of the debt to pay for a qualified medical expense. C makes no principal payments on the debt during 1987. During 1988 and 1989, C makes principal payments of $1,000 per year. The average balance of the debt during 1988 is $9,500 and the average balance during 1989 is $8,500.

(ii) Under paragraph (n)(1)(iii) of this section, C determines the amount of qualified indebtedness for 1988 as follows:

Average balance...	$9,500	
Amount of debt used to pay for qualified medical expenses..	$4,000	
Less payments of principal before 1988..............	$0	
Net qualified expenses......................................	$4,000	

The amount of qualified indebtedness for 1988 is, therefore, $4,000 (lesser of $9,500 average balance or $4,000 net qualified expenses). This amount may be added to the adjusted purchase price of C's principal residence under paragraph (e)(2)(i)(B) of this section for purposes of computing the applicable debt limit for this debt and any other debt subsequently secured by the principal residence.

(iii) C determines the amount of qualified indebtedness for 1989 as follows:

Average balance...		$8,500
Amount of debt used to pay for qualified medical		
expenses..	$4,000	
5 Less payments of principal before 1988..............	$1,000	
Net qualified expenses..		$3,000

The amount of qualified indebtedness for 1989 is, therefore, $3,000 (lesser of $8,500
10 average balance or $3,000 net qualified expenses).
(v) *Prevention of double counting in year of refinancing*--(A) *In general*. A debt used to
pay for qualified medical or educational expenses is refinanced if some or all of the
outstanding balance of the debt (the ``original debt") is repaid out of the proceeds of a
second debt (the ``replacement debt"). If, in the year of a refinancing, the combined
15 qualified indebtedness of the original debt and the replacement debt exceeds the
combined qualified expenses of such debts, the amount of qualified indebtedness for
each such debt shall be determined by multiplying the amount of qualified indebtedness
for each such debt by a fraction, the numerator of which is the combined qualified
expenses and the denominator of which is the combined qualified indebtedness.
20 (B) *Definitions*. For purposes of paragraph (n)(1)(v)(A) of this section--
(1) The term ``combined qualified indebtedness" means the sum of the qualified
indebtedness (determined without regard to paragraph (n)(1)(v) of this section) for the
original debt and the replacement debt.
(2) The term ``combined qualified expenses" means the amount of the proceeds of
25 the original debt used to pay for qualified medical and educational expenses through the
end of the current taxable year, reduced by any principal payments on the debt before the
first day of the current taxable year, and increased by the amount, if any, of the proceeds
of the replacement debt used to pay such expenses through the end of the current
taxable year other than as part of the refinancing.
30 (C) *Example*. (i) On August 11, 1987, C incurs a $8,000 debt secured by a principal
residence. C uses (within the meaning of paragraph (n)(2)(i) of this section) $5,000 of the
proceeds of the debt to pay for qualified educational expenses. C makes no principal
payments on the debt. On July 1, 1988, C incurs a new debt in the amount of $8,000
secured by C's principal residence and uses all of the proceeds of the new debt to repay
35 the original debt. Under paragraph (n)(2)(ii) of this section $5,000 of the new debt is
treated as being used to pay for qualified educational expenses. C makes no principal
payments (other than the refinancing) during 1987 or 1988 on either debt and pays all
accrued interest monthly. The average balance of each debt in 1988 is $4,000.
(ii) Under paragraph (n)(1)(iii) of this section, the amount of qualified indebtedness for
40 1988 with respect to the original debt is $4,000 (the lesser of its average balance
($4,000) and the amount of the debt used to pay for qualified medical and educational
expenses ($5,000)). Similarly, the amount of qualified indebtedness for 1988 with respect
to the replacement debt is also $4,000. Both debts, however, are subject in 1988 to the
limitation in paragraph (n)(1)(v)(A) of this section. The combined qualified indebtedness,
45 determined without regard to the limitation, is $8,000 ($4,000 of qualified indebtedness
from each debt). The combined qualified expenses are $5,000 ($5,000 from the original
debt and $0 from the replacement debt). The amount of qualified indebtedness from each
debt must, therefore, be reduced by a fraction, the numerator of which is $5,000 (the
combined qualified expenses) and the denominator of which is $8,000 (the combined
50 qualified indebtedness). After application of the limitation, the amount of qualified
indebtedness for the original debt is $2,500 ($4,000 x5/8). Similarly, the amount of

qualified indebtedness for the replacement debt is $2,500. Note that the total qualified indebtedness for both the original and the replacement debt is $5,000 ($2,500 + $2,500). Therefore, C is entitled to the same amount of qualified indebtedness as C would have been entitled to if C had not refinanced the debt.

(vi) *Special rule for principal payments in excess of qualified expenses.* For purposes of paragraph (n)(1)(iii)(B), (n)(1)(v)(B)(2) and (n)(2)(ii) of this section, a principal payment is taken into account only to the extent that the payment, when added to all prior payments, does not exceed the amount used on or before the date of the payment to pay for qualified medical and educational expenses.

(2) *Debt used to pay for qualified medical or educational expenses--(i) In general.* For purposes of this section, the proceeds of a debt are used to pay for qualified medical or educational expenses to the extent that--

(A) The taxpayer pays qualified medical or educational expenses within 90 days before or after the date that amounts are actually borrowed with respect to the debt, the proceeds of the debt are not directly allocable to another expense under § 1.163-8T(c)(3) (allocation of debt; proceeds not disbursed to borrower) and the proceeds of any other debt are not allocable to the medical or educational expenses under § 1.163-8T(c)(3), or

(B) The proceeds of the debt are otherwise allocated to such expenditures under § 1.163-8T.

(ii) *Special rule for refinancings.* For purposes of this section, the proceeds of a debt are used to pay for qualified medical and educational expenses to the extent that the proceeds of the debt are allocated under § 1.163-8T to the repayment of another debt (the ``original debt"), but only to the extent of the amount of the original debt used to pay for qualified medical and educational expenses, reduced by any principal payments on such debt up to the time of the refinancing.

(iii) *Other special rules.* The following special rules apply for purposes of this section.

(A) Proceeds of a debt are used to pay for qualified medical or educational expenses as of the later of the taxable year in which such proceeds are borrowed or the taxable year in which such expenses are paid.

(B) The amount of debt which may be treated as being used to pay for qualified medical or educational expenses may not exceed the amount of such expenses.

(C) Proceeds of a debt may not be treated as being used to pay for qualified medical or educational expenses to the extent that:

(1) The proceeds have been repaid as of the time the expense is paid;

(2) The proceeds are actually borrowed before August 17, 1986; or

(3) The medical or educational expenses are paid before August 17, 1986.

(iv) *Examples--*

Example (1). A pays a $5,000 qualified educational expense from a checking account that A maintains at Bank 1 on November 9, 1987. On January 1, 1988, A incurs a $20,000 debt that is secured by A's residence and places the proceeds of the debt in a savings account that A also maintains at Bank 1. A pays another $5,000 qualified educations expense on March 15 from a checking account that A maintains at Bank 2. Under paragraph (n)(2) of this section, the debt proceeds are used to pay for both educational expenses, regardless of other deposits to, or expenditures from, the accounts, because both expenditures are made within 90 days before or after the debt was incurred.

Example (2). B pays a $5,000 qualified educational expense from a checking account on November 1, 1987. On November 30, 1987, B incurs a debt secured by B's residence, and the lender disburses the debt proceeds directly to a person who sells B a new car. Although the educational expense is paid within 90 days of the date the debt is incurred, the proceeds of the debt are not used to pay for the educational expense because the proceeds are directly allocable to the purchase of the new car under § 1.163-8T(c)(3).

Example (3). On November 1, 1987, C borrows $5,000 from C's college. The proceeds of this debt are not disbursed to C, but rather are used to pay tuition fees for C's attendance at the college. On November 30, 1987, C incurs a second debt and secures the debt by C's residence. Although the $5,000 educational expense is paid within 90
5 days before the second debt is incurred, the proceeds of the second debt are not used to pay for the educational expense, because the proceeds of the first debt are directly allocable to the educational expense under § 1.163-8T(c)(3).

Example (4). On January 1, 1988, D incurs a $20,000 debt secured by a qualified residence. D places the proceeds of the debt in a separate account (i.e., the proceeds of
10 the debt are the only deposit in the account). D makes payments of $5,000 each for qualified educational expenses on September 1, 1988, September 1, 1989, September 1, 1990, and September 1, 1991. Because the debt proceeds are allocated to educational expenses as of the date the expenses are paid, under the rules of § 1.163-8T(c)(4), the following amounts of the debt proceeds are used to pay for qualified educational
15 expenses as of the end of each year:

> 1988: $5,000
> 1989: $10,000
> 1990: $15,000
20 > 1991: $20,000

Example (5). During 1987 E incurs a $10,000 debt secured by a principal residence. E uses (within the meaning of paragraph (n)(2)(i) of this section) all of the proceeds of the debt to pay for qualified educational expenses. On August 20, 1988, at which time the
25 balance of the debt is $9,500, E incurs a new debt in the amount of $9,500 secured by E's principal residence and uses all of the proceeds of the new debt to repay the original debt. Under paragraph (n)(2)(ii) of this section, all of the proceeds of the new debt are used to pay for qualified educational expenses.

(3) *Qualified medical expenses*. Qualified medical expenses are amounts that are
30 paid for medical care (within the meaning of section 213(d)(1) (A) and (B)) for the taxpayer, the taxpayer's spouse, or a dependent of the taxpayer (within the meaning of section 152), and that are not compensated for by insurance or otherwise.

(4) *Qualified educational expenses*. Qualified educational expenses are amounts that are paid for tuition, fees, books, supplies and equipment required for enrollment,
35 attendance or courses of instruction at an educational organization described in section 170(b) (1)(A)(ii) and for any reasonable living expenses while away from home while in attendance at such an institution, for the taxpayer, the taxpayer's spouse or a dependent of the taxpayer (within the meaning of section 152) and that are not reimbursed by scholarship or otherwise.

40 (o) *Secured debt*--(1) *In general*. For purposes of this section, the term ``secured debt'' means a debt that is on the security of any instrument (such as a mortgage, deed of trust, or land contract)--

(i) That makes the interest of the debtor in the qualified residence specific security for the payment of the debt,
45 (ii) Under which, in the event of default, the residence could be subjected to the satisfaction of the debt with the same priority as a mortgage or deed of trust in the jurisdiction in which the property is situated, and

(iii) That is recorded, where permitted, or is otherwise perfected in accordance with applicable State law.
50 A debt will not be considered to be secured by a qualified residence if it is secured solely by virtue of a lien upon the general assets of the taxpayer or by a security interest, such

Sec. 163. Interest

as a mechanic's lien or judgment lien, that attaches to the property without the consent of the debtor.

(2) *Special rule for debt in certain States.* Debt will not fail to be treated as secured solely because, under an applicable State or local homestead law or other debtor protection law in effect on August 16, 1986, the security interest is ineffective or the enforceability of the security interest is restricted.

(3) *Times at which debt is treated as secured.* For purposes of this section, a debt is treated as secured as of the date on which each of the requirements of paragraph (o)(1) of this section are satisfied, regardless of when amounts are actually borrowed with respect to the debt. For purposes of this paragraph (o)(3), if the instrument is recorded within a commercially reasonable time after the security interest is granted, the instrument will be treated as recorded on the date that the security interest was granted.

(4) *Partially secured debt*--(i) *In general.* If the security interest is limited to a prescribed maximum amount or portion of the residence, and the average balance of the debt exceeds such amount or the value of such portion, such excess shall not be treated as secured debt for purposes of this section.

(ii) *Example.* T borrows $80,000 on January 1, 1991. T secures the debt with a principal residence. The security in the residence for the debt, however, is limited to $20,000. T pays $8,000 in interest on the debt in 1991 and the average balance of the debt in that year is $80,000. Because the average balance of the debt exceeds the maximum amount of the security interest, such excess is not treated as secured debt. Therefore, for purposes of applying the limitation on qualified residence interest, the average balance of the secured debt is $20,000 (the maximum amount of the security interest) and the interest paid or accrued on the secured debt is $2,000 (the total interest paid on the debt multiplied by the ratio of the average balance of the secured debt ($20,000) and the average balance of the total debt ($80,000)).

(5) *Election to treat debt as not secured by a qualified residence*--(i) *In general.* For purposes of this section, a taxpayer may elect to treat any debt that is secured by a qualified residence as not secured by the qualified residence. An election made under this paragraph shall be effective for the taxable year for which the election is made and for all subsequent taxable years unless revoked with the consent of the Commissioner.

(ii) *Example.* T owns a principal residence with a fair market value of $75,000 and an adjusted purchase price of $40,000. In 1988, debt A, the proceeds of which were used to purchase the residence, has an average balance of $15,000. The proceeds of debt B, which is secured by a second mortgage on the property, are allocable to T's trade or business under § 1.163-8T and has an average balance of $25,000. In 1988, T incurs debt C, which is also secured by T's principal residence and which has an average balance in 1988 of $5,000. In the absence of an election to treat debt B as unsecured, the applicable debt limit for debt C in 1988 under paragraph (e) of this section would be zero dollars ($40,000-$15,000-$25,000) and none of the interest paid on debt C would be qualified residence interest. If, however, T makes or has previously made an election pursuant to paragraph (o)(5)(i) of this section to treat debt B as not secured by the residence, the applicable debt limit for debt C would be $25,000 ($40,000-$15,000), and all of the interest paid on debt C during the taxable year would be qualified residence interest. Since the proceeds of debt B are allocable to T's trade or business under § 1.163-8T, interest on debt B may be deductible under other sections of the Internal Revenue Code.

(iii) *Allocation of debt secured by two qualified residences.* [Reserved]

(p) *Definition of qualified residence*--(1) *In general.* The term ``qualified residence" means the taxpayer's principal residence (as defined in paragraph (p)(2) of this section), or the taxpayer's second residence (as defined in paragraph (p)(3) of this section).

Sec. 163. Interest

(2) *Principal residence.* The term ``principal residence" means the taxpayer's principal residence within the meaning of section 1034. For purposes of this section, a taxpayer cannot have more than one principal residence at any one time.

(3) *Second residence*--(i) *In general.* The term ``second residence" means--

5   (A) A residence within the meaning of paragraph (p)(3)(ii) of this section,

(B) That the taxpayer uses as a residence within the meaning of paragraph (p)(3)(iii) of this section, and

(C) That the taxpayer elects to treat as a second residence pursuant to paragraph (p)(3)(iv) of this section.

10 A taxpayer cannot have more than one second residence at any time.

(ii) *Definition of residence.* Whether property is a residence shall be determined based on all the facts and circumstances, including the good faith of the taxpayer. A residence generally includes a house, condominium, mobile home, boat, or house trailer, that contains sleeping space and toilet and cooking facilities. A residence does not include

15 personal property, such as furniture or a television, that, in accordance with the applicable local law, is not a fixture.

(iii) *Use as a residence.* If a residence is rented at any time during the taxable year, it is considered to be used as a residence only if the taxpayer uses it during the taxable year as a residence within the meaning of section 280A(d). If a residence is not rented at

20 any time during the taxable year, it shall be considered to be used as a residence. For purposes of the preceding sentence, a residence will be deemed to be rented during any period that the taxpayer holds the residence out for rental or resale or repairs or renovates the residence with the intention of holding it out for rental or resale.

(iv) *Election of second residence.* A taxpayer may elect a different residence (other

25 than the taxpayer's principal residence) to be the taxpayer's second residence for each taxable year. A taxpayer may not elect different residences as second residences at different times of the same taxable year except as provided below--

(A) If the taxpayer acquires a new residence during the taxable year, the taxpayer may elect the new residence as a taxpayer's second residence as of the date acquired;

30   (B) If property that was the taxpayer's principal residence during the taxable year ceases to qualify as the taxpayer's principal residence, the taxpayer may elect that property as the taxpayer's second residence as of the date that the property ceases to be the taxpayer's principal residence; or

(C) If property that was the taxpayer's second residence is sold during the taxable

35 year or becomes the taxpayer's principal residence, the taxpayer may elect a new second residence as of such day.

(4) *Allocations between residence and other property*--(i) *In general.* For purposes of this section, the adjusted purchase price and fair market value of property must be allocated between the portion of the property that is a qualified residence and the portion

40 that is not a qualified residence. Neither the average balance of the secured debt nor the interest paid or accrued on secured debt is so allocated. Property that is not used for residential purposes does not qualify as a residence. For example, if a portion of the property is used as an office in the taxpayer's trade or business, that portion of the property does not qualify as a residence.

45   (ii) *Special rule for rental of residence.* If a taxpayer rents a portion of his or her principal or second residence to another person (a ``tenant"), such portion may be treated as used by the taxpayer for residential purposes if, but only if--

(A) Such rented portion is used by the tenant primarily for residential purposes,

(B) The rented portion is not a self-contained residential unit containing separate

50 sleeping space and toilet and cooking facilities, and

(C) The total number of tenants renting (directly or by sublease) the same or different portions of the residence at any time during the taxable year does not exceed two. For this purpose, if two persons (and the dependents, as defined by section 152, of either of them) share the same sleeping quarters, they shall be treated as a single tenant.

(iii) *Examples.*

Example (1). D, a dentist, uses a room in D's principal residence as an office which qualifies under section 280A(c)(1)(B) as a portion of the dwelling unit used exclusively on a regular basis as a place of business for meeting with patients in the normal course of D's trade or business. D's adjusted purchase price of the property is $65,000; $10,000 of which is allocable under paragraph (o)(4)(i) of this section to the room used as an office. For purposes of this section, D's residence does not include the room used as an office. The adjusted purchase price of the residence is, accordingly, $55,000. Similarly, the fair market value of D's residence must be allocated between the office and the remainder of the property.

Example (2). J rents out the basement of property that is otherwise used as J's principal residence. The basement is a self-contained residential unit, with sleeping space and toilet and cooking facilities. The adjusted purchase price of the property is $100,000; $15,000 of which is allocable under paragraph (o)(4)(i) of this section to the basement. For purposes of this section, J's residence does not include the basement and the adjusted purchase price of the residence is $85,000. Similarly, the fair market value of the residence must be allocated between the basement unit and the remainder of the property.

(5) *Residence under construction*--(i) *In general.* A taxpayer may treat a residence under construction as a qualified residence for a period of up to 24 months, but only if the residence becomes a qualified residence, without regard to this paragraph (p)(5)(i), as of the time that the residence is ready for occupancy.

(ii) *Example.* X owns a residential lot suitable for the construction of a vacation home. On April 20, 1987, X obtains a mortgage secured by the lot and any property to be constructed on the lot. On August 9, 1987, X begins construction of a residence on the lot. The residence is ready for occupancy on November 9, 1989. The residence is used as a residence within the meaning of paragraph (p)(3)(iii) of this section during 1989 and X elects to treat the residence as his second residence for the period November 9, 1989, through December 31, 1989. Since the residence under construction is a qualified residence as of the first day that the residence is ready for occupancy (November 9, 1987), X may treat the residence as his second residence under paragraph (p)(5)(i) of this section for up to 24 months of the period during which the residence is under construction, commencing on or after the date that construction is begun (August 9, 1987). If X treats the residence under construction as X's second residence beginning on August 9, 1987, the residence under construction would cease to qualify as a qualified residence under paragraph (p)(5)(i) on August 8, 1989. The residence's status as a qualified residence for future periods would be determined without regard to paragraph (p)(5)(i) of this section.

(6) *Special rule for time-sharing arrangements.* Property that is otherwise a qualified residence will not fail to qualify as such solely because the taxpayer's interest in or right to use the property is restricted by an arrangement whereby two or more persons with interests in the property agree to exercise control over the property for different periods during the taxable year. For purposes of determining the use of a residence under paragraph (p)(3)(iii) of this section, a taxpayer will not be considered to have used or rented a residence during any period that the taxpayer does not have the right to use the property or to receive any benefits from the rental of the property.

(q) *Special rules for tenant-stockholders in cooperative housing corporations*--(1) *In general.* For purposes of this section, a residence includes stock in a cooperative housing

Sec. 163. Interest

corporation owned by a tenant-stockholder if the house or apartment which the tenant-stockholder is entitled to occupy by virtue of owning such stock is a residence within the meaning of paragraph (p)(3)(ii) of this section.

(2) *Special rule where stock may not be used to secure debt.* For purposes of this section, if stock described in paragraph (q)(1) of this section may not be used to secure debt because of restrictions under local or State law or because of restrictions in the cooperative agreement (other than restrictions the principal purpose of which is to permit the tenant-stockholder to treat unsecured debt as secured debt under this paragraph (q)(2)), debt may be treated as secured by such stock to the extent that the proceeds of the debt are allocated to the purchase of the stock under the rules of § 1.163-8T. For purposes of this paragraph (q)(2), proceeds of debt incurred prior to January 1, 1987, may be treated as allocated to the purchase of such stock to the extent that the tenant-stockholder has properly and consistently deducted interest expense on such debt as home mortgage interest attributable to such stock on Schedule A of Form 1040 in determining his taxable income for taxable years beginning before January 1, 1987. For purposes of this paragraph (q)(2), amended returns filed after December 22, 1987, are disregarded.

(3) *Treatment of interest expense of the cooperative described in section 216(a)(2).* For purposes of section 163(h) and § 1.163-9T (disallowance of deduction for personal interest) and section 163(d) (limitation on investment interest), any amount allowable as a deduction to a tenant-stockholder under section 216(a)(2) shall be treated as interest paid or accrued by the tenant-stockholder. If a tenant-stockholder's stock in a cooperative housing corporation is a qualified residence of the tenant-shareholder, any amount allowable as a deduction to the tenant-stockholder under section 216(a)(2) is qualified residence interest.

(4) *Special rule to prevent tax avoidance.* If the amount treated as qualified residence interest under this section exceeds the amount which would be so treated if the tenant-stockholder were treated as directly owning his proportionate share of the assets and liabilities of the cooperative and one of the principal purposes of the cooperative arrangement is to permit the tenant-stockholder to increase the amount of qualified residence interest, the district director may determine that such excess is not qualified residence interest.

(5) *Other definitions.* For purposes of this section, the terms ``tenant-stockholder,'' ``cooperative housing corporation'' and ``proportionate share'' shall have the meaning given by section 216 and the regulations thereunder.

***

[T.D. 6500, 25 FR 11402, Nov. 26, 1960. T.D. 6821, 30 FR 6216, May 4, 1965; T.D. 6873, 31 FR 941, Jan. 25, 1966; T.D. 7408, 41 FR 9547, Mar. 5, 1976; T.D. 8145, 52 FR 24999, July 2, 1987; T.D. 8145, 62 FR 40270, July 28, 1997; T.D. 8168, 52 FR 48410, Dec. 22, 1987]

Sec. 164. Taxes

(a) **General rule.** -- Except as otherwise provided in this section, the following taxes shall be allowed as a deduction for the taxable year within which paid or accrued:

(1) State and local, and foreign, real property taxes.

(2) State and local personal property taxes.

(3) State and local, and foreign, income, war profits, and excess profits taxes.

In addition, there shall be allowed as a deduction State and local, and foreign, taxes not described in the preceding sentence which are paid or accrued within the taxable year in carrying on a trade

Sec. 164. Taxes

or business or an activity described in section 212 (relating to expenses for production of income). Notwithstanding the preceding sentence, any tax (not described in the first sentence of this subsection) which is paid or accrued by the taxpayer in connection with an acquisition or disposition of property shall be treated as part of the cost of the acquired property or, in the case of a disposition, as a reduction in the amount realized on the disposition. 5

(b) Definitions and special rules. -- For purposes of this section--

(1) Personal property taxes. -- The term "personal property tax" means an ad valorem tax which is imposed on an annual basis in respect of personal property.

(2) State or local taxes. -- A State or local tax includes only a tax imposed by a State, a possession of the United States, or a political subdivision of any of the foregoing, or by the 10 District of Columbia.

***

(5) General sales taxes. -- For purposes of subsection (a) -

(A) Election to deduct State and local sales taxes in lieu of State and local income taxes. -- 15

(i) In general. -- At the election of the taxpayer for the taxable year, subsection (a) shall be applied--

(I) without regard to the reference to State and local income taxes, and

(II) as if State and local general sales taxes were referred to in a paragraph thereof. 20

(B) Definition of general sales tax. -- The term "general sales tax" means a tax imposed at one rate with respect to the sale at retail of a broad range of classes of items.

(C) Special rules for food, etc. -- In the case of items of food, clothing, medical supplies, and motor vehicles--

(i) the fact that the tax does not apply with respect to some or all of such items shall 25 not be taken into account in determining whether the tax applies with respect to a broad range of classes of items, and

(ii) the fact that the rate of tax applicable with respect to some or all of such items is lower than the general rate of tax shall not be taken into account in determining whether the tax is imposed at one rate. 30

(D) Items taxed at different rates. -- Except in the case of a lower rate of tax applicable with respect to an item described in subparagraph (C), no deduction shall be allowed under this paragraph for any general sales tax imposed with respect to an item at a rate other than the general rate of tax.

(E) Compensating use taxes. -- A compensating use tax with respect to an item shall be 35 treated as a general sales tax. For purposes of the preceding sentence, the term "compensating use tax" means, with respect to any item, a tax which--

(i) is imposed on the use, storage, or consumption of such item, and

(ii) is complementary to a general sales tax, but only if a deduction is allowable under this paragraph with respect to items sold at retail in the taxing jurisdiction which 40 are similar to such item.

(F) Special rule for motor vehicles. -- In the case of motor vehicles, if the rate of tax exceeds the general rate, such excess shall be disregarded and the general rate shall be treated as the rate of tax.

(G) Separately stated general sales taxes. -- If the amount of any general sales tax is 45 separately stated, then, to the extent that the amount so stated is paid by the consumer

Sec. 164. Taxes

(other than in connection with the consumer's trade or business) to the seller, such amount shall be treated as a tax imposed on, and paid by, such consumer.

(H) Amount of deduction may be determined under tables. --

(i) In general. -- At the election of the taxpayer for the taxable year, the amount of the deduction allowed under this paragraph for such year shall be--

(I) the amount determined under this paragraph (without regard to this subparagraph) with respect to motor vehicles, boats, and other items specified by the Secretary, and

(II) the amount determined under tables prescribed by the Secretary with respect to items to which subclause (I) does not apply.

(ii) Requirements for tables. -- The tables prescribed under clause (i)--

(I) shall reflect the provisions of this paragraph,

(II) shall be based on the average consumption by taxpayers on a State-by-State basis (as determined by the Secretary) of items to which clause (i)(I) does not apply, taking into account filing status, number of dependents, adjusted gross income, and rates of State and local general sales taxation, and

(III) need only be determined with respect to adjusted gross incomes up to the applicable amount (as determined under section 68(b)).

(I) Application of paragraph. -- This paragraph shall apply to taxable years beginning after December 31, 2003, and before January 1, 2008.

(c) Deduction denied in case of certain taxes. -- No deduction shall be allowed for the following taxes:

(1) Taxes assessed against local benefits of a kind tending to increase the value of the property assessed; but this paragraph shall not prevent the deduction of so much of such taxes as is properly allocable to maintenance or interest charges.

(2) Taxes on real property, to the extent that subsection (d) requires such taxes to be treated as imposed on another taxpayer.

(d) Apportionment of taxes on real property between seller and purchaser. --

(1) General rule. -- For purposes of subsection (a), if real property is sold during any real property tax year, then--

(A) so much of the real property tax as is properly allocable to that part of such year which ends on the day before the date of the sale shall be treated as a tax imposed on the seller, and

(B) so much of such tax as is properly allocable to that part of such year which begins on the date of the sale shall be treated as a tax imposed on the purchaser.

Sec. 165. Losses

(a) General rule. -- There shall be allowed as a deduction any loss sustained during the taxable year and not compensated for by insurance or otherwise.

(b) Amount of deduction. -- For purposes of subsection (a), the basis for determining the amount of the deduction for any loss shall be the adjusted basis provided in section 1011 for determining the loss from the sale or other disposition of property.

(c) Limitation on losses of individuals. -- In the case of an individual, the deduction under subsection (a) shall be limited to--

Sec. 165.   Losses

(1) losses incurred in a trade or business;

(2) losses incurred in any transaction entered into for profit, though not connected with a trade or business; and

(3) except as provided in subsection (h), losses of property not connected with a trade or business or a transaction entered into for profit, if such losses arise from fire, storm, shipwreck, 5 or other casualty, or from theft.

(d) Wagering losses. -- Losses from wagering transactions shall be allowed only to the extent of the gains from such transactions.

(e) Theft losses. -- For purposes of subsection (a), any loss arising from theft shall be treated as sustained during the taxable year in which the taxpayer discovers such loss.   10

(f) Capital losses. -- Losses from sales or exchanges of capital assets shall be allowed only to the extent allowed in sections 1211 and 1212.

(g) Worthless securities. --

(1) General rule. -- If any security which is a capital asset becomes worthless during the taxable year, the loss resulting therefrom shall, for purposes of this subtitle, be treated as a loss 15 from the sale or exchange, on the last day of the taxable year, of a capital asset.

(2) Security defined. -- For purposes of this subsection, the term "security" means -

(A) a share of stock in a corporation;

(B) a right to subscribe for, or to receive, a share of stock in a corporation; or

(C) a bond, debenture, note, or certificate, or other evidence of indebtedness, issued by a 20 corporation or by a government or political subdivision thereof, with interest coupons or in registered form.

(h) Treatment of casualty gains and losses. --

(1) $100 limitation per casualty. -- Any loss of an individual described in subsection (c)(3) shall be allowed only to the extent that the amount of the loss to such individual arising from 25 each casualty, or from each theft, exceeds $100.

(2) Net casualty loss allowed only to the extent it exceeds 10 percent of adjusted gross income. --

(A) In general. -- If the personal casualty losses for any taxable year exceed the personal casualty gains for such taxable year, such losses shall be allowed for the taxable year only 30 to the extent of the sum of--

(i) the amount of the personal casualty gains for the taxable year, plus

(ii) so much of such excess as exceeds 10 percent of the adjusted gross income of the individual.

(B) Special rule where personal casualty gains exceed personal casualty losses. -- If 35 the personal casualty gains for any taxable year exceed the personal casualty losses for such taxable year--

(i) all such gains shall be treated as gains from sales or exchanges of capital assets, and

(ii) all such losses shall be treated as losses from sales or exchanges of capital assets.   40

(3) Definitions of personal casualty gain and personal casualty loss. -- For purposes of this subsection--

(A) Personal casualty gain. -- The term "personal casualty gain" means the recognized gain from any involuntary conversion of property which is described in subsection (c)(3) arising from fire, storm, shipwreck, or other casualty, or from theft.   45

Sec. 165. Losses

(B) **Personal casualty loss.** -- The term "personal casualty loss" means any loss described in subsection (c)(3). For purposes of paragraph (2), the amount of any personal casualty loss shall be determined after the application of paragraph (1).

(4) **Special rules.** --

(A) **Personal casualty losses allowable in computing adjusted gross income to the extent of personal casualty gains.** -- In any case to which paragraph (2)(A) applies, the deduction for personal casualty losses for any taxable year shall be treated as a deduction allowable in computing adjusted gross income to the extent such losses do not exceed the personal casualty gains for the taxable year.

(B) **Joint returns.** -- For purposes of this subsection, a husband and wife making a joint return for the taxable year shall be treated as 1 individual.

***

(E) **Claim required to be filed in certain cases.** -- Any loss of an individual described in subsection (c)(3) to the extent covered by insurance shall be taken into account under this section only if the individual files a timely insurance claim with respect to such loss.

(i) **Disaster losses.** --

(1) **Election to take deduction for preceding year.** -- Notwithstanding the provisions of subsection (a), any loss attributable to a disaster occurring in an area subsequently determined by the President of the United States to warrant assistance by the Federal Government under the Robert T. Stafford Disaster Relief and Emergency Assistance Act may, at the election of the taxpayer, be taken into account for the taxable year immediately preceding the taxable year in which the disaster occurred.

(2) **Year of loss.** -- If an election is made under this subsection, the casualty resulting in the loss shall be treated for purposes of this title as having occurred in the taxable year for which the deduction is claimed.

(3) **Amount of loss.** -- The amount of the loss taken into account in the preceding taxable year by reason of paragraph (1) shall not exceed the uncompensated amount determined on the basis of the facts existing at the date the taxpayer claims the loss.

(4) **Use of disaster loan appraisals to establish amount of loss.** -- Nothing in this title shall be construed to prohibit the Secretary from prescribing regulations or other guidance under which an appraisal for the purpose of obtaining a loan of Federal funds or a loan guarantee from the Federal Government as a result of a Presidentially declared disaster (as defined by section 1033(h)(3)) may be used to establish the amount of any loss described in paragraph (1) or (2).

(j) **Denial of deduction for losses on certain obligations not in registered form.** --

(1) **In general.** -- Nothing in subsection (a) or in any other provision of law shall be construed to provide a deduction for any loss sustained on any registration-required obligation unless such obligation is in registered form (or the issuance of such obligation was subject to tax under section 4701).

(2) **Definitions.** -- For purposes of this subsection--

(A) **Registration-required obligation.** -- The term "registration-required obligation" has the meaning given to such term by section 163(f)(2) except that clause (iv) of subparagraph (A), and subparagraph (B), of such section shall not apply.

***

(k) **Treatment as disaster loss where taxpayer ordered to demolish or relocate residence in disaster area because of disaster.** -- In the case of a taxpayer whose residence is located in an area which has been determined by the President of the United States to warrant assistance by the

Sec. 165.   Losses

Federal Government under the Robert T. Stafford Disaster Relief and Emergency Assistance Act, if--

> **(1)** not later than the 120th day after the date of such determination, the taxpayer is ordered, by the government of the State or any political subdivision thereof in which such residence is located, to demolish or relocate such residence, and

5

> **(2)** the residence has been rendered unsafe for use as a residence by reason of the disaster,

any loss attributable to such disaster shall be treated as a loss which arises from a casualty and which is described in subsection (i).

Reg. § 1.165-1   Losses.

10

(a) *Allowance of deduction.* Section 165(a) provides that, in computing taxable income under section 63, any loss actually sustained during the taxable year and not made good by insurance or some other form of compensation shall be allowed as a deduction subject to any provision of the internal revenue laws which prohibits or limits the amount of the deduction. This deduction for losses sustained shall be taken in accordance with 15 section 165 and the regulations thereunder. For the disallowance of deductions for worthless securities issued by a political party, see § 1.271-1.

(b) *Nature of loss allowable.* To be allowable as a deduction under section 165(a), a loss must be evidenced by closed and completed transactions, fixed by identifiable events, and, except as otherwise provided in section 165(h) and § 1.165-11, relating to 20 disaster losses, actually sustained during the taxable year. Only a bona fide loss is allowable. Substance and not mere form shall govern in determining a deductible loss.

(c) *Amount deductible.* (1) The amount of loss allowable as a deduction under section 165(a) shall not exceed the amount prescribed by § 1.1011-1 as the adjusted basis for determining the loss from the sale or other disposition of the property involved. In the 25 case of each such deduction claimed, therefore, the basis of the property must be properly adjusted as prescribed by § 1.1011-1 for such items as expenditures, receipts, or losses, properly chargeable to capital account, and for such items as depreciation, obsolescence, amortization, and depletion, in order to determine the amount of loss allowable as a deduction. To determine the allowable loss in the case of property 30 acquired before March 1, 1913, see also paragraph (b) of § 1.1053-1.

(2) The amount of loss recognized upon the sale or exchange of property shall be determined for purposes of section 165(a) in accordance with § 1.1002-1.

(3) A loss from the sale or exchange of a capital asset shall be allowed as a deduction under section 165(a) but only to the extent allowed in section 1211 (relating to limitation 35 on capital losses) and section 1212 (relating to capital loss carrybacks and carryovers), and in the regulations under those sections.

(4) In determining the amount of loss actually sustained for purposes of section 165(a), proper adjustment shall be made for any salvage value and for any insurance or other compensation received.

40

(d) *Year of deduction.* (1) A loss shall be allowed as a deduction under section 165(a) only for the taxable year in which the loss is sustained. For this purpose, a loss shall be treated as sustained during the taxable year in which the loss occurs as evidenced by closed and completed transactions and as fixed by identifiable events occurring in such taxable year. For provisions relating to situations where a loss attributable to a disaster 45 will be treated as sustained in the taxable year immediately preceding the taxable year in which the disaster actually occurred, see section 165(h) and § 1.165-11.

(2)(i) If a casualty or other event occurs which may result in a loss and, in the year of such casualty or event, there exists a claim for reimbursement with respect to which there is a reasonable prospect of recovery, no portion of the loss with respect to which 50

413

reimbursement may be received is sustained, for purposes of section 165, until it can be ascertained with reasonable certainty whether or not such reimbursement will be received. Whether a reasonable prospect of recovery exists with respect to a claim for reimbursement of a loss is a question of fact to be determined upon an examination of all
5 facts and circumstances. Whether or not such reimbursement will be received may be ascertained with reasonable certainty, for example, by a settlement of the claim, by an adjudication of the claim, or by an abandonment of the claim. When a taxpayer claims that the taxable year in which a loss is sustained is fixed by his abandonment of the claim for reimbursement, he must be able to produce objective evidence of his having
10 abandoned the claim, such as the execution of a release.

(ii) If in the year of the casualty or other event a portion of the loss is not covered by a claim for reimbursement with respect to which there is a reasonable prospect of recovery, then such portion of the loss is sustained during the taxable year in which the casualty or other event occurs. For example, if property having an adjusted basis of $10,000 is
15 completely destroyed by fire in 1961, and if the taxpayer's only claim for reimbursement consists of an insurance claim for $8,000 which is settled in 1962, the taxpayer sustains a loss of $2,000 in 1961. However, if the taxpayer's automobile is completely destroyed in 1961 as a result of the negligence of another person and there exists a reasonable prospect of recovery on a claim for the full value of the automobile against such person,
20 the taxpayer does not sustain any loss until the taxable year in which the claim is adjudicated or otherwise settled. If the automobile had an adjusted basis of $5,000 and the taxpayer secures a judgment of $4,000 in 1962, $1,000 is deductible for the taxable year 1962. If in 1963 it becomes reasonably certain that only $3,500 can ever be collected on such judgment, $500 is deductible for the taxable year 1963.
25 (iii) If the taxpayer deducted a loss in accordance with the provisions of this paragraph and in a subsequent taxable year receives reimbursement for such loss, he does not recompute the tax for the taxable year in which the deduction was taken but includes the amount of such reimbursement in his gross income for the taxable year in which received, subject to the provisions of section 111, relating to recovery of amounts
30 previously deducted.

(3) Any loss arising from theft shall be treated as sustained during the taxable year in which the taxpayer discovers the loss (see § 1.165-8, relating to theft losses). However, if in the year of discovery there exists a claim for reimbursement with respect to which there is a reasonable prospect of recovery, no portion of the loss with respect to which
35 reimbursement may be received is sustained, for purposes of section 165, until the taxable year in which it can be ascertained with reasonable certainty whether or not such reimbursement will be received.

(4) The rules of this paragraph are applicable with respect to a casualty or other event which may result in a loss and which occurs after January 16, 1960. If the casualty or
40 other event occurs on or before such date, a taxpayer may treat any loss resulting therefrom in accordance with the rules then applicable, or, if he so desires, in accordance with the provisions of this paragraph; but no provision of this paragraph shall be construed to permit a deduction of the same loss or any part thereof in more than one taxable year or to extend the period of limitations within which a claim for credit or refund
45 may be filed under section 6511.

(e) *Limitation on losses of individuals.* In the case of an individual, the deduction for losses granted by section 165(a) shall, subject to the provisions of section 165(c) and paragraph (a) of this section, be limited to:

(1) Losses incurred in a trade or business;
50 (2) Losses incurred in any transaction entered into for profit, though not connected with a trade or business; and

Sec. 165. Losses

(3) Losses of property not connected with a trade or business and not incurred in any transaction entered into for profit, if such losses arise from fire, storm, shipwreck, or other casualty, or from theft, and if the loss involved has not been allowed for estate tax purposes in the estate tax return. For additional provisions pertaining to the allowance of casualty and theft losses, see §§ 1.165-7 and 1.165-8, respectively.

For special rules relating to an election by a taxpayer to deduct disaster losses in the taxable year immediately preceding the taxable year in which the disaster occurred, see section 165(h) and § 1.165-11.

Reg. § 1.165-3   Demolition of buildings.

(a) Intent to demolish formed at time of purchase. (1) Except as provided in subparagraph (2) of this paragraph, the following rule shall apply when, in the course of a trade or business or in a transaction entered into for profit, real property is purchased with the intention of demolishing either immediately or subsequently the buildings situated thereon: No deduction shall be allowed under section 165(a) on account of the demolition of the old buildings even though any demolition originally planned is subsequently deferred or abandoned. The entire basis of the property so purchased shall, notwithstanding the provisions of § 1.167(a)-5, be allocated to the land only. Such basis shall be increased by the net cost of demolition or decreased by the net proceeds from demolition.

(2)(i) If the property is purchased with the intention of demolishing the buildings and the buildings are used in a trade or business or held for the production of income before their demolition, a portion of the basis of the property may be allocated to such buildings and depreciated over the period during which they are so used or held. The fact that the taxpayer intends to demolish the buildings shall be taken into account in making the apportionment of basis between the land and buildings under § 1.167(a)-5. In any event, the portion of the purchase price which may be allocated to the buildings shall not exceed the present value of the right to receive rentals from the buildings over the period of their intended use. The present value of such right shall be determined at the time that the buildings are first used in the trade or business or first held for the production of income. If the taxpayer does not rent the buildings, but uses them in his own trade or business or in the production of his income, the present value of such right shall be determined by reference to the rentals which could be realized during such period of intended use. The fact that the taxpayer intends to rent or use the buildings for a limited period before their demolition shall also be taken into account in computing the useful life in accordance with paragraph (b) of § 1.167(a)-1.

(ii) Any portion of the purchase price which is allocated to the buildings in accordance with this subparagraph shall not be included in the basis of the land computed under subparagraph (1) of this paragraph, and any portion of the basis of the buildings which has not been recovered through depreciation or otherwise at the time of the demolition of the buildings is allowable as a deduction under section 165.

(iii) The application of this subparagraph may be illustrated by the following example:

Example. In January 1958, A purchased land and a building for $60,000 with the intention of demolishing the building. In the following April, A concludes that he will be unable to commence the construction of a proposed new building for a period of more than 3 years. Accordingly, on June 1, 1958, he leased the building for a period of 3 years at an annual rental of $1,200. A intends to demolish the building upon expiration of the lease. A may allocate a portion of the $60,000 basis of the property to the building to be depreciated over the 3-year period. That portion is equal to the present value of the right to receive $3,600 (3 times $1,200). Assuming that the present value of that right determined as of June 1, 1958, is $2,850, A may allocate that amount to the building and,

415

Sec. 165. Losses

if A files his return on the basis of a taxable year ending May 31, 1959, A may take a depreciation deduction with respect to such building of $950 for such taxable year. The basis of the land to A as determined under subparagraph (1) of this paragraph is reduced by $2,850. If on June 1, 1960, A ceases to rent the building and demolishes it, the
5 balance of the undepreciated portion allocated to the buildings, $950, may be deducted from gross income under section 165.

(3) The basis of any building acquired in replacement of the old buildings shall not include any part of the basis of the property originally purchased even though such part was, at the time of purchase, allocated to the buildings to be demolished for purposes of
10 determining allowable depreciation for the period before demolition.

(b) *Intent to demolish formed subsequent to the time of acquisition.* (1) Except as provided in subparagraph (2) of this paragraph, the loss incurred in a trade or business or in a transaction entered into for profit and arising from a demolition of old buildings shall be allowed as a deduction under section 165(a) if the demolition occurs as a result of a
15 plan formed subsequent to the acquisition of the buildings demolished. The amount of the loss shall be the adjusted basis of the buildings demolished increased by the net cost of demolition or decreased by the net proceeds from demolition. See paragraph (c) of § 1.165-1 relating to amount deductible under section 165. The basis of any building acquired in replacement of the old buildings shall not include any part of the basis of the
20 property demolished.

(2) If a lessor or lessee of real property demolishes the buildings situated thereon pursuant to a lease or an agreement which resulted in a lease, under which either the lessor was required or the lessee was required or permitted to demolish such buildings, no deduction shall be allowed to the lessor under section 165(a) on account of the
25 demolition of the old buildings. However, the adjusted basis of the demolished buildings, increased by the net cost of demolition or decreased by the net proceeds from demolition, shall be considered as a part of the cost of the lease to be amortized over the remaining term thereof.

(c) *Evidence of intention.* (1) Whether real property has been purchased with the
30 intention of demolishing the buildings thereon or whether the demolition of the buildings occurs as a result of a plan formed subsequent to their acquisition is a question of fact, and the answer depends upon an examination of all the surrounding facts and circumstances. The answer to the question does not depend solely upon the statements of the taxpayer at the time he acquired the property or demolished the buildings, but such
35 statements, if made, are relevant and will be considered. Certain other relevant facts and circumstances that exist in some cases and the inferences that might reasonably be drawn from them are described in subparagraphs (2) and (3) of this paragraph. The question as to the taxpayer's intention is not answered by any inference that is drawn from any one fact or circumstance but can be answered only by a consideration of all
40 relevant facts and circumstances and the reasonable inferences to be drawn therefrom.

(2) An intention at the time of acquisition to demolish may be suggested by:

(i) A short delay between the date of acquisition and the date of demolition;

(ii) Evidence of prohibitive remodeling costs determined at the time of acquisition;

(iii) Existence of municipal regulations at the time of acquisition which would prohibit
45 the continued use of the buildings for profit purposes;

(iv) Unsuitability of the buildings for the taxpayer's trade or business at the time of acquisition; or

(v) Inability at the time of acquisition to realize a reasonable income from the buildings.
50 (3) The fact that the demolition occurred pursuant to a plan formed subsequent to the acquisition of the property may be suggested by:

Sec. 165. Losses

(i) Substantial improvement of the buildings immediately after their acquisition;

(ii) Prolonged use of the buildings for business purposes after their acquisition;

(iii) Suitability of the buildings for investment purposes at the time of acquisition;

(iv) Substantial change in economic or business conditions after the date of acquisition;

(v) Loss of useful value occurring after the date of acquisition;

(vi) Substantial damage to the buildings occurring after their acquisition;

(vii) Discovery of latent structural defects in the buildings after their acquisition;

(viii) Decline in the taxpayer's business after the date of acquisition;

(ix) Condemnation of the property by municipal authorities after the date of acquisition; or

(x) Inability after acquisition to obtain building material necessary for the improvement of the property.

Reg. § 1.165-5 Worthless securities.

(a) *Definition of security.* As used in section 165(g) and this section, the term ``security" means:

(1) A share of stock in a corporation;

(2) A right to subscribe for, or to receive, a share of stock in a corporation; or

(3) A bond, debenture, note, or certificate, or other evidence of indebtedness to pay a fixed or determinable sum of money, which has been issued with interest coupons or in registered form by a domestic or foreign corporation or by any government or political subdivision thereof.

(b) *Ordinary loss.* If any security which is not a capital asset becomes wholly worthless during the taxable year, the loss resulting therefrom may be deducted under section 165(a) as an ordinary loss.

(c) *Capital loss.* If any security which is a capital asset becomes wholly worthless at any time during the taxable year, the loss resulting therefrom may be deducted under section 165(a) but only as though it were a loss from a sale or exchange, on the last day of the taxable year, of a capital asset. See section 165(g)(1). The amount so allowed as a deduction shall be subject to the limitations upon capital losses described in paragraph (c)(3) of § 1.165-1.

(d) *Loss on worthless securities of an affiliated corporation--*(1) *Deductible as an ordinary loss.* If a taxpayer which is a domestic corporation owns any security of a domestic or foreign corporation which is affiliated with the taxpayer within the meaning of subparagraph (2) of this paragraph and such security becomes wholly worthless during the taxable year, the loss resulting therefrom may be deducted under section 165(a) as an ordinary loss in accordance with paragraph (b) of this section. The fact that the security is in fact a capital asset of the taxpayer is immaterial for this purpose, since section 165(g)(3) provides that such security shall be treated as though it were not a capital asset for the purposes of section 165(g)(1). A debt which becomes wholly worthless during the taxable year shall be as an ordinary loss in accordance with the provisions of this subparagraph, to the extent that such debt is a security within the meaning of paragraph (a)(3) of this section.

(2) *Affiliated corporation defined.* For purposes of this paragraph, a corporation shall be treated as affiliated with the taxpayer owning the security if--

(i)(a) In the case of a taxable year beginning on or after January 1, 1970, the taxpayer owns directly--

(1) Stock possessing at least 80 percent of the voting power of all classes of such corporation's stock, and

Sec. 165. Losses

(2) At least 80 percent of each class of such corporation's nonvoting stock excluding for purposes of this subdivision (i)(a) nonvoting stock which is limited and preferred as to dividends (see section 1504(a)), or

(b) In the case of a taxable year beginning before January 1, 1970, the taxpayer owns
5 directly at least 95 percent of each class of the stock of such corporation;

(ii) None of the stock of such corporation was acquired by the taxpayer solely for the purpose of converting a capital loss sustained by reason of the worthlessness of any such stock into an ordinary loss under section 165(g)(3), and

(iii) More than 90 percent of the aggregate of the gross receipts of such corporation
10 for all the taxable years during which it has been in existence has been from sources other than royalties, rents (except rents derived from rental of properties to employees of such corporation in the ordinary course of its operating business), dividends, interest (except interest received on the deferred purchase price of operating assets sold), annuities, and gains from sales or exchanges of stocks and securities. For this purpose,
15 the term ``gross receipts" means total receipts determined without any deduction for cost of goods sold, and gross receipts from sales or exchanges of stocks and securities shall be taken into account only to the extent of gains from such sales or exchanges.

(e) *Bonds issued by an insolvent corporation.* A bond of an insolvent corporation secured only by a mortgage from which nothing is realized for the bondholders on
20 foreclosure shall be regarded as having become worthless not later than the year of the foreclosure sale, and no deduction in respect of the loss shall be allowed under section 165(a) in computing a bondholder's taxable income for a subsequent year. See also paragraph (d) of § 1.165-1.

(f) *Decline in market value.* A taxpayer possessing a security to which this section
25 relates shall not be allowed any deduction under section 165(a) on account of mere market fluctuation in the value of such security. See also § 1.165-4.

(g) *Application to inventories.* This section does not apply to any loss upon the worthlessness of any security reflected in inventories required to be taken by a dealer in securities under section 471. See § 1.471-5.

30 (h) *Special rules for banks.* For special rules applicable under this section to worthless securities of a bank, including securities issued by an affiliated bank, see § 1.582-1.

(i) *Examples.* The provisions of this section may be illustrated by the following examples:

Example (1). (i) X Corporation, a domestic manufacturing corporation which makes its
35 return on the basis of the calendar year, owns 100 percent of each class of the stock of Y Corporation; and, in addition, 19 percent of the common stock (the only class of stock) of Z Corporation, which it acquired in 1948. Y Corporation, a domestic manufacturing corporation which makes its return on the basis of the calendar year, owns 81 percent of the common stock of Z Corporation, which it acquired in 1946. It is established that the
40 stock of Z Corporation, which has from its inception derived all of its gross receipts from manufacturing operations, became worthless during 1971.

(ii) Since the stock of Z Corporation which is owned by X Corporation is a capital asset and since X Corporation does not directly own at least 80 percent of the stock of Z Corporation, any loss sustained by X Corporation upon the worthlessness of such stock
45 shall be deducted under section 165(g)(1) and paragraph (c) of this section as a loss from a sale or exchange on December 31, 1971, of a capital asset. The loss so sustained by X Corporation shall be considered a long-term capital loss under the provisions of section 1222(4), since the stock was held by that corporation for more than 6 months.

(iii) Since Z Corporation is considered to be affiliated with Y Corporation under the
50 provisions of paragraph (d)(2) of this section, any loss sustained by Y Corporation upon the worthlessness of the stock of Z Corporation shall be deducted in 1971 under section

165(g)(3) and paragraph (d)(1) of this section as an ordinary loss.

Example (2). (i) On January 1, 1971, X Corporation, a domestic manufacturing corporation which makes its return on the basis of the calendar year, owns 60 percent of each class of the stock of Y Corporation, a foreign corporation, which it acquired in 1950. Y Corporation has, from the date of its incorporation, derived all of its gross receipts from 5 manufacturing operations. It is established that the stock of Y Corporation became worthless on June 30, 1971. On August 1, 1971, X Corporation acquires the balance of the stock of Y Corporation for the purpose of obtaining the benefit of section 165(g)(3) with respect to the loss it has sustained on the worthlessness of the stock of Y Corporation. 10

(ii) Since the stock of Y Corporation which is owned by X Corporation is a capital asset and since Y Corporation is not to be treated as affiliated with X Corporation under the provisions of paragraph (d)(2) of this section, notwithstanding the fact that, at the close of 1971, X Corporation owns 100 percent of each class of stock of Y Corporation, any loss sustained by X Corporation upon the worthlessness of such stock shall be 15 deducted under the provisions of section 165(g)(1) and paragraph (c) of this section as a loss from a sale or exchange on December 31, 1971, of a capital asset.

Example (3). (i) X Corporation, a domestic manufacturing corporation which makes its return on the basis of the calendar year, owns 80 percent of each class of the stock of Y Corporation, which from its inception has derived all of its gross receipts from 20 manufacturing operations. As one of its capital assets, X Corporation owns $100,000 in registered bonds issued by Y Corporation payable at maturity on December 31, 1974. It is established that these bonds became worthless during 1971.

(ii) Since Y Corporation is considered to be affiliated with X Corporation under the provisions of paragraph (d)(2) of this section, any loss sustained by X Corporation upon 25 the worthlessness of these bonds may be deducted in 1971 under section 165(g)(3) and paragraph (d)(1) of this section as an ordinary loss. The loss may not be deducted under section 166 as a bad debt. See section 166(e).

Reg. § 1.165-7 Casualty losses. 30

(a) *In general--*(1) *Allowance of deduction.* Except as otherwise provided in paragraphs (b)(4) and (c) of this section, any loss arising from fire, storm, shipwreck, or other casualty is allowable as a deduction under section 165(a) for the taxable year in which the loss is sustained. However, see § 1.165-6, relating to farming losses, and § 1.165-11, relating to an election by a taxpayer to deduct disaster losses in the taxable 35 year immediately preceding the taxable year in which the disaster occurred. The manner of determining the amount of a casualty loss allowable as a deduction in computing taxable income under section 63 is the same whether the loss has been incurred in a trade or business or in any transaction entered into for profit, or whether it has been a loss of property not connected with a trade or business and not incurred in any 40 transaction entered into for profit. The amount of a casualty loss shall be determined in accordance with paragraph (b) of this section. For other rules relating to the treatment of deductible casualty losses, see § 1.1231-1, relating to the involuntary conversion of property.

(2) *Method of valuation.* (i) In determining the amount of loss deductible under this 45 section, the fair market value of the property immediately before and immediately after the casualty shall generally be ascertained by competent appraisal. This appraisal must recognize the effects of any general market decline affecting undamaged as well as damaged property which may occur simultaneously with the casualty, in order that any deduction under this section shall be limited to the actual loss resulting from damage to 50 the property.

Sec. 165. Losses

(ii) The cost of repairs to the property damaged is acceptable as evidence of the loss of value if the taxpayer shows that (a) the repairs are necessary to restore the property to its condition immediately before the casualty, (b) the amount spent for such repairs is not excessive, (c) the repairs do not care for more than the damage suffered, and (d) the
5 value of the property after the repairs does not as a result of the repairs exceed the value of the property immediately before the casualty.

(3) *Damage to automobiles.* An automobile owned by the taxpayer, whether used for business purposes or maintained for recreation or pleasure, may be the subject of a casualty loss, including those losses specifically referred to in subparagraph (1) of this
10 paragraph. In addition, a casualty loss occurs when an automobile owned by the taxpayer is damaged and when:

(i) The damage results from the faulty driving of the taxpayer or other person operating the automobile but is not due to the willful act or willful negligence of the taxpayer or of one acting in his behalf or
15 (ii) The damage results from the faulty driving of the operator of the vehicle with which the automobile of the taxpayer collides.

(4) *Application to inventories.* This section does not apply to a casualty loss reflected in the inventories of the taxpayer. For provisions relating to inventories, see section 471 and the regulations thereunder.
20 (5) *Property converted from personal use.* In the case of property which originally was not used in the trade or business or for income-producing purposes and which is thereafter converted to either of such uses, the fair market value of the property on the date of conversion, if less than the adjusted basis of the property at such time, shall be used, after making proper adjustments in respect of basis, as the basis for determining
25 the amount of loss under paragraph (b)(1) of this section. See paragraph (b) of § 1.165-9, and § 1.167(g)-1.

(6) *Theft losses.* A loss which arises from theft is not considered a casualty loss for purposes of this section. See § 1.165-8, relating to theft losses.

(b) *Amount deductible--*(1) *General rule.* In the case of any casualty loss whether or
30 not incurred in a trade or business or in any transaction entered into for profit, the amount of loss to be taken into account for purposes of section 165(a) shall be the lesser of either--

(i) The amount which is equal to the fair market value of the property immediately before the casualty reduced by the fair market value of the property immediately after the
35 casualty; or

(ii) The amount of the adjusted basis prescribed in § 1.1011-1 for determining the loss from the sale or other disposition of the property involved.

However, if property used in a trade or business or held for the production of income is totally destroyed by casualty, and if the fair market value of such property immediately
40 before the casualty is less than the adjusted basis of such property, the amount of the adjusted basis of such property shall be treated as the amount of the loss for purposes of section 165(a).

(2) *Aggregation of property for computing loss.* (i) A loss incurred in a trade or business or in any transaction entered into for profit shall be determined under subparagraph (1) of
45 this paragraph by reference to the single, identifiable property damaged or destroyed. Thus, for example, in determining the fair market value of the property before and after the casualty in a case where damage by casualty has occurred to a building and ornamental or fruit trees used in a trade or business, the decrease in value shall be measured by taking the building and trees into account separately, and not together as
50 an integral part of the realty, and separate losses shall be determined for such building and trees.

Sec. 165. Losses

(ii) In determining a casualty loss involving real property and improvements thereon not used in a trade or business or in any transaction entered into for profit, the improvements (such as buildings and ornamental trees and shrubbery) to the property damaged or destroyed shall be considered an integral part of the property, for purposes of subparagraph (1) of this paragraph, and no separate basis need be apportioned to such improvements.

(3) *Examples.* The application of this paragraph may be illustrated by the following examples:

Example (1). In 1956 B purchases for $3,600 an automobile which he uses for nonbusiness purposes. In 1959 the automobile is damaged in an accidental collision with another automobile. The fair market value of B's automobile is $2,000 immediately before the collision and $1,500 immediately after the collision. B receives insurance proceeds of $300 to cover the loss. The amount of the deduction allowable under section 165(a) for the taxable year 1959 is $200, computed as follows:

Value of automobile immediately before casualty..................	$2,000
Less: Value of automobile immediately after casualty..........	1,500
Value of property actually destroyed.......................................	500
Loss to be taken into account for purposes of section 165(a): Lesser amount of property actually destroyed ($500) or adjusted basis of property ($3,600)...	500
Less: Insurance received...	300
Deduction allowable...	200

Example (2). In 1958 A purchases land containing an office building for the lump sum of $90,000. The purchase price is allocated between the land ($18,000) and the building ($72,000) for purposes of determining basis. After the purchase A planted trees and ornamental shrubs on the grounds surrounding the building. In 1961 the land, building, trees, and shrubs are damaged by hurricane. At the time of the casualty the adjusted basis of the land is $18,000 and the adjusted basis of the building is $66,000. At that time the trees and shrubs have an adjusted basis of $1,200. The fair market value of the land and building immediately before the casualty is $18,000 and $70,000, respectively, and immediately after the casualty is $18,000 and $52,000, respectively. The fair market value of the trees and shrubs immediately before the casualty is $2,000 and immediately after the casualty is $400. In 1961 insurance of $5,000 is received to cover the loss to the building. A has no other gains or losses in 1961 subject to section 1231 and § 1.1231-1. The amount of the deduction allowable under section 165(a) with respect to the building for the taxable year 1961 is $13,000, computed as follows:

Value of property immediately before casualty......................	$70,000
Less: Value of property immediately after casualty..............	52,000
Value of property actually destroyed.......................................	18,000
Less: Insurance received...	5,000
Loss to be taken into account for purposes of section 165(a): Lesser amount of property actually destroyed ($18,000) or adjusted basis of property ($66,000)...	18,000
Less: Insurance received...	5,000
Deduction allowable...	13,000

Sec. 165. Losses

The amount of the deduction allowable under section 165(a) with respect to the trees and shrubs for the taxable year 1961 is $1,200, computed as follows:

Value of property immediately before casualty......................	$2,000
Less: Value of property immediately after casualty..............	$400
Value of property actually destroyed....................................	1,600
Loss to be taken into account for purposes of section 165(a):	
Lesser amount of property actually destroyed ($1,600) or	
adjusted basis of property ($1,200).....................................	1,200

Example (3). Assume the same facts as in example (2) except that A purchases land containing a house instead of an office building. The house is used as his private residence. Since the property is used for personal purposes, no allocation of the purchase price is necessary for the land and house. Likewise, no individual determination of thefair market values of the land, house, trees, and shrubs is necessary. The amount of the deduction allowable under section 165(a) with respect to the land, house, trees, and shrubs for the taxable year 1961 is $14,600, computed as follows:

Value of property immediately before casualty......................	$90,000
Less: Value of property immediately after casualty..............	70,400
Value of property actually destroyed....................................	19,600
Less: Insurance received..	5,000
Deduction allowable...	14,600

(4) *Limitation on certain losses sustained by individuals after December 31, 1963.* (i) Pursuant to section 165(c)(3), the deduction allowable under section 165(a) in respect of a loss sustained--

(a) After December 31, 1963, in a taxable year ending after such date,

(b) In respect of property not used in a trade or business or for income producing purposes, and

(c) From a single casualty shall be limited to that portion of the loss which is in excess of $100. The nondeductibility of the first $100 of loss applies to a loss sustained after December 31, 1963, without regard to when the casualty occurred. Thus, if property not used in a trade or business or for income producing purposes is damaged or destroyed by a casualty which occurred prior to January 1, 1964, and loss resulting therefrom is sustained after December 31, 1963, the $100 limitation applies.

(ii) The $100 limitation applies separately in respect of each casualty and applies to the entire loss sustained from each casualty. Thus, if as a result of a particular casualty occurring in 1964, a taxpayer sustains in 1964 a loss of $40 and in 1965 a loss of $250, no deduction is allowable for the loss sustained in 1964 and the loss sustained in 1965 must be reduced by $60 ($100-$40). The determination of whether damage to, or destruction of, property resulted from a single casualty or from two or more separate casualties will be made upon the basis of the particular facts of each case. However, events which are closely related in origin generally give rise to a single casualty. For example, if a storm damages a taxpayer's residence and his automobile parked in his driveway, any loss sustained results from a single casualty. Similarly, if a hurricane causes high waves, all wind and flood damage to a taxpayer's property caused by the hurricane and the waves results from a single casualty.

(iii) Except as otherwise provided in this subdivision, the $100 limitation applies separately to each individual taxpayer who sustains a loss even though the property

Sec. 165. Losses

damaged or destroyed is owned by two or more individuals. Thus, if a house occupied by two sisters and jointly owned by them is damaged or destroyed, the $100 limitation applies separately to each sister in respect of any loss sustained by her. However, for purposes of applying the $100 limitation, a husband and wife who file a joint return for the first taxable year in which the loss is allowable as a deduction are treated as one 5 individual taxpayer. Accordingly, if property jointly owned by a husband and wife, or property separately owned by the husband or by the wife, is damaged or destroyed by a single casualty in 1964, and a loss is sustained in that year by either or both the husband or wife, only one $100 limitation applies if a joint return is filed for 1964. If, however, the husband and wife file separate returns for 1964, the $100 limitation applies separately in 10 respect of any loss sustained by the husband and in respect of any loss sustained by the wife. Where losses from a single casualty are sustained in two or more separate tax years, the husband and wife shall, for purposes of applying the $100 limitation to such losses, be treated as one individual for all such years if they file a joint return for the first year in which a loss is sustained from the casualty; they shall be treated as separate 15 individuals for all such years if they file separate returns for the first such year. If a joint return is filed in the first loss year but separate returns are filed in a subsequent year, any unused portion of the $100 limitation shall be allocated equally between the husband and wife in the latter year.

(iv) If a loss is sustained in respect of property used partially for business and partially 20 for nonbusiness purposes, the $100 limitation applies only to that portion of the loss properly attributable to the nonbusiness use. For example, if a taxpayer sustains a $1,000 loss in respect of an automobile which he uses 60 percent for business and 40 percent for nonbusiness, the loss is allocated 60 percent to business use and 40 percent to nonbusiness use. The $100 limitation applies to the portion of the loss allocable to the 25 nonbusiness loss.

(c) *Loss sustained by an estate.* A casualty loss of property not connected with a trade or business and not incurred in any transaction entered into for profit which is sustained during the settlement of an estate shall be allowed as a deduction under sections 165(a) and 641(b) in computing the taxable income of the estate if the loss has not been allowed 30 under section 2054 in computing the taxable estate of the decedent and if the statement has been filed in accordance with § 1.642(g)-1. See section 165(c)(3).

(d) *Loss treated as though attributable to a trade or business.* For the rule treating a casualty loss not connected with a trade or business as though it were a deduction attributable to a trade or business for purposes of computing a net operating loss, see 35 paragraph (a)(3)(iii) of § 1.172-3.

***

Reg. § 1.165-9 Sale of residential property.

(a) *Losses not allowed.* A loss sustained on the sale of residential property purchased or constructed by the taxpayer for use as his personal residence and so used by him up 40 to the time of the sale is not deductible under section 165(a).

(b) *Property converted from personal use.* (1) If property purchased or constructed by the taxpayer for use as his personal residence is, prior to its sale, rented or otherwise appropriated to income-producing purposes and is used for such purposes up to the time of its sale, a loss sustained on the sale of the property shall be allowed as a deduction 45 under section 165(a).

(2) The loss allowed under this paragraph upon the sale of the property shall be the excess of the adjusted basis prescribed in § 1.1011-1 for determining loss over the amount realized from the sale. For this purpose, the adjusted basis for determining loss shall be the lesser of either of the following amounts, adjusted as prescribed in § 50

Sec. 165. Losses

1.1011-1 for the period subsequent to the conversion of the property to income-producing purposes:

(i) The fair market value of the property at the time of conversion, or

(ii) The adjusted basis for loss, at the time of conversion, determined under § 1.1011-1 but without reference to the fair market value.

(3) For rules relating to casualty losses of property converted from personal use, see paragraph (a)(5) of § 1.165-7. To determine the basis for depreciation in the case of such property, see § 1.167(g)-1. For limitations on the loss from the sale of a capital asset, see paragraph (c)(3) of § 1.165-1.

(c) *Examples.* The application of paragraph (b) of this section may be illustrated by the following examples:

Example (1). Residential property is purchased by the taxpayer in 1943 for use as his personal residence at a cost of $25,000, of which $15,000 is allocable to the building. The taxpayer uses the property as his personal residence until January 1, 1952, at which time its fair market value is $22,000, of which $12,000 is allocable to the building. The taxpayer rents the property from January 1,1952, until January 1, 1955, at which time it is sold for $16,000. On January 1, 1952, the building has an estimated useful life of 20 years. It is assumed that the building has no estimated salvage value and that there are no adjustments in respect of basis other than depreciation, which is computed on the straight-line method. The loss to be taken into account for purposes of section 165(a) for the taxable year 1955 is $4,200, computed as follows:

Basis of property at time of conversion for purposes of this section (that is, the lesser of $25,000 cost or $22,000 fair market value)...	$22,000
Less: Depreciation allowable from January 1, 1952, to January 1, 1955 (3 years at 5 percent based on $12,000, the value of the building at time of conversion, as prescribed by § 1.167(g)-1)...	1,800
Adjusted basis prescribed in § 1.1011-1 for determining loss on sale of the property...	20,200
Less: Amount realized on sale...	16,000
Loss to be taken into account for purposes of section 165(a)..	4,200

In this example the value of the building at the time of conversion is used as the basis for computing depreciation. See example (2) of this paragraph wherein the adjusted basis of the building is required to be used for such purpose.

Example (2). Residential property is purchased by the taxpayer in 1940 for use as his personal residence at a cost of $23,000, of which $10,000 is allocable to the building. The taxpayer uses the property as his personal residence until January 1, 1953, at which time its fair market value is $20,000, of which $12,000 is allocable to the building. The taxpayer rents the property from January 1, 1953, until January 1, 1957, at which time it is sold for $17,000. On January 1, 1953, the building has an estimated useful life of 20 years. It is assumed that the building has no estimated salvage value and that there are no adjustments in respect of basis other than depreciation, which is computed on the straight-line method. The loss to be taken into account for purposes of section 165(a) for the taxable year 1957 is $1,000, computed as follows:

Basis of property at time of conversion for purposes of this section (that is, the lesser of $23,000 cost or $20,000 fair market value)..	$20,000	
Less: Depreciation allowable from January 1, 1953, to January 1, 1957 (4 years at 5 percent based on $10,000, the cost of the building, as prescribed by §1.167(g)-1......	2,000	5
Adjusted basis prescribed in § 1.1011-1 for determining loss on sale of the property...	$18,000	
Less: Amount realized on sale...	17,000	10
Loss to be taken into account for purposes of section 165(a)...	1,000	

Reg. § 1.162-11   Rentals.   15

(a) *Acquisition of a leasehold.* If a leasehold is acquired for business purposes for a specified sum, the purchaser may take as a deduction in his return an aliquot part of such sum each year, based on the number of years the lease has to run. Taxes paid by a tenant to or for a landlord for business property are additional rent and constitute a deductible item to the tenant and taxable income to the landlord, the amount of the tax 20 being deductible by the latter. For disallowance of deduction for income taxes paid by a lessee corporation pursuant to a lease arrangement with the lessor corporation, see section 110 and the regulations thereunder. See section 178 and the regulations thereunder for rules governing the effect to be given renewal options in amortizing the costs incurred after July 28, 1958 of acquiring a lease. See § 1.197-2 for rules governing 25 the amortization of costs to acquire limited interests in section 197 intangibles.

(b) *Improvements by lessee on lessor's property.* (1) The cost to a lessee of erecting buildings or making permanent improvements on property of which he is the lessee is a capital investment, and is not deductible as a business expense. If the estimated useful life in the hands of the taxpayer of the building erected or of the improvements made, 30 determined without regard to the terms of the lease, is longer than the remaining period of the lease, an annual deduction may be made from gross income of an amount equal to the total cost of such improvements divided by the number of years remaining in the term of the lease, and such deduction shall be in lieu of a deduction for depreciation. If, on the other hand, the useful life of such buildings or improvements in the hands of the taxpayer 35 is equal to or shorter than the remaining period of the lease, this deduction shall be computed under the provisions of section 167 (relating to depreciation).

(2) If the lessee began improvements on leased property before July 28, 1958, or if the lessee was on such date and at all times thereafter under a binding legal obligation to make such improvements, the matter of spreading the cost of erecting buildings or 40 making permanent improvements over the term of the original lease, together with the renewal period or periods depends upon the facts in the particular case, including the presence or absence of an obligation of renewal and the relationship between the parties. As a general rule, unless the lease has been renewed or the facts show with reasonable certainty that the lease will be renewed, the cost or other basis of the lease, or the cost of 45 improvements shall be spread only over the number of years the lease has to run without taking into account any right of renewal. The provisions of this subparagraph may be illustrated by the following examples:

Example (1). A subsidiary corporation leases land from its parent at a fair rental for a 25-year period. The subsidiary erects on the land valuable factory buildings having an 50 estimated useful life of 50 years. These facts show with reasonable certainty that the lease will be renewed, even though the lease contains no option of renewal. Therefore, the cost of the buildings shall be depreciated over the estimated useful life of the buildings in accordance with section 167 and the regulations thereunder.

Example (2). A retail merchandising corporation leases land at a fair rental from an unrelated lessor for the longest period that the lessor is willing to lease the land (30 years). The lessee erects on the land a department store having an estimated useful life of 40 years. These facts do not show with reasonable certainty that the lease will be renewed. Therefore, the cost of the building shall be spread over the remaining term of the lease. An annual deduction may be made of an amount equal to the cost of the building divided by the number of years remaining in the term of the lease, and such deduction shall be in lieu of a deduction for depreciation.

(3) See section 178 and the regulations thereunder for rules governing the effect to be given renewal options where a lessee begins improvements on leased property after July 28, 1958, other than improvements which on such date and at all times thereafter, the lessee was under a binding legal obligation to make.

Reg. § 1.165-10   Wagering losses.

Losses sustained during the taxable year on wagering transactions shall be allowed as a deduction but only to the extent of the gains during the taxable year from such transactions. In the case of a husband and wife making a joint return for the taxable year, the combined losses of the spouses from wagering transactions shall be allowed to the extent of the combined gains of the spouses from wagering transactions.

[T.D. 6500, 25 FR 11402, Nov. 26, 1960; 25 FR 14021, Dec. 31, 1960; T.D. 6520, 25 FR 13692, Dec. 24, 1960; T.D. 6712, 29 FR 3652, Mar. 24, 1964; T.D. 6735, 29 FR 6493, May 19, 1964; T.D. 6786, 29 FR 18501, Dec. 29, 1964; T.D. 6996, 34 FR 835, Jan. 18, 1969; T.D. 7224, 37 FR 25928, Dec. 6, 1972; T.D. 7301, 39 FR 963, Jan. 4, 1974; T.D. 7474, 41 FR 55710, Dec. 22, 1976; T.D. 7522, 42 FR 63411, Dec. 16, 1977; T.D. 8867, 65 FR 3825, Jan. 25, 2000]

Sec. 166.   Bad debts

(a) General rule. --

(1) Wholly worthless debts. -- There shall be allowed as a deduction any debt which becomes worthless within the taxable year.

(2) Partially worthless debts. -- When satisfied that a debt is recoverable only in part, the Secretary may allow such debt, in an amount not in excess of the part charged off within the taxable year, as a deduction.

(b) Amount of deduction. -- For purposes of subsection (a), the basis for determining the amount of the deduction for any bad debt shall be the adjusted basis provided in section 1011 for determining the loss from the sale or other disposition of property.

***

(d) Nonbusiness debts. --

(1) General rule. -- In the case of a taxpayer other than a corporation--

(A) subsection (a) shall not apply to any nonbusiness debt; and

(B) where any nonbusiness debt becomes worthless within the taxable year, the loss resulting therefrom shall be considered a loss from the sale or exchange, during the taxable year, of a capital asset held for not more than 1 year.

(2) Nonbusiness debt defined. -- For purposes of paragraph (1), the term "nonbusiness

Sec. 166. Bad debts

debt" means a debt other than--

> **(A)** a debt created or acquired (as the case may be) in connection with a trade or business of the taxpayer; or

> **(B)** a debt the loss from the worthlessness of which is incurred in the taxpayer's trade or business.

    (e) Worthless securities. -- This section shall not apply to a debt which is evidenced by a security as defined in section 165(g)(2)(C).

Reg. § 1.166-1 Bad debts.

    (a) *Allowance of deduction.* Section 166 provides that, in computing taxable income under section 63, a deduction shall be allowed in respect of bad debts owed to the taxpayer. For this purpose, bad debts shall, subject to the provisions of section 166 and the regulations thereunder, be taken into account either as--

    (1) A deduction in respect of debts which become worthless in whole or in part; or as

    (2) A deduction for a reasonable addition to a reserve for bad debts.

    (b) *Manner of selecting method.* (1) A taxpayer filing a return of income for the first taxable year for which he is entitled to a bad debt deduction may select either of the two methods prescribed by paragraph (a) of this section for treating bad debts, but such selection is subject to the approval of the district director upon examination of the return. If the method so selected is approved, it shall be used in returns for all subsequent taxable years unless the Commissioner grants permission to use the other method. A statement of facts substantiating any deduction claimed under section 166 on account of bad debts shall accompany each return of income.

    (2) Taxpayers who have properly selected one of the two methods for treating bad debts under provisions of prior law corresponding to section 166 shall continue to use that method for all subsequent taxable years unless the Commissioner grants permission to use the other method.

    (3)(i) For taxable years beginning after December 31, 1959, application for permission to change the method of treating bad debts shall be made in accordance with section 446(e) and paragraph (e)(3) of § 1.446-1.

    (ii) For taxable years beginning before January 1, 1960, application for permission to change the method of treating bad debts shall be made at least 30 days before the close of the taxable year for which the change is effective.

    (4) Notwithstanding paragraphs (b)(1), (2), and (3) of this section, a dealer in property currently employing the accrual method of accounting and currently maintaining a reserve for bad debts under section 166(c) (which may have included guaranteed debt obligations described in section 166(f)(1)(A)) may establish a reserve for section 166(f)(1)(A) guaranteed debt obligations for a taxable year ending after October 21, 1965 under section 166(f) and § 1.166-10 by filing on or before April 17, 1986 an amended return indicating that such a reserve has been established. The establishment of such a reserve will not be considered a change in method of accounting for purposes of section 446(e). However, an election by a taxpayer to establish a reserve for bad debts under section 166(c) shall be treated as a change in method of accounting. See also § 1.166-4, relating to reserve for bad debts, and § 1.166-10, relating to reserve for guaranteed debt obligations.

    (c) *Bona fide debt required.* Only a bona fide debt qualifies for purposes of section 166. A bona fide debt is a debt which arises from a debtor-creditor relationship based upon a valid and enforceable obligation to pay a fixed or determinable sum of money. A debt arising out of the receivables of an accrual method taxpayer is deemed to be an enforceable obligation for purposes of the preceding sentence to the extent that the

Sec. 166. Bad debts

income such debt represents have been included in the return of income for the year for which the deduction as a bad debt is claimed or for a prior taxable year. For example, a debt arising out of gambling receivables that are unenforceable under state or local law, which an accrual method taxpayer includes in income under section 61, is an enforceable
5 obligation for purposes of this paragraph. A gift or contribution to capital shall not be considered a debt for purposes of section 166. The fact that a bad debt its not due at the time of deduction shall not of itself prevent is allowance under section 166. For the disallowance of deductions for bad debts owed by a political party, see § 1.271-1.

(d) *Amount deductible*--(1) *General rule.* Except in the case of a deduction for a
10 reasonable addition to a reserve for bad debts, the basis for determining the amount of deduction under section 166 in respect of a bad debt shall be the same as the adjusted basis prescribed by § 1.1011-1 for determining the loss from the sale or other disposition of property. To determine the allowable deduction in the case of obligations acquired before March 1, 1913, see also paragraph (b) of § 1.1053-1.

15   (2) *Specific cases.* Subject to any provision of section 166 and the regulations thereunder which provides to the contrary, the following amounts are deductible as bad debts:

(i) *Notes or accounts receivable.* (a) If, in computing taxable income, a taxpayer values his notes or accounts receivable at their fair market value when received, the
20 amount deductible as a bad debt under section 166 in respect of such receivables shall be limited to such fair market value even though it is less than their face value.

(b) A purchaser of accounts receivable which become worthless during the taxable year shall be entitled under section 166 to a deduction which is based upon the price he paid for such receivables but not upon their face value.

25   (ii) *Bankruptcy claim.* Only the difference between the amount received in distribution of the assets of a bankrupt and the amount of the claim may be deducted under section 166 as a bad debt.

(iii) *Claim against decedent's estate.* The excess of the amount of the claim over the amount received by a creditor of a decedent in distribution of the assets of the decedent's
30 estate may be considered a worthless debt under section 166.

(e) *Prior inclusion in income required.* Worthless debts arising from unpaid wages, salaries, fees, rents, and similar items of taxable income shall not be allowed as a deduction under section 166 unless the income such items represent has been included in the return of income for the year for which the deduction as a bad debt is claimed or for
35 a prior taxable year.

(f) *Recovery of bad debts.* Any amount attributable to the recovery during the taxable year of a bad debt, or of a part of a bad debt, which was allowed as a deduction from gross income in a prior taxable year shall be included in gross income for the taxable year of recovery, except to the extent that the recovery is excluded from gross income
40 under the provisions of § 1.111-1, relating to the recovery of certain items previously deducted or credited. This paragraph shall not apply, however, to a bad debt which was previously charged against a reserve by a taxpayer on the reserve method of treating bad debts.

(g) *Worthless securities.* (1) Section 166 and the regulations thereunder do not apply
45 to a debt which is evidenced by a bond, debenture, note, or certificate, or other evidence of indebtedness, issued by a corporation or by a government or political subdivision thereof, with interest coupons or in registered form. See section 166(e). For provisions allowing the deduction of a loss resulting from the worthlessness of such a debt, § 1.165-5.

50   (2) The provisions of subparagraph (1) of this paragraph do not apply to any loss sustained by a bank and resulting from the worthlessness of a security described in

Sec. 166. Bad debts

section 165(g)(2)(C). See paragraph (a) of § 1.582-1.

Reg. § 1.166-2 Evidence of worthlessness.

(a) *General rule.* In determining whether a debt is worthless in whole or in part the district director will consider all pertinent evidence, including the value of the collateral, if 5 any, securing the debt and the financial condition of the debtor.

(b) *Legal action not required.* Where the surrounding circumstances indicate that a debt is worthless and uncollectible and that legal action to enforce payment would in all probability not result in the satisfaction of execution on a judgment, a showing of these facts will be sufficient evidence of the worthlessness of the debt for purposes of the 10 deduction under section 166.

(c) *Bankruptcy*--(1) *General rule.* Bankruptcy is generally an indication of the worthlessness of at least a part of an unsecured and unpreferred debt.

(2) *Year of deduction.* In bankruptcy cases a debt may become worthless before settlement in some instances; and in others, only when a settlement in bankruptcy has 15 been reached. In either case, the mere fact that bankruptcy proceedings instituted against the debtor are terminated in a later year, thereby confirming the conclusion that the debt is worthless, shall not authorize the shifting of the deduction under section 166 to such later year.

(d) *Banks and other regulated corporations*--(1) *Worthlessness presumed in year of* 20 *charge-off.* If a bank or other corporation which is subject to supervision by Federal authorities, or by State authorities maintaining substantially equivalent standards, charges off a debt in whole or in part, either--

(i) In obedience to the specific orders of such authorities, or

(ii) In accordance with established policies of such authorities, and, upon their first 25 audit of the bank or other corporation subsequent to the charge-off, such authorities confirm in writing that the charge-off would have been subject to such specific orders if the audit had been made on the date of the charge-off, then the debt shall, to the extent charged off during the taxable year, be conclusively presumed to have become worthless, or worthless only in part, as the case may be, during such taxable year. But no 30 such debt shall be so conclusively presumed to be worthless, or worthless only in part, as the case may be, if the amount so charged off is not claimed as a deduction by the taxpayer at the time of filing the return for the taxable year in which the charge-off takes place.

(2) *Evidence of worthlessness in later taxable year.* If such a bank or other corporation 35 does not claim a deduction for such a totally or partially worthless debt in its return for the taxable year in which the charge-off takes place, but claims the deduction for a later taxable year, then the charge-off in the prior taxable year shall be deemed to have been involuntary and the deduction under section 166 shall be allowed for the taxable year for which claimed, provided that the taxpayer produces sufficient evidence to show that-- 40

(i) The debt became wholly worthless in the later taxable year, or became recoverable only in part subsequent to the taxable year of the involuntary charge-off, as the case may be; and,

(ii) To the extent that the deduction claimed in the later taxable year for a debt partially worthless was not involuntarily charged off in prior taxable years, it was charged off in the 45 later taxable year.

(3) *Conformity election*--(i) *Eligibility for election.* In lieu of applying paragraphs (d)(1) and (2) of this section, a bank (as defined in paragraph (d)(4)(i) of this section) that is subject to supervision by Federal authorities, or by state authorities maintaining substantially equivalent standards, may elect under this paragraph (d)(3) to use a method 50 of accounting that establishes a conclusive presumption of worthlessness for debts,

Sec. 166. Bad debts

provided that the bank meets the express determination requirement of paragraph (d)(3)
(iii)(D) of this section for the taxable year of the election.

(ii) *Conclusive presumption--(A)* *In general.* If a bank satisfies the express
determination requirement of paragraph (d)(3)(iii)(D) of this section and elects to use the
5 method of accounting under this paragraph (d)(3)--

(1) Debts charged off, in whole or in part, for regulatory purposes during a taxable
year are conclusively presumed to have become worthless, or worthless only in part, as
the case may be, during that year, but only if the charge-off results from a specific order
of the bank's supervisory authority or corresponds to the bank's classification of the debt,
10 in whole or in part, as a loss asset, as described in paragraph (d)(3)(ii)(C) of this section;
and

(2) A bad debt deduction for a debt that is subject to regulatory loss classification
standards is allowed for a taxable year only to the extent that the debt is conclusively
presumed to have become worthless under paragraph (d)(3)(ii)(A)(1) of this section
15 during that year.

(B) *Charge-off should have been made in earlier year.* The conclusive presumption
that a debt is worthless in the year that it is charged off for regulatory purposes applies
even if the bank's supervisory authority determines in a subsequent year that the charge-
off should have been made in an earlier year. A pattern of charge-offs in the wrong year,
20 however, may result in revocation of the bank's election by the Commissioner pursuant to
paragraph (d)(3)(iv)(D) of this section.

(C) *Loss asset defined.* A debt is classified as a loss asset by a bank if the bank
assigns the debt to a class that corresponds to a loss asset classification under the
standards set forth in the ``Uniform Agreement on the Classification of Assets and
25 Securities Held by Banks" (See Attachment to Comptroller of the Currency Banking
Circular No. 127, Rev. 4-26-91, Comptroller of the Currency, Communications
Department, Washington, DC 20219) or similar guidance issued by the Office of the
Comptroller of the Currency, the Federal Deposit Insurance Corporation, the Board of
Governors of the Federal Reserve, or the Farm Credit Administration; or for institutions
30 under the supervision of the Office of Thrift Supervision, 12 CFR 563.160(b)(3).

***

(4) *Definitions.* For purposes of this paragraph (d)--

(i) *Bank.* The term bank has the meaning assigned to it by section 581. The term bank
also includes any corporation that would be a bank within the meaning of section 581
35 except for the fact that it is a foreign corporation, but this paragraph (d) applies only with
respect to loans the interest on which is effectively connected with the conduct of a
banking business within the United States. In addition, the term bank includes a Farm
Credit System institution that is subject to supervision by the Farm Credit Administration.

(ii) *Charge-off.* For banks regulated by the Office of Thrift Supervision, the term
40 charge-off includes the establishment of specific allowances for loan losses in the amount
of 100 percent of the portion of the debt classified as loss.

Reg. § 1.166-5 Nonbusiness debts.

(a) *Allowance of deduction as capital loss.* (1) The loss resulting from any
45 nonbusiness debt's becoming partially or wholly worthless within the taxable year shall
not be allowed as a deduction under either section 166(a) or section 166(c) in
determining the taxable income of a taxpayer other than a corporation. See section
166(d)(1)(A).

(2) If, in the case of a taxpayer other than a corporation, a nonbusiness debt becomes
50 wholly worthless within the taxable year, the loss resulting therefrom shall be treated as a
loss from the sale or exchange, during the taxable year, of a capital asset held for not

Sec. 166. Bad debts

more than 1 year (6 months for taxable years beginning before 1977; 9 months for taxable years beginning in 1977). Such a loss is subject to the limitations provided in section 1211, relating to the limitation on capital losses, and section 1212, relating to the capital loss carryover, and in the regulations under those sections. A loss on a nonbusiness debt shall be treated as sustained only if and when the debt has become 5 totally worthless, and no deduction shall be allowed for a nonbusiness debt which is recoverable in part during the taxable year.

(b) *Nonbusiness debt defined.* For purposes of section 166 and this section, a nonbusiness debt is any debt other than--

(1) A debt which is created, or acquired, in the course of a trade or business of the 10 taxpayer, determined without regard to the relationship of the debt to a trade or business of the taxpayer at the time when the debt becomes worthless; or

(2) A debt the loss from the worthlessness of which is incurred in the taxpayer's trade or business.

The question whether a debt is a nonbusiness debt is a question of fact in each particular 15 case. The determination of whether the loss on a debt's becoming worthless has been incurred in a trade or business of the taxpayer shall, for this purpose, be made in substantially the same manner for determining whether a loss has been incurred in a trade or business for purposes of section 165(c)(1). For purposes of subparagraph (2) of this paragraph, the character of the debt is to be determined by the relation which the 20 loss resulting from the debt's becoming worthless bears to the trade or business of the taxpayer. If that relation is a proximate one in the conduct of the trade or business in which the taxpayer is engaged at the time the debt becomes worthless, the debt comes within the exception provided by that subparagraph. The use to which the borrowed funds are put by the debtor is of no consequence in making a determination under this 25 paragraph. For purposes of section 166 and this section, a nonbusiness debt does not include a debt described in section 165(g)(2)(C). See § 1.165-5, relating to losses on worthless securities.

(c) *Guaranty of obligations.* For provisions treating a loss sustained by a guarantor of obligations as a loss resulting from the worthlessness of a debt, see §§ 1.166-8 and 30 1.166-9.

(d) *Examples.* The application of this section may be illustrated by the following examples involving a case where A, an individual who is engaged in the grocery business and who makes his return on the basis of the calendar year, extends credit to B in 1955 on an open account: 35

Example (1). In 1956 A sells the business but retains the claim against B. The claim becomes worthless in A's hands in 1957. A's loss is not controlled by the nonbusiness debt provisions, since the original consideration has been advanced by A in his trade or business.

Example (2). In 1956 A sells the business to C but sells the claim against B to the 40 taxpayer, D. The claim becomes worthless in D's hands in 1957. During 1956 and 1957, D is not engaged in any trade or business. D's loss is controlled by the nonbusiness debt provisions even though the original consideration has been advanced by A in his trade or business, since the debt has not been created or acquired in connection with a trade or business of D and since in 1957 D is not engaged in a trade or business incident to the 45 conduct of which a loss from the worthlessness of such claim is a proximate result.

Example (3). In 1956 A dies, leaving the business, including the accounts receivable, to his son, C, the taxpayer. The claim against B becomes worthless in C's hands in 1957. C's loss is not controlled by the nonbusiness debt provisions. While C does not advance any consideration for the claim, or create or acquire it in connection with his trade or 50 business, the loss is sustained as a proximate incident to the conduct of the trade or business in which he is engaged at the time the debt becomes worthless.

Example (4). In 1956 A dies, leaving the business to his son, C, but leaving the claim against B to his son, D, the taxpayer. The claim against B becomes worthless in D's hands in 1957. During 1956 and 1957, D is not engaged in any trade or business. D's
5 loss is controlled by the nonbusiness debt provisions even though the original consideration has been advanced by A in his trade or business, since the debt has not been created or acquired in connection with a trade or business of D and since in 1957 D is not engaged in a trade or business incident to the conduct of which a loss from the worthlessness of such claim is a proximate result.
10   *Example (5)*. In 1956 A dies; and, while his executor, C, is carrying on the business, the claim against B becomes worthless in 1957. The loss sustained by A's estate is not controlled by the nonbusiness debt provisions. While C does not advance any consideration for the claim on behalf of the estate, or create or acquire it in connection with a trade or business in which the estate is engaged, the loss is sustained as a
15 proximate incident to the conduct of the trade or business in which the estate is engaged at the time the debt becomes worthless.

Example (6). In 1956, A, in liquidating the business, attempts to collect the claim against B but finds that it has become worthless. A's loss is not controlled by the nonbusiness debt provisions, since the original consideration has been advanced by A in
20 his trade or business and since a loss incurred in liquidating a trade or business is a proximate incident to the conduct thereof.

Reg. § 1.166-9   Losses of guarantors, endorsers, and indemnitors incurred, on agreements made after December 31, 1975, in taxable years beginning after such
25 **date.**

(a) *Payment treated as worthless business debt*. This paragraph applies to taxpayers who, after December 31, 1975, enter into an agreement in the course of their trade or business to act as (or in a manner essentially equivalent to) a guarantor, endorser, or indemnitor of (or other secondary obligor upon) a debt obligation. Subject to the
30 provisions of paragraphs (c), (d), and (e) of this section, a payment of principal or interest made during a taxable year beginning after December 31, 1975, by the taxpayer in discharge of part or all of the taxpayer's obligation as a guarantor, endorser, or idemnitor is treated as a business debt becoming worthless in the taxable year in which the payment is made or in the taxable year described in paragraph (e)(2) of this section.
35 Neither section 163 (relating to interest) nor section 165 (relating to losses) shall apply with respect to such a payment.

(b) *Payment treated as worthless nonbusiness debt*. This paragraph applies to taxpayers (other than corporations) who, after December 31, 1975, enter into a transaction for profit, but not in the course of their trade or business, to act as (or in a
40 manner essentially equivalent to) a guarantor, endorser, or indemnitor of (or other secondary obligor upon) a debt obligation. Subject to the provisions of paragraphs (c), (d), and (e) of this section, a payment ofprincipal or interest made during a taxable year beginning after December 31, 1975, by the taxpayer in discharge of part or all of the taxpayer's obligation as a guarantor, endorser, or indemnitor is treated as a worthless
45 nonbusiness debt in the taxable year in which the payment is made or in the taxable year described in paragraph (e)(2) of this section. Neither section 163 nor section 165 shall apply with respect to such a payment.

(c) *Obligations issued by corporations*. No treatment as a worthless debt is allowed with respect to a payment made by the taxpayer in discharge of part or all of the
50 taxpayer's obligation as a guarantor, endorser, or indemnitor of an obligation issued by a corporation if, on the basis of the facts and circumstances at the time the obligation was

Sec. 166. Bad debts

entered into, the payment constitutes a contribution to capital by a shareholder. The rule of this paragraph (c) applies to payments whenever made (see paragraph (f) of this section).

(d) *Certain payments treated as worthless debts.* A payment in discharge of part or all of taxpayer's agreement to act as guarantor, endorser, or indemnitor of an obligation is to be treated as a worthless debt only if--

(1) The agreement was entered into in the course of the taxpayer's trade or business or a transaction for profit;

(2) There was an enforceable legal duty upon the taxpayer to make the payment (except that legal action need not have been brought against the taxpayer); and

(3) The agreement was entered into before the obligation became worthless (or partially worthless in the case of an agreement entered into in the course of the taxpayer's trade or business). See §§ 1.166-2 and 1.166-3 for rules on worthless and partially worthless debts. For purposes of this paragraph (d)(3), an agreement is considered as entered into before the obligation became worthless (or partially worthless) if there was a reasonable expectation on the part of the taxpayer at the time the agreement was entered into that the taxpayer would not be called upon to pay the debt (subject to such agreement) without full reimbursement from the issuer of the obligation.

(e) *Special rules*--(1) *Reasonable consideration required.* Treatment as a worthless debt of a payment made by a taxpayer in discharge of part or all of the taxpayer's agreement to act as a guarantor, endorser, or indemnitor of an obligation is allowed only if the taxpayer demonstrates that reasonable consideration was received for entering into the agreement. For purposes of this paragraph (e)(1), reasonable consideration is not limited to direct consideration in the form of cash or property. Thus, where a taxpayer can demonstrate that the agreement was given without direct consideration in the form of cash or property but in accordance with normal business practice or for a good faith business purpose, worthless debt treatment is allowed with respect to a payment in discharge of part or all of the agreement if the conditions of this section are met. However, consideration received from a taxpayer's spouse or any individual listed in section 152(a) must be direct consideration in the form of cash or property.

(2) *Right of subrogation.* With respect to a payment made by a taxpayer in discharge of part or all of the taxpayer's agreement to act as a guarantor, endorser, or indemnitor where the agreement provides for a right of subrogation or other similar right against the issuer, treatment as a worthless debt is not allowed until the taxable year in which the right of subrogation or other similar right becomes totally worthless (or partially worthless in the case of an agreement which arose in the course of the taxpayer's trade or business).

(3) *Other applicable provisions.* Unless inconsistent with this section, other Internal Revenue laws concerning worthless debts, such as section 111 relating to the recovery of bad debts, apply to any payment which, under the provisions of this section, is treated as giving rise to a worthless debt.

(4) *Taxpayer defined.* For purposes of this section, except as otherwise provided, the term ``taxpayer'' means any taxpayer and includes individuals, corporations, partnerships, trusts and estates.

***

[T.D. 6500, 25 FR 11402, Nov. 26, 1960; 25 FR 14021, Dec. 31, 1960; T.D. 6996, 34 FR 835, Jan. 18, 1969; T.D. 7254, 38 FR 2418, Jan. 26, 1973; T.D. 7657, 44 FR 68464, Nov. 29, 1979; T.D. 7728, 45 FR 72650, Nov. 3, 1980; T.D. 7902, 48 FR 33260, July 21, 1983; T.D. 7920, 48 FR 50712, Nov. 3, 1983; T.D. 8071, 51 FR 2479, Jan. 17, 1986; T.D. 8396, 57 FR 6294, Feb. 24, 1992; T.D. 8441, 57 FR 45569, Oct. 2, 1992; T.D. 8492, 58 FR 53658, Oct. 18, 1993]

Sec. 167. Depreciation

(a) **General rule.** --There shall be allowed as a depreciation deduction a reasonable allowance for the exhaustion, wear and tear (including a reasonable allowance for obsolescence) -

    (1) of property used in the trade or business, or

    (2) of property held for the production of income.

5   **(b) Cross reference.** -- For determination of depreciation deduction in case of property to which section 168 applies, see section 168.

    (c) Basis for depreciation. --

    (1) In general. -- The basis on which exhaustion, wear and tear, and obsolescence are to be allowed in respect of any property shall be the adjusted basis provided in section 1011, for the 10   purpose of determining the gain on the sale or other disposition of such property.

    (2) Special rule for property subject to lease. -- If any property is acquired subject to a lease--

    (A) no portion of the adjusted basis shall be allocated to the leasehold interest, and

    (B) the entire adjusted basis shall be taken into account in determining the depreciation 15   deduction (if any) with respect to the property subject to the lease.

    (d) Life tenants and beneficiaries of trusts and estates. -- In the case of property held by one person for life with remainder to another person, the deduction shall be computed as if the life tenant were the absolute owner of the property and shall be allowed to the life tenant. In the case of property held in trust, the allowable deduction shall be apportioned between the income 20 beneficiaries and the trustee in accordance with the pertinent provisions of the instrument creating the trust, or, in the absence of such provisions, on the basis of the trust income allocable to each. In the case of an estate, the allowable deduction shall be apportioned between the estate and the heirs, legatees, and devisees on the basis of the income of the estate allocable to each.

    (f) Treatment of certain property excluded from section 197. --

25   **(1) Computer software.** --

    (A) In general. -- If a depreciation deduction is allowable under subsection (a) with respect to any computer software, such deduction shall be computed by using the straight line method and a useful life of 36 months.

    (B) Computer software. -- For purposes of this section, the term "computer software" 30   has the meaning given to such term by section 197(e)(3)(B); except that such term shall not include any such software which is an amortizable section 197 intangible.

***

    (g) Depreciation under income forecast method. --

***

35   **(6) Limitation on property for which income forecast method may be used.** -- The depreciation deduction allowable under this section may be determined under the income forecast method or any similar method only with respect to--

    (A) property described in paragraph (3) or (4) of section 168(f),

    (B) copyrights,

40   **(C)** books,

    (D) patents, and

    (E) other property specified in regulations.

Such methods may not be used with respect to any amortizable section 197 intangible (as defined in section 197(c)).

Sec. 167. Depreciation

***

(8) Special rules for certain musical works and copyrights. --

(A) In general. -- If an election is in effect under this paragraph for any taxable year, then, notwithstanding paragraph (1), any expense which--

(i) is paid or incurred by the taxpayer in creating or acquiring any applicable musical property placed in service during the taxable year, and

(ii) is otherwise properly chargeable to capital account, shall be amortized ratably over the 5-year period beginning with the month in which the property was placed in service. The preceding sentence shall not apply to any expense which, without regard to this paragraph, would not be allowable as a deduction.

(B) Exclusive method. -- Except as provided in this paragraph, no depreciation or amortization deduction shall be allowed with respect to any expense to which subparagraph (A) applies.

(C) Applicable musical property. -- For purposes of this paragraph--

(i) In general. -- The term `applicable musical property' means any musical composition (including any accompanying words), or any copyright with respect to a musical composition, which is property to which this subsection applies without regard to this paragraph.

(ii) Exceptions. -- Such term shall not include any property--

(I) with respect to which expenses are treated as qualified creative expenses to which section 263A(h) applies,

(II) to which a simplified procedure established under section 263A(i)(2) applies, or

(III) which is an amortizable section 197 intangible (as defined in section 197(c)).

(D) Election. -- An election under this paragraph shall be made at such time and in such form as the Secretary may prescribe and shall apply to all applicable musical property placed in service during the taxable year for which the election applies.

(E) Termination. -- An election may not be made under this paragraph for any taxable year beginning after December 31, 201

(h) Amortization of Geological and Geophysical Expenditures. --

(1) In general. -- Any geological and geophysical expenses paid or incurred in connection with the exploration for, or development of, oil or gas within the United States (as defined in section 638) shall be allowed as a deduction ratably over the 24-month period beginning on the date that such expense was paid or incurred.

(2) Half-year convention. -- For purposes of paragraph (1), any payment paid or incurred during the taxable year shall be treated as paid or incurred on the mid-point of such taxable year.

(3) Exclusive method. -- Except as provided in this subsection, no depreciation or amortization deduction shall be allowed with respect to such payments.

(4) Treatment upon abandonment. -- If any property with respect to which geological and geophysical expenses are paid or incurred is retired or abandoned during the 24-month period described in paragraph (1), no deduction shall be allowed on account of such retirement or abandonment and the amortization deduction under this subsection shall continue with respect to such payment.

(5) Special rule for major integrated oil companies. --

Sec. 167. Depreciation

(A) **In general.** -- In the case of a major integrated oil company, paragraphs (1) and (4) shall be applied by substituting `5-year' for `24 month'.

(B) **Major integrated oil company.** -- For purposes of this paragraph, the term `major integrated oil company' means, with respect to any taxable year, a producer of crude oil--

(i) which has an average daily worldwide production of crude oil of at least 500,000 barrels for the taxable year,

(ii) which had gross receipts in excess of $1,000,000,000 for its last taxable year ending during calendar year 2005, and

(iii) to which subsection (c) of section 613A does not apply by reason of paragraph (4) of section 613A(d), determined--

(I) by substituting `15 percent' for `5 percent' each place it occurs in paragraph (3) of section 613A(d), and

(II) without regard to whether subsection (c) of section 613A does not apply by reason of paragraph (2) of section 613A(d).

For purposes of clauses (i) and (ii), all persons treated as a single employer under subsections (a) and (b) of section 52 shall be treated as 1 person and, in case of a short taxable year, the rule under section 448(c)(3)(B) shall apply.

Reg. § 1.167(a)-1 Depreciation in general.

(a) *Reasonable allowance*. Section 167(a) provides that a reasonable allowance for the exhaustion, wear and tear, and obsolescence of property used in the trade or business or of property held by the taxpayer for the production of income shall be allowed as a depreciation deduction. The allowance is that amount which should be set aside for the taxable year in accordance with a reasonably consistent plan (not necessarily at a uniform rate), so that the aggregate of the amounts set aside, plus the salvage value, will, at the end of the estimated useful life of the depreciable property, equal the cost or other basis of the property as provided in section 167(g) and § 1.167(g)-1. An asset shall not be depreciated below a reasonable salvage value under any method of computing depreciation. However, see section 167(f) and § 1.167(f)-1 for rules which permit a reduction in the amount of salvage value to be taken into account for certain personal property acquired after October 16, 1962. See also paragraph (c) of this section for definition of salvage. The allowance shall not reflect amounts representing a mere reduction in market value. See section 179 and § 1.179-1 for a further description of the term ``reasonable allowance."

(b) *Useful life*. For the purpose of section 167 the estimated useful life of an asset is not necessarily the useful life inherent in the asset but is the period over which the asset may reasonably be expected to be useful to the taxpayer in his trade or business or in the production of his income. This period shall be determined by reference to his experience with similar property taking into account present conditions and probable future developments. Some of the factors to be considered in determining this period are (1) wear and tear and decay or decline from natural causes, (2) the normal progress of the art, economic changes, inventions, and current developments within the industry and the taxpayer's trade or business, (3) the climatic and other local conditions peculiar to the taxpayer's trade or business, and (4) the taxpayer's policy as to repairs, renewals, and replacements. Salvage value is not a factor for the purpose of determining useful life. If the taxpayer's experience is inadequate, the general experience in the industry may be used until such time as the taxpayer's own experience forms an adequate basis for making the determination. The estimated remaining useful life may be subject to modification by reason of conditions known to exist at the end of the taxable year and

Sec. 167. Depreciation

shall be redetermined when necessary regardless of the method of computing depreciation. However, estimated remaining useful life shall be redetermined only when the change in the useful life is significant and there is a clear and convincing basis for the redetermination. For rules covering agreements with respect to useful life, see section 167(d) and § 1.167(d)-1. If a taxpayer claims an investment credit with respect to an 5 asset for a taxable year preceding the taxable year in which the asset is considered as placed in service under § 1.167(a)-10(b) or § 1.167(a)-11(e), the useful life of the asset under this paragraph shall be the same useful life assigned to the asset under § 1.46-3(e).

(c) *Salvage.* (1) Salvage value is the amount (determined at the time of acquisition) 10 which is estimated will be realizable upon sale or other disposition of an asset when it is no longer useful in the taxpayer's trade or business or in the production of his income and is to be retired from service by the taxpayer. Salvage value shall not be changed at any time after the determination made at the time of acquisition merely because of changes in price levels. However, if there is a redetermination of useful life under the rules of 15 paragraph (b) of this section, salvage value may be redetermined based upon facts known at the time of such redetermination of useful life. Salvage, when reduced by the cost of removal, is referred to as net salvage. The time at which an asset is retired from service may vary according to the policy of the taxpayer. If the taxpayer's policy is to dispose of assets which are still in good operating condition, the salvage value may 20 represent a relatively large proportion of the original basis of the asset. However, if the taxpayer customarily uses an asset until its inherent useful life has been substantially exhausted, salvage value may represent no more than junk value. Salvage value must be taken into account in determining the depreciation deduction either by a reduction of the amount subject to depreciation or by a reduction in the rate of depreciation, but in no 25 event shall an asset (or an account) be depreciated below a reasonable salvage value. See, however, paragraph (a) of § 1.167(b)-2 for the treatment of salvage under the declining balance method, and § 1.179-1 for the treatment of salvage in computing the additional first-year depreciation allowance. The taxpayer may use either salvage or net salvage in determining depreciation allowances but such practice must be consistently 30 followed and the treatment of the costs of removal must be consistent with the practice adopted. For specific treatment of salvage value, see §§ 1.167(b)-1, 1.167(b)-2, and 1.167(b)-3. When an asset is retired or disposed of, appropriate adjustments shall be made in the asset and depreciation reserve accounts. For example, the amount of the salvage adjusted for the costs of removal may be credited to the depreciation reserve.   35

***

Reg. § 1.167(a)-2 Tangible property.

The depreciation allowance in the case of tangible property applies only to that part of the property which is subject to wear and tear, to decay or decline from natural causes, to exhaustion, and to obsolescence. The allowance does not apply to inventories or stock in 40 trade, or to land apart from the improvements or physical development added to it. The allowance does not apply to natural resources which are subject to the allowance for depletion provided in section 611. No deduction for depreciation shall be allowed on automobiles or other vehicles used solely for pleasure, on a building used by the taxpayer solely as his residence, or on furniture or furnishings therein, personal effects, or 45 clothing; but properties and costumes used exclusively in a business, such as a theatrical business, may be depreciated.

Reg. § 1.167(a)-3 Intangibles.

(a) *In general.* If an intangible asset is known from experience or other factors to be of 50 use in the business or in the production of income for only a limited period, the length of

Sec. 167. Depreciation

which can be estimated with reasonable accuracy, such an intangible asset may be the subject of a depreciation allowance. Examples are patents and copyrights. An intangible asset, the useful life of which is not limited, is not subject to the allowance for depreciation. No allowance will be permitted merely because, in the unsupported opinion
5 of the taxpayer, the intangible asset has a limited useful life. No deduction for depreciation is allowable with respect to goodwill. For rules with respect to organizational expenditures, see section 248 and the regulations thereunder. For rules with respect to trademark and trade name expenditures, see section 177 and the regulations thereunder. See sections 197 and 167(f) and, to the extent applicable, §§ 1.197-2 and 1.167(a)-14 for
10 amortization of goodwill and certain other intangibles acquired after August 10, 1993, or after July 25, 1991, if a valid retroactive election under § 1.197-1T has been made.

(b) *Safe harbor amortization for certain intangible assets*--(1) *Useful life.* Solely for purposes of determining the depreciation allowance referred to in paragraph (a) of this section, a taxpayer may treat an intangible asset as having a useful life equal to 15 years
15 unless--

(i) An amortization period or useful life for the intangible asset is specifically prescribed or prohibited by the Internal Revenue Code, the regulations thereunder (other than by this paragraph (b)), or other published guidance in the Internal Revenue Bulletin (see § 601.601(d)(2) of this chapter);
20 (ii) The intangible asset is described in § 1.263(a)-4(c) (relating to intangibles acquired from another person) or § 1.263(a)-4(d)(2) (relating to created financial interests);

(iii) The intangible asset has a useful life the length of which can be estimated with reasonable accuracy; or

(iv) The intangible asset is described in § 1.263(a)-4(d)(8) (relating to certain benefits
25 arising from the provision, production, or improvement of real property), in which case the taxpayer may treat the intangible asset as having a useful life equal to 25 years solely for purposes of determining the depreciation allowance referred to in paragraph (a) of this section.

(2) *Applicability to acquisitions of a trade or business, changes in the capital structure*
30 *of a business entity, and certain other transactions.* The safe harbor useful life provided by paragraph (b)(1) of this section does not apply to an amount required to be capitalized by § 1.263(a)-5 (relating to amounts paid to facilitate an acquisition of a trade or business, a change in the capital structure of a business entity, and certain other transactions).
35 (3) *Depreciation method.* A taxpayer that determines its depreciation allowance for an intangible asset using the 15-year useful life prescribed by paragraph (b)(1) of this section (or the 25-year useful life in the case of an intangible asset described in § 1.263(a)-4(d)(8)) must determine the allowance by amortizing the basis of the intangible asset (as determined under section 167(c) and without regard to salvage value) ratably
40 over the useful life beginning on the first day of the month in which the intangible asset is placed in service by the taxpayer. The intangible asset is not eligible for amortization in the month of disposition.

***

Reg. § 1.167(a)-10   When depreciation deduction is allowable.
45 (a) A taxpayer should deduct the proper depreciation allowance each year and may not increase his depreciation allowances in later years by reason of his failure to deduct any depreciation allowance or of his action in deducting an allowance plainly inadequate under the known facts in prior years. The inadequacy of the depreciation allowance for property in prior years shall be determined on the basis of the allowable method of
50 depreciation used by the taxpayer for such property or under the straight line method if no allowance has ever been claimed for such property. The preceding sentence shall not

be construed as precluding application of any method provided in section 167(b) if taxpayer's failure to claim any allowance for depreciation was due solely to erroneously treating as a deductible expense an item properly chargeable to capital account. For rules relating to adjustments to basis, see section 1016 and the regulations thereunder.

(b) The period for depreciation of an asset shall begin when the asset is placed in service and shall end when the asset is retired from service. A proportionate part of one year's depreciation is allowable for that part of the first and last year during which the asset was in service. However, in the case of a multiple asset account, the amount of depreciation may be determined by using what is commonly described as an ``averaging convention'', that is, by using an assumed timing of additions and retirements. For example, it might be assumed that all additions and retirements to the asset account occur uniformly throughout the taxable year, in which case depreciation is computed on the average of the beginning and ending balances of the asset account for the taxable year. See example (3) under paragraph (b) of § 1.167(b)-1. Among still other averaging conventions which may be used is the one under which it is assumed that all additions and retirements during the first half of a given year were made on the first day of that year and that all additions and retirements during the second half of the year were made on the first day of the following year. Thus, a full year's depreciation would be taken on additions in the first half of the year and no depreciation would be taken on additions in the second half. Moreover, under this convention, no depreciation would be taken on retirements in the first half of the year and a full year's depreciation would be taken on the retirements in the second half. An averaging convention, if used, must be consistently followed as to the account or accounts for which it is adopted, and must be applied to both additions and retirements. In any year in which an averaging convention substantially distorts the depreciation allowance for the taxable year, it may not be used.

Reg. § 1.167(b)-1 Straight line method.

(a) *In general.* Under the straight line method the cost or other basis of the property less its estimated salvage value is deductible in equal annual amounts over the period of the estimated useful life of the property. The allowance for depreciation for the taxable year is determined by dividing the adjusted basis of the property at the beginning of the taxable year, less salvage value, by the remaining useful life of the property at such time. For convenience, the allowance so determined may be reduced to a percentage or fraction. The straight line method may be used in determining a reasonable allowance for depreciation for any property which is subject to depreciation under section 167 and it shall be used in all cases where the taxpayer has not adopted a different acceptable method with respect to such property.

(b) *Illustrations.* The straight line method is illustrated by the following examples:
Example (1). Under the straight line method items may be depreciated separately:

Year and item	Cost or other basis less salaries	Useful life (years)	Depreciation allowable 1954	1955	1956
1954:					
Asset A......................	$1,600	4	[1]$200	$400	$400
Asset B......................	12,000	40	[1] 150	300	300

[1] In this example it is assumed that the assets were placed in service on July 1, 1954.

Sec. 167. Depreciation

Example (2). In group, classified, or composite accounting, a number of assets with the same or different useful lives may be combined into one account, and a single rate of depreciation, i.e., the group, classified, or composite rate used for the entire account. In the case of group accounts, i.e., accounts containing assets which are similar in kind and
5 which have approximately the same estimated useful lives, the group rate is determined from the average of the useful lives of the assets. In the case of classified or composite accounts, the classified or composite rate is generally computed by determining the amount of one year's depreciation for each item or each group of similar items, and by dividing the total depreciation thus obtained by the total cost or other basis of the assets.
10 The average rate so obtained is to be used as long as subsequent additions, retirements, or replacements do not substantially alter the relative proportions of different types of assets in the account. An example of the computation of a classified or composite rate follows:

Cost or other basis	Estimated useful life (years)	Annual depreciation
$10,000	5	$2,000
10,000	15	667
20,000		2,667

20
Average rate is 13.33 percent ($2,667/$20,000) unadjusted for salvage. Assuming the estimated salvage value is 10 percent of the cost or other basis, the rate adjusted for salvage will be 13.33 percent minus 10 percent of 13.33 percent (13.33%-1.33%), or 12 percent.
25   *Example (3)*. The use of the straight line method for group, classified, or composite accounts is illustrated by the following example: A taxpayer filing his returns on a calendar year basis maintains an asset account for which a group rate of 20 percent has been determined, before adjustment for salvage. Estimated salvage is determined to be 6-2/3 percent, resulting in an adjusted rate of 18.67 percent. During the years illustrated,
30 the initial investment, additions, retirements, and salvage recoveries, which were determined not to change the composition of the group sufficiently to require a change in rate, were assumed to have been made as follows:

   1954--Initial investment of $12,000.
35   1957--Retirement $2,000, salvage realized $200.
   1958--Retirement $2,000, salvage realized $200.
   1959--Retirement $4,000, salvage realized $400.
   1959--Additions $10,000.
   1960--Retirement $2,000, no salvage realized.
40   1961--Retirement $2,000, no salvage realized.

440

Sec. 167. Depreciation

Depreciable Asset Account and Depreciation Computation on Average Balances

Year	Asset balance Jan. 1	Current additions	Current retirements	Asset balance Dec. 31	Average balance	Rate (percent)	Allowable depreciation
1954	....	$12,000	....	$12,000	$6,000	18.67	$1,120
1955	$12,000	....	....	12,000	12,000	18.67	2,240
1956	12,000	....	....	12,000	12,000	18.67	2,240
1957	12,000	....	$2,000	10,000	11,000	18.67	2,054
1958	10,000	....	2,000	8,000	9,000	18.67	1,680
1959	8,000	10,000	4,000	14,000	11,000	18.67	2,054
1960	14,000	....	2,000	12,000	13,000	18.67	2,427
1961	12,000	....	2,000	10,000	11,000	18.67	2,054

Corresponding Depreciation Reserve Account

Year	Depreciation reserve Jan. 1	Depreciation allowable	Current retirements	Salvage realized	Depreciation reserve Dec. 31
1954	....	$1,120	....	....	$1,120
1955	$1,120	2,240	....	....	3,360
1956	3,360	2,240	....	....	5,600
1957	5,600	2,054	$2,000	$200	5,854
1958	5,854	1,680	2,000	200	5,734
1959	5,734	2,054	4,000	400	4,188
1960	4,188	2,427	2,000	....	4,615
1961	4,615	2,054	2,000	....	4,669

Reg. § 1.167(b)-2 Declining balance method.

(a) *Application of method.* Under the declining balance method a uniform rate is applied each year to the unrecovered cost or other basis of the property. The unrecovered cost or other basis is the basis provided by section 167(g), adjusted for depreciation previously allowed or allowable, and for all other adjustments provided by section 1016 and other applicable provisions of law. The declining balance rate may be determined without resort to formula. Such rate determined under section 167(b)(2) shall not exceed twice the appropriate straight line rate computed without adjustment for salvage. While salvage is not taken into account in determining the annual allowances under this method, in no event shall an asset (or an account) be depreciated below a reasonable salvage value. However, see section 167(f) and § 1.167(f)-1 for rules which permit a reduction in the amount of salvage value to be taken into account for certain personal property acquired after October 16, 1962. Also, see section 167(c) and § 1.167(c)-1 for restrictions on the use of the declining balance method.

(b) *Illustrations.* The declining balance method is illustrated by the following examples:

Example (1). A new asset having an estimated useful life of 20 years was purchased on January 1, 1954, for $1,000. The normal straight line rate (without adjustment for salvage) is 5 percent, and the declining balance rate at twice the normal straight line rate is 10 percent. The annual depreciation allowances for 1954, 1955, and 1956 are as follows:

Sec. 167. Depreciation

Year	Basis	Declining balance rate (percent)	Depreciation allowance
1954	$1,000	10	$100
1955	900	10	90
1956	810	10	81

Example (2). A taxpayer filing his returns on a calendar year basis maintains a group account to which a 5 year life and a 40 percent declining balance rate are applicable. Original investment, additions, retirements, and salvage recoveries are the same as those set forth in example (3) of paragraph (b) of § 1.167(b)-1. Although salvage value is not taken into consideration in computing a declining balance rate, it must be recognized and accounted for when assets are retired.

Depreciable Asset Account and Depreciation Computation Using Average Asset and Reserve Balances

Year	Asset balance Jan. 1	Current additions	Current retirements	Average Asset balance Dec. 31	Average	reserve before depreciation	Net depreciable balance	Rate (pct.)	Allowable depreciation
1954	....	$12,000	....	$12,000	$6,000	....	$6,000	40	$2,400
1955	$12,000	....	....	12,000	12,000	$2,400	9,600	40	3,840
1956	12,000	....	....	12,000	12,000	6,240	5,760	40	2,304
1957	12,000	....	$2,000	10,000	11,000	7,644	3,356	40	1,342
1958	10,000	....	2,000	8,000	9,000	7,186	1,814	40	726
1959	8,000	10,000	4,000	14,000	11,000	5,212	5,788	40	2,315
1960	14,000	....	2,000	12,000	13,000	4,727	8,273	40	3,309
1961	12,000	....	2,000	10,000	11,000	6,036	4,964	40	1,986

Depreciation Reserve

Year	Reserve Jan. 1	Current retirements	Salvage realized	Reserve Dec. 31, before depreciation	Average reserve before depreciation	Allowable depreciation	Reserve Dec. 31, after depreciation
1954	....	....	....	....	....	$2,400	$2,400
1955	$2,400	....	....	$2,400	$2,400	3,840	6,240
1956	6,240	....	....	6,240	6,240	2,304	8,544
1957	8,544	$2,000	$200	6,744	7,644	1,342	8,086
1958	8,086	2,000	200	6,286	7,186	726	7,012
1959	7,012	4,000	400	3,412	5,212	2,315	5,727
1960	5,727	2,000	....	3,727	4,727	3,309	7,036
1961	7,036	2,000	....	5,036	6,036	1,986	7,022

Where separate depreciation accounts are maintained by year of acquisition and there is an unrecovered balance at the time of the last retirement, such unrecovered balance may be deducted as part of the depreciation allowance for the year of such retirement. Thus, if the taxpayer had kept separate depreciation accounts by year of acquisition and all the retirements shown in the example above were from 1954 acquisitions, depreciation would be computed on the 1954 and 1959 acquisitions as follows:

442

Sec. 167. Depreciation

1954 Acquisitions

Year	Asset balance Jan. 1	Acquisitions	Current retirements	Asset balance Dec. 31	Average balance	Avg. reserve before depreciation	Net depreciable balance	Rate (percent)	Allowable depreciation	
1954	....	$12,000	....	$12,000	$6,000	....	$6,000	40	$2,400	5
1955	$12,000	....	....	12,000	12,000	$2,400	9,600	40	3,840	
1956	12,000	....	....	12,000	12,000	6,240	5,760	40	2,304	10
1957	12,000	....	$2,000	10,000	11,000	7,644	3,356	40	1,342	
1958	10,000	....	2,000	8,000	9,000	7,186	1,814	40	726	
1959	8,000	....	4,000	4,000	6,000	5,212	788	40	315	
1960	4,000	....	2,000	2,000	3,000	2,727	273	40	109	
1961	2,000	....	2,000	....	1,000	836	164	....	[1]164	15

[1] Balance allowable as depreciation in the year of retirement of the last survivor of the 1954 acquisitions.

Depreciation Reserve for 1954 Acquisitions 20

Year	Reserve Jan. 1	Current retirements	Salvage realized	Average Reserve Dec. 31, before depreciation	Reserve before depreciation	Allowable depreciation	Reserve Dec. 31, after depreciation	
1954	....	....	....	....	....	$2,400	$2,400	25
1955	$2,400	....	....	$2,400	$2,400	3,840	6,240	
1956	6,240	....	....	6,240	6,240	2,304	8,544	
1957	8,544	$2,000	$200	6,744	7,644	1,342	8,086	30
1958	8,086	2,000	200	6,286	7,186	726	7,012	
1959	7,012	4,000	400	3,412	5,212	315	3,727	
1960	3,727	2,000	....	1,727	2,727	109	1,836	
1961	1,836	2,000	....	(164)	836	164	....	35

1959 Acquisitions 40

Year	Asset balance Jan. 1	Acquisition	Asset balance Dec. 31	Avg. balance	Reserve Dec. 31, before depreciation	Net depreciable balance	Rate percent	Allowable depreciation	Reserve Dec. 31, after depreciation	
1959	....	$10,000	$10,000	$5,000	None	$5,000	40	$2,000	$2,000	45
1960	$10,000	....	10,000	10,000	$2,000	8,000	40	3,200	5,200	
1961	10,000	....	10,000	10,000	5,200	4,800	40	1,920	7,120	

In the above example, the allowable depreciation on the 1954 acquisitions totals $11,200. This amount when increased by salvage realized in the amount of $800, equals the entire cost or other basis of the 1954 acquisitions ($12,000). 50

(c) *Change in estimated useful life.* In the declining balance method when a change is justified in the useful life estimated for an account, subsequent computations shall be made as though the revised useful life had been originally estimated. For example, assume that an account has an estimated useful life of ten years and that a declining 55 balance rate of 20 percent is applicable. If, at the end of the sixth year, it is determined that the remaining useful life of the account is six years, computations shall be made as though the estimated useful life was originally determined as twelve years. Accordingly, the applicable depreciation rate will be 16-2/3 percent. This rate is thereafter applied to the unrecovered cost or other basis. 60

Reg. § 1.167(g)-1 Basis for depreciation.

The basis upon which the allowance for depreciation is to be computed with respect to any property shall be the adjusted basis provided in section 1011 for the purpose of determining gain on the sale or other disposition of such property. In the case of property 65 which has not been used in the trade or business or held for the production of income and which is thereafter converted to such use, the fair market value on the date of such conversion, if less than the adjusted basis of the property at that time, is the basis for computing depreciation.

Sec. 167. Depreciation

[T.D. 6500, 25 FR 11402, Nov. 26, 1960; 25 FR 14021, Dec. 21, 1960; T.D. 6712, 29 FR 3653, Mar. 24, 1964; T.D. 7203, 37 FR 17133, Aug. 25, 1972; T.D. 8867, 65 FR 3825, Jan. 25, 2000; T.D. 9107, 69 FR 444, Jan. 5, 2004]

Sec. 168. Accelerated cost recovery system

(a) General rule. -- Except as otherwise provided in this section, the depreciation deduction provided by section 167(a) for any tangible property shall be determined by using -

(1) the applicable depreciation method,

(2) the applicable recovery period, and

(3) the applicable convention.

(b) Applicable depreciation method. -- For purposes of this section--

(1) In general. -- Except as provided in paragraphs (2) and (3), the applicable depreciation method is -

(A) the 200 percent declining balance method,

(B) switching to the straight line method for the 1st taxable year for which using the straight line method with respect to the adjusted basis as of the beginning of such year will yield a larger allowance.

(2) 150 percent declining balance method in certain cases. -- Paragraph (1) shall be applied by substituting "150 percent" for "200 percent" in the case of--

(A) any 15-year or 20-year property not referred to in paragraph (3),

(B) any property used in a farming business (within the meaning of section 263A(e)(4)), or

(C) any property (other than property described in paragraph (3)) with respect to which the taxpayer elects under paragraph (5) to have the provisions of this paragraph apply.

(3) Property to which straight line method applies. -- The applicable depreciation method shall be the straight line method in the case of the following property:

(A) Nonresidential real property.

(B) Residential rental property.

(C) Any railroad grading or tunnel bore.

(D) Property with respect to which the taxpayer elects under paragraph (5) to have the provisions of this paragraph apply.

(E) Property described in subsection (e)(3)(D)(ii).

(F) Water utility property described in subsection (e)(5).

(G) Qualified leasehold improvement property described in subsection (e)(6).

(H) Qualified restaurant property described in subsection (e)(7).

(4) Salvage value treated as zero. -- Salvage value shall be treated as zero.

(5) Election. -- An election under paragraph (2)(C) or (3)(D) may be made with respect to 1 or more classes of property for any taxable year and once made with respect to any class shall apply to all property in such class placed in service during such taxable year. Such an election, once made, shall be irrevocable.

(c) Applicable recovery period. -- For purposes of this section, the applicable recovery period shall be determined in accordance with the following table:

Sec. 168. Accelerated cost recovery system

In the case of:	The applicable recovery period is:	
3-year property	3 years	
5-year property	5 years	
7-year property	7 years	5
10-year property	10 years	
15-year property	15 years	
20-year property	20 years	
Water utility property	25 years	
Residential rental property	27.5 years	10
Nonresidential real property	39 years.	
Any railroad grading or tunnel bore	50 years.	

(d) Applicable convention. -- For purposes of this section--

  (1) In general. -- Except as otherwise provided in this subsection, the applicable convention 15 is the half-year convention.

  (2) Real property. -- In the case of--

    (A) nonresidential real property,

    (B) residential rental property, and

    (C) any railroad grading or tunnel bore, 20
the applicable convention is the mid-month convention.

  (3) Special rule where substantial property placed in service during last 3 months of taxable year. --

    (A) In general. -- Except as provided in regulations, if during any taxable year--

      (i) the aggregate bases of property to which this section applies placed in service 25 during the last 3 months of the taxable year, exceed

      (ii) 40 percent of the aggregate bases of property to which this section applies placed in service during such taxable year,
the applicable convention for all property to which this section applies placed in service during such taxable year shall be the mid-quarter convention. 30

    (B) Certain property not taken into account. -- For purposes of subparagraph (A), there shall not be taken into account--

      (i) any nonresidential real property, residential rental property, and railroad grading or tunnel bore, and

      (ii) any other property placed in service and disposed of during the same taxable 35 year.

  (4) Definitions. --

    (A) Half-year convention. -- The half-year convention is a convention which treats all property placed in service during any taxable year (or disposed of during any taxable year) as placed in service (or disposed of) on the mid-point of such taxable year. 40

    (B) Mid-month convention. -- The mid-month convention is a convention which treats all property placed in service during any month (or disposed of during any month) as placed in service (or disposed of) on the mid-point of such month.

    (C) Mid-quarter convention. -- The mid-quarter convention is a convention which treats all property placed in service during any quarter of a taxable year (or disposed of 45 during any quarter of a taxable year) as placed in service (or disposed of) on the mid-point of such quarter.

Sec. 168. Accelerated cost recovery system

(e) Classification of property. -- For purposes of this section--

(1) In general. -- Except as otherwise provided in this subsection, property shall be classified under the following table:

Property shall be treated as:	If such property has a class life (in years) of:
3-year property..	4 or less
5-year property..	More than 4 but less than 10
7-year property..	10 or more but less than 16
10-year property..................................	16 or more but less than 20
15-year property..................................	20 or more but less than 25
20-year property..................................	25 or more.

(2) Residential rental or nonresidential real property. --

    (A) Residential rental property. --

        (i) Residential rental property. -- The term "residential rental property" means any building or structure if 80 percent or more of the gross rental income from such building or structure for the taxable year is rental income from dwelling units.

        (ii) Definitions. -- For purposes of clause (i)--

            (I) the term "dwelling unit" means a house or apartment used to provide living accommodations in a building or structure, but does not include a unit in a hotel, motel, or other establishment more than one-half of the units in which are used on a transient basis, and

            (II) if any portion of the building or structure is occupied by the taxpayer, the gross rental income from such building or structure shall include the rental value of the portion so occupied.

    (B) Nonresidential real property. -- The term "nonresidential real property" means section 1250 property which is not--

        (i) residential rental property, or

        (ii) property with a class life of less than 27.5 years.

(3) Classification of certain property. --

    (A) 3-year property. -- The term "3-year property" includes--

        (i) any race horse which is more than 2 years old at the time it is placed in service,

        (ii) any horse other than a race horse which is more than 12 years old at the time it is placed in service, and

        (iii) any qualified rent-to-own property.

    (B) 5-year property. -- The term "5-year property" includes--

        (i) any automobile or light general purpose truck,

        (ii) any semi-conductor manufacturing equipment,

        (iii) any computer-based telephone central office switching equipment,

        (iv) any qualified technological equipment,

        (v) any section 1245 property used in connection with research and experimentation, and...

    (C) 7-year property. -- The term "7-year property" includes--

        (i) any railroad track,

***

Sec. 168. Accelerated cost recovery system

(v) any property which -

   (I) does not have a class life, and

   (II) is not otherwise classified under paragraph (2) or this paragraph.

(D) 10-year property. -- The term "10-year property" includes -

   (i) any single purpose agricultural or horticultural structure (within the meaning of 5 subsection (i)(13)), and

   (ii) any tree or vine bearing fruit or nuts.

(E) 15-year property. -- The term "15-year property" includes--

   (i) any municipal wastewater treatment plant,

   (ii) any telephone distribution plant and comparable equipment used for 2-way 10 exchange of voice and data communications,

   (iii) any section 1250 property which is a retail motor fuels outlet (whether or not food or other convenience items are sold at the outlet)

***

(F) 20-year property. -- The term "20-year property" means initial clearing and grading 15 land improvements with respect to any electric utility transmission and distribution plant.

(4) Railroad grading or tunnel bore. -- The term "railroad grading or tunnel bore" means all improvements resulting from excavations (including tunneling), construction of embankments, clearings, diversions of roads and streams, sodding of slopes, and from similar work necessary to provide, construct, reconstruct, alter, protect, improve, replace, or restore a 20 roadbed or right-of-way for railroad track.

(f) Property to which section does not apply. -- This section shall not apply to--

   (1) Certain methods of depreciation. -- Any property if--

   (A) the taxpayer elects to exclude such property from the application of this section, and

   (B) for the 1st taxable year for which a depreciation deduction would be allowable with 25 respect to such property in the hands of the taxpayer, the property is properly depreciated under the unit-of-production method or any method of depreciation not expressed in a term of years (other than the retirement-replacement-betterment method or similar method).

***

   (3) Films and video tape. -- Any motion picture film or video tape.   30

   (4) Sound recordings. -- Any works which result from the fixation of a series of musical, spoken, or other sounds, regardless of the nature of the material (such as discs, tapes, or other phonorecordings) in which such sounds are embodied.

(g) Alternative depreciation system for certain property. --

***   35

   (2) Alternative depreciation system. -- For purposes of paragraph (1), the alternative depreciation system is depreciation determined by using--

   (A) the straight line method (without regard to salvage value),

   (B) the applicable convention determined under subsection (d), and

                                                                                                40

447

(C) a recovery period determined under the following table:

In the case of:	The recovery period shall be:
(i) Property not described in clause (ii) or (iii)	The class life.
(ii) Personal property with no class life	12 years.
(iii) Nonresidential real and residential rental property	40 years.
(iv) Any railroad grading or tunnel bore or water utility property	50 years.

(3) Special rules for determining class life. --

***

(B) Special rule for certain property assigned to classes. -- For purposes of paragraph (2), in the case of property described in any of the following subparagraphs of subsection (e)(3), the class life shall be determined as follows:

If property is described in subparagraph:	The class life is:
(A)(iii)	4
(B)(ii)	5
(B)(iii)	9.5
(C)(i)	10
(C)(iii)	22
(D)(i)	15
(D)(ii)	20
(E)(i)	24
(E)(ii)	24
(E)(iii)	20
(E)(iv)	39
(E)(v)	39
(E)(vi)	20
(E)(vii)	30
(F)	25.

(C) Qualified technological equipment. -- In the case of any qualified technological equipment, the recovery period used for purposes of paragraph (2) shall be 5 years.

(D) Automobiles, etc. -- In the case of any automobile or light general purpose truck, the recovery period used for purposes of paragraph (2) shall be 5 years.

(7) Election to use alternative depreciation system. --

(A) In general. -- If the taxpayer makes an election under this paragraph with respect to any class of property for any taxable year, the alternative depreciation system under this subsection shall apply to all property in such class placed in service during such taxable year. Notwithstanding the preceding sentence, in the case of nonresidential real property or residential rental property, such election may be made separately with respect to each property.

(B) Election irrevocable. -- An election under subparagraph (A), once made, shall be irrevocable.

***

(i) Definitions and special rules. -- For purposes of this section--

Sec. 168. Accelerated cost recovery system

(1) Class life. -- Except as provided in this section, the term "class life" means the class life (if any) which would be applicable with respect to any property as of January 1, 1986, under subsection (m) of section 167 (determined without regard to paragraph (4) and as if the taxpayer had made an election under such subsection). The Secretary, through an office established in the Treasury, shall monitor and analyze actual experience with respect to all 5 depreciable assets. The reference in this paragraph to subsection (m) of section 167 shall be treated as a reference to such subsection as in effect on the day before the date of the enactment of the Revenue Reconciliation Act of 1990.

***

(k) Special allowance for certain property acquired after December 31, 2007, and before 10 January 1, 2009.

(1) Additional allowance. -- In the case of any qualified property--

(A) the depreciation deduction provided by section 167(a) for the taxable year in which such property is placed in service shall include an allowance equal to 50 percent of the adjusted basis of the qualified property, and 15

(B) the adjusted basis of the qualified property shall be reduced by the amount of such deduction before computing the amount otherwise allowable as a depreciation deduction under this chapter for such taxable year and any subsequent taxable year.

(2) Qualified property. -- For purposes of this subsection--

(A) In general. -- The term "qualified property" means property-- 20

(i)(I) to which this section applies which has a recovery period of 20 years or less,

(II) which is computer software (as defined in section 167(f)(1)(B)) for which a deduction is allowable under section 167(a) without regard to this subsection,

(III) which is water utility property, or

(IV) which is qualified leasehold improvement property, 25

(ii) the original use of which commences with the taxpayer after December 31, 2007,

(iii) which is--

(I) acquired by the taxpayer after December 31, 2007, and before January 1 2009, but only if no written binding contract for the acquisition was in effect before January 1, 2008, or 30

(II) acquired by the taxpayer pursuant to a written binding contract which was entered into after December 31, 2007, and before January 1, 2008, and

(iv) which is placed in service by the taxpayer before January 1, 2009, or, in the case of property described in subparagraphs (B) and (C), before January 1, 2010.

(B) Certain property having longer production periods treated as qualified 35 property. --

(i) In general. -- The term "qualified property" includes any property if such property--

(I) meets the requirements of clauses (i), (ii), (iii), and (iv) of subparagraph (A),

(II) has a recovery period of at least 10 years or is transportation property, 40

(III) is subject to section 263A, and

(IV) meets the requirements of clause (iii) of section 263A(f)(1)(B) (determined as if such clauses also apply to property which has a long useful life (within the meaning of section 263A(f))).

(ii) Only pre-January 1, 2009, basis eligible for additional allowance. -- 45

Sec. 168. Accelerated cost recovery system

In the case of property which is qualified property solely by reason of clause (i), paragraph (1) shall apply only to the extent of the adjusted basis thereof attributable to manufacture, construction, or production before January 1, 2009.

***

(D) Exceptions. --

(i) Alternative depreciation property. -- The term "qualified property" shall not include any property to which the alternative depreciation system under subsection (g) applies, determined -

(I) without regard to paragraph (7) of subsection (g) (relating to election to have system apply), and

(II) after application of section 280F(b) (relating to listed property with limited business use).

***

(E) Special rules. --

(i) Self-constructed property. -- In the case of a taxpayer manufacturing, constructing, or producing property for the taxpayer's own use, the requirements of clause (iii) of subparagraph (A) shall be treated as met if the taxpayer begins manufacturing, constructing, or producing the property after December 31, 2007, and before January 1, 2009.

***

(iv) Limitations related to users and related parties. -- The term "qualified property" shall not include any property if--

(I) the user of such property (as of the date on which such property is originally placed in service) or a person which is related (within the meaning of section 267(b) or 707(b)) to such user or to the taxpayer had a written binding contract in effect for the acquisition of such property at any time on or before December 31, 2007, or

(II) in the case of property manufactured, constructed, or produced for such user's or person's own use, the manufacture, construction, or production of such property began at any time on or before December 31, 2007.

(F) Coordination with section 280F. -- For purposes of section 280F--

(i) Automobiles. -- In the case of a passenger automobile (as defined in section 280F(d)(5)) which is qualified property, the Secretary shall increase the limitation under section 280F(a)(1)(A)(i) by $8,000.

(ii) Listed property. -- The deduction allowable under paragraph (1) shall be taken into account in computing any recapture amount under section 280F(b)(2).

(G) Deduction allowed in computing minimum tax. -- For purposes of determining alternative minimum taxable income under section 55, the deduction under subsection (a) for qualified property shall be determined under this section without regard to any adjustment under section 56.

(3) Qualified leasehold improvement property. -- For purposes of this subsection--

(A) In general. -- The term "qualified leasehold improvement property" means any improvement to an interior portion of a building which is nonresidential real property if--

(i) such improvement is made under or pursuant to a lease (as defined in subsection (h)(7))--

(I) by the lessee (or any sublessee) of such portion, or

(II) by the lessor of such portion,

Sec. 168. Accelerated cost recovery system

(ii) such portion is to be occupied exclusively by the lessee (or any sublessee) of such portion, and

(iii) such improvement is placed in service more than 3 years after the date the building was first placed in service.

***

5

Sec. 169. Amortization of pollution control facilities

(a) Allowance of deduction. -- Every person, at his election, shall be entitled to a deduction with respect to the amortization of the amortizable basis of any certified pollution control facility (as defined in subsection (d)), based on a period of 60 months. Such amortization deduction shall be an amount, with respect to each month of such period within the taxable year, equal to the 10 amortizable basis of the pollution control facility at the end of such month divided by the number of months (including the month for which the deduction is computed) remaining in the period. Such amortizable basis at the end of the month shall be computed without regard to the amortization deduction for such month. The amortization deduction provided by this section with respect to any month shall be in lieu of the depreciation deduction with respect to such pollution 15 control facility for such month provided by section 167. The 60-month period shall begin, as to any pollution control facility, at the election of the taxpayer, with the month following the month in which such facility was completed or acquired, or with the succeeding taxable year.

***

20

Sec. 170. Charitable, etc., contributions and gifts

(a) Allowance of deduction. --

(1) General rule. -- There shall be allowed as a deduction any charitable contribution (as defined in subsection (c)) payment of which is made within the taxable year. A charitable contribution shall be allowable as a deduction only if verified under regulations prescribed by the Secretary.

25

***

(b) Percentage limitations. --

(1) Individuals. -- In the case of an individual, the deduction provided in subsection (a) shall be limited as provided in the succeeding subparagraphs.

(A) General rule. -- Any charitable contribution to--

30

(i) a church or a convention or association of churches,

(ii) an educational organization which normally maintains a regular faculty and curriculum and normally has a regularly enrolled body of pupils or students in attendance at the place where its educational activities are regularly carried on,

(iii) an organization the principal purpose or functions of which are the providing of 35 medical or hospital care or medical education or medical research, if the organization is a hospital, or if the organization is a medical research organization directly engaged in the continuous active conduct of medical research in conjunction with a hospital, and during the calendar year in which the contribution is made such organization is committed to spend such contributions for such research before January 1 of the fifth 40 calendar year which begins after the date such contribution is made,

(iv) an organization which normally receives a substantial part of its support (exclusive of income received in the exercise or performance by such organization of its charitable, educational, or other purpose or function constituting the basis for its exemption under section 501(a)) from the United States or any State or political 45

451

subdivision thereof or from direct or indirect contributions from the general public, and which is organized and operated exclusively to receive, hold, invest, and administer property and to make expenditures to or for the benefit of a college or university which is an organization referred to in clause (ii) of this subparagraph and which is an agency or instrumentality of a State or political subdivision thereof, or which is owned or operated by a State or political subdivision thereof or by an agency or instrumentality of one or more States or political subdivisions,

(v) a governmental unit referred to in subsection (c)(1),

(vi) an organization referred to in subsection (c)(2) which normally receives a substantial part of its support (exclusive of income received in the exercise or performance by such organization of its charitable, educational, or other purpose or function constituting the basis for its exemption under section 501(a)) from a governmental unit referred to in subsection (c)(1) or from direct or indirect contributions from the general public,

(vii) a private foundation described in subparagraph (F),or

(viii) an organization described in section 509(a)(2) or (3),

shall be allowed to the extent that the aggregate of such contributions does not exceed 50 percent of the taxpayer's contribution base for the taxable year.

(B) Other contributions. -- Any charitable contribution other than a charitable contribution to which subparagraph (A) applies shall be allowed to the extent that the aggregate of such contributions does not exceed the lesser of --

(i) 30 percent of the taxpayer's contribution base for the taxable year, or

(ii) the excess of 50 percent of the taxpayer's contribution base for the taxable year over the amount of charitable contributions allowable under subparagraph (A) (determined without regard to subparagraph (C)).

If the aggregate of such contributions exceeds the limitation of the preceding sentence, such excess shall be treated (in a manner consistent with the rules of subsection (d)(1)) as a charitable contribution (to which subparagraph (A) does not apply) in each of the 5 succeeding taxable years in order of time.

(C) Special limitation with respect to contributions described in subparagraph (A) of certain capital gain property. --

(i) In the case of charitable contributions described in subparagraph (A) of capital gain property to which subsection (e)(1)(B) does not apply, the total amount of contributions of such property which may be taken into account under subsection (a) for any taxable year shall not exceed 30 percent of the taxpayer's contribution base for such year. For purposes of this subsection, contributions of capital gain property to which this subparagraph applies shall be taken into account after all other charitable contributions (other than charitable contributions to which subparagraph (D) applies).

(ii) If charitable contributions described in subparagraph (A) of capital gain property to which clause (i) applies exceeds 30 percent of the taxpayer's contribution base for any taxable year, such excess shall be treated, in a manner consistent with the rules of subsection (d)(1), as a charitable contribution of capital gain property to which clause (i) applies in each of the 5 succeeding taxable years in order of time.

(iii) At the election of the taxpayer (made at such time and in such manner as the Secretary prescribes by regulations), subsection (e)(1) shall apply to all contributions of capital gain property (to which subsection (e)(1)(B) does not otherwise apply) made by the taxpayer during the taxable year. If such an election is made, clauses (i) and (ii) shall not apply to contributions of capital gain property made during the taxable year, and, in applying subsection (d)(1) for such taxable year with respect to contributions of capital gain property made in any prior contribution year for which an election was not made under this clause, such contributions shall be reduced as if subsection (e)(1) had applied to such contributions in the year in which made.

(iv) For purposes of this paragraph, the term "capital gain property" means, with 5 respect to any contribution, any capital asset the sale of which at its fair market value at the time of the contribution would have resulted in gain which would have been long-term capital gain. For purposes of the preceding sentence, any property which is property used in the trade or business (as defined in section 1231(b)) shall be treated as a capital asset.   10

(D) Special limitation with respect to contributions of capital gain property to organizations not described in subparagraph (A). --

(i) **In general.** -- In the case of charitable contributions (other than charitable contributions to which subparagraph (A) applies) of capital gain property, the total amount of such contributions of such property taken into account under subsection (a) 15 for any taxable year shall not exceed the lesser of--

(I) 20 percent of the taxpayer's contribution base for the taxable year, or

(II) the excess of 30 percent of the taxpayer's contribution base for the taxable year over the amount of the contributions of capital gain property to which subparagraph (C) applies.   20

For purposes of this subsection, contributions of capital gain property to which this subparagraph applies shall be taken into account after all other charitable contributions.

(ii) **Carryover.** -- If the aggregate amount of contributions described in clause (i) exceeds the limitation of clause (i), such excess shall be treated (in a manner consistent with the rules of subsection (d)(1)) as a charitable contribution of capital gain property 25 to which clause (i) applies in each of the 5 succeeding taxable years in order of time.

(E) Contributions of qualified conservation contributions. --

(i) **In general.** -- Any qualified conservation contribution (as defined in subsection (h)(1)) shall be allowed to the extent the aggregate of such contributions does not exceed the excess of 50 percent of the taxpayer's contribution base over the amount of 30 all other charitable contributions allowable under this paragraph.

(ii) **Carryover.** -- If the aggregate amount of contributions described in clause (i) exceeds the limitation of clause (i), such excess shall be treated (in a manner consistent with the rules of subsection (d)(1)) as a charitable contribution to which clause (i) applies in each of the 15 succeeding years in order of time.   35

(iii) **Coordination with other subparagraphs.** -- For purposes of applying this subsection and subsection (d)(1), contributions described in clause (i) shall not be treated as described in subparagraph (A), (B), (C), or (D) and such subparagraphs shall apply without regard to such contributions.

(iv) **Special rule for contribution of property used in agriculture or livestock** 40 **production. --**

(I) In general. -- If the individual is a qualified farmer or rancher for the taxable year for which the contribution is made, clause (i) shall be applied by substituting `100 percent' for `50 percent'.

(II) Exception. -- Subclause (I) shall not apply to any contribution of 45 property made after the date of the enactment of this subparagraph which is used in agriculture or livestock production (or available for such production) unless

Sec. 170. Charitable, etc., contributions and gifts

such contribution is subject to a restriction that such property remain available for such production. This subparagraph shall be applied separately with respect to property to which subclause (I) does not apply by reason of the preceding sentence prior to its application to property to which subclause (I) does apply.

(v) Definition. -- For purposes of clause (iv), the term `qualified farmer or rancher' means a taxpayer whose gross income from the trade or business of farming (within the meaning of section 2032A(e)(5)) is greater than 50 percent of the taxpayer's gross income for the taxable year.

(vi) Termination. -- This subparagraph shall not apply to any contribution made in taxable years beginning after December 31, 2007.

(F) Certain private foundations. -- The private foundations referred to in subparagraph (A)(vii) and subsection (e)(1)(B) are--

(i) a private operating foundation (as defined in section 4942(j)(3)),

(ii) any other private foundation (as defined in section 509(a)) which, not later than the 15th day of the third month after the close of the foundation's taxable year in which contributions are received, makes qualifying distributions (as defined in section 4942(g), without regard to paragraph (3) thereof), which are treated, after the application of section 4942(g)(3), as distributions out of corpus (in accordance with section 4942(h)) in an amount equal to 100 percent of such contributions, and with respect to which the taxpayer obtains adequate records or other sufficient evidence from the foundation showing that the foundation made such qualifying distributions, and

(iii) a private foundation all of the contributions to which are pooled in a common fund and which would be described in section 509(a)(3) but for the right of any substantial contributor (hereafter in this clause called "donor") or his spouse to designate annually the recipients, from among organizations described in paragraph (1) of section 509(a), of the income attributable to the donor's contribution to the fund and to direct (by deed or by will) the payment, to an organization described in such paragraph (1), of the corpus in the common fund attributable to the donor's contribution; but this clause shall apply only if all of the income of the common fund is required to be (and is) distributed to one or more organizations described in such paragraph (1) not later than the 15th day of the third month after the close of the taxable year in which the income is realized by the fund and only if all of the corpus attributable to any donor's contribution to the fund is required to be (and is) distributed to one or more of such organizations not later than one year after his death or after the death of his surviving spouse if she has the right to designate the recipients of such corpus.

(G) Contribution base defined. -- For purposes of this section, the term "contribution base" means adjusted gross income (computed without regard to any net operating loss carryback to the taxable year under section 172).

(2) Corporations. -- In the case of a corporation--

(A) In general. -- The total deductions under subsection (a) for any taxable year (other than for contributions to which subparagraph (B) applies) shall not exceed 10 percent of the taxpayer's taxable income.

(B) Qualified conservation contributions by certain corporate farmers and ranchers. --

(i) In general. -- Any qualified conservation contribution (as defined in subsection (h)(1))--

454

Sec. 170. Charitable, etc., contributions and gifts

(I) which is made by a corporation which, for the taxable year during which the contribution is made, is a qualified farmer or rancher (as defined in paragraph (1)(E)(v)) and the stock of which is not readily tradable on an established securities market at any time during such year, and

(II) which, in the case of contributions made after the date of the 5 enactment of this subparagraph, is a contribution of property which is used in agriculture or livestock production (or available for such production) and which is subject to a restriction such property remain available for such production, shall be allowed to the extent the aggregate of such contributions does not exceed the excess of the taxpayer's taxable income over the amount of charitable contributions 10 allowable under subparagraph (A).

(ii)   **Carryover.** -- If the aggregate amount of contributions described in clause (i) exceeds the limitation of clause (i), such excess shall be treated (in a manner consistent with the rules of subsection (d)(2)) as a charitable contribution to which clause (i) applies in each of the 15 succeeding years in order of time.   15

(iii) **Termination.** -- This subparagraph shall not apply to any contribution made in taxable years beginning after December 31, 2007.

(C) Taxable income. -- For purposes of this paragraph, taxable income shall be computed without regard to--

(i) this section,   20

(ii) part VIII (except section 248),

(iii) any net operating loss carryback to the taxable year under section 172,

(iv) section 199, and

(v) any capital loss carryback to the taxable year under section 1212(a)(1).

(c) Charitable contribution defined. -- For purposes of this section, the term "charitable 25 contribution" means a contribution or gift to or for the use of -

(1) A State, a possession of the United States, or any political subdivision of any of the foregoing, or the United States or the District of Columbia, but only if the contribution or gift is made for exclusively public purposes.

(2) A corporation, trust, or community chest, fund, or foundation -   30

(A) created or organized in the United States or in any possession thereof, or under the law of the United States, any State, the District of Columbia, or any possession of the United States;

(B) organized and operated exclusively for religious, charitable, scientific, literary, or educational purposes, or to foster national or international amateur sports competition (but 35 only if no part of its activities involve the provision of athletic facilities or equipment), or for the prevention of cruelty to children or animals;

(C) no part of the net earnings of which inures to the benefit of any private shareholder or individual; and

(D) which is not disqualified for tax exemption under section 501(c)(3) by reason of 40 attempting to influence legislation, and which does not participate in, or intervene in (including the publishing or distributing of statements), any political campaign on behalf of (or in opposition to) any candidate for public office.

A contribution or gift by a corporation to a trust, chest, fund, or foundation shall be deductible by reason of this paragraph only if it is to be used within the United States or any of its 45 possessions exclusively for purposes specified in subparagraph (B). Rules similar to the rules of section 501(j) shall apply for purposes of this paragraph.

Sec. 170. Charitable, etc., contributions and gifts

(3) A post or organization of war veterans, or an auxiliary unit or society of, or trust or foundation for, any such post or organization -

(A) organized in the United States or any of its possessions, and

(B) no part of the net earnings of which inures to the benefit of any private shareholder or individual.

(4) In the case of a contribution or gift by an individual, a domestic fraternal society, order, or association, operating under the lodge system, but only if such contribution or gift is to be used exclusively for religious, charitable, scientific, literary, or educational purposes, or for the prevention of cruelty to children or animals.

(5) A cemetery company owned and operated exclusively for the benefit of its members, or any corporation chartered solely for burial purposes as a cemetery corporation and not permitted by its charter to engage in any business not necessarily incident to that purpose, if such company or corporation is not operated for profit and no part of the net earnings of such company or corporation inures to the benefit of any private shareholder or individual.

For purposes of this section, the term "charitable contribution" also means an amount treated under subsection (g) as paid for the use of an organization described in paragraph (2), (3), or (4).

(d) Carryovers of excess contributions. --

(1) Individuals. --

(A) In general. -- In the case of an individual, if the amount of charitable contributions described in subsection (b)(1)(A) payment of which is made within a taxable year (hereinafter in this paragraph referred to as the "contribution year") exceeds 50 percent of the taxpayer's contribution base for such year, such excess shall be treated as a charitable contribution described in subsection (b)(1)(A) paid in each of the 5 succeeding taxable years in order of time, but, with respect to any such succeeding taxable year, only to the extent of the lesser of the two following amounts:

(i) the amount by which 50 percent of the taxpayer's contribution base for such succeeding taxable year exceeds the sum of the charitable contributions described in subsection (b)(1)(A) payment of which is made by the taxpayer within such succeeding taxable year (determined without regard to this subparagraph) and the charitable contributions described in subsection (b)(1)(A) payment of which was made in taxable years before the contribution year which are treated under this subparagraph as having been paid in such succeeding taxable year; or

(ii) in the case of the first succeeding taxable year, the amount of such excess, and in the case of the second, third, fourth, or fifth succeeding taxable year, the portion of such excess not treated under this subparagraph as a charitable contribution described in subsection (b)(1)(A) paid in any taxable year intervening between the contribution year and such succeeding taxable year.

(B) Special rule for net operating loss carryovers. -- In applying subparagraph (A), the excess determined under subparagraph (A) for the contribution year shall be reduced to the extent that such excess reduces taxable income (as computed for purposes of the second sentence of section 172(b)(2)) and increases the net operating loss deduction for a taxable year succeeding the contribution year.

(2) Corporations. --

(A) In general. -- Any contribution made by a corporation in a taxable year (hereinafter in this paragraph referred to as the "contribution year") in excess of the amount deductible for such year under subsection (b)(2)(A) shall be deductible for each of the 5 succeeding taxable years in order of time, but only to the extent of the lesser of the two following amounts: (i) the excess of the maximum amount deductible for such succeeding taxable

456

year under subsection (b)(2)(A) over the sum of the contributions made in such year plus the aggregate of the excess contributions which were made in taxable years before the contribution year and which are deductible under this subparagraph for such succeeding taxable year; or (ii) in the case of the first succeeding taxable year, the amount of such excess contribution, and in the case of the second, third, fourth, or fifth succeeding taxable 5 year, the portion of such excess contribution not deductible under this subparagraph for any taxable year intervening between the contribution year and such succeeding taxable year.

(B) Special rule for net operating loss carryovers. -- For purposes of subparagraph (A), the excess of -

> **(i)** the contributions made by a corporation in a taxable year to which this section 10 applies, over

> **(ii)** the amount deductible in such year under the limitation in subsection (b)(2)(A), shall be reduced to the extent that such excess reduces taxable income (as computed for purposes of the second sentence of section 172(b)(2)) and increases a net operating loss carryover under section 172 to a succeeding taxable year. 15

(e) Certain contributions of ordinary income and capital gain property. --

(1) General rule. -- The amount of any charitable contribution of property otherwise taken into account under this section shall be reduced by the sum of -

(A) the amount of gain which would not have been long-term capital gain (determined without regard to section 1221(b)(3))if the property contributed had been sold by the 20 taxpayer at its fair market value (determined at the time of such contribution), and

(B) in the case of a charitable contribution -

> **(i)** f tangible personal property--

>> **(I)** if the use by the donee is unrelated to the purpose or function constituting the basis for its exemption under section 501 (or, in the case of a 25 governmental unit, to any purpose or function described in subsection (c)), or

>> **(II)** which is applicable property (as defined in paragraph (7)(C), but without regard to clause (ii) thereof) which is sold, exchanged, or otherwise disposed of by the donee before the last day of the taxable year in which the contribution was made and with respect to which the donee has not made a certification in accordance with 30 paragraph (7)(D),

> **(ii)** to or for the use of a private foundation (as defined in section 509(a)), other than a private foundation described in subsection (b)(1)(F),

> **(iii)** of any patent, copyright (other than a copyright described in section 1221(a)(3) or 1231(b)(1)(C)), trademark, trade name, trade secret, know-how, software (other than 35 software described in section 197(e)(3)(A)(i)), or similar property, or applications or registrations of such property,

***

the amount of gain which would have been long-term capital gain if the property contributed had been sold by the taxpayer at its fair market value (determined at the time of 40 such contribution).

For purposes of applying this paragraph (other than in the case of gain to which section 617(d)(1), 1245(a), 1250(a), 1252(a), or 1254(a) applies), property which is property used in the trade or business (as defined in section 1231(b)) shall be treated as a capital asset.

(2) Allocation of basis. -- For purposes of paragraph (1), in the case of a charitable 45 contribution of less than the taxpayer's entire interest in the property contributed, the taxpayer's adjusted basis in such property shall be allocated between the interest contributed and any

Sec. 170. Charitable, etc., contributions and gifts

interest not contributed in accordance with regulations prescribed by the Secretary.

(3) Special rule for certain contributions of inventory and other property. --

(A) Qualified contributions. -- For purposes of this paragraph, a qualified contribution shall mean a charitable contribution of property described in paragraph (1) or (2) of section 1221(a), by a corporation (other than a corporation which is an S corporation) to an organization which is described in section 501(c)(3) and is exempt under section 501(a) (other than a private foundation, as defined in section 509(a), which is not an operating foundation, as defined in section 4942(j)(3)), but only if -

(i) the use of the property by the donee is related to the purpose or function constituting the basis for its exemption under section 501 and the property is to be used by the donee solely for the care of the ill, the needy, or infants;

(ii) the property is not transferred by the donee in exchange for money, other property, or services;

(iii) the taxpayer receives from the donee a written statement representing that its use and disposition of the property will be in accordance with the provisions of clauses (i) and (ii); and

(iv) in the case where the property is subject to regulation under the Federal Food, Drug, and Cosmetic Act, as amended, such property must fully satisfy the applicable requirements of such Act and regulations promulgated thereunder on the date of transfer and for one hundred and eighty days prior thereto.

(B) Amount of reduction. -- The reduction under paragraph (1)(A) for any qualified contribution (as defined in subparagraph (A)) shall be no greater than the sum of -

(i) one-half of the amount computed under paragraph (1)(A) (computed without regard to this paragraph), and

(ii) the amount (if any) by which the charitable contribution deduction under this section for any qualified contribution (computed by taking into account the amount determined in clause (i), but without regard to this clause) exceeds twice the basis of such property.

***

(E) This paragraph shall not apply to so much of the amount of the gain described in paragraph (1)(A) which would be long-term capital gain but for the application of sections 617, 1245, 1250, or 1252.

***

(4) Special rule for contributions of scientific property used for research. --

(A) Limit on reduction. -- In the case of a qualified research contribution, the reduction under paragraph (1)(A) shall be no greater than the amount determined under paragraph (3) (B).

(B) Qualified research contributions. -- For purposes of this paragraph, the term "qualified research contribution" means a charitable contribution by a corporation of tangible personal property described in paragraph (1) of section 1221(a), but only if--

(i) the contribution is to an organization described in subparagraph (A) or subparagraph (B) of section 41(e)(6),

(ii) the property is constructed or assembled by the taxpayer,

(iii) the contribution is made not later than 2 years after the date the construction or assembly of the property is substantially completed,

(iv) the original use of the property is by the donee,

Sec. 170. Charitable, etc., contributions and gifts

(v) the property is scientific equipment or apparatus substantially all of the use of which by the donee is for research or experimentation (within the meaning of section 174), or for research training, in the United States in physical or biological sciences,

(vi) the property is not transferred by the donee in exchange for money, other property, or services, and

(vii) the taxpayer receives from the donee a written statement representing that its use and disposition of the property will be in accordance with the provisions of clauses (v) and (vi).

(C) Construction of property by taxpayer. -- For purposes of this paragraph, property shall be treated as constructed by the taxpayer only if the cost of the parts used in the construction of such property (other than parts manufactured by the taxpayer or a related person) do not exceed 50 percent of the taxpayer's basis in such property.

***

(7) Recapture of deduction on certain dispositions of exempt use property. --

(A) In general. -- In the case of an applicable disposition of applicable property, there shall be included in the income of the donor of such property for the taxable year of such donor in which the applicable disposition occurs an amount equal to the excess (if any) of--

(i) the amount of the deduction allowed to the donor under this section with respect to such property, over

(ii) the donor's basis in such property at the time such property was contributed.

(B) Applicable disposition. -- For purposes of this paragraph, the term `applicable disposition' means any sale, exchange, or other disposition by the donee of applicable property--

(i) after the last day of the taxable year of the donor in which such property was contributed, and

(ii) before the last day of the 3-year period beginning on the date of the contribution of such property, unless the donee makes a certification in accordance with subparagraph (D).

(C) Applicable property. -- For purposes of this paragraph, the term `applicable property' means charitable deduction property (as defined in section 6050L(a)(2)(A))--

(i) which is tangible personal property the use of which is identified by the donee as related to the purpose or function constituting the basis of the donee's exemption under section 501, and

(ii) for which a deduction in excess of the donor's basis is allowed.

(D) Certification. -- A certification meets the requirements of this subparagraph if it is a written statement which is signed under penalty of perjury by an officer of the donee organization and--

(i) which --

(I) certifies that the use of the property by the donee was substantial and related to the purpose or function constituting the basis for the donee's exemption under section 501, and

(II) describes how the property was used and how such use furthered such purpose or function, or

(ii) which--

(I) states the intended use of the property by the donee at the time of the contribution, and

459

Sec. 170.   Charitable, etc., contributions and gifts

(II) certifies that such intended use has become impossible or infeasible to implement.

(f) Disallowance of deduction in certain cases and special rules. --

***

(3) Denial of   deduction   in case of certain   contributions of partial interests   in property. --

(A) **In general.** -- In the case of a contribution (not made by a transfer in trust) of an interest in property which consists of less than the taxpayer's entire interest in such property, a deduction shall be allowed under this section only to the extent that the value of the interest contributed would be allowable as a deduction under this section if such interest had been transferred in trust. For purposes of this subparagraph, a contribution by a taxpayer of the right to use property shall be treated as a contribution of less than the taxpayer's entire interest in such property.

***

(5) Reduction for certain interest. -- If, in connection with any charitable contribution, a liability is assumed by the recipient or by any other person, or if a charitable contribution is of property which is subject to a liability, then, to the extent necessary to avoid the duplication of amounts, the amount taken into account for purposes of this section as the amount of the charitable contribution--

(A) shall be reduced for interest (i) which has been paid (or is to be paid) by the taxpayer, (ii) which is attributable to the liability, and (iii) which is attributable to any period after the making of the contribution, and

(B) in the case of a bond, shall be further reduced for interest (i) which has been paid (or is to be paid) by the taxpayer on indebtedness incurred or continued to purchase or carry such bond, and (ii) which is attributable to any period before the making of the contribution.

The reduction pursuant to subparagraph (B) shall not exceed the interest (including interest equivalent) on the bond which is attributable to any period before the making of the contribution and which is not (under the taxpayer's method of accounting) includible in the gross income of the taxpayer for any taxable year. For purposes of this paragraph, the term "bond" means any bond, debenture, note, or certificate or other evidence of indebtedness.

(6) Deductions for out-of-pocket expenditures. -- No deduction shall be allowed under this section for an out-of-pocket expenditure made by any person on behalf of an organization described in subsection (c) (other than an organization described in section 501(h)(5) (relating to churches, etc.)) if the expenditure is made for the purpose of influencing legislation (within the meaning of section 501(c)(3)).

***

(8) Substantiation requirement for certain contributions. --

(A) **General rule.** -- No deduction shall be allowed under subsection (a) for any contribution of $250 or more unless the taxpayer substantiates the contribution by a contemporaneous written acknowledgment of the contribution by the donee organization that meets the requirements of subparagraph (B).

(B) **Content of acknowledgement.** -- An acknowledgement meets the requirements of this subparagraph if it includes the following information:

(i) The amount of cash and a description (but not value) of any property other than cash contributed.

(ii) Whether the donee organization provided any goods or services in consideration,

460

in whole or in part, for any property described in clause (i).

(iii) A description and good faith estimate of the value of any goods or services referred to in clause (ii) or, if such goods or services consist solely of intangible religious benefits, a statement to that effect.

For purposes of this subparagraph, the term "intangible religious benefit" means any 5 intangible religious benefit which is provided by an organization organized exclusively for religious purposes and which generally is not sold in commercial transaction outside the donative context.

(C) Contemporaneous. -- For purposes of subparagraph (A), an acknowledgment shall be considered to be contemporaneous if the taxpayer obtains the acknowledgment on or 10 before the earlier of--

(i) the date on which the taxpayer files a return for the taxable year in which the contribution was made, or

(ii) the due date (including extensions) for filing such return.

(D) Substantiation not required for contributions reported by the donee 15 **organization.** -- Subparagraph (A) shall not apply to a contribution if the donee organization files a return, on such form and in accordance with such regulations as the Secretary may prescribe, which includes the information described in subparagraph (B) with respect to the contribution.

(E) Regulations. -- The Secretary shall prescribe such regulations as may be necessary 20 or appropriate to carry out the purposes of this paragraph, including regulations that may provide that some or all of the requirements of this paragraph do not apply in appropriate cases.

***

(9) Denial of deduction where contribution for lobbying activities. -- No deduction shall 25 be allowed under this section for a contribution to an organization which conducts activities to which section 162(e)(1) applies on matters of direct financial interest to the donor's trade or business, if a principal purpose of the contribution was to avoid Federal income tax by securing a deduction for such activities under this section which would be disallowed by reason of section 162(e) if the donor had conducted such activities directly. No deduction shall 30 be allowed under section 162(a) for any amount for which a deduction is disallowed under the preceding sentence.

***

(11) Qualified appraisal and other documentation for certain contributions. --

(A) In general. --   35

(i) Denial of deduction. -- In the case of an individual, partnership, or corporation, no deduction shall be allowed under subsection (a) for any contribution of property for which a deduction of more than $500 is claimed unless such person meets the requirements of subparagraphs (B), (C), and (D), as the case may be, with respect to such contribution.   40

(ii) Exceptions. --

(I) Readily valued property. -- Subparagraphs (C) and (D) shall not apply to cash, property described in subsection (e)(1)(B)(iii) or section 1221(a)(1), publicly traded securities (as defined in section 6050L(a)(2)(B)), and any qualified vehicle described in paragraph (12)(A)(ii) for which an acknowledgement under paragraph 45 (12)(B)(iii) is provided.

(II) Reasonable cause. -- Clause (i) shall not apply if it is shown that the failure

Sec. 170. Charitable, etc., contributions and gifts

to meet such requirements is due to reasonable cause and not to willful neglect.

(B) Property description for contributions of more than $500. -- In the case of contributions of property for which a deduction of more than $500 is claimed, the requirements of this subparagraph are met if the individual, partnership or corporation includes with the return for the taxable year in which the contribution is made a description of such property and such other information as the Secretary may require. The requirements of this subparagraph shall not apply to a C corporation which is not a personal service corporation or a closely held C corporation.

(C) Qualified appraisal for contributions of more than $5,000. -- In the case of contributions of property for which a deduction of more than $5,000 is claimed, the requirements of this subparagraph are met if the individual, partnership, or corporation obtains a qualified appraisal of such property and attaches to the return for the taxable year in which such contribution is made such information regarding such property and such appraisal as the Secretary may require.

(D) Substantiation for contributions of more than $500,000. -- In the case of contributions of property for which a deduction of more than $500,000 is claimed, the requirements of this subparagraph are met if the individual, partnership, or corporation attaches to the return for the taxable year a qualified appraisal of such property.

(E) Qualified appraisal. -- For purposes of this paragraph, the term "qualified appraisal" means, with respect to any property, an appraisal of such property which is treated for purposes of this paragraph as a qualified appraisal under regulations or other guidance prescribed by the Secretary.

(F) Aggregation of similar items of property. -- For purposes of determining thresholds under this paragraph, property and all similar items of property donated to 1 or more donees shall be treated as 1 property.

(12) Contributions of used motor vehicles, boats, and airplanes. --

(A) In general. -- In the case of a contribution of a qualified vehicle the claimed value of which exceeds $500--

(i) paragraph (8) shall not apply and no deduction shall be allowed under subsection (a) for such contribution unless the taxpayer substantiates the contribution by a contemporaneous written acknowledgement of the contribution by the donee organization that meets the requirements of subparagraph (B) and includes the acknowledgement with the taxpayer's return of tax which includes the deduction, and

(ii) if the organization sells the vehicle without any significant intervening use or material improvement of such vehicle by the organization, the amount of the deduction allowed under subsection (a) shall not exceed the gross proceeds received from such sale.

(B) Content of acknowledgement. -- An acknowledgement meets the requirements of this subparagraph if it includes the following information:

(i) The name and taxpayer identification number of the donor.

(ii) The vehicle identification number or similar number.

(iii) In the case of a qualified vehicle to which subparagraph (A)(ii) applies--

(I) a certification that the vehicle was sold in an arm's length transaction between unrelated parties,

(II) the gross proceeds from the sale, and

(III) a statement that the deductible amount may not exceed the amount of such gross proceeds.

462

(iv) In the case of a qualified vehicle to which subparagraph (A)(ii) does not apply--

(I) a certification of the intended use or material improvement of the vehicle and the intended duration of such use, and

(II) a certification that the vehicle would not be transferred in exchange for money, other property, or services before completion of such use or improvement.   5

(C) Contemporaneous. -- For purposes of subparagraph (A), an acknowledgement shall be considered to be contemporaneous if the donee organization provides it within 30 days of--

(i) the sale of the qualified vehicle, or

(ii) in the case of an acknowledgement including a certification described in   10 subparagraph (B)(iv), the contribution of the qualified vehicle.

(D) Information to Secretary. -- A donee organization required to provide an acknowledgement under this paragraph shall provide to the Secretary the information contained in the acknowledgement. Such information shall be provided at such time and in such manner as the Secretary may prescribe.   15

(E) Qualified vehicle. -- For purposes of this paragraph, the term "qualified vehicle" means any--

(i) motor vehicle manufactured primarily for use on public streets, roads, and highways,

(ii) boat, or   20

(iii) airplane.

Such term shall not include any property which is described in section 1221(a)(1).

(F) Regulations or other guidance. -- The Secretary shall prescribe such regulations or other guidance as may be necessary to carry out the purposes of this paragraph. The Secretary may prescribe regulations or other guidance which exempts sales by the donee   25 organization which are in direct furtherance of such organization's charitable purpose from the requirements of subparagraphs (A)(ii) and (B)(iv)(II).

***

(16) Contributions of clothing and household items. --

(A) In general. -- In the case of an individual, partnership, or corporation, no deduction   30 shall be allowed under subsection (a) for any contribution of clothing or a household item unless such clothing or ousehold item is in good used condition or better.

(B) Items of minimal value. -- Notwithstanding subparagraph (A), the Secretary may by regulation deny a deduction under subsection (a) for any contribution of clothing or a household item which has minimal monetary value.   35

(C) Exception for certain property. -- Subparagraphs (A) and (B) shall not apply to any contribution of a single item of clothing or a household item for which a deduction of more than $500 is claimed if the taxpayer includes with the taxpayer's return a qualified appraisal with respect to the property.

(D) Household items. -- For purposes of this paragraph--   40

(i) In general. -- The term `household items' includes furniture, furnishings, electronics, appliances, linens, and other similar items.

(ii) Excluded items. -- Such term does not include--

(I) food,

(II) paintings, antiques, and other objects of art,   45

(III) jewelry and gems, and

(IV) collections.

(17) **Recordkeeping.** -- No deduction shall be allowed under nsection (a) for any contribution of a cash, check, or other monetary gift unless the donor maintains as a record of such contribution a bank record or a written communication from the donee showing the name of the donee organization, the date of the contribution, and the amount of the contribution.

***

(g) Amounts paid to maintain certain students as members of taxpayer's household. --

(1) In general. -- Subject to the limitations provided by paragraph (2), amounts paid by the taxpayer to maintain an individual (other than a dependent, as defined in section 152 (determined without regard to subsections (b)(1), (b)(2), and (d)(1)(B) thereof), or a relative of the taxpayer) as a member of his household during the period that such individual is--

(A) a member of the taxpayer's household under a written agreement between the taxpayer and an organization described in paragraph (2), (3), or (4) of subsection (c) to implement a program of the organization to provide educational opportunities for pupils or students in private homes, and

(B) a full-time pupil or student in the twelfth or any lower grade at an educational organization described in section 170(b)(1)(A)(ii) located in the United States, shall be treated as amounts paid for the use of the organization.

(2) Limitations. --

(A) **Amount.** -- Paragraph (1) shall apply to amounts paid within the taxable year only to the extent that such amounts do not exceed $50 multiplied by the number of full calendar months during the taxable year which fall within the period described in paragraph (1). For purposes of the preceding sentence, if 15 or more days of a calendar month fall within such period such month shall be considered as a full calendar month.

(B) **Compensation or reimbursement.** -- Paragraph (1) shall not apply to any amount paid by the taxpayer within the taxable year if the taxpayer receives any money or other property as compensation or reimbursement for maintaining the individual in his household during the period described in paragraph (1).

(3) **Relative defined.** -- For purposes of paragraph (1), the term "relative of the taxpayer" means an individual who, with respect to the taxpayer, bears any of the relationships described in subparagraphs (A) through (G) of section 152(d)(2).

(4) **No other amount allowed as deduction.** -- No deduction shall be allowed under subsection (a) for any amount paid by a taxpayer to maintain an individual as a member of his household under a program described in paragraph (1)(A) except as provided in this subsection.

***

(l) Treatment of certain amounts paid to or for the benefit of institutions of higher education. --

(1) In general. -- For purposes of this section, 80 percent of any amount described in paragraph (2) shall be treated as a charitable contribution.

(2) Amount described. -- For purposes of paragraph (1), an amount is described in this paragraph if--

(A) the amount is paid by the taxpayer to or for the benefit of an educational organization--

(i) which is described in subsection (b)(1)(A)(ii), and

Sec. 170. Charitable, etc., contributions and gifts

(ii) which is an institution of higher education (as defined in section 3304(f)), and

(B) such amount would be allowable as a deduction under this section but for the fact that the taxpayer receives (directly or indirectly) as a result of paying such amount the right to purchase tickets for seating at an athletic event in an athletic stadium of such institution. If any portion of a payment is for the purchase of such tickets, such portion and the remaining portion (if any) of such payment shall be treated as separate amounts for purposes of this subsection.

(m) Certain donee income from intellectual property treated as an additional charitable contribution. --

(1) Treatment as additional contribution. -- In the case of a taxpayer who makes a qualified intellectual property contribution, the deduction allowed under subsection (a) for each taxable year of the taxpayer ending on or after the date of such contribution shall be increased (subject to the limitations under subsection (b)) by the applicable percentage of qualified donee income with respect to such contribution which is properly allocable to such year under this subsection.

(2) Reduction in additional deductions to extent of initial deduction. -- With respect to any qualified intellectual property contribution, the deduction allowed under subsection (a) shall be increased under paragraph (1) only to the extent that the aggregate amount of such increases with respect to such contribution exceed the amount allowed as a deduction under subsection (a) with respect to such contribution determined without regard to this subsection.

(3) Qualified donee income. -- For purposes of this subsection, the term "qualified donee income" means any net income received by or accrued to the donee which is properly allocable to the qualified intellectual property.

(4) Allocation of qualified donee income to taxable years of donor. -- For purposes of this subsection, qualified donee income shall be treated as properly allocable to a taxable year of the donor if such income is received by or accrued to the donee for the taxable year of the donee which ends within or with such taxable year of the donor.

(5) 10-year limitation. -- Income shall not be treated as properly allocable to qualified intellectual property for purposes of this subsection if such income is received by or accrued to the donee after the 10-year period beginning on the date of the contribution of such property.

(6) Benefit limited to life of intellectual property. -- Income shall not be treated as properly allocable to qualified intellectual property for purposes of this subsection if such income is received by or accrued to the donee after the expiration of the legal life of such property.

(7) Applicable percentage. -- For purposes of this subsection, the term "applicable percentage" means the percentage determined under the following table which corresponds to a taxable year of the donor ending on or after the date of the qualified intellectual property contribution:

465

Sec. 170. Charitable, etc., contributions and gifts

Taxable Year of Donor
Ending on or After
Date of Contribution:

	Applicable Percentage:
1st	100
2nd	100
3rd	90
4th	80
5th	70
6th	60
7th	50
8th	40
9th	30
10th	20
11th	10
12th	10.

(8) Qualified intellectual property contribution. -- For purposes of this subsection, the term "qualified intellectual property contribution" means any charitable contribution of qualified intellectual property--

(A) the amount of which taken into account under this section is reduced by reason of subsection (e)(1), and

(B) with respect to which the donor informs the donee at the time of such contribution that the donor intends to treat such contribution as a qualified intellectual property contribution for purposes of this subsection and section 6050L.

(9) Qualified intellectual property. -- For purposes of this subsection, the term "qualified intellectual property" means property described in subsection (e)(1)(B)(iii) (other than property contributed to or for the use of an organization described in subsection (e)(1)(B)(ii)).

***

Reg. § 1.170A-1 Charitable, etc., contributions and gifts; allowance of deduction.

(a) *Allowance of deduction.* Any charitable contribution, as defined in section 170(c), actually paid during the taxable year is allowable as a deduction in computing taxable income irrespective of the method of accounting employed or of the date on which the contribution is pledged. However, charitable contributions by corporations may under certain circumstances be deductible even though not paid during the taxable year as provided in section 170(a)(2) and § 1.170A-11. For rules relating to recordkeeping and return requirements in support of deductions for charitable contributions (whether by an itemizing or nonitemizing taxpayer) see § 1.170A-13. The deduction is subject to the limitations of section 170(b) and § 1.170A-8 or § 1.170A-11. Subject to the provisions of section 170(d) and §§ 1.170A-10 and 1.170A-11, certain excess charitable contributions made by individuals and corporations shall be treated as paid in certain succeeding taxable years. For provisions relating to direct charitable deductions under section 63 by nonitemizers, see section 63(b)(1)(C) and (i) and section 170(i). For rules relating to the determination of, and the deduction for, amounts paid to maintain certain students as members of the taxpayer's household and treated under section 170(g) as paid for the use of an organization described in section 170(c) (2), (3), or (4), see § 1.170A-2. For the reduction of any charitable contributions for interest on certain indebtedness, see section 170(f)(5) and § 1.170A-3. For a special rule relating to the computation of the amount of the deduction with respect to a charitable contribution of certain ordinary income or

Sec. 170. Charitable, etc., contributions and gifts

capital gain property, see section 170(e) and §§ 1.170A-4 and 1.170A-4A. For rules for postponing the time for deduction of a charitable contribution of a future interest in tangible personal property, see section 170(a)(3) and § 1.170A-5. For rules with respect to transfers in trust and of partial interests in property, see section 170(e), section 170(f) (2) and (3), §§ 1.170A-4, 1.170A-6, and 1.170A-7. For definition of the term section 170(b)(1)(A) organization, see § 1.170A-9. For valuation of a remainder interest in real property, see section 170(f)(4) and the regulations thereunder. The deduction for charitable contributions is subject to verification by the district director.

(b) *Time of making contribution.* Ordinarily, a contribution is made at the time delivery is effected. The unconditional delivery or mailing of a check which subsequently clears in due course will constitute an effective contribution on the date of delivery or mailing. If a taxpayer unconditionally delivers or mails a properly endorsed stock certificate to a charitable donee or the donee's agent, the gift is completed on the date of delivery or, if such certificate is received in the ordinary course of the mails, on the date of mailing. If the donor delivers the stock certificate to his bank or broker as the donor's agent, or to the issuing corporation or its agent, for transfer into the name of the donee, the gift is completed on the date the stock is transferred on the books of the corporation. For rules relating to the date of payment of a contribution consisting of a future interest in tangible personal property, see section 170(a)(3) and § 1.170A-5.

(c) *Value of a contribution in property.* (1) If a charitable contribution is made in property other than money, the amount of the contribution is the fair market value of the property at the time of the contribution reduced as provided in section 170(e)(1) and paragraph (a) of § 1.170A-4, or section 170(e)(3) and paragraph (c) of § 1.170A-4A.

(2) The fair market value is the price at which the property would change hands between a willing buyer and a willing seller, neither being under any compulsion to buy or sell and both having reasonable knowledge of relevant facts. If the contribution is made in property of a type which the taxpayer sells in the course of his business, the fair market value is the price which the taxpayer would have received if he had sold the contributed property in the usual market in which he customarily sells, at the time and place of the contribution and, in the case of a contribution of goods in quantity, in the quantity contributed. The usual market of a manufacturer or other producer consists of the wholesalers or other distributors to or through whom he customarily sells, but if he sells only at retail the usual market consists of his retail customers.

(3) If a donor makes a charitable contribution of property, such as stock in trade, at a time when he could not reasonably have been expected to realize its usual selling price, the value of the gift is not the usual selling price but is the amount for which the quantity of property contributed would have been sold by the donor at the time of the contribution.

(4) Any costs and expenses pertaining to the contributed property which were incurred in taxable years preceding the year of contribution and are properly reflected in the opening inventory for the year of contribution must be removed from inventory and are not a part of the cost of goods sold for purposes of determining gross income for the year of contribution. Any costs and expenses pertaining to the contributed property which are incurred in the year of contribution and would, under the method of accounting used, be properly reflected in the cost of goods sold for such year are to be treated as part of the costs of goods sold for such year. If costs and expenses incurred in producing or acquiring the contributed property are, under the method of accounting used, properly deducted under section 162 or other section of the Code, such costs and expenses will be allowed as deductions for the taxable year in which they are paid or incurred whether or not such year is the year of the contribution. Any such costs and expenses which are treated as part of the cost of goods sold for the year of contribution, and any such costs and expenses which are properly deducted under section 162 or other section of the

Sec. 170. Charitable, etc., contributions and gifts

Code, are not to be treated under any section of the Code as resulting in any basis for the contributed property. Thus, for example, the contributed property has no basis for purposes of determining under section 170(e)(1)(A) and paragraph (a) of § 1.170A-4 the amount of gain which would have been recognized if such property had been sold by the
5 donor at its fair market value at the time of its contribution. The amount of any charitable contribution for the taxable year is not to be reduced by the amount of any costs or expenses pertaining to the contributed property which was properly deducted under section 162 or other section of the Code for any taxable year preceding the year of the contribution. This subparagraph applies only to property which was held by the taxpayer
10 for sale in the course of a trade or business. The application of this subparagraph may be illustrated by the following examples:

Example 1. In 1970, A, an individual using the calendar year as the taxable year and the accrual method of accounting, contributed to a church property from inventory having a fair market value of $600. The closing inventory at the end of 1969 properly included
15 $400 of costs attributable to the acquisition of such property, and in 1969 A properly deducted under section 162 $50 of administrative and other expenses attributable to such property. Under section 170(e)(1)(A) and paragraph (a) of § 1.170A-4, the amount of the charitable contribution allowed for 1970 is $400 ($600-[$600-$400]). Pursuant to this subparagraph, the cost of goods sold to be used in determining gross income for
20 1970 may not include the $400 which was included in opening inventory for that year.

Example 2. The facts are the same as in Example 1 except that the contributed property was acquired in 1970 at a cost of $400. The $400 cost of the property is included in determining the cost of goods sold for 1970, and $50 is allowed as a deduction for that year under section 162. A is not allowed any deduction under section
25 170 for the contributed property, since under section 170(e)(1)(A) and paragraph (a) of § 1.170A-4 the amount of the charitable contribution is reduced to zero ($600-[$600-$0]).

Example 3. In 1970, B, an individual using the calendar year as the taxable year and the accrual method of accounting, contributed to a church property from inventory having a fair market value of $600. Under § 1.471-3(c), the closing inventory at the end of 1969
30 properly included $450 costs attributable to the production of such property, including $50 of administrative and other indirect expenses which, under his method of accounting, was properly added to inventory rather than deducted as a business expense. Under section 170(e)(1)(A) and paragraph (a) of § 1.170A-4, the amount of the charitable contribution allowed for 1970 is $450 ($600-[$600-$450]). Pursuant to this subparagraph, the cost of
35 goods sold to be used in determining gross income for 1970 may not include the $450 which was included in opening inventory for that year.

Example 4. The facts are the same as in Example 3 except that the contributed property was produced in 1970 at a cost of $450, including $50 of administrative and other indirect expenses. The $450 cost of the property is included in determining the cost
40 of goods sold for 1970. B is not allowed any deduction under section 170 for the contributed property, since under section 170(e)(1)(A) and paragraph (a) of § 1.170A-4 the amount of the charitable contribution is reduced to zero ($600-[$600-$0]).

Example 5. In 1970, C, a farmer using the cash method of accounting and the calendar year as the taxable year, contributed to a church a quantity of grain which he
45 had raised having a fair market value of $600. In 1969, C paid expenses of $450 in raising the property which he properly deducted for such year under section 162. Under section 170(e)(1)(A) and paragraph (a) of § 1.170A-4, the amount of the charitable contribution in 1970 is reduced to zero ($600-[$600-$0]). Accordingly, C is not allowed any deduction under section 170 for the contributed property.
50 *Example 6.* The facts are the same as in Example 5 except that the $450 expenses incurred in raising the contributed property were paid in 1970. The result is the same as

in Example 5, except the amount of $450 is deductible under section 162 for 1970.

(5) Transfers of property to an organization described in section 170(c) which bear a direct relationship to the taxpayer's trade or business and which are made with a reasonable expectation of financial return commensurate with the amount of the transfer may constitute allowable deductions as trade or business expenses rather than as charitable contributions. See section 162 and the regulations thereunder.

(d) *Purchase of an annuity*. (1) In the case of an annuity or portion thereof purchased from an organization described in section 170(c), there shall be allowed as a deduction the excess of the amount paid over the value at the time of purchase of the annuity or portion purchased.

(2) The value of the annuity or portion is the value of the annuity determined in accordance with paragraph (e)(1)(iii)(b)(2) of § 1.101-2.

(3) For determining gain on any such transaction constituting a bargain sale, see section 1011(b) and § 1.1011-2.

(e) *Transfers subject to a condition or power*. If as of the date of a gift a transfer for charitable purposes is dependent upon the performance of some act or the happening of a precedent event in order that it might become effective, no deduction is allowable unless the possibility that the charitable transfer will not become effective is so remote as to be negligible. If an interest in property passes to, or is vested in, charity on the date of the gift and the interest would be defeated by the subsequent performance of some act or the happening of some event, the possibility of occurrence of which appears on the date of the gift to be so remote as to be negligible, the deduction is allowable. For example, A transfers land to a city government for as long as the land is used by the city for a public park. If on the date of the gift the city does plan to use the land for a park and the possibility that the city will not use the land for a public park is so remote as to be negligible, A is entitled to a deduction under section 170 for his charitable contribution.

***

(g) *Contributions of services*. No deduction is allowable under section 170 for a contribution of services. However, unreimbursed expenditures made incident to the rendition of services to an organization contributions to which are deductible may constitute a deductible contribution. For example, the cost of a uniform without general utility which is required to be worn in performing donated services is deductible. Similarly, out-of-pocket transportation expenses necessarily incurred in performing donated services are deductible. Reasonable expenditures for meals and lodging necessarily incurred while away from home in the course of performing donated services also are deductible. For the purposes of this paragraph, the phrase while away from home has the same meaning as that phrase is used for purposes of section 162 and the regulations thereunder.

(h) *Payment in exchange for consideration*--(1) *Burden on taxpayer to show that all or part of payment is a charitable contribution or gift*. No part of a payment that a taxpayer makes to or for the use of an organization described in section 170(c) that is in consideration for (as defined in § 1.170A-13(f)(6)) goods or services (as defined in § 1.170A-13(f)(5)) is a contribution or gift within the meaning of section 170(c) unless the taxpayer--

(i) Intends to make a payment in an amount that exceeds the fair market value of the goods or services; and

(ii) Makes a payment in an amount that exceeds the fair market value of the goods or services.

(2) *Limitation on amount deductible*--(i) *In general*. The charitable contribution deduction under section 170(a) for a payment a taxpayer makes partly in consideration for goods or services may not exceed the excess of--

Sec. 170. Charitable, etc., contributions and gifts

(A) The amount of any cash paid and the fair market value of any property (other than cash) transferred by the taxpayer to an organization described in section 170(c); over

(B) The fair market value of the goods or services the organization provides in return.

(ii) *Special rules.* For special limits on the deduction for charitable contributions of
5   ordinary income and capital gain property, see section 170(e) and §§ 1.170A-4 and 1.170A-4A.

(3) *Certain goods or services disregarded.* For purposes of section 170(a) and paragraphs (h)(1) and (h)(2) of this section, goods or services described in § 1.170A-13(f) (8)(i) or § 1.170A-13(f)(9)(i) are disregarded.
10   (4) *Donee estimates of the value of goods or services may be treated as fair market value--*(i) *In general.* For purposes of section 170(a), a taxpayer may rely on either a contemporaneous written acknowledgment provided under section 170(f)(8) and § 1.170A-13(f) or a written disclosure statement provided under section 6115 for the fair market value of any goods or services provided to the taxpayer by the donee
15   organization.

(ii) *Exception.* A taxpayer may not treat an estimate of the value of goods or services as their fair market value if the taxpayer knows, or has reason to know, that such treatment is unreasonable. For example, if a taxpayer knows, or has reason to know, that there is an error in an estimate provided by an organization described in section 170(c)
20   pertaining to goods or services that have a readily ascertainable value, it is unreasonable for the taxpayer to treat the estimate as the fair market value of the goods or services. Similarly, if a taxpayer is a dealer in the type of goods or services provided in consideration for the taxpayer's payment and knows, or has reason to know, that the estimate is in error, it is unreasonable for the taxpayer to treat the estimate as the fair
25   market value of the goods or services.

(5) *Examples.* The following examples illustrate the rules of this paragraph (h).

Example 1. Certain goods or services disregarded. Taxpayer makes a $50 payment to Charity B, an organization described in section 170(c), in exchange for a family membership. The family membership entitles Taxpayer and members of Taxpayer's family
30   to certain benefits. These benefits include free admission to weekly poetry readings, discounts on merchandise sold by B in its gift shop or by mail order, and invitations to special events for members only, such as lectures or informal receptions. When B first offers its membership package for the year, B reasonably projects that each special event for members will have a cost to B, excluding any allocable overhead, of $5 or less per
35   person attending the event. Because the family membership benefits are disregarded pursuant to § 1.170A-13(f)(8)(i), Taxpayer may treat the $50 payment as a contribution or gift within the meaning of section 170(c), regardless of Taxpayer's intent and whether or not the payment exceeds the fair market value of the goods or services. Furthermore, any charitable contribution deduction available to Taxpayer may be calculated without
40   regard to the membership benefits.

Example 2. Treatment of good faith estimate at auction as the fair market value. Taxpayer attends an auction held by Charity C, an organization described in section 170(c). Prior to the auction, C publishes a catalog that meets the requirements for a written disclosure statement under section 6115(a) (including C's good faith estimate of
45   the value of items that will be available for bidding). A representative of C gives a copy of the catalog to each individual (including Taxpayer) who attends the auction. Taxpayer notes that in the catalog C's estimate of the value of a vase is $100. Taxpayer has no reason to doubt the accuracy of this estimate. Taxpayer successfully bids and pays $500 for the vase. Because Taxpayer knew, prior to making her payment, that the estimate in
50   the catalog was less than the amount of her payment, Taxpayer satisfies the requirement of paragraph (h)(1)(i) of this section. Because Taxpayer makes a payment in an amount

Sec. 170. Charitable, etc., contributions and gifts

that exceeds that estimate, Taxpayer satisfies the requirements of paragraph (h)(1)(ii) of this section. Taxpayer may treat C's estimate of the value of the vase as its fair market value in determining the amount of her charitable contribution deduction.

Example 3. Good faith estimate not in error. Taxpayer makes a $200 payment to Charity D, an organization described in section 170(c). In return for Taxpayer's payment, D gives Taxpayer a book that Taxpayer could buy at retail prices typically ranging from $18 to $25. D provides Taxpayer with a good faith estimate, in a written disclosure statement under section 6115(a), of $20 for the value of the book. Because the estimate is within the range of typical retail prices for the book, the estimate contained in the written disclosure statement is not in error. Although Taxpayer knows that the book is sold for as much as $25, Taxpayer may treat the estimate of $20 as the fair market value of the book in determining the amount of his charitable contribution deduction.

***

(j) *Exceptions and other rules.* (1) The provisions of section 170 do not apply to contributions by an estate; nor do they apply to a trust unless the trust is a private foundation which, pursuant to section 642(c)(6) and § 1.642(c)-4, is allowed a deduction under section 170 subject to the provisions applicable to individuals.

(2) No deduction shall be allowed under section 170 for a charitable contribution to or for the use of an organization or trust described in section 508(d) or 4948(c)(4), subject to the conditions specified in such sections and the regulations thereunder.

(3) For disallowance of deductions for contributions to or for the use of communist controlled organizations, see section 11(a) of the Internal Security Act of 1950, as amended (50 U.S.C. 790).

(4) For denial of deductions for charitable contributions as trade or business expenses and rules with respect to treatment of payments to organizations other than those described in section 170(c), see section 162 and the regulations thereunder.

(5) No deduction shall be allowed under section 170 for amounts paid to an organization:

(i) Which is disqualified for tax exemption under section 501(c)(3) by reason of attempting to influence legislation, or

(ii) Which participates in, or intervenes in (including the publishing or distribution of statements), any political campaign on behalf of or in opposition to any candidate for public office.

For purposes of determining whether an organization is attempting to influence legislation or is engaging in political activities, see sections 501(c)(3), 501(h), 4911 and the regulations thereunder.

(6) No deduction shall be allowed under section 170 for expenditures for lobbying purposes, the promotion or defeat of legislation, etc. See also the regulations under sections 162 and 4945.

***

(11) No deduction shall be allowed under section 170 for out-of-pocket expenditures on behalf of an eligible organization (within the meaning of § 1.501(h)-2(b)(1)) if the expenditure is made in connection with influencing legislation (within the meaning of section 501(c)(3) or § 56.4911-2), or in connection with the payment of the organization's tax liability under section 4911. For the treatment of similar expenditures on behalf of other organizations see paragraph (h)(6) of this section.

***

Reg. § 1.170A-4   Reduction in amount of charitable contributions of certain appreciated property.

(a) *Amount of reduction.* Section 170(e)(1) requires that the amount of the charitable

Sec. 170. Charitable, etc., contributions and gifts

contribution which would be taken into account under section 170(a) without regard to section 170(e) shall be reduced before applying the percentage limitations under section 170(b):

    (1) In the case of a contribution by an individual or by a corporation of ordinary income property, as defined in paragraph (b)(1) of this section, by the amount of gain (hereinafter in this section referred to as ordinary income) which would have been recognized as gain which is not long-term capital gain if the property had been sold by the donor at its fair market value at the time of its contribution to the charitable organization,

    (2) In the case of a contribution by an individual of section 170(e) capital gain property, as defined in paragraph (b)(2) of this section, by 50 percent of the amount of gain (hereinafter in this section referred to as long-term capital gain) which would have been recognized as long-term capital gain if the property had been sold by the donor at its fair market value at the time of its contribution to the charitable organization, and

    (3) In the case of a contribution by a corporation of section 170(e) capital gain property, as defined in paragraph (b)(2) of this section, by 62-1/2 percent of the amount of gain (hereinafter in this section referred to as long-term capital gain) which would have been recognized as long-term capital gain if the property had been sold by the donor at its fair market value at the time of its contribution to the charitable organization.

Section 170(e)(1) and this paragraph do not apply to reduce the amount of the charitable contribution where, by reason of the transfer of the contributed property, ordinary income or capital gain is recognized by the donor in the same taxable year in which the contribution is made. Thus, where income or gain is recognized under section 453(d) upon the transfer of an installment obligation to a charitable organization, or under section 454(b) upon the transfer of an obligation issued at a discount to such an organization, or upon the assignment of income to such an organization, section 170(e) (1) and this paragraph do not apply if recognition of the income or gain occurs in the same taxable year in which the contribution is made. Section 170(e)(1) and this paragraph apply to a charitable contribution of an interest in ordinary income property or section 170(e) capital gain property which is described in paragraph (b) of § 1.170A-6, or paragraph (b) of § 1.170A-7. For purposes of applying section 170(e)(1) and this paragraph it is immaterial whether the charitable contribution is made ``to" the charitable organization or whether it is made ``for the use of" the charitable organization. See § 1.170A-8(a)(2).

    (b) *Definitions and other rules.* For purposes of this section:

    (1) *Ordinary income property.* The term ordinary income property means property any portion of the gain on which would not have been long term capital gain if the property had been sold by the donor at its fair market value at the time of its contribution to the charitable organization. Such term includes, for example, property held by the donor primarily for sale to customers in the ordinary course of his trade or business, a work of art created by the donor, a manuscript prepared by the donor, letters and memorandums prepared by or for the donor, a capital asset held by the donor for not more than 1 year (6 months for taxable years beginning before 1977; 9 months for taxable years beginning in 1977), and stock described in section 306(a), 341(a), or 1248(a) to the extent that, after applying such section, gain on its disposition would not have been long-term capital gain. The term does not include an income interest in respect of which a deduction is allowed under section 170(f)(2)(B) and paragraph (c) of § 1.170A-6.

    (2) *Section 170(e) capital gain property.* The term section 170(e) capital gain property means property any portion of the gain on which would have been treated as long-term capital gain if the property had been sold by the donor at its fair market value at the time of its contribution to the charitable organization and which:

    (i) Is contributed to or for the use of a private foundation, as defined in section 509(a) and the regulations thereunder, other than a private foundation described in section 170(b)(1)(E),

(ii) Constitutes tangible personal property contributed to or for the use of a charitable organization, other than a private foundation to which subdivision (i) of this subparagraph applies, which is put to an unrelated use by the charitable organization within the 5 meaning of subparagraph (3) of this paragraph, or

(iii) Constitutes property not described in subdivision (i) or (ii) of this subparagraph which is 30-percent capital gain property to which an election under paragraph (d)(2) of § 1.170A-8 applies.

For purposes of this subparagraph a fixture which is intended to be severed from real 10 property shall be treated as tangible personal property.

(3) *Unrelated use--*(i) *In general.* The term unrelated use means a use which is unrelated to the purpose or function constituting the basis of the charitable organization's exemption under section 501 or, in the case of a contribution of property to a governmental unit, the use of such property by such unit for other than exclusively public 15 purposes. For example, if a painting contributed to an educational institution is used by that organization for educational purposes by being placed in its library for display and study by art students, the use is not an unrelated use; but if the painting is sold and the proceeds used by the organization for educational purposes, the use of the property is an unrelated use. If furnishings contributed to a charitable organization are used by it in its 20 offices and buildings in the course of carrying out its functions, the use of the property is not an unrelated use. If a set or collection of items of tangible personal property is contributed to a charitable organization or governmental unit, the use of the set or collection is not an unrelated use if the donee sells or otherwise disposes of only an insubstantial portion of the set or collection. The use by a trust of tangible personal 25 property contributed to it for the benefit of a charitable organization is an unrelated use if the use by the trust is one which would have been unrelated if made by the charitable organization.

(ii) *Proof of use.* For purposes of applying subparagraph (2)(ii) of this paragraph, a taxpayer who makes a charitable contribution of tangible personal property to or for the 30 use of a charitable organization or governmental unit may treat such property as not being put to an unrelated use by the donee if:

(a) He establishes that the property is not in fact put to an unrelated use by the donee, or

(b) At the time of the contribution or at the time the contribution is treated as made, it 35 is reasonable to anticipate that the property will not be put to an unrelated use by the donee. In the case of a contribution of tangible personal property to or for the use of a museum, if the object donated is of a general type normally retained by such museum or other museums for museum purposes, it will be reasonable for the donor to anticipate, unless he has actual knowledge to the contrary, that the object will not be put to an 40 unrelated use by the donee, whether or not the object is later sold or exchanged by the donee.

(4) *Property used in trade or business.* For purposes of applying subparagraphs (1) and (2) of this paragraph, property which is used in the trade or business, as defined in section 1231(b), shall be treated as a capital asset, except that any gain in respect of 45 such property which would have been recognized if the property had been sold by the donor at its fair market value at the time of its contribution to the charitable organization shall be treated as ordinary income to the extent that such gain would have constituted ordinary income by reason of the application of section 617 (d)(1), 1245(a), 1250(a), 1251(c), 1252(a), or 1254(a). 50

***

473

Sec. 170. Charitable, etc., contributions and gifts

(c) *Allocation of basis and gain--(1)* *In general.* Except as provided in subparagraph (2) of this paragraph:

(i) If a taxpayer makes a charitable contribution of less than his entire interest in appreciated property, whether or not the transfer is made in trust, as, for example, in the
5 case of a transfer of appreciated property to a pooled income fund described in section 642(c)(5) and § 1.642(c)-5, and is allowed a deduction under section 170 for a portion of the fair market value of such property, then for purposes of applying the reduction rules of section 170(e)(1) and this section to the contributed portion of the property the taxpayer's adjusted basis in such property at the time of the contribution shall be allocated under
10 section 170(e)(2) between the contributed portion of the property and the noncontributed portion.

(ii) The adjusted basis of the contributed portion of the property shall be that portion of the adjusted basis of the entire property which bears the same ratio to the total adjusted basis as the fair market value of the contributed portion of the property bears to the fair
15 market value of the entire property.

(iii) The ordinary income and the long-term capital gain which shall be taken into account in applying section 170(e)(1) and paragraph (a) of this section to the contributed portion of the property shall be the amount of gain which would have been recognized as ordinary income and long-term capital gain if such contributed portion had been sold by
20 the donor at its fair market value at the time of its contribution to the charitable organization.

(2) *Bargain sale.* (i) Section 1011(b) and § 1.1011-2 apply to bargain sales of property to charitable organizations. For purposes of applying the reduction rules of section 170(e) (1) and this section to the contributed portion of the property in the case of a bargain sale,
25 there shall be allocated under section 1011(b) to the contributed portion of the property that portion of the adjusted basis of the entire property that bears the same ratio to the total adjusted basis as the fair market value of the contributed portion of the property bears to the fair market value of the entire property. For purposes of applying section 170(e)(1) and paragraph (a) of this section to the contributed portion of the property in
30 such a case, there shall be allocated to the contributed portion the amount of gain that is not recognized on the bargain sale but that would have been recognized if such contributed portion had been sold by the donor at its fair market value at the time of its contribution to the charitable organization.

(ii) The term bargain sale, as used in this subparagraph, means a transfer of property
35 which is in part a sale or exchange of the property and in part a charitable contribution, as defined in section 170(c), of the property.

(3) *Ratio of ordinary income and capital gain.* For purposes of applying subparagraphs (1)(iii) and (2)(i) of this paragraph, the amount of ordinary income (or long-term capital gain) which would have been recognized if the contributed portion of the property had
40 been sold by the donor at its fair market value at the time of its contribution shall be that amount which bears the same ratio to the ordinary income (or long-term capital gain) which would have been recognized if the entire property had been sold by the donor at its fair market value at the time of its contribution as (i) the fair market value of the contributed portion at such time bears to (ii) the fair market value of the entire property at
45 such time. In the case of a bargain sale, the fair market value of the contributed portion for purposes of subdivision (i) is the amount determined by subtracting from the fair market value of the entire property the amount realized on the sale.

(4) *Donee's basis of property acquired.* The adjusted basis of the contributed portion of the property, as determined under subparagraph (1) or (2) of this paragraph, shall be
50 used by the donee in applying to the contributed portion such provisions as section 514(a)(1), relating to adjusted basis of debt-financed property; section 1015(a), relating to

basis of property acquired by gift; section 4940(c)(4), relating to capital gains and losses in determination of net investment income; and section 4942(f)(2)(B), relating to net short-term capital gain in determination of tax on failure to distribute income. The fair market value of the contributed portion of the property at the time of the contribution shall not be used by the donee as the basis of such contributed portion. $\quad$ 5

(d) *Illustrations.* The application of this section may be illustrated by the following examples:

Example 1. (a) On July 1, 1970, C, an individual, makes the following charitable contributions, all of which are made to a church except in the case of the stock (as indicated): $\quad$ 10

Property	Fair market value	Adjusted basis	Recognized gain sold
Ordinary income property................	$50,000	$35,000	$15,000
Property which, if sold, would produce long-term capital gain:			
(1) Stock held more than 6 months contributed to--			
(i) A church..................................	25,000	21,000	4,000
(ii) A private foundation not described in section 170(b)(1)(E).	15,000	10,000	5,000
(2) Tangible personal property held more than 6 months (put to unrelated use by church)...............	12,000	6,000	6,000
Total..	102,000	72,000	30,000

15

20

25

(b) After making the reductions required by paragraph (a) of this section, the amount of charitable contributions allowed (before application of section 170(b) limitations) is as 30 follows:

Property	Fair market value	Reduction	Contribution allowed
Ordinary income property............	$50,000	$15,000	$35,000
Property which, if sold, would produce long-term capital gain:			
(1) Stock contributed to:			
(i) The church..........................	25,000	....	25,000
(ii) The private foundation........	15,000	2,500	2,500
(2) Tangible personal property..	12,000	3,000	9,000
Total..	102,000	20,500	81,500

35

40

(c) If C were a corporation, rather than an individual, the amount of charitable 45 contributions allowed (before application of section 170(b) limitation) would be as follows:

Sec. 170. Charitable, etc., contributions and gifts

Property	Fair market value	Reduction	Contribution allowed
5 Ordinary income property.............	$50,000	$15,000	$35,000
Property which, if sold, would produce long-term capital gain:			
(1) Stock contributed to:			
(i) The church...........................	25,000	....	25,000
10 (ii) The private foundation........	15,000	3,125	11,875
(2) Tangible personal property...	12,000	3,750	8,250
Total...	102,000	21,875	80,125

Example 2. On March 1, 1970, D, an individual, contributes to a church intangible
15 property to which section 1245 applies which has a fair market value of $60,000 and an adjusted basis of $10,000. At the time of the contribution D has used the property in his business for more than 6 months. If the property had been sold by D at its fair market value at the time of its contribution, it is assumed that under section 1245 $20,000 of the gain of $50,000 would have been treated as ordinary income and $30,000 would have
20 been long-term capital gain. Under paragraph (a)(1) of this section, D's contribution of $60,000 is reduced by $20,000.

Example 3. The facts are the same as in Example 2 except that the property is contributed to a private foundation not described in section 170(b)(1)(E). Under paragraph (a) (1) and (2) of this section, D's contribution is reduced by $35,000 (100
25 percent of the ordinary income of $20,000 and 50 percent of the long-term capital gain of $30,000).

Example 4. (a) In 1971, E, an individual calendar-year taxpayer, contributes to a church stock held for more than 6 months which has a fair market value of $90,000 and an adjusted basis of $10,000. In 1972, E also contributes to a church stock held for more
30 than 6 months which has a fair market value of $20,000 and an adjusted basis of $10,000. E's contribution base for 1971 is $200,000; and for 1972, is $150,000. E makes no other charitable contributions for these 2 taxable years.

(b) For 1971 the amount of the contribution which may be taken into account under section 170(a) is limited by section 170(b)(1)(D)(i) to $60,000 ($200,000x30%), and A is
35 allowed a deduction for $60,000. Under section 170(b)(1)(D)(ii), E has a $30,000 carryover to 1972 of 30-percent capital gain property, as defined in paragraph (d)(3) of § 1.170A-8. For 1972 the amount of the charitable contributions deduction is $45,000 (total contributions of $50,000 [$30,000+$20,000] but not to exceed 30% of $150,000).

(c) Assuming, however, that in 1972 E elects under section 170(b)(1)(D)(iii) and
40 paragraph (d)(2) of § 1.170A-8 to have section 170(e)(1)(B) apply to his contributions and carryovers of 30-percent capital gain property, he must apply section 170(d)(1) as if section 170(e)(1)(B) had applied to the contribution for 1971. If section 170(e)(1)(B) had applied in 1971 to his contributions of 30-percent capital gain property, E's contribution would have been reduced from $90,000 to $50,000, the reduction of $40,000 being 50
45 percent of the gain of $80,000 ($90,000-$10,000) which would have been recognized as long-term capital gain if the property had been sold by E at its fair market value at the time of its contribution to the church. Accordingly, by taking the election into account, E has no carryover of 30-percent capital gain property to 1972 since the charitable contributions deduction of $60,000 allowed for 1971 in respect of that property exceeds
50 the reduced contribution of $50,000 for 1971 which may be taken into account by reason of the election. The charitable contributions deduction of $60,000 allowed for 1971 is not

Sec. 170. Charitable, etc., contributions and gifts

reduced by reason of the election.

(d) Since by reason of the election E is allowed under paragraph (a)(2) of this section a charitable contributions deduction for 1972 of $15,000 ($20,000-[($20,000-$10,000)x50%]) and since the $30,000 carryover from 1971 is eliminated, it would not be to E's advantage to make the election under section 170(b)(1)(D)(iii) in 1972.　　　5

Example 5. In 1970, F, an individual calendar-year taxpayer, sells to a church for $4,000 ordinary income property with a fair market value of $10,000 and an adjusted basis of $4,000. F's contribution base for 1970 is $20,000, and F makes no other charitable contributions in 1970. Thus, F makes a charitable contribution to the church of $6,000 ($10,000-$4,000 amount realized), which is 60% of the value of the property. The　10 amount realized on the bargain sale is 40% ($4,000/$10,000) of the value of the property. In applying section 1011(b) to the bargain sale, adjusted basis in the amount of $1,600 ($4,000 adjusted basis x 40%) is allocated under § 1.1011-2(b) to the noncontributed portion of the property, and F recognizes $2,400 ($4,000 amount realized less $1,600 adjusted basis) of ordinary income. Under paragraphs (a)(1) and (c)(2)(i) of this section,　15 F's contribution of $6,000 is reduced by $3,600 ($6,000 - [$4,000 adjusted basis x 60%]) (i.e., the amount of ordinary income that would have been recognized on the contributed portion had the property been sold). The reduced contribution of $2,400 consists of the portion ($4,000 x 60%) of the adjusted basis not allocated to the noncontributed portion of the property. That is, the reduced contribution consists of the portion of the adjusted　20 basis allocated to the contributed portion. Under sections 1012 and 1015(a) the basis of the property to the church is $6,400 ($4,000 + $2,400).

Example 6. In 1970, G, an individual calendar-year taxpayer, sells to a church for $6,000 ordinary income property with a fair market value of $10,000 and an adjusted basis of $4,000. G's contribution base for 1970 is $20,000, and G makes no other　25 charitable contributions in 1970. Thus, G makes a charitable contribution to the church of $4,000 ($10,000 - $6,000 amount realized), which is 40% of the value of the property. The amount realized on the bargain sale is 60% ($6,000/$10,000) of the value of the property. In applying section 1011(b) to the bargain sale, adjusted basis in the amount of $2,400 ($4,000 adjusted basis x 60%) is allocated under § 1.1011-2(b) to the　30 noncontributed portion of the property, and G recognizes $3,600 ($6,000 amount realized less $2,400 adjusted basis) of ordinary income. Under paragraphs (a)(1) and (c)(2)(i) of this section, G's contribution of $4,000 is reduced by $2,400 ($4,000 - [$4,000 adjusted basis x 40%]) (i.e., the amount of ordinary income that would have been recognized on the contributed portion had the property been sold). The reduced contribution of $1,600　35 consist of the portion ($4,000x40%) of the adjusted basis not allocated to the noncontributed portion of the property. That is, the reduced contribution consists of the portion of the adjusted basis allocated to the contributed portion. Under sections 1012 and 1015(a) the basis of the property to the church is $7,600 ($6,000+$1,600).

Example 7. In 1970, H, an individual calendar-year taxpayer, sells to a church for　40 $2,000 stock held for not more than 6 months which has an adjusted basis of $4,000 and a fair market value of $10,000. H's contribution base for 1970 is $20,000, and H makes no other charitable contributions in 1970. Thus, H makes a charitable contribution to the church of $8,000 ($10,000-$2,000 amount realized), which is 80% of the value of the property. The amount realized on the bargain sale is 20% ($2,000/$10,000) of the value　45 of the property. In applying section 1011(b) to the bargain sale, adjusted basis in the amount of $800 ($4,000 adjusted basis x 20%) is allocated under § 1.1011-2(b) to the noncontributed portion of the property, and H recognizes $1,200 ($2,000 amount realized less $800 adjusted basis) of ordinary income. Under paragraphs (a)(1) and (c)(2)(i) of this section, H's contribution of $8,000 is reduced by $4,800 ($8,000 - [$4,000 adjusted　50 basisx80%]) (i.e., the amount of ordinary income that would have been recognized on the contributed portion had the property been sold). The reduced contribution of $3,200 consists of the portion ($4,000x80%) of the adjusted basis not allocated to the noncontributed portion of the property. That is, the reduced contribution consists of the portion of the adjusted basis allocated to the contributed portion. Under sections 1012 and 1015(a) the basis of the property to the church is $5,200 ($2,000+$3,200).

Example 8. In 1970, F, an individual calendar-year taxpayer, sells for $4,000 to a private foundation not described in section 170(b)(1)(E) property to which section 1245 applies which has a fair market value of $10,000 and an adjusted basis of $4,000. F's contribution base for 1970 is $20,000, and F makes no other charitable contributions in 1970. At the time of the bargain sale, F has used the property in his business for more than 6 months. Thus F makes a charitable contribution of $6,000 ($10,000-$4,000 amount realized), which is 60% of the value of the property. The amount realized on the bargain sale is 40% ($4,000/$10,000) of the value of the property. If the property had been sold by F at its fair market value at the time of its contribution, it is assumed that under section 1245 $4,000 of the gain of $6,000 ($10,000-$4,000 adjusted basis) would have been treated as ordinary income and $2,000 would have been long-term capital gain. In applying section 1011(b) to the bargain sale, adjusted basis in the amount of $1,600 ($4,000 adjusted basis x 40%) is allocated under § 1.1011-2(b) to the noncontributed portion of the property, and F's recognized gain of $2,400 ($4,000 amount realized less $1,600 adjusted basis) consists of $1,600 ($4,000x40%) of ordinary income and $800 ($2,000x40%) of long-term capital gain. Under paragraphs (a) and (c)(2)(i) of this section, F's contribution of $6,000 is reduced by $3,000 (the sum of $2,400 ($4,000x60%) of ordinary income and $600 ([$2,000x60%] x 50%) of long-term capital gain) (i.e., the amount of gain that would have been recognized on the contributed portion had the property been sold). The reduced contribution of $3,000 consists of $2,400 ($4,000x60%) of adjusted basis and $600 ([$2,000x60%] x 50%) of long-term capital gain not used as a reduction under paragraph (a)(2) of this section. Under sections 1012 and 1015(a) the basis of the property to the private foundation is $6,400 ($4,000+$2,400).

Example 9. On January 1, 1970, A, an individual, transfers to a charitable remainder annuity trust described in section 664 (d)(1) stock which he has held for more than 6 months and which has a fair market value of $250,000 and an adjusted basis of $50,000, an irrevocable remainder interest in the property being contributed to a private foundation not described in section 170(b)(1)(E). The trusts provides that an annuity of $12,500 a year is payable to A at the end of each year for 20 years. By reference to § 20.2031-7A(c) of this chapter (Estate Tax Regulations) the figure in column (2) opposite 20 years is 11.4699. Therefore, under § 1.664-2 the fair market value of the gift of the remainder interest to charity is $106,626.25 ($250,000 - [$12,500x11.4699]). Under paragraph (c)(1) (ii) of this section, the adjusted basis allocated to the contributed portion of the property is $21,325.25 ($50,000x$106,626.25/$250,000). Under paragraphs (a)(2) and (c)(1) of this section, A's contribution is reduced by $42,650.50 (50 percent x [$106,626.25-$21,325.25]) to $63,975.75 ($106,626.25-$42,650.50). If, however, the irrevocable remainder interest in the property had been contributed to a section 170(b)(1)(A) organization, A's contribution of $106,626.25 would not be reduced under paragraph (a) of this section.

Example 10. (a) On July 1, 1970, B, a calendar-year individual taxpayer, sells to a church for $75,000 intangible property to which section 1245 applies which has a fair market value of $250,000 and an adjusted basis of $75,000. Thus, B makes a charitable contribution to the church of $175,000 ($250,000-$75,000 amount realized), which is 70% ($175,000/$250,000) of the value of the property, the amount realized on the bargain sale is 30% ($75,000/$250,000) of the value of the property. At the time of the bargain sale, B has used the property in his business for more than 6 months. B's contribution base for 1970 is $500,000, and B makes no other charitable contributions in 1970. If the property had been sold by B at its fair market value at the time of its contribution, it is assumed that under section 1245 $105,000 of the gain of $175,000 ($250,000-$75,000 adjusted basis) would have been treated as ordinary income and $70,000 would have been long-term capital gain. In applying section 1011(b) to the bargain sale, adjusted basis in the amount of $22,500 ($75,000 adjusted basis x 30%) is allocated under § 1.1011-2(b) to the noncontributed portion of the property and B's recognized gain of $52,500 ($75,000 amount realized less $22,500 adjusted basis) consists of $31,500 ($105,000x30%) of ordinary income and $21,000 ($70,000x30%) of long term capital gain.

(b) Under paragraphs (a)(1) and (c)(2)(i) of this section B's contribution of $175,000 is reduced by $73,500 ($105,000x70%) (i.e., the amount of ordinary income that would have been recognized on the contributed portion had the property been sold). The reduced contribution of $101,500 consists of $52,500 [$75,000x70%] of adjusted basis allocated to the contributed portion of the property and $49,000 [$70,000x70%] of long-term capital gain allocated to the contributed portion. Under sections 1012 and 1015(a) the basis of the property to the church is $127,500 ($75,000+$52,500).

***

Reg § 1.170A-8   Limitations on charitable deductions by individuals.

(a) *Percentage limitations*--(1) *In general.* An individual's charitable contributions deduction is subject to 20-, 30-, and 50-percent limitations unless the individual qualifies for the unlimited charitable contributions deduction under section 170(b)(1)(C). For a discussion of these limitations and examples of their application, see paragraphs (b) through (f) of this section. If a husband and wife make a joint return, the deduction for contributions is the aggregate of the contributions made by the spouses, and the limitations in section 170(b) and this section are based on the aggregate contribution base of the spouses. A charitable contribution by an individual to or for the use of an organization described in section 170(c) may be deductible even though all, or some portion, of the funds of the organization may be used in foreign countries for charitable or educational purposes.

(2) ``To'' or ``for the use of'' defined. For purposes of section 170, a contribution of an income interest in property, whether or not such contributed interest is transferred in trust, for which a deduction is allowed under section 170(f)(2)(B) or (3)(A) shall be considered as made ``for the use of'' rather than ``to'' the charitable organization. A contribution of a remainder interest in property, whether or not such contributed interest is transferred in trust, for which a deduction is allowed under section 170(f)(2)(A) or (3)(A), shall be considered as made ``to'' the charitable organization except that, if such interest is transferred in trust and, pursuant to the terms of the trust instrument, the interest contributed is, upon termination of the predecessor estate, to be held in trust for the benefit of such organization, the contribution shall be considered as made ``for the use of'' such organization. Thus, for example, assume that A transfers property to a charitable remainder annuity trust described in section 664(d)(1) which is required to pay to B for life an annuity equal to 5 percent of the initial fair market value of the property transferred in trust. The trust instrument provides that after B's death the remainder interest in the trust is to be transferred to M Church or, in the event M Church is not an organization described in section 170(c) when the amount is to be irrevocably transferred to such church, to an organization which is described in section 170(c) at that time. The contribution by A of the remainder interest shall be considered as made ``to'' M Church. However, if in the trust instrument A had directed that after B's death the remainder interest is to be held in trust for the benefit of M Church, the contribution shall be considered as made ``for the use of'' M Church. This subparagraph does not apply to the

479

contribution of a partial interest in property, or of an undivided portion of such partial interest, if such partial interest is the donor's entire interest in the property and such entire interest was not created to avoid section 170(f)(2) or (3)(A). See paragraph (a)(2) of § 1.170A-6 and paragraphs (a)(2)(i) and (b)(1) of § 1.170A-7.

5   (b) *50-percent limitation.* An individual may deduct charitable contributions made during a taxable year to any one or more section 170(b)(1)(A) organizations, as defined in § 1.170A-9, to the extent that such contributions in the aggregate do not exceed 50 percent of his contribution base, as defined in section 170(b)(1)(F) and paragraph (e) of this section, for the taxable year. However, see paragraph (d) of this section for a
10 limitation on the amount of charitable contributions of 30-percent capital gain property. To qualify for the 50-percent limitation the contributions must be made ``to,'' and not merely ``for the use of,'' one of the specified organizations. A contribution to an organization referred to in section 170(c)(2), other than a section 170(b)(1)(A) organization, will not qualify for the 50-percent limitation even though such organization makes the contribution
15 available to an organization which is a section 170 (b)(1)(A) organization. For provisions relating to the carryover of contributions in excess of 50-percent of an individual's contribution base see section 170(d)(1) and paragraph (b) of § 1.170A-10.

    (c) *20-percent limitation.* (1) An individual may deduct charitable contributions made during a taxable year:
20   (i) To any one or more charitable organizations described in section 170(c) other than section 170(b)(1)(A) organizations, as defined in § 1.170A-9, and,

    (ii) For the use of any charitable organization described in section 170(c), to the extent that such contributions in the aggregate do not exceed the lesser of the limitations under subparagraph (2) of this paragraph.
25   (2) For purposes of subparagraph (1) of this paragraph the limitations are:

    (i) 20 percent of the individual's contribution base, as defined in paragraph (e) of this section, for the taxable year, or

    (ii) The excess of 50 percent of the individual's contribution base, as so defined, for the taxable year over the total amount of the charitable contributions allowed under
30 section 170(b)(1)(A) and paragraph (b) of this section, determined by first reducing the amount of such contributions under section 170(e)(1) and paragraph (a) of § 1.170A-4 but without applying the 30-percent limitation under section 170(b)(1)(D)(i) and paragraph (d)(1) of this section. However, see paragraph (d) of this section for a limitation on the amount of charitable contributions of 30-percent capital gain property. If an election under
35 section 170(b)(1)(D)(iii) and paragraph (d)(2) of this section applies to any contributions of 30-percent capital gain property made during the taxable year or carried over to the taxable year, the amount allowed for the taxable year under paragraph (b) of this section with respect to such contributions for purposes of applying subdivision (ii) of this subparagraph shall be the reduced amount of such contributions determined by applying
40 paragraph (d)(2) of this section.

    (d) *30-percent limitation*--(1) *In general.* An individual may deduct charitable contributions of 30-percent capital gain property, as defined in subparagraph (3) of this paragraph, made during a taxable year to or for the use of any charitable organization described in section 170(c) to the extent that such contributions in the aggregate do not
45 exceed 30-percent of his contribution base, as defined in paragraph (e) of this section, subject, however, to the 50- and 20-percent limitations prescribed by paragraphs (b) and (c) of this section. For purposes of applying the 50-percent and 20-percent limitations described in paragraphs (b) and (c) of this section, charitable contributions of 30-percent capital gain property paid during the taxable year, and limited as provided by this
50 subparagraph, shall be taken into account after all other charitable contributions paid during the taxable year. For provisions relating to the carryover of certain contributions of

Sec. 170. Charitable, etc., contributions and gifts

30-percent capital gain property in excess of 30-percent of an individual's contribution base, see section 170(b)(1)(D)(ii) and paragraph (c) of § 1.170A-10.

(2) *Election by an individual to have section 170(e)(1)(B) apply to contributions--(i) In general.* (A) An individual may elect under section 170(b)(1)(D)(iii) for any taxable year to have the reduction rule of section 170(e)(1)(B) and paragraph (a) of § 1.170A-4 apply to 5 all his charitable contributions of 30-percent capital gain property made during such taxable year or carried over to such taxable year from a taxable year beginning after December 31, 1969. If such election is made such contributions shall be treated as contributions of section 170(e) capital gain property in accordance with paragraph (b)(2) (iii) of § 1.170A-4. The election may be made with respect to contributions of 30-percent 10 capital gain property carried over to the taxable year even though the individual has not made any contribution of 30-percent capital gain property in such year. If such an election is made, section 170(b)(1)(D)(i) and (ii) and subparagraph (1) of this paragraph shall not apply to such contributions made during such year. However, such contributions must be reduced as required under section 170(e)(1)(B) and paragraph (a) of § 1.170A-4.   15

(B) If there are carryovers to such taxable year of charitable contributions of 30-percent capital gain property made in preceding taxable years beginning after December 31, 1969, the amount of such contributions in each such preceding year shall be reduced as if section 170(e)(1)(B) had applied to them in the preceding year and shall be carried over to the taxable year and succeeding taxable years under section 170(d)(1) and 20 paragraph (b) of § 1.170A-10 as contributions of property other than 30-percent capital gain property. For purposes of applying the immediately preceding sentence, the percentage limitations under section 170(b) for the preceding taxable year and for any taxable years intervening between such year and the year of the election shall not be redetermined and the amount of any deduction allowed for such years under section 170 25 in respect of the charitable contributions of 30-percent capital gain property in the preceding taxable year shall not be redetermined. However, the amount of the deduction so allowed under section 170 in the preceding taxable year must be subtracted from the reduced amount of the charitable contributions made in such year in order to determine the excess amount which is carried over from such year under section 170(d)(1). If the 30 amount of the deduction so allowed in the preceding taxable year equals or exceeds the reduced amount of the charitable contributions, there shall be no carryover from such year to the year of the election.

(C) An election under this subparagraph may be made for each taxable year in which charitable contributions of 30-percent capital gain property are made or to which they are 35 carried over under section 170(b)(1)(D)(ii). If there are also carryovers under section 170(d)(1) to the year of the election by reason of an election made under this subparagraph for a previous taxable year, such carryovers under section 170(d)(1) shall not be redetermined by reason of the subsequent election.

(ii) *Husband and wife making joint return.* If a husband and wife make a joint return of 40 income for a contribution year and one of the spouses elects under this subparagraph in a later year when he files a separate return, or if a spouse dies after a contribution year for which a joint return is made, any excess contribution of 30-percent capital gain property which is carried over to the election year from the contribution year shall be allocated between the husband and wife as provided in paragraph (d)(4)(i) and (iii) of § 45 1.170A-10. If a husband and wife file separate returns in a contribution year, any election under this subparagraph in a later year when a joint return is filed shall be applicable to any excess contributions of 30-percent capital gain property of either taxpayer carried over from the contribution year to the election year. The immediately preceding sentence shall also apply where two single individuals are subsequently married and file a joint 50 return. A remarried individual who filed a joint return with his former spouse for a

481

contribution year and thereafter files a joint return with his present spouse shall treat the carryover to the election year as provided in paragraph (d)(4)(ii) of § 1.170A-10.

(iii) *Manner of making election.* The election under subdivision (i) of this subparagraph shall be made by attaching to the income tax return for the election year a statement
5 indicating that the election under section 170(b)(1)(D)(iii) and this subparagraph is being made. If there is a carryover to the taxable year of any charitable contributions of 30-percent capital gain property from a previous taxable year or years, the statement shall show a recomputation, in accordance with this subparagraph and § 1.170A-4, of such carryover, setting forth sufficient information with respect to the previous taxable year or
10 any intervening year to show the basis of the recomputation. The statement shall indicate the district director, or the director of the internal revenue service center, with whom the return for the previous taxable year or years was filed, the name or names in which such return or returns were filed, and whether each such return was a joint or separate return.

(3) *30-percent capital gain property defined.* If there is a charitable contribution of a
15 capital asset which, if it were sold by the donor at its fair market value at the time of its contribution, would result in the recognition of gain all, or any portion, of which would be long-term capital gain and if the amount of such contribution is not required to be reduced under section 170(e)(1)(B) and § 1.170A-4(a)(2), such capital asset shall be treated as ``30-percent capital gain property'' for purposes of section 170 and the regulations
20 thereunder. For such purposes any property which is property used in the trade or business, as defined in section 1231(b), shall be treated as a capital asset. However, see paragraph (b)(4) of § 1.170A-4. For the treatment of such property as section 170(e) capital gain property, see paragraph (b)(2)(iii) of § 1.170A-4.

(e) *Contribution base defined.* For purposes of section 170 the term contribution base
25 means adjusted gross income under section 62, computed without regard to any net operating loss carryback to the taxable year under section 172. See section 170(b)(1)(F).

(f) *Illustrations.* The application of this section may be illustrated by the following examples:

Example 1. B, an individual, reports his income on the calendar-year basis and for
30 1970 has a contribution base of $100,000. During 1970 he makes charitable contributions of $70,000 in cash, of which $40,000 is given to section 170(b)(1)(A) organizations and $30,000 is given to other organizations described in section 170(c). Accordingly, B is allowed a charitable contributions deduction of $50,000 (50% of $100,000), which consists of the $40,000 contributed to section 170(b)(1)(A) organizations and $10,000 of
35 the $30,000 contributed to the other organizations. Under paragraph (c) of this section, only $10,000 of the $30,000 contributed to the other organizations is allowed as a deduction since such contribution of $30,000 is allowed to the extent of the lesser of $20,000 (20% of $100,000) or $10,000 ([50% of $100,000]-$40,000 (contributions allowed under section 170(b)(1)(A) and paragraph (b) of this section)). Under section 170
40 (b)(1)(D)(ii) and (d)(1) and § 1.170A-10, B is not allowed a carryover to 1971 or to any other taxable year for any of the $20,000 ($30,000-$10,000) not deductible under section 170(b)(1)(B) and paragraph (c) of this section.

Example 2. C, an individual, reports his income on the calendar-year basis and for 1970 has a contribution base of $100,000. During 1970 he makes charitable contributions
45 of $40,000 in 30-percent capital gain property to section 170(b)(1)(A) organizations and of $30,000 in cash to other organizations described in section 170(c). The 20-percent limitation in section 170(b)(1)(B) and paragraph (c) of this section is applied before the 30-percent limitation in section 170(b)(1)(D)(i) and paragraph (d) of this section; accordingly section 170(b)(1)(B)(ii) limits the deduction for the $30,000 cash contribution
50 to $10,000 ([50% of $100,000]- $40,000). The amount of the contribution of 30-percent capital gain property is limited by section 170(b)(1)(D)(i) and paragraph (d) of this section

to $30,000 (30% of $100,000). Accordingly, C's charitable contributions deduction for 1970 is limited to $40,000 ($10,000+$30,000). Under section 170 (b)(1)(D)(ii) and paragraph (c) of § 1.170A-10, C is allowed a carryover to 1971 of $10,000 ($40,000-$30,000) in respect of his contributions of 30-percent capital gain property. C is not allowed a carryover to 1971 or to any other taxable year for any of the $20,000 cash ($30,000-$10,000) not deductible under section 170(b)(1)(B) and paragraph (c) of this section.

Example 3. (a) D, an individual, reports his income on the calendar-year basis and for 1970 has a contribution base of $100,000. During 1970 he makes charitable contributions of $70,000 in cash, of which $40,000 is given to section 170(b)(1)(A) organizations and $30,000 is given to other organizations described in section 170(c). During 1971 D makes charitable contributions to a section 170(b)(1)(A) organization of $12,000, consisting of cash of $1,000 and $11,000 in 30-percent capital gain property. His contribution base for 1971 is $10,000.

(b) For 1970, D is allowed a charitable contributions deduction of $50,000 (50% of $100,000), which consists of the $40,000 contributed to section 170(b)(1)(A) organizations and $10,000 of the $30,000 contributed to the other organizations. Under paragraph (c) of this section, only $10,000 of the $30,000 contributed to the other organizations is allowed as a deduction since such contribution of $30,000 is allowed to the extent of the lesser of $20,000 (20% of $100,000) or $10,000 ([50% of $100,000]- $40,000 (contributions allowed under section 170(b)(1)(A) and paragraph (b) of this section)). D is not allowed a carryover to 1971 or to any other taxable year for any of the $20,000 ($30,000-$10,000) not deductible under section 170(b)(1)(B) and paragraph (c) of this section.

(c) For 1971, D is allowed a charitable contributions deduction of $4,000, consisting of $1,000 cash and $3,000 of the 30-percent capital gain property (30% of $10,000). Under section 170(b)(1)(D)(ii) and paragraph (c) of § 1.170A-10, D is allowed a carryover to 1972 of $8,000 ($11,000-$3,000) in respect of his contribution of 30-percent capital gain property in 1971.

Example 4. (a) E, an individual, reports his income on the calendar-year basis and for 1970 has a contribution base of $100,000. During 1970 he makes charitable contributions of $70,000 in cash, of which $40,000 is given to section 170(b)(1)(A) organizations and $30,000 is given to other organizations described in section 170(c). During 1971 E makes charitable contributions to a section 170(b)(1)(A) organization of $14,000 consisting of cash of $3,000 and $11,000 in 30-percent capital gain property. His contribution base for 1971 is $10,000.

(b) For 1970, E is allowed a charitable contributions deduction of $50,000 (50% of $100,000), which consists of the $40,000 contributed to section 170(b)(1)(A) organizations and $10,000 of the $30,000 contributed to the other organizations. Under paragraph (c) of this section, only $10,000 of the $30,000 contributed to the other organizations is allowed as a deduction since such contribution of $30,000 is allowed to the extent of the lesser of $20,000 (20% of $100,000) or ($10,000 ([50% of $100,000]- $40,000 (contributions allowed under section 170(b)(1)(A) and paragraph (b) of this section)). E is not allowed a carryover to 1971 or to any other taxable year for any of the $20,000 ($30,000-$10,000) not deductible under section 170(b)(1)(B) and paragraph (c) of this section.

(c) For 1971, E is allowed a charitable contributions deduction of $5,000 (50% of $10,000), consisting of $3,000 cash and $2,000 of the $3,000 (30% of $10,000) 30-percent capital gain property which is taken into account. This result is reached because, as provided in section 170(b)(1)(D)(i) and paragraph (d)(1) of this section, cash contributions are taken into account before charitable contributions of 30-percent capital gain property. Under section 170(b)(1)(D)(ii) and (d)(1) and paragraphs (b) and (c) of § 1.170A-10, E is allowed a carryover of $9,000 ([$11,000-$3,000] plus [$6,000 -$5,000]) to 1972 in respect of his contribution of 30-percent capital gain property in 1971.

Example 5. In 1970, C, a calendar-year individual taxpayer, contributes to section
5 170(b)(1)(A) organizations the amount of $8,000, consisting of $3,000 in cash and $5,000 in 30-percent capital gain property. In 1970, C also makes charitable contributions of $8,500 in 30 percent capital gain property to other organizations described in section 170(c). C's contribution base for 1970 is $20,000. The 20-percent limitation in section 170(b)(1)(B) and paragraph (c) of this section is applied before the 30-percent limitation
10 in section 170(b)(1)(D)(i) and paragraph (d) of this section; accordingly, section 170(b)(1) (B)(ii) limits the deduction for the $8,500 of contributions to the other organizations described in section 170(c) to $2,000 ([50% of $20,000]-[$3,000+$5,000]). However, the total amount of contributions of 30-percent capital gain property which is allowed as a deduction for 1970 is limited by section 170(b)(1)(D)(i) and paragraph (d) of this section
15 to $6,000 (30% of $20,000), consisting of the $5,000 contribution to the section 170(b)(1) (A) organizations and $1,000 of the contributions to the other organizations described in section 170(c). Accordingly C is allowed a charitable contributions deduction for 1970 of $9,000, which consists of $3,000 cash and $6,000 of the $13,500 of 30-percent capital gain property. C is not allowed to carryover to 1971 or any other year the remaining
20 $7,500 because his contributions of 30-percent capital gain property for 1970 to section 170(b)(1)(A) organizations amount only to $5,000 and do not exceed $6,000 (30% of $20,000). Thus, the requirement of section 170(b)(1)(D)(ii) is not satisfied.

Example 6. During 1971, D, a calendar-year individual taxpayer, makes a charitable contribution to a church of $8,000, consisting of $5,000 in cash and $3,000 in 30-percent
25 capital gain property. For such year, D's contribution base is $10,000. Accordingly, D is allowed a charitable contributions deduction for 1971 of $5,000 (50% of $10,000) of cash. Under section 170(d)(1) and paragraph (b) of § 1.170A-10, D is allowed a carryover to 1972 of his $3,000 contribution of 30-percent capital gain property, even though such amount does not exceed 30 percent of his contribution base for 1971.

30 *Example 7.* In 1970, E, a calendar-year individual taxpayer, makes a charitable contribution to a section 170(b)(1)(A) organization in the amount of $10,000, consisting of $8,000 in 30-percent capital gain property and of $2,000 (after reduction under section 170(e)) in other property. E's contribution base of 1970 is $20,000. Accordingly, E is allowed a charitable contributions deduction for 1970 of $8,000, consisting of the $2,000
35 of property the amount of which was reduced under section 170(e) and $6,000 (30% of $20,000) of the 30-percent capital gain property. Under section 170(b)(1)(D)(ii) and paragraph (c) of § 1.170A-10, E is allowed to carryover to 1971 $2,000 ($8,000-$6,000) of his contribution of 30-percent capital gain property.

Example 8. (a) In 1972, F, calendar-year individual taxpayer, makes a charitable
40 contribution to a church of $4,000, consisting of $1,000 in cash and $3,000 in 30-percent capital gain property. In addition, F makes a charitable contribution in 1972 of $2,000 in cash to an organization described in section 170(c)(4). F also has a carryover from 1971 under section 170(d)(1) of $5,000 (none of which consists of contributions of 30-percent capital gain property) and a carryover from 1971 under section 170(b)(1)(D)(ii) of $6,000
45 of contributions of 30-percent capital gain property. F's contribution base for 1972 is $11,000.

Accordingly, F is allowed a charitable contributions deduction for 1972 of $5,500 (50% of $11,000), which consists of $1,000 cash contributed in 1972 to the church, $3,000 of 30-percent capital gain property contributed in 1972 to the church, and $1,500 (carryover
50 of $5,000 but not to exceed [$5,500-($1,000 +$3,000)]) of the carryover from 1971 under section 170(d)(1).

Sec. 170. Charitable, etc., contributions and gifts

(b) No deduction is allowed for 1972 for the contribution in that year of $2,000 cash to the section 170(c)(4) organization since section 170(b)(1)(B)(ii) and paragraph (c) of this section limit the deduction for such contribution to $0([50% of $11,000]-[$1,000 +$1,500+ $3,000]). Moreover, F is not allowed a carryover to 1973 or to any other year for any of such $2,000 cash contributed to the section 170(c)(4) organization.   5

(c) Under section 170(d)(1) and paragraph (b) of § 1.170A-10, F is allowed a carryover to 1973 from 1971 of $3,500 ($5,000-$1,500) of contributions of other than 30-percent capital gain property. Under section 170(b)(1)(D)(ii) and paragraph (c) of § 1.170A-10, F is allowed a carryover to 1973 from 1971 of $6,000 ($6,000-$0 of such carryover treated as paid in 1972) of contributions of 30-percent capital gain property.   10 The portion of such $6,000 carryover from 1971 which is treated as paid in 1972 is $0 ([50% of $11,000]-[$4,000 contributions to the church in 1972 plus $1,500 of section 170(d)(1) carryover treated as paid in 1972]).

Example 9. (a) In 1970, A, a calendar-year individual taxpayer, makes a charitable contribution to a church of 30-percent capital gain property having a fair market value of   15 $60,000 and an adjusted basis of $10,000. A's contribution base for 1970 is $50,000, and he makes no other charitable contributions in that year. A does not elect for 1970 under paragraph (d)(2) of this section to have section 170(e)(1)(B) apply to such contribution. Accordingly, under section 170(b)(1)(D)(i) and paragraph (d) of this section, A is allowed a charitable contributions deduction for 1970 of $15,000 (30% of $50,000). Under section   20 170(b)(1)(D)(ii) and paragraph (c) of § 1.170A-10, A is allowed a carryover to 1971 of $45,000 ($60,000-$15,000) for his contribution of 30-percent capital gain property.

(b) In 1971, A makes a charitable contribution to a church of 30-percent capital gain property having a fair market value of $11,000 and an adjusted basis of $10,000. A's contribution base for 1971 is $60,000, and he makes no other charitable contributions in   25 that year. A elects for 1971 under paragraph (d)(2) of this section to have section 170(e) (1)(B) and § 1.170A-4 apply to his contribution of $11,000 in that year and to his carryover of $45,000 from 1970. Accordingly, he is required to recompute his carryover from 1970 as if section 170(e)(1)(B) had applied to his contribution of 30-percent capital gain property in that year.   30

(c) If section 170(e)(1)(B) had applied in 1970 to his contribution of 30-percent capital gain property, A's contribution would have been reduced from $60,000 to $35,000, the reduction of $25,000 being 50 percent of the gain of $50,000 ($60,000-$10,000) which would have been recognized as long-term capital gain if the property had been sold by A at its fair market value at the time of the contribution in 1970. Accordingly, by taking the   35 election under paragraph (d)(2) of this section into account, A has a recomputed carryover to 1971 of $20,000 ($35,000- $15,000) of his contribution of 30-percent capital gain property in 1970. However, A's charitable contributions deduction of $15,000 allowed for 1970 is not recomputed by reason of the election.

(d) Pursuant to the election for 1971, the contribution of 30-percent capital gain   40 property for 1971 is reduced from $11,000 to $10,500, the reduction of $500 being 50 percent of the gain of $1,000 ($11,000-$10,000) which would have been recognized as long-term capital gain if the property had been sold by A at its fair market value at the time of its contribution in 1971.

(e) Accordingly, A is allowed a charitable contributions deduction for 1971 of $30,000   45 (total contributions of $30,500 [$20,000+ $10,500] but not to exceed 50% of $60,000).

(f) Under section 170(d)(1) and paragraph (b) of § 1.170A-10, A is allowed a carryover of $500 ($30,500-$30,000) to 1972 and the 3 succeeding taxable years. The $500 carryover, which by reason of the election is no longer treated as a contribution of 30-percent capital gain property, is treated as carried over under paragraph (b) of §   50 1.170A-10 from 1970 since in 1971 current year contributions are deducted before

485

contributions which are carried over from preceding taxable years.

Example 10. The facts are the same as in Example 9 except that A also makes a charitable contribution in 1971 of $2,000 cash to a private foundation not described in section 170(b)(1)(E) and that A's contribution base for that year is $62,000, instead of
5 $60,000. Accordingly, A is allowed a charitable contributions deduction for 1971 of $31,000, determined in the following manner Under section 170(b)(1)(A) and paragraph (b) of this section, A is allowed a charitable contributions deduction for 1971 of $30,500, consisting of $10,500 of property contributed to the church in 1971 and of $20,000 (carryover of $20,000 but not to exceed [($62,000x50%)-$10,500]) of contributions of
10 property carried over to 1971 under section 170(d)(1) and paragraph (b) of § 1.170A-10. Under section 170(b)(1)(B) and paragraph (c) of this section, A is allowed a charitable contributions deduction for 1971 of $500 ([50% of $62,000]-[$10,500+ $20,000]) of cash contributed to the private foundation in that year. A is not allowed a carryover to 1972 or to any other taxable year for any of the $1,500 ($2,000-$500) cash not deductible in 1971
15 under section 170(b)(1)(B) and paragraph (c) of this section.

Example 11. The facts are the same as in Example 9 except that A's contribution base for 1970 is $120,000. Thus, before making the election under paragraph (d)(2) of this section for 1971, A is allowed a charitable contributions deduction for 1970 of $36,000 (30% of $120,000) and is allowed a carryover to 1971 of $24,000 ($60,000-$36,000). By
20 making the election for 1971, A is required to recompute the carryover from 1970, which is reduced from $24,000 to zero, since the charitable contributions deduction of $36,000 allowed for 1970 exceeds the reduced $35,000 contribution for 1970 which iay be taken into account by reason of the election for 1971. Accordingly, A is allowed a deduction for 1971 of $10,500 and is allowed no carryover to 1972, since the reduced contribution for
25 1971 ($10,500) does not exceed the limitation of $30,000 (50% of $60,000) for 1971 which applies under section 170(d)(1) and paragraph (b) of § 1.170A-10. A's charitable contributions deduction of $36,000 allowed for 1970 is not recomputed by reason of the election. Thus, it is not to A's advantage to make the election under paragraph (d)(2) of this section.

30 *Example 12*. (a) B, an individual, reports his income on the calendar-year basis and for 1970 has a contribution base of $100,000. During 1970 he makes charitable contributions of $70,000, consisting of $50,000 in 30-percent capital gain property contributed to a church and $20,000 in cash contributed to a private foundation not described in section 170(b)(1)(E). For 1971, B's contribution base is $40,000, and in that year he makes a
35 charitable contribution of $5,000 in cash to such private foundation. During the years involved B makes no other charitable contributions.

(b) The amount of the contribution of 30-percent capital gain property which may be taken into account for 1970 is limited by section 170(b)(1)(D)(i) and paragraph (d) of this section to $30,000 (30% of $100,000). Accordingly, under section 170(b)(1)(A) and
40 paragraph (b) of this section B is allowed a deduction for 1970 of $30,000 of 30-percent capital gain property (contribution of $30,000 but not to exceed $50,000 [50% of $100,000]). No deduction is allowed for 1970 for the contribution in that year of $20,000 of cash to the private foundation since section 170(b)(1)(B)(ii) and paragraph (c) of this section limit the deduction for such contribution to $0 ([50% of $100,000]- $50,000, the
45 amount of the contribution of 30-percent capital gain property).

(c) Under section 170(b)(1)(D)(ii) and paragraph (c) of § 1.170A-10, B is allowed a carryover to 1971 of $20,000 ($50,000-[30% of $100,000]) of his contribution in 1970 of 30-percent capital gain property. B is not allowed a carryover to 1971 or to any other taxable year for any of the $20,000 cash contribution in 1970 which is not deductible
50 under section 170(b)(1)(B) and paragraph (c) of this section.

(d) The amount of the contribution of 30-percent capital gain property which may be taken into account for 1971 is limited by section 170(b)(1)(D)(i) and paragraph (d) of this section to $12,000 (30% of $40,000).

Accordingly, under section 170(b)(1)(A) and paragraph (b) of this section B is allowed a deduction for 1971 of $12,000 of 30-percent capital gain property (contribution of $12,000 but not to exceed $20,000 [50% of $40,000]). No deduction is allowed for 1971 for the contribution in that year of $5,000 of cash to the private foundation, since section 170(b)(1)(B)(ii) and paragraph (c) of this section limit the deduction for such contribution to $0 ([50% of $40,000]-$20,000 carryover of 30-percent capital gain property from 1970).

(e) Under section 170(b)(1)(D)(ii) and paragraph (c) of § 1.170A-10, B is allowed a carryover to 1972 of $8,000 ($20,000-[30% of $40,000]) of his contribution in 1970 of 30-percent capital gain property. B is not allowed a carryover to 1972 or to any other taxable year for any of the $5,000 cash contribution for 1971 which is not deductible under section 170(b)(1)(B) and paragraph (c) of this section.

Example 13. D, an individual, reports his income on the calendar-year basis and for 1970 has a contribution base of $100,000. On March 1, 1970, he contributes to a church intangible property to which section 1245 applies which has a fair market value of $60,000 and an adjusted basis of $10,000. At the time of the contribution D has used the property in his business for more than 6 months. If the property had been sold by D at its fair market value at the time of its contribution, it is assumed that under section 1245 $20,000 of the gain of $50,000 would have been treated as ordinary income and $30,000 would have been long-term capital gain. Since the property contributed is ordinary income property within the meaning of paragraph (b)(1) of § 1.170A-4, D's contribution of $60,000 is reduced under paragraph (a)(1) of such section to $40,000 ($60,000-$20,000 ordinary income). However, since the property contributed is also 30-percent capital gain property within the meaning of paragraph (d)(3) of this section, D's deduction for 1970 is limited by section 170(b)(1)(D)(i) and paragraph (d) of this section to $30,000 (30% of $100,000). Under section 170(b)(1)(D)(ii) and paragraph (c) of § 1.170A-10, D is allowed to carry over to 1971 $10,000 ($40,000-$30,000) of his contribution of 30-percent capital gain property.

Example 14. C, an individual, reports his income on the calendar-year basis and for 1970 has a contribution base of $50,000. During 1970 he makes charitable contributions to a church of $57,000, consisting of $2,000 cash and of 30-percent capital gain property with a fair market value of $55,000 and an adjusted basis of $15,000. In addition, C contributes $3,000 cash in 1970 to a private foundation not described in section 170(b)(1) (E). For 1970, C elects under paragraph (d)(2) of this section to have section 170(e)(1)(B) and § 1.170A-4(a) apply to his contribution of property to the church. Accordingly, for 1970 C's contribution of property to the church is reduced from $55,000 to $35,000, the reduction of $20,000 being 50 percent of the gain of $40,000 ($55,000 -$15,000) which would have been recognized as long-term capital gain if the property had been sold by C at its fair market value at the time of its contribution to the church. Under section 170(b) (1)(A) and paragraph (b) of this section, C is allowed a charitable contributions deduction for 1970 of $25,000 ([$2,000+$35,000] but not to exceed [$50,000x50%]). Under section 170(d)(1) and paragraph (b) of § 1.170A-10, C is allowed a carryover from 1970 to 1971 of $12,000 ($37,000-$25,000). No deduction is allowed for 1970 for the contribution in that year of $3,000 cash to the private foundation since section 170(b)(1)(B) and paragraph (c) of this section limit the deduction for such contribution to the smaller of $10,000 ($50,000x20%) or $0 ([$50,000x50%]-$25,000). C is not allowed a carryover from 1970 for any of the $3,000 cash contribution in that year which is not deductible under section 170(b)(1)(B) and paragraph (c) of this section.

Example 15. (a) D, an individual, reports his income on the calendar-year basis and for

Sec. 170. Charitable, etc., contributions and gifts

1970 has a contribution base of $100,000. During 1970 he makes a charitable contribution to a church of 30-percent capital gain property with a fair market value of $40,000 and an adjusted basis of $21,000. In addition, he contributes $23,000 cash in 1970 to a private foundation not described in section 170(b)(1)(E). For 1970, D elects
5 under paragraph (d)(2) of this section to have section 170(e)(1)(B) and § 1.170A-4(a) apply to his contribution of property to the church. Accordingly, for 1970 D's contribution of property to the church is reduced from $40,000 to $30,500, the reduction of $9,500 being 50 percent of the gain of $19,000 ($40,000-$21,000) which would have been recognized as long-term capital gain if the property had been sold by D at its fair market
10 value at the time of its contribution to the church. Under section 170(b)(1)(A) and paragraph (b) of this section, D is allowed a charitable contributions deduction for 1970 of $30,500 for the property contributed to the church. In addition, under section 170(b)(1)(B) and paragraph (c) of this section D is allowed a deduction of $19,500 for the cash contributed to the private foundation, since such contribution of $23,000 is allowed to the
15 extent of the lesser of $20,000 (20% of $100,000) or $19,500 ([$100,000x50%]-$30,500). D is not allowed a carryover to 1971 or to any other taxable year for any of the $3,500 ($23,000-$19,500) of cash not deductible under section 170(b)(1)(B) and paragraph (c) of this section.

(b) If D had not made the election under paragraph (d)(2) of this section for 1970, his
20 deduction for 1970 under section 170(a) for the $40,000 contribution of property to the church would have been limited by section 170(b)(1)(D)(i) and paragraph (d) of this section to $30,000 (30% of $100,000), and under section 170(b)(1)(D)(ii) and paragraph (c) of § 1.170A-10 he would have been allowed a carryover to 1971 of $10,000 ($40,000-$30,000) for his contribution of such property. In addition, he would have been allowed
25 under section 170(b)(1)(B)(ii) and paragraph (c) of this section for 1970 a charitable contributions deduction of $10,000 ([$100,000x50%]-$40,000) for the cash contributed to the private foundation. In such case, D would not have been allowed a carryover to 1971 or to any other taxable year for any of the $13,000 ($23,000-$10,000) of cash not deductible under section 170(b)(1)(B) and paragraph (c) of this section.

30 ***

Reg. § 1.170A-13   Recordkeeping and return requirements for deductions for charitable contributions.

(a) *Charitable contributions of money made in taxable years beginning after*
35 *December 31, 1982--(1) In general.* If a taxpayer makes a charitable contribution of money in a taxable year beginning after December 31, 1982, the taxpayer shall maintain for each contribution one of the following:

(i) A canceled check.

(ii) A receipt from the donee charitable organization showing the name of the donee,
40 the date of the contribution, and the amount of the contribution. A letter or other communication from the donee charitable organization acknowledging receipt of a contribution and showing the date and amount of the contribution constitutes a receipt for purposes of this paragraph (a).

(iii) In the absence of a canceled check or receipt from the donee charitable
45 organization, other reliable written records showing the name of the donee, the date of the contribution, and the amount of the contribution.

(2) *Special rules--(i) Reliability of records.* The reliability of the written records described in paragraph (a)(1)(iii) of this section is to be determined on the basis of all of the facts and circumstances of a particular case. In all events, however, the burden shall
50 be on the taxpayer to establish reliability. Factors indicating that the written records are reliable include, but are not limited to:

Sec. 170. Charitable, etc., contributions and gifts

(A) The contemporaneous nature of the writing evidencing the contribution.

(B) The regularity of the taxpayer's recordkeeping procedures. For example, a contemporaneous diary entry stating the amount and date of the donation and the name of the donee charitable organization made by a taxpayer who regularly makes such diary entries would generally be considered reliable.

(C) In the case of a contribution of a small amount, the existence of any written or other evidence from the donee charitable organization evidencing receipt of a donation that would not otherwise constitute a receipt under paragraph (a)(1)(ii) of this section (including an emblem, button, or other token traditionally associated with a charitable organization and regularly given by the organization to persons making cash donations).

(ii) *Information stated in income tax return*. The information required by paragraph (a)(1)(iii) of this section shall be stated in the taxpayer's income tax return if required by the return form or its instructions.

***

(b) *Charitable contributions of property other than money made in taxable years beginning after December 31, 1982--(1) In general.* Except in the case of certain charitable contributions of property made after December 31, 1984, to which paragraph (c) of this section applies, any taxpayer who makes a charitable contribution of property other than money in a taxable year beginning after December 31, 1982, shall maintain for each contribution a receipt from the donee showing the following information:

(i) The name of the donee.

(ii) The date and location of the contribution.

(iii) A description of the property in detail reasonably sufficient under the circumstances. Although the fair market value of the property is one of the circumstances to be taken into account in determining the amount of detail to be included on the receipt, such value need not be stated on the receipt. A letter or other written communication from the donee acknowledging receipt of the contribution, showing the date of the contribution, and containing the required description of the property contributed constitutes a receipt for purposes of this paragraph. A receipt is not required if the contribution is made in circumstances where it is impractical to obtain a receipt (e.g., by depositing property at a charity's unattended drop site). In such cases, however, the taxpayer shall maintain reliable written records with respect to each item of donated property that include the information required by paragraph (b)(2)(ii) of this section.

(2) *Special rules--(i) Reliability of records*. The rules described in paragraph (a)(2)(i) of this section also apply to this paragraph (b) for determining the reliability of the written records described in paragraph (b)(1) of this section

(ii) Content of records. The written records described in paragraph (b)(1) of this section shall include the following information and such information shall be stated in the taxpayers income tax return if required by the return form or its instructions:

(A) The name and address of the donee organization to which the contribution was made.

(B) The date and location of the contribution.

(C) A description of the property in detail reasonable under the circumstances (including the value of the property), and, in the case of securities, the name of the issuer, the type of security, and whether or not such security is regularly traded on a stock exchange or in an over-the-counter market.

(D) The fair market value of the property at the time the contribution was made, the method utilized in determining the fair market value, and, if the valuation was determined by appraisal, a copy of the signed report of the appraiser.

(E) In the case of property to which section 170(e) applies, the cost or other basis, adjusted as provided by section 1016, the reduction by reason of section 170(e)(1) in the

Sec. 170. Charitable, etc., contributions and gifts

amount of the charitable contribution otherwise taken into account, and the manner in which such reduction was determined. A taxpayer who elects under paragraph (d)(2) of § 1.170A-8 to apply section 170(e)(1) to contributions and carryovers of 30 percent capital gain property shall maintain a written record indicating the years for which the election
5 was made and showing the contributions in the current year and carryovers from preceding years to which it applies. For the definition of the term ``30-percent capital gain property,'' see paragraph (d)(3) of § 1.170A-8.

(F) If less than the entire interest in the property is contributed during the taxable year, the total amount claimed as a deduction for the taxable year due to the contribution of the
10 property, and the amount claimed as a deduction in any prior year or years for contributions of other interests in such property, the name and address of each organization to which any such contribution was made, the place where any such property which is tangible property is located or kept, and the name of any person, other than the organization to which the property giving rise to the deduction was contributed,
15 having actual possession of the property.

(G) The terms of any agreement or understanding entered into by or on behalf of the taxpayer which relates to the use, sale, or other disposition of the property contributed, including for example, the terms of any agreement or understanding which:

(1) Restricts temporarily or permanently the donee's right to use or dispose of the
20 donated property,

(2) Reserves to, or confers upon, anyone (other than the donee organization or an organization participating with the donee organization in cooperative fundraising) any right to the income from the donated property or to the possession of the property, including the right to vote donated securities, to acquire the property by purchase or
25 otherwise, or to designate the person having such income, possession, or right to acquire, or

(3) Earmarks donated property for a particular use.

(3) Deductions in excess of $500 claimed for a charitable contribution of property other than money--(i) In general. In addition to the information required under paragraph (b)(2)
30 (ii) of this section, if a taxpayer makes a charitable contribution of property other than money in a taxable year beginning after December 31, 1982, and claims a deduction in excess of $500 in respect of the contribution of such item, the taxpayer shall maintain written records that include the following information with respect to such item of donated property, and shall state such information in his or her income tax return if required by the
35 return form or its instructions:

(A) The manner of acquisition, as for example by purchase, gift bequest, inheritance, or exchange, and the approximate date of acquisition of the property by the taxpayer or, if the property was created, produced, or manufactured by or for the taxpayer, the approximate date the property was substantially completed.
40 (B) The cost or other basis, adjusted as provided by section 1016, of property, other than publicly traded securities, held by the taxpayer for a period of less than 12 months (6 months for property contributed in taxable years beginning after December 31, 1982, and on or before June 6, 1988, immediately preceding the date on which the contribution was made and, when the information is available, of property, other than publicly traded
45 securities, held for a period of 12 months or more (6 months or more for property contributed in taxable years beginning after December 31, 1982, and on or before June 6, 1988, preceding the date on which the contribution was made.

(ii) *Information on acquisition date or cost basis not available.* If the return form or its instructions require the taxpayer to provide information on either the acquisition date of
50 the property or the cost basis as described in paragraph (b)(3)(i) (A) and (B), respectively, of this section, and the taxpayer has reasonable cause for not being able to provide such

Sec. 170. Charitable, etc., contributions and gifts

information, the taxpayer shall attach an explanatory statement to the return. If a taxpayer has reasonable cause for not being able to provide such information, the taxpayer shall not be disallowed a charitable contribution deduction under section 170 for failure to comply with paragraph (b)(3)(i) (A) and (B) of the section.

(4) Taxpayer option to apply paragraph (d) (1) and (2) to pre-1985 contributions. See 5 paragraph (d) (1) and (2) of this section with regard to contributions of property made on or before December 31, 1984.

(c) *Deductions in excess of $5,000 for certain charitable contributions of property made after December 31, 1984--(1) General Rule--(i) In general.* This paragraph applies to any charitable contribution made after December 31, 1984, by an individual, closely 10 held corporation, personal service corporation, partnership, or S corporation of an item of property (other than money and publicly traded securities to which § 1.170A-13(c)(7)(xi) (B) does not apply if the amount claimed or reported as a deduction under section 170 with respect to such item exceeds $5,000. This paragraph also applies to charitable contributions by C corporations (as defined in section 1361(a)(2) of the Code) to the 15 extent described in paragraph (c)(2)(ii) of this section. No deduction under section 170 shall be allowed with respect to a charitable contribution to which this paragraph applies unless the substantiation requirements described in paragraph (c)(2) of this section are met. For purposes of this paragraph (c), the amount claimed or reported as a deduction for an item of property is the aggregate amount claimed or reported as a deduction for a 20 charitable contribution under section 170 for such items of property and all similar items of property (as defined in paragraph (c)(7)(iii) of this section) by the same donor for the same taxable year (whether or not donated to the same donee).

(ii) *Special rule for property to which section 170(e)(3) or (4) applies.* For purposes of this paragraph (c), in computing the amount claimed or reported as a deduction for 25 donated property to which section 170(e)(3) or (4) applies (pertaining to certain contributions of inventory and scientific equipment) there shall be taken into account only the amount claimed or reported as a deduction in excess of the amount which would have been taken into account for tax purposes by the donor as costs of goods sold if the donor had sold the contributed property to the donee. For example, assume that a donor 30 makes a contribution from inventory of clothing for the care of the needy to which section 170(e)(3) applies. The cost of the property to the donor was $5,000, and, pursuant to section 170(e)(3)(B), the donor claims a charitable contribution deduction of $8,000 with respect to the property. Therefore, $3,000 ($8,000-$5,000) is the amount taken into account for purposes of determining whether the $5,000 threshold of this paragraph (c) 35 (1) is met.

(2) *Substantiation requirements--(i) In general.* Except as provided in paragraph (c)(2) (ii) of this section, a donor who claims or reports a deduction with respect to a charitable contribution to which this paragraph (c) applies must comply with the following three requirements: 40

(A) Obtain a qualified appraisal (as defined in paragraph (c)(3) of this section) for such property contributed. If the contributed property is a partial interest, the appraisal shall be of the partial interest.

(B) Attach a fully completed appraisal summary (as defined in paragraph (c)(4) of this section) to the tax return (or, in the case of a donor that is a partnership or S corporation, 45 the information return) on which the deduction for the contribution is first claimed (or reported) by the donor.

(C) Maintain records containing the information required by paragraph (b)(2) ii) of this section.

(ii) Special rules for certain nonpublicly traded stock, certain publicly traded securities, 50 and contributions by certain C corporations. (A) In cases described in paragraph (c)(2)(ii)

Sec. 170. Charitable, etc., contributions and gifts

(B) of this section, a qualified appraisal is not required, and only a partially completed appraisal summary form (as described in paragraph (c)(4)(iv)(A) of this section) is required to be attached to the tax or information return specified in paragraph (c)(2)(i)(B) of this section. However, in all cases donors must maintain records containing the information required by paragraph (b)(2)(ii) of this section.

 (B) This paragraph (c)(2)(ii) applies in each of the following cases:

 (1) The contribution of nonpublicly traded stock, if the amount claimed or reported as a deduction for the charitable contribution of such stock is greater than $5,000 but does not exceed $10,000;

 (2) The contribution of a security to which paragraph (c)(7)(xi)(B) of this section applies; and

 (3) The contribution of an item of property or of similar items of property described in paragraph (c)(1) of this section made after June 6, 1988, by a C corporation (as defined in section 1361(a)(2) of the Code), other than a closely held corporation or a personal service corporation.

 (3) *Qualified appraisal*--(i) *In general.* For purposes of this paragraph (c), the term ``qualified appraisal" means an appraisal document that--

 (A) Relates to an appraisal that is made not earlier than 60 days prior to the date of contribution of the appraised property nor later than the date specified in paragraph (c)(3) (iv)(B) of this section;

 (B) Is prepared, signed, and dated by a qualified appraiser (within the meaning of paragraph (c)(5) of this section);

 (C) Includes the information required by paragraph (c)(3)(ii) of this section; and

 (D) Does not involve an appraisal fee prohibited by paragraph (c)(6) of this section.

 (ii) Information included in qualified appraisal. A qualified appraisal shall include the following information:

 (A) A description of the property in sufficient detail for a person who is not generally familiar with the type of property to ascertain that the property that was appraised is the property that was (or will be) contributed;

 (B) In the case of tangible property, the physical condition of the property;

 (C) The date (or expected date) of contribution to the donee;

 (D) The terms of any agreement or understanding entered into (or expected to be entered into) by or on behalf of the donor or donee that relates to the use, sale, or other disposition of the property contributed, including, for example, the terms of any agreement or understanding that--

 (1) Restricts temporarily or permanently a donee's right to use or dispose of the donated property,

 (2) Reserves to, or confers upon, anyone (other than a donee organization or an organization participating with a donee organization in cooperative fundraising) any right to the income from the contributed property or to the possession of the property, including the right to vote donated securities, to acquire the property by purchase or otherwise, or to designate the person having such income, possession, or right to acquire, or

 (3) Earmarks donated property for a particular use;

 (E) The name, address, and (if a taxpayer identification number is otherwise required by section 6109 and the regulations thereunder) the identifying number of the qualified appraiser; and, if the qualified appraiser is acting in his or her capacity as a partner in a partnership, an employee of any person (whether an individual, corporation, or partnerships), or an independent contractor engaged by a person other than the donor, the name, address, and taxpayer identification number (if a number is otherwise required by section 6109 and the regulations thereunder) of the partnership or the person who employs or engages the qualified appraiser;

(F) The qualifications of the qualified appraiser who signs the appraisal, including the appraiser's background, experience, education, and membership, if any, in professional appraisal associations;

(G) A statement that the appraisal was prepared for income tax purposes;

(H) The date (or dates) on which the property was appraised;

(I) The appraised fair market value (within the meaning of § 1.170A-1 (c)(2)) of the property on the date (or expected date) of contribution;

(J) The method of valuation used to determine the fair market value, such as the income approach, the market-data approach, and the replacement-cost-less-depreciation approach; and

(K) The specific basis for the valuation, such as specific comparable sales transactions or statistical sampling, including a justification for using sampling and an explanation of the sampling procedure employed.

(iii) *Effect of signature of the qualified appraiser.* Any appraiser who falsely or fraudulently overstates the value of the contributed property referred to in a qualified appraisal or appraisal summary (as defined in paragraphs (c) (3) and (4), respectively, of this section) that the appraiser has signed may be subject to a civil penalty under section 6701 for aiding and abetting an understatement of tax liability and, moreover, may have appraisals disregarded pursuant to 31 U.S.C. 330(c).

(iv) *Special rules--*(A) *Number of qualified appraisals.* For purposes of paragraph (c) (2)(i)(A) of this section, a separate qualified appraisal is required for each item of property that is not included in a group of similar items of property. See paragraph (c)(7)(iii) of this section for the definition of similar items of property. Only one qualified appraisal is required for a group of similar items of property contributed in the same taxable year of the donor, although a donor may obtain separate qualified appraisals for each item of property. A qualified appraisal prepared with respect to a group of similar items of property shall provide all the information required by paragraph (c)(3)(ii) of this section for each item of similar property, except that the appraiser may select any items whose aggregate value is appraised at $100 or less and provide a group description of such items.

(B) *Time of receipt of qualified appraisal.* The qualified appraisal must be received by the donor before the due date (including extensions) of the return on which a deduction is first claimed (or reported in the case of a donor that is a partnership or S corporation) under section 170 with respect to the donated property, or, in the case of a deduction first claimed (or reported) on an amended return, the date on which the return is filed.

(C) *Retention of qualified appraisal.* The donor must retain the qualified appraisal in the donor's records for so long as it may be relevant in the administration of any internal revenue law.

(D) *Appraisal disregarded pursuant to 31 U.S.C. 330(c).* If an appraisal is disregarded pursuant to 31 U.S.C. 330(c) it shall have no probative effect as to the value of the appraised property. Such appraisal will, however, otherwise constitute a ``qualified appraisal" for purposes of this paragraph (c) if the appraisal summary includes the declaration described in paragraph (c)(4)(ii)(L)(2) and the taxpayer had no knowledge that such declaration was false as of the time described in paragraph (c)(4)(i)(B) of this section.

(4) *Appraisal summary--*(i) *In general.* For purposes of this paragraph (c), except as provided in paragraph (c)(4)(iv)(A) of this section, the term appraisal summary means a summary of a qualified appraisal that--

(A) Is made on the form prescribed by the Internal Revenue Service;

(B) Is signed and dated (as described in paragraph (c)(4)(iii) of this section) by the donee (or presented to the donee for signature in cases described in paragraph (c)(4)(iv)

(C)(2) of this section);

(C) Is signed and dated by the qualified appraiser (within the meaning of paragraph (c)(5) of this section) who prepared the qualified appraisal (within the meaning of paragraph (c)(3) of this section); and

5   (D) Includes the information required by paragraph (c)(4)(ii) of this section.

(ii) Information included in an appraisal summary. An appraisal summary shall include the following information:

(A) The name and taxpayer identification number of the donor (social security number if the donor is an individual or employer identification number if the donor is a partnership 10 or corporation);

(B) A description of the property in sufficient detail for a person who is not generally familiar with the type of property to ascertain that the property that was appraised is the property that was contributed;

(C) In the case of tangible property, a brief summary of the overall physical condition 15 of the property at the time of the contribution;

(D) The manner of acquisition (e.g., purchase, exchange, gift, or bequest) and the date of acquisition of the property by the donor, or, if the property was created, produced, or manufactured by or for the donor, a statement to that effect and the approximate date the property was substantially completed;

20   (E) The cost or other basis of the property adjusted as provided by section 1016;

(F) The name, address, and taxpayer identification number of the donee;

(G) The date the donee received the property;

(H) For charitable contributions made after June 6, 1988, a statement explaining whether or not the charitable contribution was made by means of a bargain sale and the 25 amount of any consideration received from the donee for the contribution;

(I) The name, address, and (if a taxpayer identification number is otherwise required by section 6109 and the regulations thereunder) the identifying number of the qualified appraiser who signs the appraisal summary and of other persons as required by paragraph (c)(3)(ii)(E) of this section;

30   (J) The appraised fair market value of the property on the date of contribution;

(K) The declaration by the appraiser described in paragraph (c)(5)(i) of this section;

(L) A declaration by the appraiser stating that--

(1) The fee charged for the appraisal is not of a type prohibited by paragraph (c)(6) of this section; and

35   (2) Appraisals prepared by the appraiser are not being disregarded pursuant to 31 U.S.C. 330(c) on the date the appraisal summary is signed by the appraiser; and

(M) Such other information as may be specified by the form.

(iii) *Signature of the original donee.* The person who signs the appraisal summary for the donee shall be an official authorized to sign the tax or information returns of the 40 donee, or a person specifically authorized to sign appraisal summaries by an official authorized to sign the tax or information returns of such done. In the case of a donee that is a governmental unit, the person who signs the appraisal summary for such donee shall be the official authorized by such donee to sign appraisal summaries. The signature of the donee on the appraisal summary does not represent concurrence in the appraised 45 value of the contributed property. Rather, it represents acknowledgment of receipt of the property described in the appraisal summary on the date specified in the appraisal summary and that the donee understands the information reporting requirements imposed by section 6050L and § 1.6050L-1. In general, § 1.6050L-1 requires the donee to file an information return with the Internal Revenue Service in the event the donee 50 sells, exchanges, consumes, or otherwise disposes of the property (or any portion thereof) described in the appraisal summary within 2 years after the date of the donor's contribution of such property.

(iv) *Special rules*--(A) *Content of appraisal summary required in certain cases.* With respect to contributions of nonpublicly traded stock described in paragraph (c)(2)(ii)(B)(1) of this section, contributions of securities described in paragraph (c)(7)(xi)(B) of this section, and contributions by C corporations described in paragraph (c)(2)(ii)(B)(3) of this section, the term appraisal summary means a document that--

(1) Complies with the requirements of paragraph (c)(4)(i) (A) and (B) of this section,

(2) Includes the information required by paragraph (c)(4)(ii) (A) through (H) of this section,

(3) Includes the amount claimed or reported as a charitable contribution deduction, and

(4) In the case of securities described in paragraph (c)(7)(xi)(B) of this section, also includes the pertinent average trading price (as described in paragraph (c)(7)(xi)(B)(2)(iii) of this section).

(B) *Number of appraisal summaries.* A separate appraisal summary for each item of property described in paragraph (c)(1) of this section must be attached to the donor's return. If, during the donor's taxable year, the donor contributes similar items of property described in paragraph (c)(1) of this section to more than one donee, the donor shall attach to the donor's return a separate appraisal summary for each donee. See paragraph (c)(7)(iii) of this section for the definition of similar items of property. If, however, during the donor's taxable year, a donor contributes similar items of property described in paragraph (c)(1) of this section to the same donee, the donor may attach to the donor's return a single appraisal summary with respect to all similar items of property contributed to the same donee. Such an appraisal summary shall provide all the information required by paragraph (c)(4)(ii) of this section for each item of property, except that the appraiser may select any items whose aggregate value is appraised at $100 or less and provide a group description for such items.

(C) *Manner of acquisition, cost basis and donee's signature.* (1) If a taxpayer has reasonable cause for being unable to provide the information required by paragraph (c)(4)(ii) (D) and (E) of this section (relating to the manner of acquisition and basis of the contributed property), an appropriate explanation should be attached to the appraisal summary. The taxpayer's deduction will not be disallowed simply because of the inability (for reasonable cause) to provide these items of information.

(2) In rare and unusual circumstances in which it is impossible for the taxpayer to obtain the signature of the donee on the appraisal summary as required by paragraph (c) (4)(i)(B) of this section, the taxpayer's deduction will not be disallowed for that reason provided that the taxpayer attaches a statement to the appraisal summary explaining, in detail, why it was not possible to obtain the donee's signature. For example, if the donee ceases to exist as an entity subsequent to the date of the contribution and prior to the date when the appraisal summary must be signed, and the donor acted reasonably in not obtaining the donee's signature at the time of the contribution, relief under this paragraph (c)(4)(iv)(C)(2) would generally be appropriate.

(D) *Information excluded from certain appraisal summaries.* The information required by paragraph (c)(4)(i)(C), paragraph (c)(4)(ii) (D), (E), (H) through (M), and paragraph (c) (4)(iv)(A)(3), and the average trading price referred to in paragraph (c)(4)(iv)(A)(4) of this section do not have to be included on the appraisal summary at the time it is signed by the donee or a copy is provided to the donee pursuant to paragraph (c)(4)(iv)(E) of this section.

(E) *Statement to be furnished by donors to donees.* Every donor who presents an appraisal summary to a donee for signature after June 6, 1988, in order to comply with paragraph (c)(4)(i)(B) of this section shall furnish a copy of the appraisal summary to

Sec. 170. Charitable, etc., contributions and gifts

such donee.

(F) *Appraisal summary requitred to be provided to partners and S corporation shareholders.* If the donor is a partnership or S corporation, the donor shall provide a copy of the appraisal summary to every partner or shareholder, respectively, who
5 receives an allocation of a charitable contribution deduction under section 170 with respect to the property described in the appraisal summary.

(G) *Partners and S corporation shareholders.* A partner of a partnership or shareholder of an S corporation who receives an allocation of a deduction under section 170 for a charitable contribution of property to which this paragraph (c) applies must
10 attach a copy of the partnership's or S corporation's appraisal summary to the tax return on which the deduction for the contribution is first claimed. If such appraisal summary is not attached, the partner's or shareholder's deduction shall not be allowed except as provided for in paragraph (c)(4)(iv)(H) of this section.

(H) *Failure to attach appraisal summary.* In the event that a donor fails to attach to the
15 donor's return an appraisal summary as required by paragraph (c)(2)(i)(B) of this section, the Internal Revenue Service may request that the donor submit the appraisal summary within 90 days of the request. If such a request is made and the donor complies with the request within the 90-day period, the deduction under section 170 shall not be disallowed for failure to attach the appraisal summary, provided that the donor's failure to attach the
20 appraisal summary was a good faith omission and the requirements of paragraph (c) (3) and (4) of this section are met (including the completion of the qualified appraisal prior to the date specified in paragraph (c)(3)(iv)(B) of this section).

(5) *Qualified appraiser*--(i) *In general.* The term qualified appraiser means an individual (other than a person described in paragraph (c)(5)(iv) of this section) who
25 includes on the appraisal summary (described in paragraph (c)(4) of this section), a declaration that--

(A) The individual either holds himself or herself out to the public as an appraiser or performs appraisals on a regular basis;

(B) Because of the appraiser's qualifications as described in the appraisal (pursuant to
30 paragraph (c)(3)(ii)(F) of this section), the appraiser is qualified to make appraisals of the type of property being valued;

(C) The appraiser is not one of the persons described in paragraph (c)(5)(iv) of this section; and

(D) The appraiser understands that an intentionally false or fraudulent overstatement
35 of the value of the property described in the qualified appraisal or appraisal summary may subject the appraiser to a civil penalty under section 6701 for aiding and abetting an understatement of tax liability, and, moreover, the appraiser may have appraisals disregarded pursuant to 31 U.S.C. 330(c) (see paragraph (c)(3)(iii) of this section).

(ii) *Exception.* An individual is not a qualified appraiser with respect to a particular
40 donation, even if the declaration specified in paragraph (c)(5)(i) of this section is provided in the appraisal summary, if the donor had knowledge of facts that would cause a reasonable person to expect the appraiser falsely to overstate the value of the donated property (e.g., the donor and the appraiser make an agreement concerning the amount at which the property will be valued and the donor knows that such amount exceeds the fair
45 market value of the property).

(iii) *Numbers of appraisers.* More than one appraiser may appraise the donated property. If more than one appraiser appraises the property, the donor does not have to use each appraiser's appraisal for purposes of substantiating the charitable contribution deduction pursuant to this paragraph (c). If the donor uses the appraisal of more than one
50 appraiser, or if two or more appraisers contribute to a single appraisal, each appraiser shall comply with the requirements of this paragraph (c), including signing the qualified

496

appraisal and appraisal summary as required by paragraphs (c)(3)(i)(B) and (c)(4)(i)(C) of this section, respectively.

(iv) *Qualified appraiser exclusions.* The following persons cannot be qualified appraisers with respect to particular property:

(A) The donor or the taxpayer who claims or reports a deductions under section 170 5 for the contribution of the property that is being appraised.

(B) A party to the transaction in which the donor acquired the property being appraised (i.e., the person who sold, exchanged, or gave the property to the donor, or any person who acted as an agent for the transferor or for the donor with respect to such sale, exchange, or gift), unless the property is donated within 2 months of the date of 10 acquisition and its appraised value does not exceed its acquisition price.

(C) The donee of the property.

(D) Any person employed by any of the foregoing persons (e.g., if the donor acquired a painting from an art dealer, neither the art dealer nor persons employed by the dealer can be qualified appraisers with respect to that painting).   15

(E) Any person related to any of the foregoing persons under section 267(b), or, with respect to appraisals made after June 6, 1988, married to a person who is in a relationship described in section 267(b) with any of the foregoing persons.

(F) An appraiser who is regularly used by any person described in paragraph (c)(5)(iv) (A), (B), or (C) of this section and who does not perform a majority of his or her 20 appraisals made during his or her taxable year for other persons.

(6) *Appraisal fees--*(i) *In general.* Except as otherwise provided in paragraph (c)(6)(ii) of this section, no part of the fee arrangement for a qualified appraisal can be based, in effect, on a percentage (or set of percentages) of the appraised value of the property. If a fee arrangement for an appraisal is based in whole or in part on the amount of the 25 appraised value of the property, if any, that is allowed as a deduction under section 170, after Internal Revenue Service examination or otherwise, it shall be treated as a fee based on a percentage of the appraised value of the property. For example, an appraiser's fee that is subject to reduction by the same percentage as the appraised value may be reduced by the Internal Revenue Service would be treated as a fee that 30 violates this paragraph (c)(6).

(ii) *Exception.* Paragraph (c)(6)(i) of this section does not apply to a fee paid to a generally recognized association that regulates appraisers provided all of the following requirements are met:

(A) The association is not organized for profit and no part of the net earnings of the 35 association inures to the benefit of any private shareholder or individual (these terms have the same meaning as in section 501(c)),

(B) The appraiser does not receive any compensation from the association or any other persons for making the appraisal, and

(C) The fee arrangement is not based in whole or in part on the amount of the 40 appraised value of the donated property, if any, that is allowed as a deduction under section 170 after Internal Revenue Service examination or otherwise.

(7) *Meaning of terms.* For purposes of this paragraph (c)--

(i) *Closely held corporation.* The term closely held corporation means any corporation (other than an S corporation) with respect to which the stock ownership requirement of 45 paragraph (2) of section 542(a) of the Code is met.

(ii) *Personal service corporation.* The term personal service corporation means any corporation (other than an S corporation) which is a service organization (within the meaning of section 414(m)(3) of the Code).

(iii) *Similar items of property.* The phrase similar items of property means property of 50 the same generic category or type, such as stamp collections (including philatelic

Sec. 170. Charitable, etc., contributions and gifts

supplies and books on stamp collecting), coin collections (including numismatic supplies and books on coin collecting), lithographs, paintings, photographs, books, nonpublicly traded stock, nonpublicly traded securities other than nonpublicly trade stock, land, buildings, clothing, jewelry, funiture, electronic equipment, household appliances, toys,
5 everyday kitchenware, china, crystal, or silver. For example, if a donor claims on her return for the year deductions of $2,000 for books given by her to College A, $2,500 for books given by her to College B, and $900 for books given by her to College C, the $5,000 threshold of paragraph (c)(1) of this section is exceeded. Therefore, the donor must obtain a qualified appraisal for the books and attach to her return three appraisal
10 summaries for the books donated to A, B, and C. For rules regarding the number of qualified appraisals and appraisal summaries required when similar items of property are contributed, see paragraphs (c)(3)(iv)(A) and (c)(4)(iv)(B), respectively, of this section.

(iv) *Donor.* The term donor means a person or entity (other than an organization described in section 170(c) to which the donated property was previously contributed)
15 that makes a charitable contribution of property.

(v) *Donee.* The term donee means--

(A) Except as provided in paragraph (c)(7)(v)(B) and (C) of this section, an organization described in section 170(c) to which property is contributed,

(B) Except as provided in paragraph (c)(7)(v)(C) of this section, in the case of a
20 charitable contribution of property placed in trust for the benefit of an organization described in section 170(c), the trust, or

(C) In the case of a charitable contribution of property placed in trust for the benefit of an organization described in section 170(c) made on or before June 6, 1988, the beneficiary that is an organization described in section 170(c), or if the trust has assumed
25 the duties of a donee by signing the appraisal summary pursuant to paragraph (c)(4)(i)(B) of this section, the trust.

In general, the term, refers only to the original donee. However, with respect to paragraph (c)(3)(ii)(D), the last sentence of paragraph (c)(4)(iii), and paragraph (c)(5)(iv)(C) of this section, the term donee means the original donee and all successor donees in cases
30 where the original donee transfers the contributed property to a successor donee after July 5, 1988.

(vi) *Original donee.* The term original donee means the donee to or for which property is initially donated by a donor.

(vii) *Successor donee.* The term successor donee means any donee of property other
35 than its original donee (i.e., a transferee of property for less than fair market value from an original donee or another successor donee).

(viii) *Fair market value.* For the meaning of the term fair market value, see § 1.170A-1(c)(2).

(ix) *Nonpublicly traded securities.* The term nonpublicly traded securities means
40 securities (within the meaning of section 165(g)(2) of the Code) which are not publicly traded securities as defined in paragraph (c)(7)(xi) of this section.

(x) *Nonpublicly traded stock.* The term nonpublicly traded stock means any stock of a corporation (evidence by a stock certificate) which is not a publicly traded security. The term stock does not include a debenture or any other evidence of indebtedness.
45 (xi) *Publicly traded securities--(A) In general.* Except as provided in paragraph (c)(7) (xi)(C) of this section, the term publicly traded securities means securities (within the meaning of section 165(g)(2) of the Code) for which (as of the date of the contribution) market quotations are readily available on an established securities market. For purposes of this section, market quotations are readily available on an established securities
50 market with respect to a security if:

(1) The security is listed on the New York Stock Exchange, the American Stock

498

Sec. 170. Charitable, etc., contributions and gifts

Exchange, or any city or regional exchange in which quotations are published on a daily basis, including foreign securities listed on a recognized foreign, national, or regional exchange in which quotations are published on a daily basis;

(2) The security is regularly traded in the national or regional over-the-counter market, for which published quotations are available; or   5

(3) The security is a share of an open-end investment company (commonly known as a mutual fund) registered under the Investment Company Act of 1940, as amended (15 U.S.C. 80a-1 to 80b-2), for which quotations are published on a daily basis in a newspaper of general circulation throughout the United States.

(If the market value of an issue of a security is reflected only on an interdealer quotation   10 system, the issue shall not be considered to be publicly traded unless the special rule described in paragraph (c)(7)(xi)(B) of this section is satisfied.)

(B) *Special rule*--(1) *In General.* An issue of a security that does not satisfy the requirements of paragraph (c)(7)(xi)(A)(1), (2), or (3) of this section shall nonetheless be considered to have market quotations readily available on an established securities   15 market for purposes of paragraph (c)(7)(xi)(A) of this section if all of the following five requirements are met:

(i) The issue is regularly traded during the computational period (as defined in paragraph (c)(7)(xi)(B)(2)(iv) of this section) in a market that is reflected by the existence of an interdealer quotation system for the issue,   20

(ii) The issuer or an agent of the issuer computes the average trading price (as defined in paragraph (c)(7)(xi)(B)(2)(iii) of this section) for the issue for the computational period,

(iii) The average trading price and total volume of the issue during the computational period are published in a newspaper of general circulation throughout the United States   25 not later than the last day of the month following the end of the calendar quarter in which the computational period ends,

(iv) The issuer or its agent keeps books and records that list for each transaction during the computational period involving each issue covered by this procedure the date of the settlement of the transaction, the name and address of the broker or dealer making   30 the market in which the transaction occurred, and the trading price and volume, and

(v) The issuer or its agent permits the Internal Revenue Service to review the books and records described in paragraph (c)(7)(xi)(B)(1)(iv) of this section with respect to transactions during the computational period upon giving reasonable notice to the issuer or agent.   35

(2) *Definitions.* For purposes of this paragraph (c)(7)(xi)(B)--

(i) *Issue of a security.* The term issue of a security means a class of debt securities with the same obligor and identical terms except as to their relative denominations (amounts) or a class of stock having identical rights.

(ii) *Interdealer quotation system.* The term interdealer quotation system means any   40 system of general circulation to brokers and dealers that regularly disseminates quotations of obligations by two or more identified brokers or dealers, who are not related to either the issuer of the security or to the issuer's agent, who compute the average trading price of the security. A quotation sheet prepared and distributed by a broker or dealer in the regular course of its business and containing only quotations of such broker   45 or dealer is not an interdealer quotation system.

(iii) *Average trading price.* The term average trading price means the mean price of all transactions (weighted by volume), other than original issue or redemption transactions, conducted through a United States office of a broker or dealer who maintains a market in the issue of the security during the computational period. For this purpose, bid and asked   50 quotations are not taken into account.

(iv) *Computational period*. For calendar quarters beginning on or after June 6, 1988, the term computational period means weekly during October through December (beginning with the first Monday in October and ending with the first Sunday following the last Monday in December) and monthly during January through September (beginning
5 January 1). For calendar quarters beginning before June 6, 1988, the term computational period means weekly during October through December and monthly during January through September.

(C) *Exception*. Securities described in paragraph (c)(7)(xi) (A) or (B) of this section shall not be considered publicly traded securities if--
10   (1) The securities are subject to any restrictions that materially affect the value of the securities to the donor or prevent the securities from being freely traded, or

(2) If the amount claimed or reported as a deduction with respect to the contribution of the securities is different than the amount listed in the market quotations that are readily available on an established securities market pursuant to paragraph (c)(7)(xi) (A) or (B) of
15 this section.

(D) *Market quotations and fair market value*. The fair market value of a publicly traded security, as defined in this paragraph (c)(7)(xi), is not necessarily equal to its market quotation, its average trading price (as defined in paragraph (c)(7)(xi)(B)(2)(iii) of this section), or its face value, if any. See § 1.170A-1(c)(2) for the definition of fair market
20 value.

***

(f) *Substantiation of charitable contributions of $250 or more--(1) In general*. No deduction is allowed under section 170(a) for all or part of any contribution of $250 or more unless the taxpayer substantiates the contribution with a contemporaneous written
25 acknowledgment from the donee organization. A taxpayer who makes more than one contribution of $250 or more to a donee organization in a taxable year may substantiate the contributions with one or more contemporaneous written acknowledgments. Section 170(f)(8) does not apply to a payment of $250 or more if the amount contributed (as determined under § 1.170A-1(h)) is less than $250. Separate contributions of less than
30 $250 are not subject to the requirements of section 170(f)(8), regardless of whether the sum of the contributions made by a taxpayer to a donee organization during a taxable year equals $250 or more.

(2) *Written acknowledgment*. Except as otherwise provided in paragraphs (f)(8) through (f)(11) and (f)(13) of this section, a written acknowledgment from a donee
35 organization must provide the following information--

(i) The amount of any cash the taxpayer paid and a description (but not necessarily the value) of any property other than cash the taxpayer transferred to the donee organization;

(ii) A statement of whether or not the donee organization provides any goods or
40 services in consideration, in whole or in part, for any of the cash or other property transferred to the donee organization;

(iii) If the donee organization provides any goods or services other than intangible religious benefits (as described in section 170(f)(8)), a description and good faith estimate of the value of those goods or services; and
45   (iv) If the donee organization provides any intangible religious benefits, a statement to that effect.

(3) *Contemporaneous*. A written acknowledgment is contemporaneous if it is obtained by the taxpayer on or before the earlier of--

(i) The date the taxpayer files the original return for the taxable year in which the
50 contribution was made; or

(ii) The due date (including extensions) for filing the taxpayer's original return for that year.

(4) *Donee organization.* For purposes of this paragraph (f), a donee organization is an organization described in section 170(c).

(5) *Goods or services.* Goods or services means cash, property, services, benefits, and privileges.   5

(6) In consideration for. A donee organization provides goods or services in consideration for a taxpayer's payment if, at the time the taxpayer makes the payment to the donee organization, the taxpayer receives or expects to receive goods or services in exchange for that payment. Goods or services a donee organization provides in consideration for a payment by a taxpayer include goods or services provided in a year   10 other than the year in which the taxpayer makes the payment to the donee organization.

(7) *Good faith estimate.* For purposes of this section, good faith estimate means a donee organization's estimate of the fair market value of any goods or services, without regard to the manner in which the organization in fact made that estimate. See § 1.170A-1(h)(4) for rules regarding when a taxpayer may treat a donee organization's   15 estimate of the value of goods or services as the fair market value.

(8) *Certain goods or services disregarded--(i) In general.* For purposes of section 170(f)(8), the following goods or services are disregarded--

(A) Goods or services that have insubstantial value under the guidelines provided in Revenue Procedures 90-12, 1990-1 C.B. 471, 92-49, 1992-1 C.B. 987, and any   20 successor documents. (See § 601.601(d)(2)(ii) of the Statement of Procedural Rules, 26 CFR part 601.); and

(B) Annual membership benefits offered to a taxpayer in exchange for a payment of $75 or less per year that consist of--

(1) Any rights or privileges, other than those described in section 170(l), that the   25 taxpayer can exercise frequently during the membership period. Examples of such rights and privileges may include, but are not limited to, free or discounted admission to the organization's facilities or events, free or discounted parking, preferred access to goods or services, and discounts on the purchase of goods or services; and

(2) Admission to events during the membership period that are open only to members   30 of a donee organization and for which the donee organization reasonably projects that the cost per person (excluding any allocable overhead) attending each such event is within the limits established for ``low cost articles'' under section 513(h)(2). The projected cost to the donee organization is determined at the time the organization first offers its membership package for the year (using section 3.07 of Revenue Procedure 90-12, or   35 any successor documents, to determine the cost of any items or services that are donated).

(ii) *Examples.* The following examples illustrate the rules of this paragraph (f)(8).

Example 1. Membership benefits disregarded. Performing Arts Center E is an organization described in section 170(c). In return for a payment of $75, E offers a   40 package of basic membership benefits that includes the right to purchase tickets to performances one week before they go on sale to the general public, free parking in E's garage during evening and weekend performances, and a 10% discount on merchandise sold in E's gift shop. In return for a payment of $150, E offers a package of preferred membership benefits that includes all of the benefits in the $75 package as well as a   45 poster that is sold in E's gift shop for $20. The basic membership and the preferred membership are each valid for twelve months, and there are approximately 50 performances of various productions at E during a twelve-month period. E's gift shop is open for several hours each week and at performance times. F, a patron of the arts, is solicited by E to make a contribution. E offers F the preferred membership benefits in   50 return for a payment of $150 or more. F makes a payment of $300 to E. F can satisfy the substantiation requirement of section 170(f)(8) by obtaining a contemporaneous written acknowledgment from E that includes a description of the poster and a good faith estimate of its fair market value ($20) and disregards the remaining membership benefits.

Example 2. Contemporaneous written acknowledgment need not mention rights or
5 *privileges that can be disregarded.* The facts are the same as in Example 1, except that F made a payment of $300 and received only a basic membership. F can satisfy the section 170(f)(8) substantiation requirement with a contemporaneous written acknowledgment stating that no goods or services were provided.

Example 3. Rights or privileges that cannot be exercised frequently. Community
10 Theater Group G is an organization described in section 170(c). Every summer, G performs four different plays. Each play is performed two times. In return for a membership fee of $60, G offers its members free admission to any of its performances. Non-members may purchase tickets on a performance by performance basis for $15 a ticket. H, an individual who is a sponsor of the theater, is solicited by G to make a
15 contribution. G tells H that the membership benefit will be provided in return for any payment of $60 or more. H chooses to make a payment of $350 to G and receives in return the membership benefit. G's membership benefit of free admission is not described in paragraph (f)(8)(i)(B) of this section because it is not a privilege that can be exercised frequently (due to the limited number of performances offered by G). Therefore, to meet
20 the requirements of section 170(f)(8), a contemporaneous written acknowledgment of H's $350 payment must include a description of the free admission benefit and a good faith estimate of its value.

Example 4. Multiple memberships. In December of each year, K, an individual, gives each of her six grandchildren a junior membership in Dinosaur Museum, an organization
25 described in section 170(c). Each junior membership costs $50, and K makes a single payment of $300 for all six memberships. A junior member is entitled to free admission to the museum and to weekly films, slide shows, and lectures about dinosaurs. In addition, each junior member receives a bi-monthly, non-commercial quality newsletter with information about dinosaurs and upcoming events. K's contemporaneous written
30 acknowledgment from Dinosaur Museum may state that no goods or services were provided in exchange for K's payment.

(9) *Goods or services provided to employees or partners of donors--*(i) *Certain goods or services disregarded.* For purposes of section 170(f)(8), goods or services provided by a donee organization to employees of a donor, or to partners of a partnership that is a
35 donor, in return for a payment to the organization may be disregarded to the extent that the goods or services provided to each employee or partner are the same as those described in paragraph (f)(8)(i) of this section.

(ii) No good faith estimate required for other goods or services. If a taxpayer makes a contribution of $250 or more to a donee organization and, in return, the donee
40 organization offers the taxpayer's employees or partners goods or services other than those described in paragraph (f)(9)(i) of this section, the contemporaneous written acknowledgment of the taxpayer's contribution is not required to include a good faith estimate of the value of such goods or services but must include a description of those goods or services.

45 (iii) *Example.* The following example illustrates the rules of this paragraph (f)(9).

Example. Museum J is an organization described in section 170(c). For a payment of $40, J offers a package of basic membership benefits that includes free admission and a 10% discount on merchandise sold in J's gift shop. J's other membership categories are for supporters who contribute $100 or more. Corporation K makes a payment of $50,000
50 to J and, in return, J offers K's employees free admission for one year, a tee-shirt with J's logo that costs J $4.50, and a gift shop discount of 25% for one year. The free admission

for K's employees is the same as the benefit made available to holders of the $40 membership and is otherwise described in paragraph (f)(8)(i)(B) of this section. The tee-shirt given to each of K's employees is described in paragraph (f)(8)(i)(A) of this section. Therefore, the contemporaneous written acknowledgment of K's payment is not required to include a description or good faith estimate of the value of the free admission or the 5 tee-shirts. However, because the gift shop discount offered to K's employees is different than that offered to those who purchase the $40 membership, the discount is not described in paragraph (f)(8)(i) of this section. Therefore, the contemporaneous written acknowledgment of K's payment is required to include a description of the 25% discount offered to K's employees. 10

(10) *Substantiation of out-of-pocket expenses.* A taxpayer who incurs unreimbursed expenditures incident to the rendition of services, within the meaning of § 1.170A-1(g), is treated as having obtained a contemporaneous written acknowledgment of those expenditures if the taxpayer--

(i) Has adequate records under paragraph (a) of this section to substantiate the 15 amount of the expenditures; and

(ii) Obtains by the date prescribed in paragraph (f)(3) of this section a statement prepared by the donee organization containing--

(A) A description of the services provided by the taxpayer;

(B) A statement of whether or not the donee organization provides any goods or 20 services in consideration, in whole or in part, for the unreimbursed expenditures; and

(C) The information required by paragraphs (f)(2)(iii) and (iv) of this section.

(11) Contributions made by payroll deduction--(i) Form of substantiation. A contribution made by means of withholding from a taxpayer's wages and payment by the taxpayer's employer to a donee organization may be substantiated, for purposes of section 170(f) 25 (8), by both--

(A) A pay stub, Form W-2, or other document furnished by the employer that sets forth the amount withheld by the employer for the purpose of payment to a donee organization; and

(B) A pledge card or other document prepared by or at the direction of the donee 30 organization that includes a statement to the effect that the organization does not provide goods or services in whole or partial consideration for any contributions made to the organization by payroll deduction.

(ii) *Application of $250 threshold.* For the purpose of applying the $250 threshold provided in section 170(f)(8)(A) to contributions made by the means described in 35 paragraph (f)(11)(i) of this section, the amount withheld from each payment of wages to a taxpayer is treated as a separate contribution.

(12) *Distributing organizations as donees.* An organization described in section 170(c), or an organization described in 5 CFR 950.105 (a Principal Combined Fund Organization for purposes of the Combined Federal Campaign) and acting in that capacity, that 40 receives a payment made as a contribution is treated as a donee organization solely for purposes of section 170(f)(8), even if the organization (pursuant to the donor's instructions or otherwise) distributes the amount received to one or more organizations described in section 170(c). This paragraph (f)(12) does not apply, however, to a case in which the distributee organization provides goods or services as part of a transaction 45 structured with a view to avoid taking the goods or services into account in determining the amount of the deduction to which the donor is entitled under section 170.

(13) *Transfers to certain trusts.* Section 170(f)(8) does not apply to a transfer of property to a trust described in section 170(f)(2)(B), a charitable remainder annuity trust (as defined in section 664(d)(1)), or a charitable remainder unitrust (as defined in section 50 664(d)(2) or (d)(3) or § 1.664(3)(a)(1)(i)(b)). Section 170(f)(8) does apply, however, to a

transfer to a pooled income fund (as defined in section 642(c)(5)); for such a transfer, the contemporaneous written acknowledgment must state that the contribution was transferred to the donee organization's pooled income fund and indicate whether any goods or services (in addition to an income interest in the fund) were provided in
5 exchange for the transfer. The contemporaneous written acknowledgment is not required to include a good faith estimate of the income interest.

(14) *Substantiation of payments to a college or university for the right to purchase tickets to athletic events.* For purposes of paragraph (f)(2)(iii) of this section, the right to purchase tickets for seating at an athletic event in exchange for a payment described in
10 section 170(l) is treated as having a value equal to twenty percent of such payment. For example, when a taxpayer makes a payment of $312.50 for the right to purchase tickets for seating at an athletic event, the right to purchase tickets is treated as having a value of $62.50. The remaining $250 is treated as a charitable contribution, which the taxpayer must substantiate in accordance with the requirements of this section.

15 (15) *Substantiation of charitable contributions made by a partnership or an S corporation.* If a partnership or an S corporation makes a charitable contribution of $250 or more, the partnership or S corporation will be treated as the taxpayer for purposes of section 170(f)(8). Therefore, the partnership or S corporation must substantiate the contribution with a contemporaneous written acknowledgment from the donee
20 organization before reporting the contribution on its income tax return for the year in which the contribution was made and must maintain the contemporaneous written acknowledgment in its records. A partner of a partnership or a shareholder of an S corporation is not required to obtain any additional substantiation for his or her share of the partnership's or S corporation's charitable contribution.

25 (16) *Purchase of an annuity.* If a taxpayer purchases an annuity from a charitable organization and claims a charitable contribution deduction of $250 or more for the excess of the amount paid over the value of the annuity, the contemporaneous written acknowledgment must state whether any goods or services in addition to the annuity were provided to the taxpayer. The contemporaneous written acknowledgment is not
30 required to include a good faith estimate of the value of the annuity. See § 1.170A-1(d)(2) for guidance in determining the value of the annuity.

(17) *Substantiation of matched payments*--(i) *In general.* For purposes of section 170, if a taxpayer's payment to a donee organization is matched, in whole or in part, by another payor, and the taxpayer receives goods or services in consideration for its
35 payment and some or all of the matching payment, those goods or services will be treated as provided in consideration for the taxpayer's payment and not in consideration for the matching payment.

(ii) *Example.* The following example illustrates the rules of this paragraph (f)(17).

Example. Taxpayer makes a $400 payment to Charity L, a donee organization.
40 Pursuant to a matching payment plan, Taxpayer's employer matches Taxpayer's $400 payment with an additional payment of $400. In consideration for the combined payments of $800, L gives Taxpayer an item that it estimates has a fair market value of $100. L does not give the employer any goods or services in consideration for its contribution. The contemporaneous written acknowledgment provided to the employer must include a
45 statement that no goods or services were provided in consideration for the employer's $400 payment. The contemporaneous written acknowledgment provided to Taxpayer must include a statement of the amount of Taxpayer's payment, a description of the item received by Taxpayer, and a statement that L's good faith estimate of the value of the item received by Taxpayer is $100.

***

50
[T.D. 7207, 37 FR 20776, Oct. 4, 1972; 37 FR 22982, Oct. 27, 1972; T.D. 7340, 40 FR

504

Sec. 170. Charitable, etc., contributions and gifts

1238, Jan. 7, 1975; T.D. 7728, 45 FR 72650, Nov. 3, 1980; T.D. 7807, 47 FR 4510, Feb. 1, 1982; T.D. 8002, 49 FR 50666, Dec. 31, 1984; T.D. 8003, 49 FR 50659, Dec. 31, 1984;T.D. 8069, 51 FR 1499, Jan. 14, 1986; 51 FR 5322, Feb. 13, 1986; 51 FR 6219, Feb. 21, 1986; T.D. 8176, 53 FR 5569, Feb. 25, 1988; T.D. 8199, 53 FR 16085, May 5, 1988; T.D. 8308, 55 FR 35587, Aug. 31, 1990; T.D. 8540, 59 FR 30102, June 10, 1994; T.D. 8623, 60 FR 53128, Oct. 12, 1995; T.D. 8690, 61 FR 65951, Dec. 16, 1996; T.D. 8819, 64 FR 23228, Apr. 30, 1999; T. D. 9194, 70 FR 18928, Apr. 11, 2005]

Sec. 171. Amortizable bond premium

(a) General rule. -- In the case of any bond, as defined in subsection (d), the following rules shall apply to the amortizable bond premium (determined under subsection (b)) on the bond:

(1) Taxable bonds. -- In the case of a bond (other than a bond the interest on which is excludable from gross income), the amount of the amortizable bond premium for the taxable year shall be allowed as a deduction.

(2) Tax-exempt bonds. -- In the case of any bond the interest on which is excludable from gross income, no deduction shall be allowed for the amortizable bond premium for the taxable year.

(3) Cross reference. -- For adjustment to basis on account of amortizable bond premium, see section 1016(a)(5).

(b) Amortizable bond premium. --

(1) Amount of bond premium. -- For purposes of paragraph (2), the amount of bond premium, in the case of the holder of any bond, shall be determined--

(A) with reference to the amount of the basis (for determining loss on sale or exchange) of such bond,

(B)(i) with reference to the amount payable on maturity or on earlier call date, in the case of any bond other than a bond to which clause (ii) applies, or

(ii) with reference to the amount payable on maturity (or if it results in a smaller amortizable bond premium attributable to the period to earlier call date, with reference to the amount payable on earlier call date), in the case of any bond described in subsection (a)(1) which is acquired after December 31, 1957, and

(C) with adjustments proper to reflect unamortized bond premium, with respect to the bond, for the period before the date as of which subsection (a) becomes applicable with respect to the taxpayer with respect to such bond.
In no case shall the amount of bond premium on a convertible bond include any amount attributable to the conversion features of the bond.

(2) Amount amortizable. -- The amortizable bond premium of the taxable year shall be the amount of the bond premium attributable to such year. In the case of a bond to which paragraph (1)(B)(ii) applies and which has a call date, the amount of bond premium attributable to the taxable year in which the bond is called shall include an amount equal to the excess of the amount of the adjusted basis (for determining loss on sale or exchange) of such bond as of the beginning of the taxable year over the amount received on redemption of the bond or (if greater) the amount payable on maturity.

(3) Method of determination. --

(A) In general. -- Except as provided in regulations prescribed by the Secretary, the determinations required under paragraphs (1) and (2) shall be made on the basis of the taxpayer's yield to maturity determined by -

(i) using the taxpayer's basis (for purposes of determining loss on sale or exchange)

Sec. 171. Amortizable bond premium

of the obligation, and

(ii) compounding at the close of each accrual period (as defined in section 1272(a)(5)).

(B) **Special rule where earlier call date is used.** -- For purposes of subparagraph (A), if the amount payable on an earlier call date is used under paragraph (1)(B)(ii) in determining the amortizable bond premium attributable to the period before the earlier call date, such bond shall be treated as maturing on such date for the amount so payable and then reissued on such date for the amount so payable.

***

(4) **Treatment of certain bonds acquired in exchange for other property.** --

(A) **In general.** -- If -

(i) a bond is acquired by any person in exchange for other property, and

(ii) the basis of such bond is determined (in whole or in part) by reference to the basis of such other property,

for purposes of applying this subsection to such bond while held by such person, the basis of such bond shall not exceed its fair market value immediately after the exchange. A similar rule shall apply in the case of such bond while held by any other person whose basis is determined (in whole or in part) by reference to the basis in the hands of the person referred to in clause (i).

(B) **Special rule where bond exchanged in reorganization.** -- Subparagraph (A) shall not apply to an exchange by the taxpayer of a bond for another bond if such exchange is a part of a reorganization (as defined in section 368). If any portion of the basis of the taxpayer in a bond transferred in such an exchange is not taken into account in determining bond premium by reason of this paragraph, such portion shall not be taken into account in determining the amount of bond premium on any bond received in the exchange.

(c) **Election as to taxable bonds.** --

(1) **Eligibility to elect; bonds with respect to which election permitted.** -- In the case of bonds the interest on which is not excludible from gross income, this section shall apply only if the taxpayer has so elected.

(2) **Manner and effect of election.** -- The election authorized under this subsection shall be made in accordance with such regulations as the Secretary shall prescribe. If such election is made with respect to any bond (described in paragraph (1)) of the taxpayer, it shall also apply to all such bonds held by the taxpayer at the beginning of the first taxable year to which the election applies and to all such bonds thereafter acquired by him and shall be binding for all subsequent taxable years with respect to all such bonds of the taxpayer, unless, on application by the taxpayer, the Secretary permits him, subject to such conditions as the Secretary deems necessary, to revoke such election. In the case of bonds held by a common trust fund, as defined in section 584(a), the election authorized under this subsection shall be exercisable with respect to such bonds only by the common trust fund. In case of bonds held by an estate or trust, the election authorized under this subsection shall be exercisable with respect to such bonds only by the fiduciary.

(d) **Bond defined.** -- For purposes of this section, the term "bond" means any bond, debenture, note, or certificate or other evidence of indebtedness, but does not include any such obligation which constitutes stock in trade of the taxpayer or any such obligation of a kind which would properly be included in the inventory of the taxpayer if on hand at the close of the taxable year, or any such obligation held by the taxpayer primarily for sale to customers in the ordinary course of his trade or business.

Sec. 171. Amortizable bond premium

(e) Treatment as offset to interest payments. -- Except as provided in regulations, in the case of any taxable bond -

(1) the amount of any bond premium shall be allocated among the interest payments on the bond under rules similar to the rules of subsection (b)(3), and

(2) in lieu of any deduction under subsection (a), the amount of any premium so allocated to any interest payment shall be applied against (and operate to reduce) the amount of such interest payment.

For purposes of the preceding sentence, the term "taxable bond" means any bond the interest of which is not excludable from gross income.

Sec. 172. Net operating loss deduction

(a) Deduction allowed. -- There shall be allowed as a deduction for the taxable year an amount equal to the aggregate of (1) the net operating loss carryovers to such year, plus (2) the net operating loss carrybacks to such year. For purposes of this subtitle, the term "net operating loss deduction" means the deduction allowed by this subsection.

(b) Net operating loss carrybacks and carryovers. --

(1) Years to which loss may be carried. --

(A) General rule. -- Except as otherwise provided in this paragraph, a net operating loss for any taxable year--

(i) shall be a net operating loss carryback to each of the 2 taxable years preceding the taxable year of such loss, and

(ii) shall be a net operating loss carryover to each of the 20 taxable years following the taxable year of the loss.

***

(F) Retention of 3-year carryback in certain cases. --

(i) In general. -- Subparagraph (A)(i) shall be applied by substituting "3 taxable years" for "2 taxable years" with respect to the portion of the net operating loss for the taxable year which is an eligible loss with respect to the taxpayer.

(ii) Eligible loss. -- For purposes of clause (i), the term "eligible loss" means -

(I) in the case of an individual, losses of property arising from fire, storm, shipwreck, or other casualty, or from theft,

(II) in the case of a taxpayer which is a small business, net operating losses attributable to Presidentially declared disasters (as defined in section 1033(h)(3)), and

(III) in the case of a taxpayer engaged in the trade or business of farming (as defined in section 263A(e)(4)), net operating losses attributable to such Presidentially declared disasters.

Such term shall not include any farming loss (as defined in subsection (i)).

(iii) Small business. -- For purposes of this subparagraph, the term "small business" means a corporation or partnership which meets the gross receipts test of section 448(c) for the taxable year in which the loss arose (or, in the case of a sole proprietorship, which would meet such test if such proprietorship were a corporation).

(iv) Coordination with paragraph (2). -- For purposes of applying paragraph (2), an eligible loss for any taxable year shall be treated in a manner similar to the manner in which a specified liability loss is treated.

Sec. 172. Net operating loss deduction

(G) Farming losses. -- In the case of a taxpayer which has a farming loss (as defined in subsection (i)) for a taxable year, such farming loss shall be a net operating loss carryback to each of the 5 taxable years preceding the taxable year of such loss.

(H) In the case of a net operating loss for any taxable year ending during 2001 or 2002, subparagraph (A)(i) shall be applied by substituting "5" for "2" and subparagraph (F) shall not apply.

***

(2) Amount of carrybacks and carryovers. -- The entire amount of the net operating loss for any taxable year (hereinafter in this section referred to as the "loss year") shall be carried to the earliest of the taxable years to which (by reason of paragraph (1)) such loss may be carried. The portion of such loss which shall be carried to each of the other taxable years shall be the excess, if any, of the amount of such loss over the sum of the taxable income for each of the prior taxable years to which such loss may be carried. For purposes of the preceding sentence, the taxable income for any such prior taxable year shall be computed -

(A) with the modifications specified in subsection (d) other than paragraphs (1), (4), and (5) thereof, and

(B) by determining the amount of the net operating loss deduction without regard to the net operating loss for the loss year or for any taxable year thereafter,

and the taxable income so computed shall not be considered to be less than zero.

(3) Election to waive carryback. -- Any taxpayer entitled to a carryback period under paragraph (1) may elect to relinquish the entire carryback period with respect to a net operating loss for any taxable year. Such election shall be made in such manner as may be prescribed by the Secretary, and shall be made by the due date (including extensions of time) for filing the taxpayer's return for the taxable year of the net operating loss for which the election is to be in effect. Such election, once made for any taxable year, shall be irrevocable for such taxable year.

(c) Net operating loss defined. -- For purposes of this section, the term "net operating loss" means the excess of the deductions allowed by this chapter over the gross income. Such excess shall be computed with the modifications specified in subsection (d).

(d) Modifications. -- The modifications referred to in this section are as follows:

(1) Net operating loss deduction. -- No net operating loss deduction shall be allowed.

(2) Capital gains and losses of taxpayers other than corporations. -- In the case of a taxpayer other than a corporation--

(A) the amount deductible on account of losses from sales or exchanges of capital assets shall not exceed the amount includable on account of gains from sales or exchanges of capital assets; and

(B) the exclusion provided by section 1202 shall not be allowed.

(3) Deduction for personal exemptions. -- No deduction shall be allowed under section 151 (relating to personal exemptions). No deduction in lieu of any such deduction shall be allowed.

(4) Nonbusiness deductions of taxpayers other than corporations. -- In the case of a taxpayer other than a corporation, the deductions allowable by this chapter which are not attributable to a taxpayer's trade or business shall be allowed only to the extent of the amount of the gross income not derived from such trade or business. For purposes of the preceding sentence--

(A) any gain or loss from the sale or other disposition of--

(i) property, used in the trade or business, of a character which is subject to the

508

Sec. 172. Net operating loss deduction

allowance for depreciation provided in section 167, or

    (ii) real property used in the trade or business,

shall be treated as attributable to the trade or business;

    (B) the modifications specified in paragraphs (1), (2)(B), and (3) shall be taken into account; 5

    (C) any deduction for casualty or theft losses allowable under paragraph (2) or (3) of section 165(c) shall be treated as attributable to the trade or business; and

    (D) any deduction allowed under section 404 to the extent attributable to contributions which are made on behalf of an individual who is an employee within the meaning of section 401(c)(1) shall not be treated as attributable to the trade or business of such 10 individual.

Reg. § 1.172-5 Taxable income which is subtracted from net operating loss to determine carryback or carryover.

(a) *Taxable year subject to the Internal Revenue Code of 1954.* The taxable income 15 for any taxable year subject to the Internal Revenue Code of 1954 which is subtracted from the net operating loss for any other taxable year to determine the portion of such net operating loss which is a carryback or a carryover to a particular taxable year is computed with the modifications prescribed in this paragraph. These modifications shall be made independently of, and without reference to, the modifications required by §§ 20 1.172-2(a) and 1.172-3(a) for purposes of computing the net operating loss itself.

(1) Modifications applicable to unincorporated taxpayers only. In the case of a taxpayer other than a corporation, in computing taxable income and adjusted gross income:

(i) No deduction shall be allowed under section 151 for the personal exemptions (or 25 under any other section which grants a deduction in lieu of the deductions allowed by section 151) and under section 1202 in respect of the net long-term capital gain.

(ii) The amount deductible on account of losses from sales or exchanges of capital assets shall not exceed the amount includible on account of gains from sales or exchanges of capital assets. 30

(2) *Modifications applicable to all taxpayers.* In the case either of a corporation or of a taxpayer other than a corporation:

(i) *Net operating loss deduction.* The net operating loss deduction for such taxable year shall be computed by taking into account only such net operating losses otherwise allowable as carrybacks or carryovers to such taxable year as were sustained in taxable 35 years preceding the taxable year in which the taxpayer sustained the net operating loss from which the taxable income is to be deducted. Thus, for such purposes, the net operating loss for the loss year or any taxable year thereafter shall not be taken into account.

Example. The taxpayer's income tax returns are made on the basis of the calendar 40 year. In computing the net operating loss deduction for 1954, the taxpayer has a carryover from 1952 of $9,000, a carryover from 1953 of $6,000, a carryback from 1955 of $18,000, and a carryback from 1956 of $10,000, or an aggregate of $43,000 in carryovers and carrybacks. Thus, the net operating loss deduction for 1954, for purposes of determining the tax liability for 1954, is $43,000. However, in computing the taxable 45 income for 1954 which is subtracted from the net operating loss for 1955 for the purpose of determining the portion of such loss which may be carried over to subsequent taxable years, the net operating loss deduction for 1954 is $15,000, that is, the aggregate of the $9,000 carryover from 1952 and the $6,000 carryover from 1953. In computing the net operating loss deduction for such purpose, the $18,000 carryback from 1955 and the 50

Sec. 172. Net operating loss deduction

$10,000 carryback from 1956 are disregarded. In computing the taxable income for 1954, however, which is subtracted from the net operating loss for 1956 for the purpose of determining the portion of such loss which may be carried over to subsequent taxable years, the net operating loss deduction for 1954 is $33,000, that is, the aggregate of the
5 $9,000 carryover from 1952, the $6,000 carryover from 1953, and the $18,000 carryback from 1955. In computing the net operating loss deduction for such purpose, the $10,000 carryback from 1956 is disregarded.

(ii) *Recomputation of percentage limitations.* Unless otherwise specifically provided in this subchapter, any deduction which is limited in amount to a percentage of the
10 taxpayer's taxable income or adjusted gross income shall be recomputed upon the basis of the taxable income or adjusted gross income, as the case may be, determined with the modifications prescribed in this paragraph. Thus, in the case of an individual the deduction for medical expenses would be recomputed after making all the modifications prescribed in this paragraph, whereas the deduction for charitable contributions would be
15 determined without regard to any net operating loss carryback but with regard to any other modifications so prescribed. See, however, the regulations under paragraph (g) of § 1.170-2 (relating to charitable contributions carryover of individuals) and paragraph (c) of § 1.170-3 (relating to charitable contributions carryover of corporations) for special rules regarding charitable contributions in excess of the percentage limitations which may be
20 treated as paid in succeeding taxable years.

Example 1. For the calendar year 1954 the taxpayer, an individual, files a return showing taxable income of $4,800, computed as follows:

Salary..		$5,000
25 Net long-term capital gain.............................		4,000
Total gross income..................................		9,000
Less: Deduction allowed by section 1202		
in respect of net long-term capital gain.......		2,000
Adjusted gross income...............................		7,000
30 Less:		
Deduction for personal exemption.................	$600	
Deduction for medical expense ($410 actually paid but allowable only to extent in excess of 3 percent of adjusted gross income)............	200	
35 Deduction for charitable contributions ($2,000 actually paid but allowable only to extent not in excess of 20 percent of adjusted gross income)...	$1,400	$2,200
Taxable income..		4,800

40
In 1955 the taxpayer undertakes the operation of a trade or business and sustains therein a net operating loss of $3,000. Under section 172(b)(2), it is determined that the entire $3,000 is a carryback to 1954. In 1956 he sustains a net operating loss of $10,000 in the operation of the business. In determining the amount of the carryover of the 1956 loss to
45 1957, the taxable income for 1954 as computed under this paragraph is $3,970, determined as follows:

Salary..	$5,000	
Net long-term capital gain................................	4,000	
Total gross income.......................................	9,000	5
Less: Deduction for carryback		
of 1955 net operating loss..............................	3,000	
Adjusted gross income.....................................	6,000	
Less:		
Deduction for medical expense ($410 actually		10
paid but allowable only to extent in excess of		
3 percent of adjusted gross income as modified		
under this paragraph).......................................	$230	
Deduction for charitable contributions ($2,000		
actually paid but allowable only to extent not		15
in excess of 20 percent of adjusted gross		
income determined with all the modifications		
prescribed in this paragraph other than the net		
operating loss carryback)................................	1,800	
	2,030	20
Taxable income...	3,970	

Example 2. For the calendar year 1959 the taxpayer, an individual, files a return showing taxable income of $5,700, computed as follows:

Salary..	$5,000	25
Net long-term capital gain................................	4,000	
Total gross income.......................................	9,000	
Less: Deduction allowed by section 1202		
in respect of net long-term capital gain............	2,000	
Adjusted gross income.....................................	7,000	30
Less:		
Deduction for personal exemption......................	$600 .	
Standard deduction allowed by section 141......	$700 $1,300	
Taxable income...	5,700	

35

In 1960 the taxpayer undertakes the operation of a trade or business and sustains therein a net operating loss of $4,700. In 1961 he sustains a net operating loss of $10,000 in the operation of the business. Under section 172(b)(2), it is determined that the entire amount of each loss, $4,700 and $10,000, is a carryback to 1959. In determining the amount of the carryover of the 1961 loss to 1962, the taxable income for 1959 as 40 computed under this paragraph is $3,870, determined as follows:

Sec. 172. Net operating loss deduction

Salary..	$5,000
Net long-term capital gain.................................	4,000
5 Total gross income..	9,000
Less: Deduction for carryback of	
1960 net operating loss....................................	4,700
Adjusted gross income.....................................	4,300
Less: Standard deduction.................................	430
10 Taxable income..	3,870

(iii) *Minimum limitation.* The taxable income, as modified under this paragraph, shall in no case be considered less than zero.

(3) *Electing small business corporations.* For special rule applicable to corporations
15 which were electing small business corporations under Subchapter S (section 1361 and following), Chapter 1 of the Code, during one or more of the taxable years described in section 172(b)(1), see paragraph (f) of § 1.172-1.

(4) *Qualified real estate investment trust.* Where a net operating loss is carried over to a qualified taxable year (as defined in § 1.172-10(b)) ending after October 4, 1976, the
20 real estate investment trust taxable income (as defined in section 857(b)(2)) shall be used as the ``taxable income" for that taxable year to determine, under section 172(b)(2), the balance of the net operating loss available as a carryover to a subsequent taxable year. The real estate investment trust taxable income, however, is computed by applying the rules applicable to corporations in paragraph (a)(2) of this section. Thus, in computing
25 real estate investment trust taxable income for purposes of section 172(b)(2), the net operating loss deduction for the taxable year shall be computed in accordance with paragraph (a)(2)(i) of this section. The principles of this subparagraph may be illustrated by the following examples:

Example 1. Corporation X, a calendar year taxpayer, is formed on January 1, 1977. X
30 incurs a net operating loss of $100,000 for its taxable year 1977, which under section 172(b)(2), is a carryover to 1978. For 1978 X is a qualified real estate investment trust (as defined in § 1.172-10(b)) and has real estate investment trust taxable income (determined without regard to the deduction for dividends paid or the net operating loss deduction) of $150,000, all of which consists of ordinary income. X pays dividends in
35 1978 totaling $120,000 that qualify for the deduction for dividends paid under section 857(b)(2)(B). The portion of the 1977 net operating loss available as a carryover to 1979 and subsequent years is $70,000 (i.e., the excess of the amount of the net operating loss ($100,000) over the amount of the real estate investment trust taxable income for 1978 ($30,000), determined by taking into account the deduction for dividends paid allowable
40 under section 857(b)(2)(B) and without taking into account the net operating loss of 1977).

Example 2. (i) Assume the same facts as in Example 1, except that the $150,000 of real estate investment trust taxable income (determined without the net operating loss deduction or the dividends paid deduction) consists of $80,000 of ordinary income and
45 $70,000 of net capital gain. The amount of capital gain dividends which may be paid for 1978 is limited to $50,000, that is, the amount of the real estate investment trust taxable income for 1978, determined by taking into account the net operating loss deduction for the taxable year, but not the deduction for dividends paid ($150,000 minus $100,000). See § 1.857-6(e)(1)(ii).
50   (ii) X designated $50,000 of the $120,000 of dividends paid as capital gains dividends (as defined in section 857(b)(3)(C) and § 1.857-6(e)). Thus, $70,000 is an ordinary

dividend. Since both ordinary dividends and capital gains dividends are taken into account in computing the deduction for dividends paid under section 857(b)(2)(B), the result will be the same as in Example 1; that is, the portion of the 1977 net operating loss available as a carryover to 1979 and subsequent years is $70,000.

***

[T.D. 6500, 25 FR 11402, Nov. 26, 1960; T.D. 6862, 30 FR 14428, Nov. 18, 1965; T.D. 6900, 31 FR 14641, Nov. 17, 1966; T.D. 7767, 46 FR 11263, Feb. 6, 1981; T.D. 8107, 51 FR 43346, Dec. 2, 1986]

Sec. 173. Circulation expenditures

(a) **General rule.** -- Notwithstanding section 263, all expenditures (other than expenditures for the purchase of land or depreciable property or for the acquisition of circulation through the purchase of any part of the business of another publisher of a newspaper, magazine, or other periodical) to establish, maintain, or increase the circulation of a newspaper, magazine, or other periodical shall be allowed as a deduction; except that the deduction shall not be allowed with respect to the portion of such expenditures as, under regulations prescribed by the Secretary, is chargeable to capital account if the taxpayer elects, in accordance with such regulations, to treat such portion as so chargeable. Such election, if made, must be for the total amount of such portion of the expenditures which is so chargeable to capital account, and shall be binding for all subsequent taxable years unless, upon application by the taxpayer, the Secretary permits a revocation of such election subject to such conditions as he deems necessary.

Sec. 174. Research and experimental expenditures

(a) **Treatment as expenses.** --

(1) **In general.** -- A taxpayer may treat research or experimental expenditures which are paid or incurred by him during the taxable year in connection with his trade or business as expenses which are not chargeable to capital account. The expenditures so treated shall be allowed as a deduction.

(2) **When method may be adopted.** --

(A) **Without consent.** -- A taxpayer may, without the consent of the Secretary, adopt the method provided in this subsection for his first taxable year--

(i) which begins after December 31, 1953, and ends after August 16, 1954, and

(ii) for which expenditures described in paragraph (1) are paid or incurred.

(B) **With consent.** -- A taxpayer may, with the consent of the Secretary, adopt at any time the method provided in this subsection.

(3) **Scope.** -- The method adopted under this subsection shall apply to all expenditures described in paragraph (1). The method adopted shall be adhered to in computing taxable income for the taxable year and for all subsequent taxable years unless, with the approval of the Secretary, a change to a different method is authorized with respect to part or all of such expenditures.

(b) **Amortization of certain research and experimental expenditures.** --

(1) **In general.** -- At the election of the taxpayer, made in accordance with regulations prescribed by the Secretary, research or experimental expenditures which are--

(A) paid or incurred by the taxpayer in connection with his trade or business,

(B) not treated as expenses under subsection (a), and

Sec. 174. Research and experimental expenditures

    (C) chargeable to capital account but not chargeable to property of a character which is subject to the allowance under section 167 (relating to allowance for depreciation, etc.) or section 611 (relating to allowance for depletion),

may be treated as deferred expenses. In computing taxable income, such deferred expenses shall be allowed as a deduction ratably over such period of not less than 60 months as may be selected by the taxpayer (beginning with the month in which the taxpayer first realizes benefits from such expenditures). Such deferred expenses are expenditures properly chargeable to capital account for purposes of section 1016(a)(1) (relating to adjustments to basis of property).

    (2) Time for and scope of election. -- The election provided by paragraph (1) may be made for any taxable year beginning after December 31, 1953, but only if made not later than the time prescribed by law for filing the return for such taxable year (including extensions thereof). The method so elected, and the period selected by the taxpayer, shall be adhered to in computing taxable income for the taxable year for which the election is made and for all subsequent taxable years unless, with the approval of the Secretary, a change to a different method (or to a different period) is authorized with respect to part or all of such expenditures. The election shall not apply to any expenditure paid or incurred during any taxable year before the taxable year for which the taxpayer makes the election.

    (c) Land and other property. -- This section shall not apply to any expenditure for the acquisition or improvement of land, or for the acquisition or improvement of property to be used in connection with the research or experimentation and of a character which is subject to the allowance under section 167 (relating to allowance for depreciation, etc.) or section 611 (relating to allowance for depletion); but for purposes of this section allowances under section 167, and allowances under section 611, shall be considered as expenditures.

    (d) Exploration expenditures. -- This section shall not apply to any expenditure paid or incurred for the purpose of ascertaining the existence, location, extent, or quality of any deposit of ore or other mineral (including oil and gas).

    (e) Only reasonable research expenditures eligible. -- This section shall apply to a research or experimental expenditure only to the extent that the amount thereof is reasonable under the circumstances.

    (f) Cross references. --

    (1) For adjustments to basis of property for amounts allowed as deductions as deferred expenses under subsection (b), see section 1016(a)(14).

Sec. 175. Soil and water conservation expenditures

    (a) In general. -- A taxpayer engaged in the business of farming may treat expenditures which are paid or incurred by him during the taxable year for the purpose of soil or water conservation in respect of land used in farming, or for the prevention of erosion of land used in farming, as expenses which are not chargeable to capital account. The expenditures so treated shall be allowed as a deduction.

***

Sec. 179. Election to expense certain depreciable business assets

    (a) Treatment as expenses. -- A taxpayer may elect to treat the cost of any section 179 property as an expense which is not chargeable to capital account. Any cost so treated shall be allowed as a deduction for the taxable year in which the section 179 property is placed in service.

    (b) Limitations. --

514

Sec. 179. Election to expense certain depreciable business assets

(1) Dollar limitation. -- The aggregate cost which may be taken into account under subsection (a) for any taxable year shall not exceed $25,000 ($100,000 in the case of taxable years beginning after 2002 and before 2010).

(2) Reduction in limitation. -- The limitation under paragraph (1) for any taxable year shall be reduced (but not below zero) by the amount by which the cost of section 179 property 5 placed in service during such taxable year exceeds $200,000 ($400,000 in the case of taxable years beginning after 2002 and before 2010).

(3) Limitation based on income from trade or business. --

(A) In general. -- The amount allowed as a deduction under subsection (a) for any taxable year (determined after the application of paragraphs (1) and (2)) shall not exceed 10 the aggregate amount of taxable income of the taxpayer for such taxable year which is derived from the active conduct by the taxpayer of any trade or business during such taxable year.

(B) Carryover of disallowed deduction. -- The amount allowable as a deduction under subsection (a) for any taxable year shall be increased by the lesser of-- 15

(i) the aggregate amount disallowed under subparagraph (A) for all prior taxable years (to the extent not previously allowed as a deduction by reason of this subparagraph), or

(ii) the excess (if any) of--

(I) the limitation of paragraphs (1) and (2) (or if lesser, the aggregate amount of 20 taxable income referred to in subparagraph (A)), over

(II) the amount allowable as a deduction under subsection (a) for such taxable year without regard to this subparagraph.

(C) Computation of taxable income. -- For purposes of this paragraph, taxable income derived from the conduct of a trade or business shall be computed without regard to the 25 deduction allowable under this section.

(4) Married individuals filing separately. -- In the case of a husband and wife filing separate returns for the taxable year--

(A) such individuals shall be treated as 1 taxpayer for purposes of paragraphs (1) and (2), and 30

(B) unless such individuals elect otherwise, 50 percent of the cost which may be taken into account under subsection (a) for such taxable year (before application of paragraph (3)) shall be allocated to each such individual.

(5) Inflation adjustments. --

(A) In general. -- In the case of any taxable year beginning in a calendar year after 2003 35 and before 2010, the $100,000 and $400,000 amounts in paragraphs (1) and (2) shall each be increased by an amount equal to--

(i) such dollar amount, multiplied by

(ii) the cost-of-living adjustment determined under section 1(f)(3) for the calendar year in which the taxable year begins, by substituting "calendar year 2002" for 40 "calendar year 1992" in subparagraph (B) thereof.

(B) Rounding. --

(i) Dollar limitation. -- If the amount in paragraph (1) as increased under subparagraph (A) is not a multiple of $1,000, such amount shall be rounded to the nearest multiple of $1,000. 45

(ii) Phaseout amount. -- If the amount in paragraph (2) as increased under

Sec. 179. Election to expense certain depreciable business assets

subparagraph (A) is not a multiple of $10,000, such amount shall be rounded to the nearest multiple of $10,000.

(6) Limitation on cost taken into account for certain passenger vehicles. --

(A) In general. -- The cost of any sport utility vehicle for any taxable year which may be taken into account under this section shall not exceed $25,000.

(B) Sport utility vehicle. -- For purposes of subparagraph (A)--

(i) In general. -- The term "sport utility vehicle" means any 4-wheeled vehicle -

(I) which is primarily designed or which can be used to carry passengers over public streets, roads, or highways (except any vehicle operated exclusively on a rail or rails),

(II) which is not subject to section 280F, and

(III) which is rated at not more than 14,000 pounds gross vehicle weight.

(ii) Certain vehicles excluded. -- Such term does not include any vehicle which--

(I) is designed to have a seating capacity of more than 9 persons behind the driver's seat,

(II) is equipped with a cargo area of at least 6 feet in interior length which is an open area or is designed for use as an open area but is enclosed by a cap and is not readily accessible directly from the passenger compartment,or

(III) has an integral enclosure, fully enclosing the driver compartment and load carrying device, does not have seating rearward of the driver's seat, and has no body section protruding more than 30 inches ahead of the leading edge of the windshield.

(7) Increase in limitations for 2008. -- In the case of any taxable year beginning in 2008 —

(A) the dollar limitation under paragraph (1) shall be $250,000,

(B) the dollar limitation under paragraph (2) shall be $800,000, and

(C) the amounts described in subparagraphs (A) and (B) shall not be adjusted under paragraph (5).

(c) Election. --

(1) In general. -- An election under this section for any taxable year shall--

(A) specify the items of section 179 property to which the election applies and the portion of the cost of each of such items which is to be taken into account under subsection (a), and

(B) be made on the taxpayer's return of the tax imposed by this chapter for the taxable year.

Such election shall be made in such manner as the Secretary may by regulations prescribe.

(2) Election irrevocable. -- Any election made under this section, and any specification contained in any such election, may not be revoked except with the consent of the Secretary. Any such election or specification with respect to any taxable year beginning after 2002 and before 2010 may be revoked by the taxpayer with respect to any property,and such revocation, once made, shall be irrevocable.

(d) Definitions and special rules. --

(1) Section 179 property. -- For purposes of this section, the term "section 179 property" means property--

(A) which is -

(i) tangible property (to which section 168 applies), or

(ii) computer software (as defined in section 197(e)(3)(B)) which is described in

Sec. 179. Election to expense certain depreciable business assets

section 197(e)(3)(A)(i), to which section 167 applies, and which is placed in service in a taxable year beginning after 2002 and before 2010,

(B) which is section 1245 property (as defined in section1245(a)(3)), and

(C) which is acquired by purchase for use in the active conduct of a trade or business. Such term shall not include any property described in section 50(b) and shall not include air conditioning or heating units.

(2) Purchase defined. -- For purposes of paragraph (1), the term "purchase" means any acquisition of property, but only if--

(A) the property is not acquired from a person whose relationship to the person acquiring it would result in the disallowance of losses under section 267 or 707(b) (but, in applying section 267(b) and (c) for purposes of this section, paragraph (4) of section 267(c) shall be treated as providing that the family of an individual shall include only his spouse, ancestors, and lineal descendants),

(B) the property is not acquired by one component member of a controlled group from another component member of the same controlled group, and

(C) the basis of the property in the hands of the person acquiring it is not determined -

(i) in whole or in part by reference to the adjusted basis of such property in the hands of the person from whom acquired, or

(ii) under section 1014(a) (relating to property acquired from a decedent).

(3) Cost. -- For purposes of this section, the cost of property does not include so much of the basis of such property as is determined by reference to the basis of other property held at any time by the person acquiring such property.

***

(5) Section not to apply to certain noncorporate lessors. -- This section shall not apply to any section 179 property which is purchased by a person who is not a corporation and with respect to which such person is the lessor unless--

(A) the property subject to the lease has been manufactured or produced by the lessor, or

(B) the term of the lease (taking into account options to renew) is less than 50 percent of the class life of the property (as defined in section 168(i)(1)), and for the period consisting of the first 12 months after the date on which the property is transferred to the lessee the sum of the deductions with respect to such property which are allowable to the lessor solely by reason of section 162 (other than rents and reimbursed amounts with respect to such property) exceeds 15 percent of the rental income produced by such property.

***

(9) Coordination with section 38. -- No credit shall be allowed under section 38 with respect to any amount for which a deduction is allowed under subsection (a).

(10) Recapture in certain cases. -- The Secretary shall, by regulations, provide for recapturing the benefit under any deduction allowable under subsection (a) with respect to any property which is not used predominantly in a trade or business at any time.

Sec. 179C. Election to expense certain refineries

(a) Treatment as Expenses. -- A taxpayer may elect to treat 50 percent of the cost of any qualified refinery property as an expense which is not chargeable to capital account. Any cost so treated shall be allowed as a deduction for the taxable year in which the qualified

Sec. 179C. Election to expense certain refineries

refinery property is placed in service.

***

Sec. 179D. Energy efficient commercial buildings deduction

(a) In General. -- There shall be allowed as a deduction an amount equal to the cost of energy efficient commercial building property placed in service during the taxable year.

(b) Maximum Amount of Deduction. -- The deduction under subsection (a) with respect to any building for any taxable year shall not exceed the excess (if any) of --

(1) the product of --

(A) $1.80, and

(B) the square footage of the building, over

(2) the aggregate amount of the deductions under subsection (a) with respect to the building for all prior taxable years.

***

Sec. 180. Expenditures by farmers for fertilizer, etc.

(a) In general. -- A taxpayer engaged in the business of farming may elect to treat as expenses which are not chargeable to capital account expenditures (otherwise chargeable to capital account) which are paid or incurred by him during the taxable year for the purchase or acquisition of fertilizer, lime, ground limestone, marl, or other materials to enrich, neutralize, or condition land used in farming, or for the application of such materials to such land. The expenditures so treated shall be allowed as a deduction.

***

Sec. 183. Activities not engaged in for profit

(a) General rule. -- In the case of an activity engaged in by an individual or an S corporation, if such activity is not engaged in for profit, no deduction attributable to such activity shall be allowed under this chapter except as provided in this section.

(b) Deductions allowable. -- In the case of an activity not engaged in for profit to which subsection (a) applies, there shall be allowed--

(1) the deductions which would be allowable under this chapter for the taxable year without regard to whether or not such activity is engaged in for profit, and

(2) a deduction equal to the amount of the deductions which would be allowable under this chapter for the taxable year only if such activity were engaged in for profit, but only to the extent that the gross income derived from such activity for the taxable year exceeds the deductions allowable by reason of paragraph (1).

(c) Activity not engaged in for profit defined. -- For purposes of this section, the term "activity not engaged in for profit" means any activity other than one with respect to which deductions are allowable for the taxable year under section 162 or under paragraph (1) or (2) of section 212.

(d) Presumption. -- If the gross income derived from an activity for 3 or more of the taxable years in the period of 5 consecutive taxable years which ends with the taxable year exceeds the deductions attributable to such activity (determined without regard to whether or not such activity is engaged in for profit), then, unless the Secretary establishes to the contrary, such activity shall be presumed for purposes of this chapter for such taxable year to be an activity engaged in for

Sec. 183. Activities not engaged in for profit

profit. In the case of an activity which consists in major part of the breeding, training, showing, or racing of horses, the preceding sentence shall be applied by substituting "2" for "3" and "7" for "5".

(e) Special rule. --

(1) In general. -- A determination as to whether the presumption provided by subsection (d) applies with respect to any activity shall, if the taxpayer so elects, not be made before the close of the fourth taxable year (sixth taxable year, in the case of an activity described in the last sentence of such subsection) following the taxable year in which the taxpayer first engages in the activity.

For purposes of the preceding sentence, a taxpayer shall be treated as not having engaged in an activity during any taxable year beginning before January 1, 1970.

(2) Initial period. -- If the taxpayer makes an election under paragraph (1), the presumption provided by subsection (d) shall apply to each taxable year in the 5-taxable year (or 7-taxable year) period beginning with the taxable year in which the taxpayer first engages in the activity, if the gross income derived from the activity for 3 (or 2 if applicable) or more of the taxable years in such period exceeds the deductions attributable to the activity (determined without regard to whether or not the activity is engaged in for profit).

(3) Election. -- An election under paragraph (1) shall be made at such time and manner, and subject to such terms and conditions, as the Secretary may prescribe.

(4) Time for assessing deficiency attributable to activity. -- If a taxpayer makes an election under paragraph (1) with respect to an activity, the statutory period for the assessment of any deficiency attributable to such activity shall not expire before the expiration of 2 years after the date prescribed by law (determined without extensions) for filing the return of tax under chapter 1 for the last taxable year in the period of 5 taxable years (or 7 taxable years) to which the election relates. Such deficiency may be assessed notwithstanding the provisions of any law or rule of law which would otherwise prevent such an assessment.

Reg. § 1.183-1 Activities not engaged in for profit.

(a) *In general.* Section 183 provides rules relating to the allowance of deductions in the case of activities (whether active or passive in character) not engaged in for profit by individuals and electing small business corporations, creates a presumption that an activity is engaged in for profit if certain requirements are met, and permits the taxpayer to elect to postpone determination of whether such presumption applies until he has engaged in the activity for at least 5 taxable years, or, in certain cases, 7 taxable years. Whether an activity is engaged in for profit is determined under section 162 and section 212(1) and (2) except insofar as section 183(d) creates a presumption that the activity is engaged in for profit. If deductions are not allowable under sections 162 and 212(1) and (2), the deduction allowance rules of section 183(b) and this section apply. Pursuant to section 641(b), the taxable income of an estate or trust is computed in the same manner as in the case of an individual, with certain exceptions not here relevant. Accordingly, where an estate or trust engages in an activity or activities which are not for profit, the rules of section 183 and this section apply in computing the allowable deductions of such trust or estate. No inference is to be drawn from the provisions of section 183 and the regulations thereunder that any activity of a corporation (other than an electing small business corporation) is or is not a business or engaged in for profit. For rules relating to the deductions that may be taken into account by taxable membership organizations which are operated primarily to furnish services, facilities, or goods to members, see section 277 and the regulations thereunder. For the definition of an activity not engaged in for profit, see § 1.183-2. For rules relating to the election contained in section 183(e),

Sec. 183. Activities not engaged in for profit

see § 1.183-3.

(b) *Deductions allowable*--(1) *Manner and extent.* If an activity is not engaged in for profit, deductions are allowable under section 183(b) in the following order and only to the following extent:

5   (i) Amounts allowable as deductions during the taxable year under Chapter 1 of the Code without regard to whether the activity giving rise to such amounts was engaged in for profit are allowable to the full extent allowed by the relevant sections of the Code, determined after taking into account any limitations or exceptions with respect to the allowability of such amounts. For example, the allowability-of-interest expenses incurred

10 with respect to activities not engaged in for profit is limited by the rules contained in section 163(d).

(ii) Amounts otherwise allowable as deductions during the taxable year under Chapter 1 of the Code, but only if such allowance does not result in an adjustment to the basis of property, determined as if the activity giving rise to such amounts was engaged in for

15 profit, are allowed only to the extent the gross income attributable to such activity exceeds the deductions allowed or allowable under subdivision (i) of this subparagraph.

(iii) Amounts otherwise allowable as deductions for the taxable year under Chapter 1 of the Code which result in (or if otherwise allowed would have resulted in) an adjustment to the basis of property, determined as if the activity giving rise to such deductions was

20 engaged in for profit, are allowed only to the extent the gross income attributable to such activity exceeds the deductions allowed or allowable under subdivisions (i) and (ii) of this subparagraph. Deductions falling within this subdivision include such items as depreciation, partial losses with respect to property, partially worthless debts, amortization, and amortizable bond premium.

25   (2) *Rule for deductions involving basis adjustments*--(i) *In general.* If deductions are allowed under subparagraph (1)(iii) of this paragraph, and such deductions are allowed with respect to more than one asset, the deduction allowed with respect to each asset shall be determined separately in accordance with the computation set forth in subdivision (ii) of this subparagraph.

30   (ii) *Basis adjustment fractio*n. The deduction allowed under subparagraph (1)(iii) of this paragraph is computed by multiplying the amount which would have been allowed, had the activity been engaged in for profit, as a deduction with respect to each particular asset which involves a basis adjustment, by the basis adjustment fraction:

(a) The numerator of which is the total of deductions allowable under subparagraph

35 (1)(iii) of this paragraph, and

(b) The denominator of which is the total of deductions which involve basis adjustments which would have been allowed with respect to the activity had the activity been engaged in for profit. The amount resulting from this computation is the deduction allowed under subparagraph (1)(iii) of this paragraph with respect to the particular asset.

40 The basis of such asset is adjusted only to the extent of such deduction.

(3) *Examples.* The provisions of subparagraphs (1) and (2) of this paragraph may be illustrated by the following examples:

Example 1. A, an individual, maintains a herd of dairy cattle, which is an ``activity not engaged in for profit" within the meaning of section 183(c). A sold milk for $1,000 during

45 the year. During the year A paid $300 State taxes on gasoline used to transport the cows, milk, etc., and paid $1,200 for feed for the cows. For the year A also had a casualty loss attributable to this activity of $500. A determines the amount of his allowable deductions under section 183 as follows:

(i) First, A computes his deductions allowable under subparagraph (1)(i) of this

50 paragraph as follows:

State gasoline taxes specifically allowed under section 164(a)(5) without regard to whether the activity is engaged in for profit.................................	$300	5
Casualty loss specifically allowed under section 165(c)(3) without regard to whether the activity is engaged in for profit ($500 less $100 limitation)...	400	
Deductions allowable under subparagraph (1)(i) of this paragraph....................................	700	10

(ii) Second, A computes his deductions allowable under subparagraph (1)(ii) of this paragraph (deductions which would be allowed under chapter 1 of the Code if the activity were engaged in for profit and which do not involve basis adjustments) as follows: Maximum amount of deductions allowable under subparagraph (1)(ii) of this paragraph: 15

Income from milk sales...	$1,000	
Gross income from activity...	1,000	
Less: deductions allowable under subparagraph (1)(i) paragraph..	700	20
Maximum amount of deductions allowable under subparagraph (1)(ii) of this paragraph.............................	300	
Feed for cows..	1,200	
Deduction allowed under subparagraph (1)(ii) of this paragraph..	300	25

$900 of the feed expense is not allowed as a deduction under section 183 because the total feed expense ($1,200) exceeds the maximum amount of deductions allowable under subparagraph (1)(ii) of this paragraph ($300). In view of these circumstances, it is not necessary to determine deductions allowable under subparagraph (1)(iii) of this 30 paragraph which would be allowable under chapter 1 of the Code if the activity were engaged in for profit and which involve basis adjustment (the $100 of casualty loss not allowable under subparagraph (1)(i) of this paragraph because of the limitation in section 165(c)(3)) because none of such amount will be allowed as a deduction under section 183. 35

Example 2. Assume the same facts as in Example 1, except that A also had income from sales of hay grown on the farm of $1,200 and that depreciation of $750 with respect to a barn, and $650 with respect to a tractor would have been allowed with respect to the activity had it been engaged in for profit. A determines the amount of his allowable deductions under section 183 as follows: 40

(i) First, A computes his deductions allowable under subparagraph (1)(i) of this paragraph as follows:

State gasoline taxes specifically allowed under section
164(a)(5) without regard to whether the activity is engaged
5 in for profit... $300
Casualty loss specifically allowed under section
165(c)(3) without regard to whether the activity is
engaged in for profit ($500 less $100 limitation)..........   <u>400</u>
Deductions allowable under subparagraph (1)(i)
10 of this paragraph...   700

    (ii) Second, A computes his deductions allowable under subparagraph (1)(ii) of this paragraph (deductions which would be allowable under chapter 1 of the Code if the activity were engaged in for profit and which do not involve basis adjustments) as follows:

15

Maximum amount of deductions allowable under subparagraph (1)(ii) of this paragraph:

Income from milk sales... $1,000
Income from hay sales..   <u>1,200</u>
20 Gross income from activity..   2,200
Less: deductions allowable under subparagraph
(1)(i) of this paragraph..   <u>700</u>
Maximum amount of deductions allowable under
subparagraph (1)(ii) of this paragraph......................   1,500
25 Feed for cows..   1,200

    The entire $1,200 of expenses relating to feed for cows is allowable as a deduction under subparagraph (1)(ii) of this paragraph, since it does not exceed the maximum amount of deductions allowable under such subparagraph.
30   (iii) Last, A computes the deductions allowable under subparagraph (1)(iii) of this paragraph (deductions which would be allowable under chapter 1 of the Code if the activity were engaged in for profit and which involve basis adjustments) as follows:
    Maximum amount of deductions allowable under subparagraph (1)(iii) of this paragraph:

35

Gross income from farming................................ .... $2,200
Less: Deductions allowed under subparagraph
(1)(i) of this paragraph...................................... $700
Deductions allowed under subparagraph (1)(ii) of
40 this paragraph... <u>1,200</u>   <u>1,900</u>
    1,900

Maximum amount of deductions allowable under
subparagraph (1)(iii) of this paragraph..............   300

45   (iv) Since the total of A's deductions under chapter 1 of the Code (determined as if the activity was engaged in for profit) which involve basis adjustments ($750 with respect to barn, $650 with respect to tractor, and $100 with respect to limitation on casualty loss) exceeds the maximum amount of the deductions allowable under subparagraph (1)(iii) of this paragraph ($300), A computes his allowable deductions with respect to such assets
50 as follows:

Sec. 183. Activities not engaged in for profit

A first computes his basis adjustment fraction under subparagraph (2)(ii) of this paragraph as follows:

The numerator of the fraction is the maximum of deductions
 allowable under subparagraph (1)(iii) of this paragraph
 which involve basis adjustments.. $300
The denominator of the fraction is the total of deductions
 that involve basis adjustments which would have been allowed
 with respect to the activity had the activity been engaged
 in for profit.. 1,500

The basis adjustment fraction is then applied to the amount of each deduction which would have been allowable if the activity were engaged in for profit and which involves a basis adjustment as follows:

Depreciation allowed with respect to barn (300/1,500x$750)...... $150
Depreciation allowed with respect to tractor (300/1,500x$650)... 130
Deduction allowed with respect to limitation on casualty loss
 (300/1,500x$100).. 20

    The basis of the barn and of the tractor are adjusted only by the amount of depreciation actually allowed under section 183 with respect to each (as determined by the above computation). The basis of the asset with regard to which the casualty loss was suffered is adjusted only to the extent of the amount of the casualty loss actually allowed as a deduction under subparagraph (1) (i) and (iii) of this paragraph.
    (4) *Rule for capital gains and losses*--(i) *In general*. For purposes of section 183 and the regulations thereunder, the gross income from any activity not engaged in for profit includes the total of all capital gains attributable to such activity determined without regard to the section 1202 deduction. Amounts attributable to an activity not engaged in for profit which would be allowable as a deduction under section 1202, without regard to section 183, shall be allowable as a deduction under section 183(b)(1) in accordance with the rules stated in this subparagraph.
    (ii) *Cases where deduction not allowed under section 183*. No deduction is allowable under section 183(b)(1) with respect to capital gains attributable to an activity not engaged in for profit if:
    (a) Without regard to section 183 and the regulations thereunder, there is no excess of net long-term capital gain over net short-term capital loss for the year, or
    (b) There is no excess of net long-term capital gain attributable to the activity over net short-term capital loss attributable to the activity.
    (iii) *Allocation of deduction*. If there is:
    (a) An excess of net long-term capital gain over net short-term capital loss attributable to an activity not engaged in for profit, and
    (b) Such an excess attributable to all activities, determined without regard to section 183 and the regulations thereunder, the deduction allowable under section 183(b)(1) attributable to capital gains with respect to each activity not engaged in for profit (with respect to which there is an excess of net long-term capital gain over net short-term capital loss for the year) shall be an amount equal to the deduction allowable under section 1202 for the taxable year (determined without regard to section 183) multiplied by a fraction the numerator of which is the excess of the net long-term capital gain attributable to the activity over the net short-term capital loss attributable to the activity and the denominator of which is an amount equal to the total excess of net long-term

Sec. 183. Activities not engaged in for profit

capital gain over net short-term capital loss for all activities with respect to which there is such excess. The amount of the total section 1202 deduction allowable for the year shall be reduced by the amount determined to be allocable to activities not engaged in for profit and accordingly allowed as a deduction under section 183(b)(1).

5   (iv) *Example*. The provisions of this subparagraph may be illustrated by the following example:

Example. A, an individual who uses the cash receipts and disbursement method of accounting and the calendar year as the taxable year, has three activities not engaged in for profit. For his taxable year ending on December 31, 1973, A has a $200 net long-term

10   capital gain from activity No. 1, a $100 net short-term capital loss from activity No. 2, and a $300 net long-term capital gain from activity No. 3. In addition, A has a $500 net long-term capital gain from another activity which he engages in for profit. A computes his deductions for capital gains for calendar year 1973 as follows:

15   Section 1202 deduction without regard to section 183 is determined as follows:

Net long-term capital gain from activity No. 1..................	$200
Net long-term capital gain from activity No. 3..................	300
Net long-term capital gain from activity engaged in for	
20 profit...	500
Total net long-term capital gain from all activities........	1,000
Less: Net short-term capital loss attributable to activity	
No. 2..	100
Aggregate net long-term capital gain over net short-term	
25 capital loss from all activities..	900
Section 1202 deduction determined without regard to	
section 183 (one-half of $900).......................................	$450

Allocation of the total section 1202 deduction among A's various activities:

30

Portion allocable to activity No. 1 which is deductible under section 183(b)(1) (Excess net long-term capital gain attributable to activity No. 1 ($200) over total excess net long-term capital gain attributable to all of A's activities	
35 with respect to which there is such an excess ($1,000) times amount of section 1202 deduction ($450))..............	90
Portion allocable to activity No. 3 which is deductible under section 183(b)(1) (Excess net long-term capital gain attributable to activity No. 3 ($300) over total excess net	
40 long-term capital gain attributable to all of A's activities with respect to which there is such an excess ($1,000) a times mount of section 1202 deduction ($450))..............	135
Portion allocable to all activities engaged in for profit (total section 1202 deduction ($450) less section 1202	
45 deduction allowable to activities Nos. 1 and 3 ($225)).......	225
Total section 1202 deduction deductible under sections 1202 and 183(b)(1)..	450

(c) Presumption that activity is engaged in for profit--(1) *In general*. If for:

50   (i) Any 2 of 7 consecutive taxable years, in the case of an activity which consists in major part of the breeding, training, showing, or racing of horses, or

Sec. 183. Activities not engaged in for profit

(ii) Any 2 of 5 consecutive taxable years, in the case of any other activity, the gross income derived from an activity exceeds the deductions attributable to such activity which would be allowed or allowable if the activity were engaged in for profit, such activity is presumed, unless the Commissioner establishes to the contrary, to be engaged in for profit. For purposes of this determination the deduction permitted by section 1202 shall 5 not be taken into account. Such presumption applies with respect to the second profit year and all years subsequent to the second profit year within the 5- or 7-year period beginning with the first profit year. This presumption arises only if the activity is substantially the same activity for each of the relevant taxable years, including the taxable year in question. If the taxpayer does not meet the requirements of section 183(d) 10 and this paragraph, no inference that the activity is not engaged in for profit shall arise by reason of the provisions of section 183. For purposes of this paragraph, a net operating loss deduction is not taken into account as a deduction. For purposes of this subparagraph a short taxable year constitutes a taxable year.

(2) *Examples.* The provisions of subparagraph (1) of this paragraph may be illustrated 15 by the following examples, in each of which it is assumed that the taxpayer has not elected, in accordance with section 183(e), to postpone determination of whether the presumption described in section 183(d) and this paragraph is applicable.

Example 1. For taxable years 1970-74, A, an individual who uses the cash receipts and disbursement method of accounting and the calendar year as the taxable year, is 20 engaged in the activity of farming. In taxable years 1971, 1973, and 1974, A's deductible expenditures with respect to such activity exceed his gross income from the activity. In taxable years 1970 and 1972 A has income from the sale of farm produce of $30,000 for each year. In each of such years A had expenses for feed for his livestock of $10,000, depreciation of equipment of $10,000, and fertilizer cost of $5,000 which he elects to take 25 as a deduction. A also has a net operating loss carryover to taxable year 1970 of $6,000. A is presumed, for taxable years 1972, 1973, and 1974, to have engaged in the activity of farming for profit, since for 2 years of a 5-consecutive-year period the gross income from the activity ($30,000 for each year) exceeded the deductions (computed without regard to the net operating loss) which are allowable in the case of the activity ($25,000 for each 30 year).

Example 2. For the taxable years 1970 and 1971, B, an individual who uses the cash receipts and disbursement method of accounting and the calendar year as taxable year, engaged in raising pure-bred Charolais cattle for breeding purposes. The operation showed a loss during 1970. At the end of 1971, B sold a substantial portion of his herd 35 and the cattle operation showed a profit for that year. For all subsequent relevant taxable years B continued to keep a few Charolais bulls at stud. In 1972, B started to raise Tennessee Walking Horses for breeding and show purposes, utilizing substantially the same pasture land, barns, and (with structural modifications) the same stalls. The Walking Horse operations showed a small profit in 1973 and losses in 1972 and 1974 40 through 1976.

(i) Assuming that under paragraph (d)(1) of this section the raising of cattle and raising of horses are determined to be separate activities, no presumption that the Walking Horse operation was carried on for profit arises under section 183(d) and this paragraph since this activity was not the same activity that generated the profit in 1971 and there 45 are not, therefore, 2 profit years attributable to the horse activity.

(ii) Assuming the same facts as in (i) above, if there were no stud fees received in 1972 with respect to Charolais bulls, but for 1973 stud fees with respect to such bulls exceed deductions attributable to maintenance of the bulls in that year, the presumption will arise under section 183(d) and this paragraph with respect to the activity of raising 50 and maintaining Charolais cattle for 1973 and for all subsequent years within the 5-year

period beginning with taxable year 1971, since the activity of raising and maintaining Charolais cattle is the same activity in 1971 and in 1973, although carried on by B on a much reduced basis and in a different manner. Since it has been assumed that the horse and cattle operations are separate activities, no presumption will arise with respect to the
5 Walking Horse operation because there are not 2 profit years attributable to such horse operation during the period in question.

(iii) Assuming, alternatively, that the raising of cattle and raising of horses would be considered a single activity under paragraph (d)(1) of this section, B would receive the benefit of the presumption beginning in 1973 with respect to both the cattle and horses
10 since there were profits in 1971 and 1973. The presumption would be effective through 1977 (and longer if there is an excess of income over deductions in this activity in 1974, 1975, 1976, or 1977 which would extend the presumption) if, under section 183(d) and subparagraph (3) of this paragraph, it was determined that the activity consists in major part of the breeding, training, showing, or racing of horses. Otherwise, the presumption
15 would be effective only through 1975 (assuming no excess of income over deductions in this activity in 1974 or 1975 which would extend the presumption).

(3) *Activity which consists in major part of the breeding, training, showing, or racing of horses.* For purposes of this paragraph an activity consists in major part of the breeding, training, showing, or racing of horses for the taxable year if the average of the portion of
20 expenditures attributable to breeding, training, showing, and racing of horses for the 3 taxable years preceding the taxable year (or, in the case of an activity which has not been conducted by the taxpayer for 3 years, for so long as it has been carried on by him) was at least 50 percent of the total expenditures attributable to the activity for such prior taxable years.
25
***

(5) *Cross reference.* For rules relating to section 183(e) which permits a taxpayer to elect to postpone determination of whether any activity shall be presumed to be ``an activity engaged in for profit'' by operation of the presumption described in section 183(d) and this paragraph until after the close of the fourth taxable year (sixth taxable year, in
30 the case of activity which consists in major part of breeding, training, showing, or racing of horses) following the taxable year in which the taxpayer first engages in the activity, see § 1.183-3.

(d) *Activity defined*--(1) *Ascertainment of activity.* In order to determine whether, and to what extent, section 183 and the regulations thereunder apply, the activity or activities
35 of the taxpayer must be ascertained. For instance, where the taxpayer is engaged in several undertakings, each of these may be a separate activity, or several undertakings may constitute one activity. In ascertaining the activity or activities of the taxpayer, all the facts and circumstances of the case must be taken into account. Generally, the most significant facts and circumstances in making this determination are the degree of
40 organizational and economic interrelationship of various undertakings, the business purpose which is (or might be) served by carrying on the various undertakings separately or together in a trade or business or in an investment setting, and the similarity of various undertakings. Generally, the Commissioner will accept the characterization by the taxpayer of several undertakings either as a single activity or as separate activities. The
45 taxpayer's characterization will not be accepted, however, when it appears that his characterization is artificial and cannot be reasonably supported under the facts and circumstances of the case. If the taxpayer engages in two or more separate activities, deductions and income from each separate activity are not aggregated either in determining whether a particular activity is engaged in for profit or in applying section
50 183. Where land is purchased or held primarily with the intent to profit from increase in its value, and the taxpayer also engages in farming on such land, the farming and the

Sec. 183. Activities not engaged in for profit

holding of the land will ordinarily be considered a single activity only if the farming activity reduces the net cost of carrying the land for its appreciation in value. Thus, the farming and holding of the land will be considered a single activity only if the income derived from farming exceeds the deductions attributable to the farming activity which are not directly attributable to the holding of the land (that is, deductions other than those directly attributable to the holding of the land such as interest on a mortgage secured by the land, annual property taxes attributable to the land and improvements, and depreciation of improvements to the land).

(2) *Rules for allocation of expenses.* If the taxpayer is engaged in more than one activity, an item of deduction or income may be allocated between two or more of these activities. Where property is used in several activities, and one or more of such activities is determined not to be engaged in for profit, deductions relating to such property must be allocated between the various activities on a reasonable and consistently applied basis.

(3) *Example.* The provisions of this paragraph may be illustrated by the following example:

Example. (i) A, an individual, owns a small house located near the beach in a resort community. Visitors come to the area for recreational purposes during only 3 months of the year. During the remaining 9 months of the year houses such as A's are not rented. Customarily, A arranges that the house will be leased for 2 months of 3-month recreational season to vacationers and reserves the house for his own vacation during the remaining month of the recreational season. In 1971, A leases the house for 2 months for $1,000 per month and actually uses the house for his own vacation during the other month of the recreational season. For 1971, the expenses attributable to the house are $1,200 interest, $600 real estate taxes, $600 maintenance, $300 utilities, and $1,200 which would have been allowed as depreciation had the activity been engaged in for profit. Under these facts and circumstances, A is engaged in a single activity, holding the beach house primarily for personal purposes, which is an ``activity not engaged in for profit'' within the meaning of section 183(c). See paragraph (b)(9) of § 1.183-2.

(ii) Since the $1,200 of interest and the $600 of real estate taxes are specifically allowable as deductions under sections 163 and 164(a) without regard to whether the beach house activity is engaged in for profit, no allocation of these expenses between the uses of the beach house is necessary. However, since section 262 specifically disallows personal, living, and family expenses as deductions, the maintenance and utilities expenses and the depreciation from the activity must be allocated between the rental use and the personal use of the beach house. Under the particular facts and circumstances, 2/3 (2 months of rental use over 3 months of total use) of each of these expenses are allocated to the rental use, and 1/3 (1 month of personal use over 3 months of total use) of each of these expenses are allocated to the personal use as follows:

	Rental use 2/3-- expenses allocable to section 183(b)(2)	Personal use 1/3-- expenses allocable to section 262
Maintenance expense $600........................	$400	$200
Utilities expense $300.............................	200	100
Depreciation $1,200.................................	800	400
Total..	1,400	700

Sec. 183. Activities not engaged in for profit

The $700 of expenses and depreciation allocated to the personal use of the beach house are disallowed as a deduction under section 262. In addition, the allowability of each of the expenses and the depreciation allocated to section 183(b)(2) is determined under paragraph (b)(1)(ii) and (iii) of this section. Thus, the maximum amount allowable as a
5 deduction under section 183(b)(2) is $200 ($2,000 gross income from activity, less $1,800 deductions under section 183(b)(1)). Since the amounts described in section 183(b)(2) ($1,400) exceed the maximum amount allowable ($200), and since the amounts described in paragraph (b)(1)(ii) of this section ($600) exceed such maximum amount allowable ($200), none of the depreciation (an amount described in paragraph (b)
10 (1)(iii) of this section) is allowable as a deduction.

(e) *Gross income from activity not engaged in for profit defined.* For purposes of section 183 and the regulations thereunder, gross income derived from an activity not engaged in for profit includes the total of all gains from the sale, exchange, or other disposition of property, and all other gross receipts derived from such activity. Such gross
15 income shall include, for instance, capital gains, and rents received for the use of property which is held in connection with the activity. The taxpayer may determine gross income from any activity by subtracting the cost of goods sold from the gross receipts so long as he consistently does so and follows generally accepted methods of accounting in determining such gross income.

20 ***

Reg. § 1.183-2   Activity not engaged in for profit defined.

(a) *In general.* For purposes of section 183 and the regulations thereunder, the term activity not engaged in for profit means any activity other than one with respect to which deductions are allowable for the taxable year under section 162 or under paragraph (1) or
25 (2) of section 212. Deductions are allowable under section 162 for expenses of carrying on activities which constitute a trade or business of the taxpayer and under section 212 for expenses incurred in connection with activities engaged in for the production or collection of income or for the management, conservation, or maintenance of property held for the production of income. Except as provided in section 183 and § 1.183-1, no
30 deductions are allowable for expenses incurred in connection with activities which are not engaged in for profit. Thus, for example, deductions are not allowable under section 162 or 212 for activities which are carried on primarily as a sport, hobby, or for recreation. The determination whether an activity is engaged in for profit is to be made by reference to objective standards, taking into account all of the facts and circumstances of each case.
35 Although a reasonable expectation of profit is not required, the facts and circumstances must indicate that the taxpayer entered into the activity, or continued the activity, with the objective of making a profit. In determining whether such an objective exists, it may be sufficient that there is a small chance of making a large profit. Thus it may be found that an investor in a wildcat oil well who incurs very substantial expenditures is in the venture
40 for profit even though the expectation of a profit might be considered unreasonable. In determining whether an activity is engaged in for profit, greater weight is given to objective facts than to the taxpayer's mere statement of his intent.

(b) *Relevant factors.* In determining whether an activity is engaged in for profit, all facts and circumstances with respect to the activity are to be taken into account. No one
45 factor is determinative in making this determination. In addition, it is not intended that only the factors described in this paragraph are to be taken into account in making the determination, or that a determination is to be made on the basis that the number of factors (whether or not listed in this paragraph) indicating a lack of profit objective exceeds the number of factors indicating a profit objective, or vice versa. Among the
50 factors which should normally be taken into account are the following:

Sec. 183. Activities not engaged in for profit

(1) M*anner in which the taxpayer carries on the activity*. The fact that the taxpayer carries on the activity in a businesslike manner and maintains complete and accurate books and records may indicate that the activity is engaged in for profit. Similarly, where an activity is carried on in a manner substantially similar to other activities of the same nature which are profitable, a profit motive may be indicated. A change of operating 5 methods, adoption of new techniques or abandonment of unprofitable methods in a manner consistent with an intent to improve profitability may also indicate a profit motive.

(2) *The expertise of the taxpayer or his advisors*. Preparation for the activity by extensive study of its accepted business, economic, and scientific practices, or consultation with those who are expert therein, may indicate that the taxpayer has a profit 10 motive where the taxpayer carries on the activity in accordance with such practices. Where a taxpayer has such preparation or procures such expert advice, but does not carry on the activity in accordance with such practices, a lack of intent to derive profit may be indicated unless it appears that the taxpayer is attempting to develop new or superior techniques which may result in profits from the activity. 15

(3) *The time and effort expended by the taxpayer in carrying on the activity*. The fact that the taxpayer devotes much of his personal time and effort to carrying on an activity, particularly if the activity does not have substantial personal or recreational aspects, may indicate an intention to derive a profit. A taxpayer's withdrawal from another occupation to devote most of his energies to the activity may also be evidence that the activity is 20 engaged in for profit. The fact that the taxpayer devotes a limited amount of time to an activity does not necessarily indicate a lack of profit motive where the taxpayer employs competent and qualified persons to carry on such activity.

(4) *Expectation that assets used in activity may appreciate in value*. The term profit encompasses appreciation in the value of assets, such as land, used in the activity. Thus, 25 the taxpayer may intend to derive a profit from the operation of the activity, and may also intend that, even if no profit from current operations is derived, an overall profit will result when appreciation in the value of land used in the activity is realized since income from the activity together with the appreciation of land will exceed expenses of operation. See, however, paragraph (d) of § 1.183-1 for definition of an activity in this connection. 30

(5) *The success of the taxpayer in carrying on other similar or dissimilar activities*. The fact that the taxpayer has engaged in similar activities in the past and converted them from unprofitable to profitable enterprises may indicate that he is engaged in the present activity for profit, even though the activity is presently unprofitable.

(6) *The taxpayer's history of income or losses with respect to the activity*. A series of 35 losses during the initial or start-up stage of an activity may not necessarily be an indication that the activity is not engaged in for profit. However, where losses continue to be sustained beyond the period which customarily is necessary to bring the operation to profitable status such continued losses, if not explainable, as due to customary business risks or reverses, may be indicative that the activity is not being engaged in for profit. If 40 losses are sustained because of unforeseen or fortuitous circumstances which are beyond the control of the taxpayer, such as drought, disease, fire, theft, weather damages, other involuntary conversions, or depressed market conditions, such losses would not be an indication that the activity is not engaged in for profit. A series of years in which net income was realized would of course be strong evidence that the activity is 45 engaged in for profit.

(7) *The amount of occasional profits, if any, which are earned*. The amount of profits in relation to the amount of losses incurred, and in relation to the amount of the taxpayer's investment and the value of the assets used in the activity, may provide useful criteria in determining the taxpayer's intent. An occasional small profit from an activity 50 generating large losses, or from an activity in which the taxpayer has made a large

Sec. 183. Activities not engaged in for profit

investment, would not generally be determinative that the activity is engaged in for profit. However, substantial profit, though only occasional, would generally be indicative that an activity is engaged in for profit, where the investment or losses are comparatively small. Moreover, an opportunity to earn a substantial ultimate profit in a highly speculative
5 venture is ordinarily sufficient to indicate that the activity is engaged in for profit even though losses or only occasional small profits are actually generated.

(8) *The financial status of the taxpayer.* The fact that the taxpayer does not have substantial income or capital from sources other than the activity may indicate that an activity is engaged in for profit. Substantial income from sources other than the activity
10 (particularly if the losses from the activity generate substantial tax benefits) may indicate that the activity is not engaged in for profit especially if there are personal or recreational elements involved.

(9) *Elements of personal pleasure or recreation.* The presence of personal motives in carrying on of an activity may indicate that the activity is not engaged in for profit,
15 especially where there are recreational or personal elements involved. On the other hand, a profit motivation may be indicated where an activity lacks any appeal other than profit. It is not, however, necessary that an activity be engaged in with the exclusive intention of deriving a profit or with the intention of maximizing profits. For example, the availability of other investments which would yield a higher return, or which would be
20 more likely to be profitable, is not evidence that an activity is not engaged in for profit. An activity will not be treated as not engaged in for profit merely because the taxpayer has purposes or motivations other than solely to make a profit. Also, the fact that the taxpayer derives personal pleasure from engaging in the activity is not sufficient to cause the activity to be classified as not engaged in for profit if the activity is in fact engaged in for
25 profit as evidenced by other factors whether or not listed in this paragraph.

(c) *Examples.* The provisions of this section may be illustrated by the following examples:

Example 1. The taxpayer inherited a farm from her husband in an area which was becoming largely residential, and is now nearly all so. The farm had never made a profit
30 before the taxpayer inherited it, and the farm has since had substantial losses in each year. The decedent from whom the taxpayer inherited the farm was a stockbroker, and he also left the taxpayer substantial stock holdings which yield large income from dividends. The taxpayer lives on an area of the farm which is set aside exclusively for living purposes. A farm manager is employed to operate the farm, but modern methods are not
35 used in operating the farm. The taxpayer was born and raised on a farm, and expresses a strong preference for living on a farm. The taxpayer's activity of farming, based on all the facts and circumstances, could be found not to be engaged in for profit.

Example 2. The taxpayer is a wealthy individual who is greatly interested in philosophy. During the past 30 years he has written and published at his own expense several
40 pamphlets, and he has engaged in extensive lecturing activity, advocating and disseminating his ideas. He has made a profit from these activities in only occasional years, and the profits in those years were small in relation to the amounts of the losses in all other years. The taxpayer has very sizable income from securities (dividends and capital gains) which constitutes the principal source of his livelihood. The activity of
45 lecturing, publishing pamphlets, and disseminating his ideas is not an activity engaged in by the taxpayer for profit.

Example 3. The taxpayer, very successful in the business of retailing soft drinks, raises dogs and horses. He began raising a particular breed of dogs many years ago in the belief that the breed was in danger of declining, and he has raised and sold the dogs in
50 each year since. The taxpayer recently began raising and racing thoroughbred horses. The losses from the taxpayer's dog and horse activities have increased in magnitude

Sec. 183. Activities not engaged in for profit

over the years, and he has not made a profit on these operations during any of the last 15 years. The taxpayer generally sells the dogs only to friends, does not advertise the dogs for sale, and shows the dogs only infrequently. The taxpayer races his horses only at the ``prestige" tracks at which he combines his racing activities with social and recreational activities. The horse and dog operations are conducted at a large residential 5 property on which the taxpayer also lives, which includes substantial living quarters and attractive recreational facilities for the taxpayer and his family. Since (i) the activity of raising dogs and horses and racing the horses is of a sporting and recreational nature, (ii) the taxpayer has substantial income from his business activities of retailing soft drinks, (iii) the horse and dog operations are not conducted in a businesslike manner, and (iv) 10 such operations have a continuous record of losses, it could be determined that the horse and dog activities of the taxpayer are not engaged in for profit.

Example 4. The taxpayer inherited a farm of 65 acres from his parents when they died 6 years ago. The taxpayer moved to the farm from his house in a small nearby town, and he operates it in the same manner as his parents operated the farm before they died. The 15 taxpayer is employed as a skilled machine operator in a nearby factory, for which he is paid approximately $8,500 per year. The farm has not been profitable for the past 15 years because of rising costs of operating farms in general, and because of the decline in the price of the produce of this farm in particular. The taxpayer consults the local agent of the State agricultural service from time to time, and the suggestions of the agent have 20 generally been followed. The manner in which the farm is operated by the taxpayer is substantially similar to the manner in which farms of similar size, and which grow similar crops in the area, are operated. Many of these other farms do not make profits. The taxpayer does much of the required labor around the farm himself, such as fixing fences, planting crops, etc. The activity of farming could be found, based on all the facts and 25 circumstances, to be engaged in by the taxpayer for profit.

Example 5. A, an independent oil and gas operator, frequently engages in the activity of searching for oil on undeveloped and unexplored land which is not near proven fields. He does so in a manner substantially similar to that of others who engage in the same activity. The chances, based on the experience of A and others who engaged in this 30 activity, are strong that A will not find a commercially profitable oil deposit when he drills on land not established geologically to be proven oil bearing land. However, on the rare occasions that these activities do result in discovering a well, the operator generally realizes a very large return from such activity. Thus, there is a small chance that A will make a large profit from his soil exploration activity. Under these circumstances, A is 35 engaged in the activity of oil drilling for profit.

Example 6. C, a chemist, is employed by a large chemical company and is engaged in a wide variety of basic research projects for his employer. Although he does no work for his employer with respect to the development of new plastics, he has always been interested in such development and has outfitted a workshop in his home at his own 40 expense which he uses to experiment in the field. He has patented several developments at his own expense but as yet has realized no income from his inventions or from such patents. C conducts his research on a regular, systematic basis, incurs fees to secure consultation on his projects from time to time, and makes extensive efforts to ``market" his developments. C has devoted substantial time and expense in an effort to develop a 45 plastic sufficiently hard, durable, and malleable that it could be used in lieu of sheet steel in many major applications, such as automobile bodies. Although there may be only a small chance that C will invent new plastics, the return from any such development would be so large that it induces C to incur the costs of his experimental work. C is sufficiently qualified by his background that there is some reasonable basis for his experimental 50 activities. C's experimental work does not involve substantial personal or recreational

531

aspects and is conducted in an effort to find practical applications for his work. Under these circumstances, C may be found to be engaged in the experimental activities for profit.

5 [T.D. 7198, 37 FR 13683, July 13, 1972]

Sec. 186. Recoveries of damages for antitrust violations, etc.

(a) Allowance of deduction. -- If a compensatory amount which is included in gross income is received or accrued during the taxable year for a compensable injury, there shall be allowed as a
10 deduction for the taxable year an amount equal to the lesser of--

   (1) the amount of such compensatory amount, or

   (2) the amount of the unrecovered losses sustained as a result of such compensable injury.

(b) Compensable injury. -- For purposes of this section, the term "compensable injury" means-

   (1) injuries sustained as a result of an infringement of a patent issued by the United States,

15   **(2)** injuries sustained as a result of a breach of contract or a breach of fiduciary duty or relationship, or

   (3) injuries sustained in business, or to property, by reason of any conduct forbidden in the antitrust laws for which a civil action may be brought under section 4 of the Act ... (commonly known as the Clayton Act).

20 **(c) Compensatory amount.** -- For purposes of this section, the term "compensatory amount" means the amount received or accrued during the taxable year as damages as a result of an award in, or in settlement of, a civil action for recovery for a compensable injury, reduced by any amounts paid or incurred in the taxable year in securing such award or settlement.

   (d) Unrecovered losses. --
25   **(1) In general.** -- For purposes of this section, the amount of any unrecovered loss sustained as a result of any compensable injury is--

      (A) the sum of the amount of the net operating losses (as determined under section 172) for each taxable year in whole or in part within the injury period, to the extent that such net operating losses are attributable to such compensable injury, reduced by

30   **(B)** the sum of--

         (i) the amount of the net operating losses described in subparagraph (A) which were allowed for any prior taxable year as a deduction under section 172 as a net operating loss carryback or carryover to such taxable year, and (ii) the amounts allowed as a deduction under subsection (a) for any prior taxable year for prior recoveries of
35   compensatory amounts for such compensable injury.

***

(2) Injury period. -- For purposes of paragraph (1), the injury period is--

   (A) with respect to any infringement of a patent, the period in which such infringement occurred,

40   **(B)** with respect to a breach of contract or breach of fiduciary duty or relationship, the period during which amounts would have been received or accrued but for the breach of contract or breach of fiduciary duty or relationship, and

   (C) with respect to injuries sustained by reason of any conduct forbidden in the antitrust laws, the period in which such injuries were sustained.

45 ***

Sec. 186. Recoveries of damages for antitrust violations, etc.

Reg. § 1.186-1 Recoveries of damages for antitrust violations, etc.

(a) *Allowance of deduction.* Under section 186, when a compensatory amount which is included in gross income is received or accrued during a taxable year for a compensable injury, a deduction is allowed in an amount equal to the lesser of (1) such compensatory amount, or (2) the unrecovered losses sustained as a result of such 5 compensable injury.

(b) *Compensable injury*--(1) *In general.* For purposes of this section, the term compensable injury means any of the injuries described in subparagraph (2), (3), or (4) of this paragraph.

(2) *Patent infringement.* An injury sustained as a result of an infringement of a patent 10 issued by the United States (whether or not issued to the taxpayer or another person or persons) constitutes a compensable injury. The term patent issued by the United States means any patent issued or granted by the United States under the authority of the Commissioner of Patents pursuant to 35 U.S.C. 153.

(3) *Breach of contract or of fiduciary duty or relationship.* An injury sustained as a 15 result of a breach of contract (including an injury sustained by a third party beneficiary) or a breach of fiduciary duty or relationship constitutes a compensable injury.

(4) *Injury suffered under certain antitrust law violations.* An injury sustained in business, or to property, by reason of any conduct forbidden in the antitrust laws for which a civil action may be brought under section 4 of the Act of October 15, 1914 (15 20 U.S.C. 15), commonly known as the Clayton Act, constitutes a compensable injury.

(c) *Compensatory amount*--(1) *In general.* For purposes of this section, the term, compensatory amount means any amount received or accrued during the taxable year as damages as a result of an award in, or in settlement of, a civil action for recovery for a compensable injury, reduced by any amounts paid or incurred in the taxable year in 25 securing such award or settlement. The term compensatory amount includes only amounts compensating for actual economic injury. Thus, additional amounts representing punitive, exemplary, or treble damages are not included within the term. Where, for example, a taxpayer recovers treble damages under section 4 of the Clayton Act, only one-third of the recovery representing economic injury constitutes a compensatory 30 amount. In the absence of any indication to the contrary, amounts received in settlement of an action shall be deemed to be a recovery for an actual economic injury except to the extent such settlement amounts exceed actual damages claimed by the taxpayer in such action.

(2) *Interest on a compensatory amount.* Interest attributable to a compensatory 35 amount shall not be included within the term compensatory amount.

(3) *Settlement of a civil action for damages*--(i) *Necessity for an action.* The term compensatory amount does not include an amount received or accrued in settlement of a claim for a compensable injury if the amount is received or accrued prior to institution of an action. An action shall be considered as instituted upon completion of service of 40 process, in accordance with the laws and rules of the court in which the action has been commenced or to which the action has been removed, upon all defendants who pay or incur an obligation to pay a compensatory amount.

(ii) *Specifications of the parties.* If an action for a compensable injury is settled, the specifications of the parties will generally determine compensatory amounts unless such 45 specifications are not reasonably supported by the facts and circumstances of the case. For example, the parties may provide that the sum of $1,000 represents actual damages sustained as the result of antitrust violations and that the total amount of the settlement after the trebling of damages is $3,000. In such case, only the sum of $1,000 would be a compensatory amount. In the absence of specifications of the parties, the complaint filed 50 by the taxpayer may be considered in determining what portion of the amount of the

533

Sec. 186. Recoveries of damages for antitrust violations, etc.

settlement is a compensatory amount.

(4) Amounts paid or incurred in securing the award or settlement. For purposes of this section, the term amounts paid or incurred in the taxable year in securing such award or settlement shall include legal expenses such as attorney's fees, witness fees, accountant fees, and court costs. Expenses incurred in securing a recovery of both a compensatory amount and other amounts from the same action shall be allocated among such amounts in the ratio each of such amounts bears to the total recovery. For instance, where a taxpayerincurs attorney's fees and other expenses of $3,000 in recovering $10,000 as a compensatory amount, $5,000 as a return of capital, and $25,000 as punitive damages from the same action, the taxpayer shall allocate $750 of the expenses to the compensatory amount (10,000/40,000x3,000), $375 to the return of capital (5,000/40,000x3,000), and $1,875 to the punitive damages (25,000/40,000x 3,000).

(d) *Unrecovered losses*--(1) *In general*. For purposes of this section, the term unrecovered losses sustained as a result of such compensable injury means the sum of the amounts of the net operating losses for each taxable year in whole or in part within the injury period, to the extent that such net operating losses are attributable to such compensable injury, reduced by (i) the sum of any amounts of such net operating losses which were allowed as a net operating loss carryback or carryover for any prior taxable year under the provisions of section 172, and (ii) the sum of any amounts allowed as deductions under section 186(a) and this section for all prior taxable years with respect to the same compensable injury. Accordingly, a deduction is permitted under section 186(a) and this section with respect to net operating losses whether or not the period for carryover under section 172 has expired.

(2) *Injury period*. For purposes of this section, the term injury period means (i) with respect to an infringement of a patent, the period during which the infringement of the patent continued, (ii) with respect to a breach of contract or breach of fiduciary duty or relationship, the period during which amounts would have been received or accrued but for such breach of contract or breach of fiduciary duty or relationship, or (iii) with respect to injuries sustained by reason of a violation of section 4 of the Clayton Act, the period during which such injuries were sustained. The injury period will be determined on the basis of the facts and circumstances of the taxpayer's situation. The injury period may include a periods before and after the period covered by the civil action instituted.

(3) *Net operating losses attributable to compensable injuries*. A net operating loss for any taxable year shall be treated as attributable (whether actually attributable or not) to a compensable injury to the extent the compensable injury is sustained during the taxable year. For purposes of determining the extent of the compensable injury sustained during a taxable year, a judgment for a compensable injury apportioning the amount of the recovery (not reduced by any amounts paid or incurred in securing such recovery) to specific taxable years within the injury period will be conclusive. If a judgment for a compensable injury does not apportion the amount of the recovery to specific taxable years within the injury period, the amount of the recovery will be prorated among the years within the injury period in the proportion that the net operating loss sustained in each of such years bear to the total net operating losses sustained for all such years. If an action is settled, the specifications of the parties will generally determine the apportionment of the amount of the recovery unless such specifications are not reasonably supported by the facts and circumstances of the case. In the absence of specifications of the parties, the amount of the recovery will be prorated among the years within the injury period in the proportion that the net operating loss sustained in each of such years bears to the total net operating losses sustained for all such years.

(4) *Application of losses attributable to a compensable injury*. If only a portion of a net operating loss for any taxable year is attributable to a compensable injury, such portion

Sec. 186. Recoveries of damages for antitrust violations, etc.

shall (in applying section 172 for purposes of this section) be considered to be a separate net operating loss for such year to be applied after the other portion of such net operating loss. If, for example, in the year of the compensable injury the net operating loss was $1,000 and the amount of the compensable injury was $600, the amount of $400 not attributable to the compensable injury would be used first to offset profits in the carryover 5 or carryback periods as prescribed by section 172. After the amount not attributable to the compensable injury is used to offset profits in other years, then the amount attributable to the compensable injury will be applied against profits in the carryover or carryback periods.

(e) *Effect on net operating loss carryovers*--(1) *In general.* Under section 186 (e) if for 10 the taxable year in which a compensatory amount is received or accrued any portion of the net operating loss carryovers to such year is attributable to the compensable injury for which such amount is received or accrued, such portion of the net operating loss carryovers must be reduced by the excess, if any, of (i) the amount computed under section 186(e)(1) with respect to such compensatory amount, over (ii) the amount 15 computed under section 186(e)(2) with respect to such compensable injury.

(2) *Amount computed under section 186(e)(1).* The amount computed under section 186(e)(1) is equal to the deduction allowed under section 186(a) with respect to the compensatory amount received or accrued for the taxable year.

(3) *Amount computed under section 186(e)(2).* The amount computed under section 20 186(e)(2) is equal to that portion of the unrecovered losses sustained as a result of the compensable injury with respect to which, as of the beginning of the taxable year, the period for carryover under section 172 has expired without benefit to the taxpayer, but only to the extent that such portion of the unrecovered losses did not reduce an amount computed under section 186(e)(1) for any prior taxable year.   25

(4) *Increase in income under section 172(b)(2).* If there is a reduction for any taxable year under subparagraph (1) of this paragraph in the portion of the net operating loss carryovers to such year attributable to a compensable injury, then, solely for purposes of determining the amount of such portion which may be carried to subsequent taxable years, the income of such taxable year, as computed under section 172(b)(2), shall be 30 increased by the amount of the reduction computed under subparagraph (1) of this paragraph, for such year.

(f) *Illustration.* The provisions of section 186 and this section may be illustrated by the following example:

Example. (i) As of the beginning of his taxable year 1969, taxpayer A has a net 35 operating loss carryover from his taxable year 1966 of $550 of which $250 is attributable to a compensable injury. In addition, he has a net operating loss attributable to the compensable injury of $150 with respect to which the period for carryover under section 172 has expired without benefit to the taxpayer. In 1969, he receives a $100 compensatory amount with respect to that injury and he has $75 in other income. Thus, A 40 has gross income of $175 and he is entitled to a $100 deduction (the compensatory amount received) under section 186(a) and this section since this amount is less than the unrecovered losses sustained as a result of the compensable injury ($250+$150=$400). No portion of the net operating loss carryover to the current taxable year attributable to the compensable injury is reduced under section 186(e) since the amount determined 45 under section 186(e)(1) ($100) does not exceed the amount determined under section 186(e)(2) ($150). Therefore, A applies a net operating loss carryover of $550 against his remaining income of $75 and retains a net operating loss carryover of $475 to following years of which amount $250 remains attributable to the compensable injury. In addition, he retains $50 of net operating losses attributable to the compensable injury with respect 50 to which the period for carryover under section 172 has expired without benefit to the taxpayer.

(ii) In 1970, A receives a $200 compensatory amount with respect to the same compensable injury and has $75 of other income. Thus, A has gross income of $275 and he is entitled to a $200 deduction (the compensatory amount received) under section 186(a) and this section since this amount is less than the remaining unrecovered loss sustained as a result of the compensable injury ($250+$50=$300). The net operating loss carryover to the current taxable year of $250 attributable to the compensable injury is reduced under section 186(e) by $150, which is the excess of the amount determined under section 186(e)(1) ($200) over the amount determined under section 186(e)(2) ($50). Therefore, A applies net operating loss carryovers of $325 ($225 not attributable to the compensable injury, +$100 attributable to such injury) against his remaining income of $75. A retains net operating loss carryovers of $250 for following years, of which amount $100 is attributable to the compensable injury. A has used all of his net operating losses attributable to the compensable injury with respect to which the period for carryover under section 172 has expired without benefit to the taxpayer.

(iii) In 1971, A receives a $200 compensatory amount with respect to the same compensable injury and has $75 of other income. Thus, A has gross income of $275 and he is entitled to a $100 deduction (the amount of unrecovered losses) under section 186(a) and this section since this amount is less than the compensatory amount received ($200). The net operating loss carryover to the current taxable year of $100 attributable to the compensable injury is reduced under section 186(e) by $100, which is the excess of the amount determined under section 186(e)(1) ($100) over the amount determined under section 186(e)(2) ($0). Therefore, A applies net operating loss carryovers of $150 against his remaining income of $175 ($100 compensatory amount plus $75 other income) which leaves $25 taxable income. No net operating loss carryover remains for following years.

***

[T.D. 7220, 37 FR 24744, Nov. 21, 1972]

Sec. 190. Expenditures to remove architectural and transportation barriers to the handicapped and elderly

(a) Treatment as expenses. --

(1) In general. -- A taxpayer may elect to treat qualified architectural and transportation barrier removal expenses which are paid or incurred by him during the taxable year as expenses which are not chargeable to capital account. The expenditures so treated shall be allowed as a deduction.

***

Sec. 193. Tertiary injectants

(a) Allowance of deduction. -- There shall be allowed as a deduction for the taxable year an amount equal to the qualified tertiary injectant expenses of the taxpayer for tertiary injectants injected during such taxable year.

***

Sec. 194. Treatment of reforestation expenditures

(a) Allowance of deduction. -- In the case of any qualified timber property with respect to which the taxpayer has made (in accordance with regulations prescribed by the Secretary) an

Sec. 194. Treatment of reforestation expenditures

election under this subsection, the taxpayer shall be entitled to a deduction with respect to the amortization of the amortizable basis of qualified timber property based on a period of 84 months. Such amortization deduction shall be an amount, with respect to each month of such period within the taxable year, equal to the amortizable basis at the end of such month divided by the number of months (including the month for which the deduction is computed) remaining in the period. Such 5 amortizable basis at the end of the month shall be computed without regard to the amortization deduction for such month. The 84-month period shall begin on the first day of the first month of the second half of the taxable year in which the amortizable basis is acquired.

(b) Treatment as expenses. --

    (1) Election to treat certain reforestation expenditures as expenses. -- 10

        (A) In general. -- In the case of any qualified timber property with respect to which the taxpayer has made (in accordance with regulations prescribed by the Secretary) an election under this subsection, the taxpayer shall treat reforestation expenditures which are paid or incurred during the taxable year with respect to such property as an expense which is not chargeable to capital account. The reforestation expenditures so treated shall be allowed as 15 a deduction.

        (B) Dollar limitation. -- The aggregate amount of reforestation expenditures which maybe taken into account under subparagraph (A) with respect to each qualified timber property or any taxable year shall not exceed $10,000 ($5,000 in the case of a separate return by a married individual (as defined in section 7703)). 20

            ***

(c) Definitions and special rule. -- For purposes of this section--

    (1) Qualified timber property. -- The term "qualified timber property" means a woodlot or other site located in the United States which will contain trees in significant commercial quantities and which is held by the taxpayer for the planting, cultivating, caring for, and cutting 25 of trees for sale or use in the commercial production of timber products.

    (2) Amortizable basis. -- The term "amortizable basis" means that portion of the basis of the qualified timber property attributable to reforestation expenditures which have not been taken into account under subsection (b).

    (3) Reforestation expenditures. -- 30

        (A) In general. -- The term "reforestation expenditures" means direct costs incurred in connection with forestation or reforestation by planting or artificial or natural seeding, including costs--

            (i) for the preparation of the site;

            (ii) of seeds or seedlings; and 35

            (iii) for labor and tools, including depreciation of equipment such as tractors, trucks, tree planters, and similar machines used in planting or seeding.

            ***

Sec. 195. Start-up expenditures

(a) Capitalization of expenditures. -- Except as otherwise provided in this section, no 40 deduction shall be allowed for start-up expenditures.

(b) Election to deduct. --

    (1) Allowance of deduction. -- If a taxpayer elects the application of this subsection with respect to any start-up expenditures--

        (A) the taxpayer shall be allowed a deduction for the taxable year in which the active 45

Sec. 195. Start-up expenditures

trade or business begins in an amount equal to the lesser of -

(i) the amount of start-up expenditures with respect to the active trade or business, or

(ii) $5,000, reduced (but not below zero) by the amount by which such start-up expenditures exceed $50,000, and

5

(B) the remainder of such start-up expenditures shall be allowed as a deduction ratably over the 180-month period beginning with the month in which the active trade or business begins.

(2) **Dispositions before close of amortization period.** -- In any case in which a trade or business is completely disposed of by the taxpayer before the end of the period to which paragraph (1) applies, any deferred expenses attributable to such trade or business which were not allowed as a deduction by reason of this section may be deducted to the extent allowable under section 165.

10

(c) **Definitions.** -- For purposes of this section--

(1) **Start-up expenditures.** -- The term "start-up expenditure" means any amount--

15

(A) paid or incurred in connection with--

(i) investigating the creation or acquisition of an active trade or business, or

(ii) creating an active trade or business, or

(iii) any activity engaged in for profit and for the production of income before the day on which the active trade or business begins, in anticipation of such activity becoming an active trade or business, and

20

(B) which, if paid or incurred in connection with the operation of an existing active trade or business (in the same field as the trade or business referred to in subparagraph (A)), would be allowable as a deduction for the taxable year in which paid or incurred. The term "start-up expenditure" does not include any amount with respect to which a deduction is allowable under section 163(a), 164, or 174.

25

(2) **Beginning of trade or business.** --

(A) **In general.** -- Except as provided in subparagraph (B), the determination of when an active trade or business begins shall be made in accordance with such regulations as the Secretary may prescribe.

30

(B) **Acquired trade or business.** -- An acquired active trade or business shall be treated as beginning when the taxpayer acquires it.

(d) **Election.** --

(1) **Time for making election.** -- An election under subsection (b) shall be made not later than the time prescribed by law for filing the return for the taxable year in which the trade or business begins (including extensions thereof).

35

(2) **Scope of election.** -- The period selected under subsection (b) shall be adhered to in computing taxable income for the taxable year for which the election is made and all subsequent taxable years.

40 **Reg. § 1.195-1 Election to amortize start-up expenditures.**

(a) *In general.* Under section 195(b), a taxpayer may elect to amortize start-up expenditures (as defined in section 195(c)(1)). A taxpayer who elects to amortize start-up expenditures must, at the time of the election, select an amortization period of not less than 60 months, beginning with the month in which the active trade or business begins.

45 The election applies to all of the taxpayer's start-up expenditures with respect to the trade or business. The election to amortize start-up expenditures is irrevocable, and the

Sec. 195. Start-up expenditures

amortization period selected by the taxpayer in making the election may not subsequently be changed.

(b) *Time and manner of making election.* The election to amortize start-up expenditures under section 195 shall be made by attaching a statement containing the information described in paragraph (c) of this section to the taxpayer's return. The statement must be filed no later than the date prescribed by law for filing the return (including any extensions of time) for the taxable year in which the active trade or business begins. The statement may be filed with a return for any taxable year prior to the year in which the taxpayer's active trade or business begins, but no later than the date prescribed in the preceding sentence. Accordingly, an election under section 195 filed for any taxable year prior to the year in which the taxpayer's active trade or business begins (and pursuant to which the taxpayer commenced amortizing start-up expenditures in that prior year) will become effective in the month of the year in which the taxpayer's active trade or business begins.

(c) *Information required.* The statement shall set forth a description of the trade or business to which it relates with sufficient detail so that expenses relating to the trade or business can be identified properly for the taxable year in which the statement is filed and for all future taxable years to which it relates. The statement also shall include the number of months (not less than 60) over which the expenditures are to be amortized, and to the extent known at the time the statement is filed, a description of each start-up expenditure incurred (whether or not paid) and the month in which the active trade or business began (or was acquired). A revised statement may be filed to include any start-up expenditures not included in the taxpayer's original election statement, but the revised statement may not include any expenditures for which the taxpayer had previously taken a position on a return inconsistent with their treatment as start-up expenditures. The revised statement may be filed with a return filed after the return that contained the election.

***

[T.D. 8797, 63 FR 69555, Dec. 17, 1998]

Sec. 197. Amortization of goodwill and certain other intangibles

(a) **General rule.** -- A taxpayer shall be entitled to an amortization deduction with respect to any amortizable section 197 intangible. The amount of such deduction shall be determined by amortizing the adjusted basis (for purposes of determining gain) of such intangible ratably over the 15-year period beginning with the month in which such intangible was acquired.

(b) **No other depreciation or amortization deduction allowable.** -- Except as provided in subsection (a), no depreciation or amortization deduction shall be allowable with respect to an amortizable section 197 intangible.

(c) **Amortizable section 197 intangible.** -- For purposes of this section--

(1) **In general.** -- Except as otherwise provided in this section, the term "amortizable section 197 intangible" means any section 197 intangible--

(A) which is acquired by the taxpayer after the date of the enactment of this section, and

(B) which is held in connection with the conduct of a trade or business or an activity described in section 212.

(2) **Exclusion of self-created intangibles, etc.** -- The term "amortizable section 197 intangible" shall not include any section 197 intangible--

(A) which is not described in subparagraph (D), (E), or (F) of subsection (d)(1), and

(B) which is created by the taxpayer.

539

Sec. 197. Amortization of goodwill and certain other intangibles

This paragraph shall not apply if the intangible is created in connection with a transaction (or series of related transactions) involving the acquisition of assets constituting a trade or business or substantial portion thereof.

***

5   **(d) Section 197 intangible.** -- For purposes of this section--

(1) In general. -- Except as otherwise provided in this section, the term "section197 intangible" means--

(A) goodwill,

(B) going concern value,

10   **(C)** any of the following intangible items:

(i) workforce in place including its composition and terms and conditions (contractual or otherwise) of its employment,

(ii) business books and records, operating systems, or any other information base (including lists or other information with respect to current or prospective customers),

15   **(iii)** any patent, copyright, formula, process, design, pattern, knowhow, format, or other similar item,

(iv) any customer-based intangible,

(v) any supplier-based intangible, and

(vi) any other similar item,

20   **(D)** any license, permit, or other right granted by a governmental unit or an agency or instrumentality thereof,

(E) any covenant not to compete (or other arrangement to the extent such arrangement has substantially the same effect as a covenant not to compete) entered into in connection with an acquisition (directly or indirectly) of an interest in a trade or business or substantial

25   portion thereof, and

(F) any franchise, trademark, or trade name.

(2) Customer-based intangible. --

(A) In general. -- The term "customer-based intangible" means--

(i) composition of market,

30   **(ii)** market share, and

(iii) any other value resulting from future provision of goods or services pursuant to relationships (contractual or otherwise) in the ordinary course of business with customers.

(B) Special rule for financial institutions. -- In the case of a financial institution, the

35   term "customer-based intangible" includes deposit base and similar items.

(3) Supplier-based intangible. -- The term "supplier-based intangible" means any value resulting from future acquisitions of goods or services pursuant to relationships (contractual or otherwise) in the ordinary course of business with suppliers of goods or services to be used or sold by the taxpayer.

40   **(e) Exceptions.** -- For purposes of this section, the term "section 197 intangible" shall not include any of the following:

(1) Financial interests. -- Any interest--

(A) in a corporation, partnership, trust, or estate, or **(B)** under an existing futures contract, foreign currency contract, notional principal contract, or other similar financial

45   contract.

Sec. 197. Amortization of goodwill and certain other intangibles

(2) Land. -- Any interest in land.

(3) Computer software. --

(A) In general. -- Any--

(i) computer software which is readily available for purchase by the general public, is subject to a nonexclusive license, and has not been substantially modified, and

(ii) other computer software which is not acquired in a transaction (or series of related transactions) involving the acquisition of assets constituting a trade or business or substantial portion thereof.

(B) Computer software defined. -- For purposes of subparagraph (A), the term "computer software" means any program designed to cause a computer to perform a desired function. Such term shall not include any data base or similar item unless the data base or item is in the public domain and is incidental to the operation of otherwise qualifying computer software.

(4) Certain interests or rights acquired separately. -- Any of the following not acquired in a transaction (or series of related transactions) involving the acquisition of assets constituting a trade business or substantial portion thereof:

(A) Any interest in a film, sound recording, video tape, book, or similar property.

(B) Any right to receive tangible property or services under a contract or granted by a governmental unit or agency or instrumentality thereof.

(C) Any interest in a patent or copyright.

(D) To the extent provided in regulations, any right under a contract (or granted by a governmental unit or an agency or instrumentality thereof) if such right--

(i) has a fixed duration of less than 15 years, or

(ii) is fixed as to amount and, without regard to this section, would be recoverable under a method similar to the unit-of-production method.

(5) Interests under leases and debt instruments. -- Any interest under--

(A) an existing lease of tangible property, or

(B) except as provided in subsection (d)(2)(B), any existing indebtedness.

(6) Mortgage servicing. -- Any right to service indebtedness which is secured by residential real property unless such right is acquired in a transaction (or series of related transactions) involving the acquisition of assets (other than rights described in this paragraph) constituting a trade or business or substantial portion thereof.

(7) Certain transaction costs. -- Any fees for professional services, and any transaction costs, incurred by parties to a transaction with respect to which any portion of the gain or loss is not recognized under part III of subchapter C.

(f) Special rules. --

(1) Treatment of certain dispositions, etc. --

(A) In general. -- If there is a disposition of any amortizable section 197 intangible acquired in a transaction or series of related transactions (or any such intangible becomes worthless) and one or more other amortizable section 197 intangibles acquired in such transaction or series of related transactions are retained--

(i) no loss shall be recognized by reason of such disposition (or such worthlessness), and

(ii) appropriate adjustments to the adjusted bases of such retained intangibles shall be made for any loss not recognized under clause (i).

Sec. 197. Amortization of goodwill and certain other intangibles

(B) Special rule for covenants not to compete. -- In the case of any section 197 intangible which is a covenant not to compete (or other arrangement) described in subsection (d)(1)(E), in no event shall such covenant or other arrangement be treated as disposed of (or becoming worthless) before the disposition of the entire interest described in such subsection in connection with which such covenant (or other arrangement) was entered into.

***

(3) Treatment of amounts paid pursuant to covenants not to compete, etc. -- Any amount paid or incurred pursuant to a covenant or arrangement referred to in subsection (d)(1) (E) shall be treate as an amount chargeable to capital account.

***

(7) Treatment as depreciable. -- For purposes of this chapter, any amortizable section 197 intangible shall be treated as property which is of a character subject to the allowance for depreciation provided in section 167.

***

Sec. 198. Expensing of environmental remediation costs

(a) In general. -- A taxpayer may elect to treat any qualified environmental remediation expenditure which is paid or incurred by the taxpayer as an expense which is not chargeable to capital account. Any expenditure which is so treated shall be allowed as a deduction for the taxable year in which it is paid or incurred.

(b) Qualified environmental remediation expenditure. -- For purposes of this section -

(1) In general. -- The term "qualified environmental remediation expenditure" means any expenditure--

(A) which is otherwise chargeable to capital account, and

(B) which is paid or incurred in connection with the abatement or control of hazardous substances at a qualified contaminated site.

***

Sec. 211. Allowance of deductions

In computing taxable income under section 63, there shall be allowed as deductions the items specified in this part, subject to the exceptions provided in part IX (section 261 and following, relating to items not deductible).

Sec. 212. Expenses for production of income

In the case of an individual, there shall be allowed as a deduction all the ordinary and necessary expenses paid or incurred during the taxable year--

(1) for the production or collection of income;

(2) for the management, conservation, or maintenance of property held for the production of income; or

(3) in connection with the determination, collection, or refund of any tax.

542

Sec. 212.   Expenses for production of income

Reg. § 1.212-1   Nontrade or nonbusiness expenses.

(a) An expense may be deducted under section 212 only if:

(1) It has been paid or incurred by the taxpayer during the taxable year (i) for the production or collection of income which, if and when realized, will be required to be included in income for Federal income tax purposes, or (ii) for the management, conservation, or maintenance of property held for the production of such income, or (iii) in connection with the determination, collection, or refund of any tax; and

(2) It is an ordinary and necessary expense for any of the purposes stated in subparagraph (1) of this paragraph.

(b) The term income for the purpose of section 212 includes not merely income of the taxable year but also income which the taxpayer has realized in a prior taxable year or may realize in subsequent taxable years; and is not confined to recurring income but applies as well to gains from the disposition of property. For example, if defaulted bonds, the interest from which if received would be includible in income, are purchased with the expectation of realizing capital gain on their resale, even though no current yield thereon is anticipated, ordinary and necessary expenses thereafter paid or incurred in connection with such bonds are deductible. Similarly, ordinary and necessary expenses paid or incurred in the management, conservation, or maintenance of a building devoted to rental purposes are deductible notwithstanding that there is actually no income therefrom in the taxable year, and regardless of the manner in which or the purpose for which the property in question was acquired. Expenses paid or incurred in managing, conserving, or maintaining property held for investment may be deductible under section 212 even though the property is not currently productive and there is no likelihood that the property will be sold at a profit or will otherwise be productive of income and even though the property is held merely to minimize a loss with respect thereto.

(c) In the case of taxable years beginning before January 1, 1970, expenses of carrying on transactions which do not constitute a trade or business of the taxpayer and are not carried on for the production or collection of income or for the management, conservation, or maintenance of property held for the production of income, but which are carried on primarily as a sport, hobby, or recreation are not allowable as nontrade or nonbusiness expenses. The question whether or not a transaction is carried on primarily for the production of income or for the management, conservation, or maintenance of property held for the production or collection of income, rather than primarily as a sport, hobby, or recreation, is not to be determined solely from the intention of the taxpayer but rather from all the circumstances of the case. For example, consideration will be given to the record of prior gain or loss of the taxpayer in the activity, the relation between the type of activity and the principal occupation of the taxpayer, and the uses to which the property or what it produces is put by the taxpayer. For provisions relating to activities not engaged in for profit applicable to taxable years beginning after December 31, 1969, see section 183 and the regulations thereunder.

(d) Expenses, to be deductible under section 212, must be ``ordinary and necessary''. Thus, such expenses must be reasonable in amount and must bear a reasonable and proximate relation tothe production or collection of taxable income or to the management, conservation, or maintenance of property held for the production of income.

(e) A deduction under section 212 is subject to the restrictions and limitations in part IX (section 261 and following), subchapter B, chapter 1 of the Code, relating to items not deductible. Thus, no deduction is allowable under section 212 for any amount allocable to the production or collection of one or more classes of income which are not includible in gross income, or for any amount allocable to the management, conservation, or maintenance of property held for the production of income which is not included in gross income. See section 265. Nor does section 212 allow the deduction of any expenses

543

Sec. 212. Expenses for production of income

which are disallowed by any of the provisions of subtitle A of the Code, even though such expenses may be paid or incurred for one of the purposes specified in section 212.

(f) Among expenditures not allowable as deductions under section 212 are the following: Commuter's expenses; expenses of taking special courses or training;
5 expenses for improving personal appearance; the cost of rental of a safe-deposit box for storing jewelry and other personal effects; expenses such as those paid or incurred in seeking employment or in placing oneself in a position to begin rendering personal services for compensation, campaign expenses of a candidate for public office, bar examination fees and other expenses paid or incurred in securing admission to the bar,
10 and corresponding fees and expenses paid or incurred by physicians, dentists, accountants, and other taxpayers for securing the right to practice their respective professions. See, however, section 162 and the regulations thereunder.

(g) Fees for services of investment counsel, custodial fees, clerical help, office rent, and similar expenses paid or incurred by a taxpayer in connection with investments held
15 by him are deductible under section 212 only if (1) they are paid or incurred by the taxpayer for the production or collection of income or for the management, conservation, or maintenance of investments held by him for the production of income; and (2) they are ordinary and necessary under all the circumstances, having regard to the type of investment and to the relation of the taxpayer to such investment.
20 (h) Ordinary and necessary expenses paid or incurred in connection with the management, conservation, or maintenance of property held for use as a residence by the taxpayer are not deductible. However, ordinary and necessary expenses paid or incurred in connection with the management, conservation, or maintenance of property held by the taxpayer as rental property are deductible even though such property was
25 formerly held by the taxpayer for use as a home.

(i) Reasonable amounts paid or incurred by the fiduciary of an estate or trust on account of administration expenses, including fiduciaries' fees and expenses of litigation, which are ordinary and necessary in connection with the performance of the duties of administration are deductible under section 212, notwithstanding that the estate or trust is
30 not engaged in a trade or business, except to the extent that such expenses are allocable to the production or collection of tax-exempt income. But see section 642 (g) and the regulations thereunder for disallowance of such deductions to an estate where such items are allowed as a deduction under section 2053 or 2054 in computing the net estate subject to the estate tax.
35 (j) Reasonable amounts paid or incurred for the services of a guardian or committee for a ward or minor, and other expenses of guardians and committees which are ordinary and necessary, in connection with the production or collection of income inuring to the ward or minor, or in connection with the management, conservation, or maintenance of property, held for the production of income, belonging to the ward or minor, are
40 deductible.

(k) Expenses paid or incurred in defending or perfecting title to property, in recovering property (other than investment property and amounts of income which, if and when recovered, must be included in gross income), or in developing or improving property, constitute a part of the cost of the property and are not deductible expenses. Attorneys'
45 fees paid in a suit to quiet title to lands are not deductible; but if the suit is also to collect accrued rents thereon, that portion of such fees is deductible which is properly allocable to the services rendered in collecting such rents. Expenses paid or incurred in protecting or asserting one's right to property of a decedent as heir or legatee, or as beneficiary under a testamentary trust, are not deductible.
50 (l) Expenses paid or incurred by an individual in connection with the determination, collection, or refund of any tax, whether the taxing authority be Federal, State, or

544

Sec. 212. Expenses for production of income

municipal, and whether the tax be income, estate, gift, property, or any other tax, are deductible. Thus, expenses paid or incurred by a taxpayer for tax counsel or expenses paid or incurred in connection with the preparation of his tax returns or in connection with any proceedings involved in determining the extent of his tax liability or in contesting his tax liability are deductible.

(m) An expense (not otherwise deductible) paid or incurred by an individual in determining or contesting a liability asserted against him does not become deductible by reason of the fact that property held by him for the production of income may be required to be used or sold for the purpose of satisfying such liability.

(n) Capital expenditures are not allowable as nontrade or nonbusiness expenses. The deduction of an item otherwise allowable under section 212 will not be disallowed simply because the taxpayer was entitled under Subtitle A of the Code to treat such item as a capital expenditure, rather than to deduct it as an expense. For example, see section 266. Where, however, the item may properly be treated only as a capital expenditure or where it was properly so treated under an option granted in Subtitle A of the Code, no deduction is allowable under section 212; and this is true regardless of whether any basis adjustment is allowed under any other provision of the Code.

(o) The provisions of section 212 are not intended in any way to disallow expenses which would otherwise be allowable under section 162 and the regulations thereunder. Double deductions are not permitted. Amounts deducted under one provision of the Internal Revenue Code of 1954 cannot again be deducted under any other provision thereof.

(p) Frustration of public policy. The deduction of a payment will be disallowed under section 212 if the payment is of a type for which a deduction would be disallowed under section 162(c), (f), or (g) and the regulations thereunder in the case of a business expense.

[T.D. 6500, 25 FR 11402, Nov. 26, 1960; 25 FR 14021, Dec. 12, 1960; T.D. 7198, 37 FR 13685, July 13, 1972; T.D. 7345, 40 FR 7439, Feb. 20, 1975]

Sec. 213. Medical, dental, etc., expenses

(a) **Allowance of deduction.** -- There shall be allowed as a deduction the expenses paid during the taxable year, not compensated for by insurance or otherwise, for medical care of the taxpayer, his spouse, or a dependent (as defined in section 152, determined without regard to subsections (b)(1), (b)(2), and (d)(1)(B) thereof), to the extent that such expenses exceed 7.5 percent of adjusted gross income.

(b) **Limitation with respect to medicine and drugs.** -- An amount paid during the taxable year for medicine or a drug shall be taken into account under subsection (a) only if such medicine or drug is a prescribed drug or is insulin.

***

(d) **Definitions.** -- For purposes of this section--

(1) The term "medical care" means amounts paid -

(A) for the diagnosis, cure, mitigation, treatment, or prevention of disease, or for the purpose of affecting any structure or function of the body,

(B) for transportation primarily for and essential to medical care referred to in subparagraph (A),

(C) for qualified long-term care services (as defined in section 7702B(c)), or

545

Sec. 213. Medical, dental, etc., expenses

(D) for insurance (including amounts paid as premiums under part B of title XVIII of the Social Security Act, relating to supplementary medical insurance for the aged) covering medical care referred to in subparagraphs (A) and (B) or for any qualified long-term care insurance contract (as defined in section 7702B(b)).

In the case of a qualified long-term care insurance contract (as defined in section 7702B(b)), only eligible long-term care premiums (as defined in paragraph (10)) shall be taken into account under subparagraph (D).

(2) Amounts paid for certain lodging away from home treated as paid for medical care. -- Amounts paid for lodging (not lavish or extravagant under the circumstances) while away from home primarily for and essential to medical care referred to in paragraph (1)(A) shall be treated as amounts paid for medical care if--

(A) the medical care referred to in paragraph (1)(A) is provided by a physician in a licensed hospital (or in a medica care facility which is related to, or the equivalent of, a licensed hospital), and

(B) there is no significant element of personal pleasure, recreation, or vacation in the travel away from home.

The amount taken into account under the preceding sentence shall not exceed $50 for each night for each individual.

(3) Prescribed drug. -- The term "prescribed drug" means a drug or biological which requires a prescription of a physician for its use by an individual.

(4) Physician. -- The term "physician" has the meaning given to such term by section 1861(r) of the Social Security Act (42 U.S.C. 1395x(r)).

(5) Special rule in the case of child of divorced parents, etc. -- Any child to whom section 152(e) applies shall be treated as a dependent of both parents for purposes of this section.

(6) In the case of an insurance contract under which amounts are payable for other than medical care referred to in subparagraphs (A), (B), and (C) of paragraph (1)--

(A) no amount shall be treated as paid for insurance to which paragraph (1)(D) applies unless the charge for such insurance is either separately stated in the contract, or furnished to the policyholder by the insurance company in a separate statement,

(B) the amount taken into account as the amount paid for such insurance shall not exceed such charge, and

(C) no amount shall be treated as paid for such insurance if the amount specified in the contract (or furnished to the policyholder by the insurance company in a separate statement) as the charge for such insurance is unreasonably large in relation to the total charges under the contract.

(7) Subject to the limitations of paragraph (6), premiums paid during the taxable year by a taxpayer before he attains the age of 65 for insurance covering medical care (within the meaning of subparagraphs (A), (B), and (C) of paragraph (1)) for the taxpayer, his spouse, or a dependent after the taxpayer attains the age of 65 shall be treated as expenses paid during the taxable year for insurance which constitutes medical care if premiums for such insurance are payable (on a level payment basis) under the contract for a period of 10 years or more or until the year in which the taxpayer attains the age of 65 (but in no case for a period of less than 5 years).

(8) The determination of whether an individual is married at any time during the taxable year shall be made in accordance with the provisions of section 6013(d) (relating to determination of status as husband and wife).

(9) Cosmetic surgery. --

Sec. 213. Medical, dental, etc., expenses

(A) In general. -- The term "medical care" does not include cosmetic surgery or other similar procedures, unless the surgery or procedure is necessary to ameliorate a deformity arising from, or directly related to, a congenital abnormality, a personal injury resulting from an accident or trauma, or disfiguring disease.

(B) Cosmetic surgery defined. -- For purposes of this paragraph, the term "cosmetic surgery" means any procedure which is directed at improving the patient's appearance and does not meaningfully promote the proper function of the body or prevent or treat illness or disease.

(10) Eligible long-term care premiums. --

(A) In general. -- For purposes of this section, the term "eligible long-term care premiums" means the amount paid during a taxable year for any qualified long-term care insurance contract (as defined in section 7702B(b)) covering an individual, to the extent such amount does not exceed the limitation determined under the following table:

In the case of an individual with an attained age before the close of the taxable year of:	The limitation is:
40 or less..	$ 200
More than 40 but not more than 50..................	375
More than 50 but not more than 60..................	750
More than 60 but not more than 70..................	2,000
More than 70...	2,500.

(B) Indexing. --

(i) In general. -- In the case of any taxable year beginning in a calendar year after 1997, each dollar amount contained in subparagraph (A) shall be increased by the medical care cost adjustment of such amount for such calendar year. If any increase determined under the preceding sentence is not a multiple of $10, such increase shall be rounded to the nearest multiple of $10.

(ii) Medical care cost adjustment. -- For purposes of clause (i), the medical care cost adjustment for any calendar year is the percentage (if any) by which--

(I) the medical care component of the Consumer Price Index (as defined in section 1(f)(5)) for August of the preceding calendar year, exceeds

(II) such component for August of 1996.

The Secretary shall, in consultation with the Secretary of Health and Human Services, prescribe an adjustment which the Secretary determines is more appropriate for purposes of this paragraph than the adjustment described in the preceding sentence, and the adjustment so prescribed shall apply in lieu of the adjustment described in the preceding sentence.

(11) Certain payments to relatives treated as not paid for medical care. -- An amount paid for a qualified long-term care service (as defined in section 7702B(c)) provided to an individual shall be treated as not paid for medical care if such service is provided--

(A) by the spouse of the individual or by a relative (directly or through a partnership, corporation, or other entity) unless the service is provided by a licensed professional with respect to such service, or

(B) by a corporation or partnership which is related (within the meaning of section 267(b) or 707(b)) to the individual.

For purposes of this paragraph, the term "relative" means an individual bearing a relationship

547

Sec. 213.   Medical, dental, etc., expenses

to the individual which is described in any of subparagraphs (A) through (G) of section152(d) (2). This paragraph shall not apply for purposes of section 105(b) with respect to reimbursements through insurance.

(e) Exclusion of amounts allowed for care of certain dependents. -- Any expense allowed as
5 a credit under section 21 shall not be treated as an expense paid for medical care.

Reg. § 1.213-1   Medical, dental, etc., expenses.

(a) *Allowance of deduction.* (1) Section 213 permits a deduction of payments for certain medical expenses (including expenses for medicine and drugs). Except as
10 provided in paragraph (d) of this section (relating to special rule for decedents) a deduction is allowable only to individuals and only with respect to medical expenses actually paid during the taxable year, regardless of when the incident or event which occasioned the expenses occurred and regardless of the method of accounting employed by the taxpayer in making his income tax return. Thus, if the medical expenses are
15 incurred but not paid during the taxable year, no deduction for such expenses shall be allowed for such

year.

(2) Except as provided in subparagraphs (4)(i) and (5)(i) of this paragraph, only such medical expenses (including the allowable expenses for medicine and drugs) are
20 deductible as exceed 3 percent of the adjusted gross income for the taxable year. For taxable years beginning after December 31, 1966, the amounts paid during the taxable year for insurance that constitute expenses paid for medical care shall, for purposes of computing total medical expenses, be reduced by the amount determined under subparagraph (5)(i) of this paragraph. For the amounts paid during the taxable year for
25 medicine and drugs which may be taken into account in computing total medical expenses, see paragraph (b) of this section. For the maximum deduction allowable under section 213 in the case of certain taxable years, see paragraph (c) of this section. As to what constitutes ``adjusted gross income'', see section 62 and the regulations thereunder.

30 (3)(i) For medical expenses paid (including expenses paid for medicine and drugs) to be deductible, they must be for medical care of the taxpayer, his spouse, or a dependent of the taxpayer and not be compensated for by insurance or otherwise. Expenses paid for the medical care of a dependent, as defined in section 152 and the regulations thereunder, are deductible under this section even though the dependent has gross
35 income equal to or in excess of the amount determined pursuant to § 1.151-2 applicable to the calendar year in which the taxable year of the taxpayer begins. Where such expenses are paid by two or more persons and the conditions of section 152(c) and the regulations thereunder are met, the medical expenses are deductible only by the person designated in the multiple support agreement filed by such persons and such deduction
40 is limited to the amount of medical expenses paid by such person.

(ii) An amount excluded from gross income under section 105 (c) or (d) (relating to amounts received under accident and health plans) and the regulations thereunder shall not constitute compensation for expenses paid for medical care. Exclusion of such amounts from gross income will not affect the treatment of expenses paid for medical
45 care.

(iii) The application of the rule allowing a deduction for medical expenses to the extent not compensated for by insurance or otherwise may be illustrated by the following example in which it is assumed that neither the taxpayer nor his wife has attained the age of 65:

50 *Example.* Taxpayer H, married to W and having one dependent child, had adjusted

548

Sec. 213. Medical, dental, etc., expenses

gross income for 1956 of $3,000. During 1956 he paid $300 for medical care, of which $100 was for treatment of his dependent child and $200 for an operation on W which was performed in September 1955. In 1956 he received a payment of $50 for health insurance to cover a portion of the cost of W's operation performed during 1955. The deduction allowable under section 213 for the calendar year 1956, provided the taxpayer itemizes his deductions and does not compute his tax under section 3 by use of the tax table, is $160, computed as follows:

Payments in 1956 for medical care.......................................	$300
Less: Amount of insurance received in 1956........................	50
Payments in 1956 for medical care not compensated for during 1956..	250
Less: 3 percent of $3,000 (adjusted gross income)..............	90
Excess, allowable as a deduction for 1956........................	160

***

(5)(i) For taxable years beginning after December 31, 1966, there may be deducted without regard to the 3-percent limitation the lesser of--(a) One-half of the amounts paid during the taxable year for insurance which constitute expenses for medical care for the taxpayer, his spouse, and dependents; or (b) $150.

(ii) The application of subdivision (i) of this subparagraph may be illustrated by the following example:

Example. H and W made a joint return for the calendar year 1967. The adjusted gross income of H and W for 1967 was $10,000 and they paid in such year $370 for medical care of which amount $350 was paid for insurance which constitutes medical care for H and W. No part of the payment was for medicine and drugs or was compensated for by insurance or otherwise. The allowable deduction under section 213 for medical expenses paid in 1967 is $150, computed as follows:

(1) Lesser of $175 (one-half of amounts paid for insurance) or $150...	$150
(2) Payments for medical care...	$370
(3) Less line 1..	150
(4) Medical expenses to be taken into account under 3-percent limitation (line 2 minus line 3)...............................	$220
(5) Less: 3 percent of $10,000 (adjusted gross income).......	300
(6) Excess allowable as a deduction for 1967 (excess of line 4 over line 5)..	0
(7) Allowable medical expense deduction for 1967 (line 1 plus line 6)..	$150

(b) Limitation with respect to medicine and drugs--

***

(2) *Taxable years beginning after December 31, 1963.* (i) Except as otherwise provided in subdivision (ii) of this subparagraph, amounts paid during taxable years beginning after December 31, 1963, for medicine and drugs are to be taken into account in computing the allowable deduction for medical expenses paid during the taxable year only to the extent that the aggregate of such amounts exceeds 1 percent of the adjusted gross income for the taxable year. Thus, if the aggregate of the amounts paid for medicine and drugs which are subject to the 1-percent limitation exceeds 1 percent of adjusted gross income, the excess is added to other medical expenses for the purpose of computing the

Sec. 213. Medical, dental, etc., expenses

medical expense deduction.

***

(iii) The application of this subparagraph may be illustrated by the following examples:

Example 1. H and W, who have a dependent child, C, were both under 65 years of age
5 at the close of the calendar year 1964 and made a joint return for that calendar year.
During the year 1964, H's mother, M, attained the age of 65, and was a dependent (as
defined in section 152) of H. The adjusted gross income of H and W in 1964 was
$12,000. During 1964 H and W paid the following amounts for medical care: (i) $600 for
doctors and hospital expenses and $120 for medicine and drugs for themselves; (ii) $350
10 for doctors and hospital expenses and $60 for medicine and drugs for C; and (iii) $400 for
doctors and hospital expenses and $100 for medicine and drugs for M. These payments
were not compensated for by insurance or otherwise. The deduction allowable under
section 213(a) (1) for medical expenses paid in 1964 is $1,150, computed as follows:

15 H, W, and C:

Payments for doctors and hospital...........................		$950
Payments for medicine and drugs...........................	$180	
Less: 1 percent of $12,000 (adjusted gross income)...	120	60
20 Total medical expenses..		1,010
Less: 3 percent of $12,000 (adjusted gross income)...		360
Medical expenses of H, W, and C to be taken into account...		$650
25 M:		
Payments for doctors and hospitals.........................	400	
Payments for medicine and drugs...........................	100	
Medical expenses of M to be taken into account...		500
Allowable deduction for 1964....................................		1,150

30

Example 2. H and W, who have a dependent child, C, made a joint return for the
calendar year 1964, and reported adjusted gross income of $12,000. H became 65 years
of age on January 23, 1964. F, the 87 year old father of W, was a dependent of H. During
1964, H and W paid the following amounts for medical care: (i) $400 for doctors and
35 hospital expenses and $75 for medicine and drugs for H; (ii) $200 for doctors and
hospital expenses and $100 for medicine and drugs for W; (iii) $200 for doctors and
hospital expenses and $175 for medicine and drugs for C; and (iv) $700 for doctors and
hospital expenses and $150 for medicine and drugs for F. These payments were not
compensated for by insurance or otherwise. The deduction allowable under section
40 213(a) (2) for medical expenses paid in 1964 is $1,625, computed as follows:

Sec. 213. Medical, dental, etc., expenses

H and W:
Payments for doctors and hospital..........................	$600	
Payments for medicine and drugs..........................	175	
Medical expenses for H and W to be taken into account..		$775	5

F:
Payments for doctors and hospital..........................	700	
Payments for medicine and drugs..........................	150	
Medical expenses for F to be taken into account..		850	10

C:
Payments for doctors and hospital..........................	200	
Payments for medicine and drugs..........................	$175	
Less: 1 percent of $12,000 (adjusted gross income)...	120	15
55		
Total medical expenses.......................................	255	
Less: 3 percent of $12,000 (adjusted gross income)...	360	
Medical expenses for C to be taken into account..	0	20
Allowable deduction for 1964...............................	1,625	

Example 3. Assume the same facts as example (2) except that the calendar year of the return is 1967 and the amounts paid for medical care were paid during 1967. The 25 deduction allowable under section 213(a) for medical expenses paid in 1967 is $1,520, computed as follows:

Sec. 213. Medical, dental, etc., expenses

Payments for doctors and hospitals:

H.	$400
W.	200
C.	200
5 F.	700
	$1,500

Payments for medicine and drugs:

H.	75
W.	100
10 C.	175
F.	150
	$500

Less: 1 percent of $12,000
(adjusted gross income). 120

15   380

Medical expenses to be
taken into account......... $1,880
Less: 3 percent of $12,000
(adjusted gross income). 360
20 Allowable medical expense
deduction for 1967......... 1,520

(3) Definition of medicine and drugs. For definition of medicine and drugs, see paragraph (e) (2) of this section.

25   (c) Maximum limitations. (1) For taxable years beginning after December 31, 1966, there shall be no maximum limitation on the amount of the deduction allowable for payment of medical expenses.

    (2) Except as provided in section 213(g) and § 1.213-2 (relating to maximum limitations with respect to certain aged and disabled individuals for taxable years 30 beginning before January 1, 1967), for taxable years beginning after December 31, 1961, and before January 1, 1967, the maximum deduction allowable for medical expenses paid in any one taxable year is the lesser of:

    (i) $5,000 multiplied by the number of exemptions allowed under section 151 (exclusive of exemptions allowed under section 151(c) for a taxpayer or spouse attaining 35 the age of 65, or section 151(d) for a taxpayer who is blind or a spouse who is blind);

    (ii) $10,000, if the taxpayer is single, not the head of a household (as defined in section 1(b)(2)) and not a surviving spouse (as defined in section 2(b)), or is married and files a separate return; or

    (iii) $20,000 if the taxpayer is married and files a joint return with his spouse under 40 section 6013, or is the head of a household (as defined in section 1(b)(2)), or a surviving spouse (as defined in section 2(b)).

    (3) The application of subparagraph (2) of this paragraph may be illustrated by the following example:

    Example. H and W made a joint return for the calendar year 1962 and were allowed 45 five exemptions (exclusive of exemptions under sec. 151(c) and (d)), one for each taxpayer and three for their dependents. The adjusted gross income of H and W in 1962 was $80,000. They paid during such year $26,000 for medical care, no part of which is compensated for by insurance or otherwise. The deduction allowable under section 213 for the calendar year 1962 is $20,000, computed as follows:

50

Sec. 213. Medical, dental, etc., expenses

Payments for medical care in 1962..	$26,000
Less: 3 percent of $80,000 (adjusted gross income)...........	2,400
Excess of medical expenses in 1962 over 3 percent	
of adjusted gross income..	23,600
Allowable deduction for 1962 ($5,000 multiplied by five	
exemptions allowed under sec. 151 (b) and (e) but not in	
excess of $20,000)..	20,000

***

(d) *Special rule for decedents.* (1) For the purpose of section 213(a), expenses for medical care of the taxpayer which are paid out of his estate during the 1-year period beginning with the day after the date of his death shall be treated as paid by the taxpayer at the time the medical services were rendered. However, no credit or refund of tax shall be allowed for any taxable year for which the statutory period for filing a claim has expired. See section 6511 and the regulations thereunder.

(2) The rule prescribed in subparagraph (1) of this paragraph shall not apply where the amount so paid is allowable under section 2053 as a deduction in computing the taxable estate of the decedent unless there is filed in duplicate (i) a statement that such amount has not been allowed as a deduction under section 2053 in computing the taxable estate of the decedent and (ii) a waiver of the right to have such amount allowed at any time as a deduction under section 2053. The statement and waiver shall be filed with or for association with the return, amended return, or claim for credit or refund for the decedent for any taxable year for which such an amount is claimed as a deduction.

(e) *Definitions*--(1) *General.* (i) The term medical care includes the diagnosis, cure, mitigation, treatment, or prevention of disease. Expenses paid for ``medical care" shall include those paid for the purpose of affecting any structure or function of the body or for transportation primarily for and essential to medical care. See subparagraph (4) of this paragraph for provisions relating to medical insurance.

(ii) Amounts paid for operations or treatments affecting any portion of the body, including obstetrical expenses and expenses of therapy or X-ray treatments, are deemed to be for the purpose of affecting any structure or function of the body and are therefore paid for medical care. Amounts expended for illegal operations or treatments are not deductible. Deductions for expenditures for medical care allowable under section 213 will be confined strictly to expenses incurred primarily for the prevention or alleviation of a physical or mental defect or illness. Thus, payments for the following are payments for medical care: hospital services, nursing services (including nurses' board where paid by the taxpayer), medical, laboratory, surgical, dental and other diagnostic and healing services, X-rays, medicine and drugs (as defined in subparagraph (2) of this paragraph, subject to the 1-percent limitation in paragraph (b) of this section), artificial teeth or limbs, and ambulance hire. However, an expenditure which is merely beneficial to the general health of an individual, such as an expenditure for a vacation, is not an expenditure for medical care.

(iii) Capital expenditures are generally not deductible for Federal income tax purposes. See section 263 and the regulations thereunder. However, an expenditure which otherwise qualifies as a medical expense under section 213 shall not be disqualified merely because it is a capital expenditure. For purposes of section 213 and this paragraph, a capital expenditure made by the taxpayer may qualify as a medical expense, if it has as its primary purpose the medical care (as defined in subdivisions (i) and (ii) of this subparagraph) of the taxpayer, his spouse, or his dependent. Thus, a capital expenditure which is related only to the sick person and is not related to permanent improvement or betterment of property, if it otherwise qualifies as an expenditure for medical care, shall be deductible; for example, an expenditure for eye

553

glasses, a seeing eye dog, artificial teeth and limbs, a wheel chair, crutches, an inclinator or an air conditioner which is detachable from the property and purchased only for the use of a sick person, etc. Moreover, a capital expenditure for permanent improvement or betterment of property which would not ordinarily be for the purpose of medical care

5 (within the meaning of this paragraph) may, nevertheless, qualify as a medical expense to the extent that the expenditure exceeds the increase in the value of the related property, if the particular expenditure is related directly to medical care. Such a situation could arise, for example, where a taxpayer is advised by a physician to install an elevator in his residence so that the taxpayer's wife who is afflicted with heart disease will not be

10 required to climb stairs. If the cost of installing the elevator is $1,000 and the increase in the value of the residence is determined to be only $700, the difference of $300, which is the amount in excess of the value enhancement, is deductible as a medical expense. If, however, by reason of this expenditure, it is determined that the value of the residence has not been increased, the entire cost of installing the elevator would qualify as a

15 medical expense. Expenditures made for the operation or maintenance of a capital asset are likewise deductible medical expenses if they have as their primary purpose the medical care (as defined in subdivisions (i) and (ii) of this subparagraph) of the taxpayer, his spouse, or his dependent. Normally, if a capital expenditure qualifies as a medical expense, expenditures for the operation or maintenance of the capital asset would also

20 qualify provided that the medical reason for the capital expenditure still exists. The entire amount of such operation and maintenance expenditures qualifies, even if none or only a portion of the original cost of the capital asset itself qualified.

(iv) Expenses paid for transportation primarily for and essential to the rendition of the medical care are expenses paid for medical care. However, an amount allowable as a

25 deduction for ``transportation primarily for and essential to medical care" shall not include the cost of any meals and lodging while away from home receiving medical treatment. For example, if a doctor prescribes that a taxpayer go to a warm climate in order to alleviate a specific chronic ailment, the cost of meals and lodging while there would not be deductible. On the other hand, if the travel is undertaken merely for the general

30 improvement of a taxpayer's health, neither the cost of transportation nor the cost of meals and lodging would be deductible. If a doctor prescribes an operation or other medical care, and the taxpayer chooses for purely personal considerations to travel to another locality (such as a resort area) for the operation or the other medical care, neither the cost of transportation nor the cost of meals and lodging (except where paid as part of

35 a hospital bill) is deductible.

(v) The cost of in-patient hospital care (including the cost of meals and lodging therein) is an expenditure for medical care. The extent to which expenses for care in an institution other than a hospital shall constitute medical care is primarily a question of fact which depends upon the condition of the individual and the nature of the services he

40 receives (rather than the nature of the institution). A private establishment which is regularly engaged in providing the types of care or services outlined in this subdivision shall be considered an institution for purposes of the rules provided herein. In general, the following rules will be applied:

(a) Where an individual is in an institution because his condition 6is such that the

45 availability of medical care (as defined in subdivisions (i) and (ii) of this subparagraph) in such institution is a principal reason for his presence there, and meals and lodging are furnished as a necessary incident to such care, the entire cost of medical care and meals and lodging at the institution, which are furnished while the individual requires continual medical care, shall constitute an expense for medical care. For example, medical care

50 includes the entire cost of institutional care for a person who is mentally ill and unsafe when left alone. While ordinary education is not medical care, the cost of medical care

includes the cost of attending a special school for a mentally or physically handicapped individual, if his condition is such that the resources of the institution for alleviating such mental or physical handicap are a principal reason for his presence there. In such a case, the cost of attending such a special school will include the cost of meals and lodging, if supplied, and the cost of ordinary education furnished which is incidental to the special 5 services furnished by the school. Thus, the cost of medical care includes the cost of attending a special school designed to compensate for or overcome a physical handicap, in order to qualify the individual for future normal education or for normal living, such as a school for the teaching of braille or lip reading. Similarly, the cost of care and supervision, or of treatment and training, of a mentally retarded or physically handicapped individual at 10 an institution is within the meaning of the term medical care.

(b) Where an individual is in an institution, and his condition is such that the availability of medical care in such institution is not a principal reason for his presence there, only that part of the cost of care in the institution as is attributable to medical care (as defined in subdivisions (i) and (ii) of this subparagraph) shall be considered as a cost 15 of medical care; meals and lodging at the institution in such a case are not considered a cost of medical care for purposes of this section. For example, an individual is in a home for the aged for personal or family considerations and not because he requires medical or nursing attention. In such case, medical care consists only of that part of the cost for care in the home which is attributable to medical care or nursing attention furnished to him; his 20 meals and lodging at the home are not considered a cost of medical care.

(c) It is immaterial for purposes of this subdivision whether the medical care is furnished in a Federal or State institution or in a private institution.

(vi) See section 262 and the regulations thereunder for disallowance of deduction for personal living, and family expenses not falling within the definition of medical care. 25

(2) *Medicine and drugs.* The term medicine and drugs shall include only items which are legally procured and which are generally accepted as falling within the category of medicine and drugs (whether or not requiring a prescription). Such term shall not include toiletries or similar preparations (such as toothpaste, shaving lotion, shaving cream, etc.) nor shall it include cosmetics (such as face creams, deodorants, hand lotions, etc., or any 30 similar preparation used for ordinary cosmetic purposes) or sundry items. Amounts expended for items which, under this subparagraph, are excluded from the term medicine and drugs shall not constitute amounts expended for ``medical care''.

(3) *Status as spouse or dependent.* In the case of medical expenses for the care of a person who is the taxpayer's spouse or dependent, the deduction under section 213 is 35 allowable if the status of such person as ``spouse'' or ``dependent'' of the taxpayer exists either at the time the medical services were rendered or at the time the expenses were paid. In determining whether such status as ``spouse'' exists, a taxpayer who is legally separated from his spouse under a decree of separate maintenance is not considered as married. Thus, payments made in June 1956 by A, for medical services rendered in 1955 40 to B, his wife, may be deducted by A for 1956 even though, before the payments were made, B may have died or in 1956 secured a divorce. Payments made in July 1956 by C, for medical services rendered to D in 1955 may be deducted by C for 1956 even though C and D were not married until June 1956.

(4) *Medical insurance.* (i)(a) For taxable years beginning after December 31, 1966, 45 expenditures for insurance shall constitute expenses paid for medical care only to the extent that such amounts are paid for insurance covering expenses of medical care referred to in subparagraph (1) of this paragraph. In the case of an insurance contract under which amounts are payable for other than medical care (as, for example, a policy providing an indemnity for loss of income or for loss of life, limb, or sight): 50

(1) No amount shall be treated as paid for insurance covering expenses of medical

Sec. 213. Medical, dental, etc., expenses

care referred to in subparagraph (1) of this paragraph unless the charge for such insurance is either separately stated in the contract or furnished to the policyholder by the insurer in a separate statement,

    (2) The amount taken into account as the amount paid for such medical insurance
5 shall not exceed such charge, and

    (3) No amount shall be treated as paid for such medical insurance if the amount specified in the contract (or furnished to the policyholder by the insurer in a separate statement) as the charge for such insurance is unreasonably large in relation to the total charges under the contract.

10 For purposes of the preceding sentence, amounts will be considered payable for other than medical care under the contract if the contract provides for the waiver of premiums upon the occurrence of an event. In determining whether a separately stated charge for insurance covering expenses of medical care is unreasonably large in relation to the total premium, the relationship of the coverages under the contract together with all of the
15 facts and circumstances shall be considered. In determining whether a contract constitutes an ``insurance'' contract it is irrelevant whether the benefits are payable in cash or in services. For example, amounts paid for hospitalization insurance, for membership in an association furnishing cooperative or so-called free-choice medical service, or for group hospitalization and clinical care are expenses paid for medical care.
20 Premiums paid under Part B, Title XVIII of the Social Security Act (42 U.S.C. 1395j-1395w), relating to supplementary medical insurance benefits for the aged, are amounts paid for insurance covering expenses of medical care. Taxes imposed by any governmental unit do not, however, constitute amounts paid for such medical insurance.

    (b) For taxable years beginning after December 31, 1966, subject to the rules of (a) of
25 this subdivision, premiums paid during a taxable year by a taxpayer under the age of 65 for insurance covering expenses of medical care for the taxpayer, his spouse, or a dependent after the taxpayer attains the age of 65 are to be treated as expenses paid during the taxable year for insurance covering expenses of medical care if the premiums for such insurance are payable (on a level payment basis) under the contract:

30   (1) For a period of 10 years or more, or

    (2) Until the year in which the taxpayer attains the age of 65 (but in no case for a period of less than 5 years).

For purposes of this subdivision (b), premiums will be considered payable on a level payment basis if the total premium under the contract is payable in equal annual or more
35 frequent installments. Thus, a total premium of $10,000 payable over a period of 10 years at $1,000 a year shall be considered payable on a level payment basis.

***

    (f) *Exclusion of amounts allowed for care of certain dependents.* Amounts taken into account under section 44A in computing a credit for the care of certain dependents shall
40 not be treated as expenses paid for medical care.

    (g) *Reimbursement for expenses paid in prior years.* (1) Where reimbursement, from insurance or otherwise, for medical expenses is received in a taxable year subsequent to a year in which a deduction was claimed on account of such expenses, the reimbursement must be included in gross income in such subsequent year to the extent
45 attributable to (and not in excess of) deductions allowed under section 213 for any prior taxable year. See section 104, relating to compensation for injuries or sickness, and section 105(b), relating to amounts expended for medical care, and the regulations thereunder, with regard to amounts in excess of or not attributable to deductions allowed.

    (2) If no medical expense deduction was taken in an earlier year, for example, if the
50 standard deduction under section 141 was taken for the earlier year, the reimbursement received in the taxable year for the medical expense of the earlier year is not includible in

Sec. 213. Medical, dental, etc., expenses

gross income.

(3) In order to allow the same aggregate medical expense deductions as if the reimbursement received in a subsequent year or years had been received in the year in which the payments for medical care were made, the following rules shall be followed:

(i) If the amount of the reimbursement is equal to or less than the amount which was deducted in a prior year, the entire amount of the reimbursement shall be considered attributable to the deduction taken in such prior year (and hence includible in gross income); or

(ii) If the amount of the reimbursement received in such subsequent year or years is greater than the amount which was deducted for the prior year, that portion of the reimbursement received which is equal in amount to the deduction taken in the prior year shall be considered as attributable to such deduction (and hence includible in gross income); but

(iii) If the deduction for the prior year would have been greater but for the limitations on the maximum amount of such deduction provided by section 213 (c), then the amount of the reimbursement attributable to such deduction (and hence includible in gross income) shall be the amount of the reimbursement received in a subsequent year or years reduced by the amount disallowed as a deduction because of the maximum limitation, but not in excess of the deduction allowed for the previous year.

(4) The application of subparagraphs (1), (2), and (3) of this paragraph may be illustrated by the following examples.

***

Example 1. Taxpayer A, a single individual (not the head of a household and not a surviving spouse) with one dependent, is entitled to two exemptions under the provisions of section 151. He had an adjusted gross income of $35,000 for the calendar year 1962. During 1962 he paid $16,000 for medical care. A received no reimbursement for such medical expenses in 1962, but in 1963 he received $6,000 upon an insurance policy covering the medical expenses which he paid in 1962. A was allowed a deduction of $10,000 (the maximum) from his adjusted gross income for 1962. The amount which A must include in his gross income for 1963 is $1,050, and the amount to be excluded from gross income for 1963 is $4,950, computed as follows:

Payments for medical care in 1962 (not reimbursed in 1962)...	$16,000	
Less: 3 percent of $35,000 (adjusted gross income)................	1,050	
Excess of medical expenses not reimbursed in 1962 over 3 percent of adjusted gross income..	10,000	
Allowable deduction for 1962..	10,000	
Amount by which the medical deductions for 1962 would have been greater than $10,000 but for the limitations on the maximum amount provided by section 213..............................	4,950	
Reimbursement received in 1963...	$6,000	
Less: Amount by which the medical deduction for 1962 would have been greater than $10,000 but for the limitation on the maximum amount provided by section 213...........................	4,950	
Reimbursement received in 1963 reduced by the amount by which the medical deduction for 1962 would have been greater than $10,000 but for the limitations on the maximum amount provided by section 213..	1,050	
Amount attributed to medical deduction taken for 1962............	1,050	

557

Sec. 213. Medical, dental, etc., expenses

Amount to be included in gross income for 1963..........................	1,050
Amount to be excluded from gross income for 1963 ($6,000 less $1,050)..	4,950

5   *Example 2.* Assuming that A, in example (1), received $15,000 in 1963 as reimbursement for the medical expenses which he paid in 1962, the amount which A must include in his gross income for 1963 is $10,000, and the amount to be excluded from gross income for 1963 is $5,000, computed as follows:

10 Reimbursement received in 1963...	$15,000
Less: Amount by which the medical deduction for 1962 would have been greater than $10,000 but for the limitations on the maximum amount provided by section 213........................	4,950
15 Reimbursement received in 1963 reduced by the amount by which the medical deduction for 1962 would have been greater than $10,000 but for the limitations on the maximum amount provided by section 213...........................	10,050
Deduction allowable for 1962..	10,000
20 Amount of reimbursement received in 1963 to be included in gross income for 1963 as attributable to deduction allowable for 1962..	10,000
Amount to be excluded from gross income for 1963 ($15,000 less $10,000)...	5,000

25   ***

(h) *Substantiation of deductions.* In connection with claims for deductions under section 213, the taxpayer shall furnish the name and address of each person to whom payment for medical expenses was made and the amount and date of the payment thereof in each case. If payment was made in kind, such fact shall be so reflected. Claims
30 for deductions must be substantiated, when requested by the district director, by a statement or itemized invoice from the individual or entity to which payment for medical expenses was made showing the nature of the service rendered, and to or for whom rendered; the nature of any other item of expense and for whom incurred and for what specific purpose, the amount paid therefor and the date of the payment thereof; and by
35 such other information as the district director may deem necessary.

[T.D. 6500, 25 FR 11402, Nov. 26, 1960]

Sec. 215. Alimony, etc., payments

(a) **General rule.** -- In the case of an individual, there shall be allowed as a deduction an
40 amount equal to the alimony or separate maintenance payments paid during such individual's taxable year.

(b) **Alimony or separate maintenance payments defined.** -- For purposes of this section, the term "alimony or separate maintenance payment" means any alimony or separate maintenance payment (as defined in section 71(b)) which is includible in the gross income of the recipient
45 under section 71.

(c) **Requirement of identification number.** -- The Secretary may prescribe regulations under which--

Sec. 215. Alimony, etc., payments

    (1) any individual receiving alimony or separate maintenance payments is required to furnish such individual's taxpayer
identification number to the individual making such payments, and

    (2) the individual making such payments is required to include such taxpayer identification number on such individual's return for the taxable year in which such payments are made.   5

  (d) Coordination with section 682. -- No deduction shall be allowed under this section with respect to any payment if, by reason of section 682 (relating to income of alimony trusts), the amount thereof is not includible in such individual's gross income.

          10

Sec. 216. Deduction of taxes, interest, and business depreciation by cooperative housing corporation tenant-stockholder

  (a) Allowance of deduction. -- In the case of a tenant-stockholder (as defined in subsection (b)(2)), there shall be allowed as a deduction amounts (not otherwise deductible) paid or accrued to a cooperative housing corporation within the taxable year, but only to the extent that such amounts represent the tenant-stockholder's proportionate share of--

    (1) the real estate taxes allowable as a deduction to the corporation under section 164 which 15 are paid or incurred by the corporation on the houses or apartment building and on the land on which such houses (or building) are situated, or

    (2) the interest allowable as a deduction to the corporation under section 163 which is paid or incurred by the corporation on its indebtedness contracted -

        (A) in the acquisition, construction, alteration, rehabilitation, or maintenance of the 20 houses or apartment building, or

        (B) in the acquisition of the land on which the houses (or apartment building) are situated.

***

          25

Sec. 217. Moving expenses

  (a) Deduction allowed. -- There shall be allowed as a deduction moving expenses paid or incurred during the taxable year in connection with the commencement of work by the taxpayer as an employee or as a self- employed individual at a new principal place of work.

  (b) Definition of moving expenses. --

    (1) In general. -- For purposes of this section, the term "moving expenses" means only the 30 reasonable expenses--

        (A) of moving household goods and personal effects from the former residence to the new residence, and

        (B) of traveling (including lodging) from the former residence to the new place of residence.   35

  Such term shall not include any expenses for meals.

    (2) Individuals other than taxpayer. -- In the case of any individual other than the taxpayer, expenses referred to in paragraph (1) shall be taken into account only if such individual has both the former residence and the new residence as his principal place of abode and is a member of the taxpayer's household.   40

  (c) Conditions for allowance. -- No deduction shall be allowed under this section unless -

    (1) the taxpayer's new principal place of work -

559

Sec. 217. Moving expenses

(A) is at least 50 miles farther from his former residence than was his former principal place of work, or

(B) if he had no former principal place of work, is at least 50 miles from his former residence, and

(2) either -

(A) during the 12-month period immediately following his arrival in the general location of his new principal place of work, the taxpayer is a full-time employee, in such general location, during at least 39 weeks, or

(B) during the 24-month period immediately following his arrival in the general location of his new principal place of work, the taxpayer is a full-time employee or performs services as a self-employed individual on a full-time basis, in such general location, during at least 78 weeks, of which not less than 39 weeks are during the 12-month period referred to in subparagraph (A).

For purposes of paragraph (1), the distance between two points shall be the shortest of the more commonly traveled routes between such two points.

(d) **Rules for application of subsection (c)(2).** --

(1) The condition of subsection (c)(2) shall not apply if the taxpayer is unable to satisfy such condition by reason of -

(A) death or disability, or

(B) involuntary separation (other than for willful misconduct) from the service of, or transfer for the benefit of, an employer after obtaining full-time employment in which the taxpayer could reasonably have been expected to satisfy such condition.

(2) If a taxpayer has not satisfied the condition of subsection (c)(2) before the time prescribed by law (including extensions thereof) for filing the return for the taxable year during which he paid or incurred moving expenses which would otherwise be deductible under this section, but may still satisfy such condition, then such expenses may (at the election of the taxpayer) be deducted for such taxable year notwithstanding subsection (c)(2).

(3) If--

(A) for any taxable year moving expenses have been deducted in accordance with the rule provided in paragraph (2), and

(B) the condition of subsection (c)(2) cannot be satisfied at the close of a subsequent taxable year, then an amount equal to the expenses which were so deducted shall be included in gross income for the first such subsequent taxable year.

***

(f) **Self-employed individual.** -- For purposes of this section, the term "self-employed individual" means an individual who performs personal services--

(1) as the owner of the entire interest in an unincorporated trade or business, or

(2) as a partner in a partnership carrying on a trade or business.

(g) **Rules for members of the Armed Forces of the United States.** -- In the case of a member of the Armed Forces of the United States on active duty who moves pursuant to a military order and incident to a permanent change of station--

(1) the limitations under subsection (c) shall not apply;

(2) any moving and storage expenses which are furnished in kind (or for which reimbursement or an allowance is provided, but only to the extent of the expenses paid or incurred) to such member, his spouse, or his dependents, shall not be includible in gross income, and no reporting with respect to such expenses shall be required by the Secretary of

560

Sec. 217. Moving expenses

Defense or the Secretary of Transportation, as the case may be; and

(3) if moving and storage expenses are furnished in kind (or if reimbursement or an allowance for such expenses is provided) to such member's spouse and his dependents with regard to moving to a location other than the one to which such member moves (or from a location other than the one from which such member moves), this section shall apply with 5 respect to the moving expenses of his spouse and dependents--

    (A) as if his spouse commenced work as an employee at a new principal place of work at such location; and

    (B) without regard to the limitations under subsection (c).

(h) Special rules for foreign moves. --   10

    (1) Allowance of certain storage fees. -- In the case of a foreign move, for purposes of this section, the moving expenses described in subsection (b)(1)(A) include the reasonable expenses--

        (A) of moving household goods and personal effects to and from storage, and

        (B) of storing such goods and effects for part or all of the period during which the new 15 place of work continues to be the taxpayer's principal place of work.

    (2) Foreign move. -- For purposes of this subsection, the term "foreign move" means the commencement of work by the taxpayer at a new principal place of work located outside the United States.

    (3) United States defined. -- For purposes of this subsection and subsection (i), the term 20 "United States" includes the possessions of the United States.

(i) Allowance of deductions in case of retirees or decedents who were working abroad. --

    (1) In general. -- In the case of any qualified retiree moving expenses or qualified survivor moving expenses--

        (A) this section (other than subsection (h)) shall be applied with respect to such expenses 25 as if they were incurred in connection with the commencement of work by the taxpayer as an employee at a new principal place of work located within the United States, and

        (B) the limitations of subsection (c)(2) shall not apply.

    (2) Qualified retiree moving expenses. -- For purposes of paragraph (1), the term "qualified retiree moving expenses" means any moving expenses--   30

        (A) which are incurred by an individual whose former principal place of work and former residence were outside the United States, and

        (B) which are incurred for a move to a new residence in the United States in connection with the bona fide retirement of the individual.

    (3) Qualified survivor moving expenses. -- For purposes of paragraph (1), the term 35 "qualified survivor moving expenses" means moving expenses--

        (A) which are paid or incurred by the spouse or any dependent of any decedent who (as of the time of his death) had a principal place of work outside the United States, and

        (B) which are incurred for a move which begins within 6 months after the death of such decedent and which is to a residence in the United States from a former residence outside 40 the United States which (as of the time of the decedent's death) was the residence of such decedent and the individual paying or incurring the expense.

***

Reg. § 1.217-2   Deduction for moving expenses paid or incurred in taxable years beginning after December 31, 1969.   45

    (a) Allowance of deduction--(1) In general. Section 217(a) allows a deduction from

Sec. 217. Moving expenses

gross income for moving expenses paid or incurred by the taxpayer during the taxable year in connection with his commencement of work as an employee or as a self-employed individual at a new principal place of work. For purposes of this section, amounts are considered as being paid or incurred by an individual whether goods or
5 services are furnished to the taxpayer directly (by an employer, a client, a customer, or similar person) or indirectly (paid to a third party on behalf of the taxpayer by an employer, a client, a customer, or similar person). A cash basis taxpayer will treat moving expenses as being paid for purposes of section 217 and this section in the year in which the taxpayer is considered to have received such payment under section 82 and §
10 1.82-1. No deduction is allowable under section 162 for any expenses incurred by the taxpayer in connection with moving from one residence to another residence unless such expenses are deductible under section 162 without regard to such change in residence. To qualify for the deduction under section 217 the expenses must meet the definition of the term moving expenses provided in section 217(b) and the taxpayer must meet the
15 conditions set forth in section 217(c). The term employee as used in this section has the same meaning as in § 31.3401(c)-1 of this chapter (Employment Tax Regulations). The term self-employed individual as used in this section is defined in paragraph (f)(1) of this section.

(2) Expenses paid in a taxable year other than the taxable year in which
20 reimbursement representing such expenses is received. In general, moving expenses are deductible in the year paid or incurred. If a taxpayer who uses the cash receipts and disbursements method of accounting receives reimbursement for a moving expense in a taxable year other than the taxable year the taxpayer pays such expense, he may elect to deduct such expense in the taxable year that he receives such reimbursement, rather
25 than the taxable year when he paid such expense in any case where:

(i) The expense is paid in a taxable year prior to the taxable year in which the reimbursement is received, or

(ii) The expense is paid in the taxable year immediately following the taxable year in which the reimbursement is received, provided that such expense is paid on or before the
30 due date prescribed for filing the return (determined with regard to any extension of time for such filing) for the taxable year in which the reimbursement is received.

An election to deduct moving expenses in the taxable year that the reimbursement is received shall be made by claiming the deduction on the return, amended return, or claim for refund for the taxable year in which the reimbursement is received.
35 (3) *Commencement of work.* (i) To be deductible the moving expenses must be paid or incurred by the taxpayer in connection with his commencement of work at a new principal place of work (see paragraph (c)(3) of this section for a discussion of the term principal place of work). Except for those expenses described in section 217(b)(1) (C) and (D) it is not necessary for the taxpayer to have made arrangements to work prior to
40 his moving to a new location; however, a deduction is not allowable unless employment or self-employment actually does occur. The term commencement includes (a) the beginning of work by a taxpayer as an employee or as a self-employed individual for the first time or after a substantial period of unemployment or part-time employment, (b) the beginning of work by a taxpayer for a different employer or in the case of a self-employed
45 individual in a new trade or business, or (c) the beginning of work by a taxpayer for the same employer or in the case of a self-employed individual in the same trade or business at a new location. To qualify as being in connection with the commencement of work, the move must bear a reasonable proximity both in time and place to such commencement at the new principal place of work. In general, moving expenses incurred within 1 year of the
50 date of the commencement of work are considered to be reasonably proximate in time to such commencement. Moving expenses incurred after the 1-year period may be

Sec. 217. Moving expenses

considered reasonably proximate in time if it can be shown that circumstances existed which prevented the taxpayer from incurring the expenses of moving within the 1-year period allowed. Whether circumstances existed which prevented the taxpayer from incurring the expenses of moving within the period allowed is dependent upon the facts and circumstances of each case. The length of the delay and the fact that the taxpayer 5 may have incurred part of the expenses of the move within the 1-year period allowed shall be taken into account in determining whether expenses incurred after such period are allowable. In general, a move is not considered to be reasonably proximate in place to the commencement of work at the new principal place of work where the distance between the taxpayer's new residence and his new principal place of work exceeds the 10 distance between his former residence and his new principal place of work. A move to a new residence which does not satisfy this test may, however, be considered reasonably proximate in place to the commencement of work if the taxpayer can demonstrate, for example, that he is required to live at such residence as a condition of employment or that living at such residence will result in an actual decrease in commuting time or 15 expense. For example, assume that in 1977 A is transferred by his employer to a new principal place of work and the distance between his former residence and his new principal place of work is 35 miles greater than was the distance between his former residence and his former principal place of work. However, the distance between his new residence and his new principal place of work is 10 miles greater than was the distance 20 between his former residence and his new principal place of work. Although the minimum distance requirement of section 217(c)(1) is met the expenses of moving to the new residence are not considered as incurred in connection with A's commencement of work at his new principal place of work since the new residence is not proximate in place to the new place of work. If, however, A can demonstrate, for example, that he is required to live 25 at such new residence as a condition of employment or if living at such new residence will result in an actual decrease in commuting time or expense, the expenses of the move may be considered as incurred in connection with A's commencement of work at his new principal place of work.

(ii) The provisions of subdivision (i) of this subparagraph may be illustrated by the 30 following examples

Example 1. Assume that A is transferred by his employer from Boston, MA, to Washington, DC. A moves to a new residence in Washington, DC, and commences work on February 1, 1971. A's wife and his two children remain in Boston until June 1972 in order to allow A's children to complete their grade school education in Boston. On June 1, 35 1972, A sells his home in Boston and his wife and children move to the new residence in Washington, DC. The expenses incurred on June 1, 1972, in selling the old residence and in moving A's family, their household goods, and personal effects to the new residence in Washington are allowable as a deduction although they were incurred 16 months after the date of the commencement of work by A since A has moved to and 40 established a new residence in Washington, DC, and thus incurred part of the total expenses of the move prior to the expiration of the 1-year period.

Example 2. Assume that A is transferred by his employer from Washington, DC, to Baltimore, MD. A commences work on January 1, 1971, in Baltimore. A commutes from his residence in Washington to his new principal place of work in Baltimore for a period of 45 18 months. On July 1, 1972, A decides to move to and establish a new residence in Baltimore. None of the moving expenses otherwise allowable under section 217 may be deducted since A neither incurred the expenses within 1 year nor has shown circumstances under which he was prevented from moving within such period.

(b) *Definition of moving expenses*--(1) *In general.* Section 217(b) defines the term 50 moving expenses to mean only the reasonable expenses (i) of moving household goods

Sec. 217. Moving expenses

and personal effects from the taxpayer's former residence to his new residence, (ii) of traveling (including meals and lodging) from the taxpayer's former residence to his new place of residence, (iii) of traveling (including meals and lodging), after obtaining employment, from the taxpayer's former residence to the general location of his new
5 principal place of work and return, for the principal purpose of searching for a new residence, (iv) of meals and lodging while occupying temporary quarters in the general location of the new principal place of work during any period of 30 consecutive days after obtaining employment, or (v) of a nature constituting qualified residence sale, purchase, or lease expenses. Thus, the test of deductibility is whether the expenses are reasonable
10 and are incurred for the items set forth in subdivisions (i) through (v) of this subparagraph.

(2) *Reasonable expenses.* (i) The term moving expenses includes only those expenses which are reasonable under the circumstances of the particular move. Expenses paid or incurred in excess of a reasonable amount are not deductible.
15 Generally, expenses paid or incurred for movement of household goods and personal effects or for travel (including meals and lodging) are reasonable only to the extent that they are paid or incurred for such movement or travel by the shortest and most direct route available from the former residence to the new residence by the conventional mode or modes of transportation actually used and in the shortest period of time commonly
20 required to travel the distance involved by such mode. Thus, if moving or travel arrangements are made to provide a circuitous route for scenic, stopover, or other similar reasons, additional expenses resulting therefrom are not deductible since they are not reasonable nor related to the commencement of work at the new principal place of work. In addition, expenses paid or incurred for meals and lodging while traveling from the
25 former residence to the new place of residence or to the general location of the new principal place of work and return or occupying temporary quarters in the general location of the new principal place of work are reasonable only if under the facts and circumstances involved such expenses are not lavish or extravagant.

(ii) The application of this subparagraph may be illustrated by the following example:
30 *Example. A*, an employee of the M Company works and maintains his residence in Boston, MA. Upon receiving orders from his employer that he is to be transferred to M's Los Angeles, CA, office, A motors to Los Angeles with his family with stopovers at various cities between Boston and Los Angeles to visit friends and relatives. In addition, A detours into Mexico for sightseeing. Because of the stopovers and tour into Mexico, A's
35 travel time and distance are increased over what they would have been had he proceeded directly to Los Angeles. To the extent that A's route of travel between Boston and Los Angeles is in a generally southwesterly direction it may be said that he is traveling by the shortest and most direct route available by motor vehicle. Since A's excursion into Mexico is away from the usual Boston-Los Angeles route, the portion of
40 the expenses paid or incurred attributable to such excursion is not deductible. Likewise, that portion of the expenses attributable to A's delay en route in visiting personal friends and sightseeing are not deductible.

(3) Expense of moving household goods and personal effects. Expenses of moving household goods and personal effects include expenses of transporting such goods and
45 effects from the taxpayer's former residence to his new residence, and expenses of packing, crating, and in-transit storage and insurance for such goods and effects. Such expenses also include any costs of connecting or disconnecting utilities required because of the moving of household goods, appliances, or personal effects. Expenses of storing and insuring household goods and personal effects constitute in-transit expenses if
50 incurred within any consecutive 30-day period after the day such goods and effects are moved from the taxpayer's former residence and prior to delivery at the taxpayer's new

residence. Expenses paid or incurred in moving household goods and personal effects to the taxpayer's new residence from a place other than his former residence are allowable, but only to the extent that such expenses do not exceed the amount which would be allowable had such goods and effects been moved from the taxpayer's former residence. Expenses of moving household goods and personal effects do not include, for example, storage charges (other than in-transit), costs incurred in the acquisition of property, costs incurred and losses sustained in the disposition of property, penalties for breaking leases, mortgage penalties, expenses of refitting rugs or draperies, losses sustained on the disposal of memberships in clubs, tuition fees, and similar items. The above expenses may, however, be described in other provisions of section 217(b) and if so a deduction may be allowed for them subject to the allowable dollar limitations.

(4) *Expenses of traveling from the former residence to the new place of residence.* Expenses of traveling from the former residence to the new place of residence include the cost of transportation and of meals and lodging en route (including the date of arrival) from the taxpayer's former residence to his new place of residence. Expenses of meals and lodging incurred in the general location of the former residence within 1 day after the former residence is no longer suitable for occupancy because of the removal of household goods and personal effects shall be considered as expenses of traveling for purposes of this subparagraph. The date of arrival is the day the taxpayer secures lodging at the new place of residence, even if on a temporary basis. Expenses of traveling from the taxpayer's former residence to his new place of residence do not include, for example, living or other expenses following the date of arrival at the new place of residence and while waiting to enter the new residence or waiting for household goods to arrive, expenses in connection with house or apartment hunting, living expenses preceding date of departure for the new place of residence (other than expenses of meals and lodging incurred within 1 day after the former residence is no longer suitable for occupancy), expenses of trips for purposes of selling property, expenses of trips to the former residence by the taxpayer pending the move by his family to the new place of residence, or any allowance for depreciation. The above expenses may, however, be described in other provisions of section 217(b) and if so a deduction may be allowed for them subject to the allowable dollar limitations. The deduction for traveling expenses from the former residence to the new place of residence is allowable for only one trip made by the taxpayer and members of his household; however, it is not necessary that the taxpayer and all members of his household travel together or at the same time.

(5) *Expenses of traveling for the principal purpose of looking for a new residence.* Expenses of traveling, after obtaining employment, from the former residence to the general location of the new principal place of work and return, for the principal purpose of searching for a new residence include the cost of transportation and meals and lodging during such travel and while at the general location of the new place of work for the principal purpose of searching for a new residence. However, such expenses do not include, for example, expenses of meals and lodging of the taxpayer and members of his household before departing for the new principal place of work, expenses for trips for purposes of selling property, expenses of trips to the former residence by the taxpayer pending the move by his family to the place of residence, or any allowance for depreciation. The above expenses may, however, be described in other provisions of section 217(b) and if so a deduction may be allowed for them. The deduction for expenses of traveling for the principal purpose of looking for a new residence is not limited to any number of trips by the taxpayer and by members of his household. In addition, the taxpayer and all members of his household need not travel together or at the same time. Moreover, a trip need not result in acquisition of a lease of property or purchase of property. An employee is considered to have obtained employment in the

Sec. 217. Moving expenses

general location of the new principal place of work after he has obtained a contract or agreement of employment. A self-employed individual is considered to have obtained employment when he has made substantial arrangements to commence work at the new principal place of work (see paragraph (f)(2) of this section for a discussion of the term
5 made substantial arrangements to commence to work).

(6) *Expenses of occupying temporary quarters.* Expenses of occupying temporary quarters include only the cost of meals and lodging while occupying temporary quarters in the general location of the new principal place of work during any period of 30 consecutive days after the taxpayer has obtained employment in such general location.
10 Thus, expenses of occupying temporary quarters do not include, for example, the cost of entertainment, laundry, transportation, or other personal, living family expenses, or expenses of occupying temporary quarters in the general location of the former place of work. The 30 consecutive day period is any one period of 30 consecutive days which can begin, at the option of the taxpayer, on any day after the day the taxpayer obtains
15 employment in the general location of the new principal place of work.

(7) *Qualified residence sale, purchase, or lease expenses.* Qualified residence sale, purchase, or lease expenses (hereinafter ``qualified real estate expenses") are only reasonable amounts paid or incurred for any of the following purposes:

(i) Expenses incident to the sale or exchange by the taxpayer or his spouse of the
20 taxpayer's former residence which, but for section 217 (b) and (e), would be taken into account in determining the amount realized on the sale or exchange of the residence. These expenses include real estate commissions, attorneys' fees, title fees, escrow fees, so called ``points" or loan placement charges which the seller is required to pay, State transfer taxes and similar expenses paid or incurred in connection with the sale or
25 exchange. No deduction, however, is permitted under section 217 and this section for the cost of physical improvements intended to enhance salability by improving the condition or appearance of the residence.

(ii) Expenses incident to the purchase by the taxpayer or his spouse of a new residence in the general location of the new principal place of work which, but for section
30 217 (b) and (e), would be taken into account in determining either the adjusted basis of the new residence or the cost of a loan. These expenses include attorney's fees, escrow fees, appraisal fees, title costs, so-called ``points" or loan placement charges not representing payments or prepayments of interest, and similar expenses paid or incurred in connection with the purchase of the new residence. No deduction, however, is
35 permitted under section 217 and this section for any portion of real estate taxes or insurance, so-called ``points" or loan placement charges which are, in essence, prepayments of interest, or the purchase price of the residence.

(iii) Expenses incident to the settlement of an unexpired lease held by the taxpayer or his spouse on property used by the taxpayer as his former residence. These expenses
40 include consideration paid to a lessor to obtain a release from a lease, attorneys' fees, real estate commissions, or similar expenses incident to obtaining a release from a lease or to obtaining an assignee or a sublessee such as the difference between rent paid under a primary lease and rent received under a sublease. No deduction, however, is permitted under section 217 and this section for the cost of physical improvement
45 intended to enhance marketability of the leasehold by improving the condition or appearance of the residence.

(iv) Expenses incident to the acquisition of a lease by the taxpayer or his spouse. These expenses include the cost of fees or commissions for obtaining a lease, a sublease, or an assignment of an interest in property used by the taxpayer as his new
50 residence in the general location of the new principal place of work. No deduction, however, is permitted under section 217 and this section for payments or prepayments of

rent or payments representing the cost of a security or other similar deposit. Qualified real estate expenses do not include losses sustained on the disposition of property or mortgage penalties, to the extent that such penalties are otherwise deductible as interest.

(8) *Residence*. The term former residence refers to the taxpayer's principal residence before his departure for his new principal place of work. The term new residence refers to the taxpayer's principal residence within the general location of his new principal place of work. Thus, neither term includes other residences owned or maintained by the taxpayer or members of his family or seasonal residences such as a summer beach cottage. Whether or not property is used by the taxpayer as his principal residence depends upon all the facts and circumstances in each case. Property used by the taxpayer as his principal residence may include a houseboat, a housetrailer, or similar dwelling. The term new place of residence generally includes the area within which the taxpayer might reasonably be expected to commute to his new principal place of work.

(9) *Dollar limitations*. (i) Expenses described in subparagraphs (A) and (B) of section 217(b)(1) are not subject to an overall dollar limitation. Thus, assuming all other requirements of section 217 are satisfied, a taxpayer who, in connection with his commencement of work at a new principal place of work, pays or incurs reasonable expenses of moving household goods and personal effects from his former residence to his new place of residence and reasonable expenses of traveling, including meals and lodging, from his former residence to his new place of residence is permitted to deduct the entire amount of these expenses.

(ii) Expenses described in subparagraphs (C), (D), and (E) of section 217(b)(1) are subject to an overall dollar limitation for each commencement of work of 3,000 ($2,500 in the case of a commencement of work in a taxable year beginning before January 1, 1977), of which the expenses described in subparagraphs (C) and (D) of section 217(b)(1) cannot exceed $1,500 ($1,000 in the case of a commencement of work in a taxable year beginning before January 1, 1977). The dollar limitation applies to the amount of expenses paid or incurred in connection with each commencement of work and not to the amount of expenses paid or incurred in each taxable year. Thus, for example, a taxpayer who paid or incurred $2,000 of expenses described in subparagraphs (C), (D), and (E) of section 217(b)(1) in taxable year 1977 in connection with his commencement of work at a principal place of work and paid or incurred an additional $2,000 of such expenses in taxable year 1978 in connection with the same commencement of work is permitted to deduct the $2,000 of such expenses paid or incurred in taxable year 1977 and only $1,000 of such expenses paid or incurred in taxable year 1978.

(iii) A taxpayer who pays or incurs expenses described in subparagraphs (C), (D), and (E) of section 217(b)(1) in connection with the same commencement of work may choose to deduct any combination of such expenses within the dollar amounts specified in subdivision (ii) of this subparagraph. For example, a taxpayer who pays or incurs such expenses in connection with the same commencement of work may either choose to deduct: (a) Expenses described in subparagraphs (C) and (D) of section 217(b)(1) to the extent of $1,500 ($1,000 in the case of a commencement of work in a taxable year beginning before January 1, 1977) before deducting any of the expenses described in subparagraph (E) of such section, or (b) expenses described in subparagraph (E) of section 217(b)(1) to the extent of $3,000 ($2,500 in the case of a commencement of work in a taxable year beginning before January 1, 1977) before deducting any of the expenses described in subparagraphs (C) and (D) of such section.

(iv) For the purpose of computing the dollar limitation contained in subparagraph (A) of section 217(b)(3) a commencement of work by a taxpayer at a new principal place of work and a commencement of work by his spouse at a new principal place of work which

Sec. 217. Moving expenses

are in the same general location constitute a single commencement of work. Two principal places of work are treated as being in the same general location where the taxpayer and his spouse reside together and commute to their principal places of work. Two principal places of work are not treated as being in the same general location where,

5 as of the close of the taxable year, the taxpayer and his spouse have not shared the same new residence nor made specific plans to share the same new residence within a determinable time. Under such circumstances, the separate commencements of work by a taxpayer and his spouse will be considered separately in assigning the dollar limitations and expenses to the appropriate return in the manner described in subdivisions (v) and

10 (vi) of this subparagraph.

(v) Moving expenses (described in subparagraphs (C), (D), and (E) of section 217(b)(1)), paid or incurred with respect to the commencement of work by both a husband and wife which is considered a single commencement of work under subdivision (iv) of this subparagraph are subject to an overall dollar limitation of $3,000 ($2,500 in the case of a

15 commencement of work in a taxable year beginning before January 1, 1977), per move of which the expenses described in subparagraphs (C) and (D) of section 217(b)(1) cannot exceed $1,500 ($1,000 in the case of a commencement of work in a taxable year beginning before January 1, 1977). If separate returns are filed with respect to the commencement of work by both a husband and wife which is considered a single

20 commencement of work under subdivision (iv) of this subparagraph, moving expenses (described in subparagraphs (C), (D), and (E) of section 217(b)(1)) are subject to an overall dollar limitation of $1,500 ($1,250 in the case of a commencement of work in a taxable year beginning before January 1, 1977), per move of which the expenses described in subparagraphs (C) and (D) of section 217(b)(1) cannot exceed $750 ($500

25 in the case of a commencement of work in a taxable year beginning before January 1, 1977) with respect to each return. Where moving expenses are paid or incurred in more than 1 taxable year with respect to a single commencement of work by a husband and wife they shall, for purposes of applying the dollar limitations to such move, be subject to a $3,000 and $1,500 limitation ($2,500 and $1,000, respectively, in the case of a

30 commencement of work in a taxable year beginning before January 1, 1977) for all such years that they file a joint return and shall be subject to a separate $1,500 and $750 limitation ($1,250 and $500, respectively, in the case of a commencement of work in a taxable year beginning before January 1, 1977) for all such years that they file separate returns. If a joint return is filed for the first taxable year moving expenses are paid or

35 incurred with respect to a move but separate returns are filed in a subsequent year, the unused portion of the amount which may be deducted shall be allocated equally between the husband and wife in the later year. If separate returns are filed for the first taxable year such moving expenses are paid or incurred but a joint return is filed in a subsequent year, the deductions claimed on their separate returns shall be aggregated for purposes

40 of determining the unused portion of the amount which may be deducted in the later year.

(vi) The application of subdivisions (iv) and (v) of this subparagraph may be illustrated by the following examples:

Example 1. A, who was transferred by his employer, effective January 15, 1977, moved from Boston, MA, to Washington, DC. A's wife was transferred by her employer, effective

45 January 15, 1977, from Boston, MA, to Baltimore, MD. A and his wife reside together at the same new residence. A and his wife are cash basis taxpayers and file a joint return for taxable year 1977. Because A and his wife reside together at the new residence, the commencement of work by both is considered a single commencement of work under subdivision (iv) of this subparagraph. They are permitted to deduct with respect to their

50 commencement of work in Washington and Baltimore up to $3,000 of the expenses described in subparagraphs (C), (D), and (E) of section 217(b)(1) of which the expenses

Sec. 217. Moving expenses

described in subparagraphs (C) and (D) of such section cannot exceed $1,500.

Example 2. Assume the same facts as in Example 1 except that for taxable year 1977, A and his wife file separate returns. Because A and his wife reside together, the commencement of work by both is considered a single commencement of work under subdivision (iv) of this subparagraph. A is permitted to deduct with respect to his 5 commencement of work in Washington up to $1,500 of the expenses described in subparagraphs (C), (D), and (E) of section 217(b)(1) of which the expenses described in subparagraphs (C) and (D) cannot exceed $750. A is not permitted to deduct any of the expenses described in subparagraphs (C), (D), and (E) of section 217(b)(1) paid by his wife in connection with her commencement of work at a new principal place of work. A's 10 wife is permitted to deduct with respect to her commencement of work in Baltimore up to $1,500 of the expenses described in subparagraphs (C), (D), and (E) of section 217(b)(1) that are paid by her of which the expenses described in subparagraphs (C) and (D) cannot exceed $750. A's wife is not permitted to deduct any of the expenses described in subparagraphs (C), (D), and (E) of section 217(b)(1) paid by A in connection with his 15 commencement of work in Washington, DC.

Example 3. Assume the same facts as in Example 1 except that A and his wife take up separate residences in Washington and Baltimore, do not reside together during the entire taxable year, and have no specific plans to reside together. The commencement of work by A in Washington, DC, and by his wife in Baltimore are considered separate 20 commencements of work since their principal places of work are not treated as being in the same general location. If A and his wife file a joint return for taxable year 1977, the moving expenses described in subparagraphs (C), (D), and (E) of section 217(b)(1) paid in connection with the commencement of work by A in Washington, DC, and his wife in Baltimore, MD, are subject to an overall limitation of $6,000 of which the expenses 25 described in subparagrahs (C) and (D) cannot exceed $3,000. If A and his wife file separate returns for taxable year 1977, A may deduct up to $3,000 of the expenses described in subparagraphs (C), (D), and (E) of which the expenses described in subparagraphs (C) and (D) cannot exceed $1,500. A's wife may deduct up to $3,000 of the expenses described in subparagraphs (C), (D), and (E) of which the expenses 30 described in subparagraphs (C) and (D) cannot exceed $1,500.

(10) *Individuals other than taxpayer.* (i) In addition to the expenses set forth in subparagraphs (A) through (D) of section 217(b)(1) attributable to the taxpayer alone, the same type of expenses attributable to certain individuals other than the taxpayer, if paid or incurred by the taxpayer, are deductible. These other individuals must be members of 35 the taxpayer's household, and have both the taxpayer's former residence and his new residence as their principal place of abode. A member of the taxpayer's household includes any individual residing at the taxpayer's residence who is neither a tenant nor an employee of the taxpayer. Thus, for example, a member of the taxpayer's household may not be an individual such as a servant, governess, chauffeur, nurse, valet, or personal 40 attendant.

However, for purposes of this paragraph, a tenant or employee will be considered a member of the taxpayer's household where the tenant or employee is a dependent of the taxpayer as defined in section 152.

(ii) In addition to the expenses set forth in section 217(b)(2) paid or incurred by the 45 taxpayer attributable to property sold, purchased, or leased by the taxpayer alone, the same type of expenses paid or incurred by the taxpayer attributable to property sold, purchased, or leased by the taxpayer's spouse or by the taxpayer and his spouse are deductible providing such property is used by the taxpayer as his principal place of residence. 50

(c) *Conditions for allowance*--(1) *In general.* Section 217(c) provides two conditions

Sec. 217. Moving expenses

which must be satisfied in order for a deduction of moving expenses to be allowed under section 217(a). The first is a minimum distance condition prescribed by section 217(c)(1), and the second is a minimum period of employment condition prescribed by section 217(c)(2).

5 (2) *Minimum distance.* For purposes of applying the minimum distance condition of section 217(c)(1) all taxpayers are divided into one or the other of the following categories: Taxpayers having a former principal place of work, and taxpayers not having a former principal place of work. Included in this latter category are individuals who are seeking fulltime employment for the first time either as an employee or on a self-
10 employed basis (for example, recent high school or college graduates), or individuals who are reentering the labor force after a substantial period of unemployment or part-time employment.

(i) In the case of a taxpayer having a former principal place of work, section 217(c)(1) (A) provides that no deduction is allowable unless the distance between the former
15 residence and the new principal place of work exceeds by at least 35 miles (50 miles in the case of expenses paid or incurred in taxable years beginning before January 1, 1977) the distance between the former residence and the former principal place of work.

(ii) In the case of a taxpayer not having a former principal place of work, section 217(c)(1)(B) provides that no deduction is allowable unless the distance between the
20 former residence and the new principal place of work is at least 35 miles (50 miles in the case of expenses paid or incurred in taxable years beginning before January 1, 1977).

(iii) For purposes of measuring distances under section 217(c)(1) the distance between two geographic points is measured by the shortest of the more commonly traveled routes between such points. The shortest of the more commonly traveled routes
25 refers to the line of travel and the mode or modes of transportation commonly used to go between two geographic points comprising the shortest distance between such points irrespective of the route used by the taxpayer.

(3) *Principal place of work.* (i) A taxpayer's principal place of work usually is the place where he spends most of his working time. The principal place of work of a taxpayer who
30 performs services as an employee is his employer's plant, office, shop, store, or other property. The principal place of work of a taxpayer who is self-employed is the plant, office, shop, store, or other property which serves as the center of his business activities. However, a taxpayer may have a principal place of work even if there is no one place where he spends a substantial portion of his working time. In such case, the taxpayer's
35 principal place of work is the place where his business activities are centered--for example, because he reports there for work, or is required either by his employer or the nature of his employment to ``base" his employment there. Thus, while a member of a railroad crew may spend most of his working time aboard a train, his principal place of work is his home terminal, station, or other such central point where he reports in, checks
40 out, or receives instructions. The principal place of work of a taxpayer who is employed by a number of employers on a relatively short-term basis, and secures employment by means of a union hall system (such as a construction or building trades worker) would be the union hall.

(ii) Where a taxpayer has more than one employment (i.e., the taxpayer is employed
45 by more than one employer, or is self-employed in more than one trade or business, or is an employee and is self-employed at any particular time) his principal place of work is determined with reference to his principal employment. The location of a taxpayer's principal place of work is a question of fact determined on the basis of the particular circumstances in each case. The more important factors to be considered in making this
50 determination are (a) the total time ordinarily spent by the taxpayer at each place, (b) the degree of the taxpayer's business activity at each place, and (c) the relative significance

Sec. 217. Moving expenses

of the financial return to the taxpayer from each place.

(iii) Where a taxpayer maintains inconsistent positions by claiming a deduction for expenses of meals and lodging while away from home (incurred in the general location of the new principal place of work) under section 162 (relating to trade or business expenses) and by claiming a deduction under this section for moving expenses incurred 5 in connection with the commencement of work at such place of work, it will be a question of facts and circumstances as to whether such new place of work will be considered a principal place of work, and accordingly, which category of deductions he will be allowed.

(4) *Minimum period of employment.* (i) Under section 217(c)(2) no deduction is allowed unless: 10

(a) Where a taxpayer is an employee, during the 12-month period immediately following his arrival in the general location of the new principal place of work, he is a full-time employee, in such general location, during at least 39 weeks, or

(b) Where a taxpayer is a self-employed individual (including a taxpayer who is also an employee, but is unable to satisfy the requirements of the 39-week test of (a) of this 15 subdivision (i)), during the 24-month period immediately following his arrival in the general location of the new principal place of work, he is a full-time employee or performs services as a self-employed individual on a full-time basis, in such general location, during at least 78 weeks, of which not less than 39 weeks are during the 12-month period referred to above. Where a taxpayer works as an employee and at the same time 20 performs services as a self-employed individual his principal employment (determined according to subdivision (i) of subparagraph (3) of this paragraph) governs whether the 39-week or 78-week test is applicable.

(ii) The 12-month period and the 39- week period set forth in subparagraph (A) of section 217(c)(2) and the 12- and 24-month periods as well as 39- and 78- week periods 25 set forth in subparagraph (B) of such section are measured from the date of the taxpayer's arrival in the general location of the new principal place of work. Generally, date of arrival is the date of the termination of the last trip preceding the taxpayer's commencement of work on a regular basis and is not the date the taxpayer's family or household goods and effects arrive. 30

(iii) The taxpayer need not remain in the employ of the same employer or remain self-employed in the same trade or business for the required number of weeks. However, he must be employed in the same general location of the new principal place of work during such period. The general location of the new principal place of work refers to a general commutation area and is usually the same area as the ``new place of residence''; see 35 paragraph (b)(8) of this section.

(iv) Only those weeks during which the taxpayer is a full-time employee or during which he performs services as a self-employed individual on a full-time basis qualify as a week of work for purposes of the minimum period of employment condition of section 217(c)(2). 40

(a) Whether an employee is a full-time employee during any particular week depends upon the customary practices of the occupation in the geographic area in which the taxpayer works. Where employment is on a seasonal basis, weeks occurring in the off-season when no work is required or available may be counted as weeks of full-time employment only if the employee's contract or agreement of employment covers the off- 45 season period and such period is less than 6 months. Thus, for example, a schoolteacher whose employment contract covers a 12-month period and who teaches on a full-time basis for more than 6 months is considered a full-time employee during the entire 12-month period. A taxpayer will be treated as a full-time employee during any week of involuntary temporary absence from work because of illness, strikes, shutouts, layoffs, 50 natural disasters, etc. A taxpayer will, also, be treated as a full-time employee during any

Sec. 217. Moving expenses

week in which he voluntarily absents himself from work for leave or vacation provided for in his contract or agreement of employment.

(b) Whether a taxpayer performs services as a self-employed individual on a full-time basis during any particular week depends on the practices of the trade or business in the
5 geographic area in which the taxpayer works. For example, a self-employed dentist maintaining office hours 4 days a week is considered to perform services as a self-employed individual on a full-time basis providing it is not unusual for other self-employed dentists in the geographic area in which the taxpayer works to maintain office hours only 4 days a week. Where a trade or business is seasonal, weeks occurring during the off-
10 season when no work is required or available may be counted as weeks of performance of services on a full-time basis only if the off-season is less than 6 months and the taxpayer performs services on a full-time basis both before and after the off-season. For example, a taxpayer who owns and operates a motel at a beach resort is considered to perform services as a self-employed individual on a full-time basis if the motel is closed
15 for a period not exceeding 6 months during the off-season and if he performs services on a full-time basis as the operator of a motel both before and after the off-season. A taxpayer will be treated as performing services as a self-employed individual on a full-time basis during any week of involuntary temporary absence from work because of illness, strikes, natural disasters, etc.
20 (v) Where taxpayers file a joint return, either spouse may satisfy the minimum period of employment condition. However, weeks worked by one spouse may not be added to weeks worked by the other spouse in order to satisfy such condition. The taxpayer seeking to satisfy the minimum period of employment condition must satisfy the condition applicable to him. Thus, if a taxpayer is subject to the 39-week condition and his spouse
25 is subject to the 78-week condition and the taxpayer satisfies the 39-week condition, his spouse need not satisfy the 78-week condition. On the other hand, if the taxpayer does not satisfy the 39-week condition, his spouse in such case must satisfy the 78-week condition.

(vi) The application of this subparagraph may be illustrated by the following examples:
30 *Example 1.* A is an electrician residing in New York City. He moves himself, his family, and his household goods and personal effects, at his own expense, to Denver where he commences employment with the M Aircraft Corporation. After working full-time for 30 weeks he voluntarily leaves his job, and he subsequently moves to and commences employment in Los Angeles, CA, which employment lasts for more than 39 weeks. Since
35 A was not employed in the general location of his new principal place of employment in Denver for at least 39 weeks, no deduction is allowable for moving expenses paid or incurred between New York City and Denver. A will be allowed to deduct only those moving expenses attributable to his move from Denver to Los Angeles, assuming all other conditions of section 217 are met.
40 *Example 2.* Assume the same facts as in Example 1, except that A's wife commences employment in Denver at the same time as A, and that she continues to work in Denver for at least 9 weeks after A's departure for Los Angeles. Since she has met the 39-week requirement in Denver, and assuming all other requirements of section 217 are met, the moving expenses paid by A attributable to the move from New York City to Denver will be
45 allowed as a deduction, provided A and his wife file a joint return. If A and his wife file separate returns moving expenses paid by A's wife attributable to the move from New York City to Denver will be allowed as a deduction on A's wife's return.

Example 3. Assume the same facts as in Example 1, except that A's wife commences employment in Denver on the same day that A departs for Los Angeles, and continues to
50 work in Denver for 9 weeks thereafter. Since neither A (who has worked 30 weeks) nor his wife (who has worked 9 weeks) has independently satisfied the 39-week requirement,

Sec. 217. Moving expenses

no deduction for moving expenses attributable to the move from New York City to Denver is allowable.

(d) *Rules for application of section 217(c)(2)--(1) Inapplicability of minimum period of employment condition in certain cases.* Section 217(d)(1) provides that the minimum period of employment condition of section 217(c)(2) does not apply in the case of a taxpayer who is unable to meet such condition by reason of:

(i) Death or disability, or

(ii) Involuntary separation (other than for willfull misconduct) from the service of an employer or separation by reason of transfer for the benefit of an employer after obtaining full-time employment in which the taxpayer could reasonably have been expected to satisfy such condition.

For purposes of subdivision (i) of this paragraph disability shall be determined according to the rules in section 72(m)(7) and § 1.72-17(f). Subdivision (ii) of this subparagraph applies only where the taxpayer has obtained full-time employment in which he could reasonably have been expected to satisfy the minimum period of employment condition. A taxpayer could reasonably have been expected to satisfy the minimum period of employment condition if at the time he commences work at the new principal place of work he could have been expected, based upon the facts known to him at such time, to satisfy such condition. Thus, for example, if the taxpayer at the time of transfer was not advised by his employer that he planned to transfer him within 6 months to another principal place of work, the taxpayer could, in the absence of other factors, reasonably have been expected to satisfy the minimum employment period condition at the time of the first transfer. On the other hand, a taxpayer could not reasonably have been expected to satisfy the minimum employment condition if at the time of the commencement of the move he knew that his employer's retirement age policy would prevent his satisfying the minimum employment period condition.

(2) *Election of deduction before minimum period of employment condition is satisfied.* (i) Paragraph (2) of section 217(d) provides a rule which applies where a taxpayer paid or incurred, in a taxable year, moving expenses which would be deductible in that taxable year except that the minimum period of employment condition of section 217(c)(2) has not been satisfied before the time prescribed by law for filing the return for such taxable year. The rule provides that where a taxpayer has paid or incurred moving expenses and as of the date prescribed by section 6072 for filing his return for such taxable year (determined with regard to extensions of time for filing) there remains unexpired a sufficient portion of the 12-month or the 24-month period so that it is still possible for the taxpayer to satisfy the applicable period of employment condition, the taxpayer may elect to claim a deduction for such moving expenses on the return for such taxable year. The election is exercised by taking the deduction on the return.

(ii) Where a taxpayer does not elect to claim a deduction for moving expenses on the return for the taxable year in which such expenses were paid or incurred in accordance with subdivision (i) of this subparagraph and the applicable minimum period of employment condition of section 217(c)(2) (as well as all other requirements of section 217) is subsequently satisfied, the taxpayer may file an amended return or a claim for refund for the taxable year such moving expenses were paid or incurred on which he may claim a deduction under section 217.

(iii) The application of this subparagraph may be illustrated by the following examples:

Example 1. A is transferred by his employer from Boston, MA, to Cleveland, OH. He begins working there on November 1, 1970. Moving expenses are paid by A in 1970 in connection with this move. On April 15, 1971, when he files his income tax return for the year 1970, A has been a full-time employee in Cleveland for approximately 24 weeks. Although he has not satisfied the 39-week employment condition at this time, A may elect

573

Sec. 217. Moving expenses

to claim his 1970 moving expenses on his 1970 income tax return as there is still sufficient time remaining before November 1, 1971, to satisfy such condition.

Example 2. Assume the same facts as in Example 1, except that on April 15, 1971, A has voluntarily left his employer and is looking for other employment in Cleveland. A may
5 not be sure he will be able to meet the 39-week employment condition by November 1, 1971. Thus, he may if he wishes wait until such condition is met and file an amended return claiming as a deduction the expenses paid in 1970. Instead of filing an amended return A may file a claim for refund based on a deduction for such expenses. If A fails to meet the 39-week employment condition on or before November 1, 1971, no deduction is
10 allowable for such expenses.

Example 3. B is a self-employed accountant. He moves from Rochester, NY, to New York, NY, and begins to work there on December 1, 1970. Moving expenses are paid by B in 1970 and 1971 in connection with this move. On April 15, 1971, when he files his income tax return for the year 1970, B has been performing services as a self-employed
15 individual on a full-time basis in New York City for approximately 20 weeks. Although he has not satisfied the 78-week employment condition at this time, A may elect to claim his 1970 moving expenses on his 1970 income tax return as there is still sufficient time remaining before December 1, 1972, to satisfy such condition. On April 15, 1972, when he files his income tax return for the year 1971, B has been performing services as a self-
20 employed individual on a full-time basis in New York City for approximately 72 weeks. Although he has not met the 78-week employment condition at this time, B may elect to claim his 1971 moving expenses on his 1971 income tax return as there is still sufficient time remaining before December 1, 1972, to satisfy such requirement.

(3) *Recapture of deduction.* Paragraph (3) of section 217(d) provides a rule which
25 applies where a taxpayer has deducted moving expenses under the election provided in section 217(d)(2) prior to satisfying the applicable minimum period of employment condition and such condition cannot be satisfied at the close of a subsequent taxable year. In such cases an amount equal to the expenses deducted must be included in the taxpayer's gross income for the taxable year in which the taxpayer is no longer able to
30 satisfy such minimum period of employment condition. Where the taxpayer has deducted moving expenses under the election provided in section 217(d)(2) for the taxable year and subsequently files an amended return for such year on which he does not claim the deduction, such expenses are not treated as having been deducted for purposes of the recapture rule of the preceding sentence.

35 (e) *Denial of double benefit--*(1) *In general.* Section 217(e) provides a rule for computing the amount realized and the basis where qualified real estate expenses are allowed as a deduction under section 217(a).

(2) *Sale or exchange of residence.* Section 217(e) provides that the amount realized on the sale or exchange of a residence owned by the taxpayer, by the taxpayer's spouse,
40 or by the taxpayer and his spouse and used by the taxpayer as his principal place of residence is not decreased by the amount of any expenses described in subparagraph (A) of section 217(b)(2) and deducted under section 217(a). For the purposes of section 217(e) and of this paragraph the term amount realized" has the same meaning as under section 1001(b) and the regulations thereunder. Thus, for example, if the taxpayer sells a
45 residence used as his principal place of residence and real estate commissions or similar expenses described in subparagraph (A) of section 217(b)(2) are deducted by him pursuant to section 217(a), the amount realized on the sale of the residence is not reduced by the amount of such real estate commissions or such similar expenses described in subparagraph (A) of section 217(b)(2).

50 (3) *Purchase of a residence.* Section 217(e) provides that the basis of a residence purchased or received in exchange for other property by the taxpayer, by the taxpayer's

Sec. 217. Moving expenses

spouse, or by the taxpayer and his spouse and used by the taxpayer as his principal place of residence is not increased by the amount of any expenses described in subparagraph (B) of section 217(b)(2) and deducted under section 217(a). For the purposes of section 217(e) and of this paragraph the term basis has the same meaning as under section 1011 and the regulations thereunder. Thus, for example, if a taxpayer 5 purchases a residence to be used as his principal place of residence and attorneys' fees or similar expenses described in subparagraph (B) of section 217(b)(2) are deducted pursuant to section 217(a), the basis of such residence is not increased by the amount of such attorneys' fees or such similar expenses described in subparagraph (B) of section 217(b)(2). 10

(4) *Inapplicability of section 217(e).* (i) Section 217(e) and subparagraphs (1) through (3) of this paragraph do not apply to any expenses with respect to which an amount is included in gross income under section 217(d)(3). Thus, the amount of any expenses describedin subparagraph (A) of section 217(b)(2) deducted in the year paid or incurred pursuant to the election under section 217(d)(2) and subsequently recaptured pursuant to 15 section 217(d)(3) may be taken into account in computing the amount realized on the sale or exchange of the residence described in such subparagraph. Also, the amount of expenses described in subparagraph (B) of section 217(b)(2) deducted in the year paid or incurred pursuant to such election under section 217(d)(2) and subsequently recaptured pursuant to section 217(d)(3) may be taken into account as an adjustment to 20 the basis of the residence described in such subparagraph.

(ii) The application of subdivision (i) of this subparagraph may be illustrated by the following examples:

Example 1. A was notified of his transfer effective December 15, 1972, from Seattle, WA, to Philadelphia, PA. In connection with the transfer A sold his house in Seattle on 25 November 10, 1972. Expenses incident to the sale of the house of $2,500 were paid by A prior to or at the time of the closing of the contract of sale on December 10, 1972. The amount realized on the sale of the house was $47,500 and the adjusted basis of the house was $30,000. Pursuant to the election provided in section 217(d)(2), A deducted the expenses of moving from Seattle to Philadelphia including the expenses incident to 30 the sale of his former residence in taxable year 1972. Dissatisfied with his position with his employer in Philadelphia, A took a position with an employer in Chicago, IL, on July 15, 1973. Since A was no longer able to satisfy the minimum period employment condition at the close of taxable year 1973 he included an amount equal to the amount deducted as moving expenses including the expenses incident to the sale of his former 35 residence in gross income for taxable year 1973. A is permitted to decrease the amount realized on the sale of the house by the amount of the expenses incident to the sale of the house deducted from gross income and subsequently included in gross income. Thus, the amount realized on the sale of the house is decreased from $47,500 to $45,000 and thus, the gain on the sale of the house is reduced from $17,500 to $15,000. 40 A is allowed to file an amended return or a claim for refund in order to reflect the recomputation of the amount realized.

Example 2. B, who is self-employed decided to move from Washington, DC, to Los Angeles, CA. In connection with the commencement of work in Los Angeles on March 1, 1973, B purchased a house in a suburb of Los Angeles for $65,000. Expenses incident to 45 the purchase of the house in the amount of $1,500 were paid by B prior to or at the time of the closing of the contract of sale on September 15, 1973. Pursuant to the election provided in section 217(d)(2), B deducted the expenses of moving from Washington to Los Angeles including the expenses incident to the purchase of his new residence in taxable year 1973. Dissatisfied with his prospects in Los Angeles, B moved back to 50 Washington on July 1, 1974. Since B was no longer able to satisfy the minimum period of

Sec. 217. Moving expenses

employment condition at the close of taxable year 1974 he included an amount equal to the amount deducted as moving expenses incident to the purchase of the former residence in gross income for taxable year 1974. B is permitted to increase the basis of the house by the amount of the expenses incident to the purchase of the house deducted
5 from gross income and subsequently included in gross income. Thus, the basis of the house is increased to $66,500.

(f) *Rules for self-employed individuals--*(1) *Definition.* Section 217(f)(1) defines the term self-employed individual for purposes of section 217 to mean an individual who performs personal services either as the owner of the entire interest in an unincorporated
10 trade or business or as a partner in a partnership carrying on a trade or business. The term self-employed individual does not include the semiretired, part-time students, or other similarly situated taxpayers who work only a few hours each week. The application of this subparagraph may be illustrated by the following example:

Example. A is the owner of the entire interest in an unincorporated construction
15 business. A hires a manager who performs all of the daily functions of the business including the negotiation of contracts with customers, the hiring and firing of employees, the purchasing of materials used on the projects, and other similar services. A and his manager discuss the operations of the business about once a week over the telephone. Otherwise A does not perform any managerial services for the business. For the
20 purposes of section 217, A is not considered to be a self-employed individual.

(2) *Rule for application of subsection (b)(1) (C) and (D).* Section 217(f)(2) provides that for purposes of subparagraphs (C) and (D) of section 217(b)(1) an individual who commences work at a new principal place of work as a self-employed individual is treated as having obtained employment when he has made substantial arrangements to
25 commence such work. Whether the taxpayer has made substantial arrangements to commence work at a new principal place of work is determined on the basis of all the facts and circumstances in each case. The factors to be considered in this determination depend upon the nature of the taxpayer's trade or business and include such considerations as whether the taxpayer has: (i) Leased or purchased a plant, office, shop,
30 store, equipment, or other property to be used in the trade or business, (ii) made arrangements to purchase inventory or supplies to be used in connection with the operation of the trade or business, (iii) entered into commitments with individuals to be employed in the trade or business, and (iv) made arrangements to contact customers or clients in order to advertise the business in the general location of the new principal place
35 of work. The application of this subparagraph may be illustrated by the following examples:

Example 1. A, a partner in a growing chain of drug stores decided to move from Houston, TX, to Dallas, TX, in order to open a drug store in Dallas. A made several trips to Dallas for the purpose of looking for a site for the drug store. After the signing of a
40 lease on a building in a shopping plaza, suppliers were contacted, equipment was purchased, and employees were hired. Shortly before the opening of the store A and his wife moved from Houston to Dallas and took up temporary quarters in a motel until the time their apartment was available. By the time he and his wife took up temporary quarters in the motel A was considered to have made substantial arrangements to
45 commence work at the new principal place of work.

Example 2. B, who is a partner in a securities brokerage firm in New York, NY, decided to move to Rochester, NY, to become the resident partner in the firm's new Rochester office. After a lease was signed on an office in downtown Rochester B moved to Rochester and took up temporary quarters in a motel until his apartment became
50 available. Before the opening of the office B supervised the decoration of the office, the purchase of equipment and supplies necessary for the operation of the office, the hiring

Sec. 217. Moving expenses

of personnel for the office, as well as other similar activities. By the time B took up temporary quarters in the motel he was considered to have made substantial arrangements to commence to work at the new principal place of work.

Example 3. C, who is about to complete his residency in ophthalmology at a hospital in Pittsburgh, PA, decided to fly to Philadelphia, PA, for the purpose of looking into opportunities for practicing in that city. Following his arrival in Philadelphia C decided to establish his practice in that city. He leased an office and an apartment. At the time he departed Pittsburgh for Philadelphia C was not considered to have made substantial arrangements to commence work at the new principal place of work, and, therefore, is not allowed to deduct expenses described in subparagraph (C) of section 217(b)(1) (relating to expenses of traveling (including meals and lodging), after obtaining employment, from the former residence to the general location of the new principal place of work and return, for the principal purpose of searching for a new residence).

(g) *Rules for members of the Armed Forces of the United States*--(1) *In general.* The rules in paragraphs (a)(1) and (2), (b), and (e) of this section apply to moving expenses paid or incurred by members of the Armed Forces of the United States on active duty who move pursuant to a military order and incident to a permanent change of station, except as provided in this paragraph (g). However, if the moving expenses are not paid or incurred incident to a permanent change of station, this paragraph (g) does not apply, but all other paragraphs of this section do apply. The provisions of this paragraph apply to taxable years beginning December 31, 1975.

(2) *Treatment of services or reimbursement provided by Government*--(i) *Services in kind.* The value of any moving or storage services furnished by the United States Government to members of the Armed Forces, their spouses, or their dependents in connection with a permanent change of station is not includible in gross income. The Secretary of Defense and (in cases involving members of the peacetime Coast Guard) the Secretary of Transportation are not required to report or withhold taxes with respect to those services. Services furnished by the Government include services rendered directly by the Government or rendered by a third party who is compensated directly by the Government for the services.

(ii) *Reimbursements.* The following rules apply to reimbursements or allowances by the Government to members of the Armed Forces, their spouses, or their dependents for moving or storage expenses paid or incurred by them in connection with a permanent change of station. If the reimbursement or allowance exceeds the actual expenses paid or incurred, the excess is includible in the gross income of the member, and the Secretary of Defense or Secretary of Transportation must report the excess as payment of wages and withhold income taxes under section 3402 and the employee taxes under section 3102 with respect to that excess. If the reimbursement or allowance does not exceed the actual expenses, the reimbursement or allowance in not includible in gross income, and no reporting or withholding by the Secretary of Defense or Secretary of Transportation is required. If the actual expenses, as limited by paragraph (b)(9) of this section, exceed the reimbursement of allowance, the member may deduct the excess if the other requirements of this section, as modified by this paragraph, are met. The determination of the limitation on actual expenses under paragraph (b)(9) of this section is made without regard to any services in kind furnished by the Government.

(3) *Permanent change of station.* For purposes of this section, the term permanent change of station includes the following situations.

(i) A move from home to the first post of duty when appointed, reappointed, reinstated, or inducted.

(ii) A move from the last post of duty to home or a nearer point in the United States in connection with retirement, discharge, resignation, separation under honorable

Sec. 217. Moving expenses

conditions, transfer, relief from active duty, temporary disability retirement, or transfer to a Fleet Reserve, if such move occurs within 1 year of such termination of active duty or within the period prescribed by the Joint Travel Regulations promulgated under the authority contained in sections 404 through 411 of Title 37 of the United States Code.

5   (iii) A move from one permanent post of duty to another permanent post of duty at a different duty station, even if the member separates from the Armed Forces immediately or shortly after the move.

The term permanent, post of duty, duty station, and honorable have the meanings given them in appropriate Department of Defense or Department of Transportation rules and 10 regulations.

    (4) *Storage expenses.* This paragraph applies to storage expenses as well as to moving expenses described in paragraph (b)(1) of this section. the term storage expenses means the cost of storing personal effects of members of the Armed Forces, their spouses, and their dependents.

15   (5) *Moves of spouses and dependents.* (i) The following special rule applies for purposes of paragraphs (b)(9) and (10) of this section, if the spouse or dependents of a member of the Armed Forces move to or from a different location than does the member. In this case, the spouse is considered to have commenced work as an employee at a new principal place of work that is within the same general location as the location to 20 which the member moves.

    (ii) The following special rule applies for purposes of this paragraph to moves by spouses or dependents of members of the Armed Forces who die, are imprisoned, or desert while on active duty. In these cases, a move to a member's place of enlistment or induction or the member's, spouse's, or dependent's home of record or nearer point in the 25 United States is considered incident to a permanent change of station.

    (6) *Disallowance of deduction.* No deduction is allowed under this section for any moving or storage expense reimbursed by an allowance that is excluded from gross income.

    (h) *Special rules for foreign moves--(1) Increase in limitations.* In the case of a foreign 30 move (as defined in paragraph (h)(3) of this section), paragraph (b)(6) of this section shall be applied by substituting ``90 consecutive" for ``30 consecutive" each time it appears. Paragraph (b)(9)(ii), (iii) and (v) of this section shall be applied by substituting ``$6,000" for ``$3,000" each time it appears and by substituting ``$4,500" for ``$1,500" each time it appears. Paragraph (b)(9)(ii) of this section shall be applied by substituting ``$5,000" for 35 ``$2,000" each time it appears and by substituting ``1979" for ``1977" and ``1980" for ``1978" each time they appear in the last sentence. Paragraph (b)(9)(v) of this section shall be applied by substituting ``$2,250" for ``$750" each time it appears. Paragraph (b)(9)(vi) of this section does not apply.

    (2) *Allowance of certain storage fees.* In the case of a foreign move, for purposes of 40 this section, the moving expenses described in paragraph (b)(3) of this section shall include the reasonable expenses of moving household goods and personal effects to and from storage, and of storing such goods and effects for part or all of the period during which the new place of work continues to be the taxpayer's principal place of work.

    (3) *Foreign move.* For purposes of this paragraph, the term foreign move means a 45 move in connection with the commencement of work by the taxpayer at a new principal place of work located outside the United States. Thus, a move from the United States to a foreign country or from one foreign country to another foreign country qualifies as a foreign move. A move within a foreign country also qualifies as a foreign move. A move from a foreign country to the United States does not qualify as a foreign move.

50   (4) *United States.* For purposes of this paragraph, the term United States includes the possessions of the United States.

Sec. 217. Moving expenses

***

(i) **Allowance of deductions in case of retirees or decedents who were working abroad**--(1) *In general.* In the case of any qualified retiree moving expenses or qualified survivor moving expenses, this section (other than paragraph (h)) shall be applied to such expenses as if they were incurred in connection with the commencement of work by the taxpayer as an employee at a new principal place of work located within the United States and the limitations of paragraph (c)(4) of this section (relating to the minimum period of employment) shall not apply.

(2) *Qualified retiree moving expenses.* For purposes of this paragraph, the term qualified retiree moving expenses means any moving expenses which are incurred by an individual whose former principal place of work and former residence were outside the United States and which are incurred for a move to a new residence in the United States in connection with the bona fide retirement of the individual. Bona fide retirement means the permanent withdrawal from gainful full-time employment and self-employment. An individual who at the time of withdrawal from gainful full-time employment or self-employment, intends the withdrawal to be permanent shall be considered to be a bona fide retiree even though the individual ultimately resumes gainful full-time employment or self-employment. An individual's intention may be evidenced by relevant facts and circumstances which include the age and health of the individual, the customary retirement age of employees engaged in similar work, whether the individual is receiving a retirement allowance under a pension annuity, retirement or similar fund or system, and the length of time before resuming full-time employment or self-employment.

(3) *Qualified survivor moving expenses.* (i) For purposes of this paragraph, the term qualified survivor moving expenses means any moving expenses:

(A) Which are paid or incurred by the spouse or any dependent (as defined in section 152) of any decedent who (as of the time of his death) had a principal place of work outside the United States, and

(B) Which are incurred for a move which begins within 6 months after the death of the decedent and which is to a residence in the United States from a former residence outside the United States which (as of the time of the decedent's death) was the residence of such decedent and the individual paying or incurring the expense.

(ii) For purposes of paragraph (i)(3)(i)(B) of this section, a move begins when:

(A) The taxpayer contracts for the moving of his or her household goods and personal effects to a residence in the United States but only if the move is completed within a reasonable time thereafter;

(B) The taxpayer's household goods and personal effects are packed and in transit to a residence in the United States; or

(C) The taxpayer leaves the former residence to travel to a new place of residence in the United States.

(4) *United States.* For purposes of this paragraph, the term United States includes the possessions of the United States.

***

[T.D. 7195, 37 FR 13535, July 11, 1972, 37 FR 14230, July 18, 1972; T.D. 7578 43 FR 59355, Dec. 20, 1978; T.D. 7605, 44 FR 18970, Mar. 30, 1979; T.D. 7689, 45 FR 20796, Mar. 31, 1980; T.D. 7810, 47 FR 6003, Feb. 10, 1982; T.D. 8607, 60 FR 40077, Aug. 7, 1995]

Sec. 219. Retirement savings

(a) **Allowance of deduction.** -- In the case of an individual, there shall be allowed as a

Sec. 219. Retirement savings

deduction an amount equal to the qualified retirement contributions of the individual for the taxable year.

(b) Maximum amount of deduction. --

(1) In general. -- The amount allowable as a deduction under subsection (a) to any individual for any taxable year shall not exceed the lesser of--

(A) the deductible amount, or

(B) an amount equal to the compensation includible in the individual's gross income for such taxable year.

***

(5) Deductible amount. -- For purposes of paragraph (1)(A)--

(A) In general. -- The deductible amount shall be determined in accordance with the following table:

For taxable years beginning in:	The deductible amount is:
2002 through 2004	$3,000
2005 through 2007	$4,000
2008 and thereafter	$5,000.

(B) Catch-up contributions for individuals 50 or older. --

(i) In general. -- In the case of an individual who has attained the age of 50 before the close of the taxable year, the deductible amount for such taxable year shall be increased by the applicable amount.

(ii) Applicable amount. -- For purposes of clause (i), the applicable amount shall be the amount determined in accordance with the following table:

For taxable years beginning in:	The applicable amount is:
2002 through 2005.........................	$500
2006 and thereafter........................	$1,000.

***

(D) Cost-of-living adjustment. --

(i) In general. -- In the case of any taxable year beginning in a calendar year after 2008, the $5,000 amount under subparagraph (A) shall be increased by an amount equal to--

(I) such dollar amount, multiplied by

(II) the cost-of-living adjustment determined under section 1(f)(3) for the calendar year in which the taxable year begins, determined by substituting "calendar year 2007" for "calendar year 1992" in subparagraph (B) thereof.

(ii) Rounding rules. -- If any amount after adjustment under clause (i) is not a multiple of $500, such amount shall be rounded to the next lower multiple of $500.

(c) Special rules for certain married individuals. --

(1) In general. -- In the case of an individual to whom this paragraph applies for the taxable year, the limitation of paragraph (1) of subsection (b) shall be equal to the lesser of--

Sec. 219. Retirement savings

(A) the dollar amount in effect under subsection (b)(1)(A) for the taxable year, or

(B) the sum of--

    (i) the compensation includible in such individual's gross income for the taxable year, plus

    (ii) the compensation includible in the gross income of such individual's spouse for the taxable year reduced by -

        (I) the amount allowed as a deduction under subsection (a) to such spouse for such taxable year,

        (II) the amount of any designated nondeductible contribution (as defined in section 408(o)) on behalf of such spouse for such taxable year, and

        (III) the amount of any contribution on behalf of such spouse to a Roth IRA under section 408A for such taxable year.

(2) Individuals to whom paragraph (1) applies. -- Paragraph (1) shall apply to any individual if--

    (A) such individual files a joint return for the taxable year, and

    (B) the amount of compensation (if any) includible in such individual's gross income for the taxable year is less than the compensation includible in the gross income of such individual's spouse for the taxable year.

(d) Other limitations and restrictions. --

(1) Beneficiary must be under age 70 1/2 . -- No deduction shall be allowed under this section with respect to any qualified retirement contribution for the benefit of an individual if such individual has attained age 70 1/2 before the close of such individual's taxable year for which the   contribution was made.

***

(e) Qualified retirement contribution. -- For purposes of this section, the term "qualified retirement contribution" means--

(1) any amount paid in cash for the taxable year by or on behalf of an individual to an individual retirement plan for such individual's benefit, and

(2) any amount contributed on behalf of any individual to a plan described in section 501(c)(18).

(f) Other definitions and special rules. --

(1) Compensation. -- For purposes of this section, the term "compensation" includes earned income (as defined in section 401(c)(2)). The term "compensation" does not include any amount received as a pension or annuity and does not include any amount received as deferred compensation. The term "compensation" shall include any amount includible in the individual's gross income under section 71 with respect to a divorce or separation instrument described in subparagraph (A) of section 71(b)(2). For purposes of this paragraph, section 401(c)(2) shall be applied as if the term trade or business for purposes of section 1402 included service described in subsection (c)(6).

(2) Married individuals. -- The maximum deduction under subsection (b) shall be computed separately for each individual, and this section shall be applied without regard to any community property laws.

(3) Time when contributions deemed made. -- For purposes of this section, a taxpayer shall be deemed to have made a contribution to an individual retirement plan on the last day of the preceding taxable year if the contribution is made on account of such taxable year and is made not later than the time prescribed by law for filing the return for such taxable year (not

Sec. 219.   Retirement savings

including extensions thereof).

* * *

(5) Employer payments. -- For purposes of this title, any amount paid by an employer to an individual retirement plan shall be treated as payment of compensation to the employee (other than a self-employed individual who is an employee within the meaning of section 401(c)(1)) includible in his gross income in the taxable year for which the amount was contributed, whether or not a deduction for such payment is allowable under this section to the employee.

(6) Excess contributions treated as contribution made during subsequent year for which there is an unused limitation. --

   (A) In general. -- If for the taxable year the maximum amount allowable as a deduction under this section for contributions to an individual retirement plan exceeds the amount contributed, then the taxpayer shall be treated as having made an additional contribution for the taxable year in an amount equal to the lesser of--

   (i) the amount of such excess, or

   (ii) the amount of the excess contributions for such taxable year (determined under section 4973(b)(2) without regard to subparagraph (C) thereof).

   (B) Amount contributed. -- For purposes of this paragraph, the amount contributed -

   (i) shall be determined without regard to this paragraph, and

   (ii) shall not include any rollover contribution.

* * *

(g) Limitation on deduction for active participants in certain pension plans. --

   (1) In general. -- If (for any part of any plan year ending with or within a taxable year) an individual or the individual's spouse is an active participant, each of the dollar limitations contained in subsections (b)(1)(A) and (c)(1)(A) for such taxable year shall be reduced (but not below zero) by the amount determined under paragraph (2).

   (2) Amount of reduction. --

   (A) In general. -- The amount determined under this paragraph with respect to any dollar limitation shall be the amount which bears the same ratio to such limitation as -

   (i) the excess of--

   (I) the taxpayer's adjusted gross income for such taxable year, over

   (II) the applicable dollar amount, bears to

   (ii) $10,000 ($20,000 in the case of a joint return for a taxable year beginning after December 31, 2006).

   (B) No reduction below $200 until complete phase-out. -- No dollar limitation shall be reduced below $200 under paragraph (1) unless (without regard to this subparagraph) such limitation is reduced to zero.

   (C) Rounding. -- Any amount determined under this paragraph which is not a multiple of $10 shall be rounded to the next lowest $10.

   (3) Adjusted gross income; applicable dollar amount. -- For purposes of this subsection -

   (A) Adjusted gross income. -- Adjusted gross income of any taxpayer shall be determined--

   (i) after application of sections 86 and 469, and

   (ii) without regard to sections 135, 137, 199, 221, 222, and 911 or the deduction allowable under this section.

   (B) Applicable dollar amount. -- The term "applicable dollar amount" means the

582

Sec. 219.   Retirement savings

following:

(i) In the case of a taxpayer filing a joint return:

For taxable years beginning in:	The applicable dollar amount is:
***	
2007 and thereafter.............................	$80,000.

(ii) In the case of any other taxpayer (other than a married individual filing a separate return):

For taxable years beginning in:	The applicable dollar amount is:
***	
2005 and thereafter.............................	$50,000.

(iii) In the case of a married individual filing a separate return, zero.

(4) Special rule for married individuals filing separately and living apart. -- A husband and wife who -

(A) file separate returns for any taxable year, and

(B) live apart at all times during such taxable year, shall not be treated as married individuals for purposes of this subsection.

(5) Active participant. -- For purposes of this subsection, the term "active participant" means, with respect to any plan year, an individual--

(A) who is an active participant in -

(i) a plan described in section 401(a) which includes a trust exempt from tax under section 501(a),

(ii) an annuity plan described in section 403(a),

(iii) a plan established for its employees by the United States, by a State or political subdivision thereof, or by an agency or instrumentality of any of the foregoing,

(iv) an annuity contract described in section 403(b),

(v) a simplified employee pension (within the meaning of section 408(k)), or

(vi) any simple retirement account (within the meaning of section 408(p)), or

(B) who makes deductible contributions to a trust described in section 501(c)(18).

The determination of whether an individual is an active participant shall be made without regard to whether or not such individual's rights under a plan, trust, or contract are nonforfeitable. An eligible deferred compensation plan (within the meaning of section 457(b)) shall not be treated as a plan described in subparagraph (A)(iii).

(6) Certain individuals not treated as active participants. -- For purposes of this subsection, any individual described in any of the following subparagraphs shall not be treated as an active participant for any taxable year solely because of any participation so described:

(A) **Members of reserve components.** -- Participation in a plan described in subparagraph (A)(iii) of paragraph (5) by reason of service as a member of a reserve component of the Armed Forces (as defined in section 10101 of title 10), unless such

Sec. 219. Retirement savings

individual has served in excess of 90 days on active duty (other than active duty for training) during the year.

    (B) Volunteer firefighters. -- A volunteer firefighter--

        (i) who is a participant in a plan described in subparagraph (A)(iii) of paragraph (5) based on his activity as a volunteer firefighter, and

        (ii) whose accrued benefit as of the beginning of the taxable year is not more than an annual benefit of $1,800 (when expressed as a single life annuity commencing at age 65).

    (7) Special rule for spouses who are not active participants. -- If this subsection applies to an individual for any taxable year solely because their spouse is an active participant, then, in applying this subsection to the individual (but not their spouse)--

        (A) the applicable dollar amount under paragraph (3)(B)(i) shall be $150,000; and

        (B) the amount applicable under paragraph (2)(A)(ii) shall be $10,000.

    (8) Inflation adjustment. -- In the case of any taxable year beginning in a calendar year after 2006, the dollar amount in the last row of the table contained in paragraph (3)(B)(i), the dollar amount in the last row of the table contained in paragraph (3)(B)(ii), and the dollar amount contained in paragraph (7)(A), shall each be increased by an amount equal to--

        (A) such dollar amount, multiplied by

        (B) the cost-of-living adjustment determined under section 1(f)(3) for the calendar year in which the taxable year begins, determined by substituting `calendar year 2005' for `calendar year 1992' in subparagraph (B) thereof.

Any increase determined under the preceding sentence shall be rounded to the nearest multiple of $1,000.

***

Sec. 220. Archer MSAs

    (a) Deduction allowed. -- In the case of an individual who is an eligible individual for any month during the taxable year, there shall be allowed as a deduction for the taxable year an amount equal to the aggregate amount paid in cash during such taxable year by such individual to an Archer MSA of such individual.

    (b) Limitations. --

    (1) In general. -- The amount allowable as a deduction under subsection (a) to an individual for the taxable year shall not exceed the sum of the monthly limitations for months during such taxable year that the individual is an eligible individual.

    (2) Monthly limitation. -- The monthly limitation for any month is the amount equal to 1/12 of -

        (A) in the case of an individual who has self-only coverage under the high deductible health plan as of the first day of such month, 65 percent of the annual deductible under such coverage, and

        (B) in the case of an individual who has family coverage under the high deductible health plan as of the first day of such month, 75 percent of the annual deductible under such coverage.

    (3) Special rule for married individuals. -- In the case of individuals who are married to each other, if either spouse has family coverage--

        (A) both spouses shall be treated as having only such family coverage (and if such spouses each have family coverage under different plans, as having the family coverage

584

with the lowest annual deductible), and

(B) the limitation under paragraph (1) (after the application of subparagraph (A) of this paragraph) shall be divided equally between them unless they agree on a different division.

(4) Deduction not to exceed compensation. --

(A) Employees. -- The deduction allowed under subsection (a) for contributions as an eligible individual described in subclause (I) of subsection (c)(1)(A)(iii) shall not exceed such individual's wages, salaries, tips, and other employee compensation which are attributable to such individual's employment by the employer referred to in such subclause.

(B) Self-employed individuals. -- The deduction allowed under subsection (a) for contributions as an eligible individual described in subclause (II) of subsection (c)(1)(A) (iii) shall not exceed such individual's earned income (as defined in section 401(c)(1)) derived by the taxpayer from the trade or business with respect to which the high deductible health plan is established.

(C) Community property laws not to apply. -- The limitations under this paragraph shall be determined without regard to community property laws.

(5) Coordination with exclusion for employer contributions. -- No deduction shall be allowed under this section for any amount paid for any taxable year to an Archer MSA of an individual if--

(A) any amount is contributed to any Archer MSA of such individual for such year which is excludable from gross income under section 106(b), or

(B) if such individual's spouse is covered under the high deductible health plan covering such individual, any amount is contributed for such year to any Archer MSA of such spouse which is so excludable.

(6) Denial of deduction to dependents. -- No deduction shall be allowed under this section to any individual with respect to whom a deduction under section 151 is allowable to another taxpayer for a taxable year beginning in the calendar year in which such individual's taxable year begins.

(7) Medicare eligible individuals. -- The limitation under this subsection for any month with respect to an individual shall be zero for the first month such individual is entitled to benefits under title XVIII of the Social Security Act and for each month thereafter.

(c) Definitions. -- For purposes of this section -

(1) Eligible individual. --

(A) In general. -- the term "eligible individual" means, with respect to any month, any individual if -

(i) such individual is covered under a high deductible health plan as of the 1st day of such month,

(ii) such individual is not, while covered under a high deductible health plan, covered under any health plan--

(I) which is not a high deductible health plan, and

(II) which provides coverage for any benefit which is covered under the high deductible health plan, and

(iii)(I) the high deductible health plan covering such individual is established and maintained by the employer of such individual or of the spouse of such individual and such employer is a small employer, or

(II) such individual is an employee (within the meaning of section 401(c)(1)) or the spouse of such an employee and the high deductible health plan covering such

585

individual is not established or maintained by any employer of such individual or spouse.

(B) Certain coverage disregarded. -- Subparagraph (A)(ii) shall be applied without regard to--

(i) coverage for any benefit provided by permitted insurance, and

(ii) coverage (whether through insurance or otherwise) for accidents, disability, dental care, vision care, or long-term care.

(C) Continued eligibility of employee and spouse establishing Archer MSAs. -- If, while an employer is a small employer--

(i) any amount is contributed to an Archer MSA of an individual who is an employee of such employer or the spouse of such an employee, and

(ii) such amount is excludable from gross income under section 106(b) or allowable as a deduction under this section,

such individual shall not cease to meet the requirement of subparagraph (A)(iii)(I) by reason of such employer ceasing to be a small employer so long as such employee continues to be an employee of such employer.

(D) Limitations on eligibility. -- For limitations on number of taxpayers who are eligible to have Archer MSAs, see subsection (i).

(2) High deductible health plan. --

(A) In general. -- The term "high deductible health plan" means a health plan--

(i) in the case of self-only coverage, which has an annual deductible which is not less than $1,500 and not more than $2,250,

(ii) in the case of family coverage, which has an annual deductible which is not less than $3,000 and not more than $4,500, and

(iii) the annual out-of-pocket expenses required to be paid under the plan (other than for premiums) for covered benefits does not exceed--

(I) $3,000 for self-only coverage, and

(II) $5,500 for family coverage.

(B) Special rules. --

(i) **Exclusion of certain plans.** -- Such term does not include a health plan if substantially all of its coverage is coverage described in paragraph (1)(B).

(ii) **Safe harbor for absence of preventive care deductible.** -- A plan shall not fail to be treated as a high deductible health plan by reason of failing to have a deductible for preventive care if the absence of a deductible for such care is required by State law.

(3) Permitted insurance. -- The term "permitted insurance" means--

(A) insurance if substantially all of the coverage provided under such insurance relates to--

(i) liabilities incurred under workers' compensation laws,

(ii) tort liabilities,

(iii) liabilities relating to ownership or use of property,or

(iv) such other similar liabilities as the Secretary may specify by regulations,

(B) insurance for a specified disease or illness, and

(C) insurance paying a fixed amount per day (or other period) of hospitalization.

(4) Small employer. --

    (A) In general. -- The term "small employer" means, with respect to any calendar year, any employer if such employer employed an average of 50 or fewer employees on business days during either of the 2 preceding calendar years. For purposes of the preceding sentence, a preceding calendar year may be taken into account only if the employer was in 5 existence throughout such year.

    (B) Employers not in existence in preceding year. -- In the case of an employer which was not in existence throughout the 1st preceding calendar year, the determination under subparagraph (A) shall be based on the average number of employees that it is reasonably expected such employer will employ on business days in the current calendar year. 10

    (C) Certain growing employers retain treatment as small employer. -- The term "small employer" includes, with respect to any calendar year, any employer if--

        (i) such employer met the requirement of subparagraph (A) (determined without regard to subparagraph (B)) for any preceding calendar year after 1996,

        (ii) any amount was contributed to the Archer MSA of any employee of such 15 employer with respect to coverage of such employee under a high deductible health plan of such employer during such preceding calendar year and such amount was excludable from gross income under section 106(b) or allowable as a deduction under this section, and

        (iii) such employer employed an average of 200 or fewer employees on business 20 days during each preceding calendar year after 1996.

***

    (5) Family coverage. -- The term "family coverage" means any coverage other than self-only coverage.

(d) Archer MSA. -- For purposes of this section-- 25

    (1) Archer MSA. -- The term "Archer MSA" means a trust created or organized in the United States as a medical savings account exclusively for the purpose of paying the qualified medical expenses of the account holder, but only if the written governing instrument creating the trust meets the following requirements:

    (A) Except in the case of a rollover contribution described in subsection (f)(5), no 30 contribution will be accepted -

        (i) unless it is in cash, or

        (ii) to the extent such contribution, when added to previous contributions to the trust for the calendar year, exceeds 75 percent of the highest annual limit deductible permitted under subsection (c)(2)(A)(ii) for such calendar year. 35

    (B) The trustee is a bank (as defined in section 408(n)), an insurance company (as defined in section 816), or another person who demonstrates to the satisfaction of the Secretary that the manner in which such person will administer the trust will be consistent with the requirements of this section.

    (C) No part of the trust assets will be invested in life insurance contracts. 40

    (D) The assets of the trust will not be commingled with other property except in a common trust fund or common investment fund.

    (E) The interest of an individual in the balance in his account is nonforfeitable.

Sec. 220. Archer MSAs

(2) Qualified medical expenses. --

(A) In general. -- The term "qualified medical expenses" means, with respect to an account holder, amounts paid by such holder for medical care (as defined in section 213(d)) for such individual, the spouse of such individual, and any dependent (as defined in section 152, determined without regard to subsections (b)(1), (b)(2), and (d)(1)(B) thereof) of such individual, but only to the extent such amounts are not compensated for by insurance or otherwise.

(B) Health insurance may not be purchased from account. --

(i) In general. -- Subparagraph (A) shall not apply to any payment for insurance.

(ii) Exceptions. -- Clause (i) shall not apply to any expense for coverage under--

(I) a health plan during any period of continuation coverage required under any Federal law,

(II) a qualified long-term care insurance contract (as defined in section 7702B(b)), or

(III) a health plan during a period in which the individual is receiving unemployment compensation under any Federal or State law.

(C) Medical expenses of individuals who are not eligible individuals. -- Subparagraph (A) shall apply to an amount paid by an account holder for medical care of an individual who is not described in clauses (i) and (ii) of subsection (c)(1)(A) for the month in which the expense for such care is incurred only if no amount is contributed (other than a rollover contribution) to any Archer MSA of such account holder for the taxable year which includes such month. This subparagraph shall not apply to any expense for coverage described in subclause (I) or (III) of subparagraph (B)(ii).

(3) Account holder. -- The term "account holder" means the individual on whose behalf the Archer MSA was established.

***

(e) Tax treatment of accounts. --

(1) In general. -- An Archer MSA is exempt from taxation under this subtitle unless such account has ceased to be an Archer MSA.

Notwithstanding the preceding sentence, any such account is subject to the taxes imposed by section 511 (relating to imposition of tax on unrelated business income of charitable, etc. organizations).

***

(f) Tax treatment of distributions. --

(1) Amounts used for qualified medical expenses. -- Any amount paid or distributed out of an Archer MSA which is used exclusively to pay qualified medical expenses of any account holder shall not be includible in gross income.

(2) Inclusion of amounts not used for qualified medical expenses. -- Any amount paid or distributed out of an Archer MSA which is not used exclusively to pay the qualified medical expenses of the account holder shall be included in the gross income of such holder.

(3) Excess contributions returned before due date of return. --

(A) In general. -- If any excess contribution is contributed for a taxable year to any Archer MSA of an individual, paragraph (2) shall not apply to distributions from the Archer MSAs of such individual (to the extent such distributions do not exceed the aggregate excess contributions to all such accounts of such individual for such year) if--

588

(i) such distribution is received by the individual on or before the last day prescribed by law (including extensions of time) for filing such individual's return for such taxable year, and

(ii) such distribution is accompanied by the amount of net income attributable to such excess contribution.

Any net income described in clause (ii) shall be included in the gross income of the individual for the taxable year in which it is received.

(B) Excess contribution. -- For purposes of subparagraph (A), the term "excess contribution" means any contribution (other than a rollover contribution) which is neither excludable from gross income under section 106(b) nor deductible under this section.

(4) Additional tax on distributions not used for qualified medical expenses. --

(A) In general. -- The tax imposed by this chapter on the account holder for any taxable year in which there is a payment or distribution from an Archer MSA of such holder which is includible in gross income under paragraph (2) shall be increased by 15 percent of the amount which is so includible.

(B) Exception for disability or death. -- Subparagraph (A) shall not apply if the payment or distribution is made after the account holder becomes disabled within the meaning of section 72(m)(7) or dies.

(C) Exception for distributions after medicare eligibility. -- Subparagraph (A) shall not apply to any payment or distribution after the date on which the account holder attains the age specified in section 1811 of the Social Security Act.

(5) Rollover contribution. -- An amount is described in this paragraph as a rollover contribution if it meets the requirements of subparagraphs (A) and (B).

(A) In general. -- Paragraph (2) shall not apply to any amount paid or distributed from an Archer MSA to the account holder to the extent the amount received is paid into an Archer MSA or a health savings account (as defined in section 223(d)) for the benefit of such holder not later than the 60th day after the day on which the holder receives the payment or distribution.

(B) Limitation. -- This paragraph shall not apply to any amount described in subparagraph (A) received by an individual from an Archer MSA if, at any time during the 1-year period ending on the day of such receipt, such individual received any other amount described in subparagraph (A) from an Archer MSA which was not includible in the individual's gross income because of the application of this paragraph.

(6) Coordination with medical expense deduction. -- For purposes of determining the amount of the deduction under section 213, any payment or distribution out of an Archer MSA for qualified medical expenses shall not be treated as an expense paid for medical care.

(7) Transfer of account incident to divorce. -- The transfer of an individual's interest in an Archer MSA to an individual's spouse or former spouse under a divorce or separation instrument described in subparagraph (A) of section 71(b)(2) shall not be considered a taxable transfer made by such individual notwithstanding any other provision of this subtitle, and such interest shall, after such transfer, be treated as an Archer MSA with respect to which such spouse is the account holder.

(8) Treatment after death of account holder. --

(A) Treatment if designated beneficiary is spouse. -- If the account holder's surviving spouse acquires such holder's interest in an Archer MSA by reason of being the designated beneficiary of such account at the death of the account holder, such Archer MSA shall be treated as if the spouse were the account holder.

Sec. 220. Archer MSAs

(B) Other cases. --

(i) In general. -- If, by reason of the death of the account holder, any person acquires the account holder's interest in an Archer MSA in a case to which subparagraph (A) does not apply--

(I) such account shall cease to be an Archer MSA as of the date of death, and

(II) an amount equal to the fair market value of the assets in such account on such date shall be includible if such person is not the estate of such holder, in such person's gross income for the taxable year which includes such date, or if such person is the estate of such holder, in such holder's gross income for the last taxable year of such holder.

(ii) Special rules. --

(I) Reduction of inclusion for pre-death expenses. -- The amount includible in gross income under clause (i) by any person (other than the estate) shall be reduced by the amount of qualified medical expenses which were incurred by the decedent before the date of the decedent's death and paid by such person within 1 year after such date.

(II) Deduction for estate taxes. -- An appropriate deduction shall be allowed under section 691(c) to any person (other than the decedent or the decedent's spouse) with respect to amounts included in gross income under clause (i) by such person.

(g) Cost-of-living adjustment. -- In the case of any taxable year beginning in a calendar year after 1998, each dollar amount in subsection (c)(2) shall be increased by an amount equal to -

(1) such dollar amount, multiplied by. --

(2) the cost-of-living adjustment determined under section1(f)(3) for the calendar year in which such taxable year begins by substituting "calendar year 1997" for "calendar year 1992" in subparagraph (B) thereof.

If any increase under the preceding sentence is not a multiple of $50, such increase shall be rounded to the nearest multiple of $50.

(h) Reports. -- The Secretary may require the trustee of an Archer MSA to make such reports regarding such account to the Secretary and to the account holder with respect to contributions, distributions, and such other matters as the Secretary determines appropriate. The reports required by this subsection shall be filed at such time and in such manner and furnished to such individuals at such time and in such manner as may be required by the Secretary.

(i) Limitation on number of taxpayers having Archer MSAs. --

(1) In general. -- Except as provided in paragraph (5), no individual shall be treated as an eligible individual for any taxable year beginning after the cut-off year unless--

(A) such individual was an active MSA participant for any taxable year ending on or before the close of the cut-off year,or

(B) such individual first became an active MSA participant for a taxable year ending after the cut-off year by reason of coverage under a high deductible health plan of an MSA-participating employer.

(2) Cut-off year. -- For purposes of paragraph (1), the term "cut-off year" means the earlier of--

(A) calendar year 2007, or

(B) the first calendar year before 2007 for which the Secretary determines under subsection

590

Sec. 220.   Archer MSAs

(j) that the numerical limitation for such year has been exceeded. --

(3) Active MSA participant. -- For purposes of this subsection--

(A) In general. -- The term "active MSA participant" means, with respect to any taxable year, any individual who is the account holder of any Archer MSA into which any contribution was made which was excludable from gross income under section 106(b), or allowable as a deduction under this section, for such taxable year.

***

(C) Cut-off date. -- For purposes of subparagraph (B)--

(i) In general. -- Except as otherwise provided in this subparagraph, the cut-off date is October 1 of the cut-off year.

(ii) Employees with enrollment periods after October 1. -- In the case of an individual described in subclause (I) of subsection (c)(1)(A)(iii), if the regularly scheduled enrollment period for health plans of the individual's employer occurs during the last 3 months of the cut-off year, the cut-off date is December 31 of the cut-off year.

(iii) Self-employed individuals. -- In the case of an individual described in subclause (II) of subsection (c)(1)(A)(iii), the cut-off date is November 1 of the cut-off year.

***

(4) MSA-participating employer. -- For purposes of this subsection, the term "MSA-participating employer" means any small employer if--

(A) such employer made any contribution to the Archer MSA of any employee during the cut-off year or any preceding calendar year which was excludable from gross income under section 106(b), or

(B) at least 20 percent of the employees of such employer who are eligible individuals for any month of the cut-off year by reason of coverage under a high deductible health plan of such employer each made a contribution of at least $100 to their Archer MSAs for any taxable year ending with or within the cut- off year which was allowable as a deduction under this section.

(5) Additional eligibility after cut-off year. -- If the Secretary determines under subsection (j)(2)(A) that the numerical limit for the calendar year following a cut-off year described in paragraph (2)(B) has not been exceeded--

(A) this subsection shall not apply to any otherwise eligible individual who is covered under a high deductible health plan during the first 6 months of the second calendar year following the cut-off year (and such individual shall be treated as an active MSA participant for purposes of this subsection if a contribution is made to any Archer MSA with respect to such coverage), and

(B) any employer who offers coverage under a high deductible health plan to any employee during such 6-month period shall be treated as an MSA-participating employer for purposes of this subsection if the requirements of paragraph (4) are met with respect to such coverage.

For purposes of this paragraph, subsection (j)(2)(A) shall be applied for 1998 by substituting "750,000" for "600,000".

(j) Determination of whether numerical limits are exceeded. --

***

(2) Determination of whether limit exceeded for 1998, 1999, 2001, 2002, 2004, 2005, or 2006. --

Sec. 220. Archer MSAs

(A) In general. -- The numerical limitation for 1998, 1999, 2001, 2002, 2004, 2005, or 2006 is exceeded if the sum of--

(i) the number of MSA returns filed on or before April 15 of such calendar year for taxable years ending with or within the preceding calendar year, plus

(ii) the Secretary's estimate (determined on the basis of the returns described in clause (i)) of the number of MSA returns for such taxable years which will be filed after such date,

exceeds 750,000 (600,000 in the case of 1998). For purposes of the preceding sentence, the term "MSA return" means any return on which any exclusion is claimed under section 106(b) or any deduction is claimed under this section.

(B) Alternative computation of limitation. -- The numerical limitation for 1998, 1999, 2001, 2002, 2004, 2005, or 2006 is also exceeded if the sum of--

(i) 90 percent of the sum determined under subparagraph (A) for such calendar year, plus

(ii) the product of 2.5 and the number of Archer MSAs established during the portion of such year preceding July 1 (based on the reports required under paragraph (4)) for taxable years beginning in such year,

exceeds 750,000.

(C) No limitation for 2000 or 2003. -- The numerical limitation shall not apply for 2000 or 2003.

(3) Previously uninsured individuals not included in determination. --

(A) In general. -- The determination of whether any calendar year is a cut-off year shall be made by not counting the Archer MSA of any previously uninsured individual.

(B) Previously uninsured individual. -- For purposes of this subsection, the term "previously uninsured individual" means, with respect to any Archer MSA, any individual who had no health plan coverage (other than coverage referred to in subsection (c)(1)(B)) at any time during the 6-month period before the date such individual's coverage under the high deductible health plan commences.

***

(5) Date of making determinations. -- Any determination under this subsection that a calendar year is a cut-off year shall be made by the Secretary and shall be published not later than October 1 of such year.

Sec. 221. Interest on education loans

(a) Allowance of deduction. -- In the case of an individual, there shall be allowed as a deduction for the taxable year an amount equal to the interest paid by the taxpayer during the taxable year on any qualified education loan.

(b) Maximum deduction. --

(1) In general. -- Except as provided in paragraph (2), the deduction allowed by subsection (a) for the taxable year shall not exceed the amount determined in accordance with the following table:

Sec. 221.   Interest on education loans

In the case of taxable years beginning in:	The dollar amount is:	
***		
2001 or thereafter...................................	$2,500.	5

(2) Limitation based on modified adjusted gross income. --

(A) In general. -- The amount which would (but for this paragraph) be allowable as a deduction under this section shall be reduced (but not below zero) by the amount determined under subparagraph (B).   10

(B) Amount of reduction. -- The amount determined under this subparagraph is the amount which bears the same ratio to the amount which would be so taken into account as -

(i) the excess of--

(I) the taxpayer's modified adjusted gross income for such taxable year, over

(II) $50,000 ($100,000 in the case of a joint return), bears to   15

(ii) $15,000 ($30,000 in the case of a joint return).

(C) Modified adjusted gross income. -- The term "modified adjusted gross income" means adjusted gross income determined--

(i) without regard to this section and sections 199, 222, 911, 931, and 933, and

(ii) after application of sections 86, 135, 137, 219, and 469.   20

(c) Dependents not eligible for deduction. -- No deduction shall be allowed by this section to an individual for the taxable year if a deduction under section 151 with respect to such individual is allowed to another taxpayer for the taxable year beginning in the calendar year in which such individual's taxable year begins.

(d) Definitions. -- For purposes of this section--   25

(1) Qualified education loan. -- The term "qualified education loan" means any indebtedness incurred by the taxpayer solely to pay qualified higher education expenses -

(A) which are incurred on behalf of the taxpayer, the taxpayer's spouse, or any dependent of the taxpayer as of the time the indebtedness was incurred,

(B) which are paid or incurred within a reasonable period of time before or after the 30 indebtedness is incurred, and

(C) which are attributable to education furnished during a period during which the recipient was an eligible student,

Such term includes indebtedness used to refinance indebtedness which qualifies as a qualified education loan. The term "qualified education loan" shall not include any indebtedness owed to 35 a person who is related (within the meaning of section 267(b) or 707(b)(1)) to the taxpayer or to any person by reason of a loan under any qualified employer plan (as defined in section 72(p)(4)) or under any contract referred to in section 72(p)(5).

(2) Qualified higher education expenses. -- The term "qualified higher education expenses" means the cost of attendance (as defined in section 472 of the Higher Education Act 40 of 1965, 20 U.S.C. 1087ll, as in effect on the day before the date of the enactment of this Act) at an eligible educational institution, reduced by the sum of -

(A) the amount excluded from gross income under section 127, 135, 529, or 530 by reason of such expenses, and

(B) the amount of any scholarship, allowance, or payment described in section 25A(g) 45 (2).

Sec. 221.   Interest on education loans

For purposes of the preceding sentence, the term "eligible educational institution" has the same meaning given such term by section 25A(f)(2), except that such term shall also include an institution conducting an internship or residency program leading to a degree or certificate awarded by an institution of higher education, a hospital, or a health care facility which offers postgraduate training.

(3) Eligible student. -- The term "eligible student" has the meaning given such term by section 25A(b)(3).

(4) Dependent. -- The term "dependent" has the meaning given such term by section 152 (determined without regard to subsections (b)(1), (b)(2), and (d)(1)(B) thereof).

(e) Special rules. --

(1) Denial of double benefit. -- No deduction shall be allowed under this section for any amount for which a deduction is allowable under any other provision of this chapter.

(2) Married couples must file joint return. -- If the taxpayer is married at the close of the taxable year, the deduction shall be allowed under subsection (a) only if the taxpayer and the taxpayer's spouse file a joint return for the taxable year.

(3) Marital status. -- Marital status shall be determined in accordance with section 7703.

(f) Inflation adjustments. --

(1) In general. -- In the case of a taxable year beginning after 2002, the $50,000 and $100,000 amounts in subsection (b)(2) shall each be increased by an amount equal to -

(A) such dollar amount, multiplied by

(B) the cost-of-living adjustment determined under section 1(f)(3) for the calendar year in which the taxable year begins, determined by substituting "calendar year 2001" for "calendar year 1992" in subparagraph (B) thereof.

(2) Rounding. -- If any amount as adjusted under paragraph (1) is not a multiple of $5,000, such amount shall be rounded to the next lowest multiple of $5,000.

Reg. § 1.221-1   Deduction for interest paid on qualified education loans after December 31, 2001.

***

(b) *Eligibility*--(1) Taxpayer must have a legal obligation to make interest payments. A taxpayer is entitled to a deduction under section 221 only if the taxpayer has a legal obligation to make interest payments under the terms of the qualified education loan.

(2) *Claimed dependents not eligible*--(i) *In general.* An individual is not entitled to a deduction under section 221 for a taxable year if the individual is a dependent (as defined in section 152) for whom another taxpayer is allowed a deduction under section 151 on a Federal income tax return for the same taxable year (or, in the case of a fiscal year taxpayer, the taxable year beginning in the same calendar year as the individual's taxable year).

(ii) Examples. The following examples illustrate the rules of this paragraph (b)(2):

Example 1. Student not claimed as dependent. Student B pays $750 of interest on qualified education loans during 2003. Student B's parents are not allowed a deduction for her as a dependent for 2003. Assuming fulfillment of all other relevant requirements, Student B may deduct under section 221 the $750 of interest paid in 2003.

Example 2. Student claimed as dependent. Student C pays $750 of interest on qualified education loans during 2003. Only Student C has the legal obligation to make the payments. Student C's parent claims him as a dependent and is allowed a deduction under section 151 with respect to Student C in computing the parent's 2003 Federal income tax. Student C is not entitled to a deduction under section 221 for the $750 of

594

Sec. 221. Interest on education loans

interest paid in 2003. Because Student C's parent was not legally obligated to make the payments, Student C's parent also is not entitled to a deduction for the interest.

(3) *Married taxpayers.* If a taxpayer is married as of the close of a taxable year, he or she is entitled to a deduction under this section only if the taxpayer and the taxpayer's spouse file a joint return for that taxable year. 5

(4) *Payments of interest by a third party--(i) In general.* If a third party who is not legally obligated to make a payment of interest on a qualified education loan makes a payment of interest on behalf of a taxpayer who is legally obligated to make the payment, then the taxpayer is treated as receiving the payment from the third party and, in turn, paying the interest. 10

(ii) *Examples.* The following examples illustrate the rules of this paragraph (b)(4):

Example 1. Payment by employer. Student D obtains a qualified education loan to attend college. Upon Student D's graduation from college, Student D works as an intern for a non-profit organization during which time Student D's loan is in deferment and Student D makes no interest payments. As part of the internship program, the non-profit 15 organization makes an interest payment on behalf of Student D after the deferment period. This payment is not excluded from Student D's income under section 108(f) and is treated as additional compensation includible in Student D's gross income. Assuming fulfillment of all other requirements of section 221, Student D may deduct this payment of interest for Federal income tax purposes. 20

Example 2. Payment by parent. Student E obtains a qualified education loan to attend college. Upon graduation from college, Student E makes legally required monthly payments of principal and interest. Student E's mother makes a required monthly payment of interest as a gift to Student E. A deduction for Student E as a dependent is not allowed on another taxpayer's tax return for that taxable year. Assuming fulfillment of 25 all other requirements of section 221, Student E may deduct this payment of interest for Federal income tax purposes.

(c) *Maximum deduction.* The amount allowed as a deduction under section 221 for any taxable year may not exceed $2,500.

(d) *Limitation based on modified adjusted gross income--(1) In general.* The deduction 30 allowed under section 221 is phased out ratably for taxpayers with modified adjusted gross income between $50,000 and $65,000 ($100,000 and $130,000 for married individuals who file a joint return). Section 221 does not allow a deduction for taxpayers with modified adjusted gross income of $65,000 or above ($130,000 or above for married individuals who file a joint return). See paragraph (d)(3) of this section for inflation 35 adjustment of amounts in this paragraph (d)(1).

(2) *Modified adjusted gross income defined.* The term modified adjusted gross income means the adjusted gross income (as defined in section 62) of the taxpayer for the taxable year increased by any amount excluded from gross income under section 911, 931, or 933 (relating to income earned abroad or from certain United States possessions 40 or Puerto Rico). Modified adjusted gross income must be determined under this section after taking into account the inclusions, exclusions, deductions, and limitations provided by sections 86 (social security and tier 1 railroad retirement benefits), 135 (redemption of qualified United States savings bonds), 137 (adoption assistance programs), 219 (deductible qualified retirement contributions), and 469 (limitation on passive activity 45 losses and credits), but before taking into account the deductions provided by sections 221 and 222 (qualified tuition and related expenses).

(3) *Inflation adjustment.* For taxable years beginning after 2002, the amounts in paragraph (d)(1) of this section will be increased for inflation occurring after 2001 in accordance with section 221(f)(1). If any amount adjusted under section 221(f)(1) is not a 50 multiple of $5,000, the amount will be rounded to the next lowest multiple of $5,000.

595

Sec. 221.   Interest on education loans

(e) *Definitions*--(1) *Eligible educational institution.* In general, an eligible educational institution means any college, university, vocational school, or other postsecondary educational institution described in section 481 of the Higher Education Act of 1965 (20 U.S.C. 1088), as in effect on August 5, 1997, and certified by the U.S. Department of
5 Education as eligible to participate in student aid programs administered by the Department, as described in section 25A(f)(2) and § 1.25A-2(b). For purposes of this section, an eligible educational institution also includes an institution that conducts an internship or residency program leading to a degree or certificate awarded by an institution, a hospital, or a health care facility that offers postgraduate training.
10 (2) *Qualified higher education expenses*--(i) *In general.* Qualified higher education expenses means the cost of attendance (as defined in section 472 of the Higher Education Act of 1965, 20 U.S.C. 1087ll, as in effect on August 4, 1997), at an eligible educational institution, reduced by the amounts described in paragraph (e)(2)(ii) of this section. Consistent with section 472 of the Higher Education Act of 1965, a student's cost
15 of attendance is determined by the eligible educational institution and includes tuition and fees normally assessed a student carrying the same academic workload as the student, an allowance for room and board, and an allowance for books, supplies, transportation, and miscellaneous expenses of the student.

(ii) *Reductions.* Qualified higher education expenses are reduced by any amount that
20 is paid to or on behalf of a student with respect to such expenses and that is--

(A) A qualified scholarship that is excludable from income under section 117;

(B) An educational assistance allowance for a veteran or member of the armed forces under chapter 30, 31, 32, 34 or 35 of title 38, United States Code, or under chapter 1606 of title 10, United States Code;
25 (C) Employer-provided educational assistance that is excludable from income under section 127;

(D) Any other amount that is described in section 25A(g)(2)(C) (relating to amounts excludable from gross income as educational assistance);

(E) Any otherwise includible amount excluded from gross income under section 135
30 (relating to the redemption of United States savings bonds);

(F) Any otherwise includible amount distributed from a Coverdell education savings account and excluded from gross income under section 530(d)(2); or

(G) Any otherwise includible amount distributed from a qualified tuition program and excluded from gross income under section 529(c)(3)(B).
35 (3) *Qualified education loan*--(i) *In general.* A qualified education loan means indebtedness incurred by a taxpayer solely to pay qualified higher education expenses that are--

(A) Incurred on behalf of a student who is the taxpayer, the taxpayer's spouse, or a dependent (as defined in section 152) of the taxpayer at the time the taxpayer incurs the
40 indebtedness;

(B) Attributable to education provided during an academic period, as described in section 25A and the regulations thereunder, when the student is an eligible student as defined in section 25A(b)(3) (requiring that the student be a degree candidate carrying at least half the normal full-time workload); and
45 (C) Paid or incurred within a reasonable period of time before or after the taxpayer incurs the indebtedness.

(ii) *Reasonable period.* Except as otherwise provided in this paragraph (e)(3)(ii), what constitutes a reasonable period of time for purposes of paragraph (e)(3)(i)(C) of this section generally is determined based on all the relevant facts and circumstances.
50 However, qualified higher education expenses are treated as paid or incurred within a reasonable period of time before or after the taxpayer incurs the indebtedness if--

Sec. 221. Interest on education loans

(A) The expenses are paid with the proceeds of education loans that are part of a Federal postsecondary education loan program; or

(B) The expenses relate to a particular academic period and the loan proceeds used to pay the expenses are disbursed within a period that begins 90 days prior to the start of that academic period and ends 90 days after the end of that academic period.   5

(iii) *Related party.* A qualified education loan does not include any indebtedness owed to a person who is related to the taxpayer, within the meaning of section 267(b) or 707(b)(1). For example, a parent or grandparent of the taxpayer is a related person. In addition, a qualified education loan does not include a loan made under any qualified employer plan as defined in section 72(p)(4) or under any contract referred to in section 72(p)(5).   10

(iv) *Federal issuance or guarantee not required.* A loan does not have to be issued or guaranteed under a Federal postsecondary education loan program to be a qualified education loan.

(v) *Refinanced and consolidated indebtedness--*(A) *In general.* A qualified education loan includes indebtedness incurred solely to refinance a qualified education loan. A   15 qualified education loan includes a single, consolidated indebtedness incurred solely to refinance two or more qualified education loans of a borrower.

(B) *Treatment of refinanced and consolidated indebtedness.* [Reserved]

(4) *Examples.* The following examples illustrate the rules of this paragraph (e):

Example 1. Eligible educational institution. University F is a postsecondary   20 educational institution described in section 481 of the Higher Education Act of 1965. The U.S. Department of Education has certified that University F is eligible to participate in federal financial aid programs administered by that Department, although University F chooses not to participate. University F is an eligible educational institution.

Example 2. Qualified higher education expenses. Student G receives a $3,000   25 qualified scholarship for the 2003 fall semester that is excludable from Student G's gross income under section 117. Student G receives no other forms of financial assistance with respect to the 2003 fall semester. Student G's cost of attendance for the 2003 fall semester, as determined by Student G's eligible educational institution for purposes of calculating a student's financial need in accordance with section 472 of the Higher   30 Education Act, is $16,000. For the 2003 fall semester, Student G has qualified higher education expenses of $13,000 (the cost of attendance as determined by the institution ($16,000) reduced by the qualified scholarship proceeds excludable from gross income ($3,000)).

Example 3. Qualified education loan. Student H borrows money from a commercial   35 bank to pay qualified higher education expenses related to his enrollment on a half-time basis in a graduate program at an eligible educational institution. Student H uses all the loan proceeds to pay qualified higher education expenses incurred within a reasonable period of time after incurring the indebtedness. The loan is not federally guaranteed. The commercial bank is not related to Student H within the meaning of section 267(b) or   40 707(b)(1). Student H's loan is a qualified education loan within the meaning of section 221.

Example 4. Qualified education loan. Student I signs a promissory note for a loan on August 15, 2003, to pay for qualified higher education expenses for the 2003 fall and 2004 spring semesters. On August 20, 2003, the lender disburses loan proceeds to   45 Student I's college. The college credits them to Student I's account to pay qualified higher education expenses for the 2003 fall semester, which begins on August 25, 2003. On January 26, 2004, the lender disburses additional loan proceeds to Student I's college. The college credits them to Student I's account to pay qualified higher education expenses for the 2004 spring semester, which began on January 12, 2004. Student I's   50 qualified higher education expenses for the two semesters are paid within a reasonable period of time, as the first loan disbursement occurred within the 90 days prior to the start of the fall 2003 semester and the second loan disbursement occurred during the spring 2004 semester.

Example 5. Qualified education loan. The facts are the same as in Example 4 except that in 2005 the college is not an eligible educational institution because it loses its eligibility to participate in certain federal financial aid programs administered by the U.S. Department of Education. The qualification of Student I's loan, which was used to pay for qualified higher education expenses for the 2003 fall and 2004 spring semesters, as a qualified education loan is not affected by the college's subsequent loss of eligibility.

Example 6. Mixed-use loans. Student J signs a promissory note for a loan secured by Student J's personal residence. Student J will use part of the loan proceeds to pay for certain improvements to Student J's residence and part of the loan proceeds to pay qualified higher education expenses of Student J's spouse. Because Student J obtains the loan not solely to pay qualified higher education expenses, the loan is not a qualified education loan.

(f) *Interest*--(1) *In general.* Amounts paid on a qualified education loan are deductible under section 221 if the amounts are interest for Federal income tax purposes. For example, interest includes--

(i) Qualified stated interest (as defined in § 1.1273-1(c)); and

(ii) Original issue discount, which generally includes capitalized interest. For purposes of section 221, capitalized interest means any accrued and unpaid interest on a qualified education loan that, in accordance with the terms of the loan, is added by the lender to the outstanding principal balance of the loan.

(2) *Operative rules for original issue discount*--(i) *In general.* The rules to determine the amount of original issue discount on a loan and the accruals of the discount are in sections 163(e), 1271 through 1275, and the regulations thereunder. In general, original issue discount is the excess of a loan's stated redemption price at maturity (all payments due under the loan other than qualified stated interest payments) over its issue price (the amount loaned). Although original issue discount generally is deductible as it accrues under section 163(e) and § 1.163-7, original issue discount on a qualified education loan is not deductible until paid. See paragraph (f)(3) of this section to determine when original issue discount is paid.

(ii) *Treatment of loan origination fees by the borrower.* If a loan origination fee is paid by the borrower other than for property or services provided by the lender, the fee reduces the issue price of the loan, which creates original issue discount (or additional original issue discount) on the loan in an amount equal to the fee. See § 1.1273-2(g). For an example of how a loan origination fee is taken into account, see Example 2 of paragraph (f)(4) of this section.

(3) *Allocation of payments.* See §§ 1.446-2(e) and 1.1275-2(a) for rules on allocating payments between interest and principal. In general, these rules treat a payment first as a payment of interest to the extent of the interest that has accrued and remains unpaid as of the date the payment is due, and second as a payment of principal. The characterization of a payment as either interest or principal under these rules applies regardless of how the parties label the payment (either as interest or principal). Accordingly, the taxpayer may deduct the portion of a payment labeled as principal that these rules treat as a payment of interest on the loan, including any portion attributable to capitalized interest or loan origination fees.

(4) *Examples.* The following examples illustrate the rules of this paragraph (f). In the examples, assume that the institution the student attends is an eligible educational institution, the loan is a qualified education loan, the student is legally obligated to make interest payments under the terms of the loan, and any other applicable requirements, if

not otherwise specified, are fulfilled. The examples are as follows:

Example 1. Capitalized interest. Interest on Student K's loan accrues while Student K is in school, but Student K is not required to make any payments on the loan until six months after he graduates or otherwise leaves school. At that time, the lender capitalizes all accrued but unpaid interest and adds it to the outstanding principal amount of the loan. 5 Thereafter, Student K is required to make monthly payments of interest and principal on the loan. The interest payable on the loan, including the capitalized interest, is original issue discount. See section 1273 and the regulations thereunder. Therefore, in determining the total amount of interest paid on the loan each taxable year, Student K may deduct any payments that § 1.1275-2(a) treats as payments of interest, including 10 any principal payments that are treated as payments of capitalized interest. See paragraph (f)(3) of this section.

Example 2. Allocation of payments. The facts are the same as in Example 1, except that, in addition, the lender charges Student K a loan origination fee, which is not for any property or services provided by the lender. Under § 1.1273-2(g), the loan origination fee 15 reduces the issue price of the loan, which reduction increases the amount of original issue discount on the loan by the amount of the fee. The amount of original issue discount (which includes the capitalized interest and loan origination fee) that accrues each year is determined under section 1272 and § 1.1272-1. In effect, the loan origination fee accrues over the entire term of the loan. Because the loan has original issue 20 discount, the payment ordering rules in § 1.1275-2(a) must be used to determine how much of each payment is interest for federal tax purposes. See paragraph (f)(3) of this section. Under § 1.1275-2(a), each payment (regardless of its designation by the parties as either interest or principal) generally is treated first as a payment of original issue discount, to the extent of the original issue discount that has accrued as of the date the 25 payment is due and has not been allocated to prior payments, and second as a payment of principal. Therefore, in determining the total amount of interest paid on the qualified education loan for a taxable year, Student K may deduct any payments that the parties label as principal but that are treated as payments of original issue discount under § 1.1275-2(a). 30

(g) *Additional Rules--(1) Payment of interest made during period when interest payment not required.* Payments of interest on a qualified education loan to which this section is applicable are deductible even if the payments are made during a period when interest payments are not required because, for example, the loan has not yet entered repayment status or is in a period of deferment or forbearance. 35

(2) Denial of double benefit. No deduction is allowed under this section for any amount for which a deduction is allowable under another provision of Chapter 1 of the Internal Revenue Code. No deduction is allowed under this section for any amount for which an exclusion is allowable under section 108(f) (relating to cancellation of indebtedness). 40

(3) *Examples.* The following examples illustrate the rules of this paragraph (g). In the examples, assume that the institution the student attends is an eligible educational institution, the loan is a qualified education loan, and the student is legally obligated to make interest payments under the terms of the loan:

Example 1. Voluntary payment of interest before loan has entered repayment status. 45 Student L obtains a loan to attend college. The terms of the loan provide that interest accrues on the loan while Student L earns his undergraduate degree but that Student L is not required to begin making payments of interest until six full calendar months after he graduates or otherwise leaves school. Nevertheless, Student L voluntarily pays interest on the loan during 2003, while enrolled in college. Assuming all other relevant 50 requirements are met, Student L is allowed a deduction for interest paid while attending

Sec. 221. Interest on education loans

college even though the payments were made before interest payments were required.

Example 2. Voluntary payment during period of deferment or forbearance. The facts are the same as in Example 2, except that Student L makes no payments on the loan while enrolled in college. Student L graduates in June 2003 and begins making monthly
5 payments of principal and interest on the loan in January 2004, as required by the terms of the loan. In August 2004, Student L enrolls in graduate school on a full-time basis. Under the terms of the loan, Student L may apply for deferment of the loan payments while Student L is enrolled in graduate school. Student L applies for and receives a deferment on the outstanding loan. However, Student L continues to make some monthly
10 payments of interest during graduate school. Student L may deduct interest paid on the loan during the period beginning in January 2004, including interest paid while Student L is enrolled in graduate school.

[T.D. 9125, 69 FR 25492, May 7, 2004]
15

Sec. 222. Qualified tuition and related expenses

(a) **Allowance of deduction.** -- In the case of an individual, there shall be allowed as a deduction an amount equal to the qualified tuition and related expenses paid by the taxpayer during the taxable year.

(b) **Dollar limitations.** --

20   (1) **In general.** -- The amount allowed as a deduction under subsection (a) with respect to the taxpayer for any taxable year shall not exceed the applicable dollar limit.

    (2) **Applicable dollar limit.** --

***

        (B) **After 2003.** -- In the case of any taxable year beginning after 2003, the applicable
25   dollar amount shall be equal to--

            (i) in the case of a taxpayer whose adjusted gross income for the taxable year does not exceed $65,000 ($130,000 in the case of a joint return), $4,000,

            (ii) in the case of a taxpayer not described in clause (i) whose adjusted gross income for the taxable year does not exceed $80,000 ($160,000 in the case of a joint return),
30     $2,000, and

            (iii) in the case of any other taxpayer, zero.

        (C) **Adjusted gross income.** -- For purposes of this paragraph, adjusted gross income shall be determined--

            (i) without regard to this section and sections 199, 911, 931, and 933, and
35   (ii) after application of sections 86, 135, 137, 219, 221, and 469.

(c) **No double benefit.** --

    (1) **In general.** -- No deduction shall be allowed under subsection (a) for any expense for which a deduction is allowed to the taxpayer under any other provision of this chapter.

    (2) **Coordination with other education incentives.** --

40   (A) **Denial of deduction if credit elected.** -- No deduction shall be allowed under subsection (a) for a taxable year with respect to the qualified tuition and related expenses with respect to an individual if the taxpayer or any other person elects to have section 25A apply with respect to such individual for such year.

        (B) **Coordination with exclusions.** -- The total amount of qualified tuition and related
45   expenses shall be reduced by the amount of such expenses taken into account in

Sec. 222. Qualified tuition and related expenses

determining any amount excluded under section 135, 529(c)(1), or 530(d)(2). For purposes of the preceding sentence, the amount taken into account in determining the amount excluded under section 529(c)(1) shall not include that portion of the distribution which represents a return of any contributions to the plan.

(3) Dependents. -- No deduction shall be allowed under subsection (a) to any individual with respect to whom a deduction under section 151 is allowable to another taxpayer for a taxable year beginning in the calendar year in which such individual's taxable year begins.

(d) Definitions and special rules. -- For purposes of this section--

(1) Qualified tuition and related expenses. -- The term "qualified tuition and related expenses" has the meaning given such term by section 25A(f). Such expenses shall be reduced in the same manner as under section 25A(g)(2).

(2) Identification requirement. -- No deduction shall be allowed under subsection (a) to a taxpayer with respect to the qualified tuition and related expenses of an individual unless the taxpayer includes the name and taxpayer identification number of the individual on the return of tax for the taxable year.

(3) Limitation on taxable year of deduction. --

(A) In general. -- A deduction shall be allowed under subsection (a) for qualified tuition and related expenses for any taxable year only to the extent such expenses are in connection with enrollment at an institution of higher education during the taxable year.

(B) Certain prepayments allowed. -- Subparagraph (A) shall not apply to qualified tuition and related expenses paid during a taxable year if such expenses are in connection with an academic term beginning during such taxable year or during the first 3 months of the next taxable year.

(4) No deduction for married individuals filing separate returns. -- If the taxpayer is a married individual (within the meaning of section 7703), this section shall apply only if the taxpayer and the taxpayer's spouse file a joint return for the taxable year.

(5) Nonresident aliens. -- If the taxpayer is a nonresident alien individual for any portion of the taxable year, this section shall apply only if such individual is treated as a resident alien of the United States for purposes of this chapter by reason of an election under subsection (g) or (h) of section 6013.

***

(e) Termination. -- This section shall not apply to taxable years beginning after December 31, 2007.

Sec. 223. Health savings accounts

(a) Deduction allowed. -- In the case of an individual who is an eligible individual for any month during the taxable year, there shall be allowed as a deduction for the taxable year an amount equal to the aggregate amount paid in cash during such taxable year by or on behalf of such individual to a health savings account of such individual.

(b) Limitations. --

(1) In general. -- The amount allowable as a deduction under subsection (a) to an individual for the taxable year shall not exceed the sum of the monthly limitations for months during such taxable year that the individual is an eligible individual.

(2) Monthly limitation. -- The monthly limitation for any month is 1/12 of -

(A) in the case of an eligible individual who has self-only coverage under a high

Sec. 223. Health savings accounts

deductible health plan as of the first day of such month, $2,250, or

(B) in the case of an eligible individual who has family coverage under a high deductible health plan as of the first day of such month, $4,500.

(3) Additional contributions for individuals 55 or older. --

(A) In general. -- In the case of an individual who has attained age 55 before the close of the taxable year, the applicable limitation under subparagraphs (A) and (B) of paragraph (2) shall be increased by the additional contribution amount.

(B) Additional contribution amount. -- For purposes of this section, the additional contribution amount is the amount determined in accordance with the following table:

For taxable years beginning in:	The additional contribution amount is:
***	
2008.....................................	$900
2009 and thereafter.............	$1,000.

(4) Coordination with other contributions. -- The limitation which would (but for this paragraph) apply under this subsection to an individual for any taxable year shall be reduced (but not below zero) by the sum of--

(A) the aggregate amount paid for such taxable year to Archer MSAs of such individual,

(B) the aggregate amount contributed to health savings accounts of such individual which is excludable from the taxpayer's gross income for such taxable year under section 106(d) (and such amount shall not be allowed as a deduction under subsection (a)), and

(C) the aggregate amount contributed to health savings accounts of such individual for such taxable year under section 408(d)(9) (and such amount shall not be allowed as a deduction under subsection (a)).

Subparagraph (A) shall not apply with respect to any individual to whom paragraph (5) applies.

(5) Special rule for married individuals. -- In the case of individuals who are married to each other, if either spouse has family coverage--

(A) both spouses shall be treated as having only such family coverage (and if such spouses each have family coverage under different plans, as having the family coverage with the lowest annual deductible), and

(B) the limitation under paragraph (1) (after the application of subparagraph (A) and without regard to any additional contribution amount under paragraph (3)) -

(i) shall be reduced by the aggregate amount paid to Archer MSAs of such spouses for the taxable year, and

(ii) after such reduction, shall be divided equally between them unless they agree on a different division.

(6) Denial of deduction to dependents. -- No deduction shall be allowed under this section to any individual with respect to whom a deduction under section 151 is allowable to another taxpayer for a taxable year beginning in the calendar year in which such individual's taxable year begins.

(7) Medicare eligible individuals. -- The limitation under this subsection for any month with respect to an individual shall be zero for the first month such individual is entitled to benefits under title XVIII of the Social Security Act and for each month thereafter.

Sec. 223. Health savings accounts

(8) Increase in limit for individuals becoming eligible individuals after the beginning of the year.--

    (A) In general.--For purposes of computing the limitation under paragraph (1) for any taxable year, an individual who is an eligible individual during the last month of such taxable year shall be treated--

        (i) as having been an eligible individual during each of the months in such taxable year, and

        (ii) as having been enrolled, during each of the months such individual is treated as an eligible individual solely by reason of clause (i), in the same high deductible health plan in which the individual was enrolled for the last month of such taxable year.

    (B) Failure to maintain high deductible health plan coverage. --

        (i) In general. -- If, at any time during the testing period, the individual is not an eligible individual, then--

            (I) gross income of the individual for the taxable year in which occurs the first month in the testing period for which such individual is not an eligible individual is increased by the aggregate amount of all contributions to the health savings account of the individual which could not have been made but for subparagraph (A), and

            (II) the tax imposed by this chapter for any taxable year on the individual shall be increased by 10 percent of the amount of such increase.

        (ii) Exception for disability or death. -- Subclauses (I) and (II) of clause (i) shall not apply if the individual ceased to be an eligible individual by reason of the death of the individual or the individual becoming disabled (within the meaning of section 72(m)(7)).

        (iii) Testing period.--The term `testing period' means the period beginning with the last month of the taxable year referred to in subparagraph (A) and ending on the last day of the 12th month following such month.

  (c) Definitions and special rules. -- For purposes of this section--

  (1) Eligible individual. --

    (A) In general. --   The term "eligible individual" means, with respect to any month, any individual if -

        (i) such individual is covered under a high deductible health plan as of the 1st day of such month, and

        (ii) such individual is not, while covered under a high deductible health plan, covered under any health plan -

            (I) which is not a high deductible health plan,

            (II) which provides coverage for any benefit which is covered under the high deductible health plan, and

        (iii) for taxable years beginning after December 31, 2006, coverage under a health flexible spending arrangement during any period immediately following the end of a plan year of such arrangement during which unused benefits or contributions remaining at the end of such plan year may be paid or reimbursed to plan participants for qualified benefit expenses incurred during such period if--

            (I) the balance in such arrangement at the end of such plan year is zero, or

            (II) the individual is making a qualified HSA distribution (as defined in section 106(e)) in an amount equal to the remaining balance in such arrangement as of the end of such plan year, in accordance with rules prescribed by the Secretary.

(B) Certain coverage disregarded. -- Subparagraph (A)(ii) shall be applied without regard to--

(i) coverage for any benefit provided by permitted insurance, and

(ii) coverage (whether through insurance or otherwise) for accidents, disability, dental care, vision care, or long-term care.

(2) High deductible health plan. --

(A) In general. -- The term "high deductible health plan" means a health plan -

(i) which has an annual deductible which is not less than -

(I) $1,000 for self-only coverage, and

(II) twice the dollar amount in subclause (I) for family coverage, and

(ii) the sum of the annual deductible and the other annual out-of-pocket expenses required to be paid under the plan (other than for premiums) for covered benefits does not exceed--

(I) $5,000 for self-only coverage, and

(II) twice the dollar amount in subclause (I) for family coverage.

(B) Exclusion of certain plans. -- Such term does not include a health plan if substantially all of its coverage is coverage described in paragraph (1)(B).

(C) Safe harbor for absence of preventive care deductible. -- A plan shall not fail to be treated as a high deductible health plan by reason of failing to have a deductible for preventive care (within the meaning of section 1871 of the Social Security Act, except as otherwise provided by the Secretary).

(D) Special rules for network plans. -- In the case of a plan using a network of providers--

(i) **Annual out-of-pocket limitation.** -- Such plan shall not fail to be treated as a high deductible health plan by reason of having an out-of-pocket limitation for services provided outside of such network which exceeds the applicable limitation under subparagraph (A)(ii).

(ii) **Annual deductible.** -- Such plan's annual deductible for services provided outside of such network shall not be taken into account for purposes of subsection (b) (2).

(3) Permitted insurance. -- The term "permitted insurance" means--

(A) insurance if substantially all of the coverage provided under such insurance relates to -

(i) liabilities incurred under workers' compensation laws,

(ii) tort liabilities,

(iii) liabilities relating to ownership or use of property, or

(iv) such other similar liabilities as the Secretary may specify by regulations,

(B) insurance for a specified disease or illness, and

(C) insurance paying a fixed amount per day (or other period) of hospitalization.

(4) Family coverage. -- The term "family coverage" means any coverage other than self-only coverage.

(5) Archer MSA. -- The term "Archer MSA" has the meaning given such term in section 220(d).

Sec. 223. Health savings accounts

(d) Health savings account. -- For purposes of this section--

(1) In general. -- The term "health savings account" means a trust created or organized in the United States as a health savings account exclusively for the purpose of paying the qualified medical expenses of the account beneficiary, but only if the written governing instrument creating the trust meets the following requirements: 5

(A) Except in the case of a rollover contribution described in subsection (f)(5) or section 220(f)(5), no contribution will be accepted--

(i) unless it is in cash, or

(ii) to the extent such contribution, when added to previous contributions to the trust for the calendar year, exceeds the sum of--   10

(I) the dollar amount in effect under subsection (b)(2)(B), and

(II) the dollar amount in effect under subsection (b)(3)(B).

(B) The trustee is a bank (as defined in section 408(n)), an insurance company (as defined in section 816), or another person who demonstrates to the satisfaction of the Secretary that the manner in which such person will administer the trust will be consistent 15 with the requirements of this section.

(C) No part of the trust assets will be invested in life insurance contracts.

(D) The assets of the trust will not be commingled with other property except in a common trust fund or common investment fund.

(E) The interest of an individual in the balance in his account is nonforfeitable.   20

(2) Qualified medical expenses. --

(A) In general. -- The term "qualified medical expenses" means, with respect to an account beneficiary, amounts paid by such beneficiary for medical care (as defined in section 213(d) for such individual, the spouse of such individual, and any dependent (as defined in section 152) of such individual, but only to the extent such amounts are not 25 compensated for by insurance or otherwise.

(B) Health insurance may not be purchased from account. -- Subparagraph (A) shall not apply to any payment for insurance.

(C) Exceptions. -- Subparagraph (B) shall not apply to any expense for coverage under -

(i) a health plan during any period of continuation coverage required under any 30 Federal law,

(ii) a qualified long-term care insurance contract (as defined in section 7702B(b)),

(iii) a health plan during a period in which the individual is receiving unemployment compensation under any Federal or State law, or

(iv) in the case of an account beneficiary who has attained the age specified in 35 section 1811 of the Social Security Act, any health insurance other than a medicare supplemental policy (as defined in section 1882 of the Social Security Act).

(3) Account beneficiary. -- The term "account beneficiary" means the individual on whose behalf the health savings account was established.

(4) Certain rules to apply. -- Rules similar to the following rules shall apply for purposes 40 of this section:

(A) Section 219(d)(2) (relating to no deduction for rollovers).

(B) Section 219(f)(3) (relating to time when contributions deemed made).

(C) Except as provided in section 106(d), section 219(f)(5) (relating to employer payments).   45

Sec. 223. Health savings accounts

(D) Section 408(g) (relating to community property laws).

(E) Section 408(h) (relating to custodial accounts).

(e) Tax treatment of accounts. --

(1) In general. -- A health savings account is exempt from taxation under this subtitle unless such account has ceased to be a health savings account. Notwithstanding the preceding sentence, any such account is subject to the taxes imposed by section 511 (relating to imposition of tax on unrelated business income of charitable, etc. organizations).

(2) Account terminations. -- Rules similar to the rules of paragraphs (2) and (4) of section 408(e) shall apply to health savings accounts, and any amount treated as distributed under such rules shall be treated as not used to pay qualified medical expenses.

(f) Tax treatment of distributions. --

(1) Amounts used for qualified medical expenses. -- Any amount paid or distributed out of a health savings account which is used exclusively to pay qualified medical expenses of any account beneficiary shall not be includible in gross income.

(2) Inclusion of amounts not used for qualified medical expenses. -- Any amount paid or distributed out of a health savings account which is not used exclusively to pay the qualified medical expenses of the account beneficiary shall be included in the gross income of such beneficiary.

(3) Excess contributions returned before due date of return. --

(A) In general. -- If any excess contribution is contributed for a taxable year to any health savings account of an individual, paragraph (2) shall not apply to distributions from the health savings accounts of such individual (to the extent such distributions do not exceed the aggregate excess contributions to all such accounts of such individual for such year) if -

(i) such distribution is received by the individual on or before the last day prescribed by law (including extensions of time) for filing such individual's return for such taxable year, and

(ii) such distribution is accompanied by the amount of net income attributable to such excess contribution.

Any net income described in clause (ii) shall be included in the gross income of the individual for the taxable year in which it is received.

(B) Excess contribution. -- For purposes of subparagraph (A), the term "excess contribution" means any contribution (other than a rollover contribution described in paragraph (5) or section 220(f)(5)) which is neither excludable from gross income under section 106(d) nor deductible under this section.

(4) Additional tax on distributions not used for qualified medical expenses. --

(A) In general. -- The tax imposed by this chapter on the account beneficiary for any taxable year in which there is a payment or distribution from a health savings account of such beneficiary which is includible in gross income under paragraph (2) shall be increased by 10 percent of the amount which is so includible.

(B) Exception for disability or death. -- Subparagraph (A) shall not apply if the payment or distribution is made after the account beneficiary becomes disabled within the meaning of section 72(m)(7) or dies.

(C) Exception for distributions after medicare eligibility. -- Subparagraph (A) shall not apply to any payment or distribution after the date on which the account beneficiary attains the age specified in section 1811 of the Social Security Act.

Sec. 223. Health savings accounts

(5) Rollover contribution. -- An amount is described in this paragraph as a rollover contribution if it meets the requirements of subparagraphs (A) and (B).

   (A) In general. -- Paragraph (2) shall not apply to any amount paid or distributed from a health savings account to the account beneficiary to the extent the amount received is paid into a health savings account for the benefit of such beneficiary not later than the 60th day 5 after the day on which the beneficiary receives the payment or distribution.

   (B) Limitation. -- This paragraph shall not apply to any amount described in subparagraph (A) received by an individual from a health savings account if, at any time during the 1-year period ending on the day of such receipt, such individual received any other amount described in subparagraph (A) from a health savings account which was not 10 includible in the individual's gross income because of the application of this paragraph.

(6) Coordination with medical expense deduction. -- For purposes of determining the amount of the deduction under section 213, any payment or distribution out of a health savings account for qualified medical expenses shall not be treated as an   expense paid for medical care. 15

(7) Transfer of account incident to divorce. -- The transfer of an individual's interest in a health savings account to an individual's spouse or former spouse under divorce or separation instrument described in subparagraph (A) of section 71(b)(2) shall not be considered a taxable transfer made by such individual notwithstanding any other provision of this subtitle, and such interest shall, after such transfer, be treated as a health savings account with respect to which 20 such spouse is the account beneficiary.

(8) Treatment after death of account beneficiary. --

   (A) Treatment if designated beneficiary is spouse. -- If the account beneficiary's surviving spouse acquires such beneficiary's interest in a health savings account by reason of being the designated beneficiary of such account at the death of the account beneficiary, 25 such health savings account shall be treated as if the spouse were the account beneficiary.

   (B) Other cases. --

      (i) In general. -- If, by reason of the death of the account beneficiary, any person acquires the account beneficiary's interest in a health savings account in a case to which subparagraph (A) does not apply-- 30

         (I) such account shall cease to be a health savings account as of the date of death, and

         (II) an amount equal to the fair market value of the assets in such account on such date shall be includible if such person is not the estate of such beneficiary, in such person's gross income for the taxable year which includes such date, or if such 35 person is the estate of such beneficiary, in such beneficiary's gross income for the last taxable year of such beneficiary.

      (ii) Special rules. --

         (I) Reduction of inclusion for predeath expenses. -- The amount includible in gross income under clause (i) by any person (other than the estate) shall be reduced 40 by the amount of qualified medical expenses which were incurred by the decedent before the date of the decedent's death and paid by such person within 1 year after such date.

         (II) Deduction for estate taxes. -- An appropriate deduction shall be allowed under section 691(c) to any person (other than the decedent or the decedent's 45 spouse) with respect to amounts included in gross income under clause (i) by such person.

Sec. 223.   Health savings accounts

(g) Cost-of-living adjustment. --

(1) In general. -- Each dollar amount in subsections (b)(2) and (c)(2)(A) shall be increased by an amount equal to -

(A) such dollar amount, multiplied by

(B) the cost-of-living adjustment determined under section 1(f)(3) for the calendar year in which such taxable year begins determined by substituting for "calendar year 1992" in subparagraph (B) thereof--

(i) except as provided in clause (ii), "calendar year 1997", and

(ii) in the case of each dollar amount in subsection (c)(2)(A), "calendar year 2003".

In the case of adjustments made for any taxable year beginning after 2007, section 1(f)(4) shall be applied for purposes of this paragraph by substituting `March 31' for `August 31', and the Secretary shall publish the adjusted amounts under subsections (b)(2) and (c)(2)(A) for taxable years beginning in any calendar year no later than June 1 of the preceding calendar year.

(2) Rounding. -- If any increase under paragraph (1) is not a multiple of $50, such increase shall be rounded to the nearest multiple of $50.

***

Sec. 243.   Dividends received by corporations

(a) General rule. -- In the case of a corporation, there shall be allowed as a deduction an amount equal to the following percentages of the amount received as dividends from a domestic corporation which is subject to taxation under this chapter:

(1) 70 percent, in the case of dividends other than dividends described in paragraph (2) or (3);

(2) 100 percent, in the case of dividends received by a small business investment company operating under the Small Business Investment Act of 1958 (15 U.S.C. 661 and following); and

(3) 100 percent, in the case of qualifying dividends (as defined in subsection (b)(1)).

***

Sec. 248.   Organizational expenditures

(a) Election to deduct. -- If a corporation elects the application of this subsection (in accordance with regulations prescribed by the Secretary) with respect to any organizational expenditures--

(1) the corporation shall be allowed a deduction for the taxable year in which the corporation begins business in an amount equal to the lesser of--

(A) the amount of organizational expenditures with respect to the taxpayer, or

(B) $5,000, reduced (but not below zero) by the amount by which such organizational expenditures exceed $50,000, and

(2) the remainder of such organizational expenditures shall be allowed as a deduction ratably over the 180-month period beginning with the month in which the corporation begins business.

(b) Organizational expenditures defined. -- The term "organizational expenditures" means any expenditure which--

(1) is incident to the creation of the corporation;

(2) is chargeable to capital account; and

608

Sec. 248.   Organizational expenditures

(3) is of a character which, if expended incident to the creation of a corporation having a limited life, would be amortizable over such life.

Sec. 261.   General rule for disallowance of deductions

In computing taxable income no deduction shall in any case be allowed in respect of the items specified in this part.

Reg. § 1.261-1   General rule for disallowance of deductions.

In computing taxable income, no deduction shall be allowed, except as otherwise expressly provided in Chapter 1 of the Code, in respect of any of the items specified in Part IX (section 262 and following), Subchapter B, Chapter 1 of the Code, and the regulations thereunder.

Sec. 262.   Personal, living, and family expenses

(a) General rule. -- Except as otherwise expressly provided in this chapter, no deduction shall be allowed for personal, living, or family expenses.

(b) Treatment of certain phone expenses. -- For purposes of subsection (a), in the case of an individual, any charge (including taxes thereon) for basic local telephone service with respect to the 1st telephone line provided to any residence of the taxpayer shall be treated as a personal expense.

Reg. § 1.262-1   Personal, living, and family expenses.

(a) *In general.* In computing taxable income, no deduction shall be allowed, except as otherwise expressly provided in chapter 1 of the Code, for personal, living, and family expenses.

(b) *Examples of personal, living, and family expenses.* Personal, living, and family expenses are illustrated in the following examples:

(1) Premiums paid for life insurance by the insured are not deductible. See also section 264 and the regulations thereunder.

(2) The cost of insuring a dwelling owned and occupied by the taxpayer as a personal residence is not deductible.

(3) Expenses of maintaining a household, including amounts paid for rent, water, utilities, domestic service, and the like, are not deductible. A taxpayer who rents a property for residential purposes, but incidentally conducts business there (his place of business being elsewhere) shall not deduct any part of the rent. If, however, he uses part of the house as his place of business, such portion of the rent and other similar expenses as is properly attributable to such place of business is deductible as a business expense.

(4) Losses sustained by the taxpayer upon the sale or other disposition of property held for personal, living, and family purposes are not deductible. But see section 165 and the regulations thereunder for deduction of losses sustained to such property by reason of casualty, etc.

(5) Expenses incurred in traveling away from home (which include transportation expenses, meals, and lodging) and any other transportation expenses are not deductible unless they qualify as expenses deductible under section 162, § 1.162-2, and paragraph (d) of § 1.162-5 (relating to trade or business expenses), section 170 and paragraph (a) (2) of § 1.170-2 or paragraph (g) of § 1.170A-1 (relating to charitable contributions),

Sec. 262.   Personal, living, and family expenses

section 212 and § 1.212-1 (relating to expenses for production of income), section 213(e) and paragraph (e) of § 1.213-1 (relating to medical expenses) or section 217(a) and paragraph (a) of § 1.217-1 (relating to moving expenses). The taxpayer's costs of commuting to his place of business or employment are personal expenses and do not
5   qualify as deductible expenses. The costs of the taxpayer's lodging not incurred in traveling away from home are personal expenses and are not deductible unless they qualify as deductible expenses under section 217. Except as permitted under section 162, 212, or 217, the costs of the taxpayer's meals not incurred in traveling away from home are personal expenses.
10   (6) Amounts paid as damages for breach of promise to marry, and attorney's fees and other costs of suit to recover such damages, are not deductible.

   (7) Generally, attorney's fees and other costs paid in connection with a divorce, separation, or decree for support are not deductible by either the husband or the wife. However, the part of an attorney's fee and the part of the other costs paid in connection
15   with a divorce, legal separation, written separation agreement, or a decree for support, which are properly attributable to the production or collection of amounts includible in gross income under section 71 are deductible by the wife under section 212.

   (8) The cost of equipment of a member of the armed services is deductible only to the extent that it exceeds nontaxable allowances received for such equipment and to the
20   extent that such equipment is especially required by his profession and does not merely take the place of articles required in civilian life. For example, the cost of a sword is an allowable deduction in computing taxable income, but the cost of a uniform is not. However, amounts expended by a reservist for the purchase and maintenance of uniforms which may be worn only when on active duty for training for temporary periods,
25   when attending service school courses, or when attending training assemblies are deductible except to the extent that nontaxable allowances are received for such amounts.

   (9) Expenditures made by a taxpayer in obtaining an education or in furthering his education are not deductible unless they qualify under section 162 and § 1.162-5
30   (relating to trade or business expenses).

   (c) *Cross references.* Certain items of a personal, living, or family nature are deductible to the extent expressly provided under the following sections, and the regulations under those sections:
   (1) Section 163 (interest).
35   (2) Section 164 (taxes).
   (3) Section 165 (losses).
   (4) Section 166 (bad debts).
   (5) Section 170 (charitable, etc., contributions and gifts).
   (6) Section 213 (medical, dental, etc., expenses).
40   (7) Section 214 (expenses for care of certain dependents).
   (8) Section 215 (alimony, etc., payments).
   (9) Section 216 (amounts representing taxes and interest paid to cooperative housing corporation).
   (10) Section 217 (moving expenses).
45

[T.D. 6500, 25 FR 11402, Nov. 26, 1960; T.D. 6796, 30 FR 1041, Feb. 2, 1965; T.D. 6918, 32 FR 6681, May 2, 1967; T.D. 7207, 37 FR 20795, Oct. 4, 1972]

Sec. 263.   Capital expenditures

   (a) **General rule.** -- No deduction shall be allowed for--

Sec. 263. Capital expenditures

(1) Any amount paid out for new buildings or for permanent improvements or betterments made to increase the value of any property or estate. This paragraph shall not apply to--

***

(B) research and experimental expenditures deductible under section 174,

(C) soil and water conservation expenditures deductible under section 175,

(D) expenditures by farmers for fertilizer, etc., deductible under section 180,

***

(G) expenditures for which a deduction is allowed under section 179,

***

(J) expenditures for which a deduction is allowed under section 179C,

(K) expenditures for which a deduction is allowed under section 179D

***

(2) Any amount expended in restoring property or in making good the exhaustion thereof for which an allowance is or has been made.

***

(c) Intangible drilling and development costs in the case of oil and gas wells and geothermal wells. -- Notwithstanding subsection (a), and except as provided in subsection (i), regulations shall be prescribed by the Secretar under this subtitle corresponding to the regulations which granted the option to deduct as expenses intangible drilling and development costs in the case of oil and gas wells and which were recognized and approved by the Congress in House Concurrent Resolution 50, Seventy-ninth Congress. Such regulations shall also grant the option to deduct as expenses intangible drilling and development costs in the case of wells drilled for any geothermal deposit (as defined in section 613(e)(2)) to the same extent and in the same manner as such expenses are deductible in the case of oil and gas wells. This subsection shall not apply with respect to any costs to which any deduction is allowed under section 59(e) or 291.

***

Reg. § 1.263(a)-1 Capital expenditures; In general.

(a) Except as otherwise provided in chapter 1 of the Code, no deduction shall be allowed for:

(1) Any amount paid out for new buildings or for permanent improvements or betterments made to increase the value of any property or estate, or

(2) Any amount expended in restoring property or in making good the exhaustion thereof for which an allowance is or has been made in the form of a deduction for depreciation, amortization, or depletion.

(b) In general, the amounts referred to in paragraph (a) of this section include amounts paid or incurred (1) to add to the value, or substantially prolong the useful life, of property owned by the taxpayer, such as plant or equipment, or (2) to adapt property to a new or different use. Amounts paid or incurred for incidental repairs and maintenance of property are not capital expenditures within the meaning of subparagraphs (1) and (2) of this paragraph. See section 162 and § 1.162-4. See section 263A and the regulations thereunder for cost capitalization rules which apply to amounts referred to in paragraph (a) of this section with respect to the production of real and tangible personal property (as defined in § 1.263A-1T(a)(5)(iii)), including films, sound recordings, video tapes, books, or similar properties. An amount referred to in paragraph (a) of this section is a capital expenditure that is taken into account through inclusion in inventory costs or a charge to capital accounts or basis no earlier than the taxable year during which the amount is incurred within the meaning of § 1.446-1(c)(1)(ii). See section 263A and the regulations

Sec. 263. Capital expenditures

thereunder for cost capitalization rules that apply to amounts referred to in paragraph (a) of this section with respect to the production of real and tangible personal property (as defined in § 1.263A-2(a)(2)), including films, sound recordings, video tapes, books, or similar properties.

5   (c) The provisions of paragraph (a) (1) of this section shall not apply to expenditures deductible under:

    (1) Section 616 and §§ 1.616-1 through 1.616-3, relating to the development of mines or deposits,

    (2) Section 174 and §§ 1.174-1 through 1.174-4, relating to research and 10 experimentation,

    (3) Section 175 and §§ 1.175-1 through 1.175-6, relating to soil and water conservation,

    (4) Section 179 and §§ 1.179-1 through 1.179-5, relating to election to expense certain depreciable business assets,

15   (5) Section 180 and §§ 1.180-1 and 1.180-2, relating to expenditures by farmers for fertilizer, lime, etc., and

    (6) Section 182 and §§ 1.182-1 through 1.182-6, relating to expenditures by farmers for clearing land.

20 **Reg. § 1.263(a)-2 Examples of capital expenditures.**

    The following paragraphs of this section include examples of capital expenditures:

    (a) The cost of acquisition, construction, or erection of buildings, machinery and equipment, furniture and fixtures, and similar property having a useful life substantially beyond the taxable year.

25   (b) Amounts expended for securing a copyright and plates, which remain the property of the person making the payments. See section 263A and the regulations thereunder for capitalization rules which apply to amounts expended in securing and producing a copyrightand plates in connection with the production of property, including films, sound recordings, video tapes, books, or similar properties.

30   (c) The cost of defending or perfecting title to property.

    (d) The amount expended for architect's services.

    (e) Commissions paid in purchasing securities. Commissions paid in selling securities are an offset against the selling price, except that in the case of dealers in securities such commissions may be treated as an ordinary and necessary business expense.

35   (f) Amounts assessed and paid under an agreement between bondholders or shareholders of a corporation to be used in a reorganization of the corporation or voluntary contributions by shareholders to the capital of the corporation for any corporate purpose. Such amounts are capital investments and are not deductible. See section 118 and § 1.118-1.

40   (g) A holding company which guarantees dividends at a specified rate on the stock of a subsidiary corporation for the purpose of securing new capital for the subsidiary and increasing the value of its stockholdings in the subsidiary shall not deduct amounts paid in carrying out this guaranty in computing its taxable income, but such payments are capital expenditures to be added to the cost of its stock in the subsidiary.

45   (h) The cost of good will in connection with the acquisition of the assets of a going concern is a capital expenditure.

Reg. § 1.263(a)-3 Election to deduct or capitalize certain expenditures.

    (a) Under certain provisions of the Code, taxpayers may elect to treat capital 50 expenditures as deductible expenses or as deferred expenses, or to treat deductible expenses as capital expenditures.

Sec. 263. Capital expenditures

(b) The sections referred to in paragraph (a) of this section include:

(1) Section 173 (circulation expenditures).

(2) Section 174 (research and experimental expenditures).

(3) Section 175 (soil and water conservation expenditures).

(4) Section 177 (trademark and trade name expenditures).

(5) Section 179 (election to expense certain depreciable business assets).

(6) Section 180 (expenditures by farmers for fertilizer, lime, etc.).

(7) Section 182 (expenditures by farmers for clearing land).

(8) Section 248 (organizational expenditures of a corporation).

(9) Section 266 (carrying charges).

(10) Section 615 (exploration expenditures).

(11) Section 616 (development expenditures).

Reg. § 1.263(a)-4 Amounts paid to acquire or create intangibles.

(a) *Overview.* This section provides rules for applying section 263(a) to amounts paid to acquire or create intangibles. Except to the extent provided in paragraph (d)(8) of this section, the rules provided by this section do not apply to amounts paid to acquire or create tangible assets. Paragraph (b) of this section provides a general principle of capitalization. Paragraphs (c) and (d) of this section identify intangibles for which capitalization is specifically required under the general principle. Paragraph (e) of this section provides rules for determining the extent to which taxpayers must capitalize transaction costs. Paragraph (f) of this section provides a 12-month rule intended to simplify the application of the general principle to certain payments that create benefits of a brief duration. Additional rules and examples relating to these provisions are provided in paragraphs (g) through (n) of this section. The applicability date of the rules in this section is provided in paragraph (o) of this section. Paragraph (p) of this section provides rules applicable to changes in methods of accounting made to comply with this section.

(b) *Capitalization with respect to intangibles*--(1) *In general.* Except as otherwise provided in this section, a taxpayer must capitalize--

(i) An amount paid to acquire an intangible (see paragraph (c) of this section);

(ii) An amount paid to create an intangible described in paragraph (d) of this section;

(iii) An amount paid to create or enhance a separate and distinct intangible asset within the meaning of paragraph (b)(3) of this section;

(iv) An amount paid to create or enhance a future benefit identified in published guidance in the Federal Register or in the Internal Revenue Bulletin (see § 601.601(d)(2) (ii) of this chapter) as an intangible for which capitalization is required under this section; and

(v) An amount paid to facilitate (within the meaning of paragraph (e)(1) of this section) an acquisition or creation of an intangible described in paragraph (b)(1)(i), (ii), (iii) or (iv) of this section.

(2) *Published guidance.* Any published guidance identifying a future benefit as an intangible for which capitalization is required under paragraph (b)(1)(iv) of this section applies only to amounts paid on or after the date of publication of the guidance.

(3) *Separate and distinct intangible asset*--(i) *Definition.* The term separate and distinct intangible asset means a property interest of ascertainable and measurable value in money's worth that is subject to protection under applicable State, Federal or foreign law and the possession and control of which is intrinsically capable of being sold, transferred or pledged (ignoring any restrictions imposed on assignability) separate and apart from a trade or business. In addition, for purposes of this section, a fund (or similar account) is treated as a separate and distinct intangible asset of the taxpayer if amounts in the fund (or account) may revert to the taxpayer. The determination of whether a payment creates

Sec. 263. Capital expenditures

a separate and distinct intangible asset is made based on all of the facts and circumstances existing during the taxable year in which the payment is made.

(ii) *Creation or termination of contract rights.* Amounts paid to another party to create, originate, enter into, renew or renegotiate an agreement with that party that produces

5 rights or benefits for the taxpayer (and amounts paid to facilitate the creation, origination, enhancement, renewal or renegotiation of such an agreement) are treated as amounts that do not create (or facilitate the creation of) a separate and distinct intangible asset within the meaning of this paragraph (b)(3). Further, amounts paid to another party to terminate (or facilitate the termination of) an agreement with that party are treated as

10 amounts that do not create a separate and distinct intangible asset within the meaning of this paragraph (b)(3). See paragraphs (d)(2), (d)(6), and (d)(7) of this section for rules that specifically require capitalization of amounts paid to create or terminate certain agreements.

(iii) *Amounts paid in performing services.* Amounts paid in performing services under

15 an agreement are treated as amounts that do not create a separate and distinct intangible asset within the meaning of this paragraph (b)(3), regardless of whether the amounts result in the creation of an income stream under the agreement.

(iv) *Creation of computer software.* Except as otherwise provided in the Internal Revenue Code, the regulations thereunder, or other published guidance in the Federal

20 Register or in the Internal Revenue Bulletin (see § 601.601(d)(2)(ii) of this chapter), amounts paid to develop computer software are treated as amounts that do not create a separate and distinct intangible asset within the meaning of this paragraph (b)(3).

(v) *Creation of package design.* Amounts paid to develop a package design are treated as amounts that do not create a separate and distinct intangible asset within the

25 meaning of this paragraph (b)(3). For purposes of this section, the term package design means the specific graphic arrangement or design of shapes, colors, words, pictures, lettering, and other elements on a given product package, or the design of a container with respect to its shape or function.

(4) *Coordination with other provisions of the Internal Revenue Code--*(i) In general.

30 Nothing in this section changes the treatment of an amount that is specifically provided for under any other provision of the Internal Revenue Code (other than section 162(a) or 212) or the regulations thereunder.

***

(c) *Acquired intangibles--*(1) *In general.* A taxpayer must capitalize amounts paid to

35 another party to acquire any intangible from that party in a purchase or similar transaction. Examples of intangibles within the scope of this paragraph (c) include, but are not limited to, the following (if acquired from another party in a purchase or similar transaction):

(i) An ownership interest in a corporation, partnership, trust, estate, limited liability

40 company, or other entity.

(ii) A debt instrument, deposit, stripped bond, stripped coupon (including a servicing right treated for federal income tax purposes as a stripped coupon), regular interest in a REMIC or FASIT, or any other intangible treated as debt for federal income tax purposes.

(iii) A financial instrument, such as--

45 (A) A notional principal contract;

(B) A foreign currency contract;

(C) A futures contract;

(D) A forward contract (including an agreement under which the taxpayer has the right and obligation to provide or to acquire property (or to be compensated for such property,

50 regardless of whether the taxpayer provides or acquires the property));

(E) An option (including an agreement under which the taxpayer has the right to

614

Sec. 263. Capital expenditures

provide or to acquire property (or to be compensated for such property, regardless of whether the taxpayer provides or acquires the property)); and

(F) Any other financial derivative.

(iv) An endowment contract, annuity contract, or insurance contract.

(v) Non-functional currency. 5

(vi) A lease.

(vii) A patent or copyright.

(viii) A franchise, trademark or tradename (as defined in § 1.197-2(b)(10)).

(ix) An assembled workforce (as defined in § 1.197-2(b)(3)).

(x) Goodwill (as defined in § 1.197-2(b)(1)) or going concern value (as defined in § 10 1.197-2(b)(2)).

(xi) A customer list.

(xii) A servicing right (for example, a mortgage servicing right that is not treated for Federal income tax purposes as a stripped coupon).

(xiii) A customer-based intangible (as defined in § 1.197-2(b)(6)) or supplier-based 15 intangible (as defined in § 1.197-2(b)(7)).

(xiv) Computer software.

(xv) An agreement providing either party the right to use, possess or sell an intangible described in paragraphs (c)(1)(i) through (v) of this section.

(2) *Readily available software.* An amount paid to obtain a nonexclusive license for 20 software that is (or has been) readily available to the general public on similar terms and has not been substantially modified (within the meaning of § 1.197-2(c)(4)) is treated for purposes of this paragraph (c) as an amount paid to another party to acquire an intangible from that party in a purchase or similar transaction.

(3) *Intangibles acquired from an employee.* Amounts paid to an employee to acquire 25 an intangible from that employee are not required to be capitalized under this section if the amounts are includible in the employee's income in connection with the performance of services under section 61 or 83. For purposes of this section, whether an individual is an employee is determined in accordance with the rules contained in section 3401(c) and the regulations thereunder. 30

***

(d) *Created intangibles*--(1) *In general.* Except as provided in paragraph (f) of this section (relating to the 12-month rule), a taxpayer must capitalize amounts paid to create an intangible described in this paragraph (d). The determination of whether an amount is paid to create an intangible described in this paragraph (d) is to be made based on all of 35 the facts and circumstances, disregarding distinctions between the labels used in this paragraph (d) to describe the intangible and the labels used by the taxpayer and other parties to the transaction.

(2) *Financial interests*--(i) *In general.* A taxpayer must capitalize amounts paid to another party to create, originate, enter into, renew or renegotiate with that party any of 40 the following financial interests, whether or not the interest is regularly traded on an established market:

(A) An ownership interest in a corporation, partnership, trust, estate, limited liability company, or other entity.

(B) A debt instrument, deposit, stripped bond, stripped coupon (including a servicing 45 right treated for federal income tax purposes as a stripped coupon), regular interest in a REMIC or FASIT, or any other intangible treated as debt for Federal income tax purposes.

(C) A financial instrument, such as--

(1) A letter of credit;

(2) A credit card agreement; 50

615

Sec. 263. Capital expenditures

(3) A notional principal contract;

(4) A foreign currency contract;

(5) A futures contract;

(6) A forward contract (including an agreement under which the taxpayer has the right and obligation to provide or to acquire property (or to be compensated for such property, regardless of whether the taxpayer provides or acquires the property));

(7) An option (including an agreement under which the taxpayer has the right to provide or to acquire property (or to be compensated for such property, regardless of whether the taxpayer provides or acquires the property)); and

(8) Any other financial derivative.

(D) An endowment contract, annuity contract, or insurance contract that has or may have cash value.

(E) Non-functional currency.

(F) An agreement providing either party the right to use, possess or sell a financial interest described in this paragraph (d)(2).

(ii) *Amounts paid to create, originate, enter into, renew or renegotiate.* An amount paid to another party is not paid to create, originate, enter into, renew or renegotiate a financial interest with that party if the payment is made with the mere hope or expectation of developing or maintaining a business relationship with that party and is not contingent on the origination, renewal or renegotiation of a financial interest with that party.

(iii) *Renegotiate.* A taxpayer is treated as renegotiating a financial interest if the terms of the financial interest are modified. A taxpayer also is treated as renegotiating a financial interest if the taxpayer enters into a new financial interest with the same party (or substantially the same parties) to a terminated financial interest, the taxpayer could not cancel the terminated financial interest without the consent of the other party (or parties), and the other party (or parties) would not have consented to the cancellation unless the taxpayer entered into the new financial interest. A taxpayer is treated as unable to cancel a financial interest without the consent of the other party (or parties) if, under the terms of the financial interest, the taxpayer is subject to a termination penalty and the other party (or parties) to the financial interest modifies the terms of the penalty.

(iv) *Coordination with other provisions of this paragraph (d).* An amount described in this paragraph (d)(2) that is also described elsewhere in paragraph (d) of this section is treated as described only in this paragraph (d)(2).

(v) *Coordination with § 1.263(a)-5.* See § 1.263(a)-5 for the treatment of borrowing costs and the treatment of amounts paid by an option writer.

***

(3) *Prepaid expenses--*(i) *In general.* A taxpayer must capitalize prepaid expenses.

***

(5) *Certain rights obtained from a governmental agency--*(i) *In general.* A taxpayer must capitalize amounts paid to a governmental agency to obtain, renew, renegotiate, or upgrade its rights under a trademark, trade name, copyright, license, permit, franchise, or other similar right granted by that governmental agency.

***

(6) *Certain contract rights--*(i) *In general.* Except as otherwise provided in this paragraph (d)(6), a taxpayer must capitalize amounts paid to another party to create, originate, enter into, renew or renegotiate with that party--

(A) An agreement providing the taxpayer the right to use tangible or intangible property or the right to be compensated for the use of tangible or intangible property;

(B) An agreement providing the taxpayer the right to provide or to receive services (or the right to be compensated for services regardless of whether the taxpayer provides

616

Sec. 263.   Capital expenditures

such services);

(C) A covenant not to compete or an agreement having substantially the same effect as a covenant not to compete (except, in the case of an agreement that requires the performance of services, to the extent that the amount represents reasonable compensation for services actually rendered);   5

(D) An agreement not to acquire additional ownership interests in the taxpayer; or

(E) An agreement providing the taxpayer (as the covered party) with an annuity, an endowment, or insurance coverage.

(ii) *Amounts paid to create, originate, enter into, renew or renegotiate.* An amount paid to another party is not paid to create, originate, enter into, renew or renegotiate an   10 agreement with that party if the payment is made with the mere hope or expectation of developing or maintaining a business relationship with that party and is not contingent on the origination, renewal or renegotiation of an agreement with that party.

(iii) *Renegotiate.* A taxpayer is treated as renegotiating an agreement if the terms of the agreement are modified. A taxpayer also is treated as renegotiating an agreement if   15 the taxpayer enters into a new agreement with the same party (or substantially the same parties) to a terminated agreement, the taxpayer could not cancel the terminated agreement without the consent of the other party (or parties), and the other party (or parties) would not have consented to the cancellation unless the taxpayer entered into the new agreement. A taxpayer is treated as unable to cancel an agreement without the   20 consent of the other party (or parties) if, under the terms of the agreement, the taxpayer is subject to a termination penalty and the other party (or parties) to the agreement modifies the terms of the penalty.

(iv) *Right.* An agreement does not provide the taxpayer a right to use property or to provide or receive services if the agreement may be terminated at will by the other party   25 (or parties) to the agreement before the end of the period prescribed by paragraph (f)(1) of this section. An agreement is not terminable at will if the other party (or parties) to the agreement is economically compelled not to terminate the agreement until the end of the period prescribed by paragraph (f)(1) of this section. All of the facts and circumstances will be considered in determining whether the other party (or parties) to an agreement is   30 economically compelled not to terminate the agreement. An agreement also does not provide the taxpayer the right to provide services if the agreement merely provides that the taxpayer will stand ready to provide services if requested, but places no obligation on another person to request or pay for the taxpayer's services.

(v) *De minimis amounts.* A taxpayer is not required to capitalize amounts paid to   35 another party (or parties) to create, originate, enter into, renew or renegotiate with that party (or those parties) an agreement described in paragraph (d)(6)(i) of this section if the aggregate of all amounts paid to that party (or those parties) with respect to the agreement does not exceed $5,000. If the aggregate of all amounts paid to the other party (or parties) with respect to that agreement exceeds $5,000, then all amounts must   40 be capitalized. For purposes of this paragraph (d)(6), an amount paid in the form of property is valued at its fair market value at the time of the payment. In general, a taxpayer must determine whether the rules of this paragraph (d)(6)(v) apply by accounting for the specific amounts paid with respect to each agreement. However, a taxpayer that reasonably expects to create, originate, enter into, renew or renegotiate at   45 least 25 similar agreements during the taxable year may establish a pool of agreements for purposes of determining the amounts paid with respect to the agreements in the pool. Under this pooling method, the amount paid with respect to each agreement included in the pool is equal to the average amount paid with respect to all agreements included in the pool. A taxpayer computes the average amount paid with respect to all agreements   50 included in the pool by dividing the sum of all amounts paid with respect to all agreements included in the pool by the number of agreements included in the pool. See paragraph (h) of this section for additional rules relating to pooling.

***

(7) *Certain contract terminations*--(i) *In general.* A taxpayer must capitalize amounts
5 paid to another party to terminate--
(A) A lease of real or tangible personal property between the taxpayer (as lessor) and that party (as lessee);
(B) An agreement that grants that party the exclusive right to acquire or use the taxpayer's property or services or to conduct the taxpayer's business (other than an
10 intangible described in paragraph (c)(1)(i) through (iv) of this section or a financial interest described in paragraph (d)(2) of this section); or
(C) An agreement that prohibits the taxpayer from competing with that party or from acquiring property or services from a competitor of that party.

***

15   (8) *Certain benefits arising from the provision, production, or improvement of real property*--(i) *In general.* A taxpayer must capitalize amounts paid for real property if the taxpayer transfers ownership of the real property to another person (except to the extent the real property is sold for fair market value) and if the real property can reasonably be expected to produce significant economic benefits to the taxpayer after the transfer. A
20 taxpayer also must capitalize amounts paid to produce or improve real property owned by another (except to the extent the taxpayer is selling services at fair market value to produce or improve the real property) if the real property can reasonably be expected to produce significant economic benefits for the taxpayer.
(ii) *Exclusions.* A taxpayer is not required to capitalize an amount under paragraph (d)
25 (8)(i) of this section if the taxpayer transfers real property or pays an amount to produce or improve real property owned by another in exchange for services, the purchase or use of property, or the creation of an intangible described in paragraph (d) of this section (other than in this paragraph (d)(8)). The preceding sentence does not apply to the extent the taxpayer does not receive fair market value consideration for the real property that is
30 relinquished or for the amounts that are paid by the taxpayer to produce or improve real property owned by another.
(iii) *Real property.* For purposes of this paragraph (d)(8), real property includes property that is affixed to real property and that will ordinarily remain affixed for an indefinite period of time, such as roads, bridges, tunnels, pavements, wharves and docks,
35 breakwaters and sea walls, elevators, power generation and transmission facilities, and pollution control facilities.
(iv) *Impact fees and dedicated improvements.* Paragraph (d)(8)(i) of this section does not apply to amounts paid to satisfy one-time charges imposed by a State or local government against new development (or expansion of existing development) to finance
40 specific offsite capital improvements for general public use that are necessitated by the new or expanded development. In addition, paragraph (d)(8)(i) of this section does not apply to amounts paid for real property or improvements to real property constructed by the taxpayer where the real property or improvements benefit new development or expansion of existing development, are immediately transferred to a State or local
45 government for dedication to the general public use, and are maintained by the State or local government. See section 263A and the regulations thereunder for capitalization rules that apply to amounts referred to in this paragraph (d)(8)(iv).

***

(9) *Defense or perfection of title to intangible property*--(i) *In general.* A taxpayer must
50 capitalize amounts paid to another party to defend or perfect title to intangible property if

Sec. 263. Capital expenditures

that other party challenges the taxpayer's title to the intangible property.

***

(e) *Transaction costs*--(1) *Scope of facilitate*--(i) *In general.* Except as otherwise provided in this section, an amount is paid to facilitate the acquisition or creation of an intangible (the transaction) if the amount is paid in the process of investigating or 5 otherwise pursuing the transaction. Whether an amount is paid in the process of investigating or otherwise pursuing the transaction is determined based on all of the facts and circumstances. In determining whether an amount is paid to facilitate a transaction, the fact that the amount would (or would not) have been paid but for the transaction is relevant, but is not determinative. An amount paid to determine the value or price of an 10 intangible is an amount paid in the process of investigating or otherwise pursuing the transaction.

(ii) *Treatment of termination payments.* An amount paid to terminate (or facilitate the termination of) an existing agreement does not facilitate the acquisition or creation of another agreement under this section. See paragraph (d)(6)(iii) of this section for the 15 treatment of termination fees paid to the other party (or parties) of a renegotiated agreement.

(iii) *Special rule for contracts.* An amount is treated as not paid in the process of investigating or otherwise pursuing the creation of an agreement described in paragraph (d)(2) or (d)(6) of this section if the amount relates to activities performed before the 20 earlier of the date the taxpayer begins preparing its bid for the agreement or the date the taxpayer begins discussing or negotiating the agreement with another party to the agreement.

(iv) *Borrowing costs.* An amount paid to facilitate a borrowing does not facilitate an acquisition or creation of an intangible described in paragraphs (b)(1)(i) through (iv) of 25 this section. See §§ 1.263(a)-5 and 1.446-5 for the treatment of an amount paid to facilitate a borrowing.

***

(2) *Coordination with paragraph (d) of this section.* In the case of an amount paid to facilitate the creation of an intangible described in paragraph (d) of this section, the 30 provisions of this paragraph (e) apply regardless of whether a payment described in paragraph (d) is made.

(3) *Transaction.* For purposes of this section, the term transaction means all of the factual elements comprising an acquisition or creation of an intangible and includes a series of steps carried out as part of a single plan. Thus, a transaction can involve more 35 than one invoice and more than one intangible. For example, a purchase of intangibles under one purchase agreement constitutes a single transaction, notwithstanding the fact that the acquisition involves multiple intangibles and the amounts paid to facilitate the acquisition are capable of being allocated among the various intangibles acquired.

(4) *Simplifying conventions*--(i) *In general.* For purposes of this section, employee 40 compensation (within the meaning of paragraph (e)(4)(ii) of this section), overhead, and de minimis costs (within the meaning of paragraph (e)(4)(iii) of this section) are treated as amounts that do not facilitate the acquisition or creation of an intangible.

(ii) Employee compensation--(A) In general. The term employee compensation means compensation (including salary, bonuses and commissions) paid to an employee of the 45 taxpayer. For purposes of this section, whether an individual is an employee is determined in accordance with the rules contained in section 3401(c) and the regulations thereunder.

(B) *Certain amounts treated as employee compensation.* For purposes of this section, a guaranteed payment to a partner in a partnership is treated as employee 50 compensation. For purposes of this section, annual compensation paid to a director of a corporation is treated as employee compensation. For example, an amount paid to a director of a corporation for attendance at a regular meeting of the board of directors (or committee thereof) is treated as employee compensation for purposes of this section.

5 However, an amount paid to a director for attendance at a special meeting of the board of directors (or committee thereof) is not treated as employee compensation. An amount paid to a person that is not an employee of the taxpayer (including the employer of the individual who performs the services) is treated as employee compensation for purposes of this section only if the amount is paid for secretarial, clerical, or similar administrative

10 support services. In the case of an affiliated group of corporations filing a consolidated Federal income tax return, a payment by one member of the group to a second member of the group for services performed by an employee of the second member is treated as employee compensation if the services provided by the employee are provided at a time during which both members are affiliated.

15 (iii) *De minimis costs*--(A) *In general.* Except as provided in paragraph (e)(4)(iii)(B) of this section, the term de minimis costs means amounts (other than employee compensation and overhead) paid in the process of investigating or otherwise pursuing a transaction if, in the aggregate, the amounts do not exceed $5,000 (or such greater amount as may be set forth in published guidance). If the amounts exceed $5,000 (or

20 such greater amount as may be set forth in published guidance), none of the amounts are de minimis costs within the meaning of this paragraph (e)(4)(iii)(A). For purposes of this paragraph (e)(4)(iii), an amount paid in the form of property is valued at its fair market value at the time of the payment. In determining the amount of transaction costs paid in the process of investigating or otherwise pursuing a transaction, a taxpayer generally

25 must account for the specific costs paid with respect to each transaction. However, a taxpayer that reasonably expects to enter into at least 25 similar transactions during the taxable year may establish a pool of similar transactions for purposes of determining the amount of transaction costs paid in the process of investigating or otherwise pursuing the transactions in the pool. Under this pooling method, the amount of transaction costs paid

30 in the process of investigating or otherwise pursuing each transaction included in the pool is equal to the average transaction costs paid in the process of investigating or otherwise pursuing all transactions included in the pool. A taxpayer computes the average transaction costs paid in the process of investigating or otherwise pursuing all transactions included in the pool by dividing the sum of all transaction costs paid in the

35 process of investigating or otherwise pursuing all transactions included in the pool by the number of transactions included in the pool. See paragraph (h) of this section for additional rules relating to pooling.

(B) *Treatment of commissions.* The term de minimis costs does not include commissions paid to facilitate the acquisition of an intangible described in paragraphs (c)

40 (1)(i) through (v) of this section or to facilitate the creation, origination, entrance into, renewal or renegotiation of an intangible described in paragraph (d)(2)(i) of this section.

(iv) *Election to capitalize.* A taxpayer may elect to treat employee compensation, overhead, or de minimis costs paid in the process of investigating or otherwise pursuing a transaction as amounts that facilitate the transaction. The election is made separately for

45 each transaction and applies to employee compensation, overhead, or de minimis costs, or to any combination thereof. For example, a taxpayer may elect to treat overhead and de minimis costs, but not employee compensation, as amounts that facilitate the transaction. A taxpayer makes the election by treating the amounts to which the election applies as amounts that facilitate the transaction in the taxpayer's timely filed original

50 Federal income tax return (including extensions) for the taxable year during which the amounts are paid. In the case of an affiliated group of corporations filing a consolidated

Sec. 263. Capital expenditures

return, the election is made separately with respect to each member of the group, and not with respect to the group as a whole. In the case of an S corporation or partnership, the election is made by the S corporation or by the partnership, and not by the shareholders or partners. An election made under this paragraph (e)(4)(iv) is revocable with respect to each taxable year for which made only with the consent of the Commissioner. 5

***

(f) *12-month rule*--(1) *In general.* Except as otherwise provided in this paragraph (f), a taxpayer is not required to capitalize under this section amounts paid to create (or to facilitate the creation of) any right or benefit for the taxpayer that does not extend beyond the earlier of-- 10

(i) 12 months after the first date on which the taxpayer realizes the right or benefit; or

(ii) The end of the taxable year following the taxable year in which the payment is made.

(2) *Duration of benefit for contract terminations.* For purposes of this paragraph (f), amounts paid to terminate a contract or other agreement described in paragraph (d)(7)(i) 15 of this section prior to its expiration date (or amounts paid to facilitate such termination) create a benefit for the taxpayer that lasts for the unexpired term of the agreement immediately before the date of the termination. If the terms of a contract or other agreement described in paragraph (d)(7)(i) of this section permit the taxpayer to terminate the contract or agreement after a notice period, amounts paid by the taxpayer 20 to terminate the contract or agreement before the end of the notice period create a benefit for the taxpayer that lasts for the amount of time by which the notice period is shortened.

(3) *Inapplicability to created financial interests and self-created amortizable section 197 intangibles.* Paragraph (f)(1) of this section does not apply to amounts paid to create 25 (or facilitate the creation of) an intangible described in paragraph (d)(2) of this section (relating to amounts paid to create financial interests) or to amounts paid to create (or facilitate the creation of) an intangible that constitutes an amortizable section 197 intangible within the meaning of section 197(c).

(4) *Inapplicability to rights of indefinite duration.* Paragraph (f)(1) of this section does 30 not apply to amounts paid to create (or facilitate the creation of) an intangible of indefinite duration. A right has an indefinite duration if it has no period of duration fixed by agreement or by law, or if it is not based on a period of time, such as a right attributable to an agreement to provide or receive a fixed amount of goods or services. For example, a license granted by a governmental agency that permits the taxpayer to operate a 35 business conveys a right of indefinite duration if the license may be revoked only upon the taxpayer's violation of the terms of the license.

(5) *Rights subject to renewal*--(i) *In general.* For purposes of paragraph (f)(1) of this section, the duration of a right includes any renewal period if all of the facts and circumstances in existence during the taxable year in which the right is created indicate a 40 reasonable expectancy of renewal.

***

(6) *Coordination with section 461.* In the case of a taxpayer using an accrual method of accounting, the rules of this paragraph (f) do not affect the determination of whether a liability is incurred during the taxable year, including the determination of whether 45 economic performance has occurred with respect to the liability. See § 1.461-4 for rules relating to economic performance.

(7) *Election to capitalize.* A taxpayer may elect not to apply the rule contained in paragraph (f)(1) of this section. An election made under this paragraph (f)(7) applies to all similar transactions during the taxable year to which paragraph (f)(1) of this section would 50

621

Sec. 263. Capital expenditures

apply (but for the election under this paragraph (f)(7)). For example, a taxpayer may elect under this paragraph (f)(7) to capitalize its costs of prepaying insurance contracts for 12 months, but may continue to apply the rule in paragraph (f)(1) to its costs of entering into non-renewable, 12-month service contracts. A taxpayer makes the election by treating
5 the amounts as capital expenditures in its timely filed original federal income tax return (including extensions) for the taxable year during which the amounts are paid. In the case of an affiliated group of corporations filing a consolidated return, the election is made separately with respect to each member of the group, and not with respect to the group as a whole. In the case of an S corporation or partnership, the election is made by the S
10 corporation or by the partnership, and not by the shareholders or partners. An election made under this paragraph (f)(7) is revocable with respect to each taxable year for which made only with the consent of the Commissioner.

(8) *Examples.* The rules of this paragraph (f) are illustrated by the following examples, in which it is assumed (unless otherwise stated) that the taxpayer is a calendar year,
15 accrual method taxpayer that does not have a short taxable year in any taxable year and has not made an election under paragraph (f)(7) of this section:

Example 1. Prepaid expenses. On December 1, 2005, N corporation pays a $10,000 insurance premium to obtain a property insurance policy (with no cash value) with a 1-year term that begins on February 1, 2006. The amount paid by N is a prepaid expense
20 described in paragraph (d)(3) of this section and not paragraph (d)(2) of this section. Because the right or benefit attributable to the $10,000 payment extends beyond the end of the taxable year following the taxable year in which the payment is made, the 12-month rule provided by this paragraph (f) does not apply. N must capitalize the $10,000 payment.

25 *Example 2. Prepaid expenses.* (i) Assume the same facts as in Example 1, except that the policy has a term beginning on December 15, 2005. The 12-month rule of this paragraph (f) applies to the $10,000 payment because the right or benefit attributable to the payment neither extends more than 12 months beyond December 15, 2005 (the first date the benefit is realized by the taxpayer) nor beyond the end of the taxable year
30 following the taxable year in which the payment is made. Accordingly, N is not required to capitalize the $10,000 payment.

(ii) Alternatively, assume N capitalizes prepaid expenses for financial accounting and reporting purposes and elects under paragraph (f)(7) of this section not to apply the 12-month rule contained in paragraph (f)(1) of this section. N must capitalize the $10,000
35 payment for Federal income tax purposes.

Example 3. Financial interests. On October 1, 2005, X corporation makes a 9-month loan to B in the principal amount of $250,000. The principal amount of the loan to B constitutes an amount paid to create or originate a financial interest under paragraph (d) (2)(i)(B) of this section. The 9-month term of the loan does not extend beyond the period
40 prescribed by paragraph (f)(1) of this section. However, as provided by paragraph (f)(3) of this section, the rules of this paragraph (f) do not apply to intangibles described in paragraph (d)(2) of this section. Accordingly, X must capitalize the $250,000 loan amount.

Example 4. Financial interests. X corporation owns all of the outstanding stock of Z corporation. On December 1, 2005, Y corporation pays X $1,000,000 in exchange for X's
45 grant of a 9-month call option to Y permitting Y to purchase all of the outstanding stock of Z. Y's payment to X constitutes an amount paid to create or originate an option with X under paragraph (d)(2)(i)(C)(7) of this section. The 9-month term of the option does not extend beyond the period prescribed by paragraph (f)(1) of this section. However, as provided by paragraph (f)(3) of this section, the rules of this paragraph (f) do not apply to
50 intangibles described in paragraph (d)(2) of this section. Accordingly, Y must capitalize the $1,000,000 payment.

Sec. 263. Capital expenditures

Example 5. License. (i) On July 1, 2005, R corporation pays $10,000 to state X to obtain a license to operate a business in state X for a period of 5 years. The terms of the license require R to pay state X an annual fee of $500 due on July 1, 2005, and each of the succeeding four years. R pays the $500 fee on July 1 as required by the license.

(ii) R's payment of $10,000 is an amount paid to a governmental agency for a license 5 granted by that agency to which paragraph (d)(5) of this section applies. Because R's payment creates rights or benefits for R that extend beyond 12 months after the first date on which R realizes the rights or benefits attributable to the payment and beyond the end of 2006 (the taxable year following the taxable year in which the payment is made), the rules of this paragraph (f) do not apply to R's payment. Accordingly, R must capitalize the 10 $10,000 payment.

(iii) R's payment of each $500 annual fee is a prepaid expense described in paragraph (d)(3) of this section. R is not required to capitalize the $500 fee in each taxable year. The rules of this paragraph (f) apply to each such payment because each payment provides a right or benefit to R that does not extend beyond 12 months after the first date on which 15 R realizes the rights or benefits attributable to the payment and does not extend beyond the end of the taxable year following the taxable year in which the payment is made.

Example 6. Lease. On December 1, 2005, W corporation enters into a lease agreement with X corporation under which W agrees to lease property to X for a period of 9 months, beginning on December 1, 2005. W pays its outside counsel $7,000 for legal 20 services rendered in drafting the lease agreement and negotiating with X. The agreement between W and X is an agreement providing W the right to be compensated for the use of property, as described in paragraph (d)(6)(i)(A) of this section. W's $7,000 payment to its outside counsel is an amount paid to facilitate W's creation of the lease as described in paragraph (e)(1)(i) of this section. The 12-month rule of this paragraph (f) applies to the 25 $7,000 payment because the right or benefit that the $7,000 payment facilitates the creation of neither extends more than 12 months beyond December 1, 2005 (the first date the benefit is realized by the taxpayer) nor beyond the end of the taxable year following the taxable year in which the payment is made. Accordingly, W is not required to capitalize its payment to its outside counsel. 30

Example 7. Certain contract terminations. V corporation owns real property that it has leased to A for a period of 15 years. When the lease has a remaining unexpired term of 5 years, V and A agree to terminate the lease, enabling V to use the property in its trade or business. V pays A $100,000 in exchange for A's agreement to terminate the lease. V's payment to A to terminate the lease is described in paragraph (d)(7)(i)(A) of this section. 35 Under paragraph (f)(2) of this section, V's payment creates a benefit for V with a duration of 5 years, the remaining unexpired term of the lease as of the date of the termination. Because the benefit attributable to the expenditure extends beyond 12 months after the first date on which V realizes the rights or benefits attributable to the payment and beyond the end of the taxable year following the taxable year in which the payment is 40 made, the rules of this paragraph (f) do not apply to the payment. V must capitalize the $100,000 payment.

Example 8. Certain contract terminations. Assume the same facts as in Example 7, except that the lease is terminated when it has a remaining unexpired term of 10 months. Under paragraph (f)(2) of this section, V's payment creates a benefit for V with a duration 45 of 10 months. The 12-month rule of this paragraph (f) applies to the payment because the benefit attributable to the payment neither extends more than 12 months beyond the date of termination (the first date the benefit is realized by V) nor beyond the end of the taxable year following the taxable year in which the payment is made. Accordingly, V is not required to capitalize the $100,000 payment. 50

Example 9. Certain contract terminations. Assume the same facts as in Example 7,

623

Sec. 263. Capital expenditures

except that either party can terminate the lease upon 12 months notice. When the lease has a remaining unexpired term of 5 years, V wants to terminate the lease, however, V does not want to wait another 12 months. V pays A $50,000 for the ability to terminate the lease with one month's notice. V's payment to A to terminate the lease is described in
5 paragraph (d)(7)(i)(A) of this section. Under paragraph (f)(2) of this section, V's payment creates a benefit for V with a duration of 11 months, the time by which the notice period is shortened. The 12-month rule of this paragraph (f) applies to V's $50,000 payment because the benefit attributable to the payment neither extends more than 12 months beyond the date of termination (the first date the benefit is realized by V) nor beyond the
10 end of the taxable year following the taxable year in which the payment is made. Accordingly, V is not required to capitalize the $50,000 payment.

Example 10. Coordination with section 461. (i) U corporation leases office space from W corporation at a monthly rental rate of $2,000. On August 1, 2005, U prepays its office rent expense for the first six months of 2006 in the amount of $12,000. For purposes of
15 this example, it is assumed that the recurring item exception provided by § 1.461-5 does not apply and that the lease between W and U is not a section 467 rental agreement as defined in section 467(d).

(ii) Under § 1.461-4(d)(3), U's prepayment of rent is a payment for the use of property by U for which economic performance occurs ratably over the period of time U is entitled
20 to use the property. Accordingly, because economic performance with respect to U's prepayment of rent does not occur until 2006, U's prepaid rent is not incurred in 2005 and therefore is not properly taken into account through capitalization, deduction, or otherwise in 2005. Thus, the rules of this paragraph (f) do not apply to U's prepayment of its rent.

(iii) Alternatively, assume that U uses the cash method of accounting and the
25 economic performance rules in § 1.461-4 therefore do not apply to U. The 12-month rule of this paragraph (f) applies to the $12,000 payment because the rights or benefits attributable to U's prepayment of its rent do not extend beyond December 31, 2006. Accordingly, U is not required to capitalize its prepaid rent.

Example 11. Coordination with section 461. N corporation pays R corporation, an
30 advertising and marketing firm, $40,000 on August 1, 2005, for advertising and marketing services to be provided to N throughout calendar year 2006. For purposes of this example, it is assumed that the recurring item exception provided by § 1.461-5 does not apply. Under § 1.461-4(d)(2), N's payment arises out of the provision of services to N by R for which economic performance occurs as the services are provided. Accordingly,
35 because economic performance with respect to N's prepaid advertising expense does not occur until 2006, N's prepaid advertising expense is not incurred in 2005 and therefore is not properly taken into account through capitalization, deduction, or otherwise in 2005. Thus, the rules of this paragraph (f) do not apply to N's payment.

(g) *Treatment of capitalized costs*--(1) *In general.* An amount required to be capitalized
40 by this section is not currently deductible under section 162. Instead, the amount generally is added to the basis of the intangible acquired or created. See section 1012.

***

(j) *Application to accrual method taxpayers.* For purposes of this section, the terms amount paid and payment mean, in the case of a taxpayer using an accrual method of
45 accounting, a liability incurred (within the meaning of § 1.446-1(c)(1)(ii)). A liability may not be taken into account under this section prior to the taxable year during which the liability is incurred.

***

(l) *Examples.* The rules of this section are illustrated by the following examples in
50 which it is assumed that the Internal Revenue Service has not published guidance that

Sec. 263. Capital expenditures

requires capitalization under paragraph (b)(1)(iv) of this section (relating to amounts paid to create or enhance a future benefit that is identified in published guidance as an intangible for which capitalization is required):

***

Example 3. Covenant not to compete. (i) On December 1, 2005, N corporation, a 5 calendar year taxpayer, enters into a covenant not to compete with B, a key employee that is leaving the employ of N. The covenant not to compete is not entered into in connection with the acquisition of an interest in a trade or business. The covenant not to compete prohibits B from competing with N for a period of 9 months, beginning December 1, 2005. N pays B $25,000 in full consideration for B's agreement not to 10 compete. In addition, N pays its outside counsel $6,000 to facilitate the creation of the covenant not to compete with B. N does not have a short taxable year in 2005 or 2006.

(ii) Under paragraph (d)(6)(i)(C) of this section, N's payment of $25,000 is an amount paid to another party to induce that party to enter into a covenant not to compete with N. However, because the covenant not to compete has a duration that does not extend 15 beyond 12 months after the first date on which N realizes the rights attributable to its payment (i.e., December 1, 2005) or beyond the end of the taxable year following the taxable year in which payment is made, the 12-month rule contained in paragraph (f)(1) of this section applies. Accordingly, N is not required to capitalize its $25,000 payment to B or its $6,000 payment to facilitate the creation of the covenant not to compete. 20

Example 4. Demand-side management. (i) X corporation, a public utility engaged in generating and distributing electrical energy, provides programs to its customers to promote energy conservation and energy efficiency. These programs are aimed at reducing electrical costs to X's customers, building goodwill with X's customers, and reducing X's future operating and capital costs. X provides these programs without 25 obligating any of its customers participating in the programs to purchase power from X in the future. Under these programs, X pays a consultant to help industrial customers design energy-efficient manufacturing processes, to conduct ``energy efficiency audits" that serve to identify for customers inefficiencies in their energy usage patterns, and to provide cash allowances to encourage residential customers to replace existing 30 appliances with more energy efficient appliances.

(ii) The amounts paid by X to the consultant are not amounts to acquire or create an intangible under paragraph (c) or (d) of this section or to facilitate such an acquisition or creation. In addition, the amounts do not create a separate and distinct intangible asset within the meaning of paragraph (b)(3) of this section. Accordingly, the amounts paid to 35 the consultant are not required to be capitalized under this section. While the amounts may serve to reduce future operating and capital costs and create goodwill with customers, these benefits, without more, are not intangibles for which capitalization is required under this section.

*** 40

Example 6. Defense of business reputation. (i) X, an investment adviser, serves as the fund manager of a money market investment fund. X, like its competitors in the industry, strives to maintain a constant net asset value for its money market fund of $1.00 per share. During 2005, in the course of managing the fund assets, X incorrectly predicts the direction of market interest rates, resulting in significant investment losses to the fund. 45 Due to these significant losses, X is faced with the prospect of reporting a net asset value that is less than $1.00 per share. X is not aware of any investment adviser in its industry that has ever reported a net asset value for its money market fund of less than $1.00 per share. X is concerned that reporting a net asset value of less than $1.00 per share will significantly harm its reputation as an investment adviser, and could lead to litigation by 50

625

shareholders. X decides to contribute $2,000,000 to the fund in order to raise the net asset value of the fund to $1.00 per share. This contribution is not a loan to the fund and does not give X any ownership interest in the fund.

    (ii) The $2,000,000 contribution is not an amount paid to acquire or create an
5 intangible under paragraph (c) or (d) of this section or to facilitate such an acquisition or creation. In addition, the amount does not create a separate and distinct intangible asset within the meaning of paragraph (b)(3) of this section. Accordingly, the amount contributed to the fund is not required to be capitalized under this section. While the amount serves to protect the business reputation of the taxpayer and may protect the
10 taxpayer from litigation by shareholders, these benefits, without more, are not intangibles for which capitalization is required under this section.

    Example 7. Product launch costs. (i) R corporation, a manufacturer of pharmaceutical products, is required by law to obtain regulatory approval before selling its products. While awaiting regulatory approval on Product A, R pays to develop and implement a
15 marketing strategy and an advertising campaign to raise consumer awareness of the purported need for Product A. R also pays to train health care professionals and other distributors in the proper use of Product A.

    (ii) The amounts paid by R are not amounts paid to acquire or create an intangible under paragraph (c) or (d) of this section or to facilitate such an acquisition or creation. In
20 addition, the amounts do not create a separate and distinct intangible asset within the meaning of paragraph (b)(3) of this section. Accordingly, R is not required to capitalize these amounts under this section. While the amounts may benefit R by creating consumer demand for Product A and increasing awareness of Product A among distributors, these benefits, without more, are not intangibles for which capitalization is
25 required under this section.

***

    Example 9. Package design costs. (i) Z corporation manufactures and markets personal care products. Z pays $100,000 to a consultant to develop a package design for Z's newest product, Product A. Z also pays a fee to a government agency to obtain
30 trademark and copyright protection on certain elements of the package design. Z pays its outside legal counsel $10,000 for services rendered in preparing and filing the trademark and copyright applications and for other services rendered in securing the trademark and copyright protection.

    (ii) The $100,000 paid by Z to the consultant for development of the package design is
35 not an amount paid to acquire or create an intangible under paragraph (c) or (d) of this section or to facilitate such an acquisition or creation. In addition, as provided in paragraph (b)(3)(v) of this section, amounts paid to develop a package design are treated as amounts that do not create a separate and distinct intangible asset. Accordingly, Z is not required to capitalize the $100,000 payment under this section.

40   (iii) The amounts paid by Z to the government agency to obtain trademark and copyright protection are amounts paid to a government agency for a right granted by that agency. Accordingly, Z must capitalize the payment. In addition, the $10,000 paid by Z to its outside counsel is an amount paid to facilitate the creation of the trademark and copyright. Because the aggregate amounts paid to facilitate the transaction exceed
45 $5,000, the amounts are not de minimis as defined in paragraph (e)(4)(iii)(A) of this section. Accordingly, Z must capitalize the $10,000 payment to its outside counsel under paragraph (b)(1)(v) of this section.

    (iv) Alternatively, assume that Z acquires an existing package design for Product A as part of an acquisition of a trade or business that constitutes an applicable asset
50 acquisition within the meaning of section 1060(c). Assume further that $100,000 of the consideration paid by N in the acquisition is properly allocable to the package design for

Sec. 263. Capital expenditures

Product A. Under paragraph (c)(1) of this section, Z must capitalize the $100,000 payment.

Example 10. Contract to provide services. (i) Q corporation, a financial planning firm, provides financial advisory services on a fee-only basis. During 2005, Q and several other financial planning firms submit separate bids to R corporation for a contract to become one of three providers of financial advisory services to R's employees. Q pays $2,000 to a printing company to develop and produce materials for its sales presentation to R's management. Q also pays $6,000 to travel to R's corporate headquarters to make the sales presentation, and $20,000 of salaries to its employees for services performed in preparing the bid and making the presentation to R's management. Q's bid is successful and Q enters into an agreement with R in 2005 under which Q agrees to provide financial advisory services to R's employees, and R agrees to pay Q's fee on behalf of each employee who chooses to utilize such services. R enters into similar agreements with two other financial planning firms, and R's employees may choose to use the services of any one of the three firms. Based on its past experience, Q reasonably expects to provide services to at least 5 percent of R's employees.

(ii) Q's agreement with R is not an agreement providing Q the right to provide services, as described in paragraph (d)(6)(i)(B) of this section. Under paragraph (d)(6)(iv) the agreement places no obligation on another person to request or pay for Q's services. Accordingly, Q is not required to capitalize any of the amounts paid in the process of pursuing the agreement with R.

***

Reg. § 1.263(b)-1 Expenditures for advertising or promotion of good will (8/21/2006).

See § 1.162-14 for the rules applicable to a corporation which has elected to capitalize expenditures for advertising or the promotion of good will under the provisions of section 733 or section 451 of the Internal Revenue Code of 1939, in computing its excess profits tax credit under Subchapter E, Chapter 2, or Subchapter D, Chapter 1, of the Internal Revenue Code of 1939.

[T.D. 6500, 25 FR 11402, Nov. 26, 1960; 59 FR 3318, 3319, Jan. 21, 1994; T.D. 6794, 30 FR 792, Jan. 26, 1965; T.D. 8121, 52 FR 414, Jan. 6, 1987; T.D. 8121, 52 FR 414, Jan. 6, 1987; T.D. 8131, 52 FR 10084, Mar. 30, 1987; T.D. 8408, 57 FR 12419, Apr. 10, 1992; T.D. 8482, 58 FR 42207, Aug. 9, 1993; T.D. 8584, 59 FR 67197, Dec. 29, 1994; T.D. 9107, 69 FR 446, Jan. 5, 2004; T.D. 9217, 70 FR 44469, Aug. 3, 2005; 71 FR 48589, August 21, 2006; T.D. 9318, 72 FR 14677, Mar. 29, 2007]

Prop. § 1.263(a)-2 Amounts paid to acquire or produce tangible property (8/21/2006).

***

(d) *Acquired or produced tangible property--*

***

(4) *12-month rule--*(i) *In general.* Except as otherwise provided in this paragraph (d) (4), an amount paid for the acquisition or production (including any amount paid to facilitate the acquisition or production) of a unit of property (as determined under § 1.263(a)-3(d)(2)) with an economic useful life (as defined in § 1.263(a)-3(f)(2)) of 12 months or less is not a capital expenditure under paragraph (d) of this section.

***

Sec. 263. Capital expenditures

Prop. § 1.263(a)-3 Amounts paid to improve tangible property (8/21/2006).

***

(b) *Definitions*. For purposes this section, the following definitions apply:

(1) *Amount paid*. In the case of a taxpayer using an accrual method of *accounting*,
5 the terms amounts paid and payment mean a liability incurred (within the meaning of §
1.446-1(c)(1)(ii)). A liability may not be taken into account under this section prior to the
taxable year during which the liability is incurred.

***

(d) *Improved property*--(1) *Capitalization rule*. Except as provided in the repair
10 allowance method in paragraph (g) of this section, a taxpayer must capitalize the
aggregate of related amounts paid to improve a unit of property (including a unit of
property for which the acquisition or production costs were deducted under the 12-month
rule in § 1.263(a)-2(d)(4)), whether the improvements are made by the taxpayer or by a
third party. See section 263A for the scope of costs required to be capitalized to property
15 produced by the taxpayer or to property acquired for resale; section 1016 for adding
capitalized amounts to the basis of the unit of property; and section 168(i)(6) for the
treatment of additions or improvements to a unit of property. For purposes of this
paragraph (d), a unit of property is improved if the amounts paid--

(i) Materially increase the value of the unit of property (see paragraph (e) of this
20 section); or

(ii) Restore the unit of property (see paragraph (f) of this section).

***

(e) *Value*--(1) *In general*. A taxpayer must capitalize amounts paid that materially
increase the value of a unit of property. An amount paid materially increases the value of
25 a unit of property only if it--

(i) Ameliorates a condition or defect that either existed prior to the taxpayer's
acquisition of the unit of property or arose during the production of the unit of property,
whether or not the taxpayer was aware of the condition or defect at the time of acquisition
or production;

30 (ii) Is for work performed prior to the date the property is placed in service by the
taxpayer (without regard to any applicable convention under section 168(d));

(iii) Adapts the unit of property to a new or different use (including a permanent
structural alteration to the unit of property);

(iv) Results in a betterment (including a material increase in quality or strength) or a
35 material addition (including an enlargement, expansion, or extension) to the unit of
property; or

(v) Results in a material increase in capacity (including additional cubic or square
space), productivity, efficiency, or quality of output of the unit of property.

(2) *Exception*. Notwithstanding the rules in paragraph (e)(1)(i) through (e)(1)(v) of this
40 section, an amount paid does not result in a material increase in value to a unit of
property if the economic useful life (as defined in § 1.263(a)-3(f)(2)) of the unit of property
is 12 months or less and the taxpayer did not elect to capitalize the amounts paid
originally for the unit of property.

(3) *Appropriate comparison*. For purposes of paragraphs (e)(1)(iv) and (e)(1)(v) of this
45 section, in cases in which a particular event necessitates an expenditure, the
determination of whether the amount paid materially increases the value of the unit of
property is made by comparing the condition of the property immediately after the
expenditure with the condition of the property immediately prior to the event necessitating
the expenditure. When the event necessitating the expenditure is normal wear and tear to
50 the unit of property, the condition of the property immediately prior to the event

necessitating the expenditure is the condition of the property after the last time the taxpayer corrected the effects of normal wear and tear (whether the amounts paid were for maintenance or improvements) or, if the taxpayer has not previously corrected the effects of normal wear and tear, the condition of the property when placed in service by the taxpayer.   5

(4) *Examples.* The following examples illustrate the rules of this paragraph (e) and assume that the amounts paid are not required to be capitalized under any other provision of this section (paragraph (f), for example):

Example 1. Pre-existing condition. In 2008, X purchased a store located on 10 acres of land that contained underground gasoline storage tanks left by prior occupants. The   10 tanks had leaked, causing soil contamination. X was not aware of the contamination at the time of purchase. When X discovered the contamination, it incurred costs to remediate the soil. For purposes of this Example 1, assume the 10 acres of land is the appropriate unit of property. The amounts paid for soil remediation must be capitalized as an improvement to the land because they ameliorated a condition or defect that existed   15 prior to the taxpayer's acquisition of the land. The comparison rule in paragraph (e)(3) of this section does not apply to these amounts paid.

Example 2. Not a pre-existing condition; repair performed during an improvement. (i) X owned land on which it constructed a building in 1969 for use as a bank. The building was constructed with asbestos-containing materials. The health dangers of asbestos   20 were not widely known when the building was constructed. The presence of asbestos did not necessarily endanger the health of building occupants. The danger arises when asbestos-containing materials are damaged or disturbed, thereby releasing asbestos fibers into the air (where they can be inhaled). In 1971, Federal regulatory agencies designated asbestos a hazardous substance. In 2008, X determined it needed additional   25 space in its building to accommodate additional operations at its branch and decided to remodel the building. However, any remodeling work could not be undertaken without disturbing the asbestos-containing materials. The governmental regulations required that asbestos be removed if any remodeling was undertaking that would disturb asbestos-containing materials. Therefore, X decided to remove the asbestos-containing materials   30 from the building in coordination with the overall remodeling project.

(ii) For purposes of this Example 2, assume that the building is the appropriate unit of property and that the amounts paid to remodel are required to be capitalized under § 1.263(a)-3. The amounts paid to remove the asbestos are not required to be capitalized as a separate improvement under paragraph (e)(1)(i) of this section because the   35 asbestos, although later determined to be unsafe under certain circumstances, was not an inherent defect to the property. The removal of the asbestos, by itself, also did not result in a material increase in value under paragraphs (e)(1)(ii) through (e)(1)(v) of this section. Under paragraph (d)(5)(i) of this section, repairs that do not directly benefit or are not incurred by reason of an improvement are not required to be capitalized under   40 section 263(a). Under section 263A, all indirect costs, including otherwise deductible repair costs, that directly benefit or are incurred by reason of the improvement must be capitalized as part of the improvement. The amounts paid to remove the asbestos were incurred by reason of the remodeling project, which was an improvement. Therefore, X must capitalize under section 263A to the remodeling improvement amounts paid to   45 remove the asbestos.

Example 3. Work performed prior to placing the property in service. In 2008, X purchased a building for use as a business office. The building was in a state of disrepair. In 2009, X incurred costs to repair cement steps; shore up parts of the first and second floors; replace electrical wiring; remove and replace old plumbing; and paint the outside   50 and inside of the building. Assume all the work was performed on the building or its

Sec. 263. Capital expenditures

structural components. In 2010, X placed the building in service and began using the building as its business office. For purposes of this Example 3, assume the building and its structural components are the appropriate unit of property. The amounts paid must be capitalized as an improvement to the building because they were for work performed
5 prior to X's placing the building in service. The comparison rule in paragraph (e)(3) of this section does not apply to these amounts paid.

Example 4. Work performed prior to placing the property in service. In January 2008, X purchased new machinery for use in an existing production line of its manufacturing business. After the machinery was installed, X performed critical testing on the machinery
10 to ensure that it was operational. On November 1, 2008, the new machinery became operational and, thus, the machinery was placed in service on November 1, 2008 (although X continued to perform testing for quality control). The amounts paid must be capitalized as an improvement to the machinery because they were for work performed prior to X's placing the machinery in service. The comparison rule in paragraph (e)(3) of
15 this section does not apply to these amounts paid.

Example 5. New or different use. X is an interior decorating company and manufactures its own designs. In 2008, X decides to stop manufacturing and converts the manufacturing facility into a showroom for X's business. To convert the facility, X removes certain load-bearing walls and builds new load-bearing walls to provide a better layout for
20 the showroom and its offices. As part of building the new walls, X moves or replaces electrical, cable, and telephone wiring and paints the walls. X also repairs the floors, builds a fire escape, and performs small carpentry jobs related to making the showroom accessible, including installing ramps and widening doorways. For purposes of this Example 5, assume the building and its structural components are the unit of property
25 and that the work is performed on the structural components. The amounts paid by X to convert the manufacturing facility into a showroom must be capitalized as an improvement to the building because they adapted the building to a new or different use. The comparison rule in paragraph (e)(3) of this section does not apply to these amounts paid.

30 *Example 6. New or different use.* X owned a building consisting of five separate retail stores, each of which it rented to different tenants. In 2008, two of the stores rented became vacant and remained vacant for several months. One of the remaining tenants agreed to expand its occupancy to the two vacant stores, which adjoined its own retail store. X incurred costs to break down walls between the existing stores and construct an
35 additional rear entrance. For purposes of this Example 6, assume the building and its structural components are the appropriate unit of property. The amounts paid by X to convert three retail stores into one larger store must be capitalized because they resulted in a permanent structural alteration, and thus a new or different use, to the building. The comparison rule in paragraph (e)(3) of this section does not apply to these amounts paid.

40 *Example 7. Not a new or different use.* X owns a building for rental purposes and decides to sell it. In preparation of selling, X paints the interior walls, cleans the gutters, repairs cracks in the porch, and refinishes the hardwood floors. For purposes of this Example 7, assume the building and its structural components are the unit of property. Amounts paid for work done in anticipation of selling the building are not required to be
45 capitalized unless the amounts paid materially increase the value as defined in paragraph (e)(3) of this section or prolong the economic useful life as defined in paragraph (f)(3). The amounts paid by X are not transaction costs paid to facilitate the sale of property under § 1.263(a)-1(c), nor do they materially increase the value of the building. Although the amounts were paid for the purpose of selling the building, the sale does not constitute
50 a new or different use. Therefore, X is not required to capitalize as an improvement under paragraph (e) of this section the amounts paid for work performed on the building. The

Sec. 263. Capital expenditures

comparison rule in paragraph (e)(3) of this section does not apply to these amounts paid.

***

Example 11. Not a material increase in value; replacement with same part. X owns a small retail shop. In 2008, a storm damaged the roof of X's shop by displacing numerous wooden shingles. X decides to replace all the wooden shingles on the roof and hired a 5 contractor to replace all the shingles on the roof with new wooden shingles. No part of the sheathing, rafters, or joists was replaced. For purposes of this Example 11, assume the shop and its structural components are the appropriate unit of property. The event necessitating the expenditure was the storm. Prior to the storm, the retail shop was functioning for its intended use. The expenditure did not result in a material addition, 10 betterment, or material increase in capacity, productivity, efficiency, or quality of output of the shop compared to the condition of the shop prior to the storm, nor did it adapt the shop to a new or different use. Therefore, the amounts paid by X to reshingle the roof with wooden shingles do not materially increase the value of the shop. X is not required to capitalize as an improvement under paragraph (e) of this section amounts paid to 15 replace the shingles.

Example 12. Not a material increase in value; replacement with comparable part. Assume the same facts as in Example 11, except that wooden shingles are not available on the market. X decides to replace all the wooden shingles with comparable asphalt shingles. The amounts paid by X to reshingle the roof with asphalt shingles do not 20 materially increase the value of the shop, even though the asphalt shingles may be an improvement over the wooden shingles. Because the wooden shingles could not practicably be replaced with new wooden shingles, the replacement of the old shingles with comparable asphalt shingles does not, by itself, result in an improvement to the shop. X is not required to capitalize as an improvement under paragraph (e) of this 25 section amounts paid to replace the shingles.

Example 13. Betterment; replacement with improved parts. Assume the same facts as in Example 11, except that, instead of replacing the wooden shingles with asphalt shingles, X decides to replace all the wooden shingles with shingles made of lightweight composite materials that are maintenance-free and do not absorb moisture. The new 30 shingles have a 50-year warranty and a Class A fire rating. X must capitalize as an improvement amounts paid to reshingle the roof because they result in a betterment to the shop.

Example 14. Material increase in capacity. X owns a factory building with a storage area on the second floor. In 2008, X replaces the columns and girders supporting the 35 second floor to permit storage of supplies with a gross weight 50 percent greater than the previous load-carrying capacity of the storage area. For purposes of this Example 14, assume the factory building and its structural components are the appropriate unit of property. X must capitalize as an improvement amounts paid for the columns and girders because they result in a material increase in the load-carrying capacity of the building. 40 The comparison rule in paragraph (e)(3) of this section does not apply to these amounts paid because the expenditure was not necessitated by a particular event.

Example 15. Material increase in capacity. In 2008, X purchased harbor facilities consisting of a slip for the loading and unloading of barges and a channel leading from the slip to the river. At the time of purchase, the channel was 150 feet wide, 1,000 feet 45 long, and 10 feet deep. To allow for ingress and egress and for the unloading of its barges, X needed to deepen the channel to a depth of 20 feet. X hired a contractor to dredge the channel to the required depth. For purposes of this Example 15, assume the channel is the appropriate unit of property. X must capitalize as an improvement amounts paid for the dredging because it resulted in a material increase in the capacity of the 50 channel. The comparison rule in paragraph (e)(3) of this section does not apply to these

631

Sec. 263. Capital expenditures

amounts paid because the expenditure was not necessitated by a particular event.

Example 16. Not a material increase in capacity. Assume the same facts as in Example 15, except that the channel was susceptible to siltation and, by 2009, the channel depth had been reduced to 18 feet. X hired a contractor to redredge the channel
5 to a depth of 20 feet. The event necessitating the expenditure was the siltation of the channel. Both prior to the siltation and after the redredging, the depth of the channel was 20 feet. Therefore, the amounts paid by X for redredging the channel did not materially increase the capacity of the unit of property. X is not required to capitalize as an improvement under paragraph (e) of this section amounts paid to redredge.
10 *Example 17. Not a material increase in capacity.* X owns a building used in its trade or business. The first floor has a drop-ceiling. X decides to remove the drop-ceiling and repaint the original ceiling. For purposes of this Example 17, assume the building and its structural components are the appropriate unit of property. The removal of the drop-ceiling does not create additional capacity in the building that was not there prior to the
15 removal. Therefore, the amounts paid by X to remove the drop-ceiling and repaint the original ceiling did not materially increase the capacity of the unit of property. X is not required to capitalize as an improvement under paragraph (e) of this section amounts paid related to removing the drop-ceiling. The comparison rule in paragraph (e)(3) of this section does not apply to these amounts paid because the expenditure was not
20 necessitated by a particular event.

(f) *Restoration--(1) In general.* A taxpayer must capitalize amounts paid that restore a unit of property. Amounts paid restore property if the amounts paid substantially (as defined in paragraph (f)(3) of this section) prolong the economic useful life of the unit of property.
25 (2) *Economic useful life--(i) Taxpayers with an applicable financial statement.* For taxpayers with an applicable financial statement (as defined in paragraph (f)(2)(iii) of this section), the economic useful life of a unit of property generally is presumed to be the same as the useful life used by the taxpayer for purposes of determining (at the time the property is originally acquired or produced by the taxpayer) depreciation in its applicable
30 financial statement, regardless of any salvage value of the property. A taxpayer may rebut this presumption only if there is a clear and convincing basis that the economic useful life (as defined in paragraph (f)(2)(ii) of this section for taxpayers without an applicable financial statement) of the unit of property is significantly different than the useful life used by the taxpayer for purposes of determining depreciation in its applicable financial
35 statement. If a taxpayer does not have an applicable financial statement at the time the property was originally acquired or produced, but does have an applicable financial statement at some later date, the economic useful life of the unit of property must be determined under paragraph (f)(2)(ii) of this section. Further, if a taxpayer treats amounts paid for a unit of property as an expense in its applicable financial statement on a basis
40 other than the property having a useful life of one year or less, the economic useful life of the unit of property must be determined under paragraph (f)(2)(ii) of this section. For example, if a taxpayer has a policy of treating as an expense on its applicable financial statement amounts paid for property costing less than a certain dollar amount, notwithstanding that the property has a useful life of more than one year, the economic
45 useful life of the property must be determined under paragraph (f)(2)(ii) of this section.

(ii) *Taxpayers without an applicable financial statement.* For taxpayers that do not have an applicable financial statement (as defined in paragraph (f)(2)(iii) of this section), the economic useful life of a unit of property is not necessarily the useful life inherent in the property but is the period over which the property may reasonably be expected to be
50 useful to the taxpayer or, if the taxpayer is engaged in a trade or business or an activity for the production of *income*, the period over which the property may reasonably be

632

Sec. 263. Capital expenditures

expected to be useful to the taxpayer in its trade or business or for the production of *income*, as applicable. This period is determined by reference to the taxpayer's experience with similar property, taking into account present conditions and probable future developments. Factors to be considered in determining this period include, but are not limited to--　5

(A) Wear and tear and decay or decline from natural causes;

(B) The normal progress of the art, economic changes, inventions, and current developments within the industry and the taxpayer's trade or business;

(C) The climatic and other local conditions peculiar to the taxpayer's trade or business; and　10

(D) The taxpayer's policy as to repairs, renewals, and replacements.

(iii) *Definition of ``applicable financial statement''*. The taxpayer's applicable financial statement is the taxpayer's financial statement listed in paragraphs (f)(2)(ii)(A) through (C) of this section that has the highest priority (including within paragraph (f)(2)(ii)(B) of this section). The financial statements are, in descending priority--　15

(A) A financial statement required to be filed with the Securities and Exchange Commission (SEC) (the 10-K or the Annual Statement to Shareholders);

(B) A certified audited financial statement that is accompanied by the report of an independent CPA (or in the case of a foreign entity, by the report of a similarly qualified independent professional), that is used for--　20

(1) Credit purposes,

(2) Reporting to shareholders, partners, or similar persons; or

(3) Any other substantial non-*tax* purpose; or

(C) A financial statement (other than a *tax* return) required to be provided to the Federal or a state government or any Federal or state agencies (other than the SEC or 　25 the Internal Revenue Service).

(3) *Substantially prolonging economic useful life*--(i) *In general.* An amount paid substantially prolongs the economic useful life of the unit of property if it extends the period over which the property may reasonably be expected to be useful to the taxpayer in its trade or business or for the production of *income*, as applicable (or, if the taxpayer 　30 is not engaged in a trade or business or an activity for the production of *income*, the period over which the property may reasonably be expected to be useful to the taxpayer) beyond the end of the taxable year immediately succeeding the taxable year in which the economic useful life of the unit of property was originally expected to cease, or if the property's economic useful life was previously prolonged (as determined under this 　35 paragraph (e)(3)(i)), the end of the taxable year immediately succeeding the taxable year in which the prolonged economic useful life was expected to cease.

(ii) *Replacements.* Amounts paid will be deemed to substantially prolong the economic useful life of the unit of property if a major component or a substantial structural part of the unit of property is replaced with either a new part or a part that has been restored to 　40 like-new condition as described in paragraph (f)(3)(iii) of this section. Thus, the replacement of a part with another part that is not new or is not in like-new condition (for example, a used or reconditioned part) does not constitute the replacement of a major component or substantial structural part of the unit of property under this paragraph (f)(3) (ii). Further, replacement of a relatively minor portion of the physical structure of the unit 　45 of property or a relatively minor portion of any of its major parts, even if those parts are new, does not constitute the replacement of a major component or substantial structural part of the unit of property.

(iii) *Restoration to like-new condition.* Amounts paid will be deemed to substantially prolong the economic useful life of the unit of property if they result in the unit of property 　50 or a major component or substantial structural part of the unit of property being restored

633

Sec. 263. Capital expenditures

to a like-new condition (including bringing the unit of property or a major component or substantial structural part of the property to the status of new, rebuilt, remanufactured, or similar status under the terms of any Federal regulatory guideline or the manufacturer's original specifications).

5   (iv) *Restoration after a casualty loss.* Amounts paid will be deemed to substantially prolong the useful life of the unit of property if the taxpayer properly deducts a casualty loss under section 165 with respect to the unit of property and the amounts paid restore the unit of property to a condition that is the same or better than before the casualty.

    (4) *Examples.* The following examples illustrate the rules of this paragraph (f) and,
10 except as otherwise provided, assume that the amounts paid would not be required to be capitalized under any other provision of this section (paragraph (e), for example):

    Example 1. Prolonged economic useful life. X is a Class I railroad that owns a fleet of locomotives. In 1989, X purchased a new locomotive with an economic useful life (as defined in paragraph (f)(2) of this section) of 22 years (from 1989-2011). X performs
15 substantially the same cyclical maintenance on its locomotives approximately every 6 years. X performed cyclical maintenance on the locomotive in 1995, in 2001, and in 2007. Assume that the locomotive (which includes the engine) is the appropriate unit of property and that none of the cyclical maintenance projects resulted in a restoration under paragraph (f)(3)(ii) or (f)(3)(iii) of this section. Amounts paid for cyclical
20 maintenance in 1995 and 2001 do not substantially prolong the economic useful life of the locomotive. However, the cyclical maintenance performed in 2007 will prolong the economic useful life of the locomotive to 2013, which is beyond the end of the next succeeding taxable year after the economic useful life of the locomotive ceases (2011). Therefore, under paragraphs (f)(1) and (f)(3)(i) of this section, X must capitalize as an
25 improvement to the locomotive amounts paid for the cyclical maintenance performed in 2007, regardless of whether X was required to capitalize the amounts paid in previous years for cyclical maintenance.

    Example 2. Economic useful life not prolonged. Assume the same facts as in Example 1, except that in 2009, X replaces a filter in the locomotive engine. X generally replaces
30 this type of filter every 4 years. Although the filter itself would last beyond the end of the locomotive's economic useful life in 2011, the amount paid for the filter does not substantially prolong the economic useful life of the locomotive because the filter will not extend beyond 2009 the period over which the locomotive may reasonably be expected to be useful to X in its trade or business. Additionally, although the filter is a necessary
35 component of the locomotive, the filter is not a substantial structural part or major component of the locomotive. Therefore, the amount paid to replace the filter does not substantially prolong the economic useful life of the locomotive.

    Example 3. Minor part replacement. X owns a small retail shop. In 2008, a storm damaged the roof of X's shop by displacing numerous wooden shingles. X decides to
40 replace all the wooden shingles on the roof and hires a contractor to replace all the shingles on the roof with new wooden shingles. No part of the sheathing, rafters, or joists was replaced. For purposes of this Example 3, assume the shop and its structural components are the appropriate unit of property. The replacement of the shingles did not extend the useful life of the shop under paragraph (f)(3)(i) of this section. The portion of
45 the roof replaced is not a substantial structural part of the shop, nor does the replacement of the shingles restore to a like-new condition a major component or substantial structural part of the shop. Therefore, the amounts paid by X to reshingle the roof with wooden shingles do not substantially prolong the economic useful life of the shop.

    Example 4. Major component or substantial structural part. Assume the same facts as
50 in Example 3, except that when the contractor began work on the shingles, the contractor discovered that a major portion of the sheathing had rotted, and the rafters were

Sec. 263.   Capital expenditures

weakened as well. The contractor replaced all the sheathing and a significant portion of the rafters. The roof (including the shingles, sheathing, rafters, and joists) is a substantial structural part of a building. The replacement of the shingles, sheathing, and rafters restored to a like-new condition a substantial structural part of the shop. Therefore, under paragraphs (f)(1) and (f)(3)(iii) of this section, X must capitalize as an improvement to the shop amounts paid to replace the roof of the shop. 5

Example 5. Not a major component or structural part. X uses a car in providing a taxi service. X purchased the car in 2008. Assume that the unit of property is the car. The car has an economic useful life of 5 years. In 2011, the battery dies and X takes the car to a repair shop, which replaces the battery. Although the battery itself may last beyond the 10 end of the car's economic useful life, the amount paid for the battery does not substantially prolong the economic useful life of the car because the battery will not extend beyond 2013 the period over which the car may reasonably be expected to be useful to X in its trade or business. Although the battery is a necessary component of the car, the battery is not a substantial structural part or major component of the car. 15 Therefore, the amount paid to replace the battery does not substantially prolong the economic useful life of the car.

Example 6. Major component or structural part. Assume the same facts as Example 5, except rather than the battery dying, the car overheats and causes so much damage that the engine has to be rebuilt. The engine is a major component of the car. Therefore, X is 20 required to capitalize as an improvement to the car under paragraphs (f)(1) and (f)(3)(iii) of this section the amounts paid to rebuild the engine.

Example 7. Repair performed during an improvement; coordination with section 263A. Assume the same facts as Example 6, except that X has a broken taillight fixed at the same time that the engine was rebuilt. The repair to the taillight was not incurred because 25 the engine was rebuilt, nor did it benefit the rebuild of the engine. The repair of the broken taillight is a deductible expense under § 1.162-4. Under section 263A, all indirect costs, including otherwise deductible repair and maintenance costs that directly benefit or are incurred by reason of the improvement must be capitalized as part of the improvement. Therefore, all amounts paid that are incurred by reason of the engine being 30 rebuilt must be capitalized, including, for example, amounts paid for activities that would usually be deductible maintenance expenses, such as refilling the engine with oil and radiator fluid. Amounts paid to repair the broken taillight, however, are not incurred by reason of the engine being rebuilt, nor do the amounts paid directly benefit the engine rebuild, despite being repaired at the same time. Thus, X is not required to capitalize to 35 the improvement of the car (the rebuild of the engine) the amounts paid to repair the broken taillight.

***

Sec. 263A.   Capitalization and inclusion in inventory costs of certain expenses

(a) Nondeductibility of certain direct and indirect costs. -- 40

    (1) In general. -- In the case of any property to which this section applies, any costs described in paragraph (2)--

        (A) in the case of property which is inventory in the hands of the taxpayer, shall be included in inventory costs, and

        (B) in the case of any other property, shall be capitalized. 45

    (2) Allocable costs. -- The costs described in this paragraph with respect to any property

Sec. 263A. Capitalization and inclusion in inventory costs of certain expenses

are-

   (A) the direct costs of such property, and

   (B) such property's proper share of those indirect costs (including taxes) part or all of which are allocable to such property.

5 Any cost which (but for this subsection) could not be taken into account in computing taxable income for any taxable year shall not be treated as a cost described in this paragraph.

   (b) Property to which section applies. -- Except as otherwise provided in this section, this section shall apply to--

   (1) Property produced by taxpayer. -- Real or tangible personal property produced by the
10 taxpayer.

   (2) Property acquired for resale. --

   (A) In general. -- Real or personal property described in section 1221(a)(1) which is acquired by the taxpayer for resale.

   (B) Exception for taxpayer with gross receipts of $10,000,000 or less. --
15 Subparagraph (A) shall not apply to any personal property acquired during any taxable year by the taxpayer for resale if the average annual gross receipts of the taxpayer (or any predecessor) for the 3-taxable year period ending with the taxable year preceding such taxable year do not exceed $10,000,000.

***

20 For purposes of paragraph (1), the term "tangible personal property" shall include a film, sound recording, video tape, book, or similar property.

   (c) General exceptions. --

   (1) Personal use property. -- This section shall not apply to any property produced by the taxpayer for use by the taxpayer other than in a trade or business or an activity conducted for
25 profit.

   (2) Research and experimental expenditures. -- This section shall not apply to any amount allowable as a deduction under section 174.

   (3) Certain development and other costs of oil and gas wells or other mineral property.-- This section shall not apply to any cost allowable as a deduction under section
30 179B, 263(c), 263(i), 291(b)(2), 616, or 617.

***

   (f) Special rules for allocation of interest to property produced by the taxpayer. --

   (1) Interest capitalized only in certain cases. -- Subsection (a) shall only apply to interest costs which are--

35   (A) paid or incurred during the production period, and

   (B) allocable to property which is described in subsection (b)(1) and which has -

      (i) a long useful life,

      (ii) an estimated production period exceeding 2 years, or

      (iii) an estimated production period exceeding 1 year and a cost exceeding
40       $1,000,000.

   (2) Allocation rules. --

   (A) In general. -- In determining the amount of interest required to be capitalized under subsection (a) with respect to any property--

      (i) interest on any indebtedness directly attributable to production expenditures with

636

Sec. 263A. Capitalization and inclusion in inventory costs of certain expenses

respect to such property shall be assigned to such property, and

(ii) interest on any other indebtedness shall be assigned to such property to the extent that the taxpayer's interest costs could have been reduced if production expenditures (not attributable to indebtedness described in clause (i)) had not been incurred.

(B) Exception for qualified residence interest. -- Subparagraph (A) shall not apply to 5 any qualified residence interest (within the meaning of section 163(h)).

***

(3) Interest relating to property used to produce property. -- This subsection shall apply to any interest on indebtedness allocable (as determined under paragraph (2)) to property used to produce property to which this subsection applies to the extent such interest is allocable (as 10 so determined) to the produced property.

(4) Definitions. -- For purposes of this subsection--

(A) **Long useful life.** -- Property has a long useful life if such property is--

(i) real property, or

(ii) property with a class life of 20 years or more (as determined under section 168). 15

(B) **Production period.** -- The term "production period" means, when used with respect to any property, the period--

(i) beginning on the date on which production of the property begins, and

(ii) ending on the date on which the property is ready to be placed in service or is ready to be held for sale. 20

(C) **Production expenditures.** -- The term "production expenditures" means the costs (whether or not incurred during the production period) required to be capitalized under subsection (a) with respect to the property.

(g) Production. -- For purposes of this section--

(1) In general. -- The term "produce" includes construct, build, install, manufacture, 25 develop, or improve.

(2) Treatment of property produced under contract for the taxpayer. -- The taxpayer shall be treated as producing any property produced for the taxpayer under a contract with the taxpayer; except that only costs paid or incurred by the taxpayer (whether under such contract or otherwise) shall be taken into account in applying subsection (a) to the taxpayer. 30

(h) Exemption for free lance authors, photographers, and artists. --

(1) In general. -- Nothing in this section shall require the capitalization of any qualified creative expense.

(2) Qualified creative expense. -- For purposes of this subsection, the term "qualified creative expense" means any expense-- 35

(A) which is paid or incurred by an individual in the trade or business of such individual (other than as an employee) of being a writer, photographer, or artist, and

(B) which, without regard to this section, would be allowable as a deduction for the taxable year.

Such term does not include any expense related to printing, photographic plates, motion 40 picture films, video tapes, or similar items.

(3) Definitions. -- For purposes of this subsection--

(A) **Writer.** -- The term "writer" means any individual if the personal efforts of such individual create (or may reasonably be expected to create) a literary manuscript, musical

637

Sec. 263A. Capitalization and inclusion in inventory costs of certain expenses

composition (including any accompanying words), or dance score.

(B) Photographer. -- The term "photographer" means any individual if the personal efforts of such individual create (or may reasonably be expected to create) a photograph or photographic negative or transparency.

5   **(C) Artist.** --

(i) In general. -- The term "artist" means any individual if the personal efforts of such individual create (or may reasonably be expected to create) a picture, painting, sculpture, statue, etching, drawing, cartoon, graphic design, or original print edition.

(ii) Criteria. -- In determining whether any expense is paid or incurred in the trade or 10   business of being an artist, the following criteria shall be taken into account:

(I) The originality and uniqueness of the item created (or to be created).

(II) The predominance of aesthetic value over utilitarian value of the item created (or to be created).

***

15 **Reg. § 1.263A-1   Uniform capitalization of costs.**

***

(c) *General operation of section 263A*--(1) *Allocations.* Under section 263A, taxpayers must capitalize their direct costs and a properly allocable share of their indirect costs to property produced or property acquired for resale. In order to determine these 20 capitalizable costs, taxpayers must allocate or apportion costs to various activities, including production or resale activities. After section 263A costs are allocated to the appropriate production or resale activities, these costs are generally allocated to the items of property produced or property acquired for resale during the taxable year and capitalized to the items that remain on hand at the end of the taxable year. See however, 25 the simplified production method and the simplified resale method in §§ 1.263A-2(b) and 1.263A-3(d).

(2) *Otherwise deductible.* (i) Any cost which (but for section 263A and the regulations thereunder) may not be taken into account in computing taxable income for any taxable year is not treated as a cost properly allocable to property produced or acquired for 30 resale under section 263A and the regulations thereunder. Thus, for example, if a business meal deduction is limited by section 274(n) to 80 percent of the cost of the meal, the amount properly allocable to property produced or acquired for resale under section 263A is also limited to 80 percent of the cost of the meal.

(ii) The amount of any cost required to be capitalized under section 263A may not be 35 included in inventory or charged to capital accounts or basis any earlier than the taxable year during which the amount is incurred within the meaning of § 1.446-1(c)(1)(ii).

(3) *Capitalize.* Capitalize means, in the case of property that is inventory in the hands of a taxpayer, to include in inventory costs and, in the case of other property, to charge to a capital account or basis.

40   (4) *Recovery of capitalized costs.* Costs that are capitalized under section 263A are recovered through depreciation, amortization, cost of goods sold, or by an adjustment to basis at the time the property is used, sold, placed in service, or otherwise disposed of by the taxpayer. Cost recovery is determined by the applicable Internal Revenue Code and regulation provisions relating to the use, sale, or disposition of property.

45   ***

(e) *Types of costs subject to capitalization*--(1) *In general.* Taxpayers subject to section 263A must capitalize all direct costs and certain indirect costs properly allocable to property produced or property acquired for resale. This paragraph (e) describes the types of costs subject to section 263A.

(2) *Direct costs*--(i) *Producers.* Producers must capitalize direct material costs and direct labor costs.

(A) Direct material costs include the costs of those materials that become an integral 5 part of specific property produced and those materials that are consumed in the ordinary course of production and that can be identified or associated with particular units or groups of units of property produced.

(B) Direct labor costs include the costs of labor that can be identified or associated with particular units or groups of units of specific property produced. For this purpose, 10 labor encompasses full-time and part-time employees, as well as contract employees and independent contractors. Direct labor costs include all elements of compensation other than employee benefit costs described in paragraph (e)(3)(ii)(D) of this section. Elements of direct labor costs include basic compensation, overtime pay, vacation pay, holiday pay, sick leave pay (other than payments pursuant to a wage continuation plan under section 15 105(d) as it existed prior to its repeal in 1983), shift differential, payroll taxes, and payments to a supplemental unemployment benefit plan.

(ii) *Resellers.* Resellers must capitalize the acquisition costs of property acquired for resale. In the case of inventory, the acquisition cost is the cost described in § 1.471-3(b).

(3) *Indirect costs*--(i) *In general.* Indirect costs are defined as all costs other than direct 20 material costs and direct labor costs (in the case of property produced) or acquisition costs (in the case of property acquired for resale). Taxpayers subject to section 263A must capitalize all indirect costs properly allocable to property produced or property acquired for resale. Indirect costs are properly allocable to property produced or property acquired for resale when the costs directly benefit or are incurred by reason of the 25 performance of production or resale activities. Indirect costs may be allocable to both production and resale activities, as well as to other activities that are not subject to section 263A. Taxpayers subject to section 263A must make a reasonable allocation of indirect costs between production, resale, and other activities.

(ii) *Examples of indirect costs required to be capitalized.* The following are examples 30 of indirect costs that must be capitalized to the extent they are properly allocable to property produced or property acquired for resale:

(A) *Indirect labor costs.* Indirect labor costs include all labor costs (including the elements of labor costs set forth in paragraph (e)(2)(i) of this section) that cannot be directly identified or associated with particular units or groups of units of specific property 35 produced or property acquired for resale (e.g., factory labor that is not direct labor). As in the case of direct labor, indirect labor encompasses full-time and part-time employees, as well as contract employees and independent contractors.

(B) *Officers' compensation.* Officers' compensation includes compensation paid to officers of the taxpayer.   40

(C) *Pension and other related costs.* Pension and other related costs include contributions paid to or made under any stock bonus, pension, profit-sharing or annuity plan, or other plan deferring the receipt of compensation, whether or not the plan qualifies under section 401(a). Contributions to employee plans representing past services must be capitalized in the same manner (and in the same proportion to property currently 45 being acquired or produced) as amounts contributed for current service.

(D) *Employee benefit expenses.* Employee benefit expenses include all other employee benefit expenses (not described in paragraph (e)(3)(ii)(C) of this section) to the extent such expenses are otherwise allowable as deductions under chapter 1 of the Internal Revenue Code. These other employee benefit expenses include: worker's 50

compensation; amounts otherwise deductible or allowable in reducing earnings and profits under section 404A; payments pursuant to a wage continuation plan under section 105(d) as it existed prior to its repeal in 1983; amounts includible in the gross income of employees under a method or arrangement of employer contributions or compensation
5 that has the effect of a stock bonus, pension, profit-sharing or annuity plan, or other plan deferring receipt of compensation or providing deferred benefits; premiums on life and health insurance; and miscellaneous benefits provided for employees such as safety, medical treatment, recreational and eating facilities, membership dues, etc. Employee benefit expenses do not, however, include direct labor costs described in paragraph (e)
10 (2)(i) of this section.

(E) *Indirect material costs.* Indirect material costs include the cost of materials that are not an integral part of specific property produced and the cost of materials that are consumed in the ordinary course of performing production or resale activities that cannot be identified or associated with particular units or groups of units of property. Thus, for
15 example, a cost described in § 1.162-3, relating to the cost of a material or supply, is an indirect material cost.

(F) *Purchasing costs.* Purchasing costs include costs attributable to purchasing activities. See § 1.263A-3(c)(3) for a further discussion of purchasing costs.

(G) *Handling costs.* Handling costs include costs attributable to processing,
20 assembling, repackaging and transporting goods, and other similar activities. See § 1.263A-3(c)(4) for a further discussion of handling costs.

(H) *Storage costs.* Storage costs include the costs of carrying, storing, or warehousing property. See § 1.263A-3(c)(5) for a further discussion of storage costs.

(I) *Cost recovery.* Cost recovery includes depreciation, amortization, and cost
25 recovery allowances on equipment and facilities (including depreciation or amortization of self-constructed assets or other previously produced or acquired property to which section 263A or section 263 applies).

(J) *Depletion.* Depletion includes allowances for depletion, whether or not in excess of cost. Depletion is, however, only properly allocable to property that has been sold (i.e., for
30 purposes of determining gain or loss on the sale of the property).

(K) *Rent.* Rent includes the cost of renting or leasing equipment, facilities, or land.

(L) *Taxes.* Taxes include those taxes (other than taxes described in paragraph (e)(3) (iii)(F) of this section) that are otherwise allowable as a deduction to the extent such taxes are attributable to labor, materials, supplies, equipment, land, or facilities used in
35 production or resale activities.

(M) *Insurance.* Insurance includes the cost of insurance on plant or facility, machinery, equipment, materials, property produced, or property acquired for resale.

(N) *Utilities.* Utilities include the cost of electricity, gas, and water.

(O) *Repairs and maintenance.* Repairs and maintenance include the cost of repairing
40 and maintaining equipment or facilities.

(P) *Engineering and design costs.* Engineering and design costs include pre-production costs, such as costs attributable to research, experimental, engineering, and design activities (to the extent that such amounts are not research and experimental expenditures as described in section 174 and the regulations thereunder).
45 (Q) *Spoilage.* Spoilage includes the costs of rework labor, scrap, and spoilage.

(R) *Tools and equipment.* Tools and equipment include the costs of tools and equipment which are not otherwise capitalized.

(S) *Quality control.* Quality control includes the costs of quality control and inspection.

(T) *Bidding costs.* Bidding costs are costs incurred in the solicitation of contracts
50 (including contracts pertaining to property acquired for resale) ultimately awarded to the

Sec. 263A. Capitalization and inclusion in inventory costs of certain expenses

taxpayer. The taxpayer must defer all bidding costs paid or incurred in the solicitation of a particular contract until the contract is awarded. If the contract is awarded to the taxpayer, the bidding costs become part of the indirect costs allocated to the subject matter of the contract. If the contract is not awarded to the taxpayer, bidding costs are deductible in the taxable year that the contract is awarded to another party, or in the taxable year that the 5 taxpayer is notified in writing that no contract will be awarded and that the contract (or a similar or related contract) will not be rebid, or in the taxable year that the taxpayer abandons its bid or proposal, whichever occurs first. Abandoning a bid does not include modifying, supplementing, or changing the original bid or proposal. If the taxpayer is awarded only part of the bid (for example, the taxpayer submitted one bid to build each of 10 two different types of products, and the taxpayer was awarded a contract to build only one of the two types of products), the taxpayer shall deduct the portion of the bidding costs related to the portion of the bid not awarded to the taxpayer. In the case of a bid or proposal for a multi-unit contract, all bidding costs must be included in the costs allocated to the subject matter of the contract awarded to the taxpayer to produce or acquire for 15 resale any of such units. For example, where the taxpayer submits one bid to produce three similar turbines and the taxpayer is awarded a contract to produce only two of the three turbines, all bidding costs must be included in the cost of the two turbines. For purposes of this paragraph (e)(3)(ii)(T), a contract means--

(1) In the case of a specific unit of property, any agreement under which the taxpayer 20 would produce or sell property to another party if the agreement is entered into before the taxpayer produces or acquires the specific unit of property to be delivered to the party under the agreement; and

(2) In the case of fungible property, any agreement to the extent that, at the time the agreement is entered into, the taxpayer has on hand an insufficient quantity of completed 25 fungible items of such property that may be used to satisfy the agreement (plus any other production or sales agreements of the taxpayer).

(U) *Licensing and franchise costs.* Licensing and franchise costs include fees incurred in securing the contractual right to use a trademark, corporate plan, manufacturing procedure, special recipe, or other similar right associated with property produced or 30 property acquired for resale. These costs include the otherwise deductible portion (e.g., amortization) of the initial fees incurred to obtain the license or franchise and any minimum annual payments and royalties that are incurred by a licensee or a franchisee.

(V) *Interest.* Interest includes interest on debt incurred or continued during the production period to finance the production of real property or tangible personal property 35 to which section 263A(f) applies.

(W) *Capitalizable service costs.* Service costs that are required to be capitalized include capitalizable service costs and capitalizable mixed service costs as defined in paragraph (e)(4) of this section.

(iii) *Indirect costs not capitalized.* The following indirect costs are not required to be 40 capitalized under section 263A:

(A) *Selling and distribution costs.* These costs are marketing, selling, advertising, and distribution costs.

(B) *Research and experimental expenditures.* Research and experimental expenditures are expenditures described in section 174 and the regulations thereunder. 45

(C) Section 179 costs. Section 179 costs are expenses for certain depreciable assets deductible at the election of the taxpayer under section 179 and the regulations thereunder.

(D) *Section 165 losses.* Section 165 losses are losses under section 165 and the regulations thereunder. 50

Sec. 263A.   Capitalization and inclusion in inventory costs of certain expenses

(E) *Cost recovery allowances on temporarily idle equipment and facilities--(1) In general.* Cost recovery allowances on temporarily idle equipment and facilities include only depreciation, amortization, and cost recovery allowances on equipment and facilities that have been placed in service but are temporarily idle. Equipment and facilities are

5 temporarily idle when a taxpayer takes them out of service for a finite period. However, equipment and facilities are not considered temporarily idle--

(i) During worker breaks, non-working hours, or on regularly scheduled non-working days (such as holidays or weekends);

(ii) During normal interruptions in the operation of the equipment or facilities;

10 (iii) When equipment is en route to or located at a job site; or

(iv) When under normal operating conditions, the equipment is used or operated only during certain shifts.

(2) *Examples.* The provisions of this paragraph (e)(3)(iii)(E) are illustrated by the following examples:

15 *Example 1.* Equipment operated only during certain shifts. Taxpayer A manufactures widgets. Although A's manufacturing facility operates 24 hours each day in three shifts, A only operates its stamping machine during one shift each day. Because A only operates its stamping machine during certain shifts, A's stamping machine is not considered temporarily idle during the two shifts that it is not operated.

20 *Example 2.* Facility shut down for retooling. Taxpayer B owns and operates a manufacturing facility. B closes its manufacturing facility for two weeks to retool its assembly line. B's manufacturing facility is considered temporarily idle during this two-week period.

(F) *Taxes assessed on the basis of income.* Taxes assessed on the basis of income

25 include only state, local, and foreign income taxes, and franchise taxes that are assessed on the taxpayer based on income.

(G) *Strike expenses.* Strike expenses include only costs associated with hiring employees to replace striking personnel (but not wages of replacement personnel), costs of security, and legal fees associated with settling strikes.

30 (H) *Warranty and product liability costs.* Warranty costs and product liability costs are costs incurred in fulfilling product warranty obligations for products that have been sold and costs incurred for product liability insurance.

(I) *On-site storage costs.* On-site storage costs are storage and warehousing costs incurred by a taxpayer at an on-site storage facility, as defined in § 1.263A-3(c)(5)(ii)(A),

35 with respect to property produced or property acquired for resale.

(J) *Unsuccessful bidding expenses.* Unsuccessful bidding costs are bidding expenses incurred in the solicitation of contracts not awarded to the taxpayer.

(K) *Deductible service costs.* Service costs that are not required to be capitalized include deductible service costs and deductible mixed service costs as defined in

40 paragraph (e)(4) of this section.

(4) *Service costs--(i) Introduction.* This paragraph (e)(4) provides definitions and categories of service costs. Paragraph (g)(4) of this section provides specific rules for determining the amount of service costs allocable to property produced or property acquired for resale. In addition, paragraph (h) of this section provides a simplified method

45 for determining the amount of service costs that must be capitalized.

(A) *Definition of service costs.* Service costs are defined as a type of indirect costs (e.g., general and administrative costs) that can be identified specifically with a service department or function or that directly benefit or are incurred by reason of a service department or function.

642

Sec. 263A. Capitalization and inclusion in inventory costs of certain expenses

(B) *Definition of service departments.* Service departments are defined as administrative, service, or support departments that incur service costs. The facts and circumstances of the taxpayer's activities and business organization control whether a department is a service department. For example, service departments include personnel, accounting, data processing, security, legal, and other similar departments.   5

(ii) *Various service cost categories--*(A) *Capitalizable service costs.* Capitalizable service costs are defined as service costs that directly benefit or are incurred by reason of the performance of the production or resale activities of the taxpayer. Therefore, these service costs are required to be capitalized under section 263A. Examples of service departments or functions that incur capitalizable service costs are provided in paragraph 10 (e)(4)(iii) of this section.

(B) *Deductible service costs.* Deductible service costs are defined as service costs that do not directly benefit or are not incurred by reason of the performance of the production or resale activities of the taxpayer, and therefore, are not required to be capitalized under section 263A. Deductible service costs generally include costs incurred 15 by reason of the taxpayer's overall management or policy guidance functions. In addition, deductible service costs include costs incurred by reason of the marketing, selling, advertising, and distribution activities of the taxpayer. Examples of service departments or functions that incur deductible service costs are provided in paragraph (e)(4)(iv) of this section.   20

(C) *Mixed service costs.* Mixed service costs are defined as service costs that are partially allocable to production or resale activities (capitalizable mixed service costs) and partially allocable to non-production or non-resale activities (deductible mixed service costs). For example, a personnel department may incur costs to recruit factory workers, the costs of which are allocable to production activities, and it may incur costs to develop 25 wage, salary, and benefit policies, the costs of which are allocable to non-production activities.

(iii) *Examples of capitalizable service costs.* Costs incurred in the following departments or functions are generally allocated among production or resale activities:

(A) The administration and coordination of production or resale activities (wherever 30 performed in the business organization of the taxpayer).

(B) Personnel operations, including the cost of recruiting, hiring, relocating, assigning, and maintaining personnel records or employees.

(C) Purchasing operations, including purchasing materials and equipment, scheduling and coordinating delivery of materials and equipment to or from factories or job sites, and 35 expediting and follow-up.

(D) Materials handling and warehousing and storage operations.

(E) Accounting and data services operations, including, for example, cost accounting, accounts payable, disbursements, and payroll functions (but excluding accounts receivable and customer billing functions).   40

(F) Data processing.

(G) Security services.

(H) Legal services.

(iv) *Examples of deductible service costs.* Costs incurred in the following departments or functions are not generally allocated to production or resale activities: 45

(A) Departments or functions responsible for overall management of the taxpayer or for setting overall policy for all of the taxpayer's activities or trades or businesses, such as the board of directors (including their immediate staff), and the chief executive, financial, accounting, and legal officers (including their immediate staff) of the taxpayer, provided that no substantial part of the cost of such departments or functions benefits a particular 50

Sec. 263A. Capitalization and inclusion in inventory costs of certain expenses

production or resale activity.

(B) Strategic business planning.

(C) General financial accounting.

(D) General financial planning (including general budgeting) and financial
5 management (including bank relations and cash management).

(E) Personnel policy (such as establishing and managing personnel policy in general;
developing wage, salary, and benefit policies; developing employee training programs
unrelated to particular production or resale activities; negotiating with labor unions; and
maintaining relations with retired workers).

10 (F) Quality control policy.

(G) Safety engineering policy.

(H) Insurance or risk management policy (but not including bid or performance bonds
or insurance related to activities associated with property produced or property acquired
for resale).

15 (I) Environmental management policy (except to the extent that the costs of any
system or procedure benefits a particular production or resale activity).

(J) General economic analysis and forecasting.

(K) Internal audit.

(L) Shareholder, public, and industrial relations.

20 (M) Tax services.

(N) Marketing, selling, or advertising.

***

Reg. § 1.263A-2 Rules relating to property produced by the taxpayer.

(a) *In general.* Section 263A applies to real property and tangible personal property
25 produced by a taxpayer for use in its trade or business or for sale to its customers. In
addition, section 263A applies to property produced for a taxpayer under a contract with
another party. The principal terms related to the scope of section 263A with respect to
producers are provided in this paragraph (a). See § 1.263A-1(b)(11) for an exception in
the case of certain de minimis property provided to customers incident to the provision of
30 services.

(1) *Produce--(i) In general.* For purposes of section 263A, produce includes the
following: construct, build, install, manufacture, develop, improve, create, raise, or grow.

***

(2) *Tangible personal property--(i) General rule.* In general, section 263A applies to the
35 costs of producing tangible personal property, and not to the costs of producing intangible
property. For example, section 263A applies to the costs manufacturers incur to produce
goods, but does not apply to the costs financial institutions incur to originate loans.

(ii) *Intellectual or creative property.* For purposes of determining whether a taxpayer
producing intellectual or creative property is producing tangible personal property or
40 intangible property, the term tangible personal property includes films, sound recordings,
video tapes, books, and other similar property embodying words, ideas, concepts,
images, or sounds by the creator thereof. Other similar property for this purpose
generally means intellectual or creative property for which, as costs are incurred in
producing the property, it is intended (or is reasonably likely) that any tangible medium in
45 which the property is embodied will be mass distributed by the creator or any one or more
third parties in a form that is not substantially altered. However, any intellectual or
creative property that is embodied in a tangible medium that is mass distributed merely
incident to the distribution of a principal product or good of the creator is not other similar
property for these purposes.

644

Sec. 263A. Capitalization and inclusion in inventory costs of certain expenses

(A) *Intellectual or creative property that is tangible personal property*. Section 263A applies to tangible personal property defined in this paragraph (a)(2) without regard to whether such property is treated as tangible or intangible property under other sections of the Internal Revenue Code. Thus, for example, section 263A applies to the costs of producing a motion picture or researching and writing a book even though these assets 5 may be considered intangible for other purposes of the Internal Revenue Code. Tangible personal property includes, for example, the following:

(1) *Books*. The costs of producing and developing books (including teaching aids and other literary works) required to be capitalized under this section include costs incurred by an author in researching, preparing, and writing the book. (However, see section 10 263A(h), which provides an exemption from the capitalization requirements of section 263A in the case of certain free-lance authors.) In addition, the costs of producing and developing books include prepublication expenditures incurred by publishers, including payments made to authors (other than commissions for sales of books that have already taken place), as well as costs incurred by publishers in writing, editing, compiling, 15 illustrating, designing, and developing the books. The costs of producing a book also include the costs of producing the underlying manuscript, copyright, or license. (These costs are distinguished from the separately capitalizable costs of printing and binding the tangible medium embodying the book (e.g., paper and ink).) See § 1.174-2(a)(1), which provides that the term research or experimental expenditures does not include 20 expenditures incurred for research in connection with literary, historical, or similar projects.

(2) *Sound recordings*. A sound recording is a work that results from the fixation of a series of musical, spoken, or other sounds, regardless of the nature of the material objects, such as discs, tapes, or other phono recordings, in which such sounds are 25 embodied.

(B) Intellectual or creative property that is not tangible personal property. Items that are not considered tangible personal property within the meaning of section 263A(b) and paragraph (a)(2)(ii) of this section include:

(1) *Evidences of value*. Tangible personal property does not include property that is 30 representative or evidence of value, such as stock, securities, debt instruments, mortgages, or loans.

(2) *Property provided incident to services*. Tangible personal property does not include de minimis property provided to a client or customer incident to the provision of services, such as wills prepared by attorneys, or blueprints prepared by architects. See § 35 1.263A-1(b)(11).

(3) *Costs required to be capitalized by producers*--(i) *In general*. Except as specifically provided in section 263A(f) with respect to interest costs, producers must capitalize direct and indirect costs properly allocable to property produced under section 263A, without regard to whether those costs are incurred before, during, or after the production period 40 (as defined in section 263A(f)(4)(B)).

(ii) *Pre-production costs*. If property is held for future production, taxpayers must capitalize direct and indirect costs allocable to such property (e.g., purchasing, storage, handling, and other costs), even though production has not begun. If property is not held for production, indirect costs incurred prior to the beginning of the production period must 45 be allocated to the property and capitalized if, at the time the costs are incurred, it is reasonably likely that production will occur at some future date. Thus, for example, a manufacturer must capitalize the costs of storing and handling raw materials before the raw materials are committed to production. In addition, a real estate developer must capitalize property taxes incurred with respect to property if, at the time the taxes are 50

Sec. 263A. Capitalization and inclusion in inventory costs of certain expenses

incurred, it is reasonably likely that the property will be subsequently developed.

(iii) *Post-production costs.* Generally, producers must capitalize all indirect costs incurred subsequent to completion of production that are properly allocable to the property produced. Thus, for example, storage and handling costs incurred while holding the property produced for sale after production must be capitalized to the property to the extent properly allocable to the property. However, see § 1.263A-3(c) for exceptions.

***

[T.D. 8482, 58 FR 42219, Aug. 9, 1993; 59 FR 3318, 3319, Jan. 21, 1994; T.D. 8584, 59 FR 67197, Dec. 29, 1994; T.D. 9217, 70 FR 44469, Aug. 3, 2005; T.D. 9318, 72 FR 14677, Mar. 29, 2007]

Sec. 264. Certain amounts paid in connection with insurance contracts

(a) General rule. -- No deduction shall be allowed for--

(1) Premiums on any life insurance policy, or endowment or annuity contract, if the taxpayer is directly or indirectly a beneficiary under the policy or contract.

(2) Any amount paid or accrued on indebtedness incurred or continued to purchase or carry a single premium life insurance, endowment, or annuity contract.

(3) Except as provided in subsection (d), any amount paid or accrued on indebtedness incurred or continued to purchase or carry a life insurance, endowment, or annuity contract (other than a single premium contract or a contract treated as a single premium contract) pursuant to a plan of purchase which contemplates the systematic direct or indirect borrowing of part or all of the increases in the cash value of such contract (either from the insurer or otherwise).

(4) Except as provided in subsection (e), any interest paid or accrued on any indebtedness with respect to 1 or more life insurance policies owned by the taxpayer covering the life of any individual, or any endowment or annuity contracts owned by the taxpayer covering any individual.

***

(f) Pro rata allocation of interest expense to policy cash values. --

(1) In general. -- No deduction shall be allowed for that portion of the taxpayer's interest expense which is allocable to unborrowed policy cash values.

(2) Allocation. -- For purposes of paragraph (1), the portion of the taxpayer's interest expense which is allocable to unborrowed policy cash values is an amount which bears the same ratio to such interest expense as--

(A) the taxpayer's average unborrowed policy cash values of life insurance policies, and annuity and endowment contracts, issued after June 8, 1997, bears to

(B) the sum of--

(i) in the case of assets of the taxpayer which are life insurance policies or annuity or endowment contracts, the average unborrowed policy cash values of such policies and contracts, and

(ii) in the case of assets of the taxpayer not described in clause (i), the average adjusted bases (within the meaning of section 1016) of such assets.

(3) Unborrowed policy cash value. -- For purposes of this subsection, the term "unborrowed policy cash value" means, with respect to any life insurance policy or annuity or endowment contract, the excess of--

Sec. 264. Certain amounts paid in connection with insurance contracts

(A) the cash surrender value of such policy or contract determined without regard to any surrender charge, over

(B) the amount of any loan with respect to such policy or contract. -- If the amount described in subparagraph (A) with respect to any policy or contract does not reasonably approximate its actual value, the amount taken into account under subparagraph (A) shall be the greater of the amount of the insurance company liability or the insurance company reserve with respect to such policy or contract (as determined for purposes of the annual statement approved by the National Association of Insurance Commissioners) or shall be such other amount as is determined by the Secretary.

***

(6) Special rules. --

(A) Coordination with subsection (a) and section 265. -- If interest on any indebtedness is disallowed under subsection (a) or section 265--

(i) such disallowed interest shall not be taken into account for purposes of applying this subsection, and

(ii) the amount otherwise taken into account under paragraph (2)(B) shall be reduced (but not below zero) by the amount of such indebtedness.

(B) Coordination with section 263A. -- This subsection shall be applied before the application of section 263A (relating to capitalization of certain expenses where taxpayer produces property).

(7) Interest expense. -- The term "interest expense" means the aggregate amount allowable to the taxpayer as a deduction for interest (within the meaning of section 265(b)(4)) for the taxable year (determined without regard to this subsection, section 265(b), and section 291).

***

Sec. 265. Expenses and interest relating to tax-exempt income

(a) General rule. -- No deduction shall be allowed for--

(1) Expenses. -- Any amount otherwise allowable as a deduction which is allocable to one or more classes of income other than interest (whether or not any amount of income of that class or classes is received or accrued) wholly exempt from the taxes imposed by this subtitle, or any amount otherwise allowable under section 212 (relating to expenses for production of income) which is allocable to interest (whether or not any amount of such interest is received or accrued) wholly exempt from the taxes imposed by this subtitle.

(2) Interest. -- Interest on indebtedness incurred or continued to purchase or carry obligations the interest on which is wholly exempt from the taxes imposed by this subtitle.

***

(4) Interest related to exempt-interest dividends. -- Interest on indebtedness incurred or continued to purchase or carry shares of stock of a regulated investment company which during the taxable year of the holder thereof distributes exempt- interest dividends.

***

(b) Pro rata allocation of interest expense of financial institutions to tax-exempt interest. --

(1) In general. -- In the case of a financial institution, no deduction shall be allowed for that portion of the taxpayer's interest expense which is allocable to tax-exempt interest.

(2) Allocation. -- For purposes of paragraph (1), the portion of the taxpayer's interest expense which is allocable to tax-exempt interest is an amount which bears the same ratio to such interest expense as--

Sec. 265. Expenses and interest relating to tax-exempt income

(A) the taxpayer's average adjusted bases (within the meaning of section 1016) of tax-exempt obligations acquired after August 7, 1986, bears to

(B) such average adjusted bases for all assets of the taxpayer.

***

(4) Definitions. -- For purposes of this subsection--

(A) Interest expense. -- The term "interest expense" means the aggregate amount allowable to the taxpayer as a deduction for interest for the taxable year (determined without regard to this subsection, section 264, and section 291). For purposes of the preceding sentence, the term "interest" includes amounts (whether or not designated as interest) paid in respect of deposits, investment certificates, or withdrawable or repurchasable shares.

(B) Tax-exempt obligation. -- The term "tax-exempt obligation" means any obligation the interest on which is wholly exempt from taxes imposed by this subtitle. Such term includes shares of stock of a regulated investment company which during the taxable year of the holder thereof distributes exempt-interest dividends.

(5) Financial institution. -- For purposes of this subsection, the term "financial institution" means any person who--

(A) accepts deposits from the public in the ordinary course of such person's trade or business, and is subject to Federal or State supervision as a financial institution, or

(B) is a corporation described in section 585(a)(2).

(6) Special rules. --

(A) Coordination with subsection (a). -- If interest on any indebtedness is disallowed under subsection (a) with respect to any tax-exempt obligation -

(i) such disallowed interest shall not be taken into account for purposes of applying this subsection, and

(ii) for purposes of applying paragraph (2), the adjusted basis of such tax-exempt obligation shall be reduced (but not below zero) by the amount of such indebtedness.

(B) Coordination with section 263A. -- This section shall be applied before the application of section 263A (relating to capitalization of certain expenses where taxpayer produces property).

Reg. § 1.265-1 Expenses relating to tax-exempt income.

(a) *Nondeductibility of expenses allocable to exempt income.* (1) No amount shall be allowed as a deduction under any provision of the Code for any expense or amount which is otherwise allowable as a deduction and which is allocable to a class or classes of exempt income other than a class or classes of exempt interest income.

(2) No amount shall be allowed as a deduction under section 212 (relating to expenses for production of income) for any expense or amount which is otherwise allowable as a deduction and which is allocable to a class or classes of exempt interest income.

(b) *Exempt income and nonexempt income.* (1) As used in this section, the term class of exempt income means any class of income (whether or not any amount of income of such class is received or accrued) wholly exempt from the taxes imposed by Subtitle A of the Code. For purposes of this section, a class of income which is considered as wholly exempt from the taxes imposed by subtitle A includes any class of income which is:

(i) Wholly excluded from gross income under any provision of Subtitle A, or

(ii) Wholly exempt from the taxes imposed by Subtitle A under the provisions of any other law.

Sec. 265. Expenses and interest relating to tax-exempt income

(2) As used in this section the term nonexempt income means any income which is required to be included in gross income.

(c) *Allocation of expenses to a class or classes of exempt income.* Expenses and amounts otherwise allowable which are directly allocable to any class or classes of exempt income shall be allocated thereto; and expenses and amounts directly allocable 5 to any class or classes of nonexempt income shall be allocated thereto. If an expense or amount otherwise allowable is indirectly allocable to both a class of nonexempt income and a class of exempt income, a reasonable proportion thereof determined in the light of all the facts and circumstances in each case shall be allocated to each.

(d) *Statement of classes of exempt income; records.* (1) A taxpayer receiving any 10 class of exempt income or holding any property or engaging in any activity the income from which is exempt shall submit with his return as a part thereof an itemized statement, in detail, showing (i) the amount of each class of exempt income, and (ii) the amount of expenses and amounts otherwise allowable allocated to each such class (the amount allocated by apportionment being shown separately) as required by paragraph (c) of this 15 section. If an item is apportioned between a class of exempt income and a class of nonexempt income, the statement shall show the basis of the apportionment. Such statemen tshall also recite that each deduction claimed in the return is not in any way attributable to a class of exempt income.

(2) The taxpayer shall keep such records as will enable him to make the allocations 20 required by this section. See section 6001 and the regulations thereunder.

Sec. 266. Carrying charges

No deduction shall be allowed for amounts paid or accrued for such taxes and carrying charges as, under regulations prescribed by the Secretary, are chargeable to capital account with respect to property, if the taxpayer elects, in accordance with such regulations, to treat such taxes or charges 25 as so chargeable.

Sec. 267. Losses, expenses, and interest with respect to transactions between related taxpayers

(a) In general. --

(1) **Deduction for losses disallowed.** -- No deduction shall be allowed in respect of any loss from the sale or exchange of property, directly or indirectly, between persons specified in any 30 of the paragraphs of subsection (b). The preceding sentence shall not apply to any loss of the distributing corporation (or the distributee) in the case of a distribution in complete liquidation.

(2) Matching of deduction and payee income item in the case of expenses and interest If -

(A) by reason of the method of accounting of the person to whom the payment is to be 35 made, the amount thereof is not (unless paid) includible in the gross income of such person, and

(B) at the close of the taxable year of the taxpayer for which (but for this paragraph) the amount would be deductible under this chapter, both the taxpayer and the person to whom the payment is to be made are persons specified in any of the paragraphs of subsection (b), 40 then any deduction allowable under this chapter in respect of such amount shall be allowable as of the day as of which such amount is includible in the gross income of the person to whom the payment is made (or, if later, as of the day on which it would be so allowable but for this paragraph). For purposes of this paragraph, in the case of a personal service corporation (within the meaning of section 441(i)(2)), such corporation and any employee-owner (within the meaning of section 269A(b)(2), as modified by section 441(i)(2)) shall be treated as persons specified in subsection (b).

***

(b) Relationships. -- The persons referred to in subsection (a) are:

(1) Members of a family, as defined in subsection (c)(4);

(2) An individual and a corporation more than 50 percent in value of the outstanding stock of which is owned, directly or indirectly, by or for such individual;

(3) Two corporations which are members of the same controlled group (as defined in subsection (f));

(4) A grantor and a fiduciary of any trust;

(5) A fiduciary of a trust and a fiduciary of another trust, if the same person is a grantor of both trusts;

(6) A fiduciary of a trust and a beneficiary of such trust;

(7) A fiduciary of a trust and a beneficiary of another trust, if the same person is a grantor of both trusts;

(8) A fiduciary of a trust and a corporation more than 50 percent in value of the outstanding stock of which is owned, directly or indirectly, by or for the trust or by or for a person who is a grantor of the trust;

(9) A person and an organization to which section 501 (relating to certain educational and charitable organizations which are exempt from tax) applies and which is controlled directly or indirectly by such person or (if such person is an individual) by members of the family of such individual;

(10) A corporation and a partnership if the same persons own--

(A) more than 50 percent in value of the outstanding stock of the corporation, and

(B) more than 50 percent of the capital interest, or the profits interest, in the partnership;

***

(d) Amount of gain where loss previously disallowed. -- If--

(1) in the case of a sale or exchange of property to the taxpayer a loss sustained by the transferor is not allowable to the transferor as a deduction by reason of subsection (a)(1) (or by reason of section 24(b) of the Internal Revenue Code of 1939); and

(2) after December 31, 1953, the taxpayer sells or otherwise disposes of such property (or of other property the basis of which in his hands is determined directly or indirectly by reference to such property) at a gain then such gain shall be recognized only to the extent that it exceeds so much of such loss as is properly allocable to the property sold or otherwise disposed of by the taxpayer.

***

(g) Coordination with section 1041. -- Subsection (a)(1) shall not apply to any transfer described in section 1041(a) (relating to transfers of property between spouses or incident to divorce).

Reg. § 1.267(d)-1 Amount of gain where loss previously disallowed.

(a) **General rule**. (1) If a taxpayer acquires property by purchase or exchange from a transferor who, on the transaction, sustained a loss not allowable as a deduction by reason of section 267(a)(1) (or by reason of section 24(b) of the Internal Revenue Code

Sec. 267.   Losses, expenses, and interest with respect to transactions between related taxpayers

of 1939), then any gain realized by the taxpayer on a sale or other disposition of the property after December 31, 1953, shall be recognized only to the extent that the gain exceeds the amount of such loss as is properly allocable to the property sold or otherwise disposed of by the taxpayer.

(2) The general rule is also applicable to a sale or other disposition of property by a 5 taxpayer when the basis of such property in the taxpayer's hands is determined directly or indirectly by reference to other property acquired by the taxpayer from a transferor through a sale or exchange in which a loss sustained by the transferor was not allowable. Therefore, section 267(d) applies to a sale or other disposition of property after a series of transactions if the basis of the property acquired in each transaction is determined by 10 reference to the basis of the property transferred, and if the original property was acquired in a transaction in which a loss to a transferor was not allowable by reason of section 267(a)(1) (or by reason of section 24(b) of the Internal Revenue Code of 1939).

(3) The benefit of the general rule is available only to the original transferee but does not apply to any original transferee (e.g., a donee) who acquired the property in any 15 manner other than by purchase or exchange.

(4) The application of the provisions of this paragraph may be illustrated by the following examples:

Example 1. H sells to his wife, W, for $500, certain corporate stock with an adjusted basis for determining loss to him of $800. The loss of $300 is not allowable to H by 20 reason of section 267(a)(1) and paragraph (a) of § 1.267(a)-1. W later sells this stock for $1,000. Although W's realized gain is $500 ($1,000 minus $500, her basis), her recognized gain under section 267(d) is only $200, the excess of the realized gain of $500 over the loss of $300 not allowable to H. In determining capital gain or loss W's holding period commences on the date of the sale from H to W.   25

Example 2. Assume the same facts as in Example 1 except that W later sells her stock for $300 instead of $1,000. Her recognized loss is $200 and not $500 since section 267(d) applies only to the nonrecognition of gain and does not affect basis.

Example 3. Assume the same facts as in Example 1 except that W transfers her stock as a gift to X. The basis of the stock in the hands of X for the purpose of determining 30 gain, under the provisions of section 1015, is the same as W's, or $500. If X later sells the stock for $1,000 the entire $500 gain is taxed to him.

Example 4. H sells to his wife, W, for $5,500, farmland, with an adjusted basis for determining loss to him of $8,000. The loss of $2,500 is not allowable to H by reason of section 267(a)(1) and paragraph (a) of § 1.267(a)-1. W exchanges the farmland, held for 35 investment purposes, with S, an unrelated individual, for two city lots, also held for investment purposes. The basis of the city lots in the hands of W ($5,500) is a substituted basis determined under section 1031(d) by reference to the basis of the farmland. Later W sells the city lots for $10,000. Although W's realized gain is $4,500 (10,000 minus $5,500), her recognized gain under section 267(d) is only $2,000, the excess of the 40 realized gain of $4,500 over the loss of $2,500 not allowable to H.

(b) *Determination of basis and gain with respect to divisible property*--(1) *Taxpayer's basis.* When the taxpayer acquires divisible property or property that consists of several items or classes of items by a purchase or exchange on which loss is not allowable to the transferor, the basis in the taxpayer's hands of a particular part, item, or class of such 45 property shall be determined (if the taxpayer's basis for that part is not known) by allocating to the particular part, item, or class a portion of the taxpayer's basis for the entire property in the proportion that the fair market value of the particular part, item, or class bears to the fair market value of the entire property at the time of the taxpayer's acquisition of the property.   50

Sec. 267. Losses, expenses, and interest with respect to transactions between related taxpayers

(2) *Taxpayer's recognized gain.* Gain realized by the taxpayer on sales or other dispositions after December 31, 1953, of a part, item, or class of the property shall be recognized only to the extent that such gain exceeds the amount of loss attributable to such part, item, or class of property not allowable to the taxpayer's transferor on the
5 latter's sale or exchange of such property to the taxpayer.

(3) *Transferor's loss not allowable.* (i) The transferor's loss on the sale or exchange of a part, item, or class of the property to the taxpayer shall be the excess of the transferor's adjusted basis for determining loss on the part, item, or class of the property over the amount realized by the transferor on the sale or exchange of the part, item, or class. The
10 amount realized by the transferor on the part, item, or class shall be determined (if such amount is not known) in the same manner that the taxpayer's basis for such part, item, or class is determined. See subparagraph (1) of this paragraph.

(ii) If the transferor's basis for determining loss on the part, item, or class cannot be determined, the transferor's loss on the particular part, item, or class transferred to the
15 taxpayer shall be determined by allocating to the part, item, or class a portion of his loss on the entire property in the proportion that the fair market value of such part, item, or class bears to the fair market value of the entire property on the date of the taxpayer's acquisition of the entire property.

(4) *Examples.* The application of the provisions of this paragraph may be illustrated by
20 the following examples:

Example 1. During 1953, H sold class A stock which had cost him $1,100, and common stock which had cost him $2,000, to his wife W for a lump sum of $1,500. Under section 24(b)(1)(A) of the 1939 Code, the loss of $1,600 on the transaction was not allowable to H. At the time the stocks were purchased by W, the fair market value of class
25 A stock was $900 and the fair market value of common stock was $600. In 1954, W sold the class A stock for $2,500. W's recognized gain is determined as follows:

Amount realized by W on sale of class A stock.........................	$2,500
Less: Basis allocated to class A stock--$900/$1,500 x $1,500.	900
30 Realized gain on transaction...	1,600
Less: Loss sustained by H on sale of class A stock to W not	
allowable as a deduction:	
Basis to H of class A stock..	$1,100
Amount realized by H on class A stock--	
35 $900/$1,500 x $1,500...	900
Unallowable loss to H on sale of class A stock....................	200
Recognized gain on sale of class A stock by W.....................	1,400

Example 2. Assume the same facts as those stated in Example 1 of this subparagraph
40 except that H originally purchased both classes of stock for a lump sum of $3,100. The unallowable loss to H on the sale of all the stock to W is $1,600 ($3,100 minus $1,500). An exact determination of the unallowable loss sustained by H on sale to W of class A stock cannot be made because H's basis for class A stock cannot be determined. Therefore, a determination of the unallowable loss is made by allocating to class A stock
45 a portion of H's loss on the entire property transferred to W in the proportion that the fair market value of class A stock at the time acquired by W ($900) bears to the fair market value of both classes of stock at that time ($1,500). The allocated portion is $900/$1,500 x $1,600, or $960. W's recognized gain is, therefore, $640 (W's realized gain of $1,600 minus $960).

50   c) Special rules. (1) Section 267(d) does not affect the basis of property for

652

Sec. 267. Losses, expenses, and interest with respect to transactions between related taxpayers

determining gain. Depreciation and other items which depend on such basis are also not affected.

(2) The provisions of section 267(d) shall not apply if the loss sustained by the transferor is not allowable to the transferor as a deduction by reason of section 1091, or section 118 of the Internal Revenue Code of 1939, which relate to losses from wash sales 5 of stock or securities.

(3) In determining the holding period in the hands of the transferee of property received in an exchange with a transferor with respect to whom a loss on the exchange is not allowable by reason of section 267, section 1223(2) does not apply to include the period during which the property was held by the transferor. In determining such holding 10 period, however, section 1223(1) may apply to include the period during which the transferee held the property which he exchanged where, for example, he exchanged a capital asset in a transaction which, as to him, was nontaxable under section 1031 and the property received in the exchange has the same basis as the property exchanged.

15

Sec. 269. Acquisitions made to evade or avoid income tax

(a) In general. -- If -

(1) any person or persons acquire, or acquired on or after October 8, 1940, directly or indirectly, control of a corporation, or

(2) any corporation acquires, or acquired on or after October 8, 1940, directly or indirectly, 20 property of another corporation, not controlled, directly or indirectly, immediately before such acquisition, by such acquiring corporation or its stockholders, the basis of which property, in the hands of the acquiring corporation, is determined by reference to the basis in the hands of the transferor corporation,

and the principal purpose for which such acquisition was made is evasion or avoidance of Federal 25 income tax by securing the benefit of a deduction, credit, or other allowance which such person or corporation would not otherwise enjoy, then the Secretary may disallow such deduction, credit, or other allowance. For purposes of paragraphs (1) and (2), control means the ownership of stock possessing at least 50 percent of the total combined voting power of all classes of stock entitled to vote or at least 50 percent of the total value of shares of all classes of stock of the corporation. 30

***

Sec. 269A. Personal service corporations formed or availed of to avoid or evade income tax

(a) General rule. -- If--

(1) substantially all of the services of a personal service corporation are performed for (or on behalf of) 1 other corporation, partnership, or other entity, and 35

(2) the principal purpose for forming, or availing of, such personal service corporation is the avoidance or evasion of Federal income tax by reducing the income of, or securing the benefit of any expense, deduction, credit, exclusion, or other allowance for, any employee-owner which would not otherwise be available,

then the Secretary may allocate all income, deductions, credits, exclusions, and other allowances 40 between such personal service corporation and its employee-owners, if such allocation is necessary to prevent avoidance or evasion of Federal income tax or clearly to reflect the income of the personal service corporation or any of its employee-owners.

653

Sec. 269A. Personal service corporations formed or availed of to avoid or evade income tax

(b) **Definitions.** -- For purposes of this section--

(1) **Personal service corporation.** -- The term "personal service corporation" means a corporation the principal activity of which is the performance of personal services and such services are substantially performed by employee-owners.

***

Sec. 274. Disallowance of certain entertainment, etc., expenses

(a) **Entertainment, amusement, or recreation.** --

(1) **In general.** -- No deduction otherwise allowable under this chapter shall be allowed for any item--

(A) **Activity.** -- With respect to an activity which is of a type generally considered to constitute entertainment, amusement, or recreation, unless the taxpayer establishes that the item was directly related to, or, in the case of an item directly preceding or following a substantial and bona fide business discussion (including business meetings at a convention or otherwise), that such item was associated with, the active conduct of the taxpayer's trade or business, or

(B) **Facility.** -- With respect to a facility used in connection with an activity referred to in subparagraph (A).

In the case of an item described in subparagraph (A), the deduction shall in no event exceed the portion of such item which meets the requirements of subparagraph (A).

(2) **Special rules.** -- For purposes of applying paragraph (1)--

(A) Dues or fees to any social, athletic, or sporting club or organization shall be treated as items with respect to facilities.

(B) An activity described in section 212 shall be treated as a trade or business.

(C) In the case of a club, paragraph (1)(B) shall apply unless the taxpayer establishes that the facility was used primarily for the furtherance of the taxpayer's trade or business and that the item was directly related to the active conduct of such trade or business.

(3) **Denial of deduction for club dues.** -- Notwithstanding the preceding provisions of this subsection, no deduction shall be allowed under this chapter for amounts paid or incurred for membership in any club organized for business, pleasure, recreation, or other social purpose.

(b) **Gifts.** --

(1) **Limitation.** -- No deduction shall be allowed under section 162 or section 212 for any expense for gifts made directly or indirectly to any individual to the extent that such expense, when added to prior expenses of the taxpayer for gifts made to such individual during the same taxable year, exceeds $25. For purposes of this section, the term "gift" means any item excludable from gross income of the recipient under section 102 which is not excludable from his gross income under any other provision of this chapter, but such term does not include--

(A) an item having a cost to the taxpayer not in excess of $4.00 on which the name of the taxpayer is clearly and permanently imprinted and which is one of a number of identical items distributed generally by the taxpayer, or

(B) a sign, display rack, or other promotional material to be used on the business premises of the recipient.

(2) **Special rules.** --

(A) In the case of a gift by a partnership, the limitation contained in paragraph (1) shall apply to the partnership as well as to each member thereof.

(B) For purposes of paragraph (1), a husband and wife shall be treated as one taxpayer.

654

Sec. 274.   Disallowance of certain entertainment, etc., expenses

(c) Certain foreign travel. --

(1) In general. -- In the case of any individual who travels outside the United States away from home in pursuit of a trade or business or in pursuit of an activity described in section 212, no deduction shall be allowed under section 162, or section 212 for that portion of the expenses of such travel otherwise allowable under such section which, under regulations 5 prescribed by the Secretary, is not allocable to such trade or business or to such activity.

(2) Exception. -- Paragraph (1) shall not apply to the expenses of any travel outside the United States away from home if--

(A) such travel does not exceed one week, or

(B) the portion of the time of travel outside the United States away from home which is 10 not attributable to the pursuit of the taxpayer's trade or business or an activity described in section 212 is less than 25 percent of the total time on such travel.

(3) Domestic travel excluded. -- For purposes of this subsection, travel outside the United States does not include any travel from one point in the United States to another point in the United States.   15

(d) Substantiation required. -- No deduction or credit shall be allowed--

(1) under section 162 or 212 for any traveling expense (including meals and lodging while away from home),

(2) for any item with respect to an activity which is of a type generally considered to constitute entertainment, amusement, or recreation, or with respect to a facility used in 20 connection with such an activity,

(3) for any expense for gifts, or

(4) with respect to any listed property (as defined in section 280F(d)(4)),

unless the taxpayer substantiates by adequate records or by sufficient evidence corroborating the taxpayer's own statement (A) the amount of such expense or other item, (B) the time and place of 25 the travel, entertainment, amusement, recreation, or use of the facility or property, or the date and description of the gift, (C) the business purpose of the expense or other item, and (D) the business relationship to the taxpayer of persons entertained, using the facility or property, or receiving the gift. The Secretary may by regulations provide that some or all of the requirements of the preceding sentence shall not apply in the case of an expense which does not exceed an amount 30 prescribed pursuant to such regulations. This subsection shall not apply to any qualified nonpersonal use vehicle (as defined in subsection (i)).

(e) Specific exceptions to application of subsection (a). -- Subsection (a) shall not apply to--

(1) Food and beverages for employees. -- Expenses for food and beverages (and facilities used in connection therewith) furnished on the business premises of the taxpayer primarily for 35 his employees.

(2) Expenses treated as compensation. --

(A) In general. -- Except as provided in subparagraph (B), expenses for goods, services, and facilities, to the extent that the expenses are treated by the taxpayer, with respect to the recipient of the entertainment, amusement, or recreation, as compensation to an employee 40 on the taxpayer's return of tax under this chapter and as wages to such employee for purposes of chapter 24 (relating to withholding of income tax at source on wages).

(B) Specified individuals. --

(i) In general. -- In the case of a recipient who is a specified individual, subparagraph (A) and paragraph (9) shall each be applied by substituting "to the extent 45 that the expenses do not exceed the amount of the expenses which" for "to the extent that the expenses".

655

Sec. 274. Disallowance of certain entertainment, etc., expenses

  (ii) Specified individual .-- For purposes of clause (i), the term "specified individual" means any individual who--

    (I) is subject to the requirements of section 16(a) of the Securities Exchange Act of 1934 with respect to the taxpayer, or

    (II) would be subject to such requirements if the taxpayer were an issuer of equity securities referred to in such section.

  (3) Reimbursed expenses. -- Expenses paid or incurred by the taxpayer, in connection with the performance by him of services for another person (whether or not such other person is his employer), under a reimbursement or other expense allowance arrangement with such other person, but this paragraph shall apply--

    (A) where the services are performed for an employer, only if the employer has not treated such expenses in the manner provided in paragraph (2), or

    (B) where the services are performed for a person other than an employer, only if the taxpayer accounts (to the extent provided by subsection (d)) to such person.

  (4) Recreational, etc., expenses for employees. -- Expenses for recreational, social, or similar activities (including facilities therefor) primarily for the benefit of employees (other than employees who are highly compensated employees (within the meaning of section 414(q))). For purposes of this paragraph, an individual owning less than a 10-percent interest in the taxpayer's trade or business shall not be considered a shareholder or other owner, and for such purposes an individual shall be treated as owning any interest owned by a member of his family (within the meaning of section 267(c)(4)). This paragraph shall not apply for purposes of subsection (a)(3).

  (5) Employees, stockholder, etc., business meetings. -- Expenses incurred by a taxpayer which are directly related to business meetings of his employees, stockholders, agents, or directors.

  (6) Meetings of business leagues, etc. -- Expenses directly related and necessary to attendance at a business meeting or convention of any organization described in section 501(c)(6) (relating to business leagues, chambers of commerce, real estate boards, and boards of trade) and exempt from taxation under section 501(a).

  (7) Items available to public. -- Expenses for goods, services, and facilities made available by the taxpayer to the general public.

  (8) Entertainment sold to customers. -- Expenses for goods or services (including the use of facilities) which are sold by the taxpayer in a bona fide transaction for an adequate and full consideration in money or money's worth.

  (9) Expenses includible in income of persons who are not employees. -- Expenses paid or incurred by the taxpayer for goods, services, and facilities to the extent that the expenses are includible in the gross income of a recipient of the entertainment, amusement, or recreation who is not an employee of the taxpayer as compensation for services rendered or as a prize or award under section 74. The preceding sentence shall not apply to any amount paid or incurred by the taxpayer if such amount is required to be included (or would be so required except that the amount is less than $600) in any information return filed by such taxpayer under part III of subchapter A of chapter 61 and is not so included.

For purposes of this subsection, any item referred to in subsection (a) shall be treated as an expense.

  (f) Interest, taxes, casualty losses, etc. -- This section shall not apply to any deduction allowable to the taxpayer without regard to its connection with his trade or business (or with his income-producing activity). In the case of a taxpayer which is not an individual, the preceding sentence shall be applied as if it were an individual.

Sec. 274. Disallowance of certain entertainment, etc., expenses

(g) Treatment of entertainment, etc., type facility. -- For purposes of this chapter, if deductions are disallowed under subsection (a) with respect to any portion of a facility, such portion shall be treated as an asset which is used for personal, living, and family purposes (and not as an asset used in the trade or business).

(h) Attendance at conventions, etc. --

(1) In general. -- In the case of any individual who attends a convention, seminar, or similar meeting which is held outside the North American area, no deduction shall be allowed under section 162 for expenses allocable to such meeting unless the taxpayer establishes that the meeting is directly related to the active conduct of his trade or business and that, after taking into account in the manner provided by regulations prescribed by the Secretary--

(A) the purpose of such meeting and the activities taking place at such meeting,

(B) the purposes and activities of the sponsoring organizations or groups,

(C) the residences of the active members of the sponsoring organization and the places at which other meetings of the sponsoring organization or groups have been held or will be held, and

(D) such other relevant factors as the taxpayer may present,it is as reasonable for the meeting to be held outside the North American area as within the North American area.

(2) Conventions on cruise ships. -- In the case of any individual who attends a convention, seminar, or other meeting which is held on any cruise ship, no deduction shall be allowed under section 162 for expenses allocable to such meeting, unless the taxpayer meets the requirements of paragraph (5) and establishes that the meeting is directly related to the active conduct of his trade or business and that--

(A) the cruise ship is a vessel registered in the United States; and

(B) all ports of call of such cruise ship are located in the United States or in possessions of the United States.

With respect to cruises beginning in any calendar year, not more than $2,000 of the expenses attributable to an individual attending one or more meetings may be taken into account under section 162 by reason of the preceding sentence.

(3) Definitions. -- For purposes of this subsection--

(A) North American area. -- The term "North American area" means the United States, its possessions, and the Trust Territory of the Pacific Islands, and Canada and Mexico.

(B) Cruise ship. -- The term "cruise ship" means any vessel sailing within or without the territorial waters of the United States.

(4) Subsection to apply to employer as well as to traveler. --

(A) Except as provided in subparagraph (B), this subsection shall apply to deductions otherwise allowable under section 162 to any person, whether or not such person is the individual attending the convention, seminar, or similar meeting.

(B) This subsection shall not deny a deduction to any person other than the individual attending the convention, seminar, or similar meeting with respect to any amount paid by such person to or on behalf of such individual if includible in the gross income of such individual. The preceding sentence shall not apply if the amount is required to be included in any information return filed by such person under part III of subchapter A of chapter 61 and is not so included.

(5) Reporting requirements. -- No deduction shall be allowed under section 162 for expenses allocable to attendance at a convention, seminar, or similar meeting on any cruise ship unless the taxpayer claiming the deduction attaches to the return of tax on which the deduction is claimed--

Sec. 274. Disallowance of certain entertainment, etc., expenses

(A) a written statement signed by the individual attending the meeting which includes -

(i) information with respect to the total days of the trip, excluding the days of transportation to and from the cruise ship port, and the number of hours of each day of the trip which such individual devoted to scheduled business activities,

(ii) a program of the scheduled business activities of the meeting, and

(iii) such other information as may be required in regulations prescribed by the Secretary; and

(B) a written statement signed by an officer of the organization or group sponsoring the meeting which includes -

(i) a schedule of the business activities of each day of the meeting,

(ii) the number of hours which the individual attending the meeting attended such scheduled business activities, and

(iii) such other information as may be required in regulations prescribed by the Secretary.

(6) Treatment of conventions in certain Caribbean countries. --

(A) In general. -- For purposes of this subsection, the term "North American area" includes, with respect to any convention, seminar, or similar meeting, any beneficiary country if (as of the time such meeting begins)--

(i) there is in effect a bilateral or multilateral agreement described in subparagraph (C) between such country and the United States providing for the exchange of information between the United States and such country, and

(ii) there is not in effect a finding by the Secretary that the tax laws of such country discriminate against convention held in the United States.

(B) Beneficiary country. -- For purposes of this paragraph, the term "beneficiary country" has the meaning given to such term by section 212(a)(1)(A) of the Caribbean Basin Economic Recovery Act; except that such term shall include Bermuda.

***

(7) Seminars, etc. for section 212 purposes. -- No deduction shall be allowed under section 212 for expenses allocable to a convention, seminar, or similar meeting.

(i) Qualified nonpersonal use vehicle. -- For purposes of subsection (d), the term "qualified nonpersonal use vehicle" means any vehicle which, by reason of its nature, isnot likely to be used more than a de minimis amount for personal purposes.

(j) Employee achievement awards. --

(1) General rule. -- No deduction shall be allowed under section 162 or section 212 for the cost of an employee achievement award except to the extent that such cost does not exceed the deduction limitations of paragraph (2).

(2) Deduction limitations. -- The deduction for the cost of an employee achievement award made by an employer to an employee--

(A) which is not a qualified plan award, when added to the cost to the employer for all other employee achievement awards made to such employee during the taxable year which are not qualified plan awards, shall not exceed $400, and

(B) which is a qualified plan award, when added to the cost to the employer for all other employee achievement awards made to such employee during the taxable year (including employee achievement awards which are not qualified plan awards), shall not exceed $1,600.

Sec. 274.   Disallowance of certain entertainment, etc., expenses

(3) Definitions. -- For purposes of this subsection--

(A) Employee achievement award. -- The term "employee achievement award" means an item of tangible personal property which is--

(i) transferred by an employer to an employee for length of service achievement or safety achievement   5

(ii) awarded as part of a meaningful presentation, and

(iii) awarded under conditions and circumstances that do not create a significant likelihood of the payment of disguised compensation.

(B) Qualified plan award. --

(i) **In general.** -- The term "qualified plan award" means an employee achievement   10
award awarded as part of an established written plan or program of the taxpayer which does not discriminate in favor of highly compensated employees (within the meaning of section 414(q)) as to eligibility or benefits.

(ii) **Limitation.** -- An employee achievement award shall not be treated as a qualified plan award for any taxable year if the average cost of all employee achievement awards   15 which are provided by the employer during the year, and which would be qualified plan awards but for this subparagraph, exceeds $400. For purposes of the preceding sentence, average cost shall be determined by including the entire cost of qualified plan awards, without taking into account employee achievement awards of nominal value.

***   20

(k) Business meals. --

(1) In general. -- No deduction shall be allowed under this chapter for the expense of any food or beverages unless--

(A) such expense is not lavish or extravagant under the circumstances, and

(B) the taxpayer (or an employee of the taxpayer) is present at the furnishing of such   25 food or beverages.

(2) Exceptions. -- Paragraph (1) shall not apply to--

(A) any expense described in paragraph (2), (3), (4), (7), (8), or (9) of subsection (e), and

(B) any other expense to the extent provided in regulations.   30

(l) Additional limitations on entertainment tickets. --

(1) Entertainment tickets. --

(A) In general. -- In determining the amount allowable as a deduction under this chapter for any ticket for any activity or facility described in subsection (d)(2), the amount taken into account shall not exceed the face value of such ticket.   35

(B) Exception for certain charitable sports events. -- Subparagraph (A) shall not apply to any ticket for any sports event--

(i) which is organized for the primary purpose of benefiting an organization which is described in section 501(c)(3) and exempt from tax under section 501(a),

(ii) all of the net proceeds of which are contributed to such organization, and   40

(iii) which utilizes volunteers for substantially all of the work performed in carrying out such event.

(2) Skyboxes, etc. -- In the case of a skybox or other private luxury box leased for more than 1 event, the amount allowable as a deduction under this chapter with respect to such events shall not exceed the sum of the face value of non-luxury box seat tickets for the seats in   45

659

Sec. 274. Disallowance of certain entertainment, etc., expenses

such box covered by the lease. For purposes of the preceding sentence, 2 or more related leases shall be treated as 1 lease.

(m) Additional limitations on travel expenses. --

(1) Luxury water transportation. --

(A) In general. -- No deduction shall be allowed under this chapter for expenses incurred for transportation by water to the extent such expenses exceed twice the aggregate per diem amounts for days of such transportation. For purposes of the preceding sentence, the term "per diem amounts" means the highest amount generally allowable with respect to a day to employees of the executive branch of the Federal Government for per diem while away from home but serving in the United States.

(B) Exceptions. -- Subparagraph (A) shall not apply to--

(i) any expense allocable to a convention, seminar, or other meeting which is held on any cruise ship, and

(ii) any expense described in paragraph (2), (3), (4), (7), (8), or (9) of subsection (e).

(2) Travel as form of education. -- No deduction shall be allowed under this chapter for expenses for travel as a form of education.

(3) Travel expenses of spouse, dependent, or others. -- No deduction shall be allowed under this chapter (other than section 217) for travel expenses paid or incurred with respect to a spouse, dependent, or other individual accompanying the taxpayer (or an officer or employee of the taxpayer) on business travel, unless--

(A) the spouse, dependent, or other individual is an employee of the taxpayer,

(B) the travel of the spouse, dependent, or other individual is for a bona fide business purpose, and

(C) such expenses would otherwise be deductible by the spouse, dependent, or other individual.

(n) Only 50 percent of meal and entertainment expenses allowed as deduction. --

(1) In general. -- The amount allowable as a deduction under this chapter for--

(A) any expense for food or beverages, and

(B) any item with respect to an activity which is of a type generally considered to constitute entertainment, amusement, or recreation, or with respect to a facility used in connection with such activity,

shall not exceed 50 percent of the amount of such expense or item which would (but for this paragraph) be allowable as a deduction under this chapter.

(2) Exceptions. -- Paragraph (1) shall not apply to any expense if--

(A) such expense is described in paragraph (2), (3), (4), (7), (8), or (9) of subsection (e),

(B) in the case of an expense for food or beverages, such expense is excludable from the gross income of the recipient under section 132 by reason of subsection (e) thereof (relating to de minimis fringes),

(C) such expense is covered by a package involving a ticket described in subsection (l) (1)(B),

(D) in the case of an employer who pays or reimburses moving expenses of an employee, such expenses are includible in the income of the employee under section 82, or

(E) such expense is for food or beverages--

(i) required by any Federal law to be provided to crew members of a commercial vessel,

660

Sec. 274. Disallowance of certain entertainment, etc., expenses

(ii) provided to crew members of a commercial vessel--

(I) which is operating on the Great Lakes, the Saint Lawrence Seaway, or any inland waterway of the United States, and

(II) which is of a kind which would be required by Federal law to provide food and beverages to crew membersif it were operated at sea, 5

(iii) provided on an oil or gas platform or drilling rig if the platform or rig is located offshore, or

(iv) provided on an oil or gas platform or drilling rig, or at a support camp which is in proximity and integral to such platform or rig, if the platform or rig is located in the United States north of 54 degrees north latitude. 10

Clauses (i) and (ii) of subparagraph (E) shall not apply to vessels primarily engaged in providing luxury water transportation (determined under the principles of subsection m)). In the case of the employee, the exception of subparagraph(A) shall not apply to expenses described in subparagraph (D).

*** 15

(o) Regulatory authority. -- The Secretary shall prescribe such regulations as he may deem necessary to carry out the purposes of this section, including regulations prescribing whether subsection (a) or subsection (b) applies in cases where both such subsections would otherwise apply.

20

Reg. § 1.274-1   Disallowance of certain entertainment, gift and travel expenses.

Section 274 disallows in whole, or in part, certain expenditures for entertainment, gifts and travel which would otherwise be allowable under Chapter 1 of the Code. The requirements imposed by section 274 are in addition to the requirements for deductibility imposed by other provisions of the Code. If a deduction is claimed for an expenditure for 25 entertainment, gifts, or travel, the taxpayer must first establish that it is otherwise allowable as a deduction under Chapter 1 of the Code before the provisions of section 274 become applicable. An expenditure for entertainment, to the extent it is lavish or extravagant, shall not be allowable as a deduction. The taxpayer should then substantiate such an expenditure in accordance with the rules under section 274(d). See 30 § 1.274-5. Section 274 is a disallowance provision exclusively, and does not make deductible any expense which is disallowed under any other provision of the Code. Similarly, section 274 does not affect the includability of an item in, or the excludability of an item from, the gross income of any taxpayer. For specific provisions with respect to the deductibility of expenditures: for an activity of a type generally considered to 35 constitute entertainment, amusement, or recreation, and for a facility used in connection with such an activity, as well as certain travel expenses of a spouse, etc., see § 1.274-2; for expenses for gifts, see § 1.274-3; for expenses for foreign travel, see § 1.274-4; for expenditures deductible without regard to business activity, see § 1.274-6; and for treatment of personal portion of entertainment facility, see § 1.274-7. 40

Reg. § 1.274-2   Disallowance of deductions for certain expenses for entertainment, amusement, recreation, or travel.

(a) *General rules*--(1) *Entertainment activity*. Except as provided in this section, no deduction otherwise allowable under Chapter 1 of the Code shall be allowed for any 45 expenditure with respect to entertainment unless the taxpayer establishes:

(i) That the expenditure was directly related to the active conduct of the taxpayer's trade or business, or

(ii) In the case of an expenditure directly preceding or following a substantial and bona

661

fide business discussion (including business meetings at a convention or otherwise), that the expenditure was associated with the active conduct of the taxpayer's trade or business. Such deduction shall not exceed the portion of the expenditure directly related to (or in the case of an expenditure described in subdivision (ii) of this subparagraph, the
5 portion of the expenditure associated with) the active conduct of the taxpayer's trade or business.

(2) *Entertainment facilities--(i) Expenditures paid or incurred after December 31, 1978, and not with respect to a club.* Except as provided in this section with respect to a club, no deduction otherwise allowable under chapter 1 of the Code shall be allowed for any
10 expenditure paid or incurred after December 31, 1978, with respect to a facility used in connection with entertainment.

***

(iii) *Expenditures paid or incurred after December 31, 1993, with respect to a club--(a) In general.* No deduction otherwise allowable under chapter 1 of the Internal Revenue
15 Code shall be allowed for amounts paid or incurred after December 31, 1993, for membership in any club organized for business, pleasure, recreation, or other social purpose. The purposes and activities of a club, and not its name, determine whether it is organized for business, pleasure, recreation, or other social purpose. Clubs organized for business, pleasure, recreation, or other social purpose include any membership
20 organization if a principal purpose of the organization is to conduct entertainment activities for members of the organization or their guests or to provide members or their guests with access to entertainment facilities within the meaning of paragraph (e)(2) of this section. Clubs organized for business, pleasure, recreation, or other social purpose include, but are not limited to, country clubs, golf and athletic clubs, airline clubs, hotel
25 clubs, and clubs operated to provide meals under circumstances generally considered to be conducive to business discussion.

(b) *Exceptions.* Unless a principal purpose of the organization is to conduct entertainment activities for members or their guests or to provide members or their guests with access to entertainment facilities, business leagues, trade associations,
30 chambers of commerce, boards of trade, real estate boards, professional organizations (such as bar associations and medical associations), and civic or public service organizations will not be treated as clubs organized for business, pleasure, recreation, or other social purpose.

(3) *Cross references.* For definition of the term entertainment, see paragraph (b)(1) of
35 this section. For the disallowance of deductions for the cost of admission to a dinner or program any part of the proceeds of which inures to the use of a political party or political candidate, and cost of admission to an inaugural event or similar event identified with any political party or political candidate, see § 1.276-1. For rules and definitions with respect to:
40 (i) ``Directly related entertainment", see paragraph (c) of this section,

(ii) ``Associated entertainment", see paragraph (d) of this section,

(iii) ``Expenditures paid or incurred before January 1, 1979, with respect to entertainment facilities or before January 1, 1994, with respect to clubs", see paragraph (e) of this section, and
45 (iv) ``Specific exceptions" to the disallowance rules of this section, see paragraph (f) of this section.

(b) *Definitions--(1) Entertainment defined--(i) In general.* For purposes of this section, the term entertainment means any activity which is of a type generally considered to constitute entertainment, amusement, or recreation, such as entertaining at night clubs,
50 cocktail lounges, theaters, country clubs, golf and athletic clubs, sporting events, and on hunting, fishing, vacation and similar trips, including such activity relating solely to the

Sec. 274. Disallowance of certain entertainment, etc., expenses

taxpayer or the taxpayer's family. The term entertainment may include an activity, the cost of which is claimed as a business expense by the taxpayer, which satisfies the personal, living, or family needs of any individual, such as providing food and beverages, a hotel suite, or an automobile to a business customer or his family. The term entertainment does not include activities which, although satisfying personal, living, or family needs of an individual, are clearly not regarded as constituting entertainment, such as (a) supper money provided by an employer to his employee working overtime, (b) a hotel room maintained by an employer for lodging of his employees while in business travel status, or (c) an automobile used in the active conduct of trade or business even though used for routine personal purposes such as commuting to and from work. On the other hand, the providing of a hotel room or an automobile by an employer to his employee who is on vacation would constitute entertainment of the employee.

(ii) *Objective test.* An objective test shall be used to determine whether an activity is of a type generally considered to constitute entertainment. Thus, if an activity is generally considered to be entertainment, it will constitute entertainment for purposes of this section and section 274(a) regardless of whether the expenditure can also be described otherwise, and even though the expenditure relates to the taxpayer alone. This objective test precludes arguments such as that entertainment means only entertainment of others or that an expenditure for entertainment should be characterized as an expenditure for advertising or public relations. However, in applying this test the taxpayer's trade or business shall be considered. Thus, although attending a theatrical performance would generally be considered entertainment, it would not be so considered in the case of a professional theater critic, attending in his professional capacity. Similarly, if a manufacturer of dresses conducts a fashion show to introduce his products to a group of store buyers, the show would not be generally considered to constitute entertainment. However, if an appliance distributor conducts a fashion show for the wives of his retailers, the fashion show would be generally considered to constitute entertainment.

(iii) *Special definitional rules*--(a) *In general.* Except as otherwise provided in (b) or (c) of this subdivision, any expenditure which might generally be considered either for a gift or entertainment, or considered either for travel or entertainment, shall be considered an expenditure for entertainment rather than for a gift or travel.

(b) *Expenditures deemed gifts.* An expenditure described in (a) of this subdivision shall be deemed for a gift to which this section does not apply if it is:

(1) An expenditure for packaged food or beverages transferred directly or indirectly to another person intended for consumption at a later time.

(2) An expenditure for tickets of admission to a place of entertainment transferred to another person if the taxpayer does not accompany the recipient to the entertainment unless the taxpayer treats the expenditure as entertainment. The taxpayer may change his treatment of such an expenditure as either a gift or entertainment at any time within the period prescribed for assessment of tax as provided in section 6501 of the Code and the regulations thereunder.

(3) Such other specific classes of expenditure generally considered to be for a gift as the Commissioner, in his discretion, may prescribe.

(c) *Expenditures deemed travel.* An expenditure described in (a) of this subdivision shall be deemed for travel to which this section does not apply if it is:

(1) With respect to a transportation type facility (such as an automobile or an airplane), even though used on other occasions in connection with an activity of a type generally considered to constitute entertainment, to the extent the facility is used in pursuit of a trade or business for purposes of transportation not in connection with entertainment. See also paragraph (e)(3)(iii)(b) of this section for provisions covering nonentertainment expenditures with respect to such facilities.

663

Sec. 274. Disallowance of certain entertainment, etc., expenses

(2) Such other specific classes of expenditure generally considered to be for travel as the Commissioner, in his discretion, may prescribe.

(2) *Other definitions*--(i) *Expenditure.* The term expenditure as used in this section shall include expenses paid or incurred for goods, services, facilities, and items (including items such as losses and depreciation).

(ii) Expenses for production of income. For purposes of this section, any reference to trade or business shall include any activity described in section 212.

(iii) *Business associate.* The term business associate as used in this section means a person with whom the taxpayer could reasonably expect to engage or deal in the active conduct of the taxpayer's trade or business such as the taxpayer's customer, client, supplier, employee, agent, partner, or professional adviser, whether established or prospective.

(c) *Directly related entertainment*--(1) *In general.* Except as otherwise provided in paragraph (d) of this section (relating to associated entertainment) or under paragraph (f) of this section (relating to business meals and other specific exceptions), no deduction shall be allowed for any expenditure for entertainment unless the taxpayer establishes that the expenditure was directly related to the active conduct of his trade or business within the meaning of this paragraph.

(2) *Directly related entertainment defined.* Any expenditure for entertainment, if it is otherwise allowable as a deduction under chapter 1 of the Code, shall be considered directly related to the active conduct of the taxpayer's trade or business if it meets the requirements of any one of subparagraphs (3), (4), (5), or (6) of this paragraph.

(3) *Directly related in general.* Except as provided in subparagraph (7) of this paragraph, an expenditure for entertainment shall be considered directly related to the active conduct of the taxpayer's trade or business if it is established that it meets all of the requirements of subdivisions (i), (ii), (iii) and (iv) of this subparagraph.

(i) At the time the taxpayer made the entertainment expenditure (or committed himself to make the expenditure), the taxpayer had more than a general expectation of deriving some income or other specific trade or business benefit (other than the goodwill of the person or persons entertained) at some indefinite future time from the making of the expenditure. A taxpayer, however, shall not be required to show that income or other business benefit actually resulted from each and every expenditure for which a deduction is claimed.

(ii) During the entertainment period to which the expenditure related, the taxpayer actively engaged in a business meeting, negotiation, discussion, or other bona fide business transaction, other than entertainment, for the purpose of obtaining such income or other specific trade or business benefit (or, at the time the taxpayer made the expenditure or committed himself to the expenditure, it was reasonable for the taxpayer to expect that he would have done so, although such was not the case solely for reasons beyond the taxpayer's control).

(iii) In light of all the facts and circumstances of the case, the principal character or aspect of the combined business and entertainment to which the expenditure related was the active conduct of the taxpayer's trade or business (or at the time the taxpayer made the expenditure or committed himself to the expenditure, it was reasonable for the taxpayer to expect that the active conduct of trade or business would have been the principal character or aspect of the entertainment, although such was not the case solely for reasons beyond the taxpayer's control). It is not necessary that more time be devoted to business than to entertainment to meet this requirement. The active conduct of trade or business is considered not to be the principal character or aspect of combined business and entertainment activity on hunting or fishing trips or on yachts and other pleasure boats unless the taxpayer clearly establishes to the contrary.

664

Sec. 274. Disallowance of certain entertainment, etc., expenses

(iv) The expenditure was allocable to the taxpayer and a person or persons with whom the taxpayer engaged in the active conduct of trade or business during the entertainment or with whom the taxpayer establishes he would have engaged in such active conduct of trade or business if it were not for circumstances beyond the taxpayer's control. For expenditures closely connected with directly related entertainment, see paragraph (d)(4) 5 of this section.

(4) *Expenditures in clear business setting.* An expenditure for entertainment shall be considered directly related to the active conduct of the taxpayer's trade or business if it is established that the expenditure was for entertainment occurring in a clear business setting directly in furtherance of the taxpayer's trade or business. Generally, 10 entertainment shall not be considered to have occurred in a clear business setting unless the taxpayer clearly establishes that any recipient of the entertainment would have reasonably known that the taxpayer had no significant motive, in incurring the expenditure, other than directly furthering his trade or business. Objective rather than subjective standards will be determinative. Thus, entertainment which occurred under 15 any circumstances described in subparagraph (7)(ii) of this paragraph ordinarily will not be considered as occurring in a clear business setting. Such entertainment will generally be considered to be socially rather than commercially motivated. Expenditures made for the furtherance of a taxpayer's trade or business in providing a ``hospitality room" at a convention (described in paragraph (d)(3)(i)(b) of this section) at which goodwill is 20 created through display or discussion of the taxpayer's products, will, however, be treated as directly related. In addition, entertainment of a clear business nature which occurred under circumstances where there was no meaningful personal or social relationship between the taxpayer and the recipients of the entertainment may be considered to have occurred in a clear business setting. For example, entertainment of business 25 representatives and civic leaders at the opening of a new hotel or theatrical production, where the clear purpose of the taxpayer is to obtain business publicity rather than to create or maintain the goodwill of the recipients of the entertainment, would generally be considered to be in a clear business setting. Also, entertainment which has the principal effect of a price rebate in connection with the sale of the taxpayer's products generally 30 will be considered to have occurred in a clear business setting. Such would be the case, for example, if a taxpayer owning a hotel were to provide occasional free dinners at the hotel for a customer who patronized the hotel.

(5) *Expenditures for services performed.* An expenditure shall be considered directly related to the active conduct of the taxpayer's trade or business if it is established that the 35 expenditure was made directly or indirectly by the taxpayer for the benefit of an individual (other than an employee), and if such expenditure was in the nature of compensation for services rendered or was paid as a prize or award which is required to be included in gross income under section 74 and the regulations thereunder. For example, if a manufacturer of products provides a vacation trip for retailers of his products who exceed 40 sales quotas as a prize or award which is includible in gross income, the expenditure will be considered directly related to the active conduct of the taxpayer's trade or business.

(6) *Club dues, etc., allocable to business meals.* An expenditure shall be considered directly related to the active conduct of the taxpayer's trade or business if it is established that the expenditure was with respect to a facility (as described in paragraph (e) of this 45 section) used by the taxpayer for the furnishing of food or beverages under circumstances described in paragraph (f)(2)(i) of this section (relating to business meals and similar expenditures), to the extent allocable to the furnishing of such food or beverages. This paragraph (c)(6) applies to club dues paid or incurred before January 1, 1987. 50

(7) *Expenditures generally considered not directly related.* Expenditures for

Sec. 274. Disallowance of certain entertainment, etc., expenses

entertainment, even if connected with the taxpayer's trade or business, will generally be considered not directly related to the active conduct of the taxpayer's trade or business, if the entertainment occurred under circumstances where there was little or no possibility of engaging in the active conduct of trade or business. The following circumstances will

5 generally be considered circumstances where there was little or no possibility of engaging in the active conduct of a trade or business:

(i) The taxpayer was not present;

(ii) The distractions were substantial, such as:

(a) A meeting or discussion at night clubs, theaters, and sporting events, or during

10 essentially social gatherings such as cocktail parties, or

(b) A meeting or discussion, if the taxpayer meets with a group which includes persons other than business associates, at places such as cocktail lounges, country clubs, golf and athletic clubs, or at vacation resorts.

An expenditure for entertainment in any such case is considered not to be directly related

15 to the active conduct of the taxpayer's trade or business unless the taxpayer clearly establishes to the contrary.

(d) *Associated entertainment*--(1) *In general.* Except as provided in paragraph (f) of this section (relating to business meals and other specific exceptions) and subparagraph (4) of this paragraph (relating to expenditures closely connected with directly related

20 entertainment), any expenditure for entertainment which is not directly related to the active conduct of the taxpayer's trade or business will not be allowable as a deduction unless:

(i) It was associated with the active conduct of trade or business as defined in subparagraph (2) of this paragraph, and

25 (ii) The entertainment directly preceded or followed a substantial and bona fide business discussion as defined in subparagraph (3) of this paragraph.

(2) *Associated entertainment defined.* Generally, any expenditure for entertainment, if it is otherwise allowable under Chapter 1 of the Code, shall be considered associated with the active conduct of the taxpayer's trade or business if the taxpayer establishes that

30 he had a clear business purpose in making the expenditure, such as to obtain new business or to encourage the continuation of an existing business relationship. However, any portion of an expenditure allocable to a person who was not closely connected with a person who engaged in the substantial and bona fide business discussion (as defined in subparagraph (3)(i) of this paragraph) shall not be considered associated with the active

35 conduct of the taxpayer's trade or business. The portion of an expenditure allocable to the spouse of a person who engaged in the discussion will, if it is otherwise allowable under chapter 1 of the Code, be considered associated with the active conduct of the taxpayer's trade or business.

(3) *Directly preceding or following a substantial and bona fide business discussion*

40 *defined*--(i) *Substantial and bona fide business discussion*--(a) *In general.* Whether any meeting, negotiation or discussion constitutes a ``substantial and bona fide business discussion" within the meaning of this section depends upon the facts and circumstances of each case. It must be established, however, that the taxpayer actively engaged in a business meeting, negotiation, discussion, or other bona fide business transaction, other

45 than entertainment, for the purpose of obtaining income or other specific trade or business benefit. In addition, it must be established that such a business meeting, negotiation, discussion, or transaction was substantial in relation to the entertainment. This requirement will be satisfied if the principal character or aspect of the combined entertainment and business activity was the active conduct of business. However, it is not

50 necessary that more time be devoted to business than to entertainment to meet this requirement.

Sec. 274. Disallowance of certain entertainment, etc., expenses

(b) *Meetings at conventions, etc.* Any meeting officially scheduled in connection with a program at a convention or similar general assembly, or at a bona fide trade or business meeting sponsored and conducted by business or professional organizations, shall be considered to constitute a substantial and bona fide business discussion within the meaning of this section provided:

(1) *Expenses necessary to taxpayer's attendance.* The expenses necessary to the attendance of the taxpayer at the convention, general assembly, or trade or business meeting, were ordinary and necessary within the meaning of section 162 or 212;

(2) *Convention program.* The organization which sponsored the convention, or trade or business meeting had scheduled a program of business activities (including committee meetings or presentation of lectures, panel discussions, display of products, or other similar activities), and that such program was the principal activity of the convention, general assembly, or trade or business meeting.

(ii) *Directly preceding or following.* Entertainment which occurs on the same day as a substantial and bona fide business discussion (as defined in subdivision (i) of this subparagraph) will be considered to directly precede or follow such discussion. If the entertainment and the business discussion do not occur on the same day, the facts and circumstances of each case are to be considered, including the place, date and duration of the business discussion, whether the taxpayer or his business associates are from out of town, and, if so, the date of arrival and departure, and the reasons the entertainment did not take place on the day of the business discussion. For example, if a group of business associates comes from out of town to the taxpayer's place of business to hold a substantial business discussion, the entertainment of such business guests and their wives on the evening prior to, or on the evening of the day following, the business discussion would generally be regarded as directly preceding or following such discussion.

(4) *Expenses closely connected with directly related entertainment.* If any portion of an expenditure meets the requirements of paragraph (c)(3) of this section (relating to directly related entertainment in general), the remaining portion of the expenditure, if it is otherwise allowable under Chapter 1 of the Code, shall be considered associated with the active conduct of the taxpayer's trade or business to the extent allocable to a person or persons closely connected with a person referred to in paragraph (c)(3)(iv) of this section. The spouse of a person referred to in paragraph(c)(3)(iv) of this section will be considered closely connected to such a person for purposes of this subparagraph. Thus, if a taxpayer and his wife entertain a business customer and the customer's wife under circumstances where the entertainment of the customer is considered directly related to the active conduct of the taxpayer's trade or business (within the meaning of paragraph (c)(3) of this section) the portion of the expenditure allocable to both wives will be considered associated with the active conduct of the taxpayer's trade or business under this subparagraph.

***

(2) *Facilities used in connection with entertainment--*(i) *In general.* Any item of personal or real property owned, rented, or used by a taxpayer shall (unless otherwise provided under the rules of subdivision (ii) of this subparagraph) be considered to constitute a facility used in connection with entertainment if it is used during the taxable year for, or in connection with, entertainment (as defined in paragraph (b)(1) of this section). Examples of facilities which might be used for, or in connection with, entertainment include yachts, hunting lodges, fishing camps, swimming pools, tennis courts, bowling alleys, automobiles, airplanes, apartments, hotel suites, and homes in vacation resorts.

(ii) *Facilities used incidentally for entertainment.* A facility used only incidentally during

Sec. 274. Disallowance of certain entertainment, etc., expenses

a taxable year in connection with entertainment, if such use is insubstantial, will not be considered a ``facility used in connection with entertainment'' for purposes of this section or for purposes of the recordkeeping requirements of section 274(d). See § 1.274-5(c)(6) (iii).

5   (3) *Expenditures with respect to a facility used in connection with entertainment--(i) In general.* The phrase expenditures with respect to a facility used in connection with entertainment includes depreciation and operating costs, such as rent and utility charges (for example, water or electricity), expenses for the maintenance, preservation or protection of a facility (for example, repairs, painting, insurance charges), and salaries or
10 expenses for subsistence paid to caretakers or watchmen. In addition, the phrase includes losses realized on the sale or other disposition of a facility.

***

    (b) *Club dues paid or incurred after December 31, 1993.* See paragraph (a)(2)(iii) of this section with reference to the disallowance of deductions for club dues paid or
15 incurred after December 31, 1993.

    (iii) *Expenditures not with respect to a facility.* The following expenditures shall not be considered to constitute expenditures with respect to a facility used in connection with entertainment:

    (a) *Out of pocket expenditures.* Expenses (exclusive of operating costs and other
20 expenses referred to in subdivision (i) of this subparagraph) incurred at the time of an entertainment activity, even though in connection with the use of facility for entertainment purposes, such as expenses for food and beverages, or expenses for catering, or expenses for gasoline and fishing bait consumed on a fishing trip;

    (b) *Non-entertainment expenditures.* Expenses or items attributable to the use of a
25 facility for other than entertainment purposes such as expenses for an automobile when not used for entertainment; and

    (c) *Expenditures otherwise deductible.* Expenses allowable as a deduction without regard to their connection with a taxpayer's trade or business such as taxes, interest, and casualty losses. The provisions of this subdivision shall be applied in the case of a
30 taxpayer which is not an individual as if it were an individual. See also § 1.274-6.

    (iv) *Cross reference.* For other rules with respect to treatment of certain expenditures for entertainment-type facilities, see § 1.274-7.

    (4) *Determination of primary use--(i) In general.* A facility used in connection with entertainment shall be considered as used primarily for the furtherance of the taxpayer's
35 trade or business only if it is established that the primary use of the facility during the taxable year was for purposes considered ordinary and necessary within the meaning of sections 162 and 212 and the regulations thereunder. All of the facts and circumstances of each case shall be considered in determining the primary use of a facility. Generally, it is the actual use of the facility which establishes the deductibility of expenditures with
40 respect to the facility; not its availability for use and not the taxpayer's principal purpose in acquiring the facility. Objective rather than subjective standards will be determinative. If membership entitles the member's entire family to use of a facility, such as a country club, their use will be considered in determining whether business use of the facility exceeds personal use. The factors to be considered include the nature of each use, the
45 frequency and duration of use for business purposes as compared with other purposes, and the amount of expenditures incurred during use for business compared with amount of expenditures incurred during use for other purposes. No single standard of comparison, or quantitative measurement, as to the significance of any such factor, however, is necessarily appropriate for all classes or types of facilities. For example, an
50 appropriate standard for determining the primary use of a country club during a taxable year will not necessarily be appropriate for determining the primary use of an airplane.

Sec. 274. Disallowance of certain entertainment, etc., expenses

However, a taxpayer shall be deemed to have established that a facility was used primarily for the furtherance of his trade or business if he establishes such primary use in accordance with subdivision (ii) or (iii) of this subparagraph. Subdivisions (ii) and (iii) of this subparagraph shall not preclude a taxpayer from otherwise establishing the primary use of a facility under the general provisions of this subdivision.   5

(ii) *Certain transportation facilities.* A taxpayer shall be deemed to have established that a facility of a type described in this subdivision was used primarily for the furtherance of his trade or business if:

(a) *Automobiles.* In the case of an automobile, the taxpayer establishes that more than 50 percent of mileage driven during the taxable year was in connection with travel 10 considered to be ordinary and necessary within the meaning of section 162 or 212 and the regulations thereunder.

(b) *Airplanes.* In the case of an airplane, the taxpayer establishes that more than 50 percent of hours flown during the taxable year was in connection with travel considered to be ordinary and necessary within the meaning of section 162 or 212 and the regulations 15 thereunder.

(iii) *Entertainment facilities in general.* A taxpayer shall be deemed to have established that:

(a) A facility used in connection with entertainment, such as a yacht or other pleasure boat, hunting lodge, fishing camp, summer home or vacation cottage, hotel suite, country 20 club, golf club or similar social, athletic, or sporting club or organization, bowling alley, tennis court, or swimming pool, or,

(b) A facility for employees not falling within the scope of section 274(e) (2) or (5) was used primarily for the furtherance of his trade or business if he establishes that more than 50 percent of the total calendar days of use of the facility by, or under authority of, the 25 taxpayer during the taxable year were days of business use. Any use of a facility (of a type described in this subdivision) during one calendar day shall be considered to constitute a ``day of business use'' if the primary use of the facility on such day was ordinary and necessary within the meaning of section 162 or 212 and the regulations thereunder. For the purposes of this subdivision, a facility shall be deemed to have been 30 primarily used for such purposes on any one calendar day if the facility was used for the conduct of a substantial and bona fide business discussion (as defined in paragraph (d) (3)(i) of this section) notwithstanding that the facility may also have been used on the same day for personal or family use by the taxpayer or any member of the taxpayer's family not involving entertainment of others by, or under the authority of, the taxpayer.   35

(f) *Specific exceptions to application of this section*--(1) *In general.* The provisions of paragraphs (a) through (e) of this section (imposing limitations on deductions for entertainment expenses) are not applicable in the case of expenditures set forth in subparagraph (2) of this paragraph. Such expenditures are deductible to the extent allowable under chapter 1 of the Code. This paragraph shall not be construed to affect 40 the allowability or nonallowability of a deduction under section 162 or 212 and the regulations thereunder. The fact that an expenditure is not covered by a specific exception provided for in this paragraph shall not be determinative of the allowability or nonallowability of the expenditure under paragraphs (a) through (e) of this section. Expenditures described in subparagraph (2) of this paragraph are subject to the 45 substantiation requirements of section 274(d) to the extent provided in § 1.274-5.

(2) *Exceptions.* The expenditures referred to in subparagraph (1) of this paragraph are set forth in subdivisions (i) through (ix) of this subparagraph.

***

(ii) *Food and beverages for employees.* Any expenditure by a taxpayer for food and 50 beverages (or for use of a facility in connection therewith) furnished on the taxpayer's

Sec. 274. Disallowance of certain entertainment, etc., expenses

business premises primarily for his employees is not subject to the limitations on allowability of deductions provided for in paragraphs (a) through (e) of this section. This exception applies not only to expenditures for food or beverages furnished in a typical company cafeteria or an executive dining room, but also to expenditures with respect to
5 the operation of such facilities. This exception applies even though guests are occasionally served in the cafeteria or dining room.

(iii) *Certain entertainment and travel expenses treated as compensation*--(A) *In general.* Any expenditure by a taxpayer for entertainment (or for use of a facility in connection therewith) or for travel described in section 274(m)(3), if an employee is the
10 recipient of the entertainment or travel, is not subject to the limitations on allowability of deductions provided for in paragraphs (a) through (e) of this section to the extent that the expenditure is treated by the taxpayer--

(1) On the taxpayer's income tax return as originally filed, as compensation paid to the employee; and
15 (2) As wages to the employee for purposes of withholding under chapter 24 (relating to collection of income tax at source on wages).

(B) *Expenses includible in income of persons who are not employees.* Any expenditure by a taxpayer for entertainment (or for use of a facility in connection therewith), or for travel described in section 274(m)(3), is not subject to the limitations on
20 allowability of deductions provided for in paragraphs (a) through (e) of this section to the extent the expenditure is includible in gross income as compensation for services rendered, or as a prize or award under section 74, by a recipient of the expenditure who is not an employee of the taxpayer. The preceding sentence shall not apply to any amount paid or incurred by the taxpayer if such amount is required to be included (or
25 would be so required except that the amount is less that $600) in any information return filed by such taxpayer under part III of subchapter A of chapter 61 and is not so included. See section 274(e)(9).

***

(iv) *Reimbursed entertainment expenses*--(a) *Introductory.* In the case of any
30 expenditure for entertainment paid or incurred by one person in connection with the performance by him of services for another person (whether or not such other person is an employer) under a reimbursement or other expense allowance arrangement, the limitations on allowability of deductions provided for in paragraphs (a) through (e) of this section shall be applied only once, either (1) to the person who makes the expenditure or
35 (2) to the person who actually bears the expense, but not to both. For purposes of this subdivision (iv), the term reimbursement or other expense allowance arrangement has the same meaning as it has in section 62(2)(A), but without regard to whether the taxpayer is the employee of a person for whom services are performed. If an expenditure of a type described in this subdivision properly constitutes a dividend paid to a
40 shareholder, unreasonable compensation paid to an employee, or a personal, living or family expense, nothing in this exception prevents disallowance of the expenditure to the taxpayer under other provisions of the Code.

(b) *Reimbursement arrangements between employee and employer.* In the case of an expenditure for entertainment paid or incurred by an employee under a reimbursement or
45 other expense allowance arrangement with his employer, the limitations on deductions provided for in paragraphs (a) through (e) of this section shall not apply:

(1) *Employees.* To the employee except to the extent his employer has treated the expenditure on the employer's income tax return as originally filed as compensation paid to the employee and as wages to such employee for purposes of withholding under
50 Chapter 24 (relating to collection of income tax at source on wages).

(2) *Employers.* To the employer to the extent he has treated the expenditure as

670

Sec. 274. Disallowance of certain entertainment, etc., expenses

compensation and wages paid to an employee in the manner provided in (b)(1) of this subdivision.

(c) *Reimbursement arrangements between independent contractors and clients or customers.* In the case of an expenditure for entertainment paid or incurred by one person (hereinafter termed ``independent contractor") under a reimbursement or other expense allowance arrangement with another person other than an employer (hereinafter termed ``client or customer"), the limitations on deductions provided for in paragraphs (a) through (e) of this section shall not apply:

(1) *Independent contractors.* To the independent contractor to the extent he accounts to his client or customer within the meaning of section 274(d) and the regulations thereunder. See § 1.274-5.

(2) *Clients or customers.* To the client or customer if the expenditure is disallowed to the independent contractor under paragraphs (a) through (e) of this section.

(v) *Recreational expenses for employees generally.* Any expenditure by a taxpayer for a recreational, social, or similar activity (or for use of a facility in connection therewith), primarily for the benefit of his employees generally, is not subject to the limitations on allowability of deductions provided for in paragraphs (a) through (e) of this section. This exception applies only to expenditures made primarily for the benefit of employees of the taxpayer other than employees who are officers, shareholders on other owners who own a 10-percent or greater interest in the business, or other highly compensated employees. For purposes of the preceding sentence, an employee shall be treated as owning any interest owned by a member of his family (within the meaning of section 267(c)(4) and the regulations thereunder). Ordinarily, this exception applies to usual employee benefit programs such as expenses of a taxpayer (a) in holding Christmas parties, annual picnics, or summer outings, for his employees generally, or (b) of maintaining a swimming pool, baseball diamond, bowling alley, or golf course available to his employees generally. Any expenditure for an activity which is made under circumstances which discriminate in favor of employees who are officers, shareholders or other owners, or highly compensated employees shall not be considered made primarily for the benefit of employees generally. On the other hand, an expenditure for an activity will not be considered outside of this exception merely because, due to the large number of employees involved, the activity is intended to benefit only a limited number of such employees at one time, provided the activity does not discriminate in favor of officers, shareholders, other owners, or highly compensated employees.

(vi) *Employee, stockholder, etc., business meetings.* Any expenditure by a taxpayer for entertainment which is directly related to bona fide business meetings of the taxpayer's employees, stockholders, agents, or directors held principally for discussion of trade or business is not subject to the limitations on allowability of deductions provided for in paragraphs (a) through (e) of this section. For purposes of this exception, a partnership is to be considered a taxpayer and a member of a partnership is to be considered an agent. For example, an expenditure by a taxpayer to furnish refreshments to his employees at a bona fide meeting, sponsored by the taxpayer for the principal purpose of instructing them with respect to a new procedure for conducting his business, would be within the provisions of this exception. A similar expenditure made at a bona fide meeting of stockholders of the taxpayer for the election of directors and discussion of corporate affairs would also be within the provisions of this exception. While this exception will apply to bona fide business meetings even though some social activities are provided, it will not apply to meetings which are primarily for social or nonbusiness purposes rather than for the transaction of the taxpayer's business. A meeting under circumstances where there was little or no possibility of engaging in the active conduct of trade or business (as described in paragraph (c)(7) of this section) generally will not be considered a business

671

Sec. 274. Disallowance of certain entertainment, etc., expenses

meeting for purposes of this subdivision. This exception will not apply to a meeting or convention of employees or agents, or similar meeting for directors, partners or others for the principal purpose of rewarding them for their services to the taxpayer. However, such a meeting or convention of employees might come within the scope of subdivisions (iii) or
5 (v) of this subparagraph.

(vii) *Meetings of business leagues, etc.* Any expenditure for entertainment directly related and necessary to attendance at bona fide business meetings or conventions of organizations exempt from taxation under section 501(c)(6) of the Code, such as business leagues, chambers of commerce, real estate boards, boards of trade, and
10 certain professional associations, is not subject to the limitations on allowability of deductions provided in paragraphs (a) through (e) of this section.

(viii) *Items available to the public.* Any expenditure by a taxpayer for entertainment (or for a facility in connection therewith) to the extent the entertainment is made available to the general public is not subject to the limitations on allowability of deductions provided
15 for in paragraphs (a) through (e) of this section. Expenditures for entertainment of the general public by means of television, radio, newspapers and the like, will come within this exception, as will expenditures for distributing samples to the general public. Similarly, expenditures for maintaining private parks, golf courses and similar facilities, to the extent that they are available for public use, will come within this exception. For
20 example, if a corporation maintains a swimming pool which it makes available for a period of time each week to children participating in a local public recreational program, the portion of the expense relating to such public use of the pool will come within this exception.

(ix) *Entertainment sold to customers.* Any expenditure by a taxpayer for entertainment
25 (or for use of a facility in connection therewith) to the extent the entertainment is sold to customers in a bona fide transaction for an adequate and full consideration in money or money's worth is not subject to the limitations on allowability of deductions provided for in paragraphs (a) through (e) of this section. Thus, the cost of producing night club entertainment (such as salaries paid to employees of night clubs and amounts paid to
30 performers) for sale to customers or the cost of operating a pleasure cruise ship as a business will come within this exception.

(g) *Additional provisions of section 274--travel of spouse, dependent or others.* Section 274(m)(3) provides that no deduction shall be allowed under this chapter (except section 217) for travel expenses paid or incurred with respect to a spouse, dependent, or
35 other individual accompanying the taxpayer (or an officer or employee of the taxpayer) on business travel, unless certain conditions are met. As provided in section 274(m)(3), the term other individual does not include a business associate (as defined in paragraph (b) (2)(iii) of this section) who otherwise meets the requirements of sections 274(m)(3)(B) and (C).
40

Reg. § 1.274-3 Disallowance of deduction for gifts.

(a) *In general.* No deduction shall be allowed under section 162 or 212 for any expense for a gift made directly or indirectly by a taxpayer to any individual to the extent that such expense, when added to prior expenses of the taxpayer for gifts made to such
45 individual during the taxpayer's taxable year, exceeds $25.

(b) *Gift defined--*(1) *In general.* Except as provided in subparagraph (2) of this paragraph the term gift, for purposes of this section, means any item excludable from the gross income of the recipient under section 102 which is not excludable from his gross income under any other provision of chapter 1 of the Code. Thus, a payment by an
50 employer to a deceased employee's widow is not a gift, for purposes of this section, to the extent the payment constitutes an employee's death benefit excludable by the

Sec. 274.   Disallowance of certain entertainment, etc., expenses

recipient under section 101(b). Similarly, a scholarship which is excludable from a recipient's gross income under section 117, and a prize or award which is excludable from a recipient's gross income under section 74(b), are not subject to the provisions of this section.

(2) *Items not treated as gifts.* The term gift, for purposes of this section, does not 5 include the following:

(i) An item having a cost to the taxpayer not in excess of $4.00 on which the name of the taxpayer is clearly and permanently imprinted and which is one of a number of identical items distributed generally by such a taxpayer.

(ii) A sign, display rack, or other promotional material to be used on the business 10 premises of the recipient,

***

(c) *Expense for a gift.* For purposes of this section, the term expense for a gift means the cost of the gift to the taxpayer, other than incidental costs such as for customary engraving on jewelry, or for packaging, insurance, and mailing or other delivery. A related 15 cost will be considered ``incidental'' only if it does not add substantial value to the gift. Although the cost of customary gift wrapping will be considered an incidental cost, the purchase of an ornamental basket for packaging fruit will not be considered an incidental cost of packaging if the basket has a value which is substantial in relation to the value of the fruit. 20

(d) *Qualified plan award*--(1) *In general.* Except as provided in subparagraph (2) of this paragraph the term qualified plan award, for purposes of this section, means an item of tangible personal property that is awarded to an employee by reason of the employee's length of service (including retirement), productivity, or safety achievement, and that is awarded pursuant to a permanent, written award plan or program of the taxpayer that 25 does not discriminate as to eligibility or benefits in favor of employees who are officers, shareholders, or highly compensated employees. The ``permanency'' of an award plan shall be determined from all the facts and circumstances of the particular case, including the taxpayer's ability to continue to make the awards as required by the award plan. Although the taxpayer may reserve the right to change or to terminate an award plan, the 30 actual termination of the award plan for any reason other than business necessity within a few years after it has taken effect may be evidence that the award plan from its inception was not a ``permanent'' award plan. Whether or not an award plan is discriminatory shall be determined from all the facts and circumstances of the particular case. An award plan may fail to qualify because it is discriminatory in its actual operation 35 even though the written provisions of the award plan are not discriminatory.

(2) *Items not treated as qualified plan awards.* The term qualified plan award, for purposes of this section, does not include an item qualifying under paragraph (d)(1) of this section to the extent that the cost of the item exceeds $1,600. In addition, that term does not include any items qualifying under paragraph (d)(1) of this section if the average 40 cost of all items (whether or not tangible personal property) awarded during the taxable year by the taxpayer under any plan described in paragraph (d)(1) of this section exceeds $400. The average cost of those items shall be computed by dividing (i) the sum of the costs for those items (including amounts in excess of the $1,600 limitation) by (ii) the total number of those items. 45

(e) *Gifts made indirectly to an individual*--(1) *Gift to spouse or member of family.* If a taxpayer makes a gift to the wife of a man who has a business connection with the taxpayer, the gift generally will be considered as made indirectly to the husband. However, if the wife has a bona fide business connection with the taxpayer independently of her relationship to her husband, a gift to her generally will not be considered as made 50 indirectly to her husband unless the gift is intended for his eventual use or benefit. Thus,

673

Sec. 274. Disallowance of certain entertainment, etc., expenses

if a taxpayer makes a gift to a wife who is engaged with her husband in the active conduct of a partnership business, the gift to the wife will not be considered an indirect gift to her husband unless it is intended for his eventual use or benefit. The same rules apply to gifts to any other member of the family of an individual who has a business
5 connection with the taxpayer.

(2) *Gift to corporation or other business entity.* If a taxpayer makes a gift to a corporation or other business entity intended for the eventual personal use or benefit of an individual who is an employee, stockholder, or other owner of the corporation or business entity, the gift generally will be considered as made indirectly to such individual.
10 Thus, if a taxpayer provides theater tickets to a closely held corporation for eventual use by any one of the stockholders of the corporation, and if such tickets are gifts, the gifts will be considered as made indirectly to the individual who eventually uses such ticket. On the other hand, a gift to a business organization of property to be used in connection with the business of the organization (for example, a technical manual) will not be
15 considered as a gift to an individual, even though, in practice, the book will be used principally by a readily identifiable individual employee. A gift for the eventual personal use or benefit of some undesignated member of a large group of individuals generally will not be considered as made indirectly to the individual who eventually uses, or benefits from, such gifts unless, under the circumstances of the case, it is reasonably practicable
20 for the taxpayer to ascertain the ultimate recipient of the gift. Thus, if a taxpayer provides several baseball tickets to a corporation for the eventual use by any one of a large number of employees or customers of the corporation, and if such tickets are gifts, the gifts generally will not be treated as made indirectly to the individuals who use such tickets.

25 (f) *Special rules--(1) Partnership.* In the case of a gift by a partnership, the $25 annual limitation contained in paragraph (a) of this section shall apply to the partnership as well as to each member of the partnership. Thus, in the case of a gift made by a partner with respect to the business of the partnership, the $25 limitation will be applied at the partnership level as well as at the level of the individual partner. Consequently,
30 deductions for gifts made with respect to partnership business will not exceed $25 annually for each recipient, regardless of the number of partners.

(2) *Husband and wife.* For purposes of applying the $25 annual limitation contained in paragraph (a) of this section, a husband and wife shall be treated as one taxpayer. Thus, in the case of gifts to an individual by a husband and wife, the spouses will be treated as
35 one donor; and they are limited to a deduction of $25 annually for each recipient. This rule applies regardless of whether the husband and wife file a joint return or whether the husband and wife make separate gifts to an individual with respect to separate businesses. Since the term taxpayer in paragraph (a) of this section refers only to the donor of a gift, this special rule does not apply to treat a husband and wife as one
40 individual where each is a recipient of a gift. See paragraph (e)(1) of this section.

(g) *Cross reference.* For rules with respect to whether this section or § 1.274-2 applies, see § 1.274-2(b)(1) (iii).

Reg. § 1.274-4 Disallowance of certain foreign travel expenses.
45 (a) *Introductory.* Section 274(c) and this section impose certain restrictions on the deductibility of travel expenses incurred in the case of an individual who, while traveling outside the United States away from home in the pursuit of trade or business (hereinafter termed ``business activity"), engages in substantial personal activity not attributable to such trade or business (hereinafter termed ``nonbusiness activity"). Section 274(c) and
50 this section are limited in their application to individuals (whether or not an employee or other person traveling under a reimbursement or other expense allowance arrangement)

who engage in nonbusiness activity while traveling outside the United States away from home, and do not impose restrictions on the deductibility of travel expenses incurred by an employer or client under an advance, reimbursement, or other arrangement with the individual who engages in nonbusiness activity. For purposes of this section, the term United States includes only the States and the District of Columbia, and any reference to ``trade or business'' or ``business activity'' includes any activity described in section 212. For rules governing the determination of travel outside the United States away from home, see paragraph (e) of this section. For rules governing the disallowance of travel expense to which this section applies, see paragraph (f) of this section.

(b) *Limitations on application of section.* The restrictions on deductibility of travel expenses contained in paragraph (f) of this section are applicable only if:

(1) The travel expense is otherwise deductible under section 162 or 212 and the regulations thereunder,

(2) The travel expense is for travel outside the United States away from home which exceeds 1 week (as determined under paragraph (c) of this section), and

(3) The time outside the United States away from home attributable to nonbusiness activity (as determined under paragraph (d) of this section) constitutes 25 percent or more of the total time on such travel.

(c) *Travel in excess of 1 week.* This section does not apply to an expense of travel unless the expense is for travel outside the United States away from home which exceeds 1 week. For purposes of this section, 1 week means 7 consecutive days. The day in which travel outside the United States away from home begins shall not be considered, but the day in which such travel ends shall be considered, in determining whether a taxpayer is outside the United States away from home for more than 7 consecutive days. For example, if a taxpayer departs on travel outside the United States away from home on a Wednesday morning and ends such travel the following Wednesday evening, he shall be considered as being outside the United States away from home only 7 consecutive days. In such a case, this section would not apply because the taxpayer was not outside the United States away from home for more than 7 consecutive days. However, if the taxpayer travels outside the United States away from home for more than 7 consecutive days, both the day such travel begins and the day such travel ends shall be considered a ``business day'' or a ``nonbusiness day'', as the case may be, for purposes of determining whether nonbusiness activity constituted 25 percent or more of travel time under paragraph (d) of this section and for purposes of allocating expenses under paragraph (f) of this section. For purposes of determining whether travel is outside the United States away from home, see paragraph (e) of this section.

(d) *Nonbusiness activity constituting 25 percent or more of travel time--(1) In general.* This section does not apply to any expense of travel outside the United States away from home unless the portion of time outside the United States away from home attributable to nonbusiness activity constitutes 25 percent or more of the total time on such travel.

(2) *Allocation on per day basis.* The total time traveling outside the United States away from home will be allocated on a day-by-day basis to (i) days of business activity or (ii) days of nonbusiness activity (hereinafter termed ``business days'' or ``nonbusiness days'' respectively) unless the taxpayer establishes that a different method of allocation more clearly reflects the portion of time outside the United States away from home which is attributable to nonbusiness activity. For purposes of this section, a day spent outside the United States away from home shall be deemed entirely a business day even though spent only in part on business activity if the taxpayer establishes:

(i) *Transportation days.* That on such day the taxpayer was traveling to or returning from a destination outside the United States away from home in the pursuit of trade or

business. However, if for purposes of engaging in nonbusiness activity, the taxpayer while traveling outside the United States away from home does not travel by a reasonably direct route, only that number of days shall be considered business days as would be required for the taxpayer, using the same mode of transportation, to travel to or
5 return from the same destination by a reasonably direct route. Also, if, while so traveling, the taxpayer interrupts the normal course of travel by engaging in substantial diversions for nonbusiness reasons of his own choosing, only that number of days shall be considered business days as equals the number of days required for the taxpayer, using the same mode of transportation, to travel to or return from the same destination without
10 engaging in such diversion. For example, if a taxpayer residing in New York departs on an evening on a direct flight to Quebec for a business meeting to be held in Quebec the next morning, for purposes of determining whether nonbusiness activity constituted 25 percent or more of his travel time, the entire day of his departure shall be considered a business day. On the other hand, if a taxpayer travels by automobile from New York to
15 Quebec to attend a business meeting and while en route spends 2 days in Ottawa and 1 day in Montreal on nonbusiness activities of his personal choice, only that number of days outside the United States shall be considered business days as would have been required for the taxpayer to drive by a reasonably direct route to Quebec, taking into account normal periods for rest and meals.
20   (ii) *Presence required.* That on such day his presence outside the United States away from home was required at a particular place for a specific and bona fide business purpose. For example, if a taxpayer is instructed by his employer to attend a specific business meeting, the day of the meeting shall be considered a business day even though, because of the scheduled length of the meeting, the taxpayer spends more time
25 during normal working hours of the day on nonbusiness activity than on business activity.
   (iii) *Days primarily business.* That during hours normally considered to be appropriate for business activity, his principal activity on such day was the pursuit of trade or business.
   (iv) *Circumstances beyond control.* That on such day he was prevented from engaging
30 in the conduct of trade or business as his principal activity due to circumstances beyond his control.
   (v) *Weekends, holidays, etc.* That such day was a Saturday, Sunday, legal holiday, or other reasonably necessary standby day which intervened during that course of the taxpayer's trade or business while outside the United States away from home which the
35 taxpayer endeavored to conduct with reasonable dispatch. For example, if a taxpayer travels from New York to London to take part in business negotiations beginning on a Wednesday and concluding on the following Tuesday, the intervening Saturday and Sunday shall be considered business days whether or not business is conducted on either of such days. Similarly, if in the above case the meetings which concluded on
40 Tuesday evening were followed by business meetings with another business group in London on the immediately succeeding Thursday and Friday, the intervening Wednesday will be deemed a business day. However, if at the conclusion of the business meetings on Friday, the taxpayer stays in London for an additional week for personal purposes, the Saturday and Sunday following the conclusion of the business meeting will not be
45 considered business days.
   (e) *Domestic travel excluded--*(1) *In general.* For purposes of this section, travel outside the United States away from home does not include any travel from one point in the United States to another point in the United States. However, travel which is not from one point in the United States to another point in the United States shall be considered
50 travel outside the United States. If a taxpayer travels from a place within the United States to a place outside the United States, the portion, if any, of such travel which is

Sec. 274. Disallowance of certain entertainment, etc., expenses

from one point in the United States to another point in the United States is to be disregarded for purposes of determining:

(i) Whether the taxpayer's travel outside the United States away from home exceeds 1 week (see paragraph (c) of this section),

(ii) Whether the time outside the United States away from home attributable to 5 nonbusiness activity constitutes 25 percent or more of the total time on such travel (see paragraph (d) of this section), or

(iii) The amount of travel expense subject to the allocation rules of this section (see paragraph (f) of this section).

(2) *Determination of travel from one point in the United States to another point in the* 10 *United States.* In the case of the following means of transportation, travel from one point in the United States to another point in the United States shall be determined as follows:

(i) Travel by public transportation. In the case of travel by public transportation, any place in the United States at which the vehicle makes a scheduled stop for the purpose of adding or discharging passengers shall be considered a point in the United States. 15

(ii) *Travel by private automobile*. In the case of travel by private automobile, any such travel which is within the United States shall be considered travel from one point in the United States to another point in the United States.

(iii) *Travel by private airplane*. In the case of travel by private airplane, any flight, whether or not constituting the entire trip, where both the takeoff and the landing are 20 within the United States shall be considered travel from one point in the United States to another point in the United States.

(3) *Examples*. The provisions of subparagraph (2) may be illustrated by the following examples:

Example 1. Taxpayer A flies from Los Angeles to Puerto Rico with a brief scheduled 25 stopover in Miami for the purpose of adding and discharging passengers and A returns by airplane nonstop to Los Angeles. The travel from Los Angeles to Miami is considered travel from one point in the United States to another point in the United States. The travel from Miami to Puerto Rico and from Puerto Rico to Los Angeles is not considered travel from one point in the United States to another point in the United States and, thus, is 30 considered to be travel outside the United States away from home.

Example 2. Taxpayer B travels by train from New York to Montreal. The travel from New York to the last place in the United States where the train is stopped for the purpose of adding or discharging passengers is considered to be travel from one point in the United States to another point in the United States. 35

Example 3. Taxpayer C travels by automobile from Tulsa to Mexico City and back. All travel in the United States is considered to be travel from one point in the United States to another point in the United States.

Example 4. Taxpayer D flies nonstop from Seattle to Juneau. Although the flight passes over Canada, the trip is considered to be travel from one point in the United States to 40 another point in the United States.

Example 5. If in Example 4 above, the airplane makes a scheduled landing in Vancouver, the time spent in traveling from Seattle to Juneau is considered to be travel outside the United States away from home. However, the time spent in Juneau is not considered to be travel outside the United States away from home. 45

(f) *Application of disallowance rules*--(1) *In general*. In the case of expense for travel outside the United States away from home by an individual to which this section applies, except as otherwise provided in subparagraph (4) or (5) of this paragraph, no deduction shall be allowed for that amount of travel expense specified in subparagraph (2) or (3) of this paragraph (whichever is applicable) which is obtained by multiplying the total of such 50 travel expense by a fraction:

Sec. 274. Disallowance of certain entertainment, etc., expenses

(i) The numerator of which is the number of nonbusiness days during such travel, and

(ii) The denominator of which is the total number of business days and nonbusiness days during such travel.

For determination of ``business days'' and ``nonbusiness days'', see paragraph (d)(2) of this section.

(2) *Nonbusiness activity at, near, or beyond business destination.* If the place at which the individual engages in nonbusiness activity (hereinafter termed ``nonbusiness destination'') is at, near, or beyond the place to which he travels in the pursuit of a trade or business (hereinafter termed ``business destination''), the amount of travel expense referred to in subparagraph (1) of this paragraph shall be the amount of travel expense, otherwise allowable as a deduction under section 162 or section 212, which would have been incurred in traveling from the place where travel outside the United States away from home begins to the business destination, and returning. Thus, if the individual travels from New York to London on business, and then takes a vacation in Paris before returning to New York, the amount of the travel expense subject to allocation is the expense which would have been incurred in traveling from New York to London and returning.

(3) *Nonbusiness activity on the route to or from business destination.* If the nonbusiness destination is on the route to or from the business destination, the amount of the travel expense referred to in subparagraph (1) of this paragraph shall be the amount of travel expense, otherwise allowable as a deduction under section 162 or 212, which would have been incurred in traveling from the place where travel outside the United States away from home begins to the nonbusiness destination and returning. Thus, if the individual travels on business from Chicago to Rio de Janeiro, Brazil with a scheduled stop in New York for the purpose of adding and discharging passengers, and while en route stops in Caracas, Venezuela for a vacation and returns to Chicago from Rio de Janeiro with another scheduled stop in New York for the purpose of adding and discharging passengers, the amount of travel expense subject to allocation is the expense which would have been incurred in traveling from New York to Caracas and returning.

(4) *Other allocation method.* If a taxpayer establishes that a method other than allocation on a day-by-day basis (as determined under paragraph (d)(2) of this section) more clearly reflects the portion of time outside the United States away from home which is attributable to nonbusiness activity, the amount of travel expense for which no deduction shall be allowed shall be determined by such other method.

(5) *Travel expense deemed entirely allocable to business activity.* Expenses of travel shall be considered allocable in full to business activity, and no portion of such expense shall be subject to disallowance under this section, if incurred under circumstances provided for in subdivision (i) or (ii) of this subparagraph.

(i) *Lack of control over travel.* Expenses of travel otherwise deductible under section 162 or 212 shall be considered fully allocable to business activity if, considering all the facts and circumstances, the individual incurring such expenses did not have substantial control over the arranging of the business trip. A person who is required to travel to a business destination will not be considered to have substantial control over the arranging of the business trip merely because he has control over the timing of the trip. Any individual who travels on behalf of his employer under a reimbursement or other expense allowance arrangement shall be considered not to have had substantial control over the arranging of his business trip, provided the employee is not:

(a) A managing executive of the employer for whom he is traveling (and for this purpose the term managing executive includes only an employee who, by reason of his authority and responsibility, is authorized, without effective veto procedures, to decide upon the necessity for his business trip), or

(b) Related to his employer within the meaning of section 267(b) but for this purpose the percentage referred to in section 267(b)(2) shall be 10 percent.

(ii) *Lack of major consideration to obtain a vacation.* Any expense of travel, which qualifies for deduction under section 162 or 212, shall be considered fully allocable to 5 business activity if the individual incurring such expenses can establish that, considering all the facts and circumstances, he did not have a major consideration, in determining to make the trip, of obtaining a personal vacation or holiday. If such a major consideration were present, the provisions of subparagraphs (1) through (4) of this paragraph shall apply. However, if the trip were primarily personal in nature, the traveling expenses to and 10 from the destination are not deductible even though the taxpayer engages in business activities while at such destination. See paragraph (b) of § 1.162-2.

(g) *Examples.* The application of this section may be illustrated by the following examples:

Example 1. Individual A flew from New York to Paris where he conducted business for 15 1 day. He spent the next 2 days sightseeing in Paris and then flew back to New York. The entire trip, including 2 days for travel en route, took 5 days. Since the time outside the United States away from home during the trip did not exceed 1 week, the disallowance rules of this section do not apply.

Example 2. Individual B flew from Tampa to Honolulu (from one point in the United 20 States to another point in the United States) for a business meeting which lasted 3 days and for personal matters which took 10 days. He then flew to Melbourne, Australia where he conducted business for 2 days and went sightseeing for 1 day. Immediately thereafter he flew back to Tampa, with a scheduled landing in Honolulu for the purpose of adding and discharging passengers. Although the trip exceeded 1 week, the time spent outside 25 the United States away from home, including 2 days for traveling from Honolulu to Melbourne and return, was 5 days. Since the time outside the United States away from home during the trip did not exceed 1 week, the disallowance rules of this section do not apply.

Example 3. Individual C flew from Los Angeles to New York where he spent 5 days. He 30 then flew to Brussels where he spent 14 days on business and 5 days on personal matters. He then flew back to Los Angeles by way of New York. The entire trip, including 4 days for travel en route, took 28 days. However, the 2 days spent traveling from Los Angeles to New York and return, and the 5 days spent in New York are not considered travel outside the United States away from home and, thus, are disregarded for purposes 35 of this section. Although the time spent outside the United States away from home exceeded 1 week, the time outside the United States away from home attributable to nonbusiness activities (5 days out of 21) was less than 25 percent of the total time outside the United States away from home during the trip. Therefore, the disallowance rules of this section do not apply.   40

Example 4. D, an employee of Y Company, who is neither a managing executive of, nor related to, Y Company within the meaning of paragraph (f)(5)(i) of this section, traveled outside the United States away from home on behalf of his employer and was reimbursed by Y for his traveling expense to and from the business destination. The trip took more than a week and D took advantage of the opportunity to enjoy a personal 45 vacation which exceeded 25 percent of the total time on the trip. Since D, traveling under a reimbursement arrangement, is not a managing executive of, or related to, Y Company, he is not considered to have substantial control over the arranging of the business trip, and the travel expenses shall be considered fully allocable to business activity

Example 5. E, a managing executive and principal shareholder of X Company, travels 50 from New York to Stockholm, Sweden, to attend a series of business meetings. At the

conclusion of the series of meetings, which last 1 week, E spends 1 week on a personal vacation in Stockholm. If E establishes either that he did not have substantial control over the arranging of the trip or that a major consideration in his determining to make the trip was not to provide an opportunity for taking a personal vacation, the entire travel expense
5 to and from Stockholm shall be considered fully allocable to business activity.

    Example 6. F, a self-employed professional man, flew from New York to Copenhagen, Denmark, to attend a convention sponsored by a professional society. The trip lasted 3 weeks, of which 2 weeks were spent on vacation in Europe. F generally would be regarded as having substantial control over arranging this business trip. Unless F can
10 establish that obtaining a vacation was not a major consideration in determining to make the trip, the disallowance rules of this section apply.

    Example 7. Taxpayer G flew from Chicago to New York where he spent 6 days on business. He then flew to London where he conducted business for 2 days. G then flew to Paris for a 5 day vacation after which he flew back to Chicago, with a scheduled
15 landing in New York for the purpose of adding and discharging passengers. G would not have made the trip except for the business he had to conduct in London. The travel outside the United States away from home, including 2 days for travel en route, exceeded a week and the time devoted to nonbusiness activities was not less than 25 percent of the total time on such travel. The 2 days spent traveling from Chicago to New York and
20 return, and the 6 days spent in New York are disregarded for purposes of determining whether the travel outside the United States away from home exceeded a week and whether the time devoted to nonbusiness activities was less than 25 percent of the total time outside the United States away from home. If G is unable to establish either that he did not have substantial control over the arranging of the business trip or that an
25 opportunity for taking a personal vacation was not a major consideration in his determining to make the trip, 5/9ths (5 days devoted to nonbusiness activities out of a total 9 days outside the United States away from home on the trip) of the expenses attributable to transportation and food from New York to London and from London to New York will be disallowed (unless G
30 establishes that a different method of allocation more clearly reflects the portion of time outside the United States away from home which is attributable to nonbusiness activity).

    (h) *Cross reference*. For rules with respect to whether an expense is travel or entertainment, see paragraph (b)(1)(iii) of § 1.274-2.

35 **Reg. § 1.274-5 Substantiation requirements.**

***

    (c) *Rules of substantiation--*

***

    (2) *Substantiation by adequate records--*
40   (iii) *Documentary evidence--*(A) Except as provided in paragraph (c)(2)(iii)(B), documentary evidence, such as receipts, paid bills, or similar evidence sufficient to support an expenditure, is required for--

    (1) Any expenditure for lodging while traveling away from home, and

    (2) Any other expenditure of $75 or more except, for transportation charges,
45 documentary evidence will not be required if not readily available.

    (B) The Commissioner, in his or her discretion, may prescribe rules waiving the documentary evidence requirements in circumstances where it is impracticable for such documentary evidence to be required. Ordinarily, documentary evidence will be considered adequate to support an expenditure if it includes sufficient information to
50 establish the amount, date, place, and the essential character of the expenditure. For

example, a hotel receipt is sufficient to support expenditures for business travel if it contains the following: name, location, date, and separate amounts for charges such as for lodging, meals, and telephone. Similarly, a restaurant receipt is sufficient to support an expenditure for a business meal if it contains the following: name and location of the restaurant, the date and amount of the expenditure, the number of people served, and, if 5 a charge is made for an item other than meals and beverages, an indication that such is the case. A document may be indicative of only one (or part of one) element of an expenditure. Thus, a canceled check, together with a bill from the payee, ordinarily would establish the element of cost. In contrast, a canceled check drawn payable to a named payee would not by itself support a business expenditure without other evidence showing 10 that the check was used for a certain business purpose.

(iv)-(v) [Reserved]. For further guidance, see § 1.274-5T(c)(2)(iv) and (v).

(3)-(7) [Reserved]. For further guidance, see § 1.274-5T(c)(3) through (7).

(d)-(e) [Reserved]. For further guidance, see § 1.274-5T(d) and (e). 15

(f) *Reporting and substantiation of expenses of certain employees for travel, entertainment, gifts, and with respect to listed property*--(1) through (3) [Reserved]. For further guidance, see § 1.274-5T(f)(1) through (3).

(4) *Definition of an adequate accounting to the employer*--(i) *In general.* For purposes of this paragraph (f) an adequate accounting means the submission to the employer of an 20 account book, diary, log, statement of expense, trip sheet, or similar record maintained by the employee in which the information as to each element of an expenditure or use (described in paragraph (b) of this section) is recorded at or near the time of the expenditure or use, together with supporting documentary evidence, in a manner that conforms to all the adequate records requirements of paragraph (c)(2) of this section. An 25 adequate accounting requires that the employee account for all amounts received from the employer during the taxable year as advances, reimbursements, or allowances (including those charged directly or indirectly to the employer through credit cards or otherwise) for travel, entertainment, gifts, and the use of listed property. The methods of substantiation allowed under paragraph (c)(4) or (c)(5) of this section also will be 30 considered to be an adequate accounting if the employer accepts an employee's substantiation and establishes that such substantiation meets the requirements of paragraph (c)(4) or (c)(5). For purposes of an adequate accounting, the method of substantiation allowed under paragraph (c)(3) of this section will not be permitted.

(ii) *Procedures for adequate accounting without documentary evidence.* The 35 Commissioner may, in his or her discretion, prescribe rules under which an employee may make an adequate accounting to an employer by submitting an account book, log, diary, etc., alone, without submitting documentary evidence.

(iii) *Employer.* For purposes of this section, the term employer includes an agent of the employer or a third party payor who pays amounts to an employee under a 40 reimbursement or other expense allowance arrangement.

(5) [Reserved]. For further guidance, see § 1.274-5T(f)(5).

(g) *Substantiation by reimbursement arrangements or per diem, mileage, and other traveling allowances*--(1) *In general.* The Commissioner may, in his or her discretion, prescribe rules in pronouncements of general applicability under which allowances for 45 expenses described in paragraph (g)(2) of this section will, if in accordance with reasonable business practice, be regarded as equivalent to substantiation by adequate records or other sufficient evidence, for purposes of paragraph (c) of this section, of the amount of the expenses and as satisfying, with respect to the amount of the expenses, the requirements of an adequate accounting to the employer for purposes of paragraph 50 (f)(4) of this section. If the total allowance received exceeds the deductible expenses paid or incurred by the employee, such excess must be reported as income on the employee's return. See paragraph (j)(1) of this section relating to the substantiation of meal expenses while traveling away from home, and paragraph (j)(2) of this section relating to the substantiation of expenses for the business use of a vehicle.

5   (2) *Allowances for expenses described.* An allowance for expenses is described in this paragraph (g)(2) if it is a--

(i) Reimbursement arrangement covering ordinary and necessary expenses of traveling away from home (exclusive of transportation expenses to and from destination);

(ii) Per diem allowance providing for ordinary and necessary expenses of traveling 10 away from home (exclusive of transportation costs to and from destination); or

(iii) Mileage allowance providing for ordinary and necessary expenses of local transportation and transportation to, from, and at the destination while traveling away from home.

(h) [Reserved]. For further guidance, see § 1.274-5T(h).

15   (i) [Reserved]

(j) *Authority for optional methods of computing certain expenses*--(1) *Meal expenses while traveling away from home.* The Commissioner may establish a method under which a taxpayer may use a specified amount or amounts for meals while traveling away from home in lieu of substantiating the actual cost of meals. The taxpayer will not be relieved 20 of the requirement to substantiate the actual cost of other travel expenses as well as the time, place, and business purpose of the travel. See paragraphs (b)(2) and (c) of this section.

(2) *Use of mileage rates for vehicle expenses.* The Commissioner may establish a method under which a taxpayer may use mileage rates to determine the amount of the 25 ordinary and necessary expenses of using a vehicle for local transportation and transportation to, from, and at the destination while traveling away from home in lieu of substantiating the actual costs. The method may include appropriate limitations and conditions in order to reflect more accurately vehicle expenses over the entire period of usage. The taxpayer will not be relieved of the requirement to substantiate the amount of 30 each business use (i.e., the business mileage), or the time and business purpose of each use. See paragraphs (b)(2) and (c) of this section.

(3) *Incidental expenses while traveling away from home.* The Commissioner may establish a method under which a taxpayer may use a specified amount or amounts for incidental expenses paid or incurred while traveling away from home in lieu of 35 substantiating the actual cost of incidental expenses. The taxpayer will not be relieved of the requirement to substantiate the actual cost of other travel expenses as well as the time, place, and business purpose of the travel.

(k)-(l) [Reserved]. For further guidance, see § 1.274-5T(k) and (l).

***

40 **Reg. § 1.274-5T   Substantiation requirements (temporary).**

(a) *In general.* For taxable years beginning on or after January 1, 1986, no deduction or credit shall be allowed with respect to--

(1) Traveling away from home (including meals and lodging),

(2) Any activity which is of a type generally considered to constitute entertainment, 45 amusement, or recreation, or with respect to a facility used in connection with such an activity, including the items specified in section 274(e),

(3) Gifts defined in section 274(b), or

(4) Any listed property (as defined in section 280F(d)(4) and § 1.280F-6T(b)), unless the taxpayer substantiates each element of the expenditure or use (as described in 50 paragraph (b) of this section) in the manner provided in paragraph (c) of this section. This limitation supersedes the doctrine found in Cohan v. Commissioner, 39 F. 2d 540 (2d Cir.

Sec. 274. Disallowance of certain entertainment, etc., expenses

1930). The decision held that, where the evidence indicated a taxpayer incurred deductible travel or entertainment expenses but the exact amount could not be determined, the court should make a close approximation and not disallow the deduction entirely. Section 274(d) contemplates that no deduction or credit shall be allowed a taxpayer on the basis of such approximations or unsupported testimony of the taxpayer. 5 For purposes of this section, the term entertainment means entertainment, amusement, or recreation, and use of a facility therefor; and the term expenditure includes expenses and items (including items such as losses and depreciation).

(b) *Elements of an expenditure or use*--(1) *In general.* Section 274(d) and this section contemplate that no deduction or credit shall be allowed for travel, entertainment, a gift, 10 or with respect to listed property unless the taxpayer substantiates the requisite elements of each expenditure or use as set forth in this paragraph (b).

(2) *Travel away from home.* The elements to be provided with respect to an expenditure for travel away from home are--

(i) *Amount.* Amount of each separate expenditure for traveling away from home, such 15 as cost of transportation or lodging, except that the daily cost of the traveler's own breakfast, lunch, and dinner and of expenditures incidental to such travel may be aggregated, if set forth in reasonable categories, such as for meals, for gasoline and oil, and for taxi fares;

(ii) *Time.* Dates of departure and return for each trip away from home, and number of 20 days away from home spent on business;

(iii) *Place.* Destinations or locality of travel, described by name of city or town or other similar designation; and

(iv) *Business purpose.* Business reason for travel or nature of the business benefit derived or expected to be derived as a result of travel. 25

(3) *Entertainment in general.* The elements to be proved with respect to an expenditure for entertainment are--

(i) *Amount.* Amount of each separate expenditure for entertainment, except that such incidental items as taxi fares or telephone calls may be aggregated on a daily basis;

(ii) *Time.* Date of entertainment; 30

(iii) *Place.* Name, if any, address or location, and destination of type of entertainment, such as dinner or theater, if such information is not apparent from the designation of the place;

(iv) *Business purpose.* Business reason for the entertainment or nature of business benefit derived or expected to be derived as a result of the entertainment and, except in 35 the case of business meals described in section 274(e)(1), the nature of any business discussion or activity;

(v) *Business relationship.* Occupation or other information relating to the person or persons entertained, including name, title, or other designation, sufficient to establish business relationship to the taxpayer. 40

(4) *Entertainment directly preceding or following a substantial and bona fide business discussion.* If a taxpayer claims a deduction for entertainment directly preceding or following a substantial and bona fide business discussion on the ground that such entertainment was associated with the active conduct of the taxpayer's trade or business, the elements to be proved with respect to such expenditure, in addition to those 45 enumerated in paragraph (b)(3)(i), (ii), (iii), and (v) of this section are--

(i) *Time.* Date and duration of business discussion;

(ii) *Place.* Place of business discussion;

(iii) *Business purpose.* Nature of business discussion, and business reason for the entertainment or nature of business benefit derived or expected to be derived as the 50 result of the entertainment.

(iv) *Business relationship*. Identification of those persons entertained who participated in the business discussion.

(5) *Gifts*. The elements to be proved with respect to an expenditure for a gift are--

(i) *Amount*. Cost of the gift to the taxpayer;

5   (ii) *Time*. Date of the gift;

(iii) *Description*. Description of the gift;

(iv) *Business purpose*. Business reason for the gift or nature of business benefit derived or expected to be derived as a result of the gift; and

(v) *Business relationship*. Occupation or other information relating to the recipient of 10 the gift, including name, title, or other designation, sufficient to establish business relationship to the taxpayer.

(6) *Listed property*. The elements to be proved with respect to any listed property are--

(i) *Amount*--(A) *Expenditures*. The amount of each separate expenditure with respect to an item of listed property, such as the cost of acquisition, the cost of capital 15 improvements, lease payments, the cost of maintenance and repairs, or other expenditures, and

(B) *Uses*. The amount of each business/investment use (as defined in § 1.280F-6T (d) (3) and (e)), based on the appropriate measure (i.e., mileage for automobiles and other means of transportation and time for other listed property, unless the Commissioner 20 approves an alternative method), and the total use of the listed property for the taxable period.

(ii) *Time*. Date of the expenditure or use with respect to listed property, and

(iii) *Business or investment purpose*. The business purpose for an expenditure or use with respect to any listed property (see § 1.274-5T(c)(6)(i)(B) and (C) for special rules for 25 the aggregation of expenditures and business use and § 1.280F-6T(d)(2) for the distinction between qualified business use and business/investment use). See also § 1.274-5T(e) relating to the substantiation of business use of employer-provided listed property and § 1.274-6T for special rules for substantiating the business/investment use of certain types of listed property.

30   (c) *Rules of substantiation*--(1) *In general*. Except as otherwise provided in this section and § 1.274-6T, a taxpayer must substantiate each element of an expenditure or use (described in paragraph (b) of this section) by adequate records or by sufficient evidence corroborating his own statement. Section 274(d) contemplates that a taxpayer will maintain and produce such substantiation as will constitute proof of each expenditure or 35 use referred to in section 274. Written evidence has considerably more probative value than oral evidence alone. In addition, the probative value of written evidence is greater the closer in time it relates to the expenditure or use. A contemporaneous log is not required, but a record of the elements of an expenditure or of a business use of listed property made at or near the time of the expenditure or use, supported by sufficient 40 documentary evidence, has a high degree of credibility not present with respect to a statement prepared subsequent thereto when generally there is a lack of accurate recall. Thus, the corroborative evidence required to support a statement not make at or near the time of the expenditure or use must have a high degree of probative value to elevate such statement and evidence to the level of credibility reflected by a record made at or 45 near the time of the expenditure or use supported by sufficient documentary evidence. The substantiation requirements of section 274(d) are designed to encourage taxpayers to maintain the records, together with documentary evidence, as provided in paragraph (c)(2) of this section.

(2) *Substantiation by adequate records*--(i) *In general*. To meet the ``adequate 50 records" requirements of section 274(d), a taxpayer shall maintain an account book, diary, log, statement of expense, trip sheets, or similar record (as provided in paragraph

Sec. 274. Disallowance of certain entertainment, etc., expenses

(c)(2)(ii) of this section), and documentary evidence (as provided in paragraph (c)(2)(iii) of this section) which, in combination, are sufficient to establish each element of an expenditure or use specified in paragraph (b) of this section. It is not necessary to record information in an account book, diary, log, statement of expense, trip sheet, or similar record which duplicates information reflected on a receipt so long as the account book, etc. and receipt complement each other in an orderly manner.

(ii) *Account book, diary, etc.* An account book, diary, log, statement of expense, trip sheet, or similar record must be prepared or maintained in such manner that each recording of an element of an expenditure or use is made at or near the time of the expenditure or use.

(A) *Made at or near the time of the expenditure or use.* For purposes of this section, the phrase made at or near the time of the expenditure or use means the element of an expenditure or use are recorded at a time when, in relation to the use or making of an expenditure, the taxpayer has full present knowledge of each element of the expenditure or use, such as the amount, time, place, and business purpose of the expenditure and business relationship. An expense account statement which is a transcription of an account book, diary, log, or similar record prepared or maintained in accordance with the provisions of this paragraph (c)(2)(ii) shall be considered a record prepared or maintained in the manner prescribed in the preceding sentence if such expense account statement is submitted by an employee to his employer or by an independent contractor to his client or customer in the regular course of good business practice. For example, a log maintained on a weekly basis, which accounts for use during the week, shall be considered a record made at or near the time of such use.

(B) *Substantiation of business purpose.* In order to constitute an adequate record of business purpose within the meaning of section 274(d) and this paragraph (c)(2), a written statement of business purpose generally is required. However, the degree of substantiation necessary to establish business purpose will vary depending upon the facts and circumstances of each case. Where the business purpose is evident from the surrounding facts and circumstances, a written explanation of such business purpose will not be required. For example, in the case of a salesman calling on customers on an established sales route, a written explanation of the business purpose of such travel ordinarily will not be required. Similarly, in the case of a business meal described in section 274(e)(1), if the business purpose of such meal is evident from the business relationship to the taxpayer of the persons entertained and other surrounding circumstances, a written explanation of such business purpose will not be required.

(C) *Substantiation of business use of listed property*--(1) *Degree of substantiation.* In order to constitute an adequate record (within the meaning of section 274(d) and this paragraph (c)(2)(ii)), which substantiates business/investment use of listed property (as defined in § 1.280F-6T(d)(3)), the record must contain sufficient information as to each element of every business/investment use. However, the level of detail required in an adequate record to substantiate business/investment use may vary depending upon the facts and circumstances. For example, a taxpayer who uses a truck for both business and personal purposes and whose only business use of a truck is to make deliveries to customers on an established route may satisfy the adequate record requirement by recording the total number miles driven during the taxable year, the length of the delivery route once, and the date of each trip at or near the time of the trips. Alternatively, the taxpayer may establish the date of each trip with a receipt, record of delivery, or other documentary evidence.

(2) *Written record.* Generally, an adequate record must be written. However, a record of the business use of listed property, such as a computer or automobile, prepared in a

computer memory device with the aid of a logging program will constitute an adequate record.

(D) *Confidential information.* If any information relating to the elements of an expenditure or use, such as place, business purpose, or business relationship, is of a
5 confidential nature, such information need not be set forth in the account book, diary, log, statement of expense, trip sheet, or similar record, provided such information is recorded at or near the time of the expenditure or use and is elsewhere available to the district director to substantiate such element of the expenditure or use.

(iii) [Reserved]. For further guidance, see § 1.274-5(c)(2)(iii).
10 (iv) *Retention of written evidence.* The Commissioner may, in his discretion, prescribe rules under which an employer may dispose of the adequate records and documentary evidence submitted to him by employees who are required to, and do, make an adequate accounting to the employer (within the meaning of paragraph (f)(4) of this section) if the employer maintains adequate accounting procedures with respect to such employees
15 (within the meaning of paragraph (f)(5) of this section.

(v) *Substantial compliance.* If a taxpayer has not fully substantiated a particular element of an expenditure or use, but the taxpayer establishes to the satisfaction of the district director that he has substantially complied with the ``adequate records'' requirements of this paragraph (c)(2) with respect to the expenditure or use, the taxpayer
20 may be permitted to establish such element by evidence which the district director shall deem adequate.

(3) *Substantiation by other sufficient evidence--*(i) *In general.* If a taxpayer fails to establish to the satisfaction of the district director that he has substantially complied with the ``adequate records'' requirements of paragraph (c)(2) of this section with respect to
25 an element of an expenditure or use, then, except as otherwise provided in this paragraph, the taxpayer must establish such element--

(A) By his own statement, whether written or oral, containing specific information in detail as to such element; and

(B) By other corroborative evidence sufficient to establish such element.
30 If such element is the description of a gift, or the cost or amount, time, place, or date of an expenditure or use, the corroborative evidence shall be direct evidence, such as a statement in writing or the oral testimony of persons entertained or other witnesses setting forth detailed information about such element, or the documentary evidence described in paragraph (c)(2) of this section. If such element is either the business
35 relationship to the taxpayer of persons entertained, or the business purpose of an expenditure, the corroborative evidence may be circumstantial evidence.

(ii) *Sampling--*(A) *In general.* Except as provided in paragraph (c)(3)(ii)(B) of this section, a taxpayer may maintain an adequate record for portions of a taxable year and use that record to substantiate the business/investment use of listed property for all or a
40 portion of the taxable year if the taxpayer can demonstrate by other evidence that the periods for which an adequate record is maintained are representative of the use for the taxable year or a portion thereof.

(B) *Exception for pooled vehicles.* The sampling method of paragraph (c)(3)(ii)(A) of this section may not be used to substantiate the business/investment use of an
45 automobile or other vehicle of an employer that is made available for use by more than one employee for all or a portion of a taxable year.

(C) *Examples.* The following examples illustrate this paragraph (c)(3)(ii).

Example 1. A, a sole proprietor and calendar year taxpayer, operates an interior decorating business out of her home. A uses an automobile for local business travel to
50 visit the homes or offices of clients, to meet with suppliers and other subcontractors, and to pick up and deliver certain items to clients when feasible. There is no other business

686

Sec. 274. Disallowance of certain entertainment, etc., expenses

use of the automobile but A and other members of her family also use the automobile for personal purposes. A maintains adequate records for the first three months of 1986 that indicate that 75 percent of the use of the automobile was in A's business. Invoices from subcontractors and paid bills indicate that A's business continued at approximately the same rate for the remainder of 1986. If other circumstances do not change (e.g., A does 5 not obtain a second car for exclusive use in her business), the determination that the business/investment use of the automobile for the taxable year is 75 percent is based on sufficient corroborative evidence.

Example 2. The facts are the same as in Example 1, except that A maintains adequate records during the first week of every month, which indicate that 75 percent of the use of 10 the automobile is in A's business. The invoices from A's business indicate that A's business continued at the same rate during the subsequent weeks of each month so that A's weekly records are representative of each month's business use of the automobile. Thus, the determination that the business/investment use of the automobile for the taxable year is 75 percent is based on sufficient corroborative evidence.   15

Example 3. B, a sole proprietor and calendar year taxpayer, is a salesman in a large metropolitan area for a company that manufactures household products. For the first three weeks of each month, B uses his own automobile occasionally to travel within the metropolitan area on business. During these three weeks, B's use of the automobile for business purposes does not follow a consistent pattern from day to day or week to week. 20 During the fourth week of each month, B delivers to his customers all the orders taken during the previous month. B's use of his automobile for business purposes, as substantiated by adequate records, is 70 percent of the total use during that fourth week. In this example, a determination based on the records maintained during that fourth week that the business/investment use of the automobile for the taxable year is 70 percent is 25 not based on sufficient corroborative evidence because use during this week is not representative of use during other periods.

(iii) *Special rules.* See § 1.274-6T for special rules for substantiation by sufficient corroborating evidence with respect to certain listed property.

(4) *Substantiation in exceptional circumstances.* If a taxpayer establishes that, by 30 reason of the inherent nature of the situation--

(i) He was unable to obtain evidence with respect to an element of the expenditure or use which conforms fully to the ``adequate records'' requirements of paragraph (c)(2) of this section,

(ii) He is unable to obtain evidence with respect to such element which conforms fully 35 to the ``other sufficient evidence'' requirements of paragraph (c)(3) of this section, and

(iii) He has presented other evidence, with respect to such element, which possesses the highest degree of probative value possible under the circumstances, such other evidence shall be considered to satisfy the substantiation requirements of section 274(d) and this paragraph.   40

(5) *Loss of records due to circumstances beyond control of the taxpayer.* Where the taxpayer establishes that the failure to produce adequate records is due to the loss of such records through circumstances beyond the taxpayer's control, such as destruction by fire, flood, earthquake, or other casualty, the taxpayer shall have a right to substantiate a deduction by reasonable reconstruction of his expenditures or use.   45

(6) *Special rules--*(i) *Separate expenditure or use--*(A) *In general.* For the purposes of this section, each separate payment or use by the taxpayer shall ordinarily be considered to constitute a separate expenditure. However, concurrent or repetitious expenses or uses may be substantiated as a single item. To illustrate the above rules, where a taxpayer entertains a business guest at dinner and thereafter at the theater, the payment 50 for dinner shall be considered to constitute one expenditure and the payment for the

tickets for the theater shall be considered to constitute a separate expenditure. Similarly, if during a day of business travel a taxpayer makes separate payments for breakfast, lunch, and dinner, he shall be considered to have made three separate expenditures. However, if during entertainment at a cocktail lounge the taxpayer pays separately for
5 each serving of refreshments, the total amount expended for the refreshments will be treated as a single expenditure. A tip may be treated as a separate expenditure.

(B) *Aggregation of expenditures*. Except as otherwise provided in this section, the account book, diary, log, statement of expense, trip sheet, or similar record required by paragraph (c)(2)(ii) of this section shall be maintained with respect to each separate
10 expenditure and not with respect to aggregate amounts for two or more expenditures. Thus, each expenditure for such items as lodging and air or rail travel shall be recorded as a separate item and not aggregated. However, at the option of the taxpayer, amounts expended for breakfast, lunch, or dinner, may be aggregated. A tip or gratuity which is related to an underlying expense may be aggregated with such expense. In addition,
15 amounts expended in connection with the use of listed property during a taxable year, such as for gasoline or repairs for an automobile, may be aggregated. If these expenses are aggregated, the taxpayer must establish the date and amount, but need not prove the business purpose of each expenditure. Instead, the taxpayer may prorate the expenses based on the total business use of the listed property. For other provisions permitting
20 recording of aggregate amounts in an account book, diary, log, statement of expense, trip sheet, or similar record, see paragraphs (b)(2)(i) and (b)(3) of this section (relating to incidental costs of travel and entertainment).

(C) *Aggregation of business use*. Uses which may be considered part of a single use, for example, a round trip or uninterrupted business use, may be accounted for by a single
25 record. For example, use of a truck to make deliveries at several different locations which begins and ends at the business premises and which may include a stop at the business premises in between two deliveries may be accounted for by a single record of miles driven. In addition, use of a passenger automobile by a salesman for a business trip away from home over a period of time may be accounted for by a single record of miles
30 traveled. De minimis personal use (such as a stop for lunch on the way between two business stops) is not an interruption of business use.

(ii) *Allocation of expenditure*. For purposes of this section, if a taxpayer has established the amount of an expenditure, but is unable to establish the portion of such amount which is attributable to each person participating in the event giving rise to the
35 expenditure, such amount shall ordinarily be allocated to each participant on a pro rata basis, if such determination is material. Accordingly, the total number of persons for whom a travel or entertainment expenditure is incurred must be established in order to compute the portion of the expenditure allocable to such person.

***

40 (iv) *Additional information*. In a case where it is necessary to obtain additional information, either--

(A) To clarify information contained in records, statements, testimony, or documentary evidence submitted by a taxpayer under the provisions of paragraph (c)(2) or (c)(3) of this section, or
45 (B) To establish the reliability or accuracy of such records, statements, testimony, or documentary evidence, the district director may, notwithstanding any other provision of this section, obtain such additional information by personal interview or otherwise as he determines necessary to implement properly the provisions of section 274 and the regulations thereunder.
50 (7) *Specific exceptions*. Except as otherwise prescribed by the Commissioner, substantiation otherwise required by this paragraph is not required for--

Sec. 274. Disallowance of certain entertainment, etc., expenses

(i) Expenses described in section 274(e)(2) relating to food and beverages for employees, section 274(e)(3) relating to expenses treated as compensation, section 274(e)(8) relating to items available to the public, and section 274(e)(9) relating to entertainment sold to customers, and

(ii) Expenses described in section 274(e)(5) relating to recreational, etc., expenses for employees, except that a taxpayer shall keep such records or other evidence as shall establish that such expenses were for activities (or facilities used in connection therewith) primarily for the benefit of employees other than employees who are officers, shareholders or other owners (as defined in section 274(e)(5)), or highly compensated employees.

(d) *Disclosure on returns*--(1) *In general.* The Commissioner may, in his discretion, prescribe rules under which any taxpayer claiming a deduction or credit for entertainment, gifts, travel, or with respect to listed property, or any other person receiving advances, reimbursements, or allowances for such items, shall make disclosure on his tax return with respect to such items. The provisions of this paragraph shall apply notwithstanding the provisions of paragraph (f) of this section.

(2) *Business use of passenger automobiles and other vehicles.* (i) On returns for taxable years beginning after December 31, 1984, taxpayers that claim a deduction or credit with respect to any vehicle are required to answer certain questions providing information about the use of the vehicle. The information required on the tax return relates to mileage (total, business, commuting, and other personal mileage), percentage of business use, date placed in service, use of other vehicles, after-work use, whether the taxpayer has evidence to support the business use claimed on the return, and whether or not the evidence is written.

(ii) Any employer that provides the use of a vehicle to an employee must obtain information from the employee sufficient to complete the employer's tax return. Any employer that provides more than five vehicles to its employees need not include any information on its return. The employer, instead, must obtain the information from its employees, indicate on its return that it has obtained the information, and retain the information received. Any employer--

(A) That can satisfy the requirements of § 1.274-6T(a)(2), relating to vehicles not used for personal purposes,

(B) That can satisfy the requirements of § 1.274-6T(a)(3), relating to vehicles not used for personal purposes other than commuting, or

(C) That treats all use of vehicles by employees as personal use need not obtain information with respect to those vehicles, but instead must indicate on its return that it has vehicles exempt from the requirements of this paragraph (d)(2).

(3) *Business use of other listed property.* On returns for taxable years beginning after December 31, 1984, taxpayers that claim a deduction or credit with respect to any listed property other than a vehicle (for example, a yacht, airplane, or certain computers) are required to provide the following information:

(i) The date that the property was placed in service,

(ii) The percentage of business use,

(iii) Whether evidence is available to support the percentage of business use claimed on the return, and

(iv) Whether the evidence is written.

(e) *Substantiation of the business use of listed property made available by an employer for use by an employee*--(1) *Employee*--(i) *In general.* An employee may not exclude from gross income as a working condition fringe any amount of the value of the availability of listed property provided by an employer to the employee, unless the employee substantiates for the period of availability the amount of the exclusion in

Sec. 274. Disallowance of certain entertainment, etc., expenses

accordance with the requirements of section 274(d) and either this section or § 1.274-6T.

(ii) Vehicles treated as used entirely for personal purposes. If an employer includes the value of the availability of a vehicle (as defined in § 1.61-21(e)(2)) in an employee's gross income without taking into account any exclusion for a working condition fringe
5 allowable under section 132 and the regulations thereunder with respect to the vehicle, the employee must substantiate any deduction claimed under §§ 1.162-25 and 1.162-25T for the business/investment use of the vehicle in accordance with the requirements of section 274(d) and either this section or § 1.274-6T.

(2) *Employer*--(i) *In general.* An employer substantiates its business/investment use of
10 listed property by showing either--

(A) That, based on evidence that satisfies the requirements of section 274(d) or statements submitted by employees that summarize such evidence, all or a portion of the use of the listed property is by employees in the employer's trade or business and, if any employee used the property for personal purposes, the employer included an appropriate
15 amount in the employee's income, or

(B) In the case of a vehicle, the employer treats all use by employees as personal use and includes an appropriate amount in the employees' income.

(ii) *Reliance on employee records.* For purposes of substantiating the business/investment use of listed property that an employer provides to an employee and
20 for purposes of the information required by paragraph (d)(2) and (3) of this section, the employer may rely on adequate records maintained by the employee or on the employee's own statement if corroborated by other sufficient evidence unless the employer knows or has reason to know that the statement, records, or other evidence are not accurate. The employer must retain a copy of the adequate records maintained by the
25 employee or the other sufficient evidence, if available. Alternatively, the employer may rely on a statement submitted by the employee that provides sufficient information to allow the employer to determine the business/investment use of the property unless the employer knows or has reason to know that the statement is not based on adequate records or on the employee's own statement corroborated by other sufficient evidence. If
30 the employer relies on the employee's statement, the employer must retain only a copy of the statement. The employee must retain a copy of the adequate records or other evidence.

(f) *Reporting and substantiation of expenses of certain employees for travel, entertainment, gifts, and with respect to listed property*--(1) *In general.* The purpose of
35 this paragraph is to provide rules for reporting and substantiation of certain expenses paid or incurred by employees in connection with the performance of services as employees. For purposes of this paragraph, the term business expenses means ordinary and necessary expenses for travel, entertainment, gifts, or with respect to listed property which are deductible under section 162, and the regulations thereunder, to the extent not
40 disallowed by section 262, 274(c), and 280F. Thus, the term business expenses does not include personal, living, or family expenses disallowed by section 262, travel expenses disallowed by section 274(c), or cost recovery deductions and credits with respect to listed property disallowed by section 280F(d)(3) because the use of such property is not for the convenience of the employer and required as a condition of employment. Except
45 as provided in paragraph (f)(2), advances, reimbursements, or allowances for such expenditures must be reported as income by the employee.

(2) *Reporting of expenses for which the employee is required to make an adequate accounting to his employer*--(i) *Reimbursements equal to expenses.* For purposes of computing tax liability, an employee need not report on his tax return business expenses
50 for travel, transportation, entertainment, gifts, or with respect to listed property, paid or incurred by him solely for the benefit of his employer for which he is required to, and

Sec. 274. Disallowance of certain entertainment, etc., expenses

does, make an adequate accounting to his employer (as defined in paragraph (f)(4) of this section) and which are charged directly or indirectly to the employer (for example, through credit cards) or for which the employee is paid through advances, reimbursements, or otherwise, provided that the total amount of such advances, reimbursements, and charges is equal to such expenses.   5

(ii) *Reimbursements in excess of expenses.* In case the total of the amounts charged directly or indirectly to the employer or received from the employer as advances, reimbursements, or otherwise, exceeds the business expenses paid or incurred by the employee and the employee is required to, and does, make an adequate accounting to his employer for such expenses, the employee must include such excess (including 10 amounts received for expenditures not deductible by him) in income.

(iii) *Expenses in excess of reimbursements.* If an employee incurs deductible business expenses on behalf of his employer which exceed the total of the amounts charged directly or indirectly to the employer and received from the employer as advances, reimbursements, or otherwise, and the employee makes an adequate accounting to his 15 employer, the employee must be able to substantiate any deduction for such excess with such records and supporting evidence as will substantiate each element of an expenditure (described in paragraph (b) of this section) in accordance with paragraph (c) of this section.

(3) *Reporting of expenses for which the employee is not required to make an* 20 *adequate accounting to his employer.* If the employee is not required to make an adequate accounting to his employer for his business expenses or, though required, fails to make an adequate accounting for such expenses, he must submit, as a part of his tax return, the appropriate form issued by the Internal Revenue Service for claiming deductions for employee business expenses (e.g., Form 2106, Employee Business 25 Expenses, for 1985) and provide the information requested on that form, including the information required by paragraph (d)(2) and (3) of this section if the employee's business expenses are with respect to the use of listed property. In addition, the employee must maintain such records and supporting evidence as will substantiate each element of an expenditure or use (described in paragraph (b) of this section) in accordance with 30 paragraph (c) of this section.

(4) [Reserved]. For further guidance, see § 1.274-5(f)(4).

(5) *Substantiation of expenditures by certain employees.* An employee who makes an adequate accounting to his employer within the meaning of this paragraph will not again be required to substantiate such expense account information except in the following 35 cases:

(i) An employee whose business expenses exceed the total of amounts charged to his employer and amounts received through advances, reimbursements or otherwise and who claims a deduction on his return for such excess,

(ii) An employee who is related to his employer within the meaning of section 267(b), 40 but for this purpose the percentage referred to in section 267(b)(2) shall be 10 percent, and

(iii) Employees in cases where it is determined that the accounting procedures used by the employer for the reporting and substantiation of expenses by such employees are not adequate, or where it cannot be determined that such procedures are adequate. The 45 district director will determine whether the employer's accounting procedures are adequate by considering the facts and circumstances of each case, including the use of proper internal controls. For example, an employer should require that an expense account be verified and approved by a reasonable person other than the person incurring such expenses. Accounting procedures will be considered inadequate to the extent that 50 the employer does not require an adequate accounting from his employees as defined in

691

paragraph (f)(4) of this section, or does not maintain such substantiation. To the extent an employer fails to maintain adequate accounting procedures he will thereby obligate his employees to substantiate separately their expense account information.

(g) [Reserved]. For further guidance, see § 1.274-5(g).

5   (h) *Reporting and substantiation of certain reimbursements of persons other than employees--(1) In general.* The purpose of this paragraph is to provide rules for the reporting and substantiation of certain expenses for travel, entertainment, gifts, or with respect to listed property paid or incurred by one person (hereinafter termed ``independent contractor") in connection with services performed for another person 10  other than an employer (hereinafter termed ``client or customer") under a reimbursement or other expense allowance arrangement with such client or customer. For purposes of this paragraph, the term business expenses means ordinary and necessary expenses for travel, entertainment, gifts, or with respect to listed property which are deductible under section 162, and the regulations thereunder, to the extent not disallowed by sections 262 15 and 274(c). Thus, the term business expenses does not include personal, living, or family expenses disallowed by section 262 or travel expenses disallowed by section 274(c), and reimbursements for such expenditures must be reported as income by the independent contractor. For purposes of this paragraph, the term reimbursements means advances, allowances, or reimbursements received by an independent contractor for travel, 20 entertainment, gifts, or with respect to listed property in connection with the performance by him of services for his client or customer, under a reimbursement or other expense allowance arrangement with his client or customer, and includes amounts charged directly or indirectly to the client or customer through credit card systems or otherwise. See paragraph (j) of this section relating to the substantiation of meal expenses while 25 traveling away from home.

(2) *Substantiation by independent contractors.* An independent contractor shall substantiate, with respect to his reimbursements, each element of an expenditure (described in paragraph (b) of this section) in accordance with the requirements of paragraph (c) of this section; and, to the extent he does not so substantiate, he shall 30 include such reimbursements in income. An independent contractor shall so substantiate a reimbursement for entertainment regardless of whether he accounts (within the meaning of paragraph (h)(3) of this section) for such entertainment.

(3) *Accounting to a client or customer under section 274(e)(4)(B).* Section 274(e)(4) (B) provides that section 274(a) (relating to disallowance of expenses for entertainment) 35 shall not apply to expenditures for entertainment for which an independent contractor has been reimbursed if the independent contractor accounts to his client or customer, to the extent provided by section 274(d). For purposes of section 274(e)(4)(B), an independent contractor shall be considered to account to his client or customer for an expense paid or incurred under a reimbursement or other expense allowance arrangement with his client 40 or customer if, with respect to such expense for entertainment, he submits to his client or customer adequate records or other sufficient evidence conforming to the requirements of paragraph (c) of this section.

(4) *Substantiation by client or customer.* A client or customer shall not be required to substantiate, in accordance with the requirements of paragraph (c) of this section, 45 reimbursements to an independent contractor for travel and gifts, or for entertainment unless the independent contractor has accounted to him (within the meaning of section 274(e)(4)(B) and paragraph (h)(3) of this section) for such entertainment. If an independent contractor has so accounted to a client or customer for entertainment, the client or customer shall substantiate each element of the expenditure (as described in 50 paragraph (b) of this section) in accordance with the requirements of paragraph (c) of this section.

Sec. 274. Disallowance of certain entertainment, etc., expenses

(i) [Reserved]

(j) [Reserved]. For further guidance, see § 1.274-5(j).

(k) *Exceptions for qualified nonpersonal use vehicles--*(1) *In general.* The substantiation requirements of section 274(d) and this section do not apply to any qualified nonpersonal use vehicle (as defined in paragraph (k)(2) of this section). 5

(2) *Qualified nonpersonal use vehicle--*(i) *In general.* For purposes of section 274(d) and this section, the term qualified nonpersonal use vehicle means any vehicle which, by reason of its nature (i.e., design), is not likely to be used more than a de minimis amount for personal purposes.

(ii) *List of vehicles.* Vehicles which are qualified nonpersonal use vehicles include the 10 following--

(A) Clearly marked police and fire vehicles (as defined and to the extent provided in paragraph (k)(3) of this section),

(B) Ambulances used as such or hearses used as such,

(C) Any vehicle designed to carry cargo with a loaded gross vehicle weight over 15 14,000 pounds,

(D) Bucket trucks (``cherry pickers''),

(E) Cement mixers,

(F) Combines,

(G) Cranes and derricks, 20

(H) Delivery trucks with seating only for the driver, or only for the driver plus a folding jump seat,

(I) Dump trucks (including garbage trucks),

(J) Flatbed trucks,

(K) Forklifts, 25

(L) Passenger buses used as such with a capacity of at least 20 passengers,

(M) Qualified moving vans (as defined in paragraph (k)(4) of this section),

(N) Qualified specialized utility repair trucks (as defined in paragraph (k)(5) of this section),

(O) Refrigerated trucks, 30

(P) School buses (as defined in section 4221(d)(7)(C)),

(Q) Tractors and other special purpose farm vehicles,

(R) Unmarked vehicles used by law enforcement officers (as defined in paragraph (k) (6) of this section) if the use is officially authorized, and

(S) Such other vehicles as the Commissioner may designate. 35

(3) *Clearly marked police or fire vehicles.* A police or fire vehicle is a vehicle, owned or leased by a governmental unit, or any agency or instrumentality thereof, that is required to be used for commuting by a police officer or fire fighter who, when not on a regular shift, is on call at all times, provided that any personal use (other than commuting) of the vehicle outside the limit of the police officer's arrest powers or the fire fighter's obligation 40 to respond to an emergency is prohibited by such governmental unit. A police or fire vehicle is clearly marked if, through painted insignia or words, it is readily apparent that the vehicle is a police or fire vehicle. A marking on a license plate is not a clear marking for purposes of this paragraph (k).

(4) *Qualified moving van.* The term qualified moving van means any truck or van used 45 by a professional moving company in the trade or business of moving household or business goods if--

(i) No personal use of the van is allowed other than for travel to and from a move site (or for de minimis personal use, such as a stop for lunch on the way between two move sites), 50

(ii) Personal use for travel to and from a move site is an irregular practice (i.e., not more than five times a month on average), and

(iii) Personal use is limited to situations in which it is more convenient to the employer, because of the location of the employee's residence in relation to the location of the move site, for the van not to be returned to the employer's business location.

5   (5) *Qualified specialized utility repair truck.* The term qualified specialized utility repair truck means any truck (not including a van or pickup truck) specifically designed and used to carry heavy tools, testing equipment, or parts if--

(i) The shelves, racks, or other permanent interior construction which has been installed to carry and store such heavy items is such that it is unlikely that the truck will be
10 used more than a de minimis amount for personal purposes, and

(ii) The employer requires the employee to drive the truck home in order to be able to respond in emergency situations for purposes of restoring or maintaining electricity, gas, telephone, water, sewer, or steam utility services.

(6) *Unmarked law enforcement vehicles--*(i) *In general.* The substantiation
15 requirements of section 274(d) and this section do not apply to officially authorized uses of an unmarked vehicle by a ``law enforcement officer''. To qualify for this exception, any personal use must be authorized by the Federal, State, county, or local governmental agency or department that owns or leases the vehicle and employs the officer, and must be incident to law-enforcement functions, such as being able to report directly from home
20 to a stakeout or surveillance site, or to an emergency situation. Use of an unmarked vehicle for vacation or recreation trips cannot qualify as an authorized use.

(ii) *Law enforcement officer.* The term law enforcement officer means an individual who is employed on a full-time basis by a governmental unit that is responsible for the prevention or investigation of crime involving injury to persons or property (including
25 apprehension or detention of persons for such crimes), who is authorized by law to carry firearms, execute search warrants, and to make arrests (other than merely a citizen's arrest), and who regularly carries firearms (except when it is not possible to do so because of the requirements of undercover work). The term law enforcement officer may include an arson investigator if the investigator otherwise meets the requirements of this
30 paragraph (k)(6)(ii), but does not include Internal Revenue Service special agents.

(7) *Trucks and vans.* The substantiation requirements of section 274(d) and this section apply generally to any pickup truck or van, unless the truck or van has been specially modified with the result that it is not likely to be used more than a de minimis amount for personal purposes. For example, a van that has only a front bench for
35 seating, in which permanent shelving that fills most of the cargo area has been installed, that constantly carries merchandise or equipment, and that has been specially painted with advertising or the company's name, is a vehicle not likely to be used more than a de minimis amount for personal purposes.

(8) *Examples.* The following examples illustrate the provisions of paragraph (k)(3) and
40 (6) of this section:

Example 1. Detective C, who is a ``law enforcement officer'' employed by a state police department, headquartered in city M, is provided with an unmarked vehicle (equipped with radio communication) for use during off-duty hours because C must be able to communicate with headquarters and be available for duty at any time (for
45 example, to report to a surveillance or crime site). The police department generally has officially authorized personal use of the vehicle by C but has prohibited use of the vehicle for recreational purposes or for personal purposes outside the state. Thus, C's use of the vehicle for commuting between headquarters or a surveillance site and home and for personal errands is authorized personal use as described in paragraph (k)(6)(i) of this
50 section. With respect to these authorized uses, the vehicle is not subject to the substantiation requirements of section 274(d) and the value of these uses is not included

Sec. 274. Disallowance of certain entertainment, etc., expenses

in C's gross income.

Example 2. Detective T is a ``law enforcement officer'' employed by city M. T is authorized to make arrests only within M's city limits. T, along with all other officers on the force, is ordinarily on duty for eight hours each work day and on call during the other sixteen hours. T is provided with the use of a clearly marked police vehicle in which T is required to commute to his home in city M. The police department's official policy regarding marked police vehicles prohibits personal use (other than commuting) of the vehicles outside the city limits. When not using the vehicle on the job, T uses the vehicle only for commuting, personal errands on the way between work and home, and personal errands within city M. All use of the vehicle by T conforms to the requirements of paragraph (k)(3) of this section. Therefore, the value of that use is excluded from T's gross income as a working condition fringe and the vehicle is not subject to the substantiation requirements of section 274(d).

(l) *Definitions.* For purposes of section 274(d) and this section, the terms automobile and vehicle have the same meanings as prescribed in § 1.61-21(d)(1)(ii) and § 1.61-21(e) (2), respectively. Also, for purposes of section 274(d) and this section, the terms employer, employee, and personal use have the same meanings as prescribed in § 1.274-6T(e).

***

[T.D. 6659, 28 FR 6505, June 25, 1963; T.D. 6758, 29 FR 12768, Sept. 10, 1964; T.D. 6996, 34 FR 835, Jan. 18, 1969; T.D. 8051, 50 FR 36576, Sept. 9, 1985; T.D. 8061, 50 FR 46014, Nov. 6, 1985; T.D. 8063, 50 FR 52312, Dec. 23, 1985; T.D. 8230, 53 FR 36451, Sept. 20, 1988; T.D. 8276, 54 FR 51027, Dec. 12, 1989; T.D. 8451, 57 FR 57669, Dec. 7, 1992; T.D. 8601, 60 FR 36995, July 19, 1995; T.D. 8666, 61 FR 27006, May 30, 1996; T.D. 8715, 62 FR 13990, Mar. 25, 1997; T.D. 8864, 65 FR 4123, Jan. 26, 2000; T.D. 9020, 67 FR 68513, Nov. 12, 2002; T.D. 9020, 67 FR 72273, Dec. 4, 2002; T.D. 9064, July 1, 2003]

Sec. 275. Certain taxes

(a) **General rule.** -- No deduction shall be allowed for the following taxes:

(1) Federal income taxes, including--

(A) the tax imposed by section 3101 (relating to the tax on employees under the Federal Insurance Contributions Act);

(B) the taxes imposed by sections 3201 and 3211 (relating to the taxes on railroad employees and railroad employee representatives); and

(C) the tax withheld at source on wages under section 3402.

(2) Federal war profits and excess profits taxes.

(3) Estate, inheritance, legacy, succession, and gift taxes.

***

(5) Taxes on real property, to the extent that section 164(d) requires such taxes to be treated as imposed on another taxpayer.

***

Paragraph (1) shall not apply to any taxes to the extent such taxes are allowable as a deduction under section 164(f).

Sec. 275. Certain taxes

(b) Cross reference. -- For disallowance of certain other taxes, see section 164(c).

Sec. 276. Certain indirect contributions to political parties

(a) Disallowance of deduction. -- No deduction otherwise allowable under this chapter shall be allowed for any amount paid or incurred for--

(1) advertising in a convention program of a political party, or in any other publication if any part of the proceeds of such publication directly or indirectly inures (or is intended to inure) to or for the use of a political party or a political candidate,

(2) admission to any dinner or program, if any part of the proceeds of such dinner or program directly or indirectly inures(or is intended to inure) to or for the use of a political party or a political candidate, or

(3) admission to an inaugural ball, inaugural gala, inaugural parade, or inaugural concert, or to any similar event which is identified with a political party or a political candidate.

***

Sec. 280A. Disallowance of certain expenses in connection with business use of home, rental of vacation homes, etc.

(a) General rule. -- Except as otherwise provided in this section, in the case of a taxpayer who is an individual or an S corporation, no deduction otherwise allowable under this chapter shall be allowed with respect to the use of a dwelling unit which is used by the taxpayer during the taxable year as a residence.

(b) Exception for interest, taxes, casualty losses, etc. -- Subsection (a) shall not apply to any deduction allowable to the taxpayer without regard to its connection with his trade or business (or with his income-producing activity).

(c) Exceptions for certain business or rental use; limitation on deductions for such use. --

(1) Certain business use. -- Subsection (a) shall not apply to any item to the extent such item is allocable to a portion of the dwelling unit which is exclusively used on a regular basis -

(A) as the principal place of business for any trade or business of the taxpayer,

(B) as a place of business which is used by patients, clients, or customers in meeting or dealing with the taxpayer in the normal course of his trade or business, or

(C) in the case of a separate structure which is not attached to the dwelling unit, in connection with the taxpayer's trade or business.

In the case of an employee, the preceding sentence shall apply only if the exclusive use referred to in the preceding sentence is for the convenience of his employer. For purposes of subparagraph (A), the term "principal place of business" includes a place of business which is used by the taxpayer for the administrative or management activities of any trade or business of the taxpayer if there is no other fixed location of such trade or business where the taxpayer conducts substantial administrative or management activities of such trade or business.

(2) Certain storage use. -- Subsection (a) shall not apply to any item to the extent such item is allocable to space within the dwelling unit which is used on a regular basis as a storage unit for the inventory or product samples of the taxpayer held for use in the taxpayer's trade or business of selling products at retail or wholesale, but only if the dwelling unit is the sole fixed location of such trade or business.

(3) Rental use. -- Subsection (a) shall not apply to any item which is attributable to the rental of the dwelling unit or portion thereof (determined after the application of subsection

Sec. 280A. Disallowance of certain expenses in connection with business use of home, rental of vacation homes, etc.

(e)).

(4) Use in providing day care services. --

(A) In general. -- Subsection (a) shall not apply to any item to the extent that such item is allocable to the use of any portion of the dwelling unit on a regular basis in the taxpayer's trade or business of providing day care for children, for individuals who have attained age 5 65, or for individuals who are physically or mentally incapable of caring for themselves.

***

(C) Allocation formula. -- If a portion of the taxpayer's dwelling unit used for the purposes described in subparagraph (A) is not used exclusively for those purposes, the amount of the expenses attributable to that portion shall not exceed an amount which bears 10 the same ratio to the total amount of the items allocable to such portion as the number of hours the portion is used for such purposes bears to the number of hours the portion is available for use.

(5) Limitation on deductions. -- In the case of a use described in paragraph (1), (2), or (4), and in the case of a use described in paragraph (3) where the dwelling unit is used by the 15 taxpayer during the taxable year as a residence, the deductions allowed under this chapter for the taxable year by reason of being attributed to such use shall not exceed the excess of--

(A) the gross income derived from such use for the taxable year, over

(B) the sum of--

(i) the deductions allocable to such use which are allowable under this chapter for the 20 taxable year whether or not such unit (or portion thereof) was so used, and

(ii) the deductions allocable to the trade or business (or rental activity) in which such use occurs (but which are not allocable to such use) for such taxable year.

Any amount not allowable as a deduction under this chapter by reason of the preceding sentence shall be taken into account as a deduction (allocable to such use) under this chapter 25 for the succeeding taxable year. Any amount taken into account for any taxable year under the preceding sentence shall be subject to the limitation of the 1st sentence of this paragraph whether or not the dwelling unit is used as a residence during such taxable year.

(6) Treatment of rental to employer. -- Paragraphs (1) and (3) shall not apply to any item which is attributable to the rental of the dwelling unit (or any portion thereof) by the taxpayer 30 to his employer during any period in which the taxpayer uses the dwelling unit (or portion) in performing services as an employee of the employer.

(d) Use as residence. --

(1) In general. -- For purposes of this section, a taxpayer uses a dwelling unit during the taxable year as a residence if he uses such unit (or portion thereof) for personal purposes for a 35 number of days which exceeds the greater of--

(A) 14 days, or

(B) 10 percent of the number of days during such year for which such unit is rented at a fair rental.

For purposes of subparagraph (B), a unit shall not be treated as rented at a fair rental for any 40 day for which it is used for personal purposes.

(2) Personal use of unit. -- For purposes of this section, the taxpayer shall be deemed to have used a dwelling unit for personal purposes for a day if, for any part of such day, the unit is used--

(A) for personal purposes by the taxpayer or any other person who has an interest in such 45 unit, or by any member of the family (as defined in section 267(c)(4)) of the taxpayer or such other person;

   (B) by any individual who uses the unit under an arrangement which enables the taxpayer to use some other dwelling unit (whether or not a rental is charged for the use of such other unit); or

   (C) by any individual (other than an employee with respect to whose use section 119 applies), unless for such day the dwelling unit is rented for a rental which, under the facts and circumstances, is fair rental.

The Secretary shall prescribe regulations with respect to the circumstances under which use of the unit for repairs and annual maintenance will not constitute personal use under this paragraph, except that if the taxpayer is engaged in repair and maintenance on a substantially full time basis for any day, such authority shall not allow the Secretary to treat a dwelling unit as being used for personal use by the taxpayer on such day merely because other individuals who are on the premises on such day are not so engaged.

   (3) Rental to family member, etc., for use as principal residence. --

   (A) In general. -- A taxpayer shall not be treated as using a dwelling unit for personal purposes by reason of a rental arrangement for any period if for such period such dwelling unit is rented, at a fair rental, to any person for use as such person's principal residence.

   (B) Special rules for rental to person having interest in unit. --

   (i) Rental must be pursuant to shared equity financing agreement. -- Subparagraph (A) shall apply to a rental to a person who has an interest in the dwelling unit only if such rental is pursuant to a shared equity financing agreement.

   (ii) Determination of fair rental. -- In the case of a rental pursuant to a shared equity financing agreement, fair rental shall be determined as of the time the agreement is entered into and by taking into account the occupant's qualified ownership interest.

   (C) Shared equity financing agreement. -- For purposes of this paragraph, the term "shared equity financing agreement" means an agreement under which--

   (i) 2 or more persons acquire qualified ownership interests in a dwelling unit, and

   (ii) the person (or persons) holding 1 or more of such interests--

   (I) is entitled to occupy the dwelling unit for use as a   principal residence, and

   (II) is required to pay rent to 1 or more other persons holding qualified ownership interests in the dwelling unit.

   (D) Qualified ownership interest. -- For purposes of this paragraph, the term "qualified ownership interest" means an undivided interest for more than 50 years in the entire dwelling unit and appurtenant land being acquired in the transaction to which the shared equity financing agreement relates.

   (4) Rental of principal residence. --

   (A) In general. -- For purposes of applying subsection (c)(5) to deductions allocable to a qualified rental period, a taxpayer shall not be considered to have used a dwelling unit for personal purposes for any day during the taxable year which occurs before or after a qualified rental period described in subparagraph (B)(i), or before a qualified rental period described in subparagraph (B)(ii), if with respect to such day such unit constitutes the principal residence (within the meaning of section 121) of the taxpayer.

   (B) Qualified rental period. -- For purposes of subparagraph (A), the term "qualified rental period" means a consecutive period of--

Sec. 280A. Disallowance of certain expenses in connection with business use of home, rental of vacation homes, etc.

      (i) 12 or more months which begins or ends in such taxable year, or

      (ii) less than 12 months which begins in such taxable year and at the end of which such dwelling unit is sold oo exchanged, and for which such unit is rented, or is held for rental, at a fair rental.

(e) **Expenses attributable to rental.** --

      (1) **In general.** -- In any case where a taxpayer who is an individual or an S corporation uses a dwelling unit for personal purposes on any day during the taxable year (whether or not he is treated under this section as using such unit as a residence), the amount deductible under this chapter with respect to expenses attributable to the rental of the unit (or portion thereof) for the taxable year shall not exceed an amount which bears the same relationship to such expenses as the number of days during each year that the unit (or portion thereof) is rented at a fair rental bears to the total number of days during such year that the unit (or portion thereof) is used.

      (2) **Exception for deductions otherwise allowable.** -- This subsection shall not apply with respect to deductions which would be allowable under this chapter for the taxable year whether or not such unit (or portion thereof) was rented.

(f) **Definitions and special rules.** --

      (1) **Dwelling unit defined.** -- For purposes of this section--

        (A) **In general.** -- The term "dwelling unit" includes a house, apartment, condominium, mobile home, boat, or similar property, and all structures or other property appurtenant to such dwelling unit.

        (B) **Exception.** -- The term "dwelling unit" does not include that portion of a unit which is used exclusively as a hotel, motel, inn, or similar establishment.

      (2) **Personal use by shareholders of S corporation.** -- In the case of an S corporation, subparagraphs (A) and (B) of subsection (d)(2) shall be applied by substituting "and shareholder of the S corporation" for "the taxpayer" each place it appears.

      (3) **Coordination with section 183.** -- If subsection (a) applies with respect to any dwelling unit (or portion thereof) for the taxable year--

        (A) section 183 (relating to activities not engaged in for profit) shall not apply to such unit (or portion thereof) for such year, but

        (B) such year shall be taken into account as a taxable year for purposes of applying subsection (d) of section 183 (relating to 5-year presumption).

      (4) **Coordination with section 162(a)(2).** -- Nothing in this section shall be construed to disallow any deduction allowable under section 162(a)(2) (or any deduction which meets the tests of section 162(a)(2) but is allowable under another provision of this title) by reason of the taxpayer's being away from home in the pursuit of a trade or business (other than the trade or business of renting dwelling units).

(g) **Special rule for certain rental use.** -- Notwithstanding any other provision of this section or section 183, if a dwelling unit is used during the taxable year by the taxpayer as a residence and such dwelling unit is actually rented for less than 15 days during the taxable year, then--

      (1) no deduction otherwise allowable under this chapter because of the rental use of such dwelling unit shall be allowed, and

Sec. 280A.   Disallowance of certain expenses in connection with business use of home, rental of vacation homes, etc.

(2) the income derived from such use for the taxable year shall not be included in the gross income of such taxpayer under section 61.

Prop. § 1.280A-1.   Limitations on deductions with respect to a dwelling unit which
5 **is used by the taxpayer during the taxable year as a residence, (7/21/83)**

***

(c) *Dwelling unit*-(1) *In general.*--For purposes of this section and §§1.280A-2 and 1.280A-3, the term "dwelling unit" includes a house, apartment, condominium, mobile home, boat, or similar property, which provides basic living accommodations such as
10 sleeping space, toilet, and cooking facilities. A single structure may contain more than one dwelling unit. For example, each apartment in an apartment building is a separate dwelling unit. Similarly, if the basement of a house contains basic living accommodations, the basement constitutes a separate dwelling unit. All structures and other property appurtenant to a dwelling unit which do not themselves constitute dwelling units are
15 considered part of the unit. For example, an individual who rents to another person space in a garage which is appurtenant to a house which the individual owns and occupies may claim deductions with respect to that rental activity only to the extent allowed under section 280A, paragraph (b) of this section, and § 1.280A-3.

(2) *Exception.*--Notwithstanding the provisions of paragraph (c) (1) of this section, the
20 term "dwelling unit" does not include any unit or portion of a unit which is used exclusively as a hotel, motel, inn, or similar establishment. Property is so used only if it is regularly available for occupancy by paying customers and only if no person having an interest in the property is deemed under the rules of this section to have used the unit (or the portion of the unit) as a residence during the taxable year. Thus, this exception may apply
25 to a portion of a home used to furnish lodging to tourists or to long-term boarders such as students. This exception may also apply to a unit entered in a rental pool (see §§ 1.280A-3 (e)) if the owner of the unit does not use it as a residence during the taxable year.

***

30
Prop. § 1.280A-2 Deductibility of expenses attributable to business use of a dwelling unit used as a residence. (5/20/94)

***

(h) *Use on a regular basis.*--The determination whether a taxpayer has used a portion
35 of a dwelling unit for a particular purpose on a regular basis must be made in light of all the facts and circumstances.

(i) *Limitation on deductions.*

***

(5) *Order of deductions.*--Business deductions with respect to the business use of a
40 dwelling unit are allowable in the following order and only to the following extent:

(i) The allocable portions of amounts allowable as deductions for the taxable year under chapter 1 of the Code with respect to the dwelling unit without regard to any use of the unit in trade or business, e.g., mortgage interest and real estate taxes, are allowable as business deductions to the extent of the gross income derived from use of the unit.
45   (ii) Amounts otherwise allowable as deductions for the taxable year under chapter 1 of the Code by reason of the business use of the dwelling unit (other than those which would result in an adjustment to the basis of property) are allowable to the extent the

gross income derived from use of the unit exceeds the deductions allowed or allowable under subdivision (i) of this subparagraph.

(iii) Amounts otherwise allowable as deductions for the taxable year under chapter 1 of the Code by reason of the business use of the dwelling unit which would result in an adjustment to the basis of property are allowable to the extent the gross income derived 5 from use of the unit exceeds the deductions allowed or allowable under subdivisions (i) and (ii) of this subparagraph.

(6) *Cross reference.*--For rules with respect to the deductions to be taken into account in computing adjusted gross income in the case of employees, see section 62 and the regulations prescribed thereunder. 10

(7) *Example.*--The provisions of this subparagraph may be illustrated by the following example:

Example. A, a self-employed individual, uses an office in the home on a regular basis as a place of business for meeting with clients of A's consulting service. A makes no other use of the office during the taxable year and uses no other premises for the consulting 15 activity. A has a special telephone line for the office and occasionally employs secretarial assistance. A also has a gardener care for the lawn around the home during the year. A determines that 10% of the general expenses for the dwelling unit are allocable to the office. On the basis of the following figures, A determines that the sum of the allowable business deductions for the use of the office is $1,050. 20

Gross income from consulting services......................		$1,900	
Expense for secretary..	$ 500		
Business telephone...	150		
Supplies..	200		25
Total expenditures not allocable to use of unit........		850	
Gross income derived from use of unit.......................		$1,050	

Deductions allowable under subparagraph (5)(i) of this paragraph:

30

	Allocable to	
	Total	Office
Mortgage interest............................	$5,000	$500
Real estate taxes..............................	2,000	200
Amount allowable...............................		700
Limit on further deductions...................................		$350

35

Deductions allowable under subparagraph (5)(ii) of this paragraph:

	Allocable to		40
	Total	Office	
Insurance...	$600	$60	
Utilities (other than residential telephone)......................................	900	90	
Lawn care...	500	0	45
Amount allowable..............................		150	
Limit on further deductions.................................		$200	

Sec. 280A. Disallowance of certain expenses in connection with business use of home, rental of vacation homes, etc.

Deductions allowable under subparagraph (5)(iii) of this paragraph:

		Allocable to	
		Total	Office
5	Depreciation......................................	$3,200	$320
	Amount allowable..		$200

No portion of the lawn care expense is allocable to the business use of the dwelling unit. A may claim the remaining $6,300 paid for mortgage interest and real estate taxes as 10 itemized deductions.

Sec. 280B. Demolition of structures

In the case of the demolition of any structure--

(1) no deduction otherwise allowable under this chapter shall be allowed to the owner or 15 lessee of such structure for--

(A) any amount expended for such demolition, or

(B) any loss sustained on account of such demolition; and

(2) amounts described in paragraph (1) shall be treated as properly chargeable to capital account with respect to the land on which the demolished structure was located.

20

Sec. 280E. Expenditures in connection with the illegal sale of drugs

No deduction or credit shall be allowed for any amount paid or incurred during the taxable year in carrying on any trade or business if such trade or business (or the activities which comprise such trade or business) consists of trafficking i controlled substances (within the meaning of schedule I and II of the Controlled Substances Act) which is prohibited by Federal law or the law of any State 25 in which such trade or business is conducted.

Sec. 280F. Limitation on depreciation for luxury automobiles; limitation where certain property used for personal purposes

(a) Limitation on amount of depreciation for luxury automobiles. --

(1) Depreciation. --

(A) Limitation. -- The amount of the depreciation deduction for any taxable year for any 30 passenger automobile shall not exceed--

(i) $2,560 for the 1st taxable year in the recovery period,

(ii) $4,100 for the 2nd taxable year in the recovery period,

(iii) $2,450 for the 3rd taxable year in the recovery period, and

(iv) $1,475 for each succeeding taxable year in the recovery period.

35 **(B) Disallowed deductions allowed for years after recovery period. --**

(i) In general. -- Except as provided in clause (ii), the unrecovered basis of any passenger automobile shall be treated as an expense for the 1st taxable year after the recovery period. Any excess of the unrecovered basis over the limitation of clause (ii) shall be treated as an expense in the succeeding taxable year.

702

Sec. 280F.   Limitation on depreciation for luxury automobiles; limitation where certain property used for personal purposes

(ii) $1,475 limitation. -- The amount treated as an expense under clause (i) for any taxable year shall not exceed $1,475.

(iii) Property must be depreciable. -- No amount shall be allowable as a deduction by reason of this subparagraph with respect to any property for any taxable year unless a depreciation deduction would be allowable with respect to such property for such taxable year.

(iv) Amount treated as depreciation deduction. -- For purposes of this subtitle, any amount allowable as a deduction by reason of this subparagraph shall be treated a a depreciation deduction allowable under section 168.

(C) Special rule for certain clean-fuel passenger automobiles. --

(i) Modified automobiles. -- In the case of a passenger automobile which is propelled by a fuel which is not a clean-burning fuel and to which is installed qualified clean-fuel vehicle property (as defined in section 179A(c)(1)(A)) for purposes of permitting such vehicle to be propelled by a clean burning fuel (as defined in section 179A(e)(1)), subparagraph (A) shall not apply to the cost of the installed qualified clean burning vehicle property.

(ii) Purpose built passenger vehicles. -- In the case of a purpose built passenger vehicle (as defined in section 4001(a)(2)(C)(ii)), each of the annual limitations specified in subparagraphs (A) and (B) shall be tripled.

(iii) Application of subparagraph. -- This subparagraph shall apply to property placed in service after August 5, 1997, and before January 1, 2007.

(2) Coordination with reductions in amount allowable by reason of personal use, etc. -- This subsection shall be applied before--

(A) the application of subsection (b), and

(B) the application of any other reduction in the amount of any depreciation deduction allowable under section 168 by reason of any use not qualifying the property for such credit or depreciation deduction.

(b) Limitation where business use of listed property not greater than 50 percent. --

(1) Depreciation. -- If any listed property is not predominantly used in a qualified business use for any taxable year, the deduction allowed under section 168 with respect to such property for such taxable year and any subsequent taxable year shall be determined under section 168(g) (relating to alternative depreciation system).

(2) Recapture. --

(A) Where business use percentage does not exceed 50 percent. -- If--

(i) property is predominantly used in a qualified business use in a taxable year in which it is placed in service, and

(ii) such property is not predominantly used in a qualified business use for any subsequent taxable year,

then any excess depreciation shall be included in gross income for the taxable year referred to in clause (ii), and the depreciation deduction for the taxable year referred to in clause (ii) and any subsequent taxable years shall be determined under section 168(g) (relating to alternative depreciation system).

(B) Excess depreciation. -- For purposes of subparagraph (A), the term "excess depreciation" means the excess (if any) of -

(i) the amount of the depreciation deductions allowable with respect to the property

703

Sec. 280F. Limitation on depreciation for luxury automobiles; limitation where certain property used for personal purposes

for taxable years before the 1st taxable year in which the property was not predominantly usedin a qualified business use, over

(ii) the amount which would have been so allowable if the property had not been predominantly used in a qualified business use for the taxable year in which it was placed in service.

(3) Property predominantly used in qualified business use. -- For purposes of this subsection, property shall be treated as predominantly used in a qualified business use for any taxable year if the business use percentage for such taxable year exceeds 50 percent.

(c) Treatment of leases. --

(1) Lessor's deductions not affected. -- This section shall not apply to any listed property leased or held for leasing by any person regularly engaged in the business of leasing such property.

(2) Lessee's deductions reduced. -- For purposes of determining the amount allowable as a deduction under this chapter for rentals or other payments under a lease for a period of 30 days or more of listed property, only the allowable percentage of such payments shall be taken into account.

(3) Allowable percentage. -- For purposes of paragraph (2), the allowable percentage shall be determined under tables prescribed by the Secretary. Such tables shall be prescribed so that the reduction in the deduction under paragraph (2) is substantially equivalent to the applicable restrictions contained in subsections (a) and (b).

(4) Lease term. -- In determining the term of any lease for purposes of paragraph (2), the rules of section 168(i)(3)(A) shall apply.

(5) Lessee recapture. -- Under regulations prescribed by the Secretary, rules similar to the rules of subsection (b)(3) shall apply to any lessee to which paragraph (2) applies.

(d) Definitions and special rules. -- For purposes of this section--

(1) Coordination with section 179. -- Any deduction allowable under section 179 with respect to any listed property shall be subject to the limitations of subsections (a) and (b), and the limitation of paragraph (3) of this subsection, in the same manner as if it were a depreciation deduction allowable under section 168.

(2) Subsequent depreciation deductions reduced for deductions allocable to personal use. -- Solely for purposes of determining the amount of the depreciation deduction for subsequent taxable years, if less than 100 percent of the use of any listed property during any taxable year is use in a trade or business (including the holding for the production of income), all of the use of such property during such taxable year shall be treated as use so described.

(3) Deductions of employee. --

(A) In general. -- Any employee use of listed property shall not be treated as use in a trade or business for purposes of determining the amount of any depreciation deduction allowable to the employee (or the amount of any deduction allowable to the employee for rentals or other payments under a lease of listed property) unless such use is for the convenience of the employer and required as a condition of employment.

(B) Employee use. -- For purposes of subparagraph (A), the term "employee use" means any use in connection with the performance of services as an employee.

(4) Listed property. --

(A) In general. -- Except as provided in subparagraph (B), the term "listed property" means--

(i) any passenger automobile,

Sec. 280F. Limitation on depreciation for luxury automobiles; limitation where certain property used for personal purposes

   (ii) any other property used as a means of transportation,

   (iii) any property of a type generally used for purposes of entertainment, recreation, or amusement,

   (iv) any computer or peripheral equipment (as defined in section 168(i)(2)(B)),

   (v) any cellular telephone (or other similar telecommunications equipment), and   5

   (vi) any other property of a type specified by the Secretary by regulations.

   (B) Exception for certain computers. -- The term "listed property" shall not include any computer or peripheral equipment (as so defined) used exclusively at a regular business establishment and owned or leased by the person operating such establishment. For purposes of the preceding sentence, any portion of a dwelling unit shall be treated as a   10 regular business establishment if (and only if) the requirements of section 280A(c)(1) are met with respect to such portion.

   (C) Exception for property used in business of transporting persons or property. -- Except to the extent provided in regulations, clause (ii) of subparagraph (A) shall not apply to any property substantially all of the use of which is in a trade or business of providing to   15 unrelated persons services consisting of the transportation of persons or property for compensation or hire.

(5) Passenger automobile. --

   (A) In general. -- Except as provided in subparagraph (B), the term "passenger automobile" means any 4-wheeled vehicle--   20

   (i) which is manufactured primarily for use on public streets, roads, and highways, and

   (ii) which is rated at 6,000 pounds unloaded gross vehicle weight or less.

In the case of a truck or van, clause (ii) shall be applied by substituting "gross vehicle weight" for "unloaded gross vehicle weight".   25

   (B) Exception for certain vehicles. -- The term "passenger automobile" shall not include--

   (i) any ambulance, hearse, or combination ambulance-hearse used by the taxpayer directly in a trade or business,

   (ii) any vehicle used by the taxpayer directly in the trade or business of transporting   30 persons or property for compensation or hire, and

   (iii) under regulations, any truck or van.

(6) Business use percentage. --

   (A) In general. -- The term "business use percentage" means the percentage of the use of any listed property during any taxable year which is a qualified business use.   35

   (B) Qualified business use. -- Except as provided in subparagraph (C), the term "qualified business use" means any use in a trade or business of th taxpayer.

   (C) Exception for certain use by 5-percent owners and related persons. --

   (i) In general. -- The term "qualified business use" shall not include--

   (I) leasing property to any 5-percent owner or related person,   40

   (II) use of property provided as compensation for the performance of services by a 5-percent owner or related person, or

   (III) use of property provided as compensation for the performance of services by any person not described in subclause (II) unless an amount is included in the gross

Sec. 280F. Limitation on depreciation for luxury automobiles; limitation where certain property used for personal purposes

income of such person with respect to such use, and, where required, there was withholding under chapter 24.

(ii) **Special rule for aircraft.** -- Clause (i) shall not apply with respect to any aircraft if at least 25 percent of the total use of the aircraft during the taxable year consists of qualified business use not described in clause (i).

(D) **Definitions.** -- For purposes of this paragraph--

(i) **5-percent owner.** -- The term "5-percent owner" means any person who is a 5-percent owner with respect to the taxpayer (as defined in section 416(i)(1)(B)(i)).

(ii) **Related person.** -- The term "related person" means any person related to the taxpayer (within the meaning of section 267(b)).

(7) **Automobile price inflation adjustment.** --

(A) **In general.** -- In the case of any passenger automobile placed in service after 1988, subsection (a) shall be applied by increasing each dollar amount contained in such subsection by the automobile price inflation adjustment for the calendar year in which such automobile is placed in service. Any increase under the preceding sentence shall be rounded to the nearest multiple of $100 (or if the increase is a multiple of $50, such increase shall be increased to the next higher multiple of $100).

(B) **Automobile price inflation adjustment.** -- For purposes of this paragraph--

(i) **In general.** -- The automobile price inflation adjustment for any calendar year is the percentage (if any) by which--

(I) the CPI automobile component for October of the preceding calendar year, exceeds

(II) the CPI automobile component for October of 1987.

(ii) **CPI automobile component.** -- The term "CPI automobile component" means the automobile component of the Consumer Price Index for All Urban Consumers published by the Department of Labor.

(8) **Unrecovered basis.** -- For purposes of subsection (a)(2), the term "unrecovered basis" means the adjusted basis of the passenger automobile determined after the application of subsection (a) and as if all use during the recovery period were use in a trade or business (including the holding of property for the production of income).

***

(10) **Special rule for property acquired in nonrecognition transactions.** -- For purposes of subsection (a)(2) any property acquired in a nonrecognition transaction shall be treated as a single property originally placed in service in the taxable year in which it was placed in service after being so acquired.

***

Reg. § 1.280F-2T Limitations on recovery deductions and the investment tax credit for certain passenger automobiles (temporary).

***

(b) *Limitations on allowable recovery deductions--(1) Recovery deduction for year passenger automobile is placed in service.* For the taxable year that a taxpayer places a passenger automobile in service, the allowable recovery deduction under section 168(a) shall not exceed $4,000. See paragraph (b)(3) of this section for the adjustment to this limitation.

(2) *Recovery deduction for remaining taxable years during the recovery period.* For any taxable year during the recovery period remaining after the year that the property is

placed in service, the allowable recovery deduction under section 168(a) shall not exceed $6,000. See paragraph (b)(3) of this section for the adjustment to this limitation.

(3) *Adjustment to limitation by reason of automobile price inflation adjustment.* The limitations on the allowable recovery deductions prescribed in paragraph (b) (1) and (2) of this section are increased by the automobile price inflation adjustment (as defined in 5 section 280F(d)(7)) for the calendar year in which the automobile is placed in service.

(4) *Coordination with section 179.* For purposes of section 280F(a) and this section, any deduction allowable under section 179 (relating to the election to expense certain depreciable trade or business assets) is treated as if that deduction were a recovery deduction under section 168. Thus, the amount of the section 179 deduction is subject to 10 the limitations described in paragraph (b) (1) and (2) of this section.

(c) *Disallowed recovery deductions allowed for years subsequent to the recovery period*--(1) *In general.* (i) Except as otherwise provided in this paragraph (c), the "unrecovered basis" (as defined in paragraph (c)(1)(ii) of this section) of any passenger automobile is treated as a deductible expense in the first taxable year succeeding the 15 end of the recovery period.

(ii) The term unrecovered basis means the excess (if any) of:

(A) The unadjusted basis (as defined in section 168(d)(1)(A), except that there is no reduction by reason of an election to expense a portion of the basis under section 179) of the passenger automobile, over   20

(B) The amount of the recovery deductions (including any section 179 deduction elected by the taxpayer) which would have been allowable for taxable years in the recovery period (determined after the application of section 280F (a) and paragraph (b) of this section and as if all use during the recovery period were used described in section 168(c)(1)).   25

(2) *Special rule when taxpayer elects to use the section 168(b)(3) optional recovery percentages.* If the taxpayer elects to use the optional recovery percentages under section 168(b)(3) or must use the straight line method over the earnings and profits life (as defined and described in § 1.280F-3T(f)), the second succeeding taxable year after the end of the recovery period is treated as the first succeeding taxable year after the end 30 of the recovery period for purposes of this paragraph (c) because of the half-year convention. For example, assume a calendar-year taxpayer places in service on July 1, 1984, a passenger automobile (i.e., 3-year recovery property) and elects under section 168(b)(3) to recover its cost over 5 years using the straight line optional percentages. Based on these facts, calendar year 1990 is treated as the first succeeding taxable year 35 after the end of the recovery period.

(3) *Deduction limited to $6,000 for any taxable year.* The amount that may be treated as a deductible expense under this paragraph (c) in the first taxable year succeeding the recovery period shall not exceed $6,000. Any excess shall be treated as an expense for the succeeding taxable years. However, in no event may any deduction in a succeeding 40 taxable year exceed $6,000. The limitation on amounts deductible as an expense under this paragraph (c) with respect to any passenger automobile is increased by the automobile price inflation adjustment (as defined in section 280F(d)(7)) for the calendar year in which such automobile is placed in service.

(4) *Deduction treated as a section 168 recovery deduction.* Any amount allowable as 45 an expense in a taxable year after the recovery period by reason of this paragraph (c) shall be treated as a recovery deduction allowable under section 168. However, a deduction is allowable by reason of this paragraph (c) with respect to any passenger automobile for a taxable year only to the extent that a deduction under section 168 would be allowable with respect to the automobile for that year. For example, no recovery 50

Sec. 280F. Limitation on depreciation for luxury automobiles; limitation where certain property used for personal purposes

deduction is allowable for a year during which a passenger automobile is disposed of or is used exclusively for personal purposes.

***

[T.D. 7986, 49 FR 42704, Oct. 24, 1984; T.D. 9133, 69 FR 35514, June 25, 2004]

Sec. 280G. Golden parachute payments

5   **(a) General rule.** -- No deduction shall be allowed under this chapter for any excess parachute payment.

   (b) Excess parachute payment. -- For purposes of this section--

     (1) In general. -- The term "excess parachute payment" means an amount equal to the excess of any parachute payment over the portion of the base amount allocated to such
10   payment.

     (2) Parachute payment defined. --

       (A) In general. -- The term "parachute payment" means any payment in the nature of compensation to (or for the benefit of) a disqualified individual if--

         (i) such payment is contingent on a change--

15   **(I)** in the ownership or effective control of the corporation, or

           (II) in the ownership of a substantial portion of the assets of the corporation, and

         (ii) the aggregate present value of the payments in the nature of compensation to (or for the benefit of) such individual which are contingent on such change equals or exceeds an amount equal to 3 times the base amount.

20   **(3) Base amount.** --

       (A) In general. -- The term "base amount" means the individual's annualized includible compensation for the base period.

       (B) Allocation. -- The portion of the base amount allocated to any parachute payment shall be an amount which bears the same ratio to the base amount as--

25   **(i)** the present value of such payment, bears to

         (ii) the aggregate present value of all such payments.

     (4) Treatment of amounts which taxpayer establishes as reasonable compensation. -- In the case of any payment described in paragraph (2)(A)--

       (A) the amount treated as a parachute payment shall not include the portion of such
30   payment which the taxpayer establishes by clear and convincing evidence is reasonable compensation for personal services to be rendered on or after the date of the change described in paragraph (2)(A)(i), and

       (B) the amount treated as an excess parachute payment shall be reduced by the portion of such payment which the taxpayer establishes by clear and convincing evidence is
35   reasonable compensation for personal services actually rendered before the date of the change described in paragraph (2)(A)(i).

For purposes of subparagraph (B), reasonable compensation for services actually rendered before the date of the change described in paragraph (2)(A)(i) shall be first offset against the base amount.

40 <center>***</center>

   (c) Disqualified individuals. -- For purposes of this section, the term "disqualified individual" means any individual who is--

     (1) an employee, independent contractor, or other person specified in regulations by the

708

Sec. 280G. Golden parachute payments

Secretary who performs personal services for any corporation, and

    (2) is an officer, shareholder, or highly-compensated individual.

For purposes of this section, a personal service corporation (or similar entity) shall be treated as an individual. For purposes of paragraph (2), the term "highly-compensated individual" only includes an individual who is (or would be if the individual were an employee) a member of the group 5 consisting of the highest paid 1 percent of the employees of the corporation or, if less, the highest paid 250 employees of the corporation.

  (d) Other definitions and special rules. -- For purposes of this section--

    (1) Annualized includible compensation for base period. -- The term "annualized includible compensation for the base period" means the average annual compensation which--   10

      (A) was payable by the corporation with respect to which the change in ownership or control described in paragraph (2)(A) of subsection (b) occurs, and

      (B) was includible in the gross income of the disqualified individual for taxable years in the base period.

    (2) Base period. -- The term "base period" means the period consisting of the most recent 5   15 taxable years ending before the date on which the change in ownership or control described in paragraph (2)(A) of subsection (b) occurs (or such portion of such period during which the disqualified individual performed personal services for the corporation).

    (3) Property transfers. -- Any transfer of property--

      (A) shall be treated as a payment, and   20

      (B) shall be taken into account as its fair market value.

    (4) Present value. -- Present value shall be determined by using a discount rate equal to 120 percent of the applicable Federal rate (determined under section 1274(d)), compounded semiannually.

  25

Sec. 291. Special rules relating to corporate preference items

  (a) Reduction in certain preference items, etc. -- For purposes of this subtitle, in the case of a corporation--

    (1) Section 1250 capital gain treatment. -- In the case of section 1250 property which is disposed of during the taxable year, 20 percent of the excess (if any) of--

      (A) the amount which would be treated as ordinary income if such property was section 30 1245 property, over

      (B) the amount treated as ordinary income under section 1250 (determined without regard to this paragraph),

shall be treated as gain which is ordinary income under section 1250 and shall be recognized notwithstanding any other provision of this title. Under regulations prescribed by the Secretary, 35 the provisions of this paragraph shall not apply to the disposition of any property to the extent section 1250(a) does not apply to such disposition by reason of section 1250(d).

    (2) Reduction in percentage depletion. -- In the case of iron ore and coal (including lignite), the amount allowable as a deduction under section 613 with respect to any property (as defined in section 614) shall be reduced by 20 percent of the amount of the excess (if any) 40 of -

      (A) the amount of the deduction allowable under section 613 for the taxable year (determined without regard to this paragraph), over

      (B) the adjusted basis of the property at the close of the taxable year (determined without regard to the depletion deduction for the taxable year).   45

Sec. 291. Special rules relating to corporate preference items

***

(4) Amortization of pollution control facilities. -- If an election is made under section 169 with respect to any certified pollution control facility, the amortizable basis of such facility for purposes of such section shall be reduced by 20 percent.

(b) Special rules for treatment of intangible drilling costs and mineral exploration and development costs. -- For purposes of this subtitle, in the case of a corporation--

    (1) In general. -- The amount allowable as a deduction for any taxable year (determined without regard to this section)--

        (A) under section 263(c) in the case of an integrated oil company, or

        (B) under section 616(a) or 617(a),

shall be reduced by 30 percent.

    (2) Amortization of amounts not allowable as deductions under paragraph (1). -- The amount not allowable as a deduction under section 263(c), 616(a), or 617(a) (as the case may be) for any taxable year by reason of paragraph (1) shall be allowable as a deduction ratably over the 60-month period beginning with the month in which the costs are paid or incurred.

    (3) Dispositions. -- For purposes of section 1254, any deduction under paragraph (2) shall be treated as a deduction allowable under section 263(c), 616(a), or 617(a) (whichever is appropriate).

    (4) Integrated oil company defined. -- For purposes of this subsection, the term "integrated oil company" means, with respect to any taxable year, any producer of crude oil to whom subsection (c) of section 613A does not apply by reason of paragraph (2) or (4) of section 613A(d).

    (5) Coordination with cost depletion. -- The portion of the adjusted basis of any property which is attributable to amounts to which paragraph (1) applied shall not be taken into account for purposes of determining depletion under section 611.

***

(e) Definitions. -- For purposes of this section -

***

    (2) Section 1245 and 1250 property. -- The terms "section 1245 property" and "section 1250 property" have the meanings given such terms by sections 1245(a)(3) and 1250(c), respectively.

Sec. 301. Distributions of property

(a) In general. -- Except as otherwise provided in this chapter, a distribution of property (as defined in section 317(a)) made by a corporation to a shareholder with respect to its stock shall be treated in the manner provided in subsection (c).

(b) Amount distributed. --

    (1) General rule. -- For purposes of this section, the amount of any distribution shall be the amount of money received, plus the fair market value of the other property received.

***

    (3) Determination of fair market value. -- For purposes of this section, fair market value shall be determined as of the date of the distribution.

(c) Amount taxable. -- In the case of a distribution to which subsection (a) applies--

710

Sec. 301. Distributions of property

(1) Amount constituting dividend. -- That portion of the distribution which is a dividend (as defined in section 316) shall be included in gross income.

(2) Amount applied against basis. -- That portion of the distribution which is not a dividend shall be applied against and reduce the adjusted basis of the stock.

(3) Amount in excess of basis. --

>   **(A) In general.** -- Except as provided in subparagraph (B), that portion of the distribution which is not a dividend, to the extent that it exceeds the adjusted basis of the stock, shall be treated as gain from the sale or exchange of property.

***

(d) Basis. -- The basis of property received in a distribution to which subsection (a) applies shall be the fair market value of such property.

Sec. 302. Distributions in redemption of stock

(a) General rule. -- If a corporation redeems its stock (within the meaning of section 317(b)), and if paragraph (1), (2), (3), or (4) of subsection (b) applies, such redemption shall be treated as a distribution in part or full payment in exchange for the stock.

***

Sec. 312. Effect on earnings and profits

***

(n) Adjustments to earnings and profits to more accurately reflect economic gain and loss. --

***

(2) Intangible drilling costs and mineral exploration and development costs. --

>   **(A) Intangible drilling costs.** -- Any amount allowable as a deduction under section 263(c) in determining taxable income (other than costs incurred in connection with a nonproductive well)--

>   >   **(i)** shall be capitalized, and

>   >   **(ii)** shall be allowed as a deduction ratably over the 60- month period beginning with the month in which such amount was paid or incurred.

***

Sec. 316. Dividend defined

(a) General rule. -- For purposes of this subtitle, the term "dividend" means any distribution of property made by a corporation to its shareholders--

(1) out of its earnings and profits accumulated after February 28, 1913, or

(2) out of its earnings and profits of the taxable year (computed as of the close of the taxable year without diminution by reason of any distributions made during the taxable year), without regard to the amount of the earnings and profits at the time the distribution was made.

Except as otherwise provided in this subtitle, every distribution is made out of earnings and profits to the extent thereof, and from the most recently accumulated earnings and profits. To the extent that any distribution is, under any provision of this subchapter, treated as a distribution of property

711

Sec. 316. Dividend defined

to which section 301 applies,such distribution shall be treated as a distribution of property for purposes of this subsection.

Sec. 318. Constructive ownership of stock

5   **(a) General rule.** -- For purposes of those provisions of this subchapter to which the rules contained in this section are expressly made applicable--

(1) Members of family. --

(A) In general. -- An individual shall be considered as owning the stock owned, directly or indirectly, by or for--

10   **(i)** his spouse (other than a spouse who is legally separated from the individual under a decree of divorce or separate maintenance), and

(ii) his children, grandchildren, and parents.

(B) Effect of adoption. -- For purposes of subparagraph (A)(ii), a legally adopted child of an individual shall be treated as a child of such individual by blood.

15   **(2) Attribution from partnerships, estates, trusts, and corporations.** --

(A) From partnerships and estates. -- Stock owned, directly or indirectly, by or for a partnership or estate shall be considered as owned proportionately by its partners or beneficiaries.

(B) From trusts. --

20   **(i)** Stock owned, directly or indirectly, by or for a trust (other than an employees' trust described in section 401(a) which is exempt from tax under section 501(a)) shall be considered as owned by its beneficiaries in proportion to the actuarial interest of such beneficiaries in such trust.

(ii) Stock owned, directly or indirectly, by or for any portion of a trust of which a 25   person is considered the owner under subpart E of part I of subchapter J (relating to grantors and others treated as substantial owners) shall be considered as owned by such person.

(C) From corporations. -- If 50 percent or more in value of the stock in a corporation is owned, directly or indirectly, by or for any person, such person shall be considered as 30   owning the stock owned, directly or indirectly, by or for such corporation, in that proportion which the value of the stock which such person so owns bears to the value of all the stock in such corporation.

(3) Attribution to partnerships, estates, trusts, and corporations. --

(A) To partnerships and estates. -- Stock owned, directly or indirectly, by or for a 35   partner or a beneficiary of an estate shall be considered as owned by the partnership or estate.

(B) To trusts. --

(i) Stock owned, directly or indirectly, by or for a beneficiary of a trust (other than an employees' trust described in section 401(a) which is exempt from tax under section 40   501(a)) shall be considered as owned by the trust, unless such beneficiary's interest in the trust is a remote contingent interest. For purposes of this clause, a contingent interest of a beneficiary in a trust shall be considered remote if, under the maximum exercise of discretion by the trustee in favor of such beneficiary, the value of such interest, computed actuarially, is 5 percent or less of the value of the trust property.

45   **(ii)** Stock owned, directly or indirectly, by or for a person who is considered the

Sec. 318. Constructive ownership of stock

owner of any portion of a trust under subpart E of part I of subchapter J (relating to grantors and others treated as substantial owners), shall be considered as owned by the trust.

   (C) To corporations. -- If 50 percent or more in value of the stock in a corporation is owned, directly or indirectly, by or for any person, such corporation shall be considered as 5 owning the stock owned, directly or indirectly, by or for such person.

  (4) Options. -- If any person has an option to acquire stock, such stock shall be considered as owned by such person. For purposes of this paragraph, an option to acquire such an option, and each one of a series of such options, shall be considered as an option to acquire such stock.

  (5) Operating rules. --   10

   (A) In general. -- Except as provided in subparagraphs (B) and (C), stock constructively owned by a person by reason of the application of paragraph (1), (2), (3), or (4), shall, for purposes of applying paragraphs (1), (2), (3), and (4), be considered as actually owned by such person.

   (B) Members of family. -- Stock constructively owned by an individual by reason of the 15 application of paragraph (1) shall not be considered as owned by him for purposes of again applying paragraph (1) in order to make another the constructive owner of such stock.

   (C) Partnerships, estates, trusts, and corporations. -- Stock constructively owned by a partnership, estate, trust, or corporation by reason of the application of paragraph (3) shall not be considered as owned by it for purposes of applying paragraph (2) in order to make 20 another the constructive owner of such stock.

   (D) Option rule in lieu of family rule. -- For purposes of this paragraph, if stock may be considered as owned by an individual under paragraph (1) or (4), it shall be considered as owned by him under paragraph (4).

   (E) S corporation treated as partnership. -- For purposes of this subsection--   25

    (i) an S corporation shall be treated as a partnership, and

    (ii) any shareholder of the S corporation shall be treated as a partner of such partnership.

The preceding sentence shall not apply for purposes of determining whether stock in the S corporation is constructively owned by any person.   30

***

Sec. 331. Gain or loss to shareholders in corporate liquidations

  (a) Distributions in complete liquidation treated as exchanges. -- Amounts received by a shareholder in a distribution in complete liquidation of a corporation shall be treated as in full payment in exchange for the stock.   35

***

Sec. 401. Qualified pension, profit-sharing, and stock bonus plans

  (a) Requirements for qualification. -- A trust created or organized in the United States and forming part of a stock bonus, pension, or profit-sharing plan of an employer for the exclusive benefit of his employees or their beneficiaries shall constitute a qualified trust under this section-- 40

  (1) if contributions are made to the trust by such employer, or employees, or both, or by another employer who is entitled to deduct his contributions under section 404(a)(3)(B) (relating to deduction for contributions to profit-sharing and stock bonus plans), or by a charitable remainder trust pursuant to a qualified gratuitous transfer (as defined in section

713

Sec. 401. Qualified pension, profit-sharing, and stock bonus plans

664(g)(1)), for the purpose of distributing to such employees or their beneficiaries the corpus and income of the fund accumulated by the trust in accordance with such plan;

(2) if under the trust instrument it is impossible, at any time prior to the satisfaction of all liabilities with respect to employees and their beneficiaries under the trust, for any part of the corpus or income to be (within the taxable year or thereafter) used for, or diverted to, purposes other than for the exclusive benefit of his employees or their beneficiaries (but this paragraph shall not be construed, in the case of a multiemployer plan, to prohibit the return of a contribution within 6 months after the plan administrator determines that the contribution was made by a mistake of fact or law (other than a mistake relating to whether the plan is described in section 401(a) or the trust which is part of such plan is exempt from taxation under section 501(a), or the return of any withdrawal liability payment determined to be an overpayment within 6 months of such determination).

(3) if the plan of which such trust is a part satisfies the requirements of section 410 (relating to minimum participation standards); and

(4) if the contributions or benefits provided under the plan do not discriminate in favor of highly compensated employees (within the meaning of section 414(q)).

***

(5) Special rules relating to nondiscrimination requirements. --

***

(B) Contributions and benefits may bear uniform relationship to compensation. -- A plan shall not be considered discriminatory within the meaning of paragraph (4) merely because the contributions or benefits of, or on behalf of, the employees under the plan bear a uniform relationship to the compensation (within the meaning of section 414(s)) of such employees.

***

(7) A trust shall not constitute a qualified trust under this section unless the plan of which such trust is a part satisfies the requirements of section 411 (relating to minimum vesting standards).

***

(9) Required distributions. --

(A) In general. -- A trust shall not constitute a qualified trust under this subsection unless the plan provides that the entire interest of each employee--

(i) will be distributed to such employee not later than the required beginning date, or

(ii) will be distributed, beginning not later than the required beginning date, in accordance with regulations, over the life of such employee or over the lives of such employee and a designated beneficiary (or over a period not extending beyond the life expectancy of such employee or the life expectancy of such employee and a designated beneficiary).

***

(C) Required beginning date. -- For purposes of this paragraph--

(i) In general. -- The term "required beginning date" means April 1 of the calendar year following the later of--

(I) the calendar year in which the employee attains age 70 1/2 , or

(II) the calendar year in which the employee retires.

***

(20) A trust forming part of a pension plan shall not be treated as failing to constitute a

714

Sec. 401. Qualified pension, profit-sharing, and stock bonus plans

qualified trust under this section merely because the pension plan of which such trust is a part makes 1 or more distributions within 1 taxable year to a distributee on account of a termination of the plan of which the trust is a part, or in the case of a profit-sharing or stock bonus plan, a complete discontinuance of contributions under such plan. This paragraph shall not apply to a defined benefit plan unless the employer maintaining such plan files a notice with the Pension 5 Benefit Guaranty Corporation (at the time and in the manner prescribed by the Pension Benefit Guaranty Corporation) notifying the Corporation of such payment or distribution and the Corporation has approved such payment or distribution or, within 90 days after the date on which such notice was filed, has failed to disapprove such payment or distribution. For purposes of this paragraph, rules similar to the rules of section 402(a)(6)(B) (as in effect before 10 its repeal by section 521 of the Unemployment Compensation Amendments of 1992) shall apply.

***

(26) Additional participation requirements. --

(A) In general. -- In the case of a trust which is a part of a defined benefit plan, such 15 trust shall not constitute a qualified trust under this subsection unless on each day of the plan year such trust benefits at least the lesser of--

(i) 50 employees of the employer, or

(ii) the greater of -

(I) 40 percent of all employees of the employer, or 20

(II) 2 employees (or if there is only 1 employee, such employee).

***

(c) Definitions and rules relating to self-employed individuals and owner-employees. -- For purposes of this section -

(1) Self-employed individual treated as employee. -- 25

(A) In general. -- The term "employee" includes, for any taxable year, an individual who is a self-employed individual for such taxable year.

(B) Self-employed individual. -- The term "self-employed individual" means, with respect to any taxable year, an individual who has earned income (as defined in paragraph (2)) for such taxable year. To the extent provided in regulations prescribed by the Secretary, 30 such term also includes, for any taxable year--

(i) an individual who would be a self-employed individual within the meaning of the preceding sentence but for the fact that the trade or business carried on by such individual did not have net profits for the taxable year, and

(ii) an individual who has been a self-employed individual within the meaning of the 35 preceding sentence for any prior taxable year.

(2) Earned income. --

(A) In general. -- The term "earned income" means the net earnings from self-employment (as defined in section 1402(a)), but such net earnings shall be determined -

(i) only with respect to a trade or business in which personal services of the taxpayer 40 are a material income- producing factor,

(ii) without regard to paragraphs (4) and (5) of section 1402(c),

(iii) in the case of any individual who is treated as an employee under sections 3121(d)(3)(A), (C), or (D), without regard to paragraph (2) of section 1402(c),

(iv) without regard to items which are not included in gross income for purposes of 45 this chapter, and the deductions properly allocable to or chargeable against such items,

715

Sec. 401. Qualified pension, profit-sharing, and stock bonus plans

(v) with regard to the deductions allowed by section 404 to the taxpayer, and

(vi) with regard to the deduction allowed to the taxpayer by section 164(f).

***

(k) Cash or deferred arrangements. --

(1) General rule. -- A profit-sharing or stock bonus plan, a pre-ERISA money purchase plan, or a rural cooperative plan shall not be considered as not satisfying the requirements of subsection (a) merely because the plan includes a qualified cash or deferred arrangement.

***

(l) Permitted disparity in plan contributions or benefits. --

(1) In general. -- The requirements of this subsection are met with respect to a plan if--

(A) in the case of a defined contribution plan, the requirements of paragraph (2) are met, and

(B) in the case of a defined benefit plan, the requirements of paragraph (3) are met.

(2) Defined contribution plan. --

(A) In general. -- A defined contribution plan meets the requirements of this paragraph if the excess contribution percentage does not exceed the base contribution percentage by more than the lesser of--

(i) the base contribution percentage, or

(ii) the greater of--

(I) 5.7 percentage points, or

(II) the percentage equal to the portion of the rate of tax under section 3111(a) (in effect as of the beginning of the year) which is attributable to old-age insurance.

(B) Contribution percentages. -- For purposes of this paragraph--

(i) Excess contribution percentage. -- The term "excess contribution percentage" means the percentage of compensation which is contributed by the employer under the plan with respect to that portion of each participant's compensation in excess of the integration level.

(ii) Base contribution percentage. -- The term "base contribution percentage" means the percentage of compensation contributed by the employer under the plan with respect to that portion of each participant's compensation not in excess of the integration level.

(3) Defined benefit plan. -- A defined benefit plan meets the requirements of this paragraph if-

(A) Excess plans. --

(i) In general. -- In the case of a plan other than an offset plan--

(I) the excess benefit percentage does not exceed the base benefit percentage by more than the maximum excess allowance,

(II) any optional form of benefit, preretirement benefit, actuarial factor, or other benefit or feature provided with respect to compensation in excess of the integration level is provided with respect to compensation not in excess of such level, and

(III) benefits are based on average annual compensation.

(ii) Benefit percentages. -- For purposes of this subparagraph, the excess and base benefit percentages shall be computed in the same manner as the excess and base contribution percentages under paragraph (2)(B), except that such determination shall be made on the basis of benefits attributable to employer contributions rather than contributions.

716

Sec. 401. Qualified pension, profit-sharing, and stock bonus plans

***

Sec. 402. Taxability of beneficiary of employees' trust

(a) Taxability of beneficiary of exempt trust. -- Except as otherwise provided in this section, any amount actually distributed to any distributee by any employees' trust described in section 401(a) which is exempt from tax under section 501(a) shall be taxable to the distributee, in the taxable year of the distributee in which distributed, under section 72 (relating to annuities).   5

***

Sec. 404. Deduction for contributions of an employer to an employees' trust or annuity plan and compensation under a deferred-payment plan

(a) General rule. --

***

(5) Other plans. -- If the plan is not one included in paragraph (1), (2), or (3), in the taxable 10 year in which an amount attributable to the contribution is includible in the gross income of employees participating in the plan, but, in the case of a plan in which more than one employee participates only if separate accounts are maintained for each employee. For purposes of this section, any vacation pay which is treated as deferred compensation shall be deductible for the taxable year of the employer in which paid to the employee.   15

***

Sec. 408. Individual retirement accounts

(a) Individual retirement account. -- For purposes of this section, the term "individual retirement account" means a trust created or organized in the United States for the exclusive benefit of an individual or his beneficiaries, but only if the written governing instrument creating 20 the trust meets the following requirements:

    (1) Except in the case of a rollover contribution described in subsection (d)(3) in (!1) section 402(c), 403(a)(4), 403(b)(8), or 457(e)(16), no contribution will be accepted unless it is in cash, and contributions will not be accepted for the taxable year on behalf of any individual in excess of the amount in effect for such taxable year under section 219(b)(1)(A).   25

    (2) The trustee is a bank (as defined in subsection (n)) or such other person who demonstrates to the satisfaction of the Secretary that the manner in which such other person will administer the trust will be consistent with the requirements of this section.

    (3) No part of the trust funds will be invested in life insurance contracts.

    (4) The interest of an individual in the balance in his account is nonforfeitable.   30

    (5) The assets of the trust will not be commingled with other property except in a common trust fund or common investment fund.

    (6) Under regulations prescribed by the Secretary, rules similar to the rules of section 401(a) (9) and the incidental death benefit requirements of section 401(a) shall apply to the distribution of the entire interest of an individual for whose benefit the trust is maintained.   35

***

(d) Tax treatment of distributions. --

    (1) In general. -- Except as otherwise provided in this subsection, any amount paid or distributed out of an individual retirement plan shall be included in gross income by the payee or distributee, as the case may be, in the manner provided under section 72.   40

***

Sec. 408. Individual retirement accounts

(6) Transfer of account incident to divorce. -- The transfer of an individual's interest in an individual retirement account or an individual retirement annuity to his spouse or former spouse under a divorce or separation instrument described in subparagraph (A) of section 71(b)(2) is not to be considered a taxable transfer made by such individual notwithstanding any other provision of this subtitle, and such interest at the time of the transfer is to be treated as an individual retirement account of such spouse, and not of such individual. Thereafter such account or annuity for purposes of this subtitle is to be treated as maintained for the benefit of such spouse.

***

(e) Tax treatment of accounts and annuities. --

(1) Exemption from tax. -- Any individual retirement account is exempt from taxation under this subtitle unless such account has ceased to be an individual retirement account by reason of paragraph (2) or (3). Notwithstanding the preceding sentence, any such account is subject to the taxes imposed by section 511 (relating to imposition of tax on unrelated business income of charitable, etc. organizations).

***

(g) Community property laws. -- This section shall be applied without regard to any community property laws.

***

(o) Definitions and rules relating to nondeductible contributions to individual retirement plans. --

(1) In general. -- Subject to the provisions of this subsection, designated nondeductible contributions may be made on behalf of a individual to an individual retirement plan.

(2) Limits on amounts which may be contributed. --

(A) In general. -- The amount of the designated nondeductible contributions made on behalf of any individual for any taxable year shall not exceed the nondeductible limit for such taxable year.

(B) Nondeductible limit. -- For purposes of this paragraph--

(i) In general. -- The term "nondeductible limit" means the excess of--

(I) the amount allowable as a deduction under section 219 (determined without regard to section 219(g)), over

(II) the amount allowable as a deduction under section 219 (determined with regard to section 219(g)).

(ii) Taxpayer may elect to treat deductible contributions as nondeductible. -- If a taxpayer elects not to deduct an amount which (without regard to this clause) is allowable as a deduction under section 219 for any taxable year, the nondeductible limit for such taxable year shall be increased by such amount.

***

Sec. 408A. Roth IRAs

(a) General rule. -- Except as provided in this section, a Roth IRA shall be treated for purposes of this title in the same manner as an individual retirement plan.

(b) Roth IRA. -- For purposes of this title, the term "Roth IRA" means an individual retirement plan (as defined in section 7701(a)(37)) which is designated (in such manner as the Secretary may prescribe) at the time of establishment of the plan as a Roth IRA. Such designation shall be made in such manner as the Secretary may prescribe.

718

Sec. 408A. Roth IRAs

(c) Treatment of contributions. --

(1) No deduction allowed. -- No deduction shall be allowed under section 219 for a contribution to a Roth IRA.

(2) Contribution limit. -- The aggregate amount of contributions for any taxable year to all Roth IRAs maintained for the benefit of an individual shall not exceed the excess (if any) of--

(A) the maximum amount allowable as a deduction under section 219 with respect to such individual for such taxable year (computed without regard to subsection (d)(1) or (g) of such section), over

(B) the aggregate amount of contributions for such taxable year to all other individual retirement plans (other than Roth IRAs) maintained for the benefit of the individual.

(3) Limits based on modified adjusted gross income. --

(A) Dollar limit. -- The amount determined under paragraph (2) for any taxable year shall not exceed an amount equal to the amount determined under paragraph (2)(A) for such taxable year, reduced (but not below zero) by the amount which bears the same ratio to such amount as--

(i) the excess of--

(I) the taxpayer's adjusted gross income for such taxable year, over

(II) the applicable dollar amount, bears to

(ii) $15,000 ($10,000 in the case of a joint return or a married individual filing a separate return).

The rules of subparagraphs (B) and (C) of section 219(g)(2) shall apply to any reduction under this subparagraph.

(B) Definitions. -- For purposes of this paragraph--

(i) adjusted gross income shall be determined in the same manner as under section 219(g)(3), except that any amount included in gross income under subsection (d)(3) shall not be taken into account; and

(ii) the applicable dollar amount is--

(I) in the case of a taxpayer filing a joint return, $150,000,

(II) in the case of any other taxpayer (other than a married individual filing a separate return), $95,000, and

(III) in the case of a married individual filing a separate return, zero.

(C) Marital status. -- Section 219(g)(4) shall apply for purposes of this paragraph.

(4) Contributions permitted after age 70 1/2. -- Contributions to a Roth IRA may be made even after the individual for whom the account is maintained has attained age 701/2 .

***

(d) Distribution rules. -- For purposes of this title--

(1) Exclusion. -- Any qualified distribution from a Roth IRA shall not be includible in gross income.

(2) Qualified distribution. -- For purposes of this subsection--

(A) In general. -- The term "qualified distribution" means any payment or distribution -

(i) made on or after the date on which the individual attains age 59 1/2 ,

(ii) made to a beneficiary (or to the estate of the individual) on or after the death of the individual,

(iii) attributable to the individual's being disabled (within the meaning of section

72(m)(7)), or

(iv) which is a qualified special purpose distribution.

(B) Distributions within nonexclusion period. -- A payment or distribution from a Roth IRA shall not be treated as a qualified distribution under subparagraph (A) if such payment or distribution is made within the 5-taxable year period beginning with the first taxable year for which the individual made a contribution to a Roth IRA (or such individual's spouse made a contribution to a Roth IRA) established for such individual.

(C) Distributions of excess contributions and earnings. -- The term "qualified distribution" shall not include any distribution of any contribution described in section 408(d)(4) and any net income allocable to the contribution.

(3) Rollovers from an IRA other than a Roth IRA. --

(A) In general. -- Notwithstanding section 408(d)(3), in the case of any distribution to which this paragraph applies--

(i) there shall be included in gross income any amount which would be includible were it not part of a qualified rollover contribution,

(ii) section 72(t) shall not apply, and

(iii) unless the taxpayer elects not to have this clause apply, any amount required to be included in gross income for any taxable year beginning in 2010 by reason of this paragraph shall be so included ratably over the 2-taxable-year period beginning with the first taxable year beginning in 2011.

Any election under clause (iii) for any distributions during a taxable year may not be changed after the due date for such taxable year.

(B) Distributions to which paragraph applies. -- This paragraph shall apply to a distribution from an individual retirement plan (other than a Roth IRA) maintained for the benefit of an individual which is contributed to a Roth IRA maintained for the benefit of such individual in a qualified rollover contribution.

(C) Conversions. -- The conversion of an individual retirement plan (other than a Roth IRA) to a Roth IRA shall be treated for purposes of this paragraph as a distribution to which this paragraph applies.

***

Sec. 409A.   Inclusion in gross income of deferred compensation under nonqualified deferred compensation plans

(a) Rules relating to constructive receipt. --

(1) Plan failures. --

(A) Gross income inclusion. --

(i) In general. -- If at any time during a taxable year a nonqualified deferred compensation plan--

(I) fails to meet the requirements of paragraphs (2), (3), and (4), or

(II) is not operated in accordance with such requirements,

all compensation deferred under the plan for the taxable year and all preceding taxable years shall be includible in gross income for the taxable year to the extent not subject to a substantial risk of forfeiture and not previously included in gross income.

(ii) Application only to affected participants. -- Clause (i) shall only apply with respect to all compensation deferred under the plan for participants with respect to whom the failure relates.

Sec. 409A. Inclusion in gross income of deferred compensation under nonqualified deferred compensation plans

(B) Interest and additional tax payable with respect to previously deferred compensation. --

(i) In general. -- If compensation is required to be included in gross income under subparagraph (A) for a taxable year, the tax imposed by this chapter for the taxable year shall be increased by the sum of-- 5

(I) the amount of interest determined under clause (ii), and

(II) an amount equal to 20 percent of the compensation which is required to be included in gross income.

(ii) Interest. -- For purposes of clause (i), the interest determined under this clause for any taxable year is the amount of interest at the underpayment rate plus 1 10 percentage point on the underpayments that would have occurred had the deferred compensation been includible in gross income for the taxable year in which first deferred or, if later, the first taxable year in which such deferred compensation is not subject to a substantial risk of forfeiture.

(2) Distributions. -- 15

(A) In general. -- The requirements of this paragraph are met if the plan provides that compensation deferred under the plan may not be distributed earlier than--

(i) separation from service as determined by the Secretary (except as provided in subparagraph (B)(i)),

(ii) the date the participant becomes disabled (within the meaning of subparagraph 20 (C)),

(iii) death,

(iv) a specified time (or pursuant to a fixed schedule) specified under the plan at the date of the deferral of such compensation,

(v) to the extent provided by the Secretary, a change in the ownership or effective 25 control of the corporation, or in the ownership of a substantial portion of the assets of the corporation, or

(vi) the occurrence of an unforeseeable emergency.

(B) Special rules. --

(i) Specified employees. -- In the case of any specified employee, the requirement of 30 subparagraph (A)(i) is met only if distributions may not be made before the date which is 6 months after the date of separation from service (or, if earlier, the date of death of the employee). For purposes of the preceding sentence, a specified employee is a key employee (as defined in section 416(i) without regard to paragraph (5) thereof) of a corporation any stock in which is publicly traded on an established securities market or 35 otherwise.

(ii) Unforeseeable emergency. -- For purposes of subparagraph (A)(vi)--

(I) In general. -- The term "unforeseeable emergency" means a severe financial hardship to the participant resulting from an illness or accident of the participant, the participant's spouse, or a dependent (as defined in section 152(a)) of the 40 participant, loss of the participant's property due to casualty, or other similar extraordinary and unforeseeable circumstances arising as a result of events beyond the control of the participant.

(II) Limitation on distributions. -- The requirement of subparagraph (A)(vi) is met only if, as determined under regulations of the Secretary, the amounts 45 distributed with respect to an emergency do not exceed the amounts necessary to

Sec. 409A. Inclusion in gross income of deferred compensation under nonqualified deferred compensation plans

satisfy such emergency plus amounts necessary to pay taxes reasonably anticipated as a result of the distribution, after taking into account the extent to which such hardship is or may be relieved through reimbursement or compensation by insurance or otherwise or by liquidation of the participant's assets (to the extent the liquidation of such assets would not itself cause severe financial hardship).

(C) **Disabled.** -- For purposes of subparagraph (A)(ii), a participant shall be considered disabled if the participant--

(i) is unable to engage in any substantial gainful activity by reason of any medically determinable physical or mental impairment which can be expected to result in death or can be expected to last for a continuous period of not less than 12 months, or

(ii) is, by reason of any medically determinable physical or mental impairment which can be expected to result in death or can be expected to last for a continuous period of not less than 12 months, receiving income replacement benefits for a period of not less than 3 months under an accident and health plan covering employees of the participant's employer.

(3) **Acceleration of benefits.** -- The requirements of this paragraph are met if the plan does not permit the acceleration of the time or schedule of any payment under the plan, except as provided in regulations by the Secretary.

(4) **Elections.** --

(A) **In general.** -- The requirements of this paragraph are met if the requirements of subparagraphs (B) and (C) are met.

(B) **Initial deferral decision.** --

(i) **In general.** -- The requirements of this subparagraph are met if the plan provides that compensation for services performed during a taxable year may be deferred at the participant's election only if the election to defer such compensation is made not later than the close of the preceding taxable year or at such other time as provided in regulations.

(ii) **First year of eligibility.** -- In the case of the first year in which a participant becomes eligible to participate in the plan, such election may be made with respect to services to be performed subsequent to the election within 30 days after the date the participant becomes eligible to participate in such plan.

(iii) **Performance-based compensation.** -- In the case of any performance-based compensation based on services performed over a period of at least 12 months, such election may be made no later than 6 months before the end of the period.

(C) **Changes in time and form of distribution.** -- The requirements of this subparagraph are met if, in the case of a plan which permits under a subsequent election a delay in a payment or a change in the form of payment--

(i) the plan requires that such election may not take effect until at least 12 months after the date on which the election is made,

(ii) in the case of an election related to a payment not described in clause (ii), (iii), or (vi) of paragraph (2)(A), the plan requires that the first payment with respect to which such election is made be deferred for a period of not less than 5 years from the date such payment would otherwise have been made, and

(iii) the plan requires that any election related to a payment described in paragraph (2)(A)(iv) may not be made less than 12 months prior to the date of the first scheduled payment under such paragraph.

Sec. 409A. Inclusion in gross income of deferred compensation under nonqualified deferred compensation plans

(b) Rules relating to funding. --

   (1) Offshore property in a trust. -- In the case of assets set aside (directly or indirectly) in a trust (or other arrangement determined by the Secretary) for purposes of paying deferred compensation under a nonqualified deferred compensation plan, for purposes of section 83 such assets shall be treated as property transferred in connection with the performance of 5 services whether or not such assets are available to satisfy claims of general creditors--

   (A) at the time set aside if such assets (or such trust or other arrangement) are located outside of the United States, or

   (B) at the time transferred if such assets (or such trust or other arrangement) are subsequently transferred outside of the United States. 10

This paragraph shall not apply to assets located in a foreign jurisdiction if substantially all of the services to which the nonqualified deferred compensation relates are performed in such jurisdiction.

   (2) Employer's financial health. -- In the case of compensation deferred under a nonqualified deferred compensation plan, there is a transfer of property within the meaning of 15 section 83 with respect to such compensation as of the earlier of--

   (A) the date on which the plan first provides that assets will become restricted to the provision of benefits under the plan in connection with a change in the employer's financial health, or

   (B) the date on which assets are so restricted, whether or not such assets are available to 20 satisfy claims of general creditors.

   (3) Income inclusion for offshore trusts and employer's financial health. -- For each taxable year that assets treated as transferred under this subsection remain set aside in a trust or other arrangement subject to paragraph (1) or (2), any increase in value in, or earnings with respect to, such assets shall be treated as an additional transfer of property under this 25 subsection (to the extent not previously included in income).

   (4) Interest on tax liability payable with respect to transferred property. --

   (A) In general. -- If amounts are required to be included in gross income by reason of paragraph (1) or (2) for a taxable year, the tax imposed by this chapter for such taxable year shall be increased by the sum of-- 30

   (i) the amount of interest determined under subparagraph (B), and

   (ii) an amount equal to 20 percent of the amounts required to be included in gross income.

   (B) Interest. -- For purposes of subparagraph (A), the interest determined under this subparagraph for any taxable year is the amount of interest at the underpayment rate plus 1 35 percentage point on the underpayments that would have occurred had the amounts so required to be included in gross income by paragraph (1) or (2) been includible in gross income for the taxable year in which first deferred or, if later, the first taxable year in which such amounts are not subject to a substantial risk of forfeiture.

(c) No inference on earlier income inclusion or requirement of later inclusion. -- Nothing in 40 this section shall be construed to prevent the inclusion of amounts in gross income under any other provision of this chapter or any other rule of law earlier than the time provided in this section. Any amount included in gross income under this section shall not be required to be included in gross income under any other provision of this chapter or any other rule of law later than the time provided in this section. 45

(d) Other definitions and special rules. -- For purposes of this section:

Sec. 409A. Inclusion in gross income of deferred compensation under nonqualified deferred compensation plans

(1) Nonqualified deferred compensation plan. -- The term "nonqualified deferred compensation plan" means any plan that provides for the deferral of compensation, other than--

> **(A)** a qualified employer plan, and

> **(B)** any bona fide vacation leave, sick leave, compensatory time, disability pay, or death benefit plan.

(2) Qualified employer plan. -- The term "qualified employer plan" means--

> **(A)** any plan, contract, pension, account, or trust described in subparagraph (A) or (B) of section 219(g)(5) (without regard to subparagraph (A)(iii)),

> **(B)** any eligible deferred compensation plan (within the meaning of section 457(b)), and

> **(C)** any plan described in section 415(m).

(3) Plan includes arrangements, etc. -- The term "plan" includes any agreement or arrangement, including an agreement or arrangement that includes one person.

(4) Substantial risk of forfeiture. -- The rights of a person to compensation are subject to a substantial risk of forfeiture if such person's rights to such compensation are conditioned upon the future performance of substantial services by any individual.

(5) Treatment of earnings. -- References to deferred compensation shall be treated as including references to income (whether actual or notional) attributable to such compensation or such income.

***

(e) Regulations. -- The Secretary shall prescribe such regulations as may be necessary or appropriate to carry out the purposes of this section, including regulations--

> **(1)** providing for the determination of amounts of deferral in the case of a nonqualified deferred compensation plan which is a defined benefit plan,

> **(2)** relating to changes in the ownership and control of a corporation or assets of a corporation for purposes of subsection (a)(2)(A)(v),

> **(3)** exempting arrangements from the application of subsection (b) if such arrangements will not result in an improper deferral of United States tax and will not result in assets being effectively beyond the reach of creditors,

> **(4)** defining financial health for purposes of subsection (b)(2), and

> **(5)** disregarding a substantial risk of forfeiture in cases where necessary to carry out the purposes of this section.

Reg. § 1.409A-1 Definitions and covered plans.

***

(b) *Deferral of compensation*--(1) *In general.* Except as otherwise provided in paragraphs (b)(3) through (b)(12) of this section, a plan provides for the deferral of compensation if, under the terms of the plan and the relevant facts and circumstances, the service provider has a legally binding right during a taxable year to compensation that, pursuant to the terms of the plan, is or may be payable to (or on behalf of) the service provider in a later taxable year. Such compensation is deferred compensation for purposes of section 409A, this section and §§ 1.409A-2 through 1.409A-6. A legally binding right to an amount that will be excluded from income when and if received does not constitute a deferral of compensation, unless the service provider has received the right in exchange for, or has the right to exchange the right for, an amount that will be includible in income (other than due to participation in a cafeteria plan described in section 125). A service provider does not have a legally binding right to compensation to the extent that compensation may be reduced unilaterally or eliminated by the service recipient or other person after the services creating the right to the compensation have been performed. However, if the facts and circumstances indicate that the discretion to reduce or eliminate the compensation is available or exercisable only upon a condition, or 5 the discretion to reduce or eliminate the compensation lacks substantive significance, a service provider will be considered to have a legally binding right to the compensation. Whether the discretion to reduce or eliminate the compensation lacks substantive significance depends on all the relevant facts and circumstances. However, where the service provider to whom the compensation may be paid has effective control of the 10 person retaining the discretion to reduce or eliminate the compensation, or has effective control over any portion of the compensation of the person retaining the discretion to reduce or eliminate the compensation, or is a member of the family (as defined in section 267(c)(4) applied as if the family of an individual includes the spouse of any member of the family) of the person retaining the discretion to reduce or eliminate the compensation, 15 the discretion to reduce or eliminate the compensation will not be treated as having substantive significance. For this purpose, compensation is not considered subject to unilateral reduction or elimination merely because it may be reduced or eliminated by operation of the objective terms of the plan, such as the application of a nondiscretionary, objective provision creating a substantial risk of forfeiture. Similarly, a service provider 20 does not fail to have a legally binding right to compensation merely because the amount of compensation is determined under a formula that provides for benefits to be offset by benefits provided under another plan (including a plan that is qualified under section 401(a)), or because benefits are reduced due to actual or notional investment losses, or, in a final average pay plan, subsequent decreases in compensation. 25

***

(3) *Compensation payable pursuant to the service recipient's customary payment timing arrangement.* A deferral of compensation does not occur solely because compensation is paid after the last day of the service provider's taxable year pursuant to the timing arrangement under which the service recipient normally compensates service 30 providers for services performed during a payroll period described in section 3401(b), or with respect to a non-employee service provider, a period not longer than the payroll period described in section 3401(b) or if no such payroll period exists, a period not longer than the earlier of the normal timing arrangement under which the service provider normally compensates non-employee service providers or 30 days after the end of the 35 service provider's taxable year.

(4) *Short-term deferrals*--(i) I*n general*. A deferral of compensation does not occur if the plan under which a payment (as defined in § 1.409A-2(b)(2)) is made does not provide for a deferred payment and the service provider actually or constructively receives such payment on or before the last day of the applicable 2-1/2 month period. 40 The following rules apply for purposes of this paragraph (b)(4)(i):

(A) The applicable 2-1/2 month period is the period ending on the later of the 15th day of the third month following the end of the service provider's first taxable year in which the right to the payment is no longer subject to a substantial risk of forfeiture or the 15th day of the third month following the end of the service recipient's first taxable year in which 45 the right to the payment is no longer subject to a substantial risk of forfeiture.

***

(5) *Stock options, stock appreciation rights, and other equity-based compensation*--(i) *Stock rights*--(A) *Nonstatutory stock options not providing for the deferral of*

compensation. An option to purchase service recipient stock does not provide for a deferral of compensation if--

(1) The exercise price may never be less than the fair market value of the underlying stock (disregarding lapse restrictions as defined in § 1.83-3(i)) on the date the option is granted and the number of shares subject to the option is fixed on the original date of grant of the option;

(2) The transfer or exercise of the option is subject to taxation under section 83 and § 1.83-7; and

(3) The option does not include any feature for the deferral of compensation other than the deferral of recognition of income until the later of the following:

(i) The exercise or disposition of the option under § 1.83-7.

(ii) The time the stock acquired pursuant to the exercise of the option first becomes substantially vested (as defined in § 1.83-3(b)).

***

(iv) *Determination of the fair market value of service recipient stock--(A) Stock readily tradable on an established securities market.* For purposes of paragraph (b)(5)(i) of this section, in the case of service recipient stock that is readily tradable on an established securities market, the fair market value of the stock may be determined based upon the last sale before or the first sale after the grant, the closing price on the trading day before or the trading day of the grant, the arithmetic mean of the high and low prices on the trading day before or the trading day of the grant, or any other reasonable method using actual transactions in such stock as reported by such market. The determination of fair market value also may be determined using an average selling price during a specified period that is within 30 days before or 30 days after the applicable valuation date, provided that the program under which the stock right is granted, including a program with a single participant, must irrevocably specify the commitment to grant the stock right with an exercise price set using such an average selling price before the beginning of the specified period. For this purpose, the term average selling price refers to the arithmetic mean of such selling prices on all trading days during the specified period, or the average of such prices over the specified period weighted based on the volume of trading of such stock on each trading day during such specified period. To satisfy this requirement, the service recipient must designate the recipient of the stock right, the number and class of shares of stock that are subject to the stock right, and the method for determining the exercise price including the period over which the averaging will occur, before the beginning of the specified averaging period.

***

(B) *Stock not readily tradable on an established securities market--(1) In general.* For purposes of paragraph (b)(5)(i) of this section, in the case of service recipient stock that is not readily tradable on an established securities market, the fair market value of the stock as of a valuation date means a value determined by the reasonable application of a reasonable valuation method. The determination whether a valuation method is reasonable, or whether an application of a valuation method is reasonable, is made based on the facts and circumstances as of the valuation date. Factors to be considered under a reasonable valuation method include, as applicable, the value of tangible and intangible assets of the corporation, the present value of anticipated future cash-flows of the corporation, the market value of stock or equity interests in similar corporations and other entities engaged in trades or businesses substantially similar to those engaged in by the corporation the stock of which is to be valued, the value of which can be readily determined through nondiscretionary, objective means (such as through trading prices on

726

Sec. 409A. Inclusion in gross income of deferred compensation under nonqualified deferred compensation plans

an established securities market or an amount paid in an arm's length private transaction), recent arm's length transactions involving the sale or transfer of such stock or equity interests, and other relevant factors such as control premiums or discounts for lack of marketability and whether the valuation method is used for other purposes that have a material economic effect on the service recipient, its stockholders, or its creditors. 5 The use of a valuation method is not reasonable if such valuation method does not take into consideration in applying its methodology all available information material to the value of the corporation. Similarly, the use of a value previously calculated under a valuation method is not reasonable as of a later date if such calculation fails to reflect information available after the date of the calculation that may materially affect the value 10 of the corporation (for example, the resolution of material litigation or the issuance of a patent) or the value was calculated with respect to a date that is more than 12 months earlier than the date for which the valuation is being used. The service recipient's consistent use of a valuation method to determine the value of its stock or assets for other purposes, including for purposes unrelated to compensation of service providers, is 15 also a factor supporting the reasonableness of such valuation method.

(2) *Presumption of reasonableness*. For purposes of this paragraph (b)(5)(iv)(B), the use of any of the following methods of valuation is presumed to result in a reasonable valuation, provided that the Commissioner may rebut such a presumption upon a showing that either the valuation method or the application of such method was grossly 20 unreasonable:

(i) A valuation of a class of stock determined by an independent appraisal that meets the requirements of section 401(a)(28)(C) and the regulations as of a date that is no more than 12 months before the relevant transaction to which the valuation is applied (for example, the date of grant of a stock option). 25

(ii) A valuation based upon a formula that, if used as part of a nonlapse restriction (as defined in § 1.83-3(h)) with respect to the stock, would be considered to be the fair market value of the stock pursuant to § 1.83-5, provided that such stock is valued in the same manner for purposes of any nonlapse restriction applicable to the transfer of any shares of such class of stock (or any substantially similar class of stock) to the issuer or 30 any person that owns stock possessing more than 10 percent of the total combined voting power of all classes of stock of the issuer (applying the stock attribution rules of § 1.424-1(d)), other than an arm's length transaction involving the sale of all or substantially all of the outstanding stock of the issuer, and such valuation method is used consistently for all such purposes, and provided further that this paragraph (b)(5)(iv)(B)(2)(ii) does not 35 apply with respect to stock subject to a stock right payable in stock, where the stock acquired pursuant to the exercise of the stock right is transferable other than through the operation of a nonlapse restriction.

(iii) A valuation, made reasonably and in good faith and evidenced by a written report that takes into account the relevant factors described in paragraph (b)(5)(iv)(B)(1) of this 40 section, of illiquid stock of a start-up corporation. For this purpose, illiquid stock of a start-up corporation means service recipient stock of a corporation that has no material trade or business that it or any predecessor to it has conducted for a period of 10 years or more and has no class of equity securities that are traded on an established securities market (as defined in paragraph (k) of this section), where such stock is not subject to 45 any put, call, or other right or obligation of the service recipient or other person to purchase such stock (other than a right of first refusal upon an offer to purchase by a third party that is unrelated to the service recipient or service provider and other than a right or obligation that constitutes a lapse restriction as defined in § 1.83-3(i)), and provided that this paragraph (b)(5)(iv)(B)(2)(iii) does not apply to the valuation of any stock if the 50

Sec. 409A. Inclusion in gross income of deferred compensation under nonqualified deferred compensation plans

service recipient or service provider may reasonably anticipate, as of the time the valuation is applied, that the service recipient will undergo a change in control event as described in § 1.409A-3(i)(5)(v) or § 1.409A-3(i)(5)(vii) within the 90 days following the action to which the valuation is applied, or make a public offering of securities within the
5 180 days following the action to which the valuation is applied. For purposes of this paragraph (b)(5)(iv)(B)(2)(iii), a valuation will not be treated as made reasonably and in good faith unless the valuation is performed by a person or persons that the corporation reasonably determines is qualified to perform such a valuation based on the person's or persons" significant knowledge, experience, education, or training. Generally, a person
10 will be qualified to perform such a valuation if a reasonable individual, upon being apprised of such knowledge, experience, education, and training, would reasonably rely on the advice of such person with respect to valuation in deciding whether to accept an offer to purchase or sell the stock being valued. For this purpose, significant experience generally means at least five years of relevant experience in business valuation or
15 appraisal, financial accounting, investment banking, private equity, secured lending, or other comparable experience in the line of business or industry in which the service recipient operates.

(3) *Use of alternative methods.* For purposes of this paragraph (b)(5), a different valuation method may be used for each separate action for which a valuation is relevant,
20 provided that a single valuation method is used for each separate action and, once used, may not retroactively be altered. For example, one valuation method may be used to establish the exercise price of a stock option, and a different valuation method may be used to determine the value at the date of the repurchase of stock pursuant to a put or call right. However, once an exercise price or amount to be paid has been established,
25 the exercise price or amount to be paid may not be changed through the retroactive use of another valuation method. In addition, notwithstanding the foregoing, where after the date of grant, but before the date of exercise or transfer, of the stock right, the service recipient stock to which the stock right relates becomes readily tradable on an established securities market, the service recipient must use the valuation method set
30 forth in paragraph (b)(5)(iv)(A) of this section for purposes of determining the payment at the date of exercise or the purchase of the stock, as applicable.

***

[T.D. 9321 72 C.F.R. 19233, Apr. 17, 2007]

Sec. 414. Definitions and special rules

35 **(a) Service for predecessor employer.** -- For purposes of this part--

(1) in any case in which the employer maintains a plan of a predecessor employer, service for such predecessor shall be treated as service for the employer, and

(2) in any case in which the employer maintains a plan which is not the plan maintained by a predecessor employer, service for such predecessor shall, to the extent provided in regulations
40 prescribed by the Secretary, be treated as service for the employer.

***

(i) Defined contribution plan. -- For purposes of this part, the term "defined contribution plan" means a plan which provides for an individual account for each participant and for benefits based solely on the amount contributed to the participant's account, and any income, expenses, gains and
45 losses, and any forfeitures of accounts of other participants which may be allocated to such participant's account.

Sec. 414. Definitions and special rules

(j) Defined benefit plan. -- For purposes of this part, the term "defined benefit plan" means any plan which is not a defined contribution plan.

(k) Certain plans. -- A defined benefit plan which provides a benefit derived from employer contributions which is based partly on the balance of the separate account of a participant shall--

(1) for purposes of section 410 (relating to minimum participation standards), be treated as a 5
defined contribution plan.

(2) for purposes of sections 72(d) (relating to treatment of employee contributions as separate contract), 411(a)(7)(A) (relating to minimum vesting standards), 415 (relating to limitations on benefits and contributions under qualified plans), and 401(m) (relating to nondiscrimination tests for matching requirements and employee contributions), be treated as 10 consisting of a defined contribution plan to the extent benefits are based on the separate account of a participant and as a defined benefit plan with respect to the remaining portion of benefits under the plan, and

(3) for purposes of section 4975 (relating to tax on prohibited transactions), be treated as a defined benefit plan.   15

***

(q) Highly compensated employee. --

(1) In general. -- The term "highly compensated employee" means any employee who--

(A) was a 5-percent owner at any time during the year or the preceding year, or

(B) for the preceding year--   20

(i) had compensation from the employer in excess of $80,000, and

(ii) if the employer elects the application of this clause for such preceding year, was in the top-paid group of employees for such preceding year.

The Secretary shall adjust the $80,000 amount under subparagraph (B) at the same time and in the same manner as under section 415(d), except that the base period shall be the 25 calendar quarter ending September 30, 1996.

(2) 5-percent owner. -- An employee shall be treated as a 5-percent owner for any year if at any time during such year such employee was a 5-percent owner (as defined in section 416(i) (1)) of the employer.

(3) Top-paid group. -- An employee is in the top-paid group of employees for any year if 30 such employee is in the group consisting of the top 20 percent of the employees when ranked on the basis of compensation paid during such year.

(4) Compensation. -- For purposes of this subsection, the term "compensation" has the meaning given such term by section 415(c)(3).

(5) Excluded employees. -- For purposes of subsection (r) and for purposes of determining 35 the number of employees in the top-paid group, the following employees shall be excluded--

(A) employees who have not completed 6 months of service,

(B) employees who normally work less than 17 1/2 hours per week,

(C) employees who normally work during not more than 6 months during any year,

(D) employees who have not attained age 21, and   40

(E) except to the extent provided in regulations, employees who are included in a unit of employees covered by an agreement which the Secretary of Labor finds to be a collective bargaining agreement between employee representatives and the employer.

Except as provided by the Secretary, the employer may elect to apply subparagraph (A), (B), (C), or (D) by substituting a shorter period of service, smaller number of hours or months, or 45

Sec. 414. Definitions and special rules

lower age for the period of service, number of hours or months, or age (as the case may be) than that specified in such subparagraph.

(6) Former employees. -- A former employee shall be treated as a highly compensated employee if--

5   **(A)** such employee was a highly compensated employee when such employee separated from service, or

     (B) such employee was a highly compensated employee at any time after attaining age 55.

(7) Coordination with other provisions. -- Subsections (b), (c), (m), (n), and (o) shall be
10   applied before the application of this subsection.

***

Sec. 415. Limitations on benefits and contribution under qualified plans

(a) General rule. --

     (1) Trusts. -- A trust which is a part of a pension, profit sharing, or stock bonus plan shall not constitute a qualified trust under section 401(a) if--

15   **(A)** in the case of a defined benefit plan, the plan provides for the payment of benefits with respect to a participant which exceed the limitation of subsection (b), or

     (B) in the case of a defined contribution plan, contributions and other additions under the plan with respect to any participant for any taxable year exceed the limitation of subsection (c).

20 ***

(b) Limitation for defined benefit plans. --

     (1) In general. -- Benefits with respect to a participant exceed the limitation of this subsection if, when expressed as an annual benefit (within the meaning of paragraph (2)), such annual benefit is greater than the lesser of--

25   **(A)** $160,000, or

     (B) 100 percent of the participant's average compensation for his high 3 years.

     (2) Annual benefit. --

     (A) In general. -- For purposes of paragraph (1), the term "annual benefit" means a benefit payable annually in the form of a straight life annuity (with no ancillary benefits)
30   under a plan to which employees do not contribute and under which no rollover contributions (as defined in sections 402(c), 403(a)(4), 403(b)(8), 408(d)(3), and 457(e) (16)) are made.

     (B) Adjustment for certain other forms of benefit. -- If the benefit under the plan is payable in any form other than the form described in subparagraph (A), or if the employees
35   contribute to the plan or make rollover contributions (as defined in sections 402(c), 403(a) (4), 403(b)(8), 408(d)(3), and 457(e)(16)), the determinations as to whether the limitation described in paragraph (1) has been satisfied shall be made, in accordance with regulations prescribed by the Secretary by adjusting such benefit so that it is equivalent to the benefit described in subparagraph (A). For purposes of this subparagraph, any ancillary benefit
40   which is not directly related to retirement income benefits shall not be taken into account; and that portion of any joint and survivor annuity which constitutes a qualified joint and survivor annuity (as defined in section 417) shall not be taken into account.

     (C) Adjustment to $160,000 limit where benefit begins before age 62. -- If the retirement income benefit under the plan begins before age 62, the determination as to
45   whether the $160,000 limitation set forth in paragraph (1)(A) has been satisfied shall be

730

Sec. 415. Limitations on benefits and contribution under qualified plans

made, in accordance with regulations prescribed by the Secretary, by reducing the limitation of paragraph (1)(A) so that such limitation (as so reduced) equals an annual benefit (beginning when such retirement income benefit begins) which is equivalent to a $160,000 annual benefit beginning at age 62.

(D) Adjustment to $160,000 limit where benefit begins after age 65. -- If the retirement income benefit under the plan begins after age 65, the determination as to whether the $160,000 limitation set forth in paragraph (1)(A) has been satisfied shall be made, in accordance with regulations prescribed by the Secretary, by increasing the limitation of paragraph (1)(A) so that such limitation (as so increased) equals an annual benefit (beginning when such retirement income benefit begins) which is equivalent to a $160,000 annual benefit beginning at age 65.

***

(c) Limitation for defined contribution plans. --

(1) In general. -- Contributions and other additions with respect to a participant exceed the limitation of this subsection if, when expressed as an annual addition (within the meaning of paragraph (2)) to the participant's account, such annual addition is greater than the lesser of--

(A) $40,000, or

(B) 100 percent of the participant's compensation.

(2) Annual addition. -- For purposes of paragraph (1), the term "annual addition" means the sum of any year of--

(A) employer contributions,

(B) the employee contributions, and

(C) forfeitures.

For the purposes of this paragraph, employee contributions under subparagraph (B) are determined without regard to any rollover contributions (as defined in sections 402(c), 403(a) (4), 403(b)(8), 408(d)(3), and 457(e)(16)) without regard to employee contributions to a simplified employee pension which are excludable from gross income under section 408(k)(6). Subparagraph (B) of paragraph (1) shall not apply to any contribution for medical benefits (within the meaning of section 419A(f)(2)) after separation from service which is treated as an annual addition.

(3) Participant's compensation. -- For purposes of paragraph (1)--

(A) In general. -- The term "participant's compensation" means the compensation of the participant from the employer for the year.

(B) Special rule for self-employed individuals. -- In the case of an employee within the meaning of section 401(c)(1), subparagraph (A) shall be applied by substituting "the participant's earned income (within the meaning of section 401(c)(2) but determined without regard to any exclusion under section 911)" for "compensation of the participant from the employer".

(C) Special rules for permanent and total disability. -- In the case of a participant in any defined contribution plan--

(i) who is permanently and totally disabled (as defined in section 22(e)(3)),

(ii) who is not a highly compensated employee (within the meaning of section 414(q)), and

(iii) with respect to whom the employer elects, at such time and in such manner as the Secretary may prescribe, to have this subparagraph apply, the term "participant's compensation" means the compensation the participant would have received for the

Sec. 415. Limitations on benefits and contribution under qualified plans

year if the participant was paid at the rate of compensation paid immediately before becoming permanently and totally disabled.

This subparagraph shall apply only if contributions made with respect to amounts treated as compensation under this subparagraph are nonforfeitable when made. If a defined contribution plan provides for the continuation of contributions on behalf of all participants described in clause (i) for a fixed or determinable period, this subparagraph shall be applied without regard to clauses (ii) and (iii).

***

(d) Cost-of-living adjustments. --

    (1) In general. -- The Secretary shall adjust annually--

        (A) the $160,000 amount in subsection (b)(1)(A),

        (B) in the case of a participant who is separated from service, the amount taken into account under subsection b)(1)(B), and

        (C) the $40,000 amount in subsection (c)(1)(A),

for increases in the cost-of-living in accordance with regulations prescribed by the Secretary.

Sec. 416. Special rules for top-heavy plans

(a) General rule. -- A trust shall not constitute a qualified trust under section 401(a) for any plan year if the plan of which it is a part is a top- heavy plan for such plan year unless such plan meets--

    (1) the vesting requirements of subsection (b), and

    (2) the minimum benefit requirements of subsection (c).

***

(i) Definitions. -- For purposes of this section--

    (1) Key employee. --

        (A) In general. -- The term "key employee" means an employee who, at any time during the plan year, is--

            (i) an officer of the employer having an annual compensation greater than $130,000,

            (ii) a 5-percent owner of the employer, or

            (iii) a 1-percent owner of the employer having an annual compensation from the employer of more than $150,000.

For purposes of clause (i), no more than 50 employees (or, if lesser, the greater of 3 or 10 percent of the employees) shall be treated as officers. In the case of plan years beginning after December 31, 2002, the $130,000 amount in clause (i) shall be adjusted at the same time and in the same manner as under section 415(d), except that the base period shall be the calendar quarter beginning July 1, 2001, and any increase under this sentence which is not a multiple of $5,000 shall be rounded to the next lower multiple of $5,000. Such term shall not include any officer or employee of an entity referred to in section 414(d) (relating to governmental plans). For purposes of determining the number of officers taken into account under clause (i), employees described in section 414(q)(5) shall be excluded.

        (B) Percentage owners. --

            (i) 5-percent owner. -- For purposes of this paragraph, the term "5-percent owner" means--

                (I) if the employer is a corporation, any person who owns (or is considered as owning within the meaning of section 318) more than 5 percent of the outstanding stock of the corporation or stock possessing more than 5 percent of the total combined voting power of all stock of the corporation, or

    (II) if the employer is not a corporation, any person who owns more than 5 percent of the capital or profits interest in the employer.

    (ii) 1-percent owner. -- For purposes of this paragraph, the term "1-percent owner" means any person who would be described in clause (i) if "1 percent" were substituted for "5 percent" each place it appears in clause (i).

    (iii) Constructive ownership rules. -- For purposes of this subparagraph--

    (I) subparagraph (C) of section 318(a)(2) shall be applied by substituting "5 percent" for "50 percent", and

    (II) in the case of any employer which is not a corporation, ownership in such employer shall be determined in accordance with regulations prescribed by the Secretary which shall be based on principles similar to the principles of section 318 (as modified by subclause (I)).

    (C) Aggregation rules do not apply for purposes of determining ownership in the employer. -- The rules of subsections (b), (c), and (m) of section 414 shall not apply for purposes of determining ownership in the employer.

    (D) Compensation. -- For purposes of this paragraph, the term "compensation" has the meaning given such term by section 414(q)(4).

    (2) Non-key employee. -- The term "non-key employee" means any employee who is not a key employee.

    (3) Self-employed individuals. -- In the case of a self-employed individual described in section 401(c)(1)--

    (A) such individual shall be treated as an employee, and

    (B) such individual's earned income (within the meaning of section 401(c)(2)) shall be treated as compensation.

***

    (5) Treatment of beneficiaries. -- The terms "employee'" and "key employee" include their beneficiaries.

***

Sec. 421. General rules

    (a) Effect of qualifying transfer. -- If a share of stock is transferred to an individual in a transfer in respect of which the requirements of section 422(a) or 423(a) are met--

    (1) no income shall result at the time of the transfer of such share to the individual upon his exercise of the option with respect to such share;

    (2) no deduction under section 162 (relating to trade or business expenses) shall be allowable at any time to the employer corporation, a parent or subsidiary corporation of such corporation, or a corporation issuing or assuming a stock option in a transaction to which section 424(a) applies, with respect to the share so transferred; and

    (3) no amount other than the price paid under the option shall be considered as received by any of such corporations for the share so transferred.

    (b) Effect of disqualifying disposition. -- If the transfer of a share of stock to an individual pursuant to his exercise of an option would otherwise meet the requirements of section 422(a) or 423(a) except that there is a failure to meet any of the holding period requirements of section

Sec. 421. General rules

422(a)(1) or 423(a)(1), then any increase in the income of such individual or deduction from the income of his employer corporation for the taxable year in which such exercise occurred attributable to such disposition, shall be treated as an increase in income or a deduction from income in the taxable year of such individual or of such employer corporation in which such disposition occurred. No amount shall be required to be deducted and withheld under chapter 24 with respect to any increase in income attributable to a disposition described in the preceding sentence.

***

Sec. 422. Incentive stock options

(a) **In general.** -- Section 421(a) shall apply with respect to the transfer of a share of stock to an individual pursuant to his exercise of an incentive stock option if--

> **(1)** no disposition of such share is made by him within 2 years from the date of the granting of the option nor within 1 year after the transfer of such share to him, and

> **(2)** at all times during the period beginning on the date of the granting of the option and ending on the day 3 months before the date of such exercise, such individual was an employee of either the corporation granting such option, a parent or subsidiary corporation of such corporation, or a corporation or a parent or subsidiary corporation of such corporation issuing or assuming a stock option in a transaction to which section 424(a) applies.

(b) **Incentive stock option.** -- For purposes of this part, the term "incentive stock option" means an option granted to an individual for any reason connected with his employment by a corporation, if granted by the employer corporation or its parent or subsidiary corporation, to purchase stock of any of such corporations, but only if--

> **(1)** the option is granted pursuant to a plan which includes the aggregate number of shares which may be issued under options and the employees (or class of employees) eligible to receive options, and which is approved by the stockholders of the granting corporation within 12 months before or after the date such plan is adopted;

> **(2)** such option is granted within 10 years from the date such plan is adopted, or the date such plan is approved by the stockholders, whichever is earlier;

> **(3)** such option by its terms is not exercisable after the expiration of 10 years from the date such option is granted;

> **(4)** the option price is not less than the fair market value of the stock at the time such option is granted;

> **(5)** such option by its terms is not transferable by such individual otherwise than by will or the laws of descent and distribution, and is exercisable, during his lifetime, only by him; and

> **(6)** such individual, at the time the option is granted, does not own stock possessing more than 10 percent of the total combined voting power of all classes of stock of the employer corporation or of its parent or subsidiary corporation.

Such term shall not include any option if (as of the time the option is granted) the terms of such option provide that it will not be treated as an incentive stock option.

(c) **Special rules.** --

***

> **(2)** Certain disqualifying dispositions where amount realized is less than value at exercise If--

> > **(A)** an individual who has acquired a share of stock by the exercise of an incentive stock option makes a disposition of such share within either of the periods described in

734

Sec. 422. Incentive stock options

subsection (a)(1), and

    (B) such disposition is a sale or exchange with respect to which a loss (if sustained) would be recognized to such individual,

then the amount which is includible in the gross income of such individual, and the amount which is deductible from the income of his employer corporation, as compensation attributable to the 5 exercise of such option shall not exceed the excess (if any) of the amount realized on such sale or exchange over the adjusted basis of such share.

***

(d) $100,000 per year limitation. --

    (1) In general. -- To the extent that the aggregate fair market value of stock with respect to 10 which incentive stock options (determined without regard to this subsection) are exercisable for the 1st time by any individual during any calendar year (under all plans of the individual's employer corporation and its parent and subsidiary corporations) exceeds $100,000, such options shall be treated as options which are not incentive stock options.

    (2) Ordering rule. -- Paragraph (1) shall be applied by taking options into account in the 15 order in which they were granted.

    (3) Determination of fair market value. -- For purposes of paragraph (1), the fair market value of any stock shall be determined as of the time the option with respect to such stock is granted.

20

Sec. 441. Period for computation of taxable income

    (a) Computation of taxable income. -- Taxable income shall be computed on the basis of the taxpayer's taxable year.

    (b) Taxable year. -- For purposes of this subtitle, the term "taxable year" means--

    (1) the taxpayer's annual accounting period, if it is a calendar year or a fiscal year;

    (2) the calendar year, if subsection (g) applies;   25

    (3) the period for which the return is made, if a return is made for a period of less than 12 months; or

    (4) in the case of a FSC or DISC filing a return for a period of at least 12 months, the period determined under subsection (h).

    (c) Annual accounting period. -- For purposes of this subtitle, the term "annual accounting 30 period" means the annual period on the basis of which the taxpayer regularly computes his income in keeping his books.

    (d) Calendar year. -- For purposes of this subtitle, the term "calendar year" means a period of 12 months ending on December 31.

    (e) Fiscal year. -- For purposes of this subtitle, the term "fiscal year" means a period of 12 35 months ending on the last day of any month other than December. In the case of any taxpayer who has made the election provided by subsection (f) the term means the annual period (varying from 52 to 53 weeks) so elected.

    (f) Election of year consisting of 52-53 weeks. --

    (1) General rule. -- A taxpayer who, in keeping his books, regularly computes his income 40 on the basis of an annual period which varies from 52 to 53 weeks and ends always on the same day of the week and ends always--

    (A) on whatever date such same day of the week last occurs in a calendar month, or

Sec. 441.   Period for computation of taxable income

(B) on whatever date such same day of the week falls which is nearest to the last day of a calendar month,

may (in accordance with the regulations prescribed under paragraph (3)) elect to compute his taxable income for purposes of this subtitle on the basis of such annual period. This paragraph shall apply to taxable years ending after the date of the enactment of this title.

(2) Special rules for 52-53-week year. --

(A) Effective dates. -- In any case in which the effective date or the applicability of any provision of this title is expressed in terms of taxable years beginning, including, or ending with reference to a specified date which is the first or last day of a month, a taxable year described in paragraph (1) shall (except for purposes of the computation under section 15) be treated--

(i) as beginning with the first day of the calendar month beginning nearest to the first day of such taxable year, or

(ii) as ending with the last day of the calendar month ending nearest to the last day of such taxable year, as the case may be.

***

(g) No books kept; no accounting period. -- Except as provided in section 443 (relating to returns for periods of less than 12 months), the taxpayer's taxable year shall be the calendar year if--

(1) the taxpayer keeps no books;

(2) the taxpayer does not have an annual accounting period; or

(3) the taxpayer has an annual accounting period, but such period does not qualify as a fiscal year.

***

(i) Taxable year of personal service corporations. --

(1) In general. -- For purposes of this subtitle, the taxable year of any personal service corporation shall be the calendar year unless the corporation establishes, to the satisfaction of the Secretary, a business purpose for having a different period for its taxable year. For purposes of this paragraph, any deferral of income to shareholders shall not be treated as a business purpose.

(2) Personal service corporation. -- For purposes of this subsection, the term "personal service corporation" has the meaning given such term by section 269A(b)(1), except that section 269A(b)(2) shall be applied--

(A) by substituting "any" for "more than 10 percent", and

(B) by substituting "any" for "50 percent or more in value" in section 318(a)(2)(C).

A corporation shall not be treated as a personal service corporation unless more than 10 percent of the stock (by value) in such corporation is held by employee-owners (within the meaning of section 269A(b)(2), as modified by the preceding sentence). If a corporation is a member of an affiliated group filing a consolidated return, all members of such group shall be taken into account in determining whether such corporation is a personal service corporation.

Sec. 443.   Returns for a period of less than 12 months

(a) Returns for short period. -- A return for a period of less than 12 months (referred to in this section as "short period") shall be made under any of the following circumstances:

***

Sec. 443.   Returns for a period of less than 12 months

(2) Taxpayer not in existence for entire taxable year. -- When the taxpayer is in existence during only part of what would otherwise be his taxable year.

***

(d) Adjustment in computing minimum tax and tax preferences. -- If a return is made for a short period by reason of subsection (a)--   5

(1) the alternative minimum taxable income for the short period shall be placed on an annual basis by multiplying such amount by 12 and dividing the result by the number of months in the short period, and

(2) the amount computed under paragraph (1) of section 55(a) shall bear the same relation to the tax computed on the annual basis as the number of months in the short period bears to 12.   10

Sec. 446.   General rule for methods of accounting

(a) General rule. -- Taxable income shall be computed under the method of accounting on the basis of which the taxpayer regularly computes his income in keeping his books.

(b) Exceptions. -- If no method of accounting has been regularly used by the taxpayer, or if the   15 method used does not clearly reflect income, the computation of taxable income shall be made under such method as, in the opinion of the Secretary, does clearly reflect income.

(c) Permissible methods. -- Subject to the provisions of subsections (a) and (b), a taxpayer may compute taxable income under any of the following methods of accounting--

(1) the cash receipts and disbursements method;   20

(2) an accrual method;

(3) any other method permitted by this chapter; or

(4) any combination of the foregoing methods permitted under regulations prescribed by the Secretary.

(d) Taxpayer engaged in more than one business. -- A taxpayer engaged in more than one   25 trade or business may, in computing taxable income, use a different method of accounting for each trade or business.

(e) Requirement respecting change of accounting method. -- Except as otherwise expressly provided in this chapter, a taxpayer who changes the method of accounting on the basis of which he regularly computes his income in keeping his books shall, before computing his taxable income   30 under the new method, secure the consent of the Secretary.

(f) Failure to request change of method of accounting. -- If the taxpayer does not file with the Secretary a request to change the method of accounting, the absence of the consent of the Secretary to a change in the method of accounting shall not be taken into account--

(1) to prevent the imposition of any penalty, or the addition of any amount to tax, under this   35 title, or

(2) to diminish the amount of such penalty or addition to tax.

Reg. § 1.446-1   General rule for methods of accounting.

(a) *General rule.* (1) Section 446(a) provides that taxable income shall be computed   40 under the method of accounting on the basis of which a taxpayer regularly computes his income in keeping his books. The term ``method of accounting'' includes not only the overall method of accounting of the taxpayer but also the accounting treatment of any item. Examples of such over-all methods are the cash receipts and disbursements method, an accrual method, combinations of such methods, and combinations of the   45

foregoing with various methods provided for the accounting treatment of special items. These methods of accounting for special items include the accounting treatment prescribed for research and experimental expenditures, soil and water conservation expenditures, depreciation, net operating losses, etc. Except for deviations permitted or
5 required by such special accounting treatment, taxable income shall be computed under the method of accounting on the basis of which the taxpayer regularly computes his income in keeping his books. For requirement respecting the adoption or change of accounting method, see section 446(e) and paragraph (e) of this section.

(2) It is recognized that no uniform method of accounting can be prescribed for all
10 taxpayers. Each taxpayer shall adopt such forms and systems as are, in his judgment, best suited to his needs. However, no method of accounting is acceptable unless, in the opinion of the Commissioner, it clearly reflects income. A method of accounting which reflects the consistent application of generally accepted accounting principles in a particular trade or business in accordance with accepted conditions or practices in that
15 trade or business will ordinarily be regarded as clearly reflecting income, provided all items of gross income and expense are treated consistently from year to year.

(3) Items of gross income and expenditures which are elements in the computation of taxable income need not be in the form of cash. It is sufficient that such items can be valued in terms of money. For general rules relating to the taxable year for inclusion of
20 income and for taking deductions, see sections 451 and 461, and the regulations thereunder.

(4) Each taxpayer is required to make a return of his taxable income for each taxable year and must maintain such accounting records as will enable him to file a correct return. See section 6001 and the regulations thereunder. Accounting records include the
25 taxpayer's regular books of account and such other records and data as may be necessary to support the entries on his books of account and on his return, as for example, a reconciliation of any differences between such books and his return. The following are among the essential features that must be considered in maintaining such records:
30   (i) In all cases in which the production, purchase, or sale of merchandise of any kind is an income-producing factor, merchandise on hand (including finished goods, work in process, raw materials, and supplies) at the beginning and end of the year shall be taken into account in computing the taxable income of the year. (For rules relating to computation of inventories, see section 263A, 471, and 472 and the regulations
35 thereunder.)
(ii) Expenditures made during the year shall be properly classified as between capital and expense. For example, expenditures for such items as plant and equipment, which have a useful life extending substantially beyond the taxable year, shall be charged to a capital account and not to an expense account.
40   (iii) In any case in which there is allowable with respect to an asset a deduction for depreciation, amortization, or depletion, any expenditures (other than ordinary repairs) made to restore the asset or prolong its useful life shall be added to the asset account or charged against the appropriate reserve.

(b) *Exceptions.* (1) If the taxpayer does not regularly employ a method of accounting
45 which clearly reflects his income, the computation of taxable income shall be made in a manner which, in the opinion of the Commissioner, does clearly reflect income.

(2) A taxpayer whose sole source of income is wages need not keep formal books in order to have an accounting method. Tax returns, copies thereof, or other records may be sufficient to establish the use of the method of accounting used in the preparation of the
50 taxpayer's income tax returns.

(c) *Permissible methods--*(1) *In general.* Subject to the provisions of paragraphs (a)

Sec. 446. General rule for methods of accounting

and (b) of this section, a taxpayer may compute his taxable income under any of the following methods of accounting:

(i) *Cash receipts and disbursements method.* Generally, under the cash receipts and disbursements method in the computation of taxable income, all items which constitute gross income (whether in the form of cash, property, or services) are to be included for 5 the taxable year in which actually or constructively received. Expenditures are to be deducted for the taxable year in which actually made. For rules relating to constructive receipt, see § 1.451-2. For treatment of an expenditure attributable to more than one taxable year, see section 461(a) and paragraph (a)(1) of § 1.461-1.

(ii) *Accrual method.* (A) Generally, under an accrual method, income is to be included 10 for the taxable year when all the events have occurred that fix the right to receive the income and the amount of the income can be determined with reasonable accuracy. Under such a method, a liability is incurred, and generally is taken into account for Federal income tax purposes, in the taxable year in which all the events have occurred that establish the fact of the liability, the amount of the liability can be determined with 15 reasonable accuracy, and economic performance has occurred with respect to the liability. (See paragraph (a)(2)(iii)(A) of § 1.461-1 for examples of liabilities that may not be taken into account until after the taxable year incurred, and see §§ 1.461-4 through 1.461-6 for rules relating to economic performance.) Applicable provisions of the Code, the Income Tax Regulations, and other guidance published by the Secretary prescribe 20 the manner in which a liability that has been incurred is taken into account. For example, section 162 provides that a deductible liability generally is taken into account in the taxable year incurred through a deduction from gross income. As a further example, under section 263 or 263A, a liability that relates to the creation of an asset having a useful life extending substantially beyond the close of the taxable year is taken into 25 account in the taxable year incurred through capitalization (within the meaning of § 1.263A-1(c)(3)) and may later affect the computation of taxable income through depreciation or otherwise over a period including subsequent taxable years, in accordance with applicable Internal Revenue Code sections and related guidance.

(B) The term ``liability'' includes any item allowable as a deduction, cost, or expense 30 for Federal income tax purposes. In addition to allowable deductions, the term includes any amount otherwise allowable as a capitalized cost, as a cost taken into account in computing cost of goods sold, as a cost allocable to a long-term contract, or as any other cost or expense. Thus, for example, an amount that a taxpayer expends or will expend for capital improvements to property must be incurred before the taxpayer may take the 35 amount into account in computing its basis in the property. The term ``liability'' is not limited to items for which a legal obligation to pay exists at the time of payment. Thus, for example, amounts prepaid for goods or services and amounts paid without a legal obligation to do so may not be taken into account by an accrual basis taxpayer any earlier than the taxable year in which those amounts are incurred.   40

(C) No method of accounting is acceptable unless, in the opinion of the Commissioner, it clearly reflects income. The method used by the taxpayer in determining when income is to be accounted for will generally be acceptable if it accords with generally accepted accounting principles, is consistently used by the taxpayer from year to year, and is consistent with the Income Tax Regulations. For example, a taxpayer 45 engaged in a manufacturing business may account for sales of the taxpayer's product when the goods are shipped, when the product is delivered or accepted, or when title to the goods passes to the customers, whether or not billed, depending on the method regularly employed in keeping the taxpayer's books.

(iii) *Other permissible methods.* Special methods of accounting are described 50 elsewhere in chapter 1 of the Code and the regulations thereunder. For example, see the

739

Sec. 446. General rule for methods of accounting

following sections and the regulations thereunder: Sections 61 and 162, relating to the crop method of accounting; section 453, relating to the installment method; section 460, relating to the long-term contract methods. In addition, special methods of accounting for particular items of income and expense are provided under other sections of chapter 1.
5 For example, see section 174, relating to research and experimental expenditures, and section 175, relating to soil and water conservation expenditures.

(iv) *Combinations of the foregoing methods.* (a) In accordance with the following rules, any combination of the foregoing methods of accounting will be permitted in connection with a trade or business if such combination clearly reflects income and is consistently
10 used. Where a combination of methods of accounting includes any special methods, such as those referred to in subdivision (iii) of this subparagraph, the taxpayer must comply with the requirements relating to such special methods. A taxpayer using an accrual method of accounting with respect to purchases and sales may use the cash method in computing all other items of income and expense. However, a taxpayer who
15 uses the cash method of accounting in computing gross income from his trade or business shall use the cash method in computing expenses of such trade or business. Similarly, a taxpayer who uses an accrual method of accounting in computing business expenses shall use an accrual method in computing items affecting gross income from his trade or business.
20 (b) A taxpayer using one method of accounting in computing items of income and deductions of his trade or business may compute other items of income and deductions not connected with his trade or business under a different method of accounting.

(2) *Special rules.* (i) In any case in which it is necessary to use an inventory the accrual method of accounting must be used with regard to purchases and sales unless
25 otherwise authorized under subdivision (ii) of this subparagraph.

(ii) No method of accounting will be regarded as clearly reflecting income unless all items of gross profit and deductions are treated with consistency from year to year. The Commissioner may authorize a taxpayer to adopt or change to a method of accounting permitted by this chapter although the method is not specifically described in the
30 regulations in this part if, in the opinion of the Commissioner, income is clearly reflected by the use of such method. Further, the Commissioner may authorize a taxpayer to continue the use of a method of accounting consistently used by the taxpayer, even though not specifically authorized by the regulations in this part, if, in the opinion of the Commissioner, income is clearly reflected by the use of such method. See section 446(a)
35 and paragraph (a) of this section, which require that taxable income shall be computed under the method of accounting on the basis of which the taxpayer regularly computes his income in keeping his books, and section 446(e) and paragraph (e) of this section, which require the prior approval of the Commissioner in the case of changes in accounting method.
40 (iii) The timing rules of § 1.1502-13 are a method of accounting for intercompany transactions (as defined in § 1.1502-13(b)(1)(i)), to be applied by each member of a consolidated group in addition to the member's other methods of accounting. See § 1.1502-13(a)(3)(i). This paragraph (c)(2)(iii) is applicable to consolidated return years beginning on or after November 7, 2001.
45 (d) *Taxpayer engaged in more than one business.* (1) Where a taxpayer has two or more separate and distinct trades or businesses, a different method of accounting may be used for each trade or business, provided the method used for each trade or business clearly reflects the income of that particular trade or business. For example, a taxpayer may account for the operations of a personal service business on the cash receipts and
50 disbursements method and of a manufacturing business on an accrual method, provided such businesses are separate and distinct and the methods used for each clearly reflect

Sec. 446. General rule for methods of accounting

income. The method first used in accounting for business income and deductions in connection with each trade or business, as evidenced in the taxpayer's income tax return in which such income or deductions are first reported, must be consistently followed thereafter.

*** 5

(e) *Requirement respecting the adoption or change of accounting method.* (1) A taxpayer filing his first return may adopt any permissible method of accounting in computing taxable income for the taxable year covered by such return. See section 446(c) and paragraph (c) of this section for permissible methods. Moreover, a taxpayer may adopt any permissible method of accounting in connection with each separate and 10 distinct trade or business, the income from which is reported for the first time. See section 446(d) and paragraph (d) of this section. See also section 446(a) and paragraph (a) of this section.

(2)(i) Except as otherwise expressly provided in chapter 1 of the Code and the regulations thereunder, a taxpayer who changes the method of accounting employed in 15 keeping his books shall, before computing his income upon such new method for purposes of taxation, secure the consent of the Commissioner. Consent must be secured whether or not such method is proper or is permitted under the Internal Revenue Code or the regulations thereunder.

(ii) (a) A change in the method of accounting includes a change in the overall plan of 20 accounting for gross income or deductions or a change in the treatment of any material item used in such overall plan. Although a method of accounting may exist under this definition without the necessity of a pattern of consistent treatment of an item, in most instances a method of accounting is not established for an item without such consistent treatment. A material item is any item that involves the proper time for the inclusion of the 25 item in income or the taking of a deduction. Changes in method of accounting include a change from the cash receipts and disbursement method to an accrual method, or vice versa, a change involving the method or basis used in the valuation of inventories (see sections 471 and 472 and the regulations under sections 471 and 472), a change from the cash or accrual method to a long-term contract method, or vice versa (see § 1.460-4), 30 certain changes in computing depreciation or amortization (see paragraph (e)(2)(ii)(d) of this section), a change involving the adoption, use or discontinuance of any other specialized method of computing taxable income, such as the crop method, and a change where the Internal Revenue Code and regulations under the Internal Revenue Code specifically require that the consent of the Commissioner must be obtained before 35 adopting such.

***

[T.D. 6500, 25 FR 11708, Nov. 26, 1960; T.D. 7073, 35 FR 17710, Nov. 18, 1970; T.D. 7285, 38 FR 26184, Sept. 19, 1973; T.D. 8067, 51 FR 378, Jan. 6, 1986; T.D. 8131, 52 FR 10084, Mar. 30, 1987; T.D. 8408, 57 FR 12419, Apr. 10, 1992; T.D. 8482, 58 FR 40 42233, Aug. 9, 1993; T.D. 8608, 60 FR 40078, Aug. 7, 1995; T.D. 8719, 62 FR 26741, May 15, 1997; T.D. 8742, 62 FR 68169, Dec. 31, 1997; T.D. 8929, 66 FR 2223, Jan. 11, 2001; T.D. 9025, 67 FR 76985, Dec. 16, 2002; T.D. 9105, 69 FR 8, Jan. 2, 2004; T.D. 9307, 71 FR 78068, Dec. 28, 2006]

45

Sec. 448. Limitation on use of cash method of accounting

(a) **General rule.** -- Except as otherwise provided in this section, in the case of a--

(1) C corporation,

(2) partnership which has a C corporation as a partner, or

741

Sec. 448.   Limitation on use of cash method of accounting

(3) tax shelter,

taxable income shall not be computed under the cash receipts and disbursements method of accounting.

(b) Exceptions. --

(1) Farming business. -- Paragraphs (1) and (2) of subsection (a) shall not apply to any farming business.

(2) Qualified personal service corporations. -- Paragraphs (1) and (2) of subsection (a) shall not apply to a qualified personal service corporation, and such a corporation shall be treated as an individual for purposes of determining whether paragraph (2) of subsection (a) applies to any partnership.

(3) Entities with gross receipts of not more than $5,000,000. -- Paragraphs (1) and (2) of subsection (a) shall not apply to any corporation or partnership for any taxable year if, for all prior taxable years beginning after December 31, 1985, such entity (or any predecessor) met the $5,000,000 gross receipts test of subsection (c).

(c) $5,000,000 gross receipts test. -- For purposes of this section--

(1) In general. -- A corporation or partnership meets the $5,000,000 gross receipts test of this subsection for any prior taxable year if the average annual gross receipts of such entity for the 3-taxable-year period ending with such prior taxable year does not exceed $5,000,000.

(2) Aggregation rules. -- All persons treated as a single employer under subsection (a) or (b) of section 52 or subsection (m) or (o) of section 414 shall be treated as one person for purposes of paragraph (1).

(3) Special rules. -- For purposes of this subsection--

(A) Not in existence for entire 3-year period. -- If the entity was not in existence for the entire 3-year period referred to in paragraph (1), such paragraph shall be applied on the basis of the period during which such entity (or trade or business) was in existence.

(B) Short taxable years. -- Gross receipts for any taxable year of less than 12 months shall be annualized by multiplying the gross receipts for the short period by 12 and dividing the result by the number of months in the short period.

***

(d) Definitions and special rules. -- For purposes of this section--

(1) Farming business. --

(A) In general. -- The term "farming business" means the trade or business of farming (within the meaning of section 263A(e)(4)).

(B) Timber and ornamental trees. -- The term "farming business" includes the raising, harvesting, or growing of trees to which section 263A(c)(5) applies.

(2) Qualified personal service corporation. -- The term "qualified personal service corporation" means any corporation--

(A) substantially all of the activities of which involve the performance of services in the fields of health, law, engineering, architecture, accounting, actuarial science, performing arts, or consulting, and

(B) substantially all of the stock of which (by value) is held directly (or indirectly through 1 or more partnerships, S corporations, or qualified personal service corporations not described in paragraph (2) or (3) of subsection (a)) by--

(i) employees performing services for such corporation in connection with the activities involving a field referred to in subparagraph (A),

(ii) retired employees who had performed such services for such corporation,

742

Sec. 448. Limitation on use of cash method of accounting

(iii) the estate of any individual described in clause (i) or (ii), or

(iv) any other person who acquired such stock by reason of the death of an individual described in clause (i) or (ii) (but only for the 2-year period beginning on the date of the death of such individual).

To the extent provided in regulations which shall be prescribed by the Secretary, indirect 5
holdings through a trust shall be taken into account under subparagraph (B).

(3) Tax shelter defined. -- The term "tax shelter" has the meaning given such term by section 461(i)(3) (determined after application of paragraph (4) thereof). An S corporation shall not be treated as a tax shelter for purposes of this section merely by reason of being required to file a notice of exemption from registration with a State agency described in section 10
461(i)(3)(A), but only if there is a   requirement applicable to all corporations offering securities for sale in the State that to be exempt from such registration the corporation must file such a notice.

(4) Special rules for application of paragraph (2). -- For purposes of paragraph (2)--

(A) community property laws shall be disregarded,   15

***

Sec. 451. General rule for taxable year of inclusion

(a) General rule. -- The amount of any item of gross income shall be included in the gross income for the taxable year in which received by the taxpayer, unless, under the method of accounting used in computing taxable income, such amount is to be properly accounted for as of a different period.   20

(b) Special rule in case of death. -- In the case of the death of a taxpayer whose taxable income is computed under an accrual method of accounting, any amount accrued only by reason of the death of the taxpayer shall not be included in computing taxable income for the period in which falls the date of the taxpayer's death.

(c) Special rule for employee tips. -- For purposes of subsection (a), tips included in a written 25
statement furnished an employer by an employee pursuant to section 6053(a) shall be deemed to be received at the time the written statement including such tips is furnished to the employer.

***

(h) Special rule for cash options for receipt of qualified prizes. --

(1) In general. -- For purposes of this title, in the case of an individual on the cash receipts 30
and disbursements method of accounting, a qualified prize option shall be disregarded in determining the taxable year for which any portion of the qualified prize is properly includible in gross income of the taxpayer.

Reg. § 1.451-1   General rule for taxable year of inclusion.   35

(a) *General rule.* Gains, profits, and income are to be included in gross income for the taxable year in which they are actually or constructively received by the taxpayer unless includible for a different year in accordance with the taxpayer's method of accounting. Under an accrual method of accounting, income is includible in gross income when all the events have occurred which fix the right to receive such income and the amount thereof 40
can be determined with reasonable accuracy. Therefore, under such a method of accounting if, in the case of compensation for services, no determination can be made as to the right to such compensation or the amount thereof until the services are completed, the amount of compensation is ordinarily income for the taxable year in which the determination can be made. Under the cash receipts and disbursements method of 45
accounting, such an amount is includible in gross income when actually or constructively

Sec. 451. General rule for taxable year of inclusion

received. Where an amount of income is properly accrued on the basis of a reasonable estimate and the exact amount is subsequently determined, the difference, if any, shall be taken into account for the taxable year in which such determination is made. To the extent that income is attributable to the recovery of bad debts for accounts charged off in prior
5 years, it is includible in the year of recovery in accordance with the taxpayer's method of accounting, regardless of the date when the amounts were charged off. For treatment of bad debts and bad debt recoveries, see sections 166 and 111 and the regulations thereunder. For rules relating to the treatment of amounts received in crop shares, see section 61 and the regulations thereunder. For the year in which a partner must include
10 his distributive share of partnership income, see section 706(a) and paragraph (a) of § 1.706-1. If a taxpayer ascertains that an item should have been included in gross income in a prior taxable year, he should, if within the period of limitation, file an amended return and pay any additional tax due. Similarly, if a taxpayer ascertains that an item was improperly included in gross income in a prior taxable year, he should, if within the period
15 of limitation, file claim for credit or refund of any overpayment of tax arising therefrom.

(b) *Special rule in case of death.* (1) A taxpayer's taxable year ends on the date of his death. See section 443(a)(2) and paragraph (a)(2) of § 1.443-1. In computing taxable income for such year, there shall be included only amounts properly includible under the method of accounting used by the taxpayer. However, if the taxpayer used an accrual
20 method of accounting, amounts accrued only by reason of his death shall not be included in computing taxable income for such year. If the taxpayer uses no regular accounting method, only amounts actually or constructively received during such year shall be included. (For rules relating to the inclusion of partnership income in the return of a decedent partner, see subchapter K, chapter 1 of the Code, and the regulations
25 thereunder.)

(2) If the decedent owned an installment obligation the income from which was taxable to him under section 453, no income is required to be reported in the return of the decedent by reason of the transmission at death of such obligation. See section 453(d) (3). For the treatment of installment obligations acquired by the decedent's estate or by
30 any person by bequest, devise, or inheritance from the decedent, see section 691(a)(4) and the regulations thereunder.

(c) *Special rule for employee tips.* Tips reported by an employee to his employer in a written statement furnished to the employer pursuant to section 6053(a) shall be included in gross income of the employee for the taxable year in which the written statement is
35 furnished the employer.

***

Reg. § 1.451-2 Constructive receipt of income.

(a) *General rule.* Income although not actually reduced to a taxpayer's possession is constructively received by him in the taxable year during which it is credited to his
40 account, set apart for him, or otherwise made available so that he may draw upon it at any time, or so that he could have drawn upon it during the taxable year if notice of intention to withdraw had been given. However, income is not constructively received if the taxpayer's control of its receipt is subject to substantial limitations or restrictions. Thus, if a corporation credits its employees with bonus stock, but the stock is not
45 available to such employees until some future date, the mere crediting on the books of the corporation does not constitute receipt. In the case of interest, dividends, or other earnings (whether or not credited) payable in respect of any deposit or account in a bank, building and loan association, savings and loan association, or similar institution, the following are not substantial limitations or restrictions on the taxpayer's control over the
50 receipt of such earnings:

(1) A requirement that the deposit or account, and the earnings thereon, must be

Sec. 451. General rule for taxable year of inclusion

withdrawn in multiples of even amounts;

(2) The fact that the taxpayer would, by withdrawing the earnings during the taxable year, receive earnings that are not substantially less in comparison with the earnings for the corresponding period to which the taxpayer would be entitled had he left the account on deposit until a later date (for example, if an amount equal to three months' interest 5 must be forfeited upon withdrawal or redemption before maturity of a one year or less certificate of deposit, time deposit, bonus plan, or other deposit arrangement then the earnings payable on premature withdrawal or redemption would be substantially less when compared with the earnings available at maturity);

(3) A requirement that the earnings may be withdrawn only upon a withdrawal of all or 10 part of the deposit or account. However, the mere fact that such institutions may pay earnings on withdrawals, total or partial, made during the last three business days of any calendar month ending a regular quarterly or semiannual earnings period at the applicable rate calculated to the end of such calendar month shall not constitute constructive receipt of income by any depositor or account holder in any such institution 15 who has not made a withdrawal during such period;

(4) A requirement that a notice of intention to withdraw must be given in advance of the withdrawal. In any case when the rate of earnings payable in respect of such a deposit or account depends on the amount of notice of intention to withdraw that is given, earnings at the maximum rate are constructively received during the taxable year 20 regardless of how long the deposit or account was held during the year or whether, in fact, any notice of intention to withdraw is given during the year. However, if in the taxable year of withdrawal the depositor or account holder receives a lower rate of earnings because he failed to give the required notice of intention to withdraw, he shall be allowed an ordinary loss in such taxable year in an amount equal to the difference between the 25 amount of earnings previously included in gross income and the amount of earnings actually received. See section 165 and the regulations thereunder.

***

Reg. § 1.451-5 Advance payments for goods and long-term contracts.

(a) *Advance payment defined.* (1) For purposes of this section, the term ``advance 30 payment" means any amount which is received in a taxable year by a taxpayer using an accrual method of accounting for purchases and sales or a long-term contract method of accounting (described in § 1.451-3), pursuant to, and to be applied against, an agreement:

(i) For the sale or other disposition in a future taxable year of goods held by the 35 taxpayer primarily for sale to customers in the ordinary course of his trade or business, or

(ii) For the building, installing, constructing or manufacturing by the taxpayer of items where the agreement is not completed within such taxable year.

(2) For purposes of subparagraph (1) of this paragraph:

(i) The term ``agreement" includes (a) a gift certificate that can be redeemed for 40 goods, and (b) an agreement which obligates a taxpayer to perform activities described in subparagraph (1)(i) or (ii) of this paragraph and which also contains an obligation to perform services that are to be performed as an integral part of such activities; and

(ii) Amounts due and payable are considered ``received".

(3) If a taxpayer (described in subparagraph (1) of this paragraph) receives an amount 45 pursuant to, and to be applied against, an agreement that not only obligates the taxpayer to perform the activities described in subparagraph (1) (i) and (ii) of this paragraph, but also obligates the taxpayer to perform services that are not to be performed as an integral part of such activities, such amount will be treated as an ``advance payment" (as defined in subparagraph (1) of this paragraph) only to the extent such amount is properly 50 allocable to the obligation to perform the activities described in subparagraph (1) (i) and

Sec. 451. General rule for taxable year of inclusion

(ii) of this paragraph. The portion of the amount not so allocable will not be considered an ``advance payment'' to which this section applies. If, however, the amount not so allocable is less than 5 percent of the total contract price, such amount will be treated as so allocable except that such treatment cannot result in delaying the time at which the

5 taxpayer would otherwise accrue the amounts attributable to the activities described in subparagraph (1) (i) and (ii) of this paragraph.

(b) *Taxable year of inclusion--*(1) *In general.* Advance payments must be included in income either--

(i) In the taxable year of receipt; or

10 (ii) Except as provided in paragraph (c) of this section.

(a) In the taxable year in which properly accruable under the taxpayer's method of accounting for tax purposes if such method results in including advance payments in gross receipts no later than the time such advance payments are included in gross receipts for purposes of all of his reports (including consolidated financial statements) to

15 shareholders, partners, beneficiaries, other proprietors, and for credit purposes, or

(b) If the taxpayer's method of accounting for purposes of such reports results in advance payments (or any portion of such payments) being included in gross receipts earlier than for tax purposes, in the taxable year in which includible in gross receipts pursuant to his method of accounting for purposes of such reports.

20   ***

(c) *Exception for inventoriable goods.* (1)(i) If a taxpayer receives an advance payment in a taxable year with respect to an agreement for the sale of goods properly includible in his inventory, or with respect to an agreement (such as a gift certificate) which can be satisfied with goods or a type of goods that cannot be identified in such

25 taxable year, and on the last day of such taxable year the taxpayer--

(a) Is accounting for advance payments pursuant to a method described in paragraph (b)(1)(ii) of this section for tax purposes,

(b) Has received ``substantial advance payments'' (as defined in subparagraph (3) of this paragraph) with respect to such agreement, and

30 (c) Has on hand (or available to him in such year through his normal source

of supply) goods of substantially similar kind and in sufficient quantity to satisfy the agreement in such year, then all advance payments received with respect to such agreement by the last day of the second taxable year following the year in which such substantial advance payments are received, and not previously included in income in

35 accordance with the taxpayer's accrual method of accounting, must be included in income in such second taxable year.

(ii) If advance payments are required to be included in income in a taxable year solely by reason of subdivision (i) of this subparagraph, the taxpayer must take into account in such taxable year the costs and expenditures included in inventory at the end of such

40 year with respect to such goods (or substantially similar goods) on hand or, if no such goods are on hand by the last day of such second taxable year, the estimated cost of goods necessary to satisfy the agreement.

(iii) Subdivision (ii) of this subparagraph does not apply if the goods or type of goods with respect to which the advance payment is received are not identifiable in the year the

45 advance payments are required to be included in income by reason of subdivision (i) of this subparagraph (for example, where an amount is received for a gift certificate).

(2) If subparagraph (1)(i) of this paragraph is applicable to advance payments received with respect to an agreement, any advance payments received with respect to such agreement subsequent to such second taxable year must be included in gross

50 income in the taxable year of receipt. To the extent estimated costs of goods are taken into account in a taxable year pursuant to subparagraph (1)(ii) of this paragraph, such

Sec. 451. General rule for taxable year of inclusion

costs may not again be taken into account in another year. In addition, any variances between the costs or estimated costs taken into account pursuant to subparagraph (1)(ii) of this paragraph and the costs actually incurred in fulfilling the taxpayer's obligations under the agreement must be taken into account as an adjustment to the cost of goods sold in the year the taxpayer completes his obligations under such agreement.   5

(3) For purposes of subparagraph (1) of this paragraph, a taxpayer will be considered to have received ``substantial advance payments'' with respect to an agreement by the last day of a taxable year if the advance payments received with respect to such agreement during such taxable year plus the advance payments received prior to such taxable year pursuant to such agreement, equal or exceed the total costs and 10 expenditures reasonably estimated as includible in inventory with respect to such agreement. Advance payments received in a taxable year with respect to an agreement (such as a gift certificate) under which the goods or type of goods to be sold are not identifiable in such year shall be treated as ``substantial advance payments'' when received.   15

***

[T.D. 6500, 25 FR 11709, Nov. 26, 1960; T.D. 6723, 29 FR 5342, Apr. 21, 1964; T.D. 7001, 34 FR 997, Jan. 23, 1969; T.D. 7103, 36 FR 5495, Mar. 24, 1971; T.D. 7154, 36 FR 24996, Dec. 28, 1971; 43 FR 59357, Dec. 20, 1978; T.D. 7397, 41 FR 2641, Jan. 19, 1976; T.D. 7663, 44 FR 76782, Dec. 28, 1979; T.D. 8067, 51 FR 393, Jan. 6, 1986; T.D. 20 8491, 58 FR 53135, Oct. 14, 1993; T.D. 8820, 64 FR 26851, May 18, 1999; T.D. 8929, 66 FR 2224, Jan. 11, 2001]

Sec. 453. Installment method

(a) **General rule.** -- Except as otherwise provided in this section, income from an installment sale shall be taken into account for purposes of this title under the installment method.   25

(b) **Installment sale defined.** -- For purposes of this section--

(1) **In general.** -- The term "installment sale" means a disposition of property where at least 1 payment is to be received after the close of the taxable year in which the disposition occurs.

(2) **Exceptions.** -- The term "installment sale" does not include--

(A) **Dealer dispositions.** -- Any dealer disposition (as defined in subsection (l)).   30

(B) **Inventories of personal property.** -- A disposition of personal property of a kind which is required to be included in the inventory of the taxpayer if on hand at the close of the taxable year.

(c) **Installment method defined.** -- For purposes of this section, the term "installment method" means a method under which the income recognized for any taxable year from a disposition is that 35 proportion of the payments received in that year which the gross profit (realized or to be realized when payment is completed) bears to the total contract price.

(d) **Election out.** --

(1) **In general.** -- Subsection (a) shall not apply to any disposition if the taxpayer elects to have subsection (a) not apply to such disposition.   40

(2) **Time and manner for making election.** -- Except as otherwise provided by regulations, an election under paragraph (1) with respect to a disposition may be made only on or before the due date prescribed by law (including extensions) for filing the taxpayer's return of the tax imposed by this chapter for the taxable year in which the disposition occurs. Such an election shall be made in the manner prescribed by regulations.   45

(3) **Election revocable only with consent.** -- An election under paragraph (1) with respect

Sec. 453. Installment method

to any disposition may be revoked only with the consent of the Secretary.

(e) Second dispositions by related persons. --

(1) In general. -- If--

(A) any person disposes of property to a related person (hereinafter in this subsection referred to as the "first disposition"), and

(B) before the person making the first disposition receives all payments with respect to such disposition, the related person disposes of the property (hereinafter in this subsection referred to as the "second disposition"), then, for purposes of this section, the amount realized with respect to such second disposition shall be treated as received at the time of the second disposition by the person making the first disposition.

(2) 2-Year cutoff for property other than marketable securities. --

(A) In general. -- Except in the case of marketable securities, paragraph (1) shall apply only if the date of the second disposition is not more than 2 years after the date of the first disposition.

(B) Substantial diminishing of risk of ownership. -- The running of the 2-year period set forth in subparagraph (A) shall be suspended with respect to any property for any period during which the related person's risk of loss with respect to the property is substantially diminished by -

(i) the holding of a put with respect to such property (or similar property),

(ii) the holding by another person of a right to acquire the property, or

(iii) a short sale or any other transaction.

(3) Limitation on amount treated as received. -- The amount treated for any taxable year as received by the person making the first disposition by reason of paragraph (1) shall not exceed the excess of--

(A) the lesser of--

(i) the total amount realized with respect to any second disposition of the property occurring before the close of the taxable year, or

(ii) the total contract price for the first disposition, over

(B) the sum of -

(i) the aggregate amount of payments received with respect to the first disposition before the close of such year, plus

(ii) the aggregate amount treated as received with respect to the first disposition for prior taxable years by reason of this subsection.

(4) Fair market value where disposition is not sale or exchange. -- For purposes of this subsection, if the second disposition is not a sale or exchange, an amount equal to the fair market value of the property disposed of shall be substituted for the amount realized.

(5) Later payments treated as receipt of tax paid amounts. -- If paragraph (1) applies for any taxable year, payments received in subsequent taxable years by the person making the first disposition shall not be treated as the receipt of payments with respect to the first disposition to the extent that the aggregate of such payments does not exceed the amount treated as received by reason of paragraph (1).

(6) Exception for certain dispositions. -- For purposes of this subsection--

(A) Reacquisitions of stock by issuing corporation not treated as first dispositions.-- Any sale or exchange of stock to the issuing corporation shall not be treated as a first disposition.

748

Sec. 453. Installment method

(B) Involuntary conversions not treated as second dispositions. -- A compulsory or involuntary conversion (within the meaning of section 1033) and any transfer thereafter shall not be treated as a second disposition if the first disposition occurred before the threat or imminence of the conversion.

(C) Dispositions after death. -- Any transfer after the earlier of-- 5

(i) the death of the person making the first disposition, or

(ii) the death of the person acquiring the property in the first disposition,

and any transfer thereafter shall not be treated as a second disposition.

(7) Exception where tax avoidance not a principal purpose. -- This subsection shall not apply to a second disposition (and any transfer thereafter) if it is established to the satisfaction 10 of the Secretary that neither the first disposition nor the second disposition had as one of its principal purposes the avoidance of Federal income tax.

(8) Extension of statute of limitations. -- The period for assessing a deficiency with respect to a first disposition (to the extent such deficiency is attributable to the application of this subsection) shall not expire before the day which is 2 years after the date on which the person 15 making the first disposition furnishes (in such manner as the Secretary may by regulations prescribe) a notice that there was a second disposition of the property to which this subsection may have applied. Such deficiency may be assessed notwithstanding the provisions of any law or rule of law which would otherwise prevent such assessment.

(f) Definitions and special rules. -- For purposes of this section-- 20

(1) Related person. -- Except for purposes of subsections (g) and (h), the term "related person" means--

(A) a person whose stock would be attributed under section 318(a) (other than paragraph (4) thereof) to the person first disposing of the property, or

(B) a person who bears a relationship described in section 267(b) to the person first 25 disposing of the property.

(2) Marketable securities. -- The term "marketable securities" means any security for which, as of the date of the disposition, there was a market on an established securities market or otherwise.

(3) Payment. -- Except as provided in paragraph (4), the term "payment" does not include 30 the receipt of evidences of indebtedness of the person acquiring the property (whether or not payment of such indebtedness is guaranteed by another person).

(4) Purchaser evidences of indebtedness payable on demand or readily tradable. -- Receipt of a bond or other evidence of indebtedness which--

(A) is payable on demand, or 35

(B) is readily tradable,

shall be treated as receipt of payment.

(5) Readily tradable defined. -- For purposes of paragraph (4), the term "readily tradable" means a bond or other evidence of indebtedness which is issued--

(A) with interest coupons attached or in registered form (other than one in registered 40 form which the taxpayer establishes will not be readily tradable in an established securities market), or

(B) in any other form designed to render such bond or other evidence of indebtedness readily tradable in an established securities market.

(6) Like-kind exchanges. -- In the case of any exchange described in section 1031(b)-- 45

(A) the total contract price shall be reduced to take into account the amount of any

Sec. 453. Installment method

property permitted to be received in such exchange without recognition of gain,

    (B) the gross profit from such exchange shall be reduced to take into account any amount not recognized by reason of section 1031(b), and

    (C) the term "payment", when used in any provision of this section other than subsection (b)(1), shall not include any property permitted to be received in such exchange without recognition of gain.

Similar rules shall apply in the case of an exchange which is described in section 356(a) and is not treated as a dividend.

    (7) Depreciable property. -- The term "depreciable property" means property of a character which (in the hands of the transferee) is subject to the allowance for depreciation provided in section 167.

    (8) Payments to be received defined. -- The term "payments to be received" includes--

        (A) the aggregate amount of all payments which are not contingent as to amount, and

        (B) the fair market value of any payments which are contingent as to amount.

(g) Sale of depreciable property to controlled entity. --

    (1) In general. -- In the case of an installment sale of depreciable property between related persons--

        (A) subsection (a) shall not apply,

        (B) for purposes of this title--

            (i) except as provided in clause (ii), all payments to be received shall be treated as received in the year of the disposition, and

            (ii) in the case of any payments which are contingent as to the amount but with respect to which the fair market value may not be reasonably ascertained, the basis shall be recovered ratably, and

        (C) the purchaser may not increase the basis of any property acquired in such sale by any amount before the time such amount is includible in the gross income of the seller.

    (2) Exception where tax avoidance not a principal purpose. -- Paragraph (1) shall not apply if it is established to the satisfaction of the Secretary that the disposition did not have as one of its principal purposes the avoidance of Federal income tax.

    (3) Related persons. -- For purposes of this subsection, the term "related persons" has the meaning given to such term by section 1239(b), except that such term shall include 2 or more partnerships having a relationship to each other described in section 707(b)(1)(B).

***

(i) Recognition of recapture income in year of disposition. --

    (1) In general. -- In the case of any installment sale of property to which subsection (a) applies--

        (A) notwithstanding subsection (a), any recapture income shall be recognized in the year of the disposition, and

        (B) any gain in excess of the recapture income shall be taken into account under the installment method.

    (2) Recapture income. -- For purposes of paragraph (1), the term "recapture income" means, with respect to any installment sale, the aggregate amount which would be treated as ordinary income under (or so much of section 751 as relates to section 1245 or 1250) for the taxable year of the disposition if all payments to be received were received in the taxable year of disposition.

Sec. 453.   Installment method

(j) Regulations. --

(1) In general. -- The Secretary shall prescribe such regulations as may be necessary or appropriate to carry out the provisions of this section.

(2) Selling price not readily ascertainable. -- The regulations prescribed under paragraph (1) shall include regulations providing for ratable basis recovery in transactions where the gross profit or the total contract price (or both) cannot be readily ascertained.

(k) Current inclusion in case of revolving credit plans, etc. -- In the case of--

(1) any disposition of personal property under a revolving credit plan, or

(2) any installment obligation arising out of a sale of -

(A) stock or securities which are traded on an established securities market, or

(B) to the extent provided in regulations, property (other than stock or securities) of a kind regularly traded on an established market,

subsection (a) shall not apply, and, for purposes of this title, all payments to be received shall be treated as received in the year of disposition. The Secretary may provide for the application of this subsection in whole or in part for transactions in which the rules of this subsection otherwise would be avoided through the use of related parties, pass-thru entities, or intermediaries.

(l) Dealer dispositions. -- For purposes of subsection (b)(2)(A)--

(1) In general. -- The term "dealer disposition" means any of the following dispositions:

(A) Personal property. -- Any disposition of personal property by a person who regularly sells or otherwise disposes of personal property of the same type on the installment plan.

(B) Real property. -- Any disposition of real property which is held by the taxpayer for sale to customers in the ordinary course of the taxpayer's trade or business.

(2) Exceptions. -- The term "dealer disposition" does not include--

(A) Farm property. -- The disposition on the installment plan of any property used or produced in the trade or business of farming (within the meaning of section 2032A(e)(4) or (5)).

***

Reg. § 1.453-4   Sale of real property involving deferred periodic payments.

***

(c) *Determination of ``selling price''.* In the sale of mortgaged property the amount of the mortgage, whether the property is merely taken subject to the mortgage or whether the mortgage is assumed by the purchaser, shall, for the purpose of determining whether a sale is on the installment plan, be included as a part of the ``selling price''; and for the purpose of determining the payments and the total contract price as those terms are used in section 453, and §§ 1.453-1 through 1.453-7, the amount of such mortgage shall be included only to the extent that it exceeds the basis of the property. The term ``payments'' does not include amounts received by the vendor in the year of sale from the disposition to a third person of notes given by the vendee as part of the purchase price which are due and payable in subsequent years. Commissions and other selling expenses paid or incurred by the vendor shall not reduce the amount of the payments, the total contract price, or the selling price.

Reg. § 1.453-5   Sale of real property treated on installment method.

***

(b) *Defaults and repossessions*--(1) *Effective date.* This paragraph shall apply only with respect to taxable years beginning before September 3, 1964, in respect of which an

Sec. 453. Installment method

election has not been properly made to have the provisions of section 1038 apply. For rules applicable to taxable years beginning after September 2, 1964, and for taxable years beginning after December 31, 1957, to which such an election applies, see section 1038, and §§ 1.1038-1 through 1.1038-3.

5   (2) *Gain or loss on reacquisition of property.* If the purchaser of real property on the installment plan defaults in any of his payments, and the vendor returning income on the installment method reacquires the property sold, whether title thereto had been retained by the vendor or transferred to the purchaser, gain or loss for the year in which the reacquisition occurs is to be computed upon any installment obligations of the purchaser
10 which are satisfied or discharged upon the reacquisition or are applied by the vendor to the purchase or bid price of the property. Such gain or loss is to be measured by the difference between the fair market value at the date of reacquisition of the property reacquired (including the fair market value of any fixed improvements placed on the property by the purchaser) and the basis in the hands of the vendor of the obligations of
15 the purchaser which are so satisfied, discharged, or applied, with proper adjustment for any other amounts realized or costs incurred in connection with the reacquisition.

(3) *Fair market value of reacquired property.* If the property reacquired is bid in by the vendor at a foreclosure sale, the fair market value of the property shall be presumed to be the purchase or bid price thereof in the absence of clear and convincing proof to the
20 contrary.

(4) *Basis of obligations.* The basis in the hands of the vendor of the obligations of the purchaser satisfied, discharged, or applied upon the reacquisition of the property will be the excess of the face value of such obligations over an amount equal to the income which would be returnable were the obligations paid in full. For definition of the basis of
25 an installment obligation, see section 453(d)(2) and paragraph (b)(2) of § 1.453-9.

(5) *Bad debt deduction.* No deduction for a bad debt shall in any case be taken on account of any portion of the obligations of the purchaser which are treated by the vendor as not having been satisfied, discharged, or applied upon the reacquisition of the property, unless it is clearly shown that after the property was reacquired the purchaser
30 remained liable for such portion; and in no event shall the amount of the deduction exceed the basis in the hands of the vendor of the portion of the obligations with respect to which the purchaser remained liable after the reacquisition. See section 166 and the regulations thereunder.

(6) *Basis of reacquired property.* If the property reacquired is subsequently sold, the
35 basis for determining gain or loss is the fair market value of the property at the date of reacquisition, including the fair market value of any fixed improvements placed on the property by the purchaser.

Reg. § 1.453-9 Gain or loss on disposition of installment obligations.
40   ***

(b) *Computation of gain or loss.* (1) The amount of gain or loss resulting under paragraph (a) of this section is the difference between the basis of the obligation and (i) the amount realized, in the case of satisfaction at other than face value or in the case of a sale or exchange, or (ii) the fair market value of the obligation at the time of disposition, if
45 such disposition is other than by sale or exchange.

(2) The basis of an installment obligation shall be the excess of the face value of the obligation over an amount equal to the income which would be returnable were the obligation satisfied in full.

(3) The application of subparagraphs (1) and (2) of this paragraph may be illustrated
50 by the following examples:

Example (1). In 1960 the M Corporation sold a piece of unimproved real estate to B

Sec. 453. Installment method

for $20,000. The company acquired the property in 1948 at a cost of $10,000. During 1960 the company received $5,000 cash and vendee's notes for the remainder of the selling price, or $15,000, payable in subsequent years. In 1962, before the vendee made any further payments, the company sold the notes for $13,000 in cash. The corporation makes its returns on the calendar year basis. The income to be reported for 1962 is $5,500, computed as follows:

Proceeds of sale of notes............................		$13,000
Selling price of property.............................	$20,000	
Cost of property.......................................	10,000	
Total profit..	10,000	
Total contract price...............................	20,000	
Percent of profit, or proportion of each payment returnable as income, $10,000 divided by $20,000, 50 percent.		
Face value of notes...................................	15,000	
Amount of income returnable were the notes satisfied in full, 50 percent of $15,000...	7,500	
Basis of obligation--excess of face value of notes over amount of income returnable were the notes satisfied in full.......................	7,500	
Taxable income to be reported for 1962	5,500	

Example (2). Suppose in example (1) the M Corporation, instead of selling the notes, distributed them in 1962 to its shareholders as a dividend, and at the time of such distribution, the fair market value of the notes was $14,000. The income to be reported for 1962 is $6,500, computed as follows:

Fair market value of notes....................................	$14,000
Basis of obligation--excess of face value of notes over amount of income returnable were the notes satisfied in full(computed as in example (1))......	7,500
Taxable income to be reported for 1962..............	6,500

***

Reg. § 1.453-12   Allocation of unrecaptured section 1250 gain reported on the installment method.

(a) *General rule.* Unrecaptured section 1250 gain, as defined in section 1(h)(7), is reported on the installment method if that method otherwise applies under section 453 or 453A and the corresponding regulations. If gain from an installment sale includes unrecaptured section 1250 gain and adjusted net capital gain (as defined in section 1(h) (4)), the unrecaptured section 1250 gain is taken into account before the adjusted net capital gain.

***

(d) *Examples.* In each example, the taxpayer, an individual whose taxable year is the calendar year, does not elect out of the installment method. The installment obligation bears adequate stated interest, and the property sold is real property held in a trade or business that qualifies as both section 1231 property and section 1250 property. In all taxable years, the taxpayer's marginal tax rate on ordinary income is 28 percent. The following examples illustrate the rules of this section:

Example 1. General rule. This example illustrates the rule of paragraph (a) of this

5   section as follows:

(i) In 1999, A sells property for $10,000, to be paid in ten equal annual installments beginning on December 1, 1999. A originally purchased the property for $5000, held the property for several years, and took straight-line depreciation deductions in the amount of $3000. In each of the years 1999-2008, A has no other capital or section 1231 gains or

10   losses.

(ii) A's adjusted basis at the time of the sale is $2000. Of A's $8000 of section 1231 gain on the sale of the property, $3000 is attributable to prior straight-line depreciation deductions and is unrecaptured section 1250 gain. The gain on each installment payment is $800.

15   (iii) As illustrated in the table in this paragraph (iii) of this Example 1., A takes into account the unrecaptured section 1250 gain first. Therefore, the gain on A's first three payments, received in 1999, 2000, and 2001, is taxed at 25 percent. Of the $800 of gain on the fourth payment, received in 2002, $600 is taxed at 25 percent and the remaining $200 is taxed at 20 percent. The gain on A's remaining six installment payments is taxed

20   at 20 percent. The table is as follows:

	1999	2000	2001	2002	2003	2004-2008	Total gain
Installment gain...................	800	800	800	800	800	4000	8000
Taxed at 25%........................	800	800	800	600	....	....	3000
Taxed at 20%........................	....	....	....	200	800	4000	5000
Remaining to be taxed at 25%	....	2200	1400	600	....	....	....

30   *Example 2.* Installment payments from sales prior to May 7, 1997. This example illustrates the rule of paragraph (b) of this section as follows:

(i) The facts are the same as in Example 1 except that A sold the property in 1994, received the first of the ten annual installment payments on December 1, 1994, and had no other capital or section 1231 gains or losses in the years 1994-2003.

35   (ii) As in Example 1, of A's $8000 of gain on the sale of the property, $3000 was attributable to prior straight-line depreciation deductions and is unrecaptured section 1250 gain.

(iii) As illustrated in the following table, A's first three payments, in 1994, 1995, and 1996, were received before May 7, 1997, and taxed at 28 percent. Under the rule

40   described in paragraph (b) of this section, A determines the allocation of unrecaptured section 1250 gain for each installment payment after May 6, 1997, by taking unrecaptured section 1250 gain into account first, treating the general rule of paragraph (a) of this section as having applied since the time the property was sold, in 1994. Consequently, of the $800 of gain on the fourth payment, received in 1997, $600 is taxed

45   at 25 percent and the remaining $200 is taxed at 20 percent. The gain on A's remaining six installment payments is taxed at 20 percent. The table is as follows:

	1994	1995	1996	1997	1998	1999-2003	Total gain
Installment gain....................	800	800	800	800	800	4000	8000
Taxed at 28%........................	800	800	800	....	....	....	2400
Taxed at 25%........................	....	....	....	600	....	....	600
Taxed at 20%........................	....	....	....	200	800	4000	5000

Remaining to be taxed at 25% 2200   1400   600   ....

Example 3. Effect of section 1231(c) recapture. This example illustrates the rule of paragraph (a) of this section when there are non-recaptured net section 1231 losses, as defined in section 1231(c)(2), from prior years as follows:

(i) The facts are the same as in Example 1, except that in 1999 A has non-recaptured net section 1231 losses from the previous four years of $1000.

(ii) As illustrated in the table in paragraph (iv) of this Example 3, in 1999, all of A's $800 installment gain is recaptured as ordinary income under section 1231(c). Under the rule described in paragraph (a) of this section, for purposes of determining the amount of unrecaptured section 1250 gain remaining to be taken into account, the $800 recaptured as ordinary income under section 1231(c) is treated as reducing unrecaptured section 1250 gain, rather than adjusted net capital gain. Therefore, A has $2200 of unrecaptured section 1250 gain remaining to be taken into account.

(iii) In the year 2000, A's installment gain is taxed at two rates. First, $200 is recaptured as ordinary income under section 1231(c). Second, the remaining $600 of gain on A's year 2000 installment payment is taxed at 25 percent. Because the full $800 of gain reduces unrecaptured section 1250 gain, A has $1400 of unrecaptured section 1250 gain remaining to be taken into account.

(iv) The gain on A's installment payment received in 2001 is taxed at 25 percent. Of the $800 of gain on the fourth payment, received in 2002, $600 is taxed at 25 percent and the remaining $200 is taxed at 20 percent. The gain on A's remaining six installment payments is taxed at 20 percent. The table is as follows:

	1999	2000	2001	2002	2003	2004-2008	Total gain
Installment gain...................	800	800	800	800	800	4000	8000
Taxed at ordinary rates under section 1231(c)..................	800	200	....	....	....	....	1000
Taxed at 25%........................	....	600	800	600	....	....	2000
Taxed at 20%........................	....	....	....	200	800	4000	5000
Remaining non-recaptured net section 1231 losses..............	200	....	....	....	....	....	
Remaining to be taxed at 25%		2200	1400	600	....	....	....

Example 4. Effect of a net section 1231 loss. This example Illustrates the application of paragraph (a) of this section when there is a net section 1231 loss as follows:

(i) The facts are the same as in Example 1 except that A has section 1231 losses of $1000 in 1999.

(ii) In 1999, A's section 1231 installment gain of $800 does not exceed A's section 1231 losses of $1000. Therefore, A has a net section 1231 loss of $200. As a result, under section 1231(a) all of A's section 1231 gains and losses are treated as ordinary gains and losses. As illustrated in the following table, A's entire $800 of installment gain is ordinary gain. Under the rule described in paragraph (a) of this section, for purposes of determining the amount of unrecaptured section 1250 gain remaining to be taken into account, A's $800 of ordinary section 1231 installment gain in 1999 is treated as reducing unrecaptured section 1250 gain. Therefore, A has $2200 of unrecaptured section 1250 gain remaining to be taken into account.

(iii) In the year 2000, A has $800 of section 1231 installment gain, resulting in a net section 1231 gain of $800. A also has $200 of non-recaptured net section 1231 losses. The $800 gain is taxed at two rates. First, $200 is taxed at ordinary rates under section 1231(c), recapturing the $200 net section 1231 loss sustained in 1999. Second, the remaining $600 of gain on A's year 2000 installment payment is taxed at 25 percent. As in Example 3, the $200 of section 1231(c) gain is treated as reducing unrecaptured section 1250 gain, rather than adjusted net capital gain. Therefore, A has $1400 of unrecaptured section 1250 gain remaining to be taken into account.

5 (iv) The gain on A's installment payment received in 2001 is taxed at 25 percent, reducing the remaining unrecaptured section 1250 gain to $600. Of the $800 of gain on the fourth payment, received in 2002, $600 is taxed at 25 percent and the remaining $200 is taxed at 20 percent. The gain on A's remaining six installment payments is taxed at 20 percent. The table is as follows:

10

	1999	2000	2001	2002	2003	2004-2008	Total gain
Installment gain..................	800	800	800	800	800	4000	8000
Ordinary gain under section 1231(a).................	800	....	....	....	....	....	800
Taxed at ordinary rates under section 1231(c)..................	....	200	....	....	....	....	200
Taxed at 25%.......................	....	600	800	600	....	....	2000
Taxed at 20%........................	....	....	....	200	800	4000	5000
Net section 1231 loss.............	200	....	....	....	....	....	....
Remaining to be taxed at 25%	2200	1400	600	....	....	....	....

***

25 **Reg. § 15a.453-1 Installment method reporting for sales of real property and casual sales of personal property (Temporary).**

(a). *In general* Unless the taxpayer otherwise elects in the manner prescribed in paragraph (d)(3) of this section, income from a sale of real property or a casual sale of personal property, where any payment is to be received in a taxable year after the year of 30 sale, is to be reported on the installment method.

(b) *Installment sale defined*--(1) *In general.* The term ``installment sale" means a disposition of property (except as provided in paragraph (b)(4) of this section) where at least one payment is to be received after the close of the taxable year in which the disposition occurs. The term ``installment sale" includes dispositions from which payment 35 is to be received in a lump sum in a taxable year subsequent to the year of sale. For purposes of this paragraph, the taxable year in which payments are to be received is to be determined without regard to section 453(e) (relating to related party sales), section (f) (3) (relating to the definition of a ``payment") and section (g) (relating to sales of depreciable property to a spouse or 80-percent-owned entity).

40 (2) Installment method defined--(i) *In general.* Under the installment method, the amount of any payment which is income to the taxpayer is that portion of the installment payment received in that year which the gross profit realized or to be realized bears to the total contract price (the ``gross profit ratio"). See paragraph (c) of this section for rules describing installment method reporting of contingent payment sales.

45 (ii) *Selling price defined.* The term ``selling price" means the gross selling price without reduction to reflect any existing mortgage or other encumbrance on the property (whether assumed or taken subject to by the buyer) and, for installment sales in taxable years ending after October 19, 1980, without reduction to reflect any selling expenses. Neither interest, whether stated or unstated, nor original issue discount is considered to 50 be a part of the selling price. See paragraph (c) of this section for rules describing installment method reporting of contingent payment sales.

(iii) *Contract price defined.* The term ``contract price" means the total contract price equal to selling price reduced by that portion of any qualifying indebtedness (as defined

Sec. 453. Installment method

in paragraph (b)(2)(iv) of this section), assumed or taken subject to by the buyer, which does not exceed the seller's basis in the property (adjusted, for installment sales in taxable years ending after October 19, 1980, to reflect commissions and other selling expenses as provided in paragraph (b)(2)(v) of this section). See paragraph (c) of this section for rules describing installment method reporting of contingent payment sales.   5

(iv) *Qualifying indebtedness.* The term ``qualifying indebtedness" means a mortgage or other indebtedness encumbering the property and indebtedness, not secured by the property but incurred or assumed by the purchaser incident to the purchaser's acquisition, holding, or operation in the ordinary course of business or investment, of the property. The term ``qualifying indebtedness" does not include an obligation of the 10 taxpayer incurred incident to the disposition of the property (e.g., legal fees relating to the taxpayer's sale of the property) or an obligation functionally unrelated to the acquisition, holding, or operating of the property (e.g., the taxpayer's medical bill). Any obligation created subsequent to the taxpayer's acquisition of the property and incurred or assumed by the taxpayer or placed as an encumbrance on the property in contemplation of 15 disposition of the property is not qualifying indebtedness if the arrangement results in accelerating recovery of the taxpayer's basis in the installment sale.

(v) *Gross profit defined.* The term ``gross profit" means the selling price less the adjusted basis as defined in section 1011 and the regulations thereunder. For sales in taxable years ending after October 19, 1980, in the case of sales of real property by a 20 person other than a dealer and casual sales of personal property, commissions and other selling expenses shall be added to basis for purposes of determining the proportion of payments which is gross profit attributable to the disposition. Such additions to basis will not be deemed to affect the taxpayer's holding period in the transferred property.

(3) Payment--(i) *In general.* Except as provided in paragraph (e) of this section 25 (relating to purchaser evidences of indebtedness payable on demand or readily tradable), the term ``payment" does not include the receipt of evidences of indebtedness of the person acquiring the property (``installment obligation"), whether or not payment of such indebtedness is guaranteed by a third party (including a government agency). For special rules regarding the receipt of an evidence of indebtedness of a transferee of a qualified 30 intermediary, see §§ 1.1031(b)-2(b) and 1.1031(k)-1(j)(2)(iii) of this chapter. A standby letter of credit (as defined in paragraph (b)(3)(iii) of this section) shall be treated as a third party guarantee. Payments include amounts actually or constructively received in the taxable year under an installment obligation. For a special rule regarding a transfer of property to a qualified intermediary followed by the sale of such property by the qualified 35 intermediary, see § 1.1031(k)-1(j)(2)(ii) of this chapter. Receipt of an evidence of indebtedness which is secured directly or indirectly by cash or a cash equivalent, such as a bank certificate of deposit or a treasury note, will be treated as the receipt of payment. For a special rule regarding a transfer of property in exchange for an obligation that is secured by cash or a cash equivalent held in a qualified escrow account or a qualified 40 trust, see § 1.1031(k)-1(j)(2)(i) of this chapter. Payment may be received in cash or other property, including foreign currency, marketable securities, and evidences or indebtedness which are payable on demand or readily tradable. However, for special rules relating to the receipt of certain property with respect to which gain is not recognized, see paragraph (f) of this section (relating to transactions described in 45 sections 351, 356(a) and 1031). Except as provided in § 15a.453-2 of these regulations (relating to distributions of installment obligations in corporate liquidations described in section 337), payment includes receipt of an evidence of indebtedness of a person other than the person acquiring the property from the taxpayer. For purposes of determining the amount of payment received in the taxable year, the amount of qualifying 50 indebtedness (as defined in paragraph (b)(2)(iv) of this section) assumed or taken subject

Sec. 453. Installment method

to by the person acquiring the property shall be included only to the extent that it exceeds the basis of the property (determined after adjustment to reflect selling expenses). For purposes of the preceding sentence, an arrangement under which the taxpayer's liability on qualifying indebtedness is eliminated incident to the disposition (e.g., a novation) shall
5 be treated as an assumption of the qualifying indebtedness. If the taxpayer sells property to a creditor of the taxpayer and indebtedness of the taxpayer is cancelled in consideration of the sale, such cancellation shall be treated as payment. To the extent that cancellation is not in consideration of the sale, see §§ 1.61-12(b)(1) and 1.1001-2(a) (2) relating to discharges of indebtedness. If the taxpayer sells property which is
10 encumbered by a mortgage or other indebtedness on which the taxpayer is not personally liable, and the person acquiring the property is the obligee, the taxpayer shall be treated as having received payment in the amount of such indebtedness.

    (ii) *Wrap-around mortgage.* This paragraph (b)(3)(ii) shall apply generally to any installment sale after March 4, 1981 unless the installment sale was completed before
15 June 1, 1981 pursuant to a written obligation binding on the seller that was executed on or before March 4, 1981. A ``wrap-around mortgage'' means an agreement in which the buyer initially does not assume and purportedly does not take subject to part or all of the mortgage or other indebtedness encumbering the property (``wrapped indebtedness'') and, instead, the buyer issues to the seller an installment obligation the principal amount
20 of which reflects such wrapped indebtedness. Ordinarily, the seller will use payments received on the installment obligation to service the wrapped indebtedness. The wrapped indebtedness shall be deemed to have been taken subject to even though title to the property has not passed in the year of sale and even though the seller remains liable for payments on the wrapped indebtedness. In the hands of the seller, the wrap-around
25 installment obligation shall have a basis equal to the seller's basis in the property which was the subject of the installment sale, increased by the amount of gain recognized in the year of sale, and decreased by the amount of cash and the fair market value of other nonqualifying property received in the year of sale. For purposes of this paragraph (b)(3) (ii), the amount of any indebtedness assumed or taken subject to by the buyer (other than
30 wrapped indebtedness) is to be treated as cash received by the seller in the year of sale. Therefore, except as otherwise required by section 483 or 1232, the gross profit ratio with respect to the wrap-around installment obligation is a fraction, the numerator of which is the face value of the obligation less the taxpayer's basis in the obligation and the denominator of which is the face value of the obligation.

35   (iii) *Standby letter of credit.* The term ``standby letter of credit'' means a non-negotiable, non-transferable (except together with the evidence of indebtedness which it secures) letter of credit, issued by a bank or other financial institution, which serves as a guarantee of the evidence of indebtedness which is secured by the letter of credit. Whether or not the letter of credit explicitly states it is non-negotiable and
40 nontransferable, it will be treated as non-negotiable and nontransferable if applicable local law so provides. The mere right of the secured party (under applicable local law) to transfer the proceeds of a letter of credit shall be disregarded in determining whether the instrument qualifies as a standby letter of credit. A letter of credit is not a standby letter of credit if it may be drawn upon in the absence of default in payment of the underlying
45 evidence of indebtedness.

    (4) *Exceptions.* The term ``installment sale'' does not include, and the provisions of section 453 do not apply to, dispositions of personal property on the installment plan by a person who regularly sells or otherwise disposes of personal property on the installment plan, or to dispositions of personal property of a kind which is required to be included in
50 the inventory of the taxpayer if on hand at the close of the taxable year. See section 453A and the regulations thereunder for rules relating to installment sales by dealers in

Sec. 453. Installment method

personal property. A dealer in real property or a farmer who is not required under his method of accounting to maintain inventories may report the gain on the installment method under section 453.

(5) *Examples.* The following examples illustrate installment method reporting under this section:

Example (1). In 1980, A, a calendar year taxpayer, sells Blackacre, an unencumbered capital asset in A's hands, to B for $100,000: $10,000 down and the remainder payable in equal annual installments over the next 9 years, together with adequate stated interest. A's basis in Blackacre, exclusive of selling expenses, is $38,000. Selling expenses paid by A are $2,000. Therefore, the gross profit is $60,000 ($100,000 selling price-$40,000 basis inclusive of selling expenses). The gross profit ratio is 3/5 (gross profit of $60,000 divided by $100,000 contract price). Accordingly, $6,000 3/5 of ($10,000) of each $10,000 payment received is gain attributable to the sale and $4,000 ($10,000-$6,000) is recovery of basis. The interest received in addition to principal is ordinary income to A.

Example (2). C sells Whiteacre to D for a selling price of $160,000. Whiteacre is encumbered by a longstanding mortgage in the principal amount of $60,000. D will assume or take subject to the $60,000 mortgage and pay the remaining $100,000 in 10 equal annual installments together with adequate stated interest. C's basis in Whiteacre is $90,000. There are no selling expenses. The contract price is $100,000, the $160,000 selling price reduced by the mortgage of $60,000 assumed or taken subject to. Gross profit is $70,000 ($160,000 selling price less C's basis of $90,000). C's gross profit ratio is 7/10 (gross profit of $70,000 divided by $100,000 contract price). Thus, $7,000 (7/10 of $10,000) of each $10,000 annual payment is gain attributable to the sale, and $3,000 ($10,000-$7,000) is recovery of basis.

Example (3). The facts are the same as in example (2), except that C's basis in the land is $40,000. In the year of the sale C is deemed to have received payment of $20,000 ($60,000-$40,000, the amount by which the mortgage D assumed or took subject to exceeds C's basis). Since basis is fully recovered in the year of sale, the gross profit ratio is 1 ($120,000/$120,000) and C will report 100% of the $20,000 deemed payment in the year of sale and each $10,000 annual payment as gain attributable to the sale.

Example (4). E sells Blackacre, an unencumbered capital gain property in E's hands, to F on January 2, 1981. F makes a cash down payment of $500,000 and issues a note to E obliging F to pay an additional $500,000 on the fifth anniversary date. The note does not require a payment of interest. In determining selling price, section 483 will apply to recharacterize as interest a portion of the $500,000 future payment. Assume that under section 483 and the applicable regulations $193,045 is treated as total unstated interest, and the selling price is $806,955 ($1 million less unstated interest). Assuming E's basis (including selling expenses) in Blackacre is $200,000) gross profit is $606,955 ($806,955-$200,000) and the gross profit ratio is 75.21547%. Accordingly, of the $500,000 cash down payment received by E in 1981, $376,077 (75.21547% of $500,000) is gain attributable to the sale and $123,923 is recovery of basis ($500,000-$376,077).

Example (5). In 1982, G sells to H Blackacre, which is encumbered by a first mortgage with a principal amount of $500,000 and a second mortgage with a principal amount of $400,000, for a selling price of $2 million. G's basis in Blackacre is $700,000. Under the agreement between G and H, passage of title is deferred and H does not assume and purportedly does not take subject to either mortgage in the year of sale. H pays G $200,000 in cash and issues a wrap-around mortgage note with a principal amount of $1,800,000 bearing adequate stated interest. H is deemed to have acquired Blackacre subject to the first and second mortgages (wrapped indebtedness) totaling $900,000. The contract price is $1,300,000 (selling price of $2 million less $700,000 mortgages within the seller's basis assumed or taken subject to). Gross profit is also $1,300,000 (selling

price of $2 million less $700,000 basis). Accordingly in the year of sale, the gross profit ratio is 1 ($1,300,000/$1,300,000). Payment in the year of sale is $400,000 ($200,000 cash received plus $200,000 mortgage in excess of basis ($900,000-$700,000)). Therefore, G recognizes $400,000 gain in the year of sale ($400,000x1). In the hands of
5 G the wrap-around installment obligation has a basis of $900,000, equal to G's basis in Blackacre ($700,000) increased by the gain recognized by G in the year of sale ($400,000) reduced by the cash received by G in the year of sale ($200,000). G's gross profit with respect to the note is $900,000 ($1,800,000 face amount less $900,000 basis in the note) and G's contract price with respect to the note is its face amount of
10 $1,800,000. Therefore, the gross profit ratio with respect to the note is 1/2 ($900,000/$1,800,000).

    Example (6). The facts are the same as example (5) except that under the terms of the agreement H assumes the $500,000 first mortgage on Blackacre. H does not assume and purportedly does not take subject to the $400,000 second mortgage on Blackacre.
15 The wrap-around installment obligation issued by H to G has a face amount of $1,300,000. The tax results in the year of sale to G are the same as example (5) ($400,000 payment received and gain recognized). In the hands of G, basis in the wrap-around installment obligation is $400,000 ($700,000 basis in Blackacre plus $400,000 gain recognized in the year of sale minus $700,000 ($200,000 cash received and
20 $500,000 treated as cash received as a result of H's assumption of the first mortgage)). G's gross profit with respect to the note is $900,000 ($1,300,000 face amount of the wrap-around installment obligation less $400,000 basis in that note) and G's contract price with respect to the note is its face value of $1,300,000. Therefore, the gross profit ratio with respect to the note is 9/13 ($900,000/$1,300,000).

25   *Example (7).* A sells the stock of X corporation to B for a $1 million installment obligation payable in equal annual installments over the next 10 years with adequate stated interest. The installment obligation is secured by a standby letter of credit (within the meaning of paragraph (b)(3)(iii) of this section) issued by M bank. Under the agreement between B and M bank, B is required to maintain a compensating balance in
30 an account B maintains with M bank and is required by the M bank to post additional collateral, which may include cash or a cash equivalent, with M bank. Under neither the standby letter of credit nor any other agreement or arrangement is A granted a direct lien upon or other security interest in such cash or cash equivalent collateral. Receipt of B's installment obligation secured by the standby letter of credit will not be treated as the
35 receipt of payment by A.

    Example (8). The facts are the same as in example (7) except that the standby letter of credit is in the drawable sum of $600,000. To secure fully its $1 million note issued to A, B deposits in escrow $400,000 in cash and Treasury bills. Under the escrow agreement, upon default in payment of the note A may look directly to the escrowed
40 collateral. Receipt of B's installment obligation will be treated as the receipt payment by A in the sum of $400,000.

    (c) *Contingent payment sales*--(1) *In general.* Unless the taxpayer otherwise elects in the manner prescribed in paragraph (d)(3) of this section, contingent payment sales are to be reported on the installment method. As used in this section, the term ``contingent
45 payment sale" means a sale or other disposition of property in which the aggregate selling price cannot be determined by the close of the taxable year in which such sale or other disposition occurs. The term ``contingent payment sale" does not include transactions with respect to which the installment obligation represents, under applicable principles of tax law, a retained interest in the property which is the subject of the
50 transaction, an interest in a joint venture or a partnership, an equity interest in a corporation or similar transactions, regardless of the existence of a stated maximum

Sec. 453. Installment method

selling price or a fixed payment term. See paragraph (c)(8) of this section, describing the extent to which the regulations under section 385 apply to the determination of whether an installment obligation represents an equity interest in a corporation. This paragraph prescribes the rules to be applied in allocating the taxpayer's basis (including selling expenses except for selling expenses of dealers in real estate) to payments received and 5 to be received in a contingent payment sale. The rules are designed appropriately to distinguish contingent payment sales for which a maximum selling price is determinable, sales for which a maximum selling price is not determinable but the time over which payments will be received is determinable, and sales for which neither a maximum selling price nor a definite payment term is determinable. In addition, rules are prescribed under 10 which, in appropriate circumstances, the taxpayer will be permitted to recover basis under an income forecast computation.

(2) *Stated maximum selling price*--(i) In general. (A) contingent payment sale will be treated as having a stated maximum selling price if, under the terms of the agreement, the maximum amount of sale proceeds that may be received by the taxpayer can be 15 determined as of the end of the taxable year in which the sale or other disposition occurs. The stated maximum selling price shall be determined by assuming that all of the contingencies contemplated by the agreement are met or otherwise resolved in a manner that will maximize the selling price and accelerate payments to the earliest date or dates permitted under the agreement. Except as provided in paragraph (c)(2)(ii) and (7) of this 20 section (relating to certain payment recomputations), the taxpayer's basis shall be allocated to payments received and to be received under a stated maximum selling price agreement by treating the stated maximum selling price as the selling price for purposes of paragraph (b) of this section. The stated maximum selling price, as initially determined, shall thereafter be treated as the selling price unless and until that maximum amount is 25 reduced, whether pursuant to the terms of the original agreement, by subsequent amendment, by application of the payment recharacterization rule (described in paragraph (c)(2)(ii) of this section), or by a subsequent supervening event such as bankruptcy of the obligor. When the maximum amount is subsequently reduced, the gross profit ratio will be recomputed with respect to payments received in or after the 30 taxable year in which an event requiring reduction occurs. If, however, application of the foregoing rules in a particular case would substantially and inappropriately accelerate or defer recovery of the taxpayer's basis, a special rule will apply. See paragraph (c)(7) of this section.

(B) The following examples illustrate the provisions of paragraph (e)(2)(i) of this 35 section. In each example, it is assumed that application of the rules illustrated will not substantially and inappropriately defer or accelerate recovery of the taxpayer's basis.

Example (1). A sells all of the stock of X corporation to B for $100,000 payable at closing plus an amount equal to 5% of the net profits of X for each of the next nine years, the contingent payments to be made annually together with adequate stated interest. The 40 agreement provides that the maximum amount A may receive, inclusive of the $100,000 down payment but exclusive of interest, shall be $2,000,000. A's basis in the stock of X inclusive of selling expenses, is $200,000. Selling price and contract price are considered to be $2,000,000. Gross profit is $1,800,000, and the gross profit ratio is 9/10 ($1,800,000/$2,000,000). Accordingly, of the $100,000 received by A in the year of sale, 45 $90,000 is reportable as gain attributable to the sale and $10,000 is recovery of basis.

Example (2). C owns Blackacre which is encumbered by a long-standing mortgage of $100,000. On January 15, 1981, C sells Blackacre to D under the following payment arrangement: $100,000 in cash on closing; nine equal annual installment payments of $100,000 commencing January 15, 1982; and nine annual payments (the first to be made 50 on March 30, 1982) equal to 5% of the gross annual rental receipts from Blackacre

761

generated during the preceding calendar year. The agreement provides that each deferred payment shall be accompanied by a payment of interest calculated at the rate of 12% per annum and that the maximum amount payable to C under the agreement (exclusive of interest) shall be $2,100,000. The agreement also specifies that D will
5 assume the long-standing mortgage. C's basis (inclusive of selling expenses) in Blackacre is $300,000. Accordingly, selling price is $2,100,000 and contract price is $2,000,000 (selling price of $2,100,000 less the $100,000 mortgage). The gross profit ratio is 9/10 (gross profit of $1,800,000 divided by $2,000,000 contract price). Of the $100,000 cash payment received by C in 1981, $90,000 is gain attributable to the sale of
10 Blackacre and $10,000 is recovery of basis.

(ii) *Certain interest recomputations.* When interest is stated in the contingent price sale agreement at a rate equal to or greater than the applicable prescribed test rate referred to in § 1.483-1(d)(1)(ii) and such stated interest is payable in addition to the amounts otherwise payable under the agreement, such stated interest is not considered
15 a part of the selling price. In other circumstances (i.e., section 483 is applicable because no interest is stated or interest is stated below the applicable test rate, or interest is stated under a payment recharacterization provision of the sale agreement), the special rule set forth in this (ii) shall be applied in the initial computation and subsequent recomputations of selling price, contract price, and gross profit ratio. The special rule is
20 referred to in this section as the ``price-interest recomputation rule." As used in this section, the term ``payment recharacterization" refers to a contractual arrangement under which a computed amount otherwise payable as part of the selling price is denominated an interest payment. The amount of unstated interest determined under section 483 or (if section 483 is inapplicable in the particular case) the amount of interest determined under
25 a payment recharacterization arrangement is collectively referred to in this section as ``internal interest" amounts. The price-interest recomputation rule is applicable to any stated maximum selling price agreement which contemplates receipt of internal interest by the taxpayer. Under the rule, stated maximum selling price will be determined as of the end of the taxpayer's taxable year in which the sale or other disposition occurs, taking
30 into account all events which have occurred and are subject to prompt subsequent calculation and verification and assuming that all amounts that may become payable under the agreement will be paid on the earliest date or dates permitted under the agreement. With respect to the year of sale, the amount (if any) of internal interest then shall be determined taking account of the respective components of that calculation. The
35 maximum amount initially calculated, minus the internal interest so determined, is the initial stated maximum selling price under the price-interest recomputation rule. For each subsequent taxable year, stated maximum selling price (and thus selling price, contract price, and gross profit ratio) shall be recomputed, taking into account all events which have occurred and are subject to prompt subsequent calculation and verification and
40 assuming that all amounts that may become payable under the agreement will be paid on the earliest date or dates permitted under the agreement. The redetermined gross profit ratio, adjusted to reflect payments received and gain recognized in prior taxable years, shall be applied to payments received in that taxable year.

(iii) *Examples.* The following examples illustrate installment method reporting of a
45 contingent payment sale under which there is a stated maximum selling price. In each example, it is assumed that application of the rules described will not substantially and inappropriately defer or accelerate recovery of the taxpayer's basis.

Example (1). A owns all of the stock of X corporation with a basis to A of $20 million. On July 1, 1981, A sells the stock of X to B under an agreement calling for fifteen annual
50 payments respectively equal to 5% of the net profits of X earned in the immediately preceding fiscal year beginning with the fiscal year ending March 31, 1982. Each

Sec. 453.   Installment method

payment is to be made on the following June 15th, commencing June 15, 1982, together with adequate stated interest. The agreement specifies that the maximum amount (exclusive of interest) payable to A shall not exceed $60 million. Since stated interest is payable as an addition to the selling price and the specified rate is not below the section 483 test rate, there is no internal interest under the agreement. The stated maximum selling price is $60 million. The gross profit ratio is 2/3 (gross profit of $40 million divided by $60 million contract price). Thus, if on June 15, 1982, A receives a payment of $3 million (exclusive of interest) under the agreement, in that year A will report $2 million ($3 million x 2/3) as gain attributable to the sale, and $1 million as recovery of basis.

Example (2). (i) The facts are the same as in example (1) except that the agreement does not call for the payment of any stated interest but does provide for an initial cash payment of $3 million on July 1, 1981. The maximum amount payable, including the $3 million initial payment, remains $60 million. Since section 483 will apply to each payment received by A more than one year following the date of sale (section 483 is inapplicable to the contingent payment that will be received on June 15, 1982 since that date is within one year following the July 1, 1981 sale date), the agreement contemplates internal interest and the price-interest recomputation rule is applicable. Under the rule, an initial determination must be made for A's taxable year 1981. On December 31, 1981, the last day of the taxable year, no events with regard to the first fiscal year have occurred which are subject to prompt subsequent calculation and verification because that fiscal year will end March 31, 1982. Under the price-interest recomputation rule, on December 31, 1981 A is required to assume that the maximum amount subsequently payable under the agreement ($57 million, equal to $60 million less the $3 million initial cash payment received by A in 1981) will be paid on the earliest date permissible under the agreement, i.e., on June 15, 1982. Since no part of a payment received on that date would be treated as interest under section 483, the initial stated maximum selling price, applicable to A's 1981 tax calculations, is deemed to be $60 million. Thus, the 1981 gross profit ratio is 2/3 and for the taxable year 1981 A will report $2 million as gain attributable to the sale.

(ii) The net profits of X for its fiscal year ending March 31, 1982 are $120 million. On June 15, 1982 A receives a payment from B equal to 5% of that amount, or $6 million. On December 31, 1982, A knows that the maximum amount he may subsequently receive under the agreement is $51 million, and A is required to assume that this amount will be paid to him on the earliest permissible date, June 15, 1983. Section 483 does not treat as interest any part of the $6 million received by A on June 15, 1982, but section 483 will treat as unstated interest a computed part of the $51 million it is assumed A will receive on June 15, 1983. Assuming that under the tables in the regulations under section 483, it is determined that the principal component of a payment received more than 21 months but less than 27 months after the date of sale is considered to be .82270, $41,957,700 of the presumed $51 million payment will be treated as principal. The balance of $9,042,300 is interest. Accordingly, in A's 1982 tax calculations stated maximum selling price will be $50,957,700, which amount is equal to the stated maximum selling price that was determined in the 1981 tax calculations ($60 million) reduced by the section 483 interest component of the $6 million payment received by A in 1982 ($0) and further reduced by the section 483 interest component of the $51 million presumed payment to be received by A on June 15, 1983 ($9,042,300). Similarly, in determining gross profit for 1982 tax calculations, the gross profit of $40 million determined in the 1981 tax calculations must be reduced by the same section 483 interest amounts, yielding a recomputed gross profit of $30,957,700 ($40,000,000-$9,042,300). Further, since prior to 1982 A received payment under the agreement (1981 payment of $3 million of which $2 million was profit), the appropriate amounts must be subtracted in the 1982 tax calculation. The total previously received selling price payment of $3 million is subtracted from the recomputed

maximum selling price of $50,957,700, yielding an adjusted selling price of $47,957,700. The total previously recognized gain of $2 million is subtracted from the recomputed maximum gross profit of $30,957,700, yielding an adjusted gross profit of $28,957,700. The gross profit percentage applicable to 1982 tax calculations thus is determined to be
5   60.38175%, equal to the quotient of dividing the adjusted gross profit of $28,957,700 by the adjusted selling price of $47,957,700. Accordingly, of the $6 million received by A in 1982, no part of which is unstated interest under section 483, A will report $3,622,905 (60.38175% of $6 million) as gain attributable to the sale and $2,377,095 ($6,000,000-$3,622,905) as recovery of basis.
10   (iii) The net profits of X for its fiscal year ending March 31, 1983 are $200 million. On June 15, 1983 A receives a payment from B equal to $10 million. On December 31, 1983, A knows that the maximum amount he may subsequently receive under the agreement is $41 million, and A is required to assume that this amount will be paid to him on the earliest permissible date, June 15, 1984. Assuming that under the tables in the
15   regulations under section 483 it is determined that the principal component of a payment received more than 33 months but less than 39 months after the date of sale is .74622, $30,595,020 of the presumed $41 million ($51 million-$10 million) payment will be treated as principal and $10,404,980 is interest. Based upon the assumed factor for 21 months but less than 27 months (.82270) $8,227,000 of the $10 million payment is principal and
20    $1,773,000 is interest. Accordingly, in A's 1983 tax calculations stated maximum selling price will be $47,822,020, which amount is equal to the stated maximum selling price determined in the 1981 calculation ($60 million) reduced by the section 483 interest component of the $6 million 1982 payment ($0), the section 483 interest component of the 1983 payment ($1,773,000) and by the section 483 interest component of the
25   presumed $41 million payment to be received in 1984 ($10,404,980). The recomputed gross profit is $27,822,020 ($40 million-$10,404,980-$1,773,000). The previously reported payments must be deducted for the 1983 calculation. Selling price is reduced to $38,822,020 by subtracting the $3 million 1981 payment and the $6 million 1982 payment ($47,822,020-$9 million) and gross profit is reduced to $22,199,115 by subtracting the
30   1981 profit of $2 million and the 1982 profit of $3,622,905 ($27,822,020-$5,622,905), yielding a gross profit percentage of 57.18176% ($22,199,115/$38,822,020). Accordingly, of the $10 million received in 1983, A will report $1,773,000 as interest under section 483, and of the remaining principal component of $8,227,000, $4,704,343 as gain attributable to the sale ($8,227,000x57.18176%) and $3,522,657 ($8,227,000-$4,704,343) as
35   recovery of basis.
     Example (3). The facts are the same as in example (2) except that X is a collapsible corporation as defined in section 341(b)(1) and no limitation or exception under section 341 (d), (e), or (f) is applicable. Under section 341(a), all of A's gain on the sale will be ordinary income. Accordingly, section 483 will not apply to treat as interest any part of the
40   payments to be received by A under his agreement with B. See section 483(f)(3). Therefore, the price-interest recomputation rule is inapplicable and the tax results to A in each year in which payment is received will be determined in a manner consistent with example (1).
     Example (4). The facts are the same as in example (2) (maximum amount payable
45   under the agreement $60 million) except that the agreement between A and B contains the following ``payment recharacterization" provision:
     ``Any payment made more than one year after the (July 1, 1981) date of sale shall be composed of an interest element and a principal element, the interest element being computed on the principal element at an interest rate of 9% per annum computed from
50   the date of sale to the date of payment."
     The results reached in example (2), with respect to the $3 million initial cash payment

received by A in 1981 remain the same because, under the payment recharacterization formula, no amount received or assumed to be received prior to July 1, 1982 is treated as interest. The 1982 tax computation method described in example (2) is equally applicable to the $6 million payment received in 1982. However, the adjusted gross profit ratio determined in this example (4) will differ from the ratio determined in example (2). The 5 difference is attributable to the difference between a 9% stated interest rate calculation (in this example (4)) and the compound rate of unstated interest required under section 483 and used in calculating the results in example (2).

Example (5). The facts are the same as in example (1). In 1992 X is adjudged a bankrupt and it is determined that, in and after 1992, B will not be required to make any 10 further payments under the agreement, i.e., B's contingent payment obligation held by A now has become worthless. Assume that A previously received aggregate payments (exclusive of interest) of $45 million and out of those payments recovered $15 million of A's total $20 million basis. For 1992 A will report a loss of $5 million attributable to the sale, taken at the time determined to be appropriate under the rules generally applicable 15 to worthless debts.

Example (6). (i) C owns all of the stock of Z corporation, a calendar year taxpayer. On July 1, 1981, C sells the stock of Z to D under an agreement calling for payment, each year for the next ten years, of an amount equal to 10% of the net profits of Z earned in the immediately preceding calendar year beginning with the year ending December 31, 20 1981. Each payment is to be made on the following April 1st, commencing April 1, 1982. In addition, C is to receive a payment of $5 million on closing. The agreement specifies that the maximum amount payable to C, including the $5 million cash payment at closing, is $24 million. The agreement does not call for the payment of any stated interest. Since section 483 will apply to each payment received by C more than one year following the 25 date of sale (section 483 is inapplicable to the payment that will be received on April 1, 1982, since that date is within one year following the July 1, 1981 sale date), the agreement contemplates internal interest and the price interest recomputation rule is applicable. Under that rule, C must make an initial determination for his taxable year 1981.   30

(ii) On December 31, 1981, the exact amount of Z's 1981 net profit is not known, since it normally takes a number of weeks to compile the relevant information. However, the events which will determine the amount of the payment C will receive on April 1, 1982 have already occurred, and the information (Z's 1981 financial statement) will be promptly calculated and verified and will be available prior to the time C's 1981 tax return is timely 35 filed. On March 15, 1982, Z reports net income of $14 million, and on April 1, 1982 D pays C $1.4 million.

(iii) Under the price-interest recomputation rule, C is required to determine the gross profit ratio for the 1981 $5 million payment on the basis of the events which occurred by the close of that taxable year and which are verifiable before the due date of the 1981 40 return. Because at the end of C's 1981 taxable year all events which will determine the amount of the April 1, 1982 payment have occurred and because the actual facts are known prior to the due date of C's return, C will take those facts into account when calculating the gross profit ratio. Thus, because C knows that the 1982 payment is $1.4 million, C knows that the remaining amount to be recovered under the contract is $17.6 45 million ($24 million - ($5 million + $1.4 million)). For purposes of this paragraph C must assume that the entire $17.6 million will be paid on the earliest possible date, April 1, 1983. Because section 483 will apply to that payment, and assuming that under the tables in the regulations under section 483 the principal component of a payment received 21 months after the date of sale is considered to be .86384, $15,203,584 of the 50 $17.6 million would be principal and $2,396,416 ($17,600,000 - $15,203,584) would be

Sec. 453. Installment method

interest. Therefore, C must assume, for purposes of reporting the $5 million payment received in 1981, that the selling price is $21,603,584 calculated as follows:

Total selling price...	$24,000,000
5 Interest component of the $17,600,000 payment which C must assume will be made April 1, 1983...........................	-2,396,416
Adjusted selling price to be used when reporting the 1981 payment..	21,603,584

10   (iv) Assume that on March 15, 1982, Z reports net income of $15 million for 1982 and that on April 1, 1983 D pays C $1.5 million. Because section 483 will apply to that payment, and assuming that under the tables in the regulations under section 483 the principal component of a payment received 21 months after the date of sale is considered to be .86384, $1,295,760 of the $1,500,000 payment will be principal and $204,240
15 ($1,500,000 - $1,295,760) will be interest. Because C knows the amount of the 1983 payment when filing the 1982 tax return, C must assume that the remaining amount to be received under the contract, $16.1 million ($24 million - ($5 million + $1.4 million + $1.5 million)), will be received as a lump sum on April 1, 1984. Because section 483 will again apply, and assuming that the principal component of a payment made 34 months after
20 the date of the sale is .74622, $12,014,142 of the $16.1 million would be principal, and $4,085,858 ($16,100,000 - $12,014,142) would be interest. Therefore, C must assume, for purpose of reporting the $1.4 million payment made April 1, 1982, that the adjusted selling price (within the meaning of example (2)) is $14,709,902, calculated as follows:

25 Total selling price...	$24,000,000
Interest component of the $1,500,000 payment made April 1, 1983..	-204,240
Interest component of the $16,100,000 payment which C must assume will be made April 1, 1984...........................	-4,085,858
30 Payment made in 1981...	-5,000,000
Adjusted selling price for calculations for reporting the 1982 payment..	14,709,902

(3) *Fixed period*--(i) *In general.* When a stated maximum selling price cannot be
35 determined as of the close of the taxable year in which the sale or other disposition occurs, but the maximum period over which payments may be received under the contingent sale price agreement is fixed, the taxpayer's basis (inclusive of selling expenses) shall be allocated to the taxable years in which payment may be received under the agreement in equal annual increments. In making the allocation it is not
40 relevant whether the buyer is required to pay adequate stated interest. However, if the terms of the agreement incorporate an arithmetic component that is not identical for all taxable years, basis shall be allocated among the taxable years to accord with that component unless, taking into account all of the payment terms of the agreement, it is inappropriate to presume that payments under the contract are likely to accord with the
45 variable component. If in any taxable year no payment is received or the amount of payment received (exclusive of interest) is less than the basis allocated to that taxable year, no loss shall be allowed unless the taxable year is the final payment year under the agreement or unless it is otherwise determined in accordance with the rules generally applicable to worthless debts that the future payment obligation under the agreement has
50 become worthless. When no loss is allowed, the unrecovered portion of basis allocated to the taxable year shall be carried forward to the next succeeding taxable year. If

Sec. 453. Installment method

application of the foregoing rules to a particular case would substantially and inappropriately defer or accelerate recovery of the taxpayer's basis, a special rule will apply. See paragraph (c)(7) of this section.

(ii) *Examples.* The following examples illustrate the rules for recovery of basis in a contingent payment sale in which stated maximum selling price cannot be determined but the period over which payments are to be received under the agreement is fixed. In each case, it is assumed that application of the described rules will not substantially and inappropriately defer or accelerate recovery of the taxpayer's basis.

Example (1). A sells Blackacre to B for 10 percent of Blackacre's gross yield for each of the next 5 years. A's basis in Blackacre is $5 million. Since the sales price is indefinite and the maximum selling price is not ascertainable from the terms of the contract, basis is recovered ratably over the period during which payment may be received under the contract. Thus, assuming A receives the payments (exclusive of interest) listed in the following table, A will report the following:

Year	Payment	Basis recovered	Gain attributable to the sale
1	$1,300,000	$1,000,000	$300,000
2	1,500,000	1,000,000	500,000
3	1,400,000	1,000,000	400,000
4	1,800,000	1,000,000	800,000
5	2,100,000	1,000,000	1,100,000

Example (2). The facts are the same as in example (1), except that the payment in year 1 is only $900,000. Since the installment payment is less than the amount of basis allocated to that year, the unrecovered basis, $100,000, is carried forward to year 2.

Year	Payment	Basis recovered	Gain attributable to the sale
1	$900,000	$900,000	....
2	1,500,000	1,100,000	$400,000
3	1,400,000	1,000,000	400,000
4	1,800,000	1,000,000	800,000
5	2,100,000	1,000,000	1,100,000

Example (3). C owns all of the stock of X corporation with a basis of $100,000 (inclusive of selling expenses). D purchases the X stock from C and agrees to make four payments computed in accordance with the following formula: 40% of the net profits of X in year 1, 30% in year 2, 20% in year 3, and 10% in year 4. Accordingly, C's basis is allocated as follows: $40,000 to year 1, $30,000 to year 2, $20,000 to year 3, and $10,000 to year 4.

Example (4). The facts are the same as in example (3), but the agreement also requires that D make fixed installment payments in accordance with the following schedule: no payment in year 1, $100,000 in year 2, $200,000 in year 3, $300,000 in year 4, and $400,000 in year 5. Thus, while it is reasonable to project that the contingent component of the payments will decrease each year, the fixed component of the payments will increase each year. Accordingly, C is required to allocate $20,000 of basis to each of the taxable years 1 through 5.

(4) *Neither stated maximum selling price nor fixed period.* If the agreement neither

Sec. 453. Installment method

specifies a maximum selling price nor limits payments to a fixed period, a question arises whether a sale realistically has occurred or whether, in economic effect, payments received under the agreement are in the nature of rent or royalty income. Arrangements of this sort will be closely scrutinized. If, taking into account all of the pertinent facts,
5 including the nature of the property, the arrangement is determined to qualify as a sale, the taxpayer's basis (including selling expenses) shall be recovered in equal annual increments over a period of 15 years commencing with the date of sale. However, if in any taxable year no payment is received or the amount of payment received (exclusive of interest) is less than basis allocated to the year, no loss shall be allowed unless it is
10 otherwise determined in accordance with the timing rules generally applicable to worthless debts that the future payment obligation under the agreement has become worthless; instead the excess basis shall be reallocated in level amounts over the balance of the 15 year term. Any basis not recovered at the end of the 15th year shall be carried forward to the next succeeding year, and to the extent unrecovered thereafter
15 shall be carried forward from year to year until all basis has been recovered or the future payment obligation is determined to be worthless. The general rule requiring initial level allocation of basis over 15 years shall not apply if the taxpayer can establish to the satisfaction of the Internal Revenue Service that application of the general rule would substantially and inappropriately defer recovery of the taxpayer's basis. See paragraph
20 (c)(7) of this section. If the Service determines that initially allocating basis in level amounts over the first 15 years will substantially and inappropriately accelerate recovery of the taxpayer's basis in early years of that 15-year term, the Service may require that basis be reallocated within the 15-year term but the Service will not require that basis initially be allocated over more than 15 years. See paragraph (c)(7) of this section.
25   (5) *Foreign currency and other fungible payment units*--(i) *In general*. An installment sale may call for payment in foreign currency. For federal income tax purposes, foreign currency is property. Because the value of foreign currency will vary over time in relation to the United States dollar, an installment sale requiring payment in foreign currency is a contingent payment sale. However, when the consideration payable under an installment
30 sale agreement is specified in foreign currency, the taxpayer's basis (including selling expenses) shall be recovered in the same manner as basis would have been recovered had the agreement called for payment in United States dollars. This rule is equally applicable to any installment sale in which the agreement specifies that payment shall be made in identified, fungible units of property the value of which will or may vary over time
35 in relation to the dollar (e.g., bushels of wheat or ounces of gold).
    (ii) *Example*. The following example illustrates the provisions of this subparagraph:
    Example. A sells Blackacre to B for 4 million Swiss francs payable 1 million in year 2 and 3 million in year 3, together with adequate stated interest. A's basis (including selling expenses) in Blackacre is $100,000. Twenty five thousand dollars of A's basis (1/4 of total
40 basis) is allocable to the year 2 payment of 1 million Swiss francs and
$75,000 of A's basis is allocable to the year 3 payment of 3 million Swiss francs.
    (6) *Income forecast method for basis recovery*--(i) *In general*. The rules for ratable recovery of basis set forth in paragraph (c) (2) through (4) of this section focus on the *In genera* payment terms of the contingent selling price agreement. Except to the extent
45 contemplated by paragraph(c)(7) of this section (relating to a special rule to prevent substantial distortion of basis recovery), the nature and productivity of the property sold is not independently relevant to the basis to be recovered in any payment year. The special rule for an income forecast method of basis recovery set forth in paragraph (c)(6) of this section recognizes that there are cases in which failure to take account of the nature or
50 productivity of the property sold may be expected to result in distortion of the taxpayer's income over time. Specifically, when the property sold is depreciable property of a type

Sec. 453. Installment method

normally eligible for depreciation on the income forecast method, or is depletable property of a type normally eligible for cost depletion in which total future production must be estimated, and payments under the contingent selling price agreement are based upon receipts or units produced by or from the property, the taxpayer's basis may appropriately be recovered by using an income forecast method.   5

(ii) *Availability of method.* In lieu of applying the rules set forth in paragraph (c) (2) through (4) of this section, in an appropriate case the taxpayer may elect (on its tax return timely filed for the first year under the contingent payment agreement in which a payment is received) to recover basis using the income forecast method of basis recovery. No special form of election is prescribed. An appropriate case is one meeting the criteria set 10 forth in paragraph (c)(6)(i) of this section in which the property sold is a mineral property, a motion picture film, a television film, or a taped television show. The Internal Revenue Service may from time to time specify other properties of a similar character which, in appropriate circumstances, will be eligible for recovery of basis on the income forecast method. In addition, a taxpayer may seek a ruling from the Service as to whether a 15 specific property qualifies as property of a similar character eligible, in appropriate circumstances, for income forecast recovery of basis.

(iii) *Required calculations.* The income forecast method requires application of a fraction, the numerator of which is the payment (exclusive of interest) received in the taxable year under a contingent payment agreement, and the denominator of which is the 20 forecast or estimated total payments (exclusive of interest) to be received under the agreement. This fraction is multiplied by the taxpayer's basis in the property sold to determine the basis recovered with respect to the payment received in the taxable year. If in a subsequent year it is found that the income forecast was substantially overestimated or underestimated by reason of circumstances occurring in such subsequent year, an 25 adjustment of the income forecast of such subsequent year shall be made. In such case, the formula for computing recovery of basis would be as follows: payment received in the taxable year (exclusive of interest) divided by the revised estimated total payments (exclusive of interest) then and thereafter to be made under the agreement (the current year's payment and total estimated future payments), multiplied by the taxpayer's 30 unrecovered basis remaining as of the beginning of the taxable year. If the agreement contemplates internal interest (as defined in paragraph (c)(2)(ii) of this section), in making the initial income forecast computation and in making any required subsequent recomputation the amount of internal interest (which shall not be treated as payment under the agreement) shall be calculated by assuming that each future contingent selling 35 price payment will be made in the amount and at the time forecast. The total forecast of estimated payments to be received under the agreement shall be based on the conditions known to exist at the end of the taxable year for which the return is filed. If a subsequent upward or downward revision of this estimate is required, the revision shall be made at the end of the subsequent taxable year based on additional information which 40 became available after the last prior estimate. No loss shall be allowed unless   the taxable year is the final payment year under the agreement or unless it is otherwise determined in accordance with the rules generally applicable to the time a debt becomes worthless that the future payment obligation under the agreement has become worthless.

(iv) *Examples.* The following examples illustrate the income forecast method of basis 45 recovery:

Example (1). A sells a television film to B for 5% of annual gross receipts from the exploitation of the film. The film is an ordinary income asset in the hands of A. A reasonably forecasts that total payments to be received under the contingent selling price agreement will be $1,200,000, and that A will be paid $600,000 in year 1, $150,000 in 50 year 2, $300,000 in year 3, $100,000 in year 4, and $50,000 in year 5. A reasonably

Sec. 453. Installment method

anticipates no or only insignificant receipts thereafter. A's basis in the film is $100,000. Under the income forecast method, A's basis initially is allocated to the five taxable years of forecasted payment as follows:

	Year	Percentage	Basis
1		50.00	$50,000
2		12.50	12,500
3		25.00	25,000
4		8.33	8,333
5		4.17	4,167

Payments are received and A reports the sale under the installment method as follows:

Year	Payment received	Basis recovered	Gain on sale
1	$600,000	$50,000	$550,000
2	150,000	12,500	137,500
3	300,000	25,000	275,000
4	100,000	8,333	91,667
5	50,000	4,167	45,833

Example (2). The facts are the same as in example (1), except that in year 2 A receives no payment. In year 3 A receives a payment of $300,000 and reasonably estimates that in subsequent years he will receive total additional payments of only $100,000. In year 2 A will be allowed no loss. At the beginning of year 3 A's unrecovered basis is $50,000. In year 3 A must recompute the applicable basis recovery fraction based upon facts known and forecast as at the end of year 3: year 3 payment of $300,000 divided by estimated current and future payments of $400,000, equaling 75%. Thus, in year 3 A recovers $37,500 (75% of $50,000) of A's previously unrecovered basis.

(7) *Special rule to avoid substantial distortion*--(i) *In general.* The normal basis recovery rules set forth in paragraph (c)(2) through (4) of this section may, with respect to a particular contingent payment sale, substantially and inappropriately defer or accelerate recovery of the taxpayer's basis.

(ii) *Substantial and inappropriate deferral.* The taxpayer may use an alternative method of basis recovery if the taxpayer is able to demonstrate prior to the due date of the return including extensions for the taxable year in which the first payment is received, that application of the normal basis recovery rule will substantially and inappropriately defer recovery of basis. To demonstrate that application of the normal basis recovery rule will substantially and inappropriately defer recovery of basis, the taxpayer must show (A) that the alternative method is a reasonable method of ratably recovering basis and, (B) that, under that method, it is reasonable to conclude that over time the taxpayer likely will recover basis at a rate twice as fast as the rate at which basis would have been recovered under the otherwise applicable normal basis recovery rule. The taxpayer must receive a ruling from the Internal Revenue Service before using an alternative method of basis recovery described in paragraph (c)(7)(ii) of this section. The request for a ruling shall be made in accordance with all applicable procedural rules set forth in the Statement of Procedural Rules (26 CFR part 601) and any applicable revenue procedures relating to submission of ruling requests. The request shall be submitted to the Commissioner of Internal Revenue, Attention: Assistant Commissioner (Technical), Washington, DC 20224. The taxpayer must file a request for a ruling prior to the due date

Sec. 453. Installment method

for the return including extensions. In demonstrating that application of the normal basis recovery rule would substantially and inappropriately defer recovery of the taxpayer's basis, the taxpayer in appropriate circumstances may rely upon contemporaneous or immediate past relevant sales, profit, or other factual data that are subject to verification. The taxpayer ordinarily is not permitted to rely upon projections of future productivity, 5 receipts, profits, or the like. However, in special circumstances a reasonable projection may be acceptable if the projection is based upon a specific event that already has occurred (e.g., corporate stock has been sold for future payments contingent on profits and an inadequately insured major plant facility of the corporation has been destroyed).

(iii) *Substantial and inappropriate acceleration.* Notwithstanding the other provisions of 10 this paragraph, the Internal Revenue Service may find that the normal basis recovery rule will substantially and inappropriately accelerate recovery of basis. In such a case, the Service may require an alternate method of basis recovery, unless the taxpayer is able to demonstrate either (A) that the method of basis recovery required by the Service is not a reasonable method of ratable recovery, or (B) that it is not reasonable to conclude that 15 the taxpayer over time is likely to recover basis at a rate twice as fast under the normally applicable basis recovery rule as the rate at which basis would be recovered under the method proposed by the Service. In making such demonstrations the taxpayer may rely in appropriate circumstances upon contemporaneous or immediate past relevant sales, profit, or other factual data subject to verification. In special circumstances a reasonable 20 projection may be acceptable, but only with the consent of the Service, if the projection is based upon a specific event that has already occurred.

(iv) *Subsequent recomputation.* A contingent payment sale may initially and properly have been reported under the normally applicable basis recovery rule and, during the term of the agreement, circumstances may show that continued reporting on the original 25 method will substantially and inappropriately defer or accelerate recovery of the unrecovered balance of the taxpayer's basis. In this event, the special rule provided in this paragraph is applicable.

(v) *Examples.* The following examples illustrate the application of the special rule of this paragraph. In examples (1) and (2) it is assumed that rulings consistent with 30 paragraph (c)(7)(ii) of this section have been requested.

Example (1). A owns all of the stock of X corporation with a basis of $100,000. A sells the stock of X to B for a cash down payment of $1,800,000 and B's agreement to pay A an amount equal to 1% of the net profits of X in each of the next 10 years (together with adequate stated interest). The agreement further specifies that the maximum amount that 35 may be paid to A (exclusive of interest) shall not exceed $10 million. A is able to demonstrate that current and recent profits of X have approximated $2 million annually, and that there is no reason to anticipate a major increase in the annual profits of X during the next 10 years. One percent of $2 million annual profits is $20,000, a total of $200,000 over 10 years. Under the basis recovery rule normally applicable to a maximum 40 contingent selling price agreement, in the year of sale A would recover $18,000 of A's total $100,000 basis, and would not recover more than a minor part of the balance until the final year under the agreement. On a $2 million selling price ($200,000 plus $1,800,000 down payment), A would recover $90,000 of A's total $100,000 basis in the year of sale and 5% of each payment ($100,000/$2,000,000) received up to a maximum 45 of $10,000 over the next ten years. Since the rate of basis recovery under the demonstrated method is more than twice the rate under the normal rule, A will be permitted to recover $90,000 basis in the year of sale.

Example (2). The facts are the same as in example (1) except that no maximum contingent selling price is stated in the agreement. Under the basis recovery rule 50 normally applicable when no maximum amount is stated but the payment term is fixed, in

771

the year of sale and in each subsequent year A would recover approximately $9,100 (1/11 of $100,000) of A's total basis. A will be permitted to recover $90,000 of A's total basis in the year of sale.

Example (3). The facts are the same as in example (1) except that A sells the X stock
5 to B on the following terms: 1% of the annual net profits of X in each of the next 10 years and a cash payment of $1,800,000 in the eleventh year, all payments to be made together with adequate stated interest. No maximum contingent selling price is stated. Under the normally applicable basis recovery rule, A would recover 1/11 of A's total $100,000 basis in each of the 11 payment years under the agreement. On the facts (see
10 example (1)), A cannot demonstrate that application of the normal rule would not substantially and inappropriately accelerate recovery of A's basis. Accordingly, A will be allowed to recover only $1,000 of A's total basis in each of the 10 contingent payment years under the agreement, and will recover the $90,000 balance of A's basis in the final year in which the large fixed cash payment will be made.

15   ***

(d) *Election not to report an installment sale on the installment method--*(1) In general. An installment sale is to be reported on the installment method unless the taxpayer elects otherwise in accordance with the rules set forth in paragraph (d)(3) of this section.

(2) *Treatment of an installment sale when a taxpayer elects not to report on the*
20 *installment method--*(i) *In general.* A taxpayer who elects not to report an installment sale on the installment method must recognize gain on the sale in accordance with the taxpayer's method of accounting. The fair market value of an installment obligation shall be determined in accordance with paragraph (d)(2)(ii) and (iii) of this section. In making such determination, any provision of contract or local law restricting the transferability of
25 the installment obligation shall be disregarded. Receipt of an installment obligation shall be treated as a receipt of property, in an amount equal to the fair market value of the installment obligation, whether or not such obligation is the equivalent of cash. An installment obligation is considered to be property and is subject to valuation, as provided in paragraph (d)(2)(ii) and (iii) of this section, without regard to whether the obligation is
30 embodied in a note, an executory contract, or any other instrument, or is an oral promise enforceable under local law.

(ii) *Fixed amount obligations.* (A) A fixed amount obligation means an installment obligation the amount payable under which is fixed. Solely for the purpose of determining whether the amount payable under an installment obligation is fixed, the provisions of
35 section 483 and any ``payment recharacterization" arrangement (as defined in paragraph (c)(2)(ii) of this section) shall be disregarded. If the fixed amount payable is stated in identified, fungible units of property the value of which will or may vary over time in relation to the United States dollar (e.g., foreign currency, ounces of gold, or bushels of wheat), such units shall be converted to United States dollars at the rate of exchange or
40 dollar value on the date the installment sale is made. A taxpayer using the cash receipts and disbursements methods of accounting shall treat as an amount realized in the year of sale the fair market value of the installment obligation. In no event will the fair market value of the installment obligation be considered to be less than the fair market value of the property sold (minus any other consideration received by the taxpayer on the sale). A
45 taxpayer using the accrual method of accounting shall treat as an amount realized in the year of sale the total amount payable under the installment obligation. For this purpose, neither interest (whether stated or unstated) nor original issue discount is considered to be part of the amount payable. If the amount payable is otherwise fixed, but because the time over which payments may be made is contingent, a portion of the fixed amount will
50 or may be treated as internal interest (as defined in paragraph (c)(2)(ii) of this section), the amount payable shall be determined by applying the price interest recomputation rule

Sec. 453. Installment method

(described in paragraph (c)(2)(ii) of this section). Under no circumstances will an installment sale for a fixed amount obligation be considered an ``open" transaction. For purposes of this (ii), remote or incidental contingencies are not to be taken into account.

***

(e) *Purchaser evidences of indebtedness payable on demand or readily tradable--(1)* 5 *Treatment as payment--(i) In general.* A bond or other evidence of indebtedness (hereinafter in this section referred to as an obligation) issued by any person and payable on demand shall be treated as a payment in the year received, not as installment obligations payable in future years. In addition, an obligation issued by a corporation or a government or political subdivision thereof-- 10
   (A) With interest coupons attached (whether or not the obligation is readily tradable in an established securities market),
   (B) In registered form (other than an obligation issued in registered form which the taxpayer establishes will not be readily tradable in an established securities market), or
   (C) In any other form designed to render such obligation readily tradable in an 15 established securities market, shall be treated as a payment in the year received, not as an installment obligation payable in future years. For purposes of this paragraph, an obligation is to be considered in registered form if it is registered as to principal, interest, or both and if its transfer must be effected by the surrender of the old instrument and either the reissuance by the corporation of the old instrument to the new holder or the 20 issuance by the corporation of a new instrument to the new holder.
   (ii) *Examples.* The rules stated in this paragraph may be illustrated by the following examples:
   Example (1). On July 1, 1981, A, an individual on the cash method of accounting reporting on a calendar year basis, transferred all of his stock in corporation X (traded on 25 an established securities market and having a fair market value of $1,000,000) to corporation Y in exchange for 250 of Y's registered bonds (which are traded in an over-the-counter-market) each with a principal amount and fair market value of $1,000 (with interest payable at the rate of 12 percent per year), and Y's unsecured promissory note with a principal amount of $750,000. At the time of such exchange A's basis in the X 30 stock is $900,000. The promissory note is payable at the rate of $75,000 annually, due on July 1 of each year following 1981 until the principal balance is paid. The note provides for the payment of interest at the rate of 12 percent per year also payable on July 1 of each year. Under the rule stated in paragraph (e)(1)(i) of this section, the 250 registered bonds of Y are treated as a payment in 1981 in the amount of the value of the bonds, 35 $250,000.
   Example (2). Assume the same facts as in example (1). Assume further that on July 1, 1982, Y makes its first installment payment to A under the terms of the unsecured promissory note with 75 more of its $1,000 registered bonds. A must include $7,500 (i.e., 10 percent gross profit percentage times $75,000) A's gross income for calendar year 40 1982. In addition, A includes the interest payment made by Y on July 1 in A's gross income for 1982.
   (2) *Amounts treated as payment.* If under paragraph (e)(1) of this section an obligation is treated as a payment in the year received, the amount realized by reason of such payment shall be determined in accordance with the taxpayer's method of accounting. If 45 the taxpayer uses the cash receipts and disbursements method of accounting, the amount realized on such payment is the fair market value of the obligation. If the taxpayer uses the accrual method of accounting, the amount realized on receipt of an obligation payable on demand is the face amount of the obligation, and the amount realized on receipt of an obligation with coupons attached or a readily tradable obligation is the 50 stated redemption price at maturity less any original issue discount (as defined in section

Sec. 453. Installment method

1232(b)(1)) or, if there is no original issue discount, the amount realized is the stated redemption price at maturity appropriately discounted to reflect total unstated interest (as defined in section 483(b)), if any.

(3) *Payable on demand.* An obligation shall be treated as payable on demand only if 5 the obligation is treated as payable on demand under applicable state or local law.

(4) Designed to be readily tradable in an established securities market--(i) In general. Obligations issued by a corporation or government or political subdivision thereof will be deemed to be in a form designed to render such obligations readily tradable in an established securities market if--

10 (A) Steps necessary to create a market for them are taken at the time of issuance (or later, if taken pursuant to an expressed or implied agreement or understanding which existed at the time of issuance),

(B) If they are treated as readily tradable in an established securities market under paragraph (e)(4)(ii) of this section, or

15 (C) If they are convertible obligations to which paragraph (e)(5) of this section applies.

(ii) Readily tradable in an established securities market. An obligation will be treated as readily tradable in an established securities market if--

(A) The obligation is part of an issue or series of issues which are readily tradable in an established securities market, or

20 (B) The corporation issuing the obligation has other obligations of a comparable character which are described in paragraph (e)(4)(ii)(A) of this section. For purposes of paragraph (e)(4)(ii)(B) of this section, the determination as to whether there exist obligations of a comparable character depends upon the particular facts and circumstances. Factors to be considered in making such determination include, but are 25 not limited to, substantial similarity with respect to the presence and nature of security for the obligation, the number of obligations issued (or to be issued), the number of holders of such obligation, the principal amount of the obligation, and other relevant factors.

(iii) *Readily tradable.* For purposes of paragraph (e)(4)(ii)(A) of this section, an obligation shall be treated as readily tradable if it is regularly quoted by brokers or dealers 30 making a market in such obligation or is part of an issue a portion of which is in fact traded in an established securities market.

(iv) *Established securities market.* For purposes of this paragraph, the term ``established securities market'' includes (A) a national securities exchange which is registered under section 6 of the Securities Exchange Act of 1934 (15 U.S.C. 78f), (B) an 35 exchange which is exempted from registration under section 5 of the Securities Exchange Act of 1934 (15 U.S.C. 78e) because of the limited volume of transactions, and (c) any over-the-counter market. For purposes of this (iv), an over-the-counter market is reflected by the existence of an interdealer quotation system. An interdealer quotation system is any system of general circulation to brokers and dealers which regularly 40 disseminates quotations of obligations by identified brokers or dealers, other than a quotation sheet prepared and distributed by a broker or dealer in the regular course of business and containing only quotations of such broker or dealer.

(v) *Examples.* The rules stated in this paragraph may be illustrated by the following examples:

45 *Example (1).* On June 1, 1982, 25 individuals owning equal interests in a tract of land with a fair market value of $1 million sell the land to corporation Y. The $1 million sales price is represented by 25 bonds issued by Y, each having a face value of $40,000. The bonds are not in registered form and do not have interest coupons attached, and, in addition, are payable in 120 equal installments, each due on the first business day of 50 each month. In addition, the bonds are negotiable and may be assigned by the holder to any other person. However, the bonds are not quoted by any brokers or dealers who deal

Sec. 453. Installment method

in corporate bonds, and, furthermore, there are no comparable obligations of Y (determined with reference to the characteristics set forth in paragraph (e)(2) of this section) which are so quoted. Therefore, the bonds are not treated as readily tradable in an established securities market. In addition, under the particular facts and circumstances stated, the bonds will not be considered to be in a form designed to render 5 them readily tradable in an established securities market. The receipt of such bonds by the holder is not treated as a payment for purposes of section 453(f)(4), notwithstanding that they are freely assignable.

Example (2). On April 1, 1981, corporation M purchases in a casual sale of personal property a fleet of trucks from corporation N in exchange for M's negotiable notes, not in 10 registered form and without coupons attached. The M notes are comparable to earlier notes issued by M, which notes are quoted in the Eastern Bond section of the National Daily Quotation Sheet, which is an interdealer quotation system. Both issues of notes are unsecured, held by more than 100 holders, have a maturity date of more than 5 years, and were issued for a comparable principal amount. On the basis of these similar 15 characteristics it appears that the latest notes will also be readily tradable. Since an interdealer system reflects an over-the-counter market, the earlier notes are treated as readily tradable in an established securities market. Since the later notes are obligations comparable to the earlier ones, which are treated as readily tradable in an established securities market, the later notes are also treated as readily tradable in an established 20 securities market (whether or not such notes are actually traded).

***

[T.D. 6500, 25 FR 11718, Nov. 26, 1960; 6590, 27 FR 1319, Feb. 13, 1962; T.D. 6916, 32 FR 5923, Apr. 13, 1967; T.D. 7084, 36 FR 267, Jan. 8, 1971; T.D. 7418, 41 FR 18812, May 7, 1976; T.D. 7768, 46 FR 10709, Feb. 4, 1981; 46 FR 13688, Feb. 24, 1981; 46 FR 25 43036, Aug. 26, 1981;T.D. 7788, 46 FR 48920, Oct. 5, 1981; T.D. 8269, 54 FR 46375, Nov. 3, 1989; T.D. 8535, 59 FR 18751, Apr. 20, 1994; T.D. 8586, 60 FR 2500, Jan. 10, 1995; T.D. 8836, 64 FR 45875, Aug. 23, 1999]

Sec. 453A. Special rules for nondealers

(a) **General rule.** -- In the case of an installment obligation to which this section applies-- 30

(1) interest shall be paid on the deferred tax liability with respect to such obligation in the manner provided under subsection (c), and

(2) the pledging rules under subsection (d) shall apply.

(b) **Installment obligations to which section applies.** --

(1) **In general.** -- This section shall apply to any obligation which arises from the 35 disposition of any property under the installment method, but only if the sales price of such property exceeds $150,000.

(2) **Special rule for interest payments.** -- For purposes of subsection (a)(1), this section shall apply to an obligation described in paragraph (1) arising during a taxable year only if--

(A) such obligation is outstanding as of the close of such taxable year, and 40

(B) the face amount of all such obligations held by the taxpayer which arose during, and are outstanding as of the close of, such taxable year exceeds $5,000,000.

Except as provided in regulations, all persons treated as a single employer under subsection (a) or (b) of section 52 shall be treated as one person for purposes of this paragraph and subsection (c) (4). 45

(3) **Exception for personal use and farm property.** -- An installment obligation shall not be treated as described in paragraph (1) if it arises from the disposition--

775

Sec. 453A. Special rules for nondealers

(A) by an individual of personal use property (within the meaning of section 1275(b)(3)), or

(B) of any property used or produced in the trade or business of farming (within the meaning of section 2032A(e)(4) or (5)).

(4) Special rule for timeshares and residential lots. -- An installment obligation shall not be treated as described in paragraph (1) if it arises from a disposition described in section 453(l)(2)(B), but the provisions of section 453(l)(3) (relating to interest payments on timeshares and residential lots) shall apply to such obligation.

(5) Sales price. -- For purposes of paragraph (1), all sales or exchanges which are part of the same transaction (or a series of related transactions) shall be treated as 1 sale or exchange.

(c) Interest on deferred tax liability. --

(1) In general. -- If an obligation to which this section applies is outstanding as of the close of any taxable year, the tax imposed by this chapter for such taxable year shall be increased by the amount of interest determined in the manner provided under paragraph (2).

(2) Computation of interest. -- For purposes of paragraph (1), the interest for any taxable year shall be an amount equal to the product of--

(A) the applicable percentage of the deferred tax liability with respect to such obligation, multiplied by

(B) the underpayment rate in effect under section 6621(a)(2) for the month with or within which the taxable year ends.

(3) Deferred tax liability. -- For purposes of this section, the term "deferred tax liability" means, with respect to any taxable year, the product of--

(A) the amount of gain with respect to an obligation which has not been recognized as of the close of such taxable year, multiplied by

(B) the maximum rate of tax in effect under section 1 or 11, whichever is appropriate, for such taxable year.

For purposes of applying the preceding sentence with respect to so much of the gain which, when recognized, will be treated as long-term capital gain, the maximum rate on net capital gain under section 1(h) or 1201 (whichever is appropriate) shall be taken into account.

(4) Applicable percentage. -- For purposes of this subsection, the term "applicable percentage" means, with respect to obligations arising in any taxable year, the percentage determined by dividing--

(A) the portion of the aggregate face amount of such obligations outstanding as of the close of such taxable year in excess of $5,000,000, by

(B) the aggregate face amount of such obligations outstanding as of the close of such taxable year.

(5) Treatment as interest. -- Any amount payable under this subsection shall be taken into account in computing the amount of any deduction allowable to the taxpayer for interest paid or accrued during the taxable year.

***

(d) Pledges, etc., of installment obligations. --

(1) In general. -- For purposes of section 453, if any indebtedness (hereinafter in this subsection referred to as "secured indebtedness") is secured by an installment obligation to which this section applies, the net proceeds of the secured indebtedness shall be treated as a payment received on such installment obligation as of the later of--

(A) the time the indebtedness becomes secured indebtedness, or

Sec. 453A. Special rules for nondealers

(B) the time the proceeds of such indebtedness are received by the taxpayer.

(2) Limitation based on total contract price. -- The amount treated as received under paragraph (1) by reason of any secured indebtedness shall not exceed the excess (if any) of--

(A) the total contract price, over

(B) any portion of the total contract price received under the contract before the later of the times referred to in subparagraph (A) or (B) of paragraph (1) (including amounts previously treated as received under paragraph (1) but not including amounts not taken into account by reason of paragraph (3)).

(3) Later payments treated as receipt of tax paid amounts. -- If any amount is treated as received under paragraph (1) with respect to any installment obligation, subsequent payments received on such obligation shall not be taken into account for purposes of section 453 to the extent that the aggregate of such subsequent payments does not exceed the aggregate amount treated as received under paragraph (1).

(4) Secured indebtedness. -- For purposes of this subsection indebtedness is secured by an installment obligation to the extent that payment of principal or interest on such indebtedness is directly secured (under the terms of the indebtedness or any underlying arrangements) by any interest in such installment obligation. A payment shall be treated as directly secured by an interest in an installment obligation to the extent an arrangement allows the taxpayer to satisfy all or a portion of the indebtedness with the installment obligation.

(e) Regulations. -- The Secretary shall prescribe such regulations as may be necessary to carry out the purposes of this section, including regulations--

(1) disallowing the use of the installment method in whole or in part for transactions in which the rules of this section otherwise would be avoided through the use of related persons, pass-thru entities, or intermediaries, and

(2) providing that the sale of an interest in a partnership or other pass-thru entity will be treated as a sale of the proportionate share of the assets of the partnership or other entity.

Sec. 453B. Gain or loss disposition of installment obligations

(a) General rule. -- If an installment obligation is satisfied at other than its face value or distributed, transmitted, sold, or otherwise disposed of, gain or loss shall result to the extent of the difference between the basis of the obligation and--

(1) the amount realized, in the case of satisfaction at other than face value or a sale or exchange, or

(2) the fair market value of the obligation at the time of distribution, transmission, or disposition, in the case of the distribution, transmission, or disposition otherwise than by sale or exchange. any gain or loss so resulting shall be considered as resulting from the sale or exchange of the property in respect of which the installment obligation was received.

(b) Basis of obligation. -- The basis of an installment obligation shall be the excess of the face value of the obligation over an amount equal to the income which would be returnable were the obligation satisfied in full..

(c) Special rule for transmission at death. -- Except as provided in section 691 (relating to recipients of income in respect of decedents), this section shall not apply to the transmission of installment obligations at death.

***

(f) Obligation becomes unenforceable. -- For purposes of this section, if any installment obligation is canceled or otherwise becomes unenforceable--

Sec. 453B. Gain or loss disposition of installment obligations

(1) the obligation shall be treated as if it were disposed of in a transaction other than a sale or exchange, and

(2) if the obligor and obligee are related persons (within the meaning of section 453(f)(1)), the fair market value of the obligation shall be treated as not less than its face amount.

(g) **Transfers between spouses or incident to divorce.** -- In the case of any transfer described in subsection (a) of section 1041 (other than a transfer in trust)--

(1) subsection (a) of this section shall not apply, and

(2) the same tax treatment with respect to the transferred installment obligation shall apply to the transferee as would have applied to the transferor.

***

Sec. 454. Obligations issued at discount

***

(c) Matured United States savings bonds. -- In the case of a taxpayer who--

(1) holds a series E United States savings bond at the date of maturity, and

(2) pursuant to regulations prescribed under chapter 31 of title 31 (A) retains his investment in such series E bond in an obligation of the United States, other than a current income obligation, or (B) exchanges such series E bond for another nontransferable obligation of the United States in an exchange upon which gain or loss is not recognized because of section 1037 (or so much of section 1031 as relates to section 1037), the increase in redemption value (to the extent not previously includible in gross income) in excess of the amount paid for such series E bond shall be includible in gross income in the taxable year in which the obligation is finally redeemed or in the taxable year of final maturity, whichever is earlier. This subsection shall not apply to a corporation, and shall not apply in the case of any taxable year for which the taxpayer's taxable income is computed under an accrual method of accounting or for which an election made by the taxpayer under subsection (a) applies.

Reg. § 1.454-1 Obligations issued at discount.

(a) *Certain non-interest-bearing obligations issued at discount*--(1) *Election to include increase in income currently.* If a taxpayer owns--

(i) A non-interest-bearing obligation issued at a discount and redeemable for fixed amounts increasing at stated intervals (other than an obligation issued by a corporation after May 27, 1969, as to which ratable inclusion of original issue discount is required under section 1232(a)(3)), or

(ii) An obligation of the United States, other than a current income obligation, in which he retains his investment in a matured series E U.S. savings bond, or

(iii) A nontransferable obligation (whether or not a current income obligation) of the United States for which a series E U.S. savings bond was exchanged (whether or not at final maturity) in an exchange upon which gain is not recognized because of section 1037(a) (or so much of section 1031(b) as relates to section 1037), and if the increase, if any, in redemption price of such obligation described in subdivision (i), (ii), or (iii) of this subparagraph during the taxable year (as described in subparagraph (2) of this paragraph) does not constitute income for such year under the method of accounting used in computing his taxable income, then the taxpayer may, at his election, treat the increase as constituting income for the year in which such increase occurs. If the election is not made and section 1037 (or so much of section 1031 as relates to section 1037) does not apply, the taxpayer shall treat the increase as constituting income for the year in which the obligation is redeemed or disposed of, or finally matures, whichever is earlier.

Sec. 454. Obligations issued at discount

Any such election must be made in the taxpayer's return and may be made for any taxable year. If an election is made with respect to any such obligation described in subdivision (i), (ii), or (iii) of this subparagraph, it shall apply also to all other obligations of the type described in such subdivisions owned by the taxpayer at the beginning of the first taxable year to which the election applies, and to those thereafter acquired by him, and shall be binding for the taxable year for which the return is filed and for all subsequent taxable years, unless the Commissioner permits the taxpayer to change to a different method of reporting income from such obligations. See section 446(e) and paragraph (e) of § 1.446-1, relating to requirement respecting a change of accounting method. Although the election once made is binding upon the taxpayer, it does not apply to a transferee of the taxpayer.

(2) *Amount of increase in case of non-interest-bearing obligations.* In any case in which an election is made under section 454, the amount which accrues in any taxable year to which the election applies is measured by the actual increase in the redemption price occurring in that year. This amount does not accrue ratably between the dates on which the redemption price changes. For example, if two dates on which the redemption price increases (February 1 and August 1) fall within a taxable year and if the redemption price increases in the amount of 50 cents on each such date, the amount accruing in that year would be $1 ($0.50 on February 1 and $0.50 on August 1). If the taxpayer owns a non-interest-bearing obligation of the character described in subdivision (i), (ii), or (iii) of subparagraph (1) of this paragraph acquired prior to the first taxable year to which his election applies, he must also include in gross income for such first taxable year (i) the increase in the redemption price of such obligation occurring between the date of acquisition of the obligation and the first day of such first taxable year and (ii), in a case where a series E bond was exchanged for such obligation, the increase in the redemption price of such series E bond occurring between the date of acquisition of such series E bond and the date of the exchange.

(3) *Amount of increase in case of current income obligations.* If an election is made under section 454 and the taxpayer owns, at the beginning of the first taxable year to which the election applies, a current income obligation of the character described in subparagraph (1)(iii) of this paragraph acquired prior to such taxable year, he must also include in gross income for such first taxable year the increase in the redemption price of the series E bond which was surrendered to the United States in exchange for such current income obligation; the amount of the increase is that occurring between the date of acquisition of the series E bond and the date of the exchange.

(4) *Illustrations.* The application of this paragraph may be illustrated by the following examples:

Example (1). Throughout the calendar year 1954, a taxpayer who uses the cash receipts and disbursements method of accounting holds series E U.S. savings bonds having a maturity value of $5,000 and a redemption value at the beginning of the year 1954 of $4,050 and at the end of the year 1954 of $4,150. He purchased the bonds on January 1, 1949, for $3,750, and holds no other obligation of the type described in this section. If the taxpayer exercises the election in his return for the calendar year 1954, he is required to include $400 in taxable income with respect to such bonds. Of this amount, $300 represents the increase in the redemption price before 1954 and $100 represents the increase in the redemption price in 1954. The increases in redemption value occurring in subsequent taxable years are includible in gross income for such taxable years.

Example (2). In 1958 B, a taxpayer who uses the cash receipts and disbursements method of accounting and the calendar year as his taxable year, purchased for $7,500 a series E United States savings bond with a face value of $10,000. In 1965, when the

779

Sec. 454. Obligations issued at discount

stated redemption value of the series E bond is $9,760, B surrenders it to the United States in exchange solely for a $10,000 series H U.S. current income savings bond in an exchange qualifying under section 1037(a), after paying $240 additional consideration. On the exchange of the series E bond for the series H bond in 1965, B realizes a gain of $2,260 ($9,760 less $7,500), none of which is recognized for that year by reason of section 1037(a). B retains the series H bond and redeems it at maturity in 1975 for $10,000, but in 1966 he exercises the election under section 454(a) in his return for that year with respect to five series E bonds he purchased in 1960. B is required to include in gross income for 1966 the increase in redemption price occurring before 1966 and in 1966 with respect to the series E bonds purchased in 1960; he is also required to include in gross income for 1966 the $2,260 increase in redemption price of the series E bond which was exchanged in 1965 for the series H bond.

(b) *Short-term obligations issued on a discount basis.* In the case of obligations of the United States or any of its possessions, or of a State, or Territory, or any political subdivision thereof, or of the District of Columbia, issued on a discount basis and payable without interest at a fixed maturity date not exceeding one year from the date of issue, the amount of discount at which such obligation originally sold does not accrue until the date on which such obligation is redeemed, sold, or otherwise disposed of. This rule applies regardless of the method of accounting used by the taxpayer. For examples illustrating rules for computation of income from sale or other disposition of certain obligations of the type described in this paragraph, see section 1221 and the regulations thereunder.

(c) *Matured U.S. savings bonds--*(1) *Inclusion of increase in income upon redemption or final maturity.* If a taxpayer (other than a corporation) holds--

(i) A matured series E U.S. savings bond,

(ii) An obligation of the United States, other than a current income obligation, in which he retains his investment in a matured series E U.S. savings bond, or

(iii) A nontransferable obligation (whether or not a current income obligation) of the United States for which a series E U.S. savings bond was exchanged (whether or not at final maturity) in an exchange upon which gain is not recognized because of section 1037(a) (or so much of section 1031(b) as relates to section 1037(a)),the increase in redemption price of the series E bond in excess of the amount paid for such series E bond shall be included in the gross income of such taxpayer for the taxable year in which the obligation described in subdivision (i), (ii), or (iii) of this subparagraph is redeemed or disposed of, or finally matures, whichever is earlier, but only to the extent such increase has not previously been includible in the gross income of such taxpayer or any other taxpayer. If such obligation is partially redeemed before final maturity, or partially disposed of by being partially reissued to another owner, such increase in redemption price shall be included in the gross income of such taxpayer for such taxable year on a basis proportional to the total denomination of obligations redeemed or disposed of. The provisions of section 454 (c) and of this subparagraph shall not apply in the case of any taxable year for which the taxpayer's taxable income is computed under an accrual method of accounting or for a taxable year for which an election made by the taxpayer under section 454(a) and paragraph (a) of this section applies. For rules respecting the character of the gain realized upon the disposition or redemption of an obligation described in subdivision (iii) of this subparagraph, see paragraph (b) of § 1.1037-1.

***

[T.D. 6500, 25 FR 11719, Nov. 26, 1960; T.D. 6935, 32 FR 15820, Nov. 17, 1967; T.D. 7154, 36 FR 24997, Dec. 28, 1971]

Sec. 455.   Prepaid subscription income

(a) **Year in which included.** -- Prepaid subscription income to which this section applies shall be included in gross income for the taxable years during which the liability described in subsection (d)(2) exists.

***

(d) **Definitions.** -- For purposes of this section--   5

***

(2) **Liability.** -- The term "liability" means a liability to furnish or deliver a newspaper, magazine, or other periodical.

(3) **Receipt of prepaid subscription income.** -- Prepaid subscription income shall be treated as received during the taxable year for which it is includible in gross income under 10 section 451 (without regard to this section).

Sec. 461.   General rule for taxable year of deduction

(a) **General rule.** -- The amount of any deduction or credit allowed by this subtitle shall be taken for the taxable year which is the proper taxable year under the method of accounting used in computing taxable income.   15

(b) **Special rule in case of death.** -- In the case of the death of a taxpayer whose taxable income is computed under an accrual method of accounting, any amount accrued as a deduction or credit only by reason of the death of the taxpayer shall not be allowed in computing taxable income for the period in which falls the date of the taxpayer's death.

(c) **Accrual of real property taxes.** --   20

(1) **In general.** -- If the taxable income is computed under an accrual method of accounting, then, at the election of the taxpayer, any real property tax which is related to a definite period of time shall be accrued ratably over that period.

***

(d) **Limitation on acceleration of accrual of taxes.** --   25

(1) **General rule.** -- In the case of a taxpayer whose taxable income is computed under an accrual method of accounting, to the extent that the time for accruing taxes is earlier than it would be but for any action of any taxing jurisdiction taken after December 31, 1960, then, under regulations prescribed by the Secretary, such taxes shall be treated as accruing at the time they would have accrued but for such action by such taxing jurisdiction.   30

(2) **Limitation.** -- Under regulations prescribed by the Secretary, paragraph (1) shall be inapplicable to any item of tax to the extent that its application would (but for this paragraph) prevent all persons (including successors in interest) from ever taking such item into account.

(e) **Dividends or interest paid on certain deposits or withdrawable accounts.** -- Except as provided in regulations prescribed by the Secretary, amounts paid to, or credited to the accounts 35 of, depositors or holders of accounts as dividends or interest on their deposits or withdrawable accounts (if such amounts paid or credited are withdrawable on demand subject only to customary notice to withdraw) by a mutual savings bank not having capital stock represented by shares, a domestic building and loan association, or a cooperative bank shall not be allowed as a deduction for the taxable year to the extent such amounts are paid or credited for periods representing more 40 than 12 months. Any such amount not allowed as a deduction as the result of the application of the preceding sentence shall be allowed as a deduction for such other taxable year as the Secretary determines to be consistent with the preceding sentence.

(f) **Contested liabilities.** - If--

781

Sec. 461. General rule for taxable year of deduction

(1) the taxpayer contests an asserted liability,

(2) the taxpayer transfers money or other property to provide for the satisfaction of the asserted liability,

(3) the contest with respect to the asserted liability exists after the time of the transfer, and

(4) but for the fact that the asserted liability is contested, a deduction would be allowed for the taxable year of the transfer (or for an earlier taxable year) determined after application of subsection (h),

then the deduction shall be allowed for the taxable year of the transfer. This subsection shall not apply in respect of the deduction for income, war profits, and excess profits taxes imposed by the authority of any foreign country or possession of the United States.

(g) Prepaid interest. --

(1) In general. -- If the taxable income of the taxpayer is computed under the cash receipts and disbursements method of accounting, interest paid by the taxpayer which, under regulations prescribed by the Secretary, is properly allocable to any period--

(A) with respect to which the interest represents a charge for the use or forbearance of money, and

(B) which is after the close of the taxable year in which paid,

shall be charged to capital account and shall be treated as paid in the period to which so allocable.

(2) Exception. -- This subsection shall not apply to points paid in respect of any indebtedness incurred in connection with the purchase or improvement of, and secured by, the principal residence of the taxpayer to the extent that, under regulations prescribed by the Secretary, such payment of points is an established business practice in the area in which such indebtedness is incurred, and the amount of such payment does not exceed the amount generally charged in such area.

(h) Certain liabilities not incurred before economic performance. --

(1) In general. -- For purposes of this title, in determining whether an amount has been incurred with respect to any item during any taxable year, the all events test shall not be treated as met any earlier than when economic performance with respect to such item occurs.

(2) Time when economic performance occurs. -- Except as provided in regulations prescribed by the Secretary, the time when economic performance occurs shall be determined under the following principles:

(A) Services and property provided to the taxpayer. -- If the liability of the taxpayer arises out of -

(i) the providing of services to the taxpayer by another person, economic performance occurs as such person provides such services,

(ii) the providing of property to the taxpayer by another person, economic performance occurs as the person provides such property, or

(iii) the use of property by the taxpayer, economic performance occurs as the taxpayer uses such property.

(B) Services and property provided by the taxpayer. -- If the liability of the taxpayer requires the taxpayer to provide property or services, economic performance occurs as the taxpayer provides such property or services.

(C) Workers compensation and tort liabilities of the taxpayer. -- If the liability of the taxpayer requires a payment to another person and--

(i) arises under any workers compensation act, or

Sec. 461. General rule for taxable year of deduction

(ii) arises out of any tort,

economic performance occurs as the payments to such person are made. Subparagraphs (A) and (B) shall not apply to any liability described in the preceding sentence.

(D) Other items. -- In the case of any other liability of the taxpayer, economic performance occurs at the time determined under regulations prescribed by the Secretary.   5

(3) Exception for certain recurring items. --

(A) In general. -- Notwithstanding paragraph (1) an item shall be treated as incurred during any taxable year if--

(i) the all events test with respect to such item is met during such taxable year (determined without regard to paragraph (1)),   10

(ii) economic performance with respect to such item occurs within the shorter of -

(I) a reasonable period after the close of such taxable year, or

(II) 8 1/2 months after the close of such taxable year,

(iii) such item is recurring in nature and the taxpayer consistently treats items of such kind as incurred in the taxable year in which the requirements of clause (i) are met, and   15

(iv) either--

(I) such item is not a material item, or

(II) the accrual of such item in the taxable year in which the requirements of clause (i) are met results in a more proper match against income than accruing such item in the taxable year in which economic performance occurs.   20

(B) Financial statements considered under subparagraph (A)(iv). -- In making a determination under subparagraph (A)(iv), the treatment of such item on financial statements shall be taken into account.

(C) Paragraph not to apply to workers compensation and tort liabilities. -- This paragraph shall not apply to any item described in subparagraph (C) of paragraph (2).   25

(4) All events test. -- For purposes of this subsection, the all events test is met with respect to any item if all events have occurred which determine the fact of liability and the amount of such liability can be determined with reasonable accuracy.

(5) Subsection not to apply to certain items. -- This subsection shall not apply to any item for which a deduction is allowable under a provision of this title which specifically provides   30 for a deduction for a reserve for estimated expenses.

(i) Special rules for tax shelters. --

(1) Recurring item exception not to apply. -- In the case of a tax shelter, economic performance shall be determined without regard to paragraph (3) of subsection (h).

(2) Special rule for spudding of oil or gas wells. --   35

(A) In general. -- In the case of a tax shelter, economic performance with respect to amounts paid during the taxable year for drilling an oil or gas well shall be treated as having occurred within a taxable year if drilling of the well commences before the close of the 90th day after the close of the taxable year.

(B) Deduction limited to cash basis. --   40

(i) Tax shelter partnerships. -- In the case of a tax shelter which is a partnership, in applying section 704(d) to a deduction or loss for any taxable year attributable to an item which is deductible by reason of subparagraph (A), the term "cash basis" shall be substituted for the term "adjusted basis".

(ii) Other tax shelters. -- Under regulations prescribed by the Secretary, in the case   45

Sec. 461. General rule for taxable year of deduction

of a tax shelter other than a partnership, the aggregate amount of the deductions allowable by reason of subparagraph (A) for any taxable year shall be limited in a manner similar to the limitation under clause (i).

(C) Cash basis defined. -- For purposes of subparagraph (B), a partner's cash basis in a partnership shall be equal to the adjusted basis of such partner's interest in the partnership, determined without regard to--

(i) any liability of the partnership, and

(ii) any amount borrowed by the partner with respect to such partnership which -

(I) was arranged by the partnership or by any person who participated in the organization, sale, or management of the partnership (or any person related to such person within the meaning of section 465(b)(3)(C)), or

(II) was secured by any asset of the partnership.

(3) Tax shelter defined. -- For purposes of this subsection, the term "tax shelter" means--

(A) any enterprise (other than a C corporation) if at any time interests in such enterprise have been offered for sale in any offering required to be registered with any Federal or State agency having the authority to regulate the offering of securities for sale,

(B) any syndicate (within the meaning of section 1256(e)(3)(B)), and

(C) any tax shelter (as defined in section 6662(d)(2)(C)(iii)).

(4) Special rules for farming. -- In the case of the trade or business of farming (as defined in section 464(e)), in determining whether an entity is a tax shelter, the definition of farming syndicate in section 464(c) shall be substituted for subparagraphs (A) and (B) of paragraph (3).

(5) Economic performance. -- For purposes of this subsection, the term "economic performance" has the meaning given such term by subsection (h).

Reg. § 1.461-1   General rule for taxable year of deduction.

(a) *General rule*--(1) *Taxpayer using cash receipts and disbursements method.* Under the cash receipts and disbursements method of accounting, amounts representing allowable deductions shall, as a general rule, be taken into account for the taxable year in which paid. Further, a taxpayer using this method may also be entitled to certain deductions in the computation of taxable income which do not involve cash disbursements during the taxable year, such as the deductions for depreciation, depletion, and losses under sections 167, 611, and 165, respectively. If an expenditure results in the creation of an asset having a useful life which extends substantially beyond the close of the taxable year, such an expenditure may not be deductible, or may be deductible only in part, for the taxable year in which made. An example is an expenditure for the construction of improvements by the lessee on leased property where the estimated life of the improvements is in excess of the remaining period of the lease. In such a case, in lieu of the allowance for depreciation provided by section 167, the basis shall be amortized ratably over the remaining period of the lease. See section 178 and the regulations thereunder for rules governing the effect to be given renewal options in determining whether the useful life of the improvements exceeds the remaining term of the lease where a lessee begins improvements on leased property after July 28, 1958, other than improvements which on such date and at all times thereafter, the lessee was under a binding legal obligation to make. See section 263 and the regulations thereunder for rules relating to capital expenditures. See section 467 and the regulations thereunder for rules under which a liability arising out of the use of property pursuant to a section 467 rental agreement is taken into account.

Sec. 461. General rule for taxable year of deduction

(2) *Taxpayer using an accrual method*--(i) *In general*. Under an accrual method of accounting, a liability (as defined in § 1.446-1(c)(1)(ii)(B)) is incurred, and generally is taken into account for Federal income tax purposes, in the taxable year in which all the events have occurred that establish the fact of the liability, the amount of the liability can be determined with reasonable accuracy, and economic performance has occurred with 5 respect to the liability. (See paragraph (a)(2)(iii)(A) of this section for examples of liabilities that may not be taken into account until a taxable year subsequent to the taxable year incurred, and see §§ 1.461-4 through 1.461-6 for rules relating to economic performance.) Applicable provisions of the Code, the Income Tax Regulations, and other guidance published by the Secretary prescribe the manner in which a liability that has 10 been incurred is taken into account. For example, section 162 provides that the deductible liability generally is taken into account in the taxable year incurred through a deduction from gross income. As a further example, under section 263 or 263A, a liability that relates to the creation of an asset having a useful life extending substantially beyond the close of the taxable year is taken into account in the taxable year incurred through 15 capitalization (within the meaning of § 1.263A-1(c)(3)), and may later affect the computation of taxable income through depreciation or otherwise over a period including subsequent taxable years, in accordance with applicable Internal Revenue Code sections and guidance published by the Secretary. The principles of this paragraph (a)(2) also apply in the calculation of earnings and profits and accumulated earnings and profits.   20

(ii) *Uncertainty as to the amount of a liability*. While no liability shall be taken into account before economic performance and all of the events that fix the liability have occurred, the fact that the exact amount of the liability cannot be determined does not prevent a taxpayer from taking into account that portion of the amount of the liability which can be computed with reasonable accuracy within the taxable year. For example, A 25 renders services to B during the taxable year for which A charges $10,000. B admits a liability to A for $6,000 but contests the remainder. B may take into account only $6,000 as an expense for the taxable year in which the services were rendered.

(iii) *Alternative timing rules*. (A) If any provision of the Code requires a liability to be taken into account in a taxable year later than the taxable year provided in paragraph (a) 30 (2)(i) of this section, the liability is taken into account as prescribed in that Code provision. See, for example, section 267 (transactions between related parties) and section 464 (farming syndicates).

(B) If the liability of a taxpayer is subject to section 170 (charitable contributions), section 192 (black lung benefit trusts), section 194A (employer liability trusts), section 468 35 (mining and solid waste disposal reclamation and closing costs), or section 468A (certain nuclear decommissioning costs), the liability is taken into account as determined under that section and not under section 461 or the regulations thereunder. For special rules relating to certain loss deductions, see sections 165(e), 165(i), and 165(l), relating to theft losses, disaster losses, and losses from certain deposits in qualified financial institutions.   40

(C) Section 461 and the regulations thereunder do not apply to any amount allowable under a provision of the Code as a deduction for a reserve for estimated expenses.

(D) Except as otherwise provided in any Internal Revenue regulations, revenue procedure, or revenue ruling, the economic performance requirement of section 461(h) and the regulations thereunder is satisfied to the extent that any amount is otherwise 45 deductible under section 404 (employer contributions to a plan of deferred compensation), section 404A (certain foreign deferred compensation plans), or section 419 (welfare benefit funds). See § 1.461-4(d)(2)(iii).

(E) Except as otherwise provided by regulations or other published guidance issued by the Commissioner (See § 601.601(b)(2) of this chapter), in the case of a liability 50 arising out of the use of property pursuant to a section 467 rental agreement, the all

Sec. 461. General rule for taxable year of deduction

events test (including economic performance) is considered met in the taxable year in which the liability is to be taken into account under section 467 and the regulations thereunder.

    (3) *Effect in current taxable year of improperly accounting for a liability in a prior*
5 *taxable year.* Each year's return should be complete in itself, and taxpayers shall ascertain the facts necessary to make a correct return. The expenses, liabilities, or loss of one year generally cannot be used to reduce the income of a subsequent year. A taxpayer may not take into account in a return for a subsequent taxable year liabilities that, under the taxpayer's method of accounting, should have been taken into account in
10 a prior taxable year. If a taxpayer ascertains that a liability should have been taken into account in a prior taxable year, the taxpayer should, if within the period of limitation, file a claim for credit or refund of any overpayment of tax arising therefrom. Similarly, if a taxpayer ascertains that a liability was improperly taken into account in a prior taxable year, the taxpayer should, if within the period of limitation, file an amended return and pay
15 any additional tax due. However, except as provided in section 905(c) and the regulations thereunder, if a liability is properly taken into account in an amount based on a computation made with reasonable accuracy and the exact amount of the liability is subsequently determined in a later taxable year, the difference, if any, between such amounts shall be taken into account for the later taxable year.

20 <center>***</center>

    (b) *Special rule in case of death.* A taxpayer's taxable year ends on the date of his death. See section 443(a)(2) and paragraph (a)(2) of § 1.443-1. In computing taxable income for such year, there shall be deducted only amounts properly deductible under the method of accounting used by the taxpayer. However, if the taxpayer used an accrual
25 method of accounting, no deduction shall be allowed for amounts accrued only by reason of his death. For rules relating to the inclusion of items of partnership deduction, loss, or credit in the return of a decedent partner, see subchapter K, chapter 1 of the Code, and the regulations thereunder.

    (c) A*ccrual of real property taxes--*(1) *In general.* If the accrual of real property taxes is
30 proper in connection with one of the methods of accounting described in section 446(c), any taxpayer using such a method of accounting may elect to accrue any real property tax, which is related to a definite period of time, ratably over that period in the manner described in this paragraph. For example, assume that such an election is made by a calendar-year taxpayer whose real property taxes, applicable to the period from July 1,
35 1955, to June 30, 1956, amount to $1,200. Under section 461(c), $600 of such taxes accrue in the calendar year 1955, and the balance accrues in 1956. For special rule in the case of certain contested real property taxes in respect of which the taxpayer transfers money or other property to provide for the satisfaction of the contested tax, see § 1.461-2. For general rules relating to deductions for taxes, see section 164 and the
40 regulations thereunder,

***

Reg. § 1.461-4 Economic performance.
    (a) *Introduction--*(1) *In general.* For purposes of determining whether an accrual basis taxpayer can treat the amount of any liability (as defined in § 1.446-1(c)(1)(ii)(B)) as
45 incurred, the all events test is not treated as met any earlier than the taxable year in which economic performance occurs with respect to the liability.

***

    (g) *Certain liabilities for which payment is economic performance--*(1) *In general--*(i) *Person to which payment must be made.* In the case of liabilities described in paragraphs
50 (g) 2) through (7) of this section, economic performance occurs when, and to the extent

786

Sec. 461.   General rule for taxable year of deduction

that, payment is made to the person to which the liability is owed. Thus, except as otherwise provided in paragraph (g)(1)(iv) of this section and § 1.461-6, economic performance does not occur as a taxpayer makes payments in connection with such a liability to any other person, including a trust, escrow account, court-administered fund, or any similar arrangement, unless the payments constitute payment to the person to which 5 the liability is owed under paragraph (g)(1)(ii)(B) of this section. Instead, economic performance occurs as payments are made from that other person or fund to the person to which the liability is owed. The amount of economic performance that occurs as payment is made from the other person or fund to the person to which the liability is owed may not exceed the amount the taxpayer transferred to the other person or fund. For 10 special rules relating to the taxation of amounts transferred to ``qualified settlement funds," see section 468B and the regulations thereunder. The Commissioner may provide additional rules in regulations, revenue procedures, and revenue rulings concerning the time at which economic performance occurs for items described in this paragraph (g).

(ii) *Payment to person to which liability is owed.* Paragraph (d)(6) of this section 15 provides that for purposes of paragraph (d) of this section (relating to the provision of services or property to the taxpayer) in certain cases a taxpayer may treat services or property as provided to the taxpayer as the taxpayer makes payments to the person providing the services or property. In addition, this paragraph (g) provides that in the case of certain liabilities of a taxpayer, economic performance occurs as the taxpayer makes 20 payment to persons specified therein. For these and all other purposes of section 461(h) and the regulations thereunder:

(A) *Payment.* The term payment has the same meaning as is used when determining whether a taxpayer using the cash receipts and disbursements method of accounting has made a payment. Thus, for example, payment includes the furnishing of cash or cash 25 equivalents and the netting of offsetting accounts. Payment does not include the furnishing of a note or other evidence of indebtedness of the taxpayer, whether or not the evidence is guaranteed by any other instrument (including a standby letter of credit) or by any third party (including a government agency). As a further example, payment does not include a promise of the taxpayer to provide services or property in the future (whether or 30 not the promise is evidenced by a contract or other written agreement). In addition, payment does not include an amount transferred as a loan, refundable deposit, or contingent payment.

(B) *Person to which payment is made.* Payment to a particular person is accomplished if paragraph (g)(1)(ii)(A) of this section is satisfied and a cash basis 35 taxpayer in the position of that person would be treated as having actually or constructively received the amount of the payment as gross income under the principles of section 451 (without regard to section 104(a) or any other provision that specifically excludes the amount from gross income). Thus, for example, the purchase of an annuity contract or any other asset generally does not constitute payment to the person to which 40 a liability is owed unless the ownership of the contract or other asset is transferred to that person.

(C) *Liabilities that are assumed in connection with the sale of a trade or business.* Paragraph (d)(5) of this section provides rules that determine when economic performance occurs in the case of liabilities that are assumed in connection with the sale 45 of a trade or business. The provisions of paragraph (d)(5) of this section also apply to any liability described in paragraph (g)(2) through (7) of this section that the purchaser expressly assumes in connection with the sale or exchange of a trade or business by a taxpayer, provided the taxpayer (but for the economic performance requirement) would have been entitled to incur the liability as of the date of the sale.   50

(iii) *Person.* For purposes of this paragraph (g), ``person" has the same meaning as in

Sec. 461. General rule for taxable year of deduction

section 7701(a)(1), except that it also includes any foreign state, the United States, any State or political subdivision thereof, any possession of the United States, and any agency or instrumentality of any of the foregoing.

(iv) *Assignments*. If a person that has a right to receive payment in satisfaction of a
5 liability described in paragraphs (g) (2) through (7) of this section makes a valid assignment of that right to a second person, or if the right is assigned to the second person through operation of law, then payment to the second person in satisfaction of that liability constitutes payment to the person to which the liability is owed.

(2) *Liabilities arising under a workers compensation act or out of any tort, breach of*
10 *contract, or violation of law*. If the liability of a taxpayer requires a payment or series of payments to another person and arises under any workers compensation act or out of any tort, breach of contract, or violation of law, economic performance occurs as payment is made to the person to which the liability is owed. See Example 1 of paragraph (g)(8) of this section. For purposes of this paragraph (g)(2)--
15 (i) A liability to make payments for services, property, or other consideration provided under a contract is not a liability arising out of a breach of that contract unless the payments are in the nature of incidental, consequential, or liquidated damages; and

(ii) A liability arising out of a tort, breach of contract, or violation of law includes a liability arising out of the settlement of a dispute in which a tort, breach of contract, or
20 violation of law, respectively, is alleged.

(3) *Rebates and refunds*. If the liability of a taxpayer is to pay a rebate, refund, or similar payment to another person (whether paid in property, money, or as a reduction in the price of goods or services to be provided in the future by the taxpayer), economic performance occurs as payment is made to the person to which the liability is owed. This
25 paragraph (g)(3) applies to all rebates, refunds, and payments or transfers in the nature of a rebate or refund regardless of whether they are characterized as a deduction from gross income, an adjustment to gross receipts or total sales, or an adjustment or addition to cost of goods sold. In the case of a rebate or refund made as a reduction in the price of goods or services to be provided in the future by the taxpayer, ``payment" is deemed to
30 occur as the taxpayer would otherwise be required to recognize income resulting from a disposition at an unreduced price. See Example 2 of paragraph (g)(8) of this section. For purposes of determining whether the recurring item exception of § 1.461-5 applies, a liability that arises out of a tort, breach of contract, or violation of law is not considered a rebate or refund.
35 (4) *Awards, prizes, and jackpots*. If the liability of a taxpayer is to provide an award, prize, jackpot, or other similar payment to another person, economic performance occurs as payment is made to the person to which the liability is owed. See Examples 3 and 4 of paragraph (g)(8) of this section.

(5) *Insurance, warranty, and service contracts*. If the liability of a taxpayer arises out of
40 the provision to the taxpayer of insurance, or a warranty or service contract, economic performance occurs as payment is made to the person to which the liability is owed. See Examples 5 through 7 of paragraph (g)(8) of this section. For purposes of this paragraph (g)(5)--

(i) A warranty or service contract is a contract that a taxpayer enters into in connection
45 with property bought or leased by the taxpayer, pursuant to which the other party to the contract promises to replace or repair the property under specified circumstances.

(ii) The term ``insurance" has the same meaning as is used when determining the deductibility of amounts paid or incurred for insurance under section 162.

(6) *Taxes*--(i) *In general*. Except as otherwise provided in this paragraph (g)(6), if the
50 liability of a taxpayer is to pay a tax, economic performance occurs as the tax is paid to the governmental authority that imposed the tax. For purposes of this paragraph (g)(6),

788

Sec. 461. General rule for taxable year of deduction

payment includes payments of estimated income tax and payments of tax where the taxpayer subsequently files a claim for credit or refund. In addition, for purposes of this paragraph (g)(6), a tax does not include a charge collected by a governmental authority for specific extraordinary services or property provided to a taxpayer by the governmental authority. Examples of such a charge include the purchase price of a parcel of land sold to a taxpayer by a governmental authority and a charge for labor engaged in by government employees to improve that parcel. In certain cases, a liability to pay a tax is permitted to be taken into account in the taxable year before the taxable year during which economic performance occurs under the recurring item exception of § 1.461-5. See Example 8 of paragraph (g)(8) of this section.

(ii) *Licensing fees.* If the liability of a taxpayer is to pay a licensing or permit fee required by a governmental authority, economic performance occurs as the fee is paid to the governmental authority, or as payment is made to any other person at the direction of the governmental authority.

(iii) *Exceptions*--(A) *Real property taxes.* If a taxpayer has made a valid election under section 461(c), the taxpayer's accrual for real property taxes is determined under section 461(c). Otherwise, economic performance with respect to a property tax liability occurs as the tax is paid, as specified in paragraph (g)(6)(i) of this section.

(B) *Certain foreign taxes.* If the liability of a taxpayer is to pay an income, war profits, or excess profits tax that is imposed by the authority of any foreign country or possession of the United States and is creditable under section 901 (including a creditable tax described in section 903 that is paid in lieu of such a tax), economic performance occurs when the requirements of the all events test (as described in § 1.446-1(c)(1)(ii)) other than economic performance are met, whether or not the taxpayer elects to credit such taxes under section 901(a).

(7) *Other liabilities.* In the case of a taxpayer's liability for which economic performance rules are not provided elsewhere in this section or in any other Internal Revenue regulation, revenue ruling or revenue procedure, economic performance occurs as the taxpayer makes payments in satisfaction of the liability to the person to which the liability is owed. This paragraph (g)(7) applies only if the liability cannot properly be characterized as a liability covered by rules provided elsewhere in this section. If a liability may properly be characterized as, for example, a liability arising from the provision of services or property to, or by, a taxpayer, the determination as to when economic performance occurs with respect to that liability is made under paragraph (d) of this section and not under this paragraph (g)(7).

(8) *Examples.* The following examples illustrate the principles of this paragraph (g). For purposes of these examples, it is assumed that the requirements of the all events test other than economic performance have been met and, except as otherwise provided, that the recurring item exception is not used.

Example 1. Liabilities arising out of a tort. (i) During the period 1970 through 1975, Z corporation, a calendar year, accrual method taxpayer, manufactured and distributed industrial products that contained carcinogenic substances. In 1992, a number of lawsuits are filed against Z alleging damages due to exposure to these products. In settlement of a lawsuit maintained by A, Z agrees to purchase an annuity contract that will provide annual payments to A of $50,000 for a period of 25 years. On December 15, 1992, Z pays W, an unrelated life insurance company, $491,129 for such an annuity contract. Z retains ownership of the annuity contract.

(ii) Under paragraph (g)(2) of this section, economic performance with respect to Z's liability to A occurs as each payment is made to A. Consequently, $50,000 is incurred by Z for each taxable year that a payment is made to A under the annuity contract. (Z must also include in income a portion of amounts paid under the annuity, pursuant to section

Sec. 461. General rule for taxable year of deduction

72.) The result is the same if in 1992 Z secures its obligation with a standby letter of credit.

(iii) If Z later transfers ownership of the annuity contract to A, an amount equal to the fair market value of the annuity on the date of transfer is incurred by Z in the taxable year
5 of the transfer (see paragraph (g)(1)(ii)(B) of this section). In addition, the transfer constitutes a transaction to which section 1001 applies.

Example 2. Rebates and refunds. (i) X corporation, a calendar year, accrual method taxpayer, manufactures and sells hardware products. X enters into agreements that entitle each of its distributors to a rebate (or discount on future purchases) from X based
10 on the amount of purchases made by the distributor from X during any calendar year. During the 1992 calendar year, X becomes liable to pay a $2,000 rebate to distributor A. X pays A $1,200 of the rebate on January 15, 1993, and the remaining $800 on October 15, 1993. Assume the rebate is deductible (or allowable as an adjustment to gross receipts or cost of goods sold) when incurred.

15 (ii) If X does not adopt the recurring item exception described in § 1.461-5 with respect to rebates and refunds, then under paragraph (g)(3) of this section, economic performance with respect to the $2,000 rebate liability occurs in 1993. However, if X has made a proper election under § 1.461-5, and as of December 31, 1992, all events have occurred that determine the fact of the rebate liability, X incurs $1,200 for the 1992
20 taxable year. Because economic performance (payment) with respect to the remaining $800 does not occur until October 15, 1993 (more than 8-1/2 months after the end of 1992), X cannot use the recurring item exception for this portion of the liability (see § 1.461-5). Thus, the $800 is not incurred by X until the 1993 taxable year. If, instead of making the cash payments to A during 1993, X adjusts the price of hardware purchased
25 by A that is delivered to A during 1993, X's ``payment" occurs as X would otherwise be required to recognize income resulting from a disposition at an unreduced price.

Example 3. Awards, prizes, and jackpots. (i) W corporation, a calendar year, accrual method taxpayer, produces and sells breakfast cereal. W conducts a contest pursuant to which the winner is entitled to $10,000 per year for a period of 20 years. On December 1,
30 1992, A is declared the winner of the contest and is paid $10,000 by W. In addition, on December 1 of each of the next nineteen years, W pays $10,000 to A.

(ii) Under paragraph (g)(4) of this section, economic performance with respect to the $200,000Subsec contest liability occurs as each of the $10,000 payments is made by W to A. Consequently, $10,000 is incurred by W for the 1992 taxable year and for each of
35 the succeeding nineteen taxable years.

Example 4. Awards, prizes, and jackpots. (i) Y corporation, a calendar year, accrual method taxpayer, owns a casino that contains progressive slot machines. A progressive slot machine provides a guaranteed jackpot amount that increases as money is gambled through the machine until the jackpot is won or until a maximum predetermined amount is
40 reached. On July 1, 1993, the guaranteed jackpot amount on one of Y's slot machines reaches the maximum predetermined amount of $50,000. On October 1, 1994, the $50,000 jackpot is paid to B.

(ii) Under paragraph (g)(4) of this section, economic performance with respect to the $50,000 jackpot liability occurs on the date the jackpot is paid to B. Consequently,
45 $50,000 is incurred by Y for the 1994 taxable year.

Example 5. Insurance, warranty, and service contracts. (i) V corporation, a calendar year, accrual method taxpayer, manufactures toys. V enters into a contract with W, an unrelated insurance company, on December 15, 1992. The contract obligates V to pay W a premium of $500,000 before the end of 1995. The contract obligates W to satisfy any
50 liability of V resulting from claims made during 1993 or 1994 against V by any third party for damages attributable to defects in toys manufactured by V. Pursuant to the contract, V

Sec. 461. General rule for taxable year of deduction

pays W a premium of $500,000 on October 1, 1995.

(ii) Assuming the arrangement constitutes insurance, under paragraph (g)(5) of this section economic performance occurs as the premium is paid. Thus, $500,000 is incurred by V for the 1995 taxable year.

Example 6. Insurance, warranty, and service contracts. (i) Y corporation, a calendar 5 year, accrual method taxpayer, is a common carrier. On December 15, 1992, Y enters into a contract with Z, an unrelated insurance company, under which Z must satisfy any liability of Y that arises during the succeeding 5 years for damages under a workers compensation act or out of any tort, provided the event that causes the damages occurs during 1993 or 1994. Under the contract, Y pays $360,000 to Z on December 31, 1993. 10

(ii) Assuming the arrangement constitutes insurance, under paragraph (g)(5) of this section economic performance occurs as the premium is paid. Consequently, $360,000 is incurred by Y for the 1993 taxable year. The period for which the $360,000 amount is permitted to be taken into account is determined under the capitalization rules because the insurance contract is an asset having a useful life extending substantially beyond the 15 close of the taxable year.

Example 7. Insurance, warranty, and service contracts. Assume the same facts as in Example 6, except that Y is obligated to pay the first $5,000 of any damages covered by the arrangement with Z. Y is, in effect, self-insured to the extent of this $5,000 ``deductible." Thus, under paragraph (g)(2) of this section, economic performance with 20 respect to the $5,000 liability does not occur until the amount is paid to the person to which the tort or workers compensation liability is owed.

Example 8. Taxes. (i) The laws of State A provide that every person owning personal property located in State A on the first day of January shall be liable for tax thereon and that a lien for the tax shall attach as of that date. In addition, the laws of State A provide 25 that 60% of the tax is due on the first day of December following the lien date and the remaining 40% is due on the first day of July of the succeeding year. On January 1, 1992, X corporation, a calendar year, accrual method taxpayer, owns personal property located in State A. State A imposes a $10,000 tax on S with respect to that property on January 1, 1992. X pays State A $6,000 of the tax on December 1, 1992, and the remaining 30 $4,000 on July 1, 1993.

(ii) Under paragraph (g)(6) of this section, economic performance with respect to $6,000 of the tax liability occurs on December 1, 1992. Consequently, $6,000 is incurred by X for the 1992 taxable year. Economic performance with respect to the remaining $4,000 of the tax liability occurs on July 1, 1993. If X has adopted the recurring item 35 exception described in § 1.461-5 as a method of accounting for taxes, and as of December 31, 1992, all events have occurred that determine the liability of X for the remaining $4,000, X also incurs $4,000 for the 1992 taxable year. If X does not adopt the recurring item exception method, the $4,000 is not incurred by X until the 1993 taxable year. 40

***

Reg. § 1.461-5 Recurring item exception.

(a) *In general.* Except as otherwise provided in paragraph (c) of this section, a taxpayer using an accrual method of accounting may adopt the recurring item exception described in paragraph (b) of this section as method of accounting for one or more types 45 of recurring items incurred by the taxpayer. In the case of the ``other payment liabilities" described in § 1.461-4(g)(7), the Commissioner may provide for the application of the recurring item exception by regulation, revenue procedure or revenue ruling.

(b) *Requirements for use of the exception*--(1) *General rule.* Under the recurring item exception, a liability is treated as incurred for a taxable year if-- 50

(i) As of the end of that taxable year, all events have occurred that establish the fact of

Sec. 461. General rule for taxable year of deduction

the liability and the amount of the liability can be determined with reasonable accuracy;
    (ii) Economic performance with respect to the liability occurs on or before the earlier of--
        (A) The date the taxpayer files a timely (including extensions) return for that taxable
5 year; or
        (B) The 15th day of the 9th calendar month after the close of that taxable year;
    (iii) The liability is recurring in nature; and
    (iv) Either--
        (A) The amount of the liability is not material; or
10   (B) The accrual of the liability for that taxable year results in a better matching of the
    liability with the income to which it relates than would result from accruing the liability for
    the taxable year in which economic performance occurs.
    (2) *Amended returns.* A taxpayer may file an amended return treating a liability as
incurred under the recurring item exception for a taxable year if economic performance
15 with respect to the liability occurs after the taxpayer files a return for that year, but within
8-1/2 months after the close of that year.
    (3) *Liabilities that are recurring in nature.* A liability is recurring if it can generally be
expected to be incurred from one taxable year to the next. However, a taxpayer may treat
such a liability as recurring in nature even if it is not incurred by the taxpayer in each
20 taxable year. In addition, a liability that has never previously been incurred by a taxpayer
may be treated as recurring if it is reasonable to expect that the liability will be incurred on
a recurring basis in the future.
    (4) *Materiality requirement.* For purposes of this paragraph (b):
    (i) In determining whether a liability is material, consideration shall be given to the
25 amount of the liability in absolute terms and in relation to the amount of other items of
income and expense attributable to the same activity.
    (ii) A liability is material if it is material for financial statement purposes under generally
accepted accounting principles.
    (iii) A liability that is immaterial for financial statement purposes under generally
30 accepted accounting principles may be material for purposes of this paragraph (b).
    (5) Matching requirement. (i) In determining whether the matching requirement of
paragraph (b)(1)(iv)(B) of this section is satisfied, generally accepted accounting
principles are an important factor, but are not dispositive.
    (ii) In the case of a liability described in paragraph (g)(3) (rebates and refunds),
35 paragraph (g)(4) (awards, prizes, and jackpots), paragraph (g)(5) (insurance, warranty,
and service contracts), paragraph (g)(6) (taxes), or paragraph (h) (continuing fees under
the Nuclear Waste Policy Act of 1982) of § 1.461-4, the matching requirement of
paragraph (b)(1)(iv)(B) of this section shall be deemed satisfied.
    (c) Types of liabilities not eligible for treatment under the recurring item exception. The
40 recurring item exception does not apply to any liability of a taxpayer described in
paragraph (e) (interest), paragraph (g)(2) (workers compensation, tort, breach of contract,
and violation of law), or paragraph (g)(7) (other liabilities) of § 1.461-4. Moreover, the
recurring item exception does not apply to any liability incurred by a tax shelter, as
defined in section 461(i) and § 1.448-1T(b).
45   ***

    (e) *Examples.* The following examples illustrate the principles of this section:
    Example 1. Requirements for use of the recurring item exception. (i) Y corporation, a
calendar year, accrual method taxpayer, manufactures and distributes video cassette
recorders. Y timely files its federal income tax return for each taxable year on the
50 extended due date for the return (September 15, of the following taxable year). Y offers to
refund the price of a recorder to any purchaser not satisfied with the recorder. During

792

Sec. 461. General rule for taxable year of deduction

1992, 100 purchasers request a refund of the $500 purchase price. Y refunds $30,000 on or before September 15, 1993, and the remaining $20,000 after such date but before the end of 1993.

(ii) Under paragraph (g)(3) of § 1.461-4, economic performance with respect to $30,000 of the refund liability occurs on September 15, 1993. Assume the refund is deductible (or allowable as an adjustment to gross receipts or cost of goods sold) when incurred. If Y does not adopt the recurring item exception with respect to rebates and refunds, the $30,000 refund is incurred by Y for the 1993 taxable year. However, if Y has properly adopted the recurring item exception method of accounting under this section, and as of December 31, 1992, all events have occurred that determine the fact of the liability for the $30,000 refund, Y incurs that amount for the 1992 taxable year. Because economic performance (payment) with respect to the remaining $20,000 occurs after September 15, 1993 (more than 8-1/2 months after the end of 1992), that amount is not eligible for recurring item treatment under this section. Thus, the $20,000 amount is not incurred by Y until the 1993 taxable year.

Example 2. Requirements for use of the recurring item exception; amended returns. The facts are the same as in Example 2, except that Y files its income tax return for 1992 on March 15, 1993, and Y does not refund the price of any recorder before that date. Under paragraph (b)(1) of this section, the refund liability is not eligible for the recurring item exception because economic performance with respect to the refund does not occur before Y files a return for the taxable year for which the item would have been incurred under the exception. However, since economic performance occurs within 8-1/2 months after 1992, Y may file an amended return claiming the $30,000 as incurred for its 1992 taxable year (see paragraph (b)(2) of this section).

[T.D. 6500, 25 FR 11720, Nov. 26, 1960; T.D. 6520, 25 FR 13692, Dec. 24, 1960; T.D. 6710, 29 FR 3473, Mar. 18, 1964; T.D. 6735, 29 FR 6494, May 19, 1964; T.D. 6772, 29 FR 15753, Nov. 24, 1964; T.D. 6917, 32 FR 6682, May 2, 1967; T.D. 8408, 57 FR 12420, Apr. 10, 1992; T.D. 8482, 58 FR 42233, Aug. 9, 1993; T.D. 8491, 58 FR 53135, Oct. 14, 1993; T.D. 8554, 59 FR 36360, July 18, 1994; T.D. 8593, 60 FR 18743, Apr. 13, 1995; T.D. 8820, 64 FR 26851, May 18, 1999; T.D. 8408, 69 FR 44597, July 27, 2004]

Sec. 465. Deductions limited to amount at risk

(a) **Limitation to amount at risk.** --

    (1) **In general.** -- In the case of--

        (A) an individual, and

        (B) a C corporation with respect to which the stock ownership requirement of paragraph (2) of section 542(a) is met, engaged in an activity to which this section applies, any loss from such activity for the taxable year shall be allowed only to the extent of the aggregate amount with respect to which the taxpayer is at risk (within the meaning of subsection (b)) for such activity at the close of the taxable year.

    (2) **Deduction in succeeding year.** -- Any loss from an activity to which this section applies not allowed under this section for the taxable year shall be treated as a deduction allocable to such activity in the first succeeding taxable year.

    (3) **Special rules for applying paragraph (1)(B).** -- For purposes of paragraph (1)(B)--

        (A) section 544(a)(2) shall be applied as if such section did not contain the phrase "or by or for his partner"; and

Sec. 465. Deductions limited to amount at risk

(B) sections 544(a)(4)(A) and 544(b)(1) shall be applied by substituting "the corporation meet the stock ownership requirements of section 542(a)(2)" for "the corporation a personal holding company".

(b) Amounts considered at risk. --

(1) In general. -- For purposes of this section, a taxpayer shall be considered at risk for an activity with respect to amounts including--

(A) the amount of money and the adjusted basis of other property contributed by the taxpayer to the activity, and

(B) amounts borrowed with respect to such activity (as determined under paragraph (2)).

(2) Borrowed amounts. -- For purposes of this section, a taxpayer shall be considered at risk with respect to amounts borrowed for use in an activity to the extent that he--

(A) is personally liable for the repayment of such amounts, or

(B) has pledged property, other than property used in such activity, as security for such borrowed amount (to the extent of the net fair market value of the taxpayer's interest in such property).

No property shall be taken into account as security if such property is directly or indirectly financed by indebtedness which is secured by property described in paragraph (1).

(3) Certain borrowed amounts excluded. --

(A) In general. -- Except to the extent provided in regulations, for purposes of paragraph (1)(B), amounts borrowed shall not be considered to be at risk with respect to an activity if such amounts are borrowed from any person who has an interest in such activity or from a related person to a person (other than the taxpayer) having such an interest.

(B) Exceptions. --

(i) Interest as creditor. -- Subparagraph (A) shall not apply to an interest as a creditor in the activity.

(ii) Interest as shareholder with respect to amounts borrowed by corporation. -- In the case of amounts borrowed by a corporation from a shareholder, subparagraph (A) shall not apply to an interest as a shareholder.

(C) Related person. -- For purposes of this subsection, a person (hereinafter in this paragraph referred to as the "related person") is related to any person if--

(i) the related person bears a relationship to such person specified in section 267(b) or section 707(b)(1), or

(ii) the related person and such person are engaged in trades or business under common control (within the meaning of subsections (a) and (b) of section 52).

For purposes of clause (i), in applying section 267(b) or 707(b)(1), "10 percent" shall be substituted for "50 percent".

(4) Exception. -- Notwithstanding any other provision of this section, a taxpayer shall not be considered at risk with respect to amounts protected against loss through nonrecourse financing, guarantees, stop loss agreements, or other similar arrangements.

(5) Amounts at risk in subsequent years. -- If in any taxable year the taxpayer has a loss from an activity to which subsection (a) applies, the amount with respect to which a taxpayer is considered to be at risk (within the meaning of subsection (b)) in subsequent taxable years with respect to that activity shall be reduced by that portion of the loss which (after the application of subsection (a)) is allowable as a deduction.

(6) Qualified nonrecourse financing treated as amount at risk. -- For purposes of this section--

Sec. 465. Deductions limited to amount at risk

(A) **In general.** -- Notwithstanding any other provision of this subsection, in the case of an activity of holding real property, a taxpayer shall be considered at risk with respect to the taxpayer's share of any qualified nonrecourse financing which is secured by real property used in such activity.

(B) **Qualified nonrecourse financing.** -- For purposes of this paragraph, the term "qualified nonrecourse financing" means any financing--

    (i) which is borrowed by the taxpayer with respect to the activity of holding real property,

    (ii) which is borrowed by the taxpayer from a qualified person or represents a loan from any Federal, State, or local government or instrumentality thereof, or is guaranteed by any Federal, State, or local government,

    (iii) except to the extent provided in regulations, with respect to which no person is personally liable for repayment, and

    (iv) which is not convertible debt.

***

(D) **Qualified person defined.** -- For purposes of this paragraph--

    (i) **In general.** -- The term "qualified person" has the meaning given such term by section 49(a)(1)(D)(iv).

    (ii) **Certain commercially reasonable financing from related persons.** -- For purposes of clause (i), section 49(a)(1)(D)(iv) shall be applied without regard to subclause (I) thereof (relating to financing from related persons) if the financing from the related person is commercially reasonable and on substantially the same terms as loans involving unrelated persons.

(E) **Activity of holding real property.** -- For purposes of this paragraph--

    (i) **Incidental personal property and services.** -- The activity of holding real property includes the holding of personal property and the providing of services which are incidental to making real property available as living accommodations.

    (ii) **Mineral property.** -- The activity of holding real property shall not include the holding of mineral property.

(c) **Activities to which section applies.** --

***

(3) **Extension to other activities.** --

(A) **In general.** -- In the case of taxable years beginning after December 31, 1978, this section also applies to each activity--

    (i) engaged in by the taxpayer in carrying on a trade or business or for the production of income, and

    (ii) which is not described in paragraph (1).

(B) **Aggregation of activities where taxpayer actively participates in management of trade or business.** -- Except as provided in subparagraph (C), for purposes of this section, activities described in subparagraph (A) which constitute a trade or business shall be treated as one activity if--

    (i) the taxpayer actively participates in the management of such trade or business, or

    (ii) such trade or business is carried on by a partnership or an S corporation and 65 percent or more of the losses for the taxable year is allocable to persons who actively participate in the management of the trade or business.

795

Sec. 465. Deductions limited to amount at risk

(C) Aggregation or separation of activities under regulations. -- The Secretary shall prescribe regulations under which activities described in subparagraph (A) shall be aggregated or treated as separate activities.

(D) Application of subsection (b)(3). -- In the case of an activity described in subparagraph (A), subsection (b)(3) shall apply only to the extent provided in regulations prescribed by the Secretary.

***

(7) Exclusion of active businesses of qualified C corporations. --

(A) In general. -- In the case of a taxpayer which is a qualified C corporation--

(i) each qualifying business carried on by such taxpayer shall be treated as a separate activity, and

(ii) subsection (a) shall not apply to losses from such business.

(B) Qualified C corporation. -- For purposes of subparagraph (A), the term "qualified C corporation" means any corporation described in subparagraph (B) of subsection (a)(1) which is no--

(i) a personal holding company (as defined in section 542(a)), or

(ii) a personal service corporation (as defined in section 269A(b) but determined by substituting "5 percent" for "10 percent" in section 269A(b)(2)).

(C) Qualifying business. -- For purposes of this paragraph, the term "qualifying business" means any active business if--

(i) during the entire 12-month period ending on the last day of the taxable year, such corporation had at least 1 full- time employee substantially all the services of whom were in the active management of such business,

(ii) during the entire 12-month period ending on the last day of the taxable year, such corporation had at least 3 full- time, nonowner employees substantially all of the services of whom were services directly related to such business,

(iii) the amount of the deductions attributable to such business which are allowable to the taxpayer solely by reason of sections 162 and 404 for the taxable year exceeds 15 percent of the gross income from such business for such year, and

(iv) such business is not an excluded business.

***

(E) Definitions. -- For purposes of this paragraph--

(i) Non-owner employee. -- The term "non-owner employee" means any employee who does not own, at any time during the taxable year, more than 5 percent in value of the outstanding stock of the taxpayer. For purposes of the preceding sentence, section 318 shall apply, except that "5 percent" shall be substituted for "50 percent" in section 318(a)(2)(C).

(ii) Excluded business. -- The term "excluded business" means--

(I) equipment leasing (as defined in paragraph (6)), and

(II) any business involving the use, exploitation, sale, lease, or other disposition of master sound recordings, motion picture films, video tapes, or tangible or intangible assets associated with literary, artistic, musical, or similar properties.

(iii) Special rules relating to communications industry, etc. --

(I) Business not excluded where taxpayer not completely at risk. -- A business involving the use, exploitation, sale, lease, or other disposition of property described

Sec. 465. Deductions limited to amount at risk

in subclause (II) of clause (ii) shall not constitute an excluded business by reason of such subclause if the taxpayer is at risk with respect to all amounts paid or incurred (or chargeable to capital account) in such business.

(II) Certain licensed businesses not excluded. -- For purposes of subclause (II) of clause (ii), the provision of radio, television, cable television, or similar services 5 pursuant to a license or franchise granted by the Federal Communications Commission or any other Federal, State, or local authority shall not constitute an excluded business by reason of such subclause.

(F) Affiliated group treated as 1 taxpayer. -- For purposes of this paragraph--

(i) In general. -- Except as provided in subparagraph (G), the component members 10 of an affiliated group of corporations shall be treated as a single taxpayer.

(ii) Affiliated group of corporations. -- The term "affiliated group of corporations" means an affiliated group (as defined in section 1504(a)) which files or is required to file consolidated income tax returns.

(iii) Component member. -- The term "component member" means an includible 15 corporation (as defined in section 1504) which is a member of the affiliated group.

(G) Loss of 1 member of affiliated group may not offset income of personal holding company or personal service corporation. -- Nothing in this paragraph shall permit any loss of a member of an affiliated group to be used as an offset against the income of any other member of such group which is a personal holding company (as defined in section 20 542(a)) or a personal service corporation (as defined in section 269A(b) but determined by substituting "5 percent" for "10 percent" in section 269A(b)(2)).

(d) Definition of loss. -- For purposes of this section, the term "loss" means the excess of the deductions allowable under this chapter for the taxable year (determined without regard to the first sentence of subsection (a)) and allocable to an activity to which this section applies over the 25 income received or accrued by the taxpayer during the taxable year from such activity (determined without regard to subsection (e)(1)(A)).

(e) Recapture of losses where amount at risk is less than zero. --

(1) In general. -- If zero exceeds the amount for which the taxpayer is at risk in any activity at the close of any taxable year-- 30

(A) the taxpayer shall include in his gross income for such taxable year (as income from such activity) an amount equal to such excess, and

(B) an amount equal to the amount so included in gross income shall be treated as a deduction allocable to such activity for the first succeeding taxable year.

(2) Limitation. -- The excess referred to in paragraph (1) shall not exceed - 35

(A) the aggregate amount of the reductions required by subsection (b)(5) with respect to the activity by reason of losses for all prior taxable years beginning after December 31, 1978, reduced by

(B) the amounts previously included in gross income with respect to such activity under this subsection. 40

Sec. 467. Certain payments for the use of property or services

(a) Accrual method on present value basis. -- In the case of the lessor or lessee under any section 467 rental agreement, there shall be taken into account for purposes of this title for any taxable year the sum of-- 45

Sec. 467. Certain payments for the use of property or services

(1) the amount of the rent which accrues during such taxable year as determined under subsection (b), and

(2) interest for the year on the amounts which were taken into account under this subsection for prior taxable years and which are unpaid.

(b) Accrual of rental payments. --

(1) Allocation follows agreement. -- Except as provided in paragraph (2), the determination of the amount of the rent under any section 467 rental agreement which accrues during any taxable year shall be made--

(A) by allocating rents in accordance with the agreement, and

(B) by taking into account any rent to be paid after the close of the period in an amount determined under regulations which shall be based on present value concepts.

(2) Constant rental accrual in case of certain tax avoidance transactions, etc. -- In the case of any section 467 rental agreement to which this paragraph applies, the portion of the rent which accrues during any taxable year shall be that portion of the constant rental amount with respect to such agreement which is allocable to such taxable year.

(3) Agreements to which paragraph (2) applies. -- Paragraph (2) applies to any rental payment agreement if--

(A) such agreement is a disqualified leaseback or long-term agreement, or

(B) such agreement does not provide for the allocation referred to in paragraph (1)(A).

(4) Disqualified leaseback or long-term agreement. -- For purposes of this subsection, the term "disqualified leaseback or long-term agreement" means any section 467 rental agreement if--

(A) such agreement is part of a leaseback transaction or such agreement is for a term in excess of 75 percent of the statutory recovery period for the property, and

(B) a principal purpose for providing increasing rents under the agreement is the avoidance of tax imposed by this subtitle.

(5) Exceptions to disqualification in certain cases. -- The Secretary shall prescribe regulations setting forth circumstances under which agreements will not be treated as disqualified leaseback or long-term agreements, including circumstances relating to--

(A) changes in amounts paid determined by reference to price indices,

(B) rents based on a fixed percentage of lessee receipts or similar amounts,

(C) reasonable rent holidays, or

(D) changes in amounts paid to unrelated 3rd parties.

(c) Recapture of prior understated inclusions under leaseback or long-term agreements. --

(1) In general. -- If--

(A) the lessor under any section 467 rental agreement disposes of any property subject to such agreement during the term of such agreement, and

(B) such agreement is a leaseback or long-term agreement to which paragraph (2) of subsection (b) did not apply,

the recapture amount shall be treated as ordinary income. Such gain shall be recognized notwithstanding any other provision of this subtitle.

(2) Recapture amount. -- For purposes of paragraph (1), the term "recapture amount" means the lesser of--

(A) the prior understated inclusions, or

(B) the excess of the amount realized (or in the case of a disposition other than a sale,

Sec. 467.   Certain payments for the use of property or services

exchange, or involuntary conversion, the fair market value of the property) over the adjusted basis of such property.

The amount determined under subparagraph (B) shall be reduced by the amount of any gain treated as ordinary income on the disposition under any other provision of this subtitle.

(3) **Prior understated inclusions.** -- For purposes of this subsection, the term "prior 5 understated inclusion" means the excess (if any) of--

(A) the amount which would have been taken into account by the lessor under subsection (a) for periods before the disposition if subsection (b)(2) had applied to the agreement, over

(B) the amount taken into account under subsection (a) by the lessor for periods before 10 the disposition.

(4) **Leaseback or long-term agreement.** -- For purposes of this subsection, the term "leaseback or long- term agreement" means any agreement described in subsection (b)(4)(A).

(5) **Special rules.** -- Under regulations prescribed by the Secretary--

(A) exceptions similar to the exceptions applicable under section 1245 or 1250 15 (whichever is appropriate) shall apply for purposes of this subsection,

(B) any transferee in a disposition excepted by reason of subparagraph (A) who has a transferred basis in the property shall be treated in the same manner as the transferor, and

(C) for purposes of sections 170(e) and 751(c), amounts treated as ordinary income under this section shall be treated in the same manner as amounts treated as ordinary 20 income under section 1245 or 1250.

(d) **Section 467 rental agreements.** --

(1) **In general.** -- Except as otherwise provided in this subsection, the term "section 467 rental agreements" means any rental agreement for the use of tangible property under which--

(A) there is at least one amount allocable to the use of property during a calendar year 25 which is to be paid after the close of the calendar year following the calendar year in which such use occurs, or

(B) there are increases in the amount to be paid as rent under the agreement.

(2) Section not to apply to agreements involving payments of $250,000 or less. -- This section shall not apply to any amount to be paid for the use of property if the sum of the 30 following amounts does not exceed $250,000--

(A) the aggregate amount of payments received as consideration for such use of property, and

(B) the aggregate value of any other consideration to be received for such use of property. 35

For purposes of the preceding sentence, rules similar to the rules of clauses (ii) and (iii) of section 1274(c)(4)(C) shall apply.

(e) **Definitions.** -- For purposes of this section--

(1) **Constant rental amount.** -- The term "constant rental amount" means, with respect to any section 467 rental agreement, the amount which, if paid as of the close of each lease period 40 under the agreement, would result in an aggregate present value equal to the present value of the aggregate payments required under the agreement.

(2) **Leaseback transaction.** -- A transaction is a leaseback transaction if it involves a leaseback to any person who had an interest in such property at any time within 2 years before such leaseback (or to a related person). 45

(3) **Statutory recovery period.** --

Sec. 467. Certain payments for the use of property or services

(A) In general. --

	The statutory recovery period is:
In the case of:	
3-year property.....................................	3 years
5-year property.....................................	5 years
7-year property.....................................	7 years
10-year property.....................................	10 years
15-year and 20-year property............................	15 years
Residential rental property and nonresidential real property...............................	19 years
Any railroad grading or tunnel bore...................	50 years.

(B) Special rule for property not depreciable under section 168. -- In the case of property to which section 168 does not apply, subparagraph (A) shall be applied as if section 168 applies to such property.

(4) Discount and interest rate. -- For purposes of computing present value and interest under subsection (a)(2), the rate used shall be equal to 110 percent of the applicable Federal rate determined under section 1274(d) (compounded semiannually) which is in effect at the time the agreement is entered into with respect to debt instruments having a maturity equal to the term of the agreement.

(5) Related person. -- The term "related person" has the meaning given to such term by section 465(b)(3)(C).

(6) Certain options of lessee to renew not taken into account. -- Except as provided in regulations prescribed by the Secretary, there shall not be taken into account in computing the term of any agreement for purposes of this section any extension which is solely at the option of the lessee.

(f) Comparable rules where agreement for decreasing payments. -- Under regulations prescribed by the Secretary, rules comparable to the rules of this section shall also apply in the case of any agreement where the amount paid under the agreement for the use of property decreases during the term of the agreement.

(g) Comparable rules for services. -- Under regulations prescribed by the Secretary, rules comparable to the rules of subsection (a)(2) shall also apply in the case of payments for services which meet requirements comparable to the requirements of subsection (d). The preceding sentence shall not apply to any amount to which section 404 or 404A (or any other provision specified in regulations) applies.

(h) Regulations. -- The Secretary shall prescribe such regulations as may be appropriate to carry out the purposes of this section, including regulations providing for the application of this section in the case of contingent payments.

Sec. 469. Passive activity losses and credits limited

(a) Disallowance. --

(1) In general. -- If for any taxable year the taxpayer is described in paragraph (2), neither -

(A) the passive activity loss, nor

(B) the passive activity credit,

for the taxable year shall be allowed.

(2) Persons described. -- The following are described in this paragraph:

800

Sec. 469. Passive activity losses and credits limited

(A) any individual, estate, or trust,

(B) any closely held C corporation, and

(C) any personal service corporation.

(b) Disallowed loss or credit carried to next year. -- Except as otherwise provided in this section, any loss or credit from an activity which is disallowed under subsection (a) shall be treated as a deduction or credit allocable to such activity in the next taxable year.

(c) Passive activity defined. -- For purposes of this section -

(1) In general. -- The term "passive activity" means any activity--

(A) which involves the conduct of any trade or business, and

(B) in which the taxpayer does not materially participate.

(2) Passive activity includes any rental activity. -- Except as provided in paragraph (7), the term "passive activity" includes any rental activity.

(3) Working interests in oil and gas property. --

(A) In general. -- The term "passive activity" shall not include any working interest in any oil or gas property which the taxpayer holds directly or through an entity which does not limit the liability of the taxpayer with respect to such interest.

(B) Income in subsequent years. -- If any taxpayer has any loss for any taxable year from a working interest in any oil or gas property which is treated as a loss which is not from a passive activity, then any net income from such property (or any property the basis of which is determined in whole or in part by reference to the basis of such property) for any succeeding taxable year shall be treated as income of the taxpayer which is not from a passive activity.

If the preceding sentence applies to the net income from any property for any taxable year, any credits allowable under subpart B (other than section 27(a)) or D of part IV of subchapter A for such taxable year which are attributable to such property shall be treated as credits not from a passive activity to the extent the amount of such credits does not exceed the regular tax liability of the taxpayer for the taxable year which is allocable to such net income.

(4) Material participation not required for paragraphs (2) and (3). -- Paragraphs (2) and (3) shall be applied without regard to whether or not the taxpayer materially participates in the activity.

(5) Trade or business includes research and experimentation activity. -- For purposes of paragraph (1)(A), the term "trade or business" includes any activity involving research or experimentation (within the meaning of section 174).

(6) Activity in connection with trade or business or production of income. -- To the extent provided in regulations, for purposes of paragraph (1)(A), the term "trade or business" include--

(A) any activity in connection with a trade or business, or

(B) any activity with respect to which expenses are allowable as a deduction under section 212.

(7) Special rules for taxpayers in real property business. --

(A) In general. -- If this paragraph applies to any taxpayer for a taxable year--

(i) paragraph (2) shall not apply to any rental real estate activity of such taxpayer for such taxable year, and

(ii) this section shall be applied as if each interest of the taxpayer in rental real estate were a separate activity.

Sec. 469. Passive activity losses and credits limited

Notwithstanding clause (ii), a taxpayer may elect to treat all interests in rental real estate as one activity. Nothing in the preceding provisions of this subparagraph shall be construed as affecting the determination of whether the taxpayer materially participates with respect to any interest in a limited partnership as a limited partner.

(B) Taxpayers to whom paragraph applies. -- This paragraph shall apply to a taxpayer for a taxable year if--

(i) more than one-half of the personal services performed in trades or businesses by the taxpayer during such taxable year are performed in real property trades or businesses in which the taxpayer materially participates, and

(ii) such taxpayer performs more than 750 hours of services during the taxable year in real property trades or businesses in which the taxpayer materially participates.

In the case of a joint return, the requirements of the preceding sentence are satisfied if and only if either spouse separately satisfies such requirements. For purposes of the preceding sentence, activities in which a spouse materially participates shall be determined under subsection (h).

(C) Real property trade or business. -- For purposes of this paragraph, the term "real property trade or business" means any real property development, redevelopment, construction, reconstruction, acquisition, conversion, rental, operation, management, leasing, or brokerage trade or business.

(D) Special rules for subparagraph (B). --

(i) Closely held C corporations. -- In the case of a closely held C corporation, the requirements of subparagraph (B) shall be treated as met for any taxable year if more than 50 percent of the gross receipts of such corporation for such taxable year are derived from real property trades or businesses in which the corporation materially participates.

(ii) Personal services as an employee. -- For purposes of subparagraph (B), personal services performed as an employee shall not be treated as performed in real property trades or businesses. The preceding sentence shall not apply if such employee is a 5-percent owner (as defined in section 416(i)(1)(B)) in the employer.

(d) Passive activity loss and credit defined. -- For purposes of this section -

(1) Passive activity loss. -- The term "passive activity loss" means the amount (if any) by which--

(A) the aggregate losses from all passive activities for the taxable year, exceed

(B) the aggregate income from all passive activities for such year.

(2) Passive activity credit. -- The term "passive activity credit" means the amount (if any) by which--

(A) the sum of the credits from all passive activities allowable for the taxable year under-

(i) subpart D of part IV of subchapter A, or

(ii) subpart B (other than section 27(a)) of such part IV, exceeds

(B) the regular tax liability of the taxpayer for the taxable year allocable to all passive activities.

(e) Special rules for determining income or loss from a passive activity. -- For purposes of this section--

(1) Certain income not treated as income from passive activity. -- In determining the income or loss from any activity--

802

Sec. 469. Passive activity losses and credits limited

(A) In general. -- There shall not be taken into account--

(i) any--

(I) gross income from interest, dividends, annuities, or royalties not derived in the ordinary course of a trade or business,

(II) expenses (other than interest) which are clearly and directly allocable to such 5 gross income, and

(III) interest expense properly allocable to such gross income, and

(ii) gain or loss not derived in the ordinary course of a trade or business which is attributable to the disposition of property--

(I) producing income of a type described in clause (i), or 10

(II) held for investment.

For purposes of clause (ii), any interest in a passive activity shall not be treated as property held for investment.

(B) Return on working capital. -- For purposes of subparagraph (A), any income, gain, or loss which is attributable to an investment of working capital shall be treated as not 15 derived in the ordinary course of a trade or business.

(2) Passive losses of certain closely held corporations may offset active income. --

(A) In general. -- If a closely held C corporation (other than a personal service corporation) has net active income for any taxable year, the passive activity loss of such taxpayer for such taxable year (determined without regard to this paragraph)-- 20

(i) shall be allowable as a deduction against net active income, and

(ii) shall not be taken into account under subsection (a) to the extent so allowable as a deduction.

A similar rule shall apply in the case of any passive activity credit of the taxpayer.

(B) Net active income. -- For purposes of this paragraph, the term "net active income" 25 means the taxable income of the taxpayer for the taxable year determined without regard to--

(i) any income or loss from a passive activity, and

(ii) any item of gross income, expense, gain, or loss described in paragraph (1)(A).

(3) Compensation for personal services. -- Earned income (within the meaning of section 30 911(d)(2)(A)) shall not be taken into account in computing the income or loss from a passive activity for any taxable year.

(4) Dividends reduced by dividends received deduction. -- For purposes of paragraphs (1) and (2), income from dividends shall be reduced by the amount of any dividends received deduction under section 243, 244, or 245. 35

(f) Treatment of former passive activities. -- For purposes of this section--

(1) In general. -- If an activity is a former passive activity for any taxable year--

(A) any unused deduction allocable to such activity under subsection (b) shall be offset against the income from such activity for the taxable year,

(B) any unused credit allocable to such activity under subsection (b) shall be offset 40 against the regular tax liability (computed after the application of paragraph (1)) allocable to such activity for the taxable year, and

(C) any such deduction or credit remaining after the application of subparagraphs (A) and (B) shall continue to be treated as arising from a passive activity.

(2) Change in status of closely held C corporation or personal service corporation. -- If 45

803

Sec. 469. Passive activity losses and credits limited

a taxpayer ceases for any taxable year to be a closely held C corporation or personal service corporation, this section shall continue to apply to losses and credits to which this section applied for any preceding taxable year in the same manner as if such taxpayer continued to be a closely held C corporation or personal service corporation, whichever is applicable.

(3) Former passive activity. -- The term "former passive activity" means any activity which, with respect to the taxpayer--

(A) is not a passive activity for the taxable year, but

(B) was a passive activity for any prior taxable year.

(g) Dispositions of entire interest in passive activity. -- If during the taxable year a taxpayer disposes of his entire interest in any passive activity (or former passive activity), the following rules shall apply:

(1) Fully taxable transaction. --

(A) In general. -- If all gain or loss realized on such disposition is recognized, the excess of--

(i) any loss from such activity for such taxable year (determined after the application of subsection (b)), over

(ii) any net income or gain for such taxable year from all other passive activities (determined after the application of subsection (b)),

shall be treated as a loss which is not from a passive activity.

(B) Subparagraph (A) not to apply to disposition involving related party. -- If the taxpayer and the person acquiring the interest bear a relationship to each other described in section 267(b) or section 707(b)(1), then subparagraph (A) shall not apply to any loss of the taxpayer until the taxable year in which such interest is acquired (in a transaction described in subparagraph (A)) by another person who does not bear such a relationship to the taxpayer.

(C) Income from prior years. -- To the extent provided in regulations, income or gain from the activity for preceding taxable years shall be taken into account under subparagraph (A)(ii) for the taxable year to the extent necessary to prevent the avoidance of this section.

(2) Disposition by death. -- If an interest in the activity is transferred by reason of the death of the taxpayer--

(A) paragraph (1)(A) shall apply to losses described in paragraph (1)(A) to the extent such losses are greater than the excess (if any) of--

(i) the basis of such property in the hands of the transferee, over

(ii) the adjusted basis of such property immediately before the death of the taxpayer, and

(B) any losses to the extent of the excess described in subparagraph (A) shall not be allowed as a deduction for any taxable year.

(3) Installment sale of entire interest. -- In the case of an installment sale of an entire interest in an activity to which section 453 applies, paragraph (1) shall apply to the portion of such losses for each taxable year which bears the same ratio to all such losses as the gain recognized on such sale during such taxable year bears to the gross profit from such sale (realized or to be realized when payment is completed).

(h) Material participation defined. -- For purposes of this section--

(1) In general. -- A taxpayer shall be treated as materially participating in an activity only if the taxpayer is involved in the operations of the activity on a basis which is--

Sec. 469. Passive activity losses and credits limited

(A) regular,

(B) continuous, and

(C) substantial.

(2) Interests in limited partnerships. -- Except as provided in regulations, no interest in a limited partnership as a limited partner shall be treated as an interest with respect to which a taxpayer materially participates.

(3) Treatment of certain retired individuals and surviving spouses. -- A taxpayer shall be treated as materially participating in any farming activity for a taxable year if paragraph (4) or (5) of section 2032A(b) would cause the requirements of section 2032A(b)(1)(C)(ii) to be met with respect to real property used in such activity if such taxpayer had died during the taxable year.

(4) Certain closely held C corporations and personal service corporations. -- A closely held C corporation or personal service corporation shall be treated as materially participating in an activity only if--

(A) 1 or more shareholders holding stock representing more than 50 percent (by value) of the outstanding stock of such corporation materially participate in such activity, or

(B) in the case of a closely held C corporation (other than a personal service corporation), the requirements of section 465(c)(7)(C) (without regard to clause (iv)) are met with respect to such activity.

(5) Participation by spouse. -- In determining whether a taxpayer materially participates, the participation of the spouse of the taxpayer shall be taken into account.

(i) $25,000 offset for rental real estate activities. --

(1) In general. -- In the case of any natural person, subsection (a) shall not apply to that portion of the passive activity loss or the deduction equivalent (within the meaning of subsection (j)(5)) of the passive activity credit for any taxable year which is attributable to all rental real estate activities with respect to which such individual actively participated in such taxable year (and if any portion of such loss or credit arose in another taxable year, in such other taxable year).

(2) Dollar limitation. -- The aggregate amount to which paragraph (1) applies for any taxable year shall not exceed $25,000.

(3) Phase-out of exemption. --

(A) **In general.** -- In the case of any taxpayer, the $25,000 amount under paragraph (2) shall be reduced (but not below zero) by 50 percent of the amount by which the adjusted gross income of the taxpayer for the taxable year exceeds $100,000.

(B) **Special phase-out of rehabilitation credit.** -- In the case of any portion of the passive activity credit for any taxable year which is attributable to the rehabilitation credit determined under section 47, subparagraph (A) shall be applied by substituting "$200,000" for "$100,000".

(C) **Exception for commercial revitalization deduction.** -- Subparagraph (A) shall not apply to any portion of the passive activity loss for any taxable year which is attributable to the commercial revitalization deduction under section 1400I.

(D) **Exception for low-income housing credit.** -- Subparagraph (A) shall not apply to any portion of the passive activity credit for any taxable year which is attributable to any credit determined under section 42.

(E) **Ordering rules to reflect exceptions and separate phase- outs.** -- If subparagraph (B), (C), or (D) applies for a taxable year, paragraph (1) shall be applied--

805

Sec. 469. Passive activity losses and credits limited

(i) first to the portion of the passive activity loss to which subparagraph (C) does not apply,

(ii) second to the portion of such loss to which subparagraph (C) applies,

(iii) third to the portion of the passive activity credit to which subparagraph (B) or (D) does not apply,

(iv) fourth to the portion of such credit to which subparagraph (B) applies, and

(v) then to the portion of such credit to which subparagraph (D) applies.

(F) **Adjusted gross income.** -- For purposes of this paragraph, adjusted gross income shall be determined without regard to--

(i) any amount includible in gross income under section 86,

(ii) the amounts excludable from gross income under sections 135 and 137,

(iii) the amounts allowable as a deduction under sections 199, 219, 221, and 222, and

(iv) any passive activity loss or any loss allowable by reason of subsection (c)(7).

(4) **Special rule for estates.** --

(A) **In general.** -- In the case of taxable years of an estate ending less than 2 years after the date of the death of the decedent, this subsection shall apply to all rental real estate activities with respect to which such decedent actively participated before his death.

(B) **Reduction for surviving spouse's exemption.** -- For purposes of subparagraph (A), the $25,000 amount under paragraph (2) shall be reduced by the amount of the exemption under paragraph (1) (without regard to paragraph (3)) allowable to the surviving spouse of the decedent for the taxable year ending with or within the taxable year of the estate.

(5) **Married individuals filing separately.** --

(A) **In general.** -- Except as provided in subparagraph (B), in the case of any married individual filing a separate return, this subsection shall be applied by substituting--

(i) "$12,500" for "$25,000" each place it appears,

(ii) "$50,000" for "$100,000" in paragraph (3)(A), and

(iii) "$100,000" for "$200,000" in paragraph (3)(B).

(B) **Taxpayers not living apart.** -- This subsection shall not apply to a taxpayer who--

(i) is a married individual filing a separate return for any taxable year, and

(ii) does not live apart from his spouse at all times during such taxable year.

(6) **Active participation.** --

(A) **In general.** -- An individual shall not be treated as actively participating with respect to any interest in any rental real estate activity for any period if, at any time during such period, such interest (including any interest of the spouse of the individual) is less than 10 percent (by value) of all interests in such activity.

(B) **No participation requirement for low-income housing, rehabilitation credit, or commercial revitalization deduction.** -- Paragraphs (1) and (4)(A) shall be applied without regard to the active participation requirement in the case of--

(i) any credit determined under section 42 for any taxable year,

(ii) any rehabilitation credit determined under section 47, or

(iii) any deduction under section 1400I (relating to commercial revitalization deduction).

(C) **Interest as a limited partner.** -- Except as provided in regulations, no interest as a

Sec. 469. Passive activity losses and credits limited

limited partner in a limited partnership shall be treated as an interest with respect to which the taxpayer actively participates.

(D) Participation by spouse. -- In determining whether a taxpayer actively participates, the participation of the spouse of the taxpayer shall be taken into account.

(j) Other definitions and special rules. -- For purposes of this section--   5

(1) Closely held C corporation. -- The term "closely held C corporation" means any C corporation described in section 465(a)(1)(B).

(2) Personal service corporation. --   The term "personal service corporation" has the meaning given such term by section 269A(b)(1), except that section 269A(b)(2) shall be applied--   10

(A) by substituting "any" for "more than 10 percent", and

(B) by substituting "any" for "50 percent or more in value" in section 318(a)(2)(C).

A corporation shall not be treated as a personal service corporation unless more than 10 percent of the stock (by value) in such corporation is held by employee-owners (within the meaning of section 269A(b)(2), as modified by the preceding sentence).   15

(3) Regular tax liability. -- The term "regular tax liability" has the meaning given such term by section 26(b).

(4) Allocation of passive activity loss and credit. -- The passive activity loss and the passive activity credit (and the $25,000 amount under subsection (i)) shall be allocated to activities, and within activities, on a pro rata basis in such manner as the Secretary may 20 prescribe.

(5) Deduction equivalent. -- The deduction equivalent of credits from a passive activity for any taxable year is the amount which (if allowed as a deduction) would reduce the regular tax liability for such taxable year by an amount equal to such credits.

(6) Special rule for gifts. -- In the case of a disposition of any interest in a passive activity 25 by gift --

(A) the basis of such interest immediately before the transfer shall be increased by the amount of any passive activity losses allocable to such interest with respect to which a deduction has not been allowed by reason of subsection (a), and

(B) such losses shall not be allowable as a deduction for any taxable year.   30

(7) Qualified residence interest. -- The passive activity loss of a taxpayer shall be computed without regard to qualified residence interest (within the meaning of section 163(h)(3)).

(8) Rental activity. -- The term "rental activity" means any activity where payments are principally for the use of tangible property.   35

(9) Election to increase basis of property by amount of   disallowed credit. -- For purposes of determining gain or loss from a disposition of any property to which subsection (g)(1) applies, the transferor may elect to increase the basis of such property immediately before the transfer by an amount equal to the portion of any unused credit allowable under this chapter which reduced the basis of such property for the taxable year in which such credit 40 arose. If the taxpayer elects the application of this paragraph, such portion of the passive activity credit of such taxpayer shall not be allowed for any taxable year.

(10) Coordination with section 280A. -- If a passive activity involves the use of a dwelling unit to which section 280A(c)(5) applies for any taxable year, any income, deduction, gain, or loss allocable to such use shall not be taken into account for purposes of this section for such 45 taxable year.

807

Sec. 469. Passive activity losses and credits limited

(11) Aggregation of members of affiliated groups. -- Except as provided in regulations, all members of an affiliated group which files a consolidated return shall be treated as 1 corporation.

***

5   **(k) Separate application of section in case of publicly traded partnerships.** --

(1) In general. -- This section shall be applied separately with respect to items attributable to each publicly traded partnership (and subsection (i) shall not apply with respect to items attributable to any such partnership). The preceding sentence shall not apply to any credit determined under section 42, or any rehabilitation credit determined under section 47,
10   attributable to a publicly traded partnership to the extent the amount of any such credits exceeds the regular tax liability attributable to income from such partnership.

(2) Publicly traded partnership. -- For purposes of this section, the term "publicly traded partnership" means any partnership if--

(A) interests in such partnership are traded on an established securities market, or

15   **(B)** interests in such partnership are readily tradable on a secondary market (or the substantial equivalent thereof).

(3) Coordination with subsection (g). -- For purposes of subsection (g), a taxpayer shall not be treated as having disposed of his entire interest in an activity of a publicly traded partnership until he disposes of his entire interest in such partnership.

20   **(4) Application to regulated investment companies.** -- For purposes of this section, a regulated investment company (as defined in section 851) holding an interest in a qualified publicly traded partnership (as defined in section 851(h)) shall be treated as a taxpayer described in subsection (a)(2) with respect to items attributable to such interest.

(l) Regulations. -- The Secretary shall prescribe such regulations as may be necessary or
25 appropriate to carry out provisions of this section, including regulations--

(1) which specify what constitutes an activity, material participation, or active participation for purposes of this section,

(2) which provide that certain items of gross income will not be taken into account in determining income or loss from any activity (and the treatment of expenses allocable to such
30   income),

(3) requiring net income or gain from a limited partnership or other passive activity to be treated as not from a passive activity,

(4) which provide for the determination of the allocation of interest expense for purposes of this section, and

35   **(5)** which deal with changes in marital status and changes between joint returns and separate returns.

***

Reg. § 1.469-1T General rules (temporary).

***

40   (e) Definition of ``passive activity''--(1) In general. Except as otherwise provided in this paragraph (e), an activity is a passive activity of the taxpayer for a taxable year if and only if the activity--

(i) Is a trade or business activity (within the meaning of paragraph (e)(2) of this section) in which the taxpayer does not materially participate for such taxable year; or
45   (ii) Is a rental activity (within the meaning of paragraph (e)(3) of this section), without regard to whether or to what extent the taxpayer participates in such activity.

***

Sec. 469. Passive activity losses and credits limited

(3) *Rental activity*--(i) *In general*. Except as otherwise provided in this paragraph (e)(3), an activity is a rental activity for a taxable year if--

(A) During such taxable year, tangible property held in connection with the activity is used by customers or held for use by customers; and

(B) The gross income attributable to the conduct of the activity during such taxable year represents (or, in the case of an activity in which property is held for use by customers, the expected gross income from the conduct of the activity will represent) amounts paid or to be paid principally for the use of such tangible property (without regard to whether the use of the property by customers is pursuant to a lease or pursuant to a service contract or other arrangement that is not denominated a lease).

(ii) *Exceptions*. For purposes of this paragraph (e)(3), an activity involving the use of tangible property is not a rental activity for a taxable year if for such taxable year--

(A) The average period of customer use for such property is seven days or less;

(B) The average period of customer use for such property is 30 days or less, and significant personal services (within the meaning of paragraph (e)(3)(iv) of this section) are provided by or on behalf of the owner of the property in connection with making the property available for use by customers;

(C) Extraordinary personal services (within the meaning of paragraph (e)(3)(v) of this section) are provided by or on behalf of the owner of the property in connection with making such property available for use by customers (without regard to the average period of customer use);

(D) The rental of such property is treated as incidental to a nonrental activity of the taxpayer under paragraph (e)(3)(vi) of this section;

(E) The taxpayer customarily makes the property available during defined business hours for nonexclusive use by various customers; or

(F) The provision of the property for use in an activity conducted by a partnership, S corporation, or joint venture in which the taxpayer owns an interest is not a rental activity under paragraph (e)(3)(vii) of this section.

(iii) *Average period of customer use*. [Reserved]. See § 1.469-1(e)(3)(iii) for rules relating to this paragraph.

(iv) *Significant personal services*--(A) *In general*. For purposes of paragraph (e)(3)(ii)(B) of this section, personal services include only services performed by individuals, and do not include excluded services (within the meaning of paragraph (e)(3)(iv)(B) of this section). In determining whether personal services provided in connection with making property available for use by customers are significant, all of the relevant facts and circumstances shall be taken into account. Relevant facts and circumstances include the frequency with which such services are provided, the type and amount of labor required to perform such services, and the value of such services relative to the amount charged for the use of the property.

(B) *Excluded services*. For purposes of paragraph (e)(3)(iv)(A) of this section, the term ``excluded services'' means, with respect to any property made available for use by customers--

(1) Services necessary to permit the lawful use of the property;

(2) Services performed in connection with the construction of improvements to the property, or in connection with the performance of repairs that extend the property's useful life for a period substantially longer than the average period for which such property is used by customers; and

(3) Services, provided in connection with the use of any improved real property, that are similar to those commonly provided in connection with long-term rentals of high-grade commercial or residential real property (e.g., cleaning and maintenance of common areas, routine repairs, trash collection, elevator service, and security at entrances or

perimeters).

(v) *Extraordinary personal services.* For purposes of paragraph (e)(3)(ii)(C) of this section, extraordinary personal services are provided in connection with making property available for use by customers only if the services provided in connection with the use of
5 the property are performed by individuals, and the use by customers of the property is incidental to their receipt of such services. For example, the use by patients of a hospital's boarding facilities generally is incidental to their receipt of the personal services provided by the hospital's medical and nursing staff. Similarly, the use by students of a boarding school's dormitories generally is incidental to their receipt of the personal
10 services provided by the school's teaching staff.

(vi) *Rental of property incidental to a nonrental activity of the taxpayer--(A) In general.* For purposes of paragraph (e)(3)(ii)(D) of this section, the rental of property shall be treated as incidental to a nonrental activity of the taxpayer only to the extent provided in this paragraph (e)(3)(vi).
15 (B) *Property held for investment.* The rental of property during a taxable year shall be treated as incidental to an activity of holding such property for investment if and only if--

(1) The principal purpose for holding the property during such taxable year is to realize gain from the appreciation of the property (without regard to whether it is expected that such gain will be realized from the sale or exchange of the property in its current state of
20 development); and

(2) The gross rental income from the property for such taxable year is less than two percent of the lesser of--

(i) The unadjusted basis of such property; and

(ii) The fair market value of such property.
25 (C) *Property used in a trade or business.* The rental of property during a taxable year shall be treated as incidental to a trade or business activity (within the meaning of paragraph (e)(2) of this section) if and only if--

(1) The taxpayer owns an interest in such trade or business activity during the taxable year;
30 (2) The property was predominantly used in such trade or business activity during the taxable year or during at least two of the five taxable years that immediately precede the taxable year; and

(3) The gross rental income from such property for the taxable year is less than two percent of the lesser of--
35 (i) The unadjusted basis of such property; and

(ii) The fair market value of such property.

***

(viii) *Examples.* The following examples illustrate the application of this paragraph (e) (3):
40 *Example (1).* The taxpayer is engaged in an activity of leasing photocopying equipment. The average period of customer use for the equipment exceeds 30 days. Pursuant to the lease agreements, skilled technicians employed by the taxpayer maintain the equipment and service malfunctioning equipment for no additional charge. Service calls occur frequently (three times per week on average) and require substantial labor.
45 The value of the maintenance and repair services (measured by the cost to the taxpayer of employees performing these services) exceeds 50 percent of the amount charged for the use of the equipment. Under these facts, services performed by individuals are provided in connection with the use of the photocopying equipment, but the customers' use of the photocopying equipment is not incidental to their receipt of the services.
50 Therefore, extraordinary personal services (within the meaning of paragraph (e)(3)(v) of this section) are not provided in connection with making the photocopying equipment

available for use by customers, and the activity is a rental activity.

Example (2). The facts are the same as in example (1), except that the average period of customer use for the photocopying equipment exceeds seven days but does not exceed 30 days. Under these facts, significant personal services (within the meaning of paragraph (e)(3)(iv) of this section) are provided in connection with making the photocopying equipment available for use by customers and, under paragraph (e)(3)(ii) (B) of this section, the activity is not a rental activity.

Example (3). The taxpayer is engaged in an activity of transporting goods for customers. In conducting the activity, the taxpayer provides tractor-trailers to transport goods for customers pursuant to arrangements under which the tractor-trailers are selected by the taxpayer, may be replaced at the sole option of the taxpayer, and are operated and maintained by drivers and mechanics employed by the taxpayer. The average period of customer use for the tractor-trailers exceeds 30 days. Under these facts, the use of tractor-trailers by the taxpayer's customers is incidental to their receipt of personal services provided by the taxpayer. Accordingly, the services performed in the activity are extraordinary personal services (within the meaning of paragraph (e)(3)(v) of this section) and, under paragraph (e)(3)(ii)(C) of this section, the activity is not a rental activity.

Example (4). The taxpayer is engaged in an activity of owning and operating a residential apartment hotel. For the taxable year, the average period of customer use for apartments exceeds seven days but does not exceed 30 days. In addition to cleaning public entrances, exists, stairways, and lobbies, and collecting and removing trash, the taxpayer provides a daily maid and linen service at no additional charge. All of the services other than maid and linen service are excluded services (within the meaning of paragraph (e)(3)(iv)(B) of this section), because such services are similar to those commonly provided in connection with long-term rentals of high-grade residential real property. The value of the maid and linen services (measured by the cost to the taxpayer of employees performing such services) is less than 10 percent of the amount charged to tenants for occupancy of apartments. Under these facts, neither significant personal services (within the meaning of paragraph (e)(3)(iv) of this section) nor extraordinary personal services (within the meaning of paragraph (e)(3)(v) of this section) are provided in connection with making apartments available for use by customers. Accordingly, the activity is a rental activity.

***

Example (9). The taxpayer owns a taxicab which the taxpayer operates during the day and leases to another driver for use at night under a one-year lease. Under the terms of the lease, the other driver is charged a fixed rental for use of the taxicab. Assume that, under the rules to be contained in § 1.469-4T, the taxpayer is engaged in two separate activities, an activity of operating the taxicab and an activity of making the taxicab available for use by the other driver. Under these facts, the period for which the other driver uses the taxicab exceeds 30 days, and the taxpayer does not provide extraordinary personal services in connection with making the taxicab available to the other driver. Accordingly, the lease of the taxicab is a rental activity.

Example (10). The taxpayer operates a golf course. Some customers of the golf course pay green fees upon each use of the golf course, while other customers purchase weekly, monthly, or annual passes. The golf course is open to all customers from sunrise to sunset every day of the year except certain holidays and days on which the taxpayer determines that the course is too wet for play. The taxpayer thus makes the golf course available during prescribed hours for nonexclusive use by various customers. Accordingly, under paragraph (e)(3)(ii)(E) of this section, the taxpayer is not engaged in a rental activity, without regard to the average period of customer use for the golf course.

Sec. 469. Passive activity losses and credits limited

***

(j) *Spouses filing joint return*--(1) *In general.* Except as otherwise provided in the regulations under section 469, spouses filing a joint return for a taxable year shall be treated for such year as one taxpayer for purposes of section 469 and the regulations
5 thereunder Thus, for example, spouses filing a joint return are treated as one taxpayer for purposes of--

(i) Section 1.469-2T (relating generally to the computation of such taxpayer's passive activity loss); and

(ii) Paragraph (f) of this section (relating to the allocation of such taxpayer's disallowed
10 passive activity loss and passive activity credit among activities and the identification of disallowed passive activity deductions and credits from passive activities).

(2) *Exceptions to treatment as one taxpayer*--(i) *Identification of disallowed deductions and credits.* For purposes of paragraphs (f)(2)(iii) and (3)(iii) of this section, spouses filing a joint return for the taxable year must account separately for the deductions and credits
15 attributable to the interests of each spouse in any activity.

(ii) *Treatment of deductions disallowed under sections 704(d), 1366(d), and 465.* Notwithstanding any other provision of this section or § 1.469-2T, this paragraph (j) shall not affect the application of section 704(d), section 1366(d), or section 465 to taxpayers filing a joint return for the taxable year.
20   (iii) *Treatment of losses from working interests.* Paragraph (e)(4) of this section (relating to losses and credits from certain interests in oil and gas wells) shall be applied by treating a husband and wife (whether or not filing a joint return) as separate taxpayers.

(3) *Joint return no longer filed.* If an individual--

(A) Does not file a joint return for the taxable years; and
25   (B) Filed a joint return for the immediately preceding taxable year;
then the passive activity deductions and credits allocable to such individual's activities for the taxable year under paragraph (f)(4) of this section shall be determined by taking into account the items of deduction and credit attributable to such individual's interests in passive activities for the immediately preceding taxable year. See paragraph (j)(2)(i) of
30 this section.

(4) *Participation of spouses.* Rules treating an individual's participation in an activity as participation of such individual's spouse in such activity (without regard to whether the spouses file a joint return) are contained in § 1.469-5T(f)(3).

***

35 **Reg. § 1.469-2T   Passive activity loss (temporary).**

***

(c) *Passive activity gross income*--(1) *In general.* Except as otherwise provided in the regulations under section 469, passive activity gross income for a taxable year includes an item of gross income if and only if such income is from a passive activity.
40   (2) *Treatment of gain from disposition of an interest in an activity or an interest in property used in an activity*--(i) *In general*--(A) *Treatment of gain.* Except as otherwise provided in the regulations under section 469, any gain recognized upon the sale, exchange or other disposition (a ``disposition") of an interest in property used in an activity at the time of the disposition or of an interest in an activity held through a
45 partnership or S corporation is treated in the following manner:

(1) The gain is treated as gross income from such activity for the taxable year or years in which it is recognized;

(2) If the activity is a passive activity of the taxpayer for the taxable year of the disposition, the gain is treated as passive activity gross income for the taxable year or
50 years in which it is recognized; and

812

Sec. 469. Passive activity losses and credits limited

(3) If the activity is not a passive activity of the taxpayer for the taxable year of the disposition, the gain is treated as not from a passive activity.

***

(3) *Items of portfolio income specifically excluded--*(i) *In general.* Passive activity gross income does not include portfolio income. For purposes of the preceding sentence, 5 portfolio income includes all gross income, other than income derived in the ordinary course of a trade or business (within the meaning of paragraph (c)(3)(ii) of this section), that is attributable to--

(A) Interest (including amounts treated as interest under paragraph (e)(2)(ii) of this section, relating to certain payments to partners for the use of capital); annuities; royalties 10 (including fees and other payments for the use of intangible property); dividends on C corporation stock; and income (including dividends) from a real estate investment trust (within the meaning of section 856), regulated investment company (within the meaning of section 851), real estate mortgage investment conduit (within the meaning of section 860D), common trust fund (within the meaning of section 584), controlled foreign 15 corporation (within the meaning of section 957), qualified electing fund (within the meaning of section 1295(a)), or cooperative (within the meaning of section 1381(a));

(B) Dividends on S corporation stock (within the meaning of section 1368(c)(2);

(C) The disposition of property that produces income of a type described in paragraph (c)(3)(i)(A) of this section; and   20

(D) The disposition of property held for investment (within the meaning of section 163 (d)).

(ii) *Gross income derived in the ordinary course of a trade or business.* Solely for purposes of paragraph (c)(3)(i) of this section, gross income derived in the ordinary course of a trade or business includes only--   25

(A) Interest income on loans and investments made in the ordinary course of a trade or business of lending money;

(B) Interest on accounts receivable arising from the performance of services or the sale of property in the ordinary course of a trade or business of performing such services or selling such property, but only if credit is customarily offered to customers of the 30 business;

(C) Income from investments made in the ordinary course of a trade or business of furnishing insurance or annuity contracts or reinsuring risks underwritten by insurance companies;

(D) Income or gain derived in the ordinary course of an activity of trading or dealing in 35 any property if such activity constitutes a trade or business (but see paragraph (c)(3)(iii) (A) of this section);

(E) Royalties derived by the taxpayer in the ordinary course of a trade or business of licensing intangible property (within the meaning of paragraph (c)(3)(iii)(B) of this section);   40

(F) Amount included in the gross income of a patron of a cooperative (within the meaning of section 1381(a), without regard to paragraph (2)(A) or (C) thereof) by reason of any payment or allocation to the patron based on patronage occurring with respect to a trade or business of the patron; and

(G) Other income identified by the Commissioner as income derived by the taxpayer 45 in the ordinary course of a trade or business.

(iii) *Special rules--*(A) *Income from property held for investment by dealer.* For purposes of paragraph (c)(3)(i) of this section, a dealer's income or gain from an item of property is not derived by the dealer in the ordinary course of a trade or business of dealing in such property if the dealer held the property for investment at any time before 50 such income or gain is recognized.

(B) *Royalties derived in the ordinary course of the trade or business of licensing intangible property--(1) In general.* Royalties received by any person with respect to a license or other transfer of any rights in intangible property shall be considered to be derived in the ordinary course of the trade or business of licensing such property only if
5 such person--

(i) Created such property; or

(ii) Performed substantial services or incurred substantial costs with respect to the development or marketing of such property.

(2) *Substantial services or costs--(i) In general.* Except as provided in paragraph (c)(3)
10 (iii)(B)(2)(ii) of this section, the determination of whether a person has performed substantial services or incurred substantial costs with respect to the development or marketing of an item of intangible property shall be made on the basis of all the facts and circumstances.

(ii) *Exception.* A person has performed substantial services or incurred substantial
15 costs for a taxable year with respect to the development or marketing of an item of intangible property if--

(a) The expenditures reasonably incurred by such person in such taxable year with respect to the development or marketing of the property exceed 50 percent of the gross royalties from licensing such property that are includible in such person's gross income
20 for the taxable year; or

(b) The expenditures reasonably incurred by such person in such taxable year and all prior taxable years with respect to the development or marketing of the property exceed 25 percent of the aggregate capital expenditures (without any adjustment of amortization) made by such person with respect to the property in all such taxable years.

25 (iii) Expenditures taken into account. For purposes of paragraph (c)(3)(iii)(B)(2)(ii) of this section, expenditures in a taxable year include amounts chargeable to capital account for such year without regard to the year or years (if any) in which any deduction for such expenditure is allowed.

(3) *Passthrough entities.* For purposes of this paragraph (c)(3)(iii)(B), in the case of
30 any intangible property held by a partnership, S corporation, estate, or trust, the determination of whether royalties from such property are derived in the ordinary course of a trade or business shall be made by applying the rules of this paragraph (c)(3)(iii)(B) to such entity and not to any holder of an interest in such entity.

(4) *Cross reference.* For special rules applicable to certain gross income from a trade
35 or business of licensing intangible property, see paragraph (f)(7) of this section.

***

(4) *Items of personal service income specifically excluded--(i) In general.* Passive activity gross income does not include compensation paid to or on behalf of an individual for personal services performed or to be performed by such individual at any time. For
40 purposes of this paragraph (c)(4), compensation for personal services includes only--

(A) Earned income (within the meaning of section 911(d)(2)(A)), including gross income from a payment described in paragraph (e)(2) of this section that represents compensation for the performance of services by a partner;

(B) Amounts includible in gross income under section 83;

45 (C) Amounts includible in gross income under sections 402 and 403;

(D) Amounts (other than amounts described in paragraph (c)(4)(i)(C) of this section) paid pursuant to retirement, pension, and other arrangements for deferred compensation for services;

(E) Social security benefits (within the meaning of section 86(d)) includible in gross
50 income under section 86; and

(F) Other income identified by the Commissioner as income derived by the taxpayer

Sec. 469. Passive activity losses and credits limited

from personal services;
provided, however, that no portion of a partner's distributive share of partnership income (within the meaning of section 704(b)) or a shareholder's pro rata share of income from an S corporation (within the meaning of section 1377(a)) shall be treated as compensation for personal services. 5

(ii) *Example*. The following example illustrates the application of this paragraph (c)(4):

Example. C owns 50 percent of the stock of X, an S corporation. X owns rental real estate, which it manages. X pays C a salary for services performed by C on behalf of X in connection with the management of X's rental properties. Under this paragraph (c)(4), although C's pro rata share of X's gross rental income is passive activity gross income 10 (even if the salary paid to C is less than the fair market value of C's services), the salary paid to C does not constitute passive activity gross income.

***

(d) P*assive activity deductions*--(1) *In general*. Except as otherwise provided in section 469 and the regulations thereunder, a deduction is a passive activity deduction for 15 a taxable year if and only if such deduction--

(i) Arises (within the meaning of paragraph (d)(8) of this section) in connection with the conduct of an activity that is a passive activity for the taxable year;

***

(2) *Exceptions*. Passive activity deductions do not include-- 20

(i) A deduction for an item of expense (other than interest) that is clearly and directly allocable (within the meaning of paragraph (d)(4) of this section) to portfolio income (within the meaning of paragraph (c)(3)(i) of this section);

***

(iii) Interest expense (other than interest expense described in paragraph (d)(3) of this 25 section);

(iv) A deduction for a loss from the disposition of property of a type that produces portfolio income (within the meaning of paragraph (c)(3)(i) of this section);

(v) A deduction that, under section 469(g) and § 1.469-6T (relating to the allowance of passive activity losses upon certain dispositions of interests in passive activities), is 30 treated as a deduction that is not a passive activity deduction;

(vi) A deduction for any state, local, or foreign income, war profits, or excess profits tax;

(vii) A miscellaneous itemized deduction (within the meaning of section 67(b)) that is subject to disallowance in whole or in part under section 67(a) (without regard to whether 35 any amount of such deduction is disallowed under section 67);

(viii) A deduction allowed under section 170 for a charitable contribution;

***

(3) *Interest expense*. Except as otherwise provided in the regulations under section 469, interest expense is taken into account as a passive activity deduction if and only if 40 such interest expense--

(i) Is allocated under § 1.163-8T to a passive activity expenditure (within the meaning of § 1.163-8T(b)(4)); and

(ii) Is not--

(A) Qualified residence interest (within the meaning of § 1.163-10T); or 45

(B) Capitalized pursuant to a capitalization provision (within the meaning of § 1.163-8T(m)(7)(i)).

(4) *Clearly and directly allocable expenses*. For purposes of section 469 and the regulations thereunder, an expense (other than interest expense) is clearly and directly allocable to portfolio income (within the meaning of paragraph (c)(3)(i) of this section) if 50

and only if such expense is incurred as a result of, or incident to, an activity in which such gross income is derived or in connection with property from which such gross income is derived. For example, general and administrative expenses and compensation paid to officers attributable to the performance of services that do not directly benefit or are not
5 incurred by reason of a particular activity or particular property are not clearly and directly allocable to portfolio income (within the meaning of paragraph (c)(3)(i) of this section).

(5) *Treatment of loss from disposition--*(i) *In general.* Except as otherwise provided in the regulations under section 469--

(A) Any loss recognized in any year upon the sale, exchange, or other disposition (a
10 ``disposition'') of an interest in property used in an activity at the time of the disposition or of an interest in an activity held through a partnership or S corporation and any deduction allowed on account of the abandonment or worthlessness of such an interest is treated as a deduction from such activity; and

(B) Any such deduction is a passive activity deduction if and only if the activity is a
15 passive activity of the taxpayer for the taxable year of the disposition (or other event giving rise to the deduction).

(ii) *Disposition of property used in more than one activity in 12-month period preceding disposition.* In the case of a disposition of an interest in property that is used in more than one activity during the 12-month period ending on the date of the disposition,
20 the amount realized from the disposition and the adjusted basis of such interest must be allocated among such activities in the manner described in paragraph (c)(2)(ii) of this section.

(iii) *Other applicable rules--*(A) *Applicability of rules in paragraph (c)(2).* [Reserved]. See § 1.469-2(d)(5)(iii)(A) for rules relating to this paragraph.
25 (B) *Dispositions of partnership interests and S corporation stock.* A partnership interest or S corporation stock is not property used in an activity for purposes of this paragraph (d)(5). See paragraph (e)(3) of this section for rules treating the loss recognized upon the disposition of a partnership interest or S corporation stock as loss from the disposition of interests in the activities in which the partnership or S corporation
30 has an interest.

(6) *Coordination with other limitations on deductions that apply before section 469--*(i) *In general.* An item of deduction from a passive activity that is disallowed for a taxable year under section 704(d), 1366(d), or 465 is not a passive activity deduction for the taxable year. Paragraphs (d)(6) (ii) and (iii) of this section provide rules for determining
35 the extent to which items of deduction from a passive activity are disallowed for a taxable year under sections 704(d), 1366(d), and 465.

***

(iv) *Coordination of basis and at-risk limitations.* The portion of any item of deduction or loss that is disallowed for the taxable year under section 704(d) or 1366(d) is not taken
40 into account for the taxable year in determining the loss from an activity (within the meaning of section 465(c)) for purposes of applying section 465.

***

(f) *Recharacterization of passive income in certain situations--*(1) *In general.* This paragraph (f) sets forth rules that require income from certain passive activities to be
45 treated as income that is not from a passive activity (regardless of whether such income is treated as passive activity gross income under section 469 or any other provision of he regulations thereunder). For definitions of certain terms used in this paragraph (f), see paragraph (f)(9) of this section.

(2) *Special rule for significant participation--*(i) *In general.* An amount of the taxpayer's
50 gross income from each significant participation passive activity for the taxable year

Sec. 469. Passive activity losses and credits limited

equal to a ratable portion of the taxpayer's net passive income from such activity for the taxable year shall be treated as not from a passive activity if the taxpayer's passive activity gross income from all significant participation passive activities for the taxable year (determined without regard to paragraphs (f) (2) through (4) of this section) exceeds the taxpayer's passive activity deductions from all such activities for such year. For 5 purposes of this paragraph (f)(2), the ratable portion of the net passive income from an activity is determined by multiplying the amount of such income by the fraction obtained by dividing--
  (A) The amount of the excess described in the preceding sentence; by
  (B) The amount of the excess described in the preceding sentence taking into account 10 only significant participation passive activities from which the taxpayer has net passive income for the taxable year.
  (ii) *Significant participation passive activity*. For purposes of this paragraph (f)(2), the term ``significant participation passive activity'' means any trade or business activity (within the meaning of § 1.469-1T(e)(2)) in which the taxpayer significantly participates 15 (within the meaning of § 1.469-5T(c)(2)) for the taxable year but in which the taxpayer does not materially participate (within the meaning of § 1.469-5T) for such year.

***

  (3) *Rental of nondepreciable property*. If less than 30 percent of the unadjusted basis of the property used or held for use by customers in a rental activity (within the meaning 20 of § 1.469-1T(e)(3)) during the taxable year is subject to the allowance for depreciation under section 167, an amount of the taxpayer's gross income from the activity equal to the taxpayer's net passive income from the activity shall be treated as not from a passive activity. For purposes of this paragraph (f)(3), the term ``unadjusted basis'' means adjusted basis determined without regard to any adjustment described in section 1016 25 that decreases basis.

***

Reg. § 1.469-4 Definition of activity.
  (a) *Scope and purpose*. This section sets forth the rules for grouping a taxpayer's trade or business activities and rental activities for purposes of applying the passive 30 activity loss and credit limitation rules of section 469. A taxpayer's activities include those conducted through C corporations that are subject to section 469, S corporations, and partnerships.
  (b) *Definitions*. The following definitions apply for purposes of this section--
  (1) *Trade or business activities*. Trade or business activities are activities, other than 35 rental activities or activities that are treated under § 1.469-1T(e)(3)(vi)(B) as incidental to an activity of holding property for investment, that--
  (i) Involve the conduct of a trade or business (within the meaning of section 162);
  (ii) Are conducted in anticipation of the commencement of a trade or business; or
  (iii) Involve research or experimental expenditures that are deductible under section 40 174 (or would be deductible if the taxpayer adopted the method described in section 174(a)).
  (2) *Rental activities*. Rental activities are activities that constitute rental activities within the meaning of § 1.469-1T(e)(3).
  (c) *General rules for grouping activities*--(1) *Appropriate economic unit*. One or more 45 trade or business activities or rental activities may be treated as a single activity if the activities constitute an appropriate economic unit for the measurement of gain or loss for purposes of section 469.
  (2) *Facts and circumstances test*. Except as otherwise provided in this section, whether activities constitute an appropriate economic unit and, therefore, may be treated 50

Sec. 469. Passive activity losses and credits limited

as a single activity depends upon all the relevant facts and circumstances. A taxpayer may use any reasonable method of applying the relevant facts and circumstances in grouping activities. The factors listed below, not all of which are necessary for a taxpayer to treat more than one activity as a single activity, are given the greatest weight in determining whether activities constitute an appropriate economic unit for the measurement of gain or loss for purposes of section 469--

(i) Similarities and differences in types of trades or businesses;

(ii) The extent of common control;

(iii) The extent of common ownership;

(iv) Geographical location; and

(v) Interdependencies between or among the activities (for example, the extent to which the activities purchase or sell goods between or among themselves, involve products or services that are normally provided together, have the same customers, have the same employees, or are accounted for with a single set of books and records).

***

(d) *Limitation on grouping certain activities.* The grouping of activities under this section is subject to the following limitations:

(1) *Grouping rental activities with other trade or business activities*--(i) *Rule.* A rental activity may not be grouped with a trade or business activity unless the activities being grouped together constitute an appropriate economic unit under paragraph (c) of this section and--

(A) The rental activity is insubstantial in relation to the trade or business activity;

(B) The trade or business activity is insubstantial in relation to the rental activity; or

(C) Each owner of the trade or business activity has the same proportionate ownership interest in the rental activity, in which case the portion of the rental activity that involves the rental of items of property for use in the trade or business activity may be grouped with the trade or business activity.

***

(2) *Grouping real property rentals and personal property rentals prohibited.* An activity involving the rental of real property and an activity involving the rental of personal property (other than personal property provided in connection with the real property or real property provided in connection with the personal property) may not be treated as a single activity.

***

Reg. § 1.469-5T   Material participation (temporary).

(a) *In general.* Except as provided in paragraphs (e) and (h)(2) of this section, an individual shall be treated, for purposes of section 469 and the regulations thereunder, as materially participating in an activity for the taxable year if and only if--

(1) The individual participates in the activity for more than 500 hours during such year;

(2) The individual's participation in the activity for the taxable year constitutes substantially all of the participation in such activity of all individuals (including individuals who are not owners of interests in the activity) for such year;

(3) The individual participates in the activity for more than 100 hours during the taxable year, and such individual's participation in the activity for the taxable year is not less than the participation in the activity of any other individual (including individuals who are not owners of interests in the activity) for such year;

(4) The activity is a significant participation activity (within the meaning of paragraph (c) of this section) for the taxable year, and the individual's aggregate participation in all significant participation activities during such year exceeds 500 hours;

(5) The individual materially participated in the activity (determined without regard to

this paragraph (a)(5)) for any five taxable years (whether or not consecutive) during the ten taxable years that immediately precede the taxable year;

(6) The activity is a personal service activity (within the meaning of paragraph (d) of this section), and the individual materially participated in the activity for any three taxable years (whether or not consecutive) preceding the taxable year; or

(7) Based on all of the facts and circumstances (taking into account the rules in paragraph (b) of this section), the individual participates in the activity on a regular, continuous, and substantial basis during such year.

(b) *Facts and circumstances--*(1) *In general.* [Reserved]

(2) *Certain participation insufficient to constitute material participation under this paragraph (b)--*(i) *Participation satisfying standards not contained in section 469.* Except as provided in section 469(h)(3) and paragraph (h)(2) of this section (relating to certain retired individuals and surviving spouses in the case of farming activities), the fact that an individual satisfies the requirements of any participation standard (whether or not referred to as ``material participation") under any provision (including sections 1402 and 2032A and the regulations thereunder) other than section 469 and the regulations thereunder shall not be taken into account in determining whether such individual materially participates in any activity for any taxable year for purposes of section 469 and the regulations thereunder.

(ii) *Certain management activities.* An individual's services performed in the management of an activity shall not be taken into account in determining whether such individual is treated as materially participating in such activity for the taxable year under paragraph (a)(7) of this section unless, for such taxable year--

(A) No person (other than such individual) who performs services in connection with the management of the activity receives compensation described in section 911(d)(2)(A) in consideration for such services; and

(B) No individual performs services in connection with the management of the activity that exceed (by hours) the amount of such services performed by such individual.

(iii) *Participation less than 100 hours.* If an individual participates in an activity for 100 hours or less during the taxable year, such individual shall not be treated as materially participating in such activity for the taxable year under paragraph (a)(7) of this section.

(c) *Significant participation activity--*(1) *In general.* For purposes of paragraph (a)(4) of this section, an activity is a significant participation activity of an individual if and only if such activity--

(i) Is a trade or business activity (within the meaning of § 1.469-1T(e)(2)) in which the individual significantly participates for the taxable year; and

(ii) Would be an activity in which the individual does not materially participate for the taxable year if material participation for such year were determined without regard to paragraph (a)(4) of this section.

(2) *Significant participation.* An individual is treated as significantly participating in an activity for a taxable year if and only if the individual participates in the activity for more than 100 hours during such year.

(d) *Personal service activity.* An activity constitutes a personal service activity for purposes of paragraph (a)(6) of this section if such activity involves the performance of personal services in--

(1) The fields of health, law, engineering, architecture, accounting, actuarial science, performing arts, or consulting; or

(2) Any other trade or business in which capital is not a material income-producing factor.

(e) *Treatment of limited partners--*(1) *General rule.* Except as otherwise provided in this paragraph (e), an individual shall not be treated as materially participating in any activity of a limited partnership for purposes of applying section 469 and the regulations thereunder to--

(i) The individual's share of any income, gain, loss, deduction, or credit from such activity that is attributable to a limited partnership interest in the partnership; and

5 (ii) Any gain or loss from such activity recognized upon a sale or exchange of such an interest.

(2) *Exceptions.* Paragraph (e)(1) of this section shall not apply to an individual's share of income, gain, loss, deduction, and credit for a taxable year from any activity in which the individual would be treated as materially participating for the taxable year under 10 paragraph (a)(1), (5), or (6) of this section if the individual were not a limited partner for such taxable year.

***

(f) *Participation*--(1) [Reserved].

(2) *Exceptions*--(i) *Certain work not customarily done by owners.* Work done in 15 connection with an activity shall not be treated as participation in the activity for purposes of this section if--

(A) Such work is not of a type that is customarily done by an owner of such an activity; and

(B) One of the principal purposes for the performance of such work is to avoid the 20 disallowance, under section 469 and the regulations thereunder, of any loss or credit from such activity.

(ii) *Participation as an investor*--(A) *In general.* Work done by an individual in the individual's capacity as an investor in an activity shall not be treated as participation in the activity for purposes of this section unless the individual is directly involved in the day-to- 25 day management or operations of the activity.

(B) *Work done in individual's capacity as an investor.* For purposes of this paragraph (f)(2)(ii), work done by an individual in the individual's capacity as an investor in an activity includes--

(1) Studying and reviewing financial statements or reports on operations of the 30 activity;

(2) Preparing or compiling summaries or analyses of the finances or operations of the activity for the individual's own use; and

(3) Monitoring the finances or operations of the activity in a non-managerial capacity.

(3) *Participation of spouse.* In the case of any person who is a married individual 35 (within the meaning of section 7703) for the taxable year, any participation by such person's spouse in the activity during the taxable year (without regard to whether the spouse owns an interest in the activity and without regard to whether the spouses file a joint return for the taxable year) shall be treated, for purposes of applying section 469 and the regulations thereunder to such person, as participation by such person in the activity 40 during the taxable year.

(4) *Methods of proof.* The extent of an individual's participation in an activity may be established by any reasonable means. Contemporaneous daily time reports, logs, or similar documents are not required if the extent of such participation may be established by other reasonable means. Reasonable means for purposes of this paragraph may 45 include but are not limited to the identification of services performed over a period of time and the approximate number of hours spent performing such services during such period, based on appointment books, calendars, or narrative summaries.

***

[T.D. 8175, 53 FR 5725, Feb. 25, 1988; 53 FR 15494, Apr. 29, 1988; T.D. 8253, 54 FR 50 20565, May 12, 1989; T.D. 8290, 55 FR 6981, Feb. 28, 1990; T.D. 8318, 55 FR 48108,

Sec. 469. Passive activity losses and credits limited

Nov. 19, 1990; 55 FR 51688, Dec. 17, 1990; T.D. 8319, 55 FR 49038, Nov. 26, 1990; T.D. 8417, 57 FR 20753, May 15, 1992; 58 FR 29536, May 21, 1993; 58 FR 45059, Aug. 26, 1993; 59 FR 17478, Apr. 13, 1994; T.D. 8417, 57 FR 20759, May 15, 1992; 61 FR 14247, Apr. 1, 1996; T.D. 8477, 58 FR 11538, Feb. 26, 1993; T.D. 8495, 58 FR 58788, Nov. 4, 1993; T.D. 8560, 59 FR 41674, Aug. 15, 1994; T.D. 8565, 59 FR 50487, Oct. 4, 1994; T.D. 5 8597, 60 FR 36685, July 18, 1995;T.D. 8645, 60 FR 66499, Dec. 22, 1995; T.D. 8996, 67 FR 35012, May 17, 2002]

Sec. 471. General rule for inventories

(a) **General rule.** -- Whenever in the opinion of the Secretary the use of inventories is necessary in order clearly to determine the income of any taxpayer, inventories shall be taken by such 10 taxpayer on such basis as the Secretary may prescribe as conforming as nearly as may be to the best accounting practice in the trade or business and as most clearly reflecting the income.

(b) **Estimates of inventory shrinkage permitted.** -- A method of determining inventories shall not be treated as failing to clearly reflect income solely because it utilizes estimates of inventory shrinkage that are confirmed by a physical count only after the last day of the taxable year if-- 15

    (1) the taxpayer normally does a physical count of inventories at each location on a regular and consistent basis, and

    (2) the taxpayer makes proper adjustments to such inventories and to its estimating methods to the extent such estimates are greater than or less than the actual shrinkage.

(c) **Cross reference.** -- For rules relating to capitalization of direct and indirect costs of property, 20 see section 263A.

Reg. § 1.471-1 Need for inventories.

In order to reflect taxable income correctly, inventories at the beginning and end of each taxable year are necessary in every case in which the production, purchase, or sale 25 of merchandise is an income-producing factor. The inventory should include all finished or partly finished goods and, in the case of raw materials and supplies, only those which have been acquired for sale or which will physically become a part of merchandise intended for sale, in which class fall containers, such as kegs, bottles, and cases, whether returnable or not, if title thereto will pass to the purchaser of the product to be 30 sold therein. Merchandise should be included in the inventory only if title thereto is vested in the taxpayer. Accordingly, the seller should include in his inventory goods under contract for sale but not yet segregated and applied to the contract and goods out upon consignment, but should exclude from inventory goods sold (including containers), title to which has passed to the purchaser. A purchaser should include in inventory merchandise 35 purchased (including containers), title to which has passed to him, although such merchandise is in transit or for other reasons has not been reduced to physical possession, but should not include goods ordered for future delivery, transfer of title to which has not yet been effected.

***
    40

Reg. § 1.471-2 Valuation of inventories.

(a) Section 471 provides two tests to which each inventory must conform:

(1) It must conform as nearly as may be to the best accounting practice in the trade or business, and

(2) It must clearly reflect the income. 45

(b) It follows, therefore, that inventory rules cannot be uniform but must give effect to trade customs which come within the scope of the best accounting practice in the particular trade or business. In order to clearly reflect income, the inventory practice of a

821

Sec. 471. General rule for inventories

taxpayer should be consistent from year to year, and greater weight is to be given to consistency than to any particular method of inventorying or basis of valuation so long as the method or basis used is in accord with §§ 1.471-1 through 1.471-11.

(c) The bases of valuation most commonly used by business concerns and which
5 meet the requirements of section 471 are (1) cost and (2) cost or market, whichever is lower. (For inventories by dealers in securities, see § 1.471-5.) Any goods in an inventory which are unsalable at normal prices or unusable in the normal way because of damage, imperfections, shop wear, changes of style, odd or broken lots, or other similar causes, including second-hand goods taken in exchange, should be valued at bona fide selling
10 prices less direct cost of disposition, whether subparagraph (1) or (2) of this paragraph is used, or if such goods consist of raw materials or partly finished goods held for use or consumption, they shall be valued upon a reasonable basis, taking into consideration the usability and the condition of the goods, but in no case shall such value be less than the scrap value. Bona fide selling price means actual offering of goods during a period
15 ending not later than 30 days after inventory date. The burden of proof will rest upon the taxpayer to show that such exceptional goods as are valued upon such selling basis come within the classifications indicated above, and he shall maintain such records of the disposition of the goods as will enable a verification of the inventory to be made.

***

20 **Reg. § 1.471-3   Inventories at cost.**

Cost means:

(a) In the case of merchandise on hand at the beginning of the taxable year, the inventory price of such goods.

(b) In the case of merchandise purchased since the beginning of the taxable year, the
25 invoice price less trade or other discounts, except strictly cash discounts approximating a fair interest rate, which may be deducted or not at the option of the taxpayer, provided a consistent course is followed. To this net invoice price should be added transportation or other necessary charges incurred in acquiring possession of the goods. For taxpayers acquiring merchandise for resale that are subject to the provisions of section 263A, see
30 §§ 1.263A-1 and 1.263A-3 for additional amounts that must be included in inventory costs.

(c) In the case of merchandise produced by the taxpayer since the beginning of the taxable year, (1) the cost of raw materials and supplies entering into or consumed in connection with the product, (2) expenditures for direct labor, and (3) indirect production
35 costs incident to and necessary for the production of the particular article, including in such indirect production costs an appropriate portion of management expenses, but not including any cost of selling or return on capital, whether by way of interest or profit. See §§ 1.263A-1 and 1.263A-2 for more specific rules regarding the treatment of production costs.

40 (d) In any industry in which the usual rules for computation of cost of production are inapplicable, costs may be approximated upon such basis as may be reasonable and in conformity with established trade practice in the particular industry. Among such cases are:

(1) Farmers and raisers of livestock (see § 1.471-6);
45 (2) Miners and manufacturers who by a single process or uniform series of processes derive a product of two or more kinds, sizes, or grades, the unit cost of which is substantially alike (see § 1.471-7); and

(3) Retail merchants who use what is known as the ``retail method" in ascertaining approximate cost (see § 1.471-8).

50

Sec. 471. General rule for inventories

Notwithstanding the other rules of this section, cost shall not include an amount which is of a type for which a deduction would be disallowed under section 162(c), (f), or (g) and the regulations thereunder in the case of a business expense.

Reg. § 1.471-4 Inventories at cost or market, whichever is lower.
(a) *In general*--(1) *Market definition.* Under ordinary circumstances and for normal goods in an inventory, market means the aggregate of the current bid prices prevailing at 5 the date of the inventory of the basic elements of cost reflected in inventories of goods purchased and on hand, goods in process of manufacture, and finished manufactured goods on hand. The basic elements of cost include direct materials, direct labor, and indirect costs required to be included in inventories by the taxpayer (e.g., under section 263A and its underlying regulations for taxpayers subject to that section). For taxpayers 10 to which section 263A applies, for example, the basic elements of cost must reflect all direct costs and all indirect costs properly allocable to goods on hand at the inventory date at the current bid price of those costs, including but not limited to the cost of purchasing, handling, and storage activities conducted by the taxpayer, both prior to and subsequent to acquisition or production of the goods. The determination of the current bid 15 price of the basic elements of costs reflected in goods on hand at the inventory date must be based on the usual volume of particular cost elements purchased (or incurred) by the taxpayer.

*** 5

(b) *Inactive markets.* Where no open market exists or where quotations are nominal, due to inactive market conditions, the taxpayer must use such evidence of a fair market price at the date or dates nearest the inventory as may be available, such as specific purchases or sales by the taxpayer or others in reasonable volume and made in good faith, or compensation paid for cancellation of contracts for purchase commitments. 10 Where the taxpayer in the regular course of business has offered for sale such merchandise at prices lower than the current price as above defined, the inventory may be valued at such prices less direct cost of disposition, and the correctness of such prices will be determined by reference to the actual sales of the taxpayer for a reasonable period before and after the date of the inventory. Prices which vary materially from the 15 actual prices so ascertained will not be accepted as reflecting the market.
(c) *Comparison of cost and market.* Where the inventory is valued upon the basis of cost or market, whichever is lower, the market value of each article on hand at the inventory date shall be compared with the cost of the article, and the lower of such values shall be taken as the inventory value of the article. 10

***

Reg. § 1.471-5 Inventories by dealers in securities.
A dealer in securities who in his books of account regularly inventories unsold 10 securities on hand either--
(a) At cost,
(b) At cost or market, whichever is lower, or
(c) At market value, may make his return upon the basis upon which his accounts are kept, provided that a description of the method employed is included in or attached to the return, that all the securities are inventoried by the same method, and that such method 15 is adhered to in subsequent years, unless another method is authorized by the Commissioner pursuant to a written application therefor filed as provided in paragraph (e) of § 1.446-1. A dealer in securities in whose books of account separate computations of the gain or loss from the sale of the various lots of securities sold are made on the basis of the cost of each lot shall be regarded, for the purposes of this section, as regularly 20

823

Sec. 471.   General rule for inventories

inventorying his securities at cost. For the purposes of this section, a dealer in securities is a merchant of securities, whether an individual, partnership, or corporation, with an established place of business, regularly engaged in the purchase of securities and their resale to customers; that is, one who as a merchant buys securities and sells them to
5 customers with a view to the gains and profits that may be derived therefrom. If such business is simply a branch of the activities carried on by such person, the securities inventoried as provided in this section may include only those held for purposes of resale and not for investment. Taxpayers who buy and sell or hold securities for investment or speculation, irrespective of whether such buying or selling constitutes the carrying on of a
10 trade or business, and officers of corporations and members of partnerships who in their individual capacities buy and sell securities, are not dealers in securities within the meaning of this section. See §§ 1.263A-1 and 1.263A-3 for rules regarding the treatment of costs with respect to property acquired for resale.

Reg. § 1.471-6   Inventories of livestock raisers and other farmers.

(a) A farmer may make his return upon an inventory method instead of the cash
5 receipts and disbursements method. It is optional with the taxpayer which of these methods of accounting is used but, having elected one method, the option so exercised will be binding upon the taxpayer for the year for which the option is exercised and for subsequent years unless another method is authorized by the Commissioner as provided in paragraph (e) of § 1.446-1.
5   (b) In any change of accounting method from the cash receipts and disbursements method to an inventory method, adjustments shall be made as provided in section 481 (relating to adjustments required by change in method of accounting) and the regulations thereunder.

(c) Because of the difficulty of ascertaining actual cost of livestock and other farm products, farmers who render their returns upon an inventory method may value their inventories according to the "farm-price method", and farmers raising livestock may value their inventories of animals according to either the "farm-price method" or the "unit-
10 livestock-price method". In addition, these inventory methods may be used to account for the costs of property produced in a farming business that are required to be capitalized under section 263A regardless of whether the property being produced is otherwise treated as inventory by the taxpayer, and regardless of whether the taxpayer is otherwise using the cash or an accrual method of accounting.

(d) The "farm-price method" provides for the valuation of inventories at market price less direct cost of disposition. If this method of valuation is used, it generally must be applied to all property produced by the taxpayer in the trade or business of farming,
10 except as to livestock accounted for, at the taxpayer's election, under the unit livestock method of accounting. However, see § 1.263A-4(c)(3) for an exception to this rule. If the use of the "farm-price method" of valuing inventories for any taxable year involves a change in method of valuing inventories from that employed in prior years, permission for such change shall first be secured from the Commissioner as provided in paragraph (e)
15 of § 1.446-1.

(e) The "unit-livestock-price method" provides for the valuation of the different classes of animals in the inventory at a standard unit price for each animal within a class. A
10 livestock raiser electing this method of valuing his animals must adopt a reasonable classification of the animals in his inventory with respect to the age and kind included so that the unit prices assigned to the several classes will reasonably account for the normal costs incurred in producing the animals within such classes. Thus, if a cattle raiser determines that it costs approximately $15 to produce a calf, and $7.50 each year to
15 raise the calf to maturity, his classifications and unit prices would be as follows: Calves,

Sec. 471.   General rule for inventories

$15; yearlings, $22.50; 2-year olds, $30; mature animals, $37.50. The classification selected by the livestock raiser, and the unit prices assigned to the several classes, are subject to approval by the district director upon examination of the taxpayer's return.

(f) A taxpayer that elects to use the "unit-livestock-price method" must apply it to all livestock raised, whether for sale or for draft, breeding, or dairy purposes. The inventoriable costs of animals raised for draft, breeding, or dairy purposes can, at the election of the livestock raiser, be included in inventory or treated as property used in a 5 trade or business subject to depreciation after maturity. See § 1.263A-4 for rules regarding the computation of inventoriable costs for purposes of the unit-livestock-price method. Once established, the methods of accounting used by the taxpayer to determine unit prices and to classify animals must be consistently applied in all subsequent taxable years. A taxpayer that uses the unit-livestock-price method must annually reevaluate its 10 unit prices and adjust the prices either upward to reflect increases, or downward to reflect decreases, in the costs of raising livestock. The consent of the Commissioner is not required to make such upward or downward adjustments. No other changes in the classification of animals or unit prices may be made without the consent of the Commissioner. See § 1.446-1(e) for procedures for obtaining the consent of the 15 Commissioner.

***

(g) A livestock raiser who uses the "unit-livestock-price method" must include in his inventory at cost any livestock purchased, except that animals purchased for draft, 5 breeding, or dairy purposes can, at the election of the livestock raiser, be included in inventory or be treated as property used in a trade or business subject to depreciation after maturity. If the animals purchased are not mature at the time of purchase, the cost should be increased at the end of each taxable year in accordance with the established unit prices, except that no increase is to be made in the taxable year of purchase if the 10 animal is acquired during the last six months of that year. If the records maintained permit identification of a purchased animal, the cost of such animal will be eliminated from the closing inventory in the event of its sale or loss. Otherwise, the first-in, first-out method of valuing inventories must be applied.

(h) If a taxpayer using the "farm-price method" desires to adopt the ``unit-livestock- 5 price method" in valuing his inventories of livestock, permission for the change shall first be secured from the Commissioner as provided in paragraph (e) of § 1.446-1. However, a taxpayer who has filed returns on the basis of inventories at cost, or cost or market whichever is lower, may adopt the "unit-livestock-price method" for valuing his inventories of livestock without formal application for permission, but the classifications and unit 10 prices selected are subject to approval by the district director upon examination of the taxpayer's return. A livestock raiser who has adopted a constant unit-price method of valuing livestock inventories and filed returns on that basis will be considered as having elected the"`unit-livestock-price method".

(i) If returns have been made in which the taxable income has been computed upon incomplete inventories, the abnormality should be corrected by submitting with the return for the current taxable year a statement for the preceding taxable year. In this statement such adjustments shall be made as are necessary to bring the closing inventory for the preceding taxable year into agreement with the opening complete inventory for the 10 current taxable year. If necessary clearly to reflect income, similar adjustments may be made as at the beginning of the preceding year or years, and the tax, if any be due, shall be assessed and paid at the rate of tax in effect for such year or years.

Reg. § 1.471-11   Inventories of manufacturers.

(a) *Use of full absorption method of inventory costing.* In order to conform as nearly as

825

Sec. 471.   General rule for inventories

may be possible to the best accounting practices and to clearly reflect income (as required by section 471 of the Code), both direct and indirect production costs must be taken into account in the computation of inventoriable costs in accordance with the ``full absorption" method of inventory costing. Under the full absorption method of inventory
5   costing production costs must be allocated to goods produced during the taxable year, whether sold during the taxable year or in inventory at the close of the taxable year determined in accordance with the taxpayer's method of identifying goods in inventory. Thus, the taxpayer must include as inventoriable costs all direct production costs and, to the extent provided by paragraphs (c) and (d) of this section, all indirect production costs.
10   For purposes of this section, the term ``financial reports" means financial reports (including consolidated financial statements) to shareholders, partners, beneficiaries or other proprietors and for credit purposes. See also § 1.263A-1T with respect to the treatment of production costs incurred in taxable years beginning after December 31, 1986, and before January 1, 1994. See also §§ 1.263A-1 and 1.263A-2 with respect to
15   the treatment of production costs incurred in taxable years beginning after December 31, 1993.

(b) *Production costs--(1) In general.* Costs are considered to be production costs to the extent that they are incident to and necessary for production or manufacturing operations or processes. Production costs include direct production costs and fixed and
5   variable indirect production costs.

(2) *Direct production costs.* (i) Costs classified as ``direct production costs" are generally those costs which are incident to and necessary for production or
5   manufacturing operations or processes and are components of the cost of either direct material or direct labor. Direct material costs include the cost of those materials which become an integral part of the specific product and those materials which are consumed in the ordinary course of manufacturing and can be identified or associated with particular units or groups of units of that product. See § 1.471-3 for the elements of direct material
10   costs. Direct labor costs include the cost of labor which can be identified or associated with particular units or groups of units of a specific product. The elements of direct labor costs include such items as basic compensation, overtime pay, vacation and holiday pay, sick leave pay (other than payments pursuant to a wage continuation plan under section 105(d)), shift differential, payroll taxes and payments to a supplemental unemployment
15   benefit plan paid or incurred on behalf of employees engaged in direct labor. For the treatment of rework labor, scrap, spoilage costs, and any other costs not specifically described as direct production costs see § 1.471-11(c)(2).

(ii) Under the full absorption method, a taxpayer must take into account all items of
5   direct production cost in his inventoriable costs. Nevertheless, a taxpayer will not be treated as using an incorrect method of inventory costing if he treats any direct production costs as indirect production costs, provided such costs are allocated to the taxpayer's ending inventory to the extent provided by paragraph (d) of this section. Thus, for example, a taxpayer may treat direct labor costs as part of indirect production costs
10   (for example, by use of the conversion cost method), provided all such costs are allocated to ending inventory to the extent provided by paragraph (d) of this section.

5   (3) *Indirect production costs--(i) In general.* The term ``indirect production costs" includes all costs which are incident to and necessary for production or manufacturing operations or processes other than direct production costs (as defined in subparagraph (2) of this paragraph). Indirect production costs may be classified as to kind or type in accordance with acceptable accounting principles so as to enable convenient
10   identification with various production or manufacturing activities or functions and to facilitate reasonable groupings of such costs for purposes of determining unit product costs.

Sec. 471. General rule for inventories

(ii) *Fixed and variable classifications.* For purposes of this section, fixed indirect production costs are generally those costs which do not vary significantly with changes in the amount of goods produced at any given level of production capacity. These fixed costs may include, among other costs, rent and property taxes on buildings and machinery incident to and necessary for manufacturing operations or processes. On the other hand, variable indirect production costs are generally those costs which do vary significantly with changes in the amount of goods produced at any given level of production capacity. These variable costs may include, among other costs, indirect materials, factory janitorial supplies, and utilities. Where a particular cost contains both fixed and variable elements, these elements should be segregated into fixed and variable classifications to the extent necessary under the taxpayer's method of allocation, such as for the application of the practical capacity concept (as described in paragraph (d)(4) of this section).

(c) *Certain indirect and production costs*--(1) *General rule.* Except as provided in paragraph (c)(3) of this section and in paragraph (d)(6)(v) of § 1.451-3, in order to determine whether indirect production costs referred to in paragraph (b) of this section must be included in a taxpayer's computation of the amount of inventoriable costs, three categories of costs have been provided in subparagraph (2) of this paragraph. Costs described in subparagraph (2)(i) of this paragraph must be included in the taxpayer's computation of the amount of inventoriable costs, regardless of their treatment by the taxpayer in his financial reports. Costs described in subparagraph (2)(ii) of this paragraph need not enter into the taxpayer's computation of the amount of inventoriable costs, regardless of their treatment by the taxpayer in his financial reports. Costs described in subparagraph (2)(iii) of this paragraph must be included in or excluded from the taxpayer's computation of the amount inventoriable costs in accordance with the treatment of such costs by the taxpayer in his financial reports and generally accepted accounting principles. For the treatment of indirect production costs described in subparagraph (2) of this paragraph in the case of a taxpayer who is not using comparable methods of accounting for such costs for tax and financial reporting see paragraph (c)(3) of this section. For contracts entered into after December 31, 1982, notwithstanding this section, taxpayers who use an inventory method of accounting for extended period long-term contracts (as defined in paragraph (b)(3) of § 1.451-3) for tax purposes may be required to use the cost allocation rules provided in paragraph (d)(6) of § 1.451-3 rather than the cost allocation rules provided in this section. See paragraph (d)(6)(v) of § 1.451-3. After a taxpayer has determined which costs must be treated as indirect production costs includible in the computation of the amount of inventoriable costs, such costs must be allocated to a taxpayer's ending inventory in a manner prescribed by paragraph (d) of this section.

(2) *Includibility of certain indirect production costs*--(i) *Indirect production costs included in inventoriable costs.* Indirect production costs which must enter into the computation of the amount of inventoriable costs (regardless of their treatment by a taxpayer in his financial reports) include:

(a) Repair expenses,

(b) Maintenance,

(c) Utilities, such as heat, power and light,

(d) Rent,

(e) Indirect labor and production supervisory wages, including basic compensation, overtime pay, vacation and holiday pay, sick leave pay (other than payments pursuant to a wage continuation plan under section 105(d), shift differential, payroll taxes and contributions to a supplemental unemployment benefit plan,

(f) Indirect materials and supplies,

Sec. 471. General rule for inventories

(g) Tools and equipment not capitalized, and

(h) Costs of quality control and inspection, to the extent, and only to the extent, such costs are incident to and necessary for production or manufacturing operations or processes.

(ii) *Costs not included in inventoriable costs.* Costs which are not required to be included for tax purposes in the computation of the amount of inventoriable costs (regardless of their treatment by a taxpayer in his financial reports) include:

(a) Marketing expenses,

(b) Advertising expenses,

(c) Selling expenses,

(d) Other distribution expenses,

(e) Interest,

(f) Research and experimental expenses including engineering and product development expenses,

(g) Losses under section 165 and the regulations thereunder,

(h) Percentage depletion in excess of cost depletion,

(i) Depreciation and amortization reported for Federal income tax purposes in excess of depreciation reported by the taxpayer in his financial reports,

(j) Income taxes attributable to income received on the sale of inventory,

(k) Pension contributions to the extent that they represent past services cost,

(l) General and administrative expenses incident to and necessary for the taxpayer's activities as a whole rather than to production or manufacturing operations or processes, and

(m) Salaries paid to officers attributable to the performance of services which are incident to and necessary for the taxpayer's activities taken as a whole rather than to production or manufacturing operations or processes.

Notwithstanding the preceding sentence, if a taxpayer consistently includes in his computation of the amount of inventoriable costs any of the costs described in the preceding sentence, a change in such method of inclusion shall be considered a change in method of accounting within the meaning of sections 446, 481, and paragraph (e)(4) of this section.

(iii) *Indirect production costs includible in inventoriable costs depending upon treatment in taxpayer's financial reports.* In the case of costs listed in this subdivision, the inclusion or exclusion of such costs from the amount of inventoriable costs for purposes of a taxpayer's financial reports shall determine whether such costs must be included in or excluded from the computation of inventoriable costs for tax purposes, but only if such treatment is not inconsistent with generally accepted accounting principles. In the case of costs which are not included in subdivision (i) or (ii) of this subparagraph, nor listed in this subdivision, whether such costs must be included in or excluded from the computation of inventoriable costs for tax purposes depends upon the extent to which such costs are similar to costs included in subdivision (i) or (ii), and if such costs are dissimilar to costs in subdivision (i) or (ii), such costs shall be treated as included in or excludable from the amount of inventoriable costs in accordance with this subdivision. The costs listed in this subdivision are:

(a) *Taxes.* Taxes otherwise allowable as a deduction under section 164 (other than State and local and foreign income taxes) attributable to assets incident to and necessary for production or manufacturing operations or processes. Thus, for example, the cost of State and local property taxes imposed on a factory or other production facility and any State and local taxes imposed on inventory must be included in or excluded from the computation of the amount of inventoriable costs for tax purposes depending upon their treatment by a taxpayer in his financial reports.

Sec. 471.   General rule for inventories

(b) *Depreciation and depletion*. Depreciation reported in financial reports and cost depletion on assets incident to and necessary for production or manufacturing operations or processes. In computing cost depletion under this section, the adjusted basis of such assets shall be reduced by cost depletion and not by percentage depletion taken thereon.

(c) Employee benefits. Pension and profit-sharing contributions representing current 5 service costs otherwise allowable as a deduction under section 404, and other employee benefits incurred on behalf of labor incident to and necessary for production or manufacturing operations or processes. These other benefits include workmen's compensation expenses, payments under a wage continuation plan described in section 105(d), amounts of a type which would be includible in the gross income of employees 10 under non-qualified pension, profit-sharing and stock bonus plans, premiums on life and health insurance and miscellaneous benefits provided for employees such as safety, medical treatment, cafeteria, recreational facilities, membership dues, etc., which are otherwise allowable as deductions under chapter 1 of the Code.

(d) *Costs attributable to strikes, rework labor, scrap and spoilage*. Costs attributable to 15 rework labor, scrap and spoilage which are incident to and necessary for production or manufacturing operations or processes and costs attributable to strikes incident to production or manufacturing operation or processes.

(e) *Factory administrative expenses*. Administrative costs of production (but not including any cost of selling or any return on capital) incident to and necessary for 20 production or manufacturing operations or processes.

(f) *Officers' salaries*. Salaries paid to officers attributable to services performed incident to and necessary for production or manufacturing operations or processes.

(g) *Insurance costs*. Insurance costs incident to and necessary for production or manufacturing operations or processes such as insurance on production machinery and 25 equipment. A change in the taxpayer's treatment in his financial reports of costs described in this subdivision which results in a change in treatment of such costs for tax purposes shall constitute a change in method of accounting within the meaning of sections 446 and 481 to which paragraph (e) applies.

***

30

[T.D. 6500, 25 FR 11726, Nov. 26, 1960; T.D. 7285, 38 FR 26185, Sept. 19, 1973; T.D. 7345, 40 FR 7439, Feb. 20, 1975;T.D. 8067, 51 FR 393, Jan. 6, 1986; T.D. 8131, 52 FR 10084, Mar. 30, 1987; T.D. 8482, 58 FR 42234, Aug. 9, 1993; T.D. 8729, 62 FR 44551, Aug. 22, 1997; T.D. 8897, 65 FR 50650, Aug. 21, 2000; T.D. 9019, 67 FR 65698, Oct. 28, 2002]

35

Sec. 472.   Last-in, first-out inventories

(a) **Authorization.** -- A taxpayer may use the method provided in subsection (b) (whether or not such method has been prescribed under section 471) in inventorying goods specified in an application to use such method filed at such time and in such manner as the Secretary may prescribe. The change to, and the use of, such method shall be in accordance with such regulations 40 as the Secretary may prescribe as necessary in order that the use of such method may clearly reflect income.

(b) **Method applicable.** -- In inventorying goods specified in the application described in subsection (a), the taxpayer shall:

(1) Treat those remaining on hand at the close of the taxable year as being: First, those 45 included in the opening inventory of the taxable year (in the order of acquisition) to the extent thereof; and second, those acquired in the taxable year;

(2) Inventory them at cost; and

Sec. 472.   Last-in, first-out inventories

(3) Treat those included in the opening inventory of the taxable year in which such method is first used as having been acquired at the same time and determine their cost by the average cost method.

(c) Condition. -- Subsection (a) shall apply only if the taxpayer establishes to the satisfaction of
5 the Secretary that the taxpayer has used no procedure other than that specified in paragraphs (1) and (3) of subsection (b) in inventorying such goods to ascertain the income, profit, or loss of the first taxable year for which the method described in subsection (b) is to be used, for the purpose of a report or statement covering such taxable year--

   (1) to shareholders, partners, or other proprietors, or to beneficiaries, or

10   **(2)** for credit purposes.

***

(e) Subsequent inventories. -- If a taxpayer, having complied with subsection (a), uses the method described in subsection (b) for any taxable year, then such method shall be used in all subsequent taxable years unless -

15   **(1)** with the approval of the Secretary a change to a different method is authorized; or,

   (2) the Secretary determines that the taxpayer has used for any such subsequent taxable year some procedure other than that specified in paragraph (1) of subsection (b) in inventorying the goods specified in the application to ascertain the income, profit, or loss of such subsequent taxable year for the purpose of a report or statement covering such taxable year (A) to
20   shareholders, partners, or other proprietors, or beneficiaries, or (B) for credit purposes; and requires a change to a method different from that prescribed in subsection (b) beginning with such subsequent taxable year or any taxable year thereafter.

If paragraph (1) or (2) of this subsection applies, the change to, and the use of, the different method shall be in accordance with such regulations as the Secretary may prescribe as necessary
25 in order that the use of such method may clearly reflect income.

Sec. 482.   Allocation of income and deductions among taxpayers

In any case of two or more organizations, trades, or businesses (whether or not incorporated, whether or not organized in the United States, and whether or not affiliated) owned or controlled
30 directly or indirectly by the same interests, the Secretary may distribute, apportion, or allocate gross income, deductions, credits, or allowances between or among such organizations, trades, or businesses, if he determines that such distribution, apportionment, or allocation is necessary in order to prevent evasion of taxes or clearly to reflect the income of any of such organizations, trades, or businesses. In the case of any transfer (or license) of intangible property (within the
35 meaning of section 936(h)(3)(B)), the income with respect to such transfer or license shall be commensurate with the income attributable to the intangible.

Sec. 483.   Interest on certain deferred payments

(a) Amount constituting interest. -- For purposes of this title, in the case of any payment -

40   **(1)** under any contract for the sale or exchange of any property, and

   (2) to which this section applies,

there shall be treated as interest that portion of the total unstated interest under such contract which, as determined in a manner consistent with the method of computing interest under section 1272(a), is properly allocable to such payment.

Sec. 483. Interest on certain deferred payments

(b) Total unstated interest. -- For purposes of this section, the term "total unstated interest" means, with respect to a contract for the sale or exchange of property, an amount equal to the excess of--

    (1) the sum of the payments to which this section applies which are due under the contract, over   5

    (2) the sum of the present values of such payments and the present values of any interest payments due under the contract.

For purposes of the preceding sentence, the present value of a payment shall be determined under the rules of section 1274(b)(2) using a discount rate equal to the applicable Federal rate determined under section 1274(d).   10

(c) Payments to which subsection (a) applies. --

    (1) In general. -- Except as provided in subsection (d), this section shall apply to any payment on account of the sale or exchange of property which constitutes part or all of the sales price and which is due more than 6 months after the date of such sale or exchange under a contract -   15

        (A) under which some or all of the payments are due more than 1 year after the date of such sale or exchange, and

        (B) under which there is total unstated interest.

    (2) Treatment of other debt instruments. -- For purposes of this section, a debt instrument of the purchaser which is given in consideration for the sale or exchange of property shall not 20 be treated as a payment, and any payment due under such debt instrument shall be treated as due under the contract for the sale or exchange.

    (3) Debt instrument defined. -- For purposes of this subsection, the term "debt instrument" has the meaning given such term by section 1275(a)(1).

(d) Exceptions and limitations. --   25

    (1) Coordination with original issue discount rules. -- This section shall not apply to any debt instrument for which an issue price is determined under section 1273(b) (other than paragraph (4) thereof) or section 1274.

    (2) Sales prices of $3,000 or less. -- This section shall not apply to any payment on account of the sale or exchange of property if it can be determined at the time of such sale or exchange 30 that the sales price cannot exceed $3,000.

    (3) Carrying charges. -- In the case of the purchaser, the tax treatment of amounts paid on account of the sale or exchange of property shall be made without regard to this section if any such amounts are treated under section 163(b) as if they included interest.

    (4) Certain sales of patents. -- In the case of any transfer described in section 1235(a) 35 (relating to sale or exchange of patents), this section shall not apply to any amount contingent on the productivity, use, or disposition of the property transferred.

(e) Maximum rate of interest on certain transfers of land between related parties. --

    (1) In general. -- In the case of any qualified sale, the discount rate used in determining the total unstated interest rate under subsection (b) shall not exceed 6 percent, compounded 40 semiannually.

    (2) Qualified sale. -- For purposes of this subsection, the term "qualified sale" means any sale or exchange of land by an individual to a member of such individual's family (within the meaning of section 267(c)(4)).

    (3) $500,000 limitation. -- Paragraph (1) shall not apply to any qualified sale between 45 individuals made during any calendar year to the extent that the sales price for such sale (when

Sec. 483. Interest on certain deferred payments

added to the aggregate sales price for prior qualified sales between such individuals during the calendar year) exceeds $500,000.

***

    (f) Regulations. -- The Secretary shall prescribe such regulations as may be necessary or
5 appropriate to carry out the purposes of this section including regulations providing for the application of this section in the case of -

    (1) any contract for the sale or exchange of property under which the liability for, or the amount or due date of, a payment cannot be determined at the time of the sale or exchange, or

    (2) any change in the liability for, or the amount or due date of, any payment (including
10 interest) under a contract for the sale or exchange of property.

***

Reg. § 1.483-1   Interest on certain deferred payments.

    (a) *Amount constituting interest in certain deferred payment transactions*--(1) *In general.* Except as provided in paragraph (c) of this section, section 483 applies to a
15 contract for the sale or exchange of property if the contract provides for one or more payments due more than 1 year after the date of the sale or exchange, and the contract does not provide for adequate stated interest. In general, a contract has adequate stated interest if the contract provides for a stated rate of interest that is at least equal to the test rate (determined under § 1.483-3) and the interest is paid or compounded at least
20 annually. Section 483 may apply to a contract whether the contract is express (written or oral) or implied. For purposes of section 483, a sale or exchange is any transaction treated as a sale or exchange for tax purposes. In addition, for purposes of section 483, property includes debt instruments and investment units, but does not include money, services, or the right to use property.
25   ***

    (2) *Treatment of contracts to which section 483 applies*--(i) *Treatment of unstated interest.* If section 483 applies to a contract, unstated interest under the contract is treated as interest for tax purposes. Thus, for example, unstated interest is not treated as part of the amount realized from the sale or exchange of property (in the case of the
30 seller), and is not included in the purchaser's basis in the property acquired in the sale or exchange.

    (ii) *Method of accounting for interest on contracts subject to section 483.* Any stated or unstated interest on a contract subject to section 483 is taken into account by a taxpayer under the taxpayer's regular method of accounting (e.g., an accrual method or the cash
35 receipts and disbursements method). See §§ 1.446-1, 1.451-1, and 1.461-1. For purposes of the preceding sentence, the amount of interest (including unstated interest) allocable to a payment under a contract to which section 483 applies is determined under § 1.446-2(e).

    (b) *Definitions*--(1) *Deferred payments.* For purposes of the regulations under section
40 483, a deferred payment means any payment that constitutes all or a part of the sales price (as defined in paragraph (b)(2) of this section), and that is due more than 6 months after the date of the sale or exchange. Except as provided in section 483(c)(2) (relating to the treatment of a debt instrument of the purchaser), a payment may be made in the form of cash, stock or securities, or other property.
45   (2) *Sales price.* For purposes of section 483, the sales price for any sale or exchange is the sum of the amount due under the contract (other than stated interest) and the amount of any liability included in the amount realized from the sale or exchange. See § 1.1001-2. Thus, the sales price for any sale or exchange includes any amount of unstated interest under the contract.

Sec. 483. Interest on certain deferred payments

(c) *Exceptions to and limitations on the application of section 483--*(1) *In general.* Sections 483(d), 1274(c)(4), and 1275(b) contain exceptions to and limitations on the application of section 483.

(2) *Sales price of $3,000 or less.* Section 483(d)(2) applies only if it can be determined at the time of the sale or exchange that the sales price cannot exceed $3,000, regardless 5 of whether the sales price eventually paid for the property is less than $3,000.

(3) *Other exceptions and limitations--*(i) *Certain transfers subject to section 1041.* Section 483 does not apply to any transfer of property subject to section 1041 (relating to transfers of property between spouses or incident to divorce).

(ii) *Treatment of certain obligees.* Section 483 does not apply to an obligee under a 10 contract for the sale or exchange of personal use property (within the meaning of section 1275(b)(3)) in the hands of the obligor and that evidences a below-market loan described in section 7872(c)(1).

(iii) *Transactions involving certain demand loans.* Section 483 does not apply to any payment under a contract that evidences a demand loan that is a below-market loan 15 described in section 7872(c)(1).

(iv) *Transactions involving certain annuity contracts.* Section 483 does not apply to any payment under an annuity contract described in section 1275(a)(1)(B) (relating to annuity contracts excluded from the definition of debt instrument).

(v) *Options.* Section 483 does not apply to any payment under an option to buy or sell 20 property.

(d) *Assumptions.* If a debt instrument is assumed, or property is taken subject to a debt instrument, in connection with a sale or exchange of property, the debt instrument is treated for purposes of section 483 in a manner consistent with the rules of § 1.1274-5.

(e) *Aggregation rule.* For purposes of section 483, all sales or exchanges that are part 25 of the same transaction (or a series of related transactions) are treated as a single sale or exchange, and all contracts calling for deferred payments arising from the same transaction (or a series of related transactions) are treated as a single contract. This rule, however, generally only applies to contracts and to sales or exchanges involving a single buyer and a single seller. 30

***

[T.D. 8517, 59 FR 4805, Feb. 2, 1994]

Sec. 501. Exemption from tax on corporations, certain trusts, etc.

(a) **Exemption from taxation.** -- An organization described in subsection (c) or (d) or section 401(a) shall be exempt from taxation under this subtitle unless such exemption is denied under 35 section 502 or 503.

(b) **Tax on unrelated business income and certain other activities.** -- An organization exempt from taxation under subsection (a) shall be subject to tax to the extent provided in parts II, III, and VI of this subchapter, but (notwithstanding parts II, III, and VI of this subchapter) shall be considered an organization exempt from income taxes for the purpose of any law which refers to 40 organizations exempt from income taxes.

(c) **List of exempt organizations.** -- The following organizations are referred to in subsection (a):

(1) Any corporation organized under Act of Congress which is an instrumentality of the United States but only if such corporation-- 45

(A) is exempt from Federal income taxes--

(i) under such Act as amended and supplemented before July 18, 1984, or

Sec. 501. Exemption from tax on corporations, certain trusts, etc.

        (ii) under this title without regard to any provision of law which is not contained in this title and which is not contained in a revenue Act, or

        (B) is described in subsection (l).

    (2) Corporations organized for the exclusive purpose of holding title to property, collecting income therefrom, and turning over the entire amount thereof, less expenses, to an organization which itself is exempt under this section. Rules similar to the rules of subparagraph (G) of paragraph (25) shall apply for purposes of this paragraph.

    (3) Corporations, and any community chest, fund, or foundation, organized and operated exclusively for religious, charitable, scientific, testing for public safety, literary, or educational purposes, or to foster national or international amateur sports competition (but only if no part of its activities involve the provision of athletic facilities or equipment), or for the prevention of cruelty to children or animals, no part of the net earnings of which inures to the benefit of any private shareholder or individual, no substantial part of the activities of which is carrying on propaganda, or otherwise attempting, to influence legislation (except as otherwise provided in subsection (h)), and which does not participate in, or intervene in (including the publishing or distributing of statements), any political campaign on behalf of (or in opposition to) any candidate for public office.

    (4)(A) Civic leagues or organizations not organized for profit but operated exclusively for the promotion of social welfare, or local associations of employees, the membership of which is limited to the employees of a designated person or persons in a particular municipality, and the net earnings of which are devoted exclusively to charitable, educational, or recreational purposes.

    (B) Subparagraph (A) shall not apply to an entity unless no part of the net earnings of such entity inures to the benefit of any private shareholder or individual.

    (5) Labor, agricultural, or horticultural organizations.

    (6) Business leagues, chambers of commerce, real-estate boards, boards of trade, or professional football leagues (whether or not administering a pension fund for football players), not organized for profit and no part of the net earnings of which inures to the benefit of any private shareholder or individual.

    (7) Clubs organized for pleasure, recreation, and other nonprofitable purposes, substantially all of the activities of which are for such purposes and no part of the net earnings of which inures to the benefit of any private shareholder.

    (8) Fraternal beneficiary societies, orders, or associations--

    (A) operating under the lodge system or for the exclusive benefit of the members of a fraternity itself operating under the lodge system, and

    (B) providing for the payment of life, sick, accident, or other benefits to the members of such society, order, or association or their dependents.

    (9) Voluntary employees' beneficiary associations providing for the payment of life, sick, accident, or other benefits to the members of such association or their dependents or designated beneficiaries, if no part of the net earnings of such association inures (other than through such payments) to the benefit of any private shareholder or individual.

    (10) Domestic fraternal societies, orders, or associations, operating under the lodge system--

    (A) the net earnings of which are devoted exclusively to religious, charitable, scientific, literary, educational, and fraternal purposes, and

    (B) which do not provide for the payment of life, sick, accident, or other benefits.

    (11) Teachers' retirement fund associations of a purely local character, if--

    (A) no part of their net earnings inures (other than through payment of retirement

Sec. 501. Exemption from tax on corporations, certain trusts, etc.

benefits) to the benefit of any private shareholder or individual, and

(B) the income consists solely of amounts received from public taxation, amounts received from assessments on the teaching salaries of members, and income in respect of investments.

(12)(A) Benevolent life insurance associations of a purely local character, mutual ditch or irrigation companies, mutual or cooperative telephone companies,

***

(13) Cemetery companies owned and operated exclusively for the benefit of their members or which are not operated for profit; and any corporation chartered solely for the purpose of the disposal of bodies by burial or cremation which is not permitted by its charter to engage in any business not necessarily incident to that purpose and no part of the net earnings of which inures to the benefit of any private shareholder or individual.

(14)(A) Credit unions without capital stock organized and operated for mutual purposes and without profit.

(B) Corporations or associations without capital stock organized before September 1, 1957, and operated for mutual purposes and without profit for the purpose of providing reserve funds for, and insurance of shares or deposits in--

(i) domestic building and loan associations,

(ii) cooperative banks without capital stock organized and operated for mutual purposes and without profit,

(iii) mutual savings banks not having capital stock represented by shares, or

(iv) mutual savings banks described in section 591(b).

***

(15)(A) Insurance companies (as defined in section 816(a)) other than life (including interinsurers and reciprocal underwriters) if--

(i)(I) the gross receipts for the taxable year do not exceed $600,000, and

(II) more than 50 percent of such gross receipts consist of premiums, or

(ii) in the case of a mutual insurance company--

(I) the gross receipts of which for the taxable year do not exceed $150,000, and

(II) more than 35 percent of such gross receipts consist of premiums.

Clause (ii) shall not apply to a company if any employee of the company, or a member of the employee's family (as defined in section 2032A(e)(2)), is an employee of another company exempt from taxation by reason of this paragraph (or would be so exempt but for this sentence).

(B) For purposes of subparagraph (A), in determining whether any company or association is described in subparagraph (A), such company or association shall be treated as receiving during the taxable year amounts described in subparagraph (A) which are received during such year by all other companies or associations which are members of the same controlled group as the insurance company or association for which the determination is being made.

(C) For purposes of subparagraph (B), the term "controlled group" has the meaning given such term by section 831(b)(2)(B)(ii), except that in applying section 831(b)(2)(B)(ii) for purposes of this subparagraph, subparagraphs (B) and (C) of section 1563(b)(2) shall be disregarded.

(16) Corporations organized by an association subject to part IV of this subchapter or members thereof, for the purpose of financing the ordinary crop operations of such members or other producers, and operated in conjunction with such association.

Sec. 501. Exemption from tax on corporations, certain trusts, etc.

***

(17)(A) A trust or trusts forming part of a plan providing for the payment of supplemental unemployment compensation benefits, if--

(i) under the plan, it is impossible, at any time prior to the satisfaction of all liabilities, with respect to employees under the plan, for any part of the corpus or income to be (within the taxable year or thereafter) used for, or diverted to, any purpose other than the providing of supplemental unemployment compensation benefits,

(ii) such benefits are payable to employees under a classification which is set forth in the plan and which is found by the Secretary not to be discriminatory in favor of employees who are highly compensated employees (within the meaning of section 414(q)), and

(iii) such benefits do not discriminate in favor of employees who are highly compensated employees (within the meaning of section 414(q)). A plan shall not be considered discriminatory within the meaning of this clause merely because the benefits received under the plan bear a uniform relationship to the total compensation, or the basic or regular rate of compensation, of the employees covered by the plan.

(B) In determining whether a plan meets the requirements of subparagraph (A), any benefits provided under any other plan shall not be taken into consideration, except that a plan shall not be considered discriminatory -

(i) merely because the benefits under the plan which are first determined in a nondiscriminatory manner within the meaning of subparagraph (A) are then reduced by any sick, accident, or unemployment compensation benefits received under State or Federal law (or reduced by a portion of such benefits if determined in a nondiscriminatory manner), or

(ii) merely because the plan provides only for employees who are not eligible to receive sick, accident, or unemployment compensation benefits under State or Federal law the same benefits (or a portion of such benefits if determined in a nondiscriminatory manner) which such employees would receive under such laws if such employees were eligible for such benefits, or

(iii) merely because the plan provides only for employees who are not eligible under another plan (which meets the requirements of subparagraph (A)) of supplemental unemployment compensation benefits provided wholly by the employer the same benefits (or a portion of such benefits if determined in a nondiscriminatory manner) which such employees would receive under such other plan if such employees were eligible under such other plan, but only if the employees eligible under both plans would make a classification which would be nondiscriminatory within the meaning of subparagraph (A).

(C) A plan shall be considered to meet the requirements of subparagraph (A) during the whole of any year of the plan if on one day in each quarter it satisfies such requirements.

(D) The term "supplemental unemployment compensation benefits" means only--

(i) benefits which are paid to an employee because of his involuntary separation from the employment of the employer (whether or not such separation is temporary) resulting directly from a reduction in force, the discontinuance of a plant or operation, or other similar conditions, and

(ii) sick and accident benefits subordinate to the benefits described in clause (i).

(E) Exemption shall not be denied under subsection (a) to any organization entitled to such exemption as an association described in paragraph (9) of this subsection merely because such organization provides for the payment of supplemental unemployment benefits (as defined in subparagraph (D)(i)).

***

Sec. 501. Exemption from tax on corporations, certain trusts, etc.

(19) A post or organization of past or present members of the Armed Forces of the United States, or an auxiliary unit or society of, or a trust or foundation for, any such post or organization--

   (A) organized in the United States or any of its possessions,

   (B) at least 75 percent of the members of which are past or present members of the 5 Armed Forces of the United States and substantially all of the other members of which are individuals who are cadets or are spouses, widows, widowers, ancestors, or lineal descendants of past or present members of the Armed Forces of the United States or of cadets, and

   (C) no part of the net earnings of which inures to the benefit of any private shareholder 10 or individual.

(20) an organization or trust created or organized in the United States, the exclusive function of which is to form part of a qualified group legal services plan or plans, within the meaning of section 120. An organization or trust which receives contributions because of section 120(c)(5) (C) shall not be prevented from qualifying as an organization described in this paragraph 15 merely because it provides legal services or indemnification against the cost of legal services unassociated with a qualified group legal services plan.

(21)(A) A trust or trusts established in writing, created or organized in the United States, and contributed to by any person (except an insurance company) if--

   (i) the purpose of such trust or trusts is exclusively--   20

      (I) to satisfy, in whole or in part, the liability of such person for, or with respect to, claims for compensation for disability or death due to pneumoconiosis under Black Lung Acts,

      (II) to pay premiums for insurance exclusively covering such liability,

      (III) to pay administrative and other incidental expenses of such trust in connection 25 with the operation of the trust and the processing of claims against such person under Black Lung Acts, and

      (IV) to pay accident or health benefits for retired miners and their spouses and dependents (including administrative and other incidental expenses of such trust in connection therewith) or premiums for insurance exclusively covering such benefits; 30 and

   (ii) no part of the assets of the trust may be used for, or diverted to, any purpose other than--

      (I) the purposes described in clause (i),

      (II) investment (but only to the extent that the trustee determines that a portion of the 35 assets is not currently needed for the purposes described in clause (i)) in qualified investments, or

      (III) payment into the Black Lung Disability Trust Fund established under section 9501, or into the general fund of the United States Treasury (other than in satisfaction of any tax or other civil or criminal liability of the person established or contributed to 40 the trust).

   (B) No deduction shall be allowed under this chapter for any payment described in subparagraph (A)(i)(IV) from such trust.

   (C) Payments described in subparagraph (A)(i)(IV) may be made from such trust during a taxable year only to the extent that the aggregate amount of such payments during such taxable 45 year does not exceed the lesser of -

      (i) the excess (if any) (as of the close of the preceding taxable year) of--

(I) the fair market value of the assets of the trust, over

(II) 110 percent of the present value of the liability described in subparagraph (A)(i)(I) of such person, or

(ii) the excess (if any) of--

(I) the sum of a similar excess determined as of the close of the last taxable year ending before the date of the enactment of this subparagraph plus earnings thereon as of the close of the taxable year preceding the taxable year involved, over

(II) the aggregate payments described in subparagraph (A)(i)(IV) made from the trust during all taxable years beginning after the date of the enactment of this subparagraph.

The determinations under the preceding sentence shall be made by an independent actuary using actuarial methods and assumptions (not inconsistent with the regulations prescribed under section 192(c)(1)(A)) each of which is reasonable and which are reasonable in the aggregate.

***

(22) A trust created or organized in the United States and established in writing by the plan sponsors of multiemployer plans if--

(A) the purpose of such trust is exclusively -

(i) to pay any amount described in section 4223(c) or (h) of the Employee Retirement Income Security Act of 1974, and

(ii) to pay reasonable and necessary administrative expenses in connection with the establishment and operation of the trust and the processing of claims against the trust,

(B) no part of the assets of the trust may be used for, or diverted to, any purpose other than -

(i) the purposes described in subparagraph (A), or

(ii) the investment in securities, obligations, or time or demand deposits described in clause (ii) of paragraph (21)(B),

(C) such trust meets the requirements of paragraphs (2), (3), and (4) of section 4223(b), 4223(h), or, if applicable, section 4223(c) of the Employee Retirement Income Security Act of 1974, and

(D) the trust instrument provides that, on dissolution of the trust, assets of the trust may not be paid other than to plans which have participated in the plan or, in the case of a trust established under section 4223(h) of such Act, to plans with respect to which employers have participated in the fund.

***

(25)(A) Any corporation or trust which--

(i) has no more than 35 shareholders or beneficiaries,

(ii) has only 1 class of stock or beneficial interest, and

(iii) is organized for the exclusive purposes of--

(I) acquiring real property and holding title to, and collecting income from, such property, and

(II) remitting the entire amount of income from such property (less expenses) to 1 or more organizations described in subparagraph (C) which are shareholders of such corporation or beneficiaries of such trust.

***

Sec. 501. Exemption from tax on corporations, certain trusts, etc.

(C) An organization is described in this subparagraph if such organization is--

(i) a qualified pension, profit sharing, or stock bonus plan that meets the requirements of section 401(a),

(ii) a governmental plan (within the meaning of section 414(d)),

(iii) the United States, any State or political subdivision thereof, or any agency or instrumentality of any of the foregoing, or

(iv) any organization described in paragraph (3).

***

(26) Any membership organization if--

(A) such organization is established by a State exclusively to provide coverage for medical care (as defined in section 213(d)) on a not-for-profit basis to individuals described in subparagraph (B) through -

(i) insurance issued by the organization, or

(ii) a health maintenance organization under an arrangement with the organization,

(B) the only individuals receiving such coverage through the organization are individuals-

(i) who are residents of such State, and

(ii) who, by reason of the existence or history of a medical condition--

(I) are unable to acquire medical care coverage for such condition through insurance or from a health maintenance organization, or

(II) are able to acquire such coverage only at a rate which is substantially in excess of the rate for such coverage through the membership organization,

(C) the composition of the membership in such organization is specified by such State, and

(D) no part of the net earnings of the organization inures to the benefit of any private shareholder or individual.

A spouse and any qualifying child (as defined in section 24(c)) of an individual described in subparagraph (B) (without regard to this sentence) shall be treated as described in subparagraph (B).

(27)(A) Any membership organization if--

(i) such organization is established before June 1, 1996, by a State exclusively to reimburse its members for losses arising under workmen's compensation acts,

(ii) such State requires that the membership of such organization consist of--

(I) all persons who issue insurance covering workmen's compensation losses in such State, and

(II) all persons and governmental entities who self-insure against such losses, and

(iii) such organization operates as a non-profit organization by--

(I) returning surplus income to its members or workmen's compensation policyholders on a periodic basis, and

(II) reducing initial premiums in anticipation of investment income.

(B) Any organization (including a mutual insurance company) if--

(i) such organization is created by State law and is organized and operated under State law exclusively to--

(I) provide workmen's compensation insurance which is required by State law or

Sec. 501. Exemption from tax on corporations, certain trusts, etc.

with respect to which State law provides significant disincentives if such insurance is not purchased by an employer, and

(II) provide related coverage which is incidental to workmen's compensation insurance,

(ii) such organization must provide workmen's compensation insurance to any employer in the State (for employees in the State or temporarily assigned out-of-State) which seeks such insurance and meets other reasonable requirements relating thereto,

(iii)(I) the State makes a financial commitment with respect to such organization either by extending the full faith and credit of the State to the initial debt of such organization or by providing the initial operating capital of such organization, and (II) in the case of periods after the date of enactment of this subparagraph, the assets of such organization revert to the State upon dissolution or State law does not permit the dissolution of such organization, and

(iv) the majority of the board of directors or oversight body of such organization are appointed by the chief executive officer or other executive branch official of the State, by the State legislature, or by both.

***

(h) Expenditures by public charities to influence legislation. --

(1) General rule. -- In the case of an organization to which this subsection applies, exemption from taxation under subsection (a) shall be denied because a substantial part of the activities of such organization consists of carrying on propaganda, or otherwise attempting, to influence legislation, but only if such organization normally--

(A) makes lobbying expenditures in excess of the lobbying ceiling amount for such organization for each taxable year, or

(B) makes grass roots expenditures in excess of the grass roots ceiling amount for such organization for each taxable year.

(2) Definitions. -- For purposes of this subsection--

(A) Lobbying expenditures. -- The term "lobbying expenditures" means expenditures for the purpose of influencing legislation (as defined in section 4911(d)).

(B) Lobbying ceiling amount. -- The lobbying ceiling amount for any organization for any taxable year is 150 percent of the lobbying nontaxable amount for such organization for such taxable year, determined under section 4911.

(C) Grass roots expenditures. -- The term "grass roots expenditures" means expenditures for the purpose of influencing legislation (as defined in section 4911(d) without regard to paragraph (1)(B) thereof).

(D) Grass roots ceiling amount. -- The grass roots ceiling amount for any organization for any taxable year is 150 percent of the grass roots nontaxable amount for such organization for such taxable year, determined under section 4911.

(3) Organizations to which this subsection applies. -- This subsection shall apply to any organization which has elected (in such manner and at such time as the Secretary may prescribe) to have the provisions of this subsection apply to such organization and which, for the taxable year which includes the date the election is made, is described in subsection (c)(3) and--

(A) is described in paragraph (4), and

(B) is not a disqualified organization under paragraph (5).

(4) Organizations permitted to elect to have this subsection apply. -- An organization is

Sec. 501. Exemption from tax on corporations, certain trusts, etc.

described in this paragraph if it is described in--

   (A) section 170(b)(1)(A)(ii) (relating to educational institutions),

   (B) section 170(b)(1)(A)(iii) (relating to hospitals and medical research organizations),

   (C) section 170(b)(1)(A)(iv) (relating to organizations supporting government schools),

   (D) section 170(b)(1)(A)(vi) (relating to organizations publicly supported by charitable 5 contributions),

   (E) section 509(a)(2) (relating to organizations publicly supported by admissions, sales, etc.), or

   (F) section 509(a)(3) (relating to organizations supporting certain types of public charities) except that for purposes of this subparagraph, section 509(a)(3) shall be applied 10 without regard to the last sentence of section 509(a).

   (5) Disqualified organizations. -- For purposes of paragraph (3) an organization is a disqualified organization if it is--

   (A) described in section 170(b)(1)(A)(i) (relating to churches),

   (B) an integrated auxiliary of a church or of a convention or association of churches, or   15

   (C) a member of an affiliated group of organizations (within the meaning of section 4911(f)(2)) if one or more members of such group is described in subparagraph (A) or (B).

***

   (k) Treatment of certain organizations providing child care. -- For purposes of subsection (c) (3) of this section and sections 170(c)(2), 2055(a)(2), and 2522(a)(2), the term "educational 20 purposes" includes the providing of care of children away from their homes if--

   (1) substantially all of the care provided by the organization is for purposes of enabling individuals to be gainfully employed, and

   (2) the services provided by the organization are available to the general public.

***   25

Sec. 509.   Private foundation defined

   (a) General rule. -- For purposes of this title, the term "private foundation" means a domestic or foreign organization described in section 501(c)(3) other than--

   (1) an organization described in section 170(b)(1)(A) (other than in clauses (vii) and (viii));

   (2) an organization which--   30

   (A) normally receives more than one-third of its support in each taxable year from any combination of -

   (i) gifts, grants, contributions, or membership fees, and

   (ii) gross receipts from admissions, sales of merchandise, performance of services, or furnishing of facilities, in an activity which is not an unrelated trade or business (within 35 the meaning of section 513), not including such receipts from any person, or from any bureau or similar agency of a governmental unit (as described in section 170(c)(1)), in any taxable year to the extent such receipts exceed the greater of $5,000 or 1 percent of the organization's support in such taxable year, from persons other than disqualified persons (as defined in section 4946) with respect to the organization, from 40 governmental units described in section 170(c)(1), or from organizations described in section 170(b)(1)(A) (other than in clauses (vii) and (viii)), and

   (B) normally receives not more than one-third of its support in each taxable year from the sum of -

841

Sec. 509. Private foundation defined

(i) gross investment income (as defined in subsection (e)) and

(ii) the excess (if any) of the amount of the unrelated business taxable income (as defined in section 512) over the amount of the tax imposed by section 511;

(3) an organization which--

(A) is organized, and at all times thereafter is operated, exclusively for the benefit of, to perform the functions of, or to carry out the purposes of one or more specified organizations described in paragraph (1) or (2),

(B) is--

(i) operated, supervised, or controlled by one or more organizations described in paragraph (1) or (2),

(ii) supervised or controlled in connection with one or more such organizations, or

(iii) operated in connection with one or more such organizations, and

(C) is not controlled directly or indirectly by one or more disqualified persons (as defined in section 4946) other than foundation managers and other than one or more organizations described in paragraph (1) or (2); and (4) an organization which is organized and operated exclusively for testing for public safety.

For purposes of paragraph (3), an organization described in paragraph (2) shall be deemed to include an organization described in section 501(c)(4), (5), or (6) which would be described in paragraph (2) if it were an organization described in section 501(c)(3).

***

(d) **Definition of support.** -- For purposes of this part and chapter 42, the term "support" includes (but is not limited to)--

(1) gifts, grants, contributions, or membership fees,

(2) gross receipts from admissions, sales of merchandise, performance of services, or furnishing of facilities in any activity which is not an unrelated trade or business (within the meaning of section 513),

(3) net income from unrelated business activities, whether or not such activities are carried on regularly as a trade or business,

(4) gross investment income (as defined in subsection (e)),

(5) tax revenues levied for the benefit of an organization and either paid to or expended on behalf of such organization, and

(6) the value of services or facilities (exclusive of services or facilities generally furnished to the public without charge) furnished by a governmental unit referred to in section 170(c)(1) to an organization without charge.

Such term does not include any gain from the sale or other disposition of property which would be considered as gain from the sale or exchange of a capital asset, or the value of exemption from any Federal, State, or local tax or any similar benefit.

(e) **Definition of gross investment income.** -- For purposes of subsection (d), the term "gross investment income" means the gross amount of income from interest, dividends, payments with respect to securities loans (as defined in section 512(a)(5)), rents, and royalties, but not including any such income to the extent included in computing the tax imposed by section 511. Such term shall also include income from sources similar to those in the preceding sentence.

(f) **Requirements for Supporting Organizations.** --

(1) **Type iii supporting organizations.** -- For purposes of subsection (a)(3)(B)(iii), an organization shall not be considered to be operated in connection with any organization described in paragraph (1) or (2) of subsection (a) unless such organization meets the

Sec. 509. Private foundation defined

following requirements:

    (A) Responsiveness. -- For each taxable year beginning after the date of the enactment of this subsection, the organization provides to each supported organization such information as the Secretary may require to ensure that such organization is responsive to the needs or demands of the supported organization.   5

    (B) Foreign supported organizations. --

        (i) In general. -- The organization is not operated in connection with any supported organization that is not organized in the United States.

        (ii) Transition rule for existing organizations. -- If the organization is operated in connection with an organization that is not organized in the United States on the date of 10 the enactment of this subsection, clause (i) shall not apply until the first day of the third taxable year of the organization beginning after the date of the enactment of this subsection.

(2) Organizations controlled by donors. --

    (A) In general. -- For purposes of subsection (a)(3)(B), an organization shall not be 15 considered to be--

        (i) operated, supervised, or controlled by any organization described in paragraph (1) or (2) of subsection (a), or

        (ii) operated in connection with any organization described in paragraph (1) or (2) of subsection (a), if such organization accepts any gift or contribution from any person 20 described in subparagraph (B).

    (B) Person described. -- A person is described in this subparagraph if, with respect to a supported organization of an organization described in subparagraph (A), such person is--

        (i) a person (other than an organization described in paragraph (1), (2), or (4) of section 509(a)) who directly or indirectly controls, either alone or together with persons 25 described in clauses (ii) and (iii), the governing body of such supported organization,

        (ii) a member of the family (determined under section 4958(f)(4)) of an individual described in clause (i), or

        (iii) a 35-percent controlled entity (as defined in section 4958(f)(3) by substituting `persons described in clause (i) or (ii) of section 509(f)(2)(B)' for `persons described in 30 subparagraph (A) or (B) of paragraph (1)' in subparagraph (A)(i) thereof).

(3) Supported organization. -- For purposes of this subsection, the term `supported organization' means, with respect to an organization described in subsection (a)(3), an organization described in paragraph (1) or (2) of subsection (a)--

    (A) for whose benefit the organization described in subsection (a)(3) is organized and 35 operated, or

    (B) with respect to which the organization performs the functions of, or carries out the purposes of.

Sec. 529. Qualified tuition programs

    (a) General rule. -- A qualified tuition program shall be exempt from taxation under this 40 subtitle. Notwithstanding the preceding sentence, such program shall be subject to the taxes imposed by section 511 (relating to imposition of tax on unrelated business income of charitable organizations).

    (b) Qualified tuition program. -- For purposes of this section--

    (1) In general. -- The term "qualified tuition program" means a program established and 45

Sec. 529. Qualified tuition programs

maintained by a State or agency or instrumentality thereof or by 1 or more eligible educational institutions -

    (A) under which a person--

        (i) may purchase tuition credits or certificates on behalf of a designated beneficiary which entitle the beneficiary to the waiver or payment of qualified higher education expenses of the beneficiary, or

        (ii) in the case of a program established and maintained by a State or agency or instrumentality thereof, may make contributions to an account which is established for the purpose of meeting the qualified higher education expenses of the designated beneficiary of the account, and

    (B) which meets the other requirements of this subsection.

Except to the extent provided in regulations, a program established and maintained by 1 or more eligible educational institutions shall not be treated as a qualified tuition program unless such program provides that amounts are held in a qualified trust and such program has received a ruling or determination that such program meets the applicable requirements for a qualified tuition program. For purposes of the preceding sentence, the term "qualified trust" means a trust which is created or organized in the United States for the exclusive benefit of designated beneficiaries and with respect to which the requirements of paragraphs (2) and (5) of section 408(a) are met.

    (2) Cash contributions. -- A program shall not be treated as a qualified tuition program unless it provides that purchases or contributions may only be made in cash.

    (3) Separate accounting. -- A program shall not be treated as a qualified tuition program unless it provides separate accounting for each designated beneficiary.

    (4) No investment direction. -- A program shall not be treated as a qualified tuition program unless it provides that any contributor to, or designated beneficiary under, such program may not directly or indirectly direct the investment of any contributions to the program (or any earnings thereon).

    (5) No pledging of interest as security. -- A program shall not be treated as a qualified tuition program if it allows any interest in the program or any portion thereof to be used as security for a loan.

    (6) Prohibition on excess contributions. -- A program shall not be treated as a qualified tuition program unless it provides adequate safeguards to prevent contributions on behalf of a designated beneficiary in excess of those necessary to provide for the qualified higher education expenses of the beneficiary.

(c) Tax treatment of designated beneficiaries and contributors. --

    (1) In general. -- Except as otherwise provided in this subsection, no amount shall be includible in gross income of--

    (A) a designated beneficiary under a qualified tuition program, or

    (B) a contributor to such program on behalf of a designated beneficiary,

with respect to any distribution or earnings under such program.

    (2) Gift tax treatment of contributions. -- For purposes of chapters 12 and 13--

    (A) In general. -- Any contribution to a qualified tuition program on behalf of any designated beneficiary--

        (i) shall be treated as a completed gift to such beneficiary which is not a future interest in property, and

        (ii) shall not be treated as a qualified transfer under section 2503(e).

Sec. 529.   Qualified tuition programs

(B) Treatment of excess contributions. -- If the aggregate amount of contributions described in subparagraph (A) during the calendar year by a donor exceeds the limitation for such year under section 2503(b), such aggregate amount shall, at the election of the donor, be taken into account for purposes of such section ratably over the 5-year period beginning with such calendar year.   5

(3) Distributions. --

(A) In general. -- Any distribution under a qualified tuition program shall be includible in the gross income of the distributee in the manner as provided under section 72 to the extent not excluded from gross income under any other provision of this chapter.

(B) Distributions for qualified higher education expenses. -- For purposes of this 10 paragraph--

(i) In-kind distributions. -- No amount shall be includible in gross income under subparagraph (A) by reason of a distribution which consists of providing a benefit to the distributee which, if paid for by the distributee, would constitute payment of a qualified higher education expense.   15

(ii) Cash distributions. -- In the case of distributions not described in clause (i), if--

(I) such distributions do not exceed the qualified higher education expenses (reduced by expenses described in clause (i)), no amount shall be includible in gross income, and

(II) in any other case, the amount otherwise includible in gross income shall be 20 reduced by an amount which bears the same ratio to such amount as such expenses bear to such distributions.

***

(iv) Treatment as distributions. -- Any benefit furnished to a designated beneficiary under a qualified tuition program shall be treated as a distribution to the beneficiary for 25 purposes of this paragraph.

(v) Coordination with Hope and Lifetime Learning credits. -- The total amount of qualified higher education expenses with respect to an individual for the taxable year shall be reduced--

(I) as provided in section 25A(g)(2), and   30

(II) by the amount of such expenses which were taken into account in determining the credit allowed to the taxpayer or any other person under section 25A.

(vi) Coordination with Coverdell education savings accounts. -- If, with respect to an individual for any taxable year--   35

(I) the aggregate distributions to which clauses (i) and (ii) and section 530(d)(2) (A) apply, exceed

(II) the total amount of qualified higher education expenses otherwise taken into account under clauses (i) and (ii) (after the application of clause (v)) for such year,

the taxpayer shall allocate such expenses among such distributions for purposes of 40 determining the amount of the exclusion under clauses (i) and (ii) and section 530(d)(2) (A).

(C) Change in beneficiaries or programs. --

(i) Rollovers. -- Subparagraph (A) shall not apply to that portion of any distribution which, within 60 days of such distribution, is transferred--   45

Sec. 529. Qualified tuition programs

        (I) to another qualified tuition program for the benefit of the designated beneficiary, or

        (II) to the credit of another designated beneficiary under a qualified tuition program who is a member of the family of the designated beneficiary with respect to which the distribution was made.

    (ii) Change in designated beneficiaries. -- Any change in the designated beneficiary of an interest in a qualified tuition program shall not be treated as a distribution for purposes of subparagraph (A) if the new beneficiary is a member of the family of the old beneficiary.

    (iii) Limitation on certain rollovers. -- Clause (i)(I) shall not apply to any transfer if such transfer occurs within 12 months from the date of a previous transfer to any qualified tuition program for the benefit of the designated beneficiary.

  (D) Operating rules. -- For purposes of applying section 72--

    (i) to the extent provided by the Secretary, all qualified tuition programs of which an individual is a designated beneficiary shall be treated as one program,

    (ii) except to the extent provided by the Secretary, all distributions during a taxable year shall be treated as one distribution, and

    (iii) except to the extent provided by the Secretary, the value of the contract, income on the contract, and investment in the contract shall be computed as of the close of the calendar year in which the taxable year begins.

***

(e) Other definitions and special rules. -- For purposes of this section--

  (1) Designated beneficiary. -- The term "designated beneficiary" means--

    (A) the individual designated at the commencement of participation in the qualified tuition program as the beneficiary of amounts paid (or to be paid) to the program,

    (B) in the case of a change in beneficiaries described in subsection (c)(3)(C), the individual who is the new beneficiary, and

    (C) in the case of an interest in a qualified tuition program purchased by a State or local government (or agency or instrumentality thereof) or an organization described in section 501(c)(3) and exempt from taxation under section 501(a) as part of a scholarship program operated by such government or organization, the individual receiving such interest as a scholarship.

  (2) Member of family. -- The term "member of the family" means, with respect to any designated beneficiary--

    (A) the spouse of such beneficiary;

    (B) an individual who bears a relationship to such beneficiary which is described in subparagraphs (A) through (G) of section 152(d)(2);

    (C) the spouse of any individual described in subparagraph (B); and

    (D) any first cousin of such beneficiary.

  (3) Qualified higher education expenses. --

    (A) In general. -- The term "qualified higher education expenses" means--

      (i) tuition, fees, books, supplies, and equipment required for the enrollment or attendance of a designated beneficiary at an eligible educational institution; and

      (ii) expenses for special needs services in the case of a special needs beneficiary which are incurred in connection with such enrollment or attendance.

Sec. 529. Qualified tuition programs

(B) Room and board included for students who are at least half- time. --

(i) In general. -- In the case of an individual who is an eligible student (as defined in section 25A(b)(3)) for any academic period, such term shall also include reasonable costs for such period (as determined under the qualified tuition program) incurred by the designated beneficiary for room and board while attending such institution. For 5 purposes of subsection (b)(6), a designated beneficiary shall be treated as meeting the requirements of this clause.

(ii) Limitation. -- The amount treated as qualified higher education expenses by reason of clause (i) shall not exceed--

(I) the allowance (applicable to the student) for room and board included in the 10 cost of attendance (as defined in section 472 of the Higher Education Act of 1965 (20 U.S.C. 1087ll), as in effect on the date of the enactment of the Economic Growth and Tax Relief Reconciliation Act of 2001) as determined by the eligible educational institution for such period, or

(II) if greater, the actual invoice amount the student residing in housing owned or 15 operated by the eligible educational institution is charged by such institution for room and board costs for such period.

(4) Application of section 514. -- An interest in a qualified tuition program shall not be treated as debt for purposes of section 514.

(5) Eligible educational institution. -- The term "eligible educational institution" means an 20 institution--

(A) which is described in section 481 of the Higher Education Act of 1965 (20 U.S.C. 1088), as in effect on the date of the enactment of this paragraph, and

(B) which is eligible to participate in a program under title IV of such Act.

***

25

Sec. 530. Coverdell education savings accounts

(a) General rule. -- A Coverdell education savings account shall be exempt from taxation under this subtitle. Notwithstanding the preceding sentence, the Coverdell education savings account shall be subject to the taxes imposed by section 511 (relating to imposition of tax on unrelated business income of charitable organizations). 30

(b) Definitions and special rules. -- For purposes of this section--

(1) Coverdell education savings account. -- The term "Coverdell education savings account" means a trust created or organized in the United States exclusively for the purpose of paying the qualified education expenses of an individual who is the designated beneficiary of the trust (and designated as a Coverdell education savings account at the time created or 35 organized), but only if the written governing instrument creating the trust meets the following requirements:

(A) No contribution will be accepted--

(i) unless it is in cash,

(ii) after the date on which such beneficiary attains age 18, or 40

(iii) except in the case of rollover contributions, if such contribution would result in aggregate contributions for the taxable year exceeding $2,000.

(B) The trustee is a bank (as defined in section 408(n)) or another person who demonstrates to the satisfaction of the Secretary that the manner in which that person will administer the trust will be consistent with the requirements of this section or who has so 45

847

Sec. 530. Coverdell education savings accounts

demonstrated with respect to any individual retirement plan.

(C) No part of the trust assets will be invested in life insurance contracts.

(D) The assets of the trust shall not be commingled with other property except in a common trust fund or common investment fund.

(E) Except as provided in subsection (d)(7), any balance to the credit of the designated beneficiary on the date on which the beneficiary attains age 30 shall be distributed within 30 days after such date to the beneficiary or, if the beneficiary dies before attaining age 30, shall be distributed within 30 days after the date of death of such beneficiary.

The age limitations in subparagraphs (A)(ii) and (E), and paragraphs (5) and (6) of subsection (d), shall not apply to any designated beneficiary with special needs (as determined under regulations prescribed by the Secretary).

(2) Qualified education expenses. --

(A) In general. -- The term "qualified education expenses" means--

(i) qualified higher education expenses (as defined in section 529(e)(3)), and

(ii) qualified elementary and secondary education expenses (as defined in paragraph (4)).

(B) Qualified tuition programs. -- Such term shall include any contribution to a qualified tuition program (as defined in section 529(b)) on behalf of the designated beneficiary (as defined in section 529(e)(1)); but there shall be no increase in the investment in the contract for purposes of applying section 72 by reason of any portion of such contribution which is not includible in gross income by reason of subsection (d)(2).

(3) Eligible educational institution. -- The term "eligible educational institution" has the meaning given such term by section 529(e)(5).

(4) Qualified elementary and secondary education expenses. --

(A) In general. -- The term "qualified elementary and secondary education expenses" means--

(i) expenses for tuition, fees, academic tutoring, special needs services in the case of a special needs beneficiary, books, supplies, and other equipment which are incurred in connection with the enrollment or attendance of the designated beneficiary of the trust as an elementary or secondary school student at a public, private, or religious school,

(ii) expenses for room and board, uniforms, transportation, and supplementary items and services (including extended day programs) which are required or provided by a public, private, or religious school in connection with such enrollment or attendance, and

(iii) expenses for the purchase of any computer technology or equipment (as defined in section 170(e)(6)(F)(i)) or Internet access and related services, if such technology, equipment, or services are to be used by the beneficiary and the beneficiary's family during any of the years the beneficiary is in school.

Clause (iii) shall not include expenses for computer software designed for sports, games, or hobbies unless the software is predominantly educational in nature.

(B) School. -- The term "school" means any school which provides elementary education or secondary education (kindergarten through grade 12), as determined under State law.

(5) Time when contributions deemed made. -- An individual shall be deemed to have made a contribution to an education individual retirement account on the last day of the preceding taxable year if the contribution is made on account of such taxable year and is made

Sec. 530. Coverdell education savings accounts

not later than the time prescribed by law for filing the return for such taxable year (not including extensions thereof).

(c) Reduction in permitted contributions based on adjusted gross income. --

(1) In general. -- In the case of a contributor who is an individual, the maximum amount the contributor could otherwise make to an account under this section shall be reduced by an amount which bears the same ratio to such maximum amount as-- 5

(A) the excess of--

(i) the contributor's modified adjusted gross income for such taxable year, over

(ii) $95,000 ($190,000 in the case of a joint return), bears to

(B) $15,000 ($30,000 in the case of a joint return). -- 10

(2) Modified adjusted gross income. -- For purposes of paragraph (1), the term "modified adjusted gross income" means the adjusted gross income of the taxpayer for the taxable year increased by any amount excluded from gross income under section 911, 931, or 933.

(d) Tax treatment of distributions. --

(1) In general. -- Any distribution shall be includible in the gross income of the distributee 15 in the manner as provided in section 72.

(2) Distributions for qualified education expenses. --

(A) In general. -- No amount shall be includible in gross income under paragraph (1) if the qualified education expenses of the designated beneficiary during the taxable year are not less than the aggregate distributions during the taxable year. 20

(B) Distributions in excess of expenses. -- If such aggregate distributions exceed such expenses during the taxable year, the amount otherwise includible in gross income under paragraph (1) shall be reduced by the amount which bears the same ratio to the amount which would be includible in gross income under paragraph (1) (without regard to this subparagraph) as the qualified education expenses bear to such aggregate distributions. 25

(C) Coordination with Hope and Lifetime Learning credits and qualified tuition programs. -- For purposes of subparagraph (A)--

(i) Credit coordination. -- The total amount of qualified education expenses with respect to an individual for the taxable year shall be reduced--

(I) as provided in section 25A(g)(2), and 30

(II) by the amount of such expenses which were taken into account in determining the credit allowed to the taxpayer or any other person under section 25A.

(ii) Coordination with qualified tuition programs. -- If, with respect to an individual for any taxable year-- 35

(I) the aggregate distributions during such year to which subparagraph (A) and section 529(c)(3)(B) apply, exceed

(II) the total amount of qualified education expenses (after the application of clause (i)) for such year,

the taxpayer shall allocate such expenses among such distributions for purposes of 40 determining the amount of the exclusion under subparagraph (A) and section 529(c)(3) (B).

(D) Disallowance of excluded amounts as deduction, credit, or exclusion. -- No deduction, credit, or exclusion shall be allowed to the taxpayer under any other section of this chapter for any qualified education expenses to the extent taken into account in 45 determining the amount of the exclusion under this paragraph.

849

Sec. 530. Coverdell education savings accounts

***

(4) Additional tax for distributions not used for educational expenses. --

   (A) In general. -- The tax imposed by this chapter for any taxable year on any taxpayer who receives a payment or distribution from a Coverdell education savings account which is includible in gross income shall be increased by 10 percent of the amount which is so includible.

   (B) Exceptions. -- Subparagraph (A) shall not apply if the payment or distribution is--

     (i) made to a beneficiary (or to the estate of the designated beneficiary) on or after the death of the designated beneficiary,

     (ii) attributable to the designated beneficiary's being disabled (within the meaning of section 72(m)(7)),

     (iii) made on account of a scholarship, allowance, or payment described in section 25A(g)(2) received by the designated beneficiary to the extent the amount of the payment or distribution does not exceed the amount of the scholarship, allowance, or payment,

     (iv) made on account of the attendance of the designated beneficiary at the United States Military Academy, the United States Naval Academy, the United States Air Force Academy, the United States Coast Guard Academy, or the United States Merchant Marine Academy, to the extent that the amount of the payment or distribution does not exceed the costs of advanced education (as defined by section 2005(e)(3) of title 10, United States Code, as in effect on the date of the enactment of this section) attributable to such attendance, or

     (v) an amount which is includible in gross income solely by application of paragraph (2)(C)(i)(II) for the taxable year.

***

   (7) Special rules for death and divorce. -- Rules similar to the rules of paragraphs (7) and (8) of section 220(f) shall apply. In applying the preceding sentence, members of the family (as so defined) of the designated beneficiary shall be treated in the same manner as the spouse under such paragraph (8).

   (8) Deemed distribution on required distribution date. -- In any case in which a distribution is required under subsection (b)(1)(E), any balance to the credit of a designated beneficiary as of the close of the 30-day period referred to in such subsection for making such distribution shall be deemed distributed at the close of such period.

   (e) Tax treatment of accounts. -- Rules similar to the rules of paragraphs (2) and (4) of section 408(e) shall apply to any Coverdell education savings account.

   (f) Community property laws. -- This section shall be applied without regard to any community property laws.

***

Sec. 542. Definition of personal holding company

   (a) General rule. -- For purposes of this subtitle, the term "personal holding company" means any corporation (other than a corporation described in subsection (c)) if--

   (1) Adjusted ordinary gross income requirement. -- At least 60 percent of its adjusted ordinary gross income (as defined in section 543(b)(2)) for the taxable year is personal holding company income (as defined in section 543(a)), and

   (2) Stock ownership requirement. -- At any time during the last half of the taxable year more than 50 percent in value of its outstanding stock is owned, directly or indirectly, by or for

850

not more than 5 individuals. For purposes of this paragraph, an organization described in section 401(a), 501(c)(17), or 509(a) or a portion of a trust permanently set aside or to be used exclusively for the purposes described in section 642(c) or a corresponding provision of a prior income tax law shall be considered an individual.

***

5

Sec. 611. Allowance of deduction for depletion

(a) **General rule.** -- In the case of mines, oil and gas wells, other natural deposits, and timber, there shall be allowed as a deduction in computing taxable income a reasonable allowance for depletion and for depreciation of improvements, according to the peculiar conditions in each case; such reasonable allowance in all cases to be made under regulations prescribed by the Secretary. 10 For purposes of this part, the term "mines" includes deposits of waste or residue, the extraction of ores or minerals from which is treated as mining under section 613(c). In any case in which it is ascertained as a result of operations or of development work that the recoverable units are greater or less than the prior estimate thereof, then such prior estimate (but not the basis for depletion) shall be revised and the allowance under this section for subsequent taxable years shall be based 15 on such revised estimate.

***

Sec. 612. Basis for cost depletion

Except as otherwise provided in this subchapter, the basis on which depletion is to be allowed in respect of any property shall be the adjusted basis provided in section 1011 for the purpose of 20 determining the gain upon the sale or other disposition of such property.

Sec. 613. Percentage depletion

(a) **General rule.** -- In the case of the mines, wells, and other natural deposits listed in subsection (b), the allowance for depletion under section 611 shall be the percentage, specified in 25 subsection (b), of the gross income from the property excluding from such gross income an amount equal to any rents or royalties paid or incurred by the taxpayer in respect of the property. Such allowance shall not exceed 50 percent (100 percent in the case of oil and gas properties) of the taxpayer's taxable income from the property (computed without allowance for depletion and without the deduction under section 199). For purposes of the preceding sentence, the allowable 30 deductions taken into account with respect to expenses of mining in computing the taxable income from the property shall be decreased by an amount equal to so much of any gain which (1) is treated under section 1245 (relating to gain from disposition of certain depreciable property) as ordinary income, and (2) is properly allocable to the property. In no case shall the allowance for depletion under section 611 be less than it would be if computed without reference to this section. 35

(b) **Percentage depletion rates.** -- The mines, wells, and other natural deposits, and the percentages, referred to in subsection (a) are as follows:

(1) **22 percent.** --

(A) sulphur and uranium; and

(B) if from deposits in the United States - anorthosite, clay, laterite, and nephelite syenite 40 (to the extent that alumina and aluminum compounds are extracted therefrom), asbestos, bauxite, celestite, chromite, corundum, fluorspar, graphite, ilmenite, kyanite, mica, olivine, quartz crystals (radio grade), rutile, block steatite talc, and zircon, and ores of the following metals: antimony, beryllium, bismuth, cadmium, cobalt, columbium, lead, lithium,

Sec. 613.   Percentage depletion

manganese, mercury, molybdenum, nickel, platinum and platinum group metals, tantalum, thorium, tin, titanium, tungsten, vanadium, and zinc.

(2) 15 percent. -- If from deposits in the United States--

   (A) gold, silver, copper, and iron ore, and

   (B) oil shale (except shale described in paragraph (5)).

(3) 14 percent. --

   (A) metal mines (if paragraph (1)(B) or (2)(A) does not apply),   rock asphalt, and vermiculite; and

   (B) if paragraph (1)(B), (5), or (6)(B) does not apply, ball clay, bentonite, china clay, sagger clay, and clay used or sold for use for purposes dependent on its refractory properties.

(4) 10 percent. -- Asbestos (if paragraph (1)(B) does not apply), brucite, coal, lignite, perlite, sodium chloride, and wollastonite.

(5) 7 1/2 percent. -- Clay and shale used or sold for use in the manufacture of sewer pipe or brick, and clay, shale, and slate used or sold for use as sintered or burned lightweight aggregates.

(6) 5 percent. --

   (A) gravel, peat, pumice, sand, scoria, shale (except shale described in paragraph (2)(B) or (5)), and stone (except stone described in paragraph (7));

   (B) clay used, or sold for use, in the manufacture of drainage and roofing tile, flower pots, and kindred products; and

   (C) if from brine wells - bromine, calcium chloride, and magnesium chloride.

(7) 14 percent. -- All other minerals, including, but not limited to, aplite, barite, borax, calcium carbonates, diatomaceous earth, dolomite, feldspar, fullers earth, garnet, gilsonite, granite, limestone, magnesite, magnesium carbonates, marble, mollusk shells (including clam shells and oyster shells), phosphate rock, potash, quartzite, slate, soapstone, stone (used or sold for use by the mine owner or operator as dimension stone or ornamental stone), thenardite, tripoli, trona, and (if paragraph (1)(B) does not apply) bauxite, flake graphite, fluorspar, lepidolite, mica, spodumene, and talc (including pyrophyllite), except that, unless sold on bid in direct competition with a bona fide bid to sell a mineral listed in paragraph (3), the percentage shall be 5 percent for any such other mineral (other than slate to which paragraph (5) applies) when used, or sold for use, by the mine owner or operator as rip rap, ballast, road material, rubble, concrete aggregates, or for similar purposes. For purposes of this paragraph, the term "all other minerals" does not include -

   (A) soil, sod, dirt, turf, water, or mosses;

   (B) minerals from sea water, the air, or similar inexhaustible sources; or

   (C) oil and gas wells.

For the purposes of this subsection, minerals (other than sodium chloride) extracted from brines pumped from a saline perennial lake within the United States shall not be considered minerals from an inexhaustible source.

***

(d) Denial of percentage depletion in case of oil and gas wells. -- Except as provided in section 613A, in the case of any oil or gas well, the allowance for depletion shall be computed without reference to this section.

(e) Percentage depletion for geothermal deposits. --

   (1) In general. -- In the case of geothermal deposits located in the United States or in a

852

Sec. 613.   Percentage depletion

possession of the United States, for purposes of subsection (a)--

    (A) such deposits shall be treated as listed in subsection (b), and

    (B) 15 percent shall be deemed to be the percentage specified in subsection (b).

***

Sec. 613A.   Limitations on percentage depletion in case of oil and gas wells

    (a) General rule. -- Except as otherwise provided in this section, the allowance for depletion under section 611 with respect to any oil or gas well shall be computed without regard to section 613.

    (b) Exemption for certain domestic gas wells. --

        (1) In general. -- The allowance for depletion under section 611 shall be computed in accordance with section 613 with respect to--

        (A) regulated natural gas, and

        (B) natural gas sold under a fixed contract,

and 22 percent shall be deemed to be specified in subsection (b) of section 613 for purposes of subsection (a) of that section.

***

    (c) Exemption for independent producers and royalty owners. --

        (1) In general. -- Except as provided in subsection (d), the allowance for depletion under section 611 shall be computed in accordance with section 613 with respect to--

        (A) so much of the taxpayer's average daily production of domestic crude oil as does not exceed the taxpayer's depletable oil quantity; and

        (B) so much of the taxpayer's average daily production of domestic natural gas as does not exceed the taxpayer's depletable natural gas quantity;

and 15 percent shall be deemed to be specified in subsection (b) of section 613 for purposes of subsection (a) of that section.

***

Sec. 616.   Development expenditures

    (a) In general. -- Except as provided in subsections (b) and (d), there shall be allowed as a deduction in computing taxable income all expenditures paid or incurred during the taxable year for the development of a mine or other natural deposit (other than an oil or gas well) if paid or incurred after the existence of ores or minerals in commercially marketable quantities has been disclosed. This section shall not apply to expenditures for the acquisition or improvement of property of a character which is subject to the allowance for depreciation provided in section 167, but allowances for depreciation shall be considered, for purposes of this section, as expenditures.

***

Sec. 617.   Deduction and recapture of certain mining exploration expenditures

    (a) Allowance of deduction. --

        (1) General rule. -- At the election of the taxpayer, expenditures paid or incurred during the taxable year for the purpose of ascertaining the existence, location, extent, or quality of any deposit of ore or other mineral, and paid or incurred before the beginning of the development

853

Sec. 617. Deduction and recapture of certain mining exploration expenditures

stage of the mine, shall be allowed as a deduction in computing taxable income. This subsection shall apply only with respect to the amount of such expenditures which, but for this subsection, would not be allowable as a deduction for the taxable year. This subsection shall not apply to expenditures for the acquisition or improvement of property of a character which is subject to the allowance for depreciation provided in section 167, but allowances for depreciation shall be considered, for purposes of this subsection, as expenditures paid or incurred. In no case shall this subsection apply with respect to amounts paid or incurred for the purpose of ascertaining the existence, location, extent, or quality of any deposit of oil or gas or of any mineral with respect to which a deduction for percentage depletion is not allowable under section 613.

***

Sec. 631. Gain or loss in the case of timber, coal, or domestic iron ore

(a) Election to consider cutting as sale or exchange. -- If the taxpayer so elects on his return for a taxable year, the cutting of timber (for sale or for use in the taxpayer's trade or business) during such year by the taxpayer who owns, or has a contract right to cut, such timber (providing he has owned such timber or has held such contract right for a period of more than 1 year) shall be considered as a sale or exchange of such timber cut during such year. If such election has been made, gain or loss to the taxpayer shall be recognized in an amount equal to the difference between the fair market value of such timber, and the adjusted basis for depletion of such timber in the hands of the taxpayer. Such fair market value shall be the fair market value as of the first day of the taxable year in which such timber is cut, and shall thereafter be considered as the cost of such cut timber to the taxpayer for all purposes for which such cost is a necessary factor. If a taxpayer makes an election under this subsection, such election shall apply with respect to all timber which is owned by the taxpayer or which the taxpayer has a contract right to cut and shall be binding on the taxpayer for the taxable year for which the election is made and for all subsequent years, unless the Secretary, on showing of undue hardship, permits the taxpayer to revoke his election; such revocation, however, shall preclude any further elections under this subsection except with the consent of the Secretary. For purposes of this subsection and subsection (b), the term "timber" includes evergreen trees which are more than 6 years old at the time severed from the roots and are sold for ornamental purposes.

***

Sec. 641. Imposition of tax

(a) Application of tax. -- The tax imposed by section 1(e) shall apply to the taxable income of estates or of any kind of property held in trust, including--

(1) income accumulated in trust for the benefit of unborn or unascertained persons or persons with contingent interests, and income accumulated or held for future distribution under the terms of the will or trust;

(2) income which is to be distributed currently by the fiduciary to the beneficiaries, and income collected by a guardian of an infant which is to be held or distributed as the court may direct;

(3) income received by estates of deceased persons during the period of administration or settlement of the estate; and

(4) income which, in the discretion of the fiduciary, may be either distributed to the beneficiaries or accumulated.

***

Sec. 642.   Special rules for credits and deductions

***

(b) Deduction for personal exemption. --

    (1) Estates. -- An estate shall be allowed a deduction of $600.

    (2) Trusts. --

        (A) In general. -- Except as otherwise provided in this paragraph, a trust shall be allowed a deduction of $100.

        (B) Trusts distributing income currently. -- A trust which, under its governing instrument, is required to distribute all of its income currently shall be allowed a deduction of $300.

***

    (3) Deductions in lieu of personal exemption. -- The deductions allowed by this subsection shall be in lieu of the deductions allowed under section 151 (relating to deduction for personal exemption).

(c) Deduction for amounts paid or permanently set aside for a charitable purpose. --

    (1) General rule. -- In the case of an estate or trust (other than a trust meeting the specifications of subpart B), there shall be allowed as a deduction in computing its taxable income (in lieu of the deduction allowed by section 170(a), relating to deduction for charitable, etc., contributions and gifts) any amount of the gross income, without limitation, which pursuant to the terms of the governing instrument is, during the taxable year, paid for a purpose specified in section 170(c) (determined without regard to section 170(c)(2)(A)). If a charitable contribution is paid after the close of such taxable year and on or before the last day of the year following the close of such taxable year, then the trustee or administrator may elect to treat such contribution as paid during such taxable year. The election shall be made at such time and in such manner as the Secretary prescribes by regulations.

***

(d) Net operating loss deduction. -- The benefit of the deduction for net operating losses provided by section 172 shall be allowed to estates and trusts under regulations prescribed by the Secretary.

(e) Deduction for depreciation and depletion. -- An estate or trust shall be allowed the deduction for depreciation and depletion only to the extent not allowable to beneficiaries under section 167(d) and 611(b).

(f) Amortization deductions. -- The benefit of the deductions for amortization provided by sections 169 and 197 shall be allowed to estates and trusts in the same manner as in the case of an individual. The allowable deduction shall be apportioned between the income beneficiaries and the fiduciary under regulations prescribed by the Secretary.

***

Sec. 651.   Deduction for trusts distributing current income only

(a) Deduction. -- In the case of any trust the terms of which--

    (1) provide that all of its income is required to be distributed currently, and

    (2) do not provide that any amounts are to be paid, permanently set aside, or used for the purposes specified in section 642(c) (relating to deduction for charitable, etc., purposes),

there shall be allowed as a deduction in computing the taxable income of the trust the amount of the income for the taxable year which is required to be distributed currently. This section shall not

855

Sec. 651. Deduction for trusts distributing current income only

apply in any taxable year in which the trust distributes amounts other than amounts of income described in paragraph (1).

    (b) Limitation on deduction. -- If the amount of income required to be distributed currently exceeds the distributable net income of the trust for the taxable year, the deduction shall be limited
5 to the amount of the distributable net income. For this purpose, the computation of distributable net income shall not include items of income which are not included in the gross income of the trust and the deductions allocable thereto.

Reg. § 1.651(b)-1 Deduction for distributions to beneficiaries.
10   In computing its taxable income, a simple trust is allowed a deduction for the amount of income which is required under the terms of the trust instrument to be distributed currently to beneficiaries. If the amount of income required to be distributed currently exceeds the distributable net income, the deduction allowable to the trust is limited to the amount of the distributable net income. For this purpose the amount of income required
15 to be distributed currently, or distributable net income, whichever is applicable, does not include items of trust income (adjusted for deductions allocable thereto) which are not included in the gross income of the trust. For determination of the character of the income required to be distributed currently, see § 1.652(b)-2. Accordingly, for the purposes of determining the deduction allowable to the trust under section 651, distributable net
20 income is computed without the modifications specified in paragraphs (5), (6), and (7) of section 643(a), relating to tax-exempt interest, foreign income, and excluded dividends. For example: Assume that the distributable net income of a trust as computed under section 643(a) amounts to $99,000 but includes nontaxable income of $9,000. Then distributable net income for the purpose of determining the deduction allowable under
25 section 651 is $90,000 ($99,000 less $9,000 nontaxable income).

Sec. 652. Inclusion of amounts in gross income of beneficiaries of trusts distributing current income only

    (a) Inclusion. -- Subject to subsection (b), the amount of income for the taxable year required to be distributed currently by a trust described in section 651 shall be included in the gross income of the beneficiaries to whom the income is required to be distributed, whether distributed or not. If
30 such amount exceeds the distributable net income, there shall be included in the gross income of each beneficiary an amount which bears the same ratio to distributable net income as the amount of income required to be distributed to such beneficiary bears to the amount of income required to be distributed to all beneficiaries.

    (b) Character of amounts. -- The amounts specified in subsection (a) shall have the same
35 character in the hands of the beneficiary as in the hands of the trust. For this purpose, the amounts shall be treated as consisting of the same proportion of each class of items entering into the computation of distributable net income of the trust as the total of each class bears to the total distributable net income of the trust, unless the terms of the trust specifically allocate different classes of income to different beneficiaries. In the application of the preceding sentence, the items
40 of deduction entering into the computation of distributable net income shall be allocated among the items of distributable net income in accordance with regulations prescribed by the Secretary.

***

Reg. § 1.652(a)-1 Simple trusts; inclusion of amounts in income of beneficiaries.
    Subject to the rules in §§ 1.652(a)-2 and 1.652(b)-1, a beneficiary of a simple trust
45 includes in his gross income for the taxable year the amounts of income required to be distributed to him for such year, whether or not distributed. Thus, the income of a simple trust is includible in the beneficiary's gross income for the taxable year in which the

Sec. 652. Inclusion of amounts in gross income of beneficiaries of trusts distributing current income only

income is required to be distributed currently even though, as a matter of practical necessity, the income is not distributed until after the close of the taxable year of the trust. See § 1.642(a)(3)-2 with respect to time of receipt of dividends. See § 1.652(c)-1 for treatment of amounts required to be distributed where a beneficiary and the trust have different taxable years. The term income required to be distributed currently includes 5 income required to be distributed currently which is in fact used to discharge or satisfy any person's legal obligation as that term is used in § 1.662(a)-4.

Reg. § 1.652(b)-1 Character of amounts.

In determining the gross income of a beneficiary, the amounts includible under § 10 1.652(a)-1 have the same character in the hands of the beneficiary as in the hands of the trust. For example, to the extent that the amounts specified in § 1.652(a)-1 consist of income exempt from tax under section 103, such amounts are not included in the beneficiary's gross income. Similarly, dividends distributed to a beneficiary retain their original character in the beneficiary's hands for purposes of determining the availability to 15 the beneficiary of the dividends received credit under section 34 (for dividends received on or before December 31, 1964) and the dividend exclusion under section 116. Also, to the extent that the amounts specified in § 1.652(a)-1 consist of ``earned income" in the hands of the trust under the provisions of section 1348 such amount shall be treated under section 1348 as ``earned income" in the hands of the beneficiary. Similarly, to the 20 extent such amounts consist of an amount received as a part of a lump sum distribution from a qualified plan and to which the provisions of section 72(n) would apply in the hands of the trust, such amount shall be treated as subject to such section in the hands of the beneficiary except where such amount is deemed under section 666(a) to have been distributed in a preceding taxable year of the trust and the partial tax described in 25 section 668(a)(2) is determined under section 668(b)(1)(B). The tax treatment of amounts determined under § 1.652(a)-1 depends upon the beneficiary's status with respect to them not upon the status of the trust. Thus, if a beneficiary is deemed to have received foreign income of a foreign trust, the includibility of such income in his gross income depends upon his taxable status with respect to that income.   30

Reg. § 1.652(b)-2 Allocation of income items.

(a) The amounts specified in § 1.652(a)-1 which are required to be included in the gross income of a beneficiary are treated as consisting of the same proportion of each class of items entering into distributable net income of the trust (as defined in section 643(a)) as the total of each class bears to such distributable net income, unless the terms 35 of the trust specifically allocate different classes of income to different beneficiaries, or unless local law requires such an allocation. For example: Assume that under the terms of the governing instrument, beneficiary A is to receive currently one-half of the trust income and beneficiaries B and C are each to receive currently one-quarter, and the distributable net income of the trust (after allocation of expenses) consists of dividends of 40 $10,000, taxable interest of $10,000, and tax-exempt interest of $4,000. A will be deemed to have received $5,000 of dividends, $5,000 of taxable interest, and $2,000 of tax-exempt interest; B and C will each be deemed to have received $2,500 of dividends, $2,500 of taxable interest, and $1,000 of tax-exempt interest. However, if the terms of the trust specifically allocate different classes of income to different beneficiaries, entirely or 45 in part, or if local law requires such an allocation, each beneficiary will be deemed to have received those items of income specifically allocated to him.

(b) The terms of the trust are considered specifically to allocate different classes of income to different beneficiaries only to the extent that the allocation is required in the trust instrument, and only to the extent that it has an economic effect independent of the 50

857

Sec. 652. Inclusion of amounts in gross income of beneficiaries of trusts distributing current income only

income tax consequences of the allocation. For example:

(1) Allocation pursuant to a provision in a trust instrument granting the trustee discretion to allocate different classes of income to different beneficiaries is not a specific allocation by the terms of the trust.

(2) Allocation pursuant to a provision directing the trustee to pay all of one income to A, or $10,000 out of the income to A, and the balance of the income to B, but directing the trustee first to allocate a specific class of income to A's share (to the extent there is income of that class and to the extent it does not exceed A's share) is not a specific allocation by the terms of the trust.

(3) Allocation pursuant to a provision directing the trustee to pay half the class of income (whatever it may be) to A, and the balance of the income to B, is a specific allocation by the terms of the trust.

[T.D. 7204, 37 FR 17134, Aug. 25, 1972]

Sec. 661. Deduction for estates and trusts accumulating income or distributing corpus

(a) **Deduction.** -- In any taxable year there shall be allowed as a deduction in computing the taxable income of an estate or trust (other than a trust to which subpart B applies), the sum of--

(1) any amount of income for such taxable year required to be distributed currently (including any amount required to be distributed which may be paid out of income or corpus to the extent such amount is paid out of income for such taxable year); and

(2) any other amounts properly paid or credited or required to be distributed for such taxable year;

but such deduction shall not exceed the distributable net income of the estate or trust.

(b) Character of amounts distributed. -- The amount determined under subsection (a) shall be treated as consisting of the same proportion of each class of items entering into the computation of distributable net income of the estate or trust as the total of each class bears to the total distributable net income of the estate or trust in the absence of the allocation of different classes of income under the specific terms of the governing instrument. In the application of the preceding sentence, the items of deduction entering into the computation of distributable net income (including the deduction allowed under section 642(c)) shall be allocated among the items of distributable net income in accordance with regulations prescribed by the Secretary.

(c) **Limitation on deduction.** -- No deduction shall be allowed under subsection (a) in respect of any portion of the amount allowed as a deduction under that subsection (without regard to this subsection) which is treated under subsection (b) as consisting of any item of distributable net income which is not included in the gross income of the estate or trust.

Sec. 662. Inclusion of amounts in gross income of beneficiaries of estates and trusts accumulating income or distributing corpus

(a) **Inclusion.** -- Subject to subsection (b), there shall be included in the gross income of a beneficiary to whom an amount specified in section 661(a) is paid, credited, or required to be distributed (by an estate or trust described in section 661), the sum of the following amounts:

(1) **Amounts required to be distributed currently.** -- The amount of income for the taxable year required to be distributed currently to such beneficiary, whether distributed or not.

858

Sec. 662. Inclusion of amounts in gross income of beneficiaries of estates and trusts accumulating income or distributing corpus

If the amount of income required to be distributed currently to all beneficiaries exceeds the distributable net income (computed without the deduction allowed by section 642(c), relating to deduction for charitable, etc., purposes) of the estate or trust, then, in lieu of the amount provided in the preceding sentence, there shall be included in the gross income of the beneficiary an amount which bears the same ratio to distributable net income (as so computed) 5 as the amount of income required to be distributed currently to such beneficiary bears to the amount required to be distributed currently to all beneficiaries. For purposes of this section, the phrase "the amount of income for the taxable year required to be distributed currently" includes any amount required to be paid out of income or corpus to the extent such amount is paid out of income for such taxable year. 10

(2) **Other amounts distributed.** -- All other amounts properly paid, credited, or required to be distributed to such beneficiary for the taxable year. If the sum of--

(A) the amount of income for the taxable year required to be distributed currently to all beneficiaries, and

(B) all other amounts properly paid, credited, or required to be distributed to all 15 beneficiaries

exceeds the distributable net income of the estate or trust, then, in lieu of the amount provided in the preceding sentence, there shall be included in the gross income of the beneficiary an amount which bears the same ratio to distributable net income (reduced by the amounts specified in (A)) as the other amounts properly paid, credited or required to be distributed to 20 the beneficiary bear to the other amounts properly paid, credited, or required to be distributed to all beneficiaries.

(b) **Character of amounts.** -- The amounts determined under subsection (a) shall have the same character in the hands of the beneficiary as in the hands of the estate or trust. For this purpose, the amounts shall be treated as consisting of the same proportion of each class of items entering into 25 the computation of distributable net income as the total of each class bears to the total distributable net income of the estate or trust unless the terms of the governing instrument specifically allocate different classes of income to different beneficiaries. In the application of the preceding sentence, the items of deduction entering into the computation of distributable net income (including the deduction allowed under section 642(c)) shall be allocated among the items of distributable net 30 income in accordance with regulations prescribed by the Secretary. In the application of this subsection to the amount determined under paragraph (1) of subsection (a), distributable net income shall be computed without regard to any portion of the deduction under section 642(c) which is not attributable to income of the taxable year.

*** 35

Reg. § 1.662(a)-4 Amounts used in discharge of a legal obligation.

Any amount which, pursuant to the terms of a will or trust instrument, is used in full or partial discharge or satisfaction of a legal obligation of any person is included in the gross income of such person under section 662(a) (1) or (2), whichever is applicable, as though directly distributed to him as a beneficiary, except in cases to which section 71 (relating to 40 alimony payments) or section 682 (relating to income of a trust in case of divorce, etc.) applies. The term legal obligation includes a legal obligation to support another person if, and only if, the obligation is not affected by the adequacy of the dependent's own resources. For example, a parent has a ``legal obligation" within the meaning of the preceding sentence to support his minor child if under local law property or income from 45 property owned by the child cannot be used for his support so long as his parent is able to support him. On the other hand, if under local law a mother may use the resources of a child for the child's support in lieu of supporting him herself, no obligation of support exists within the meaning of this paragraph, whether or not income is actually used for

support. Similarly, since under local law a child ordinarily is obligated to support his parent only if the parent's earnings and resources are insufficient for the purpose, no obligation exists whether or not the parent's earnings and resources are sufficient. In any event the amount of trust income which is included in the gross income of a person
5 obligated to support a dependent is limited by the extent of his legal obligation under local law. In the case of a parent's obligation to support his child, to the extent that the parent's legal obligation of support, including education, is determined under local law by the family's station in life and by the means of the parent, it is to be determined without consideration of the trust income in question.
10

Reg. § 1.662(b)-1   Character of amounts; when no charitable contributions are made.

In determining the amount includible in the gross income of a beneficiary, the amounts which are determined under section 662(a) and §§ 1.662(a)-1 through 1.662(a)-4 shall
15 have the same character in the hands of the beneficiary as in the hands of the estate or trust. The amounts are treated as consisting of the same proportion of each class of items entering into the computation of distributable net income as the total of each class bears to the total distributable net income of the estate or trust unless the terms of the governing instrument specifically allocate different classes of income to different
20 beneficiaries, or unless local law requires such an allocation. For this purpose, the principles contained in § 1.652(b)-1 shall apply.

Sec. 674.   Power to control beneficial enjoyment

(a) **General rule**. -- The grantor shall be treated as the owner of any portion of a trust in respect
25 of which the beneficial enjoyment of the corpus or the income therefrom is subject to a power of disposition, exercisable by the grantor or a nonadverse party, or both, without the approval or consent of any adverse party.

***

Reg. § 1.674(b)-1   Excepted powers exercisable by any person.
30   (a) Paragraph (b)(1) through (8) of this section sets forth a number of powers which may be exercisable by any person without causing the grantor to be treated as an owner of a trust under section 674(a). Further, with the exception of powers described in paragraph (b)(1) of this section, it is immaterial whether these powers are held in the capacity of trustee. It makes no difference under section 674(b) that the person holding
35 the power is the grantor, or a related or subordinate party (with the qualifications noted in paragraph (b)(1) and (3) of this section).
(b) The exceptions referred to in paragraph (a) of this section are as follows (see, however, the limitations set forth in § 1.674(d)-2):
(1) *Powers to apply income to support of a dependent*. Section 674(b)(1) provides, in
40 effect, that regardless of the general rule of section 674(a), the income of a trust will not be considered as taxable to the grantor merely because in the discretion of any person (other than a grantor who is not acting as a trustee or cotrustee) it may be used for the support of a beneficiary whom the grantor is legally obligated to support, except to the extent that it is in fact used for that purpose. See section 677(b) and the regulations
45 thereunder.
(2) *Powers affecting beneficial enjoyment only after a period*. Section 674(b)(2) provides an exception to section 674(a) if the exercise of a power can only affect the beneficial enjoyment of the income of a trust received after a period of time which is such

Sec. 674. Power to control beneficial enjoyment

that a grantor would not be treated as an owner under section 673 if the power were a reversionary interest. See §§ 1.673(a)-1 and 1.673(b)-1. For example, if a trust created on January 1, 1955, provides for the payment of income to the grantor's son, and the grantor reserves the power to substitute other beneficiaries of income or corpus in lieu of his son on or after January 1, 1965, the grantor is not treated under section 674 as the owner of the trust with respect to ordinary income received before January 1, 1965. But the grantor will be treated as an owner on and after that date unless the power is relinquished. If the beginning of the period during which the grantor may substitute beneficiaries is postponed, the rules set forth in § 1.673(d)-1 are applicable in order to determine whether the grantor should be treated as an owner during the period following the postponement.

(3) *Testamentary powers.* Under paragraph (3) of section 674(b) a power in any person to control beneficial enjoyment exercisable only by will does not cause a grantor to be treated as an owner under section 674(a). However, this exception does not apply to income accumulated for testamentary disposition by the grantor or to income which may be accumulated for such distribution in the discretion of the grantor or a nonadverse party, or both, without the approval or consent of any adverse party. For example, if a trust instrument provides that the income is to be accumulated during the grantor's life and that the grantor may appoint the accumulated income by will, the grantor is treated as the owner of the trust. Moreover, if a trust instrument provides that the income is payable to another person for his life, but the grantor has a testamentary power of appointment over the remainder, and under the trust instrument and local law capital gains are added to corpus, the grantor is treated as the owner of a portion of the trust and capital gains and losses are included in that portion. (See § 1.671-3.)

(4) *Powers to determine beneficial enjoyment of charitable beneficiaries.* Under paragraph (4) of section 674(b) a power in any person to determine the beneficial enjoyment of corpus or income which is irrevocably payable (currently or in the future) for purposes specified in section 170(c) (relating to definition of charitable contributions) will not cause the grantor to be treated as an owner under section 674(a). For example, if a grantor creates a trust, the income of which is irrevocably payable solely to educational or other organizations that qualify under section 170(c), he is not treated as an owner under section 674 although he retains the power to allocate the income among such organizations.

(5) *Powers to distribute corpu*s. Paragraph (5) of section 674(b) provides an exception to section 674(a) for powers to distribute corpus, subject to certain limitations, as follows:

(i) If the power is limited by a reasonably definite standard which is set forth in the trust instrument, it may extend to corpus distributions to any beneficiary or beneficiaries or class of beneficiaries (whether income beneficiaries or remaindermen) without causing the grantor to be treated as an owner under section 674. See section 674(b)(5)(A). It is not required that the standard consist of the needs and circumstances of the beneficiary. A clearly measurable standard under which the holder of a power is legally accountable is deemed a reasonably definite standard for this purpose. For instance, a power to distribute corpus for the education, support, maintenance, or health of the beneficiary; for his reasonable support and comfort; or to enable him to maintain his accustomed standard of living; or to meet an emergency, would be limited by a reasonably definite standard. However, a power to distribute corpus for the pleasure, desire, or happiness of a beneficiary is not limited by a reasonably definite standard. The entire context of a provision of a trust instrument granting a power must be considered in determining whether the power is limited by a reasonably definite standard. For example, if a trust instrument provides that the determination of the trustee shall be conclusive with respect to the exercise or nonexercise of a power, the power is not limited by a reasonably definite standard. However, the fact that the governing instrument is phrased in discretionary terms is not in itself an indication that no reasonably definite standard exists.

(ii) If the power is not limited by a reasonably definite standard set forth in the trust
5 instrument, the exception applies only if distributions of corpus may be made solely in favor of current income beneficiaries, and any corpus distribution to the current income beneficiary must be chargeable against the proportionate part of corpus held in trust for payment of income to that beneficiary as if it constituted a separate trust (whether or not physically segregated). See section 674(b)(5)(B).

10   (iii) This subparagraph may be illustrated by the following examples:

Example 1. A trust instrument provides for payment of the income to the grantor's two brothers for life, and for payment of the corpus to the grantor's nephews in equal shares. The grantor reserves the power to distribute corpus to pay medical expenses that may be incurred by his brothers or nephews. The grantor is not treated as an owner by reason of
15 this power because section 674(b)(5)(A) excepts a power, exercisable by any person, to invade corpus for any beneficiary, including a remainderman, if the power is limited by a reasonably definite standard which is set forth in the trust instrument. However, if the power were also exercisable in favor of a person (for example, a sister) who was not otherwise a beneficiary of the trust, section 674(b)(5)(A) would not be applicable.

20   *Example* 2. The facts are the same as in example 1 except that the grantor reserves the power to distribute any part of the corpus to his brothers or to his nephews for their happiness. The grantor is treated as the owner of the trust. Paragraph (5)(A) of section 674(b) is inapplicable because the power is not limited by a reasonably definite standard. Paragraph (5)(B) is inapplicable because the power to distribute corpus permits a
25 distribution of corpus to persons other than current income beneficiaries.

Example 3. A trust instrument provides for payment of the income to the grantor's two adult sons in equal shares for 10 years, after which the corpus is to be distributed to his grandchildren in equal shares. The grantor reserves the power to pay over to each son up to one-half of the corpus during the 10-year period, but any such payment shall
30 proportionately reduce subsequent income and corpus payments made to the son receiving the corpus. Thus, if one-half of the corpus is paid to one son, all the income from the remaining half is thereafter payable to the other son. The grantor is not treated as an owner under section 674(a) by reason of this power because it qualifies under the exception of section 674(b)(5)(B).

35   (6) *Powers to withhold income temporarily.* (i) Section 674(b)(6) excepts a power which, in general, enables the holder merely to effect a postponement in the time when the ordinary income is enjoyed by a current income beneficiary. Specifically, there is excepted a power to distribute or apply ordinary income to or for a current income beneficiary or to accumulate the income, if the accumulated income must ultimately be
40 payable either:

(a) To the beneficiary from whom it was withheld, his estate, or his appointees (or persons designated by name, as a class, or otherwise as alternate takers in default of appointment) under a power of appointment held by the beneficiary which does not exclude from the class of possible appointees any person other than the beneficiary, his
45 estate, his creditors, or the creditors of his estate (section 674(b)(6)(A));

(b) To the beneficiary from whom it was withheld, or if he does not survive a date of distribution which could reasonably be expected to occur within his lifetime, to his appointees (or alternate takers in default of appointment) under any power of appointment, general or special, or if he has no power of appointment to one or more
50 designated alternate takers (other than the grantor of the grantor's estate) whose shares have been irrevocably specified in the trust instrument (section 674(b)(6)(A) and the flush

Sec. 674. Power to control beneficial enjoyment

material following); or

(c) On termination of the trust, or in conjunction with a distribution of corpus which is augmented by the accumulated income, to the current income beneficiaries in shares which have been irrevocably specified in the trust instrument, or if any beneficiary does not survive a date of distribution which would reasonably be expected to occur within his 5 lifetime, to his appointees (or alternate takers in default of appointment) under any power of appointment, general or special, or if he has no power of appointment to one or more designated alternate takers (other than the grantor or the grantor's estate) whose shares have been irrevocably specified in the trust instrument (section 674(b)(6)(B) and the flush material following). 10
(In the application of (a) of this subdivision, if the accumulated income of a trust is ultimately payable to the estate of the current income beneficiary or is ultimately payable to his appointees or takers in default of appointment, under a power of the type described in (a) of this subdivision, it need not be payable to the beneficiary from whom it was withheld under any circumstances. Furthermore, if a trust otherwise qualifies for the 15 exception in (a) of this subdivision the trust income will not be considered to be taxable to the grantor under section 677 by reason of the existence of the power of appointment referred to in (a) of this subdivision.) In general, the exception in section 674(b)(6) is not applicable if the power is in substance one to shift ordinary income from one beneficiary to another. Thus, a power will not qualify for this exception if ordinary income may be 20 distributed to beneficiary A, or may be added to corpus which is ultimately payable to beneficiary B, a remainderman who is not a current income beneficiary. However, section 674(b)(6)(B), and (c) of this subdivision, permit a limited power to shift ordinary income among current income beneficiaries, as illustrated in example 1 of this subparagraph.

(ii) The application of section 674(b)(6) may be illustrated by the following examples: 25
Example 1. A trust instrument provides that the income shall be paid in equal shares to the grantor's two adult daughters but the grantor reserves the power to withhold from either beneficiary any part of that beneficiary's share of income and to add it to the corpus of the trust until the younger daughter reaches the age of 30 years. When the younger daughter reaches the age of 30, the trust is to terminate and the corpus is to be divided 30 equally between the two daughters or their estates. Although exercise of this power may permit the shifting of accumulated income from one beneficiary to the other (since the corpus with the accumulations is to be divided equally) the power is excepted under section 674(b)(6)(B) and subdivision (i)(c) of this subparagraph.
Example 2. The facts are the same as in example 1, except that the grantor of the trust 35 reserves the power to distribute accumulated income to the beneficiaries in such shares as he chooses. The combined powers are not excepted by section 674(b)(6)(B) since income accumulated pursuant to the first power is neither required to be payable only in conjunction with a corpus distribution nor required to be payable in shares specified in the trust instrument. See, however, section 674(c) and § 1.674(c)-1 for the effect of such a 40 power if it is exercisable only by independent trustees.
Example 3. A trust provides for payment of income to the grantor's adult son with the grantor retaining the power to accumulate the income until the grantor's death, when all accumulations are to be paid to the son. If the son predeceases the grantor, all accumulations are, at the death of the grantor, to be paid to his daughter, or if she is not 45 living, to alternate takers (which do not include the grantor's estate) in specified shares. The power is excepted under section 674(b)(6)(A) since the date of distribution (the date of the grantor's death) may, in the usual case, reasonably be expected to occur during the beneficiary's (the son's) lifetime. It is not necessary that the accumulations be payable to the son's estate or his appointees if he should predecease the grantor for this 50 exception to apply.

Sec. 674. Power to control beneficial enjoyment

(7) *Power to withhold income during disability.* Section 674(b)(7) provides an exception for a power which, in general, will permit ordinary income to be withheld during the legal disability of an income beneficiary or while he is under 21. Specifically, there is excepted a power, exercisable only during the existence of a legal disability of any
5 current income beneficiary or the period during which any income beneficiary is under the age of 21 years, to distribute or apply ordinary income to or for that beneficiary or to accumulate the income and add it to corpus. To qualify under this exception it is not necessary that the income ultimately be payable to the income beneficiary from whom it was withheld, his estate, or his appointees; that is, the accumulated income may be
10 added to corpus and ultimately distributed to others. For example, the grantor is not treated as an owner under section 674 if the income of a trust is payable to his son for life, remainder to his grandchildren, although he reserves the power to accumulate income and add it to corpus while his son is under 21.

(8) *Powers to allocate between corpus and income.* Paragraph (8) of section 674(b)
15 provides that a power to allocate receipts and disbursements between corpus and income, even though expressed in broad language, will not cause the grantor to be treated as an owner under the general rule of section 674(a).

Reg. § 1.674(d)-1 Excepted powers exercisable by any trustee other than grantor
20 **or spouse.**

Section 674(d) provides an additional exception to the general rule of section 674(a) for a power to distribute, apportion, or accumulate income to or for a beneficiary or beneficiaries or to, for, or within a class of beneficiaries, whether or not the conditions of section 674(b) (6) or (7) are satisfied, if the power is solely exercisable (without the
25 approval or consent of any other person) by a trustee or trustees none of whom is the grantor or spouse living with the grantor, and if the power is limited by a reasonably definite external standard set forth in the trust instrument (see paragraph (b)(5) of § 1.674(b)-1 with respect to what constitutes a reasonably definite standard). See, however, the limitations set forth in § 1.674(d)-2.
30

Sec. 678. Person other than grantor treated as substantial owner

(a) **General rule.** -- A person other than the grantor shall be treated as the owner of any portion of a trust with respect to which:

(1) such person has a power exercisable solely by himself to vest the corpus or the income
35 therefrom in himself, or

(2) such person has previously partially released or otherwise modified such a power and after the release or modification retains such control as would, within the principles of sections 671 to 677, inclusive, subject to grantor of a trust to treatment as the owner thereof.

***

40 **Reg. § 1.678(c)-1 Trusts for support.**

(a) Section 678(a) does not apply to a power which enables the holder, in the capacity of trustee or cotrustee, to apply the income of the trust to the support or maintenance of a person whom the holder is obligated to support, except to the extent the income is so applied. See paragraphs (a), (b), and (c) of § 1.677(b)-1 for applicable principles where
45 any amount is applied for the support or maintenance of a person whom the holder is obligated to support.

(b) The general rule in section 678(a) (and not the exception in section 678(c)) is applicable in any case in which the holder of a power exercisable solely by himself is

Sec. 678.   Person other than grantor treated as substantial owner

able, in any capacity other than that of trustee or cotrustee, to apply the income in discharge of his obligation of support or maintenance.

(c) Section 678(c) is concerned with the taxability of income subject to a power described in section 678(a). It has no application to the taxability of income which is either required to be applied pursuant to the terms of the trust instrument or is applied 5 pursuant to a power which is not described in section 678(a), the taxability of such income being governed by other provisions of the Code. See § 1.662(a)-4.

Sec. 682.   Income of an estate or trust in case of divorce, etc.

(a) Inclusion in gross income of wife. -- There shall be included in the gross income of a wife 10 who is divorced or legally separated under a decree of divorce or of separate maintenance (or who is separated from her husband under a written separation agreement) the amount of the income of any trust which such wife is entitled to receive and which, except for this section, would be includible in the gross income of her husband, and such amount shall not, despite any other provision of this subtitle, be includible in the gross income of such husband. This subsection shall 15 not apply to that part of any such income of the trust which the terms of the decree, written separation agreement, or trust instrument fix, in terms of an amount of money or a portion of such income, as a sum which is payable for the support of minor children of such husband. In case such income is less than the amount specified in the decree, agreement, or instrument, for the purpose of applying the preceding sentence, such income, to the extent of such sum payable for such 20 support, shall be considered a payment for such support.

(b) Wife considered a beneficiary. -- For purposes of computing the taxable income of the estate or trust and the taxable income of a wife to whom subsection (a) applies, such wife shall be considered as the beneficiary specified in this part.

(c) Cross reference. -- For definitions of "husband" and "wife", as used in this section, see 25 section 7701(a)(17).

Sec. 691.   Recipients of income in respect of decedents

(a) Inclusion in gross income. --

(1) General rule. -- The amount of all items of gross income in respect of a decedent which 30 are not properly includible in respect of the taxable period in which falls the date of his death or a prior period (including the amount of all items of gross income in respect of a prior decedent, if the right to receive such amount was acquired by reason of the death of the prior decedent or by bequest, devise, or inheritance from the prior decedent) shall be included in the gross income, for the taxable year when received, of: 35

(A) the estate of the decedent, if the right to receive the amount is acquired by the decedent's estate from the decedent;

(B) the person who, by reason of the death of the decedent, acquires the right to receive the amount, if the right to receive the amount is not acquired by the decedent's estate from the decedent; or 40

(C) the person who acquires from the decedent the right to receive the amount by bequest, devise, or inheritance, if the amount is received after a distribution by the decedent's estate of such right.

(2) Income in case of sale, etc. -- If a right, described in paragraph (1), to receive an amount is transferred by the estate of the decedent or a person who received such right by reason of the 45 death of the decedent or by bequest, devise, or inheritance from the decedent, there shall be

865

Sec. 691. Recipients of income in respect of decedents

included in the gross income of the estate or such person, as the case may be, for the taxable period in which the transfer occurs, the fair market value of such right at the time of such transfer plus the amount by which any consideration for the transfer exceeds such fair market value. For purposes of this paragraph, the term "transfer" includes sale, exchange, or other disposition, or the satisfaction of an installment obligation at other than face value, but does not include transmission at death to the estate of the decedent or a transfer to a person pursuant to the right of such person to receive such amount by reason of the death of the decedent or by bequest, devise, or inheritance from the decedent.

(3) Character of income determined by reference to decedent. -- The right, described in paragraph (1), to receive an amount shall be treated, in the hands of the estate of the decedent or any person who acquired such right by reason of the death of the decedent, or by bequest, devise, or inheritance from the decedent, as if it had been acquired by the estate or such person in the transaction in which the right to receive the income was originally derived and the amount includible in gross income under paragraph (1) or (2) shall be considered in the hands of the estate or such person to have the character which it would have had in the hands of the decedent if the decedent had lived and received such amount.

(4) Installment obligations acquired from decedent. -- In the case of an installment obligation reportable by the decedent on the installment method under section 453, if such obligation is acquired by the decedent's estate from the decedent or by any person by reason of the death of the decedent or by bequest, devise, or inheritance from the decedent--

    (A) an amount equal to the excess of the face amount of such obligation over the basis of the obligation in the hands of the decedent (determined under section 453B) shall, for the purpose of paragraph (1), be considered as an item of gross income in respect of the decedent; and

    (B) such obligation shall, for purposes of paragraphs (2) and (3), be considered a right to receive an item of gross income in respect of the decedent, but the amount includible in gross income under paragraph (2) shall be reduced by an amount equal to the basis of the obligation in the hands of the decedent (determined under section 453B).

(5) Other rules relating to installment obligations. --

    (A) In general. -- In the case of an installment obligation reportable by the decedent on the installment method under section 453, for purposes of paragraph (2)--

        (i) the second sentence of paragraph (2) shall be applied by inserting "(other than the obligor)" after "or a transfer to a person",

        (ii) any cancellation of such an obligation shall be treated as a transfer, and

        (iii) any cancellation of such an obligation occurring at the death of the decedent shall be treated as a transfer by the estate of the decedent (or, if held by a person other than the decedent before the death of the decedent, by such person).

    (B) Face amount treated as fair market value in certain cases. -- In any case to which the first sentence of paragraph (2) applies by reason of subparagraph (A), if the decedent and the obligor were related persons (within the meaning of section 453(f)(1)), the fair market value of the installment obligation shall be treated as not less than its face amount.

    (C) Cancellation includes becoming unenforceable. -- For purposes of subparagraph (A), an installment obligation which becomes unenforceable shall be treated as if it were canceled.

(b) Allowance of deductions and credit. -- The amount of any deduction specified in section 162, 163, 164, 212, or 611 (relating to deductions for expenses, interest, taxes, and depletion) or credit specified in section 27 (relating to foreign tax credit), in respect of a decedent which is not

Sec. 691. Recipients of income in respect of decedents

properly allowable to the decedent in respect of the taxable period in which falls the date of his death, or a prior period, shall be allowed:

    (1) Expenses, interest, and taxes. -- In the case of a deduction specified in sections 162, 163, 164, or 212 and a credit specified in section 27, in the taxable year when paid -

        (A) to the estate of the decedent; except that   5

        (B) if the estate of the decedent is not liable to discharge the obligation to which the deduction or credit relates, to the person who, by reason of the death of the decedent or by bequest, devise, or inheritance acquires, subject to such obligation, from the decedent an interest in property of the decedent.

    (2) Depletion. -- In the case of the deduction specified in section 611, to the person 10 described in subsection (a)(1)(A), (B), or (C) who, in the manner described therein, receives the income to which the deduction relates, in the taxable year when such income is received.

(c) Deduction for estate tax. --

    (1) Allowance of deduction. --

        (A) General rule. -- A person who includes an amount in gross income under subsection 15 (a) shall be allowed, for the same taxable year, as a deduction an amount which bears the same ratio to the estate tax attributable to the net value for estate tax purposes of all the items described in subsection (a)(1) as the value for estate tax purposes of the items of gross income or portions thereof in respect of which such person included the amount in gross income (or the amount included in gross income, whichever is lower) bears to the 20 value for estate tax purposes of all the items described in subsection (a)(1).

        (B) Estates and trusts. -- In the case of an estate or trust, the amount allowed as a deduction under subparagraph (A) shall be computed by excluding from the gross income of the estate or trust the portion (if any) of the items described in subsection (a)(1) which is properly paid, credited, or to be distributed to the beneficiaries during the taxable year.   25

    (2) Method of computing deduction. -- For purposes of paragraph (1)--

        (A) The term "estate tax" means the tax imposed on the estate of the decedent or any prior decedent under section 2001 or 2101, reduced by the credits against such tax.

        (B) The net value for estate tax purposes of all the items described in subsection (a)(1) shall be the excess of the value for estate tax purposes of all the items described in 30 subsection (a)(1) over the deductions from the gross estate in respect of claims which represent the deductions and credit described in subsection (b). Such net value shall be determined with respect to the provisions of section 421(c)(2), relating to the deduction for estate tax with respect to stock options to which part II of subchapter D applies.

    (C) The estate tax attributable to such net value shall be an amount equal to the excess of the 35 estate tax over the estate tax computed without including in the gross estate such net value.***

For purposes of sections 1(h), 1201, 1202, and 1211, the amount taken into account with respect to any item described in subsection (a)(1) shall be reduced (but not below zero) by the amount of the deduction allowable under paragraph (1) of this subsection with respect to such item.

                           ***   40

Reg. § 1.691(a)-1 Income in respect of a decedent.

    (a) *Scope of section 691.* In general, the regulations under section 691 cover: (1) The provisions requiring that amounts which are not includible in gross income for the decedent's last taxable year or for a prior taxable year be included in the gross income of the estate or persons receiving such income to the extent that such amounts constitute 45 ``income in respect of a decedent''; (2) the taxable effect of a transfer of the right to such income; (3) the treatment of certain deductions and credit in respect of a decedent which

Sec. 691.   Recipients of income in respect of decedents

are not allowable to the decedent for the taxable period ending with his death or for a prior taxable year; (4) the allowance to a recipient of income in respect of a decedent of a deduction for estate taxes attributable to the inclusion of the value of the right to such income in the decedent's estate; (5) special provisions with respect to installment
5   obligations acquired from a decedent and with respect to the allowance of a deduction for estate taxes to a surviving annuitant under a joint and survivor annuity contract; and (6) special provisions relating to installment obligations transmitted at death when prior law applied to the transmission.

(b) *General definition.* In general, the term income in respect of a decedent refers to
10   those amounts to which a decedent was entitled as gross income but which were not properly includible in computing his taxable income for the taxable year ending with the date of his death or for a previous taxable year under the method of accounting employed by the decedent. See the regulations under section 451. Thus, the term includes:

(1) All accrued income of a decedent who reported his income by use of the cash
15   receipts and disbursements method;

(2) Income accrued solely by reason of the decedent's death in case of a decedent who reports his income by use of an accrual method of accounting; and

(3) Income to which the decedent had a contingent claim at the time of his death.

***

20   (c) *Prior decedent.* The term income in respect of a decedent also includes the amount of all items of gross income in respect of a prior decedent, if (1) the right to receive such amount was acquired by the decedent by reason of the death of the prior decedent or by bequest, devise, or inheritance from the prior decedent and if (2) the amount of gross income in respect of the prior decedent was not properly includible in
25   computing the decedent's taxable income for the taxable year ending with the date of his death or for a previous taxable year. See example 2 of paragraph (b) of § 1.691(a)-2.

(d) *Items excluded from gross income.* Section 691 applies only to the amount of items of gross income in respect of a decedent, and items which are excluded from gross income under subtitle A of the Code are not within the provisions of section 691.
30   ***

Reg. § 1.691(a)-2 Inclusion in gross income by recipients.

(a) Under section 691(a)(1), income in respect of a decedent shall be included in the gross income, for the taxable year when received, of:

(1) The estate of the decedent, if the right to receive the amount is acquired by the
35   decedent's estate from the decedent;

(2) The person who, by reason of the death of the decedent, acquires the right to receive the amount, if the right to receive the amount is not acquired by the decedent's estate from the decedent; or

(3) The person who acquires from the decedent the right to receive the amount by
40   bequest, devise, or inheritance, if the amount is received after a distribution by the decedent's estate of such right. These amounts are included in the income of the estate or of such persons when received by them whether or not they report income by use of the cash receipts and disbursements methods.

(b) The application of paragraph (a) of this section may be illustrated by the following
45   examples, in each of which it is assumed that the decedent kept his books by use of the cash receipts and disbursements method.

Example 1. The decedent was entitled at the date of his death to a large salary payment to be made in equal annual installments over five years. His estate, after collecting two installments, distributed the right to the remaining installment payments to
50   the residuary legatee of the estate. The estate must include in its gross income the two

installments received by it, and the legatee must include in his gross income each of the three installments received by him.

Example 2. A widow acquired, by bequest from her husband, the right to receive renewal commissions on life insurance sold by him in his lifetime, which commissions were payable over a period of years. The widow died before having received all of such 5 commissions, and her son inherited the right to receive the rest of the commissions. The commissions received by the widow were includible in her gross income. The commissions received by the son were not includible in the widow's gross income but must be included in the gross income of the son.

Example 3. The decedent owned a Series E United States savings bond, with his wife 10 as co-owner or beneficiary, but died before the payment of such bond. The entire amount of interest accruing on the bond and not includible in income by the decedent, not just the amount accruing after the death of the decedent, would be treated as income to his wife when the bond is paid.

Example 4. A, prior to his death, acquired 10,000 shares of the capital stock of the X 15 Corporation at a cost of $100 per share. During his lifetime, A had entered into an agreement with X Corporation whereby X Corporation agreed to purchase and the decedent agreed that his executor would sell the 10,000 shares of X Corporation stock owned by him at the book value of the stock at the date of A's death. Upon A's death, the shares are sold by A's executor for $500 a share pursuant to the agreement. Since the 20 sale of stock is consummated after A's death, there is no income in respect of a decedent with respect to the appreciation in value of A's stock to the date of his death. If, in this example, A had in fact sold the stock during his lifetime but payment had not been received before his death, any gain on the sale would constitute income in respect of a decedent when the proceeds were received. 25

Example 5. (1) A owned and operated an apple orchard. During his lifetime, A sold and delivered 1,000 bushels of apples to X, a canning factory, but did not receive payment before his death. A also entered into negotiations to sell 3,000 bushels of apples to Y, a canning factory, but did not complete the sale before his death. After A's death, the executor received payment from X. He also completed the sale to Y and transferred to Y 30 1,200 bushels of apples on hand at A's death and harvested and transferred an additional 1,800 bushels. The gain from the sale of apples by A to X constitutes income in respect of a decedent when received. On the other hand, the gain from the sale of apples by the executor to Y does not.

(2) Assume that, instead of the transaction entered into with Y, A had disposed of the 35 1,200 bushels of harvested apples by delivering them to Z, a cooperative association, for processing and sale. Each year the association commingles the fruit received from all of its members into a pool and assigns to each member a percentage interest in the pool based on the fruit delivered by him. After the fruit is processed and the products are sold, the association distributes the net proceeds from the pool to its members in proportion to 40 their interests in the pool. After A's death, the association made distributions to the executor with respect to A's share of the proceeds from the pool in which A had in interest. Under such circumstances, the proceeds from the disposition of the 1,200 bushels of apples constitute income in respect of a decedent.

45

Reg. § 1.691(a)-3   Character of gross income.

(a) The right to receive an amount of income in respect of a decedent shall be treated in the hands of the estate, or by the person entitled to receive such amount by bequest, devise, or inheritance from the decedent or by reason of his death, as if it had been acquired in the transaction by which the decedent (or a prior decedent) acquired such 50 right, and shall be considered as having the same character it would have had if the

Sec. 691.   Recipients of income in respect of decedents

decedent (or a prior decedent) had lived and received such amount. The provisions of section 1014(a), relating to the basis of property acquired from a decedent, do not apply to these amounts in the hands of the estate and such persons. See section 1014(c).

(b) The application of paragraph (a) of this section may be illustrated by the following:

5 (1) If the income would have been capital gain to the decedent, if he had lived and had received it, from the sale of property, held for more than 1 year (6 months for taxable years beginning before 1977; 9 months for taxable years beginning in 1977), the income, when received, shall be treated in the hands of the estate or of such person as capital gain from the sale of the property, held for more than 1 year (6 months for taxable years

10 beginning before 1977; 9 months for taxable years beginning in 1977), in the same manner as if such person had held the property for the period the decedent held it, and had made the sale.

(2) If the income is interest on United States obligations which were owned by the decedent, such income shall be treated as interest on United States obligations in the

15 hands of the person receiving it, for the purpose of determining the credit provided by section 35, as if such person had owned the obligations with respect to which such interest is paid.

***

20 [T.D. 6500, 25 FR 11814, Nov. 26, 1960; T.D. 6808, 30 FR 3435, Mar. 16, 1965; T.D. 6885, 31 FR 7803, June 2, 1966; T.D. 7728, 45 FR 72650, Nov. 3, 1980]

Sec. 701.   Partners, not partnership, subject to tax

A partnership as such shall not be subject to the income tax imposed by this chapter. Persons
25 carrying on business as partners shall be liable for income tax only in their separate or individual capacities.

Sec. 702.   Income and credits of partner

(a) **General rule.** -- In determining his income tax, each partner shall take into account
30 separately his distributive share of the partnership's--

(1) gains and losses from sales or exchanges of capital assets held for not more than 1 year,

(2) gains and losses from sales or exchanges of capital assets held for more than 1 year,

(3) gains and losses from sales or exchanges of property described in section 1231 (relating
35 to certain property used in a trade or business and involuntary conversions),

(4) charitable contributions (as defined in section 170(c)),

(5) dividends with respect to which section 1(h)(11) or part VIII of subchapter B applies,

(6) taxes, described in section 901, paid or accrued to foreign countries and to possessions of the United States,

40 (7) other items of income, gain, loss, deduction, or credit, to the extent provided by regulations prescribed by the Secretary, and

(8) taxable income or loss, exclusive of items requiring separate computation under other paragraphs of this subsection.

(b) **Character of items constituting distributive share.** -- The character of any item of

Sec. 702. Income and credits of partner

income, gain, loss, deduction, or credit included in a partner's distributive share under paragraphs (1) through (7) of subsection (a) shall be determined as if such item were realized directly from the source from which realized by the partnership, or incurred in the same manner as incurred by the partnership.

    (c) Gross income of a partner. -- In any case where it is necessary to determine the gross income of a partner for purposes of this title, such amount shall include his distributive share of the gross income of the partnership.

Sec. 911. Citizens or residents of the United States living abroad

***

    (d) Definitions and special rules. --

***

    (2) Earned income. --

        (A) In general. -- The term "earned income" means wages, salaries, or professional fees, and other amounts received as compensation for personal services actually rendered, but does not include that part of the compensation derived by the taxpayer for personal services rendered by him to a corporation which represents a distribution of earnings or profits rather than a reasonable allowance as compensation for the personal services actually rendered.

        (B) Taxpayer engaged in trade or business. -- In the case of a taxpayer engaged in a trade or business in which both personal services and capital are material income-producing factors, under regulations prescribed by the Secretary, a reasonable allowance as compensation for the personal services rendered by the taxpayer, not in excess of 30 percent of his share of the net profits of such trade or business, shall be considered as earned income.

***

Sec. 1001. Determination of amount of and recognition of gain or loss

    (a) Computation of gain or loss. -- The gain from the sale or other disposition of property shall be the excess of the amount realized therefrom over the adjusted basis provided in section 1011 for determining gain, and the loss shall be the excess of the adjusted basis provided in such section for determining loss over the amount realized.

    (b) Amount realized. -- The amount realized from the sale or other disposition of property shall be the sum of any money received plus the fair market value of the property (other than money) received. In determining the amount realized -

    (1) there shall not be taken into account any amount received as reimbursement for real property taxes which are treated under section 164(d) as imposed on the purchaser, and

    (2) there shall be taken into account amounts representing real property taxes which are treated under section 164(d) as imposed on the taxpayer if such taxes are to be paid by the purchaser.

    (c) Recognition of gain or loss. -- Except as otherwise provided in this subtitle, the entire amount of the gain or loss, determined under this section, on the sale or exchange of property shall be recognized.

    (d) Installment sales. -- Nothing in this section shall be construed to prevent (in the case of property sold under contract providing for payment in installments) the taxation of that portion of any installment payment representing gain or profit in the year in which such payment is received.

Sec. 1001. Determination of amount of and recognition of gain or loss

(e) Certain term interests. --

(1) In general. -- In determining gain or loss from the sale or other disposition of a term interest in property, that portion of the adjusted basis of such interest which is determined pursuant to section 1014, 1015, or 1041 (to the extent that such adjusted basis is a portion of the entire adjusted basis of the property) shall be disregarded.

(2) Term interest in property defined. -- For purposes of paragraph (1), the term "term interest in property" means--

(A) a life interest in property,

(B) an interest in property for a term of years, or

(C) an income interest in a trust.

(3) Exception. -- Paragraph (1) shall not apply to a sale or other disposition which is a part of a transaction in which the entire interest in property is transferred to any person or persons.

Reg. § 1.1001-1 Computation of gain or loss.

(a) *General rule.* Except as otherwise provided in subtitle A of the Code, the gain or loss realized from the conversion of property into cash, or from the exchange of property for other property differing materially either in kind or in extent, is treated as income or as loss sustained. The amount realized from a sale or other disposition of property is the sum of any money received plus the fair market value of any property (other than money) received. The fair market value of property is a question of fact, but only in rare and extraordinary cases will property be considered to have no fair market value. The general method of computing such gain or loss is prescribed by section 1001 (a) through (d) which contemplates that from the amount realized upon the sale or exchange there shall be withdrawn a sum sufficient to restore the adjusted basis prescribed by section 1011 and the regulations thereunder (i.e., the cost or other basis adjusted for receipts, expenditures, losses, allowances, and other items chargeable against and applicable to such cost or other basis). The amount which remains after the adjusted basis has been restored to the taxpayer constitutes the realized gain. If the amount realized upon the sale or exchange is insufficient to restore to the taxpayer the adjusted basis of the property, a loss is sustained to the extent of the difference between such adjusted basis and the amount realized. The basis may be different depending upon whether gain or loss is being computed. For example, see section 1015(a) and the regulations thereunder. Section 1001(e) and paragraph (f) of this section prescribe the method of computing gain or loss upon the sale or other disposition of a term interest in property the adjusted basis (or a portion) of which is determined pursuant, or by reference, to section 1014 (relating to the basis of property acquired from a decedent) or section 1015 (relating to the basis of property acquired by gift or by a transfer in trust).

(b) *Real estate taxes as amounts received.* (1) Section 1001(b) and section 1012 state rules applicable in making an adjustment upon a sale of real property with respect to the real property taxes apportioned between seller and purchaser under section 164(d). Thus, if the seller pays (or agrees to pay) real property taxes attributable to the real property tax year in which the sale occurs, he shall not take into account, in determining the amount realized from the sale under section 1001(b), any amount received as reimbursement for taxes which are treated under section 164(d) as imposed upon the purchaser. Similarly, in computing the cost of the property under section 1012, the purchaser shall not take into account any amount paid to the seller as reimbursement for real property taxes which are treated under section 164(d) as imposed upon the purchaser. These rules apply whether or not the contract of sale calls for the purchaser to reimburse the seller for such real property taxes paid or to be paid by the seller.

Sec. 1001. Determination of amount of and recognition of gain or loss

(2) *On the other hand*, if the purchaser pays (or is to pay) an amount representing real property taxes which are treated under section 164(d) as imposed upon the seller, that amount shall be taken into account both in determining the amount realized from the sale under section 1001(b) and in computing the cost of the property under section 1012. It is immaterial whether or not the contract of sale specifies that the sale price has been reduced by, or is in any way intended to reflect, the taxes allocable to the seller. See also paragraph (b) of § 1.1012-1.

(3) Subparagraph (1) of this paragraph shall not apply to a seller who, in a taxable year prior to the taxable year of sale, pays an amount representing real property taxes which are treated under section 164(d) as imposed on the purchaser, if such seller has elected to capitalize such amount in accordance with section 266 and the regulations thereunder (relating to election to capitalize certain carrying charges and taxes).

(4) The application of this paragraph may be illustrated by the following examples:

Example 1. Assume that the contract price on the sale of a parcel of real estate is $50,000 and that real property taxes thereon in the amount of $1,000 for the real property tax year in which occurred the date of sale were previously paid by the seller. Assume further that $750 of the taxes are treated under section 164(d) as imposed upon the purchaser and that he reimburses the seller in that amount in addition to the contract price. The amount realized by the seller is $50,000. Similarly, $50,000 is the purchaser's cost. If, in this example, the purchaser made no payment other than the contract price of $50,000, the amount realized by the seller would be $49,250, since the sales price would be deemed to include $750 paid to the seller in reimbursement for real property taxes imposed upon the purchaser. Similarly, $49,250 would be the purchaser's cost.

Example 2. Assume that the purchaser in example (1), above, paid all of the real property taxes. Assume further that $250 of the taxes are treated under section 164(d) as imposed upon the seller. The amount realized by the seller is $50,250. Similarly, $50,250 is the purchaser's cost, regardless of the taxable year in which the purchaser makes actual payment of the taxes.

Example 3. Assume that the seller described in the first part of example (1), above, paid the real property taxes of $1,000 in the taxable year prior to the taxable year of sale and elected under section 266 to capitalize the $1,000 of taxes. In such a case, the amount realized is $50,750. Moreover, regardless of whether the seller elected to capitalize the real property taxes, the purchaser in that case could elect under section 266 to capitalize the $750 of taxes treated under section 164(d) as imposed upon him, in which case his adjusted basis would be $50,750 (cost of $50,000 plus capitalized taxes of $570).

(c) *Other rules.* (1) Even though property is not sold or otherwise disposed of, gain is realized if the sum of all the amounts received which are required by section 1016 and other applicable provisions of subtitle A of the Code to be applied against the basis of the property exceeds such basis. Except as otherwise provided in section 301(c)(3)(B) with respect to distributions out of increase in value of property accrued prior to March 1, 1913, such gain is includible in gross income under section 61 as ``income from whatever source derived''. On the other hand, a loss is not ordinarily sustained prior to the sale or other disposition of the property, for the reason that until such sale or other disposition occurs there remains the possibility that the taxpayer may recover or recoup the adjusted basis of the property. Until some identifiable event fixes the actual sustaining of a loss and the amount thereof, it is not taken into account.

(2) The provisions of subparagraph (1) of this paragraph may be illustrated by the following example:

Example: A, an individual on a calendar year basis, purchased certain shares of stock subsequent to February 28, 1913, for $10,000. On January 1, 1954, A's adjusted basis

Sec. 1001. Determination of amount of and recognition of gain or loss

for the stock had been reduced to $1,000 by reason of receipts and distributions described in sections 1016(a)(1) and 1016(a)(4). He received in 1954 a further distribution of $5,000, being a distribution covered by section 1016(a)(4), other than a distribution out of increase of value of property accrued prior to March 1, 1913. This
5 distribution applied against the adjusted basis as required by section 1016(a)(4) exceeds that basis by $4,000. The $4,000 excess is a gain realized by A in 1954 and is includible in gross income in his return for that calendar year. In computing gain from the stock, as in adjusting basis, no distinction is made between items of receipts or distributions described in section 1016. If A sells the stock in 1955 for $5,000, he realizes in 1955 a
10 gain of $5,000, since the adjusted basis of the stock for the purpose of computing gain or loss from the sale is zero.

(d) *Installment sales.* In the case of property sold on the installment plan, special rules for the taxation of the gain are prescribed in section 453.

(e) *Transfers in part a sale and in part a gift.* (1) Where a transfer of property is in part
15 a sale and in part a gift, the transferor has a gain to the extent that the amount realized by him exceeds his adjusted basis in the property. However, no loss is sustained on such a transfer if the amount realized is less than the adjusted basis. For the determination of basis of property in the hands of the transferee, see § 1.1015-4. For the allocation of the adjusted basis of property in the case of a bargain sale to a charitable organization, see §
20 1.1011-2.

(2) *Examples.* The provisions of subparagraph (1) may be illustrated by the following examples:

Example 1. A transfers property to his son for $60,000. Such property in the hands of A has an adjusted basis of $30,000 (and a fair market value of $90,000). A's gain is
25 $30,000, the excess of $60,000, the amount realized, over the adjusted basis, $30,000. He has made a gift of $30,000, the excess of $90,000, the fair market value, over the amount realized, $60,000.

Example 2. A transfers property to his son for $30,000. Such property in the hands of A has an adjusted basis of $60,000 (and a fair market value of $90,000). A has no gain or
30 loss, and has made a gift of $60,000, the excess of $90,000, the fair market value, over the amount realized, $30,000.

Example 3. A transfers property to his son for $30,000. Such property in A's hands has an adjusted basis of $30,000 (and a fair market value of $60,000). A has no gain and has made a gift of $30,000, the excess of $60,000, the fair market value, over the amount
35 realized, $30,000.

Example 4. A transfers property to his son for $30,000. Such property in A's hands has an adjusted basis of $90,000 (and a fair market value of $60,000). A has sustained no loss, and has made a gift of $30,000, the excess of $60,000, the fair market value, over the amount realized, $30,000.
40 (f) *Sale or other disposition of a term interest in property--*(1) *General rule.* Except as otherwise provided in subparagraph (3) of this paragraph, for purposes of determining gain or loss from the sale or other disposition after October 9, 1969, of a term interest in property (as defined in subparagraph (2) of this paragraph) a taxpayer shall not take into account that portion of the adjusted basis of such interest which is determined pursuant,
45 or by reference, to section 1014 (relating to the basis of property acquired from a decedent) or section 1015 (relating to the basis of property acquired by gift or by a transfer in trust) to the extent that such adjusted basis is a portion of the adjusted uniform basis of the entire property (as defined in § 1.1014-5). Where a term interest in property is transferred to a corporation in connection with a transaction to which section 351
50 applies and the adjusted basis of the term interest (i) is determined pursuant to section 1014 or 1015 and (ii) is also a portion of the adjusted uniform basis of the entire property,

Sec. 1001. Determination of amount of and recognition of gain or loss

a subsequent sale or other disposition of such term interest by the corporation will be subject to the provisions of section 1001(e) and this paragraph to the extent that the basis of the term interest so sold or otherwise disposed of is determined by reference to its basis in the hands of the transferor as provided by section 362(a). See subparagraph (2) of this paragraph for rules relating to the characterization of stock received by the transferor of a term interest in property in connection with a transaction to which section 351 applies. That portion of the adjusted uniform basis of the entire property which is assignable to such interest at the time of its sale or other disposition shall be determined under the rules provided in § 1.1014-5. Thus, gain or loss realized from a sale or other disposition of a term interest in property shall be determined by comparing the amount of the proceeds of such sale with that part of the adjusted basis of such interest which is not a portion of the adjusted uniform basis of the entire property.

(2) *Term interest defined.* For purposes of section 1001(e) and this paragraph, a term interest in property means--

(i) A life interest in property,

(ii) An interest in property for a term of years, or

(iii) An income interest in a trust.

Generally, subdivisions (i), (ii), and (iii) refer to an interest, present or future, in the income from property or the right to use property which will terminate or fail on the lapse of time, on the occurrence of an event or contingency, or on the failure of an event or contingency to occur. Such divisions do not refer to remainder or reversionary interests in the property itself or other interests in the property which will ripen into ownership of the entire property upon termination or failure of a preceding term interest. A term interest in property also includes any property received upon a sale or other disposition of a life interest in property, an interest in property for a term of years, or an income interest in a trust by the original holder of such interest, but only to the extent that the adjusted basis of the property received is determined by reference to the adjusted basis of the term interest so transferred.

(3) *Exception.* Paragraph (1) of section 1001(e) and subparagraph (1) of this paragraph shall not apply to a sale or other disposition of a term interest in property as a part of a single transaction in which the entire interest in the property is transferred to a third person or to two or more other persons, including persons who acquire such entire interest as joint tenants, tenants by the entirety, or tenants in common. See § 1.1014-5 for computation of gain or loss upon such a sale or other disposition where the property has been acquired from a decedent or by gift or transfer in trust.

(4) *Illustrations.* For examples illustrating the application of this paragraph, see paragraph (c) of § 1.1014-5.

(g) *Debt instruments issued in exchange for property*--(1) *In general.* If a debt instrument is issued in exchange for property, the amount realized attributable to the debt instrument is the issue price of the debt instrument as determined under § 1.1273-2 or § 1.1274-2, whichever is applicable. If, however, the issue price of the debt instrument is determined under section 1273(b)(4), the amount realized attributable to the debt instrument is its stated principal amount reduced by any unstated interest (as determined under section 483).

(2) *Certain debt instruments that provide for contingent payments*--(i) *In general.* Paragraph (g)(1) of this section does not apply to a debt instrument subject to either § 1.483-4 or § 1.1275-4(c) (certain contingent payment debt instruments issued for nonpublicly traded property).

(ii) *Special rule to determine amount realized.* If a debt instrument subject to § 1.1275-4(c) is issued in exchange for property, and the income from the exchange is not reported under the installment method of section 453, the amount realized attributable to

the debt instrument is the issue price of the debt instrument as determined under §
1.1274-2(g), increased by the fair market value of the contingent payments payable on
the debt instrument. If a debt instrument subject to § 1.483-4 is issued in exchange for
property, and the income from the exchange is not reported under the installment method
5 of section 453, the amount realized attributable to the debt instrument is its stated
principal amount, reduced by any unstated interest (as determined under section 483),
and increased by the fair market value of the contingent payments payable on the debt
instrument. This paragraph (g)(2)(ii), however, does not apply to a debt instrument if the
fair market value of the contingent payments is not reasonably ascertainable. Only in rare
10 and extraordinary cases will the fair market value of the contingent payments be treated
as not reasonably ascertainable.

(3) *Coordination with section 453.* If a debt instrument is issued in exchange for
property, and the income from the exchange is not reported under the installment method
of section 453, this paragraph (g) applies rather than § 15a.453-1(d)(2) to determine the
15 taxpayer's amount realized attributable to the debt instrument.

***

Reg. § 1.1001-2 Discharge of liabilities.

(a) *Inclusion in amount realized*--(1) *In general.* Except as provided in paragraph (a)
(2) and (3) of this section, the amount realized from a sale or other disposition of property
20 includes the amount of liabilities from which the transferor is discharged as a result of the
sale or disposition.

(2) *Discharge of indebtedness.* The amount realized on a sale or other disposition of
property that secures a recourse liability does not include amounts that are (or would be if
realized and recognized) income from the discharge of indebtedness under section 61(a)
25 (12). For situations where amounts arising from the discharge of indebtedness are not
realized and recognized, see section 108 and § 1.61-12(b)(1).

(3) *Liability incurred on acquisition.* In the case of a liability incurred by reason of the
acquisition of the property, this section does not apply to the extent that such liability was
not taken into account in determining the transferor's basis for such property.
30 (4) *Special rules.* For purposes of this section--
(i) The sale or other disposition of property that secures a nonrecourse liability
discharges the transferor from the liability;
(ii) The sale or other disposition of property that secures a recourse liability discharges
the transferor from the liability if another person agrees to pay the liability (whether or not
35 the transferor is in fact released from liability);
(iii) A disposition of property includes a gift of the property or a transfer of the property
in satisfaction of liabilities to which it is subject;
(iv) Contributions and distributions of property between a partner and a partnership
are not sales or other dispositions of property; and
40 (v) The liabilities from which a transferor is discharged as a result of the sale or
disposition of a partnership interest include the transferor's share of the liabilities of the
partnership.

(b) *Effect of fair market value of security.* The fair market value of the security at the
time of sale or disposition is not relevant for purposes of determining under paragraph (a)
45 of this section the amount of liabilities from which the taxpayer is discharged or treated as
discharged. Thus, the fact that the fair market value of the property is less than the
amount of the liabilities it secures does not prevent the full amount of those liabilities from
being treated as money received from the sale or other disposition of the property.
However, see paragraph (a)(2) of this section for a rule relating to certain income from
50 discharge of indebtedness.

(c) *Examples.* The provisions of this section may be illustrated by the following

Sec. 1001. Determination of amount of and recognition of gain or loss

examples. In each example assume the taxpayer uses the cash receipts and disbursements method of accounting, makes a return on the basis of the calendar year, and sells or disposes of all property which is security for a given liability.

Example 1. In 1976 A purchases an asset for $10,000. A pays the seller $1,000 in cash and signs a note payable to the seller for $9,000. A is personally liable for repayment with the seller having full recourse in the event of default. In addition, the asset which was purchased is pledged as security. During the years 1976 and 1977, A takes depreciation deductions on the asset in the amount of $3,100. During this same time period A reduces the outstanding principal on the note to $7,600. At the beginning of 1978 A sells the asset. The buyer pays A $1,600 in cash and assumes personal liability for the $7,600 outstanding liability. A becomes secondarily liable for repayment of the liability. A's amount realized is $9,200 ($1,600 + $7,600). Since A's adjusted basis in the asset is $6,900 ($10,000 - $3,100) A realizes a gain of $2,300 ($9,200 - $6,900).

Example 2. Assume the same facts as in example (1) except that A is not personally liable on the $9,000 note given to the seller and in the event of default the seller's only recourse is to the asset. In addition, on the sale of the asset by A, the purchaser takes the asset subject to the liability. Nevertheless, A's amount realized is $9,200 and A's gain realized is $2,300 on the sale.

***

Example 7. In 1974 E purchases a herd of cattle for breeding purposes. The purchase price is $20,000 consisting of $1,000 cash and a $19,000 note. E is not personally liable for repayment of the liability and the seller's only recourse in the event of default is to the herd of cattle. In 1977 E transfers the herd back to the original seller thereby satisfying the indebtedness pursuant to a provision in the original sales agreement. At the time of the transfer the fair market value of the herd is $15,000 and the remaining principal balance on the note is $19,000. At that time E's adjusted basis in the herd is $16,500 due to a deductible loss incurred when a portion of the herd died as a result of disease. As a result of the indebtedness being satisfied, E's amount realized is $19,000 notwithstanding the fact that the fair market value of the herd was less than $19,000. E's realized gain is $2,500 ($19,000 - $16,500).

Example 8. In 1980, F transfers to a creditor an asset with a fair market value of $6,000 and the creditor discharges $7,500 of indebtedness for which F is personally liable. The amount realized on the disposition of the asset is its fair market value ($6,000). In addition, F has income from the discharge of indebtedness of $1,500 ($7,500 - $6,000).

Reg. § 1.1001-3 Modifications of debt instruments.

(a) *Scope*--(1) *In general.* This section provides rules for determining whether a modification of the terms of a debt instrument results in an exchange for purposes of § 1.1001-1(a). This section applies to any modification of a debt instrument, regardless of the form of the modification. For example, this section applies to an exchange of a new instrument for an existing debt instrument, or to an amendment of an existing debt instrument. This section also applies to a modification of a debt instrument that the issuer and holder accomplish indirectly through one or more transactions with third parties. This section, however, does not apply to exchanges of debt instruments between holders.

***

(b) *General rule.* For purposes of § 1.1001-1(a), a significant modification of a debt instrument, within the meaning of this section, results in an exchange of the original debt instrument for a modified instrument that differs materially either in kind or in extent. A modification that is not a significant modification is not an exchange for purposes of § 1.1001-1(a).

Sec. 1001. Determination of amount of and recognition of gain or loss

1.1001-1(a). Paragraphs (c) and (d) of this section define the term modification and contain examples illustrating the application of the rule. Paragraphs (e) and (f) of this section provide rules for determining when a modification is a significant modification. Paragraph (g) of this section contains examples illustrating the application of the rules in
5 paragraphs (e) and (f) of this section.

***

(e) Significant modifications.

***

(1) *General rule.* Except as otherwise provided in paragraphs (e)(2) through (e)(6) of
10 this section, a modification is a significant modification only if, based on all facts and circumstances, the legal rights or obligations that are altered and the degree to which they are altered are economically significant. In making a determination under this paragraph (e)(1), all modifications to the debt instrument (other than modifications subject to paragraphs (e) (2) through (6) of this section) are considered collectively, so that a
15 series of such modifications may be significant when considered together although each modification, if considered alone, would not be significant.

(2) *Change in yield*--(i) *Scope of rule.* This paragraph (e)(2) applies to debt instruments that provide for only fixed payments, debt instruments with alternative payment schedules subject to § 1.1272-1(c), debt instruments that provide for a fixed
20 yield subject to § 1.1272-1(d) (such as certain demand loans), and variable rate debt instruments. Whether a change in the yield of other debt instruments (for example, a contingent payment debt instrument) is a significant modification is determined under paragraph (e)(1) of this section.

(ii) *In general.* A change in the yield of a debt instrument is a significant modification if
25 the yield computed under paragraph (e)(2)(iii) of this section varies from the annual yield on the unmodified instrument (determined as of the date of the modification) by more than the greater of--

(A) 1/4 of one percent (25 basis points); or

(B) 5 percent of the annual yield of the unmodified instrument (.05 x annual yield).
30 (iii) Yield of the modified instrument--(A) In general. The yield computed under this paragraph (e)(2)(iii) is the annual yield of a debt instrument with--

(1) An issue price equal to the adjusted issue price of the unmodified instrument on the date of the modification (increased by any accrued but unpaid interest and decreased by any accrued bond issuance premium not yet taken into account, and increased or
35 decreased, respectively, to reflect payments made to the issuer or to the holder as consideration for the modification); and

(2) Payments equal to the payments on the modified debt instrument from the date of the modification.

(B) *Prepayment penalty.* For purposes of this paragraph (e)(2)(iii), a commercially
40 reasonable prepayment penalty for a pro rata prepayment (as defined in § 1.1275-2(f)) is not consideration for a modification of a debt instrument and is not taken into account in determining the yield of the modified instrument.

(iv) *Variable rate debt instruments.* For purposes of this paragraph (e)(2), the annual yield of a variable rate debt instrument is the annual yield of the equivalent fixed rate debt
45 instrument (as defined in § 1.1275-5(e)) which is constructed based on the terms of the instrument (either modified or unmodified, whichever is applicable) as of the date of the modification.

(3) *Changes in timing of payments*--(i) *In general.* A modification that changes the timing of payments (including any resulting change in the amount of payments) due
50 under a debt instrument is a significant modification if it results in the material deferral of

Sec. 1001. Determination of amount of and recognition of gain or loss

scheduled payments. The deferral may occur either through an extension of the final maturity date of an instrument or through a deferral of payments due prior to maturity. The materiality of the deferral depends on all the facts and circumstances, including the length of the deferral, the original term of the instrument, the amounts of the payments that are deferred, and the time period between the modification and the actual deferral of 5 payments.

(ii) *Safe-harbor period*. The deferral of one or more scheduled payments within the safe-harbor period is not a material deferral if the deferred payments are unconditionally payable no later than at the end of the safe-harbor period. The safe-harbor period begins on the original due date of the first scheduled payment that is deferred and extends for a 10 period equal to the lesser of five years or 50 percent of the original term of the instrument. For purposes of this paragraph (e)(3)(ii), the term of an instrument is determined without regard to any option to extend the original maturity and deferrals of de minimis payments are ignored. If the period during which payments are deferred is less than the full safe-harbor period, the unused portion of the period remains a safe- 15 harbor period for any subsequent deferral of payments on the instrument.

(4) *Change in obligor or security--*

***

(ii) *Substitution of a new obligor on nonrecourse debt instruments*. The substitution of a new obligor on a nonrecourse debt instrument is not a significant modification.   20

***

(iv) *Change in security or credit enhancement--*(A) R*ecourse debt instruments*. A modification that releases, substitutes, adds or otherwise alters the collateral for, a guarantee on, or other form of credit enhancement for a recourse debt instrument is a significant modification if the modification results in a change in payment expectations.   25

(B) *Nonrecourse debt instruments*. A modification that releases, substitutes, adds or otherwise alters a substantial amount of the collateral for, a guarantee on, or other form of credit enhancement for a nonrecourse debt instrument is a significant modification. A substitution of collateral is not a significant modification, however, if the collateral is fungible or otherwise of a type where the particular units pledged are unimportant (for 30 example, government securities or financial instruments of a particular type and rating). In addition, the substitution of a similar commercially available credit enhancement contract is not a significant modification, and an improvement to the property securing a nonrecourse debt instrument does not result in a significant modification.

(v) *Change in priority of debt*. A change in the priority of a debt instrument relative to 35 other debt of the issuer is a significant modification if it results in a change in payment expectations.

(vi) C*hange in payment expectations--*(A) *In general*. For purposes of this section, a change in payment expectations occurs if, as a result of a transaction--

(1) There is a substantial enhancement of the obligor's capacity to meet the payment 40 obligations under a debt instrument and that capacity was primarily speculative prior to the modification and is adequate after the modification; or

(2) There is a substantial impairment of the obligor's capacity to meet the payment obligations under a debt instrument and that capacity was adequate prior to the modification and is primarily speculative after the modification.   45

(B) *Obligor's capacity*. The obligor's capacity includes any source for payment, including collateral, guarantees, or other credit enhancement.

(5) *Changes in the nature of a debt instrument--*

***

(ii) *Change in recourse nature--*(A) *In general*. Except as provided in paragraph (e)(5) 50

879

(ii)(B) of this section, a change in the nature of a debt instrument from recourse (or substantially all recourse) to nonrecourse (or substantially all nonrecourse) is a significant modification. Thus, for example, a legal defeasance of a debt instrument in which the issuer is released from all liability to make payments on the debt instrument (including an
5 obligation to contribute additional securities to a trust if necessary to provide sufficient funds to meet all scheduled payments on the instrument) is a significant modification. Similarly, a change in the nature of the debt instrument from nonrecourse (or substantially all nonrecourse) to recourse (or substantially all recourse) is a significant modification. If an instrument is not substantially all recourse or not substantially all nonrecourse either
10 before or after a modification, the significance of the modification is determined under paragraph (e)(1) of this section.
  (B) *Exceptions--*

***

  (2) *Original collateral.* A modification that changes a recourse debt instrument to a
15 nonrecourse debt instrument is not a significant modification if the instrument continues to be secured only by the original collateral and the modification does not result in a change in payment expectations. For this purpose, if the original collateral is fungible or otherwise of a type where the particular units pledged are unimportant (for example, government securities or financial instruments of a particular type and rating),
20 replacement of some or all units of the original collateral with other units of the same or similar type and aggregate value is not considered a change in the original collateral.
  (6) *Accounting or financial covenants.* A modification that adds, deletes, or alters customary accounting or financial covenants is not a significant modification.

***

25 [T.D. 6500, 25 FR 11910, Nov. 26, 1960; T.D. 7142, 36 FR 18950, Sept. 24, 1971; T.D. 7207, 37 FR 20797, Oct. 5, 1972; T.D. 7213, 37 FR 21992, Oct. 18, 1972; T.D. 7741, 45 FR 81744, Dec. 12, 1980; T.D. 8517, 59 FR 4807, Feb. 2, 1994; T.D. 8674, 61 FR 30139, June 14, 1996; T.D. 8675, 61 FR 32930, June 26, 1996; 61 FR 47822, Sept. 11, 1996]

30 **Reg. § 1.1002-1 Sales or exchanges.**
  (a) *General rule.* The general rule with respect to gain or loss realized upon the sale or exchange of property as determined under section 1001 is that the entire amount of such gain or loss is recognized except in cases where specific provisions of subtitle A of the code provide otherwise.
35 (b) *Strict construction of exceptions from general rule.* The exceptions from the general rule requiring the recognition of all gains and losses, like other exceptions from a rule of taxation of general and uniform application, are strictly construed and do not extend either beyond the words or the underlying assumptions and purposes of the exception. Nonrecognition is accorded by the Code only if the exchange is one which
40 satisfies both (1) the specific description in the Code of an excepted exchange, and (2) the underlying purpose for which such exchange is excepted from the general rule. The exchange must be germane to, and a necessary incident of, the investment or enterprise in hand. The relationship of the exchange to the venture or enterprise is always material, and the surrounding facts and circumstances must be shown. As elsewhere, the taxpayer
45 claiming the benefit of the exception must show himself within the exception.
  (c) *Certain exceptions to general rule.* Exceptions to the general rule are made, for example, by sections 351(a), 354, 361(a), 371(a)(1), 371(b)(1), 721, 1031, 1035 and 1036. These sections describe certain specific exchanges of property in which at the time of the exchange particular differences exist between the property parted with and the
50 property acquired, but such differences are more formal than substantial. As to these, the

Sec. 1001. Determination of amount of and recognition of gain or loss

Code provides that such differences shall not be deemed controlling, and that gain or loss shall not be recognized at the time of the exchange. The underlying assumption of these exceptions is that the new property is substantially a continuation of the old investment still unliquidated; and, in the case of reorganizations, that the new enterprise, the new corporate structure, and the new property are substantially continuations of the old still unliquidated.

(d) *Exchange*. Ordinarily, to constitute an exchange, the transaction must be a reciprocal transfer of property, as distinguished from a transfer of property for a money consideration only.

Sec. 1011. Adjusted basis for determining gain or loss

(a) General rule. -- The adjusted basis for determining the gain or loss from the sale or other disposition of property, whenever acquired, shall be the basis (determined under section 1012 or other applicable sections of this subchapter and subchapters C (relating to corporate distributions and adjustments), K (relating to partners and partnerships), and P (relating to capital gains and losses)), adjusted as provided in section 1016.

(b) Bargain sale to a charitable organization. -- If a deduction is allowable under section 170 (relating to charitable contributions) by reason of a sale, then the adjusted basis for determining the gain from such sale shall be that portion of the adjusted basis which bears the same ratio to the adjusted basis as the amount realized bears to the fair market value of the property.

Reg. § 1.1011-2 Bargain sale to a charitable organization.

(a) *In general.* (1) If for the taxable year a charitable contributions deduction is allowable under section 170 by reason of a sale or exchange of property, the taxpayer's adjusted basis of such property for purposes of determining gain from such sale or exchange must be computed as provided in section 1011(b) and paragraph (b) of this section. If after applying the provisions of section 170 for the taxable year, including the percentage limitations of section 170(b), no deduction is allowable under that section by reason of the sale or exchange of the property, section 1011(b) does not apply and the adjusted basis of the property is not required to be apportioned pursuant to paragraph (b) of this section. In such case the entire adjusted basis of the property is to be taken into account in determining gain from the sale or exchange, as provided in § 1.1011-1(e). In ascertaining whether or not a charitable contributions deduction is allowable under section 170 for the taxable year for such purposes, that section is to be applied without regard to this section and the amount by which the contributed portion of the property must be reduced under section 170(e)(1) is the amount determined by taking into account the amount of gain which would have been ordinary income or long-term capital gain if the contributed portion of the property had been sold by the donor at its fair market value at the time of the sale or exchange.

(2) If in the taxable year there is a sale or exchange of property which gives rise to a charitable contribution which is carried over under section 170(b)(1)(D)(ii) or section 170(d) to a subsequent taxable year or is postponed under section 170(a)(3) to a subsequent taxable year, section 1011(b) and paragraph (b) of this section must be applied for purposes of apportioning the adjusted basis of the property for the year of the sale or exchange, whether or not such contribution is allowable as a deduction under section 170 in such subsequent year.

(3) If property is transferred subject to an indebtedness, the amount of the indebtedness must be treated as an amount realized for purposes of determining whether there is a sale or exchange to which section 1011(b) and this section apply, even though

Sec. 1011. Adjusted basis for determining gain or loss

the transferee does not agree to assume or pay the indebtedness.

***

(b) *Apportionment of adjusted basis.* For purposes of determining gain on a sale or exchange to which this paragraph applies, the adjusted basis of the property which is
5 sold or exchanged shall be that portion of the adjusted basis of the entire property which bears the same ratio to the adjusted basis as the amount realized bears to the fair market value of the entire property. The amount of such gain which shall be treated as ordinary income (or long-term capital gain) shall be that amount which bears the same ratio to the ordinary income (or long-term capital gain) which would have been recognized if the
10 entire property had been sold by the donor at its fair market value at the time of the sale or exchange as the amount realized on the sale or exchange bears to the fair market value of the entire property at such time. The terms ordinary income and long-term capital gain, as used in this section, have the same meaning as they have in paragraph (a) of § 1.170A-4. For determining the portion of the adjusted basis, ordinary income, and long-
15 term capital gain allocated to the contributed portion of the property for purposes of applying section 170(e)(1) and paragraph (a) of § 1.170A-4 to the contributed portion of the property, and for determining the donee's basis in such contributed portion, see paragraph (c) (2) and (4) of § 1.170A-4. For determining the holding period of such contributed portion, see section 1223(2) and the regulations thereunder.
20 (c) *Illustrations.* The application of this section may be illustrated by the following examples, which are supplemented by other examples in paragraph (d) of § 1.170A-4:

Example 1. In 1970, A, a calendar-year individual taxpayer, sells to a church for $4,000 stock held for more than 6 months which has an adjusted basis of $4,000 and a fair market value of $10,000. A's contribution base for 1970, as defined in section 170(b)
25 (1)(F), is $100,000, and during that year he makes no other charitable contributions. Thus, A makes a charitable contribution to the church of $6,000 ($10,000 value -$4,000 amount realized). Without regard to this section, A is allowed a deduction under section 170 of $6,000 for his charitable contribution to the church, since there is no reduction under section 170(e)(1) with respect to the long-term capital gain. Accordingly, under
30 paragraph (b) of this section the adjusted basis for determining gain on the bargain sale is $1,600 ($4,000 adjusted basis x $4,000 amount realized / $10,000 value of property). A has recognized long-term capital gain of $2,400 ($4,000 amount realized - $1,600 adjusted basis) on the bargain sale.

Example 2. The facts are the same as in example (1) except that A also makes a
35 charitable contribution in 1970 of $50,000 cash to the church. By reason of section 170(b) (1)(A), the deduction allowed under section 170 for 1970 is $50,000 for the amount of cash contributed to the church; however, the $6,000 contribution of property is carried over to 1971 under section 170(d). Under paragraphs (a)(2) and (b) of this section the adjusted basis for determining gain for 1970 on the bargain sale in that year is $1,600
40 ($4,000 x $4,000 / $10,000). A has a recognized long-term capital gain for 1970 of $2,400 ($4,000 - $1,600) on the sale.

Example 3. In 1970, C, a calendar-year individual taxpayer, makes a charitable contribution of $50,000 cash to a church. In addition, he sells for $4,000 to a private foundation not described in section 170(b)(1)(E) stock held for more than 6 months which
45 has an adjusted basis of $4,000 and a fair market value of $10,000. Thus, C makes a charitable contribution of $6,000 of such property to the private foundation ($10,000 value - $4,000 amount realized). C's contribution base for 1970, as defined in section 170(b)(1) (F), is $100,000, and during that year he makes no other charitable contributions. By reason of section 170(b)(1)(A), the deduction allowed under section 170 for 1970 is
50 $50,000 for the amount of cash contributed to the church. Under section 170(e)(1)(B)(ii) and paragraphs (a)(1) and (c)(2)(i) of § 1.170A-4, the $6,000 contribution of stock is

Sec. 1011. Adjusted basis for determining gain or loss

reduced to $4,800 ($6,000 - [50% x ($6,000 value of contributed portion of stock - $3,600 adjusted basis)]). However, by reason of section 170(b)(1)(B)(ii), applied without regard to section 1011(b), no deduction is allowed under section 170 for 1970 or any other year for the reduced contribution of $4,800 to the private foundation. Accordingly, paragraph (b) of this section does not apply for purposes of apportioning the adjusted basis of the stock sold to the private foundation, and under § 1.1011-1(e) the recognized gain on the bargain sale is $0 ($4,000 amount realized - $4,000 adjusted basis).

***

[T.D. 7207, 37 FR 20798, Oct. 5, 1972; T.D. 7741, 45 FR 81745, Dec. 12, 1980; T.D. 8176, 53 FR 5570, Feb. 25, 1988; 53 FR 11002, Apr. 4, 1988; T.D. 8540, 59 FR 30148, June 10, 1994]

Sec. 1012. Basis of property - cost

The basis of property shall be the cost of such property, except as otherwise provided in this subchapter and subchapters C (relating to corporate distributions and adjustments), K (relating to partners and partnerships), and P (relating to capital gains and losses). The cost of real property shall not include any amount in respect of real property taxes which are treated under section 164(d) as imposed on the taxpayer.

Reg. § 1.1012-1 Basis of property.

(a) *General rule.* In general, the basis of property is the cost thereof. The cost is the amount paid for such property in cash or other property. This general rule is subject to exceptions stated in subchapter O (relating to gain or loss on the disposition of property), subchapter C (relating to corporate distributions and adjustments), subchapter K (relating to partners and partnerships), and subchapter P (relating to capital gains and losses), chapter 1 of the code.

(b) *Real estate taxes as part of cost.* In computing the cost of real property, the purchaser shall not take into account any amount paid to the seller as reimbursement for real property taxes which are treated under section 164(d) as imposed upon the purchaser. This rule applies whether or not the contract of sale calls for the purchaser to reimburse the seller for such real estate taxes paid or to be paid by the seller. On the other hand, where the purchaser pays (or assumes liability for) real estate taxes which are treated under section 164(d) as imposed upon the seller, such taxes shall be considered part of the cost of the property. It is immaterial whether or not the contract of sale specifies that the sale price has been reduced by, or is in any way intended to reflect, real estate taxes allocable to the seller under section 164(d). For illustrations of the application of this paragraph, see paragraph (b) of § 1.1001-1.

(c) *Sale of stock*--(1) *In general.* If shares of stock in a corporation are sold or transferred by a taxpayer who purchased or acquired lots of stock on different dates or at different prices, and the lot from which the stock was sold or transferred cannot be adequately identified, the stock sold or transferred shall be charged against the earliest of such lots purchased or acquired in order to determine the cost or other basis of such stock and in order to determine the holding period of such stock for purposes of subchapter P, chapter 1 of the code. If, on the other hand, the lot from which the stock is sold or transferred can be adequately identified, the rule stated in the preceding sentence is not applicable. As to what constitutes ``adequate identification'', see subparagraphs (2), (3), and (4) of this paragraph.

(2) *Identification of stock.* An adequate identification is made if it is shown that certificates representing shares of stock from a lot which was purchased or acquired on a

certain date or for a certain price were delivered to the taxpayer's transferee. Except as otherwise provided in subparagraph (3) or (4) of this paragraph, such stock certificates delivered to the transferee constitute the stock sold or transferred by the taxpayer. Thus, unless the requirements of subparagraph (3) or (4) of this paragraph are met, the stock
5 sold or transferred is charged to the lot to which the certificates delivered to the transferee belong, whether or not the taxpayer intends, or instructs his broker or other agent, to sell or transfer stock from a lot purchased or acquired on a different date or for a different price.

(3) *Identification on confirmation document.* (i) Where the stock is left in the custody of
10 a broker or other agent, an adequate identification is made if--

(a) At the time of the sale or transfer, the taxpayer specifies to such broker or other agent having custody of the stock the particular stock to be sold or transferred, and

(b) Within a reasonable time thereafter, confirmation of such specification is set forth in a written document from such broker or other agent.
15 Stock identified pursuant to this subdivision is the stock sold or transferred by the taxpayer, even though stock certificates from a different lot are delivered to the taxpayer's transferee.

(ii) Where a single stock certificate represents stock from different lots, where such certificate is held by the taxpayer rather than his broker or other agent, and where the
20 taxpayer sells a part of the stock represented by such certificate through a broker or other agent, an adequate identification is made if--

(a) At the time of the delivery of the certificate to the broker or other agent, the taxpayer specifies to such broker or other agent the particular stock to be sold or transferred, and
25 (b) Within a reasonable time thereafter, confirmation of such specification is set forth in a written document from such broker or agent.

Where part of the stock represented by a single certificate is sold or transferred directly by the taxpayer to the purchaser or transferee instead of through a broker or other agent, an adequate identification is made if the taxpayer maintains a written record of the
30 particular stock which he intended to sell or transfer.

***

(5) *Subsequent sales.* If stock identified under subparagraph (3) or (4) of this paragraph as belonging to a particular lot is sold, transferred, or distributed, the stock so identified shall be deemed to have been sold, transferred, or distributed, and such sale,
35 transfer, or distribution will be taken into consideration in identifying the taxpayer's remaining stock for purposes of subsequent sales, transfers, or distributions.

***

(7) *Book-entry securities.* (i) In applying the provisions of subparagraph (3)(i)(a) of this paragraph in the case of a sale or transfer of a book-entry security (as defined in
40 subdivision (iii) (a) of this subparagraph) which is made after December 31, 1970, pursuant to a written instruction by the taxpayer, a specification by the taxpayer of the unique lot number which he has assigned to the lot which contains the securities being sold or transferred shall constitute specification as required by such subparagraph. The specification of the lot number shall be made either--
45 (a) In such written instruction, or

(b) In the case of a taxpayer in whose name the book entry by the Reserve Bank is made, in a list of lot numbers with respect to all book-entry securities on the books of the Reserve Bank sold or transferred on that date by the taxpayer, provided such list is mailed to or received by the Reserve Bank on or before the Reserve Bank's next
50 business day.

Sec. 1012. Basis of property - cost

This subdivision shall apply only if the taxpayer assigns lot numbers in numerical sequence to successive purchases of securities of the same loan title (series) and maturity date, except that securities of the same loan title (series) and maturity date which are purchased at the same price on the same date may be included within the same lot.   5

(ii) In applying the provisions of subparagraph (3)(i)(b) of this paragraph in the case of a sale or transfer of a book-entry security which is made pursuant to a written instruction by the taxpayer, a confirmation as required by such subparagraph shall be deemed made by--

(a) In the case of a sale or transfer made after December 31, 1970, the furnishing to 10 the taxpayer of a written advice of transaction, by the Reserve Bank or the person through whom the taxpayer sells or transfers the securities, which specifies the amount and description of the securities sold or transferred and the date of the transaction,

***

(b) The term other security of the United States means a bond, note, certificate of 15 indebtedness, bill, debenture, or similar obligation which is subject to the provisions of 31 CFR part 306 or other comparable Federal regulations and which is issued by (1) any department or agency of the Government of the United States, or (2) the Federal National Mortgage Association, the Federal Home Loan Banks, the Federal Home Loan Mortgage Corporation, the Federal Land Banks, the Federal Intermediate Credit Banks, the Banks 20 for Cooperatives, or the Tennessee Valley Authority;

***

(e) *Election as to certain regulated investment company stock*--(1) General rule--(i) *In general.* Notwithstanding paragraph (c) of this section, and except as provided in subdivision (ii) of this subparagraph, if--   25

(a) Shares of stock of a regulated investment company (as defined in subparagraph (5) of this paragraph) are left by a taxpayer in the custody of a custodian or agent in an account maintained for the acquisition or redemption of shares of such company, and

(b) The taxpayer purchased or acquired shares of stock held in the account at different prices or bases, the taxpayer may elect to determine the cost or other basis of shares of 30 stock he sells or transfers from such account by using one of the methods described in subparagraphs (3) and (4) of this paragraph. The cost or other basis determined in accordance with either of such methods shall be known as the average basis. For purposes of this paragraph, securities issued by unit investment trusts shall be treated as shares of stock and the term share or shares shall include fractions of a share.   35

(ii) *Certain gift shares.* (a) Except as provided in subdivision (b) of this subdivision (ii), this paragraph shall not apply to any account which contains shares which were acquired by the taxpayer by gift after December 31, 1920, if the basis of such shares (adjusted for the period before the date of the gift as provided in section 1016) in the hands of the donor or the last preceding owner by whom it was not acquired by gift was greater than 40 the fair market value of such shares at the time of the gift. However, shares acquired by a taxpayer as a result of a taxable dividend or a capital gain distribution from such an account may be included in an account to which this paragraph applies.

(b) Notwithstanding the provisions of subdivision (a) of this subdivision (ii), this paragraph shall apply with respect to accounts containing gift shares described in such 45 subdivision (a) if, at the time the election described in this paragraph is made in the manner prescribed in subparagraph (6) of this paragraph, the taxpayer includes a statement, in writing, indicating that the basis of such gift shares shall be the fair market value of such gift shares at the time they were acquired by the taxpayer by gift and that such basis shall be used in computing average basis in the manner described in 50

885

subparagraph (3) or (4) of this paragraph. Such statement shall be effective with respect to gift shares acquired prior to making such election and with respect to gift shares acquired after such time and shall remain in effect so long as such election remains in effect.

5   (2) *Determination of average basis.* Average basis shall be determined using either the method described in subparagraph (3) of this paragraph (the double-category method) or the method described in subparagraph (4) of this paragraph (the single-category method). The taxpayer shall specify, in the manner described in subparagraph (6) of this paragraph, the method used. Such method shall be used with respect to an

10 account until such time as the election is revoked with the consent of the Commissioner. Although a taxpayer may specify different methods with respect to accounts in different regulated investment companies, the same method shall be used with respect to all of the taxpayer's accounts in the same regulated investment company.

(3) *Double-category method*--(i) *In general.* In determining average basis using the

15 double category method, all shares in an account at the time of each sale or transfer shall be divided into two categories. The first category shall include all shares in such account having, at the time of the sale or transfer, a holding period of more than 1-year (6-months for taxable years beginning before 1977; 9-months for taxable years beginning in 1977) (the ``more-than 1-year (6-months for taxable years beginning before 1977; 9-months for

20 taxable years beginning in 1977)'' category), and the second category shall include all shares in such account having, at such time, a holding period of 1-year (6-months for taxable years beginning before 1977; 9-months for taxable years beginning in 1977) or less (the ``1-year (6-months for taxable years beginning before 1977; 9-months for taxable years beginning in 1977)-or-less'' category). The cost or other basis of each

25 share in a category shall be an amount equal to the remaining aggregate cost or other basis of all shares in that category at the time of the sale or transfer divided by the aggregate number of shares in that category at such time.

(ii) Order of disposition of shares old or transferred. Prior to a sale or transfer of shares from such an account, the taxpayer may specify, to the custodian or agent having

30 custody of the account, from which category (described in subdivision (i) of this subparagraph) the shares are to be sold or transferred. Shares shall be deemed sold or transferred from the category specified without regard to the stock certificates, if any, actually delivered if, within a reasonable time thereafter, confirmation of such specification is set forth in a written document from the custodian or agent having custody

35 of the account. In the absence of such specification or confirmation, shares sold or transferred shall be charged against the more-than-1-year (6-months for taxable years beginning before 1977; 9-months for taxable years beginning in 1977) category. However, if the number of shares sold or transferred exceeds the number in such category, the additional shares sold or transferred shall be charged against the shares in

40 the 1-year (6-months for taxable years beginning before 1977; 9-months for taxable years beginning in 1977)-or-less category. Any gain or loss attributable to a sale or transfer which is charged against shares in the more-than-1-year (6-months for taxable years beginning before 1977; 9-months for taxable years beginning in 1977) category shall constitute long-term gain or loss, and any gain or loss attributable to a sale or transfer

45 which is charged against shares in the 1-year (6-months for taxable years beginning before 1977; 9-months for taxable years beginning in 1977)-or-less category shall constitute short-term gain or loss. As to adjustments from wash sales, see section 1091(d) and subdivisions (iii)(c) and (d) of this subparagraph.

(iii) *Special rules with respect to shares from the 1 year-or-less category.* (a) After the

50 taxpayer's holding period with respect to a share is more than 1-year (6-months for taxable years beginning before 1977; 9-months for taxable years beginning in 1977),

Sec. 1012. Basis of property - cost

such share shall be changed from the 1-year (6-months for taxable years beginning before 1977; 9-months for taxable years beginning in 1977)-or-less category to the more-than 1-year (6-months for taxable years beginning before 1977; 9-months for taxable years beginning in 1977) category. For purposes of such change, the basis of a changed share shall be its actual cost or other basis to the taxpayer or its basis determined in accordance with the rules contained in subdivision (b)(2) of this subdivision (iii) if the rules of such subdivision (b)(2) are applicable.

(b) If, during the period that shares are in the 1-year (6-months for taxable years beginning before 1977; 9-months for taxable years beginning in 1977)-or-less category some but not all of the shares in such category are sold or transferred, then--

(1) The shares sold or transferred (the basis of which was determined in the manner prescribed by subdivision (i) of this subparagraph) shall be assumed to be those shares in such category which were earliest purchased or acquired, and

(2) The basis of those shares which are not sold or transferred and which are changed from the 1-year (6-months for taxable years beginning before 1977; 9-months for taxable years beginning in 1977)-or-less category to the more-than-1-year (6-months for taxable years beginning before 1977; 9-months for taxable years beginning in 1977) category shall be the average basis of the shares in the 1-year (6-months for taxable years beginning before 1977; 9-months for taxable years beginning in 1977)-or-less category at the time of the most recent sale or transfer of shares from such category. For such purposes, the average basis shall be determined in the manner prescribed in subdivision (i) of this subparagraph.

***

(6) *Election.* (i) An election to adopt one of the methods described in this paragraph shall be made in an income tax return for the first taxable year ending on or after December 31, 1970, for which the taxpayer desires the election to apply. If the taxpayer does not file a timely return (taking into account extensions of the time for filing) for such taxable year, the election shall be filed at the time the taxpayer files his first return for such year. The election may be made with an amended return only if such amended return is filed no later than the time prescribed by law (including extensions thereof) for filing the return for such taxable year. If the election is made, the taxpayer shall clearly indicate on his income tax return for each year to which the election is applicable that an average basis has been used in reporting gain or loss from the sale or transfer of shares sold or transferred. In addition, the taxpayer shall specify on such return the method (either the single-category method or the double-category method) used in determining average basis. The taxpayer shall also indicate in a statement described in subparagraph (1)(ii)(b) of this paragraph if the election is to apply to accounts described in subparagraph (1)(ii) of this paragraph. Such statement shall be attached to, or incorporated in, such return. A taxpayer making the election shall maintain such records as are necessary to substantiate the average basis (or bases) used on his income tax return.

(ii) An election made with respect to some of the shares of a regulated investment company sold or transferred from an account described in subparagraph (1)(i) of this paragraph applies to all such shares in the account. Such election also applies to all shares of that regulated investment company held in other such accounts (i.e., those described in subparagraph (1)(i) of this paragraph) by the electing taxpayer for his own benefit. Thus, the election shall apply to all shares of the regulated investment company held by the electing taxpayer (for his own benefit) in such accounts on or after the first day of the first taxable year for which the election is made. Such election does not apply to shares held in accounts described in subparagraph (1)(ii) of this paragraph unless the taxpayer indicates, in the manner described in subdivision (i) of this subparagraph, that

Sec. 1012. Basis of property - cost

the election is to apply to shares held in such accounts. An election made pursuant to the provisions of this paragraph may not be revoked without the prior written permission of the Commissioner.

(7) *Examples.* The provisions of this paragraph may be illustrated by the following examples:

Example 1. (i) On January 11, 1971, taxpayer A, who files his income tax return on a calendar year basis, enters into an agreement with the W Bank establishing an account for the periodic acquisition of shares of the Y Company, an open-end mutual fund. The agreement provides (1) that the bank is to purchase, for A, shares of Y stock as A may from time to time direct, (2) that all shares in the account are to be left in the custody of the bank, and (3) that the bank is to reinvest any dividends paid by Y (including capital gain dividends) in additional shares of Y stock. Pursuant to the agreement, on January 11, 1971, February 1, 1971, and March 1, 1971, respectively, the bank purchases, at A's direction, 100 shares of Y stock for a total of $1,880, 20 shares of Y stock for a total of $400, and 20 shares of Y stock for a total of $410. On March 15, 1971, the bank reinvests a $1-per-share capital gain dividend (that is, a total of $140) in seven additional shares of Y stock. The acquisitions to A's account, are, therefore, as follows:

Date	Number of shares	Basis
January 11, 1971	100	$1,880
February 1, 1971	20	400
March 1, 1971	20	410
March 15, 1971	7	140

On August 20, 1971, at A's direction, the bank redeems (i.e., sells) 40 shares of Y stock, and on September 20, 1971, 30 shares. A elects to determine the gain or loss from the sales of the stock by reference to its average basis using the double-category method of determining average basis. A did not specify from which category the sales were to take place, and therefore, each sale is deemed to have been made from the more-than-6-months category.

(ii) The average basis for the shares sold on August 20, 1971, is $19, and the total average basis for the 40 shares which are sold is $760, computed as follows:

Number of shares in the more-than-6-months category at the time of sale	Basis
100	$1,880
20	400
Total 120	2,280

Average cost or other basis: $2,280 / 120 = $19.40 shares x $19 each = $760, total average basis. Therefore, after the sale on August 20, 1971, 80 shares remain in the more-than-6-months category, and their remaining aggregate cost is $1,520.

(iii) The average basis for the shares sold on September 20, 1971, must reflect the sale which was made on August 20, 1971. Accordingly, such average basis would be $19.35 and may be computed as follows:

888

Sec. 1012. Basis of property - cost

Number of shares in the more-than-6-months category at the time of sale	Basis
80	$1,520
20	410
7	140
Total 107	2,070

Average cost or other basis: $2,070 / 107 shares = $19.35 (to the nearest cent).

Example 2. Taxpayer B, who files his income tax returns on a calendar year basis, enters into an agreement with the X Bank establishing an account for the periodic acquisition of shares of the Z Company, an open-end mutual fund. X acquired for B's account shares of Z on the following dates in the designated amounts:

January 15, 1971	50 shares.
February 16, 1971	30 shares.
March 15, 1971	25 shares.

Pursuant to B's direction, the Bank redeemed (i.e., sold) 25 shares from the account on February 1, 1971, and 20 shares on April 1, 1971, for a total of 45 shares. All of such shares had been held for less than 6 months. B elects to determine the gain or loss from the sales of the stock by reference to its average basis using the double-category method of determining average basis. Thus, the 45 shares which were sold are assumed to be from the 50 shares which were purchased on January 15, 1971. Accordingly, on July 16, 1971, only five shares from those shares which had been purchased on January 15, 1971, remain to be transferred from the 6-months-or-less category to the more- than-6-months category. The basis of such five shares for purposes of the change to the more-than-6-months category would be the average basis of the shares in the 6-months- or-less category at the time of the sale on April 1, 1971.

Example 3. Assume the same facts as in example (2), except that an additional sale of 18 shares was made on May 3, 1971. There were, therefore, a total of 63 shares sold during the 6-month period beginning on January 15, 1971, the date of the earliest purchase. Fifty of the shares which were sold during such period shall be assumed to be the shares purchased on January 15, 1971, and the remaining 13 shares shall be assumed to be from the shares which were purchased on February 16, 1971. Thus, none of the shares which were purchased on January 15, 1971, remain to be changed from the 6-months-or-less category to the more-than-6-months category. In the absence of further dispositions of shares during the 6-month holding period for the shares purchased on February 16, 1971, there would be 17 of such shares to be changed over after the expiration of that period since 13 of the shares sold on May 3, 1971, were assumed to be from the shares purchased on February 16, 1971. The basis of the 17 shares for purposes of the change to the more-than-6-months category would be the average basis of the shares in the 6-months-or-less category at the time of the sale on May 3, 1971.

Example 4. Taxpayer C, who files his income tax returns on a calendar year basis, enters into an agreement with Y Bank establishing an account for the periodic acquisition of XYZ Company, a closed-end mutual fund. Y acquired for B's account shares of XYZ on the following dates in the designated amounts:

Sec. 1012. Basis of property - cost

Date	Number of shares	Cost
January 8, 1971......................................	25	$200
February 8, 1971..................................	24	200
March 8, 1971......................................	23	200
April 8, 1971..	23	200

Pursuant to C's direction, the bank redeemed (i.e., sold) 40 shares from the account on July 15, 1971, for $10 per share or a total of $400. C elects to determine the gain or loss from the sale of the stock by reference to its average basis using the single-category method of determining average basis. The average basis for the shares sold on July 15, 1971 (determined by dividing the total number of shares in the account at such time (95) into the aggregate cost of such shares ($800)) is $8.42 (to the nearest cent). Under the rules of subparagraph (4) of this paragraph the shares sold would be deemed to be those first acquired. Thus, C would realize a $39.50 ($1.58 x 25) long-term capital gain with respect to the 25 shares acquired on January 8, 1971, and he would realize a $23.70 ($1.58 x 15 short-term capital gain with respect to 15 of the shares acquired on February 8, 1971. The next sale occurred on August 16, 1971. At that time, absent further intervening acquisitions or dispositions, the account contained nine shares (the 24 shares acquired on February 8, 1971, less 15 of such shares which were sold on July 15, 1971) with a holding period of more than 6 months, and 46 shares with a holding period of 6 months or less.

Example 5. Taxpayer D owns four separate accounts (D-1, D-2, D-3, and D-4) for the periodic acquisition of shares of the Y Company, an open-end mutual fund. Account D-4 contains shares which D acquired by gift on April 15, 1970. These shares had an adjusted basis in the hands of the donor which was greater than the fair market value of the donated shares on such date. For his taxable year ending on December 31, 1971, D elects to use an average basis for shares sold from account D-1 during such year using the single-category method of determining average basis. Under the provisions of subparagraph (1)(ii) of this paragraph, D may use an average basis for shares sold or transferred from account D-4 if he includes with his statement of election a statement, in writing, indicating that the basis of such gift shares in account D-4 shall be the fair market value of such shares at the time he acquired such shares and that such basis shall be used in computing the average basis of shares in account D-4. In addition, since D elected to use an average basis for shares sold from account D-1, he must also use an average basis for all shares sold or transferred from accounts D-2 and D-3 (as well as account D-1) for his taxable year ending on December 31, 1971, and for all subsequent years until he revokes (with the consent of the Commissioner) his election to use an average basis for such accounts. Further, D must use the single-category method of determining average basis with respect to accounts D-2, D-3 (and D-4 if the above-mentioned statement is filed).

***

[T.D. 6500, 25 FR 11910, Nov. 26, 1960]

Sec. 1014. Basis of property acquired from a decedent

(a) In general. -- Except as otherwise provided in this section, the basis of property in the hands of a person acquiring the property from a decedent or to whom the property passed from a decedent shall, if not sold, exchanged, or otherwise disposed of before the decedent's death by such person, be--

Sec. 1014. Basis of property acquired from a decedent

(1) the fair market value of the property at the date of the decedent's death,

(2) in the case of an election under either section 2032 or section 811(j) of the Internal Revenue Code of 1939 where the   decedent died after October 21, 1942, its value at the applicable valuation date prescribed by those sections,

(3) in the case of an election under section 2032A, its value determined under such section, or

(4) to the extent of the applicability of the exclusion described in section 2031(c), the basis in the hands of the decedent.

(b) Property acquired from the decedent. -- For purposes of subsection (a), the following property shall be considered to have been acquired from or to have passed from the decedent:

(1) Property acquired by bequest, devise, or inheritance, or by the decedent's estate from the decedent;

(2) Property transferred by the decedent during his lifetime in trust to pay the income for life to or on the order or direction of the decedent, with the right reserved to the decedent at all times before his death to revoke the trust;

(3) In the case of decedents dying after December 31, 1951, property transferred by the decedent during his lifetime in trust to pay the income for life to or on the order or direction of the decedent with the right reserved to the decedent at all times before his death to make any change in the enjoyment thereof through the exercise of a power to alter, amend, or terminate the trust;

(4) Property passing without full and adequate consideration under a general power of appointment exercised by the decedent by will;

***

(6) In the case of decedents dying after December 31, 1947, property which represents the surviving spouse's one-half share of community property held by the decedent and the surviving spouse under the community property laws of any State, or possession of the United States or any foreign country, if at least one-half of the whole of the community interest in such property was includible in determining the value of the decedent's gross estate under chapter 11 of subtitle B (section 2001 and following, relating to estate tax) or section 811 of the Internal Revenue Code of 1939;

***

(9) In the case of decedents dying after December 31, 1953, property acquired from the decedent by reason of death, form of ownership, or other conditions (including property acquired through the exercise or non-exercise of a power of appointment), if by reason thereof the property is required to be included in determining the value of the decedent's gross estate under chapter 11 of subtitle B or under the Internal Revenue Code of 1939. In such case, if the property is acquired before the death of the decedent, the basis shall be the amount determined under subsection (a) reduced by the amount allowed to the taxpayer as deductions in computing taxable income under this subtitle or prior income tax laws for exhaustion, wear and tear, obsolescence, amortization, and depletion on such property before the death of the decedent. Such basis shall be applicable to the property commencing on the death of the decedent. This paragraph shall not apply to -

(A) annuities described in section 72;

(B) property to which paragraph (5) would apply if the property had been acquired by bequest; and

(C) property described in any other paragraph of this subsection.

(10) Property includible in the gross estate of the decedent under section 2044 (relating to

Sec. 1014. Basis of property acquired from a decedent

certain property for which marital deduction was previously allowed). In any such case, the last 3 sentences of paragraph (9) shall apply as if such property were described in the first sentence of paragraph (9).

    (c) Property representing income in respect of a decedent. -- This section shall not apply to
5 property which constitutes a right to receive an item of income in respect of a decedent under section 691.

***

    (e) Appreciated property acquired by decedent by gift within 1 year of death. --

      (1) In general. -- In the case of a decedent dying after December 31, 1981, if--

10   **(A)** appreciated property was acquired by the decedent by gift during the 1-year period ending on the date of the decedent's death, and

        (B) such property is acquired from the decedent by (or passes from the decedent to) the donor of such property (or the spouse of such donor), the basis of such property in the hands of such donor (or spouse) shall be the adjusted basis of such property in the hands of
15 the decedent immediately before the death of the decedent.

      (2) Definitions. -- For purposes of paragraph (1)--

        (A) Appreciated property. -- The term "appreciated property" means any property if the fair market value of such property on the day it was transferred to the decedent by gift exceeds its adjusted basis.

20   **(B) Treatment of certain property sold by estate.** -- In the case of any appreciated property described in subparagraph (A) of paragraph (1) sold by the estate of the decedent or by a trust of which the decedent was the grantor, rules similar to the rules of paragraph (1) shall apply to the extent the donor of such property (or the spouse of such donor) is entitled to the proceeds from such sale.

25   **(f) Termination.** -- This section shall not apply with respect to decedents dying after December 31, 2009.

Reg. § 1.1014-2 Property acquired from a decedent.

    (a) *In general*. The following property, except where otherwise indicated, is considered
30 to have been acquired from a decedent and the basis thereof is determined in accordance with the general rule in § 1.1014-1:

    (1) Without regard to the date of the decedent's death, property acquired by bequest, devise, or inheritance, or by the decedent's estate from the decedent, whether the property was acquired under the decedent's will or under the law governing the descent
35 and distribution of the property of decedents. However, see paragraph (c)(1) of this section if the property was acquired by bequest or inheritance from a decedent dying after August 26, 1937, and if such property consists of stock or securities of a foreign personal holding company.

    (2) Without regard to the date of the decedent's death, property transferred by the
40 decedent during his lifetime in trust to pay the income for life to or on the order or direction of the decedent, with the right reserved to the decedent at all times before his death to revoke the trust.

    (3) In the case of decedents dying after December 31, 1951, property transferred by the decedent during his lifetime in trust to pay the income for life to or on the order or
45 direction of the decedent with the right reserved to the decedent at all times before his death to make any change in the enjoyment thereof through the exercise of a power to alter, amend, or terminate the trust.

    (4) Without regard to the date of the decedent's death, property passing without full

Sec. 1014. Basis of property acquired from a decedent

and adequate consideration under a general power of appointment exercised by the decedent by will. (See section 2041(b) for definition of general power of appointment.)

(5) In the case of decedents dying after December 31, 1947, property which represents the surviving spouse's one-half share of community property held by the decedent and the surviving spouse under the community property laws of any State, 5 Territory, or possession of the United States or any foreign country, if at least one-half of the whole of the community interest in that property was includible in determining the value of the decedent's gross estate under part III, chapter 11 of the Internal Revenue Code of 1954 (relating to the estate tax) or section 811 of the Internal Revenue Code of 1939. It is not necessary for the application of this subparagraph that an estate tax return 10 be required to be filed for the estate of the decedent or that an estate tax be payable.

***

(b) *Property acquired from a decedent dying after December 31, 1953*--(1) *In general.* In addition to the property described in paragraph (a) of this section, and except as otherwise provided in subparagraph (3) of this paragraph, in the case of a decedent dying 15 after December 31, 1953, property shall also be considered to have been acquired from the decedent to the extent that both of the following conditions are met: (i) The property was acquired from the decedent by reason of death, form of ownership, or other conditions (including property acquired through the exercise or non-exercise of a power of appointment), and (ii) the property is includible in the decedent's gross estate under 20 the provisions of the Internal Revenue Code of 1954, or the Internal Revenue Code of 1939, because of such acquisition. The basis of such property in the hands of the person who acquired it from the decedent shall be determined in accordance with the general rule in § 1.1014-1. See, however, § 1.1014-6 for special adjustments if such property is acquired before the death of the decedent. See also subparagraph (3) of this paragraph 25 for a description of property not within the scope of this paragraph.

(2) *Rules for the application of subparagraph (1) of this paragraph.* Except as provided in subparagraph (3) of this paragraph, this paragraph generally includes all property acquired from a decedent, which is includible in the gross estate of the decedent if the decedent died after December 31, 1953. It is not necessary for the application of this 30 paragraph that an estate tax return be required to be filed for the estate of the decedent or that an estate tax be payable. Property acquired prior to the death of a decedent which is includible in the decedent's gross estate, such as property transferred by a decedent in contemplation of death, and property held by a taxpayer and the decedent as joint tenants or as tenants by the entireties is within the scope of this paragraph. Also, this 35 paragraph includes property acquired through the exercise or nonexercise of a power of appointment where such property is includible in the decedent's gross estate. It does not include property not includible in the decedent's gross estate such as property not situated in the United States acquired from a nonresident who is not a citizen of the United States.   40

***

Reg. § 1.1014-3 Other basis rules.

(a) *Fair market value.* For purposes of this section and § 1.1014-1, the value of property as of the date of the decedent's death as appraised for the purpose of the 45 Federal estate tax or the alternate value as appraised for such purpose, whichever is applicable, shall be deemed to be its fair market value. If no estate tax return is required to be filed under section 6018 (or under section 821 or 864 of the Internal Revenue Code of 1939), the value of the property appraised as of the date of the decedent's death for the purpose of State inheritance or transmission taxes shall be deemed to be its fair 50

Sec. 1014. Basis of property acquired from a decedent

market value and no alternate valuation date shall be applicable.

***

(d) *Reinvestments of property transferred during life.* Where property is transferred by a decedent during life and the property is sold, exchanged, or otherwise disposed of
5 before the decedent's death by the person who acquired the property from the decedent, the general rule stated in paragraph (a) of § 1.1014-1 shall not apply to such property. However, in such a case, the basis of any property acquired by such donee in exchange for the original property, or of any property acquired by the donee through reinvesting the proceeds of the sale of the original property, shall be the fair market value of the property
10 thus acquired at the date of the decedent's death (or applicable alternate valuation date) if the property thus acquired is properly included in the decedent's gross estate for Federal estate tax purposes. These rules also apply to property acquired by the donee in any further exchanges or in further reinvestments. For example, on January 1, 1956, the decedent made a gift of real property to a trust for the benefit of his children, reserving to
15 himself the power to revoke the trust at will. Prior to the decedent's death, the trustee sold the real property and invested the proceeds in stock of the Y company at $50 per share. At the time of the decedent's death, the value of such stock was $75 per share. The corpus of the trust was required to be included in the decedent's gross estate owing to his reservation of the power of revocation. The basis of the Y company stock following the
20 decedent's death is $75 per share. Moreover, if the trustee sold the Y Company stock before the decedent's death for $65 a share and reinvested the proceeds in Z company stock which increased in value to $85 per share at the time of the decedent's death, the basis of the Z company stock following the decedent's death would be $85 per share.

***

25 **Reg. § 1.1014-5 Gain or loss.**

(a) *Sale or other disposition of a life interest, remainder interest, or other interest in property acquired from a decedent.* (1) Except as provided in paragraph (b) of this section with respect to the sale or other disposition after October 9, 1969, of a term interest in property, gain or loss from a sale or other disposition of a life interest,
30 remainder interest, or other interest in property acquired from a decedent is determined by comparing the amount of the proceeds with the amount of that part of the adjusted uniform basis which is assignable to the interest so transferred. The adjusted uniform basis is the uniform basis of the entire property adjusted to the date of sale or other disposition of any such interest as required by sections 1016 and 1017. The uniform
35 basis is the unadjusted basis of the entire property determined immediately after the decedent's death under the applicable sections of part II of subchapter O of chapter 1 of the Code.

(2) Except as provided in paragraph (b) of this section, the proper measure of gain or loss resulting from a sale or other disposition of an interest in property acquired from a
40 decedent is so much of the increase or decrease in the value of the entire property as is reflected in such sale or other disposition. Hence, in ascertaining the basis of a life interest, remainder interest, or other interest which has been so transferred, the uniform basis rule contemplates that proper adjustments will be made to reflect the change in relative value of the interests on account of the passage of time.

45 ***

(b) *Sale or other disposition of certain term interests.* In determining gain or loss from the sale or other disposition after October 9, 1969, of a term interest in property (as defined in paragraph (f)(2) of § 1.1001-1) the adjusted basis of which is determined pursuant, or by reference, to section 1014 (relating to the basis of property acquired from
50 a decedent) or section 1015 (relating to the basis of property acquired by gift or by a

894

Sec. 1014. Basis of property acquired from a decedent

transfer in trust), that part of the adjusted uniform basis assignable under the rules of paragraph (a) of this section to the interest sold or otherwise disposed of shall be disregarded to the extent and in the manner provided by section 1001(e) and paragraph (f) of § 1.1001-1.

(c) *Illustrations.* The application of this section may be illustrated by the following examples, in which references are made to the actuarial tables contained in part 20 of this chapter (Estate Tax Regulations):

Example 1. Securities worth $500,000 at the date of decedent's death on January 1, 1971, are bequeathed to his wife, W, for life, with remainder over to his son, S. W is 48 years of age when the life interest is acquired. The estate does not elect the alternate valuation allowed by section 2032. By reference to § 20.2031-7A(c), the life estate factor for age 48, female, is found to be 0.77488 and the remainder factor for such age is found to be 0.22512. Therefore, the present value of the portion of the uniform basis assigned to W's life interest is $387,440 ($500,000 x 0.77488), and the present value of the portion of the uniform basis assigned to S's remainder interest is $112,560 ($500,000 x 0.22512). W sells her life interest to her nephew, A, on February 1, 1971, for $370,000, at which time W is still 48 years of age. Pursuant to section 1001(e), W realizes no loss; her gain is $370,000, the amount realized from the sale. A has a basis of $370,000 which he can recover by amortization deductions over W's life expectancy.

Example 2. The facts are the same as in example (1) except that W retains the life interest for 12 years, until she is 60 years of age, and then sells it to A on February 1, 1983, when the fair market value of the securities has increased to $650,000. By reference to § 20.2031-7A(c), the life estate factor for age 60, female, is found to be 0.63226 and the remainder factor for such age is found to be 0.36774. Therefore, the present value on February 1, 1983, of the portion of the uniform basis assigned to W's life interest is $316,130 ($500,000 x 0.63226) and the present value on that date of the portion of the uniform basis assigned to S's remainder interest is $183,870 ($500,000 x 0.36774). W sells her life interest for $410,969, that being the commuted value of her remaining life interest in the securities as appreciated ($650,000 x 0.63226). Pursuant to section 1001(e), W's gain is $410,969, the amount realized. A has a basis of $410,969 which he can recover by amortization deductions over W's life expectancy.

[T.D. 7142, 36 FR 18951, Sept. 24, 1971; T.D. 8540, 59 FR 30102, June 10, 1994]

Sec. 1015. Basis of property acquired by gifts and transfers in trust

(a) **Gifts after December 31, 1920.** -- If the property was acquired by gift after December 31, 1920, the basis shall be the same as it would be in the hands of the donor or the last preceding owner by whom it was not acquired by gift, except that if such basis (adjusted for the period before the date of the gift as provided in section 1016) is greater than the fair market value of the property at the time of the gift, then for the purpose of determining loss the basis shall be such fair market value. If the facts necessary to determine the basis in the hands of the donor or the last preceding owner are unknown to the donee, the Secretary shall, if possible, obtain such facts from such donor or last preceding owner, or any other person cognizant thereof. Ifthe Secretary finds it impossible to obtain such facts, the basis in the hands of such donor or last preceding owner shall be the fair market value of such property as found by the Secretary as of the date or approximate date at which, according to the best information that the Secretary is able to obtain, such property was acquired by such donor or last preceding owner.

(b) **Transfer in trust after December 31, 1920.** -- If the property was acquired after December 31, 1920, by a transfer in trust (other than by a transfer in trust by a gift, bequest, or devise), the

Sec. 1015. Basis of property acquired by gifts and transfers in trust

basis shall be the same as it would be in the hands of the grantor increased in the amount of gain or decreased in the amount of loss recognized to the grantor on such transfer under the law applicable to the year in which the transfer was made.

***

5   **(d) Increased basis for gift tax paid.** --

   (1) In general. -- If--

      (A) the property is acquired by gift on or after September 2, 1958, the basis shall be the basis determined under subsection (a), increased (but not above the fair market value of the property at the time of the gift) by the amount of gift tax paid with respect to such gift, or

10   **(B)** the property was acquired by gift before September 2,1958, and has not been sold, exchanged, or otherwise disposed of before such date, the basis of the property shall be increased on such date by the amount of gift tax paid with respect to such gift, but such increase shall not exceed an amount equal to the amount by which the fair market value of the property at the time of the gift exceeded the basis of the property in the hands of the

15   donor at the time of the gift.

   (2) Amount of tax paid with respect to gift. -- For purposes of paragraph (1), the amount of gift tax paid with respect to any gift is an amount which bears the same ratio to the amount of gift tax paid under chapter 12 with respect to all gifts made by the donor for the calendar year (or preceding calendar period) in which such gift is made as the amount of such gift bears

20   to the taxable gifts (as defined in section 2503(a) but computed without the deduction allowed by section 2521) made by the donor during such calendar year or period. For purposes of the preceding sentence, the amount of any gift shall be the amount included with respect to such gift in determining (for the purposes of section 2503(a)) the total amount of gifts made during the calendar year or period, reduced by the amount of any deduction allowed with respect to

25   such gift under section 2522 (relating to charitable deduction) or under section 2523 (relating to marital deduction).

   (3) Gifts treated as made one-half by each spouse. -- For purposes of paragraph (1), where the donor and his spouse elected, under section 2513 to have the gift considered as made one-half by each, the amount of gift tax paid with respect to such gift under chapter 12 shall be

30   the sum of the amounts of tax paid with respect to each half of such gift (computed in the manner provided in paragraph (2)).

   (4) Treatment as adjustment to basis. -- For purposes of section 1016(b), an increase in basis under paragraph (1) shall be treated as an adjustment under section1016(a).

***

35   **(e) Gifts between spouses.** -- In the case of any property acquired by gift in a transfer described in section 1041(a), the basis of such property in the hands of the transferee shall be determined under section 1041(b)(2) and not this section.

Reg. § 1.1015-1 Basis of property acquired by gift after December 31, 1920.

40   (a) *General rule*. (1) In the case of property acquired by gift after December 31, 1920 (whether by a transfer in trust or otherwise), the basis of the property for the purpose of determining gain is the same as it would be in the hands of the donor or the last preceding owner by whom it was not acquired by gift. The same rule applies in determining loss unless the basis (adjusted for the period prior to the date of gift in

45   accordance with sections 1016 and 1017) is greater than the fair market value of the property at the time of the gift. In such case, the basis for determining loss is the fair market value at the time of the gift.

      (2) The provisions of subparagraph (1) of this paragraph may be illustrated by the

Sec. 1015. Basis of property acquired by gifts and transfers in trust

following example.

Example: A acquires by gift income-producing property which has an adjusted basis of $100,000 at the date of gift. The fair market value of the property at the date of gift is $90,000. A later sells the property for $95,000. In such case there is neither gain nor loss. The basis for determining loss is $90,000; therefore, there is no loss. Furthermore, there is no gain, since the basis for determining gain is $100,000.

(3) If the facts necessary to determine the basis of property in the hands of the donor or the last preceding owner by whom it was not acquired by gift are unknown to the donee, the district director shall, if possible, obtain such facts from such donor or last preceding owner, or any other person cognizant thereof. If the district director finds it impossible to obtain such facts, the basis in the hands of such donor or last preceding owner shall be the fair market value of such property as found by the district director as of the date or approximate date at which, according to the best information the district director is able to obtain, such property was acquired by such donor or last preceding owner. See paragraph (e) of this section for rules relating to fair market value.

(b) *Uniform basis; proportionate parts of.* Property acquired by gift has a single or uniform basis although more than one person may acquire an interest in such property. The uniform basis of the property remains fixed subject to proper adjustment for items under sections 1016 and 1017. However, the value of the proportionate parts of the uniform basis represented, for instance, by the respective interests of the life tenant and remainderman are adjustable to reflect the change in the relative values of such interest on account of the lapse of time. The portion of the basis attributable to an interest at the time of its sale or other disposition shall be determined under the rules provided in § 1.1014-5. In determining gain or loss from the sale or other disposition after October 9, 1969, of a term interest in property (as defined in § 1.1001-1(f)(2)) the adjusted basis of which is determined pursuant, or by reference, to section 1015, that part of the adjusted uniform basis assignable under the rules of § 1.1014-5(a) to the interest sold or otherwise disposed of shall be disregarded to the extent and in the manner provided by section 1001(e) and § 1.1001-1(f).

(c) *Time of acquisition.* The date that the donee acquires an interest in property by gift is when the donor relinquishes dominion over the property and not necessarily when title to the property is acquired by the donee. Thus, the date that the donee acquires an interest in property by gift where he is a successor in interest, such as in the case of a remainderman of a life estate or a beneficiary of the distribution of the corpus of a trust, is the date such interests are created by the donor and not the date the property is actually acquired.

(d) *Property acquired by gift from a decedent dying after December 31, 1953.* If an interest in property was acquired by the taxpayer by gift from a donor dying after December 31, 1953, under conditions which required the inclusion of the property in the donor's gross estate for estate tax purposes, and the property had not been sold, exchanged, or otherwise disposed of by the taxpayer before the donor's death, see the rules prescribed in section 1014 and the regulations thereunder.

(e) *Fair market value.* For the purposes of this section, the value of property as appraised for the purpose of the Federal gift tax, or, if the gift is not subject to such tax, its value as appraised for the purpose of a State gift tax, shall be deemed to be the fair market value of the property at the time of the gift.

(f) *Reinvestments by fiduciary.* If the property is an investment by the fiduciary under the terms of the gift (as, for example, in the case of a sale by the fiduciary of property transferred under the terms of the gift, and the reinvestment of the proceeds), the cost or other basis to the fiduciary is taken in lieu of the basis specified in paragraph (a) of this section.

Sec. 1015. Basis of property acquired by gifts and transfers in trust

(g) *Records*. To insure a fair and adequate determination of the proper basis under section 1015, persons making or receiving gifts of property should preserve and keep accessible a record of the facts necessary to determine the cost of the property and, if pertinent, its fair market value as of March 1, 1913, or its fair market value as of the date
5 of the gift.

Reg. § 1.1015-4 Transfers in part a gift and in part a sale.

(a) **General rule**. Where a transfer of property is in part a sale and in part a gift, the unadjusted basis of the property in the hands of the transferee is the sum of--
10 (1) Whichever of the following is the greater:
(i) The amount paid by the transferee for the property, or
(ii) The transferor's adjusted basis for the property at the time of the transfer, and
(2) The amount of increase, if any, in basis authorized by section 1015(d) for gift tax paid (see § 1.1015-5).
15 For determining loss, the unadjusted basis of the property in the hands of the transferee shall not be greater than the fair market value of the property at the time of such transfer. For determination of gain or loss of the transferor, see § 1.1001-1(e) and § 1.1011-2. For special rule where there has been a charitable contribution of less than a taxpayer's entire interest in property, see section 170(e)(2) and § 1.170A-4(c).
20 (b) *Examples*. The rule of paragraph (a) of this section is illustrated by the following examples:
Example 1. If A transfers property to his son for $30,000, and such property at the time of the transfer has an adjusted basis of $30,000 in A's hands (and a fair market value of $60,000), the unadjusted basis of the property in the hands of the son is
25 $30,000.
Example 2. If A transfers property to his son for $60,000, and such property at the time of transfer has an adjusted basis of $30,000 in A's hands (and a fair market value of $90,000), the unadjusted basis of such property in the hands of the son is $60,000.
Example 3. If A transfers property to his son for $30,000, and such property at the
30 time of transfer has an adjusted basis in A's hands of $60,000 (and a fair market value of $90,000), the unadjusted basis of such property in the hands of the son is $60,000.
Example 4. If A transfers property to his son for $30,000 and such property at the time of transfer has an adjusted basis of $90,000 in A's hands (and a fair market value of $60,000), the unadjusted basis of the property in the hands of the son ins $90,000.
35 However, since the adjusted basis of the property in A's hands at the time of the transfer was greater than the fair market value at that time, for the purpose of determining any loss on a later sale or other disposition of the property by the son its unadjusted basis in his hands is $60,000.

40 [T.D. 6500, 25 FR 11910, Nov. 26, 1960; T.D. 6693, 28 FR 12818, Dec. 3, 1963; T.D. 6693, 28 FR 12818, Dec. 3, 1963; T.D. 7142, 36 FR 18952, Sept. 24, 1971; T.D. 7207, 37 FR 20799, Oct. 5, 1972]

Sec. 1016. Adjustments to basis

(a) **General rule.** -- Proper adjustment in respect of the property shall in all cases be made--
45 (1) for expenditures, receipts, losses, or other items, properly chargeable to capital account, but no such adjustment shall be made -
(A) for taxes or other carrying charges described in section 266, or
(B) for expenditures described in section 173 (relating to circulation expenditures),

Sec. 1016. Adjustments to basis

for which deductions have been taken by the taxpayer in determining taxable income for the taxable year or prior taxable years;

(2) in respect of any period since February 28, 1913, for exhaustion, wear and tear, obsolescence, amortization, and depletion, to the extent of the amount--

(A) allowed as deductions in computing taxable income under this subtitle or prior income tax laws, and

(B) resulting (by reason of the deductions so allowed) in a reduction for any taxable year of the taxpayer's taxes under this subtitle (other than chapter 2, relating to tax on self-employment income), or prior income, war-profits, or excess-profits tax laws,

but not less than the amount allowable under this subtitle or prior income tax laws. Where no method has been adopted under section 167 (relating to depreciation deduction), the amount allowable shall be determined under the straight line method. Subparagraph (B) of this paragraph shall not apply in respect of any period since February 28, 1913, and before January 1, 1952, unless an election has been made under section 1020 (as in effect before the date of the enactment of the Tax Reform Act of 1976). Where for any taxable year before the taxable year 1932 the depletion allowance was based on discovery value or a percentage of income, then the adjustment for depletion for such year shall be based on the depletion which would have been allowable for such year if computed without reference to discovery value or a percentage of income;

(3) in respect of any period--

(A) before March 1, 1913,

(B) since February 28, 1913, during which such property was held by a person or an organization not subject to income taxation under this chapter or prior income tax laws,

***

and

(D) since February 28, 1913, during which such property was held by a person subject to tax under part II of subchapter L (or the corresponding provisions of prior income tax laws), to the extent that paragraph (2) does not apply, for exhaustion, wear and tear, obsolescence, amortization, and depletion, to the extent sustained;

(4) in the case of stock (to the extent not provided for in the foregoing paragraphs) for the amount of distributions previously made which, under the law applicable to the year in which the distribution was made, either were tax-free or were applicable in reduction of basis (not including distributions made by a corporation which was classified as a personal service corporation under the provisions of the Revenue Act of 1918 (40 Stat. 1057), or the Revenue Act of 1921 (42 Stat. 227), out of its earnings or profits which were taxable in accordance with the provisions of section 218 of the Revenue Act of 1918 or 1921);

(5) in the case of any bond (as defined in section 171(d)) the interest on which is wholly exempt from the tax imposed by this subtitle, to the extent of the amortizable bond premium disallowable as a deduction pursuant to section 171(a)(2), and in the case of any other bond (as defined in section 171(d)) to the extent of the deductions allowable pursuant to section 171(a)(1) (or the amount applied to reduce interest payments under section 171(e)(2)) with respect thereto;

***

(7) in the case of a residence the acquisition of which resulted, under section 1034 (as in effect on the day before the date of the enactment of the Taxpayer Relief Act of 1997), in the nonrecognition of any part of the gain realized on the sale, exchange, or involuntary conversion of another residence, to the extent provided in section 1034(e) (as so in effect);

Sec. 1016. Adjustments to basis

***

(9) for amounts allowed as deductions as deferred expenses under section 616(b) (relating to certain expenditures in the development of mines) and resulting in a reduction of the taxpayer's taxes under this subtitle, but not less than the amounts allowable under such section for the taxable year and prior years;

***

(14) for amounts allowed as deductions as deferred expenses under section 174(b)(1) (relating to research and experimental expenditures) and resulting in a reduction of the taxpayers' taxes under this subtitle, but not less than the amounts allowable under such section for the taxable year and prior years;

***

(19) to the extent provided in section 50(c), in the case of expenditures with respect to which a credit has been allowed under section 38;

(20) for amounts allowed as deductions under section 59(e) (relating to optional 10-year writeoff of certain tax preferences);

***

(24) to the extent provided in section 179A(e)(6)(A),

***

(31) to the extent provided in section 179D(e).

***

(35) to the extent provided in section 30B(h)(4), and.

***

(b) **Substituted basis.** -- Whenever it appears that the basis of property in the hands of the taxpayer is a substituted basis, then the adjustments provided in subsection (a) shall be made after first making in respect of such substituted basis proper adjustments of a similar nature in respect of the period during which the property was held by the transferor, donor, or grantor, or during which the other property was held by the person for whom the basis is to be determined. A similar rule shall be applied in the case of a series of substituted bases.

(c) **Increase in basis of property on which additional estate tax is imposed.** --

(1) **Tax imposed with respect to entire interest.** -- If an additional estate tax is imposed under section 2032A(c)(1) with respect to any interest in property and the qualified heir makes an election under this subsection with respect to the imposition of such tax, the adjusted basis of such interest shall be increased by an amount equal to the excess of--

(A) the fair market value of such interest on the date of the decedent's death (or the alternate valuation date under section 2032, if the executor of the decedent's estate elected the application of such section), over

(B) the value of such interest determined under section 2032A(a).

(2) **Partial dispositions.** --

(A) **In general.** -- In the case of any partial disposition for which an election under this subsection is made, the increase in basis under paragraph (1) shall be an amount--

(i) which bears the same ratio to the increase which would be determined under paragraph (1) (without regard to this paragraph) with respect to the entire interest, as

(ii) the amount of the tax imposed under section 2032A(c)(1) with respect to such disposition bears to the adjusted tax difference attributable to the entire interest (as determined under section 2032A(c)(2)(B)).

Sec. 1016. Adjustments to basis

(B) Partial disposition. -- For purposes of subparagraph (A), the term "partial disposition" means any disposition or cessation to which subsection (c)(2)(D), (h)(1)(B), or (i)(1)(B) of section 2032A applies.

(3) Time adjustment made. -- Any increase in basis under this subsection shall be deemed to have occurred immediately before the disposition or cessation resulting in the imposition of the tax under section 2032A(c)(1).

***

(5) Election. --

(A) In general. -- An election under this subsection shall be made at such time and in such manner as the Secretary shall by regulations prescribe. Such an election, once made, shall be irrevocable.

(B) Interest on recaptured amount. -- If an election is made under this subsection with respect to any additional estate tax imposed under section 2032A(c)(1), for purposes of section 6601 (relating to interest on underpayments), the last date prescribed for payment of such tax shall be deemed to be the last date prescribed for payment of the tax imposed by section 2001 with respect to the estate of the decedent (as determined for purposes of section 6601).

***

Sec. 1017. Discharge of indebtedness

(a) General rule. -- If--

(1) an amount is excluded from gross income under subsection (a) of section 108 (relating to discharge of indebtedness), and

(2) under subsection (b)(2)(E), (b)(5), or (c)(1) of section 108, any portion of such amount is to be applied to reduce basis, then such portion shall be applied in reduction of the basis of any property held by the taxpayer at the beginning of the taxable year following the taxable year in which the discharge occurs.

(b) Amount and properties determined under regulations. --

(1) In general. -- The amount of reduction to be applied under subsection (a) (not in excess of the portion referred to in subsection (a)), and the particular properties the bases of which are to be reduced, shall be determined under regulations prescribed by the Secretary.

(2) Limitation in title 11 case or insolvency. -- In the case of a discharge to which subparagraph (A) or (B) of section 108(a)(1) applies, the reduction in basis under subsection (a) of this section shall not exceed the excess of--

(A) the aggregate of the bases of the property held by the taxpayer immediately after the discharge, over

(B) the aggregate of the liabilities of the taxpayer immediately after the discharge.

The preceding sentence shall not apply to any reduction in basis by reason of an election under section 108(b)(5).

(3) Certain reductions may only be made in the basis of depreciable property. --

(A) In general. -- Any amount which under subsection (b)(5) or (c)(1) of section 108 is to be applied to reduce basis shall be applied only to reduce the basis of depreciable property held by the taxpayer.

(B) Depreciable property. -- For purposes of this section, the term "depreciable property" means any property of a character subject to the allowance for depreciation, but only if a basis reduction under subsection (a) will reduce the amount of depreciation or

901

Sec. 1017. Discharge of indebtedness

amortization which otherwise would be allowable for the period immediately following such reduction.

(C) Special rule for partnership interests. -- For purposes of this section, any interest of a partner in a partnership shall be treated as depreciable property to the extent of such partner's proportionate interest in the depreciable property held by such partnership. The preceding sentence shall apply only if there is a corresponding reduction in the partnership's basis in depreciable property with respect to such partner.

(D) Special rule in case of affiliated group. -- For purposes of this section, if--

(i) a corporation holds stock in another corporation (hereinafter in this subparagraph referred to as the "subsidiary"), and

(ii) such corporations are members of the same affiliated group which file a consolidated return under section 1501 for the taxable year in which the discharge occurs,

then such stock shall be treated as depreciable property to the extent that such subsidiary consents to a corresponding reduction in the basis of its depreciable property.

(E) Election to treat certain inventory as depreciable property. --

(i) In general. -- At the election of the taxpayer, for purposes of this section, the term "depreciable property" includes any real property which is described in section 1221(a)(1).

(ii) Election. -- An election under clause (i) shall be made on the taxpayer's return for the taxable year in which the discharge occurs or at such other time as may be permitted in regulations prescribed by the Secretary. Such an election, once made, may be revoked only with the consent of the Secretary.

(F) Special rules for qualified real property business indebtedness. -- In the case of any amount which under section 108(c)(1) is to be applied to reduce basis--

(i) depreciable property shall only include depreciable real property for purposes of subparagraphs (A) and (C),

(ii) subparagraph (E) shall not apply, and

(iii) in the case of property taken into account under section 108(c)(2)(B), the reduction with respect to such property shall be made as of the time immediately before disposition if earlier than the time under subsection (a).

(4) Special rules for qualified farm indebtedness. --

(A) In general. -- Any amount which under subsection (b)(2)(E) of section 108 is to be applied to reduce basis and which is attributable to an amount excluded under subsection (a)(1)(C) of section 108--

(i) shall be applied only to reduce the basis of qualified property held by the taxpayer, and

(ii) shall be applied to reduce the basis of qualified property in the following order:

(I) First the basis of qualified property which is depreciable property.

(II) Second the basis of qualified property which is land used or held for use in the trade or business of farming.

(III) Then the basis of other qualified property.

(B) Qualified property. -- For purposes of this paragraph, the term "qualified property" has the meaning given to such term by section 108(g)(3)(C).

(C) Certain rules made applicable. -- Rules similar to the rules of subparagraphs (C), (D), and (E) of paragraph (3) shall apply for purposes of this paragraph and section 108(g).

Sec. 1017. Discharge of indebtedness

(c) Special rules. --

(1) Reduction not to be made in exempt property. -- In the case of an amount excluded from gross income under section 108(a)(1)(A), no reduction in basis shall be made under this section in the basis of property which the debtor treats as exempt property under section 522 of title 11 of the United States Code.   5

(2) Reductions in basis not treated as dispositions. -- For purposes of this title, a reduction in basis under this section shall not be treated as a disposition.

(d) Recapture of reductions. --

(1) In general. -- For purposes of sections 1245 and 1250--

(A) any property the basis of which is reduced under this section and which is neither 10 section 1245 property nor section 1250 property shall be treated as section 1245 property, and

(B) any reduction under this section shall be treated as a deduction allowed for depreciation.

(2) Special rule for section 1250. -- For purposes of section 1250(b), the determination of 15 what would have been the depreciation adjustments under the straight line method shall be made as if there had been no reduction under this section.

Sec. 1019. Property on which lessee has made improvements

Neither the basis nor the adjusted basis of any portion of real property shall, in the case of the lessor of such property, be increased or diminished on account of income derived by the lessor in 20 respect of such property and excludable from gross income under section 109 (relating to improvements by lessee on lessor's property). If an amount representing any part of the value of real property attributable to buildings erected or other improvements made by a lessee in respect of such property was included in gross income of the lessor for any taxable year beginning before January1, 1942, the basis of each portion of such property shall be properly adjusted for the 25 amount so included in gross income.

Sec. 1022. Treatment of property acquired from a decedent dying after December 31, 2009

(a) In general. -- Except as otherwise provided in this section--

(1) property acquired from a decedent dying after December 31, 2009, shall be treated for 30 purposes of this subtitle as transferred by gift, and

(2) the basis of the person acquiring property from such a decedent shall be the lesser of -

(A) the adjusted basis of the decedent, or

(B) the fair market value of the property at the date of the decedent's death.

(b) Basis increase for certain property. --   35

(1) In general. -- In the case of property to which this subsection applies, the basis of such property under subsection (a) shall be increased by its basis increase under this subsection.

(2) Basis increase. -- For purposes of this subsection--

(A) In general. -- The basis increase under this subsection for any property is the portion of the aggregate basis increase which is allocated to the property pursuant to this section.   40

(B) Aggregate basis increase. -- In the case of any estate, the aggregate basis increase

903

under this subsection is $1,300,000.

(C) Limit increased by unused built-in losses and loss carryovers. -- The limitation under subparagraph (B) shall be increased by--

(i) the sum of the amount of any capital loss carryover under section 1212(b), and the amount of any net operating loss carryover under section 172, which would (but for the decedent's death) be carried from the decedent's last taxable year to a later taxable year of the decedent, plus

(ii) the sum of the amount of any losses that would have been allowable under section 165 if the property acquired from the decedent had been sold at fair market value immediately before the decedent's death.

(3) Decedent nonresidents who are not citizens of the United States. -- In the case of a decedent nonresident not a citizen of the United States--

(A) paragraph (2)(B) shall be applied by substituting "$60,000" for "$1,300,000", and

(B) paragraph (2)(C) shall not apply.

(c) Additional basis increase for property acquired by surviving spouse. --

(1) In general. -- In the case of property to which this subsection applies and which is qualified spousal property, the basis of such property under subsection (a) (as increased under subsection (b)) shall be increased by its spousal property basis increase.

(2) Spousal property basis increase. -- For purposes of this subsection--

(A) In general. -- The spousal property basis increase for property referred to in paragraph (1) is the portion of the aggregate spousal property basis increase which is allocated to the property pursuant to this section.

(B) Aggregate spousal property basis increase. -- In the case of any estate, the aggregate spousal property basis increase is $3,000,000.

(3) Qualified spousal property. -- For purposes of this subsection, the term "qualified spousal property" means--

(A) outright transfer property, and

(B) qualified terminable interest property.

(4) Outright transfer property. -- For purposes of this subsection--

(A) In general. -- The term "outright transfer property" means any interest in property acquired from the decedent by the decedent's surviving spouse.

(B) Exception. -- Subparagraph (A) shall not apply where, on the lapse of time, on the occurrence of an event or contingency, or on the failure of an event or contingency to occur, an interest passing to the surviving spouse will terminate or fail--

(i)(I) if an interest in such property passes or has passed (for less than an adequate and full consideration in money or money's worth) from the decedent to any person other than such surviving spouse (or the estate of such spouse), and

(II) if by reason of such passing such person (or his heirs or assigns) may possess or enjoy any part of such property after such termination or failure of the interest so passing to the surviving spouse, or

(ii) if such interest is to be acquired for the surviving spouse, pursuant to directions of the decedent, by his executor or by the trustee of a trust.

For purposes of this subparagraph, an interest shall not be considered as an interest which will terminate or fail merely because it is the ownership of a bond, note, or similar contractual obligation, the discharge of which would not have the effect of an annuity for

Sec. 1022. Treatment of property acquired from a decedent dying after December 31, 2009

life or for a term.

(C) Interest of spouse conditional on survival for limited period. -- For purposes of this paragraph, an interest passing to the surviving spouse shall not be considered as an interest which will terminate or fail on the death of such spouse if--

(i) such death will cause a termination or failure of such interest only if it occurs 5 within a period not exceeding 6 months after the decedent's death, or only if it occurs as a result of a common disaster resulting in the death of the decedent and the surviving spouse, or only if it occurs in the case of either such event, and

(ii) such termination or failure does not in fact occur.

(5) Qualified terminable interest property. -- For purposes of this subsection-- 10

(A) In general. -- The term "qualified terminable interest property" means property--

(i) which passes from the decedent, and

(ii) in which the surviving spouse has a qualifying income interest for life.

(B) Qualifying income interest for life. -- The surviving spouse has a qualifying income interest for life if-- 15

(i) the surviving spouse is entitled to all the income from the property, payable annually or at more frequent intervals, or has a usufruct interest for life in the property, and

(ii) no person has a power to appoint any part of the property to any person other than the surviving spouse. 20

Clause (ii) shall not apply to a power exercisable only at or after the death of the surviving spouse. To the extent provided in regulations, an annuity shall be treated in a manner similar to an income interest in property (regardless of whether the property from which the annuity is payable can be separately identified).

(C) Property includes interest therein. -- The term "property" includes an interest in 25 property.

(D) Specific portion treated as separate property. -- A specific portion of property shall be treated as separate property. For purposes of the preceding sentence, the term "specific portion" only includes a portion determined on a fractional or percentage basis.

(d) Definitions and special rules for application of subsections (b) and (c). -- 30

(1) Property to which subsections (b) and (c) apply. --

(A) In general. -- The basis of property acquired from a decedent may be increased under subsection (b) or (c) only if the property was owned by the decedent at the time of death.

(B) Rules relating to ownership. -- 35

(i) Jointly held property. -- In the case of property which was owned by the decedent and another person as joint tenants with right of survivorship or tenants by the entirety--

(I) if the only such other person is the surviving spouse, the decedent shall be treated as the owner of only 50 percent of the property, 40

(II) in any case (to which subclause (I) does not apply) in which the decedent furnished consideration for the acquisition of the property, the decedent shall be treated as the owner to the extent of the portion of the property which is proportionate to such consideration, and

(III) in any case (to which subclause (I) does not apply) in which the property 45

Sec. 1022.   Treatment of property acquired from a decedent dying after December 31, 2009

has been acquired by gift, bequest, devise, or inheritance by the decedent and any other person as joint tenants with right of survivorship and their interests are not otherwise specified or fixed by law, the decedent shall be treated as the owner to the extent of the value of a fractional part to be determined by dividing the value of the property by the number of joint tenants with right of survivorship.

(ii) Revocable trusts. -- The decedent shall be treated as owning property transferred by the decedent during life to a qualified revocable trust (as defined in section 645(b)(1)).

(iii) Powers of appointment. -- The decedent shall not be treated as owning any property by reason of holding a power of appointment with respect to such property.

(iv) Community property. -- Property which represents the surviving spouse's one-half share of community property held by the decedent and the surviving spouse under the community property laws of any State or possession of the United States or any foreign country shall be treated for purposes of this section as owned by, and acquired from, the decedent if at least one- half of the whole of the community interest in such property is treated as owned by, and acquired from, the decedent without regard to this clause.

(C) Property acquired by decedent by gift within 3 years of death. --

(i) In general. -- Subsections (b) and (c) shall not apply to property acquired by the decedent by gift or by inter vivos transfer for less than adequate and full consideration in money or money's worth during the 3-year period ending on the date of the decedent's death.

(ii) Exception for certain gifts from spouse. -- Clause (i) shall not apply to property acquired by the decedent from the decedent's spouse unless, during such 3-year period, such spouse acquired the property in whole or in part by gift or by inter vivos transfer for less than adequate and full consideration in money or money's worth.

***

(2) Fair market value limitation. -- The adjustments under subsections (b) and (c) shall not increase the basis of any interest in property acquired from the decedent above its fair market value in the hands of the decedent as of the date of the decedent's death.

(3) Allocation rules. --

(A) In general. -- The executor shall allocate the adjustments under subsections (b) and (c) on the return required by section 6018.

(B) Changes in allocation. -- Any allocation made pursuant to subparagraph (A) may be changed only as provided by the Secretary.

(4) Inflation adjustment of basis adjustment amounts. --

(A) In general. -- In the case of decedents dying in a calendar year after 2010, the $1,300,000, $60,000, and $3,000,000 dollar amounts in subsections (b) and (c)(2)(B) shall each be increased by an amount equal to the product of--

(i) such dollar amount, and

(ii) the cost-of-living adjustment determined under section 1(f)(3) for such calendar year, determined by substituting "2009" for "1992" in subparagraph (B) thereof.

(B) Rounding. -- If any increase determined under subparagraph (A) is not a multiple of--

(i) $100,000 in the case of the $1,300,000 amount,

Sec. 1022. Treatment of property acquired from a decedent dying after December 31, 2009

        (ii) $5,000 in the case of the $60,000 amount, and

        (iii) $250,000 in the case of the $3,000,000 amount,

such increase shall be rounded to the next lowest multiple thereof.

  (e) Property acquired from the decedent. -- For purposes of this section, the following property shall be considered to have been acquired from the decedent:

    (1) Property acquired by bequest, devise, or inheritance, or by the decedent's estate from the decedent.

    (2) Property transferred by the decedent during his lifetime--

        (A) to a qualified revocable trust (as defined in section 645(b)(1)), or

        (B) to any other trust with respect to which the decedent reserved the right to make any change in the enjoyment thereof through the exercise of a power to alter, amend, or terminate the trust.

    (3) Any other property passing from the decedent by reason of death to the extent that such property passed without consideration.

  (f) Coordination with section 691. -- This section shall not apply to property which constitutes a right to receive an item of income in respect of a decedent under section 691.

  (g) Certain liabilities disregarded. --

    (1) In general. -- In determining whether gain is recognized on the acquisition of property--

        (A) from a decedent by a decedent's estate or any beneficiary other than a tax-exempt beneficiary, and

        (B) from the decedent's estate by any beneficiary other than a tax-exempt beneficiary,

and in determining the adjusted basis of such property, liabilities in excess of basis shall be disregarded.

    (2) Tax-exempt beneficiary. -- For purposes of paragraph (1), the term "tax-exempt beneficiary" means--

        (A) the United States, any State or political subdivision thereof, any possession of the United States, any Indian tribal government (within the meaning of section 7871), or any agency or instrumentality of any of the foregoing,

        (B) an organization (other than a cooperative described in section 521) which is exempt from tax imposed by chapter 1,

        (C) any foreign person or entity (within the meaning of section 168(h)(2)), and

        (D) to the extent provided in regulations, any person to whom property is transferred for the principal purpose of tax avoidance.

***

Sec. 1031. Exchange of property held for productive use or investment

  (a) Nonrecognition of gain or loss from exchanges solely in kind. --

    (1) In general. -- No gain or loss shall be recognized on the exchange of property held for productive use in a trade or business or for investment if such property is exchanged solely for property of like kind which is to be held either for productive use in a trade or business or for investment.

    (2) Exception. -- This subsection shall not apply to any exchange of--

        (A) stock in trade or other property held primarily for sale,

Sec. 1031. Exchange of property held for productive use or investment

   (B) stocks, bonds, or notes,

   (C) other securities or evidences of indebtedness or interest,

   (D) interests in a partnership,

   (E) certificates of trust or beneficial interests, or

   (F) choses in action.

For purposes of this section, an interest in a partnership which has in effect a valid election under section 761(a) to be excluded from the application of all of subchapter K shall be treated as an interest in each of the assets of such partnership and not as an interest in a partnership.

  (3) Requirement that property be identified and that exchange be completed not more than 180 days after transfer of exchanged property. -- For purposes of this subsection, any property received by the taxpayer shall be treated as property which is not like-kind property if--

   (A) such property is not identified as property to be received in the exchange on or before the day which is 45 days after the date on which the taxpayer transfers the property relinquished in the exchange, or

   (B) such property is received after the earlier of--

    (i) the day which is 180 days after the date on which the taxpayer transfers the property relinquished in the exchange, or

    (ii) the due date (determined with regard to extension) for the transferor's return of the tax imposed by this chapter for the taxable year in which the transfer of the relinquished property occurs.

  (b) Gain from exchanges not solely in kind. -- If an exchange would be within the provisions of subsection (a), of section 1035(a), of section 1036(a), or of section 1037(a), if it were not for the fact that the property received in exchange consists not only of property permitted by such provisions to be received without the recognition of gain, but also of other property or money, then the gain, if any, to the recipient shall be recognized, but in an amount not in excess of the sum of such money and the fair market value of such other property.

  (c) Loss from exchanges not solely in kind. -- If an exchange would be within the provisions of subsection (a), of section 1035(a), of section 1036(a), or of section 1037(a), if it were not for the fact that the property received in exchange consists not only of property permitted by such provisions to be received without the recognition of gain or loss, but also of other property or money, then no loss from the exchange shall be recognized.

  (d) Basis. -- If property was acquired on an exchange described in this section, section 1035(a), section 1036(a), or section 1037(a), then the basis shall be the same as that of the property exchanged, decreased in the amount of any money received by the taxpayer and increased in the amount of gain or decreased in the amount of loss to the taxpayer that was recognized on such exchange. If the property so acquired consisted in part of the type of property permitted by this section, section 1035(a), section 1036(a), or section 1037(a), to be received without the recognition of gain or loss, and in part of other property, the basis provided in this subsection shall be allocated between the properties (other than money) received, and for the purpose of the allocation there shall be assigned to such other property an amount equivalent to its fair market value at the date of the exchange. For purposes of this section, section 1035(a), and section 1036(a), where as part of the consideration to the taxpayer another party to the exchange assumed (as determined under section 357(d)) a liability of the taxpayer, such assumption shall be considered as money received by the taxpayer on the exchange.

  (e) Exchanges of livestock of different sexes. -- For purposes of this section, livestock of different sexes are not property of a like kind.

Sec. 1031. Exchange of property held for productive use or investment

(f) Special rules for exchanges between related persons. --

(1) In general. -- If--

(A) a taxpayer exchanges property with a related person,

(B) there is nonrecognition of gain or loss to the taxpayer under this section with respect to the exchange of such property (determined without regard to this subsection), and   5

(C) before the date 2 years after the date of the last transfer which was part of such exchange--

(i) the related person disposes of such property, or

(ii) the taxpayer disposes of the property received in the exchange from the related person which was of like kind to the property transferred by the taxpayer, there shall be   10 no nonrecognition of gain or loss under this section to the taxpayer with respect to such exchange; except that any gain or loss recognized by the taxpayer by reason of this subsection shall be taken into account as of the date on which the disposition referred to in subparagraph (C) occurs.

(2) Certain dispositions not taken into account. -- For purposes of paragraph (1)(C), there   15 shall not be taken into account any disposition--

(A) after the earlier of the death of the taxpayer or the death of the related person,

(B) in a compulsory or involuntary conversion (within the meaning of section 1033) if the exchange occurred before the threat or imminence of such conversion, or

(C) with respect to which it is established to the satisfaction of the Secretary that neither   20 the exchange nor such disposition had as one of its principal purposes the avoidance of Federal income tax.

(3) Related person. -- For purposes of this subsection, the term "related person" means any person bearing a relationship to the taxpayer described in section 267(b) or 707(b)(1).

(4) Treatment of certain transactions. -- This section shall not apply to any exchange   25 which is part of a transaction (or series of transactions) structured to avoid the purposes of this subsection.

(g) Special rule where substantial diminution of risk. --

(1) In general. -- If paragraph (2) applies to any property for any period, the running of the period set forth in subsection (f)(1)(C) with respect to such property shall be suspended during   30 such period.

(2) Property to which subsection applies. -- This paragraph shall apply to any property for any period during which the holder's risk of loss with respect to the property is substantially diminished by--

(A) the holding of a put with respect to such property,   35

(B) the holding by another person of a right to acquire such property, or

(C) a short sale or any other transaction.

(h) Special rules for foreign real and personal property. -- For purposes of this section -

(1) Real property. -- Real property located in the United States and real property located outside the United States are not property of a like kind.   40

(2) Personal property. --

(A) In general. -- Personal property used predominantly within the United States and personal property used predominantly outside the United States are not property of a like kind.

(B) Predominant use. -- Except as provided in subparagraph (!1) (C) and (D), the   45 predominant use of any property shall be determined based on--

(i) in the case of the property relinquished in the exchange, the 2-year period ending on the date of such relinquishment, and

(ii) in the case of the property acquired in the exchange,

5   the 2-year period beginning on the date of such acquisition.

(C) Property held for less than 2 years. -- Except in the case of an exchange which is part of a transaction (or series of transactions) structured to avoid the purposes of this subsection--

(i) only the periods the property was held by the person relinquishing the property (or
10   any related person) shall be taken into account under subparagraph (B)(i), and

(ii) only the periods the property was held by the person acquiring the property (or any related person) shall be taken into account under subparagraph (B)(ii).

(D) Special rule for certain property. -- Property described in any subparagraph of section 168(g)(4) shall be treated as used predominantly in the United States.

15

Reg. § 1.1031(a)-1   Property held for productive use in trade or business or for investment.

(a) *In general*--(1) *Exchanges of property solely for property of a like kind.* Section 1031(a)(1) provides an exception from the general rule requiring the recognition of gain
20 or loss upon the sale or exchange of property. Under section 1031(a)(1), no gain or loss is recognized if property held for productive use in a trade or business or for investment is exchanged solely for property of a like kind to be held either for productive use in a trade or business or for investment. Under section 1031(a)(1), property held for productive use in a trade or business may be exchanged for property held for investment. Similarly,
25 under section 1031(a)(1), property held for investment may be exchanged for property held for productive use in a trade or business. However, section 1031(a)(2) provides that section 1031(a)(1) does not apply to any exchange of--

(i) Stock in trade or other property held primarily for sale;

(ii) Stocks, bonds, or notes;
30 (iii) Other securities or evidences of indebtedness or interest;

(iv) Interests in a partnership;

(v) Certificates of trust or beneficial interests; or

(vi) Choses in action.

Section 1031(a)(1) does not apply to any exchange of interests in a partnership
35 regardless of whether the interests exchanged are general or limited partnership interests or are interests in the same partnership or in different partnerships. An interest in a partnership that has in effect a valid election under section 761(a) to be excluded from the application of all of subchapter K is treated as an interest in each of the assets of the partnership and not as an interest in a partnership for purposes of section 1031(a)(2)(D)
40 and paragraph (a)(1)(iv) of this section. An exchange of an interest in such a partnership does not qualify for nonrecognition of gain or loss under section 1031 with respect to any asset of the partnership that is described in section 1031(a)(2) or to the extent the exchange of assets of the partnership does not otherwise satisfy the requirements of section 1031(a).
45 (2) *Exchanges of property not solely for property of a like kind.* A transfer is not within the provisions of section 1031(a) if, as part of the consideration, the taxpayer receives money or property which does not meet the requirements of section 1031(a), but the transfer, if otherwise qualified, will be within the provisions of either section 1031 (b) or (c). Similarly, a transfer is not within the provisions of section 1031(a) if, as part of the

Sec. 1031. Exchange of property held for productive use or investment

consideration, the other party to the exchange assumes a liability of the taxpayer (or acquires property from the taxpayer that is subject to a liability), but the transfer, if otherwise qualified, will be within the provisions of either section 1031 (b) or (c). A transfer of property meeting the requirements of section 1031(a) may be within the provisions of section 1031(a) even though the taxpayer transfers in addition property not 5 meeting the requirements of section 1031(a) or money. However, the nonrecognition treatment provided by section 1031(a) does not apply to the property transferred which does not meet the requirements of section 1031(a).

(b) *Definition of ``like kind."* As used in section 1031(a), the words like kind have reference to the nature or character of the property and not to its grade or quality. One 10 kind or class of property may not, under that section, be exchanged for property of a different kind or class. The fact that any real estate involved is improved or unimproved is not material, for that fact relates only to the grade or quality of the property and not to its kind or class. Unproductive real estate held by one other than a dealer for future use or future realization of the increment in value is held for investment and not primarily for 15 sale. For additional rules for exchanges of personal property, see § 1.1031 (a)-2.

(c) *Examples of exchanges of property of a ``like kind."* No gain or loss is recognized if (1) a taxpayer exchanges property held for productive use in his trade or business, together with cash, for other property of like kind for the same use, such as a truck for a new truck or a passenger automobile for a new passenger automobile to be used for a 20 like purpose; or (2) a taxpayer who is not a dealer in real estate exchanges city real estate for a ranch or farm, or exchanges a leasehold of a fee with 30 years or more to run for real estate, or exchanges improved real estate for unimproved real estate; or (3) a taxpayer exchanges investment property and cash for investment property of a like kind.

(d) *Examples of exchanges not solely in kind.* Gain or loss is recognized if, for 25 instance, a taxpayer exchanges (1) Treasury bonds maturing March 15, 1958, for Treasury bonds maturing December 15, 1968, unless section 1037(a) (or so much of section 1031 as relates to section 1037(a)) applies to such exchange, or (2) a real estate mortgage for consolidated farm loan bonds.

***

30

Reg. § 1.1031(a)-2 Additional rules for exchanges of personal property.

(a) *Introduction.* Section 1.1031(a)-1(b) provides that the nonrecognition rules of section 1031 do not apply to an exchange of one kind or class of property for property of a different kind or class. This section contains additional rules for determining whether personal property has been exchanged for property of a like kind or like class. Personal 35 properties of a like class are considered to be of a ``like kind" for purposes of section 1031. In addition, an exchange of properties of a like kind may qualify under section 1031 regardless of whether the properties are also of a like class. In determining whether exchanged properties are of a like kind, no inference is to be drawn from the fact that the properties are not of a like class. Under paragraph (b) of this section, depreciable 40 tangible personal properties are of a like class if they are either within the same General Asset Class (as defined in paragraph (b)(2) of this section) or within the same Product Class (as defined in paragraph (b)(3) of this section). Paragraph (c) of this section provides rules for exchanges of intangible personal property and nondepreciable personal property. 45

(b) *Depreciable tangible personal property--(1) General rule.* Depreciable tangible personal property is exchanged for property of a ``like kind" under section 1031 if the property is exchanged for property of a like kind or like class. Depreciable tangible personal property is of a like class to other depreciable tangible personal property if the exchanged properties are either within the same General Asset Class or within the same 50 Product Class. A single property may not be classified within more than one General

911

Sec. 1031. Exchange of property held for productive use or investment

Asset Class or within more than one Product Class. In addition, property classified within any General Asset Class may not be classified within a Product Class. A property's General Asset Class or Product Class is determined as of the date of the exchange.

(2) *General Asset Classes.* Except as provided in paragraphs (b)(4) and (b)(5) of this
5 section, property within a General Asset Class consists of depreciable tangible personal property described in one of asset classes 00.11 through 00.28 and 00.4 of Rev. Proc. 87-56, 1987-2 C.B. 674. These General Asset Classes describe types of depreciable tangible personal property that frequently are used in many businesses. The General Asset Classes are as follows:

10   (i) Office furniture, fixtures, and equipment (asset class 00.11),

    (ii) Information systems (computers and peripheral equipment) (asset class 00.12),

    (iii) Data handling equipment, except computers (asset class 00.13),

    (iv) Airplanes (airframes and engines), except those used in commercial or contract carrying of passengers or freight, and all helicopters (airframes and engines) (asset class
15 00.21),

    (v) Automobiles, taxis (asset class 00.22),

    (vi) Buses (asset class 00.23),

    (vii) Light general purpose trucks (asset class 00.241),

    (viii) Heavy general purpose trucks (asset class 00.242),

20   (ix) Railroad cars and locomotives, except those owned by railroad transportation companies (asset class 00.25),

    (x) Tractor units for use over-the-road (asset class 00.26),

    (xi) Trailers and trailer-mounted containers (asset class 00.27),

    (xii) Vessels, barges, tugs, and similar water-transportation equipment, except those
25 used in marine construction (asset class 00.28), and

    (xiii) Industrial steam and electric generation and/or distribution systems (asset class 00.4).

(3) *Product classes.* Except as provided in paragraphs (b)(4) and (5) of this section, or as provided by the Commissioner in published guidance of general applicability, property
30 within a product class consists of depreciable tangible personal property that is described in a 6-digit product class within Sectors 31, 32, and 33 (pertaining to manufacturing industries) of the North American Industry Classification System (NAICS), set forth in Executive Office of the President, Office of Management and Budget, North American Industry Classification System, United States, 2002 (NAICS Manual), as periodically
35 updated. Copies of the NAICS Manual may be obtained from the National Technical Information Service, an agency of the U.S. Department of Commerce, and may be accessed on the internet. Sectors 31 through 33 of the NAICS Manual contain listings of specialized industries for the manufacture of described products and equipment. For this purpose, any 6-digit NAICS product class with a last digit of 9 (a miscellaneous category)
40 is not a product class for purposes of this section. If a property is listed in more than one product class, the property is treated as listed in any one of those product classes. A property's 6-digit product class is referred to as the property's NAICS code.

(4) *Modifications of NAICS product classes.* The product classes of the NAICS Manual may be updated or otherwise modified from time to time as the manual is updated,
45 effective on or after the date of the modification. The NAICS Manual generally is modified every five years, in years ending in a 2 or 7 (such as 2002, 2007, and 2012). The applicability date of the modified NAICS Manual is announced in the Federal Register and generally is January 1 of the year the NAICS Manual is modified. Taxpayers may rely on these modifications as they become effective in structuring exchanges under this
50 section. Taxpayers may rely on the previous NAICS Manual for transfers of property made by a taxpayer during the one-year period following the effective date of the

Sec. 1031. Exchange of property held for productive use or investment

modification. For transfers of property made by a taxpayer on or after January 1, 1997, and on or before January 1, 2003, the NAICS Manual of 1997 may be used for determining product classes of the exchanged property.

(5) *Administrative procedures for revising general asset classes and product classes.* The Commissioner may, through published guidance of general applicability, supplement, modify, clarify, or update the guidance relating to the classification of properties provided in this paragraph (b). (See § 601.601(d)(2) of this chapter.) For example, the Commissioner may determine not to follow (in whole or in part) a general asset class for purposes of identifying property of like class, may determine not to follow (in whole or in part) any modification of product classes published in the NAICS Manual, or may determine that other properties not listed within the same or in any product class or general asset class nevertheless are of a like class. The Commissioner also may determine that two items of property that are listed in separate product classes or in product classes with a last digit of 9 are of a like class, or that an item of property that has a NAICS code is of a like class to an item of property that does not have a NAICS code.

(6) *No inference outside of section 1031.* The rules provided in this section concerning the use of general asset classes or product classes are limited to exchanges under section 1031. No inference is intended with respect to the classification of property for other purposes, such as depreciation.

(7) *Examples.* The application of this paragraph (b) may be illustrated by the following examples:

Example 1. Taxpayer A transfers a personal computer (asset class 00.12) to B in exchange for a printer (asset class 00.12). With respect to A, the properties exchanged are within the same General Asset Class and therefore are of a like class.

Example 2. Taxpayer C transfers an airplane (asset class 00.21) to D in exchange for a heavy general purpose truck (asset class 00.242). The properties exchanged are not of a like class because they are within different General Asset Classes. Because each of the properties is within a General Asset Class, the properties may not be classified within a Product Class. The airplane and heavy general purpose truck are also not of a like kind. Therefore, the exchange does not qualify for nonrecognition of gain or loss under section 1031.

Example 3. Taxpayer E transfers a grader to F in exchange for a scraper. Neither property is within any of the general asset classes. However, both properties are within the same product class (NAICS code 333120). The grader and scraper are of a like class and deemed to be of a like kind for purposes of section 1031.

Example 4. Taxpayer G transfers a personal computer (asset class 00.12), an airplane (asset class 00.21) and a sanding machine (NAICS code 333210), to H in exchange for a printer (asset class 00.12), a heavy general purpose truck (asset class 00.242) and a lathe (NAICS code 333210). The personal computer and the printer are of a like class because they are within the same general asset class. The sanding machine and the lathe are of a like class because they are within the same product class (although neither property is within any of the general asset classes). The airplane and the heavy general purpose truck are neither within the same general asset class nor within the same product class, and are not of a like kind.

(8) *Transition rule.* Properties within the same product classes based on the 4-digit codes contained in Division D of the Executive Office of the President, Office of Management and Budget, Standard Industrial Classification Manual (1987), will be treated as property of a like class for transfers of property made by taxpayers on or before May 19, 2005.

(c) *Intangible personal property and nondepreciable personal property--(1) General rule.* An exchange of intangible personal property of nondepreciable personal property

Sec. 1031. Exchange of property held for productive use or investment

qualifies for nonrecognition of gain or loss under section 1031 only if the exchanged properties are of a like kind. No like classes are provided for these properties. Whether intangible personal property is of a like kind to other intangible personal property generally depends on the nature or character of the rights involved (e.g., a patent or a
5 copyright) and also on the nature or character of the underlying property to which the intangible personal property relates.

(2) *Goodwill and going concern value.* The goodwill or going concern value of a business is not of a like kind to the goodwill or going concern value of another business.

(3) *Examples.* The application of this paragraph (c) may be illustrated by the following
10 examples:

Example 1. Taxpayer K exchanges a copyright on a novel for a copyright on a different novel. The properties exchanged are of a like kind.

Example 2. Taxpayer J exchanges a copyright on a novel for a copyright on a song. The properties exchanged are not of a like kind.
15

Reg. § 1.1031(b)-1 Receipt of other property or money in tax-free exchange.

(a) If the taxpayer receives other property (in addition to property permitted to be received without recognition of gain) or money--

(1) In an exchange described in section 1031(a) of property held for investment or
20 productive use in trade or business for property of like kind to be held either for productive use or for investment,

(2) In an exchange described in section 1035(a) of insurance policies or annuity contracts,

(3) In an exchange described in section 1036(a) of common stock for common stock,
25 or preferred stock for preferred stock, in the same corporation and not in connection with a corporate reorganization, or

(4) In an exchange described in section 1037(a) of obligations of the United States, issued under the Second Liberty Bond Act (31 U.S.C. 774 (2)), solely for other obligations issued under such Act, the gain, if any, to the taxpayer will be recognized under section
30 1031(b) in an amount not in excess of the sum of the money and the fair market value of the other property, but the loss, if any, to the taxpayer from such an exchange will not be recognized under section 1031(c) to any extent.

(b) The application of this section may be illustrated by the following examples:

Example 1. A, who is not a dealer in real estate, in 1954 exchanges real estate held
35 for investment, which he purchased in 1940 for $5,000, for other real estate (to be held for productive use in trade or business) which has a fair market value of $6,000, and $2,000 in cash. The gain from the transaction is $3,000, but is recognized only to the extent of the cash received of $2,000.

Example 2. (a) B, who uses the cash receipts and disbursements method of
40 accounting and the calendar year as his taxable year, has never elected under section 454(a) to include in gross income currently the annual increase in the redemption price of non-interest-bearing obligations issued at a discount. In 1943, for $750 each, B purchased four $1,000 series E U.S. savings bonds bearing an issue date of March 1, 1943.
45   (b) On October 1, 1963, the redemption value of each such bond was $1,396, and the total redemption value of the four bonds was $5,584. On that date B submitted the four $1,000 series E bonds to the United States in a transaction in which one of such $1,000 bonds was reissued by issuing four $100 series E U.S. savings bonds bearing an issue date of March 1, 1943, and by considering six $100 series E bonds bearing an issue date
50 of March 1, 1943, to have been issued. The redemption value of each such $100 series E bond was $139.60 on October 1, 1963. Then, as part of the transaction, the six $100

914

Sec. 1031. Exchange of property held for productive use or investment

series E bonds so considered to have been issued and the three $1,000 series E bonds were exchanged, in an exchange qualifying under section 1037(a), for five $1,000 series H U.S. savings bonds plus $25.60 in cash.

(c) The gain realized on the exchange qualifying under section 1037(a) is $2,325.60, determined as follows:

Amount realized:	
Par value of five series H bonds............................	$5,000.00
Cash received..	25.60
Total realized..	5,025.60
Less: Adjusted basis of series E bonds surrendered in the exchange:	
Three $1,000 series E bonds..............................	$2,250.00
Six $100 series E bonds at $75 each...................	450.00
	2,700.00
Gain realized..	2,325.60

(d) Pursuant to section 1031(b), only $25.60 (the money received) of the total gain of $2,325.60 realized on the exchange is recognized at the time of exchange and must be included in B's gross income for 1963. The $2,300 balance of the gain ($2,325.60 less $25.60) must be included in B's gross income for the taxable year in which the series H bonds are redeemed or disposed of, or reach final maturity, whichever is earlier, as provided in paragraph (c) of § 1.454-1.

(e) The gain on the four $100 series E bonds, determined by using $75 as a basis for each such bond, must be included in B's gross income for the taxable year in which such bonds are redeemed or disposed of, or reach final maturity, whichever is earlier.

Example 3. (a) The facts are the same as in example (2), except that, as part of the transaction, the $1,000 series E bond is reissued by considering ten $100 series E bonds bearing an issue date of March 1, 1943, to have been issued. Six of the $100 series E bonds so considered to have been issued are surrendered to the United States as part of the exchange qualifying under section 1037(a) and the other four are immediately redeemed.

(b) Pursuant to section 1031(b), only $25.60 (the money received) of the total gain of $2,325.60 realized on the exchange qualifying under section 1037(a) is recognized at the time of the exchange and must be included in B's gross income for 1963. The $2,300 balance of the gain ($2,325.60 less $25.60) realized on such exchange must be included in B's gross income for the taxable year in which the series H bonds are redeemed or disposed of, or reach final maturity, whichever is earlier, as provided in paragraph (c) of § 1.454-1.

(c) The redemption on October 1, 1963, of the four $100 series E bonds considered to have been issued at such time results in gain of $258.40, which is then recognized and must be included in B's gross income for 1963. This gain of $258.40 is the difference between the $558.40 redemption value of such bonds on the date of the exchange and the $300 (4x$75) paid for such series E bonds in 1943.

Example 4. On November 1, 1963, C purchased for $91 a marketable U.S. bond which was originally issued at its par value of $100 under the Second Liberty Bond Act. On February 1, 1964, in an exchange qualifying under section 1037(a), C surrendered the bond to the United States for another marketable U.S. bond, which then had a fair market value of $92, and $1.85 in cash, $0.85 of which was interest. The $0.85 interest received is includible in gross income for the taxable year of the exchange, but the $2 gain ($93 less $91) realized on the exchange is recognized for such year under section 1031(b) to

Sec. 1031. Exchange of property held for productive use or investment

the extent of $1 (the money received). Under section 1031(d), C's basis in the bond received in exchange is $91 (his basis of $91 in the bond surrendered, reduced by the $1 money received and increased by the $1 gain recognized).

    (c) *Consideration received in the form of an assumption of liabilities (or a transfer*
5 *subject to a liability) is to be treated as other property or money for the purposes of section 1031(b).* Where, on an exchange described in section 1031(b), each party to the exchange either assumes a liability of the other party or acquires property subject to a liability, then, in determining the amount of other property or money for purposes of section 1031(b), consideration given in the form of an assumption of liabilities (or a
10 receipt of property subject to a liability) shall be offset against consideration received in the form of an assumption of liabilities (or a transfer subject to a liability). See § 1.1031(d)-2, examples (1) and (2).

Reg. § 1.1031(d)-1   Property acquired upon a tax-free exchange.

15   (a) If, in an exchange of property solely of the type described in section 1031, section 1035(a), section 1036(a), or section 1037(a), no part of the gain or loss was recognized under the law applicable to the year in which the exchange was made, the basis of the property acquired is the same as the basis of the property transferred by the taxpayer with proper adjustments to the date of the exchange. If additional consideration is given
20 by the taxpayer in the exchange, the basis of the property acquired shall be the same as the property transferred increased by the amount of additional consideration given (see section 1016 and the regulations thereunder).

    (b) If, in an exchange of properties of the type indicated in section 1031, section 1035(a), section 1036(a), or section 1037(a), gain to the taxpayer was recognized under
25 the provisions of section 1031(b) or a similar provision of a prior revenue law, on account of the receipt of money in the transaction, the basis of the property acquired is the basis of the property transferred (adjusted to the date of the exchange), decreased by the amount of money received and increased by the amount of gain recognized on the exchange. The application of this paragaph may be illustrated by the following example:
30   *Example*: A, an individual in the moving and storage business, in 1954 transfers one of his moving trucks with an adjusted basis in his hands of $2,500 to B in exchange for a truck (to be used in A's business) with a fair market value of $2,400 and $200 in cash. A realizes a gain of $100 upon the exchange, all of which is recognized under section 1031(b). The basis of the truck acquired by A is determined as follows:
35

Adjusted basis of A's former truck	$2,500
Less: Amount of money received	200
Difference	2,300
Plus: Amount of gain recognized	100
40 Basis of truck acquired by A	2,400

    (c) If, upon an exchange of properties of the type described in section 1031, section 1035(a), section 1036(a), or section 1037(a), the taxpayer received other property (not permitted to be received without the recognition of gain) and gain from the transaction
45 was recognized as required under section 1031(b), or a similar provision of a prior revenue law, the basis (adjusted to the date of the exchange) of the property transferred by the taxpayer, decreased by the amount of any money received and increased by the amount of gain recognized, must be allocated to and is the basis of the properties (other than money) received on the exchange. For the purpose of the allocation of the basis of
50 the properties received, there must be assigned to such other property an amount

Sec. 1031. Exchange of property held for productive use or investment

equivalent to its fair market value at the date of the exchange. The application of this paragraph may be illustrated by the following example:

Example: A, who is not a dealer in real estate, in 1954 transfers real estate held for investment which he purchased in 1940 for $10,000 in exchange for other real estate (to be held for investment) which has a fair market value of $9,000, an automobile which has 5 a fair market value of $2,000, and $1,500 in cash. A realizes a gain of $2,500, all of which is recognized under section 1031(b). The basis of the property received in exchange is the basis of the real estate A transfers ($10,000) decreased by the amount of money received ($1,500) and increased in the amount of gain that was recognized ($2,500), which results in a basis for the property received of $11,000. This basis of $11,000 is 10 allocated between the automobile and the real estate received by A, the basis of the automobile being its fair market value at the date of the exchange, $2,000, and the basis of the real estate received being the remainder, $9,000.

(d) Section 1031(c) and, with respect to section 1031 and section 1036(a), similar provisions of prior revenue laws provide that no loss may be recognized on an exchange 15 of properties of a type described in section 1031, section 1035(a), section 1036(a), or section 1037(a), although the taxpayer receives other property or money from the transaction. However, the basis of the property or properties (other than money) received by the taxpayer is the basis (adjusted to the date of the exchange) of the property transferred, decreased by the amount of money received. This basis must be allocated to 20 the properties received, and for this purpose there must be allocated to such other property an amount of such basis equivalent to its fair market value at the date of the exchange.

(e) If, upon an exchange of properties of the type described in section 1031, section 1035(a), section 1036(a), or section 1037(a), the taxpayer also exchanged other property 25 (not permitted to be transferred without the recognition of gain or loss) and gain or loss from the transaction is recognized under section 1002 or a similar provision of a prior revenue law, the basis of the property acquired is the total basis of the properties transferred (adjusted to the date of the exchange) increased by the amount of gain and decreased by the amount of loss recognized on the other property. For purposes of this 30 rule, the taxpayer is deemed to have received in exchange for such other property an amount equal to its fair market value on the date of the exchange. The application of this paragraph may be illustrated by the following example:

Example: A exchanges real estate held for investment plus stock for real estate to be held for investment. The real estate transferred has an adjusted basis of $10,000 and a 35 fair market value of $11,000. The stock transferred has an adjusted basis of $4,000 and a fair market value of $2,000. The real estate acquired has a fair market value of $13,000. A is deemed to have received a $2,000 portion of the acquired real estate in exchange for the stock, since $2,000 is the fair market value of the stock at the time of the exchange. A $2,000 loss is recognized under section 1002 on the exchange of the stock for real 40 estate. No gain or loss is recognized on the exchange of the real estate since the property received is of the type permitted to be received without recognition of gain or loss. The basis of the real estate acquired by A is determined as follows:

Adjusted basis of real estate transferred..........................	$10,000	45
Adjusted basis of stock transferred................................	4,000	
	14,000	
Less: Loss recognized on transfer of stock......................	2,000	
Basis of real estate acquired upon the exchange.......	12,000	
		50

Sec. 1031. Exchange of property held for productive use or investment

Reg. § 1.1031(d)-2 Treatment of assumption of liabilities.

For the purposes of section 1031(d), the amount of any liabilities of the taxpayer assumed by the other party to the exchange (or of any liabilities to which the property exchanged by the taxpayer is subject) is to be treated as money received by the taxpayer
5 upon the exchange, whether or not the assumption resulted in a recognition of gain or loss to the taxpayer under the law applicable to the year in which the exchange was made. The application of this section may be illustrated by the following examples:

Example 1. B, an individual, owns an apartment house which has an adjusted basis in his hands of $500,000, but which is subject to a mortgage of $150,000. On September 1,
10 1954, he transfers the apartment house to C, receiving in exchange therefor $50,000 in cash and another apartment house with a fair market value on that date of $600,000. The transfer to C is made subject to the $150,000 mortgage. B realizes a gain of $300,000 on the exchange, computed as follows:

15 | | |
|---|---:|
| Value of property received... | $600,000 |
| Cash.. | 50,000 |
| Liabilities subject to which old property was transferred... | 150,000 |
| Less: Adjusted basis of property transferred..................... | 500,000 |
| Gain realized.. | 300,000 |

20

Under section 1031(b), $200,000 of the $300,000 gain is recognized. The basis of the apartment house acquired by B upon the exchange is $500,000, computed as follows:

Adjusted basis of property transferred.....................		500,000
25	Less: Amount of money received:		
Cash..	$50,000	
Amount of liabilities subject to which		
property was transferred......................................	150,000	
		200,000
30			
Difference..		300,000
Plus: Amount of gain recognized upon the exchange		200,000
Basis of property acquired upon the exchange.....		500,000

35

Example 2. (a) D, an individual, owns an apartment house. On December 1, 1955, the apartment house owned by D has an adjusted basis in his hands of $100,000, a fair market value of $220,000, but is subject to a mortgage of $80,000. E, an individual, also owns an apartment house. On December 1, 1955, the apartment house owned by E has
40 an adjusted basis of $175,000, a fair market value of $250,000, but is subject to a mortgage of $150,000. On December 1, 1955, D transfers his apartment house to E, receiving in exchange therefore $40,000 in cash and the apartment house owned by E. Each apartment house is transferred subject to the mortgage on it.

(b) D realizes a gain of $120,000 on the exchange, computed as follows:

918

Sec. 1031. Exchange of property held for productive use or investment

Value of property received..	$250,000	
Cash..	40,000	
Liabilities subject to which old property was transferred...	80,000	5
Total consideration received.................................	370,000	
Less:		
Adjusted basis of property transferred.................... $100,000		
Liabilities to which new property is subject............. 150,000		
	250,000	10
Gain realized...	120,000	

For purposes of section 1031(b), the amount of other property or money received by D is $40,000. (Consideration received by D in the form of a transfer subject to a liability of $80,000 is offset by consideration given in the form of a receipt of property subject to a 15 $150,000 liability. Thus, only the consideration received in the form of cash, $40,000, is treated as other property or money for purposes of section 1031(b).) Accordingly, under section 1031(b), $40,000 of the $120,000 gain is recognized. The basis of the apartment house acquired by D is $170,000, computed as follows:

20

Adjusted basis of property transferred..........................	$100,000	
Liabilities to which new property is subject...................	150,000	
Total...	250,000	
Less: Amount of money		
received: Cash... $40,000		25
Amount of liabilities subject to which property		
was transferred.. 80,000		
	120,000	
Difference...	130,000	30
Plus: Amount of gain recognized upon the exchange.	40,000	
Basis of property acquired upon the exchange..	170,000	

(c) E realizes a gain of $75,000 on the exchange, computed as follows:

Value of property received...		$220,000
Liabilities subject to which old property was transferred...		150,000
Total consideration received..................................		370,000
Less:		
Adjusted basis of property transferred...	$175,000	
Cash..	40,000	
Liabilities to which new property is subject	80,000	
		295,000
Gain realized...		75,000

For purposes of section 1031(b), the amount of other property or money received by E is $30,000. (Consideration received by E in the form of a transfer subject to a liability of $150,000 is offset by consideration given in the form of a receipt of property subject to an $80,000 liability and by the $40,000 cash paid by E. Although consideration received in the form of cash or other property is not offset by consideration given in the form of an assumption of liabilities or a receipt of property subject to a liability, consideration given in the form of cash or other property is offset against consideration received in the form of an assumption of liabilities or a transfer of property subject to a liability.) Accordingly, under section 1031(b), $30,000 of the $75,000 gain is recognized. The basis of the apartment house acquired by E is $175,000, computed as follows:

Adjusted basis of property transferred......................	$175,000
Cash..	40,000
Liabilities to which new property is subject...............	80,000
Total..	295,000
Less: Amount of money received: Amount of liabilities subject to which property was transferred...	$150,000
	150,000
Difference...	145,000
Plus: Amount of gain recognized upon the exchange	30,000
Basis of property acquired upon the exchange.	175,000

Reg. § 1.1031(j)-1 Exchanges of multiple properties.

(a) *Introduction*--(1) *Overview.* As a general rule, the application of section 1031 requires a property-by-property comparison for computing the gain recognized and basis of property received in a like-kind exchange. This section provides an exception to this general rule in the case of an exchange of multiple properties. An exchange is an exchange of multiple properties if, under paragraph (b)(2) of this section, more than one exchange group is created. In addition, an exchange is an exchange of multiple properties if only one exchange group is created but there is more than one property being transferred or received within that exchange group. Paragraph (b) of this section provides rules for computing the amount of gain recognized in an exchange of multiple properties qualifying for nonrecognition of gain or loss under section 1031. Paragraph (c) of this section provides rules for computing the basis of properties received in an

Sec. 1031. Exchange of property held for productive use or investment

exchange of multiple properties qualifying for nonrecognition of gain or loss under section 1031.

(2) *General approach*--(i) *In general*, the amount of gain recognized in an exchange of multiple properties is computed by first separating the properties transferred and the properties received by the taxpayer in the exchange into exchange groups in the manner described in paragraph (b)(2) of this section. The separation of the properties transferred and the properties received in the exchange into exchange groups involves matching up properties of a like kind of like class to the extent possible. Next, all liabilities assumed by the taxpayer as part of the transaction are offset by all liabilities of which the taxpayer is relieved as part of the transaction, with the excess liabilities assumed or relieved allocated in accordance with paragraph (b)(2)(ii) of this section. Then, the rules of section 1031 and the regulations thereunder are applied separately to each exchange group to determine the amount of gain recognized in the exchange. See §§ 1.1031(b)-1 and 1.1031(c)-1. Finally, the rules of section 1031 and the regulations thereunder are applied separately to each exchange group to determine the basis of the properties received in the exchange. See §§ 1.1031(d)-1 and 1.1031(d)-2.

(ii) For purposes of this section, the exchanges are assumed to be made at arms' length, so that the aggregate fair market value of the property received in the exchange equals the aggregate fair market value of the property transferred. Thus, the amount realized with respect to the properties transferred in each exchange group is assumed to equal their aggregate fair market value.

(b) *Computation of gain recognized*--(1) *In general.* In computing the amount of gain recognized in an exchange of multiple properties, the fair market value must be determined for each property transferred and for each property received by the taxpayer in the exchange. In addition, the adjusted basis must be determined for each property transferred by the taxpayer in the exchange.

(2) *Exchange groups and residual group.* The properties transferred and the properties received by the taxpayer in the exchange are separated into exchange groups and a residual group to the extent provided in this paragraph (b)(2).

(i) *Exchange groups.* Each exchange group consists of the properties transferred and received in the exchange, all of which are of a like kind or like class. If a property could be included in more than one exchange group, the taxpayer may include the property in any of those exchange groups. Property eligible for inclusion within an exchange group does not include money or property described in section 1031(a)(2) (i.e., stock in trade or other property held primarily for sale, stocks, bonds, notes, other securities or evidences of indebtedness or interest, interests in a partnership, certificates of trust or beneficial interests, or choses in action). For example, an exchange group may consist of all exchanged properties that are within the same General Asset Class or within the same Product Class (as defined in § 1.1031(a)-2(b)). Each exchange group must consist of at least one property transferred and at least one property received in the exchange.

(ii) *Treatment of liabilities.* (A) All liabilities assumed by the taxpayer as part of the exchange are offset against all liabilities of which the taxpayer is relieved as part of the exchange, regardless of whether the liabilities are recourse or nonrecourse and regardless of whether the liabilities are secured by or otherwise relate to specific property transferred or received as part of the exchange. See §§ 1.1031 (b)-1(c) and 1.1031(d)-2. For purposes of this section, liabilities assumed by the taxpayer as part of the exchange consist of liabilities of the other party to the exchange assumed by the taxpayer and liabilities subject to which the other party's property is transferred in the exchange. Similarly, liabilities of which the taxpayer is relieved as part of the exchange consist of liabilities of the taxpayer assumed by the other party to the exchange and liabilities subject to which the taxpayer's property is transferred.

921

(B) If there are excess liabilities assumed by the taxpayer as part of the exchange (i.e., the amount of liabilities assumed by the taxpayer exceeds the amount of liabilities of which the taxpayer is relieved), the excess is allocated among the exchange groups (but not to the residual group) in proportion to the aggregate fair market value of the
5 properties received by the taxpayer in the exchange groups. The amount of excess liabilities assumed by the taxpayer that are allocated to each exchange group may not exceed the aggregate fair market value of the properties received in the exchange group.

(C) If there are excess liabilities of which the taxpayer is relieved as part of the exchange (i.e., the amount of liabilities of which the taxpayer is relieved exceeds the
10 amount of liabilities assumed by the taxpayer), the excess is treated as a Class I asset for purposes of making allocations to the residual group under paragraph (b)(2)(iii) of this section.

(D) Paragraphs (b)(2)(ii)(A), (B), and (C) of this section are applied in the same manner even if section 1031 and this section apply to only a portion of a larger
15 transaction (such as a transaction described in section 1060(c) and § 1.1060-1T(b)). In that event, the amount of excess liabilities assumed by the taxpayer or the amount of excess liabilities of which the taxpayer is relieved is determined based on all liabilities assumed by the taxpayer and all liabilities of which the taxpayer is relieve as part of the larger transaction.

20   (iii) *Residual group*. If the aggregate fair market value of the properties transferred in all of the exchange groups differs from the aggregate fair market value of the properties received in all of the exchange groups (taking liabilities into account in the manner described in paragraph (b)(2)(ii) of this section), a residual group is created. The residual group consists of an amount of money or other property having an aggregate fair market
25 value equal to that difference. The residual group consists of either money or other property transferred in the exchange or money or other property received in the exchange, but not both. For this purpose, other property includes property described in section 1031(a)(2) (i.e., stock in trade or other property held primarily for sale, stocks, bonds, notes, other securities or evidences of indebtedness or interest, interests in a
30 partnership, certificates of trust or beneficial interests, or choses in action), property transferred that is not of a like kind or like class with any property received, and property received that is not of a like kind or like class with any property transferred. The money and properties that are allocated to the residual group are considered to come from the following assets in the following order: first from Class I assets, then from Class II assets,
35 then from Class III assets, and then from Class IV assets. The terms Class I assets, Class II assets, Class III assets, and Class IV assets have the same meanings as in § 1.338-6(b), to which reference is made by § 1.1060-1(c)(2). Within each Class, taxpayers may choose which properties are allocated to the residual group.

(iv) *Exchange group surplus and deficiency*. For each of the exchange groups
40 described in this section, an ``exchange group surplus'' or ``exchange group deficiency,'' if any, must be determined. An exchange group surplus is the excess of the aggregate fair market value of the properties received (less the amount of any excess liabilities assumed by the taxpayer that are allocated to that exchange group), in an exchange group over the aggregate fair market value of the properties transferred in that exchange
45 group. An exchange group deficiency is the excess of the aggregate fair market value of the properties transferred in an exchange group over the aggregate fair market value of the properties received (less the amount of any excess liabilities assumed by the taxpayer that are allocated to that exchange group) in that exchange group.

(3) *Amount of gain recognized*. (i) For purposes of this section, the amount of gain or
50 loss realized with respect to each exchange group and the residual group is the difference between the aggregate fair market value of the properties transferred in that

Sec. 1031. Exchange of property held for productive use or investment

exchange group or residual group and the properties' aggregate adjusted basis. The gain realized with respect to each exchange group is recognized to the extent of the lesser of the gain realized and the amount of the exchange group deficiency, if any. Losses realized with respect to an exchange group are not recognized. See section 1031 (a) and (c). The total amount of gain recognized under section 1031 in the exchange is the sum of the amount of gain recognized with respect to each exchange group. With respect to the residual group, the gain or loss realized (as determined under this section) is recognized as provided in section 1001 or other applicable provision of the Code.

(ii) The amount of gain or loss realized and recognized with respect to properties transferred by the taxpayer that are not within any exchange group or the residual group is determined under section 1001 and other applicable provisions of the Code, with proper adjustments made for all liabilities not allocated to the exchange groups or the residual group.

(c) *Computation of basis of properties received.* In an exchange of multiple properties qualifying for nonrecognition of gain or loss under section 1031 and this section, the aggregate basis of properties received in each of the exchange groups is the aggregate adjusted basis of the properties transferred by the taxpayer within that exchange group, increased by the amount of gain recognized by the taxpayer with respect to that exchange group, increased by the amount of the exchange group surplus or decreased by the amount of the exchange group deficiency, and increased by the amount, if any, of excess liabilities assumed by the taxpayer that are allocated to that exchange group. The resulting aggregate basis of each exchange group is allocated proportionately to each property received in the exchange group in accordance with its fair market value. The basis of each property received within the residual group (other than money) is equal to its fair market value.

(d) *Examples.* The application of this section may be illustrated by the following examples:

***

Example 3. (i) J and H enter into an exchange of the following properties. All of the property (except for the inventory) transferred by J was held for productive use in J's business. All of the property received by J will be held by J for productive use in its business.

J Transfers: H Transfers:

Property	Adjusted basis	Fair market value	Property	Fair market value
Computer A	$1,500	$5,000	Computer Z	$4,500
Computer B	500	3,000	Printer Y	2,500
Printer C	2,000	1,500	Real Estate X	1,000
Real Estate D	1,200	2,000	Real Estate W	4,000
Real Estate E	0	1,800	Grader V	2,000
Scraper F	3,300	2,500	Truck T	1,700
Inventory	1,000	1,700	Cash	1,800
Total	9,500	17,500		17,500

(ii) Under paragraph (b)(2) of this section, the properties exchanged are separated into exchange groups as follows:

(A) The first exchange group consists of computer A, computer B, printer C, computer Z, and printer Y (all are within the same General Asset Class) and, as to J, has an exchange group deficiency of $2500 (($5000 + $3000 + $1500) - ($4500 + $2500)).

(B) The second exchange group consists of real estate D, E, X and W (all are of a like kind) and, as to J, has an exchange group surplus of $1200 (($1000 + $4000) - ($2000 + $1800)).

923

(C) The third exchange group consists of scraper F and grader V (both are within the same Product Class (NAICS code 333120)) and, as to J, has an exchange group deficiency of $500 ($2500 - $2000).

(D) Because the aggregate fair market value of the properties transferred by J in the
5 exchange groups ($15,800) exceeds the aggregate fair market value of the properties received by J in the exchange groups ($14,000) by $1800, there is a residual group in that amount consisting of the $1800 cash (a Class I asset).

(E) The transaction also includes a taxable exchange of inventory (which is property described in section 1031 (a)(2)) for truck T (which is not of a like kind or like class to any
10 property transferred in the exchange).

(iii) J recognizes gain on the transaction as follows:

(A) With respect to the first exchange group, the amount of gain realized is the excess of the aggregate fair market value of the properties transferred in the exchange group ($9500) over the aggregate adjusted basis ($4000), or $5500. The amount of gain
15 recognized is the lesser of the gain realized ($5500) and the exchange group deficiency ($2500), or $2500.

(B) With respect to the second exchange group, the amount of gain realized is the excess of the aggregate fair market value of the properties transferred in the exchange group ($3800) over the aggregate adjusted basis ($1200), or $2600. The amount of gain
20 recognized is the lesser of the gain realized ($2600) and the exchange group deficiency ($0), or $0.

(C) With respect to the third exchange group, a loss is realized in the amount of $800 because the fair market value of the property transferred in the exchange group ($2500) is less than its adjusted basis ($3300). Although a loss of $800 was realized, under
25 section 1031 (a) and (c) losses are not recognized.

(D) No property transferred by J was allocated to the residual group. Therefore, J does not recognize gain or loss with respect to the residual group.

(E) With respect to the taxable exchange of inventory for truck T, gain of $700 is realized and recognized by J (amount realized of $1700 (the fair market value of truck T)
30 less the adjusted basis of the inventory ($1000)).

(iv) The total amount of gain recognized by J in the transaction is the sum of the gains recognized under section 1031 with respect to each exchange group ($2500 + $0 + $0) and any gain recognized outside of section 1031 ($700), or $3200.

(v) The bases of the property received by J in the exchange are determined in the
35 following manner:

(A) The aggregate basis of the properties received in the first exchange group is the adjusted basis of the properties transferred within that exchange group ($4000), increased by the amount of gain recognized with respect to that exchange group ($2500), decreased by the amount of the exchange group deficiency ($2500), and increased by
40 the amount of excess liabilities assumed allocated to that exchange group ($0), or $4000. This $4000 of basis is allocated proportionately among the assets received within the first exchange group in accordance with their fair market values: Computer Z's basis is $2571 ($4000 x $4500/$7000); printer Y's basis is $1429 ($4000 x $2500/$7000).

(B) The aggregate basis of the properties received in the second exchange group is
45 the adjusted basis of the properties transferred within that exchange group ($1200), increased by the amount of gain recognized with respect to that exchange group ($0), increased by the amount of the exchange group surplus ($1200), and increased by the amount of excess liabilities assumed allocated to that exchange group ($0), or $2400. This $2400 of basis is allocated proportionately among the assets received within the
50 second exchange group in accordance with their fair market values: Real estate X's basis is $480 ($2400 x $1000/$5000); real estate W's basis is $1920 ($2400 x $4000/$5000).

Sec. 1031. Exchange of property held for productive use or investment

(c) The basis of the property received in the third exchange group is the adjusted basis of the property transferred within that exchange group ($3300), increased by the amount of gain recognized with respect to that exchange group ($0), decreased by the amount of the exchange group deficiency ($500), and increased by the amount of excess liabilities assumed allocated to that exchange group ($0), or $2800. Because grader V 5 was the only property received within the third exchange group, the entire basis of $2800 is allocated to grader V.

(D) Cash of $1800 is received within the residual group.

(E) The basis of the property received in the taxable exchange (truck T) is equal to its cost of $1700.   10

Reg. § 1.1031(k)-1 Treatment of deferred exchanges.

(a) *Overview.* This section provides rules for the application of section 1031 and the regulations thereunder in the case of a ``deferred exchange." For purposes of section 1031 and this section, a deferred exchange is defined as an exchange in which, pursuant  15 to an agreement, the taxpayer transfers property held for productive use in a trade or business or for investment (the ``relinquished property") and subsequently receives property to be held either for productive use in a trade or business or for investment (the ``replacement property"). In the case of a deferred exchange, if the requirements set forth in paragraphs (b), (c), and (d) of this section (relating to identification and receipt of 20 replacement property) are not satisfied, the replacement property received by the taxpayer will be treated as property which is not of a like kind to the relinquished property. In order to constitute a deferred exchange, the transaction must be an exchange (i.e., a transfer of property for property, as distinguished from a transfer of property for money). For example, a sale of property followed by a purchase of property of a like kind does not 25 qualify for nonrecognition of gain or loss under section 1031 regardless of whether the identification and receipt requirements of section 1031(a)(3) and paragraphs (b), (c), and (d) of this section are satisfied. The transfer of relinquished property in a deferred exchange is not within the provisions of section 1031(a) if, as part of the consideration, the taxpayer receives money or property which does not meet the requirements of 30 section 1031(a), but the transfer, if otherwise qualified, will be within the provisions of either section 1031(b) or (c). See § 1.1031(a)-1(a)(2). In addition, in the case of a transfer of relinquished property in a deferred exchange, gain or loss may be recognized if the taxpayer actually or constructively receives money or property which does not meet the requirements of section 1031(a) before the taxpayer actually receives like-kind 35 replacement property. If the taxpayer actually or constructively receives money or property which does not meet the requirements of section 1031(a) in the full amount of the consideration for the relinquished property, the transaction will constitute a sale, and not a deferred exchange, even though the taxpayer may ultimately receive like-kind replacement property. For purposes of this section, property which does not meet the 40 requirements of section 1031(a) (whether by being described in section 1031(a)(2) or otherwise) is referred to as ``other property." For rules regarding actual and constructive receipt, and safe harbors therefrom, see paragraphs (f) and (g), respectively, of this section. For rules regarding the determination of gain or loss recognized and the basis of property received in a deferred exchange, see paragraph (j) of this section.   45

(b) *Identification and receipt requirements*--(1) *In general.* In the case of a deferred exchange, any replacement property received by the taxpayer will be treated as property which is not of a like kind to the relinquished property if--

(i) The replacement property is not ``identified" before the end of the ``identification period," or   50

(ii) The identified replacement property is not received before the end of the

Sec. 1031. Exchange of property held for productive use or investment

``exchange period."

(2) Identification period and exchange period. (i) The identification period begins on the date the taxpayer transfers the relinquished property and ends at midnight on the 45th day thereafter.

5   (ii) The exchange period begins on the date the taxpayer transfers the relinquished property and ends at midnight on the earlier of the 180th day thereafter or the due date (including extensions) for the taxpayer's return of the tax imposed by chapter 1 of subtitle A of the Code for the taxable year in which the transfer of the relinquished property occurs.

10   (iii) If, as part of the same deferred exchange, the taxpayer transfers more than one relinquished property and the relinquished properties are transferred on different dates, the identification period and the exchange period are determined by reference to the earliest date on which any of the properties are transferred.

(iv) For purposes of this paragraph (b)(2), property is transferred when the property is
15 disposed of within the meaning of section 1001(a).

***

(c) *Identification of replacement property before the end of the identification period--*
(1) *In general.* For purposes of paragraph (b)(1)(i) of this section (relating to the identification requirement), replacement property is identified before the end of the
20 identification period only if the requirements of this paragraph (c) are satisfied with respect to the replacement property. However, any replacement property that is received by the taxpayer before the end of the identification period will in all events be treated as identified before the end of the identification period.

(2) *Manner of identifying replacement property.* Replacement property is identified
25 only if it is designated as replacement property in a written document signed by the taxpayer and hand delivered, mailed, telecopied, or otherwise sent before the end of the identification period to either--

(i) The person obligated to transfer the replacement property to the taxpayer (regardless of whether that person is a disqualified person as defined in paragraph (k) of
30 this section); or

(ii) Any other person involved in the exchange other than the taxpayer or a disqualified person (as defined in paragraph (k) of this section).
Examples of persons involved in the exchange include any of the parties to the exchange, an intermediary, an escrow agent, and a title company. An identification of
35 replacement property made in a written agreement for the exchange of properties signed by all parties thereto before the end of the identification period will be treated as satisfying the requirements of this paragraph (c)(2).

***

(d) *Receipt of identified replacement property--*(1) *In general.* For purposes of
40 paragraph (b)(1)(ii) of this section (relating to the receipt requirement), the identified replacement property is received before the end of the exchange period only if the requriements of this paragraph (d) are satisfied with respect to the replacement property. In the case of a deferred exchange, the identified replacement property is received before the end of the exchange period if--

45   (i) The taxpayer receives the replacement property before the end of the exchange period, and

(ii) The replacement property received is substantially the same property as identified.
If the taxpayer has identified more than one replacement property, section 1031(a)(3)(B) and this paragraph (d) are applied separately to each replacement property.

50   ***

926

Sec. 1031. Exchange of property held for productive use or investment

(e) *Special rules for identification and receipt of replacement property to be produced--*(1) *In general.* A transfer of relinquished property in a deferred exchange will not fail to qualify for nonrecognition of gain or loss under section 1031 merely because the replacement property is not in existence or is being produced at the time the property is identified as replacement property. For purposes of this paragraph (e), the terms ``produced'' and ``production'' have the same meanings as provided in section 263A(g) (1) and the regulations thereunder.

(2) *Identification of replacement property to be produced.* (i) In the case of replacement property that is to be produced, the replacement property must be identified as provided in paragraph (c) of this section (relating to identification of replacement property). For example, if the identified replacement property consists of improved real property where the improvements are to be constructed, the description of the replacement property satisfies the requirements of paragraph (c)(3) of this section (relating to description of replacement property) if a legal description is provided for the underlying land and as much detail is provided regarding construction of the improvements as is practicable at the time the identification is made.

(ii) For purposes of paragraphs (c)(4)(i)(B) and (c)(5) of this section (relating to the 200-percent rule and incidental property), the fair market value of replacement property that is to be produced is its estimated fair market value as of the date it is expected to be received by the taxpayer.

(3) *Receipt of replacement property to be produced.* (i) For purposes of paragraph (d) (1)(ii) of this section (relating to receipt of the identified replacement property), in determining whether the replacement property received by the taxpayer is substantially the same property as identified where the identified replacement property is property to be produced, variations due to usual or typical production changes are not taken into account. However, if substantial changes are made in the property to be produced, the replacement property received will not be considered to be substantially the same property as identified.

(ii) If the identified replacement property is personal property to be produced, the replacement property received will not be considered to be substantially the same property as identified unless production of the replacement property received is completed on or before the date the property is received by the taxpayer.

(iii) If the identified replacement property is real property to be produced and the production of the property is not completed on or before the date the taxpayer receives the property, the property received will be considered to be substantially the same property as identified only if, had production been completed on or before the date the taxpayer receives the replacement property, the property received would have been considered to be substantially the same property as identified. Even so, the property received is considered to be substantially the same property as identified only to the extent the property received constitutes real property under local law.

***

(f) *Receipt of money or other property--*(1) *In general.* A transfer of relinquished property in a deferred exchange is not within the provisions of section 1031(a) if, as part of the consideration, the taxpayer receives money or other property. However, such a transfer, if otherwise qualified, will be within the provisions of either section 1031(b) or (c). See § 1.1031(a)-1(a)(2). In addition, in the case of a transfer of relinquished property in a deferred exchange, gain or loss may be recognized if the taxpayer actually or constructively receives money or other property before the taxpayer actually receives like-kind replacement property. If the taxpayer actually or constructively receives money or other property in the full amount of the consideration for the relinquished property before the taxpayer actually receives like-kind replacement property, the transaction will constitute a sale and not a deferred exchange, even though the taxpayer may ultimately receive like-kind replacement property.

(2) *Actual and constructive receipt.* Except as provided in paragraph (g) of this section (relating to safe harbors), for purposes of section 1031 and this section, the determination
5 of whether (or the extent to which) the taxpayer is in actual or constructive receipt of money or other property before the taxpayer actually receives like-kind replacement property is made under the general rules concerning actual and constructive receipt and without regard to the taxpayer's method of accounting. The taxpayer is in actual receipt of money or property at the time the taxpayer actually receives the money or property or
10 receives the economic benefit of the money or property. The taxpayer is in constructive receipt of money or property at the time the money or property is credited to the taxpayer's account, set apart for the taxpayer, or otherwise made available so that the taxpayer may draw upon it at any time or so that the taxpayer can draw upon it if notice of intention to draw is given. Although the taxpayer is not in constructive receipt of money or
15 property if the taxpayer's control of its receipt is subject to substantial limitations or restrictions, the taxpayer is in constructive receipt of the money or property at the time the limitations or restrictions lapse, expire, or are waived. In addition, actual or constructive receipt of money or property by an agent of the taxpayer (determined without regard to paragraph (k) of this section) is actual or constructive receipt by the taxpayer.
20 (3) *Example.* This paragraph (f) may be illustrated by the following example.

Example: (i) B, a calendar year taxpayer, and C agree to enter into a deferred exchange. Pursuant to the agreement, on May 17, 1991, B transfers real property X to C. Real property X, which has been held by B for investment, is unencumbered and has a fair market value on May 17, 1991, of $100,000. On or before July 1, 1991 (the end of the
25 identification period), B is to identify replacement property that is of a like kind to real property X. On or before November 13, 1991 (the end of the exchange period), C is required to purchase the property identified by B and to transfer that property to B. At any time after May 17, 1991, and before C has purchased the replacement property, B has the right, upon notice, to demand that C pay $100,000 in lieu of acquiring and transferring
30 the replacement property. Pursuant to the agreement, B identifies replacement property, and C purchases the replacement property and transfers it to B.

(ii) Under the agreement, B has the unrestricted right to demand the payment of $100,000 as of May 17, 1991. B is therefore in constructive receipt of $100,000 on that date. Because B is in constructive receipt of money in the full amount of the consideration
35 for the relinquished property before B actually receives the like-kind replacement property, the transaction constitutes a sale, and the transfer of real property X does not qualify for nonrecognition of gain or loss under section 1031. B is treated as if B received the $100,000 in consideration for the sale of real property X and then purchased the like-kind replacement property.
40 (iii) If B's right to demand payment of the $100,000 were subject to a substantial limitation or restriction (e.g., the agreement provided that B had no right to demand payment before November 14, 1991 (the end of the exchange period)), then, for purposes of this section, B would not be in actual or constructive receipt of the money unless (or until) the limitation or restriction lapsed, expired, or was waived.
45 (g) *Safe harbors--*(1) *In general.* Paragraphs (g)(2) through (g)(5) of this section set forth four safe harbors the use of which will result in a determination that the taxpayer is not in actual or constructive receipt of money or other property for purposes of section 1031 and this section. More than one safe harbor can be used in the same deferred exchange, but the terms and conditions of each must be separately satisfied. For
50 purposes of the safe harbor rules, the term ``taxpayer'' does not include a person or entity utilized in a safe harbor (e.g., a qualified intermediary). See paragraph (g)(8),

Example 3(v), of this section.

(2) *Security or guarantee arrangements.* (i) In the case of a deferred exchange, the determination of whether the taxpayer is in actual or constructive receipt of money or other property before the taxpayer actually receives like-kind replacement property will be made without regard to the fact that the obligation of the taxpayer's transferee to transfer 5 the replacement property to the taxpayer is or may be secured or guaranteed by one or more of the following--

(A) A mortgage, deed of trust, or other security interest in property (other than cash or a cash equivalent),

(B) A standby letter of credit which satisfies all of the requirements of § 15A.453-1 (b) 10 (3)(iii) and which may not be drawn upon in the absence of a default of the transferee's obligation to transfer like-kind replacement property to the taxpayer, or

(C) A guarantee of a third party.

(ii) Paragraph (g)(2)(i) of this section ceases to apply at the time the taxpayer has an immediate ability or unrestricted right to receive money or other property pursuant to the 15 security or guarantee arrangement.

(3) *Qualified escrow accounts and qualified trusts.* (i) In the case of a deferred exchange, the determination of whether the taxpayer is in actual or constructive receipt of money or other property before the taxpayer actually receives like-kind replacement property will be made without regard to the fact that the obligation of the taxpayer's 20 transferee to transfer the replacement property to the taxpayer is or may be secured by cash or a cash equivalent if the cash or cash equivalent is held in a qualified escrow account or in a qualified trust.

(ii) A qualified escrow account is an escrow account wherein--

(A) The escrow holder is not the taxpayer or a disqualified person (as defined in 25 paragraph (k) of this section), and

(B) The escrow agreement expressly limits the taxpayer's rights to receive, pledge, borrow, or otherwise obtain the benefits of the cash or cash equivalent held in the escrow account as provided in paragraph (g)(6) of this section.

(iii) A qualified trust is a trust wherein--   30

(A) The trustee is not the taxpayer or a disqualified person (as defined in paragraph (k) of this section, except that for this purpose the relationship between the taxpayer and the trustee created by the qualified trust will not be considered a relationship under section 267(b)), and

(B) The trust agreement expressly limits the taxpayer's rights to receive, pledge, 35 borrow, or otherwise obtain the benefits of the cash or cash equivalent held by the trustee as provided in paragraph (g)(6) of this section.

(iv) Paragraph (g)(3)(i) of this section ceases to apply at the time the taxpayer has an immediate ability or unrestricted right to receive, pledge, borrow, or otherwise obtain the benefits of the cash or cash equivalent held in the qualified escrow account or qualified 40 trust. Rights conferred upon the taxpayer under state law to terminate or dismiss the escrow holder of a qualified escrow account or the trustee of a qualified trust are disregarded for this purpose.

(v) A taxpayer may receive money or other property directly from a party to the exchange, but not from a qualified escrow account or a qualified trust, without affecting 45 the application of paragraph (g)(3)(i) of this section.

(4) *Qualified intermediaries.* (i) In the case of a taxpayer's transfer of relinquished property involving a qualified intermediary, the qualified intermediary is not considered the agent of the taxpayer for purposes of section 1031(a). In such a case, the taxpayer's transfer of relinquished property and subsequent receipt of like-kind replacement property 50 is treated as an exchange, and the determination of whether the taxpayer is in actual or

Sec. 1031. Exchange of property held for productive use or investment

constructive receipt of money or other property before the taxpayer actually receives like-kind replacement property is made as if the qualified intermediary is not the agent of the taxpayer.

    (ii) Paragraph (g)(4)(i) of this section applies only if the agreement between the
5 taxpayer and the qualified intermediary expressly limits the taxpayer's rights to receive, pledge, borrow, or otherwise obtain the benefits of money or other property held by the qualified intermediary as provided in paragraph (g)(6) of this section.

    (iii) A qualified intermediary is a person who--

    (A) Is not the taxpayer or a disqualified person (as defined in paragraph (k) of this
10 section), and

    (B) Enters into a written agreement with the taxpayer (the ``exchange agreement") and, as required by the exchange agreement, acquires the relinquished property from the taxpayer, transfers the relinquished property, acquires the replacement property, and transfers the replacement property to the taxpayer.

15   (iv) Regardless of whether an intermediary acquires and transfers property under general tax principals, solely for purposes of paragraph (g)(4)(iii)(B) of this section--

    (A) An intermediary is treated as acquiring and transferring property if the intermediary acquires and transfers legal title to that property,

    (B) An intermediary is treated as acquiring and transferring the relinquished property if
20 the intermediary (either on its own behalf or as the agent of any party to the transaction) enters into an agreement with a person other than the taxpayer for the transfer of the relinquished property to that person and, pursuant to that agreement, the relinquished property is transferred to that person, and

    (C) An intermediary is treated as acquiring and transferring replacement property if the
25 intermediary (either on its own behalf or as the agent of any party to the transaction) enters into an agreement with the owner of the replacement property for the transfer of that property and, pursuant to that agreement, the replacement property is transferred to the taxpayer.

    (v) Solely for purposes of paragraphs (g)(4)(iii) and (g)(4)(iv) of this section, an
30 intermediary is treated as entering into an agreement if the rights of a party to the agreement are assigned to the intermediary and all parties to that agreement are notified in writing of the assignment on or before the date of the relevant transfer of property. For example, if a taxpayer enters into an agreement for the transfer of relinquished property and thereafter assigns its rights in that agreement to an intermediary and all parties to
35 that agreement are notified in writing of the assignment on or before the date of the transfer of the relinquished property, the intermediary is treated as entering into that agreement. If the relinquished property is transferred pursuant to that agreement, the intermediary is treated as having acquired and transferred the relinquished property.

    (vi) Paragraph (g)(4)(i) of this section ceases to apply at the time the taxpayer has an
40 immediate ability or unrestricted right to receive, pledge, borrow, or otherwise obtain the benefits of money or other property held by the qualified intermediary. Rights conferred upon the taxpayer under state law to terminate or dismiss the qualified intermediary are disregarded for this purpose.

    (vii) A taxpayer may receive money or other property directly from a party to the
45 transaction other than the qualified intermediary without affecting the application of paragraph (g)(4)(i) of this section.

    (5) *Interest and growth factors.* In the case of a deferred exchange, the determination of whether the taxpayer is in actual or constructive receipt of money or other property before the taxpayer actually receives the like-kind replacement property will be made
50 without regard to the fact that the taxpayer is or may be entitled to receive any interest or growth factor with respect to the deferred exchange. The preceding sentence applies

Sec. 1031. Exchange of property held for productive use or investment

only if the agreement pursuant to which the taxpayer is or may be entitled to the interest or growth factor expressly limits the taxpayer's rights to receive the interest or growth factor as provided in paragragh (g)(6) of this section. For additional rules concerning interest or growth factors, see paragraph (h) of this section.

***

5

(k) *Definition of disqualified person.* (1) For purposes of this section, a disqualified person is a person described in paragraph (k)(2), (k)(3), or (k)(4) of this section.

(2) The person is the agent of the taxpayer at the time of the transaction. For this purpose, a person who has acted as the taxpayer's employee, attorney, accountant, investment banker or broker, or real estate agent or broker within the 2-year period 10 ending on the date of the transfer of the first of the relinquished properties is treated as an agent of the taxpayer at the time of the transaction. Solely for purposes of this paragraph (k)(2), performance of the following services will not be taken into account--

(i) Services for the taxpayer with respect to exchanges of property intended to qualify for nonrecognition of gain or loss under section 1031; and   15

(ii) Routine financial, title insurance, escrow, or trust services for the taxpayer by a financial institution, title insurance company, or escrow company.

(3) The person and the taxpayer bear a relationship described in either section 267(b) or section 707(b) (determined by substituting in each section ``10 percent'' for ``50 percent'' each place it appears).   20

(4)(i) Except as provided in paragraph (k)(4)(ii) of this section, the person and a person described in paragraph (k)(2) of this section bear a relationship described in either section 267(b) or 707(b) (determined by substituting in each section ``10 percent'' for ``50 percent'' each place it appears).

(ii) In the case of a transfer of relinquished property made by a taxpayer on or after 25 January 17, 2001, paragraph (k)(4)(i) of this section does not apply to a bank (as defined in section 581) or a bank affiliate if, but for this paragraph (k)(4)(ii), the bank or bank affiliate would be a disqualified person under paragraph (k)(4)(i) of this section solely because it is a member of the same controlled group (as determined under section 267(f) (1), substituting ``10 percent'' for ``50 percent' where it appears) as a person that has 30 provided investment banking or brokerage services to the taxpayer within the 2-year period described in paragraph (k)(2) of this section. For purposes of this paragraph (k)(4) (ii), a bank affiliate is a corporation whose principal activity is rendering services to facilitate exchanges of property intended to qualify for nonrecognition of gain under section 1031 and all of whose stock is owned by either a bank or a bank holding 35 company (within the meaning of section 2(a) of the Bank Holding Company Act of 1956 (12 U.S.C. 1841(a)).

[T.D. 6500, 25 FR 11910, Nov. 26, 1960, 32 FR 15823, Nov. 17, 1967; T.D. 6935, 32 FR 15822, Nov. 17, 1967; T.D. 8343, 56 FR 14855, Apr. 12, 1991; T.D. 8346, 56 FR 19937, 40 May 1, 1991; T.D. 8535, 59 FR 18749, Apr. 20, 1994; T.D. 8858, 65 FR 1237, Jan. 7, 2000; T.D. 8940, 66 FR 9929, Feb. 13, 2001; T.D. 8982, 67 FR 4909, Feb. 1, 2002; T.D. 9151, 69 FR 50068, Aug. 13, 2004; T.D. 9202, 70 FR 28820, May 19, 2005; T.D. 9202, 70 FR 28819, May 19, 2005]

45

Sec. 1033. Involuntary conversions

(a) **General rule.** -- If property (as a result of its destruction in whole or in part, theft, seizure, or requisition or condemnation or threat or imminence thereof) is compulsorily or involuntarily converted--

(1) **Conversion into similar property.** -- Into property similar or related in service or use to

Sec. 1033. Involuntary conversions

the property so converted, no gain shall be recognized.

(2) Conversion into money. -- Into money or into property not similar or related in service or use to the converted property, the gain (if any) shall be recognized except to the extent hereinafter provided in this paragraph:

(A) Nonrecognition of gain. -- If the taxpayer during the period specified in subparagraph (B), for the purpose of replacing the property so converted, purchases other property similar or related in service or use to the property so converted, or purchases stock in the acquisition of control of a corporation owning such other property, at the election of the taxpayer the gain shall be recognized only to the extent that the amount realized upon such conversion (regardless of whether such amount is received in one or more taxable years) exceeds the cost of such other property or such stock. Such election shall be made at such time and in such manner as the Secretary may by regulations prescribe. For purposes of this paragraph -

(i) no property or stock acquired before the disposition of the converted property shall be considered to have been acquired for the purpose of replacing such converted property unless held by the taxpayer on the date of such disposition; and

(ii) the taxpayer shall be considered to have purchased property or stock only if, but for the provisions of subsection (b) of this section, the unadjusted basis of such property or stock would be its cost within the meaning of section 1012.

(B) Period within which property must be replaced. -- The period referred to in subparagraph (A) shall be the period beginning with the date of the disposition of the converted property, or the earliest date of the threat or imminence of requisition or condemnation of the converted property, whichever is the earlier, and ending--

(i) 2 years after the close of the first taxable year in which any part of the gain upon the conversion is realized, or

(ii) subject to such terms and conditions as may be specified by the Secretary, at the close of such later date as the Secretary may designate on application by the taxpayer. Such application shall be made at such time and in such manner as the Secretary may by regulations prescribe.

(C) Time for assessment of deficiency attributable to gain upon conversion. -- If a taxpayer has made the election provided in subparagraph (A), then--

(i) the statutory period for the assessment of any deficiency, for any taxable year in which any part of the gain on such conversion is realized, attributable to such gain shall not expire prior to the expiration of 3 years from the date the Secretary is notified by the taxpayer (in such manner as the Secretary may by regulations prescribe) of the replacement of the converted property or of an intention not to replace, and

(ii) such deficiency may be assessed before the expiration of such 3-year period notwithstanding the provisions of section 6212(c) or the provisions of any other law or rule of law which would otherwise prevent such assessment.

(D) Time for assessment of other deficiencies attributable to election. -- If the election provided in subparagraph (A) is made by the taxpayer and such other property or such stock was purchased before the beginning of the last taxable year in which any part of the gain upon such conversion is realized, any deficiency, to the extent resulting from such election, for any taxable year ending before such last taxable year may be assessed (notwithstanding the provisions of section 6212(c) or 6501 or the provisions of any other law or rule of law which would otherwise prevent such assessment) at any time before the expiration of the period within which a deficiency for such last taxable year may be assessed.

Sec. 1033. Involuntary conversions

(E) Definitions. -- For purposes of this paragraph--

    (i) Control. -- The term "control" means the ownership of stock possessing at least 80 percent of the total combined voting power of all classes of stock entitled to vote and at least 80 percent of the total number of shares of all other classes of stock of the corporation.

    (ii) Disposition of the converted property. -- The term "disposition of the converted property" means the destruction, theft, seizure, requisition, or condemnation of the converted property, or the sale or exchange of such property under threat or imminence of requisition or condemnation.

(b) Basis of property acquired through involuntary conversion. --

(1) Conversions described in subsection (a)(1). -- If the property was acquired as the result of a compulsory or involuntary conversion described in subsection (a)(1), the basis shall be the same as in the case of the property so converted--

    (A) decreased in the amount of any money received by the taxpayer which was not expended in accordance with the provisions of law (applicable to the year in which such conversion was made) determining the taxable status of the gain or loss upon such conversion, and

    (B) increased in the amount of gain or decreased in the amount of loss to the taxpayer recognized upon such conversion under the law applicable to the year in which such conversion was made.

(2) Conversions described in subsection (a)(2). -- In the case of property purchased by the taxpayer in a transaction described in subsection (a)(2) which resulted in the nonrecognition of any part of the gain realized as the result of a compulsory or involuntary conversion, the basis shall be the cost of such property decreased in the amount of the gain not so recognized; and if the property purchased consists of more than 1 piece of property, the basis determined under this sentence shall be allocated to the purchased properties in proportion to their respective costs.

(3) Property held by corporation the stock of which is replacement property. --

    (A) In general. -- If the basis of stock in a corporation is decreased under paragraph (2), an amount equal to such decrease shall also be applied to reduce the basis of property held by the corporation at the time the taxpayer acquired control (as defined in subsection (a)(2)(E)) of such corporation.

    (B) Limitation. -- Subparagraph (A) shall not apply to the extent that it would (but for this subparagraph) require a reduction in the aggregate adjusted bases of the property of the corporation below the taxpayer's adjusted basis of the stock in the corporation (determined immediately after such basis is decreased under paragraph (2)).

    (C) Allocation of basis reduction. -- The decrease required under subparagraph (A) shall be allocated--

        (i) first to property which is similar or related in service or use to the converted property,

        (ii) second to depreciable property (as defined in section1017(b)(3)(B)) not described in clause (i), and

        (iii) then to other property.

    (D) Special rules. --

        (i) Reduction not to exceed adjusted basis of property. -- No reduction in the basis of any property under this paragraph shall exceed the adjusted basis of such property (determined without regard to such reduction).

(ii) **Allocation of reduction among properties.** -- If more than 1 property is described in a clause of subparagraph (C), the reduction under this paragraph shall be allocated among such property in proportion to the adjusted bases of such property (as so determined).

(c) Property sold pursuant to reclamation laws. -- For purposes of this subtitle, if property lying within an irrigation project is sold or otherwise disposed of in order to conform to the acreage limitation provisions of Federal reclamation laws, such sale or disposition shall be treated as an involuntary conversion to which this section applies.

(d) Livestock destroyed by disease. -- For purposes of this subtitle, if livestock are destroyed by or on account of disease, or are sold or exchanged because of disease, such destruction or such sale or exchange shall be treated as an involuntary conversion to which this section applies.

(e) Livestock sold on account of drought, flood, or other weather- related conditions. --

(1) In general. -- For purposes of this subtitle, the sale or exchange of livestock (other than poultry) held by a taxpayer for draft, breeding, or dairy purposes in excess of the number the taxpayer would sell if he followed his usual business practices shall be treated as an involuntary conversion to which this section applies if such livestock are sold or exchanged by the taxpayer solely on account of drought, flood, or other weather-related conditions.

(2) Extension of replacement period. --

(A) In general. -- In the case of drought, flood, or other weather-related conditions described in paragraph (1) which result in the area being designated as eligible for assistance by the Federal Government, subsection (a)(2)(B) shall be applied with respect to any converted property by substituting "4 years" for "2 years".

(B) Further extension by Secretary. -- The Secretary may extend on a regional basis the period for replacement under this section (after the application of subparagraph (A)) for such additional time as the Secretary determines appropriate if the weather-related conditions which resulted in such application continue for more than 3 years.

(f) Replacement of livestock with other farm property in certain cases. -- For purposes of subsection (a), if, because of drought, flood, or other weather-related conditions, or soil contamination or other environmental contamination, it is not feasible for the taxpayer to reinvest the proceeds from compulsorily or involuntarily converted livestock in property similar or related in use to the livestock so converted, other property (including real property in the case of soil contamination or other environmental contamination) used for farming purposes shall be treated as property similar or related in service or use to the livestock so converted.

(g) Condemnation of real property held for productive use in trade or business or for investment. --

(1) Special rule. -- For purposes of subsection (a), if real property (not including stock in trade or other property held primarily for sale) held for productive use in trade or business or for investment is (as the result of its seizure, requisition, or condemnation, or threat or imminence thereof) compulsorily or involuntarily converted, property of a like kind to be held either for productive use in trade or business or for investment shall be treated as property similar or related in service or use to the property so converted.

(2) Limitations. -- Paragraph (1) shall not apply to the purchase of stock in the acquisition of control of a corporation described in subsection (a)(2)(A).

(3) Election to treat outdoor advertising displays as real property. --

(A) In general. -- A taxpayer may elect, at such time and in such manner as the Secretary may prescribe, to treat property which constitutes an outdoor advertising display as real property for purposes of this chapter. The election provided by this subparagraph may not be made with respect to any property with respect to which an election under

934

Sec. 1033. Involuntary conversions

section 179(a) (relating to election to expense certain depreciable business assets) is in effect.

(B) Election. -- An election made under subparagraph (A) may not be revoked without the consent of the Secretary.

(C) Outdoor advertising display. -- For purposes of this paragraph, the term "outdoor advertising display" means a rigidly assembled sign, display, or device permanently affixed to the ground or permanently attached to a building or other inherently permanent structure constituting, or used for the display of, a commercial or other advertisement to the public.

(D) Character of replacement property. -- For purposes of this subsection, an interest in real property purchased as replacement property for a compulsorily or involuntarily converted outdoor advertising display defined in subparagraph (C) (and treated by the taxpayer as real property) shall be considered property of a like kind as the property converted without regard to whether the taxpayer's interest in the replacement property is the same kind of interest the taxpayer held in the converted property.

(4) Special rule. -- In the case of a compulsory or involuntary conversion described in paragraph (1), subsection (a)(2)(B)(i) shall be applied by substituting "3 years" for "2 years".

(h) Special rules for property damaged by Presidentially declared disasters. --

(1) Principal residences. -- If the taxpayer's principal residence or any of its contents is compulsorily or involuntarily converted as a result of a Presidentially declared disaster--

(A) Treatment of insurance proceeds. --

(i) Exclusion for unscheduled personal property. -- No gain shall be recognized by reason of the receipt of any insurance proceeds for personal property which was part of such contents and which was not scheduled property for purposes of such insurance.

(ii) Other proceeds treated as common fund. -- In the case of any insurance proceeds (not described in clause (i)) for such residence or contents--

(I) such proceeds shall be treated as received for the conversion of a single item of property, and

(II) any property which is similar or related in service or use to the residence so converted (or contents thereof) shall be treated for purposes of subsection (a)(2) as property similar or related in service or use to such single item of property.

(B) Extension of replacement period. -- Subsection (a)(2)(B) shall be applied with respect to any property so converted by substituting "4 years" for "2 years".

(2) Trade or business and investment property. -- If a taxpayer's property held for productive use in a trade or business or for investment is compulsorily or involuntarily converted as a result of a Presidentially declared disaster, tangible property of a type held for productive use in a trade or business shall be treated for purposes of subsection (a) as property similar or related in service or use to the property so converted.

(3) Presidentially declared disaster. -- For purposes of this subsection, the term "Presidentially declared disaster" means any disaster which, with respect to the area in which the property is located, resulted in a subsequent determination by the President that such area warrants assistance by the Federal Government under the Robert T. Stafford Disaster Relief and Emergency Assistance Act.

(4) Principal residence. -- For purposes of this subsection, the term "principal residence" has the same meaning as when used in section 121, except that such term shall include a residence not treated as a principal residence solely because the taxpayer does not own the residence.

(i) Replacement property must be acquired from unrelated person in certain cases. --

935

Sec. 1033. Involuntary conversions

(1) In general. -- If the property which is involuntarily converted is held by a taxpayer to which this subsection applies, subsection (a) shall not apply if the replacement property or stock is acquired from a related person. The preceding sentence shall not apply to the extent that the related person acquired the replacement property or stock from an unrelated person during the period applicable under subsection (a)(2)(B).

(2) Taxpayers to which subsection applies. -- This subsection shall apply to--

(A) a C corporation,

(B) a partnership in which 1 or more C corporations own, directly or indirectly (determined in accordance with section 707(b)(3)), more than 50 percent of the capital interest, or   profits interest, in such partnership at the time of the involuntary conversion, and

(C) any other taxpayer if, with respect to property which is involuntarily converted during the taxable year, the aggregate of the amount of realized gain on such property on which there is realized gain exceeds $100,000.

In the case of a partnership, subparagraph (C) shall apply with respect to the partnership and with respect to each partner. A similar rule shall apply in the case of an S corporation and its shareholders.

(3) Related person. -- For purposes of this subsection, a person is related to another person if the person bears a relationship to the other person described in section 267(b) or 707(b)(1).

***

(k) Cross references. --

(1) For determination of the period for which the taxpayer has held property involuntarily converted, see section 1223.

(2) For treatment of gains from involuntary conversions as capital gains in certain cases, see section 1231(a).

(3) For exclusion from gross income of gain from involuntary conversion of principal residence, see section 121.

Sec. 1038. Certain reacquisitions of real property

(a) General rule. -- If--

(1) a sale of real property gives rise to indebtedness to the seller which is secured by the real property sold, and

(2) the seller of such property reacquires such property in partial or full satisfaction of such indebtedness, then, except as provided in subsections (b) and (d), no gain or loss shall result to the seller from such reacquisition, and no debt shall become worthless or partially worthless as a result of such reacquisition.

(b) Amount of gain resulting. --

(1) In general. -- In the case of a reacquisition of real property to which subsection (a) applies, gain shall result from such reacquisition to the extent that--

(A) the amount of money and the fair market value of other property (other than obligations of the purchaser) received, prior to such reacquisition, with respect to the sale of such property, exceeds

(B) the amount of the gain on the sale of such property returned as income for periods prior to such reacquisition.

(2) Limitation. -- The amount of gain determined under paragraph (1) resulting from a

936

Sec. 1038. Certain reacquisitions of real property

reacquisition during any taxable year beginning after the date of the enactment of this section shall not exceed the amount by which the price at which the real property was sold exceeded its adjusted basis, reduced by the sum of -

(A) the amount of the gain on the sale of such property returned as income for periods prior to the reacquisition of such property, and 5

(B) the amount of money and the fair market value of other property (other than obligations of the purchaser received with respect to the sale of such property) paid or transferred by the seller in connection with the reacquisition of such property.

For purposes of this paragraph, the price at which real property is sold is the gross sales price reduced by the selling commissions, legal fees, and other expenses incident to the sale of such 10 property which are properly taken into account in determining gain or loss on such sale.

(3) **Gain recognized.** -- Except as provided in this section, the gain determined under this subsection resulting from a reacquisition to which subsection (a) applies shall be recognized, notwithstanding any other provision of this subtitle.

(c) **Basis of reacquired real property.** -- If subsection (a) applies to the reacquisition of any 15 real property, the basis of such property upon such reacquisition shall be the adjusted basis of the indebtedness to the seller secured by such property (determined as of the date of reacquisition), increased by the sum of -

(1) the amount of the gain determined under subsection (b) resulting from such reacquisition, and 20

(2) the amount described in subsection (b)(2)(B).
If any indebtedness to the seller secured by such property is not discharged upon the reacquisition of such property, the basis of such indebtedness shall be zero.

(d) Indebtedness treated as worthless prior to reacquisition. -- If, prior to a reacquisition of real property to which subsection (a) applies, the seller has treated indebtedness secured by such 25 property as having become worthless or partially worthless--

(1) such seller shall be considered as receiving, upon the reacquisition of such property, an amount equal to the amount of such indebtedness treated by him as having become worthless, and

(2) the adjusted basis of such indebtedness shall be increased (as of the date of reacquisition) 30 by an amount equal to the amount so considered as received by such seller.

(e) **Principal residences.** -- If--

(1) subsection (a) applies to a reacquisition of real property with respect to the sale of which gain was not recognized under section 121 (relating to gain on sale of principal residence); and

(2) within 1 year after the date of the reacquisition of such property by the seller, such 35 property is resold by him,

then, under regulations prescribed by the Secretary, subsections (b), (c), and (d) of this section shall not apply to the reacquisition of such property and, for purposes of applying section 121, the resale of such property shall be treated as a part of the transaction constituting the original sale of such property. 40

***

Sec. 1041. Transfers of property between spouses or incident to divorce

(a) **General rule.** -- No gain or loss shall be recognized on a transfer of property from an individual to (or in trust for the benefit of)--

(1) a spouse, or 45

937

Sec. 1041. Transfers of property between spouses or incident to divorce

(2) a former spouse, but only if the transfer is incident to the divorce.

(b) Transfer treated as gift; transferee has transferor's basis. -- In the case of any transfer of property described in subsection (a)--

(1) for purposes of this subtitle, the property shall be treated as acquired by the transferee by gift, and

(2) the basis of the transferee in the property shall be the adjusted basis of the transferor.

(c) Incident to divorce. -- For purposes of subsection (a)(2), a transfer of property is incident to the divorce if such transfer--

(1) occurs within 1 year after the date on which the marriage ceases, or

(2) is related to the cessation of the marriage.

(d) Special rule where spouse is nonresident alien. -- Subsection (a) shall not apply if the spouse (or former spouse) of the individual making the transfer is a nonresident alien.

(e) Transfers in trust where liability exceeds basis. -- Subsection (a) shall not apply to the transfer of property in trust to the extent that--

(1) the sum of the amount of the liabilities assumed, plus the amount of the liabilities to which the property is subject,

exceeds

(2) the total of the adjusted basis of the property transferred.

Proper adjustment shall be made under subsection (b) in the basis of the transferee in such property to take into account gain recognized by reason of the preceding sentence.

Reg. § 1.1041-1T Treatment of transfer of property between spouses or incident to divorce (temporary).

Q-1: How is the transfer of property between spouses treated under section 1041?

A-1: Generally, no gain or loss is recognized on a transfer of property from an individual to (or in trust for the benefit of) a spouse or, if the transfer is incident to a divorce, a former spouse. The following questions and answers describe more fully the scope, tax consequences and other rules which apply to transfers of property under section 1041.

(a) *Scope of section 1041 in general.*

Q-2: Does section 1041 apply only to transfers of property incident to divorce?

A-2: No. Section 1041 is not limited to transfers of property incident to divorce. Section 1041 applies to any transfer of property between spouses regardless of whether the transfer is a gift or is a sale or exchange between spouses acting at arm's length (including a transfer in exchange for the relinquishment of property or marital rights or an exchange otherwise governed by another nonrecognition provision of the Code). A divorce or legal separation need not be contemplated between the spouses at the time of the transfer nor must a divorce or legal separation ever occur.

Example 1. A and B are married and file a joint return. A is the sole owner of a condominium unit. A sale or gift of the condominium from A to B is a transfer which is subject to the rules of section 1041.

Example 2. A and B are married and file separate returns. A is the owner of an independent sole proprietorship, X Company. In the ordinary course of business, X Company makes a sale of property to B. This sale is a transfer of property between spouses and is subject to the rules of section 1041.

Example 3. Assume the same facts as in example (2), except that X Company is a corporation wholly owned by A. This sale is not a sale between spouses subject to the rules of section 1041. However, in appropriate circumstances, general tax principles,

Sec. 1041. Transfers of property between spouses or incident to divorce

including the step-transaction doctrine, may be applicable in recharacterizing the transaction.

***

Q-4: What kinds of transfers are governed by section 1041?

A-4: Only transfers of property (whether real or personal, tangible or intangible) are 5 governed by section 1041. Transfers of services are not subject to the rules of section 1041.

Q-5: Must the property transferred to a former spouse have been owned by the transferor spouse during the marriage?

A-5: No. A transfer of property acquired after the marriage ceases may be governed by 10 section 1041.

(b) Transfer incident to the divorce.

Q-6: When is a transfer of property incident to the divorce?

A-6: A transfer of property is incident to the divorce in either of the following 2 circumstances-- 15

(1) The transfer occurs not more than one year after the date on which the marriage ceases, or

(2) The transfer is related to the cessation of the marriage.

Thus, a transfer of property occurring not more than one year after the date on which the marriage ceases need not be related to the cessation of the marriage to qualify for 20 section 1041 treatment. (See A-7 for transfers occurring more than one year after the cessation of the marriage.)

Q-7: When is a transfer of property related to the cessation of the marriage?

A-7: A transfer of property is treated as related to the cessation of the marriage if the transfer is pursuant to a divorce or separation instrument, as defined in section 71(b)(2), 25 and the transfer occurs not more than 6 years after the date on which the marriage ceases. A divorce or separation instrument includes a modification or amendment to such decree or instrument. Any transfer not pursuant to a divorce or separation instrument and any transfer occurring more than 6 years after the cessation of the marriage is presumed to be not related to the cessation of the marriage. This presumption may be rebutted only 30 by showing that the transfer was made to effect the division of property owned by the former spouses at the time of the cessation of the marriage. For example, the presumption may be rebutted by showing that (a) the transfer was not made within the one- and six-year periods described above because of factors which hampered an earlier transfer of the property, such as legal or business impediments to transfer or disputes 35 concerning the value of the property owned at the time of the cessation of the marriage, and (b) the transfer is effected promptly after the impediment to transfer is removed.

Q-8: Do annulments and the cessations of marriages that are void ab initio due to violations of state law constitute divorces for purposes of section 1041?

A-8: Yes. 40

(c) Transfers on behalf of a spouse.

Q-9: May transfers of property to third parties on behalf of a spouse (or former spouse) qualify under section 1041?

A-9: Yes. There are three situations in which a transfer of property to a third party on behalf of a spouse (or former spouse) will qualify under section 1041, provided all other 45 requirements of the section are satisfied. The first situation is where the transfer to the third party is required by a divorce or separation instrument. The second situation is where the transfer to the third party is pursuant to the written request of the other spouse (or former spouse). The third situation is where the transferor receives from the other spouse (or former spouse) a written consent or ratification of the transfer to the third 50 party. Such consent or ratification must state that the parties intend the transfer to be

939

Sec. 1041. Transfers of property between spouses or incident to divorce

treated as a transfer to the nontransferring spouse (or former spouse) subject to the rules of section 1041 and must be received by the transferor prior to the date of filing of the transferor's first return of tax for the taxable year in which the transfer was made. In the three situations described above, the transfer of property will be treated as made directly
5 to the nontransferring spouse (or former spouse) and the nontransferring spouse will be treated as immediately transferring the property to the third party. The deemed transfer from the nontransferring spouse (or former spouse) to the third party is not a transaction that qualifies for nonrecognition of gain under section 1041. This A-9 shall not apply to transfers to which § 1.1041-2 applies.
10   (d) Tax consequences of transfers subject to section 1041.
    Q-10: How is the transferor of property under section 1041 treated for income tax purposes?
    A-10: The transferor of property under section 1041 recognizes no gain or loss on the transfer even if the transfer was in exchange for the release of marital rights or other
15 consideration. This rule applies regardless of whether the transfer is of property separately owned by the transferor or is a division (equal or unequal) of community property. Thus, the result under section 1041 differs from the result in United States v. Davis, 370 U.S. 65 (1962).
    Q-11: How is the transferee of property under section 1041 treated for income tax
20 purposes?
    A-11: The transferee of property under section 1041 recognizes no gain or loss upon receipt of the transferred property. In all cases, the basis of the transferred property in the hands of the transferee is the adjusted basis of such property in the hands of the transferor immediately before the transfer. Even if the transfer is a bona fide sale, the
25 transferee does not acquire a basis in the transferred property equal to the transferee's cost (the fair market value). This carryover basis rule applies whether the adjusted basis of the transferred property is less than, equal to, or greater than its fair market value at the time of transfer (or the value of any consideration provided by the transferee) and applies for purposes of determining loss as well as gain upon the subsequent disposition
30 of the property by the transferee. Thus, this rule is different from the rule applied in section 1015(a) for determining the basis of property acquired by gift.
    Q-12: Do the rules described in A-10 and A-11 apply even if the transferred property is subject to liabilities which exceed the adjusted basis of the property?
    A-12: Yes. For example, assume A owns property having a fair market value of
35 $10,000 and an adjusted basis of $1,000. In contemplation of making a transfer of this property incident to a divorce from B, A borrows $5,000 from a bank, using the property as security for the borrowing. A then transfers the property to B and B assumes, or takes the property subject to, the liability to pay the $5,000 debt. Under section 1041, A recognizes no gain or loss upon the transfer of the property, and the adjusted basis of the
40 property in the hands of B is $1,000.

***

[T.D. 7973, 49 FR 34452, Aug. 31, 1984; T.D. 9035, 68 FR 1536, Jan. 13, 2003]

Sec. 1045. Rollover of gain from qualified small business stock to another qualified small business stock

    (a) Nonrecognition of gain. -- In the case of any sale of qualified small business stock held by
45 a taxpayer other than a corporation for more than 6 months and with respect to which such taxpayer elects the application of this section, gain from such sale shall be recognized only to the extent that the amount realized on such sale exceeds--

Sec. 1045.   Rollover of gain from qualified small business stock to another qualified small business stock

    (1) the cost of any qualified small business stock purchased by the taxpayer during the 60-day period beginning on the date of such sale, reduced by

    (2) any portion of such cost previously taken into account under this section.

This section shall not apply to any gain which is treated as ordinary income for purposes of this title.

  (b) Definitions and special rules. -- For purposes of this section--

    (1) Qualified small business stock. -- The term "qualified small business stock" has the meaning given such term by section 1202(c).

    (2) Purchase. -- A taxpayer shall be treated as having purchased any property if, but for paragraph (3), the unadjusted basis of such property in the hands of the taxpayer would be its cost (within the meaning of section 1012).

    (3) Basis adjustments. -- If gain from any sale is not recognized by reason of subsection (a), such gain shall be applied to reduce (in the order acquired) the basis for determining gain or loss of any qualified small business stock which is purchased by the taxpayer during the 60-day period described in subsection (a).

    (4) Holding period. -- For purposes of determining whether the nonrecognition of gain under subsection (a) applies to stock which is sold--

      (A) the taxpayer's holding period for such stock and the stock referred to in subsection (a)(1) shall be determined without regard to section 1223, and

      (B) only the first 6 months of the taxpayer's holding period for the stock referred to in subsection (a)(1) shall be taken into account for purposes of applying section 1202(c)(2).

    (5) Certain rules to apply. -- Rules similar to the rules of subsections (f), (g), (h), (i), (j), and (k) of section 1202 shall apply.

Sec. 1060.   Special allocation rules for certain asset acquisitions

  (a) General rule. -- In the case of any applicable asset acquisition, for purposes of determining both--

    (1) the transferee's basis in such assets, and

    (2) the gain or loss of the transferor with respect to such acquisition,

the consideration received for such assets shall be allocated among such assets acquired in such acquisition in the same manner as amounts are allocated to assets under section 338(b)(5). If in connection with an applicable asset acquisition, the transferee and transferor agree in writing as to the allocation of any consideration, or as to the fair market value of any of the assets, such agreement shall be binding on both the transferee and transferor unless the Secretary determines that such allocation (or fair market value) is not appropriate.

          ***

  (c) Applicable asset acquisition. -- For purposes of this section, the term "applicable asset acquisition" means any transfer (whether directly or indirectly)--

    (1) of assets which constitute a trade or business, and

    (2) with respect to which the transferee's basis in such assets is determined wholly by reference to the consideration paid for such assets.

A transfer shall not be treated as failing to be an applicable asset acquisition merely because section 1031 applies to a portion of the assets transferred.

Sec. 1060.   Special allocation rules for certain asset acquisitions

***

Sec. 1091.   Loss from wash sales of stock or securities

(a) Disallowance of loss deduction. -- In the case of any loss claimed to have been sustained from any sale or other disposition of shares of stock or securities where it appears that, within a period beginning 30 days before the date of such sale or disposition and ending 30 days after such date, the taxpayer has acquired (by purchase or by an exchange on which the entire amount of gain or loss was recognized by law), or has entered into a contract or option so to acquire, substantially identical stock or securities, then no deduction shall be allowed under section 165 unless the taxpayer is a dealer in stock or securities and the loss is sustained in a transaction made in the ordinary course of such business. For purposes of this section, the term "stock or securities" shall, except as provided in regulations, include contracts or options to acquire or sell stock or securities.

(b) Stock acquired less than stock sold. -- If the amount of stock or securities acquired (or covered by the contract or option to acquire) is less than the amount of stock or securities sold or otherwise disposed of, then the particular shares of stock or securities the loss from the sale or other disposition of which is not deductible shall be determined under regulations prescribed by the Secretary.

(c) Stock acquired not less than stock sold. -- If the amount of stock or securities acquired (or covered by the contract or option to acquire) is not less than the amount of stock or securities sold or otherwise disposed of, then the particular shares of stock or securities the acquisition of which (or the contract or option to acquire which) resulted in the nondeductibility of the loss shall be determined under regulations prescribed by the Secretary.

(d) Unadjusted basis in case of wash sale of stock. -- If the property consists of stock or securities the acquisition of which (or the contract or option to acquire which) resulted in the nondeductibility (under this section or corresponding provisions of prior internal revenue laws) of the loss from the sale or other disposition of substantially identical stock or securities, then the basis shall be the basis of the stock or securities so sold or disposed of, increased or decreased, as the case may be, by the difference, if any, between the price at which the property was acquired and the price at which such substantially identical stock or securities were sold or otherwise disposed of.

(e) Certain short sales of stock or securities and securities futures contracts to sell. -- Rules similar to the rules of subsection (a) shall apply to any loss realized on the closing of a short sale of (or the sale, exchange, or termination of a securities futures contract to sell) stock or securities if, within a period beginning 30 days before the date of such closing and ending 30 days after such date -

(1) substantially identical stock or securities were sold, or

(2) another short sale of (or securities futures contracts to sell) substantially identical stock or securities was entered into.

For purposes of this subsection, the term "securities futures contract" has the meaning provided by section 1234B(c).

(f) Cash settlement. -- This section shall not fail to apply to a contract or option to acquire or sell stock or securities solely by reason of the fact that the contract or option settles in (or could be settled in) cash or property other than such stock or securities.

Reg. § 1.1091-1   Losses from wash sales of stock or securities.

(a) A taxpayer cannot deduct any loss claimed to have been sustained from the sale or other disposition of stock or securities if, within a period beginning 30 days before the date of such sale or disposition and ending 30 days after such date (referred to in this

Sec. 1091.   Loss from wash sales of stock or securities

section as the 61-day period), he has acquired (by purchase or by an exchange upon which the entire amount of gain or loss was recognized by law), or has entered into a contract or option so to acquire, substantially identical stock or securities. However, this prohibition does not apply (1) in the case of a taxpayer, not a corporation, if the sale or other disposition of stock or securities is made in connection with the taxpayer's trade or 5 business, or (2) in the case of a corporation, a dealer in stock or securities, if the sale or other disposition of stock or securities is made in the ordinary course of its business as such dealer.

(b) Where more than one loss is claimed to have been sustained within the taxable year from the sale or other disposition of stock or securities, the provisions of this section 10 shall be applied to the losses in the order in which the stock or securities the disposition of which resulted in the respective losses were disposed of (beginning with the earliest disposition). If the order of disposition of stock or securities disposed of at a loss on the same day cannot be determined, the stock or securities will be considered to have been disposed of in the order in which they were originally acquired (beginning with the earliest 15 acquisition).

(c) Where the amount of stock or securities acquired within the 61-day period is less than the amount of stock or securities sold or otherwise disposed of, then the particular shares of stock or securities the loss from the sale or other disposition of which is not deductible shall be those with which the stock or securities acquired are matched in 20 accordance with the following rule: The stock or securities acquired will be matched in accordance with the order of their acquisition (beginning with the earliest acquisition) with an equal number of the shares of stock or securities sold or otherwise disposed of.

(d) Where the amount of stock or securities acquired within the 61-day period is not less than the amount of stock or securities sold or otherwise disposed of, then the 25 particular shares of stock or securities the acquisition of which resulted in the nondeductibility of the loss shall be those with which the stock or securities disposed of are matched in accordance with the following rule: The stock or securities sold or otherwise disposed of will be matched with an equal number of the shares of stock or securities acquired in accordance with the order of acquisition (beginning with the earliest 30 acquisition) of the stock or securities acquired.

(e) The acquisition of any share of stock or any security which results in the nondeductibility of a loss under the provisions of this section shall be disregarded in determining the deductibility of any other loss.

(f) The word acquired as used in this section means acquired by purchase or by an 35 exchange upon which the entire amount of gain or loss was recognized by law, and comprehends cases where the taxpayer has entered into a contract or option within the 61-day period to acquire by purchase or by such an exchange.

(g) For purposes of determining under this section the 61-day period applicable to a short sale of stock or securities, the principles of paragraph (a) of § 1.1233-1 for 40 determining the consummation of a short sale shall generally apply except that the date of entering into the short sale shall be deemed to be the date of sale if, on the date of entering into the short sale, the taxpayer owns (or on or before such date has entered into a contract or option to acquire) stock or securities identical to those sold short and subsequently delivers such stock or securities to close the short sale.   45

(h) The following examples illustrate the application of this section:

Example 1. A, whose taxable year is the calendar year, on December 1, 1954, purchased 100 shares of common stock in the M Company for $10,000 and on December 15, 1954, purchased 100 additional shares for $9,000. On January 3, 1955, he sold the 100 shares purchased on December 1, 1954, for $9,000. Because of the 50 provisions of section 1091, no loss from the sale is allowable as a deduction.

Sec. 1091. Loss from wash sales of stock or securities

Example 2. A, whose taxable year is the calendar year, on September 21, 1954, purchased 100 shares of the common stock of the M Company for $5,000. On December 21, 1954, he purchased 50 shares of substantially identical stock for $2,750, and on December 27, 1954, he purchased 25 additional shares of such stock for $1,125. On
5 January 3, 1955, he sold for $4,000 the 100 shares purchased on September 21, 1954. There is an indicated loss of $1,000 on the sale of the 100 shares. Since, within the 61-day period, A purchased 75 shares of substantially identical stock, the loss on the sale of 75 of the shares ($3,750-$3,000, or $750) is not allowable as a deduction because of the provisions of section 1091. The loss on the sale of the remaining 25 shares ($1,250-
10 $1,000, or $250) is deductible subject to the limitations provided in sections 267 and 1211. The basis of the 50 shares purchased December 21, 1954, the acquisition of which resulted in the nondeductibility of the loss ($500) sustained on 50 of the 100 shares sold on January 3, 1955, is $2,500 (the cost of 50 of the shares sold on January 3, 1955) + $750 (the difference between the purchase price ($2,750) of the 50 shares acquired on
15 December 21, 1954, and the selling price ($2,000) of 50 of the shares sold on January 3, 1955), or $3,250. Similarly, the basis of the 25 shares purchased on December 27, 1954, the acquisition of which resulted in the nondeductibility of the loss ($250) sustained on 25 of the shares sold on January 3, 1955, is $1,250+$125, or $1,375. See § 1.1091-2.

Example 3. A, whose taxable year is the calendar year, on September 15, 1954,
20 purchased 100 shares of the stock of the M Company for $5,000. He sold these shares on February 1, 1956, for $4,000. On each of the four days from February 15, 1956, to February 18, 1956, inclusive, he purchased 50 shares of substantially identical stock for $2,000. There is an indicated loss of $1,000 from the sale of the 100 shares on February 1, 1956, but, since within the 61-day period A purchased not less than 100 shares of
25 substantially identical stock, the loss is not deductible. The particular shares of stock the purchase of which resulted in the nondeductibility of the loss are the first 100 shares purchased within such period, that is, the 50 shares purchased on February 15, 1956, and the 50 shares purchased on February 16, 1956. In determining the period for which the 50 shares purchased on February 15, 1956, and the 50 shares purchased on
30 February 16, 1956, were held, there is to be included the period for which the 100 shares purchased on September 15, 1954, and sold on February 1, 1956, were held.

Reg. § 1.1091-2 Basis of stock or securities acquired in ``wash sales''.

(a) *In general.* The application of section 1091(d) may be illustrated by the following
35 examples:

Example 1. A purchased a share of common stock of the X Corporation for $100 in 1935, which he sold January 15, 1955, for $80. On February 1, 1955, he purchased a share of common stock of the same corporation for $90. No loss from the sale is recognized under section 1091. The basis of the new share is $110; that is, the basis of
40 the old share ($100) increased by $10, the excess of the price at which the new share was acquired ($90) over the price at which the old share was sold ($80).

Example 2. A purchased a share of common stock of the Y Corporation for $100 in 1935, which he sold January 15, 1955, for $80. On February 1, 1955, he purchased a share of common stock of the same corporation for $70. No loss from the sale is
45 recognized under section 1091. The basis of the new share is $90; that is, the basis of the old share ($100) decreased by $10, the excess of the price at which the old share was sold ($80) over the price at which the new share was acquired ($70).

[T.D. 6500, 25 FR 11910, Nov. 26, 1960; T.D. 6926, 32 FR 11468, Aug. 9, 1967; T.D.
50 7129, 36 FR 12738, July 7, 1971]

Sec. 1091. Loss from wash sales of stock or securities

Sec. 1092. Straddles

(a) **Recognition of loss in case of straddles, etc.** --

   (1) **Limitation on recognition of loss.** --

   (A) **In general.** -- Any loss with respect to 1 or more positions shall be taken into account for any taxable year only to the extent that the amount of such loss exceeds the 5 unrecognized gain (if any) with respect to 1 or more positions which were offsetting positions with respect to 1 or more positions from which the loss arose.

   (B) **Carryover of loss.** -- Any loss which may not be taken into account under subparagraph (A) for any taxable year shall, subject to the limitations under subparagraph (A), be treated as sustained in the succeeding taxable year. 10

   (2) **Special rule for identified straddles.** --

   (A) **In general.** -- In the case of any straddle which is an identified straddle--

   (i) paragraph (1) shall not apply with respect to positions comprising the identified straddle,

   (ii) if there is any loss with respect to any position of the identified straddle, the 15 basis of each of the offsetting positions in the identified straddle shall be increased by an amount which bears the same ratio to the loss as the unrecognized gain with respect to such offsetting position bears to the aggregate unrecognized gain with respect to all such offsetting positions,

   (iii) if the application of clause (ii) does not result in an increase in the basis of any 20 offsetting position in the identified straddle, the basis of each of the offsetting positions in the identified straddle shall be increased in a manner which--

   (I) is reasonable, consistent with the purposes of this paragraph, and consistently applied by the taxpayer, and

   (II) results in an aggregate increase in the basis of such offsetting positions which 25 is equal to the loss described in clause (ii), and

   (iv) any loss described in clause (ii) shall not otherwise be taken into account for purposes of this title.

   (B) **Identified straddle.** -- The term "identified straddle" means any straddle --

   (i) which is clearly identified on the taxpayer's records as an identified straddle 30 before the earlier of--

   (I) the close of the day on which the straddle is acquired, or

   (II) such time as the Secretary may prescribe by regulations.

   (ii) to the extent provided by regulations, the value of each position of which (in the hands of the taxpayer immediately before the creation of the straddle) is not less than 35 the basis of such position in the hands of the taxpayer at the time the straddle is created, and

   (iii) which is not part of a larger straddle.

A straddle shall be treated as clearly identified for purposes of clause (i) only if such identification includes an identification of the positions in the straddle which are offsetting 40 with respect other positions in the straddle.

   (C) **Application to liabilities and obligations**. -- Except as otherwise provided by the Secretary, rules similar to the rules of clauses (ii) and (iii) of subparagraph (A) shall apply for purposes of this paragraph with respect to any position which is, or has been, a liability or obligation.

(D) Regulations. -- The Secretary shall prescribe regulations which specify the proper methods for clearly identifying a straddle as an identified straddle (and the positions comprising such straddle), which specify the rules for the application of this section for a taxpayer which fails to properly identify the positions of an identified straddle, the rules for the application of this section to a position which is or has been a liability or obligation, methods of loss allocation which satisfy the requirements of subparagraph (A)(iii), and the ordering rules in cases where a taxpayer disposes of less than an entire position which is part of an identified straddle.

(3) Unrecognized gain. -- For purposes of this subsection--

(A) In general. -- The term "unrecognized gain" means--

(i) in the case of any position held by the taxpayer as of the close of the taxable year, the amount of gain which would be taken into account with respect to such position if such position were sold on the last business day of such taxable year at its fair market value, and

(ii) in the case of any position with respect to which, as of the close of the taxable year, gain has been realized but not recognized, the amount of gain so realized.

(B) Special rule for identified straddles. -- For purposes of paragraph (2)(A)(ii), the unrecognized gain with respect to any offsetting position shall be the excess of the fair market value of the position at the time of the determination over the fair market value of the position at the time the taxpayer identified the position as a position in an identified straddle.

(C) Reporting of gain. --

(i) In general. -- Each taxpayer shall disclose to the Secretary, at such time and in such manner and form as the Secretary may prescribe by regulations--

(I) each position (whether or not part of a straddle) with respect to which, as of the close of the taxable year, there is unrecognized gain, and

(II) the amount of such unrecognized gain.

(ii) Reports not required in certain cases. -- Clause (i) shall not apply--

(I) to any position which is part of an identified straddle,

(II) to any position which, with respect to the taxpayer, is property described in paragraph (1) or (2) of section 1221(a) or to any position which is part of a hedging transaction (as defined in section 1256(e)), or

(III) with respect to any taxable year if no loss on a position (including a regulated futures contract) has been sustained during such taxable year or if the only loss sustained on such position is a loss described in subclause (II).

***

(c) Straddle defined. --

(1) In general. -- The term "straddle" means offsetting positions with respect to personal property.

(2) Offsetting positions. --

(A) In general. -- A taxpayer holds offsetting positions with respect to personal property if there is a substantial diminution of the taxpayer's risk of loss from holding any position with respect to personal property by reason of his holding 1 or more other positions with respect to personal property (whether or not of the same kind).

(B) Special rule for identified straddles. -- In the case of any position which is not part of an identified straddle (within the meaning of subsection (a)(2)(B)), such position shall not be treated as offsetting with respect to any position which is part of an identified straddle.

(3) Presumption. --

(A) In general. -- For purposes of paragraph (2), 2 or more positions shall be presumed 5 to be offsetting if--

(i) the positions are in the same personal property (whether established in such property or a contract for such property),

(ii) the positions are in the same personal property, even though such property may be in a substantially altered form, 10

(iii) the positions are in debt instruments of a similar maturity or other debt instruments described in regulations prescribed by the Secretary,

(iv) the positions are sold or marketed as offsetting positions (whether or not such positions are called a straddle, spread, butterfly, or any similar name),

(v) the aggregate margin requirement for such positions is lower than the sum of the 15 margin requirements for each such position (if held separately), or

(vi) there are such other factors (or satisfaction of subjective or objective tests) as the Secretary may by regulations prescribe as indicating that such positions are offsetting.

For purposes of the preceding sentence, 2 or more positions shall be treated as described in clause (i), (ii), (iii), or (vi) only if the value of 1 or more of such positions ordinarily varies 20 inversely with the value of 1 or more other such positions.

(B) Presumption may be rebutted. -- Any presumption established pursuant to subparagraph (A) may be rebutted.

(4) Exception for certain straddles consisting of qualified covered call options and the optioned stock. -- 25

(A) In general. -- If--

(i) all the offsetting positions making up any straddle consist of 1 or more qualified covered call options and the stock to be purchased from the taxpayer under such options, and

(ii) such straddle is not part of a larger straddle, such straddle shall not be treated as 30 a straddle for purposes of this section and section 263(g).

(B) Qualified covered call option defined. -- For purposes of subparagraph (A), the term "qualified covered call option" means any option granted by the taxpayer to purchase stock held by the taxpayer (or stock acquired by the taxpayer in connection with the granting of the option) but only if-- 35

(i) such option is traded on a national securities exchange which is registered with the Securities and Exchange Commission or other market which the Secretary determines has rules adequate to carry out the purposes of this paragraph,

(ii) such option is granted more than 30 days before the day on which the option expires, 40

(iii) such option is not a deep-in-the-money option,

(iv) such option is not granted by an options dealer (within the meaning of section 1256(g)(8)) in connection with his activity of dealing in options, and

(v) gain or loss with respect to such option is not ordinary income or loss.

(C) Deep-in-the-money option. -- For purposes of subparagraph (B), the term "deep-in- 45 the-money option" means an option having a strike price lower than the lowest qualified

Sec. 1092. Straddles

bench mark.

(D) Lowest qualified bench mark. --

    (i) In general. -- Except as otherwise provided in this subparagraph, for purposes of subparagraph (C), the term "lowest qualified bench mark" means the highest available strike price which is less than the applicable stock price.

    (ii) Special rule where option is for period more than 90 days and strike price exceeds $50. -- In the case of an option--

        (I) which is granted more than 90 days before the date on which such option expires, and

        (II) with respect to which the strike price is more than $50,

the lowest qualified bench mark is the second highest available strike price which is less than the applicable stock price.

    (iii) 85 percent rule where applicable stock price $25 or less. -- If--

        (I) the applicable stock price is $25 or less, and

        (II) but for this clause, the lowest qualified bench mark would be less than 85 percent of the applicable stock price,

the lowest qualified bench mark shall be treated as equal to 85 percent of the applicable stock price.

    (iv) Limitation where applicable stock price $150 or less. -- If--

        (I) the applicable stock price is $150 or less, and

        (II) but for this clause, the lowest qualified bench mark would be less than the applicable stock price reduced by $10,

the lowest qualified bench mark shall be treated as equal to the applicable stock price reduced by $10.

    (E) Special year-end rule. -- Subparagraph (A) shall not apply to any straddle for purposes of section 1092(a) if--

    (i) the qualified covered call options referred to in such subparagraph are closed or the stock is disposed of at a loss during any taxable year,

    (ii) gain on disposition of the stock to be purchased from the taxpayer under such options or gains on such options are includible in gross income for a later taxable year, and

    (iii) such stock or option was not held by the taxpayer for 30 days or more after the closing of such options or the disposition of such stock.

For purposes of the preceding sentence, the rules of paragraphs (3) (other than subparagraph (B) thereof) and (4) of section 246(c) shall apply in determining the period for which the taxpayer holds the stock.

    (F) Strike price. -- For purposes of this paragraph, the term "strike price" means the price at which the option is exercisable.

    (G) Applicable stock price. -- For purposes of subparagraph (D), the term "applicable stock price" means, with respect to any stock for which an option has been granted -

    (i) the closing price of such stock on the most recent day on which such stock was traded before the date on which such option was granted, or

    (ii) the opening price of such stock on the day on which such option was granted, but only if such price is greater than 110 percent of the price determined under clause (i).

***

Sec. 1092.   Straddles

(d) Definitions and special rules. -- For purposes of this section--

    (1) Personal property. -- The term "personal property" means any personal property of a type which is actively traded.

    (2) Position. -- The term "position" means an interest (including a futures or forward contract or option) in personal property.

***

Sec. 1201.   Alternative tax for corporations

    (a) General rule. -- If for any taxable year a corporation has a net capital gain and any rate of tax imposed by section 11, 511, or 831(a) or (b) (whichever is applicable) exceeds 35 percent (determined without regard to the last 2 sentences of section 11(b)(1)), then, in lieu of any such tax, there is hereby imposed a tax (if such tax is less than the tax imposed by such sections) which shall consist of the sum of -

    (1) a tax computed on the taxable income reduced by the amount of the net capital gain, at the rates and in the manner as if this subsection had not been enacted, plus

    (2) a tax of 35 percent of the net capital gain (or, if less, taxable income).

***

Sec. 1202.   Partial exclusion for gain from certain small business stock

    (a) Exclusion. --

    (1) In general. -- In the case of a taxpayer other than a corporation, gross income shall not include 50 percent of any gain from the sale or exchange of qualified small business stock held for more than 5 years.

***

(c) Qualified small business stock. -- For purposes of this section--

    (1) In general. -- Except as otherwise provided in this section, the term "qualified small business stock" means any stock in a C corporation which is originally issued after the date of the enactment of the Revenue Reconciliation Act of 1993, if -

    (A) as of the date of issuance, such corporation is a qualified small business, and

    (B) except as provided in subsections (f) and (h), such stock is acquired by the taxpayer at its original issue (directly or through an underwriter)-

        (i) in exchange for money or other property (not including stock), or

        (ii) as compensation for services provided to such corporation (other than services performed as an underwriter of such stock).

***

(d) Qualified small business. -- For purposes of this section -

    (1) In general. -- The term "qualified small business" means any domestic corporation which is a C corporation if--

    (A) the aggregate gross assets of such corporation (or any predecessor thereof) at all times on or after the date of the enactment of the Revenue Reconciliation Act of 1993 and before the issuance did not exceed $50,000,000,

    (B) the aggregate gross assets of such corporation immediately after the issuance (determined by taking into account amounts received in the issuance) do not exceed $50,000,000, and

    (C) such corporation agrees to submit such reports to the Secretary and to shareholders as the Secretary may require to carry out the purposes of this section.

949

Sec. 1202. Partial exclusion for gain from certain small business stock

(2) Aggregate gross assets. --

(A) In general. -- For purposes of paragraph (1), the term "aggregate gross assets" means the amount of cash and the aggregate adjusted bases of other property held by the corporation.

5

***

Sec. 1211. Limitation on capital losses

(a) Corporations. -- In the case of a corporation, losses from sales or exchanges of capital assets shall be allowed only to the extent of gains from such sales or exchanges.

(b) Other taxpayers. -- In the case of a taxpayer other than a corporation, losses from sales or
10 exchanges of capital assets shall be allowed only to the extent of the gains from such sales or exchanges, plus (if such losses exceed such gains) the lower of -

(1) $3,000 ($1,500 in the case of a married individual filing a separate return), or

(2) the excess of such losses over such gains.

15

Sec. 1212. Capital loss carrybacks and carryovers

(a) Corporations. --

(1) In general. -- If a corporation has a net capital loss for any taxable year (hereinafter in this paragraph referred to as the "loss year"), the amount thereof shall be--

(A) a capital loss carryback to each of the 3 taxable years preceding the loss year, but
20 only to the extent -

(i) such loss is not attributable to a foreign expropriation capital loss, and

(ii) the carryback of such loss does not increase or produce a net operating loss (as defined in section 172(c)) for the taxable year to which it is being carried back;

(B) except as provided in subparagraph (C), a capital loss carryover to each of the 5
25 taxable years succeeding the loss year; and

(C) a capital loss carryover--

(i) in the case of a regulated investment company (as defined in section 851) to each of the 8 taxable years succeeding the loss year, and

(ii) to the extent such loss is attributable to a foreign expropriation capital loss, to
30 each of the 10 taxable years succeeding the loss year.

and shall be treated as a short-term capital loss in each such taxable year. The entire amount of the net capital loss for any taxable year shall be carried to the earliest of the taxable years to which such loss may be carried, and the portion of such loss which shall be carried to each of the other taxable years to which such loss may be carried shall be the excess, if any, of such
35 loss over the total of the capital gain net income for each of the prior taxable years to which such loss may be carried. For purposes of the preceding sentence, the capital gain net income for any such prior taxable year shall be computed without regard to the net capital loss for the loss year or for any taxable year thereafter. In the case of any net capital loss which cannot be carried back in full to a preceding taxable year by reason of clause (ii) of subparagraph (A), the
40 capital gain net income for such prior taxable year shall in no case be treated as greater than the amount of such loss which can be carried back to such preceding taxable year upon the application of such clause (ii).

***

950

Sec. 1212. Capital loss carrybacks and carryovers

(b) Other taxpayers. --

(1) In general. -- If a taxpayer other than a corporation has a net capital loss for any taxable year--

(A) the excess of the net short-term capital loss over the net long-term capital gain for such year shall be a short-term capital loss in the succeeding taxable year, and 5

(B) the excess of the net long-term capital loss over the net short-term capital gain for such year shall be a long-term capital loss in the succeeding taxable year.

(2) Treatment of amounts allowed under section 1211(b)(1) or (2). --

(A) In general. -- For purposes of determining the excess referred to in subparagraph (A) or (B) of paragraph (1), there shall be treated as a short-term capital gain in the taxable 10 year an amount equal to the lesser of--

(i) the amount allowed for the taxable year under paragraph (1) or (2) of section 1211(b), or

(ii) the adjusted taxable income for such taxable year.

(B) Adjusted taxable income. -- For purposes of subparagraph (A), the term "adjusted 15 taxable income" means taxable income increased by the sum of--

(i) the amount allowed for the taxable year under paragraph (1) or (2) of section 1211(b), and

(ii) the deduction allowed for such year under section 151 or any deduction in lieu thereof. 20

For purposes of the preceding sentence, any excess of the deductions allowed for the taxable year over the gross income for such year shall be taken into account as negative taxable income.

***

25

Sec. 1221. Capital asset defined

(a) In general. -- For purposes of this subtitle, the term "capital asset" means property held by the taxpayer (whether or not connected with his trade or business), but does not include--

(1) stock in trade of the taxpayer or other property of a kind which would properly be included in the inventory of the taxpayer if on hand at the close of the taxable year, or property held by the taxpayer primarily for sale to customers in the ordinary course of his trade or 30 business;

(2) property, used in his trade or business, of a character which is subject to the allowance for depreciation provided in section 167, or real property used in his trade or business;

(3) a copyright, a literary, musical, or artistic composition, a letter or memorandum, or similar property, held by-- 35

(A) a taxpayer whose personal efforts created such property,

(B) in the case of a letter, memorandum, or similar property, a taxpayer for whom such property was prepared or produced, or

(C) a taxpayer in whose hands the basis of such property is determined, for purposes of determining gain from a sale or exchange, in whole or part by reference to the basis of such 40 property in the hands of a taxpayer described in subparagraph (A) or (B);

(4) accounts or notes receivable acquired in the ordinary course of trade or business for services rendered or from the sale of property described in paragraph (1);

(5) a publication of the United States Government (including the Congressional Record)

Sec. 1221. Capital asset defined

which is received from the United States Government or any agency thereof, other than by purchase at the price at which it is offered for sale to the public, and which is held by--

(A) a taxpayer who so received such publication, or

(B) a taxpayer in whose hands the basis of such publication is determined, for purposes of determining gain from a sale or exchange, in whole or in part by reference to the basis of such publication in the hands of a taxpayer described in subparagraph (A);

(6) any commodities derivative financial instrument held by a commodities derivatives dealer, unless--

(A) it is established to the satisfaction of the Secretary that such instrument has no connection to the activities of such dealer as a dealer, and

(B) such instrument is clearly identified in such dealer's records as being described in subparagraph (A) before the close of the day on which it was acquired, originated, or entered into (or such other time as the Secretary may by regulations prescribe);

(7) any hedging transaction which is clearly identified as such before the close of the day on which it was acquired, originated, or entered into (or such other time as the Secretary may by regulations prescribe); or

(8) supplies of a type regularly used or consumed by the taxpayer in the ordinary course of a trade or business of the taxpayer.

(b) **Definitions and special rules.** --

(1) **Commodities derivative financial instruments.** -- For purposes of subsection (a)(6)--

(A) **Commodities derivatives dealer.** -- The term "commodities derivatives dealer" means a person which regularly offers to enter into, assume, offset, assign, or terminate positions in commodities derivative financial instruments with customers in the ordinary course of a trade or business.

(B) **Commodities derivative financial instrument.** --

(i) **In general.** -- The term "commodities derivative financial instrument" means any contract or financial instrument with respect to commodities (other than a share of stock in a corporation, a beneficial interest in a partnership or trust, a note, bond, debenture, or other evidence of indebtedness, or a section 1256 contract (as defined in section 1256(b))), the value or settlement price of which is calculated by or determined by reference to a specified index.

(ii) **Specified index.** -- The term "specified index" means any one or more or any combination of--

(I) a fixed rate, price, or amount, or

(II) a variable rate, price, or amount, which is based on any current, objectively determinable financial or economic information with respect to commodities which is not within the control of any of the parties to the contract or instrument and is not unique to any of the parties' circumstances.

(2) **Hedging transaction.** --

(A) **In general.** -- For purposes of this section, the term "hedging transaction" means any transaction entered into by the taxpayer in the normal course of the taxpayer's trade or business primarily--

(i) to manage risk of price changes or currency fluctuations with respect to ordinary property which is held or to be held by the taxpayer,

(ii) to manage risk of interest rate or price changes or currency fluctuations with respect to borrowings made or to be made, or ordinary obligations incurred or to be

Sec. 1221. Capital asset defined

incurred, by the taxpayer, or

    (iii) to manage such other risks as the Secretary may prescribe in regulations.

    (B) Treatment of nonidentification or improper identification of hedging transactions. -- Notwithstanding subsection (a)(7), the Secretary shall prescribe regulations to properly characterize any income, gain, expense, or loss arising from a 5 transaction--

    (i) which is a hedging transaction but which was not identified as such in accordance with subsection (a)(7), or

    (ii) which was so identified but is not a hedging transaction.

***

    (3) Sale or exchange of self-created musical works. -- At the election of the taxpayer, paragraphs (1) and (3) of subsection (a) shall not apply to musical compositions or copyrights in musical works sold or exchanged by a taxpayer described in subsection (a)(3).

***

Reg. § 1.1221-2 Hedging transactions.

***

    (f) *Identification and recordkeeping*--(1) *Same-day identification of hedging transactions.* Under section 1221(a)(7), a taxpayer that enters into a hedging transaction (including recycling an existing hedging transaction) must clearly identify it as a hedging transaction before the close of the day on which the taxpayer acquired, originated, or entered into the transaction (or recycled the existing hedging transaction).

    (2) *Substantially contemporaneous identification of hedged item*--(i) *Content of the identification.* A taxpayer that enters into a hedging transaction must identify the item, items, or aggregate risk being hedged. Identification of an item being hedged generally involves identifying a transaction that creates risk, and the type of risk that the transaction creates. For example, if a taxpayer is hedging the price risk with respect to its June purchases of corn inventory, the transaction being hedged is the June purchase of corn and the risk is price movements in the market where the taxpayer buys its corn. For additional rules concerning the content of this identification, see paragraph (f)(3) of this section.

***

[T.D. 8985, 67 FR 12865, Mar. 20, 2002; T.D. 9264, 71 FR 30602, May 30, 2006]

Sec. 1222. Other terms relating to capital gains and losses

For purposes of this subtitle -

    (1) Short-term capital gain. -- The term "short-term capital gain" means gain from the sale or exchange of a capital asset held for not more than 1 year, if and to the extent such gain is taken into account in computing gross income.

    (2) Short-term capital loss. -- The term "short-term capital loss" means loss from the sale or exchange of a capital asset held for not more than 1 year, if and to the extent that such loss is taken into account in computing taxable income.

    (3) Long-term capital gain. -- The term "long-term capital gain" means gain from the sale or exchange of a capital asset held for more than 1 year, if and to the extent such gain is taken into account in computing gross income.

    (4) Long-term capital loss. -- The term "long-term capital loss" means loss from the sale or exchange of a capital asset held for more than 1 year, if and to the extent that such loss is taken into account in computing taxable income.

Sec. 1222. Other terms relating to capital gains and losses

(5) Net short-term capital gain. -- The term "net short-term capital gain" means the excess of short-term capital gains for the taxable year over the short-term capital losses for such year.

(6) Net short-term capital loss. -- The term "net short-term capital loss" means the excess of short-term capital losses for the taxable year over the short- term capital gains for such year.

(7) Net long-term capital gain. -- The term "net long-term capital gain" means the excess of long-term capital gains for the taxable year over the long-term capital losses for such year.

(8) Net long-term capital loss. -- The term "net long-term capital loss" means the excess of long-term capital losses for the taxable year over the long-term capital gains for such year.

(9) Capital gain net income. -- The term "capital gain net income" means the excess of the gains from sales or exchanges of capital assets over the losses from such sales or exchanges.

(10) Net capital loss. -- The term "net capital loss" means the excess of the losses from sales or exchanges of capital assets over the sum allowed under section 1211. In the case of a corporation, for the purpose of determining losses under this paragraph, amounts which are short-term capital losses under section 1212 shall be excluded.

(11) Net capital gain. -- The term "net capital gain" means the excess of the net long-term capital gain for the taxable year over the net short-term capital loss for such year.

For purposes of this subtitle, in the case of futures transactions in any commodity subject to the rules of a board of trade or commodity exchange, the length of the holding period taken into account under this section or under any other section amended by section 1402 of the Tax Reform Act of 1976 shall be determined without regard to the amendments made by subsections (a) and (b) of such section 1402.

Sec. 1223. Holding period of property

For purposes of this subtitle -

(1) In determining the period for which the taxpayer has held property received in an exchange, there shall be included the period for which he held the property exchanged if, under this chapter, the property has, for the purpose of determining gain or loss from a sale or exchange, the same basis in whole or in part in his hands as the property exchanged, and, in the case of such exchanges after March 1, 1954, the property exchanged at the time of such exchange was a capital asset as defined in section 1221 or property described in section 1231. For purposes of this paragraph--

(A) an involuntary conversion described in section 1033 shall be considered an exchange of the property converted for the property acquired, and

(B) a distribution to which section 355 (or so much of section 356 as relates to section 355) applies shall be treated as an exchange.

(2) In determining the period for which the taxpayer has held property however acquired there shall be included the period for which such property was held by any other person, if under this chapter such property has, for the purpose of determining gain or loss from a sale or exchange, the same basis in whole or in part in his hands as it would have in the hands of such other person.

***

(4) In determining the period for which the taxpayer has held stock or securities the acquisition of which (or the contract or option to acquire which) resulted in the nondeductibility (under section 1091 relating to wash sales) of the loss from the sale or other disposition of substantially identical stock or securities, there shall be included the period for which he held the stock or securities the loss from.

954

Sec. 1223.   Holding period of property

***

(7) In determining the period for which the taxpayer has held a residence, the acquisition of which resulted under section 1034 (as in effect on the day before the date of the enactment of the Taxpayer Relief Act of 1997) in the nonrecognition of any part of the gain realized on the sale or exchange of another residence, there shall be included the period for which such other 5 residence had been held as of the date of such sale or exchange.

***

(8) In determining the period for which the taxpayer has held a commodity acquired in satisfaction of a commodity futures contract (other than a commodity futures contract to which section 1256 applies) there shall be included the period for which he held the commodity 10 futures contract if such commodity futures contract was a capital asset in his hands.

***

(10) In the case of a person acquiring property from a decedent or to whom property passed from a decedent (within the meaning of section 1014(b)), if--

 (A) the basis of such property in the hands of such person is determined under section 15 1014, and

 (B) such property is sold or otherwise disposed of by such person within 1 year after the decedent's death,

then such person shall be considered to have held such property for more than 1 year.

***   20

(14) Except for purposes of sections 1202(a)(2), 1202(c)(2)(A), 1400B(b), and 1400F(b), in determining the period for which the taxpayer has held property the acquisition of which resulted under section 1045 or 1397B in the nonrecognition of any part of the gain realized on the sale of other property, there shall be included the period for which such other property has been held as of the date of such sale.   25

(15) If the security to which a securities futures contract (as defined in section 1234B) relates (other than a contract to which section 1256 applies) is acquired in satisfaction of such contract, in determining the period for which the taxpayer has held such security, there shall be included the period for which the taxpayer held such contract if such contract was a capital asset in the hands of the taxpayer.   30

***

Reg. § 1.1223-1   Determination of period for which capital assets are held.

(a) The holding period of property received in an exchange by a taxpayer includes the period for which the property which he exchanged was held by him, if the property received has the same basis in whole or in part for determining gain or loss in the hands 35 of the taxpayer as the property exchanged. However, this rule shall apply, in the case of exchanges after March 1, 1954, only if the property exchanged was at the time of the exchange a capital asset in the hands of the taxpayer or property used in his trade or business as defined in section 1231(b). For the purposes of this paragraph, the term exchange includes the following transactions: 40

(1) An involuntary conversion described in section 1033, and

(2) A distribution to which section 355 (or so much of section 356 as relates to section 355) applies.

Thus, if property acquired as the result of a compulsory or involuntary conversion of other property of the taxpayer has under section 1033(c) the same basis in whole or in part in 45 the hands of the taxpayer as the property so converted, its acquisition is treated as an exchange and the holding period of the newly acquired property shall include the period during which the converted property was held by the taxpayer. Thus, also, where stock of

Sec. 1223. Holding period of property

a controlled corporation is received by a taxpayer pursuant to a distribution to which section 355 (or so much of section 356 as relates to section 355) applies, the distribution is treated as an exchange and the period for which the taxpayer has held the stock of the controlled corporation shall include the period for which he held the stock of the
5 distributing corporation with respect to which such distribution was made.

(b) The holding period of property in the hands of a taxpayer shall include the period during which the property was held by any other person, if such property has the same basis in whole or in part in the hands of the taxpayer for determining gain or loss from a sale or exchange as it would have in the hands of such other person. For example, the
10 period for which property acquired by gift after December 31, 1920, was held by the donor must be included in determining the period for which the property was held by the taxpayer if, under the provisions of section 1015, such property has, for the purpose of determining gain or loss from the sale or exchange, the same basis in the hands of the taxpayer as it would have in the hands of the donor.

15   (c) In determining the period for which the taxpayer has held stock or securities received upon a distribution where no gain was recognized to the distributee under section 1081(c) (or under section 112(g) of the Revenue Act of 1928 (45 Stat. 818) or the Revenue Act of 1932 (47 Stat. 197)), there shall be included the period for which he held the stock or securities in the distributing corporation before the receipt of the stock or
20 securities on such distribution.

(d) If the acquisition of stock or securities resulted in the nondeductibility (under section 1091, relating to wash sales) of the loss from the sale or other disposition of substantially identical stock or securities, the holding period of the newly acquired securities shall include the period for which the taxpayer held the securities with respect
25 to which the loss was not allowable.

(e) The period for which the taxpayer has held stock, or stock subscription rights, received on a distribution shall be determined as though the stock dividend, or stock right, as the case may be, were the stock in respect of which the dividend was issued if the basis for determining gain or loss upon the sale or other disposition of such stock
30 dividend or stock right is determined under section 307. If the basis of stock received by a taxpayer pursuant to a spin-off is determined under so much of section 1052(c) as refers to section 113(a)(23) of the Internal Revenue Code of 1939, and such stock is sold or otherwise disposed of in a taxable year which is subject to the Internal Revenue Code of 1954, the period for which the taxpayer has held the stock received in such spin-off shall
35 include the period for which he held the stock of the distributing corporation with respect to which such distribution was made.

(f) The period for which the taxpayer has held stock or securities issued to him by a corporation pursuant to the exercise by him of rights to acquire such stock or securities from the corporation will, in every case and whether or not the receipt of taxable gain was
40 recognized in connection with the distribution of the rights, begin with and include the day upon which the rights to acquire such stock or securities were exercised. A taxpayer will be deemed to have exercised rights received from a corporation to acquire stock or securities therein where there is an expression of assent to the terms of such rights made by the taxpayer in the manner requested or authorized by the corporation.

45   (g) The period for which the taxpayer has held a residence, the acquisition of which resulted under the provisions of section 1034 in the nonrecognition of any part of the gain realized on the sale or exchange of another residence, shall include the period for which such other residence had been held as of the date of such sale or exchange. See § 1.1034-1. For purposes of this paragraph, the term sale or exchange includes an
50 involuntary conversion occurring after December 31, 1950, and before January 1, 1954.

(h) If a taxpayer accepts delivery of a commodity in satisfaction of a commodity

Sec. 1223. Holding period of property

futures contract, the holding period of the commodity shall include the period for which the taxpayer held the commodity futures contract, if such futures contract was a capital asset in his hands.

(i) If shares of stock in a corporation are sold from lots purchased at different dates or at different prices and the identity of the lots cannot be determined, the rules prescribed by the regulations under section 1012 for determining the cost or other basis of such stocks so sold or transferred shall also apply for the purpose of determining the holding period of such stock.

(j) In the case of a person acquiring property, or to whom property passed, from a decedent (within the meaning of section 1014(b)) dying after December 31, 1970, such person shall be considered to have held the property for more than 1 year (6 months for taxable years beginning before 1977; 9 months for taxable years beginning in 1977) if the property:

(1) Has a basis in the hands of such person which is determined in whole or in part under section 1014, and

(2) Is sold or otherwise disposed of by such person within 6 months after the decedent's death.

The provisions of this paragraph apply to sales of such property included in the decedent's gross estate for the purposes of the estate tax by the executor or administrator of the estate and to sales of such property by other persons who have acquired property from the decedent. The provisions of this paragraph may also be applicable to cases involving joint tenancies, community property, and properties transferred in contemplation of death. Thus, if a surviving joint tenant, who acquired property by right of survivorship, sells or otherwise disposes of such property within 6 months after the date of the decedent's death, and the basis of the property in his hands is determined in whole or in part under section 1014, the property shall be considered to have been held by the surviving joint tenant for more than 6 months. Similarly, a surviving spouse's share of community property shall be considered to have been held by her for more than 6 months if it is sold or otherwise disposed of within 6 months after the date of the decedent's death, regardless of when the property was actually acquired by the marital community. For the purposes of this paragraph, it is immaterial that the sale or other disposition produces gain or loss. If property is considered to have been held for more than 6 months by reason of this paragraph, it also is considered to have been held for that period for purposes of section 1231 (if that section is otherwise applicable).

***

[T.D. 6500, 25 FR 12005, Nov. 26, 1960; T.D. 7238, 37 FR 28717, Dec. 29, 1972; T.D. 7728, 45 FR 72650, Nov. 3, 1980]

Sec. 1231. Property used in the trade or business and involuntary conversions

(a) General rule. --

(1) Gains exceed losses. -- If--

(A) the section 1231 gains for any taxable year, exceed

(B) the section 1231 losses for such taxable year,

such gains and losses shall be treated as long-term capital gains or long-term capital losses, as the case may be.

(2) Gains do not exceed losses. -- If--

(A) the section 1231 gains for any taxable year, do not exceed

Sec. 1231. Property used in the trade or business and involuntary conversions

(B) the section 1231 losses for such taxable year,

such gains and losses shall not be treated as gains and losses from sales or exchanges of capital assets.

(3) Section 1231 gains and losses. -- For purposes of this subsection--

(A) Section 1231 gain. -- The term "section 1231 gain" means--

(i) any recognized gain on the sale or exchange of property used in the trade or business, and

(ii) any recognized gain from the compulsory or involuntary conversion (as a result of destruction in whole or in part, theft or seizure, or an exercise of the power of requisition or condemnation or the threat or imminence thereof) into other property or money of--

(I) property used in the trade or business, or

(II) any capital asset which is held for more than 1 year and is held in connection with a trade or business or a transaction entered into for profit.

(B) Section 1231 loss. -- The term "section 1231 loss" means any recognized loss from a sale or exchange or conversion described in subparagraph (A).

(4) Special rules. -- For purposes of this subsection--

(A) In determining under this subsection whether gains exceed losses--

(i) the section 1231 gains shall be included only if and to the extent taken into account in computing gross income, and

(ii) the section 1231 losses shall be included only if and to the extent taken into account in computing taxable income, except that section 1211 shall not apply.

(B) Losses (including losses not compensated for by insurance or otherwise) on the destruction, in whole or in part, theft or seizure, or requisition or condemnation of--

(i) property used in the trade or business, or

(ii) capital assets which are held for more than 1 year and are held in connection with a trade or business or a transaction entered into for profit,

shall be treated as losses from a compulsory or involuntary conversion.

(C) In the case of any involuntary conversion (subject to the provisions of this subsection but for this sentence) arising from fire, storm, shipwreck, or other casualty, or from theft, of any--

(i) property used in the trade or business, or

(ii) any capital asset which is held for more than 1 year and is held in connection with a trade or business or a transaction entered into for profit,

this subsection shall not apply to such conversion (whether resulting in gain or loss) if during the taxable year the recognized losses from such conversions exceed the recognized gains from such conversions.

(b) Definition of property used in the trade or business. -- For purposes of this section--

(1) General rule. -- The term "property used in the trade or business" means property used in the trade or business, of a character which is subject to the allowance for depreciation provided in section 167, held for more than 1 year, and real property used in the trade or business, held for more than 1 year, which is not -

(A) property of a kind which would properly be includible in the inventory of the taxpayer if on hand at the close of the taxable year,

Sec. 1231. Property used in the trade or business and involuntary conversions

    (B) property held by the taxpayer primarily for sale to customers in the ordinary course of his trade or business,

    (C) a copyright, a literary, musical, or artistic composition, a letter or memorandum, or similar property, held by a taxpayer described in paragraph (3) of section 1221(a), or

    (D) a publication of the United States Government (including the Congressional Record) which is received from the United States Government, or any agency thereof, other than by purchase at the price at which it is offered for sale to the public, and which is held by a taxpayer described in paragraph (5) of section 1221(a).

    (2) Timber, coal, or domestic iron ore. -- Such term includes timber, coal, and iron ore with respect to which section 631 applies.

    (3) Livestock. -- Such term includes--

    (A) cattle and horses, regardless of age, held by the taxpayer for draft, breeding, dairy, or sporting purposes, and held by him for 24 months or more from the date of acquisition, and

    (B) other livestock, regardless of age, held by the taxpayer for draft, breeding, dairy, or sporting purposes, and held by him for 12 months or more from the date of acquisition.

Such term does not include poultry.

    (4) Unharvested crop. -- In the case of an unharvested crop on land used in the trade or business and held for more than 1 year, if the crop and the land are sold or exchanged (or compulsorily or involuntarily converted) at the same time and to the same person, the crop shall be considered as "property used in the trade or business."

(c) Recapture of net ordinary losses. --

    (1) In general. -- The net section 1231 gain for any taxable year shall be treated as ordinary income to the extent such gain does not exceed the non-recaptured net section 1231 losses.

    (2) Non-recaptured net section 1231 losses. -- For purposes of this subsection, the term "non-recaptured net section 1231 losses" means the excess of--

    (A) the aggregate amount of the net section 1231 losses for the 5 most recent preceding taxable years beginning after December 31, 1981, over

    (B) the portion of such losses taken into account under paragraph (1) for such preceding taxable years.

    (3) Net section 1231 gain. -- For purposes of this subsection, the term "net section 1231 gain" means the excess of--

    (A) the section 1231 gains, over

    (B) the section 1231 losses.

    (4) Net section 1231 loss. -- For purposes of this subsection, the term "net section 1231 loss" means the excess of--

    (A) the section 1231 losses, over

    (B) the section 1231 gains.

    (5) Special rules. -- For purposes of determining the amount of the net section 1231 gain or loss for any taxable year, the rules of paragraph (4) of subsection (a) shall apply.

Sec. 1233. Gains and losses from short sales

    (a) Capital assets. -- For purposes of this subtitle, gain or loss from the short sale of property

959

Sec. 1233. Gains and losses from short sales

shall be considered as gain or loss from the sale or exchange of a capital asset to the extent that the property, including a commodity future, used to close the short sale constitutes a capital asset in the hands of the taxpayer.

(b) Short-term gains and holding periods. -- If gain or loss from a short sale is considered as
5 gain or loss from the sale or exchange of a capital asset under subsection (a) and if on the date of such short sale substantially identical property has been held by the taxpayer for not more than 1 year (determined without regard to the effect, under paragraph (2) of this subsection, of such short sale on the holding period), or if substantially identical property is acquired by the taxpayer after such short sale and on or before the date of the closing thereof--

10   **(1)** any gain on the closing of such short sale shall be considered as a gain on the sale or exchange of a capital asset held for not more than 1 year (notwithstanding the period of time any property used to close such short sale has been held); and

    (2) the holding period of such substantially identical property shall be considered to begin (notwithstanding section 1223, relating to the holding period of property) on the date of the
15   closing of the short sale, or on the date of a sale, gift, or other disposition of such property, whichever date occurs first. This paragraph shall apply to such substantially identical property in the order of the dates of the acquisition of such property, but only to so much of such property as does not exceed the quantity sold short.

For purposes of this subsection, the acquisition of an option to sell property at a fixed price shall
20 be considered as a short sale, and the exercise or failure to exercise such option shall be considered as a closing of such short sale.

(c) Certain options to sell. -- Subsection (b) shall not include an option to sell property at a fixed price acquired on the same day on which the property identified as intended to be used in exercising such option is acquired and which, if exercised, is exercised through the sale of the
25 property so identified. If the option is not exercised, the cost of the option shall be added to the basis of the property with which the option is identified. This subsection shall apply only to options acquired after August 16, 1954.

(d) Long-term losses. -- If on the date of such short sale substantially identical property has been held by the taxpayer for more than 1 year, any loss on the closing of such short sale shall be
30 considered as a loss on the sale or exchange of a capital asset held for more than 1 year (notwithstanding the period of time any property used to close such short sale has been held, and notwithstanding section 1234).

(e) Rules for application of section. --

    (1) Subsection (b)(1) or (d) shall not apply to the gain or loss, respectively, on any quantity
35   of property used to close such short sale which is in excess of the quantity of the substantially identical property referred to in the applicable subsection.

    (2) For purposes of subsections (b) and (d)--

        (A) the term "property" includes only stocks and securities (including stocks and securities dealt with on a "when issued" basis), and commodity futures, which are capital
40   assets in the hands of the taxpayer, but does not include any position to which section 1092(b) applies;

        (B) in the case of futures transactions in any commodity on or subject to the rules of a board of trade or commodity exchange, a commodity future requiring delivery in 1 calendar month shall not be considered as property substantially identical to another
45   commodity future requiring delivery in a different calendar month;

        (C) in the case of a short sale of property by an individual, the term "taxpayer", in the application of this subsection and subsections (b) and (d), shall be read as "taxpayer or his spouse"; but an individual who is legally separated from the taxpayer under a decree of

Sec. 1233.   Gains and losses from short sales

divorce or of separate maintenance shall not be considered as the spouse of the taxpayer;

(D) a securities futures contract (as defined in section 1234B) to acquire substantially identical property shall be treated as substantially identical property; and

(E) entering into a securities futures contract (as so defined) to sell shall be considered to be a short sale, and the settlement of such contract shall be considered to be the closing 5 of such short sale.

(3) Where the taxpayer enters into 2 commodity futures transactions on the same day, one requiring delivery by him in one market and the other requiring delivery to him of the same (or substantially identical) commodity in the same calendar month in a different market, and the taxpayer subsequently closes both such transactions on the same day, subsections (b) and (d) 10 shall have no application to so much of the commodity involved in either such transaction as does not exceed in quantity the commodity involved in the other.

(4)(A) In the case of a taxpayer who is a dealer in securities (within the meaning of section 1236)--

(i) if, on the date of a short sale of stock, substantially identical property which is a 15 capital asset in the hands of the taxpayer has been held for not more than 1 year, and

(ii) if such short sale is closed more than 20 days after the date on which it was made, subsection (b)(2) shall apply in respect of the holding period of such substantially identical property.

(B) For purposes of subparagraph (A)-- 20

(i) the last sentence of subsection (b) applies; and

(ii) the term "stock" means any share or certificate of stock in a corporation, any bond or other evidence of indebtedness which is convertible into any such share or certificate, or any evidence of an interest in, or right to subscribe to or purchase, any of the foregoing.

(f) Arbitrage operations in securities. -- In the case of a short sale which had been entered into 25 as an arbitrage operation, to which sale the rule of subsection (b)(2) would apply except as otherwise provided in this subsection--

(1) subsection (b)(2) shall apply first to substantially identical assets acquired for arbitrage operations held at the close of business on the day such sale is made, and only to the extent that the quantity sold short exceeds the substantially identical assets acquired for arbitrage 30 operations held at the close of business on the day such sale is made, shall the holding period of any other such identical assets held by the taxpayer be affected;

(2) in the event that assets acquired for arbitrage operations are disposed of in such manner as to create a net short position in assets acquired for arbitrage operations, such net short position shall be deemed to constitute a short sale made on that day; 35

(3) for the purpose of paragraphs (1) and (2) of this subsection the taxpayer will be deemed as of the close of any business day to hold property which he is or will be entitled to receive or acquire by virtue of any other asset acquired for arbitrage operations or by virtue of any contract he has entered into in an arbitrage operation; and

(4) for the purpose of this subsection arbitrage operations are   transactions involving the 40 purchase and sale of assets for the purpose of profiting from a current difference between the price of the asset purchased and the price of the asset sold, and in which the asset purchased, if not identical to the asset sold, is such that by virtue thereof the taxpayer is, or will be, entitled to acquire assets identical to the assets sold. Such operations must be clearly identified by the taxpayer in his records as arbitrage operations on the day of the transaction or as soon 45 thereafter as may be practicable. Assets acquired for arbitrage operations will include stocks and securities and the right to acquire stocks and securities.

Sec. 1233. Gains and losses from short sales

(g) Hedging transactions. -- This section shall not apply in the case of a hedging transaction in commodity futures.

(h) Short sales of property which becomes substantially worthless. --

(1) In general. -- If--

(A) the taxpayer enters into a short sale of property, and

(B) such property becomes substantially worthless, the taxpayer shall recognize gain in the same manner as if the short sale were closed when the property becomes substantially worthless. To the extent provided in regulations prescribed by the Secretary, the preceding sentence also shall apply with respect to any option with respect to property, any offsetting notional principal contract with respect to property, any futures or forward contract to deliver any property, and any other similar transaction.

(2) Statute of limitations. -- If property becomes substantially worthless during a taxable year and any short sale of such property remains open at the time such property becomes substantially worthless, then--

(A) the statutory period for the assessment of any deficiency attributable to any part of the gain on such transaction shall not expire before the earlier of--

(i) the date which is 3 years after the date the Secretary is notified by the taxpayer (in such manner as the Secretary may by regulations prescribe) of the substantial worthlessness of such property, or

(ii) the date which is 6 years after the date the return for such taxable year is filed, and

(B) such deficiency may be assessed before the date applicable under subparagraph (A) notwithstanding the provisions of any other law or rule of law which would otherwise prevent such assessment.

Sec. 1234. Options to buy or sell

(a) Treatment of gain or loss in the case of the purchaser. --

(1) General rule. -- Gain or loss attributable to the sale or exchange of, or loss attributable to failure to exercise, an option to buy or sell property shall be considered gain or loss from the sale or exchange of property which has the same character as the property to which the option relates has in the hands of the taxpayer (or would have in the hands of the taxpayer if acquired by him).

(2) Special rule for loss attributable to failure to exercise option. -- For purposes of paragraph (1), if loss is attributable to failure to exercise an option, the option shall be deemed to have been sold or exchanged on the day it expired.

(3) Nonapplication of subsection. -- This subsection shall not apply to--

(A) an option which constitutes property described in paragraph (1) of section 1221(a);

(B) in the case of gain attributable to the sale or exchange of an option, any income derived in connection with such option which, without regard to this subsection, is treated as other than gain from the sale or exchange of a capital asset; and

(C) a loss attributable to failure to exercise an option described in section 1233(c).

(b) Treatment of grantor of option in the case of stock, securities, or commodities. --

(1) General rule. -- In the case of the grantor of the option, gain or loss from any closing transaction with respect to, and gain on lapse of, an option in property shall be treated as a gain or loss from the sale or exchange of a capital asset held not more than 1 year.

Sec. 1234. Options to buy or sell

(2) Definitions. -- For purposes of this subsection--

(A) Closing transaction. -- The term "closing transaction" means any termination of the taxpayer's obligation under an option in property other than through the exercise or lapse of the option.

(B) Property. -- The term "property" means stocks and securities (including stocks and securities dealt with on a "when issued" basis), commodities, and commodity futures.

(3) Nonapplication of subsection. -- This subsection shall not apply to any option granted in the ordinary course of the taxpayer's trade or business of granting options.

(c) Treatment of options on section 1256 contracts and cash settlement options. --

(1) Section 1256 contracts. -- Gain or loss shall be recognized on the exercise of an option on a section 1256 contract (within the meaning of section 1256(b)).

(2) Treatment of cash settlement options. --

(A) In general. -- For purposes of subsections (a) and (b), a cash settlement option shall be treated as an option to buy or sell property.

(B) Cash settlement option. -- For purposes of subparagraph (A), the term "cash settlement option" means any option which on exercise settles in (or could be settled in) cash or property other than the underlying property.

Sec. 1234A. Gains or losses from certain terminations

Gain or loss attributable to the cancellation, lapse, expiration, or other termination of--

(1) a right or obligation (other than a securities futures contract, as defined in section 1234B) with respect to property which is (or on acquisition would be) a capital asset in the hands of the taxpayer, or

(2) a section 1256 contract (as defined in section 1256) not described in paragraph (1) which is a capital asset in the hands of the taxpayer,

shall be treated as gain or loss from the sale of a capital asset. The preceding sentence shall not apply to the retirement of any debt instrument (whether or not through a trust or other participation arrangement).

Sec. 1234B. Gains or losses from securities futures contracts

(a) Treatment of gain or loss. --

(1) In general. -- Gain or loss attributable to the sale, exchange, or termination of a securities futures contract shall be considered gain or loss from the sale or exchange of property which has the same character as the property to which the contract relates has in the hands of the taxpayer (or would have in the hands of the taxpayer if acquired by the taxpayer).

(2) Nonapplication of subsection. -- This subsection shall not apply to--

(A) a contract which constitutes property described in paragraph (1) or (7) of section 1221(a), and

(B) any income derived in connection with a contract which, without regard to this subsection, is treated as other than gain from the sale or exchange of a capital asset.

(b) Short-term gains and losses. -- Except as provided in the regulations under section 1092(b) or this section, or in section 1233, if gain or loss on the sale, exchange, or termination of a

Sec. 1234B. Gains or losses from securities futures contracts

securities futures contract to sell property is considered as gain or loss from the sale or exchange of a capital asset, such gain or loss shall be treated as short-term capital gain or loss.

(c) **Securities futures contract.** -- For purposes of this section, the term "securities futures contract" means any security future (as defined in section 3(a)(55)(A) of the Securities Exchange Act of 1934, as in effect on the date of the enactment of this section). The Secretary may prescribe regulations regarding the status of contracts the values of which are determined directly or indirectly by reference to any index which becomes (or ceases to be) a narrow-based security index (as defined for purposes of section 1256(g)(6)).

(d) **Contracts not treated as commodity futures contracts.** -- For purposes of this title, a securities futures contract shall not be treated as a commodity futures contract.

(e) **Regulations.** -- The Secretary shall prescribe such regulations as may be appropriate to provide for the proper treatment of securities futures contracts under this title.

(f) **Cross reference.** -- For special rules relating to dealer securities futures contracts, see section 1256.

Sec. 1235. Sale or exchange of patents

(a) **General.** -- A transfer (other than by gift, inheritance, or devise) of property consisting of all substantial rights to a patent, or an undivided interest therein which includes a part of all such rights, by any holder shall be considered the sale or exchange of a capital asset held for more than 1 year, regardless of whether or not payments in consideration of such transfer are -

(1) payable periodically over a period generally coterminous with the transferee's use of the patent, or

(2) contingent on the productivity, use, or disposition of the property transferred.

(b) **"Holder" defined.** -- For purposes of this section, the term "holder" means--

(1) any individual whose efforts created such property, or

(2) any other individual who has acquired his interest in such property in exchange for consideration in money or money's worth paid to such creator prior to actual reduction to practice of the invention covered by the patent, if such individual is neither -

(A) the employer of such creator, nor

(B) related to such creator (within the meaning of subsection (d)).

***

(d) **Related persons.** -- Subsection (a) shall not apply to any transfer, directly or indirectly, between persons specified within any one of the paragraphs of section 267(b) or persons described in section 707(b); except that, in applying section 267(b) and (c) and section 707(b) for purposes of this section--

(1) the phrase "25 percent or more" shall be substituted for the phrase "more than 50 percent" each place it appears in section 267(b) or 707(b), and

(2) paragraph (4) of section 267(c) shall be treated as providing that the family of an individual shall include only his spouse, ancestors, and lineal descendants.

***

Sec. 1236. Dealers in securities

(a) **Capital gains.** -- Gain by a dealer in securities from the sale or exchange of any security shall in no event be considered as gain from the sale or exchange of a capital asset unless--

964

Sec. 1236. Dealers in securities

(1) the security was, before the close of the day on which it was acquired (or such earlier time as the Secretary may prescribe by regulations), clearly identified in the dealer's records as a security held for investment; and

(2) the security was not, at any time after the close of such day (or such earlier time), held by such dealer primarily for sale to customers in the ordinary course of his trade or business. 5

(b) Ordinary losses. -- Loss by a dealer in securities from the sale or exchange of any security shall, except as otherwise provided in section 582(c), (relating to bond, etc., losses of banks), in no event be considered as ordinary loss if at any time after November 19, 1951, the security was clearly identified in the dealer's records as a security held for investment.

(c) Definition of security. -- For purposes of this section, the term "security" means any share 10 of stock in any corporation, certificate of stock or interest in any corporation, note, bond, debenture, or evidence of indebtedness, or any evidence of an interest in or right to subscribe to or purchase any of the foregoing.

(d) Special rule for floor specialists. --

(1) In general. -- In the case of a floor specialist (but only with respect to acquisitions, in 15 connection with his duties on an exchange, of stock in which the specialist is registered with the exchange), subsection (a) shall be applied--

(A) by inserting "the 7th business day following" before "the day" the first place it appears in paragraph (1) and by inserting "7th business" before "day" in paragraph (2), and

(B) by striking the parenthetical phrase in paragraph (1). 20

(2) Floor specialist. -- The term "floor specialist" means a person who is--

(A) a member of a national securities exchange,

(B) is registered as a specialist with the exchange, and

(C) meets the requirements for specialists established by the Securities and Exchange Commission. 25

(e) Special rule for options. -- For purposes of subsection (a), any security acquired by a dealer pursuant to an option held by such dealer may be treated as held for investment only if the dealer, before the close of the day on which the option was acquired, clearly identified the option on his records as held for investment. For purposes of the preceding sentence, the term "option" includes the right to subscribe to or purchase any security. 30

Reg. § 1.1236-1 Dealers in securities.

(a) *Capital gains.* Section 1236(a) provides that gain realized by a dealer in securities from the sale or exchange of a security (as defined in paragraph (c) of this section) shall not be considered as gain from the sale or exchange of a capital asset unless: 35

(1) The security is, before the expiration of the thirtieth day after the date of its acquisition, clearly identified in the dealer's records as a security held for investment or, if acquired before October 20, 1951, was so identified before November 20, 1951; and

(2) The security is not held by the dealer primarily for sale to customers in the ordinary course of his trade or business at any time after the identification referred to in 40 subparagraph (1) of this paragraph has been made.
Unless both of these requirements are met, the gain is considered as gain from the sale of assets held by the dealer primarily for sale to customers in the course of his business.

(b) *Ordinary losses.* Section 1236(b) provides that a loss sustained by a dealer in securities from the sale or exchange of a security shall not be considered a loss from the 45 sale or exchange of property which is not a capital asset if at any time after November 19, 1951, the security has been clearly identified in the dealer's records as a security held for investment. Once a security has been identified after November 19, 1951, as being

Sec. 1236. Dealers in securities

held by the dealer for investment, it shall retain that character for purposes of determining loss on its ultimate disposition, even though at the time of its disposition the dealer holds it primarily for sale to his customers in the ordinary course of his business. However, section 1236 has no application to the extent that section 582(c) applies to losses of banks.

(c) *Definitions*--(1) *Security*. For the purposes of this section, the term security means any share of stock in any corporation, any certificate of stock or interest in any corporation, any note, bond, debenture, or other evidence of indebtedness, or any evidence of any interest in, or right to subscribe to or purchase, any of the foregoing.

(2) *Dealer in securities*. For definition of a dealer in securities, see the regulations under section 471.

(d) *Identification of security in dealer's records*. (1) A security is clearly identified in the dealer's records as a security held for investment when there is an accounting separation of the security from other securities, as by making appropriate entries in the dealer's books of account to distinguish the security from inventories and to designate it as an investment and by (i) indicating with such entries, to the extent feasible, the individual serial number of, or other characteristic symbol imprinted upon, the individual security, or (ii) adopting any other method of identification satisfactory to the Commissioner.

(2) In computing the 30-day period prescribed by section 1236(a), the first day of the period is the day following the date of acquisition. Thus, in the case of a security acquired on March 18, 1957, the 30-day period expires at midnight on April 17, 1957.

[T.D. 6500, 25 FR 12015, Nov. 26, 1960; T.D. 6726, 29 FR 5667, Apr. 29, 1964]

Sec. 1237. Real property subdivided for sale

(a) **General.** -- Any lot or parcel which is part of a tract of real property in the hands of a taxpayer other than a C corporation shall not be deemed to be held primarily for sale to customers in the ordinary course of trade or business at the time of sale solely because of the taxpayer having subdivided such tract for purposes of sale or because of any activity incident to such subdivision or sale, if--

(1) such tract, or any lot or parcel thereof, had not previously been held by such taxpayer primarily for sale to customers in the ordinary course of trade or business (unless such tract at such previous time would have been covered by this section) and, in the same taxable year in which the sale occurs, such taxpayer does not so hold any other real property; and

(2) no substantial improvement that substantially enhances the value of the lot or parcel sold is made by the taxpayer on such tract while held by the taxpayer or is made pursuant to a contract of sale entered into between the taxpayer and the buyer. For purposes of this paragraph, an improvement shall be deemed to be made by the taxpayer if such improvement was made by--

(A) the taxpayer or members of his family (as defined in section 267(c)(4)), by a corporation controlled by the taxpayer, an S corporation which included the taxpayer as a shareholder, or by a partnership which included the taxpayer as a partner; or

(B) a lessee, but only if the improvement constitutes income to the taxpayer; or

(C) Federal, State, or local government, or political subdivision thereof, but only if the improvement constitutes an addition to basis for the taxpayer; and

(3) such lot or parcel, except in the case of real property acquired by inheritance or devise, is held by the taxpayer for a period of 5 years.

(b) **Special rules for application of section.** --

Sec. 1237. Real property subdivided for sale

(1) Gains. -- If more than 5 lots or parcels contained in the same tract of real property are sold or exchanged, gain from any sale or exchange (which occurs in or after the taxable year in which the sixth lot or parcel is sold or exchanged) of any lot or parcel which comes within the provisions of paragraphs (1), (2) and (3) of subsection (a) of this section shall be deemed to be gain from the sale of property held primarily for sale to customers in the ordinary course of the   5 trade or business to the extent of 5 percent of the selling price.

(2) Expenditures of sale. -- For the purpose of computing gain under paragraph (1) of this subsection, expenditures incurred in connection with the sale or exchange of any lot or parcel shall neither be allowed as a deduction in computing taxable income, nor treated as reducing the amount realized on such sale or exchange; but so much of such expenditures as does not   10 exceed the portion of gain deemed under paragraph (1) of this subsection to be gain from the sale of property held primarily for sale to customers in the ordinary course of trade or business shall be so allowed as a deduction, and the remainder, if any, shall be treated as reducing the amount realized on such sale or exchange.

(3) Necessary improvements. -- No improvement shall be deemed a substantial   15 improvement for purposes of subsection (a) if the lot or parcel is held by the taxpayer for a period of 10 years and if--

(A) such improvement is the building or installation of water, sewer, or drainage facilities or roads (if such improvement would except for this paragraph constitute a substantial improvement);   20

(B) it is shown to the satisfaction of the Secretary that the lot or parcel, the value of which was substantially enhanced by such improvement, would not have been marketable at the prevailing local price for similar building sites without such improvement; and

(C) the taxpayer elects, in accordance with regulations prescribed by the Secretary, to make no adjustment to basis of the lot or parcel, or of any other property owned by the   25 taxpayer, on account of the expenditures for such improvements. Such election shall not make any item deductible which would not otherwise be deductible.

(c) Tract defined. -- For purposes of this section, the term "tract of real property" means a single piece of real property, except that 2 or more pieces of real property shall be considered a tract if at any time they were contiguous in the hands of the taxpayer or if they would be   30 contiguous except for the interposition of a road, street, railroad, stream, or similar property. If, following the sale or exchange of any lot or parcel from a tract of real property, no further sales or exchanges of any other lots or parcels from the remainder of such tract are made for a period of 5 years, such remainder shall be deemed a tract.

  35

Reg. §. 1.1237-1   Real property subdivided for sale.
(a) General rule--

***

(4) Section 1237 not exclusive. (i) The rule in section 1237 is not exclusive in its application. Section 1237 has no application in determining whether or not real property   40 is held by a taxpayer primarily for sale in his business if any requirement under the section is not met. Also, even though the conditions of section 1237 are met, the rules of section 1237 are not applicable if without regard to section 1237 the real property sold would not have been considered real property held primarily for sale to customers in the ordinary course of his business. Thus, the district director may at all times conclude from   45 convincing evidence that the taxpayer held the real property solely as an investment. Furthermore, whether or not the conditions of section 1237 are met, the section has no application to losses realized upon the sale of realty from subdivided property.

(ii) If, owing solely to the application of section 1237, the real property sold is deemed

Sec. 1237. Real property subdivided for sale

not to have been held primarily for sale in the ordinary course of business, any gain realized uponsuch sale shall be treated as ordinary income to the extent provided in section 1237(b)(1) and (2) and paragraph (e) of this section. Any additional gain realized upon the sale shall be treated as gain arising from the sale of a capital asset or, if the
5 circumstances so indicate, as gain arising from the sale of real property used in the trade or business as defined in section 1231(b)(1). For the relationship between sections 1237 and 1231, see paragraph (f) of this section.

Sec. 1239. Gain from sale of depreciable property between certain related taxpayers

(a) Treatment of gain as ordinary income. -- In the case of a sale or exchange of property,
10 directly or indirectly, between related persons, any gain recognized to the transferor shall be treated as ordinary income if such property is, in the hands of the transferee, of a character which is subject to the allowance for depreciation provided in section 167.

(b) Related persons. -- For purposes of subsection (a), the term "related persons" means--

(1) a person and all entities which are controlled entities with respect to such person,

15 **(2)** a taxpayer and any trust in which such taxpayer (or his spouse) is a beneficiary, unless such beneficiary's interest in the trust is a remote contingent interest (within the meaning of section 318(a)(3)(B)(i)), and

(3) except in the case of a sale or exchange in satisfaction of a pecuniary bequest, an executor of an estate and a beneficiary of such estate.

20 **(c) Controlled entity defined.** --

(1) General rule. -- For purposes of this section, the term "controlled entity" means, with respect to any person--

(A) a corporation more than 50 percent of the value of the outstanding stock of which is owned (directly or indirectly) by or for such person,

25 **(B)** a partnership more than 50 percent of the capital interest or profits interest in which is owned (directly or indirectly) by or for such person, and

(C) any entity which is a related person to such person under paragraph (3), (10), (11), or (12) of section 267(b).

(2) Constructive ownership. -- For purposes of this section, ownership shall be determined
30 in accordance with rules similar to the rules under section 267(c) (other than paragraph (3) thereof).

(d) Employer and related employee association. -- For purposes of subsection (a), the term "related person" also includes--

(1) an employer and any person related to the employer (within the meaning of subsection
35 (b)), and

(2) a welfare benefit fund (within the meaning of section 419(e)) which is controlled directly or indirectly by persons referred to in paragraph (1).

(e) Patent applications treated as depreciable property. -- For purposes of this section, a patent application shall be treated as property which, in the hands of the transferee, is of a
40 character which is subject to the allowance for depreciation provided in section 167.

Sec. 1241. Cancellation of lease or distributor's agreement

(11) Special rules for certain combination contracts providing long-term care insurance.--

Sec. 1241. Cancellation of lease or distributor's agreement

Notwithstanding paragraphs (2), (5)(C), and (10), in the case of any charge against the cash value of an annuity contract or the cash surrender value of a life insurance contract made as payment for coverage under a qualified long-term care insurance contract which is part of or a rider on such annuity or life insurance contract--

    (A) the investment in the contract shall be reduced (but not below zero) by such charge, 5 and

    (B) such charge shall not be includible in gross income.

Amounts received by a lessee for the cancellation of a lease, or by a distributor of goods for the cancellation of a distributor's agreement (if the distributor has a substantial capital investment in the distributorship), shall be considered as amounts received in exchange for such lease or 10 agreement.

Sec. 1242. Losses on small business investment company stock

If--

    (1) a loss is on stock in a small business investment company operating under the Small 15 Business Investment Act of 1958, and

    (2) such loss would (but for this section) be a loss from the sale or exchange of a capital asset,

then such loss shall be treated as an ordinary loss. For purposes of section 172 (relating to the net operating loss deduction) any amount of loss treated by reason of this section as an ordinary loss 20 shall be treated as attributable to a trade or business of the taxpayer.

Sec. 1243. Loss of small business investment company

In the case of a small business investment company operating under the Small Business Investment Act of 1958, if--   25

    (1) a loss is on stock received pursuant to the conversion privilege of convertible debentures acquired pursuant to section 304 of the Small Business Investment Act of 1958, and

    (2) such loss would (but for this section) be a loss from the sale or exchange of a capital asset,

then such loss shall be treated as an ordinary loss.   30

Sec. 1244. Losses on small business stock

    (a) General rule. -- In the case of an individual, a loss on section 1244 stock issued to such individual or to a partnership which would (but for this section) be treated as a loss from the sale or exchange of a capital asset shall, to the extent provided in this section, be treated as an ordinary 35 loss.

    (b) Maximum amount for any taxable year. -- For any taxable year the aggregate amount treated by the taxpayer by reason of this section as an ordinary loss shall not exceed--

    (1) $50,000, or

    (2) $100,000, in the case of a husband and wife filing a joint return for such year under 40 section 6013.

    (c) Section 1244 stock defined. --

Sec. 1244. Losses on small business stock

(1) **In general.** -- For purposes of this section, the term "section 1244 stock" means stock in a domestic corporation if--

  (A) at the time such stock is issued, such corporation was a small business corporation,

  (B) such stock was issued by such corporation for money or other property (other than stock and securities), and

  (C) such corporation, during the period of its 5 most recent taxable years ending before the date the loss on such stock was sustained, derived more than 50 percent of its aggregate gross receipts from sources other than royalties, rents, dividends, interests, annuities, and sales or exchanges of stocks or securities.

(2) **Rules for application of paragraph (1)(C).** --

  (A) **Period taken into account with respect to new corporations.** -- For purposes of paragraph (1)(C), if the corporation has not been in existence for 5 taxable years ending before the date the loss on the stock was sustained, there shall be substituted for such 5-year period--

    (i) the period of the corporation's taxable years ending before such date, or

    (ii) if the corporation has not been in existence for 1 taxable year ending before such date, the period such corporation has been in existence before such date.

  (B) **Gross receipts from sales of securities.** -- For purposes of paragraph (1)(C), gross receipts from the sales or exchanges of stock or securities shall be taken into account only to the extent of gains therefrom.

  (C) **Nonapplication where deductions exceed gross income.** -- Paragraph (1)(C) shall not apply with respect to any corporation if, for the period taken into account for purposes of paragraph (1)(C), the amount of the deductions allowed by this chapter (other than by sections 172, 243, 244, and 245) exceeds the amount of gross income.

(3) **Small business corporation defined.** --

  (A) **In general.** -- For purposes of this section, a corporation shall be treated as a small business corporation if the aggregate amount of money and other property received by the corporation for stock, as a contribution to capital, and as paid-in surplus, does not exceed $1,000,000. The determination under the preceding sentence shall be made as of the time of the issuance of the stock in question but shall include amounts received for such stock and for all stock theretofore issued.

  (B) **Amount taken into account with respect to property.** -- For purposes of subparagraph (A), the amount taken into account with respect to any property other than money shall be the amount equal to the adjusted basis to the corporation of such property for determining gain, reduced by any liability to which the property was subject or which was assumed by the corporation. The determination under the preceding sentence shall be made as of the time the property was received by the corporation.

(d) **Special rules.** --

(1) **Limitations on amount of ordinary loss.** --

  (A) **Contributions of property having basis in excess of value.** -- If--

    (i) section 1244 stock was issued in exchange for property,

    (ii) the basis of such stock in the hands of the taxpayer is determined by reference to the basis in his hands of such property, and

    (iii) the adjusted basis (for determining loss) of such property immediately before the exchange exceeded its fair market value at such time,

  then in computing the amount of the loss on such stock for purposes of this section the

970

basis of such stock shall be reduced by an amount equal to the excess described in clause (iii).

(B) Increases in basis. -- In computing the amount of the loss on stock for purposes of this section, any increase in the basis of such stock (through contributions to the capital of the corporation, or otherwise) shall be treated as allocable to stock which is not section 1244 stock.

(2) Recapitalizations, changes in name, etc. -- To the extent provided in regulations prescribed by the Secretary, stock in a corporation, the basis of which (in the hands of a taxpayer) is determined in whole or in part by reference to the basis in his hands of stock in such corporation which meets the requirements of subsection (c)(1) (other than subparagraph (C) thereof), or which is received in a reorganization described in section 368(a)(1)(F) in exchange for stock which meets such requirements, shall be treated as meeting such requirements. For purposes of paragraphs (1)(C) and (3)(A) of subsection (c), a successor corporation in a reorganization described in section 368(a)(1)(F) shall be treated as the same corporation as its predecessor.

(3) Relationship to net operating loss deduction. -- For purposes of section 172 (relating to the net operating loss deduction), any amount of loss treated by reason of this section as an ordinary loss shall be treated as attributable to a trade or business of the taxpayer.

***

Sec. 1245.   Gain from dispositions of certain depreciable property

(a) General rule. --

(1) Ordinary income. -- Except as otherwise provided in this section, if section 1245 property is disposed of the amount by which the lower of--

(A) the recomputed basis of the property, or

(B)(i) in the case of a sale, exchange, or involuntary conversion, the amount realized, or

(ii) in the case of any other disposition, the fair market value of such property,

exceeds the adjusted basis of such property shall be treated as ordinary income. Such gain shall be recognized notwithstanding any other provision of this subtitle.

(2) Recomputed basis. -- For purposes of this section -

(A) In general. -- The term "recomputed basis" means, with respect to any property, its adjusted basis recomputed by adding thereto all adjustments reflected in such adjusted basis on account of deductions (whether in respect of the same or other property) allowed or allowable to the taxpayer or to any other person for depreciation or amortization.

(B) Taxpayer may establish amount allowed. -- For purposes of subparagraph (A), if the taxpayer can establish by adequate records or other sufficient evidence that the amount allowed for depreciation or amortization for any period was less than the amount allowable, the amount added for such period shall be the amount allowed.

(C) Certain deductions treated as amortization. -- Any deduction allowable under section 179, 179A, 179B, 179C, 179D, 179E, 181, 190, 193, or 194 shall be treated as if it were a deduction allowable for amortization.

(3) Section 1245 property. -- For purposes of this section, the term "section 1245 property" means any property which is or has been property of a character subject to the allowance for depreciation provided in section 167 and is either -

(A) personal property,

(B) other property (not including a building or its structural components) but only if such

Sec. 1245. Gain from dispositions of certain depreciable property

other property is tangible and has an adjusted basis in which there are reflected adjustments described in paragraph (2) for a period in which such property (or other property)--

    (i) was used as an integral part of manufacturing, production, or extraction or of furnishing transportation, communications, electrical energy, gas, water, or sewage disposal services,

    (ii) constituted a research facility used in connection with any of the activities referred to in clause (i), or

    (iii) constituted a facility used in connection with any of the activities referred to in clause (i) for the bulk storage of fungible commodities (including commodities in a liquid or gaseous state),

(C) so much of any real property (other than any property described in subparagraph (B)) which has an adjusted basis in which there are reflected adjustments for amortization under section 169, 179, 179A, 179B, 179C, 179D, 179E, 185, 188 (as in effect before its repeal by the Revenue Reconciliation Act of 1990), 190, 193, or 194,

(D) a single purpose agricultural or horticultural structure (as defined in section 168(i) (13)),

(E) a storage facility (not including a building or its structural components) used in connection with the distribution of petroleum or any primary product of petroleum, or

(F) any railroad grading or tunnel bore (as defined in section 168(e)(4)).

(b) Exceptions and limitations. --

(1) Gifts. -- Subsection (a) shall not apply to a disposition by gift.

(2) Transfers at death. -- Except as provided in section 691 (relating to income in respect of a decedent), subsection (a) shall not apply to a transfer at death.

***

(4) Like kind exchanges; involuntary conversions, etc. -- If property is disposed of and gain (determined without regard to this section) is not recognized in whole or in part under section 1031 or 1033, then the amount of gain taken into account by the transferor under subsection (a)(1) shall not exceed the sum of--

(A) the amount of gain recognized on such disposition (determined without regard to this section), plus

(B) the fair market value of property acquired which is not section 1245 property and which is not taken into account under subparagraph (A).

***

(9) Disposition of amortizable section 197 intangibles.--

(A) **In general. --** If a taxpayer disposes of more than 1 amortizable section 197 intangible (as defined in section 197(c)) in a transaction or a series of related transactions, all such amortizable 197 intangibles shall be treated as 1 section 1245 property for purposes of this section.

(B) **Exception. --** Subparagraph (A) shall not apply to any amortizable section 197 intangible (as so defined) with respect to which the adjusted basis exceeds the fair market value.

(c) **Adjustments to basis. --** The Secretary shall prescribe such regulations as he may deem necessary to provide for adjustments to the basis of property to reflect gain recognized under subsection (a).

Sec. 1245. Gain from dispositions of certain depreciable property

(d) Application of section. -- This section shall apply notwithstanding any other provision of this subtitle.

Reg. § 1.1245-1 General rule for treatment of gain from dispositions of certain depreciable property.

(a) *General.* (1) In general, section 1245(a)(1) provides that, upon a disposition of an item of section 1245 property, the amount by which the lower of (i) the recomputed basis of the property, or (ii) the amount realized on a sale, exchange, or involuntary conversion (or the fair market value of the property on any other disposition), exceeds the adjusted basis of the property shall be treated as gain from the sale or exchange of property which 10 is neither a capital asset nor property described in section 1231 (that is, shall be recognized as ordinary income). The amount of such gain shall be determined separately for each item of section 1245 property. In general, the term recomputed basis means the adjusted basis of property plus all adjustments reflected in such adjusted basis on account of depreciation allowed or allowable for all periods after December 31, 1961. See 15 section 1245(a)(2) and § 1.1245-2. Generally, the ordinary income treatment applies even though in the absence of section 1245 no gain would be recognized under the Code. For example, if a corporation distributes section 1245 property as a dividend, gain may be recognized as ordinary income to the corporation even though, in the absence of section 1245, section 311(a) would preclude any recognition of gain to the corporation. 20 For the definition of section 1245 property, see section 1245(a)(3) and § 1.1245-3. For exceptions and limitations to the application of section 1245(a)(1), see section 1245(b) and § 1.1245-4.

***

(b) *Sale, exchange, or involuntary conversion.* (1) In the case of a sale, exchange, or 25 involuntary conversion of section 1245 property, the gain to which section 1245(a)(1) applies is the amount by which (i) the lower of the amount realized upon the disposition of the property or the recomputed basis of the property, exceeds (ii) the adjusted basis of the property.

(2) The provisions of this paragraph may be illustrated by the following examples: 30

Example 1. On January 1, 1964, Brown purchases section 1245 property for use in his manufacturing business. The property has a basis for depreciation of $3,300. After taking depreciation deductions of $1,300 (the amount allowable), Brown realizes after selling expenses the amount of $2,900 upon sale of the property on January 1, 1969. Brown's gain is $900 ($2,900 amount realized minus $2,000 adjusted basis). Since the 35 amount realized upon disposition of the property ($2,900) is lower than its recomputed basis ($3,300, i.e., $2,000 adjusted basis plus $1,300 in depreciation deductions), the entire gain is treated as ordinary income under section 1245(a)(1) and not as gain from the sale or exchange of property described in section 1231.

Example 2. Assume the same facts as in example (1) except that Brown exchanges 40 the section 1245 property for land which has a fair market value of $3,700, thereby realizing a gain of $1,700 ($3,700 amount realized minus $2,000 adjusted basis). Since the recomputed basis of the property ($3,300) is lower than the amount realized upon its disposition ($3,700), the excess of recomputed basis over adjusted basis, or $1,300, is treated as ordinary income under section 1245(a)(1). The remaining $400 of the gain 45 may be treated as gain from the sale or exchange of property described in section 1231.

(c) *Other dispositions.* (1) In the case of a disposition of section 1245 property other than by way of a sale, exchange, or involuntary conversion, the gain to which section 1245(a)(1) applies is the amount by which (i) the lower of the fair market value of the property on the date of disposition or the recomputed basis of the property, exceeds (ii) 50

Sec. 1245. Gain from dispositions of certain depreciable property

the adjusted basis of the property. If property is transferred by a corporation to a shareholder for an amount less than its fair market value in a sale or exchange, for purposes of applying section 1245 such transfer shall be treated as a disposition other than by way of a sale, exchange, or involuntary conversion.

5   (2) The provisions of this paragraph may be illustrated by the following examples:

Example 1. X Corporation distributes section 1245 property to its shareholders as a dividend. The property has an adjusted basis of $2,000 to the corporation, a recomputed basis of $3,300, and a fair market value of $3,100. Since the fair market value of the property ($3,100) is lower than its recomputed basis ($3,300), the excess of fair market
10 value over adjusted basis, or $1,100, is treated under section 1245(a)(1) as ordinary income to the corporation even though, in the absence of section 1245, section 311(a) would preclude recognition of gain to the corporation.

Example 2. Assume the same facts as in example (1) except that X Corporation distributes the section 1245 property to its shareholders in complete liquidation of the
15 corporation. Assume further that section 1245(b)(3) does not apply and that the fair market value of the property is $3,800 at the time of the distribution. Since the recomputed basis of the property ($3,300) is lower than its fair market value ($3,800), the excess of recomputed basis over adjusted basis, or $1,300, is treated under section 1245(a)(1) as ordinary income to the corporation even though, in the absence of section
20 1245, section 336 would preclude recognition of gain to the corporation.

(d) *Losses.* Section 1245(a)(1) does not apply to losses. Thus, section 1245(a)(1) does not apply if a loss is realized upon a sale, exchange, or involuntary conversion of property, all of which is considered section 1245 property, nor does the section apply to a disposition of such property other than by way of sale, exchange, or involuntary
25 conversion if at the time of the disposition the fair market value of such property is not greater than its adjusted basis.

***

Reg. § 1.1245-2 Definition of recomputed basis.

(a) *General rule*--(1) *Recomputed basis defined.* The term recomputed basis means,
30 with respect to any property, an amount equal to the sum of:

(i) The adjusted basis of the property, as defined in section 1011, plus

(ii) The amount of the adjustments reflected in the adjusted basis.

(2) *Definition of adjustments reflected in adjusted basis.* The term adjustments reflected in the adjusted basis means:

35 (i) With respect to any property other than property described in subdivision (ii), (iii), or (iv) of this subparagraph, the amount of the adjustments attributable to periods after December 31, 1961,

(ii) With respect to an elevator or escalator, the amount of the adjustments attributable to periods after June 30, 1963,

40 (iii) With respect to livestock (described in subparagraph (4) of § 1.1245-3(a)), the amount of the adjustments attributable to periods after December 31, 1969, or

(iv) [Reserved]

which are reflected in the adjusted basis of such property on account of deductions allowed or allowable for depreciation or amortization (within the meaning of subparagraph
45 (3) of this paragraph). For cases where the taxpayer can establish that the amount allowed for any period was less than the amount allowable, see subparagraph (7) of this paragraph. For determination of adjusted basis of property in a multiple asset account, see paragraph (c)(3) of § 1.167(a)-8.

(3) *Meaning of depreciation or amortization.* (i) For purposes of subparagraph (2) of
50 this paragraph, the term depreciation or amortization includes allowances (and amounts treated as allowances) for depreciation (or amortization in lieu thereof), and deductions

Sec. 1245. Gain from dispositions of certain depreciable property

for amortization of emergency facilities under section 168. Thus, for example, such term includes a reasonable allowance for exhaustion, wear and tear (including a reasonable allowance for obsolescence) under section 167, an expense allowance (additional first-year depreciation allowance for property placed in service before January 1, 1981), under section 179, an expenditure treated as an amount allowed under section 167 by reason 5 of the application of section 182(d)(2)(B) (relating to expenditures by farmers for clearing land), and a deduction for depreciation of improvements under section 611 (relating to depletion). For further examples, the term depreciation or amortization includes periodic deductions referred to in § 1.162-11 in respect of a specified sum paid for the acquisition of a leasehold and in respect of the cost to a lessee of improvements on property of 10 which he is the lessee. However, such term does not include deductions for the periodic payment of rent.

(ii) The provisions of this subparagraph may be illustrated by the following example:

Example: On January 1, 1966, Smith purchases for $1,000, and places in service, an item of property described in section 1245(a)(3)(A). Smith deducts an additional first-year 15 allowance for depreciation under section 179 of $200. Accordingly, the basis of the property for purposes of depreciation is $800 on January 1, 1966. Between that date and January 1, 1974, Smith deducts $640 in depreciation (the amount allowable) with respect to the property, thereby reducing its adjusted basis to $160. Since this adjusted basis reflects deductions for depreciation and amortization (within the meaning of this 20 subparagraph) amounting to $840 ($200 plus $640), the recomputed basis of the property is $1,000 ($160 plus $840).

***

(7) *Depreciation or amortization allowed or allowable.* For purposes of determining recomputed basis, generally all adjustments (for periods after Dec. 31, 1961, or, in the 25 case of property described in subparagraph (2) (ii), (iii), or (iv) of this paragraph, for periods after the applicable date) attributable to allowed or allowable depreciation or amortization must be taken into account. See section 1016(a)(2) and the regulations thereunder for the meaning of allowed and allowable. However, if a taxpayer can establish by adequate records or other sufficient evidence that the amount allowed for 30 depreciation or amortization for any period was less than the amount allowable for such period, the amount to be taken into account for such period shall be the amount allowed. No adjustment is to be made on account of the tax imposed by section 56 (relating to the minimum tax for tax preferences). See paragraph (b) of this section (relating to records to be kept and information to be filed). For example, assume that in the year 1967 it 35 becomes necessary to determine the recomputed basis of property, the $500 adjusted basis of which reflects adjustments of $1,000 with respect to depreciation deductions allowable for periods after December 31, 1961. If the taxpayer can establish by adequate records or other sufficient evidence that he had been allowed deductions amounting to only $800 for the period, then in determining recomputed basis the amount added to 40 adjusted basis with respect to the $1,000 adjustments to basis for the period will be only $800.

***

Reg. § 1.1245-6   Relation of section 1245 to other sections.

(a) *General.* The provisions of section 1245 apply notwithstanding any other provision 45 of subtitle A of the Code. Thus, unless an exception or limitation under section 1245(b) applies, gain under section 1245(a)(1) is recognized notwithstanding any contrary nonrecognition provision or income characterizing provision. For example, since section 1245 overrides section 1231 (relating to property used in the trade or business), the gain recognized under section 1245(a)(1) upon a disposition will be treated as ordinary 50

Sec. 1245. Gain from dispositions of certain depreciable property

income and only the remaining gain, if any, from the disposition may be considered as gain from the sale or exchange of a capital asset if section 1231 is applicable. See example (2) of paragraph (b)(2) of § 1.1245-1. For effect of section 1245 on basis provisions of the Code, see § 1.1245-5.

5   (b) *Nonrecognition sections overridden.* The nonrecognition provisions of subtitle A of the Code which section 1245 overrides include, but are not limited to, sections 267(d), 311(a), 336, 337, 501(a), 512(b)(5), and 1039. See section 1245(b) for the extent to which section 1245(a)(1) overrides sections 332, 351, 361, 371(a), 374(a), 721, 731, 1031, 1033, 1071, and 1081(b)(1) and (d)(1)(A). For limitation on amount of adjustments

10 reflected in adjusted basis of property disposed of by an organization exempt from income taxes (within the meaning of section 501(a)), see paragraph (a)(8) of § 1.1245-2.

***

[T.D. 6832, 30 FR 8578, July 7, 1965; T.D. 7084, 36 FR 268, Jan. 8, 1971; T.D. 7141, 36 FR 18793, Sept. 22, 1971; 36 FR 19160, Sept. 30, 1971; T.D. 7400, 41 FR 5101, Feb. 4,

15 1976; T.D. 7564, 43 FR 40496, Sept. 12, 1978; T.D. 8121, 52 FR 414, Jan. 6, 1987; T.D. 8730, 62 FR 44216, Aug. 20, 1997]

Sec. 1250. Gain from dispositions of certain depreciable realty

    (a) General rule. -- Except as otherwise provided in this section--

        (1) Additional depreciation after December 31, 1975. --

20   **(A) In general.** -- If section 1250 property is disposed of after December 31, 1975, then the applicable percentage of the lower of--

                (i) that portion of the additional depreciation (as defined in subsection (b)(1) or (4)) attributable to periods after December 31, 1975, in respect of the property, or

25   **(ii)** the excess of the amount realized (in the case of a sale, exchange, or involuntary conversion), or the fair market value of such property (in the case of any other disposition), over the adjusted basis of such property, shall be treated as gain which is ordinary income. Such gain shall be recognized notwithstanding any other provision of this subtitle.

            (B) Applicable percentage. -- For purposes of subparagraph (A), the term "applicable
30 percentage" means--

***

                (v) in the case of all other section 1250 property, 100 percent.

***

    (b) Additional depreciation defined. -- For purposes of this section--

35   **(1) In general.** -- The term "additional depreciation" means, in the case of any property, the depreciation adjustments in respect of such property; except that, in the case of property held more than one year, it means such adjustments only to the extent that they exceed the amount of the depreciation adjustments which would have resulted if such adjustments had been determined for each taxable year under the straight line method of adjustment.

40 ***

        (5) Method of computing straight line adjustments. -- For purposes of paragraph (1), the depreciation adjustments which would have resulted for any taxable year under the straight line method shall be determined--

            (A) in the case of property to which section 168 applies, by determining the adjustments
45   which would have resulted for such year if the taxpayer had elected the straight line

976

Sec. 1250. Gain from dispositions of certain depreciable realty

method for such year using the recovery period applicable to such property, and

    (B) in the case any property to which section 168 does not apply, if a useful life (or salvage value) was used in determining the amount allowable as a deduction for any taxable year, by using such life (or value).

(c) Section 1250 property. -- For purposes of this section, the term "section 1250 property" means any real property (other than section 1245 property, as defined in section 1245(a)(3)) which is or has been property of a character subject to the allowance for depreciation provided in section 167.

(d) Exceptions and limitations. --

    (1) Gifts. -- Subsection (a) shall not apply to a disposition by gift.

    (2) Transfers at death. -- Except as provided in section 691 (relating to income in respect of a decedent), subsection (a) shall not apply to a transfer at death.

***

    (4) Like kind exchanges; involuntary conversions, etc. --

        (A) Recognition limit. -- If property is disposed of and gain (determined without regard to this section) is not recognized in whole or in part under section 1031 or 1033, then the amount of gain taken into account by the transferor under subsection (a) shall not exceed the greater of the following:

            (i) the amount of gain recognized on the disposition (determined without regard to this section), increased as provided in subparagraph (B), or

            (ii) the amount determined under subparagraph (C).

        (B) Increase for certain stock. -- With respect to any transaction, the increase provided by this subparagraph is the amount equal to the fair market value of any stock purchased in a corporation which (but for this paragraph) would result in nonrecognition of gain under section 1033(a)(2)(A).

        (C) Adjustment where insufficient section 1250 property is acquired. -- With respect to any transaction, the amount determined under this subparagraph shall be the excess of--

            (i) the amount of gain which would (but for this paragraph) be taken into account under subsection (a), over

            (ii) the fair market value (or cost in the case of a transaction described in section 1033(a)(2)) of the section 1250 property acquired in the transaction.

        (D) Basis of property acquired. -- In the case of property purchased by the taxpayer in a transaction described in section 1033(a)(2), in applying section 1033(b)(2), such sentence shall be applied--

            (i) first solely to section 1250 properties and to the amount of gain not taken into account under subsection (a) by reason of this paragraph, and

            (ii) then to all purchased properties to which such sentence applies and to the remaining gain not recognized on the transaction as if the cost of the section 1250 properties were the basis of such properties computed under clause (i).

In the case of property acquired in any other transaction to which this paragraph applies, rules consistent with the preceding sentence shall be applied under regulations prescribed by the Secretary.

        (E) Additional depreciation with respect to property disposed of. -- In the case of any transaction described in section 1031 or 1033, the additional depreciation in respect of the section 1250 property acquired which is attributable to the section 1250 property disposed of shall be an amount equal to the amount of the gain which was not taken into account

977

Sec. 1250. Gain from dispositions of certain depreciable realty

under subsection (a) by reason of the application of this paragraph.

***

(g) Adjustments to basis. -- The Secretary shall prescribe such regulations as he may deem necessary to provide for adjustments to the basis of property to reflect gain recognized under subsection (a).

(h) Application of section. -- This section shall apply notwithstanding any other provision of this subtitle.

Sec. 1252. Gain from disposition of farm land

(a) General rule. --

    (1) Ordinary income. -- Except as otherwise provided in this section, if farm land which the taxpayer has held for less than 10 years is disposed of during a taxable year beginning after December 31, 1969, the lower of--

        (A) the applicable percentage of the aggregate of the deductions allowed under sections 175 (relating to soil and water conservation expenditures) and 182 (relating to expenditures by farmers for clearing land) for expenditures made by the taxpayer after December 31, 1969, with respect to the farm land or

        (B) the excess of--

            (i) the amount realized (in the case of a sale, exchange, or involuntary conversion), or the fair market value of the farm land (in the case of any other disposition), over

            (ii) the adjusted basis of such land,

shall be treated as ordinary income. Such gain shall be recognized notwithstanding any other provision of this subtitle.

    (2) Farm land. -- For purposes of this section, the term "farm land" means any land with respect to which deductions have been allowed under sections 175 (relating to soil and water conservation expenditures) or 182 (as in effect on the day before the date of the enactment of the Tax Reform Act of 1986).

    (3) Applicable percentage. -- For purposes of this section--

If the farm land is disposed of -	The applicable percentage is -
Within 5 years after the date it was acquire............	100 percent.
Within the sixth year after it was acquired.............	80 percent.
Within the seventh year after it was acquire...........	60 percent.
Within the eighth year after it was acquired..........	40 percent.
Within the ninth year after it was acquired.............	20 percent.
10 years or more years after it was acquired...........	0 percent.

(b) Special rules. -- Under regulations prescribed by the Secretary, rules similar to the rules of section 1245 shall be applied for purposes of this section.

Sec. 1253. Transfers of franchises, trademarks, and trade names

(a) General rule. -- A transfer of a franchise, trademark, or trade name shall not be treated as a sale or exchange of a capital asset if the transferor retains any significant power, right, or continuing interest with respect to the subject matter of the franchise, trademark, or trade name.

Sec. 1253.   Transfers of franchises, trademarks, and trade names

(b) Definitions. -- For purposes of this section--

(1) Franchise. -- The term "franchise" includes an agreement which gives one of the parties to the agreement the right to distribute, sell, or provide goods, services, or facilities, within a specified area.

(2) Significant power, right, or continuing interest. -- The term "significant power, right, or continuing interest" includes, but is not limited to, the following rights with respect to the interest transferred:

(A) A right to disapprove any assignment of such interest, or any part thereof.

(B) A right to terminate at will.

(C) A right to prescribe the standards of quality of products used or sold, or of services furnished, and of the equipment and facilities used to promote such products or services.

(D) A right to require that the transferee sell or advertise only products or services of the transferor.

(E) A right to require that the transferee purchase substantially all of his supplies and equipment from the transferor.

(F) A right to payments contingent on the productivity, use, or disposition of the subject matter of the interest transferred, if such payments constitute a substantial element under the transfer agreement.

(3) Transfer. -- The term "transfer" includes the renewal of a franchise, trademark, or trade name.

(c) Treatment of contingent payments by transferor. -- Amounts received or accrued on account of a transfer, sale, or other disposition of a franchise, trademark, or trade name which are contingent on the productivity, use, or disposition of the franchise, trademark, or trade name transferred shall be treated as amounts received or accrued from the sale or other disposition of property which is not a capital asset.

(d) Treatment of payments by transferee. --

(1) Contingent serial payments. --

(A) In general. -- Any amount described in subparagraph (B) which is paid or incurred during the taxable year on account of a transfer, sale, or other disposition of a franchise, trademark, or trade name shall be allowed as a deduction under section 162(a) (relating to trade or business expenses).

(B) Amounts to which paragraph applies. -- An amount is described in this subparagraph if it--

(i) is contingent on the productivity, use, or disposition of the franchise, trademark, or trade name, and

(ii) is paid as part of a series of payments--

(I) which are payable not less frequently than annually throughout the entire term of the transfer agreement, and

(II) which are substantially equal in amount (or payable under a fixed formula).

(2) Other payments. -- Any amount paid or incurred on account of a transfer, sale, or other disposition of a franchise, trademark, or trade name to which paragraph (1) does not apply shall be treated as an amount chargeable to capital account.

(3) Renewals, etc. -- For purposes of determining the term of a transfer agreement under this section, there shall be taken into account all renewal options (and any other period for which the parties reasonably expect the agreement to be renewed).

Sec. 1253. Transfers of franchises, trademarks, and trade names

Sec. 1254. Gain from disposition of interest in oil, gas, geothermal, or other mineral properties

(a) General rule. --

(1) **Ordinary income.** -- If any section 1254 property is disposed of, the lesser of--

(A) the aggregate amount of--

(i) expenditures which have been deducted by the taxpayer or any person under section 263, 616, or 617 with respect to such property and which, but for such deduction, would have been included in the adjusted basis of such property, and

(ii) the deductions for depletion under section 611 which reduced the adjusted basis of such property, or

(B) the excess of--

(i) in the case of--

(I) a sale, exchange, or involuntary conversion, the amount realized, or

(II) in the case of any other disposition, the fair market value of such property, over

(ii) the adjusted basis of such property,

shall be treated as gain which is ordinary income. Such gain shall be recognized notwithstanding any other provision of this subtitle.

(2) **Disposition of portion of property.** -- For purposes of paragraph (1)--

(A) In the case of the disposition of a portion of section 1254 property (other than an undivided interest), the entire amount of the aggregate expenditures or deductions described in paragraph (1)(A) with respect to such property shall be treated as allocable to such portion to the extent of the amount of the gain to which paragraph (1) applies.

(B) In the case of the disposition of an undivided interest in a section 1254 property (or a portion thereof), a proportionate part of the expenditures or deductions described in paragraph (1)(A) with respect to such property shall be treated as allocable to such undivided interest to the extent of the amount of the gain to which paragraph (1) applies.

This paragraph shall not apply to any expenditures to the extent the taxpayer establishes to the satisfaction of the Secretary that such expenditures do not relate to the portion (or interest therein) disposed of.

(3) **Section 1254 property.** -- The term "section 1254 property" means any property (within the meaning of section 614) if--

(A) any expenditures described in paragraph (1)(A) are properly chargeable to such property, or

(B) the adjusted basis of such property includes adjustments for deductions for depletion under section 611.

(4) **Adjustment for amounts included in gross income under section 617(b)(1)(A).** -- The amount of the expenditures referred to in paragraph (1)(A)(i) shall be properly adjusted for amounts included in gross income under section 617(b)(1)(A).

***

Sec. 1256. Section 1256 contracts marked to market

(a) General rule. -- For purposes of this subtitle--

Sec. 1256. Section 1256 contracts marked to market

(1) each section 1256 contract held by the taxpayer at the close of the taxable year shall be treated as sold for its fair market value on the last business day of such taxable year (and any gain or loss shall be taken into account for the taxable year),

(2) proper adjustment shall be made in the amount of any gain or loss subsequently realized for gain or loss taken into account by reason of paragraph (1),   5

(3) any gain or loss with respect to a section 1256 contract shall be treated as--

   (A) short-term capital gain or loss, to the extent of 40 percent of such gain or loss, and

   (B) long-term capital gain or loss, to the extent of 60 percent of such gain or loss, and

(4) if all the offsetting positions making up any straddle consist of section 1256 contracts to which this section applies (and such straddle is not part of a larger straddle), sections 1092 and 10 263(g) shall not apply with respect to such straddle.

(b) Section 1256 contract defined. -- For purposes of this section, the term "section 1256 contract" means--

(1) any regulated futures contract,

(2) any foreign currency contract,   15

(3) any nonequity option,

(4) any dealer equity option, and

(5) any dealer securities futures contract.

The term "section 1256 contract" shall not include any securities futures contract or option on such a contract unless such contract or option is a dealer securities futures contract.   20

(c) Terminations, etc. --

(1) In general. -- The rules of paragraphs (1), (2), and (3) of subsection (a) shall also apply to the termination (or transfer) during the taxable year of the taxpayer's obligation (or rights) with respect to a section 1256 contract by offsetting, by taking or making delivery, by exercise or being exercised, by assignment or being assigned, by lapse, or otherwise.   25

(2) Special rule where taxpayer takes delivery on or exercises part of straddle. -- If--

   (A) 2 or more section 1256 contracts are part of a straddle (as defined in section 1092(c)), and

   (B) the taxpayer takes delivery under or exercises any of such contracts,

then, for purposes of this section, each of the other such contracts shall be treated as terminated 30 on the day on which the taxpayer took delivery.

(3) Fair market value taken into account. -- For purposes of this subsection, fair market value at the time of the termination (or transfer) shall be taken into account.

(d) Elections with respect to mixed straddles. --

(1) Election. -- The taxpayer may elect to have this section not to apply to all section 1256 35 contracts which are part of a mixed straddle.

(2) Time and manner. -- An election under paragraph (1) shall be made at such time and in such manner as the Secretary may by regulations prescribe.

(3) Election revocable only with consent. -- An election under paragraph (1) shall apply to the taxpayer's taxable year for which made and to all subsequent taxable years, unless the 40 Secretary consents to a revocation of such election.

(4) Mixed straddle. -- For purposes of this subsection, the term "mixed straddle" means any straddle (as defined in section 1092(c))--

   (A) at least 1 (but not all) of the positions of which are section 1256 contracts, and

Sec. 1256. Section 1256 contracts marked to market

(B) with respect to which each position forming part of such straddle is clearly identified, before the close of the day on which the first section 1256 contract forming part of the straddle is acquired (or such earlier time as the Secretary may prescribe by regulations), as being part of such straddle.

(e) Mark to market not to apply to hedging transactions. --

(1) Section not to apply. -- Subsection (a) shall not apply in the case of a hedging transaction.

(2) Definition of hedging transaction. -- For purposes of this subsection, the term "hedging transaction" means any hedging transaction (as defined in section 1221(b)(2)(A)) if, before the close of the day on which such transaction was entered into (or such earlier time as the Secretary may prescribe by regulations), the taxpayer clearly identifies such transaction as being a hedging transaction.

(3) Special rule for syndicates. --

(A) In general. -- Notwithstanding paragraph (2), the term "hedging transaction" shall not include any transaction entered into by or for a syndicate.

(B) Syndicate defined. -- For purposes of subparagraph (A), the term "syndicate" means any partnership or other entity (other than a corporation which is not an S corporation) if more than 35 percent of the losses of such entity during the taxable year are allocable to limited partners or limited entrepreneurs (within the meaning of section 464(e)(2)).

(C) Holdings attributable to active management. -- For purposes of subparagraph (B), an interest in an entity shall not be treated as held by a limited partner or a limited entrepreneur (within the meaning of section 464(e)(2))--

(i) for any period if during such period such interest is held by an individual who actively participates at all times during such period in the management of such entity,

(ii) for any period if during such period such interest is held by the spouse, children, grandchildren, and parents of an individual who actively participates at all times during such period in the management of such entity,

(iii) if such interest is held by an individual who actively participated in the management of such entity for a period of not less than 5 years,

(iv) if such interest is held by the estate of an individual who actively participated in the management of such entity or is held by the estate of an individual if with respect to such individual such interest was at any time described in clause (ii), or

(v) if the Secretary determines (by regulations or otherwise) that such interest should be treated as held by an individual who actively participates in the management of such entity, and that such entity and such interest are not used (or to be used) for tax-avoidance purposes.

For purposes of this subparagraph, a legally adopted child of an individual shall be treated as a child of such individual by blood.

(4) Limitation on losses from hedging transactions. --

(A) In general. --

(i) Limitation. -- Any hedging loss for a taxable year which is allocable to any limited partner or limited entrepreneur (within the meaning of paragraph (3)) shall be allowed only to the extent of the taxable income of such limited partner or entrepreneur for such taxable year attributable to the trade or business in which the hedging transactions were entered into. For purposes of the preceding sentence, taxable income shall be determined by not taking into account items attributable to hedging transactions.

982

Sec. 1256. Section 1256 contracts marked to market

(ii) Carryover of disallowed loss. -- Any hedging loss disallowed under clause (i) shall be treated as a deduction attributable to a hedging transaction allowable in the first succeeding taxable year.

(B) Exception where economic loss. -- Subparagraph (A)(i) shall not apply to any hedging loss to the extent that such loss exceeds the aggregate unrecognized gains from hedging transactions as of the close of the taxable year attributable to the trade or business in which the hedging transactions were entered into.

(C) Exception for certain hedging transactions. -- In the case of any hedging transaction relating to property other than stock or securities, this paragraph shall apply only in the case of a taxpayer described in section 465(a)(1).

(D) Hedging loss. -- The term "hedging loss" means the excess of--

(i) the deductions allowable under this chapter for the taxable year attributable to hedging transactions (determined without regard to subparagraph (A)(i)), over

(ii) income received or accrued by the taxpayer during such taxable year from such transactions.

(E) Unrecognized gain. -- The term "unrecognized gain" has the meaning given to such term by section 1092(a)(3).

(f) Special rules. --

(1) Denial of capital gains treatment for property identified as part of a hedging transaction. -- For purposes of this title, gain from any property shall in no event be considered as gain from the sale or exchange of a capital asset if such property was at any time personal property (as defined in section 1092(d)(1)) identified under subsection (e)(2)(C) by the taxpayer as being part of a hedging transaction.

(2) Subsection (a)(3) not to apply to ordinary income property. -- Paragraph (3) of subsection (a) shall not apply to any gain or loss which, but for such paragraph, would be ordinary income or loss.

(3) Capital gain treatment for traders in section 1256 contracts. --

(A) In general. -- For purposes of this title, gain or loss from trading of section 1256 contracts shall be treated as gain or loss from the sale or exchange of a capital asset.

(B) Exception for certain hedging transactions. -- Subparagraph (A) shall not apply to any section 1256 contract to the extent such contract is held for purposes of hedging property if any loss with respect to such property in the hands of the taxpayer would be ordinary loss.

(C) Treatment of underlying property. -- For purposes of determining whether gain or loss with respect to any property is ordinary income or loss, the fact that the taxpayer is actively engaged in dealing in or trading section1256 contracts related to such property shall not be taken into account.

(4) Special rule for dealer equity options and dealer securities futures contracts of limited partners or limited entrepreneurs. -- In the case of any gain or loss with respect to dealer equity options, or dealer securities futures contracts, which are allocable to limited partners or limited entrepreneurs (within the meaning of subsection (e)(3))--

(A) paragraph (3) of subsection (a) shall not apply to any such gain or loss, and

(B) all such gains or losses shall be treated as short-term capital gains or losses, as the case may be.

(5) Special rule related to losses. -- Section 1091 (relating to loss from wash sales of stock or securities) shall not apply to any loss taken into account by reason of paragraph (1) of subsection (a).

Sec. 1256.   Section 1256 contracts marked to market

(g) Definitions. -- For purposes of this section--

(1) Regulated futures contracts defined. -- The term "regulated futures contract" means a contract--

(A) with respect to which the amount required to be deposited and the amount which may be withdrawn depends on a system of marking to market, and

(B) which is traded on or subject to the rules of a qualified board or exchange.

(2) Foreign currency contract defined. --

(A) Foreign currency contract. -- The term "foreign currency contract" means a contract--

(i) which requires delivery of, or the settlement of which depends on the value of, a foreign currency which is a currency in which positions are also traded through regulated futures contracts,

(ii) which is traded in the interbank market, and

(iii) which is entered into at arm's length at a price determined by reference to the price in the interbank market.

***

(3) Nonequity option. -- The term "nonequity option" means any listed option which is not an equity option.

(4) Dealer equity option. -- The term "dealer equity option" means, with respect to an options dealer, any listed option which--

(A) is an equity option,

(B) is purchased or granted by such options dealer in the normal course of his activity of dealing in options, and

(C) is listed on the qualified board or exchange on which such options dealer is registered.

(5) Listed option. -- The term "listed option" means any option (other than a right to acquire stock from the issuer) which is traded on (or subject to the rules of) a qualified board or exchange.

(6) Equity option. -- The term "equity option" means any option--

(A) to buy or sell stock, or

(B) the value of which is determined directly or indirectly by reference to any stock or any narrow-based security index (as defined in section 3(a)(55) of the Securities Exchange Act of 1934, as in effect on the date of the enactment of this paragraph).

The term "equity option" includes such an option on a group of stocks only if such group meets the requirements for a narrow-based security index (as so defined). The Secretary may prescribe regulations regarding the status of options the values of which are determined directly or indirectly by reference to any index which becomes (or ceases to be) a narrow-based security index (as so defined).

(7) Qualified board or exchange. -- The term "qualified board or exchange" means--

(A) a national securities exchange which is registered with the Securities and Exchange Commission,

(B) a domestic board of trade designated as a contract market by the Commodity Futures Trading Commission, or

(C) any other exchange, board of trade, or other market which the Secretary determines has rules adequate to carry out the purposes of this section.

Sec. 1256.   Section 1256 contracts marked to market

(8) Options dealer. --

(A) In general. -- The term "options dealer" means any person registered with an appropriate national securities exchange as a market maker or specialist in listed options.

(B) Persons trading in other markets. -- In any case in which the Secretary makes a determination under subparagraph (C) of paragraph (7), the term "options dealer" also 5 includes any person whom the Secretary determines performs functions similar to the persons described in subparagraph (A). Such determinations shall be made to the extent appropriate to carry out the purposes of this section.

(9) Dealer securities futures contract. --

(A) In general. -- The term "dealer securities futures contract" means, with respect to 10 any dealer, any securities futures contract, and an option on such a contract, which--

(i) is entered into by such dealer (or, in the case of an option, is purchased or granted by such dealer) in the normal course of his activity of dealing in such contracts or options, as the case may be, and

(ii) is traded on a qualified board or exchange. 15

(B) Dealer. -- For purposes of subparagraph (A), a person shall be treated as a dealer in securities futures contracts or options on such contracts if the Secretary determines that such person performs, with respect to such contracts or options, as the case may be, functions similar to the functions performed by persons described in paragraph (8)(A). Such determination shall be made to the extent appropriate to carry out the purposes of this 20 section.

(C) Securities futures contract. -- The term "securities futures contract" has the meaning given to such term by section 1234B.Sec. 1258.   Recharacterization of gain from certain financial transactions

(a) General rule. -- In the case of any gain-- 25

(1) which (but for this section) would be treated as gain from the sale or exchange of a capital asset, and

(2) which is recognized on the disposition or other termination of any position which was held as part of a conversion transaction,

such gain (to the extent such gain does not exceed the applicable imputed income amount) shall be 30 treated as ordinary income.

(b) Applicable imputed income amount. -- For purposes of subsection (a), the term "applicable imputed income amount" means, with respect to any disposition or other termination referred to in subsection (a), an amount equal to--

(1) the amount of interest which would have accrued on the taxpayer's net investment in the 35 conversion transaction for the period ending on the date of such disposition or other termination (or, if earlier, the date on which the requirements of subsection (c) ceased to be satisfied) at a rate equal to 120 percent of the applicable rate, reduced by

(2) the amount treated as ordinary income under subsection (a) with respect to any prior disposition or other termination of a position which was held as a part of such transaction.   40

The Secretary shall by regulations provide for such reductions in the applicable imputed income amount as may be appropriate by reason of amounts capitalized under section 263(g), ordinary income received, or otherwise.

(c) Conversion transaction. -- For purposes of this section, the term "conversion transaction" means any transaction-- 45

(1) substantially all of the taxpayer's expected return from which is attributable to the time

Sec. 1256. Section 1256 contracts marked to market

value of the taxpayer's net investment in such transaction, and

(2) which is--

(A) the holding of any property (whether or not actively traded), and the entering into a contract to sell such property (or substantially identical property) at a price determined in accordance with such contract, but only if such property was acquired and such contract was entered into on a substantially contemporaneous basis,

(B) an applicable straddle,

(C) any other transaction which is marketed or sold as producing capital gains from a transaction described in paragraph (1), or

(D) any other transaction specified in regulations prescribed by the Secretary.

(d) Definitions and special rules. -- For purposes of this section--

(1) Applicable straddle. -- The term "applicable straddle" means any straddle (within the meaning of section 1092(c)).

(2) Applicable rate. -- The term "applicable rate" means--

(A) the applicable Federal rate determined under section 1274(d) (compounded semiannually) as if the conversion transaction were a debt instrument, or

(B) if the term of the conversion transaction is indefinite, the Federal short-term rates in effect under section 6621(b) during the period of the conversion transaction (compounded daily).

(3) Treatment of built-in losses. --

(A) In general. -- If any position with a built-in loss becomes part of a conversion transaction--

(i) for purposes of applying this subtitle to such position for periods after such position becomes part of such transaction, such position shall be taken into account at its fair market value as of the time it became part of such transaction, except that

(ii) upon the disposition or other termination of such position in a transaction in which gain or loss is recognized, such built-in loss shall be recognized and shall have a character determined without regard to this section.

(B) Built-in loss. -- For purposes of subparagraph (A), the term "built-in loss" means the loss (if any) which would have been realized if the position had been disposed of or otherwise terminated at its fair market value as of the time such position became part of the conversion transaction.

(4) Position taken into account at fair market value. -- In determining the taxpayer's net investment in any conversion transaction, there shall be included the fair market value of any position which becomes part of such transaction (determined as of the time such position became part of such transaction).

(5) Special rule for options dealers and commodities traders. --

(A) In general. -- Subsection (a) shall not apply to transactions--

(i) of an options dealer in the normal course of the dealer's trade or business of dealing in options, or

(ii) of a commodities trader in the normal course of the trader's trade or business of trading section 1256 contracts.

(B) Definitions. -- For purposes of this paragraph--

(i) Options dealer. -- The term "options dealer" has the meaning given such term by section 1256(g)(8).

Sec. 1256. Section 1256 contracts marked to market

(ii) **Commodities trader.** -- The term "commodities trader" means any person who is a member (or, except as otherwise provided in regulations, is entitled to trade as a member) of a domestic board of trade which is designated as a contract market by the Commodity Futures Trading Commission.

(C) **Limited partners and limited entrepreneurs.** -- In the case of any gain from a transaction recognized by an entity which is allocable to a limited partner or limited entrepreneur (within the meaning of section 464(e)(2)), subparagraph (A) shall not apply if-- 5

(i) substantially all of the limited partner's (or limited entrepreneur's) expected return from the entity is attributable to the time value of the partner's (or entrepreneur's) net investment in such entity, 10

(ii) the transaction (or the interest in the entity) was marketed or sold as producing capital gains treatment from a transaction described in subsection (c)(1), or

(iii) the transaction (or the interest in the entity) is a transaction (or interest) specified in regulations prescribed by the Secretary. 15

Sec. 1271. Treatment of amounts received on retirement or sale or exchange of debt instruments

(a) **General rule.** -- For purposes of this title--

(1) **Retirement.** -- Amounts received by the holder on retirement of any debt instrument shall be considered as amounts received in exchange therefor. 20

(2) **Ordinary income on sale or exchange where intention to call before maturity.** --

(A) **In general.** -- If at the time of original issue there was an intention to call a debt instrument before maturity, any gain realized on the sale or exchange thereof which does not exceed an amount equal to--

(i) the original issue discount, reduced by 25

(ii) the portion of original issue discount previously includible in the gross income of any holder (without regard to subsection (a)(7) or (b)(4) of section 1272 (or the corresponding provisions of prior law)), shall be treated as ordinary income.

(B) **Exceptions.** -- This paragraph (and paragraph (2) of subsection (c)) shall not apply to-- 30

(i) any tax-exempt obligation, or

(ii) any holder who has purchased the debt instrument at a premium.

(3) **Certain short-term Government obligations.** --

(A) **In general.** -- On the sale or exchange of any short-term Government obligation, any gain realized which does not exceed an amount equal to the ratable share of the acquisition discount shall be treated as ordinary income. 35

(B) **Short-term Government obligation.** -- For purposes of this paragraph, the term "short-term Government obligation" means any obligation of the United States or any of its possessions, or of a State or any political subdivision thereof, or of the District of Columbia, which has a fixed maturity date not more than 1 year from the date of issue. 40 Such term does not include any tax-exempt obligation.

(C) **Acquisition discount.** -- For purposes of this paragraph, the term "acquisition discount" means the excess of the stated redemption price at maturity over the taxpayer's basis for the obligation.

Sec. 1271. Treatment of amounts received on retirement or sale or exchange of debt instruments

    (D) Ratable share. -- For purposes of this paragraph, except as provided in subparagraph (E), the ratable share of the acquisition discount is an amount which bears the same ratio to such discount as--

        (i) the number of days which the taxpayer held the obligation, bears to

        (ii) the number of days after the date the taxpayer acquired the obligation and up to (and including) the date of its maturity.

    (E) Election of accrual on basis of constant interest rate. -- At the election of the taxpayer with respect to any obligation, the ratable share of the acquisition discount is the portion of the acquisition discount accruing while the taxpayer held the obligation determined (under regulations prescribed by the Secretary) on the basis of--

        (i) the taxpayer's yield to maturity based on the taxpayer's cost of acquiring the obligation, and

        (ii) compounding daily.

An election under this subparagraph, once made with respect to any obligation, shall be irrevocable.

    (4) Certain short-term nongovernment obligations. --

    (A) In general. -- On the sale or exchange of any short-term nongovernment obligation, any gain realized which does not exceed an amount equal to the ratable share of the original issue discount shall be treated as ordinary income.

    (B) Short-term nongovernment obligation. -- For purposes of this paragraph, the term "short-term nongovernment obligation" means any obligation which--

        (i) has a fixed maturity date not more than 1 year from the date of the issue, and

        (ii) is not a short-term Government obligation (as defined in paragraph (3)(B) without regard to the last sentence thereof).

    (C) Ratable share. -- For purposes of this paragraph, except as provided in subparagraph (D), the ratable share of the original issue discount is an amount which bears the same ratio to such discount as--

        (i) the number of days which the taxpayer held the obligation, bears to

        (ii) the number of days after the date of original issue and up to (and including) the date of its maturity.

    (D) Election of accrual on basis of constant interest rate. -- At the election of the taxpayer with respect to any obligation, the ratable share of the original issue discount is the portion of the original issue discount accruing while the taxpayer held the obligation determined (under regulations prescribed by the Secretary) on the basis of--

        (i) the yield to maturity based on the issue price of the obligation, and

        (ii) compounding daily.

***

    (d) Double inclusion in income not required. -- This section and sections 1272 and 1286 shall not require the inclusion of any amount previously includible in gross income.

Sec. 1272. Current inclusion in income of original issue discount

    (a) Original issue discount on debt instruments issued after July 1, 1982, included in income on basis of constant interest rate. --

    (1) General rule. -- For purposes of this title, there shall be included in the gross income of

988

Sec. 1272. Current inclusion in income of original issue discount

the holder of any debt instrument having original issue discount issued after July 1, 1982, an amount equal to the sum of the daily portions of the original issue discount for each day during the taxable year on which such holder held such debt instrument.

(2) **Exceptions.** -- Paragraph (1) shall not apply to--

(A) **Tax-exempt obligations.** -- Any tax-exempt obligation.   5

(B) **United States savings bonds.** -- Any United States savings bond.

(C) **Short-term obligations.** -- Any debt instrument which has a fixed maturity date not more than 1 year from the date of issue.

(D) **Obligations issued by natural persons before March 2, 1984.** -- Any obligation issued by a natural person before March 2, 1984.   10

(E) **Loans between natural persons.** --

(i) **In general.** -- Any loan made by a natural person to another natural person if--

(I) such loan is not made in the course of a trade or business of the lender, and

(II) the amount of such loan (when increased by the outstanding amount of prior loans by such natural person to such other natural person) does not exceed $10,000.   15

(ii) **Clause (i) not to apply where tax avoidance a principal purpose.** -- Clause (i) shall not apply if the loan has as 1 of its principal purposes the avoidance of any Federal tax.

(iii) **Treatment of husband and wife.** -- For purposes of this subparagraph, a husband and wife shall be treated as 1 person. The preceding sentence shall not apply 20 where the spouses lived apart at all times during the taxable year in which the loan is made.

(3) **Determination of daily portions.** -- For purposes of paragraph (1), the daily portion of the original issue discount on any debt instrument shall be determined by allocating to each day in any accrual period its ratable portion of the increase during such accrual period in the 25 adjusted issue price of the debt instrument. For purposes of the preceding sentence, the increase in the adjusted issue price for any accrual period shall be an amount equal to the excess (if any) of--

(A) the product of--

(i) the adjusted issue price of the debt instrument at the beginning of such accrual 30 period, and

(ii) the yield to maturity (determined on the basis of compounding at the close of each accrual period and properly adjusted for the length of the accrual period), over

(B) the sum of the amounts payable as interest on such debt instrument during such accrual period.   35

(4) **Adjusted issue price.** -- For purposes of this subsection, the adjusted issue price of any debt instrument at the beginning of any accrual period is the sum of--

(A) the issue price of such debt instrument, plus

(B) the adjustments under this subsection to such issue price for all periods before the first day of such accrual period.   40

(5) **Accrual period.** -- Except as otherwise provided in regulations prescribed by the Secretary, the term "accrual period" means a 6-month period (or shorter period from the date of original issue of the debt instrument) which ends on a day in the calendar year corresponding to the maturity date of the debt instrument or the date 6 months before such maturity date.

(6) **Determination of daily portions where principal subject to acceleration.** --   45

989

Sec. 1272. Current inclusion in income of original issue discount

(A) In general. -- In the case of any debt instrument to which this paragraph applies, the daily portion of the original issue discount shall be determined by allocating to each day in any accrual period its ratable portion of the excess (if any) of--

(i) the sum of (I) the present value determined under subparagraph (B) of all remaining payments under the debt instrument as of the close of such period, and (II) the payments during the accrual period of amounts included in the stated redemption price of the debt instrument, over

(ii) the adjusted issue price of such debt instrument at the beginning of such period.

(B) Determination of present value. -- For purposes of subparagraph (A), the present value shall be determined on the basis of--

(i) the original yield to maturity (determined on the basis of compounding at the close of each accrual period and properly adjusted for the length of the accrual period),

(ii) events which have occurred before the close of the accrual period, and

(iii) a prepayment assumption determined in the manner prescribed by regulations.

(C) Debt instruments to which paragraph applies. -- This paragraph applies to--

(i) any regular interest in a REMIC or qualified mortgage held by a REMIC,

(ii) any other debt instrument if payments under such deb instrument may be accelerated by reason of prepayments of other obligations securing such debt instrument (or, to the extent provided in regulations, by reason of other events), or

(iii) any pool of debt instruments the yield on which may be affected by reason of prepayments (or to the extent provided in regulations, by reason of other events).

To the extent provided in regulations prescribed by the Secretary, in the case of a small business engaged in the trade or business of selling tangible personal property at retail, clause (iii) shall not apply to debt instruments incurred in the ordinary course of such trade or business while held by such business.

(7) Reduction where subsequent holder pays acquisition premium. --

(A) Reduction. -- For purposes of this subsection, in the case of any purchase after its original issue of a debt instrument to which this subsection applies, the daily portion for any day shall be reduced by an amount equal to the amount which would be the daily portion for such day (without regard to this paragraph) multiplied by the fraction determined under subparagraph (B).

(B) Determination of fraction. -- For purposes of subparagraph (A), the fraction determined under this subparagraph is a fraction--

(i) the numerator of which is the excess (if any) of--

(I) the cost of such debt instrument incurred by the purchaser, over

(II) the issue price of such debt instrument, increased by the portion of original issue discount previously includible in the gross income of any holder (computed without regard to this paragraph), and

(ii) the denominator of which is the sum of the daily portions for such debt instrument for all days after the date of such purchase and ending on the stated maturity date (computed without regard to this paragraph).

***

(c) Exceptions. -- This section shall not apply to any holder--

(1) who has purchased the debt instrument at a premium,

***

Sec. 1272. Current inclusion in income of original issue discount

(d) Definition and special rule. --

(1) Purchase defined. -- For purposes of this section, the term "purchase" means--

(A) any acquisition of a debt instrument, where

(B) the basis of the debt instrument is not determined in whole or in part by reference to the adjusted basis of such debt instrument in the hands of the person from whom acquired. 5

(2) Basis adjustment. -- The basis of any debt instrument in the hands of the holder thereof shall be increased by the amount included in his gross income pursuant to this section.

Sec. 1273. Determination of amount of original issue discount

(a) General rule. -- For purposes of this subpart-- 10

(1) In general. -- The term "original issue discount" means the excess (if any) of --

(A) the stated redemption price at maturity, over

(B) the issue price.

(2) Stated redemption price at maturity. -- The term "stated redemption price at maturity" means the amount fixed by the last modification of the purchase agreement and includes 15 interest and other amounts payable at that time (other than any interest based on a fixed rate, and payable unconditionally at fixed periodic intervals of 1 year or less during the entire term of the debt instrument).

(3) 1/4 of 1 percent de minimis rule. -- If the original issue discount determined under paragraph (1) is less than-- 20

(A) 1/4 of 1 percent of the stated redemption price at maturity, multiplied by

(B) the number of complete years to maturity,

then the original issue discount shall be treated as zero.

(b) Issue price. -- For purposes of this subpart--

(1) Publicly offered debt instruments not issued for property. -- In the case of any issue of 25 debt instruments--

(A) publicly offered, and

(B) not issued for property,

the issue price is the initial offering price to the public (excluding bond houses and brokers) at which price a substantial amount of such debt instruments was sold. 30

(2) Other debt instruments not issued for property. -- In the case of any issue of debt instruments not issued for property and not publicly offered, the issue price of each such instrument is the price paid by the first buyer of such debt instrument.

(3) Debt instruments issued for property where there is public trading. -- In the case of a debt instrument which is issued for property and which-- 35

(A) is part of an issue a portion of which is traded on an established securities market, or

(B)(i) is issued for stock or securities which are traded on an established securities market, or

(ii) to the extent provided in regulations, is issued for property (other than stock or securities) of a kind regularly traded on an established market, 40

the issue price of such debt instrument shall be the fair market value of such property.

(4) Other cases. -- Except in any case--

(A) to which paragraph (1), (2), or (3) of this subsection applies, or

991

Sec. 1273. Determination of amount of original issue discount

      (B) to which section 1274 applies,

the issue price of a debt instrument which is issued for property shall be the stated redemption price at maturity.

      (5) Property. -- In applying this subsection, the term "property" includes services and the right to use property, but such term does not include money.

    (c) Special rules for applying subsection (b). -- For purposes of subsection (b)--

      (1) Initial offering price; price paid by the first buyer. -- The terms "initial offering price" and "price paid by the first buyer" include the aggregate payments made by the purchaser under the purchase agreement, including modifications thereof.

      (2) Treatment of investment units. -- In the case of any debt instrument and an option, security, or other property issued together as an investment unit--

          (A) the issue price for such unit shall be determined in accordance with the rules of this subsection and subsection (b) as if it were a debt instrument,

          (B) the issue price determined for such unit shall be allocated to each element of such unit on the basis of the relationship of the fair market value of such element to the fair market value of all elements in such unit, and

          (C) the issue price of any debt instrument included in such unit shall be the portion of the issue price of the unit allocated to the debt instrument under subparagraph (B).

Sec. 1274. Determination of issue price in the case of certain debt instruments issued for property

    (a) In general. -- In the case of any debt instrument to which this section applies, for purposes of this subpart, the issue price shall be--

      (1) where there is adequate stated interest, the stated principal amount, or

      (2) in any other case, the imputed principal amount.

    (b) Imputed principal amount. -- For purposes of this section--

      (1) In general. -- Except as provided in paragraph (3), the imputed principal amount of any debt instrument shall be equal to the sum of the present values of all payments due under such debt instrument.

      (2) Determination of present value. -- For purposes of paragraph (1), the present value of a payment shall be determined in the manner provided by regulations prescribed by the Secretary -

          (A) as of the date of the sale or exchange, and

          (B) by using a discount rate equal to the applicable Federal rate, compounded semiannually.

      (3) Fair market value rule in potentially abusive situations. --

          (A) In general. -- In the case of any potentially abusive situation, the imputed principal amount of any debt instrument received in exchange for property shall be the fair market value of such property adjusted to take into account other consideration involved in the transaction.

          (B) Potentially abusive situation defined. -- For purposes of subparagraph (A), the term "potentially abusive situation" means--

              (i) a tax shelter (as defined in section 6662(d)(2)(C)(iii)), and

              (ii) any other situation which, by reason of--

Sec. 1274. Determination of issue price in the case of certain debt instruments issued for property

(I) recent sales transactions,

(II) nonrecourse financing,

(III) financing with a term in excess of the economic life of the property, or

(IV) other circumstances,

is of a type which the Secretary specifies by regulations as having potential for tax 5 avoidance.

(c) Debt instruments to which section applies. --

(1) In general. -- Except as otherwise provided in this subsection, this section shall apply to any debt instrument given in consideration for the sale or exchange of property if--

(A) the stated redemption price at maturity for such debt instrument exceeds--   10

(i) where there is adequate stated interest, the stated principal amount, or

(ii) in any other case, the imputed principal amount of such debt instrument determined under subsection (b), and

(B) some or all of the payments due under such debt instrument are due more than 6 months after the date of such sale or exchange.   15

(2) Adequate stated interest. -- For purposes of this section, there is adequate stated interest with respect to any debt instrument if the stated principal amount for such debt instrument is less than or equal to the imputed principal amount of such debt instrument determined under subsection (b).

(3) Exceptions. -- This section shall not apply to --   20

(A) Sales for $1,000,000 or less of farms by individuals or small businesses. --

(i) In general. -- Any debt instrument arising from the sale or exchange of a farm (within the meaning of section 6420(c)(2))--

(I) by an individual, estate, or testamentary trust,

(II) by a corporation which as of the date of the sale or exchange is a small 25 business corporation (as defined in section 1244(c)(3)), or

(III) by a partnership which as of the date of the sale or exchange meets requirements similar to those of section 1244(c)(3).

(ii) $1,000,000 limitation. -- Clause (i) shall apply only if it can be determined at the time of the sale or exchange that the sales price cannot exceed $1,000,000. For 30 purposes of the preceding sentence, all sales and exchanges which are part of the same transaction (or a series of related transactions) shall be treated as 1 sale or exchange.

(B) Sales of principal residences. -- Any debt instrument arising from the sale or exchange by an individual of his principal residence (within the meaning of section 121).

(C) Sales involving total payments of $250,000 or less. --   35

(i) In general. -- Any debt instrument arising from the sale or exchange of property if the sum of the following amounts does not exceed $250,000:

(I) the aggregate amount of the payments due under such debt instrument and all other debt instruments received as consideration for the sale or exchange, and

(II) the aggregate amount of any other consideration to be received for the sale or 40 exchange.

(ii) Consideration other than debt instrument taken into account at fair market value. -- For purposes of clause (i), any consideration (other than a debt instrument) shall be taken into account at its fair market value.

993

Sec. 1274. Determination of issue price in the case of certain debt instruments issued for property

        (iii) Aggregation of transactions. -- For purposes of this subparagraph, all sales and exchanges which are part of the same transaction (or a series of related transactions) shall be treated as 1 sale or exchange.

     (D) Debt instruments which are publicly traded or issued for publicly traded property. -- Any debt instrument to which section 1273(b)(3) applies.

     (E) Certain sales of patents. -- In the case of any transfer described in section 1235(a) (relating to sale or exchange of patents), any amount contingent on the productivity, use, or disposition of the property transferred.

     (F) Sales or exchanges to which section 483(e) applies. -- Any debt instrument to the extent section 483(e) (relating to certain land transfers between related persons) applies to such instrument.

   (4) Exception for assumptions. -- If any person--

     (A) in connection with the sale or exchange of property, assumes any debt instrument, or

     (B) acquires any property subject to any debt instrument, in determining whether this section or section 483 applies to such debt instrument, such assumption (or such acquisition) shall not be taken into account unless the terms and conditions of such debt instrument are modified (or the nature of the transaction is changed) in connection with the assumption (or acquisition).

 (d) Determination of applicable Federal rate. -- For purposes of this section--

   (1) Applicable Federal rate. --

     (A) In general. --

In the case of a debt instrument with a term of:	The applicable Federal rate is:
Not over 3 years..	The Federal short-term rate.
Over 3 years but not over 9 years..............	The Federal mid-term rate.
Over 9 years...	The Federal long-term rate.

     (B) Determination of rates. -- During each calendar month, the Secretary shall determine the Federal short-term rate, mid-term rate, and long-term rate which shall apply during the following calendar month.

     (C) Federal rate for any calendar month. -- For purposes of this paragraph--

       (i) Federal short-term rate. -- The Federal short-term rate shall be the rate determined by the Secretary based on the average market yield (during any 1- month period selected by the Secretary and ending in the calendar month in which the determination is made) on outstanding marketable obligations of the United States with remaining periods to maturity of 3 years or less.

       (ii) Federal mid-term and long-term rates. -- The Federal mid-term and long-term rate shall be determined in accordance with the principles of clause (i).

     (D) Lower rate permitted in certain cases. -- The Secretary may by regulations permit a rate to be used with respect to any debt instrument which is lower than the applicable Federal rate if the taxpayer establishes to the satisfaction of the Secretary that such lower rate is based on the same principles as the applicable Federal rate and is appropriate for the term of such instrument.

   (2) Lowest 3-month rate applicable to any sale or exchange. --

Sec. 1274. Determination of issue price in the case of certain debt instruments issued for property

(A) In general. -- In the case of any sale or exchange, the applicable Federal rate shall be the lowest 3-month rate.

(B) Lowest 3-month rate. -- For purposes of subparagraph (A), the term "lowest 3-month rate" means the lowest of the applicable Federal rates in effect for any month in the 3-calendar-month period ending with   the 1st calendar month in which there is a binding contract in writing for such sale or exchange.

(3) Term of debt instrument. -- In determining the term of a debt instrument for purposes of this subsection, under regulations prescribed by the Secretary, there shall be taken into account options to renew or extend.

(e) 110 Percent rate where sale-leaseback involved. --

(1) In general. -- In the case of any debt instrument to which this subsection applies, the discount rate used under subsection (b)(2)(B) or section 483(b) shall be 110 percent of the applicable Federal rate, compounded semiannually.

(2) Lower discount rates shall not apply. -- Section 1274A shall not apply to any debt instrument to which this subsection applies.

(3) Debt instruments to which this subsection applies. -- This subsection shall apply to any debt instrument given in consideration for the sale or exchange of any property if pursuant to a plan, the transferor or any related person leases a portion of such property after such sale or exchange.

Reg. § 1.1274-2 Issue price of debt instruments to which section 1274 applies.

***

(b) *Issue price--(1) Debt instruments that provide for adequate stated interest; stated principal amount.* The issue price of a debt instrument that provides for adequate stated interest is the stated principal amount of the debt instrument. For purposes of section 1274, the stated principal amount of a debt instrument is the aggregate amount of all payments due under the debt instrument, excluding any amount of stated interest. Under § 1.1273-2(g)(2)(ii), however, the stated principal amount of a debt instrument is reduced by any payment from the buyer- borrower to the seller-lender that is designated as interest or points. See Example 2 of § 1.1273-2(g)(5).

(2) *Debt instruments that do not provide for adequate stated interest; imputed principal amount.* The issue price of a debt instrument that does not provide for adequate stated interest is the imputed principal amount of the debt instrument.

(3) *Debt instruments issued in a potentially abusive situation; fair market value.* Notwithstanding paragraphs (b)(1) and (b)(2) of this section, in the case of a debt instrument issued in a potentially abusive situation (as defined in § 1.1274-3), the issue price of the debt instrument is the fair market value of the property received in exchange for the debt instrument, reduced by the fair market value of any consideration other than the debt instrument issued in consideration for the sale or exchange.

***

[T.D. 8517, 59 FR 4821, Feb. 2, 1994; T.D. 8674, 61 FR 30141, June 14, 1996]

Sec. 1274A. Special rules for certain transactions where stated principal amount does not exceed $2,800,000

(a) **Lower discount rate.** -- In the case of any qualified debt instrument, the discount rate used for purposes of sections 483 and 1274 shall not exceed 9 percent, compounded semiannually.

Sec. 1274A. Special rules for certain transactions where stated principal amount does not exceed $2,800,000

(b) Qualified debt instrument defined. -- For purposes of this section, the term "qualified debt instrument" means any debt instrument given in consideration for the sale or exchange of property (other than new section 38 property within the meaning of section 48(b), as in effect on th day before the date of the enactment of the Revenue Reconciliation Act of 1990) if the stated principal amount of such instrument does not exceed $2,800,000.

(c) Election to use cash method where stated principal amount does not exceed $2,000,000. --

(1) In general. -- In the case of any cash method debt instrument--

(A) section 1274 shall not apply, and

(B) interest on such debt instrument shall be taken into account by both the borrower and the lender under the cash receipts and disbursements method of accounting.

(2) Cash method debt instrument. -- For purposes of paragraph (1), the term "cash method debt instrument" means any qualified debt instrument if--

(A) the stated principal amount does not exceed $2,000,000,

(B) the lender does not use an accrual method of accounting and is not a dealer with respect to the property sold or exchanged,

(C) section 1274 would have applied to such instrument but for an election under this subsection, and

(D) an election under this subsection is jointly made with respect to such debt instrument by the borrower and lender.

(3) Successors bound by election. --

(A) In general. -- Except as provided in subparagraph (B), paragraph (1) shall apply to any successor to the borrower or lender with respect to a cash method debt instrument.

(B) Exception where lender transfers debt instrument to accrual method taxpayer. -- If the lender (or any successor) transfers any cash method debt instrument to a taxpayer who uses an accrual method of accounting, this paragraph shall not apply with respect to such instrument for periods after such transfer.

(4) Fair market value rule in potentially abusive situations. -- In the case of any cash method debt instrument, section 483 shall be applied as if it included provisions similar to the provisions of section 1274(b)(3).

(d) Other special rules. --

(1) Aggregation rules. -- For purposes of this section--

(A) all sales or exchanges which are part of the same transaction (or a series of related transactions) shall be treated as 1 sale or exchange, and

(B) all debt instruments arising from the same transaction (or a series of related transactions) shall be treated as 1 debt instrument.

(2) Inflation adjustments. --

(A) In general. -- In the case of any debt instrument arising out of a sale or exchange during any calendar year after 1989, each dollar amount contained in the preceding provisions of this section shall be increased by the inflation adjustment for such calendar year. Any increase under the preceding sentence shall be rounded to the nearest multiple of $100 (or, if such increase is a multiple of $50, such increase shall be increased to the nearest multiple of $100).

(B) Inflation adjustment. -- For purposes of subparagraph (A), the inflation adjustment for any calendar year is the percentage (if any) by which--

996

Sec. 1274A. Special rules for certain transactions where stated principal amount does not exceed $2,800,000

      (i) the CPI for the preceding calendar year exceeds

      (ii) the CPI for calendar year 1988.

For purposes of the preceding sentence, the CPI for any calendar year is the average of the Consumer Price Index as of the close of the 12-month period ending on September 30 of such calendar year.   5

***

Sec. 1275. Other definitions and special rules

(a) Definitions. -- For purposes of this subpart--

  (1) Debt instrument. --

    (A) In general. -- Except as provided in subparagraph (B), the term "debt instrument" 10 means a bond, debenture, note, or certificate or other evidence of indebtedness.

    (B) Exception for certain annuity contracts. -- The term "debt instrument" shall not include any annuity contract to which section 72 applies and which--

      (i) depends (in whole or in substantial part) on the life expectancy of 1 or more individuals, or   15

      (ii) is issued by an insurance company subject to tax under subchapter L (or by an entity described in section 501(c) and exempt from tax under section 501(a) which would be subject to tax under subchapter L were it not so exempt) -

        (I) in a transaction in which there is no consideration other than cash or another annuity contract meeting the requirements of this clause,   20

        (II) pursuant to the exercise of an election under an insurance contract by a beneficiary thereof on the death of the insured party under such contract, o

        (III) in a transaction involving a qualified pension or employee benefit plan.

  (2) Issue date. --

    (A) Publicly offered debt instruments. -- In the case of any debt instrument which is 25 publicly offered, the term "date of original issue" means the date on which the issue was first issued to the public.

    (B) Issues not publicly offered and not issued for property. -- In the case of any debt instrument to which section1273(b)(2) applies, the term "date of original issue" means the date on which the debt instrument was sold by the issuer.   30

    (C) Other debt instruments. -- In the case of any debt instrument not described in subparagraph (A) or (B), the term "date of original issue" means the date on which the debt instrument was issued in a sale or exchange.

  (3) Tax-exempt obligation. -- The term "tax-exempt obligation" means any obligation if--

    (A) the interest on such obligation is not includible in gross income under section 103, or 35

    (B) the interest on such obligation is exempt from tax (without regard to the identity of the holder) under any other provision of law.

  (4) Treatment of obligations distributed by corporations. -- Any debt obligation of a corporation distributed by such corporation with respect to its stock shall be treated as if it had been issued by such corporation for property.   40

(b) Treatment of borrower in the case of certain loans for personal use. --

  (1) Sections 1274 and 483 not to apply. -- In the case of the obligor under any debt instrument given in consideration for the sale or exchange of property, sections 1274 and 483

997

Sec. 1275. Other definitions and special rules

shall not apply if such property is personal use property.

(2) Original issue discount deducted on cash basis in certain cases. -- In the case of any debt instrument, if--

(A) such instrument--

(i) is incurred in connection with the acquisition or carrying of personal use property, and

(ii) has original issue discount (determined after the application of paragraph (1)), and

(B) the obligor under such instrument uses the cash receipts and disbursements method of accounting,

notwithstanding section 163(e), the original issue discount on such instrument shall be deductible only when paid.

(3) Personal use property. -- For purposes of this subsection, the term "personal use property" means any property substantially all of the use of which by the taxpayer is not in connection with a trade or business of the taxpayer or an activity described in section 212. The determination of whether property is described in the preceding sentence shall be made as of the time of issuance of the debt instrument.

(c) Information requirements. --

***

(2) Information required to be submitted to Secretary. -- In the case of any issue of publicly offered debt instruments having original issue discount, the issuer shall (at such time and in such manner as the Secretary shall by regulation prescribe) furnish the Secretary the following information:

(A) The amount of the original issue discount.

(B) The issue date.

(C) Such other information with respect to the issue as the Secretary may by regulations require.

For purposes of the preceding sentence, any person who makes a public offering of stripped bonds (or stripped coupons) shall be treated as the issuer of a publicly offered debt instrument having original issue discount.

(3) Exceptions. -- This subsection shall not apply to any obligation referred to in section 1272(a)(2) (relating to exceptions from current inclusion of original issue discount).

(4) Cross reference. -- For civil penalty for failure to meet requirements of this subsection, see section 6706.

(d) Regulation authority. -- The Secretary may prescribe regulations providing that where, by reason of varying rates of interest, put or call options, indefinite maturities, contingent payments, assumptions of debt instruments, or other circumstances, the tax treatment under this subpart (or section 163(e)) does not carry out the purposes of this subpart (or section 163(e)), such treatment shall be modified to the extent appropriate to carry out the purposes of this subpart (or section 163(e)).

Sec. 1276. Disposition gain representing accrued market discount treated as ordinary income

(a) Ordinary income. --

(1) In general. -- Except as otherwise provided in this section, gain on the disposition of

Sec. 1276. Disposition gain representing accrued market discount treated as ordinary income

any market discount bond shall be treated as ordinary income to the extent it does not exceed the accrued market discount on such bond. Such gain shall be recognized notwithstanding any other provision of this subtitle.

(2) Dispositions other than sales, etc. -- For purposes of paragraph (1), a person disposing of any market discount bond in any transaction other than a sale, exchange, or involuntary conversion shall be treated as realizing an amount equal to the fair market value of the bond.

(3) Treatment of partial principal payments. --

(A) In general. -- Any partial principal payment on a market discount bond shall be included in gross income as ordinary income to the extent such payment does not exceed the accrued market discount on such bond.

(B) Adjustment. -- If subparagraph (A) applies to any partial principal payment on any market discount bond, for purposes of applying this section to any disposition of (or subsequent partial principal payment on) such bond, the amount of accrued market discount shall be reduced by the amount of such partial principal payment included in gross income under subparagraph (A).

(4) Gain treated as interest for certain purposes. -- Except for purposes of sections 103, 871(a), 881, 1441, 1442, and 6049 (and such other provisions as may be specified in regulations), any amount treated as ordinary income under paragraph (1) or (3) shall be treated as interest for purposes of this title.

(b) Accrued market discount. -- For purposes of this section--

(1) Ratable accrual. -- Except as otherwise provided in this subsection or subsection (c), the accrued market discount on any bond shall be an amount which bears the same ratio to the market discount on such bond as -

(A) the number of days which the taxpayer held the bond, bears to

(B) the number of days after the date the taxpayer acquired the bond and up to (and including) the date of its maturity.

(2) Election of accrual on basis of constant interest rate (in lieu of ratable accrual). --

(A) In general. -- At the election of the taxpayer with respect to any bond, the accrued market discount on such bond shall be the aggregate amount which would have been includible in the gross income of the taxpayer under section 1272(a) (determined without regard to paragraph (2) thereof) with respect to such bond for all periods during which the bond was held by the taxpayer if such bond had been--

(i) originally issued on the date on which such bond was acquired by the taxpayer,

(ii) for an issue price equal to the basis of the taxpayer in such bond immediately after its acquisition.

(B) Coordination where bond has original issue discount. -- In the case of any bond having original issue discount, for purposes of applying subparagraph (A)--

(i) the stated redemption price at maturity of such bond shall be treated as equal to its revised issue price, and

(ii) the determination of the portion of the original issue discount which would have been includible in the gross income of the taxpayer under section 1272(a) shall be made under regulations prescribed by the Secretary.

(C) Election irrevocable. -- An election under subparagraph (A), once made with respect to any bond, shall be irrevocable.

(3) Special rule where partial principal payments. -- In the case of a bond the principal of which may be paid in 2 or more payments, the amount of accrued market discount shall be

999

Sec. 1276. Disposition gain representing accrued market discount treated as ordinary income

determined under regulations prescribed by the Secretary.

(c) Treatment of nonrecognition transactions. -- Under regulations prescribed by the Secretary-

(1) Transferred basis property. -- If a market discount bond is transferred in a nonrecognition transaction and such bond is transferred basis property in the hands of the transferee, for purposes of determining the amount of the accrued market discount with respect to the transferee--

(A) the transferee shall be treated as having acquired the bond on the date on which it was acquired by the transferor for an amount equal to the basis of the transferor, and

(B) proper adjustments shall be made for gain recognized by the transferor on such transfer (and for any original issue discount or market discount included in the gross income of the transferor).

(2) Exchanged basis property. -- If any market discount bond is disposed of by the taxpayer in a nonrecognition transaction and paragraph (1) does not apply to such transaction, any accrued market discount determined with respect to the property disposed of to the extent not theretofore treated as ordinary income under subsection (a)--

(A) shall be treated as accrued market discount with respect to the exchanged basis property received by the taxpayer in such transaction if such property is a market discount bond, and

(B) shall be treated as ordinary income on the disposition of the exchanged basis property received by the taxpayer in such exchange if such property is not a market discount bond.

***

(d) Special rules. -- Under regulations prescribed by the Secretary -

(1) rules similar to the rules of subsection (b) of section1245 shall apply for purposes of this section;

***

(2) appropriate adjustments shall be made to the basis of any property to reflect gain recognized under subsection (a).

Sec. 1277. Deferral of interest deduction allocable to accrued market discount

(a) General rule. -- Except as otherwise provided in this section, the net direct interest expense with respect to any market discount bond shall be allowed as a deduction for the taxable year only to the extent that such expense exceeds the portion of the market discount allocable to the days during the taxable year on which such bond was held by the taxpayer (as determined under the rules of section 1276(b)).

(b) Disallowed deduction allowed for later years. --

(1) Election to take into account in later year where net interest income from bond. --

(A) In general. -- If--

(i) there is net interest income for any taxable year with respect to any market discount bond, and

(ii) the taxpayer makes an election under this subparagraph with respect to such bond,

Sec. 1277. Deferral of interest deduction allocable to accrued market discount

any disallowed interest expense with respect to such bond shall be treated as interest paid or accrued by the taxpayer during such taxable year to the extent such disallowed interest expense does not exceed the net interest income with respect to such bond.

   (B) Determination of disallowed interest expense. -- For purposes of subparagraph (A), the amount of the disallowed interest expense--
(i) shall be determined as of the close of the preceding taxable year, and
(ii) shall not include any amount previously taken into account under subparagraph (A).

   (C) Net interest income. -- For purposes of this paragraph, the term "net interest income" means the excess of the amount determined under paragraph (2) of subsection (c) over the amount determined under paragraph (1) of subsection (c).

(2) Remainder of disallowed interest expense allowed for year of disposition. --

   (A) In general. -- Except as otherwise provided in this paragraph, the amount of the disallowed interest expense with respect to any market discount bond shall be treated as interest paid or accrued by the taxpayer in the taxable year in which such bond is disposed of.

   (B) Nonrecognition transactions. -- If any market discount bond is disposed of in a nonrecognition transaction--

      (i) the disallowed interest expense with respect to such bond shall be treated as interest paid or accrued in the year of disposition only to the extent of the amount of gain recognized on such disposition, and

      (ii) the disallowed interest expense with respect to such property (to the extent not so treated) shall be treated as disallowed interest expense--

         (I) in the case of a transaction described in section1276(c)(1), of the transferee with respect to the transferred basis property, or

         (II) in the case of a transaction described in section 1276(c)(2), with respect to the exchanged basis property.

   (C) Disallowed interest expense reduced for amounts previously taken into account under paragraph (1)
For purposes of this paragraph, the amount of the disallowed interest expense shall not include any amount previously taken into account under paragraph (1).

   (3) Disallowed interest expense. -- For purposes of this subsection, the term "disallowed interest expense" means the aggregate amount disallowed under subsection (a) with respect to the market discount bond.

(c) Net direct interest expense. -- For purposes of this section, the term "net direct interest expense" means, with respect to any market discount bond, the excess (if any) of--

   (1) the amount of interest paid or accrued during the taxable year on indebtedness which is incurred or continued to purchase or carry such bond, over

   (2) the aggregate amount of interest (including original issue discount) includible in gross income for the taxable year with respect to such bond.

In the case of any financial institution which is a bank (as defined in section 585(a)(2)), the determination of whether interest is described in paragraph (1) shall be made under principles similar to the principles of section 291(e)(1)(B)(ii). Under rules similar to the rules of section 265(a)(5), short sale expenses shall be treated as interest for purposes of determining net direct interest expense.

Sec. 1278. Definitions and special rules

(a) **In general.** -- For purposes of this part--

(1) **Market discount bond.** --

(A) **In general.** -- Except as provided in subparagraph (B), the term "market discount bond" means any bond having market discount.

5   (B) **Exceptions.** -- The term "market discount bond" shall not include--

(i) **Short-term obligations.** -- Any obligation with a fixed maturity date not exceeding 6 months from the date of issue.

(ii) **United States savings bonds.** -- Any United States savings bond.

(iii) **Installment obligations.** -- Any installment obligation to which section 453B
10   applies.

(C) **Section 1277 not applicable to tax-exempt obligations.** -- For purposes of section 1277, the term "market discount bond" shall not include any tax-exempt obligation (as defined in section 1275(a)(3)).

(D) **Treatment of bonds acquired at original issue.** --

15   (i) **In general.** -- Except as otherwise provided in this subparagraph or in regulations, the term "market discount bond" shall not include any bond acquired by the taxpayer at its original issue.

(ii) **Treatment of bonds acquired for less than issue price.** -- Clause (i) shall not apply to any bond if--

20   (I) the basis of the taxpayer in such bond is determined under section 1012, and

(II) such basis is less than the issue price of such bond determined under subpart A of this part.

(iii) **Bonds acquired in certain reorganizations.** -- Clause (i) shall not apply to any bond issued pursuant to a plan of reorganization (within the meaning of section 368(a)
25   (1)) in exchange for another bond having market discount. Solely for purposes of section 1276, the preceding sentence shall not apply if such other bond was issued on or before July 18, 1984 (the date of the enactment of section 1276) and if the bond issued pursuant to such plan of reorganization has the same term and the same interest rate as such other bond had.

30   (iv) **Treatment of certain transferred basis property.** -- For purposes of clause (i), if the adjusted basis of any bond in the hands of the taxpayer is determined by reference to the adjusted basis of such bond in the hands of a person who acquired such bond at its original issue, such bond shall be treated as acquired by the taxpayer at its original issue.

35   (2) **Market discount.** --

(A) **In general.** -- The term "market discount" means the excess (if any) of--

(i) the stated redemption price of the bond at maturity, over

(ii) the basis of such bond immediately after its acquisition by the taxpayer.

(B) **Coordination where bond has original issue discount.** -- In the case of any bond
40   having original issue discount, for purposes of subparagraph (A), the stated redemption price of such bond at maturity shall be treated as equal to its revised issue price.

(C) **De minimis rule.** -- If the market discount is less than 1/4 of 1 percent of the stated redemption price of the bond at maturity multiplied by the number of complete years to maturity (after the taxpayer acquired the bond), then the market discount shall be

Sec. 1278. Definitions and special rules

considered to be zero.

(3) Bond. -- The term "bond" means any bond, debenture, note, certificate, or other evidence of indebtedness.

(4) Revised issue price. -- The term "revised issue price" means the sum of--

    (A) the issue price of the bond, and

    (B) the aggregate amount of the original issue discount includible in the gross income of all holders for periods before the acquisition of the bond by the taxpayer (determined without regard to section 1272(a)(7) or (b)(4)) or, in the case of a tax-exempt obligation, the aggregate amount of the original issue discount which accrued in the manner provided by section 1272(a) (determined without regard to paragraph (7) thereof) during periods before the acquisition of the bond by the taxpayer.

(5) Original issue discount, etc. -- The terms "original issue discount", "stated redemption price at maturity", and "issue price" have the respective meanings given such terms by subpart A of this part.

(b) Election to include market discount currently. --

    (1) In general. -- If the taxpayer makes an election under this subsection--

        (A) sections 1276 and 1277 shall not apply, and

        (B) market discount on any market discount bond shall be included in the gross income of the taxpayer for the taxable years to which it is attributable (as determined under the rules of subsection (b) of section 1276).

Except for purposes of sections 103, 871(a), 881, 1441, 1442, and 6049 (and such other provisions as may be specified in regulations), any amount included in gross income under subparagraph (B) shall be treated as interest for purposes of this title.

    (2) Scope of election. -- An election under this subsection shall apply to all market discount bonds acquired by the taxpayer on or after the 1st day of the 1st taxable year to which such election applies.

    (3) Period to which election applies. -- An election under this subsection shall apply to the taxable year for which it is made and for all subsequent taxable years, unless the taxpayer secures the consent of the Secretary to the revocation of such election.

    (4) Basis adjustment. -- The basis of any bond in the hands of the taxpayer shall be increased by the amount included in gross income pursuant to this subsection.

(c) Regulations. -- The Secretary shall prescribe such regulations as may be necessary to carry out the purposes of this subpart, including regulations providing proper adjustments in the case of a bond the principal of which may be paid in 2 or more payments.

Sec. 1281. Current inclusion in income of discount on certain short- term obligations

(a) General rule. -- In the case of any short-term obligation to which this section applies, for purposes of this title--

    (1) there shall be included in the gross income of the holder an amount equal to the sum of the daily portions of the acquisition discount for each day during the taxable year on which such holder held such obligation, and

    (2) any interest payable on the obligation (other than interest taken into account in determining the amount of the acquisition discount) shall be included in gross income as it accrues.

Sec. 1281. Current inclusion in income of discount on certain short- term obligations

   (b) Short-term obligations to which section applies. --

   (1) In general. -- This section shall apply to any short-term obligation which--

   (A) is held by a taxpayer using an accrual method of accounting,

   (B) is held primarily for sale to customers in the ordinary course of the taxpayer's trade or business,

   (C) is held by a bank (as defined in section 581),

   (D) is held by a regulated investment company or a common trust fund,

   (E) is identified by the taxpayer under section 1256(e)(2) as being part of a hedging transaction, or

   (F) is a stripped bond or stripped coupon held by the person who stripped the bond or coupon (or by any other person whose basis is determined by reference to the basis in the hands of such person).

   (2) Treatment of obligations held by pass-thru entities. --

   (A) In general. -- This section shall apply also to--

   (i) any short-term obligation which is held by a pass-thru entity which is formed or availed of for purposes of avoiding the provisions of this section, and

   (ii) any short-term obligation which is acquired by a pass- thru entity (not described in clause (i)) during the required accrual period.

   (B) Required accrual period. -- For purposes of subparagraph (A), the term "required accrual period" means the period--

   (i) which begins with the first taxable year for which the ownership test of subparagraph (C) is met with respect to the pass-thru entity (or a predecessor), and

   (ii) which ends with the first taxable year after the taxable year referred to in clause (i) for which the ownership test of subparagraph (C) is not met and with respect to which the Secretary consents to the termination of the required accrual period.

   (C) Ownership test. -- The ownership test of this subparagraph is met for any taxable year if, on at least 90 days during the taxable year, 20 percent or more of the value of the interests in the pass-thru entity are held by persons described in paragraph (1) or by other pass-thru entities to which subparagraph (A) applies.

   (D) Pass-thru entity. -- The term "pass-thru entity" means any partnership, S corporation, trust, or other pass-thru entity.

   (c) Cross reference. -- For special rules limiting the application of this section to original issue discount in the case of nongovernmental obligations, see section 1283(c).

Sec. 1283. Definitions and special rules

   (a) Definitions. -- For purposes of this subpart--

   (1) Short-term obligation. --

   (A) In general. -- Except as provided in subparagraph (B), the term "short-term obligation" means any bond, debenture, note, certificate, or other evidence of indebtedness which has a fixed maturity date not more than 1 year from the date of issue.

   (B) Exceptions for tax-exempt obligations. -- The term "short-term obligation" shall not include any tax- exempt obligation (as defined in section 1275(a)(3)).

Sec. 1283. Definitions and special rules

(2) Acquisition discount. -- The term "acquisition discount" means the excess of--

(A) the stated redemption price at maturity (as defined in section 1273), over

(B) the taxpayer's basis for the obligation.

(b) Daily portion. -- For purposes of this subpart--

(1) Ratable accrual. -- Except as otherwise provided in this subsection, the daily portion of 5 the acquisition discount is an amount equal to--

(A) the amount of such discount, divided by

(B) the number of days after the day on which the taxpayer acquired the obligation and up to (and including) the day of its maturity.

(2) Election of accrual on basis of constant interest rate (in lieu of ratable accrual). --   10

(A) In general. -- At the election of the taxpayer with respect to any obligation, the daily portion of the acquisition discount for any day is the portion of the acquisition discount accruing on such day determined (under regulations prescribed by the Secretary) on the basis of--

(i) the taxpayer's yield to maturity based on the taxpayer's cost of acquiring the 15 obligation, and

(ii) compounding daily.

(B) Election irrevocable. -- An election under subparagraph (A), once made with respect to any obligation, shall be irrevocable.

(c) Special rules for nongovernmental obligations. --   20

(1) In general. -- In the case of any short-term obligation which is not a short-term Government obligation (as defined in section 1271(a)(3)(B))--

(A) sections 1281 and 1282 shall be applied by taking into account original issue discount in lieu of acquisition discount, and

(B) appropriate adjustments shall be made in the application of subsection (b) of this 25 section.

(2) Election to have paragraph (1) not apply. --

(A) In general. -- A taxpayer may make an election under this paragraph to have paragraph (1) not apply to all obligations acquired by the taxpayer on or after the first day of the first taxable year to which such election applies.   30

(B) Period to which election applies. -- An election under this paragraph shall apply to the taxable year for which it is made and for all subsequent taxable years, unless the taxpayer secures the consent of the Secretary to the revocation of such election.

(d) Other special rules. --

(1) Basis adjustments. -- The basis of any short-term obligation in the hands of the holder 35 thereof shall be increased by the amount included in his gross income pursuant to section 1281.

(2) Double inclusion in income not required. -- Section 1281 shall not require the inclusion of any amount previously includible in gross income.

(3) Coordination with other provisions. -- Section 454(b) and paragraphs (3) and (4) of section 1271(a) shall not apply to any short-term obligation to which section 1281 applies.   40

Sec. 1286. Tax treatment of stripped bonds

(a) Inclusion in income as if bond and coupons were original issue discount bonds. -- If any person purchases after July 1, 1982, a stripped bond or a stripped coupon, then such bond or

Sec. 1286. Tax treatment of stripped bonds

coupon while held by such purchaser (or by any other person whose basis is determined by reference to the basis in the hands of such purchaser) shall be treated for purposes of this part as a bond originally issued on the purchase date and having an original issue discount equal to the excess (if any) of--

(1) the stated redemption price at maturity (or, in the case of coupon, the amount payable on the due date of such coupon), over

(2) such bond's or coupon's ratable share of the purchase price.

For purposes of paragraph (2), ratable shares shall be determined on the basis of their respective fair market values on the date of purchase.

(b) Tax treatment of person stripping bond. -- For purposes of this subtitle, if any person strips 1 or more coupons from a bond and after July 1, 1982, disposes of the bond or such coupon--

(1) such person shall include in gross income an amount equal to the sum of--

(A) the interest accrued on such bond while held by such person and before the time such coupon or bond was disposed of (to the extent such interest has not theretofore been included in such person's gross income), and

(B) the accrued market discount on such bond determined as of the time such coupon or bond was disposed of (to the extent such discount has not theretofore been included in such person's gross income),

(2) the basis of the bond and coupons shall be increased by the amount included in gross income under paragraph (1),

(3) the basis of the bond and coupons immediately before the disposition (as adjusted pursuant to paragraph (2)) shall be allocated among the items retained by such person and the items disposed of by such person on the basis of their respective fair market values, and

(4) for purposes of subsection (a), such person shall be treated as having purchased on the date of such disposition each such item which he retains for an amount equal to the basis allocated to such item under paragraph (3).

A rule similar to the rule of paragraph (4) shall apply in the case of any person whose basis in any bond or coupon is determined by reference to the basis of the person described in the preceding sentence.

***

(d) Special rules for tax-exempt obligations. --

(1) In general. -- In the case of any tax-exempt obligation (as defined in section1275(a)(3)) from which 1 or more coupons have been stripped--

(A) the amount of the original issue discount determined under subsection (a) with respect to any stripped bond or stripped coupon--

(i) shall be treated as original issue discount on a tax- exempt obligation to the extent such discount does not exceed the tax-exempt portion of such discount, and

(ii) shall be treated as original issue discount on an obligation which is not a tax-exempt obligation to the extent such discount exceeds the tax-exempt portion of such discount,

(B) subsection (b)(1)(A) shall not apply, and

(C) subsection (b)(2) shall be applied by increasing the basis of the bond or coupon by the sum of--

(i) the interest accrued but not paid before such bond or coupon was disposed of (and not previously reflected in basis), plus

(ii) the amount included in gross income under subsection (b)(1)(B).

Sec. 1286.   Tax treatment of stripped bonds

(2) Tax-exempt portion. -- For purposes of paragraph (1), the tax-exempt portion of the original issue discount determined under subsection (a) is the excess of--

(A) the amount referred to in subsection (a)(1), over

(B) an issue price which would produce a yield to maturity as of the purchase date equal to the lower of-- 5

(i) the coupon rate of interest on the obligation from which the coupons were separated, or

(ii) the yield to maturity (on the basis of the purchase price) of the stripped obligation or coupon.

The purchaser of any stripped obligation or coupon may elect to apply clause (i) by 10 substituting "original yield to maturity of" for "coupon rate of interest on".

(e) Definitions and special rules. -- For purposes of this section--

(1) Bond. -- The term "bond" means a bond, debenture, note, or certificate or other evidence of indebtedness.

(2) Stripped bond. -- The term "stripped bond" means a bond issued at any time with 15 interest coupons where there is a separation in ownership between the bond and any coupon which has not yet become payable.

(3) Stripped coupon. -- The term "stripped coupon" means any coupon relating to a stripped bond.

(4) Stated redemption price at maturity. -- The term "stated redemption price at maturity" 20 has the meaning given such term by section 1273(a)(2).

(5) Coupon. -- The term "coupon" includes any right to receive interest on a bond (whether or not evidenced by a coupon).

***

(6) Purchase. -- The term "purchase" has the meaning given such term by section 1272(d) 25 (1).

***

(g) Regulation authority. - The Secretary may prescribe regulations providing that where, by reason of varying rates of interest, put or call options, or other circumstances, the tax treatment under this section does not accurately reflect the income of the holder of a stripped coupon or 30 stripped bond, or of the person disposing of such bond or coupon, as the case may be, for any period, such treatment shall be modified to require that the proper amount of income be included for such period.

Sec. 1288.   Treatment of original issue discount on tax-exempt obligations

(a) General rule. -- Original issue discount on any tax-exempt obligation shall be treated as 35 accruing--

(1) for purposes of section 163, in the manner provided by section 1272(a) (determined without regard to paragraph (7) thereof), and

(2) for purposes of determining the adjusted basis of the holder, in the manner provided by section 1272(a) (determined with regard to paragraph (7) thereof). 40

***

Sec. 1311.   Correction of error

(a) General rule. -- If a determination (as defined in section 1313) is described in one or more

1007

Sec. 1311.   Correction of error

of the paragraphs of section 1312 and, on the date of the determination, correction of the effect of the error referred to in the applicable paragraph of section 1312 is prevented by the operation of any law or rule of law, other than this part and other than section 7122 (relating to compromises), then the effect of the error shall be corrected by an adjustment made in the amount and in the
5 manner specified in section 1314.

   (b) Conditions necessary for adjustment. --

   (1) Maintenance of an inconsistent position. -- Except in cases described in paragraphs (3) (B) and (4) of section 1312, an adjustment shall be made under this part only if--

      (A) in case the amount of the adjustment would be credited or refunded in the same
10   manner as an overpayment under section1314, there is adopted in the determination a position maintained by the Secretary, or

      (B) in case the amount of the adjustment would be assessed and collected in the same manner as a deficiency under section1314, there is adopted in the determination a position maintained by the taxpayer with respect to whom the determination is made,

15 and the position maintained by the Secretary in the case described in subparagraph (A) or maintained by the taxpayer in the case described in subparagraph (B) is inconsistent with the erroneous inclusion, exclusion, omission, allowance, disallowance, recognition, or non-recognition, as the case may be.

   (2) Correction not barred at time of erroneous action. --

20   **(A) Determination described in section 1312(3)(B).** -- In the case of a determination described in section 1312(3)(B) (relating to certain exclusions from income), adjustment shall be made under this part only if assessment of a deficiency for the taxable year in which the item is includible or against the related taxpayer was not barred, by any law or rule of law, at the time the Secretary first maintained, in a notice of deficiency sent
25   pursuant to section 6212 or before the Tax Court that the item described in section 1312(3) (B) should be included in the gross income of the taxpayer for the taxable year to which the determination relates.

      (B) Determination described in section 1312(4). -- In the case of a determination described in section 1312(4) (relating to disallowance of certain deductions and credits),
30   adjustment shall be made under this part only if credit or refund of the overpayment attributable to the deduction or credit described in such section which should have been allowed to the taxpayer or related taxpayer was not barred, by any law or rule of law, at the time the taxpayer first maintained before the Secretary or before the Tax Court, in writing, that he was entitled to such deduction or credit for the taxable year to which the
35   determination relates.

   (3) Existence of relationship. -- In case the amount of the adjustment would be assessed and collected in the same manner as a deficiency (except for cases described in section 1312(3) (B)), the adjustment shall not be made with respect to a related taxpayer unless he stands in such relationship to the taxpayer at the time the latter first maintains the inconsistent position
40 in a return, claim for refund, or petition (or amended petition) to the Tax Court for the taxable year with respect to which the determination is made, or if such position is not so maintained, then at the time of the determination.

Sec. 1312.   Circumstances of adjustment

   The circumstances under which the adjustment provided in section 1311 is authorized are as
45 follows:

   (1) Double inclusion of an item of gross income. -- The determination requires the

Sec. 1312.   Circumstances of adjustment

inclusion in gross income of an item which was erroneously included in the gross income of the taxpayer for another taxable year or in the gross income of a related taxpayer.

(2) Double allowance of a deduction or credit. -- The determination allows a deduction or credit which was erroneously allowed to the taxpayer for another taxable year or to a related taxpayer.

(3) Double exclusion of an item of gross income. --

(A) Items included in income. -- The determination requires the exclusion from gross income of an item included in a return filed by the taxpayer or with respect to which tax was paid and which was erroneously excluded or omitted from the gross income of the taxpayer for another taxable year, or from the gross income of a related taxpayer; or

(B) Items not included in income. -- The determination requires the exclusion from gross income of an item not included in a return filed by the taxpayer and with respect to which the tax was not paid but which is includible in the gross income of the taxpayer for another taxable year or in the gross income of a related taxpayer.

(4) Double disallowance of a deduction or credit. -- The determination disallows a deduction or credit which should have been allowed to, but was not allowed to, the taxpayer for another taxable year, or to a related taxpayer.

(5) Correlative deductions and inclusions for trusts or estates and legatees, beneficiaries, or heirs. -- The determination allows or disallows any of the additional deductions allowable in computing the taxable income of estates or trusts, or requires or denies any of the inclusions in the computation of taxable income of beneficiaries, heirs, or legatees, specified in subparts A to E, inclusive (secs. 641 and following, relating to estates, trusts, and beneficiaries) of part I of subchapter J of this chapter, or corresponding provisions of prior internal revenue laws, and the correlative inclusion or deduction, as the case may be, has been erroneously excluded, omitted, or included, or disallowed, omitted, or allowed, as the case may be, in respect of the related taxpayer.

(6) Correlative deductions and credits for certain related corporations. -- The determination allows or disallows a deduction (including a credit) in computing the taxable income (or, as the case may be, net income, normal tax net income, or surtax net income) of a corporation, and a correlative deduction or credit has been erroneously allowed, omitted, or disallowed, as the case may be, in respect of a related taxpayer described in section 1313(c)(7).

(7) Basis of property after erroneous treatment of a prior transaction. --

(A) General rule. -- The determination determines the basis of property, and in respect of any transaction on which such basis depends, or in respect of any transaction which was erroneously treated as affecting such basis, there occurred, with respect to a taxpayer described in subparagraph (B) of this paragraph, any of the errors described in subparagraph (C) of this paragraph.

(B) Taxpayers with respect to whom the erroneous treatment occurred. -- The taxpayer with respect to whom the erroneous treatment occurred must be--

(i) the taxpayer with respect to whom the determination is made,

(ii) a taxpayer who acquired title to the property in the transaction and from whom, mediately or immediately, the taxpayer with respect to whom the determination is made derived title, or

(iii) a taxpayer who had title to the property at the time of the transaction and from whom, mediately or immediately, the taxpayer with respect to whom the determination is made derived title, if the basis of the property in the hands of the taxpayer with respect to whom the determination is made is determined under section 1015(a) (relating to the basis of property acquired by gift).

Sec. 1312.   Circumstances of adjustment

    (C) Prior erroneous treatment. -- With respect to a taxpayer described in subparagraph (B) of this paragraph--

        (i) there was an erroneous inclusion in, or omission from, gross income,

        (ii) there was an erroneous recognition, or nonrecognition, of gain or loss, or

        (iii) there was an erroneous deduction of an item properly chargeable to capital account or an erroneous charge to capital account of an item properly deductible.

Sec. 1313.   Definitions.

    (a) Determination. -- For purposes of this part, the term "determination" means--

    (1) a decision by the Tax Court or a judgment, decree, or other order by any court of competent jurisdiction, which has become final;

    (2) a closing agreement made under section 7121;

    (3) a final disposition by the Secretary of a claim for refund.

For purposes of this part, a claim for refund shall be deemed finally disposed of by the Secretary -

    (A) as to items with respect to which the claim was allowed, on the date of allowance of refund or credit or on the date of mailing notice of disallowance (by reason of offsetting items) of the claim for refund, and

    (B) as to items with respect to which the claim was disallowed, in whole or in part, or as to items applied by the Secretary in reduction of the refund or credit, on expiration of the time for instituting suit with respect thereto (unless suit is instituted before the expiration of such time); or

    (4) under regulations prescribed by the Secretary, an agreement for purposes of this part, signed by the Secretary and by any person, relating to the liability of such person (or the person for whom he acts) in respect of a tax under this subtitle for any taxable period.

    (b) Taxpayer. -- Notwithstanding section 7701(a)(14), the term "taxpayer" means any person subject to a tax under the applicable revenue law.

    (c) Related taxpayer. -- For purposes of this part, the term "related taxpayer" means a taxpayer who, with the taxpayer with respect to whom   determination is made, stood, in the taxable year with respect to which the erroneous inclusion, exclusion, omission, allowance, or disallowance was made, in one of the following relationships:

    (1) husband and wife,

    (2) grantor and fiduciary,

    (3) grantor and beneficiary,

    (4) fiduciary and beneficiary, legatee, or heir,

    (5) decedent and decedent's estate,

    (6) partner, or

    (7) member of an affiliated group of corporations (as defined in section 1504).

Sec. 1314.   Amount and method of adjustment

    (a) Ascertainment of amount of adjustment. -- In computing the amount of an adjustment under this part thereshall first be ascertained the tax previously determined for the taxable year with respect to which the error was made. The amount of the tax previously determined shall be the excess of -

Sec. 1314.   Amount and method of adjustment

(1) the sum of--

(A) the amount shown as the tax by the taxpayer on his return (determined as provided in section 6211(b)(1), (3), and (4), relating to the definition of deficiency), if a return was made by the taxpayer and an amount was shown as the tax by the taxpayer thereon, plus

(B) the amounts previously assessed (or collected without assessment) as a deficiency, 5 over--

(2) the amount of rebates, as defined in section 6211(b)(2), made.

There shall then be ascertained the increase or decrease in tax previously determined which results solely from the correct treatment of the item which was the subject of the error (with due regard given to the effect of the item in the computation of gross income, taxable income, and other 10 matters under this subtitle). A similar computation shall be made for any other taxable year affected, or treated as affected, by a net operating loss deduction (as defined in section 172) or by a capital loss carryback or carryover (as defined in section 1212), determined with reference to the taxable year with respect to which the error was made. The amount so ascertained (together with any amounts wrongfully collected as additions to the tax or interest, as a result of such error) for 15 each taxable year shall be the amount of the adjustment for that taxable year.

(b) Method of adjustment. -- The adjustment authorized in section 1311(a) shall be made by assessing and collecting, or refunding or crediting, the amount thereof in the same manner as if it were a deficiency determined by the Secretary with respect to the taxpayer as to whom the error was made or an overpayment claimed by such taxpayer, as the case may be, for the taxable year or 20 years with respect to which an amount is ascertained under subsection (a), and as if on the date of the determination one year remained before the expiration of the periods of limitation upon assessment or filing claim for refund for such taxable year or years. If, as a result of a determination described in section 1313(a)(4), an adjustment has been made by the assessment and collection of a deficiency or the refund or credit of an overpayment, and subsequently such 25 determination is altered or revoked, the amount of the adjustment ascertained under subsection (a) of this section shall be redetermined on the basis of such alteration or revocation and any overpayment or deficiency resulting from such redetermination shall be refunded or credited, or assessed and collected, as the case may be, as an adjustment under this part. In the case of an adjustment resulting from an increase or decrease in a net operating loss or net capital loss which 30 is carried back to the year of adjustment, interest shall not be collected or paid for any period prior to the close of the taxable year in which the net operating loss or net capital loss arises.

(c) Adjustment unaffected by other items. -- The amount to be assessed and collected in the same manner as a deficiency, or to be refunded or credited in the same manner as an overpayment, under this part, shall not be diminished by any credit or set-off based upon any item other than the 35 one which was the subject of the adjustment. The amount of the adjustment under this part, if paid, shall not be recovered by a claim or suit for refund or suit for erroneous refund based upon any item other than the one which was the subject of the adjustment.

(d) Periods for which adjustments may be made. -- No adjustment shall be made under this part in respect of any taxable year beginning prior to January 1, 1932.   40

(e) Taxes imposed by subtitle C. -- This part shall not apply to any tax imposed by subtitle C (sec.3101 and following relating to employment taxes).

Sec. 1341.   Computation of tax where taxpayer restores substantial amount held under claim of right

(a) General rule. -- If--   45

(1) an item was included in gross income for a prior taxable year (or years) because it

Sec. 1341. Computation of tax where taxpayer restores substantial amount held under claim of right

appeared that the taxpayer had an unrestricted right to such item;

    (2) a deduction is allowable for the taxable year because it was established after the close of such prior taxable year (o years) that the taxpayer did not have an unrestricted right to such item or to a portion of such item; and

5   **(3)** the amount of such deduction exceeds $3,000,

then the tax imposed by this chapter for the taxable year shall be the lesser of the following:

    (4) the tax for the taxable year computed with such deduction; or

    (5) an amount equal to--

        (A) the tax for the taxable year computed without such deduction, minus

10   **(B)** the decrease in tax under this chapter (or the corresponding provisions of prior revenue laws) for the prior taxable year (or years) which would result solely from the exclusion of such item (or portion thereof) from gross income for such prior taxable year (or years).

For purposes of paragraph (5)(B), the corresponding provisions of the Internal Revenue Code 15 of 1939 shall be chapter 1 of such code (other than subchapter E, relating to self-employment income) and subchapter E of chapter 2 of such code.

(b) Special rules. --

    (1) If the decrease in tax ascertained under subsection (a)(5)(B) exceeds the tax imposed by this chapter for the taxable year (computed without the deduction) such excess shall be 20 considered to be a payment of tax on the last day prescribed by law for the payment of tax for the taxable year, and shall be refunded or credited in the same manner as if it were an overpayment for such taxable year.

    (2) Subsection (a) does not apply to any deduction allowable with respect to an item which was included in gross income by reason of the sale or other disposition of stock in trade of the 25 taxpayer (or other property of a kind which would properly have been included in the inventory of the taxpayer if on hand at the close of the prior taxable year) or property held by the taxpayer primarily for sale to customers in the ordinary course of his trade or business. This paragraph shall not apply if the deduction arises out of refunds or repayments with respect to rates made by a regulated public utility (as defined in section 7701(a)(33) without regard to 30 the limitation contained in the last two sentences thereof) if such refunds or repayments are required to be made by the Government, political subdivision, agency, or instrumentality referred to in such section, or by an order of a court, or are made in settlement of litigation or under threat or imminence of litigation.

    (3) If the tax imposed by this chapter for the taxable year is the amount determined under 35 subsection (a)(5), then the deduction referred to in subsection (a)(2) shall not be taken into account for any purpose of this subtitle other than this section.

    (4) For purposes of determining whether paragraph (4) or paragraph (5) of subsection (a) applies--

        (A) in any case where the deduction referred to in paragraph (4) of subsection (a) results 40 in a net operating loss, such loss shall, for purposes of computing the tax for the taxable year under such paragraph (4), be carried back to the same extent and in the same manner as is provided under section 172; and

        (B) in any case where the exclusion referred to in paragraph (5)(B) of subsection (a) results in a net operating loss or capital loss for the prior taxable year (or years), such loss 45 shall, for purposes of computing the decrease in tax for the prior taxable year (or years) under such paragraph (5) (B), be carried back and carried over to the same extent and in the

Sec. 1341. Computation of tax where taxpayer restores substantial amount held under claim of right

same manner as is provided under section 172 or section 1212, except that no carryover beyond the taxable year shall be taken into account.

(5) For purposes of this chapter, the net operating loss described in paragraph (4)(A) of this subsection, or the net operating loss or capital loss described in paragraph (4)(B) of this subsection, as the case may be, shall (after the application of paragraph (4) or (5)(B) of 5 subsection (a) for the taxable year) be taken into account under section 172 or 1212 for taxable years after the taxable year to the same extent and in the same manner as--

    (A) a net operating loss sustained for the taxable year, if paragraph (4) of subsection (a) applied, or

    (B) a net operating loss or capital loss sustained for the prior taxable year (or years), if 10 paragraph (5)(B) of subsection (a) applied.

Reg. § 1.1341-1 Restoration of amounts received or accrued under claim of right.

(a) *In general.* (1) If, during the taxable year, the taxpayer is entitled under other provisions of chapter 1 of the Internal Revenue Code of 1954 to a deduction of more than 15 $3,000 because of the restoration to another of an item which was included in the taxpayer's gross income for a prior taxable year (or years) under a claim of right, the tax imposed by chapter 1 of the Internal Revenue Code of 1954 for the taxable year shall be the tax provided in paragraph (b) of this section.

(2) For the purpose of this section income included under a claim of right means an 20 item included in gross income because it appeared from all the facts available in the year of inclusion that the taxpayer had an unrestricted right to such item, and restoration to another means a restoration resulting because it was established after the close of such prior taxable year (or years) that the taxpayer did not have an unrestricted right to such item (or portion thereof). 25

(3) For purposes of determining whether the amount of a deduction described in section 1341(a)(2) exceeds $3,000 for the taxable year, there shall be taken into account the aggregate of all such deductions with respect to each item of income (described in section 1341(a)(1)) of the same class.

(b) *Determination of tax.* (1) Under the circumstances described in paragraph (a) of 30 this section, the tax imposed by chapter 1 of the Internal Revenue Code of 1954 for the taxable year shall be the lesser of:

(i) The tax for the taxable year computed under section 1341(a)(4), that is, with the deduction taken into account, or

(ii) The tax for the taxable year computed under section 1341(a)(5), that is, without 35 taking such deduction into account, minus the decrease in tax (net of any increase in tax imposed by section 56, relating to the minimum tax for tax preferences) (under chapter 1 of the Internal Revenue Code of 1954, under chapter 1 (other than subchapter E) and subchapter E of chapter 2 of the Internal Revenue Code of 1939, or under the corresponding provisions of prior revenue laws) for the prior taxable year (or years) which 40 would result solely from the exclusion from gross income of all or that portion of the income included under a claim of right to which the deduction is attributable. For the purpose of this subdivision, the amount of the decrease in tax is not limited to the amount of the tax for the taxable year. See paragraph (i) of this section where the decrease in tax for the prior taxable year (or years) exceeds the tax for the taxable year. 45

(iii) For purposes of computing, under section 1341(a)(4) and subdivision (i) of this subparagraph, the tax for a taxable year beginning after December 31, 1961, if the deduction of the amount of the restoration results in a net operating loss for the taxable year of restoration, such net operating loss shall, pursuant to section 1341(b)(4)(A), be

Sec. 1341. Computation of tax where taxpayer restores substantial amount held under claim of right

carried back to the same extent and in the same manner as is provided under section 172 (relating to the net operating loss deduction) and the regulations thereunder. If the aggregate decrease in tax for the taxable year (or years) to which such net operating loss is carried back is greater than the excess of:

5   (a) The amount of decrease in tax for a prior taxable year (or years) computed under section 1341(a)(5)(B), over

(b) The tax for the taxable year computed under section 1341(a)(5)(A).

The tax imposed for the taxable year under chapter 1 shall be the tax determined under section 1341(a)(4) and subdivision (i) of this subparagraph. If the tax imposed for the

10 taxable year is determined under section 1341(a)(4) and subdivision (i) of this subparagraph, the decrease in tax for the taxable year (or years) to which the net operating loss is carried back shall be an overpayment of tax for the taxable year (or years) to which the net operating loss is carried back and shall be refunded or credited as an overpayment for such taxable year (or years). See section 6511(d)(2), relating to

15 special period of limitation with respect to net operating loss carrybacks.

(2) Except as otherwise provided in section 1341(b)(4)(B) and paragraph (d)(1)(ii) and (4)(ii) of this section, if the taxpayer computes his tax for the taxable year under the provisions of section 1341(a)(5) and subparagraph (1)(ii) of this paragraph, the amount of the restoration shall not be taken into account in computing taxable income or loss for the

20 taxable year, including the computation of any net operating loss carryback or carryover or any capital loss carryover. However, the amount of such restoration shall be taken into account in adjusting earnings and profits for the current taxable year.

(3) If the tax determined under subparagraph (1)(i) of this paragraph is the same as the tax determined under subparagraph (1)(ii) of this paragraph, the tax imposed for the

25 taxable year under chapter 1 shall be the tax determined under subparagraph (1)(i) of this paragraph, and section 1341 and this section shall not otherwise apply.

(4) After it has been determined whether the tax imposed for a taxable year of restoration beginning after December 31, 1961, shall be computed under the provisions of section 1341(a)(4) or under the provisions of section 1341(a)(5), the net operating loss,

30 if any, which remains after the application of section 1341(b)(4)(A) or the net operating loss or capital loss, if any, which remains after the application of section 1341(b)(4)(B) shall be taken into account in accordance with the following rules:

(i) If it is determined that section 1341(a)(4) and subparagraph (1)(i) of this paragraph apply, then that portion, if any, of the net operating loss for the taxable year which

35 remains after the application of section 1341(b)(4)(A) and subparagraph (1)(iii) of this paragraph shall be taken into account under section 172 for taxable years subsequent to the taxable year of restoration to the same extent and in the same manner as a net operating loss sustained in such taxable year of restoration. Thus, if the net operating loss for the taxable year of restoration (computed with the deduction referred to in section

40 1341(a)(4)) exceeds the taxable income (computed with the modifications prescribed in section 172) for the taxable year (or years) to which it is carried back, such excess shall be available as a carryover to taxable years subsequent to the taxable year of restoration.

(ii) If it is determined that section 1341(a)(5) and subparagraph (1)(ii) of this paragraph

45 apply, then that portion, if any, of a net operating loss or capital loss which remains after the application of section 1341(b)(4)(B) and paragraph (d)(4) of this section shall be taken into account under section 172 or 1212, as the case may be, for taxable years subsequent to the taxable year of restoration to the same extent and in the same manner as a net operating loss or capital loss sustained in the prior taxable year (or years). For

50 example, if the net operating loss for the prior taxable year (computed with the exclusion

Sec. 1341. Computation of tax where taxpayer restores substantial amount held under claim of right

referred to in section 1341(a)(5)(B)) exceeds the taxable income (computed with the modifications prescribed in section 172) for prior taxable years to which such net operating loss is carried back or carried over (including for this purpose the taxable year of restoration), such excess shall be available as a carryover to taxable years subsequent to the taxable year of restoration in accordance with the rules prescribed in section 172 which are applicable to such prior taxable year (or years).

(c) *Application to deductions which are capital in nature.* Section 1341 and this section shall also apply to a deduction which is capital in nature otherwise allowable in the taxable year. If the deduction otherwise allowable is capital in nature, the determination of whether the taxpayer is entitled to the benefits of section 1341 and this section shall be made without regard to the net capital loss limitation imposed by section 1211. For example, if a taxpayer restores $4,000 in the taxable year and such amount is a long-term capital loss, the taxpayer will, nevertheless, be considered to have met the $3,000 deduction requirement for purposes of applying this section, although the full amount of the loss might not be allowable as a deduction for the taxable year. However, if the tax for the taxable year is computed with the deduction taken into account, the deduction allowable will be subject to the limitation on capital losses provided in section 1211, and the capital loss carryover provided in section 1212.

(d) *Determination of decrease in tax for prior taxable years*--(1) *Prior taxable years.* (i) Except as otherwise provided in subdivision (ii) of this subparagraph, the prior taxable year (or years) referred to in paragraph (b) of this section is the year (or years) in which the item to which the deduction is attributable was included in gross income under a claim of right and, in addition, any other prior taxable year (or years) the tax for which will be affected by the exclusion from gross income in such prior taxable year (or years) of such income.

(ii) For purposes of applying section 1341(b)(4)(B) in computing the amount of the decrease referred to in paragraph (b)(1)(ii) of this section for any taxable year beginning after December 31, 1961, the term prior taxable year (or years) includes the taxable year of restoration. Under section 1341(b)(4)(B), for taxable years of restoration beginning after December 31, 1961, in any case where the exclusion referred to in section 1341(a) (5)(B) and paragraph (b)(1)(ii) of this section results in a net operating loss or capital loss for the prior taxable year (or years), such loss shall, for purposes of computing the decrease in tax for the prior taxable year (or years) under such section 1341(a)(5)(B) and such paragraph (b)(1)(ii) of this section, be carried back and carried over to the same extent and in the same manner as is provided under section 172 (relating to the net operating loss deduction) or section 1212 (relating to capital loss carryover), except that no carryover beyond the taxable year shall be taken into account. See subparagraph (4) of this paragraph for rules relating to the computation of the amount of decrease in tax.

(2) *Amount of exclusion from gross income in prior taxable years.* (i) The amount to be excluded from gross income for the prior taxable year (or years) in determining the decrease in tax under section 1341(a)(5)(B) and paragraph (b)(1)(ii) of this section shall be the amount restored in the taxable year, but shall not exceed the amount included in gross income in the prior taxable year (or years) under the claim of right to which the deduction for the restoration is attributable, and shall be adjusted as provided in subdivision (ii) of this subparagraph.

(ii) If the amount included in gross income for the prior taxable year (or years) under the claim of right in question was reduced in such year (or years) by a deduction allowed under section 1202 (or section 117 (b) of the Internal Revenue Code of 1939 or corresponding provisions of prior revenue laws), then the amount determined under subdivision (i) of this subparagraph to be excluded from gross income for such year (or

Sec. 1341. Computation of tax where taxpayer restores substantial amount held under claim of right

years) shall be reduced in the same proportion that the amount included in gross income under a claim of right was reduced.

(iii) The determination of the amount of the exclusion from gross income of the prior taxable year shall be made without regard to the capital loss limitation contained in section 1211 applicable in computing taxable income for the current taxable year. The amount of the exclusion from gross income in a prior taxable year (or years) shall not exceed the amount which would, but for the application of section 1211, be allowable as a deduction in the taxable year of restoration.

***

(3) *Determination of amount of deduction attributable to prior taxable years.* (i) If the deduction otherwise allowable for the taxable year relates to income included in gross income under a claim of right in more than one prior taxable year and the amount attributable to each such prior taxable year cannot be readily identified, then the portion attributable to each such prior taxable year shall be that proportion of the deduction otherwise allowable for the taxable year which the amount of the income included under the claim of right in question for the prior taxable year bears to the total of all such income included under the claim of right for all such prior taxable years.

***

(4) *Computation of amount of decrease in tax.* (i) In computing the amount of decrease in tax for a prior taxable year (or years) resulting from the exclusion from gross income of the income included under a claim of right, there must first be ascertained the amount of tax previously determined for the taxpayer for such prior taxable year (or years). The tax previously determined shall be the sum of the amounts shown by the taxpayer on his return or returns, plus any amounts which have been previously assessed (or collected without assessment) as deficiencies or which appropriately should be assessed or collected, reduced by the amount of any refunds or credits which have previously been made or which appropriately should be made. For taxable years beginning after December 31,1961, if the provisions of section 1341(b)(4)(B) are applicable, the tax previously determined shall include the tax for the taxable year of restoration computed without taking the deduction for the amount of the restoration into account. After the tax previously determined has been ascertained, a recomputation must then be made to determine the decrease in tax, if any, resulting from the exclusion from gross income of all or that portion of the income included under a claim of right to which the deduction otherwise allowable in the taxable year is attributable.

(ii) No item other than the exclusion of the income previously included under a claim of right shall be considered in computing the amount of decrease in tax if reconsideration of such other item is prevented by the operation of any provision of the internal revenue laws or any other rule of law. However, if the amounts of other items in the return are dependent upon the amount of adjusted gross income, taxable income, or net income (such as charitable contributions, foreign tax credit, deductions for depletion, and net operating loss), appropriate adjustment shall be made as part of the computation of the decrease in tax. For the purpose of determining the decrease in tax for the prior taxable year (or years) which would result from the exclusion from gross income of the item included under a claim of right, the exclusion of such item shall be given effect not only in the prior taxable year in which it was included in gross income but in all other prior taxable years (including the taxable year of restoration if such year begins after December 31, 1961, and section 1341(b)(4)(B) applies, see subparagraph (1)(ii) of this paragraph) affected by the inclusion of the item (for example, prior taxable years affected by a net operating loss carryback or carryover or capital loss carryover).

Sec. 1341. Computation of tax where taxpayer restores substantial amount held under claim of right

***

(e) *Method of accounting.* The provisions of section 1341 and this section shall be applicable in the case of a taxpayer on the cash receipts and disbursements method of accounting only to the taxable year in which the item of income included in a prior year (or years) under a claim of right is actually repaid. However, in the case of a taxpayer on the cash receipts and disbursements method of accounting who constructively received an item of income under a claim of right and included such item of income in gross income in a prior year (or years), the provisions of section 1341 and this section shall be applicable to the taxable year in which the taxpayer is required to relinquish his right to receive such item of income. Such provisions shall be applicable in the case of other taxpayers only to the taxable year which is the proper taxable year (under the method of accounting used by the taxpayer in computing taxable income) for taking into account the deduction resulting from the restoration of the item of income included in a prior year (or years) under a claim of right. For example, if the taxpayer is on an accrual method of accounting, the provisions of this section shall apply to the year in which the obligation properly accrues for the repayment of the item included under a claim of right.

(f) *Inventory items, stock in trade, and property held primarily for sale in the ordinary course of trade or business.* (1) Except for amounts specified in subparagraphs (2) and (3) of this paragraph, the provisions of section 1341 and this section do not apply to deductions attributable to items which were included in gross income by reason of the sale or other disposition of stock in trade of the taxpayer (or other property of a kind which would properly have been included in the inventory of the taxpayer if on hand at the close of the prior taxable year) or property held by the taxpayer primarily for sale to customers in the ordinary course of the taxpayer's trade or business. This section is, therefore, not applicable to sales returns and allowances and similar items.

***

(g) *Bad debts.* The provisions of sections 1341 and this section do not apply to deductions attributable to bad debts.

(h) *Legal fees and other expenses.* Section 1341 and this section do not apply to legal fees or other expenses incurred by a taxpayer in contesting the restoration of an item previously included in income.

***

(i) *Refunds.* If the decrease in tax for the prior taxable year (or years) determined under section 1341(a)(5)(B) and paragraph (b)(1)(ii) of this section exceeds the tax imposed by chapter 1 of the Code for the taxable year computed without the deduction, and for taxable years beginning after December 31, 1961, if such excess is greater than the decrease in tax for the taxable year (or years) to which the net operating loss described in section 1341(b)(4)(A) and paragraph (b)(1)(iii) of this section is carried back, such excess shall be considered to be a payment of tax for the taxable year of restoration. Such payment is deemed to have been made on the last day prescribed by law for the payment of tax for the taxable year and shall be refunded or credited in the same manner as if it were an overpayment of tax for such taxable year. However, no interest shall be allowed or paid if such an excess results from the application of section 1341(a)(5)(B) in the case of a deduction described in paragraph (f)(3) of this section (relating to payments or repayments pursuant to price redetermination). If the tax for the taxable year of restoration is computed under section 1341(a)(4) and results in a decrease in tax for the taxable year (or years) to which a net operating loss described in section 1341(b)(4)(A) is carried back, see paragraph (b)(1)(iii) of this section.

Sec. 1341. Computation of tax where taxpayer restores substantial amount held under claim of right

[T.D. 6500, 25 FR 12049, Nov. 26, 1960, as amended by T.D. 6617, 27 FR 10824, Nov. 7, 1962; T.D. 6747, 29 FR 9790, July 21, 1964; T.D. 7244, 37 FR 28897, Dec. 30, 1972; T.D. 7564, 43 FR 40496, Sept. 12, 1978; T.D. 8677, 61 FR 33323, June 27, 1996]

Sec. 1361. S corporation defined

(a) S corporation defined. --

(1) In general. -- For purposes of this title, the term "S corporation" means, with respect to any taxable year, a small business corporation for which an election under section 1362(a) is in effect for such year.

(2) C corporation. -- For purposes of this title, the term "C corporation" means, with respect to any taxable year, a corporation which is not an S corporation for such year.

(b) Small business corporation. --

(1) In general. -- For purposes of this subchapter, the term "small business corporation" means a domestic corporation which is not an ineligible corporation and which does not -

(A) have more than 100 shareholders,

(B) have as a shareholder a person (other than an estate, a trust described in subsection (c)(2), or an organization described in subsection (c)(6)) who is not an individual,

(C) have a nonresident alien as a shareholder, and

(D) have more than 1 class of stock.

(2) Ineligible corporation defined. -- For purposes of paragraph (1), the term "ineligible corporation" means any corporation which is -

(A) a financial institution which uses the reserve method of accounting for bad debts described in section 585,

(B) an insurance company subject to tax under subchapter L,

(C) a corporation to which an election under section 936 applies, or

(D) a DISC or former DISC.

***

Sec. 1363. Effect of election on corporation

(a) General rule. -- Except as otherwise provided in this subchapter, an S corporation shall not be subject to the taxes imposed by this chapter.

***

Sec. 1366. Pass-thru of items to shareholders

(a) Determination of shareholder's tax liability. --

(1) In general. -- In determining the tax under this chapter of a shareholder for the shareholder's taxable year in which the taxable year of the S corporation ends (or for the final taxable year of a shareholder who dies, or of a trust or estate which terminates, before the end of the corporation's taxable year), there shall be taken into account the shareholder's pro rata share of the corporation's--

(A) items of income (including tax-exempt income), loss, deduction, or credit the separate treatment of which could affect the liability for tax of any shareholder, and

(B) nonseparately computed income or loss.

For purposes of the preceding sentence, the items referred to in subparagraph (A) shall include

Sec. 1366. Pass-thru of items to shareholders

amounts described in paragraph (4) or (6) of section 702(a).

    (2) Nonseparately computed income or loss defined. -- For purposes of this subchapter, the term "nonseparately computed income or loss" means gross income minus the deductions allowed to the corporation under this chapter, determined by excluding all items described in paragraph (1)(A).   5

    (b) Character passed thru. -- The character of any item included in a shareholder's pro rata share under paragraph (1) of subsection (a) shall be determined as if such item were realized directly from the source from which realized by the corporation, or incurred in the same manner as incurred by the corporation.

∗∗∗   10

Sec. 1402. Definitions

    (a) Net earnings from self-employment. -- The term "net earnings from self-employment" means the gross income derived by an individual from any trade or business carried on by such individual, less the deductions allowed by this subtitle which are attributable to such trade or business, plus his distributive share (whether or not distributed) of income or loss described in section 702(a)(8) from any trade or business carried on by a partnership of which he is a member; 15 except that in computing such gross income and deductions and such distributive share of partnership ordinary income or loss--

    (1) there shall be excluded rentals from real estate and from personal property leased with the real estate (including such rentals paid in crop shares) together with the deductions attributable thereto, unless such rentals are received in the course of a trade or business as a 20 real estate dealer; except that the preceding provisions of this paragraph shall not apply to any income derived by the owner or tenant of land if (A) such income is derived under an arrangement, between the owner or tenant and another individual, which provides that such other individual shall produce agricultural or horticultural commodities (including livestock, bees, poultry, and fur-bearing animals and wildlife) on such land, and that there shall be 25 material participation by the owner or tenant (as determined without regard to any activities of an agent of such owner or tenant) in the production or the management of the production of such agricultural or horticultural commodities, and (B) there is material participation by the owner or tenant (as determined without regard to any activities of an agent of such owner or tenant) with respect to any such agricultural or horticultural commodity; 30

    (2) there shall be excluded dividends on any share of stock, and interest on any bond, debenture, note, or certificate, or other evidence of indebtedness, issued with interest coupons or in registered form by any corporation (including one issued by a government or political subdivision thereof), unless such dividends and interest are received in the course of a trade or business as a dealer in stocks or securities; 35

    (3) there shall be excluded any gain or loss--

        (A) which is considered as gain or loss from the sale or exchange of a capital asset,

        (B) from the cutting of timber, or the disposal of timber, coal, or iron ore, if section 631 applies to such gain or loss, or

        (C) from the sale, exchange, involuntary conversion, or other disposition of property if 40 such property is neither -

            (i) stock in trade or other property of a kind which would properly be includible in inventory if on hand at the close of the taxable year, nor

            (ii) property held primarily for sale to customers in the ordinary course of the trade or business; 45

    (4) the deduction for net operating losses provided in section 172 shall not be allowed;

1019

Sec. 1402. Definitions

(5) if--

(A) any of the income derived from a trade or business (other than a trade or business carried on by a partnership) is community income under community property laws applicable to such income, the gross income and deductions attributable to such trade or business shall be treated as the gross income and deductions of the spouse carrying on such trade or business or, if such trade or business is jointly operated, treated as the gross income and deductions of each spouse on the basis of their respective distributive share of the gross income and deductions;

***

(7) the deduction for personal exemptions provided in section 151 shall not be allowed;

***

(12) in lieu of the deduction provided by section 164(f) (relating to deduction for one-half of self-employment taxes), there shall be allowed a deduction equal to the product of--

(A) the taxpayer's net earnings from self-employment for the taxable year (determined without regard to this paragraph), and

(B) one-half of the sum of the rates imposed by subsections (a) and (b) of section 1401 for such year;

***

(b) Self-employment income. -- The term "self-employment income" means the net earnings from self-employment derived by an individual (other than a nonresident alien individual, except as provided by an agreement under section 233 of the Social Security Act) during any taxable year; except that such term shall not include--

(1) in the case of the tax imposed by section 1401(a), that part of the net earnings from self-employment which is in excess of (i) an amount equal to the contribution and benefit base (as determined under section 230 of the Social Security Act) which is effective for the calendar year in which such taxable year begins, minus (ii) the amount of the wages paid to such individual during such taxable years; or

(2) the net earnings from self-employment, if such net earnings for the taxable year are less than $400.

For purposes of paragraph (1), the term "wages" (A) includes such remuneration paid to an employee for services included under an agreement entered into pursuant to the provisions of section 3121(l) (relating to coverage of citizens of the United States who are employees of foreign affiliates of American employers), as would be wages under section 3121(a) if such services constituted employment under section 3121(b), and (B) includes compensation which is subject to the tax imposed by section 3201 or 3211. An individual who is not a citizen of the United States but who is a resident of the Commonwealth of Puerto Rico, the Virgin Islands, Guam, or American Samoa shall not, for purposes of this chapter be considered to be a nonresident alien individual. In the case of church employee income, the special rules of subsection (j)(2) shall apply for purposes of paragraph (2).

(c) Trade or business. -- The term "trade or business", when used with reference to self-employment income or net earnings from self-employment, shall have the same meaning as when used in section 162 (relating to trade or business expenses), except that such term shall not include--

(1) the performance of the functions of a public office, other than the functions of a public office of a State or a political subdivision thereof with respect to fees received in any period in which the functions are performed in a position compensated solely on a fee basis and in which

Sec. 1402. Definitions

such functions are not covered under an agreement entered into by such State and the Commissioner of Social Security pursuant to section 218 of the Social Security Act;

   (2) the performance of service by an individual as an employee, other than--

***

Sec. 1504. Definitions

   (a) Affiliated group defined. -- For purposes of this subtitle--

   (1) In general. -- The term "affiliated group" means--

   (A) 1 or more chains of includible corporations connected through stock ownership with a common parent corporation which is an includible corporation, but only if--

   (B)(i) the common parent owns directly stock meeting the requirements of paragraph (2) in at least 1 of the other includible corporations, and

   (ii) stock meeting the requirements of paragraph (2) in each of the includible corporations (except the common parent) is owned directly by 1 or more of the other includible corporations.

   (2) 80-percent voting and value test. -- The ownership of stock of any corporation meets the requirements of this paragraph if it--

   (A) possesses at least 80 percent of the total voting power of the stock of such corporation, and

   (B) has a value equal to at least 80 percent of the total value of the stock of such corporation.

***

Sec. 2031. Definition of gross estate

   (a) General. -- The value of the gross estate of the decedent shall be determined by including to the extent provided for in this part, the value at the time of his death of all property, real or personal, tangible or intangible, wherever situated.

***

Reg. § 20.2031-1   Definition of gross estate; valuation of property.

***

   (b) *Valuation of property in general.* The value of every item of property includible in a decedent's gross estate under sections 2031 through 2044 is its fair market value at the time of the decedent's death, except that if the executor elects the alternate valuation method under section 2032, it is the fair market value thereof at the date, and with the adjustments, prescribed in that section. The fair market value is the price at which the property would change hands between a willing buyer and a willing seller, neither being under any compulsion to buy or to sell and both having reasonable knowledge of relevant facts. The fair market value of a particular item of property includible in the decedent's gross estate is not to be determined by a forced sale price. Nor is the fair market value of an item of property to be determined by the sale price of the item in a market other than that in which such item is most commonly sold to the public, taking into account the location of the item wherever appropriate. Thus, in the case of an item of property includible in the decedent's gross estate, which is generally obtained by the public in the retail market, the fair market value of such an item of property is the price at which the item or a comparable item would be sold at retail. For example, the fair market value of an automobile (an article generally obtained by the public in the retail market) includible in the decedent's gross estate is the price for which an automobile of the same or

1021

approximately the same description, make, model, age, condition, etc., could be purchased by a member of the general public and not the price for which the particular automobile of the decedent would be purchased by a dealer in used automobiles. Examples of items of property which are generally sold to the public at retail may be
5 found in §§ 20.2031-6 and 20.2031-8. The value is generally to be determined by ascertaining as a basis the fair market value as of the applicable valuation date of each unit of property. For example, in the case of shares of stock or bonds, such unit of property is generally a share of stock or a bond. Livestock, farm machinery, harvested and growing crops must generally be itemized and the value of each item separately
10 returned. Property shall not be returned at the value at which it is assessed for local tax purposes unless that value represents the fair market value as of the applicable valuation date. All relevant facts and elements of value as of the applicable valuation date shall be considered in every case. The value of items of property which were held by the decedent for sale in the course of a business generally should be reflected in the value of
15 the business. For valuation of interests in businesses, see § 20.2031-3. See § 20.2031-2 and Secs. 20.2031-4 through 20.2031-8 for further information concerning the valuation of other particular kinds of property. For certain circumstances under which the sale of an item of property at a price below its fair market value may result in a deduction for the estate, see paragraph (d)(2) of § 20.2053-3.
20   ***

Reg. § 20.2031-7   Valuation of annuities, interests for life or term of years, and remainder or reversionary interests.

   (a) *In general.* Except as otherwise provided in paragraph (b) of this section and §
20.7520-3(b) (pertaining to certain limitations on the use of prescribed tables), the fair
25 market value of annuities, life estates, terms of years, remainders, and reversionary interests for estates of decedents is the present value of such interests, determined under paragraph (d) of this section. The regulations in this and in related sections provide tables with standard actuarial factors and examples that illustrate how to use the tables to compute the present value of ordinary annuity, life, and remainder interests in property.
30 These sections also refer to standard and special actuarial factors that may be necessary to compute the present value of similar interests in more unusual fact situations.

   (b) *Commercial annuities and insurance contracts.* The value of annuities issued by companies regularly engaged in their sale, and of insurance policies on the lives of persons other than the decedent, is determined under § 20.2031-8. See § 20.2042-1 with
35 respect to insurance policies on the decedent's life.

   (c) *Actuarial valuations.* The present value of annuities, life estates, terms of years, remainders, and reversions for estates of decedents for which the valuation date of the gross estate is after April 30, 1999, is determined under paragraph (d) of this section. The present value of annuities, life estates, terms of years, remainders, and reversions for
40 estates of decedents for which the valuation date of the gross estate is before May 1, 1999, is determined under the following sections:

Sec. 2031. Definition of gross estate

Valuation date		Applicable regulations
After	Before	
	01-01-52	20.2031-7A(a)
12-31-51............................	01-01-71	20.2031-7A(b)
12-31-70............................	12-01-83	20.2031-7A(c)
11-30-83............................	05-01-89	20.2031-7A(d)
04-30-89............................	05-01-99	20.2031-7A(e)

(d) *Actuarial valuations after April 30, 1999--(1) In general*. Except as otherwise provided in paragraph (b) of this section and § 20.7520-3(b) (pertaining to certain limitations on the use of prescribed tables), if the valuation date for the gross estate of the decedent is after April 30, 1999, the fair market value of annuities, life estates, terms of years, remainders, and reversionary interests is the present value determined by use of standard or special section 7520 actuarial factors. These factors are derived by using the appropriate section 7520 interest rate and, if applicable, the mortality component for the valuation date of the interest that is being valued. For purposes of the computations described in this section, the age of an individual is the age of that individual at the individual's nearest birthday. See §§ 20.7520-1 through 20.7520-4.

(2) *Specific interests--(i) Charitable remainder trusts*. The fair market value of a remainder interest in a pooled income fund, as defined in § 1.642(c)-5 of this chapter, is its value determined under § 1.642(c)-6(e) of this chapter. The fair market value of a remainder interest in a charitable remainder annuity trust, as defined in § 1.664-2(a) of this chapter, is the present value determined under § 1.664-2(c) of this chapter. The fair market value of a remainder interest in a charitable remainder unitrust, as defined in § 1.664-3 of this chapter, is its present value determined under § 1.664-4(e) of this chapter. The fair market value of a life interest or term of years in a charitable remainder unitrust is the fair market value of the property as of the date of valuation less the fair market value of the remainder interest on that date determined under § 1.664-4(e)(4) and (5) of this chapter.

(ii) *Ordinary remainder and reversionary interests*. If the interest to be valued is to take effect after a definite number of years or after the death of one individual, the present value of the interest is computed by multiplying the value of the property by the appropriate remainder interest actuarial factor (that corresponds to the applicable section 7520 interest rate and remainder interest period) in Table B (for a term certain) or the appropriate Table S (for one measuring life), as the case may be. Table B is contained in paragraph (d)(6) of this section and Table S (for one measuring life when the valuation date is after April 30, 1999) is contained in paragraph (d)(7) of this section and in Internal Revenue Service Publication 1457. For information about obtaining actuarial factors for other types of remainder interests, see paragraph (d)(4) of this section.

(iii) *Ordinary term-of-years and life interests*. If the interest to be valued is the right of a person to receive the income of certain property, or to use certain non income-producing property, for a term of years or for the life of one individual, the present value of the interest is computed by multiplying the value of the property by the appropriate term-of-years or life interest actuarial factor (that corresponds to the applicable section 7520 interest rate and term-of-years or life interest period). Internal Revenue Service Publication 1457 includes actuarial factors for an interest for a term of years in Table B and for the life of one individual in Table S (for one measuring life when the valuation date is after April 30, 1999). However, term-of-years and life interest actuarial factors are not

Sec. 2031. Definition of gross estate

included in Table B in paragraph (d)(6) of this section or Table S in paragraph (d)(7) of this section. If Internal Revenue Service Publication 1457 (or any other reliable source of term-of-years and life interest actuarial factors) is not conveniently available, an actuarial factor for the interest may be derived mathematically. This actuarial factor may be derived
5 by subtracting the correlative remainder factor (that corresponds to the applicable section 7520 interest rate and the term of years or the life) in Table B (for a term of years) in paragraph (d)(6) of this section or in Table S (for the life of one individual) in paragraph (d)(7) of this section, as the case may be, from 1.000000. For information about obtaining actuarial factors for other types of term-of-years and life interests, see paragraph (d)(4) of
10 this section.

    (iv) *Annuities.* (A) If the interest to be valued is the right of a person to receive an annuity that is payable at the end of each year for a term of years or for the life of one individual, the present value of the interest is computed by multiplying the aggregate amount payable annually by the appropriate annuity actuarial factor (that corresponds to
15 the applicable section 7520 interest rate and annuity period). Internal Revenue Publication 1457 includes actuarial factors in Table B (for an annuity payable for a term of years) and in Table S (for an annuity payable for the life of one individual when the valuation date is after April 30, 1999). However, annuity actuarial factors are not included in Table B in paragraph (d)(6) of this section or Table S in paragraph (d)(7) of this section.
20 If Internal Revenue Service Publication 1457 (or any other reliable source of annuity actuarial factors) is not conveniently available, a required annuity factor for a term of years or for one life may be mathematically derived. This annuity factor may be derived by subtracting the applicable remainder factor (that corresponds to the applicable section 7520 interest rate and annuity period) in Table B (in the case of a term-of-years annuity)
25 in paragraph (d)(6) of this section or in Table S (in the case of a one-life annuity when the valuation date is after April 30, 1999) in paragraph (d)(7) of this section, as the case may be, from 1.000000 and then dividing the result by the applicable section 7520 interest rate expressed as a decimal number.

    (B) If the annuity is payable at the end of semiannual, quarterly, monthly, or weekly
30 periods, the product obtained by multiplying the annuity factor by the aggregate amount payable annually is then multiplied by the applicable adjustment factor as contained in Table K in paragraph (d)(6) of this section for payments made at the end of the specified periods. The provisions of this paragraph (d)(2)(iv)(B) are illustrated by the following example:
35   *Example.* At the time of the decedent's death, the survivor/annuitant, age 72, is entitled to receive an annuity of $15,000 a year for life payable in equal monthly installments at the end of each period. The section 7520 rate for the month in which the decedent died is 9.6 percent. Under Table S in paragraph (d)(7) of this section, the remainder factor at 9.6 percent for an individual aged 72 is .38438. By converting the
40 remainder factor to an annuity factor, as described above, the annuity factor at 9.6 percent for an individual aged 72 is 6.4127 (1.00000 minus .38438, divided by .096). Under Table K in paragraph (d)(6) of this section, the adjustment factor under the column for payments made at the end of each monthly period at the rate of 9.6 percent is 1.0433. The aggregate annual amount, $15,000, is multiplied by the factor 6.4127 and the
45 product multiplied by 1.0433. The present value of the annuity at the date of the decedent's death is, therefore, $100,355.55 ($15,000 x 6.4127 x 1.0433).

    (C) If an annuity is payable at the beginning of annual, semiannual, quarterly, monthly, or weekly periods for a term of years, the value of the annuity is computed by multiplying the aggregate amount payable annually by the annuity factor described in paragraph (d)
50 (2)(iv)(A) of this section; and the product so obtained is then multiplied by the adjustment factor in Table J in paragraph (d)(6) of this section at the appropriate interest rate

component for payments made at the beginning of specified periods. If an annuity is payable at the beginning of annual, semiannual, quarterly, monthly, or weekly periods for one or more lives, the value of the annuity is the sum of the first payment plus the present value of a similar annuity, the first payment of which is not to be made until the end of the payment period, determined as provided in this paragraph (d)(2)(iv).   5

(v) Annuity and unitrust interests for a term of years or until the prior death of an individual. See § 25.2512-5(d)(2)(v) of this chapter for examples explaining how to compute the present value of an annuity or unitrust interest that is payable until the earlier of the lapse of a specific number of years or the death of an individual.

*** 10

(4) *Publications and actuarial computations by the Internal Revenue Service.* Many standard actuarial factors not included in paragraphs (d)(6) or (d)(7) of this section are included in Internal Revenue Service Publication 1457, ``Actuarial Values, Book Aleph,'' (7-1999). Publication 1457 also includes examples that illustrate how to compute many special factors for more unusual situations. A copy of this publication is available for 15 purchase from the Superintendent of Documents, United States Government Printing Office, Washington, DC 20402. See § 20.2031-7A for publications containing actuarial factors for valuing interests for which the valuation date is before May 1, 1999. If a special factor is required in the case of an actual decedent, the Internal Revenue Service may furnish the factor to the executor upon a request for a ruling. The request for a ruling 20 must be accompanied by a recitation of the facts including a statement of the date of birth for each measuring life, the date of the decedent's death, any other applicable dates, and a copy of the will, trust, or other relevant documents. A request for a ruling must comply with the instructions for requesting a ruling published periodically in the Internal Revenue Bulletin (see §§ 601.201 and 601.601(d)(2)(ii)(b) of this chapter) and include payment of 25 the required user fee.

(5) *Examples.* The provisions of this section are illustrated by the following examples:

Example 1. Remainder payable at an individual's death. The decedent, or the decedent's estate, was entitled to receive certain property worth $50,000 upon the death of A, to whom the income was bequeathed for life. At the time of the decedent's death, A 30 was 47 years 5 months old. In the month in which the decedent died, the section 7520 rate was 9.8 percent. Under Table S in paragraph (d)(7) of this section, the remainder factor at 9.8 percent for determining the present value of the remainder interest due at the death of a person aged 47, the number of years nearest A's actual age at the decedent's death, is .10317. The present value of the remainder interest at the date of 35 the decedent's death is, therefore, $5,158.50 ($50,000 x .10317).

Example 2. Income payable for an individual's life. A's parent bequeathed an income interest in property to A for life, with the remainder interest passing to B at A's death. At the time of the parent's death, the value of the property was $50,000 and A was 30 years 10 months old. The section 7520 rate at the time of the parent's death was 10.2 percent. 40 Under Table S in paragraph (d)(7) of this section, the remainder factor at 10.2 percent for determining the present value of the remainder interest due at the death of a person aged 31, the number of years closest to A's age at the decedent's death, is .03583. Converting this remainder factor to an income factor, as described in paragraph (d)(2)(iii) of this section, the factor for determining the present value of an income interest for the life of a 45 person aged 31 is .96417. The present value of A's interest at the time of the parent's death is, therefore, $48,208.50 ($50,000 x .96417).

Example 3. Annuity payable for an individual's life. A purchased an annuity for the benefit of both A and B. Under the terms of the annuity contract, at A's death, a survivor annuity of $10,000 a year payable in equal semiannual installments made at the end of 50 each interval is payable to B for life. At A's death, B was 45 years 7 months old. Also, at

Sec. 2031. Definition of gross estate

A's death, the section 7520 rate was 9.6 percent. Under Table S in paragraph (d)(7) of this section, the factor at 9.6 percent for determining the present value of the remainder interest at the death of a person age 46 (the number of years nearest B's actual age) is . 10013. By converting the factor to an annuity factor, as described in paragraph (d)(2)(iv)
5 (A) of this section, the factor for the present value of an annuity payable until the death of a person age 46 is 9.3736 (1.00000 minus .10013, divided by .096). The adjustment factor from Table K in paragraph (d)(6) of this section at an interest rate of 9.6 percent for semiannual annuity payments made at the end of the period is 1.0235. The present value of the annuity at the date of A's death is, therefore, $95,938.80 ($10,000 x 9.3736 x
10 1.0235).

Example 4. Annuity payable for a term of years. The decedent, or the decedent's estate, was entitled to receive an annuity of $10,000 a year payable in equal quarterly installments at the end of each quarter throughout a term certain. At the time of the decedent's death, the section 7520 rate was 9.8 percent. A quarterly payment had just
15 been made prior to the decedent's death and payments were to continue for 5 more years. Under Table B in paragraph (d)(6) of this section for the interest rate of 9.8 percent, the factor for the present value of a remainder interest due after a term of 5 years is .626597. Converting the factor to an annuity factor, as described in paragraph (d) (2)(iv)(A) of this section, the factor for the present value of an annuity for a term of 5
20 years is 3.8102. The adjustment factor from Table K in paragraph (d)(6) of this section at an interest rate of 9.8 percent for quarterly annuity payments made at the end of the period is 1.0360. The present value of the annuity is, therefore, $39,473.67 ($10,000 x 3.8102 x 1.0360).

(6) **Actuarial Table B, Table J, and Table K where the valuation date is after April**
25 **30, 1989**. Except as provided in § 20.7520-3(b) (pertaining to certain limitations on prescribed tables), for determination of the present value of an interest that is dependent on a term of years, the tables in this paragraph (d)(6) must be used in the application of the provisions of this section when the section 7520 interest rate component is between 4.2 and 14 percent.

30

Table B--Term Certain Remainder Factors Applicable After April 30, 1989

Interest rate

Years	4.2%	4.4%	4.6%	4.8%	5.0%	5.2%	5.4%	5.6%	5.8%	6.0%
1	.959693	.957854	.956023	.954198	.952381	.950570	.948767	.946970	.945180	.943396
2	.921010	.917485	.913980	.910495	.907029	.903584	.900158	.896752	.893364	.889996
3	.883887	.878817	.873786	.868793	.863838	.858920	.854040	.849197	.844390	.839619
4	.848260	.841779	.835359	.829001	.822702	.816464	.810285	.804163	.798100	.792094
5	.814069	.806302	.798623	.791031	.783526	.776106	.768771	.761518	.754348	.747258
6	.781257	.772320	.763501	.754801	.746215	.737744	.729384	.721135	.712994	.704961
7	.749766	.739770	.729925	.720230	.710681	.701277	.692015	.682893	.673908	.665057
8	.719545	.708592	.697825	.687242	.676839	.666613	.656561	.646679	.636964	.627412
9	.690543	.678728	.667137	.655765	.644609	.633663	.622923	.612385	.602045	.591898
10	.662709	.650122	.637798	.625730	.613913	.602341	.591009	.579910	.569041	.558395
11	.635997	.622722	.609750	.597071	.584679	.572568	.560729	.549157	.537846	.526788
12	.610362	.596477	.582935	.569724	.556837	.544266	.532001	.520035	.508361	.496969
13	.585760	.571339	.557299	.543630	.530321	.517363	.504745	.492458	.480492	.468839
14	.562150	.547259	.532790	.518731	.505068	.491790	.478885	.466343	.454151	.442301
15	.539491	.524195	.509360	.494972	.481017	.467481	.454350	.441612	.429255	.417265
16	.517746	.502102	.486960	.472302	.458112	.444374	.431072	.418194	.405723	.393646
17	.496877	.480941	.465545	.450670	.436297	.422408	.408987	.396017	.383481	.371364
18	.476849	.460671	.445071	.430028	.415521	.401529	.388033	.375016	.362458	.350344
19	.457629	.441256	.425498	.410332	.395734	.381681	.368153	.355129	.342588	.330513
20	.439183	.422659	.406786	.391538	.376889	.362815	.349291	.336296	.323807	.311805
21	.421481	.404846	.388897	.373605	.358942	.344881	.331396	.318462	.306056	.294155
22	.404492	.387783	.371794	.356494	.341850	.327834	.314417	.301574	.289278	.277505
23	.388188	.371440	.355444	.340166	.325571	.311629	.298309	.285581	.273420	.261797
24	.372542	.355785	.339813	.324586	.310068	.296225	.283025	.270437	.258431	.246979
25	.357526	.340791	.324869	.309719	.295303	.281583	.268525	.256096	.244263	.232999
26	.343115	.326428	.310582	.295533	.281241	.267664	.254768	.242515	.230873	.219810
27	.329285	.312670	.296923	.281998	.267848	.254434	.241715	.229654	.218216	.207368
28	.316012	.299493	.283866	.269082	.255094	.241857	.229331	.217475	.206253	.195630
29	.303275	.286870	.271382	.256757	.242946	.229902	.217582	.205943	.194947	.184557

30	.291051	.274780	.259447	.244997	.231377	.218538	.206434	.195021	.184260	.174110
31	.279319	.263199	.248038	.233776	.220359	.207736	.195858	.184679	.174158	.164255
32	.268061	.252106	.237130	.223069	.209866	.197468	.185823	.174886	.164611	.154957
33	.257256	.241481	.226702	.212852	.199873	.187707	.176303	.165612	.155587	.146186
34	.246887	.231304	.216732	.203103	.190355	.178429	.167270	.156829	.147058	.137912
35	.236935	.221556	.207201	.193801	.181290	.169609	.158701	.148512	.138996	.130105
36	.227385	.212218	.198089	.184924	.172657	.161225	.150570	.140637	.131376	.122741
37	.218220	.203274	.189377	.176454	.164436	.153256	.142856	.133179	.124174	.115793
38	.209424	.194707	.181049	.168373	.156605	.145681	.135537	.126116	.117367	.109239
39	.200983	.186501	.173087	.160661	.149148	.138480	.128593	.119428	.110933	.103056
40	.192882	.178641	.165475	.153302	.142046	.131635	.122004	.113095	.104851	.097222
41	.185107	.171112	.158198	.146281	.135282	.125128	.115754	.107098	.099103	.091719
42	.177646	.163900	.151241	.139581	.128840	.118943	.109823	.101418	.093670	.086527
43	.170486	.156992	.144590	.133188	.122704	.113064	.104197	.096040	.088535	.081630
44	.163614	.150376	.138231	.127088	.116861	.107475	.098858	.090947	.083682	.077009
45	.157019	.144038	.132152	.121267	.111297	.102163	.093793	.086124	.079094	.072650
46	.150690	.137968	.126340	.115713	.105997	.097113	.088988	.081557	.074758	.068538
47	.144616	.132153	.120784	.110413	.100949	.092312	.084429	.077232	.070660	.064658
48	.138787	.126583	.115473	.105356	.096142	.087749	.080103	.073136	.066786	.060998
49	.133193	.121248	.110395	.100530	.091564	.083412	.075999	.069258	.063125	.057546
50	.127824	.116138	.105540	.095926	.087204	.079289	.072106	.065585	.059665	.054288
51	.122672	.111243	.100898	.091532	.083051	.075370	.068411	.062107	.056394	.051215
52	.117728	.106555	.096461	.087340	.079096	.071644	.064907	.058813	.053302	.048316
53	.112982	.102064	.092219	.083340	.075330	.068103	.061581	.055695	.050380	.045582
54	.108428	.097763	.088164	.079523	.071743	.064737	.058426	.052741	.047618	.043001
55	.104058	.093642	.084286	.075880	.068326	.061537	.055433	.049944	.045008	.040567
56	.099864	.089696	.080580	.072405	.065073	.058495	.052593	.047296	.042541	.038271
57	.095839	.085916	.077036	.069089	.061974	.055604	.049898	.044787	.040208	.036105
58	.091976	.082295	.073648	.065924	.059023	.052855	.047342	.042412	.038004	.034061
59	.088268	.078826	.070409	.062905	.056212	.050243	.044916	.040163	.035921	.032133

Table B--Term Certain Remainder Factors Applicable After April 30, 1989

Interest rate

Years	6.2%	6.4%	6.6%	6.8%	7.0%	7.2%	7.4%	7.6%	7.8%	8.0%
1	.941620	.939850	.938086	.936330	.934579	.932836	.931099	.929368	.927644	.925926
2	.886647	.883317	.880006	.876713	.873439	.870183	.866945	.863725	.860523	.857339
3	.834885	.830185	.825521	.820892	.816298	.811738	.807211	.802718	.798259	.793832
4	.786144	.780249	.774410	.768626	.762895	.757218	.751593	.746021	.740500	.735030
5	.740248	.733317	.726464	.719687	.712986	.706360	.699808	.693328	.686920	.680583
6	.697032	.689208	.681486	.673864	.666342	.658918	.651590	.644357	.637217	.630170
7	.656339	.647752	.639292	.630959	.622750	.614662	.606694	.598845	.591111	.583490
8	.618022	.608789	.599711	.590786	.582009	.573379	.564892	.556547	.548340	.540269
9	.581942	.572170	.562581	.553170	.543934	.534868	.525971	.517237	.508664	.500249
10	.547968	.537754	.527750	.517950	.508349	.498944	.489731	.480704	.471859	.463193
11	.515977	.505408	.495075	.484972	.475093	.465433	.455987	.446750	.437717	.428883
12	.485854	.475007	.464423	.454093	.444012	.434173	.424569	.415196	.406046	.397114
13	.457490	.446436	.435669	.425181	.414964	.405012	.395316	.385870	.376666	.367698
14	.430781	.419582	.408695	.398109	.387817	.377810	.368078	.358615	.349412	.340461
15	.405632	.394344	.383391	.372762	.362446	.352434	.342717	.333285	.324130	.315242
16	.381951	.370624	.359654	.349028	.338735	.328763	.319103	.309745	.300677	.291890
17	.359653	.348331	.337386	.326805	.316574	.306682	.297117	.287867	.278921	.270269
18	.338656	.327379	.316498	.305997	.295864	.286084	.276645	.267534	.258739	.250249
19	.318885	.307687	.296902	.286514	.276508	.266870	.257584	.248638	.240018	.231712
20	.300268	.289179	.278520	.268272	.258419	.248946	.239836	.231076	.222651	.214548
21	.282739	.271785	.261276	.251191	.241513	.232225	.223311	.214755	.206541	.198656
22	.266232	.255437	.245099	.235197	.225713	.216628	.207925	.199586	.191596	.183941
23	.250689	.240073	.229924	.220222	.210947	.202078	.193598	.185489	.177733	.170315
24	.236054	.225632	.215689	.206201	.197147	.188506	.180259	.172387	.164873	.157699
25	.222273	.212060	.202334	.193072	.184249	.175845	.167839	.160211	.152943	.146018
26	.209297	.199305	.189807	.180779	.172195	.164035	.156275	.148895	.141877	.135202
27	.197078	.187317	.178056	.169269	.160930	.153017	.145507	.138379	.131611	.125187
28	.185572	.176049	.167031	.158491	.150402	.142740	.135482	.128605	.122088	.115914
29	.174739	.165460	.156690	.148400	.140563	.133153	.126147	.119521	.113255	.107328
30	.164537	.155507	.146989	.138951	.131367	.124210	.117455	.111079	.105060	.099377
31	.154932	.146154	.137888	.130104	.122773	.115868	.109362	.103233	.097458	.092016
32	.145887	.137362	.129351	.121820	.114741	.108085	.101827	.095942	.090406	.085200
33	.137370	.129100	.121342	.114064	.107235	.100826	.094811	.089165	.083865	.078889
34	.129350	.121335	.113830	.106802	.100219	.094054	.088278	.082867	.077797	.073045
35	.121798	.114036	.106782	.100001	.093663	.087737	.082196	.077014	.072168	.067635
36	.114688	.107177	.100171	.093634	.087535	.081844	.076532	.071574	.066946	.062625
37	.107992	.100730	.093969	.087673	.081809	.076347	.071259	.066519	.062102	.057986
38	.101688	.094671	.088151	.082090	.076457	.071219	.066349	.061821	.057609	.053690
39	.095751	.088977	.082693	.076864	.071455	.066436	.061778	.057454	.053440	.049713
40	.090161	.083625	.077573	.071970	.066780	.061974	.057521	.053396	.049573	.046031
41	.084897	.078595	.072770	.067387	.062412	.057811	.053558	.049625	.045987	.042621
42	.079941	.073867	.068265	.063097	.058329	.053929	.049868	.046120	.042659	.039464
43	.075274	.069424	.064038	.059079	.054513	.050307	.046432	.042862	.039572	.036541
44	.070880	.065248	.060074	.055318	.050946	.046928	.043233	.039835	.036709	.033834
45	.066742	.061323	.056354	.051796	.047613	.043776	.040254	.037021	.034053	.031328
46	.062845	.057635	.052865	.048498	.044499	.040836	.037480	.034406	.031589	.029007
47	.059176	.054168	.049592	.045410	.041587	.038093	.034898	.031976	.029303	.026859
48	.055722	.050910	.046522	.042519	.038867	.035535	.032493	.029717	.027183	.024869
49	.052469	.047848	.043641	.039812	.036324	.033148	.030255	.027618	.025216	.023027

Sec. 2031. Definition of gross estate

50	.049405	.044970	.040939	.037277	.033948	.030922	.028170	.025668	.023392	.021321
51	.046521	.042265	.038405	.034903	.031727	.028845	.026229	.023855	.021699	.019742
52	.043805	.039722	.036027	.032681	.029651	.026907	.024422	.022170	.020129	.018280
53	.041248	.037333	.033796	.030600	.027711	.025100	.022739	.020604	.018673	.016925
54	.038840	.035087	.031704	.028652	.025899	.023414	.021172	.019149	.017322	.015672
55	.036572	.032977	.029741	.026828	.024204	.021842	.019714	.017796	.016068	.014511
56	.034437	.030993	.027900	.025119	.022621	.020375	.018355	.016539	.014906	.013436
57	.032427	.029129	.026172	.023520	.021141	.019006	.017091	.015371	.013827	.012441
58	.030534	.027377	.024552	.022023	.019758	.017730	.015913	.014285	.012827	.011519
59	.028751	.025730	.023032	.020620	.018465	.016539	.014817	.013276	.011899	.010666
60	.027073	.024183	.021606	.019307	.017257	.015428	.013796	.012339	.011038	

Table B--Term Certain Remainder Factors Applicable After April 30, 1989

Interest rate

Years	8.2%	8.4%	8.6%	8.8%	9.0%	9.2%	9.4%	9.6%	9.8%	10%
1	.924214	.922509	.920810	.919118	.917431	.915751	.914077	.912409	.910747	.909091
2	.854172	.851023	.847892	.844777	.841680	.838600	.835536	.832490	.829460	.826446
3	.789438	.785077	.780747	.776450	.772183	.767948	.763744	.759571	.755428	.751315
4	.729610	.724241	.718920	.713649	.708425	.703250	.698121	.693039	.688003	.683013
5	.674316	.668119	.661989	.655927	.649931	.644001	.638136	.632335	.626597	.620921
6	.623213	.616346	.609566	.602874	.596267	.589745	.583305	.576948	.570671	.564474
7	.575982	.568585	.561295	.554112	.547034	.540059	.533186	.526412	.519737	.513158
8	.532331	.524524	.516846	.509294	.501866	.494560	.487373	.480303	.473349	.466507
9	.491988	.483879	.475917	.468101	.460428	.452894	.445496	.438233	.431101	.424098
10	.454703	.446383	.438230	.430240	.422411	.414738	.407218	.399848	.392624	.385543
11	.420243	.411792	.403526	.395441	.387533	.379797	.372228	.364824	.357581	.350494
12	.388394	.379882	.371571	.363457	.355535	.347799	.340245	.332869	.325666	.318631
13	.358960	.350445	.342147	.334060	.326179	.318497	.311010	.303713	.296599	.289664
14	.331756	.323288	.315052	.307040	.299246	.291664	.284287	.277110	.270127	.263331
15	.306613	.298236	.290103	.282206	.274538	.267092	.259860	.252838	.246017	.239392
16	.283376	.275126	.267130	.259381	.251870	.244589	.237532	.230691	.224059	.217629
17	.261901	.253806	.245976	.238401	.231073	.223983	.217123	.210485	.204061	.197845
18	.242052	.234139	.226497	.219119	.211994	.205113	.198467	.192048	.185848	.179859
19	.223708	.215995	.208561	.201396	.194490	.187832	.181414	.175226	.169260	.163508
20	.206754	.199257	.192045	.185107	.178431	.172007	.165826	.159878	.154153	.148644
21	.191085	.183817	.176837	.170135	.163698	.157516	.151578	.145874	.140395	.135131
22	.176604	.169573	.162834	.156374	.150182	.144245	.138554	.133097	.127864	.122846
23	.163220	.156432	.149939	.143726	.137781	.132093	.126649	.121439	.116452	.111678
24	.150850	.144310	.138065	.132101	.126405	.120964	.115767	.110802	.106058	.101526
25	.139418	.133128	.127132	.121416	.115968	.110773	.105820	.101097	.096592	.092296
26	.128852	.122811	.117064	.111596	.106393	.101441	.096727	.092241	.087971	.083905
27	.119087	.113295	.107794	.102570	.097608	.092894	.088416	.084162	.080119	.076278
28	.110062	.104515	.099258	.094274	.089548	.085068	.080819	.076790	.072968	.069343
29	.101721	.096416	.091398	.086649	.082155	.077901	.073875	.070064	.066456	.063039
30	.094012	.088945	.084160	.079640	.075371	.071338	.067527	.063927	.060524	.057309
31	.086887	.082053	.077495	.073199	.069148	.065328	.061725	.058327	.055122	.052099
32	.080302	.075694	.071358	.067278	.063438	.059824	.056422	.053218	.050202	.047362
33	.074216	.069829	.065708	.061837	.058200	.054784	.051574	.048557	.045722	.043057
34	.068592	.064418	.060504	.056835	.053395	.050168	.047142	.044304	.041641	.039143
35	.063394	.059426	.055713	.052238	.048986	.045942	.043092	.040423	.037924	.035584
36	.058589	.054821	.051301	.048013	.044941	.042071	.039389	.036882	.034539	.032349
37	.054149	.050573	.047239	.044130	.041231	.038527	.036005	.033652	.031457	.029408
38	.050045	.046654	.043498	.040560	.037826	.035281	.032911	.030704	.028649	.026735
39	.046253	.043039	.040053	.037280	.034703	.032309	.030083	.028015	.026092	.024304
40	.042747	.039703	.036881	.034264	.031838	.029587	.027498	.025561	.023763	.022095
41	.039508	.036627	.033961	.031493	.029209	.027094	.025136	.023322	.021642	.020086
42	.036514	.033789	.031271	.028946	.026797	.024811	.022976	.021279	.019711	.018260
43	.033746	.031170	.028795	.026605	.024584	.022721	.021002	.019415	.017951	.016600
44	.031189	.028755	.026515	.024453	.022555	.020807	.019197	.017715	.016349	.015091
45	.028825	.026527	.024415	.022475	.020692	.019054	.017548	.016163	.014890	.013719
46	.026641	.024471	.022482	.020657	.018984	.017449	.016040	.014747	.013561	.012472
47	.024622	.022575	.020701	.018986	.017416	.015978	.014662	.013456	.012351	.011338
48	.022756	.020825	.019062	.017451	.015978	.014632	.013402	.012277	.011248	.010307
49	.021031	.019212	.017552	.016039	.014659	.013400	.012250	.011202	.010244	.009370
50	.019437	.017723	.016163	.014742	.013449	.012271	.011198	.010221	.009330	.008519
51	.017964	.016350	.014883	.013550	.012338	.011237	.010236	.009325	.008497	.007744
52	.016603	.015083	.013704	.012454	.011319	.010290	.009356	.008508	.007739	.007040
53	.015345	.013914	.012619	.011446	.010385	.009423	.008552	.007763	.007048	.006400
54	.014182	.012836	.011620	.010521	.009527	.008629	.007817	.007083	.006419	.005818
55	.013107	.011841	.010699	.009670	.008741	.007902	.007146	.006463	.005846	.005289
56	.012114	.010923	.009852	.008888	.008019	.007237	.006532	.005897	.005324	.004809
57	.011196	.010077	.009072	.008169	.007357	.006627	.005971	.005380	.004849	.004371
58	.010347	.009296	.008354	.007508	.006749	.006069	.005458	.004909	.004416	.003974
59	.009563	.008576	.007692	.006901	.006192	.005557	.004989	.004479	.004022	.003613
60	.008838	.007911	.007083	.006343	.005681	.005089	.004560	.004087	.003663	

Sec. 2031. Definition of gross estate

Table B--Term Certain Remainder Factors Applicable After April 30, 1989

Interest rate

Years	10.2%	10.4%	10.6%	10.8%	11.0%	11.2%	11.4%	11.6%	11.8%	12.0%
1	.907441	.905797	.904159	.902527	.900901	.899281	.897666	.896057	.894454	.892857
2	.823449	.820468	.817504	.814555	.811622	.808706	.805804	.802919	.800049	.797194
3	.747232	.743178	.739153	.735158	.731191	.727253	.723343	.719461	.715607	.711780
4	.678069	.673168	.668312	.663500	.658731	.654005	.649321	.644679	.640078	.635518
5	.615307	.609754	.604261	.598827	.593451	.588134	.582873	.577669	.572520	.567427
6	.558355	.552313	.546348	.540457	.534641	.528897	.523225	.517625	.512093	.506631
7	.506674	.500284	.493985	.487777	.481658	.475627	.469682	.463821	.458044	.452349
8	.459777	.453156	.446641	.440232	.433926	.427722	.421617	.415610	.409700	.403883
9	.417221	.410467	.403835	.397322	.390925	.384642	.378472	.372411	.366458	.360610
10	.378603	.371800	.365131	.358593	.352184	.345901	.339741	.333701	.327780	.321973
11	.343560	.336775	.330137	.323640	.317283	.311062	.304974	.299016	.293184	.287476
12	.311760	.305050	.298496	.292094	.285841	.279732	.273765	.267935	.262240	.256675
13	.282904	.276313	.269888	.263623	.257514	.251558	.245749	.240085	.234561	.229174
14	.256719	.250284	.244022	.237927	.231995	.226221	.220601	.215130	.209804	.204620
15	.232957	.226706	.220634	.214735	.209004	.203436	.198026	.192769	.187661	.182696
16	.211395	.205350	.199489	.193804	.188292	.182946	.177761	.172732	.167854	.163122
17	.191828	.186005	.180369	.174914	.169633	.164520	.159570	.154778	.150138	.145644
18	.174073	.168483	.163083	.157864	.152822	.147950	.143241	.138690	.134291	.130040
19	.157961	.152612	.147453	.142477	.137678	.133048	.128582	.124274	.120117	.116107
20	.143340	.138235	.133321	.128589	.124034	.119648	.115424	.111357	.107439	.103667
21	.130073	.125213	.120543	.116055	.111742	.107597	.103612	.099782	.096100	.092560
22	.118033	.113418	.108990	.104743	.100669	.096760	.093009	.089410	.085957	.082643
23	.107108	.102733	.098544	.094533	.090693	.087014	.083491	.080117	.076884	.073788
24	.097195	.093056	.089100	.085319	.081705	.078250	.074947	.071789	.068770	.065882
25	.088198	.084289	.080560	.077003	.073608	.070369	.067278	.064327	.061511	.058823
26	.080035	.076349	.072839	.069497	.066314	.063281	.060393	.057641	.055019	.052521
27	.072627	.069157	.065858	.062723	.059742	.056908	.054213	.051650	.049212	.046894
28	.065905	.062642	.059547	.056609	.053822	.051176	.048665	.046281	.044018	.041869
29	.059804	.056741	.053840	.051091	.048488	.046022	.043685	.041470	.039372	.037383
30	.054269	.051396	.048680	.046111	.043683	.041386	.039214	.037160	.035216	.033378
31	.049246	.046554	.044014	.041617	.039354	.037218	.035201	.033297	.031500	.029802
32	.044688	.042169	.039796	.037560	.035454	.033469	.031599	.029836	.028175	.026609
33	.040552	.038196	.035982	.033899	.031940	.030098	.028365	.026735	.025201	.023758
34	.036798	.034598	.032533	.030595	.028775	.027067	.025463	.023956	.022541	.021212
35	.033392	.031339	.029415	.027613	.025924	.024341	.022857	.021466	.020162	.018940
36	.030301	.028387	.026596	.024921	.023355	.021889	.020518	.019235	.018034	.016910
37	.027497	.025712	.024047	.022492	.021040	.019684	.018418	.017236	.016131	.015098
38	.024952	.023290	.021742	.020300	.018955	.017702	.016533	.015444	.014428	.013481
39	.022642	.021096	.019658	.018321	.017077	.015919	.014841	.013839	.012905	.012036
40	.020546	.019109	.017774	.016535	.015384	.014316	.013323	.012400	.011543	.010747
41	.018645	.017309	.016071	.014923	.013860	.012874	.011959	.011111	.010325	.009595
42	.016919	.015678	.014531	.013469	.012486	.011577	.010735	.009956	.009235	.008567
43	.015353	.014201	.013138	.012156	.011249	.010411	.009637	.008922	.008260	.007649
44	.013932	.012864	.011879	.010971	.010134	.009362	.008651	.007994	.007389	.006830
45	.012642	.011652	.010740	.009902	.009130	.008419	.007765	.007163	.006609	.006098
46	.011472	.010554	.009711	.008937	.008225	.007571	.006971	.006419	.005911	.005445
47	.010410	.009560	.008780	.008065	.007410	.006809	.006257	.005752	.005287	.004861
48	.009447	.008659	.007939	.007279	.006676	.006123	.005617	.005154	.004729	.004340
49	.008572	.007844	.007178	.006570	.006014	.005506	.005042	.004618	.004230	.003875
50	.007779	.007105	.006490	.005929	.005418	.004952	.004526	.004138	.003784	.003460
51	.007059	.006435	.005868	.005351	.004881	.004453	.004063	.003708	.003384	.003089
52	.006406	.005829	.005306	.004830	.004397	.004005	.003647	.003322	.003027	.002758
53	.005813	.005280	.004797	.004359	.003962	.003601	.003274	.002977	.002708	.002463
54	.005275	.004783	.004337	.003934	.003569	.003238	.002939	.002668	.002422	.002199
55	.004786	.004332	.003922	.003551	.003215	.002912	.002638	.002390	.002166	.001963
56	.004343	.003924	.003546	.003205	.002897	.002619	.002368	.002142	.001938	.001753
57	.003941	.003554	.003206	.002892	.002610	.002355	.002126	.001919	.001733	.001565
58	.003577	.003220	.002899	.002610	.002351	.002118	.001908	.001720	.001550	.001398
59	.003246	.002916	.002621	.002356	.002118	.001905	.001713	.001541	.001387	.001248
60	.002945	.002642	.002370	.002126	.001908	.001713	.001538	.001381	.001240	.001114

Table B--Term Certain Remainder Factors Applicable After April 30, 1989

Interest rate

Years	12.2%	12.4%	12.6%	12.8%	13.0%	13.2%	13.4%	13.6%	13.8%	14.0%
1	.891266	.889680	.888099	.886525	884956	.883392	.881834	.880282	.878735	.877193
2	.794354	.791530	.788721	.785926	.783147	.780382	.777632	.774896	.772175	.769468
3	.707981	.704208	.700462	.696743	.693050	.689383	.685742	.682127	.678536	.674972
4	.630999	.626520	.622080	.617680	.613319	.608996	.604711	.600464	.596254	.592080
5	.562388	.557402	.552469	.547589	.542760	.537982	.533255	.528577	.523949	.519369
6	.501237	.495909	.490648	.485451	.480319	.475249	.470242	.465297	.460412	.455587
7	.446735	.441200	.435744	.430364	.425061	.419831	.414676	.409592	.404580	.399637
8	.398160	.392527	.386984	.381529	.376160	.370876	.365675	.360557	.355518	.350559
9	.354866	.349223	.343680	.338235	.332885	.327629	.322465	.317391	.312406	.307508
10	.316280	.310697	.305222	.299853	.294588	.289425	.284361	.279394	.274522	.269744
11	.281889	.276421	.271068	.265827	.260698	.255676	.250759	.245945	.241232	.236617
12	.251238	.245926	.240735	.235663	.230706	.225862	.221128	.216501	.211979	.207559
13	.223920	.218795	.213797	.208921	.204165	.199525	.194998	.190582	.186273	.182069

Sec. 2031.   Definition of gross estate

Line	Age									
	14	.199572	.194658	.189873	.185213	.180677	.176258	.171956	.167766	.163685	.159710
	15	.177872	.173183	.168626	.164196	.159891	.155705	.151637	.147681	.143835	.140096
	16	.158531	.154077	.149757	.145564	.141496	.137549	.133718	.130001	.126393	.122892
	17	.141293	.137080	.132999	.129046	.125218	.121510	.117917	.114438	.111066	.107800
5	18	.125930	.121957	.118116	.114403	.110812	.107341	.103984	.100737	.097598	.094561
	19	.112237	.108503	.104899	.101421	.098064	.094824	.091696	.088677	.085762	.082948
	20	.100033	.096533	.093161	.089912	.086782	.083767	.080861	.078061	.075362	.072762
	21	.089156	.085883	.082736	.079709	.076798	.073999	.071306	.068716	.066224	.063826
	22	.079462	.076408	.073478	.070664	.067963	.065370	.062880	.060489	.058193	.055988
10	23	.070821	.067979	.065255	.062646	.060144	.057747	.055450	.053247	.051136	.049112
	24	.063121	.060480	.057953	.055537	.053225	.051014	.048898	.046873	.044935	.043081
	25	.056257	.053807	.051468	.049235	.047102	.045065	.043119	.041261	.039486	.037790
	26	.050140	.047871	.045709	.043648	.041683	.039810	.038024	.036321	.034698	.033149
	27	.044688	.042590	.040594	.038695	.036888	.035168	.033531	.031973	.030490	.029078
15	28	.039829	.037892	.036052	.034304	.032644	.031067	.029569	.028145	.026793	.025507
	29	.035498	.033711	.032017	.030411	.028889	.027444	.026075	.024776	.023544	.022375
	30	.031638	.029992	.028435	.026960	.025565	.024244	.022994	.021810	.020689	.019627
	31	.028198	.026684	.025253	.023901	.022624	.021417	.020277	.019199	.018180	.017217
	32	.025132	.023740	.022427	.021189	.020021	.018920	.017881	.016900	.015975	.015102
20	33	.022399	.021121	.019917	.018785	.017718	.016714	.015768	.014877	.014038	.013248
	34	.019964	.018791	.017689	.016653	.015680	.014765	.013905	.013096	.012336	.011621
	35	.017793	.016718	.015709	.014763	.013876	.013043	.012261	.011528	.010840	.010194
	36	.015858	.014873	.013951	.013088	.012279	.011522	.010813	.010148	.009525	.008942
	37	.014134	.013233	.012390	.011603	.010867	.010178	.009535	.008933	.008370	.007844
25	38	.012597	.011773	.011004	.010286	.009617	.008992	.008408	.007864	.007355	.006880
	39	.011227	.010474	.009772	.009119	.008510	.007943	.007415	.006922	.006463	.006035
	40	.010007	.009319	.008679	.008084	.007531	.007017	.006538	.006093	.005679	.005294
	41	.008919	.008291	.007708	.007167	.006665	.006199	.005766	.005364	.004991	.004644
	42	.007949	.007376	.006845	.006354	.005898	.005476	.005085	.004722	.004386	.004074
30	43	.007084	.006562	.006079	.005633	.005219	.004837	.004484	.004157	.003854	.003573
	44	.006314	.005838	.005399	.004993	.004619	.004273	.003954	.003659	.003386	.003135
	45	.005628	.005194	.004795	.004427	.004088	.003775	.003487	.003221	.002976	.002750
	46	.005016	.004621	.004258	.003924	.003617	.003335	.003075	.002835	.002615	.002412
	47	.004470	.004111	.003782	.003479	.003201	.002946	.002711	.002496	.002298	.002116
35	48	.003984	.003658	.003359	.003084	.002833	.002602	.002391	.002197	.002019	.001856
	49	.003551	.003254	.002983	.002734	.002507	.002299	.002108	.001934	.001774	.001628
	50	.003165	.002895	.002649	.002424	.002219	.002031	.001859	.001702	.001559	.001428
	51	.002821	.002576	.002353	.002149	.001963	.001794	.001640	.001499	.001370	.001253
	52	.002514	.002292	.002089	.001905	.001737	.001585	.001446	.001319	.001204	.001099
40	53	.002241	.002039	.001856	.001689	.001538	.001400	.001275	.001161	.001058	.000964
	54	.001997	.001814	.001648	.001497	.001361	.001237	.001124	.001022	.000930	.000846
	55	.001780	.001614	.001463	.001327	.001204	.001093	.000991	.000900	.000817	.000742
	56	.001586	.001436	.001300	.001177	.001066	.000965	.000874	.000792	.000718	.000651
	57	.001414	.001277	.001154	.001043	.000943	.000853	.000771	.000697	.000631	.000571
45	58	.001260	.001136	.001025	.000925	.000835	.000753	.000680	.000614	.000554	.000501
	59	.001123	.001011	.000910	.000820	.000739	.000665	.000600	.000540	.000487	.000439
	60	.001001	.000900	.000809	.000727	.000654	.000588	.000529	.000476	.000428	.000385

Table J--Adjustment Factors for Term Certain Annuities Payable at the Beginning of Each Interval Applicable Aer April 30, 1989

Line	Interest rate	Annually	Semi annually	Quarterly	Monthly	Weekly
50			[Frequency of payments]			
55	4.2	1.0420	1.0314	1.0261	1.0226	1.0213
	4.4	1.0440	1.0329	1.0274	1.0237	1.0223
	4.6	1.0460	1.0344	1.0286	1.0247	1.0233
	4.8	1.0480	1.0359	1.0298	1.0258	1.0243
	5.0	1.0500	1.0373	1.0311	1.0269	1.0253
60	5.2	1.0520	1.0388	1.0323	1.0279	1.0263
	5.4	1.0540	1.0403	1.0335	1.0290	1.0273
	5.6	1.0560	1.0418	1.0348	1.0301	1.0283
	5.8	1.0580	1.0433	1.0360	1.0311	1.0293
	6.0	1.0600	1.0448	1.0372	1.0322	1.0303
65	6.2	1.0620	1.0463	1.0385	1.0333	1.0313
	6.4	1.0640	1.0478	1.0397	1.0343	1.0323
	6.6	1.0660	1.0492	1.0409	1.0354	1.0333
	6.8	1.0680	1.0507	1.0422	1.0365	1.0343
	7.0	1.0700	1.0522	1.0434	1.0375	1.0353
70	7.2	1.0720	1.0537	1.0446	1.0386	1.0363
	7.4	1.0740	1.0552	1.0458	1.0396	1.0373
	7.6	1.0760	1.0567	1.0471	1.0407	1.0383
	7.8	1.0780	1.0581	1.0483	1.0418	1.0393
	8.0	1.0800	1.0596	1.0495	1.0428	1.0403
75	8.2	1.0820	1.0611	1.0507	1.0439	1.0413
	8.4	1.0840	1.0626	1.0520	1.0449	1.0422
	8.6	1.0860	1.0641	1.0532	1.0460	1.0432
	8.8	1.0880	1.0655	1.0544	1.0471	1.0442
	9.0	1.0900	1.0670	1.0556	1.0481	1.0452
80	9.2	1.0920	1.0685	1.0569	1.0492	1.0462
	9.4	1.0940	1.0700	1.0581	1.0502	1.0472
	9.6	1.0960	1.0715	1.0593	1.0513	1.0482
	9.8	1.0980	1.0729	1.0605	1.0523	1.0492
	10.0	1.1000	1.0744	1.0618	1.0534	1.0502
85	10.2	1.1020	1.0759	1.0630	1.0544	1.0512
	10.4	1.1040	1.0774	1.0642	1.0555	1.0521

10.6	1.1060	1.0788	1.0654	1.0565	1.0531
10.8	1.1080	1.0803	1.0666	1.0576	1.0541
11.0	1.1100	1.0818	1.0679	1.0586	1.0551
11.2	1.1120	1.0833	1.0691	1.0597	1.0561
11.4	1.1140	1.0847	1.0703	1.0607	1.0571
11.6	1.1160	1.0862	1.0715	1.0618	1.0581
11.8	1.1180	1.0877	1.0727	1.0628	1.0590
12.0	1.1200	1.0892	1.0739	1.0639	1.0600
12.2	1.1220	1.0906	1.0752	1.0649	1.0610
12.4	1.1240	1.0921	1.0764	1.0660	1.0620
12.6	1.1260	1.0936	1.0776	1.0670	1.0630
12.8	1.1280	1.0950	1.0788	1.0681	1.0639
13.0	1.1300	1.0965	1.0800	1.0691	1.0649
13.2	1.1320	1.0980	1.0812	1.0701	1.0659
13.4	1.1340	1.0994	1.0824	1.0712	1.0669
13.6	1.1360	1.1009	1.0836	1.0722	1.0679
13.8	1.1380	1.1024	1.0849	1.0733	1.0688
14.0	1.1400	1.1039	1.0861	1.0743	1.0698

Table K--Adjustment Factors For Annuities Payable At The End Of Each Interval Applicable After April 30, 1989

[Frequency of Payments]

Interest Rate	Annually	Semi annually	Quarterly	Monthly	Weekly
4.2	1.0000	1.0104	1.0156	1.0191	1.0205
4.4	1.0000	1.0109	1.0164	1.0200	1.0214
4.6	1.0000	1.0114	1.0171	1.0209	1.0224
4.8	1.0000	1.0119	1.0178	1.0218	1.0234
5.0	1.0000	1.0123	1.0186	1.0227	1.0243
5.2	1.0000	1.0128	1.0193	1.0236	1.0253
5.4	1.0000	1.0133	1.0200	1.0245	1.0262
5.6	1.0000	1.0138	1.0208	1.0254	1.0272
5.8	1.0000	1.0143	1.0215	1.0263	1.0282
6.0	1.0000	1.0148	1.0222	1.0272	1.0291
6.2	1.0000	1.0153	1.0230	1.0281	1.0301
6.4	1.0000	1.0158	1.0237	1.0290	1.0311
6.6	1.0000	1.0162	1.0244	1.0299	1.0320
6.8	1.0000	1.0167	1.0252	1.0308	1.0330
7.0	1.0000	1.0172	1.0259	1.0317	1.0339
7.2	1.0000	1.0177	1.0266	1.0326	1.0349
7.4	1.0000	1.0182	1.0273	1.0335	1.0358
7.6	1.0000	1.0187	1.0281	1.0344	1.0368
7.8	1.0000	1.0191	1.0288	1.0353	1.0378
8.0	1.0000	1.0196	1.0295	1.0362	1.0387
8.2	1.0000	1.0201	1.0302	1.0370	1.0397
8.4	1.0000	1.0206	1.0310	1.0379	1.0406
8.6	1.0000	1.0211	1.0317	1.0388	1.0416
8.8	1.0000	1.0215	1.0324	1.0397	1.0425
9.0	1.0000	1.0220	1.0331	1.0406	1.0435
9.2	1.0000	1.0225	1.0339	1.0415	1.0444
9.4	1.0000	1.0230	1.0346	1.0424	1.0454
9.6	1.0000	1.0235	1.0353	1.0433	1.0463
9.8	1.0000	1.0239	1.0360	1.0442	1.0473
10.0	1.0000	1.0244	1.0368	1.0450	1.0482
10.2	1.0000	1.0249	1.0375	1.0459	1.0492
10.4	1.0000	1.0254	1.0382	1.0468	1.0501
10.6	1.0000	1.0258	1.0389	1.0477	1.0511
10.8	1.0000	1.0263	1.0396	1.0486	1.0520
11.0	1.0000	1.0268	1.0404	1.0495	1.0530
11.2	1.0000	1.0273	1.0411	1.0503	1.0539
11.4	1.0000	1.0277	1.0418	1.0512	1.0549
11.6	1.0000	1.0282	1.0425	1.0521	1.0558
11.8	1.0000	1.0287	1.0432	1.0530	1.0568
12.0	1.0000	1.0292	1.0439	1.0539	1.0577
12.2	1.0000	1.0296	1.0447	1.0548	1.0587
12.4	1.0000	1.0301	1.0454	1.0556	1.0596
12.6	1.0000	1.0306	1.0461	1.0565	1.0605
12.8	1.0000	1.0310	1.0468	1.0574	1.0615
13.0	1.0000	1.0315	1.0475	1.0583	1.0624
13.2	1.0000	1.0320	1.0482	1.0591	1.0634
13.4	1.0000	1.0324	1.0489	1.0600	1.0643
13.6	1.0000	1.0329	1.0496	1.0609	1.0652
13.8	1.0000	1.0334	1.0504	1.0618	1.0662
14.0	1.0000	1.0339	1.0511	1.0626	1.0671

(7) *Actuarial Table S and Table 90CM where the valuation date is after April 30, 1999.* Except as provided in § 20.7520-2(b) (pertaining to certain limitations on the use of prescribed tables), for determination of the present value of an interest that is dependent on the termination of a life interest, Table 90CM and Table S, single life remainder factors applicable where the valuation date is after April 30, 1999, contained in this paragraph (d)

Sec. 2031. Definition of gross estate

(7) (or Table S and Table 80CNSMT contained in § 20.2031-7A(e)(4) for valuation dates after April 30, 1989, and before May 1, 1999) and Table J and Table K contained in paragraph (d)(6) of this section, must be used in the application of the provisions of this section when the section 7520 interest rate component is between 4.2 and 14 percent.

5

Table S--Based on Life Table 90CM Single Life Remainder Factors Applicable After April 30, 1999
[Interest rate]

Age	4.2%	4.4%	4.6%	4.8%	5.0%	5.2%	5.4%	5.6%	5.8%	6.0%
0	.06752	.06130	.05586	.05109	.04691	.04322	.03998	.03711	.03458	.03233
1	.06137	.05495	.04932	.04438	.04003	.03620	.03283	.02985	.02721	.02487
2	.06325	.05667	.05088	.04580	.04132	.03737	.03388	.03079	.02806	.02563
3	.06545	.05869	.05275	.04752	.04291	.03883	.03523	.03203	.02920	.02668
4	.06784	.06092	.05482	.04944	.04469	.04048	.03676	.03346	.03052	.02791
5	.07040	.06331	.05705	.05152	.04662	.04229	.03845	.03503	.03199	.02928
6	.07310	.06583	.05941	.05372	.04869	.04422	.04025	.03672	.03357	.03076
7	.07594	.06849	.06191	.05607	.05089	.04628	.04219	.03854	.03528	.03236
8	.07891	.07129	.06453	.05853	.05321	.04846	.04424	.04046	.03709	.03407
9	.08203	.07423	.06731	.06115	.05567	.05079	.04643	.04253	.03904	.03592
10	.08532	.07734	.07024	.06392	.05829	.05326	.04877	.04474	.04114	.03790
11	.08875	.08059	.07331	.06683	.06104	.05587	.05124	.04709	.04336	.04002
12	.09233	.08398	.07653	.06989	.06394	.05862	.05385	.04957	.04572	.04226
13	.09601	.08748	.07985	.07304	.06693	.06146	.05655	.05214	.04816	.04458
14	.09974	.09102	.08322	.07624	.06997	.06435	.05929	.05474	.05064	.04694
15	.10350	.09460	.08661	.07946	.07303	.06725	.06204	.05735	.05312	.04930
16	.10728	.09818	.09001	.08268	.07608	.07014	.06479	.05996	.05559	.05164
17	.11108	.10179	.09344	.08592	.07916	.07306	.06755	.06257	.05807	.05399
18	.11494	.10545	.09691	.08921	.08227	.07601	.07034	.06521	.06057	.05636
19	.11889	.10921	.10047	.09259	.08548	.07904	.07322	.06794	.06315	.05880
20	.12298	.11310	.10417	.09610	.08881	.08220	.07622	.07078	.06584	.06135
21	.12722	.11713	.10801	.09976	.09228	.08550	.07935	.07375	.06866	.06403
22	.13159	.12130	.11199	.10354	.09588	.08893	.08260	.07685	.07160	.06682
23	.13613	.12563	.11612	.10748	.09964	.09250	.08601	.08009	.07468	.06975
24	.14084	.13014	.12043	.11160	.10357	.09625	.08958	.08349	.07793	.07284
25	.14574	.13484	.12493	.11591	.10768	.10018	.09334	.08708	.08135	.07611
26	.15084	.13974	.12963	.12041	.11199	.10431	.09728	.09085	.08496	.07956
27	.15615	.14485	.13454	.12513	.11652	.10865	.10144	.09484	.08878	.08322
28	.16166	.15016	.13965	.13004	.12124	.11319	.10580	.09901	.09279	.08706
29	.16737	.15567	.14497	.13516	.12617	.11792	.11035	.10339	.09699	.09109
30	.17328	.16138	.15048	.14047	.13129	.12286	.11510	.10796	.10138	.09532
31	.17938	.16728	.15618	.14599	.13661	.12799	.12004	.11272	.10597	.09974
32	.18568	.17339	.16210	.15171	.14214	.13333	.12520	.11769	.11076	.10435
33	.19220	.17972	.16824	.15766	.14790	.13889	.13058	.12289	.11578	.10920
34	.19894	.18627	.17460	.16383	.15388	.14468	.13618	.12831	.12102	.11426
35	.20592	.19307	.18121	.17025	.16011	.15073	.14204	.13399	.12652	.11958
36	.21312	.20010	.18805	.17691	.16658	.15701	.14814	.13990	.13225	.12514
37	.22057	.20737	.19514	.18382	.17331	.16356	.15450	.14608	.13825	.13096
38	.22827	.21490	.20251	.19100	.18031	.17038	.16113	.15253	.14452	.13705
39	.23623	.22270	.21013	.19845	.18759	.17747	.16805	.15927	.15108	.14344
40	.24446	.23078	.21805	.20620	.19516	.18487	.17527	.16631	.15795	.15013
41	.25298	.23915	.22626	.21425	.20305	.19259	.18282	.17368	.16514	.15715
42	.26178	.24782	.23478	.22262	.21125	.20062	.19069	.18138	.17267	.16450
43	.27087	.25678	.24360	.23129	.21977	.20898	.19888	.18941	.18053	.17220
44	.28025	.26603	.25273	.24027	.22860	.21766	.20740	.19777	.18873	.18023
45	.28987	.27555	.26212	.24953	.23772	.22664	.21622	.20644	.19724	.18858
46	.29976	.28533	.27179	.25908	.24714	.23591	.22536	.21542	.20606	.19725
47	.30987	.29535	.28171	.26889	.25682	.24546	.23476	.22468	.21518	.20621
48	.32023	.30563	.29190	.27897	.26678	.25530	.24447	.23425	.22460	.21549
49	.33082	.31615	.30234	.28931	.27702	.26543	.25447	.24412	.23434	.22509
50	.34166	.32694	.31306	.29995	.28756	.27586	.26479	.25432	.24441	.23502
51	.35274	.33798	.32404	.31085	.29838	.28658	.27541	.26482	.25479	.24528
52	.36402	.34924	.33525	.32200	.30946	.29757	.28630	.27561	.26547	.25584
53	.37550	.36070	.34668	.33339	.32078	.30882	.29746	.28667	.27643	.26669
54	.38717	.37237	.35833	.34500	.33234	.32031	.30888	.29801	.28766	.27782
55	.39903	.38424	.37019	.35683	.34413	.33205	.32056	.30961	.29918	.28925
56	.41108	.39631	.38227	.36890	.35617	.34405	.33250	.32149	.31099	.30097
57	.42330	.40857	.39455	.38118	.36844	.35629	.34469	.33363	.32306	.31297
58	.43566	.42098	.40699	.39364	.38089	.36873	.35710	.34600	.33538	.32522
59	.44811	.43351	.41956	.40623	.39350	.38133	.36968	.35855	.34789	.33768
60	.46066	.44613	.43224	.41896	.40624	.39408	.38243	.37127	.36058	.35033
61	.47330	.45887	.44505	.43182	.41914	.40699	.39535	.38418	.37347	.36318
62	.48608	.47175	.45802	.44485	.43223	.42011	.40848	.39732	.38660	.37629
63	.49898	.48478	.47115	.45807	.44550	.43343	.42184	.41069	.39997	.38966
64	.51200	.49793	.48442	.47143	.45895	.44694	.43539	.42427	.41357	.40326
65	.52512	.51121	.49782	.48495	.47255	.46062	.44912	.43805	.42738	.41709
66	.53835	.52461	.51137	.49862	.48634	.47449	.46307	.45206	.44143	.43118
67	.55174	.53818	.52511	.51250	.50034	.48860	.47727	.46633	.45576	.44556
68	.56524	.55188	.53899	.52654	.51452	.50291	.49168	.48083	.47034	.46020
69	.57882	.56568	.55299	.54071	.52885	.51737	.50627	.49552	.48513	.47506
70	.59242	.57951	.56703	.55495	.54325	.53193	.52096	.51034	.50004	.49007
71	.60598	.59332	.58106	.56918	.55767	.54651	.53569	.52520	.51503	.50516

1032

Sec. 2031. Definition of gross estate

Age											
72	.61948	.60707	.59504	.58338	.57206	.56108	.55043	.54009	.53004	.52029	
73	.63287	.62073	.60895	.59751	.58640	.57561	.56513	.55495	.54505	.53543	
74	.64621	.63435	.62282	.61162	.60073	.59015	.57985	.56984	.56009	.55061	
75	.65953	.64796	.63671	.62575	.61510	.60473	.59463	.58480	.57523	.56591	
76	.67287	.66160	.65063	.63995	.62954	.61940	.60952	.59989	.59050	.58135	5
77	.68622	.67526	.66459	.65419	.64404	.63415	.62450	.61509	.60590	.59694	
78	.69954	.68892	.67856	.66845	.65858	.64895	.63955	.63036	.62140	.61264	
79	.71278	.70250	.69246	.68265	.67308	.66372	.65457	.64563	.63690	.62836	
80	.72581	.71588	.70618	.69668	.68740	.67833	.66945	.66077	.65227	.64396	
81	.73857	.72899	.71962	.71045	.70147	.69268	.68408	.67566	.66741	.65933	10
82	.75101	.74178	.73274	.72389	.71522	.70672	.69840	.69024	.68225	.67441	
83	.76311	.75423	.74553	.73700	.72864	.72044	.71240	.70451	.69678	.68919	
84	.77497	.76645	.75809	.74988	.74183	.73393	.72618	.71857	.71110	.70377	
85	.78665	.77848	.77047	.76260	.75487	.74728	.73982	.73250	.72530	.71823	
86	.79805	.79025	.78258	.77504	.76764	.76036	.75320	.74617	.73925	.73245	15
87	.80904	.80159	.79427	.78706	.77998	.77301	.76615	.75940	.75277	.74624	
88	.81962	.81251	.80552	.79865	.79188	.78521	.77865	.77220	.76584	.75958	
89	.82978	.82302	.81636	.80980	.80335	.79699	.79072	.78455	.77847	.77248	
90	.83952	.83309	.82676	.82052	.81437	.80831	.80234	.79645	.79064	.78492	
91	.84870	.84260	.83658	.83064	.82479	.81902	.81332	.80771	.80217	.79671	20
92	.85716	.85136	.84563	.83998	.83441	.82891	.82348	.81812	.81283	.80761	
93	.86494	.85942	.85396	.84858	.84326	.83801	.83283	.82771	.82266	.81767	
94	.87216	.86690	.86170	.85657	.85149	.84648	.84153	.83664	.83181	.82704	
95	.87898	.87397	.86902	.86412	.85928	.85450	.84977	.84510	.84049	.83592	
96	.88537	.88060	.87587	.87121	.86659	.86203	.85751	.85305	.84864	.84427	25
97	.89127	.88672	.88221	.87775	.87335	.86898	.86467	.86040	.85618	.85200	
98	.89680	.89245	.88815	.88389	.87968	.87551	.87138	.86730	.86326	.85926	
99	.90217	.89803	.89393	.88987	.88585	.88187	.87793	.87402	.87016	.86633	
100	.90738	.90344	.89953	.89567	.89183	.88804	.88428	.88056	.87687	.87322	
101	.91250	.90876	.90504	.90137	.89772	.89412	.89054	.88699	.88348	.88000	30
102	.91751	.91396	.91045	.90696	.90350	.90007	.89668	.89331	.88997	.88666	
103	.92247	.91912	.91579	.91249	.90922	.90598	.90276	.89957	.89640	.89326	
104	.92775	.92460	.92148	.91839	.91532	.91227	.90924	.90624	.90326	.90031	
105	.93290	.92996	.92704	.92415	.92127	.91841	.91558	.91276	.90997	.90719	
106	.93948	.93680	.93415	.93151	.92889	.92628	.92370	.92113	.91857	.91604	35
107	.94739	.94504	.94271	.94039	.93808	.93579	.93351	.93124	.92899	.92675	
108	.95950	.95767	.95585	.95404	.95224	.95045	.94867	.94689	.94512	.94336	
109	.97985	.97893	.97801	.97710	.97619	.97529	.97438	.97348	.97259	.97170	

40

Age	6.2%	6.4%	6.6%	6.8%	7.0%	7.2%	7.4%	7.6%	7.8%	8.0%	
0	.03034	.02857	.02700	.02559	.02433	.02321	.02220	.02129	.02047	.01973	
1	.02279	.02094	.01929	.01782	.01650	.01533	.01427	.01331	.01246	.01168	
2	.02347	.02155	.01983	.01829	.01692	.01569	.01458	.01358	.01268	.01187	
3	.02444	.02243	.02065	.01905	.01761	.01632	.01516	.01412	.01317	.01232	45
4	.02558	.02349	.02163	.01996	.01846	.01712	.01590	.01481	.01382	.01292	
5	.02686	.02469	.02275	.02101	.01945	.01804	.01677	.01562	.01458	.01364	
6	.02825	.02600	.02398	.02217	.02053	.01906	.01773	.01653	.01544	.01445	
7	.02976	.02742	.02532	.02343	.02172	.02019	.01880	.01755	.01640	.01536	
8	.03137	.02894	.02675	.02479	.02301	.02140	.01995	.01864	.01744	.01635	50
9	.03311	.03059	.02832	.02627	.02442	.02274	.02122	.01985	.01859	.01745	
10	.03499	.03237	.03001	.02788	.02595	.02420	.02262	.02118	.01987	.01867	
11	.03700	.03428	.03183	.02961	.02760	.02578	.02413	.02262	.02125	.02000	
12	.03913	.03632	.03377	.03146	.02937	.02748	.02575	.02418	.02275	.02144	
13	.04135	.03843	.03579	.03339	.03122	.02924	.02744	.02580	.02431	.02294	55
14	.04359	.04057	.03783	.03534	.03308	.03102	.02915	.02744	.02587	.02444	
15	.04584	.04270	.03986	.03728	.03493	.03279	.03083	.02905	.02742	.02593	
16	.04806	.04482	.04187	.03919	.03674	.03452	.03248	.03063	.02892	.02736	
17	.05029	.04692	.04387	.04108	.03855	.03623	.03411	.03218	.03040	.02877	
18	.05253	.04905	.04588	.04299	.04036	.03795	.03574	.03373	.03187	.03017	60
19	.05484	.05124	.04796	.04496	.04222	.03972	.03742	.03532	.03339	.03161	
20	.05726	.05354	.05013	.04702	.04418	.04158	.03919	.03700	.03498	.03313	
21	.05980	.05595	.05242	.04920	.04625	.04354	.04105	.03877	.03667	.03473	
22	.06246	.05847	.05482	.05147	.04841	.04559	.04301	.04063	.03844	.03642	
23	.06524	.06112	.05734	.05387	.05069	.04777	.04508	.04260	.04032	.03821	65
24	.06819	.06392	.06001	.05642	.05312	.05008	.04728	.04470	.04232	.04012	
25	.07131	.06690	.06285	.05913	.05570	.05255	.04964	.04695	.04447	.04218	
26	.07460	.07005	.06586	.06200	.05845	.05518	.05215	.04936	.04677	.04438	
27	.07810	.07340	.06907	.06508	.06140	.05800	.05485	.05195	.04925	.04676	
28	.08179	.07693	.07246	.06833	.06451	.06098	.05772	.05469	.05189	.04929	70
29	.08566	.08065	.07603	.07176	.06780	.06414	.06075	.05761	.05469	.05198	
30	.08973	.08456	.07978	.07536	.07127	.06748	.06396	.06069	.05766	.05483	
31	.09398	.08865	.08372	.07915	.07491	.07098	.06733	.06394	.06078	.05785	
32	.09843	.09294	.08785	.08313	.07875	.07468	.07089	.06737	.06409	.06103	
33	.10310	.09745	.09220	.08732	.08279	.07858	.07466	.07100	.06759	.06441	75
34	.10799	.10217	.09676	.09173	.08705	.08269	.07862	.07483	.07129	.06798	
35	.11314	.10715	.10157	.09638	.09155	.08704	.08283	.07890	.07522	.07179	
36	.11852	.11236	.10662	.10127	.09628	.09162	.08726	.08319	.07938	.07581	
37	.12416	.11783	.11193	.10641	.10126	.09645	.09194	.08772	.08377	.08006	
38	.13009	.12359	.11751	.11183	.10652	.10155	.09689	.09253	.08843	.08459	80
39	.13629	.12962	.12338	.11753	.11206	.10693	.10212	.09761	.09337	.08938	
40	.14281	.13597	.12955	.12355	.11791	.11262	.10766	.10299	.09860	.09447	
41	.14966	.14264	.13606	.12989	.12409	.11864	.11352	.10870	.10417	.09989	
42	.15685	.14966	.14291	.13657	.13061	.12500	.11972	.11475	.11006	.10564	
43	.16437	.15702	.15010	.14360	.13747	.13171	.12627	.12115	.11631	.11174	85
44	.17224	.16472	.15764	.15098	.14469	.13876	.13317	.12789	.12290	.11819	

	45	.18042	.17274	.16550	.15867	.15223	.14615	.14040	.13496	.12982	.12496
	46	.18893	.18110	.17370	.16671	.16011	.15387	.14796	.14238	.13708	.13207
	47	.19775	.18975	.18220	.17505	.16830	.16190	.15584	.15010	.14466	.13950
	48	.20688	.19873	.19102	.18373	.17682	.17027	.16406	.15817	.15258	.14727
5	49	.21633	.20804	.20018	.19274	.18568	.17898	.17262	.16658	.16084	.15539
	50	.22612	.21769	.20969	.20210	.19490	.18805	.18155	.17536	.16948	.16388
	51	.23625	.22769	.21955	.21182	.20448	.19749	.19084	.18452	.17849	.17275
	52	.24669	.23799	.22973	.22186	.21438	.20726	.20047	.19400	.18784	.18196
	53	.25742	.24861	.24022	.23222	.22461	.21735	.21043	.20383	.19753	.19151
10	54	.26845	.25952	.25101	.24290	.23516	.22777	.22072	.21399	.20756	.20140
	55	.27978	.27074	.26212	.25389	.24604	.23853	.23136	.22450	.21793	.21166
	56	.29140	.28227	.27355	.26522	.25725	.24963	.24233	.23535	.22867	.22227
	57	.30333	.29411	.28529	.27686	.26879	.26106	.25365	.24656	.23976	.23324
	58	.31551	.30621	.29731	.28878	.28061	.27278	.26528	.25807	.25116	.24453
15	59	.32790	.31854	.30956	.30095	.29269	.28477	.27716	.26986	.26284	.25610
	60	.34050	.33107	.32202	.31334	.30500	.29699	.28929	.28190	.27478	.26794
	61	.35331	.34384	.33473	.32598	.31757	.30948	.30170	.29422	.28701	.28007
	62	.36639	.35688	.34772	.33892	.33044	.32229	.31443	.30687	.29958	.29255
	63	.37974	.37020	.36101	.35216	.34363	.33542	.32750	.31986	.31250	.30539
20	64	.39334	.38378	.37456	.36568	.35711	.34884	.34087	.33317	.32574	.31857
	65	.40718	.39761	.38838	.37947	.37087	.36257	.35455	.34681	.33932	.33208
	66	.42128	.41172	.40249	.39357	.38496	.37663	.36858	.36079	.35326	.34597
	67	.43569	.42616	.41694	.40803	.39941	.39107	.38299	.37518	.36761	.36028
	68	.45038	.44089	.43170	.42281	.41419	.40585	.39777	.38994	.38235	.37499
25	69	.46531	.45587	.44672	.43786	.42927	.42094	.41286	.40503	.39743	.39006
	70	.48040	.47103	.46194	.45312	.44456	.43626	.42820	.42038	.41278	.40540
	71	.49558	.48629	.47727	.46851	.46000	.45174	.44371	.43591	.42832	.42095
	72	.51082	.50162	.49268	.48399	.47554	.46733	.45934	.45157	.44401	.43666
	73	.52607	.51697	.50813	.49952	.49114	.48299	.47506	.46733	.45981	.45249
30	74	.54139	.53241	.52367	.51515	.50686	.49879	.49092	.48325	.47578	.46849
	75	.55683	.54798	.53936	.53095	.52276	.51477	.50698	.49938	.49197	.48474
	76	.57243	.56373	.55524	.54696	.53888	.53100	.52330	.51579	.50846	.50130
	77	.58819	.57965	.57132	.56318	.55523	.54747	.53988	.53247	.52523	.51815
	78	.60408	.59572	.58755	.57957	.57177	.56414	.55668	.54939	.54225	.53527
35	79	.62001	.61184	.60385	.59604	.58840	.58092	.57360	.56644	.55943	.55256
	80	.63582	.62786	.62007	.61244	.60497	.59765	.59048	.58347	.57659	.56985
	81	.65142	.64367	.63608	.62864	.62135	.61421	.60721	.60034	.59361	.58701
	82	.66673	.65920	.65182	.64458	.63748	.63052	.62368	.61698	.61041	.60395
	83	.68175	.67444	.66728	.66024	.65334	.64656	.63991	.63338	.62696	.62066
40	84	.69657	.68950	.68256	.67574	.66904	.66246	.65599	.64964	.64340	.63727
	85	.71128	.70446	.69775	.69116	.68467	.67830	.67204	.66587	.65982	.65386
	86	.72576	.71919	.71272	.70636	.70010	.69394	.68789	.68193	.67606	.67029
	87	.73981	.73349	.72726	.72114	.71511	.70917	.70333	.69757	.69190	.68632
	88	.75342	.74735	.74137	.73548	.72968	.72396	.71833	.71279	.70732	.70194
45	89	.76658	.76076	.75503	.74938	.74381	.73832	.73290	.72757	.72231	.71712
	90	.77928	.77371	.76823	.76281	.75748	.75221	.74702	.74190	.73684	.73186
	91	.79131	.78600	.78075	.77557	.77046	.76542	.76044	.75553	.75068	.74589
	92	.80246	.79737	.79235	.78740	.78250	.77767	.77290	.76818	.76353	.75893
	93	.81274	.80788	.80307	.79832	.79363	.78899	.78441	.77989	.77542	.77100
50	94	.82232	.81766	.81306	.80850	.80401	.79956	.79517	.79082	.78653	.78228
	95	.83141	.82695	.82254	.81818	.81387	.80961	.80539	.80122	.79710	.79302
	96	.83996	.83569	.83147	.82729	.82316	.81907	.81503	.81103	.80707	.80315
	97	.84787	.84378	.83973	.83573	.83176	.82784	.82396	.82012	.81632	.81255
	98	.85530	.85138	.84750	.84366	.83985	.83609	.83236	.82867	.82502	.82140
55	99	.86255	.85880	.85508	.85140	.84776	.84415	.84057	.83703	.83353	.83005
	100	.86960	.86601	.86246	.85894	.85546	.85200	.84858	.84519	.84183	.83849
	101	.87655	.87313	.86974	.86638	.86305	.85975	.85648	.85324	.85003	.84684
	102	.88338	.88012	.87689	.87369	.87052	.86738	.86426	.86116	.85809	.85505
	103	.89015	.88706	.88399	.88095	.87793	.87494	.87197	.86903	.86611	.86321
60	104	.89737	.89446	.89157	.88871	.88586	.88304	.88024	.87745	.87469	.87195
	105	.90443	.90170	.89898	.89628	.89360	.89094	.88830	.88568	.88307	.88049
	106	.91351	.91101	.90852	.90605	.90359	.90115	.89873	.89632	.89392	.89154
	107	.92452	.92230	.92010	.91791	.91573	.91356	.91141	.90927	.90714	.90502
	108	.94161	.93987	.93814	.93641	.93469	.93298	.93128	.92958	.92790	.92622
65	109	.97081	.96992	.96904	.96816	.96729	.96642	.96555	.96468	.96382	.96296

	Age	8.2%	8.4%	8.6%	8.8%	9.0%	9.2%	9.4%	9.6%	9.8%	10.0%
	0	.01906	.01845	.01790	.01740	.01694	.01652	.01613	.01578	.01546	.01516
70	1	.01098	.01034	.00977	.00924	.00876	.00833	.00793	.00756	.00722	.00691
	2	.01113	.01046	.00986	.00930	.00880	.00834	.00791	.00753	.00717	.00684
	3	.01155	.01084	.01020	.00962	.00909	.00860	.00816	.00775	.00737	.00702
	4	.01211	.01137	.01069	.01008	.00952	.00900	.00853	.00810	.00770	.00733
	5	.01279	.01201	.01130	.01065	.01006	.00952	.00902	.00856	.00814	.00775
75	6	.01356	.01274	.01199	.01131	.01068	.01011	.00959	.00910	.00865	.00824
	7	.01442	.01356	.01277	.01205	.01140	.01079	.01023	.00972	.00925	.00881
	8	.01536	.01446	.01363	.01287	.01218	.01154	.01096	.01041	.00991	.00945
	9	.01641	.01546	.01460	.01380	.01307	.01240	.01178	.01120	.01068	.01019
	10	.01758	.01659	.01567	.01484	.01407	.01336	.01270	.01210	.01154	.01103
80	11	.01886	.01781	.01686	.01598	.01517	.01442	.01373	.01310	.01251	.01196
	12	.02024	.01915	.01814	.01721	.01636	.01558	.01485	.01419	.01357	.01299
	13	.02168	.02054	.01948	.01851	.01762	.01679	.01603	.01533	.01467	.01407
	14	.02313	.02193	.02083	.01981	.01887	.01801	.01721	.01646	.01578	.01514
	15	.02456	.02330	.02214	.02107	.02009	.01918	.01834	.01756	.01684	.01617
85	16	.02593	.02462	.02340	.02229	.02126	.02030	.01942	.01860	.01785	.01714
	17	.02728	.02590	.02463	.02346	.02238	.02138	.02046	.01960	.01880	.01806

Sec. 2031. Definition of gross estate

18	02861	.02717	.02584	.02462	.02348	.02243	.02146	.02056	.01972	.01894	
19	02998	.02847	.02708	.02580	.02461	.02351	.02249	.02154	.02066	.01984	
20	03142	.02984	.02839	.02704	.02580	.02465	.02357	.02258	.02165	.02079	
21	03295	.03130	.02978	.02837	.02706	.02585	.02473	.02368	.02271	.02180	
22	03455	.03283	.03124	.02976	.02839	.02712	.02594	.02484	.02382	.02286	5
23	03626	.03446	.03279	.03124	.02981	.02847	.02723	.02608	.02500	.02400	
24	03809	.03620	.03446	.03283	.03133	.02993	.02863	.02741	.02628	.02522	
25	04005	.03808	.03625	.03456	.03298	.03151	.03014	.02887	.02768	.02656	
26	04216	.04010	.03819	.03641	.03476	.03322	.03178	.03044	.02919	.02802	
27	04444	.04229	.04029	.03843	.03670	.03508	.03357	.03217	.03085	.02962	10
28	04687	.04463	.04254	.04059	.03877	.03708	.03550	.03402	.03263	.03133	
29	04946	.04712	.04493	.04289	.04099	.03922	.03756	.03600	.03455	.03318	
30	05221	.04976	.04748	.04534	.04335	.04149	.03975	.03812	.03659	.03515	
31	05511	.05255	.05017	.04794	.04585	.04390	.04208	.04037	.03876	.03725	
32	05818	.05551	.05302	.05069	.04851	.04647	.04455	.04276	.04107	.03948	15
33	06144	.05866	.05606	.05363	.05135	.04921	.04720	.04532	.04355	.04188	
34	06489	.06200	.05928	.05674	.05436	.05212	.05002	.04805	.04619	.04444	
35	06857	.06555	.06273	.06007	.05758	.05524	.05304	.05097	.04902	.04718	
36	07246	.06932	.06638	.06361	.06101	.05856	.05626	.05409	.05205	.05012	
37	07659	.07332	.07025	.06737	.06466	.06210	.05969	.05742	.05528	.05325	20
38	08098	.07758	.07439	.07138	.06855	.06588	.06336	.06099	.05874	.05662	
39	08563	.08210	.07878	.07565	.07270	.06992	.06729	.06480	.06245	.06023	
40	09059	.08692	.08347	.08021	.07714	.07423	.07149	.06889	.06643	.06411	
41	09586	.09206	.08848	.08509	.08189	.07886	.07600	.07329	.07072	.06828	
42	10147	.09753	.09381	.09029	.08696	.08381	.08083	.07800	.07531	.07277	25
43	10742	.10334	.09948	.09583	.09237	.08909	.08598	.08304	.08024	.07758	
44	11373	.10950	.10551	.10172	.09813	.09472	.09148	.08841	.08549	.08272	
45	12035	.11599	.11185	.10792	.10420	.10066	.09730	.09410	.09106	.08817	
46	12732	.12281	.11853	.11447	.11061	.10694	.10345	.10013	.09696	.09395	
47	13460	.12995	.12553	.12133	.11733	.11353	.10991	.10646	.10317	.10004	30
48	14223	.13743	.13287	.12853	.12439	.12046	.11671	.11313	.10972	.10646	
49	15020	.14526	.14056	.13608	.13181	.12774	.12385	.12015	.11661	.11322	
50	15855	.15347	.14862	.14401	.13960	.13540	.13138	.12754	.12388	.12037	
51	16727	.16205	.15707	.15232	.14777	.14344	.13929	.13532	.13153	.12789	
52	17634	.17098	.16587	.16097	.15630	.15183	.14755	.14345	.13953	.13577	35
53	18576	.18027	.17501	.16999	.16518	.16057	.15616	.15194	.14789	.14400	
54	19552	.18990	.18451	.17935	.17441	.16968	.16514	.16078	.15661	.15260	
55	20564	.19989	.19437	.18908	.18402	.17915	.17449	.17001	.16571	.16157	
56	21613	.21025	.20461	.19919	.19400	.18901	.18422	.17962	.17519	.17093	
57	22698	.22098	.21522	.20968	.20436	.19925	.19434	.18961	.18507	.18069	40
58	23816	.23204	.22616	.22051	.21507	.20984	.20481	.19996	.19530	.19080	
59	24962	.24339	.23740	.23163	.22608	.22073	.21558	.21062	.20584	.20123	
60	26136	.25502	.24892	.24304	.23738	.23192	.22666	.22158	.21669	.21196	
61	27339	.26695	.26075	.25477	.24900	.24343	.23806	.23288	.22787	.22304	
62	28578	.27925	.27295	.26687	.26100	.25533	.24985	.24456	.23945	.23451	45
63	29854	.29192	.28553	.27935	.27339	.26762	.26205	.25666	.25145	.24641	
64	31164	.30494	.29846	.29221	.28615	.28030	.27463	.26915	.26384	.25870	
65	32508	.31831	.31177	.30543	.29930	.29336	.28761	.28203	.27663	.27140	
66	33891	.33208	.32547	.31906	.31285	.30684	.30101	.29536	.28987	.28456	
67	35318	.34630	.33963	.33316	.32689	.32081	.31491	.30918	.30363	.29823	50
68	36785	.36093	.35422	.34770	.34138	.33524	.32928	.32349	.31787	.31240	
69	38290	.37595	.36920	.36265	.35628	.35009	.34408	.33824	.33256	.32703	
70	39823	.39127	.38450	.37791	.37151	.36529	.35924	.35335	.34762	.34204	
71	41378	.40681	.40003	.39343	.38701	.38076	.37467	.36875	.36298	.35736	
72	42950	.42253	.41575	.40914	.40271	.39644	.39034	.38438	.37858	.37293	55
73	44535	.43840	.43162	.42502	.41858	.41231	.40619	.40022	.39440	.38872	
74	46139	.45446	.44771	.44112	.43469	.42842	.42230	.41632	.41049	.40479	
75	47769	.47080	.46408	.45752	.45111	.44485	.43874	.43277	.42693	.42123	
76	49430	.48747	.48079	.47427	.46790	.46167	.45558	.44963	.44380	.43811	
77	51123	.50447	.49786	.49139	.48506	.47888	.47282	.46690	.46111	.45543	60
78	52845	.52177	.51523	.50884	.50257	.49645	.49044	.48457	.47881	.47317	
79	54584	.53926	.53282	.52650	.52032	.51426	.50833	.50251	.49681	.49122	
80	56325	.55678	.55044	.54423	.53813	.53216	.52630	.52056	.51492	.50939	
81	58054	.57419	.56797	.56186	.55587	.54999	.54422	.53856	.53300	.52754	
82	59762	.59140	.58530	.57931	.57343	.56766	.56198	.55641	.55094	.54557	65
83	61448	.60840	.60243	.59657	.59081	.58515	.57958	.57411	.56874	.56346	
84	63124	.62531	.61949	.61376	.60813	.60259	.59715	.59179	.58652	.58134	
85	64800	.64224	.63657	.63099	.62550	.62010	.61478	.60955	.60441	.59934	
86	66461	.65902	.65351	.64810	.64276	.63751	.63233	.62724	.62222	.61728	
87	68083	.67541	.67008	.66483	.65965	.65455	.64953	.64458	.63970	.63489	70
88	69663	.69140	.68624	.68116	.67615	.67121	.66634	.66154	.65680	.65213	
89	71201	.70696	.70199	.69708	.69224	.68747	.68276	.67811	.67353	.66900	
90	72694	.72209	.71730	.71257	.70791	.70330	.69876	.69427	.68984	.68547	
91	74117	.73650	.73190	.72735	.72286	.71842	.71404	.70972	.70545	.70123	
92	75439	.74991	.74548	.74110	.73678	.73251	.72829	.72412	.72000	.71593	75
93	76664	.76233	.75806	.75385	.74969	.74557	.74150	.73748	.73350	.72957	
94	77809	.77394	.76983	.76578	.76177	.75780	.75388	.75000	.74616	.74237	
95	78899	.78500	.78106	.77715	.77329	.76947	.76569	.76195	.75826	.75460	
96	79928	.79544	.79165	.78790	.78418	.78050	.77686	.77326	.76970	.76617	
97	80883	.80514	.80149	.79787	.79430	.79075	.78725	.78377	.78033	.77693	80
98	81781	.81427	.81075	.80727	.80382	.80041	.79703	.79368	.79036	.78708	
99	82661	.82320	.81982	.81648	.81316	.80988	.80662	.80340	.80020	.79704	
100	83519	.83192	.82868	.82547	.82228	.81913	.81600	.81290	.80982	.80678	
101	84368	.84055	.83744	.83437	.83131	.82829	.82529	.82231	.81936	.81643	
102	85203	.84904	.84607	.84313	.84021	.83731	.83444	.83159	.82876	.82596	85
103	86034	.85748	.85465	.85184	.84906	.84629	.84355	.84082	.83812	.83544	

104	86923	.86653	.86385	.86119	.85855	.85593	.85333	.85074	.84818	.84563
105	87792	.87537	.87283	.87032	.86782	.86534	.86287	.86042	.85799	.85557
106	88918	.88683	.88450	.88218	.87987	.87758	.87530	.87304	.87079	.86855
107	90291	.90082	.89873	.89666	.89460	.89255	.89051	.88849	.88647	.88447
108	92455	.92288	.92123	.91958	.91794	.91630	.91468	.91306	.91145	.90984
109	96211	.96125	.96041	.95956	.95872	.95788	.95704	.95620	.95537	.95455

Age	10.2%	10.4%	10.6%	0.8%	11.0%	11.2%	11.4%	11.6%	11.8%	12.0%
0	.01488	.01463	.01439	.01417	.01396	.01377	.01359	.01343	.01327	.01312
1	.00662	.00636	.00612	.00589	.00568	.00548	.00530	.00513	.00497	.00482
2	.00654	.00626	.00600	.00576	.00554	.00533	.00514	.00496	.00479	.00463
3	.00670	.00641	.00613	.00588	.00564	.00542	.00522	.00502	.00484	.00468
4	.00699	.00668	.00639	.00612	.00587	.00563	.00542	.00521	.00502	.00484
5	.00739	.00706	.00675	.00646	.00620	.00595	.00571	.00550	.00529	.00510
6	.00786	.00751	.00718	.00687	.00659	.00633	.00608	.00585	.00563	.00543
7	.00841	.00803	.00769	.00736	.00706	.00678	.00652	.00627	.00604	.00582
8	.00902	.00863	.00826	.00791	.00759	.00730	.00702	.00675	.00651	.00628
9	.00973	.00931	.00892	.00856	.00822	.00790	.00760	.00733	.00706	.00682
10	.01055	.01010	.00969	.00930	.00894	.00861	.00829	.00799	.00772	.00746
11	.01146	.01099	.01055	.01014	.00976	.00940	.00907	.00875	.00846	.00818
12	.01246	.01196	.01150	.01106	.01066	.01028	.00993	.00960	.00928	.00899
13	.01351	.01298	.01249	.01204	.01161	.01121	.01084	.01049	.01016	.00985
14	.01455	.01400	.01348	.01300	.01255	.01213	.01173	.01136	.01102	.01069
15	.01555	.01497	.01443	.01392	.01345	.01300	.01259	.01220	.01183	.01148
16	.01648	.01587	.01530	.01477	.01427	.01380	.01336	.01295	.01257	.01220
17	.01737	.01673	.01612	.01556	.01504	.01455	.01408	.01365	.01324	.01286
18	.01822	.01754	.01691	.01632	.01576	.01525	.01476	.01430	.01387	.01347
19	.01908	.01837	.01770	.01708	.01650	.01595	.01544	.01495	.01450	.01407
20	.01999	.01924	.01854	.01788	.01726	.01669	.01615	.01564	.01516	.01471
21	.02096	.02017	.01943	.01874	.01809	.01748	.01691	.01637	.01586	.01539
22	.02197	.02114	.02036	.01963	.01895	.01830	.01770	.01713	.01660	.01610
23	.02306	.02218	.02136	.02059	.01987	.01919	.01855	.01795	.01739	.01686
24	.02424	.02331	.02245	.02163	.02087	.02016	.01948	.01885	.01825	.01769
25	.02552	.02455	.02364	.02278	.02197	.02122	.02051	.01984	.01920	.01861
26	.02692	.02589	.02493	.02403	.02318	.02238	.02162	.02091	.02025	.01961
27	.02846	.02738	.02636	.02541	.02451	.02367	.02287	.02212	.02141	.02074
28	.03012	.02898	.02791	.02690	.02595	.02506	.02422	.02342	.02267	.02196
29	.03190	.03070	.02957	.02851	.02751	.02656	.02567	.02483	.02404	.02329
30	.03381	.03254	.03135	.03023	.02917	.02817	.02723	.02634	.02551	.02471
31	.03583	.03450	.03324	.03206	.03094	.02989	.02890	.02796	.02707	.02623
32	.03799	.03659	.03527	.03402	.03284	.03173	.03068	.02968	.02874	.02785
33	.04031	.03883	.03744	.03612	.03488	.03371	.03260	.03155	.03055	.02961
34	.04279	.04123	.03976	.03838	.03707	.03583	.03465	.03354	.03249	.03149
35	.04545	.04382	.04227	.04081	.03943	.03812	.03688	.03571	.03459	.03354
36	.04830	.04658	.04495	.04341	.04196	.04058	.03927	.03803	.03685	.03573
37	.05134	.04953	.04782	.04620	.04467	.04321	.04183	.04052	.03928	.03809
38	.05462	.05272	.05092	.04921	.04760	.04606	.04461	.04322	.04191	.04066
39	.05812	.05613	.05424	.05245	.05075	.04913	.04760	.04614	.04475	.04343
40	.06190	.05981	.05782	.05594	.05415	.05245	.05083	.04929	.04783	.04643
41	.06597	.06378	.06170	.05972	.05784	.05605	.05435	.05272	.05118	.04970
42	.07035	.06806	.06587	.06380	.06182	.05994	.05815	.05644	.05481	.05326
43	.07505	.07265	.07036	.06818	.06611	.06414	.06225	.06045	.05874	.05710
44	.08008	.07757	.07518	.07290	.07072	.06865	.06667	.06478	.06298	.06125
45	.08542	.08279	.08029	.07791	.07563	.07346	.07138	.06940	.06750	.06569
46	.09108	.08834	.08573	.08324	.08085	.07858	.07640	.07432	.07233	.07043
47	.09705	.09419	.09147	.08886	.08637	.08399	.08172	.07954	.07745	.07545
48	.10335	.10038	.09754	.09482	.09222	.08973	.08735	.08507	.08288	.08078
49	.10999	.10690	.10394	.10111	.09840	.09581	.09332	.09093	.08864	.08644
50	.11701	.11380	.11073	.10778	.10496	.10225	.09965	.09716	.09477	.09247
51	.12441	.12108	.11789	.11482	.11189	.10907	.10636	.10376	.10126	.09886
52	.13217	.12871	.12540	.12222	.11916	.11623	.11341	.11071	.10810	.10560
53	.14028	.13670	.13327	.12997	.12680	.12375	.12082	.11801	.11529	.11268
54	.14875	.14505	.14150	.13808	.13480	.13163	.12859	.12566	.12284	.12012
55	.15760	.15378	.15011	.14657	.14317	.13989	.13674	.13370	.13077	.12794
56	.16684	.16290	.15911	.15546	.15194	.14855	.14528	.14213	.13909	.13615
57	.17648	.17242	.16851	.16474	.16111	.15760	.15422	.15096	.14781	.14477
58	.18647	.18229	.17827	.17438	.17064	.16702	.16353	.16015	.15689	.15374
59	.19678	.19249	.18835	.18435	.18049	.17676	.17316	.16968	.16631	.16305
60	.20740	.20300	.19875	.19464	.19066	.18682	.18311	.17952	.17604	.17268
61	.21837	.21385	.20949	.20527	.20119	.19724	.19341	.18971	.18613	.18266
62	.22973	.22511	.22064	.21631	.21212	.20807	.20414	.20033	.19664	.19306
63	.24152	.23680	.23222	.22779	.22350	.21934	.21530	.21139	.20760	.20392
64	.25372	.24890	.24422	.23969	.23529	.23103	.22690	.22289	.21899	.21521
65	.26633	.26141	.25664	.25201	.24752	.24316	.23893	.23482	.23083	.22695
66	.27940	.27439	.26953	.26481	.26023	.25577	.25145	.24724	.24316	.23918
67	.29299	.28790	.28296	.27815	.27348	.26894	.26453	.26024	.25606	.25200
68	.30709	.30193	.29691	.29202	.28728	.28265	.27816	.27378	.26952	.26537
69	.32166	.31643	.31134	.30639	.30157	.29687	.29230	.28785	.28351	.27928
70	.33661	.33133	.32618	.32116	.31628	.31152	.30688	.30235	.29794	.29364
71	.35188	.34654	.34134	.33627	.33133	.32651	.32181	.31722	.31275	.30838
72	.36742	.36204	.35679	.35168	.34668	.34181	.33706	.33241	.32788	.32345
73	.38317	.37776	.37248	.36733	.36229	.35738	.35257	.34788	.34330	.33882
74	.39923	.39380	.38849	.38330	.37823	.37328	.36844	.36370	.35908	.35455
75	.41566	.41021	.40489	.39968	.39459	.38961	.38474	.37997	.37531	.37074
76	.43254	.42709	.42176	.41655	.41144	.40645	.40156	.39677	.39208	.38749

77	.44988	.44444	.43912	.43391	.42880	.42380	.41891	.41411	.40940	.40479
78	.46765	.46224	.45694	.45174	.44665	.44166	.43677	.43197	.42726	.42265
79	.48574	.48037	.47510	.46993	.46487	.45990	.45502	.45024	.44554	.44094
80	.50397	.49865	.49343	.48830	.48327	.47834	.47349	.46873	.46406	.45947
81	.52219	.51693	.51176	.50669	.50171	.49682	.49201	.48729	.48265	.47809
82	.54029	.53510	.53000	.52499	.52007	.51523	.51047	.50580	.50120	.49667
83	.55826	.55315	.54813	.54319	.53834	.53356	.52886	.52424	.51969	.51522
84	.57624	.57123	.56629	.56144	.55666	.55195	.54732	.54277	.53828	.53386
85	.59435	.58944	.58460	.57984	.57516	.57054	.56599	.56151	.55710	.55275
86	.61241	.60762	.60289	.59824	.59365	.58913	.58468	.58029	.57596	.57170
87	.63015	.62548	.62087	.61633	.61185	.60744	.60309	.59880	.59456	.59039
88	.64753	.64299	.63851	.63409	.62973	.62543	.62118	.61700	.61287	.60879
89	.66454	.66013	.65579	.65150	.64726	.64308	.63895	.63488	.63086	.62689
90	.68115	.67689	.67268	.66853	.66442	.66037	.65637	.65241	.64851	.64465
91	.69706	.69294	.68887	.68486	.68089	.67696	.67309	.66925	.66547	.66173
92	.71190	.70792	.70399	.70011	.69627	.69247	.68872	.68501	.68134	.67771
93	.72569	.72184	.71804	.71429	.71057	.70689	.70326	.69967	.69611	.69259
94	.73861	.73490	.73123	.72759	.72400	.72044	.71692	.71344	.71000	.70659
95	.75097	.74739	.74384	.74033	.73686	.73342	.73002	.72665	.72331	.72001
96	.76267	.75922	.75579	.75240	.74905	.74572	.74243	.73917	.73595	.73275
97	.77356	.77022	.76691	.76363	.76039	.75718	.75399	.75084	.74772	.74463
98	.78382	.78059	.77740	.77423	.77110	.76799	.76491	.76186	.75884	.75584
99	.79390	.79079	.78771	.78465	.78162	.77862	.77565	.77270	.76978	.76688
100	.80376	.80076	.79779	.79485	.79193	.78904	.78617	.78333	.78051	.77771
101	.81353	.81066	.80780	.80497	.80217	.79938	.79662	.79388	.79117	.78847
102	.82318	.82042	.81768	.81496	.81227	.80960	.80694	.80431	.80170	.79911
103	.83278	.83014	.82752	.82491	.82233	.81977	.81723	.81470	.81220	.80971
104	.84310	.84059	.83810	.83563	.83317	.83073	.82831	.82591	.82352	.82115
105	.85318	.85079	.84843	.84607	.84374	.84142	.83911	.83682	.83455	.83229
106	.86633	.86413	.86193	.85975	.85758	.85543	.85329	.85116	.84904	.84694
107	.88247	.88049	.87852	.87656	.87460	.87266	.87073	.86881	.86690	.86500
108	.90825	.90666	.90507	.90350	.90193	.90037	.89881	.89727	.89572	.89419
109	.95372	.95290	.95208	.95126	.95045	.94964	.94883	.94803	.94723	.94643

Age	12.2%	12.4%	12.6%	12.8%	13.0%	13.2%	13.4%	13.6%	13.8%	14.0%
0	.01298	.01285	.01273	.01261	.01250	.01240	.01230	.01221	.01212	.01203
1	.00468	.00455	.00443	.00431	.00420	.00410	.00400	.00391	.00382	.00374
2	.00448	.00435	.00421	.00409	.00398	.00387	.00376	.00366	.00357	.00348
3	.00452	.00437	.00423	.00410	.00398	.00386	.00375	.00365	.00355	.00345
4	.00468	.00452	.00437	.00423	.00410	.00397	.00386	.00375	.00364	.00354
5	.00493	.00476	.00460	.00445	.00431	.00418	.00405	.00393	.00382	.00371
6	.00524	.00506	.00489	.00473	.00458	.00444	.00430	.00418	.00406	.00394
7	.00562	.00543	.00525	.00508	.00492	.00477	.00462	.00449	.00436	.00423
8	.00606	.00586	.00566	.00548	.00531	.00515	.00499	.00485	.00471	.00458
9	.00659	.00637	.00616	.00597	.00579	.00561	.00545	.00529	.00514	.00500
10	.00721	.00698	.00676	.00655	.00636	.00617	.00600	.00583	.00567	.00552
11	.00792	.00767	.00744	.00722	.00701	.00682	.00663	.00645	.00628	.00612
12	.00871	.00845	.00821	.00797	.00775	.00754	.00735	.00716	.00698	.00681
13	.00955	.00928	.00902	.00877	.00854	.00831	.00810	.00790	.00771	.00753
14	.01038	.01009	.00981	.00955	.00930	.00907	.00885	.00864	.00843	.00824
15	.01116	.01085	.01056	.01028	.01002	.00977	.00954	.00932	.00910	.00890
16	.01186	.01153	.01123	.01094	.01066	.01040	.01015	.00992	.00969	.00948
17	.01250	.01215	.01183	.01152	.01124	.01096	.01070	.01045	.01022	.00999
18	.01308	.01272	.01238	.01206	.01175	.01147	.01119	.01093	.01068	.01044
19	.01367	.01329	.01293	.01259	.01227	.01196	.01167	.01140	.01113	.01088
20	.01428	.01388	.01350	.01314	.01280	.01248	.01217	.01188	.01161	.01134
21	.01494	.01451	.01411	.01373	.01337	.01303	.01271	.01240	.01211	.01183
22	.01562	.01517	.01475	.01435	.01397	.01361	.01326	.01294	.01263	.01233
23	.01635	.01588	.01543	.01501	.01460	.01422	.01386	.01351	.01319	.01287
24	.01716	.01665	.01618	.01573	.01530	.01489	.01451	.01415	.01380	.01347
25	.01804	.01751	.01701	.01653	.01608	.01565	.01524	.01485	.01448	.01413
26	.01902	.01845	.01792	.01741	.01693	.01648	.01604	.01563	.01524	.01487
27	.02011	.01951	.01895	.01841	.01790	.01742	.01696	.01652	.01610	.01571
28	.02129	.02066	.02006	.01949	.01895	.01844	.01795	.01748	.01704	.01662
29	.02258	.02191	.02127	.02067	.02009	.01955	.01903	.01853	.01806	.01762
30	.02396	.02325	.02257	.02193	.02132	.02074	.02019	.01966	.01916	.01869
31	.02543	.02467	.02396	.02328	.02263	.02201	.02143	.02087	.02034	.01983
32	.02701	.02621	.02545	.02472	.02404	.02338	.02276	.02217	.02160	.02106
33	.02871	.02786	.02706	.02629	.02556	.02487	.02420	.02357	.02297	.02240
34	.03054	.02964	.02879	.02797	.02720	.02646	.02576	.02509	.02445	.02383
35	.03253	.03158	.03067	.02981	.02898	.02820	.02745	.02674	.02606	.02541
36	.03467	.03366	.03269	.03178	.03090	.03007	.02928	.02852	.02779	.02710
37	.03697	.03590	.03488	.03391	.03298	.03209	.03125	.03044	.02967	.02893
38	.03947	.03833	.03725	.03622	.03524	.03430	.03340	.03254	.03172	.03094
39	.04217	.04096	.03982	.03873	.03768	.03669	.03573	.03482	.03395	.03312
40	.04510	.04383	.04262	.04146	.04035	.03930	.03828	.03732	.03639	.03550
41	.04830	.04695	.04567	.04445	.04327	.04215	.04108	.04005	.03907	.03812
42	.05177	.05035	.04900	.04770	.04646	.04527	.04413	.04304	.04200	.04100
43	.05553	.05404	.05261	.05123	.04992	.04866	.04746	.04630	.04520	.04413
44	.05960	.05802	.05651	.05506	.05368	.05235	.05107	.04985	.04868	.04754
45	.06395	.06229	.06069	.05917	.05770	.05630	.05495	.05365	.05241	.05121
46	.06860	.06685	.06517	.06356	.06202	.06053	.05911	.05774	.05643	.05516
47	.07353	.07169	.06992	.06823	.06660	.06504	.06353	.06209	.06070	.05936
48	.07877	.07684	.07498	.07320	.07149	.06984	.06826	.06673	.06527	.06385
49	.08433	.08231	.08036	.07849	.07669	.07495	.07329	.07168	.07013	.06864

Age										
50	.09026	.08814	.08609	.08413	.08224	.08042	.07867	.07698	.07535	.07378
51	.09655	.09433	.09219	.09013	.08815	.08624	.08440	.08262	.08091	.07926
52	.10318	.10086	.09863	.09647	.09439	.09239	.09046	.08860	.08680	.08506
53	.11017	.10774	.10541	.10315	.10098	.09888	.09686	.09491	.09302	.09120
54	.11750	.11498	.11254	.11019	.10792	.10572	.10361	.10156	.09958	.09767
55	.12522	.12258	.12005	.11759	.11522	.11294	.11072	.10859	.10652	.10451
56	.13332	.13059	.12794	.12539	.12292	.12054	.11823	.11599	.11383	.11174
57	.14183	.13899	.13624	.13359	.13102	.12853	.12613	.12380	.12154	.11936
58	.15070	.14775	.14490	.14215	.13948	.13689	.13439	.13197	.12962	.12734
59	.15990	.15685	.15389	.15103	.14826	.14558	.14298	.14046	.13801	.13564
60	.16942	.16626	.16321	.16024	.15737	.15459	.15189	.14927	.14673	.14426
61	.17929	.17603	.17287	.16981	.16684	.16395	.16115	.15844	.15580	.15324
62	.18960	.18623	.18297	.17980	.17673	.17375	.17085	.16803	.16530	.16264
63	.20035	.19688	.19352	.19025	.18708	.18400	.18100	.17809	.17525	.17250
64	.21154	.20797	.20451	.20114	.19787	.19469	.19159	.18859	.18566	.18281
65	.22318	.21951	.21595	.21249	.20912	.20584	.20265	.19955	.19652	.19358
66	.23532	.23156	.22790	.22434	.22088	.21751	.21422	.21102	.20791	.20487
67	.24804	.24419	.24044	.23679	.23324	.22977	.22640	.22311	.21990	.21678
68	.26133	.25740	.25356	.24983	.24618	.24263	.23917	.23579	.23250	.22929
69	.27516	.27114	.26723	.26341	.25969	.25605	.25251	.24905	.24567	.24237
70	.28945	.28536	.28137	.27747	.27367	.26996	.26633	.26279	.25934	.25596
71	.30412	.29996	.29590	.29193	.28806	.28427	.28057	.27696	.27343	.26998
72	.31913	.31491	.31078	.30675	.30281	.29895	.29519	.29150	.28790	.28438
73	.33444	.33016	.32597	.32188	.31788	.31396	.31013	.30638	.30271	.29913
74	.35012	.34579	.34155	.33741	.33335	.32938	.32549	.32168	.31795	.31430
75	.36628	.36190	.35762	.35343	.34932	.34530	.34136	.33750	.33372	.33001
76	.38299	.37858	.37427	.37004	.36589	.36183	.35784	.35394	.35011	.34636
77	.40028	.39585	.39151	.38725	.38307	.37898	.37496	.37103	.36716	.36337
78	.41812	.41368	.40933	.40506	.40086	.39675	.39271	.38874	.38485	.38103
79	.43641	.43198	.42762	.42334	.41914	.41502	.41096	.40698	.40308	.39924
80	.45496	.45054	.44619	.44192	.43772	.43360	.42954	.42556	.42164	.41779
81	.47360	.46920	.46487	.46061	.45643	.45231	.44827	.44429	.44038	.43653
82	.49223	.48785	.48355	.47932	.47516	.47106	.46703	.46307	.45916	.45532
83	.51081	.50648	.50221	.49802	.49388	.48982	.48581	.48187	.47799	.47416
84	.52951	.52523	.52101	.51686	.51277	.50874	.50477	.50086	.49701	.49321
85	.54847	.54425	.54009	.53600	.53196	.52798	.52406	.52019	.51638	.51262
86	.56749	.56335	.55926	.55523	.55126	.54734	.54348	.53966	.53591	.53220
87	.58627	.58221	.57820	.57425	.57035	.56650	.56270	.55895	.55526	.55161
88	.60477	.60079	.59688	.59301	.58919	.58542	.58170	.57802	.57439	.57081
89	.62297	.61909	.61527	.61149	.60776	.60408	.60044	.59685	.59330	.58979
90	.64084	.63707	.63335	.62968	.62604	.62246	.61891	.61540	.61194	.60851
91	.65803	.65437	.65076	.64719	.64366	.64017	.63672	.63330	.62993	.62659
92	.67412	.67058	.66707	.66360	.66017	.65678	.65342	.65010	.64682	.64357
93	.68911	.68567	.68227	.67890	.67557	.67227	.66901	.66578	.66258	.65942
94	.70321	.69988	.69657	.69330	.69006	.68686	.68369	.68055	.67744	.67437
95	.71674	.71351	.71031	.70713	.70399	.70088	.69781	.69476	.69174	.68875
96	.72959	.72646	.72335	.72028	.71724	.71422	.71123	.70828	.70534	.70244
97	.74156	.73853	.73552	.73254	.72959	.72666	.72376	.72089	.71804	.71522
98	.75287	.74993	.74702	.74413	.74126	.73842	.73561	.73282	.73006	.72732
99	.76401	.76117	.75834	.75555	.75277	.75002	.74730	.74459	.74191	.73926
100	.77494	.77219	.76946	.76676	.76408	.76142	.75878	.75616	.75357	.75099
101	.78580	.78315	.78052	.77791	.77532	.77275	.77021	.76768	.76517	.76268
102	.79654	.79399	.79146	.78894	.78645	.78397	.78152	.77908	.77666	.77426
103	.80724	.80479	.80236	.79994	.79755	.79517	.79280	.79046	.78813	.78582
104	.81879	.81646	.81413	.81183	.80954	.80726	.80501	.80276	.80054	.79832
105	.83005	.82782	.82560	.82340	.82121	.81904	.81688	.81474	.81260	.81049
106	.84485	.84277	.84071	.83866	.83662	.83459	.83257	.83057	.82857	.82659
107	.86311	.86124	.85937	.85751	.85566	.85382	.85199	.85017	.84835	.84655
108	.89266	.89114	.88963	.88812	.88662	.88513	.88364	.88216	.88068	.87922
109	.94563	.94484	.94405	.94326	.94248	.94170	.94092	.94014	.93937	.93860

Table 90CM--Life Table Applicable After April 30, 1999

Age x (1)	l(x) (2)	Age x (1)	l(x) (2)	Age x (1)	l(x) (2)
0	100000	37	95969	74	62852
1	99064	38	95780	75	60449
2	98992	39	95581	76	57955
3	98944	40	95373	77	55373
4	98907	41	95156	78	52704
5	98877	42	94928	79	49943
6	98850	43	94687	80	47084
7	98826	44	94431	81	44129
8	98803	45	94154	82	41091
9	98783	46	93855	83	37994
10	98766	47	93528	84	34876
11	98750	48	93173	85	31770
12	98734	49	92787	86	28687
13	98713	50	92370	87	25638
14	98681	51	91918	88	22658
15	98635	52	91424	89	19783
16	98573	53	90885	90	17046
17	98497	54	90297	91	14466
18	98409	55	89658	92	12066
19	98314	56	88965	93	9884
20	98215	57	88214	94	7951

21	98113	58	87397	95	6282
22	98006	59	86506	96	4868
23	97896	60	85537	97	3694
24	97784	61	84490	98	2745
25	97671	62	83368	99	1999
26	97556	63	82169	100	1424
27	97441	64	80887	101	991
28	97322	65	79519	102	672
29	97199	66	78066	103	443
30	97070	67	76531	104	284
31	96934	68	74907	105	175
32	96791	69	73186	106	105
33	96642	70	71357	107	60
34	96485	71	69411	108	33
35	96322	72	67344	109	17
36	96150	73	65154	110	0

[T.D. 6296, 23 FR 4529, June 24, 1958; T.D. 6684, 28 FR 11408, Oct. 24, 1963; T.D. 6826, 30 FR 7708, June 15, 1965; T.D. 8540, 59 FR 30152, June 10, 1994; T.D. 8819, 64 FR 23212, Apr. 30, 1999; T.D. 8886, 65 FR 36929, June 12, 2000]

Sec. 2512. Valuation of gifts

(a) If the gift is made in property, the value thereof at the date of the gift shall be considered the amount of the gift.

***

Reg. § 25.2512-5 Valuation of annuities, unitrust interests, interests for life or term of years, and remainder or reversionary interests.

(a) *In general.* Except as otherwise provided in paragraph (b) of this section and § 25.7520-3(b), the fair market value of annuities, unitrust interests, life estates, terms of years, remainders, and reversions transferred by gift is the present value of the interests determined under paragraph (d) of this section. Section 20.2031-7 of this chapter (Estate Tax Regulations) and related sections provide tables with standard actuarial factors and examples that illustrate how to use the tables to compute the present value of ordinary annuity, life, and remainder interests in property. These sections also refer to standard and special actuarial factors that may be necessary to compute the present value of similar interests in more unusual fact situations. These factors and examples are also generally applicable for gift tax purposes in computing the values of taxable gifts.

(b) *Commercial annuities and insurance contracts.* The value of life insurance contracts and contracts for the payment of annuities issued by companies regularly engaged in their sale is determined under § 25.2512-6.

(c) *Actuarial valuations.* The present value of annuities, unitrust interests, life estates, terms of years, remainders, and reversions transferred by gift after April 30, 1999, is determined under paragraph (d) of this section. The present value of annuities, unitrust interests, life estates, terms of years, remainders, and reversions transferred by gift before May 1, 1999, is determined under the following sections:

Transfers		Applicable regulations
After	Before	
	01-01-52	25.2512-5A(a)
12-31-51	01-01-71	25.2512-5A(b)
12-31-70	12-01-83	25.2512-5A(c)
11-30-83	05-01-89	25.2512-5A(d)
04-30-89	05-01-99	25.2512-5A(e)

Sec. 2512. Valuation of gifts

(d) *Actuarial valuations after April 30, 1999--*(1) *In general.* Except as otherwise provided in paragraph (b) of this section and § 25.7520-3(b) (relating to exceptions to the use of prescribed tables under certain circumstances), if the valuation date for the gift is after April 30, 1999, the fair market value of annuities, life estates, terms of years,
5 remainders, and reversions transferred after April 30, 1999, is the present value of such interests determined under paragraph (d)(2) of this section and by use of standard or special section 7520 actuarial factors. These factors are derived by using the appropriate section 7520 interest rate and, if applicable, the mortality component for the valuation date of the interest that is being valued. See §§ 25.7520-1 through 25.7520-4. The fair
10 market value of a qualified annuity interest described in section 2702(b)(1) and a qualified unitrust interest described in section 2702(b)(2) is the present value of such interests determined under § 25.7520-1(c).

(2) *Specific interests.* When the donor transfers property in trust or otherwise and retains an interest therein, generally, the value of the gift is the value of the property
15 transferred less the value of the donor's retained interest. However, if the donor transfers property after October 8, 1990, to or for the benefit of a member of the donor's family, the value of the gift is the value of the property transferred less the value of the donor's retained interest as determined under section 2702. If the donor assigns or relinquishes an annuity, life estate, remainder, or reversion that the donor holds by virtue of a transfer
20 previously made by the donor or another, the value of the gift is the value of the interest transferred. However, see section 2519 for a special rule in the case of the assignment of an income interest by a person who received the interest from a spouse.

(i) *Charitable remainder trusts.* The fair market value of a remainder interest in a pooled income fund, as defined in § 1.642(c)-5 of this chapter, is its value determined
25 under § 1.642(c)-6(e) of this chapter (see § 1.642(c)-6A for certain prior periods). The fair market value of a remainder interest in a charitable remainder annuity trust, as described in § 1.664-2(a) of this chapter, is its present value determined under § 1.664-2(c) of this chapter. The fair market value of a remainder interest in a charitable remainder unitrust, as defined in § 1.664-3 of this chapter, is its present value determined under § 1.664-4(e)
30 of this chapter. The fair market value of a life interest or term for years in a charitable remainder unitrust is the fair market value of the property as of the date of transfer less the fair market value of the remainder interest, determined under § 1.664-4(e)(4) and (5) of this chapter.

(ii) *Ordinary remainder and reversionary interests.* If the interest to be valued is to take
35 effect after a definite number of years or after the death of one individual, the present value of the interest is computed by multiplying the value of the property by the appropriate remainder interest actuarial factor (that corresponds to the applicable section 7520 interest rate and remainder interest period) in Table B (for a term certain) or the appropriate Table S (for one measuring life), as the case may be. Table B is contained in
40 § 20.2031-7(d)(6) of this chapter and Table S (for one measuring life when the valuation date is after April 30, 1999) is included in § 20.2031-7(d)(7) of this chapter and Internal Revenue Service Publication 1457. See § 20.2031-7A(e)(4) of this chapter containing Table S and Life Table 80CNSMT for valuation of interests after April 30, 1989, and before May 1, 1999. For information about obtaining actuarial factors for other types of
45 remainder interests, see paragraph (d)(4) of this section.

(iii) *Ordinary term-of-years and life interests.* If the interest to be valued is the right of a person to receive the income of certain property, or to use certain nonincome-producing property, for a term of years or for the life of one individual, the present value of the interest is computed by multiplying the value of the property by the appropriate term-of-
50 years or life interest actuarial factor (that corresponds to the applicable section 7520 interest rate and term-of-years or life interest period). Internal Revenue Service

Sec. 2512. Valuation of gifts

Publication 1457 includes actuarial factors for an interest for a term of years in Table B and for the life of one individual in Table S (for one measuring life when the valuation date is after April 30, 1999). However, term-of-years and life interest actuarial factors are not included in Table B in § 20.2031-7(d)(6) or Table S in § 20.2031-7(d)(7) (or in § 20.2031-7A(e)(4)) of this chapter. If Internal Revenue Service Publication 1457 (or any other reliable source of term-of-years and life interest actuarial factors) is not conveniently available, an actuarial factor for the interest may be derived mathematically. This actuarial factor may be derived by subtracting the correlative remainder factor (that corresponds to the applicable section 7520 interest rate) in Table B (for a term of years) in § 20.2031-7(d)(6) of this chapter or in Table S (for the life of one individual) in § 20.2031-7(d)(7) of this chapter, as the case may be, from 1.000000. For information about obtaining actuarial factors for other types of term-of-years and life interests, see paragraph (d)(4) of this section.

(iv) *Annuities.* (A) If the interest to be valued is the right of a person to receive an annuity that is payable at the end of each year for a term of years or for the life of one individual, the present value of the interest is computed by multiplying the aggregate amount payable annually by the appropriate annuity actuarial factor (that corresponds to the applicable section 7520 interest rate and annuity period). Internal Revenue Service Publication 1457 includes actuarial factors in Table B (for an annuity payable for a term of years) and in Table S (for an annuity payable for the life of one individual when the valuation date is after April 30, 1999). However, annuity actuarial factors are not included in Table B in § 20.2031-7(d)(6) of this chapter or Table S in § 20.2031-7(d)(7) (or in § 20.2031-7A(e)(4)) of this chapter. If Internal Revenue Service Publication 1457 (or any other reliable source of annuity actuarial factors) is not conveniently available, an annuity factor for a term of years or for one life may be derived mathematically. This annuity factor may be derived by subtracting the applicable remainder factor (that corresponds to the applicable section 7520 interest rate and annuity period) in Table B (in the case of a term-of-years annuity) in § 20.2031-7(d)(6) of this chapter or in Table S (in the case of a one-life annuity) in § 20.2031-7(d)(7) of this chapter, as the case may be, from 1.000000 and then dividing the result by the applicable section 7520 interest rate expressed as a decimal number. See § 20.2031-7(d)(2)(iv) of this chapter for an example that illustrates the computation of the present value of an annuity.

(B) If the annuity is payable at the end of semiannual, quarterly, monthly, or weekly periods, the product obtained by multiplying the annuity factor by the aggregate amount payable annually is then multiplied by the applicable adjustment factor set forth in Table K in § 20.2031-7(d)(6) of this chapter at the appropriate interest rate component for payments made at the end of the specified periods. The provisions of this paragraph (d) (2)(iv)(B) are illustrated by the following example:

Example. In July, the donor agreed to pay the annuitant the sum of $10,000 per year, payable in equal semiannual installments at the end of each period. The semiannual installments are to be made on each December 31st and June 30th. The annuity is payable until the annuitant's death. On the date of the agreement, the annuitant is 68 years and 5 months old. The donee annuitant's age is treated as 68 for purposes of computing the present value of the annuity. The section 7520 rate on the date of the agreement is 10.6 percent. Under Table S in § 20.2031-7(d)(7) of this chapter, the factor at 10.6 percent for determining the present value of a remainder interest payable at the death of an individual aged 68 is .29691. Converting the remainder factor to an annuity factor, as described above, the annuity factor for determining the present value of an annuity transferred to an individual age 68 is 6.6329 (1.00000 minus .29691 divided by . 106). The adjustment factor from Table K in § 20.2031-7(d)(6) of this chapter in the column for payments made at the end of each semiannual period at the rate of 10.6

Sec. 2512. Valuation of gifts

percent is 1.0258. The aggregate annual amount of the annuity, $10,000, is multiplied by the factor 6.6329 and the product multiplied by 1.0258. The present value of the donee's annuity is, therefore, $68,040.29 ($10,000 x 6.6329 x 1.0258).

(C) If an annuity is payable at the beginning of annual, semiannual, quarterly, monthly,
5 or weekly periods for a term of years, the value of the annuity is computed by multiplying the aggregate amount payable annually by the annuity factor described in paragraph (d) (2)(iv)(A) of this section; and the product so obtained is then multiplied by the adjustment factor in Table J in § 20.2031-7(d)(6) of this chapter at the appropriate interest rate component for payments made at the beginning of specified periods. If an annuity is
10 payable at the beginning of annual, semiannual, quarterly, monthly, or weekly periods for one or more lives, the value of the annuity is the sum of the first payment plus the present value of a similar annuity, the first payment of which is not to be made until the end of the payment period, determined as provided in paragraph (d)(2)(iv)(B) of this section.

***

15 [T.D. 8540, 59 FR 30174, June 10, 1994; T.D. 8819, 64 FR 23224, Apr. 30, 1999; T.D. 8886, 65 FR 36940, June 12, 2000; 65 FR 39470, June 26, 2000; 65 FR 58222, Sept. 28, 2000]

Sec. 3401. Definitions

20   (a) Wages. -- For purposes of this chapter, the term "wages" means all remuneration (other than fees paid to a public official) for services performed by an employee for his employer, including the cash value of all remuneration (including benefits) paid in any medium other than cash; except that

***

25

Reg. § 31.3401(a)-1 Wages.

(a) *In general.* (1) The term ``wages'' means all remuneration for services performed by an employee for his employer unless specifically excepted under section 3401(a) or excepted under section 3402(e).
30   (2) The name by which the remuneration for services is designated is immaterial. Thus, salaries, fees, bonuses, commissions on sales or on insurance premiums, pensions, and retired pay are wages within the meaning of the statute if paid as compensation for services performed by the employee for his employer.

(3) The basis upon which the remuneration is paid is immaterial in determining
35 whether the remuneration constitutes wages. Thus, it may be paid on the basis of piecework, or a percentage of profits; and may be paid hourly, daily, weekly, monthly, or annually.

(4) Generally the medium in which remuneration is paid is also immaterial. It may be paid in cash or in something other than cash, as for example, stocks, bonds, or other
40 forms of property. (See, however, § 31.3401(a)(11)-1, relating to the exclusion from wages of remuneration paid in any medium other than cash for services not in the course of the employer's trade or business, and § 31.3401(a)(16)-1, relating to the exclusion from wages of tips paid in any medium other than cash.) If services are paid for in a medium other than cash, the fair market value of the thing taken in payment is the
45 amount to be included as wages. If the services were rendered at a stipulated price, in the absence of evidence to the contrary, such price will be presumed to be the fair value of the remuneration received. If a corporation transfers to its employees its own stock as remuneration for services rendered by the employee, the amount of such remuneration is the fair market value of the stock at the time of the transfer.

Sec. 3401. Definitions

(5) Remuneration for services, unless such remuneration is specifically excepted by the statute, constitutes wages even though at the time paid the relationship of employer and employee no longer exists between the person in whose employ the services were performed and the individual who performed them.

Example. A is employed by R during the month of January 1955 and is entitled to 5 receive remuneration of $100 for the services performed for R, the employer, during the month. A leaves the employ of R at the close of business on January 31, 1955. On February 15, 1955 (when A is no longer an employee of R), R pays A the remuneration of $100 which was earned for the services performed in January. The $100 is wages within the meaning of the statute.   10

(b) *Certain specific items*--(1) *Pensions and retirement pay.* (i) In general, pensions and retired pay are wages subject to withholding. However, no withholding is required with respect to amounts paid to an employee upon retirement which are taxable as annuities under the provisions of section 72 or 403. So-called pensions awarded by one to whom no services have been rendered are mere gifts or gratuities and do not 15 constitute wages. Those payments of pensions or other benefits by the Federal Government under Title 38 of the United States Code which are excluded from gross income are not wages subject to withholding.

(ii) Amounts received as retirement pay for service in the Armed Forces of the United States, the Coast and Geodetic Survey, or the Public Health Service or as a disability 20 annuity paid under the provisions of section 831 of the Foreign Service Act of 1946, as amended (22) U.S.C. 1081; 60 Stat. 1021), are subject to withholding unless such pay or disability annuity is excluded from gross income under section 104(a)(4), or is taxable as an annuity under the provisions of section 72. Where such retirement pay or disability annuity (not excluded from gross income under section 104(a)(4) and not taxable as an 25 annuity under the provisions of section 72) is paid to a nonresident alien individual, withholding is required only in the case of such amounts paid to a nonresident alien individual who is a resident of Puerto Rico.

(2) *Traveling and other expenses.* Amounts paid specifically--either as advances or reimbursements--for traveling or other bona fide ordinary and necessary expenses 30 incurred or reasonably expected to be incurred in the business of the employer are not wages and are not subject to withholding. Traveling and other reimbursed expenses must be identified either by making a separate payment or by specifically indicating the separate amounts where both wages and expense allowances are combined in a single payment. For amounts that are received by an employee on or after July 1, 1990, with 35 respect to expenses paid or incurred on or after July 1, 1990, see § 31.3401 (a)-4.

(3) *Vacation allowances.* Amounts of so-called ``vacation allowances" paid to an employee constitute wages. Thus, the salary of an employee on vacation, paid notwithstanding his absence from work, constitutes wages.

(4) *Dismissal payments.* Any payments made by an employer to an employee on 40 account of dismissal, that is, involuntary separation from the service of the employer, constitute wages regardless of whether the employer is legally bound by contract, statute, or otherwise to make such payments.

(5) *Deductions by employer from remuneration of an employee.* Any amount deducted by an employer from the remuneration of an employee is considered to be a part of the 45 employee's remuneration and is considered to be paid to the employee as remuneration at the time that the deduction is made. It is immaterial that any act of Congress, or the law of any State or of Puerto Rico, requires or permits such deductions and the payment of the amounts thereof to the United States, a State, a Territory, Puerto Rico, or the District of Columbia, or any political subdivision of any one or more of the foregoing.   50

(6) *Payment by an employer of employee's tax, or employee's contributions under a*

Sec. 3401. Definitions

State law. The term ``wages'' includes the amount paid by an employer on behalf of an employee (without deduction from the remuneration of, or other reimbursement from, the employee) on account of any payment required from an employee under a State unemployment compensation law, or on account of any tax imposed upon the employee
5 by any taxing authority, including the taxes imposed by sections 3101 and 3201.

(7) *Remuneration for services as employee of nonresident alien individual or foreign entity.* The term ``wages'' includes remuneration for services performed by a citizen or resident (including, in regard to wages paid after February 28, 1979, an individual treated as a resident under section 6013(g) or (h)) of the United States as an employee of a
10 nonresident alien individual, foreign partnership, or foreign corporation whether or not such alien individual or foreign entity is engaged in trade or business within the United States. Any person paying wages on behalf of a nonresident alien individual, foreign partnership, or foreign corporation, not engaged in trade or business within the United States (including Puerto Rico as if a part of the United States), is subject to all the
15 provisions of law and regulations applicable with respect to an employer. See § 31.3401(d)-1, relating to the term ``employer'', and § 31.3401(a)(8)(C)-1, relating to remuneration paid for services performed by a citizen of the United States in Puerto Rico.

(8) *Amounts paid under accident or health plans*--(i) *Amounts paid in taxable years beginning on or after January 1, 1977*--(a) *In general.* Withholding is required on all
20 payments of amounts includible in gross income under section 105(a) and § 1.105-1 (relating to amounts attributable to employer contributions), made in taxable years beginning on or after January 1, 1977, to an employee under an accident or health plan for a period of absence from work on account of personal injuries or sickness. Payments on which withholding is required by this subdivision are wages as defined in section
25 3401(a), and the employer shall deduct and withhold in accordance with the requirements of chapter 24 of subtitle C of the Code. Third party payments of sick pay, as defined in section 3402(o) and the regulations thereunder, are not wages for purposes of this section.

***

30 (c) *Exceptions to withholding.* (1) Withholding is not required on payments that are specifically excepted under the numbered paragraphs of section 3401(a) (relating to the definition of wages), under section 3402(e) (relating to included and excluded wages), or under section 3402(n) (relating to employees incurring no income tax liability).

(2) Withholding is not required on disability payments to the extent that the payments
35 are excludable from gross income under section 105(d). In determining the excludable portion of the disability payments, the employer may assume that payments that the employer makes to the employee are the employee's sole source of income. This exception applies only if the employee furnishes the employer with adequate verification of disability. A certificate from a qualified physician attesting that the employee is
40 permanently and totally disabled (within the meaning of section 105(d)) shall be deemed to constitute adequate verification. This exception does not affect the requirement that a statement (which includes any amount paid under section 105(d)) be furnished under either section 6041 (relating to information at source) or section 6051 (relating to receipts for employees) and the regulations thereunder.

45 ***

(9) *Value of meals and lodging.* The value of any meals or lodging furnished to an employee by his employer is not subject to withholding if the value of the meals or lodging is excludable from the gross income of the employee. See § 1.119-1 of this chapter (Income Tax Regulations).
50 (10) *Facilities or privileges.* Ordinarily, facilities or privileges (such as entertainment,

1044

Sec. 3401. Definitions

medical services, or so-called ``courtesy'' discounts on purchases), furnished or offered by an employer to his employees generally, are not considered as wages subject to withholding if such facilities or privileges are of relatively small value and are offered or furnished by the employer merely as a means of promoting the health, good will, contentment, or efficiency of his employees.   5

***

(14) *Supplemental unemployment compensation benefits.* (i) Supplemental unemployment compensation benefits paid to an individual after December 31, 1970, shall be treated (for purposes of the provisions of Subparts E, F, and G of this part which relate to withholding of income tax) as if they were wages, to the extent such benefits are 10 includible in the gross income of such individual.

(ii) For purposes of this subparagraph, the term ``supplemental unemployment compensation benefits'' means amounts which are paid to an employee, pursuant to a plan to which the employer is a party, because of the employee's involuntary separation from the employment of the employer, whether or not such separation is temporary, but 15 only when such separation is one resulting directly from a reduction in force, the discontinuance of a plant or operation, or other similar conditions.

(iii) For the meanings of the terms ``involuntary separation from the employment of the employer'' and ``other similar conditions'', see subparagraphs (3) and (4) of § 1.501(c) (17)-1(b) of this chapter (Income Tax Regulations).   20

(iv) As used in this subparagraph, the term ``employee'' means an employee within the meaning of paragraph (a) of § 31.3401(c)-1, the term ``employer'' means an employer within the meaning of paragraph (a) of § 31.3401(d)-1, and the term ``employment'' means employment as defined under the usual common law rules.

***   25

Reg. § 31.3401(b)-1   Payroll period.

(a) The term payroll period means the period of service for which a payment of wages is ordinarily made to an employee by his employer. It is immaterial that the wages are not always paid at regular intervals. For example, if an employer ordinarily pays a particular employee for each calendar week at the end of the week, but if for some reason the 30 employee in a given week receives a payment in the middle of the week for the portion of the week already elapsed and receives the remainder at the end of the week, the payroll period is still the calendar week; or if, instead, that employee is sent on a 3-week trip by his employer and receives at the end of the trip a single wage payment for three weeks' services, the payroll period is still the calendar week, and the wage payment shall be 35 treated as though it were three separate weekly wage payments.

(b) For the purpose of section 3402, an employee can have but one payroll period with respect to wages paid by any one employer. Thus, if an employee is paid a regular wage for a weekly payroll period and in addition thereto is paid supplemental wages (for example, bonuses) determined with respect to a different period, the payroll period is the 40 weekly payroll period. For computation of tax on supplemental wage payments, see § 31.3402(g)-1.

(c) The term payroll period also means the period of accrual of supplemental unemployment compensation benefits for which a payment of such benefits is ordinarily made. Thus if benefits are ordinarily accrued and paid on a monthly basis, the payroll 45 period is deemed to be monthly.

(d) The term miscellaneous payroll period means a payroll period other than a daily, weekly, biweekly, semi-monthly, monthly, quarterly, semiannual, or annual payroll period.

Sec. 3401. Definitions

Reg. § 31.3401(c)-1 Employee.

(a) The term employee includes every individual performing services if the relationship between him and the person for whom he performs such services is the legal relationship of employer and employee. The term includes officers and employees, whether elected or
5 appointed, of the United States, a State, Territory, Puerto Rico, or any political subdivision thereof, or the District of Columbia, or any agency or instrumentality of any one or more of the foregoing.

(b) Generally the relationship of employer and employee exists when the person for whom services are performed has the right to control and direct the individual who
10 performs the services, not only as to the result to be accomplished by the work but also as to the details and means by which that result is accomplished. That is, an employee is subject to the will and control of the employer not only as to what shall be done but how it shall be done. In this connection, it is not necessary that the employer actually direct or control the manner in which the services are performed; it is sufficient if he has the right
15 to do so. The right to discharge is also an important factor indicating that the person possessing that right is an employer. Other factors characteristic of an employer, but not necessarily present in every case, are the furnishing of tools and the furnishing of a place to work to the individual who performs the services. In general, if an individual is subject to the control or direction of another merely as to the result to be accomplished by the
20 work and not as to the means and methods for accomplishing the result, he is not an employee.

(c) Generally, physicians, lawyers, dentists, veterinarians, contractors, subcontractors, public stenographers, auctioneers, and others who follow an independent trade, business, or profession, in which they offer their services to the public, are not
25 employees.

(d) Whether the relationship of employer and employee exists will in doubtful cases be determined upon an examination of the particular facts of each case.

(e) If the relationship of employer and employee exists, the designation or description of the relationship by the parties as anything other than that of employer and employee is
30 immaterial. Thus, if such relationship exists, it is of no consequence that the employee is designated as a partner, coadventurer, agent, independent contractor, or the like.

(f) All classes or grades of employees are included within the relationship of employer and employee. Thus, superintendents, managers and other supervisory personnel are employees. Generally, an officer of a corporation is an employee of the corporation.
35 However, an officer of a corporation who as such does not perform any services or performs only minor services and who neither receives nor is entitled to receive, directly or indirectly, any remuneration is not considered to be an employee of the corporation. A director of a corporation in his capacity as such is not an employee of the corporation.

(g) The term employee includes every individual who receives a supplemental
40 unemployment compensation benefit which is treated under paragraph (b)(14) of § 31.3401(a)-1 as if it were wages.

(h) Although an individual may be an employee under this section, his services may be of such a nature, or performed under such circumstances, that the remuneration paid for such services does not constitute wages within the meaning of section 3401(a).
45

[T.D. 6516, 25 FR 13032, Dec. 20, 1960; T.D. 6654, 28 FR 5251, May 28, 1963; T.D. 6908, 31 FR 16775, Dec. 31, 1966; T.D. 7001, 34 FR 1000, Jan. 23, 1969; T.D. 7068, 35 FR 17328, Nov. 11, 1970; T.D. 7277, 38 FR 12742, May 15, 1973; T.D. 7493, 42 FR 33728, July 1, 1977; T.D. 7670, 45 FR 6932, Jan. 31, 1980; T.D. 7888, 48 FR 17587, Apr.
50 25, 1983; T.D. 8276, 54 FR 51028, Dec. 12, 1989; T.D. 8324, 55 FR 51697, Dec. 17, 1990; T.D. 9092, 68 FR 54361, Sept. 17, 2003; T.D. 9276, 71 FR 42054, July 25, 2006]

Sec. 3402. Income tax collected at source

Sec. 3402. Income tax collected at source

(a) Requirement of withholding. --

(1) In general. -- Except as otherwise provided in this section, every employer making payment of wages shall deduct and withhold upon such wages a tax determined in accordance with tables or computational procedures prescribed by the Secretary. Any tables or procedures prescribed under this paragraph shall--

    (A) apply with respect to the amount of wages paid during such periods as the Secretary may prescribe, and

    (B) be in such form, and provide for such amounts to be deducted and withheld, as the Secretary determines to be most appropriate to carry out the purposes of this chapter and to reflect the provisions of chapter 1 applicable to such periods.

(2) Amount of wages. -- For purposes of applying tables or procedures prescribed under paragraph (1), the term "the amount of wages" means the amount by which the wages exceed the number of withholding exemptions claimed multiplied by the amount of one such exemption. The amount of each withholding exemption shall be equal to the amount of one personal exemption provided in section 151(b), prorated to the payroll period. The maximum number of withholding exemptions permitted shall be calculated in accordance with regulations prescribed by the Secretary under this section, taking into account any reduction in withholding to which an employee is entitled under this section.

(b) Percentage method of withholding. --

(1) If wages are paid with respect to a period which is not a payroll period, the withholding exemption allowable with respect to each payment of such wages shall be the exemption allowed for a miscellaneous payroll period containing a number of days (including Sundays and holidays) equal to the number of days in the period with respect to which such wages are paid.

(2) In any case in which wages are paid by an employer without regard to any payroll period or other period, the withholding exemption allowable with respect to each payment of such wages shall be the exemption allowed for a miscellaneous payroll period containing a number of days equal to the number of days (including Sundays and holidays) which have elapsed since the date of the last payment of such wages by such employer during the calendar year, or the date of commencement of employment with such employer during such year, or January 1 of such year, whichever is the later.

(3) In any case in which the period, or the time described in paragraph (2), in respect of any wages is less than one week, the Secretary, under regulations prescribed by him, may authorize an employer to compute the tax to be deducted and withheld as if the aggregate of the wages paid to the employee during the calendar week were paid for a weekly payroll period.

(4) In determining the amount to be deducted and withheld under this subsection, the wages may, at the election of the employer, be computed to the nearest dollar.

(c) Wage bracket withholding. --

(1) At the election of the employer with respect to any employee, the employer shall deduct and withhold upon the wages paid to such employee a tax (in lieu of the tax required to be deducted and withheld under subsection (a)) determined in accordance with tables prescribed by the Secretary in accordance with paragraph (6).

(2) If wages are paid with respect to a period which is not a payroll period, the amount to be deducted and withheld shall be that applicable in the case of a miscellaneous payroll period containing a number of days (including Sundays and holidays) equal to the number of days in the period with respect to which such wages are paid.

Sec. 3402.   Income tax collected at source

(3) In any case in which wages are paid by an employer without regard to any payroll period or other period, the amount to be deducted and withheld shall be that applicable in the case of a miscellaneous payroll period containing a number of days equal to the number of days (including Sundays and holidays) which have elapsed since the date of the last payment of such wages by such employer during the calendar year, or the date of commencement of employment with such employer during such year, or January 1 of such year, whichever is the later.

(4) In any case in which the period, or the time described in paragraph (3), in respect of any wages is less than one week, the Secretary, under regulations prescribed by him, may authorize an employer to determine the amount to be deducted and withheld under the tables applicable in the case of a weekly payroll period, in which case the aggregate of the wages paid to the employee during the calendar week shall be considered the weekly wages.

(5) If the wages exceed the highest wage bracket, in determining the amount to be deducted and withheld under this subsection, the wages may, at the election of the employer, be computed to the nearest dollar.

(6) In the case of wages paid after December 31, 1969, the amount deducted and withheld under paragraph (1) shall be determined in accordance with tables prescribed by the Secretary. In the tables so prescribed, the amounts set forth as amounts of wages and amounts of income tax to be deducted and withheld shall be computed on the basis of the table for an annual payroll period prescribed pursuant to subsection (a).

(d) Tax paid by recipient. -- If the employer, in violation of the provisions of this chapter, fails to deduct and withhold the tax under this chapter, and thereafter the tax against which such tax may be credited is paid, the tax so required to be deducted and withheld shall not be collected from the employer; but this subsection shall in no case relieve the employer from liability for any penalties or additions to the tax otherwise applicable in respect of such failure to deduct and withhold.

***

(f) Withholding exemptions. --

(1) In general. -- An employee receiving wages shall on any day be entitled to the following withholding exemptions:

(A) an exemption for himself unless he is an individual described in section 151(d)(2);

(B) if the employee is married, any exemption to which his spouse is entitled, or would be entitled if such spouse were an employee receiving wages, under subparagraph (A) or (D), but only if such spouse does not have in effect a withholding exemption certificate claiming such exemption;

(C) an exemption for each individual with respect to whom, on the basis of facts existing at the beginning of such day, there may reasonably be expected to be allowable an exemption under section 151(c) for the taxable year under subtitle A in respect of which amounts deducted and withheld under this chapter in the calendar year in which such day falls are allowed as a credit;

(D) any allowance to which he is entitled under subsection (m), but only if his spouse does not have in effect a withholding exemption certificate claiming such allowance; and

(E) a standard deduction allowance which shall be an amount equal to one exemption (or more than one exemption if so prescribed by the Secretary) unless (i) he is married (as determined under section 7703) and his spouse is an employee receiving wages subject to withholding or (ii) he has withholding exemption certificates in effect with respect to more than one employer.

For purposes of this title, any standard deduction allowance under subparagraph (E) shall be treated as if it were denominated a withholding exemption.

Sec. 3402. Income tax collected at source

***

(h) Alternative methods of computing amount to be withheld. -- The Secretary may, under regulations prescribed by him, authorize--

(1) Withholding on basis of average wages. -- An employer--

(A) to estimate the wages which will be paid to any employee in any quarter of the calendar year, 5

(B) to determine the amount to be deducted and withheld upon each payment of wages to such employee during such quarter as if the appropriate average of the wages so estimated constituted the actual wages paid, and

(C) to deduct and withhold upon any payment of wages to such employee during such 10 quarter (and, in the case of tips referred to in subsection (k), within 30 days thereafter) such amount as may be necessary to adjust the amount actually deducted and withheld upon the wages of such employee during such quarter to the amount required to be deducted and withheld during such quarter without regard to this subsection.

(2) Withholding on basis of annualized wages. -- An employer to determine the amount of 15 tax to be deducted and withheld upon a payment of wages to an employee for a payroll period by--

(A) multiplying the amount of an employee's wages for a payroll period by the number of such payroll periods in the calendar year,

(B) determining the amount of tax which would be required to be deducted and withheld 20 upon the amount determined under subparagraph (A) if such amount constituted the actual wages for the calendar year and the payroll period of the employee were an annual payroll period, and

(C) dividing the amount of tax determined under subparagraph (B) by the number of payroll periods (described in subparagraph (A)) in the calendar year. 25

(3) Withholding on basis of cumulative wages. -- An employer, in the case of any employee who requests to have the amount of tax to be withheld from his wages computed on the basis of his cumulative wages, to--

(A) add the amount of the wages to be paid to the employee for the payroll period to the total amount of wages paid by the employer to the employee during the calendar year, 30

(B) divide the aggregate amount of wages computed under subparagraph (A) by the number of payroll periods to which such aggregate amount of wages relates,

(C) compute the total amount of tax that would have been required to be deducted and withheld under subsection (a) if the average amount of wages (as computed under subparagraph (B)) had been paid to the employee for the number of payroll periods to 35 which the aggregate amount of wages (computed under subparagraph (A)) relates,

(D) determine the excess, if any, of the amount of tax computed under subparagraph (C) over the total amount of tax deducted and withheld by the employer from wages paid to the employee during the calendar year, and

(E) deduct and withhold upon the payment of wages (referred to in subparagraph (A)) to 40 the employee an amount equal to the excess (if any) computed under subparagraph (D).

(4) Other methods. -- An employer to determine the amount of tax to be deducted and withheld upon the wages paid to an employee by any other method which will require the employer to deduct and withhold upon such wages substantially the same amount as would be required to be deducted and withheld by applying subsection (a) or (c), either with respect to a 45 payroll period or with respect to the entire taxable year.

Sec. 4911.   Tax on excess expenditures to influence legislation

(a) Tax imposed. --

(1) In general. -- There is hereby imposed on the excess lobbying expenditures of any organization to which this section applies a tax equal to 25 percent of the amount of the excess lobbying expenditures for the taxable year.

(2) Organizations to which this section applies. -- This section applies to any organization with respect to which an election under section 501(h) (relating to lobbying expenditures by public charities) is in effect for the taxable year.

(b) Excess lobbying expenditures. -- For purposes of this section, the term "excess lobbying expenditures" means, for a taxable year, the greater of--

(1) the amount by which the lobbying expenditures made by the organization during the taxable year exceed the lobbying nontaxable amount for such organization for such taxable year, or

(2) the amount by which the grass roots expenditures made by the organization during the taxable year exceed the grass roots nontaxable amount for such organization for such taxable year.

(c) Definitions. -- For purposes of this section--

(1) Lobbying expenditures. -- The term "lobbying expenditures" means expenditures for the purpose of influencing legislation (as defined in subsection (d)).

(2) Lobbying nontaxable amount. -- The lobbying nontaxable amount for any organization for any taxable year is the lesser of (A) $1,000,000 or (B) the amount determined under the following table:

If the exempt purpose expenditures are -	The lobbying nontaxable amount is -
Not over $500,00...	20 percent of the exempt purpose expenditures.
Over $500,000 but not over $1,000,000....	$100,000, plus 15 percent of the excess of the exempt purpose expenditures over $500,000.
Over $1,000,000 but not over..;................ $1,500,000	$175,000 plus 10 percent of the excess of the exempt purpose expenditures over $1,000,000.
Over $1,500,000..	$225,000 plus 5 percent of the excess of the exempt purpose expenditures over $1,500,000.

(3) Grass roots expenditures. -- The term "grass roots expenditures" means expenditures for the purpose of influencing legislation (as defined in subsection (d) without regard to paragraph (1)(B) thereof).

(4) Grass roots nontaxable amount. -- The grass roots nontaxable amount for any organization for any taxable year is 25 percent of the lobbying nontaxable amount (determined under paragraph (2)) for such organization for such taxable year.

(d) Influencing legislation. --

(1) General rule. -- Except as otherwise provided in paragraph (2), for purposes of this section, the term "influencing legislation" means--

(A) any attempt to influence any legislation through an attempt to affect the opinions of

Sec. 4911. Tax on excess expenditures to influence legislation

the general public or any segment thereof, and

(B) any attempt to influence any legislation through communication with any member or employee of a legislative body, or with any government official or employee who may participate in the formulation of the legislation.

(2) Exceptions. -- For purposes of this section, the term "influencing legislation", with respect to an organization, does not include--   5

(A) making available the results of nonpartisan analysis, study, or research;

(B) providing of technical advice or assistance (where such advice would otherwise constitute the influencing of legislation) to a governmental body or to a committee or other subdivision thereof in response to a written request by such body or subdivision, as the case   10 may be;

(C) appearances before, or communications to, any legislative body with respect to a possible decision of such body which might affect the existence of the organization, its powers and duties, tax-exempt status, or the deduction of contributions to the organization;

(D) communications between the organization and its bona fide members with respect to   15 legislation or proposed legislation of direct interest to the organization and such members, other than communications described in paragraph (3); and

(E) any communication with a governmental official or employee, other than--

(i) a communication with a member or employee of a legislative body (where such communication would otherwise constitute the influencing of legislation), or   20

(ii) a communication the principal purpose of which is to influence legislation.

(3) Communications with members. --

(A) A communication between an organization and any bona fide member of such organization to directly encourage such member to communicate as provided in paragraph (1)(B) shall be treated as a communication described in paragraph (1)(B).   25

(B) A communication between an organization and any bona fide member of such organization to directly encourage such member to urge persons other than members to communicate as provided in either subparagraph (A) or subparagraph (B) of paragraph (1) shall be treated as a communication described in paragraph (1)(A).

(e) Other definitions and special rules. -- For purposes of this section--   30

(1) Exempt purpose expenditures. --

(A) In general. -- The term "exempt purpose expenditures" means, with respect to any organization for any taxable year, the total of the amounts paid or incurred by such organization to accomplish purposes described in section 170(c)(2)(B) (relating to religious, charitable, educational, etc., purposes).   35

(B) Certain amounts included. -- The term "exempt purpose expenditures" includes--

(i) administrative expenses paid or incurred for purposes described in section 170(c)(2)(B), and

(ii) amounts paid or incurred for the purpose of influencing legislation (whether or not for purposes described in section 170(c)(2)(B)).   40

(C) Certain amounts excluded. -- The term "exempt purpose expenditures" does not include amounts paid or incurred to or for -

(i) a separate fundraising unit of such organization, or

(ii) one or more other organizations, if such amounts are paid or incurred primarily for fundraising.   45

Sec. 4911. Tax on excess expenditures to influence legislation

(2) Legislation. -- The term "legislation" includes action with respect to Acts, bills, resolutions, or similar items by the Congress, any State legislature, any local council, or similar governing body, or by the public in a referendum, initiative, constitutional amendment, or similar procedure.

(3) Action. -- The term "action" is limited to the introduction, amendment, enactment, defeat, or repeal of Acts, bills, resolutions, or similar items.

***

Sec. 6001. Notice or regulations requiring records, statements, and special returns

Every person liable for any tax imposed by this title, or for the collection thereof, shall keep such records, render such statements, make such returns, and comply with such rules and regulations as the Secretary may from time to time prescribe. Whenever in the judgment of the Secretary it is necessary, he may require any person, by notice served upon such person or by regulations, to make such returns, render such statements, or keep such records, as the Secretary deems sufficient to show whether or not such person is liable for tax under this title. The only records which an employer shall be required to keep under this section in connection with charged tips shall be charge receipts, records necessary to comply with section 6053(c), and copies of statements furnished by employees under section 6053(a).

Reg. § 1.6001-1 Records.

(a) *In general.* Except as provided in paragraph (b) of this section, any person subject to tax under subtitle A of the Code (including a qualified State individual income tax which is treated pursuant to section 6361(a) as if it were imposed by chapter 1 of subtitle A), or any person required to file a return of information with respect to income, shall keep such permanent books of account or records, including inventories, as are sufficient to establish the amount of gross income, deductions, credits, or other matters required to be shown by such person in any return of such tax or information.

***

(e) *Retention of records.* The books or records required by this section shall be kept at all times available for inspection by authorized internal revenue officers or employees, and shall be retained so long as the contents thereof may become material in the administration of any internal revenue law.

[T.D. 6500, 25 FR 12108, Nov. 26, 1960; T.D. 7122, 36 FR 11025, June 8, 1971; T.D. 7577, 43 FR 59357, Dec. 20, 1978; T.D. 8308, 55 FR 35593, Aug. 31, 1990]

Sec. 6011. General requirement of return, statement, or list

(a) General rule. -- When required by regulations prescribed by the Secretary any person made liable for any tax imposed by this title, or with respect to the collection thereof, shall make a return or statement according to the forms and regulations prescribed by the Secretary. Every person required to make a return or statement shall include therein the information required by such forms or regulations.

(b) Identification of taxpayer. -- The Secretary is authorized to require such information with respect to persons subject to the taxes imposed by chapter 21 or chapter 24 as is necessary or helpful in securing proper identification of such persons.

***

Sec. 6011. General requirement of return, statement, or list

Reg. § 1.6011-4 Requirement of statement disclosing participation in certain transactions by taxpayers.

(a) *In general.* Every taxpayer that has participated, as described in paragraph (c)(3) of this section, in a reportable transaction within the meaning of paragraph (b) of this section and who is required to file a tax return must file within the time prescribed in 5 paragraph (e) of this section a disclosure statement in the form prescribed by paragraph (d) of this section. The fact that a transaction is a reportable transaction shall not affect the legal determination of whether the taxpayer's treatment of the transaction is proper.

(b) *Reportable transactions*--(1) *In general.* A reportable transaction is a transaction described in any of the paragraphs (b)(2) through (7) of this section. The term transaction 10 includes all of the factual elements relevant to the expected tax treatment of any investment, entity, plan, or arrangement, and includes any series of steps carried out as part of a plan.

(2) *Listed transactions.* A listed transaction is a transaction that is the same as or substantially similar to one of the types of transactions that the Internal Revenue Service 15 (IRS) has determined to be a tax avoidance transaction and identified by notice, regulation, or other form of published guidance as a listed transaction.

(3) *Confidential transactions*--(i) *In general.* A confidential transaction is a transaction that is offered to a taxpayer under conditions of confidentiality and for which the taxpayer has paid an advisor a minimum fee. 20

(ii) *Conditions of confidentiality.* A transaction is considered to be offered to a taxpayer under conditions of confidentiality if the advisor who is paid the minimum fee places a limitation on disclosure by the taxpayer of the tax treatment or tax structure of the transaction and the limitation on disclosure protects the confidentiality of that advisor's tax strategies. A transaction is treated as confidential even if the conditions of confidentiality 25 are not legally binding on the taxpayer. A claim that a transaction is proprietary or exclusive is not treated as a limitation on disclosure if the advisor confirms to the taxpayer that there is no limitation on disclosure of the tax treatment or tax structure of the transaction.

(iii) *Minimum fee.* For purposes of this paragraph (b)(3), the minimum fee is -- 30
(A) $250,000 for a transaction if the taxpayer is a corporation;
(B) $50,000 for all other transactions unless the taxpayer is a partnership or trust, all of the owners or beneficiaries of which are corporations (looking through any partners or beneficiaries that are themselves partnerships or trusts), in which case the minimum fee is $250,000. 35

(iv) *Determination of minimum fee.* For purposes of this paragraph (b)(3), in determining the minimum fee, all fees for a tax strategy or for services for advice (whether or not tax advice) or for the implementation of a transaction are taken into account. Fees include consideration in whatever form paid, whether in cash or in kind, for services to analyze the transaction (whether or not related to the tax consequences of the 40 transaction), for services to implement the transaction, for services to document the transaction, and for services to prepare tax returns to the extent return preparation fees are unreasonable in light of the facts and circumstances. For purposes of this paragraph (b)(3), a taxpayer also is treated as paying fees to an advisor if the taxpayer knows or should know that the amount it pays will be paid indirectly to the advisor, such as through 45 a referral fee or fee-sharing arrangement. A fee does not include amounts paid to a person, including an advisor, in that person's capacity as a party to the transaction. For example, a fee does not include reasonable charges for the use of capital or the sale or use of property. The IRS will scrutinize carefully all of the facts and circumstances in determining whether consideration received in connection with a confidential transaction 50 constitutes fees.

Sec. 6011. General requirement of return, statement, or list

(v) *Related parties.* For purposes of this paragraph (b)(3), persons who bear a relationship to each other as described in section 267(b) or 707(b) will be treated as the same person.

5　(4) Transactions with contractual protection--(i) In general. A transaction with contractual protection is a transaction for which the taxpayer or a related party (as described in section 267(b) or 707(b)) has the right to a full or partial refund of fees (as described in paragraph (b)(4)(ii) of this section) if all or part of the intended tax consequences from the transaction are not sustained. A transaction with contractual protection also is a transaction for which fees (as described in paragraph (b)(4)(ii) of this
10　section) are contingent on the taxpayer's realization of tax benefits from the transaction. All the facts and circumstances relating to the transaction will be considered when determining whether a fee is refundable or contingent, including the right to reimbursements of amounts that the parties to the transaction have not designated as fees or any agreement to provide services without reasonable compensation.

15　(ii) *Fees.* Paragraph (b)(4)(i) of this section only applies with respect to fees paid by or on behalf of the taxpayer or a related party to any person who makes or provides a statement, oral or written, to the taxpayer or related party (or for whose benefit a statement is made or provided to the taxpayer or related party) as to the potential tax consequences that may result from the transaction.

20　(iii) *Exceptions--(A) Termination of transaction.* A transaction is not considered to have contractual protection solely because a party to the transaction has the right to terminate the transaction upon the happening of an event affecting the taxation of one or more parties to the transaction.

(B) *Previously reported transaction.* If a person makes or provides a statement to a
25　taxpayer as to the potential tax consequences that may result from a transaction only after the taxpayer has entered into the transaction and reported the consequences of the transaction on a filed tax return, and the person has not previously received fees from the taxpayer relating to the transaction, then any refundable or contingent fees are not taken into account in determining whether the transaction has contractual protection. This
30　paragraph (b)(4) does not provide any substantive rules regarding when a person may charge refundable or contingent fees with respect to a transaction. See Circular 230, 31 CFR Part 10, for the regulations governing practice before the IRS.

(5) *Loss transactions---(i) In general.* A loss transaction is any transaction resulting in the taxpayer claiming a loss under section 165 of at least --

35　(A) $10 million in any single taxable year or $20 million in any combination of taxable years for corporations;

(B) $10 million in any single taxable year or $20 million in any combination of taxable years for partnerships that have only corporations as partners (looking through any partners that are themselves partnerships), whether or not any losses flow through to one
40　or more partners; or

(C) $2 million in any single taxable year or $4 million in any combination of taxable years for all other partnerships, whether or not any losses flow through to one or more partners;

(D) $2 million in any single taxable year or $4 million in any combination of taxable
45　years for individuals, S corporations, or trusts, whether or not any losses flow through to one or more shareholders or beneficiaries; or

(E) $50,000 in any single taxable year for individuals or trusts, whether or not the loss flows through from an S corporation or partnership, if the loss arises with respect to a section 988 transaction (as defined in section 988(c)(1) relating to foreign currency
50　transactions).

(ii) *Cumulative losses.* In determining whether a transaction results in a taxpayer

1054

Sec. 6011.   General requirement of return, statement, or list

claiming a loss that meets the threshold amounts over a combination of taxable years as described in paragraph (b)(5)(i) of this section, only losses claimed in the taxable year that the transaction is entered into and the five succeeding taxable years are combined.

(iii) Section 165 loss--(A) For purposes of this section, in determining the thresholds in paragraph (b)(5)(i) of this section, the amount of a section 165 loss is adjusted for any 5 salvage value and for any insurance or other compensation received. See §1.165-1(c)(4). However, a section 165 loss does not take into account offsetting gains, or other income or limitations. For example, a section 165 loss does not take into account the limitation in section 165(d) (relating to wagering losses) or the limitations in sections 165(f), 1211, and 1212 (relating to capital losses). The full amount of a section 165 loss is taken into 10 account for the year in which the loss is sustained, regardless of whether all or part of the loss enters into the computation of a net operating loss under section 172 or a net capital loss under section 1212 that is a carryback or carryover to another year. A section 165 loss does not include any portion of a loss, attributable to a capital loss carryback or carryover from another year, that is treated as a deemed capital loss under section 1212. 15

(B) For purposes of this section, a section 165 loss includes an amount deductible pursuant to a provision that treats a transaction as a sale or other disposition, or otherwise results in a deduction under section 165. A section 165 loss includes, for example, a loss resulting from a sale or exchange of a partnership interest under section 741 and a loss resulting from a section 988 transaction. 20

(6) *Transactions of interest.* A transaction of interest is a transaction that is the same as or substantially similar to one of the types of transactions that the IRS has identified by notice, regulation, or other form of published guidance as a transaction of interest.

(7) [*Reserved*].

(8) *Exceptions*--(i) *In general.* A transaction will not be considered a reportable 25 transaction, or will be excluded from any individual category of reportable transaction under paragraphs (b)(3) through (7) of this section, if the Commissioner makes a determination by published guidance that the transaction is not subject to the reporting requirements of this section. The Commissioner may make a determination by individual letter ruling under paragraph (f) of this section that an individual letter ruling request on a 30 specific transaction satisfies the reporting requirements of this section with regard to that transaction for the taxpayer who requests the individual letter ruling.

(ii) *Special rule for RICs.* For purposes of this section, a regulated investment company (RIC) as defined in section 851 or an investment vehicle that is owned 95 percent or more by one or more RICs at all times during the course of the transaction is 35 not required to disclose a transaction that is described in any of paragraphs (b)(3) through (5) and (b)(7) of this section unless the transaction is also a listed transaction or a transaction of interest.

(c) Definitions. For purposes of this section, the following definitions apply:

(1) Taxpayer . The term taxpayer means any person described in section 7701(a)(1), 40 including S corporations. Except as otherwise specifically provided in this section, the term taxpayer also includes an affiliated group of corporations that joins in the filing of a consolidated return under section 1501.

(2) *Corporation.* When used specifically in this section, the term *corporation* means an entity that is required to file a return for a taxable year on any 1120 series form, or 45 successor form, excluding S corporations.

(3) *Participation*--(i) *In general*--(A) *Listed transactions.* A taxpayer has participated in a listed transaction if the taxpayer's tax return reflects tax consequences or a tax strategy described in the published guidance that lists the transaction under paragraph (b)(2) of this section. A taxpayer also has participated in a listed transaction if the taxpayer knows 50 or has reason to know that the taxpayer's tax benefits are derived directly or indirectly

from tax consequences or a tax strategy described in published guidance that lists a transaction under paragraph (b)(2) of this section. Published guidance may identify other types or classes of persons that will be treated as participants in a listed transaction. Published guidance also may identify types or classes of persons that will not be treated
5 as participants in a listed transaction.

     (B) *Confidential transactions.* A taxpayer has participated in a confidential transaction if the taxpayer's tax return reflects a tax benefit from the transaction and the taxpayer's disclosure of the tax treatment or tax structure of the transaction is limited in the manner described in paragraph (b)(3) of this section. If a partnership's, S corporation's or trust's
10 disclosure is limited, and the partner's, shareholder's, or beneficiary's disclosure is not limited, then the partnership, S corporation, or trust, and not the partner, shareholder, or beneficiary, has participated in the confidential transaction.

     (C) *Transactions with contractual protection.* A taxpayer has participated in a transaction with contractual protection if the taxpayer's tax return reflects a tax benefit
15 from the transaction and, as described in paragraph (b)(4) of this section, the taxpayer has the right to the full or partial refund of fees or the fees are contingent. If a partnership, S corporation, or trust has the right to a full or partial refund of fees or has a contingent fee arrangement, and the partner, shareholder, or beneficiary does not individually have the right to the refund of fees or a contingent fee arrangement, then the partnership, S
20 corporation, or trust, and not the partner, shareholder, or beneficiary, has participated in the transaction with contractual protection.

     (D) *Loss transactions.* A taxpayer has participated in a loss transaction if the taxpayer's tax return reflects a section 165 loss and the amount of the section 165 loss equals or exceeds the threshold amount applicable to the taxpayer as described in
25 paragraph (b)(5)(i) of this section. If a taxpayer is a partner in a partnership, shareholder in an S corporation, or beneficiary of a trust and a section 165 loss as described in paragraph (b)(5) of this section flows through the entity to the taxpayer (disregarding netting at the entity level), the taxpayer has participated in a loss transaction if the taxpayer's tax return reflects a section 165 loss and the amount of the section 165 loss
30 that flows through to the taxpayer equals or exceeds the threshold amounts applicable to the taxpayer as described in paragraph (b)(5)(i) of this section. For this purpose, a tax return is deemed to reflect the full amount of a section 165 loss described in paragraph (b)(5) of this section allocable to the taxpayer under this paragraph (c)(3)(i)(D), regardless of whether all or part of the loss enters into the computation of a net operating
35 loss under section 172 or net capital loss under section 1212 that the taxpayer may carry back or carry over to another year.

     (E) *Transactions of interest.* A taxpayer has participated in a transaction of interest if the taxpayer is one of the types or classes of persons identified as participants in the transaction in the published guidance describing the transaction of interest.
40   (F) [*Reserved*].

     (G) *Shareholders of foreign corporations--*(1) *In general.* A reporting shareholder of a foreign corporation participates in a transaction described in paragraphs (b)(2) through (5) and (b)(7) of this section if the foreign corporation would be considered to participate in the transaction under the rules of this paragraph (c)(3) if it were a domestic corporation
45 filing a tax return that reflects the items from the transaction. A reporting shareholder of a foreign corporation participates in a transaction described in paragraph (b)(6) of this section only if the published guidance identifying the transaction includes the reporting shareholder among the types or classes of persons identified as participants. A reporting shareholder (and any successor in interest) is considered to participate in a transaction
50 under this paragraph (c)(3)(i)(G) only for its first taxable year with or within which ends the first taxable year of the foreign corporation in which the foreign corporation

participates in the transaction, and for the reporting shareholder's five succeeding taxable years.

(2) *Reporting shareholder.* The term reporting shareholder means a United States shareholder (as defined in section 951(b)) in a controlled foreign corporation (as defined in section 957) or a 10 percent shareholder (by vote or value) of a qualified electing fund 5 (as defined in section 1295).

(ii) *Examples.* The following examples illustrate the provisions of paragraph (c)(3)(i) of this section:

***

Example 2. XYZ is a limited liability company treated as a partnership for tax 10 purposes. X, Y, and Z are members of XYZ. X is an individual, Y is an S corporation, and Z is a partnership. XYZ enters into a confidential transaction under paragraph (b)(3) of this section. XYZ and X are bound by the confidentiality agreement, but Y and Z are not bound by the agreement. As a result of the transaction, XYZ, X, Y, and Z all reflect a tax benefit on their tax returns. Because XYZ's and X's disclosure of the tax treatment and 15 tax structure are limited in the manner described in paragraph (b)(3) of this section and their tax returns reflect a tax benefit from the transaction, both XYZ and X have participated in the confidential transaction. Neither Y nor Z has participated in the confidential transaction because they are not subject to the confidentiality agreement.

Example 3. P, a corporation, has an 80% partnership interest in PS, and S, an 20 individual, has a 20% partnership interest in PS. P, S, and PS are calendar year taxpayers. In 2006, PS enters into a transaction and incurs a section 165 loss (that does not meet any of the exceptions to a section 165 loss identified in published guidance) of $12 million and offsetting gain of $3 million. On PS' 2006 tax return, PS includes the section 165 loss and the corresponding gain. PS must disclose the transaction under this 25 section because PS' section 165 loss of $12 million is equal to or greater than $2 million. P is allocated $9.6 million of the section 165 loss and $2.4 million of the offsetting gain. P does not have to disclose the transaction under this section because P's section 165 loss of $9.6 million is not equal to or greater than $10 million. S is allocated $2.4 million of the section 165 loss and $600,000 of the offsetting gain. S must disclose the transaction 30 under this section because S's section 165 loss of $2.4 million is equal to or greater than $2 million.

(4) *Substantially similar.* The term *substantially similar* includes any transaction that is expected to obtain the same or similar types of tax consequences and that is either factually similar or based on the same or similar tax strategy. Receipt of an opinion 35 regarding the tax consequences of the transaction is not relevant to the determination of whether the transaction is the same as or substantially similar to another transaction. Further, the term *substantially similar* must be broadly construed in favor of disclosure. For example, a transaction may be substantially similar to a listed transaction even though it involves different entities or uses different Internal Revenue Code provisions   40

***

(5) *Tax.* The term *tax* means Federal income tax.

(6) *Tax benefit.* A tax benefit includes deductions, exclusions from gross income, nonrecognition of gain, tax credits, adjustments (or the absence of adjustments) to the basis of property, status as an entity exempt from Federal income taxation, and any other 45 tax consequences that may reduce a taxpayer's Federal income tax liability by affecting the amount, timing, character, or source of any item of income, gain, expense, loss, or credit.

(7) *Tax return.* The term *tax return* means a Federal income tax return and a Federal information return.   50

(8) *Tax treatment.* The tax treatment of a transaction is the purported or claimed

Sec. 6011. General requirement of return, statement, or list

Federal income tax treatment of the transaction.

(9) *Tax structure.* The tax structure of a transaction is any fact that may be relevant to understanding the purported or claimed Federal income tax treatment of the transaction.

(d) *Form and content of disclosure statement.* A taxpayer required to file a disclosure
5 statement under this section must file a completed Form 8886, "Reportable Transaction Disclosure Statement" (or a successor form), in accordance with this paragraph (d) and the instructions to the form. The Form 8886 (or a successor form) is the disclosure statement required under this section. The form must be attached to the appropriate tax return(s) as provided in paragraph (e) of this section. If a copy of a disclosure statement
10 is required to be sent to the Office of Tax Shelter Analysis (OTSA) under paragraph (e) of this section, it must be sent in accordance with the instructions to the form. To be considered complete, the information provided on the form must describe the expected tax treatment and all potential tax benefits expected to result from the transaction, describe any tax result protection (as defined in § 301.6111-3(c)(12) of this chapter) with
15 respect to the transaction, and identify and describe the transaction in sufficient detail for the IRS to be able to understand the tax structure of the reportable transaction and the identity of all parties involved in the transaction. An incomplete Form 8886 (or a successor form) containing a statement that information will be provided upon request is not considered a complete disclosure statement. If the form is not completed in
20 accordance with the provisions in this paragraph (d) and the instructions to the form, the taxpayer will not be considered to have complied with the disclosure requirements of this section. If a taxpayer receives one or more reportable transaction numbers for a reportable transaction, the taxpayer must include the reportable transaction number(s) on the Form 8886 (or a successor form). See § 301.6111-3(d)(2) of this chapter.

25 (e) *Time of providing disclosure--*(1) *In general.* The disclosure statement for a reportable transaction must be attached to the taxpayer's tax return for each taxable year for which a taxpayer participates in a reportable transaction. In addition, a disclosure statement for a reportable transaction must be attached to each amended return that reflects a taxpayer's participation in a reportable transaction. A copy of the disclosure
30 statement must be sent to OTSA at the same time that any disclosure statement is first filed by the taxpayer pertaining to a particular reportable transaction. If a reportable transaction results in a loss which is carried back to a prior year, the disclosure statement for the reportable transaction must be attached to the taxpayer's application for tentative refund or amended tax return for that prior year. In the case of a taxpayer that is a partner
35 in a partnership, a shareholder in an S corporation, or a beneficiary of a trust, the disclosure statement for a reportable transaction must be attached to the partnership, S corporation, or trust's tax return for each taxable year in which the partnership, S corporation, or trust participates in the transaction under the rules of paragraph (c)(3)(i) of this section. If a taxpayer who is a partner in a partnership, a shareholder in an S
40 corporation, or a beneficiary of a trust receives a timely Schedule K-1 less than 10 calendar days before the due date of the taxpayer's return (including extensions) and, based on receipt of the timely Schedule K-1, the taxpayer determines that the taxpayer participated in a reportable transaction within the meaning of paragraph (c)(3) of this section, the disclosure statement will not be considered late if the taxpayer discloses the
45 reportable transaction by filing a disclosure statement with OTSA within 60 calendar days after the due date of the taxpayer's return (including extensions). The Commissioner in his discretion may issue in published guidance other provisions for disclosure under § 1.6011-4.

(2) *Special rules--*(i) *Listed transactions and transactions of interest.* In general, if a
50 transaction becomes a listed transaction or a transaction of interest after the filing of a taxpayer's tax return (including an amended return) reflecting the taxpayer's participation

Sec. 6011. General requirement of return, statement, or list

in the listed transaction or transaction of interest and before the end of the period of limitations for assessment of tax for any taxable year in which the taxpayer participated in the listed transaction or transaction of interest, then a disclosure statement must be filed, regardless of whether the taxpayer participated in the transaction in the year the transaction became a listed transaction or a transaction of interest, with OTSA within 90   5 calendar days after the date on which the transaction became a listed transaction or a transaction of interest. The Commissioner also may determine the time for disclosure of listed transactions and transactions of interest in the published guidance identifying the transaction.

(ii) *Loss transactions.* If a transaction becomes a loss transaction because the losses   10 equal or exceed the threshold amounts as described in paragraph (b)(5)(i) of this section, a disclosure statement must be filed as an attachment to the taxpayer=s tax return for the first taxable year in which the threshold amount is reached and to any subsequent tax return that reflects any amount of section 165 loss from the transaction.

(3) *Multiple disclosures.* The taxpayer must disclose the transaction in the time and   15 manner provided for under the provisions of this section regardless of whether the taxpayer also plans to disclose the transaction under other published guidance, for example, § 1.6662-3(c)(2).

(4) *Example.* The following example illustrates the application of this paragraph (e):

Example. In January of 2008, F, a calendar year taxpayer, enters into a transaction   20 that at the time is not a listed transaction and is not a transaction described in any of the paragraphs (b)(3) through (7) of this section. All the tax benefits from the transaction are reported on F's 2008 tax return filed timely in April 2009. On May 2, 2011, the IRS publishes a notice identifying the transaction as a listed transaction described in paragraph (b)(2) of this section. Upon issuance of the May 2, 2011 notice, the transaction   25 becomes a reportable transaction described in paragraph (b) of this section. The period of limitations on assessment for F's 2008 taxable year is still open. F is required to file Form 8886 for the transaction with OTSA within 90 calendar days after May 2, 2011.

(f) *Rulings and protective disclosures*--(1) *Rulings.* If a taxpayer requests a ruling on the merits of a specific transaction on or before the date that disclosure would otherwise   30 be required under this section, and receives a favorable ruling as to the transaction, the disclosure rules under this section will be deemed to have been satisfied by that taxpayer with regard to that transaction, so long as the request fully discloses all relevant facts relating to the transaction which would otherwise be required to be disclosed under this section. If a taxpayer requests a ruling as to whether a specific transaction is a reportable   35 transaction on or before the date that disclosure would otherwise be required under this section, the Commissioner in his discretion may determine that the submission satisfies the disclosure rules under this section for the taxpayer requesting the ruling for that transaction if the request fully discloses all relevant facts relating to the transaction which would otherwise be required to be disclosed under this section. The potential obligation of   40 the taxpayer to disclose the transaction under this section will not be suspended during the period that the ruling request is pending.

(2) *Protective disclosures.* If a taxpayer is uncertain whether a transaction must be disclosed under this section, the taxpayer may disclose the transaction in accordance with the requirements of this section and comply with all the provisions of this section,   45 and indicate on the disclosure statement that the disclosure statement is being filed on a protective basis. The IRS will not treat disclosure statements filed on a protective basis any differently than other disclosure statements filed under this section. For a protective disclosure to be effective, the taxpayer must comply with these disclosure regulations by providing to the IRS all information requested by the IRS under this section.   50

(g) *Retention of documents.* (1) In accordance with the instructions to Form 8886 (or a

Sec. 6011. General requirement of return, statement, or list

successor form), the taxpayer must retain a copy of all documents and other records related to a transaction subject to disclosure under this section that are material to an understanding of the tax treatment or tax structure of the transaction. The documents must be retained until the expiration of the statute of limitations applicable to the final
5 taxable year for which disclosure of the transaction was required under this section. (This document retention requirement is in addition to any document retention requirements that section 6001 generally imposes on the taxpayer.) The documents may include the following:

  (i) Marketing materials related to the transaction;
10 (ii) Written analyses used in decision-making related to the transaction;
  (iii) Correspondence and agreements between the taxpayer and any advisor, lender, or other party to the reportable transaction that relate to the transaction;
  (iv) Documents discussing, referring to, or demonstrating the purported or claimed tax benefits arising from the reportable transaction; and documents, if any, referring to the
15 business purposes for the reportable transaction.

  (2) A taxpayer is not required to retain earlier drafts of a document if the taxpayer retains a copy of the final document (or, if there is no final document, the most recent draft of the document) and the final document (or most recent draft) contains all the information in the earlier drafts of the document that is material to an understanding of
20 the purported tax treatment or tax structure of the transaction.

***

[T.D. 9046, 68 FR 10163, Mar. 4, 2003; T.D. 9108, 68 FR 75130, Dec. 30, 2003; T.D. 9295, 71 FR 64459, Nov. 2, 2006; T.D. 9350, 8/31/2007]

Sec. 6012. Persons required to make returns of income

25 **(a) General rule.** -- Returns with respect to income taxes under subtitle A shall be made by the following:

  (1)(A) Every individual having for the taxable year gross income which equals or exceeds the exemption amount, except that a return shall not be required of an individual--

  (i) who is not married (determined by applying section 7703), is not a surviving spouse
30 (as defined in section 2(a)), is not a head of a household (as defined in section 2(b)), and for the taxable year has gross income of less than the sum of the exemption amount plus the basic standard deduction applicable to such an individual,

  (ii) who is a head of a household (as so defined) and for the taxable year has gross income of less than the sum of the exemption amount plus the basic standard deduction
35 applicable to such an individual,

  (iii) who is a surviving spouse (as so defined) and for the taxable year has gross income of less than the sum of the exemption amount plus the basic standard deduction applicable to such an individual, or

  (iv) who is entitled to make a joint return and whose gross income, when combined with
40 the gross income of his spouse, is, for the taxable year, less than the sum of twice the exemption amount plus the basic standard deduction applicable to a joint return, but only if such individual and his spouse, at the close of the taxable year, had the same household as their home.

  Clause (iv) shall not apply if for the taxable year such spouse makes a separate return or any
45 other taxpayer is entitled to an exemption for such spouse under section 151(c).

  (B) The amount specified in clause (i), (ii), or (iii) of subparagraph (A) shall be increased by the amount of 1 additional standard deduction (within the meaning of section 63(c)(3)) in the

1060

Sec. 6012. Persons required to make returns of income

case of an individual entitled to such deduction by reason of section 63(f)(1)(A) (relating to individuals age 65 or more), and the amount specified in clause (iv) of subparagraph (A) shall be increased by the amount of the additional standard deduction for each additional standard deduction to which the individual or his spouse is entitled by reason of section 63(f)(1).

    (C) The exception under subparagraph (A) shall not apply to any individual--   5

        (i) who is described in section 63(c)(5) and who has--

            (I) income (other than earned income) in excess of the sum of the amount in effect under section 63(c)(5)(A) plus the additional standard deduction (if any) to which the individual is entitled, or

            (II) total gross income in excess of the standard deduction, or   10

        (ii) for whom the standard deduction is zero under section 63(c)(6).

    (D) For purposes of this subsection--

        (i) The terms "standard deduction", "basic standard deduction" and "additional standard deduction" have the respective meanings given such terms by section 63(c).

        (ii) The term "exemption amount" has the meaning given such term by section 151(d). In   15 the case of an individual described in section 151(d)(2), the exemption amount shall be zero.

    (2) Every corporation subject to taxation under subtitle A;

    (3) Every estate the gross income of which for the taxable year is $600 or more;

    (4) Every trust having for the taxable year any taxable income, or having gross income of   20 $600 or over, regardless of the amount of taxable income;

***

Sec. 6013. Joint returns of income tax by husband and wife

    (a) **Joint returns.** -- A husband and wife may make a single return jointly of income taxes under subtitle A, even though one of the spouses has neither gross income nor deductions, except as   25 provided below:

    (1) no joint return shall be made if either the husband or wife at any time during the taxable year is a nonresident alien;

    (2) no joint return shall be made if the husband and wife have different taxable years; except that if such taxable years begin on the same day and end on different days because of the death   30 of either or both, then the joint return may be made with respect to the taxable year of each. The above exception shall not apply if the surviving spouse remarries before the close of his taxable year, nor if the taxable year of either spouse is a fractional part of a year under section 443(a)(1);

    (3) in the case of death of one spouse or both spouses the joint return with respect to the   35 decedent may be made only by his executor or administrator; except that in the case of the death of one spouse the joint return may be made by the surviving spouse with respect to both himself and the decedent if no return for the taxable year has been made by the decedent, no executor or administrator has been appointed, and no executor or administrator is appointed before the last day prescribed by law for filing the return of the surviving spouse. If an   40 executor or administrator of the decedent is appointed after the making of the joint return by the surviving spouse, the executor or administrator may disaffirm such joint return by making, within 1 year after the last day prescribed by law for filing the return of the surviving spouse, a separate return for the taxable year of the decedent with respect to which the joint return was made, in which case the return made by the survivor shall constitute his separate return.   45

1061

Sec. 6013. Joint returns of income tax by husband and wife

(b) Joint return after filing separate return. --

(1) In general. -- Except as provided in paragraph (2), if an individual has filed a separate return for a taxable year for which a joint return could have been made by him and his spouse under subsection (a) and the time prescribed by law for filing the return for such taxable year has expired, such individual and his spouse may nevertheless make a joint return for such taxable year. A joint return filed by the husband and wife under this subsection shall constitute the return of the husband and wife for such taxable year, and all payments, credits, refunds, or other repayments made or allowed with respect to the separate return of either spouse for such taxable year shall be taken into account in determining the extent to which the tax based upon the joint return has been paid. If a joint return is made under this subsection, any election (other than the election to file a separate return) made by either spouse in his separate return for such taxable year with respect to the treatment of any income, deduction, or credit of such spouse shall not be changed in the making of the joint return where such election would have been irrevocable if the joint return had not been made. If a joint return is made under this subsection after the death of either spouse, such return with respect to the decedent can be made only by his executor or administrator.

(2) Limitations for making of election. -- The election provided for in paragraph (1) may not be made--

(A) after the expiration of 3 years from the last date prescribed by law for filing the return for such taxable year (determined without regard to any extension of time granted to either spouse); or

(B) after there has been mailed to either spouse, with respect to such taxable year, a notice of deficiency under section 6212, if the spouse, as to such notice, files a petition with the Tax Court within the time prescribed in section 6213; or

(C) after either spouse has commenced a suit in any court for the recovery of any part of the tax for such taxable year; or

(D) after either spouse has entered into a closing agreement under section 7121 with respect to such taxable year, or after any civil or criminal case arising against either spouse with respect to such taxable year has been compromised under section 7122.

***

Sec. 6015. Relief from joint and several liability on joint return

(a) In general. -- Notwithstanding section 6013(d)(3)--

(1) an individual who has made a joint return may elect to seek relief under the procedures prescribed under subsection (b); and

(2) if such individual is eligible to elect the application of subsection (c), such individual may, in addition to any election under paragraph (1), elect to limit such individual's liability for any deficiency with respect to such joint return in the manner prescribed under subsection (c). Any determination under this section shall be made without regard to community property laws.

(b) Procedures for relief from liability applicable to all joint filers. --

(1) In general. -- Under procedures prescribed by the Secretary, if--

(A) a joint return has been made for a taxable year;

(B) on such return there is an understatement of tax attributable to erroneous items of one individual filing the joint return;

(C) the other individual filing the joint return establishes that in signing the return he or she did not know, and had no reason to know, that there was such understatement;

Sec. 6015. Relief from joint and several liability on joint return

(D) taking into account all the facts and circumstances, it is inequitable to hold the other individual liable for the deficiency in tax for such taxable year attributable to such understatement; and

(E) the other individual elects (in such form as the Secretary may prescribe) the benefits of this subsection not later than the date which is 2 years after the date the Secretary has 5 begun collection activities with respect to the individual making the election, then the other individual shall be relieved of liability for tax (including interest, penalties, and other amounts) for such taxable year to the extent such liability is attributable to such understatement.

(2) Apportionment of relief. -- If an individual who, but for paragraph (1)(C), would be 10 relieved of liability under paragraph (1), establishes that in signing the return such individual did not know, and had no reason to know, the extent of such understatement, then such individual shall be relieved of liability for tax (including interest, penalties, and other amounts) for such taxable year to the extent that such liability is attributable to the portion of such understatement of which such individual did not know and had no reason to know. 15

(3) Understatement. -- For purposes of this subsection, the term "understatement" has the meaning given to such term by section 6662(d)(2)(A).

(c) Procedures to limit liability for taxpayers no longer married or taxpayers legally separated or not living together. --

(1) In general. -- Except as provided in this subsection, if an individual who has made a 20 joint return for any taxable year elects the application of this subsection, the individual's liability for any deficiency which is assessed with respect to the return shall not exceed the portion of such deficiency properly allocable to the individual under subsection (d).

(2) Burden of proof. -- Except as provided in subparagraph (A)(ii) or (C) of paragraph (3), each individual who elects the application of this subsection shall have the burden of proof 25 with respect to establishing the portion of any deficiency allocable to such individual.

(3) Election. --

(A) Individuals eligible to make election. --

(i) In general. -- An individual shall only be eligible to elect the application of this subsection if-- 30

(I) at the time such election is filed, such individual is no longer married to, or is legally separated from, the individual with whom such individual filed the joint return to which the election relates; or

(II) such individual was not a member of the same household as the individual with whom such joint return was filed at any time during the 12-month period 35 ending on the date such election is filed.

(ii) Certain taxpayers ineligible to elect. -- If the Secretary demonstrates that assets were transferred between individuals filing a joint return as part of a fraudulent scheme by such individuals, an election under this subsection by either individual shall be invalid (and section 6013(d)(3) shall apply to the joint return). 40

(B) Time for election. -- An election under this subsection for any taxable year may be made at any time after a deficiency for such year is asserted but not later than 2 years after the date on which the Secretary has begun collection activities with respect to the individual making the election.

(C) Election not valid with respect to certain deficiencies. -- If the Secretary 45 demonstrates that an individual making an election under this subsection had actual knowledge, at the time such individual signed the return, of any item giving rise to a deficiency (or portion thereof) which is not allocable to such individual under subsection (d), such election shall not apply to such deficiency (or portion). This subparagraph shall not apply where the individual with actual knowledge establishes that such individual signed the return under duress.

(4) Liability increased by reason of transfers of property to avoid tax. --

(A) In general. -- Notwithstanding any other provision of this subsection, the portion of the deficiency for which the individual electing the application of this subsection is liable (without regard to this paragraph) shall be increased by the value of any disqualified asset transferred to the individual.

(B) Disqualified asset. -- For purposes of this paragraph--

(i) In general. -- The term "disqualified asset" means any property or right to property transferred to an individual making the election under this subsection with respect to a joint return by the other individual filing such joint return if the principal purpose of the transfer was the avoidance of tax or payment of tax.

(ii) Presumption. --

(I) In general. -- For purposes of clause (i), except as provided in subclause (II), any transfer which is made after the date which is 1 year before the date on which the first letter of proposed deficiency which allows the taxpayer an opportunity for administrative review in the Internal Revenue Service Office of Appeals is sent shall be presumed to have as its principal purpose the avoidance of tax or payment of tax.

(II) Exceptions. -- Subclause (I) shall not apply to any transfer pursuant to a decree of divorce or separate maintenance or a written instrument incident to such a decree or to any transfer which an individual establishes did not have as its principal purpose the avoidance of tax or payment of tax.

(d) Allocation of deficiency. -- For purposes of subsection (c) -

(1) In general. -- The portion of any deficiency on a joint return allocated to an individual shall be the amount which bears the same ratio to such deficiency as the net amount of items taken into account in computing the deficiency and allocable to the individual under paragraph (3) bears to the net amount of all items taken into account in computing the deficiency.

(2) Separate treatment of certain items. -- If a deficiency (or portion thereof) is attributable to--

(A) the disallowance of a credit; or

(B) any tax (other than tax imposed by section 1 or 55) required to be included with the joint return; and such item is allocated to one individual under paragraph (3), such deficiency (or portion) shall be allocated to such individual. Any such item shall not be taken into account under paragraph (1).

(3) Allocation of items giving rise to the deficiency. -- For purposes of this subsection--

(A) In general. -- Except as provided in paragraphs (4) and (5), any item giving rise to a deficiency on a joint return shall be allocated to individuals filing the return in the same manner as it would have been allocated if the individuals had filed separate returns for the taxable year.

(B) Exception where other spouse benefits. -- Under rules prescribed by the Secretary, an item otherwise allocable to an individual under subparagraph (A) shall be allocated to the other individual filing the joint return to the extent the item gave rise to a tax benefit on the joint return to the other individual.

(C) Exception for fraud. -- The Secretary may provide for an allocation of any item in a manner not prescribed by subparagraph (A) if the Secretary establishes that such allocation

Sec. 6015.   Relief from joint and several liability on joint return

is appropriate due to fraud of one or both individuals.

(4) Limitations on separate returns disregarded. -- If an item of deduction or credit is disallowed in its entirety solely because a separate return is filed, such disallowance shall be disregarded and the item shall be computed as if a joint return had been filed and then allocated between the spouses appropriately. A similar rule shall apply for purposes of section 86.

(5) Child's liability. -- If the liability of a child of a taxpayer is included on a joint return, such liability shall be disregarded in computing the separate liability of either spouse and such liability shall be allocated appropriately between the spouses.

***

(f) Equitable relief. -- Under procedures prescribed by the Secretary, if--

(1) taking into account all the facts and circumstances, it is inequitable to hold the individual liable for any unpaid tax or any deficiency (or any portion of either); and

(2) relief is not available to such individual under subsection (b) or (c),

the Secretary may relieve such individual of such liability.

***

Sec. 6041.   Information at source

(a) Payments of $600 or more. -- All persons engaged in a trade or business and making payment in the course of such trade or business to another person, of rent, salaries, wages, premiums, annuities, compensations, remunerations, emoluments, or other fixed or determinable gains, profits, and income (other than payments to which section 6042(a)(1), 6044(a)(1), 6047(e), 6049(a), or 6050N(a) applies, and other than payments with respect to which a statement is required under the authority of section 6042(a)(2), 6044(a)(2), or 6045), of $600 or more in any taxable year, or, in the case of such payments made by the United States, the officers or employees of the United States having information as to such payments and required to make returns in regard thereto by the regulations hereinafter provided for, shall render a true and accurate return to the Secretary, under such regulations and in such form and manner and to such extent as may be prescribed by the Secretary, setting forth the amount of such gains, profits, and income, and the name and address of the recipient of such payment.

***

Sec. 6041A.   Returns regarding payments of remuneration for services and direct sales

(a) Returns regarding remuneration for services. -- If--

(1) any service-recipient engaged in a trade or business pays in the course of such trade or business during any calendar year remuneration to any person for services performed by such person, and

(2) the aggregate of such remuneration paid to such person during such calendar year is $600 or more,

then the service-recipient shall make a return, according to the forms or regulations prescribed by the Secretary, setting forth the aggregate amount of such payments and the name and address of the recipient of such payments. For purposes of the preceding sentence, the term "service-recipient" means the person for whom the service is performed.

***

Sec. 6042. Returns regarding payments of dividends and corporate earnings and profits

Sec. 6042. Returns regarding payments of dividends and corporate earnings and profits

(a) **Requirement of reporting.** --

    (1) In general. -- Every person--

        (A) who makes payments of dividends aggregating $10 or more to any other person during any calendar year, or

5   **(B)** who receives payments of dividends as a nominee and who makes payments aggregating $10 or more during any calendar year to any other person with respect to the dividends so received, shall make a return according to the forms or regulations prescribed by the Secretary, setting forth the aggregate amount of such payments and the name and address of the person to whom paid.

10   **(2) Returns required by the Secretary.** -- Every person who makes payments of dividends aggregating less than $10 to any other person during any calendar year shall, when required by the Secretary, make a return setting forth the aggregate amount of such payments, and the name and address of the person to whom paid.

(b) **Dividend defined.** --

15   **(1) General rule.** -- For purposes of this section, the term "dividend" means--

        (A) any distribution by a corporation which is a dividend (as defined in section 316); and

        (B) any payment made by a stockbroker to any person as a substitute for a dividend (as so defined).

***

Sec. 6045. Returns of brokers

20 (a) **General rule.** -- Every person doing business as a broker shall, when required by the Secretary, make a return, in accordance with such regulations as the Secretary may prescribe, showing the name and address of each customer, with such details regarding gross proceeds and such other information as the Secretary may by forms or regulations require with respect to such business.

25 ***

(c) **Definitions.** -- For purposes of this section -

    (1) Broker. -- The term "broker" includes--

        (A) a dealer,

        (B) a barter exchange, and

30   **(C)** any other person who (for a consideration) regularly acts as a middleman with respect to property or services.

A person shall not be treated as a broker with respect to activities consisting of managing a farm on behalf of another person.

    (2) Customer. -- The term "customer" means any person for whom the broker has transacted
35 any business.

    (3) Barter exchange. -- The term "barter exchange" means any organization of members providing property or services who jointly contract to trade or barter such property or services.

    (4) Person. -- The term "person" includes any governmental unit and any agency or instrumentality thereof.

Sec. 6045. Returns of brokers

***

(e) Return required in the case of real estate transactions. --

(1) In general. -- In the case of a real estate transaction, the real estate reporting person shall file a return under subsection (a) and a statement under subsection (b) with respect to such transaction.   5

(2) Real estate reporting person. -- For purposes of this subsection, the term "real estate reporting person" means any of the following persons involved in a real estate transaction in the following order:

(A) the person (including any attorney or title company) responsible for closing the transaction,   10

(B) the mortgage lender,

(C) the seller's broker,

(D) the buyer's broker, or

(E) such other person designated in regulations prescribed by the Secretary.

Any person treated as a real estate reporting person under the preceding sentence shall be 15 treated as a broker for purposes of subsection (c)(1).

(3) Prohibition of separate charge for filing return. -- It shall be unlawful for any real estate reporting person to separately charge any customer for complying with any requirement of paragraph (1). Nothing in this paragraph shall be construed to prohibit the real estate reporting person from taking into account its cost of complying with such requirement in 20 establishing its charge (other than a separate charge for complying with such requirement) to any customer for performing services in the case of a real estate transaction.

(4) Additional information required. -- In the case of a real estate transaction involving a residence, the real estate reporting person shall include the following information on the return under subsection (a) and on the statement under subsection (b):   25

(A) The portion of any real property tax which is treated as a tax imposed on the purchaser by reason of section 164(d)(1)(B).

(B) Whether or not the financing (if any) of the seller was federally-subsidized indebtedness (as defined in section 143(m)(3)).

(5) Exception for sales or exchanges of certain principal residences. --   30

(A) In general. -- Paragraph (1) shall not apply to any sale or exchange of a residence for $250,000 or less if the person referred to in paragraph (2) receives written assurance in a form acceptable to the Secretary from the seller that--

(i) such residence is the principal residence (within the meaning of section 121) of the seller,   35

(ii) if the Secretary requires the inclusion on the return under subsection (a) of information as to whether there is federally subsidized mortgage financing assistance with respect to the mortgage on residences, that there is no such assistance with respect to the mortgage on such residence, and

(iii) the full amount of the gain on such sale or exchange is excludable from gross 40 income under section 121.

If such assurance includes an assurance that the seller is married, the preceding sentence shall be applied by substituting "$500,000" for "$250,000".

The Secretary may by regulation increase the dollar amounts under this subparagraph if the Secretary determines that such an increase will not materially reduce revenues to the Treasury.   45

(B) Seller. -- For purposes of this paragraph, the term "seller" includes the person

Sec. 6045. Returns of brokers

relinquishing the residence in an exchange.

(f) Return required in the case of payments to attorneys. --

(1) In general. -- Any person engaged in a trade or business and making a payment (in the course of such trade or business) to which this subsection applies shall file a return under subsection (a) and a statement under subsection (b) with respect to such payment.

(2) Application of subsection. --

(A) In general. -- This subsection shall apply to any payment to an attorney in connection with legal services (whether or not such services are performed for the payor).

(B) Exception. -- This subsection shall not apply to the portion of any payment which is required to be reported under section 6041(a) (or would be so required but for the dollar limitation contained therein) or section 6051.

Reg. § 1.6045-1 Returns of information of brokers and barter exchanges.

(a) *Definitions*. The following definitions apply for purposes of this section and § 1.6045-2:

***

(4) The term barter exchange means any person with members or clients that contract either with each other or with such person to trade or barter property or services either directly or through such person. The term does not include arrangements that provide solely for the informal exchange of similar services on a noncommercial basis.

***

[T.D. 7873, 48 FR 10304, Mar. 11, 1983; T.D. 7932, 48 FR 57485, Dec. 30, 1983; 49 FR 2469, Jan. 20, 1984; T.D. 7960, 49 FR 22283, May 29, 1984; T.D. 8445, 57 FR 53032, Nov. 6, 1992; T.D. 8452, 57 FR 58984, Dec. 14, 1992; T.D. 8683, 61 FR 53060, Oct. 10, 1996; T.D. 8734, 62 FR 53476, Oct. 14, 1997; T.D. 8445, 63 FR 12410, Mar. 13, 1998; T.D. 8770, 63 FR 35519, June 30, 1998; T.D. 8804, 63 FR 72186, 72188, Dec. 31, 1998; T.D. 8856, 64 FR 73411, 73412, Dec. 30, 1999; T.D. 8881, 65 FR 32206, 32212, May 22, 2000; T.D. 8895, 65 FR 50407, Aug. 18, 2000; 66 FR 18189, Apr. 6, 2001; T.D. 9010, 67 FR 48758, July 26, 2002; T.D. 9241, 71 FR 4025, Jan. 24, 2006]

Sec. 6053. Reporting of tips

(a) Reports by employees. -- Every employee who, in the course of his employment by an employer, receives in any calendar month tips which are wages (as defined in section 3121(a) or section 3401(a)) or which are compensation (as defined in section 3231(e)) shall report all such tips in one or more written statements furnished to his employer on or before the 10th day following such month. Such statements shall be furnished by the employee under such regulations, at such other times before such 10th day, and in such form and manner, as may be prescribed by the Secretary.

(b) Statements furnished by employers. -- If the tax imposed by section 3101 or section 3201 (as the case may be) with respect to tips reported by an employee pursuant to subsection (a) exceeds the tax which can be collected by the employer pursuant to section 3102 or section 3202 (as the case may be), the employer shall furnish to the employee a written statement showing the amount of such excess. The statement required to be furnished pursuant to this subsection shall be furnished at such time, shall contain such other information, and shall be in such form as the Secretary may by regulations prescribe. When required by such regulations, a duplicate of any such statement shall be filed with the Secretary.

(c) Reporting requirements relating to certain large food or beverage establishments. --

Sec. 6053. Reporting of tips

(1) Report to Secretary. -- In the case of a large food or beverage establishment, each employer shall report to the Secretary, at such time and manner as the Secretary may prescribe by regulation, the following information with respect to each calendar year:

(A) The gross receipts of such establishment from the provision of food and beverages (other than nonallocable receipts).

(B) The aggregate amount of charge receipts (other than nonallocable receipts).

(C) The aggregate amount of charged tips shown on such charge receipts.

(D) The sum of--

(i) the aggregate amount reported by employees to the employer under subsection (a), plus

(ii) the amount the employer is required to report under section 6051 with respect to service charges of less than 10 percent.

(E) With respect to each employee, the amount allocated to such employee under paragraph (3).

(2) Furnishing of statement to employees. -- Each employer described in paragraph (1) shall furnish, in such manner as the Secretary may prescribe by regulations, to each employee of the large food or beverage establishment a written statement for each calendar year showing the following information:

(A) The name and address of such employer.

(B) The name of the employee.

(C) The amount allocated to the employee under paragraph (3) for all payroll periods ending within the calendar year.

Any statement under this paragraph shall be furnished to the employee during January of the calendar year following the calendar year for which such statement is made.

(3) Employee allocation of 8 percent of gross receipts. --

(A) In general. -- For purposes of paragraphs (1)(E) and (2)(C), the employer of a large food or beverage establishment shall allocate (as tips for purposes of the requirements of this subsection) among employees performing services during any payroll period who customarily receive tip income an amount equal to the excess of--

(i) 8 percent of the gross receipts (other than nonallocable receipts) of such establishment for the payroll period, over

(ii) the aggregate amount reported by such employees to the employer under subsection (a) for such period.

(B) Method of allocation. -- The employer shall allocate the amount under subparagraph (A)--

(i) on the basis of a good faith agreement by the employer and the employees, or

(ii) in the absence of an agreement under clause (i), in the manner determined under regulations prescribed by the Secretary.

(C) The Secretary may lower the percentage required to be allocated. -- Upon the petition of the employer or the majority of employees of such employer, the Secretary may reduce (but not below 2 percent) the percentage of gross receipts required to be allocated under subparagraph (A) where he determines that the percentage of gross receipts constituting tips is less than 8 percent.

(4) Large food or beverage establishment. -- For purposes of this subsection, the term "large food or beverage establishment" means any trade or business (or portion thereof)--

Sec. 6053. Reporting of tips

(A) which provides food or beverages,

(B) with respect to which the tipping of employees serving food or beverages by customers is customary, and

(C) which normally employed more than 10 employees on a typical business day during the preceding calendar year.

For purposes of subparagraph (C), rules similar to the rules of subsections (a) and (b) of section 52 shall apply under regulations prescribed by the Secretary, and an individual who owns 50 percent or more in value of the stock of the corporation operating the establishment shall not be treated as an employee.

(5) Employer not to be liable for wrong allocations. -- The employer shall not be liable to any person if any amount is improperly allocated under paragraph (3)(B) if such allocation is done in accordance with the regulations prescribed under paragraph (3)(B).

(6) Nonallocable receipts defined. -- For purposes of this subsection, the term "nonallocable receipts" means receipts which are allocable to--

(A) carryout sales, or

(B) services with respect to which a service charge of 10 percent or more is added.

(7) Application to new businesses. -- The Secretary shall prescribe regulations for the application of this subsection to new businesses.

Sec. 6061. Signing of returns and other documents

(a) General rule. -- Except as otherwise provided by subsection (b) and sections 6062 and 6063, any return, statement, or other document required to be made under any provision of the internal revenue laws or regulations shall be signed in accordance with forms or regulations prescribed by the Secretary.

***

Sec. 6071. Time for filing returns and other documents

(a) General rule. -- When not otherwise provided for by this title, the Secretary shall by regulations prescribe the time for filing any return, statement, or other document required by this title or by regulations.

***

Reg. § 31.6071(a)-1 Time for filing returns and other documents.

(a) *Federal Insurance Contributions Act and income tax withheld from wages and from nonpayroll payments--(1) Quarterly or annual returns.* Except as provided in subparagraph (4) of this paragraph, each return required to be made under §§ 31.6011(a)-1 and 31.6011(a)-1T, in respect of the taxes imposed by the Federal Insurance Contributions Act (26 U.S.C. 3101-3128), or required to be made under §§ 31.6011(a)-4 and 31.6011(a)-4T, in respect of income tax withheld, shall be filed on or before the last day of the first calendar month following the period for which it is made. However, a return may be filed on or before the 10th day of the second calendar month following such period if timely deposits under section 6302(c) of the Code and the regulations thereunder have been made in full payment of such taxes due for the period. For the purpose of the preceding sentence, a deposit which is not required by such regulations in respect of the return period may be made on or before the last day of the first calendar month following the close of such period, and the timeliness of any deposit will be determined by the earliest date stamped on the applicable deposit form by an authorized financial institution.

(2) *Monthly tax returns.* Each return in respect of the taxes imposed by the Federal Insurance Contributions Act or of income tax withheld which is required to be made under paragraph (a) of § 31.6011(a)-5 shall be filed on or before the fifteenth day of the first calendar month following the period for which it is made.   5

(3) *Information returns*--(i) *General rule.* Each information return in respect of wages as defined in the Federal Insurance Contributions Act or of income tax withheld from wages which is required to be made under § 31.6051-2 shall be filed on or before the last day of February (March 31 if filed electronically) of the year following the calendar year for which it is made, except that, if a tax return under § 31.6011(a)-5(a) is filed as a final return for a   10 period ending prior to December 31, the information statement shall be filed on or before the last day of the second calendar month following the period for which the tax return is filed.

(ii) *Expedited filing*--(A) *General rule.* If an employer who is required to make a return pursuant to § 31.6011(a)-1 or § 31.6011(a)-4 is required to make a final return on Form   15 941, or a variation thereof, under § 31.6011(a)-6(a)(1) (relating to the final return for Federal Insurance Contributions Act taxes and income tax withholding from wages), the return which is required to be made under § 31.6051-2 must be filed on or before the last day of the second calendar month following the period for which the final return is filed. The requirements set forth in this paragraph (a)(3)(ii) do not apply to employers with   20 respect to employees whose wages are for domestic service in the private home of the employer. See § 31.6011(a)-1(a)(3).

***

(4) *Employee returns under Federal Insurance Contributions Act.* A return of employee tax under section 3101 required under paragraph (d) of § 31.6011(a)-1 to be made by an   25 individual for a calendar year on Form 1040 shall be filed on or before the due date of such individual's return of income (see § 1.6012-1 of this chapter (Income Tax Regulations)) for the calendar year, or, if the individual makes his return of income on a fiscal year basis, on or before the due date of his return of income for the fiscal year beginning in the calendar year for which a return of employee tax is required. A return of   30 employee tax under section 3101 required under paragraph (d) of § 31.601(a)-1 to be made for a calendar year--

(i) On Form 1040SS or Form 1040PR, or

(ii) On Form 1040 by an individual who is not required to make a return of income for the calendar year or for a fiscal year beginning in such calendar year, shall be filed on or   35 before the 15th day of the fourth month following the close of the calendar year.

(b) *Railroad Retirement Tax Act.* Each return of the taxes imposed by the Railroad Retirement Tax Act required to be made under § 31.6011(a)-2 shall be filed on or before the last day of the second calendar month following the period for which it is made.

(c) *Federal Unemployment Tax Act.* Each return of the tax imposed by the Federal   40 Unemployment Tax Act required to be made under § 31.6011(a)-3 shall be filed on or before the last day of the first calendar month following the period for which it is made. However, a return for a period which ends after December 31, 1970, may be filed on or before the 10th day of the second calendar month following such period if timely deposits under section 6302(c) of the Code and the regulations thereunder have been made in full   45 payment of such tax due for the period. For the purpose of the preceding sentence, a deposit which is not required by such regulations in respect of the return period may be made on or before the last day of the first calendar month following the close of such period, and the timeliness of any deposit will be determined by the date the deposit is received (or is deemed received under section 7502(e)) by an authorized financial   50 institution whichever is earlier.

Sec. 6071.   Time for filing returns and other documents

(d) *Last day for filing.* For provisions relating to the time for filing a return when the prescribed due date falls on Saturday, Sunday, or a legal holiday, see the provisions of § 301.7503-1 of this chapter (Regulations on Procedure and Administration).

(e) *Late filing.* For additions to the tax in case of failure to file a return within the prescribed time, see the provisions of § 301.6651-1 of this chapter (Regulations on Procedure and Administration).

***

[T.D. 6516, 25 FR 13032, Dec. 20, 1960; T.D. 6941, 32 FR 18041, Dec. 16, 1967; T.D. 7001, 34 FR 1005, Jan. 23, 1969; T.D. 7078, 35 FR 18525, Dec. 5, 1970; T.D. 7351, 40 FR 17146, Apr. 17, 1975; T.D. 7953, 49 FR 19644, May 9, 1984; T.D. 8504, 58 FR 68035, Dec. 23, 1993; T.D. 8895, 65 FR 50408, Aug. 18, 2000; T.D. 8952, 66 FR 33832, June 26, 2001; T.D. 9239, 71 FR 14, Jan. 3, 2006]

Sec. 6072.   Time for filing income tax returns

(a) **General rule.** -- In the case of returns under section 6012, 6013, 6017, or 6031 (relating to income tax under subtitle A), returns made on the basis of the calendar year shall be filed on or before the 15th day of April following the close of the calendar year and returns made on the basis of a fiscal year shall be filed on or before the 15th day of the fourth month following the close of the fiscal year, except as otherwise provided in the following subsections of this section.

(b) **Returns of corporations.** -- Returns of corporations under section 6012 made on the basis of the calendar year shall be filed on or before the 15th day of March following the close of the calendar year, and such returns made on the basis of a fiscal year shall be filed on or before the 15th day of the third month following the close of the fiscal year. Returns required for a taxable year by section 6011(e)(2) (relating to returns of a DISC) shall be filed on or before the fifteenth day of the ninth month following the close of the taxable year.

Sec. 6103.   Confidentiality and disclosure of returns and return information

(a) **General rule.** -- Returns and return information shall be confidential, and except as authorized by this title--

(1) no officer or employee of the United States,

(2) no officer or employee of any State, any local law enforcement agency receiving information under subsection (i)(7)(A), any local child support enforcement agency, or any local agency administering a program listed in subsection (l)(7)(D) who has or had access to returns or return information under this section, and

(3) no other person (or officer or employee thereof) who has or had access to returns or return information under subsection (e)(1)(D)(iii), paragraph (6), (12), (16), (19), or (20) of subsection (l), paragraph (2) or (4)(B) of subsection (m), or subsection (n),

shall disclose any return or return information obtained by him in any manner in connection with his service as such an officer or an employee or otherwise or under the provisions of this section. For purposes of this subsection, the term "officer or employee" includes a former officer or employee.

***

Sec. 6109. Identifying numbers

(a) **Supplying of identifying numbers.** -- When required by regulations prescribed by the Secretary:

(1) **Inclusion in returns.** -- Any person required under the authority of this title to make a return, statement, or other document shall include in such return, statement, or other document such identifying number as may be prescribed for securing proper identification of such 5 person.

(2) **Furnishing number to other persons.** -- Any person with respect to whom a return, statement, or other document is required under the authority of this title to be made by another person or whose identifying number is required to be shown on a return of another person shall furnish to such other person such identifying number as may be prescribed for securing his 10 proper identification.

***

Reg. § 301.6110-1 Public inspection of written determinations and background file documents.

(a) *General rule.* Except as provided in § 301.6110-3, relating to deletion of certain 15 information, § 301.6110-5(b), relating to actions to restrain disclosure, paragraph (b)(2) of this section, relating to technical advice memoranda involving civil fraud and criminal investigations, and jeopardy and termination assessments, and paragraph (b)(3) of this section, relating to general written determinations relating to accounting or funding periods and methods, the text of any written determination (as defined in § 20 301.6110-2(a)) issued pursuant to a request postmarked or hand delivered after October 31, 1976, shall be open to public inspection in the places provided in paragraph (c)(1) of this section. The text of any written determination issued pursuant to a request postmarked or hand delivered before November 1, 1976, shall be open to public inspection pursuant to section 6110(h) and § 301.6110-6, when funds are appropriated by 25 Congress for such purpose. The procedures and rules set forth in §§ 301.6110-1 through 301.6110-5 and 301.6110-7 do not apply to written determinations issued pursuant to requests postmarked or hand delivered before November 1, 1976, unless § 301.6110-6 states otherwise. There shall also be open to public inspection in each place of public inspection an index to the written determinations open or subject to inspection at such 30 place. Each such index shall be arranged by section of the Internal Revenue Code, related statute, or tax treaty and by subject matter description with such section in such manner as the Commissioner may from time to time provide. The Commissioner shall not be required to make any written determination or background file document open to public inspection pursuant to section 6110 or refrain from disclosure of any such 35 documents or any information therein, except as provided by section 6110 or with respect to a discovery order made in connection with a judicial proceeding. The provisions of section 6110 shall not apply to matters for which the determination of whether public inspection should occur is made pursuant to section 6104. Matters within the ambit of section 6104 include: Any application filed with the Internal Revenue Service with respect 40 to the qualification or exempt status of an organization, plan, or account described in section 6104(a)(1), whether the plan or account has more than 25 or less than 26 participants; any document issued by the Internal Revenue Service in which the qualification or exempt status of an organization, plan, or account described in section 6104 (a)(1) is granted, denied or revoked or the portion of any document in which 45 technical advice with respect thereto is given to a district director; any application filed, and any document issued by the Internal Revenue Service, with respect to the qualification or status of master, prototype, and pattern employee plans; the portion of

Sec. 6109. Identifying numbers

any document issued by the Internal Revenue Service in which is discussed the effect on the qualification or exempt status of an organization, plan, or account described in section 6104(a)(1) of proposed transactions by such organization, plan, or account; and any document issued by the Internal Revenue Service in which is discussed the
5 qualification or status of an organization described in section 509(a) or 4942(j)(3), but not including any document issued to nonexempt charitable trusts described in section 4947(a)(1).

(b) *Items that may be inspected only under certain circumstances*--(1) *Background file documents.* A background file document (as such term is defined in § 301.6110-2(g))
10 relating to a particular written determination issued pursuant to a request postmarked or hand delivered after October 31, 1976, shall not be subject to inspection until such written determination is open to public inspection or available for inspection pursuant to paragraph (b)(2) or (3) of this section, and then only if a written request pursuant to paragraph (c)(4) of this section is made for inspection of such background file document.
15 Background file documents relating to written determinations issued pursuant to requests postmarked or hand delivered before November 1, 1976, shall be subject to inspection pursuant to section 6110(h) and § 301.6110-6, when funds are appropriated by Congress for such purpose. The version of the background file document which is available for inspection shall be the version originally made available for inspection, as modified by
20 any additional disclosure pursuant to sections 6110(d)(3) and (f)(4).

(2) *Technical advice memoranda involving civil fraud and criminal investigations, jeopardy and termination assessments.* Any technical advice memorandum (as such term is defined in § 301.6110-2(f) involving any matter that is the subject of a civil fraud or criminal investigation, a jeopardy assessment (as such term is defined in section 6861),
25 or a termination assessment (as such term is defined in section 6851) shall not be subject to inspection until all actions relating to such investigation or assessment are completed and then only if a written request pursuant to paragraph (c)(4) of this section is made for inspection of such technical advice memorandum. A ``civil fraud investigation" is any administrative step or judicial proceeding in which an issue for determination is
30 whether the Commissioner should impose additional tax pursuant to section 6653(b). A ``criminal investigation" is any administrative step or judicial proceeding in which an issue for determination is whether a taxpayer should be charged with or is guilty of criminal conduct. An action relating to a civil fraud or criminal investigation includes any such administrative step or judicial proceeding, the review of subsequent related activities and
35 related returns of the taxpayer or related taxpayers, and any other administrative step or judicial procedure or proceeding or appellate process that is initiated as a consequence of the facts and circumstances disclosed by such investigation. An action relating to a jeopardy or termination assessment includes any administrative step or judicial proceeding that is initiated to determine whether to make such assessment, that is
40 brought pursuant to section 7429 to determine the appropriateness or reasonableness of such assessment, or that is brought to resolve the legal consequences of the tax status or liability issue underlying the making of such assessment. Any action relating to a civil fraud or criminal investigation, a jeopardy assessment, or a termination assessment is not completed until all available administrative steps and judicial proceedings and
45 remedies, including appeals, have been completed.

(3) *Written determinations with respect to adoption of or change in certain accounting or funding periods and methods.* Any general written determination (as defined in § 301.6110-2(c) that relates solely to approval of any adoption of or change in--
(i) The funding method or plan year of a plan under section 412.
50 (ii) A taxpayer's annual accounting period under section 442.
(iii) A taxpayer's method of accounting under section 446(e), or

Sec. 6109. Identifying numbers

(iv) A partnership's or partner's taxable year under section 706 shall not be subject to inspection until such written determination would, but for this paragraph (b)(3), be open to public inspection pursuant to § 301.6110-5(c) and then only if a written request pursuant to paragraph (c)(4) of this section is made for inspection of such written determination.

(c) *Procedure for public inspection*--(1) *Place of public inspection*. The text of any 5 ruling (as such term is defined in § 301.6110-2(d) or technical advice memorandum that is open to public inspection pursuant to section 6110 shall be located in the National Office Reading Room. The text of any determination letter (as such term is defined in § 301.6110-2(e)) that is open to public inspection pursuant to section 6110 shall be located in the Reading Room of the Regional Office in which is located the district office that 10 issued such determination letter. Inspection of any written determination subject to inspection only upon written request shall be requested from the National Office Reading Room. Inspection of any background file document shall be requested only from the reading room in which the related written determination is either open to public inspection or subject to inspection upon written request. The locations and mailing addresses of the 15 reading rooms are set forth in § 601.702(b)(3)(ii) of this chapter.

(2) *Time and manner of public inspection*. The inspection authorized by section 6110 will be allowed only in the place provided for such inspection in the presence of an Internal Revenue officer or employee and only during the regular hours of business of the Internal Revenue Service office in which the reading room is located. The public will not 20 be allowed to remove any record from a reading room. A person who wishes to inspect reading room material without visiting a reading room may submit a written request pursuant to paragraph (c)(4) of this section for copies of any such material to the Internal Revenue Service reading room in which is located such material.

(3) *Copies*. Notes may be taken of any material open to public inspection under 25 section 6110, and copies may be made manually. Copies of any material open to public inspection or subject to inspection upon written request will be furnished by the Internal Revenue Service to any person making requests therefor pursuant to paragraph (c)(4) of this section. If made at the time of inspection the request for copies need not be in writing, unless the material is not immediately available for copying. The Commissioner 30 may prescribe fees pursuant to section 6110(j) for furnishing copies of material open or subject to inspection.

(4) *Requests*. Any request for copies of written determinations, for inspection of general written determinations relating to accounting or funding periods and methods or technical advice memoranda involving civil fraud and criminal investigations, and 35 jeopardy and termination assessments, for inspection or copies of background file documents, and for copies of the index shall be submitted to the reading room in which is located the requested material. If made in person, the request may be submitted to the internal revenue employee supervising the reading room. The request shall contain:

(i) Authorization for the Internal Revenue Service to charge the person making such 40 request for making copies, searching for material, and making deletions therefrom;

(ii) The maximum amount of charges which the Internal Revenue Service may incur without further authorization from the person making such request;

(iii) With respect to requests for inspection and copies of background file documents, the file number of the written determination to which such background file document 45 relates and a specific identification of the nature or type of the background file document requested;

(iv) With respect to requests for inspections of general written determinations relating to accounting or funding periods and methods, the day, week, or month of issuance of such written determination, and the applicable category as selected from a special 50 summary listing of categories prepared by the Internal Revenue Service;

Sec. 6109. Identifying numbers

(v) With respect to requests for copies of written determinations, the file number of the written determination to be copied, which can be ascertained in the reading room or from the index;

(vi) With respect to requests for copies of portions of the index, the section of the Internal Revenue Code, related statute or tax treaty in which the person making such request is interested;

(vii) With respect to material which is to be mailed, the name, address, and telephone number of the person making such request and the address to which copies of the requested material should be sent; and

(viii) Such other information as the Internal Revenue Service may from time to time require in its operation of reading rooms.

[T.D. 7524, 42 FR 63412, Dec. 16, 1977]

Sec. 6111. Disclosure of reportable transactions

(a) In general. -- Each material advisor with respect to any reportable transaction shall make a return (in such form as the Secretary may prescribe) setting forth--

(1) information identifying and describing the transaction,

(2) information describing any potential tax benefits expected to result from the transaction, and

(3) such other information as the Secretary may prescribe.

Such return shall be filed not later than the date specified by the Secretary.

(b) Definitions. -- For purposes of this section:

(1) Material advisor. --

(A) In general. -- The term "material advisor" means any person--

(i) who provides any material aid, assistance, or advice with respect to organizing, managing, promoting, selling, implementing, insuring, or carrying out any reportable transaction, and

(ii) who directly or indirectly derives gross income in excess of the threshold amount (or such other amount as may be prescribed by the Secretary) for such advice or assistance.

(B) Threshold amount. -- For purposes of subparagraph (A), the threshold amount is--

(i) $50,000 in the case of a reportable transaction substantially all of the tax benefits from which are provided to natural persons, and

(ii) $250,000 in any other case.

(2) Reportable transaction. -- The term "reportable transaction" has the meaning given to such term by section 6707A(c).

(c) Regulations. -- The Secretary may prescribe regulations which provide--

(1) that only 1 person shall be required to meet the requirements of subsection (a) in cases in which 2 or more persons would otherwise be required to meet such requirements,

(2) exemptions from the requirements of this section, and

(3) such rules as may be necessary or appropriate to carry out the purposes of this section.

***

Sec. 6115.   Disclosure related to quid pro quo contributions

(a) **Disclosure requirement.** -- If an organization described in section 170(c) (other than paragraph (1) thereof) receives a quid pro quo contribution in excess of $75, the organization shall, in connection with the solicitation or receipt of the contribution, provide a written statement which-

    (1) informs the donor that the amount of the contribution that is deductible for Federal 5 income tax purposes is limited to the excess of the amount of any money and the value of any property other than money contributed by the donor over the value of the goods or services provided by the organization, and

    (2) provides the donor with a good faith estimate of the value of such goods or services.

(b) **Quid pro quo contribution.** -- For purposes of this section, the term "quid pro quo 10 contribution" means a payment made partly as a contribution and partly in consideration for goods or services provided to the payor by the donee organization. A quid pro quo contribution does not include any payment made to an organization, organized exclusively for religious purposes, in return for which the taxpayer receives solely an intangible religious benefit that generally is not sold in a commercial transaction outside the donative context. 15

***

Sec. 6151.   Time and place for paying tax shown on returns

(a) **General rule.** -- Except as otherwise provided in this subchapter, when a return of tax is required under this title or regulations, the person required to make such return shall, without assessment or notice and demand from the Secretary, pay such tax to the internal revenue officer 20 with whom the return is filed, and shall pay such tax at the time and place fixed for filing the return (determined without regard to any extension of time for filing the return).

***

Sec. 6201.   Assessment authority

(a) **Authority of Secretary.** -- The Secretary is authorized and required to make the inquiries, 25 determinations, and assessments of all taxes (including interest, additional amounts, additions to the tax, and assessable penalties) imposed by this title, or accruing under any former internal revenue law, which have not been duly paid by stamp at the time and in the manner provided by law. Such authority shall extend to and include the following:

    (1) **Taxes shown on return.** -- The Secretary shall assess all taxes determined by the 30 taxpayer or by the Secretary as to which returns or lists are made under this title.

***

Reg. § 301.6203-1   Method of assessment.

The district director and the director of the regional service center shall appoint one or more assessment officers. The district director shall also appoint assessment officers in a 35 Service Center servicing his district. The assessment shall be made by an assessment officer signing the summary record of assessment. The summary record, through supporting records, shall provide identification of the taxpayer, the character of the liability assessed, the taxable period, if applicable, and the amount of the assessment. The amount of the assessment shall, in the case of tax shown on a return by the taxpayer, be 40 the amount so shown, and in all other cases the amount of the assessment shall be the amount shown on the supporting list or record. The date of the assessment is the date the summary record is signed by an assessment officer. If the taxpayer requests a copy of the record of assessment, he shall be furnished a copy of the pertinent parts of the assessment which set forth the name of the taxpayer, the date of assessment, the 45 character of the liability assessed, the taxable period, if applicable, and the amounts assessed.

Sec. 6211. Definition of a deficiency

5   **(a) In general.** -- For purposes of this title in the case of income, estate, and gift taxes imposed by subtitles A and B and excise taxes imposed by chapters 41, 42, 43, and 44 the term "deficiency" means the amount by which the tax imposed by subtitle A or B, or chapter 41, 42, 43, or 44 exceeds the excess of--

    (1) the sum of

10   **(A)** the amount shown as the tax by the taxpayer upon his return, if a return was made by the taxpayer and an amount was shown as the tax by the taxpayer thereon, plus

        (B) the amounts previously assessed (or collected without assessment) as a deficiency, over--

    (2) the amount of rebates, as defined in subsection (b)(2), made.

15   **(b) Rules for application of subsection (a).** -- For purposes of this section--

    (1) The tax imposed by subtitle A and the tax shown on the return shall both be determined without regard to payments on account of estimated tax, without regard to the credit under section 31, without regard to the credit under section 33, and without regard to any credits resulting from the collection of amounts assessed under section 6851 or 6852 (relating to 20 termination assessments).

The term "rebate" means so much of an abatement, credit, refund, or other repayment, as was made on the ground that the tax imposed by subtitle A or B or chapter 41, 42, 43, or 44 was less than the excess of the amount specified in subsection (a)(1) over the rebates previously made.

25   **(3)** The computation by the Secretary, pursuant to section 6014, of the tax imposed by chapter 1 shall be considered as having been made by the taxpayer and the tax so computed considered as shown by the taxpayer upon his return.

    (4) For purposes of subsection (a)--

        (A) any excess of the sum of the credits allowable under sections 24(d), 32, and 34 over 30 the tax imposed by subtitle A (determined without regard to such credits), and

        (B) any excess of the sum of such credits as shown by the taxpayer on his return over the amount shown as the tax by the taxpayer on such return (determined without regard to such credits),

shall be taken into account as negative amounts of tax.

35   ***

Sec. 6213. Restrictions applicable to deficiencies; petition to Tax Court

    (a) Time for filing petition and restriction on assessment. -- Within 90 days, or 150 days if the notice is addressed to a person outside the United States, after the notice of deficiency authorized in section 6212 is mailed (not counting Saturday, Sunday, or a legal holiday in the District of Columbia as the last day), the taxpayer may file a petition with the Tax Court for a 40 redetermination of the deficiency. Except as otherwise provided in section 6851, 6852, or 6861 no assessment of a deficiency in respect of any tax imposed by subtitle A, or B, chapter 41, 42, 43, or 44 and no levy or proceeding in court for its collection shall be made, begun, or prosecuted until such notice has been mailed to the taxpayer, nor until the expiration of such 90-day or 150-day

Sec. 6213. Restrictions applicable to deficiencies; petition to Tax Court

period, as the case may be, nor, if a petition has been filed with the Tax Court, until the decision of the Tax Court has become final. Notwithstanding the provisions of section 7421(a), the making of such assessment or the beginning of such proceeding or levy during the time such prohibition is in force may be enjoined by a proceeding in the proper court, including the Tax Court, and a refund may be ordered by such court of any amount collected within the period during which the 5 Secretary is prohibited from collecting by levy or through a proceeding in court under the provisions of this subsection. The Tax Court shall have no jurisdiction to enjoin any action or proceeding or order any refund under this subsection unless a timely petition for a redetermination of the deficiency has been filed and then only in respect of the deficiency that is the subject of such petition. Any petition filed with the Tax Court on or before the last date specified for filing 10 such petition by the Secretary in the notice of deficiency shall be treated as timely filed.

***

Reg. § 301.6213-1 Restrictions applicable to deficiencies; petition to Tax Court.

(a) *Time for filing petition and restrictions on assessment--*(1) *Time for filing petition.* 15 Within 90 days after notice of the deficiency is mailed (or within 150 days after mailing in the case of such notice addressed to a person outside the States of the Union and the District of Columbia), as provided in section 6212, a petition may be filed with the Tax Court of the United States for a redetermination of the deficiency. In determining such 90-day or 150-day period, Saturday, Sunday, or a legal holiday in the District of Columbia is 20 not counted as the 90th or 150th day. In determining the time for filing a petition with the Tax Court in the case of a notice of deficiency mailed to a resident of Alaska prior to 12:01 p.m., e.s.t., January 3, 1959, and in the case of a notice of deficiency mailed to a resident of Hawaii prior to 4 p.m., e.d.s.t., August 21, 1959, the term ``States of the Union" does not include Alaska or Hawaii, respectively, and the 150-day period applies. 25 In determining the time within which a petition to the Tax Court may be filed in the case of a notice of deficiency mailed to a resident of Alaska after 12:01 p.m., e.s.t., January 3, 1959, and in the case of a notice of deficiency mailed to a resident of Hawaii after 4 p.m., e.d.s.t., August 21, 1959, the term ``States of the Union" includes Alaska and Hawaii, respectively, and the 90-day period applies. 30

(2) *Restrictions on assessment.* Except as otherwise provided by this section, by sections 6851, 6852, and 6861(a) (relating to termination and jeopardy assessments), by section 6871(a) (relating to immediate assessment of claims for income, estate, and gift taxes in bankruptcy and receivership cases), or by section 7485 (in case taxpayer petitions for a review of a Tax Court decision without filing bond), no assessment of a 35 deficiency in respect of a tax imposed by subtitle A or B or chapter 41, 42, 43, or 44 of the Code and no levy or proceeding in court for its collection shall be made until notice of deficiency has been mailed to the taxpayer, nor until the expiration of the 90-day or 150-day period within which a petition may be filed with the Tax Court, nor, if a petition has been filed with the Tax Court, until the decision of the Tax Court has become final. As to 40 the date on which a decision of the Tax court becomes final, see section 7481. Notwithstanding the provisions of section 7421(a), the making of an assessment or the beginning of a proceeding or levy which is forbidden by this paragraph may be enjoined by a proceeding in the proper court. In any case where the running of the time prescribed for filing a petition in the Tax Court with respect to a tax imposed by chapter 42 or 43 is 45 suspended under section 6213(e), no assessment of a deficiency in respect of such tax shall be made until expiration of the entire period for filing the petition.

(b) *Exceptions to restrictions on assessment of deficiencies--*(1) *Mathematical errors.* If a taxpayer is notified of an additional amount of tax due on account of a mathematical error appearing upon the return, such notice is not deemed a notice of deficiency, and the 50 taxpayer has no right to file a petition with the Tax Court upon the basis of such notice, nor is the assessment of such additional amount prohibited by section 6213(a).

(2) *Tentative carryback adjustments.* (i) If the district director or the director of the regional service center determines that any amount applied, credited, or refunded under
5 section 6411(b) with respect to an application for a tentative carryback adjustment is in excess of the overassessment properly attributable to the carryback upon which such application was based, the district director or the director of the regional service center may assess the amount of the excess as a deficiency as if such deficiency were due to a mathematical error appearing on the return. That is, the district director or the director of
10 the regional service center may assess an amount equal to the excess, and such amount may be collected, without regard to the restrictions on assessment and collection imposed by section 6213(a). Thus, the district director or the director of the regional service center may assess such amount without regard to whether the taxpayer has been mailed a prior notice of deficiency. Either before or after assessing such an amount, the
15 district director or the director of the regional service center will notify the taxpayer that such assessment has been or will be made. Such notice will not constitute a notice of deficiency, and the taxpayer may not file a petition with the Tax Court of the United States based on such notice. However, the taxpayer, within the applicable period of limitation, may file a regular claim for credit or refund based on the carryback, if he has not already
20 filed such a claim, and may maintain a suit based on such claim if it is disallowed or if it is not acted upon by the Internal Revenue Service within 6 months from the date the claim was filed.

(ii) The method provided in subdivision (i) of this subparagraph to recover any amount applied, credited, or refunded in respect of an application for a tentative carryback
25 adjustment which should not have been so applied, credited, or refunded is not an exclusive method. Two other methods are available to recover such amount: (a) By way of a deficiency notice under section 6212; or (b) by a suit to recover an erroneous refund under section 7405. Any one or more of the three available methods may be used to recover any amount which was improperly applied, credited, or refunded in respect of an
30 application for a tentative carryback adjustment.

(3) *Assessment of amount paid.* Any payment made after the mailing of a notice of deficiency which is made by the taxpayer as a payment with respect to the proposed deficiency may be assessed without regard to the restrictions on assessment and collection imposed by section 6213(a) even though the taxpayer has not filed a waiver of
35 restrictions on assessment as provided in section 6213(d). A payment of all or part of the deficiency asserted in the notice together with the assessment of the amount so paid will not affect the jurisdiction of the Tax Court. If any payment is made before the mailing of a notice of deficiency, the district director or the director of the regional service center is not prohibited by section 6213(a) from assessing such amount, and such amount may be
40 assessed if such action is deemed to be proper. If such amount is assessed, the assessment is taken into account in determining whether or not there is a deficiency for which a notice of deficiency must be issued. Thus, if such a payment satisfies the taxpayer's tax liability, no notice of deficiency will be mailed and the Tax Court will have no jurisdiction over the matter. In any case in which there is a controversy as to the
45 correct amount of the tax liability, the assessment of any amount pursuant to the provisions of section 6213(b)(3) shall in no way be considered to be the acceptance of an offer by the taxpayer to settle such controversy.

(4) *Jeopardy.* If the district director believes that the assessment or collection of a deficiency will be jeopardized by delay, such deficiency shall be assessed immediately,
50 as provided in section 6861(a).

(c) *Failure to file petition.* If no petition is filed with the Tax Court within the period

Sec. 6213. Restrictions applicable to deficiencies; petition to Tax Court

prescribed in section 6213(a), the district director or the director of the regional service center shall assess the amount determined as the deficiency and of which the taxpayer was notified by registered or certified mail and the taxpayer shall pay the same upon notice and demand therefor. In such case the district director will not be precluded from determining a further deficiency and notifying the taxpayer thereof by registered or 5 certified mail. If a petition is filed with the Tax Court the taxpayer should notify the district director who issued the notice of deficiency that the petition has been filed in order to prevent an assessment of the amount determined to be the deficiency.

(d) *Waiver of restrictions.* The taxpayer may at any time by a signed notice in writing filed with the district director waive the restrictions on the assessment and collection of 10 the whole or any part of the deficiency. The notice must in all cases be filed with the district director or other authorized official under whose jurisdiction the audit or other consideration of the return in question is being conducted. The filing of such notice with the Tax Court does not constitute filing with the district director within the meaning of the Code. After such waiver has been acted upon by the district director and the assessment 15 has been made in accordance with its terms, the waiver cannot be withdrawn.

***

[32 FR 15241, Nov. 3, 1967; T.D. 7838, 47 FR 44250, Oct. 7, 1982; T.D. 8084, 51 FR 16035, May 2, 1986; T.D. 8628, 60 FR 62212, Dec. 5, 1995; T.D. 8920, 66 FR 2171, Jan. 10, 2001]   20

Sec. 6215. Assessment of deficiency found by Tax Court

(a) **General rule.** -- If the taxpayer files a petition with the Tax Court, the entire amount redetermined as the deficiency by the decision of the Tax Court which has become final shall be assessed and shall be paid upon notice and demand from the Secretary. No part of the amount 25 determined as a deficiency by the Secretary but disallowed as such by the decision of the Tax Court which has become final shall be assessed or be collected by levy or by proceeding in court with or without assessment.

***
                                                                                                30

Sec. 6401. Amounts treated as overpayments

(a) **Assessment and collection after limitation period.** -- The term "overpayment" includes that part of the amount of the payment of any internal revenue tax which is assessed or collected after the expiration of the period of limitation properly applicable thereto.

***
                                                                                                35

Reg. § 301.6402-3 Special rules applicable to income tax.
(a) In the case of a claim for credit or refund filed after June 30, 1976--

(1) In general, in the case of an overpayment of income taxes, a claim for credit or refund of such overpayment shall be made on the appropriate income tax return.

(2) In the case of an overpayment of income taxes for a taxable year of an individual 40 for which a Form 1040 or 1040A has been filed, a claim for refund shall be made on Form 1040X (``Amended U.S. Individual Income Tax Return").

(3) In the case of an overpayment of income taxes for a taxable year of a corporation for which a Form 1120 has been filed, a claim for refund shall be made on Form 1120X (``Amended U.S. Corporation Income Tax Return").   45

(4) In the case of an overpayment of income taxes for a taxable year for which a form other than Form 1040, 1040A, or 1120 was filed (such as Form 1041 (U.S. Fiduciary

Sec. 6401. Amounts treated as overpayments

Income Tax Return) or Form 990T (Exempt Organization Business Income Tax Return)), a claim for credit or refund shall be made on the appropriate amended income tax return.

(5) A properly executed individual, fiduciary, or corporation original income tax return or an amended return (on 1040X or 1120X if applicable) shall constitute a claim for refund 5 or credit within the meaning of section 6402 and section 6511 for the amount of the overpayment disclosed by such return (or amended return). For purposes of section 6511, such claim shall be considered as filed on the date on which such return (or amended return) is considered as filed, except that if the requirements of § 301.7502-1, relating to timely mailing treated as timely filing are met, the claim shall be considered to 10 be filed on the date of the postmark stamped on the cover in which the return (or amended return) was mailed. A return or amended return shall constitute a claim for refund or credit if it contains a statement setting forth the amount determined as an overpayment and advising whether such amount shall be refunded to the taxpayer or shall be applied as a credit against the taxpayer's estimated income tax for the taxable 15 year immediately succeeding the taxable year for which such return (or amended return) is filed. If the taxpayer indicates on its return (or amended return) that all or part of the overpayment shown by its return (or amended return) is to be applied to its estimated income tax for its succeeding taxable year, such indication shall constitute an election to so apply such overpayment, and no interest shall be allowed on such portion of the 20 overpayment credited and such amount shall be applied as a payment on account of the estimated income tax for such year or the installments thereof.

(6) Notwithstanding paragraph (a)(5) of this section, the Internal Revenue Service, within the applicable period of limitations, may credit any overpayment of individual, fiduciary, or corporation income tax, including interest thereon, against--
25   (i) First, any outstanding liability for any tax (or for any interest, additional amount, additions to the tax, or assessable penalty) owed by the taxpayer making the overpayment;

(ii) Second, in the case of an individual taxpayer, amounts of past-due support assigned to a State under section 402(a)(26) or 471(a)(17) of the Social Security Act 30 under procedures set forth in the regulations under section 6402(c);

(iii) Third, past-due and legally enforceable debt under procedures set forth in the regulations under section 6402(d); and

(iv) Fourth, qualifying amounts of past-due support not assigned to a State under procedures set forth in the regulations under section 6402 (c).
35 Only the balance, if any, of the overpayment remaining after credits described in this paragraph (a)(6) shall be treated in the manner so elected.

***

(c) The filing of a properly executed income tax return shall, in any case in which the taxpayer is not required to show his tax on such form (see section 6014 and the 40 regulations thereunder), be treated as a claim for refund (or for claims filed before July 1, 1976, constitute an election by the taxpayer to have the return treated as a claim for refund), and such return shall constitute a claim for refund within the meaning of section 6402 and section 6511 for the amount of the overpayment shown by the computation of the tax made by the district director or the director of the regional service center on the 45 basis of the return. For purposes of section 6511, such claim shall be considered as filed on the date on which such return is considered as filed, except that if the requirements of § 301.7502-1, relating to timely mailing treated as timely filing, are met the claim shall be considered to be filed on the date of the postmark stamped on the cover in which the return was mailed.
50   (d) In any case in which a taxpayer elects to have an overpayment refunded to him he may not thereafter change his election to have the overpayment applied as a payment on

Sec. 6401. Amounts treated as overpayments

account of his estimated income tax.

***

[32 FR 15241, Nov. 3, 1967; T.D. 7102, 36 FR 5498, Mar. 24, 1971; T.D. 7234, 37 FR 28163, Dec. 21, 1972; T.D. 7293, 38 FR 32804, Nov. 28, 1973; T.D. 7298, 38 FR 35234, Dec. 26, 1973; T.D. 7410, 41 FR 11020, Mar. 16, 1976; T.D. 7808, 47 FR 5714, Feb. 8, 1982; T.D. 8053, 50 FR 39662, Sept. 30, 1985; T.D. 8734, 62 FR 53495, Oct. 14, 1997]

Sec. 6501. Limitations on assessment and collection

(a) **General rule.** -- Except as otherwise provided in this section, the amount of any tax imposed by this title shall be assessed within 3 years after the return was filed (whether or not such return was filed on or after the date prescribed) or, if the tax is payable by stamp, at any time after such tax became due and before the expiration of 3 years after the date on which any part of such tax was paid, and no proceeding in court without assessment for the collection of such tax shall be begun after the expiration of such period. For purposes of this chapter, the term "return" means the return required to be filed by the taxpayer (and does not include a return of any person from whom the taxpayer has received an item of income, gain, loss, deduction, or credit).

***

(c) **Exceptions.** --

(1) **False return.** -- In the case of a false or fraudulent return with the intent to evade tax, the tax may be assessed, or a proceeding in court for collection of such tax may be begun without assessment, at any time.

(2) **Willful attempt to evade tax.** -- In case of a willful attempt in any manner to defeat or evade tax imposed by this title (other than tax imposed by subtitle A or B), the tax may be assessed, or a proceeding in court for the collection of such tax may be begun without assessment, at any time.

(3) **No return.** -- In the case of failure to file a return, the tax may be assessed, or a proceeding in court for the collection of such tax
may be begun without assessment, at any time.

(4) **Extension by agreement.** --

(A) **In general.** -- Where, before the expiration of the time prescribed in this section for the assessment of any tax imposed by this title, except the estate tax provided in chapter 11, both the Secretary and the taxpayer have consented in writing to its assessment after such time, the tax may be assessed at any time prior to the expiration of the period agreed upon. The period so agreed upon may be extended by subsequent agreements in writing made before the expiration of the period previously agreed upon.

***

(7) **Special rule for certain amended returns.** -- Where, within the 60-day period ending on the day on which the time prescribed in this section for the assessment of any tax imposed by subtitle A for any taxable year would otherwise expire, the Secretary receives a written document signed by the taxpayer showing that the taxpayer owes an additional amount of such tax for such taxable year, the period for the assessment of such additional amount shall not expire before the day 60 days after the day on which the Secretary receives such document.

***

(10) **Listed transactions.** -- If a taxpayer fails to include on any return or statement for any taxable year any information with respect to a listed transaction (as defined in section 6707A(c)(2)) which is required under section 6011 to be included with such return or

Sec. 6501. Limitations on assessment and collection

statement, the time for assessment of any tax imposed by this title with respect to such transaction shall not expire before the date which is 1 year after the earlier of -

   (A) the date on which the Secretary is furnished the information so required, or

   (B) the date that a material advisor (as defined in section 6111) meets the requirements of section 6112 with respect to a request by the Secretary under section 6112(b) relating to such transaction with respect to such taxpayer.

***

   (e) Substantial omission of items. -- Except as otherwise provided in subsection (c)--

   (1) Income taxes. -- In the case of any tax imposed by subtitle A--

      (A) General rule. -- If the taxpayer omits from gross income an amount properly includible therein which is in excess of 25 percent of the amount of gross income stated in the return, the tax may be assessed, or a proceeding in court for the collection of such tax may be begun without assessment, at any time within 6 years after the return was filed. For purposes of this subparagraph -

         (i) In the case of a trade or business, the term "gross income" means the total of the amounts received or accrued from the sale of goods or services (if such amounts are required to be shown on the return) prior to diminution by the cost of such sales or services; and

         (ii) In determining the amount omitted from gross income, there shall not be taken into account any amount which is omitted from gross income stated in the return if such amount is disclosed in the return, or in a statement attached to the return, in a manner adequate to apprise the Secretary of the nature and amount of such item.

***

   (h) Net operating loss or capital loss carrybacks. -- In the case of a deficiency attributable to the application to the taxpayer of a net operating loss carryback or a capital loss carryback (including deficiencies which may be assessed pursuant to the provisions of section 6213(b)(3)), such deficiency may be assessed at any time before the expiration of the period within which a deficiency for the taxable year of the net operating loss or net capital loss which results in such carryback may be assessed.

***

Sec. 6511. Limitations on credit or refund

   (a) Period of limitation on filing claim. -- Claim for credit or refund of an overpayment of any tax imposed by this title in respect of which tax the taxpayer is required to file a return shall be filed by the taxpayer within 3 years from the time the return was filed or 2 years from the time the tax was paid, whichever of such periods expires the later, or if no return was filed by the taxpayer, within 2 years from the time the tax was paid. Claim for credit or refund of an overpayment of any tax imposed by this title which is required to be paid by means of a stamp shall be filed by the taxpayer within 3 years from the time the tax was paid.

   (b) Limitation on allowance of credits and refunds. --

      (1) Filing of claim within prescribed period. -- No credit or refund shall be allowed or made after the expiration of the period of limitation prescribed in subsection (a) for the filing of a claim for credit or refund, unless a claim for credit or refund is filed by the taxpayer within such period.

      (2) Limit on amount of credit or refund. --

         (A) Limit where claim filed within 3-year period. -- If the claim was filed by the taxpayer during the 3-year period prescribed in subsection (a), the amount of the credit or refund shall not exceed the portion of the tax paid within the period, immediately preceding the filing of the claim, equal to 3 years plus the period of any extension of time for filing the return. If the tax was required to be paid by means of a stamp, the amount of the credit or refund shall not exceed the portion of the tax paid within the 3 years immediately 5 preceding the filing of the claim.

(B) Limit where claim not filed within 3-year period. -- If the claim was not filed within such 3-year period, the amount of the credit or refund shall not exceed the portion of the tax paid during the 2 years immediately preceding the filing of the claim.

(C) Limit if no claim filed. -- If no claim was filed, the credit or refund shall not exceed 10 the amount which would be allowable under subparagraph (A) or (B), as the case may be, if claim was filed on the date the credit or refund is allowed.

(c) Special rules applicable in case of extension of time by agreement. -- If an agreement under the provisions of section 6501(c)(4) extending the period for assessment of a tax imposed by this title is made within the period prescribed in subsection (a) for the filing of a claim for credit or 15 refund -

(1) Time for filing claim. -- The period for filing claim for credit or refund or for making credit or refund if no claim is filed, provided in subsections (a) and (b)(1), shall not expire prior to 6 months after the expiration of the period within which an assessment may be made pursuant to the agreement or any extension thereof under section 6501(c)(4).   20

(2) Limit on amount. -- If a claim is filed, or a credit or refund is allowed when no claim was filed, after the execution of the agreement and within 6 months after the expiration of the period within which an assessment may be made pursuant to the agreement or any extension thereof, the amount of the credit or refund shall not exceed the portion of the tax paid after the execution of the agreement and before the filing of the claim or the making of the credit or 25 refund, as the case may be, plus the portion of the tax paid within the period which would be applicable under subsection (b)(2) if a claim had been filed on the date the agreement was executed.

(3) Claims not subject to special rule. -- This subsection shall not apply in the case of a claim filed, or credit or refund allowed if no claim is filed, either--   30

(A) prior to the execution of the agreement or

(B) more than 6 months after the expiration of the period within which an assessment may be made pursuant to the agreement or any extension thereof.

(d) Special rules applicable to income taxes. --

(1) Seven-year period of limitation with respect to bad debts and worthless securities. -- 35 If the claim for credit or refund relates to an overpayment of tax imposed by subtitle A on account of--

(A) The deductibility by the taxpayer, under section 166 or section 832(c), of a debt as a debt which became worthless, or, under section 165(g), of a loss from worthlessness of a security, or   40

(B) The effect that the deductibility of a debt or loss described in subparagraph (A) has on the application to the taxpayer of a carryover,

in lieu of the 3-year period of limitation prescribed in subsection (a), the period shall be 7 years from the date prescribed by law for filing the return for the year with respect to which the claim is made. If the claim for credit or refund relates to an overpayment on account of the 45 effect that the deductibility of such a debt or loss has on the application to the taxpayer of a carryback, the period shall be either 7 years from the date prescribed by law for filing the return for the year of the net operating loss which results in such carryback or the period

Sec. 6511. Limitations on credit or refund

prescribed in paragraph (2) of this subsection, whichever expires the later. In the case of a claim described in this paragraph the amount of the credit or refund may exceed the portion of the tax paid within the period prescribed in subsection (b)(2) or (c), whichever is applicable, to the extent of the amount of the overpayment attributable to the deductibility of items described in this paragraph.

(2) Special period of limitation with respect to net operating loss or capital loss carrybacks. --

(A) Period of limitation. -- If the claim for credit or refund relates to an overpayment attributable to a net operating loss carryback or a capital loss carryback, in lieu of the 3-year period of limitation prescribed in subsection (a), the period shall be that period which ends 3 years after the time prescribed by law for filing the return (including extensions thereof) for the taxable year of the net operating loss or net capital loss which results in such carryback, or the period prescribed in subsection (c) in respect of such taxable year, whichever expires later. In the case of such a claim, the amount of the credit or refund may exceed the portion of the tax paid within the period provided in subsection (b)(2) or (c), whichever is applicable, to the extent of the amount of the overpayment attributable to such carryback.

(B) Applicable rules. --

(i) In general. -- If the allowance of a credit or refund of an overpayment of tax attributable to a net operating loss carryback or a capital loss carryback is otherwise prevented by the operation of any law or rule of law other than section 7122 (relating to compromises), such credit or refund may be allowed or made, if claim therefor is filed within the period provided in subparagraph (A) of this paragraph.

(ii) Tentative carryback adjustments. -- If the allowance of an application, credit, or refund of a decrease in tax determined under section 6411(b) is otherwise prevented by the operation of any law or rule of law other than section 7122, such application, credit, or refund may be allowed or made if application for a tentative carryback adjustment is made within the period provided in section 6411(a).

(iii) Determinations by courts to be conclusive. -- In the case of any such claim for credit or refund or any such application for a tentative carryback adjustment, the determination by any court, including the Tax Court, in any proceeding in which the decision of the court has become final, shall be conclusive except with respect to -

(I) the net operating loss deduction and the effect of such deduction, and

(II) the determination of a short-term capital loss and the effect of such short-term capital loss, to the extent that such deduction or short-term capital loss is affected by a carryback which was not an issue in such proceeding.

***

(h) Running of periods of limitation suspended while taxpayer is unable to manage financial affairs due to disability. --

(1) In general. -- In the case of an individual, the running of the periods specified in subsections (a), (b), and (c) shall be suspended during any period of such individual's life that such individual is financially disabled.

(2) Financially disabled. --

(A) In general. -- For purposes of paragraph (1), an individual is financially disabled if such individual is unable to manage his financial affairs by reason of a medically determinable physical or mental impairment of the individual which can be expected to result in death or which has lasted or can be expected to last for a continuous period of not less than 12 months. An individual shall not be considered to have such an impairment

Sec. 6511.   Limitations on credit or refund

unless proof of the existence thereof is furnished in such form and manner as the Secretary may require.

(B) Exception where individual has guardian, etc. -- An individual shall not be treated as financially disabled during any period that such individual's spouse or any other person is authorized to act on behalf of such individual in financial matters. 5

(i) Cross references. --

(1) For time return deemed filed and tax considered paid, see section 6513.

(2) For limitations with respect to certain credits against estate tax, see sections 2014(b) and 2015.

(3) For limitations in case of floor stocks refunds, see section 6412. 10

(4) For a period of limitations for credit or refund in the case of joint income returns after separate returns have been filed, see section 6013(b)(3).

(5) For limitations in case of payments under section 6420 (relating to gasoline used on farms), see section 6420(b).

(6) For limitations in case of payments under section 6421 (relating to gasoline used for 15 certain nonhighway purposes or by local transit systems), see section 6421(d).

(7) For a period of limitations for refund of an overpayment of penalties imposed under section 6694 or 6695, see section 6696(d)(2).

20

Sec. 6601.   Interest on underpayment, nonpayment, or extensions of time for payment, of tax

(a) General rule. -- If any amount of tax imposed by this title (whether required to be shown on a return, or to be paid by stamp or by some other method) is not paid on or before the last date prescribed for payment, interest on such amount at the underpayment rate established under section 6621 shall be paid for the period from such last date to the date paid.

(b) Last date prescribed for payment. -- For purposes of this section, the last date prescribed 25 for payment of the tax shall be determined under chapter 62 with the application of the following rules:

(1) Extensions of time disregarded. -- The last date prescribed for payment shall be determined without regard to any extension of time for payment or any installment agreement entered into under section 6159. 30

(2) Installment payments. -- In the case of an election under section 6156(a) to pay the tax in installments -

(A) The date prescribed for payment of each installment of the tax shown on the return shall be determined under section 6156(b),(!1) and

(B) The last date prescribed for payment of the first installment shall be deemed the last 35 date prescribed for payment of any portion of the tax not shown on the return.

(3) Jeopardy. -- The last date prescribed for payment shall be determined without regard to any notice and demand for payment issued, by reason of jeopardy (as provided in chapter 70), prior to the last date otherwise prescribed for such payment.

(4) Accumulated earnings tax. -- In the case of the tax imposed by section 531 for any 40 taxable year, the last date prescribed for payment shall be deemed to be the due date (without regard to extensions) for the return of tax imposed by subtitle A for such taxable year.

(5) Last date for payment not otherwise prescribed. -- In the case of taxes payable by stamp and in all other cases in which the last date for payment is not otherwise prescribed, the

Sec. 6601. Interest on underpayment, nonpayment, or extensions of time for payment, of tax

last date for payment shall be deemed to be the date the liability for tax arises (and in no event shall be later than the date notice and demand for the tax is made by the Secretary).

(c) Suspension of interest in certain income, estate, gift, and certain excise tax cases. -- In the case of a deficiency as defined in section 6211 (relating to income, estate, gift, and certain excise taxes), if a waiver of restrictions under section 6213(d) on the assessment of such deficiency has been filed, and if notice and demand by the Secretary for payment of such deficiency is not made within 30 days after the filing of such waiver, interest shall not be imposed on such deficiency for the period beginning immediately after such 30th day and ending with the date of notice and demand and interest shall not be imposed during such period on any interest with respect to such deficiency for any prior period. In the case of a settlement under section 6224(c) which results in the conversion of partnership items to nonpartnership items pursuant to section 6231(b)(1)(C), the preceding sentence shall apply to a computational adjustment resulting from such settlement in the same manner as if such adjustment were a deficiency and such settlement were a waiver referred to in the preceding sentence.

(d) Income tax reduced by carryback or adjustment for certain unused deductions. --

(1) Net operating loss or capital loss carryback. -- If the amount of any tax imposed by subtitle A is reduced by reason of a carryback of a net operating loss or net capital loss, such reduction in tax shall not affect the computation ofinterest under this section for the period ending with the filing date for the taxable year in which the net operating loss or net capital loss arises.

***

(3) Certain credit carrybacks. --

(A) In general. -- If any credit allowed for any taxable year is increased by reason of a credit carryback, such increase shall not affect the computation of interest under this section for the period ending with the filing date for the taxable year in which the credit carryback arises, or, with respect to any portion of a credit carryback from a taxable year attributable to a net operating loss carryback, capital loss carryback, or other credit carryback from a subsequent taxable year, such increase shall not affect the computation of interest under this section for the period ending with the filing date for such subsequent taxable year.

(B) Credit carryback defined. -- For purposes of this paragraph, the term "credit carryback" has the meaning given such term by section 6511(d)(4)(C).

(4) Filing date. -- For purposes of this subsection, the term "filing date" has the meaning given to such term by section 6611(f)(3)(A).

(e) Applicable rules. -- Except as otherwise provided in this title--

(1) Interest treated as tax. -- Interest prescribed under this section on any tax shall be paid upon notice and demand, and shall be assessed, collected, and paid in the same manner as taxes. Any reference to this title (except subchapter B of chapter 63, relating to deficiency procedures) to any tax imposed by this title shall be deemed also to refer to interest imposed by this section on such tax.

(2) Interest on penalties, additional amounts, or additions to the tax. --

(A) In general. -- Interest shall be imposed under subsection (a) in respect of any assessable penalty, additional amount, or addition to the tax (other than an addition to tax imposed under section 6651(a)(1) or 6653 or under part II of subchapter A of chapter 68) only if such assessable penalty, additional amount, or addition to the tax is not paid within 21 calendar days from the date of notice and demand therefor (10 business days if the amount for which such notice and demand is made equals or exceeds $100,000), and in

Sec. 6601.   Interest on underpayment, nonpayment, or extensions of time for payment, of tax

such case interest shall be imposed only for the period from the date of the notice and demand to the date of payment.

(B) Interest on certain additions to tax. -- Interest shall be imposed under this section with respect to any addition to tax imposed by section 6651(a)(1) or 6653 or under part II of subchapter A of chapter 68 for the period which--   5

(i) begins on the date on which the return of the tax with respect to which such addition to tax is imposed is required to be filed (including any extensions), and

(ii) ends on the date of payment of such addition to tax.

(3) Payments made within specified period after notice and demand. -- If notice and demand is made for payment of any amount and if such amount is paid within 21 calendar 10 days (10 business days if the amount for which such notice and demand is made equals or exceeds $100,000) after the date of such notice and demand,interest under this section on the amount so paid shall not be imposed for the period after the date of such notice and demand.

(f) Satisfaction by credits. -- If any portion of a tax is satisfied by credit of an overpayment, then no interest shall be imposed under this section on the portion of the tax so satisfied for any 15 period during which, if the credit had not been made, interest would have been allowable with respect to such overpayment. The preceding sentence shall not apply to the extent that section 6621(d) applies.

(g) Limitation on assessment and collection. -- Interest prescribed under this section on any tax may be assessed and collected at any time during the period within which the tax to which such 20 interest relates may be collected.

(h) Exception as to estimated tax. -- This section shall not apply to any failure to pay any estimated tax required to be paid by section 6654 or 6655.

***

(k) No interest on certain adjustments. -- For provisions prohibiting interest on certain 25 adjustments in tax, see section 6205(a).

Sec. 6611.   Interest on overpayments

(a) Rate. -- Interest shall be allowed and paid upon any overpayment in respect of any internal revenue tax at the overpayment rate established under section 6621.   30

(b) Period. -- Such interest shall be allowed and paid as follows:

(1) Credits. -- In the case of a credit, from the date of the overpayment to the due date of the amount against which the credit is taken.

(2) Refunds. -- In the case of a refund, from the date of the overpayment to a date (to be determined by the Secretary) preceding the date of the refund check by not more than 30 days, 35 whether or not such refund check is accepted by the taxpayer after tender of such check to the taxpayer. The acceptance of such check shall be without prejudice to any right of the taxpayer to claim any additional overpayment and interest thereon.

(3) Late returns. -- Notwithstanding paragraph (1) or (2) in the case of a return of tax which is filed after the last date prescribed for filing such return (determined with regard to 40 extensions), no interest shall be allowed or paid for any day before the date on which the return is filed.

***

(d) Advance payment of tax, payment of estimated tax, and credit for income tax

1089

Sec. 6611. Interest on overpayments

withholding. -- The provisions of section 6513 (except the provisions of subsection (c) thereof, applicable in determining the date of payment of tax for purposes of determining the period of limitation on credit or refund, shall be applicable in determining the date of payment for purposes of subsection (a).

(e) Disallowance of interest on certain overpayments. --

(1) Refunds within 45 days after return is filed. -- If any overpayment of tax imposed by this title is refunded within 45 days after the last day prescribed for filing the return of such tax (determined without regard to any extension of time for filing the return) or, in the case of a return filed after such last date, is refunded within 45 days after the date the return is filed, no interest shall be allowed under subsection (a) on such overpayment.

(2) Refunds after claim for credit or refund. -- If--

(A) the taxpayer files a claim for a credit or refund for any overpayment of tax imposed by this title, and

(B) such overpayment is refunded within 45 days after such claim is filed,

no interest shall be allowed on such overpayment from the date the claim is filed until the day the refund is made.

(3) IRS initiated adjustments. -- If an adjustment initiated by the Secretary, results in a refund or credit of an overpayment, interest on such overpayment shall be computed by subtracting 45 days from the number of days interest would otherwise be allowed with respect to such overpayment.

(f) Refund of income tax caused by carryback or adjustment for certain unused deductions. --

(1) Net operating loss or capital loss carryback. -- For purposes of subsection (a), if any overpayment of tax imposed by subtitle A results from a carryback of a net operating loss or net capital loss, such overpayment shall be deemed not to have been made prior to the filing date for the taxable year in which such net operating loss or net capital loss arises.

(2) Foreign tax credit carrybacks. -- For purposes of subsection (a), if any overpayment of tax imposed by subtitle A results from a carryback of tax paid or accrued to foreign countries or possessions of the United States, such overpayment shall be deemed not to have been made before the filing date for the taxable year in which such taxes were in fact paid or accrued, or, with respect to any portion of such credit carryback from a taxable year attributable to a net operating loss carryback or a capital loss carryback from a subsequent taxable year, such overpayment shall be deemed not to have been made before the filing date for such subsequent taxable year.

(3) Certain credit carrybacks. --

(A) In general. -- For purposes of subsection (a), if any overpayment of tax imposed by subtitle A results from a credit carryback, such overpayment shall be deemed not to have been made before the filing date for the taxable year in which such credit carryback arises, or, with respect to any portion of a credit carryback from a taxable year attributable to a net operating loss carryback, capital loss carryback, or other credit carryback from a subsequent taxable year, such overpayment shall be deemed not to have been made before the filing date for such subsequent taxable year.

(B) Credit carryback defined. -- For purposes of this paragraph, the term "credit carryback" has the meaning given such term by section 6511(d)(4)(C).

(4) Special rules for paragraphs (1), (2), and (3). --

(A) Filing date. -- For purposes of this subsection, the term "filing date" means the last date prescribed for filing the return of tax imposed by subtitle A for the taxable year

Sec. 6611. Interest on overpayments

(determined without regard to extensions).

   (B) Coordination with subsection (e). --

   (i) In general. -- For purposes of subsection (e)--

   (I) any overpayment described in paragraph (1), (2), or (3) shall be treated as an overpayment for the loss year,

   (II) such subsection shall be applied with respect to such overpayment by treating the return for the loss year as not filed before claim for such overpayment is filed.

   (ii) Loss year. -- For purposes of this subparagraph, the term "loss year" means--

   (I) in the case of a carryback of a net operating loss or net capital loss, the taxable year in which such loss arises,

   (II) in the case of a carryback of taxes paid or accrued to foreign countries or possessions of the United States, the taxable year in which such taxes were in fact paid or accrued (or, with respect to any portion of such carryback from a taxable year attributable to a net operating loss carryback or a capital loss carryback from a subsequent taxable year, such subsequent taxable year), and

   (III) in the case of a credit carryback (as defined in paragraph (3)(B)), the taxable year in which such credit carryback arises (or, with respect to any portion of a credit carryback from a taxable year attributable to a net operating loss carryback, a capital loss carryback, or other credit carryback from a subsequent taxable year, such subsequent taxable year).

   (C) Application of subparagraph (B) where section 6411(a) claim filed. -- For purposes of subparagraph (B)(i)(II), if a taxpayer--

   (i) files a claim for refund of any overpayment described in paragraph (1), (2), or (3) with respect to the taxable year to which a loss or credit is carried back, and

   (ii) subsequently files an application under section 6411(a) with respect to such overpayment,

then the claim for overpayment shall be treated as having been filed on the date the application under section 6411(a) was filed.

(g) No interest until return in processible form. --

   (1) For purposes of subsections (b)(3) and (e), a return shall not be treated as filed until it is filed in processible form.

   (2) For purposes of paragraph (1), a return is in a processible form if--

   (A) such return is filed on a permitted form, and

   (B) such return contains--

   (i) the taxpayer's name, address, and identifying number and the required signature, and

   (ii) sufficient required information (whether on the return or on required attachments) to permit the mathematical verification of tax liability shown on the return.

(h) Prohibition of administrative review. -- For prohibition of administrative review, see section 6406.

Sec. 6651. Failure to file tax return or to pay tax

(a) Addition to the tax. -- In case of failure -

   (1) to file any return required under authority of subchapter A of chapter 61 (other than part III thereof), subchapter A of chapter 51 (relating to distilled spirits, wines, and beer), or of

Sec. 6651. Failure to file tax return or to pay tax

subchapter A of chapter 52 (relating to tobacco, cigars, cigarettes, and cigarette papers and tubes), or of subchapter A of chapter 53 (relating to machine guns and certain other firearms), on the date prescribed therefor (determined with regard to any extension of time for filing), unless it is shown that such failure is due to reasonable cause and not due to willful neglect, there shall be added to the amount required to be shown as tax on such return 5 percent of the amount of such tax if the failure is for not more than 1 month, with an additional 5 percent for each additional month or fraction thereof during which such failure continues, not exceeding 25 percent in the aggregate;

    (2) to pay the amount shown on tax on any return specified in paragraph (1) on or before the date prescribed for payment of such tax (determined with regard to any extension of time for payment), unless it is shown that such failure is due to reasonable cause and not due to willful neglect, there shall be added to the amount shown as tax on such return 0.5 percent of the amount of such tax if the failure is for not more than 1 month, with an additional 0.5 percent for each additional month or fraction thereof during which such failure continues, not exceeding 25 percent in the aggregate; or

    (3) to pay any amount in respect of any tax required to be shown on a return specified in paragraph (1) which is not so shown (including an assessment made pursuant to section 6213(b)) within 21 calendar days from the date of notice and demand therefor (10 business days if the amount for which such notice and demand is made equals or exceeds $100,000), unless it is shown that such failure is due to reasonable cause and not due to willful neglect, there shall be added to the amount of tax stated in such notice and demand 0.5 percent of the amount of such tax if the failure is for not more than 1 month, with an additional 0.5 percent for each additional month or fraction thereof during which such failure continues, not exceeding 25 percent in the aggregate.

In the case of a failure to file a return of tax imposed by chapter 1 within 60 days of the date prescribed for filing of such return (determined with regard to any extensions of time for filing), unless it is shown that such failure is due to reasonable cause and not due to willful neglect, the addition to tax under paragraph (1) shall not be less than the lesser of $100 or 100 percent of the amount required to be shown as tax on such return.

(b) Penalty imposed on net amount due. -- For purposes of--

    (1) subsection (a)(1), the amount of tax required to be shown on the return shall be reduced by the amount of any part of the tax which is paid on or before the date prescribed for payment of the tax and by the amount of any credit against the tax which may be claimed on the return,

    (2) subsection (a)(2), the amount of tax shown on the return shall, for purposes of computing the addition for any month, be reduced by the amount of any part of the tax which is paid on or before the beginning of such month and by the amount of any credit against the tax which may be claimed on the return, and

    (3) subsection (a)(3), the amount of tax stated in the notice and demand shall, for the purpose of computing the addition for any month, be reduced by the amount of any part of the tax which is paid before the beginning of such month.

(c) Limitations and special rule. --

    (1) Additions under more than one paragraph. -- With respect to any return, the amount of the addition under paragraph (1) of subsection (a) shall be reduced by the amount of the addition under paragraph (2) of subsection (a) for any month (or fraction thereof) to which an addition to tax applies under both paragraphs (1) and (2). In any case described in the last sentence of subsection (a), the amount of the addition under paragraph (1) of subsection (a) shall not be reduced under the preceding sentence below the amount provided in such last sentence.

    (2) Amounts of tax shown more than amount required to be shown. -- If the amount

Sec. 6651. Failure to file tax return or to pay tax

required to be shown as tax on a return is less than the amount shown as tax on such return, subsections (a)(2) and (b)(2) shall be applied by substituting such lower amount.

(d) Increase in penalty for failure to pay tax in certain cases. --

(1) In general. -- In the case of each month (or fraction thereof) beginning after the day described in paragraph (2) of this subsection, paragraphs (2) and (3) of subsection (a) shall be applied by substituting "1 percent" for "0.5 percent" each place it appears.

(2) Description. -- For purposes of paragraph (1), the day described in this paragraph is the earlier of--

(A) the day 10 days after the date on which notice is given under section 6331(d), or

(B) the day on which notice and demand for immediate payment is given under the last sentence of section 6331(a).

(e) Exception for estimated tax. -- This section shall not apply to any failure to pay any estimated tax required to be paid by section 6654 or 6655.

(f) Increase in penalty for fraudulent failure to file. -- If any failure to file any return is fraudulent, paragraph (1) of subsection (a) shall be applied--

(1) by substituting "15 percent" for "5 percent" each place it appears, and

(2) by substituting "75 percent" for "25 percent".

***

(h) Limitation on penalty on individual's failure to pay for months during period of installment agreement. -- In the case of an individual who files a return of tax on or before the due date for the return (including extensions), paragraphs (2) and (3) of subsection (a) shall each be applied by substituting "0.25" for "0.5" each place it appears for purposes of determining the addition to tax for any month during which an installment agreement under section 6159 is in effect for the payment of such tax.

Sec. 6654. Failure by individual to pay estimated income tax

(a) Addition to the tax. -- Except as otherwise provided in this section, in the case of any underpayment of estimated tax by an individual, there shall be added to the tax under chapter 1 and the tax under chapter 2 for the taxable year an amount determined by applying--

(1) the underpayment rate established under section 6621,

(2) to the amount of the underpayment,

(3) for the period of the underpayment.

(b) Amount of underpayment; period of underpayment. -- For purposes of subsection (a) -

(1) Amount. -- The amount of the underpayment shall be the excess of--

(A) the required installment, over

(B) the amount (if any) of the installment paid on or before the due date for the installment.

(2) Period of underpayment. -- The period of the underpayment shall run from the due date for the installment to whichever of the following dates is the earlier--

(A) the 15th day of the 4th month following the close of the taxable year, or

(B) with respect to any portion of the underpayment, the date on which such portion is paid.

(3) Order of crediting payments. -- For purposes of paragraph (2)(B), a payment of estimated tax shall be credited against unpaid required installments in the order in which such

Sec. 6654. Failure by individual to pay estimated income tax

installments are required to be paid.

(c) Number of required installments; due dates. -- For purposes of this section--

(1) Payable in 4 installments. -- There shall be 4 required installments for each taxable year.

(2) Time for payment of installments. --

In the case of the following required installments:	The due date is:
1st..	April 15
2nd...	June 15
3rd..	September 15
4th..	January 15 of the following taxable year.

(d) Amount of required installments. -- For purposes of this section -

(1) Amount. --

(A) In general. -- Except as provided in paragraph (2), the amount of any required installment shall be 25 percent of the required annual payment.

(B) Required annual payment. -- For purposes of subparagraph (A), the term "required annual payment" means the lesser of -

(i) 90 percent of the tax shown on the return for the taxable year (or, if no return is filed, 90 percent of the tax for such year), or

(ii) 100 percent of the tax shown on the return of the individual for the preceding taxable year.

Clause (ii) shall not apply if the preceding taxable year was not a taxable year of 12 months or if the individual did not file a return for such preceding taxable year.

(C) Limitation on use of preceding year's tax. --

(i) In general. -- If the adjusted gross income shown on the return of the individual for the preceding taxable year beginning in any calendar year exceeds $150,000, clause (ii) of subparagraph (B) shall be applied by substituting the applicable percentage for "100 percent". For purposes of the preceding sentence, the applicable percentage shall be determined in accordance with the following table:

If the preceding taxable year begins in:	The applicable percentage is:
***	
2002 or thereafter	110.

This clause shall not apply in the case of a preceding taxable year beginning in calendar year 1997.

(ii) Separate returns. -- In the case of a married individual (within the meaning of section 7703) who files a separate return for the taxable year for which the amount of the installment is being determined, clause (i) shall be applied by substituting "$75,000" for "$150,000".

(iii) Special rule. -- In the case of an estate or trust, adjusted gross income shall be determined as provided in section 67(e).

(2) Lower required installment where annualized income installment is less than amount determined under paragraph (1)

1094

Sec. 6654.   Failure by individual to pay estimated income tax

(A) In general. -- In the case of any required installment, if the individual establishes that the annualized income installment is less than the amount determined under paragraph (1)--

(i) the amount of such required installment shall be the annualized income installment, and   5

(ii) any reduction in a required installment resulting from the application of this subparagraph shall be recaptured by increasing the amount of the next required installment determined under paragraph (1) by the amount of such reduction (and by increasing subsequent required installments to the extent that the reduction has not previously been recaptured under this clause).   10

(B) Determination of annualized income installment. -- In the case of any required installment, the annualized income installment is the excess (if any) of--

(i) an amount equal to the applicable percentage of the tax for the taxable year computed by placing on an annualized basis the taxable income, alternative minimum taxable income, and adjusted self-employment income for months in the taxable year 15 ending before the due date for the installment, over

(ii) the aggregate amount of any prior required installments for the taxable year.

(C) Special rules. -- For purposes of this paragraph--

(i) Annualization. -- The taxable income, alternative minimum taxable income, and adjusted self-employment income shall be placed on an annualized basis under 20 regulations prescribed by the Secretary.

(ii) Applicable percentage. --

In the case of the following required installments:	The applicable percentage is:	
1st	22.5	25
2nd	45	
3rd	67.5	
4th	90.	
		30

(iii) Adjusted self-employment income. -- The term "adjusted self-employment income" means self- employment income (as defined in section 1402(b)); except that section 1402(b) shall be applied by placing wages (within the meaning of section 1402(b)) for months in the taxable year ending before the due date for the installment on an annualized basis consistent with clause (i).   35

***

(e) Exceptions. --

(1) Where tax is small amount. -- No addition to tax shall be imposed under subsection (a) for any taxable year if the tax shown on the return for such taxable year (or, if no return is filed, the tax), reduced by the credit allowable under section 31, is less than $1,000.   40

(2) Where no tax liability for preceding taxable year. -- No addition to tax shall be imposed under subsection (a) for any taxable year if--

(A) the preceding taxable year was a taxable year of 12 months,

(B) the individual did not have any liability for tax for the preceding taxable year, and

(C) the individual was a citizen or resident of the United States throughout the preceding 45 taxable year.

(3) Waiver in certain cases. --

Sec. 6654.   Failure by individual to pay estimated income tax

(A) **In general.** -- No addition to tax shall be imposed under subsection (a) with respect to any underpayment to the extent the Secretary determines that by reason of casualty, disaster, or other unusual circumstances the imposition of such addition to tax would be against equity and good conscience.

(B) **Newly retired or disabled individuals.** -- No addition to tax shall be imposed under subsection (a) with respect to any underpayment if the Secretary determines that--

(i) the taxpayer--

(I) retired after having attained age 62, or

(II) became disabled,

in the taxable year for which estimated payments were required to be made or in the taxable year preceding such taxable year, and

(ii) such underpayment was due to reasonable cause and not to willful neglect.

(f) **Tax computed after application of credits against tax.** -- For purposes of this section, the term "tax" means--

(1) the tax imposed by chapter 1 (other than any increase in such tax by reason of section 143(m)), plus

(2) the tax imposed by chapter 2, minus

(3) the credits against tax provided by part IV of subchapter A of chapter 1, other than the credit against tax provided by section 31 (relating to tax withheld on wages).

(g) **Application of section in case of tax withheld on wages.** --

(1) **In general.** -- For purposes of applying this section, the amount of the credit allowed under section 31 for the taxable year shall be deemed a payment of estimated tax, and an equal part of such amount shall be deemed paid on each due date for such taxable year, unless the taxpayer establishes the dates on which all amounts were actually withheld, in which case the amounts so withheld shall be deemed payments of estimated tax on the dates on which such amounts were actually withheld.

(2) **Separate application.** -- The taxpayer may apply paragraph (1) separately with respect to--

(A) wage withholding, and

(B) all other amounts withheld for which credit is allowed under section 31.

(h) **Special rule where return filed on or before January 31.** -- If, on or before January 31 of the following taxable year, the taxpayer files a return for the taxable year and pays in full the amount computed on the return as payable, then no addition to tax shall be imposed under subsection (a) with respect to any underpayment of the 4th required installment for the taxable year.

***

Sec. 6662.   Imposition of accuracy-related penalty on underpayments

(a) **Imposition of penalty.** -- If this section applies to any portion of an underpayment of tax required to be shown on a return, there shall be added to the tax an amount equal to 20 percent of the portion of the underpayment to which this section applies.

(b) **Portion of underpayment to which section applies.** -- This section shall apply to the portion of any underpayment which is attributable to 1 or more of the following:

(1) Negligence or disregard of rules or regulations.

(2) Any substantial understatement of income tax.

Sec. 6662. Imposition of accuracy-related penalty on underpayments

(3) Any substantial valuation misstatement under chapter 1.

***

This section shall not apply to any portion of an underpayment on which a penalty is imposed under section 6663.

(c) Negligence. -- For purposes of this section, the term "negligence" includes any failure to make a reasonable attempt to comply with the provisions of this title, and the term "disregard" includes any careless, reckless, or intentional disregard.

(d) Substantial understatement of income tax. --

(1) Substantial understatement. --

(A) In general. -- For purposes of this section, there is a substantial understatement of income tax for any taxable year if the amount of the understatement for the taxable year exceeds the greater of--

(i) 10 percent of the tax required to be shown on the return for the taxable year, or

(ii) $5,000.

(B) Special rule for corporations. -- In the case of a corporation other than an S corporation or a personal holding company (as defined in section 542), there is a substantial understatement of income tax for any taxable year if the amount of the understatement for the taxable year exceeds the lesser of--

(i) 10 percent of the tax required to be shown on the return for the taxable year (or, if greater, $10,000), or

(ii) $10,000,000.

(2) Understatement. --

(A) In general. -- For purposes of paragraph (1), the term "understatement" means the excess of--

(i) the amount of the tax required to be shown on the return for the taxable year, over

(ii) the amount of the tax imposed which is shown on the return, reduced by any rebate (within the meaning of section 6211(b)(2)).

The excess under the preceding sentence shall be determined without regard to items to which section 6662A applies.

(B) Reduction for understatement due to position of taxpayer or disclosed item. -- The amount of the understatement under subparagraph (A) shall be reduced by that portion of the understatement which is attributable to--

(i) the tax treatment of any item by the taxpayer if there is or was substantial authority for such treatment, or

(ii) any item if--

(I) the relevant facts affecting the item's tax treatment are adequately disclosed in the return or in a statement attached to the return, and

(II) there is a reasonable basis for the tax treatment of such item by the taxpayer.

For purposes of clause (ii)(II), in no event shall a corporation be treated as having a reasonable basis for its tax treatment of an item attributable to a multiple-party financing transaction if such treatment does not clearly reflect the income of the corporation.

(C) Reduction not to apply to tax shelters. --

(i) In general. -- Subparagraph (B) shall not apply to any item attributable to a tax shelter.

(ii) Tax shelter. -- For purposes of clause (i), the term "tax shelter" means--

Sec. 6662. Imposition of accuracy-related penalty on underpayments

(I) a partnership or other entity,

(II) any investment plan or arrangement, or

(III) any other plan or arrangement,

if a significant purpose of such partnership, entity, plan, or arrangement is the avoidance or evasion of Federal income tax.

(3) Secretarial list. -- The Secretary may prescribe a list of positions which the Secretary believes do not meet the 1 or more of the standards specified in paragraph (2)(B)(i), section 6664(d)(2), and section 6694(a)(1). Such list (and any revisions thereof)shall be published in the Federal Register or the Internal Revenue Bulletin.

(e) Substantial valuation misstatement under chapter 1. --

(1) In general. -- For purposes of this section, there is a substantial valuation misstatement under chapter 1 if--

(A) the value of any property (or the adjusted basis of any property) claimed on any return of tax imposed by chapter 1 is 150 percent or more of the amount determined to be the correct amount of such valuation or adjusted basis (as the case may be), or

(B)(i) the price for any property or services (or for the use of property) claimed on any such return in connection with any transaction between persons described in section 482 is 200 percent or more (or 50 percent or less) of the amount determined under section 482 to be the correct amount of such price, or

(ii) the net section 482 transfer price adjustment for the taxable year exceeds the lesser of $5,000,000 or 10 percent of the taxpayer's gross receipts.

(2) Limitation. -- No penalty shall be imposed by reason of subsection (b)(3) unless the portion of the underpayment for the taxable year attributable to substantial valuation misstatements under chapter 1 exceeds $5,000 ($10,000 in the case of a corporation other than an S corporation or a personal holding company (as defined in section 542)).

(3) Net section 482 transfer price adjustment. -- For purposes of this subsection--

(A) In general. -- The term "net section 482 transfer price adjustment" means, with respect to any taxable year, the net increase in taxable income for the taxable year (determined without regard to any amount carried to such taxable year from another taxable year) resulting from adjustments under section 482 in the price for any property or services (or for the use of property).

(B) Certain adjustments excluded in determining threshold. -- For purposes of determining whether the threshold requirements of paragraph (1)(B)(ii) are met, the following shall be excluded:

(i) Any portion of the net increase in taxable income referred to in subparagraph (A) which is attributable to any redetermination of a price if--

(I) it is established that the taxpayer determined such price in accordance with a specific pricing method set forth in the regulations prescribed under section 482 and that the taxpayer's use of such method was reasonable,

(II) the taxpayer has documentation (which was in existence as of the time of filing the return) which sets forth the determination of such price in accordance with such a method and which establishes that the use of such method was reasonable, and

(III) the taxpayer provides such documentation to the Secretary within 30 days of a request for such documentation.

(ii) Any portion of the net increase in taxable income referred to in subparagraph (A) which is attributable to a redetermination of price where such price was not determined in accordance with such a specific pricing method if -

    (I) the taxpayer establishes that none of such pricing methods was likely to result in a price that would clearly reflect income, the taxpayer used another pricing method to determine such price, and such other pricing method was likely to result in a price that would clearly reflect income,

    (II) the taxpayer has documentation (which was in existence as of the time of filing the return) which sets forth the determination of such price in accordance with such other method and which establishes that the requirements of subclause (I) were satisfied, and

    (III) the taxpayer provides such documentation to the Secretary within 30 days of request for such documentation.

  (iii) Any portion of such net increase which is attributable to any transaction solely between foreign corporations unless, in the case of any such corporations, the treatment of such transaction affects the determination of income from sources within the United States or taxable income effectively connected with the conduct of a trade or business within the United States.

(C) Special rule. -- If the regular tax (as defined in section 55(c)) imposed by chapter 1 on the taxpayer is determined by reference to an amount other than taxable income, such amount shall be treated as the taxable income of such taxpayer for purposes of this paragraph.

(D) Coordination with reasonable cause exception. -- For purposes of section 6664(c) the taxpayer shall not be treated as having reasonable cause for any portion of an underpayment attributable to a net section 482 transfer price adjustment unless such taxpayer meets the requirements of clause (i), (ii), or (iii) of subparagraph (B) with respect to such portion.

***

(h) Increase in penalty in case of gross valuation misstatements. --

  (1) In general. -- To the extent that a portion of the underpayment to which this section applies is attributable to one or more gross valuation misstatements, subsection (a) shall be applied with respect to such portion by substituting "40 percent" for "20 percent".

  (2) Gross valuation misstatements. -- The term "gross valuation misstatements" means -

    (A) any substantial valuation misstatement under chapter 1 as determined under subsection (e) by substituting--

      (i) "400 percent" for "200 percent" each place it appears,

      (ii) "25 percent" for "50 percent", and

      (iii) in paragraph (1)(B)(ii) -

        (I) "$20,000,000" for "$5,000,000", and

        (II) "20 percent" for "10 percent".

    (B) any substantial overstatement of pension liabilities as determined under subsection (f) by substituting "400 percent" for "200 percent", and

    (C) any substantial estate or gift tax valuation understatement as determined under subsection (g) by substituting "25 percent" for "50 percent".

Reg. § 1.6662-3 Negligence or disregard of rules or regulations.

  (a) *In general.* If any portion of an underpayment, as defined in section 6664(a) and §

1099

Sec. 6662. Imposition of accuracy-related penalty on underpayments

1.6664-2, of any income tax imposed under subtitle A of the Internal Revenue Code that is required to be shown on a return is attributable to negligence or disregard of rules or regulations, there is added to the tax an amount equal to 20 percent of such portion. The penalty for disregarding rules or regulations does not apply, however, if the requirements
5 of paragraph (c)(1) of this section are satisfied and the position in question is adequately disclosed as provided in paragraph (c)(2) of this section (and, if the position relates to a reportable transaction as defined in § 1.6011-4(b) (or § 1.6011-4T(b), as applicable), the transaction is disclosed in accordance with § 1.6011-4 (or § 1.6011-4T, as applicable)), or to the extent that the reasonable cause and good faith exception to this penalty set forth
10 in § 1.6664-4 applies. In addition, if a position with respect to an item (other than with respect to a reportable transaction, as defined in § 1.6011-4(b) or § 1.6011-4T(b), as applicable) is contrary to a revenue ruling or notice (other than a notice of proposed rulemaking) issued by the Internal Revenue Service and published in the Internal Revenue Bulletin (see § 601.601(d)(2) of this chapter), this penalty does not apply if the
15 position has a realistic possibility of being sustained on its merits. See § 1.6694-2(b) of the income tax return preparer penalty regulations for a description of the realistic possibility standard.

(b) *Definitions and rules*--(1) *Negligence.* The term negligence includes any failure to make a reasonable attempt to comply with the provisions of the internal revenue laws or
20 to exercise ordinary and reasonable care in the preparation of a tax return. ``Negligence" also includes any failure by the taxpayer to keep adequate books and records or to substantiate items properly. A return position that has a reasonable basis as defined in paragraph (b)(3) of this section is not attributable to negligence. Negligence is strongly indicated where--
25 (i) A taxpayer fails to include on an income tax return an amount of income shown on an information return, as defined in section 6724(d)(1);

(ii) A taxpayer fails to make a reasonable attempt to ascertain the correctness of a deduction, credit or exclusion on a return which would seem to a reasonable and prudent person to be ``too good to be true" under the circumstances;
30 (iii) A partner fails to comply with the requirements of section 6222, which requires that a partner treat partnership items on its return in a manner that is consistent with the treatment of such items on the partnership return (or notify the Secretary of the inconsistency); or

(iv) A shareholder fails to comply with the requirements of section 6242, which
35 requires that an S corporation shareholder treat subchapter S items on its return in a manner that is consistent with the treatment of such items on the corporation's return (or notify the Secretary of the inconsistency).

(2) *Disregard of rules or regulations.* The term disregard includes any careless, reckless or intentional disregard of rules or regulations. The term ``rules or regulations"
40 includes the provisions of the Internal Revenue Code, temporary or final Treasury regulations issued under the Code, and revenue rulings or notices (other than notices of proposed rulemaking) issued by the Internal Revenue Service and published in the Internal Revenue Bulletin. A disregard of rules or regulations is ``careless" if the taxpayer does not exercise reasonable diligence to determine the correctness of a return position
45 that is contrary to the rule or regulation. A disregard is ``reckless" if the taxpayer makes little or no effort to determine whether a rule or regulation exists, under circumstances which demonstrate a substantial deviation from the standard of conduct that a reasonable person would observe. A disregard is ``intentional" if the taxpayer knows of the rule or regulation that is disregarded. Nevertheless, a taxpayer who takes a position (other than
50 with respect to a reportable transaction, as defined in § 1.6011-4(b) or § 1.6011-4T(b), as applicable) contrary to a revenue ruling or notice has not disregarded the ruling or notice

Sec. 6662. Imposition of accuracy-related penalty on underpayments

if the contrary position has a realistic possibility of being sustained on its merits.

(3) *Reasonable basis.* Reasonable basis is a relatively high standard of tax reporting, that is, significantly higher than not frivolous or not patently improper. The reasonable basis standard is not satisfied by a return position that is merely arguable or that is merely a colorable claim. If a return position is reasonably based on one or more of the authorities set forth in § 1.6662-4(d)(3)(iii) (taking into account the relevance and persuasiveness of the authorities, and subsequent developments), the return position will generally satisfy the reasonable basis standard even though it may not satisfy the substantial authority standard as defined in § 1.6662-4(d)(2). (See § 1.6662-4(d)(3)(ii) for rules with respect to relevance, persuasiveness, subsequent developments, and use of a well-reasoned construction of an applicable statutory provision for purposes of the substantial understatement penalty.) In addition, the reasonable cause and good faith exception in § 1.6664-4 may provide relief from the penalty for negligence or disregard of rules or regulations, even if a return position does not satisfy the reasonable basis standard.

(c) *Exception for adequate disclosure--*(1) *In general.* No penalty under section 6662(b)(1) may be imposed on any portion of an underpayment that is attributable to a position contrary to a rule or regulation if the position is disclosed in accordance with the rules of paragraph (c)(2) of this section (and, if the position relates to a reportable transaction as defined in § 1.6011-4(b) (or § 1.6011-4T(b), as applicable), the transaction is disclosed in accordance with § 1.6011-4 (or § 1.6011-4T, as applicable)) and, in case of a position contrary to a regulation, the position represents a good faith challenge to the validity of the regulation. This disclosure exception does not apply, however, in the case of a position that does not have a reasonable basis or where the taxpayer fails to keep adequate books and records or to substantiate items properly.

(2) *Method of disclosure.* Disclosure is adequate for purposes of the penalty for disregarding rules or regulations if made in accordance with the provisions of §§ 1.6662-4(f)(1), (3), (4), and (5), which permit disclosure on a properly completed and filed Form 8275 or 8275-R, as appropriate. In addition, the statutory or regulatory provision or ruling in question must be adequately identified on the Form 8275 or 8275-R, as appropriate. The provisions of § 1.6662-4(f)(2), which permit disclosure in accordance with an annual revenue procedure for purposes of the substantial understatement penalty, do not apply for purposes of this section.

(d) *Special rules in the case of carrybacks and carryovers--*(1) *In general.* The penalty for negligence or disregard of rules or regulations applies to any portion of an underpayment for a year to which a loss, deduction or credit is carried, which portion is attributable to negligence or disregard of rules or regulations in the year in which the carryback or carryover of the loss, deduction or credit arises (the ``loss or credit year'').

***

(3) *Example.* The following example illustrates the provisions of paragraph (d) of this section. This example does not take into account the reasonable cause exception under § 1.6664-4.

Example. Corporation M is a C corporation. In 1990, M had a loss of $200,000 before taking into account a deduction of $350,000 that M claimed as an expense in careless disregard of the capitalization requirements of section 263 of the Code. M failed to make adequate disclosure of the item for 1990. M reported a $550,000 loss for 1990 and carried back the loss to 1987 and 1988. M had reported taxable income of $400,000 for 1987 and $200,000 for 1988, before application of the carryback. The carryback eliminated all of M's taxable income for 1987 and $150,000 of taxable income for 1988. After disallowance of the $350,000 expense deduction and allowance of a $35,000 depreciation deduction with respect to the capitalized amount, the correct loss for 1990 was determined to be $235,000. Because there is no underpayment for 1990, the penalty for negligence or disregard of rules or regulations does not apply for 1990. However, as a result of the 1990 adjustments, the loss carried back to 1987 is reduced from $550,000 to $235,000. After application of the $235,000 carryback, M has taxable income of $165,000 for 1987 and $200,000 for 1988. This adjustment results in underpayments for 1987 and 1988 that are attributable to the disregard of rules or regulations on the 1990 return. Therefore, the 20 percent penalty rate applies to the 1987 and 1988 underpayments attributable to the disallowed carryback.

[T.D. 8381, 56 FR 67498, Dec. 31, 1991; T.D. 8617, 60 FR 45664, Sept. 1, 1995; T.D. 8790, 63 FR 66434, Dec. 2, 1998; T.D. 9109, 68 FR 75127, Dec. 30, 2003]

Sec. 6662A.   Imposition of accuracy-related penalty on understatements with respect to reportable transactions

(a) **Imposition of penalty.** -- If a taxpayer has a reportable transaction understatement for any taxable year, there shall be added to the tax an amount equal to 20 percent of the amount of such understatement.

(b) **Reportable transaction understatement.** -- For purposes of this section--

(1) **In general.** -- The term "reportable transaction understatement" means the sum of--

(A) the product of--

(i) the amount of the increase (if any) in taxable income which results from a difference between the proper tax treatment of an item to which this section applies and the taxpayer's treatment of such item (as shown on the taxpayer's return of tax), and

(ii) the highest rate of tax imposed by section 1 (section 11 in the case of a taxpayer which is a corporation), and

(B) the amount of the decrease (if any) in the aggregate amount of credits determined under subtitle A which results from a difference between the taxpayer's treatment of an item to which this section applies (as shown on the taxpayer's return of tax) and the proper tax treatment of such item.

For purposes of subparagraph (A), any reduction of the excess of deductions allowed for the taxable year over gross income for such year, and any reduction in the amount of capital losses which would (without regard to section 1211) be allowed for such year, shall be treated as an increase in taxable income.

(2) **Items to which section applies.** -- This section shall apply to any item which is attributable to--

(A) any listed transaction, and

(B) any reportable transaction (other than a listed transaction) if a significant purpose of such transaction is the avoidance or evasion of Federal income tax.

(c) **Higher penalty for nondisclosed listed and other avoidance transactions.** -- Subsection (a) shall be applied by substituting "30 percent" for "20 percent" with respect to the portion of any reportable transaction understatement with respect to which the requirement of section 6664(d)(2) (A) is not met.

(d) **Definitions of reportable and listed transactions.** -- For purposes of this section, the terms "reportable transaction" and "listed transaction" have the respective meanings given to such terms by section 6707A(c).

(e) **Special rules.** --

(1) **Coordination with penalties, etc., on other understatements.** -- In the case of an

Sec. 6662A. Imposition of accuracy-related penalty on understatements with respect to reportable transactions

understatement (as defined in section 6662(d)(2))--

    (A) the amount of such understatement (determined without regard to this paragraph) shall be increased by the aggregate amount of reportable transaction understatements for purposes of determining whether such understatement is a substantial understatement under section 6662(d)(1), and

    (B) the addition to tax under section 6662(a) shall apply only to the excess of the amount of the substantial understatement (if any) after the application of subparagraph (A) over the aggregate amount of reportable transaction understatements.

  (2) Coordination with other penalties. --

    (A) Application of fraud penalty. -- References to an underpayment in section 6663 shall be treated as including references to a reportable transaction understatement.

    (B) No double penalty. -- This section shall not apply to any portion of an understatement on which a penalty is imposed under section 6663.

    (C) Coordination with valuation penalties. --

      (i) Section 6662(e). -- Section 6662(e) shall not apply to any portion of an understatement on which a penalty is imposed under this section.

      (ii) Section 6662(h). -- This section shall not apply to any portion of an understatement on which a penalty is imposed under section 6662(h).

  (3) Special rule for amended returns. -- Except as provided in regulations, in no event shall any tax treatment included with an amendment or supplement to a return of tax be taken into account in determining the amount of any reportable transaction understatement if the amendment or supplement is filed after the earlier of the date the taxpayer is first contacted by the Secretary regarding the examination of the return or such other date as is specified by the Secretary.

Sec. 6663. Imposition of fraud penalty

  (a) Imposition of penalty. -- If any part of any underpayment of tax required to be shown on a return is due to fraud, there shall be added to the tax an amount equal to 75 percent of the portion of the underpayment which is attributable to fraud.

  (b) Determination of portion attributable to fraud. -- If the Secretary establishes that any portion of an underpayment is attributable to fraud, the entire underpayment shall be treated as attributable to fraud, except with respect to any portion of the underpayment which the taxpayer establishes (by a preponderance of the evidence) is not attributable to fraud.

  (c) Special rule for joint returns. -- In the case of a joint return, this section shall not apply with respect to a spouse unless some part of the underpayment is due to the fraud of such spouse.

Reg. § 1.6664-3 Ordering rules for determining the total amount of penalties imposed.

  (a) *In general.* This section provides rules for determining the order in which adjustments to a return are taken into account for the purpose of computing the total amount of penalties imposed under sections 6662 and 6663, where--

  (1) There is at least one adjustment with respect to which no penalty has been imposed and at least one with respect to which a penalty has been imposed, or

  (2) There are at least two adjustments with respect to which penalties have been imposed and they have been imposed at different rates.

Sec. 6663. Imposition of fraud penalty

This section also provides rules for allocating unclaimed prepayment credits to adjustments to a return.

(b) *Order in which adjustments are taken into account.* In computing the portions of an underpayment subject to penalties imposed under sections 6662 and 6663, adjustments
5 to a return are considered made in the following order:

(1) Those with respect to which no penalties have been imposed.

(2) Those with respect to which a penalty has been imposed at a 20 percent rate (i.e., a penalty for negligence or disregard of rules or regulations, substantial understatement of income tax, or substantial valuation misstatement, under sections 6662(b)(1) through
10 6662(b)(3), respectively).

(3) Those with respect to which a penalty has been imposed at a 40 percent rate (i.e., a penalty for a gross valuation misstatement under sections 6662 (b)(3) and (h)).

(4) Those with respect to which a penalty has been imposed at a 75 percent rate (i.e., a penalty for fraud under section 6663).

15 ***

Reg. § 1.6664-4 Reasonable cause and good faith exception to section 6662 penalties.

(a) *In general.* No penalty may be imposed under section 6662 with respect to any portion of an underpayment upon a showing by the taxpayer that there was reasonable
20 cause for, and the taxpayer acted in good faith with respect to, such portion. Rules for determining whether the reasonable cause and good faith exception applies are set forth in paragraphs (b) through (h) of this section.

(b) *Facts and circumstances taken into account--*(1) *In general.* The determination of whether a taxpayer acted with reasonable cause and in good faith is made on a case-by-
25 case basis, taking into account all pertinent facts and circumstances. (See paragraph (e) of this section for certain rules relating to a substantial understatement penalty attributable to tax shelter items of corporations.) Generally, the most important factor is the extent of the taxpayer's effort to assess the taxpayer's proper tax liability. Circumstances that may indicate reasonable cause and good faith include an honest
30 misunderstanding of fact or law that is reasonable in light of all of the facts and circumstances, including the experience, knowledge, and education of the taxpayer. An isolated computational or transcriptional error generally is not inconsistent with reasonable cause and good faith. Reliance on an information return or on the advice of a professional tax advisor or an appraiser does not necessarily demonstrate reasonable
35 cause and good faith. Similarly, reasonable cause and good faith is not necessarily indicated by reliance on facts that, unknown to the taxpayer, are incorrect. Reliance on an information return, professional advice, or other facts, however, constitutes reasonable cause and good faith if, under all the circumstances, such reliance was reasonable and the taxpayer acted in good faith. (See paragraph (c) of this section for certain rules
40 relating to reliance on the advice of others.) For example, reliance on erroneous information (such as an error relating to the cost or adjusted basis of property, the date property was placed in service, or the amount of opening or closing inventory) inadvertently included in data compiled by the various divisions of a multidivisional corporation or in financial books and records prepared by those divisions generally
45 indicates reasonable cause and good faith, provided the corporation employed internal controls and procedures, reasonable under the circumstances, that were designed to identify such factual errors. Reasonable cause and good faith ordinarily is not indicated by the mere fact that there is an appraisal of the value of property. Other factors to consider include the methodology and assumptions underlying the appraisal, the
50 appraised value, the relationship between appraised value and purchase price, the circumstances under which the appraisal was obtained, and the appraiser's relationship

1104

Sec. 6663. Imposition of fraud penalty

to the taxpayer or to the activity in which the property is used. (See paragraph (g) of this section for certain rules relating to appraisals for charitable deduction property.) A taxpayer's reliance on erroneous information reported on a Form W-2, Form 1099, or other information return indicates reasonable cause and good faith, provided the taxpayer did not know or have reason to know that the information was incorrect. Generally, a 5 taxpayer knows, or has reason to know, that the information on an information return is incorrect if such information is inconsistent with other information reported or otherwise furnished to the taxpayer, or with the taxpayer's knowledge of the transaction. This knowledge includes, for example, the taxpayer's knowledge of the terms of his employment relationship or of the rate of return on a payor's obligation. 10

(2) *Examples.* The following examples illustrate this paragraph (b). They do not involve tax shelter items. (See paragraph (e) of this section for certain rules relating to the substantial understatement penalty attributable to the tax shelter items of corporations.)

Example 1. A, an individual calendar year taxpayer, engages B, a professional tax advisor, to give A advice concerning the deductibility of certain state and local taxes. A 15 provides B with full details concerning the taxes at issue. B advises A that the taxes are fully deductible. A, in preparing his own tax return, claims a deduction for the taxes. Absent other facts, and assuming the facts and circumstances surrounding B's advice and A's reliance on such advice satisfy the requirements of paragraph (c) of this section, A is considered to have demonstrated good faith by seeking the advice of a professional 20 tax advisor, and to have shown reasonable cause for any underpayment attributable to the deduction claimed for the taxes. However, if A had sought advice from someone that A knew, or should have known, lacked knowledge in the relevant aspects of Federal tax law, or if other facts demonstrate that A failed to act reasonably or in good faith, A would not be considered to have shown reasonable cause or to have acted in good faith. 25

Example 2. C, an individual, sought advice from D, a friend who was not a tax professional, as to how C might reduce his Federal tax obligations. D advised C that, for a nominal investment in Corporation X, D had received certain tax benefits which virtually eliminated D's Federal tax liability. D also named other investors who had received similar benefits. Without further inquiry, C invested in X and claimed the benefits that he had 30 been assured by D were due him. In this case, C did not make any good faith attempt to ascertain the correctness of what D had advised him concerning his tax matters, and is not considered to have reasonable cause for the underpayment attributable to the benefits claimed.

Example 3. E, an individual, worked for Company X doing odd jobs and filling in for 35 other employees when necessary. E worked irregular hours and was paid by the hour. The amount of E's pay check differed from week to week. The Form W-2 furnished to E reflected wages for 1990 in the amount of $29,729. It did not, however, include compensation of $1,467 paid for some hours E worked. Relying on the Form W-2, E filed a return reporting wages of $29,729. E had no reason to know that the amount reported 40 on the Form W-2 was incorrect. Under the circumstances, E is considered to have acted in good faith in relying on the Form W-2 and to have reasonable cause for the underpayment attributable to the unreported wages.

Example 4. H, an individual, did not enjoy preparing his tax returns and procrastinated in doing so until April 15th. On April 15th, H hurriedly gathered together his tax records 45 and materials, prepared a return, and mailed it before midnight. The return contained numerous errors, some of which were in H's favor and some of which were not. The net result of all the adjustments, however, was an underpayment of tax by H. Under these circumstances, H is not considered to have reasonable cause for the underpayment or to have acted in good faith in attempting to file an accurate return. 50

(c) *Reliance on opinion or advice*--(1) *Facts and circumstances; minimum*

Sec. 6663. Imposition of fraud penalty

requirements. All facts and circumstances must be taken into account in determining whether a taxpayer has reasonably relied in good faith on advice (including the opinion of a professional tax advisor) as to the treatment of the taxpayer (or any entity, plan, or arrangement) under Federal tax law. For example, the taxpayer's education,
5 sophistication and business experience will be relevant in determining whether the taxpayer's reliance on tax advice was reasonable and made in good faith. In no event will a taxpayer be considered to have reasonably relied in good faith on advice (including an opinion) unless the requirements of this paragraph (c)(1) are satisfied. The fact that these requirements are satisfied, however, will not necessarily establish that the taxpayer
10 reasonably relied on the advice (including the opinion of a tax advisor) in good faith. For example, reliance may not be reasonable or in good faith if the taxpayer knew, or reasonably should have known, that the advisor lacked knowledge in the relevant aspects of Federal tax law.

   (i) *All facts and circumstances considered.* The advice must be based upon all
15 pertinent facts and circumstances and the law as it relates to those facts and circumstances. For example, the advice must take into account the taxpayer's purposes (and the relative weight of such purposes) for entering into a transaction and for structuring a transaction in a particular manner. In addition, the requirements of this paragraph (c)(1) are not satisfied if the taxpayer fails to disclose a fact that it knows, or
20 reasonably should know, to be relevant to the proper tax treatment of an item.

   (ii) *No unreasonable assumptions.* The advice must not be based on unreasonable factual or legal assumptions (including assumptions as to future events) and must not unreasonably rely on the representations, statements, findings, or agreements of the taxpayer or any other person. For example, the advice must not be based upon a
25 representation or assumption which the taxpayer knows, or has reason to know, is unlikely to be true, such as an inaccurate representation or assumption as to the taxpayer's purposes for entering into a transaction or for structuring a transaction in a particular manner.

   (iii) *Reliance on the invalidity of a regulation.* A taxpayer may not rely on an opinion or
30 advice that a regulation is invalid to establish that the taxpayer acted with reasonable cause and good faith unless the taxpayer adequately disclosed, in accordance with § 1.6662-3(c)(2), the position that the regulation in question is invalid.

   (2) *Advice defined.* Advice is any communication, including the opinion of a professional tax advisor, setting forth the analysis or conclusion of a person, other than
35 the taxpayer, provided to (or for the benefit of) the taxpayer and on which the taxpayer relies, directly or indirectly, with respect to the imposition of the section 6662 accuracy-related penalty. Advice does not have to be in any particular form.

   (3) *Cross-reference.* For rules applicable to advisors, see e.g., §§ 1.6694-1 through 1.6694-3 (regarding preparer penalties), 31 CFR 10.22 (regarding diligence as to
40 accuracy), 31 CFR 10.33 (regarding tax shelter opinions), and 31 CFR 10.34 (regarding standards for advising with respect to tax return positions and for preparing or signing returns).

   (d) U*nderpayments attributable to reportable transactions.* If any portion of an underpayment is attributable to a reportable transaction, as defined in § 1.6011-4(b) (or §
45 1.6011-4T(b), as applicable), then failure by the taxpayer to disclose the transaction in accordance with § 1.6011-4 (or § 1.6011-4T, as applicable) is a strong indication that the taxpayer did not act in good faith with respect to the portion of the underpayment attributable to the reportable transaction.

   (e) *Pass-through items.* The determination of whether a taxpayer acted with
50 reasonable cause and in good faith with respect to an underpayment that is related to an item reflected on the return of a pass-through entity is made on the basis of all pertinent

Sec. 6663.   Imposition of fraud penalty

facts and circumstances, including the taxpayer's own actions, as well as the actions of the pass-through entity.

(f) *Special rules for substantial understatement penalty attributable to tax shelter items of corporations--(1) In general; facts and circumstances.* The determination of whether a corporation acted with reasonable cause and in good faith in its treatment of a tax shelter item (as defined in § 1.6662-4(g)(3)) is based on all pertinent facts and circumstances. Paragraphs (f)(2), (3), and (4) of this section set forth rules that apply, in the case of a penalty attributable to a substantial understatement of income tax (within the meaning of section 6662(d)), in determining whether a corporation acted with reasonable cause and in good faith with respect to a tax shelter item.

(2) *Reasonable cause based on legal justification--(i) Minimum requirements.* A corporation's legal justification (as defined in paragraph (f)(2)(ii) of this section) may be taken into account, as appropriate, in establishing that the corporation acted with reasonable cause and in good faith in its treatment of a tax shelter item only if the authority requirement of paragraph (f)(2)(i)(A) of this section and the belief requirement of paragraph (f)(2)(i)(B) of this section are satisfied (the minimum requirements). Thus, a failure to satisfy the minimum requirements will preclude a finding of reasonable cause and good faith based (in whole or in part) on the corporation's legal justification.

(A) *Authority requirement.* The authority requirement is satisfied only if there is substantial authority (within the meaning of § 1.6662-4(d)) for the tax treatment of the item.

(B) *Belief requirement.* The belief requirement is satisfied only if, based on all facts and circumstances, the corporation reasonably believed, at the time the return was filed, that the tax treatment of the item was more likely than not the proper treatment. For purposes of the preceding sentence, a corporation is considered reasonably to believe that the tax treatment of an item is more likely than not the proper tax treatment if (without taking into account the possibility that a return will not be audited, that an issue will not be raised on audit, or that an issue will be settled)--

(1) The corporation analyzes the pertinent facts and authorities in the manner described in § 1.6662-4(d)(3)(ii), and in reliance upon that analysis, reasonably concludes in good faith that there is a greater than 50-percent likelihood that the tax treatment of the item will be upheld if challenged by the Internal Revenue Service; or

(2) The corporation reasonably relies in good faith on the opinion of a professional tax advisor, if the opinion is based on the tax advisor's analysis of the pertinent facts and authorities in the manner described in § 1.6662-4(d)(3)(ii) and unambiguously states that the tax advisor concludes that there is a greater than 50-percent likelihood that the tax treatment of the item will be upheld if challenged by the Internal Revenue Service. (For this purpose, the requirements of paragraph (c) of this section must be met with respect to the opinion of a professional tax advisor.)

(ii) *Legal justification defined.* For purposes of this paragraph (e), legal justification includes any justification relating to the treatment or characterization under the Federal tax law of the tax shelter item or of the entity, plan, or arrangement that gave rise to the item. Thus, a taxpayer's belief (whether independently formed or based on the advice of others) as to the merits of the taxpayer's underlying position is a legal justification.

(3) *Minimum requirements not dispositive.* Satisfaction of the minimum requirements of paragraph (f)(2) of this section is an important factor to be considered in determining whether a corporate taxpayer acted with reasonable cause and in good faith, but is not necessarily dispositive. For example, depending on the circumstances, satisfaction of the minimum requirements may not be dispositive if the taxpayer's participation in the tax shelter lacked significant business purpose, if the taxpayer claimed tax benefits that are unreasonable in comparison to the taxpayer's investment in the tax shelter, or if the

Sec. 6663. Imposition of fraud penalty

taxpayer agreed with the organizer or promoter of the tax shelter that the taxpayer would protect the confidentiality of the tax aspects of the structure of the tax shelter.

(4) *Other factors.* Facts and circumstances other than a corporation's legal justification may be taken into account, as appropriate, in determining whether the corporation acted
5   with reasonable cause and in good faith with respect to a tax shelter item regardless of whether the minimum requirements of paragraph (f)(2) of this section are satisfied.

***

(h) *Valuation misstatements of charitable deduction property*--(1) *In general.* There may be reasonable cause and good faith with respect to a portion of an underpayment that is attributable to a substantial (or gross) valuation misstatement of charitable
10 deduction property (as defined in paragraph (h)(2) of this section) only if--

(i) The claimed value of the property was based on a qualified appraisal (as defined in paragraph (h)(2) of this section) by a qualified appraiser (as defined in paragraph (h)(2) of this section); and

15   (ii) In addition to obtaining a qualified appraisal, the taxpayer made a good faith investigation of the value of the contributed property.

(2) *Definitions.* For purposes of this paragraph (h):

Charitable deduction property means any property (other than money or publicly traded securities, as defined in § 1.170A-13(c)(7)(xi)) contributed by the taxpayer in a
20 contribution for which a deduction was claimed under section 170.

Qualified appraisal means a qualified appraisal as defined in § 1.170A-13(c)(3).

Qualified appraiser means a qualified appraiser as defined in § 1.170A-13(c)(5).

(3) *Special rules.* The rules of this paragraph (h) apply regardless of whether § 1.170A-13 permits a taxpayer to claim a charitable contribution deduction for the property
25 without obtaining a qualified appraisal. The rules of this paragraph (h) apply in addition to the generally applicable rules concerning reasonable cause and good faith.

[T.D. 8381, 56 FR 67508, Dec. 31, 1991; T.D. 8381, 57 FR 6166, Feb. 20, 1992; T.D. 8617, 60 FR 45666, Sept. 1, 1995; T.D. 8790, 63 FR 66435, Dec. 2, 1998; T.D. 9109, 68
30 FR 75128, Dec. 30, 2003]

Reg. § 1.6694-2 Penalty for understatement due to an unrealistic position.

(a) *In general*--(1) *Proscribed conduct.* Except as otherwise provided in this section, if any part of an understatement of liability relating to a return of tax under subtitle A of the
35 Internal Revenue Code or claim for refund of tax under subtitle A of the Internal Revenue Code is due to a position for which there was not a realistic possibility of being sustained on its merits, any person who is a preparer with respect to such return or claim for refund who knew or reasonably should have known of such position is subject to a penalty of $250 with respect to such return or claim for refund.
40   (2) *Special rule for employers and partnerships.* An employer or partnership of a preparer subject to penalty under section 6694(a) is also subject to penalty only if--

(i) One or more members of the principal management (or principal officers) of the firm or a branch office participated in or knew of the conduct proscribed by section 6694(a);

(ii) The employer or partnership failed to provide reasonable and appropriate
45 procedures for review of the position for which the penalty is imposed; or

(iii) Such review procedures were disregarded in the formulation of the advice, or the preparation of the return or claim for refund, that included the position for which the penalty is imposed.

(b) *Realistic possibility of being sustained on its merits*--(1) *In general.* A position is
50 considered to have a realistic possibility of being sustained on its merits if a reasonable and well-informed analysis by a person knowledgeable in the tax law would lead such a

Sec. 6663. Imposition of fraud penalty

person to conclude that the position has approximately a one in three, or greater, likelihood of being sustained on its merits (realistic possibility standard). In making this determination, the possibility that the position will not be challenged by the Internal Revenue Service (e.g., because the taxpayer's return may not be audited or because the issue may not be raised on audit) is not to be taken into account. The analysis prescribed 5 by § 1.6662-4(d)(3)(ii) for purposes of determining whether substantial authority is present applies for purposes of determining whether the realistic possibility standard is satisfied.

(2) *Authorities.* The authorities considered in determining whether a position satisfies the realistic possibility standard are those authorities provided in § 1.6662-4(d)(3)(iii). 10

(3) *Examples.* The provisions of paragraphs (b)(1) and (b)(2) of this section are illustrated by the following examples:

Example 1. A new statute is unclear as to whether a certain transaction that a taxpayer has engaged in will result in favorable tax treatment. Prior law, however, supported the taxpayer's position. There are no regulations under the new statute and no 15 authority other than the statutory language and committee reports. The committee reports state that the intent was not to adversely affect transactions similar to the taxpayer's transaction. The taxpayer's position satisfies the realistic possibility standard.

Example 2. A taxpayer has engaged in a transaction that is adversely affected by a new statutory provision. Prior law supported a position favorable to the taxpayer. The 20 preparer believes that the new statute is inequitable as applied to the taxpayer's situation. The statutory language is unambiguous as it applies to the transaction (e.g., it applies to all manufacturers and the taxpayer is a manufacturer of widgets). The committee reports do not specifically address the taxpayer's situation. A position contrary to the statute does not satisfy the realistic possibility standard. 25

Example 3. The facts are the same as in Example 2, except the committee reports indicate that Congress did not intend to apply the new statutory provision to the taxpayer's transaction (e.g., to a manufacturer of widgets). Thus, there is a conflict between the general language of the statute, which adversely affects the taxpayer's transaction, and a specific statement in the committee reports that transactions such as 30 the taxpayer's are not adversely affected. A position consistent with either the statute or the committee reports satisfies the realistic possibility standard. However, a position consistent with the committee reports constitutes a disregard of a rule or regulation and, therefore, must be adequately disclosed in order to avoid the section 6694(b) penalty.

Example 4. The instructions to an item on a tax form published by the Internal 35 Revenue Service are incorrect and are clearly contrary to the regulations. Before the return is prepared, the Internal Revenue Service publishes an announcement acknowledging the error and providing the correct instruction. Under these facts, a position taken on a return which is consistent with the regulations satisfies the realistic possibility standard. On the other hand, a position taken on a return which is consistent 40 with the incorrect instructions does not satisfy the realistic possibility standard. However, if the preparer relied on the incorrect instructions and was not aware of the announcement or the regulations, the reasonable cause and good faith exception may apply depending on all facts and circumstances. See § 1.6694-2(d).

Example 5. A statute is silent as to whether a taxpayer may take a certain position on 45 the taxpayer's 1991 Federal income tax return. Three private letter rulings issued to other taxpayers in 1987 and 1988 support the taxpayer's position. However, proposed regulations issued in 1990 are clearly contrary to the taxpayer's position. After the issuance of the proposed regulations, the earlier private letter rulings cease to be authorities and are not taken into account in determining whether the taxpayer's position 50 satisfies the realistic possibility standard. See § 1.6694-2(b)(2) and § 1.6662-4(d)(3)(iii).

Sec. 6663. Imposition of fraud penalty

The taxpayer's position may or may not satisfy the realistic possibility standard, depending on an analysis of all the relevant authorities.

Example 6. In the course of researching whether a particular position has a realistic possibility of being sustained on its merits, a preparer discovers that a taxpayer took the
5 same position on a return several years ago and that the return was audited by the Service. The taxpayer tells the preparer that the revenue agent who conducted the audit was aware of the position and decided that the treatment on the return was correct. The revenue agent's report, however, made no mention of the position. The determination by the revenue agent is not authority for purposes of the realistic possibility standard.
10 However, the preparer's reliance on the revenue agent's determination in the audit may qualify for the reasonable cause and good faith exception depending on all facts and circumstances. See § 1.6694-2(d). Also see § 1.6694-2(b)(4) and § 1.6662-4(d)(3)(iv)(A) regarding affirmative statements in a revenue agent's report.

Example 7. In the course of researching whether an interpretation of a phrase
15 incorporated in the Internal Revenue Code has a realistic possibility of being sustained on its merits, a preparer discovers that identical language in the taxing statute of another jurisdiction (e.g., a state or foreign country) has been authoritatively construed by a court of that jurisdiction in a manner which would be favorable to the taxpayer, if the same interpretation were applied to the phrase applicable to the taxpayer's situation. The
20 construction of the statute of the other jurisdiction is not authority for purposes of determining whether the position satisfies the realistic possibility standard. See § 1.6694-2(b)(2) and § 1.6662-4(d)(3)(iii). However, as in the case of conclusions reached in treatises and legal periodicals, the authorities underlying the court's opinion, if relevant to the taxpayer's situation, may give a position favorable to the taxpayer a realistic
25 possibility of being sustained on its merits. See § 1.6694-2(b)(2) and § 1.6662-4(d)(3)(iii).

Example 8. In the course of researching whether an interpretation of a statutory phrase has a realistic possibility of being sustained on its merits, a preparer discovers that identical language appearing in another place in the Internal Revenue Code has consistently been interpreted by the courts and by the Service in a manner which would
30 be favorable to the taxpayer, if the same interpretation were applied to the phrase applicable to the taxpayer's situation. No authority has interpreted the phrase applicable to the taxpayer's situation. The interpretations of the identical language are relevant in arriving at a well reasoned construction of the language at issue, but the context in which the language arises also must be taken into account in determining whether the realistic
35 possibility standard is satisfied.

Example 9. A new statutory provision is silent on the tax treatment of an item under the provision. However, the committee reports explaining the provision direct the Treasury to issue regulations interpreting the provision in a specified way. No regulations have been issued at the time the preparer must recommend a position on the tax treatment of the
40 item, and no other authorities exist. The position supported by the committee reports satisfies the realistic possibility standard.

(4) Written determinations. To the extent a position has substantial authority with respect to the taxpayer by virtue of a ``written determination'' as provided in § 1.6662-4(d)(3)(iv)(A), such position will be considered to satisfy the realistic possibility standard with
45 respect to the taxpayer's preparer for purposes of section 6694(a).

(5) When ``realistic possibility'' determined. For purposes of this section, the requirement that a position satisfy the realistic possibility standard must be satisfied on the date prescribed by paragraph (b)(5)(i) or (b)(5)(ii) of this section, whichever is applicable.
50 (i) Signing preparers--(A) In the case of a signing preparer, the relevant date is the date the preparer signs and dates the return or claim for refund.

1110

Sec. 6663. Imposition of fraud penalty

(B) If the preparer did not date the return or claim for refund, the relevant date is the date the taxpayer signed and dated the return or claim for refund. If the taxpayer also did not date the return or claim for refund, the relevant date is the date the return or claim for refund was filed.

(ii) *Nonsigning preparers.* In the case of a nonsigning preparer, the relevant date is the 5 date the preparer provides the advice. That date will be determined based on all the facts and circumstances.

(c) *Exception for adequate disclosure of nonfrivolous positions--*(1) *In general.* The section 6694(a) penalty will not be imposed on a preparer if the position taken is not frivolous and is adequately disclosed. For an exception to the section 6694(a) penalty for 10 reasonable cause and good faith, see paragraph (d) of this section.

(2) *Frivolous.* For purposes of this section, a ``frivolous" position with respect to an item is one that is patently improper.

(3) *Adequate disclosure--*(i) *Signing preparers.* In the case of a signing preparer, disclosure of a position that does not satisfy the realistic possibility standard is adequate 15 only if the disclosure is made in accordance with § 1.6662-4(f) (which permits disclosure on a properly completed and filed Form 8275 or 8275-R, as appropriate, or on the return in accordance with an annual revenue procedure).

(ii) *Nonsigning preparers.* In the case of a nonsigning preparer, disclosure of a position that does not satisfy the realistic possibility standard is adequate if the position is 20 disclosed in accordance with § 1.6662-4(f) (which permits disclosure on a properly completed and filed Form 8275 or 8275-R, as appropriate, or on the return in accordance with an annual revenue procedure). In addition, disclosure of a position is adequate in the case of a nonsigning preparer if, with respect to that position, the preparer complies with the provisions of paragraph (c)(3)(ii)(A) or (B) of this section, whichever is applicable.   25

(A) *Advice to taxpayers.* If a nonsigning preparer provides advice to the taxpayer with respect to a position that does not satisfy the realistic possibility standard, disclosure of that position is adequate if the advice includes a statement that the position lacks substantial authority and, therefore, may be subject to penalty under section 6662(d) unless adequately disclosed in the manner provided in § 1.6662-4(f) (or in the case of a 30 tax shelter item, that the position lacks substantial authority and, therefore, may be subject to penalty under section 6662(d) regardless of disclosure). If the advice with respect to the position is in writing, the statement concerning disclosure (or the statement regarding possible penalty under section 6662(d)) also must be in writing. If the advice with respect to the position is oral, advice to the taxpayer concerning the need to disclose 35 (or the advice regarding possible penalty under section 6662(d)) also may be oral. The determination as to whether oral advice as to disclosure (or the oral advice regarding possible penalty under section 6662(d)) was in fact given is based on all facts and circumstances. Contemporaneously prepared documentation of the oral advice regarding disclosure (or the oral advice regarding possible penalty under section 6662(d)) generally 40 is sufficient to establish that the advice was given to the taxpayer.

(B) *Advice to another preparer.* If a nonsigning preparer provides advice to another preparer with respect to a position that does not satisfy the realistic possibility standard, disclosure of that position is adequate if the advice includes a statement that disclosure under section 6694(a) is required. If the advice with respect to the position is in writing, 45 the statement concerning disclosure also must be in writing. If the advice with respect to the position is oral, advice to the preparer concerning the need to disclose also may be oral. The determination as to whether oral advice as to diclosure was in fact given is based on all facts and circumstances. Contemporaneously prepared documentation of the oral advice regarding disclosure generally is sufficient to establish that the advice 50 regarding disclosure was given to the other preparer.

Sec. 6663. Imposition of fraud penalty

(d) *Exception for reasonable cause and good faith*. The penalty under section 6694(a) will not be imposed if considering all the facts and circumstances, it is determined that the understatement was due to reasonable cause and that the preparer acted in good faith. Factors to consider include:

5   (1) *Nature of the error causing the understatement*. Whether the error resulted from a provision that was so complex, uncommon, or highly technical that a competent preparer of returns or claims of the type at issue reasonably could have made the error. The reasonable cause and good faith exception does not apply to an error that would have been apparent from a general review of the return or claim for refund by the preparer.

10   (2) *Frequency of errors*. Whether the understatement was the result of an isolated error (such as an inadvertent mathematical or clerical error) rather than a number of errors. Although the reasonable cause and good faith exception generally applies to an isolated error, it does not apply if the isolated error is so obvious, flagrant or material that it should have been discovered during a review of the return or claim. Furthermore, the

15 reasonable cause and good faith exception does not apply if there is a pattern of errors on a return or claim for refund even though any one error, in isolation, would have qualified for the reasonable cause and good faith exception.

(3) *Materiality of errors*. Whether the understatement was material in relation to the correct tax liability. The reasonable cause and good faith exception generally applies if

20 the understatement is of a relatively immaterial amount. Nevertheless, even an immaterial understatement may not qualify for the reasonable cause and good faith exception if the error or errors creating the understatement are sufficiently obvious or numerous.

(4) *Preparer's normal office practice*. Whether the preparer's normal office practice,

25 when considered together with other facts and circumstances such as the knowledge of the preparer, indicates that the error in question would rarely occur and the normal office practice was followed in preparing the return or claim in question. Such a normal office practice must be a system for promoting accuracy and consistency in the preparation of returns or claims and generally would include, in the case of a signing preparer,

30 checklists, methods for obtaining necessary information from the taxpayer, a review of the prior year's return, and review procedures. Notwithstanding the above, the reasonable cause and good faith exception does not apply if there is a flagrant error on a return or claim for refund, a pattern of errors on a return or claim for refund, or a repetition of the same or similar errors on numerous returns or claims.

35   (5) *Reliance on advice of another preparer*. Whether the preparer relied on the advice of or schedules prepared by (``advice") another preparer as defined in § 1.6694-1(b). The reasonable cause and good faith exception applies if the preparer relied in good faith on the advice of another preparer (or a person who would be considered a preparer under § 1.6694-1(b) had the advice constituted preparation of a substantial portion of the return or

40 claim for refund) who the preparer had reason to believe was competent to render such advice. A preparer is not considered to have relied in good faith if--

(i) The advice is unreasonable on its face;

(ii) The preparer knew or should have known that the other preparer was not aware of all relevant facts; or

45   (iii) The preparer knew or should have known (given the nature of the preparer's practice), at the time the return or claim for refund was prepared, that the advice was no longer reliable due to developments in the law since the time the advice was given.

The advice may be written or oral, but in either case the burden of establishing that the advice was received is on the preparer.

50   (e) *Burden of proof*. In any proceeding with respect to the penalty imposed by section 6694(a), the issues on which the preparer bears the burden of proof include whether--

1112

Sec. 6663. Imposition of fraud penalty

(1) The preparer knew or reasonably should have known that the questioned position was taken on the return;

(2) There is reasonable cause and good faith with respect to such position; and

(3) The position was disclosed adequately in accordance with paragraph (c) of this section.

5

[T.D. 8382, 56 FR 67516, Dec. 31, 1991; T.D. 8382, 57 FR 6061, Feb. 19, 1992]

Sec. 6700. Promoting abusive tax shelters, etc.

(a) Imposition of penalty. -- Any person who--

10

    (1)(A) organizes (or assists in the organization of)--

        (i) a partnership or other entity,

        (ii) any investment plan or arrangement, or

        (iii) any other plan or arrangement, or

    (B) participates (directly or indirectly) in the sale of any interest in an entity or plan or arrangement referred to in subparagraph (A), and

15

    (2) makes or furnishes or causes another person to make or furnish (in connection with such organization or sale)--

        (A) a statement with respect to the allowability of any deduction or credit, the excludability of any income, or the securing of any other tax benefit by reason of holding an interest in the entity or participating in the plan or arrangement which the person knows or has reason to known is false or fraudulent as to any material matter, or

20

        (B) a gross valuation overstatement as to any material matter,

shall pay, with respect to each activity described in paragraph (1), a penalty equal to the $1,000 or, if the person establishes that it is lesser, 100 percent of the gross income derived (or to be derived) by such person from such activity. For purposes of the preceding sentence, activities described in paragraph (1)(A) with respect to each entity or arrangement shall be treated as a separate activity and participation in each sale described in paragraph (1)(B) shall be so treated. Notwithstanding the first sentence, if an activity with respect to which a penalty imposed under this subsection involves a statement described in paragraph (2)(A), the amount of the penalty shall be equal to 50 percent of the gross income derived (or to be derived) from such activity by the person on which the penalty is imposed.

25

30

(b) Rules relating to penalty for gross valuation overstatements. --

    (1) Gross valuation overstatement defined. -- For purposes of this section, the term "gross valuation overstatement" means any statement as to the value of any property or services if -

35

        (A) the value so stated exceeds 200 percent of the amount determined to be the correct valuation, and

        (B) the value of such property or services is directly related to the amount of any deduction or credit allowable under chapter 1 to any participant.

    (2) Authority to waive. -- The Secretary may waive all or any part of the penalty provided by subsection (a) with respect to any gross valuation overstatement on a showing that there was a reasonable basis for the valuation and that such valuation was made in good faith.

40

(c) Penalty in addition to other penalties. -- The penalty imposed by this section shall be in addition to any other penalty provided by law.

45

Sec. 6700.   Promoting abusive tax shelters, etc.

Sec. 6701.   Penalties for aiding and abetting understatement of tax liability

(a) Imposition of penalty. -- Any person--

(1) who aids or assists in, procures, or advises with respect to, the preparation or presentation of any portion of a return, affidavit, claim, or other document,

(2) who knows (or has reason to believe) that such portion will be used in connection with any material matter arising under the internal revenue laws, and

(3) who knows that such portion (if so used) would result in an understatement of the liability for tax of another person,

shall pay a penalty with respect to each such document in the amount determined under subsection (b).

(b) Amount of penalty. --

(1) In general. -- Except as provided in paragraph (2), the amount of the penalty imposed by subsection (a) shall be $1,000.

(2) Corporations. -- If the return, affidavit, claim, or other document relates to the tax liability of a corporation, the amount of the penalty imposed by subsection (a) shall be $10,000.

(3) Only 1 penalty per person per period. -- If any person is subject to a penalty under subsection (a) with respect to any document relating to any taxpayer for any taxable period (or where there is no taxable period, any taxable event), such person shall not be subject to a penalty under subsection (a) with respect to any other document relating to such taxpayer for such taxable period (or event).

(c) Activities of subordinates. --

(1) In general. -- For purposes of subsection (a), the term "procures" includes--

(A) ordering (or otherwise causing) a subordinate to do an act, and

(B) knowing of, and not attempting to prevent, participation by a subordinate in an act.

(2) Subordinate. -- For purposes of paragraph (1), the term "subordinate" means any other person (whether or not a director, officer, employee, or agent of the taxpayer involved) over whose activities the person has direction, supervision, or control.

(d) Taxpayer not required to have knowledge. -- Subsection (a) shall apply whether or not the understatement is with the knowledge or consent of the persons authorized or required to present the return, affidavit, claim, or other document.

(e) Certain actions not treated as aid or assistance. -- For purposes of subsection (a)(1), a person furnishing typing, reproducing, or other mechanical assistance with respect to a document shall not be treated as having aided or assisted in the preparation of such document by reason of such assistance.

(f) Penalty in addition to other penalties. --

(1) In general. -- Except as provided by paragraphs (2) and (3), the penalty imposed by this section shall be in addition to any other penalty provided by law.

(2) Coordination with return preparer penalties. -- No penalty shall be assessed under subsection (a) or (b) of section 6694 on any person with respect to any document for which a penalty is assessed on such person under subsection (a).

(3) Coordination with section 6700. -- No penalty shall be assessed under section 6700 on any person with respect to any document for which a penalty is assessed on such person under subsection (a).

Sec. 6701.   Penalties for aiding and abetting understatement of tax liability

Sec. 6702.   Frivolous Tax Submissions

(a) **Civil Penalty for Frivolous Tax Returns.** -- A person shall pay a penalty of $5,000 if--

(1) such person files what purports to be a return of a tax imposed by this title but which--

(A) does not contain information on which the substantial correctness of the self- 5 assessment may be judged, or

(B) contains information that on its face indicates that the self-assessment is substantially incorrect, and

(2) the conduct referred to in paragraph (1)--

(A) is based on a position which the Secretary has identified as frivolous under 10 subsection (c), or

(B) reflects a desire to delay or impede the administration of Federal tax laws.

(b) **Civil Penalty for Specified Frivolous Submissions.** --

(1) **Imposition of penalty.** -- Except as provided in paragraph (3), any person who submits a specified frivolous submission shall pay a penalty of $5,000.   15

(2) **Specified frivolous submission.** -- For purposes of this section--

(A) **Specified frivolous submission.** --The term `specified frivolous submission' means a specified submission if any portion of such submission--

(i) is based on a position which the Secretary has identified as frivolous under

subsection (c), or   20

(ii) reflects a desire to delay or impede the administration of Federal tax laws.

(B) **Specified submission.** -- The term `specified submission' means--

(i) a request for a hearing under--

(I) section 6320 (relating to notice and opportunity for hearing upon filing of notice of lien), or   25

(II) section 6330 (relating to notice and opportunity for hearing before levy), and

(ii) an application under--

(I) section 6159 (relating to agreements for payment of tax liability in installments),

(II) section 7122 (relating to compromises), or   30

(III) section 7811 (relating to taxpayer assistance orders).

(3) **Opportunity to withdraw submission.** -- If the Secretary provides a person with notice that a submission is a specified frivolous submission and such person withdraws such submission within 30 days after such notice, the penalty imposed under paragraph (1) shall not apply with respect to such submission.   35

(c) **Listing of Frivolous Positions.** -- The Secretary shall prescribe and periodically revise) a list of positions which the Secretary has identified as being frivolous for purposes of this subsection. The Secretary shall not include in such list any position that the Secretary determines meets the requirement of section 6662(d)(2)(B)(ii)(II).

(d) **Reduction of Penalty.** -- The Secretary may reduce the amount of any penalty imposed 40 under this section if the Secretary determines that such reduction would promote compliance with and administration of the Federal tax laws.

Sec. 6702. Frivolous Tax Submissions

(e) Penalties in Addition to Other Penalties. -- The penalties imposed by this section shall be in addition to any other penalty provided by law.

Sec. 6707. Failure to furnish information regarding reportable transactions

(a) In general. -- If a person who is required to file a return under section 6111(a) with respect to any reportable transaction--

5

(1) fails to file such return on or before the date prescribed therefor, or

(2) files false or incomplete information with the Secretary with respect to such transaction,

such person shall pay a penalty with respect to such return in the amount determined under subsection (b).

10   **(b) Amount of penalty.** --

(1) In general. -- Except as provided in paragraph (2), the penalty imposed under subsection (a) with respect to any failure shall be $50,000.

(2) Listed transactions. -- The penalty imposed under subsection (a) with respect to any listed transaction shall be an amount equal to the greater of--

15

(A) $200,000, or

(B) 50 percent of the gross income derived by such person with respect to aid, assistance, or advice which is provided with respect to the listed transaction before the date the return is filed under section 6111.

Subparagraph (B) shall be applied by substituting "75 percent" for "50 percent" in the case of

20   an intentional failure or act described in subsection (a).

(c) Rescission authority. -- The provisions of section 6707A(d) (relating to authority of Commissioner to rescind penalty) shall apply to any penalty imposed under this section.

(d) Reportable and listed transactions. -- For purposes of this section, the terms "reportable transaction" and "listed transaction" have the respective meanings given to such terms by section

25   6707A(c).

Sec. 6707A. Penalty for failure to include reportable transaction information with return

(a) Imposition of penalty. -- Any person who fails to include on any return or statement any information with respect to a reportable transaction which is required under section 6011 to be

30   included with such return or statement shall pay a penalty in the amount determined under subsection (b).

(b) Amount of penalty. --

(1) In general. -- Except as provided in paragraph (2), the amount of the penalty under subsection (a) shall be--

35

(A) $10,000 in the case of a natural person, and

(B) $50,000 in any other case.

(2) Listed transaction. -- The amount of the penalty under subsection (a) with respect to a listed transaction shall be -

(A) $100,000 in the case of a natural person, and

40

(B) $200,000 in any other case.

Sec. 6707A. Penalty for failure to include reportable transaction information with return

(c) **Definitions.** -- For purposes of this section:

(1) **Reportable transaction.** -- The term "reportable transaction" means any transaction with respect to which information is required to be included with a return or statement because, as determined under regulations prescribed under section 6011, such transaction is of a type which the Secretary determines as having a potential for tax avoidance or evasion.   5

(2) **Listed transaction.** -- The term "listed transaction" means a reportable transaction which is the same as, or substantially similar to, a transaction specifically identified by the Secretary as a tax avoidance transaction for purposes of section 6011.

***

(f) **Coordination with other penalties.** -- The penalty imposed by this section shall be in   10 addition to any other penalty imposed by this title.

Sec. 7121. Closing agreements

(a) **Authorization.** -- The Secretary is authorized to enter into an agreement in writing with any person relating to the liability of such person (or of the person or estate for whom he acts) in   15 respect of any internal revenue tax for any taxable period.

***

Reg. § 301.7121-1 Closing agreements.

(a) *In general.* The Commissioner may enter into a written agreement with any person relating to the liability of such person (or of the person or estate for whom he acts) in   20 respect of any internal revenue tax for any taxable period ending prior or subsequent to the date of such agreement. A closing agreement may be entered into in any case in which there appears to be an advantage in having the case permanently and conclusively closed, or if good and sufficient reasons are shown by the taxpayer for desiring a closing agreement and it is determined by the Commissioner that the United States will sustain   25 no disadvantage through consummation of such an agreement.

(b) *Scope of closing agreement*--(1) *In general.* A closing agreement may be executed even though under the agreement the taxpayer is not liable for any tax for the period to which the agreement relates. There may be a series of closing agreements relating to the tax liability for a single period.   30

(2) *Taxable periods ended prior to date of closing agreement.* Closing agreements with respect to taxable periods ended prior to the date of the agreement may relate to the total tax liability of the taxpayer or to one or more separate items affecting the tax liability of the taxpayer, as, for example, the amount of gross income, deduction for losses, depreciation, depletion, the year in which an item of income is to be included in gross   35 income, the year in which an item of loss is to be deducted, or the value of property on a specific date. A closing agreement may also be entered into for the purpose of allowing a deficiency dividend deduction under section 547. In addition, a closing agreement constitutes a determination as defined by section 1313.

(3) *Taxable periods ending subsequent to date of closing agreement.* Closing   40 agreements with respect to taxable periods ending subsequent to the date of the agreement may relate to one or more separate items affecting the tax liability of the taxpayer.

(4) *Illustration.* The provisions of this paragraph may be illustrated by the following example: 45

Example. A owns 500 shares of stock in the XYZ Corporation which he purchased prior to March 1, 1913. A is considering selling 200 shares of such stock but is uncertain as to the basis of the stock for the purpose of computing gain. Either prior or subsequent to the sale, a closing agreement may be entered into determining the market value of such stock as of March 1, 1913, which represents the basis for determining gain if it exceeds the adjusted basis otherwise determined as of such date. Not only may the closing agreement determine the basis for computing gain on the sale of the 200 shares of stock, but such an agreement may also determine the basis (unless or until the law is changed to require the use of some other factor to determine basis) of the remaining 300 shares of stock upon which gain will be computed in a subsequent sale.

(c) *Finality.* A closing agreement which is approved within such time as may be stated in such agreement, or later agreed to, shall be final and conclusive, and, except upon a showing of fraud or malfeasance, or misrepresentation of a material fact:

(1) The case shall not be reopened as to the matters agreed upon or the agreement modified by any officer, employee, or agent of the United States, and

(2) In any suit, action, or proceeding, such agreement, or any determination, assessment, collection, payment, abatement, refund, or credit made in accordance therewith, shall not be annulled, modified, set aside, or disregarded. However, a closing agreement with respect to a taxable period ending subsequent to the date of the agreement is subject to any change in, or modification of, the law enacted subsequent to the date of the agreement and made applicable to such taxable period, and each closing agreement shall so recite.

(d) *Procedure with respect to closing agreements--*(1) *Submission of request.* A request for a closing agreement which relates to a prior taxable period may be submitted at any time before a case with respect to the tax liability involved is docketed in the Tax Court of the United States. All closing agreements shall be executed on forms prescribed by the Internal Revenue Service. The procedure with respect to requests for closing agreements shall be under such rules as may be prescribed from time to time by the Commissioner in accordance with the regulations under this section.

(2) *Collection, credit, or refund.* Any tax or deficiency in tax determined pursuant to a closing agreement shall be assessed and collected, and any overpayment determined pursuant thereto shall be credited or refunded, in accordance with the applicable provisions of law.

Sec. 7122. Compromises

(a) **Authorization.** -- The Secretary may compromise any civil or criminal case arising under the internal revenue laws prior to reference to the Department of Justice for prosecution or defense; and the Attorney General or his delegate may compromise any such case after reference to the Department of Justice for prosecution or defense.

***

Reg. § 301.7122-1 Compromises.

(a) *In general--*(1) If the Secretary determines that there are grounds for compromise under this section, the Secretary may, at the Secretary's discretion, compromise any civil or criminal liability arising under the internal revenue laws prior to reference of a case involving such a liability to the Department of Justice for prosecution or defense.

(2) An agreement to compromise may relate to a civil or criminal liability for taxes, interest, or penalties. Unless the terms of the offer and acceptance expressly provide otherwise, acceptance of an offer to compromise a civil liability does not remit a criminal liability, nor does acceptance of an offer to compromise a criminal liability remit a civil liability.

(b) *Grounds for compromise--*(1) Doubt as to liability. Doubt as to liability exists where

Sec. 7122. Compromises

there is a genuine dispute as to the existence or amount of the correct tax liability under the law. Doubt as to liability does not exist where the liability has been established by a final court decision or judgment concerning the existence or amount of the liability. See paragraph (f)(4) of this section for special rules applicable to rejection of offers in cases where the Internal Revenue Service (IRS) is unable to locate the taxpayer's return or 5 return information to verify the liability.

(2) *Doubt as to collectibility*. Doubt as to collectibility exists in any case where the taxpayer's assets and income are less than the full amount of the liability.

(3) *Promote effective tax administration*. (i) A compromise may be entered into to promote effective tax administration when the Secretary determines that, although 10 collection in full could be achieved, collection of the full liability would cause the taxpayer economic hardship within the meaning of § 301.6343-1.

(ii) If there are no grounds for compromise under paragraphs (b)(1), (2), or (3)(i) of this section, the IRS may compromise to promote effective tax administration where compelling public policy or equity considerations identified by the taxpayer provide a 15 sufficient basis for compromising the liability. Compromise will be justified only where, due to exceptional circumstances, collection of the full liability would undermine public confidence that the tax laws are being administered in a fair and equitable manner. A taxpayer proposing compromise under this paragraph (b)(3)(ii) will be expected to demonstrate circumstances that justify compromise even though a similarly situated 20 taxpayer may have paid his liability in full.

(iii) No compromise to promote effective tax administration may be entered into if compromise of the liability would undermine compliance by taxpayers with the tax laws.

(c) *Special rules for evaluating offers to compromise*--(1) *In general*. Once a basis for compromise under paragraph (b) of this section has been identified, the decision to 25 accept or reject an offer to compromise, as well as the terms and conditions agreed to, is left to the discretion of the Secretary. The determination whether to accept or reject an offer to compromise will be based upon consideration of all the facts and circumstances, including whether the circumstances of a particular case warrant acceptance of an amount that might not otherwise be acceptable under the Secretary's policies and 30 procedures.

(2) *Doubt as to collectibility*--(i) *Allowable expenses*. A determination of doubt as to collectibility will include a determination of ability to pay. In determining ability to pay, the Secretary will permit taxpayers to retain sufficient funds to pay basic living expenses. The determination of the amount of such basic living expenses will be founded upon an 35 evaluation of the individual facts and circumstances presented by the taxpayer's case. To guide this determination, guidelines published by the Secretary on national and local living expense standards will be taken into account.

(ii) *Nonliable spouses*--(A) *In general*. Where a taxpayer is offering to compromise a liability for which the taxpayer's spouse has no liability, the assets and income of the 40 nonliable spouse will not be considered in determining the amount of an adequate offer. The assets and income of a nonliable spouse may be considered, however, to the extent property has been transferred by the taxpayer to the nonliable spouse under circumstances that would permit the IRS to effect collection of the taxpayer's liability from such property (e.g., property that was conveyed in fraud of creditors), property has been 45 transferred by the taxpayer to the nonliable spouse for the purpose of removing the property from consideration by the IRS in evaluating the compromise, or as provided in paragraph (c)(2)(ii)(B) of this section. The IRS also may request information regarding the assets and income of the nonliable spouse for the purpose of verifying the amount of and responsibility for expenses claimed by the taxpayer. 50

(B) *Exception*. Where collection of the taxpayer's liability from the assets and income

Sec. 7122. Compromises

of the nonliable spouse is permitted by applicable state law (e.g., under state community property laws), the assets and income of the nonliable spouse will be considered in determining the amount of an adequate offer except to the extent that the taxpayer and the nonliable spouse demonstrate that collection of such assets and income would have
5 a material and adverse impact on the standard of living of the taxpayer, the nonliable spouse, and their dependents.

(3) *Compromises to promote effective tax administration*--(i) Factors supporting (but not conclusive of) a determination that collection would cause economic hardship within the meaning of paragraph (b)(3)(i) of this section include, but are not limited to--
10   (A) Taxpayer is incapable of earning a living because of a long term illness, medical condition, or disability, and it is reasonably foreseeable that taxpayer's financial resources will be exhausted providing for care and support during the course of the condition;

(B) Although taxpayer has certain monthly income, that income is exhausted each month in providing for the care of dependents with no other means of support; and
15   (C) Although taxpayer has certain assets, the taxpayer is unable to borrow against the equity in those assets and liquidation of those assets to pay outstanding tax liabilities would render the taxpayer unable to meet basic living expenses.

(ii) Factors supporting (but not conclusive of) a determination that compromise would undermine compliance within the meaning of paragraph (b)(3)(iii) of this section include,
20 but are not limited to--

(A) Taxpayer has a history of noncompliance with the filing and payment requirements of the Internal Revenue Code;

(B) Taxpayer has taken deliberate actions to avoid the payment of taxes; and

(C) Taxpayer has encouraged others to refuse to comply with the tax laws.
25   (iii) The following examples illustrate the types of cases that may be compromised by the Secretary, at the Secretary's discretion, under the economic hardship provisions of paragraph (b)(3)(i) of this section:

Example 1. The taxpayer has assets sufficient to satisfy the tax liability. The taxpayer provides full time care and assistance to her dependent child, who has a serious long-
30 term illness. It is expected that the taxpayer will need to use the equity in his assets to provide for adequate basic living expenses and medical care for his child. The taxpayer's overall compliance history does not weigh against compromise.

Example 2. The taxpayer is retired and his only income is from a pension. The taxpayer's only asset is a retirement account, and the funds in the account are sufficient
35 to satisfy the liability. Liquidation of the retirement account would leave the taxpayer without an adequate means to provide for basic living expenses. The taxpayer's overall compliance history does not weigh against compromise.

Example 3. The taxpayer is disabled and lives on a fixed income that will not, after allowance of basic living expenses, permit full payment of his liability under an installment
40 agreement. The taxpayer also owns a modest house that has been specially equipped to accommodate his disability. The taxpayer's equity in the house is sufficient to permit payment of the liability he owes. However, because of his disability and limited earning potential, the taxpayer is unable to obtain a mortgage or otherwise borrow against this equity. In addition, because the taxpayer's home has been specially equipped to
45 accommodate his disability, forced sale of the taxpayer's residence would create severe adverse consequences for the taxpayer. The taxpayer's overall compliance history does not weigh against compromise.

(iv) The following examples illustrate the types of cases that may be compromised by the Secretary, at the Secretary's discretion, under the public policy and equity provisions
50 of paragraph (b)(3)(ii) of this section:

Example 1. In October of 1986, the taxpayer developed a serious illness that resulted

1120

in almost continuous hospitalizations for a number of years. The taxpayer's medical condition was such that during this period the taxpayer was unable to manage any of his financial affairs. The taxpayer has not filed tax returns since that time. The taxpayer's health has now improved and he has promptly begun to attend to his tax affairs. He discovers that the IRS prepared a substitute for return for the 1986 tax year on the basis 5 of information returns it had received and had assessed a tax deficiency. When the taxpayer discovered the liability, with penalties and interest, the tax bill is more than three times the original tax liability. The taxpayer's overall compliance history does not weigh against compromise.

Example 2. The taxpayer is a salaried sales manager at a department store who has 10 been able to place $2,000 in a tax-deductible IRA account for each of the last two years. The taxpayer learns that he can earn a higher rate of interest on his IRA savings by moving those savings from a money management account to a certificate of deposit at a different financial institution. Prior to transferring his savings, the taxpayer submits an e-mail inquiry to the IRS at its Web Page, requesting information about the steps he must 15 take to preserve the tax benefits he has enjoyed and to avoid penalties. The IRS responds in an answering e-mail that the taxpayer may withdraw his IRA savings from his neighborhood bank, but he must redeposit those savings in a new IRA account within 90 days. The taxpayer withdraws the funds and redeposits them in a new IRA account 63 days later. Upon audit, the taxpayer learns that he has been misinformed about the 20 required rollover period and that he is liable for additional taxes, penalties and additions to tax for not having redeposited the amount within 60 days. Had it not been for the erroneous advice that is reflected in the taxpayer's retained copy of the IRS e-mail response to his inquiry, the taxpayer would have redeposited the amount within the required 60-day period. The taxpayer's overall compliance history does not weigh against 25 compromise.

(d) *Procedures for submission and consideration of offers--*(1) *In general.* An offer to compromise a tax liability pursuant to section 7122 must be submitted according to the procedures, and in the form and manner, prescribed by the Secretary. An offer to compromise a tax liability must be made in writing, must be signed by the taxpayer under 30 penalty of perjury, and must contain all of the information prescribed or requested by the Secretary. However, taxpayers submitting offers to compromise liabilities solely on the basis of doubt as to liability will not be required to provide financial statements.

(2) *When offers become pending and return of offers.* An offer to compromise becomes pending when it is accepted for processing. The IRS may not accept for 35 processing any offer to compromise a liability following reference of a case involving such liability to the Department of Justice for prosecution or defense. If an offer accepted for processing does not contain sufficient information to permit the IRS to evaluate whether the offer should be accepted, the IRS will request that the taxpayer provide the needed additional information. If the taxpayer does not submit the additional information that the 40 IRS has requested within a reasonable time period after such a request, the IRS may return the offer to the taxpayer. The IRS may also return an offer to compromise a tax liability if it determines that the offer was submitted solely to delay collection or was otherwise nonprocessable. An offer returned following acceptance for processing is deemed pending only for the period between the date the offer is accepted for processing 45 and the date the IRS returns the offer to the taxpayer. See paragraphs (f)(5)(ii) and (g)(4) of this section for rules regarding the effect of such returns of offers.

(3) *Withdrawal.* An offer to compromise a tax liability may be withdrawn by the taxpayer or the taxpayer's representative at any time prior to the IRS' acceptance of the offer to compromise. An offer ill be considered withdrawn upon the IRS' receipt of written 50 notification of the withdrawal of the offer either by personal delivery or certified mail, or

Sec. 7122. Compromises

upon issuance of a letter by the IRS confirming the taxpayer's intent to withdraw the offer.

(e) *Acceptance of an offer to compromise a tax liability.*--(1) An offer to compromise has not been accepted until the IRS issues a written notification of acceptance to the taxpayer or the taxpayer's representative.

5   (2) As additional consideration for the acceptance of an offer to compromise, the IRS may request that taxpayer enter into any collateral agreement or post any security which is deemed necessary for the protection of the interests of the United States.

(3) Offers may be accepted when they provide for payment of compromised amounts in one or more equal or unequal installments.

10   (4) If the final payment on an accepted offer to compromise is contingent upon the immediate and simultaneous release of a tax lien in whole or in part, such payment must be made in accordance with the forms, instructions, or procedures prescribed by the Secretary.

(5) Acceptance of an offer to compromise will conclusively settle the liability of the 15 taxpayer specified in the offer. Compromise with one taxpayer does not extinguish the liability of, nor prevent the IRS from taking action to collect from, any person not named in the offer who is also liable for the tax to which the compromise relates. Neither the taxpayer nor the Government will, following acceptance of an offer to compromise, be permitted to reopen the case except in instances where--

20   (i) False information or documents are supplied in conjunction with the offer;

(ii) The ability to pay or the assets of the taxpayer are concealed; or

(iii) A mutual mistake of material fact sufficient to cause the offer agreement to be reformed or set aside is discovered.

(6) *Opinion of Chief Counsel.* Except as otherwise provided in this paragraph (e)(6), if 25 an offer to compromise is accepted, there will be placed on file the opinion of the Chief Counsel for the IRS with respect to such compromise, along with the reasons therefor. However, no such opinion will be required with respect to the compromise of any civil case in which the unpaid amount of tax assessed (including any interest, additional amount, addition to the tax, or assessable penalty) is less than $50,000. Also placed on 30 file will be a statement of--

(i) The amount of tax assessed;

(ii) The amount of interest, additional amount, addition to the tax, or assessable penalty, imposed by law on the person against whom the tax is assessed; and

(iii) The amount actually paid in accordance with the terms of the compromise.

35   (f) Rejection of an offer to compromise. (1) An offer to compromise has not been rejected until the IRS issues a written notice to the taxpayer or his representative, advising of the rejection, the reason(s) for rejection, and the right to an appeal.

(2) The IRS may not notify a taxpayer or taxpayer's representative of the rejection of an offer to compromise until an independent administrative review of the proposed 40 rejection is completed.

(3) No offer to compromise may be rejected solely on the basis of the amount of the offer without evaluating that offer under the provisions of this section and the Secretary's policies and procedures regarding the compromise of cases.

(4) *Offers based upon doubt as to liability.* Offers submitted on the basis of doubt as to 45 liability cannot be rejected solely because the IRS is unable to locate the taxpayer's return or return information for verification of the liability.

(5) *Appeal of rejection of an offer to compromise*--(i) *In general.* The taxpayer may administratively appeal a rejection of an offer to compromise to the IRS Office of Appeals (Appeals) if, within the 30-day period commencing the day after the date on the letter of 50 rejection, the taxpayer requests such an administrative review in the manner provided by the Secretary.

Sec. 7122. Compromises

(ii) *Offer to compromise returned following a determination that the offer was nonprocessable, a failure by the taxpayer to provide requested information, or a determination that the offer was submitted for purposes of delay.* Where a determination is made to return offer documents because the offer to compromise was nonprocessable, because the taxpayer failed to provide requested information, or because the IRS 5 determined that the offer to compromise was submitted solely for purposes of delay under paragraph (d)(2) of this section, the return of the offer does not constitute a rejection of the offer for purposes of this provision and does not entitle the taxpayer to appeal the matter to Appeals under the provisions of this paragraph (f)(5). However, if the offer is returned because the taxpayer failed to provide requested financial information, 10 the offer will not be returned until a managerial review of the proposed return is completed.

(g) *Effect of offer to compromise on collection activity*--(1) *In general.* The IRS will not levy against the property or rights to property of a taxpayer who submits an offer to compromise, to collect the liability that is the subject of the offer, during the period the 15 offer is pending, for 30 days immediately following the rejection of the offer, and for any period when a timely filed appeal from the rejection is being considered by Appeals.

(2) *Revised offers submitted following rejection.* If, following the rejection of an offer to compromise, the taxpayer makes a good faith revision of that offer and submits the revised offer within 30 days after the date of rejection, the IRS will not levy to collect from 20 the taxpayer the liability that is the subject of the revised offer to compromise while that revised offer is pending.

(3) *Jeopardy.* The IRS may levy to collect the liability that is the subject of an offer to compromise during the period the IRS is evaluating whether that offer will be accepted if it determines that collection of the liability is in jeopardy.   25

(4) *Offers to compromise determined by IRS to be nonprocessable or submitted solely for purposes of delay.* If the IRS determines, under paragraph (d)(2) of this section, that a pending offer did not contain sufficient information to permit evaluation of whether the offer should be accepted, that the offer was submitted solely to delay collection, or that the offer was otherwise nonprocessable, then the IRS may levy to collect the liability that 30 is the subject of that offer at any time after it returns the offer to the taxpayer.

(5) *Offsets under section 6402.* Notwithstanding the evaluation and processing of an offer to compromise, the IRS may, in accordance with section 6402, credit any overpayments made by the taxpayer against a liability that is the subject of an offer to compromise and may offset such overpayments against other liabilities owed by the 35 taxpayer to the extent authorized by section 6402.

(6) *Proceedings in court.* Except as otherwise provided in this paragraph (g)(6), the IRS will not refer a case to the Department of Justice for the commencement of a proceeding in court, against a person named in a pending offer to compromise, if levy to collect the liability is prohibited by paragraph (g)(1) of this section. Without regard to 40 whether a person is named in a pending offer to compromise, however, the IRS may authorize the Department of Justice to file a counterclaim or third-party complaint in a refund action or to join that person in any other proceeding in which liability for the tax that is the subject of the pending offer to compromise may be established or disputed, including a suit against the United States under 28 U.S.C. 2410. In addition, the United 45 States may file a claim in any bankruptcy proceeding or insolvency action brought by or against such person.

(h) *Deposits.* Sums submitted with an offer to compromise a liability or during the pendency of an offer to compromise are considered deposits and will not be applied to the liability until the offer is accepted unless the taxpayer provides written authorization 50 for application of the payments. If an offer to compromise is withdrawn, is determined to

Sec. 7122. Compromises

be nonprocessable, or is submitted solely for purposes of delay and returned to the taxpayer, any amount tendered with the offer, including all installments paid on the offer, will be refunded without interest. If an offer is rejected, any amount tendered with the offer, including all installments paid on the offer, will be refunded, without interest, after

5 the conclusion of any review sought by the taxpayer with Appeals. Refund will not be required if the taxpayer has agreed in writing that amounts tendered pursuant to the offer may be applied to the liability for which the offer was submitted.

(i) *Statute of limitations*--(1) *Suspension of the statute of limitations on collection.* The statute of limitations on collection will be suspended while levy is prohibited under

10 paragraph (g)(1) of this section.

(2) *Extension of the statute of limitations on assessment.* For any offer to compromise, the IRS may require, where appropriate, the extension of the statute of limitations on assessment. However, in any case where waiver of the running of the statutory period of limitations on assessment is sought, the taxpayer must be notified of the right to refuse to

15 extend the period of limitations or to limit the extension to particular issues or particular periods of time.

***

[T.D. 9007, 67 FR 48029, July 23, 2002; 67 FR 53879, Aug. 20, 2002]

Sec. 7201. Attempt to evade or defeat tax

Any person who willfully attempts in any manner to evade or defeat any tax imposed by this

20 title or the payment thereof shall, in addition to other penalties provided by law, be guilty of a felony and, upon conviction thereof, shall be fined not more than $100,000 ($500,000 in the case of a corporation), or imprisoned not more than 5 years, or both, together with the costs of prosecution.

Sec. 7202. Willful failure to collect or pay over tax

25 Any person required under this title to collect, account for, and pay over any tax imposed by this title who willfully fails to collect or truthfully account for and pay over such tax shall, in addition to other penalties provided by law, be guilty of a felony and, upon conviction thereof, shall be fined not more than $10,000, or imprisoned not more than 5 years, or both, together with the costs of prosecution.

30

Sec. 7203. Willful failure to file return, supply information, or pay tax

Any person required under this title to pay any estimated tax or tax, or required by this title or by regulations made under authority thereof to make a return, keep any records, or supply any information, who willfully fails to pay such estimated tax or tax, make such return, keep such

35 records, or supply such information, at the time or times required by law or regulations, shall, in addition to other penalties provided by law, be guilty of a misdemeanor and, upon conviction thereof, shall be fined not more than $25,000 ($100,000 in the case of a corporation), or imprisoned not more than 1 year, or both, together with the costs of prosecution. In the case of any person with respect to whom there is a failure to pay any estimated tax, this section shall not apply

40 to such person with respect to such failure if there is no addition to tax under section 6654 or 6655 with respect to such failure. In the case of a willful violation of any provision of section 6050I, the first sentence of this section shall be applied by substituting "felony" for "misdemeanor" and "5 years" for "1 year".

Sec. 7206. Fraud and false statements

Any person who -

(1) Declaration under penalties of perjury. -- Willfully makes and subscribes any return, statement, or other document, which contains or is verified by a written declaration that it is made under the penalties of perjury, and which he does not believe to be true and correct as to every material matter; or   5

(2) Aid or assistance. -- Willfully aids or assists in, or procures, counsels, or advises the preparation or presentation under, or in connection with any matter arising under, the internal revenue laws, of a return, affidavit, claim, or other document, which is fraudulent or is false as to any material matter, whether or not such falsity or fraud is with the knowledge or consent of the person authorized or required to present such return, affidavit, claim, or document; or   10

(3) Fraudulent bonds, permits, and entries. -- Simulates or falsely or fraudulently executes or signs any bond, permit, entry, or other document required by the provisions of the internal revenue laws, or by any regulation made in pursuance thereof, or procures the same to be falsely or fraudulently executed, or advises, aids in, or connives at such execution thereof; or   15

(4) Removal or concealment with intent to defraud. -- Removes, deposits, or conceals, or is concerned in removing, depositing, or concealing, any goods or commodities for or in respect whereof any tax is or shall be imposed, or any property upon which levy is authorized by section 6331, with intent to evade or defeat the assessment or collection of any tax imposed by this title;   20

***

shall be guilty of a felony and, upon conviction thereof, shall be fined not more than $100,000 ($500,000 in the case of a corporation), or imprisoned not more than 3 years, or both, together with the costs of prosecution.

25

Sec. 7217. Prohibition on executive branch influence over taxpayer audits and other investigations

(a) Prohibition. -- It shall be unlawful for any applicable person to request, directly or indirectly, any officer or employee of the Internal Revenue Service to conduct or terminate an audit or other investigation of any particular taxpayer with respect to the tax liability of such taxpayer.   30

***

(c) Exceptions. -- Subsection (a) shall not apply to any written request made-

(1) to an applicable person by or on behalf of the taxpayer and forwarded by such applicable person to the Internal Revenue Service;

(2) by an applicable person for disclosure of return or return   35
information under section 6103 if such request is made in accordance with the requirements of such section; or

(3) by the Secretary of the Treasury as a consequence of the implementation of a change in tax policy.

(d) Penalty. -- Any person who willfully violates subsection (a) or fails to report under   40
subsection (b) shall be punished upon conviction by a fine in any amount not exceeding $5,000, or imprisonment of not more than 5 years, or both, together with the costs of prosecution.

Sec. 7217. Prohibition on executive branch influence over taxpayer audits and other investigations

(e) Applicable person. -- For purposes of this section, the term "applicable person" means--

    (1) the President, the Vice President, any employee of the executive office of the President, and any employee of the executive office of the Vice President; and

    (2) any individual (other than the Attorney General of the United States) serving in a position specified in section 5312 of title 5, United States Code.

Sec. 7408. Actions to enjoin specified conduct related to tax shelters and reportable transactions

    (a) Authority to seek injunction. -- A civil action in the name of the United States to enjoin any person from further engaging in specified conduct may be commenced at the request of the Secretary. Any action under this section shall be brought in the district court of the United States for the district in which such person resides, has his principal place of business, or has engaged in specified conduct. The court may exercise its jurisdiction over such action (as provided in section 7402(a)) separate and apart from any other action brought by the United States against such person.

    (b) Adjudication and decree. -- In any action under subsection (a), if the court finds--

        (1) that the person has engaged in any specified conduct, and

        (2) that injunctive relief is appropriate to prevent recurrence of such conduct,

the court may enjoin such person from engaging in such conduct or in any other activity subject to penalty under this title.

    (c) Specified conduct. -- For purposes of this section, the term "specified conduct" means any action, or failure to take action, which is--

        (1) subject to penalty under section 6700, 6701, 6707, or 6708, or

        (2) in violation of any requirement under regulations issued under section 330 of title 31, United States Code.

    (d) Citizens and residents outside the United States. -- If any citizen or resident of the United States does not reside in, and does not have his principal place of business in, any United States judicial district, such citizen or resident shall be treated for purposes of this section as residing in the District of Columbia.

Sec. 7421. Prohibition of suits to restrain assessment or collection

    (a) Tax. -- Except as provided in sections 6015(e), 6212(a) and (c), 6213(a), 6225(b), 6246(b), 6330(e)(1), 6331(i), 6672(c), 6694(c), and 7426(a) and (b)(1), 7429(b), and 7436, no suit for the purpose of restraining the assessment or collection of any tax shall be maintained in any court by any person, whether or not such person is the person against whom such tax was assessed.

***

Sec. 7422. Civil actions for refund

    (a) No suit prior to filing claim for refund. -- No suit or proceeding shall be maintained in any court for the recovery of any internal revenue tax alleged to have been erroneously or illegally assessed or collected, or of any penalty claimed to have been collected without authority, or of any sum alleged to have been excessive or in any manner wrongfully collected, until a claim for refund or credit has been duly filed with the Secretary, according to the provisions of law in that regard, and the regulations of the Secretary established in pursuance thereof.

Sec. 7422. Civil actions for refund

(b) Protest or duress. -- Such suit or proceeding may be maintained whether or not such tax, penalty, or sum has been paid under protest or duress.

(c) Suits against collection officer a bar. -- A suit against any officer or employee of the United States (or former officer or employee) or his personal representative for the recovery of any internal revenue tax alleged to have been erroneously or illegally assessed or collected, or of   5
any penalty claimed to have been collected without authority, or of any sum alleged to have been excessive or in any manner wrongfully collected shall be treated as if the United States had been a party to such suit in applying the doctrine of res judicata in all suits in respect of any internal revenue tax, and in all proceedings in the Tax Court and on review of decisions of the Tax Court.

(d) Credit treated as payment. -- The credit of an overpayment of any tax in satisfaction of   10
any tax liability shall, for the purpose of any suit for refund of such tax liability so satisfied, be deemed to be a payment in respect of such tax liability at the time such credit is allowed.

(e) Stay of proceedings. -- If the Secretary prior to the hearing of a suit brought by a taxpayer in a district court or the United States Court of Federal Claims for the recovery of any income tax, estate tax, gift tax, or tax imposed by chapter 41, 42, 43, or 44 (or any penalty relating to such   15
taxes) mails to the taxpayer a notice that a deficiency has been determined in respect of the tax which is the subject matter of taxpayer's suit, the proceedings in taxpayer's suit shall be stayed during the period of time in which the taxpayer may file a   petition with the Tax Court for a redetermination of the asserted deficiency, and for 60 days thereafter. If the taxpayer files a petition with the Tax Court, the district court or the United States Court of Federal Claims, as the   20
case may be, shall lose jurisdiction of taxpayer's suit to whatever extent jurisdiction is acquired by the Tax Court of the subject matter of taxpayer's suit for refund. If the taxpayer does not file a petition with the Tax Court for a redetermination of the asserted deficiency, the United States may counterclaim in the taxpayer's suit, or intervene in the event of a suit as described in subsection (c) (relating to suits against officers or employees of the United States), within the period of the stay   25
of proceedings notwithstanding that the time for such pleading may have otherwise expired. The taxpayer shall have the burden of proof with respect to the issues raised by such counterclaim or intervention of the United States except as to the issue of whether the taxpayer has been guilty of fraud with intent to evade tax. This subsection shall not apply to a suit by a taxpayer which, prior to the date of enactment of this title, is commenced, instituted, or pending in a district court or the   30
United States Court of Federal Claims for the recovery of any income tax, estate tax, or gift tax (or any penalty relating to such taxes).

(f) Limitation on right of action for refund. --

    (1) General rule. -- A suit or proceeding referred to in subsection (a) may be maintained only against the United States and not against any officer or employee of the United States (or   35
    former officer or employee) or his personal representative. Such suit or proceeding may be maintained against the United States notwithstanding the provisions of section 2502 of title 28 of the United States Code (relating to aliens' privilege to sue) and notwithstanding the provisions of section 1502 of such title 28 (relating to certain treaty cases).

    (2) Misjoinder and change of venue. -- If a suit or proceeding brought in a United States   40
    district court against an officer or employee of the United States (or former officer or employee) or his personal representative is improperly brought solely by virtue of paragraph (1), the court shall order, upon such terms as are just, that the pleadings be amended to substitute the United States as a party for such officer or employee as of the time such action commenced, upon proper service of process on the United States. Such suit or proceeding   45
    shall upon request by the United States be transferred to the district or division where it should have been brought if such action initially had been brought against the United States.

***

    (i) Special rule for actions with respect to tax shelter promoter and

Sec. 7422. Civil actions for refund

understatement penalties. -- No action or proceeding may be brought in the United States Court of Federal Claims for any refund or credit of a penalty imposed by section 6700 (relating to penalty for promoting abusive tax shelters, etc.) or section 6701 (relating to penalties for aiding and abetting understatement of tax liability).

***

(k) Cross references. --

(1) For provisions relating generally to claims for refund or credit, see chapter 65 (relating to abatements, credit, and refund) and chapter 66 (relating to limitations).

(2) For duty of United States attorneys to defend suits, see section 507 of Title 28 of the United States Code.

(3) For jurisdiction of United States district courts, see section 1346 of Title 28 of the United States Code.

(4) For payment by the Treasury of judgments against internal revenue officers or employees, upon certificate of probable cause, see section 2006 of Title 28 of the United States Code.

Sec. 7430. Awarding of costs and certain fees

(a) In general. -- In any administrative or court proceeding which is brought by or against the United States in connection with the determination, collection, or refund of any tax, interest, or penalty under this title, the prevailing party may be awarded a judgment or a settlement for--

(1) reasonable administrative costs incurred in connection with such administrative proceeding within the Internal Revenue Service, and

(2) reasonable litigation costs incurred in connection with such court proceeding.

(b) Limitations. --

(1) Requirement that administrative remedies be exhausted. -- A judgment for reasonable litigation costs shall not be awarded under subsection (a) in any court proceeding unless the court determines that the prevailing party has exhausted the administrative remedies available to such party within the Internal Revenue Service. Any failure to agree to an extension of the time for the assessment of any tax shall not be taken into account for purposes of determining whether the prevailing party meets the requirements of the preceding sentence.

(2) Only costs allocable to the United States. -- An award under subsection (a) shall be made only for reasonable litigation and administrative costs which are allocable to the United States and not to any other party.

(3) Costs denied where party prevailing protracts proceedings. -- No award for reasonable litigation and administrative costs may be made under subsection (a) with respect to any portion of the administrative or court proceeding during which the prevailing party has unreasonably protracted such proceeding.

(4) Period for applying to IRS for administrative costs. -- An award may be made under subsection (a) by the Internal Revenue Service for reasonable administrative costs only if the prevailing party files an application with the Internal Revenue Service for such costs before the 91st day after the date on which the final decision of the Internal Revenue Service as to the determination of the tax, interest, or penalty is mailed to such party.

(c) Definitions. -- For purposes of this section--

(1) Reasonable litigation costs. -- The term "reasonable litigation costs" includes--

(A) reasonable court costs, and

Sec. 7430. Awarding of costs and certain fees

(B) based upon prevailing market rates for the kind or quality of services furnished--

(i) the reasonable expenses of expert witnesses in connection with a court proceeding, except that no expert witness shall be compensated at a rate in excess of the highest rate of compensation for expert witnesses paid by the United States,

(ii) the reasonable cost of any study, analysis, engineering report, test, or project 5 which is found by the court to be necessary for the preparation of the party's case, and

(iii) reasonable fees paid or incurred for the services of attorneys in connection with the court proceeding, except that such fees shall not be in excess of $125 per hour unless the court determines that a special factor, such as the limited availability of qualified attorneys for such proceeding, the difficulty of the issues presented in the 10 case, or the local availability of tax expertise, justifies a higher rate.

In the case of any calendar year beginning after 1996, the dollar amount referred to in clause (iii) shall be increased by an amount equal to such dollar amount multiplied by the cost-of- living adjustment determined under section 1(f)(3) for such calendar year, by substituting "calendar year 1995" for "calendar year 1992" in subparagraph (B) thereof. If 15 any dollar amount after being increased under the preceding sentence is not a multiple of $10, such dollar amount shall be rounded to the nearest multiple of $10.

(2) Reasonable administrative costs. -- The term "reasonable administrative costs" means -

(A) any administrative fees or similar charges imposed by the Internal Revenue Service, and 20

(B) expenses, costs, and fees described in paragraph (1)(B), except that any determination made by the court under clause (ii) or (iii) thereof shall be made by the Internal Revenue Service in cases where the determination under paragraph (4)(C) of the awarding of reasonable administrative costs is made by the Internal Revenue Service.

Such term shall only include costs incurred on or after whichever of the following is the 25 earliest: (i) the date of the receipt by the taxpayer of the notice of the decision of the Internal Revenue Service Office of Appeals; (ii) the date of the notice of deficiency; or (iii) the date on which the first letter of proposed deficiency which allows the taxpayer an opportunity for administrative review in the Internal Revenue Service Office of Appeals is sent.

(3) Attorneys' fees. -- 30

(A) In general. -- For purposes of paragraphs (1) and (2), fees for the services of an individual (whether or not an attorney) who is authorized to practice before the Tax Court or before the Internal Revenue Service shall be treated as fees for the services of an attorney.

(B) Pro bono services. -- The court may award reasonable attorneys' fees under 35 subsection (a) in excess of the attorneys' fees paid or incurred if such fees are less than the reasonable attorneys' fees because an individual is representing the prevailing party for no fee or for a fee which (taking into account all the facts and circumstances) is no more than a nominal fee. This subparagraph shall apply only if such award is paid to such individual or such individual's employer. 40

(4) Prevailing party. --

(A) In general. -- The term "prevailing party" means any party in any proceeding to which subsection (a) applies (other than the United States or any creditor of the taxpayer involved)--

(i) which-- 45

(I) has substantially prevailed with respect to the amount in controversy, or

(II) has substantially prevailed with respect to the most significant issue or set of

Sec. 7430. Awarding of costs and certain fees

issues presented, and

(ii) which meets the requirements of the 1st sentence of section 2412(d)(1)(B) of title 28, United States Code (as in effect on October 22, 1986) except to the extent differing procedures are established by rule of court and meets the requirements of section 2412(d)(2)(B) of such title 28 (as so in effect).

(B) Exception if United States establishes that its position was substantially justified. --

(i) **General rule.** -- A party shall not be treated as the prevailing party in a proceeding to which subsection (a) applies if the United States establishes that the position of the United States in the proceeding was substantially justified.

(ii) **Presumption of no justification if Internal Revenue Service did not follow certain published guidance.** -- For purposes of clause (i), the position of the United States shall be presumed not to be substantially justified if the Internal Revenue Service did not follow its applicable published guidance in the administrative proceeding. Such presumption may be rebutted.

(iii) **Effect of losing on substantially similar issues.** -- In determining for purposes of clause (i) whether the position of the United States was substantially justified, the court shall take into account whether the United States has lost in courts of appeal for other circuits on substantially similar issues.

(iv) **Applicable published guidance.** -- For purposes of clause (ii), the term "applicable published guidance" means--

(I) regulations, revenue rulings, revenue procedures, information releases, notices, and announcements, and

(II) any of the following which are issued to the taxpayer: private letter rulings, technical advice memoranda, and determination letters.

(C) Determination as to prevailing party. -- Any determination under this paragraph as to whether a party is a prevailing party shall be made by agreement of the parties or--

(i) in the case where the final determination with respect to the tax, interest, or penalty is made at the administrative level, by the Internal Revenue Service, or

(ii) in the case where such final determination is made by a court, the court.

(D) Special rules for applying net worth requirement. -- In applying the requirements of section 2412(d)(2)(B) of title 28, United States Code, for purposes of subparagraph (A)(ii) of this paragraph--

(i) the net worth limitation in clause (i) of such section shall apply to--

(I) an estate but shall be determined as of the date of the decedent's death, and

(II) a trust but shall be determined as of the last day of the taxable year involved in the proceeding, and

(ii) individuals filing a joint return shall be treated as separate individuals for purposes of clause (i) of such section.

(E) Special rules where judgment less than taxpayer's offer. --

(i) **In general.** -- A party to a court proceeding meeting the requirements of subparagraph (A)(ii) shall be treated as the prevailing party if the liability of the taxpayer pursuant to the judgment in the proceeding (determined without regard to interest) is equal to or less than the liability of the taxpayer which would have been so determined if the United States had accepted a qualified offer of the party under subsection (g).

Sec. 7430. Awarding of costs and certain fees

      (ii) Exceptions. -- This subparagraph shall not apply to--

        (I) any judgment issued pursuant to a settlement; or

        (II) any proceeding in which the amount of tax liability is not in issue, including any declaratory judgment proceeding, any proceeding to enforce or quash any summons issued pursuant to this title, and any action to restrain disclosure under section 6110(f). 5

      (iii) Special rules. -- If this subparagraph applies to any court proceeding--

        (I) the determination under clause (i) shall be made by reference to the last qualified offer made with respect to the tax liability at issue in the proceeding; and

        (II) reasonable administrative and litigation costs shall only include costs incurred on and after the date of such offer. 10

      (iv) Coordination. -- This subparagraph shall not apply to a party which is a prevailing party under any other provision of this paragraph.

    (5) Administrative proceedings. -- The term "administrative proceeding" means any procedure or other action before the Internal Revenue Service. 15

    (6) Court proceedings. -- The term "court proceeding" means any civil action brought in a court of the United States (including the Tax Court and the United States Court of Federal Claims).

    (7) Position of United States. -- The term "position of the United States" means--

      (A) the position taken by the United States in a judicial proceeding to which subsection (a) applies, and 20

      (B) the position taken in an administrative proceeding to which subsection (a) applies as of the earlier of--

        (i) the date of the receipt by the taxpayer of the notice of the decision of the Internal Revenue Service Office of Appeals, or 25

        (ii) the date of the notice of deficiency.

***

(e) Multiple actions. -- For purposes of this section, in the case of--

    (1) multiple actions which could have been joined or consolidated, or

    (2) a case or cases involving a return or returns of the same taxpayer (including joint returns of married individuals) which could have been joined in a single court proceeding in the same court, 30

such actions or cases shall be treated as 1 court proceeding regardless of whether such joinder or consolidation actually occurs, unless the court in which such action is brought determines, in its discretion, that it would be inappropriate to treat such actions or cases as joined or consolidated. 35

(f) Right of appeal. --

    (1) Court proceedings. -- An order granting or denying (in whole or in part) an award for reasonable litigation or administrative costs under subsection (a) in a court proceeding, may be incorporated as a part of the decision or judgment in the court proceeding and shall be subject to appeal in the same manner as the decision or judgment. 40

    (2) Administrative proceedings. -- A decision granting or denying (in whole or in part) an award for reasonable administrative costs under subsection (a) by the Internal Revenue Service shall be subject to the filing of a petition for review with the Tax Court under rules similar to the rules under section 7463 (without regard to the amount in dispute). If the Secretary sends by certified or registered mail a notice of such decision to the petitioner, no proceeding in the 45 Tax Court may be initiated under this paragraph unless such petition is filed before the 91st day after the date of such mailing.

(3) **Appeal of Tax Court decision.** -- An order of the Tax Court disposing of a petition under paragraph (2) shall be reviewable in the same manner as a decision of the Tax Court, but only with respect to the matters determined in such order.

5   (g) **Qualified offer.** -- For purposes of subsection (c)(4)--

(1) **In general.** -- The term "qualified offer" means a written offer which--

(A) is made by the taxpayer to the United States during the qualified offer period;

(B) specifies the offered amount of the taxpayer's liability (determined without regard to interest);

10   (C) is designated at the time it is made as a qualified offer for purposes of this section; and

(D) remains open during the period beginning on the date it is made and ending on the earliest of the date the offer is rejected, the date the trial begins, or the 90th day after the date the offer is made.

15   (2) **Qualified offer period.** -- For purposes of this subsection, the term "qualified offer period" means the period--

(A) beginning on the date on which the first letter of proposed deficiency which allows the taxpayer an opportunity for administrative review in the Internal Revenue Service Office of Appeals is sent, and

20   (B) ending on the date which is 30 days before the date the case is first set for trial.

Reg. § 301.7430-1 Exhaustion of administrative remedies.

(a) *In general.* Section 7430(b)(1) provides that a court shall not award reasonable litigation costs in any civil tax proceeding under section 7430(a) unless the court
25 determines that the prevailing party has exhausted the administrative remedies available to the party within the Internal Revenue Service. This section sets forth the circumstances in which such administrative remedies shall be deemed to have been exhausted.

(b) *Requirements*--(1) *In general.* A party has not exhausted the administrative remedies available within the Internal Revenue Service with respect to any tax matter for
30 which an Appeals office conference is available under §§ 601.105 and 601.106 of this chapter (other than a tax matter described in paragraph (c) of this section) unless--

(i) The party, prior to filing a petition in the Tax Court or a civil action for refund in a court of the United States (including the Court of Federal Claims), participates, either in person or through a qualified representative described in § 601.502 of this chapter, in an
35 Appeals office conference; or

(ii) If no Appeals office conference is granted, the party, prior to the issuance of a statutory notice in the case of a petition in the Tax Court or the issuance of a notice of disallowance in the case of a civil action for refund in a court of the United States (including the Court of Federal Claims)--

40   (A) Requests an Appeals office conference in accordance with §§ 601.105 and 601.106 of this chapter; and

(B) Files a written protest if a written protest is required to obtain an Appeals office conference.

(2) *Participates.* For purposes of this section, a party or qualified representative of the
45 party described in § 601.502 of this chapter participates in an Appeals office conference if the party or qualified representative discloses to the Appeals office all relevant information regarding the party's tax matter to the extent such information and its relevance were known or should have been known to the party or qualified representative

Sec. 7430. Awarding of costs and certain fees

at the time of such conference.

(3) *Tax matter.* For purposes of this section, ``tax matter'' means a matter in connection with the determination, collection or refund of any tax, interest, penalty, addition to tax or additional amount under the Internal Revenue Code.

(4) *Failure to agree to extension of time for assessments.* Any failure by the prevailing 5 party to agree to an extension of the time for the assessment of any tax will not be taken into account for purposes of determining whether the prevailing party has exhausted the administrative remedies available to the party within the Internal Revenue Service.

(c) *Revocation of a determination that an organization is described in section 501(c) (3).* A party has not exhausted the administrative remedies available within the Internal 10 Revenue Service with respect to a revocation of a determination that it is an organization described in section 501(c)(3) unless, prior to filing a declaratory judgment action under section 7428, the party has exhausted its administrative remedies in accordance with section 7428, and any regulations, rules, and revenue procedures thereunder.

(d) *Actions involving summonses, levies, liens, jeopardy and termination* 15 *assessments, etc.* (1) A party has not exhausted the administrative remedies available within the Internal Revenue Service with respect to a matter other than one to which paragraph (b) or (c) of this section applies (including summonses, levies, liens, and jeopardy and termination assessments) unless, prior to filing an action in a court of the United States (including the Tax Court and the Court of Federal Claims)-- 20

(i) The party submits to the district director of the district having jurisdiction over the dispute a written claim for relief reciting facts and circumstances sufficient to show the nature of the relief requested and that the party is entitled to such relief; and

(ii) The district director has denied the claim for relief in writing or failed to act on the claim within a reasonable period after such claim is received by the district director. 25

(2) For purposes of this paragraph (d)(2), a reasonable period is--

(i) The 5-day period preceding the filing of a petition to quash an administrative summons issued under section 7609;

(ii) The 5-day period preceding the filing of a wrongful levy action in which a demand for the return of property is made; 30

(iii) The period expressly provided for administrative review of the party's claim by an applicable provision of the Internal Revenue Code that expressly provides for the pursuit of administrative remedies (such as the 16-day period provided under section 7429(b)(1) (B) relating to review of jeopardy assessment procedures); or

(iv) The 60-day period following receipt of the claim for relief in all other cases. 35

(e) *Actions involving willful violations of the automatic stay under section 362 or the discharge provisions under section 524 of the Bankruptcy Code*--(1) *Section 7433 claims.* A party has not exhausted administrative remedies within the Internal Revenue Service with respect to asserted violations of the automatic stay under section 362 of the Bankruptcy Code or the discharge provisions under section 524 of the Bankruptcy Code 40 unless it files an administrative claim for damages or for relief from a violation of section 362 or 524 of the Bankruptcy Code with the Chief, Local Insolvency Unit, for the judicial district in which the bankruptcy petition that is the basis for the asserted automatic stay or discharge violation was filed pursuant to § 301.7433-2(e) and satisfies the other conditions set forth in § 301.7433-2(d) prior to filing a petition under section 7433. 45

(2) *Section 362(h) claims.* A party has not exhausted administrative remedies within the Internal Revenue Service with respect to asserted violations of the automatic stay under section 362 of the Bankruptcy Code unless it files an administrative claim for relief from a violation of section 362 of the Bankruptcy Code with the Chief, Local Insolvency Unit, for the judicial district in which the bankruptcy petition that is the basis for the 50 asserted automatic stay violation was filed pursuant to § 301.7433-2(e) and satisfies the

Sec. 7430. Awarding of costs and certain fees

other conditions set forth in § 301.7433-2(d) prior to filing a petition under section 362(h) of the Bankruptcy Code.

(f) *Exception to requirement that party pursue administrative remedies.* If the conditions set forth in paragraph (f)(1), (f)(2), (f)(3), or (f)(4) of this section are satisfied, a party's administrative remedies within the Internal Revenue Service shall be deemed to have been exhausted for purposes of section 7430.

(1) The Internal Revenue Service notifies the party in writing that the pursuit of administrative remedies in accordance with paragraphs (b), (c), and (d) of this section is unnecessary.

(2) In the case of a petition in the Tax Court--

(i) The party did not receive a notice of proposed deficiency (30-day letter) prior to the issuance of the statutory notice and the failure to receive such notice was not due to actions of the party (such as a failure to supply requested information or a current mailing address to the district director or service center having jurisdiction over the tax matter); and

(ii) The party does not refuse to participate in an Appeals office conference while the case is in docketed status.

(3) In the case of a civil action for refund involving a tax matter other than a tax matter described in paragraph (e)(4) of this section, the party--

(i) Participates in an Appeals office conference with respect to the tax matter prior to issuance of a statutory notice of deficiency with respect to such tax matter; or

(ii) Did not receive written notification that an Appeals office conference was available prior to issuance of a notice of disallowance and the failure to receive such a notification was not due to the actions of the party (such as the failure to supply requested information or a current mailing address to the district director or service center having jurisdiction over the tax matter); or

(iii) Did not receive either written or oral notification that an Appeals office conference had been granted within six months from the date of the filing of the claim for refund and the failure to receive such notice was not due to actions of the party (such as the failure to supply requested information or a current mailing address to the district director or service center having jurisdiction over the tax matter).

(4) In the case of a civil action for refund involving a tax matter under sections 6703 or 6694--

(i) The party did not receive a notice of proposed disallowance prior to issuance of a notice of disallowance and the failure to receive such notice was not due to actions of the party (such as the failure to supply requested information or a current mailing address to the district director or service center having jurisdiction over the tax matter); or

(ii) During the six-month period following the day on which the party's claim for refund is filed, the party's claim for refund is not denied, and the Internal Revenue Service has failed to process the claim with due diligence.

(g) *Examples.* The provisions of this section may be illustrated by the following examples:

Example 1. Taxpayer A exchanges property held for investment for similar property and claims that the gain on the exchange is not recognized under section 1031. The Internal Revenue Service conducts a field examination and determines that there has not been a like-kind exchange. No agreement is reached on the matter and a notice of proposed deficiency (30-day letter) is sent to A. A does not file a request for an Appeals office conference. A pays the amount of the proposed deficiency and files a claim for refund. A notice of proposed disallowance is issued by the Internal Revenue Service. A does not request an Appeals office conference and, instead, files a civil action for refund in a United States District Court. A has not exhausted the administrative remedies available within the Internal Revenue Service.

Example 2. Assume the same facts as in Example 1 except that, after receiving the notice of proposed deficiency (30-day letter), A files a request for an Appeals office conference. No agreement is reached at the conference. A pays the amount of the proposed deficiency and files a claim for refund. A notice of proposed disallowance is 5 issued by the Internal Revenue Service. A does not request an Appeals office conference and files a civil action for refund in a United States District Court. A has exhausted the administrative remedies available within the Internal Revenue Service.

Example 3. Assume the same facts as in Example 1 except A first requests an Appeals office conference after A's receipt of the notice of proposed disallowance. A is 10 granted an Appeals office conference and A participates in such conference. A has exhausted the administrative remedies available within the Internal Revenue Service.

Example 4. Taxpayer B receives a notice of proposed deficiency (30-day letter) after completion of a field examination. B provided to the Internal Revenue Service during the examination all relevant information under the taxpayer's control and all relevant legal 15 arguments supporting the taxpayer's position. B properly requests an Appeals office conference. The Appeals office, to obtain an additional period of time to consider the tax matter, requests that B sign Form 872 to extend the time for an assessment of tax, but B declines. Appeals then denies the request for a conference and issues a notice of deficiency. B has exhausted the administrative remedies available within the Internal 20 Revenue Service.

Example 5. Taxpayer C receives a notice of proposed deficiency (30-day letter) and a written statement that C need not file a written protest or request an Appeals office conference since a conference will not be granted. C files a petition in the Tax Court after receiving the statutory notice of deficiency. C's administrative remedies within the Internal 25 Revenue Service are deemed to have been exhausted.

Example 6. On January 2, the Internal Revenue Service serves a summons issued under section 7609 on third-party recordkeeper D to produce records of taxpayer E. On January 5, notice of the summons is given to E. The last day on which E may file a petition in a court of the United States to quash the summons is January 25. Thereafter, E 30 files a written claim for relief with the district director having jurisdiction over the matter together with a copy of the summons. The claim and copy are received by the district director on January 20. On January 25, E files a petition to quash the summons. E has exhausted the administrative remedies available within the Internal Revenue Service.

Example 7. A notice of Federal tax lien is filed in County M on March 3, in the name of 35 F. On April 2, F pays the entire liability thereby satisfying the lien. On May 2, F files a written claim with the district director having jurisdiction over the tax matter demanding a certificate of release of lien. Thereafter, F provides the district director with a copy of the notice of Federal tax lien and a copy of the canceled check in satisfaction of the lien, which are received by the district director on May 15. F's claim is deemed to have been 40 filed on May 15. Accordingly, F must wait until after July 14 (60 days following the filing of the claim for relief on May 15) to commence an action, in order to have exhausted the administrative remedies available within the Internal Revenue Service.

45

Example 8. A revenue officer seizes an automobile to effect collection of G's liability on January 10. On January 22, H submits a written claim to the district director having jurisdiction over the tax matter claiming that H purchased the automobile from G for an adequate consideration before the tax lien against G arose, and demands immediate return of the automobile. A copy of the title certificate and H's canceled check are 50 submitted with the claim. The claim is received by the district director on January 25. On

Sec. 7430. Awarding of costs and certain fees

January 30, H brings a wrongful levy action. H has exhausted the administrative remedies available within the Internal Revenue Service.

Example 9. The Internal Revenue Service issues a revenue ruling which holds that ear piercing does not affect a function or structure of the body within the meaning of
5 section 213 and therefore is not deductible. Taxpayer I deducts the costs of ear piercing and, following an examination, receives a notice of proposed deficiency (30-day letter) disallowing the treatment of such costs. Because of the revenue ruling, I believes a conference would not aid in the resolution of the tax dispute. Accordingly, I does not request an Appeals office conference. After receiving a statutory notice of deficiency, I
10 files a petition in the Tax Court. I has not exhausted the administrative remedies available within the Internal Revenue Service. The issuance of a revenue ruling covering the same fact situation but taking a contrary position does not constitute notification by the Internal Revenue Service to I that the pursuit of administrative remedies is unnecessary. Similarly, the issuance to I of a private letter ruling or technical advice does not constitute
15 notification by the Internal Revenue Service that the pursuit of administrative remedies is unnecessary.

Example 10. Taxpayer J is assessed a penalty under section 6701 for aiding in the understatement of the tax liability of another person. J pays 15% of the penalty in accordance with section 6703 and files a claim for refund on June 15. J is not issued a
20 notice of proposed disallowance and thus cannot participate in an Appeals office conference within six months of the filing of the claim for refund. J brings an action on December 23. J has exhausted the administrative remedies available within the Internal Revenue Service.

Example 11. Taxpayer K receives a notice of proposed deficiency (30-day letter) and
25 neither requests nor participates in an Appeals office conference. The Service then issues a statutory notice of deficiency (90-day letter). Upon receiving the statutory notice, and after filing a petition with the Tax Court, K requests an Appeals office conference. K has not exhausted the administrative remedies available within the Internal Revenue Service because the request for an Appeals office conference was made after the
30 issuance of the statutory notice.

***

[T.D. 8543, 59 FR 29357, June 7, 1994; T.D. 8725, 62 FR 39118, July 22, 1997; T.D. 9050, 68 FR 14319, Mar. 25, 2003; T.D. 9050, 68 FR 16351, Apr. 3, 2003]

35
Sec. 7454. Burden of proof in fraud, foundation manager, and transferee cases

(a) Fraud. -- In any proceeding involving the issue whether the petitioner has been guilty of fraud with intent to evade tax, the burden of proof in respect of such issue shall be upon the Secretary.

***

40
Sec. 7463. Disputes involving $50,000 or less

(a) In general. -- In the case of any petition filed with the Tax Court for a redetermination of a deficiency where neither the amount of the deficiency placed in dispute, nor the amount of any claimed overpayment, exceeds--

(1) $50,000 for any one taxable year, in the case of the taxes imposed by subtitle A,

45   (2) $50,000, in the case of the tax imposed by chapter 11,

(3) $50,000 for any one calendar year, in the case of the tax imposed by chapter 12, or

(4) $50,000 for any 1 taxable period (or, if there is no taxable period, taxable event) in the case of any tax imposed by subtitle D which is described in section 6212(a) (relating to a notice of deficiency),

at the option of the taxpayer concurred in by the Tax Court or a division thereof before the hearing of the case, proceedings in the case shall be conducted under this section. Notwithstanding the provisions of section 7453, such proceedings shall be conducted in accordance with such rules of evidence, practice, and procedure as the Tax Court may prescribe. A decision, together with a brief summary of the reasons therefor, in any such case shall satisfy the requirements of sections 7459(b) and 7460.

***

Sec. 7482. Courts of review

(a) Jurisdiction. --

(1) In general. -- The United States Courts of Appeals (other than the United States Court of Appeals for the Federal Circuit) shall have exclusive jurisdiction to review the decisions of the Tax Court, except as provided in section 1254 of Title 28 of the United States Code, in the same manner and to the same extent as decisions of the district courts in civil actions tried without a jury; and the judgment of any such court shall be final, except that it shall be subject to review by the Supreme Court of the United States upon certiorari, in the manner provided in section 1254 of Title 28 of the United States Code.

***

(b) Venue. --

(1) In general. -- Except as otherwise provided in paragraphs (2) and (3), such decisions may be reviewed by the United States court of appeals for the circuit in which is located--

(A) in the case of a petitioner seeking redetermination of tax liability other than a corporation, the legal residence of the petitioner,

(B) in the case of a corporation seeking redetermination of tax liability, the principal place of business or principal office or agency of the corporation, or, if it has no principal place of business or principal office or agency in any judicial circuit, then the office to which was made the return of the tax in respect of which the liability arises,

(C) in the case of a person seeking a declaratory decision under section 7476, the principal place of business, or principal office or agency of the employer,

(D) in the case of an organization seeking a declaratory decision under section 7428, the principal office or agency of the organization,

(E) in the case of a petition under section 6226, 6228(a), 6247, or 6252, the principal place of business of the partnership, or

(F) in the case of a petition under section 6234(c)--

(i) the legal residence of the petitioner if the petitioner is not a corporation, and

(ii) the place or office applicable under subparagraph (B) if the petitioner is a corporation.

If for any reason no subparagraph of the preceding sentence applies, then such decisions may be reviewed by the Court of Appeals for the District of Columbia. For purposes of this paragraph, the legal residence, principal place of business, or principal office or agency referred to herein shall be determined as of the time the petition seeking redetermination of tax liability was filed with the Tax Court or as of the time the petition seeking a declaratory

1137

Sec. 7482. Courts of review

decision under section 7428 or 7476 or the petition under section 6226, 6228(a), or 6234(c), was filed with the Tax Court.

(2) By agreement. -- Notwithstanding the provisions of paragraph (1), such decisions   may be reviewed by any United States Court of Appeals which may be designated by the Secretary and the taxpayer by stipulation in writing.

***

(c) Powers. --

(1) To affirm, modify, or reverse. -- Upon such review, such courts shall have power to affirm or, if the decision of the Tax Court is not in accordance with law, to modify or to reverse the decision of the Tax Court, with or without remanding the case for a rehearing, as justice may require.

(2) To make rules. -- Rules for review of decisions of the Tax Court shall be those prescribed by the Supreme Court under section 2072 of title 28 of the United States Code.

(3) To require additional security. -- Nothing in section 7483 shall be construed as relieving the petitioner from making or filing such undertakings as the court may require as a condition of or in connection with the review.

(4) To impose penalties. -- The United States Court of Appeals and the Supreme Court shall have the power to require the taxpayer to pay to the United States a penalty in any case where the decision of the Tax Court is affirmed and it appears that the appeal was instituted or maintained primarily for delay or that the taxpayer's position in the appeal is frivolous or groundless.

***

Sec. 7491. Burden of proof

(a) Burden shifts where taxpayer produces credible evidence. --

(1) General rule. -- If, in any court proceeding, a taxpayer introduces credible evidence with respect to any factual issue relevant to ascertaining the liability of the taxpayer for any tax imposed by subtitle A or B, the Secretary shall have the burden of proof with respect to such issue.

***

Sec. 7502. Timely mailing treated as timely filing and paying

(a) General rule. --

(1) Date of delivery. -- If any return, claim, statement, or other document required to be filed, or any payment required to be made, within a prescribed period or on or before a prescribed date under authority of any provision of the internal revenue laws is, after such period or such date, delivered by United States mail to the agency, officer, or office with which such return, claim, statement, or other document is required to be filed, or to which such payment is required to be made, the date of the United States postmark stamped on the cover in which such return, claim, statement, or other document, or payment, is mailed shall be deemed to be the date of delivery or the date of payment, as the case may be.

***

Sec. 7503. Time for performance of acts where last day falls on Saturday, Sunday, or legal holiday

When the last day prescribed under authority of the internal revenue laws for performing any act falls on Saturday, Sunday, or a legal holiday, the performance of such act shall be considered

1138

Sec. 7503. Time for performance of acts where last day falls on Saturday, Sunday, or legal holiday

timely if it is performed on the next succeeding day which is not a Saturday, Sunday, or a legal holiday. For purposes of this section, the last day for the performance of any act shall be determined by including any authorized extension of time; the term "legal holiday" means a legal holiday in the District of Columbia; and in the case of any return, statement, or other document required to be filed, or any other act required under authority of the internal revenue laws to be 5 performed, at any office of the Secretary or at any other office of the United States or any agency thereof, located outside the District of Columbia but within an internal revenue district, the term "legal holiday" also means a Statewide legal holiday in the State where such office is located.

10

Sec. 7504. Fractional parts of a dollar

The Secretary may by regulations provide that in the allowance of any amount as a credit or refund, or in the collection of any amount as a deficiency or underpayment, of any tax imposed by this title, a fractional part of a dollar shall be disregarded, unless it amounts to 50 cents or more, in which case it shall be increased to 1 dollar.

15

Sec. 7602. Examination of books and witnesses

(a) **Authority to summon, etc.** -- For the purpose of ascertaining the correctness of any return, making a return where none has been made, determining the liability of any person for any internal revenue tax or the liability at law or in equity of any transferee or fiduciary of any person in respect of any internal revenue tax, or collecting any such liability, the Secretary is authorized-- 20

(1) To examine any books, papers, records, or other data which may be relevant or material to such inquiry;

(2) To summon the person liable for tax or required to perform the act, or any officer or employee of such person, or any person having possession, custody, or care of books of account containing entries relating to the business of the person liable for tax or required to 25 perform the act, or any other person the Secretary may deem proper, to appear before the Secretary at a time and place named in the summons and to produce such books, papers, records, or other data, and to give such testimony, under oath, as may be relevant or material to such inquiry; and

(3) To take such testimony of the person concerned, under oath, as may be relevant or 30 material to such inquiry.

***

Sec. 7701. Definitions

(a) When used in this title, where not otherwise distinctly expressed or manifestly incompatible with the intent thereof-- 35

(1) **Person.** -- The term "person" shall be construed to mean and include an individual, a trust, estate, partnership, association, company or corporation.

(2) **Partnership and partner.** -- The term "partnership" includes a syndicate, group, pool, joint venture, or other unincorporated organization, through or by means of which any business, financial operation, or venture is carried on, and which is not, within the meaning of 40 this title, a trust or estate or a corporation; and the term "partner" include a member in such a syndicate, group, pool, joint venture, or organization.

(3) **Corporation.** -- The term "corporation" includes associations, joint-stock companies,

1139

Sec. 7701.   Definitions

and insurance companies.

(4) Domestic. -- The term "domestic" when applied to a corporation or partnership means created or organized in the United States or under the law of the United States or of any State unless, in the case of a partnership, the Secretary provides otherwise by regulations.

(5) Foreign. -- The term "foreign" when applied to a corporation or partnership means a corporation or partnership which is not domestic.

(6) Fiduciary. -- The term "fiduciary" means a guardian, trustee, executor, administrator, receiver, conservator, or any person acting in any fiduciary capacity for any person.

(7) Stock. -- The term "stock" includes shares in an association, joint-stock company, or insurance company.

(8) Shareholder. -- The term "shareholder" includes a member in an association, joint-stock company, or insurance company.

(9) United States. -- The term "United States" when used in a geographical sense includes only the States and the District of Columbia.

(10) State. -- The term "State" shall be construed to include the District of Columbia, where such construction is necessary to carry out provisions of this title.

(11) Secretary of the Treasury and Secretary. --

(A) Secretary of the Treasury. -- The term "Secretary of the Treasury" means the Secretary of the Treasury, personally, and shall not include any delegate of his.

(B) Secretary. -- The term "Secretary" means the Secretary of the Treasury or his delegate.

(12) Delegate. --

(A) In general. -- The term "or his delegate"--

(i) when used with reference to the Secretary of the Treasury, means any officer, employee, or agency of the Treasury Department duly authorized by the Secretary of the Treasury directly, or indirectly by one or more redelegations of authority, to perform the function mentioned or described in the context; and

(ii) when used with reference to any other official of the United States, shall be similarly construed.

***

(13) Commissioner. -- The term "Commissioner" means the Commissioner of Internal Revenue.

(14) Taxpayer. -- The term "taxpayer" means any person subject to any internal revenue tax.

(15) Military or naval forces and armed forces of the United States. -- The term "military or naval forces of the United States" and the term "Armed Forces of the United States" each includes all regular and reserve components of the uniformed services which are subject to the jurisdiction of the Secretary of Defense, the Secretary of the Army, the Secretary of the Navy, or the Secretary of the Air Force, and each term also includes the Coast Guard. The members of such forces include commissioned officers and personnel below the grade of commissioned officers in such forces.

(16) Withholding agent. -- The term "withholding agent" means any person required to deduct and withhold any tax under the provisions of section 1441, 1442, 1443, or 1461.

(17) Husband and wife. -- As used in sections 682 and 2516, if the husband and wife therein referred to are divorced, wherever appropriate to the meaning of such sections, the term "wife" shall be read "former wife" and the term "husband" shall be read "former husband"; and, if the payments described in such sections are made by or on behalf of the wife or former wife to the husband or former husband instead of vice versa, wherever appropriate to the meaning of such sections, the term "husband" shall be read "wife" and the term "wife" shall be read "husband."

***

(20) Employee. -- For the purpose of applying the provisions of section 79 with respect to 5 group-term life insurance purchased for employees, for the purpose of applying the provisions of sections 104, 105, and106 with respect to accident and health insurance or accident and health plans, and for the purpose of applying the provisions of subtitle A with respect to contributions to or under a stock bonus, pension, profit-sharing, or annuity plan, and with respect to distributions under such a plan, or by a trust forming part of such a plan, and for 10 purposes of applying section 125 with respect to cafeteria plans, the term "employee" shall include a full-time life insurance salesman who is considered an employee for the purpose of chapter 21, or in the case of services performed before January 1, 1951, who would be considered an employee if his services were performed during 1951.

(21) Levy. -- The term "levy" includes the power of distraint and seizure by any means.   15

(22) Attorney General. -- The term "Attorney General" means the Attorney General of the United States.

(23) Taxable year. -- The term "taxable year" means the calendar year, or the fiscal year ending during such calendar year, upon the basis of which the taxable income is computed under subtitle A. "Taxable year" means, in the case of a return made for a fractional part of a 20 year under the provisions of subtitle A or under regulations prescribed by the Secretary, the period for which such return is made.

(24) Fiscal year. -- The term "fiscal year" means an accounting period of 12 months ending on the last day of any month other than December.

(25) Paid or incurred, paid or accrued. -- The terms "paid or incurred" and "paid or 25 accrued" shall be construed according to the method of accounting upon the basis of which the taxable income is computed under subtitle A.

(26) Trade or business. -- The term "trade or business" includes the performance of the functions of a public office.

(27) Tax Court. -- The term "Tax Court" means the United States Tax Court.   30

(28) Other terms. -- Any term used in this subtitle with respect to the application of, or in connection with, the provisions of any other subtitle of this title shall have the same meaning as in such provisions.

(29) Internal Revenue Code. -- The term "Internal Revenue Code of 1986" means this title, and the term "Internal Revenue Code of 1939" means the Internal Revenue Code enacted 35 February 10, 1939, as amended.

(30) United States person. -- The term "United States person" means--

(A) a citizen or resident of the United States,

(B) a domestic partnership,

(C) a domestic corporation,   40

(D) any estate (other than a foreign estate, within the meaning of paragraph (31)), and

(E) any trust if -

(i) a court within the United States is able to exercise primary supervision over the administration of the trust, and

(ii) one or more United States persons have the authority to control all substantial 45 decisions of the trust.

Sec. 7701. Definitions

***

(36) Income tax return preparer. --

    (A) In general. -- The term "income tax return preparer" means any person who prepares for compensation, or who employs one or more persons to prepare for compensation, any return of tax imposed by subtitle A or any claim for refund of tax imposed by subtitle A. For purposes of the preceding sentence, the preparation of a substantial portion of a return or claim for refund shall be treated as if it were the preparation of such return or claim for refund.

    (B) Exceptions. -- A person shall not be an "income tax return preparer" merely because such person--

        (i) furnishes typing, reproducing, or other mechanical assistance,

        (ii) prepares a return or claim for refund of the employer (or of an officer or employee of the employer) by whom he is regularly and continuously employed,

        (iii) prepares as a fiduciary a return or claim for refund for any person,

***

(37) Individual retirement plan. -- The term "individual retirement plan" means--

    (A) an individual retirement account described in section 408(a), and

    (B) an individual retirement annuity described in section 408(b).

(38) Joint return. -- The term "joint return" means a single return made jointly under section 6013 by a husband and wife.

(39) Persons residing outside United States. -- If any citizen or resident of the United States does not reside in (and is not found in) any United States judicial district, such citizen or resident shall be treated as residing in the District of Columbia for purposes of any provision of this title relating to--

    (A) jurisdiction of courts, or

    (B) enforcement of summons.

(41) TIN. -- The term "TIN" means the identifying number assigned to a person under section 6109.

(42) Substituted basis property. -- The term "substituted basis property" means property which is--

    (A) transferred basis property, or

    (B) exchanged basis property.

(43) Transferred basis property. -- The term "transferred basis property" means property having a basis determined under any provision of subtitle A (or under any corresponding provision of prior income tax law) providing that the basis shall be determined in whole or in part by reference to the basis in the hands of the donor, grantor, or other transferor.

(44) Exchanged basis property. -- The term "exchanged basis property" means property having a basis determined under any provision of subtitle A (or under any corresponding provision of prior income tax law) providing that the basis shall be determined in whole or in part by reference to other property held at any time by the person for whom the basis is to be determined.

(45) Nonrecognition transaction. -- The term "nonrecognition transaction" means any disposition of property in a transaction in which gain or loss is not recognized in whole or in part for purposes of subtitle A.

***

1142

Sec. 7701. Definitions

(47) Executor. -- The term "executor" means the executor or administrator of the decedent, or, if there is no executor or administrator appointed, qualified, and acting within the United States, then any person in actual or constructive possession of any property of the decedent.

***

(c) Includes and including. -- The terms "includes" and "including" when used in a definition contained in this title shall not be deemed to exclude other things otherwise within the meaning of the term defined.

(d) Commonwealth of Puerto Rico. -- Where not otherwise distinctly expressed or manifestly incompatible with the intent thereof, references in this title to possessions of the United States shall be treated as also referring to the Commonwealth of Puerto Rico.

(e) Treatment of certain contracts for providing services, etc. -- For purposes of chapter 1--

(1) In general. -- A contract which purports to be a service contract shall be treated as a lease of property if such contract is properly treated as a lease of property, taking into account all relevant factors including whether or not--

(A) the service recipient is in physical possession of the property,

(B) the service recipient controls the property,

(C) the service recipient has a significant economic or possessory interest in the property,

(D) the service provider does not bear any risk of substantially diminished receipts or substantially increased expenditures if there is nonperformance under the contract,

(E) the service provider does not use the property concurrently to provide significant services to entities unrelated to the service recipient, and

(F) the total contract price does not substantially exceed the rental value of the property for the contract period.

(2) Other arrangements. -- An arrangement (including a partnership or other pass-thru entity) which is not described in paragraph (1) shall be treated as a lease if such arrangement is properly treated as a lease, taking into account all relevant factors including factors similar to those set forth in paragraph (1).

***

(g) Clarification of fair market value in the case of nonrecourse indebtedness. -- For purposes of subtitle A, in determining the amount of gain or loss (or deemed gain or loss) with respect to any property, the fair market value of such property shall be treated as being not less than the amount of any nonrecourse indebtedness to which such property is subject.

***

(o) Cross references. --

(1) Other definitions.-- For other definitions, see the following sections of Title 1 of the United States Code:

(1) Singular as including plural, section 1.

(2) Plural as including singular, section 1.

(3) Masculine as including feminine, section 1.

(4) Officer, section 1.

(5) Oath as including affirmation, section 1.

(6) County as including parish, section 2.

(7) Vessel as including all means of water transportation, section 3.

(8) Vehicle as including all means of land transportation, section 4.

Sec. 7701. Definitions

(9) Company or association as including successors and assigns, section 5.

(2) Effect of cross references. -- For effect of cross references in this title, see section 7806(a).

Sec. 7702. Life insurance contract defined

(a) General rule. -- For purposes of this title, the term "life insurance contract" means any contract which is a life insurance contract under the applicable law, but only if such contract--

(1) meets the cash value accumulation test of subsection (b), or

(2)(A) meets the guideline premium requirements of subsection (c), and

(B) falls within the cash value corridor of subsection (d).

(b) Cash value accumulation test for subsection (a)(1). --

(1) In general. -- A contract meets the cash value accumulation test of this subsection if, by the terms of the contract, the cash surrender value of such contract may not at any time exceed the net single premium which would have to be paid at such time to fund future benefits under the contract.

***

(c) Guideline premium requirements. -- For purposes of this section--

(1) In general. -- A contract meets the guideline premium requirements of this subsection if the sum of the premiums paid under such contract does not at any time exceed the guideline premium limitation as of such time.

(2) Guideline premium limitation. -- The term "guideline premium limitation" means, as of any date, the greater of--

(A) the guideline single premium, or

(B) the sum of the guideline level premiums to such date.

(3) Guideline single premium. --

(A) In general. -- The term "guideline single premium" means the premium at issue with respect to future benefits under the contract.

(B) Basis on which determination is made. -- The determination under subparagraph (A) shall be based on--

(i) reasonable mortality charges which meet the requirements (if any) prescribed in regulations and which (except as provided in regulations) do not exceed the mortality charges specified in the prevailing commissioners' standard tables (as defined in section 807(d)(5)) as of the time the contract is issued,

(ii) any reasonable charges (other than mortality charges) which (on the basis of the company's experience, if any, with respect to similar contracts) are reasonably expected to be actually paid, and

(iii) interest at the greater of an annual effective rate of 6 percent or the rate or rates guaranteed on issuance of the contract.

(C) When determination made. -- Except as provided in subsection (f)(7), the determination under subparagraph (A) shall be made as of the time the contract is issued.

(D) Special rules for subparagraph (B)(ii). --

(i) Charges not specified in the contract. -- If any charge is not specified in the contract, the amount taken into account under subparagraph (B)(ii) for such charge shall be zero.

Sec. 7702. Life insurance contract defined

(ii) New companies, etc. -- If any company does not have adequate experience for purposes of the determination under subparagraph (B)(ii), to the extent provided in regulations, such determination shall be made on the basis of the industry-wide experience.

(4) Guideline level premium. -- The term "guideline level premium" means the level annual amount, payable over a period not ending before the insured attains age 95, computed on the same basis as the guideline single premium, except that paragraph (3)(B)(iii) shall be applied by substituting "4 percent" for "6 percent".

(d) Cash value corridor for purposes of subsection (a)(2)(B). -- For purposes of this section -

(1) In general. -- A contract falls within the cash value corridor of this subsection if the death benefit under the contract at any time is not less than the applicable percentage of the cash surrender value.

(2) Applicable percentage. --

In the case of an insured with an attained age as of the beginning of the contract year of:		The applicable percentage shall decrease by a ratable portion for each full year:	
More than:	**But not more than:**	**From:**	**To:**
0	40	250	250
40	45	250	215
45	50	215	185
50	55	185	150
55	60	150	130
60	65	130	120
65	70	120	115
70	75	115	105
75	90	105	105
90	95	105	100.

***

(g) Treatment of contracts which do not meet subsection (a) test. --

(1) Income inclusion. --

(A) In general. -- If at any time any contract which is a life insurance contract under the applicable law does not meet the definition of life insurance contract under subsection (a), the income on the contract for any taxable year of the policyholder shall be treated as ordinary income received or accrued by the policyholder during such year.

(B) Income on the contract. -- For purposes of this paragraph, the term "income on the contract" means, with respect to any taxable year of the policyholder, the excess of -

(i) the sum of -

(I) the increase in the net surrender value of the contract during the taxable year, and

(II) the cost of life insurance protection provided under the contract during the taxable year, over

(ii) the premiums paid (as defined in subsection (f)(1)) under the contract during the taxable year.

Sec. 7702. Life insurance contract defined

(C) Contracts which cease to meet definition. -- If, during any taxable year of the policyholder, a contract which is a life insurance contract under the applicable law ceases to meet the definition of life insurance contract under subsection (a), the income on the contract for all prior taxable years shall be treated as received or accrued during the taxable year in which such cessation occurs.

(D) Cost of life insurance protection. -- For purposes of this paragraph, the cost of life insurance protection provided under the contract shall be the lesser of--

(i) the cost of individual insurance on the life of the insured as determined on the basis of uniform premiums (computed on the basis of 5-year age brackets) prescribed by the Secretary by regulations, or

(ii) the mortality charge (if any) stated in the contract.

(2) Treatment of amount paid on death of insured. -- If any contract which is a life insurance contract under the applicable law does not meet the definition of life insurance contract under subsection (a), the excess of the amount paid by the reason of the death of the insured over the net surrender value of the contract shall be deemed to be paid under a life insurance contract for purposes of section 101 and subtitle B.

(3) Contract continues to be treated as insurance contract. -- If any contract which is a life insurance contract under the applicable law does not meet the definition of life insurance contract under subsection (a), such contract shall, notwithstanding such failure, be treated as an insurance contract for purposes of this title.

***

Sec. 7702A. Modified endowment contract defined

(a) General. -- For purposes of section 72, the term "modified endowment contract" means any contract meeting the requirements of section 7702 -

(1) which -

(A) is entered into on or after June 21, 1988, and

(B) fails to meet the 7-pay test of subsection (b), or

(2) which is received in exchange for a contract described in paragraph (1) or this paragraph.

(b) 7-pay test. -- For purposes of subsection (a), a contract fails to meet the 7- pay test of this subsection if the accumulated amount paid under the contract at any time during the 1st 7 contract years exceeds the sum of the net level premiums which would have been paid on or before such time if the contract provided for paid-up future benefits after the payment of 7 level annual premiums.

***

Sec. 7702B. Treatment of qualified long-term care insurance

(a) In general. -- For purposes of this title--

(1) a qualified long-term care insurance contract shall be treated as an accident and health insurance contract,

(2) amounts (other than policyholder dividends, as defined in section 808, or premium refunds) received under a qualified long-term care insurance contract shall be treated as amounts received for personal injuries and sickness and shall be treated as reimbursement for expenses actually incurred for medical care (as defined in section 213(d)),

(3) any plan of an employer providing coverage under a qualified long-term care insurance contract shall be treated as an accident and health plan with respect to such coverage,

Sec. 7702B. Treatment of qualified long-term care insurance

(4) except as provided in subsection (e)(3), amounts paid for a qualified long-term care insurance contract providing the benefits described in subsection (b)(2)(A) shall be treated as payments made for insurance for purposes of section 213(d)(1)(D), and

(5) a qualified long-term care insurance contract shall be treated as a guaranteed renewable contract subject to the rules of section 816(e).   5

(b) Qualified long-term care insurance contract. -- For purposes of this title--

(1) In general. -- The term "qualified long-term care insurance contract" means any insurance contract if--

   (A) the only insurance protection provided under such contract is coverage of qualified long-term care services,   10

   (B) such contract does not pay or reimburse expenses incurred for services or items to the extent that such expenses are reimbursable under title XVIII of the Social Security Act or would be so reimbursable but for the application of a deductible or coinsurance amount,

   (C) such contract is guaranteed renewable,

   (D) such contract does not provide for a cash surrender value or other money that can be- 15

      (i) paid, assigned, or pledged as collateral for a loan, or

      (ii) borrowed,

other than as provided in subparagraph (E) or paragraph (2)(C),

   (E) all refunds of premiums, and all policyholder dividends or similar amounts, under such contract are to be applied as a reduction in future premiums or to increase future 20 benefits, and

   (F) such contract meets the requirements of subsection (g).

(2) Special rules. --

   (A) Per diem, etc. payments permitted. -- A contract shall not fail to be described in subparagraph (A) or (B) of paragraph (1) by reason of payments being made on a per diem 25 or other periodic basis without regard to the expenses incurred during the period to which the payments relate.

   (B) Special rules relating to medicare. --

      (i) Paragraph (1)(B) shall not apply to expenses which are reimbursable under title XVIII of the Social Security Act only as a secondary payor.   30

      (ii) No provision of law shall be construed or applied so as to prohibit the offering of a qualified long-term care insurance contract on the basis that the contract coordinates its benefits with those provided under such title.

   (C) Refunds of premiums. -- Paragraph (1)(E) shall not apply to any refund on the death of the insured, or on a complete surrender or cancellation of the contract, which 35 cannot exceed the aggregate premiums paid under the contract. Any refund on a complete surrender or cancellation of the contract shall be includible in gross income to the extent that any deduction or exclusion was allowable with respect to the premiums.

(c) Qualified long-term care services. -- For purposes of this section--

(1) In general. -- The term "qualified long-term care services" means necessary diagnostic, 40 preventive, therapeutic, curing, treating, mitigating, and rehabilitative services, and maintenance or personal care services, which--

   (A) are required by a chronically ill individual, and

   (B) are provided pursuant to a plan of care prescribed by a licensed health care practitioner.   45

Sec. 7702B. Treatment of qualified long-term care insurance

(2) Chronically ill individual. --

(A) In general. -- The term "chronically ill individual" means any individual who has been certified by a licensed health care practitioner as--

(i) being unable to perform (without substantial assistance from another individual) at least 2 activities of daily living for a period of at least 90 days due to a loss of functional capacity,

(ii) having a level of disability similar (as determined under regulations prescribed by the Secretary in consultation with the Secretary of Health and Human Services) to the level of disability described in clause (i), or

(iii) requiring substantial supervision to protect such individual from threats to health and safety due to severe cognitive impairment.

Such term shall not include any individual otherwise meeting the requirements of the preceding sentence unless within the preceding 12-month period a licensed health care practitioner has certified that such individual meets such requirements.

(B) Activities of daily living. -- For purposes of subparagraph (A), each of the following is an activity of daily living:

(i) Eating.

(ii) Toileting.

(iii) Transferring.

(iv) Bathing.

(v) Dressing.

(vi) Continence.

A contract shall not be treated as a qualified long-term care insurance contract unless the determination of whether an individual is a chronically ill individual described in subparagraph (A)(i) takes into account at least 5 of such activities.

(3) Maintenance or personal care services. -- The term "maintenance or personal care services" means any care the primary purpose of which is the provision of needed assistance with any of the disabilities as a result of which the individual is a chronically ill individual (including the protection from threats to health and safety due to severe cognitive impairment).

(4) Licensed health care practitioner. -- The term "licensed health care practitioner" means any physician (as defined in section 1861(r)(1) of the Social Security Act) and any registered professional nurse, licensed social worker, or other individual who meets such requirements as may be prescribed by the Secretary.

(d) Aggregate payments in excess of limits. --

(1) In general. -- If the aggregate of--

(A) the periodic payments received for any period under all qualified long-term care insurance contracts which are treated as made for qualified long-term care services for an insured, and

(B) the periodic payments received for such period which are treated under section 101(g) as paid by reason of the death of such insured,

exceeds the per diem limitation for such period, such excess shall be includible in gross income without regard to section 72. A payment shall not be taken into account under subparagraph (B) if the insured is a terminally ill individual (as defined in section 101(g)) at the time the payment is received.

(2) Per diem limitation. -- For purposes of paragraph (1), the per diem limitation for any period is an amount equal to the excess (if any) of--

1148

Sec. 7702B. Treatment of qualified long-term care insurance

(A) the greater of -

   (i) the dollar amount in effect for such period under paragraph (4), or

   (ii) the costs incurred for qualified long-term care services provided for the insured for such period, over

(B) the aggregate payments received as reimbursements (through insurance or otherwise) for qualified long-term care services provided for the insured during such period.

(3) Aggregation rules. -- For purposes of this subsection--

   (A) all persons receiving periodic payments described in paragraph (1) with respect to the same insured shall be treated as 1 person, and

   (B) the per diem limitation determined under paragraph (2) shall be allocated first to the insured and any remaining limitation shall be allocated among the other such persons in such manner as the Secretary shall prescribe.

(4) Dollar amount. -- The dollar amount in effect under this subsection shall be $175 per day (or the equivalent amount in the case of payments on another periodic basis).

(5) Inflation adjustment. -- In the case of a calendar year after 1997, the dollar amount contained in paragraph (4) shall be increased at the same time and in the same manner as amounts are increased pursuant to section 213(d)(10).

(6) Periodic payments. -- For purposes of this subsection, the term "periodic payment" means any payment (whether on a periodic basis or otherwise) made without regard to the extent of the costs incurred by the payee for qualified long-term care services.

(e) Treatment of coverage provided as part of a life insurance contract. -- Except as otherwise provided in regulations prescribed by the Secretary, in the case of any long-term care insurance coverage (whether or not qualified) provided by a rider on or as part of a life insurance contract -

(1) In general. -- This section shall apply as if the portion of the contract providing such coverage is a separate contract.

(2) Application of section 7702. -- Section 7702(c)(2) (relating to the guideline premium limitation) shall be applied by increasing the guideline premium limitation with respect to a life insurance contract, as of any date--

   (A) by the sum of any charges (but not premium payments) against the life insurance contract's cash surrender value (within the meaning of section 7702(f)(2)(A)) for such coverage made to that date under the contract, less

   (B) any such charges the imposition of which reduces the premiums paid for the contract (within the meaning of section 7702(f)(1)).

(3) Application of section 213. -- No deduction shall be allowed under section 213(a) for charges against the life insurance contract's cash surrender value described in paragraph (2), unless such charges are includible in income as a result of the application of section 72(e)(10) and the rider is a qualified long-term care insurance contract under subsection (b).

(4) Portion defined. -- For purposes of this subsection, the term "portion" means only the terms and benefits under a life insurance contract that are in addition to the terms and benefits under the contract without regard to long-term care insurance coverage.

              ***

Sec. 7703. Determination of marital status

(a) General rule. -- For purposes of part V of subchapter B of chapter 1 and those provisions of this title which refer to this subsection--

   (1) the determination of whether an individual is married shall be made as of the close of his

Sec. 7703. Determination of marital status

taxable year; except that if his spouse dies during his taxable year such determination shall be made as of the time of such death; and

(2) an individual legally separated from his spouse under a decree of divorce or of separate maintenance shall not be considered as married.

(b) Certain married individuals living apart. -- For purposes of those provisions of this title which refer to this subsection, if--

(1) an individual who is married (within the meaning of subsection (a)) and who files a separate return maintains as his home a household which constitutes for more than one-half of the taxable year the principal place of abode of a child (within the meaning of section 152(f)(1)) with respect to whom such individual is entitled to a deduction for the taxable year under section 151 (or would be so entitled but for section 152(e)),

(2) such individual furnishes over one-half of the cost of maintaining such household during the taxable year, and

(3) during the last 6 months of the taxable year, such individual's spouse is not a member of such household, such individual shall not be considered as married.

Sec. 7704. Certain publicly traded partnerships treated as corporations

(a) General rule. -- For purposes of this title, except as provided in subsection (c), a publicly traded partnership shall be treated as a corporation.

***

(c) Exception for partnerships with passive-type income. --

(1) In general. -- Subsection (a) shall not apply to any publicly traded partnership for any taxable year if such partnership met the gross income requirements of paragraph (2) for such taxable year and each preceding taxable year beginning after December 31, 1987, during which the partnership (or any predecessor) was in existence. For purposes of the preceding sentence, a partnership shall not be treated as being in existence during any period before the 1st taxable year in which such partnership (or a predecessor) was a publicly traded partnership.

(2) Gross income requirements. -- A partnership meets the gross income requirements of this paragraph for any taxable year if 90 percent or more of the gross income of such partnership for such taxable year consists of qualifying income.

***

(d) Qualifying income. -- For purposes of this section--

(1) In general. -- Except as otherwise provided in this subsection, the term "qualifying income" means--

(A) interest,

(B) dividends,

(C) real property rents,

(D) gain from the sale or other disposition of real property (including property described in section 1221(a)(1)),

(E) income and gains derived from the exploration, development, mining or production, processing, refining, transportation (including pipelines transporting gas, oil, or products thereof), or the marketing of any mineral or natural resource (including fertilizer, geothermal energy, and timber),

(F) any gain from the sale or disposition of a capital asset (or property described in section 1231(b)) held for the production of income described in any of the foregoing subparagraphs of this paragraph, and

Sec. 7703. Determination of marital status

(G) in the case of a partnership described in the second sentence of subsection (c)(3), income and gains from commodities (not described in section 1221(a)(1)) or futures, forwards, and options with respect to commodities.

For purposes of subparagraph (E), the term "mineral or natural resource" means any product of a character with respect to which a deduction for depletion is allowable under section 611; except that such term shall not include any product described in subparagraph (A) or (B) of section 613(b)(7).

(2) Certain interest not qualified. -- Interest shall not be treated as qualifying income if--

(A) such interest is derived in the conduct of a financial or insurance business, or

(B) such interest would be excluded from the term "interest" under section 856(f).

(3) Real property rent. -- The term "real property rent" means amounts which would qualify as rent from real property under section 856(d) if--

(A) such section were applied without regard to paragraph (2)(C) thereof (relating to independent contractor requirements), and

(B) stock owned, directly or indirectly, by or for a partner would not be considered as owned under section 318(a)(3)(A) by the partnership unless 5 percent or more (by value) of the interests in such partnership are owned, directly or indirectly, by or for such partner.

(4) Certain income qualifying under regulated investment company or real estate trust provisions. -- The term "qualifying income" also includes any income which would qualify under section 851(b)(2)(A) or 856(c)(2).

(5) Special rule for determining gross income from certain real property sales. -- In the case of the sale or other disposition of real property described in section 1221(a)(1), gross income shall not be reduced by inventory costs.

***

Sec. 7805. Rules and regulations

(a) Authorization. -- Except where such authority is expressly given by this title to any person other than an officer or employee of the Treasury Department, the Secretary shall prescribe all needful rules and regulations for the enforcement of this title, including all rules and regulations as may be necessary by reason of any alteration of law in relation to internal revenue.

(b) Retroactivity of regulations. --

(1) In general. -- Except as otherwise provided in this subsection, no temporary, proposed, or final regulation relating to the internal revenue laws shall apply to any taxable period ending before the earliest of the following dates:

(A) The date on which such regulation is filed with the Federal Register.

(B) In the case of any final regulation, the date on which any proposed or temporary regulation to which such final regulation relates was filed with the Federal Register.

(C) The date on which any notice substantially describing the expected contents of any temporary, proposed, or final regulation is issued to the public.

(2) Exception for promptly issued regulations. -- Paragraph (1) shall not apply to regulations filed or issued within 18 months of the date of the enactment of the statutory provision to which the regulation relates.

(3) Prevention of abuse. -- The Secretary may provide that any regulation may take effect or apply retroactively to prevent abuse.

Sec. 7805. Rules and regulations

(4) Correction of procedural defects. -- The Secretary may provide that any regulation may apply retroactively to correct a procedural defect in the issuance of any prior regulation.

(5) Internal regulations. -- The limitation of paragraph (1) shall not apply to any regulation relating to internal Treasury Department policies, practices, or procedures.

(6) Congressional authorization. -- The limitation of paragraph (1) may be superseded by a legislative grant from Congress authorizing the Secretary to prescribe the effective date with respect to any regulation.

(7) Election to apply retroactively. -- The Secretary may provide for any taxpayer to elect to apply any regulation before the dates specified in paragraph (1).

(8) Application to rulings. -- The Secretary may prescribe the extent, if any, to which any ruling (including any judicial decision or any administrative determination other than by regulation) relating to the internal revenue laws shall be applied without retroactive effect.

(c) Preparation and distribution of regulations, forms, stamps, and other matters. -- The Secretary shall prepare and distribute all the instructions, regulations, directions, forms, blanks, stamps, and other matters pertaining to the assessment and collection of internal revenue.

(d) Manner of making elections prescribed by Secretary. -- Except to the extent otherwise provided by this title, any election under this title shall be made at such time and in such manner as the Secretary shall prescribe.

(e) Temporary regulations. --

(1) Issuance. -- Any temporary regulation issued by the Secretary shall also be issued as a proposed regulation.

(2) 3-year duration. -- Any temporary regulation shall expire within 3 years after the date of issuance of such regulation.

(f) Review of impact of regulations on small business. --

(1) Submissions to Small Business Administration. -- After publication of any proposed or temporary regulation by the Secretary, the Secretary shall submit such regulation to the Chief Counsel for Advocacy of the Small Business Administration for comment on the impact of such regulation on small business. Not later than the date 4 weeks after the date of such submission, the Chief Counsel for Advocacy shall submit comments on such regulation to the Secretary.

(2) Consideration of comments. -- In prescribing any final regulation which supersedes a proposed or temporary regulation which had been submitted under this subsection to the Chief Counsel for Advocacy of the Small Business Administration -

(A) the Secretary shall consider the comments of the Chief Counsel for Advocacy on such proposed or temporary regulation, and

(B) the Secretary shall discuss any response to such comments in the preamble of such final regulation.

(3) Submission of certain final regulations. -- In the case of the promulgation by the Secretary of any final regulation (other than a temporary regulation) which does not supersede a proposed regulation, the requirements of paragraphs (1) and (2) shall apply; except that--

(A) the submission under paragraph (1) shall be made at least 4 weeks before the date of such promulgation, and

(B) the consideration (and discussion) required under paragraph (2) shall be made in connection with the promulgation of such final regulation.

Sec. 7806.   Construction of title

(a) **Cross references.** -- The cross references in this title to other portions of the title, or other provisions of law, where the word "see" is used, are made only for convenience, and shall be given no legal effect.

(b) **Arrangement and classification.** -- No inference, implication, or presumption of legislative construction shall be drawn or made by reason of the location or grouping of any particular section 5 or provision or portion of this title, nor shall any table of contents, table of cross references, or similar outline, analysis, or descriptive matter relating to the contents of this title be given any legal effect. The preceding sentence also applies to the sidenotes and ancillary tables contained in the various prints of this Act before its enactment into law.

10

Sec. 7872.   Treatment of loans with below-market interest rates

(a) **Treatment of gift loans and demand loans.** --

(1) **In general.** -- For purposes of this title, in the case of any below-market loan to which this section applies and which is a gift loan or a demand loan, the forgone interest shall be treated as -

(A) transferred from the lender to the borrower, and   15

(B) retransferred by the borrower to the lender as interest.

(2) **Time when transfers made.** -- Except as otherwise provided in regulations prescribed by the Secretary, any forgone interest attributable to periods during any calendar year shall be treated as transferred (and retransferred) under paragraph (1) on the last day of such calendar year.   20

(b) **Treatment of other below-market loans.** --

(1) **In general.** -- For purposes of this title, in the case of any below-market loan to which this section applies and to which subsection (a)(1) does not apply, the lender shall be treated as having transferred on the date the loan was made (or, if later, on the first day on which this section applies to such loan), and the borrower shall be treated as having received on such date, 25 cash in an amount equal to the excess of--

(A) the amount loaned, over

(B) the present value of all payments which are required to be made under the terms of the loan.

(2) **Obligation treated as having original issue discount.** -- For purposes of this title--   30

(A) **In general.** -- Any below-market loan to which paragraph (1) applies shall be treated as having original issue discount in an amount equal to the excess described in paragraph (1).

(B) **Amount in addition to other original issue discount.** -- Any original issue discount which a loan is treated as having by reason of subparagraph (A) shall be in addition to any 35 other original issue discount on such loan (determined without regard to subparagraph (A)).

(c) **Below-market loans to which section applies.** --

(1) **In general.** -- Except as otherwise provided in this subsection and subsection (g), this section shall apply to--

(A) **Gifts.** -- Any below-market loan which is a gift loan.   40

(B) **Compensation-related loans.** -- Any below-market loan directly or indirectly between--

Sec. 7872. Treatment of loans with below-market interest rates

    (i) an employer and an employee, or

    (ii) an independent contractor and a person for whom such independent contractor provides services.

    (C) Corporation-shareholder loans. -- Any below-market loan directly or indirectly between a corporation and any shareholder of such corporation.

    (D) Tax avoidance loans. -- Any below-market loan 1 of the principal purposes of the interest arrangements of which is the avoidance of any Federal tax.

    (E) Other below-market loans. -- To the extent provided in regulations, any below-market loan which is not described in subparagraph (A), (B), (C), or (F) if the interest arrangements of such loan have a significant effect on any Federal tax liability of the lender or the borrower.

    (F) Loans to qualified continuing care facilities. -- Any loan to any qualified continuing care facility pursuant to a continuing care contract.

(2) $10,000 de minimis exception for gift loans between individuals. --

    (A) In general. -- In the case of any gift loan directly between individuals, this section shall not apply to any day on which the aggregate outstanding amount of loans between such individuals does not exceed $10,000.

    (B) De minimis exception not to apply to loans attributable to acquisition of income-producing assets. -- Subparagraph (A) shall not apply to any gift loan directly attributable to the purchase or carrying of income-producing assets.

    (C) Cross reference. -- For limitation on amount treated as interest where loans do not exceed $100,000, see subsection (d)(1).

(3) $10,000 de minimis exception for compensation-related and corporate-shareholder loans. --

    (A) In general. -- In the case of any loan described in subparagraph (B) or (C) of paragraph (1), this section shall not apply to any day on which the aggregate outstanding amount of loans between the borrower and lender does not exceed $10,000.

    (B) Exception not to apply where 1 of principal purposes is tax avoidance. -- Subparagraph (A) shall not apply to any loan the interest arrangements of which have as 1 of their principal purposes the avoidance of any Federal tax.

(d) Special rules for gift loans. --

(1) Limitation on interest accrual for purposes of income taxes where loans do not exceed $100,000. --

    (A) In general. -- For purposes of subtitle A, in the case of a gift loan directly between individuals, the amount treated as retransferred by the borrower to the lender as of the close of any year shall not exceed the borrower's net investment income for such year.

    (B) Limitation not to apply where 1 of principal purposes is tax avoidance. -- Subparagraph (A) shall not apply to any loan the interest arrangements of which have as 1 of their principal purposes the avoidance of any Federal tax.

    (C) Special rule where more than 1 gift loan outstanding. -- For purposes of subparagraph (A), in any case in which a borrower has outstanding more than 1 gift loan, the net investment income of such borrower shall be allocated among such loans in proportion to the respective amounts which would be treated as retransferred by the borrower without regard to this paragraph.

    (D) Limitation not to apply where aggregate amount of loans exceed $100,000. -- This paragraph shall not apply to any loan made by a lender to a borrower for any day on

Sec. 7872. Treatment of loans with below-market interest rates

which the aggregate outstanding amount of loans between the borrower and lender exceeds $100,000.

(E) Net investment income. -- For purposes of this paragraph--

(i) In general. -- The term "net investment income" has the meaning given such term by section 163(d)(4).

(ii) De minimis rule. -- If the net investment income of any borrower for any year does not exceed $1,000, the net investment income of such borrower for such year shall be treated as zero.

(iii) Additional amounts treated as interest. -- In determining the net investment income of a person for any year, any amount which would be included in the gross income of such person for such year by reason of section 1272 if such section applied to all deferred payment obligations shall be treated as interest received by such person for such year.

(iv) Deferred payment obligations. -- The term "deferred payment obligation" includes any market discount bond, short-term obligation, United States savings bond, annuity, or similar obligation.

(2) Special rule for gift tax. -- In the case of any gift loan which is a term loan, subsection (b)(1) (and not subsection (a)) shall apply for purposes of chapter 12.

(e) Definitions of below-market loan and forgone interest. -- For purposes of this section--

(1) Below-market loan. -- The term "below-market loan" means any loan if--

(A) in the case of a demand loan, interest is payable on the loan at a rate less than the applicable Federal rate, or

(B) in the case of a term loan, the amount loaned exceeds the present value of all payments due under the loan.

(2) Forgone interest. -- The term "forgone interest" means, with respect to any period during which the loan is outstanding, the excess of--

(A) the amount of interest which would have been payable on the loan for the period if interest accrued on the loan at the applicable Federal rate and were payable annually on the day referred to in subsection (a)(2), over

(B) any interest payable on the loan properly allocable to such period.

(f) Other definitions and special rules. -- For purposes of this section--

(1) Present value. -- The present value of any payment shall be determined in the manner provided by regulations prescribed by the Secretary--

(A) as of the date of the loan, and

(B) by using a discount rate equal to the applicable Federal rate.

(2) Applicable Federal rate. --

(A) Term loans. -- In the case of any term loan, the applicable Federal rate shall be the applicable Federal rate in effect under section 1274(d) (as of the day on which the loan was made), compounded semiannually.

(B) Demand loans. -- In the case of a demand loan, the applicable Federal rate shall be the Federal short-term rate in effect under section 1274(d) for the period for which the amount of forgone interest is being determined, compounded semiannually.

(3) Gift loan. -- The term "gift loan" means any below-market loan where the forgoing of interest is in the nature of a gift.

(4) Amount loaned. -- The term "amount loaned" means the amount received by the

Sec. 7872. Treatment of loans with below-market interest rates

borrower.

(5) Demand loan. -- The term "demand loan" means any loan which is payable in full at any time on the demand of the lender. Such term also includes (for purposes other than determining the applicable Federal rate under paragraph (2)) any loan if the benefits of the interest arrangements of such loan are not transferable and are conditioned on the future performance of substantial services by an individual. To the extent provided in regulations, such term also includes any loan with an indefinite maturity.

(6) Term loan. -- The term "term loan" means any loan which is not a demand loan.

(7) Husband and wife treated as 1 person. -- A husband and wife shall be treated as 1 person.

(8) Loans to which section 483, 643(i), or 1274 applies. -- This section shall not apply to any loan to which section 483, 643(i), or 1274 applies.

(9) No withholding. -- No amount shall be withheld under chapter 24 with respect to--

(A) any amount treated as transferred or retransferred under subsection (a), and

(B) any amount treated as received under subsection (b).

(10) Special rule for term loans. -- If this section applies to any term loan on any day, this section shall continue to apply to such loan notwithstanding paragraphs (2) and (3) of subsection (c). In the case of a gift loan, the preceding sentence shall only apply for purposes of chapter 12.

(11) Time for determining rate applicable to employee relocation loans. --

(A) In general. -- In the case of any term loan made by an employer to an employee the proceeds of which are used by the employee to purchase a principal residence (within the meaning of section 121), the determination of the applicable Federal rate shall be made as of the date the written contract to purchase such residence was entered into.

(B) Paragraph only to apply to cases to which section 217 applies. -- Subparagraph (A) shall only apply to the purchase of a principal residence in connection with the commencement of work by an employee or a change in the principal place of work of an employee to which section 217 applies.

(g) Exception for certain loans to qualified continuing care facilities. --

(1) In general. -- This section shall not apply for any calendar year to any below- market loan made by a lender to a qualified continuing care facility pursuant to a continuing care contract if the lender (or the lender's spouse) attains age 65 before the close of such year.

(2) $90,000 limit. -- Paragraph (1) shall apply only to the extent that the aggregate outstanding amount of any loan to which such paragraph applies (determined without regard to this paragraph), when added to the aggregate outstanding amount of all other previous loans between the lender (or the lender's spouse) and any qualified continuing care facility to which paragraph (1) applies, does not exceed $90,000.

(3) Continuing care contract. -- For purposes of this section, the term "continuing care contract" means a written contract between an individual and a qualified continuing care facility under which -

(A) the individual or individual's spouse may use a qualified continuing care facility for their life or lives,

(B) the individual or individual's spouse -

(i) will first -

(I) reside in a separate, independent living unit with additional facilities outside such unit for the providing of meals and other personal care, and

   (II) not require long-term nursing care, and

   (ii) then will be provided long-term and skilled nursing care as the health of such individual or individual's spouse requires, and

   (C) no additional substantial payment is required if such individual or individual's spouse requires increased personal care services or long-term and skilled nursing care.   5

(4) Qualified continuing care facility. --

   (A) In general. -- For purposes of this section, the term "qualified continuing care facility" means 1 or more facilities--

   (i) which are designed to provide services under continuing care contracts, and

   (ii) substantially all of the residents of which are covered by continuing care   10 contracts.

   (B) Substantially all facilities must be owned or operated by borrower. -- A facility shall not be treated as a qualified continuing care facility unless substantially all facilities which are used to provide services which are required to be provided under a continuing care contract are owned or operated by the borrower.   15

   (C) Nursing homes excluded. -- The term "qualified continuing care facility" shall not include any facility which is of a type which is traditionally considered a nursing home.

(5) Adjustment of limit for inflation. --

   (A) In general. -- In the case of any loan made during any calendar year after 1986 to which paragraph (1) applies, the dollar amount in paragraph (2) shall be increased by the   20 inflation adjustment for such calendar year. Any increase under the preceding sentence shall be rounded to the nearest multiple of $100 (or, if such increase is a multiple of $50, such increase shall be increased to the nearest multiple of $100).

   (B) Inflation adjustment. -- For purposes of subparagraph (A), the inflation adjustment for any calendar year is the percentage (if any) by which--   25

   (i) the CPI for the preceding calendar year exceeds

   (ii) the CPI for calendar year 1985.

For purposes of the preceding sentence, the CPI for any calendar year is the average of the Consumer Price Index as of the close of the 12-month period ending on September 30 of such calendar year.   30

   (6) Suspension of application. -- Paragraph (1) shall not apply for any calendar year to which subsection (h) applies. In the case of adjustments made for any taxable year beginning after 2007, section 1(f)(4) shall be applied for purposes of this paragraph by substituting `March 31' for `August 31', and the Secretary shall publish the adjusted amounts under subsections (b)(2) and (c)(2)(A) for taxable years beginning in any calendar year no later than   35 June 1 of the preceding calendar year.

Reg. § 1.7872-5T Exempted loans (temporary).

   (a) *In general*--(1) *General rule.* Except as provided in paragraph (a)(2) of this section, notwithstanding any other provision of section 7872 and the regulations thereunder,   40 section 7872 does not apply to the loans listed in paragraph (b) of this section because the interest arrangements do not have a significant effect on the Federal tax liability of the borrower or the lender.

   (2) *No exemption for tax avoidance loans.* If a taxpayer structures a transaction to be a loan described in paragraph (b) of this section and one of the principal purposes of so   45 structuring the transaction is the avoidance of Federal tax, then the transaction will be recharacterized as a tax avoidance loan as defined in section 7872(c)(1)(D).

Sec. 7872. Treatment of loans with below-market interest rates

(b) *List of exemptions*. Except as provided in paragraph (a) of this section, the following transactions are exempt from section 7872:

(1) Loans which are made available by the lender to the general public on the same terms and conditions and which are consistent with the lender's customary business
5 practice;

(2) Accounts or withdrawable shares with a bank (as defined in section 581), or an institution to which section 591 applies, or a credit union, made in the ordinary course of its business;

(3) Acquisitions of publicly traded debt obligations for an amount equal to the public
10 trading price at the time of acquisition;

(4) Loans made by a life insurance company (as defined in section 816 (a)), in the ordinary course of its business, to an insured, under a loan right contained in a life insurance policy and in which the cash surrender values are used as collateral for the loans;

15 (5) Loans subsidized by the Federal, State (including the District of Columbia), or Municipal government (or any agency or instrumentality thereof), and which are made available under a program of general application to the public;

(6) Employee-relocation loans that meet the requirements of paragraph (c)(1) of this section;

20 (7) Obligations the interest on which is excluded from gross income under section 103;

(8) Obligations of the United States government;

(9) Gift loans to a charitable organization (described in section 170(c)), but only if at no time during the taxable year will the aggregate outstanding amount of gift loans by the
25 lender to that organization exceed $250,000. Charitable organizations which are effectively controlled, within the meaning of § 1.482-1(a)(1), by the same person or persons shall be considered one charitable organization for purposes of this limitation.

***

(11) Loans made by a private foundation or other organization described in section
30 170(c), the primary purpose of which is to accomplish one or more of the purposes described in section 170(c)(2)(B);

(12) Indebtedness subject to section 482, but such indebtedness is exempt from the application of section 7872 only during the interest-free period, if any, determined under § 1.482-2(a)(1)(iii) with respect to intercompany trade receivables described in § 1.482-2(a)
35 (1)(ii)(A)(ii). See also § 1.482-2(a)(3);

(13) All money, securities, and property--

(i) Received by a futures commission merchant or registered broker/dealer or by a clearing organization (A) to margin, guarantee or secure contracts for future delivery on or subject to the rules of a qualified board or exchange (as defined in section 1256(g)(7)),
40 or (B) to purchase, margin, guarantee or secure options contracts traded on or subject to the rules of a qualified board or exchange, so long as the amounts so received to purchase, margin, guarantee or secure such contracts for future delivery or such options contracts are reasonably necessary for such purposes and so long as any commissions received by the futures commission merchant, registered broker-dealer, or clearing
45 organization are not reduced for those making deposits of money, and all money accruing to account holders as the result of such futures and options contacts or

(ii) Received by a clearing organization from a member thereof as a required deposit to a clearing fund, guaranty fund, or similar fund maintained by the clearing organization to protect it against defaults by members.

50 (14) Loans the interest arrangements of which the taxpayer is able to show have no significant effect on any Federal tax liability of the lender or the borrower, as described in

paragraph (c)(3) of this section; and

(15) Loans, described in revenue rulings or revenue procedures issued under section 7872(g)(1)(C), if the Commissioner finds that the factors justifying an exemption for such loans are sufficiently similar to the factors justifying the exemptions contained in this section.   5

(c) *Special rules--*(1) *Employee-relocation loans--*(i) *Mortgage loans.* In the case of a compensation-related loan to an employee, where such loan is secured by a mortgage on the new principal residence (within the meaning of section 217 and the regulations thereunder) of the employee, acquired in connection with the transfer of that employee to a new principal place of work (which meets the requirements in section 217(c) and the   10 regulations thereunder), the loan will be exempt from section 7872 if the following conditions are satisfied:

(A) The loan is a demand loan or is a term loan the benefits of the interest arrangements of which are not transferable by the employee and are conditioned on the future performance of substantial services by the employee;   15

(B) The employee certifies to the employer that the employee reasonably expects to be entitled to and will itemize deductions for each year the loan is outstanding; and

(C) The loan agreement requires that the loan proceeds be used only to purchase the new principal residence of the employee.

(ii) *Bridge loans.* In the case of a compensation-related loan to an employee which is   20 not described in paragraph (c)(1)(i) of this section, and which is used to purchase a new principal residence (within the meaning of section 217 and the regulations thereunder) of the employee acquired in connection with the transfer of that employee to a new principal place of work (which meets the requirements in section 217(c) and the regulations thereunder), the loan will be exempt from section 7872 if the following conditions are   25 satisfied:

(A) The conditions contained in paragraphs (c)(1)(i)(A), (B), and (C) of this section;

(B) The loan agreement provides that the loan is payable in full within 15 days after the date of the sale of the employee's immediately former principal residence;

(C) The aggregate principal amount of all outstanding loans described in this   30 paragraph (c)(1)(ii) to an employee is no greater than the employer's reasonable estimate of the amount of the equity of the employee and the employee's spouse in the employee's immediately former principal residence, and

(D) The employee's immediately former principal residence is not converted to business or investment use.   35

***

(3) *Loans without significant tax effect.* Whether a loan will be considered to be a loan the interest arrangements of which have a significant effect on any Federal tax liability of the lender or the borrower will be determined according to all of the facts and circumstances. Among the factors to be considered are--   40

(i) Whether items of income and deduction generated by the loan offset each other;

(ii) The amount of such items;

(iii) The cost to the taxpayer of complying with the provisions of section 7872 if such section were applied; and

(iv) Any non-tax reasons for deciding to structure the transaction as a below-market   45 loan rather than a loan with interest at a rate equal to or greater than the applicable Federal rate and a payment by the lender to the borrower.

[T.D. 8045, 50 FR 33520, Aug. 20, 1985; T.D. 8093, 51 FR 25033, July 10, 1986; 51 FR 28553, Aug. 8, 1986; T.D. 8204, 53 FR 18282, May 23, 1988]   50

Sec. 7872. Treatment of loans with below-market interest rates

Prop. Reg. § 1.7872-1   Introduction. (8/20/85)

(a) *Statement of purpose.*--Section 7872 generally treats certain loans in which the interest rate charged is less than the applicable Federal rate as economically equivalent to loans bearing interest at the applicable Federal rate, coupled with a payment by the
5 lender to the borrower sufficient to fund all or part of the payment of interest by the borrower. Such loans are referred to as "below-market loans." See §1.7872-3 for detailed definitions of below-market loans and the determination of the applicable Federal rate. Accordingly, section 7872 recharacterizes a below-market loan as two transactions:

(1) An arm's-length transaction in which the lender makes a loan to the borrower in
10 exchange for a note requiring the payment of interest at the applicable Federal rate; and

(2) A transfer of funds by the lender to the borrower ("imputed transfer").

The timing and the characterization of the amount of the imputed transfer by the lender to the borrower are determined in accordance with the substance of the transaction. The timing and the amount of the imputed interest payment (the excess of the amount of
15 interest required to be paid using the applicable Federal rate, over the amount of interest required to be paid according to the loan agreement) by the borrower to the lender depend on the character of the imputed transfer by the lender to the borrower and whether the loan is a term loan or a demand loan. If the imputed transfer by the lender is characterized as a gift, the provisions of chapter 12 of the Internal Revenue Code,
20 relating to gift tax, also apply. All imputed transfers under section 7872 (e.g., interest, compensation, gift) are characterized in accordance with the substance of the transaction, and, except as otherwise provided in the regulations under section 7872, are treated as so characterized for all purposes of the Code. For example, for purposes of section 170, an interest-free loan to a charity referred to in section 170 for which interest
25 is imputed under section 7872, is treated as an interest bearing loan coupled with periodic gifts to the charity in the amount of the imputed transfer, for purposes of section 170. In addition, all applicable information and reporting requirements (e.g., reporting on W-2 and Form 1099) must be satisfied.

30

I.R.S. Procedural Rules

Reg. § 601.104   Collection functions.

***

(c) *Enforcement procedure*--(1) *General.* Taxes shown to be due on returns, deficiencies in taxes, additional or delinquent taxes to be assessed, and penalties,
35 interest, and additions to taxes, are recorded by the district director or the director of the appropriate service center as ``assessments." Under the law an assessment is prima facie correct for all purposes. Generally, the taxpayer bears the burden of disproving the correctness of an assessment. Upon assessment, the district director is required to effect collection of any amounts which remain due and unpaid. Generally, payment within 10
40 days from the date of the notice and demand for payment is requested; however, payment may be required in a shorter period if collection of the tax is considered to be in jeopardy. When collection of income tax is in jeopardy, the taxpayer's taxable period may be terminated under section 6851 of the Code and assessment of the tax made expeditiously under section 6201 of the Code.

45   (2) *Levy.* If a taxpayer neglects or refuses to pay any tax within the period provided for its payment, it is lawful for the district director to make collection by levy on the taxpayer's property. However, unless collection is in jeopardy, the taxpayer must be furnished written notice of intent to levy no fewer than 10 days before the date of the levy. See section 6331 of the Code. No suit for the purpose of restraining the assessment or collection of

an internal revenue tax may be maintained in any court, except to restrain the assessment or collection of income, estate, Chapters 41 through 44, or gift taxes during the period within which the assessment or collection of deficiencies in such taxes is prohibited. See section 7421 of the Code. Property taken under authority of any revenue law of the United States is irrepleviable. 28 U.S.C. 2463. If the Service sells property, and 5 it is subsequently determined that the taxpayer had no interest in the property or that the purchaser was misled by the Service as to the value of the taxpayer's interest, immediate action will be taken to refund any money wrongfully collected if a claim is made and the pertinent facts are present. The mere fact that a taxpayer's interest in property turns out to be less valuable than the purchaser expected will not be regarded as giving the 10 purchaser any claim against the Government.

(3) *Liens.* The United States' claim for taxes is a lien on the taxpayer's property at the time of assessment. Such lien is not valid as against any purchaser, holder of a security interest, mechanic's lienor, or judgment lien creditor until notice has been filed by the district director. Despite such filing, the lien is not valid with respect to certain securities 15 as against any purchaser of such security who, at the time of purchase, did not have actual notice or knowledge of the existence of such lien and as against a holder of a security interest in such security who, at the time such interest came into existence, did not have actual notice or knowledge of the existence of such lien. Certain motor vehicle purchases are similarly protected. Even though a notice of lien has been filed, certain 20 other categories are afforded additional protection. These categories are: Retail purchases, casual sales, possessory liens, real property taxes and property assessments, small repairs and improvements, attorneys' liens, certain insurance contracts and passbook loans. A valid lien generally continues until the liability is satisfied, becomes unenforceable by reason of lapse of time or is discharged in 25 bankruptcy. A certificate of release of lien will be issued not later than 30 days after the taxpayer furnishes proper bond in lieu of the lien, or 30 days after it is determined that the liability has been satisfied, has become unenforceable by reason of lapse of time, or has been discharged in bankruptcy. If a certificate has not been issued and one of the foregoing criteria for release has been met, a certificate of release of lien will be issued 30 within 30 days after a written request by a taxpayer, specifying the grounds upon which the issuance of release is sought. The Code also contains additional provisions with respect to the discharge of specific property from the effect of the lien. Also, under certain conditions, a lien may be subordinated. The Code also contains additional provisions with respect to liens in the case of estate and gift taxes. For the specific rules with respect to 35 liens, see Subchapter C of Chapter 64 of the Code and the regulations thereunder.

(4) *Penalties.* In the case of failure to file a return within the prescribed time, a certain percentage of the amount of tax (or a minimum penalty) is, pursuant to statute, added to the tax unless the failure to file the return within the prescribed time is shown to the satisfaction of the district director or the director of the appropriate service center to be 40 due to reasonable cause and not neglect. In the case of failure to file an exempt organization information return within the prescribed time, a penalty of $10 a day for each day the return is delinquent is assessed unless the failure to file the return within the prescribed time is shown to be due to reasonable cause and not neglect. In the case of failure to pay or deposit taxes due within the prescribed time, a certain percentage of the 45 amount of tax due is, pursuant to statute, added to the tax unless the failure to pay or deposit the tax due within the prescribed time is shown to the satisfaction of the district director or the director of the appropriate service center to be due to reasonable cause and not neglect. Civil penalties are also imposed for fraudulent returns; in the case of income and gift taxes, for intentional disregard of rules and regulations or negligence; 50 and additions to the tax are imposed for the failure to comply with the requirements of law

with respect to the estimated income tax. There are also civil penalties for filing false withholding certificates, for substantial understatement of income tax, for filing a frivolous return, for organizing or participating in the sale of abusive tax shelters, and for aiding and abetting in the understatement of tax liability. See Chapter 68 of the Code. A 50

5 percent penalty, in addition to the personal liability incurred, is imposed upon any person who fails or refuses without reasonable cause to honor a levy. Criminal penalties are imposed for willful failure to make returns, keep records, supply information, etc. See Chapter 75 of the Code.

(5) *Informants' rewards.* Payments to informers are authorized for detecting and

10 bringing to trial and punishment persons guilty of violating the internal revenue laws. See section 7623 of the Code and the regulations thereunder. Claims for rewards should be made on Form 211. Relevant facts should be stated on the form, which after execution should be forwarded to the district director of internal revenue for the district in which the informer resides, or to the Commissioner of Internal Revenue, Washington, DC 20224.

15

Reg. § 601.105   Examination of returns and claims for refund, credit or abatement; determination of correct tax liability.

***

(b) *Examination of returns*--(1) *General.* The original examination of income (including

20 partnership and fiduciary), estate, gift, excise, employment, exempt organization, and information returns is a primary function of examiners in the Examination Division of the office of each district director of internal revenue. Such examiners are organized in groups, each of which is under the immediate supervision of a group supervisor designated by the district director. Revenue agents (and such other officers or employees

25 of the Internal Revenue Service as may be designated for this purpose by the Commissioner) are authorized to examine any books, papers, records, or memoranda bearing upon matters required to be included in Federal tax returns and to take testimony relative thereto and to administer oaths. See section 7602 of the Code and the regulations thereunder. There are two general types of examination. These are commonly

30 called ``office examination'' and ``field examination''. During the examination of a return a taxpayer may be represented before the examiner by an attorney, certified public accountant, or other representative. See Subpart E of this part for conference and practice requirements.

(2) *Office examination*--(i) *Adjustments by Examination Division at service center.*

35 Certain individual income tax returns identified as containing potential unallowable items are examined by Examination Divisions at regional service centers. Correspondence examination techniques are used. If the taxpayer requests an interview to discuss the proposed adjustments, the case is transferred to the taxpayer's district office. If the taxpayer does not agree to proposed adjustments, regular appellate procedures apply.

40   (ii) *Examinations at district office.* Certain returns are examined at district offices by office examination techniques. These returns include some business returns, besides the full range of nonbusiness individual income tax returns. Office examinations are conducted primarily by the interview method. Examinations are conducted by correspondence only when warranted by the nature of the questionable items and by the

45 convenience and characteristics of the taxpayer. In a correspondence examination, the taxpayer is asked to explain or send supporting evidence by mail. In an office interview examination, the taxpayer is asked to come to the district director's office for an interview and to bring certain records in support of the return. During the interview examination, the taxpayer has the right to point out to the examiner any amounts included in the return

50 which are not taxable, or any deductions which the taxpayer failed to claim on the return. If it develops that a field examination is necessary, the examiner may conduct such

1162

examination.

(3) *Field examination*. Certain returns are examined by field examination which involves an examination of the taxpayer's books and records on the taxpayer's premises. An examiner will check the entire return filed by the taxpayer and will examine all books, papers, records, and memoranda dealing with matters required to be included in the 5 return. If the return presents an engineering or appraisal problem (e.g., depreciation or depletion deductions, gains or losses upon the sale or exchange of property, or losses on account of abandonment, exhaustion, or obsolescence), it may be investigated by an engineer agent who makes a separate report.

(4) *Conclusion of examination*. At the conclusion of an office or field examination, the 10 taxpayer is given an opportunity to agree with the findings of the examiner. If the taxpayer does not agree, the examiner will inform the taxpayer of the appeal rights. If the taxpayer does agree with the proposed changes, the examiner will invite the taxpayer to execute either Form 870 or another appropriate agreement form. When the taxpayer agrees with the proposed changes but does not offer to pay any deficiency or additional tax which 15 may be due, the examiner will also invite payment (by check or money order), together with any applicable interest or penalty. If the agreed case involves income, profits, estate, gift, generation-skipping transfer, or Chapter 41, 42, 43, or 44 taxes, the agreement is evidenced by a waiver by the taxpayer of restrictions on assessment and collection of the deficiency, or an acceptance of a proposed overassessment. If the case involves excise 20 or employment taxes or 100 percent penalty, the agreement is evidenced in the form of a consent to assessment and collection of additional tax or penalty and waiver of right to file claim for abatement, or the acceptance of the proposed overassessment. Even though the taxpayer signs an acceptance of a proposed overassessment the district director or the director of the regional service center remains free to assess a deficiency. 25 On the other hand, the taxpayer who has given a waiver may still claim a refund of any part of the deficiency assessed against, and paid by, the taxpayer, or any part of the tax originally assessed and paid by the taxpayer. The taxpayer's acceptance of an agreed overassessment does not prevent the taxpayer from filing a claim and bringing a suit for an additional sum, nor does it preclude the Government from maintaining suit to recover 30 an erroneous refund. As a matter of practice, however, waivers or acceptances ordinarily result in the closing of a case insofar as the Government is concerned.

(5) *Technical advice from the National Office*--(i) *Definition and nature of technical advice*. (a) As used in this subparagraph, ``technical advice'' means advice or guidance as to the interpretation and proper application of internal revenue laws, related statutes, 35 and regulations, to a specific set of facts, furnished by the National Office upon request of a district office in connection with the examination of a taxpayer's return or consideration of a taxpayer's return claim for refund or credit. It is furnished as a means of assisting Service personnel in closing cases and establishing and maintaining consistent holdings in the several districts. It does not include memorandums on matters of general technical 40 application furnished to district offices where the issues are not raised in connection with the examination of the return of a specific taxpayer.

(b) The consideration or examination of the facts relating to a request for a determination letter is considered to be in connection with the examination or consideration of a return of the taxpayer. Thus, a district director may, in his discretion, 45 request technical advice with respect to the consideration of a request for a determination letter.

(c) If a district director is of the opinion that a ruling letter previously issued to a taxpayer should be modified or revoked, and requests the National Office to reconsider the ruling, the reference of the matter to the National Office is treated as a request for 50 technical advice and the procedures specified in subdivision (iii) of this subparagraph

should be followed in order that the National Office may consider the district director's recommendation. Only the National Office can revoke a ruling letter. Before referral to the National Office, the district director should inform the taxpayer of his opinion that the ruling letter should be revoked. The district director, after development of the facts and
5 consideration of the taxpayer's arguments, will decide whether to recommend revocation of the ruling to the National Office. For procedures relating to a request for a ruling, see § 601.201.

(d) The Assistant Commissioner (Technical), acting under a delegation of authority from the Commissioner of Internal Revenue, is exclusively responsible for providing
10 technical advice in any issue involving the establishment of basic principles and rules for the uniform interpretation and application of tax laws other than those which are under the jurisdiction of the Bureau of Alcohol, Tobacco, and Firearms. This authority has been largely redelegated to subordinate officials.

(e) The provisions of this subparagraph apply only to a case under the jurisdiction of a
15 district director but do not apply to an Employee Plans case under the jurisdiction of a key district director as provided in § 601.201(o) or to an Exempt Organization case under the jurisdiction of a key district director as provided in § 601.201(n). The technical advice provisions applicable to Employee Plans and Exempt Organization cases are set forth in § 601.201(n)(9). The provisions of this subparagraph do not apply to a case under the
20 jurisdiction of the Bureau of Alcohol, Tobacco, and Firearms. They also do not apply to a case under the jurisdiction of an Appeals office, including a case previously considered by Appeals. The technical advice provisions applicable to a case under the jurisdiction of an Appeals office, other than Employee Plans and Exempt Organizations cases, are set forth in § 601.106(f)(10). A case remains under the jurisdiction of the district director
25 even though an Appeals office has the identical issue under consideration in the case of another taxpayer (not related within the meaning of section 267 of the Code) in an entirely different transaction. Technical advice may not be requested with respect to a taxable period if a prior Appeals disposition of the same taxable period of the same taxpayer's case was based on mutual concessions (ordinarily with a Form 870-AD, Offer
30 of Waiver of Restrictions on Assessment and Collection of Deficiency in Tax and of Acceptance of Overassessment). However, technical advice may be requested by a district director on issues previously considered in a prior Appeals disposition, not based on mutual concessions, of the same taxable periods of the same taxpayer with the concurrence of the Appeals office that had the case.
35 (ii) *Areas in which technical advice may be requested.* (a) District directors may request technical advice on any technical or procedural question that develops during the audit or examination of a return, or claim for refund or credit, of a taxpayer. These procedures are applicable as provided in subdivision (i) of this subparagraph.

(b) District directors are encouraged to request technical advice on any technical or
40 procedural question arising in connection with any case of the type described in subdivision (i) of this subparagraph, which cannot be resolved on the basis of law, regulations, or a clearly applicable revenue ruling or other precedent issued by the National Office. This request should be made at the earliest possible stage of the examination process.
45 (iii) *Requesting technical advice.* (a) It is the responsibility of the district office to determine whether technical advice is to be requested on any issue before that office. However, while the case is under the jurisdiction of the district director, a taxpayer or his/her representative may request that an issue be referred to the National Office for technical advice on the grounds that a lack of uniformity exists as to the disposition of the
50 issue, or that the issue is so unusual or complex as to warrant consideration by the National Office. This request should be made at the earliest possible stage of the

examination process. While taxpayers are encouraged to make written requests setting forth the facts, law, and argument with respect to the issue, and reason for requesting National Office advice, a taxpayer may make the request orally. If, after considering the taxpayer's request, the examiner is of the opinion that the circumstances do not warrant referral of the case to the National Office, he/she will so advise the taxpayer. (See 5 subdivision (iv) of this subparagraph for taxpayer's appeal rights where the examiner declines to request technical advice.)

(b) When technical advice is to be requested, whether or not upon the request of the taxpayer, the taxpayer will be so advised, except as noted in (g) of this subdivision. If the examiner initiates the action, the taxpayer will be furnished a copy of the statement of the 10 pertinent facts and the question or questions proposed for submission to the National Office. The request for advice submitted by the district director should be so worded as to avoid possible misunderstanding, in the National Office, of the facts or of the specific point or points at issue.

(c) After receipt of the statement of facts and specific questions from the district office, 15 the taxpayer will be given 10 calendar days in which to indicate in writing the extent, if any, to which he may not be in complete agreement. An extension of time must be justified by the taxpayer in writing and approved by the Chief, Examination Division. Every effort should be made to reach agreement as to the facts and specific point at issue. If agreement cannot be reached, the taxpayer may submit, within 10 calendar days 20 after receipt of notice from the district office, a statement of his understanding as to the specific point or points at issue which will be forwarded to the National Office with the request for advice. An extension of time must be justified by the taxpayer in writing and approved by the Chief, Examination Division.

(d) If the taxpayer initiates the action to request advice, and his statement of the facts 25 and point or points at issue are not wholly acceptable to the district officials, the taxpayer will be advised in writing as to the areas of disagreement. The taxpayer will be given 10 calendar days after receipt of the written notice to reply to the district official's letter. An extension of time must be justified by the taxpayer in writing and approved by the Chief, Examination Division. If agreement cannot be reached, both the statements of the 30 taxpayer and the district official will be forwarded to the National Office.

(e)(1) In the case of requests for technical advice the taxpayer must also submit, within the 10-day period referred to in (c) and (d) of this subdivision, whichever applicable (relating to agreement by the taxpayer with the statement of facts submitted in connection with the request for technical advice), the statement described in (f) of this subdivision of 35 proposed deletions pursuant to section 6110(c) of the Code. If the statement is not submitted, the taxpayer will be informed by the district director that such a statement is required. If the district director does not receive the statement within 10 days after the taxpayer has been informed of the need for such statement, the district director may decline to submit the request for technical advice. If the district director decides to 40 request technical advice in a case where the taxpayer has not submitted the statement of proposed deletions, the National Office will make those deletions which in the judgment of the Commissioner are required by section 6110(c) of the Code.

(2) The requirements included in § 601.105(b)(5) with respect to submissions of statements and other material with respect to proposed deletions to be made from 45 technical advice memoranda before public inspection is permitted to take place do not apply to requests made by the district director before November 1, 1976, or requests for any document to which section 6104 of the Code applies.

(f) In order to assist the Internal Revenue Service in making the deletions, required by section 6110(c) of the Code, from the text of technical advice memoranda which are open 50 to public inspection pursuant to section 6110(a) of the Code, there must accompany

requests for such technical advice either a statement of the deletions proposed by the taxpayer and the statutory basis for each proposed deletion, or a statement that no information other than names, addresses, and taxpayer identifying numbers need be deleted. Such statements shall be made in a separate document. The statement of
5 proposed deletions shall be accompanied by a copy of all statements of facts and supporting documents which are submitted to the National Office pursuant to (c) or (d) of this subdivision, on which shall be indicated, by the use of brackets, the material which the taxpayer indicates should be deleted pursuant to section 6110(c) of the Code. The statement of proposed deletions shall indicate the statutory basis, under section 6110(c)
10 of the Code, for each proposed deletion. The statement of proposed deletions shall not appear or be referred to anywhere in the request for technical advice. If the taxpayer decides to request additional deletions pursuant to section 6110(c) of the Code prior to the time the National Office replies to the request for technical advice, additional statements may be submitted.

15 (g) If the taxpayer has not already done so, the taxpayer may submit a statement explaining the taxpayer's position on the issues, citing precedents which the taxpayer believes will bear on the case. This statement will be forwarded to the National Office with the request for advice. If it is received at a later date, it will be forwarded for association with the case file.

20 (h) At the time the taxpayer is informed that the matter is being referred to the National Office, the taxpayer will also be informed of the taxpayer's right to a conference in the National Office in the event an adverse decision is indicated, and will be asked to indicate whether such a conference is desired.

(i) Generally, prior to replying to the request for technical advice, the National Office
25 shall inform the taxpayer orally or in writing of the material likely to appear in the technical advice memorandum which the taxpayer proposed be deleted but which the Internal Revenue Service determined should not be deleted. If so informed, the taxpayer may submit within 10 days any further information, arguments or other material in support of the position that such material be deleted. The Internal Revenue Service will attempt, if
30 feasible, to resolve all disagreements with respect to proposed deletions prior to the time the National Office replies to the request for technical advice. However, in no event shall the taxpayer have the right to a conference with respect to resolution of any disagreements concerning material to be deleted from the text of the technical advice memorandum, but such matters may be considered at any conference otherwise
35 scheduled with respect to the request.

(j) The provisions of (a) through (i) of this subdivision, relating to the referral of issues upon request of the taxpayer, advising taxpayers of the referral of issues, the submission of proposed deletions, and the granting of conferences in the National Office, are not applicable to technical advice memoranda described in section 611(g)(5)(A) of the Code,
40 relating to cases involving criminal or civil fraud investigations and jeopardy or termination assessments. However, in such cases the taxpayer shall be allowed to provide the statement of proposed deletions to the National Office upon the completion of all proceedings with respect to the investigations or assessments, but prior to the date on which the Commissioner mails the notice pursuant to section 6110(f)(1) of the Code of
45 intention to disclose the technical advice memorandum.

(k) Form 4463, Request for Technical Advice, should be used for transmitting requests for technical advice to the National Office.

(iv) Appeal by taxpayers of determinations not to seek technical advice. (a) If the taxpayer has requested referral of an issue before a district office to the National Office
50 for technical advice, and after consideration of the request the examiner is of the opinion that the circumstances do not warrant such referral, he will so advise the taxpayer.

(b) The taxpayer may appeal the decision of the examining officer not to request technical advice by submitting to that official, within 10 calendar days after being advised of the decision, a statement of the facts, law, and arguments with respect to the issue, and the reasons why he believes the matter should be referred to the National Office for advice. An extension of time must be justified by the taxpayer in writing and approved by 5 the Chief, Examination Division.

(c) The examining officer will submit the statement of the taxpayer through channels to the Chief, Examination Division, accompanied by a statement of his reasons why the issue should not be referred to the National Office. The Chief, Examination Division, will determine, on the basis of the statements submitted, whether technical advice will be 10 requested. If he determines that technical advice is not warranted, he will inform the taxpayer in writing that he proposes to deny the request. In the letter to the taxpayer the Chief, Examination Division, will (except in unusual situations where such action would be prejudicial to the best interests of the Government) state specifically the reasons for the proposed denial. The taxpayer will be given 15 calendar days after receipt of the 15 letter in which to notify the Chief, Examination Division, whether he agrees with the proposed denial. The taxpayer may not appeal the decision of the Chief, Examination Division,

not to request technical advice from the National Office. However, if he does not agree with the proposed denial, all data relating to the issue for which technical advice has 20 been sought, including taxpayer's written request and statements, will be submitted to the National Office, Attention: Director, Examination Division, for review. After review in the National Office, the district office will be notified whether the proposed denial is approved or disapproved.

(d) While the matter is being reviewed in the National Office, the district office will 25 suspend action on the issue (except where the delay would prejudice the Government's interests) until it is notified of the National Office decision. This notification will be made within 30 days after receipt of the data in the National Office. The review will be solely on the basis of the written record and no conference will be held in the National Office.

(v) *Conference in the National Office.* (a) If, after a study of the technical advice 30 request, it appears that advice adverse to the taxpayer should be given and a conference has been requested, the taxpayer will be notified of the time and place of the conference. If conferences are being arranged with respect to more than one request for advice involving the same taxpayer, they will be so scheduled as to cause the least inconvenience to the taxpayer. The conference will be arranged by telephone, if possible, 35 and must be held within 21 calendar days after contact has been made. Extensions of time will be granted only if justified in writing by the taxpayer and approved by the appropriate Technical branch chief.

(b) A taxpayer is entitled, as a matter of right, to only one conference in the National Office unless one of the circumstances discussed in (c) of this subdivision exists. This 40 conference will usually be held at the branch level in the appropriate division (Corporation Tax Division or Individual Tax Division) in the office of the Assistant Commissioner (Technical), and will usually be attended by a person who has authority to act for the branch chief. In appropriate cases the examining officer may also attend the conference to clarify the facts in the case. If more than one subject is discussed at the conference, 45 the discussion constitutes a conference with respect to each subject. At the request of the taxpayer or his representative, the conference may be held at an earlier stage in the consideration of the case than the Service would ordinarily designate. A taxpayer has no ``right'' of appeal from an action of a branch to the director of a division or to any other National Office official. 50

(c) In the process of review of a holding proposed by a branch, it may appear that the

final answer will involve a reversal of the branch proposal with a result less favorable to the taxpayer. Or it may appear that an adverse holding proposed by a branch will be approved, but on a new or different issue or on different grounds than those on which the branch decided the case. Under either of these circumstances, the taxpayer or his
5 representative will be invited to another conference. The provisions of this subparagraph limiting the number of conferences to which a taxpayer is entitled will not foreclose inviting a taxpayer to attend further conferences when, in the opinion of National Office personnel, such need arises. All additional conferences of this type discussed are held only at the invitation of the Service.
10 (d) It is the responsibility of the taxpayer to furnish to the National Office, within 21 calendar days after the conference, a written record of any additional data, line of reasoning, precedents, etc., that were proposed by the taxpayer and discussed at the conference but were not previously or adequately presented in writing. Extensions of time will be granted only if justified in writing by the taxpayer and approved by the appropriate
15 Technical branch chief. Any additional material and a copy thereof should be addressed to and sent to the National Office which will forward the copy to the appropriate district director. The district director will be requested to give the matter his prompt attention. He may verify the additional facts and data and comment upon it to the extent he deems it appropriate.
20 (e) A taxpayer or a taxpayer's representative desiring to obtain information as to the status of the case may do so by contacting the following offices with respect to matters in the areas of their responsibility:

Official	Telephone numbers, (AreaCode 202)
25		
Director, Corporation Tax Division	566-4504, 566-4505.
Director, Individual Tax Division	566-3767 or 566-3788.

(vi) Preparation of technical advice memorandum by the National Office. (a)
30 Immediately upon receipt in the National Office, the technical employee to whom the case is assigned will analyze the file to ascertain whether it meets the requirements of subdivision (iii) of this subparagraph. If the case is not complete with respect to any requirement in subdivisions (iii) (a) through (d) of this subparagraph, appropriate steps will be taken to complete the file. If any request for technical advice does not comply with
35 the requirements of subdivision (iii)(e) of this subparagraph, relating to the statement of proposed deletions, the National Office will make those deletions from the technical advice memorandum which in the judgment of the Commissioner are required by section 6110(c) of the Code.
(b) If the taxpayer has requested a conference in the National Office, the procedures
40 in subdivision (v) of this subparagraph will be followed.
(c) Replies to requests for technical advice will be addressed to the district director and will be drafted in two parts. Each part will identify the taxpayer by name, address, identification number, and year or years involved. The first part (hereafter called the ``Technical Advice Memorandum") will contain (1) a recitation of the pertinent facts
45 having a bearing on the issue; (2) a discussion of the facts, precedents, and reasoning of the National Office; and (3) the conclusions of the National Office. The conclusions will give direct answers, whenever possible, to the specific questions of the district office. The discussion of the issues will be in such detail that the district officials are apprised of the reasoning underlying the conclusion. There shall accompany the technical advice
50 memorandum a notice pursuant to section 6110 (f)(1) of the Code of intention to disclose the technical advice memorandum (including a copy of the version proposed to be open

to public inspection and notations of third party communications pursuant to section 6110 (d) of the Code) which the district director shall forward to the taxpayer at such time that the district director furnishes a copy of the technical advice memorandum to the taxpayer pursuant to (e) of this subsection.

(d) The second part of the reply will consist of a transmittal memorandum. In the 5 unusual cases it will serve as a vehicle for providing the district office administrative information or other information which, under the nondisclosure statutes, or for other reasons, may not be discussed with the taxpayer.

(e) It is the general practice of the Service to furnish a copy of the technical advice memorandum to the taxpayer after it has been adopted by the district director. However, 10 in the case of technical advice memoranda described in section 6110(g)(5)(A) of the Code, relating to cases involving criminal or civil fraud investigations and jeopardy or termination assessments, a copy of the technical advice memorandum shall not be furnished the taxpayer until all proceedings with respect to the investigations or assessments are completed. 15

(f) After receiving the notice pursuant to section 6110(f)(1) of the Code of intention to disclose the technical advice memorandum, if the taxpayer desires to protest the disclosure of certain information in the technical advice memorandum, the taxpayer must within 20 days after the notice is mailed submit a written statement identifying those deletions not made by the Internal Revenue Service which the taxpayer believes should 20 have been made. The taxpayer shall also submit a copy of the version of the technical advice memorandum proposed to be open to public inspection on which the taxpayer indicates, by the use of brackets, the deletions proposed by the taxpayer but which have not been made by the Internal Revenue Service. Generally the Internal Revenue Service will not consider the deletion under this subparagraph of any material which the taxpayer 25 did not, prior to the time when the National Office sent its reply to the request for technical advice to the district director, propose be deleted. The Internal Revenue Service shall, within 20 days after receipt of the response by the taxpayer to the notice pursuant to section 6110(f)(1) of the Code, mail to the taxpayer its final administrative conclusion with respect to the deletions to be made. 30

(vii) Action on technical advice in district offices. (a) Unless the district director feels that the conclusions reached by the National Office in a technical advice memorandum should be reconsidered and promptly requests such reconsideration, his office will proceed to process the taxpayer's case on the basis of the conclusions expressed in the technical advice memorandum. 35

(b) The district director will furnish to the taxpayer a copy of the technical advice memorandum described in subdivision (vi)(c) of this subparagraph and the notice pursuant to section 6110(f)(1) of the Code of intention to disclose the technical advice memorandum (including a copy of the version proposed to be open to public inspection and notations of third party communications pursuant to section 6110(d) of the Code). 40 The preceding sentence shall not apply to technical advice memoranda involving civil fraud or criminal investigations, or jeopardy or termination assessments, as described in subdivision (iii)(j) of this subparagraph or to documents to which section 6104 of the Code applies.

(c) In those cases in which the National Office advises the district director that he 45 should not furnish a copy of the technical memorandum to the taxpayer, the district director will so inform the taxpayer if he requests a copy.

(viii) Effect of technical advice. (a) A technical advice memorandum represents an expression of the views of the Service as to the application of law, regulations, and precedents to the facts of a specific case, and is issued primarily as a means of assisting 50 district officials in the examination and closing of the case involved.

I.R.S. Procedural Rules

(b) Except in rare or unusual circumstances, a holding in a technical advice memorandum that is favorable to the taxpayer is applied retroactively. Moreover, since technical advice, as described in subdivision (i) of this subparagraph, is issued only on closed transactions, a holding in a technical advice memorandum that is adverse to the
5 taxpayer is also applied retroactively unless the Assistant Commissioner (Technical) exercises the discretionary authority under section 7805(b) of the Code to limit the retroactive effect of the holding. Likewise, a holding in a technical advice memorandum that modifies or revokes a holding in a prior technical advice memorandum will also be applied retroactively, with one exception. If the new holding is less favorable to the
10 taxpayer, it will generally not be applied to the period in which the taxpayer relied on the prior holding in situations involving continuing transactions of the type described in §§ 601.201(1) (7) and 601.201(1) (8).

(c) Technical advice memoranda often form the basis for revenue rulings. For the description of revenue rulings and the effect thereof, see §§ 601.601(d)(2)(i)(a) and
15 601.601(d) (2) (v).

(d) A district director may raise an issue in any taxable period, even though he or she may have asked for and been furnished technical advice with regard to the same or a similar issue in any other taxable period.

***

20 (d) *Thirty-day letters and protests*--(1) *General*. The report of the examiner, as approved after review, recommends one of four determinations:

(i) Acceptance of the return as filed and closing of the case;

(ii) Assertion of a given deficiency or additional tax;

(iii) Allowance of a given overassessment, with or without a claim for refund, credit, or
25 abatement;

(iv) Denial of a claim for refund, credit, or abatement which has been filed and is found wholly lacking in merit. When a return is accepted as filed (as in subdivision (i) of this subparagraph), the taxpayer is notified by appropriate ``no change" letter. In an unagreed case, the district director sends to the taxpayer a preliminary or ``30-day letter" if any one
30 of the last three determinations is made (except a full allowance of a claim in respect of any tax). The 30-day letter is a form letter which states the determination proposed to be made. It is accompanied by a copy of the examiner's report explaining the basis of the proposed determination. It suggests to the taxpayer that if the taxpayer concurs in the recommendation, he or she indicate agreement by executing and returning a waiver or
35 acceptance. The preliminary letter also informs the taxpayer of appeal rights available if he or she disagrees with the proposed determination. If the taxpayer does not respond to the letter within 30 days, a statutory notice of deficiency will be issued or other appropriate action taken, such as the issuance of a notice of adjustment, the denial of a claim in income, profits, estate, and gift tax cases, or an appropriate adjustment of the tax
40 liability or denial of a claim in excise and employment tax cases.

(2) *Protests*. (i) No written protest or brief written statement of disputed issues is required to obtain an Appeals office conference in office interview and correspondence examination cases.

(ii) No written protest or brief written statement of disputed issues is required to obtain
45 an Appeals office conference in a field examination case if the total amount of proposed additional tax including penalties, proposed overassessment, or claimed refund (or, in an offer in compromise, the total amount of assessed tax, penalty, and interest sought to be compromised) is $2,500 or less for any taxable period.

(iii) A written protest is required to obtain Appeals consideration in a field examination
50 case if the total amount of proposed tax including penalties, proposed overassessment,

or claimed refund (or, in an offer in compromise, the total amount of assessed tax, penalty, and interest sought to be compromised) exceeds $10,000 for any taxable period.

(iv) A written protest is optional (although a brief written statement of disputed issues is required) to obtain Appeals consideration in a field examination case if for any taxable period the total amount of proposed additional tax including penalties, proposed overassessment, or claimed refund (or, in an offer in compromise, the total amount of assessed tax, penalty,and interest sought to be compromised) exceeds $2,500 but does not exceed $10,000.

(v) Instructions for preparation of written protests are sent to the taxpayer with the transmittal (30-day) letter.

(e) *Claims for refund or credit.* (1) After payment of the tax a taxpayer may (unless he has executed an agreement to the contrary) contest the assessment by filing a claim for refund or credit for all or any part of the amount paid, except as provided in section 6512 of the Code with respect to certain taxes determined by the Tax Court, the decision of which has become final. A claim for refund or credit of income taxes shall be made on Form 1040X, 1120X, or an amended income tax return, in accordance with § 301.6402-3. In the case of taxes other than income taxes, a claim for refund or credit shall be made on Form 843. The appropriate forms are obtainable from district directors or directors of service centers. Generally, the claim, together with appropriate supporting evidence, must be filed at the location prescribed in § 301.6402-2(a) (2). A claim for refund or credit must be filed within the applicable statutory period of limitation. In certain cases, a properly executed income tax return may operate as a claim for refund or credit of the amount of the overpayment disclosed by such return. (See § 301.6402-3).

(2) When claims for refund or credit are examined by the Examination Division, substantially the same procedure is followed (including appeal rights afforded to taxpayers) as when taxpayers' returns are originally examined. But see § 601.108 for procedure for reviewing proposed overpayment exceeding $200,000 of income, estate, and gift taxes.

(3) As to suits for refund, see § 601.103 (c).

(4) [Reserved]

(5) There is also a special procedure applicable to applications for tentative carryback adjustments under section 6411 of the Code (consult Forms 1045 and 1139).

(6) For special procedure applicable to claims for payment or credit in respect of gasoline used on a farm for farming purposes, for certain nonhighway purposes, for use in commercial aircraft, or used by local transit systems, see sections 39, 6420, and 6421 of the Code and § 601.402(c)(3). For special procedure applicable to claims for payment or credit in respect of lubricating oil used otherwise than in a highway motor vehicle, see sections 39 and 6424 of the Code and § 601.402(c)(3). For special procedure applicable for credit or refund of aircraft use tax, see section 6426 of the Code and § 601.402(c)(4). For special procedure applicable for payment or credit in respect of special fuels not used for taxable purposes, see sections 39 and 6427 of the Code and § 601.402(c)(5).

(7) For special procedure applicable in certain cases to adjustment of overpayment of estimated tax by a corporation see section 6425 of the Code.

Reg. § 601.106 Appeals functions.

***

(b) *Initiation of proceedings before Appeals.* In any case in which the district director has issued a preliminary or ``30-day letter" and the taxpayer requests Appeals consideration and files a written protest when required (see paragraph (c)(1) of §§ 601.103, (c)(1) and (c)(2) of 601.105 and 601.507) against the proposed determination of

tax liability, except as to those taxes described in paragraph (a)(3) of this section, the taxpayer has the right (and will be so advised by the district director) of administrative appeal to the Appeals organization. However, the appeal procedures do not extend to cases involving solely the failure or refusal to comply with the tax laws because of moral,
5 religious, political, constitutional, conscientious, or similar grounds. Organizations such as labor unions and trade associations which have been examined by the district director to determine the amounts expended by the organization for purposes of lobbying, promotion or defeat of legislation, political campaigns, or propaganda related to those purposes are treated as ``taxpayers'' for the purpose of this right of administrative appeal. Thus, upon
10 requesting appellate consideration and filing a written protest, when required, to the district director's findings that a portion of member dues is to be disallowed as a deduction to each member because expended for such purposes, the organization will be afforded full rights of administrative appeal to the Appeals activity similar to those rights afforded to taxpayers generally. After review of any required written protest by the district
15 director, the case and its administrative record are referred to Appeals. Appeals may refuse to accept a protested nondocketed case where preliminary review indicates it requires further consideration or development. No taxpayer is required to submit a case to Appeals for consideration. Appeal is at the option of the taxpayer. After the issuance by the district director of a statutory notice of deficiency, upon the taxpayer's request,
20 Appeals may take up the case for settlement and may grant the taxpayer a conference thereon.

***

(d) *Disposition and settlement of cases before Appeals*--(1) *In general.* During consideration of a case, the Appeals office should neither reopen an issue as to which
25 the taxpayer and the office of the district director are in agreement nor raise a new issue, unless the ground for such action is a substantial one and the potential effect upon the tax liability is material. If the Appeals raises a new issue, the taxpayer or the taxpayer's representative should be so advised and offered an opportunity for discussion prior to the taking of any formal action, such as the issuance of a statutory notice of deficiency.
30 (2) *Cases not docketed in the Tax Court.* (i) If after consideration of the case by Appeals a satisfactory settlement of some or all the issues is reached with the taxpayer, the taxpayer will be requested to sign Form 870-AD or other appropriate agreement form waiving restrictions on the assessment and collection of any deficiency and accepting any overassessment resulting under the agreed settlement. In addition, in partially
35 unagreed cases, a statutory notice of deficiency will be prepared and issued in accordance with subdivision (ii) of this subparagraph with respect to the unagreed issue or issues.
(ii) If after consideration of the case by Appeals it is determined that there is a deficiency in income, profits, estate, gift tax, generation-skipping transfer, or Chapter 41,
40 42, 43, or 44 tax liability to which the taxpayer does not agree, a statutory notice of deficiency will be prepared and issued by Appeals. Officers of the Appeals office having authority for the administrative determination of tax liabilities referred to in paragraph (a) of this section are also authorized to prepare, sign on behalf of the Commissioner, and send to the taxpayer by registered or certified mail any statutory notice of deficiency
45 prescribed in sections 6212 and 6861 of the Code, and in corresponding provisions of the Internal Revenue Code of 1939. Within 90 days, or 150 days if the notice is addressed to a person outside of the States of the Union and the District of Columbia, after such a statutory notice of deficiency is mailed (not counting Saturday, Sunday, or a legal holiday in the District of Columbia as the last day), the taxpayer may file a petition with the U.S.
50 Tax Court for a redetermination of the deficiency. In addition, if a claim for refund is disallowed in full or in part by the Appelate Division and the taxpayer does not sign Form

I.R.S. Procedural Rules

2297, Appeals will prepare the statutory notice of claim disallowance and send it to the taxpayer by certified mail (or registered mail if the taxpayer is outside the United States), with a carbon copy to the taxpayer's representative by regular mail, if appropriate. In any other unagreed case, the case and its administrative file will be forwarded to the appropriate function with directions to take action with respect to the tax liability 5 determined in Appeals. Administrative appeal procedures will apply to 100-percent penalty cases, except where an assessment is made because of Chief Counsel's request to support a third-party action in a pending refund suit. See Rev. Proc. 69-26.

(iii) Taxpayers desiring to further contest unagreed excise (other than those under Chapters 41 through 44 of the Code) and employment tax cases and 100-percent penalty 10 cases must pay the additional tax (or portion thereof of divisible taxes) when assessed, file claim for refund within the applicable statutory period of limitations (ordinarily 3 years from time return was required to be filed or 2 years from payment, whichever expires later), and upon disallowance of claim or after 6 months from date claim was filed, file suit in U.S. District Court or U.S. Claims Court. Suits for refund of taxes paid are under the 15 jurisdiction of the Department of Justice.

(3) *Cases docketed in the Tax Court.* (i) If the case under consideration in Appeals is docketed in the Tax Court and agreement is reached with the taxpayer with respect to the issues involved, the disposition of the case is effected by a stipulation of agreed deficiency or overpayment to be filed with the Tax Court and in conformity with which the 20 Court will enter its order.

(ii) If the case under consideration in Appeals is docketed in the Tax Court and the issues remain unsettled after consideration and conference in Appeals, the case will be referred to the appropriate district counsel for the region for defense of the tax liability determined. 25

(iii) If the deficiency notice in a case docketed in the Tax Court was not issued by the Appeals office and no recommendation for criminal prosecution is pending, the case will be referred by the district counsel to the Appeals office for settlement as soon as it is at issue in the Tax Court. The settlement procedure shall be governed by the following rules:

(a) The Appeals office will have exclusive settlement jurisdiction for a period of 4 30 months over certain cases docketed in the Tax Court. The 4-month period will commence at the time Appeals receives the case from Counsel, which will be after the case is at issue. Appeals will arrange settlement conferences in such cases within 45 days of receipt of the case. In the event of a settlement, Appeals will prepare and forward to Counsel the necessary computations and any stipulation decisions secured. Counsel will 35 prepare any needed settlement documents for execution by the parties and filing with the Tax Court. Appeals will also have authority to settle less than all the issues in the case and to refer the unsettled issues to Counsel for disposition. In the event of a partial settlement, Appeals will inform Counsel of the agreement of the petitioner(s) and Appeals may secure and forward to Counsel a stipulation covering the agreed issues. Counsel 40 will, if necessary, prepare documents reflecting settlement of the agreed issues for execution by the parties and filing with the Tax Court at the appropriate time.

(b) At the end of the 4-month period, or before that time if Appeals determines the case is not susceptible of settlement, the case will be returned to Counsel. Thereafter, Counsel will have exclusive authority to dispose of the case. If, at the end of the 4-month 45 period, there is substantial likelihood that a settlement of the entire case can be effected in a reasonable period of time, Counsel may extend Appeals settlement jurisdiction for a period not to exceed 60 days, but not beyond the date of the receipt of a trial calendar upon which the case appears. Extensions beyond the 50-day period or after the event indicated will be granted only with the personal approval of regional counsel and will be 50 made only in those cases in which the probability of settlement of the case in its entirety by Appeals clearly outweighs the need to commence trial preparation.

(c) During the period of Appeals jurisdiction, Appeals will make available such files and information as may be necessary for Counsel to take any action required by the Court or which is in the best interests of the Government. When a case is referred by Counsel to Appeals, Counsel may indicate areas of needed factual development or areas of possible technical uncertainties. In referring a case to Counsel, Appeals will furnish its summary of the facts and the pertinent legal authorities.

(d) The Appeals office may specify that proposed Counsel settlements be referred back to Appeals for its views. Appeals may protest the proposed Counsel settlements. If Counsel disagrees with Appeals, the Regional Counsel will determine the disposition of the cases.

(e) If an offer is received at or about the time of trial in a case designated by the Appeals office for settlement consultation, Counsel will endeavor to have the case placed on a motions calendar to permit consultation with and review by Appeals in accordance with the foregoing procedures.

(f) For issues in docketed and nondocketed cases pending with Appeals which are related to issues in docketed cases over which Counsel has jurisdiction, no settlement offer will be accepted by either Appeals or Counsel unless both agree that the offer is acceptable. The protest procedure will be available to Appeals and regional counsel will have authority to resolve the issue with respect to both the Appeals and Counsel cases. If settlement of the docketed case requires approval by regional counsel or Chief Counsel, the final decision with respect to the issues under the jurisdiction of both Appeals and Counsel will be made by regional counsel or Chief Counsel. See Rev. Proc. 79-59.

(g) Cases classified as ``Small Tax" cases by the Tax Court are given expeditious consideration because such cases are not included on a Trial Status Request. These cases are considered by the Court as ready for placing on a trial calendar as soon as the answer has been filed and are given priority by the Court for trial over other docketed cases. These cases are designated by the Court as small tax cases upon request of petitioners and will include letter ``S" as part of the docket number.

***

Reg. § 601.107 Criminal investigation functions.

***

(b) *Investigative procedure.* (1) A witness when questioned in an investigation conducted by the Criminal Investigation Division may have counsel present to represent and advise him. Upon request, a copy of an affidavit or transcript of a question and answer statement will be furnished a witness promptly, except in circumstances deemed by the Regional Commissioner to necessitate temporarily withholding a copy.

(2) A taxpayer who may be the subject of a criminal recommendation will be afforded a district Criminal Investigation conference when he requests one or where the Chief, Criminal Investigation Division, makes a determination that such a conference will be in the best interests of the Government. At the conference, the IRS representative will inform the taxpayer by a general oral statement of the alleged fraudulent features of the case, to the extent consistent with protecting the Government's interests, and, at the same time, making available to the taxpayer sufficient facts and figures to acquaint him with the basis, nature, and other essential elements of the proposed criminal charges against him.

***

[32 FR 15990, Nov. 22, 1967; 32 FR 20645, Dec. 21, 1967; 33 FR 17234, Nov. 21, 1968; 34 FR 6424, Apr. 12, 1969; 35 FR 7112, May 6, 1970; 36 FR 7584, Apr. 22, 1971; 38 FR

4956, Feb. 23, 1973; 38 FR 9227, Apr. 12, 1973; 39 FR 8917; 43 FR 53029, Nov. 15, 1978; 45 FR 7251, Feb. 1, 1980; 49 FR 36499, Sept. 18, 1984; 49 FR 40809, Oct. 18, 1984; T.D. 8685, 61 FR 58008, Nov. 12, 1996]

I.R.S. Publication 946: How to Depreciate Property (2006).

Depreciation Tables

Table A-1.   3-, 5-, 7-, 10-, 15-, and 20-Year Property
             Half-Year Convention

Year	Depreciation rate for recovery period					
	3-year	5-year	7-year	10-year	15-year	20-year
1	33.33%	20.00%	14.29%	10.00%	5.00%	3.750%
2	44.45	32.00	24.49	18.00	9.50	7.219
3	14.81	19.20	17.49	14.40	8.55	6.677
4	7.41	11.52	12.49	11.52	7.70	6.177
5		11.52	8.93	9.22	6.93	5.713
6		5.76	8.92	7.37	6.23	5.285
7			8.93	6.55	5.90	4.888
8			4.46	6.55	5.90	4.522
9				6.56	5.91	4.462
10				6.55	5.90	4.461
11				3.28	5.91	4.462
12					5.90	4.461
13					5.91	4.462
14					5.90	4.461
15					5.91	4.462
16					2.95	4.461
17						4.462
18						4.461
19						4.462
20						4.461
21						2.231

Table A-2.   3-, 5-, 7-, 10-, 15-, and 20-Year Property
             Mid-Quarter Convention
             Placed in Service in First Quarter

Year	Depreciation rate for recovery period					
	3-year	5-year	7-year	10-year	15-year	20-year
1	58.33%	35.00%	25.00%	17.50%	8.75%	6.563%
2	27.78	26.00	21.43	16.50	9.13	7.000
3	12.35	15.60	15.31	13.20	8.21	6.482
4	1.54	11.01	10.93	10.56	7.39	5.996
5		11.01	8.75	8.45	6.65	5.546
6		1.38	8.74	6.76	5.99	5.130
7			8.75	6.55	5.90	4.746
8			1.09	6.55	5.91	4.459
9				6.56	5.90	4.459
10				6.55	5.91	4.459
11				0.82	5.90	4.459
12					5.91	4.460
13					5.90	4.459
14					5.91	4.460
15					5.90	4.459
16					0.74	4.460
17						4.459
18						4.460
19						4.459
20						4.460
21						0.565

Depreciation Tables

**Table A-3.   3-, 5-, 7-, 10-, 15-, and 20-Year Property
Mid-Quarter Convention
Placed in Service in Second Quarter**

Year	Depreciation rate for recovery period					
	3-year	5-year	7-year	10-year	15-year	20-year
1	41.67%	25.00%	17.85%	12.50%	6.25%	4.688%
2	38.89	30.00	23.47	17.50	9.38	7.148
3	14.14	18.00	16.76	14.00	8.44	6.612
4	5.30	11.37	11.97	11.20	7.59	6.116
5		11.37	8.87	8.96	6.83	5.658
6		4.26	8.87	7.17	6.15	5.233
7			8.87	6.55	5.91	4.841
8			3.34	6.55	5.90	4.478
9				6.56	5.91	4.463
10				6.55	5.90	4.463
11				2.46	5.91	4.463
12					5.90	4.463
13					5.91	4.463
14					5.90	4.463
15					5.91	4.462
16					2.21	4.463
17						4.462
18						4.463
19						4.462
20						4.463
21						1.673

**Table A-4.   3-, 5-, 7-, 10-, 15-, and 20-Year Property
Mid-Quarter Convention
Placed in Service in Third Quarter**

Year	Depreciation rate for recovery period					
	3-year	5-year	7-year	10-year	15-year	20-year
1	25.00%	15.00%	10.71%	7.50%	3.75%	2.813%
2	50.00	34.00	25.51	18.50	9.63	7.289
3	16.67	20.40	18.22	14.80	8.66	6.742
4	8.33	12.24	13.02	11.84	7.80	6.237
5		11.30	9.30	9.47	7.02	5.769
6		7.06	8.85	7.58	6.31	5.336
7			8.86	6.55	5.90	4.936
8			5.53	6.55	5.90	4.566
9				6.56	5.91	4.460
10				6.55	5.90	4.460
11				4.10	5.91	4.460
12					5.90	4.460
13					5.91	4.461
14					5.90	4.460
15					5.91	4.461
16					3.69	4.460
17						4.461
18						4.460
19						4.461
20						4.460
21						2.788

Depreciation Tables

Table A-5. 3-, 5-, 7-, 10-, 15-, and 20-Year Property
Mid-Quarter Convention
Placed in Service in Fourth Quarter

Year	Depreciation rate for recovery period					
	3-year	5-year	7-year	10-year	15-year	20-year
1	8.33%	5.00%	3.57%	2.50%	1.25%	0.938%
2	61.11	38.00	27.55	19.50	9.88	7.430
3	20.37	22.80	19.68	15.60	8.89	6.872
4	10.19	13.68	14.06	12.48	8.00	6.357
5		10.94	10.04	9.98	7.20	5.880
6		9.58	8.73	7.99	6.48	5.439
7			8.73	6.55	5.90	5.031
8			7.64	6.55	5.90	4.654
9				6.56	5.90	4.458
10				6.55	5.91	4.458
11				5.74	5.90	4.458
12					5.91	4.458
13					5.90	4.458
14					5.91	4.458
15					5.90	4.458
16					5.17	4.458
17						4.458
18						4.459
19						4.458
20						4.459
21						3.901

Table A-6. Residential Rental Property
Mid-Month Convention
Straight Line—27.5 Years

Year	Month property placed in service											
	1	2	3	4	5	6	7	8	9	10	11	12
1	3.485%	3.182%	2.879%	2.576%	2.273%	1.970%	1.667%	1.364%	1.061%	0.758%	0.455%	0.152%
2-9	3.636	3.636	3.636	3.636	3.636	3.636	3.636	3.636	3.636	3.636	3.636	3.636
10	3.637	3.637	3.637	3.637	3.637	3.637	3.636	3.636	3.636	3.636	3.636	3.636
11	3.636	3.636	3.636	3.636	3.636	3.636	3.637	3.637	3.637	3.637	3.637	3.637
12	3.637	3.637	3.637	3.637	3.637	3.637	3.636	3.636	3.636	3.636	3.636	3.636
13	3.636	3.636	3.636	3.636	3.636	3.636	3.637	3.637	3.637	3.637	3.637	3.637
14	3.637	3.637	3.637	3.637	3.637	3.637	3.636	3.636	3.636	3.636	3.636	3.636
15	3.636	3.636	3.636	3.636	3.636	3.636	3.637	3.637	3.637	3.637	3.637	3.637
16	3.637	3.637	3.637	3.637	3.637	3.637	3.636	3.636	3.636	3.636	3.636	3.636
17	3.636	3.636	3.636	3.636	3.636	3.636	3.637	3.637	3.637	3.637	3.637	3.637
18	3.637	3.637	3.637	3.637	3.637	3.637	3.636	3.636	3.636	3.636	3.636	3.636
19	3.636	3.636	3.636	3.636	3.636	3.636	3.637	3.637	3.637	3.637	3.637	3.637
20	3.637	3.637	3.637	3.637	3.637	3.637	3.636	3.636	3.636	3.636	3.636	3.636
21	3.636	3.636	3.636	3.636	3.636	3.636	3.637	3.637	3.637	3.637	3.637	3.637
22	3.637	3.637	3.637	3.637	3.637	3.637	3.636	3.636	3.636	3.636	3.636	3.636
23	3.636	3.636	3.636	3.636	3.636	3.636	3.637	3.637	3.637	3.637	3.637	3.637
24	3.637	3.637	3.637	3.637	3.637	3.637	3.636	3.636	3.636	3.636	3.636	3.636
25	3.636	3.636	3.636	3.636	3.636	3.636	3.637	3.637	3.637	3.637	3.637	3.637
26	3.637	3.637	3.637	3.637	3.637	3.637	3.636	3.636	3.636	3.636	3.636	3.636
27	3.636	3.636	3.636	3.636	3.636	3.636	3.637	3.637	3.637	3.637	3.637	3.637
28	1.97	2.273	2.576	2.879	3.182	3.485	3.636	3.636	3.636	3.636	3.636	3.636
29							0.152	0.455	0.758	1.061	1.364	1.667

Depreciation Tables

Table A-7a. Nonresidential Real Property
Mid-Month Convention
Straight Line—39 Years

Year	Month property placed in service											
	1	2	3	4	5	6	7	8	9	10	11	12
1	2.461%	2.247%	2.033%	1.819%	1.605%	1.391%	1.177%	0.963%	0.749%	0.535%	0.321%	0.107%
2–39	2.564	2.564	2.564	2.564	2.564	2.564	2.564	2.564	2.564	2.564	2.564	2.564
40	0.107	0.321	0.535	0.749	0.963	1.177	1.391	1.605	1.819	2.033	2.247	2.461

2008 Inflation Adjustments and Mileage Rates

Rev. Proc. 2007-66, I.R.B. 2007-45, October 18, 2007.

SECTION 3. 2008 ADJUSTED ITEMS

.01 *Tax Rate Tables.* For taxable years beginning in 2008, the tax rate tables under § 1 are as follows:

TABLE 1 - Section 1(a) - Married Individuals Filing Joint Returns and Surviving Spouses

If Taxable Income Is:	The Tax Is:
Not over $16,050	10% of the taxable income
Over $16,050 but not over $65,100	$1,605 plus 15% of the excess over $16,050
Over $65,100 but not over $131,450	$8,962.50 plus 25% of the excess over $65,100
Over $131,450 but not over $200,300	$25,550 plus 28% of the excess over $131,450
Over $200,300 but not over $357,700	$44,828 plus 33% of the excess over $200,300
Over $357,700	$96,770 plus 35% of the excess over $357,700

TABLE 2 - Section 1(b) - Heads of Households

If Taxable Income Is:	The Tax Is:
Not over $11,450	10% of the taxable income
Over $11,450 but not over $43,650	$1,145 plus 15% of the excess over $11,450
Over $43,650 but not over $112,650	$5,975 plus 25% of the excess over $43,650
Over $112,650 but not over $182,400	$23,225 plus 28% of the excess over $112,650
Over $182,400 but not over $357,700	$42,755 plus 33% of the excess over $182,400
Over $357,700	$100,604 plus 35% of the excess over $357,700

TABLE 3 - Section 1(c) - Unmarried Individuals (other than Surviving Spouses and Heads of Households).

If Taxable Income Is:	The Tax Is:
Not over $8,025	10% of the taxable income
Over $8,025 but not over $32,550	$802.50 plus 15% of the excess over $8,025
Over $32,550 but not over $78,850	$4,481.25 plus 25% of the excess over $32,550
Over $78,850 but not over $164,550	$16,056.25 plus 28% of the excess over $78,850
Over $164,550 but not over $357,70	$40,052.25 plus 33% of the excess over $164,550
Over $357,700	$103,791.75 plus 35% of the excess over $357,700

TABLE 4 - Section 1(d) - Married Individuals Filing Separate Returns

If Taxable Income Is:	The Tax Is:
Not over $8,025	10% of the taxable income
Over $8,025 but not over $32,550	$802.50 plus 15% of the excess over $8,025
Over $32,550 but not over $65,725	$4,481.25 plus 25% of the excess over $32,550
Over $65,725 but not over $100,150	$12,775 plus 28% of the excess over $65,725
Over $100,150 but not over $178,850	$22,414 plus 33% of the excess over $100,150
Over $178,850	$48,385 plus 35% of the excess over $178,850

TABLE 5 - Section 1(e) - Estates and Trusts

If Taxable Income Is:	The Tax Is:
Not over $2,200	15% of the taxable income
Over $2,200 but not over $5,150	$330 plus 25% of the excess over $2,200
Over $5,150 but not over $7,850	$1,067.50 plus 28% of the excess over $5,150
Over $7,850 but not over $10,700	$1,823.50 plus 33% of the excess over $7,850
Over $10,700	$2,764 plus 35% of the excess over $10,700

.02 *Unearned Income of Minor Children Taxed as if Parent's Income (the "Kiddie Tax")*. For taxable years beginning in 2008, the amount in § 1(g)(4)(A)(ii)(I), which is used to reduce the net unearned income reported on the child's return that is subject to the "kiddie tax," is $900. This amount is the same as the $900 standard deduction amount provided in section 3.11(2) of this revenue procedure. The same $900 amount is used for purposes of § 1(g)(7) (that is, to determine whether a parent may elect to include a child's gross income in the parent's gross income and to calculate the "kiddie tax"). For example, one of the requirements for the parental election is that a child's gross income is more than the amount referenced in §1(g)(4)(A)(ii)(I) but less than 10 times that amount; thus, a child's gross income for 2008 must be more than $900 but less than $9,000.

.03 *Adoption Credit*. For taxable years beginning in 2008, under § 23(a)(3) the credit allowed for an adoption of a child with special needs is $11,650. For taxable years beginning in 2008, under § 23(b)(1) the maximum credit allowed for other adoptions is the amount of qualified adoption expenses up to $11,650. The available adoption credit begins to phase out under § 23(b)(2)(A) for taxpayers with modified adjusted gross income in excess of $174,730 and is completely phased out for taxpayers with modified adjusted gross income of $214,730 or more. (See section 3.15 of this revenue procedure for the adjusted items relating to adoption assistance programs.)

.04 *Child Tax Credit*. For taxable years beginning in 2008, the value used in § 24(d)(1)(B)(i) to determine the amount of credit under §24 that may be refundable is $12,050.

.05 *Hope and Lifetime Learning Credits*. (1) For taxable years beginning in 2008, the Hope Scholarship Credit under § 25A(b)(1) is an amount equal to 100 percent of qualified tuition and related expenses not in excess of $1,200 plus 50 percent of those expenses in excess of $1,200, but not in excess of $2,400. Accordingly, the maximum Hope Scholarship Credit allowable under § 25A(b)(1) for taxable years beginning in 2008 is $1,800.

(2) For taxable years beginning in 2008, a taxpayer's modified adjusted gross income in excess of $48,000 ($96,000 for a joint return) is used to determine the reduction under§ 25A(d)(2)(A)(ii) in the amount of the Hope Scholarship and Lifetime Learning Credits otherwise allowable under § 25A(a).

.06 *Elective Deferrals and IRA Contributions by Certain Individuals*. For taxable years beginning in 2008, the applicable percentage under § 2B(b) is determined based on the following amounts:

Modified Adjusted Gross Income

Joint Return		Head of Household		All Other Cases		Applicable Percentage
Over	Not Over	Over	Not Over	Over	Not over	
$ 0	$32,000	$ 0	$24,000	$ 0	$16,000	50%
$32,000	$34,500	$24,000	$25,875	$16,000	$17,250	20%
$34,500	$53,000	$25,875	$39,750	$17,250	$26,500	10%
$53,000		$39,750		$26,500		0%

.07 *Earned Income Credit*.

(1) *In general*. For taxable years beginning in 2008, the following amounts are used to determine the earned income credit under § 32(b). The "earned income amount" is the amount of earned income at or above which the maximum amount of the earned income credit is allowed. The "threshold phaseout amount" is the amount of adjusted gross income (or, if greater, earned income) above which the maximum amount of the credit begins to phase out. The "completed phaseout amount" is the amount of adjusted gross income (or, if greater, earned income) at or above which no credit is allowed.

Number of Qualifying Children

Item	One	Two or More	None
Earned Income Amount	$8,580	$12,060	$5,720
Maximum Amount of Credit	$2,917	$4,824	$438
Threshold Phaseout Amount (Single, Surviving Spouse, or Head of Household)	$15,740	$15,740	$7,160
Completed Phaseout Amount (Single, Surviving Spouse, or Head of Household)	$33,995	$38,646	$12,880
Threshold Phaseout Amount (Married Filing Jointly)	$18,740	$18,740	$10,160
Completed Phaseout Amount (Married Filing Jointly)	$36,995	$41,646	$15,880

The instructions for the Form 1040 series provide tables showing the amount of the earned income credit for each type of taxpayer.

(2) *Excessive investment income*. For taxable years beginning in 2008, the earned income tax credit is not allowed under § 32(i) if the aggregate amount of certain investment income exceeds $2,950.

.08 *Low-Income Housing Credit*. For calendar year 2008, the amount used under § 42(h)(3)(C)(ii) to calculate the State housing credit ceiling for the

2008 Inflation Adjustments and Mileage Rates

low-income housing credit is the greater of (1) $2.00 multiplied by the State population, or (2) $2,325,000.

.09 *Alternative Minimum Tax Exemption for a Child Subject to the "Kiddie Tax."* For taxable years beginning in 2008, for a child to whom the § 1(g) "kiddie tax" applies, the exemption amount under §§ 55 and 59(j) for purposes of the alternative minimum tax under § 55 may not exceed the sum of (1) the child's earned income for the taxable year, plus (2) $6,400.

***

.11 *Standard Deduction.*

(1) *In general.* For taxable years beginning in 2008, the standard deduction amounts under § 63(c)(2) are as follows:

Filing Status	Standard Deduction
Married Individuals Filing Joint Returns and Surviving Spouses (§ 1(a))	$10,900
Heads of Households (§ 1(b))	$8,000
Unmarried Individuals (other than Surviving Spouses and	$5,450
Married Individuals Filing Separate Returns (§ 1(d))	$5,450

(2) *Dependent.* For taxable years beginning in 2008, the standard deduction amount under §63(c)(5) for an individual who may be claimed as a dependent by another taxpayer cannot exceed the greater of (1) $900, or (2) the sum of $300 and the individual's earned income.

(3) *Aged or blind.* For taxable years beginning in 2008, the additional standard deduction amount under § 63(f) for the aged or the blind is $1,050. These amounts are increased to $1,350 if the individual is also unmarried and not a surviving spouse.

.12 Overall Limitation on Itemized Deductions. For taxable years beginning in 2008, the "applicable amount" of adjusted gross income under §68(b), above which the amount of otherwise allowable itemized deductions is reduced under §68, is $159,950 (or $79,975 for a separate return filed by a married individual).

.13 Qualified Transportation Fringe. For taxable years beginning in 2008, the monthly limitation under § 132(f)(2)(A), regarding the aggregate fringe benefit exclusion amount for transportation in a commuter highway vehicle and any transit pass, is $115. The monthly limitation under § 132(f)(2)(B), regarding the fringe benefit exclusion amount for qualified parking, is $220.

.14 Income from United States Savings Bonds for Taxpayers Who Pay Qualified Higher Education Expenses. For taxable years beginning in 2008, the exclusion under §135, regarding income from United States savings bonds for taxpayers who pay qualified higher education expenses, begins to phase out for modified adjusted gross income above $100,650 for joint returns and $67,100 for other returns. The exclusion is completely phased out for modified adjusted gross income of $130,650 or more for joint returns and $82,100 or more for other returns.

.15 Adoption Assistance Programs. For taxable years beginning in 2008, under § 137(a)(2) the amount that can be excluded from an employee's gross income for the adoption of a child with special needs is $11,650. For taxable years beginning in 2008, under § 137(b)(1) the maximum amount that can be excluded from an employee's gross income for the amounts paid or expenses incurred by an employer for qualified adoption expenses furnished pursuant to an adoption assistance program for other adoptions by the employee is $11,650. The amount excludable from an employee's gross income begins to phase out under § 137(b)(2)(A) for taxpayers with modified adjusted gross income in excess of $174,730 and is completely phased out for taxpayers with modified adjusted gross income of $214,730 or more. (See section 3.03 of this revenue procedure for the adjusted items relating to the adoption credit.)

***

.19 *Personal Exemption.*

(1) *Exemption amount.* For taxable years beginning in 2008, the personal exemption amount under § 151(d) is $3,500. The exemption amount for taxpayers with adjusted gross income in excess of the maximum phaseout amount is $2,333 for taxable years beginning in 2008.

(2) *Phaseout.* For taxable years beginning in 2008, the personal exemption amount begins to phase out at, and reaches the maximum phaseout amount after, the following adjusted gross income amounts:

Filing Status	AGI - Beginning of Phaseout	AGI - Maximum Phaseout
Married Individuals Filing Joint Returns and Surviving Spouses (§1(a))	$239,950	$362,450
Heads of Households (§1(b))	$199,950	$322,450
Unmarried Individuals (other than Surviving Spouses and Heads of Households) (§1(c))	$159,950	$282,450
Married Individuals Filing Separate Returns (§1(d))	$119,975	$181,225

.20 Election to Expense Certain Depreciable Assets. For taxable years beginning in 2008, under § 179(b)(1) the aggregate cost of any §179 property a taxpayer may elect to treat as an expense can not exceed $128,000. Under §179(b)(2) the $128,000 limitation is reduced (but not below zero) by the amount by which the cost of §179 property placed in service during the 2008 taxable year exceeds $510,000.

.21 Eligible Long-Term Care Premiums. For taxable years beginning in 2008, the limitations under § 213(d)(10), regarding eligible long-term care premiums includible in the term "medical care," are as follows:

2008 Inflation Adjustments and Mileage Rates

Attained Age Before the Close of the Taxable Year	Limitation on Premiums
40 or less..	$310
More than 40 but not more than 50..	$580
More than 50 but not more than 60..	$1,150
More than 60 but not more than 70..	$3,080
More than 70..	$3,850

.22 Retirement Savings.

(1) For taxable years beginning in 2008, the applicable dollar amount under § 219(g)(3)(B)(i) for taxpayers filing a joint return is $85,000. If the taxpayer's spouse is not an active participant, the applicable dollar amount for the spouse under § 219(g)(3)(B)(i) is $159,000 for taxable years beginning in 2008.

(2) For taxable years beginning in 2008, the applicable dollar amount under § 219(g)(3)(B)(ii) for all other taxpayers (except for married taxpayers filing separately) is $53,000.

(3) The applicable dollar amount under § 219(g)(3)(B)(iii) for married taxpayers filing separately is $0.

.23 Medical Savings Accounts.

(1) Self-only coverage. For taxable years beginning in 2008, the term "high deductible health plan" as defined in § 220(c)(2)(A) means, for self-only coverage, a health plan that has an annual deductible that is not less than $1,950 and not more than $2,900, and under which the annual out-of-pocket expenses required to be paid (other than for premiums) for covered benefits does not exceed $3,850.

(2) Family coverage. For taxable years beginning in 2008, the term "high deductible health plan" means, for family coverage, a health plan that has an annual deductible that is not less than $3,850 and not more than $5,800, and under which the annual out-of-pocket expenses required to be paid (other than for premiums) for covered benefits does not exceed $7,050.

.24 Interest on Education Loans. For taxable years beginning in 2008, the $2,500 maximum deduction for interest paid on qualified education loans under §221 begins to phase out under §221(b)(2)(B) for taxpayers with modified adjusted gross income in excess of $55,000 ($115,000 for joint returns), and is completely phased out for taxpayers with modified adjusted gross income of $70,000 or more ($145,000 or more for joint returns).

.25 Roth IRAs.

(1) For taxable years beginning in 2008, the applicable dollar amount under § 408A(c)(3)(C)(ii)(I) for taxpayers filing a joint return is $159,000.

(2) For taxable years beginning in 2008, the applicable dollar amount under § 408A(c)(3)(C)(ii)(II) for all other taxpayers (except for married taxpayers filing separately) is $101,000.

(3) The applicable dollar amount under § 408A(c)(3)(C)(ii)(III) for married taxpayers filing separately is $0.
.26 Treatment of Dues Paid to Agricultural or Horticultural Organizations. For taxable years beginning in 2008, the limitation under § 512(d)(1), regarding the exemption of annual dues required to be paid by a member to an agricultural or horticultural organization, is $139.

.27 Insubstantial Benefit Limitations for Contributions Associated with Charitable Fund-Raising Campaigns.

(1) Low cost article. For taxable years beginning in 2008, the unrelated business income of certain exempt organizations under § 513(h)(2) does not include a "low cost article" of $9.10 or less.

(2) Other insubstantial benefits. For taxable years beginning in 2008, the $5, $25, and $50 guidelines in section 3 of Rev. Proc. 90-12, 1990-1 C.B. 471 (as amplified by Rev. Proc. 92-49, 1992-1 C.B. 987, and modified by Rev. Proc. 92-102, 1992-2 C.B. 579), for disregarding the value of insubstantial benefits received by a donor in return for a fully deductible charitable contribution under §170, are $9.10, $45.50, and $91, respectively.   ***

.32 *Annual Exclusion for Gifts.*(1) For calendar year 2008, the first $12,000 of gifts to any person (other than gifts of future interests in property) are not included in the total amount of taxable gifts under § 2503 made during that year.

(2) For calendar year 2008, the first $128,000 of gifts to a spouse who is not a citizen of the United States (other than gifts of future interests in property) are not included in the total amount of taxable gifts under §§ 2503 and 2523(i)(2) made during that year.
                                                                                              ***

.40 *Periodic Payments Received under Qualified Long-Term Care Insurance Contracts or under Certain Life Insurance Contracts.* For calendar year 2008, the stated dollar amount of the per diem limitation under § 7702B(d)(4), regarding periodic payments received under a qualified long-term care insurance contract or periodic payments received under a life insurance contract that are treated as paid by reason of the death of a chronically ill individual, is $270.

Rev. Proc. 2007-70, I.R.B. 2007-50, November 27, 2007.
                                                                                              ***

SECTION 2. SUMMARY OF STANDARD MILEAGE RATES

.01 Standard mileage rates

(1) Business (section 5 below)................................. 50.5 cents per mile

(2) Charitable contribution (section 7 below)............14 cents per mile

(3) Medical and moving (section 7 below)................19 cents per mile

.02 Determination of standard mileage rates. The business and medical and moving standard mileage rates reflected in this revenue procedure are based on an annual study of the fixed and variable costs of operating an automobile conducted on behalf of the Service by an independent contractor. The charitable contribution standard mileage rate is provided in § 170(i) of the Internal Revenue Code.
                                                                                              ***